Handbook of

PSYCHOTHERAPY AND BEHAVIOR CHANGE:

AN EMPIRICAL ANALYSIS

Handbook of

PSYCHOTHERAPY AND BEHAVIOR CHANGE:

AN EMPIRICAL ANALYSIS

ALLEN E. BERGIN and **SOL L. GARFIELD**, Editors

Department of Psychology
Brigham Young University

Department of Psychology
Washington University

JOHN WILEY & SONS, INC.

NEW YORK . LONDON . SYDNEY . TORONTO

Library of Congress Catalogue Card Number: 70-115654

ISBN 0-471-06968-X

Printed in the United States of America

10 9 8 7 6

CONTRIBUTORS

ALBERT BANDURA, Ph.D.

Professor of Psychology
Stanford University
Stanford, California

RICHARD L. BEDNAR, Ph.D.

Associate Professor of Psychology
University of Kentucky
Lexington, Kentucky

H. R. BEECH, Ph.D.

Head, Department of Psychology
Netherne Hospital
Coulsdan, Surrey, England

ALLEN E. BERGIN, Ph.D.

Professor of Psychology
Brigham Young University
Provo, Utah

GERALD C. DAVISON, Ph.D.

Associate Professor of Psychology
Coordinator, Postdoctoral Program in Behavior
*   Modification*
State University of New York at Stony Brook
Stony Brook, New York

H. J. EYSENCK, Ph.D., D.Sc.

Professor of Psychology
Department of Psychology, Institute of Psychiatry
University of London
London, England

DONALD H. FORD, Ph.D.

Dean
College of Human Development
The Pennsylvania State University
University Park, Pennsylvania

SOL L. GARFIELD, Ph.D.

Professor and Director
Clinical Psychology Program
Washington University
St. Louis, Missouri

JACK R. GIBB, Ph.D.

Consulting Psychologist
La Jolla, California

ARNOLD P. GOLDSTEIN, Ph.D.

Professor of Psychology
Syracuse University
Syracuse, New York

KENNETH HELLER, Ph.D.

Professor of Psychology
Department of Psychology
Indiana University
Bloomington, Indiana

LEONARD I. JACOBSON, Ph.D.

Assistant Professor of Psychology
Department of Psychology
University of Miami
Coral Gables, Florida

DONALD J. KIESLER, Ph.D.

Associate Professor of Clinical Psychology
Department of Psychology
Emory University
Atlanta, Georgia

LEONARD KRASNER, Ph.D.

Professor and Director of Clinical Training
Department of Psychology
State University of New York
Stony Brook, New York

PETER J. LANG, Ph.D.

Professor of Psychology
Department of Psychology
University of Wisconsin
Madison, Wisconsin

G. FRANK LAWLIS, Ph.D.

Director of Research and Assistant Professor of Psychology
Arkansas Rehabilitation Research and Training Center
University of Arkansas
Fayetteville, Arkansas

ARNOLD A. LAZARUS, Ph.D.

Professor of Psychology
Rutgers University
New Brunswick, New Jersey

EUGENE E. LEVITT, Ph.D.

Director, Section of Psychology of the Department of Psychiatry and Professor of Clinical Psychology
Indiana University School of Medicine
Indianapolis, Indiana

LESTER LUBORSKY, Ph.D.

Professor of Psychology in Psychiatry
Department of Psychiatry
University of Pennsylvania School of Medicine
Philadelphia, Pennsylvania

GERALD MARSDEN, Ed.D.

Assistant Professor
Department of Psychology and Department of Psychiatry
University of Michigan
Ann Arbor, Michigan

RUTH G. MATARAZZO, Ph.D.

Professor of Medical Psychology
University of Oregon Medical School
Portland, Oregon

PHILIP R. A. MAY, M.D.

Clinical Director and Clinical Professor of Psychiatry
Neuropsychiatric Institute
California State Department of Mental Hygiene and University of California at Los Angeles
Los Angeles, California

KEVIN M. MITCHELL, Ph.D.

Senior Research Scientist
Arkansas Rehabilitation Research and Training Center
Assistant Professor
Department of Psychology, University of Arkansas
Fayetteville, Arkansas

EDWARD J. MURRAY, Ph.D.

Professor of Psychology
Department of Psychology
University of Miami
Coral Gables, Florida

ROGER A. MYERS, Ph.D.

Professor of Psychology and Education
Counseling Psychology Program
Teachers College, Columbia University
New York, New York

GERALD R. PATTERSON, Ph.D.

Professor of Education, University of Oregon School of Education and
Research Associate, Oregon Research Institute,
Eugene, Oregon

SHELDON R. ROEN, Ph.D.

President, Human Sciences, Inc.
New York, New York

ARTHUR K. SHAPIRO, M.D.

Clinical Associate Professor and Director, Placebo Studies Laboratory
Payne Whitney Psychiatric Clinic
Cornell University Medical College
New York Hospital
New York, New York

NORMAN R. SIMONSON, Ph.D.

Assistant Professor of Psychology
Department of Psychology
Syracuse University
Syracuse, New York

DONALD P. SPENCE, Ph.D.

Associate Professor of Psychology
Research Center for Mental Health
New York University
New York, New York

CHARLES B. TRUAX, Ph.D.

Professor of Educational Psychology
University of Calgary
Calgary, Alberta, Canada

HUGH B. URBAN, Ph.D.

Director, Division of Individual and Family Studies
College of Human Development
The Pennsylvania State University
University Park, Pennsylvania

This Book is Affectionately Dedicated to

Marian and Amy

PREFACE

The current *Handbook* was conceived and planned to fulfill a somewhat unique function in the area of psychotherapy and behavior change. For most of its history, the field of psychotherapy has appeared to rely almost exclusively on clinical reports, case studies, and theoretical accounts generally organized around a particular school or approach to psychotherapy. Issues concerning therapeutic practice tended to be settled by allegiance to one school, by reference to the writings of authoritative persons in the field, or by recourse to one's own clinical experience. Although such patterns are not unusual for newly developed fields of inquiry and application, there emerges with the gradual development of more systematic knowledge and research, a greater reliance on empirically tested principles or practices. It was our conviction that sufficient empirical work had been carried out in the fields of psychotherapy and behavior change in recent years to merit a rather systematic review and appraisal of this work with the particular goal of seeing what implications such work might have for practice. In other words, we were interested in securing a comprehensive review and evaluation of the state of empirical knowledge pertaining to psychotherapy and the practical implications, if any, that one might draw from such data.

Increasingly, in the past few years, reports of research investigations on psychotherapy and of conferences on research in this area have been in evidence, and a number of collections of research publications have appeared in book form. Most of this material, however, was organized around either specific research issues or a particular research project, or was otherwise not adequately synthesized in relation to the broader problem of psychotherapeutic practice. In addition, some practitioners have criticized therapy research as having no clear implications for practice, and they have questioned the value and relevance of the entire enterprise. As a result of these factors, research in psychotherapy has had little impact on therapy in practice.

Until lately, there was indeed little to be concluded from psychotherapy research, but we think that practitioners may be somewhat surprised by what has happened in the past decade. During recent years, as traditional broad spectrum psychotherapies have begun to be broken down into part-processes and their effective mechanisms isolated, the behavioral therapies have developed to a point of promise that must be considered of breakthrough proportions; group techniques have been the subject of unparalleled ingenuity and invention (though still lacking a strong empirical base); the biology of disorder and change has begun to bear technical fruit, especially in the exciting possibilities for new psychosomatic treatments based on the instrumental conditioning of autonomic responses; and the rate of publication in the entire domain has accelerated exponentially. Today there is an atmosphere of optimism and anticipation in this field, which is diametrically opposite to the pessimism and even nihilism that was evident a decade ago. Certainly there are not yet any cure-alls, but there are enough promising leads documented herein to be encouraging to almost anyone. We hope also that the inquiring practitioner will find in this volume ample support for the notion that the synthesis of therapeutic and scientific interests is possible and fruitful.

As a consequence, we believed it would be worthwhile to prepare a handbook of psychotherapy and behavior change that would emphasize empirical results and the possible implications to be drawn from such results for practice. The need for a work of this kind appeared evident, and to our knowledge, no such published source was available. In line with this premise, we decided to exclude accounts of psychotherapy that merely described techniques or theoretical orientations. Other consequences were also evident. Reference to therapeutic schools or approaches for which there was little or no empirical data would of necessity have to be slighted. For this reason, for example, psychoanalysis may seem to be underrepresented here, even though it has unquestionably exerted tremendous influence on the practice and theories of psychotherapy. In spite of its influence, the amount of empirical investigation of psychoanalysis has been relatively modest. By contrast, behavior therapists have conducted many studies and are represented in several chapters. This variation in the amount of space devoted to specific topics should not be interpreted as a theoretical bias on our part; instead, it reflects the stated criterion of the availability of empirical data employed in the preparation of this book. Our focus, then, was on a survey and evaluation of the empirical data available in the literature on psychotherapy and behavior change.

Although we have attempted to be comprehensive, we know that every broad-scale enterprise is bound to leave something out. Some readers will perhaps miss an emphasis on the existential therapies, encounter groups, marathons, and other more esoteric techniques. These are discussed briefly, but we felt that little weight should be given them in an empirically oriented volume, despite their current in-vogue popularity. Certainly there is very little substantive evidence on which to base opinions about them. Regrettably, the small body of evidence on family and milieu therapies is not summarized here because we had inadvertently overburdened one contributor with several topics. This was impossible to correct in time for publication, and thus these areas are omitted. Otherwise, we are very fortunate in having a full complement of contributors and topics.

Even though we may be overly optimistic and inclined to overestimate our own system of values, these contributions appear to usher in a new emphasis and perhaps a new era in the domain of psychotherapy and behavior change. Several aspects of this development are discernible here. First, there is the obvious emphasis on research findings and empirical data as a frame of reference for evaluating psychotherapy. Second, the application of general psychological principles (particularly in the area of learning and social psychology) to human problems of adjustment and behavior modification is also apparent in a number of chapters. Third, the increased leadership activity of psychologists in psychotherapy and related areas contrasts with a less ascendant role in the past. Fourth, these presentations also appear to mirror what appears to be a decline in the prestige and importance of psychoanalysis and related therapies. While there is, of course, no precise way of measuring this change, the increased output of ideas, techniques, and research evident from the behavior therapies, the developing emphasis on community and social resources in the alleviation of human distress, the appearance of emergency therapies and crisis intervention for the more immediate treatment of adjustment difficulties, as well as a greater attention to cognitive variables in the modification of behavior, all point to the decreasing influence of the psychoanalytic approach on the psychotherapeutic scene. Whether this is good or bad is partly a matter of value judgment. However, as this book demonstrates, many of the newer approaches reflect a greater desire to evaluate their results empirically, to attempt to work with individuals who have tended to be slighted or passed over by traditional approaches, and to broaden their impact by utilizing a variety of other persons as therapeutic agents. These developments appear to be decidedly worthwhile.

In many ways, therefore, the work reviewed in this *Handbook* appears to reflect a definite maturation in the development of the field of psychotherapy. There is demonstrated not only a demand for some empirical verification of the effectiveness of what the psychotherapist does but also a more sophisticated awareness of the problems involved in such undertakings. At least on a theoretical level, we appear to be beyond the stage of asking the overly general and unanswerable question, "Is psychotherapy effective?" Instead, we are prepared to ask, "Under what conditions will this type of client with these particular problems be changed in what ways by specific types of therapists?" While this is a more specific and complicated question, as illustrated in Chapter 2 by Donald J. Kiesler, as well as by others, more sophisticated research designs are required and can be devised. The inadequacy of previous "one-shot" studies that are not replicated and that fail to specify in adequate detail the therapeutic procedures used, the clients treated, and the qualities of the therapists employed are apparent in the reviews presented and evaluated in many of the chapters. Are we too optimistic in believing that a corner in psychotherapy research and evaluation has been turned, and that more sophisticated and definitive evaluative studies will be forthcoming in the future? The need is clearly apparent, and we appear to be better equipped than ever to attempt such work.

It may appear also, on the basis of the work discussed here, that dogmatism in psychotherapy is on the wane and that there is more interest in experimentation, innovation, and evaluation. This is reflected not only in the variety of new approaches evaluated but also in the greater tolerance for training parents, aides, nurses, and teachers as therapeutic or behavior change agents, and in the attempt to devise techniques for working with diverse and severely disturbed individuals. It is not too unrealistic to expect that new programs for training new types of workers in this field, on a more systematic and rational basis than has been the case in the past, may be forthcoming in the decade ahead. Training in psychotherapy has had little systematic study in the past, but as Chapter 24 by Ruth Matarazzo indicates, there are many potential opportunities for real advances within our reach.

Finally, let us emphasize that some progress has been made in our understanding of what transactions appear to hold promise for effecting positive change in individuals with adjustment difficulties. Although much remains to be done, it seems clear that better planned, systematic research which is focused on significant and specified variables will ultimately expand our knowledge of what in psychotherapy is therapeutic. It appears most likely that specific approaches and techniques for particular types of problems will gradually replace the more typical universal approaches of the past. In this connection, more substantiated and particularized knowledge of relationship factors and placebo factors will not only be available but will be used in a more planned, deliberate, and knowledgeable manner. Furthermore, research increasingly will tend to guide practice so that harmful or useless methods will be discarded and the best techniques (whether they be drugs, different varieties of psychotherapy, or social intervention) will be used in the most efficient manner to help individuals overcome their problems. This, at least, is our fervent hope.

The contributions capture the wave of progressive feeling and optimism, expressed previously, exceedingly well. As editors, we found it intellectually exhilarating to be in close contact with the feelings, ideas, and projects of a large number of individuals who are at the frontier in these developments. We are unusually fortunate to have embarked on this project at this time and are doubly blessed in the quality of our collaborators in this summary of the empirical status of the field to date.

We express our deepest gratitude to our contributing authors and to our advisory editors for their efforts in our joint undertaking. In every meaning of the word, this has been a collaborative venture.

Allen E. Bergin
Sol L. Garfield

ACKNOWLEDGEMENTS

We are grateful to those who assisted the editors and contributors in completing this *Handbook*. Morton Deutsch, Cyril M. Franks, Harvey A. Hornstein, Marion Hornstein, and Alan O. Ross reviewed particular chapters for us, and this was most helpful. The Editorial Advisers, of course, did considerable reviewing and we could not have functioned nearly as well without their commentaries. We deeply appreciate their help and particularly acknowledge the unusual contribution of Dr. Joseph Matarazzo. Our secretaries, Alice Mucha, Nola Hobbs, Roberta Plybon, and Cathy Chavez, labored consistently and effectively in helping to maintain the orderliness necessary in such a complex project.

Also we are grateful to the following authors, editors, publishers, and publications for generously granting us permission to reproduce previously published materials:

C. W. Darrow
Robert Edelberg
H. J. Eysenck
American Psychological Association
American Psychiatric Association
Grass Instrument Co.
Journal of Consulting Psychology
Journal of Abnormal Psychology
American Journal of Psychiatry
McGraw-Hill Book Company
Holt, Rinehart & Winston Publishers
International Journal of Psychiatry
University of Wisconsin Press
Williams & Wilkins Co.
Howard M. Yanof
Radio Corporation of America (*Transistor Manual*)
Oxford University Press

CONTENTS

PART I:

THEORY, METHODOLOGY, AND EXPERIMENTATION

1. Some Historical and Conceptual Perspectives on Psychotherapy   3
and Behavior Change

    HUGH B. URBAN AND DONALD H. FORD

    Pennsylvania State University

2. Experimental Designs in Psychotherapy Research   36

    DONALD J. KIESLER

    Emory University

3. The Application of Psychophysiological Methods to the Study   75
of Psychotherapy and Behavior Modification

    PETER J. LANG

    University of Wisconsin, Madison

4. Laboratory Interview Research as an Analogue to Treatment   126

    KENNETH HELLER

    Indiana University

5. Social Psychological Approaches to Psychotherapy Research   154

    ARNOLD P. GOLDSTEIN AND NORMAN R. SIMONSON

    Syracuse University

6. Clinical Innovation in Research and Practice   196

    ARNOLD A. LAZARUS AND GERALD C. DAVISON

    Rutgers University   *State University of New York at Stony Brook*

PART II:

ANALYSIS OF CLIENT-CENTERED, PSYCHOANALYTIC, ECLECTIC, AND RELATED THERAPIES

7. The Evaluation of Therapeutic Outcomes   217

    ALLEN E. BERGIN

    Brigham Young University

8. Research on Client Variables in Psychotherapy   271

    SOL L. GARFIELD

    Washington University

9. Research on Certain Therapist Interpersonal Skills in Relation to Process and Outcome   299

    CHARLES B. TRUAX AND KEVIN M. MITCHELL

    University of Calgary   *University of Arkansas*

10. Content Analysis Studies of Psychotherapy: 1954 Through 1968   345

    GERALD MARSDEN

    University of Michigan

11. Quantitative Research on Psychoanalytic Therapy   408

    LESTER LUBORSKY AND DONALD P. SPENCE

    University of Pennsylvania   *New York University*

12. Placebo Effects in Medicine, Psychotherapy, and Psychoanalysis   439

    ARTHUR K. SHAPIRO

    Cornell University

13. Research on Psychotherapy with Children   474

    EUGENE E. LEVITT

    Indiana University

14. Psychotherapy and Ataraxic Drugs   495

    PHILIP R. A. MAY

    California State Department of Mental Hygiene and University of California at Los Angeles

PART III:

ANALYSIS OF BEHAVIORAL THERAPIES

15. Counterconditioning and Related Methods   543

    H. J. EYSENCK AND R. BEECH

    University of London   *Netherne Hospital, Coulsdon, Surrey, England*

16. The Operant Approach in Behavior Therapy   612

     LEONARD KRASNER

     State University of New York at Stony Brook

17. Psychotherapy Based Upon Modeling Principles   653

     ALBERT BANDURA

     Stanford University

18. The Nature of Learning in Traditional and Behavioral   709
     Psychotherapy

     EDWARD J. MURRAY AND LEONARD I. JACOBSON

     University of Miami

PART IV:

THERAPEUTIC APPROACHES TO THE HOME, FAMILY, SCHOOL, GROUP, ORGANIZATION, AND COMMUNITY

19. Behavioral Intervention Procedures in the Classroom and   751
     in the Home

     G. R. PATTERSON

     University of Oregon and
     Oregon Research Institute

20. Evaluative Research and Community Mental Health   776

     SHELDON R. ROEN

     Human Sciences, Inc.

21. Empirical Research in Group Psychotherapy   812

     RICHARD L. BEDNAR AND G. FRANK LAWLIS

     University of Kentucky

22. The Effects of Human Relations Training   839

     JACK R. GIBB

     La Jolla, California

23. Research on Educational and Vocational Counseling   863

     ROGER A. MYERS

     Columbia University

PART V:
EVALUATING THE TRAINING OF THERAPISTS

24. Research on the Teaching and Learning of Psychotherapeutic   895
     Skills

RUTH G. MATARAZZO

University of Oregon Medical School

Author Index   925

Subject Index   945

PART I

THEORY, METHODOLOGY,
AND EXPERIMENTATION

1

SOME HISTORICAL AND CONCEPTUAL PERSPECTIVES ON PSYCHOTHERAPY AND BEHAVIOR CHANGE

HUGH B. URBAN
DONALD H. FORD

PENNSYLVANIA STATE UNIVERSITY

It is customary to ascribe the initiation of psychotherapeutic practice to Sigmund Freud and his collaborator, Breuer, less than a century ago. In its formative years it was possible to conceptualize the approach to behavioral modification which was evolving, in relatively straightforward terms. This was because it was a rather circumscribed and stylized set of procedures, employed by a limited number of persons (a specialized few primarily within the medical guilds), focused upon symptom-relief, within a restricted range of persons. In its very early stages it was focused primarily upon the alleviation of symptoms in patients whose difficulties emulated those of the neurologically impaired. Moreover, it had evolved a relatively circumscribed conceptual rationale that served to guide the implementation of these remedial tactics—a viewpoint on how to look at the events of concern and understand their manner of operation, as well as some notion as to how the change-process took place.

But things never stand still; refinements, elaborations, changes, and developments of one kind or another inevitably occur. One of the directions in which development could have taken place was "vertical"; conceivably, the tactics introduced by Breuer and Freud could have been honed and refined in the direction of ever-increasing precision, until the point was reached where highly exact, systematic, and efficient procedures for the symptom-modification of hysteric patients could have been achieved. This, however, was not the primary direction in which developments in this field took place.

3

For a host of reasons, including the pre-dilections of the early investigators themselves, the development of the domain of psychotherapy has been "lateral" instead. This pattern of elaboration has been steady and progressive throughout the course of the entire twentieth century. The categories of behavioral difficulties to which the tactics became applied became wider and more heterogeneous, rather than narrower and more precise. Tactics akin to those introduced under the rubric of psychotherapy were used in order to try to produce beneficial changes across an extended array of behavioral problems—from hysteric problems to obsessive and compulsive ones as well, from neuroses to psychoses, from the socially constrained to the antisocial offender, from adults to children, and from medical-type problems to problems of living in general. Its name became changed in some circumstances, sometimes, for example, running under the label of "counseling" as opposed to psychotherapy as such. Even so, most workers recognized underlying commonalities in such approaches, frequently utilizing the labels interchangeably. Finally, the broadening and expanding horizons came to include not just those persons in whom problems of development had occurred, with the focus upon the clinical, remedial, or rehabilitative solution of such problems, but upon those persons whose lives were proceeding reasonably well, but where the prospects of improvements and enhancements of living could be foreseen. Psychotherapeutic tactics had begun to be employed in order to help render a reasonable adjustment even "better."

Thus, a steady and progressive shift has been taking place in the direction of larger and more encompassing definitions as to what it is that is in need of becoming changed, with respect to the behavioral situations of more and more different kinds of people, and in the definitions of the objectives that such tactics of intervention should achieve, that is, the kinds of behavioral patterns that should ideally take their place.

A second kind of elaboration has been simultaneously underway. More and more different kinds of tactics have been progressively employed. From the early utilization of procedures designed to facilitate extensive and unrestricted verbalization on the part of the subject through such means as hypnosis and free-association, literally hundreds of different practices and procedures have been introduced, designed to facilitate and to effect behavior change. From one-to-one working relationships, therapist and patient, tactics have been employed utilizing two therapists and one patient, two patients and one therapist, groups of therapists, groups of patients. Changes in scheduling of sessions have been advocated and employed—from an hour per day five days a week, to one hour per week, to sustained and "marathon" type sessions. Tactics vary from time-limited to open-ended and temporally indefinite treatment series. Multiple methods have been developed by which to elicit behavior so as to render the patients accessible to behavioral change, such as puppets and games, psychodrama, or role-playing procedures; these extend the psychotherapist's repertoire for eliciting techniques well beyond the early reliance upon the strictly verbal and personal characteristics of the therapist as the antecedent conditions for producing the desired sets of changes. Tactics for modification have been extended outside and beyond the confines of the professional office, with innovative methods of "shaping" the behavior of the person in the real-life circumstances in which it is found to occur. Procedures involving electrical, chemical, and mechanical devices have been introduced and heavily utilized, frequently applied concomitant with or subsequent to the behavioral patterns in which change is sought. And the experimentation with still "newer" procedures, differing in major and minor detail and with varying levels of systematization and precision, shows no sign of letup. Their number can be expected to steadily increase.

Most of these innovations have been developed within differing conceptual frameworks, to which they have been tied and related. For psychotherapy continues to be a deliberate, and in that sense planned, pattern of intervention into the behavioral circumstances of a person in order to correct or to modify some kind of presenting difficulty. What one elects to do is based upon what one believes to be wrong in the first place; one's analysis of a problem will predetermine what one decides to be necessary in the way of a remedy. Thus, one's view as to what constitutes a problem, what needs to be changed, and what it should be changed to, represents a conception (implicit or explicit) as to what constitutes problematic, inappropriate, or dysfunctional behavior, and what constitutes effective behavioral development instead. Moreover, one's decision on how to intervene is in turn based upon one's conception of how behavioral changes can and do take place, and the conditions one needs to arrange in order to effect them. The practice of psychotherapy, therefore, is always accomplished within a context of more general behavior theory—a theory of behavior disorder, a theory of normal behavioral development, and a theory of behavioral modification and change.

A proliferation in conception and theory has therefore taken place, with the development of theories which advocate different ways of looking at the complex human behavior that a psychotherapist encounters, of identifying what it is that is going amiss, and of analyzing how the problem operates and what needs to be and can be done to modify it. One can identify dozens of versions of psychoanalytic theories, phenomenological and existentialist theories, relationship theories, cognitive and attitudinal theories, behaviorist and neobehaviorist learning theories, almost *ad infinitum*. And these theories utilize differing concepts, focus upon different units of behavior, utilize differing propositions to account for the ways in which behaviors work, and suggest different arrangements and conditions which need to be established by which to effect changes in the behaviors of concern.

Finally, there has been a lateral proliferation in the number and variety of people associated with the practice of counseling and psychotherapy. From a limited number of medical practitioners, the knowledges and skills associated with the utilization of psychotherapeutic procedures has extended to social workers, clinical and counseling psychologists, corrections workers, the cleric and legal professions, guidance counselors in public schools at both the elementary and secondary levels of education, and many, many more. Such interviewing, counseling, and treatment method-

ologies have become intertwined within many human service systems far beyond the medical contexts in which they originated. Workers in all the major human service systems—education, the administration of justice, welfare, public health, and community development—are involved in the utilization of such procedures. And it has proliferated in the direction of the paraprofessional and the subprofessional as well.

One can legitimately ask at this point whether there is a definable realm of psychotherapy any longer, and what the justification is in continuing to speak of it as a field. It has become increasingly clear that these procedures which operate under the label of psychotherapy no longer represent an homogenous grouping. Psychotherapy as currently practiced is not a unitary process, applied to unitary problems, by a set of professionals with a definable background and training and a common set of criteria by which the fruits of their labors can be evaluated. What is the justification, one may well ask, of placing psychodrama or behavioral rehearsal tactics, or operant conditioning procedures, within the same domain and side-by-side with the psychoanalytic procedure of 600 hourly sessions, and regarding them as belonging to the same generic family? On the surface at least there appears to be little in the way of homogeneity; phenotypically they appear to be so dissimilar that one is impressed with the heterogeneity which characterizes the "field" instead.

One suspects that they continue to be categorized in this fashion because of a continuing conviction that they are inherently interrelated even if superficially those relationships are not all that apparent. Interrelationships ought to be there in principle, if only they can become discovered. All these approaches deal with various facets of the complex human being as he operates within complex social settings; they are all focused upon effecting some modifications in the person's behavioral state of affairs; and successful changes appear to be associated with the implementation of many, if not all, of them. In principle, for example, there ought to be some way conceptually to interrelate and thereby understand how it is that electroconvulsive therapy, extended verbal conversations, antidepressant medication, or a job-change would all appear to be effective for interrupting an ongoing depressive syndrome.

We share with a growing body of scholars the conviction that the heterogeneity of theory and method that has taken place over the last century obscures some underlying interrelationships, and that the task at this juncture is one of sorting out the interrelationships which are presumed to exist. We believe that interrelationships do exist and that they will be identified and verified if they are sought. The most likely outcome of such a search would appear to be more adequate and comprehensive theoretic formulations.

It seems reasonable to suppose that a first step in such a task would require a survey of the heterogeneity which has taken place and to seek whatever common threads or themes which are discernible in this elaboration. But, the thought of doing so (especially in the course of a single chapter) gives one pause, since a review of this diversity, if carefully enumerated, would result in a staggering and encyclopedic listing of literally hundreds of permutations and combinations of objectives, theories, procedures, and practitioners. It has, in short, become an overwhelming task to attempt to encompass this diversity in comprehensive fashion, without arbitrarily eliminating whole segments of the field of psychotherapy and behavioral change, and committing the unacceptable but tempting error of serious oversimplification. Moreover, it is not simply that they are unduly numerous, but rather that they are not easily and effectively related to one another. Many of these developments have proceeded in linear fashion, developed semi-independently, and because they have been articulated by different sets of people working from different knowledge backgrounds in different discipline contexts, they have been emerging in relatively segmented form. It is not too strong a statement to assert that this "field" we are dealing with is a multifaceted, heterogeneous aggregate of conflicting, competing, segmented and unarticulated versions of theories, practices, practitioners, and researchers.

We can no longer remain satisfied with the rich elaboration of alternatives resulting from past efforts, however, and some efforts must be made to work toward the goal of comprehensive new theories of behavior development and behavior change to which our growing assortment of therapeutic techniques can be systematically related. This chapter represents an effort, hesitant and groping in many respects, in that direction.

The purpose of this chapter, then, is to try to enunciate some general observations concerning the problems associated with this task, which the writers have formed after a decade of involvement in the field. It represents an effort to remark upon *some* of the trends that appear to be salient, and to try to articulate *some* of the implications which they would appear to hold for future development. The emphasis throughout lies on the phrase *some perspectives on*, which appears in the chapter title. There is no effort to present the developments which have taken place in detailed historical chronology, but to paint a pattern with broadened strokes; correspondingly, a concern with some of the major conceptual problems attendant upon these developments will of necessity be dealt with in a generalized, hopefully not too discursive, fashion. In this respect the chapter constitutes a commentary on the development of the field.

A treatment of historical and conceptual material in such a way as this produces more of an essay than anything else, and represents a self-conscious departure from the traditional practices of scientific writing. A corollary of this approach, for example, has been the decision to forego the convention of "documenting" each of the points, to avoid a burdensome succession of names and dates in parentheses throughout the text and an unwieldy bibliography at the end. Moreover, since this represents how the writers see the events of concern, a listing of references would all too often tend to be merely citations of others who see it in much the same way! But, such listings are also a way of acknowledging the prior work of others, and thus it is necessary, and indeed very valid, for the writers to disclaim any pretensions of primacy to the ideas herein discussed, since they have been propounded before, and many of them lie within the general professional *zeitgeist*.

PSYCHOTHERAPY
AS PROBLEM-SOLVING

One of the conclusions with which the writers have emerged is the inherently sensible inter-relationship that obtains between what has been called the "problem-solving approach" and the practice of psychotherapy. This approach is a way of conceptualizing what is involved in undertakings such as psychotherapy represents, and one that has evolved in contexts separate and distinct from psychotherapy theory and practice. The potential applicability of such developments to the business of psychotherapy and behavioral change, however, seems impressive indeed. We propose, therefore, that one of the ways to encompass the hetero-geneity that the "field" of psychotherapy represents is within the framework of the problem-solving approach.

The ancestor to "problem-solving" is typically identified to be a volume written by John Dewey in 1933, entitled *How We Think*, in which he attempted to describe the thought processes of a human when confronted with a problem. In doing so, Dewey was interested in clarifying reflective or rational thinking, goal-directed thinking, or problem-solving.

According to Dewey, problem-solving behavior (reflective thought) begins with a feeling of perplexity, doubt, or confusion; others would refer to this as a tension-state, a condition of frustration, or perhaps a lack of drive-satisfaction. The person becomes impelled to eliminate the difficulty, but in order to do this effectively he must follow a rational procedure. If he fails to do so, he can act uncritically or impulsively, leaping to inappropriate conclusions, mistaking the nature of the problem and becoming involved in searching for solutions to the "wrong" problem, and can in effect succumb to a variety of errors, each of which compromises his capacity to cope with the situation and, as a consequence, renders it more probable that the problem remains unsolved.

Effective problem-solving in Dewey's view calls for an entire behavioral organization, which entails the maintenance of a state of doubt while carrying out a systematic inquiry, deliberation, and avoidance of reliance upon a single authority or source of information to the exclusion of other possible sources, the capacity to entertain a variety of different ideas, resistance to spontaneous decisions, and most important of all—the active pursuit of a set of procedural steps in a well-defined and orderly sequence. These Dewey referred to as the Five Phases of Reflective Thinking and they included:

1. The recognition of a difficulty.
2. The definition or specification of the difficulty.
3. Raising suggestions for possible solutions, and a rational exploration of the ideas.
4. Selection of an optimal solution from among many proposals.
5. Carrying out the solution.

Subsequent to Dewey's very general formulations, a major thrust has taken place in the world of applied science, most especially in the fields of professional engineering and industrial management, in the utilization of such an orderly style of thinking, and in the progressive refinement of the approach. Throughout the world of industry and commerce, and including major governmental and military agencies, highly sophisticated patterns of operation have become developed. Sometimes these have become referred to as operations analysis and research; the developments in the domain of RPP & E are also relevant (Research, Program Planning, and Program Evaluation). Most of these, however, have become elaborated around the essential notion, *viz.* that there is a preferred model for orderly thought and action that can be laid out in progressive steps and pointed toward the accomplishment of a specific task, and that the conscientious implementation of such a model materially increases the likelihood that one's objectives can become achieved. It has been recognized, for example, that Dewey's list of five successive "phases" can be broken down into finer incremental steps and that orderly precision follows when this is done. It has also been recognized that Dewey's list failed to include the terminal aspects of the problem-solving sequence, *viz.* the necessity for evaluation of the effectiveness of the attempted solution, and the desireability of feed-back loops into the process, whereby modifications and adjustments can be made in the procedures employed at those junctures where incoming evidence reveals that the objectives that have been sought are not being fulfilled.

Many versions of the problem-solving approach have been proposed, implemented, and tested, resulting in varying "programs" of operation to be followed. It is not feasible to review these in their complexity; we merely note at this juncture that it is possible to refer to these analogous applied fields of study for sophisticated models on how to proceed, and workers in the area of psychotherapy would be well-advised to do so in our judgment. However, one abbreviated version of such a program is represented in the following:

1. The initial recognition of a difficulty.
2. The identification (specification) of the problem.
3. Analysis of the problem.
4. Summary restatement of the problem.
5. Selection of objectives which are to be effected.
6. Depiction of the criteria (values) by which solutions will be judged.
7. Consideration of possible solutions.
8. Testing proposals against criteria.
9. Selection of a single final solution.
10. Operation planning (how it is to be done and who is to do it).
11. Implementation (actuation) of the solution.
12. Subsequent evaluation.

One very significant feature of the problem-solving approach will have been apparent from an inspection of the sequence listed above, *viz.* the contingent relationships that obtain between one step of the process and another. Like any programmed sequence, the satisfactory accomplishment of one step in the process will be determined by the extent to which one has successfully traversed the one which went before. Indeed, that is one of the virtues attendant upon making such sequences explicit, since it focuses the worker's attention on precisely this factor, and where difficulties arise he has some guidelines available to help him to identify where in the preceding sequence the process may have gone awry.

The applicability of this manner of thinking

to the business of psychotherapy starts from the recognition that psychotherapy too is an applied field, and its concerns are characteristically those of task-accomplishment with people who are living and working in real-life environmental settings. Moreover, referrals to psychotherapists characteristically take place in relation to the recognition on the part of someone, whether it be the client himself or others who are concerned about him, that there is indeed a problem for which the psychotherapist's knowledges and skills may be relevant. And this is true, whether the "problem" be stated in gross and ill-defined terms reflecting perhaps a generalized dissatisfaction with some state of affairs, or in highly concrete terms, such as complaints about localized pain.

Thus, psychotherapists can be thought of as consultants to people about their problems, consultants who may elect to collaborate with those persons in the solution of their difficulties. And, one can consider the psychotherapeutic process in terms of the cooperation between one individual who has at hand information about his behavior "in the field" as it were, and another who is something of a behavior specialist, with each of them representing an area of particular knowledge. The one knows, or potentially knows, concretely what is happening with respect to himself and his behavior, but is handicapped by lack of formalized training in understanding what the difficulty is and how best it may be resolved. The other begins with a lack of concrete information about the nature of the problem and the contexts within which it is occurring, but has available some generalized information about how behavior works, and how it can best be conceptualized. He also has at hand a fund of information about varieties of solutions which can be considered for varieties of problems. Whether the problem becomes solved, then, will be a function of such things as (1) the extent to which each are willing to play their part in the collaborative process; (2) the efficacy with which they proceed with their respective tasks; (3) the general state of knowledge having to do with the behaviors in question; and (4) the feasibility of alternate solutions—whether they can be practicably implemented.

The relevance of this manner of thinking to the practice of psychotherapy is not that it is characteristically accomplished in precisely this fashion. Rather, it is proposed that the situation with respect to psychotherapy is much as Dewey suggested for problem-solving in general, *viz.* that there is a pattern of thinking inherent in the psychotherapist's approach to the resolution of behavioral difficulties, that every psychotherapist *implicitly* proceeds in some such fashion to a greater or lesser extent, and that the process would become more efficient and effective if it were (a) rendered explicit, (b) made specific, (c) laid out in an orderly and systematic progression, and (d) followed in conscientious fashion.

It provides a framework, moreover, for encompassing many of the inherent inter-relationships that have frequently been noted between various components in the therapy process—that the objectives of therapy are determined by one's analysis of what is wrong, that one's evaluation of the efficacy of therapy can only be accomplished in terms of what one has sought to accomplish, and so on. Pieced together in a sequence applicable to psychotherapy, the problem-solving approach makes salient the fact that effective psychotherapy will depend upon the systematic and detailed analysis of the presenting problem, the concrete specification of the objectives to be obtained, the selection of procedures in terms of the nature of the problem, orderly and systematic operations to implement the objectives, and some efforts to obtain an objective verification of the extent to which the goals have been achieved.

It is also suggested that many of the issues and problems with which the literature on psychotherapy has been concerned can be meaningfully categorized in relationship to these various steps in the problem-solving sequence. There have been discussions, for example, on the question of how one succeeds in facilitating the recognition of a problem in the thinking of a person who has hitherto "denied" its existence. Many a controversy can be reduced to competing proposals as to how best to define the problem, what is the preferred way in which it is to be conceptualized, what should be the goals or objectives of the treat-

ment to be instituted, in terms of whose values shall the goals be chosen, which solutions are preferable for what kinds of problems, or what are the considerations that have to be taken into account in deciding upon the feasibility of one plan of action as opposed to another. A great deal of the literature has also concerned itself with the implementation of the treatment operations themselves—how they are to be effected and the behavioral qualities of the "operator" that are necessary for their successful execution. Finally, research in psychotherapy can be recognized as an attempt to evaluate the efficacy with which the operations have been pursued.

It is not possible to review and thereby organize the entire therapy literature in the light of this paradigm, since that would represent a major undertaking. It is possible, however, to proceed in such a way as to indicate its potential utility as a framework within which to think about the problems and issues that have taken place in the development of the field of psychotherapy, and to do so by selecting what appear to be several major component steps and to focus upon these in particular. Those that we have chosen to emphasize include (1) the identification and specification of the problem and (2) the analysis of the problem. Foreshortened treatments of several others will be made: (3) the selection of goals and the evaluation of criteria; (4) the implementation or actuation of the problem solution; and (5) the subsequent evaluation focused upon the verification of observations and the validation of procedures. These would appear to be critical areas deserving of comment. The reader will recognize that they can be translated into a somewhat more homely question-form: What behaviors should be changed, based upon the identification and analysis of the presenting problem? What should it be changed to and who is to decide? How is it to be done? How will one be able to establish that the wished-for change has in actuality taken place? It will be possible to make only a limited number of points with respect to each of these topics.

The Identification of the Problem

From the problem-solving point of view the initial definition of the problem constitutes the first in a succession of very critical steps in the psychotherapeutic process, since the degree to which this becomes accomplished will determine the efficacy of the entire therapeutic undertaking.

In principle it entails the particularization of the concrete behaviors that are considered to be at fault, either the specification of the precise behaviors that are occurring which are not considered to be desirable or advantageous,or its reciprocal—the behaviors that are not taking place and that the person presenting the behavioral complaints thinks should be occurring instead. It involves the categorization of the problem in terms of some behavioral concepts (an act of identification and labeling) and an exploration of the problem in terms of its attributes. With respect to behavioral problems, the latter would lead to an exploration of the parameters of the behaviors of concern. Answers to a series of questions would thus be forthcoming: how intense, how "severe," how frequent, over what range of situations does it occur, is it becoming more intense with the passage of time, has it occurred before, and the like. Successful answers to such questions must necessarily develop; clearly, a therapist cannot help a person to resolve behavioral difficulties, or to change the problems in which he finds himself embroiled, unless he can form some idea as to what it is that is amiss.

The task for therapeutic problem-solving is to find the best way to conceptualize what it is that is going wrong. It is indeed a crucial step, since it is from this process that one emerges with a specification of what will be the focus of the treatment intervention (if one comes to be undertaken), and this in turn will form a basis for subsequent decisions as to the objectives that the therapeutic process will endeavor to accomplish, and the kinds of outcome evaluations that will be appropriate to employ. Thus, failure to accomplish this phase of the process effectively will compromise all of the steps that subsequently follow.

It is instructive at this juncture to inquire whether our difficulties in the exercise of psychotherapeutic practice are in any way the consequence of our failures to successively traverse this very first phase in the problem-solving process. It is not long before reflection

on this question reveals that, to a large extent, this has been the case for the field as a whole, indicating that many difficulties in both the practice of, and research on, problems in psychotherapy are at root conceptual difficulties. And it is these conceptual difficulties that have produced much of the heterogeneity to which we have earlier alluded, that is, the plethora of alternate proposals that have been utilized to analyze and to define behavioral problems.

Psychotherapy has become extended over the years as a resource-technique for the solution of a wider and wider range of problems of living in a progressively wider range of people. It has reached the point where people turn to psychotherapists (or more generally behavioral consultants) for help in effecting changes in tremendously varied sets of behavior, and in so doing have revealed the almost infinite variety of things that can go awry with respect to human behavioral organizations. No class of behavior, apparently, has proven immune to the inroads of dysfunction and disorder, and, apparently, behavioral problems can arise in relationship to most situations in which the human is called upon to operate. Patients request help in overcoming problems of sleeping, epigastric distress, emotional turmoil, deficits in memory, marital disharmony, ungovernable rage states, annoying motoric tics, unwanted feelings such as depression or guilt, hallucinatory experiences, academic failure, *ad infinitum*. These problem-labels we have just employed, however, may not be the most effective ways in which to conceptualize the patients' difficulties. Indeed, many psychotherapists would assert that they are not, as witness the number of competing proposals that have been made as to the preferred way to conceptualize behavioral problems. They should be recognized as faulty personifications, deficits in impulse control, errors in symbolization, conflicting self-evaluations, a rationalization, or a symptom-formation, say different spokesmen of different points of view. Thus, it is not just a question of what events are perceived to be occurring, but a question as to how they can be best conceptualized.

We are referring here to the problems occasioned by the lack of any satisfactory classificatory schema with which the field as a whole can proceed. Classification is a way of imposing order upon heterogeneous events by grouping them together on the basis of their similarities and differences. Lack of a clearly-defined, consistently-used classificatory schema leads to a host of difficulties, too manifold to enumerate in their entirety—fuzzy and confused thinking, poor communicability between patient and therapist, useless controversy, and, most important of all, ineffective therapeutic procedures. And failures to effect comparability of conception within and between therapists prevents any meaningful method-comparisons between treatment approaches in terms of their respective utility.

The proliferation of conceptual units as ways to analyze behavioral events in general, and behavioral problems in particular, has developed primarily because of the absence of any single classificatory schema that will serve as a satisfactory basis for specifying behavioral problems. Hundreds of alternatives have appeared because of the recurrent realization that no single one is able to serve. Dissatisfactions with the concept-classes that are available has led workers to develop others to take their place. Their dissatisfaction has often been quite legitimate, since many of the preferred concepts have not fulfilled the criteria of satisfactory theoretic units. Far too many have been excessively abstract, encompassing large and inclusive behavioral units, and have remained ill-defined and difficult to employ with any precision. Frequently they have had low communicative power because of their highly connotative nature, and have precluded reliable use from one worker to another, or even by the same worker on different occasions. Moreover, no one is complete, since it has been characteristic of advocates of differing approaches to focus exclusively upon the modification of certain behavioral patterns with a corresponding neglect of others; we have none that are sufficiently comprehensive to cover all of the categories of behavioral difficulties with which the psychotherapist must deal. We must have a classificatory schema that provides for neurological as well as emotional, physiological as well as cognitive, motoric as well as perceptual, problems. In a word, the field has too many

concepts with which to classify some behavioral events (but not others), overlapping concepts with corresponding difficulties in discrimination, excessively vague concepts producing imprecision—a situation that severely handicaps the development of the field, and of which most investigators have been thoroughly aware. Some workers of a theoretic bent simply proceed to develop more concepts, rather than refining and ordering the ones we already have. Others despair of the multiplicity and choose instead to narrow their focus upon a single approach, relying upon a simplified conceptual base, meanwhile ignoring others. More typical perhaps is the oft-mentioned eclectic posture, in which the failure of any one classificatory schema is explicitly recognized, and bits and pieces of many different approaches are called into service at those junctures where they would appear relevant to understanding the problem at hand. But, in doing so, one adapts to and lives with a problem, rather than endeavoring to find a way to resolve it. Finally, some eschew any attempt on the part of the therapist to arrive at a specification of the problem, relying upon that which becomes enunciated by the patient. If one adopts the view of the patient, however, one may be using a set of concepts that will not serve the problem-solving task any better than they have served the patient in identifying precisely what it is that is going wrong.

It is important to recognize that this heterogeneity can continue to unfold indefinitely, for the human being is ingenious and there are probably an infinite number of ways in which different sets of events can be construed. The present heterogeneity is likely to continue unabated until the field sets itself to the task of developing a satisfactory taxonomy with which to work. It is doubtful if much progress can take place until some ordering of the conceptual domain is accomplished.

To the writers, the need for a way of representing and classifying the multifaceted realm of human behavioral problems in a comprehensive fashion is both salient and significant. It is a complex task, but one that is in principle possible to achieve. We have at hand clearly articulated rules for effective construction of such classificatory schema, and models from other fields that can be utilized as guides. Effectively accomplished, this schema will succeed in conceptually interrelating such discrepant viewpoints as a phenomenological or existential approach with a strictly behaviorist one, presuming that the problems and concerns with which the different approaches are attempting to deal are equally legitimate and expressive of behavioral difficulties. And it will necessarily turn to and incorporate behavioral problems whose detailed specification has been arbitrarily excluded from the domain of psychotherapy and allotted to parallel professional emphases, such as special education, neuropsychiatry, or speech pathology and audiology; it will necessarily cross discipline boundaries and call upon findings in the human sciences in general. It will emerge with an effective cataloguing of the dysfunctional occurrences that can take place with respect to the behavioral organizations of the human in general.

Analysis of the Problem

The possession of a classificatory schema within which to order the events of concern and to arrive at a specific definition of a behavioral (human) problem will not suffice as a basis for intervention, however. Any attempt to correct a problem must logically derive from further analysis. Thus, one must not only be able to recognize and satisfactorily identify the behavioral problem, but one must also know how it is that it works.

The analytic step in the problem-solving process entails the development of some understanding, some way to conceptualize what it is that makes the problem function as it does. Different observers can agree about the events that are observed to be occurring, and they can even agree on the terms by which they will be named. They can, however, disagree violently in their respective conceptual analyses as to why they are occurring as they are; that is, the propositions they develop to account for the causal (functional) interrelationships that obtain between the events of concern. It is axiomatic that if one wants to change or to modify the ocurrence of an event (a problem), one must gain control of or modify the conditions that govern its occurrence. Hence, what one identifies to be the set of determining circumstances

(neurological, physiological, emotional, sociological—behavioral or situational) in turn becomes the basis upon which treatment tactics are devised and subsequently implemented. Different explanations logically lead to different tactics for intervention into that problem in order to effect a change in the manner of its operation.

The difficulty here with respect to psychotherapy reduces to a problem of theory, again a conceptual problem. To proceed through this step in the problem-solving process, a therapist needs a set of propositions concerning behavioral dysfunctions to help him to understand what it is that governs their occurrence, and accounts for how they are acquired and developed, and why they persist in spite of the fact that they are unwanted, ineffective, and inappropriate. He also needs some notions about the outcomes of such developmental sequences—for example, whether certain behavioral sequences once developed are irreversible, or whether highly varied symptoms may result from the same developmental process. If a patient complains of recurrent rage, for example, and that represents his presenting problem, one must question where it comes from (what are the antecedent determinants?), what it leads to (what are the consequents?), and with what else is it related (what other aspects are associated with it?). Answers to questions such as these require a conception as to how behavioral difficulties tend to take place; knowing in general what might be amiss puts the therapist in the position of knowing what to anticipate, what to look for, and how to conceptualize what he encounters. Working from an anxiety theory, for example, he looks for evidences of anxiety antecedent to the difficulty; subscribing to the classic Freudian conception of symptoms as compromise-formations of an id-ego (superego) conflict, he endeavors to "read" from the presenting symptom what the components of the conflict must be, since the symptom-pattern, according to the model, is a partial expression of both components in the conflict-relationship.

Thus, a set of hypotheses, propositions, or principles about human behavior that are rationally and logically interdependent is a crucial piece of conceptual equipment for the effective psychotherapist problem-solver. Unsatisfactory models for the explanation of behavioral dysfunctions will undermine the best of intentions and hours of conscientious effort. We can at this juncture ask where the field stands with respect to the conceptual models for analysis with which it is currently equipped. In this domain, we encounter as much diversity as we have earlier reviewed.

An inventory of explanatory models that have been developed results in an extensive array of alternatives and possibilities. We can list only a representative sampling. Deficiencies in the operation of behavioral organizations, that is, behavioral dysfunctions, are variously represented as (1) compensatory accommodations, which are the direct consequence of some physiological or biochemical process that has in turn followed from the person's genetic programming, or from adventitious damage, toxic intrusions, hormonal imbalances, or some disease process (the somatogenic model); (2) an accommodation to excessively high states of excitability and emotionality (the trauma model); (3) a habit acquired as a consequence of the paired occurrence of contiguous stimuli and hence automatically determined under the control of an antecedent stimulus (the Pavlovian model); (4) a substitutive pattern of behavior in the face of persistent interference with the completion of ongoing behavioral sequences (frustration theory); (5) a compromise-formation acquired in relation to behavioral patterns that are mutually incompatible and cannot simultaneously be satisfied (conflict theory); (6) a pattern of behavior designed to forestall, minimize, or reduce the occurrence of fear (anxiety theory); (7) a pattern of behavior acquired in relation to tension-states of several sorts (various tension-models); (8) instrumental behavioral patterns acquired in the service of a range of postulated needs, drives, or organizational requirements of the organism (need-satisfaction models, for example); (9) an organizational consequent of the interaction between physiological and learned compensatory mechanisms (the psychosomatic model); (10) a behavioral insufficiency in the face of situational demand and interpretable as a pattern of response to the person's situation in life (the sociogenic model). This constitutes but a brief sampling of the multiple alternatives that have been suggested as conceptual frameworks within which to analyze and to make sense of the operation of behavior problems.

Another way to appreciate the diversity extant in the field is to focus upon a particular problem and survey divergent proposals as to the antecedent conditions that govern its occurrence. For example, the literature tends to agree that peptic ulcers stem from a condition of hypersecretion of hydrochloric acid in the afflicted individual. But to what extent is this tendency toward hypersecretion hereditary, the direction a consequence of intense and protracted states of emotionality, or the product of learning? Is it the result of fear acquired in relationship to responsibilities and anticipations of threat and subsequent punishment at the hands of others, or the consequence of tension engendered by conflict? These are critical decisions for the person who elects to solve the problem; what he decides will determine what comes to be proposed in the way of intervention and treatment, and who will be asked to carry it out.

Compulsive masturbation may be "explained" as a substitute gratification for the frustration of heterosexual aspirations, as a compromise-formation in response to a conflict between sexual wishes and the inhibitions of fear or guilt, or as a way of reducing anxiety engendered by perceived failures throughout the course of the day through the exercise of fantasy and the imaginary rehearsal of sexual adventures and heterosexual success. Which of these analyses has greater utility? Are all equally possible, and the task is to find which one applies in the particular case? If so, how does one establish which model is appropriate for understanding the presenting problem at hand? Do some represent a spurious analysis of the ways in which such dysfunctions in behavior come to occur, and the task actually one of discovering which one is superior in accounting for the problem?

Investigators who choose the first of these options entertain the possibility that the same sets of behaviors can result from a variety of antecedent conditions. A headache, for example, can arise as a result of a brain tumor, sinus congestion, excessive drinking, or emotional arousal that has become translated into muscular tension. The range of antecedents is very wide—constitutional, environmental, socio-cultural, familial, interpersonal, physiological, cognitive, and emotional. Often these do not occur singly, but in combination, with behavioral problems typically representing a confluence of a number of determinants acting in relationship with one another. By implication, these different sets of conditions call for different sets of things that need to be done to alleviate the difficulty. It is this general view that has dominated the thinking of American psychiatry in this country, and that accounts for its characterization as "eclectic" and interested in the entire array of treatment procedures that can be mobilized to intervene and to effect changes in the multiple conditions that relate to, and govern the occurrences of, behavioral dysfunctions.

More typical, perhaps, in the strictly psycho-therapeutic tradition has been the tendency to develop and to pursue simplistic models to account for behavioral dysfunctions. One such view proposes, for example, that all behavioral difficulties are in principle patterns of avoidance in the face of fear, and thus serve the purpose of fear-reduction. All symptoms, regardless of their superficial dissimilarity, in actuality perform the same sets of functions; one must ignore the phenotypic differences, and look for the fundamental problem. Thus, compulsive strivings for success and deliberate efforts to fail, although superficially different and apparently serving contradictory goals, are conceived to be in principle the same—essentially patterns of avoidance behavior serving to minimize or to forestall the occurrence of fear. Another view proposes that diverse behavioral problems are all the result of distortions and denials in symbolization, stemming from the person's efforts to reduce the tension emanating from a conflict between what his bodily sensations and experience tell him is good and proper, and what he has been taught to believe. It is conceptual formulations such as these that lead their exponents to specify much the same sets of treatment objectives for their clients and to employ comparable treatment tactics regardless of the presenting difficulty.

There is too much hard empirical evidence accumulating throughout the human sciences to warrant the continued espousal of such simplistic views: the neurological deficits that apparently take place as a consequence of nutritional and cultural deprivation; the impressive association of subcortical electrical dysrhythmias in persons subject to violent and explosive episodes; the high hormonal concentrations of testosterone present in persons characterized as hostile and aggressive; and the highly suggestive evidence of critical stages of development, of "programmed" temperamental differences in children, continuous throughout their development and hitherto presumed to be a function of parent-child interactions; and the compelling influences of group membership in the neighborhood and the community. The evidence concerning multiple and confluent determinants of behavioral problems seems inescapable, requiring multiple models for analysis, and a corresponding conceptual integration of the alternatives that exist. It is suggested that, to a considerable extent, our difficulties in the execution of effective psychotherapy have stemmed from the omission of significant factors from consideration, and most especially those that have been the focus of study by other disciplines and other professional investigators. Our simplistic models cause us to leave them out of our analyses of the problem, and because it did not occur to us to include them, our efforts have been correspondingly handicapped. Moreover, the conceptions that we currently have can be seen to be a collection of part-theories that call for a conceptual synthesis. The field requires a more effective knowledge base concerning pathogenic functioning, one that will not only find a way to interrelate the models of disorder that we have already accumulated and for which there is much presumptive evidence, but that will also become effectively interdisciplinary as well. It is not that the realization of the necessity for such integration is new, nor that efforts to effect it have not been recurrently tried. It is merely that the task remains to be done, and until it is effectively accomplished, the field will be forced to proceed with the aggregate of heterogeneous, conflicting, and insufficient models that become progressively developed, with the consequent inefficiency and therapeutic failures that inevitably follow.

The Selection of Goals

Changing one set of events, characterized as problematic and in need of change, inevitably leads to the implication that other sets of events should take place in their stead. But the question occurs, which should they be? Also, by what criteria does one choose and by what process will the decision be made? The latter frequently reduces to a question of who it is that makes the decision.

Effective pursuit of the problem-solving approach calls for an explicit specification of the outcomes that one should seek. It constitutes a critical step for a variety of reasons. First of all, if one is to work effectively, one must know what outcomes he expects from his labors; unplanned change is likely to be inefficient and erratic. Moreover, the definition of the ends to be sought helps to define the means whereby they can become implemented; the specification of objectives tends to delimit and hence to indicate the procedures that are relevant to the accomplishment of those objectives. And finally, the definition of objectives constitutes the criterion against which the efficacy of the tactic for intervention comes to be evaluated. And once again, the problem-solving sequence hangs together. Any prior difficulty in the definition and analysis of a problem will produce corresponding difficulties in the selection of alternatives (the objectives), and this in turn will militate against efforts to implement solutions and to arrive at successful empirical verification as to whether the wished-for changes ultimately take place.

It is suggested that many of the difficulties occasioned within the field have arisen from failures to negotiate this step in the process effectively. The first and foremost problem relates to failures to formulate specific therapy objectives that are capable of implementation and empirical test. Far too often, in practice and in research, objectives never become formulated in the first place. Without a specification of desired outcomes to which his techniques are directed, the therapist permits changes to occur without foresight and planning, and he reconciles himself to whatever changes emerge. "Beneficial" changes that are observed to take place under circumstances such as this, however, are essentially fortuitous and cannot in any way be ascribed to deliberate and planned interventions by a therapist.

There has been difficulty in rendering the goals of therapy and behavior change explicit and sufficiently specific to permit the utilization of effective criterion measures. It is evident that a very general formulation of the goals of therapy is always possible—to enhance the patient's self-image, to alleviate his subjective distress, to effect marital harmony, or to promote insight into the effect of his behavior upon others. However, psychotherapy is like other problem-solving tasks—a knowledge of the objective helps to define the ways in which it can be accomplished, and specific and precise therapeutic operations are more likely to arise from specific and precise outcome-statements. Moreover, a commitment to global and non-specific objectives simultaneously commits one to global and diffuse evaluative indices. If the objective sought is one of reducing something as vague and generalized as the patient's "dependency," one is virtually forced into utilizing global and correspondingly imprecise methods of assessment with a high likelihood of inconclusive results.

But what should the goals of behavioral treatment come to be? Symptom-removal? A fully-functioning person? Restoration to the level of functioning prior to the advent of the behavioral difficulty? Graduation from college? Effective problem-solving in the patient himself? Should he be rendered open to experience, homosexually proficient, or reliant upon ataractic medication as opposed to his daily quota of alcohol? Should the goals be ambitious and include a thorough-going "characterological change" requiring years of sustained analytic-type sessions, or should they be circumscribed, adapted to the patient's circumstances in life and the resources he has at his command, and perhaps limited to his rapid rehabilitation to acceptable levels of functioning in society? We refer to the continuing controversies that persist in the therapy field, between the traditional analysts and those espousing brief psycho-analysis, between existential practitioners and the behavior therapists of more recent vintage, and indeed between exponents of many differing points of view. There is in fact very little agreement on what should constitute the specific aims and objectives of treatment programs, and hence very little agreement on criteria by which to judge and to evaluate the effectiveness of the treatment alternatives. The field cannot seem to arrive at any conceptual ordering of the range of objectives that have been proposed.

In one sense, *any* objective is legitimate to pursue, and in a pluralistic society espousing a relativistic ethic, one can justify the continuance of the heterogeneous objectives and goals that are espoused in writing and pursued in practice. But in reality there are a series of constraints in terms of what can empirically be done. The field is undergoing a growing realization that certain objectives may be possible to accomplish with various techniques and others not. This has been reflected in a steady desertion of the early optimism of someone like Adler, who presumed that the human person was in principle infinitely modifiable, or the guiding presumptions of the early Rogerians that nondirective therapy was good for everyone and thus no screening for treatment need be undertaken. At this juncture in the development of the field it is widely recognized that treatment interventions can benefit some patients, actually harm others, and render still others relatively unaffected.

The selection of objectives actually begins with one's conceptions of what the developmental alternatives are. One must have some notion of what is possible, in contrast to what is taking place. There is no point in attempting to accomplish something that is in principle unobtainable and where intervention will prove unprofitable. Thus, one's knowledge as to how behavioral development ideally, normally, usually, and hypothetically can occur is applicable. One's theory of normal behavioral development characterizes the behavioral alternatives that are possible and desirable to accomplish. We are suggesting that the selection of goals, therefore, is intimately a function of one's theory of normal behavior development, just as we had earlier proposed that one's analysis of the problem hinges upon one's theory of behavioral dysfunction. The reader will recognize that the two complement one another and in some respects are reciprocal, since it is difficult to determine whether some form of

disordered development has occurred unless one knows how the normal course of development proceeds.

Once more we emerge with the conclusion that problems with respect to the specification of therapeutic objectives are inherently conceptual problems, and they are directly reflective of the theoretic problems to which we have earlier alluded and with which the field is struggling.

Implementation of the Problem Solution

A decision to undertake a treatment intervention implies that something more than the person's behavior is required to effect a change. Some kind of intervention from "outside" the person is considered to be necessary; if this were not true, there would be no need for treatment. Assuming that he has decided to seek particular changes in behavior in specified directions, the psychotherapist must next proceed to arrange for the conditions under which that change will occur. When one arranges conditions, one is performing operations and carrying out a treatment plan. Thus, all forms of psychotherapy or behavior modification are planned interventions, differing only in the precision with which the plans are elaborated and subsequently carried out. Ideally, such procedures for effecting behavioral change will be formulated in orderly, systematic, and explicit fashion; the more this is done, the more successfully the same therapist can replicate them for a particular purpose, the more successfully some other person (therapist or researcher) can replicate them, and the more successfully the effects of the specific procedures can be studied. Just as efficiency in the problem-solving task as a whole is enhanced by the pursuit of a "program" of ordered and logically-sequenced operations to perform, so it is with the execution of the treatment operations themselves.

The field as a whole is replete with a collection of diverse procedures and operations that have been employed in order to effect various kinds of changes in the behavior of people. These procedures have tended to acquire labels so as to permit their ready identification; but these labels also suggest significant differences in methodologies, calling for different sets of operations to be performed in different sequences. Consider briefly the range and variety of labels that are extant in the field: psychoanalytic psychotherapy, client-centered therapy, family therapy, operant conditioning, direct analysis, sensitivity training, desensitization, vocational counseling, narcosynthesis, play therapy, psychodrama, encounter groups, rational-emotive psychotherapy, aversive conditioning, hypno-analysis, milieu therapy, residential treatment, LSD therapy, marathon groups, continuous narcosis, and didactic and reeducative procedures. And there is anecdotal (case study) evidence, at least, that favorable results have followed from the use of each of these procedures for certain sets of problems in some sets of people under some sets of conditions.

These alternative procedures have been drawn from varying conceptions as to how a behavioral change can be effected—how it occurs and the conditions one needs to arrange in order for it to take place. They rest upon different theories of behavior change.

Controversies abound within the field as to the necessary and sufficient conditions for producing behavioral change; we have a suffusion of competing theories. Some argue that conceptual (cognitive) changes are necessary antecedents to subsequent changes in concrete interpersonal behavior; one must change the way a person attends to, perceives, construes, or symbolizes himself and the events around him. Such approaches argue for the promotion of insight, understanding, elucidation of a problem, or admission of hitherto inaccessible events into conscious awareness. Others argue that changes are a function of the automatic effects of reinforcement; one must arrange for extinction or desensitization, or conditioned or reciprocal inhibition, or engage in avoidance conditioning. Still others point to changes in behavior that can be accomplished by changing the situational conditions antecedent to the behavioral problem and upon which the occurrence of the behavior depends.

It is the writers' view that there are multiple ways in which behavioral change can be effected, and that once again the field has suffered from the tendency on the part of its several investigators to develop and adhere to simplistic views. Rather than being a question of either/or, it is more a question of how these tremendously variable and yet apparently successful treatment procedures can be conceptually interrelated with one another into a more comprehensive theory of human development and behavioral change.

It is more parsimonious to presume that all changes in behavior occur as a consequence of learning, and that all learning proceeds in essentially the same fashion, that is, that the same principles govern the modification of all behavior regardless of its type or the characteristics of the person in whom they are taking place. If all behaviors—visual sensations, perceptions, motoric acts, emotional patterns, images, judgments, or eyeblinks—follow essentially the same sets of laws, then the procedures effective with one category of behavior will be effective for all. Much more in keeping with the evidence, however, is the conclusion that different behaviors operate according to differing sets of principles and that different sets of tactics are required for their modification. Treatment procedures for the modification of a conditioned phobia, then, would be different in significant respects from the treatment procedures required for the modification of the way in which a person has come to think. There is further evidence to suppose that different behaviors work according to different rules at different levels of development. Finally, it can be recognized that the concept of behavioral change encompasses a much broader rubric than the concept of learning, since its recognizes that there are many more processes involved in the reorganization of human behavior patterns over time than the concept of learning suggests. One is impelled, therefore, to search for ways in which all of the tactics productive of change can be accommodated within the same conceptual scheme.

Thus, one of the ways we know that change can be effected is by way of an intervention into the physical structures upon which behavior depends. Surgeons have reported prompt and dramatic changes in behavior after excising cortical tissue or effecting a vagotomy. Desired behavioral changes, such as the interruption of an ongoing depression, have reliably occurred following convulsive episodes, artificially induced by means of electric or chemical interventions. Radioactive treatments, recently developed, have been utilized to interrupt the untrammeled development of cellular structures that have in turn led to interruptions, fragmentations, and dysfunctions in the behavioral patterns of various persons. All of these illustrate that one of the effective modes of treatment intervention entails the alteration of the physical structures (and hence the physiological mechanisms) that provide the basis for behavioral organization.

Interventions into the ongoing functioning of the behavioral organizations themselves is an alternate mode of treatment. A large, perhaps the single largest, group of tactics for behavioral change is engineered so as to effect changes within the behavioral patterns themselves. Some of these tactics proceed by way of electrochemical interventions into the physiological systems of operation, changing the functioning of these systems, and thereby changing the functions of behavioral systems to which they are related. The variety of drugs for example, used to affect "personality" and behavior has increased dramatically since World War II. Chemicals are used to induce sleep or to keep one awake, to attenuate the intensity of emotional patterns or to amplify the person's level of arousal and activity, to alleviate pain, and to alter the condition of one's awareness and thereby provide novel sensations and experiences of oneself and one's surroundings.

In popular vogue have been the myriad techniques which rely upon verbal interventions of one sort or another to effect changes in attitudes, perceptions, thoughts, or feelings. Tactics such as these have been in man's possession since earliest times, as witness the efforts of Jesus to produce changes in the lives of people by reasoning and persuasion, or Plato's elucidation of the Socratic method. But they have become elaborated to extraordinary lengths following Breuer and Freud's discovery of the "talking cure," which in effect demonstrated that a particular pattern of verbal procedures could serve to elicit and subsequently to modify dysfunctions in behavior that had proven recalcitrant to change by other sets of treatment strategies. These talking cures have proliferated in all manner of directions, elaborated the diverse explanatory proposals that we have earlier reviewed, and utilized a wide variety of participants in various patterns and arrangements, in order to effect such changes. Despite this variability however, they all tend to rest upon a basic set of assumptions, *viz.* that a person's overall behavioral organization is governed and regulated by his cognitive functions, amplified and attenuated by the emotional patterns that have become associated with them. Changes in the ways in which a person perceives, thinks, remembers, evaluates, judges, and recalls—in effect, construes and symbolizes events with respect to himself and his surroundings—can be effected by devising ways in which he can be led to verbalize those "thoughts." Once they become elicited, they become subject to modification by a therapist, an interested friend, a sympathetic teacher, or a stranger who has been artfully introduced into a group. Since it is assumed that a person's actions are guided by such subjective behaviors, it is anticipated that if the person can be brought to think and hence feel differently, he will necessarily come to act differently as well.

Finally, by way of illustration, one can point to tactics that seek to operate upon the patterns of overt action that a person emits as well. This group of interventions operates upon an assumption that is almost the reverse of the one that went before. Here, the notion is that changes in the way a person thinks and feels about himself and his situation can be effected if changes are made in the way in which he behaves and performs. Athletic instructors have for years been engaged in the process of coaching and rehearsing players in preferred action patterns, which, if successful, result in major changes in the way in which a player regards himself and his capabilities and the way in which he comes to be viewed by other sets of people. Examination panics in college students are often alleviated by effective tutorial procedures in which students are coached to prepare for and to take their course examinations in more effective fashion. By the same token, patients with behavioral problems can be taken through tactics of behavioral rehearsal, role-playing, or explicit reeducative procedures, whereby their methods of coping with various sets of circumstances can be shaped and modified, with resulting ramifications throughout their self-evaluations and the ways in which their subsequent lives unfold.

All of the foregoing treatment strategies seek to alter the properties of the person's behavioral capabilities themselves by means of interventions into various component response systems that go to make up the individual's behavioral organization. An alternate set of treatments proceed by way of modifying (controlling) the situational circumstances that surround the person, and that in turn govern the occurrence of his behavior. Modification and control of a person's behavior can first of all be effected by interventions into the situational conditions under which the person is called upon to behave. One may alter the antecedent situational events to which his behavior is related, and thereby change the probability of response. This approach has long been relied upon heavily in therapeutic work with children. For example, a child who does poor school work and represents a disciplinary problem while in a class supervised by one teacher, may become an effective and cooperative student if he is assigned to a different class with a different teacher. Patterns of debilitating asthma have been alleviated by picking up an afflicted child and simply moving him across town and placing him within a different family context. By moving such a child, one changes the circumstances under which he lives, the people with whom he will interact, and the tasks that he faces, and thereby effects a change in the asthmatic problem. Custodial treatment has for many years been relied upon as a tactic for quick intervention into debilitating patterns in which individuals have become embroiled, such as agitated depressions and dissociative episodes. The damaging effects of a severe agitated depression can sometimes be promptly alleviated by relieving the person of job responsibilities, the frantic urgings of his family and friends, and pressures for competent performance, and placing him in a quiet, orderly, routine set of surroundings where the demands for behavioral efficiency are at a minimum. Similarly, college students who are failing because their curriculum does not match their interests and talents, may change remarkably in both mood and performance if they change to a different academic major. Present day emphases upon community mental health approaches, and tactics of intervention into school programs and procedures, or the neighborhood or community facilities, all echo this approach. Beneficial changes in people's behavior can be materially effected if one succeeds in changing the educational, sociological, and ecological circumstances under which they are called upon to respond, and which in turn significantly govern the pattern of their behavior.

A second approach of this kind involves the manipulation, governance, and control of the situational consequents to which the person's behavior characteristically leads. All of us, including the layman in the street, know that our behavior is extensively influenced by the consequences, positive and negative, that follow upon what we do. One view suggests that the situational outcomes determine our behavior immediately and automatically, whether we are aware of such contingencies or not. Another proposes that the human participates conceptually in these phenomena, with his behavior influenced by his anticipations of the consequences of his actions, tending to retain and to repeat those patterns that lead to positive, rewarding, successful and satisfying outcomes, and to abandon those patterns that persistently lead to failure, punishment, rejection by one's fellows, and the like. Both positions, however, lead to tactics that capitalize on the fact that the human's behavior is governed by the kind and timing of such outcomes, and thereby seek to effect changes in the person's behavior by operating on these consequences. Such techniques are of course centuries old, but have received recent and more sophisticated attention at the hands of the behavior therapists.

A variety of manipulations of this sort are possible. In those instances in which a desired pattern of behavior is not taking place, systematic and scheduled tactics of reward (food, candy, special privileges, tokens, or money) can be utilized to "reinforce" and thereby increase the likelihood of their occurrence. Correspondingly, negative and aversive consequences can be applied (punishment, scolding, or mild electric shock) in those instances where unwanted or undesirable behavior patterns are tending to occur. In addition, arrangements can be made whereby no obvious consequent, positive or negative, is permitted to take place. Frequently this can be employed in those instances where inappropriate or unwanted behaviors are apparently maintained because they have been leading to the unwitting reinforcement by other sets of people, as for example where a child's temper tantrums have been eliciting expressions of concern and prompt attention from otherwise neglectful parents. Finally, various combinations can be effected, as in the newly emerging systems of contingency management in institutional settings, whereby arrangements of rewards and punishments are reported to effect remarkable changes as long as they are conducted systematically, consistently, and on an institution-wide basis.

The point in quickly scanning these various options is to emphasize that all of them constitute effective methods by which to intervene and change the way a person behaves. The task that faces the therapy field is to find a way in which they can be conceptually interrelated, and then secondly to articulate the conditions under which specific tactics are appropriate for particularized sets of problems. Relating the task once again to the problem-solving framework calls for the discovery of which set of procedures is effective for what set of purposes when applied to what kinds of patients with which sets of problems and practiced by which sorts of people. The field as a whole is faced with the task of sorting all of this out, looking for systematic relationships between the kinds of behavior that require attention (modification), the explanations as to how they work, and the procedures for intervention that are relevant for producing the changes that are sought. Eventually the field will have progressed to the point at which it can succeed in analyzing a person's behavioral situation, deciding what is amiss, and selecting a treatment tactic that is relevant to the problem and that has some likelihood of making a difference.

Subsequent Evaluation

The concern at this juncture in the problem-solving process lies in establishing the extent to which the problem has been alleviated and the objectives of the treatment program have been achieved. It is of course another critical step in the overall approach; indeed, no one is more critical than any other. It is the process whereby the implementation of the treatment program is subject to monitoring, allowing for corrections to be made whenever performance deviates significantly from expectations, and for the decision to be made to terminate when it would appear that the objectives of the treatment have been achieved. To accomplish these purposes, the following elements are characteristically required: (1) the presence of a standard (the objective or the criterion); (2) the measurement of performance; and (3) a comparison of performance against the standard leading to (4) corrective or terminating action. It is a process whereby information with respect to the impact of the "solution" is generated and fed back into the system.

It will be evident, of course, that arrangements for monitoring the performance of a problem-solving program can be, and typically are, introduced at many junctures throughout the sequence, providing a corrective capability at successive intervals and rendering it more likely that the process can be kept "on target." However, we have chosen to focus on the evaluative process subsequent to the implementation of the program in order to keep the exposition of the approach within manageable proportions.

The analogy to psychotherapy should be readily apparent. Its objective is some sort of behavioral change, and the evaluative process recurs throughout the therapy sequence. When the therapist sets up the treatment sequence, planning for behavior a to be changed, followed by changes in behavior b, and subsequently behavior c, he has a situation in which he is forced to make judgments that are essentially evaluative; he must, for example, be able to determine that a has changed before he proceeds further. Correspondingly, the decision to terminate a treatment program must eventually be made—whether the desired behavior change has occurred, or whether it is unlikely to occur even if treatment were to be continued or modified. Hence, the subsequent evaluation inevitably takes place in some fashion, whether it be effected through gross and superficial judgments by the therapist and/or his client(s), or whether it be accomplished through the application of sophisticated techniques of measurement.

The evaluation requires a specification of behavioral events of concern, and these in turn are derived from the treatment objectives that hopefully had been specified at an earlier point in the problem-solving sequence. It is the process whereby a comparison is made between the performance (behavior change) and the standard (the goals of treatment). Every such evaluation hinges upon observation, and hence the quality of the observations that come to be effected will determine one's capacity for assessing the extent to which change has or has not occurred in the desired direction. The principles of measurement are basically a series of guidelines for the refinements of such observations; hence, effective evaluation depends upon the availability of independent, reliable, and objective measures of behavioral change.

Only a brief review of the field's position with respect to its capabilities for effective outcome-evaluation will be pursued at this juncture, since many of the problems have been anticipated in the discussions concerning the earlier phases of the problem-solving sequence. This is because of the inherent dependency of the process of subsequent evaluation on the steps that have gone before.

Unfortunately this is one of those places where the field as a whole stands least well-equipped, and many of our perplexities concerning what constitutes effective as opposed to ineffective problem-solving tactics stem from our failures to execute this step in a satisfactory fashion. First of all, it is often haphazardly done. Under the pressure of day-to-day treatment responsibilities in the typical human service setting, therapists and behavioral consultants are often forced to use treatment interventions without taking time to evaluate their effects carefully. A high proportion of cases merely lapse, perhaps reflecting a decision on the part of the client to discontinue, and with the therapist in effect abandoning the responsibility for making the evaluative judgment and emerging with no real knowledge as to whether the problem became satisfactorily resolved or not.

Second, it is characteristically accomplished by means of naturalistic (clinical) observation without the use of standardized evaluative procedures (measurement), and this in turn stems from the comparative absence of effective and/or relevant procedures of measurement. It is probable that if accurate and economically administered methods of assessment were available, they would become very widely used. It is not that efforts to develop them have not been made; the hundreds of devices that have been tried and reported throughout the literature are testimony to the repeated attempts of different investigators. The field has dozens of instruments from which to choose: inventories, questionnaires, personality tests, attitude scales, various forms of the semantic differential, and rating scales for use by patient, therapist, or other sets of observers; there are multiple systems for content analysis of interview material, projective techniques of many shapes and descriptions, and observational procedures of ongoing interpersonal behavior; there are measures of various aspects of physiological functioning (the palmar sweat, the GSR, and the plethysmograph); and there are performance samples, tests of intellective functioning, and interest and value inventories; the list could be extended indefinitely.

It is ordinarily supposed that the difficulties that the field has had in reliably establishing that treatment tactics have indeed resolved problems has stemmed from failures to build satisfactory instruments for this purpose. There are of course methodological problems associated with the development of psychometric indices of behavior change—ethical problems that exercise some constraints on the categories of data that can be collected on human subjects, problems of intrusive measures, repeated measures on the same subject, reactive measures, instrument decay, statistical regression and the interaction of such factors with one another. But these have to do with the *how* of measurement and in principle are perhaps not insurmountable. Even more formidable has been the problem of determining *what* to measure and in *which* instance it is appropriate to do so.

The circumstance in which the field of psychotherapy finds itself is directly analogous to that which obtains in the more general area of personality, in which methodological sophistication has outstripped the conceptual base. Experts in the area of psychometrics have often complained that their knowledges and skills concerning the construction of personality tests cannot be effectively employed unless and until personality theorists become more successful in specifying just what it is that one should measure. What one chooses to observe and to assess will depend upon one's theoretic framework and one's conception as to what is relevant and significant for assessment.

All the conceptual difficulties to which we have earlier referred coalesce at the point of evaluation. Too often the conceptual frameworks within which the process of psychotherapy is effected have resulted in failures to specify problems and treatment objectives in concrete and explicit terms, presenting a formidable barrier to subsequent evaluation. In general, the more specifically and concretely the objectives of treatment have been stated, the more readily one can devise satisfactory measures to assess the relevant changes. Where problem-oriented goals are sought, this becomes possible. Where therapy objectives remain unspecified, one has no indication of what it is that is relevant to measure. And where therapy objectives are stated in global, diffuse, and highly abstract terms, it becomes more difficult to be precise, and one remains saddled with the necessity for generalized estimates, subjective judgments, and overall ratings of multiplex behavioral events by various sets of observers.

Finally, too often instruments of evaluation have been employed that have no relevance to the evaluation of the problems at hand, stemming from the practitioner (or researcher) falling back upon those that are readily available whether appropriate or not, being led by his theory to assess certain dimensions of behavior whether they relate to the presenting problems or not, or by the presumption that comparable objectives across patients should be sought whether he has arrived at explicit agreement with his subject or not.

With this brief commentary on the evaluative aspects of the problem-solving process we verge upon the area of therapy research. The prototypic situation within the problem-solving framework is the treatment of the behavioral difficulties of a particular individual within a social context. Even the evaluation of the effects of procedures on groups of individuals ultimately reduces itself to a concern with the behavioral changes within the groups' component members. The goals of such an approach entail coming to grips with the particular problems of the individual patient, and this in turn calls for an identification and analysis of the particular problems that he presents, and the selection of procedures that are not only relevant to the modification of those problems but are also related to a host of other factors such as the characteristics of the subject, the interpersonal and cultural environment from which he stems and to which he returns, and the practicality of the treatment options that are available. It is apparent that the subsequent evaluation for subject X may, and probably will, be different in a number of respects from that which is relevant for subject Y. Such a circumstance places special constraints upon the kind of empirical verification procedures that are both possible with, and appropriate for, psychotherapeutic practice. Research on psychotherapy per se can be seen to fall into the category of problem-solving research, a style of investigation that parallels the workings of applied technology in many other fields, and that is importantly different from other categories of scientific inquiry into the behavioral properties of humans in format and design, and in methodology of execution. We speak here of research *on* psychotherapy, as opposed to research *of relevance to* psychotherapy, a distinction that is of considerable import and deserving of extensive elaboration. Our task is not to concern ourselves with problems of psychotherapy research, however, but rather with a focus upon the conceptual problems associated with the development of the field. It is consistent with this view, however, to note that the vast majority of problems with respect to research on psychotherapy are reducible to conceptual problems as well.

STEPS TOWARD A CONCEPTUAL SYNTHESIS

The utilization of the problem-solving framework as a model within which to review the heterogeneity that obtains throughout the field of psychotherapy and behavioral modification has revealed a series of deficiencies. It has served to emphasize and bring into sharp focus problems in practice and research that other writers have periodically observed. It is suggested that major progress in the field as a whole will be unlikely to occur until some way can be found to resolve these varied conceptual difficulties.

It is always easier to identify problems than it is to arrive at workable solutions, a generalization to which every psychotherapist can readily subscribe. The writers, however, feel impelled to try, and to take some hesitant steps in that direction. The general guidelines for such a solution have been spelled out at various junctures in the commentary that has gone before, representing the directions in which the writers have become persuaded that the long-range solutions ultimately lie. There appears to be every need for a comprehensive approach to all behavioral organizations, functional and dysfunctional, that characterize the human: an approach that will allow for the multiple and interacting conditions that relate to and govern these dysfunctional organizations of behavior; and that will thereby encompass the multi-varied tactics for intervention into these behavioral organizations so as to effect predictable changes in their manner of operation. An interdisciplinary approach is required, one that cuts across the usual discipline boundaries, effecting an integration of the findings from the entire range of human sciences, and thereby providing a more effective knowledge base from which to operate. A broadening of conception concerning the business of behavior change, from narrow views relying upon learning to broadened views of human development in general, is also required.

It will be clear to the reader that one's steps along such lines can be tentative at best, and that the writers will be unable to progress very far in these directions within the confines of a single chapter. The material that follows is included primarily to illustrate some of the developments that are possible, and to encourage others to pursue a similar intent.

One starts with the straightforward observation that a human's behavior is not just an aggregate of segmented response processes. There is some organization to it that provides continuity and makes possible effective action. The task is to find a conceptual framework within which one can make some sense out of the varied complexities of human behavior with which the psychotherapist and various behavioral change-agents must deal. This framework must be such as to encompass the great variety of human behavior that we know to exist, and with which behavioral specialists interested in helping people with their behavioral problems must constantly deal—including vegetative responses as particular as body temperature control, subjective responses such as emotions and thoughts, and the phenomena of human awareness, all the way up to complicated motoric patterns and sequences. And in doing so it must provide for the interrelationships between these patterns and sequences that reflect the highly organized and systematic nature of behavior, where each aspect of the organism must work in close harmony with other aspects and with its environment, in order to maintain the integrity of the entire system.

There appear to be four major component subsystems of behavior that have emerged as domains for research and theory, each with characteristics of its own, but each operating in patterned interrelationships with each other.

Biological Systems. The first major component might be thought of collectively as an organization of biological systems of behavior. This component would include all of the vegetative functions that keep the physical body alive and in working order. They represent the absolutely essential base for all of human activity. Respiration must occur. Food substances must be transformed into functional form. Blood must circulate; it must not contain too much carbon dioxide, nor too much nor too little sugar; and it must be maintained within certain limits of acidity and alkalinity. Body temperature and water balance must be maintained within narrow limits. Elimination of waste products must occur. All of these illustrate the many self-regulatory biological systems that must function in an interrelated fashion in order to maintain life.

Moreover, all other human behavior depends upon, and is therefore interrelated with, the effective functioning of these systems.

Not only do all other behaviors depend upon this behavioral-system substrate, but these biological systems may also be modified or disrupted as a consequence of what takes place within other response systems of the organism. A great deal of empirical data has been accumulated that illustrates the multiple ways in which operation of these various systems can be affected by one's activities, the range and intensity of the emotional states through which one proceeds, and the like. Even one's attention apparently affects the automaticity of these functions, as evidenced by the ways in which the smooth and automatic functioning of the cardiovascular and respiratory systems can become disrupted and rendered asynchronous by the excessive attention afforded their operation by fear-laden, hypochondriacal people.

Transactional Systems. The biological systems are not completely self-enclosed systems. Their successful functioning depends upon continual inputs of energy and information from sources outside the person. This in turn requires the capabilities for movement in and manipulation of the environment. Throughout his evolutionary development, man has evolved systems of sensory and motor apparatus that enable him to perform these functions. The term transactional system seems appropriate, since it is through this response realm that man's information about, and manipulation of, his environment must occur, and recent neurophysiological evidence of the interrelationships between sensory and motor activity argues for the utility of viewing these behavioral functions as a system organization.

The responses in this category, then, are those with which a person engages, manipulates, and utilizes his environment. It is useful to think of man's transactions with his environment in two components. The first, involving his capacity to move around in and to manipulate his environment, might be thought of as a group of motor subsystems. The second, involved in collecting information from the environment about what is there, one's relationship to it, and the consequences of one's activity on it, are frequently thought of as sensory subsystems.

(a) MOTOR SUBSYSTEMS. It seems obvious that man's capacity to move around in and physically manipulate his environment is fundamental to his survival and to his entire personal and social existence. Through these responses he can not only respond to, but can also actively shape and modify his physical and social environment in order to achieve his objectives. He can grow food, build shelters, make clothing, and develop transportation systems, thereby reconstructing his natural environment. He also responds to, and correspondingly shapes and builds, his social environment, evolving communities, informational systems, and patterns of communication. Indeed, it is man's capacity for communicating information to others through vocalization, speech, and various symbolic codes, that represents the principal motoric capability upon which our complex patterns of social behavior have come to be built. The operations of the biological systems are clearly dependent upon and interrelated with the efficiencies that characterize the operations of these motoric subsystems. This is pointedly illustrated by the person who has suffered a cerebral stroke that has destroyed the functioning of the motor subsystems and would terminate in his death were not others available to step in and provide the necessary environmental inputs with which to sustain his life. But these significant patterns of interrelationship between systems of behavior and their development can be seen in many other patterns as well. Deficiencies in motoric functioning in the cerebral palsied have far-reaching ramifications for the remainder of their lives in all domains, since these deficiencies have so much to do with the kinds of livelihoods that they can fashion for themselves, the varieties of social relationships that they can establish, the ways they come to think about themselves and others, and the sorts of feelings and emotions that they acquire. And to cite an illustration in the reverse direction, one needs only to refer to the patterns of hysteric seizure states, or the catatonic stupor, to recognize the effects that one's thoughts, feelings, and attitudes can have upon one's motoric functioning.

(b) SENSORY SUBSYSTEMS. But the motor

subsystems cannot function without feedback information about their performance. Thus, the sensory subsystems are equally crucial to man's transactions with his environment. Sensory reception is a key element in the selection and guidance of the direction that an organism's behavior follows. Such receptors provide the current news from which central selection of particular reports relevant to present and future behavior is made. Feedback through the eyes guides one's hand in picking up a desired object. Feedback through the kinesthetic and vestibular senses maintains body balance and coordinates its movements. Successful transactions with one's environment, then, require a set of systems to act upon the environment, and another set of systems to provide information about the effects of those actions.

In its simplest terms, blindness represents a deficiency in only one component of human behavioral systems. Its significance is that it denies the person certain kinds of informational feedback essential for guiding behavior, and that it requires a search for substitute or correlated sources of information. We might expect, and empirical evidence substantiates, that such a deficit has an impact on every other component in the behavioral systems, because of the inherent interrelationships that exist between them.

Arousal Systems. Human behavior is characterized by an impressive variability in the degree of arousal and level of activity. A person may be lethargic, bored, and disinterested; on the other hand, he may be excited, frenetic, or suffused with intense states such as panic or rage. He may stroll in a leisurely way down a street—or dash to catch a bus. He may gently grasp someone else's hand—or squeeze it unmercifully. These varying degrees of emotionality and physical activity would appear to be a pervasive and fundamental element in human behavior and are often recognized as having great adaptive significance. It is supposed that these two major factors—emotional arousal and activity level—may well rest upon some common physiological substrate; but from a functional standpoint they seem to operate somewhat separately and thus are often thought of as somewhat distinct patterns of events.

A great deal of relatively new information has been acquired in recent years concerning the operation of what are typically called the emotional states. First of all, habits of emotional response seem to be acquired only in an alerted organism. In many respects, emotional patterns represent an amplification or augmentation of an existing state of awareness, or, conversely, a diminution or attenuation of that state of awareness. The elevation and depression of other sets of behaviors by the operation of emotions can be seen in many ways. There is considerable evidence to suggest, for example, that moderate emotional arousal facilitates performance (as when a football team is "up" for a game) and renders the person more alert, sharpens his attention, and increases the efficiency of his processing and storing of experiential events (that is, his learning).

There is also evidence, however, that in excessive emotional arousal (such as in panic states or explosive anger), there tends to be a general disruption of conceptual activity and an interference with smoothly coordinated and controlled learning and motor performance. Moreover, different emotional states appear to have differing consequences. Some, such as fear and anxiety, augment and amplify some behavioral patterns; others, such as depression and apathy, serve to diminish or to attenuate these very same factors. Interestingly, there appear to be major individual differences at birth in the biological systems that sustain these emotional patterns; and the excitation or restriction of a particular response is strongly modified by learning.

Finally, none of these emotional states appear to occur independently of the interpretation or meaning that persons place upon the situations they encounter. Much evidence has been accumulated to demonstrate that whether a person responds emotionally (whether his behavior comes to be amplified or attenuated) will be determined by the construction he puts upon the situation that he encounters—whether he sees it as dangerous, attractive, disgusting, or thwarting. The occurrence of these patterns depends upon the person's meanings and perceptual interpretation of events.

Reference was made earlier to the varying levels of energy expenditure. We can remind ourselves that, from hour to hour, the amount of physical effort that we expend can vary considerably. It is supposed that such variations result from a behavioral arrangement in which the level of activity necessary is determined centrally by our intentions as to what we want to perform (objectives) and our perceptions as to what will be involved. The degree of activity (arousal) is determined by the degree of effort required by the situation as *interpreted* by the individual, and variations in the amplitude of response (whether the person speaks, calls, or shouts) will be dictated by the integrity of the physiological substrate upon which the behavior depends. If underlying biochemical and metabolic processes have gone awry, the degree of amplification that is possible will have been considerably attenuated.

Cognitive Systems. It isn't necessary to be a scholar to recognize that man is constantly aware of—and noticing—events that go on around him and the effects of his actions. He compares these impressions with memories of what has happened in the past. He makes guesses about what will happen in the future if he does one thing as opposed to another. He analyzes, plans, evaluates, dreams, or loses himself in a stream of reverie. He makes decisions and he plans and executes complicated courses of action.

Such complex and varied activities, extended over long periods of time and involving actions not only in terms of events present at the moment, but also in terms of past and future events, require some kind of behavioral functions that can organize and control, collect and store information, and subsequently retrieve the information and employ it in the guidance of later behavior. These events are ordinarily thought of as falling within the cognitive realm, and it seems legitimate, therefore, to think in terms of a cognitive system, with various subsystems involved in the different elements of cognitive functioning.

Beginning in the 1930's there was a decline of serious psychological theorizing and research among American psychologists in regard to such cognitive functions. However, since the 1950's a major revival of interest in conceptual learning, thought and judgment, and memory

and attention, has taken place. A major impetus to this shift in focus has occurred as a consequence of important discoveries and resultant changes in our understanding of the central nervous system organizations and how they function. This evidence refutes the earlier view of the brain systems as essentially passive receivers and transmitters of information, somewhat analogous to a telephone switchboard or digital computer, and has forced the recognition that these systems are highly active and constantly engaged in the selection, processing, and transforming of information as informational input takes place. These few comments about the growing evidence concerning the neurophysiological characteristics, structure, and function of the brain systems are designed to indicate that simplified stimulus-response understandings of human behavior are no longer consonant with, nor adequate to, our knowledge of how these brain systems work. The accumulating data suggests that the human brain is a highly active biological process that selects information for planning and guiding future behavior, and all of this is subject to, and governed by, an arrangement of regulatory mechanisms whose parameters are yet to be studied in detail and understood.

Such a view of brain systems and system-functions suggest a corresponding view of behavioral system-functions. One can think in terms of a set of subsystems concerned with the processing, storage, and retrieval of information —a set of processes traditionally referred to as memory. A good deal of evidence presently exists to support the notion that humans innately develop categories of concepts that influence the way future information becomes stored. The utilization of such categories is probably one of the most elementary forms of cognition. It has the distinct advantage of rendering it unnecessary to record each discrete experience separately—a probable impossibility in the light of the huge volumes of sensations transmitted to the brain each day.

The initial categories are not language categories, but probably represent perceptions that organize sensory information from multiple sources. The categories do not necessarily follow the rules of Aristotelian logic. In data processing terms, they may be thought of as analogous to a simple program for handling large masses of data. The categories undergo constant revision, with new ones evolving through discrimination and old ones combining through generalization. The general developmental trend seems to be toward increasingly differentiated categories, subsumed under larger organizing categories. Soon, further categories become elaborated, representing not merely aggregates of individual units of things, but also categories that reflect the interrelationships between things—what leads to what, or, more generally, what is related to what. Finally, the role of language becomes involved. Labels become attached to these varying categories, facilitating the individual's capacity to manipulate them in his thinking. He communicates them to others, acquiring new categories through the medium of language and the like.

Some of these categories become organized as symbolic representations of anticipated events. They may be as simple as the child's efforts to obtain some candy and, perhaps, are crudely represented in his cognitive organization as a category of images having to do with candy; or they may be as complex as an adult's conception of a career as a physician, or the state of marital bliss.

This category of thoughts is of basic importance because it represents the directing element in human behavior. What people represent to themselves as desirable become the objectives toward which they aspire, and this determines what they will seek to acquire in order to accomplish their objectives. And it is in terms of such objectives that they will subsequently evaluate their performance, judging themselves to have achieved, surpassed, or failed to live up to their respective aspirations. A special group of such thoughts are those self-defining conceptions that characterize the kind of person one wants to be. These seem to have a special controlling force in eliciting behaviors directed toward developing or maintaining that representation of oneself.

It is from such categories of accumulated knowledge and information that the person selects his courses of action and guides his subsequent efforts to accomplish his objectives. In his information storage he has characteristically acquired categories that deal with

methods and procedures and alternative courses of action: how to drive a car, bake a cake, write a composition, and follow parliamentary procedure. From this repertoire of capabilities, choices of action are derived. These are the thoughts that select, organize, and guide instrumental actions to achieve the goals that a person holds for himself.

Another category of thoughts can be regarded as primarily evaluative. As an individual behaves in an attempt to achieve the consequences he seeks, he must evaluate the success with which his activity is progressing. Thus, people develop habits of thinking by which they judge what they are accomplishing in relation to their goals. Moreover, they develop thoughts that define what is good or bad, acceptable or unacceptable; and in these terms they evaluate not only environmental consequences, but also their own behavior.

Still another component of these cognitive systems involves the phenomena of attention and awareness. These response processes have been out of favor in American psychology for several decades, but in recent years have been returning to prominence in both theoretical and experimental work. Attention in some respects seems to function as a selection and controlling device. There is a continual input of sensory stimulation from both within and without the person, varying in frequency, intensity, and pattern from moment to moment within each sensory subsystem. The individual attends to some of this information directly, some peripherally, and some not at all. The likelihood of its being noticed will depend in part on certain parameters of the sensory signal, but also in large part upon the goals that are controlling his behavior at any particular moment.

We have merely touched upon some of the very obvious elements involved in cognitive activity, and merely suggested ways in which they could be conceptualized in terms of functional organizations. There is of course a great deal more involved in cognitive behavior— the processes of identification and recognition, the matter of cognitive styles, and/or programmatic strategies of thinking, to mention but a few. What we have rapidly traversed, however, may be sufficient to indicate that cognitive operations and functions are necessarily involved in every single behavioral operation in which a person is engaged, that these cognitive functions are significantly and operationally interrelated with the various other system components of which a person is composed, and that a behavioral analyst or a behavioral modifier cannot effectively proceed to work with humans and their behavior without taking this into account. It also follows that disruptions in other system components will become reflected in the operation of these cognitive functions and perhaps produce a corresponding disruption in their functioning as well. Equally obvious is the realization that various kinds of disruptions (dysfunctions or faulty operations) within such cognitive systems of organization would have corresponding impact upon the person's biological functioning, his patterns of emotionality and activity, and his manner of interrelationship with his environment.

Environmental Systems. Behavior does not occur in a vacuum, and it is always partially determined by things external to the human. Thus, one cannot breathe unless one has air, one cannot drink unless one has a potable fluid, and one cannot fight unless one has an opponent, or communicate without a respondent. In the past, efforts have been made to account for human behavior and its modification purely in terms of the traits the person might have acquired, the type of personality that he appeared to represent, or the need-structure that he seemed to have developed. In a number of respects, however, the interrelationships between situational occurrences and the individual's behavior are so importantly operative that a satisfactory account of the situational factors and their *interrelationships* with the person's behavioral functions is essential to the understanding of human functioning.

First of all, the very operation of the response systems we have been discussing depends upon situational contexts. The effective functioning of the biological systems of the human requires special conditions of temperature, food, oxygen, and the like. The motor systems lose efficiency with disuse—as anyone who had a limb in a cast for several weeks rapidly discovers. The substance and functioning of the cognitive systems are built, in large part, upon the informational processing of situational events. Studies of stimulus deprivation reveal that if an individual is deprived of all external stimulation for an extended period of time, cognitive functioning progresses toward disorganization, impoverishment, and frequently complete suspension and sleep. And the arousal system, whose variability is controlled by the cognitive system, obviously depends upon external stimulation.

Not only do we shape our environment, but our environment also shapes us. The things that occur in the world around us influence the categories of information we proceed to develop. But the situational events that take place in relation to our selected lines of action represent a set of consequences that influence how we subsequently perform. They provide the circumstances that dictate whether the actions are retained within our repertoire as an effective way to accomplish the objective, or whether they become discontinued and others are selected in their place.

Most of the present theories of learning assume that it is the situational consequents of behavior that influence the acquisition and maintenance of certain behaviors in preference to others, a proposition that becomes translated into the various concepts of reinforcement. The entire enterprise of formal education assumes that it is possible to effect and to shape what a person will learn by exposing him to systematically organized and specifically selected patterns of situational events, such as lectures, recitation periods, books, or laboratories; manipulation of the situational contexts within which people are called upon to operate determines the behavior that is prompted and elicited from their system capabilities. And this is commonly accompanied by a manipulation of the consequences to which such responses lead, by arranging for positive events (such as a grade of A) when the student demonstrates that he has learned the specified material, and by arranging for negative consequences (such as a grade of F) when he fails to perform in the desired manner.

It is useful to think of situational events in at least two broad categories. The first represents the physical environment, both natural and constructed, within which a person behaves. Most attributes of the physical environment tend to be relatively stable and predictable, and therefore somewhat easier to cope with, although eliciting what one wants from the physical environment may oftentimes prove to be difficult. The second category can be represented as the social environment, wherein the behavior of people provides the significant situational events, both antecedent and consequent, to the individual person. The family context, the extended family, the neighborhood, schools, churches, and clubs illustrate the growing variety of social contexts that exercise socializing forces as an individual develops from infancy to maturity to old age. Concern over the slum neighborhood, the black ghetto, delinquent gangs, alcoholic parents, broken homes, indulgent and underdisciplined families, and the segregated school reflect the growing realization of the significance of such human contexts in their capacity to influence individual development. In particular, the social attitudes—the evaluations by other people— have a particular impact in shaping a person's behavior, so much so that some theorists have been led to suppose that the acquisition of inappropriate self-evaluations learned from others consitute the root of all emotional disorder. In contrast to the physical environment, the social surroundings within which the human behaves tend to be highly variable and frequently unpredictable.

It has long been suspected that many human problems have followed from a person's inability to develop organizations of behavior that are effectively related to the environmental situations (primarily social) in which he is called upon to respond, and that this inability may have arisen from a multitude of sources. In some instances it is apparent that circumstances have prevented him from developing the cognitive capabilities necessary to cope, for reasons of genetic, nutritional, or educational deficiencies. In other instances it has looked as though the person has been subjected to such inconsistent and variable patterns of child-rearing and education that he was unable to develop a stable pattern of behavior upon which to rely in his dealings with people. Others appear to have been encouraged to develop aspirations and objectives that are not in realistic accord with the environmental constraints and possibilities, or have not been

helped to acquire the relevant instrumental behavior-sequences with which to accomplish those objectives, presuming them to be possible of attainment. In other situations, the aspirations and capabilities are appropriate and relevant, but the people in the person's social surroundings (his family, the neighborhood, the community) either planfully or unwittingly behave in such a way as to bar him from the resources he needs to carry out his objectives, restrain him from the social interactions necessary to effect his goals, or derogate his incipient efforts to move in the direction of his aspirations. Still others have apparently developed incompatible patterns of response in relation to people—cooperative versus antagonistic, and trusting versus fearful—producing ambivalent attitudes and conflicting behaviors, making it difficult for them to interact with others in the consistent and effective partnerships that everyone requires in order to accomplish his developmental objectives.

By the same token, it is often supposed that persons with the least likelihood of encountering behavioral problems are those who have developed in such a way as to have acquired a highly flexible and richly varied repertoire of patterns of interpersonal interaction, permitting them to relate effectively with the highly variable social situations that they successively encounter. This is looking at behavioral functioning from a cross-sectional point of view. Viewing it in developmental perspective, one can recognize that the evolution of behavioral organizations that are both functional and effective calls for a comparable flexibility and modifiability. For example, a child may have learned that by screaming, crying, and pounding his head on the floor, he could get his parents to do what he wanted at home. When he starts school he is likely to try to utilize this same behavior pattern on a new adult figure. However, it will probably prove to be ineffective, thus disrupting an old behavior pattern and requiring the development of a new one.

Changing situational contexts are one of the major forces in the development and modification of behavior patterns as the individual matures and ages. The kinds of situations, particularly social situations, that confront the child are different from those that confront the adolescent. Behaviors that were acquired and were effective in a childhood context, may be embarassing and threatening when utilized in an adolescent peer culture. Similarly, the young married adult faces a very different set of situations than does the adolescent, and the elderly are again confronted with major situational changes requiring further adaptation on their part. Thus, human behavior is constantly evolving and changing, both because an individual's response capabilities change, and because the situational contexts that confront him change. The individual pattern of development, then, is a matter of continuous organization, disorganization, and reorganization of behavior patterns in relationship to the goals one keeps evolving, and the changing situational contexts within which those goals must be achieved.

Some Implications for the Field. It is difficult to perceive clearly all of the implications for psychotherapy and behavioral change that such a synthetic viewpoint would entail, partly because it has been represented in such a summary fashion with insufficient elaboration of the derivative details. Serious adoption of such a comprehensive view would require extensive specification in the direction of concrete behavioral events, something that is not promptly and readily done. It seems appropriate to note in a general way, however, a few of the ramifications that appear to follow.

Recognition that behavioral modification is in principle constantly going on, brings with it the realization that behavioral changes will inevitably occur with respect to the human whether a change-agent elects to intervene or not, and whether the tactics that he chooses to employ are instrumental in producing those changes or not. One thing that a psychotherapist can count on, for example, is that the behavior of his client will undergo a change. As most practicing psychotherapists know, it is relatively easy to "produce" behavior changes, but to ensure that they proceed in desirable and appropriate directions is an entirely different story. Changes will take place because the environmental demands, both physical and social, will require it of the person, because the person is surrounded by people who are inter-

ested in effecting such changes, and because the person who is seeking help in resolving his problems is constantly on the lookout for ways in which he can modify his environment or his behavioral sequences so as to permit him to effect the changes which he seeks. The task for the professional or semi-professional consultant who undertakes to collaborate with a person to resolve his problems is one of seeking to effect controlled and predictable change—intentional change—change that moves in the directions that the participants have agreed to seek. This is in contrast to haphazard behavioral change (development), and it is a course of action that will take little pride in the occurrence of fortuitous change—change that occurs concomitant with, but not necessarily as a direct consequence of, the interventions of the change-agent himself. This recognition places heavy demands upon the entire field of behavior modification, since it requires the clear specification of the objectives to be sought, an elaboration of techniques clearly relevant to the accomplishment of those objectives, a series of tactics by which it can be demonstrated that the wished-for changes have in fact taken place and have become a stable and functional part of the person's behavioral repertoire, and finally that the changes that have been identified and assessed are clearly related to the techniques of intervention that have been employed, and not a consequent of many other factors that are concurrently operative in the person's situation and that are producing change as well.

Another generalization of significance stems from the representation of the human as inevitably proceeding along a developmental course. This in turn forces the recognition that any change-agent who agrees to the desirability of intervening within the situation of another person, proceeds to intervene at some juncture within that developmental course. The behaviors with which he elects to deal and the situational factors with which they are related are both related to what has taken place with respect to the past and what is anticipated with respect to the future. A change-agent always intervenes within a developmental context. A fact such as this has many ramifications. It means, for example, that different objectives, techniques, and modes of behavioral assessment are necessary for different developmental phases throughout the individual life cycle. It also means that one cannot elect to intervene unless one takes into account the developmental course from which the "problem" arose and the complications that have occurred as a consequence, nor can one ignore the objectives and expectations (the person's present representation of the future course of his development) that are an integral part of the developmental problem. Efforts to help a deeply despondent and correspondingly ineffectual college student may require an analysis of his educational background and his current academic situation in order to establish whether his aspirations to become a physician are possible of achievement and whether the necessary changes in himself or his situation can be effected in order to accomplish the objective.

What this perspective serves to provide, then, is the view that all behavioral problems difficulties, dysfunctions, or disorders are, in principle, developmental problems. Biological changes, situational changes, and new learnings are continually creating some disruptions in existing response patterns, requiring the organization of "new" response components and the rearrangement of established ones. It is characteristic of individuals that they go through a continual process of organization, disorganization, and reorganization of their behavioral patterns as they proceed throughout their lives. At any one time most of the complex behavior patterns of a mature person may be relatively stable, although it is probable that some are always undergoing extensive transitions. For some individuals, circumstances may develop that represent a major challenge to many of their behavior patterns, as for example the occurrence of a divorce in a marriage of long standing. Biological functions are likewise in a constant state of change and development, and these may precipitate compensatory changes not only within other biological systems, but in the other system-components of the individual's behavioral organization as well. A satisfactory understanding of behavioral problems, then, not only requires an integrated view of the many different components of complex human behavior as it takes place within complex situational contexts and their various inter-

relationships, but also requires an understanding of the developmental patterns, functional and dysfunctional, through which these behavioral organizations proceed over the course of the individual life-span.

The utilization of such a comprehensive framework would also appear to place the heterogeneous and cross-disciplinary tactics for intervention within a slightly different perspective, bringing them into coherent interrelationship with one another. In illustrating this point, it is necessary to utilize many illustrations of strategies for behavior change drawn from a wide range of disciplines, professional contexts, and professional workers. Doing so helps to place psychotherapy more properly in the larger family of procedures for behavioral modification.

It is apparent, for example, that different approaches of today tend to emphasize different aspects of complex behavioral organization, and seek to intervene into different response organizations in order to modify the interrelationships that take place within such systems of events. Thus, some have focused upon direct modification of biological response organizations, on the assumption that changes in such systems will result in concomitant changes within other response realms. Such approaches are illustrated by the internist's efforts to bring a patient's hyperactivity under control through altering his endocrine balance, the psychistrist's efforts to amplify or to attenuate the patient's level of emotional arousal through the use of alerting or tranquilizing medications, or the nutritionist's efforts to upgrade the quality of nutrients that a youngster ingests into his system. Beneficial changes in activity level, emotional arousal, or nutritional input will have far-reaching ramifications with respect to the effective functioning of the person's behavioral organization as a whole.

Some have sought to intervene primarily within the cognitive response systems, perhaps the classic point of intervention within the psychotherapeutic tradition. Treatment strategies such as these have proceeded on the assumption that changes in the way a person perceives and construes events, in the categories of things to which he attends and concentrates, in the conceptual analysis of the problem he faces, and in his understanding of the effects of his behavior on other sets of people, will all result in corresponding changes in other response systems with which they are inter-related. Successful efforts to help a person modify his plans and objectives, for example, may produce extensive changes in what he aspires to accomplish, the behavioral situations to which he elects to expose himself, and the changes in his physical and social world that he seeks to effect. This in turn may produce self-evaluations of success as opposed to failure, resulting in modifications in the way he views himself and leading to extensive changes in his self-concept. This can be an important avenue by which feelings of incompetence and in-adequacy come to be changed, since they always stem from a person's judgment of his capabilities in relationship to some set of expectations that he has set for himself. One can only judge oneself inadequate in relationship to some standard of evaluation; hence, "feelings" of inadequacy are inevitably a function of the person's objectives. By the same token, changes in the emotional patterns may be sought by way of prior changes in the person's habits of interpreting events. As indicated earlier, emo-tional states are closely related to, and in many ways determined by, the way in which the person identifies and construes the situations in which he finds himself; hence, helping a person to change the way he "looks" at and thinks about events and people around him may dramatically change the emotional patterns that come to be aroused and correspondingly the way in which he feels.

For still others, the focus of intervention has been within the complex transactional response systems. Every coach uses a range of tactics to develop finely coordinated skills in his athletes. The rationale for the emphasis upon athletics, of course, has been the aphorism *mens sana, corpora sana*, reflecting the recognition that effective development of one's transactional capabilities has ramifications throughout the entire human system, not only enhancing the functioning efficiency of the biological systems in particular, but having a comparable effect upon the other systems as well. But intervention into such response organizations is not confined to the world of physical education and recreation

alone. Physical therapy is frequently a critical component in the rehabilitation of a patient, whether he has been incapacitated through physical injury, infectious disease, or a psy-chotic break. Frequently it is necessary to teach a youngster some manual or physical skills that will gain him entree into the world of his peers, provide him with a sense of achievement and physical capability to counteract his negative views of himself as puny, unacceptable and ineffectual, and prompt a change in his social image.

It is also apparent that other approaches of today have sought to intervene into different situational contexts, both physical and social, that surround the individual, thereby effecting a change in his behavior. Arranging for parents to provide a youngster with a room of his own is a tactic employed to good effect for solving some adjustmental problems. But more fre-quently the focus of intervention is the social situation in which the person is called upon to respond, illustrated by the frequent tactic of eschewing efforts to modify a child's behavior directly in favor of focusing upon the significant figures in his environment (such as the mother, or both parents together). By changing the factors within the child's social milieu, one thereby produces a change in the events to which the child is called upon to respond, and hence in the events that are eliciting his be-havior. Correspondingly, other approaches do not so much focus upon the social factors antecedent to the undesirable behaviors in the child, as seek to change the behavioral conse-quents to which the child's behavior typically leads. Various family-centered approaches would be illustrative of the former; the tactics of the behavior therapists frequently typify the latter. The recent emphases within the com-munity mental health thrust often represent interventions into entire social systems that surround the person, seeking to produce changes in school systems, educational pro-cedures, community facilities, or delivery systems for the provision of services to the people of an area—all stemming from the recognition that changing the situation in which people operate, will correspondingly produce changes in the behavior that occurs in relation to it.

And finally, some approaches focus directly upon the interrelationships between situations and response, when they seek to effect direct changes in these as they transpire. This is illustrated by treatment arrangements such as sensitivity and encounter groups, where, frequently, the focus lies upon the interactions that take place between persons, and the efforts of both the leader and the other participants are directed toward effecting a change in the person-to-person transactions to which they have immediate observational access.

Then again, it is apparent that, although the focus of intervention may lie within a particular organization of events (behavioral or situational), no treatment approach can ever realistically presume that its effects are restricted to that system and that system alone. Just as the researcher, interested in the reductionistic analysis of the conditioned eyeblink, could never prevent his experimental subject from observing what was going on, reaching conclusions as to what was happening, and reacting conceptually and emotionally—that is, attitudinally—to the experiment, so with a change-agent who is attempting to focus upon a particular aspect of another person's behavior. Inevitably he is indirectly affecting the patterns of events taking place within other aspects of the person's general behavioral organization, and correspondingly, what he is trying to accomplish will inevitably be affected by what is going on within the other behavioral systems with which the events of concern are interrelated.

It should also be clear that similar techniques can come to be employed to intervene in many of these different organizations of events. The supplying of positive consequences to the emission of desirable behavior can be utilized to change the way a person talks (operant verbal conditioning), to change his table manners, or to facilitate his skill in solving mathematical problems. Physical interventions can be used to change a person's environment, restrain his muscular movements, modify the sensory input he experiences, or change his diet. Tactics of behavioral rehearsal can correspondingly be employed to enhance motoric skill, facilitate informational storage and hence memory, or imprint a pattern of social usage through the mechanism of role-play. And in most practical clinical settings, the usage of such techniques is typically combined. Verbal procedures, modeling and social imitation, and behavioral rehearsal, and reinforcement are characteristically intertwined and implicitly, if not explicitly, utilized in relationship to each other. It remains probable, however, that different procedures are differentially effective in producing controlled and predictable change within the various systems of events, and the task remains of establishing the most efficient tactics for effecting changes in the different kinds of response systems.

Much has been made in recent years of distinctions between rehabilitative, preventive, and educational approaches to behavioral problems. The rehabilitative approach has been described as the traditional clinical posture, which responds to the occurrence of a problem or behavioral malfunction and endeavors to redress the balance and rehabilitate the person to a level of more effective functioning. This approach has been the most familiar posture of medicine from the standpoint of the layman. Intervention proceeds after the fact, as it were; efforts to modify the behavioral dysfunction are not made until the problem has become sufficiently troublesome that the person calls it to the attention of others and seeks their help in alleviating it. The clinical posture has led to the development of clinical centers, where professionals are located in preparation for the stream of behavioral difficulties which are brought to them. But, of course, man has never achieved control over a problem until he has achieved control over the factors responsible for producing it, and this has led to the preventive posture within medicine, and more recently in the human services fields in general. Efforts in this instance are focused upon the identification of the developmental antecedents of behavioral problems, and the generation of procedures by which to intervene so as to minimize, alleviate, or actually forestall the subsequent behavioral dysfunction. This has led to the development of procedures by which early detection of impending problems can be effected so as to permit the application of counteractive measures earlier in the game. Finally, there has been an educative emphasis, wherein the effort has been to increase the likelihood that functional, effective, and adaptive behavioral patterns and sequences can become acquired, correspondingly reducing the likelihood that ineffective, self-defeating and problem-producing behaviors will be utilized by people at large. Psychotherapy as a field of emphasis initially arose within the clinical and rehabilitative tradition, but with the growing realization that it was part and parcel of the more general problem of behavior change, came the recognition that psychotherapy fell within the larger family of procedures for effecting the modification of behavior. A developmental perspective shows that preventive and educational approaches constitute tactics of behavioral change as well; they differ merely in terms of the point within the person's developmental course at which the changes are being sought, and the categories of change that one is attempting to effect.

Finally, it will be apparent that different professional guilds have arisen in the past, associated with a focus upon different response domains and/or different procedures of treatment, and they have elaborated themselves in territorial fashion, attempting to stake out such domains in an exclusive fashion. Thus, the physician has traditionally focused upon physiological dysfunctions with his characteristic chemical, surgical, and mechanical procedures. Correspondingly, a guild of psychotherapists has tended to develop whose primary focus has been upon cognitive and emotional types of responses, utilizing predominately verbal procedures. The newly emerging behavior therapists have tried to focus upon objectively observable behaviors such as movements, talking, eating, working, and using varied techniques of environmental control. The social worker has by tradition been associated with a concern for the environmental aspects of human behavior, and in many work contexts has emphasized interventions into the person's familial, social, or employment settings. This segmentalization of the person according to selected facets of his overall functioning has taken place in the face of the fact that the complex human person in the "natural" setting is in principle "interdisciplinary," and that attempts to intervene and beneficially modify his behavioral situation on a piecemeal basis is in principle unsatisfactory. We are now at the juncture where it is patently

obvious that any single field of study—medicine or sociology or psychology or nutritional science alone—represents an unsatisfactory knowledge base upon which to operate. There are encouraging signs that the artificial boundary lines between our professional guilds are becoming progressively porous, that the respective disciplines are "stretching" and endeavoring to encompass and relate to the findings of allied human sciences, and that our training programs, in which the respective professionals are being developed, are coming to incorporate more of the knowledge background and procedural technique in related fields, which has developed in parallel fashion, but has yet to be effectively interrelated.

Perspectives for the Future

The foregoing culminates in a suggested strategy that workers in the field of behavior modification might well adopt in order to maintain their perspective and to remain free of the emotions of current controversy. It is evident that the human behavioral systems cannot be studied in their entirety, nor can their differential responsivity to varying treatment tactics become effectively investigated without pursuing a detailed analysis of the various components of human behavior and their interrelationships with equally detailed and carefully prescribed sets of events. Scientific inquiry necessarily proceeds in this analytic and reductionistic fashion. However, the necessity remains for investigation to proceed on all fronts simultaneously, and whereas a commitment to a point of view may be useful in order to advance the purposes of inquiry, it is also necessary for each worker to see how his own specialized focus fits into the larger spectrum of inquiry. Commitment to a point of view should never produce a closed mind to alternatives, and inquiry along a particular line of investigation should never be undertaken in conceptual isolation. Investigators must constantly be on their guard against the tendency to become excessively narrow, enthusiastic supporters of the validity of their own endeavors and simultaneously disparaging of the work of others.

There are likewise fads within the world of science and professional practice, just as there are fads within the worlds of art, music, fashion, and consumer products in general. Investigators must beware the fallacy of currency, reminding themselves of the undesirability of having their judgment clouded by the emotions of current controversy, as the pendulum of popularity swings from psychoanalysis to client-centered therapy, to existential psychotherapy, to behavioral therapy, and to whatever comes next.

Everyone is working on a piece of the puzzle. It would help if investigators would remain conversant with what the other fellow at the next bench is exploring, and one way in which this can occur is through reading one another's literature in order to avoid remaining encapsulated within one's own sectarian view.

But if it is necessary for the purposes of precision and analysis to hone in on a domain of events and study them in finer and finer detail, there is a simultaneous necessity for a subsequent study of their interrelationships. Just as the fields of biophysics and physical chemistry arose as interstitial disciplines in response to the necessity for studying the interrelationships between the events being explored within hitherto separate scientific disciplines, so in the field of behavioral modification there remains the necessity for some workers to set themselves the special task of developing the interrelationships between the findings of one group of investigators and those of another.

2

EXPERIMENTAL DESIGNS IN PSYCHOTHERAPY RESEARCH

DONALD J. KIESLER[1,2]

EMORY UNIVERSITY

Some Psychologists, members of a young and relatively insecure science, have been known to overemphasize F-ratios, beta weights, and the like to the point that they may not even inspect their original data, or may ignore obvious and basic questions of experimental logic and design. An assumption of this chapter is that the psychotherapy researcher needs first to be an applied logician of science, and is only secondarily an applied statistician. The following discussion, in examining experimental design in psychotherapy research, will focus on the logic of various designs within the general perspective of scientific psychology. While it limits its focus to individual psychotherapy of adult patients, many of the principles developed are also relevant to other forms of therapy.

An assumption, implicit above, is that psychotherapy research needs to be anchored in the more general *science* of human behavior. Psychotherapy is not a mysterious area of inquiry, somehow special and unique, requiring suprascientific theories or methodologies of investigation. Rather, the practice of psychotherapy needs to be an applied science of human behavior modification—no more, no less. Complexities are involved, but those complexities in no way separate behavior modification research from any other area of psychological scientific inquiry.

This chapter will first look more closely at psychotherapy research as a scientific endeavor. Next, it will briefly consider the theoretical models currently directing research and practice

[1] The preparation of this paper was supported in part by the United States Office of Education Grant No. OEC 3-7-061329-2853.

[2] The author expresses his gratitude to Drs. David Freides, John Hollender, and Joseph Matarazzo, and the editors of this volume, for their valuable critiques of his manuscript.

in psychotherapy, and suggest an alternate format for future models. Within this new framework it will restate some old problems that have plagued psychotherapy researchers. Finally, the chapter will consider in some detail possibilities of research design in behavior modification.

I. PERSPECTIVE: THE SCIENCE OF BEHAVIOR MODIFICATION

Behavior Modification in the Science of Psychology

The first perspective to be discussed is the place of a science of behavior modification in the general domain of scientific psychology. The issues developed here will have direct relevance to later discussions of both old problems in psychotherapy research and actual research designs utilized.

Since the topic of this chapter (psychotherapy) has been defined as the science of behavior modification, it would seem obvious that what is involved in psychotherapy research *is* the science of psychology (the scientific study of human behavior), with special emphasis on modification. This is the case. However, this description ignores a useful distinction among traditional science-of-psychology activities, a distinction that provides a useful framework for later design considerations.

Traditionally, psychotherapy research, as a topic area, has been closely related to the field of personality. Most of the theorists of psychotherapy have presented their formulations in the context of attempts at exhaustive theories of personality and personality development. In this tradition, therapy has been construed as personality modification. To the extent that this emphasis has prevailed, it has implied that psychotherapy research must involve itself with the study of the complex totality of an individual's behavior—that is, with the "most adequate conceptualization of a person's behavior in all its detail" (McClelland, 1959). This wide-band focus has tended to separate the psychotherapist's interest from more delimited areas of concern such as perception, learning, social influence, etc., inasmuch as these areas of psychology avowedly are not concerned with the totality of an individual's behavior.

Currently, this traditional separation is breaking down, so that we are seeing increasing attempts to apply principles from these more specialized areas (for example, learning and social influence) to explain the phenomena of psychotherapy. We are correspondingly encountering more frequently the phrase "behavior modification" rather than "psychotherapy" or "personality reintegration." This trend underlines the perspective that the real concern is behavior modification, and models from the different traditional areas of psychology may have important relevance (Goldstein, Heller, and Sechrest, 1966; Matarazzo, 1965). In the light of these developments, the distinction between behavior (personality) modification and other more delimited areas of psychological research is less and less clear or appropriate.

Because of this traditional closeness of psychotherapy and personality, another distinction within psychology can be drawn that has major relevance to the rest of the chapter. The reference is to what Cronbach (1957) describes as the "two disciplines of scientific psychology."

Cronbach documents a general historical distinction between the research interests and activities of clinicians and personality researchers, in contrast to persons in experimental areas such as perception and learning. He calls the former researchers "correlationists," the latter "generalists." The key to the distinction lies with differential emphasis regarding individual differences (IDs) in behavior. The generalist is annoyed by IDs. Since his goal is to control and manipulate behavior, any variation of scores within his treatment cells is proof that he has failed to some extent, and the deviations are cast into the domain of error variance. He would like error variance to be zero, since he is interested exclusively in the variation he himself controls. Correspondingly, he focuses on the treatment or main effects, expressed statistically as critical-ratios or F-ratios. An applied generalist would center his attention on modifying treatments to obtain the highest average performance when all subjects are treated alike—a search for the one best way.

The correlationist, on the other hand, is fascinated by IDs apparent in his data. He de-emphasizes control and manipulation, since he is confident that important trait or motivational systems show their effects across many situations. His goal is to predict variation within treatments, expressed statistically as a correlation coefficient of one form or another. He is naturalistic in focus, being primarily interested in real-life variability between subjects, social groups, or species. An applied correlationist would attempt to raise the average performance by treating persons differently—which is antagonistic to the generalist's doctrine of the one best way.

These somewhat arbitrary dichotomies reflect rather accurately the historical emphases of the experimental versus clinical personality disciplines of psychology. Cronbach argues that what is direly needed in psychology is a rapprochement between these respective emphases, so that our research designs incorporate both treatment manipulations (generalist) and organismic ID factors (correlationist) as independent variables. This argues for the use of factorial designs where two or more independent variables (one at least a treatment manipulation, and one at least an ID organismic variable) are simultaneously evaluated. The focus then shifts from primary interest in either main effects or within-treatment differences to the *interaction* of the organismic and treatment variables on the dependent variable measures. For example, instead of the focus being on the effects of manipulated stress versus no-stress on the state (temporary)-anxiety of subjects, or on the correlation between trait anxiety and various stress situations, it should instead be on the interactive effect of stress versus no-stress on the state-anxiety of HI versus LO trait-anxiety subjects.

A major thesis of this chapter is that much of the theoretical and research confusion present today is the result of confusion about the place of individual differences in our theoretical formulations and research designs. Fortunately, behavior modification as well as personality (Maddi, 1968) and experimental psychology (Gagne, 1967; Hirsch, 1962) all show indications of incorporating organismic ID variables in their theories and research designs. The author contends that these beginnings need to be nurtured and further facilitated. This point will be developed in later sections.

Psychotherapy: Artisanship versus Science

It seems extremely important to make a clear distinction between psychotherapy artisanship and the science of behavior modification. This distinction has not been drawn clearly in the past (for example, Colby, 1964), with resulting confusion regarding theoretical formulations and research strategies or methodologies.

Psychotherapy, whether "action," "insight," or "relationship" oriented (London, 1964; Patterson, 1966, p. 97), is both an artistic and a scientific endeavor. The artisans (clinicians) in the field are more or less adept at applying "laws" (currently inexplicit and vague) of behavior modification to a succession of individuals coming to them for assistance. Each artisan's "laws" or hunches are derived from various current theoretical formulations and from the relatively inexplicit residue of his previous artisan experience. The individual formulations are continually changing, loosely organized, and not subject to easy recall by the particular artisan. They represent the abstractive work of the clinician as he attempts to bring order to bear on the various individual therapy cases he has encountered. The artisan's activity is not explicitly scientific, since there is ordinarily no attempt at controlled observation or measurement, no systematic or explicit statement of the operating laws and their interrelationships, no explication of assumptions, and no attempt at systematic verification of the hypothetical constructs involved. Exceptions to this description are the several artisans who have attempted to explicate their formulations in the form of systematic statements—although we will see later that these past attempts are much less explicit than they appeared previously.

Psychotherapy as an art, then, represents whatever is being done (the artisan's behaviors toward his patients and his cognitive attempts to organize and explain his domain of human behavior change) by practicing clinicians with patients in hospitals, clinics, private offices, patient homes, and the like, throughout the world. Its practitioners apply vaguely formulated principles, with greater or less expertise, producing various degrees and kinds of results. It is a behavior domain of much heterogeneity, uniqueness, and sequential interaction of factors over time. It is a world with greater or lesser excitement, intimacy, challenge, frustration, and satisfaction—but, inevitably, a world with much "noise" in its data. The clinician by disposition, training, or various reinforcements, makes his living in that world. He seems not to be unduly upset by the pervasive "noise," and may find it a challenge, while others look and are repelled.

At the other end, we have psychotherapy as a science of behavior modification. Here we find some reflective artisans taking time out from their endeavors to extract some order from the "noise." Here we find Freud, Sullivan, Rogers, Wolpe, and the like—all originally practitioners of the art—attempting via explicit formulations to bring order out of chaos. The resulting theories more or less incorporate controlled observations and explicit statements of lawful relationships as well as the interrelationship of these laws in a form that leads to varying degrees of prediction and verification (Ford and Urban, 1964). Here, more recently, we also find individuals attempting to apply the "laws" of more traditional areas of academic psychology (personality, learning, and social influence) to behavior modification. Finally, here we find investigators who, through various quantitative approaches in the laboratory and in the field, have attempted to research psychotherapy.

The important difference at the scientific end of this art-science continuum is the explicit focus on and intent at controlled observation and measurement, generalization, explicit formulation, prediction, and verification. It is a movement away from the private world of the clinician's armchair to the public, replicable, and controlled world of science. There are varying degrees of excitement, intimacy, challenge, frustration, and satisfaction found in this scientific world—but, importantly, less "noise" in its data. The important, uniquely scientific procedure is that, through public controlled measures or manipulations, one arrives at or confirms/disconfirms predictions that clarify the lawful relationships operative in the data.

Psychotherapy as a science of behavior modification, then, represents the activity of individuals attempting explicitly to formulate the variables operative in human behavior change, or attempting through public and replicable controlled procedures to confirm or disconfirm hypotheses incorporating these variables—

conducting this activity in the various research laboratories or settings throughout the world.

There can be, obviously, a vigorous interplay along this art-science continuum. Some artisans may be adept at abstracting the relevant variables operating in this noisy domain and, if they take the trouble, of explicitly formulating their creative hunches. These hunches can be useful fodder for our research mills. Likewise, once researchers have established replicable relationships among variables, the artisan can increase his effectiveness by explicitly attempting to apply the principle established. A two-way flow is possible and desirable.

One can perform research in the artisan situation, but this requires at the very least controlled observation and measurement, which immediately moves the activity toward the science end of the continuum. Moreover, the intent of the scientist in "in situ" research is not to study or evaluate the artisan, but rather to formulate or verify theoretical formulations on artisan populations. The scientist, *qua* basic scientist, is not interested in institutional research. Needless confusion and consternation is still with us regarding the evaluative question and the outcome-criterion problem, primarily because the science-art distinction has been ignored. A later section will reinterpret these "problems" within the above framework.

II. A MODEL FOR THEORY AND RESEARCH IN BEHAVIOR MODIFICATION

The Uniformity Assumptions

One of the paradoxes of psychotherapy history is that Cronbach's "correlationists" applied a "generalist" model to their theoretical formulations about personality and psychotherapy—although their research efforts continued to be naturalistic in emphasis. The theoretical models for psychotherapy almost totally deemphasized individual difference variables. What ensued was a quest for the *one system* of therapist behavior that would produce constructive personality change for patients—the search, and later the polemic, for the one best way. With the mystique that accompanied the practice of therapy, it became easy for therapists to think of "the one" psychotherapy that would maximally benefit all patients. As the author has documented elsewhere (Kiesler, 1966), "uniformity" myths held the day. Briefly, the uniformity myths permeated the three major variables of the psychotherapy paradigm: patient, therapist, and outcome. "The patient" came to represent a uniform homogeneous group, much more alike than different, at the start of treatment. "The therapist" came to represent a uniform homogeneous treatment group, more alike than different—hence, whatever he does with "the patient" may be called "psychotherapy." "The outcome" came to represent a uniform and homogeneous patient-change dimension (such as "the process of becoming" or "personality reintegration" or "constructive personality change") that would reflect for any patient the effects of "psychotherapy."

Within this "generalist" framework, researchers came up with relatively naive generalist designs.[3] Groups of patients (almost any patients—sometimes a wide range of diagnoses) were assigned to "therapy." The dependent variable (outcome) was usually some global index of overall patient improvement. The variance analysis focused on main (treatment) effects. No organismic patient variables were considered (such as hostile versus depressed patients). In reading these various studies, it is difficult not to conclude that the treatment was considered to be homogeneous and standardized—that is, the assumption was that within (and often between) schools of therapists, there were no important IDs; one therapist could easily be substituted for another. The dependent variable was uniform, assuming that improvement meant the same thing for one patient as for another.

This theoretical-research framework could only lead to predominantly meaningless research results and perpetuate confusion. Fortunately, other researchers were beginning to consider the effects of patient and therapist IDs on what occurred in psychotherapy. It is abundantly clear currently that patients differ significantly

on important and relevant dimensions (Strupp and Bergin, 1969). Correspondingly, it is equally clear that "constructive personality change" for various types of patients may represent change in different directions on the same variables, or change on different dimensions, or different patterns of change on the same variables—or different degrees of these various changes. Finally, it is equally clear that therapists - providing - psychotherapy represents wide heterogeneity both within and between schools—apparently there are relevant personality, attitudinal, and technique differences.

Our psychotherapy research designs can no longer incorporate these uniformity myths. Rather, they need to incorporate relevant patient variables and crucial therapist trait and behavior dimensions, so that one can assess what therapist behaviors are more effective with which type of patients producing which kinds of patient change (Kiesler, 1966; Goldstein, Heller, and Sechrest, 1966; Strupp, 1964; Strupp and Bergin, 1969). This argues additionally for a merging of the generalist-correlational emphases in psychology, where researchers utilize factorial designs (as recommended by Cronbach, 1957, and Edwards and Cronbach, 1952) that incorporate patient organismic variables with various therapist treatment manipulations.

What is further clear from this analysis is that our current theoretical statements will be of little direct use in this factorial kind of research, since the current major systems (Freud, Rogers, and the behavior therapies) all are making claims to "the one best way." None of them has explicitly emphasized individual difference variables in their theoretical propositions. With the exception of some of the behavior therapies, none has specified exactly what the independent and dependent variables are. None has methodically dealt with the problems of the quality and quantity of outcome expected from the respective therapeutic interventions, or of differential outcome for different kinds of patients. None has dealt with the sampling and

---

[3] For recent summaries of these pioneering but inextricably confounded studies, see Eysenck (1961) and Cross (1964).

other methodological considerations which, remaining unspecified, make it difficult if not impossible to design a test of present constructs (Kiesler, 1966).[4]

Another correlated deficiency of current systems, certainly less the case for the behavior therapies, is that the constructs incorporated in the theoretical formulations are not easily relatable to specifiable and observable behavior on either the therapist or patient's part (Ford and Urban, 1964; Kiesler, 1966). Briefly, the point is that it is difficult to know exactly from present systems what kinds of therapist behaviors are indicated as counterparts to patient behaviors, and along which dimensions of patient change therapist behaviors will have their effects. The therapist behaviors are very likely multidimensional, and the patterning of this multidimensionality needs to be specified, and may be different at different phases of the interaction for different kinds of patients. Similarly, the patient behaviors are likely multidimensional, and the patterning of this multidimensionality needs to be clarified, and may be different at distinct phases of the interaction.

One of the central emphases and beneficial effects of the behavior therapies involves their focus on specifying exactly patient and therapist behaviors. Their theoretical formulations, crude at this time, are nevertheless moving towards greater specificity and operational anchoring, although they have not, to date, emphasized individual differences in their explicit formulations.

The point seems clear that most of our current theories can be of little further use unless they are restated or renovated in more clearly operational directions.[5] One hopes that this kind of restatement will occur, or that new formulations explicitly tying their constructs much more closely to patient and therapist

behavior, and explicitly incorporating individual difference variables, will soon emerge.

A Grid Model

The author has presented a "grid model" elsewhere (Kiesler, 1969) that attempts to exemplify the format in which theory needs to be cast. Figure 2.1 presents this grid model. Notice the three surfaces of the model described by the legend. *Surface A* reflects the necessity for specifying different kinds of patients for which separate theoretical statements are needed—an attempt to avoid the patient uniformity assumption. This simply reflects that, by whatever innovations, we need to be able to identify groups of homogeneous patients in both our theories and research designs. Certainly, our current nosological patient categories will not do this job reliably; neither will a naive "type" formulation of patients. This point has represented our traditional Achilles heel in the whole area of abnormal psychology. Perhaps, by abandoning a disease model, and adopting a more sophisticated behavior model, we will come up with more creative efforts.[6] Regardless, we cannot continue to include heterogeneous patients in our theories and designs without coming up with unfilterable noise.

Surface B in Figure 2.1 represents specification of the kind of changes that should occur in the respective homogeneous groups of patients—attempts to avoid the outcome uniformity myth. It is obvious from the figure that the issue is not "psychotherapy outcome" but rather outcome 1–5, A–E, α–ε, and so on, This shows that we clearly need to specify for patients directionality and/or degree of change on the same or different dimensions (Rogers and Dymond, 1954). Next, a distinction is made between two arenas of patient change—that which should be evident in the interview behavior of the patient (in-therapy change) and that

---

[4] More recent clinical-psychotherapy presentations, since Sullivan's beginnings (1965), have begun to explicitly discuss differential psychotherapy (Abse, 1966; Beck, 1967; Bellak and Small, 1965; Boyer and Giovacchini, 1967; Salzman, 1968; Shapiro, 1966; Tarachow, 1963; Wolberg, 1965).

[5] In Maddi's (1968) terms, theories need much more emphasis at the "periphery" in contrast to the "core" of personality.

[6] Some of the research attempts regarding behavior modification have used dimensions such as general anxiety, hostility, dependency, oral versus anal characters, and need for social approval to arrive at homogeneous patient groupings. This research will be discussed later in the chapter.

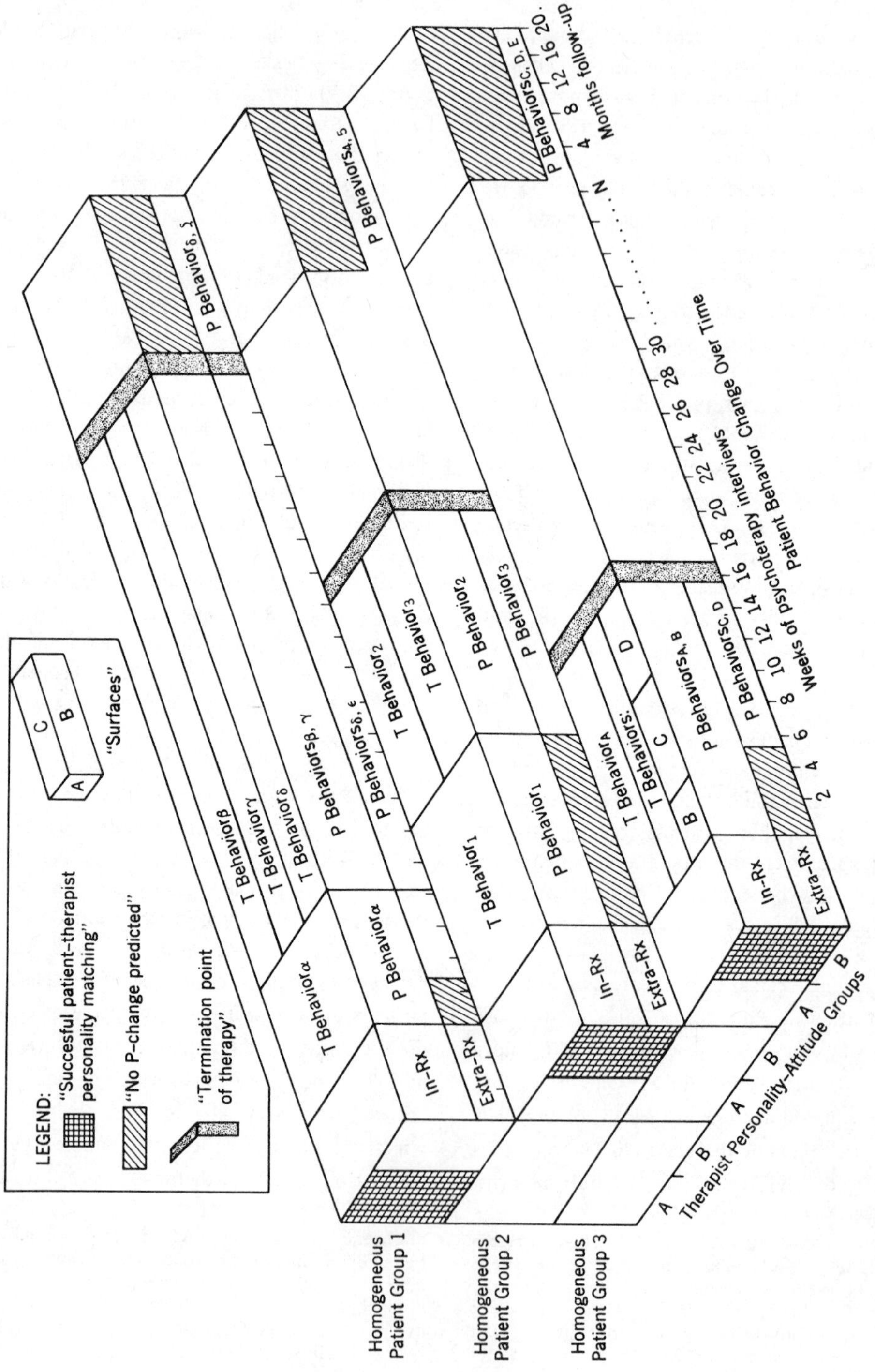

Figure 2.1 A grid model for theory and research in the psychotherapies.

which should be apparent in the patient's behavior outside of the interview—with his peers or family, on the job, and so forth (extra-therapy change). Theoretically, one needs to offer a rationale as to how, or whether, the in-therapy patient changes mediate the postulated extra-therapy changes. Further, the time dimension is specified, as well as the interaction of time with the specific patient changes and corresponding therapist behaviors. Some patient changes should occur early in the therapy sequence, while some will manifest themselves later, and some may not be expected until some time after therapy termination. Finally, the variables of dosage and duration of therapy contact are also included. This implies that for some patients the changes expected should be accomplished over, say, a four-month period; while for others two or more years of contact may be necessary. Likewise, some patients may require brief contacts daily, others may get by with an hour a week, and others may need an hour daily for several weeks with little contact until the next crisis. In any case, patient change obviously represents a complex construct. A move towards this kind of theoretical specificity will greatly aid researchers in making the operational and sampling decisions necessary to assess validly the predicted patient changes.

Surface C represents the correlated factors of therapist intervention that theoretically produce specific patient changes for the respective groups of patients—thereby attempting to avoid the therapist uniformity assumption. It may be that therapist personality type needs to be matched in some way with patient groups, as Figure 2,1 suggests (compare the "successful P–T matching" cells). It may further be the case that attitudinal "conditions," emphasized by Rogers, are important with every type of patient, and cut across patient groups. But it may also be the case that these attitudinal components are necessary but *insufficient* conditions for patient changes. To the extent that the latter is true (and that it is, seems likely) technique manipulations may be very important and may vary with different groups of patients. As the model suggests, therapist behavior is very likely multi-dimensional and certainly sequential. Inasmuch as desired patient changes are also multi-

dimensional, with different changes at different times in the interactional sequence, the therapist model needs to specify individual therapist behaviors, and their points of operation over time, which correspond to respective patient changes.

The research implications of this grid model are clear. First, and foremost, it implies the utility of factorial designs. Further, the most important first step in therapy research is the identification, by the best means available, of groups of patients homogeneous on relevant variables. Sets of homogeneous patient groups can then be assigned to therapists, varying perhaps in both personality type and specifiable technical behavior. The dependent variables of patient change utilized would have to be relevant to the patient group employed. These, or similar strategies, would then permit important conclusions regarding the interaction effect on patient changes of therapist personality and technique with various groups of patients. This factorial emphasis will be continued later when specific research designs are considered.

III. REINTERPRETATION OF SOME OLD PROBLEMS

This section will attempt to look at some old, still perplexing issues in light of the perspectives developed above. It will relook briefly at the perennial "evaluative" and the separate but related "outcome" or "criterion" problems of psychotherapy, will then turn to discuss the traditional "process-outcome" distinction, and will examine the distrust that often exists between analogue and naturalistic therapy researchers.

The Evaluative Question Restated

The evaluative question can be stated quite simply. Is psychotherapy effective? Is there any evidence that psychotherapy works (produces change)? These simple questions obscure some complex factors and mask some underlying ambiguities.

In the first place, the use of the term psychotherapy obfuscates the important distinction drawn above between psychotherapy as an artisanship and as a science of behavior modification. The question is really two questions. First, is psychotherapy as practiced by artisans throughout the world effective? This is, or should be, an important concern of society and psychotherapy practitioners. It is a question of the value of a social institution providing artisan service to members of society. It is a question very similar to: is higher education effective (Hyman and Breger, 1966)? Or is the general practice of medicine effective? Assuming that society wants to know the answer to this question, it is clear that the answer can only come from "in situ" institutional research, where whatever is done in clinics, hospitals, and the like, throughout the world, is evaluated in some manner. Further, since no knowledgeable person in the area can presently deny that heterogeneity prevails in these applied settings (patient, therapist, outcome), it is obvious that one is not evaluating a homogeneous art of "psychotherapy."

The evaluational design issues here are enormous, just as they would be for evaluating the arts of higher education or general medicine. It is obvious further that value questions are of crucial issue. Society would need to specify how much and what kinds of patient change would reflect "psychotherapy effectiveness." Some percentage of institutional cases attaining these criteria might be satisfactory evidence for society that the institution of psychotherapy should be maintained; or some percentage of cases that "improve" (that is, attain these criteria of change) without undergoing the artisan service might represent a base rate for comparing artisan effectiveness. In this regard, the much polemicized "evidence" for a two-thirds spontaneous remission rate for psychoneurosis (Eysenck, 1952, 1961) is invalid (Kiesler, 1966; Strupp, 1964; Truax and Carkhuff, 1967). In any case, if society or practitioners could specify criteria for "effectiveness" in an explicit manner, and hand the criteria to researchers as an a priori yardstick, then likely institutional research designs could be constructed to answer the question. But until that or something equivalent is done, the effectiveness of the practice of psychotherapy cannot be empirically evaluated. And to dogmatize that until its effectiveness is established, psychotherapy artisans should hang up their spikes (Eysenck, 1952, 1961; Astin, 1961) or that society should discontinue support of the psychotherapy institution is equivalent to demanding that graduate professors and general medical practitioners should go out of business until they demonstrate empirically their respective effectiveness.

The other more exciting and heuristic aspect of the evaluative question comes from its meaning in the science of behavior modification. Here the question becomes extremely important and pivotal, and is really a specific statement of the more general scientific question: what's the evidence for your theory of behavior modification? In the past, we have muddled our attempts to answer these important scientific questions by evaluative institutional research, that is, by working in the arena of the artisans of psychotherapy. Many of the early outcome studies were attempts at evaluating institutional artisanship. The studies chose available samples of patients and therapists. The subjects for these studies were any patients coming to a particular clinic over a certain period of time. These patients were then assigned to control groups (sometimes) or to "psychotherapy" with the available therapist population, as if the latter group represented a uniform, homogeneous treatment, and as if therapist differences of various sorts were irrelevant.

Obviously, this kind of institutional research cannot answer the evaluative question directed to theories of behavior modification. Such research incorporates the uniformity myths. One has little idea of the actual therapist behaviors occurring, and no notion of the relevance of the various unknown therapist behaviors to different theories of behavior modification. Basically, because of the pervasive imprecision and unspecificity of this research situation, one can conclude nothing regarding theories of behavior modification.

By restating this second meaning of the evaluative problem, it becomes clear that its answer will come from the future activities of science. What needs to be evaluated is not an amorphous "psychotherapy," but rather, specific theories of behavior modification. The program for this evaluation is no different from any other program of scientific research. One casts the theoretical statements in a form leading to predictable consequences in the observable domain, and then sets up operations that can confirm or disconfirm these predictions. The progressive and successive confirmatory operations then, over time, begin to answer this second evaluative question. One study cannot evaluate a theory of behavior change or any other theory. Evaluation is instead an increasingly productive but never-ending process, since no theory can ever be finally confirmed. Hence, the only answer to this second evaluative question is all future research in the area of behavior modification.

Thus, the question "is psychotherapy effective?" leads to some drastically different issues. The psychotherapy-as-art question can perhaps be answered, if society or practitioners can agree on values specifying criteria by which artisans are to be evaluated. This question is of no direct relevance to science. The psychotherapy - as - the - science - of - behavior - modification question can only be answered by the future of theory and research in the domain of behavior modification, and can never be finally answered. In either case, if we as scientists demand that the questions be answered immediately or soon, we are off course. Rather, as scientists we need to go ahead with theory and research in behavior modification.

The Outcome-Criterion Problem Revisited

Another issue causing much past consternation involves the "outcome-criterion problem." The past confusion with this question also derives from not making clear the science-art distinction, as well as from the inadequate theoretical models with which we have been saddled to date. Further, if one accepts the grid model perspective, then obviously there is no "outcome problem." There is no one dimension that reflects all the patient change in which we are theoretically interested. There are many outcomes corresponding to various groups of patients and correlated therapist interventions. Our search for a universal criterion of psychotherapy outcome reflects in part, therefore, the outcome uniformity myth of our theoretical structures.

The answer to the criterion problem is not complex, although it is difficult. The answer lies

in greater theoretical specificity as to the kinds or degrees of patient changes (in- and extra-therapy) that should occur with various groups of patients receiving various therapist interventions (Kiesler, 1966; Goldstein, Heller and Sechrest, 1966). In other words, there is no one answer to the criterion problem. There are as many answers as our theoretical and research ingenuity can establish. There are no best measures that one can recommend for evaluating the outcome of psychotherapy. There are as many measures as are relevant and required by the theoretically specific constructs of patient change involved.

The confusion of the two separate evaluative questions has likewise obfuscated this criterion issue. The search for *the* criterion and/or the set of measures that should be used in outcome studies occurred almost exclusively in institutional, artisan research. As mentioned above, if practitioners could agree on a criterion or criteria, psychotherapy artisanship could be evaluated. But even if it could, the resultant criteria and measures would not necessarily have direct relevance to the scientific evaluative question, that is, to the theoretical constructs of theories of behavior modification.

Process-Outcome Confusion

The distinction traditionally made between process and outcome research seems to have clouded thinking regarding research design, particularly in the latter area. The misconception seems to take the following form: process is not outcome research, and outcome is not process research. These propositions are incorrect; to some extent, process and outcome are equivalent. Typically, process studies have dealt with the therapist-patient interview interaction, while outcome studies have focused on changes in the patient as the result of therapy. Two unfortunate effects seem to have followed from this somewhat ambiguous distinction. Outcome researchers have tended to focus exclusively on pre-post patient differentiations, and patient process changes have not been considered legitimate outcome.

The exclusive reliance upon pre-post measurement in outcome designs may lead to findings that are invalid or terminate research prematurely. If patient improvement as tapped by a particular criterion measure is not a monotonic function but rather curvilinear in some lawful fashion, a focus on only two points of time may obscure or distort meaningful patient improvement. To the extent that the function of a particular outcome change is unknown, it seems that repeated-measures designs just as legitimately apply to outcome studies as to interview-by-interview process changes. Further, pre-post designs demand that one have highly reliable change measures before he can expect to tap sensitively any improvement that occurs. As Chassan (1962) observes (p. 615): "It becomes apparent that mere end-point observations for the purpose of estimating change in the patient-state after, say, the intervention of some form of treatment places generally severe limitations on the precision of the estimation of the change. For random fluctuation in the patient state can then easily be mistaken for systematic change. To overcome this difficulty, frequent repeated observations must be made of each patient in the study."

Thus, it seems that the traditional process-outcome distinction has perpetuated the relatively exclusive use of pre-post designs in outcome studies, with the unfortunate effect that information about the form of the function that represents improvement between the two end-points, as well as for follow-up periods, has not been clarified; whereas, repeated-measures designs would offer this essential type of information. Secondly, the use of only two measurement points has increased the likelihood that any differences observed may be only chance fluctuations, due to the unreliability of the measures.

The second unfortunate result of the process-outcome dichotomy has been that patient process change within the interview has not been considered explicitly as legitimate outcome. It seems clear, however, that improvement in the patient manifested in his interview behavior, is just as legitimately outcome as any extra-therapy change. Certainly, not all process investigation is equivalent to outcome—for example, if the investigator is focusing exclusively on the therapist, or on one point only of the therapy sequence. But to the extent that one is investigating in-therapy patient changes, he is concerned directly with outcome; and to the extent that one is interested in outcome, he needs to be cognizant of in-therapy patient changes. To put this differently, there seem to be two important areas of patient change: that change manifest in the therapy hours themselves, and concomitant changes observed outside the therapy interaction (in situ). The grid model presented above explicitly incorporates this distinction. Process research begins with the in-the-interview behavior of the patient; outcome investigation begins with his outside-the-interview improvement. The crucial point is that for either to be maximally useful, the other focus or perspective must be considered. It is necessary for both investigators to formulate some clear notion of the dependent variables of psychotherapy, both in- and extra-therapy, and their theoretical interrelationships.

It seems, then, that the process-outcome distinction has obscured the fact that some interview data reflects outcome (patient change); or, said differently, that some of the outcome of therapy may be evident in the interviews. Perhaps it would be helpful to discard these terms, referring instead to in-therapy (interview) studies and extra-therapy (in situ) investigations. Further, since the statistical function of these in- and extra-therapy changes is unknown, one should seriously consider repeated-measures designs in attempting to evaluate the effects of psychotherapy.

The Validity of Analogue Studies

Finally, some comments are in order about previous arguments concerning the validity of analogue as distinguished from naturalistic studies. The polemics focus on how similar laboratory-analogue studies are to "real" psychotherapy (Strupp and Luborsky, 1962). How well is "real" psychotherapy simulated by these designs of analogue researchers? Are the analogue "therapists" equivalent to real therapists? Are the analogue "patients," their problems and their motivations, similar to real patients? Clearly the referent for "real" here is psychotherapy artisanship, that is, how real live artisans operate with real live patients in clinics, hospitals, and the like.

The easiest facet to deal with is the implicit distinction in this controversy between correlationist and generalist approaches in scientific research. Analogue above all else has been manipulative (nonnaturalistic) research. Either therapist or patient behavior has been programmed and manipulated in various ways, and the statistical analyses have focused on the resulting main effects. Naturalistic research, on the other hand, by definition, insists that no manipulations of therapist or patient be made by the researcher; but rather, one studies the natural flow of these behaviors as they spontaneously occur. The focus of the latter analysis is on the natural covariations or interrelationships observed through various forms of correlational research. This distinction will be made again in the next section discussing specific research designs. The point reiterated here is that both approaches have their place in science, and a combination of the correlationist-generalist emphases is desirable.

The crucial issue lies with the generalizability of the findings of analogue research to the phenomena of psychotherapy artisanship. It can first be said that to the extent that analogue research demonstrates any kind of behavior change, it is relevant to a general theory of behavior change. Human behavior change encompasses much more than that occurring in the various traditional psychotherapies (Krasner, 1962). The research is, therefore, germane to a science of behavior change, regardless of its generalizability or relevance to the psychotherapy artisan applications. With this in mind, it becomes clearer that psychotherapy research and theory has focused on a particular domain of behavior change—that of individuals generally referred to as "emotionally disturbed." This label most parsimoniously refers to individuals who, voluntarily or not, are found in mental health clinics, hospitals, private offices, and the like. The implications of those who minimize analogue research is that the behavior change involved with "emotionally disturbed" individuals is likely of a different kind or degree, and clearly is more difficult to accomplish.

These are researchable questions; the issues cannot be decided a priori. It may be that some of the principles of behavior change that work with individuals not "emotionally disturbed" are directly relevant and effective in changing the behavior of the "emotionally disturbed."

This is one of the emphases of the recent behavior therapy approaches. On the other hand, it may be that additional or separate principles of behavior modification are required for emotionally disturbed patients. Research is the only way to resolve this issue.

Regardless, the crucial analogue question is the generalizability of the analogue change findings to "emotionally disturbed" behaviors. This issue should be of concern to any student of behavior modification. It argues for, at some point, replication studies on patient populations when the analogue study did not involve these populations. It argues further for more frequent attempts by analogists to use patient populations in manipulative studies. On the other hand, if our individual-differences measures in fact reflect a continuum along which normal and patient behaviors fall, then research findings established within areas of overlap may be reasonably expected to generalize to both ends of the continuum. In this case, replication on patient populations is not so urgent an issue, although still required in the long run. On the "therapist" side, the issue is not quite as urgent, since it has yet to be demonstrated that therapist training and experience is crucial (Truax and Carkhuff, 1967), or if so, is crucial in what ways with which groups of patients. It is of little use to have an experienced therapist unless one can specify the therapist behavior-correlates of this experience. It seems that researchers have much more leeway in utilizing various types of humans as "therapists" in manipulative studies, so long as one is careful about ethical considerations, and also so long as one can specify the programmed attitudinal or technique behaviors of his "therapist" treatments. And this latter specificity is the real challenge of researchers doing any kind of psychotherapy research.

IV. STRATEGIES AND RESEARCH DESIGNS IN BEHAVIOR MODIFICATION

This section outlines the specific ways (designs) by which researchers have studied behavior modification. The outline explicitly reflects Cronbach's distinction between "correlationist" and "generalist" traditions of psychological research, as well as his recommendation of factorial designs that amalgamate these traditions.

The remainder of the chapter, therefore, focuses on the rationales of nomothetic research in behavior modification: (1) naturalistic-correlational studies; (2) generalist-manipulative (analogue) investigations; and (3) factorial designs incorporating both organismic (ID) and manipulative independent variables. Finally, it reviews briefly the idiographic-nomothetic polemic and discusses methods of single-case study.

Studies cited in the following pages are for the most part few and briefly reported, with the intent to *represent* various research design strategies. For additional references, the reader can consult the various chapters of this volume that provide relatively exhaustive summaries of research. Critiques of the general areas of research outlined will follow the respective sections. There is no emphasis on specific critique of the studies utilized as examples. Because of space as well as author limitations, the general critiques presented are far from exhaustive. Rather, the attempt will be to focus on differentiation of designs as well as design problems and issues that seem most relevant to the author.

Various books have been devoted to experimental design in psychological research. The author considers Underwood's (1957) book as one of the better of them, and has previously applied Underwood's model of confounding in some detail to the psychotherapy situation (Kiesler, 1966). Other quite useful sources, dealing particularly with design problems in behavior modification, are Campbell and

Stanley (1963), Chassan (1967), Frank (1959), Goldstein, Heller and Sechrest (1966), Shontz (1965), and Stieper and Wiener (1965).

Correlational-Naturalistic Studies

In situ research takes the researcher out of the laboratory into various applied settings—where the action is. This research has by far dominated the psychotherapy scene since Rogers' dramatic beginnings in the 1940s. The avowed purpose of these attempts is to capture by measurements the naturally occurring events of psychotherapy. The investigator does not control precisely the therapist or patient factors in which he is interested, and is very careful that his measurement or other activity does not alter in obvious or subtle ways the natural flow of therapy events. The essential features of correlational research "are its identification of variables in terms of measurements of already existing subject characteristics, rather than in terms of manipulative operations performed by the investigator, and its use of a single, standard test situation for all subjects, rather than a different set of treatments for each research group" (Schontz, 1965, p. 132).

Traditionally, this research has been roughly categorized as process or outcome research. An equally comprehensive but more precise way of conceptualizing, as well as summarizing, the great majority of this naturalistic research can be found by a close look at the three major variables in the treatment situation: therapist, patient, and time. The various combinations of this triad cover fairly well the naturalistic research design possibilities in psychotherapy.

Figure 2.2 depicts these three parameters of the artisan therapy situation. The patient is the central figure in psychotherapy, and is

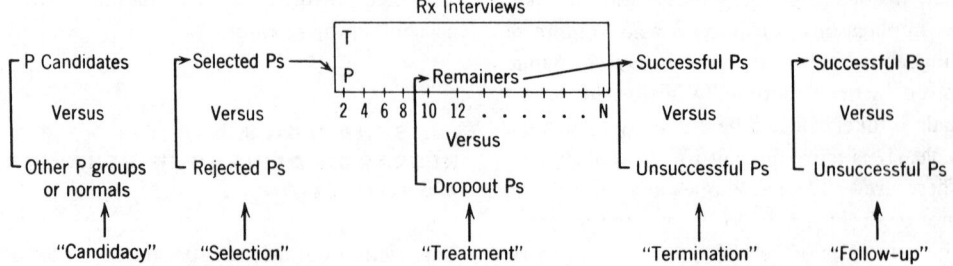

Figure 2.2 Stages of psychotherapeutic treatment, incorporating the factors of patient, therapist, and time over the interactional sequence (P = patient, T = therapist, Rx = psychotherapy).

depicted chronologically as he flows through the treatment process. The five stages depicted (candidacy, selection, treatment, termination, and follow-up) are based on an analysis by Levinson (1962). The figure also shows that at these five gross time periods, patients can be either compared with nonpatient groups or dichotomized by various criteria into respective patient group pairs: selected- rejected, remainers-dropouts, success-failures at termination, and success-failures at follow-up. Voluminous research has studied patient characteristics utilizing these dichotomies. These studies have focused primarily on patient trait measurement, dealing with such relatively enduring and general behavior systems as intelligence, neuroticism and/or trait-anxiety, extraversion-introversion, socioeconomic background (more precisely the correlated attitudinal and other behavior systems), verbal facility, sex (and its corresponding attitudinal systems), and the like.

1. Selected Versus Rejected Patients. These studies attempt to define the kind of disturbed individuals who are referred and/or selected for psychotherapeutic services by various institutions, in contrast to those disturbed subjects who are not referred or selected for psychotherapy. The designs usually contrast the two groups (selected versus rejected) on various personality, demographic, or other variables.

Examples. Hollingshead and Redlich (1958) found that both private and clinic physicians make relatively fewer referrals for treatment of patients who are diagnosed later as psychotic, in comparison to those who are neurotic. Also, in the highest social class, the patient and family are the major sources of referral, while in the lowest class the police, the court, social agencies, and clinic physicians make practically all referrals. Brill and Storrow (1960) found that patients in the upper social classes applying for therapy at a low-cost psychiatric outpatient clinic were more likely to be accepted for therapy than were those in the lower-class group. Strupp (1962, p. 460) summarizes the general thrust of this literature: "Therapists appear to have fairly definite, and probably valid, ideas of what constitutes a promising patient. In addition to being intelligent and reasonably well-educated such a person seems to possess a certain psychological-mindedness (capacity for insight), the ability to communicate about his feelings, a more or less clear recognition that his difficulties are psychological

and a willingness to be helped via psychological treatment. A number of these attributes appear to be linked to social class."

2. Remainers Versus Dropouts. These studies arbitrarily set up a criterion of psychotherapy "dropout" (such as a patient with fewer than five interviews, or one who failed to come for three or more appointments in a two-month period) and then contrast these dropouts with patients who remained in therapy until mutual termination (that is, both therapist and patient agreed that termination was desirable). The research interest usually focuses on personality differences for the two groups evidenced in initial test batteries, or on early within-interview behavior.

Examples. White, Fichtenbaum, and Dollard (1964) divided first interviews (tape-recorded) into silence units and sentence units. Utilizing Dollard and Auld's content analysis system (1959), they scored the units in categories derived from that system.

The fate of eighty-three percent of the cases was thereby predicted correctly (dropout-remain), whereas overall judgments of the interviews by a psychiatrist and a social worker yielded chance predictions. Strickland and Crowne's (1959) study suggests that one patient characteristic that is associated with early termination is the need for approval. They conclude that defensiveness and avoidance of self-criticism may constitute a major determinant of abrupt termination of psychotherapy.

3. Successes Versus Failures. A final strategy dealing with patient dichotomies involves attempts to assess which patients eventually succeed in psychotherapy, in contrast to those who remain in therapy but show no improvement. The success-failure (or more versus less successful) dichotomies are established by various outcome criteria (Zax and Klein, 1960). The outcome assessment can be made immediately after therapy termination, or at various stages of follow-up. Success and failure groups can then be contrasted vis-à-vis initial personality differences gleaned from initial test batteries or by within-interview patient, therapist, or interactional variables.

Examples. Gendlin, Jenny, and Shlien (1960) studied the association between judged success in therapy and a number of relationship factors manifest in the interviews. They devised a counselor judgment scale containing six relationship items and asked counselors to use the scale after the seventh interview and after the last interview. Three of the six items showed significant correlation with overall judged success. Wagstaff, Rice, and Butler (1960) showed that the patient's "style of participation" is related to the course and outcome of client-centered therapy. Patients' interview responses were rated in terms of level of expression, involvement, and quality of participation; then these ratings were factor-analyzed. A "success" factor was characterized by patients who explored within themselves and focused on their feelings and life experiences. "Failure" patients seemed detached and uninvolved. A "varied outcome" factor depicted patients who talked about matters that included themselves, but rarely discussed feelings.

Another category of studies shifts the attention of the investigator from the patient to the therapist. The therapist (T) appears in Figure 2 only in the treatment phase. The therapist (more exactly, some aspect of the therapist's behavior) is the treatment intervention, and ordinarily comes into contact with the patient only during the interview sessions. His intervention there is considered the vehicle of behavior-change-production in the patient, producing effects beginning at the point of intervention and continuing until termination and an undetermined period thereafter. The therapist's state and more specific interview behaviors can be measured only in that situation; while his trait as well as more general habit systems can be measured in the interview or, more likely, between interviews or any other time. The reason for flexibility with these latter measurements is that they tap relatively general and enduring therapist characteristics, which change only slowly over time.

4. Therapists Versus Nontherapists. One can study the trait or attitudinal characteristics of therapists in contrast to nontherapists. Within the profession of psychology, this approach involves differentiating clinical from other types of psychologists.

Examples. Moss et al. (1960) surveyed the attitudes and interests of 171 experienced psychologist-therapists who were members of the American Academy of Psychotherapy. Their study showed in part that those engaged in direct service activities (psychotherapy, diagnosis, and supervision) obtained higher "intuitive" scores, whereas psychologist teachers and administrators tended more toward the "objective" side. Howe and Pope (1961)

investigated the meaning-space within which psychiatrists rate therapist behavior. Factor analysis of their ratings yielded two major factors and a weak third factor which were interpreted as Professional Evaluation, Ambiguity-Passivity, and Subjectivity-Objectivity. In other words, psychiatrists judging therapist activities responded in the semantic differential rating situation with a primarily evaluative attitude (therapist behavior was either "good" or "bad"); only secondarily did they seem to concern themselves with the degree of ambiguity, activity, precision, focus, and the like, of a therapist response.

5. Therapists: Groups 1 Versus 2 Versus 3. A similar strategy attempts to contrast groups of psychotherapists of different orientations, professions, or therapy-experience on various personality, attitudinal, and other behavioral measures.

Examples. Korman (1960) asked psychologists, social workers, psychiatrists, and clinical psychology trainees to rate 11 diagnostic and 9 therapeutic concepts on 9 semantic differential scales. The results showed that the greatest intergroup differences in implicit personality theories were between psychologists and social workers, with psychiatrists occupying an intermediate position. There was greater consensus in semantic meaning between psychologists and psychiatrists than between either group and social workers. Rice (1965) studied specifiable therapist behaviors such as voice quality, freshness of words and word combinations, vocal modulation, and the like. She identified three types of therapists. Type I tended to employ commonplace language and uninflected, unmodulated vocalization. Type II differed in having a larger frequency of distorted voice quality and fewer responses in fresh, connotative language. Type III used fresh, connotative language, with two-thirds of their responses rated as having an expressive voice quality.

6. Therapists: Good Guys Versus the Losers. A much more popular research strategy is to study the characteristics of "good" versus "bad" therapists, the good-bad evaluations determined by their respective patients' outcomes (remainers-dropouts, successes-failures). One first determines groups of success and failure patients by various criteria, and then attempts to pull out from the successful and unsuccessful therapists, behaviors factors that differentiate the two groups.

Examples. Betz (1962) studied the personality characteristics of psychiatrists whose psychotherapy with schizophrenic patients was highly successful (Group A physicians, with an improvement rate of 75 percent of their patients) and those psychiatrists whose success rate was very poor (Group B physicians, with an improvement rate of only 27 percent). Betz found that Group A and Group B physicians could be differentiated independently by the Strong Vocational Interest Blank, with Group A physicians scoring high on the Lawyer scale and Group B physicians scoring high on the Math-Physical Science scale, and each group scoring low on the other scale. Rogers, Gendlin, Kiesler, and Truax (1967) related therapist attitudes or "conditions" (as measured by questionnaires filled in by both patient and therapist as well as ratings done on tape-recordings of the therapist's within-interview behavior) to successful versus unsuccessful schizophrenic psychotherapy cases. They found a significant relationship between certain measures of "empathic understanding" and "congruence" and the success-failure dichotomies, with successful therapy cases receiving significantly higher levels of these therapist conditions.

7. Matching Patients and Therapists into Congruent Dyads. The basic assumption of this group of studies is that effective psychotherapy depends upon characteristics of the patient-therapist dyad. Patient or therapist personality or behaviors considered separately are not relevant factors; instead, the central issue is the pattern or successful matching of patient and therapist. These studies have emphasized the relevance of such dyadic variables as role expectational models, interpersonal attraction, authoritarianism, and cognitive dissonance. A major advocate of this approach is Goldstein (1962).

Examples. Rogers et al. (1967) report a clear divergence of therapist views of the therapy relationship from the views of both judges (who rated tape-recordings of the interviews) and patients. There was a definite tendency for therapists to make considerably more favorable evaluations of the interaction than did their patients. However, an interesting dyadic factor emerged from examining these evaluations when the sample was divided according to therapy outcome. The data showed that in successful therapy there is a significant positive correlation between patient and therapist evaluations of the relationship, while in less successful cases, therapist and patient assessments were

more divergent, correlating negatively with one another. Levinson and Kitchener (1966) compared the effects on group treatment outcome of four different methods of pairing counselors with institutionalized delinquent boys: random assignment, a Q-sort matching method, counselor preference, and natural selection. The authors found the Q-sort method to be superior on all criterion measures: academic grades, vocational work grades, cottage adjustment grades, number of misconduct reports, number of boys paroled, and number of boys transferred.

The preceding studies focused on therapist state and specific behaviors as well as attitudinal behaviors manifest in the interview interaction itself. One can also study the corresponding patient within-interview behaviors.

8. Patient or Therapist Interview Studies: Repeated Measures. With the addition of interview data, the design possibilities increase markedly. One now can study patient or therapist interview behavior within particular therapy sessions (early to late in the 50-minute hour) or across the treatment sequence (first interview to terminal interview). These investigations take the form of repeated measures studies looking at sequential measures of the same patient or therapist behavior to assess its relative stability-consistency or instability-change over the therapy intervention.

Examples. Kiesler, Klein, and Mathieu (1965) examined the trend of patient Experiencing (a measure of depth of self-exploration) within the therapy hour. Five successive 8-minute tape-recorded segments were extracted from a therapy hour of eight normal, eight psychoneurotic, and eight schizophrenic cases—half of the hours from an early part of therapy, and half near therapy termination. The results showed that the three groups showed divergent Experiencing trends over the course of the individual therapy interview. Psychoneurotics showed a steady progression in Experiencing over the course of the interview hour, in which each consecutive segment is rated higher than the preceding one. Normals and schizophrenics, in contrast, showed no consistent or sizeable linear process movement. Rogers et al. (1967) intracorrelated therapist behaviors (attitudes or "conditions" of empathic understanding, congruence, and positive regard) interview-by-interview for a group of schizophrenics in individual psychotherapy. A 15×15 intercorrelation matrix for each of the three conditions permitted an analysis of the stability or consistency over time of each therapist behavior in the first fifteen psychotherapy interviews. Generally, the results showed that these measures of therapists' attitudes towards their patients stabilized after several interviews and remained relatively consistent thereafter.

9. Intercorrelation of Patient or Therapist Interview Behaviors. One can also look at the pattern of intercorrelation among several patient or among several therapist behavior measures at one or several points of the interviews sequence. This procedure might assess the commonalities of variance present among these concomitant measures, or might unfold patterns of relationship of theoretical relevance.

Examples. Rogers et al. (1967) examined the associations among Rogers' therapist conditions of positive regard, unconditionality, empathic understanding, and congruence from the frame of reference of a group of schizophrenic patients in individual psychotherapy. The patients filled out Barrett-Lennard Relationship Inventories (RI) on their respective therapists early in therapy and again at termination. At the initial time point, the four subscales were positively but moderately interrelated. The two subscales tapping aspects of the therapist's positive feelings toward the patient, regard and unconditionality, were highly correlated. Neither regard nor unconditionality was significantly related to the therapist's level of empathic understanding, although both correlated significantly with the total RI score. At the terminal point, there was no significant relationship among the four subscales, although regard, unconditionality, and congruence still tended to cluster. Again, all four were related significantly to the total scale score. This clustering of RI subscales for the schizophrenic patients was clearly different from that found for a sample of psychoneurotics (Barrett-Lennard, 1962). Neurotics associated therapist genuineness with his level of empathic understanding, in contrast to the schizophrenics, who tended to view genuineness and regard factors as related. The authors concluded (p. 172): "This difference may well reflect the relatively greater focus on self-exploration rather than on relationship formation occurring in the initial perception of neurotic patients, in contrast to the schizophrenic's placement of more emphasis on the therapist's potential for a genuine relationship with them."

10. Interrelationship of Patient and Therapist Interview Behavior. The immediately preceding sections focused on *either* patient or therapist measures of interview behavior respectively, looking at, for example, patient behavioral stability over time, or the interrelationships of patient behavioral measures at a particular moment in the therapy sequence. One can also look at the degree of relationship between patient *and* therapist behaviors at one or several points of the interviews sequence. This represents a more exciting research strategy in that one can assess whether supposedly effective therapist behaviors are indeed associated with patient change or state measures.

Example. Rogers et al. (1967) studied the relationship of therapist attitudes—level of Rogers' "conditions" (measured by ratings of tape-recorded segments as well as by therapist and patient questionnaire responses at several points in therapy)—with patient Experiencing as rated from tape-recorded segments. The correlational findings showed that certain therapist conditions measures (particularly rated accurate empathy and patient-perceived congruence) were associated positively and significantly with the level of Experiencing shown by patients over the total course of psychotherapy. These results confirmed the expectation that level of self-exploration or Experiencing would be higher for patients of therapists with high levels of Rogerian conditions. Speisman (1959) investigated depth of interpretation as related to verbal resistance in psychotherapy. He recorded all responses in a sequence of 5 consecutive interviews from a single case, as well as a block of 11 successive patient-therapist responses randomly selected from 21 other cases. The sample of patients was characterized as psychoneurotic, and the psychologist and psychiatrist therapists were of various orientations (Adlerian, nondirective, neoanalytic, eclectic) of 1 to 10 years of experience. The therapists' responses were rated as either superficial, moderate, or deep interpretations, while the subsequent patient responses were classified into various positive and negative categories of resistance. His results showed that both superficial and moderate interpretations were followed by more patient exploration and less resistance than were deep interpretations. Therapist shifts from deep to not-deep interpretations were followed by increased patient exploration and decreased resistance, while higher resistance followed the reverse shift. Speisman concluded that his results offer confirmatory support for Fenichel's psychoanalytic dictum to "interpret just beyond the preconscious."

Basic Methodological Issues of Interview Studies. One common factor of many of the above research strategies is that one is dealing with patient or therapist *within-interview* variables. The raw data is some representation of the interview events (tape recordings, movies, transcripts). The encoding process usually takes the form of various nominal or dimensional (rating) content-analysis systems. Many sins of omission and commission have occurred in the past with these interview or "process" studies. Several investigators (Bordin et al., 1954; Kiesler, 1966) have stressed the necessity for considering and dealing with basic methodological issues when one constructs or uses classification systems or rating scales of various sorts for within-interview measurement. Some of these issues are more obvious than others. Yet little attention has been paid to these points by previous process investigators with a few exceptions (Bordin and his group, Harway et al., 1955; Raush et al., 1956; Howe and Pope, 1961; Klein, Kiesler, and Mathieu, 1968; Matarazzo, 1968).

The basic points advocated by the above authors are summarized briefly here. (1) The researcher must develop his scale to the point that good interrater and intrarater reliability is obtained. This seems to have been accomplished best in the past when scales have been constructed carefully with much effort, when examples of scale points have been included, and when judges have been provided intensive training experiences. (2) He should be concerned at some point whether the scale is tapping a single dimension rather than several confounded dimensions. This dimensional unraveling is crucial before accurate interpretation of scale correlations is possible. The very precise work of Bordin and his associates (Harway et al., 1955; Raush et al., 1956) and Howe and Pope, (1961) has focused on this dimensionality problem. Bordin's group has applied Coombs' scaling technique, while Howe and Pope have used Osgood's semantic differential measure as vehicles for extracting and describing the dimensions that are operative in their respective therapist scales. (3) The investigator can profit from measuring the face validity of his scale. Do other clinicians consider his scale variable an operative and crucial

dimension of the therapy interaction? Would other clinicians agree with the ranking continuum explicit in his scale? (4) He can attempt to show that his scale results cannot be explained by more parsimonious variables. Is it possible that formal content variables such as the amount of patient verbalization or silence, or interruptions of silence (Matarazzo et al., 1968; Lennard and Bernstein, 1960), can explain much of the variance present in the results he obtains with his scale measure (cf., for example, Kiesler, Mathieu, and Klein, 1967). (5) Quite importantly, the researcher must define and resolve the sampling problems involved in applying his scale to the interview data of psychotherapy. This refers to the basic problem of the process-unit to which the measurement will be applied. He must first define these sampling problems in a manner appropriate for testing the theoretical system in which he is interested. There is no uniform answer to the sampling question; rather, there are different answers, depending on the questions one is asking of the data. For example, Rogers' "necessary and sufficient" therapist conditions are explicitly formulated to operate pervasively over the entire therapy encounter, to function independently of any particular problem content being discussed, and to have their effect in a cumulative way over the therapy encounter. The sampling issue is resolved rather simply, consequently, by sampling at points of the therapy interviews that would be representative of the entire therapy interaction. No previous content analysis is required—samples randomly extracted from each session would clearly suffice for valid measurement. However, working with different variables within a different theoretical framework, one could very easily make different sampling decisions. Someone dealing with Freudian constructs would likely need, initially, to edit each psychotherapy case into different problem or content areas, as well as into different interactive conditions of patient and therapist. The test of Freudian hypotheses would be limited to these specified or interactive areas in turn. Clearly, the sampling problem would be much more complex for a test of Freudian in contrast to Rogerian variables. The specific sampling issues come down to (a) the problem of sample size and location for a particular therapy hour—how large or long should the sample unit be? Should it be extracted randomly from the fifty minutes, or in some standardized fashion, such as late in the hour (for example, Kiesler, Mathieu and Klein, 1964; Kiesler, Klein and Mathieu, 1965)? and (b) the problem of sample location for the entire series of therapy interviews—which interviews (early, middle, late) in the interaction should be sampled in order to tap the variables of theoretical interest (for example, Rogers et al., 1967, pp. 136–138)? (6) He must assess the differential information loss for his scale when using different data media (typescripts versus tape-recordings versus silent movies versus "talkies"). Which data medium best provides reliable and valid measures of a particular therapeutic variable? On an a priori basis one might expect different results from the various forms of raw data. The audial dimension adds voice cues that are lost in a transcript. Movies add the visual dimension with kinesthetic, postural, and other motoric cues. Yet one cannot decide here on an a priori basis alone. The question must be submitted to empirical test. (7) He must be concerned about the potential and likely confounding arising when therapist *and* patient behavior are rated from segments where both their verbalizations are present. Take the case where separate sets of judges rate independently the "empathic understanding" of the therapist and the "experiencing" behavior of the patient (Rogers et al., 1967). Assume one finds a high positive correlation between therapist empathy and patient experiencing. Since *both* participants are present on the identical tape samples for both sets of judges, the methodological question is: were both sets of judges in effect rating the same thing—that is, only the patient's behavior? Is it possible to rate the therapist's empathic understanding from his statements alone? Or can the rating only be made in terms of the patient's response to what the therapist says (which is at some level of experiencing)? This basic problem must be dealt with empirically before findings can be interpreted unequivocally (for example, Schoeninger et al., 1967). (8) The researcher must consider the level of clinical experience required, and the degree and kind of training necessary for judges who are to make the

ratings for his particular variable. (9) The investigator might profit considerably from assessing both the patient's and the therapist's viewpoints of what is occurring in therapy, as a check on the validity of the viewpoint arrived at by judges using his scale. Interesting and marked discrepancies between these viewpoints have appeared in the literature (Feifel and Eells, 1963; Kamin and Caughlan, 1963; Keith-Spiegel and Spiegel, 1967; Muench, 1965; Rogers et al., 1967), and the discrepancies must be dealt with. (10) Finally, psychotherapy researchers must become more cognizant of each other's work and measuring instruments (Matarazzo, 1968). Process scales have multiplied with much overlap, divergent results, and little integration of closely related predecessors. Perhaps this volume will make it easier to avoid this frustrating and uneconomical ignorance of the work of others.

The upshot of this discussion seems clear: one needs to concern himself with a long-range program of methodological research when he introduces a new interview (process) scale for psychotherapy investigation. The many one-shot attempts—myriad idiosyncratic process scales—that are pervasive in the literature, can be nothing but frustrating to the serious investigator. It is only by painstaking confrontation of these basic issues, however, that psychotherapy interview research will move forward on a solid methodological foundation.

Other design possibilities are implicit in Figure 2.2, although they have been rarely considered. As an example, one could look at the intercorrelation of patient interview measures with patient extratherapy measures at one or several time points in the interviews sequence. This strategy could provide important evidence of the association (or lack of it) of patient interview behavior-change with concurrent "real life" behavior-change.

Naturalistic Studies: An Evaluation. The preceding section has taken a brief look at the many design possibilities for studying psychotherapy artisanship. These naturalistic strategies all involve studying the live, unaltered, minimally controlled, unmanipulated "natural" psychotherapy sequence—so-called "experiments of nature." They are locked securely to the correlationist tradition of psychological research (Cronbach, 1957). They all attempt to capture covariation among or between patient and therapist behaviors-in-the-raw. The statistical analyses used in these studies all theoretically could be reduced to correlation coefficients since, even when dichotomies or groups are used, the basis for grouping is an individual differences variable, with theoretical scores lying on continua of various shapes or distributions. Hence, the strengths and weaknesses of the naturalistic research reviewed above are basically those of correlational research generally.

The major advantage of correlational research is that many behavioral aspects can be studied simultaneously and their interrelationships determined with relative lack of interference with natural processes. It represents a more comprehensive strategy, potentially dealing with multiple variables—hence bowing toward the admitted complexity of real-life events. In the psychotherapy situation, one can measure several therapist behaviors and several patient behaviors over the therapy sequence and inter-correlate the measures. Since the crucial effective therapist behaviors, as well as the affected patient behaviors, are likely multidimensional, the researcher is permitted the possibility of "hooking" all the crucial elements with one "cast." The more recent factor analytic tools permit one to go further: to maximize economy by determining the minimum number of hypothesized constructs needed to explain the covariations obtained. When carefully applied, a correlational investigation can provide confirming evidence for propositions that cannot be fairly evaluated in any other way.

The major difficulty of correlational data is well known—that one can seldom make probabilistic statements about which of the factors produces the effects in the other—that is, one cannot ascertain directionality of causation. In most studies employing the correlational method, dependent and independent variables are fully interchangeable. For example, if one finds a high positive correlation between therapist empathic understanding and patient insight, one would like to infer (particularly if he is Rogerian) that the therapists' attitudinal characteristics affected the level of patient

insight observed. But it is equally possible that the patient's capacity for insight made it possible for the therapist to show high levels of empathic understanding, or that some other patient or therapist factor affected both insight and empathic understanding. Because of this interpretive ambiguity, correlational research rarely can isolate crucial variables precisely, and seldom can ascertain which factor is responsible for which effects. Partial correlation and factor analysis enable one to narrow the interpretive range, but can never really answer the causal question. The most serious error in using the correlational method, therefore, "arises from investigators' tendencies to assign it powers of proof that it does not possess and thus to draw unwarranted conclusions or inferences from the data it provides" (Shontz, 1965, p. 158).

In psychotherapy and behavior modification, the causal question is paramount: which therapist behaviors produce what kind of changes with which kinds of patients? Correlational studies provide interesting leads and permit certain predictions, but can seldom answer the crucial question. On the other hand, if one manipulates (experimentally varies) therapist behavior and looks at the subsequent patient changes, one *can* begin to answer the crucial question. In the experimental strategy, one often sacrifices some veridicality by arbitrarily isolating and restricting the experimental situation. One loses some of the complexity and excitement of the real world when he brings behavior modification into the laboratory. But much of this complexity and excitement can be regained over time as replicable and cumulative research accrues and as experimenter imagination and ingenuity blossom.

It seems clear that many of the naturalistic design strategies listed above have great potential utility for a science of behavior modification, within the limits just mentioned. For this utility to eventuate, however, certain modifications of these previous approaches are essential. Basically, these modifications would serve to avoid the various Uniformity Assumptions discussed in conjunction with the Grid Model presented earlier. These naturalistic designs can no longer ignore the pervasive patient, therapist, and patient change heterogeneity present in the artisan situations. Careful efforts will be required to restrict one's study to relatively homogeneous patient groups.[7] Care must be taken to specify quite clearly the within-interview therapist behaviors that are occurring. Imagination must be applied to finding appropriate patient change variables for the various homogeneous patient subgroups.

For example, instead of randomly assigning outpatient psychoneurotics to psychotherapy and control groups, one could restrict his focus to a study of psychotherapy of the obsessive personality (Salzman, 1968). By first carefully defining the in- and extra-therapy behaviors and attitudes that characterize the obsessive, one can attain both homogeneity and reliability of patient selection. Next, instead of assigning heterogeneous therapists with undefined techniques to these cases, one can either select therapists who claim expertise with obsessives, or can train therapists to exhibit clearly defined attitudinal and technique behaviors. Obviously one cannot totally program therapist behavior in the naturalistic setting; but one can attempt to teach a rationale of therapist behaviors that are theoretically indicated for obsessive behavior patterns. Importantly, one can, after termination, check tape recordings via judge ratings to ascertain whether the prescribed therapist behaviors were in fact carried out; or in the case of the expert therapists, to ascertain the effects of their respective approaches. Finally, one can take care to develop measures of obsessive outcome, measures which will reflect the specific changes one would expect to occur both in- and extra-therapy as a result of effective treatment. These measures could be applied at numerous points of the therapy sequence and over follow-up periods, to get a more sensitive and valid estimate of the statistical function and extent of obsessive change. Several of the large-scale cooperative studies suggested by Strupp and Bergin (1969) are in this same tradition.

If this kind of naturalistic sharpening of variables can be attained, continued artisan research will provide an exciting and heuristic function for the science of behavior modification. If not, these naturalistic research attempts will continue to be primarily institutional research with little generality or theoretical relevance.

Generalist-Manipulative Studies

The beginnings of generalist-experimental influences in psychotherapy research occurred quite recently. The first derived from the classic studies of Greenspoon (1955) and Verplanck (1955) in the area of verbal operant conditioning, and the analogue therapist studies of Strupp (1960) and Matarazzo et al. (1968). The more recent impetus came with Wolpe's (1958) publication and the resulting surge of interest and research in the behavior therapies. This experimental tradition is fortunately now entrenched. The science of behavior modification (and also artisan psychotherapy) is indebted to these individuals, not so much for the substantive findings they have so far contributed, but for the new vistas their emphases made possible.

These researchers brought psychotherapy into the laboratory and opened up controlled experimentation in behavior modification. The basic strategy of this research is to experimentally manipulate (vary) one or more variables while holding other relevant variables constant, so as to determine the differential effects of the manipulated treatment(s).

This kind of research is designed to conclude that the experimenter's manipulations of the independent variable produced or caused the observed effects in the dependent variable. If one can vary the amount of variable X (independent variable) and find that a given factor Y (dependent variable) changes in amount or magnitude, variable X can be imputed causal status vis-à-vis variable Y. Importantly, this experimental strategy does permit us to come to some answers regarding the paramount question of psychotherapy and behavior modification more generally: which therapist behaviors produce what changes in which kinds of patients?

---

[7] Attempts along these lines to date have used patient dimensions such as need for social approval (Strickland and Crowne, 1959; Kanfer and Marston, 1966), high versus low anxiety (Kaplan, 1966; Pierce and Mosher, 1967), oral versus anal character types (Noblin, Timmons, and Kael, 1966), and hostile versus friendly patients (Bandura, Lipsher, and Miller, 1960; Heller, Myers, and Kline, 1963; Heller, 1968).

One would expect of these laboratory studies that the experimenter manipulate some "therapist" behavior for groups of "patient" subjects and measure some aspect of patient change. This strategy is certainly present. But, interestingly, in many of these experimental studies, the experimenter manipulates patient variables to ascertain the effects on therapist behaviors. The experimental strategies that follow will fall under these two general categories: studies where the independent variable is some aspect of therapist behavior, and those where the manipulated factor is some aspect of patient behavior. We will first consider the design strategies that have appeared, and afterwards briefly discuss some relevant methodological considerations, attempt to evaluate this generalist research to date, and finally present the scarce examples of the multivariate-factorial design strategy advocated in the Grid Model discussion above.

1. "Patient" as the Independent Variable. The basic design in these studies is to manipulate some aspect of patient behavior and measure the effects these different manipulations or treatments have on therapist behavior. The subjects for these experiments are psychotherapists culled from graduate clinical psychology programs, from private practice, from hospitals and clinics—generally from any artisan population. In some cases, undergraduate students have been used as subjects. The manipulated patient factors are usually presented via transcripts, tape recordings, or motion picture samples of real or role-played patient behavior. In some instances, live patients (real or actors) may participate in psychotherapy interviews with therapist subjects. In any case, several different patient treatments are administered to groups of psychotherapist subjects, and some aspect of the therapist response (such as countertransference) is measured. The researcher hypothesizes that the various patient treatments will produce differential therapist effects on the therapist-variable(s) of interest. Studies are Bandura, Lipsher and Miller (1960); Beery (1967); Bohn (1965); Cutler (1958); Heller, Myers, and Kline (1963); Jenkins, Wallach, and Strupp (1962); Russell and Snyder (1966); Sommer, Mazo, and Lehner (1955); Strupp (1960); and Strupp and Wallach (1965).

Examples. Bandura, Lipsher, and Miller (1960) studied 12 advanced clinical psychology student-psychotherapists' approach-avoidance reactions to patients' expressions of hostility. Each therapist was rated independently by 3 clinical psychology staff members on various traits: hostility-anxiety, dependency, sex-inhibition, and warmth. One hundred and ten interviews of 17 of these therapists' patients were randomly selected. The transcripts were coded for several categories of patient hostility statements, and the approach-avoidance verbal behavior of the therapists recorded. Results tended to show that therapists rated less anxious regarding expression of direct hostility, and lower in need for approval, showed more verbal approach behavior toward patients' hostile expressions. The approach-avoidance therapist behaviors had significant effects on subsequent patients expressions—when therapists approached patients' hostile expressions, the patients continued to respond with verbalizations; while avoidance by the patient led to more avoidance by the patient. Heller, Myers, and Kline (1963) trained student actors to play four client roles: dominant-friendly, dominant-hostile, dependent-friendly, and dependent-hostile. Each actor-patient was presented in counterbalanced order to 34 interviewers-in-training for half-hour interviews. The interviewers were told they were seeing clients on the waiting list of the University Counseling Center. Each interview was observed through a one-way-vision-mirror by a judge trained to rate interviewer affect, control, and anxiety. Results of the 4-treatment simple analysis of variance showed that dominant client behavior (both friendly and hostile) evoked therapist friendliness. Client friendliness elicited significantly more therapist friendliness than did client hostility. Their results did not show that more therapist anxiety is elicited by a hostile client.

2. "Therapist" as the Independent Variable. The next four relatively distinct experimental research strategies fall under the area of studies manipulating some aspect of therapist or experimenter (E) behavior. The expertise and/or experience of the "therapists" can range from much to little or none. The subjects are either patients of various nosological categories or undergraduate students. The therapists or Es are typically trained to perform only certain behaviors in the interview situation with the patient-subjects—that is, the therapist roles are more or less standardized. The dependent variable is some measure of patient or S change over the time of the interview(s). The design tests the general hypothesis that therapist treatments are related to differential patient or S change over the interview(s).

(a) VERBAL OPERANT CONDITIONING STUDIES. Krasner recently reviewed this literature (1962), and does so again in the current volume (Chapter 14). Following the classic studies of Greenspoon (1955) and Verplanck (1955), the basic paradigm of this research is as follows: "In verbal operant conditioning S is required to emit verbal behavior as part of a given task, and E reinforces a preselected class of S's verbal behavior by carefully controlled verbal and/or nonverbal behavioral cues" (Krasner, 1962, p. 62). The typical E behavioral cues have been "Mmm-hmm," and "good" when S makes the correct response. The preselected patient or S response classes have covered a wide range, including the original plural nouns category, affect statements, self-reference statements, "hallucinations," "negative words," "neurotic" verbalizations, "early childhood memories," references to "mother," opinions and attitudes, "complex sentences," "acceptance of self," "confiding responses," and the like (Krasner, 1962, p. 78).

The design permits an evaluation of the general hypothesis that the patient or S behaviors reinforced by the therapist or E behaviors will increase in frequency over the interview interaction.

Examples. Taffel's (1955) verbal-conditioning procedure is frequently employed in these studies. It consists of a series of 5×7 cards with pronouns (I, We, You, She, They) printed at the top of the card and a sentence-ending at the bottom. The S's task is to choose one of the pronouns listed at the top and complete the sentence fragment below. Noblin, Timmons and Reynard (1963) used 12 patient subjects from an acute treatment ward of a psychiatric hospital (7 males, 5 females). Taffel cards were used with E reinforcing either "I, We" or "He, She, They" pronouns. Each time S chose the correct pronoun class during the conditioning trials, E read from a shuffled deck of cards one of a randomly placed series of interpretive statements. The authors concluded from their data that psychoanalytic-like

interpretations function as verbal reinforcers and that the "truth-status" or relevance of interpretations is not the central factor in whether interpretations lawfully modify verbal behavior in a conditioning situation. Waskow (1966) studied 36 undergraduate volunteers who had scores in the upper two-thirds of a manifest anxiety scale. In a preliminary interview, Ss were told to pretend that they were having their first visit to a counseling center and to discuss things they might talk about there. Each S talked for 15 minutes to a tape-recorder only, and later judges rated their responses for emphasis on content versus feelings. Ss were then placed into 12 matched triads (by their content-feeling ratings) and randomly assigned to 3 conditions: in Group F, the therapist responded to S's references to his feelings and attitudes; in Group C, to the descriptive and intellectual content of S's communication; and in Group FC, to a combination of feelings and intellectual content. In 4 interviews for each S, the therapist attempted to respond whenever the S paused at the end of a sentence or a topic, chiefly with reflective statements. Each S's tape-recorded responses were categorized as predominantly F, FC, or C. A trend analysis of variance (Edwards, 1962) showed that the different therapist reinforcement behaviors elicited different patterns of responses in the F, FC, and C treatment conditions. Although the C group showed successful conditioning, selective responding to feelings (F Group) and to combinations of feeling and content (FC Group) did not function as reinforcers. The author concludes that ". . . conditioning of subjects' verbal behavior in a therapy-like situation was not as easily achieved as one might predict on the basis of the verbal conditioning literature."

(b) OTHER BEHAVIOR THERAPY STRATEGIES. The impetus for this line of research derives from Dollard and Miller (1950), Mowrer (1950), and Salter (1949); but the greatest impact is attributed to Wolpe's (1958) introduction of reciprocal inhibition psychotherapy. Since that time, various other methods of behavior therapy have appeared. Despite the sideline polemics, research studies have emerged recently after a period dominated almost entirely by case reports.

The great value of these therapies is that all of them attempt to explicate very specific therapist behaviors that theoretically facilitate very specific patient change. The therapist does certain standardized things in relatively few interviews with patients with certain presenting symptoms. The therapist treatments are relatively clearly defined behaviors such as "desensitization," aversive conditioning, maximizing extinction, and the like. The experimental subjects are real patients or undergraduates exhibiting certain very specific behaviors—such as rat phobia, tics, stuttering, and drinking behavior. The design permits an evaluation of the general hypothesis that these various techniques "derived" from psychological learning theory will produce change in the symptom behaviors, while similar subjects not receiving treatment or receiving "traditional psychotherapy" will exhibit no change.

Examples. Gelder, Marks and Wolff (1967) report a study comparing 3 treatment methods for severely phobic patients: individual psychotherapy, group psychotherapy, and systematic desensitization. The patients were matched by age, sex, duration of illness, and also by their Cornell Index scores (severity of illness). Changes were more rapid with desensitization than with the more traditional psychotherapies in that improvement levels that took about a year to accomplish with individual treatment, and 18 months with group treatment, took only 9 months with desensitization. Also, it appeared that patients who were helped by this method were not different from those helped by the other techniques. Davison (1968) and Harrell (1968) attempted to unravel the basic effective ingredients from Wolpe's total reciprocal inhibition therapy package. Davison argues that if, as is widely assumed, the efficacy of Wolpe's procedure derives from a genuine counterconditioning process, a disruption of the pairing between graded aversive stimuli and relaxation should render the technique ineffective in modifying avoidance behavior. He used 28 volunteer female undergraduate Ss "very much afraid" of nonpoisonous snakes. The results supported his hypothesis: significant reduction in fear of snakes was observed only in desensitization Ss (relaxation paired with graded aversive stimuli), with none occurring either in matched Ss for whom relaxation was paired with irrelevant stimuli, or in matched Ss who were gradually exposed to the imaginal aversive stimuli without relaxation. Finally, Harrell (1968) argues that various learning factors are potentially operative in Wolpe's reciprocal-inhibition package: counterconditioning, operant reward, extinction, and desensitization. Using volunteer Ss afraid of laboratory rats, he applied 4 treatment conditions designed to maximize these respective components. All therapy treatments were conducted in the presence of a live rat (in contrast to the usual imaginal presentations). The results showed that all treatment groups except desensitization significantly reduced fear of rats more than the control (no therapy) conditions. The other 3 treatment groups (counterconditioning, extinction, and operant) were statistically indistinguishable on overt fear-reduction, while the extinction condition was most effective on self-report fear measures. Harrell argues that all three learning components are effective in reducing fear, and are basically confounded in Wolpe's total-package technique.

(c) "THERAPIST" TRADITIONAL INTERVIEW BEHAVIOR AS THE INDEPENDENT VARIABLE. These studies attempt to manipulate therapist behavior in interview situations with patients or undergraduates. The therapists in the various treatments are either preselected for exhibiting a particular interview behavior, or are programmed/trained to exhibit a particular therapist role. The range of therapist expertise and/or experience is quite large. The therapist variables manipulated have been derived from traditional theoretical formulations of greater or less specificity. The experimental subjects are patients or undergraduates. Studies in this tradition are Adams, Robertson, and Cooper (1966); Ashby, Ford, Guerney, and Guerney (1957); Baker (1960); Dinoff, Rickard, Salzberg, and Sipprelle (1960); Colby (1960, 1961); Craig (1966); Gendlin et al. (1968); Gendlin and Berlin (1961); Frank (1964); Crossman (1952); Heller (1968); Heller, Davis, and Myers (1966); Holder, Carkhuff, and Berenson (1967); Kanfer and Marston (1966); Martin, Lundy, and Lewin (1960); Matarazzo (1968); Mazurkiewicz (1957); Phillips and Agnew (1953); Pierce and Mosher (1967); Powell (1968); Shlien, Mosak, and Dreikurs (1960); and Tolor and Kissinger (1965).

Examples. Ashby, Ford, Guerney, and Guerney (1957) studied the effects of therapist personality and technique on client behavior. Twenty-four psychoneurotic clients (7 women, 17 men) were seen in psychotherapy by 6 advanced clinical psychology students at a psychological clinic. The therapists were trained for two different techniques—one Reflective (restatement of content, reflection of feelings, nondirective leads, and nondirective structuring responses), the other Leading (directive leads, interpretations, directive structuring, information giving, and persuasion). The clients were randomly assigned to the 6 therapists and to the two techniques, and met for at least 4 interviews (average of 12·8). The clients and therapists took batteries of tests, and the clients' dependent variable assessment included within-interview measures of dependency, openness, guardedness, resistance and defensiveness; client's self-report reactions to the relationship; and therapists' posttherapy ratings. The results provided some support for the expectation that Leading and Reflective types of therapy produce different effects on clients. Clients who were more defensive initially tended to behave more defensively with a leading, but not with a reflective, therapist. Individual therapists tended to create different effects on their clients independent of the type of therapy given. The interaction of therapist personality and technique was found to be vital, since clients felt significantly more defensive (or more positive) in one type of therapy with a particular therapist than did other clients with the same therapist in the second type of therapy. The authors' conclusion that "this study clearly illustrates the value of multivariate experimental designs . . ." surely sounds familiar by now and will be extended further in a later section. Heller, Davis, and Myers (1966) trained graduate students in speech and theater ($n = 12$) to portray 4 interviewer conditions (3 actors for each condition): active-friendly, passive-friendly, active-hostile, and passive-hostile. A total of 120 undergraduates (69 males, 51 females) were asked to participate in a model counseling situation. These Ss first listened to a short taped sample of a person talking about himself to "show what people might say in counseling," and then were randomly assigned to one of the 4 interviewer conditions to "talk to an interviewer for 15 minutes." Analysis of the last 5 minutes of the interviews showed that Ss talked more in the active than in the passive conditions, that Ss in the hostile conditions used a greater percentage of sex words while Ss in the active-friendly and passive-hostile groups used a greater percentage of family words, and that the active-friendly Es were liked best by the Ss, the passive-hostile Es least.

(d) EXPERIMENTALLY INDUCED "PATHOLOGY," WITH THERAPIST INTERVIEW BEHAVIOR AS THE INDEPENDENT VARIABLE. A final group of studies has utilized the same strategy as the research of the immediately preceding section, with one exception. In the case of the following studies, an additional manipulation is introduced: a stress or "emotional problem" is experimentally induced by E, via hypnosis or conditioning sessions, in all the subjects. The rationale is that one can thereby standardize the patient disability or "emotional problem" by uniformly inducing the problem in all subjects. Then, by subjecting Ss to differential therapist treatments, one can determine their relative effectiveness in modifying the standard "emotional problem." The impetus in this area of research apparently derived from a study by Keet (1948), despite the fact that several attempts at replication (Butler and Grummon, 1953; Heim, 1951; Merrill, 1952) failed to substantiate his results. Studies in this tradition are Gordon (1957); Gordon, Martin, and Lundy (1966); Haggard and Murray (1942); Keet (1948); Kesner (1954); Levinson, Zax, and Cohen (1961); Pomeroy (1950) and Wiener (1955).

Examples. Keet (1948) studied the differential effects of two techniques in a miniature counseling situation. 25 Ss underwent the following procedure. A word having some reference to an area of disturbance in S was found by means of a word-association test. A learning experience (retroactive inhibition paradigm) was devised in which S was likely to fail to recall the word (an analogue of repression). When the failure was established, S was administered one of two treatments. For the Expressive group, the therapist responded primarily to the feeling content and avoided the recognition of attitudes not yet expressed. For the Interpretive group, the therapist "inferred the total affective process from its partial expression and conveyed the inference to the subject." Finally, after the experimental treatment, S was again placed in a learning situation similar to the first to evaluate whether he could now recall the word that had been experimentally "repressed." If S failed to recall the word, the experimental therapy was judged to have failed. The results showed that the combined uses of expressive and interpretive methods proved consistently superior to the expressive method used alone. When the interpretive technique was applied, a sharp change occurred in the S's verbalizations, wherein much more associative content appeared in the form of related words, images, and reminiscences. Gordon (1957) studied the effects of Leading and Following techniques on hypnotically induced repression and hostility. Eighteen hypnotically susceptible Ss were assigned randomly to 9 advanced clinical psychology student therapists. While in trance, these Ss had been instructed to imagine themselves in a situation in high school in which a physical education teacher accidentally bumped into them in the hallway, then blamed S for clumsiness and threatened reprisal. S was then introduced to his therapist, rehypnotized, and told the physical education teacher looked something like his therapist. S was also told that although he would be amnesic to the high school trauma when awakened, it would bother him, and he could spend the interview hour trying to figure out what was bothering him. It was permissible for S to recall the experience during the course of the interview. The therapists were not told the Ss had been hypnotized, but each had been instructed to portray either a leading or following role. Three judges rated the typescripts for repression (different recall units) and hostility. The results indicated that leading therapist behaviors tended to be more efficient in obtaining verbalizations of the "repressed" material. The therapists' first interviews were more productive than their second, while the Ss were significantly more hostile in the second interview.

Generalist-Manipulative Studies: An Evaluation. The great advantage of manipulative research is that through control and systematic variation of variables one can arrive at cause-effect conclusions. If one's manipulations of therapist behavior, other things remaining constant, lead to reliable differential patient changes, one can conclude that his manipulations produced the observed effects. Experimentation, therefore, represents a powerful research tool.

It is important to keep in mind, however, that interpretative errors (that is, incorrectly imputing the changes to the particular independent variable one has arbitrarily defined) can occur in this kind of research. The basic interpretative problem lies with the matter of control: has one in fact held everything constant except the particular theoretical factor in which one is interested? Has one actually manipulated only the independent variable without other factors simultaneously varying? This experimental control problem is extremely important and cannot be handled at all by statistical considerations, no matter how powerful or sophisticated. The problem is a logical one, requiring critical thought by the researcher *before* he embarks on data collection. Only a few of the crucial issues that have emerged in behavior modification research will be mentioned here.

The major control problem in the experimental studies summarized in this section has to do with what Underwood (1957) calls "task confounding." Task variables refer to dimensions or aspects of the experimental apparatus, stimulus, or presentation, other than the experimenter - defined independent variable, which of themselves are relevant to and inducive of changes in the dependent variable measures. Task *confounding* occurs when factors of the experimental task on which the experimenter is not focusing (that is, aspects other than his arbitrarily defined independent variable) may actually be responsible (instead of the independent variable) for the dependent variable changes observed. If other interpretations of the results are possible and probable (that is, if one can attribute the effects to factors other than those pointed to by the investigator), then the results are confounded.

In most of the studies listed above, some aspect of the therapist's behavior (reflective versus interpretive, active versus passive, verbal reinforcements, and the like) represents the independent variable. The investigators chose experimental operations to define these theoretically relevant constructs. Their manipulations were designed to vary the therapists' behavior along these theoretical dimensions. Task confounding would occur in these studies if therapist factors other than these specific independent variables (such as therapist personality characteristics, attitudinal systems, or various other behaviors) covaried simultaneously with the E's manipulations of the defined independent variable. For example, if E wants to look at the therapist activity-passivity factor, he has to be careful that the active therapists do not differ from the passive therapists on any other variables (such as empathic ability, motivation to help, relevant personality characteristics, or number of interpretations versus reflections) that might of themselves produce differential patient effects. Again, if one's empirical hunch or theoretical framework implies that depth of interpretation is a crucial therapist dimension leading to differences in the dependent variable (such as patient insight), then one would like to conclude that in fact manipulation of therapist depth of interpretation, and it only, effected the different levels of patient insight obtained. Task confounding occurs and confuses the situation if, for example, the therapists' empathic understanding (covarying with depth of interpretation) could also be responsible for the insight differences obtained.

If empathy is related to insight, and if it is not controlled in the above situation, interpretation of the insight differences obtained will be ambiguous.

There are various ways of handling these task-confounding problems (see Underwood, 1957, pp. 154–159). One powerful method is to build in replications of therapists in the various treatment groups. The Heller, Davis, and Myers (1966) study described above used this procedure. Their intent was to vary two independent variable therapist factors, activity-passivity behavior and friendly-hostile attitudes. If they had used one therapist only to administer all four conditions to their experimental groups, they could not generalize beyond the one particular therapist. It would be quite likely also that the particular therapist's personality, motivation, or differential biases influenced the pure application of the experimental treatment. If they used a separate therapist-actor for each of the four treatment groups, they would have similar interpretative problems: Did the different therapist personalities alone produce the effects? Was one therapist dissatisfied with the treatment condition it was his job to apply? Were other factors covarying in one or more of the therapist-actor treatments, such as level of empathic understanding? Heller, Davis, and Myers instead chose to replicate therapist-actors in each of the treatment groups, by having 3 actors for each ot the 4 conditions— a total of 12 actor-therapists. By increasing the therapist Ns for each treatment, they can more legitimately argue that any of these other possibly relevant therapist factors would be randomly distributed across treatments, and hence could have no consistent effects on the dependent variable measures.

It seems that this therapist-replications procedure is a minimal requirement for experimental investigation of therapist behavior. It may be useful additionally to find measures for the potentially confounding therapist variables, so that one can further assess whether confounding was operative. For example, Heller, Davis, and Myers could have rated their actor-therapists' treatment performances on a scale of empathic understanding, or they might have taken some personality measures of their actor-therapists as further checks on their

randomization procedure. With this kind of experimental care, one is much more likely to come up with conclusions that stand the test of time. It also makes it possible to compare and cross-fertilize research of different investigators.

The same discussion applies, of course, to those studies where some aspect of patient behavior serves as the independent variable. For example, a researcher can select or construct two patient tapes, one designed to represent a friendly and the other a hostile patient. It's extremely unlikely that this is the only dimension on which the two patient tapes differ—different verbalization rates, levels of insight, other personality characteristics, and the like, are probably present. One can take care by constructing the tapes so as to hold relevant factors constant, and can assess the finished products by judges' ratings along the relevant dimensions. A safer procedure is to replicate the patient tapes, having several examples of friendly and hostile tapes respectively. One is then better able to argue that the effects of the various potentially confounding factors will randomize across treatments.

Clearly one cannot always anticipate relevant variables confounding one's results. Science advances partially by the arduous task of discovery and clarification of the confoundings present in previous research. The point is that the experimenter should be aware of these potential confoundings and attempt to control them by the best procedures available. At the very least he should not repeat the mistakes of previous research. An alternate strategy (more in line with the theme of this chapter) is to actually build one or more potentially relevant variables into the experimental design as additional independent variables. By incorporating these additional dimensions, one can not only evaluate whether the additional factor has significant effects on the dependent variable measure, but also determine the interaction effects of the added with the original independent variable.

In light of the above, it should be clear that mere arbitrary definition of one aspect of the therapist as the independent variable does not excuse an investigator from considering other therapist factors that may be concomitantly present and contributing to the results obtained.

The essential goal of any research is to "design the experiment so that the effects of the independent variables can be evaluated unambiguously." (Underwood, 1957, p. 86).

So long, however, as the investigator confronts these and other confounding problems, his experimental-manipulative research can provide answers to the central behavior modification question: which therapist behaviors produce what effects with which kinds of patients? It is, therefore, a more powerful research tool than correlational-naturalistic investigations. On the other hand, whether the results of these generalist studies are meaningful or heuristic in a more general sense is a different question (the analogue validity question) and is related to the extent to which the miniature life situation approximates the complexity and richness of real life behavior—the extent to which the laboratory is veridical vis-à-vis real life. "The fact that experimentation is sometimes not possible is only part of the reason for choosing a correlational approach. More important is the consideration that experimental manipulation is often a very poor substitute for the real thing." (Shontz, 1965, p. 156).

A few other critical statements seem in order. It seems nearsighted and off-target, in studies where the therapist is an experimental subject, to ask the therapist only to write down or choose from questionnaires of various sorts what he would say if he were a therapist confronted with a particular experimental patient. It takes such little extra effort for the therapist to provide, and the experimenter to record, vocal responses that it seems a waste to continue nonvocal behavior recording only. Next, it seems possible that greater efforts could be applied to obtaining real patients (that is, subjects with avowed "emotional problems") in these manipulative studies. One possibility is that patients on waiting lists of various psychotherapy outpatient institutions might provide a useful source of subjects for these studies. They would receive some psychotherapeutic assistance from their experimental contacts, would still be guaranteed follow-up from therapists at the original institutions, and might perhaps be given some preferential treatment in gratitude for their research cooperation. Likewise, the various psychological clinics in universities around the country could be modified more in research directions. These clinics are first and foremost training and research institutions for clinical psychology students. A portion of the patients in these clinics could be selected as homogeneous subgroups for manipulative research projects without violating either one's ethics or one's commitment to training. A final suggestion is that, so long as the experimenter can provide a specific program of interview behavior for the therapists of his study, he might reap additional benefits by using expert (at least relatively experienced) artisans to provide the therapist-manipulations rather than inexperienced trainees or students of various sorts. On the other hand, it seems equally clear that if one has to choose between inexplicit-expertise and specified-inexperience, the latter is the more desirable alternative.

With more creative research applications, it seems quite probable that experimental-manipulative strategies can offer not only statements of cause-effect relationships, but also meaningful statements directly relevant for psychotherapy artisanship as well as for the science of behavior modification.

Experimental-Naturalistic Designs

The major conclusion of the first part of this chapter, summarized in the Grid Model of Figure 2.1, was that the most heuristic payoff for behavior modification research lies with experimental designs incorporating both the correlational-naturalistic and generalist-manipulative traditions of psychological research. Operationally this means the experimenter utilizes jointly in his study at least one therapist manipulative as well as at least one organismic (individual differences) patient factor as independent variables. The use of at least two independent variable dimensions, one organismic the other environmental-manipulative, permits the possibility of analyzing the dependent variable measures for *interaction* effects. This possibility permits the ultimate answer to the crucial behavior modification question: which therapist behaviors produce what changes in which kinds of patients? The basic assumption of this strategy is that of the Grid Model—namely, that it takes different therapist behaviors to effect different changes for different kinds of patients.

This rationale will not be repeated here; rather, examples will be given of the ways this strategy has been implemented to date—admittedly not as frequently as this author judges appropriate.[8]

The research strategy involves choosing two or more groups of patients as subjects, each group made homogeneous by various procedures. The experimenter then provides two or more differential treatments (therapist-behavior conditions) to each grouping of patient-subjects. His general hypothesis is that a particular therapist-treatment (say Condition A) will be more effective with one of the patient groups (Group 1) than with other groups, while a different therapist treatment (Condition B) will be more effective with another patient group (Group 2). The statistical design is at least 2 × 2 factorial, and the investigator predicts that a significant interaction effect will occur. Studies are: Bohn, 1965; Carson, Harden, and Shows, 1964; Holder, Carkhuff, and Berenson, 1967; Kaplan, 1966; Pallone and Grande, 1965; Tolor and Kissinger, 1965; and Yulis and Kiesler, 1968.

All these studies utilize factorial designs or modifications thereof. They can be classified into two general groups: those where the dependent variable is some measure of patient behavior (patients or undergraduates serve as the experimental Ss), and those where the dependent variable is some aspect of therapist behavior (with therapists, trainees, or undergraduates serving as experimental Ss).

1. "Patient" as the Experimental Subject

Examples. Kaplan (1966) studied the effect of interview type on high and low anxious students. Her Ss were 52 undergraduate females (paid volunteers), 29 HI and 23 LO Anxious as determined by several anxiety questionnaires. The Ss were taken to an interview room and seated facing a large one-way-vision-mirror. They were asked to sit in the room alone and talk, and told they were being observed by a psychologist behind the mirror listening to them and trying to understand them. Half the Ss in each anxiety group received one of the following treatment-instructions: Free-Association

(highly unstructured with traditional instructions to say anything that came into their mind) and Problem-Focused (talk about "what you would feel you needed to talk about if you were a patient who had come to a therapist"). The dependent variable measures were Bordin's Free-Association Scale (which reflects the degree of spontaneity and affect an S shows in an interview situation), Mahl's speech-disruption ratio, a defense measure, and a modified form of Dollard and Auld's content category scoring system. The design was 2 × 2 factorial, with HI versus LO Anxious Ss receiving Free-Association versus Problem-Focused treatment instructions. The results showed a significant interaction with HI Anxious Ss responding significantly more on the various measures to the Problem-Focused interview, while LO Anxious Ss responded more to the Free-Association interview. Kaplan concluded that the LO Anxious Ss tended to be repressors and nonintrospective, whereas the HI Anxious Ss had a style of defense that permitted awareness of anxiety, that these distinctions may well be relevant to patients staying or quitting in psychotherapy, and that they may be an aid in the selection of appropriate treatment types. Tolor and Kissinger (1965) studied the effects of therapist interventions on hospitalized, mostly-schizophrenic Ss. Forty-eight Ss were selected on the basis of their extreme scores on the *Edwards Personal Preference Schedule Succorance Scale*, yielding groups of 24 HI and 24 LO Succorance patients. Each patient was exposed to 3 quasi-therapeutic sessions, the order of the 3 being systematically varied. Each session lasted about a half hour, with about a week interval between sessions. In each session S sat at a desk (alone in the room) and talked into a microphone. When S pressed a button, an operator activated a tape-recording of a "therapeutic" comment delivered through a speaker in S's room. S could make as many request for comments as he wished, although every fifth signal remained unrewarded for a 15-second period to discourage continuous signaling. The 3 classes of therapist statements used in the respective 3 sessions were Nondirective, Positive Mental Health Approach (statements in the Norman Vincent Peale tradition), and Rational-Directive Approach (statements tailored to Ellis' rational psychotherapy). All therapist comments had been prerecorded on tape by one E. Dependent variable measures were patients' favor-

---

[8] Several studies have gone half the distance recommended by this strategy, by forming relatively homogeneous subgroups of patients-subjects (for example, Kanfer and Marston, 1966; Noblin, Timmons, and Kael, 1966; and Pierce and Mosher,

1967). But these researchers did not also provide more than one experimental condition or differential treatments. Instead, all Ss (admittedly divided into homogeneous subgroups—a very positive step) received the same treatment.

able versus unfavorable ratings, change of anxiety level, change in semantic differential meanings for "Me" and "My Therapist," and frequency of pressing the button, for each of the 3 sessions. The 3×2 mixed factorial, Type 1 (Lindquist, 1953) design permitted an evaluation of the 3 therapist treatments for the HI versus LO Succorance schizophrenic patients. Although the results showed that all but 3 Ss indicated they were talking to a "real" therapist, the statistical analyses revealed no differences as a result of the 3 classes of "therapeutic interventions."

2. "Therapist" as the Experimental Subject

Examples. Bohn (1965) reports a study of counselor behavior as a function of counselor dominance, counselor experience, and client type. Sixty male counselors represented the "therapist" subjects of this study. They were classified along two therapist independent-variable dimensions: Experienced (graduate students in clinical and counseling psychology) versus Inexperienced (undergraduate students) and HI versus LO Dominance (Dominance Scale of the California Psychological Inventory). These 4 groups of therapists (15 in each group) were each presented with three 10-minute tape-recorded interviews (role-played by actors) of 3 types of clients: Typical, Dependent, and Hostile. Each of the 3 tapes had 10 stopping points following client statements. Each therapist listened to each tape, was asked to assume the role of counselor in the recordings, and at each of the 10 stopping points of each tape to select from 4 multiple-choice foil alternatives the response closest to what he would say if he were that client's therapist. The therapists' multiple-choice selections were then scored for "directiveness" (in contrast to nondirectiveness). The statistical design was a $2 \times 2 \times 3$ mixed factorial Type VI (Lindquist, 1953) with Experienced versus Inexperienced and HI versus LO Dominance counselors, and Typical versus Dependent versus Hostile patient tapes. The results showed that inexperienced counselors had higher directiveness scores than did experienced counselors. The analysis failed to confirm the expectation that HI Dominance counselors would be more directive than LO Dominance counselors. The expectation that experienced counselors would use a wider variety of therapist responses than would inexperienced counselors was not supported. Analysis of one first-order interaction effect supported the hypothesis that counselors would be most directive with the dependent client. Finally, the three client types elicited significantly different responses from the same counselors. Carson, Harden, and Shows (1964) studied Whitehorn and Betz's A–B distinction and behavior in a quasi-therapeutic situation. Assuming that the A–B SVIB Scale measures some aspect of personality, and that the particular characteristics involved may be manifested in the helping behavior of people in general (that is, not just of psychotherapists), these authors used 16 A and 16 B undergraduates as "interviewers" of 8 Distrust-Hostility-Expectancy of harm (DHH) interviewees and 8 Trust-Friendly-Expectancy of help (TFH) interviewees respectively. Each interviewer was given some instruction on interviewing techniques. An Information Outline was given to each, containing 18 modified items from Jourard's Self-Disclosure questionnaire, and the interviewer was told his task was to obtain, in the 20-minute interview, as much information as possible in the areas indicated on the Outline. Each interview was monitored by two judges who rated the amount of information obtained by the interviewer on an item-by-item basis. The design was 2×2 factorial (A versus B interviewers with DHH versus TFH interviewees). The results showed a significant interaction effect: As in relation to DHH and Bs in relation to TFH interviewees obtained relatively high amounts of information, principally by virtue of a more broad-ranging inquiry. None of the main effects was significant.

Experimental-Naturalistic Designs: An Evaluation. This chapter has argued for factorial designs in behavior modification research. At this point, however, some pessimism is inevitable, considering the quality of the experimental-naturalistic research just reviewed.

Most of this disappointment, however, springs from inadequacies that are present also in much of other behavior modification research. The constructs studied generally provoke little excitement in one experienced in psychotherapy artisanship. One wonders whether something more challenging than statements in the Norman Vincent Peale tradition might be applied as a treatment condition, particularly for schizophrenic patients (succorant or not). One can ask why studies of what therapists do when confronted with patients are so popular, when the crucial theoretical question is what effective things therapists *should* be doing. One answer, of course, is that therapist subjects are quite available and receptive for research in academic settings. One can ponder the naïveté of the dependent variable measures sometimes used;

but be aware that often what is popular and available is grasped, rather than effort being expended to develop a more theoretically relevant measure. Finally, one can be disappointed by the generally atheoretical nature of the treatment manipulations.

On the other hand, some admiration seems due investigators attempting to research theoretically relevant and complex constructs, such as empathic understanding, free-association, countertransference, and the like. This respect is enhanced further when one can find explicit attempts to develop a rationale for differential effects of the same treatment for different groups of patient subjects. Some excitement seems appropriate in response to innovative procedures such as constructing alternate therapist statements at different levels of interpretive "depth" or interpretive statements dealing or not dealing with patients' transference implications; or testing the limits of free-association instructions; or attempting to find therapist-experimenters of various levels of "therapeutic attitudes"; or programming actors to portray well-defined roles in a manner credible to patient subjects.

Clearly, only a beginning has been made, but the promise seems considerable. Perhaps specific theories of behavior change for various types of patients will gradually evolve from the findings of future factorial-design research. Maybe they will be developed independently, or in response to the challenge of this research. When explicit and precise theories of this sort arrive, the science of behavior modification will begin to come of age.

STUDY OF THE SINGLE CASE IN SCIENCE

This final research perspective relates to the idiographic-nomothetic controversy (Allport, 1962; Beck, 1953; DuMas, 1955; Eysenck, 1953; Rosenzweig, 1951; Seeman and Galanter, 1952). Emphasis on the unique individual is currently reemphasized with the emergence of humanistic and existential formulations of psychotherapy. Several authors have argued that the issue is spurious (Holt, 1962; Phillips, 1956; Shontz, 1965). The idiographic-nomothetic distinction

misleads, to the extent that it dichotomizes the approaches, rather than representing them as different emphases with some overlap and much fruitful complementarity.

Intensive study of the single case (either controlled or uncontrolled, with or without measurements) is a valuable *source of hypotheses* for the explanation of human behavior. Discovery of hypotheses is a legitimate and essential scientific activity. But idiographic study has little place in the confirmatory aspect of scientific activity, which looks for laws applying to individuals generally. Confirmatory operations ultimately are the task of the nomothetist who, through controlled observations, measurements, or manipulations, can confirm or disconfirm hypothetical statements about human behavior.

The issue also relates to the scientist-artisan distinction made earlier in the chapter. Artisans, by definition, tend to be idiographic, while scientists ultimately must be nomothetic. Idiographic-artisans and nomothetic-scientists can be of much more use to each other if they keep in mind that there is some overlap in their interests and purposes. The artisan can profit from an understanding of scientific methodology and philosophy of science. He might utilize more controlled observation where possible in his applied work, might be more sensitive to making explicit and sharing with others through publication his theoretical formulations, and might be concerned about grounding his constructs in the observable, public domain. The scientist, on the other hand, might be more concerned about devising measures and procedures of studying individual cases (Allport, 1962) as a source of fruitful hypotheses and variables. He might be more interested in a dialogue with artisans as a further check on the principles he has momentarily confirmed, might be more concerned about deviant cases in his data that seem to be exceptions to the relationships he has confirmed, and might be more concerned about modifying his research techniques in the direction of utilizing the advantages of single case data.

Single-Case Methodology. One paradox of the idiographic-nomothetic polemic is that the person arguing most for the necessity of quantitative approaches to single case study spent most of his life doing nomothetic research. In 1962, Allport explicitly listed examples of quantitative approaches meeting his criteria for idiographic study (Allport, 1962). He enumerated several data collection techniques suited to intensive individual research, calling those most suited "morphogenic" and those less-suited, but in the same tradition, "semimorphogenic." The former include the "technique of matching," which requires judges to identify, in a pool of data, performances of the same person on different tasks or in different situations. Another example is the "self-anchoring scale" (Kilpatrick and Cantril, 1960)—a rating device in which the person is asked to anchor certain extreme judgments (on a numerical scale) in his own value system. "Semimorphogenic" methods include certain modifications of traditional rating scales, adjective check lists, the Role Construct Repertory Test (Kelly, 1955), the Allport-Vernon Study of Values (1960), and Stephenson's Q-Sort (1953), among others.[9] Allport concludes, particularly regarding the morphogenic methods: "All these various examples suffice to show that it is possible to examine the internal and unique pattern of personal structure without any dependence whatsoever on universal or group norms" (Allport, 1962, p. 246).

The science of psychology has generally been explicitly cool to Allport's plea, with a few recent notable exceptions. Dukes (1965) reviewed studies of single cases in psychological research. He found 246 studies in the literature over the past 25 years, indicating clearly that although Allport did little of this research, others were certainly working on it. Dukes' theme is that "a brief scanning of general and historical accounts of psychology will dispel any doubts about their importance, revealing, as it does, many instances of pivotal research in which the observations were confined to the behavior of only one person or animal" (p. 74). He offers as legitimate rationales for $N=1$ studies the following situations: (1) when between-individual variability for the function under scrutiny is known to be negligible—hence results from a second subject may be considered

redundant; (2) when one case reported in depth parsimoniously exemplifies many; (3) when one case provides negative results—one negative case is sufficient to demand revision of a traditionally accepted hypothesis; (4) when one has limited opportunity to observe an instance of a particular behavior—rare behaviors such as multiple personality, congenital insensitivity to pain, unilateral color blindness, and the like; (5) when the research situation is greatly extended in time, requires expensive or specialized training of the subject, or entails intricate and difficult-to-administer controls; and finally (6) when a researcher simply wants to focus on a problem—by defining questions, defining variables, and indicating approaches. Dukes concludes: "Regardless of rationale and despite obvious limitations, the usefulness of $N=1$ studies in psychological research seems ... to be fairly well established" (p. 78).

Chassan (1967) also argues persuasively for the advantages of single case studies. He distinguishes "extensive" from "intensive" models of research. Although both models are based solidly on probability theory, the latter clearly refer to single-case studies, in contrast to the former groups-of-subjects investigations. Chassan argues that there are inherent limitations of extensive designs which can only be overcome with single-case strategies. Although the major focus of his book is on drug studies in clinical psychiatry, he attempts some applications to psychoanalytic psychotherapy. For example, he states that the long-term nature of psychoanalytic or intensive psychotherapy represents an ideal situation for "(1) the description of various observable and inferential components of a given patient's psychopathology in statistical terms, (2) testing for significant trends in the reduction of psychopathology in the course of treatment from one calendar period to the next, (3) testing statistically by means of occasional experimental design within the context of the ongoing psychotherapy the possible differential influence of particular therapist techniques and forms of intervention timed to test particular hypotheses regarding their effect on one or another aspect of progress, (4) testing similarly for the influence of certain

[9] The reader can check Allport's article for greater detail.

repeated intercurrent and interpersonal events as these may occur on a more or less random basis throughout the course of psychotherapy, and (5) testing statistically whether apparent reactions to such possibly significant events are altered significantly in a patient with the passage of time in treatment" (p. 213).

Finally, Shontz (1965) cogently documents the value of single-case inquiry. He asserts that idiographic study is not restricted to discovery of hypotheses, but has an additional fruitful confirmatory function regarding constructs. A major theme of his *Research Methods in Personality* is that "the measurement situation in personality research would be considerably improved if tests and examinations were validated not only through group research, but also through the intensive study of a series of individual subjects, each of whom provides an independent basis for judging the validity of the instrument" (p. 61). Shontz is explicit about procedures for implementing this confirmatory strategy. For example, he suggests that one "select, in advance, a specific subject who simply must score in certain ways on the instrument if anyone is to accept it as valid. If a test is intended to measure religiosity, it might be a good idea to find the most religious person in town and have him take the test. If that person does not achieve a high score, the instrument must certainly be useless" (p. 62). The final chapter of his book argues for use of a "representative case" strategy in confirmatory research. The method comprises "an integration of the case study approach with natural process and remote control strategies. Its aims are to test deductively derived hypotheses, through the examination of single subjects, chosen for their specific appropriateness to the research problem of interest" (p. 234). Shontz then reviews Allport's morphogenic and semimorphogenic procedures, and closes with extensive descriptions of other studies incorporating the logic of the "representative case."

Anyone seriously courting single-case research can save much time, and profit considerably, by consulting these challenging treatises. In the long pull, the science of behavior modification could derive considerable benefit from innovative and persistent quantitative study of the individual case.

Some single-case behavior-modification studies are Bellak and Chassan (1964), DiMascio and Brooks (1961), Murray (1954), Nunnally (1955), Osgood and Luria (1954), Shapiro, (1964), Subotnik (1966), and Van Kaam (1959).

Examples. Murray (1954) studied the verbal behavior of one patient in psychotherapy. The patient was a 24-year-old male college graduate, who was seen in individual psychotherapy for 17 hours at an outpatient clinic. His presenting complaint was that he had trouble getting to sleep at night—he felt that if he fell asleep he might die. He was tremendously threatened, but couldn't say what he was threatened by. The therapist was mainly supportive, but made interpretations about the defensive nature of his physical complaints and the hostility that arose when the patient became dependent. A permissive attitude toward the expression of hostility was maintained. At termination, the therapist felt that some progress had been made in the patient's ability to express his hostility, as well as to see its relationship with his dependency. Murray attempted to validate the therapist's description of patient change over the 17 interviews. He focused on the hostile and defensive behavior of the patient in the therapy sessions, and developed content measures for these constructs. The unit scored for each of the tape-recorded sessions was the statement—either a simple sentence or the meaning phrases of a more complicated sentence. Each statement in the sessions was judged by Murray, while listening to the interview recordings, as belonging to one of the several categories of hostility and defense. He then tabulated the number of statements in each of the categories for each of the 17 therapy hours. Analysis of the resultant hostility and defense scores revealed patterns of change across therapy consistent with psychoanalytic theory as well as with the therapist's evaluation of the patient's progress. Murray summarizes the pattern of content ratings that emerged as follows:

"The patient began treatment with a good deal of anxiety and subsequent defensiveness. His defensiveness decreased as a result of a combination of permissiveness about hostility and punitiveness about defenses on the part of the therapist. As this occurred he expressed strong hostility to his mother. This expression of hostility led to an increase in anxiety and defensiveness. The defense which increased was the one not previously punished by the therapist. Subsequently, hostility was displaced further and further away from his mother. Hostility to displaced objects was stronger . . . It is possible that because of the unpunished expression of hostility to the displaced objects the patient was able later in therapy ... to express hostility about his mother much more strongly, at least in the therapeutic situation."

Nunnally (1955) studied the self-conceptions of a single patient who had undergone psychotherapy. The changing modes of self-description of the subject (Miss Sun) were studied over a two-year period. The experiment was divided into three phases: (a) a pretherapy period lasting six months, during which extensive clinical interviewing and testing of Miss Sun occurred; (b) a nine-month course of client-centered therapy; and (c) an eight-month posttherapy period. The basic measurement procedure used was the Q-Sort. During the pretherapy period, she made 15 self-assessments describing herself in important situations in her life (such as "as I am generally," "as my mother regards me," and "as I act in the presence of my aunt and uncle"). These Q sorts were intercorrelated and factor-analyzed, three factors being obtained (I—aloof, cooperative, and imperturbable; II—outgoing and striving; and III—Bohemianlike escape). Next, propositions concerning how Miss Sun might change during the ensuing therapy were asserted in respect to these factors. In the posttherapy period, Miss Sun repeated the self-assessments that had defined the earlier factors. The results were obtained by comparing the separate factor analyses of the pretherapy and posttherapy Q sorts. Nunnally found that most of the propositions were supported. Miss Sun's conception of her ideal self changed markedly after therapy, with only small, if any, change in her present-self assessment. There was a definite trend toward increased congruence among her self-assessments across various situations after therapy. At follow-up she held the opinion that everyone else regarded her much as she regarded herself. Finally, there was strong support for the prediction that Miss Sun's unrealistic opinions of the way her father regarded her would fade markedly after therapy.

A FINAL STATEMENT

This chapter initially developed a scientific perspective for the study of behavior modification. It showed that differentiations of behavior modification from other traditional areas of psychology are less and less clear-cut or appropriate. It briefly reviewed current theor-etical formulations of psychotherapy, concluded that basic inadequacies are present, and suggested a Grid Model format as a guide to future theory and research. It showed that many of the difficult issues of the past are really spurious, reflecting confusion resulting from the patient, therapist, and outcome uniformity myths, from an unfortunate fusion of the scientific and artisan aspects of psychotherapy, and from irresolution regarding the place of idiography in science.

Its basic research design stance derives from the Grid Model, as well as from Cronbach's conceptualization of the two disciplines of scientific psychology. The research designs outlined and evaluated first fell into idiographic ($N=1$) versus nomothetic strategies. The latter designs were divided further into naturalistic-correlation versus generalist-manipulative traditions. A third nomothetic division, logically deriving from the rest of the chapter, involves factorial research designs incorporating both patient organismic (ID) and therapist manipulative factors as independent variables.

All these strategies have legitimate application in behavior modification research. A researcher's design first and foremost must be appropriate to the particular theoretical question he is posing. The author feels, however, that factorial designs as defined above offer the greatest precision, power, and payoff for behavior modification research.

Finally, an implicit stance of this chapter is that there is reason for much optimism in the study of behavior modification. Myths are being exploded, new paradigms are emerging, and exciting new approaches are being constructed. Careful naturalistic research is appearing. But, most importantly, it is evident that experimental studies of behavior modification are feasible and established. As scientific psychologists, psychiatrists, social workers or what have you, we can no longer fall back on pseudo-issues or supposedly insurmountable complexities as justification to avoid doing research in behavior modification. Research can be and is being done—and done well. We need only to continue, expand, and solidify these creative beginnings.

REFERENCES

Abse, D. N. *Hysteria and related mental disorders.* Baltimore: Williams and Wilkins, 1966.

Adams, H., Robertson, M., and Cooper, D. Sensory deprivation and personality change. *Journal of Nervous and Mental Disease*, 1966, **143**, 256–265.

Allport, G. W. The general and the unique in psychological science. *Journal of Personality*, 1962, **30**, 405–422. In E. A. Southwell, and M. Merbaum (Eds.), *Personality readings in theory and research.* Belmont, California: Wadsworth, 1964, 244–258.

Allport, G. W., Vernon, P. E., and Lindzey, G. *A study of values* (3rd Ed.). Boston: Houghton Mifflin, 1960.

Ashby, J. D., Ford, D. H., Guerney, B. G., Jr., and Guerney, L. F. Effects on clients of a reflective and a leading type of psychotherapy. *Psychological Monographs*, 1952, **71** (Whole No. 453).

Astin, A. W. The functional autonomy of psychotherapy. *American Psychologist*, 1961, **16**, 75–78.

Baker, E. The differential effects of two psychotherapeutic approaches on client perceptions. *Journal of Counseling Psychology*, 1960, **7**, 46–50.

Bandura, A., Lipsher, D. H., and Miller, P. E. Psychotherapists' approach-avoidance reactions to patients' expressions of hostility. *Journal of Consulting Psychology*, 1960, **24**, 1–8.

Barrett-Lennard, G. T. Dimensions of therapist response as casual factors in therapeutic change. *Psychological Monographs*, 1962, **76**, No. 43 (Whole No. 562).

Beck, A. T. *Depression: Clinical, experimental and theoretical aspects.* New York: Harper and Row, 1967.

Beck, S. J. The science of personality: Nomothetic or idiographic? *Psychological Review*, 1953, **60**, 353–359.

Beery, Judith Williams. Therapist warmth-acceptance as a function of level of therapist experience and attitude of the patient. Unpublished doctoral dissertation, University of Iowa, 1967.

Bellack, L., and Chassan, J. B. An approach to the evaluation of drug effect during psychotherapy: A double-blind study of a single case. *Journal of Nervous and Mental Disease*, 1964, **139**, 20–30.

Bellak, L., and Small, L. *Emergency psychotherapy and brief psychotherapy.* New York: Grune and Stratton, 1965.

Betz, B. J. Experiences in research in psychotherapy with schizophrenic patients. In Strupp, H. H., and Luborsky, L. (Eds.), *Research in Psychotherapy*, II. Baltimore: The French-Bray Co., 1962. Pp. 41–60.

Bohn, M. J., Jr. Counselor behavior as a function of counselor dominance, counselor experience and client type. *Journal of Counseling Psychology*, 1965, **12**, 346–352.

Bordin, E. S., Cutler, R. L., Dittmann, A. T., Harway, N. I., Raush, H. L., and Rigler, D. Measurement problems in process research on psychotherapy. *Journal of Consulting Psychology*, 1954, **18**, 79–82.

Boyer, L. B., and Giovacchini, P. L. *Psychoanalytic treatment of characterological and schizophrenic disorders.* New York: Science House, 1967.

Brill, N. Q., and Storrow, H. A. Social class and psychiatric treatment. *Archives of General Psychiatry*, 1960, **3**, 340–344.

Buss, A. H., and Durkee, A. Conditioning of hostile verbalizations in a situation resembling a clinical interview. *Journal of Consulting Psychology*, 1958, **22**, 415–418.

Butler, J. M., and Grummon, D. L. Another failure to repeat Keet's study. *Journal of Abnormal and Social Psychology*, 1953, **48**, 597.

Campbell, D. T., and Stanley, J. C. *Experimental and quasiexperimental designs for research.* Chicago: Rand McNally and Co., 1966.

Carson, R. C., Harden, J. A., and Shows, W. D. A–B distinction and behavior in quasi-therapeutic situations. *Journal of Consulting Psychology*, 1964, **28**, 426–433.

Carson, R. C., and Heine, R. W. Similarity and success in therapeutic dyads. *Journal of Consulting Psychology*, 1962, **26**, 38–43.

Chassan, J. B. Probability processes in psychoanalytic psychiatry. In J. Scher (Ed.), *Theories of the mind.* New York: Free Press of Glencoe, 1962. Pp. 598–618.

Chassan, J. B. *Research designs in clinical psychology and psychiatry.* New York: Appleton-Century-Crofts, 1967.

Colby, K. M. Experiment on the effects of an observer's presence on the image system during psychoanalytic free-association. *Behavioral Science*, 1960, **5**, 216–232.

Colby, K. M. On the greater amplifying power of causal-correlative over interrogative inputs on free-association in an experimental psychoanalytic situation. *Journal of Nervous and Mental Disease*, 1961, **133**, 233–239.

Cooke, G. Identification of the efficacious components of Reciprocal Inhibition psychotherapy. Unpublished doctoral disseration, University of Iowa, 1966.

Craig, K. Incongruities between content and temporal measures of patients' responses to confrontation with personality descriptions. *Journal of Consulting Psychology*, 1966, **30**, 550–554.

Cronbach, L. J. The two disciplines of scientific psychology. *American Psychologist*, 1957, **12**, 671–684.

Cross, H. J. The outcome of psychotherapy: A selected analysis of research findings. *Journal of Consulting Psychology*, 1964, **28**, 413–417.

Cutler, R. L. Countertransference effects in psychotherapy. *Journal of Consulting Psychology*, 1958, **22**, 349–356.

Davison, G. C. Systematic desensitization as a counterconditioning process. *Journal of Abnormal Psychology*, 1968, **73**, 91–99.

Dinoff, M., Rickard, H. C., Salzberg, H., and Sipprelle, C. N. An experimental analogue of three psychotherapeutic approaches. *Journal of Clinical Psychology*, 1960, **16**, 70–73.

DiMascio, A., and Brooks, G. Free association to a fantasied psychotherapist. *Archives of General Psychiatry*, 1961, **4**, 513–516.

Dollard, J., and Miller, N. E. *Personality and psychotherapy*. New York: McGraw-Hill Book Co., 1950.

Dukes, W. F. N=1. *Psychological Bulletin*, 1965, **64**, 74–79.

DuMas, F. M. Science and the single case. *Psychological Reports*, 1955, **1**, 65–76.

Ebel, R. L. Estimation of the reliability of ratings. *Psychometrika*, 1951, **16**, 407–424.

Edwards, A. L. *Experimental design in psychological research*. New York: Holt, Rinehart and Winston, 1962 (revised edition).

Edwards, A. L., and Cronbach, L. J. Experimental design for research in psychotherapy. *Journal of Clinical Psychology*, 1952, **8**, 51–59.

Eysenck, H. J. The science of personality: Nomothetic. *Psychological Review*, 1953, **61**, 339–342.

Eysenck, H. J. The effects of psychotherapy. In H. J. Eysenck (Ed.), *Handbook of Abnormal Psychology*. New York: Basic Books Inc., 1961. Pp. 697–725.

Feifel, H., and Eells, J. Patients and therapists assess the same psychotherapy. *Journal of Consulting Psychology*, 1963, **27**, 310–318.

Ford, D. H., and Urban, H. B. *Systems of psychotherapy: A comparative study*. New York: Wiley, 1963.

Frank, G. H. The effect of directive and nondirective statements by therapists on the content of patient verbalizations. *Journal of General Psychology*, 1964, **71**, 323–328.

Frank, J. D. Problems of control in psychotherapy as exemplified by the psychotherapy research project of the Phipps Psychiatric Clinic. In E. A. Rubinstein and M. B. Parloff (Eds.), *Research in Psychotherapy*. Washington, D. C.: American Psychological Association, Inc., 1959. Pp. 10–26.

Gagne, R. M. (Ed.) *Learning and individual differences*. Columbus, Ohio: Charles E. Merrill, 1967.

Gelder, M. G., Marks, I. M., and Wolff, H. H. Desensitization and psychotherapy in the treatment of phobic states: A controlled inquiry. *British Journal of Psychiatry*, 1967, **113**, 53–73.

Gendlin, E. T., Jenney, R. H., and Shlien, J. Counselor ratings of process and outcomes in client-centered therapy. *Journal of Clinical Psychology*, 1960, **16**, 210–213.

Gendlin, E. T., and Berlin, J. Galvanic skin response correlates of different modes of experiencing. *Journal of Clinical Psychology*, 1961, **17**, 73–77C.

Gendlin, E. T., Beebe, J., Cossens, J., Klein, M. H., and Oberlander, M. Focusing ability in psychotherapy, personality, and creativity. In J. M. Shlien, *Research in psychotherapy*. Vol. 3. Washington, D. C.: American Psychological Association, 1968. Pp. 217–241.

Goldstein, A. P. *Therapist-patient expectancies in psychotherapy*. New York: Macmillan, 1962.

Goldstein, A. P., Heller, K., and Sechrest, L. B. *Psychotherapy and the psychology of behavior change*. New York: Wiley, 1966.

Gordon, J. E. Leading and following psychotherapeutic techniques with hypnotically induced repression and hostility. *Journal of Abnormal and Social Psychology*, 1957, **54**, 405–410.

Gordon, J. E., Martin, B., and Lundy, R. M. GSRs during repression, suppression, and verbalization in psychotherapeutic interviews. In Stollak, G. B., Guerney, B. G., and Rothberg, M. (Eds.), *Psychotherapy research: Selected readings*. Chicago: Rand McNally, 1966. Pp. 420–429.

Greenspoon, J. The reinforcing effect of two spoken sounds on the frequency of two responses. *American Journal of Psychology*, 1955, **68**, 409–416.

Grossman, D. An experimental investigation of a psychotherapeutic technique. *Journal of Consulting Psychology*, 1952, **16**, 325–331.

Guilford, J. P. *Psychometric methods*. New York: McGraw-Hill, 1954 (2nd Ed.), p. 395.

Haggard, E. A., and Murray, H. A. The relative effectiveness of three "therapy" procedures on the reduction of experimentally induced anxiety. *Psychological Bulletin*, 1942, **39**, 441. (Abstract).

Harway, N. I., Dittmann, A. T., Raush, H. L., Bordin, E. T., and Rigler, D. The measurement of depth of interpretation. *Journal of Consulting Psychology*, 1955, **19**, 247–253.

Harrell, S. The effects of counterconditioning, extinction, and operant reward on a phobic reaction. Unpublished doctoral dissertation, Emory University, 1968.

Heim, R. B. An attempt to repeat the Keet counseling-comparison experiment. *American Psychologist*, 1951, **6**, 495. (Abstract)

Heine, R. W., and Trosman, H. Initial expectations of the doctor-patient interaction as a factor in the continuance of psychotherapy. *Psychiatry*, 1960, **23**, 275–278.

Heller, K. Ambiguity in the interviewer interaction. In J. M. Shlien (Ed.), *Research in psychotherapy: Vol. 3*. Washington, D. C.: American Psychological Association, 1968. Pp. 242–259.

Heller, K., Davis, J., and Myers, R. The effects of interviewer style in a standardized interview. *Journal of Consulting Psychology*, 1966, **30**, 501–508.

Heller, K., Myers, R. A., and Kline, L. V. Interviewer behavior as a function of standardized client roles. *Journal of Consulting Psychology*, 1963, **27**, 117–112.

Hirsch, J. Individual differences in behavior and their genetic basis. In E. L. Bliss (Ed.), *Roots of behavior*. NewYork: Harper, 1962. Pp. 3–23.

Holder, T., Carkhuff, R., and Berenson, B. Differential effects of the manipulation of therapeutic conditions upon high and low functioning clients. *Journal of Counseling Psychology*, 1967, **14**, 63–66.

Hollingshead, A. B., and Redlich, F. C. *Social class and mental illness*. New York: Wiley, 1958.

Horst, P. A generalized expression for the reliability of measures. *Psychometrika*, 1949, **14**, 21–31.

Howe, E. S. and Pope, B. An empirical scale of therapist verbal activity level in the initial interview. *Journal of Consulting Psychology*, 1961, **25**, 510–520.

Hyman, R., and Breger, L. Discussion. In H. J. Eysenck (Ed.), *The effects of psychotherapy*. New York: International Science Press, 1966, pp. 81–86.

Jenkins, J. W., Wallach, M. S., and Strupp, H. H. Effects of two methods of response in a quasi-therapeutic situation. *Journal of Clinical Psychology*, 1962, **18**, 220–223.

Kamin, I., and Caughlan, J. Patients report the subjective experience of outpatient psychotherapy: A follow-up study. *American Journal of Psychotherapy*, 1963, **17**, 660–668.

Kanfer, F. H. Verbal rate, eyeblink, and content in structured psychiatric interviews. *Journal of Abnormal and Social Psychology*, 1960, **61**, 341–347.

Kanfer, F. H., and Marston, A. R. Characteristics of interactional behavior in a psychotherapy analogue. In Stollak, G. E., Guerney, B. G., and Rothberg, M. (Eds.), *Psychotherapy Research: Selected Readings*. Chicago: Rand McNally, 1966. Pp. 455–469.

Kanfer, F. H., Phillips, J. S., Matarazzo, J. D., and Saslow, G. Experimental modification of interviewer content in standardized interviews. *Journal of Consulting Psychology*, 1960, **24**, 528–536.

Kaplan, F. Effects of anxiety and defense in a therapy-like situation. *Journal of Abnormal Psychology*, 1966, **71**, 449–458.

Keet, C. D. Two verbal techniques in a miniature counseling situation. *Psychological Monographs*, 1948, **62**, 1–55.

Keith-Spiegel, P., and Spiegel, D. Perceived helpfulness of others as a function of compatible intelligence levels. *Journal of Counseling Psychology*, 1967, **14**, 61–62.

Kelly, G. A. *The psychology of personal constructs*. Vol. I. New York: Norton, 1955.

Kesner, L. S. A comparison of the effectiveness of two psychotherapeutic techniques in the resolution of a post-hypnotic conflict. *Journal of Clinical and Experimental Hypnosis*, 1954, **2**, 55–75.

Kiesler, D. J. Basic methodological issues implicit in psychotherapy process research. *American Journal of Psychotherapy*, 1966, **20**, 135–155, (a).

Kiesler, D. J. Some myths of psychotherapy research and the search for a paradigm. *Psychological Bulletin*, 1966, **65**, 110–136, (b).

Kiesler, D. J. A Grid Model for theory and research in the psychotherapies. In L. D. Eron and R. Callahan (Eds.), *The relationship of theory to practice in psychotherapy*. Chicago: Aldine Publishing Co., 1969.

Kiesler, D. J., Mathieu, P. L., and Klein, M. H. Sampling from the recorded therapy interview: A comparative study of different segment lengths. *Journal of Consulting Psychology*, 1964, **28**, 349–357.

Kiesler, D. J., Klein, M. H., and Mathieu, P. L. Sampling from the recorded therapy interview: The problem of segment location. *Journal of Consulting Psychology*, 1965, **29**, 337–344.

Kiesler, D. J., Mathieu, P. L., and Klein, M. H. Patient experiencing level and interaction-chronograph variables in therapy interview segments. *Journal of Consulting Psychology*, 1967, **14**, 314–318.

Kilpatrick, F. P. and Cantril, H. Self-anchoring scale: A measure of the individual's unique reality world. *Journal of Individual Psychology*, 1960, **16**, 158–170.

Klein, Marjorie H., Mathieu, P. L., and Kiesler, D. J. *The experiencing scale: a research and training manual*. Madison, Wisconsin: Bureau of Audio-Visual Instruction, University of Wisconsin Extension, 1970.

Korman, M. Implicit personality theories of clinicians as defined by semantic structures. *Journal of Consulting Psychology*, 1960, **24**, 180–186.

Krasner, L. The therapist as a social reinforcement machine. In H. H. Strupp and L. Luborsky (eds.), *Research in psychotherapy*. Vol. 2. Washington, D. C.: American Psychological Association, Inc., 1962. Pp. 61–94.

Lang, P. J., Lazovik, A. D., and Reynolds, D. J. Desensitization, suggestibility, and pseudotherapy. *Journal of Abnormal Psychology*, 1965, **70**, 395–402.

Lennard, H. G., and Bernstein, A. *The Anatomy of Psychotherapy*. New York City: Columbia University Press, 1960.

Levinson, D. J. The psychotherapist's contribution to the patient's treatment career. In. H. H. Strupp and L. Luborsky (Eds.), *Research in psychotherapy*. Vol. 2. Washington, D. C.: American Psychological Association, 1962. Pp. 13–24.

Levinson, R., and Kitchener, H. Treatment of delinquents: comparison of four methods for assigning inmates to counselors. *Journal of Consulting Psychology*, 1966, **30**, 364.

Levison, P. K., Zax, M., and Cowen, E. L. An experimental analogue of psychotherapy for anxiety reduction. *Psychological Reports*, 1961, **8**, 171–178.

Lindquist, E. F. *Design and analysis of experiments in psychology and education*. Boston: Houghton Mifflin, 1953.

Little, K. Research etiquette in the study of clinician's behavior. *Journal of Consulting Psychology*, 1967, **31**, 16–18.

London, P. *The modes and morals of psychotherapy*. New York: Holt, Rinehart, and Winston, 1964.

Maddi, S. R. *Personality theories: A comparative analysis*. Homewood, Illinois: The Dorsey Press, 1968.

Marlowe, D. Need for social approval and the operant conditioning of meaningful verbal behavior. *Journal of Consulting Psychology*, 1962, **26**, 79–83.

Martin, B., Lundy, R. M., and Lewin, M. H. Verbal and GSR responses in experimental interviews as a function of three degrees of "therapist" communication. *Journal of Abnormal and Social Psychology*, 1960, **60**, 234–240.

Matarazzo, J. D. Psychotherapeutic processes. In *Annual Review of Psychology*, 1965, **16**, 181–224.

Matarazzo, J. D., Wiens, A. N., Matarazzo, R. G., and Saslow, G. Speech and silence behavior in clinical psychotherapy and its laboratory correlates. In J. M. Shlien, H. F. Hunt, J. D. Matarazzo, and C. Savage (Eds.), *Research in psychotherapy. Vol.* 3. Washington, D. C.: American Psychological Association, 1968. Pp. 347–394.

Mazurkiewicz, J. F. A comparison of the effect of a reflective and a leading type of psychotherapy on client concept of self, ideal, and of therapist. Unpublished doctoral dissertation, Penn State University, 1957.

McClelland, D. C. *Personality.* New York: The Dryden Press, 1951, p. 69.

McNair, D. M., Callahan, D. M., and Lorr, M. Therapist "type" and patient response to psychotherapy. *Journal of Consulting Psychology*, 1962, **26**, 425–429.

Merrill, R. M. On Keet's study, "Two verbal techniques in a miniature counseling situation." *Journal of Abnormal and Social Psychology*, 1952, **47**, 722.

Moss, C. S., Ourth, L., Auvenshine, C., and Schallenberger, P. Attitudes of experienced psychologist-therapists. *American Psychologist*, 1960, **15**, 414. (Abstract)

Mowrer, O. H. *Learning theory and personality dynamics.* New York: Ronald Press, 1950.

Muench, G. A. An investigation of the efficacy of time-limited psychotherapy. *Journal of Counseling Psychology*, 1965, **12**, 294–298.

Murray, E. J. A case study in a behavioral analysis of psychotherapy. *Journal of Abnormal and Social Psychology*, 1954, **49**, 305–310.

Nichols, R. C., and Beck, K. W. Factors in psychotherapy change. *Journal of Consulting Psychology*, 1960, **24**, 388–399.

Noblin, C. D., Timmons, E. O., and Reynard, M. C. Psychoanalytic interpretations as verbal reinforcers: Importance of interpretation content. *Journal of Clinical Psychology*, 1963, **19**, 479–481.

Noblin, C., Timmons, E., and Kael, H. Differential effects of positive and negative verbal reinforcement on psychoanalytic character types. *Journal of Personality and Social Psychology*, 1966, **4**, 224–228.

Nunnally, J. C. An investigation of some propositions of selfconception: the case of Miss Sun. *Journal of Abnormal and Social Psychology*, 1955, **50**, 87–92.

Osgood, C. E., and Luria, Z. A blind analysis of a case of multiple personality using the semantic differential. *Journal of Abnormal and Social Psychology*, 1954, **49**, 579–591.

Pallone, N. J., and Grande, P. P. Counselor verbal mode, problem relevant communication, and client rapport. *Journal of Counseling Psychology*, 1965, **12**, 359–365.

Patterson, C. H. Counseling. In *Annual Review of Psychology*, 1966, **17**, 97.

Paul, G. L. *Insight vs desensitization in psychotherapy.* Stanford, California: Stanford University Press, 1966.

Phillips, E. L. *Psychotherapy: A modern theory and practice.* Englewood Cliffs, New Jersey: Prentice-Hall, 1956, cht. 2.

Phillips, E. L., and Agnew, J. W., Jr. A study of Rogers' "reflection" hypothesis. *Journal of Clinical Psychology*, 1953, **9**, 281–284.

Pierce, W., and Mosher, D. Perceived empathy, interviewer behavior and interviewee anxiety. *Journal of Consulting Psychology*, 1967, **31**, 101.

Pomeroy, D. S. The ameliorative effects of counseling upon maze performance following experimentally induced stress. *American Psychologist*, 1950, **5**, 327. (Abstract)

Powell, W. J., Jr. Differential effectiveness of interviewer interventions in an experimental interview. *Journal of Consulting and Clinical Psychology*, 1968, **32**, 210–215.

Rachman, S. Studies in desensitization. *Behavior Research and Therapy*, 1965, **3**, 245–251.

Raush, H. L., et al. A dimensional analysis of depth of interpretation. *Journal of Consulting Psychology*, 1956, **20**, 43–48.

Rice, L. N. Therapist's style of participation and case outcome. *Journal of Consulting Psychology*, 1965, **29**, 155–160.

Rogers, C. R., and Dymond, Rosalind F. *Psychotherapy and personality change.* Chicago: University of Chicago Press, 1954.

Rogers, C. R., Gendlin, E. T., Kiesler, D. J., and Truax, C. B. *The therapeutic relationship and its impact: A study of psychotherapy with schizophrenics.* Madison: University of Wisconsin Press, 1967.

Rosenzweig, S. Idiodynamics in personality theory with special reference to projective methods. *Psychological Review*, 1951, **58**, 213–223.

Russell, P. D., and Snyder, W. U. Counselor anxiety in relation to amount of clinical experience and quality of affect demonstrated by clients. In Stollak, G. E., Guerney, B. G., and Rothberg, M. (Eds.), *Psychotherapy research: selected readings.* Chicago: Rand McNally and Co., 1966 Pp. 530–536.

Salter, A. *Conditioned Reflex therapy.* New York: Capricorn Books, 1949.

Salzman, L. *The obsessive personality.* New York: Science House, 1968.

Sarason, I. G. Interrelationships among individual difference variables, behavior in psychotherapy, and verbal conditioning. *Journal of Abnormal and Social Psychology*, 1958, **56**, 339–344.

Saslow, G., Matarazzo, J. D., and Guze, S. B. The stability of Interaction Chronograph patterns in psychiatric interviews. *Journal of Consulting Psychology*, 1955, **19**, 417–430.

Schoeninger, D. N., Klein, M. H., and Mathieu, P. L. Sampling from the recorded therapy interview: Patient experiencing ratings made with and without therapist speech cues. *Journal of Consulting Psychology*, 1967 (brief report).

Seeman, W., and Galanter, F. Objectivity in systematic and "idiodynamic" psychology. *Psychological Review*, 1952, **59**, 285–289.

Shapiro, D. *Neurotic styles*. New York: Basic Books, 1966.

Shapiro, M. B. The measurement of clinically relevant variables. *Journal of Psychosomatic Research*, 1964, **8**, 245–254.

Shlien, J. M., Mosak, H. H., and Dreikurs, R. Effect of time limits: a comparison of client-centered and Adlerian psychotherapy. *American Psychologist*, 1960, **15**, 415. (Abstract)

Shontz, F. C. *Research methods in personality*. New York: Appleton-Century-Crofts, 1965.

Sommer, G. R., Maze, B., and Lehner, G. F., Jr. An empirical investigation of therapeutic "listening." *Journal of Clinical Psychology*, 1955, **11**, 123–136.

Speisman, J. C. Depth of interpretation and verbal resistance in psychotherapy. *Journal of Consulting Psychology*, 1959, **23**, 93–99.

Stephenson, W. *The study of behavior*. Chicago: University of Chicago Press, 1953.

Strickland, B. R., and Crowne, D. P. Need for approval and the premature termination of psychotherapy. *Journal of Consulting Psychology*, 1959, **23**, 435–441.

Strupp, H. H. The psychotherapist's contribution to the treatment process: an experimental investigation. *Behavioral Science*, 1958, **3**, 34–67.

Strupp, H. H. *Psychotherapists in action*. New York: Grune and Stratton, 1960.

Strupp, H. H., and Bergin, A. E. Some empirical and conceptual bases for coordinated research in psychotherapy. *International Journal of Psychiatry*, 1969, **7**, 18–90.

Strupp, H. H. Psychotherapy. In *Annual Review of Psychology*. Palo Alto, California: Annual Reviews Inc., 1962, p. 460.

Strupp, H. H., and Luborsky, L. (Eds.). *Research in psychotherapy*. Vol. 2. Washington, D. C.: American Psychological Association, 1962.

Strupp, H. H. The outcome problem in psychotherapy revisited. *Psychotherapy: Theory, Research and Practice*. 1963, **1**, 1–13.

Subotnik, L. Transference in child therapy: A third replication. *Psychological Record*, 1966, **16**, 265–277.

Sullivan, H. S. *Collected works*. New York: Basic Books, 1965.

Taffel, C. Anxiety and the conditioning of verbal behavior. *Journal of Abnormal and Social Psychology*, 1955, **51**, 496–501.

Tarachow, S. *An introduction to psychotherapy*. New York: International Universities Press, 1963.

Tolor, A., and Kissinger, D. R. The role of the therapist's intervention in a simulated therapy situation. *Journal of Clinical Psychology*, 1965, **21**, 442–445.

Truax, C. B., and Carkhuff, R. R. *Toward Effective Counseling and Psychotherapy*. Chicago: Aldine, 1967.

Underwood, D. J. *Psychological research*. New York: Appleton-Century-Crofts, 1957.

Van Kaam, A. L. Phenomenal analysis: Exemplified by a study of the experience of "really feeling understood." *Journal of Individual Psychology*, 1959, **15**, 66–72.

Verplanck, W. S. The control of the content of conversation: Reinforcement of statements of opinion. *Journal of Abnormal and Social Psychology*, 1955, **51**, 668–676.

Vogel, J. L. Authoritarianism in the therapeutic relationship. *Journal of Consulting Psychology*, 1961, **25**, 102–108.

Wagstaff, A. K., Rice, L. N., and Butler, J. Factors of client verbal participation in therapy. *Counseling Center Discussion Papers*, University of Chicago, 1960, **6**(9), 14 pp.

Wallach, M. S., and Strupp, H. H. Dimensions of psychotherapists' activity. *Journal of Consulting Psychology*, 1964, **28**, 120–125.

Waskow, I. E. Reinforcement in a therapy-like situation through selected responding to feelings or content. In Stollak, G. E., Guerney, B. G., and Rothberg, M. (Eds.), *Psychotherapy research: selected readings*. Chicago: Rand McNally and Co., 1966, pp. 488-498.

White, A. M., Fichtenbaum, L., and Dollard, J. Measure for predicting dropping out of psychotherapy. *Journal of Consulting Psychology*, 1964, **28**, 326–332.

Wiener, M. The effects of two experimental counseling techniques on performances impaired by induced stress. *Journal of Abnormal and Social Psychology*, 1955, **51**, 565–572.

Winder, C. C., Ahmad, F. Z., Bandura, A., and Rau, L. C. Dependency of patients, psychotherapists responses, and aspects of psychotherapy. *Journal of Consulting Psychology*, 1962, **26**, 129–134.

Wolberg, L. R. (Ed.). *Short-term psychotherapy*. New York: Grune and Stratton, 1965.

Wolpe, J. *Psychotherapy by reciprocal inhibition*. Palo Alto: Stanford University Press, 1958.

Yulis, S., and Kiesler, D. J. Countertransference response as a function of therapist anxiety and content of patient talk. *Journal of Consulting and Clinical Psychology*, 1968, **32**, 413–419.

Zax, M., and Klein, A. Measurement of personality and behavior changes following psychotherapy. *Psychological Bulletin*, 1960, **57**, 435–448.

3

THE APPLICATION OF PSYCHOPHYSIOLOGICAL METHODS TO THE STUDY OF PSYCHOTHERAPY AND BEHAVIOR MODIFICATION[1]

PETER J. LANG

UNIVERSITY OF WISCONSIN, MADISON

Psychophysiology is a young discipline, that may be differentiated from the broader field of physiological psychology by the variables its investigators characteristically manipulate and measure (Stern, 1964). They do not normally employ the classic methods of the physiological psychology of animals: invasion of an organism (e.g., through brain lesion or stimulation), followed by assessment of performance and histological sequelae. On the contrary, psychophysiologists tend to study intact organisms. These subjects are of interest because of the particular stimuli to which they are exposed, because of the tasks in which they are engaged, or because of their psychological state or trait characteristics. The investigations are physiological in that coincidently recorded changes in covert, organismic events are the dependent variables of this research. Thus, experimenters in this area have studied the physiological changes in human beings associated with depression, dreaming, visual stimulation, stress,

[1] The preparation of this paper was supported in part by grants to the author from NIMH (MH-10993, MH-35324) and the Wisconsin Alumni Research Foundation.

problem solving, and a host of other analogous conditions. The goals of this research are to define relationships between the psychological and physiological domains; or more objectively stated, to study the physiological consequences of stimulus input and to explore possible interdependencies between response events (verbal, overt motor, and physiological) that will help to explain behavior.

The study of emotion has been a dominant theme in psychophysiology. This has occurred in part because of the general agreement among theorists that in emotion, physiological events represent more than the vehicle of behavior, but actually form an essential, expressive part of the emotional response. The physiologist Lange (Lange, 1922; Wenger, 1950) defended the extreme view that cardiovascular events were literally emotions, and that the verbal and behavioral manifestations were secondary consequents. Psychoanalysts hold that, when other avenues of impulse expression are blocked, organismic responses are inevitable and that their pattern is determined by the individual's psychological history (Alexander, 1950). This principle has contributed in great measure to the development of psychosmatic medicine. More recently, Schachter and Singer (1962) have proposed an interaction theory in which emotional behavior is determined jointly by physiological activation and concurrent cognitive set. Despite considerable differences in theoretical detail, all agree that the flushed face, rapid pulse, and irregular breathing of the human being under stress is no less an emotional expression than angry words or flying fists.

Psychotherapy is primarily a technique for the modification or elimination of pathological behavior. In the main, pathology involves the presence of aversive emotional states, and it is on this content that the therapist most often concentrates his efforts. It is, therefore, quite appropriate that psychophysiological methods should be employed in the study of treatment and surprising that the amount of directly relevant data is not much larger than it is. In part, this paucity may be attributed to the considerable technological demands of physiological research which must be added to those already required by the study of psychotherapy.

The investigator proposing to do a psycho-physiological study finds that he needs a good background in general physiology (not restricted to the central nervous system) as well as in psychology, and that his path is smoother if he has some knowledge and competency in electronics and computer sciences. These skills are demanded by the sophisticated tools he must employ and the quantity and complexity of the data he will obtain. Because continuous, analogue recording is routinely undertaken, the number of events measured in an experiment greatly exceeds that of most other research domains. Furthermore, compared to verbal reports or a bar press, the covert bodily changes in emotion are small and subtle. They require electronic amplifiers for their detection and high-fidelity recording equipment for their registration. Most psychophysiological research utilizes the polygraph as a central apparatus, and it will be on studies utilizing this instrument that the present review will concentrate.

The polygraph (a multichannel amplifier and recorder) is used because the potentially relevant organs of the body are so numerous (cardiovascular, gastrointestinal, striate muscle, etc.), and research suggests that the pattern of their covariation may be as important as the response of any single system. The picture is further complicated by the fact that the psychologically meaningful responses are not intuitively obvious. Cardiac activity, for example, includes a whole gamut of measurable events—electro-chemical, auditory, and mechanical—and they are essentially continuous in time, and vary in frequency, amplitude, and direction. Most of this activity is in response to vegetative needs and is irrelevant to the psychological questions that we pose. Thus, the investigator routinely faces a staggering signal-to-noise ratio, and it is not surprising that much current psychophysiological research is concerned directly or indirectly with the definition of responses. For the psychotherapy researcher, this often means that the basic parametric work in his area of interest has not been done or is controversial, and he must do his own methodological housekeeping.

Nevertheless, the potential rewards of this undertaking are great. The data have the merit of direct quantification, along inherently physical dimensions. For the student of psychotherapy, the possibility of continuously measuring emotional events, with minimal disturbance of the patient by questions or measurement tasks, is an extremely attractive goal. The information on organismic state may permit him to anticipate change in therapeutic process. At the least, it represents an important supplement to verbal or motor components of the emotional response, and in their absence it may provide the only clue to continuing change in the patient's affective state. Perhaps of most importance, there is reason to suspect that the interoceptive and exteroceptive feedback of autonomic events may directly modulate psychological state and the overt responses of emotion. Thus, efforts at the direct, behavioral control of these physiological events could become a central goal of the therapeutic enterprise.

The first part of this chapter is intended as an introduction to the methods of psychophysiological research. It is necessarily brief, and the serious, beginning investigator will need to go to the original sources listed in the bibliography for complete information. However, techniques and apparatus for recording bioelectric or transduced pressure and other biomechanical changes are considered, along with problems of the experimental environment, special populations, and sources of recording artifact. Subsequently, the central and peripheral physiology of emotion are very briefly reviewed, including a description of the autonomic nervous system, the neurohormones, and the functioning of pertinent viscera. General problems in defining psychologically meaningful physiological events are then considered, such as the effect of initial values and homeostatic mechanisms on response magnitude. The concepts of arousal and response specificity are examined in the context of current research. Finally, a systematic analysis is made of the aversive emotional response, and a strategy for its modification is described. The chapter concludes with a consideration of some current psychophysiological studies of psychotherapy and behavior change, and the use of physiological recording in the practical, clinical setting.

[2] The reader who is familiar with psychophysiological methodology may wish to skip this section of the chapter. On the other hand, the reader who wishes a more thorough grounding in recording

PHYSIOLOGICAL RECORDING[2]

Bioelectric Signals

In recent years, it has become possible to record a great number of physiological events as they occur in the intact human being. These include responses from nearly all the organ systems of the body, including the cardiovascular, cortical, respiratory, and gastrointestinal systems, as well as the sweat glands and the somatic muscles. All these organs generate bioelectric signals. When stimulated, the walls of neural and muscle cells selectively alter their permeability. The resulting rearrangement of ions on either side constitutes the "firing" of the cell, and is sensed electrically as a change in voltage polarity. This depolarization may be transmitted from cell to cell within the active organ, and evidence that such a sequence of chemoelectric events is occurring radiates through the relatively high conducting medium of the body tissue. Bioelectric assessment of an organ's functioning can thus be accomplished by placing electrodes nearby on the body surface, amplifying the sensed voltage changes and writing the result out on a stripchart recorder.

The waveform presented in Figure 3.1 is readily recognized as the changes in voltage that occur coincident with the pumping action (systole) of the heart. This electrocardiogram (EKG) was recorded from electrodes placed on the right wrist and left ankle, and is literally the

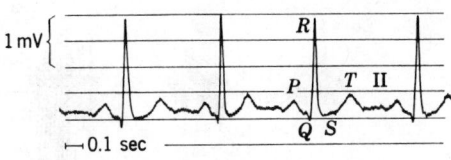

Figure 3.1 The normal electrocardiogram in man (Keele & Neil, 1965). The electrodes were placed on the right and left extremities (standard lead II).

changes in relative potential at these electrodes, as the muscle cells of the heart successively contract. The *P* wave is associated with the beginning of systole in the right atrium (the first chamber of the heart). The QRS complex is

problems than this review offers, is referred to the recent texts on this topic (Venables and Martin, 1967; Brown, 1967; Greenfield and Sternbach, 1970).

the bioelectric depolarization that initiates ventricular systole, the main pumping action that sends blood rushing to the lungs and the extremities of the body. The final *T* wave is associated with the repolarization of ventricular muscle tissue that prepares the heart for its next cycle of activity (a detailed description of the relevant cardiovascular physiology may be found in Best and Taylor, 1966, or Keele and Neil, 1965).

The EKG is a large electrical event and may be recorded from a pair of electrodes located anywhere on the body, as long as they are on opposite sides of the heart. Different placements will bisect a different plane of the electrical activity, resulting in changes in the amplitude of the different wave parts—a fact of great importance to clinical electrocardiographers (Goldman, 1960). However, the psychologist is normally interested only in a rate measure, and tends to choose a placement that emphasizes the *R* wave (from the upper right quadrant of the body to lower left). There is only one *R* wave per pumping cycle, and it is thus easy to count the number of systoles in a time unit (heart rate) or the time between pairs of systoles (heart period). The psychological significance of these measures will be considered in detail later on in this chapter.

The EKG may appear as an artifact in any bioelectric recording. However, its effect is minimized when electrodes are closely spaced and thus do not bracket the heart. Under these conditions, the relative potential of an electrode pair will be primarily influenced by the active organs that lie immediately below them. Figure 3.2 shows voltage changes that could be obtained from an electrode pair placed a few centimeters apart on the skin, over the flexor muscles of the arm. The muscles were alternately tensed and relaxed in the first part of the graph, and contraction was continuous during the second half. Rapid voltage changes clearly parallel this muscle activity. In contrast to the orderly, sequential depolarization of cells necessary to the heart's pumping action, this electromyogram (EMG) yields a random distribution of depolarization spikes, as many muscles cells fire and refire in a large, sustained contraction. The envelope of this activity is roughly proportional to the force exerted by the muscle being measured (Davis, 1952), and the voltage-time integral of the electromyogram has been shown to hold a linear relationship with voluntary contraction (Lippold, 1967). If many electrode pairs are distributed over the different muscles of the body and the total output is integrated, a good estimate of changes in overall level of tension may be obtained.

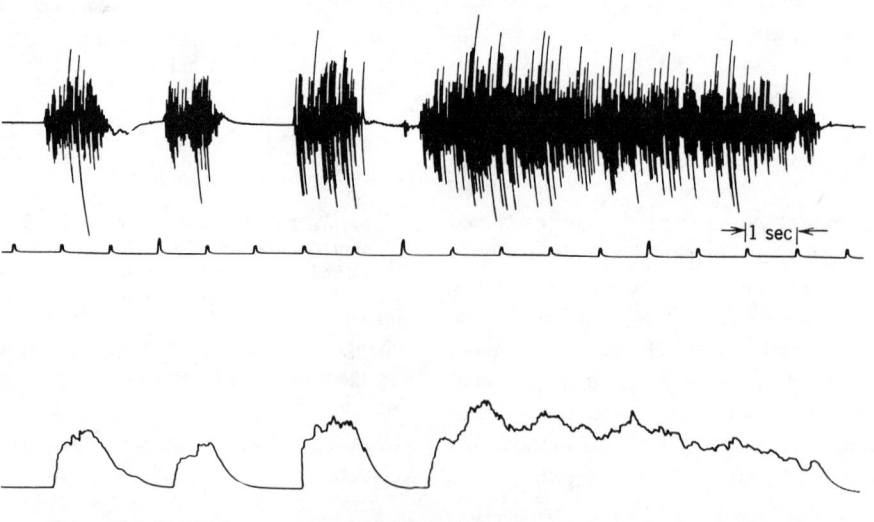

→|1 sec|←

Figure 3.2 An electromyogram recorded during bursts of muscle tension. The upper channel is a "raw" record of this activity. The lower channel shows an *RC* integration of the same signal. This latter curve approximates the envelope of the rectified voltage changes. Courtesy of the Grass Instrument Co.

In 1875, Caton demonstrated that electrodes placed on the skull of a rabbit produced characteristic electrical signals, which he held were generated by the neural activity of the brain. In the third decade of the twentieth century, Hans Berger (1929) showed a similar phenomenon in the human being, initiating the experimental and clinical study of electroencephalography (a brief history may be found in Brazier, 1958). Methods for recording the activity of neural cells are essentially the same as those employed in sensing voltage changes in striate or cardiac muscle. However, cortical signals have a lower amplitude than those from the heart or the muscles of the extremities. The voltage difference between electrodes averages about 50 microvolts (μv), and only very rarely exceeds 200 μv. Thus, the gain or amplification of the recording instrument must be increased in order to sense them clearly.

Figure 3.3 shows electroencephalograms (EEG) taken from an electrode pair similar to that used in recording the EKG and EMG. In this case, the electrodes are on the surface of the scalp over the occiput. The EEG yields an orderly pattern of voltage changes that vary with the brain area, stimulation, and organismic state. The bioelectric potential shifts between electrodes within a frequency band from 0.5 to seldom more than 30 Hz (Hertz = cycles per second). However, as many as four or five frequencies may commingle at one time, making interpretation of the EEG difficult. The most easily distinguished frequency is the alpha wave (8–13 Hz) which is primarily generated in the occipital region of the brain. Alpha waves are most easily obtained from the subject at rest, awake with eyes closed. It disappears immediately when the subject attends to a stimulus, and is replaced by higher-frequency waves at lower voltage. This "alpha blocking" has been used as a measure of arousal or orienting.

Electrodes

Many commercial firms produce equipment for registering bioelectric activity. The apparatus includes three main components: sensing electrodes, amplifier, and recorder. As the previous discussion suggested, in recording different physiological systems, electrodes vary mainly in placement. Electrode size may also be a factor when it is important to restrict the area from which signals are received. Small electrodes are necessary in sensing different but adjacent areas of the brain. Wider spacing will facilitate the sensing of deeper structures, but will increase the number of separate events that contribute to the signal. In addition to locating electrodes properly, good contact must be assured and the electrodes should not generate any potential differences of their own. The last problem is dealt with in part by making electrodes from the relatively inert precious metals. Good contact can be best achieved by burying the electrodes below the surface of the skin, and needle electrodes are available for this purpose. However, because the placing of these electrodes is often emotionally distressing to subjects (though not actually painful) and because maintaining them in a sterile condition represents an added complication, these electrodes are seldom appropriate for psychotherapy research. In general, investigators use a cup or disc electrode containing a high conduction paste, taped to the recording site. If the skin is cleaned thoroughly and lightly abraded, a low-resistance (5000 ohms or less) contact may be achieved. High-resistance contacts (usually the result of poor electrode application) are to be avoided, less because of any

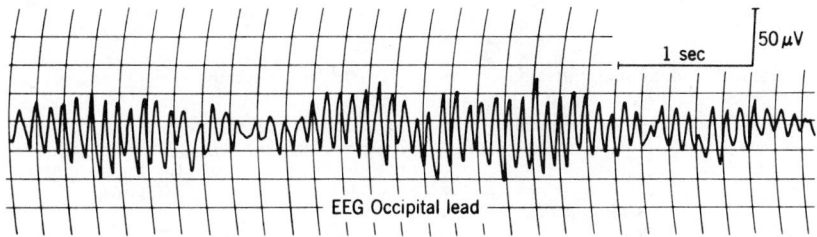

Figure 3.3 A single EEG tracing from electrodes over the occipital area of the brain. Ten-cycle-per-second alpha waves dominate this record, suggesting that the subject was awake, resting, with eyes closed. Courtesy of Grass Instrument Co.

reduction in the amplitude of the bioelectric signal that they might cause, than because of the antenna effect created by high resistance contacts which introduces electrical artifacts to the amplifier.

Amplification[3]

Electronic amplifiers are used to increase the strength of a bioelectric signal so that it may be seen and measured. Modern amplifiers accomplish this through components made of semiconducting materials, called transistors. A transistor is a kind of electronic sandwich, with semiconductor materials of one type (negative or positive) on either side of a central filling of the opposite type. The center is called the base and the two outer coverings are called the collector and the emitter. The electronic interface between the two types of materials is such that voltage changes in the base can modulate the passage of current between the outer two parts, without these latter elements greatly influencing the base itself. Thus, if the base is part of a circuit that includes the bioelectric signal, changes in this signal will evoke parallel changes in a much larger voltage circuit that includes the collector and the emitter (see Figure 3.4). Small signals in the range of a few microvolts may be thus increased to several hundred volts, through the chaining together of transistors, each one of which slightly increases the voltage level.

Most amplifiers used for bioelectric recording have two main stages that contain many transistors or tubes, as well as other electronic components. The first stage, or preamplifier accomplishes the initial signal conditioning. The second state is often called the driver, and it raises the voltage level to a point where it will operate a recorder, such as a galvanometer or servomotor. The way stages and substages of amplification are coupled together influences the signal frequency that the amplifier will pass on without distortion. When a network of capacitors and resistors form the junction between amplification stages, voltage changes are transmitted, but not voltage levels. Furthermore, the range of frequency changes that is amplified depends on a capacitor-resistance circuit characteristic called its *time constant*. Technically, the time constant is the amount of time it takes for an applied voltage to decay to 63.2 percent of its initial value. Figure 3.5 shows how capacitor circuits of varying time constants alter input waveforms.

All the bioelectric events that we have considered so far (EKG, EMG, EEG) are characterized by relatively rapid changes in voltage, and they may be recorded with resistance-capacitance or *R-C* coupled amplifiers.[4] The EKG and EMG waveforms have a fast rise time, and a short time constant (0.1 sec) is sufficient for their faithful recording. It will be recalled that the normal range of EEG frequencies extends somewhat lower and a time constant of at least 1.0 sec is necessary to minimize distortion. However, some researchers are interested in even slower phenomena that

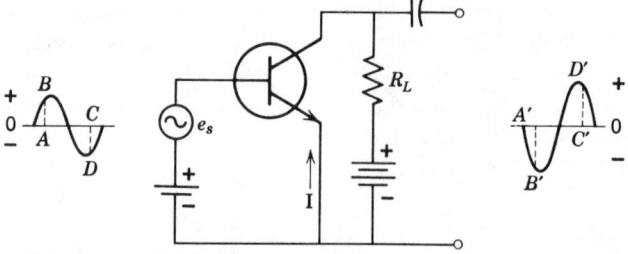

Figure 3.4 A simple, one-transistor amplifier. The input signal from the subject is at e_s, and the amplified output goes to the recorder from the two terminal leads at the right. I indicates the direction of current to the emitter of the transistor, and R_L is a load resistor. It will be noted that an output signal from this amplifier (*A'-B'*, *C'-D'*) is 180° out of phase with the input (*A-B*, *C-D*). Adapted from Yanof (1965). Courtesy of Radio Corporation of America, Harrison, New Jersey.

---

[3] More detailed discussions of electronic amplification, in the context of bioelectric recording and other research applications, may be found in Yanof (1965) or Phillips (1966).

[4] Capacitance-coupled amplifiers are also called AC (alternating current) amplifiers because they pass voltage changes, and not DC (direct current) levels.

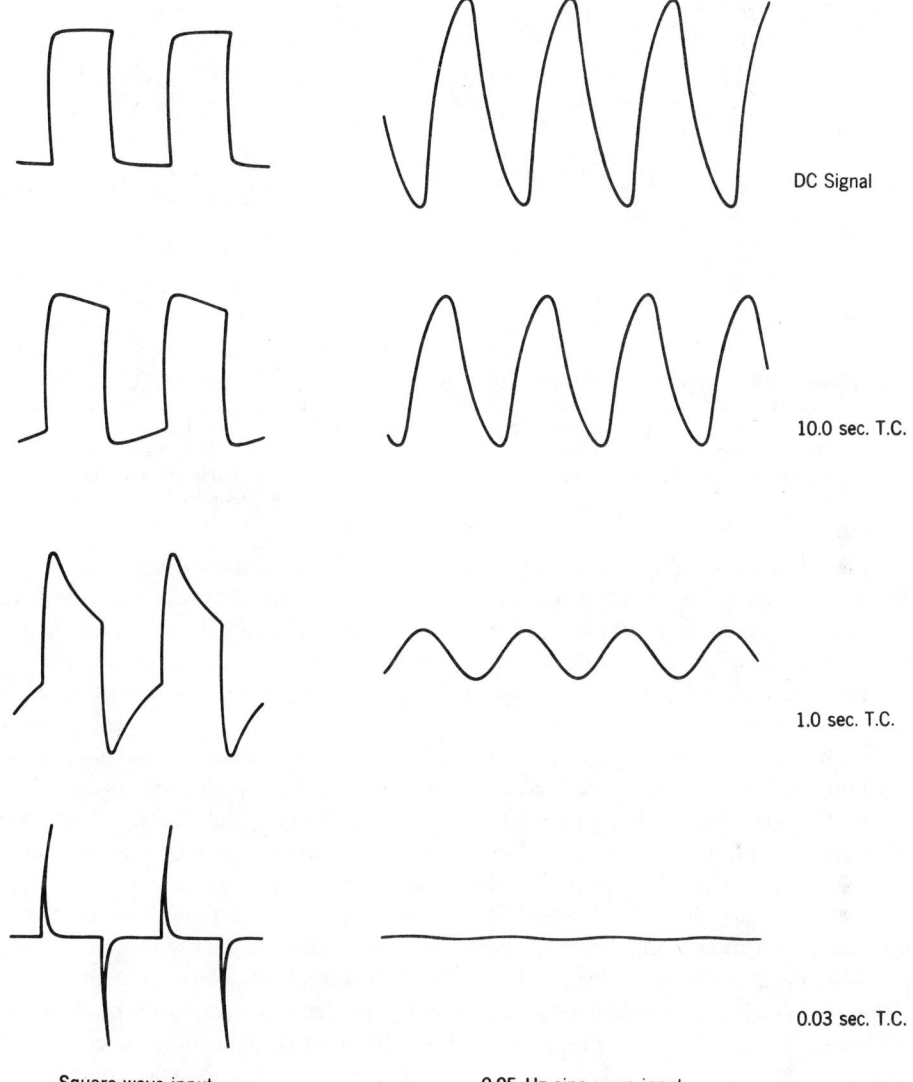

DC Signal

10.0 sec. T.C.

1.0 sec. T.C.

0.03 sec. T.C.

Square wave input   0.05 Hz sine wave input

Figure 3.5 Polygraph records of a square wave and sine wave input, as recorded at the same amplifier gain, but with various time-constant settings. The slight distortion of the D-C comparison waves is due to curvilinear recording and pen inertia. Note how the slow frequency is attenuated and phase shifted by the short (.03) time constant.

approach the point of recording direct current levels. Recently, the English neuropsychologist, W. Grey Walter (1964), pointed out that when a stimulus regularly precedes an event of interest to subjects, a very slow, negative going wave occurs in the EEG during this foreperiod. An example of such a waveform is presented in Figure 3.6, accompanied by a recording of the same signal with an *R-C* amplifier. Because most electroencephalographs are equipped only

with *R-C* channels, this slow wave phenomenon was overlooked by earlier investigators.

Events with a frequency below 1.0 Hz are amplified without distortion by direct coupled amplifiers. This may be accomplished by attaching the preceding collector circuit directly to the base of the succeeding transistor, without an intervening capacitor. However, in practice, this is sometimes an inconvenient arrangement. The high positive potential thus transferred

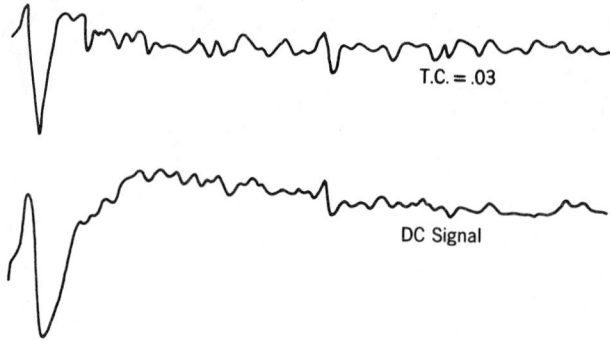

Figure 3.6 Averaged cortical evoked potentials elicited by a two-second tone, recorded from the same two electrodes, placed at the vertex of the skull and on the mastoid bone. The length of the signal on the abscissa is four seconds. A large, fast-evoked potential may be seen at onset of the tone. On the lower D-C recording, a slower, vertex negative wave may also be seen, developing immediately afterwards. With the fast time constant used in recording the upper trace, this slow wave fails to appear.

reduces the efficiency of the next stage of amplification. Furthermore, without capacitance coupling, instability in the amplifier components may generate slow drift in the signal level, an artifact difficult to distinguish from a true bioelectric event.

The DC change shown in Figure 3.6 was recorded with a so-called chopper amplifier. In this case, the DC signal is actually chopped into an amplitude modulated frequency. This frequency may, of course, be transmitted through an *R-C* network. In the next stage, the chopped signal is demodulated, filtered, and written out in the same form as the original input. This is presently the most common way of amplifying slow activity or voltage level changes.[5]

DC amplifiers are also used to record the skin potential response (SPR). This response is generated mainly by sweat gland activity, with some contribution of changes in the polarization of the epidermal membrane (Edelberg, 1967). It may be recorded from most body surfaces, but the largest potentials are obtained from the palms and soles of the feet where the eccrine sweat glands are concentrated. In placing recording electrodes, care must be taken not to abrade or break the skin surface, as the skin itself is the organ system being measured. Furthermore, the electrodes must have a low and stable difference in potential. Any back voltage generated by the electrodes themselves, would seriously distort the skin potential waveform. An example of skin potential responses are presented in Figure 3.7. The obtained waveform may be negative, occasionally positive, and most commonly multiphasic. Skin potential responses have been less studied than skin resistance, perhaps because of this response variability and uncertainty about the most suitable method of data reduction (Holmquest and Edelberg, 1964). Nevertheless, this response event has been examined with profit in studies of schizophrenic populations (Venables, 1960) and in studies of autonomic control (Crider, Shapiro, and Tursky, 1966).

Measuring the Resistance of the Skin

In 1888, the French physiologist Féré discovered that the application of a small current to the skin, yielded characteristic fluctuations in the subject's resistance to that current. Furthermore, it was soon apparent that these resistance changes related in part to the presence of emotional stimuli. What was early called the psychogalvanic response, and is now

[5] A disadvantage of this system lies in the fact that, under certain conditions, the chopper frequency itself can appear as a ripple in the amplified signal. In most recording situations this is not a serious difficulty. However, the ultimate solution to these recording problems lies in the development of inexpensive, highly stable, direct-coupled amplifiers.

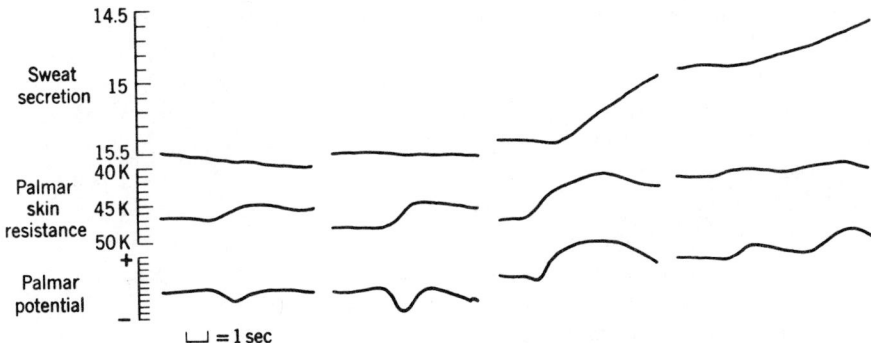

Figure 3.7 Simultaneous recording of skin potential, skin resistance, and sweat secretion (Darrow, 1964). It will be noted that the skin potential curves (lowest grouping on the ordinate) may be monophasic negative deflections, diphasic, or positive. Some tendency for diphasic and positive responses to appear with high sweat secretion is apparent.

more commonly referred to as the galvanic skin response (GSR) or skin resistance response (SRR), is the physiological event most commonly assessed in psychological research.

Skin resistance measurement differs from all other measures that we have thus far considered (EKG, EMG, EEG, and SPR) in that it is not the simple assessment of a biological voltage generated by the subject; rather we are examining the subject with an electrical probe. To accomplish this measurement, it is common to place two electrodes on the subject and pass between them a constant current, below the subject's sensory threshold and low enough to minimize tissue damage (10–20 μA/cm²). Resistance to this current lies mainly in the skin itself, the horny, durable layer that covers the highly conducting medium of the internal organs and fluids. As in skin potential measurement, we must be careful not to break the surface beneath the electrodes, or resistance will fall to near zero and changes cannot be observed. In most skin resistance recording apparatus, a bridge circuit is interposed between the subject and the recording amplifier. The subject actually forms one arm of the bridge (see Figure 3.8). A variable resistor in the adjacent arm is used to balance voltage at a null point, so that the resistance fluctuations of the subject may be read from a recorder.

The biophysics of this event are still incompletely understood. However, the frequency of resistance changes and level of activity coincide with the distribution of sweat glands on the body (Venables and Martin, 1966), and Thomas and Korr (1957), found correlations ranging from 0.4 to 0.9 between number of active sweat glands and resistance levels. Thus, it seems likely that, as with the skin potential response, sweat-gland activity is mainly responsible. Nevertheless, using an electrolysis cell for

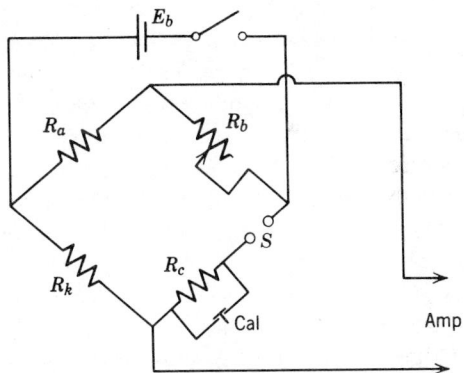

Figure 3.8 A constant-current bridge circuit providing 8 μ amp to electrode cites 1 cm². The subject is at S and bridge adjustments may be made at R_b. The voltage source at $E_b=90$ V; R_a and $R_k=11.25$ megohms each; $R_b=500$ K; $R_c=1$ K (Edelberg, 1967).

the continuous measurement of perspiration, Wilcott and Bennken (1961) found that, although correlations between sweat and skin resistance were often significant, they were quite low. Furthermore, both skin potential responses and resistance changes appear a second before sweat can be detected, and these responses may actually be recorded in the absence of palpable perspiration (Darrow, 1964). These facts argue that it is the activity of the gland that is necessary to the event, and not the presence of sweat.[6]

It has also been suggested that nonsudorific elements contribute to this response (Edelberg, 1967; Wilcott, 1967). As a result of experiments comparing resistance changes at skin sites rich and sparse in sweat glands, Edelberg and Wright (1964) concluded that variation in the permeability of an epidermal layer was a separate component of the resistance change response. They also presented evidence suggesting that the sweat gland and epidermal components may be differentially responsive to stimulus meaning (that is, whether a stimulus is an alerting signal or the signal for the execution of an act).

One of the most obvious practical problems in recording resistance changes is prompted by the broad range of possible skin resistance levels. With electrodes a few square millimeters in surface area, the between-subjects range may extend from 10,000 to 500,000 ohms. On the other hand, the size of changes, which interests an investigator, is often as small as 300 ohms. It is easy to see that, if the total signal range must be distributed over the 40 mm. width of the usual polygraph channel (or the three input volts of an instrumentation tape recorder), the resolution will not be adequate to observe responses. The obvious solution to this problem is to narrow the signal range around the present level of the subject, thus increasing response resolution. However, the experimenter must now "ride the pot," that is, rebalance the resistance bridge continuously during the experiment whenever the subject's changing resistance level moves out of the initial range. Unfortunately, this occupies the experimenter full-time, as data is not recorded if the pen is off-scale, and errors can easily be made in

estimating actual resistance levels. The "police polygraph" solves the problem with an automatic recentering device. However, in this method, information about resistance levels is irretrievably lost. A more sophisticated solution involves the use of an automatic range change preamplifier (Yellow Springs Instrument Co.). This device senses pen movement beyond the currently used scale and switches to an adjacent range of comparable sensitivity. Thus both levels and responses are preserved. A somewhat less complicated system has been proposed by Edelberg (1967). Resistance change is simultaneously amplified by both a DC amplifier and an R-C coupled amplifier. The gain differs for the two recordings: the DC channel is set at a low sensitivity, thus covering the full range of possible base resistances, and the subject's standing level of activity can be easily determined by inspection; the R-C channel is set for high gain, and records the finer-grained responses. Because this latter amplifier is capacitance-coupled, it will respond only to relatively fast events and will not move off-scale with a slow-level shift. If single responses are anticipated, a very brief time constant may be used. An amplifier time constant of 0.05 provides an output that closely approximates the skin resistance wave's first derivative. The derivative is, in turn, linearly related to peak amplitude (Edelberg, 1967). This is an excellent example of how preamplifiers of a specific type may be used to condition signals, in ways that simplify data reduction and interpretation.

Although most apparatus measure resistance, the results of experiments are usually reported in units of the reciprocal of resistance or *conductance*.[7] This is done because the skin conductance response (SCR) tends to be more normally distributed than resistance changes

---

[6] On the other hand, it should be noted that measures of sweat do not assess partially filled ducts, and these could contribute to voltage changes from the skin. Furthermore, the eruption of sweat in the ducts does appear to alter the form of the skin potential response and may sustain increments in skin conductance (Darrow, 1964). Nevertheless, chemical agents (such as atropine) that block cholinergic transmission (the mechanism of sweat gland innervation) also inhibit skin potential change and prompt increased skin resistance (Martin and Venables, 1966). Thus, the weight of evidence implicates sweat gland activity as the major contributor to the observed bioelectric responses.

[7] There are many solutions to the problems of exosomatic recording. Lykken (1968) advocates the use of a constant voltage circuit, which permits the direct measurement of apparent conductance. Recently, the Beckman Instrument Company has made available a preamplifier coupler, which may be adjusted for either constant current or constant voltage recording, and provides for either DC or R-C amplification. Furthermore, a display of both response waveform and tonic level may be combined on a single trace.

(Lacey and Siegel, 1949), and because conductance changes appear to be more consistently associated with amount of sweat production than resistance changes (Darrow, 1964). It is further argued (Montagu and Coles, 1966) that conductance measures should be expressed in log form, since "biological systems tend to obey logarithmic laws" (p. 264). Current views on initial level and response range effects will be discussed later, in dealing with the general problem of determining psychologically relevant physiological responses.

One final caution is warranted in reference to recording electrodermal events. The size and composition of the electrodes and the paste that is employed control to a considerable extent the values that will be amplified. Whereas the only serious consideration in most AC bioelectric recording is the achievement of good contact, in assessing skin conductance, we actually use the electrode and paste to build a sophisticated resistance sensor. Furthermore, this sensing device is reconstructed each time a subject is recorded. Electrodes of different sizes will yield different current densities, and thus different resistance values. If the paste dries up at differing rates or if poor application results in the paste spreading beyond the electrode, these effects contribute importantly to resistance differences and the resulting error variance in an experiment. Some metals and pastes interact to produce battery effects. The electrodes become biased, and a slow, steady change in resistance level is produced that has nothing to do with biological much less psychological events. If current is always passed between electrodes in the same direction, the regular shift in electrons will produce this biasing effect progressively, during the course of an experiment. To some extent, these problems are reduced by choosing appropriate electrode materials (Edelberg, 1967; Martin and Venables, 1966). If the direction of current is reversed periodically, biasing is reduced (when a rapid alternating current is used, *impedance* rather than resistance is being measured). However, the problems of obtaining suitable recordings remain, and the interpretation of small experimental differences obtained with this measure must be cautious.

Biological Transducers

In many cases, the bodily functions that interest researchers are sensed less effectively as bioelectric events, than as the mechanical displacement, volume, or pressure changes that are the end result of organ activity. In order to record these parameters, a device called a *transducer* must be employed, which translates mechanical energy into the electrical signals that can be sensed by a polygraph (Yanof, 1965). In measuring respiration, for example, the psychophysiologist is generally more interested in such variables as rate, or depth of inspiration, than in the chemoelectric phenomena that underlie mechanical action. A variety of devices have been employed to obtain this information. One method employs a small, temperature sensitive device called a *thermistor*, which can be mounted in the nasal passageway. The difference in temperature of inspired and expired air varies the strength of the thermistor output, and a graphic picture of respiration may be amplified and written out on a recorder. The most common type of respiration sensor employs an air bellows, circling the chest, that is attached to a volume transducer. The transducer contains a di-electric material that varies in ability to pass an electric current with change in shape. Pressure from the bellows (caused by changes in chest circumference) thus isomorphically alters current flow. This varying flow is amplified and written out on the polygraph. Other respiration transducers include a thin tube of mercury placed around the chest that varies in electrical resistance when stretched, and similar strain gauges made of other conductive materials.

The cardiovascular system is essentially a force pump operating in an enclosed hydraulic loop. While the EKG tells much about heart action, the important pressure and volume changes must be sensed with transducers. Arterial blood pressure is perhaps the cardiovascular variable of most general interest to investigators. It is directly recorded by inserting a cannula into one of the larger arteries, allowing blood to fill a vessel containing a movable diaphragm, and then measuring the excursion of the diaphragm. Of course, this direct method is more suitable to the animal laboratory than to research in psychotherapy. Regrettably, there is not yet an alternative, indirect method that provides so accurate a continuous measure of blood pressure. However, reasonable approximations of true values can be obtained.

In the physician's office, arterial pressure is assessed by the indirect, auscultatory method. A cuff is inflated to a point where it occludes the brachial artery of the arm. Pressure in the cuff is then released slowly, while the physician listens with his stethoscope for the first sound of the pumping heart. This first audible pulse of blood defines the systolic pressure in the artery (read in millimeters of mercury from a gauge attached to the cuff bladder). This is the maximum pressure occasioned by the contraction of the heart's ventricles. The cuff is released still further and the gauge reading coincident with the last heart sound is the subject's diastolic pressure, or the point of minimum pressure that occurs between ventricular systoles. This technique has been employed in psychological research (Hokanson, Burgess, and Cohen, 1963); however, it has the obvious limitations of affording only a discontinuous measure and being dependent on the auditory judgments of the examiner. A variety of efforts have been made to adapt this technique to continuous recording and provide more reliable estimates of heart sounds (Lywood, 1967; Shapiro, Tursky, Gershon, and Stern, 1969). For example, the cuff may be automatically inflated every few seconds. A microphone can be placed on the artery ahead of the cuff, to sense the heart sounds. The electrically transduced audio signal indicates to the apparatus when cuff pressure is to be recorded. Nevertheless, all methods involve some degree of occlusion of important blood vessels, even if the system is moved to the small arteries of the finger. If a cuff remained inflated on the subject for too long a period, serious tissue damage could result. With any degree of occlusion, our measuring device is altering aspects of the event we are trying to measure and others that are being simultaneously recorded. The experimenter must give these artifacts careful consideration, and decide for each experiment whether they will seriously distort his findings.

The work of Russian investigators such as Sokolov (1963) has stimulated considerable interest in recording peripheral vasomotor events. He argues that aversive stimuli differ from those to which subjects simply attend, in the changes they occasion in the distribution of blood in the body. Thus, it is held that intense aversive stimuli instigate vasoconstriction in the blood vessels of the head area and the finger, while digital constriction and cephalic vasodilation is the typical response to more moderate stimuli. Data relevant to this issue are obtained with the plethysmograph.

The plethysmograph is a device for measuring changes in the volume of a body part. In the main, these changes represent shifts in blood volume brought about by the constriction and dilation of the arteries. Measurement may be accomplished in a variety of ways, the simplest of which is to enclose the body part of interest in an air-tight container that is connected to a pressure transducer such as that used in recording respiration. A digital, volume plethysmograph system is diagrammed in Figure 3.9. Photoelectric transducers are also available for this type of measurement (Weinman, 1967) and are particularly convenient when the area of interest cannot be enclosed (e.g., the head). In this case, light is projected through or around the skin onto a light sensitive resistor. Changes in blood flow produce parallel changes in resistance, which when written out closely resemble the results obtained with a volumetric system.[8]

---

[8] All plethysmographic work involves uncertainty about the zero point on the measurement scale. In the case of volumetric methods, changes may be reported as a percent of the total volume enclosed by the oncometer. However, it must be recognized that, although blood volume shifts account for the largest part of the response, the exact proportion is unknown. If the photoelectric system is used, no absolute measure of tonic level is possible. Particular care must be taken in interpreting differences between subjects, which could easily be a function of arbitrary reference levels or recording sensitivities. Berg (1968) examined two methods for transforming photoplethysmograph scores. He concluded that neither was superior to raw scores in reducing variable error in reference level or recording sensitivity. However, if care is taken to standardize transducer attachment and recorder amplitude, meaningful differences between experimental groups may be obtained.

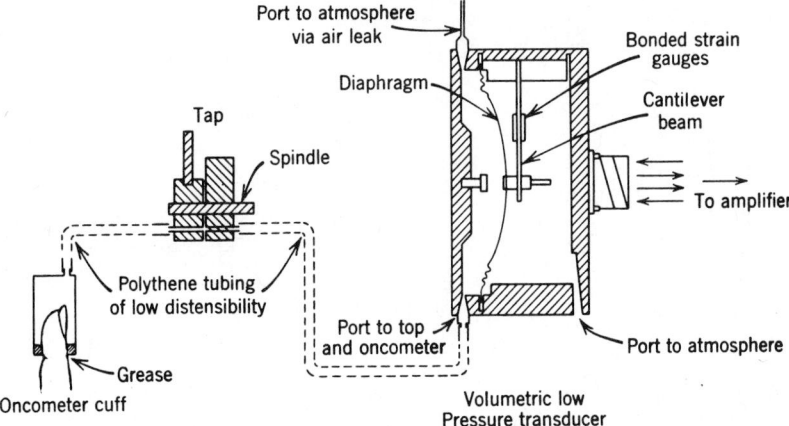

Figure 3.9 Measurement of pulse volume. The end of the finger is inserted into the oncometer (lower left). A two-way tap interrupts the tube connection to the transducer, which permits the cuff to be in communication with the atmosphere during fitting. A more complete description of this system may be found in Lader (1967b). Courtesy of Grass Instrument Co.

The above brief catalogue and description does not begin to exhaust the list of available biological transducers. Sensors have been swallowed for recording gastric motility (Wenger, 1957). Other transducers are responsive to chemical events (such as pH). Magnetic or doppler effect devices are being developed for sensing blood flow (Yanof, 1965). A host of impedance or thermocouple devices contribute to the list, which is limited only by the researcher's need and the inventiveness of the bioengineer.

A General Recording System

A modern physiological recording system is presented in block diagram in Figure 3.10. It includes recording electrodes with a master lead selector, a variety of transducers, capacitance-coupled and DC preamplifiers, and output recorders. The most basic output device is the cathode ray oscilloscope. Voltages from the physiological amplifiers deflect an electron beam within the oscilloscope display tube. The record of activity is presented as a moving, essentially inertialess spot of light. The advantage of this device is that no mechanical components distort the physiological record. If a camera is available to photograph the scope face, a permanent record of an event can be obtained.

It is, however, often more convenient to have a continuous, permanent record of an experiment written "on line," and the multichannel strip-chart recorder or polygraph is the classic output device for this purpose. The waveforms depicted in Figures 3.1, 3.2, 3.3, 3.5, and 3.7 were all taken from the polygraph. The dimensions of the Y axis for any pen is determined by the amplifier gain, and the X axis is given by the speed at which the chart paper passes beneath the pens. Because the pens are lined up in parallel, relationships between different physiological systems and stimulus or overt response events (the latter recorded on a time line) can be readily observed and interpreted. However, inspection of chart paper provides for only the most superficial analysis of the data. More profound assessment depends on conversion of the graphic wave to numerical form. This analogue to digital conversion is primitively accomplished by measuring the polygraph tracings with a millimeter rule. This same task may be achieved more quickly by a commercially available optical scanning device (such as OSCAR, Benson-Lehner Corp.). In recent years, the instrumentation tape recorder has become a common device for recording and storing bioelectric information. In order to faithfully represent frequencies from DC levels through the EMG range, it is necessary for the signal to be converted to a frequency-modulated (FM) carrier wave for storage on tape. When the information is wanted, the signal is demodulated by the recorder and may be played out onto a strip chart or oscilloscope in its

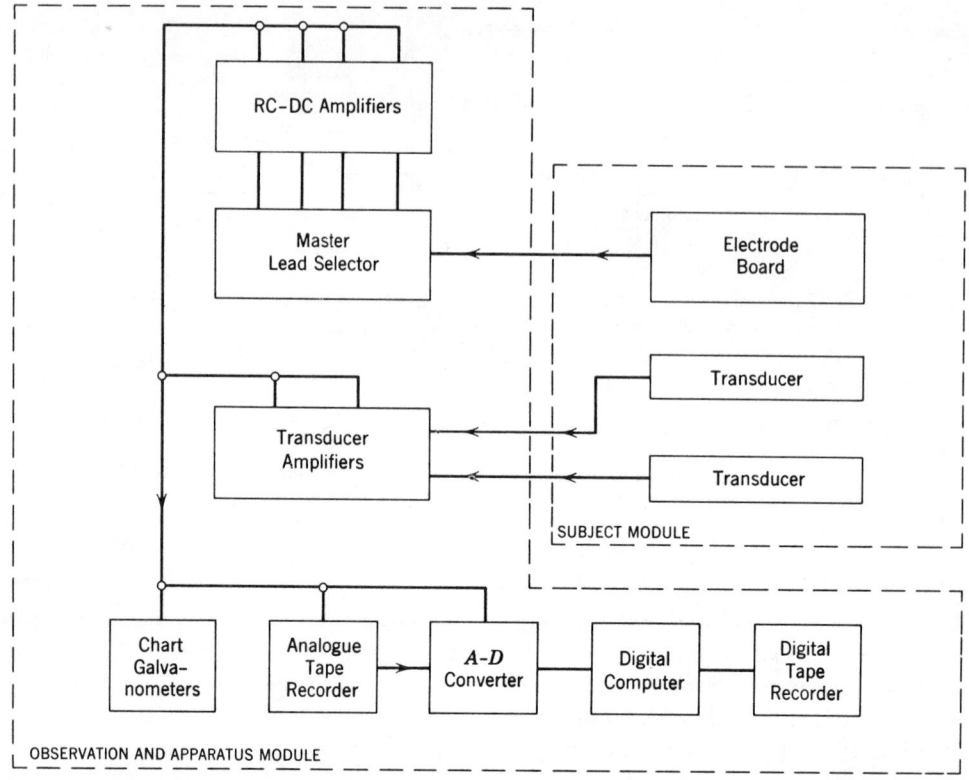

Figure 3.10 A general-purpose physiological recording system. The amplified data may be routed through the analogue-to-digital (*A-D*) converter to the computer for "on-line" processing. Alternatively, the analogue signal can be registered on the FM tape recorder for later play back to the computer. Storage of partially processed data is available on the digital tape system.

original form. Furthermore, the signal can be introduced into an electronic analogue-to-digital (A-D) converter, which will automatically produce a numerical output as a visual display, printed paper, cards, or digital magnetic tape suitable for entry into the computer. The saving in data reduction time afforded by a tape system is so great that analyses become feasible with this equipment that would be impossible if paper records had to be reduced by hand (see Ax, 1967; Zimmer, 1966).

Perhaps the most efficient, sophisticated (and expensive) method of handling physiological data is to process the amplified signal "on line" through an A-D converter and into a digital computer. This system has the advantage of eliminating error generated in the intervening tape stage, and may be necessary for experiments in which immediately processed data determine the subsequent administration of stimuli (Lang, 1969).

Recording Artifact and the Recording Environment

Part of the difficulty in recording physiological events is a result of the intrusion of other vegetative signals into the one that we are trying to measure. The body organs are adjacent and overlapping. EKG may be an interfering artifact when we are trying to record muscle activity, and muscle activity may intrude and confound our efforts to monitor the heart. If we fail to achieve a low-resistance electrode contact, the skin-potential response can contribute confusing slow waves to the EEG, or the arterial pulse may intrude, adding an artifactual frequency at the cardiac rate. Walter's anticipatory cortical slow wave is very difficult to separate from voltage changes occasioned by the slow turning of the eyeball in the ocular fluid (Connor and Lang, 1969). Careful technique and familiarity with the unique characteristics of different physiological events will reduce these problems, but they cannot be wholly eliminated.

R. C. Davis and his associates (1955) described the multitudinous responses of the body as a vast somatic sea, with waves, tides, and deep currents all commingling. If we are to follow the course of a specific event, it is wise to let this sea settle as much as possible before we begin observation. *While it sometimes seems attractive to monitor the active subject, moving about confronting "real life" situations, this seldom works out in practice. There is no technological limitation, as telemetry equipment for remote recording and transmission is available.[9] However, with the subject moving about, the psychological cockleshell is swamped in the general turbulence of gross energy demands. Fortunately, the psychotherapeutic context does not normally demand much bodily movement, and continuous monitoring is quite feasible.*

It is also important to limit the stimulus input to those signals that we hope to assess. The subject's chamber should be sound shielded. There is no appreciable difference in waveform between the skin conductance response to a "dirty word" and to a door slamming in the hall. Furthermore, the physiology is routinely responsive to a host of environmental parameters that we usually ignore, except at their extremes. Thus, subjects should be studied under conditions that include control of temperature, ambient light, and humidity (Wenger, 1962). As aspects of these ideal conditions are sacrificed to expediency, error variance increases.

Because bioelectric recording requires the assessment of very low voltages through high-impedance contacts, electrical artifact is a continuing problem. The regular beat of the sixty-cycle power line (or one of its harmonics) frequently intrudes into polygraph records. If the laboratory is located near elevator motors, diathermy machines, arcing relay contacts, or other substantial electrical equipment, this activity will be reflected in and perhaps obscure the bioelectric events under study. These problems can, however, be substantially reduced or eliminated by electrical shielding, that is, by enclosing the subject in a Faraday cage (which can be constructed of copper window screen) and attaching it to a good earth ground. Ideally, the shielding should be built into the wall so as to remain unobtrusive to the subject.

In considering artifacts, we cannot omit sources that lie within the subject himself. It is perhaps obvious to clinicians that the subject must have time and opportunity to become accustomed to the recording environment. The less it varies from the kind of "living room" atmosphere of the usual therapy context, the less the subject has to get used to. From the points of view of safety and psychological impact, recording equipment should never be placed in the same room with the subject. It may require one or two sessions before the subject has sufficiently adapted to the electrodes for adequate recordings to be taken. The electric chair is a common first association to this context, although the somewhat more benign "astronaut's couch" is increasing in frequency. Severely disturbed patients and children present special problems that will tax the clinical skills of the experimenter. It is well to remember that physiological recording itself is, at least at first, perceived as a stressor, and its effects should not be confused with the events under study. In general, more habituation time is needed with disturbed subjects, and active attention should be given to shaping the kind of quiescent behavior needed as a physiological background.

Consideration must be given to the subject's location in the diurnal cycle (and the menstrual cycle of female subjects), activity level just prior to the session, recent dietary habits, current health and medical history, and use of alcohol, drugs, and tobacco. One must beware of the "grapefruit" phenomenon; that is a situation such as that of the investigator who found reliable biochemical differences between patients and normals that turned out to be dependent on the fact that all the patients had had grapefruit for breakfast. While many of the conditions are random in large groups and thus may be ignored, the small samples to which the psychotherapy researcher is often limited will require that he give all these contingencies full consideration.

---

[9] Manufacturers producing telemetry equipment include E and M Instruments Co., Beckman Instrument Co., and Medtronic Inc.

THE AUTONOMIC NERVOUS SYSTEM[10]

Before proceeding to issues of measurement, it is appropriate to review the neurophysiology of the response events being investigated. With the exception of the EEG and the measurement of striate muscles, all the structures that we have considered so far are innervated by the autonomic nervous system (ANS). It is this system, sometimes called the vegetative or visceral system, that modulates the activities of the heart and blood vessels, the intestines and glands, and all the smooth muscle of the body. While it necessarily interacts with the central nervous system (CNS), the autonomic system is to some extent independent in its control of visceral structures. The source of this independence is both anatomical and functional. In the first place, autonomic reflex arcs differ from somatic reflexes in that the cell bodies of the motor-neurones are external to the CNS. Thus, there is a synaptic junction between the central system and the visceral organ. Furthermore, these external ganglia may be interconnected, permitting mutual influence and control outside the central system. Secondly, this system includes the capability of peripheral or neuroeffector inhibition. With non-autonomic (somatic) reflex arcs, the site of inhibition is always central. Muscles are relaxed by the action of one connector neurone on another within the CNS. However, the autonomic system postganglionic effector fibers may directly inhibit the organ to which they are connected. The best example of this phenomenon is the slowing of heart rate caused by impulses from the vagus nerve (Best and Taylor, 1966).

Characteristics of the visceral organs themselves also contribute to a remoteness from central control. Thus, the specific chemo-electric or mechanical effects of autonomic innervation seem to persist in the effector organ, after the excitatory impulse, for a longer period than in the case of somatic innervation. Furthermore, many visceral organs show spontaneous rhythmic activity that is wholly independent of neural innervation (for example, the heart and intestine).

The strict anatomical distinctions that we have drawn here concern the motor components of visceroneural connections. Visceral afferents generally find as direct a route to the central system as do the somatosensory neurones. It is of significance for the psychology of emotion that information about the viscera, from internal or even distance receptors, quickly feeds back centrally, while active control is neurologically buffered. It is tempting to see in these neuroanatomical relationships a corollary of our phenomenal observation. That is, we experience visceral events, but seem to lack conscious control over their action. Neither an emotional "feeling," nor the associated tachycardia, sweating, and stomach upset can be easily restrained.

Autonomic connections with the central nervous system occur at three separate loci: via specific cranial nerves (III, VII, IX and X), along the thoracic and first two lumbar segments of the spinal cord, and at the second and third sacral segments of the cord. From a functional point of view, the cranial and sacral components are considered together as the parasympathetic system, while the thoracic-lumbar connections that lie between are called the sympathetic nervous system. These two autonomic subsystems normally operate in a reciprocal fashion. Nearly all organs have both sympathetic *and* parasympathetic connections, varying in role for different viscera, one system acting to increase functioning while the other tends to inhibit activity. Thus, vagal (parasympathetic) impulses to the heart tend to reduce heartbeat rate, while sympathetic innervation increases it (Ruch et al., 1965).

Broadly conceived, the autonomic nervous system is a regulatory mechanism that functions to maintain a constant *milieu interne*, in the face of a changing external environment and the varying metabolic demands of an active organism. The anatomical characteristics of the sympathetic and parasympathetic systems fit them for their roles in this task. Thus, the

---

[10] A more complete description of the autonomic nervous system and the viscera that it controls may be found in any physiological text (such as Best and Taylor, 1966; Keele and Neil, 1965). Netter (1957) provides an excellent illustrated anatomy. A review of neurohormonal transmission in the autonomic system is provided by Goodman and Gilman (1966).

parasympathetic synaptic junctions are often remote from the cord, with few interconnections. Organ innervation is more specific in this system, as would be required to accommodate well-differentiated vegetative functions. In point of fact, the parasympathetic system tends to be dominant during periods of low stress, when it controls digestive and other routine body processes. The sympathetic ganglia differ from the parasympathetic in being highly interconnected along the spinal cord. Thus, the sympathetic system tends to act in a more diffuse and unitary way. It tends to dominate the viscera in periods of stress, acting to inhibit the digestive processes (such as peristalsis and enzyme secretion), increase the pumping action of the heart, constrict vessels at the periphery, and move blood to the striate muscles. Sympathetic innervation is roughly correlated with behavioral activity level and with electrocortical measures of activation.

The reciprocal relationship of the two autonomic subsystems has prompted a number of psychophysiological theories concerning individual differences in their relative dominance. Since shortly after the turn of the last century, efforts have been made to classify patients as maintaining a primary sympathetic tonus or parasympathetic tonus (vagotonic) based on their response to drugs that excite or inhibit one or the other system (Eppinger and Hess, 1915). Wenger (1941, 1947) developed the concept of autonomic balance as a normally distributed trait. He factor-analyzed a number of tests of autonomic functioning. This permitted a grouping of measures according to common variance, and the assignment of weights to the variables consistent with their factor relevance. Thus, autonomic balance scores ($\bar{A}$) could be derived for individual subjects. He reported that subjects at the sympathetic end of the scale tended to be more emotionally excitable, less patient, and less orderly than subjects at the parasympathetic extreme. Gellhorn (1967) has emphasized the role of the hypothalamus as the neural site regulating balance. He holds that this balance may shift with differential stimulation of anterior and posterior hypothalamus. Thus, the organism may be tuned sympathetically or parasympathetically, and this state will selectively modulate the direction and amplitude of the subject's response to stressors.

While most viscera are dually and reciprocally innervated by the two autonomic subsystems, the adrenal gland, the sweat glands, and perhaps the peripheral arterioles have only sympathetic connections. Thus, to the extent that peripheral vasoconstriction and particular sweat gland activity function as a unit, they provide an excellent indication of general sympathetic arousal, uncomplicated by any reflexive parasympathetic effects. Measuring the latter phenomenon is particularly useful because sweat-gland activation is exclusively neural, and the paths of innervation can be traced back through the sympathetic system to powerful excitatory centers in the anterior hypothalamus and inhibitory centers in the reticular formation (Wang, 1964). Furthermore, there are no homeostatic hormonal or mechanical modulators, as in the case of the cardiovascular system. Thus, we are in some ways on firmer ground in evaluating the psychophysiological relevance of sweat gland changes (and the related bioelectric phenomenon of skin conductance) than in considering other visceral events.

In addition to their anatomical and functional differences, the sympathetic and parasympathetic systems also differ in the pharmacology of organ innervation. Thus, for the sympathetic system, the chemical transmitter present at the junction between postganglionic fiber and effector is noradrenalin (also called norepinephrine). However, in the case of parasympathetic effector junctions, acetylcholine serves this transmitter function. A few exceptions to this scheme exist; the most notable being the sympathetic innervation of the sweat glands, which is cholinergically mediated. Thus, despite the advantages of the skin conductance response as an indicant of general sympathetic activity (to which we have already alluded), this pharmacological anomaly complicates its interpretation. In point of fact, sweat-gland activity measures such as skin conductance often seem to be more responsive when measured at low tonic levels of activation than when assessed in the context of strong emotion. This could represent some general dampening of cholinergic structures, when levels of adrenergic activity are high.

Because they figure so importantly in psycho-physiological theories of emotion, we must give consideration to the circulating hormones that are associated with sympathetic arousal. General sympathetic arousal includes the innervation of the medulla of the adrenal gland. This causes the gland to secrete the catecholamines, adrenalin and noradrenalin directly into the blood stream. While the proportion of these substances varies from organism to organism, the medullary secretions are mainly adrenalin in man. Adrenalin affects all the organs normally innervated by the sympathetic system, and acts to enhance and sustain the usual neural effects. Thus, circulating adrenalin increases heart rate and systolic blood pressure, constricts the peripheral vessels, and dilates the pupil. It also increases the metabolism of cells without direct sympathetic connections. It acts on skeletal muscle to increase the force of contraction, and appears to have central effects, activating the ascending reticular system. Under stress or in strong emotion, the secretion of adrenalin contributes to the intensity and persistence of these states, and is a further example of visceral independence from rapid neural inhibitory control (Keele and Neil, 1965).

The two catecholamines appear to have somewhat different effects and, as we will see, investigators have related their special actions to differences between emotional states. Norepinephrine, which is the main secretion of the adrenergic synapse, is a more powerful hypertensive or pressor agent on the cardiovascular system than is adrenalin. Thus, it acts to constrict both peripheral and skeletal muscle blood vessels, while adrenalin dilates the muscle arteries. Noradrenalin dominance tends to increase both systolic and diastolic blood pressure while only the former is increased by adrenaline. The catechols also differ in their degree of effect on oxygen consumption, blood sugar, and muscular tremor.

Efforts to explain the different effects of the two catechols has led to the theory of two types of chemically sensitive cells at effector sites—alpha and beta receptors. These receptors were hypothesized to account for the finding that specific chemical antagonists blocked the functions of some adrenergic viscera and not others. Presently, it appears that norepinephrine affects mainly only alpha receptors, while epinephrine influences both alpha and beta receptors. Furthermore, synthetic catechols have been found which have specifically alpha or beta actions. Both alpha and beta receptors are associated with excitation and inhibition of functioning. Thus, intestinal relaxation and vasoconstriction are mediated by alpha receptors; cardio-acceleration and bronchial relaxation are beta-receptor effects (Goodman and Gilman, 1966).

Obviously, the relative dominance of one hormone over the other in the body should produce different patterns of visceral, and perhaps also somatic and cortical activity. Efforts have been made to relate these physiological patterns to emotional states of interest to the psychotherapist. The classic study in this area was accomplished by Ax (1953) and extended by J. Schachter (1957). Both investigators found significant differences in subjects' physiological response to situations designed to induce fear and anger. While their results are not unequivocal (see chapter 6, Buss, 1961), the data suggest that anger situations may prompt a physiological pattern more like that obtained with the infusion of norepinephrine (Wenger, et al., 1960), while epinephrine-like effects dominate in fear. Thus, in both the Ax and Schachter studies diastolic and systolic blood pressure increased markedly in the anger context, while consistent with an epinephrine effect, the diastolic increments were less marked with the fearful situation. Funkenstein, Greenblatt, and Solomon (1951), and Funkenstein, King, and Drolette (1954) have also shown similar phenomena in psychiatric patients.

Silverman and Cohen (1960) have provided parallel data from catechol assays of urine, following the apparent induction of anger and fear states in human subjects. However, other research, in which assays of blood or urine provided the dependent variable, prompts a less simplistic interpretation of the data. Mason et al (1961) found that epinephrine levels in rhesus monkeys increased relative to norepinephrine when noxious stimuli were presented in a more ambiguous and unpredictable context. Euler and Lundberg (1954) reported that, while epinephrine levels increased for both passengers and aircraft pilots during a somewhat stressful flight, norepinephrine increased only for the pilots. These and similar data have led Schild-kraut and Kety (1967, p. 23) to conclude:

Increased epinephrine excretion seems to occur in states of anxiety or in threatening situations of uncertain or unpredictable nature in which active coping behavior may be required but has not been achieved. In contrast, norepinephrine excretion may occur in states of anger or aggression or in situations which are challenging but predictable and which allow active and appropriate behavioral responses to the challenge.

In interpreting data relevant to this issue, we need to be sensitive to the problem of controlling for the relative intensity of emotional stimuli and the behavior they evoke. The separate tasks used in studies of this phenomenon may have differed in their gross energy requirements. Thus, the muscular activity and related cardiovascular demands of coping behaviors may require increased norepinephrine secretion, whereas this kind of physiological mobilization is not necessary to the passive helplessness of fear. In brief, this argument suggests that specific neurohormones are not directly responsive to emotional stimuli or states, but rather that they vary with the nature and extent of subsequent activity. These questions auger a consideration of the interaction between physiological, verbal-cognitive, and behavioral responses that will be taken up shortly.[11]

The above discussion has focused on the neurohormones that interact directly with the autonomic nervous system. However, the emotional response includes broader endocrinological effects. Thus, while the catecholamines are secreted by the adrenal medulla, the outer cortex of the gland releases a great variety of other compounds that have hormonal effects. These adrenocortical steroids participate in the organism's reaction to stress, influencing metabolic rate and modulating vascular and cellular responses to injury.

Unlike the medullae, the adrenal cortex is not innervated neurally, but is controlled by the anterior pituitary gland through its secretion of the adrenocorticotrophic hormone (ACTH). Nevertheless, both parts of the gland are influenced by the same brain area. The pituitary gland is prompted to release ACTH when it is chemically stimulated by the hypothalamus—the same brain region that figures so importantly in autonomic activity.

During the "alarm reaction" (Selye, 1956), the catechols appear to produce more immediate defensive consequences, because of their neural innervation. The activation of the adrenal cortex is much slower, due to the dependence on chemical mediators; however, it appears to be important to sustained energy mobilization and healing processes, and it is the cortical steroids that are necessary to life.

Considerable psychophysiological research has been undertaken in which the levels of corticoids and their metabolites (hydroxycorticoids, 17-ketosteroids, 17-ketogenicsteroids) in blood or urine have provided the dependent variables. An excellent review of this area of study has been provided by Mason (1968). Nevertheless, the recovery and measurement of corticoids is far from an easy task. This fact, and the difficulties involved in obtaining continuous or frequent periodic samples of either the catechols or the cortical hormones, limits their value in psychophysiological studies of psychotherapy.

THE PSYCHOPHYSIOLOGICAL RESPONSE AND PROBLEMS IN ITS MEASUREMENT

The advantage of polygraphic measurement over other methods of physiological sampling lies in the continuous character of assessment and in the multiplicity of functions that are

[11] Interest in biochemical determinants of emotional states continues, and two promising approaches to the physiology of anxiety have recently been described. Frohlick et al. (1969) have shown that some patients with tension and panic attacks may be effectively treated by the injection of beta-blocking agents such as propranol hydrochloride. It is speculated that a syndrome that includes heart palpitations, hypertension, and associated emotional upset represents beta-receptor hyperresponsiveness, and furthermore "that beta-adrenergic stimulation may be the mechanism whereby cardiac symptoms are produced in certain anxious individuals" (p. 6). A parallel line of investigation has implicated blood lactate level in anxiety neuroses (Pitts et al., 1967; Pitts, 1969). Lactate is a normal product of exercise and is incremented when high levels of circulating adrenalin are present.

simultaneously recorded. However, to the beginning investigator this asset often seems like a Pyrrhic victory over ignorance, as he faces the miles of paper or magnetic tape records that can result from a single experiment. Obviously, all this information is not directly relevant to the psychological stimulus or state that prompted the investigation. As we have already suggested, events in the peripheral physiology that correlate with psychological processes are relatively subtle, accounting for a small proportion of the total variance in the system. Thus, the initial problem of psychophysiological research concerns the definition of responses, and considerable effort has been directed to this task.

Skinner (1959) has suggested that response events are those features of the organism's total behavior that show regular correlative relationships with stimulus input. Our interest in the bar press or the word association test depends on this relationship, and a similar definitional criterion exists in psychophysiological investigations. However, response-response correlations are also meaningful, and many studies are concerned with the physiological events that precede or coincide with gross motor responses (avoidance or approach behaviour) and verbal report (such as the statement "I am depressed").

While all behavior of living organisms may be viewed as part of a continuous process, this impression is pressed with particular vigor on the physiological investigator by the data he examines. The heart, the brain, and the lungs must respond continuously in a more or less stereotyped way if the organism is to survive. Thus, the researcher is always picking responses out of a repetitive flow of events. Often the rate and quality of this flow represents background noise that must be defined and partialed out of a measurement, so that the small signal deviations can be clearly apprehended. At other times it is the relatively persistent characteristics of the background itself that is the focus of investigation. From a temporal perspective, physiological data are often divided into *tonic* and *phasic* activity. The former refers to events that have relatively long continuity in time— states of the organism or effects of gross or persistent stimulation. Phasic events are more rapid changes, often the consequence of discrete stimulus input. While the distinction is in some ways arbitrary, and carries with it no absolute temporal definition, it is a useful way to organize physiological data in considering relationships to psychological phenomena.

The tonic level of activity in the viscera is of interest in assessing states of the organism. We assume some continuity of functioning during rest, exercise, repetitive physical stress, mental work, and a host of other conditions of persisting stimulation or activity. In these cases data are averaged over time. If the phenomenon presents itself as a frequency (such as heart rate), we can simply count pulses and divide by time. Signals that vary mainly in amplitude (like skin conductance) will need to be sampled periodically and the samples averaged. The frequency of sampling depends on the variance of the phenomenon. Thus, if we permit a subject 15 minutes of inactivity in order to evaluate his functioning at rest, we would not want to limit our assessment to the first 5 minutes (further adaptation may take place). Similarly, if the system tends to show periodic fluctuation (for example, the sinus arrythmia that appears in pulse rate), we would not want the sample to be so restricted that only part of the period of a cycle was noted. In brief, tonic activity is often described by a mean value obtained from samples more frequent than the period of the phenomenon (to which the careful investigator also appends some indication of associated variance). This statistic is held to represent the level of functioning of the organ system.

Differences in tonic activity are of interest in a great variety of investigations. Thus, we might investigate muscle tension levels in subjects trained in muscle relaxation compared to subjects who were administered a control procedure. An evaluation of a patient's average heart rate or blood pressure during different therapy sessions would also be a study of tonic levels. However, such within-subject comparisons raise issues of measurement that merit consideration.

In the same sense that subjects vary greatly in external physical characteristics, they vary broadly in the functioning of internal organ systems (Williams, 1963). Of particular interest here are differences in the range of possible tonic levels that a viscus might yield across a variety of states and stimulus conditions. It is clear that some subjects, for particular organ systems, may have a very narrow range of responding, while others may be extremely labile. Lykken, Rose, Luther, and Maley (1966) have suggested that physiological response measures should be corrected for range—that a response estimate should be reported as a percent of the subjects' potential range of responding. Thus, subjects whose tonic heart-rate scores over a variety of conditions extended from 40 to 120 and 80 to 120 B/M, respectively, would be considered at the same level of relative activity if a given stimulus condition yielded scores of 80 and 100 B/M for these same two subjects. Lykken and his associates suggest that this method greatly reduces error variance in studies of pathological populations.

The range correction seems intuitively appropriate when within-subject comparisons of state are being made. It is often inappropriate if we are using physiological measures to study individual differences. In this latter case, the absolute differences under a common condition and the range differences over a spectrum of tasks is not artifact, but the central fact of the investigation. Furthermore, correcting for range involves certain technical difficulties. It is rare that we have data on subjects about extreme conditions of stimulation. In studying skin conductance, Lykken et al. (1966) suggested that having a subject blow up a rubber balloon to explosion would provide an estimate of maximum activity in this system. However, this procedure might not seem sufficient to all investigators. It could be argued that, ideally the subject's activity level in the experimental context should be considered relative to his own unique distribution of scores over some standard set of intensity ordered conditions. However, the practicalities of research and treatment suggest that such precision will not be routinely achieved.

Often investigators are interested in change in system tonus. Thus, differences in peripheral vasoconstriction (plethysmograph measurement) might be studied during a brief period of rest and a succeeding period of comparable length, during which the subject exercised. In this case, the investigator may need to consider the absolute level of the resting score in interpreting the change that has occurred with exercise. All organ systems function within definable limits, and thus, responses are necessarily truncated when initial values are near the upper extremes. Furthermore, in most visceral systems, a variety of homeostatic feedback mechanisms insure a graduated dampening effect on response amplitude along the entire range of functioning. For example, increases in blood pressure initiate the carotid sinus reflex, which includes vagal slowing of the heart, and that response in turn causes a reduction in blood pressure. To some extent, the response level is always a correlative function of the initial level. Wilder (1967, p. VIII) describes this phenomenon as the law of initial values, which he most recently stated as follows:

Given a standard stimulus and a standard period of time, the extent and direction of response of a physiological function at rest depends to a large measure on its initial (pre-experimental) level. The relations are as follows: the higher the initial value, the smaller the response to function-raising, the larger the response to function-depressing stimuli. Beyond a certain medium range of initial values, there is a tendency to paradoxic (reversed) responses, increasing with the extremeness of initial values.

From this perspective, all stimuli are really "second stimuli" which land on top of a "first" response. Interpretation of the *S-R* relationship under investigation depends on some method of partialing out the confounding contribution of this ubiquitous "first" response.

A variety of investigators have sought a statistical solution to this problem. In 1956, Lacey proposed that all physiological responses should be stated as Autonomic Lability Scores. This score expresses the subject's magnitude of response as a deviation from the score predicted by the correlation between base level and stimulus level scores. The population of pre- and post-stimulus scores may be obtained from many trials within an individual subject (which is the ideal circumstance) or from the grouped single trials of all the subjects under investigation. Essentially, the technique is that of the analysis of covariance (Benjamin, 1963, 1967), and if the assumptions of that technique are met, it is a straightforward solution to a perplexing problem. However, certain circumstances argue against its use. One cannot expect covariance to handle systematic differences in the initial values of two groups when the level differences were generated by the experimental treatment itself (Evans and Anastasio, 1968). For example, an experiment designed to assess the attenuating effect of tranquilizing medication on the skin conductance response to fearful stimuli might take the following form: a tranquilizer is administered to one group and a placebo to the other; after a suitable period of time, fear stimuli are presented to both groups; change in skin conductance level is measured. However, if it were found that the tranquilizer was effective in reducing skin conductance level, we would then have systematic differences between groups in our experimental variable before the fear stimulus was applied. The law of initial values then predicts that the tranquilized group would show the largest response (just opposite of our treatment prediction!).

There is no obvious way out of the above dilemma. However, the problem is not really statistical, but lies in the psychological meaning attributed, often arbitrarily, to physiological events. It may be that the subject's absolute tonic level, post-stimulus, is a more meaningful measure of a stressor's psychological impact on the system than the change score. That is to say, while the lower initial value may prompt greater change in the tranquilized group, the absolute level occasioned by an effective drug may still be well below that of untreated subjects. Problems analogous to that of our example also arise when an effort is made to compare the amplitude of physiological responses of psychiatric groups (such as schizophrenic and normals), or developmental levels that differ in base autonomic activity (Heath and Oken, 1965; Lord, 1969). In this context, the investigator must also carefully consider physiological as well as the psychological determinants of his response measures.

From an experimental design point of view, the best way to handle initial level differences is to not have them in the first place. While they may not be avoidable in the designs just described, in many cases level differences can be significantly reduced or eliminated. Proper spacing of trials is an obvious help in avoiding

this difficulty within subjects. At least a minute is necessary for most autonomic functions to return to an initial base line, following moderate stimulation. In the case of intense stressors, the period may be considerably longer. Efforts to hurry the experiment, to fit in more trials per hour, only confound the data. It is wise to know the recovery cycle of the response (which is itself a measure of interest) to the stimuli being explored and plan the experiment accordingly.

Obviously, initial level differences are reduced if care is taken to control variables such as time of the experiment, temperature, diet of subjects, and the like, and particularly, to make sure that there are no differences between groups along these dimensions. Sometimes it is possible to match subjects on initial level, and thus eliminate the problem prior to the presentation of stimuli.

There are no set rules for applying range or initial value corrections. Like the transformations often used in the statistical analysis of skin conductance (reciprocal, square root, or log value), they tend to normalize the distribution of scores and reduce error variance. However, each adjustment moves the observer another step farther from his basic data, with a parallel increase in problems of interpretation. Furthermore, psychologically relevant events other than amplitude change often are not correlated with tonic level. Keen, Chase, and Graham (1965), for example, reported that the latency of maximum acceleration was free from this bias in studies of infant heart rate change. Thus, the investigator must base his decision to apply a statistical corrective on his specific data sample, and not blindly transform every set of physiological scores that he acquires.

Phasic Activity. We have been concerned in the previous discussion with average levels of organ functioning or changes in tonic level of activity. The response is essentially an average of samples or a single sample which is taken to be representative of a persistent level of functioning. This procedure is generally appropriate to the concept of tonicity, but often fails to provide a suitable estimate of phasic events. These briefer responses are often unique in form to the organ system being measured and may vary in complex ways with changes in the stimuli that evoke them. Thus, responses are not invariably smooth descents from a flat plateau to an equally unwavering valley, or an elevator rise from the valley floor to the surrounding tableland. The phasic response is often a complex waveform that may be difficult to detect within the ongoing flow of vegetative activity.

For a number of years considerable controversy existed as to the direction of cardiac rate change in response to non-signal stimuli and during the CS-UCS interval of classical conditioning. Investigators variously argued that it was acceleratory (Dykman, et al., 1960), mainly deceleratory (Davis, et al., 1955), or that there were two types of responders, subjects who accelerated to stimuli and another group that decelerated (Beir, 1940; Gantt, 1958). Most researchers reported data as average rates or differences in average rates pre- and post-stimulus (Shearn, 1961). The poststimulus measures were sometimes taken immediately following the onset of the CS or just before the onset of the UCS, or represented an average of the entire CS-UCS period. Few investigators questioned the hypothesis that the response was a simple unidirectional event, similar to a tonic level change. In point of fact, the most com-

monly found heart rate response resembles the waveform in Figure 3.11. It is easy to see how this triphasic event misled students of cardiac conditioning. Depending on where the elephant was grasped, a different unidirectional event was uncovered. Furthermore, with a constant point of measurement (poststimulus) and individual differences in the time scale of this response, the data might well suggest that some subjects were accelerators and others decelerators.

This basic waveform was described by a number of investigators (Davis, et al., 1955; Zeaman, et al., 1954; Lang and Hnatiow, 1962), but problems of measurement led to its neglect. Unfortunately, the waveform is seldom clearly apparent in a single trial. The cardiovascular system is so noisy, from the point of view of psychological relevance, that many trials must be averaged before the response form emerges.

The phasic, cardiac rate response is now under intensive investigation in a number of laboratories, and much progress has been made in decoding the physiological and psychological relevance of its subcomponents. Thus, the initial acceleration may be accentuated by muscle tension or synchronous inspiration,

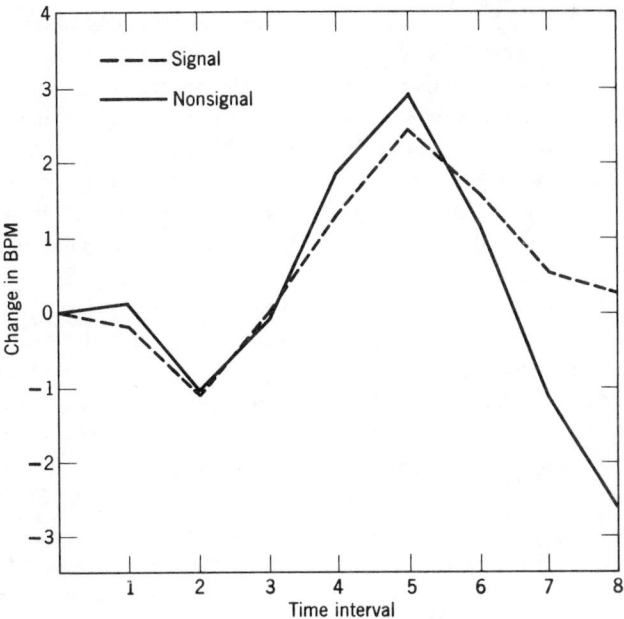

Figure 3.11 The averaged cardiac-rate response to a two-second auditory tone. Onset is just previous to second "1." For the signal series only, the initial tone was followed by another tone at second "8." The subject was told to react to the onset of this second tone by pressing a reaction-time key.

intense stimulation, and preparation for energy release, but none of these factors wholly account for its presence (Obrist, 1967, 1968; Connor and Lang, 1969; Chase, Graham, and Graham, 1968). The second deceleratory limb is reduced by habituation trials, but is reinstated with conditioning (Geer, 1964). Graham and Clifton (1966) relate the various components of the response to Sokolov's theory of orienting and defense, and propose that the deceleration is associated with attention to external stimuli of moderate intensity, while cardiac acceleration indicates the presence of the defensive reflex (a stimulus rejecting "set"). Other experiments suggest that the deceleration response is correlated with response certainty in a judgment task (Bull and Lang, 1970) and threat of aversive shock (Geer and Klein, 1969).

The technique used to uncover the cardiac rate waveform is essentially the same as that used in studies of the evoked potential in the brain. In this latter case, EEG activity time-locked to a stimulus is averaged over repeated trials. The individual trial events that are unrepeated (and thus, random) average to zero, while those events reliably associated with the stimulus are retained and become more accentuated in the response as more trials are added.

It may be useful here to comment also on the limitations and potential errors that are associated with the use of averaging. As Brazier (1967) has pointed out, if the time scale of the response is extended or collapsed, or components drop out or are added, the averaging technique will tend to obscure these changes. The investigator is prompted to suspect such metamorphosis by an increment in variance around the separate points of the averaged curve. If variance is pronounced and general, polynomial analysis of the curve would not yield significant components. The problem can be attacked experimentally by averaging smaller samples of trials at different points in the experiment. Alternatively, if the wave has a reliable form within the sample of subjects being tested, individual trials can be averaged across subjects.

The present discussion of phasic responses may mislead the reader into thinking that they are always locked to specific stimulus events. On the contrary, there is much interest in so-called spontaneous activity. Lacey and Lacey (1958a) called attention to this phenomenon of autonomic activity in connection with studies of temperamental differences between subjects. Although findings have not been consistent, Barratt (1963) and Levy and Lang (1966) did find significant relationships between heart rate variability and perceptual, psychomotor, and questionnaire indices of impulsivity. Frequency of spontaneous responses in skin conductance has been associated with "arousal level" (Lader, 1967a). Furthermore, the study of spontaneous phasic behavior is by no means limited to autonomic systems. The spontaneous "K complex"[12] is of considerable interest to students of the EEG, as are phases (saccadic or following) of rapid eye movement (REM).

In concluding this consideration of response measurement, it should be noted again that the distinction between phasic and tonic activity is more convenience than reality, and one dimension blends into the other with no clear point of demarcation. In the same vein, a distinction between the study of spontaneous phasic responses and the investigation of biological rhythms (Wieland and Mefferd, 1969) would be difficult to draw. With reference to the *S-R* context, phasic events may be somewhat less subject to initial values than tonic level change. Thus, Hord, Johnson, and Lubin (1964) found no relationship between base heart rate and the Lang-Hnatiow measure of the phasic response; however, Geer (1964) did find a low but significant correlation. This relationship must be explored for each measure under consideration. Furthermore, in some cases phasic responses should be corrected for range of amplitudes, as the Lykken study suggests, and some investigations could require correction for frequency of spontaneous activity. Geer (1966) found the number of spontaneous SCRs to be positively correlated with number of discrete responses to repetitive stimuli, and Lader and Wing (1966) reported a similar relationship with the slope of habituation gradients to intense, pure tones. In summary, we cannot be far wrong in con-

---

[12] A slow vertex wave followed by fast activity, which may appear spontaneously in sleep (Hill and Parr, 1963).

cluding that individual response estimates are most sensibly interpreted, when considered relative to the spontaneous frequency of these events in the subject's record, the tonic level of the viscera's functioning, and the ranges and distributions of response latencies or amplitudes that are generated by similar stimuli.

RESPONSE SPECIFICITY AND MULTIPLE SYSTEM MEASUREMENT

Investigators originally hoped that single measures of autonomic functioning would have a simple indicant relationship to the psychological constructs in vogue. However, it became apparent very soon that skin conductance increase, for example, did not equal "anxiety" or "drive" nor was it relationship to these constructs simple or fixed. In point of fact, a great variety of situations and events will evoke skin conductance changes, ranging from the closing of a door or the sound of a friendly voice, through a whole gamut of emotional and physiological stressors. Nearly all physiological responses can be generated by a great variety of internal and external stimuli, and it seems unlikely that any physiological event could be used in an exact substitutive way, as an index of psychological state. Thus, by observing the physiology of an organism, we are not able to go backwards and reconstruct the stimulus input or the psychological state that contributed to its generation. To assume this kind of reciprocal relationship is the classic *indicant fallacy*. It is this fallacy that prompts the criminal to confess when faced with the lie detection apparatus. However, the polygraph does not detect lies. A lie is a complex psychosocial event that has no distinct physiology, and must be understood, in the main, within its own domain of expression. Thus, the polygraph has no special power to validate (except in the sense of construct validity) suppositions about the intentions or emotional state of human subjects. As Lacey pointed out in his 1959 review of psychophysiological research on psychotherapy, physiological data must be *interpreted* in a transactional context. These interpretations depend on an understanding of the stimulus context in which the measurements were taken,

knowledge of the physiology of the system measured, and the assessment of other response events that may be simultaneously occurring.

As information relevant to these three factors is increased, the "meaning" of a given somatic or autonomic event becomes more *specific*. That is to say, we have clearer evidence of the response's relationship to a particular psychological variable or construct.

Even when we know much about the environmental transaction within which a response occurred, few physiological events can be clearly interpreted if they are considered alone, independent of other ongoing responses. Skin conductance, for example, is a unidirectional response, and is therefore restricted to a "more or less" dimension. Stimulation prompts an increase in conductance, and at moderate levels of input, more intense stimulation will yield yet larger responses. However, beyond this intensity relationship, the response is too simple to carry much information. Heart rate, on the other hand, is bidirectional and, as we have already noted, its phasic response may potentially encode a greater variety of psychological variables. However, some of these changes can be artifacts of changes in other physiological events, and our confidence in the psychological importance of a heart-rate permutation is increased when simultaneous measurement has permitted the partialing out of this latter source of variance.

It has been routine for psychophysiological investigators to record a variety of physiological systems simultaneously, and this practice soon led to a search for psychological relevance in the pattern of change, as well as the change in single measures.

The correlation among physiological measures, change scores, or tonic levels, under conditions of rest or stress, traditionally has been found to be relatively low. Thus, it is unusual for one physiological variable to account for as much as 10 percent of the variance in predicting the response of another system. In part, these poor relationships can be ascribed to the use of inappropriate measures in assessing specific systems, or the intercorrelation of different types of formal measures (phasic with tonic responses; level data with change scores). However, even when full consideration is given to such errors of experimentation, the dearth of high correlations remains impressive. To the naive investigator, this lack of simple concordance in the peripheral physiology is particularly discouraging. It is impressive evidence that there is no unitary physiological response, indexed by a host of interchangeable measures. However, to the student of physiology, this comes as no surprise. He is aware that different systems have different functions—that under any given condition of the organism, in mobilizing for a response or attending to vegetative functions, some organs will become active, others will decrease their action, and other systems may be little affected. Furthermore, he knows that there are enormous individual differences in the degree and pattern of these effects.

In their 1958 article on measurement problems, Lacey and Lacey (1958b) documented the considerable variability of individual physiological response patterns evoked by the same stressor. Thus, although many subjects showed concordant heart rate and skin conductance increases when alerted for an oncoming stress, a substantial number show marked activity in only one system. The Laceys referred to the reliable repetition of such individual patterns of responding in the *same* or similar stimulus contexts, as *intra-stressor* stereotypy. Furthermore, these individual response effects may be highly consistent across stimulus situations. Thus, some subjects may have a typical pattern that is relatively invariant regardless of the stressor applied. This phenomenon is called *inter-stressor* stereotypy. Both dispositions are closely related to Malmo's concept of "symptom specificity." This latter term refers to the finding that among psychiatric patients psychological stressors prompt exaggerated responses in those physiological systems associated with somatic complaints. Thus, Malmo and his associates (1949, 1950) reported that stressful interviews produced differentially greater muscle tension in the neck muscles of a patient complaining of headache, and that the bodily distribution of muscle tension varied reliably with interview content.

Both inter and intrastressor stereotypes were found to account for part of the variance in the experimental situation (Engel, 1960; Schnore, 1959). The degree of physiological concordance across differing psychological stressors may be important to the understanding of psychosomatic disorder. It has been postulated that those patients with high concordance tend to overwork certain systems, which are then more susceptible to systemic or infectious disease. Conversely, it has been shown that patterns are less fixed among children than normal adults (Elliott, 1964). Furthermore, it has been suggested that gross discordance may be a characteristic of general personality disorganization, as in psychosis (Reynolds, 1961).

Individual differences in pattern are difficult to assimilate in studies designed to compare the stress response of groups. No adequate statistical techniques presently exist for accomplishing multiple profile analyses and testing differences. As a temporary solution, Lacey (1959) proposed that the subject's "peak or maximal arousal" be used to describe an individual's degree of overall autonomic arousal. In this method each of the subject's physiological responses is expressed as a T-score, and the maximum T-score is used to represent his autonomic response, regardless of the physiological system in which it occurs. Thus, one subject's heart rate would be averaged with another subject's skin conductance or stomach motility. While this system has yielded significant correlations with stressors, and significant differences between experimental groups, it should be employed with caution. It is quite possible that the situationally meaningful pattern of responding changes with the intensity of the stimulus and with the extent of the subject's "psychological" response. Thus, it is possible that certain systems, which at lower stimulus levels vary with small increments in the input level, may be unresponsive to intense stimulation. In a parallel fashion, some response systems may not "kick in" until a certain level of input has been achieved. Even more complex interrelations between variables are not only possible, but highly likely and the maximal-arousal method would tend to obscure such relationships. Presently, there is no generally accepted method for assigning weights to different measures, for the simple reason that there is neither agreement on the psychological construct of arousal nor adequate information about its physiological indices. It would seem wise at this point for the investigator not to limit his report to "arousal peak" data.

Situational Stereotypy. The "maximal-arousal" method assumes that all peripheral, physiological measures encode only one type of information. They are held to vary only along a simple activation or arousal dimension. Differences in the organ-system's sensitivity to this continuum is taken to be an accident of individual variability. A very different point of view is represented by those who argue that specific psychological states have unique physiological characteristics. This latter phenomenon is called situational stereotypy, and has been a major focus of research in psychophysiology. We have already referred to the work of Ax (1953), Schachter (1957), and Fukenstein et al. (1951, 1954), who reported differences in the physiological response to fear and anger stimuli. The early work of R. C. Davis is also of importance in supporting this view. Davis (1957) found that the pattern of physiological events differed considerably in tasks requiring simple motor responses, temperature stimulation, or attention to emotionally toned slides. Of particular interest was the fact that, despite the arousing nature of some of the stimuli, not all systems responded in a sympathetic direction. Thus, male subjects observing slides of female nudes show skin-conductance increase and heart-rate decrement. Lacey et al. (1963) has since demonstrated such "directional fractionation" in a variety of other situations and has proposed a theory relating pattern of autonomic responding to the quality of the organism's transactions with the environment. Thus, he asserts that under conditions of environmental intake (visual scanning or attentive listening) both heart rate and blood pressure will be relatively low, while a set for environmental rejection (prompted by aversive stimulation or internalized problem solving) is accompanied by increased cardiovascular activity. Lacey (1967) holds that the cognitive and behavioral tasks associated with these sets are facilitated by feedback from the autonomic system which thus participates directly in the psychological event. While such feedback mechanisms have been demonstrated in the neurophysiological laboratory (Bonvallet, Dell, and Hiebel, 1954), there is also conflicting evidence showing that per-

formance does not deteriorate when important autonomic feedback paths are pharmacologically blocked (Obrist, Wood, and Perez-Reyes, 1965).

Elliot (1969), Campos and Johnson (1966), and Obrist, Webb, and Sutterer (1969) attribute the obtained patterns of cardiovascular change to the differential energy requirements of tasks and the varying involvement of somatic-muscle activity. Thus, the latter investigator has found that in situations that involve the intake set (e.g., the reaction-time foreperiod), phasic heart-rate deceleration is accompanied by a reduction in respiratory activity and muscle tension. Elliot (1969) reviewed research on motivation that involved the recording of automatic activity. He concluded that, unlike skin conductance, tonic heart-rate acceleration is generally associated with either a set to respond or actual motor events.

Despite these unresolved theoretical differences, the fact that different stimulus contexts may occasion characteristic and reliable patterns of autonomic responses appears to have considerable experimental support. However, this evidence for situational sterotypy should not be taken to mean that there exists exact physiological *indicants* of experiential states, feelings, and the like (see pages 99–100). What has been shown is that groups of subjects may yield a similiar physiological pattern, if assessed in a similar stimulus context. This does not imply that the physiological output of any individual subject can be recognized to have been generated in this setting and no other (the indicant test). While it is possible that such two-way prediction could be achieved for very narrow S-R relationships, at the level of clinically meaningful events, neither the current precision of psychological description nor the state of psychophysiological methodology are adequate to the task.

The Psychophysiology of Emotion

It is traditional for discussions of emotion to begin with the theoretical speculations of William James (1884, 1890). The great New England philosopher-psychologist conceptualized the problem within the framework of the introspective psychology of his time. He never doubted the substantive reality of feeling states, but sought their explanation in the physiological events that normally accompanied them.[13] James departed from the commonsensical view of emotion in suggesting that feelings were percepts of physiological change. In other words, he reversed the popular assumption that psychological state preceded physiological state. He speculated that the latter condition was evoked directly by affective stimuli, and the phenomenal experience came after as the subject perceived and evaluated the changes in his own bodily processes. James' great antagonist was the physiologist W. B. Cannon (1927, 1931). He criticized James' approach, arguing that the peripheral viscera were not fundamental to emotional feeling or expression. Cannon marshalled a host of logical and laboratory demonstrations in support of his view. The evidence that seemed most damaging to Jamesian theory was the finding that surgical separation of the viscera from the central nervous system did not eliminate emotional behavior. While neither Sherrington's (1900) nor Cannon's (1927) procedure for accomplishing this completely severed all interconnections, the operations were extreme enough (complete transection of the spinal cord and removal of the sympathetic chain), that the failure to find altered emotional expression raised a serious question about the relevance of visceral feedback. Cannon proposed a thalamic theory of emotion as a substitute for James' visceral theory. Cannon concluded from studies of decorticated animals that the thalamus was the brain center where sensory impulses received an emotional *quality*. Impulses from the sense organs are routed to this subcortical center, which then, via the hypothalamus, initiates excitation both in the direction of the viscera and to the cortex. The cortex was further held to have an inhibitory effect on thalamic centers, normally preventing the uncontrolled expression of affect, but ineffective in the face of strong stimulus input.

The consequent of Cannon's work and the elaboration of his theory by Bard (1934a, 1934b) was to focus physiological psychology on the brain, to the neglect of the associated visceral

phenomena. Thus, the next step, taken by Papez (1937, 1939), was to try to delineate the specific cortical mechanisms that participated in the regulation of emotional behavior. Papez held that the cingulate gyrus was the receptive region for impulses coming from lower brain centers, which in turn radiated from this gyrus to lend emotional tone to other cortical processes. Maclean (1949) similarly emphasized the importance of the cortex in differentiating feeling states, but focused attention on the hippocampus and amygdala of the limbic system (the olfactory brain of more primitive organisms) and their roles in visceral control and emotional states. Thus, he suggested that the amygdala might be predominantly parasympathetic in its effects and participate in the regulation of more sedentary, vegetative processes. He suggested that outflow from the hippocampus was mainly sympathetic, and thus active in states of emotional arousal. The advent of techniques of chemical and electrical brain stimulation and for recording electrical events from deep structures has provided tools for the exploration of this theory and its derivations in animals. While the implications of this work for the psychology of human emotion are potentially enormous, its application to current human behavioral data is not yet clear.

The study of the reticular formation and the relationship of its functioning to the EEG has, on the other hand, been of considerable value in interpreting behavioral and psychophysiological studies of human subjects. In 1949, Moruzzi and Magoun reported that stimulation of the brainstem reticular formation of the cat produced increments in cortical EEG frequency, along with autonomic and muscular responses associated with states of emotion. Soon after, Lindsley (1951) proposed an *activation theory* of emotion, in which emotional and motivational intensity were related to degree of cortical arousal. Thus, the lowest level of activation, sleep, was characterized by slow frequencies of relatively large amplitude. Waking states of inactivity yielded "alpha waves" (8–13 Hz), which were blocked by stimuli that aroused the organism's attention or interest. Increases in emotion or

---

[13] In this introspective emphasis, James differed from the physiologist Lange, with whom he is often linked. Lange's approach (1885) was more narrowly biological, and visceral activity was held to be the direct determinant of emotion.

motivation were held to be associated with still faster cortical activity, with states of violent rage producing low-amplitude, desynchronized activity of high frequency. According to Lindsley (1957), in addition to the classical or specific sensory pathways to the cortex, there is a second, nonspecific sensory system, which is rooted in the reticular formation of the lower brainstem. Visceral and somatic afferents are routed through this reticular projection system, which includes hypothalamic stimulation of waking centers in the diencephalon and, via the thalamus, general activation of the cortex.

Behavioral theorists and clinicians seized on activation theory (and its reticular system) as a physiological analogue of unitary "drive" and "anxiety" theories of emotional and pathological behavior (Malmo, 1958, 1966). Thus, activation theory has become heir to the same problems of explanation that beset these other views. If activation varies only along a continuum of intensity, how can it explain the important qualitative differences in emotional states, and their markedly different behavioral consequences? Hebb (1955) answered this question by suggesting that motivational and emotional states are composed of two elements, an arousal or energizing function and a cue function that provides behavioral direction. Thus, an emotion, such as fear, involves high arousal, with the addition of mediational processes (of cortical origin) that tend to produce avoidance and flight. A grossly similar approach has been taken by Duffy (1962) and Pribram (1967), with the latter author giving even greater emphasis to the planning and organizational function of the cortex in emotion.

In the social-psychological context, Schachter has developed this two-factor theory in a way that has far-reaching repercussions for research on emotion (Schachter, 1964). He follows Cannon in his argument that emotional states are undifferentiated in autonomic pattern. However, instead of searching for brain mechanisms that might mediate distinctions among emotional states or behaviors, he suggests that cognitive set determines the unique character of an emotional response.

... given a state of physiological arousal for which an individual has no immediate explanation, he will "label" this state and describe his feelings in terms of the cognitions available to him. To the extent that cognitive factors are potent determiners of emotional states, it could be anticipated that precisely the same state of physiological arousal could be labeled "joy" or "fury" or any of a great diversity of emotional labels, depending on the cognitive aspects of the situation (p. 53).

Schachter was apparently prompted to this speculation by earlier research on the effects of injected epinephrine on human subjects (Marañon, 1924; Wenger, 1960). Subjects in these studies usually reported that they sensed their physiological arousal, but seldom had full experience of emotion, unless it was triggered by specific memories or environmental circumstances (for example, discussion of an emotionally laden topic).

In a series of now-classical experiments, Schachter studied the interaction between subcutaneous injection of epinephrine, and instructional or behavioral manipulations to respond emotionally (Schachter and Singer, 1962; Schachter and Wheeler, 1962). He found that, when subjects were misled as to the effects of epinephrine and exposed to emotionally arousing situations, they tended to show verbal and overt-motor behavior consonant with the emotional context. Thus, such subjects found comic movies funnier than did control observers; imitated an experimental confederate's hostile, verbal derision of the experiment; or were provoked into hypomanic, playful behavior by the acts of another accomplice. On the other hand, the emotional response of the participants was considerably less in the absence of epinephrine (placebo condition), or when the effects to be anticipated from epinephrine were explained to the injected subjects.

Schachter concluded that two factors were necessary to the production of emotional states: (1) an undifferentiated state of arousal, and (2) the presence of cognitive labels that would direct the state of arousal and associated behavior along emotional lines. If either were absent, so would be the affective character of the behavior. Schachter and his students have expanded the domain of this hypothesis, researching its implications for the maintenance of obesity (Schachter, 1967) and psychopathy (Schachter and Latané, 1964), and as an explanation of effects obtained in systematic-desensitization therapy (Valins and Ray, 1967).

Schachter's theory is attractive to psychophysiologists for a variety of reasons. It does not focus on brain mechanisms to the exclusion of verbal (cognitive) and autonomically mediated response events. It may be examined by laboratory experiment. Furthermore, it is interactive; that is, it does not assume a one-way path of influence, in which either the viscera or the higher centers command behavior throughout the organism. On the other hand, it is too narrow a conception to handle much of the relevant data, and the experiments in its support are open to serious criticism. Thus, the influence of physiological arousal is described in exclusively exteroceptive terms. The individual's perception of visceral activity gives rise to "evaluative needs"; the subsequent search for an explanation is resolved in favor of emotion if the stimulus context prompts such behavior. However, there is reason to believe that visceral feedback influences central cortical activity through pathways that short-circuit awareness, and do not involve the kind of internal dialogue Schachter's theory implies. Bonvallet, Dell, and Hiebel (1954) have shown that distension of the sinus of the carotid artery leads to a decrease in cortical EEG frequency. Lacey (1967) suggests that changes in blood pressure in the intact organism may thus modulate levels of cortical activity, motor responses, and the temperament characteristics of subjects. This feedback can be much faster in its effects than would be possible for the "cognitive-evaluative" system of Schachter. For example, both Birren, et al. (1963) and Calloway (1965) found that reaction-time latency varied with the point in the cardiovascular cycle when stimuli were presented. Emotional reactions may be very rapid in their onset. To the extent that peripheral physiological states are pertinent, sudden emotions are more likely to be determined by direct, interoceptive feedback than by a slower, cognitive-exteroceptive system.

Schachter's theory implies that a competing cognitive set easily overrides the emotional impetus of physiological arousal; that is, when the subject knows he has received an adrenalin injection, he interprets his bodily changes in that light, and fails to show emotional behavior. However, a host of clinical examples suggest that this may be a very short-term inhibitory effect that is overemphasized by the relatively low epinephrine dosage and brief experimental format employed in Schachter's research. Somewhat more persistent physiological states occasioned by chronic administration of drugs (Jaffe, 1966), menstrual cycle (Ivey and Bardwick, 1968), or physical disease (Frohlich, et al., 1969) may have strong emotional correlates that are reliable, and persist despite the fact that the afflicted person has received an excellent explanation of the stressor's physiological effects. Psychotherapists will see in the above an analogue to the failures of interpretation sometimes encountered in psychoanalysis. While the analyst assumes that this occurs when his explanation is not apt (or when the patient is not receptive), from the point of view of emotional control, it is quite possible that the primarily physiological origins of some emotional responses render the cognitive elements superfluous.

In considering the experimental support for Schachter's view, a question may be raised about his physiological manipulation: does subcutaneous injection of adrenalin produce the normal physiological substrate of emotion? As we have already noted, other catechols have other autonomic effects, and different emotions are associated with their action. Furthermore, consequences for the cardiovascular system are very different when adrenalin is rapidly injected and when it is slowly infused into the vein at a rate comparable to that of glandular secretion (Keele and Neil, 1965). Schachter assumes a rather crude unitary arousal throughout the autonomic system. Thus, his supporting experiments usually include only one autonomic measure. However, Lacey (1967) has shown conclusively that autonomic subsystems fractionate—that not all autonomic responses are prompted in a sympathetic direction by an arousing circumstance, and that different activating conditions may generate directionally opposite changes in the same system (for example, heart rate).

Another relevant data source is a study by Hohmann (1966) of patients with spinal cord injury. Consistent with Schachter (1964), the higher the cord transection (and thus the greater the possible loss of autonomic feedback), the more frequently patients report attenuated experiences of emotion. However, there is also a suggestion that specific lesions may differentially affect the quality of specific emotions. Thus, nearly all patients with sacral lesions reported attenuation of sexual feelings, but three of five reported an increase in feelings of fear. Hohmann raises the hypothesis that this may be attributed to postinjury accidents related to the patient's handicap. However, it is also possible that this represents a loss of sacral-parasympathetic feedback, which functioned to attenuate rather than augment sympathetically dominant emotional experiences.

A more elaborate model than has been yet proposed is needed to accommodate the available findings on the psychophysiology of the emotional response. While few would question that a dimension of arousal or activation can be specified at the behavioral, cortical, subcortical, and autonomic levels, it seems unlikely that this is the only relevant dimension in any of these systems. Activation theorists (Malmo and Belanger, 1967) have recognized the need to revise and elaborate arousal theory in the light of recent conflicting findings (Lacey, 1967). As we have already suggested, considerable progress has been made in describing brain areas related to both the general energizing of behavior and activation in terms of specific incentives. Routtenberg (1968) has recently proposed a two-arousal hypothesis, in which the reticular formation is held to be of primary importance in maintaining tonic alertness and in orienting the organism to incoming stimuli, while the limbic system is held responsible for specific, stimulation-produced positive and negative reward effects.

It is reasonable to assume that, as activity is analyzed at lower levels of the brain and finally at the autonomic system (or the organs that it innervates), differentiation must become less refined and subtle. However, even here a wealth of data summarized by Gellhorn (1967) suggests that active processes of inhibition and excitation contend for control of organ functioning. To assume that visceral responses reflect only a single behavioral dimension or that autonomic feedback can only increment cortical activity is inconsistent with the available data.

A Conception of the Emotional Response and Its Modification

For both the therapist and the scientist, it is reasonable to consider the emotional response to be a complex of three measurable systems: verbal-cognitive, overt-motor, and physiological (autonomically innervated organs and tonic muscle activity). All systems are modulated by neural centers within the brain, but intercorrelations between their outputs are surprisingly low. From an empirical point of view, the behaviors are partially independent. Nevertheless, these systems are also highly interactive, and appear to mutually augment, sustain, or attenuate each other in ways that we are just beginning to understand.

System Interaction. The experiments of S. Schachter and his associates illustrate some important aspects of intersystem influence. Instructional set (information that permits the subjects to interpret exteroceptively perceived autonomic change) will block an emotional response that would have resulted from the coincidence of an appropriate external stimulus and sympathetic arousal. Lazarus and his colleagues (Lazarus and Opton, 1966; Lazarus, Speisman, Mordkoff, and Davison, 1962) have shown similar effects when external emotional stimuli are presented without the catechol supplement. In their studies, autonomic responses were recorded while subjects watched a stressful film (such as a film dealing with the subincision rites of Australian aborigines). They found that tonic autonomic activity was reduced if subjects are encouraged to intellectualize or deny the painful circumstances of the operation.

On the other hand, if the organism is cognitively set to be angry or afraid, autonomic activity or appropriate external stimuli will prompt a more intense response. Under the right conditions, instructions alone can lead to both the physiological and behavioral output of emotion. Thus, Graham and his colleagues (Graham, Kabler, and Graham, 1962) gave normal subjects waking or hypnotic suggestions to assume emotional attitudes previously found to be associated with specific psychosomatic syndromes. They found physiological change appearing in their subjects, in the same organ systems that were afflicted in the parallel patient group. Sternbach (1964) found that gastric motility (as measured by the movement of an ingested magnet) varied with instructions concerning a pill he administered to a small group of subjects. Those told that it would relax the stomach showed a reduction in activity relative to an uninformed group, while subjects told it was a gastric stimulant showed a significant increase in motility. In our own laboratory, Melamed (1969) found that instructional set grossly altered the physiological tonus and habituation rate of subjects to filmed fear stimuli, and that these changes were correlated with subsequent verbal reports of fear reduction. Thus, subjects instructed to intensify their emotional experience showed greatest autonomic arousal and least post-experiment change in fear; subjects instructed in muscular relaxation showed lower levels of arousal and more fear reduction.

It is also clear from clinical data that a mutually augmenting feedback loop may be generated between systems. Thus, the patient who is "set" to be distressed may become aware of autonomic feedback (such as heart rate increase) that confirms the cognition. A rapid pulse may then achieve the status of a discriminative stimulus for further anxious cognitions. In this manner, tachycardia begets tachycardia. A recent study by Lang, Sroufe, and Hastings (1967) suggests that such feedback effects are not dependent on awareness. In this experiment subjects tracked a meter, pressing a button when the pointer passed specific numbers on the meter face. They were unaware that the movements of the pointer were determined by their own heart rate. These subjects showed a significant increase in heart-rate variability during the task, relative to simultaneously run, yoked control subjects. This latter control group worked with the same meter display, but the meter was driven by their yokemates' heart rate rather than their own. The experiment clearly shows changes in an autonomic response which are a direct result of the subject's participation (albeit unaware) in an exteroceptively mediated feedback loop. It is reasonable to assume that such interactions may develop spontaneously, with important consequences for the development and maintenance of emotional behavior.

We have already alluded to neurophysiological evidence that suggests that autonomic activity may feed back *interoceptively* to influence striate-muscle reflexes and cortical activity. Such feedback is potentially disruptive, and in emotion, could contribute to the unskillful execution or blocking of motor acts. Furthermore, such failure of psychomotor functioning is *exteroceptively* perceived, and its negative valence can add to an ascending spiral of verbal, behavioral, and autonomic activation and disorganization.

Stimuli that prompt affects are less likely to instigate a general, disorganizing emotion when psychomotor responses are not disrupted. If an act is well-practiced, the individual may maintain good motor control, despite the presence of excessive autonomic arousal or anxious cognitions. Furthermore, repeated successes in generating effective behavior in the face of provocative stimuli break the link between augmenting systems. Under these conditions, it becomes possible to adapt out or unlearn the unsuitable emotional self-instruction and the associated physiological activity. Athletes, actors, musicians, and students have long used overlearning to reduce or prevent the debilitating effects of stress. Recently, this method has become a more explicit part of psychotherapeutic treatment (Wolpe and Lazarus, 1966). Social behaviors are practiced and overpracticed with the therapist. After these role-playing sessions, the patient begins supervised trials in the natural environment, proceeding on a regular schedule from low-stress to high-stress situations.

Jacobson (1938), Gellhorn (1964), Wolpe (1958), and Schultze and Luthe (1959) have all advocated the retraining of the peripheral physiological system as the best method to break the emotional-response loop. It is assumed that feedback of autonomic events is an integral part of emotion, and that efforts to attenuate this source of stimulation will favorably modify motor and cognitive response components.

Jacobson and Wolpe emphasize muscle relaxation as the vehicle for change. Instructional control of striate muscles is first achieved, and then employed to reduce tonus throughout the body. It is assumed that somatic-autonomic connections will function to reduce levels of sympathetic activity in the viscera. Schultze and Luthe's method is more similar to hypnosis, in that direct suggestions are made to reduce activity in specific body parts.

Recently, techniques have developed for the direct training of autonomic systems through the use of exteroceptive feedback and operant shaping techniques. Shearn (1962) first showed the operant conditioning of heart rate acceler- ations, and subsequent studies have also demonstrated shaping of tonic deceleration (Brenner, 1966; Engel and Hanson, 1966). Other experiments suggest that blood pressure (Hnatiow, 1968; Shapiro et al., 1969), sweat- gland activity (Crider, Shapiro, and Tursky, 1966), and blood volume (Lisina, 1958) may be similarly influenced.

In our own laboratory, exteroceptive feed- back has been used in training human subjects to reduce sinus arrythmia and stabilize their heart rates within narrowly defined limits (Hnatiow and Lang, 1965; Lang, Sroufe, and Hastings, 1967). In these experiments subjects observed a meterlike display that was in parallel circuit with a cardiotachometer (thus, pointer movements indicated beat-by-beat changes in rate). When provided with this display and given instructions to enter the pointer on the scale within a six B/M area, subjects signifi- cantly increased the total time their heart rate fell in the target area. Furthermore, they showed significantly greater reduction in heart rate standard deviation than uninstructed or non- feedback controls.

More recent experiments from our laboratory suggest that these effects may be achieved with respiration experimentally controlled (Sroufe, 1969). Furthermore, systematic changes in the P-R interval of the EKG waveform appear to be associated with learned stabilization (Hnatiow, 1968). This would suggest that such heart-rate control is effected neurally (that is, through variation in vagal inhibitory impulses to the heart) and is perhaps independent of striate mediators. Animal experiments accomplished by Miller and his associates (Miller and DiCarra, 1967; Miller, 1969) support this latter hypoth- esis. In their research, rats were curarized and artificially respirated. Positive brain stimulation was then employed to reinforce either increases

or decreases in heart rate. The appropriate directional changes shown by the shaped subjects greatly exceeded those of control animals. These investigators also reported P-wave changes in the EKG to be associated with experimental modification of heart rate.

Although autonomic feedback effects may not depend on muscle or respiratory mediation, Lisina (1958) suggests that the use of "volun- tary" striate mediators early in training facili- tates autonomic learning, and that these somatic responses then drop out when control is well learned. In a recent experiment we found some support for Lisina's first hypothesis; sub- jects given explicit instruction in relevant respiration patterns achieved rapid control of heart rate, which readily transferred to non- feedback conditions (Sroufe, Hnatiow, and Lang, 1967). Stoyva (1968) has reported success in producing states of general psychophysio- logical relaxation using electromyograph feed- back from striate muscles. The interaction of somatic and autonomic systems in the context of learned physiological control merits con- tinued study.

Recently, the investigation of operant- feedback control of EEG frequency has been undertaken. In this research, a band-pass filter is used to separate out the frequency to be incremented from the total cortical signal. A predetermined amplitude of this frequency triggers an auditory stimulus. Subjects are instructed that task success is determined by the total time they can keep on the auditory stimulus. Kamiya (1962, 1968) reports that the proportion of the EEG falling within the alpha range may be significantly increased by this method. Furthermore, the psychophysiological state accompanying alpha increase involves a reduction in tonic autonomic levels, a verbal report of lessened anxiety, and an increased sense of well-being.

Much research remains to be done before the mechanism of change or the clinical value of operant-feedback methods of physiological control is clearly established. However, these techniques show promise of providing an avenue for modifying the physiological sub- strate of emotion. While drugs have long been used for this purpose, their effectiveness is often lessened by lack of specificity, unwanted side effects, and an absence of positive transfer to the non-drug state. If the persistence of emotional states is dependent even in part on physiological feedback, the retraining of the critical organ systems in the direction of reduced sympathetic activity could become a powerful new therapeutic intervention.

System Independence. It is proposed that emotional behaviors are multiple system responses—verbal-cognitive, motor, and physiological events that interact through interoceptive (neural and hormonal) and exteroceptive channels of communication. All systems are controlled or influenced by brain mechanisms, but the level of the important centers of influence (cortical or subcortical, limbic or brainstem) are varied, and like the resulting behaviors, partially independent. Because of this imperfect coupling, it is possible and even usual to generate emotional cognitions without autonomic arousal, aggressive behavior without a hostile motive, or the autonomic and avoidant behavior of fear without insight (proper labeling).

A coincidence of activity in more than one system is what we most confidently refer to as an emotion, and a highly general response characterizes states of intense affect. Perhaps the most obvious examples of system independence are apparent when emotion is attenuated. With a reduction in intensity, systems are often diminished in an unbalanced way, and evidence of arousal may actually disappear from one system and not another. So-called mild feeling states may involve no more than the verbal report, and we might find little specific activity in the autonomic or behavioral sphere. This points up the additional fact that systems differ in their sensitivity and the subtlety of their response. For example, the verbal behavior of a human being is capable of reflecting gradations of affect, to which the cruder autonomic system may be completely insensitive (Lang, Geer, and Hnatiow, 1963).

A variety of empirical data (Eriksen, 1958; Lang, 1968; Mischel, 1968) support the hypothesis that the behavior systems that we have described as active in the emotional response are partially independent. In our own work on the desensitization of phobias (Lang and Lazovik, 1963), we have found repeatedly that some subjects will show rapid change in overt behavior (for example, show less avoidance of the phobic object), but no initial lessening of fear in questionnaires or interview report. Later this verbal system often "catches up." On the other hand, some subjects report diminution of fear, but continue to show performance deficit. Similarly, the low correlations found between physiological and behavioral data are legion (see Lacey, 1959; Martin, 1961; Martin and Sroufe, in press). While it is possible to assume that the poor relationships obtained are attributable to inadequate measurement, they have appeared so often as to merit serious consideration as real phenomena. From this perspective, these findings argue that behavioral systems are to some extent capable of independent change—they can be shaped separately by environmental influence.

With reference to the development of normal and pathological emotion, this theoretical position implies that most affects do not arise all of a piece—with a viewing of the primal scene (Freud, 1938) or the hearing of loud noises near small animals (Watson and Rayner, 1920). It suggests that emotional responses may be constructed element by element as the organism develops. We have already described the operant-feedback training of the autonomic nervous system. Similar effects may occur in nature, as they have been shown to do in the laboratory. Thus, states of general or organ-specific sympathetic activity could develop through a fortuitous occurrence of negative or positive reinforcers in the environment, in concert with specifically vulnerable developmental stages. The systematic delay of food or attention until heart-rate and blood-pressure variability increase, could produce a chronically hyperactive cardiovascular system. As Miller (1969) has suggested, such unintended but specific operant schedules may determine the development of psychosomatic disease. Furthermore, Russian studies of interoceptive conditioning suggest that conditioned stimuli can impinge on autonomically innervated organs (for example, the intestinal wall), and through contiguity with an aversive event, come to mediate widespread autonomic change (Razran, 1961). In these cases, no explicit language behavior or motor acts may be attached to the stimulus-response sequence. Nevertheless, stimulation of the gut produces an aversive psychophysiological state. Of course, language components could be added to the sequence later through further conditioning, or as a function of behavioral or semantic generalization from emotional learning in other situations.

On the other hand, individuals may develop emotional responses out of primarily verbal learning experiences. Thus, parents may reinforce the statement "I am afraid" in specific stimulus contexts. The child may learn to emit the language response reliably. However, whether the verbal statement becomes associated with behavioral acts or autonomic activity, depends on other learning. Similarly, it is possible that emotions might be started from overt aggressive acts or avoidance behavior, and the language and autonomic activity added later.

That the language system comes to catalogue, and to some extent control and direct, other behaviors is clear (although the method by which this is accomplished is not). However, it is also true that considerable independence is maintained. Emotions, almost by definition, are events that are outside the control of language (that is, conscious motives or intent). Furthermore, the breadth and tonicity of a subject's verbal emotional gradient may be considerably at variance with the same dimension's characteristics in another response system. Thus, some individuals have learned to signal anxiety as intense, when only minimal sympathetic arousal or behavioral deficit can be measured. In these cases, treatment might be directed primarily at the alteration of verbal-adaptation levels, and the acceptance of some upset as a normal part of living. On the other hand, some patients fail to note the debilitating effects of stress despite gross changes in performance or physiological deterioration. They may need an opposite, sensitization therapy, so they can begin to cope earlier in the sequence of emotion-generating events.

This analysis suggests that we are unlikely to find in the autonomic system an isomorphic representation of verbal report of feelings, or reliable precursors of emotional acts. It further suggests that human behavior may not be so smoothly integrated as introspective analysis sometimes prompts us to think. If we insist on locating a controlling homunculus in the cortex of man, we must also recognize the limitations of the beast. He is not going to have awareness of many important behaviors—much learning and unlearning is going to take place without and despite him. Furthermore, it does not seem reasonable to solve the problem by inventing another homunculus (that is, the unconscious), contenting ourselves that a sensitive bedside manner can alone encourage an internal dialogue. We will need to confine ourselves to measurable behaviors in all systems, and discover the laws that determine their interaction. The data suggest that we must deal with each behavior system in its own terms. Treatment programs will have to be tailored to each behavior, in the light of what we know about its educability. Thus, a patient who reports anxiety, fails to cope or perform effectively under stress, and evidences autonomic activity that varies widely from the practical energy demands of the situation, needs to receive treatment for all these disorders. He should be administered a treatment directed simultaneously at shaping verbal sets (so as to reduce reported stress over the variety of situations in which it appears), assisted in building effective coping behaviors and practicing them in appropriate contexts, and finally, administered a program for attenuating autonomic arousal and excessive muscle tonus, with the goal of reducing the distraction and interference of peripheral physiological feedback. In short, psychotherapy should be a vigorous multisystem training program, tailored to the unique behavioral topography presented by the patient. Fortunately, it is not infrequent that successes in the control of one system seem to precipitate broad change throughout the individual's behavioral repertoire. It may come about through a new insightful conceptualization, or relief from aversive autonomic feedback, or the generation of a new, active coping behaviour. However, all these things may be required to achieve a lasting cure. At this stage of development we know too little about the interaction between response systems to depend on the broad generalization of narrow therapeutic programs.

PSYCHOPHYSIOLOGICAL ANALYSIS OF PSYCHOTHERAPY

Traditional psychotherapies take place in the context of an unstructured dyadic interview. The reader is now aware that relative to the usual requirements of a psychophysiological experiment, this is a poorly controlled environmental transaction. Nevertheless, a number of investigators have attempted the physiological analysis of the therapy process. Lacey's (1959) excellent paper critically reviewed research undertaken in the early and middle fifties. He described a variety of interview studies demonstrating correlations between autonomic or somatic responses of patients and, for example, specific interview content (Malmo, Shagass, and Davis, 1950), the judged importance or emotional intensity of the session (Mowrer, Light, Luria, and Seleny, 1953), and the physiological changes of the therapist (Coleman, Greenblatt, and Solomon, 1956).

Subsequent experiments have found similar relationships between interview process and autonomic events (most frequently the physiological variable is skin resistance and occasionally heart rate). Thus, Dibner (1958) studied forty neuropsychiatric patients during interviews in which the therapist either guided the interviewee to a discussion of conflict areas or failed to provide such structure. A positive relationship (of borderline significance) was found between resistance decrease and the degree of interview ambiguity. Auld, Dreyer, and Dollard (1958) also measured skin resistance during therapy interviews, and reported positive relationships between emotional content and resistance decrease.

In a more systematic experiment, Gordon, Martin, and Lundy (1959) hypnotized ten female subjects and instructed them to recall conflicts with their parents. The effects of three posthypnotic suggestions on a subsequent interview were evaluated. The suggestions were: (1) repression—subjects were told not to think about these conflicts; (2) suppression—they were told to think about them, but not discuss the conflict material; and (3) verbalization—they were instructed to tell the interviewer about this material. Scoring of the tape-recorded sessions for references to parents and parent conflicts

indicated that the subjects followed instructions. For all groups, skin conductance increased throughout the interview session, but no difference was found between the repression- and suppressionlike conditions. Nevertheless, a significantly steeper conductance rise was observed for the suppression interview than for the session in which subjects were to verbalize their conflicts.

Panek and Martin (1959) studied the relationship between skin resistance and interview speech disturbances for four therapy clients. Mahl's (1956) speech-disturbance categories (number of "ahs" and repetitions) were scored from tape recordings of the interviews at 30-second intervals. Electrodermal activity was synchronized with tapes, and the investigators located those places in the interviews where large resistance decreases occurred. Analysis of trend confirmed that these resistance "dips" were associated with increased speech disturbances.

In a third experiment, Martin joined with Lundy and Lewin (1960) to evaluate skin-resistance change associated with three levels of therapist communicativeness. Twenty-seven subjects talked about their personal life either (1) to a therapist who responded verbally or (2) to a therapist who responded only with nods or facial expressions of interest, or (3) to a tape recorder without a therapist present. The subjects' verbal content was rated in terms of degree of approach or avoidance to emotionally important contents. The no-therapist group showed a progressive decrease in emotional content and in skin resistance change over sessions. Subjects who interacted with the nonverbal therapist manifested little resistance change and little increase in content. The verbal-therapist-group showed an initial increase and then a decrease in resistance, while approach to emotional content increased progressively over all sessions. The authors suggested that the pattern of skin resistance activity shown by the verbal-therapist-group indicated that they were anxious about discussing emotional content in early sessions, but were increasingly comfortable with self-revelation near the termination of treatment.

Gendlin and Berlin (1961) asessed skin resistance increments in subjects instructed to engage in different modes of "experiencing." Subjects were told, for example, to think about problems, or just talk out loud, or concentrate their attention on objects in the room. Not suprisingly, greater, more linear increments in resistance occurred during silences than when the subject was speaking. The authors further suggested that silences that were "self-interrupted or externally focused" showed less of a resistance increment than was obtained when the subject was simply "experiencing" a problem.

Kaplan (1963) examined skin-resistance changes in 37 group psychotherapy sessions. Two schizophrenic patients and a nurse therapist participated. The treatment sessions were observed and coded into 11 social categories. Significant correlations were found between group members' frequency and amplitude of skin resistance change and their social responses, stated attitudes, and position in the group. More recently, Kaplan (1967) utilized a similar procedure in studying affect in small nonpatient groups. Again a host of relationships were observed between skin resistance and descriptive asessment of the social interaction.

A few researchers have studied cardiovascular rather than sweat-gland activity during interviews. Murray (1963) evaluated the responses of college student subjects who participated in an argumentative debate with a lawyer, concerning the subjects' philosophy of life. Subjects' tonic heart rate appeared to track many phases of the discussion. Thus, when most subjects were criticizing the lawyer, average heart rate was higher than when the subjects were being criticized. However, when most subjects were being insulted, their average heart rate was no different than when the interpersonal atmosphere was more friendly. In general, subjects' heart rate correlated positively with variables like *vocal-verbal* intensity and *task-involvement*, but failed to correlate significantly with rated anxiety.

Weiner (1962) also found relationships between active responding and cardiovascular events in a study of TAT administration. He reports that when subjects were asked to "think up" a story, but not required to tell it, they showed no appreciable increment in blood pressure or heart rate. However, when subjects composed a story that they told after a delay,

heart rate and blood pressure incremented during this "anticipatory"period. These findings seem consistent with nonclinical data obtained by Campos and Johnson (1966). These latter authors found that tonic heart rate increased during stimulus presentation, only when subjects were required to make a subsequent verbal report.

The above studies are difficult to summarize. It seems clear that skin resistance changes may be associated with a multiplicity of events in therapy process. These include the extent or ambiguity of the therapist's response to the patient, increments in speech disturbances, silences, anxiety, different "modes of experiencing," and the like. Unfortunately, many of these variables appear to be confounded with covarying changes in physical stimulus intensity or in the energy requirements of the task. Thus, we might expect that silence would occasion less skin-conductance activity than speech, and Auld et al. (1958) could report: "Typically, when a patient is basking in regressive thoughts and appears relaxed, there are no GRSs" (p. 14). However, as Lacey (1957) pointed out in reviewing the previous literature, the problem lies in the appended interpretation (in this case, the "basking in regressive thoughts") that are often frankly *post hoc* and for which there is seldom confirming data. Thus, while many of these experiments ceratinly prompt the hypothesis that "anxiety" or social conflict is reflected in the observed GSR changes, given the complexity of the interview context, other interpretations often have equal claim to validity. In point of fact, the plethora of relationships between different behaviors and electrodermal events, seriously devalues this latter response when employed as a single measure of autonomic activity.

To some extent, tonic cardiovascular change appears to have a narrower psychological relevance than the skin-resistance response. Thus, heart rate (HR) tended to increase in the interview when overt behavior was either ongoing or anticipated by the subject; simple relationships with anxiety ratings were less frequently obtained. This should not be taken as evidence that cardiovascular activity does not covary with fear or anxiety stimuli in the absence of action. Lang, Melamed, and Hart

(1970) showed a strong relationship between the order of hierarchically arranged fear stimuli, anxiety ratings, and heart rate. However, these subjects had previously been trained in muscle relaxation and were in a tonic relaxed state at the time of testing. It may be that the subtler relationships of HR to emotional content are masked by muscular activity (which makes great demands for oxygen consumption). Taylor and Epstein (1967) have made a similar suggestion in attempting to account for variation among autonomic measures in emotion.

The reader will note that we are now reconsidering issues of situational stereotypy that are far from resolved in the non-clinical laboratory. Furthermore, in nearly all these interview studies we are trying to view the organism's state through an extremely narrow physiological window. A single variable (electrodermal *or* heart-rate recording) is all that is provided. In addition, we are examining treatments that are often conceptualized in experiential or introspective terms. Thus, we have the exceedingly difficult problem of interpreting state variables that seldom meet the operational requirements of a scientific experiment.

Leaving aside the latter philosophical cavil, it is still obvious that the best context in which to study the physiology of emotional change is *not* the relatively free-swinging, two-person interaction, which is the format of classical psychotherapies. Because of its spontaneity, the uncontrolled and often unknown temporal, physical, and psychological impact of stimuli, the input characteristics of an interview, are often impossible to specify. Furthermore, affective vocal communication is exceedingly complex (Ostwald, 1963), and two-way conversation involves kinesthesis as well as speech (Elkman and Friesen, 1968). Thus, the output of the subject constitutes an interaction of all three behavior systems. Efforts are being made to study these relationships: A recent experiment explored subjects' affect statements and concurrent changes in the respiratory apparatus as it meets the requirements of vocalization (Heim, Knapp, Vachon, Globus, and Memtz, 1968). Dittman and Llewellyn (1969) examined interactions between speech rhythm and body movement. Another investigator has looked at the stimulus properties of different voices as they affect physiological responding (Gaviria, 1967). However, many studies of the interview still invite the reader to make a simplistic interpretation of skin conductance or heart rate, while they fail to report even a word count or a measure of gross body movement. Perhaps the greatest problem in psychophysiological studies of the interview is that content is often specified only by therapists' or raters' judgment. We are provided with a general impression, rather than a catalogue of specific stimuli. While this level of description may be useful in pilot work, it does not provide the basis for experimental replication. I do not mean to suggest that there is no value at all in the physiological monitoring of interviews. Malmo's explorations of interview content and the distribution of myograph responses led to the useful notion of "symptom specificity" (Malmo et al., 1949, 1950). Furthermore, we will suggest later that technological advances may soon permit the "on-line," psychophysiological analysis of complex interactions. However, for the time being the interview is a bad testing ground, even for hypotheses relevant to interview behavior.

If the broad analysis of interview process is not currently feasible, it is nevertheless possible to follow the development and outcome of therapy through adjunctive sessions, in which a simpler, controlled experimental context permits systematic physiological analysis. One task that shows considerable promise for this purpose is the habituation of the orienting response to simple stimuli.

Lader and Wing (1966) have suggested that subjects' reaction to simple stimuli may relate significantly to more general patterns of reaction, which are in turn important to the development of psychological disorder. They postulate "an interaction between stimulus power, stimulus duration, and rate of habituation (p. 143)." The process of habituation is a fundamental part of any environmental transaction (Sokolov, 1963). Thus, while new stimuli will alert a subject (prompt an orienting response), the regular, noncontingent repetition of the same stimulus will be accompanied by a reduced reaction in both physiological and behavioral systems. This process of habituation is obviously a useful and necessary characteristic of organisms; without it they would remain in a constant state of alertness, attentive victims of every irrelevant stimulus in the environment. Lader suggests that there are individual differences in habituation rates, which may be in part genetically determined. He further suggests that individuals afflicted with behavioral disorders (for example, anxiety neurotics and psychotics) are defective in their ability to habituate, and this physiologically defined hyperalertness is, in effect, an analogue of experienced anxiety.

, Certain characteristics of external stimuli will alter habituation rate. In general, more intense stimuli will adapt out more slowly. Furthermore, if previous stimuli have raised the background level of arousal, new inputs will habituate less quickly than if they were presented when the organism was less activated. Lader postulates a positive-feedback loop in slow-habituating subjects, in which repeated stimulation generates ever-increasing levels of physiological activation. This may be attributable to a slow recovery cycle as described by Freeman (1948), which prompts a steplike increase in autonomic and somatic output. A similar mechanism was suggested by Mednick (1958) in an attempt to account for the psychological deficit of schizophrenics.

Lader's laboratory situation involves the recording of resting levels of physiological activity in a controlled environment and then the assessment of skin-conductance change in response to a series of 20 identical auditory stimuli (100-DB intensity, 1000 Hz). The number of spontaneous skin-conductance responses is recorded, and the rate of habituation to the auditory stimuli is calculated by regression analysis.

Recent experiments suggest that habituation rates are faster and background activity less in normal subjects than in neurotics (Lader, 1967a). Furthermore, there is evidence that increments in pathology within the disturbed population (for example, from focused phobias to generalized anxiety neurosis) are tracked by this assessment method. Sedative drugs tend to reduce both background activity and increase habituation rate (Lader and Wing, 1966). Furthermore, research suggests that such drugs are more valuable in the treatment of depressives with high spontaneous SCRs than with depressives showing low activity levels. Lader, Gelder, and Marks (1967) have also provided data that suggest that the rate of habituation predicts response to desensitization therapy, with the rapid habituators having the best prognosis.

The habituation situation is thus sensitive to pathology and at least some methods for its amelioration. It would be quite possible to provide sessions of this kind at regular intervals during therapy as a method of assessing change. It would be useful to look at stimuli other than pure tones, particularly specific, therapy-relevant contents that could be presented in the habituation format. Melamed (1969) has found that phobic subjects show similar habituation rates to auditory stimuli and brief film clips (10 sec) of relevant fear objects. This merits further study as a potentially useful assessment device.

While habituation is a promising context for adjunct sessions, other tasks may serve as well. Fenz and Steffy (1968) studied changes in the electrodermal response of regressed schizophrenic females to various physical stimuli in a controlled social interaction, concurrent with an intensive treatment program. They found an increment in skin-conductance activity, particularly in response to social stimuli and periods of stimulus anticipation, coincident with behavioral indices of improved responsiveness to the environment.

Paul (1966) studied the relative effectiveness of dynamic therapy, desensitization, and a placebo treatment in improving speaking performance and reducing associated anxiety. He assessed verbal report, overt performance, and physiological measures of change. The latter assessment included manual recording of pulse rate and the palmar-sweat index. These measures were taken while the subject waited to deliver a speech. Although the recording technique was less refined than the polygraph can provide, it has the advantage of being less obtrusive. The obtained measures were sufficiently reliable to discriminate between therapies—with desensitization showing the greatest reduction in autonomic response posttreatment.

If psychophysiological measurement is to be used to assess therapeutic outcome, everything depends on the validity of the experimental task. In the case of stimulus habituation, its usefulness is dependent on an empirically demonstrated relationship to other criteria. Paul's task (1966) had high face validity, in that it related directly to the goal of his therapeutic procedures. Even here, however, care must be taken not to overinterpret the physiological findings. They are meaningful to the extent that they are evaluated with performance and verbal-report criteria. Isolated instances of physiological change may be grossly misleading. Thus, Lacey (1959) gave the example of an experimental demonstration of reduced SCR to emotion-laden words, following brief psychotherapy (Cohen et al., 1956). However, examination of the results suggested that the effect was specific to those words and that experimental context. Change in a broad emotional response had not been demonstrated, but only a change in orienting to specific language.

The validity of an emotional response is ultimately tested by its reliability across situations, as well as its generality within the subject's response repertoire. Thus, we become convinced a subject is not dissembling in a verbal report of emotion if it is evoked consistently in a variety of contexts; that is, if the subject makes the same report to the same or different sex interrogator, peer or superior, regardless of how the question is posed, and how many times it is asked. The more consistent a report, the more intense we are likely to judge the emotion. The same considerations apply in the evaluation of physiological responses. The investigator would be wise to employ multiple-assessment situations and carefully consider the social-psychological context of each.

Modifying Emotion in the Laboratory. The complexity of social interactions has encouraged investigators to study their process through laboratory analogues, which abstract one or two elements from the overall transaction for examination in a controlled environment. Data obtained from these studies must be interpreted cautiously. Simplification necessarily involves distortion, and the research result may not actually bear on the phenomenon that prompted the experiment. However, this method has provided much useful data for personality theorists, and is likely to be increasingly applied to the study of psychotherapy.

Recently, a number of investigators have examined the physiological response of subjects to laboratory-instigated aggression, and the change in the response with psychological catharsis. Using a physician's sphygmomanometer, Hokanson and his colleagues (1961, 1962) showed that systolic blood pressure incremented when subjects were under attack. Furthermore, male subjects displayed a rapid decrease in systolic blood pressure when permitted to counteraggress. In contrast, systolic pressure was absent when only fantasy aggression (TAT stories) was permitted, and when the aggression-instigating agent was a high-status person (Hokanson and Burgess, 1962; Baker and Schaie, 1969). These findings can be interpreted as consistent with the catharsis hypothesis (Dollard, Doob, Miller, Mowrer, and Sears, 1939), which holds that the angered subject can only reduce arousal by aggressing. However, Stone and Hokanson (1969, p. 72) have recently argued

. . . that the arousal-reducing properties of counter-aggression are only a special case of a more general class of behavioral-autonomic learning processes. In this broader context, *any* social response can be viewed as having arousal-reducing concomitants, if that response has been previously instrumental in terminating or avoiding aggression from others.

In support of this position, they point out that college females did not show reduction in systolic pressure with counter-aggression (as do males), and in fact, they showed a more rapid return to previous autonomic levels when they made a friendly counterresponse (Hokanson, Willers, and Koropsak, 1968). Presumably, females in our culture are reinforced for this style of coping and not for attack.

Stone and Hokanson (1969) examined their instrumental response interpretation, using a controlled two-person interaction paradigm. Specifically, they tested the hypothesis that reinforcing self-punitive behavior with shock avoidance would increment the rate of self-punitive behavior. Furthermore, they held that the occurrence of the latter would result in a reduction in sympathetically innervated vascular activity. The experimental context involved the subject with a "confederate" of the experimenter, who behaved as if he were a naive participant. The subject was told that he was participating in an analogue of a social situation. He would be stimulated and could respond to his "fellow subject" in a manner parallel "to 'real life' interpersonal affairs." Thus, he had the option of hurting his associate by delivering a painful shock, being friendly by giving him points, or taking it out on himself with a self-administered shock. The stimuli of the confederate were preprogrammed so that during a conditioning period, for 90 percent of the trials, a shock from the "confederate" followed the subject's administration of either shock or reward. However, the subject received a reward point for every self-shock (at 3/4 of the pain level). Under these conditions, the subject learned to administer shocks to himself, and this self-punitive behavior was associated with a shorter latency recovery from vasoconstriction than was extrapunitive shock. This could be interpreted as a cathartic effect arising from intropunitive behavior, and suggests a possible paradigm for the development of the masochistic response.

A recent experiment by Gambaro and Rabin (1969) explored the relationship of a personality characteristic to similar post-aggression vascular changes. Subjects in their experiment were divided into high- and low-guilt groups, according to the Mosher Incomplete Sentences Test. Shocking a frustrator produced blood-pressure reductions, with low-guilt subjects showing greater pressure decrease than high-guilt subjects. However, with post-frustration aggression against a relatively neutral party, only the low-guilt subjects showed blood-pressure reduction; the high-guilt subjects displayed a "slight" increase.

These data are reminiscent of Funkenstein's studies of blood-pressure changes in so-called Anger-in and Anger-out patients. Funkenstein, et al. (1954) held that the tendency to express hostility against others was associated with a norepinephrine-mediated change in blood pressure, whereas the intrapunitive patient showed an epinephrine-type response. Silverman and Cohen (1960) reported a similar relationship between relatively higher urinary assays of

norepinephrine with aggression, and a greater proportion of epinephrine with fear and low stress tolerance. We have already indicated that the psychophysiology of specific emotions is a highly controversial area; however, the tighter social-interaction analogues used by more recent researchers could lead to important progress in this difficult enterprise.

On the other hand, while the behavioral context used by these researchers is highly sophisticated, the physiological assessment is less laudatory. In general, the new catharsis experiments suffer from a too restricted assessment of the subject's physiology. Thus, Hokanson's earlier papers report blood pressure, but tell us nothing about gross body movement or level of muscle tension—behaviors which will have much to do with changes in vascular flow. A recent study by Baker and Schaie (1969) provides some evidence that the catharsis effect is specific to vascular pressure (parallel changes in respiration or pulse rate were not found); however, muscle activity is again unreported. The Gambaro and Rabin experiment, referred to earlier, adds another confusing element to the physiological picture. They obtained effects for diastolic rather than systolic pressure. Their use of a mechanical transducer to record blood pressure was different from the manual asculatory method employed by Hokanson and Burgess (1962). Differences in the reliability or accuracy of these two methods could have contributed to the discrepant results. However, in the absence of broader physiological assessment, the difference between the experiments is not readily understood.

In the most recent published experiment of the Hokanson group (Stone and Hokanson, 1969) blood pressure was *not* reported, and the digital-plethysmograph response was offered as an interchangeable equivalent. However, in both the character of their functional changes and their underlying neurochemical innervation, digital blood volume and arterial pressure vary widely in response to internal or external stimulation. The distributions of alpha and beta receptors (in the cutaneous vascular bed and the arteries of the large muscles) are such that epinephrine and norepinephrine can have very different effects on these systems (Goodman and Gillman, 1965). Davis et al. (1957) found vasoconstriction of the finger to be a relatively consistent response to a broad range of stimuli that included slides of nude females, intense auditory tones, rhythmic tapping, and cutaneous stimulation. Over these same input events, pressure pulse from the brachial artery (approximately an average of systolic and diastolic pressure) varied from unitary increases or decreases to biphasic responses. The digital plethysmograph and main-artery blood pressure clearly do not yeild equivalent data. Research on emotional change could be greatly improved if such equivalence was not casually assumed, and investigators recorded and independently assessed a broader spectrum of physiological events.

Laboratory Analogues of Psychological Treatment. While brief interaction analogues can provide much insight into therapeutic process, the assessment of change across sessions, and the study of relationships between process and outcome, depend on the development of more complex laboratory therapies. In recent years, some progress has been made in this enterprise, which holds the promise of greater gains in the future.

Clinical treatments that can be described in behavioral terms lend themselves better to laboratory investigation than do dynamic formulations. Thus, in our own laboratory we have been able to generate analogue treatments of desensitization that involve considerable routinization and control, but that are nevertheless effective vehicles for the reduction of human fear (Lazovik and Lang, 1960; Lang and Lazovik, 1963; Lang, Lazovik, and Reynolds, 1965). This approach has been taken successfully by others (Paul, 1966; Davison, 1968), and the value of complex analogues in the investigation of behavior modification seems clearly established.

Recently, our specific interest in the psychophysiological study of the fear-reduction process led to the development of an electromechanical apparatus for the administration of desensitization (Lang, Melamed, and Hart, 1970). The original device for automated desensitization (DAD) consisted of two dual-channel tape playback decks with a simple tape search mechanism, keyed to pulses recorded

on one of the channels. All instructions to subjects, hierarchy items, and interrogations concerning the vividness or fearfulness of scenes were recorded on the second audio channel. A "hard-wired" logic package programmed the presentation of these materials, modifying sequence according to input from the subject's switch console. Thus, the apparatus permitted us to approach the environmental control and stimulus specification requirements of a psychophysiological experiment and also to generate a viable therapeutic interaction. Verbal input was consistent in content and physical properties, and temporal contingencies were exactly known. Thus, "therapist" statements, or the subject's console responses, could be easily cross-referenced to concurrent physiological events.

In our initial experiment, snake phobics were studied. Heart rate, skin conductance, and respiration were recorded throughout eleven treatment sessions. A number of important hypotheses received support. Subjects' report of fear following the visualization of a scene were associated with significant increment in sympathetic activity during the scene. However, repeated presentation of a fearful scene in the desensitization context was accompanied by a reduction in sympathetic physiological activity. As theory would predict, high-hierarchy scenes generated no more sympathetic response than did low-hierarchy items during desensitization. However, an independent experiment (with socially anxious and spider-phobic subjects) showed that sympathetic activity increased regularly with higher hierarchy position and verbal reports of fear, when the scenes were presented in a random order.

The results of our DAD experiment also suggested an interesting relationship between physiological events during therapy and post-treatment fear change (as measured independently by verbal report and avoidance test). In this sample, subjects who showed the greatest fear reduction had the highest heart rates during scenes they reported to be fearful. Furthermore, these same high fear-change subjects showed the most marked heart-rate habituation gradients with scene repetition. *Thus, consonance between verbal report and autonomic activity was characteristic of subjects who profited from therapy.* Furthermore, during sessions in which fear was reported, subjects who changed showed higher base heart rates. These data appear to parallel the frequent clinical finding that behavioral change is associated with an emotional response in the therapy session, and that the less emotionally committed subject who says the right things seldom profits from the treatment experience.

The success of DAD has prompted us to develop a more sophisticated automated therapist, built around a small digital computer (Lang, 1969). In addition to being more flexible in its response to the subjects and maintaining a larger library of fear materials, the new system will utilize a multichannel digital clock to sample and process physiological data "on-line," without in any way interrupting the therapeutic process.

This capacity will be utilized in testing hypotheses concerning the relationship of change in physiological events to change in performance or verbal report of fear. Thus, assuming that subjects are most likely to be desensitized under conditions of low autonomic arousal, specific fear stimuli may be delayed until the computer determines that these conditions exist in the subject. Similarly, the termination or continuance of a stimulus may be decided not by the subject's console response, but by his physiological state. Thus, a pattern of autonomic events that the computer has previously seen associated with fear signals can become a flag initiating a change in current stimulus input conditions. The efficiency of this procedure can be compared with the previous console response method.

We have already used the computer to help train individuals to control their own autonomic activity. For this purpose the machine has advantages over previous devices such as meters or auditory signals in that complex events may be resolved into a relatively simple display. Thus, the oscilloscope output of the LINC-8 has been used to train subjects in cardiac rate control through continuous feedback. In one program, each R-wave initiates a scan across the scope face; the next R-wave terminates the line at some point in its travers. A computer-controlled vertical line defines the target. Assuming heart rate slowing is the task, subjects are told to extend the R-R interval past the target line. After each pulse, an alpha-numeric counter on the scope face registers hits and misses for the subject. Furthermore, at given intervals a frequency histogram of previous performance may be provided. Autonomic

training through feedback may be added to the desensitization analogue to replace the less specific relaxation instructions, if subsequent research supports its effectiveness (Lang, 1969, p. 238).

While our work with the computer/subject interface has so far been focused on desensitization, the capabilities of this context are in no sense limited to that treatment format. The combination of rigor and flexibility provided by a computer controlled environment, may be applied to the investigation of any therapeutic method that can be described operationally. Thus, even the less constrained interview setting may ultimately be available to psychophysiological analysis.

A machine capable of quickly assimilating complex information (well beyond the capacity of the human experimenter), able to make decisions in the light of previous instructions, and yet adapt its responses to the changing behavior of subjects is a uniquely suitable tool for studying problems of treatment and psychopathological processes (Lang, 1969, p. 239).

PSYCHOPHYSIOLOGICAL APPLICATION IN PSYCHOLOGICAL TREATMENT

While the emphasis in this paper has been on the experimental study of psychotherapy, it is perhaps appropriate to consider the possible use of these psychophysiological techniques as vehicles of actual diagnosis and treatment. Recently Lang and Melamed (1969) undertook the treatment of a nine-month-old infant with chronic ruminative vomiting. Post-prandial emesis had persisted for over four months, resulting in a severely malnourished infant (body weight less than 12 lbs.) who appeared to risk death if the condition continued unrelieved. As other treatments had been unavailing, it was decided to condition the child to avoid vomiting by using an aversive stimulus (electric shock) contingent on the emesis. This required that an analysis be made of the regurgitation response itself, so that reinforcers could be applied promptly and specifically. The infant was thus studied for two days during emesis periods, using the electromyograph. Pairs of EMG electrodes were placed across the esophagus, from the chin to the upper chest.

This permitted the investigators to note the first wave or reverse peristalsis as it occurred, and to distinguish the emesis from externally similar chewing and sucking responses. Subsequently, during conditioning, the polygraph record in concert with behavioral observations was used to determine the timing of the avoidance schedule. After only a few conditioning sessions, the vomiting was inhibited, body weight increased, and the child returned home. There has been no remission of symptoms and the child was developing normally at six-month-, one year-, and two-year follow-ups.

The above case is one of the few in the current literature in which psychophysiological measurement played a substantial role both in assessing a pathological behavior and in guiding its treatment. This dearth is not surprising, since physiological information would not be sufficiently pertinent to most therapy cases to justify the expense and technical complications of such monitoring.

Nevertheless, as our knowledge of psychosomatic interaction increases, physiological assessment may become more broadly useful. It is possible that the computer-based modification of phobia and anxiety that we have already discussed may develop into a practical therapy. Furthermore, the treatment of other aversive emotions (such as depression and suppressed anger) might be usefully guided by the "on-line" analysis of the patient's physiology. Finally, new methods for the self-control of autonomic and cortical events are becoming available. Based on the use of exteroceptive feedback in conjunction with operant shaping schedules, they offer an avenue for the direct modification of the physiological substrata of aversive emotions. Whether such control can be achieved in the face of actual stressors, and whether laboratory successes will transfer to the environment, remains to be determined. However, the possibilities of such a therapeutic tool are certainly exciting.

In addition to the use of these techniques in treating anxiety, other, medical applications are to be considered. Forster and his associates (1965, 1966) have successfully employed EEG-guided counterconditioning in treating patients with sensory-induced epileptic seizures. The critical stimuli are presented at a subseizure threshold and gradually incremented. EEG signs of a beginning seizure prompt the discontinuation of the stimulus and the presentation of a competing nonseizure inducing input (for example, auditory clicks were used to disrupt seizure patterns due to stroboscopic stimuli). In one case, a computer was programmed to recognize seizure patterns and automatically discontinue stimulation when the EEG wave-complex was present (Forster, Booker, and Ansell, 1966). Similar EEG-based treatments could be explored in a variety of pathological conditions. Miller (1969), for example, has suggested that insomnia might be relieved by reinforcing slow high-voltage waves in the EEG.

The fact that normal subjects can control heart rate, suggests that medical patients with angina, or other cardiac syndromes that include tachycardia, might receive therapeutic benefit from such training. Engel (1969) has already helped a number of cardiac patients to reduce or eliminate pathological arrythmias through operant-feedback programs. Similarly, evidence that self-control of blood pressure can be achieved in the laboratory offers promise for a new approach to hypertension (Shapiro et al., 1969; Hnatiow, 1968). Traditionally, the therapist dealing with advanced psychosomatic disorders could only re-examine old conflicts, which, though perhaps causal, had long since become irrelevant to a physiologically autonomous disease. Operant methods seem to promise a more relevant psychological therapy.

In concluding his 1959 review of psychophysiology and psychotherapy, Lacey discussed his own research, in which "the autonomic nervous system is seen not simply as a source of indicant functions, but as part and parcel of the organic determination of behavior (p. 205)." It appears to this reviewer that the more promising developments in the succeeding decade have shared this orientation. Thus, the search for biological correlates of traditional psychotherapeutic constructs has shown little advance. On the other hand, research, focused on the manipulation and functional analysis of the physiological events themselves, is generating new therapies and perhaps new insights into the organization of pathology. Gross intervening variables such as "anxiety" or "arousal" seem to have lost explanatory power. However, our understanding of the physiology of specific environmental transactions (such as orienting, conditioning, latency tasks) and the interaction between cognitive set and autonomic functioning has significantly increased. Psychotherapy remains a complex subject for laboratory study, and the investigator who proposes to analyze its physiological process must shoulder a formidable technological load. Problems of measurement and response definition continue to beset the researcher, and few shortcuts are apparent. Nevertheless, the development of new tools, such as the on-line computer, that can simultaneously assimilate complex data and control an interactive context; the appearance of new techniques for modifying the physiology of intact organisms; and, most of all, the current trend towards the conceptualization of therapy in behavioral terms, suggests that psychophysiology will make an increasing contribution to the treatment enterprise.

REFERENCES

Alexander, F. *Psychosomatic medicine: Its principles and applications.* New York: Norton, 1950.

Auld, F., Jr., Dreyer, H. W., and Dollard, J. Measurement of electrical skin resistance during interviews. *Psychological Reports,* 1958, **4,** 11–15.

Ax, A. F. The physiological differentiation between fear and anger in humans. *Psychosomatic Medicine,* 1953, **15,** 433–442.

Ax, A. F. Electronic storage and computer analysis. In P. H. Venables and I. Martin (Eds.), *Manual of psychophysiological methods.* New York: Wiley, 1967.

Baker, J. W., and Schaie, K. W. Effects of aggression "alone" or "with another" on physiological and psychological arousal. *Journal of Personality and Social Psychology,* 1969, **12,** 80–86.

Bard, P. Emotion I. The neuro-humoral basis of emotional reactions. In C. Murchison (Ed.), *Handbook of general experimental psychology.* Worcester, Mass.: Clark University Press, 1934. (a)

Bard, P. On emotional expression after decortication with some remarks on certain theoretical views, Parts I and II. *Psychological Review,* 1934, **41,** 309–329, 424–449. (b)

Barratt, E. S. Intra-individual variability of performance: ANS and psychometric correlates, *Texas Reports,* 1963, **4,** 496–504.

Beier, C. D. Conditioned cardiovascular response and suggestions for treatment of cardiac responses. *Journal of Experimental Psychology,* 1940, **26,** 311–321.

Benjamin, L. S. Successive sampling of continuous psychological change. Paper presented at a conference entitled "Innovations in Clinical Research and Treatment," Central Wisconsin Colony, Madison, April 1967.

Berg, W. K. Vasomotor and heart rate response to non-signal auditory stimuli. Unpublished M.A. thesis, University of Wisconsin, 1968.

Berger, H. Über das electrenkephalogramm des menschen. *Arch. f. Psychiat.,* 1929, **87,** 527–570.

Best, C. H., and Taylor, N. B. (Eds.) *The physiological basis of medical practice.* Baltimore, Maryland: Williams and Wilkins, 1966.

Birren, J. E., Cardon, P. V., Jr., and Phillips, S. L. Reaction time as a function of the cardiac cycle in young adults. *Science,* 1963, **140,** 195–196.

Bonvallet, M., Dell, P., and Hiebel, G. Tonus symathique et activité electrique corticale. *EEG and Clinical Neurophysiology,* 1954, **6,** 119–144.

Brazier, M. A. B. *The electrical activity of the nervous system.* New York: Macmillan, 1958.

Brazier, M. A. B. Novelty and information theory. Brain potential signs of informational control. In I. R. Nedecký, L. Cigánek, V. Zikmund, and E. Kellerová (Eds.), *Mechanism of orienting reaction in man.* Bratislava: Publishing House of Slovak Academy of Sciences, 1967.

Brenner, J. Heart rate as an avoidance response. *Psychological Record,* 1966, **16,** 329–336.

Brown, C. C. (Ed.). *Methods in psychophysiology.* Baltimore: Williams & Wilkins, 1967.

Bull, K., and Lang, P. J. *Intensity, certainty, and physiological response amplitude.* 1970, in preparation.

Buss, H. *The psychology of aggression.* New York: Wiley, 1961.

Calloway, E. Response speed, the EEG alpha cycle, and the autonomic cardiovascular cycle. In A. T. Welford and J. E. Birren (Eds.), *Behavior, aging, and the nervous system.* Springfield, Illinois: Charles C. Thomas, 1965.

Campos, J. J., and Johnson, H. J. The effects of verbalization instructions and visual attention on heart rate and skin conductance. *Psychophysiology,* 1966, **2,** 305–310.

Cannon, W. B. The James-Lange theory of emotions: A critical examination and an alternative theory. *American Journal of Psychology,* 1927, **39,** 106–124.

Cannon, W. B. Again the James-Lange and the thalamic theories of emotion. *Psychological Review,* 1931, **38,** 281–295.

Caton, R. Interim report on investigation of the electric currents of the brain. *British Medical Journal,* 1877, Supplement Vol. 1, 62–65.

Chase, W. G., Graham, F. K., and Graham, D. T. Components of HR response in anticipation of reaction time and exercise tasks. *Journal of Experimental Psychology*, 1968, **76**, 642–648.

Cohen, S. I., Silverman, A. J., and Burch, N. R. A technique for the assessment of affect change. *Journal of Nervous and Mental Disorders*, 1956, **124**, 352–360.

Coleman, R., Greenblatt, M., and Solomon, H. C. Physiological evidence of rapport, during psychotherapeutic interviews. *Diseases of the Nervous System*, 1956, **17**, 2–8.

Connor, W. H., and Lang, P. J. Cortical slow wave and cardiac rate responses in stimulus orientation and reaction time conditions. *Journal of Experimental Psychology*, 1969, **82**, 310–320.

Crider, A., Shapiro, D., and Tursky, B. Reinforcement of spontaneous electrodermal activity. *Journal of Comparative and Physiological Psychology*, 1966, **61**, 20–27.

Darrow, C. W. The rationale for treating the change in galvanic skin response as a change in conductance. *Psychophysiology*, 1964, **1**, 31–38.

Davis, J. F. *Manual of surface electromyography*. Montreal: Laboratory for Psychological studies, Allan Memorial Institute of Psychiatry, 1952.

Davis, R. C. Response patterns. *Transactions of the New York Academy of Sciences*, 1957, **19**, 731–739.

Davis, R. C., and Buchwald, A. M. An exploration of somatic response patterns: Stimulation and sex differences. *Journal of Comparative and Physiological Psychology*, 1957, **50**, 44–52.

Davis, R. C. Buchwald, A. M. and Frankmann, R. W., Autonomic and muscular responses, and their relation to simple stimuli. *Psychological Monographs*, 1955, **69** (20, Whole No. 405).

Davis, R. C., Lundervold, A., and Miller, J. D. The pattern of somatic response during a repetitive motor task and its modification by visual stimuli. *Journal of Comparative and Physiological Psychology*, 1957, **50**, 53–60.

Davison, G. Systematic desensitization as a counter conditioning process. *Journal of Abnormal Psychology*, 1968, **73**, 91–99.

Dibner, A. S. Ambiguity and anxiety. *Journal of Abnormal and Social Psychology*, 1958, **56**, 165–174.

Dittman, A. T., and Llewellyn, I. Body movement and speech rhythm in social conversation. *Journal of Personality and Social Psychology*, 1969, **11**, 98–106.

Dollard, J., Doob, L. W., Miller, N. E., Mowrer, O. H. and Sears, R. P. *Frustration and aggression*. New Haven: Yale University Press, 1939.

Duffy, E. *Activation and behavior*. New York: Wiley, 1962.

Dykman, R. A., Reese, W. G., and Galbrecht, C. R. A method for studying psychophysiological adaptation to novel signals. *Psychiatric Research Reports*, 1960, **12**, 53–64.

Edelberg, R. Electrical properties of the skin. In C. C. Brown (Ed.), *Methods in psychophysiology*. Baltimore: Williams & Wilkins, 1967.

Edelberg, R., and Wright, D. J. Two galvanic skin response effector organs and their stimulus specificity. *Psychophysiology*, 1964, **1**, 39–47.

Ekman, P., and Friesen, W. V. Nonverbal behavior in psychotherapy research. In J. Shlien (Ed.), *Research in psychotherapy*. Volume III. Washington: American Psychological Association, 1968.

Elliot, R. Physiological activity and performance: A comparison of kindergarten children with young adults. *Psychological Monograph*, 1964, **78**, No. 10.

Elliot, R. Tonic heart rate: Experiments on the effects of collative variables lead to an hypothesis about its motivational significance. *Journal of Personality and Social Psychology*, 1969, **12**, 211–228.

Engle, B. T. Stimulus-response and individual-response specificity. *AMA Archives of General Psychiatry*, 1960, **2**, 305–313.

Engel, B. T. Personal communication, 1969.

Engel, B. T., and Hanson, S. P. Operant conditioning of heart rate slowing. *Psychophysiology*, 1966, **3**, 176–187.

Eppinger, H. and Hess, L. *Vagotonia. Mental Nervous Disorders Monograph*. 1915, No. 20.

Eriksen, C. W. Unconscious processes. In M. R. Jones (Ed.), *Nebraska Symposium on Motivation*. Lincoln: University of Nebraska Press, 1958.

Euler, U. S. V., and Lundberg, U. Effect of flying on the epinephrine excretion in Air Force personnel. *Journal of Applied Physiology*, 1954, **6**, 551–555.

Evans, S. H., and Anatasios, E. J. Misuse of analysis of covariance when treatment effect and covariate are confounded. *Psychological Review*, 1968, **69**, 225–234.

Fenz, W. D., and Steffy, R. A. Electrodermal arousal of chronically ill psychiatric patients undergoing intensive behavioral treatment. *Psychosomatic Medicine*, 1968, **30**, 423–436.

Féré, C. Note sur les modifications de la résistance électrique sous l'influence des excitations sensorielles et des émotions. *C. R. Soc. Biol. Mem.*, 1888, **40**, 217–219.

Forster, F. M., Booker, H. E., and Ansell, S. Computer automation of the conditioning therapy of stroboscopic induced seizures. *Transactions of the American Neurological Association*, 1966.

Forster, F. M., and Campos, G. B. Conditioning factors in stroboscopic induced seizures. *Epilepsia*, 1964, **5**, 156–165.

Forster, F. M., Kløve, H., Peterson, W. G., and Bengzon, A. R. Modification of musicogenic epilepsy by extinction technique. *Transactions of the American Neurological Association*, 1965.

Freeman, G. L. *The energetics of human behavior*. Ithaca: Cornell University Press, 1948.

Freud, S. *The basic writing of Sigmund Freud*. A. A. Brill (Ed.), New York: Modern Library, 1938.

Frohlich, E. D., Tarazi, R. C., and Dustan, H. P. Hyperdynamic beta-adrenergic circulatory state. *Archives of Internal Medicine*, 1969, **123**, 1–7.

Funkenstein, D. H., Greenblatt, M., and Solomon, H. C. Autonomic changes paralleling psychological changes in mentally ill patients. *Journal of Nervous and Mental Diseases*, 1951, **114**, 1–18.

Funkenstein, D., King, S. H., and Drolette, M. The direction of anger during a laboratory stress-inducing situation. *Psychosomatic Medicine*, 1954, **16**, 404–413.

Gambaro, S., and Rabin, A. I. Diastolic blood pressure responses following direct and displaced aggression after anger arousal in high- and low-guilt patients. *Journal of Personality and Social Psychology*, 1969, **12**, 87–94.

Gantt, W. H. (Ed.). *Physiological Bases of Psychiatry*. Springfield, Ill.: Charles C. Thomas, 1958.

Gaviria, B. Autonomic reaction magnitude and habituation to different voices. *Psychosomatic Medicine*, 1967, **29**, 598–605.

Geer, J. H. Measurement of the conditioned cardiac response. *Journal of Comparative and Physiological Psychology*, 1964, **57**, 426–433.

Geer, J. H. Effect of interstimulus intervals and rest-period length upon habituation of the orienting response. *Journal of Experimental Psychology*, 1966, **72**, 617–619.

Geer, J. H., and Klein, K. Effects of two independent stresses upon automic responding. *Journal of Abnormal Psychology*, 1969, **74**, 237–241.

Gellhorn, E. Motion and emotion: The role of proprioception in the physiology and pathology of the emotions. *Psychological Review*, 1964, **71**, 457–472.

Gellhorn, E. *Principles of autonomic-somatic integration; physiological basis and psychological and clinical implications*. Minneapolis: University of Minnesota Press, 1967.

Gendlin, E. T., and Berlin, J. I. Galvanic skin response correlates of different modes of experiencing. *Journal of Clinical Psychology*, 1961, **17**, 73–77.

Goldman, M. J. *Principles of Clinical Electrocardiography*. Los Altos, California: Lange Medical Publication, 1960.

Goodman, L. S., and Gilman, A. *The pharmacological basis of therapeutics*. New York: The Macmillan Co. 1965.

Gordon, J. E., Martin, B., and Lundy, R, M. GSRs during repression, suppression, and verbalization. *Journal of Consulting Psychology*, 1959, **23**, 243–251.

Graham, D. T., Kabler, J. D., and Graham, F. K. Physiological response to the suggestion of attitudes specific for hives and hypertension. *Psychosomatic Medicine*, 1962, **24**, 159–169.

Graham, F. K., and Clifton, R. K. Heart rate changes as a component of the orienting response. *Psychological Bulletin*, 1966, **65**, 305–320.

Greenfield, N., and Sternbach, R. (Eds.). *Handbook of psychophysiology*. New York: Holt, Rinehart & Winston, 1970.

Heath, H. A., and Oken, D. The quantification of "response" to experimental stimuli. *Psychosomatic Medicine*, 1965, **28**, 457–471.

Hebb, D. O. Drives and the C.N.S. (conceptual nervous system). *Psychological Review*, 1955, **62**, 243–254.

Heim, E., Knapp, P. H., Vachon, L. Globus, G., and Nemetz, S. J. Emotion, breathing and speech. *Journal of Psychosomatic Research*, 1968, **12**, 261–274.

Hill, J.D.N., and Parr, G. (Eds.) *Electroencephalography*. New York: The Macmillan Co., 1963.

Hnatiow, M, Learned control of heart rate and blood pressure. Unpublished doctoral dissertation, University of Pittsburgh, 1968.

Hnatiow, M., and Lang, P. J. Learned stabilization of cardiac rate. *Psychophysiology*, 1965, **1**, 330–336.

Hohmann, G. W. Some effects of spinal cord lesions on experienced emotional feelings. *Psychophysiology*, 1966, **3**, 143–156.

Hokanson, J. E., and Burgess, M. M. The effects of status, type of frustration and aggression on vascular processes. *Journal of Abnormal and Social Psychology*, 1962, **65**, 232–237.

Hokanson, J. E., Burgess, M. M. and Cohen, M. The effects of displaced aggression on systolic blood pressure. *Journal of Abnormal and Social Psychology*, 1963, **67**, 214–218.

Hokanson, J. E., and Edelman, E. The effects of three social responses on vascular processes. *Journal of Personality and Social Psychology*, 1966, **3**, 442–447.

Hokanson, J. E., and Shelter, S. The effects of overt aggression on physiological arousal level. *Journal of Abnormal and Social Psychology*, 1961, **63**, 446–448.

Hokanson, J. E., Willers, K. R., and Koropsak, E. Modification of autonomic responses during aggressive interchange. *Journal of Personality and Social Psychology*, 1968, **36**, 386–404.

Holmquest, D., and Edelberg, R. Problems in the analysis of the endosomatic galvanic skin response. *Psychophysiology*, 1964, **1**, 48–54.

Hord, D. J., Johnson, L. C., and Lubin, A. Differential affect of the law of initial values (LIV) on autonomic variables. *Psychophysiology*, 1964, **1**, 79–87.

Ivey, M. E., and Bardwick, J. M. Patterns of affective fluctuations in the menstrual cycle. *Psychosomatic Medicine*, 1968, **30**, 336–345.

Jacobson, E. *Progressive Relaxation*. Chicago: University of Chicago Press, 1938.

Jaffe, J. H. Drug addiction and drug abuse. In L. S. Goodman and A. Gilman (Eds.), *The pharmacological basis of therapeutics*. New York: Macmillan, 1966.

James, W. What is emotion *Mind*, 1884, **19**, 188–205.

James, W. *Principles of psychology*. New York: Holt, Rinehart, & Winston, 1890. 2 vols.

Kamiya, J. Conditioned discrimination of the EEG alpha rhythm in humans. Paper presented at the Western Psychological Association Meeting, San Francisco, April 1962.

Kamiya, J. Conscious control of brain waves. *Psychology Today*, 1968, **1**, 57–60.

Kaplan, H. B. Social interaction and GSR activity during group psychotherapy. *Pyschosomatic Medicine*, 1963, **25**, 141–145.

Kaplan, H. B. Physiological correlates (GSR) of affect in small groups. *Journal of Psychosomatic Research*, 1967, **11**, 173–179.

Keele, C., and Neil, E. *Samson Wright's Applied Physiology*. New York: Oxford University Press, 1965.

Keen, R. E., Chase, H. H., and Graham, F. K. 24 hour retention by neonates of an habituated heart rate response. *Psychonomic Science*, 1965, **2**, 265–266.

Lacey, J. I. The evaluation of autonomic responses: Toward a general solution. *Annals of the New York Academy of Science*, 1956, **67**, 123–164.

Lacey, J. I. Psychophysiological approaches to the evaluation of psychotherapeutic process and outcome. In E. A. Rubinstein and M. B. Parloff (Eds.), *Research in psychotherapy*. Vol. 1. Washington, D.C.: American Psychological Association, 1959.

Lacey, J. I. Somatic response patterning and stress: Some revisions of activation theory. In M. H. Appley and R. Trumbull (Eds.), *Psychological stress: Issues in research*. New York: Appleton-Century-Crofts, 1967.

Lacey, J. I., Kagan, J., Lacey, B. C., and Moss, H. A. The visceral level: Situational determinants and behavioral correlates of autonomic response patterns. In P. H. Knapp (Ed.), *Symposium on expression of the emotions in man*. New York: International Universities Press, 1963.

Lacey, J. I., and Lacey, B. C. The relationship of resting autonomic activity to motor impulsivity. In H. Solomon, S. Cobb, and W. Penfield (Eds.), *The brain and human behavior*. Baltimore: Williams & Wilkins, 1958. (a)

Lacey, J. I., and Lacey, B. C. Verification and extension of the principle of autonomic response-stereotypy. *American Journal of Psychology*, 1958, **71**, 51–73. (b)

Lacey, O. L., and Siegel, P. S. An analysis of the unit of measurement of the galvanic skin response. *Journal of Experimental Psychology*, 1949, **39**, 122–127.

Lader, M. H. Palmar skin conductance measures in anxiety and phobic states. *Journal of Psychosomatic Research*, 1967, **11**, 271–281. (a)

Lader, M. H. Pneumatic plethysmography. In P. H. Venables and I. Martin (Eds.), *Manual of psychophysiological methods*. New York: Wiley, 1967. (b)

Lader, M. H., Gelder, M. G., and Marks, I. M. Palmar skin conductance measures as predictors of response to desensitization. *Journal of Psychosomatic Research*, 1967, **11**, 283–290.

Lader, M. H., and Wing, L. *Physiological measures, sedative drugs, and morbid anxiety*. London: Oxford University Press, 1966.

Lang, P. J. Fear reduction and fear behavior: Problems in treating a construct. In J. M. Shlieu (Ed.), *Research in Psychotherapy*, Vol. III, Washington: American Psychological Association, 1968.

Lang, P. J. The on-line computer in behavior therapy research. *American Psychologist*, 1969, **24**, 236–239.

Lang, P. J., Geer, J., and Hnatiow, M. H. Semantic generalization of conditioned autonomic responses. *Journal of Experimental Psychology*, 1963, **65**, 552–558.

Lang, P. J., and Hnatiow, M. H. Stimulus repetition and the heart rate response. *Journal of Comparative and Physiological Psychology*, 1962, **55**, 781–785.

Lang, P. J., and Lazovik, A. D. Experimental desensitization of a phobia. *Journal of Abnormal and Social Psychology*, 1963, **66**, 519–525.

Lang, P. J., Lazovik, A. D., and Reynolds, D. J. Desensitization, suggestibility, and pseudotherapy. *Journal of Abnormal Psychology*, 1965, **70**, 395–402.

Lang, P. J., and Melamed, B. G. Case report: Avoidance conditioning therapy of an infant with chronic ruminative vomiting. *Journal of Abnormal Psychology*, 1969, **74**, 1–8.

Lang, P. J. Melamed, B. G., and Hart, J. A psychophysiological analysis of fear modification using an automated desensitization procedure. *Journal of Abnormal Psychology*, 1970, in press.

Lang, P. J., Sroufe, L. A., and Hastings, J. E. Effects of feedback and instructional set on the control of cardiac rate variability. *Journal of Experimental Psychology*, 1967, **75**, 425–431.

Lange, C. G. *On Sindsbevaegelser et psyko. fysiolog. studie*. Copenhagen: Krønar, 1885.

Lange, C. G. The emotions (Denmark, 1885). Translated by I. Haupt. In K. Dunlop (Ed.), *The emotions*. Baltimore: Williams & Wilkins, 1922.

Lazarus, R. S., and Opton, E. M. The study of psychological stress: A summary of theoretical formulations and experimental findings. In C. D. Spielberger (Ed.), *Anxiety and behavior*. New York: Academic Press, 1966.

Lazarus, R. S., Speisman, J. C., Mordkoff, A. M., and Davison, L. A. A laboratory study of psychological stress produced by a motion picture film. *Psychological Monographs*, 1962, **76** (Whole No. 553).

Lazovik, A. D., and Lang, P. J. A laboratory demonstration of systematic desensitization psychotherapy. *Journal of Psychological Studies*, 1960, **11**, 238–247.

Levy, P., and Lang, P. J. Activation, control, and the spiral aftermovement. *Journal of Personality and Social Psychology*, 1966, **3**, 105–112.

Lindsley, D. B. Emotions. In S. S. Stevens (Ed.), *Handbook of experimental psychology*. New York: Wiley, 1951.

Lindsley, D. B. Psychophysiology and emotion. In M. R. Jones (Ed.), *Nebraska Symposium on Motivation*. Lincoln: University of Nebraska Press, 1957.

Lippold, O. C. J. Electromyography. In P. H. Venables and I. Martin (Eds.), *Manual of psycho-physiological methods.* New York: Wiley, 1967.

Lisina, M. I. The role of orienting in the conversion of involuntary into voluntary reactions. In L. G. Voronin et al. (Eds.), *The orienting reflex and exploratory behavior.* Moscow: Acad. Pedag. Sci., 1958.

Lord, F. M. Statistical adjustments when comparing preexisting groups. *Psychological Bulletin*, 1969, **72**, 336–337.

Lykken, D. T. Neuropsychology and psychophysiology in personality research. In E. F. Borgatta and W. W. Lambert (Eds.), *Handbook of personality theory and research.* Chicago: Rand McNally, 1968.

Lykken, D. T., Rose, R., Luther, B., and Maley, M. Correcting psycho-physiological measures for individual differences in range. *Psychological Bulletin*, 1966, **66**, 481–484.

Lywood, D. W. Blood pressure. In P. H. Venables and I. Martin (Eds.), *Manual for psycho-physiological methods.* New York: Wiley, 1967.

MacLean, P. D. Psychosomatic disease and the "visceral brain." *Psychosomatic Medicine*, 1949, **11**, 338–353.

Mahl, G. F. Disturbances and silences in the patient's speech in psychotherapy. *Journal of Abnormal and Social Psychology*, 1956, **53**, 1–15.

Malmo, R. B. Measurement of drive: An unsolved problem in psychology. In M. R. Jones (Ed.), *Nebraska symposium on motivation.* Lincoln: University of Nebraska Press, 1958.

Malmo, R. B. Studies of anxiety: Some clinical origins of the activation concept. In C. D. Spielberger (Ed.), *Anxiety and Behavior*, New York: Academic Press, 1966.

Malmo, R. B., and Belanger, D. Related physiological and behavioral changes: What are their determinants? *Association for Research in Nervous and Mental Disease*, 1967, **45**, 288–318.

Malmo, R. B., and Shagass, C. Physiologic study of symptom mechanisms in psychiatric patients under stress. *Psychosomatic Medicine*, 1949, **11**, 25–29.

Malmo, R. B., Shagass, C., and Davis, F. H. Symptoms specificity and bodily reactions during psychiatric interview. *Psychosomatic Medicine*, 1950, **12**, 362–376.

Marañon, G. Contribution à l'étude de l'action emotive de l'adrénaline. *Rev. Francaise Endocrinol.*, 1924, **2**, 301–325.

Martin, B. The assessment of anxiety by physiological-behavioral measures. *Psychological Bulletin*, 1961, 234–255.

Martin, B., Lundy, R. M., and Lewin, M. H. Verbal and GSR responses in experimental interviews as a function of three degrees of "therapist" communication. *Journal of Abnormal and Social Psychology*, 1960, **60**, 234–240.

Martin, B., and Sroufe, L. A. Anxiety. In C. G. Costello (Ed.), *Symptoms of Psychopathology*, in press.

Martin, I., and Venables, P. H. Mechanisms of palmar skin resistance and skin potential. *Psychological Bulletin*, 1966, **65**, 347–357.

Mason, J. W. A review of psychoendocrine research on the pituitary-adrenal cortical system. *Psychosomatic Medicine*, 1968, **30**, 576–607.

Mason, J. W., Mangan, G., Brady, J. V., Conrad, D., and Rioch, D. Concurrent plasma epinephrine norepinephrine and 17-hydroxycorticosteroid levels during conditioned emotional disturbances in monkeys. *Psychosomatic Medicine*, 1961, **23**, 344–353.

Mednick, S. A. A learning theory approach to research in schizophrenia. *Psychological Bulletin*, 1958, **55**, 316–327.

Melamed, B. G. The habituation of psychophysiological responses to tones, and to filmed fear stimuli under varying conditions of instructional set. Unpublished doctoral dissertation, University of Wisconsin, 1969.

Miller, N. E. Learning of visceral and glandular responses. *Science*, 1969, **163**, 434–445.

Miller, N. E., and DiCara, L. V. Instrumental learning of heart rate changes in curarized rats: Shaping and specificity to descriminative stimulus. *Journal of Comparative and Physiological Psychology*, 1967, **63**, 12–19.

Mischel, W. *Personality and assessment.* New York: Wiley, 1968.

Montagu, J. D., and Coles, E. M. Mechanism and measurement of the galvanic skin response. *Psychological Bulletin*, 1966, **65**, 261–279.

Moos, R. H., Kopell, B. S., Melges, F. T., Yalom, I. D., Lunde, D. T., Clayton, R. B., and Hamburg, D. A. Fluctuations in symptoms and moods during the menstrual cycle. *Journal of Psychosomatic Research*, 1969, **13**, 37–44.

Moruzzi, G., and Magoun, H. W. Brain stem reticular formation and activation of the EEG. *Electroencephalography and Clinical Neurophysiology*, 1949, **1**, 455–473.

Mowrer, O. H., Light, D. H., Luria, Z., and Seleny, M. P. Tension changes during psychotherapy. In O. H. Mowrer (Ed.), *Psychotherapy: Theory and research.* New York: Ronald Press, 1953.

Murray, H. A. Studies of stressful interpersonal disputations. *American Psychologist*, 1963, **18**, 28–36.

Netter, F. H. *The CIBA collection of medical illustrations.* Vol. 1. *Nervous system.* New York: CIBA, 1957.

Obrist, P. A. Heart rate during classical conditioning in humans and dogs: Significance for psychological processes. In I. R. Nedecký, L. Cigánek, V. Zikmund, and E. Kellerová (Eds.), *Mechanisms of orienting reaction in man.* Bratislava: Publishing House of Slovak Academy of Sciences, 1967.

Obrist, P. A. Heart rate and somatic-motor coupling during classical aversive conditioning in humans. *Journal of Experimental Psychology*, 1968, **77**, 180–193.

Obrist, P. A., Webb, R. A., and Sutterer, J. A. Heart rate and somatic changes during aversive conditioning and a simple reaction time test. *Psychophysiology*, 1969, **5**, 696–723.

Obrist, P. A., Wood, D. M., and Perez-Reyes, M. Heart rate during conditioning in humans: Effects of UCS intensity, vagal blockage, and adrenergic block of vasomotor activity. *Journal of Experimental Psychology*, 1965, **70**, 32–40.

Ostwald, P. F. *Soundmaking—the acoustic communication of emotion.* Springfield: Charles C. Thomas, 1963.

Panek, D. M., and Martin, B. The relationship between GSR and speech disturbances in psychotherapy. *Journal of Abnormal and Social Psychology*, 1959, **58**, 402–405.

Papez, J. W. A proposed mechanism of emotion. *Archives of Neurology and Psychiatry* (Chicago), 1937, **38**, 725–743.

Papez, J. W. Cerebral mechanisms. *Res. Publ. Ass. Res. Nerv. Ment. Dis.*, 1939, **89**, 145–159.

Paul, G. L. *Insight versus desensitization in psychotherapy.* Stanford: Stanford University Press, 1966.

Phillips, L. F. *Electronics for experimenters in chemistry, physics and biology.* New York: Wiley, 1966.

Pitts, F. N. The biochemistry of anxiety. *Scientific American*, 1969, **220**, 69–75.

Pitts, F. N. and McClure, J. N. Lactate metabolism in anxiety neurosis. *New England Journal of Medicine*, 1967, **277**, 1329–1336.

Pribram, K. H. The new neurology and the biology of emotion: A structural approach. *American Psychologist*, 1967, **22**, 830–838.

Razran, G. The observable unconscious and inferable conscious in current Soviet psychophysiology: Interoceptive conditioning, semantic conditioning, and the orienting reflex. *Psychological Review*, 1961, **68**, 81–147.

Reynolds, D. J. An investigation of the somatic response system in chronic schizophrenia. Unpublished doctoral dissertation, University of Pittsburgh, 1961.

Routtenberg, A. The two-arousal hypothesis: Reticular formation and limbic system. *Psychological Review*, 1968, **75**, 51–80.

Ruch, T. C., Patton, H. D., Woodbury, J. W., and Towe, A. L. *Neurophysiology.* Philadelphia: W. B. Saunders Co., 1965.

Schachter, J. Pain, fear, and anger in hypertensives and normotensives. *Psychosomatic Medicine*, 1957, **19**, 17–29.

Schachter, S. The interaction of cognitive and physiological determinants of emotional state. In L. Berkowitz (Ed.), *Advances in experimental social psychology.* Vol. 1. New York: Academic Press, 1964.

Schachter, S. Cognitive effects on bodily functioning: Studies of obesity and eating. In D. C. Glass (Ed.), *Neurophysiology and emotion.* New York: Rockefeller University Press, 1967.

Schachter, S., and Latané, B. Crime, cognition and the autonomic nervous system. In D. Levine (Ed.), *Nebraska symposium on motivation.* Lincoln: University of Nebraska Press, 1964.

Schachter, S., and Singer, J. E. Cognitive, social, and physiological determinants of emotional state. *Psychological Review*, 1962, **69**, 379–399.

Schachter, S., and Wheeler, L. Epinephrine, chlorpromazine, and amusement. *Journal of Abnormal and Social Psychology*, 1962, **65**, 121–128.

Schildkraut, J. J., and Kety, S. S. Biogenic amines and emotion. *Science*, 1967, **156**, 21–30.

Schnore, M. M. Individual patterns of physiological activity as a function of task differences and degree of arousal. *Journal of Experimental Psychology*, 1959, **58**, 117–128.

Schultze, J. H., and Luthe, W. *Autogenic training: A psycho-physiologic approach in psychotherapy.* New York: Grune and Stratton, 1959.

Selyé, H. *The stress of life.* New York: McGraw-Hill, 1956.

Shapiro, D., Tursky, B., Gershon, E., and Stern, M. Effects of feedback and reinforcement on the control of human systolic blood pressure. *Science*, 1969, **163**, 588–590.

Shearn, D. W. Does the heart learn? *Psychological Bulletin*, 1961, **58**, 452–458.

Shearn, D. W. Operant conditioning of heart rate. *Science*, 1962, **137**, 530–531.

Sherrington, C. S. Experiments on the value of vascular and visceral factors for the genesis of emotion. *Proc. roy. Soc.* (London), B, 1900, **66**, 390–403.

Silverman, A. J., and Cohen, S. I. Affect and vascular correlates to catechol amines. In L. J. West and M. Greenblatt (Eds.), *Explorations in the physiology of emotions.* Washington, D. C.: Psychiatric Research Reports of the American Psychiatric Association, No. 12, January 1960.

Skinner, B. F. *Cumulative Record.* New York: Appleton-Century-Crofts, 1959.

Sokolov, E. N. *Perception and the conditioned reflex.* New York: Pergamon Press, 1963.

Sroufe, L. A. Learned stabilization of cardiac rate with respiration experimentally controlled. *Journal of Experimental Psychology*, 1969, **81**, 391–393.

Sroufe, L. A., Hnatiow, M. H. and Lang, P. J. Determinants of learned cardiovascular control. Paper presented at the 7th annual meeting of the Society for Psychophysiological Research, San Diego, California, October 1967.

Stern, J. A. Toward a definition of psychophysiology. *Psychophysiology*, 1964, **1**, 90–91.

Sternbach, R. A. The effects of instructional sets on autonomic responsivity. *Psychophysiology*, 1964, **1**, 67–72.

Stone, L. J., and Hokanson, J. E. Arousal reduction via self-punitive behavior. *Journal of Personality and Social Psychology*, 1969, **12**, 72–79.

Stoyva, J. Skinnerian Zen: Or control of physiological responses through information feedback. Paper read at Denver University Symposium on Behavior Modification, 1968.

Taylor, S. P., and Epstein, S. The measurement of autonomic arousal. *Psychosomatic Medicine*, 1967, **29**, 514–525.

Thomas, P. E., and Korr, I. M. Relationship between sweat gland activity and electrical resistance of the skin. *Journal of Applied Physiology*, 1957, **10**, 505–510.

Valins, S., and Ray, A. A. Effects of cognitive desensitization on avoidance behavior. *Journal of Personality and Social Psychology*, 1967, **7**, 345–350.

Venables, P. H. The effect of auditory and visual stimulation on the skin potential responses of schizophrenics. *Brain*, 1960, **83**, 77–92.

Venables, P. H., and Martin, I. Skin resistance and skin potential. In P. H. Venables and I. Martin (Eds.), *Manual of psycho-physiological methods*. New York: Wiley, 1967.

Venables, P. H., and Martin, I. (Eds.) *Manual of psycho-physiological methods*. New York: Wiley, 1967.

Walter, W. G. Slow potential waves in the human brain associated with expectancy, attention, and decision. *Archiv. für psychiatrie und zeitschrift f.d. ses. Neurologie*, 1964, **206**, 309–322.

Wang, G. H. *The neural control of sweating*. Madison: The University of Wisconsin Press, 1964.

Watson, J. B., and Rayner, R. Conditioned emotional reactions. *Journal of Experimental Psychology*, 1920, **3**, 1–14.

Weiner, H. Some psychological factors related to cardiovascular responses: A logical and empirical analysis. In R. Roessler and N. S. Greenfield (Eds.), *Physiological correlates of psychological disorder*. Madison: University of Wisconsin Press, 1962.

Weinman, J. Photoplethysmography. In P. H. Venables and I. Martin (Eds.), *Manual of psycho-physiological methods*, New York: Wiley, 1967.

Wenger, M. A. The measurement of individual differences in autonomic balance. *Psychosomatic Medicine*, 1941, **3**, 427–434.

Wenger, M. A. Preliminary study of the significance of measures of autonomic balance. *Psychosomatic Medicine*, 1947, **9**, 301–309.

Wenger, M. A. Emotion as visceral action: An extension of Lange's theory. In M. L. Reymert (Ed.), *Feelings and Emotions*. New York: McGraw-Hill, 1950.

Wenger, M. A. Some problems in psychophysiological research. In R. Roessler and N. S. Greenfield (Eds.), *Physiological correlates of psychological disorders*. University of Wisconsin Press: Madison, 1962.

Wenger, M. A., Clemens, T. L., Darsie, M. L., Engel, B. T., Estess, F. M., and Sonnenschein, R. R. Autonomic response patterns during intravenous infusion of epinephrine and nor-epinephrine. *Psychosomatic Medicine*, 1960, **22**, 294–307.

Wenger, M. A., Henderson, E. B., and Dinning, J. S. Magnetometer method for recording gastric motility. *Science*, 1957, **125**, 990–991.

Wieland, B., and Mefferd, R. B. Identification of periodic components in physiological measurements. *Psychophysiology*, 1969, **6**, 160–165.

Wilcott, R. C. Arousal sweating and electrodermal phenomena. *Psychological Bulletin*, 1967, **67**, 58–72.

Wilcott, R. C., and Bennken, H. G. The continuous measurement of palmar sweating. *American Journal of Psychology*, 1961, **74**, 619–624.

Wilder, J. *Stimulus and response the law of initial value*. Bristol: John Wright and Sons Ltd., 1967.

Williams, R. T. *Biochemical individuality*. New York: Wiley, 1963.

Wolpe, J. *Psychotherapy by reciprocal inhibition*. California: Stanford University Press, 1958.

Wolpe, J., and Lazarus, A. A. *Behavior therapy techniques*. New York: Pergamon Press, 1966.

Yanof, H. M. *Biomedical Electronics*. Philadelphia: F. A. Davis Co., 1965.

Zeamen, D., Deane, G., and Wegner, N. Amplitude and latency characteristics of the conditioned heart response. *Journal of Psychology*, 1954, **38**, 235–250.

Zimmer, H. *Computers in psychophysiology*. New York: Thomas, 1966.

4

LABORATORY INTERVIEW RESEARCH AS ANALOGUE TO TREATMENT

KENNETH HELLER

INDIANA UNIVERSITY[1,2]

Throughout history, the primary approach to the systematic development of knowledge has involved the careful observation and recording of naturally occurring events. The goal was the systematic ordering of phenomena that would lead to the prediction of their future occurrence. When the secrets of nature were not readily revealed through direct observation, man's drive to explain his world so as to obtain mastery of it, did not abate. Theories were developed to explain the unobservable—sometimes based on expectation, deductive logic, or partial observation intertwined with expectation and logical analysis. These early theories, some of which were quite sophisticated, served as guides to action when understanding was incomplete.

More recently, when the complexity of natural phenomena has defied understanding through direct observation, an alternative research strategy has come into prominence involving the building and testing of laboratory models that are abstractions or analogies of natural events. Laboratory analogues are constructed to isolate, quantify and experimentally manipulate factors whose direct observation in

[1] At the time of writing this chapter, the author was on sabbatical leave at the Laboratory of Community Psychiatry, Harvard Medical School, and was supported in part by Special Research Fellowship MH–40, 558 from the National Institute of Mental Health.

[2] The contribution of Robert J. Silver to the preliminary review of research is gratefully acknowledged.

situ would be obscured or would be prohibitively costly. As such, the laboratory analogue has a respectable history in science and in psychology in particular.

One can make a case for the proposition that almost every formal experiment in psychology is an analogue study, since the experimenter seeks to highlight some psychological process that his experimental situation has been constructed to represent. For example, it is the rare learning theorist whose primary interest is in white rats per se; or the rare social psychologist whose primary professional goal is the study of perceived movement in stationary lines. The former hopes to discover general laws of learning, while the latter seeks to uncover the conditions most conducive to the appearance of conformity behavior. In psychology, most of what we know today about perception, learning, social influence, conformity, and persuasibility, to take but a few examples, has been obtained through laboratory simplifications of more complex psychological processes.

Laboratory analogues are foreign to psychotherapy because knowledge in the clinical fields has been accumulated in a more naturalistic tradition. With few exceptions, the language and practice of psychotherapy is psychiatric in origin. What we know about psychotherapy is derived from the writings of men faced with the pressures of treating patients who were able to describe and reflect upon their experiences. This is as true today as it was some seventy years ago when Breuer and Freud (1937) first systematized their observations of hysterical disorders. For many of our clinicians, the clinic and the laboratory remain worlds apart; few see the possibilities of an orderly progression from one to the other.

Actually, psychologists have been in the business of trying to understand the factors responsible for the way behavior is changed for some time, and most recently, the experimental laboratory has become a serious source of competing hypotheses about the nature of therapeutic interventions. Clinical psychologists trained in academic settings have begun to wonder whether changes in therapeutic technique might be possible if, taking advantage of the experimental literature, psychotherapy became part of a broader psychology of behavior change (Goldstein, Heller, and Sechrest, 1966).

SIMPLIFICATION AS A RESEARCH STRATEGY

The clinical interview, while an excellent source of research hypotheses, is a poor testing ground for isolating factors responsible for behavior change. The varied complexity of the therapeutic interaction and the inability to specify and control therapeutic operations make it difficult to obtain reliable information concerning exact agents of change. The purpose of clinical laboratory research is to determine what factors produce change, under what conditions they operate best, and how they should be combined to produce an effective therapeutic package.

Do analogues have to be simple? In an attempt to approximate the control and precision of the physical sciences, the psychological experiment often is kept devoid of all stimuli except those manipulated by the experimenter. The intent is to make the experimental situation sterile of all influences except those introduced by the variables under study. The problem is that the variables of greatest interest in psychotherapy are often content and person variables, whose effects interact with more easily manipulated process and method factors. In focusing on only one variable at a time, the investigator may see just a part of what actually might be a complex interaction.

The essential ingredient in good research is experimental control. In no way does this imply that research should be conducted in sterile settings. If analogue research in psychotherapy is to escape the claim that precision is achieved only by a reduction to the trivial, context variables must be systematically controlled and sampled. We are beginning to realize that individual difference variables, as well as setting and task characteristics, cannot simply be written off as error variance, but need to be studied in their own right.

As Goldstein, Heller, and Sechrest (1966) have pointed out:

Complex problems call for complex research strategies. The complexities of behavioral change probably can be unraveled by a combination of approaches which oversimplify on the one hand, for example, in single variable research, and admit complexity by way of multivariate analysis on the other. There probably are simpler problems in psychology, but those persons who deliberately choose a complex field in which to study should not feel sorry for themselves. (p. 11)

A problem for analogue research that is common to all experimental studies is its generalizability (see Goldstein, Heller, and Sechrest, 1966, pp. 32–39 for a fuller discussion of this topic). To what extent can the conclusions one draws from an experiment apply to groups or situations other than the one on which the research was originally accomplished? Typically we accept as valid, findings from experiments that are in some way representative of the situation occupying our primary interest, so that as an analogue becomes further removed from the process of therapy and the conditions of treatment, the less relevant it will seem. Bordin (1965) expresses this point of view succinctly in the three rules of simplification that he offers:

1. We start from and keep in central focus the natural phenomena which aroused our curiosity and about which we wished to know more or to verify our present ideas.

2. The degree to which you can safely depart from the naturalistic setting is proportional to the amount you already know about the phenomena in question.

3. If it is not based on prior knowledge, simplification should be accompanied by the early establishing of empirical bridges between the simplification and the naturalistic phenomena to which it is intended to refer (pp. 497–498).

The difficulty with the position stated in Bordin's first two points is that it assumes that the naturalistic treatment setting is fully known and represents a valid criterion that the experimental situation must approximate. As will be illustrated later in this chapter, the current view of many analogue researchers is that their primary task is the discovery of factors that mediate change in helping relationships. As a group, they are now less concerned with whether the variables they study have a place in existing clinical practice.

The importance of "bridging" research between the experimental laboratory and the clinical consulting room, described in Bordin's third rule of simplification, has also been emphasized by the present author (Heller, 1969; Heller and Marlatt, 1969). Once therapeutic agents and the conditions under which they operate best have been identified in clinical laboratory research, they should then be studied in clinical field research to obtain information about the interaction of therapeutic ingredients with personality and setting characteristics that are part of actual treatment. Unfortunately, only after a therapeutic approach has become entrenched as a "school" with disciples committed to its perpetuation, do researchers begin to question the value of some of its therapeutic ingredients. But the reliance on psychotherapy as practiced to determine the direction of analogue research is changing. Whereas early analogue research attempted to simulate elements of already established therapies, more current research has attempted to innovate new methods of behavior change, whose practical applicability in clinical settings can then be determined.

THE SCOPE OF THIS CHAPTER

It is our point of view that studies of social influence, persuasion, attitude change, cognitive restructuring, learning, and education all have relevance for psychotherapy. All are concerned with the conditions facilitating the ability of person or persons A to change the psychological state of person or persons B. One could write a book concerned with the areas of commonality between basic psychology and psychotherapy, and indeed such a book has already been written (Goldstein, Heller, and Sechrest, 1966). In this chapter, we shall adopt the more conservative stance of reviewing only those experimental studies whose authors relate the results of their research to the practice of psychotherapy. What this means is that for the purposes of this chapter, studies will be described and labelled as "analogues" if they deal with factors mediating behavior change; utilize an experimental methodology involving the manipulation and control of variables; and are described by their authors as relevant to psychotherapy.

EARLY STUDIES:
OUTCOME ANALOGUES DERIVED
FROM CLINICAL PROCESS

The early studies were intended to mimic the actual conditions of treatment as closely as possible. Most often subjects were placed in an experimental conflict or stress situation and methods of treatment, usually derived from some major theories of therapy, were applied to remove that conflict. Cowen's (1961) definition summarizes the intent of these studies:

An experimental analogue of psychotherapy may be defined as a controlled laboratory situation involving two or more people, in which the behavior of one person (E) is designed along some relevant dimension(s) to simulate that of a psychotherapist, while in one or more ways the other person(s) is experiencing a feeling of stress or discomfort, or a "symptom," which in some way approximates that brought by a patient to an actual psychotherapeutic situation. Primarily through the medium of verbal interchange, E seeks to relieve S's "presenting difficulty." (p. 9)

Using a word association test, Keet (1948) found the most traumatic word on a list for each of his subjects. The traumatic word was then embedded in a complex word maze task that blocked its easy recall. Subjects who could not recall the traumatic word were given one of two types of therapy, after which, recall of the word list was again tested. The two techniques compared were *expressive* and *interpretive* therapy. The author served as therapist for all subjects. In the expressive condition, E encouraged S to express his frustrations at being unable to recall the missing word. E was supportive, and following a non-directive style, clarified S's feelings and encouraged catharsis. In the interpretive technique, E was as supportive as in the expressive procedure, but in addition, offered direct help in finding the missing word by suggesting to S that there must be a personal meaning involved in his forgetting. E encouraged S to describe some personal associations that might be interfering with his memory and helped S interpret the meaning of these associations in terms of their relationship to his forgetting.

Keet's results should come as no surprise. The interpretive technique was clearly superior in helping subjects recall the forgotten word. If anything, the expressive technique probably served to increase S's frustration at being interviewed by someone who was often seen by S as being in a position to offer active help, but who steadfastly declined to do so.

More important than the suspect findings concerning the efficacy of the two therapeutic techniques, Keet's experiment seemed to offer an ingenious methodology for finding circumscribed areas of conflict within relatively normal individuals, which could then be subject to experimental manipulation. Unfortunately, two attempts to replicate Keet's work (Grummon and Butler, 1953; Merrill, 1952) found that selective forgetting of traumatic words over neutral words could not be established, and little work with Keet's procedure has been attempted since.

Wiener (1955) induced stress in college students by implying that a Rorschach taken earlier indicated possible maladjustive signs. Subjects were then given a battery of personality tests both before and after experimental counseling. "Reassurance-interpretation" and "catharsis–reflection" proved equally effective in reducing stress-induced impairment in personality test performance. Both counseling methods proved superior to irrelevant discussion or rest (at the 0.05 to 0.10 levels of significance) on four of eight personality test measures, although seven of the eight measures were in the predicted direction. It would appear then that the experimental counseling had a weak but consistent effect.

Two studies induced stress by introducing a noxious stimulus after the presentation of a specific word in a word-association test. Haggard (1943) paired electric shock with a stimulus word and then compared three experimental treatments in terms of their ability to reduce GSR reactivity. "Catharsis–information therapy" proved more effective than rest or an experimental extinction procedure that involved the repeated presentation of the word association test without shock. The catharsis–information therapy was a complex treatment whose effective ingredients were confounded. Not only were subjects provided with the opportunity to talk about their experiences, but if they asked, they were told that no further shock was forthcoming.

In a similar experiment, Levinson, Zax and Cowen (1961) paired a loud noxious buzzer with a specific word in a word list. After GSR conditioning had been established, three methods of reducing GSR reactivity were compared. A "therapy" condition involved exploration of S's feelings and reactions to the conditioning task with the therapist displaying friendly and interested behavior. A "Talk-Control" condition required Ss to talk about nontask topics such as their extracurricular activities, again with a friendly and interested therapist. In a "Time-Control" condition, S remained alone in an empty room where he could either read or rest. The therapy group demonstrated a modest decrease in anxiety. There was a slight increase in anxiety for the Talk Controls and a larger increase in anxiety for the Time Controls. However, differences between groups were not statistically significant.

Gordon (1957) used a hypnotic procedure to induce a "traumatic experience" in otherwise normal college student males. Under hypnosis, S was instructed that he would not be able to recall the experience when he awoke; he could spend the interview hour trying to figure out what was bothering him; and, it was permissible to recall the experience during the interview. Two forms of treatment were compared for their efficacy in lifting the hypnotically induced "repression." Therapists were instructed to be either "Leading" (asking questions, making suggestions) or "Following" (restating, reflecting, clarifying), with each therapist appearing once in each condition in counterbalanced order. The results of the study indicated a trend (not quite significant at the 0.05 level) for greater recall to occur in the Leading condition. An unexpected finding was that therapists induced significantly greater recall in their first condition regardless of which form of therapy came first.

Some early studies compared the effectiveness of different therapeutic procedures, but without the prior induction of experimental stress. Grossman (1952) offered counseling to ten matched pairs of male college students who were chosen to exclude those who might be psychotic,

excessively neurotic, or psychopathic. For different subjects, the therapist concentrated on either "explicit" feeling statements (reflection) or "implicit" feeling statements (interpretation). Few differences between the therapies appeared, except that the subjects receiving the "deep" therapy (interpretation) and the therapist administering it, both thought these sessions to be more helpful than did subjects receiving the "surface" treatment (reflection). However, Grossman found that his groups were not really comparable pretherapy despite the matching. Subjects in the "deep" group seemed more ready for therapy, beginning their sessions focused on definite problems that they proceeded to discuss openly. Subjects in the "surface" group were less clearly focused on personal problems pretherapy.

One form of analogue is to involve S as an observer rather than as a participant in an interview interaction. The advantage of this approach is its relative safety in those instances where the effects of a therapeutic intervention are unknown and possibly dangerous, and where S's ability to withstand stress might be questioned. The purpose of the procedure is to obtain S's reactions to an experimental manipulation as he vicariously experiences it. Of course, what a person says he thinks of a procedure and how he would actually react to it are not at all synonymous. Even so, many therapy studies continue to use subjective reactions and opinions as their exclusive dependent variable.

Kounin, Polansky, Biddle, Coburn, and Fenn (1956) asked undergraduate educational psychology students to observe an interview that was role-played by professional actors. The interview scripts were developed from a survey of common problems faced by student teachers. The actor-counselors were either "relationship-centered" or "problem-centered" in their approach and were described to the audience as being in a position of power or no-power over the actor-client. The students observing the role-playing gave more positive evaluations of the interviewer when he was relationship-centered and when he was described as being in a nonpower role.

In a series of four interrelated studies marked by a rigorous methodology, Ashby, Ford, Guerney, and Guerney (1957) randomly assigned clients to one of two forms of therapy. "Reflective" therapy based on a Rogerian approach and "Leading" therapy derived from the theories of Dollard and Miller and Fromm-Reichmann were compared, with the same therapists seeing clients under both therapeutic orientations. This study is one of the few in the early analogue literature that clearly specified the exact therapist behavior required in each therapeutic orientation. Content analyses were performed based on Snyder's (1945) categories and therapists were discarded from the study if less than 2/3 of their responses were appropriate to the form of therapy they were required to administer. Four out of ten therapists were excluded from the principal statistical analyses for this reason.

The results of the Ashby et al. (1957) study were complex. Clear-cut differences between the therapies were not found. Overall, the two types of therapy produced similar effects, with only two out of 21 analyses showing statistically significant differences between the two therapies. There was some evidence that client pretherapy characteristics, in part, determined their reaction to therapy. For example, clients who were more defensive, aggressive, or deferent upon entering therapy felt more defensive in the Leading treatment. Individual therapists differed in the extent to which they induced patient guardedness, defensiveness, or openness, but these differences were not related to measured therapist personality characteristics. A subjective *post-hoc* analysis revealed the rather surprising result that the therapists whom the experimenters classified as most warm, skillful, and dynamically oriented did not produce the most positive results. On some variables their clients consistently earned the least desirable scores. For example, they produced more guardedness than therapists labelled "conversational" (friendly but nondynamic). The authors postulate that a mixture of open self-disclosure followed by subsequent guardedness may in fact be a sign of successful therapy. Also to be considered, however, is the possibility that ideal therapist characteristics may not be as universally relevant to progress in therapy as had been supposed.

Overview of Early Studies

The early analogue studies were conducted in anticipation of great promise by a group of investigators (often doctoral students) who saw in their work the rigorous application of experimental methodology to a clinical area otherwise bereft of experimentation. Here was a group of young clinical researchers who antedated the current behavior therapists in their desire to bridge the large gap between the experimentally derived findings of general psychology and the intuitively and experientially derived theories of the practicing clinician. Yet their efforts were far from successful. Statistically significant findings in their studies were rare. The disappointment engendered by their work led to a brief swing away from experimental studies of psychotherapy.

In the various studies reported above, the experimental treatments generally were found to be more effective than no-treatment controls, although comparisons between different forms of therapy rarely produced positive results. If we were to take these results seriously, we would be left with the conclusion that while intervention is better than no intervention, almost any therapeutic procedure may be just as good as any other procedure. Such a conclusion may in the long run prove to be correct, but it is not yet justified on the basis of the reported studies alone.

What may have prevented the discovery of differences between the schools of therapy investigated in these studies? It is possible that the experimental therapies constructed by the different investigators did not capture the essential qualities of each of the therapy systems. Or, might it be that the theories themselves do not accurately reflect what therapists actually do to make specific therapeutic orientations operational? Psychotherapy may be effective for reasons not yet fully incorporated into the major therapy systems. Rather than providing direct guides to practice, therapy theories may represent philosophical positions concerned with the development of personality and psychopathology, but with only minimal suggestions as to how different pathological conditions might be changed.

A more serious criticism concerns the rather naïve attitude of the early analogue researchers in expecting that their single derivatives from general theories would somehow test the value of entire therapeutic approaches. Nowhere in their studies does one see an appreciation for the complexities of behavior change. These studies show little recognition of the possibility that different components of therapy systems might in fact accomplish quite distinct goals, or that the same therapist will have difficulty administering two distinct therapies without his own personal preferences biasing his results. The above criticisms are related to what was the state of the field, for only recently have we clearly articulated the need for greater specification in our therapy theories (Kiesler, 1966). We now recognize that practitioners are not equally effective in their presentation of a given method, and therapy procedures are not equally effective for all, under all circumstances. Furthermore, we now have more sophisticated methodologies to deal with this complexity. *If analogue research has any future contribution to make, it will be in the elaboration of specific cause-effect relationships between factors of change and their behavioral effects.*

THE VERBAL CONDITIONING EXPERIMENT AND PSYCHO-THERAPY: ANALOGUE RESEARCH IN TRANSITION

The popularity of the research analogue to psychotherapy gained its greatest impetus from investigations of social influence that were called "verbal conditioning" experiments. The intent of the early workers in the field was to extend the principles of operant conditioning derived from animal research to human verbal behavior so that it would be possible to work with verbal behavior "in much the same way as experimenters have worked with the behavior of rats and pigeons" (Greenspoon, 1962, p. 511). The clinical implications of this work seemed immediately apparent, and research on the verbal conditioning experiment as an analogue to psychotherapy was launched. Krasner's (1962) challenge to the clinical world was that therapists operate as "social reinforcement

machines." Despite his disclaimer that "we are not saying psychotherapy is a reinforcement process and these are the studies that prove it" (Krasner, 1962, p. 103), his paper was interpreted by many as putting forward the claim that all forms of psychotherapy derive their effectiveness from the reinforcing power of the therapist. The verbal conditioning literature has grown voluminous and since it has been reviewed on a number of occasions (Greenspoon, 1962; Heller and Marlatt, 1969; Kanfer, 1966; Krasner, 1958 and this volume; Williams, 1964), no attempt will be made at this time to duplicate these reviews.

Did research on the verbal conditioning experiment lead to an increased understanding of the mechanisms by which behavior change occurs in psychotherapy? Heller and Marlatt (1969) note that verbal conditioning represents an example of a research area in which there are repeated demonstrations of the existence of a phenomenon without the full investigation of the parameters that effect its occurrence. Experiments were performed to demonstrate that different classes of words could be "conditioned," but few studies investigated parameters of the experimental setting. Positive effects were demonstrated only when the experimenter or interviewer remained minimally responsive. Thus, in considering the extrapolation of this research to a therapeutic setting, it would appear that the less responsive the therapist and the more ambiguous the stimulus field in which the patient must operate, the more likely would it be for the patient to follow the few orienting cues provided by the therapist. There are therapy systems in which the therapist is urged to minimize his responsiveness, and these are the situations that are most susceptible to the subtle interpersonal influence described in verbal conditioning experiments. However, since positive effects in these experiments have not been demonstrated in more interactive conversations, the usefulness of the verbal conditioning analogy to more interactive helping relationships remains limited.

Still, the work in verbal conditioning did have value. It stimulated the development of new therapeutic approaches based on operant methodologies, and it provided a research model for investigators of other theoretical persuasions. If one aspect of the therapist's behavior could be experimentally manipulated, perhaps similar experimental procedures could be used to study other aspects of the therapeutic setting.

NEW LINES OF INQUIRY

The popularity of the analogue approach in the study of factors of potential importance to psychotherapy has been increasing in recent years. Two trends are now evident. Some investigators have chosen to study factors already considered important in the therapeutic situation with the aim of more clearly specifying the exact operation of these factors. For example, there have been analogue studies of the processes of free association and interpretation, studies of therapeutic conditions as originally formulated by Rogers, and attempts to specify the important therapeutic ingredients in desensitization therapy. Also included in this group of clinically derived studies are those that study the personality characteristics of the participants as they affect the general interview transaction and the behavior of the other member. A quite distinct line of inquiry is evident in studies that investigate aspects of dyadic communication on the assumption that knowledge of the mechanisms of social influence and social interaction will have relevance for psychotherapy. This second group of studies focuses on the effects of such factors as set and expectation, the similarity between interview participants, the specificity or ambiguity of transmitted messages, the role relationships between participants, and the interpersonal characteristics of these roles. Psychotherapy is viewed by some of these investigators as one form of behavioral influence, possessing a distinct content, but at the same time sharing structural and role similarities with other forms of influence situations. There is less concern in these studies that the research analogue may not capture all the elements of therapeutic practice, since the question for these investigators is not "How does psychotherapy operate?", but rather, "Under what conditions does behavioral influence occur?" These researchers assume that if their work uncovers factors that maximize

behavioral change but are not part of therapeutic practice, then their work is not irrelevant to treatment, but rather, that standard treatment approaches may need revision.

CLINICALLY DERIVED ANALOGUES

Systematic Desensitization

Because its procedures are more easily identified and more objectively administered than other treatment methodologies, Wolpe's (1958) systematic desensitization has received considerable attention from analogue researchers. The attempt has been to discover which aspects of this complex therapeutic procedure are most responsible for patient change. Wolpe, in his theory of reciprocal inhibition, implies that all are necessary; but consider the following possibilities. The effective ingredients in systematic desensitization therapy might be found in the relaxation procedures; the use of imagery instead of the overt confrontation of fear-eliciting stimuli; the approach to feared objects in hierarchial order; the extinction of fears; the counter-conditioning of relaxation or other adaptive responses to replace fears; the neurological inhibition of fear; the therapist's explicit theoretical explanation of how symptoms are learned and how they can be removed; faith in the therapist; friendship and love provided through the therapeutic relationship; or some combination of the above. It is difficult to imagine how a proper test of the exact factors responsible for change in Wolpean psychotherapy could be made except in a controlled laboratory situation as represented by an experimental analogue.

Two studies support Wolpe's contention that his procedure works best when aversive stimuli, graded in severity, are paired with stimuli incompatible with anxiety (i.e., relaxation) although both sets of authors (Davison, 1968; Lang, Lazovik, and Reynolds, 1965) prefer to explain their results in terms of counter-conditioning rather than reciprocal inhibition. Systematic desensitization was found more effective in reducing avoidance of a feared object (snakes) than was relaxation paired with snake-irrelevant stimuli or exposure to graded aversive stimuli without relaxation (Davison,

1968). In the Lang, Lazovik, and Reynolds (1965) study, systematic desensitization was more effective in reducing fear of snakes than a "pseudotherapy" in which subjects were exposed to the same conditions as in systematic desensitization, except that the therapist steered the discussion away from the fears listed by the subject in a hierarchy of snake-related fears. Both the Davison (1968) and Lang et al. (1965) studies are well-controlled, but neither should be considered a powerful test of the systematic desensitization technique. In both studies, the comparison groups did not test meaningful alternate therapeutic components to systematic desensitization. Relaxation and hierarchy building cannot be considered effective if discussion of fears does not ensue. Similarly, relaxation paired with fear-irrelevant stimuli is not a convincing therapy. Note that relaxation, paired with training in the benefits of relaxation as a method of reducing anxiety, has been found to be as effective as full systematic desensitization in reducing interview anxiety (Zeisset, 1968). It would appear that relaxation alone and hierarchy construction alone are not effective therapeutic ingredients except when cast in a setting in which therapeutic benefit can be legitimately expected by the subject. This is not to say that expectation of therapeutic benefit is the primary ingredient in systematic desensitization, but rather that expectation is one ingredient in the technique that can either enhance or minimize the effectiveness of the other components. For example, when relaxation is paired with irrelevant activity (Davison, 1968; Lang et al., 1965) its effects are minimal. When positive expectancies are induced through instruction, relaxation becomes as effective as the entire desensitization procedure (Zeisset, 1968). Furthermore, in the absence of therapeutically oriented instructions and encouragement for progress, desensitization was found to be no more effective than a no-treatment control group (Leitenberg, Agras, Barlow, and Oliveau, 1969).[3]

Few American investigators feel comfortable in accepting the neurological underpinning of Wolpe's theory of reciprocal inhibition. Most prefer its reinterpretation in terms of counter-conditioning, which is the current dominant explanation of the effectiveness of systematic desensitization (Davison, 1968; Johnson and Sechrest, 1968; Lang et al., 1965). A simpler extinction theory is preferred by Cooke (1968), who found that the desensitization procedure without relaxation was as effective as desensitization with relaxation. However, the major competitor to a counter-conditioning theory is the cognitive position that interprets desensitization in terms of cognitive rehearsal and cognitive control. The essence of the cognitive position is that the desensitization procedure provides an opportunity for cognitive rehearsal of methods of overcoming fears, so that cognitive controls are developed over fears that are normally avoided. Two studies are reported supporting this position. Valins and Ray (1967) found that subjects who thought they were listening to their own heartbeats showed a greater approach to snakes when the experimental procedure led them to believe that they showed no internal emotional reaction to snakes. Subjects who thought that snake stimuli did not affect them internally were more likely to hold a live snake or required less urging to touch a live snake than subjects who were given no information about their internal reactions. Folkins, Lawson, Opton, and Lazarus (1968) found that subjects who received practice in imagining stressful scenes (cognitive rehearsal) showed a greater reduction in self-reported and GSR anxiety when those scenes were later shown on film than subjects who received cognitive rehearsal paired with relaxation (simulated desensitization) or subjects who received relaxation alone.

Note that the Valins and Ray (1967) and Folkins et al. (1968) studies suffer in one respect as analogues to clinical processes. Both are concerned with immunization against later stress rather than with the removal of already established fears. It may be that deeply entrenched fears require different processes for their removal.

---

[3] Also note the recent study by Marcia, Rubin, and Efran (1969), demonstrating that a pseudotherapy, in which high expectancy for success had been induced, was as effective as standard systematic desensitization, while both were more effective than no treatment or the pseudotherapy administered under a "low-expectancy" condition.

The motivation of the analogue researchers who initiated studies of systematic desensitization was to find the primary therapeutic ingredient in Wolpe's technique. It should come as no surprise that complex therapies include several factors capable of producing change, and indeed, the research evidence indicates that more than one therapeutic ingredient may be involved in the Wolpean technique. Counterconditioning, extinction, positive expectancies, and cognitive rehearsal and control have all been found to be capable of producing changes in behavior and all may be involved in the effectiveness of the desensitization procedure. *We conclude this section with what will be a recurrent theme in our review. We know a great deal about factors capable of producing behavior change, but now we must turn our attention to a clearer specification of the conditions under which each factor is optimized. This has not yet been done.*

Modeling Techniques in Psychotherapy

The desensitization studies reviewed above highlight one function of analogue research—that is, the study of complex therapies by an examination of their component parts. Another function of analogue research is the test of new therapies under controlled and comparatively safe laboratory conditions. The new procedures, though not part of any established therapeutic methodology, might be derived from the clinical literature, the clinical hunches of the researcher, or the general psychological literature. Regardless of their source, the laboratory experiment can provide the researcher with a useful and safe test of his ideas.

The research literature on imitation learning, primarily stimulated by the work of Albert Bandura and his associates (Bandura, 1962, 1965; Bandura and Walters, 1963) can be used as an example of experimental laboratory research that has come to have clinical relevance. Bandura's initial interests in imitation learning were not those of a practicing clinician. He saw weakness in reinforcement theories which assumed that learning can occur only when there are direct and immediate consequences to the individual. Bandura concluded that traditional reinforcement theories do not adequately explain the normal socialization of children, since the acquisition of new behavior sequences most often depends on the child's observation of the behavior of others, which he then attempts to copy. While reinforcement principles can account for the strengthening of already learned responses, they do not adequately explain the acquisition of novel, previously unrehearsed behavior sequences.

The acquisition of new behavior sequences is also a problem for psychotherapy, so it is not surprising that clinicians began to follow Bandura's work with great interest (Sarason and Ganzer, in press; Schwartz and Hawkins, 1965; Truax, Wargo, Carkhuff, Kodman, and Moles, 1966). The psychotherapist faces some special problems not encountered by those studying the acquisition of "normal," socially acceptable behaviors. The therapist must often deal with behaviors that are so strongly inhibited that the patient can neither act nor think about them. Even though punishment may no longer be forthcoming, response inhibition (in the form of repression) blocks appropriate reality testing. In situations where performance is blocked because the individual fears that unpleasant consequences might result from his actions, a technique that does not depend upon actual performance to demonstrate safe consequences could have much to recommend it. Techniques based on observational learning would seem perfectly suited to this problem.

There have been a number of analogue studies demonstrating that modeling procedures facilitate the discussion of personally revealing topics. Several studies conducted at Indiana University investigated the conditions that enhance a subject's willingness to talk about his worries, problems, and concerns. These studies have been described elsewhere (Heller, 1968; Heller and Marlatt, 1969) and will not be reviewed here. In summary, it has been found that modeling procedures provide an effective means of teaching role behaviors, particularly when task instructions are ambiguous (Marlatt, 1968a); modeling procedures are more effective than verbal reinforcement in eliciting and sustaining personal self-disclosure, at least over two interviews spaced one week apart (Marlatt, 1968b); modeling procedures can be useful in inducing realistic expectations of therapy even for chronic psychotic patients (Zerfas, 1965); and modeling procedures are most effective when the consequences to the model are either positive or neutral (Marlatt, Jacobson, Johnson, and Morrice, 1966). An unexpected finding in this series is that for college student volunteers, instructions to "talk about your problems" can produce as much problem discussion as the presentation of a problem-admitting model (Jacobson, 1968).

A recent study by Whalen (1969) suggests that in a group setting, neither models nor instructions alone are sufficient to increase meaningful self-disclosure. Male college student volunteers were constituted into groups of four and asked to participate in a group dynamics experiment. In a factorial design, subjects were exposed to one of four conditions: a film model of a similar group talking about themselves with openness and candor, plus detailed instructions designed to elicit interpersonal openness; a film model plus minimal instructions; detailed instructions with no film; and minimal instructions only. It was found that only subjects in the film model plus detailed instructions group talked about themselves openly. Subjects in the other three conditions devoted most of their time to impersonal discussion.

Taken together, the Jacobson (1968) and Whalen (1969) studies suggest that the context in which self-disclosure occurs is an important determinant of its appearance. The meaningful discussion of personal concerns and fears is often perceived as potentially risky and embarrassing. Within the context of a private interview conducted in the name of science, college students readily accede and need no further prompting other than detailed instructions concerning what is expected of them. In a group setting, among strangers, the risk of appearing weak and inadequate is greater and personal openness is inhibited. Neither modeling nor instructions alone are sufficient to overcome that inhibition. Instructions depicting openness as desirable and expected plus the observation of others engaged in similar behavior with positive consequences are required. The Jacobson (1968) and Whalen (1969) studies remind us that therapeutic tools are not universal panaceas, indiscriminately effective under all circumstances.

There is further evidence that under the proper circumstances, behavioral inhibitions produced by strong fear can be removed by modeling procedures (Bandura, Grusec, and Menlove, 1967; Bandura and Menlove, 1968). Though both studies were conducted with nursery school children, similar procedures might be tried with adults. In the first study, three- to five-year-old children described by their parents as fearful of dogs, were assigned to one of four treatment conditions. One group of subjects observed a fearless four-year-old boy exhibit progressively stronger approach responses to a dog within the positive context of a party. A second group observed the same modeling behavior toward the dog but in a neutral context. A third group merely observed the dog during a party with the peer model absent, while a fourth group participated in a party without any exposure to either the dog or peer model. Subjects who observed the model interact nonanxiously with the dog in either the positive or neutral contexts developed significantly greater approach responses to the dog that persisted through a one-month follow-up. The positive context did not enhance the effects of modeling. Of further interest is that the model's approach behavior toward the dog had to occur gradually. Pilot work revealed that when the model approached the dog boldly from the beginning and displayed an early close interaction with the dog, the children actively avoided looking at the model's performance and were reluctant to participate in subsequent sessions.

A further extension of this work by Bandura and Menlove (1968) revealed that filmed models interacting with dogs can be used in place of live models. Greatest effectiveness for the filmed models was achieved by a broad sampling of models and aversive stimuli. In other words, observation of different models varying in age, as they interacted with various dogs, produced greater approach behavior in fearful children than observation of a single-model single-dog interaction.

In reviewing the analogue research on modeling, we are beginning to see the emergence of a new therapeutic tool, one that deserves careful attention from clinical researchers to determine the parameters of its utility (Heller, 1969).

Rogerian Facilitative Conditions

It has always been difficult to separate and study components of a global therapeutic procedure. This is less of a problem for therapeutic strategies that rely on overt observable techniques, such as verbal conditioning or systematic desensitization. Analogues of these processes are relatively easy to build. Problems for the analogue researcher are compounded when the essential aspects of the therapeutic procedure depend on more subtle personal qualities of the therapist. It is difficult to capture the components of how one person acts toward another and present these in a controlled experimental fashion without the entire procedure beginning to look artificial. Various attempts to overcome experimental artificiality have been developed. The present section will concern itself with how this has been carried out within the Rogerian framework.

Rogers (1957) has proposed that three personal characteristics of the therapist, when communicated to the client, represent the necessary and sufficient conditions for client personality change to occur. These three conditions are that the therapist be a *genuine* person within the therapeutic hour; that he experience an *unconditional positive regard* for his client; and that he experience and communicate a sensitively *empathic understanding* of the client's personal world. Much effort was devoted to the development of reliable rating scales for the measurement of these therapeutic conditions. (The initial work of Truax and Kiesler in developing the scales for rating therapeutic conditions, along with the scales themselves, are reported in Rogers, Gendlin, Kiesler, and Truax, 1967.)

Thus far, one basic approach to the experimental manipulation of therapeutic conditions within the Rogerian framework has been developed (Truax and Carkhuff, 1965). In this procedure the interview is divided into three time periods. During the first period, the therapist attempts to maintain high therapeutic conditions. During the second period, he lowers the level of therapeutic conditions by withholding the best therapeutic response he might make. During this stage of the interview he might still be helpful (Truax and Carkhuff,

1965), or his response might appear innocuous (Holder, Carkhuff, and Berenson, 1967). The therapist's response would never be incongruous or disrespectful (Piaget, Berenson, and Carkhuff, 1967); it would simply not be as "good" as it could be. In the last third of the interview, the therapist reinstates his best responses, attempting to maintain high levels of therapeutic conditions.

In their first study utilizing this procedure (Truax and Carkhuff, 1965), one counselor conducted hour-long interviews with three hospitalized psychotic women. It was found that the rated depth of intrapersonal exploration in which the patient engaged was lowered during the middle section of the interview when therapeutic conditions were lowered.

Using the same procedure to manipulate therapeutic conditions, Holder, Carkhuff, and Berenson (1967) had one counselor see six female students who volunteered to discuss personal problems and experiences. The students were prechosen from a group that participated in the role of counselor in a prior standardized interview. The three highest-functioning students and the three lowest-functioning students in that interview were asked to participate as "clients" for the current project. It was found that depth of self-exploration was greater for high-functioning subjects than for low-functioning subjects. The high-functioning "clients" were not adversely affected by the lowering of therapeutic conditions during the middle period, but the low-functioning "clients" were. As in the Truax and Carkhuff (1965) study with hospitalized patients, the low-functioning students in this study lowered the level of their self-exploration when the therapist offered lower levels of therapeutic conditions.

In a third study using the same experimental procedure, Piaget, Berenson, and Carkhuff (1967) selected four high- and four low-functioning female subjects by the Holder et al. (1967) procedure cited above. Two counselors, one high-functioning and one moderate-functioning (as established in a previous study), were asked to lower the level of their facilitative conditions during the second fifteen minutes of a forty-five minute interview. Again it was found that high-functioning subjects maintained the level of their self-exploration throughout the interview when talking to a high-functioning counselor. When low-functioning subjects talked to a high-functioning counselor, their level of self-exploration was found to vary directly with the level of therapeutic conditions offered. The essential findings of the Holder et al. (1967) study are thus reflected here. The added feature in the present study is that the same subjects were also interviewed by a moderate-functioning counselor. In this case it was found that neither the high- nor the low-functioning subjects could maintain their levels of self-exploration once the counselor lowered his therapeutic conditions. Furthermore, the level of self-exploration continued downward in the third period, when the moderate-functioning counselor attempted to restore the level of his optimal therapeutic conditions.

Two additional studies in this series were completed but in these, the level of *client* functioning was manipulated. Carkhuff and Alexik (1967) trained a female graduate student in counselor education to serve as a client and discuss her personal problems with eight experienced counselors. Each of the counselors saw the client for a one-hour interview. In the initial and last third of the interview, the client explored her problem at deep levels. During the middle twenty minutes, "the client deliberately lowered her depth of self-exploration by introducing material irrelevant to herself and her problem and/or by reverting to a mechanical, unfeeling discussion of any personally relevant material introduced by the counselor" (p. 351). High-functioning counselors were able to maintain the level of their therapeutic conditions, but such was not the case for low-functioning counselors. This group lowered the level of therapeutic functioning during period two and did not raise their level of functioning when the client once again returned to deeper levels of self-exploration.

In a similar study, Friel, Kratochvil, and Carkhuff (1968) trained four graduate students as standard "clients," and each saw eight graduate student counselors for 45-minute interviews. As it turned out, none of the 32 counselors proved to be capable of high levels of therapeutic functioning—all operated at either moderate or low levels. Again, it was found that counselors lowered the level of their

therapeutic functioning in response to a lowering of the level of client self-exploration, and again therapeutic functioning did not recover when the clients returned to deeper levels of self-exploration.

There are some methodological problems that run through the entire series of studies: (a) the determination of the levels of therapeutic conditions and depth of client self-exploration are determined by judges' ratings. Raters are each responsible for only one judgement category and are "blind" as to the content of the study and the other rating categories. However, ratings of client statements are made with full knowledge of therapist statements and vice versa (Truax and Carkhuff, 1965). In other words, the rating of any one category is made with knowledge of the entire interaction; (b) the independence of the ratings of therapist conditions can be questioned on other grounds as well. Kiesler, Mathieu, and Klein, (see Rogers, Gendlin, Kiesler, and Truax, 1967) report that ratings of specific therapist conditions supposedly based on particular patient-therapist responses, can be confounded by the raters' assessment of the therapist's general commitment to the therapeutic relationship. Any specific rating may be tapping this more global therapist quality (p. 305); (c) defining an experimental manipulation as a therapist "withholding his best response" is not adequately specific and may prevent replication by those outside the principal investigator's immediate circle; and (d) in all studies reported in this section, except for Friel, Kratochvil, and Carkhuff (1968), each experimental condition was presented by only one person. The condition and the individual presenting it are thus confounded, a particularly serious problem in studies in which conditions are themselves "person" variables.

Despite the methodological problems, the results of these studies cannot be dismissed lightly. They offer data to explode patient and therapist uniformity myths (Kiesler, 1966). They suggest that therapists and patients vary in their personal qualities and that the qualities of each person has an effect on the behavior of the other. Since these experiments all dealt with single interviews, their results need replication over a longer series of contacts. Still, the findings are provocative. It would appear that "good" therapists and "good" patients are less capable of being influenced by subtle interpersonal cues. Good therapists may lapse into less therapeutic behavior without damaging consequences, but such may not be the case for less optimal therapists. Poor therapists may find it harder to maintain their therapeutic role behaviors when patients become more difficult (Carkhuff and Alexik, 1967; Friel et al., 1968). If a less-than-optimal therapist reduces his level of therapeutic functioning, the patient may be unable to return to meaningful discourse (Piaget et al., 1967). One can imagine a downwardly spiralling cycle that gives cause to wonder how often real therapy is marked by such instances.

The Free-Association Analogue

Perhaps it is a commentary on the nature of the field that there are few experimental studies of free-association. Those studies that are reported in the literature are more concerned with the personality of the subject than with interpersonal and situational determinants of behavior. This should not be too surprising, since the free-association task is specifically designed to keep situational pressures at a minimum so that the patient's concentration on internal ideation, affect, and sensations will be maximized.

Bordin (1966b) reviewed the literature on the relationship between personality characteristics and free association and reported three experiments of his own (Bordin, 1966a; 1966b). Subjects were either college students or schizophrenic or nonschizophrenic psychiatric patients. Contrary to expectations, little or no differences were found in associative performance among the three groups. Of a wide variety of predictor measures, only the Rorschach and Reversible Figures Tests were clearly related to free associative performance. Bordin (1966b, p. 37) concluded that a "personality in which drive and organizational elements are well represented and well balanced is able to respond more effectively in the free association task."

Kaplan (1966) compared female high- and low-anxiety subjects in a free-association task under two sets of instructions. Subjects were told either to "say anything that comes into your mind without omitting anything," or were given problem-focused instructions in which they were told to talk about "what you would feel you needed to talk about, if you were a patient who had come to a therapist." In both groups, subjects were seated alone in a chair directly facing a one-way-vision mirror behind which the experimenter sat. The problem-focused condition was clearly stressful. Yet, high-anxiety subjects spoke with more affect and spontaneity in this situation than did low-anxiety subjects. In other words, subjects whose defensive style allowed them to describe themselves negatively, did better with instructions that reinforce this tendency by making it permissible to admit personal inadequacy. No differences between anxiety groups were observed under the more neutral free-association instructions.

Taken together, these studies suggest that to be good candidates for a free-association therapy, subjects should be persons whose personality structure is fairly well balanced (Bordin, 1966a; 1966b), and who have easy access to personal concerns and anxiety-evoking experiences (Kaplan, 1966). It is the rare therapist who is fortunate to have patients of this ideal type.

PERSON CHARACTERISTICS AND INTERVIEW BEHAVIOR

The psychotherapeutic interaction is influenced by a number of factors, primary among which are patient and therapist personality characteristics. Yet our theories of therapeutic change rarely make provision for these variables in a systematic way. Implicit in our theories of therapy are patient and therapist "uniformity myths" (Kiesler, 1966), which suggest that we treat both patients and therapists as homogeneous classes of actors in the therapeutic encounter (Carson, 1967).

Specifying the manner in which the personality characteristics of the participants interact with the therapist's technique and with the nature of the patient's presenting problems is no easy task. Our current psychiatric nomenclature and standardized personality tests have provided only gross leads to understanding and predicting actual therapy behavior, although more functional personality trait descriptions do seem to hold more promise. For example, Snyder (1959) described a series of studies in which the Rorschach, MMPI, and Mooney Problem Checklist were administered to student therapy clients. One of the findings of this group of studies was that while therapy clients received higher maladjustment scores than a control group of students who did not come for therapy, the maladjustment scores of clients who dropped from therapy early could not be distinguished from the scores of those who continued therapy. The one exception to this finding was that early terminators showed less anxiety and greater defensiveness than those who continued therapy. It would appear that anxiety and defensiveness are functionally related to continuance in therapy to a greater extent than level of maladjustment.

When we turn to the measurement of therapist personality characteristics, we are confronted with an even greater series of problems. Applying standardized personality inventories to therapists has produced unimpressive results. Therapists are "test-wise" in their knowledge of the intent of personality tests and the nature of desirable responses. Compared to the standardization groups on which personality tests are typically developed, therapists represent a restricted, professionalized sample. It is not surprising that greater progress has been made in dealing with the technical aspects of the therapist's contribution than with the more elusive qualities of the therapist's personality (Strupp, 1962). The impact of the person of the therapist on the person of the patient remains largely an uncharted area.

Despite the difficulties, some progress is being made in specifying the nature of the interaction between person variables and aspects of therapeutic behavior. The analogue approach to this problem typically involves three interrelated strategies. Analogue researchers characteristically eschew global psychiatric diagnostic categories, using instead, measures of specific personality traits. Interviewers are chosen from subject populations with less clinical sophistication (and biases) than might be found among experienced psychotherapists. And, the attempt is always made to relate personality measures to actual interview performance—usually in standardized laboratory situations that reduce the complexity of the interpersonal exchange.

Therapist Type

The contribution of analogue research to the investigation of personality effects in therapy, as well as the problems involved, can be illustrated best by the research on therapist "type." Whitehorn and Betz (Betz, 1962) found that they could distinguish level of success with hospitalized schizophrenics on the basis of a scale developed from the Strong Vocational Interest Blank. The scale allowed the researchers to differentiate therapists who obtained high success rates with schizophrenic patients (Type A therapists) from therapists with low improvement rates (Type B therapists). After several years of this work, Betz concluded that "the crucial determinants of therapeutic outcome of schizophrenic patients lie in certain personal qualities in the physician" (Betz, 1962, p. 50–51).

One of the difficulties with the research on therapist type lies in determining the nature of the personal qualities involved. The scale was empirically derived and its content "defies description in terms that are even remotely related to psychotherapy" (Carson, 1967, p. 48). The scale does not correlate with other well-known personality measures. An unpublished factor-analytic study (reported by Carson, 1967) reveals that what seems to differentiate As from Bs is that As display a disinterest in mechanics and manual activities, while Bs have a higher interest in engineering.

Research by McNair, Callahan, and Lorr (1962) further complicates the picture. These authors found that for a sample of VA psychiatric outpatients, Type B therapists provided better outcomes than Type A therapists. The McNair et al. and the Whitehorn and Betz research are difficult to compare, since they differ in a number of respects. The McNair et al. patients were mostly neurotic, not schizophrenic, and came from lower socioeconomic backgrounds than did the patients in the Whitehorn and Betz research. Therapists in the McNair et al. study demonstrated a greater range of clinical experience, and the majority were psychologists. All therapists in the

Whitehorn and Betz research were psychiatric residents.

One possible explanation to account for the discrepant results cited above is that successful outcome may be a function of the interaction between the A—B therapist variable and type of patient studied. This was essentially the hypothesis that guided Carson and his co-workers in the series of analogue studies (summarized in Carson, 1967) that they initiated. In one of their reports, Carson, Harden, and Shows (1964) present two experiments in which students were selected to act as experimental therapists on the basis of their scores on the A—B Scale. In the first study, subjects were asked to respond in writing to letters purportedly written anonymously by mental patients. The content of the letters emphasized symptoms that could be described as either turning-against-others (TO), avoidance-of-others (AO), or turning-against-the-self (TS). The results of this study indicated that the authors' predictions were confirmed on one of the six rating scales used to score the subjects' written replies. As in relation to TO and AO symptoms (which involve schizoid-like defense styles) and Bs in relation to TS symptoms (involving neuroticlike defense styles) wrote therapeutic letters that were judged to be relatively interpretive and depth-oriented.

The second study by Carson et al. (1964) demonstrated more clear-cut results. Student interviewers chosen on the basis of their A—B scores were placed in an interview situation with student interviewees in whom an expectancy toward the interviewer had been induced. Half of the interviewees received a description of the interviewer designed to induce feelings of distrust, hostility, and expectancy of harm, while the remaining interviewees received a description of the interviewer designed to induce feelings of trust, friendliness, and expectancy of help. As predicted, Type A interviewers in relation to distrusting subjects and Type B interviewers in relation to trusting subjects obtained relatively high amounts of information. Thus far, the outcome studies of both Whitehorn and Betz (Betz, 1962) and McNair et al. (1962) seem confirmed. It would appear that Type A interviewers operate best with individuals who utilize distrustful-extrapunitive life

styles, while Type B interviewers operate best with individuals whose style involves a trusting-intrapunitive orientation.

The most controversial development in the research on therapist type stems from a study by Kemp (1966). In this investigation, student subjects, again chosen on the basis of their scores on the A—B Scale, listened in groups to a tape-recorded interview that was interrupted at predetermined intervals to allow the subject to respond to sets of multiple-choice alternatives. Prior to listening to the tape, half the subjects received instructions that described the patient's symptoms in terms of a "turning-against-self" (TAS) while for the remaining subjects, the tape patient was described as displaying "avoiding-of-others" (AVOS) symptoms. Subjects had little difficulty choosing the most therapeutic alternatives at each response point, and Type A and B subjects did not differ in the quality of their "therapeutic interventions." However, the unexpected findings of the study were revealed on a post-experiment questionnaire. As who listened to the AVOS patient and Bs who listened to the TAS patient reported that they found it *less* easy to choose interventions and were *less* comfortable during the recording than subjects in the other two experimental conditions.

This study, supported by additional research (Carson and Klein, 1965) raises the possibility that therapists are most capable of helping those who, for as yet unspecified reasons, produce greatest discomfort in them. There is further evidence that this tendency toward "paradoxical discomfort" is most characteristic of nonprofessional student therapists and is reduced during professional training (Kemp and Carson, 1967). One function of training may be to provide an opportunity for mastery over personal discomfort while enhancing professional competence.

The analogue research on therapist type reported thus far has been generated by the same group of investigators who conducted their original work at Duke University. Research by others is just beginning to accumulate. Kemp's key finding of "paradoxical discomfort" is challenged by Berzins and Seidman (1968), who found that Type A interviewers were more satisfied with their performance when responding to a tape-recorded patient displaying schizoidlike symptoms, while Type B interviewers found it easier to respond to a patient displaying neuroticlike symptoms. The Carson, Harden, and Shows (1964) research is supported, but no evidence of paradoxical discomfort was found. Jacob and Levine (1968) offer results in contradiction to Carson et al. (1964). In their study, A and B student interviewers were equally accurate in predicting the self-descriptions of distrustful-hostile and trustful-friendly interviewees. Both types of interviewers predicted the self-descriptions of distrustful-hostile interviewees more accurately than the self-descriptions of trustful-friendly interviewees.

Both Berzins and Seidman (1968) and Jacob and Levine (1968) describe procedural differences between their work and the earlier work of Kemp (1966) and Carson et al. (1964), research that they were purporting to replicate. Since no experiment can ever duplicate another in every detail anyway, we are left with the problem of deciding the importance of their procedural variations, an impossible task as long as "replications are attempted of experiments dealing with phenomena which are not embedded either within some theoretical framework or extensive body of systematic research" (Levy, 1969, p. 15). The research on therapist type using the A—B Scale has not yet developed to the point that would allow the successful prediction of the situational parameters that influence its appearance. Yet, if therapist type refers to an important construct, it should be treated in a manner suggested by Campbell and Fiske's (1959) multitrait-multimethod matrix for the study of construct validity. Other methods of measuring therapist type should be developed, and predictions derived from these methods should support those derived from the A—B Scale. Similarly, measures of therapist type should not correlate highly with measures of other personality variables. The ambiguity in the research on therapist type will remain until its parameters are investigated more systematically.

Therapist Experience Level

Strupp's (1960) laboratory procedure to study aspects of the therapist's contribution to the treatment process has become widely used. Strupp tried several different experimental formats (described by Strupp, 1962), but his most popular technique involved showing a filmed interview to therapist subjects. The film was interrupted at predetermined points and the title "What would you do?" was flashed on the screen, giving the subject an opportunity to respond. Using this method, Strupp compared therapists of different theoretical orientations, training backgrounds, and experience levels. For example, Strupp found that the dynamic quality of the therapist's remarks was a function of experience level for both psychiatrists and psychologists. In other words, regardless of field of work, experienced therapists gave more dynamic responses to the case material than did less experienced therapists (Strupp, 1962). But greater experience is not always best. Strupp also found that the more favorable estimates of prognosis came from rather inexperienced therapists. There was a tendency for older, more experienced therapists to have more negative attitudes toward the filmed patient and to be less sanguine about the course of therapy. Strupp suggests that there may be some validity to the observation that "analysts sometimes seem to achieve their greatest successes when they are beginners" (Strupp, 1960, p. 100).

Ornston, Cicchetti, Levine, and Fierman (1968) improved upon the Strupp technique in several important respects. The therapist on the film was eliminated, as were the predetermined film stops. The therapist subject who observed the film was allowed to choose his own response points. When the therapist wanted to speak, he operated a hand switch that stopped the movie projector and recorded the therapist's comment on tape. In comparing the responses of experienced therapists with those of first year psychiatry students, Ornston et al. (1968) used a film patient who was more disturbed and whose behavior was more bizarre than the patient filmed by Strupp. Results indicated that experienced therapists used more words but asked fewer questions than inexperienced therapists. In other words, experienced therapists "say something" rather than "ask something."

What experienced therapists say need not be directive. Bohn (1967) and Parsons and Parker

(1968) both found that experienced therapists chose alternatives that were less directive in response to tape recorded clients. An additional finding of the Bohn (1967) study was that while directiveness decreased with training when subjects responded to a "neural" or a "hostile" client, training did not decrease directiveness toward a dependent client. The stimulus pull of a dependent client in calling forth directiveness in a therapist (see also Heller, Myers, and Kline, 1963) may be so strong that it is not successfully reduced by standard therapy training.

The Effects of Contact Alone

We are so used to thinking of therapeutic interventions as involving complex factors that we sometimes neglect the more essential, basic conditions of dyadic therapy—namely, the potentiating effect that is produced by the coming together of two persons in intimate conversation. Does the meeting of patient and therapist itself have important benefits, irrespective of the content of their communications? Does contact by a therapist produce therapeutic benefit, and if so, under what settings?

Martin, Lundy, and Lewin (1960) compared three degrees of interviewer involvement. In one group, the subject talked to a tape recorder with no interviewer present. In a second group, the interviewer was present but could respond by nonverbal means only. In a third group, the interviewer was present and was permitted to comment in "an essentially client-centered fashion." Subjects, who were chosen to be high scorers on a forced choice version of the Manifest Anxiety Scale, were seen for five interview sessions, during which continuous GSR recordings were obtained. Results indicated that approach to emotionally important material was highest when the subject could talk to a fully responsive interviewer. This group showed a marked increase in approach to emotionally important material, from the first to the last half of their interviews over the course of the five sessions. The group with no interviewer showed a slight decrease in approach to emotionally important material, with the group receiving the minimally responsive interviewer (nonverbal communication only) showing scores between the other two groups. The group

receiving a fully responsive interviewer showed an increase in GSR reactivity for the first three sessions, but a decrease in the last two sessions. The no-interviewer group showed an increasing tendency to become more anxious within interviews as the five sessions progressed. Again, the reactions to the minimally responsive interviewer fell between the reactions to the other two groups.

Confirmatory evidence of the importance of the presence of another person on an individual's ability to discuss personally relevant material comes from a study by Colby (1960). Eleven male medical students participated in an experiment in free-association over a period of three weeks. During the first week, the subject lay on the couch and described aloud the "free-associative contents of his self-observation." For each session, which lasted one-half hour, he was alone in the office with a tape recorder behind the couch. During the second week, all conditions were the same except that at exactly fifteen minutes after the start of the session, the experimenter entered the room and sat as an observer in a chair behind the couch. During the first two weeks there were four sessions a week. In the third week, the subjects had two more free-associative sessions without an observer present, as in the first week. Colby found that subjects reported feeling more nervous and inhibited when he entered the room but the observer's presence actually had an activating effect. Affectively valued persons were discussed for longer periods of time during the observer's presence than during his absence. Even though the subjects reported feeling more inhibited, they spoke more meaningfully with the experimenter present.

Is the presence of an interviewer or therapist always an important facilitator of personal discussion? The research reported above might lead one to the belief that meaningful exploration cannot occur without the constant presence of a therapist. However, there is research to indicate that such is not the case. Exner (1966) assigned female patients to one of three types of therapy groups. Either the therapist met with patients regularly; the therapist met with patients on an irregular basis, attending a random half of the meetings; or the patients participated in group meetings without the presence of a therapist at all. Symptomatic improvement and hospital discharge rates were best for those groups in which the therapist attended on an irregular basis, and showed least change in those groups in which no therapist was present at all. It would appear that the therapist's constant presence can inhibit the appearance of certain topics. Other group members were always present, so unlike the previous studies, the patient never spoke in an empty room, and it may be that some of the other patients assumed quasi-therapeutic functions.

It would appear that the communication of personally significant material is enhanced by the physical presence of another person to whom a facilitative or caring role can be assigned. However, in order for therapeutic benefit to ensue, the conversation need not be dynamically "deep." Dreiblatt and Weatherly (1965) found that a series of brief, friendly, casual conversations between a staff member and a patient had beneficial effects on newly admitted psychiatric patients. These brief contacts produced a reduction in subjective anxiety, an increase in self-esteem, and a reduction in length of hospitalization compared with patients receiving regular hospital routine but without the brief staff-patient contact. Six contacts a week were more effective than three contacts a week. Significant positive change in patients was demonstrated only when the brief contacts avoided discussion of patient symptoms and pathology. A symptom-oriented brief-contact group failed to demonstrate significant improvement over control groups. For newly admitted hospital patients, brief contacts seemed best when they were ego-enhancing and supportive and when they conveyed the message to the patient that "he is accepted as a person" (Dreiblatt and Weatherly, 1965, p. 518).

THE INTERVIEW AS A SOCIAL INTERACTION ANALOGUE

The view of many early analogue researchers was that their goal should involve the construction of laboratory situations that would closely resemble psychotherapy as traditionally practiced. Variables were chosen on the basis of their presumed importance to actual practice, since the criterion against which the value of the analogue would be assessed, was how closely the experimental situation resembled "real" therapy.

As the limits of current therapeutic techniques became understood, and the search was begun to find new therapeutic procedures to reach those classified as "unsuitable" by the major therapy systems, analogue researchers began to question the wisdom of attempting to approximate a criterion that itself was changing. Rather than mimicking elements of classical psychotherapy, could analogue research be used to point toward new methods of treatment?

This changed attitude can be seen most clearly in the following comment by Krasner (1962, p. 103):

Many investigators imply that the process of psychotherapy, as now practiced, is the royal and only road to changing people's behavior. The yardstick for the acceptability for research then becomes "how close is this to the real psychotherapy process?" I feel strongly that we are losing sight of the purpose of psychotherapy, which is to change people's behavior . . . The apologetic tone in papers which experimentally investigate behavior is uncalled for. These so-called laboratory studies have important implications for the psychotherapy process and derive some of their hypotheses from psychotherapy. However, I am less and less inclined to call them "experimental analogues" of psychotherapy. Rather I see them as part of a broader psychology of behavior control . . .

This view highlights a trend in which analogue researchers have become more concerned with the discovery of factors that mediate change in helping relationships and less concerned with whether the variables studied have a place in existing clinical practice.

At the same time, another trend became apparent. Psychotherapy theorists had been concerned primarily with the interview's specialized content, a preoccupation that tended to emphasize the uniqueness of the therapy transaction. Analogue researchers were among those who recognized commonalities between psychotherapy and other forms of social interchange. They began to wonder whether emphasis on the structural characteristics of the interview exchange might now prove fruitful. Just as treatment methodologies had been derived in the past from consideration of the dynamic content of the therapeutic interview, so too, new treatment approaches might be suggested from a consideration of the interpersonal structure in which treatment occurs.

There was then a fusion of two lines of thought that together produced a new direction for analogue research. On the one hand, emphasis turned away from a study of the elements of therapeutic practice to a broader consideration of relevant change agents in helping relationships. At the same time, interest increased in the structural aspects of dyadic communication that might be common to all forms of social influence.

The Reliability and Utility of Measures of Interview Structure

Matarazzo, Saslow, and their co-workers (Saslow and Matarazzo, 1959; Matarazzo, Wiens, and Saslow, 1965; Matarazzo, Wiens, Matarazzo, and Saslow, 1968) were among the first to recognize the need to develop objective interview measures that could serve as indices of change in psychotherapy. Measures were needed that possessed reliability under unchanging interview conditions, as well as sensitivity to change as interview variables were manipulated. The early work of the Matarazzo group (summarized by Saslow and Matarazzo, 1959) involved the development of a standardized interview and the demonstration that behavior in that interview could be reliably assessed. Chapple's Interaction Chronograph (Chapple, 1949; 1956) was chosen as the main assessment device, since it allowed the observer to record the behavioral interaction of two individuals in time units that possessed a high degree of precision. Once reliability was established, studies were undertaken to investigate the effects on the interviewee of planned modifications in the interviewer's behavior. The major finding of these studies (summarized by Matarazzo, Wiens, and Saslow, 1965; and Matarazzo, Wiens, Matarazzo, and Saslow, 1968) was the demonstration of synchrony between interviewer and interviewee. For example, in initial interviews, the average dutation of interviewer and interviewee comments were found to be directly related. As the interviewer increased the duration of his

remarks, the interviewee spoke for longer periods of time; as the interviewer's remarks were shortened, the duration of the interviewee's comments also decreased. A similar concordance was found for latency and interruption measures.

In their latest report, Matarazzo et al. (1968) compared the results of their interview research with similar measures taken from naturalistic psychotherapy conducted by members of the same research group. The investigators hoped to discover that synchrony would be observed in free, naturalistic psychotherapy in a manner similar to that found in experimentally controlled initial interviews. Synchrony was observed in latency and interruption behaviors, but not in their more widely cited measure of duration of utterance. Several explanations to account for the failure to find synchrony on the duration measure were offered by Matarazzo and his collaborators. However, one may ask whether identical results should have been expected in settings that differ in important context and setting parameters. Perhaps the Matarazzo research could be viewed as an example of why one should *not* expect to find a direct correspondence between the laboratory analogue and the free-responding therapy situation (Heller, 1969; Heller and Marlatt, 1969). Context variables need to be identified and studied so that their interaction with general change factors can be predicted. In the Matarazzo paradigm, the effect of the interviewer on the interviewee had been carefully mapped out. But the factors impinging on the interviewer also must be identified if behavior in a naturalistic setting is to be predicted. As we begin to view the interview as involving reciprocal influence and interaction, we shall see that one factor impinging on the activity level of the therapist is the activity level of the patient (Heller, Myers, and Kline, 1963).

The Interview Interaction

We have been steadily moving toward a transactional model of the influence process, in which influence attempts are seen to be reciprocal in nature in that both parties expect to give and take from the interaction (Heller, in press). Our view of psychotherapeutic influence has also been moving toward a transactional model in that the behavior of each of the interview participants is seen as a partial cause as well as a partial result of the behavior of the other (Heller, 1963). One research strategy for the study of complex reciprocally contingent interactions is to reduce the interaction to an "asymmetrical contingency" (Jones and Thibaut, 1958) by standardizing the role behavior of one of the interview participants while allowing the behavior of the other to vary freely. This was essentially the strategy adopted by Heller, Myers, and Kline (1963) and Heller, Davis, and Myers (1966). In the first of the two studies, actors were trained to play the roles of specific client types and their effects on student-therapists were noted. In the second study, actors were trained to assume specific interviewer roles, whose effects were assessed by studying the ability of subjects to talk about themselves freely. These studies revealed that while the behavior of each interview participant impinges on the behavior of the other, the effects of this interpersonal influence is not fully complementary. Each participant does not influence the other in the same way. Both must

be taken into account in explaining the full interaction—a finding that may account for Matarazzo et al.'s (1968) inability to find synchrony in the duration of utterance between patient and therapist in free naturalistic psychotherapy.

The manner in which reciprocal interview influence varies (depending upon the direction of its impact) can be seen in Figure 4.1. Both Heller et al. (1966) and Matarazzo et al. (1968) found that the activity level of the interviewee covaried as a function of the activity level of the interviewer. This would lead us to postulate that in naturalistic psychotherapy, high therapist output would lead to high patient output, while low therapist output would lead to low patient output. However, this direct relationship is obscured in the naturalistic interview because the stimulus pull of the interviewee on the interviewer is exactly the reverse. Heller, Myers, and Kline (1963) found that dependent, passive interviewees pull activity and dominance from interviewers, while dominant interviewees induce interviewer passivity. We would therefore postulate that in naturalistic psychotherapy,

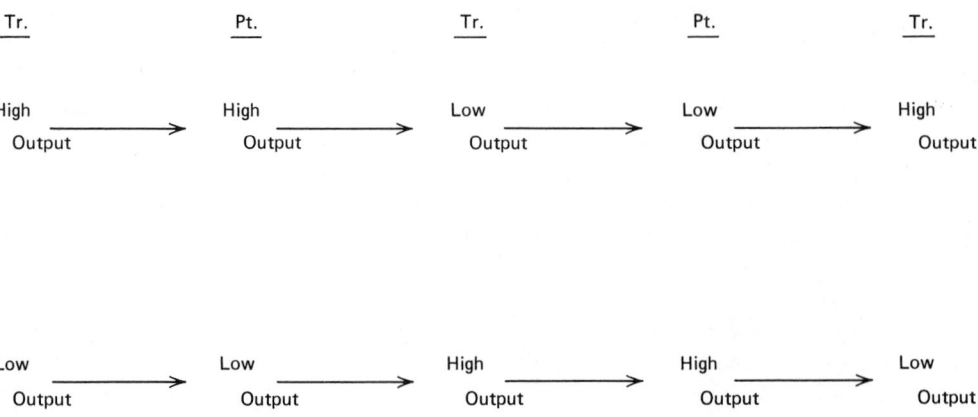

Figure 4.1 The reciprocal influence postulated to occur in naturalistic psychotherapy derived from an examination of component relationships in laboratory interview research.

high patient output would lead to low therapist output, while low patient output would lead to increased output on the part of the therapist. The same suggestion was made by Matarazzo et al. (1968) when they noted that when their patients talked little, the therapeutic set of the therapists may have led them to talk more, hoping to stimulate the patients. When their patients were already active, the therapists' tendency may have been to talk less, so as not to impede the patients' productivity.

The relationship between the activity levels of the various participants is complex, in part depending upon the source and nature of the activity. Findings with respect to the transmission of affect between interview participants reveal a more straightforward relationship. Variations in affect in one participant were found to produce synchronous affect in the other (Heller et al., 1963; Heller et al., 1966; Heller, 1968). Regardless of its source, friendly behaviors induce counterfriendliness while hostile behaviors induce counterhostility (although in the case of experienced interviewers, overt expressions of counterhostility may be suppressed). Hostile clients have been found to induce more anxiety in beginning interviewers than do friendly clients (Russell and Snyder, 1963), but the reactions of therapists to client hostility can be made more appropriate with training (Bohn, 1967).

One surprising finding of the Heller, Davis, and Myers (1966) study was that subjects with a prior set toward admitting personal inadequacies and weaknesses discussed their problems more openly when the interviewer was either passive and friendly or was completely silent. The unexpected facilitation produced by interviewer silence led Heller to concentrate more intensively on the effects of interview ambiguity (Heller, 1968).

In general, the effects of ambiguity have been found to be rather clear-cut in the psychological literature. Ambiguity retards learning (Kanfer and Marston, 1961) and increases anxiety in clinical interviews (Dibner, 1958) as well as in psychological experiments (Dittes and Zemach, 1964). Yet, despite its possible deleterious consequences, the use of ambiguity as a therapeutic tool is well entrenched in classical psychoanalysis. Primarily, this is

because ambiguity is seen as a prerequisite for the therapeutic work of free-association, and for the development and interpretation of transference phenomena. Heller's subsequent work varying the clarity with which the interviewer's message could be heard, confirmed that for subjects with a prior set toward the open disclosure of personal concerns, the interviewer condition that provided the least feedback to subjects was most facilitative of subject self-disclosure (Heller, 1968). It would appear that, at least for subjects already primed to discuss themselves openly in personal terms, the use of ambiguity to facilitate self-disclosure is supported. Also supported is the clinical use of ambiguity with "good," well-integrated, introspective patients—individuals not unlike college-student volunteers.

Further research revealed that similar effects could be produced by conditions other than unclear interviewer feedback. Heller and Jacobson (reported by Heller, in press) compared the effects of friendly and reserved interviewers. Both sets of interviewers were instructed to capture the essential message in the subject's remarks and to reflect that content back to the subject once every minute. The difference between the two conditions was completely nonverbal. Friendly interviewers appeared expressive and encouraging by smiling appropriately, nodding, leaning toward the subject and maintaining eye contact. Reserved interviewers attempted to maintain a nonresponsive demeanor except when speaking. When the subject spoke, the interviewer refrained from smiling or nodding, leaned away, and often looked away from the subject. The results revealed that highly dependent males, chosen on the basis of dependency scores derived from the Edwards Personal Preference Schedule, spoke about personal concerns and problems most freely when interacting with reserved interviewers. Since the content of the information exchange was the same in both conditions, Heller (in press) considered the possibility that interview stress might be the common ingredient in his experiments utilizing interviewer silence, ambiguous interviewer feedback, and a reserved interviewer style. He concluded that "subjects whose defensive style allows them to be more open in admitting personal concerns, do so more frequently in moderately stressful interview conditions than in more subjectively pleasant and less threatening conditions."

Confirmatory evidence for this proposition comes from two independent lines of inquiry. Working within a verbal-conditioning format, Ganzer and Sarason (1964) found that when the experimenter behaved in a hostile manner, displaying curt, disagreeable, impatient behavior, subjects were more likely to admit to qualities that reflected unfavorably upon themselves. Subjects who received warm and friendly experimenters were less likely to describe negative personal qualities. In a similar study, Sarason and Winkel (1966) found that the less favorably the interviewee rated the interviewer, the more likely it was that he would speak about personally meaningful material.

More indirect support comes from the work of Pope and Siegman (1965). These authors found that low-specificity questions and an anxiety-arousing topic elicited greater verbal productivity than did high-specificity questions or a neutral topic. Low-specificity interviewer remarks do not necessarily raise the subject's anxiety level, but do require that the subject work harder to overcome informational uncertainty (Siegman and Pope, 1965).

While moderate stress might be facilitative for college student experimental subjects who are primed to talk about themselves openly, are capable of doing so, and wish to acquiesce to the task demands of the experiment, what about subjects who are less willing and less able? The research literature offers little evidence on this question. Heller and Jacobson (reported by Heller, in press) found that neither a friendly nor a reserved interviewer style was capable of inducing independent male students to talk openly about personal problems. In another study, Heller, Silver, Bailey, and Dudgeon (reported by Heller, in press) found that chronic psychotic patients were more responsive to interviewer friendliness than to a more reserved interviewer style. If the interviewer was reserved early in the interview, patient verbal productivity was inhibited to such an extent that it did not recover later in the interview when the interviewer became more friendly. No interviewer style condition influenced the ability of the patients to talk openly about their problems. This content variable started low and continued to decrease throughout the interview.

Pope and Siegman (1968) presented female nursing students with a set of two interviews in which their female interviewers were either warm or cold. The interviewees showed higher verbal productivity when talking to a warm interviewer, but only when the warm condition appeared first in the series of two. Like the patients in the Heller, Silver, Bailey, and Dudgeon study cited above, meeting first with a cold interviewer produced verbal inhibition. The productivity of the nursing students did not recover in the second interview, even though their second interviewer was warm.

It should be clear from the above that research with other subject populations is clearly in order before many general conclusions about the interview interaction will be possible. Unfortunately, the clinical personnel who are the first to criticize "college-student research" as irrelevant to the clinical problems they face in their daily practice, are often among those who are most reluctant to allow the conduct of experimental interviews with their patients. Yet progress is being made slowly. The experimental analogue research literature has been growing (as can be seen by the number of post-1964 studies cited in this review) and research is being conducted in an ever-widening number of settings. We now know that programmed interviewer roles can be developed that appear natural in ongoing interviews, and that these roles can capture important aspects of an interviewer's interpersonal behavior. We also know that subjects are not damaged by participation in experimental interviews. It is now time to turn our attention to research that investigates the interaction of setting, task, style, and message variables with a variety of subject populations.

CONCLUDING REMARKS

This chapter has described two general approaches taken by analogue researchers. The first involves an analysis of complex therapy systems to find their most potent ingredients and the conditions under which each is optimized. Analogue studies of systematic desensitization, Rogerian facilitative conditions, and free association are examples of this trend. A second research strategy involves the investigation of aspects of dyadic communication, on the assumption that there are structural and role components of social influence situations that are common to all forms of influence, including psychotherapy. Studies of interviewer style, interviewer-interviewee synchrony, and interview stress are examples of this second trend. Both lines of inquiry are consonant with the current orientation of many psychotherapy researchers as described by Strupp and Bergin (1969). There is movement toward a "nonschool" approach to psychotherapy, with an increased concentration on specificity of techniques, and a decrease in the prominence of doctrinaire theories that describe psychotherapy as a unitary process applied to a unitary problem.

The evidence accumulated from analogue studies supports the current emphasis on specificity of factors responsible for behavior change. Complex treatments include many effective components. For example, analogue studies have found that the coming together of patient and therapist in intimate contact has therapeutic benefit, even though the conversation between the two may not be dynamically "deep" or focused on the "problems" of the patient. It has also been found that the induction of positive therapeutic expectancies can enhance the operation of almost any therapeutic method, although positive expectancies alone are usually not enough. Research has focused on the optimal combinations of patient, therapist, and treatment, but the exact pairings still elude us—our knowledge is still incomplete. We know that some therapists do better with some patients than with others. There is evidence to indicate the nature of some ideal pairings, but we still don't know why these pairings are effective. There is some support for

the proposition that some patients discuss their personal concerns more openly when confronted with moderate interview stress; for others the opposite has been found to be true. Some investigators have found that therapists do better when they are challenged or made somewhat uncomfortable by their clients. Other evidence indicates that some therapists function so poorly that they would probably be effective only with clients who are themselves optimally responsive.

Analogue research is producing evidence for the operation of factors not accounted for by classical therapy theories. If this continues to be the case, the clinician will be faced with a dilemma. Should he ignore the accumulating evidence from laboratory interviews or should he re-examine some of his previously held clinical assumptions? Our own point of view on this issue—the relevance for psychotherapy of research on behavior change—has been stated previously (Goldstein, Heller and Sechrest, 1966, pp. 8–9):

To know that solid research dealing with attitude change, learning, and a score of other research domains offering means of altering an individual's behavior exists, and to deny in an a priori manner the potential relevance of such research to the psychotherapy patient is to perform a disservice to both the advance of psychotherapy and to one's psychotherapy patients.

However, regardless of the clinician's personal opinion concerning the usefulness of extrapolating findings from laboratory interview research to psychotherapy, extrapolation attempts will prove disappointing unless research evidence is accumulated in such a way as to sample mediating variables such as context and setting factors. The promise of analogue research is only partly a function of rigorous methodology. More important will be the ability of analogue researchers to document the specific conditions under which factors of change operate.

REFERENCES

Ashby, J. D., Ford, D. H., Guerney, B. G., Jr., and Guerney, L. F. Effects on clients of a reflective and a leading type of psychotherapy. *Psychological Monographs: General and Applied*, 1957, **71**, (24, Whole No. 493), 1–32.

Bandura, A., Behavioral modification through modeling procedures. In L. Krasner and L. P. Ullmann (Eds.), *Research in behavior modification*. New York: Holt, 1965. Pp. 312–340.

Bandura, A., Social learning through imitation. In M. R. Jones (Ed.) *Nebraska Symposium on Motivation: 1962*. Lincoln: University of Nebraska Press, 1962. Pp. 211–269.

Bandura, A., Grusec, J. E., and Menlove, F. L. Vicarious extinction of avoidance behavior. *Journal of Personality and Social Psychology*, 1967, **5**, 16–23.

Bandura, A., and Menlove, F. L. Factors determining vicarious extinction of avoidance behavior through symbolic modeling. *Journal of Personality and Social Psychology*, 1968, **8**, 99–108.

Bandura, A., and Walters, R. H. *Social learning and personality development*. New York: Holt, 1963.

Berzins, J. I., and Seidman, E. Subjective reactions of A and B quasi-therapists to schizoid and neurotic communications: a replication and extension. *Journal of Consulting and Clinical Psychology*, 1968, **32**, 342–347.

Betz, B. J. Experiences in research in psychotherapy with schizophrenic patients. In H. H. Strupp and L. Luborsky (Eds.), *Research in Psychotherapy*. Vol. II. Washington, D. C.: Amer. Psychol. Assoc., 1962, 41–60.

Bohn, M. J., Jr. Therapist responses to hostility and dependency as a function of training. *Journal of Consulting Psychology*, 1967, **31**, 195–198.

Bordin, E. S. Simplification as a strategy for research in psychotherapy. *Journal of Consulting Psychology*, 1965, **29**, 493–503.

Bordin, E. S. Free association: An experimental analogue of the psychoanalytic situation. In L. A. Gottschalk and A. H. Auerback (Eds.), *Methods of Research in Psychotherapy*. New York: Appleton-Century-Crofts, 1966. (a)

Bordin, E. S. Personality and free association, *Journal of Consulting Psychology*, 1966, **30**, 30–38. (b)

Breuer, J., and Freud, S., *Studies in hysteria*. Boston: Beacon Press, 1937.

Campbell, D. T., and Fiske, D. W. Convergent and discriminant validation by the multitrait-multimethod matrix. *Psychological Bulletin*, 1959, **56**, 81–105.

Carkhuff, R. R., and Alexik, M. Effect of client depth of self-exploration upon high and low-functioning counselors. *Journal of Consulting Psychology*, 1967, **14**, 350–355.

Carson, R. C. A and B therapist "types": A possible critical variable in psychotherapy. *Journal of Nervous and Mental Disease*, 1967, **144**, 47–54.

Carson, R. C., Harden, J. A., and Shows, W. D. A–B distinction and behavior in quasi-therapeutic situations. *Journal of Consulting Psychology*, 1964, **28**, 426–433.

Carson, R. C. and Klein, S. J. The A–B therapist "type" distinction and perception of patient characteristics. Paper presented at the Southeastern Psychological Association, Atlanta, 1965.

Chapple, E. D. The interaction chronograph: its evolution and present application. *Personnel*, 1949, **25**, 295–307.

Chapple, E. D. *The interaction chronograph manual*. Norton, Conn.: E. D. Chapple Co., 1956.

Colby, K. M. Experiment on the effects of an observer's presence on the imago system during psychoanalytic free-association. *Behavioral Science*, 1960, **5**, 197–210.

Cooke, G. Evaluation of the efficacy of the components of reciprocal inhibition psychotherapy. *Journal of Abnormal Psychology*, 1968, **73**, 464–467.

Cowen, E. L. The experimental analogue: an approach to research in psychotherapy. *Psychological Reports*, 1961, **8**, 9–10.

Davison, G. C. Systematic desensitization as a counter-conditioning process. *Journal of Abnormal Psychology*, 1968, **73**, 91–99.

Dibner, A. S. Ambiguity and anxiety. *Journal of Abnormal and Social Psychology*, 1958, **56**, 165–174.

Dittes, J. E., and Zemach, M. The effect of cognitive ambiguity on anxiety and affiliative preference. Paper presented at American Psychological Association, Los Angeles, 1964.

Dreiblatt, I. S., and Weatherly, D. An evaluation of the efficacy of brief-contact therapy with hospitalized psychiatric patients. *Journal of Consulting Psychology*, 1965, **29**, 513–529.

Exner, J. E., Jr. Therapist attendance as a variable in group psychotherapy. In G. E. Stollak, B. G. Guerney, Jr., and M. Rothberg (Eds.), *Psychotherapy research: selected readings*. Chicago: Rand McNally, 1966. Pp. 372–376.

Folkins, C. H., Lawson, K. D., Opton, E. M., Jr., and Lazarus, R. S., Desensitization and the experimental reduction of threat. *Journal of Abnormal Psychology*, 1968, **73**, 100–113.

Friel, T., Kratochvil, D., and Carkhuff, R. R. The effects of the manipulation of client depth of self-exploration upon helpers of different training and experience. *Journal of Clinical Psychology*, 1968, **24**, 247–249.

Ganzer, V. J. and Sarason, I. G. Interrelationships among hostility, experimental conditions and verbal behavior. *Journal of Abnormal and Social Psychology*, 1964, **68**, 79–84.

Goldstein, A. P., Heller, K., and Sechrest, L. B. *Psychotherapy and the psychology of behavior change*. New York: Wiley, 1966.

Gordon, J. E. Leading and following psychotherapeutic techniques with hypnotically induced repression and hostility. *Journal of Abnormal and Social Psychology*, 1957, **54**, 405–410.

Greenspoon, J. Verbal conditioning and clinical psychology. In A. J. Bachrach (Ed.), *Experimental foundations of clinical psychology*. New York: Basic Books, 1962. Pp. 510–553.

Grossman, D. An experimental investigation of a psychotherapeutic technique. *Journal of Consulting Psychology*, 1952, **16**, 325–331.

Grummon, D. L., and Butler, J. M. Another failure to replicate Keet's study, "Two verbal techniques in a miniature counseling situation." *Journal of Abnormal and Social Psychology*, 1953, **48**, 597.

Haggard, E. A. Some conditions determining adjustment during and readjustment following experimentally induced stress. In S. S. Tomkins (Ed.) *Contemporary Psychopathology*. Cambridge: Harvard Univ. Press, 1943. Pp. 529–544.

Heller, K. Experimental analogues of psychotherapy: The clinical relevance of laboratory findings of social influence. *Journal of Nervous and Mental Disease*, 1963, **137**, 420–426.

Heller, K. Ambiguity in the interview interaction. In J. M. Shlien (Ed.), *Research in psychotherapy*. Vol. III. Washington, D.C.: Amer. Psychol. Assn., 1968, 242–259.

Heller, K. The effects of modeling procedures in helping relationships: a comment on the Whalen study. *Journal of Consulting and Clinical Psychology*, 1969, **33**, 522–526.

Heller, K. Interview structure and interviewer style in initial interviews. In A. Siegman and B. Pope (Eds.), *Studies in dyadic communication*. New York: Pergamon Press, in press.

Heller, K., Davis, J. D., and Myers, R. A. The effects of interviewer style in a standardized interview. *Journal of Consulting Psychology*, 1966, **30**, 501–508.

Heller, K., and Marlatt, G. A. Verbal conditioning, behavior therapy and behavior change: some problems in extrapolation. In C. M. Franks (Ed.), *Behavior therapy: Appraisal and status*. New York: McGraw-Hill, 1969, 569–588.

Heller, K., Myers, R. A., and Kline, L. V. Interviewer behavior as a function of standardized client roles. *Journal of Consulting Psychology*, 1963, **27**, 117–122.

Holder, T., Carkhuff, R. R., and Berenson, B. G. Differential effects of the manipulation of therapeutic conditions upon high- and low-functioning clients. *Journal of Counseling Psychology*, 1967, **14**, 63–66.

Jacob, T., and Levine, D. A–B distinction and prediction of interviewee self descriptions based on a quasi-therapeutic interaction. *Journal of Consulting and Clinical Psychology*, 1968, **32**, 613–615.

Jacobson, E. A. A comparison of the effects of instructions and models upon interview behavior of high-dependent and low-dependent subjects. Unpublished doctoral dissertation, Indiana University, 1968.

Johnson, S. M., and Sechrest, L. Comparison of desensitization and progressive relaxation in treating test anxiety. *Journal of Consulting and Clinical Psychology*, 1968, **32**, 280–286.

Jones, E. E., and Thibaut, J. W. Interaction goals as bases of inference in interpersonal perception. In R. Tagiuri and L. Petrullo (Eds.), *Person perception and interpersonal behavior*. Stanford: Stanford Univ. Press. 1958. Pp. 151–178.

Kanfer, F. H. Verbal conditioning: a review of its current status. Paper presented at the Kentucky Conference on Verbal Behavior, Lexington, 1966.

Kanfer, F. H., and Marston, A. R. Verbal conditioning, ambiguity and psychotherapy. *Psychological Reports*, 1961, **9**, 461–475.

Kaplan, F. Effects of anxiety and defense in a therapy-like situation. *Journal of Abnormal Psychology*, 1966, **71**, 449–458.

Keet, C. D. Two verbal techniques in a miniature counseling situation. *Psychological Monographs*, 1948, **62**, (7, Whole No. 294).

Kemp, D. E. Correlates of the Whitehorn–Betz AB scale in a quasi-therapeutic situation. *Journal of Consulting Psychology*, 1966, **30**, 509–516.

Kemp, D. E., and Carson, R. C. A–B therapist-type distinction, evaluation of patient characteristics, and professional training. Proceedings, 75th Annual Convention, A.P.A., 1967, 247–248.

Kiesler, D. J. Some myths of psychotherapy research and the search for a paradigm. *Psychological Bulletin*, 1966, **65**, 110–136.

Kounin, J., Polansky, N., Biddle, B., Coburn, H., and Fenn, A., Experimental studies of clients' reactions to initial interviews. *Human Relations*, 1956, **9**, 265–293.

Krasner, L. Studies of the conditioning of verbal behavior. *Psychological Bulletin*, 1958, **55**, 148–170.

Krasner, L. Therapists' contribution. In H. H. Strupp and L. Luborsky (Eds.), *Research in psychotherapy*. Vol. II. Washington, D. C.: American Psychological Association, 1962. Pp. 102–114.

Lang, P. J., Lazovik, A. D., and Reynolds, D. J. Desensitization, suggestibility and pseudotherapy. *Journal of Abnormal Psychology*, 1965, **70**, 395–402.

Leitenberg, H., Agras, W. S., Barlow, D. H., and Oliveau, D. C., Contribution of selective positive reinforcement and therapeutic instructions to systematic desensitization therapy. *Journal of Abnormal Psychology*, 1969, **74**, 113–118.

Levinson, P. K., Zax, M., and Cowen, E. L. An experimental analogue of psychotherapy for anxiety reduction. *Psychological Reports*, 1961, **8**, 171–178.

Levy, L. H. Reflections on replications and the experimenter bias effect. *Journal of Consulting and Clinical Psychology*, 1969, **33**, 15–17.

Marcia, J. E., Rubin, B. M., and Efran, J. S. Systematic desensitization: expectancy change or counterconditioning? *Journal of Abnormal Psychology*, 1969, 382–387.

Matarazzo, J. D., Wiens, A. N., Matarazzo, R. G., and Saslow, G. Speech and silence behavior in clinical psychotherapy and its laboratory correlates. In J. M. Shlien (Ed.), *Research in Psychotherapy*. Vol. III. Washington, D.C.: American Psychological Association, 1968. Pp. 347–394.

Matarazzo, J. D., Wiens, A. N., and Saslow, G. Studies in interview speech behavior. In L. Krasner and L. P. Ullmann (Eds.), *Research in behavior modification*. New York: Holt, 1965. Pp. 179–210.

Marlatt, G. A. Exposure to a model and task ambiguity as determinants of verbal behavior in an interview. Paper presented at Western Psychological Association, San Diego, 1968.(a)

Marlatt, G. A. Vicarious and direct reinforcement control of verbal behavior in an interview setting. Unpublished doctoral dissertation, Indiana University, 1968. (b)

Marlatt, G. A., Jacobson, E. A., Johnson, D. L., and Morrice, D. J. Effects of exposure to a model receiving varied informational feedback upon consequent behavior in an interview. Paper presented at Midwestern Psychological Associaton, Chicago, 1966.

Martin, B., Lundy, R. M., and Lewin, M. H. Verbal and GSR responses in experimental interviews as a function of three degrees of "therapist" communication. *Journal of Abnormal and Social Psychology*, 1960, **60**, 234–240.

McNair, D. M., Callahan, D. M., and Lorr, M. Therapist "type" and patient response to psychotherapy. *Journal of Consulting Psychology*, 1962, **26**, 425–429.

Merrill, R. M. On Keet's study, "Two verbal techniques in a miniature counseling situation." *Journal of Abnormal and Social Psychology*. 1952, **47**, 722.

Ornston, P. S., Cicchetti, D. V., Levine, J., and Fierman, L. B. Some parameters of verbal behavior that reliably differentiate novice from experienced psychotherapists. *Journal of Abnormal Psychology*, 1968, **73**, 240–244.

Parsons, L. B., and Parker, G. V. C. Personal attitudes, clinical appraisals, and verbal behavior of trained and untrained therapists. *Journal of Consulting and Clinical Psychology*, 1968, **32**, 64–71.

Piaget, G. W., Berenson, B. G., and Carkhuff, R. R. Differential effects of the manipulation of therapeutic conditions by high- and moderate-functioning therapists upon high- and low-functioning clients. *Journal of Consulting Psychology*, 1967, **31**, 481–486.

Pope, B., and Siegman, A. W. Interviewer specificity and topical focus in relation to interviewee productivity. *Journal of Verbal Learning and Verbal Behavior*, 1965, **4**, 188–192.

Pope, B., and Siegman, A. W. Interviewer warmth in relation to interviewee verbal behavior. *Journal of Consulting and Clinical Psychology*, 1968, **32**, 588–595.

Rogers, C. R. The necessary and sufficient conditions of therapeutic personality change. *Journal of Consulting Psychology*, 1957, **21**, 95–103.

Rogers, C. R., Gendlin, E. T., Kiesler, D. J., and Truax, C. B., (Eds.). *The therapeutic relationship and its impact; a study of psychotherapy with schizophrenics*. Madison: University of Wisconsin Press, 1967.

Russell, P. D., and Snyder, W. U. Counselor anxiety in relation to amount of clinical experience and quality of affect demonstrated by clients. *Journal of Consulting Psychology*, 1963, **27**, 358–363.

Sarason, I. G., and Ganzer, V. J. Social influence techniques in clinical and community psychology. In C. D. Spielberger (Ed.), *Current topics in Clinical and Community Psychology*. New York: Academic Press, in press.

Sarason, I. G., and Winkel, R. Individual differences among subjects and experimenters and subjects' self-descriptions. *Journal of Personality and Social Psychology*, 1966, **3**, 448–457.

Saslow, G., and Matarazzo, J. D. A technique for studying changes in interview behavior. In E. A. Rubenstein and M. B. Parloff (Eds.), *Research, in Psychotherapy*. Vol. I. Washington, D.C.: American Psychological Association, 1959. Pp. 125–159.

Schwartz, A. N., and Hawkins, H. L. Patient models and affect statements in group therapy. Proceedings, 73rd Annual Convention, APA, 1965. Pp. 265–266.

Siegman, A. W., and Pope, B. Effects of question specificity and anxiety producing messages on verbal fluency in the initial interview. *Journal of Personality and Social Psychology*, 1965, **2**, 522–530.

Snyder, W. U. An investigation of the nature of nondirective psychotherapy. *Journal of Genetic Psychology*, 1945, **33**, 193–223.

Snyder, W. U. Some investigations of relationship in psychotherapy. In E. A. Rubinstein and M. B. Parloff (Eds.), *Research in Psychotherapy*. Vol. I. Washington, D.C.: American Psychological Association, 1959. Pp. 247–259.

Strupp, H. H. *Psychotherapists in action*. New York: Grune and Stratton, 1960.

Strupp, H. H. The therapist's contribution to the treatment process: Beginnings and vagaries of a research program. In H. H. Strupp and L. Luborsky (Eds.) *Research in Psychotherapy*. Vol. II. Washington, D.C.: American Psychological Association, 1962. Pp. 25–40.

Strupp, H. H., and Bergin, A. E. Some empirical and conceptual bases for coordinated research in psychotherapy: A critical review of issues, trends and evidence. *International Journal of Psychiatry*, 1969, **7**, No. 2, 18–19.

Truax, C. B., and Carkhuff, R. R. Experimental manipulation of therapeutic conditions. *Journal of Consulting Psychology*, 1965, **29**, 119–124.

Truax, C. B., Wargo, D. G., Carkhuff, R. R., Kodman, F., Jr., and Moles, E. A. Changes in self-concepts during group psychotherapy as a function of alternate sessions and vicarious therapy pretraining in institutionalized mental patients and juvenile delinquents. *Journal of Consulting Psychology*, 1966, **30**, 309–314.

Valins, S., and Ray, A. A. Effects of cognitive desensitization on avoidance behavior. *Journal of Personality and Social Psychology*, 1967, **7**, 345–350.

Whalen, C. The effects of a model and instructions on group verbal behaviors. *Journal of Consulting and Clinical Psychology*, 1969, **33**, 509–521.

Wiener, M. The effects of two experimental counseling techniques on performance impaired by induced stress. *Journal of Abnormal and Social Psychology*, 1955, **51**, 565–572.

Williams, J. Conditioning of verbalization: A review. *Psychological Bulletin*, 1964, **62**, 383–393.

Wolpe, J. *Psychotherapy by reciprocal inhibition*. Stanford: Stanford University Press, 1958.

Zeisset, R. M. Desensitization and relaxation in the modification of psychiatric patients' interview behavior *Journal of Abnormal Psychology*, 1968, **73**, 18–24.

Zerfas, P. G. Effects of induced expectancies and therapist activity upon patient behavior in group psychotherapy. Unpublished doctoral dissertation, Indiana University, 1965.

5

SOCIAL PSYCHOLOGICAL APPROACHES TO PSYCHOTHERAPY RESEARCH

ARNOLD P. GOLDSTEIN

NORMAN R. SIMONSON

SYRACUSE UNIVERSITY

INTRODUCTION

Future historians might well regard the past decade and a half as the beginning of a major period of revisionism in psychotherapy. This revisionism began with the infusion of behavioral science into the theory and practice of psychotherapy. Investigators introduced their traditions and techniques of research to psychotherapy and suggested that they be used to examine the nature of the outcome and the process of therapy. In addition to a tradition of research, the theoretical constructs and substantive findings of all branches of behavioral science became available for use in the conceptualization and development of psychotherapy.

No doubt, historians will contend that certain sectors of a well-entrenched and powerful "psychotherapy establishment" welcomed neither the research orientation nor the theory and substantive findings of behavioral science. Some segments of the "establishment" regarded these scientists as interlopers who were not qualified to either practice or study psychotherapy. However, despite the occasionally less than warm acceptance of behavioral scientists into the domain of psychotherapy, their traditions took root, began to flourish, and eventually became influential. Some of their contributions were integrated directly into the fairly traditional and slowly evolving mainstream of psychotherapeutic thought. Other theories and substantive research findings

154

formed the core of schools of therapy that initially rivaled the more traditional modes of psychotherapy. These dissenting groups grew, obtained a broader base of support, and were gradually integrated into the new mainstream of psychotherapy. Behavioral science, then, had a revisionary impact on psychotherapy and became part of the system through routes of competition and confrontation as well as by a more direct and moderate process of assimilation.

Hindsight allows the opportunity of commenting upon the inevitability of this revisionism. After World War II, substantial governmental support was made available for the training of clinical psychologists. The well-known Boulder Conference fixed the purpose of the training and the model of the clinical psychologist. He was to be a specialist whose training and orientation would allow him to function as both clinician and scientist. It was hoped, in fact, that this specialist could effect an integration of these separate skills and orientations. In addition to being exposed to a clinical as well as a research orientation, the clinical psychologist was to be familiar with theory and empirical findings from all branches of psychology. His training was quite different from that received by more traditional psychotherapists. The traditional psychotherapist often had a very limited research orientation and only the scantiest knowledge of theory and substantive findings in behavioral science. The emergence of the clinical psychologist, as a behavioral scientist, in the therapeutic realm increased greatly during the early part of the 1950s and no doubt contributed to the beginning of the revisionary movement.

It is understandable that some conflict between this "new man" and the more conservative sectors of the establishment occurred. One of the most publicized and particularly trenchant issues raised by behavioral scientists during the early part of the 1950s involved the question of the efficacy of traditional psychotherapy. This issue was exemplified by, if not completely expressed in, Eysenck's (1952) celebrated paper. This paper can be regarded as a major expression of dissatisfaction with the scientific status and foundation of traditional psychotherapy, of which psychoanalysis was the most common. Eysenck's paper clearly underscored both the limited scientific foundation upon which the theory and practice of psychotherapy were based and the lack of scientific inquiry that was being directed towards its evaluation. In many ways, this paper served as an impetus to the emerging spirit of revisionism and the attitudes of psychotherapists, to some extent, began to polarize. Some, of course, either rejected or ignored the position represented in Eysenck's paper and continued in their tradition in a fashion that was similar to their activities of the previous decade. Others, who were sympathetic with the traditions of empirical research, either began or continued to systematically study therapeutic phenomena. Some of the research was within the paradigm of traditional forms of therapy while other scientists, unable to accept the traditional paradigm, sought to discover or implement new models of therapy that were more compatible with their own traditions of behavioral science.

Shortly after the appearance of Eysenck's article—and the ensuing exchange and controversy—a substantial number of psychotherapy research studies were reported in the professional literature. In addition to outcome studies, an increasingly large number of process studies of therapy as well as studies of the characteristics of patients and therapists began to appear. The focus of these investigations of process, patients, and therapists made them appear not unlike some of the research being done in Social Psychology. In fact, some theoretical explanations that were offered to account for therapeutic phenomena were very much like theoretical explanations offered for social psychological phenomena. This, of course, is not surprising. If the psychotherapeutic process is conceptualized primarily as a set of interpersonal events, then it is reasonable to expect that variables which are generally important in human interaction would also be relevant to psychotherapy. The theoretical constructs regarding attitude-change conformity and small group behavior, for example, are useful for conceptualizing psychotherapeutic situations that are characterized by interpersonal relations, persuasive processes, and cognitive and affective changes. The unusual and perhaps startling observation is that there was not a substantial amount of integration and explicit coalescing of research and theory in social psychology with psychotherapy. Relatively little of the theory and research findings of social psychology was utilized to explain or conceptualize psychotherapeutic events. Virtually no extrapolatory research was conducted. Group therapy, to some extent, was influenced by the work in group dynamics. Even in this domain, however, there were almost no extrapolatory studies of group dynamic phenomena in group psychotherapy.

The fact that there was not a substantial integration of social psychology and psychotherapy during the 1950s is of considerable interest to us. It is important because we advocate just such an integration and, as indicated, the course of research in these areas seemed to provide the opportunity for this synthesis. It would be helpful if those factors that prevented the integration of these domains could be identified.

The most tempting and immediate explanation would involve the suggestion that those concerned with psychotherapy were unfamiliar with the social psychological literature and vice versa. It seems, however, that the broad training received by psychologists makes this a not altogether complete or adequate explanation. It is likely that they would have enough passing familiarity with each others' literature so that a conceptual similarity could be identified and, if desired, pursued more extensively. It should be recalled, furthermore, that some of the professional journals of the era, such as the Journal of Abnormal and Social Psychology, published articles about psychotherapy and social psychological phenomena—side by side. Let us resist the temptation, then, to explain the lack of integration in terms of lack of familiarity and, rather, turn our attention to some of the philosophical and metatheoretical constructs that guided the development and maintained the organization of social psychology and of psychotherapy. It is possible that there were fundamental differences between these disciplines that made the integration of their concepts difficult to establish despite their apparent similarity.

One of the fundamental principles for many of the traditional insight-oriented psycho-

therapies was that it was inappropriate for therapy to involve any "manipulation" of a patient's environment. This prohibition included the therapist's behavior during the therapy session as well as any arrangements or alterations in the patient's daily life. This position was strongly advocated by many therapists and, for some, it virtually assumed the status of a taboo. A variety of rationales, involving both technical and ethical considerations, were offered for this taboo. Some argued that any therapeutic manipulation would necessarily be predicated upon value judgments made by the therapist. This would be unfair to the patient because, it was suggested, such a procedure would violate his integrity, interfere with his independence, and otherwise encourage a mechanistic view of human beings. From a technical point of view, it was contended that manipulative procedures would encourage an undesirable degree of patient dependence on the therapist and/or otherwise interfere with "transference" or similar processes. Still others believed that the nature of an individual's pathology and the treatment for these disorders were such that the utilization of environmental manipulations was useless and therefore inappropriate as a therapeutic intervention.

A second important assumption made by many psychotherapists was that overt disordered behavior was a symptom or some reflection of an underlying disordered process. The overt behavior was not, itself, the disorder. Accordingly, the focus of the therapeutic intervention, as well as its goal, did not typically involve a direct attempt to modify the disordered overt behavior. The goal was to correct the underlying process which, when modified, would then result in a disappearance or diminution of the troublesome overt behavior. Attempts to deal directly with the disordered behavior were generally regarded as inappropriate.

A third important assumption, which actually follows directly from the second, concerns the process of the modification of disordered behavior. Basically, it was tacitly assumed that cognitive and affective changes were antecedent to and the cause of changes in overt behavior. This assumption derived basically from a theory of psychopathology that regarded overt behavior as a symptomatic expression of a disordered underlying process. The focus of therapeutic interventions was on these affective and cognitive processes, which were often quite covert, and it was expected that a change in these processes would result in a change in overt behavior. The suggestion that a change in overt behavior could lead to a change in affective cognitive processes was alien to traditional forms of therapy. In addition to these three fundamental issues—manipulation, symptomatic focus and sequence of change—the general nature of psychotherapeutic theory might also be appropriate to consider. The theoretical aspects of most traditional psychotherapies involved elaborate and complex sets of relationships among theoretical constructs in vast nomological networks. Often there were comparatively few empirical referents, and the relationship between these referents and the nomological network was often not readily observable. The traditional psychotherapist, it appears, was neither reluctant to remain in a world of abstract thought nor preoccupied with problems of operationalism.

Now let us direct our attention to the nature of social psychology during this period. An important aspect of social psychology was the firm establishment of an empirical tradition that increasingly based its research on experimental studies of social psychological phenomena. These studies often involved the creation of miniature situations in laboratory or quasi-laboratory contexts, using experimental control and systematic manipulation of independent variables. This tradition stemmed most directly from the research of Kurt Lewin and his associates, as well as other social psychological research conducted during World War II. The most critical feature of this research, for our present purposes, was the emphasis placed on the experimental control and manipulation of independent variables and experimental situations.

A second feature that characterized much social psychology, at least until the late 1950s, derived from its emphasis on experimental empiricism. Its theoretical constructs (in comparison with psychotherapeutic theory) were rather directly and explicitly related to empirical referents. This close relationship between constructs and empirical referents moderated theory construction and prevented it from becoming as abstract and perhaps as unbridled as therapy theory. Another development in social psychology involved research findings regarding the role of an individual's overt behavior as a change agent for his own cognitive processes. Essentially, these studies explored the role of behavior change as an antecedent to rather than as a consequence of cognitive change. Investigations of the effect of overt behavior on such cognitive processes as attitude change became an important factor in the development of several theories of cognitive consistency. It should be further noted that in these studies the "overt behavior" was under direct experimental control and, clearly, was manipulated. In fact, it was often manipulated in a fashion that required a subject to behave in a manner inconsistent with or contrary to his private beliefs.

This summary of some of the characteristics of psychotherapy and social psychology during the 1950s thus suggests some of the reasons for the non-occurrence of an incorporation of social psychological theory and research findings into the mainstream of psychotherapeutic thought. For, while it is certainly true that many of the phenomena studied by the social psychologist were relevant or critical for the psychotherapist, some of the philosophical beliefs and methodological differences between these groups made integration virtually impossible.

One of the most compelling features that emerges from the comparison of social psychology and psychotherapy concerns the role of manipulative procedures. On the one hand, a major aspect of the scientific progress of social psychology involved the use of experimental procedures that employed the systematic manipulation of independent variables in carefully controlled contexts. At the same time, psychotherapists would neither permit, nor admit to, the use of manipulative procedures. Clearly then, despite any demonstrated efficacy of a technique for increasing interpersonal attraction, enhancing persuasibility, and the like, the psychotherapist could not adopt these procedures. Thus a direct extrapolation of these techniques to a clinical context would be impossible to implement, despite any similarity of phenomena or demonstrated efficacy of any technique. The routinely employed procedure of social psychologists, a procedure upon which their empirical foundation was based, involved procedures that were totally unacceptable to psychotherapists.

Although the direct implementation of manipulative techniques by psychotherapists was impossible, one might ask whether the therapist might have been able to incorporate some of the results of manipulative research into his general theory of psychotherapy. Such results might have helped to provide an empirical basis for the understanding of the nature of certain aspects of therapy, even though specific manipulative techniques did not become a part of therapeutic procedure. Two factors, however, might have decreased the probability that the psychotherapist would incorporate these findings into his general theoretical framework. First, and most critical, a "negative halo" might have surrounded experimental social psychology as far as psychotherapists were concerned. Because of their very strong negative feelings regarding the use of manipulative techniques, they might have rejected any and all aspects of such research. Secondly, they might have argued that the systematic manipulation of variables in an experimental context created situations that were artificial and not applicable to psychotherapeutic encounters. This second factor also seems to reflect their general disdain for manipulative techniques—a disdain that might have resulted in a loss of the baby along with the bath water.

It should also be recalled that experimental social psychology was a relatively recent development, and was attempting during its early years to obtain a respectable scientific identity. This meant, during the 1950s, that care was taken to concretely specify variables and operations and, more generally, such research was modeled after the more established areas of psychological inquiry. There was, despite the utilization of such concepts as attitude, attraction, and conformity, a strong spirit of behaviorism in this domain. Dependent variables and measures, as previously indicated, were carefully specified and operationalized for research purposes. It is possible that psychotherapists, whose primary concern was with underlying processes and covert behavior, could not accept the social psychologists' reliance on observable and specifiable behavior as the only legitimate indices of underlying processes. They might have believed that the specified dependent measures did not adequately reflect the very complex processes that characterized interactions in psychotherapy.

A third feature of social psychology was a trend in research that involved the role of overt behavior in attitude change studies. The research area was role playing, and it involved the attempt to alter cognitive processes, such as attitudes, through a direct manipulation of overt behavior. Sometimes this involved the requirement that a subject behave in a way that was not congruent with his private attitudes or beliefs. These studies sought to demonstrate that behaving in a certain manner would result in a modification of covert cognitive processes. This procedure assumes that cognitive change might occur as a consequent of rather than an antecedent to behavior change—a position that is the converse of the one maintained by traditional psychotherapists.

It might be further noted that during the 1950s social psychology was characterized by an empiricism that moderated theory development, while psychotherapeutic theory was highly elaborated and complex. These different levels of involvement in and complexity of theory construction could have inhibited a synthesis or integration of concepts. This particular problem began to disappear towards the end of the 1950s, with the advent of the more cognitively oriented social psychological theories. In fact, it should be noted that a recent attempt to integrate social psychological and psychotherapeutic systems (Goldstein, Heller, and Sechrest, 1966) depended to a great extent on the application of theories of cognitive dissonance to psychotherapeutic phenomena.

Thus, it seems probable that philosophical, metatheoretical, and methodological differences between social psychology and psychotherapy—manipulation, symptomatic focus, change sequence, and theory development—prevented a successful integration of these disciplines despite a similarity of subject matter. At the present time, however, we are suggesting that such an integration is more likely to be successful—more likely to appeal to psychotherapists than would have been the case during the 1950s. Several major assumptions about the nature of psychotherapy have been modified in recent years. This change is due primarily to the introduction of behavior therapy and its subsequent impact on the mainstream of psychotherapeutic thought.

The advent of the behavior therapies involved a radical departure from the more traditional modes of therapy. Some of the most basic assumptions upon which the behavior therapies were predicated were in direct conflict with the underlying assumptions and theory of traditional psychotherapy. The behavior therapies have had an impact on a substantial number of psychotherapists and have thereby altered the psychotherapeutic *Zeitgeist* in a fashion that has made it more compatible with the social psychological tradition. The assumptions and emphases of the behavior therapies are well known and we shall merely enumerate them at this time.

Firstly, the behavior therapies directly and specifically utilize manipulative techniques and procedures. This is true for all behavior therapies. Their founders and practitioners do not believe that manipulation is therapeutically or ethically "wrong," and thus they feel no need to be apologetic for these procedures.

Secondly, there is a specific emphasis on the overt behavior of an individual as opposed to an emphasis on underlying covert processes. This involves a rejection of the traditional model, which regards overt behavior as merely an indicant, reflection, or symbolic expression of an underlying disordered process. It also demands that the therapist be able to identify and specify the aspects of the patient's overt behavior that he will attempt to modify.

Thirdly, the behavior therapies were in large measure derived from and are based upon theories and research from that branch of psychology concerned with learning and conditioning. This is important for a number of reasons. Such a foundation brings with it a very strong tradition of research and explicitly indicates that the development of the behavior therapies should be guided by research findings.

While it is true that research into psychotherapy had been occurring prior to this time, the introduction of the behavior therapies further reinforced its continuation and its growth. The behavior therapies also represent a major attempt to systematically apply, on a very large scale, the theory, research, and methodology of a branch of behavioral science to psychotherapy. Its success, we believe, might invite attempts to systematically apply the theory and research of other branches of behavioral science.

A final difference between traditional psychotherapy and the behavior therapies involves the order of change sequences in the modification of behavior. Briefly, certain behavior therapies are constructed in a fashion in which the changes in overt behavior are antecedent to the changes in cognitive processes—quite the reverse of traditional psychotherapy. Traditional psychotherapy, as indicated, is conceptualized in a fashion that suggests that changes in overt behavior are consequents of cognitive change. No doubt, both of these processes can occur— the question is which of the two orders is the most effective change agent. The advent of the behavior therapies has made this a real question for therapists to consider—a number of years ago this question wasn't even raised.

Clearly, the assumptions and procedures employed by the behavior therapies are more compatible with social psychology than were the assumptions of the more traditional psychotherapies. Fortunately, the behavior therapies have also made a major impact on therapy and have, to some extent, modified the prevailing attitudes, beliefs, and implicit assumptions of many psychotherapists. It is the belief and hope of the present authors that these alterations in the attitudes and beliefs of psychotherapists will facilitate a greater exchange between them and social psychologists.

The remainder of this chapter seeks to demonstrate, in concrete form, the beginnings of this exchange. First we will present in detail one research program that is seeking to better understand and utilize the psychotherapeutic relationship by basing its hypotheses upon social psychological studies of interpersonal attraction. In succeeding sections, psychotherapeutic dimensions involving role playing and group dynamics are examined, along with their counterpart social psychological research.

INTERPERSONAL ATTRACTION AND THE PSYCHOTHERAPEUTIC RELATIONSHIP

Introduction

The historical development of individual psychotherapy, when viewed from a broad perspective, may be characterized in terms of the marked diversity of theoretical viewpoints put forth, the varied nature of specific techniques recommended, and, in general, the numerous different paths this development has followed. As examples of such psychotherapeutic diversity, one may point to the wide variety of basic concepts utilized to explain patient behavior, the time period of the patient's life focused upon, the nature of the therapist's interventions, overt and implicit characteristics of the tasks required of the patient, and the very language of the therapeutic give and take. Agreement on basic aspects of the therapeutic transaction by proponents of different approaches is far less common. On one point, however, the degree of both theoretical and operational convergence is very marked, namely the centrality accorded the interpersonal relationship between therapist and patient. The long-standing psychoanalytic emphasis upon transference and, more recently, countertransference effects; the relationship focus in Snyder's (1961) more eclectic approach to psychotherapy; the major interpersonal components in Grinker's (1961) transactional model of therapy; Jackson's (1961) interactional approach and Wolberg's (1954) directive form of treatment; and Rogerian (1961) concern with unconditional positive regard are but examples of the pervading therapeutic importance that has been accorded the patient-therapist relationship. It may also be noted in this context that interpersonal determinants of the therapeutic outcome have yet to be shown to be any less central to the success of the behavior therapies. Perhaps it will suffice here to place ourselves in agreement with Bordin (1959), who has commented (p. 235):

The key to the influence of psychotherapy on the patient is in his relationship with the therapist. Wherever psychotherapy is accepted as a significant enterprise, this statement is so widely subscribed to as to become trite. Virtually all efforts to theorize about psychotherapy are intended to describe and explain what attributes of the interactions between the therapist and the patient will account for whatever behavior change results.

It is clear then that the vast majority of theoretical approaches to psychotherapy, despite their divergence on other grounds, come together in their common emphasis on interpersonal constructs mediating between patient and therapist. However, the specific nature of these constructs remains unclear, and hence their more effective use is retarded. Transference, countertransference, interaction, transaction, relationship—these are the terms of primary concern here. Not only does their meaning differ in ways that remain to be clarified, but different writers use the same term to include differing ranges of phenomena.

A directly analogous picture emerges when one leaves the domain of theoretical statements about the therapy relationship to examine research dealing with its impact upon the therapeutic outcome. In a manner strikingly parallel to the theoretical status of "relationship," outcome studies conducted by Bown (1954), Hunt et al. (1959), Parloff (1961), Holt and Luborsky (1952), Sapolsky (1965), Truax (1961), Van der Veen (1965), and others combine to present an unequivocal demonstration of a major, positive influence of the therapy relationship upon treatment outcome. Equally apparent, however, is the scant degree of overlap in these studies in their operational definitions of "relationship." Personal Reaction Questionnaires, Q sorts, therapist ratings, Client and Therapist Affect Scales, the Picture Impressions Test, and need scales are among the several such research definitions which have been used.

Of what consequence, one may ask, is the diversity and frequent ambiguity of these various research and theoretical definitions of relationship? Since research and clinical experience combine to unequivocally demonstrate its therapeutic centrality, why need one be concerned about a lack of precision and agreement in "its" definition? Our personal view of contemporary psychotherapy is of a set of processes that are grossly inefficient in several major respects. Examples of such inefficiency are the excessive length of treatment, the grossly inadequate number of patients seen when compared with the numbers for whom psychological intervention is needed, the several classes of persons excluded from treatment altogether solely on the basis of clinical lore, and the unreasoned yielding to traditionalism by most therapeutic practitioners. If greater precision in definition and use of major psychotherapeutic variables can be achieved, treatment can be shortened, more patients can participate, a broader range of persons can be viewed as acceptable in terms of their potential for change and, of greatest consequence, the development of completely new approaches to altering patient behavior can be encouraged. It is with these aims that this section offers a start at reconceptualizing the meaning and therapeutic uses of the psychotherapeutic relationship.

At the heart of this reconceptualization lies the social-psychological construct, interpersonal attraction. We choose here to focus almost exclusively upon interpersonal attraction as the most meaningful way of viewing the therapist-patient relationship, not because of any greater parsimony implied by the construct but because, as we shall attempt to demonstrate, viewing the psychotherapeutic relationship in this manner enables us to bring to bear upon relationship a wide variety of social-psychological findings relevant to antecedents and consequents of interpersonal attraction. If research should demonstrate the appropriateness of extrapolating these parameters of interpersonal attraction from the social-psychological laboratory to the psychotherapeutic setting, then we have greatly increased our ability to understand and manipulate the therapist-patient relationship toward psychotherapeutic ends. The investigations discussed below are all concrete expressions of this extrapolatory research philosophy. These studies constitute a

research program currently being conducted by the senior author and his students.[1,2] Certain dimensions of the research philosophy underlying this series of studies should be made explicit. In keeping with the extrapolatory orientation outlined above, the hypotheses in all the studies to be discussed grew from social-psychological investigations of interpersonal attraction and had, as their clinical intent, developing procedures for enhancing the favorableness of the therapist-patient relationship. Operationally, this involved translating procedures antecedent to interpersonal attraction in the social-psychological laboratory to the clinical context and discerning if they served a similar attraction-enhancing effect. To maximize the generality or external validity of whatever findings emerge from this program, we have not only sampled varying kinds of patients and therapists, but added into our "mix" a variety of experimental designs and treatment settings. Thus, several of our studies are appropriately termed analogue studies, while several others were conducted in situ. However, our concern with broad external validity notwithstanding, we are increasingly focusing our relationship-enhancing efforts on those types of patients who, in a naturalistic sense, typically do *not* form positive therapeutic relationships. Note, thus, our increasing emphasis on prison, alcoholic clinic, mental hospital, and community psychiatric clinic settings and our decreasing emphasis on college student patient populations. Schofield (1964) has noted the major degree to which contemporary psychotherapists prefer to work with the YAVIS patient—young, attractive, verbal, intelligent, and successful. That is, patients who characteristically and without *external* intervention, can form a positive therapeutic relationship. We might, contrastingly, suggest that the ultimate interest of our research program is the HOUND patient—homely, old, unattractive, nonverbal and dumb.

The temporal focus in all the studies discussed below is the candidacy and initial stages of psychotherapy. Our concern is with develop-

[1] This research has been supported in part by Grant #MH–1072, from the National Institute of Mental Health, U.S. Public Health Service.

[2] The senior author would like to express his deep

appreciation to the many students who have been involved in this research program, for both their many cogent ideas and their continued enthusiasm and commitment to it.

ing techniques for "hooking" patients, that is, for maximizing the favorableness of the initial relationship so that the patient, at minimum, returns for further sessions and, more maximally, is open to the therapist's influence attempts. We propose no *direct* relationship between *initial* patient attraction to his therapist and the subsequent therapy outcome. Instead, we view the initial relationship as a possible potentiator or catalyst whose consequents can lead to a more favorable outcome. Specifically, and the reader will note in several studies below that we are now focusing on those processes which we hypothesize to intervene between initial attraction and favorable outcome, we speak here of openness to therapist influence attempts, disclosure, perceived similarity, self-exploration, and persuasibility. We are continuing along these lines, hopefully moving ever closer to relating our procedures to outcome criteria via these intervening processes.

Structuring

Our first ongoing series of investigations seeks to increase patient attraction to the therapist via communication to the patient, pretherapy, of messages designed to be attraction-enhancing. Perhaps one of the most frequently replicated social-psychological findings is the manner in which interpersonal attraction increases receptivity to interpersonal influence. The more A likes B, the more A is willing to be influenced by B. One of the early experimental tests of this predicted effect was conducted by Back (1951). His subjects were constituted into randomly assigned pairs and, prior to their meeting, were structured by Back for either high or low within-pair attraction. This structuring, which subsequent sociometric measurement indicated was successful, was oriented in terms of either personal liking for the future partner, task outcome, or group prestige. Prior to meeting with his partner, each subject was given a set of three pictures about which he was to write a story. Although each subject was led to believe that he and his partner had responded to the same set of pictures, there were in fact slight differences between the sets. After completion of their initial story writing, members of each pair were brought together for a discussion that was structured as an opportunity to improve

their own stories. Following this discussion, and again working apart, each subject rewrote his stories as he wished. The criterion, interpersonal influence, was reliably measured in terms of changes from the preliminary to the final stories, which were in the direction of the subject's partner's stories. Results demonstrated significantly more influence attempts and successful influence in the high attraction conditions. Burdick and Burnes (1958), Gerard (1954), Gordon (1952), Rasmussen and Zander (1954), Sapolsky (1960), Seashore (1954), and others have all independently reported concurring results. Thus, we may conclude that in the social-psychological laboratory, interpersonal attraction has a direct and robust maximizing effect upon openness to interpersonal influence. As such, it made uncommonly good sense to us to begin our extrapolatory research efforts by examining this finding in a clinical treatment setting. Our major hypothesis predicted that patients led to have high attraction toward their psychotherapist would be more receptive to the latter's influence attempts than would patients in whom low attraction to the therapist was induced. Thus, not only did we seek to examine in a psychotherapeutic context a basic and often replicated social psychological finding, but furthermore, we did so by paralleling, in effect, the social-psychological experimental procedures involved. Our subjects were 82 university students seen for psychotherapy at our Psychological Center. Five experimental conditions were constituted. As in Back's (1951) original laboratory study, these were high and low induced attraction based on the degree to which the patient would like the therapist as a person; high and low induced attraction based on the probable success of the therapy; and a control condition. All patients participated in an intake interview and a pretherapy testing session—the last of which provided the fulcrum for our structuring of attraction. For example, in our first condition (high attraction based upon liking the therapist), the last test given was called the Patient-Therapist Matching Scale, a scale consisting of items describing ways in which a therapist might behave during a therapy interview. Scale instructions were such that the respondent was requested to rate each statement in terms of how strongly he wished his as-yet-unmet therapist to behave in the manner described. In short, the scale permitted the patient to indicate the kind of therapist with whom he'd like to work. Following a fictitious scoring procedure, the intaker then delivered the high-attraction structuring to the patient:

We have carefully examined the tests you took in order to assign you to a therapist with whom you would like to work most. We usually can't match a patient and therapist the way they want most, but for you we have almost exactly the kind of therapist you described. (Intaker then shows the patient how well his Matching Scale matches one purportedly representing a composite of the judgments of many patients already seen by the therapist to whom he is to be assigned). As a matter of fact, the matching of the kind of person you wanted to work with and the kind of person your therapist is, is so close that it hardly ever happens. What's even more, he has often described the kind of patient he likes to work with most as someone just like you in many respects. You two should get along extremely well.

Our patients assigned to the low attraction (based on liking the therapist) condition were treated identically, save for the structuring tag line which was: "Frankly, we don't have anyone on our staff who fits your description closely, but Mr. —— is like your description in some ways. You and he will probably get along all right." Whereas the basis for manipulating attraction in the conditions just described was the degree to which the patient would like his therapist, the remaining experimental conditions revolved around the supposed likelihood that a given therapist would (high attraction) or would not (low attraction) be especially able to help resolve the patient's specific presenting problems.

It should be noted that patient assignment to both experimental condition and therapist were randomly conducted. The patient, following attraction structuring, then met with his therapist for the initial therapy interview. Each interview tape was then subjected to content and timing analyses according to procedures developed by Ashby et al. (1957) and Mahl (1956). These analyses provided our several dependent variable measures of patient openness to therapist influence.

Our measures of interpersonal attraction in this investigation, as well as in those to be discussed below, included (but were not limited to) the Picture Impressions Test (Libo, 1956), which is a projective technique consisting of four plates depicting therapylike situations to which the patient is requested to respond in a manner analogous to TAT administration; the Client's Personal Reaction Questionnaire, a scale developed by Ashby et al. (1957) as a measure of the client's evaluation of the therapy relationship; and the Therapist's Personal Reaction Questionnaire, an analogous relationship evaluation completed by the psychotherapist.

Our results were as follows. A series of analyses demonstrated that *as a group* our attraction inductions were unsuccessful. More specifically, while our patients processed through either type of high attraction structuring did indeed increase in attraction toward their therapist, patients structured for what we viewed as "low" attraction did not respond accordingly. Their view of their therapist, while not as favorable as was true for patients structured for high attraction, nevertheless proved more favorable than was the case for our nonstructured controls. When one considers our exact attraction-induction instructions, as they compare with those typically used in the social-psychological laboratory, a plausible basis for our failure here emerges. Our structuring for high attraction paralleled directly those found in the laboratory setting, and our results came very close to doing so also. Our low-attraction structuring, in contrast, has to materially depart from that typically provided in the laboratory context. There, subjects are characteristically told that they "will not like their partners," "will have trouble getting along with them," and so forth. We felt bound by ethical considerations to modify and moderate such low attraction structuring as it was to be delivered by us, not to laboratory subjects, but instead to psychotherapy patients. Thus we have tentatively inferred that our moderating of low-attraction structuring seriously truncated the potential spread in attraction between our high and low conditions and, accordingly, prevented us from examining in the manner we had planned the effects of interpersonal attraction upon interpersonal influence.

Up to this point our focus has been upon "induced" attraction, that is, the level of attraction a patient may hold toward his therapist as a result of our experimental structuring. A second type of attraction is relevant, however. We speak here of what might be termed "resultant" attraction, that is, the attraction with which a patient views his therapist as a result of their initial therapeutic session. The next set of questions we addressed to the data of this first study made use of our information on patient resultant attraction and sought in correlational terms to examine the attraction-influence relationship more naturalistically. Our results indicated that when patient attraction to the therapist is high, the patient (1) is less covertly resistive, (2) talks more, (3) is self-descriptively sicker, and (4) has more favorable prognostic expectancies for himself. Correspondingly, the more attracted the therapist is to the patient, (1) the more the patient talks, (2) the more open he is in the content of his communications, and (3) the less covertly and overtly resistive he is. We have here, therefore, correlational support for the association of interpersonal attraction and interpersonal influence.

This study's second hypothesis, also extrapolatory in nature, grew from Jones and Thibaut's (1958) classification of two-person interactions, and, in particular, their discussion of reciprocally contingent relationships. In such relationships, both participants function as variable responders, each alert to the incoming cues from the other, and each in turn acting as a partial cause of the other's behavior. In psychotherapy, this model may be expressed in part by the position that the therapist's behavior, rather than being largely standardized across a series of patients, is in large measure a function of specific characteristics of patients—such as their attraction to the therapist. *Thus, we hypothesized, and found support for, the prediction that patients highly attracted to their therapist would be rated as more attractive by their therapist than would patients having low attraction to their therapist— a finding that we have replicated in three other investigations in this series.* We may note in passing that this finding is consistent with the psychoanalytic law of "talion," in which transference and countertransference are held to covary. In general terms, therefore, we view the tests of our two hypotheses as providing

initial, tentative evidence to underscore the degree to which attraction remains a potentially valuable means of both defining and examining the psychotherapeutic relationship.

Again, basing both our hypotheses and experimental procedures on social-psychological findings, Land (1966), in a second attraction structuring study, drew on the attitude change studies reported by Walster and Festinger (1962) and Brock and Becker (1965). In each of these investigations, a comparison was made of two methods of presenting the study's persuasive message to subjects. In both conditions, E delivered the message verbally to an accomplice with the audio arrangement such that Ss, who were behind a one-way mirror, could also hear it. In the regular-hearing condition, all Ss were told that the discussants knew that they (the Ss) were listening. In the overhearing condition, Ss were led to believe that E and his listener did *not* know the Ss were listening in. In both studies, Ss who overheard the message changed on the relevant attitude significantly more than did Ss in the regular-hearing conditions.

The relevant attitude dimension in Land's study, as in almost all our other investigations, was patient attraction to the therapist. His subjects were 48 VA psychiatric patients who were assigned to four experimental conditions. At the start of the experiment each patient was told:

Like most VA hospitals, we do a lot of research trying to find better ways to help patients. Right now, on the 7th floor, a group of doctors from the VA Central Office are doing some research on interviewing. They are trying to find out something about the effectiveness of having two doctors at the same time talk with one patient. Now many people have pointed out that sometimes patients seem to understand other patients better than doctors do and we'd like to find out how that works. So for this study, we're asking 8th floor patients to listen in on one of the experimental interviews going on on 7 and then check off their opinions on a checklist.

Regular - hearing - condition patients, and patients in the corresponding control group, were told: "Of course, both the interviewers and the patient know you'll be listening in." Patients in the overhearing experimental and control groups were told: "Of course, the interviewers and the patient don't know you're listening in today." The patients then put on earphones which purportedly were connected to the 7th floor interview room, but which in actuality were connected to a tape recorder. The tape thus played to the two control groups (regular and overhearing) consisted of two psychiatrists interviewing a patient. All three taped voices were in actuality actors. The task requested of all patients after listening to the tape involved rating various characteristics of the interviewers and the interview conducted by them. The procedure for the two experimental conditions was identical to that described above, except that when the experimental-group patients put on the earphones, they heard only the two psychiatrist-actors chatting, and were led to believe that the patient hadn't arrived yet. This discussion between the psychiatrist-actors dealt with the rewards to patients for co-operating with the hospital staff, the positive attitudes of the staff toward the patients, and the like—that is, it was our persuasive message designed to be attraction-enhancing.

Our data analyses yielded no difference between conditions. That is, none of our several change measures of attraction indicated over-hearing to be more effective than regular delivery of the persuasive message, nor was the persuasive message effective independent of condition. Our single significant finding was of a positive association *across* conditions between patient attraction toward the interviewers and independent behavioral ratings obtained from ward nurses of patient cooperativeness.

Perhaps a major conclusion one might draw from the outcome of this investigation relates to the manner in which severe psychopathology quite possibly functions as a limiting parameter on the appropriateness of extrapolatory research of the type we have been examining. Shakow (1963), Buss (1966), McGhie and Chapman (1961), and others, in their investigations of cognitive function in schizophrenics (who constituted a large proportion of this study's sample), have demonstrated the difficulty often experienced by such subjects in handling cognitive and perceptual tasks adequately. Processes of over-inclusion, interpenetration, perseveration, and associative interference have been identified and may be pointed to by us as a probable basis for the failure of our subjects to

receive, process, and respond to our persuasive communications in a manner similar to that found by those using normal subjects in the social-psychological laboratory.

Greenberg (1968) operationalized yet a different structuring approach to attraction-enhancement. His social-psychological, extrapolatory base was studies by Asch (1946), Kelley (1950), Secord (1958), and others dealing with the manipulation of first-impression formation. Asch (1946), for example, presented two groups of subjects with identical lists of personality traits, except that one list included the trait "warm," while "cold" appeared in the other. *S*s were required to write personality sketches of the two persons described by the trait lists. Consistent differences emerged in the sketches, which clearly appeared to be associated with the warm versus cold structuring. Kelley (1950) built upon Asch's results by adding behavioral dependent variable dimensions. He arranged to have a class conducted by an instructor who had previously been described to half the students in terms of a trait list that included "warm," and to the other half with the same list, substituting the trait "cold." The students structured "warm" not only rated the instructor as more sociable, considerate, informal, and humorous, but also participated in the class discussion significantly more than did their classmates receiving "cold" structuring. Greenberg (1968) varied this warm-cold dimension, as well as experienced-inexperienced structuring in his investigation. His subjects, 112 undergraduates, were randomly assigned to the four experimental conditions thus constituted. The experimental task required *S*s to listen to a taped therapy session and rate the taped therapist on attractiveness and persuasibility dimensions. The tape used was especially constructed for the investigation so that it elicited, in prejudging, neutral judgments of the therapist on both the warm-cold and experienced-inexperienced dimensions. Immediately prior to listening to the tape, *S*s were structured both to make the procedures credible and, then, on the two dimensions predicted to be attraction-relevant. For example, *S*s assigned to the warm-experienced condition were told:

In recent years more and more people experiencing emotional and psychological problems have been seeking help from psychotherapists. We are interested in learning more about psychotherapy and the reactions of people to this treatment. Therefore, we are going to play a tape of part of an actual psychotherapy session that took place in a large city other than Syracuse and ask for your reactions to it. As you listen to the tape we would like you to put yourself in the place of the patient and imagine how you, as the patient, would react to this particular session.

The patient in this session is a college student at a large university who sought help after finding, among other things, that he was having increasing difficulty making decisions.

The therapist has been engaged in the practice of therapy for over twenty years and has lectured and taught at some of the country's leading universities and medical schools. Questionnaires submitted to the therapist's colleagues seem to reveal that he is a rather warm person, industrious, critical, practical and determined.

Remember to try to put yourself in the patient's place as you listen to the tape.

Greenberg's (1968) results strongly supported the hypothesis that Ss structured warm or experienced, as opposed to cold or inexperienced, were more attracted to the therapist, were more receptive to his influence-attempts, and evaluated his work more positively. Furthermore, Ss structured warm, rather than cold, were more willing to commit themselves to actually meeting with the therapist when told he was probably coming to campus, and were more persuaded by his communications as measured by an opinion shift questionnaire. It is worth noting that not only was Greenberg's demonstration of the effects of warm-cold structuring on attraction quite robust, but also that Simonson (1968), in a series of studies using college student Ss, and independent of the research program reported here, has successfully replicated and extended Greenberg's findings.

We noted earlier our intent in this research program to focus increasingly upon patients who naturalistically find it very difficult to form a positive psychotherapeutic relationship—to shift, as it were, from YAVIS to HOUND patients. In an investigation responsive to this sentiment, Greenberg, Goldstein, and Perry sought to replicate Greenberg's findings using an in-patient psychiatric sample. The procedures of this study formed an exact replication of Greenberg's original study, with the addition of a neutral control group whose members received no structuring for therapist warmth, coldness or experience level prior to hearing the taped session. Results once again confirmed the positive effects of prestructuring for therapist warmth. Patients receiving warm structuring were significantly more receptive to the taped therapist's influence attempts than were those receiving cold structuring. Furthermore, patients structured warm were significantly both more attracted to the taped therapist and more receptive to his influence attempts than were nonstructured (neutral condition) patients.

Therapist Status

Robert Deysach, another member of our research group, conducted the first study in what is also an ongoing series dealing with the effects of manipulated therapist status on the therapist's attractiveness to patients (Deysach, 1967). In fact, it was the findings of this particular study, originally designed for somewhat different purposes, that led to our interest in therapist status. This investigation's hypothesis grew in large measure from Adam's cognitive dissonance research on inequitable reward (1961, 1962, 1963). Adam's basic paradigm has involved comparing the productivity of two groups of Ss. Both groups are paid at the same rate for their participation in the experimental procedures. One group is led to feel qualified to earn at the given rate and is thus, from the S's perspective, equitably rewarded. The other group of Ss are led to feel markedly unqualified for the task at hand and, since they are paid at the same rate, are thus led to feel overcompensated or inequitably rewarded. Adams has consistently found, across a series of productivity criteria, that overcompensated Ss produce significantly more than do equitably rewarded Ss—a finding that he has meaningfully explained in terms of the arousal and reduction of cognitive dissonance. Since cognitive dissonance is also reducible by an increased liking for or attraction toward the dissonant position, Deysach included in his design the overcompensated and equitably compensated conditions suggested by Adam's research. More concretely, shortly before the close of the initial interview with the clients assigned to the inequitable reward condition, the therapist picked up his office phone, "called" the clinic secretary, and said to her:

Do you people up front have some coffee and donuts today? How about bringing a donut and a cup back here? You don't mind doing me a favor just once, do you? I'll expect to pay you, of course. No, it's not for myself, I just thought I'd like to buy one for (name) . . . Okay, could you check and see how long it will take? (aside to client) I've never tried this before and I think I took her by surprise. I just felt you might like some refreshments, but it . . . (to secretary) What? . . . How long will it take? . . . I guess we'll have to forget about it then. Thanks a lot anyway. (to client) I wish I had called earlier. Now, where were we?

Thus, in this, the inequitable reward condition, the therapist seeks to lead the client to believe an attempt has been made to single him out for an admittedly small but perhaps consequential reward and that the procedure is an unusual if not unique therapist behavior instituted in the client's behalf.

Clients in the equitable reward condition were treated identically, save for the fact that the therapist communicated the usualness and not uniqueness of the reward procedure, that is, "I've made it a practice with every one of the clients I see to finish our session with some coffee and a donut if I can." Our third experimental group, the reverse reward condition, was like the second in terms of purported usualness of the procedure involved, but in this instance it was made clear that the coffee and donut were for the therapist, and not the client. Finally, we also had a control, or nonreward group, for whom no reward procedure intervened during the initial interview.

Our experimental results were unequivocal but surprising. In neither of the conditions in which the client was to be rewarded was there an increment in attraction greater than for our control patients. However, when the therapist was to receive the coffee and donut, patient attraction to him increased to a very marked degree. Why the reverse-reward (therapist-reward) condition had such a strong maximizing effect on patient attraction we do not know, and can simply offer the speculation that

the effect may be related to the possible manner in which the experimental procedure involved enhanced the generalized importance of the therapist in the client's eyes, that is, a "status-spread effect."

In addition to our criteria of patient attraction, this investigation, paralleling Adam's research, examined dependent variable measures of patient productivity. Our results on these measures were consistent with cognitive dissonance theory. More specifically, inequitably rewarded patients chose to write a significantly greater number of TAT stories than did equitably rewarded patients when told that such stories might help their therapist organize their tests better and that they could respond to as many or as few TAT cards as they wished.

As noted above, we suspect that the relationship-enhancement in Deysach's study may be due to a "status-spread effect." That is, procedures that maximize the therapist's status in the patient's eyes may be causative here. This speculation gains credence from a partially successful replication of Deysach's major findings reported by Roth (1967), and by the trends of a third "status-spread" investigation— one that operationalized status quite differently than had the first two studies. Concretely, Goldstein and Walker, working in a vocational counseling center, had the three participating counselors press a buzzer under their desks when they felt there were five minutes remaining in their initial interview with a given client. The buzzer sounded in an office on the same floor, thus activating a research assistant to walk down the hall to the counselor's office. In what we termed the interruption-acceptance and interruption-rejection conditions, the interruptor (research assistant) knocked on the door of the counselor's office and, when it was opened by the counselor, the interruptor began engaging him in a conversation regarding a routine Center matter. In the interruption-rejection condition the counselor broke into the interruptor's statement and said:

Don't you see I have a client now? (Points to Do Not Disturb sign) You shouldn't just barge in like this. I thought you would know better. I'll see you later. (Counselor closes door firmly without waiting for reply from interruptor).

In the interruption-acceptance condition (that is, status-spread) the counselor participated pleasantly in three to four minutes of conversation with the interruptor and did not apologize to the client for doing so. In addition to these two conditions and a no-interruption control group, the investigators included in their design a super-status spread condition (chutzpah condition), in which the research assistant engaged yet another person in a rather loud conversation in the hallway outside the counselor's office, and the counselor got up and sought out the interruptor. Between condition differences on client attraction to his counselor were not significant, but were in the order predicted, that is, sought, accepted, rejected, control.

The results of these three "status" investigations were, we felt, sufficiently promising that a study in which therapist status was varied more fully and more systematically seemed appropriate. Since Sanford (1950), Medalia (1955) and others have found that subject authoritarianism influences his perception of the reactions to leader status, Sabalis (1968), the principal investigator for this study, used high and low authoritarian subjects. *E* conducted a structured interview centered around the Picture Impressions Test with all subjects. For half the high and half the low authoritarian *S*s, *E* presented himself as an undergraduate doing a senior thesis study. His clothes, office, and general behavior were all consistent with this low-status set. The other subjects participated in the same task, with the *same E* who, however, presented himself as a research professor and was dressed, titled, roomed, and in general behaved in a high status manner. Our usual postinterview relationship measures were obtained. The study's major predictions were that high interviewer status would be more attraction-enhancing than low interviewer status, and that this effect would be more pronounced for the high authoritarian subjects. This latter prediction was confirmed with regard to *S*'s attraction to the task, that is, psychological testing, but not with regard to his attraction toward *E*. Stated otherwise, on the measure of attraction to testing, high-authoritarian *S*s under the high-status condition, and low-authoritarian *S*s under the low-status con-

dition, yielded significantly higher attraction to testing scores than did high authoritarians under low status or low authoritarians under high status. A further finding was that, regardless of level of authoritarianism, *S*s seen under the high-status condition rated the interview as significantly less effortful than did those *S*s seen under the low-status condition. These investigations, in overview, are thus beginning to indicate the circumstances under which, and for which *S*s, high interviewer status can have attraction-enhancing effects.

Degree of Effort

Our research interests have also focused upon the implications for the therapeutic relationship of that series of cognitive dissonance studies which have demonstrated that the degree of pretask effort directly influences the level of task attractiveness, such that the greater the effort or difficulty, the greater the increment to attraction. Aronson and Mills (1959), in one of the early studies of this type, examined the effort-attraction relationship under the rubric, "severity of initiation." College women who had volunteered to participate in discussion groups were randomly assigned to one of three experimental conditions: (1) a severe (high-effort) initiation to the group, (2) a mild (low-effort) initiation, and (3) a control condition. As a precondition to joining the group, the severe-initiation condition *S*s were required to read aloud some material likely to cause feelings of marked embarrassment. *S*s assigned to the mild-initiation condition read material unlikely to cause embarrassment. No pre-admission procedures were required of control subjects. Each *S* then listened to a tape recording that appeared to be an ongoing discussion being conducted by the group, and next completed a questionnaire evaluating the discussion and the group members. Results provided clear support for their hypothesis. *S*s in the severe-initiation conditions perceived the group as being significantly more attractive than did either mild initiation or control subjects.

Zimbardo (1965) reports concurring results. He had 20 university students, all of whom were very much in favor of a numerical grading system, read a report that was a series of arguments against such a grading system. Half of the Ss read the report under high-effort conditions, half under low-effort conditions. Degree of effort was manipulated, respectively, in terms of a relatively long or a very brief duration of delayed auditory feedback while reading the report. Post-report measurement regarding attitudes toward the grading system revealed that the high-effort Ss became significantly more opposed to the numerical grading system than did the low-effort Ss. Aiken (1957), Lawrence and Festinger (1962), and Lewis (1964a, 1964b, 1965) have all similarly reported the attraction-enhancing effects of pre-task effort, even though effort was operationalized differently in each investigation.

The general theoretical position from which these studies grow, stated simply, is that high effort and low attraction are discrepant or dissonant cognitions. One likely means of dissonance reduction in this context can, and has been demonstrated to be, an increase in attraction. Since psychotherapeutic approaches naturalistically vary in the demands they place upon patients during the candidacy and initial stages of psychotherapy, our current studies seek primarily to test the extrapolatability of this proposition to the psychotherapeutic setting.

In a recently completed study, we examined this effort-attraction hypothesis by assigning patients in our University Psychological Clinic to one of three experimental conditions after their initial therapy interview. In the *low-effort* condition, the patients simply waited a week and then returned for their second therapy session. *Middle-effort* patients returned to the clinic twice during the week between their first two sessions. Each of these "between-session" visits was spent by the patient listening (alone) to the tape recording of his initial therapy session. *High-effort* patients also returned for two interposed tape review sessions. However, prior to the first such review session, the experimenter rerecorded the tape of the patient's first therapy session in such a manner that white noise was filtered in, thus making the tape difficult to understand. Our dependent variable measures consisted primarily of instruments assessing the patient's view of the favorableness of his relationship with his therapist. Our results indicated that both high-

and middle-effort patients significantly exceeded low-effort patients in the favorableness of their views of the therapy relationship.

The two patient-effort studies we initiated in response to this first investigation seek to determine if its findings may be further clarified by recourse to either consolidation or relevance explanations.

In our first study, the middle-effort patients (no white noise) yielded consistently higher mean relationship scores than did high-effort (white-noise) patients. Thus, perhaps the *relevance* to psychotherapy of the effort put forth by the patient influences its effect on the relationship—since coming to the tape review sessions *was* perceived by the study patients as relevant to their psychotherapy, but the effort due to the white noise was not. Accordingly, in this investigation, effort was held constant but the perceived relevance of the effort to, in the case of this study, the counseling relationship, was varied. This study was conducted in the vocational counseling section of our Psychological Center. Client effort was operationalized in terms of a battery of cognitive and perceptual tests developed by French (1964).

(A) Effort-Relevant Condition. Prior to their first counseling session, the 15 clients assigned to this condition were given a one-hour battery of these rather difficult tests by the Center's intake personnel. An explicit statement was made to clients in this condition to the effect that such testing was relevant to his counseling, would be seen by his counselor, should be signed, and the like.

(B) Effort-Irrelevant Condition. Clients assigned to this condition were treated the same as effort-relevant clients, save that the intaker informed them that the testing was being done under a grant contract, was only for norm collecting purposes, that they need not sign the test forms, the counselor would not see them, and so on.

(C) Control Condition. No precounseling testing. Our relevance-of-effort prediction (A > B & C) was not supported by the study's post-attraction data.

Since in our first effort investigation, patients who heard their first interview tape twice under *either* high- or middle-effort conditions became more favorable in their view of their therapy relationship than low-effort patients, the effect may have been due to factors other than effort. In a clinical paper using tape review sessions, Geocaris (1960) alludes to a consolidation effect, that is, the opportunity provided a patient when reviewing a taped therapy session to consolidate gains made, consider therapeutic events more fully, cement any budding insights, and the like. To test whether relationship gains made by patients in our first study were due to task effort or consolidation, the following three-condition study was planned and is currently in progress at our University Psychological Clinic.

(A) Consolidation Condition. Replicating our previous study's middle-effort condition, patients assigned to the consolidation condition return to our clinic twice between their first and second therapy sessions for tape review sessions of their first therapy interview.

(B) Effort Condition. These patients also return to the clinic twice between therapy sessions one and two, but the tape they hear is a recorded statement by E of the general status and nature of contemporary psychotherapy in the United States (from J. D. Frank's "Persuasion and Healing"). Such a tape has apparent relevance to psychotherapy, requires the effort of coming to the clinic twice and listening to tapes, but provides no stimuli for patient consolidation.

(C) Control Condition. Patients assigned to this condition are not reqested to visit the clinic between therapy sessions. While our data collection for this investigation is still in progress, a significant effect has already emerged such that attraction is greatest in the consolidation condition, next highest in the effort condition and lowest in the control group.

Up to this point in our discussion of our studies on interpersonal attraction and the psychotherapeutic relationship, we have primarily focused upon college student samples and three domains of potential attraction-enhancement, that is, structuring, status, and effort. Results to date in all three domains are encouraging, and thus we have begun to study further the attraction-enhancing effects of these variables and their interactions with resistive patients. Two hundred and forty outpatients at a community psychiatric clinic are being randomly assigned to twelve experimental conditions in a $2 \times 2 \times 3$ factorial design involving warm versus cold structuring, high versus low interviewer status, and effort-consolidation versus effort-no consolidation versus no effort. Following warm or cold structuring, the patient meets for an intake interview with a high or low status interviewer. All interviews are tape-recorded and will be content-analyzed for self-disclosure (Ashby et al., 1957). In the effort-consolidation condition, patients then listen to the tape of their just completed intake interview. Effort-no consolidation patients, in lieu of their own tape, hear one analogous to that used in our earlier study, a tape generally describing the nature and contemporary role of psychotherapy in the United States. No-effort patients hear no tape. All patients then complete our post-measures on attraction. Our predictions are that structured warmth, high interviewer status, and effort-consolidation will each serve as attraction and self-disclosure enhancers.

Matching

A great deal of early research focusing upon dyadic interaction, particularly that concerned with friendship and marital relationships, grappled at great length with the issues of need similarity versus need complementarity. But this quest eventually proved to be a focus upon pseudoissues, for the manner in which similarity or complementarity bases of friendship and marital choices that were sought were far too simplistic conceptually. The fact that A's dominance and B's submissiveness brings them into rapport in only a few of many ways should be no surprise in view of the complexity of interpersonal behavior. Similarly simplistic or unidimensional matching studies on patients and therapists have also failed to yield meaningful results on a variety of outcome criteria. Successful dyads, it seems likely, are composed of persons similar in some respects, complementary on others. Schutz (1958) has identified three basic dimensions of interpersonal exchanges—inclusion, affection, and control—and has devised an instrument (FIRO-B) that reliably measures interpersonal compatibility within a dyad on these dimensions. The more two people are alike in the importance that any of the three dimensions has for them, the more compatible they will be. But compatibility also requires complementarity with regard to how much the two people wish to originate or receive the need-relevant behaviors. Thus, FIRO-B measures both interpersonal similarity and complementarity as components of compatibility. Schutz (1958) has reported substantial construct validity for this measure in studies of group cohesiveness, social influence, problem-solving dyads and parent-child relationships. Sapolsky (1960) has extended the domain of its validity further and, in response to these investigations, Gassner (1968), a member of our research group, examined the appropriateness of this approach in a psychotherapeutic context.

Her subjects were 24 theological students in a 12-week summer program in pastoral counseling at a state mental hospital and an initial pool of 150 psychiatric in-patients. Each student and each patient completed the FIRO-B. The 24 patients most compatible with the therapists and the 24 least compatible were selected for the study, with the experimental procedure such that each therapist was requested to meet with his "good-match" patient and his "poor-match" patient for individual therapy sessions twice weekly. A third group of 24 patients was randomly selected from those tested and constituted a no-treatment control group. Attraction measures were obtained from all participating patients and therapists at the third and eleventh weeks of treatment. On both occasions of measurement, good-match patients were significantly more attracted to their therapists than were the poor-match or control patients. Gassner (1968) also hypothesized more favorable relationship ratings from the therapists in their good-match than in their poor-match pairings. While the data revealed a clear trend in this predicted direction, differences failed to reach statistical significance. Thus, this investigation was largely successful in manipulating dyadic attraction in an in situ therapeutic context based upon FIRO-B matching.

Modeling

Studies of modeling and vicarious learning in nonpsychotherapy contexts have been reported and examined at considerable length by Bandura and Walters (1963), de Charms and Rosenbaum (1960), and others, and need not be reviewed here. Relatively little research of this type has been conducted in therapeutic settings. Chittenden (1942), Jack (1934), and Page (1936) report the use of modeling procedures in the treatment of young children. Truax (1963), in a study of what he termed "vicarious therapy pretraining," made successful modeling usage of tape recordings of "good" patient group therapy behavior in training patient candidates to display higher levels of intrapersonal exploration.

We have responded to this research literature by designing a series of investigations of attraction-enhancement via use of modeling procedures, one of which is completed. Liberman (1969), the principal investigator on this investigation, assigned 90 alcoholic inpatients to six treatment conditions. Unlike our other tape-analogue studies in which a neutral tape was applied in a constant manner to all conditions and pretape structuring was varied, Liberman constructed four tapes of purported therapy sessions. Therapist behavior on all four tapes was identical, while patient (model) behavior varied by displaying either high or low attraction to the taped therapist and by disclosing either much or little personal information about himself. In addition to these four attraction X disclosure conditions, Liberman included in his design a neutral attraction-neutral disclosure tape control condition, and a no-tape control condition. Prior to tape listening, *all* Ss were told that the patient on the tape improved as a result of therapy, is dry, holds a job, and the like—thus equating "reward consequences to the model," which several investigators have shown has a marked effect upon the degree of modeling that occurs. In this investigation, Ss were *not* asked to rate the attractiveness of the taped therapist. Instead, immediately after the tape listening session, S participated in a structured interview with E in which the questions put to S were identical to those asked of the patients on the tape. A content analysis of S's interview responses for disclosure and his postinterview attraction ratings toward E formed the data for testing our modeling hypotheses. At the time of this writing, this study's data analysis is only partially complete. Patients exposed to the high-attraction tape were significantly more attracted to their interviewer than were no-exposure patients. The disclosure data analysis is still in progress.

Therapist Attraction

As has been obvious throughout this section, the major thrust of our attraction—enhancement research to date has been upon manipulating patient attraction to the therapist. But for therapy to succeed, we hold, Mr. HOUND must not only feel positively toward his therapist, the feeling must be reciprocated. For too long have such patients prematurely been stamped "unsuitable," never to return. Thus we are beginning to add a new, and hopefully equally active, dimension to our research program, namely studies seeking to enhance therapist attraction to patients. Other than Gassner's (1968) matching study, our single investigation of this type thus far was conducted by Beal (1969). It was, in a different sense than we have used before, a structuring study. One hundred and thirty-five advanced graduate students in clinical psychology were exposed to a 16 mm. sound movie of a psychotherapy session developed by Strupp (1960). Prior to viewing the movie, all Ss were given an intake summary on the movie patient, a summary in which his diagnosis and stated motivation for treatment were systematically varied. Concretely, in a 3×3 design, Ss were told the patient had been diagnosed neurotic or psychopathic, or no diagnosis was provided. Similarly, a high-, low- or no-motivational statement was included in the intake summary. The movie stopped at preselected points, and viewers were asked to record what they would say at that point in the session. These within-therapy responses were content-analyzed following Truax and Carkhuff's (1967) procedures for empathy and warmth. In addition, post-movie ratings were obtained from all Ss on attraction to the patient, prognosis, and "willingness to treat." Findings indicated a significant main effect for diagnosis (neurotic > psychopathic) on warmth, empathy, and attraction, and a similarly significant effect for motivation (high > low) on prognosis and willingness to treat.

We have in this section sought to describe in some detail one broad approach to the use of social psychological research for framing hypotheses relevant to the advance of psychotherapy. We feel the results of the several studies thus described are sufficiently promising to serve as a stimulus to others to don social-psychological glasses when seeking to discern more clearly means of enhancing the efficiency of psychotherapy.

ROLE PLAYING

The term "role playing" has been employed to describe or explain certain behaviors in a wide variety of contexts. These have included a number of psychotherapeutic procedures (Moreno, 1945; Moreno, 1946; Kelly, 1955; Lazarus, 1966), psychodiagnostic techniques (Borgatta, 1955; Bronfenbrenner and Newcomb, 1948), methods of inducing attitude change (Janis and King, 1954; Harvey and Beverly, 1961), and educational training programs (Schwebel, 1953; Goldberg and Hyde, 1954; Mann and Mann, 1959; Liveright, 1951). The term has also been utilized as an explanatory construct in theories of hypnosis (Sarbin, 1963), psychopathology (Cameron, 1950; Cameron and Margaret, 1951) and attitude formation (Lieberman, 1956). Because of its employment in these diverse substantive areas and by scientists of various theoretical persuasions, it is difficult to generate a single satisfactory operational definition of the term.

In a review of experimental evaluations of role playing, Mann (1956, p. 227) offered the following definition:

> . . . a situation in which an individual is explicitly asked to take a role not normally his own, or if his own in a setting not normal for the enactment of the role . . .

The focus of the present section is also on the experimental literature concerned with role playing, and thus this definition of the phrase should be adequate for our purposes. Since our interest is in the psychotherapeutic relevance of role-playing research, we shall limit our remarks to the use of role playing as a technique for the induction of personality or behavior change. Studies that evaluate the utility of role playing as a diagnostic or assessment procedure or as an explanatory construct for behavioral phenomena such as psychopathology or hypnotism will, therefore, not be discussed.

Role Playing in Psychotherapy

Role playing techniques have been used in psychotherapy for a number of years and have been employed by therapists with varied theoretical orientations. Corsini (1966) has discussed the use of role playing procedures by psychoanalysts, Adlerians, Rogerians, and eclectics. Each of these groups has made only minor use of such procedures and, when they have, the role playing has been modified to suit their own purposes and explanations regarding its appropriateness in psychotherapy. The best known system of role-playing therapy is psychodrama, which was deveolped primarily by Moreno (1945). Psychodrama appears to place a substantial emphasis on "acting-out" one's concerns, and the cathartic experience is regarded as a very important element. The therapeutic procedures are not specified or delineated to any great extent, and the approach is rather molar. The second most widely known form of role playing therapy is Kelly's (1955) fixed-role therapy. This is an approach that prescribes a general pattern of behavior for the patient to enact outside as well as during the therapy hour. This pattern of behavior is provided for him by his therapist and is not congruent with his usual manner of behaving. Kelly suggested that this new mode of behavior would present the patient with an opportunity to "explore his world" and find new and more effective ways of construing events and dealing with others. The "role" played by the patient allows his investigation to be accomplished in a relatively protected manner. This "investigatory" use of role playing is consistent with Kelly's view of "man the scientist."

These few varieties of role-playing therapy practiced during the 1950s—each with a different theoretical rationale—did share something in common. They lacked even a minimal research foundation, and comparatively little research evaluation of their efficacy was attempted. To be sure, a substantial body of literature regarding role-playing therapy emerged, but these articles dealt primarily with theory, technique, and applications of these procedures. Mann (1956) concluded that the assumption that the therapeutic use of role playing can produce personality change, had not been demonstrated. Krasner (1959) also indicated that research in role playing had barely scratched the surface of investigating role playing as a psychotherapeutic technique. Several years later, Goldstein et al. (1966) reported that there were still relatively few experimental studies regarding the efficacy of either psychodrama or fixed role therapy. It is instructive to note briefly the nature of the relatively few studies of role playing therapy that were conducted during the 1950s. An examination of these studies provides some understanding of the manner in which both role playing and the demonstration of its efficacy was conceptualized at that time. Studies by Harrow (1951) and Jones and Peters (1952) are representative. In both of these studies, groups of subjects (schizophrenics) engaged in psychodramatic sessions (25 sessions in one study and 16 weekly sessions in the other study). In both studies, pre- and posttesting was employed, change scores served as dependent measures, and untreated control groups were included in the experimental design. Harrow (1951) administered the Rorschach, MAPS, and a role test before and after the psychodramatic therapy. Although the results were not statistically significant, there were trends that suggested that the psychodrama experience helped develop a more veridical conceptualization of the world and greater interest in events occurring in their lives. Jones and Peters (1952) administered a Rorschach, Draw a Man Test, and a number of other assessment devices before and after psychodrama therapy. Although most of their results were in a direction that indicated improvement, these data also did not attain statistical significance. In a similar manner, only suggestive evidence is available regarding the efficacy of fixed-role therapy (Edwards, 1940; Robinson, 1940). These four investigations are representative of the state of psychotherapy research during the era in which they were conducted, and they add very little support for the use of such procedures in therapeutic practice.

Role Playing in the Laboratory

Let us now consider developments in theory and research in role playing offered by social psychologists during the 1950s. Their role playing techniques, as well as the procedures used to evaluate the efficacy of such techniques, contrast sharply with the procedures employed by psychotherapists at that time. The focus of social psychology was on the influence of role playing on attitude change. Most of their work involved laboratory-type experiments, in which a subject "played a role" that represented a position that was opposed to his own attitudes and beliefs. The role playing typically involved verbalizations in support of the position contrary to his own views, and pre- and post-attitude assessments were typically made. The subjects, then, were instructed to emit a fairly circumscribed pattern of behavior, and assessment procedures involved measurement of very specific shifts in attitude. The experiments were typically methodologically sound, and explanations for the phenomenon were derived from the more general theories of behavior change that were popular at the time. This approach, it should be recalled, involved the consideration of overt behavior as an antecedent to rather than as a consequence of cognitive change.

A set of studies by Janis and King (1954) and King and Janis (1956) are among the earliest systematic studies of the effects of role playing on attitude change. In their first study, college students were asked to deliver a speech, which was to be elaborated from a brief outline, and were asked to represent themselves as firm believers in the position which they advocated. They were asked to represent a position which, according to premeasures, was contrary to their private beliefs. Each subject delivered one of three communications, and passively listened to speeches about the other topics. The speeches regarding the other topics also represented positions that were contrary to the subject's private beliefs. After a subject delivered or listened to a speech, his attitudes about the topic were reassessed and compared with the premeasures that had been obtained one month earlier. Generally, subjects were more influenced by the role playing condition in which they delivered a speech than by exposure to similar speeches made by other subjects. Janis and King, speculating about the possible reasons for the effectiveness of the role-playing technique, regarded both improvisation and a subject's satisfaction with his performance as variables that should be systematically examined. They seemed to be especially interested in the potential importance of improvisation, an interest augmented by an earlier study of Kelman's (1953). Kelman conducted a study in which junior high school students wrote essays that endorsed the educational use of a comic book which they, in fact, did not privately favor. The results indicated that the group of subjects that displayed the most opinion change wrote essays which, Kelman believed, were longer, contained more improvisation, and were generally of a higher quality than essays written by other subjects.

In a second study, King and Janis (1956) sought to further examine the importance of improvisation and self-satisfaction on role-playing effectiveness. Subjects, after premeasures were obtained, were assigned to communication tasks that were contrary to their private beliefs. In one of the conditions, the subjects read a prepared speech to themselves, while in the second condition, the subjects read the prepared speech aloud. In the third experimental condition, they read the speech to themselves and then gave it aloud in an informal fashion and were encouraged to improvise during their presentation. After the subject's completion of the communication task, an assessment of his attitudes about the issue and his satisfaction with his own performance was conducted. The greatest attitude change occurred in subjects from the third group, who presented their group speeches in an informal and impromptu fashion. There were no differences in attitude change between the other experimental groups. Interestingly, however, subjects who read the speech aloud reported greater satisfaction with their performance than subjects who delivered it in the more impromptu fashion. This suggested to the authors that improvisation rather than reported satisfaction is the critical factor for attitude change in this class of role-playing situations. Improvisation, they proposed, might have generated arguments which reduced the strength of the subjects' own covert responses that impede the acceptance of contrapositional messages. Zimbardo (1965) indicated that this explanation is compatible with the position that regards improvisation as an internal debate in which the role player generates those very arguments that are most directly opposed to his private beliefs.

These explanations have evolved into what has come to be known as incentive or conflict resolution theory. According to Elms (1967), the incentive theory approach used by Janis and King (1954) was originally summarized by Hovland, Janis, and Kelly (1953, p. 11):

We assume that acceptance (of a new opinion) is contingent upon *incentives*, and that in order to change an opinion it is necessary to create a greater incentive for making the new implicit response than for making the old ones. A major basis for acceptance of a given opinion is provided by arguments or reasons which, according to the individual's own thinking habits constitute "rational" or logical support for the conclusions. In addition to supporting reasons, there are likely to be other special incentives involving anticipated rewards and punishments which motivate the individual to accept or reject a given opinion.

A more recent formulation of incentive theory for the explanation of the efficacy of role playing has been offered by Janis and Gilmore (1965, pp. 17–18). Their explanation is more specifically directed towards the "self-persuasion" that appears to occur in role playing:

According to this "incentive" theory, when a person accepts the task of improvising arguments in favor of a point of view at variance with his own personal convictions, he becomes temporarily motivated to think up all of the positive arguments he can, and at the same time suppress thoughts about the negative arguments which are supposedly irrelevant to the assigned task. This "biased scanning" increases the salience of the positive arguments and therefore increases the chances of acceptance of the new attitude position. A gain in attitude change would not be expected, however, if resentment or other interfering affective reactions were aroused by *negative* incentives in the role-playing situation.

The studies by Janis and King (1954) and King and Janis (1956), as well as a number of other studies that replicate these results, utilized issues that were not especially emotion-laden. Culbertson (1957), however, in an investigation perhaps a step closer in relevance to psychotherapy, demonstrated the efficacy of role-playing techniques in modifying attitudes that had strong affectual components. In this study, Culbertson had her subjects play the role of a Negro moving into a white neighborhood. Another group of subjects observed the role playing session. Both groups of subjects, prior to the manipulation, had maintained attitudes that were not favorable toward integration in housing. The results of this study were in accord with previous studies and indicated that greater attitude change occurred in the group that played roles than among the passive control subjects who observed the role playing session.

Scott (1957) examined the importance of social reward or reinforcement for the modification of attitudes in role-playing situations. College students were asked to participate in a debate and to adopt a position that was not in accord with their own beliefs about the issue being debated. The debate was held before a class of their peers. The subjects were led to believe that they had either won or lost the debate on the basis of a class vote. The subjects who were declared "winners" demonstrated a greater change in attitude about the debated issue than did the "losers."

In a second study by Scott (1959a), the subjects presented their debate before judges. Again, the subjects argued for positions that were contrary to their private beliefs, and the judges demonstrated a very special interest in their arguments. The attitudes of subjects who were rewarded in this fashion showed greater changes than did those of unrewarded control subjects. In a third study (Scott, 1959b), a debate before classmates was held and an apparent class vote determined the "winners" and "losers." In this study, subjects adopted positions that were either similar to their own position, contrary to their own position, or neutral with respect to the issue. The "winners" showed more attitude change towards the adopted position than did the "losers," regardless of the position that was taken.

Other studies, such as one by Harvey and Beverley (1961), replicated and extended these findings regarding the efficacy of role playing as a technique for attitude modification. In this study, subjects were asked to write an essay in favor of alcohol—which was not in accord with their own beliefs. The subjects were divided into groups of high and low authoritarians, and prior to their role-playing experience were exposed to a pro-alcohol communication. The communication was associated with either a high or a low status source. The results indicated that greater attitude change occurred among role players than among subjects in a control condition. Furthermore, high-authoritarian subjects were more influenced by role-playing procedures than low-authoritarian subjects. There were no interactions between role playing and the status of the communication source. It is interesting to note that although this study involved private rather than "public" role playing, the effectiveness of the procedures was still substantial. This study is one of the few that explicitly examines the relationship between a subject variable and role-playing procedures, a relationship of considerable relevance to the therapeutic use of role-playing procedures.

In addition to the application of incentive theory and social reinforcement theory in the explanation of the effects of role playing, dissonance theory has also been employed. In fact, Elms (1967, p. 132) has indicated that "the process of attitude change through role playing has been a mainstay of dissonance theory . . ." It should be noted at this point that perhaps the most controversial issue in the area of role playing has involved the struggle between the incentive and dissonance explanations. Festinger (1957) has reinterpreted the Janis and King (1954), King and Janis (1956), and Kelman (1953) findings in terms of dissonance theory. These findings and their explanation were subsumed under the category of forced compliance, and a number of studies were conducted by Festinger to support his position. The best known of these was conducted by Festinger and Carlsmith (1959). College student subjects performed a very boring task and were then hired to tell another student that the task was quite interesting. They were to be paid either $1 or $20 for their help in deceiving another student. It was assumed that subjects who received $1 would experience greater dissonance between their actions and their private beliefs than subjects who received $20. This was because the $1 subjects were less able than the $20 subjects to justify their behavior in terms of the monetary reward. This dissonant condition, it was further assumed, would result in efforts to reduce dissonance. It was believed that dissonance reduction would be accomplished by an alteration in attitudes that brought subjects' own attitude about the task closer to the content of the message that they had communicated. It was predicted, therefore, that because $1 subjects experienced greater dissonance than $20 subjects, they would display greater attitude change (dissonance reduction). This prediction was supported by the data and has been used to support a dissonance interpretation of role playing. As Cohen (1964, pp. 82–83) has commented:

If a person is led to express outwardly an attitude which is discrepant from his actual private attitude, a state of dissonance results. Since the behavior is fixed, dissonance in such a setting can be reduced by changing one's attitude so that it becomes consistent with the behavior one has engaged in publicly. There is no dissonance remaining because private attitude and public expression are now consistent with each other.

A number of papers have appeared during the past several years that have attempted to deal with the incentive-dissonance issue in one fashion or another. Some of these papers involve critiques of the methodology or conclusions drawn by scientists on the "other side" of the controversy and some papers involve substantive research regarding either dissonance or incentive theory explanations of the phenomena. Among the more important contributions by those who appear to favor incentive explanations are papers by Elms (1967); Rosenberg (1965); Janis and Gilmore (1965); and Elms and Janis (1965). Similar contributions by those favoring dissonance explanations have been made by Nuttin, 1966; Brehm, 1965; Collins and Blockwood, 1962; and Rabbie, Brehm and Cohen, 1959.

Studies by Carlsmith, Collins, and Helmreich (1966), and Collins and Helmreich (1966), are important because of their attempt to further clarify the focus of dissonance theory and incentive theory with respect to role-playing behavior. Collins and Helmreich (1966), for example, have suggested that dissonance theory emphasizes the *consequences* of behavior, while incentive theory emphasizes the *process* of role playing. More recently, still another theoretical position (with some substantive research) has been introduced to account for the effects of role playing (Bem, 1965; Bem, 1966; Bem, 1967). This explanation also emphasizes the effects of consequences rather than the process of role playing, but is offered as an alternative to dissonance-theory formulations. Bem's (1967) explanation is in a Skinnerian tradition and suggests that "self descriptive attitude statements can be based on the individual's observations of his own overt behavior and the external stimulus conditions under which it occurs" (Bem, 1967, p. 243). This position invites still further empirical studies of the phenomenon.

A brief description of two recent studies should be presented in order to provide an example of the nature of the current research in the area. These two studies are important because they attempt to test dissonance and incentive theory in a single study in which, fortunately, incentive theory predicts one set of findings while dissonance theory predicts opposite results.

Janis and Gilmore (1965) sought to determine the effects of favorable versus unfavorable sponsorship of the role that the subject was to enact. The subjects were college students and were asked to write an essay in which they supported the suggestion that a year of mathematics and a year of physics should be added as a requirement for all students. A 2×2 factorial design was utilized. Half of the students were told that this was part of a research program by an impartial national research organization (favorable sponsorship), while the other subjects were told that this research was being done for a publishing company that was trying to build up a market (unfavorable sponsorship). Half the subjects received, in advance, $20 for their participation, while the other half received $1. Half the subjects engaged in an overt role-playing task, while the others did not. After the completion of the role-playing task, the subjects indicated their attitude toward the proposed curriculum changes. The only statistically significant result

was an interaction predicted from an incentive-theory position. This interaction indicated that greater attitude change occurred in the overt role-playing condition when it was performed under favorable rather than under unfavorable sponsorship conditions. The results, the authors argued, offered more support for an incentive theory of attitude change rather than a dissonance position. These data, however, are not unequivocal, and the lack of a main effect due to role playing underscores the complexity of the phenomenon.

In a similar study by Elms and Janis (1965), subjects were asked to generate arguments in favor of a counter-norm attitude. The independent variables were (1) overt versus non-overt role playing, (2) unfavorable versus favorable sponsorship of the task, (3) large reward ($10) versus small reward (50 ¢) for participation in the study. The most important finding was a triple interaction which indicated that the greatest change occurred under conditions of overt roleplaying, favorable sponsorship of the task, and a large reward. This, the authors concluded, supported the incentive rather than dissonance theory of attitude change.

While these studies might offer some support for an incentive theory position, the issue is by no means resolved. A detailed examination of the controversy and the substantive research would be an important undertaking, and in fact Elms (1967) has made a major contribution in this area. We shall not attempt to examine this issue further, however, because it is somewhat removed from the purpose and scope of this chapter. There are two aspects of the dissonance-incentive theory controversy, however, that should be kept in mind. First, although many of the studies generated from this theoretical dispute were, in large part, designed to test theoretical issues, they also provide us with substantive data regarding those variables which seem to facilitate the effectiveness of role playing. This information might prove to be of greater value in the utilization of role playing as a technique in therapy than any of the theoretical issues.

Second, while there are certainly competing explanations regarding this phenomenon, one ought not to forget that there is little controversy, previous studies notwithstanding, regarding the question of its occurrence. The fact that the raging issue is not *whether* role playing, in experimental settings, is effective, but rather *how* it is effective, is not a mean achievement in the domain of behavior and personality change. It represents a significant advance and must not be forgotten amidst the polemics of competing theoretical explanations.

Role Playing and Change in Clinically Relevant Behavior

A number of other recent developments in the experimental investigation of role playing have also occurred. These are especially important because they are directly relevant to considerations of therapeutic uses of role playing. One of these developments involves a set of studies concerned with the use of role-playing techniques as a method of inducing people to discontinue cigarette smoking. They appeared during the mid 1960s and the fact of their appearance is important for a number of reasons. First, they are concerned with behaviors that are more closely akin to those of psychotherapy patients than those that have been examined in many of the other laboratory studies of role playing. Second, these procedures represent attempts to alter specific patterns of behavior rather than dealing solely with the modification of expressed attitudes. Third, emotional role-playing techniques rather than cognitive role-playing techniques are utilized. Finally, it must be noted and underscored that these studies were conducted by social psychologists. In general, they seem to provide an important substantive bridge between social psychology and psychotherapy.

Janis and Mann (1965) sought to investigate the utility of role playing in aiding an individual to reduce the extent of his smoking. They had some reservations about the effectiveness of traditional, cognitively oriented role playing in dealing with this particular behavior because of its habitual and resistant character. Specifically, they suspected that an individual might complete a cognitively oriented role in a defensively intellectualized fashion and neither become involved in his statements nor experience them as relevant for himself. These authors hoped to employ role playing in a way "that would provide an empathic contact experience similar to the type of direct contact that occasionally leads to a spectacular conversion" (Janis and Mann, 1965, pp. 84–85). Each subject was asked to improvise the role of a person who had recently undergone a series of medical tests and examinations and who now wanted to learn the diagnosis. The experimenter, in order to enhance the emotionality of the role-playing session, acted the part of the physician. He directed the conversation with the "patient" in a manner that aroused fear and apprehension in as dramatic a manner as possible. This study, the authors believed, was the first experimental attempt to examine the effectiveness of emotional role playing.

The subjects were 26 young women who were all smokers. They were not aware, however, that they had volunteered to participate in a study concerned with smoking. Subjects were randomly assigned to a role-playing condition or a control condition in which they would listen to a recording of one of the role-playing sessions. The subjects' beliefs and attitudes about smoking and cancer and their future intentions regarding smoking were assessed prior to the experimental procedures. The role-playing subjects then enacted five scenes with the experimenter—all of which were designed to arouse fear. Scene 1 involved a soliloquy in a waiting room in which the subject expressed fears regarding the outcome of the diagnosis. The second scene involved a conversation with the physician at which time she learned that she had lung cancer and that surgery was necessary. During the third scene she expressed her concern about the diagnosis and during the fourth scene she discussed the hospital arrangements and the moderate probability of a successful outcome. The fifth scene involved a conversation with the physician about the relationship between smoking and lung cancer. The control subjects, as indicated, were exposed to a tape recording of an actual role-playing session.

A questionnaire regarding the subjects' current feelings about smoking and cancer was administered immediately after the role playing session. Two weeks later, a follow-up interview was conducted in order to assess any change in cigarette consumption. It should be noted that the subjects were not advised to reduce their smoking, and care was taken to obtain as accurate an assessment of their smoking behavior as possible. The role-playing subjects showed significantly greater change than did the control subjects on all attitudinal indicators in the questionnaire. The role-playing subjects believed, more than the control subjects, that smoking led to lung cancer; were willing to try to give up smoking; and expressed the intention to stop. Two weeks after the role-playing session, the experimental subjects reported a decrease of 10.5 cigarettes per day, while the control subjects reported a decrease of 4.8 cigarettes per day. This significant difference involved 10 of the 14 role-playing subjects reporting substantial decreases in cigarette consumption, while 7 of the 12 control subjects reported no change at all. The authors suggested that the mediating variable that accounted for the success of the role playing was aroused fear.

Two follow-up interviews were conducted— 8 and 18 months after the original role-playing session (Mann and Janis, 1968). The subjects were not aware of the fact that these follow-up interviews were part of the original study. All of the original 26 subjects were contacted for the first follow-up interview, and 22 of the 26 were contacted for the second follow-up interview. The results indicated that during the entire 18-month period, the role-playing subjects reported lower cigarette consumption than the control subjects. The effects of the single role-playing session were sustained over a $1\frac{1}{2}$-year period of time. This is a very impressive account of the impact of emotional role playing on the modification of a pattern of behavior that appears to be generally quite resistant to change.

Mann (1967) sought to replicate and extend these findings. In this study his major interest involved the comparison of the effectiveness of emotional role playing with cognitive role playing. He included two kinds of emotional role playing—fear and shame—in order to further specify the effectiveness of various emotional role-playing procedures. The design also included a comparison of the performance of male and female subjects, as well as the effects of high or low opportunities for verbalization.

The subjects were 32 male and 32 female subjects who smoked more than ten cigarettes a day and who agreed to participate in a survey regarding attitudes towards smoking. Subjects were randomly assigned, within sex, to one of the three role-playing conditions and to one of the two verbalization conditions. Prior to the experimental session all subjects completed a questionnaire regarding attitudes toward smoking. After completion of these questionnaires, the verbalization manipulation was effected and the role-playing procedures were implemented. The *fear* role-playing situation involved a procedure similar to the one utilized in the Janis and Mann (1965) study. There were some modifications, which were designed to further increase the fear-provoking qualities of the role playing. The *shame* role-playing study also involved a patient-doctor conversation. In this situation, the focus was upon the likelihood of tobacco addiction and on the patient's weakness in self-control. In the *cognitive* role-playing condition, the patient played the part of a debater on the team and the experimenter served as the coach. The subject was asked to prepare for a debate in which he was to argue the resolution "Smokers should quit smoking." The subject was told to list his arguments, elaborate them, and improvise a speech with his coach. The verbalization manipulation was accomplished with a set of instructions. One group was told to be preoccupied with their thoughts and to say relatively little. The other group was told to play the part of being aroused by their thoughts and to speak a great deal. After the completion of role playing, a post measure questionnaire regarding smoking and a mood scale was administered. Two weeks later their cigarette smoking habits were reassessed. The results of the mood scale indicated that fear was effectively induced, while the attempt to induce shame was apparently not successful. An examination of the number of words employed in role taking suggested that the verbalization manipulation was successful. The cognitive role-playing condition resulted in little change in subject's desire to decrease cigarette consumption. The fear role playing led to a fairly strong desire to decrease cigarette consumption and was significantly greater than the cognitive role-playing condition. The shame role-playing condition resulted in changes in desire to decrease cigarette consumption that were between the fear and cognitive conditions, and not significantly different from the fear-condition results. Subjects in the high-verbalization group demonstrated a significantly greater desire to change their smoking habits than the low-verbalization group. There was no statistically significant effect due to the sex of the subject.

An assessment of cigarette consumption was made two weeks after the role-playing session. Sixteen of the thirty-two subjects in the fear group, four of the sixteen subjects in the shame group, and five of the sixteen subjects in the cognitive group reported a decrease in cigarette consumption. These differences are in the predicted direction, but do not attain statistical significance. An examination of the average cut in cigarettes per day indicated that the fear group smoked an average of four less per day; the cognitive group smoked three less per day; and the shame group smoked about one less per day. The difference between the fear and shame groups attained statistical significance. These data might be regarded as representing a trend that supports the efficacy of fear role playing. Further studies, with larger numbers of subjects, should be conducted in order to more fully evaluate these procedures.

The author, Mann, believed that the results of this study were consistent with the previous study by Janis and Mann (1965), and supported the utility of fear role playing for the modification of "deep-rooted" attitudes. He appropriately cautions the reader not to draw any general conclusions about the overall effectiveness of the fear type of emotional role playing. These results and the previously mentioned ones are, for this domain of behavior, however, very impressive and can be appropriately incorporated into the role-playing therapist's armentarium.

The experimental evaluation of emotional role-playing procedures provides a crucial link between traditional forms of therapeutic role playing and experimental social psychology. A consideration of affective processes makes social psychological studies of role playing more relevant to psychotherapists, and the experimental rigor of these studies makes a consideration of emotional role playing palatable to the research scientist. Emotional role playing is more akin to clinical procedures such as psychodrama than is cognitive role playing, and psychotherapists should be more responsive to its findings. It seems reasonable to suggest that emotional role playing might be a particularly appropriate treatment procedure for those problems that are characterized by the individual's attempt to insulate himself from the realities of his situation. Apparently, emotional role playing "breaks through" these defenses and serves as an impetus for action. The evidence certainly supports the use of this technique for certain problems, and there is some reason to believe that is is more effective than cognitive role playing. It seems appropriate to suggest, at this time, that both cognitive and emotional role-playing techniques be systematically studied across a variety of clinical problem areas.

It is important to emphasize the fact that cognitive role playing be studied in a variety of situations, and that the apparent success of emotional role playing not leave a cognitive approach in disuse. It is quite possible that there are problems for which emotional arousal is not necessary or specifically not advisable. It seems appropriate to explore the utility of cognitive role playing in clinical situations in which the therapeutic goal is to seek changes in self concepts, person perception, and interpersonal beliefs and attitudes.

It is interesting to note that we recommend the extrapolation of cognitive role playing to therapeutic situations with the suggestion that these techniques be used with more personally relevant issues. We are not, however, recommending that a similar extrapolation be performed with emotional role-playing procedures. This is because emotional role playing is in fact dealing with therapeutic dimensions and, in our judgement, the beginning of a synthesis has already been accomplished and we can only hope that it will continue to thrive.

There are some indications that role-playing therapy might develop in still another direction —one that appears to derive directly from the behavior therapy technique of desensitization. This variant has been called *behavior rehearsal* by Lazarus (1966), and its name clearly reflects the theoretical and substantive orientation of its author. This is a relatively new form of role-playing therapy, and Lazarus has indicated that his paper provides the first and, to our knowledge, only clinical evaluation of this technique, although it had been discussed in more general terms by Sturm (1965). Although it is still in germinal stages, it holds a great deal of promise as a bridge between role playing and behavior therapy, and its advocates strongly support a research approach for future developments in therapy.

Lazarus has indicated that the purpose of behavior rehearsal is to substitute effective patterns of social behavior for patterns that are inadequate or nonexistent. The therapy appears to be most often utilized with patients who are experiencing problems in assertiveness, although the technique seems to be appropriate for a fairly wide range of problems. The procedure involves the enactment of a variety of scenes that are relevant to a patient's particular concerns. These scenes are ordered in terms of their difficulty for the patient, and the enactments begin with the easiest sequence and progress to the more difficult ones. The therapist usually takes the role of an individual with whom the patient is attempting to be assertive. In this fashion the patient is encouraged to improvise his responses and the therapist can moderate the role playing with his own activities. He can, for example, exert some control over the patient's success and failure experiences, the level of emotionality, and the nature of the "demands" of the role. At times, the therapist might reverse roles with the patient and attempt to utilize modeling and imitation as a way of teaching the patient how he might respond in a given situation. Modeling and imitation might involve the attempt, by the patient, to duplicate a pattern of behavior that has been portrayed by the therapist. This procedure may be especially appropriate for patients with a very limited repertoire of responses.

Lazarus (1966) reports the results of a study in which a comparison of the effectiveness of behavior rehearsal, advice giving, and reflection-interpretation was performed. The study involved patients who mentioned specific social or interpersonal difficulties that were part of their overall difficulty, but not necessarily their primary concern. When these problems were mentioned, they were systematically treated by the therapist for a maximum of four 30-minute sessions. The patients were arbitrarily assigned to one of the three experimental groups, and these specific problems were treated by one of the three approaches. The criteria for success involved specific behavioral changes regarding the particular problem. Unfortunately, the evaluation was conducted by the experimenter, who also served as the therapist for all subjects, and whose own theatrical bias clearly favors behavior therapy techniques.

A total of 75 patients were involved in the study. Twenty-five were initially treated with behavior rehearsal, 25 were given advice, and 25 experienced a reflective-interpretative form of therapy. Twenty-three of the patients in the behavior-rehearsal group showed improvement. Eleven in the advice group and eight in the reflection-interpretation group showed improvement. Twenty-seven of those in the advice and reflection-interpretation group who did not improve were subsequently treated with behavior-rehearsal procedures. Twenty-two of these patients showed improvement.

This study, from a methodological point of view, clearly leaves much to be desired and must be replicated in a more rigorously controlled experiment. If these results are replicable, then they should indeed be regarded as impressive and as exciting as the results obtained by Janis and Mann (1965). This technique, like Janis and Mann's, places an emphasis on active participation by the subject, utilizes the therapist as a partner in the role-playing venture, and is concerned with the role of emotionality. Behavior rehearsal, however, is concerned with affective processes that inhibit or prevent the implementation of effective social behavior. The technique developed by Janis and Mann utilizes affective arousal as a means of penetrating the patient's defenses, which allowed him to insulate himself from certain realities that might prove detrimental for his well-being. Behavior rehearsal is primarily concerned with increasing the "instrumental value" of a patient's behavior by freeing him from the inhibiting aspects of his anxiety. In addition to its disinhibiting function, behavior rehearsal also provides an opportunity for the patient to expand his repertoire of responses through modeling and imitation processes (role reversal) and through his own improvisation.

Research Directions

In addition to the direct implementation of the reported findings, a number of other suggestions regarding therapeutic role playing might be made. These suggestions are in part based upon the reported research findings, although they are cast as hypotheses to be explored rather than as techniques to be implemented in an unqualified fashion.

It seems appropriate to utilize a second person in role-playing procedures to enhance the effectiveness of the technique. This appears to be true for both role playing that is based upon improvisation and role playing based on imitation and modeling procedures. This other "role player" can moderate the level of improvisation demanded from the patient, and is critical for modeling or imitation procedures. He can also subtly control the reinforcements experienced by a patient (he can, for example, allow the patient to win an argument). In the studies reviewed in this section, this function was assumed by the therapist. It is suggested that it might be more effective to utilize "ancillary therapists" to play these roles and allow the therapist to maintain his own professional role. In this fashion he could serve as a more objective observer of the role-playing situation and could also more directly provide social reinforcements to the patient. Similarly, he can serve as a source of reassurance for the patient in a variety of ways during the role-playing session. One way he might be influential, for example, is with the use of a "bug-in-the-ear" device. He can observe the role-playing session from a separate room and speak to the patient via a tiny radio receiver that can be worn in the patient's ear. In this fashion, the therapist can directly reassure, relax, or make suggestions to the patient. The use of a variety of "ancillary therapists" might also enhance the generalization of the results of role-playing experiences to outside-therapy situations. This would be especially appropriate for role playing that involved problems associated with deficient interpersonal skills.

In addition to the construction of hierarchies in the behavior rehearsal form of role playing, it might also be appropriate to utilize the relaxation techniques that are employed as part of the procedure of systematic desensitization. In addition to the use of the relaxation procedures in conjunction with role enactments, there might well be situations in which role playing therapy might be preceded by full-scale desensitization procedures. Such a set of procedures would be necessary for those patients who, because of their anxiety, could not assume roles—even with the use of relaxation procedures. It might be necessary to have these patients vividly *imagine* the role playing scenes while relaxed, in order to desensitize them to the role-playing behaviors. One might also want to consider the use of role-playing procedures as an alternative to systematic desensitization. In this regard it might be employed with those individuals who are unable to imagine scenes easily, or who do not become sufficiently involved with their imagery. All of the above-mentioned suggestions are currently being studied by the junior author of this chapter.

In summary of this section, let us review some of the models of therapeutic role playing that can be extracted from the experimental literature. It should be recalled that the scientific research into the adequacy of role playing was generally limited to social psychological investigations until the mid-1960s. The few studies since 1965 that have been more directly concerned with therapeutic uses of role playing have been based on social-psychological or behavior-therapy models rather than on more traditional clinical models of role-playing therapy.

The first model is one that emphasizes cognitive improvisation on the part of the subject-patient. The research based upon this model has been done primarily with topics of little immediate personal relevance. The results of these studies, however, have been replicated in many different studies in the social psychological literature, and hold promise for clinical use. It is suggested that the efficacy of such techniques be studied in situations of clinical importance, in which attempts are made to alter characteristics such as self-concept, perception of others, and empathic understanding.

A second model of role playing has come to be known as emotional role playing. The usefulness of the emotional role-playing model has been demonstrated with at least one type of problem—smoking. The results have been impressive, and it is now necessary to examine the effectiveness of this procedure in dealing with other behavioral disorders. It should be tested on a variety of problems in order to determine its "range of convenience."

The use of imitation and modeling procedures describes another model of role playing. Rather than regarding it as a competitor to improvisation, it seems to be more appropriate to delineate those conditions for which it might be more suitable than either the cognitive or emotional role-playing procedures. It has been indicated by Mann (1960), for example, that improvisation can arouse a variety of negative feelings that might interfere with role-playing success. It has further been reported (Jansen and Stolurow, 1962) that in certain training conditions, imitation was a more effective change agent than improvisation. This technique seems to be most appropriate as a treatment for deficiencies in interpersonal skills that are a function of inappropriate or inadequate learning experiences.

Another model of role-playing is the desensitization model. This seems to be appropriate to utilize in those situations in which anxiety has interfered with one's ability to act effectively. It might be a more powerful technique than just imagery because it is a closer approximation to the "real world" and provides more behavioral cues for "conditioning" than does imagery alone.

A final note is concerned with the use of reinforcement. The use of social or other reinforcement in role-playing procedures can be quite compatible with any of the four models that have been delineated. In addition to earlier work by Scott, a number of other studies regarding social reinforcement in role playing are important to mention. These include studies by Bostrum, Vlandis and Rosenbaum (1961); Wallace (1966); Greenbaum (1966); Goldstein and McGinies (1964); and Sarbin and Allen (1964). These studies provide important data regarding the effects of "reinforcement" and underscore the complexity of such procedures.

GROUP PSYCHOTHERAPY

A Priori Assumptions

The group psychotherapy literature consists largely of anecdotal, case history, and related impressionistic reports. While this level of observation is vital for its hypothesis-generating potential, it must be noted that even moderately vigorous hypothesis-testing research is far from abundant in the group-psychotherapy literature. This plateau of descriptiveness must be built upon, developed, and meaningfully fed into the clinical practice of group psychotherapy if it is to advance. We would propose that a viable source of hypotheses relevant to group psychotherapy is a major prerequisite for movement off this plateau, and that social-psychological investigations of small groups are potentially just such a source. This proposition is not new. A number of social-psychologists and group psychotherapists have, in position papers largely and necessarily lacking in supporting evidence, taken an encouraging or discouraging stance regarding this use of social-psychological, group dynamics research for generating hypotheses concerning group psychotherapy.

Cartwright (1951), drawing upon a series of small-group studies, formulated a number of principles by which group characteristics influenced the degree of attitude and behavior change in group members. Though not explicitly oriented toward therapy groups, his formulation was clearly a significant first step in bridging the conceptual gap between nontherapeutic and psychotherapeutic small groups. Bach (1954) brought the focus more directly upon group psychotherapy and proposed that such variables as cohesiveness, clique formation, norm development, status hierarchies, and so forth—all of which operate in a moderately specifiable manner in nontherapy groups—have counterpart influences in group psychotherapy. Durkin (1954) sought to distinguish between real versus apparent differences between therapy and nontherapy groups and, in so doing, cogently compared the two classes of groups in terms of their leadership structure, modes of communication, pathology of membership, and group goals. Others have entered this debate. Frank (1957), Hunt (1964), Lorr (1963), and

Schneider (1955) have all assumed a pro-extrapolation stance. Locke (1961), Lowrey (1944), Slavson (1957), and Wolf and Schwartz (1962) are among those who have held that group dynamic considerations are essentially irrelevant to the group therapeutic process. Slavson, for example comments (1957, pp. 153–154):

It is essential to differentiate between "group dynamics" and "interpersonal interactions." The first arises in groups with a goal common to all members who act by the consent of the majority. Synergy then arises and various activities are evolved to attain the common aim. At this point group dynamics arise, such as conflict, compromise, agreement, domination, and submission. These processes are characteristic of educational, social and action groups.

In the therapy groups, on the other hand, no common aim is in evidence, even though the aim in all is the same, namely, to overcome intrapsychic difficulties . . . Group cohesion has to be prevented so that each can communicate his problems and work them through.

And thus the debate continues, with papers appearing championing one position or the other, typically without evidence and thus typically with little or no movement toward closure on the issue of the appropriateness of extrapolation. Durkin (1957) and Parloff (1963) suggest that a major block to such movement grows directly from differences in orientation and language between group dynamics researchers and group psychotherapists. Of great importance, however, is the degree to which these writers stress the a priori nature of past polemics and, instead, call for research evidence with which to confirm or infirm such a research approach. Parloff notes: "The fact that therapy groups differ in many ways from the training group or the problem-solving group on which the findings of group dynamics are based is not the crucial issue. The ultimate question is whether hypotheses regarding the interrelationships among variables in one set of groups are supported in . . . therapy groups" (1963, p. 397). We unequivocally agree with this position; the ultimate contribution of social psychological studies of small groups to group psychotherapy will be discernible from appropriate research— as will answers to questions concerning limitations, parameters and qualifications on such

extrapolation—and not from a priori theorizing.

A small number of authors have gone beyond this expression of sentiment and have each proposed a series of hypotheses relevant to the advancement of group therapy, using group dynamics research as their extrapolatory base (Lakin and Carson, 1966; Goldstein, Heller, and Sechrest, 1966). The latter, for example, have drawn upon group dynamics findings to propose an extensive series of hypotheses regarding the selection of group therapy patients, their initiation into the group, the relative implications of group-centered versus leader-centered therapist behavior, as well as an array of procedures for enhancing within-group cohesiveness. But what of the actual extrapolatory research that has been conducted?

Extrapolatory Research

Interaction Process Analysis. Of the dozen or so investigations of group psychotherapy that have grown directly from the group-dynamics literature, several have focused upon Bales' (1950) Interaction Process Analysis. This rating system, as its name implies, is interaction-process centered, not content-oriented. Twelve categories of group member behavior are represented, that is, the positive and negative aspects of orientation, evaluation, control over others, decision making, tension management, and integration. The simple sentence is the unit of observation and, in its typical application, certain classes of nonverbal behavior are scored at one-minute intervals. Scores derived are primarily the number of acts of a given kind in each category (by individuals or groups) and ratios of such scores. Interrater reliability coefficients, with trained raters, have ranged from 0.75 to 0.95.

In one of the early nonclinical applications of IPA, Bales and Strodtbeck (1951) sought to identify the nature of the phases or stages through which problem-solving groups pass in their efforts at goal attainment. Their data consisted of complete protocols of 22 group problem-solving sessions. The investigators hypothesized that in sessions ". . . in which groups work toward the goal of a group decision on a full-fledged problem," group members move in their interactions from initial emphasis on interactions characterized by *orientation* to interactions of *evaluation*, and subsequently to interactions emphasizing *control*. It was further hypothesized that, concurrent with these phase transitions, the relative frequency of both positive and negative interactions would increase. Their analysis revealed a clear confirmation of the phase sequence hypothesis: the orientation-evaluation-control phase movement and the increase in both positive and negative interactions across phases were consistently in evidence.

In addition to identification of phase sequences in problem-solving groups, Bales (1955) has focused in some detail on what he terms the "equilibrium problem." Generally involved here is an attempt to identify regularities in the initiation-reaction sequences that characterize problem-solving group interactions. Sixteen meetings of five-member groups served as the source data for this study. The twelve IPA categories were grouped into four classes: (1) questions (asks orientation, asks opinion, asks suggestion), (2) attempted answers (gives orientation, gives opinion, gives suggestion), (3) positive reactions (shows solidarity, shows tension release, shows agreement), and (4) negative reactions (shows antagonism, shows tension, shows disagreement). Supporting Bales' search for interaction regularities, codification of the group protocols in this manner revealed a generally consistent pattern across group sessions:

... about one-half of all acts were Attempted Answers which moved the group toward its external goal—the solution of the problem. Such task-oriented attempts, in turn, tended to provoke Reactions—positive, negative, or questions. About one-half of the observed reactions were positive. The remaining one-half were distributed in a binary fashion: Half of them were negative, and the other half were equally divided between Questions and further Attempted Answers (1955, p. 449).

Investigations of these two phenomena, phase movement and equilibrium tendencies, as they operate in therapy groups provide us with our first opportunity to draw research based conclusions regarding group-dynamic to group-therapy extrapolation. Talland's (1955, pp. 457–458) a priori assumptions led him to predict a failure of extrapolation:

Psychotherapy groups ... differ from experimental problem-solving groups in several clearly marked respects. They meet in order to discover problems rather than to solve one neatly formulated for their attention; they neither have to reach a solution nor must they finally close a case unresolved at the end of a meeting. Insofar as the psychotherapeutic technique stresses spontaneity, the discussion is allowed a free course, whereas in the laboratory its trend is implicitly determined by the task even in the absence of directive chairmanship. Finally, discussing a hypothetical or didactic case and a transient acquaintance do not lead to deep emotional involvements that occur when patients grapple with their own and each other's personal problems; baring their inmost thoughts and experiences week after week in intimate fellowship. Consequently, the process of interaction would be expected to differ in the two situations, and more particularly in such dynamic aspects of the model as the phase sequence of acts indicated by and the equilibrium properties of the interaction system ...

His patient sample consisted of four psychotherapy groups of six to eight neurotic outpatients each. The interactions within the groups during a total of 18 ninety-minute sessions taken from the first eight weeks of therapy were observed and categorized according to the Bales IPA. Therapist responses were not included, nor were nonverbal acts. Further, because of the infrequency of occurrence (when nonverbal acts are excluded), Bales' categories 2 (shows tension release) and 11 (shows tension) were omitted from the data analysis. Talland's results failed to confirm the occurrence of either phase movement or equilibrium tendencies in the interactions of his therapy groups. More specifically, individual group-therapy sessions showed no consistent movement from orientation through evaluation to control and the problem-solving group equilibrium tendencies noted earlier also failed to appear with any degree of consistency. Thus, on two central group dynamic interactional dimensions, Talland's results demonstrate a basic dissimilarity between problem-solving and psychotherapy groups. At first glance these findings represent initial evidence suggesting that in important interactional senses, group dynamics research material may be an inappropriate basis for framing predictions relevant to group psychotherapy. Psathas (1960), however, conducted a subsequent investigation that altered a number of aspects of Talland's design and that thereby yielded a very different outcome. Specifically, in an effort to reflect more accurately the nature of group psychotherapy interactions, Psathas included in his analysis acts initiated by the therapist, nonverbal behavior, and the IPA categories of "shows tension" and "shows tension release." His subjects were eight patients in two therapy groups of four members each, who met twice weekly for 90-minute sessions over a period of one year. Nine sessions of each group were observed and IPA-recorded, an equal number of sessions being chosen from early, middle, and late periods in therapy. This is in contrast to Talland's use of the first eight weeks of therapy, a contrast of direct relevance to efforts aimed at discerning phase movement. Agreeing with Talland that there was probably little likelihood of orientation to evaluation to control movement within single group therapy sessions, Psathas hypothesized and found clear support for such phase movement more longitudinally across the full course of therapy sessions. His findings regarding equilibrium tendencies are also congruent with those reported by Bales (1955), noted earlier, as consistently operating in problem-solving groups. Thus, we may tentatively conclude that within these circumscribed areas of therapy-group interaction, the process of group-dynamic to group-psychotherapy extrapolation appears appropriate.

While we do not wish to particularly encourage method-centered as opposed to idea-centered extrapolatory research, it is worth briefly noting that a number of additional group psychotherapy studies have meaningfully used Bales' IPA (Blake, 1953; Munzer and Greenwald, 1957; Noble et al., 1961; Oakes, 1962; Roberts and Strodtbeck, 1953).

Group Cohesiveness. In an earlier section of this chapter we made major use of social psychological studies of interpersonal attraction in dyads for purposes of framing predictions relevant to the therapist-patient relationship in individual psychotherapy. In a directly analogous manner, we wish at this point to focus upon the large body of small-group studies of intermember attraction (cohesiveness) for their extrapolatory implications for group psycho-

therapy. A distillation of this small-group research clearly demonstrates cohesiveness to be a most potent variable indeed, one influencing a wide array of cognitive, interpersonal, and behavioral areas of small-group functioning. Specifically, it has been demonstrated that members of highly cohesive problem-solving groups, in contrast to members of groups low in cohesiveness, will:

1. Be more open to influence by other group members.
2. Be more accepting of member hostility.
3. Place greater value on the group's goals.
4. Find more anxiety reduction.
5. Be more equal participants in group discussion.
6. Be more active participants in group discussion.
7. Exert more pressure on deviates or marginal group members.
8. Be less susceptible to disruption as a group when a member terminates.
9. Be more in agreement regarding member status hierarchy.
10. Remain in the group longer.
11. Be absent less often from group meetings.

Whether cohesiveness in psychotherapy groups is a similarly potent variable, is, of course, an empirical question. The little research of this type that has been conducted, however, has begun to point in an affirmative direction. Truax (1961) examined the effects of cohesiveness upon depth of intrapersonal exploration. Three psychotherapy groups involving a total of thirty-nine psychiatric inpatients were his subjects. Three-minute samples of verbal interaction were randomly selected from recordings of 42 successive hours of group psychotherapy from each of the three groups. Ratings of these segments constituted the cohesiveness data, with intrapersonal exploration data being obtained from Process and Insight scales completed by independent judges. His data analysis revealed significant, positive correlations between these variables, leading Truax to conclude:

These results indicate that cohesion, long a central concept in the analysis of small group behavior, is also of importance in the analysis of group psychotherapy: successful group psychotherapy groups are cohesive. This may be a somewhat circular finding in that at least part of the attraction of the group may be due to its success in helping its members. However, these findings not only suggest the fruitfulness of applying knowledge of attitude change obtained from studies of experimental groups, but, also point to . . . one which is susceptible to external manipulation.

Encouraged by Truax's findings, and in accord with his observation regarding the manipulatability of group cohesiveness, Goldstein et al. (1967) have reported a related extrapolatory investigation. They note the frequency with which investigators in the social psychological laboratory have made use of an accomplice, cohort, or plant as an aid in implementing their independent-variable manipulation. In a number of these investigations, the plant was successfully used to enhance the group's level of cohesiveness, by serving as a deviate or model, or in some other attraction-influencing role. Following from such findings, Goldstein et al. constituted two psychotherapy groups. One consisted of six university students, the other of six psychiatric outpatients. In addition, a graduate student was planted to serve (for attraction-enhancing purposes) as a patient in each group. Sociometric and attraction-to-group questionnaire data obtained regularly from each group strongly suggested that the plants were indeed successful in consistently raising each group's level of cohesiveness. While the results of this investigation, as well as Truax's, must be considered as only suggestive, it is clear that they are a small beginning at establishing the significance of cohesiveness as a consequential variable in the success of psychotherapy groups. Myers (1961) contributes further to this positive evaluation. Working with nonpathological Ss, he found that interteam competition led to significantly higher levels of within-team cohesiveness than did an otherwise comparable noncompetitive condition. Sherif and Sherif (1953) and Wilson and Miller (1961) have reported concurring findings. In an effort to extrapolate these findings to a situation more relevant to psychotherapy, Myers (1962) divided forty-eight chronic schizophrenic patients into two-man teams and had them participate in a series of recreational tasks. Half the teams played competitively and the other half played noncompetitively. His results yielded a significant interaction between experimental condition and the level of patient pathology. Competition facilitated high levels of cohesiveness among patients in relatively good pathological condition and hindered the development of these relations among sicker patients. The opposite tendency was found in noncompetitive groups. This investigation, in addition to suggesting intergroup competition as a concrete procedure for influencing the cohesiveness of therapy groups, teaches us something about the extrapolation process. Essentially, as Durkin (1957) and Goldstein, Heller, and Sechrest (1966) have suggested elsewhere, the process of group-dynamic to group-psychotherapy extrapolation will not be unidimensionally accepted or rejected. Research evidence (such as Myers') will provide us with the bases to decide *which* group dynamic research results are relevant and which are not, under what circumstances, with which kinds of clients, and the like. Thus, Myers' success with his lesssick, but not his highly pathological, Ss concretely underscores the need for *selective*, research-based extrapolation. Directly analogous selectivity of extrapolation follows from the fact that the significant association of cohesiveness and intrapersonal exploration reported by Truax (1961) held for his two all-female groups, but not his group of all-male patients, as well as the Goldstein et al. (1967) finding that the plant was more cohesiveness-enhancing in the psychiatric outpatient group than in the group of university students.

Behavioral Selection. An enduring issue in the group psychotherapy literature concerns the procedures by which patients are to be selected and grouped. Preferred selection procedures have long revolved around the use of diagnostic interviews and psychological testing; preferred grouping criteria have for many years reflected the heterogeneity versus homogeneity controversy (for example, Furst, 1951; Slavson, 1957; Wolf and Schwartz, 1962). More recently, however, the latter has come more and more to be viewed as a pseudocontroversy, with group psychotherapists increasingly seeking to constitute "balanced" groups. Locke (1961, pp. 245–246) observes:

Groups are established by balancing active and passive patients, or by balancing diagnostic category, or personality characteristics, or whatever else the therapist regards as decisive. . . . The guiding factor is communication. . . . If the spread is too great between group members in any characteristics . . . if there is no common meeting ground because of the difference, there can be no communication and therefore no interaction.

Interview and psychodiagnostic selection procedures have not proved to be sufficiently predictive for purposes of balanced grouping; the leap from a Rorschach response to within-group patient behavior is simply too great. Locke (1961, pp. 242–243) comments:

The most fruitful procedure by which patients can be selected is not in terms of diagnosis, but rather in terms of behavior. This makes the manner in which the patient operates, the manner in which he functions, the prime consideration. When this approach is taken, the therapist cuts through the structural rigidities of nosology and comes right to the dynamics of the patient himself. . . . Such a selection is functional, not structural, as would be an approach from the point of view of diagnosis.

How, then, is such a functional or behavioral selection to be operationalized? Goldstein, Heller, and Sechrest (1966), in their examination of this behavioral approach, have suggested the use of tryout or diagnostic groups and, in doing so, had major recourse to group dynamic investigations of behavioral selection. In one such study, Borgatta and Bales (1955) used 126 Air Force enlisted men as Ss. They were divided into batches or subgroups of nine men each, and three-man group meetings were held within each batch according to a procedure that resulted in each S participating in four meetings. Rotation of Ss across groups was such that each S met with every other S in his batch only once. The sessions involved discussional and role play tasks, both of which were observed and IPA-classified. Results indicated that the interaction rate demonstrated by a given group member was an inverse function of the characteristic rates of his co-participators. More specifically, when groups were reconstituted with members—all of whom had previously demonstrated high interaction rates in different, earlier groups—the members tended to depress each others' rate of inter-

action. The converse was true for those who had been low participators in earlier sessions. The highest group interaction rates were in evidence in differentiated groups, those constituted of members high, low, and moderate in their earlier group session interactions. The investigators conclude (p. 397):

The results of this study indicate that it may be possible to use diagnostic sessions to estimate characteristic rates of particular individuals and from this information to predict certain aspects of performance of the individual in a particular group if we have estimates of the characteristic performance of each of the individuals based on previous diagnostic sessions.

Blake, Mouton, and Fruchter (1954) similarly provide evidence of the utility of behavioral observation of group sessions for predicting individual behavior in subsequent reconstituted groups. Thirty-three Ss participated in two completely independent group situations. Between-group structural differences included the tasks on which the members worked, the group composition, and the identity of the group observer. They found support for their prediction that (p. 578):

. . . reliable judgments of short-term interaction can be made even when two situations are different. Items that permit consistent assessment from both the between-and within-sessions point of view include leadership, contribution to group decision, and dominance . . . These results support the view that direct-assessment data can serve as one basis for evaluating personal and social characteristics that cannot be satisfactorily measured by other techniques.

Concurring findings have been reported by Arbous and Maree (1951), Bass (1955), Bell and French (1955), Breer (1960), and Haythorn (1955). In all of these investigations, the greater the degree of structural similarity between the predictor and criterion groups, the higher the level of predictive accuracy. Thus, in the Bass (1955) study, rated leadership behavior in a leaderless group discussion correlated 0.56 with leadership displayed in a debate, 0.48 with leadership in a personal interview, 0.47 with leadership in solving a field problem, and 0.30 with leadership in cooperatively constructing a giant toy. The implication for behavioral selection in group psychotherapy is clear: the greater the structural similarity between the diagnostic, tryout, or intake group and the criterion group, the more accurate the behavioral predictions are likely to be.

As was true of the conclusions which were drawn regarding the role of cohesiveness in psychotherapy groups, the evidence that does exist dealing with behavior selection in the group psychotherapy context provides affirmative, if tentative, support for the appropriateness of this particular extrapolation. For example, in an early investigation of nondirective group psychotherapy, Gorlow, Hoch, and Telschow (1952) reported significant relationships between each member's behavior in the first two sessions and his behavior during the remainder of psychotherapy that "suggest the feasibility of altering a group's composition on the basis of initial behavior (pp. 111–112)."

In a more direct, clinical test of diagnostic grouping, Stone, Parloff, and Frank (1954) constituted 60 consecutive patients into four intake or diagnostic groups. All sessions were observed, and both observer and therapist reliably rated each patient on a dimension of dependency - dominance. Their largely impressionistic data led the investigators to conclude ". . . that the personality patterns of dominance and dependence shown by the patients in the diagnostic groups remained essentially the same even when patients were regrouped into therapy groups and the therapist changed (p. 279)."

Deer and Silver (1962) report a relevant investigation whose intent was to demonstrate the predictive adequacy of psychometric selection procedures. Their *S*s, 24 adolescents in group psychotherapy, were each administered a number of projective tests. A subsequent attempt to demonstrate relationships between 42 scores derived from this test battery and therapist ratings of patient-within-therapy behavior was singularly unsuccessful. The investigators conclude (pp. 324–325):

. . . clinicians' failure to consistently predict group behavior on the basis of individual dynamics may be indirect evidence of the power of the group to shape and control the behavior of its members contrary to their personal predilections. If such a finding is borne out by other research it would point to the futility of making predictions about an individual's behavior in a group other than on the basis of what he does in a group similar or identical to a group in which his behavior is to be predicted.

We have briefly examined group dynamic and group psychotherapy research dealing with within-group interaction patterns, cohesiveness, and behavioral selection. In all three instances we may conclude, in a very tentative manner, that group dynamic to group psychotherapy extrapolation appears to be appropriate *if* one keeps in mind various stipulations and conditions. We find ourselves, in conclusion, in accord with Durkin (1957), who has commented:

. . . if we are to compare normal with therapeutic groups and to consider applying the experimental findings which have been made on the former to the management of the latter, then we must qualify those findings according to the specific requirements deriving from the differences between their separate goals . . . the final solution must come through further experimentation with therapeutic groups (p. 125).

. . . scientific validation should shed further light on the relationships between the group processes and the therapeutic process; minimize errors in the application of results from one type of group to another; most important increase the mutual understanding and eventual integration of the knowledge produced by these two main approaches to the understanding of the nature of groups (p. 130).

SUMMARY

We have examined three major domains of social psychological research—interpersonal attraction, role playing, and group dynamics. These domains are unique among the numerous areas of social psychological inquiry in that their findings have already begun to come under experimental scrutiny in psychotherapeutic contexts. The spirit of this chapter has urged not only further such experimentation but, by implication, the notion that many other areas of research concern to the social psychologist may potentially offer meaningful hypotheses for the advance of psychotherapy—theory, research, and practice. The list of such potentially rich extrapolatory sources is long, and has been detailed elsewhere (Goldstein, 1966; Goldstein, Heller, and Sechrest, 1966; Strong, 1968). It is perhaps sufficient to state in closing that the beginning attempts examined in this chapter are highly encouraging and, hopefully, will serve as a spur to others to turn to social psychological research when formulating hypotheses relevant to psychotherapy.

REFERENCES

Adams, J. S. The measurement of perceived equity in pay differentials. Unpublished manuscript, Behavior Research Service, General Electric Co., 1961

Adams, J. S. Toward an understanding of inequity. *Journal of Abnormal and Social Psychology*, 1963, **67**, 422–436.

Adams, J. S., and Rosenbaum, W. B. The relationship of worker productivity to cognitive dissonance. *Journal of Applied Psychology*, 1962, **46**, 161–164.

Aiken, E. G. The effort variable in the acquisition, extinction, and spontaneous recovery of an instrumental response. *Journal of Experimental Psychology*, 1957, **53**, 47–51.

Arbous, A. G., and Maree, J. Contribution of two group discussion techniques to a validated test battery. *Occupational Psychology*, 1951, **25**, 73–89.

Aronson, E. The effect of effort on the attractiveness of rewarded and unrewarded stimuli. *Journal of Abnormal and Social Psychology*, 1961, **63**, 375–380.

Aronson, E., and Mills, J. The effects of severity of initiation on liking for a group. *Journal of Abnormal and Social Psychology*, 1959, **59**, 177–181.

Asch, S. E. Forming impressions of personality. *Journal of Abnormal and Social Psychology*, 1946, **41**, 258–290.

Ashby, J. D., Ford, D. H., Guerney, B. G., and Guerney, L. F. Effect on clients of a reflective and a leading type of psychotherapy. *Psychological Monographs*, 1957, **71**, Whole No. 453.

Bach, G. R. *Intensive group psychotherapy*. New York: Ronald Press. 1954.

Back, K. W. Influence through social communication. *Journal of Abnormal and Social Psychology*, 1951, **46**, 9–23.

Bales, R. F. The equilibrium problem in small groups. In A. P. Hare, E. F. Borgatta and R. F. Bales (Eds.), *Small groups*. New York: Alfred A. Knopf, 1955. Pp. 424–456.

Bales, R. F. *Interaction process analysis: A method for the study of small groups*. Cambridge, Mass.: Addison-Wesley, 1950.

Bales, R. F., and Strodtbeck, F. L. Phases in group problem solving. *Journal of Abnormal and Social Psychology*, 1951, **46**, 485–495.

Bandura, A., and Walters, R. H. *Social learning and personality development*. New York: Holt, 1963.

Bass, B. M. *Leadership, psychology, and organizational behavior*. New York: Harper, 1960.

Beal, A. Biased therapists: The effects of prior exposure to case history material on therapist's attitudes and behavior toward patients. Unpublished doctoral dissertation, Syracuse University, 1969.

Bell, G. B., and French, R. L. Consistency of individual leadership position in small groups of varying memberships. In A. P. Hare, E. F. Borgatta, and R. F. Bales (Eds.), *Small groups*. New York: Alfred A. Knopf, 1955. Pp. 275–280.

Bem, D. J. An experimental analysis of self-persuasion. *Journal of Experimental Social Psychology*, 1965, **1**, 199–218.

Bem, D. J. Inducing belief in false confessions. *Journal of Personality and Social Psychology*, 1966, **3**, 707–710.

Bem, D. J. Self perception: an alternative interpretation of cognitive dissonance phenomena. *Psychological Review*, 1967, **74**, 238–255.

Blake, R. R. The interaction-feeling hypothesis applied to psychotherapy groups. *Sociometry*, 1953, **16**, 253–265.

Blake, R. R., Mouton, J. S., and Fruchter, B. The consistency of interpersonal behavior judgments made on the basis of short-term interaction in three-man groups. *Journal of Abnormal and Social Psychology*, 1954, **49**, 573–578.

Bordin, E. S. Inside the therapeutic hour. In E. A. Rubinstein and M. B. Parloff (Eds.), *Research in psychotherapy*. Washington: American Psychological Association, 1959. Pp. 235–346.

Borgatta, E. F. Analysis of social interaction: Actual, role-playing and projective. *Journal of Abnormal and Social Psychology*, 1955, **51**, 394–405.

Borgatta, E. F., and Bales, R. J. Interaction of individuals in reconstituted groups. In A. P. Hare, E. F. Borgatta, and R. F. Bales (Eds.), *Small groups*. New York: Alfred A. Knopf, 1955. Pp. 370–396.

Bostrum, R., Vlandis, J. and Rosenbaum, M. Grades as reinforcing contingencies and attitude change. *Journal of Educational Psychology*, 1961, **52**, 112–115.

Bown, O. H. An investigation of therapeutic relationships in client-centered psychotherapy. Unpublished doctoral dissertation, University of Chicago, 1954.

Breer, P. E. Predicting interpersonal behavior from personality and role. Unpublished doctoral dissertation, Harvard University, 1960.

Brehm, J. W. A dissonance analysis of attitude discrepant behavior. In C. I. Hovland and M. J. Rosenberg (Eds.), *Attitude organization and change*. New Haven; Yale University Press, 1960. Pp. 164–197.

Brehm, J. W. Comment on "Counter-norm attitudes induced by consonant versus dissonant conditions of role playing." *Journal of Experimental Research in Personality*, 1965, **1**, 61–64.

Brehm, J. W., and Cohen, A. R. *Explorations in cognitive dissonance*. New York: Wiley, 1962.

Brock, T. C. Cognitive restructuring and attitude change. *Journal of Abnormal and Social Psychology*, 1962, 264–271.

Brock, T. C., and Becker, L. A. Ineffectiveness of "overhead" counter propaganda. *Journal of Personality and Social Psychology*, 1965, **2**, 654–660.

Brock, T. C., and Blackwood, J. E. Dissonance reduction, social comparison, and modification of others' opinions. *Journal of Abnormal and Social Psychology*, 1962, **65**, 319–324.

Bronfenbrenner, U., and Newcomb, T. M. Improvisations: An application of psychodrama in personality diagnosis. *Sociatry*, 1948, **1**, 367–382.

Burdick, H. A., and Burnes, A. J. A test of the "strain toward symmetry" theories. *Journal of Abnormal and Social Psychology*, 1958, **57**, 367–370.

Buss, A. *Psychopathology*. New York: Wiley, 1966.

Cameron, N. A. Role concepts in behavior pathology. *American Journal of Sociology*, 1950, **55**, 464–467.

Cameron, N. A., and Magaret, A. *Behavior pathology*. Boston: Houghton-Mifflin, 1951.

Carlsmith, J. M., Collins, B. E., and Helmreich, R. K. Studies in forced compliance: I. The effect of pressure for compliance on attitude change produced by face-to-face role playing and anonymous essay writing. *Journal of Personality and Social Psychology*, 1966, **4**, 1–13.

Cartwright, D. Achieving change in people: Some applications of group dynamics theory. *Human Relations*, 1951, **4**, 381–392.

Chapanis, N. P., and Chapanis, A. Cognitive dissonance: five years later. *Psychological Bulletin*, 1964, **61**, 1–22.

Charms, R. de and Rosenbaum, M. E. Status variables and matching behavior. *Journal of Personality*, 1960, **28**, 492–502.

Chittenden, G. E. An experimental study in measuring and modifying assertive behavior in children. *Child Development*, 1942, 7, No. 31.

Cohen, A. R. *Attitude change and social influence*. New York: Basic Books, 1964.

Cohen, A. R. Attitudinal consequences of induced discrepancies between cognitions and behavior. *Public Opinion Quarterly*, 1960, **24**, 297–318.

Cohen, A. R., Brehm, J. W., and Eleming, W. H. Attitude change and justification for compliance. *Journal of Abnormal and Social Psychology*, 1958, **56**, 276–278.

Cohen, A. R., Terry, H. I., and Jones, C. B. Attitudinal effects of choice in exposure to counter-propaganda. *Journal of Abnormal and Social Psychology*, 1959, **58**, 388–391.

Collins, B, and Blockwood ,R. Attitude change and discrepant position. *Journal of Abnormal and Social Psychology*, 1961, **60**, 178–183.

Corsini, R. J. *Role playing in psychotherapy: A manual*. Chicago: Aldine, 1966.

Culbertson, F. M. Modification of an emotionally held attitude through role playing. *Journal of Abnormal and Social Psychology*, 1957, **54**, 230–233.

Davis, K., and Jones, E. E. Changes in interpersonal perception as a means of reducing cognitive dissonance. *Journal of Abnormal and Social Psychology*, 1960, **61**, 402–410.

Deer, J., and Silver, A. W. Predicting participation and behavior in group therapy from test protocols. *Journal of Clinical Psychology*, 1962, **18**, 322–325.

Deysach, R. E. The effects of a counselor favor on client attraction and openness to influence. Unpublished master's thesis, Syracuse University, 1967.

Durkin, H. E. Toward a common basis for group dynamics: Group and therapeutic processes in group psychotherapy. *International Journal of Group Psychotherapy*, 1957, **7**, 115–130.

Edwards, E. D. Observation of the use and efficacy of changing a patient's concept of his role—a psychotherapeutic device. Unpublished master's thesis, Fort Hays State College, 1940.

Elms, A. C. Influence of fantasy ability on attitude change through role playing. *Journal of Personality and Social Psychology*, 1966, **4**, 36–43.

Elms, A. C. Role playing incentive, and dissonance. *Psychological Bulletin*, 1967, **68**, 132–148.

Elms, A. C., and Janis, I. L. Counter norm attitudes induced by consonant versus dissonant conditions in role-playing. *Journal of Experimental Research in Personality*, 1965, **1**, 50–60.

Eysenck, H. J. The effects of psychotherapy: An evaluation. *Journal of Consulting Psychology*, 1952, **16**, 319–324.

Festinger, L. *A theory of cognitive dissonance*. Evanston: Row, Peterson, 1957.

Festinger, L., and Carlsmith, J. M. Cognitive consequences of forced compliance. *Journal of Abnormal and Social Psychology*, 1959, **58**, 203–210.

Frank, J. D. Some determinants, manifestations, and effects of cohesiveness in therapy groups. *International Journal of Group Psychotherapy*, 1957, **7**, 53–63.

Frank, J. D. *Persuasion and healing*. Baltimore: Johns Hopkins Press, 1961.

French, T. R. Reference kit for cognitive and perceptual tests. Princeton, New Jersey: Educational Testing Service, 1964.

Furst, W. Homogeneous versus heterogeneous groups. *International Journal of Group Psychotherapy*, 1951, **1**, 120–123.

Gassner, S. M. The relationship between patient-therapist compatability and treatment effectiveness. Unpublished doctoral dissertation, Syracuse University, 1968.

Geocaris, K. The patient as listener. *Archives of General Psychiatry*, 1960, **2**, 81–88.

Gerard, H. B. The anchorage of opinions in face-to-face groups. *Human Relations*, 1954, **7**, 313–325.

Goldberg, N., and Hyde, R. Role-playing in psychiatric training. *Journal of Social Psychology*, 1954, **39**, 63–75.

Goldstein, A. P. Psychotherapy research by extrapolation from social psychology. *Journal of Counseling Psychology*, 1966, **13**, 38–45.

Goldstein, A. P., Heller, K., and Sechrest, L. B. *Psychotherapy and the psychology of behavior change*. New York: Wiley, 1966.

Goldstein, A. P., Gassner, S. M., Greenberg, R., Gustin, A., Land, J., Liberman, B. and Streiner, D. The use of planted patients in group psychotherapy. *American Journal of Psychotherapy*, 1967, **21**, 767–773.

Goldstein, I., and McGinies, E. Compliance and attitude change under conditions of differential social reinforcement. *Journal of Abnormal and Social Psychology*, 1964, **68**, 567–570.

Gordon, R. L. Interaction between attitude and the definition of the situation in the expression of opinion. *American Sociological Review*, 1952, **17**, 50–58.

Gorlow, L., Hoch, E. L., and Telesclow, E. F. *Non-directive group psychotherapy*, New York: Teacher's College Studies in Education, Columbia University, 1952.

Gough, H. G. A sociological theory of psychopathy. *American Journal of Sociology*, 1948, **53**, 359–366.

Greenbaum, C. W. Effect of situational and personality variables on improvisation and attitude change. *Journal of Personality and Social Psychology*, 1966, **4**, 260–269.

Greenberg, R. Effects of pre-session information on perception of the therapist and receptivity to influence in a psychotherapy analogue. Unpublished doctoral dissertation, Syracuse University, 1968.

Grinker, R. R. A transactional model for psychotherapy. In M. J. Stein (Ed.), *Contemporary psychotherapies*. New York: Free Press, 1961. Pp. 190–213.

Harrow, G. S. The effects of psychodrama group therapy on role behavior of schizophrenic patients. *Group Psychotherapy*, 1951, **3**, 316–320.

Harvey, O. J., and Beverly, G. D. Some personality correlates of concept change through role playing. *Journal of Abnormal and Social Psychology*, 1961, **63**, 125–130.

Haythorn, W. The influence of individual members on the characteristics of small groups. In A. P. Hare, E. F. Borgatta, and R. F. Bales (Eds.), *Small groups*. New York: Alfred A. Knopf, 1955. Pp. 330–341.

Holt, R. R., and Luborsky, L. Research in the selection of psychiatrists. *Bulletin of the Menninger Clinic*, 1952, **16**, 125–135.

Hovland, C. I., Janis, I. L., and Kelley, H. H. *Communication and persuasion*. New York: Yale University Press, 1953.

Hunt, J. McV. Concerning the impact of group psychotherapy on psychology. *International Journal of Group Psychotherapy*, 1964, **14**, 3–31.

Hunt, J. McV., Ewing, T. N., LaForge, R., and Gilbert, W. M. An integrated approach to research on therapeutic counseling with samples of results. *Journal of Counseling Psychology*, 1959, **6**, 46–54.

Jack, L. M. An experimental study of ascendant behavior in preschool children. *University of Iowa Studies of Child Welfare*, 1934, **9**, 7–65.

Jackson, D. D. Interactional psychotherapy. In M. J. Stein (Ed.), *Contemporary psychotherapies*. New York: Free Press, 1961. Pp. 256–271.

Janis, I. L., and Gilmore, J. B. The influence of incentive conditions on the success of role playing in modifying attitudes. *Journal of Personality and Social Psychology*, 1965, **1**, 17–27.

Janis, I. L., and King, B. T. The influence of role playing on opinion change. *Journal of Abnormal and Social Psychology*, 1954, **49**, 211–218.

Janis, I., and Mann, L. Effectiveness of emotional role playing in modifying smoking habits and attitudes. *Journal of Experimental Research in Personality*, 1965, **1**, 84–90.

Jansen, M. J., and Stolurow, L. M. An experimental study of role playing. *Psychological Monographs*, 1962, **76**, No. 31.

Jones, E. E., and Thibaut, J. W. Interaction goals as a basis of inference in interpersonal perception. In R. Taguiri and L. Petrullo (Eds.), *Person perception and interpersonal behavior*. Stanford: Stanford University Press, 1958. Pp. 151–178.

Jones, F. D., and Peters, A. N. An experimental evaluation of group psychotherapy. *Journal of Abnormal and Social Psychology*, 1952, **47**, 345–353.

Kelley, H. H. Warm-cold variable in first impressions. *Journal of Personality*, 1950, **18**, 431–439.

Kelly, G. A. *The psychology of personal constructs*. New York: Norton, 1955.

Kelly, J. G., Blake, R. R., and Stromberg, C. E. The effect of role training on role reversal. *Group Psychotherapy*, 1957, **10**, 95–104.

Kelman, H. C. Attitude change as a function of response restriction. *Human Relations*, 1953, **6**, 185–214.

Kelman, H. C. The induction of action and attitude change. *Proceedings of the XIV International Congress of Applied Psychology*, 1961, **14**, 81–110.

King, B. T., and Janis, I. L. Comparison of the effectiveness of improvised versus non-improvised role-playing in producing opinion changes. *Human Relations*, 1956, **9**, 177–186.

Krasner, L. Role taking research and psychotherapy. *Research Report of VA Palo Alto*, 1959, No. 5.

Lakin, M., and Carson, R. C. A therapeutic vehicle in search of a theory of therapy. *Journal of Applied Behavioral Science*, 1966, **2**, 27–40.

Land, J. M. The use of an opinion change technique with a psychiatric patient population. Unpublished doctoral dissertation, Syracuse University, 1966.

Lazarus, A. Behaviour rehearsal versus non-directive therapy versus advice in effecting behaviour change. *Journal of Behaviour Research and Therapy*, 1966, **4**, 209–212.

Lawrence, D. H., and Festinger, L. *Deterrents and reinforcements*. Stanford: Stanford University Press, 1962.

Lewis, M. The effects of effort on choice: The value of a secondary reinforcer. *Psychological Reports*, 1965, **16**, 557–560.

Lewis, M. The effect of effort on value: An exploratory study of children. *Child Development*, 1964, **35**, 1337–1342.

Lewis, M. Some nondecremental effects of effort. *Journal of Comparative and Physiological Psychology*, 1964, **55**, 367–372.

Liberman, B. The effect of modeling procedures on attraction and disclosure in a psychotherapy analog. Unpublished doctoral dissertation, Syracuse University, in progress.

Libo, L. The projective expression of patient-therapist attraction. *Journal of Clinical Psychology*, 1957, **13**, 33–36.

Lieberman, S. The effects of changes in roles on the attitudes of role occupants. *Human Relations*, 1956, **9**, 385–402.

Liveright, A. A. Role-playing in leadership training. *Personnel Journal*, 1951, **29**, 412–416.

Locke, N. M. *Group psychoanalysis*. New York: New York University Press, 1961.

Lorr, M. Research problems in group psychotherapy. Paper read at American Group Psychotherapy Association, Washington, January, 1963.

Lowrey, L. G. Group therapy for mothers. *American Journal of Orthopsychiatry*, 1944, **14**, 589–592.

Mahl, H. F. Disturbances and silences in the patient's speech in psychotherapy. *Journal of Abnormal and Social Psychology*, 1956, **53**, 1–15.

Mann, J. H. Experimental evaluations of role playing. *Psychological Bulletin*, 1956, **53**, 227–234.

Mann, J. H. Personality and behavioral correlates of change produced by role playing experience. *Psychological Reports*, 1959, **5**, 505–526.

Mann, J. H., and Mann, C. H. The effect of role playing experience on self-ratings of interpersonal adjustment. *Group Psychotherapy*, 1958, **11**, 27–32.

Mann, J. H., and Mann, C. H. Role playing experience and interpersonal adjustment. *Journal of Counseling Psychology*, **6**, 1959, 148–152.

Mann, L. The effects of emotional role playing on desire to modify smoking habits. *Journal of Experimental Social Psychology*, 1967, **3**, 334–348.

Mann, L., and Janis, I. A follow-up study on the long-term effects of emotional role playing. *Journal of Personality and Social Psychology*, 1968, **8**, 339–342.

McGhie, A., and Chapman, J. Disorders of attention and perception in early schizophrenia. *British Journal of Medical Psychology*, 1961, **34**, 103–116.

McGuire, W. J. Inducing resistance to persuasion. In L. Berkowitz (Ed.), *Advances in Experimental Social Psychology*. Vol. 1. New York: Academic Press, 1964. Pp. 191–229.

McGuire, W. J. The current status of cognitive consistency theories. Paper presented at a conference on cognitive consistency at the University of Pennsylvania, Philadelphia, April 1965.

Medalia, N. Z. Authoritarianism, leader acceptance, and group cohesion. *Journal of Abnormal and Social Psychology*, 1955, **51**, 207–213.

Moreno, J. L. *Group psychotherapy, a symposium*. New York: Beacon, 1945.

Moreno, J. L. *Psychodrama*. New York: Beacon, 1946.

Munzer, J., and Greenwald, H. Interaction process analysis of a therapy group. *International Journal of Group Psychotherapy*, 1957, 7, 175–190.

Myers, A. Team competition, success, and the adjustment of group members. *Journal of Abnormal and Social Psychology*, 1961, **63**, 428–431.

Noble, F., Ohlsen, M., and Proff, E. A method for the quantification of psychotherapeutic interaction in counseling groups. *Journal of Counseling Psychology*, 1961, **8**, 54–61.

Nuttin, J. M., Jr. Attitude change after rewarded dissonant and consonant "forced compliance." *International Journal of Psychology*, 1966, **1**, 39–57.

Oakes, W. F. Reinforcement of Bales' categories in group discussion. *Psychological Reports*, 1962, **11**, 427–435.

Page, M. L. The modification of ascendent behavior in preschool children. *University of Iowa Studies of Child Welfare*, 1935, **12**, 1–69.

Parloff, M. B. Group dynamics and group psychotherapy: the state of the union. Paper read at American Group Psychotherapy Association, Washington, January, 1963.

Parloff, M. B. Therapist-patient relationship and outcome of psychotherapy. *Journal of Consulting Psychology*, 1961, **25**, 29–38.

Psathas, G. Phase movement and equilibrium tendencies in interaction process in psychotherapy groups. *Sociometry*, 1960, **23**, 177–194.

Rabbie, J. M., Brehm, J. W., and Cohen, A. R. Verbalization and reactions of cognitive dissonance. *Journal of Personality*, 1959, **27**, 407–417.

Rasmussen, G., and Zander, A. Group membership and self-evaluation. *Human Relations*, 1954, **7**, 239–251.

Roberts, B. H., and Strodtbeck, F. L. Interaction process differences between groups of paranoid schizophrenic and depressed patients. *International Journal of Group Psychotherapy*, 1953, **3**, 29–41.

Robinson, A. J. Further validation of role therapy. Unpublished master's thesis, Fort Hays State College, 1940.

Rogers, C. R. The characteristics of a helping relationship. In M. J. Stein (Ed.), *Contemporary psychotherapies*. New York: Free Press, 1961. Pp. 95–112.

Rosenberg, M. J. Some limits of dissonance: Toward a differentiated view of performance. In S. Feldman (Ed.), *Cognitive consistency*. New York: Academic Press, 1966. Pp. 135–170.

Roth, C. J. The effects of psychological reactance on interpersonal attraction on a quasi-psychodiagnostic task. Unpublished senior honors thesis, Syracuse University, 1967.

Sabalis, R. F. Subject authoritarianism, interviewer status, and interpersonal attraction. Unpublished master's thesis, Syracuse University, 1968.

Sanford, F. H. *Authoritarianism and leadership*. Philadelphia: Institute for Research in Human Relations, 1950.

Sapolsky, A. Effect of interpersonal relationships upon verbal conditioning. *Journal of Abnormal and Social Psychology*, 1960, **60**, 241–256.

Sapolsky, A. Relationship between patient-doctor compatibility, mutual perception, and outcome of treatment. *Journal of Abnormal Psychology*, 1965, **70**, 70–76.

Sarbin, T. R. Role theory. In G. Lindzey (Ed.), *Handbook of social psychology*. Vol. I. Cambridge: Addison-Wesley, 1954. Pp. 223–255.

Sarbin, T. R. Role theoretical interpretation of psychological change. In P. Worchel and D. Byrne (Eds.), *Personality Change*. New York: Wiley, 1964. Pp. 176–219.

Sarbin, T. R., and Allen, V. L. Role enactment, audience feedback, and attitude change. *Sociometry*, 1964, **27**, 183–193.

Sarbin, T. R., and Lim, D. T. Some evidence in support of the role taking hypothesis in hypnosis. *International Journal of Clinical and Experimental Hypnosis*, 1963, **11**, 90–103.

Schinebel, M. Role playing in counselor training. *Personnel and Guidance Journal*, 1953, **32**, 196–201.

Schneider, L. A proposed conceptual integration of group dynamics and therapy. *Journal of Social Psychology*, 1955, **42**, 173–191.

Schofield, W. *Psychotherapy, the purchase of friendship*. Englewood Cliffs, New Jersey: Prentice-Hall, 1964.

Schutz, W. *FIRO-B: A three-variable theory of interpersonal relations*. New York: Rinehart, 1958.

Scott, W. A. Attitude change through reward of verbal behavior. *Journal of Abnormal and Social Psychology*, 1957, **55**, 72–75.

Scott, W. A. Cognitive consistency, response, reinforcement, and attitude change. *Sociometry*, 1959a, **22**, 219–229.

Scott, W. A. Attitude change by response reinforcement: Replication and extension. *Sociometry*, 1959b, **22**, 328–335.

Seashore, S. E. Group cohesiveness as a factor in industrial morale and productivity. *American Psychologist*, 1954, **9**, 468.

Secord, P. F. Facial features and inference processes in interpersonal perception. In R. Taguri and L. Petrullo (Eds.), *Person perception and interpersonal behavior*. Stanford: Stanford University Press, 1958.

Shakow, D. Psychological deficit in schizophrenia. *Behavioral Science*, 1963, **8**, 275–305.

Sherif, M., and Sherif, C. W. *Groups in harmony tension*. New York: Harper, 1953.

Simonson, N. R. The impact of warm and cold self-disclosing therapists. Unpublished manuscript, Syracuse University, 1968.

Slavson, S. R. Are there "group dynamics" in therapy groups? *International Journal of Group Psychotherapy*, 1957, **7**, 131–154.

Snyder, W. V. *The psychotherapy relationship*. New York: Macmillan, 1961.

Stanley, J. C., and Klausmeier, H. J. Opinion constancy after formal role playing. *Journal of Social Psychology*, 1957, **46**, 11–18.

Stone, A. P., Parloff, M. B., and Frank, J. D. The use of "diagnostic" groups in a group therapy program. *International Journal of Group Psychotherapy*, 1954, **4**, 274–284.

Strong, S. R. Counseling: An interpersonal influence process. *Journal of Counseling Psychology*, 1968, **15**, 215–224.

Strupp, H. H. *Psychotherapists in action*. New York: Grune and Stratton, 1960.

Sturm, I. E. The behavioristic aspect of psychodrama. *Group Psychotherapy*, 1965, **18**, 50–64.

Talland, C. A. Task and interaction process: Some characteristics of therapeutic group discussion. In A. P. Hare, E. F. Borgatta, and R. F. Bales (Eds.), *Small groups*. New York: Alfred A. Knopf, 1955. Pp. 457–463.

Truax, C. B. Depth of interpersonal exploration on therapeutic process in group psychotherapy with and without vicarious therapy pretraining. Mimeograph, Wisconsin Psychiatric Institute, 1963.

Truax, C. B. The process of group psychotherapy. *Psychological Monographs*, 1961, **75**, Whole No. 511.

Truax, C. B., and Carkhuff, R. R. *Toward effective counseling and psychotherapy*. Chicago: Aldine, 1967.

Ullmann, L. P., Krasner, L., and Collins, B. J. Modification of behavior through verbal conditioning: effects in group therapy. *Journal of Abnormal and Social Psychology*, 1961, **62**, 128–132.

Van der Veen, F. Effects of the therapist and the patient on each other's therapeutic behavior. *Journal of Consulting Psychology*, 1965, **29**, 19–26.

Wallace, J. Role reward and dissonance reduction. *Journal of Personality and Social Psychology*, 1966, **3**, 305–312.

Walster, E., and Festinger, L. The effectiveness of "overheard" persuasive communications. *Journal of Abnormal and Social Psychology*, 1962, **65**, 395–402.

Wilson, W., and Miller, N. Shifts in evaluations of participants following intergroup competition. *Journal of Abnormal and Social Psychology*, 1961, **63**, 428–431.

Wolberg, L. R. *The technique of psychotherapy*. New York: Grune and Stratton, 1954.

Wolf, A., and Schwartz, E. K. *Psychoanalysis in groups*. New York: Grune and Stratton, 1962.

Yates, A. Delayed auditory feedback. *Psychological Bulletin*, 1963, **60**, 213–231.

Zimbardo, P. G. Involvement and communication discrepancy as determinants of opinion change. *Journal of Abnormal and Social Psychology*, 1960, **60**, 86–94.

Zimbardo, P. G. The effect of effort and improvisation on self persuasion produced by role-playing. *Journal of Experimental Social Psychology*, 1965, **1**, 103–120.

6

CLINICAL INNOVATION IN RESEARCH AND PRACTICE

ARNOLD A. LAZARUS

GERALD C. DAVISON

RUTGERS UNIVERSITY

STATE UNIVERSITY OF NEW YORK AT STONY BROOK

The main theme of the present chapter is that many of our greatest advances in therapeutic theory and practice come through clinical experimentation and innovation, rather than through laboratory research or controlled field trials across large samples of cases. To some, merely to think of clinical experimentation as *research* is new in itself. Many regard the laboratory and the clinic as opposite ends of a continuum. Research conducted in the laboratory is said to be precise, controlled, and uncontaminated. The ideas that flow from clinics are often regarded as woolly, riddled with bias, purely anecdotal, and even useless. The point of this chapter is that the path between the laboratory and the clinic is a two-way street. It is a statement of fact that most new methods have come from the work of creative

clinicians. Furthermore, as we hope to show, the process of discovery that is carried on within the clinical practices of some therapists is the equivalent of research.

Laboratory scientists and practicing clinicians can each offer unique contributions in their own right and can conceivably open hitherto new and unsuspected clinical-experimental dimensions for research and practice. Ideas tested in the laboratory may be applied by the practitioner who, in turn, may discover important individual nuances that remain hidden from the laboratory scientist simply because the tight environment of the experimental testing ground makes it impossible for certain behaviors to occur or for certain observations to be made. Conversely, ideas formulated in the clinic, provided that they are amenable to verification or disproof, can send scientists scurrying off into laboratories to subject the claims of efficacy to controlled tests. Cases in point will be cited further on.

Although many acts performed (or withheld) "for the sake of science" have no place in humane and service-oriented settings, the astute observer who makes use of applied scientific principles while endeavoring to alleviate suffering is often able to advance knowledge. In addition to serendipitous findings that may happen to extend the boundaries of knowledge, the clinician can deliberately set about discovering new facts and refining existing procedures. Of course, the tendency to issue authoritative statements on the basis of "clinical experience" is often viewed askance. While it is proper to guard against *ex cathedra* statements based upon flimsy and subjective evidence, it is a serious mistake to discount the importance of clinical experience *per se*. There is nothing mysterious about the fact that repeated exposure to any given set of conditions makes the recipient aware of subtle cues and contingencies in that setting which elude the scrutiny of those less familiar with the situation. Clinical experience enables a therapist to recognize problems and identify trends that are usually beyond the perceptions of novices, regardless of their general expertise. It is at this level that new ideas will come to the practitioner and often constitute breakthroughs that could not be derived from animal analogues or tightly controlled investigations. Different kinds of data and differing levels of information are obtained in the laboratory and the clinic. Each is necessary, useful, and desirable.

CLINICAL INNOVATION AND EXPERIMENTATION

A new and valuable perspective upon the clinical research enterprise should follow a concerted effort to make the process of experimentation and innovation more explicit. Innovation is the outcome of experimentation, for it is during or after experimentation that true innovators have the capacity to appreciate relationships that may go unnoticed by less observant workers. A specific excursion into one area of clinical inquiry should clarify this point of emphasis.

Most practitioners, for instance, have discovered how difficult it is to console many individuals immediately following an important loss in their lives (such as death of a friend, dismissal from a job, rejection by a lover, or a similar deprivation). The ensuing depression often remains unaltered by reassurance or even shock treatments and drugs. Supportive therapy over several weeks, notwithstanding the ever-present risk of suicide in these cases, often heralds the diminution of the patient's reported misery. In the present context, the clinical innovator is the person who addresses himself to the problem of what can be done to facilitate rapid recovery from a "reactive depression." This attitude demands some form of experimentation. The actual experimental operations will usually be determined in part by the therapist's own theoretical orientation. Those with a proclivity for organic notions will obviously be more inclined to search for an effective combination of drugs or some other biological mode of intervention. The psychologically-oriented therapist will search for more effective psychological procedures, usually limited by the restraints of his own beliefs (for instance, the "cognitive theorist" might look for newer and deeper mediating belief systems that cause subjective misery rather than for novel means of psychomotor expressiveness which those who espouse various "emotional-gut" theories might be inclined to develop). Occasionally, a sense of desperation may lead a clinician to make a response that fits neither his theoretical preconceptions nor his more usual empirical resources. Most clinical advances are preceded by what we might term a *frustration-observation* sequence.

Still confining ourselves, for illustrative purposes, to problems of "reactive depression," let us consider the practitioner who has expended energy, time, and effort to alleviate the suffering of a somewhat depressed but extremely demanding individual. The therapist has exhausted his fund of methods and techniques to no avail. Despite attempts to intervene at the sophisticated level of family relationships, to tap the underlying guilts and hostilities, and to ply the patient with appropriate medication and inspiration, the net result is a demanding and threateningly dependent person whose rapacious behavior provokes anger and anxiety in the therapist. At this stage, the harassed practitioner may advocate a course of action dictated solely by pragmatic convenience rather than by theoretical confidence. Out of keeping with his usual practices, he may confine the patient to bed for ten days and forbid any patient-therapist communication during this period. In all candor, his principal motive might simply be to "get the patient off his back" for a while. Ten days later, his patient is seen again and quite remarkably, reports feeling much better.

Unplanned or unexpected clinical improvements are often dismissed as "spontaneous remissions," but the clinical innovator is the one who carefully notes a variety of possible cause-effect sequences and thus discovers therapeutic levers that his less inquisitive colleagues are apt to overlook. A fortuitous clinical outcome might stimulate innumerable questions. In the case already mentioned, one might simply pose the obvious question: "Of what value might enforced bed rest be for certain cases of reactive depression?" Clinical trials are then feasible and experimental design, in its most rigorous sense, becomes essential. The independent variable—confining X category of patients to Y units of enforced bed rest— calls for all the salient safeguards against experimenter bias, contamination, and the like. An empirical rule might even evolve. "A period of seven to ten days of enforced bed rest can be expected to ameliorate depressive reactions in persons between the ages of fifteen to sixty years in whom the depressive reaction has been clearly precipitated by an event no more than three months previously, and in persons who have no history of chronic withdrawal reactions." Further experimentation will unearth exceptions to the rule and often call for its modification and revision. Eventually, practitioners may acquire a precise and scientific clinical rule or procedure with a predictable success-rate and clear lines of contraindication. This route is quite familiar in the practice of medicine but somewhat neglected in the practice of psychotherapy, where clinicians often seem bound to use only those methods that are justified by their theories.

Many difficulties arise when different theorists endeavor to reconcile identical empirical facts within divergent theoretical models. The efficacy of the "bed-rest hypothesis," if empirically established, will again be explained organically by organicists, psychoanalytically by psychoanalysts, behaviorally by behaviorists, and so forth. All too often, a useful method will be employed by practitioners of different theoretical persuasions only if it can be "explained" according to their own favorite theories (Weitzman, 1967). As Eysenck (1957) has pointed out, "the history of science does not deal kindly with attitudes of this kind."

A common avenue of clinical experimentation consists of the development of techniques arising out of the therapist's predilections. This was the route followed by most of the psychoanalytic offshoots. Very often, although departing from his teachings and generating independent hypotheses of their own, Freud's former pupils did not deviate very widely in matters of technique. Their patients still reclined on a couch and employed free association as their basic tool. The differences revolved entirely around points of emphasis, timing, and content of interpretations. However, Adler dispensed with the couch and substituted face-to-face discussions between patient and therapist and employed an active teaching role in place of a purely interpretive position. Stekel also added innovations in technique by frequently and actively interrupting a patient's free associations to underscore a significant point, or by advocating a different line of association as being possibly more productive. Occasional exhortation and direct advice were also employed, and the course of therapy seldom extended over more than six months. Nevertheless, the respective deviations in technique were usually dictated by the different views of man which Adler, Stekel, Sullivan, Horney, Fromm et al, espoused (although none of these individuals really evaluated the effects of their innovations). It stands to reason that a theorist who believes that emotional disturbances arise out of feelings of inferiority might develop and use different methods and techniques than a therapist who holds to a theory of unconscious sexual repression. The grave error is then to assume that if a technique proves successful in achieving its desired results, the process that gave rise to it is thereby necessarily strengthened or confirmed. For example, a Rankian might have reasoned that a depressed individual is actively reliving his birth trauma and craving for an intrauterine respite. Employing enforced bed rest as a symbolic return to the womb, and then discovering a clinical improvement in X amount of patients, the committed Rankian would be most resistant to the notion that the clinical outcome in no way strengthens his theories about the basic therapeutic process.

Some of Milton Erickson's selected papers compiled by Jay Haley (1967) represent a prime example of clinical experimentation as research. Always aware of the need for objective proof as contrasted with subjective clinical experience, Erickson devised ingenious experiments to test his hypotheses. His facility for on-the-spot inventiveness when confronted by unusual cases or challenging problems is probably unsurpassed. In reading his case reports, one sees a constant series of clinical choice points that tend to open new vistas for all inventive practitioners. Clinicians can increase and sharpen their own innovative capacities by studying Erickson's case studies and by seeking answers to such questions as, "What alerted him to the fact that the girl with the 'prostitution complex' required the therapist to play the role of a strong dictatorial father?" "What made him think of advising a young man to urinate through a bamboo pole in order to alleviate his anxiety?" He continuously stresses that "the nature and character of a single finding can often be more informative and valuable than a voluminous aggregate of data whose meaning is dependent upon statistical manipulation" (Erickson, 1953).

THEORY AND PRACTICE

The relationship between theory and clinical practice is most complicated. London (1964) has made the excellent though oft-ignored point that a sensible study of psychotherapy is best directed at what therapists DO, and only secondarily to the reasons they give for justifying their actions. *Techniques may, in fact, prove effective for reasons that do not remotely relate to the theoretical ideas that gave birth to them.* As Maher (1966) has pointed out, the history of psychotherapy is strewn with futile examples of clinical investigators building complex theoretical schemes to account for actions they have taken that prove effective. The need being emphasized is for the design of controlled studies to examine the active ingredients underlying the various techniques in clinical use. Research in desensitization over the past few years provides an excellent example of experimentally-minded clinicians beginning to ferret out the variables that operate to produce behavioral changes (for example, Davison, 1968b; Lang et al., 1965; Lang, 1969; Paul, 1969).

There is another side to this theory-practice issue, however, which we feel is sometimes dismissed. When selecting therapeutic techniques it matters very much which theoretical notions—however vague and even ultimately incorrect—a clinician espouses during the conduct of his clinical activities. For example, if one assumes that a given phobic reaction is best conceptualized as an anxiety-avoidance gradient (cf. Miller, 1959), and furthermore is not secondary to a basic underlying condition which is the proper focus for treatment, one is more likely to go ahead confidently with a technique like desensitization. Conversely, if one holds to a view that all phobias are adaptive to the extent that they protect the individual from libidinal impulses that would be devastating were they allowed expression, it would seem that the clinician might choose to dwell upon the presumed unconscious conflicts and ignore the manifest phobia. This is not to say that only one particular theoretical stance will lead to a particular mode of attack; rather, it is to say that the "set" with which a clinician approaches a problem definitely determines his own clinical behavior and his view of what occurs. This is one reason why we would advocate caution, tentativeness, and empirical testing when adopting any theoretical position. Often such positions harden commitments rather than facilitate discovery, which is the real purpose of theories.

Once one has assimilated certain theoretical constructs, it is necessary to apply these nomothetic principles to an idiographic case.

Gordon Allport (1937) has for many years been identified with the so-called "nomothetic-idiographic controversy," but we believe that Maher (1966) has recently made a convincing argument against a necessary incompatibility between these two approaches. The application of a general principle in a particular case would seem to depend not only on a familiarity with the principle but also on an accurate assessment of the given case. The example Maher uses is that of an engineer who must build a bridge across a particular river:

In order to build a bridge over a certain river, we must know the details of the soil mechanics, water flow, prevailing winds, topography, traffic usage, availability of labor and materials, and so on. When we consider all these, the total picture might not be like any other bridge that has ever been built. Nevertheless, none of the principles or assumptions that go into the final decisions could be made in contradiction to the laws of physics, economics, and the like (p. 112).

We shall return to this important issue later in this paper.

SOME CHARACTERISTICS OF CASE STUDIES AS RELATED TO RESEARCH

It would be a superhuman undertaking to try to explicate in a single chapter the processes of research in clinical innovation and experimentation with any sense of completeness. It seems expedient, therefore, to focus on our own experiences and to use the resultant methods and findings to communicate what we mean by clinical experimentation.

When a creative clinician learns new things from patients and invents new procedures to resolve difficult problems, he is conducting a form of research. There is usually a series of clinical trials or experiments in which reactions of a patient or several patients to the procedure are observed. How can clinicians make these discoveries, and how can they learn about behavior change and invent techniques for promoting it? A complete awareness of what information can and cannot be derived from case studies constitutes the first essential step

towards the achievement of any meaningful clinical innovations that deserve to be labelled "research."

There seem to us to be several characteristics unique to case studies that earn for them a firm place in psychological research. We will outline them below and then elaborate in detail upon each one:

1. A case study may cast doubt upon a general theory.

2. A case study may provide a valuable heuristic to subsequent and better-controlled research.

3. A case study may permit the investigation, although poorly controlled, of rare but important phenomena.

4. A case study can provide the opportunity to apply principles and notions in entirely new ways.

5. A case study can, under certain circumstances, provide enough experimenter control over a phenomenon to furnish "scientifically acceptable" information.

6. A case study can assist in placing "meat" on the "theoretical skeleton."

1. A Case Study May Cast Doubt Upon a General Theory.

The peculiar merit of case studies as disproofs of general theories has been recently pointed out independently by Eysenck (1964) and by Ullmann and Krasner (1965). The successful handling of a particular case may underscore an important exception to a theory. For example, a given theory may hold that a certain kind of problem is untreatable. If a therapist succeeds in making an impact upon the given problem, this would seem to cast doubt upon the tenets of the theoretical viewpoint under consideration. A particular theory may also predict that certain methods will prove antitherapeutic. To take one of the specific examples cited by Ullmann and Krasner: it has been routinely claimed from early psychoanalytic theory that the removal of a presenting problem will have negative consequences (such as psychotic breakdown or symptom substitution). Those who adhere to this notion will be wary about employing methods of "symptom removal," even when a direct approach is strongly needed. For instance, a "symptomatic" approach was recently applied in the treatment of an obese woman of 38 whose compulsive eating habits made it impossible for her to adhere to any diet. Therapy followed a technique first outlined by Lazarus (1958), in which the patient was hypnotized and instructed that whenever she strayed from her diet, she would immediately feel nauseated and also develop abdominal spasms. These hypnotic suggestions were reinforced at weekly intervals. At the same time, it was agreed that her husband would put aside $10 for each pound of weight lost towards the purchase of a second-hand automobile she very much wanted. It took almost eight months for her to lose the necessary 50 lbs. and to obtain her $500 car. A family friend who was studying psychiatry warned the patient that if she stopped overeating, she would probably turn to alcohol or drugs, or develop some other symptom in place of the one removed. We have conducted some extensive follow-ups which suggest that these untoward consequences did not occur in this case and that they generally are the exception rather than the rule. Let it be remembered that only one clearly negative instance is needed to cast doubt on any general hypothesis.

Another example from our own clinical work concerns the case of a middle-aged female physician who for many years had been extremely fearful of birds. Despite many years of psychoanalytically-oriented therapy, which had been aimed at uncovering the putative unconscious conflicts underlying the phobia, this client remained no less afraid of birds. In fact, during the year before consulting us, the phobia had been increasing in intensity. As frequently happens, she expressed concern about "symptomatic treatment." For whatever reasons, she had assimilated the widespread notion that such phobias serve a defensive function and must not be removed unless through the resolution of the "underlying conflict." With some reassurance on our part, she agreed to be desensitized to birds. Treatment was completed over 20 sessions, and generalization of improvement to the real-life setting kept pace fairly well with the progress in the consulting room. Throughout the desensitization, the client continually expressed

concern lest her fear be removed. Nevertheless she improved, and, most importantly for the present argument, did not become worse in other areas. If anything, other problems (not involving birds) were incidentally alleviated. Of course, one cannot conclude firmly from these data that it was the desensitization that alleviated the fear of birds. Fortunately, this appears to be beside the point—the fact is that she became much less fearful of birds without having any light shed on their "symbolic significance," and this was achieved without deterioration in other areas. Such evidence thus casts doubt upon the symptom substitution-relapse hypothesis and calls for more extensive testing of the issue.

2. A Case Study May Provide a Valuable Heuristic to Subsequent and Better-Controlled Research.

Case studies in clinical psychology are probably best known for suggesting new directions that might hopefully be pursued systematically by laboratory investigators. Examples here are legion, but we shall once again allude to systematic desensitization, which attracted considerable attention from the scientific psychological community primarily through the early clinical reports of Wolpe (1958, 1961) and Lazarus (1961). The fact that the desensitization procedures, however rationalized, could lead to profound changes in avoidance behavior, encouraged other investigators to subject the claims of efficacy to controlled laboratory tests (for instance, Lang and Lazovik, 1963; Paul, 1966) and to investigate the effective components of the procedure (for example, Davison, 1968b). It is uncertain whether these systematic research studies would have been undertaken without the pioneering clinical and case study reports; the fact is, at any rate, that the latter were indeed followed by the former.

This point can be illustrated in greater detail by describing the background of a current research program in which one of us is presently engaged.

In a case study published a few years ago (Lazarus, Davison, and Polefka, 1965), a child with a severe school phobia was enabled to attend school by means of a therapy that entailed his being accompanied to school by a therapist with whom he had a good relationship. The report mentioned *en passant* that a mild tranquilizer was introduced at a point when no further progress was being made by purely psychological means. After the child had taken this tranquilizer for a few mornings, he did overcome the hurdle, and the drug was discontinued. At that time it occurred to Davison that it might be beneficial to tell the child, after withdrawing the drug, that he had not "in fact" received an active tranquilizer. The idea was that if he were to be thus deprived of a drug-explanation for his clinical improvement, he might be more likely to continue acting as he had while under the drug, that is, with little anxiety. It was felt that he would have to attribute his behavior change as due *more to himself* than to an outside agent like a drug. For a variety of reasons, not the least of which was the very tricky nature of our therapeutic relationship, we did not follow through with this idea, and it lay dormant for a few years.

The opportunity to engage in some controlled research on this seemingly important question came about through the affiliation of Davison with a social psychologist, Dr. Stuart Valins. In conversations with Dr. Valins, it seemed that the vaguely formulated notion from the aforementioned case study could be meaningfully related to a larger body of social psychological theory and research, primarily the work of Stanley Schachter and his colleagues. This work stresses the central importance of cognitive variables in the generation of emotional states (for example, Schachter and Singer, 1962; Schachter and Wheeler, 1962). Perhaps of more relevance was the research by Valins which indicated the possibility of manipulating a person's cognitions and thereby *changing* his overt behavior. Thus, for example, Valins (1966) was able to increase the liking for nude photographs on the part of male undergraduates by deceiving them into thinking that their heartbeats were changing to some of the photographs and not to others. A subsequent study, by Valins and Ray (1967), indicated that one could reduce avoidance behavior in an analogous fashion. Returning to the idea arising from the school phobia case study, it seemed that the way a person explains to

himself the reason for a change in his behavior might be crucial to the maintenance of that new behavior. For specifics of the theoretical framework, the reader is referred to Davison and Valins (1969), in which two experiments describe initial confirmation of the notions arising from the case study. Briefly, all subjects were deceived into believing that their tolerance for painful electric shock had increased markedly due to the ingestion of a drug. Then half of the subjects (Placebo) were disabused of the notion that a drug had changed their behavior: they were simply told that they had been given a placebo. The control group (Drug) were told that the drug was wearing off. In other words, the first group of subjects (Placebo) went into their test for persistence of behavior-change believing that they could not have improved because of the drug, while the second group of subjects (Drug) continued to believe that the drug had influenced the behavior change. As expected from the attribution-notions, the Placebo subjects maintained their "drug-produced" improvement to a significantly greater degree than the Drug subjects.

Having demonstrated the utility of these attribution-notions in an analogue to psychoactive drug therapy, the next step will be to see whether these results will hold up using actual drugs and true drug-effects. Ultimately such laboratory research will bring us back to the starting-point, namely the clinical situation. We are just beginning experiments involving the use of actual drugs to alter "abnormal" behavior within this attribution framework.

3. A Case Study May Permit the Investigation, Although Poorly Controlled, of Rare but Important Phenomena.

Human beings are capable of harming themselves, and others, in the most unusual ways. It is the practicing clinician who is most likely to encounter the vagaries of human conduct. Unusual case reports from "field observers" can add to clinical and experimental knowledge. For example, one of us was consulted by a young married couple who practiced a most bizarre sexual perversion. As a prelude to sexual intercourse, the young man would draw blood by cutting a small incision on the palm of his wife's right hand. She would then stimulate his penis, using the blood of her right palm as a lubricant. Normal intercourse would then ensue, and the moment the wife felt her husband ejaculating, she was required to dig her nails deep into the small of his back or buttocks. Each sado-masochistic act was followed by guilt and remorse. But the most serious consequence of these abnormal practices was the fact that repeated septic wounds tended to develop. The couple in question were both intelligent college graduates who had indulged in these gory activities intermittently for 3½ years. They were vague and uncertain about the beginnings of their strange behavior. Signs of delusions, hallucinations, concrete or overinclusive thinking, and other psychotic behaviors were not present.

Knowledge, in cases such as this, can be advanced in two ways. First, a detailed study could conceivably throw light on the genesis of the problem and thereby add new insights into human aberrations. Secondly, a successful treatment strategy applied in this case may have relevance for overcoming other deviant behaviors. In regard to the first consideration, only vague and very tentative inferences could be drawn. At best, there appeared to be some associations with menstruation (probably safe vis-à-vis possible pregnancy) and the husband's frustrated desires to become a surgeon. But the connection between blood *per se* and sexual excitement remained obscure. It is possible that an extended analysis of the couple may have proved enlightening, but a remarkably simple remedy proved so successful that they were no longer motivated to undergo further therapy. When it transpired that they had desisted from engaging in their perversion since commencing treatment, but that the husband had been completely impotent, the wife was advised to obtain a harmless red dye and add it to any transparent lubricant. With the use of this mixture, the husband's potency was restored and the need for actual "blood-letting" was obviated. The same mixture applied to the husband's buttocks at the commencement of intercourse made the "ejaculatory assault" unnecessary. Thus, a harmless but unusual practice was recommended in place of a painful and harmful routine. For reasons unknown, the birth of their first child put an end to their unusual practices altogether. Here again there is tremendous potential for clinical discovery. In this case, the need to forego the understanding of etiology for purposes of practical expediency may be considered a pragmatic rule which "depth therapists" might consider.

Unlike the preceding case, in which causative factors remained obscure despite a constructive therapeutic outcome, another unusual and bizarre problem was readily reduced to simple and benign etiological factors. The patient was a 23-year-old student whose sole sexual outlets consisted of masturbation to erotic fantasies of female corpses. Despite so complex a deviation from societal norms, intensive clinical interviews revealed no psychotic features. By searching for specific and discrete areas of tension, sensitivity, and the like, a systematic and piecemeal reconstruction of his sexual pattern became possible.

From the start, his knowledge of sex was misrepresented as a form of assault which respectable women detested. His mother underscored the utter contempt with which women viewed men's sexual cravings. These negative learnings were reinforced by a female cousin who ridiculed him for having obtained an erection when they were "fooling around." Subsequently, his sense of shame was mitigated by the aggressive fantasy of murdering his cousin and ejaculating into her mouth.

His overbearing mother and two older female siblings, whom he described as "vituperative," created a passive-aggressive attitude towards women. He was inclined to inhibit the overt expression of all negative feelings towards them. His earlier attempts at self-assertion had been sharply punished by his mother and sisters.

A series of psychotherapeutic maneuvers successfully undermined his passivity to the extent that he initially overstepped his assertive prerogatives and actually came to blows with one of his sisters. He finally gained a healthier perspective concerning his interpersonal dealings, but the only change in his sexual behavior was a new-found ability to enjoy his bizarre sexual fantasies.

Much emphasis to the effect that normal women do not view sexual arousal in men with derision or contempt had no therapeutic value. How was one to institute normal heterosexual behavior? One suggestion was to administer an aversive electric shock while he was engaging in his usual masturbatory fantasies, and to terminate the shock upon his verbalizing a normal heterosexual fantasy. However, since the thought of being seen by a woman (and especially his mother) while he had an erection aroused so much tension and shame, a desensitization procedure seemed strongly indicated. The hierarchy extended from dead females to unconscious women (who could not register disgust at his sexual excitement) to women at various degrees of wakefulness: anesthetized, drunk, semiconscious, and the like. He was soon able, without negative affect, to picture himself engaging in sexual intercourse with a prostitute whose disinterest was evident and whose attention was diverted.

No doubt, the greatest therapeutic factor was his choice of a responsive female partner when he took the plunge, so to speak. "He reported his delight and astonishment at the fact that females also become sexually aroused, and he was particularly comforted to find that he had been praised and lauded for his sexual potency and ardor instead of receiving criticism and contempt" (Lazarus, 1968a).

The success of the technique does not imply anything about the nature of the complex processes that caused such strange symptoms to arise from such simple beginnings. Now that the problem is resolved, one might proceed backwards in order to try to discover the original processes.

When presenting the aforementioned case at meetings and seminars, the chief impact has been to encourage therapists to view some of their seemingly intractable cases in a more optimistic light and to attempt a more direct and economical resolution of several bizarre difficulties that ordinarily engender despair and carry a negative prognosis.

4. A Case Study Can Provide the Opportunity to Apply Principles and Notions in Entirely New Ways.

The clinical setting affords the opportunity and challenge to develop new procedures based on techniques and principles already in use. It is a truism that one will look in vain for the "textbook case." Clinicians are all too often faced with problems for which existing procedures seem unsuitable or insufficient. At the same time, certain aspects of a particular clinical problem may call for a new way of relating old principles and procedures to the resolution of the problem. This issue is not unrelated to Point 6 below, but it seems worthy of separate illustration here.

Particularly in an outpatient setting, the therapist is often faced with the necessity of exerting aversive control over the behavior of a client when in fact the client is not literally under the therapist's control, as is the case, for instance, in a hospital setting. In a recent case, the therapist was faced with the necessity of getting an obstreperous boy to stop misbehaving rather quickly so as to prevent an already deteriorating home situation from becoming irreparable. During the very first session, the therapist sensed that the boy would probably cooperate in a reasonable program to improve his relationship with his father. It appeared that a principal and most pressing problem was to get the boy to stop disobeying his father, for this invariably caused the father to become very abusive. Inasmuch as other people had probably been trying to *persuade* the boy on rational grounds to stop misbehaving, this approach was not entertained as a possibility. Rather, the therapist scanned his knowledge of the experimental literature for means by which behavior patterns can be weakened or eliminated. Naturally, one would look at the punishment literature, the presentation of aversive stimuli contingent upon an undesirable behavior. However, it was very clear that the therapist could not possibly follow the boy around and punish him or threaten him with punishment if he were to misbehave. So, while listening to him recount situations in which he would behave or misbehave, the therapist reviewed in his mind the trend in behavior therapy to proceed from actual to imaginal stimulus situations. For example, he thought of Mary Cover Jones' work (Jones, 1924) in real life with little Peter, and the shift from such *in vivo* work to systematic desensitization, which presents aversive situations in imagination. Similarly, the counterconditioning literature with homosexuals indicated a shift from actual to imaginal situations (Thorpe, Schmidt, and Castell, 1963; Davison, 1968a). A behavior analysis revealed that the boy in fact behaved very well whenever his father seemed especially angry. In keeping with the above, the boy was asked to *imagine* his father as extremely angry. He reported spontaneously that imagining this scene led to an almost immediate decrease in his tendency even to *think* about misbehaving. As the boy quickly realized, his image of an irate father created the same subjective situation that led to obedient behavior. It was also clear to him that if his behavior could be controlled by "creating" an angry father, he might be able to avoid having to face an *actual* angry father. In other words, he was being taught a means of controlling his own behavior in a way that he was not able to do before.

The second session did indeed find a dramatic improvement at home. The boy described in great detail several situations in which he had been able to use the "little trick." This change in his behavior led to the expected improvement in his relationship with the father. Therapy then continued along other lines, not the least of which was a sort of "one-downsmanship" conversation so that the boy would not become unduly suppressed or "neurotic" by controlling his behavior in this fashion. Through role playing, he learned a sense of pride in being able to accede to some of his father's unreasonable demands instead of incurring his wrath. (This case is discussed in greater detail in Davison, 1969.)

Another case, of quite a different nature, also illustrates the example of "tried and true" procedures employed in a rather novel context.

The use of deep-muscle relaxation has an extensive history in medicine, clinical psychology, and psychiatry. The pioneering work of Edmund Jacobson (1938) was concerned principally with the exploration of the Watsonian notion that thoughts and feelings were actually located in the peripheral musculature. Jacobson, a physician, also reported therapeutic benefits derived from relaxation when it was practiced by anxious people. In Europe, Schultz and Luthe (1959) were independently exploring the use of what they called "autogenic training" to reduce anxiety and foster well-being. In this country Haugen, Dixon, and Dickel (1963) outlined an entire therapy based upon deep-muscle relaxation. Mothers who have gone through natural childbirth are also familiar with muscle relaxation, not only to reduce anxiety but also to facilitate movement of the baby through the cervix (Karmel, 1959). Of course, Wolpe's technique of systematic desensitization rests upon the anxiety-inhibiting effects of striate muscle relaxation. More recently, psychologists and others interested in meditation and other eastern practices are drawing a connection between muscle relaxation and Yoga exercises (for example, Pfeiffer, 1967; Stoyva, 1968). The many and varied applications of relaxation probably share the implicit or explicit purpose of reducing subjective feelings of anxiety. In the case described below, it was possible to use relaxation in a totally different way to handle a problem that was hitherto considered unapproachable by relaxation training. Clinical innovation implies the discovery that "old" methods can be applied to new problems, as well as the discovery of new methods for overcoming common but seemingly intractable syndromes.

The case is that of a middle-aged male hospital patient diagnosed as "paranoid schizophrenic," primarily on the basis of his complaints about "pressure points" on his forehead and in other parts of his body. These "pressure points" were believed by him to be signals from outside forces impelling him towards certain decisions. The man had received treatment for two months without any change in these "pressure points." In fact, he had even managed to have the medical staff approve the removal of a cyst over his right eye in the hope that this might remove the "pressure points." Unfortunately, this had no effect upon his "paranoid delusions." Because of their theoretical orientation, the psychiatrists and residents had been restricting their clinical investigations to his past history, and, not surprisingly, were finding events in his past to which they assigned considerable etiological significance. Nonetheless, the "pressure points" remained unabated. The therapist met this man in a Grand Ward

Round in a psychiatric hospital, during which he inquired of the patient whether he would describe himself as a "tense" or "anxious" individual. This aspect of the clinical picture had been largely ignored by the presenting physician. When the patient reported that he was indeed very anxious, the therapist agreed to attempt therapy with him as a demonstration case.

During the first session, the therapist, instead of looking to past history, concentrated on clearly delineating those situations in which the man became particularly aware of his "pressure points." The patient was able to identify several such situations which were, at the same time, clearly anxiety-provoking. For example, being a truck driver, he would often get the "pressure points" when he was lost and late with a truckload of goods. He then saw them as helpful in deciding how to reach his destination. This led the therapist to inquire whether decision-making situations of any importance were, in general, anxiety-provoking. Indeed they were, and indeed they set the occasion for the most frequent occurrence of his "pressure points."

Having satisfied himself that there was a close relationship between anxiety and the "pressure points," the therapist asked the patient to extend his right arm, clench his fist, and slowly bend the wrist downwards so as to bring the closed hand toward the inside of his forearm. The intent was to produce a feeling of severe muscle tension in the forearm, and this is precisely what the patient reported. He reported also, however, that it felt very much like a "pressure point." The therapist, believing that he had a good enough relationship with the man to avoid being thrust into the patient's "delusional system" by disagreeing with him, suggested an alternative interpretation of the "pressure points": perhaps they were simply a consequence of his becoming tense and anxious in particular kinds of situations. It was suggested to the man that, in the absence of a naturalistic scientific explanation, he, like other people, tended to explain strange occurrences in somewhat supernatural or mystical terms. The patient agreed that the merit of the therapist's hypothesis was that it seemed easily amenable to verification or disproof. The means would be

to train him in deep muscle relaxation and then to determine whether the relaxation could control the occurrence of the "pressure points." The man consented to this, and relaxation training was undertaken. Conventional relaxation therapy extended over several weeks. Outside of therapy, the man was instructed to pay careful attention to the occurrence of the "pressure points" and to confirm or weaken the assumed connection between anxiety, especially in decision-making situations, and the emergence of troublesome "pressure points." The man cited enough occurrences to confirm the hypothesis, and as he was becoming more and more proficient in relaxation, he also reported some degree of control over the intensity and even the persistence of the "pressure points" by means of differential relaxation (Davison, 1965; Wolpe and Lazarus, 1966). After eight additional sessions over a nine-week period, the man was beginning to refer to the "pressure points" as "sensations," and his conversation was generally losing its "paranoid flavor."

What we have here is the application of differential relaxation as a means of testing a nonparanoid hypothesis about bodily sensations. Clearly, there is much more to the case than can be explained by relaxation principles alone. For instance, it is likely that new cognitions were induced simply via persuasion. Nevertheless, a functional analysis of the man's clinical picture led to the hypothesis that the "pressure points" were part of a general anxiety reaction to specific kinds of situations. While it is possible that they had complex symbolic meanings for the patient, simple relaxation was effective in controlling the sensations. This helped the patient to account for the sensations in terms of a tension reaction rather than as a product of external forces. That the man became "less paranoid" as therapy proceeded does suggest that the use of differential relaxation in conjunction with what might be called "cognitive restructuring" was indeed an important element in the therapy. For specifics of this therapy, the reader is referred to Davison (1966). This case report indicates both that clinicians should not become overawed by symptoms just because they seem strange, and that they should remain willing to experiment with simple, straightforward procedures.

5. A Case Study Can, Under Certain Circumstances, Provide Enough Experimenter Control Over a Phenomenon to Furnish "Scientifically Acceptable" Information.

We have at least implicitly accepted thus far the commonly held view that case reports are intrinsically uncontrolled (for instance, Maher, 1966). However, one can look to the work of the Skinnerians in both laboratories and clinical settings for apparently good disproofs of this point of view. As has been documented in many places (for example, Sidman, 1962), one can establish a reliable baseline for the occurrence of a given behavior in an individual case and then demonstrate changes that follow the alteration of a particular contingency. Then we may return the behavior to its original level by changing the contingency once again. This is the familiar A-B-A design.

For instance, it became necessary to reinstate walking behavior in a six-year-old autistic child who had regressed to the point where he crawled around on his hands and knees more than 80 percent of the time. This was achieved by instructing his teachers to offer him candy and social reinforcement (attention and praise) intermittently for walking, while completely ignoring him when crawling. Within two weeks the child walked normally and seldom crawled. One of the teachers questioned the relevance of the reinforcement contingencies and maintained that it was merely noncontingent love and approval that altered the child's behavior. To test this hypothesis, the teachers were again directed to offer "love and approval," only this time to make it coincide with crawling behavior while ignoring the child when walking. In less than a week the child had reverted to pre-treatment levels of crawling. Finally, by reversing the contingencies once more, he stopped crawling and resumed normal walking activities. The work of Montrose Wolf and his colleagues provides clear-cut instances of this typical operant conditioning approach to the control and prediction of single organism behavior (e.g., Harris et al., 1964). Another good example is the study by Gardner et al. (1968). Although our Skinnerian colleagues would probably shudder to see their research paradigm construed in terms of a case study, we nonetheless find it fruitful to do so, at least for purposes of this exposition.

Moreover, Eysenck (1965) has cited a case report described by Katsch, which provides evidence no less compelling than data derived from many laboratory experiments. Katsch described his "clinical" investigation of psychologically-based asthmatic attacks as being under the tight control of the stimulus "mother-in-law." Attack could be readily induced and relieved by manipulating the visivility of a picture of the mother-in-law. To quote Eysenck(pp. 170–171):

Katsch finally arrived at the hypothesis that the patient's mother-in-law, with whom he had many conflicts, constituted the source of the emotional trouble producing the asthmatic attacks and that a very large picture of her which hung in the bedroom of the patient was a conditioned stimulus for these attacks. Such a theory can obviously be tested by making predictions from it which can be falsified or verified. Accordingly, Katsch turned the mother-in-law's face to the wall, as it were, and immediately the asthmatic attacks ceased. They could be brought back at will, by turning the picture round again, and they could again be terminated by turning it to the wall once more; in other words, Katsch had achieved complete control over the asthmatic attacks of his patient. To say that this is merely a single case report, signifying very little if anything at all, is a complete misunderstanding of the scientific method. If Katsch had merely reported that on the basis of a conditioning type of theory he had cured a particular patient of a particular disorder, then indeed we would be justified in saying that nothing very interesting or important had been achieved, because patients have been cured by all sorts of methods ranging from the sublime to the ridiculous ... However, within a particular therapeutic session we may attempt to bring the phenomena we are dealing with under strict experimental control, as, for instance, in the case of the experiment by Katsch just mentioned; and when we achieve such a measure of control, we may quite reasonably say that we have gone beyond the simple stage of curing or not curing a neurotic, and have come to the point where very much more detailed predictions are possible and where, therefore, a much better way has been achieved of testing the general theories under which we are working.

6. A Case Study Can Assist in Placing "Meat" on the "Theoretical Skeleton."

The reader will recall our earlier discussion of the relationship between theory and clinical practice. It was pointed out that the theoretical notions to which a clinician subscribes seem to bear importantly on the specific decisions he makes in a particular case. The clinician in fact approaches his work with a given set, a framework for ordering the complex data that are his domain. But frameworks are insufficient. The clinician, like any other applied scientist, must fill out the theoretical skeleton. Individual cases present problems that always call for knowledge beyond basic psychological principles. As an example, consider what occurred during a training program that one of us conducted several years ago (Davison, 1964). During an eight - week program, undergraduates were trained to work with autistic children in the manner first suggested by Ferster (1961). The training entailed teaching the undergraduates what was known up to that time about changing the behavior of autistic children along social-learning lines. They were then exposed to an actual clinical situation where they were required to select behaviors to reinforce, extinguish, or punish, and to employ the most effective reinforcers in a given situation. The decisions about timing and other strategic choices were left pretty much up to the undergraduate therapists. The need to place "meat" on the "theoretical skeleton" arose when one of the therapists reported a case in whom the M & M's which had been effective reinforcers at one stage were losing their effectiveness. Working within a framework that necessitated an effective reinforcing event in order to have leverage over the child, the therapist searched for another reinforcer. He noticed that every time the child passed a window, she paused for a moment to look at her reflection. The therapist quickly obtained a mirror and was able to make "peeking into the mirror" the reinforcing event for obeying certain commands. Thus, the opportunity to peer into a mirror was made contingent upon various prosocial behaviors in the same *functional* way as the M & M's had been used. Guided by a general principle (reinforcement theory), the clinical situation demanded improvisation and inventiveness beyond a predetermined category of rewards (M & M's) or other primary reinforcers. It was not until a couple of years later that we came upon the work of Premack (1959), which

seemed to legitimize this procedure in learning theory terms. Premack extends the notion of reinforcement to include behaviors that have a higher probability of occurring in a given situation than the behavior one wishes to reinforce.

Further illustration of this point can be underscored by referring to desensitization procedures in general and phobic reactions in particular. The general technique of desensitization—presenting items, relaxing people, and so on—has been detailed quite specifically (for example, Wolpe and Lazarus, 1966). In fact, the procedure has been so well programmed that a Device for Automated Desensitization at the University of Wisconsin (Melamed and Lang, 1967) has already effected numerous "cures" of simple phobias. In the management of less simple and straightforward cases, however, the mechanistic sequences seldom hold up. In these instances, the "meaty" issues involve decisions about precisely what idiosyncratic variations to place on the hierarchy, whether desensitization is even appropriate to the case, and if so, whether crucial dimensions of anxiety have been properly spelled out. In placing further "meat" on the "theoretical skeleton," Lazarus (1968b) has added various cognitive procedures to the usual desensitization sequence. These additions would probably not have arisen if difficult individual cases had not called for revisions, refinements, and extensions of existing methods. Here again it is likely to be the *practitioner* who is compelled to amplify theories and techniques in order to accommodate individual variations that expose deficiencies in our existing areas of knowledge.

COMMENTS ON OBJECTIFIED SINGLE CASE STUDIES

Extensive clinical research depends mainly on averages, derived from statistical analyses of relatively large groups of patients. The unit here is based upon group averages and percentages, with the focus directed at variations between patients. Those who regard this intra- or inter-group approach as the only valid and scientific method of clinical inquiry are in error. A model not based upon variation between patients, but upon different averages or responses within a patient, need be no less valid or reliable.

The individual patient may be studied in two ways. First, he may be used as "his own control." In this connection, individual patients are studied more carefully than is usual when group comparisons are under investigation, but the findings can be added to hypotheses that still center around *group* norms. Second, in the truly intensive individual clinical design, the subject becomes his own laboratory, and hypotheses that arise are tested solely with reference to that particular individual. In the latter instance, the patient's variability and reaction patterns may be studied minute-to-minute, hour-to-hour, day-to-day, session-to-session, and so on. Statistical probabilities can be computed, and experimental design in its most rigorous sense can be applied. The patient's behavior can be described in terms of a multidimensional or multivariate probability distribution, and therapeutic progress can then be assessed in relation to these probability distributions. Symptom frequency and symptom intensity can be woven into the measures obtained and form part of the overall evaluation of treatment effects.

Much greater precision in these studies has followed the use of recordings, films, and videotapes. Since any given clinical observer is subject to his own within-rater variability, this factor seems less likely to distort and influence results when cases can be evaluated by different raters (notwithstanding problems of inter-rater reliability). Advances in telemetry and other electronic recording devices have added further impetus to objectivity and quantitative accuracy.

The general trend in clinical research is in the direction of greater specificity. Broad questions such as "Is psychotherapy effective?" are now considered quite meaningless and have been replaced by the standard scientific question: "What specific therapeutic interventions produce specific changes in specific patients under specific conditions?" (Strupp and Bergin, 1969). Yet, when aiming for specificity, the major drawback of extensive statistical designs is the fact that they yield only group norms and probabilities, and do not tell us very much about a given individual in the group. Only case studies permit one to relate therapeutic effect to specific contingent patient-characteristics.

When an individual therapeutic effect follows a sequence of treatment methods within an appropriately controlled framework, numerous patient-therapist characteristics in whose context the effect took place can be specified. One can thus narrow down the particular patient and technique variables involved. Strictly speaking, specific inferences are valid only with respect to the individual case itself, but if one relates the particular individual's most relevant characteristics to similar characteristics in other people, general theories can be formulated in terms of these common characteristics. One does not focus upon identical cases (since everyone is unique, there are no completely identical cases), but there are often sufficient similarities and obvious dissimilarities to permit the evaluation of treatment effects on the basis of these related and unrelated characteristics. The basic emphasis is upon the documentation of clinical research, with special reference to objective ratings and the statistical study of the course of a given patient's treatment, in relatively concrete and operational terms (Chassan, 1967). Dr. M. B. Shapiro of the Maudsley Hospital in London has also long been a champion of the intensive experimental single-case-study design (e.g., Shapiro, 1961a, 1961b, 1966).

THE PROCESS OF TECHNIQUE REFINEMENT

Modifications, revisions, and refinements in therapeutic techniques occupy a central role in clinical experimentation and innovation. The process can be clearly identified by tracing the extensions and variations that have accrued to the method of desensitization over the years. Initially, patients were escorted *in vivo* by the therapist, who exposed them in a graduated fashion to their feared situation (for example, Williams, 1923; Kretschmer, 1934). Next, instead of escorting patients into the actual feared situations, Salter (1949) relied exclusively upon the patient's imagination of the feared situation, employing relaxation and other counterphobic sensations. Wolpe (1954, 1961) extended the use of imaginal desensitization by employing carefully calibrated hierarchies. The clinical utility of Wolpe's technique was first confirmed by Lazarus and Rachman (1957), and the first laboratory study was conducted by Lazovik and Lang (1960).

Most therapists today consider desensitization a method that consists mainly of four separate operations. First, specific and basic tension and anxiety areas are obtained by careful and highly focused clinical inquiries. Second, the anxiety areas are divided into specific themes. Third, the items are ranked in ascending order of subjective disturbance for the patient. Fourth, the patient, while adequately relaxed and calm, is enjoined to picture each successive scene until eventually even the most distressing events cease to engender any subjective feelings of disturbance. The stage is now set for clinical experimentation and innovation.

One of the first and most obvious questions is whether imaginal desensitization procedures are applicable to phobic children. Some evidence for its pediatric utility was furnished in a clinical report (Lazarus, 1959). Here we have one of the simplest and most direct illustrations of clinical experimentation as research: a method that has some empirical support with one population (adults) was directly tested on a different population (children). Careful observation, as one might expect, led to modifications that were in keeping with the ongoing clinical demands. Thus, the use of relaxation proved less and less useful in the desensitization treatment of several phobic children. It soon became imperative to search for a more effective counterphobic response, within the desensitization framework, that would prove especially effective with children. Since most children seem capable of responding to fantasy processes more readily than to muscle-relaxation procedures, it seemed most logical to experiment with "emotive imagery" in place of relaxation (Lazarus and Abramovitz, 1962).

The use of imagery that is presumed to arouse feelings of pride, mirth, affection, self-assertion, and similar positive affective states, proved highly effective in place of relaxation. For example, a ten-year-old boy was afraid to travel in the family car ever since it was involved in a minor collision some three months previ-

ously. The use of "emotive imagery" entailed a series of imagined scenes in which the boy and his father were proudly showing the automobile to the boy's favorite cartoon characters. "And imagine that Yogi Bear is very excited and is asking your daddy to take him for a drive." The final image involved an exciting chase in which the boy and his father drove "Green Lantern" in pursuit of some bank robbers. After only two sessions, the boy willingly went for a family outing in the car and displayed no further anxiety. Having established "emotive imagery" as an effective pediatric procedure with certain fearful children, the next logical step was to examine its feasibility with adult patients. We were thus back to the original population (adults), and further clinical questions were posed and answered that again led to the modification of "emotive imagery" for use with adults (Wolpe and Lazarus, 1966).

Other obvious questions concerning desensitization methods were: (1) Is this procedure applicable to *groups* of phobic subjects? This was affirmatively answered by Lazarus (1961), who devised desensitization programs for both homogeneous and heterogeneous groups. (2) Apart from relaxation and positive imagery, what other easily applicable anti-anxiety responses can be employed within a desensitization framework? This question became fairly urgent when it was found that several people were resistant to relaxation procedures and were also having difficulty in conjuring up vivid images. Clinical experimentation again provided a tentative answer when it was found that vigorous muscular activity appeared to undermine anxiety and tension in many individuals (Lazarus, 1965). (3) What clinical effects will *combinations* of counter-phobic responses have on individual patients, specific types of problems, and various times of therapeutic intervention? Tentative conclusions point to the fact that combinations such as relaxation-plus-positive-imagery expedite therapeutic outcomes (Lazarus, 1968b).

In this manner, a wealth of useful clinical empirical information can be accumulated. Further research can readily extend the empirical data and distill some of the basic process variables involved (e.g., Davison, 1968b). And as already mentioned, any of these clinical impressions are amenable to properly controlled laboratory investigations in their own right.

Because of our therapeutic bias, we have emphasized only experiments and clinical trials that are directly related to treatment and that are intended to partially alleviate emotional suffering in a field where so many people seek help and so few ever really find it. Nevertheless, the field of clinical experimentation as research need not be involved with treatment *per se*. Studies on intermittent reinforcement, for example, were not conducted with treatment applications in mind, but the results are certainly relevant to clinical experimental investigations. Many areas of investigation are carried out with normal subjects. The basic aim of clinical experimentation is to be able to predict changes following specified experimental operations. Our own interests favor those kinds of experiments that endeavor to provide a framework of scientifically based knowledge for the treatment of specific abnormalities of behavior, or that are intended to explore particular techniques in order to either examine their validity or to improve them and to specify limiting conditions for their application (cf. Yates, 1970). Perhaps the ultimate question, as amplified by Strupp and Bergin (1969), is "in knowing how technique and therapist variables interact to influence client behavior under specifiable conditions." It is to this end that meaningful clinical experimentation should be directed.

REFERENCES

Allport, G. W. *Personality: A psychological interpretation*. New York: Holt, 1937.

Chassan, J. B. *Research design in clinical psychology and psychiatry*. New York: Appleton-Century-Crofts, 1967.

Davison, G. C. A social learning therapy programme with an autistic child. *Behaviour Research and Therapy*, 1964, **2**, 149–159.

Davison, G. C. Relative contributions of differential relaxation and graded exposure to in vivo desensitization of a neurotic fear. *Proceedings of the 73rd Annual Convention of the American Psychological Association*. Washington, D.C.: APA, 1965.

Davison, G. C. Differential relaxation and cognitive restructuring in therapy with a "paranoid schizophrenic" or "paranoid state." *Proceedings of the 74th Annual Convention of the American Psychological Association*. Washington, D.C.: APA, 1966.

Davison, G. C. Elimination of a sadistic fantasy by a client-controlled counterconditioning technique. *Journal of Abnormal Psychology*, 1968, **73**, 84–90. (a)

Davison, G. C. Systematic desensitization as a counterconditioning process. *Journal of Abnormal Psychology*, 1968b, **73**, 91–99. (b)

Davison, G. C. Self-control through "imaginal aversive contingency" and "one-downsmanship": Enabling the powerless to accommodate unreasonableness. In J. D. Krumboltz and C. E. Thoresen (Eds.), *Behavioral counseling: cases and techniques*. New York, Holt, 1969.

Davison, G. C., and Valins, S. Maintenance of self-attributed and drug-attributed behavior change. *Journal of Personality and Social Psychology*, 1969, **11**, 25–33.

Erickson, M. H. Therapy of a psychosomatic headache. *Journal of Clinical and Experimental Hypnosis*, 1953, **1**, 2–6.

Eysenck, H. J. *The dynamics of anxiety and hysteria*. London: Routledge and Kegan Paul, 1957.

Eysenck, H. J. (Ed.). *Experiments in behaviour therapy*. New York: Macmillan, 1964.

Eysenck, H. J. *Fact and fiction in psychology*. Baltimore: Penguin Books, 1965.

Ferster, C. B. Positive reinforcement and behavioral deficits in autistic children. *Child Development*, 1961, **32**, 437–456.

Gardner, J. E., Pearson, D. T., Bercovici, A. N., and Bricker, D. E. Measurement, evaluation, and modification of selected social interactions between a schizophrenic child, his parents, and his therapist. *Journal of Consulting and Clinical Psychology*, 1968, **32**, 537–542.

Haley, J. (Ed.), *Advanced techniques of hypnosis and therapy*. New York: Grune & Stratton, 1967.

Harris, F. R., Johnston, M. K., Kelley, C. S., and Wolf, M. M. Effects of positive reinforcement on regressed crawling of a nursery school child. *Journal of Educational Psychology*, 1964, **55**, 35–41.

Jacobson, E. *Progressive relaxation*. Chicago: Univ. of Chicago Press, 1938.

Jones, M. C. The elimination of children's fears. *Journal of Experimental Psychology*, 1924, **7**, 382–390.

Haugen, G. B., Dixon, H. H., and Dickel, H. A. *A therapy for anxiety tension reactions*. New York: Macmillan, 1963.

Karmel, M. *Thank you, Dr. Lamaze: A mother's experiences in painless childbirth*. Philadelphia: Lippincott, 1959.

Kretschmer, E. *Kretschmer's textbook of medical psychology*. London: Oxford University Press, 1934.

Lang, P. J., and Lazovik, A. D. Experimental desensitization of a phobia. *Journal of Abnormal and Social Psychology*, 1963, **66**, 519–525.

Lang, P. J., Lazovik, A. D., and Reynolds, D. J. Desensitization, suggestibility, and pseudotherapy. *Journal of Abnormal Psychology*, 1965, **70**, 395–402.

Lang, P. J. The mechanics of desensitization and the laboratory study of human fear. In C. M. Franks (Ed.), *Behavior therapy: appraisal and status*. New York: McGraw-Hill, 1969.

Lazarus, A. A. New methods in psychotherapy: A case study. *South African Medical Journal*, 1958, **32**, 660–664.

Lazarus, A. A. The elimination of children's phobias by deconditioning. *Medical Proceedings*, 1959, **5**, 261–265.

Lazarus, A. A. Group therapy of phobic disorders by systematic desensitization. *Journal of Abnormal and Social Psychology*, 1961, **63**, 505–510.

Lazarus, A. A. A preliminary report on the use of directed muscular activity in counter-conditioning. *Behaviour Research and Therapy*, 1965, **2**, 301–303.

Lazarus, A. A. A case of pseudonecrophilia treated by behavior therapy. *Journal of Clinical Psychology*, 1968, **24**, 113–115. (a)

Lazarus, A. A. Variations in desensitization therapy. *Psychotherapy: Theory, Research and Practice*, 1968, **5**, 50–52. (b)

Lazarus, A. A., and Abramovitz, A. The use of "emotive imagery" in the treatment of children's phobias. *Journal of Mental Science*, 1962, **108**, 191–195.

Lazarus, A. A., Davison, G. C., and Polefka, D. A. Classical and operant factors in the treatment of a school phobia. *Journal of Abnormal Psychology*, 1965, **70**, 225–229.

Lazarus, A. A., and Rachman, S. The use of systematic desensitization in psychotherapy. *South African Medical Journal*, 1957, **31**, 934–937.

Lazovik, A. D., and Lang, P. J. A laboratory demonstration of systematic desensitization psychotherapy. *Journal of Psychological Studies*, 1960, **11**, 238–247.

London, P. *The modes and morals of psychotherapy*. New York: Holt, 1964.

Maher, B. A. *Principles of psychopathology: an experimental approach*. New York: McGraw-Hill, 1966.

Melamed, B., and Lang, P. J. Study of the automated desensitization of fear. Paper presented at Midwestern Psychological Assn. Convention, Chicago, 1967.

Miller, N. E. Liberalization of basic S–R concepts: Extensions to conflict behavior, motivation, and social learning. In S. Koch (Ed.), *Psychology: a study of a science. Vol. 2*. New York: McGraw-Hill, 1959. pp. 196–292.

Paul, G. L. *Insight vs. desensitization in psychotherapy: An experiment in anxiety reduction*. Stanford: Stanford University Press, 1966.

Paul, G. L. Outcome of systematic desensitization II: Controlled investigations of individual treatment, technique variations, and current status. In C. M. Franks (Ed.), *Behavior therapy: appraisal and status*. New York: McGraw-Hill, 1969

Premack, D. Toward empirical behavior laws. I: Positive reinforcement. *Psychological Review*, 1959, **66**, 219–233.

Pfeiffer, W. M. Konzentrative selbstentspannung durch Uebungen, die sich aus der buddhistischen Atemmeditation und aus der Atemtherapie herleiten. *Zeitschrift fuer Psychotherapie und medizinische Psychologie*. 1966, **16**, 172–181.

Salter, A. *Conditioned reflex therapy*. New York: Creative Age Press, 1949.

Schachter, S., and Singer, J. E. Cognitive, social and physiological determinants of emotional state. *Psychological Review*, 1962, **69**, 379–399.

Schachter, S., and Wheeler, L. Epinephrine, chlorpromazine, and amusement. *Journal of Abnormal and Social Psychology*, 1962, **65**, 121–128.

Schultz, J. H., and Luthe, W. *Autogenic training*. New York: Grune and Stratton, 1959.

Shapiro, M. B. A method of measuring psychological changes specific to the individual psychiatric patient. *British Journal of Medical Psychology*, 1961, **34**, 151–155. (a)

Shapiro, M. B. The single case in fundamental clinical psychological research. *British Journal of Medical Psychology*, 1961, **34**, 255–262. (b)

Shapiro, M. B. The single case in clinical—psychological research. *Journal of General Psychology*. 1966, **74**, 3–23.

Sidman, M. Operant techniques. In A. J. Bachrach (Ed.), *Experimental foundations of clinical psychology*. New York: Basic Books, 1962. Pp. 170–210.

Stoyva, J. Skinnerian Zen: or control of physiological responses through information feedback. Paper read at Denver University Symposium on Behavior Modification, 1968.

Strupp, H. H., and Bergin. A. E. Critical evaluation of some empirical and conceptual bases for coordinated research in psychotherapy: a critical review of issues, trends and evidence. *International Journal of Psychiatry*, 1969, **7**, 116–168.

Thorpe, J. G., Schmidt, E., and Castell, D. A. A comparison of positive and negative (aversive) conditioning in the treatment of homosexuality. *Behaviour Research and Therapy*, 1963, **1**, 357–362.

Ullmann, L. P., and Krasner, L. (Eds.). *Case studies in behavior modification.* New York: Holt, 1965.

Valins, S. Cognitive effects of false heart-rate feedback. *Journal of Personality and Social Psychology*, 1966, **4**, 400–408.

Valins, S., and Ray, A. A. Effects of cognitive desensitization on avoidance behavior. *Journal of Personality and Social Psychology*, 1967, **7**, 345–350.

Weitzman, B. Behavior therapy and psychotherapy. *Psychological Review*, 1967, **74**, 300–317.

Williams, T. A. *Dreads and besetting fears.* Boston: Little, Brown, 1923.

Wolpe, J. Reciprocal inhibition as the main basis of psychotherapeutic effects. *Archives of Neurology and Psychiatry.* 1954, **72**, 205–226.

Wolpe, J. *Psychotherapy by reciprocal inhibition.* Stanford: Stanford University Press, 1958.

Wolpe, J. The systematic desensitization treatment of neuroses. *Journal of Nervous and Mental Disease,* 1961, **112**, 189–203.

Wolpe, J., and Lazarus, A. A. *Behavior therapy techniques.* New York: Pergamon, 1966.

Yates, A. J. *Principles and practice of behavior therapy.* New York: Wiley, 1970.

PART II

ANALYSIS OF CLIENT-CENTERED, PSYCHOANALYTIC, ECLECTIC, AND RELATED THERAPIES

7

THE EVALUATION OF THERAPEUTIC OUTCOMES[1]

ALLEN E. BERGIN

BRIGHAM YOUNG UNIVERSITY

This chapter provides an analysis of (a) classical and current studies of therapeutic outcomes, (b) spontaneous remission, (c) deterioration effects in psychotherapy, (d) research designs for evaluating outcomes of therapy, and (e) techniques for measuring the effects of psychotherapy. This overview is based upon the study and practice of traditional individual psychotherapies, such as the many variations of psychoanalytically oriented therapy, the client-centered approach, and eclectic mixtures of these and related types of intervention.

A REASSESSMENT OF SELECTED OUTCOME STUDIES

Eysenck's 1952 Survey

It is slightly amazing to find that 18 years after his original critique of therapeutic effects, Professor Hans Eysenck is still agreed and disagreed with more than any single critic on the psychotherapy scene (Eysenck, 1952; 1961; 1965; 1966; 1967). The outpouring of praise and invective, and of claims and counterclaims, has been an extraordinary phenomenon (Luborsky, 1954; Rosenzweig, 1954; Strupp, 1964;

[1] I gratefully acknowledge the support of the National Institute of Mental Health, U.S. Public Health Service, which partially supported the preparation of this manuscript through Contract No. PH-43-67-1459 and Grant No. MH 16244-01. I am also deeply indebted to the director, Mr. James Montgomery, and the staff of the New York State Psychiatric Institute Library, New York City, for substantial assistance in obtaining references. I appreciate as well the helpful assistance of Lawrence Jasper, Ellen Solomon, Cathy Day, and Mrs. Nola Hobbs in obtaining and preparing materials for the chapter.

Kiesler, 1966; Bergin, 1963, 1966, 1967a, 1967b; Strupp and Bergin, 1969b; Truax and Carkhuff, 1967).

There are probably many reasons for the endurance of this debate. My view is that three main factors have kept it alive: (a) the fact that the contest has raged around an absolutely vital question, namely, whether traditional therapies have any unique, positive effects at all, (b) the fact that most of the evidence on the subject is ambiguous enough to be subject to considerable variation in interpretation, and (c) the fact that (a) and (b) have permitted individuals to adopt highly subjective and emotionally tinged views of the subject, which are thus difficult to modify by rational argument or evidence.

It is my view that the field has now reached a stage where it is possible to turn the flame off this still rather warm pot. There are many reasons to believe that the really fertile questions and issues regarding outcome lie in new directions and lead toward new types of inquiry. This viewpoint will be fully documented and explained in the last two sections of the chapter, but it is necessary to precede that material with a review of representative outcome studies that have been done up to this point.

As suggested, a crucial contributor to our two decades of vitriol has been the ambiguity of the data in question. This deficiency is best illustrated by reference to Eysenck's surveys. Every psychology undergraduate is now familiar with the fact that Eysenck purported to show that about two-thirds of all neurotics who enter psychotherapy improve substantially within two years and that an equal proportion of neurotics who never enter therapy improve within an equivalent period. Students are also familiar with the fact that many people dispute these findings and interpretations. I would now like to show why it is impossible to resolve this debate, why it is equally feasible to take any of the several positions that have been vigorously advocated in this connection, and finally, why I believe the bases for the issue have in fact quietly died, even though some people like myself are still writing about it. I, at least, know that I am writing history, not news.

During all of the verbal forays, one important thing has not been done. No one has carefully re-reviewed the original articles on which Eysenck based his now-famous table, "Summary of Reports of the Results of Psychotherapy." This table summarizes percentages of improvement derived from 24 articles covering 8,053 cases. It originally appeared in 1952 and was reprinted in his 1961, 1965, and 1966 publications without modification. It is reprinted here as Table 7.1, for the reader's convenience.

A review of these studies reveals how ambiguous the original data are. Different percentages of improvement may be derived depending upon what criteria and what method of tabulating the reviewer uses. It is clear that Eysenck has imposed a very stringent set of criteria upon the data, which yields the lowest possible improvement rates. There is clearly nothing wrong with this. It is a matter of opinion and style. Some writers during that period, who examined the same studies, arrived at similar conclusions to those of Eysenck; others did not. To clarify the situation, I have carefully reviewed and retabulated the data from all of the 24 studies showing how investigators with differing biases can arrive at drastically different rates of improvement.

The analysis of these studies creates many difficulties that cannot be satisfactorily resolved. These include (a) lack of precisely comparable cases across studies, (b) lack of equivalent criteria of outcome, (c) large variations in the amount of therapy received and in the quality thereof, (d) differences in duration and thoroughness of follow-up, (e) variation in nature of onset and in duration of disturbance, and (f) (where comparable cases and outcome estimates appear to be used) impreciseness of definitions of disorder and criteria for improvement, to the extent of rendering their reliability questionable. Perhaps most troublesome of all is the fact that these early studies were not objective. There are no assessments of outcome made independently of the therapist's evaluations, and there are no checks on the reliability of the author's methods of tabulating the raw data.

To complicate matters further, it is frequently difficult to match the figures in the original reports with those in Dr. Eysenck's tables because (a) the original tables themselves

TABLE 7.1   Summary of Reports of the Results of Psychotherapy

	N	Cured; Much Im-proved	Slightly Improved Im-proved	Slightly Improved Im-proved	Not Im-proved; Died; Left Treat-ment	Percent Cured; Much Im-proved; Im-proved
(A) Psychoanalytic						
1. Fenichel [1920–1930]	484	104	84	99	197	39
2. Kessel and Hyman [1933]	34	16	5	4	9	62
3. Jones [1926–1936]	59	20	8	28	3	47
4. Alexander [1932–1937]	141	28	42	23	48	50
5. Knight [1941]	42	8	20	7	7	67
All cases	760	335		425		44
(B) Eclectic						
1. Huddleson [1927]	200	19	74	80	27	46
2. Matz [1929]	775	10	310	310	145	41
3. Maudsley Hospital Report [1931]	1,721	288	900	533		69
4. Maudsley Hospital Report [1935]	1,711	371	765		575	64
5. Neustatter [1935]	46	9	14	8	15	50
6. Luff and Garrod [1935]	500	140	135	26	199	55
7. Luff and Garrod [1935]	210	38	84	54	34	68
8. Ross [1936]	1,089	547	306		236	77
9. Yaskin [1936]	100	29	29		42	58
10. Curran [1937]	83	51			32	61
11. Masserman and Carmichael [1938]	50	7	20	5	18	54
12. Carmichael and Masserman [1939]	77	16	25	14	22	53
13. Schilder [1939]	35	11	11	6	7	63
14. Hamilton and Wall [1941]	100	32	34	17	17	66
15. Hamilton et al. [1942]	100	48	5	17	32	51
16. Landis [1938]	119	40	47		32	73
17. Institute Med. Psychol. (quoted Neustatter)	270	58	132	55	25	70
18. Wilder [1945]	54	3	24	16	11	50
19. Miles et al. [1951]	54	13	18	13	9	58
All cases	7,293	4,661		2,632		64

Source. Reproduced by permission from Eysenck (1952).

often include flaws, such as incorrect addition and computation of percentages; (b) in order to examine the data on neurotics, one must extract figures from tables that include information on as many as 34 different diagnostic types! Deciding which are to be included as "neurosis" is not simple, especially when nearly every author has a somewhat different set of categories; (c) to make matters worse, Eysenck

has also made some errors in transferring the original figures to his own table; (d) the confusion created in this area is further multiplied by small matters such as Eysenck's stating that "psychopathic states" are *included* in his calculations; whereas his figures can be matched with the originals only when psychopaths are *excluded*. It seems logical to exclude them from a study of neuroses, but it required many hours of labor to discover that this had been done in the original report; and (e) the ratings of outcome in different studies are based on different numbers of categories. Thus, in one study all cases may be categorized dichotomously as either improved or not improved, while another study may use as many as six different degrees of improvement. A reviewer is thus confronted with the difficult task of carefully comparing definitions of improvement and then recasting data from the various reports into a more uniform set of categories in order to make percentages of improvement comparable across studies. This is sometimes made easier in articles where brief descriptions are given of each case, but too often it is impossible to differentiate substantial from slight improvement. Eysenck has recast the data from the 24 studies he reviewed into his own system, and a new investigator must therefore cope with the double problem of interpreting the studies from his own viewpoint while also determining how Eysenck proceeded. One then usually winds up with three *different* views of the same case material (the original author's, Eysenck's, and one's own), a fact which unfortunately reduces the objectivity and credibility of the information being summarized.

To provide some indication of the complications involved in analyzing these studies and how I arrived at my interpretations of the data, a representative study is discussed below.

The Berlin Psychoanalytic Institute. The report of the first ten years of work at the Berlin Institute was difficult to find. I was finally able to obtain a copy from Dr. E. Kunzler of the Psychosomatic Clinic of the University of Heidelberg, and Miss Alice Mucha graciously translated it for me. I am most grateful to both Dr. Kunzler and Miss Mucha for their assistance.

This report was published in 1930 by the German Psychoanalytic Association under the editorship of Sandor Rado, Otto Fenichel, and Carl Muller-Braunschweig, with Fenichel providing the statistical material. It was introduced with a forward by Sigmund Freud.

The report discloses that during its first 10 years, the Institute had 1955 consultations, which led to the commencement of 721 analyses.

Of these 721 cases, 363 had concluded treatment at the time of the report:

> 241 prematurely terminated
> 117 still in progress
> 47 uncured
> 116 improved
> 89 very much improved
> 111 cured

The basic data from which these figures are derived have been reproduced in Table 7.2, which is from Fenichel's report, and Table 7.3 from Robert Knight's recasting of the same data (1941). Eysenck's tabulation is given on line one of Table 1.

The question at issue is: how shall the raw data be assembled in order to draw conclusions regarding the effects of treatment? First, we agree with Eysenck that the focus should be on neuroses, broadly defined. This requires subtracting 47 cases from the 363 who completed treatment and 73 cases from among the 241 premature terminators.

Second, we must interpret Fenichel's definitions of degrees of improvement. His criteria for success seem to be quite stringent. He states (p. 19):

We were most particular in what was to be understood as "cured." Included were only such cases where success meant not merely the disappearance of symptoms but also the manifestation of analytically acceptable personality changes and, wherever possible, confirmative follow-up. This strictness of definition demands that most of the "very much improved" cases must, for all practical purposes, be closely coordinated with the "cured" ones. "Improved" cases are those who upon termination still lack in one aspect or another, including such cases as those which had to settle, for external reasons, with an only partially successful outcome. . . .

According to this definition, I would include the improved cases among those figured in the overall percent improved, and this is where Eysenck parts company. He uses a system of four categories: (1) Cured or Much Improved, (2) Improved, (3) Slightly Improved, and (4) Not Improved, Died, or Left Treatment (see Table 7.1). Cases in the first two categories are lumped together in order to figure the *percent improved*. He classifies cases which Fenichel defined as "Improved" under "Slightly Improved," and they are thus excluded from the

TABLE 7.2 Fenichel's Report of the Berlin Psychoanalytic Institute Results: 1920–1930 [TABELLE VIII, Korrelation zwischen Diagnose, Behandlungsdauer und Ergebnis (ohne die am I. Januar 1930 noch in Behandlung befindlichen Fälle)]

| Diagnose | Zahl aller Behandlungen | abgebrochen | Behandlungsdauer bis (Monate) | | | | | | | | | | Ergebnis | | | | |
			6	12	18	24	30	36	42	48	54	60	ungeheilt	gebessert	wesentl. gebess.	geheilt	abgebrocheni
Angsthysterie	57	25	11	4	7	5	3	2	—	—	—	—	2	10	6	14	25
Asthma bronchiale	2	1	—	1	—	—	—	—	—	—	—	—	—	1	—	—	1
Charakterstörungen	37	7	7	6	11	4	1	—	1	—	—	—	4	12	8	6	7
Neurotische Depression	37	13	4	8	2	5	1	—	1	1	2	—	2	10	5	7	13
Enuresis	5	3	—	2	—	—	—	—	—	—	—	—	—	—	—	2	3
Epilepsie	6	5	—	1	—	—	—	—	—	—	—	—	1	—	—	—	5
Homosexualität	8	4	—	4	—	—	—	—	—	—	—	—	1	2	—	1	4
Hypochondrie	4	4	—	—	—	—	—	—	—	—	—	—	—	—	—	—	4
Hysterie	105	31	19	22	18	7	2	3	1	1	—	1	6	22	21	25	31
Infantilismus	12	5	—	3	1	—	1	—	2	—	—	—	1	5	—	1	5
Innersekretorische Erkrankung	3	3	—	—	—	—	—	—	—	—	—	—	—	—	—	—	3
Manisch-Depressive Störungen	14	5	1	3	1	2	1	—	—	1	—	—	2	4	2	1	5
Neurasthenie und Angstneurose	10	7	—	1	2	—	—	—	—	—	—	—	—	2	1	—	7
Neurotische Hemmungen	80	24	6	17	16	7	5	3	1	—	—	1	5	15	15	21	24
Organische Nervenerkrankung	3	3	—	—	—	—	—	—	—	—	—	—	—	—	—	—	3
Organneurose	3	1	1	—	—	—	1	—	—	—	—	—	—	—	1	1	1
Paranoia	2	1	—	1	—	—	—	—	—	—	—	—	—	1	—	—	1
Perversion	8	3	1	3	—	—	—	1	—	—	—	—	1	1	1	2	3
Psychopathie	23	18	—	3	—	—	1	1	—	—	—	—	4	—	—	1	18
Schizophrenie und Schizoïd	45	26	4	7	4	2	1	1	—	—	—	—	8	8	2	1	26
Stottern	13	3	2	3	—	3	2	—	—	—	—	—	3	3	1	3	3
Süchtigkeit	5	3	1	—	—	1	—	—	—	—	—	—	—	1	—	1	3
Traumatische Neurose	3	—	2	1	—	—	—	—	—	—	—	—	1	1	—	1	—
Tic	4	2	—	1	1	—	—	—	—	—	—	—	—	—	—	2	2
Zwangsneurose	106	35	11	17	11	15	10	4	1	—	1	1	6	18	26	21	35
Ohne Befund	2	2	—	—	—	—	—	—	—	—	—	—	—	—	—	—	2
Ohne präzise Diagnose	7	7	—	—	—	—	—	—	—	—	—	—	—	—	—	—	7
	604	241	70	108	74	51	29	15	7	3	3	3	47	116	89	111	241

percent improved. A decision like this crucially affects the ultimate results and it illustrates well how subjective bias is the only way of resolving ambiguities in the raw material. My own subjective bias in this instance is the opposite of Eysenck's and in conformity with Fenichel's description. Fenichel's definition of "Improved" seems substantial enough to me that cases so

classified should be counted among the *percent improved.*

Another issue is whether premature dropouts are to be counted as failures. Eysenck believes they should be and so tabulates them, thus automatically significantly reducing the improvement rate. I doubt the validity of this view in that individuals drop out for numerous

TABLE 7.3   Knight's Analysis of the Berlin Institute Report 1920–1930

		No. of Cases	Broken Off	Six Months or Longer	Appar- ently Cured	Much im- proved	Percent AC+MI	Im- proved	No Change or Worse	Percent I+NC
Psychoneuroses	Anxiety hysteria	57	25	32	14	6		10	2	
	Conversion hysteria	105	31	74	25	21		22	6	
	Anxiety state	—	—	—	—	—		—	—	
	Compulsion neurosis	106	35	71	21	26		18	6	
	Depression	37	13	24	7	5	62	10	2	38
	Hypochondria	4	4	0	—	—		—	—	
	Inhibitions	80	24	56	21	15		15	5	
	Traumatic neurosis	3	0	3	1	—		1	1	
	Neurasthenia and anxiety neurosis	10	7	3	—	1		2	—	
Sexual Disorders	Unclassified	8	3	5	2	1		1	1	
	Homosexuality	8	4	4	1	—		2	1	
	Transvestism	—	—	—	—	—	54·5	—	—	45·5
	Impotence	—	—	—	—	—		—	—	
	Enuresis	5	3	2	2	—		—	—	
	Character Disorders	49	12	37	7	8		17	5	
Organ Neuroses and Organic Conditions	Peptic ulcer	—	—	—	—	—		—	—	
	Gastric neurosis	—	—	—	—	—		—	—	
	Colitis	—	—	—	—	—		—	—	
	Chronic constipation	—	—	—	—	—		—	—	
	Bronchial asthma	2	1	1	—	—		1	—	
	Hay fever	—	—	—	—	—	80	—	—	20
	Skin conditions	—	—	—	—	—		—	—	
	Female disorders	—	—	—	—	—		—	—	
	Endocrine disorders	3	3	0	—	—		—	—	
	Essential hypertension	—	—	—	—	—		—	—	
	Tics	4	2	2	2	—		—	—	
	Unclassified	3	1	2	1	1		—	—	
	Epilepsies	6	5	1	—	—	—	—	1	
	Migraine	—	—	—	—	—	—	—	—	
	Stammering	13	3	10	3	1	—	3	3	
	Chronic alcoholism	5	3	2	1	—	—	1	—	
Psychoses	Psychopathies	23	18	5	1	—		—	4	
	Manic depressive	14	5	9	1	2		4	2	
	Paranoia	2	1	1	—	1	23·4	—	—	76·6
	Schizophrenia and schizoid	45	26	19	1	2		8	8	
	Totals	592	229	363	101	90	52·6	115	51	47·4

Source. Reproduced by permission from Knight (1941).

reasons, some of which have nothing to do with the therapy, and I consider it an unfair test of a method to count against it all cases where it was not fully applied.

The reader will see from Table 7.4 that differing attitudes regarding each of the preceding points yield widely differing accounts of the effects of psychoanalysis as practiced at the Berlin Institute between 1920 and 1930.

My figure of a 91 percent improvement rate may seem startling, but it is based on what I personally consider to be a logical and reasonable interpretation of the information available. In order to arrive at this figure, I (a) eliminated premature dropouts from the sample, (b) counted Fenichel's "improved" cases as improved, and (c) eliminated nonneurotics from the figures. Eysenck followed the opposite of (a) and (b) in order to arrive at his 39 percent rate.

The "Alternative A" figure of 59 percent is arrived at by including all dropouts in the

TABLE 7.4 Results of Psychotherapy—Sum of Percent Cured, Much Improved, And Improved (Excluding Slightly Improved) by Differing Criteria

	Total N	A Eysenck Dropouts Included. Improved = Much Improved	B Bergin Dropouts Excluded. Improved = Moderately Improved or Better	C Alternative A—Dropouts Included. Improved = Moderately Improved or Better	D Alternative B (Knight 1941) Dropouts Excluded. Improved = Much Improved
Psychoanalysis					
1. Fenichel (1930) (Berlin)	484	39	91 (287/316)	59	59 (186/316)
2. Kessel & Hyman (1933)[a]	25	62	68	No Dropouts Reported	89 (16/18)
Hyman (1936)[b]	30		60 (18/30)		
3. Jones (1936)[c] (London)	56	47	68 (37/56)	No Dropouts Reported	47 (26/56)
4. Alexander (1937)[d] (Chicago)	142	50	69 (70/101)	49	69 (70/101)
5. Knight (1941) (Topeka)	41	67	76 (28/37)	68	76 (28/37)
All cases	753[e]	44% (335/760)	83% (450/540)	60% (450/753)	62% (326/528)

TABLE 7.4 (continued)

		Total N	A Eysenck Dropouts Included. Improved = Much Improved	B Bergin Dropouts Excluded. Improved = Moderately Improved or Better
	Eclectic Psychotherapy			
1.	Huddleson (1927)[f]	200	46 (93/200)	46 (93/200)
2.	Matz (1929)[g]	760	41 (346/725)	42 (340/760)
3.	Maudsley (1931)[h]	1721	69 (1188/1721)	69 (1188/1721)
4.	Maudsley (1935)[h]	1711	64 (1136/1711)	64 (1136/1711)
5.	Neustatter (1935)[i]	46	50 (23/46)	50 (23/46)
6.	Luff and Garrod (1935)[j]	426	55 (275/500)	60 (253/426)
7.	Luff and Garrod (1935)[k]	210	68 (122/210)	58 (122/210)
8.	Ross (1936)[l]	1089	77 (853/1089)	78 (853/1089)
9.	Yaskin (1936)[m]	91	58 (58/100)	64 (58/91)
10.	Curran (1937)[n]	69	61 (51/83)	68 (47/69)
11.	Masserman and Carmichael (1938)[o]	30	54 (27/50)	57 (17/30)
12.	Carmichael and Masserman (1939)	70	53 (41/77)	56 (34/70)
13.	Schilder (1939)	40	63 (22/35)	60 (24/40)
14.	Hamilton and Wall (1941)[p]	100	51 (53/100)	68 (68/100)
15.	Hamilton, Varney and Wall (1942)[p]	100	66 (66/100)	83 (83/100)
16.	Landis (1937)[q]	119	73 (87/119)	87 (104/119)
17.	Institute Med. Psychol.	270	70 (190/270)	70 (190/270)
18.	Wilder (1945)[r]	54	50 (27/54)	50 (27/54)
19.	Miles, et al. (1951)	62	58 (31/53)	58 (36/62)
	All Cases	7168	64 (4661/7293)	65 (4701/7168)

a $N=25$, not 34. Kessel and Hyman begin with 33, not the 34 that Eysenck states. Seven of these are psychotics and one is alcoholic; therefore, N for neuroses $=25$.

b Follow-up of previous study, including some new cases (unreported by Eysenck).

c This report is based on 56 cases who completed more than 100 sessions at the London Clinic of Psychoanalysis between 1926 and 1936. They are, therefore, a highly selected group from among (a) the 738 patients who came to the clinic during this period and (b) the 176 who ultimately accepted treatment. Jones uses three categories of improvement: Cured, Improved, and Failed. Since there was no way to determine degree of improvement in the middle group, we simply divided them evenly between much improved and slightly improved to arrive at our *percent improved*. Neither Eysenck nor Knight's figures seem to follow logically from Jones' tables.

d Based on Knight's tables.

e Slight discrepancies between the original tables and Eysenck's compilation yields a total N of 753 here instead of Eysenck's 760.

f Poor results here are likely due to the fact that therapy consisted of an average of five 16-minute sessions—hardly a test of the effects of psychotherapy!

g These patients were *hospitalized* neurotics, thus an unusual sample. Also, there is no indication in Matz' report that they received psychotherapy in addition to routine hospital treatment. The inclusion of this report is therefore questionable.

h I was unable to obtain copies of the Maudsley Hospital reports, but analyses of them by Landis (1937) and Masserman and Carmichael (1938) appear to confirm Eysenck's figures, so they are included here as originally presented by Eysenck.

i Here, I agree with Eysenck. The 7 dropouts between sessions 2 and 10 should be included, because successes were also counted among patients seen for similarly brief periods. The 59percent figure under "D" is derived by excluding the dropouts. Neustatter himself claimed 70percent, and this was based on including the slightly improved in the total *percent improved*.

j $N=426$ instead of 500. Eysenck included 74 paranoid states, schizoid states, epileptics, alcoholics, migraines, deaths, and mentally dull cases which had been specifically excluded from prior tabulations. It should also be noted that these data are based on three-year follow-ups. Improvement rate at discharge for 426 cases was *69*.

k These figures are reported parenthetically by Luff and Garrod. They are based on 210 cases for whom they had no follow-ups, but did have end-of-treatment ratings. Eysenck's 68percent figure is incorrect and is due to an arithmetical error. Calculating even from his own table, the figure is 58percent.

l Ross reported a 70percent improvement rate and Eysenck 77percent. Both figures are based on incorrect calculations from Ross's tables. The correct figure at one-year follow-up is 78percent. These figures are based on hospitalized cases, and the nature of the therapy and of the improvement criteria are doubtful enough so that possibly these data should not be mentioned.

m Six psychotics and 3 dropouts should be subtracted from the N of 100 to obtain 91 cases for evaluation. Improvement rate at termination was 90percent, but dropped to 64percent at follow-up.

n $N=69$, not 83. Seven schizophrenics and 7 organic states should have been omitted. The author describes the therapy as being brief and superficial. The data are based on one-to-three-year follow-up questionnaires returned by 40percent of the treatment group, and are probably a biased sample.

o It is impossible to determine how Eysenck obtained 50 neurotics from the tables in this study. I could find only 30 who were followed up at one year and 36 studied at discharge.

p The figures for the two Hamilton et al. studies are reversed in Eysenck's table. Also, his totals add to 102 instead of 100 in the first study. The first study is based on four-to-fourteen-year follow-ups. Both studies are based on hospitalized neurotics. The discrepancy between my and Eysenck's percents in the second study is due to 17 cases which the authors describe as improved but which Eysenck considers unimproved.

q Eysenck misread Landis' Table. Landis reports percentages in each category of improvement which Eysenck read as raw figures; thus, his calculations for this study are erroneous. What Eysenck reads as 87 cases should read as 87percent! These were hospitalized neurotics.

r Wilder himself lumps slightly improved with other improved cases to arrive at an 83percent improvement rate. In this case, I agree with Eysenck's view. These data were based on 1.9 years of follow-up.

---

computation of the improvement rate, while still counting Fenichel's "Improved" as improved. The "Alternative B" rate, also 59 percent, is based directly upon Robert Knight's reading of the same data. He excludes dropouts but counts Fenichel's "Improved" as unimproved.[2]

[2] It should also be noted by the reader that there are errors of addition in Knight's table (e.g., numbers "apparently cured" should be 111 instead of 101) and similar errors in many of the articles summarized by Eysenck in Table 7.1. This type of

The four divergent but equally reasonable tabulations of the Berlin Institute data, as summarized in Table 7.4, clearly establish my point that there is no valid way to assess the effects of psychoanalysis from the information available. I can see no clear justification for choosing one interpretation over another, even

problem has unnecessarily complicated interpretations of some of these studies, and I have therefore attempted to make appropriate corrections when the data were retabulated in Table 7.4.

though I do have personal biases in certain directions. The ambiguity in these data cannot be resolved. My 91 percent figure is as defensible as Eysenck's 39 percent figure, and I seriously doubt that he would vigorously defend his interpretation any more than I would battle for mine. The same holds true for the other studies of psychoanalysis that are compared and for the overall average improvement of 83 percent. The matter is reduced to subjective biases whose truth value is unverifiable.

The remainder of Table 7.4 is devoted to a reanalysis of 19 studies of eclectic psychotherapy practiced in hospitals, clinics, and private offices. While there are several modest differences between my and Eysenck's evaluations of the cases so reported, the overall conclusion is virtually identical. Eysenck finds a 64 percent improvement rate, with a range from 41 to 77, and I find a 65 percent rate, with a range from 42 to 87. I analyzed eight additional studies not reviewed by Eysenck, and these yielded essentially the same mean and range of improvement (Bartlett, 1950; Bond and Braceland,

1937; Coriat, 1917; Cowen and Combs, 1950; Friess and Nelson, 1942; Kriegman, 1947; Lipkin, 1948; Wooten, 1935).[3]

It is striking that we should agree so closely on the results of eclectic psychotherapies and differ so sharply on our evaluations of psychoanalysis. This could be due to the fact that the number of dropouts reported in the psychoanalytic studies is large and Eysenck counts these as failures, whereas I do not. It could also be that the analytic results are thus based on more selected samples, which are therefore biased toward more favorable results. One might also argue that our biases differ regarding psychoanalysis and that they differentially influenced our reading of essentially ambiguous stimuli. This is difficult to support, however, since neither of us can be considered friendly toward psychoanalysis.

Another major problem with all of these percentages is the fact that they vary greatly across diagnoses and across clinics. In fact, the variation across clinics is as great as that across diagnoses, as illustrated in Table 7.5,

TABLE 7.5 Variations in Results of Psychoanalysis Across Diagnoses and Clinics—Percent Improved Based on Knight's Resume (1941)

Diagnosis	Clinical Center					
	Berlin Institute 1920–1930 $N = 316$	Hyman and Kessel $N = 18$	London Clinic 1926–1936 $N = 56$	Chicago Institute 1932–1937 $N = 101$	Menninger Clinic 1932–1941 $N = 37$	Range
Neuroses	62	87	52	63	79	35
Sexual Disorders	54	100 (n = 2)	27	50	—	73
Character Disorders	41	—	—	72	57	31
Psychosomatic Disorders	80	—	—	78	—	2
Psychoses	23	0 (n = 8)	7	40	40	40
Range	57	100	45	38	39	

which is extracted from Knight's comprehensive summary of psychoanalysis at five different centers. It is thus a misleading oversimplification to discuss "the effects of psychoanalysis or psychotherapy on psychoneuroses." Much

greater specificity is required in terms of stating what effects differing interventions have on differing syndromes.

Such an emphasis is inevitable, and it only makes more obvious the inadequacies of the

[3] The reader may wish to examine another review, by Miles, Barrabee, and Finesinger (1951), which contains tabulated results of most of the studies

included in the preceding tables and discussion. Also see Appel, Myers, and Scheflen (1953).

surveys under discussion. They simply lack information specific enough to definitively interpret the meaning of the wide variations in percentages of improvement that they yield. This problem also makes comparisons with spontaneous remission rates spurious, because if the cure rates for different diagnoses vary greatly, then it is also likely that spontaneous remission rates will vary greatly. No single spontaneous remission rate will thus suffice as a base line which therapy must exceed in order to demonstrate its efficacy. The whole question of a spontaneous remission base line is discussed at a later point in this section of the chapter. However, it should be pointed out here that the 65 percent and 83 percent improvement rates tabulated in Table 7.1 clearly exceed average spontaneous remission rates for psychoneuroses (see Table 7.8).

In general, despite the limitations of the studies published prior to 1952, the results up to that time must be considered encouraging, though certainly not dramatic.[4] It is of particular interest, however, that the longer and more intensive the treatment, the better the results. The eclectic therapy studies frequently involved very brief and superficial treatment. The least adequate therapy yielded the poorest results in these reports. Where the therapy was more intensive, the results were better; and in these latter instances, the improvement rates at the time of discharge were equivalent to those of psychoanalysis. These rates generally declined at long-term follow-up in the psychotherapy studies, whereas such follow-up studies were unavailable for the analytic cases. The difference in the overall rates for psychoanalysis and psychotherapy would thus probably disappear if the *Time in Therapy* and the *Time of Evaluation* were equated, suggesting that the same therapeutic factors operate across therapies irrespective of differences in theory.

In addition to the evidence of *some* therapeutic effect, there is also the valuable finding that results differ across personality types, crudely defined, and across therapists and clinics. This is clearly a lead into the notion of specific therapies for specific problems, which will be amplified at a later point.

Eysenck's 1966 Survey

Eysenck's recent review includes the 1952 material plus summaries of data on child therapy, behavior therapy, and controlled outcome studies of individual therapy with adult neurotics. Since child and behavior therapies are thoroughly reviewed elsewhere in this volume, I shall deal only with the controlled studies of psychotherapy and the evidence regarding its effects.

Eysenck reviewed three studies he considered to be methodologically adequate, none of which revealed any significant therapeutic effect (Powers and Witmer, 1951; Brill and Beebe, 1955; Barron and Leary, 1955). Of three other studies, considered methodologically inadequate, only one yielded positive results (Rogers and Dymond, 1954). The other two yielded negative findings (Gliedman et al., 1958; Walker and Kelley, 1960). Thus, of six studies, only one was positive, and it was considered defective.

Adding this controlled evidence to the findings from studies without control groups (Eysenck, 1952), which revealed an approximately 67 *percent improvement* rate that did not exceed a purported 67 percent spontaneous remission rate, Eysenck arrived at the following conclusion (1966, p. 40):

... The writer must admit to being somewhat surprised at the uniformly negative results issuing from all this work. In advancing his rather challenging conclusion in the 1952 report, the main motive was one of stimulating better and more worthwhile research in this important but somewhat neglected field; there was an underlying belief that while results to date had not disproved the null-hypothesis, improved methods of research would undoubtedly do so. Such a belief does not seem to be tenable any longer in this easy optimistic form, and it rather seems that psychologists and psychiatrists will have to acknowledge the fact that current psychotherapeutic procedures have not lived up to the hopes which greeted their emergence fifty years ago.

---

[4] This encouragement is based partly on the fact that improvement rates exceed the revised spontaneous remission rates tabulated later in Table 7.8.

This rather pessimistic conclusion regarding traditional therapies is set in a context of favorable evidence regarding behavioral approaches to treatment. While I too have favorable biases toward behavior modification, it would seem to me unfortunate to pass over evidence that there are also some potent variables operating in psychotherapy as traditionally practiced.

This evidence is provided by (a) additional recent outcome studies, (b) new evidence that spontaneous remission rates are actually much lower than Eysenck's estimate, and (c) indications that deterioration and numerous other processes are occurring in psychotherapy, which cast the general outcome problem in an entirely different light, namely that of specifying specific interventions for specific problems with specific outcomes.

Before moving on to that evidence, however, I would like to point out that Eysenck's critiques have had an extremely facilitative effect upon psychotherapy research. He has been a prime stimulant, if not irritant, pressing the field toward rigorous examination of its assumptions and procedures. For thus dramatically calling these issues to our attention, he is to be congratulated and not condemned as so many have been inclined to do. It is time, after all, that this field provide publicly verifiable evidence that its costly treatments have effects.

Recent Outcome Studies

Studies of therapeutic outcome have continued to increase in number during recent years, as can be seen in Figure 7.1. Represented there are controlled and uncontrolled studies and criterion measurement reports, all based on the empirical study of therapy in practice. This summary is based upon a recently compiled bibliography of research on psychotherapy (Strupp and Bergin, 1969a). It can be observed that the growth of outcome studies has closely paralleled that of process studies as depicted by Marsden in Chapter 10 of this volume, though the rate of increase for outcome is greater.

It is a practical impossibility to review thoroughly in this chapter all of the outcome studies that have appeared in the past 10 or 15 years; but a sampling is provided below which, in the author's view, represents the

empirical status of this area to date. In general, it may be stated at the outset that the picture here is similar to that already presented in regard to studies appearing prior to 1952. While the methodological sophistication and precision

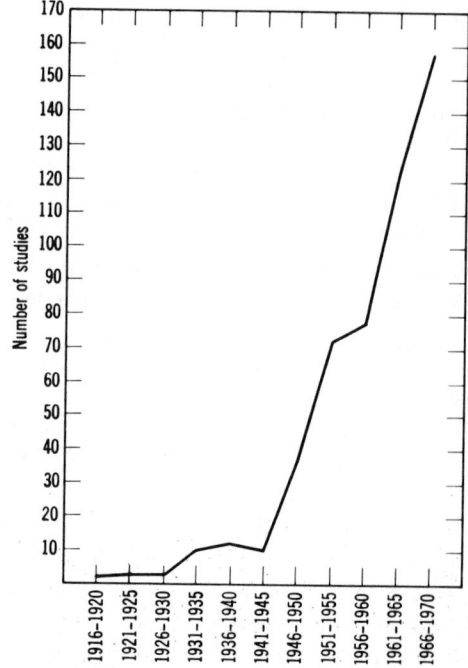

Figure 7.1 Distribution by five-year intervals of 501 outcome studies (excluding behavioral) published from 1916 through 1967. (*Note.* Data to 1967 are derived from Strupp–Bergin bibliography (1969a); 1966–1970 data are extrapolated on the basis of figures for 1966 and 1967).

of studies have improved markedly, the evidence continues to yield the general conclusion that psychotherapy, on the average, has modestly positive effects. This is based upon general tests of the effects of treatment with and without control groups, and the studies in question generally do not specify the precise nature of the therapy, nor do they usually consider specific limits to its applicability. Thus, most of these studies are quite gross in character. They are tests, for the most part, of whether therapy has any effect at all, but they usually do not examine whether specific methods have specific consequences, nor do they examine the notion that only a small proportion of therapists and patients may be accounting for the positive effects when they do occur on averaged data.

While I personally believe that there should be a moratorium on further studies of this type, it is worthwhile to briefly review what limited contributions they have to offer our thinking.

There have been several recent reviews of the outcome literature, most of which arrive at a more optimistic view of the evidence than does Eysenck. Eysenck has pointed out that the favorableness of results appears to be inversely proportional to the adequacy of the methodology. Cross (1964) for example, reviewed nine controlled studies and determined that six were favorable to therapy, whereas our own review of the same reports yielded only one that approximated adequacy, and even that one is subject to criticism (Rogers and Dymond, 1954). Dittmann (1966) added five more studies to Cross's group, considered four of them to be positive evidence, and concluded that 10 out of 14 controlled outcome studies were favorable to psychotherapy. Actually, only two of the studies indicate that psychotherapy has any effect, and neither of them would be generally acceptable as evidence (Bergin, 1967a). Thus, these authors claim *strong* support for the average cross section of therapy, whereas I would argue for a more modest conclusion.

The author of another review, yet to be published, claims in a similar vein to that of the preceding writers, that the effectiveness of psychotherapy has been clearly demonstrated:

When the evidence from controlled experiments is examined and weighed, the conclusion becomes quite clear that the effectiveness of psychotherapy with a wide variety of patient types, as ordinarily performed by journeyman therapists, has already been amply demonstrated. The research evidence to document this statement obviously cannot be presented here, but it has been steadily accumulating over the last 15 years. It now amounts to over 100 controlled outcome studies, most of which have yielded positive results (Meltzoff, 1969, p. 150; Meltzoff and Kornreich, 1970).

Upon inquiry by this writer, the above author claimed that it would be "inconvenient" to provide him with the exact references on which this conclusion is based; therefore, an independent critique of these alluded-to "evidences" is temporarily impossible. Nevertheless, assuming a viewpoint comparable to that of Cross and Dittmann, it may be surmised that

this review similarly glosses over many deficiencies of method and consequent weaknesses in the evidence.

Kellner's reviews (1965; 1967) of the same domain of inquiry yields more cautious conclusions regarding the effects of therapy. He argues that the results are frequently conflicting, that comparability of studies is usually absent, and that typically divergent processes are occurring in the diverse influences given the general label "psychotherapy." He argues that the more homogeneous the intervention and the sample of patients, and the more specific the criterion, the better the results are. He believes that psychotherapy has thus been shown to be effective under restricted, specific circumstances, but that general tests of therapeutic effects, though sometimes favorable, yield mostly ambiguity. Our own views are quite consistent with his, as will be seen from the following analysis.

Taking all of the above problems into account, there remains some modest evidence that psychotherapy "works." While most studies do not seem to yield very substantial evidence that this is so, the number that do seems to be clearly larger than would be expected by chance; therefore, something potent or efficacious must be operating in some portion of the therapy that is routinely done, even though average effects are only moderately impressive when diverse cases, therapists, and change scores are lumped together. This was brought out in our review of early, crude accountings of the *percent improved* in various studies, wherein we observed considerable variability of effects within a generally quite modest, positive set of outcomes.

The studies presented in Table 7.6 yield a similar picture. Of this cross section of 52 analyses from the literature, 22 are rated as positive, 15 in doubt, and 15 as negative evidence in relation to psychotherapy. Kellner's review yielded a similar spectrum, as did Jonckheere's (1965) also. Thus, our comprehensive view of the literature must be considered more favorable than that of Eysenck's 1966 survey, although we certainly cannot point to more than a moderately positive, average therapeutic effect.

Careful reading of these reports also reveals

TABLE 7.6 A Survey of Selected Outcome Studies Published Between 1952 and 1969[r]

Authors	Date	Population	Therapy N	Therapy Type	Average Therapy Duration
Wispe & Parloff	1965	Psychologists	55	Mixed analytic (exp.)	22 months 60 sessions
Cartwright & Lerner	1963	U. of Chicago Counseling Center	28	Client-centered (exp.)	40 sessions
Varble & Landfield	1969	Students	36	Eclectic (exp.)	8 sessions
Lorr, McNair, Michaux, & Raskin	1962	VA out-patients	133	Mixed analytic (exp.)	8 months 17 to 96 sessions
Persons	1967	Institutionalized delinquent boys	41	Group and individual (exp.)	80 hours
Jersild, Lazar, & Brodkin	1962	School teachers	111	Psychoanalysis (exp.)	600
Endicott & Endicott	1964	Outpatient neurotics	17	Analytic (one therapist—exp.)	20
Heilbrunn	1966	Outpatient neurotics (excluding psychotics)	32	Psychoanalysis (one therapist—exp.)	500
Heilbrunn	1966	Outpatient Neurotics (excluding psychotics)	48	Analytic	200
Heilbrunn	1966	Outpatient neurotics (excluding psychotics)	75	Brief analytic	50
Aronson & Weintraub	1968	Outpatient neurotics— Character disorders, borderlines	127	Psychoanalysis (exp.)	2 to 3 years
Feifel & Eells	1963	VA outpatients	63	Mixed (exp.)	50+ sessions
Rogers, Gendlin, Kiesler, & Truax	1967	Inpatient psychotics	14	Client-centered (exp.)	105
Strupp, Wallach, & Wogan	1964	Outpatient neurotics	44	Analytic (exp.)	166

Criteria	Control Group	Adequacy of Design	Percent Improved (If Given)	Outcome
Publication rate	Yes	2		Negative, but criterion questionable
Therapist rating	No	3	54	In doubt; no control
Judges' ratings	Yes	2	75	Positive, but weak compared to controls
Kelly SCRT				
Therapist and Patient ratings (Miscellaneous tests)	No	1		Modest positive
Test scores (behavior ratings, parole violations, staying in community)	Yes	1	68 to 74	Positive
Self ratings	Yes	3	50 to 90	Positive, sample highly selective. control group inadequate
Miscellaneous tests and therapist ratings	Yes	2		Negative
Therapist rating	No	3	44	Negative
Therapist rating	No	3	48	Negative
Therapist rating	No	3	45	Negative
Therapist ratings	No	3	57 to 84	Modest positive results vary by criteria and diagnosis
Patient and therapist ratings	No	2	62 to 90	Positive
Numerous tests and behaviors	Yes	1	43	Negative, with qualifications
Patient and therapist ratings on questionnaire	No	2	70 to 80	Positive, but sample favorably biased

TABLE 7.6 (continued)

Authors	Date	Population	Therapy N	Therapy Type	Average Therapy Duration
Bieber et al.	1962	Male homosexuals	106	Psychoanalysis (exp.)	200
McNair, Lorr, Young, Roth & Boyd (3-year follow-up of 1962 study)	1964	VA outpatients	81	Analytic (exp.)	60 sessions
Cattell et al.	1966	Outpatient neurotics	46	(exp.)	6 sessions
Sager, Riess, & Grendlach	1964	Out-patients, Including borderline	103	Analytic (exp.)	107 sessions
Fiske & Goodman (18-month follow-up)	1965	U. Chicago Counseling Center	69	Client-centered (mixed exp. levels)	26 sessions
Riess	1967	Outpatients, including border-line	414	Analytic (exp.)	57 sessions
Uhlenhuth & Duncan	1968	Out-patient neurotics	128	Eclectic (inexp. medical)	6 sessions
Weber, Elinson, & Moss	1965	Outpatients, all diagnoses	564	Psychoanalysis (exp. and inexp.)	
Weber, Elinson, & Moss	1965	Outpatients, all diagnoses	732	Analytic therapy (exp. and inexp.)	
Koegler & Brill	1967	Outpatients, all diagnoses	27 to 39 depending on criterion	Analytic (inexp. residents)	5.5 months
Koegler & Brill	1967	Outpatients, all diagnoses but more disturbed	162	Brief contact (inexp. residents)	10 sessions
Gottschalk, Mayerson, & Gottlieb	1967	Mostly outpatient neurotics	34	Emergency, brief therapy (exp. ?)	6 sessions

Criteria	Control Group	Adequacy of Design	Percent Improved (If Given)	Outcome
Behavior change	Yes	2	27 to 43	Positive, though sample favorably biased and control group inadequate
Tests; Patient and therapist ratings	No	1		In doubt due to small changes and no control
Cattell Scales	Yes	3		In doubt due to inadequate control group and possible placebo effects
Therapist, Patient and researcher ratings of questionnaire	No	3	25 to 59, marked improvement; 60 to 37, small improvement	Appears positive; difficult to interpret
Numerous tests, ratings, interviews and questionnaire	No	1		No change during post-therapy period
Change in income	Yes	2		Positive
Patient symptom checklist	No	2	72	Positive, but placebo effects look improved
Judges' ratings of clinic records	No	2	30	Negative
Judges' ratings of clinic records	No	2	25	Negative
Tests, patient and therapist ratings, and interview	Yes	1	87 on self-rating, but placebo group was 76 on same measure	Negative at follow-up. Change at termination, but not greater than placebo
Therapist and patient ratings	No	3	49 to 86, depending on criterion	In doubt due to criteria and lack of controls
Research interview and self-rating	Yes dropouts	2	85, but does not distinguish degree of improvement	Positive, but controls probably more disturbed

TABLE 7.6 (continued)

Authors	Date	Population	Therapy N	Therapy Type	Average Therapy Duration
Shore & Massimo	1966	Delinquent boys	10	Vocationally oriented psycho-therapy—(exp. 1 therapist)	10 months
Jonckheere	1965	Outpatient neurotics	72	Eclectic (exp.)	
Schjelderup	1955	Outpatient neurotics	28	Psychoanalysis (exp.—(1 therapist)	
Orgel	1958	Outpatient peptic ulcers	12	Psychoanalysis (exp.—(— 1 therapist)	600 sessions
Warne, Canter, & Wiznia	1953	VA outpatient neurotics	30	Eclectic—(many inexp.)	125 sessions
Warne, Canter, & Wiznia	1953	VA outpatient neurotics	30	Eclectic (exp.)	27 sessions
Shlien, Mosak, & Dreikurs; Shlien; and Henry & Shlien	1962 1965 1958	Outpatient neurotics		Client-centered and Adlerian: brief and unlimited (exp.)	20 & 37 sessions
Vorster	1966	Outpatient neurotics	65	Eclectic (exp.— (1 therapist)	27 sessions
Board	1959	Outpatients	228	Eclectic	
Rosenthal	1955	In- and out-patient neurotics	12	Eclectic (inexp. residents)	5 months
Ellis	1956	Homosexuals	40	Eclectic (exp.)	20 sessions
Graham ·	1960	Neurotics	64	Analytic (exp.)	6 months
Feldman, Lorr, & Russell	1958	VA neurotics and schizophrenics	5367	Eclectic—analytic	
Rosenbaum, Friedlander, & Kaplan	1956	Miscellaneous diagnoses	210	Analytic (inexp. residents)	
Berleman & Steinburn	1967	Potential delinquents	28	Eclectic (exp.)	5 months
Mason	1956	Neurotics	31	Analytic (exp.— 1 therapist)	
O'Connor et al.	1964	Ulcerative Colitis patients	57	Eclectic—analytic (exp. ?)	
Cappon	1964	Mixed out-patients	201	Eclectic—analytic (Exp.—1 therapist)	35 sessions

Criteria	Control Group	Adequacy of Design	Percent Improved (If Given)	Outcome
Numerous tests ratings and behavioral changes	Yes	1	70	Positive; only 30% change in controls
Therapist rating	No	3	76	In doubt; no control; liberal definition of improved
Questionnaire, therapist rating, and observer rating (Pooled)	No	2	79	Positive, criteria rigorously applied and long follow-up
Symptom removal	No	2	83	Positive, with 10 to 22 years follow-up
Ratings of case records	Yes	2	20 (slight)	Negative
Ratings of case records	Yes	2	53 (slight) 13 (great	Positive, but in doubt because controls not matched
Q sort, TAT, self-ratings	Yes	1	70 to 85 on one criterion	Positive, except time-limited at follow-up
Therapist rating	No	3	89	Positive
Therapist and patient ratings	No	3	64 to 67	In doubt
Tests, questionnaire, and research interview	No	2	42	Negative
Therapist rating	No	3	65	Positive
Therapist ratings of sexual satisfaction	Yes	2	44 to 76	Positive, but controls not equated
Therapist ratings	No	3	44 32	Negative, but difficult to interpret
Therapist ratings	No	3	68	In doubt
School discipline records	Yes	2		Negative
Therapist rating and interview at 18 months	No	3	45	Negative
Objective symptom change	Yes	1		Positive, with schizophrenic Ss deleted
Therapist, patient, and outsider ratings, and symptom change	No	3	40 to 75, depending on criterion	In doubt, but some positive evidence

TABLE 7.6 (continued)

Authors	Date	Population	Therapy N	Therapy Type	Average Therapy Duration
L. Rogers[a]	1960	Mixed outpatients patients	4081	Eclectic (exp. and inexp.)	13 sessions
Harris	1954	Neurotic out-patients	60	Eclectic (exp. ?)	
Appel, Myers, &[b] Scheflen	1953	Hospitalized neurotics	4790	Eclectic	
Rosenthal and Frank[c]	1958	Mixed out-patients	216	Eclectic (inexp. residents)	11 to 20 sessions
Imber, Nash, Stone, & Frank[d]	1968	Mostly neurotics	34	Eclectic (inexp. residents)	16 to 18 sessions 10 year f. up
Truax, Wargo, Frank, et al.[e]	1966	Outpatient neurotics	40	Eclectic (inexp. residents)	4 months
Betz	1962	Schizophrenics	421	Eclectic (inexp. residents)	
Betz	1962	Schizophrenics	432	Eclectic (inexp. residents)	
Cartwright	1957 1961	U. Chicago Counseling Center	10 19	Client-centered (exp. and inexp.)	26 37
Paul	1967 2 yr. f. up	Speech-anxious students	12	Eclectic (exp.)	5 sessions

[a] Summary of Government clinics.
[b] Summary of 14 studies.
[c] They review 3 other studies with N = 772, showing improvement rates from 19 to 39 when drop outs are counted as failures.
[d] Also Imber et al. (1957) and Stone et al. (1961).
[e] See text for further analysis of Truax studies.
[f] Variations in improvement rates within single studies are a function of differing criteria or differing diagnostic groups within the sample.

Note. Exp = Experienced Therapists; Inexp = Inexperienced Therapists. Adequacy of Design: 1 = good, 2 = fair, 3 = poor. Outcome is positive if change is greater than in control group, or (where there is no control group), percent improvement is substantially higher than 30percent spontaneous rate documented in Table 8.

that outcomes vary considerably across diagnoses, as was previously shown in Table 7.5 regarding effects of psychoanalysis. Thus, in spite of the unreliability of diagnoses, there is still evidence that there is gold to be mined in this domain. As precision of case description and differentiation increases, accuracy in predicting outcome similarly grows. This fact has been observed repeatedly by the writers of these reports from the 1920s to the present. Practically no one has believed in the "patient uniformity myth" as described by Kiesler (1966), but there has been considerable difficulty in arriving at a more precise and useful system of

Criteria	Control Group	Adequacy of Design	Percent Improved (If Given)	Outcome
Therapist ratings	No	3	71	In doubt; no control and improved ratings questionable
Therapist follow-up interviews at 1 year and patient ratings	Yes (CO_2)	2	20 to 27	Negative
Various	No	3	68	In doubt
Therapist ratings	No	2	63 (continuers); 34 (drop-outs)	In doubt
Patient ratings, and interviewer and observer rating	Yes, minimal contact therapy	1	59	In doubt; significant changes, but not greater than control
Two global ratings by patient and therapist, and three specific change indices	No	2	70, on global rating only	In doubt, due to no control and mixed results on different criteria
Research analysis of charts and Changes in overt behavior	No	2	48	Negative
Research analysis of charts and changes in overt behavior	No	2	73	Positive
Q sort	Yes	2		Both in doubt; amount of change
Q sort	Yes	2		limited and controls = normals
Behavior change and personality scales	Yes	1	25 to 50	Negative

differential description. Thus, it is not so much "mythology" that has inhibited progress in assessing differential outcomes, but rather limitations in methodology and measurement. Future progress will be achieved when we know more about which patients improve under which conditions.

Table 7.7 further analyzes possibilities of differential outcome as a function of several variables. It has been stated by many critics of psychotherapy research studies that inexperienced therapists (those captive, conveniently available subjects) are too frequently used. They argue that generalizations from such groups are limited, if not irrelevant. Our review

gives some support to this contention in that outcomes differ significantly as a function of experience level. Twenty out of 22 studies showing positive outcomes involved therapy by experienced therapists. This 91 percent figure is impressive, but reduced somewhat in significance when it is observed that experienced therapists also account for 71 percent of the negative outcomes. From another viewpoint, 53 percent of the studies involving experienced therapists (20/38) yielded positive results, while 18 percent (2/11) by inexperienced therapists were positive.

As we have stated, some opponents of psychotherapy practices have argued that the

TABLE 7.7 Outcomes of 48 Studies (52 Groups) as a Function of Quality of Design and Nature of Therapy

	Positive Outcome	In Doubt	Negative Outcome	Totals
Experienced therapists	20	8	10	38
Inexperienced therapists	2	5	4	11
Control group	11	4	8	23
No control group	11	11	7	29
Design adequacy 1	5	2	3	10
Design adequacy 2	12	4	9	25
Design adequacy 3	5	9	3	17
Brief duration (5–20)	3	5	2	10
Moderate duration (21–49)	7	5	3	15
Long duration (50–600)	9	1	6	16
Analytic therapy	11	3	8	22
Eclectic therapy	9	8	6	23
Client-centered therapy	1	4	1	6
Group of therapists	16	13	12	41
One therapist's report	6	2	3	11

Note. Totals sometimes do not add up to 52 because of missing information.

impressiveness of therapeutic results declines proportionately with the quality of the research design. We tested this question, first by examining studies with and without control groups, and found essentially no difference in positive versus negative outcomes. We next compared general thoroughness and adequacy of design with type of outcome, and found a slight tendency in the direction of more positive outcome with more rigorous design. These two analyses seem to strongly contradict the notion that experimental rigor washes out significance of results in tests of therapy effectiveness.

Duration of therapy and type of therapy appeared unrelated to outcome, though the possibilities for analysis of these variables must be considered crude and simple to date.

When studies involving a report by one therapist of his own case outcomes are compared with studies involving groups of therapists, the individual therapists clearly win out (55 percent vs. 39 percent positive outcomes).

This is most likely due to considerable selectiveness among the individual therapists. It is a rare individual who reports a rigorous analysis of his own cases, and those who do seem more likely to be the successful ones.

Another more important conclusion that can be drawn from all of the studies reviewed thus far is that it is impossible to conclude very much from gross studies of therapeutic effects. It is only when we break therapy down into its components that we begin to obtain clearer results. Thus, when we homogenize patient samples, or consider the effects of the better therapists, or specify outcomes in terms of precise criteria, or utilize exactly defined control groups, we obtain clearer results (Kellner, 1965, 1967). The fact that diverse influences and processes, some probably opposite in direction to each other, are occurring in broad tests of therapy efficacy practically insures results that are difficult to interpret.

To illustrate, the two resumes made by Betz (cf. Table 7.6) indicate markedly discrepant percentages of improvement (48 and 73), which are probably caused by differences in the two therapist samples. This is also evident in the Rogers et al. (1967) study where the effects of "high-conditions" (empathy, warmth, and the like) therapists were greater than those of "low-conditions" therapists. Ordinarily, therapists of differing characteristics and quality are lumped together in studies, and this contributes to the usual lackluster results.

In the Cappon study, the improvement percentage varied from 40 to 75, and in the Koegler and Brill study from 49 to 86, depending upon the criterion used. This supports the urgent necessity to work toward specifying precisely the change desired and developing a specific measure for it. Again, we are faced with basic problems of description and measurement.

The nature of control groups also greatly affects the nature of the results. The positive outcome of the Shore and Massimo study looks strong because the control group was carefully equated with the therapy Ss, and rigorous follow-up of both groups was conducted. The positive results in the Cartwright studies (1957, 1961) are questionable, however, because the normal controls are a poor sample for creating a spontaneous remission base line which the therapy cases should exceed. Normals change very little on typical criteria; therefore, therapy would appear to be effective even when a small amount of change has taken place. It seems much more fruitful to select a patient sample for therapy homogeneous with regard to specific dimensions, and compare them with an equivalent control group.

All of the foregoing points, and more, are developed in the succeeding sections. Before turning to them, it should be noted that several important controlled outcome studies have been omitted from the material reviewed so far.

These include:

The Cambridge-Somerville Youth Study (Powers and Witmer, 1951)

The Rogers and Dymond collection of studies (1954)

The Fairweather et al. study (1960)

The Mink Study (1959)

The Barron and Leary Study (1955)

The Cartwright and Vogel Study (1960)

The Volsky, et al. study (1965)

The Truax-Carkhuff studies (Truax and Carkhuff, 1967; Carkhuff and Berenson, 1967).

These important, well-designed projects will be referred to in the succeeding discussions.

THE PROBLEM OF SPONTANEOUS REMISSION

The Landis-Denker Data

Landis (1937) was probably the first writer to make a persuasive empirical argument for the notion of a spontaneous recovery rate for mental disturbances. His view, still a defensible one, was that to be considered efficacious, any therapeutic technique must exceed the spontaneous recovery base line by some substantial degree. He found that the discharge rate for hospitalized neurotics in New York State from 1917 to 1934 was 72 percent, and he pointed out that the improvement rates from major therapy studies to that date did not differ much from this base line. Eysenck later took up this point (1952) and referred, in addition, to the Denker study (1947), which indicated a 72 percent improvement rate over a two-year period among untreated life-insurance disability claimants. He thus argued, as we have already seen, that therapy was an unproved procedure. This spontaneous remission issue has thus become a key point of controversy in debates over whether therapy has unique effects.

There were major deficiencies in the Landis and Denker samples and in the percentages reported, which both Landis and Eysenck pointed out. These defects, and the possible misleading character of the figures, have been repeatedly and thoroughly documented and amplified by a long series of critics (Rosenzweig, 1954; Luborsky, 1954; Cartwright, 1955; Strupp, 1963, 1964). There has been an equally pointed and extended set of replies by Eysenck (1952, 1955, 1964, 1966). The history of this debate has been discussed in detail by Kiesler (1966), and the upshot of the argument (in our opinion) is that everyone agrees on the deficiencies in the Landis-Denker-Eysenck baseline, but no one has produced more accurate figures.[5] The question has thus been left in limbo because adequate longitudinal studies of the natural history of neuroses have presumably not been done. This is undoubtedly true, and such studies should be done, but in the meantime we certainly have better data than is widely believed.

"New" Evidence on Spontaneous Recovery Rates

There has actually been a substantial amount of evidence lying around for years on this question. It indicates several crucial facts: (a) so-called "spontaneous" rates vary greatly across different types of neuroses; thus, no single rate nor the usual gross comparisons of therapy and controls of unknown heterogeneity of diagnosis, are sufficient to test the effects of therapy; (b) generally, rates are lower than the Landis-Denker figures, thus justifying those critics who have emphasized the inadequacy or irrelevance of these base lines; and (c) "untreated" neurotics who are supposed to serve as controls and whose improvement rates supposedly provide a true spontaneous recovery base line, actually, on the average, seek and receive substantial therapeutic help from both professional and nonprofessional helpers; thus, they have in most cases become "treated" controls to some degree, and cannot be considered true no-treatment comparison groups.

Friess and Nelson reported as early as 1942 on a five-year follow-up of psychoneurotic patients seen in medical clinics. These patients were interviewed and examined at follow-up by Drs. Phyllis Greenacre and Emeline Hayward, who divided them into groups according to amount of therapy received. Twenty of the no-

therapy group of 70 had improved, or 29 percent. Twenty-three of the 66 *S*s with two therapy sessions had improved, or 35 percent. Thus, after 5 years and upon careful examination by skilled clinicians, these cases showed recovery rates less than half the rates reported among Landis and Denker's admittedly inadequate samples.

Shore and Massimo found that only 3 of their 10 control delinquent boys had improved, a 30 percent rate. Orgel (1958) treated 15 cases of peptic ulcer that had persisted from 4 to 15 years without change, a 0 percent remission rate. Materson (1967) found only 38 percent spontaneous recovery of adolescent disorders, and Vorster (1966) reported that only 34 percent of his neurotic sample had improved after more than three years.

Hastings (1958) found a 46 percent rate for neurotics and Graham (1960) observed a range from 34 to 40 percent for sexual problems. O'Conner's (1964a and 1964b) 57 colitis patients had symptoms that persisted without change for an average of 15 years without treatment. Cappon's (1964) cases similarly presented symptoms of 15-year duration.

Kringlen (1965) followed the course of a sample of neurotics for 13 to 20 years, and found that spontaneous changes varied with diagnosis. The overall spontaneous improvement rate was 25 percent. Endicott and Endicott (1963) conducted a rigorous study of neurotics on a 6-month waiting list. Their battery of pre- and posttests and interviews indicated that 52 percent were improved, though they included "slightly improved" in this group, which spuriously inflates the recovery rate. In the Koegler and Brill study (1967), the no-therapy

---

[5] It is impossible to resist the temptation to add one more critical observation to the tortured history of controversy over these two studies. I shall note it and then restrain the impulse to elaborate further upon this already overworked terrain. In tabulating his table of 24 studies on therapy outcome, Eysenck (1952) frequently found that authors reported results in only three categories, "cured," "improved," and "not improved." Since "improved" could mean "significantly" or "slightly," Eysenck solved the problem by the expedient of splitting the improved group and calling half "much improved" and half "slightly improved." The "slightly improved" group were lumped with the "unimproved" to arrive at the final improvement rates for these studies. Now, it so happens that the Landis data were reported in three

categories: recovered, improved, and not improved. To be consistent, it is essential that the improved group be split in half and one-half labeled as not improved. The original figures were 32 percent recovered, 40 percent improved, and 28 percent not improved. Following Eysenck's procedure, Landis' true spontaneous recovery rate should therefore be 52 percent, not 72 percent: The conclusion that Landis' 72 percent base line is spuriously high is further supported by the fact that his rates for alcoholics and psychopaths were 64 percent and 75 percent respectively—figures way out of line with clinical reality. Naturally, I consider these to be the most devastating critiques of all regarding this issue; but, of course, it is irrelevant when the many new bits of data are pieced together.

TABLE 7.8   Spontaneous Recovery Rates for Neuroses[a]

Study	Percent Improved
Friess and Nelson (1942)	29
Friess and Nelson (1942)	35
Shore and Massimo (1966)	30
Orgel (1958)	0
Materson (1967)	38
Vorster (1966)	34
Hastings (1958)	46
Graham (1960)	37
O'Connor (1964)	0
Cappon (1964)	0
Endicott and Endicott (1963)	52[b]
Koegler and Brill (1967)	0
Paul (1967)	18
Kringlen (1965)	25

[a] Note that psychosomatic (Orgel; O'Connor), sexual (Graham), and adolescent (Shore and Massimo) disorders are included here. They are closely linked with neuroses and are often included in tabulations of neuroses, as was done by Eysenck in his review, and probably by Landis and Denker as well.

[b] Inflated by including slightly improved.

wait group showed no mean change over a one-year period. A third study employing rigorous controls and extremely thorough follow-up (Paul, 1967a), showed that after two years, speech-anxious neurotic students spontaneously improved on speech anxiety at the rate of 22 percent and on more general anxiety at 18 percent.

The foregoing data from divergent sources and from studies with varying degrees of exactness provide a fascinating picture of spontaneous recovery for neuroses (see Table 7.8). *The median rate appears to be in the vicinity of 30 percent!*

Admittedly, these findings have weaknesses. They are not based upon rigorous, continuous observation of the long-term natural course of neuroses. They employ varying criteria and are based upon diverse, noncomparable samples. Thus, the rates vary from 0 to 46 percent, hardly a reliable index for any type of scientific work. The fact is that these figures, though, are based upon a much more solid base than the Landis-Denker data. They have their weaknesses, but

they are the best available to date. In addition, the wide range of figures probably roughly follows the range of prognoses for differing neurotic disturbances. Thus, we might expect a higher rate for anxieties and depressions, but lower ones for obsessions and psychosomatic disorders.

It would be unfortunate if a new 30 percent figure were to be used as a baseline for neuroses, because the number is a mere abstraction that masks a heterogeneous collection of processes. Once again, we find strong support for specificity. It is essential that future outcome research be based upon homogeneous samples, for which the specific spontaneous recovery base line is known or is concurrently studied. Rates averaged across diverse samples simply obscure, rather than reveal, facts. In any event, we hope we have thoroughly put to rest the notion of a two-thirds spontaneous remission rate. Clearly, many neuroses simply do not change at all, or possibly get worse. Our new findings seem to square more closely with clinical observations of this fact.

One might tend to conclude at this point that the difference between the average therapy improvement rate of 65 percent (Table 7.4) and the spontaneous improvement rate of 30 percent shows *strong* evidence for therapeutic efficacy rather than the *modest* evidence we have repeatedly noted on the basis of our summary in Table 7.6 and other writers' reviews (Kellner; Jonckheere). We continue to hold the modest evidence position because (a) the error of measurement in our 30 percent figure is probably large enough so that the true median may lie somewhere between 15 and 45 percent, and if the median were 45 percent, then higher figures would also occur in individual studies, and (b) studies that have employed attention-placebo controls too often yield improvement figures very close to the therapy group figures (Paul, 1966: 50 percent; Koegler and Brill, 1967: 76 percent; Imber et al., 1968: 59 percent). These factors impose caution on any tendency to conclude that therapy studies reveal strong positive findings.

What is "Spontaneous"?[6]

Despite the fact that spontaneous remission is less frequent than has been supposed, we are still confronted with the fact that the median improvement rate for untreated neurotic adult patients ranges around 30 percent. Indeed, the significant changes that occur in control groups have been major contributors to the negative findings in several very well-designed studies of the effects of therapy (Powers and Witmer, 1951; Barron and Leary, 1955; and Rogers, et al., 1967). The amount of change occurring among the therapy cases, though it is real, is matched by the amount of change occurring among controls. Though not always the case, this phenomenon underlines the existence of spontaneous personality changes. What is this mysterious process of spontaneous remission?

This widely used explanatory concept is one of very dubious value, because it explains very little. It merely labels the existence of unknown processes as "spontaneous"; therefore, the concept has retarded scientific progress by seeming to make remission a consequence of events that are unresearchable. To say that

something is spontaneous is actually simply to argue that we do not know what is happening. The thought that some events might occur randomly or for no reason at all is abhorrent to the spirit of science.

To begin with then, to identify some positive personality changes as being spontaneous is simply to acknowledge that some therapeutic processes occur "naturally," that they occur outside of the consulting room, and that they are not used or are poorly understood by therapists. No one disputes the fact that some degree of "spontaneous" change occurs in disturbed persons who do not receive formal treatment. Why do they change? This is a fascinating question which bears directly upon the issue of whether psychotherapy is a uniquely effective change agent.

No definitive evidence exists that might satisfy our curiosity completely on this issue; however, there is enough information to warrant some educated speculation.

Previous reviews of relevant data (Bergin, 1963, 1966) suggest that the majority of people who experience psychological disturbance do *not* seek out mental health professionals for treatment. Many of them seek counsel, advice, and support from a variety of helping persons who cannot be considered trained in these functions, such as spouses, friends, teachers, physicians, clergymen, and the like.

The best evidence on this point is perhaps provided by Gurin, Veroff, and Feld (1960) in their nationwide interview survey conducted for the Joint Commission on Mental Illness and Health. They found that of those persons who actively sought help for personal problems, the vast majority chose non-mental-health professionals, and generally they felt more satisfied with the help received than did those who chose psychiatrists and psychologists. These findings are reproduced in Tables 7.9 and 7.10 from Gurin et al.

It is certainly conceivable that these data describe in part the process of spontaneous remission among persons not in therapy. It may therefore consist of seeking and obtaining therapeutic help from nontherapists! To the extent that such assistance is effective, it may

---

[6] The following material is based upon a previous analysis (Bergin, 1967a).

TABLE 7.9 Source of Help Used by People Who Have Sought
Professional Help for a Personal Problem[a]

Source of Help	Percent
Clergyman	42
Doctor	29
Psychiatrist (or psychologist): private practitioner or not ascertained whether private or institutional[a]	12
Psychiatrist (or psychologist) in clinic, hospital, other agency; mental hospital	6
Marriage counselor; marriage clinic	3
Other private practitioners or social agencies for handling psychological problems	10
Social service agencies for handling nonpsychological problems (e.g., financial problems)	3
Lawyer	6
Other	11
Total	[b]
Number of people	(345)

Note. Reproduced from Gurin, Veroff and Feld, 1960, p. 307, by permission of Basic Books Inc., Publishers, New York.

[a] Actually, only six people specifically mentioned going to a private practitioner. This category should thus be looked upon as representing in the main those people who said "psychiatrist" without specifying that he was part of a mental hygiene agency.

[b] Total exceeds 100 percent due to use of more than one category by some clients.

TABLE 7.10 Relationship of Source of Help Used to Perception of
Helpfulness of Therapy (First-Mentioned Responses Only)

	Source of Help						
How Much Therapy Helped	Clergy	Doctor	Psychiatrist	Marriage Counselor	Other psychological Agencies	Non-psychological Agencies	Lawyer
Helped; helped a lot	65%	65%	46%	25%	39%	60%	62%
Helped (qualified)	13%	11%	13%	8%	33%	20%	15%
Did not help	18%	13%	24%	67%	17%	20%	15%
Don't know whether it helped	—	1%	6%	—	—	—	—
Not ascertained	4%	10%	11%	—	11%	—	8%
Total	100%	100%	100%	100%	100%	100%	100%
Number of people[a]	(130)	(89)	(46)	(12)	(18)	(10)	(13)

Source. Reproduced from Gurin, Veroff and Feld, 1960, p. 319, by permission of Basic Books Inc., Publishers, New York, New York.

[a] Does not include 27 people who mentioned "other" sources of help.

account for the change that occurs in control groups of disturbed persons who do not receive professional psychotherapy. Probably, these control subjects do not enjoy the pain of their disturbance while being detained as controls, so they seek relief elsewhere. Such a conclusion is further substantiated by Frank's finding (1961) that over a period of years, approximately 50 percent of a group who had sought psychotherapy had also sought help from a variety of non-mental-health sources. He suggests that the continued positive change that occurred among them over a long period when they were *not* in therapy was due to the effects of this non-professional "treatment." Gurin et al. comment on the significance of such phenomena (p. 341): "These findings underscore the crucial role that nonpsychiatric resources—particularly clergymen and physicians—play in the treatment process. They are the major therapeutic agents . . ." (!)

This type of analysis casts an entirely new light upon the processes that ameliorate pathology. Perhaps psychotherapy is not special after all. Perhaps selected helping persons in the "natural" social environment provide adequate or better coping conditions for neurosis than do trained mental health experts. The comparative effects of such natural cures have not been studied, but it appears evident that something has developed in our societal structure which is validly responsive to mental health problems. This is probably most obvious where it has been explicitly organized in lay mental health technologies such as Alcoholics Anonymous, Synanon, Schizophrenics Anonymous, and Neurotics Anonymous. Jane Brody, in the *New York Times* (1966), depicts the contrast between the effects of professional and lay methodologies in the following account:

Frances, a 55-year old mother of three, came to her first Neurotics Anonymous meeting as a desperate and frightened woman about to enter a mental institution for the fifth time. *After 11 years of psychiatric care, shock treatments and tranquilizers, she was still unable to function as a wife and mother.* Once a professional organist, she had had to give up her job, and her husband frequently had to stay home from his job to care for her.

Within three months, however, Frances was happy, easy to live with, and getting ready to return to her career.

"What happened to her is truly a miracle", noted another N.A. member, "the kind of miracle", he added, "that has been par for the organization throughout its two-year history."

Another illustration of a naturalistic therapy process derives from our experiences in conducting extensive personality assessments of normal persons for a governmental agency. During these evaluations, we occasionally have noted the appearance of an exceptionally effective person having come from a chaotic and ordinarily pathology-inducing family life. A young college graduate illustrates this well. He came from an extremely disturbed home setting in which every member of his family, except himself, had been hospitalized for severe mental illness, and yet he had graduated from a renowned university with honors, had starred on the football team, and was unusually popular. During his government training he was held in the highest esteem by staff members and was rated as best liked and most likely to succeed by his peers.

Needless to say, this young man's history was carefully scrutinized. It revealed that during his elementary school years he had essentially adopted a neighborhood family as his own and spent endless hours with them. Certain characteristics of this family appear most significant. They were a helping family in the sense that love emanated from them and was freely available to all. The home became a neighborhood gathering place. It might be characterized as an informal therapy agency, a kitchen clinic! Of special significance for the fellow under consideration was his relationship with a boy in the family, a year older than he, who formed for him a positive role model with whom he closely identified and followed to his considerable satisfaction. An even more crucial factor was his relationship with the mother in this family, who became his guide, counselor, and chief source of emotional nurturance. His reports indicate that while this relationship was intense, it was not symbiotic, and indeed seemed to foster his independence and self-development. This particular woman was apparently the prototypical mother, and influenced more than one stray lad toward security, resilience, and accomplishment. It is difficult to deny the potent therapeutic impact of this woman, at least as it was portrayed by her protégé's report. While there are probably few like her, she represents a dimension of socially indigenous therapy that may be more significant than is usually recognized. Certainly, it makes the possibility of "spontaneous" remission more believable.

Is it unreasonable to suppose that people in distress have simply discovered potent change agents as they exist naturally in society, and have put them to work with sufficient impact that they create changes equivalent to that appearing in psychotherapy? This is one possible explanation of spontaneous remission, and of the fact that some studies of therapy ordinarily reveal no difference between experimentals and controls. The controls are getting better because they are getting help from persons untrained in formal psychotherapy, who practice a kind of natural therapy. It could be that these agents of personality integration are actually *more* effective *as a group* than trained therapists.

The rationale for such a conclusion is that these lay therapists are probably selected by people because their ability to form therapeutic relationships and to convey wise counsel are known by word of mouth. Professionals, on the other hand, may often be selected more for their academic credentials or professional political standing than for their ability to relate and to generate insights. In other words, these lay therapists may well be a more select group with regard to dimensions relevant to the actual work of therapy than are the professionals. If this is true, and it ought to be carefully studied, then it has revolutionary implications for the training of mental health workers.

It implies that some therapeutic effects can be obtained by persons with little or no exposure to traditional training procedures, and thus suggests that selection of therapists is as important as training and experience. It also indicates that the mental health manpower problem could be solved more readily and at less cost by organizing or harnessing these indigenous change agents. That this possibility is not entirely fanciful is evidenced by Carkhuff and Truax's (1965) and Poser's (1966) remarkable findings that selected psychologically untrained mental hospital aides and student volunteers can have a significant therapeutic impact as group therapists after only a brief period of instruction. There is now enough evidence to support these innovations that entire books are being devoted to them (e.g., Guerney, 1969).

Another interpretation of spontaneous remission may be deduced from additional data presented by Gurin et al. They found that only a small minority of people who experienced personal problems admitted to seeking *any* formal help for their distress. While 464 persons from their sample of 2,460 were frank enough to admit that they had at some time felt an "impending nervous breakdown," only 29 percent of them sought formal help; 39 percent felt they could have used or might have needed external help but did not seek it, and 29 percent used self-help. Of the 106 Ss who claimed that they worried "all the time," 23 percent sought help, 24 percent felt they could have used or might have needed external help, and 49 percent utilized self-help. It is not entirely clear from the text exactly what self-help includes, but it appears to account for a considerable percentage of the responses to distress. Some suggestions of how self-help operates may be inferred from data appearing in another section of the volume. It is indicated that a significant percentage of the respondents "think things through," or "try to alleviate the situation" actively. Another significant proportion utilize denial (forgetting about worries or unhappiness) or displacement (doing something else to take one's mind off troubles). Significant percentages also use prayer or conversing with their spouse or friends, which involve somewhat greater dependence upon external sources. Gurin et al. adopt the current bias that denial and displacement are bad and classify them as passive reactions, but we question this ready assent to traditional psychodynamic interpretation. Can not these responses be considered as coping reactions which are consciously exerted, which have substantial effects, and which are not defensive in the traditional pathological sense? Is it altogether unrealistic to suppose that forgetting about worries or engaging in an activity which takes one's mind off them are beneficial? To be healthy is not to be free from troubles, but rather to be able to channel oneself toward achievements and satisfactions in spite of worries and unhappiness. Psychotherapeutically derived self-insight and personality reconstruction do not necessarily alter the troublesome facts of existence and conceivably may even cause one to ruminate excessively over things better left alone.

While there is no concrete evidence to indicate how satisfying or change-affecting such self-help responses are, they are commonly recognized reactions to stress. To the extent that they relieve anxiety and associated symptomatologies, they may account for a considerable proportion of the "spontaneous" remission noted in therapy experiments.

It is evident that several factors may account for "spontaneous" remission phenomena, that these factors have therapeutic efficacy, that many of them may occur in psychotherapy as well as naturally, but that they are not necessarily unique to the formal therapy process. This means that subjects used as control groups or to establish base line percentages of improvement for comparisons with treatment cases are not really controls at all! They are the recipients of formal, informal, and self-help procedures which are often enough identical or similar to psychotherapy, so that they cannot be justifiably used for this purpose.

Thus, we have found that not only is the spontaneous remission rate lower than expected, but also that it is probably caused to a considerable degree by actual therapy or therapylike procedures. This certainly casts psychotherapy into a more promising position than has heretofore been considered, even though formal therapy still should do better than informal therapy, which it does. It still does not mean that the general cross-section of professional therapy is uniformly dramatic in its effects, but it does suggest once again that there are some important variables at work somewhere in the process. These should not be ignored by the hardnosed academic types who tend to be skeptical of the merits of therapy.

The spontaneous remission phenomenon has also made us more convinced that psychotherapy is merely a special case of a much broader range of therapeutic phenomena that exist naturalistically in society. It will be an important task of the future to discover their characteristics and to put them to work more efficiently, perhaps within a community mental health context (Bergin, 1963, 1966, 1967a, 1967b).

DETERIORATION EFFECTS IN PSYCHOTHERAPY

When the general effects of therapy are tested, they appear to be only modestly impressive. Then, when we see variability of results occurring as a function of patient, therapist, criterion, and perhaps technique, variables, we are led inevitably toward much more precise inquiries. We stop asking "What is the effect of psychotherapy, if any?" and ask instead: "What are the specific effects of specific interventions by specified therapists upon specific symptoms or patient types?" and, "As precision of inquiry increases, do clarity and strength of results similarly increase?" (see Kiesler, 1966 and Strupp and Bergin, 1969b for elaborations of this trend).

One of several important evidences giving rise to this type of thinking and research strategy has been the observation that "While some research studies reveal little difference in the *average amount* of change occurring in experimental and control groups, a significant increase in the variability of criterion scores appears at posttesting in the treatment groups. This conclusion was drawn from seven (well-designed) psychotherapy outcome studies and was startling in that it directly implied that some treatment cases were improving while others were deteriorating, thus causing a spreading of criterion scores at the conclusion of the therapy period, which did not occur among the control subjects. Evidently there is something unique about psychotherapy which has the power to cause improvement beyond that occurring among controls, but equally evident is a contrary deteriorating impact that makes some cases worse than they were to begin with. When these contrary phenomena are lumped together in an experimental group, they cancel each other out to some extent, and the overall yield in terms of improvement (in these particular studies) is no greater than the change occurring in a control group via "spontaneous remission factors." (Bergin, 1967a, p. 184.)

We have documented this finding in two prior reviews (Bergin, 1966; 1967a; 1967b), portions of which are reproduced in Figure 7.2 and Table 7.11. Figure 7.2 is a schematic interpretation of this phenomenon, and Table 7.11 summarizes controlled studies on which this type of schema is based. There has also been a recent series of papers on the subject, beginning with two American Psychological Association papers delivered in 1962 (Bergin, 1963; Truax, 1963). The others are Bergin, 1970; Braucht, 1970; Eysenck, 1967; Frank, 1967; Matarazzo, 1967; Strupp and Bergin, 1969b; Truax and Carkhuff, 1964, 1967; and Truax and Mitchell, Chapter 9 of this volume.

This finding is exciting for three major reasons. First, it demonstrates that some portion of whatever is happening in therapy is powerful; and, like any discovery in nature, it can have beneficial or harmful effects. This is equally true of aspirin, X rays, and atomic energy. While the deteriorative effect is disturbing, its existence proves the existence of a complementary "improvement effect," thus setting some as yet unknown part of therapy beyond the effects of "spontaneous" factors. Second, evidence is now accumulating that there are specific therapist characteristics associated with deterioration and improvement (see Chapter 9 in this volume). Third, these findings have opened-up entirely new possibilities for discovering more specific change-inducing and

TABLE 7.11   Studies Demonstrating both Deterioration and Positive Change as a Result of Psychotherapy

Authors	Date	Population	N	Therapy Type	Average Therapy Duration	Relevant Criteria
Powers & Witmer	1951	Predelinquent boys	325	Directed friendship: social work counseling	6 years	Test battery Delinquency data Adjustment ratings Case record analysis
Rogers & Dymond	1954	Young adults	25	Client-centered	8 months	Q Sort; behavior ratings
Barron & Leary	1955	Outpatient neurotics	42	Eclectic-analytic	8 months	MMPI
Mink	1959	Jr. high school students	96	Client-centered (48) Directive-insight (48)	4 months	Calif. Test of Personality
Fairweather et al.	1960	Long-term psychotics; short term psychotics; nonpsychotics	72	Eclectic-analytic	3–5 months	Q Sort
Cartwright & Vogel	1960	Young adults	22	Client-centered	33 sessions	Q Sort; TAT
Truax	1963	Hospitalized Schizophrenics	16	Client-centered Electic-analytic	6 months 3½ years	Multiple tests and ward behavior
Volsky et al.	1965	College students	80	Eclectic-directive	3 sessions	Anxiety, defensiveness and problem-solving scales
Truax & Carkhuff	1965	Hospitalized psychotics	74	Lay client-centered	24 sessions	Ward behavior

Source. Reproduced by permission from Bergin (1967a).

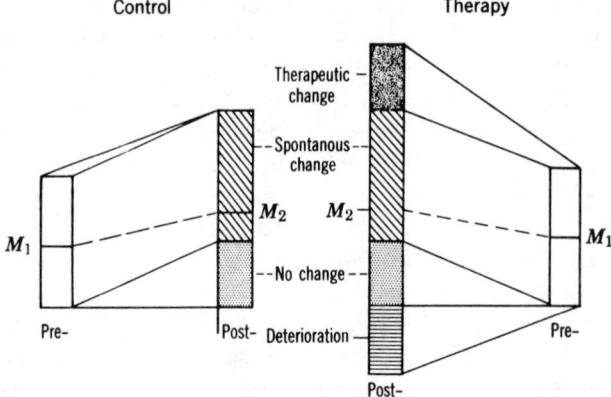

Figure 7.2 The deterioration effect. Schematic representation of pre- and post-test distributions of criterion scores in psychotherapy outcome studies. (Reproduced by permission from the *Journal of Abnormal Psychology*, 1966, **71**, 235–246.)

retarding processes than was ever possible by studying "the effects of psychotherapy" in general.

A number of questions can be raised about the deterioration phenomenon.

How well established is this finding? Tables 7.11 and 7.12 recapitulate more than 30 studies providing ample evidence that deterioration exists among patient populations.

How widespread is deterioration? In only four of the studies where I found it possible to assess the presence or absence of deterioration, was there little or no evidence of the phenomenon. There are many more outcome studies in which it is impossible to discern whether deterioration has occurred, including several that use an undifferentiated category of "not improved or worse."

It appears that deterioration occurs in a very high proportion of the samples studied, and that it is more frequent among therapy samples than control samples. A subjective reading of the material listed in Tables 7.11 and 7.12 reveals approximately a 10 percent mean rate for therapy cases and less than 5 percent for controls. This new accounting therefore requires a slight modification of Figure 7.2. While no change or slight improvement is common among controls, the possibility of a small proportion of control *S*s deteriorating must now be considered.

What causes it? It seems likely that all therapists will occasionally encounter (in some patients) a deteriorating process which they cannot reverse and which does not tend to reverse spontaneously. On the other hand, there are probably two other classes of cases who deteriorate during a therapy period because of the therapist's interventions: (a) those who are deteriorating already and who can be helped, but the therapist is inept, and they continue to get worse; and (b) those who have already attained a neurotic equilibrium that is upset by the therapist, resulting in the initiation of a new cycle of deeper deterioration. Since no one would deliberately produce deterioration in an experimental way, it is difficult to demonstrate that therapists actually *cause* it or how it is caused. There is some naturalistic evidence on this, however, which will be discussed at a later point.

Is it an artifact of criterion measurement error? This is doubtful. If it were the case, deterioration should be more common among control groups than it is, and the increased variance in experimental groups would be difficult to understand. Also, it appears that the *opposite* of regression toward the mean is occurring, which makes the nonartifactual nature of the phenomenon seem more real. Finally, it is possible to measure therapist behaviors that significantly correlate with improvement or deterioration (see Truax and Mitchell, Chapter 9 of this volume), thus further reducing the probability that the phenomenon is a random one.

Is it due to temporary regression? Psychoanalysis in particular emphasizes the importance of a temporary, deep regression in patients prior

TABLE 7.12   Additional Occurrences of Deterioration

Authors	Date	In Therapy Group	In Control Group
Wispe and Parloff	1965	Increased criterion variability, but not clear evidence of deterioration	0
Varble and Landfield	1969	2/36	0/35
Feifel and Eells	1963	5/63 Unimproved or worse—not differentiated	No control group
Rogers, Gendlin, Kiesler, and Truax	1967	Limited evidence of deterioration	0
Strupp et al.	1964	0	No control group
Aronson and Weintraub	1968	2 to 8% of 127, depending on criterion and diagnosis	No control group
Sager, Riess, and Gundlach	1964	2 to 14% of 103 same or worse, but the 2 categories lumped together	No control group
Uhlenhuth and Duncan	1968	26%, though not stated how much worse	No control group
Rosenbaum, Friedlander, and Kaplan	1956	2/210	No control group
Berleman and Steinburn (at follow-up)	1967	36% 10/28	0% 0/33
Henry and Shlien	1958	Significant mean decline at follow-up for time—limited therapy patients on TAT	0
Imber, Nash, Stone, and Frank	1968	14/34 Same or worse—not differentiated, apparently most of these were in minimal contact therapy	
Truax, Wargo, Frank, et al.	1966	2/40 on global ratings, 10/40 on discomfort scale; miscellaneous references to deterioration	No control group
Paul	1967a	4% insight therapy	5% Placebo therapy, 8% control
Weber, Elinson, and Moss	1965	5% average, though as high as 44% among psychotics ($N = 186$) in psychoanalysis	No control group
Koegler and Brill (analytic)	1967	1/27	3/116 in drug and placebo groups combined—not differentiated
Koegler and Brill (brief)	1967	5/162	No control group
Gottschalk, Mayerson, and Gottlieb	1967	2/34	4/14 among non-equivalent dropouts
Jonckheere	1965	6/72	No control group
Warne, Canter (inexp.) and Wiznia (exp.)	1953	3/30 Significantly worse, 18/30 Slightly worse 0/30 Significantly worse, 2/30 Slightly worse	4/30 Significantly worse 16/39 Slightly worse, though not a matched control
Ling, Zausmer, and Hope	1952	18% worse	No control group
Rosenthal	1955	3/12 = 25%	No control group
Kringlen	1965	5% worse at end of 2 months in hospital where treatment was mostly physical, same at 13–20 year follow-up, probably should be considered controls and not therapy Ss	

Note. Studies included in this table are only those in which the authors examined the possibility of deterioration effects, or where it was possible to assess the question from the data given regardless of the authors' intentions. Differing percents in some studies are a function of differing criteria and diagnoses examined.

to reconstructive change. This is not what is being tapped by indicators of deterioration, however, because they are always taken at the therapy termination or follow-up points. In addition, the cases showing deterioration at termination have been seen for widely varying periods from very brief therapy to long-term classical psychoanalysis.

Why does it appear on some criteria and not others in the same study (Braucht, 1970; Bergin, 1970)*?* In some studies where multiple criteria are used, deterioration is more evident on some measures than others. It seems most likely to me that this is because personality change is multidimensional, and a particular therapy does not necessarily create change on all dimensions nor at the same rate on different dimensions (see section on measurement in this chapter).

Which patients are most likely to deteriorate? There is no definitive evidence on this point, but it appears thus far that the more fragile and disturbed patients are the best candidates for getting worse. Studies of psychotherapy with psychotics often reveal deterioration. Among psychotics in psychoanalysis, Weber, et al. (1965) reported that 44 percent got worse! Nevertheless, the phenomenon is by no means confined to these cases, and the matter is quite open to question.

What should be done about it? Research on therapist and patient characteristics as they relate to deterioration is urgently needed. Special care is apparently needed with some patients, a fact that skilled clinicians have known for some time. More careful selection and evaluation of therapists will also have to become a key aspect of prevention, as will more exacting conditions for introducing neophytes into practice. Training will have to focus on these patient and therapist variables. Ultimately, when our technology is more advanced, it may become possible to intermittently evaluate and upgrade the performance of practitioners. In the meantime, training centers, supervising therapists, and certifying boards would do well to routinely use more practical and objective criteria for evaluating fledgling therapists. Perhaps their improvement rate with patients should reach a standard criterion before they are certified for practice.

Clinical Aspects of Deterioration

In recent years I have received numerous communications from both therapists and patients who have provided rich detail regarding the process of therapist-caused deterioration. I have found some of these examples most disturbing, perhaps because I have been too naive regarding the way life really is. Apparently there are many areas of error and malpractice that are regularly covered up by practitioners in every field. It seems to be an all too common procedure to ignore these incidents, no matter how serious the consequences may be for the patients involved. Indeed, I hope that one of our suicide centers might do a careful study of the possibility of therapist-precipitated suicides. In general, deterioration of various kinds is much too common to be ignored.

I wish to present two rather convincing evidences of therapist-induced deterioration. The first is a rigorous empirical analysis by a well-known writer in the field, of practice in a well-known clinical center. The second is a detailed report by a former patient of a famous practitioner.

The first is a longitudinal study of children seen for therapy during childhood and early adolescence, who have since been followed up as adults. For the time being, the author and the clinic must remain anonymous. The adult status of these patients was selected as the outcome criterion, and it was noted that therapists varied considerably in terms of adult outcomes of children they had seen. Two therapists, A and B, whose outcomes were extremely divergent but whose case samples were virtually identical, were chosen for special study. The outcomes of their cases are shown in Table 7.13. The differences here are clear and they are statistically significant.

The therapy notes on the 28 cases seen by A and B were analyzed in order to detect differences in attitude and approach. The first important finding concerned involvement. Therapist A consistently devoted more time to those cases that later turned out to be more disturbed; B did the opposite. That is, when A perceived greater disturbance in a child, he devoted more time to him, and B devoted less time to similar cases. A was very obviously interested in, liked, and had respect for the boys.

TABLE 7.13 Adult Outcome of Children Seen by Therapists A and B

	Schizophrenic				Not Schizophrenic				Total
	Chronic		Released		Socially Inadequate		Socially Adequate		
	Raw	Percent	Raw	Percent	Raw	Percent	Raw	Percent	
A	0	(0)	4	(27)	5	(33)	6	(40)	15
B	3	(23)	8	(61)	2	(15)	0	(0)	13
Total	10	(14)	24	(35)	17	(25)	17	(25)	68

Note. There are no differences in any major characteristic at the time of clinic contact between the cases seen by A and B. The only known differences between them is their adult status and the therapist they saw.

The totals shown are for all cases studied, including those seen by therapists other than A or B. This provides a rough base line of expected change.

A's work was also characterized by

... more appropriate allocation of effort, more use of resources outside the immediate therapy situation, firmness and directness in dealing with parents, support of efforts toward autonomy (and stimulation of these when they were latent), anchoring the children in reality through setting-up strong therapeutic relationships ... and the promotion of competence in handling everyday real life problems.

The author further states:

... supportive ego strengthening methods produced much more profound changes than the methods of Therapist B, who moved too precipitously into presumably deep material. Successful therapy with adolescents requires a continuous process of diagnosis, with modification of "opening up" methods, whenever the child, or the therapist, becomes incapable of coping with the material brought out.

If the results achieved by successful therapists such as A argue against the cynical belief that therapy never helps, the apparently destructive effect of intervention by Therapist B also suggests that the potential harmfulness of therapeutic efforts can hardly be ignored.

The children considered here were already experiencing nearly intolerable degrees of anxiety, vulnerability, feelings of unreality, and isolated alienation. When the therapist increased those feelings, without being at the same time able to help the boy develop ways of coping with them, he may well have played a part in the subsequent psychotic developments. Therapy may lead one into health, but it may also be a part of the complex process that ends up driving one crazy.

This study of the specifics of practice provides the kind of clinical detail that makes the deterioration process more understandable and real. Unfortunately, there has been some difficulty in obtaining permission to publish the full report.

Of the several reports I have received from patients, they are nearly all persons who felt that they were considerably disturbed by one or more therapists but were ultimately able to find effective treatment elsewhere and considered themselves much improved at the time of writing. Some of them were very bitter and extreme in their comments. I have no way of determining the accuracy of their accounts, but the truth of many of them would not surprise me, particularly in light of Strupp's finding (1960) that nearly a third of the therapists he studied might be considered to have antitherapeutic attitudes.

The report I have selected seemed to be among the more reasonable and well-articulated accounts. I shall call the patient Mrs. D (for deteriorated) and the therapist Dr. PN (for psychonoxious). Mrs. D was in therapy for three to four years on a twice-a-week basis prior to moving and finding a new therapist. Her account illustrates a number of serious negative consequences of the therapist's behavior, but she could not say "whether the negative effects outweighed the positive ... since there was no untreated control!" Subjectively, however, she seemed to feel that the total experience was weighted toward the negative side.

Her account is given essentially verbatim below:

1. He [Dr. PN] repeatedly threatened to cancel all appointments, and rejected in various ways, saying it was, for instance, useless to come unless I talked. I usually reacted with fear and crying, but the crying occurred after leaving the office.

Drinking: During the first few months, after he thus threatened desertion a number of times and I responded strongly as above, I started taking about two drinks before the session. When asked why, I replied, so that I could talk. He admitted that perhaps he was "going too fast"—the only expression of humility or modesty by an analyst whom I consider too often insufferably pompous and overly sure of himself.

He continued the rejections, the most prominent, vivid and discouraging feature of analysis with [Dr. PN].

2. "I am not here to help you; I am here only to show you what you are doing."

I do not at the moment have at hand the context of this statement by [Dr. PN], but it was a strong influence in destroying my trust. The context, if given, would not change the meaning. I reasoned that if the truth about the patient was more harmful than helpful, it should not be used, or should at least be deferred until it is not harmful. This admission on his part about not being helpful represents to me a gross distortion of personal and professional values.

3. At one point it was quite important for me to hold [an office] position which I was attempting to do. I experienced a very strong need for the psychological support of my therapist for a length of time which I arbitrarily selected as a month. By that I meant that for at least one month I wanted him not to threaten desertion or a similarly rejecting attitude. I made this as clear as possible by stating in a letter mailed to him that either he agreed to this month-long emotional support, or I would seek another therapist. He replied that if you write another letter like that, I'll tell you to leave. I was not consciously afraid of any specific threat in the absence of a therapist. Nothing would happen, except perhaps for some crying. The dependency need was present and still is today, but to a significantly lesser degree. My problem at work during this earlier interval was that because of difficulty in concentrating, my responsibilities took much longer than normally expected; I went to extremes in remaining late to complete my work.

4. He would not believe my claim about wanting children and the reason for not having them. When I later stated I did not see any future together without children, his immediate and unqualified verbatim response was "You mean you'd commit suicide?" I did not mean or imply this, and I could not help but think of the charge against psychiatrists that they "look for the worst and usually find it." Here a most vital wish was being interpreted as a death threat.

5. Pain in lower back and shoulder, assumed by me to be hysterical, developed when I left on vacation. I did not mention this as I assumed he would respond with ridicule or disbelief. During the interval of nontreatment, this pain did return in severe form, requiring bed rest for a week but gradually subsided. (Internist was consulted but gave no treatment.)

I reported to [Dr. PN] fatigue of more than moderate degree; this was met with such comments as: you are not working efficiently because you don't want to. A goodly part of this symptom, I feel sure, could have been accounted for by low blood count (7 gr. compared to a normal of 14) and a low (minus 20) basal metabolic rate, discovered after I stopped treatment. The therapist was an M.D., but never suggested a physical checkup.

Concerning [Dr. PN's] method, two physician-friends of mine were analyzed by him and came away with negative impressions. One took a training-analysis with [Dr. PN]. The other friend referred to his analysis as "sadistic."

While it would be difficult to unequivocally establish the validity of reports such as this and it would be reasonable to question the perceptions and memories of emotionally upset clients, I personally have found these accounts, of which the foregoing is but one illustration, quite believable. In light of all the objective evidence of deterioration effects, such accounts of processes that could intensify disturbances seem to make considerable sense. I therefore offer the analysis of therapists A and B and the experiences of Mrs. D as clinical annotations of this important and interesting effect.

OUTCOME RESEARCH METHODOLOGY

There have been more articles written describing how ideal outcome research should be done than there are studies attempting to match the described ideal designs (Edwards and Cronbach, 1952; Eysenck, 1966; Frank, 1959; Goldstein, Heller, and Sechrest, 1966; Hunt, 1952; Kiesler, 1966; Paul, 1967b; Rogers and Dymond, 1954;

Rogers, Gendlin, Kiesler, and Truax, 1967; Sargent, 1960; Scriven, 1959; Strupp and Bergin, 1969b; Watson, 1952a, 1952b; Watson, Mensh, and Gildea, 1951; Zubin, 1953). These proposals have rarely been implemented to any significant extent, except perhaps among the client-centered group. One reason is that they are elaborate enough to require more effort and expense than most researchers in this area have been able to provide. Another is that they assume a level of precision that has essentially not developed to date in this field. Finally, it is questionable whether these rather classical experimental designs are particularly appropriate for studying the practice of therapy.

The basic features of these classical designs are like those found in any science. There is an experimental or therapy treatment group, an equivalent control group presumably identical in every way except for not receiving treatment, and reliable procedures for measuring patient status before and after therapy and at follow-up. In addition, the effects of being tested, of waiting for therapy over varying time intervals, and the like, are controlled for by either own-control procedures or comparisons with a separate control group. Also, factorial designs for comparing two or more treatment variables and their interactions are sometimes proposed, as are additional control groups, such as attention-placebo control Ss.

Since the numerous details of these types of designs are abundantly available in the literature and are further referred to in Kiesler's chapter and elsewhere in this book, I shall not attempt a detailed exposition of them. Rather, I shall emphasize a few points that I consider to be crucial to making outcome research more useful than it has been to date.

The Need for Specificity

I seriously doubt that there is any point in doing more of the kind of outcome research that has typically been done or that has been described in the articles cited above, including my own. I believe that the present review has made it quite clear that gross tests of the effects of therapy are obsolete. Strupp and I (1969b) have recently agreed considerably with Kiesler and with Paul's view (1967b) that outcome research should be directed toward answering

"*what* treatment, by *whom*, is most effective for *this* individual with *that* specific problem, and under *which* set of circumstances" (p. 111). This attitude is strongly reinforced by our finding variability of outcome across diagnoses, criteria, and types of therapists. These findings, along with the evidence on deterioration, further support the notion that psychotherapy is such a heterogeneous collection of diverse and conflicting events that any attempt to definitively test its effect by virtue of classical pre-post-control group designs is doomed to failure. It is small wonder that such efforts have provided only the slimmest positive evidence of any effects, that results have usually been ambiguous, and that failures to replicate have been abundant.

This approach is about like asking "What are the effects of storms?" Which storms? Where? What kind of effects? What is a storm? Or it is like asking "What are the effects of medicine?" and then proceeding to collect a group of doctors practicing on patients to test for changes in "health," whatever that is.

It is essential that the entire therapeutic enterprise be broken down into specific sets of measures and operations, or in other words, be dimensionalized. Otherwise, there will continue to be little progress. What progress has occurred in recent years has come from the isolation of potent, specific variables from the broad milieu of events occurring in therapeutic practice. Two good examples are the isolation of therapist style-of-relating behaviors by the client-centered group (Rogers et al., 1967; Truax and Carkhuff, 1967), and the development of more precise interventions for specific disorders by the behavior therapists (Wolpe and Lazarus, 1966; Ullmann and Krasner, 1965). Indeed, these two lines of inquiry and innovation have so much apparent promise that they now account for a very high proportion of all studies being done on therapeutic change. The behavioral approach in particular, in spite of the fact that a few of its proponents are as closed-minded as the controllers of the psychoanalytic establishment, has stimulated an enormous new literature on specific interventions for specific problems. The appeal and potential pay-off of a specificity approach as exemplified by the behavioral therapists are signalled by the number of young professionals opting for this approach, the number of new journals being founded (at least four to date), and the radical switch in topics of articles published in general journals. A good example of the latter is the growth of behavior therapy research studies appearing in journals that appeal to the broad cross-section of clinicians, such as *The Journal of Abnormal Psychology* and *The Journal of Consulting Psychology*. Figure 7.3 shows that between 1959 and 1969, research studies of psychotherapy reported in these two journals have increased modestly and normally for traditional therapies, and with exponential drama for behavioral therapies. The important point is that these are general journals representing the whole field and are not specialized publications, such as *Behavior Research and Therapy*. If publications of the latter type were studied, of course, the rapid growth rate of behavioral studies would appear earlier and would be even more dramatic. It is of particular interest that 46 percent of the behavioral reports and only 24 percent of the traditional articles are outcome studies. Clearly, more specific approaches lend themselves more readily to less ambiguous tests of effectiveness.

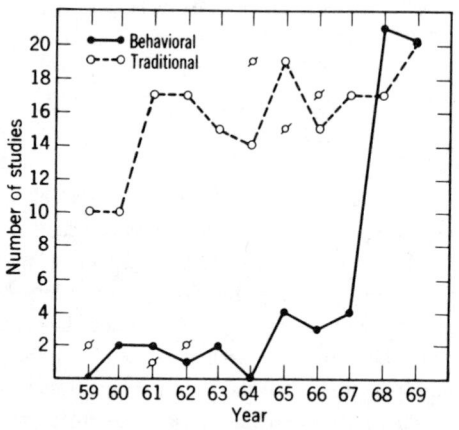

Figure 7.3 Change in rate of behavioral and traditional therapy research studies in the Journals of *Abnormal* and of *Consulting Psychology*, 1959–1969. (*Note*. The 1969 data are extrapolated from first six months' publications).

The preceding is only illustrative of the values of a specificity approach, and should not obscure the fact that there are many fertile leads yet to be extracted from traditional therapy, as our review has shown, and also from other domains, such as cognition, attitude change, group dynamics, and the like (cf. Goldstein and Simonson, Chapter 5 in this volume).

The Bugaboo of Complexity

Some critics argue that to break down, isolate, and extract variables from the therapeutic context is to drastically modify and underestimate the complexity of the phenomena under study. I feel this is irrelevant and unnecessarily inhibiting because (a) no science or applied science has ever progressed without simplifying; (b) by extracting and manipulating variables, entirely new techniques may be invented; and (c) once we understand the complex by virtue of simplifying, we may be able to put the parts back together again in order to match the complexity we are interested in, but then we will have control over it. Launching, landing, and retrieving a space ship is an enormously complex technological procedure, but it is possible because all of the relevant simpler underlying processes and mechanisms are understood and manipulatable, even within a complex context.

An Experimental Case Study Approach

Given the foregoing assumptions, there are two promising strategies of inquiry for developing new techniques and for testing their effects. One is the experimental analogue. This can be a fruitful way of simplifying and clarifying the complex, and it can stimulate ideas for technique development, though it is too far from the clinical situation to be useful for testing therapeutic effects. This approach is discussed in detail by Heller elsewhere in this volume (Chapter 4).

The other strategy is an elaborate, objectified case-study approach. It involves planning specific interventions with patients having specifiable disorders. Careful measurement is done of the presenting problem before, during, and after treatment, and an equally precise reading of the nature of the interventions is recorded. The course of change is thus thoroughly recorded and the responses to interventions pinpointed. If a technique does not seem to be having an effect, it can be continuously modified until it does. Once an effect is observed on a single case, then the procedure is replicated on equivalent cases and refined further until it is clear what kind of procedure will have certain effects on a specifiable problem or patient type. The technique is then ready for "field trials" on large samples of similar cases. This general paradigm nicely articulates a research strategy with the vicissitudes of clinical practice, and thus insures more prompt transfer of findings to practice than is usually the case. It is exemplified in part by recent behavioral technique experimentation (Ullmann and Krasner, 1965; Lovaas, 1968); by Chassan's work (1967); and by Lazarus and Davison (Chapter 6, this volume). It has been touched upon by Strupp and myself in previous publications (Strupp and Bergin, 1969b; Bergin and Strupp, 1970).

This approach seems to meet the need for specificity without entirely divorcing the procedure from the complexities of practice. It seems much more relevant than group studies, which are often based upon mean comparisons that obscure individual differences. Indeed, it is too often the case that a small minority of subjects in a group account for observed mean differences. It is precisely these individual responses that are of the most value in a developing field of inquiry, and it is to them that an objectified, experimental case study approach would be addressed.

For these reasons, I am generally distrustful of group-based multifactorial studies, and of the kinds of statistical operations that are associated with them. The results are too often of no practical use because they amount to nothing more than abstractions on top of confusion.

Controls and Placebos[7]

It now seems clear that a true no-therapy control group is essentially impossible to set up and implement, except in a carefully restricted institutional setting. This is due to the fact that clients in control groups are almost always involved in a variety of help-seeking behaviors that yield encounters with therapeutic agents existing in the community. The best control for this procedure is probably to institute a pro-

cedure for obtaining samples of the help-receiving events that are occurring among control group cases. This can be done during both therapy and follow-up periods. Counts of the frequency and duration of these events would be most helpful, not only in the life experience of controls, but also for experimental cases.

It has been clearly demonstrated that placebo effects in psychotherapy are real (Paul, 1967a; Frank, 1961; Shapiro, Chapter 12 of this volume). It is essential, whenever classical outcome studies are done, that an attention-placebo control condition be induced (as Paul did so well), and that attention be paid to the various points made by Shapiro in his chapter. I would only add that placebo processes should not necessarily be considered artifacts. If they produce change, it is essential to understand what variables or change mechanisms are operating. Once this is achieved, these processes then may be used deliberately as part of the armamentarium of techniques. Thus, the use of placebo controls should be only a temporary expedient, and not a substitute for inquiry into the specifics of placebo effects. Once fully understood, they may become part of the therapeutic procedure rather than a control method.

Many people argue that variables such as expectancy, attention, and the like, are quite powerful and are the essence of what effects change in the therapeutic transaction. Another view, and the one we are more convinced of, is that these influences are a necessary and real part of most human relationships, particularly those that focus upon helping. We view them as being facilitative, but far from the essence of therapy. It appears likely that some of the more dramatic consequences of these influences are really somewhat misleading. They appear to effect more superficial changes (moods, ratings of well-being), although they are sometimes so obvious and overt that they seem more significant than they really are. One of the defects of most previous research on outcome is that these factors have not been taken into account, and it has not been demonstrated which criteria they

---

[7] The material from this point to the summary is primarily reproduced, by permission, from the *International Journal of Psychiatry* (Strupp and Bergin, 1969b).

do and do not relate to; therefore, it has been impossible to tell exactly which therapeutic ingredients, placebo or otherwise, are doing most of the work in creating change.

Follow-Up

There have been some consistent deficiencies in follow-up procedures in therapy outcome studies. These should be easily remediable. One is that follow-up does not usually include intensive observation procedures such as those that occur during the therapy period. One therefore never really knows what the long-range effect of the therapeutic procedure is, since there is no precise determination of the intervening influences that may affect the client's status in one direction or another. There is currently enough evidence that patients, after they leave therapy, experience both strong deteriorative and therapeutic influences, such that a procedure for obtaining examples of their experiences at regular intervals seems essential in any further follow-up studies.

A second deficiency in previous follow-up studies has been the lack of long-term follow-up. This defect is relevant to both experimental and control groups. If long-term follow-up were the rule, it would be much more evident whether there are cycles in the neurotic process that follow a regular periodic interval. It would be of great interest and value in the study of therapy itself to conduct a long-range naturalistic type of inquiry into the fluctuations of pathology and distress of both neurotic control groups and experimental follow-up groups. Periodic fluctuations could then be noted and plotted, and environmental events and interpersonal encounters could be correlated with these fluctuations. The potential contribution of such an inquiry or series of inquiries would be to cast more light on the natural history of the conditions treated by psychotherapy and, thus, to reveal more precisely which changes can validly be attributed to the influence of therapy.

CRITERION MEASUREMENT ISSUES AND TECHNIQUES

As suggested repeatedly in the foregoing analyses, the development of a valid repertoire of criterion measures for testing the effects of diverse therapeutic interventions upon various syndromes and patient types is a task of high priority. It is hoped that the following synthesis will provide a substantial beginning toward that goal.

In our opinion, it is not possible at the present time to draw strong conclusions concerning the relative value of outcome criteria. The summaries provided below are, however, based upon a good deal of empirical substance and should be regarded as more than tentative. The conclusions take into account the more common issues such as (a) the low intercorrelations of many criteria and (b) the importance of values and theoretical predilections in the choice and weighting of measures.

Conclusion 1. The most obvious thing to be concluded from the various intercorrelations of therapy outcome criteria (Forsyth and Fairweather, 1961; and Cartwright, Kirtner, and Fiske, 1963) and from the divergent results obtained by using different criteria with the *same* client group (Rogers and Dymond, 1954; and Malan et al., 1967) is that the process of therapeutic change in patients is multifactorial. As simple and obvious as this sounds, it has profound implications for both research and practice. It means that divergent processes are occurring in therapeutic change, that people themselves embody divergent dimensions or phenomena, and that divergent methods of criterion measurement must be used to match the divergency in human beings and in the change processes that occur within them. This confirms the notion that any assumptions of uniformity in client characteristics or in changes thereof are simply mythical (Kiesler, 1966, 1968).

Factor analyses of multiple change criteria used in complex psychotherapy outcome studies yield generally similar findings. The main factors derived from such data tend to be closely associated with the measurement method or type of observation used rather than being identified by some conceptual variable that would be expected to cut across techniques of measurement. The most typical factors are (a) client self-evaluation, (b) therapist evaluation, (c) TAT or other fantasy evaluation,

(d) indices of concrete overt behaviors, and (e) a miscellany of factors associated with specific instruments such as interest inventories, sentence completions, personality inventories (such as subsets of MMPI and CPI scales), and the like (Cartwright, Kirtner, and Fiske, 1963; Gibson, Snyder and Ray, 1955; Forsyth and Fairweather, 1961; Nichols and Beck, 1960; Shore, Massimo and Ricks, 1965).

In addition to evidence of this type, factor-analytically derived measures of particular dimensions have been used as therapy criteria, but they tend to be confined to self-report techniques (Cattell, 1966), and are therefore limited in scope. One related technique, the Psychiatric Status Schedule, is, however, broader in scope and shows considerable promise (Spitzer, Endicott, and Cohen, 1967). It will be discussed further.

Numerous other studies report intercorrelations among two or more outcome measures; and while the results appear to sometimes confirm the factor-analytic findings, they are highly variable and difficult to interpret cogently at the present time (Ends and Page, 1957; Parloff, Kelman, and Frank, 1954; Dietze, 1966, 1967; Paul, 1966; Shore, Massimo, and Mack, 1965; Shostrom and Knapp, 1966; and Knapp, 1965). A puzzling aspect of these studies is that significant correlations between different criteria occur, in contradiction to the factor analytic evidence, but they do not occur consistently across studies. Whether this is due to chance fluctuations in the diverse data or to some more substantial factors we are as yet unable to determine.

Recommendation 1. (a) Major research effort should be expended in more carefully delineating the *divergent* processes of change that take place as a result of the extant therapies. This may best be done by studying more extensively the relationships among client characteristics, change techniques, and the specific *kinds* of change that occur. We feel quite strongly that researchers and therapists should begin to think more precisely in terms of *kinds of change* rather than in terms of a general multiform change; (b) a correlated activity would be the more rigorous and extensive development of *measures* for tapping different *kinds* of change. Some

attempts in this direction will be discussed in conclusions 2 and 3; (c) another fruitful inquiry, based directly upon the factor analytic work, would involve (1) more rigorous specification of the variables underlying client's and therapist's ratings of outcome so that it can be determined whether differences between their ratings are spurious, responses to different dimensions of the change process, or a function of differing values; and (2) careful comparison of the other outcome factors, fantasy responses, overt behavior, and inventory responses with the *process* of change, in order to detect and describe what is happening in these three domains as a result of therapy. This kind of inquiry would complement and overlap the suggestions listed under conclusions 2 and 3.

Conclusion 2. The clearest issue in criterion development and selection at the present time is whether evaluation should be based chiefly upon external behavior or internal states of experience. This issue emerges directly from the theoretical and technical controversies surrounding the confrontation between behavioral and more traditional therapies.

While behavioral indices more often correlate with follow-up measures, it is also true that follow-up measures are usually of a behavioral nature. Overt behavioral criteria are, therefore, currently more impressive, though not necessarily more important. The problem of measuring experiential phenomena with adequacy and precision remains a crucial one for future research in criterion development.

The distinction between dynamic versus symptomatic, or experiential versus behavioral, has proven valuable in the interpretation of change data. Truax and Carkhuff (1967) review a number of studies of patient characteristics and patient change in which they find that certain contradictions of outcome can be accounted for on the basis that these two types of criteria tend to be mixed together indiscriminately, or outcomes are compared between studies based on these two dimensions when they may not be actually comparable. They point out, for example, that initial level of inner disturbance is positively correlated with outcome, whereas initial level of behavioral disturbance is negatively related to outcome. Malan et al. (1967) have taken this concept one step further and devised what they call an assessment of internal or dynamic change as opposed to external change. They demonstrate that the percentage of remission in an experimental or therapy group fluctuates markedly, depending on which of these two criteria are used. They point out that the spontaneous remission rate in a control group tends to be only 33 to 50 percent on dynamic criteria, as opposed to 60 to 70 percent on external criteria. Cattell (1966) argues in favor of two major sets of factors, source traits and surface traits. Source traits refer to the underlying source of behavior or symptoms and are rated by his 16 - personality - factor questionnaire; surface traits refer to constellations or syndromes of symptoms such as are measured by the MMPI. Factor-analytic studies also reflect this dichotomy when they derive factors representing self-evaluation or TAT factors, and behavioral and other concrete factors based on posttherapy achievement or life functioning. For some years this dichotomy has been recognized implicitly in the work of Frank and his associates (Stone et al., 1961), in their focus on an overt social ineffectiveness scale and an internal discomfort scale.

Recommendation 2. (a) Since "internal" and "external" criteria measure different human characteristics, since these characteristics are significant, since changes occur in both domains during therapy, and since important decisions regarding the value of different techniques continue to be based on the extent of change induced by them, we recommend that future studies include representative measures derived from this dichotomy. Recommendations for specific measures are discussed later in this document. (b) We suggest further that specific therapist technique indices, such as those characteristic of divergent therapists, be correlated with each of these kinds of criteria in order to determine more precisely how differing types of change are effected and whether single techniques have multiple effects. (c) We encourage the refinement of work such as that being done by Malan, in which parallel systems of change measurement are being developed based on notions concerning these two domains of change. (d) We feel that energy might also be

more vigorously devoted to specifying which type of client change is more crucial in a given case, thus laying the groundwork for eventually providing the kind of therapy most appropriate to the change desired.

Conclusion 3. The possibility of tailoring change criteria to each individual in therapy is being mentioned with increasing frequency, and the idea offers intriguing alternatives for resolving several recalcitrant dilemmas in measuring change.

This notion strongly supports the development of a general trend toward *specific* rather than global improvement indices. Thus, if a person seeks help for severe depression, we would tend to measure change in depression rather than his global psychological status. Taken together, the trend to specify and the trend to individually tailor criteria offer a strong antidote to the vague and unimpressive conclusions so often reported in the outcome literature.

This implication takes several forms. First, all clients might be measured on the same criteria, but improvement could be indicated by changes in opposite directions for different clients. For example, Jewell (reported by Volsky, Magoon, Norman, and Hoyt, 1965) asked judges to evaluate client diagnostic material and determine which direction of change should be considered positive on each of three scales for each client. On the "defensiveness scale," the judges agreed that *no change* was required for 60 percent of the cases. On the "anxiety scale," it was judged that anxiety level should not be altered for 53 percent of the cases, and in 10 percent it should be increased! In relation to problem solving, it was agreed that all clients needed to increase their skill. In a correlated study by Vosbeck, reported by the same authors, it was found that in using grade-getting and degree-getting as criteria for effectiveness of college counseling, counselors were often working "against" themselves by encouraging some individuals to seek alternative goals not requiring a college degree. Volsky et al. (1965), Rogers (1963), and Mintz (1965) have also all similarly suggested that some clients *appear* equally bad off or worse as a result of therapy because they have become more open about their inadequacies and more fluid and flexible in their styles of responding, and thus *appear* less well-regulated.

Second, different standardized measures might be used for different cases, depending upon the type of change sought. Thus, for one case we might be primarily interested in measures of anxiety and depression, while for others our concern might variously focus upon compulsive defensiveness, somatic complaints, impulsivity, passivity, and the like.

Third, unique criteria could be devised for each client. This might entail the use of self-descriptive items in an idiographic Q sort which would still permit the calculation of self-ideal correlations and other computations (Shlien, 1962a, 1962b, 1965; Weiss and Schaie, 1964), or it could depend upon brief self-descriptions, which are unitized and rated (Allport, 1958). In order to make comparisons across uniquely defined client measures, standard scores could be used, or judges could use a standard scale for crudely evaluating amount of change on each criterion.

Recommendation 3. (a) We suggest that both old and new outcome studies might well be analyzed, using one or more of these techniques. The thought impresses us that the meager results of many studies may have resulted from misapplications of the same criteria to different patients. It is entirely conceivable that significant therapeutic effects have been obscured by these blanket applications and that startling new findings await the creative researcher who refines criterion estimation so as to account for the divergent processes simultaneously occurring in groups of therapy cases. (b) We feel that the evidence presented under conclusion 3, along with that presented in the first two conclusions, affirms the value of the trend noted toward the utilization of criteria specific to the change-induction technique and to the specific target symptoms. We assume that this kind of precision can be applied in even the most complex cases by the use of multiple, but specifically applied, criteria, and that the processes of change will thus be illuminated and the actual effects of psychotherapy more accurately assessed.

Conclusion and Recommendation 4. It is obvious that adequate outcome measurement in psychotherapy is dependent upon the scientific status of personality measurement in general. Given the primitive and controversial nature of this field of inquiry, it is not surprising that difficulties arise when research in this area is *applied* to clinical phenomena.

We can only applaud and encourage the present variety of efforts underway to dimensionalize human behavior in meaningful ways. We would suggest, however, two things: (a) that the dimensions of the clinical distress erupting all about us today require both a sense of urgency in this matter and the need for more programmatic efforts; and (b) that the processes of therapeutic change might themselves be a fruitful set of phenomena for measurement specialists to attend to in their research, for during personality change we might assume that the more powerful variables in human experience become salient and more readily observable.

Conclusion and Recommendation 5. The following material consists of brief commentaries on outcome criteria that have proved useful or appear promising. In light of the fact that our card file lists several hundred outcome studies, we hope the reader will charitably accept the fact that our intuition has played a dominant role in the selection of the particular measuring techniques listed here. We also hope that no one whose creative work has gone unmentioned, either in this section or elsewhere in the paper, will feel that his contributions have been slighted or inaccurately evaluated. It should also be noted that many valuable measures have been developed and tested chiefly on psychotic populations (Lorr, Wittenborn, and the like), and they will not be reviewed here.

Assessment Interviews. Several procedures have reached useful levels of development in standardizing interview evaluation of client status before, during, and after therapy. The work of Spitzer et al. (1964, 1967), Rogers et al. (1967), and Landfield (1962) all converge upon the notion that rigorous standardization of the interviewer as a diagnostic stimulus is a valuable method of clinical assessment. Thus far their views seem to be borne out.

This approach has been carried to rigorous dimensions, particularly by the Spitzer group, who have developed five procedures, the most prominent of which is the *Psychiatric Status Schedule*. This standardized interview covers factor-analytically derived dimensions of mental status in addition to a broad spectrum of behavioral manifestations of psychopathology. Interjudge reliabilities of the scores it yields are excellent. While much of the content is oriented toward in-patients, and initial experiments have revealed modest validity data, the procedure appears to be among the most promising of all evaluation measures.

The Rogers group introduced the important innovation of obtaining this type of standard interview sampling at intervals throughout the course of therapy, much as samples might be drawn from tape recordings.

A further question to be answered in this area is whether the samplings are not systematically biased by the use of *one* interviewer, who may evoke only particular kinds of information and behavior in the patient. This is similar to the patient-therapist pairing problem in therapy itself. Sampling interviews must be affected by similar variables.

MMPI. Among the traditional measures that have been used, certain *MMPI scales* repeatedly yield evidence that they are able to detect client change. Among those scales that appear to provide consistent validity as change indices are D, Pt, and Sc. Scales that correlate with these, such as Si, K, and Es, also frequently manifest change. Anxiety scales derived from the MMPI, such as the Taylor scale or the Welsh scale, also seem to be reasonable change indices, though they correlate highly with D and Pt. The sum of clinical scales has also been widely used and is of similar value (Dahlstrom and Welsh, 1960; Fulkerson and Barry, 1961). While MMPI scales thus provide some merit for future work, strong statements are being made to the effect that it is an essentially outmoded instrument. This is in part for theoretical reasons having to do with the lack of clear meaning of the scales and the items comprising them, in part because of the strongly nosological orientation of the scales, and in part because the scales are not factorially pure and are not intentionally designed with specific types of therapeutic change in mind. Despite such defects, no other paper-pencil measure of psychopathology based on self-report offers anything better to the researcher.

Behavioral Assessment. A new philosophy and methodology of diagnosis is developing within the behavioral school. It is being complemented by the work of an increasing number of eclectically oriented psychiatrists who tend to focus upon pragmatic, behavioral criteria such as being in or out of school, maintaining marriage or becoming divorced, frequency of arrest, being in or out of the hospital, and the like. While still in its infancy, this approach is having an increasing impact upon clinical assessment and upon the specification of outcome criteria for research purposes (Kanfer, 1967; Goldfried, 1967). These techniques focus upon concrete behavioral aspects of the patient's life. They include inventories of specific symptoms such as the *Fear Survey Schedule* (Lang and Lazovik, 1963) and the "Target Complaints" technique (Battle et al., 1966) developed at Johns Hopkins.

Other procedures involve rating schemes or frequency counts applied to the patient's behavior by observers. These include the "Timed Behavioral Checklist for Performance Anxiety" (Paul, 1966), the "behavior rating category system" used by Becker et al. (1967), the *Finney Therapy Scale* (Finney, 1954; Forsyth and Fairweather, 1961), and various ratings of work proficiency, interpersonal behavior, and achievement (Massimo and Shore, 1963). In addition, several ratings of social behavior based on interviews by assessors with either the patient or an informant continue to prove valuable (Social Ineffectiveness [Stone et al., 1961]; Social Adjustment [Miles, Barabee, and Finesinger, 1951; Gelder, Marks, and Wolff, 1967]; Psychiatric Status Schedule [Spitzer et al., 1967]). Measures of these types have consistently yielded high reliabilities and have sensitively reflected therapeutic change.

Self-Concept Measures. Scales measuring self-esteem or self-acceptance continue to have strong influence in psychotherapy outcome research, as described particularly by Butler

(1966) and by Truax and Carkhuff in reporting their series of studies (1967). In addition to the original Q sort devised by Butler and Haigh (1954), several instruments have been devised that are reliable and valid. They include Dymond's Q Adjustment Score (1954), Van der Veen's *Family Concept Q Sort* (1965), Gergen and Morse's new Self-Consistency Score (1967), Endler's adaptation of the *Semantic Differential* for self-descriptions (1961), and various adaptations of Kelly's *Role Construct Repertory Test*. The intercorrelations of these measures is probably high, and it is difficult to select from them on bases other than personal predilection or popularity. The factor-analytic studies reported earlier suggest that measures of this type add practically nothing to what is obtained from the MMPI or similar instruments, and vice versa. They are all basically ways of reporting subjective distress.

Thematic Stories. In general, the TAT and derivatives thereof continue to have modest, but durable, value as outcome indices. Reviews of the research evidence by Murstein (1963) and by Zubin, Eron, and Schumer (1965) confirm this conclusion, as do the factor analytic studies, which usually yield a separate TAT factor. Various scoring systems and new cards continue to be added to this venerable approach, and some have yielded rather useful criterion measures (Massimo and Shore, 1963). It is clear that the best validities are obtained when specific variables are examined via a number of cards that sample responses on that dimension, such as aggression, dependency, and the like. We strongly endorse the approach advocated by Zubin et al. to this type of instrument. They suggest "purifying" the dimensions of component parts of the TAT, broadening the range or sampling of stimuli, and rigorously accumulating normative data on responses in connection with assessments of experimenter, subject, "apparatus" (test), task, and situational characteristics. We also agree with their conclusion that the TAT, used in the classical way, cannot be considered a valid instrument; but that specific scores and sets of cards (old and new) have validity under specified conditions for given purposes, such as criterion measurement of a given dimension of experience.

Patient Checklists and Self-Ratings. Patient self-ratings of outcome are too numerous and unstandardized to list here. They are mostly simple, homemade instruments, and there is no obvious evidence that one is superior to another. There is also little evidence that they add significantly to what is measured by standardized self-report instruments such as the MMPI or Q sorts.

Several standardized checklists have been developed, which appear to be very efficient and valuable self-evaluation measures. One of these, which has already demonstrated its value in therapy research, is that by Lorr and McNair (1963), based on the Leary Interpersonal Checklist. The authors describe the instrument as follows:

The inventory items were correlated, factored, and assembled into thirteen scales. Nine of the scales could be arranged into a circular order. Supporting evidence was found in data reported by Stern, by Campbell, and in new data on the Leary Checklist. Three similar overlapping higher order factors, *dominance, affiliativeness vs. detachment*, and *compliant abasement*, accounted for the correlations in each matrix.

They suggest that this measure may be particularly useful in studies designed to clarify hypotheses concerning defense mechanisms.

Another factor-analyzed checklist, which may bear some relation to the Lorr-McNair instrument, is the new factor analysis of Gough's adjective checklist by Parker and Megargee (1967). They find that the adjective checklist in its current revised form by Gough and Heilbrun can be reduced to four primary factors. The first factor was a bipolar one labeled "positive versus negative," and is apparently very similar to the self-evaluation factors found in therapy outcome studies. The second factor is more or less an ascendance-submission factor, the third emotionality versus stolidity, and the fourth factor a representation of the total number of adjectives checked. This type of factor structure on checklists has been found a number of times across different samples and seems to be a fairly reliable finding. Adjective checklists are easy to administer and appear to have value in assessing change and in other types of evaluation.

Therapist Rating Scales. These scales have the same virtues and deficiencies that patient self-ratings do. They seem to measure an independent factor in change, or perhaps it is simply point-of-view that is being measured. A venerable global outcome measure is the nine-point rating scale developed for the Rogers and Dymond project (1954). It is still in considerable use, and correlates so highly with other more complex and sophisticated therapist ratings (Cartwright et al., 1961) that it may well be the measure of choice for this purpose. More specific and behavioral ratings are becoming more widely used, however (see Gelder, Marks, and Wolff, 1967; and Spitzer's *Psychiatric Evaluation Form*, 1967).

Factor-Analytic Batteries. General studies of personality assessment continue to yield therapy criteria. The most prominent and frequently used continue to be the *Eysenck Personality Inventory* and various measures from Cattell's *Objective-Analytic Personality Factor Battery* (experimental instrument) and *Sixteen Personality Factor Questionnaire*. The "neuroticism" and "anxiety" scores from these batteries tend to be of greatest interest to psychotherapy researchers, and it appears that they are rather well-developed measures that are sensitive to therapeutic change, though they are limited in being based solely on self-report.

Mood Scales. Another intriguing type of measurement—which has not been explored very much in therapy research except by the Frank group in their role-induction interviews, placebo studies, and long-term follow-ups—is the analysis of moods. There is increasing evidence of a fairly substantial nature that moods can be reliably studied while retaining the experiential validity of the phenomena. This is evidenced in the work of Wessman and Ricks (1966), Clyde, Nowlis, Dittmann, and McNair and Lorr. The Wessman and Ricks volume in particular contains a variety of new scales and also reveals a fact quite relevant to therapy research, namely that people can be reliably characterized by their mood levels and by their degree of stability or variability, and that there tend to be quite different mood patterns across individuals. It has been noted

by Frank et al. that moods can be dramatically affected by brief encounters with diagnostic evaluators and initial interviewers. It may be that mood scales will eventually be a good way to evaluate what might be considered the superficial effects of attention-expectancy and other placebo-related effects. If these measures can be shown to be relatively independent of other outcome measures, then we will have a way of reasonably differentiating between this type of effect and another, namely the superficial and the more substantial. On the other hand, it may also be that moods tap something much more deep and profound than is currently thought, in light of Balkin's finding (1968) that the Wessman-Ricks measures significantly differentiate groups beginning and ending therapy and that the level scores for those ending therapy are not different from scores for normals.

Personal Orientation Inventory. We are impressed with the potentialities of the *Personal Orientation Inventory* (Shostrom, 1963; Shostrom and Knapp, 1966; Knapp, 1965), which measures life-orientation, self-actualizing tendency, inner direction, and similar dimensions usually considered to be in the domain of values and health-oriented qualities. A series of studies relating it to the MMPI, the Eysenck scales, therapeutic change, and differences between diagnostic groups reveals both its validity and its ability to measure important dimensions not tapped by traditional scales. A good measure of values is sorely needed in psychotherapy research, and perhaps this is it.

Self-Regulation Measures. A trend correlated with the preceding program of research concerns the dimensions of self-control and self-regulation. A few measures have been developed that tap this area of common difficulty among modern clinic populations. This domain has been inadequately tapped in the past and is one that is relevant to several of the newer therapies such as Reality Therapy (Glasser, 1965) and Integrity Therapy (Mowrer, 1968). Studies by Ricks et al. (1964) of temporal perspective in successfully treated delinquents are relevant here, as are studies of delay of gratification (Mischel, 1966), long-range planning (Spivack and Levine, 1964), and general goal-orientation. This dimension of patient change seems important, and measures of it are arising that have substance, partly because they derive from an area of general experimentation in psychology.

Peer Ratings. Peer ratings were once touted as potentially very valuable measures, and new evidence is coming from several quarters that they may still be of more value than is suggested by the frequency with which they are used. There is some evidence from Peace Corps studies that peer ratings are among the better, if not the best, predictor of overseas performance, and there is evidence from one study, where the peer ratings were confined to an anxiety dimension, that they are of considerable value (Dildy and Liberty, 1967).

Duncan's reputation test of personality integration seems to have value similar to the peer anxiety ratings. This test, however, requires a setting in which peers have regular opportunities to observe one another's behavior. It was derived on a college campus and may be especially relevant to college students.

Miscellany. There are numerous additional measures that have possible value for psychotherapy research, and we do not demean their potentialities, but Buros' *Handbook* cannot be reproduced here. Suffice it to say that nearly any scale developed by measurement specialists has potential value as a diagnostic and therapy change evaluator. We hope that more bridge-building between these two domains will occur, and on a programmatic basis.

In addition, numerous other measures have been used in therapy research such as the Rorschach, Knight's criteria, percentage of improvement, and the like. On the basis of evidence to date, we have little faith in them as change measures.

SUMMARY AND IMPLICATIONS FOR PRACTICE

It now seems apparent that psychotherapy, as practiced over the past 40 years, has had an average effect that is modestly positive. It is clear, however, that the averaged group data on which this conclusion is based obscure the existence of a multiplicity of processes occurring in therapy, some of which are now known to be either unproductive or actually harmful.

Future progress will be more assured by reducing the complexity of therapeutic practices to more specific operations upon homogeneous syndromes. This will require a departure from gross tests of the effects of therapy and pursual of a multidimensional approach, and it will require a good deal of technique innovation and subsequent testing of each technique's specific effects. Methodologically, this may fruitfully be achieved by a judicious mix of analogue research, experimental case studies, and field trials on larger homogeneous samples.

While we have more assurance than before that there are efficacious influences present in traditional therapy, the weakness of the average effects implies that only some methods or some therapists are especially effective. It would be a task of high priority, therefore, to assiduously isolate and define those persons and methods that are most effective. Our faith is that whatever is powerful in traditional therapy resides in the work of a minority of its practitioners. It is probable that they account for whatever change is observable, rather than that all therapists cluster around a weak average effect. We assume then that there is little reason to reinforce or reassure the ordinary practitioner of psychotherapy, for we expect future research to show that his labors must be revised toward matching the behavior of a few successful peers who actually obtain most of the therapeutic results. It is also likely that observation of their styles will eventually yield completely new techniques focused around the actual therapeutic agents that are identified and extracted from their practice.

In addition, we will expect experiments of the future to focus much more on technique innovations derived from (a) the general experimental psychology of change and (b) the examination of natural therapeutic influences as they occur in everyday life. Certainly, if we had the opportunity to impose our will upon the future, we would call a moratorium on classical psychotherapy outcome studies and upon a large proportion of the traditional therapy currently practiced. This chapter could then stand as the last review of traditional outcome research.

Some of the chapters in this volume are good testimony to the value of moving in precisely these directions, and we applaud the work reported therein. Certainly, the evidence favoring the approaches of selected traditional therapists (as in Chapter 9, by Truax and Mitchell) and of behavioral therapists is

substantial enough to argue that there is little point in further promoting the average, non-specific, typical kind of therapy. What is useful in it can be extracted and put to work in a more efficient manner. Contemporary practitioners would thus do well to become empirically oriented clinical innovators. Clearly, the techniques of the near future are unlikely to be very similar to the cross-section of practice reviewed in this chapter.

REFERENCES

Alexander, F. *Five Year Report of the Chicago Institute for Psychoanalysis*, 1932–1937.

Allport, G., What Units Shall We Employ?, in G. Lindzey, Ed., *Assessment of Human Motives*. New York: Grove Press, 1958. Pp. 239–260.

Appel, K. E., Myers, J. M., and Scheflen, A. E. Prognosis in psychiatry: results of psychiatric treatment. *Archives of Neurological Psychiatry*, 1953, **70**, 459–468.

Aronson, H., and Weintraub, W. Patient changes during classical psychoanalysis as a function of initial status and duration of treatment. Unpublished manuscript, Psychiatric Institute, University of Maryland School of Medicine, 1968.

Balkin, J. L. Once more, with feeling: Psychotherapy revisited. Unpublished doctoral dissertation, Teachers College, Columbia University, 1968.

Barron, F., and Leary, T. F. Changes in psychoneurotic patients with and without psychotherapy. *Journal of Consulting Psychology*, 1955, **19**, 239–245.

Bartlett, M. R. A six month follow-up of the effects of personal adjustment counseling of veterans. *Journal of Consulting Psychology*, 1950, **14**, 393–394.

Battle, C. C., Imber, S. D., Hoehn-Saric, R., Stone, A. R., Nash, C., and Frank, J. D. Target complaints as criteria of improvement. *American Journal of Psychotherapy*, 1966, **20**, 184–192.

Becker, W. C., Madsen, C. H., Jr., Arnold, C. R., and Thomas, D. R. The contingent use of teacher attention and praise in reducing classroom behavior problems. *Journal of Special Education*, 1967, **1**, 287–307.

Bergin, A. E. The effects of psychotherapy: Negative results revisited. *Journal of Counseling Psychology*, 1963, **10**, 244–250.

Bergin, A. E. Some implications of psychotherapy research for therapeutic practice. *Journal of Abnormal Psychology*, 1966, **71**, 235–246.

Bergin, A. E. An empirical analysis of therapeutic issues. In D. Arbuckle (Ed.), *Counseling and Psychotherapy: An Overview*. McGraw-Hill, 1967. Pp. 175–208. (a)

Bergin, A. E. Further comments on psychotherapy research and therapeutic practice. *International Journal of Psychiatry*, 1967, **3**, 317–323 (b)

Bergin, A. E. The deterioration effect: A reply to Braucht. *Journal of Abnormal Psychology*, 1970, **75**, in press.

Bergin, A. E., and Strupp, H. H. The last word (?) on psychotherapy research: A reply. *International Journal of Psychiatry*, 1969, 7, 160–168.

Bergin, A. E., and Strupp, H. H. New directions in psychotherapy research. *Journal of Abnormal Psychology*, 1970, **75**, in press.

Berleman, W. C., and Steinburn, T. W. The execution and evaluation of a delinquency prevention program. *Social Problems*, 1967, **14**, 413–423.

Betz, Barbara J. Experiences in research in psychotherapy with schizophrenic patients. In H. H. Strupp and L. Luborsky (Eds.), *Research in Psychotherapy*. Vol. 2. Washington, D. C.: American Psychological Association, 1962. Pp. 41–60.

Bieber, I. *Homosexuality: A psychoanalytic study*. New York: Basic Books, 1962.

Board, F. A. Patients' and physicians' judgments of outcome of psychotherapy in an outpatient clinic. *Archives of General Psychiatry*, 1959, **1**, 185–196.

Bond, E. D., and Braceland, F. J. Prognosis in mental disease. *American Journal of Psychiatry*, 1937, **94**, 263–274.

Braucht, G. N. The deterioration effect: A reply to Bergin. *Journal of Abnormal Psychology*, 1970, **75**, in press.

Brill, N. Q., and Beebe, G. W. A follow-up study of war neuroses. Washington. *V. A. Medical Monograph*, 1955.

Brody, J. Neurotics helped by aiding others. *New York Times*, Feb. 13, 1966, section 1, p. 66.

Butler, J. M. Self-acceptance as a measure of outcome of psychotherapy. *British Journal of Social Psychiatry*, 1966, **1**, 51–62.

Butler, J. M., and Haigh, G. Changes in the relation between self-concepts and ideal concepts consequent upon client-centered counseling. In C. Rogers and R. Dymond (Eds.), *Psychotherapy and Personality Change*. Chicago: University of Chicago Press, 1954. Pp. 55–75.

Cappon, D. Results of psychotherapy. *British Journal of Psychiatry*, 1964, **110**, 35–45.

Carkhuff, R. R., and Berenson, B. G. *Beyond counseling and therapy*. New York: Holt, Rinehart, and Winston, 1967.

Carkhuff, R. R., and Truax, C. B. Lay mental health counseling: The effects of lay group counseling. *Journal of Consulting Psychology*, 1965, **29**, 426–431.

Carmichael, H. T., and Masserman, J. H. Results of treatment in a psychiatric outpatients' department. *Journal of the American Medical Association*, 1939, **113**, 2292–2298.

Cartwright, D. S. Effectiveness of psychotherapy: a critique of the spontaneous remission argument. *Journal of Counseling Psychology*, 1955, **2**, 290–296.

Cartwright, D. S. Note on "changes in psychoneurotic patients with and without psychotherapy." *Journal of Consulting Psychology*, 1956, **20**, 403–404.

Cartwright, D. S., Kirtner, W. L., and Fiske, D. W. Method factors in changes associated with psychotherapy. *Journal of Abnormal and Social Psychology*, 1963, **66**, 164–175.

Cartwright, D. S., Robertson, R. J., Fiske, D. W., and Kirtner, W. L. Length of therapy in relation to outcome and change in personal integration. *Journal of Consulting Psychology*, 1961, **25**, 84–99.

Cartwright, R. D. Effects of psychotherapy on self-consistency. *Journal of Counseling Psychology*, 1957, **4**, 15–22.

Cartwright, R. D. The effects of psychotherapy on self-consistency: a replication and extension. *Journal of Consulting Psychology*, 1961, **25**, 376–382.

Cartwright, R. D., and Lerner, B. Empathy, need to change and improvement with psychotherapy. *Journal of Consulting Psychology*, 1963, **27**, 138–144.

Cartwright, R. D., and Vogel, J. L. A comparison of changes in psychoneurotic patients during matched periods of therapy and no therapy. *Journal of Consulting Psychology*, 1960, **24**, 121–127.

Cattell, R. B. Evaluating therapy as total personality change: Theory and available instruments. *American Journal of Psychotherapy*, 1966, **20**, 69–88.

Cattell, R. B., Rickels, K., Weise, C., Gray, B., and Yee, R. The effects of psychotherapy upon measured anxiety and regression. *American Journal of Psychotherapy*, 1966, **20**, 261–269.

Chassan, J. B. *Research Design in Clinical Psychology and Psychiatry*. New York: Appleton-Century-Crofts, 1967.

Coriat, I. H. Some statistical results of the psychoanalytic treatment of the psychoneuroses. *Psychoanalytic Review*, 1917, **4**, 209–16.

Cowen, E. L. and Combs, A. W. Follow-up of 32 cases treated by nondirective psychotherapy. *Journal of Abnormal and Social Psychology*, 1950, **45**, 232–258.

Cross, H. J. The outcome of psychotherapy: A selected analysis of research findings. *Journal of Consulting Psychology*, 1964, **28**, 413–417.

Curran, D. The problem of assessing psychiatric treatment. *Lancet*, 1937, **11**, 1,005–1,009.

Dahlstrom, W. G., and Welsh, G. S. Treatment. In W. Dahlstrom and G. Welsh (Eds.), *An MMPI Handbook*. Minneapolis: University of Minnesota Press, 1960. Pp. 355–393.

Denker, P. G. Results of treatment of psychoneuroses by the general practitioner. *New York State Journal of Medicine*, 1946, **46**, 2164–2166.

Dietze, Doris. Staff and patient criteria for judgments of improvement in mental health. *Psychological Reports*, 1966, **19**, 379–387.

Dietze, Doris. Consistency and change in judgment of criteria for mental health improvement. *Journal of Clinical Psychology*, 1967, **23**, 307–310.

Dildy, L. W. and Liberty, P. G., Jr. Investigation of peer-rated anxiety. *Proceedings of the 75th Annual Convention of the American Psychological Association*. Washington, D. C.: APA, 1967. Pp. 371–372.

Dittmann, A. T. Psychotherapeutic processes. In P. R. Farnsworth, Olga McNemar, and Q. McNemar (Eds.), *Annual review of psychology*. Vol. 16. Palo Alto: Annual Reviews, 1966. Pp. 51–78.

Dymond, R. F. Adjustment changes over therapy from self-sorts. In C. R. Rogers and R. F. Dymond (Eds.), *Psychotherapy and Personality Change*. Chicago. *University of Chicago Press*, 1954. Pp. 76–89.

Edwards, A. L., and Cronbach, L. J. Experimental design for research in psychotherapy. *Journal of Clinical Psychology*, 1952, **8**, 51–59.

Ellis, A. The effectiveness of psychotherapy with individuals who have severe homosexual problems. *Journal of Consulting Psychology*, 1956, **20**, 191–195.

Endicott, N. A., and Endicott, J. "Improvement" in untreated psychiatric patients. *Archives of General Psychiatry*, 1963, **9**, 575–585.

Endicott, N. A., and Endicott, J. Changes in psychiatric patients with and without psychotherapy. Unpublished manuscript, State University of New York, Downstate Medical Center, 1964.

Endler, N. S. Changes in meaning during psychotherapy as measured by the semantic differential. *Journal of Counseling Psychology*, 1961, **8**, 105–111.

Ends, E. J., and Page, C. W. Functional relationships among measures of anxiety, ego strength, and adjustment. *Journal of Clinical Psychology*, 1957, **13**, 148–150.

Eysenck, H. J. The effects of psychotherapy. *International Journal of Psychiatry*, 1965, **1**, 97–178.

Eysenck, H. J. The non-professional psychotherapist. *International Journal of Psychiatry*, 1967, **3**, 150–153.

Eysenck, H. J. *The effects of psychotherapy*. New York: International Science Press, 1966.

Eysenck, H. J. The outcome problem in psychotherapy: A reply. *Psychotherapy*, 1964, **1**, 97–100.

Eysenck, H. J. The effects of psychotherapy: A reply. *Journal of Abnormal Psychology*, 1955, **50**, 147–148.

Eysenck, H. J. A reply to Luborsky's note. *British Journal of Psychology*, 1954, **45**, 132–133.

Eysenck, H. J. The effects of psychotherapy. In H. J. Eysenck (Ed.), *Handbook of Abnormal Psychology*. New York: Basic Books, 1961. Pp. 697–725.

Eysenck, H. J. The effects of psychotherapy: An evaluation. *Journal of Consulting Psychology*, 1952, **16**, 319–324.

Fairweather, G., Simon, R., Gebhard, M. E., Weingarten, E., Holland, J. L., Sanders, R., Stone, G. B., and Reahl, J. E. Relative effectiveness of psychotherapeutic programs: A multicriteria comparison of four programs for three different patient groups. *Psychological Monographs: General and Applied*, 1960, **74** (5, Whole No. 492).

Feifel, H., and Eells, J. Patients and therapists assess the same psychotherapy. *Journal of Consulting Psychology*, 1963, **27**, 310–318.

Feldman, R., Lorr, M., and Russell, S. B. A mental hygience clinic case survey. *Journal of Clinical Psychology*, 1958, **14**, 245–250.

Fenichel, O. *Ten years of the Berlin Psychoanalytic Institute*, 1920–1930.

Finney, B. C. A scale to measure interpersonal relationships in group psychotherapy. *International Journal of Group Psychotherapy*, 1954, **7**, 52–66.

Fiske, D. W. and Goodman, G. The posttherapy period. *Journal of Abnormal Psychology*, 1965, **70**, 169–179.

Forsyth, R., and Fairweather, G. W. Psychotherapeutic and other hospital treatment criteria. *Journal of Abnormal and Social Psychology*, 1961, **62**, 598–605.

Frank, J. D. Problems of controls in psychotherapy as exemplified by the psychotherapy research project of the Phipps Psychiatric Clinic. In E. A. Rubinstein and M. B. Parloff (Eds.), *Research in Psychotherapy*. Vol. I. Washington, D. C.: American Psychological Ass'n., 1959. Pp. 10–26.

Frank, J. D. *Persuasion and healing*. Baltimore: Johns Hopkins Press, 1961.

Frank, J. D. Does psychotherapy work? *International Journal of Psychiatry*, 1967, **3**, 153–155.

Friess, C., and Nelson, M. J. Psychoneurotics five years later. *American Journal of Mental Science*, 1942, **203**, 539–558.

Fulkerson, S. C., and Barry, J. R. Methodology and research on the prognostic use of psychological tests. *Psychological Bulletin*, 1961, **58**, 177–204.

Gelder, M. G., Marks, I. M., and Wolff, H. H. Desensitization and psychotherapy in the treatment of phobic states: A controlled inquiry. *British Journal of Psychiatry*, 1967, **113**, 53–73.

Gergen, K. J., and Morse, S. J. Self-consistency: measurement and validation. *Proceedings of the 75th Annual Convention of the American Psychological Association*, 1967, **2**, 207–208.

Gibson, R. L., Snyder, W. U., and Ray, W. S. A factor analysis of measures of change following client-centered psychotherapy. *Journal of Counseling Psychology*, 1955, **2**, 83–90.

Glasser, W. *Reality Therapy*. New York: Harper and Row, 1965.

Gliedman, L. H., Nash, E. H., Imber, S. D., Stone, A. R., and Frank, J. D. Reduction of symptoms by pharmacologically inert substances and by short term psychotherapy. *A.M.A. Archives of Neurology and Psychiatry*, 1958, **79**, 345–355.

Goldfried, M. *Assessment for Behavior Therapy*. Paper presented at the meeting of the American Psychological Association, Washington, D. C., September, 1967.

Goldstein, A. P., Heller, K., and Sechrest, L. B. *Psychotherapy and the Psychology of Behavior Change*. New York: Wiley, 1966.

Gottschalk, L. A., Mayerson, P., and Gottlieb, A. A. Prediction and evaluation of outcome in an emergency brief psychotherapy clinic. *Journal of Nervous and Mental Disease*, 1967, **144**, 77–96.

Graham, S. R. The effects of psychoanalytically oriented psychotherapy on levels of frequency and satisfaction in sexual activity. *Journal of Clinical Psychology*, 1960, **16**, 94–95.

Guerney, B. G. (Ed.). *Psychotherapeutic agents: new roles for nonprofessionals, parents, and teachers*. New York: Holt, Rinehart, and Winston, 1969.

Gurin, G., Veroff, J., and Feld, S. *Americans view their mental health*. New York: Basic Books, 1960.

Hamilton, D. M., Vanney, I. H., and Wall, T. H. Hospital treatment of patients with psychoneurotic disorder. *American Journal of Psychiatry*, 1942, **99**, 243–247.

Hamilton D. M., and Wall, T. H. Hospital treatment of patients with psychoneurotic disorder. *American Journal of Psychiatry*, 1941, **98**, 551–557.

Harris, A. A comparative study of results in neurotic patients treated by two different methods. *Journal of Mental Science*, 1954, **100**, 718–721.

Hastings, D. W. Follow-up results in psychiatric illness. *American Journal of Psychiatry*, 1958, **114**, 1057–1066.

Heilbrunn, G. Results with psychoanalytic therapy and professional commitment. *American Journal of Psychotherapy*, 1966, **20**, 89–99.

Henry, W. E., and Shlien, J. M. Affective complexity and psychotherapy: Some comparisons of time-limited and unlimited treatment. *Journal of Projective Techniques*, 1958, **22**, 153–162.

Huddleson, J. H. Psychotherapy in two hundred cases of psychoneurosis. *Military Surgeon*, 1927, **60**, 161–170.

Hunt, J. McV. Toward an integrated program of research on psychotherapy. *Journal of Consulting Psychology*, 1952, **16**, 237–246.

Hyman, H. T. The value of psychoanalysis as a therapeutic procedure. *Journal of the American Medical Association*, 1936, **107**, 326–329.

Imber, S. D., Frank, J. D., Nash, E. H., Stone, A. R., and Gliedman, L. H. Improvement and amount of therapeutic contact: An alternative to the use of no-treatment controls in psychotherapy. *Journal of Consulting Psychology*, 1957, **21**, 309–315.

Imber, S. D., Nash, E. H., Stone, A. R. and Frank, J. D. A ten-year follow-up study of treated psychiatric outpatients. In S. Lesse (Ed.), *An evaluation of the results of the psychotherapies*. New York: Charles C. Thomas, 1968.

Jersild, A. T., Lazar, E., and Brodkin, A. M. *The meaning of psychotherapy in the teachers life and work*. New York: Teachers College Bureau of Publications, 1963.

Jonckheere, P. Considerations sur la psychotherapie. *Acta Neurologica et Psychiatrica Belgica*, 1965, **65**, 667–684.

Jones, E. Report of the Clinic Work (London Clinic of Psychoanalysis): 1926–1936.

Kanfer, F. Discussion. Symposium on behavioral assessment at the meeting of the American Psychological Association, Washington, D. C., September, 1967.

Kellner, R. The efficacy of psychotherapy: The results of some controlled investigations. *Psychiatria et Neurologia*, 1965, **149**, 333–340.

Kellner, R. The evidence in favour of psychotherapy. *British Journal of Medical Psychology*, 1967, **40**, 341–358.

Kessel, L., and Hyman, H. T. The value of psychoanalysis as a therapeutic procedure. *Journal of the American Medical Association*, 1933, **101**, 1612–1615.

Kiesler, D. J., A grid model for theory and research in the psychotherapies. In L. D. Eron (Ed.), *The Relationship of Theory and Technique in Psychotherapy*. Chicago: Aldine Press, 1968.

Kiesler, D. J. Some myths of psychotherapy research and the search for a paradigm. *Psychological Bulletin*, 1966, **65**, 110–136.

Knapp, R. R. Relationship of a measure of self-actualization to neuroticism and extraversion. *Journal of Consulting Psychology*, 1965, **29**, 168–172.

Knight, R. P. Evaluation of the results of psychoanalytic therapy. *American Journal of Psychiatry*, 1941, **98**, 434–446.

Koegler, R., and Brill, Q. *Treatment of psychiatric oupatients*. New York: Appleton-Century-Crofts, 1967.

Kriegman, G., and Wright, H. B. Brief psychotherapy with enuretics in the army. *American Journal of Psychiatry*, 1947, **104**, 254–258.

Kringlen, E. Obsessional neurosis: A long-term follow-up. *British Journal of Psychiatry*, 1965, **111**, 709.

Landfield, A. W., O'Donovan, D., and Narvas, M. M. Improvement ratings by external judges and psychotherapists. *Psychological Reports*, 1962, **11**, 747–748.

Landis, C. A statistical evaluation of psychotherapeutic methods. In L. E. Hinsie (Ed.), *Concepts and Problems of Psychotherapy*. New York: Columbia University Press, 1937. Pp. 155–165.

Lang, P. J. and Lazovik, A. D. Experimental desensitization of a phobia. *Journal of Abnormal and Social Psychology*, 1963, **66**, 519–525.

Ling, T. M., Zausmer, D. M., and Hope, M. Occupational rehabilitation of psychiatric cases: a follow-up study of 115 cases. *American Journal of Psychiatry*, 1952, **109**, 172–176.

Lipkin, S. The client evaluates nondirective psychotherapy. *Journal of Consulting Psychology*, 1948, **12**, 137–146.

Lorr, M., and McNair, D. M. An interpersonal behavior circle. *Journal of Abnormal and Social Psychology*, 1963, **67**, 68–75.

Lorr, M., McNair, D. M., Michaux, W. M., and Raskin, A. Frequency of treatment and change in psychotherapy. *Journal of Abnormal and Social Psychology*, 1962, **64**, 281–292.

Luff, M. C. and Garrod, M. The after-results of psychotherapy in 500 adult cases. *British Medical Journal*, 1935, **2**, 54–59.

Lovaas, O. I. Some studies on the treatment of childhood schizophrenia. In J. M. Shlien et al. (Eds.), *Research in Psychotherapy*. Vol. III. Washington, D. C.: American Psychological Association, 1968. Pp. 103–121.

Luborsky, L. A note on Eysenck's article, "The effects of psychotherapy: An evaluation." *British Journal of Psychology*, 1954, **45**, 129–131.

Malan, D. H., Bacal, H. A., Heath, E. S., and Balfour, F. H. G. *Psychodynamic study of changes in "untreated" neurotic Patients*. Unpublished manuscript, Tavistock Clinic, London, 1967.

Mason, A. Outpatient psychotherapy under the National Health Service. *Journal of Mental Science*, 1956, **102**, 726–741.

Masserman, J. H., and Carmichael, H. T. Diagnosis and prognosis in psychiatry: with a follow-up study of the results of short-term general hospital therapy of psychiatric cases. *Journal of Mental Science*, 1938, **84**, 893–946.

Massimo, J. L., and Shore, M. F. The effectiveness of a comprehensive vocationally oriented psychotherapeutic program for adolescent delinquent boys. *American Journal of Orthopsychiatry*, 1963, **33**, 634–642.

Matarazzo, J. D. Some psychotherapists make patients worse! *International Journal of Psychiatry*, 1967, **3**, 156–157.

Materson, J. F., Jr. The symptomatic adolescent five years later: he didn't grow out of it. *American Journal of Psychiatry*, 1967, **123**, 1338–1345.

Matz, P. B. Outcome of hospital treatment of ex-service patients with nervous and mental disease in the U.S. *U.S. Veteran Bureau Medical Bulletin*, 1929, **5**, 829–842.

McNair, D. M., Lorr, M., Young, H. H., Roth, I., and Boyd, R. W. A three-year follow-up of psychotherapy patients. *Journal of Clinical Psychology*, 1964, **20**, 258–264.

Meltzoff, J., and Kornreich, M. *Research in psychotherapy*. Atherton Press, 1970.

Meltzoff, J. Effectiveness of psychotherapy is amply demonstrated. *International Journal of Psychiatry*, 1969, **7**, 149–152.

Miles, H., Barrabee, E. L., and Finesinger, J. E. Evaluation of psychotherapy. *Psychosomatic Medicine*, 1951, **13**, 83–105.

Miles, H. H. W., Barabee, E. L., and Finesinger, J. E. The problem of evaluation of psychotherapy: with a follow-up study of 62 cases of anxiety neurosis. *Journal of Nervous and Mental Disease*, 1951, **114**, 359–365.

Mink, O. G. A comparison of effectiveness of nondirective therapy and clinical counseling in the junior high school. *School Counselor*, 1959, **6**, 12–14.

Mintz, E. *Evaluation of Psychotherapy: A Three-Year Study*. Paper presented at the meeting of the Third Scientific Conference on Psychoanalysis, New York, 1965.

Mischel, W. Research and theory on delay of gratification. In B. A. Maher (Ed.), *Progress in Experimental Personality Research*. Vol. 3. New York: Academic Press, 1966. Pp. 85–132.

Mowrer, O. H. Loss and recovery of community: a guide to the theory and practice of integrity therapy. In G. M. Gazda (Ed.), *Theories and Method of Group Psychotherapy and Counseling*. Springfield, Illinois: Thomas, 1968.

Murstein, B. I. *Theory and Research in Projective Techniques*. New York: Wiley, 1963.

Neustatter, W. L. The results of fifty cases treated by psychotherapy. *Lancet*, 1935, **1**, 796–799.

Nichols, R. C., and Beck, K. W. Factors in psychotherapy change. *Journal of Consulting Psychology*, 1960, **24**, 388–399.

O'Connor, J. F., Daniels, G., Karush, A., Moses, L., Flood, C., and Stern, L. O. The effects of psychotherapy on the course of ulcerative colitis: A preliminary report. *American Journal of Psychiatry*, 1964, **120**, 738–742.

Orgel, S. Z. Effect of psychoanalysis on the course of peptic ulcer. *Psychosomatic Medicine*, 1958, **20**, 117–125.

Parker, G. V. C., and Megargee, E. I. Factor analytic studies of the adjective check list. *Proceedings of the 75th Annual Convention of the American Psychological Association*, 1967, 211–212.

Parloff, M. B., Kelman, H. C., and Frank, J. D. Comfort, effectiveness and self-awareness as criteria of improvement in psychotherapy. *American Journal of Psychiatry*, 1954, **3**, 343–351.

Paul, G. L. *Effects of insight, desensitization, and attention placebo treatment of anxiety*. Stanford, Calif.: Stanford University Press, 1966.

Paul, G. L. Insight versus desensitization in psychotherapy two years after termination. *Journal of Consulting Psychology*, 1967, **31**, 333–348. (a)

Paul, G. L. Strategy of outcome research in psychotherapy. *Journal of Consulting Psychology*, 1967, **31**, 109–118. (b)

Persons, R. W. Relationship between psychotherapy with institutionalized boys and subsequent community adjustment. *Journal of Consulting Psychology*, 1967, **31**, 137–141.

Poser, E. The effect of therapists' training on group therapeutic outcome. *Journal of Consulting Psychology*, 1966, **30**, 283–289.

Powers, E., and Witmer, H. *An experiment in the prevention of delinquency*. New York: Columbia University Press, 1951.

Ricks, D., Umbarger, C., and Mack, R. A. A measure of increased temporal perspective in successfully treated adolescent delinquent boys. *Journal of Abnormal and Social Psychology*, 1964, **69**, 685–689.

Riess, B. F. Changes in patient income concomitant with psychotherapy. *Journal of Consulting Psychology*, 1967, **31**, 430.

Rogers, C. R The concept of the fully functioning person *Psychotherapy*, 1963, **1**, 17–26

Rogers, C., and Dymond, R. *Psychotherapy and Personality Change*. Chicago: University of Chicago Press, 1954.

Rogers, C. R., Gendlin, E. T., Kiesler, D., and Truax, C. B. *The Therapeutic Relationship and Its Impact: A Study of Psychotherapy with Schizophrenics*. Madison: University of Wisconsin Press, 1967.

Rogers, L. S. Drop-out rates and results of psychotherapy in government aided mental hygiene clinics. *Journal of Clinical Psychology*, 1960, **16**, 89–92.

Rosenbaum, M., Friedlander, J., and Kaplan, S. M. Evaluation of results of psychotherapy. *Psychosomatic Medicine*, 1956, **18**, 113–132.

Rosenthal, D. Changes in some moral values following psychotherapy. *Journal of Consulting Psychology*, 1955, **19**, 431–436.

Rosenthal, D., and Frank, J. D. The fate of psychiatric clinic outpatients assigned to psychotherapy. *Journal of Nervous and Mental Disease*, 1958, **127**, 330–343.

Rosenzweig, S. A transvaluation of psychotherapy—a reply to Hans Eysenck. *Journal of Abnormal and Social Psychology*, 1954, **49**, 298–304.

Ross, T. A. *An enquiry into prognosis in the neuroses*. London: Cambridge University Press, 1936.

Sager, C. J., Riess, B. F., and Gundlach, R. Follow-up study of the results of extramural analytic psychotherapy. *American Journal of Psychotherapy*, 1964, **18**, 161–173.

Sargent, H. D. Methodological problems of follow-up studies in psychotherapy research. *American Journal of Orthopsychiatry*, 1960, **30**, 495–506.

Schilder, P. Results and problems of group psychotherapy in severe neuroses. *Mental Hygiene*, 1939, **23**, 87–98.

Schjelderup, H. Lasting effects of psychoanalytic treatment. *Psychiatry*, 1955, **18**, 109–133.

Scriven, M. The experimental investigation of psychoanalysis. In S. Hook (Ed.), *Psychoanalysis, Scientific Method, and Philosophy*. New York: New York University Press, 1959. Pp. 252–268.

Shlien, J. M., Mosak, H. H., and Dreikurs, R. Effect of time limits: a comparison of two psychotherapies. *Journal of Counseling Psychology*, 1962, **9**, 31–34. (a)

Shlien, J. M. Toward what level of abstraction in criteria? In H. H. Strupp and L. Luborsky (Eds.), *Research in Psychotherapy*. Washington, D. C.: American Psychological Association, 1962. Vol. 2. Pp. 142–154. (b)

Shlien, J. M. Cross-theoretical criteria in time-limited therapy. In *The Sixth International Congress of Psychotherapy, London, 1964, Selected Lectures*. New York: S. Karger, 1965.

Shlien, J. M. Comparison of results with different forms of psychotherapy, *American Journal of Psychotherapy*, 1964, **18**, 15–22.

Shore, M. F., Massimo, J. L., and Mack, R. The relationship between levels of guilt in thematic stories and unsocialized behavior. *The Journal of Projective Techniques and Personality Assessment*, 1964, **28**, 346–349.

Shore, M. F., Massimo, J. L., and Ricks, D. F. A factor analytic study of psychotherapeutic change in delinquent boys. *Journal of Clinical Psychology*, 1965, **21**, 208–212.

Shore, M. F. and Massimo, J. L. Comprehensive vocationally oriented psychotherapy for adolescent delinquent boys: A follow-up study. *American Journal of Orthopsychiatry*, 1966, **36**, 609–615.

Shostrom, E. L. *Personal Orientation Inventory*. San Diego: Educational and Industrial Testing Service, 1963.

Shostrom, E. L., and Knapp, R. R. The relationship of a measure of self-actualization (POI) to a measure of pathology (MMPI) and to therapeutic growth. *American Journal of Psychotherapy*, 1966, **20**, 193–202.

Spitzer, R. L., Endicott, J., and Cohen, G. *The Psychiatric Status Schedule: Technique for Evaluating Social and Role Functioning and Mental Status*. New York State Psychiatric Institute and Biometrics Research, New York, 1967.

Spitzer, R. L., Endicott, J., Cohen, G., and Hardesty, A. S. The mental status schedule: Rationale, reliability and validity. *Comprehensive Psychiatry*, 1964, **5**, 384.

Spivack, G. and Levine, M. *Self-Regulation in Acting Out and Normal Adolescents*. Devon, Pa.: The Devereux Foundation, 1964.

Stone, A. R., Frank, J. D., Nash, E. H., and Imber, S. D. An intensive five-year follow-up study of treated psychiatric outpatients. *Journal of Nervous and Mental Disease*, 1961, **133**, 410–422.

Strupp, H. H. *Psychotherapists in Action: Explorations of the Therapist's Contribution to the Treatment Process*. New York: Grune and Stratton, 1960.

Strupp, H. H. The outcome problem in psychotherapy revisited. *Psychotherapy*, 1963, **1**, 1–13.

Strupp, H. H. The outcome problem in psychotherapy: A rejoinder. *Psychotherapy*, 1964, **1**, 101.

Strupp, H. H., and Bergin, A. E. *A bibliography of research in psychotherapy*. Washington, D. C.: National Institute of Mental Health, 1969. (a)

Strupp, H. H., and Bergin, A. E. Some empirical and conceptual bases for coordinated research in psychotherapy: a critical review of issues, trends, and evidence. *International Journal of Psychiatry*, 1969, **7**, 18–90. (b)

Strupp, H. H., Wallach, M. S., and Wogan, M. Psychotherapy experience in retrospect: questionnaire survey of former patients and their therapists. *Psychological Monographs*, 1964, **78** (11, Whole No. 588).

Truax, C. B., and Carkhuff, R. R. *Toward Effective Counseling and Psychotherapy: Training and Practice*. Chicago: Aldine Press, 1967.

Truax, C. B. Effective ingredients in psychotherapy. *Journal of Counseling Psychology*, 1963, **10**, 256–263.

Truax, C. B., and Carkhuff, R. R. For better or for worse: the process of psychotherapeutic change. In *Recent advances in behavioral change*. Montreal: McGill University Press, 1964.

Truax, C. B., and Carkhuff, R. R. Personality change in hospitalized mental patients during group psychotherapy as a function of the use of alternate sessions and vicarious therapy pretraining. *Journal of Clinical Psychology*, 1965, **21**, 225–228.

Truax, C. B., Wargo, D. G., Frank, J. D., Imber, S. D., Battle, C. C., Hoehn-Saric, R., Nash, E. H., and Stone, A. R. Therapist empathy, genuineness, and warmth and patient outcome. *Journal of Consulting Psychology*, 1966, **30**, 395–401.

Uhlenhuth, E. H., and Duncan, D. B. Subjective change in psychoneurotic outpatients with medical students I. The kind, amount, and course of change. Unpublished manuscript, Johns Hopkins University, 1968.

Ullmann, L., and Krasner, L. (Eds.), *Case studies in behavior modification*. New York: Holt, Rinehart and Winston, 1965.

Van Der Veen, F. The parent's concept of the family unit and child adjustment. *Journal of Counseling Psychology*, 1965, **12**, 196–200.

Varble, D. L. and Landfield, A. W. Validity of the self-ideal discrepancy as a criterion measure for success in psychotherapy—a replication. *Journal of Counseling Psychology*, 1969 **16**, 150–156.

Volsky, T. Jr., Magoon, T. M., Norman, W. T., and Hoyt, D. P. *The outcomes of counseling and psychotherapy*. Minneapolis: University of Minnesota Press, 1965.

Vorster, D. Psychotherapy and the results of psychotherapy. *South African Medical Journal*, 1966, **40**, 934–936.

Walker, R. G., and Kelley, F. E. Short term psychotherapy with hospitalized schizophrenic patients. *Acta Psychiatrica Neurologica Scandinavica*, 1960, **35**, 34–56.

Warne, M. M., Canter, A. H., and Wiznia, B. Analysis and follow-up of patients with psychiatric disorders. *American Journal of Psychotherapy*, 1953, **7**, 278–288.

Watson, R. I. Measuring the effectiveness of psychotherapy: problems for investigation. *Journal of Clinical Psychology*, 1952, **8**, 60–64.

Watson, R. I. Research design and methodology in evaluating the results of psychotherapy. *Journal of Clinical Psychology*, 1952, **8**, 29–33.

Watson, R. I., Mensh, I. N., and Gildea, E. F. The evaluation of the effects of psychotherapy: III. Research design. *Journal of Psychology*, 1951, **32**, 293–308.

Weber, J. J., Elinson, J., and Moss, L. M. The application of ego strength scales to psychoanalytic clinic records. In G. S. Goldman and D. Shapiro (Eds.), *Developments in Psychoanalysis at Columbia University: Proceedings of the 20th Anniversary Conference*. Columbia Psychoanalytic Clinic for Training and Research, New York, 1965.

Weiss, J. M. A., and Schaie, K. W. The psychiatric evaluation index. *American Journal of Psychotherapy*, 1964, **18**, 3–14.

Wessman, A. E., and Ricks, D. F. *Mood and Personality*. New York, New York: Holt, Rinehart, and Winston, 1966.

Wilder, J. Facts and figures on psychotherapy. *Journal of Clinical Psychopathology*, 1945, **7**, 311–347.

Wispe, L. G., and Parloff, M. B. Impact of psychotherapy on the productivity of psychologists. *Journal of Abnormal Psychology*, 1965, **70**, 188–193.

Wolpe, J., and Lazarus, A. A. *Behavior Therapy Techniques*. New York: Pergamon Press, 1966.

Wooten, L. H., Armstrong, R. W., and Lilley, D. An investigation into the after-histories of discharged mental patients. *Journal of Mental Science*, 1935, **81**, 168–172.

Yaskin, J. C. The psychoneuroses and neuroses. A review of a hundred cases with special reference to treatment and results. *American Journal of Psychiatry*, 1936, **93**, 107–125.

Zubin, J. Evaluation of therapeutic outcome in mental disorders. *Journal of Nervous and Mental Disease*, 1953, **117**, 95–111.

Zubin, J., Eron, L. D., and Schumer, F. *An Experimental Approach to Projective Techniques*. New York: Wiley, 1965.

8

RESEARCH ON CLIENT VARIABLES IN PSYCHOTHERAPY

SOL L. GARFIELD

WASHINGTON UNIVERSITY

Much has been said and written about the importance of the client as a variable in psychotherapy, and a number of investigations have been concerned in some way with this matter. In attempting to survey and analyze the diverse material from varied sources that have dealt with this topic, the author has devoted primary attention to the results of empirical research investigation. Clinical and theoretical discussions that deal mainly with nosological categories or individual case studies, or narrative accounts without supporting data, were bypassed unless something of novel import for research was apparent. This selective bias is clearly justified by the specific objectives of the present volume.

In any conceptualization of the psychotherapeutic process, it is apparent that three main influences can be postulated. These are the client or patient, the therapist, and the resulting interaction of these two variables. Ideally, each of these variables should be studied in their natural interacting state and carefully evaluated in relation to significant criteria of therapy. Unfortunately, this has rarely been the case. As has been pointed out in the present volume and

elsewhere, the field of psychotherapy research has been characterized by studies of a limited number of variables and with a variety of differing criteria. In some, various client variables have been studied in relation to selected dependent variables—such as the relation of social class to length of stay in psychotherapy. In others, specific therapist attributes have been the focus of study, such as empathy, warmth, and the like. However, the study of the interaction of patient and therapist variables in relation to specific outcome criteria has been a rarity (Kiesler, 1966; Paul, 1967).

A variety of studies have attempted to relate differing client attributes to selected variables. Among the client attributes have been social class variables, personality variables, diagnostic categories, age, intelligence, motivation, and other aspects. These have been related to premature termination, outcome, length of stay in psychotherapy, and similar variables. To the extent that some research findings are relatively stable and stand up under cross-validation with new samples, we have findings that appear to have definite relevance for clinical practice and theory. However, to the extent that research reports are conflicting and offer little in the way of generalizable results, one must be cautious in what conclusions one derives from such data. Like many other areas of psychology where one is concerned with complex phenomena, research in the area of psychotherapy is beset with a number of difficulties that lead to inconsistencies in findings. Varying samples of clients and therapists are among the more obvious variables that lead to discrepant results. Different kinds of criterion measures, varying lengths of treatment, different criteria for acceptance of clients, and similar matters also lead to lack of comparability from study to study. Under such circumstances, it is not surprising that research on client variables may produce inconsistent results. While such problems limit the value of much past research, they in no way should be interpreted to mean that research on significant factors in psychotherapy can not be carried out in a meaningful manner. Rather, it may signify that our past work has been crude and has suffered from many methodological limitations that have seriously limited the value of the findings reported. At the same time, a review of past research may indicate where we are at present, what findings appear to have some tenability and application, and the direction future research should take.

The present chapter, therefore, will focus on empirical investigations in the field of psychotherapy which attempt to study client variables in relationship to some external criterion or outcome. Studies of psychotherapy process or content, unless related to some external criterion, will be omitted here. Interest is focused on the types of clients selected for psychotherapy, and client variables that appear to be related to continuation and outcome in psychotherapy. Representative samples of the available research data will be evaluated, and an attempt made to draw some implications for practice and research.

THE SELECTION OF CLIENTS FOR PSYCHOTHERAPY

One interesting aspect of psychotherapy concerns the matter of what kinds of people seek psychotherapy and to whom it is offered. This is a problem with many implications. Several kinds of data are available to help us appraise this problem, although they are admittedly incomplete. Most reports tend to come from clinics, and there is a dearth of information concerning clients who are treated by private practitioners. If we can hypothesize that there is a significant difference between those who go to low-cost clinics and those who receive long-term psychotherapy on a private basis, as seems reasonable, then it is apparent that the reported findings provide only a partial picture of who gets psychotherapy. Additional data on this problem would be of great interest.

It is apparent, at the outset, that not all individuals who apply for psychotherapeutic help receive it. At the same time, not all individuals who are offered psychotherapy accept it. With regard to the latter, two reports indicate that approximately one-third of clients judged to be in need of psychotherapy, and to whom it was offered, refused such treatment (Garfield and Kurz, 1952; Rosenthal and Frank, 1958). Comparatively little study has been made of the possible factors or variables related to this rejection of therapy. Some data are available in the study of Rosenthal and Frank (1958). They found a significant relationship between acceptance on the part of the client and the client's income, and between acceptance and rated level of motivation. Level of education was related to acceptance only at a suggestive level of significance ($p. < 10$). Thus, although the data are limited, they suggest some relationship between socioeconomic variables and the acceptance of psychotherapy on the part of patients.

Brandt (1964; Riess and Brandt, 1965) challenges the findings that about a third of those who apply to clinics for out-patient treatment reject psychotherapy, but his findings are not very convincing. In his first study, only two thirds of the subjects were contacted, and only half were willing to give complete data about whether they were receiving psychotherapy elsewhere. Furthermore, the samples used were quite different. Two of the clinics were private clinics that are primarily psychotherapy (not psychiatric) clinics, and the majority of the subjects had some college education. In a second study (Riess and Brandt, 1965) more than one fourth of the applicants did not show up for intake, and another ten percent withdrew from treatment. From that point on it is difficult to draw any firm conclusions from the published report. Nothing is said about the composition of the sample, and in a large number of cases, insufficient data were obtained. Therefore, we have little reason to reject the notion that a sizable percentage of those who apply for outpatient treatment reject psychotherapy.

The problem of who is accepted for psychotherapy on the part of clinical personnel has received somewhat more study. Schaffer and Myers (1954) found that social class status was positively related to acceptance for treatment. This finding, with minor variations, has also been reported in two more recent studies (Brill and Storrow, 1960; Cole, Branch, and Allison, 1962). A somewhat related finding is also reported by Rosenthal and Frank (1958). They examined those patients who were specifically referred for psychotherapy from the total group who were seen at the Henry Phipps Clinic during a three-year-period. Among other findings, they discovered a significant relationship between referral for psychotherapy and such variables as age, race, education, income, diagnosis, and motivation. Thus, in all four of these studies that were carried out in a medical school complex, there was some relationship between social class variables and referral or acceptance for psychotherapy. Even within a restricted range, those patients who are younger, relatively more educated, and generally more similar to the therapists, are more frequently accepted for psychotherapy.

Somewhat comparable findings have been reported in a study of a VA mental hygiene clinic (Bailey, Warshaw, and Eichler, 1959). Assignment to psychotherapy was reported to be related to high socioeconomic statues, intrapsychic complaints, age, expressed desire for psychotherapy, psychological test evaluation, and previous psychotherapy. Assignment to the psychosomatic clinic, on the other hand, was related to low socioeconomic status, somatic complaints, lack of recommendation from the psychological test evaluation, and no previous psychotherapy.

Perhaps reference should be made to another aspect of this problem before we move on to another topic. As pointed out rather dramatically by Hollingshead and Redlich (1958), different social classes appear to receive different kinds of treatment, with long-term psychoanalytic treatment given mainly to middle- and upper-class clients. It is very likely that because of income restrictions most private therapy is reserved for such patients, and that public outpatient clinics are the sources of help for lower-middle- and lower-class patients. A recent study of different kinds of clinics in New York City also indicates varying admission criteria related to social-class variables (Lorenzen, 1967). These clinics had very different criteria, with one, a psychoanalytic training clinic, being quite highly selective in terms of age, education, and relation to health professions. This particular clinic did not accept clients under 20 or over 34 years of age. The differences are also apparent in the widely different acceptance rates among the clinics. Two clinics accepted about 10 to 20 percent of applicants, whereas one clinic accepted 85 percent. Obviously, the kinds of problems and generalizations derived from such diverse samples of clients would also be expected to vary widely. It would thus appear likely that different approaches to therapy might be used in such instances, but this is far from clear. The length of therapy, however, did differ among the clinics and appeared to be related to the orientation of the clinic and its selectivity.

A somewhat similar analysis of social agencies has found *that the more sophisticated an agency's therapeutic method is, and the more qualified its workers are, the more highly selected and higher in status is the population that it serves* (Rudolph and Cumming, 1962). *Furthermore, the higher the status of the agency, the less flexible are its methods of operation and the greater the tendency to label clients as unsuitable or unmotivated. Such agencies appear to emphasize their special procedures instead of focusing on the kind of social needs that require service.*

Another interesting and related aspect of this problem pertains to the differential assignment of clients in terms of the different strata or hierarchy of therapists within a given clinical setting. Schaffer and Myers (1954) found a definite relationship between the rank of the therapist and the social class of the patients seen by him, with the senior staff members having more of the upper-class patients. While this finding was not supported in another study as far as psychiatrists and medical students were concerned, the psychiatric social workers, working largely with spouses of patients, had clients exclusively from the two lowest social classes (Cole, Branch, and Allison, 1962). It is, of course, difficult to generalize from such limited data, particularly when the personnel and clientele differ among clinics. Some clinics have an income ceiling for prospective clients, and individuals above that ceiling are referred to private practitioners. To the extent that many clinics utilize therapists in training, however, it is possible that the poorer clients receive the less experienced therapists.

It would appear then, that clinics are somewhat selective in whom they accept for treatment, that this selectivity varies according to the type of clinic, that selection is frequently related to social class criteria, and that the more expert the therapeutic staff, the more stringent are the procedures used for selection and acceptance of clients. There are two sides to this matter that are worthy of comment. Psychoanalytic or psychoanalytically oriented clinics that are looking for suitable candidates for their particular variants of psychotherapy conceivably must use some degree of selectivity in deciding which clients are best suited for treatment, and generally these are the better-educated, intelligent, verbal, and "motivated" clients. On the other hand, such selectivity does pose a serious problem when it comes to providing adequate service to the whole population.

RESEARCH PERTAINING TO CONTINUATION IN PSYCHO-THERAPY

One of the problems encountered in clinic practice concerns the number of clients who start psychotherapy but who terminate their participation relatively early. Such discontinuers, premature terminators, or dropouts constitute a sizable percentage of those who begin therapy, and a moderate number of studies have been carried out to evaluate this problem.

It may be worthwhile first to review briefly some representative findings on the nature of this problem. In Table 8.1, data are presented on the length of psychotherapy, expressed in terms of the number of interviews, for 560 patients seen at a VA mental hygiene clinic (Garfield and Kurz, 1952). This group of patients consisted of all those who had been offered and had accepted treatment at the clinic, and whose cases were officially closed at the time of the study. As is apparent in the table, the median length of treatment falls between 6 and 7 interviews, with approximately two-thirds of the cases receiving less than 10 interviews. By contrast, less than nine percent of the patients came for 25 or more interviews and only seven cases received over 50 treatment interviews.

While the data just presented are the actual findings secured with the population of one

TABLE 8.1 Length of Treatment

Number of Interviews	Number of Cases	Percentage of Cases
Less than 5	239	42.7
5–9	134	23.9
10–14	73	13.0
15–19	41	7.3
20–24	24	4.3
25 and over	49	8.8
Total	560	100.0

TABLE 8.2   Median Number of Psychotherapy Interviews in Ten Clinics

Clinic	Median Number of Interviews	Date	Source
VA Clinic, St. Louis	5	1948	Blackman
VA Clinic, Boston	10	1949	Adler, Valenstein, and Michaels
VA Clinic, Milwaukee	6	1952	Garfield and Kurz
VA Clinic, Baltimore	4	1956	Kurland
VA Clinic, Oakland	9	1958	Sullivan, Miller, and Smelser
VA Clinic, Chicago	3	1959	Affleck and Mednick
Psychiatric Clinics— General Hospitals, N.Y.C.	6	1949	N.Y.C. Commission on Mental Hygiene
Yale University Clinic	4	1954	Schaffer and Myers
Henry Phipps Clinic	6	1958	Rosenthal and Frank
Nebraska Psychiatric Institute	12	1959	Garfield and Affleck

clinic, they approximate the kinds of results secured from a number of other clinics. Table 8.2 summarizes the findings of a number of typical investigations carried out in several types of clinics. As can be seen there, a number of clinics have lost about half their therapy clients by approximately the eighth interview. Although the median length of treatment varies from three to twelve interviews for the different clinics, there is a clustering around six to eight interviews. While the methodology is not always clear or consistent among these studies, it can be emphasized that in those studies that excluded all those patients who were offered therapy but refused it, and included only actual therapy patients, the median number of interviews was between five and six (Garfield and Kurz, 1952; Schaffer and Myers, 1954; Kurland, 1956; Rosenthal and Frank, 1958). In addition, it can be pointed out that the annual statistical reports for psychiatric clinics in the states of New York and Maryland indicate that the majority of patients are seen for less than five interviews (Gordon, 1965), and a study of comparable statistics for five other states show that a majority of patients have left treatment before the eighth interview (Rogers, 1960). While these particular statistics of state clinics leave much to be desired, they do reflect the fate of the patients who are referred to them. Furthermore, on the basis of limited evidence, it appears that those who terminate

therapy early rarely go on to seek therapy elsewhere (Garfield, 1963; Riess and Brandt, 1965).

Another possible bit of information that may be of interest here, is the report of a large scale survey published by the National Center for Health Statistics (1966). According to this study, a total of 979,000 Americans consulted a psychiatrist during the twelve-month period from July 1963 to June 1964. The average number of visits per person was 4.7. The latter figure thus approximates the findings already mentioned.

On the basis of the data presented above, therefore, it is apparent that, contrary to the usual expectations concerning length of therapy, most clinic clients are done with it after only a few interviews. In practically all of the clinics studied, this pattern was viewed as a problem and was not the result of a deliberately planned brief therapy. *Rather, in most instances, the patient failed to return for a scheduled appointment.* For example, in a study by Haddock and Mensh (1957) of two university student health services and one VA mental hygiene clinic, similar findings were secured for the three separate settings. About two thirds of the patients were seen fewer than five hours, and only one patient in 20 was seen for more than twenty hours. Furthermore, over half of the veterans and a third of the students terminated treatment on their own without discussing it with the therapist.

It can be stated with some degree of confidence, therefore, that the finding of an unplanned and premature termination from psychotherapy on the part of a large number of clients is a reasonably reliable one. The apparent rejection of psychotherapy by a number of those who appear to be in need of it has been a somewhat surprising and perplexing finding that has brought forth somewhat different kinds of reactions. One type of reaction is that more careful screening should take place before clients are assigned for psychotherapy. With a scarcity of therapists, and the large demand for services, such premature terminations from psychotherapy are viewed as a waste of professional manpower. This solution thus stresses the more careful selection of cases in terms of accepting those who may be seen as being more amenable to psychotherapy, and clearly places the blame for the problem on the "unsuitable client." In essence, as will be noted later, such a view tends to favor the more educated, intelligent, psychologically sophisticated and less disturbed client as the preferred one for psychotherapy.

A second approach, less frequently mentioned but meriting attention, is that of providing some sort of pretherapy training to help prepare the client for psychotherapy, or to help prepare the therapist for such difficulties. In some instances this has called for a somewhat more active and flexible role on the part of the therapist (Baum and Felzer, 1964). This view, while focusing less blame or responsibility on the client, still does not basically question the efficacy of traditional approaches to psychotherapy. A somewhat related view, which takes cognizance of the differing expectations that clients may bring to therapy, emphasizes the need to consider the problem of expectations during the initial phase of treatment (Hoehn-Saric, Frank, Imber, Nash, Stone, and Battle, 1964; Overall and Aronson, 1962). In the study by Hoehn-Saric et al., for example, a "Role Induction Interview" was developed to give the patient appropriate expectations about certain aspects of psychotherapy, in the hope that this would facilitate the process and outcome of therapy. The Role Induction Interview basically stressed four components: (1) a general exposition of psychotherapy; (2) the expected behaviour of patient and therapist; (3) preparation for certain phenomena in therapy, such as resistance; and (4) expectation for improvement within four months of treatment. The experimental group significantly exceeded the control group in this study on six of the sixteen criterion measures used, including that of attendance at scheduled therapy sessions. The results of this carefully carried out investigation thus suggest that attempts to prepare the patient for psychotherapy have some impact on his attendance and progress in therapy.

Attempts at "vicarious therapy pretraining" have also been reported by Truax and Carkhuff (1967). They developed a 30-minute tape recording of excerpts of "good" therapy behaviour, which allows prospective clients to experience psychotherapy vicariously prior to their own therapy. While this particular approach has not been used by them with reference to the problem of continuation in psychotherapy, it has apparently had some modest beneficial effect on outcome. Attempted innovations of this kind, as well as those mentioned previously, would appear to merit further application and investigation. In this regard, the following statement by Truax and Carkhuff (1967, p. 363) appears decidedly pertinent: "If psychotherapy or counseling is indeed a process of learning and relearning, then the therapeutic process should allow for structuring what is to be learned, rather than depending on what amounts to 'incidental learning,' where the client does not have clearly in mind from the outset what it is he is supposed to learn."

Finally, the implication of premature termination for some observers has been the need for modifications in conventional psychotherapies to better meet the needs of these dropouts from psychotherapy. Thus, from one point of view these clients have been seen as undesirable clients or as failing to have the requisite attributes of candidates for psychotherapy; from another point of view, psychotherapy as practiced has been found wanting, and some changes in practice have been called for as a possible solution. We will return to a discussion of these issues later. For the present, it will be sufficient to reiterate that premature discontinuance in psychotherapy has been a frequently replicated and disturbing finding that has stimulated a moderate amount of search for associated variables. This research can be categorized for our purposes into three broad groups: (a) social class and actuarial variables; (b) psychological test data; and (c) other variables.

A. Social Class and Actuarial Variables

As indicated earlier, one group of variables that has been studied in relation to length of stay in psychotherapy concerns social class. Some investigations have simply used one of the well-known indices of social class such as that of Hollingshead, while others have studied specific components such as education, income, occupation, and the like. Those who have used the former have found a definite relationship between length of stay and social-class index. In one study, only 57.1 percent of lower-class patients stayed beyond the fourth interview, whereas 88.9 percent of middle class patients went beyond the fourth interview (Imber, Nash, and Stone, 1955). In another study, about 12 percent of the two lower-social-class groups, classified according to the Hollingshead classification, remained for over 30 interviews, as compared with 42 percent for those in the highest two social-class groups (Cole, Branch, and Allison, 1962). Gibby, Stotsky, Hiler, and Miller (1954), using primarily occupational status as a measure of social class, also found that middle-class patients remained in therapy longer than did lower-class patients.

With regard to the more specific variables such as education, the findings are slightly less consistent. While most studies have reported a positive relationship between education and length of stay (Bailey, Warshaw, and Eichler, 1959; McNair, Lorr, and Callahan, 1963; Rosenthal and Frank, 1958; Rubinstein and Lorr, 1956; Sullivan, Miller, and Smelser, 1958), some have not (Garfield and Affleck, 1959). Part of this partial lack of agreement may result from differences in the samples used, as well as the type of screening employed in selecting patients for psychotherapy. Two comments, however, may be offered at this point. It is likely that education below a certain level may be a factor in continuation in therapy. For example, in the paper by Rosenthal and Frank, the group that clearly appeared to account for the significant findings obtained was the one that had less than a ninth-grade education. The other point that is worth mentioning here is that educational level is very likely only one component of a larger factor that may include verbal ability, sophistication about psychotherapy, income, interest in receiving psychotherapy, and similar components. In any event, educational level, while not always related to length of stay, is found to have a significant relationship in most studies.

Before discussing other actuarial variables, it is of interest to comment on one other unusual investigation that has reported very atypical findings. This study was done at Tulane University (Lief, Lief, Warren, and Heath, 1961). At this clinic, in contrast to the typical findings already reported, only six percent of the clients dropped out before the sixth interview. In evaluating this report, it is clear that the population of this clinic is not typical of that found in most medical-school clinics. Most unusual, probably, is the high educational level of the subjects, which included a large number of medical students. In the clinic population studied, 82 percent of the patients had some college work, and 49 percent also had completed some graduate work. While 85 percent of the clinic population was under 35 years of age, and only two percent were Negroes, the educational level is probably the most atypical characteristic of the sample, and would appear to account for the kinds of results secured.

Besides education, the most frequently studied actuarial variables examined in relation to length of stay have been sex, age, and diagnosis. While income and occupation have also been evaluated, these have frequently been combined in estimates of social class. Furthermore, since many clinics usually have some income ceiling for their clients, it may not be too advantageous to look more specifically into these variables.

The variable of sex has been investigated in several studies with somewhat inconclusive findings (Cartwright, 1955; Garfield and Affleck, 1959; Rosenthal and Frank, 1958). A somewhat similar interpretation can be made for age of client. Although some therapists and clinics appear to show a preference for younger patients (Bailey, Warshaw, and Eichler, 1959), *age does not appear to be an important variable, at least as far as continuation in psychotherapy is concerned*

(Cartwright, 1955; Garfield and Affleck, 1959; Rosenthal and Frank, 1958; Rubinstein and Lorr, 1956). In one study where age did statistically differentiate those continuing and discontinuing psychotherapy, the mean difference in age was less than two years (Sullivan, Miller, and Smelser, 1958).

While perhaps not strictly an actuarial variable, psychiatric diagnosis has also been evaluated in terms of length of stay in outpatient psychotherapy. By and large, in spite of the time and effort devoted to placing a diagnostic label on patients, *such a means of classification appears to bear no relationship to continuation in outpatient psychotherapy* (Bailey, Warshaw, and Eichler, 1959; Garfield and Affleck, 1959; Lief, Lief, Warren, and Heath, 1961; Rosenthal and Frank, 1958).

Thus, our survey of the problem of continuation in psychotherapy indicates a likely relationship between social class and length of stay, some relationship of educational level, particularly an inverse one at the lower educational levels, and no clear relationship between length of stay and such variables as age, sex, and psychiatric diagnosis. Earlier, some mention was made of the possible significance of such findings in terms of other related variables, as these may be important in conventional approaches to psychotherapy. A few studies have discussed this matter, and we can briefly review the points presented.

In one study (Brill and Storrow, 1960), in which acceptance for psychotherapy was positively related to social-class status, an attempt was made to evaluate "psychological-mindedness" in relation to social class. Low social class was found to be significantly related to low estimated intelligence, a tendency to view the problem as physical rather than emotional, a desire for symptomatic relief, lack of understanding of the psychotherapeutic process, and lack of desire for psychotherapy. In addition, *the intake interviewer had less positive feelings for lower-class patients and saw them as less treatable by means of psychotherapy.* In terms of the data already discussed, the last statement appears to have elements of a self-fulfilling prophecy. The findings, however, do suggest some interactional effect between attributes and expectations of lower-class clients and middle-class therapists, which may play a role in length of stay in psychotherapy. Other studies, to which we will refer shortly, have attempted to investigate personality and other correlates of continuation in psychotherapy; and such variables as motivation, verbal ability, ability to introspect, and attitudes toward psychotherapy have been designated as being of importance in this regard. While such attributes have not always been evaluated in relation to social class, as the study by Brill and Storrow has shown, there may be some relationship between these two sets of variables.

Another aspect that has been commented upon by Hollingshead and Redlich (1958), as well as by others, is that therapists generally appear to prefer and be more comfortable with upper class clients, that is, clients who talk their language and are more similar to them. Thus, while several writers have been critical of existing "insight-oriented" psychotherapy for many lower-class patients (Dean, 1958; Rosenthal and Frank, 1958), and cite a need for experimentation with other forms of therapy, some appear to more tacitly accept psychotherapy as a treatment for middle- and upper-class clients (Hunt, 1960; Lief, Lief, Warren, and Heath, 1961). In fact, Lief et al. emphasize the need for selecting middle class patients "if we consider the needs of university clinics to train residents in insight therapy" (p. 208).

The relationship of social class variables to continuation in psychotherapy, thus may be a function of several variables acting independently or in interaction with each other. The attributes and expectations of the client clearly contribute one source of variance to this problem, while the personality and attitudes of the therapist contribute another. These, furthermore, may act singly or in combination. However, let us postpone further discussion of these issues until later.

B. Psychological Test Variables and Continuation in Psychotherapy

Considerable interest has been shown by psychologists in attempting to find predictive variables selected from psychological tests for assessing the matter of continuation in psychotherapy. A variety of investigations utilizing many different tests and procedures have been carried out. It should be pointed out, however, that research in psychotherapy is beset by many complexities and difficulties. Psychotherapy, in the first place, is not a uniform process that is performed in exactly the same way in every clinical setting, and the writer, like many others, is guilty of perpetuating the "uniformity myth" mentioned by Kiesler (1966), when he attempts to treat the subject in this manner. The research literature, however, does not always specify what particular therapeutic approach has been used, or else utilizes a designation such as "psycho-analytically oriented therapy," which covers a multitude of sins. In addition to possible variations in psychotherapy, other variations are also encountered. These include different samples of subjects, varying criteria, different statistical analyses and approaches to the data, different uses of the same test, and variations in therapists and therapeutic setting. Such differences, of course, complicate the problem and make replications difficult. However, the clinic is not the laboratory, and the conditions of the latter are not easily transferred to the former. While we should be aware of the probable difficulties and problems in clinical research, we should also recognize that such efforts to study problems of clinical importance in their natural setting are needed. With this, then, as an introduction, let us proceed to a review of some of the studies on psychological test variables and the problem of continuation in psychotherapy.

The Rorschach Test has been one technique which, because of its wide use in the past, has been applied a number of times to this problem with contradictory findings. An early study by Rogers, Knauss, and Hammond (1951) secured negative results with a number of Rorschach scores. However, Kotkov and Meadow (1953) found that a weighted combination of three Rorschach scores (FC-CF, R and D%), originally studied in relation to group psychotherapy, was able to significantly discriminate patients in individual therapy who continued for at least nine interviews. Auld and Eron (1953) attempted to replicate this study, but secured negative results. They further analyzed each of the three Rorschach scores in relation to continuation, and secured a significant relationship only with R (number of responses). Because of the possible correlation between R and intelligence, IQ was

then partialed out and with this the significant relationship between R and continuation disappeared. In fact, on a sample of 23 patients, the correlation between IQ and continuation was .71.

Gibby, Stotsky, Miller, and Hiler (1953) also compared two groups of patients on various Rorschach scores, and secured a number of significant findings. However, many of the separate scores were significantly correlated with the total number of responses, and they used more extreme groups of subjects. The terminators had less than six sessions, while the continuers were those who remained for 20 or more sessions. These investigators then carried out another study (Gibby, Stotsky, Hiler, and Miller, 1954) as a follow-up of their first one. Utilizing the method of discriminant function on the scores of 84 patients, they secured a formula that was then applied to 75 continuers and 110 terminators. However, in this study they utilized 19 sessions or less to designate the group of terminators, a cut-off point that differed noticeably from those used in the other studies. In this investigation, a combination of three Rorschach scores were used (R and total K and M). When applied to the second sample, 67 percent of the patients were correctly categorized. While the authors state that this measure significantly differentiated the two groups of patients, several comments are in order. In the first place, if one computes a base rate for termination on the second sample, it is close to 60 percent. Thus, the formula exceeds the base rate by only a small amount. Secondly, as the authors point out, the formula is more predictive of terminators than it is of remainers. In fact, if their cut-off score is used, it not only predicts 87 percent of the terminators correctly, but it would keep out of therapy almost 63 percent of the remainers! Finally, it appeared also that R, or number of responses alone, would have also predicted with an accuracy of 69 percent. Thus, as in most of these studies, the common Rorschach variable that appeared to account for most of the variance was R, which correlates positively with IQ. Furthermore, when separate analyses were made for IQ and R in relation to continuation, the results were quite similar. While the findings obtained here are not identical to those secured by Auld and Eron, in general, *IQ does seem to be as good or better a predictor than the best measure obtained from the Rorschach.* It might also be added as a final note here that social class also predicted continuation at a statistically significant level in this study. While correlations between IQ and social class were not reported, it would certainly appear likely on the basis of other research that a positive relationship also exists between these two variables.

It is also of interest to mention a separate investigation reported by Hiler (1958b), which was carried out on the same samples of subjects that were used in the two preceding studies. This study was concerned with the relationship of Wechsler-Bellevue IQ to continuation in outpatient psychotherapy. Terminators were defined as those quitting therapy within five sessions, and remainers as those who continued for 20 or more sessions. Remainers secured an average IQ of 112, which was 10 points higher than the average IQ of the terminators.

Another comparable study in a VA outpatient clinic has been reported by Affleck and Mednick (1959). They used a discriminant function of three Rorschach variables, including R, to predict continuation after the third interview, and cross-validated their initial findings on another sample. While the measure used would have increased the accuracy of prediction 13 percent over the base rate, its practical value appears limited, since terminators at the fourth and fifth interviews, labeled remainers in this study, would of course not have been predicted. It is of interest to mention also that the discriminant functions reported by Kotkov and Meadow (1953) and Gibby et al. (1954), to which reference has already been made, approximated the base rates for terminators in the clinic studied by Affleck and Mednick.

While interest in the Rorschach as a predictor of psychotherapy continuation appears to have diminished, a situation not necessarily to be decried, one recent study can be mentioned that points up again some of the problems evident in this field of research (Whitely and Blaine, 1967). In this study, an attempt was made to evaluate the Rorschach in relation to length of stay and outcome in psychotherapy for students at the Harvard University Health Service. Students who received short-term therapy (3 to 24 sessions) were compared with those who received long-term therapy (25 to 100 sessions). Nothing is said about the factors or decisions that led to length of therapy, and there is no indication of why some individuals received short-term therapy and others did not. Thus, one can not automatically assume that the former were terminators in the sense this term has been used in most of the previous studies. Apart from other factors, it is not surprising, therefore, that most of the Rorschach measures that were reported upon favorably in individual studies previously did not have much predictive validity in this study. The clients and the conditions were clearly different, and negative findings should not be totally unexpected.

Other testing procedures besides the Rorschach have also been used as possible predictors of continuation in psychotherapy. The Michigan Sentence Completion Test was used by Hiler (1959) in a VA clinic in which the clinic staff was considered to be "analytically oriented" and to favor long-term therapy. A set of special scoring categories based on a sample of 25 patients was tried out on a sample of 70 patients. Five scales differentiated those who remained less than six sessions from those who stayed in treatment for twenty or more sessions. The latter patients tended to be less evasive and more willing to reveal personal feelings, were more preoccupied with feelings of inadequacy, had stronger drives for achievement and status, and showed greater psychological sophistication. No data are given on the possible relationship of the attributes mentioned to social class status, nor are there reports of any further replication.

Other tests and techniques also have been tried out in relation to continuation in psychotherapy. However, there is relatively little to be gained in a review of single studies that have not been replicated. For example, Taulbee (1958), on the basis of selected MMPI and Rorschach variables, concluded that those who continue in therapy beyond the thirteenth interview are less defensive and more persistent, dependent, anxious, and introspective than are those who terminate early. However, these results were not cross-validated, and in another study no significant differences on the MMPI were found between continuers and terminators (Sullivan, Miller, and Smelser, 1958). In fact, the latter study deserves additional mention because it was a rather well-designed study, used three moderately large groups of subjects, and attempted two cross-validations of the findings secured with the initial sample of subjects. In this investigation, significant differences between the Stay and Non-Stay groups were found for several MMPI scales for each of the several groups of subjects studied. However, these scales were different for each of the groups studied, and not a single scale held up for even two of the groups. The authors concluded their report by emphasizing the necessity for cross-validation in studies of this type, a conclusion that is clearly supported by much of the research reported in this area.

Imber, Frank, Gliedman, Nash, and Stone (1956) studied the relationship of suggestibility, as measured by the sway test, to length of stay in psychotherapy. They found that 77 percent of the swayers remained for four or more interviews, whereas 54 percent of the nonswayers terminated before the fourth interview. They also found that suggestibility and social class were practically independent of each other ($r = .16$). It is again pertinent to point out the differences in the operational definition of remainers and terminators in the various studies mentioned, a problem that makes generalization difficult. Whereas Imber et al. define continuation in terms of four interviews, Hiler uses twenty interviews. As indicated in Table 8.1, very different percentages of clinic populations are included when such diverse criteria are used. Obviously, with such variation in the criterion variable, prediction will be difficult, if not impossible!

We can conclude our presentation of research studies in this area with a reference to some investigation by Lorr and his colleagues involving a number of VA outpatient clinics. This research has utilized relatively large samples of subjects, and several replications have been performed (Lorr, Katz, and Rubinstein, 1958; Rubinstein and Lorr, 1956). Both specific tests and selected hypotheses pertaining to continuation in psychotherapy were appraised. In the initial study, four short tests and questionnaires, referred to later as the TR battery, were found to be predictive of length of stay. The tests, increased to five in the second study and derived mainly from other scales, included a shortened

version of the Taylor Manifest Anxiety Scale, a 20-item F Scale, a Behavior Disturbance Scale, a 15-item Vocabulary Scale, and a brief self-rating scale. These instruments were selected on the basis of a double cross-validation on two random halves of a sample of 128 cases, and were then further evaluated on two new samples of 115 cases each. Because the total sample of patients showed a Y-shaped distribution in terms of length of therapy, those who stayed less than seven weeks were compared with those who remained more than twenty-six weeks. It is interesting that none of the tests based on the scoring keys derived from the original cross-validation differentiated the two new samples, although the scores were consistently in the predicted direction. This is, of course, a perennial problem in psychological research. However, it is of some importance, for findings based on the initial group studied become really significant only when they can be applied to other comparable groups. In this investigation, with two subsamples available, further analyses were done on one sample and then applied to the other. This did produce some statistically significant results. However, the multiple correlation of .67 for these test patterns shrank to .39 when one moved from the first subsample from which they were derived to the second subsample. While the latter correlation is statistically significant, it accounts for only a modest amount of the variance. To this extent, however, there was some support obtained for the authors' hypotheses. *Remainers were found to be more anxious, more self-dissatisfied, more willing to explore problems, more persistent and dependable, and less likely to have a history of antisocial acts.*

The above study was cross-validated on another VA sample of 282 patients with somewhat comparable results (McNair, Lorr, and Callahan, 1963). The multiple R of the TR test battery was .44, as contrasted with .39 previously. Thus, there was again some support for the hypotheses generated earlier. Furthermore, while different criteria were used in selecting terminators in the two studies, the overall accuracy of prediction was about 15 percent higher than the sample base rate. It should be emphasized that these investigators replicated their findings several times and eventually came up with somewhat stable results. While the latter may not be spectacular, they are not unimpressive when one considers the complexity of the problem.

Enough representative studies have been reviewed here to provide the reader with an adequate picture of the issue at hand. While there clearly appears to be a problem of unplanned or premature termination, the research devoted to seeking a better understanding of this problem has provided few clear answers, and conflicting or unreplicated findings have been frequent. The studies have utilized different definitions of early termination, the samples have differed, methods of appraisal have varied, therapeutic conditions and frequency of therapy have not been consistent, comparable information on certain variables has not been available, and a number of similar types of difficulties have been encountered. Such variations, of course, make reliable or clear-cut generalizations difficult. For example, the findings of Lorr et al. that remainers are more anxious, more dissatisfied, more willing to explore problems, more persistent, and the like, appear reasonable and are in agreement with other views concerning the good psychotherapy patient. However, these results were secured with an all VA outpatient population, apparently all males, and whether the same type of results would be secured with other types of populations remains to be seen. The criterion of length of stay would also have to be comparable. In contrast to the findings secured with psychological tests, social-class variables do appear to show some relationship to the phenomena being studied, are relatively easy to define, and show some consistency in terms of results. However, as indicated previously, the findings on social class may reflect both aspects of the client and therapist and clinic attitudes toward such clients.

Other psychological attributes that may or may not be related to social class have not given as consistent results, nor have they been systematically studied in relation to social class. One of the problems here is that personality variables discussed or studied in psychotherapy research are defined and measured differently in the various investigations. Thus, in some studies motivation, anxiety, or some similar variable may be found to be related to continuation, but not in others. For example, McNair et al. (1963)

found therapists' ratings of motivation related to length of stay, but in three other studies ratings of motivation were not so related (Affleck and Garfield, 1961; Garfield, Affleck, and Muffley, 1963; Siegel and Fink, 1962). In a similar vein, Hiler (1958a) reported that therapist sex, warmth, and competence were related to patient termination. He used Rorschach R as a measure of patient productivity, and found it to be related in an interactive manner with therapist attributes and duration of stay. In general, these findings, while not precisely replicated, tended not to be confirmed in two other investigations (Lorr, Katz, and Rubinstein, 1958; McNair, Lorr, and Callahan, 1963). At the present time, therefore, one has relatively few tested findings and the results of unreplicated studies can only be viewed as suggestive. The several investigations by Lorr and his coworkers, however, do provide us with a model of the value of repeated replications in this area of research.

C. Other Findings

A few other studies are also worthy of mention, particularly those that have investigated the relationship of the client's expectations concerning therapy to duration of stay. One is a report by Heine and Trosman (1960) concerning the initial expectations of the doctor-patient interaction as a factor in continuance in psychotherapy. Forty-six patients were given a questionnaire to tap attitudes toward psychiatric treatment, and the total group was dichotomized in terms of six weeks of treatment. The two groups of patients were differentiated in terms of two categories of response. The terminators tended to emphasize passive cooperation as a means of reaching their goal in treatment, and sought medicine or diagnostic information. The remainers, on the other hand, emphasized active collaboration and advice or help in changing behavior. These latter expectations were seen as being congruent with the expectations of the therapists. By contrast, the type of presenting complaint, whether somatic or emotional, or the degree of conviction that treatment would help, were unrelated to continuation. This is an interesting finding, since it does not support some clinical notions concerning the relation of the latter two attitudes and the results of psychotherapy. It may be worth mentioning here, that another recent study was also unable to find any close relationship between discussion of physical concerns and social class (White, Fichtenbaum, Cooper, and Cooper, 1966). Such discussions of somatic concerns were found to constitute only a small proportion of the therapy session.

Some related research on client expectations has also been reported by Heine and his colleagues (1962), using senior medical students as therapists. Patients who came for 12 or less interviews expressed some significantly different expectations of their therapists than did those who remained from 13 to 18 interviews (patients were limited to 18 interviews). More terminators expected specific advice on their problems in the first therapy interview than did the continuers, and the latter more frequently expected a permissive attitude on the part of the therapist than did those who discontinued. In these respects, the continuers were more similar in their expectations to the therapists than were the discontinuers. It can be added that patients who tended to leave therapy did not differentiate sharply the psychiatrist (psychotherapist) from other medical experts, and that as a consequence the discrepant expectations between some patients and their therapists may play a role in their decision to leave therapy early.

In another study, 40 lower class patients were given a questionnaire to ascertain their expectations about therapy and were re-evaluated after the first interview in terms of their perception of the interview (Overall and Aronson, 1962). The results indicated that these patients tended to expect a "medical-psychiatric" interview, with the therapist assuming an active supportive role. Furthermore, those patients whose expectations were generally least accurate in terms of therapist role were significantly less likely to return for treatment.

In a somewhat different type of study, Garfield and Wolpin (1963) attempted to evaluate the expectations of 70 patients who were referred for out-patient psychiatric treatment. The median level of education was 12 years, and none of the patients had had any previous psychiatric treatment. Several of the findings are of interest here. The patients generally saw psychotherapy as the treatment of choice (88 percent), and a majority of them saw emotional factors as being important in their difficulties. A majority also felt that an understanding of ones' difficulties is significant and helpful in terms of improvement. Thus, the group as a whole seemed to display some positive attitudes and understanding of psychotherapy. *However, over a third of them thought the therapy sessions would last 30 minutes or less, 73 percent anticipated some improvement by the fifth session, and 70 percent expected treatment to last 10 sessions or less.* The latter expectations were clearly not congruent with those held by the therapists, but appear to be not too discrepant from the median length of treatment reported by most clinics. In fact, one might even say that the clients *were* accurate in their expectations, while the therapists were not! Thus, it appears likely that the mutuality of expectations between therapist and client may be related to continuation in psychotherapy. Later in this chapter, reference will also be made to studies of client expectancies and their relationship to outcome in psychotherapy.

Heller and Goldstein (1961) report a study of client dependency and therapist expectancy as relationship maintaining variables in psychotherapy. They found a significant relationship between a measure of pretherapy client-therapist attraction on the part of the client and measures of dependency. They also secured a positive relationship between *therapists' expectancy of client improvement at the fifth interview and client attraction.* While the authors viewed their findings as offering partial support for the hypothesis that therapist expectation of change is a relationship-maintaining aspect of psychotherapy, no specific data on continuation are given. Although methodologically different, the studies by Garfield and Affleck (1961) and Affleck and Garfield (1961) are pertinent here. In the original study, ratings of therapeutic prognosis were found to be related to continuation in out-patient therapy. However, when this study was replicated on a new sample (Affleck and Garfield, 1961), the positive findings secured originally did not hold up. Here again, generalizations are compounded by sample differences, therapist differences, and different rating procedures for the variables evaluated. For the present, it would appear prudent to regard unreplicated findings as at best suggestive, and as quite likely due to chance.

It is also worth mentioning here a study pertaining to out-patient drug treatment for its potentially suggestive value for psychotherapy. While several of the findings are interesting, one particularly relates to the patient's expectations about treatment and the treatment relationship (Freedman, Engelhardt, Hankoff, Glick, Kaye, Buchwald, and Stark, 1958). In this study, the doctors' notes of the initial interview were analyzed in terms of the warmth or detachment of the relationship provided by the therapist. Although those patients who dropped out of therapy did not differ from those remaining in terms of the warmth of the doctor-patient relationship provided, when the type of relationship was matched with the patients' expectations about treatment, a significant interaction was found. Patients who denied mental illness and encountered a warm relationship tended to drop out, whereas the reverse was true with those patients who accepted their illness and were exposed to a warm relationship. This study also emphasizes the importance of examining the possible interaction between patient and therapist variables as compared with the reliance solely on separate classes of variables.

In the light of what has been said, it would be of interest to know, from the point of view of the clients themselves, their reasons for breaking off from psychotherapy. One report of such an attempt is available in a small follow-up study of 12 individuals who dropped out of psychotherapy before the seventh interview (Garfield, 1963). Eleven of the twelve cases were contacted by a social worker and, among other questions, were asked why they discontinued psychotherapy. Six of the terminators gave as their reason some external difficulty, such as lack of transportation, no babysitter, and inability to get away from work. Of the remaining five, three were dissatisfied with the results of therapy or with the therapist, and two stated that they had improved. Although long-term studies with adequate samples have not been made, on the basis of this study and one other (Riess and Brandt, 1965), it appears that very few of such terminators apply for therapy elsewhere after dropping out of therapy.

We have thus reviewed a number of variables in relation to duration of stay in psychotherapy, and have commented upon some of the diffi-culties and complexities evident in securing reliable and generalizable results. Many findings do not appear to be confirmed when applied to new samples, and conditions from clinic to clinic and study to study vary. As a result, findings that have not been cross-validated on new samples have to be viewed as suggestive at best. Some potentially significant test variables also have not been very systematically explored. For example, in several of the studies reviewed, IQ has appeared to show some relationship to length of stay (Affleck and Mednick, 1959; Auld and Eron, 1953; Gibby, Stotsky, Hiler, and Miller, 1954; Hiler, 1958b). However, in most of these studies, the analyses of IQ data have been secondary to other analyses and were carried out on a smaller number of subjects than was used in the main study. The intellectual level of the subject would appear to be of some potential significance for continuation in verbal psychotherapy *as currently practiced*, although its actual predictive value would depend to some extent on the client populations served. *One would also expect to find a positive correlation between IQ and indices of social class.*

Of the variables studied, those pertaining to social class appear to have the most consistent supporting evidence. However, while this relationship does have a fair amount of empirical support, the precise reasons advanced to explain this relationship must still be viewed tentatively until more exact studies are performed. Mutuality of expectations on the part of therapist and client is one hypothesis that has some empirical support and that appears promising. The matter of differing value systems and orientations among middle-class therapists and lower-class clients has been hypothesized as a possible explanation for the results secured (Myers and Schaffer, 1958), but systematic research on this has not been available. Research on such matters and related ones, however, may be forthcoming, particularly as we are able to manipulate therapist and client variables and to become more flexible in our therapeutic approaches. One example of such experimentation on a small scale is provided in a study by Carkhuff and Pierce (1967). Four lay counselors with special training were selected to include one upper-class white, one upper-class Negro, one lower-class white, and one lower-class Negro, and each saw 16 patients distributed equally among the four classifications represented by the counselors in terms of a Latin-square design. Taped segments of the interviews were rated according to "depth of self-exploration in interpersonal process," a patient variable that has been positively correlated with outcome in psychotherapy. Race and social class of both patient and therapist were found to be significantly related to patient depth of self-exploration, and the interaction between patient and therapist variables was also significant. In general, "the patients most similar to the race and social class of the counselor involved tended to explore themselves most, while patients most dissimilar tended to explore themselves least" (p. 634). While these findings are based on only four counselors and an initial clinical interview, they are quite interesting and deserve more systematic research follow-up.

RESEARCH ON CLIENT VARIABLES AND OUTCOME IN PSYCHOTHERAPY

While the problem of continuation in psychotherapy is of some importance, it is, of course, of secondary significance to the matter of what kind of outcome is eventually secured. In fact, the assumption is usually made that a certain (frequently unspecified) amount of contact with a therapist must be made if progress in psychotherapy is to be attained. If a client discontinues therapy before the therapist believes there has been sufficient time to affect change, then such discontinuance directly influences and limits the amount of change to be expected. It is for such a reason that early or premature termination on the part of the client is frequently viewed as a failure in psychotherapy, even though there has been practically no research evaluating the outcome of therapy in such cases. It is of interest, perhaps, to point out here that various beliefs concerning psychotherapy are frequently held with relatively little attempt made to secure research data to support or refute these beliefs. Thus, for example, while most investigators have tended to view the abrupt terminator as a failure in psychotherapy, some have viewed such individuals as post hoc successes, with the belief that

they must have changed for the better or they would have returned for psychotherapy (Garfield and Kurz, 1952). As indicated, there is little research data on this point. While some investigators have reported a positive finding between length of therapy and outcome (Lorr, McNair, Michaux, and Raskin, 1962; Bailey, Warshaw, and Eichler, 1959), detailed evaluations of the outcome of early terminators have not been made. In one follow-up study of 12 terminators and 12 remainers who had been studied more intensively for another purpose, both groups stated that they were getting along quite well, and if anything, the terminators gave more favorable reports (Garfield, 1963). However, the follow-up was based on the self-reports of the clients and no before- and- after therapy measures were used.

We can now proceed to the research that has been reported on client variables and outcome in psychotherapy. At the outset, it is probably best to say something about the difficulties evident in outcome research, even though similar comments will be made in other chapters of this volume. Among the problems encountered are variations in outcome criteria, the relative significance of these criteria, variations in the type of therapy offered, variations in the training and competence of the therapists studied, and differences in the kinds of client samples treated. Such types of problems, as we have already noted, not only place limitations on the value of any specific study, but also present serious obstacles to the drawing of reliable and valid generalizations from the plethora of published studies. With this, then, as somewhat of a *caveat*, let us now look at some representative studies. For the sake of convenience, the types of studies will again be classified into a few broad categories.

A. Test Variables Related to Outcome in Psychotherapy

Like the studies previously discussed with relationship to duration of stay, a moderate number of investigations have been concerned with the relationship of psychological test patterns of clients and outcome in psychotherapy. While length of psychotherapy as determined by the number of interviews provides a reasonably clear and objective criterion, when we turn our attention to outcome we encounter fallible and variable criteria. This may account in part for an earlier conclusion by Windle (1952), in a review of prognostic studies of test findings and outcome, that the results have been far from satisfactory. In any event, let us look at some of the research since that time.

Rosenberg (1954) examined the responses to the Wechsler-Bellevue, Rorschach, and a sentence-completion technique (unspecified) of 40 patients who received psychotherapy in a VA outpatient clinic. Twenty were judged to be definitely unimproved. The protocols of the Rorschach and the sentence completion tests for half of each of the two groups of patients were then evaluated by two psychologists and rated in terms of 23 intellectual and personality variables. On seven of these variables, as well as on the Wechsler-Bellevue IQ, the two groups were significantly differentiated. The two raters were then informed of the specific variables that had differentiated the two groups of patients, and were asked to make predictions of improvement in the remaining 20 patients. Each of them was able to make at least 15 correct predictions. On the basis of the total study, it would appear that the successful patient has superior intelligence, has the ability to produce associations easily, is not rigid, has a wide range of interests, is sensitive to his environment, feels deeply, exhibits a high energy level, and is free from bodily concerns. It should be mentioned that the patients were white and ranged in age from 25 to 35 years. While this particular investigator was critical of relying simply on formal Rorschach scores, his use of clinical evaluation and prediction limits the applicability of this study to other situations utilizing other clinicians, and may account for the lack of attempts to replicate the study.

In another study, Roberts (1954) compared 11 Rorschach indices alleged to have prognostic significance for treatment with rather careful ratings of pre- and post-treatment status by three judges. None of the measures were significantly related to the outcome criteria. A somewhat similar study was reported by Rogers and Hammond (1953). Fifty patients judged to be unimproved by their therapists "in consultation with a senior psychiatrist" were compared with 59 patients judged in a similar fashion to be "slightly improved" or "improved". Ninety-nine Rorschach signs were used, but they failed to differentiate significantly between the two groups. Three types of clinical judgments of the Rorschach records by three psychologists with three to five years of Rorschach experience also failed to differentiate the groups at a significant level of confidence. Rules for prediction obtained on an empirical basis showed some limited promise for selected cases.

Barron (1953a) also attempted to secure some test correlates of response to psychotherapy in evaluating 33 patients in an out-patient clinic, most of whom had weekly therapy sessions for six months. In part, he tried to replicate the earlier study of Harris and Christiansen (1946) by using a shortened form of the Wechsler-Bellevue Scale, the MMPI and the Rorschach. He also added the Ethnocentrism Scale. His findings illustrate the not infrequent lack of agreement between studies. Whereas Harris and Christiansen obtained positive results with their Rorschach Prognostic Index, Barron secured a correlation of .00 between it and the criterion rating of judged improvement. In a similar fashion, whereas Harris and Christiansen found no relationship between improvement and intelligence test score, Barron found a correlation of .46. Barron's total group had a higher mean IQ than that in the Harris and Christiansen group with his unimproved group's mean IQ of 112 exceeding the mean of the total group used in the other study. Here again, subject differences in the two studies may account at least in part for the differences in findings. Although Harris and Christiansen state that their 53 patients were nonpsychotic, all but two were hospitalized during therapy and were characterized as suffering from a delayed recovery from physical disease, surgery, or accident. However, there appeared to be some agreement between the two studies with reference to the MMPI, with unimproved patients securing higher scores on the Paranoid and Schizophrenia Scales. As interpreted by Barron, "the patients who are most likely to get well are those who are not very sick in the first place." As also reported by Barron (1953b) in a later study, ego strength or degree of personality integration appears to be positively related to outcome in psychotherapy.

Finally, Barron found that ethnocentrism was negatively related to change in psychotherapy.

The Barron Ego Strength Scale (ES), derived from the MMPI, has also been used in a number of other studies as a possible predictor, with conflicting results. Essentially negative results have been reported by Fiske, Cartwright, and Kirtner (1964), Gallagher (1954), Getter and Sundland (1962), Sullivan et al. (1958), and Taulbee (1958). Somewhat similar results have been reported with another index of ego strength derived from the Rorschach Test, the Rorschach Prognostic Rating Scale (RPRS) (Klopfer, Kirkner, Wisham, and Baker, 1951). Although Cartwright (1958) has reported positive results with the RPRS and psychotherapy outcome and referred to the positive results in a few other studies, a recent review of studies on the relationship of the RPRS to outcome in psychotherapy by Frank (1967) finds almost an equal number of positive and negative reports in the literature. With differences in client samples, criteria of change, and type of therapy provided, such a finding is probably not surprising.

Reference can also be made to a study by Gallagher (1954) of test indicators for prognosis in client-centered therapy. He compared a group of discontinuers with two groups judged to be the least successful and the most successful in therapy. He found no differences between the groups on the Elizur Rorschach Anxiety Scale, Productivity on the Rorschach, the Mooney Problem Check List, and as already noted, on the Barron ES Scale. The groups were differentiated on the Taylor Anxiety Scale, the Depression Scale of the MMPI, and on the number of words used by the subjects in summarizing their problems on the Mooney Check List. The findings were interpreted as supporting the hypothesis that success in client-centered therapy was positively related to the amount of overt stress and amount of verbal productivity shown on the pretherapy tests. It should be noted also that this group of clients differed considerably on the MMPI from those studied by Barron (1953a) and Harris and Christiansen (1946), particularly in having lower scores on the Pa and Sc scales, which were of some prognostic value in the other two studies. Furthermore, with reference to the positive predictive value of

high MMPI Depression scores, just the opposite results were secured by Barron (1953a).

All told, and rather surprisingly, there has not been an overabundance of research on client attributes, as measured by standard psychological tests and outcome in psychotherapy. In part, this may be due to the fact that standard psychological tests have not been viewed as providing the kinds of data required for making judgments pertaining to psychotherapy. Many investigations have simply not used tests for before and after therapy measures, or have utilized a variety of rating measures or similar methods for evaluating either the client or some aspect of the psychotherapeutic interaction or process. While some of the methods devised for specific studies may conceivably be more germane to the particular hypotheses investigated, such methods do not allow for the kinds of comparisons that can be made when standard methods are used. However, it should be pointed out that even when standard tests are used, different values or cutting points are employed from sample to sample, thus limiting comparisons.

It is difficult to generalize with any degree of confidence concerning specific test patterns of clients and their predictive significance as far as outcome is concerned. As already indicated, the variability in clients, therapeutic approaches, therapists, criteria, and absolute scores makes reliable generalization rather hazardous. Even Barron's (1953a) conclusion that those who are least disturbed show the most favorable response to psychotherapy, is not consistently supported as far as the data are concerned. In this connection, it may be pertinent to call attention to some comments by Truax and Carkhuff (1967). After mentioning that some studies appear to suggest that therapy works best with those who need it least, but that the available results are inconsistent, they go on to offer a hypothesis of their own. This is that patients with the greatest "felt disturbance" and the least overt or behavioral disturbance show the greatest therapeutic improvement. They refer to several studies of their own to support their hypothesis, in which felt disturbance is measured by some self-report inventory such as the MMPI and overt behavioral disturbance is appraised by such criteria as ward behavior ratings, length of institutionalization, and the like. This, at least, is an interesting hypothesis that merits further study and which, perhaps, might help to explain some of the discordance in current research findings.

Hopefully, we should be able to improve the level of our predictions concerning outcome in psychotherapy when psychological tests are used. However, a fairly recent review of the prognostic use of psychological tests indicates that "the variables which appear to have the strongest relationship to outcome have been nontest variables: severity and duration of illness, acuteness of onset, degree of precipitating stress, etc." (Fulkerson and Barry, 1961, p. 199).

B. Other Personality Variables Related to Outcome

In addition to some of the test variables already alluded to, a number of other types of personality variables have been mentioned in the literature on psychotherapy as being related to psychotherapeutic outcome or as having some prognostic significance. These have included such aspects as motivation for therapy, discomfort, anxiety, psychological-mindedness or sophistication, lack of defensiveness, integration, and others. Additional attributes, while manifestly referring to the therapist, such as his liking for the client, still have some implication for the client, for the therapist ostensibly may like certain kinds of clients more than others. In a more general way, as indicated previously, references are also made to the clients' "suitability for psychotherapy." In this connection, some individuals are apparently perceived as "good candidates" for psychotherapy while others are considered as unsuitable for this enterprise. Freud (1950) himself believed that psychoanalysis was suited for only certain types of individuals. Since his time, a number of others have also made similar pronouncements. However, most of these assertions have never been tested empirically. Level of intelligence, as a more readily measurable attribute, has probably received more research investigation than most. However, as we have seen, the results are far from consistent because different levels of intelligence have been used in the various studies as well as different outcome criteria, different samples of subjects, different therapists, and the like. Even where therapists appear to agree on

what are viewed as positive assets for psychotherapy, they frequently are unable to make worthwhile predictions related to therapy (Garfield and Affleck, 1961). However, some studies have been carried out, with reference to selected client variables and outcome, that report positive results, and it is worth reviewing them.

Kirtner and Cartwright (1958a, 1958b) have published two studies that have attempted to relate client personality variables to outcome in client-centered therapy. Both studies were somewhat unusual in that the clients were categorized into five groups—that is, short success, 1–12 interviews; short failure, 1–12 interviews; failure zone, 13–21 interviews; long success, over 21 interviews; and long failure, over 21 interviews. Success was determined by the therapist's rating of outcome, and 26 clients were utilized in the first study. Rating scales for six personality variables were used and were based on TAT protocols and a first therapy interview. Since only one case fell into the "long-failure" category, it was not utilized in the analyses. In general, the two success groups were significantly differentiated from the two failure groups used on one to three of the personality scales. The most frequent differences were secured between the short-success group and the short-failure group, and in general the short-success group exhibited a higher level of personality integration than that descriptive of the other groups. Specifically, they were seen as being open to their impulse life, and being less confused about their sex role than the other groups. Although the long-success group is reported as being less integrated than the short-success group and as being "anxious about their impulse life and rather confused about the meaning and place of sex in their identity," none of the comparisons between the two groups are statistically significant. How specific one should be in trying to delineate the personality features of these different groups appears somewhat questionable, since the differences were not all significant, and both success groups contained four clients each. What does seem plausible is that the relatively better-integrated clients improved, with the most integrated improving rather quickly.

The second study by Kirtner and Cartwright was concerned with the client's behavior in the first therapy interview and its relation to outcome. More specifically, what was studied was the manner in which the client conceptualizes and attempts to resolve his problems. Five types of initial therapy behaviour of the client were studied, ranging from the immediate dealing "with a feeling-in-relationship problem" and the localization of a specific area or source of difficulty, to dealing with problems as if they were entirely external to the client. Clients were categorized as in the previous study, and the same kinds of therapist ratings of improvement were employed. With a few exceptions, the successful clients tended to display different initial therapy behavior than did the failures in terms of the descriptions previously given. This categorization of first client interview behavior was used in a later study of 93 clients at the University of Chicago Counseling Center, and a statistically significant correlation of .35 was secured between this measure and therapists' ratings of improvement (Fiske, Cartwright, and Kirtner, 1964).

A few findings from the study by Rogers and Dymond (1954) can also be referred to here. Working with a group ranging in age from 21 to 40 years, they found no relationship between age and positive movement in client-centered therapy, or between the initial level of adjustment of the client and his subsequent change in therapy. Women made more significant progress than men in therapy, but all the counselors except one were males. Thus it is unclear if this result is due to the sex of the subject or to the interaction with therapists of the opposite sex. There was also a suggestion that clients low in ethnocentric attitudes benefit most from therapy.

Several studies have also been reported concerning the expectancies for being helped on the part of the patient and their effect on symptom reduction or change. While such aspects of patient behavior overlap what has commonly been referred to as the "placebo response," discussed in Chapter 12, it is worth at least some brief separate mention here.

Frank and his colleagues have published several papers pertaining to client expectancies and their relation to symptom change (Frank, 1959; Frank, Gliedman, Imber, Stone, and Nash, 1959; Rosenthal and Frank, 1956). Among other things, they have asserted that the beliefs or expectancies about therapy that the patient brings to therapy may influence the results of therapy, and that the greater the distress or need for relief, the greater the expectancy or likelihood of such relief. This has received some support from other investigators. In one study, a group of control patients showed a significant correlation between their expected and perceived improvement (Goldstein, 1960), and other studies showed a positive relationship between expectancies of improvement in patients and their judged improvement (Lennard and Bernstein, 1960; Lipkin, 1954). Goldstein and Shipman (1961) also reported a positive relationship between expectancy and perceived symptom reduction, and also between expectancy and symptom intensity after the initial psychotherapeutic interview. However, in this study the relationship between expectancy and symptom reduction was a curvilinear one—that is, those patients with very high or very low expectancies for improvement showed the smallest symptom reduction. In another study (Friedman, 1963), a direct relationship between expectancy and symptom reduction was found in 43 patients after an initial evaluation interview. The symptoms associated with anxiety and depression were the ones most affected.

The matter of the client's expectations about the psychotherapy process, their relationship to the realities of psychotherapy, and their congruence with those of the therapist was discussed previously in relationship to continuation in psychotherapy. While extensive research concerning such variables and outcome has not been carried out, several recent papers suggest that the client may be helped more when therapy is consistent with his expectations (Goin, Yamamoto, and Silverman, 1965; Hoehn-Saric et al., 1964; Levitt, 1966).

Finally, it can be noted that Goldstein (1962) has provided us with a very comprehensive account of both therapist and patient expectancies in psychotherapy and their relationship to other areas of psychological theory and research. It would appear that the client's expectancies concerning psychotherapy are of some importance for both therapy continuation and outcome, and that explicit attention should be given to them at the beginning of therapy.

Certain other qualities or attributes of clients have also been investigated in relation to outcome in psychotherapy. Isaacs and Haggard (1966) utilized the TAT to secure measures for what they termed "relatability"—"the potential capacity of an individual for object relations and interpersonal relations." Utilizing different samples of subjects who received client-centered as well as other kinds of psychotherapy, they found that high relatability is related to improvement in psychotherapy. Patient attractiveness, as measured by a dichotomous rating scale, was also found to be related to outcome in a positive manner by another group of investigators (Nash, Hoehn-Saric, Battle, Stone, Imber, and Frank, 1965).

Somewhat related to the preceeding papers have been several studies that have attempted to appraise the importance of patient likability for therapy process and outcome. Stoler (1963) had raters prepare ratings of patient likability after listening to segments of tape-recorded therapy interviews. Successful clients received significantly higher likability ratings than did the less successful clients, and the level of likability remained fairly constant from early to late interviews. One other finding is also worthy of mention. Significant correlations were also secured between the likability ratings and ratings on the Experiencing Scale, one of the Rogers Process Scales. Although these two sets of ratings were done several months apart, it would appear that both were probably influenced by some common attribute or view of the good client. A subsequent study was carried out utilizing schizophrenic patients, instead of neurotic clients as was the case in the previous study, and somewhat different findings were secured (Tomlinson and Stoler, 1967). Whereas the relationship between likability and therapy process was slightly positive in the early interviews, the relationship was significantly negative during the later interviews. Furthermore, in contrast to the previous study, the results of the present one suggests that likability, if anything, is inversely related to outcome—that is, the less successful clients were better liked than the more successful ones.

Although the findings concerning the relationship of therapists' positive feelings toward clients and outcome variables are clearly inconclusive, reference will be made to some of the results in one other study. Ehrlich and Bauer (1967), in a study of psychiatric residents at the Ohio State University Hospital, found that inexperienced therapists liked their patients less than did the relatively more experienced therapists; patients who were rated either extremely anxious or non-anxious were less well liked by their therapists; and patient prognosis was positively related to patient likability. Furthermore, patients who received low ratings in terms of likability were three times more likely to be placed on multiple drug regimes than were those who received high ratings. In addition, while neither the patient's length of stay nor type of release was associated with therapist ratings of likability, the therapists' ratings of change were positively correlated with such ratings. While one would not want to overgeneralize on the basis of such results, it does appear that the therapists' feelings toward the client constitutes a variable that is related to or interacts with other potentially significant variables in psychotherapy, including client variables. The finding of a positive correlation between the therapist's liking of the client and prognostic ratings of the client has been reported previously (Garfield and Affleck, 1961), but more data are needed concerning the relationship of such ratings and objective criteria of outcome.

The matter of client-therapist similarity or complementarity has also received some research attention, although with rather conflicting results. Carson and Heine (1962) used the MMPI to compare the therapists and clients, and reported that a curvilinear relationship existed between therapist-client similarity and rated improvement. Lichtenstein (1966), and Carson and Llewellyn (1966), however, failed to replicate these findings. Lesser (1961), utilizing a Q sort, found that similarity of self-concept between counselor and client was negatively related to therapeutic progress, whereas Levinson and Kitchener (1966), utilizing a different Q sort, secured more positive findings. Using the FIRO-B scale, Sapolsky (1965) also reported a positive correlation between patient and doctor compatibility and outcome. To make matters more complicated, mention can also be made of the study by Mendelsohn and Geller (1965), who used still another measure of compatibility, the Myers-Briggs Type Indicator, and reported a curvilinear relationship with outcome measures. In addition, some partial support for the importance of client-therapist complementarity has been offered by Swenson (1967) for one personality dimension (dominance-submission), but not for another (love-hate). *While the area of client-therapist similarities or differences would appear to be a potentially important aspect of therapy for investigation, we shall have to await more definitive research findings before any really clear conclusions can be drawn.*

Some of the studies carried out in relation to the Wisconsin program of research, under the general leadership of Carl Rogers, also have some relevance for the topic under discussion. Once again, if one examines some of the different reports, somewhat opposite findings and conclusions are forthcoming. For example, in their book, Truax and Carkhuff (1967) state rather clearly their belief that the therapeutic conditions provided by the therapist—accurate empathy, nonpossessive warmth, and congruence—are the most important variables as far as change resulting from psychotherapy is concerned. When the levels of therapeutic conditions are high, presumably all other aspects, including client variables, become of less importance, and positive change is anticipated. In this connection, reference is made to one study in which a number of hospitalized patients were allowed to seek and secure psychotherapy from a number of therapists. In this project, therefore, it was possible to secure therapy tapes of a number of therapists with the same patient, and tapes of the same therapist with different patients. All in all, while this type of therapy differs somewhat from conventional psychotherapy, it does involve a psychotherapeutic type of interaction, and the results are consequently of interest. The results indicated that a therapist tended to produce somewhat similar levels of therapeutic conditions with all patients, thus implying that the patients' impact was rather secondary. A similar conclusion is drawn from a study of the initial interview behavior of two psychiatrists, which showed significant differences between them in accurate empathy and congruence, but not in nonpossesive warmth (Truax, Wargo, Frank, Imber, Battle, Hoehn-Saric, Nash, and Stone, 1966).

On the other hand, the reanalysis of the data in the Wisconsin Project directed by Kiesler (Rogers, Gendlin, Kiesler, and Truax, 1967) leads to the tenability of just the opposite interpretation. Essentially, a number of patient variables were found to be correlated with rated therapist empathy and patient-perceived congruence, as well as with positive indices of process and outcome in psychotherapy. Among the initial patient factors related in this way were high socioeducational status, high verbal intelligence, high mental health ratings on the TAT, and a generally low level of rated manifest psychotic disturbance. "This network of initial differences suggests that more integrated therapy candidates are characterized by a more favorable prognosis, a relatively higher verbal ability, and a greater expressive productivity (Rogers et al., p. 308.).''

On the basis of the material just referred to, it appears that patient variables are of some consequence in terms of both the process and outcome in psychotherapy. Clearly, as indicated earlier in this chapter, there is an interaction between the client (or client variables) and the therapist (or therapist variables) that has to be studied and understood if we are to fully comprehend the psychotherapeutic endeavor. This point of view is summarized very succinctly by Kiesler, Mathieu, and Klein in the volume on the Wisconsin Project just referred to (Rogers et al., p. 308–309):

In those cases where the patient enters therapy with a fair degree of expressive capacity and/or motivation for self-exploration, the therapist's corresponding involvement may be enhanced. That is, the more initially expressive the patient, the richer will be the material in which the therapist can anchor his empathic efforts. The more motivated the patient for the therapeutic process, the easier it will be for the therapist to become correspondingly involved in, and committed to, the relationship. The more responsive the patient, the more likely it will be that the therapist can communicate the genuineness of his concern for, and interest in, the patient as a person. On the other hand, patients lacking these capacities for therapeutic participation will generally fail to evoke similar therapist involvement. That is, the unmotivated, defensive, and reluctant patient from a different (lower) socio-economic background may not provide the therapist sufficient opportunity to deepen the relationship, and may thus severely limit the therapist's ability to communicate and function effectively. While skillful and sensitive therapists may succeed in involving even the initially reluctant patient, and more remote or superficial therapists may dampen the motivated patient's initial enthusiasm, it seems apparent from this sample that the patient's presenting capacities and motive contribute heavily to the establishment of a climate in which the therapist can function effectively.

The problem of what kinds of clients or personality attributes of clients are related to outcome in psychotherapy is clearly a complex one that does not appear to be readily answerable by single small-scale investigations. The type of clients sampled, the therapeutic approach employed, the particular sample of therapists used, and the kinds of criterion measures utilized all have to be considered in terms of what kind of generalizations can be drawn from the separate researches. Such variations in the variables under study limit replications and contribute to the disparity in the published findings. Of special importance is the criterion problem. Personality or other variables that are related to some outcome criteria appear to be unrelated to other criteria. For example, a factor analysis of changes during psychotherapy yielded factors that were predominantly associated with the methods of measurement used (Cartwright, Kirtner, and Fiske, 1963). When these same investigators attempted to explore variables that would predict changes occuring in psychotherapy, the results were not predictable from measures derived from methods that were independent of the criterion measures (Fiske, Cartwright, and Kirtner, 1964). "It seems clear that there are reliable changes associated with psychotherapy but that none of our measures of initial status or initial assets accounts for any very appreciable proportion of the variance in such changes" (p. 425).

CONCLUSIONS AND IMPLICATIONS

We have thus reviewed some of the representative literature that has been concerned with the relationship of client variables to selection for treatment and continuation and outcome in psychotherapy. The nature of the psychotherapeutic process is admittedly complex, and research in this field is beset with numerous difficulties that have been commented upon several times in the preceding pages. There is little need to repeat these comments again. It is important, however, to emphasize that the difficulties and problems mentioned in no way imply that research efforts should be discontinued, or that the problems cannot be overcome.

The work to date suggests that more comprehensive, carefully planned, large-scale, and coordinated research efforts will have to be undertaken in the future if we are to secure more reliable and meaningful answers to our questions in the area of psychotherapy.

For the time being, however, what kind of implications or tentative conclusions can we draw from the research that exists? There would at least appear to be a few that merit consideration and possible implementation in practice. In the first place, *it seems rather clear that the more conventional dynamic, long-term orientations in psychotherapy are not effective with a large number of clients of low socioeconomic status.* As has been indicated, their expectations about treatment differ markedly from those of their middle-class counterparts and from those of their therapists. Many of these individuals have significant reality problems, lack adequate information to solve or cope with some of their difficulties, and are more concerned with the here and now of their own situation. As has been indicated earlier, some attempts have been made to modify the role of the therapist (Baum and Felzer, 1964), to pay more attention to the matter of therapeutic expectations (Overall and Aronson, 1962), and to help prepare the client for psychotherapy (Hoehn-Saric et al., 1964; Truax and Carkhuff, 1967). While these appear to be steps in the right direction, we must probably go further in modifying our therapeutic approaches in working with large segments of our society. The more traditional model of long-term psychotherapy is clearly not a suitable nor realistic model for the great majority of our population, and more efficient approaches or modifications must be sought. While this model has had tremendous influence on the writing and teaching in the area of psychotherapy, in practice—as Matarazzo (in press) has so clearly stated—it has been used with a very small and highly selected segment of the population.

Another related implication of some of the findings reviewed has to do with the apparent attitudes of therapists and clinic staffs towards different groups of patients or clients. Lower-class, relatively non-verbal, and more severely disturbed clients are not well received by many therapists, and many clinics appear to reject the applications of such individuals for treatment. In contrast, verbal, intelligent, introspective, interested, and educated clients with relatively little disturbance are eagerly sought after by therapists. While therapists may feel more comfortable and receive more personal gratification from working with the latter type of client, there appears to be a problem of serious porportions in this type of situation. This is also compounded by the tendency for the more prestigious clinics and therapists to be more highly selective in the patients they treat than are those of lesser status. Furthermore, such attitudes are conveyed to students in training in a variety of ways. Attempts are made to select training cases that are "good" cases, and not infrequently supervisors who work in clinics and hospitals will disparage the "poor-therapy" cases available and contrast them with their own private cases. Thus, such differential attitudes towards types of clients may be perpetuated, as well as the view that only certain long-term therapies are really worthwhile.

Clearly, on the basis of the research findings available concerning social class and other variables, it is possible to select clients who will remain in psychotherapy and who will prove to be rewarding in many ways to the therapists involved. However, as already indicated, this will tend to exclude from therapy a large number of people who have a variety of behavioral and personality difficulties and who are in need of help. It seems decidedly unfair and socially inequitable to favor one small segment of the population and to ignore the rest because the former appear to accommodate more readily to our techniques and *our expectations*. As behavioral scientists, we should be interested in devising ever more efficient techniques that have a greater social utility.

While progress is slow, some evidence of innovation and change is apparent. Approaches that emphasize crisis intervention, activity on the part of the therapist, attention to reality problems, time limitations in therapy, home visits, and active intervention have made their appearance and may be potentially very useful (Caplan, 1964; Darbonne, 1967; Harris, Kalis, and Freeman, 1963; Jacobson, 1965; Levine, 1966). Although many of these newer approaches have not been systematically evaluated, the clinical reports of their effectiveness are quite encouraging. Mention should be made also of the recent developments in behavior therapy that provide additional techniques for dealing with a variety of behavior disorders. While I am not aware of specific studies dealing with lower-class clients, there would appear to be little reason why behavioral methods would not be applicable in such cases. At least these methods, since they focus on the client's specific complaints and provide an active role for the therapist, appear to be more in line with conventional expectations about treatment. It seems, also, that they are not as dependent on the kinds of motivation and predisposition required in insight therapies.

It is quite likely, also, that more attention will have to be paid to social or environmental variables as contrasted with essentially intrapsychic ones, and that psychotherapy or counseling will have to go hand in hand with other attempts to alleviate the individual's distress instead of being relied upon almost exclusively to modify or remake the individual. The work of Massimo and Shore (1963) in setting up a comprehensive vocationally oriented psychotherapy program for adolescent delinquent boys, is an illustration of an experimental program in which the counselor departed from a traditional role and fulfilled many different professional functions. Meeting the clients on the level of their own problems, providing a concrete vocational focus offering realistic tasks around which other services were available, as well as providing counseling support, were some of the innovations used. In a follow-up study two to three years after termination of this program, the results clearly favored those who had participated in the program over a comparable group that received no treatment (Shore and Massimo, 1966).

The setting for psychotherapy, the period of time devoted to a therapy session, and the type of counselor or therapist selected for work with special groups of clients, may also have to be modified. For example, Gould (1967), in working with a blue collar worker, relates that he had to become more informal, more directive, and more flexible concerning the length of therapy, and that he also held some sessions in a public park. The implications for therapy of the differences in intellectual background and social class between therapist and client, alluded to previously in this chapter, is also attested to by a recent study of hospital patients concerning the perceived helpfulness of others as a function of compatible intelligence levels (Keith-Spiegel and Spiegel, 1967). In general, the higher the education and intelligence level of the patient, the more he perceived psychiatrists as most helpful, and hospital aides and other patients as least helpful. The converse was true for those of lower education and intelligence levels. One patient with an IQ of 83 and an eighth-grade education is quoted as stating: "My doctor was a nice enough guy, but I never knew what the hell he was talking about." Neighborhood storefront centers staffed by "indigenous" nonprofessionals may offer some ways of bridging such gaps in communication and understanding. *What techniques or approaches will be most effective is, of course, uncertain at this point. However, it seems clear that novel attempts at innovation and experimentation are called for.* Otherwise, we will have to admit that our techniques are suited only for working with a rather selected segment of our population. As Dumont (1968) has put it: "Psychotherapy, as generally practiced, requires a patient who is verbal, insightful, and motivated, one who can delay gratification, and who, more or less, shares the values of the therapist, thereby virtually excluding the lower-class person from treatment" (p. 25). It should be added, however, that this type of practice is becoming much less common.

The research reviewed on the outcomes of psychotherapy, while containing many deficiencies and inconsistencies, also appears to have some implications for practice. It seems more likely than not that in the past *the best therapeutic results have been obtained with those clients who are the least disturbed, or who, as some have said, are in the least need of treatment.* While this is undoubtedly true of many other areas as well, it is, nevertheless, a finding to which we must give some consideration in the future. It is clearly a problem with important social implications and one that we cannot push aside. Not only must we devise more effective techniques for dealing with serious problems of personality adjustment, but *we must not find ourselves in the position of devoting most of our professional resources to working with those who may be in least need of our help.* In the past we have been overly concerned with the client who fits our modes of psychotherapy. It appears now that we are beginning to think of devising therapeutic procedures to fit the client. This is certainly one of the challenges that faces those who work in the area of psychotherapy.

REFERENCES

Adler, M. H., Valenstein, A. F., and Michaels, J. J. A mental hygiene clinic. Its organization and operation. *Journal of Nervous and Mental Disease*, 1949, **110**, 518–533.

Affleck, D. C., and Garfield, S. L. Predictive judgments of therapists and duration of stay in psychotherapy. *Journal of Clinical Psychology*, 1961, **17**, 134–137.

Affleck, D. C., and Mednick, S. A. The use of the Rorschach Test in the prediction of the abrupt terminator in individual psychotherapy. *Journal of Consulting Psychology*, 1959, **23**, 125–128.

Auld, F., Jr., and Eron, L. D. The use of the Rorschach scores to predict whether patients will continue psychotherapy. *Journal of Consulting Psychology*, 1953, **17**, 104–109.

Bailey, M. A., Warshaw, L., and Eichler, R. M. A study of factors related to length of stay in psychotherapy. *Journal of Clinical Psychology*, 1959, **15**, 442–444.

Barron, F. Some test correlates of response to psychotherapy. *Journal of Consulting Psychology*, 1953, **17**, 234–241. (a)

Barron, F. An ego-strength scale which predicts response to psychotherapy. *Journal of Consulting Psychology*, 1953, **17**, 327–333. (b)

Baum, O. E., and Felzer, S. B. Activity in initial interviews with lower class patients. *Archives of General Psychiatry*, 1964, **10**, 345–353.

Blackman, N. Psychotherapy in a Veterans Administration mental hygiene clinic. *Psychiatric Quarterly*, 1948, **22**, 89–102.

Brandt, L. W. Rejection of Psychotherapy? The discovery of unexpected numbers of pseudorejectors. *Archives of General Psychiatry*, 1964, **10**, 310–313.

Brill, N. Q., and Storrow, H. A. Social class and psychiatric treatment. *Archives of General Psychiatry*, 1960, **3**, 340–344.

Caplan, G. *Principles of preventive psychiatry.* New York: Basic Books, 1964.

Carkhuff, R. R., and Pierce, R. Differential effects of therapist race and social class upon patient depth of self-exploration in the initial clinical interview. *Journal of Consulting Psychology*, 1967, **31**, 632–634.

Carson, R. C., and Heine, R. W. Similarity and success in therapeutic dyads. *Journal of Consulting Psychology*, 1962, **26**, 38–43.

Carson R. C., and Llewellyn, C. E. Jr. Similarity in therapeutic dyads: A re-evaluation. *Journal of Consulting Psychology*, 1966, **30**, 458.

Cartwright, D. S. Success in psychotherapy as a function of certain actuarial variables. *Journal of Consulting Psychology*, 1955, **19**, 357–363.

Cartwright, D. S., Kirtner, W. L., and Fiske, D. W. Methods factors in changes associated with psychotherapy. *Journal of Abnormal and Social Psychology*, 1963, **66**, 164–175.

Cartwright, R. D. Predicting response to client-centered therapy with the Rorschach PR Scale. *Journal of Counseling Psychology*, 1958, **5**, 11–17.

Cole, N. J., Branch, C. H., and Allison, R. B. Some relationships between social class and the practice of dynamic psychotherapy. *American Journal of Psychiatry*, 1962, **118**, 1004–1012.

Darbonne, A. R. Crisis: A review of theory, practice, and research. *Psychotherapy: Theory, Research and Practice*, 1967, **4**, 49–56.

Dean, S. I. Treatment of the reluctant client. *American Psychologist*, 1958, 627–630.

Dumont, M. *The absurd healer. Perspectives of a community psychiatrist.* New York: Science House, 1968.

Ehrlich, H. J., and Bauer, M. L. Therapists' feelings toward patients and patient treatment and outcome. *Social Science and Medicine*, 1967, **1**, 283–292.

Fiske, D. W., Cartwright, D. S., and Kirtner, W. L. Are psychotherapeutic changes predictable? *Journal of Abnormal and Social Psychology*, 1964, **69**, 418–426.

Frank, G. H. A review of research with measures of ego strength derived from the MMPI and the Rorschach. *Journal of General Psychology*, 1967, **77**, 183–206.

Frank, J. D. The dynamics of the psychotherapeutic relationship. *Psychiatry*, 1959, **22**, 17–39.

Frank, J. D., Gliedman, L. H., Imber, S. D., Stone, A. R., and Nash, E. H. Patients' expectancies and relearning as factors determining improvement in psychotherapy. *American Journal of Psychiatry*, 1959, **115**, 961–968.

Freedman, N., Engelhardt, D. M., Hankoff, L. D., Glick, B. S., Kaye, H., Buchwald, J., and Stark, P. Drop-out from outpatient psychiatric treatment. *Archives of Neurology and Psychiatry*, 1958, **80**, 657–666.

Freud, S. On psychotherapy. In *Collected Papers.* Vol. I. London: Hogarth Press and the Institute of Psycho-Analysis, 1950. Pp. 249–263.

Friedman, H. J. Patient-expectancy and symptom reduction. *Archives of General Psychiatry*, 1963, **8**, 61–67.

Fulkerson, S. C., and Barry, J. R. Methodology and research on the prognostic use of psychological tests. *Psychological Bulletin*, 1961, **58**, 177–204.

Gallagher, J. J. Test indicators for therapy prognosis. *Journal of Consulting Psychology*, 1954, **18**, 409–413.

Garfield, S. L. A note on patients' reasons for terminating therapy. *Psychological Reports*, 1963, **13**, 38.

Garfield, S. L., and Affleck, D. C. An appraisal of duration of stay in outpatient psychotherapy. *Journal of Nervous and Mental Disease*, 1959, **129**, 492–498.

Garfield, S. L., and Affleck, D. C. Therapists' judgments concerning patients considered for psychotherapy. *Journal of Consulting Psychology*, 1961, **25**, 505–509.

Garfield, S. L., Affleck, D. C., and Muffley, R. A study of psychotherapy interaction and continuation in psychotherapy. *Journal of Clinical Psychology*, 1963, **19**, 473–478.

Garfield, S. L., and Kurz, M. Evaluation of treatment and related procedures in 1216 cases referred to a mental hygiene clinic. *Psychiatric Quarterly*, 1952, **26**, 414–424.

Garfield, S. L., and Wolpin, M. Expectations regarding psychotherapy. *Journal of Nervous and Mental Disease*, 1963, **137**, 353–362.

Getter, H., and Sundland, D. M. The Barron Ego Strength Scale and psychotherapeutic outcome. *Journal of Consulting Psychology*, 1962, **26**, 195.

Gibby, R. G., Stotsky, B. A., Hiler, E. W., and Miller, D. R. Validation of Rorschach criteria for predicting duration of therapy. *Journal of Consulting Psychology*, 1954, **18**, 185–191.

Gibby, R. G., Stotsky, B. A., Miller, D. R., and Hiler, E. W. Prediction of duration of therapy from the Rorschach Test. *Journal of Consulting Psychology*, 1953, 348–354.

Goin, M. K., Yamamoto, J., and Silverman, J. Therapy congruent with class-linked expectations. *Archives of General Psychiatry*, 1965, **13**, 133–137.

Goldstein, A. P. Patients' expectancies and nonspecific therapy as a basis for (un) spontaneous remission. *Journal of Clinical Psychology*, 1960, **16**, 399–403.

Goldstein, A. P. *Therapist-patient expectancies in psychotherapy.* New York: Pergamon Press, 1962.

Goldstein, A. P., and Shipman, W. G. Patient expectancies, symptom reduction and aspects of the initial psychotherapeutic interview. *Journal of Clinical Psychology*, 1961, **17**, 129–133.

Gordon, S. Are we seeing the right patients? Child guidance intake: The sacred cow. *American Journal of Orthopsychiatry*, 1965, **35**, 131–137.

Gould, R. E. Dr. Strangeclass: Or how I stopped worrying about the theory and began treating the blue-collar worker. *American Journal of Orthopsychiatry*, 1967, **37**, 78–86.

Haddock, J. N., and Mensh, I. N. Psychotherapeutic expectations in various clinic settings. *Psychological Reports*, 1957, **3**, 109–112.

Harris M. R., Kalis, B., and Freeman, E. Precipitating stress: An approach to brief therapy. *American Journal of Psychotherapy*, 1963, **17**, 465–471.

Harris, R. E., and Christiansen, C. Prediction of response to brief psychotherapy. *Journal of Psychology*, 1946, **21**, 269–284.

Heine, R. W. (Ed.) *The student physician as psychotherapist.* Chicago: The University of Chicago Press, 1962.

Heine, R. W., and Trosman, H. Initial expectations of the doctor-patient interaction as a factor in continuance in psychotherapy. *Psychiatry*, 1960, **23**, 275–278.

Heller, K., and Goldstein, A. P. Client dependency and therapist expectancy as relationship maintaining variables in psychotherapy. *Journal of Consulting Psychology*, 1961, **25**, 371–375.

Hiler, E. W. An analysis of patient-therapist compatibility. *Journal of Consulting Psychology*, 1958, **22**, 341–347. (a)

Hiler, E. W. Wechsler-Bellevue Intelligence as a predictor of continuation in psychotherapy. *Journal of Clinical Psychology*, 1958, **14**, 192–194. (b)

Hiler, E. W. The sentence completion test as a predictor of continuation in psychotherapy. *Journal of Consulting Psychology*, 1959, **23**, 544–549.

Hoehn-Saric, R., Frank, J. D., Imber, S. D., Nash, E. H., Stone, A. R., and Battle, C. C. Systematic preparation of patients for psychotherapy. I. Effects on therapy behavior and outcome. *Journal of Psychiatric Research*, 1964, **2**, 267–281.

Hollingshead, A. B., and Redlich, F. C. *Social class and mental illness: A community study.* New York: Wiley, 1958.

Hunt, R. G. Social class in mental illness: Some implications for clinical theory and practice. *American Journal of Psychiatry*, 1960, **116**, 1065–1069.

Imber, S. D., Frank, J. D., Gliedman, L. H., Nash, E. H., and Stone, A. R. Suggestibility, social class, and the acceptance of psychotherapy. *Journal of Clinical Psychology*, 1956, **12**, 341–344.

Imber, S. D., Nash, E. H., and Stone, A. R. Social class and duration of psychotherapy. *Journal of Clinical Psychology*, 1955, **11**, 281–284.

Isaacs, K. S., and Haggard, E. A. Some methods used in the study of affect in psychotherapy. In L. A. Gottschalk and A. H. Auerbach (Eds.), *Methods of research in psychotherapy.* New York: Appleton-Century-Crofts, 1966. Pp. 226–239.

Jacobson, G. F. Crisis theory and treatment strategy: Some sociocultural and psychodynamic considerations. *Journal of Nervous and Mental Disease*, 1965, **141**, 209–218.

Keith-Spiegel, P., and Spiegel, D. E. Perceived helpfulness of others as a function of compatible intelligence levels. *Journal of Counseling Psychology*, 1967, **14**, 61–62.

Kiesler, D. J. Some myths of psychotherapy research and the search for a paradigm. *Psychological Bulletin*, 1966, **65**, 110–136.

Kirtner, W. L., and Cartwright, D. S. Success and failure in client-centered therapy as a function of client personality variables. *Journal of Consulting Psychology*, 1958, **22**, 259–264. (a)

Kirtner, W. L., and Cartwright, D. S. Success and failure in client-centered therapy as a function of initial in-therapy behavior. *Journal of Consulting Psychology*, 1958, **22**, 329–333. (b)

Klopfer, B., Kirkner, F. J., Wisham, W., and Baker, G. Rorschach Prognostic Rating Scale. *Journal of Projective Techniques*, 1951, **15**, 425–428.

Kotkov, B., and Meadow, A. Rorschach criteria for predicting continuation in individual psychotherapy. *Journal of Consulting Psychology*, 1953, **17**, 16–20.

Kurland, S. H. Length of treatment in a mental hygiene clinic. *Psychiatric Quarterly Supplement*, 1956, **30**, 83–90.

Lennard, H. L., and Bernstein, A. *The anatomy of psychotherapy. Systems of communication and expectation.* New York: Columbia University Press, 1960.

Lesser, W. M. The relationship between counseling progress and empathic understanding. *Journal of Counseling Psychology*, 1961, **8**, 330–336.

Levine, R. A. Stand-Patism versus change in psychiatric clinic practice. *American Journal of Psychiatry*, 1966, **123**, 71–77.

Levinson, R., and Kitchener, H. Treatment of delinquents: Comparison of four methods for assigning inmates to counselors. *Journal of Consulting Psychology*, 1966, **30**, 364.

Levitt, E. E. Psychotherapy research and the expectation-reality discrepancy. *Psychotherapy: Theory, Research and Practice*, 1966, **3**, 163–166.

Lichtenstein, E. Personality similarity and therapeutic success: A failure to replicate. *Journal of Consulting Psychology*, 1966, **30**, 282.

Lief, H. L., Lief, V. F., Warren, C. O., and Heath, R. G. Low dropout rate in a psychiatric clinic. *Archives of General Psychiatry*, 1961, **5**, 200–211.

Lipkin, S. Clients' feelings and attitudes in relation to the outcome of client-centered therapy. *Psychological Monographs*, 1954, **68** (Whole No. 372).

Lorenzen, I. J. Acceptance or rejection by psychiatric clinics. M. A. essay, Columbia University, 1967.

Lorr, M., Katz, M. M., and Rubinstein, E. A. The prediction of length of stay in psychotherapy. *Journal of Consulting Psychology*, 1958, **22**, 321–327.

Lorr, M., McNair, D. M., Michaux, W. W., and Raskin, A. Frequency of treatment and change in psychotherapy. *Journal of Abnormal and Social Psychology*, 1962, **64**, 281–292.

Massimo, J. L., and Shore, M. F. The effectiveness of a comprehensive, vocationally-oriented psychotherapeutic program for adolescent delinquent boys. *American Journal of Orthopsychiatry*, 1963, **33**, 634–642.

Matarazzo, J. D. The practice of psychotherapy is art and not science. In A. R. Mahrer (Ed.), *Creative developments in psychotherapy*. Cleveland, Ohio: Western Reserve Press, in press.

National Center for Health Statistics. *Characteristics of Patients of Selected Types of Medical Specialists and Practitioners: United States July 1963–June 1964*. Washington, D. C., Public Health Service Publication No. 1000, Series 10, No. 28, 1966.

McNair, D. M., Lorr, M., and Callahan, D. M. Patient and therapist influences on quitting psychotherapy. *Journal of Consulting Psychology*, 1963, **27**, 10–17.

Mendelsohn, G. A., and Geller, M. H. Structure of client attitudes toward counseling and their relation to client-counselor similarity. *Journal of Consulting Psychology*, 1965, **29**, 63–72.

Myers, J. K., and Schaffer, L. Social stratification and psychiatric practice: A study of an outpatient clinic. In E. G. Jaco (Ed.) *Patients, Physicians and Illness*. Glencoe, Ill.: The Free Press, 1958.

Nash, E. H., Hoehn-Saric, R., Battle, C. C., Stone, A. R., Imber, S. D., and Frank, J. D. Systematic preparation of patients for short-term psychotherapy. II. Relations to characteristics of patient, therapist, and the psychotherapeutic process. *Journal of Nervous and Mental Disease*, 1965, **140**, 374–383.

Overall, B., and Aronson, H. Expectations of psychotherapy in lower socioeconomic class patients. *American Journal of Orthopsychiatry*, 1962, **32**, 271–272.

Paul, G. L. Strategy of outcome research in psychotherapy. *Journal of Consulting Psychology*, 1967, **31**, 109–118.

Riess, B. F., and Brandt, L. W. What happens to applicants for psychotherapy? *Community Mental Health Journal*, 1965, **1**, 175–180.

Roberts, L. K. The failure of some Rorschach indices to predict the outcome of psychotherapy. *Journal of Consulting Psychology*, 1954, **18**, 96–98.

Rogers, C. R., and Dymond, R. F. *Psychotherapy and personality change*. Chicago: University of Chicago Press, 1954.

Rogers, C. R., Gendlin, E. T., Kiesler, D. J., and Truax, C. B. (Eds.), *The therapeutic relationship and its impact*. Madison, Wisconsin: University of Wisconsin Press, 1967.

Rogers, L. S. Drop-out rates and results of psychotherapy in government-aided mental hygiene clinics. *Journal of Clinical Psychology*, 1960, **16**, 89–92.

Rogers, L. S., and Hammond, K. R. Prediction of the results of therapy by means of the Rorschach test. *Journal of Consulting Psychology*, 1953, **17**, 8–15.

Rogers, L. S., Knauss, J., and Hammond, K. R. Predicting continuation in therapy by means of the Rorschach test. *Journal of Consulting Psychology*, 1951, **15**, 368–371.

Rosenberg, S. The relationship of certain personality factors to prognosis in psychotherapy. *Journal of Clinical Psychology*, 1954, **10**, 341–345.

Rosenthal, D., and Frank, J. D. Psychotherapy and the placebo effect. *Psychological Bulletin*, 1956, **53**, 294–302.

Rosenthal D., and Frank, J. D. The fate of psychiatric clinic outpatients assigned to psychotherapy. *Journal of Nervous and Mental Disease*, 1958, **127**, 330–343.

Rubinstein, E. A., and Lorr, M. A comparison of terminators and remainers in outpatient psychotherapy. *Journal of Clinical Psychology*, 1956, **12**, 345–349.

Rudolph, C., and Cumming, J. Where are additional psychiatric services most needed? *Social Work*, 1962, **7**, 15–20.

Sapolsky, A. Relationship between patient-doctor compatibility, mutual perception, and outcome of treatment. *Journal of Abnormal Psychology*, 1965, **70**, 70–76.

Schaffer, L., and Myers, J. K. Psychotherapy and social stratification: An empirical study of practice in a psychiatric outpatient clinic. *Psychiatry*, 1954, **17**, 83–93.

Shore, M. F., and Massimo, J. L. Comprehensive vocationally oriented psychotherapy for adolescent delinquent boys: A follow-up study. *American Journal of Orthopsychiatry*, 1966, **36**, 609–615.

Siegel, N., and Fink, M. Motivation for psychotherapy. *Comprehensive Psychiatry*, 1962, **3**, 170–173.

Stoler, N. Client likability: A variable in the study of psychotherapy. *Journal of Consulting Psychology*, 1963, **27**, 175–178.

Sullivan, P. L., Miller, C., and Smelser, W. Factors in length of stay and progress in psychotherapy. *Journal of Consulting Psychology*, 1958, **22**, 1–9.

Swenson, C. H. Psychotherapy as a special case of dyadic interaction: Some suggestions for theory and research. *Psychotherapy: Theory, Research and Practice*, 1967, **4**, 7–13.

Taulbee, E. S. Relationship between certain personality variables and continuation in psychotherapy. *Journal of Consulting Psychology*, 1958, **22**, 83–89.

The New York City Committee on Mental Hygiene of the State Charities Aid Association. *The Functioning of Psychiatric Clinics in New York City.* New York, 1949.

Tomlinson, R. M., and Stoler, N. The relationship between affective evaluation and ratings of therapy process and outcome in schizophrenics. *Psychotherapy: Theory, Research and Practice*, 1967, **4**, 14–18.

Truax, C. B., and Carkhuff, R. R. *Toward effective counseling and psychotherapy.* Chicago: Aldine, 1967.

Truax, C. B., Wargo, D. G., Frank, J. D., Imber, S. D., Battle, C. C., Hoehn-Saric, R., Nash, E. H., and Stone, A. R. The therapist's contribution to accurate empathy, non-possessive warmth, and genuiness in psychotherapy. *Journal of Clinical Psychology*, 1966, **22**, 331–334.

White, A. M., Fichtenbaum, L., Cooper, L., and Dollard, J. Physiological focus in psychiatric interviews. *Journal of Consulting Psychology*, 1966, **30**, 363.

Whitely, J. M., and Blaine, G. B. Jr. Rorschach in relation to outcome in psychotherapy with college students. *Journal of Consulting Psychology*, 1967, **31**, 595–599.

Windle, C. Psychological tests in psychopathological prognosis. *Psychological Bulletin*, 1952, **49**, 451–482.

9

RESEARCH ON CERTAIN THERAPIST INTERPERSONAL SKILLS IN RELATION TO PROCESS AND OUTCOME[1]

CHARLES B. TRUAX
UNIVERSITY OF CALGARY

KEVIN M. MITCHELL
UNIVERSITY OF ARKANSAS

Research efforts to isolate variables in the therapeutic process that effectively alter maladaptive client behavior must involve the *person* of the therapist. Whether we call him a therapist, a counselor, a doctor, a social worker, a priest, an educator, or simply a "helping person," he is officially employed as the agent or catalyst for change. Effective implementation of specific techniques must rest on his personal qualities. He is basic to the psychosocial endeavor to change the patient *for the better*. Throughout this handbook, much emphasis is given to particular techniques or procedures that are useful for inducing positive behavioral change in people. These techniques and procedures do not occur in pure form, but instead are grafted onto the existing qualities of the human being who serves as a change agent.

Obviously, the therapist is involved in transactions or interactions with the particular individuality of the client. As a result, therapist qualities will fluctuate somewhat as he interacts with different clients or patients. Just as each man is a different father to each of his children,

[1] The authors are indebted to Drs. Herbert Fine and John Pelosi for their assistance. The chapter was supported, in part, through NIMH Grant 12306-02 and by a Research and Training Center Division Grant (RT-13) from the Social and Rehabilitation Service, Department of Health, Education, and Welfare, Washington, D. C.

a different teacher to each of his students, and a different friend to each of his friends, so he will also be a different therapist to each of his patients. From a scientific point of view, the complexity of the transactional or interactional nature of the therapeutic endeavor seems at first glance to place insurmountable barriers to effective research. To gain precise scientific information and to utilize it effectively in practice would require moment-to-moment monitoring and feedback of both therapist and patient on a relatively large number of variables. In other words, human relationships are infinitely complex and, therefore, so are therapeutic relationships. Not only is there tremendous variability in clients, but there is also tremendous variability in therapists. When these two greatly varying components of the therapeutic interaction are brought together, the variability is even greater. This circumstance would seem to make impossible any attempt at precise, scientific research. But despite the methodological problems this introduces, it has been possible to identify certain prepotent therapist variables or qualities that cut across most theoretical models of therapy. Some of these identified therapist qualities have been related to both the process and the outcome of the therapeutic relationship. They will be discussed in this chapter.

Initially, this chapter was intended as a review of a number of therapist qualities or characteristics, such as the A–B categorization, therapist-client similarity, expert knowledge, experience, sex, and social class, which were thought to contribute to the therapeutic process and particularly to client outcome. It soon became apparent that such an undertaking was herculean in nature and would result in a separate book rather than a single chapter.

A review of the literature on the A–B categorization and therapist-client similarity, for example, suggested that we could take one of two approaches with respect to these variables. Either we could catalog the major studies in a relatively unintegrated fashion, or report that only two very simple-minded generalizations can be made at this time. As far as the A–B studies are concerned, the findings are often contradictory, but there seems to be a thread running through these studies suggesting that there is "something" about A and B therapists that leads to positive change in some kinds of clients, but that we have no idea what the A–B categories actually measure nor what there is about these categories that lead to client change.

Again, as far as therapist-client similarity is concerned, we could have catalogued a host of contradictory findings or reported simply that *perhaps* there is a curvilinear relationship between therapist-client similarity and positive outcome. The difficulty, however, is that this generalization depends entirely upon which therapist-client dimension we are talking about, and the fact is that most of the measures used are so diverse and unrelated from study to study that even that generalization is relatively meaningless.

As far as other therapist variables were concerned, it quickly became apparent to us that we were assuming that such variables are unitary when, in fact, they are not. Kiesler (1966) cautioned against the assumption that therapists are homogeneous. He based his concern on a large number of studies (summarized by Carkhuff and Berenson, 1967; Truax and Carkhuff, 1967; and Truax and Mitchell, 1968), which clearly demonstrated that some therapists produce positive client change, but that the majority of therapists either effect no change or client deterioration. Analogously, just as therapists are not unitary, neither are specific therapist variables. Therapists who are highly empathic, warm, and genuine, and effect client growth, are going to be affected differently by their experiences than therapists who are low on these conditions and effect either no change or client decline. Studying therapist experience as an independent variable across both groups of therapists obviously would mask the differential effect of experience. The same is true of most other therapist variables. Therefore, in our opinion, most if not all of the research dealing with therapist characteristics needs to be re-done. Moreover, much of that literature and the data dealing with counselor or therapist personality are yet to be related to client benefit. For example, a good deal of work has been based on supervisors' judgments of trainee competence. Unfortunately, supervisor judgments are highly variable and, in general, have not been related to the trainees' actual effects on clients.

We therefore decided to focus on certain interpersonal skills that have been systematically shown to be related to client outcome. This chapter, then, will be more tightly focused than originally intended. We will briefly review the earlier findings, but our major effort will be to refine some of our previous speculations about these interpersonal skills and report those studies completed since the last review (Truax and Mitchell, 1968). Throughout, we have kept outcome in clear view. In our opinion, process studies are important if and only if the process variables can be related to positive or negative client change. Psychotherapy is meant to be a change-inducing process; if client change is not central to the research, then studies are wasteful of precious energy and money.

FOR BETTER OR FOR WORSE

In spite of phenomenal growth in the field of therapeutic practice, there exists a considerable and growing amount of evidence that seems to suggest that counseling or psychotherapy is ineffective (Eysenck, 1952).

After a careful review of the relevant research literature dealing with the effects of counseling and psychotherapy, Truax and Carkhuff (1967) concluded that unfortunately Eysenck was essentially correct in saying that the *average* counseling and psychotherapy, as it is currently practiced, does not result in average client improvement greater than that observed in persons who receive no special counseling or psychotherapy treatment. Thus, in spite of the inclusion of questionable data in his early review and his indiscriminate pooling of data from reports with divergent criteria, Eysenck's general conclusion seems to have been confirmed by more recent and more adequately controlled research investigation. As Frank (1961) and others have noted, statistical studies consistently report that about two thirds of neurotic patients are improved immediately after treatment regardless of the type of psychotherapy received, but that the same improvement rate also has been found for those persons who have not received psychotherapy.

However, there also exist some relatively well-controlled studies which show that certain counselors or therapists produce beneficial effects beyond those observed in equivalent control groups. Thus, in spite of the overwhelming evidence with thousands of cases that the average counselor or therapist is not significantly more helpful in producing improvement beyond that observed in persons receiving no treatment, there are specific studies, involving specific therapists, that demonstrate positive effects of counseling and psychotherapy. In fact, a careful reexamination of the evidence reported by Eysenck (1952) and Levitt (1957) shows the same pattern. Their overall average improvement rates, which were almost identical for treatment and no treatment, were obtained by pooling studies reporting markedly different improvement rates for different therapists (Matz, 1929; Ross, 1936).

After a review of virtually all published material dealing with the effectiveness of counseling and psychotherapy, Truax and Wargo (1966), Truax and Carkhuff (1967), and Truax and Mitchell (1968) concluded that (1) the therapeutic endeavor is, on the average, quite ineffective; (2) counseling or therapy itself is a nonunitary phenomenon; (3) some counselors and therapists are significantly helpful, while others are significantly harmful, with a resulting average helpfulness not demonstrably better than the average of no professional help; (4) through close examination of existing theories and clinical writings, it is possible to identify therapeutic ingredients likely to lead to helpful and to harmful client outcomes, and, through research, to identify such ingredients; (5) it is possible to translate the research findings into training and practice; and (6) it is therefore possible to markedly enhance the average effectiveness of counseling and psychotherapy by increasing the number of helpful counselors or therapists and decreasing the number of psychonoxious or harmful practitioners.

BRIEF DEFINITIONS

The reader is probably aware of the work previously reported by Truax and his co-workers from 1962 to the present with respect to the significant and positive relationships that have been demonstrated between positive client change and at least certain minimal levels of accurate empathic understanding, nonpossessive warmth, and genuineness. These therapist conditions have been defined and their relationships to outcome delineated in a large number of studies that have been previously summarized (Truax and Carkhuff, 1967; Truax and Mitchell, 1968). We would first like to briefly define these therapist interpersonal skills that have been related significantly to client growth, present a synopsis of the past research, expand on the clinical implications of these skills, and then close with a detailed review of the more recent literature.

Three characteristics of an effective therapist emerge from the divergent viewpoints: (1) an effective therapist is nonphony, nondefensive, and authentic or *genuine* in his therapeutic encounter; (2) an effective therapist is able to provide a nonthreatening, safe, trusting, or secure atmosphere through his own acceptance, positive regard, love, valuing, or *nonpossessive warmth*, for the client; and, (3) an effective therapist is able to understand, "be with," "grasp the meaning of," or have a high degree of *accurate empathic understanding* of the client on a moment-by-moment basis. These ingredients of the psychotherapeutic relationship are aspects of human encounters that cut across the parochial theories of psychotherapy and appear to be common elements in a wide variety of psychoanalytic, client-centered, eclectic, or learning-theory approaches to psychotherapy.

PAST STUDIES

Research into the effective role of *therapist's accurate empathy*, *nonpossessive warmth*, and *genuineness* in the helping relationships grew out of both the pioneering research work of Whitehorn and Betz at Johns Hopkins Hospital (Betz, 1963; Whitehorn, 1964; Whitehorn and Betz, 1954) and the theoretical work of Carl Rogers (1967). Whitehorn and Betz's now-classic contribution was a retrospective study of seven psychiatrists who had an improvement rate of 75 percent in their schizophrenic patients, as contrasted to seven other psychiatrists of similar training who had an improvement rate of only 27 percent. Their evidence indicated that

the successful therapists were warm and attempted to understand the patient in a personal, immediate, and idiosyncratic way; whereas the less successful therapists tended to relate to the patient in a more impersonal manner, focusing upon psychopathology and a more external kind of understanding. In Betz's further delineation of successful and unsuccessful therapists (1963), the descriptions were consistent, although not identical, with the three characteristics enumerated in this chapter: empathic understanding of the patient, nonpossessive warmth for the patient, and therapist genuineness or authenticity.

From a purely client-centered viewpoint, an early study (Halkides, 1958), showed that clients rated most successful received significantly higher therapist-offered conditions of empathy, unconditional positive regard, and self-congruence than clients rated least successful. Although Hart (1960) could not replicate these results, this may have been due to the fact that the scales used in the two studies were global in nature and relied too heavily on raters' judgments exercised independently of the scales.

Studies Comparing Differential Levels of the Core Conditions

The four-year study of psychotherapy with 16 hospitalized schizophrenics conducted at the University of Wisconsin under the leadership of Rogers, Truax, Gendlin, and Kiesler, has yielded a number of studies (Rogers, 1962; Truax, 1963; Truax and Carkhuff, 1963; Truax and Carkhuff, 1967; and Rogers, Gendlin, Kiesler, and Truax, 1967). Findings from these reports indicate that (a) patients receiving psychotherapy and those receiving control conditions showed little difference in average constructive personality change and, particularly, no difference in subsequent hospitalization, but that (b) patients whose therapists offered high levels of nonpossessive warmth, genuineness, and accurate empathic understanding showed significant positive personality and behavior change on a wide variety of indices, and (c) patients whose therapists offered relatively low levels of these interpersonal skills during therapy exhibited deterioration in personality and behavioral functioning. The evidence thus indicated that the three central therapeutic ingredients were predictive of outcome, and that, since in the samples studied the number of therapists offering high levels of these conditions approximated the number offering low levels, the average therapy patient outcome was not markedly different from that of the average patient in the control group.

Truax, Carkhuff, and Kodman (1965) studied 40 hospitalized mental patients, all relatively chronic, who were given group therapy sessions twice weekly over a three-month, time-limited period. Those patients receiving high levels of accurate empathy showed improvement equal to, or greater than, that of the patients receiving relatively low levels of accurate empathy on all subscales of the Minnesota Multiphasic Personality Inventory (MMPI), which was administered pre- and post-therapy. Statistically significant differences occurred on the Pt scale, the Sc scale, and the Welsh Anxiety Index obtained from the MMPI.

The data on the therapist's genuineness were, surprisingly, in direct opposition to the prediction, although the data on nonpossessive warmth came out much like the data with communicated accurate empathy. In this study and in the Johns Hopkins study (to be discussed later), the three conditions were not all positively correlated. In the Hopkins study, warmth was negatively correlated with empathy and genuineness and, therefore, negatively related to outcome. In the present study, genuineness was negatively correlated with warmth and empathy and, therefore, negatively related to outcome. The data thus suggests that when two conditions of the therapeutic triad are highly related but the third is negatively related, then the prediction of outcome should be based on the two that are most highly related.

Studying 160 hospitalized patients, who met for only 24 sessions over a three-month period, Truax and Wargo (1967b) secured data indicating that significant differences in improvement favoring patients receiving relatively high levels of empathy, warmth, and genuineness combined, were obtained on Q-Sort measures of self-concept, the Welsh Anxiety Index, the MMPI Subscales of Mf and Sc, and particularly on time spent out of the hospital during a one-year follow-up.

In a study of 80 institutionalized juvenile delinquents receiving three months of group counseling, Truax and Wargo (1967a) reported very similar but stronger findings again indicating a significant association between the level of accurate empathy, nonpossessive warmth, and therapist genuineness offered by the group counselor, and the degree and direction of behavioral and personality change occurring in the juvenile delinquents.

Replicating the same basic design and study on a population of 80 outpatients receiving group psychotherapy, Truax and Wargo (1969) obtained essentially similar significant findings for all conditions combined. When accurate empathy, nonpossessive warmth and genuineness were analyzed separately, the data suggested that nonpossessive warmth in particular, and genuineness to a slightly lesser extent, were more critical than accurate empathy for outpatients in group therapy. In contrast to the earlier reported findings concerning deteriorative effects of low therapeutic conditions with inpatient populations, the findings from the group therapy study with outpatients suggested very little evidence of absolute deterioration from pre- to posttherapy. However, since spontaneous improvement is relatively frequent with outpatients, the effects of low conditions might be expected to reduce spontaneous improvement rather than to result in absolute deterioration.

A cross validation study of 40 outpatients treated in individual psychotherapy by resident psychiatrists at the Phipps Psychiatric Clinic at Johns Hopkins (Truax, Wargo, Frank, Imber, Battle, Hoehn-Saric, Nash, and Stone, 1966a) indicated greater improvement on two overall measures for patients seen by therapists offering high levels of combined accurate empathy, nonpossessive warmth and genuineness, in comparison with patients receiving relatively lower levels of these combined conditions. When the specific conditions of accurate empathy, nonpossessive warmth, and genuineness were analyzed separately, the data indicated identical findings for empathy and genuineness, but a reversed tendency for nonpossessive warmth, again suggesting that when one of the conditions is negatively related to the other two, predictions of outcome should be based on the two that are most highly related.

TABLE 9.1 An Overview of Findings on the Therapeutic Effectiveness of Accurate

Study	Type of Treatment (Group or Individual)	Type of Client	Number of Clients	Specific Outcome Measures Favoring Hypothesis
Truax (1963)	Ind	Hospital	28	35
Truax, Wargo, Frank, Imber Battle, Hoehn-Saric, Nash, and Stone (1966a)	Ind	Outpatient	40	2
Truax and Wargo (1967b)	Grp	Hospital	160	20
Truax and Wargo (1967a)	Grp	Delinquent	80	18
Dickenson and Truax (1966)	Grp	College Counselees	48	5
Truax, Wargo and Silber (1966)	Grp	Delinquent	70	13
Carkhuff and Truax (1965b)	Grp	Hospital	150	3
Truax, Silber, and Wargo (1966b)	Grp	Hospital	74	3
Aspy (1965)	Grp	Elementary Students	120	
Truax (1968c)	Grp	Hospital	30	
Hansen, Moore, and Carkhuff (1968)	Grp	High School Students	70	1
Bozarth and Renzaglia (1968)	Ind	Mental Retardates	40	3
Truax and Wargo (1969)	Grp	Outpatient	80	21
Truax (1969a)	Ind	Hospital	32	1
Total			992	125

Empathy, Nonpossessive Warmth and Genuineness: All Measures of Outcome

Specific Outcome Measures Against Hypothesis	Specific Outcome Measures Significantly Favoring Hypothesis ($p<0.05$)	Specific Outcome Measures Significantly Against Hypothesis ($p<0.05$)	Overall Combined Outcome Measures Favoring Hypothesis	Overall Combined Outcome Measures Against Hypothesis	Overall Combined Outcome Measures Significantly Favoring Hypothesis ($p<0.05$)	Overall Combined Outcome Measures Significantly Aagainst Hypothesis ($p<0.05$)
10	16	0	2	0	2	0
1	0	0	2	0	2	0
7	6	0	1	0	1	0
1	13	0	1	0	1	0
0	5	0				
0	7	0	1	0	1	0
0	3	0	1	0	1	0
0	3	0	1	0	1	0
			1	0	1	0
			1	0	1	0
0	1	0				
12	0	1	0	1	0	0
2	12	0				
0	0	0				
—	—	—	—	—	—	—
33	66	1	11	1	11	0

TABLE 9.2 Findings on the Therapeutic

Study	Type of Treatment (Group or Individual)	Type of Client	Number of Clients	Specific Outcome Measures Favoring Hypothesis
Truax (1961b)	Ind	Hospital	8	
Truax (1963)	Ind	Hospital	14	
Truax (1963)	Ind	Outpatient	14	
Truax (1962d)	Ind	Hospital	14	
Truax, Wargo, Frank, Imber, Battle, Hoehn-Saric, Nash and Stone (1966a)	Ind	Outpatient	40	2
Truax, Carkhuff, and Kodman (1965)	Grp	Hospital	40	16
Truax and Wargo (1967b)	Grp	Hospital	160	18
Truax and Wargo (1967a)	Grp	Delinquent	80	18
Truax (1966a)	Grp	Hospital Delinquent		
Truax (1965a)	Grp	Rehab Students	168	8
Truax (1968b)	Ind	Rehab Students	144	8
Hansen, Moore, and Carkhuff (1968)	Ind	High School Students	70	1
Stoffer (1968)	Ind	Elementary Students	35	3
Truax and Wargo (1969)	Grp	Outpatient	80	6
Totals			1099	80

Effectiveness of Accurate Empathy

Specific Outcome Measures Against Hypothesis	Specific Outcome Measures Significantly Favoring Hypothesis ($p < 0.05$)	Specific Outcome Measures Significantly Against Hypothesis ($p < 0.05$)	Overall Combined Outcome Measures Favoring Hypothesis	Overall Combined Outcome Measures Against Hypothesis	Overall Combined Outcome Measures Significantly Favoring Hypothesis ($p < 0.05$)	Overall Combined Outcome Measures Significantly Against Hypothesis ($p < 0.05$)
			1	0	1	0
			2	0	2	0
			1	0	1	0
			1	0	1	0
1	0	0	2	0	2	0
0	3	0				
9	3	0	1	0	1	0
1	13	0	1	0	1	0
			1	0	1	0
0	0	0				
0	0	0				
0	1	0				
1	2	0	1	0	1	0
17	2	0				
—	—	–	—	–	—	–
29	24	0	11	0	11	0

TABLE 9.3 Findings on the Therapeutic

Study	Type of Treatment (Group or Individual)	Type of Client	Number of Clients	Specific Outcome Measures Favoring Hypothesis
Truax (1963)	Ind	Hospital	14	
Truax, Wargo, Frank, Imber, Battle, Hoehn-Saric, Nash and Stone (1966a)	Ind	Outpatient	40	2
Truax, Carkhuff, and Kodman (1965)	Grp	Hospital	40	0
Truax and Wargo (1967b)	Grp	Hospital	160	16
Truax and Wargo (1967a)	Grp	Delinquent	80	17
Truax (1966a)	Grp	Hospital	40	
		Delinquent	40	
Hansen, Moore, and Carkhuff (1968)	Grp	High School Students	70	1
Truax and Wargo (1969)	Grp	Outpatient	80	18
Totals			564	54

TABLE 9.4 Findings on the Therapeutic

Study	Type of Treatment (Group or Individual)	Type of Client	Number of Clients	Specific Outcome Measures Favoring Hypothesis
Truax (1963)	Ind	Hospital	14	
Truax (1963)	Ind	Outpatient	14	
Truax, Wargo, Frank, Imber, Battle, Hoehn-Saric, Nash, and Stone (1966a)	Ind	Outpatient	40	3
Truax, Carkhuff, and Kodman (1965)	Grp	Hospital	40	16
Truax and Wargo (1967b)	Grp	Hospital	160	17
Truax and Wargo (1967a)	Grp	Delinquent	80	17
Truax (1966a)	Grp	Hospital	40	
		Delinquent	40	
Truax (1968a)	Grp	Rehab Students	168	8
Truax (1968b)	Ind	Rehab Students	144	8
Hansen, Moore, and Carkhuff (1968)	Grp	High School Students	70	1
Stoffer (1968)	Ind	Elementary Students	35	2
Truax and Wargo (1969)	Grp	Outpatient	80	21
Totals			925	93

Effectiveness of Genuineness

Specific Outcome Measures Against Hypothesis	Specific Outcome Measures Significantly Favoring Hypothesis ($p<0.05$)	Specific Outcome Measures Significantly Against Hypothesis ($p<0.05$)	Overall Combined Outcome Measures Favoring Hypothesis	Overall Combined Outcome Measures Against Hypothesis	Overall Combined Outcome Measures Significantly Favoring Hypothesis ($p<0.05$)	Overall Combined Outcome Measures Significantly Against Hypothesis ($p<0.05$)
			2	0	2	0
1	0	0	2	0	2	0
16	0	5				
11	4	0	1	0	0	0
1	13	0	1	0	1	0
			1	0	1	0
0	1	0				
5	2	1				
—	—	—	—	—	—	—
34	20	6	7	0	6	0

Effectiveness of Nonpossessive Warmth

Specific Outcome Measures Against Hypothesis	Specific Outcome Measures Significantly Favoring Hypothesis ($p<0.05$)	Specific Outcome Measures Significantly Against Hypothesis ($p<0.05$)	Overall Combined Outcome Measures Favoring Hypothesis	Overall Combined Outcome Measures Against Hypothesis	Overall Combined Outcome Measures Significantly Favoring Hypothesis ($p<0.05$)	Overall Combined Outcome Measures Significantly Against Hypothesis ($p<0.05$)
			2	0	2	0
			1	0	1	0
0	0	0	0	2	0	1
0	3	0				
10	3	0	1	0	0	0
1	13	0	1	0	1	0
			1	0	1	0
0	0	0				
0	0	0				
0	1	0				
2	2	0	1	0	1	0
2	12	0				
—	—	—	—	—	—	—
15	34	0	7	2	6	1

Studies Comparing Treated and Control Groups

The above studies, taken together, support the theoretical view that the level of therapist accurate empathy, nonpossessive warmth, and genuineness are related to constructive change in patients. Still, the research reported above deals with relatively successful and relatively unsuccessful cases, rather than comparisons with control groups receiving no psychotherapy. Eysenck (1952) for one has insisted on the value of comparisons with control groups by suggesting that even under the best conditions, psychotherapy might not be significantly superior to no treatment. A number of studies have now been completed utilizing control groups.

The Wisconsin study, involving 14 schizophrenics receiving individual psychotherapy and 14 carefully matched control patients (Truax and Carkhuff, 1963; Truax, 1963), found an overall significant difference in psychological functioning among patients receiving high conditions, patients receiving low conditions, and control patients. In terms of the number of patients at or above the median change in psychological functioning, the control group had a rough 50–50 split; *all* patients in the group receiving low levels of conditions were below the median; and six of the eight patients receiving high conditions showed positive change. Finally, the findings indicated that patients receiving high conditions in psychotherapy spent significantly more time out of the hospital than either the control group or patients receiving low conditions in psychotherapy, while patients who received low conditions in psychotherapy did not differ from the control population.

Working with a group of college underachievers, Dickenson and Truax (1965) found that those students receiving group counseling showed significant improvement in grade-point average over those students who did not receive counseling. One of the more striking findings from that study was that after therapy the total group of students receiving counseling functioned at the level predicted by their college entrance exam scores, and were thus no longer "underachievers," while the control population continued to achieve college grades at a level significantly below their predicted level.

A further study (Truax, Wargo, and Silber, 1966) involving juvenile delinquents in group counseling indicated that on all 12 measures obtained pre- and posttherapy, the delinquents receiving high conditions in group psychotherapy showed improvement significantly beyond that seen in the control group. Of particular importance is the fact that not only did the overall differences in the amount of time spent out of the institution significantly favor the delinquents who had received high conditions in group therapy, but the superiority over the controls extended throughout a follow-up of one year.

Summary

These studies taken together suggest that therapists or counselors who are accurately empathic, nonpossessively warm in attitude, and genuine, are indeed effective. Also, these findings seem to hold with a wide variety of therapists and counselors, regardless of their training or theoretic orientation, and with a wide variety of clients or patients, including college underachievers, juvenile delinquents, hospitalized schizophrenics, college counselees, mild to severe outpatient neurotics, and the mixed variety of hospitalized patients. Further, the evidence suggests that these findings hold in a variety of therapeutic contexts and in both individual and group psychotherapy or counseling.

Since, in reviewing any research findings, there is a natural tendency to spend more time and space discussing positive results than ambiguous results, it is useful to attempt to summarize both positive and negative findings in tabular form. An attempt to provide such overall information is presented in Tables 9.1, 9.2, 9.3, and 9.4, where the results from all studies known to the authors—published and unpublished—using the research scales are tabulated. Further, the studies themselves are arranged in order of their chronological sequence, with the earliest complete study at the top of the table and the most recent study toward the bottom.

Perhaps a clearer idea of the impact of accurate empathy, nonpossessive warmth, and genuineness can be obtained by looking at the percentage of cases in different categories of change from pre- to posttherapy. If we take the

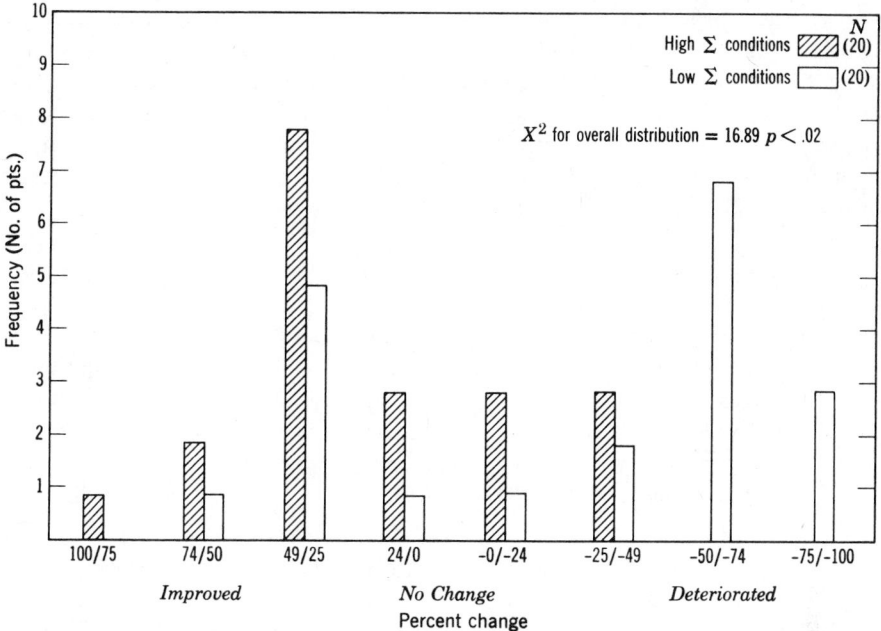

Figure 9.1 Distribution in outcome measures: Number of cases changing in higher versus lower sum of conditions for Johns Hopkins outpatients.

single individual who showed the greatest change and call that 100 percent, we can then calculate the change shown by each other individual client or patient by showing a percentage of that 100 percent change. In the data that will be presented, only measures that showed significant discriminations were used.

Figure 9.1 shows the distribution of outcome measures from the Johns Hopkins study cited earlier (Truax, Wargo, Frank, Imber, Battle,

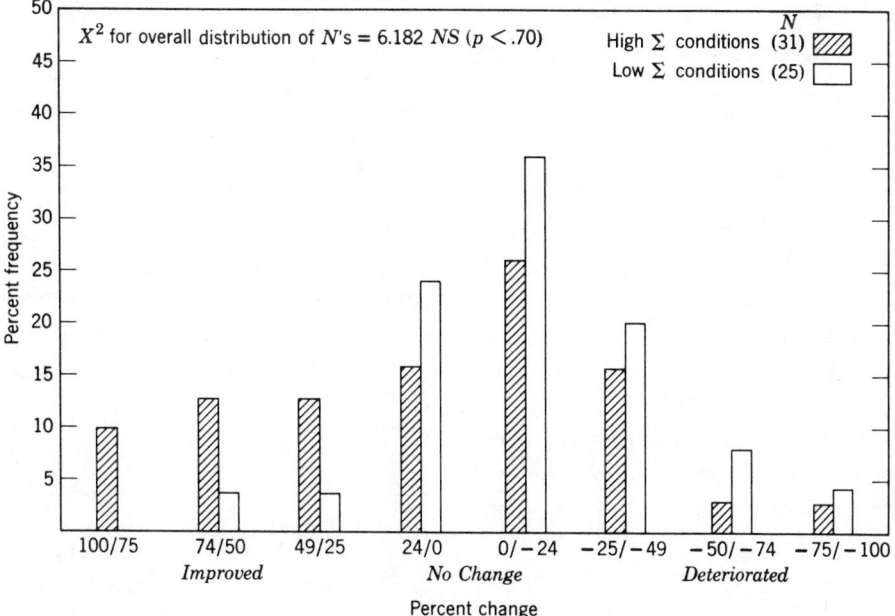

Figure 9.2 Distributions in outcome measures: Percent of cases changing in higher versus lower sum conditions for outpatients in group therapy.

Hoehn-Saric, Nash, and Stone, 1966a) combining in Z scores the therapist's global improvement scale and the patient global improvement scale. An overall chi square ($X^2 = 16.89$, $p < .02$) indicated that the distributions of patients receiving high and low levels of the combined conditions were significantly different. As can be seen, the patients seen by therapists low in accurate empathy, nonpossessive warmth, and genuineness account for the vast majority of the deteriorated cases, while therapists high in these conditions account for the majority of the benefited and the "no-change" patients.

Figure 9.2 shows a similar distribution for outpatients in group therapy (Truax and Wargo, 1969). Although the trend is in the same direction, the difference in distributions was not significant ($X^2 = 6.182$, $p < .70$). In this case the outcome measures were obtained from the MMPI by summing the Z scores representing the clinical scales (Hs, D, Hy, Pd, Pa, Pt, Sc, and Si).

Figure 9.3 indicates the distributions on change measures after summing the Z scores for change on the Q Sort (self-adjustment, self-expert correlation, ideal adjustment, the discrepancy between ideal and expert, and the

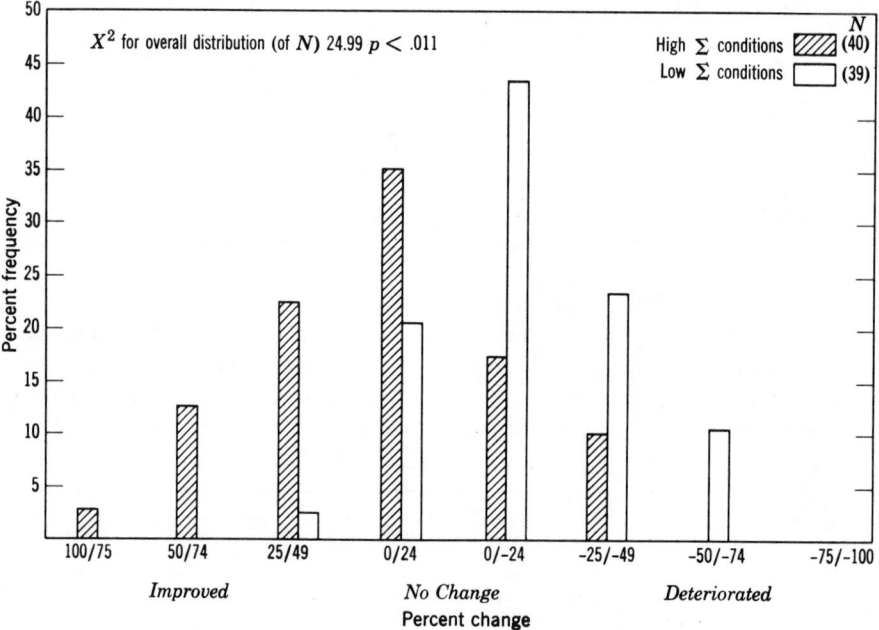

Figure 9.3 Distributions in outcome measures: Percent of cases changing in higher versus lower sum of conditions for juvenile delinquents.

correlation between self and ideal-self concepts), several scales from the Minnesota Counseling Inventory (Constructive Personality Change Index, FR, SR, R, and L), the Palo Alto Group Therapy Scale, and time out of institution during the one year follow-up (Truax and Wargo, 1967a). In this case, juvenile delinquents seen by therapists high in empathy, warmth, and genuineness tended to account for the vast bulk of the improved cases, whereas therapists low in these conditions accounted for the overwhelming majority of patients showing deterioration. The two distributions were significantly different ($X^2 = 24.99$, $p < .001$).

Finally, Figure 9.4 shows the distributions of outcome measures for control versus treated groups of the same juvenile delinquents seen in group therapy (Truax and Wargo, 1967a). Again, differences in distributions were significant ($X^2 = 17,97$, $p < .02$). Here the sum of Minnesota Counseling Inventory (FR, C), the Q Sort (self-adjustment, self-expert correlation and self-ideal correlation), and time out of institution during the one-year follow-up was used as the outcome measures after obtaining a mean Z score. Again the bulk of the deterioration was accounted for by low conditions, and the bulk of improvement was attributable almost solely to high conditions therapy.

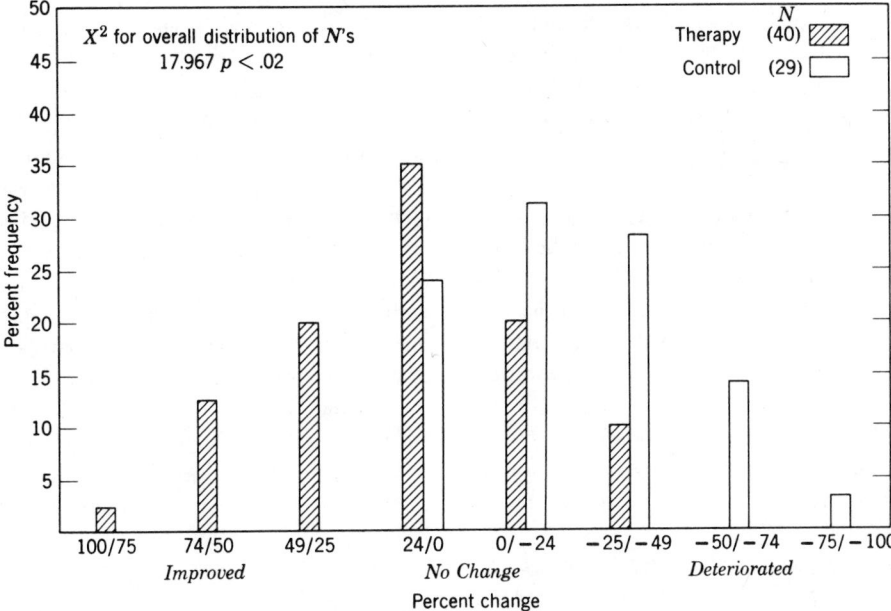

Figure 9.4 Distribution in outcome measures: Percent of cases changing in therapy versus control groups for juvenile delinquents.

It would therefore appear that, taken together, the evidence suggests that low levels of accurate empathy, nonpossessive warmth, and genuineness are important factors leading to deterioration. Similarly, extreme improvement appears to be very strongly related to high levels of these therapeutic conditions.

DEFINITIONS: THE THERAPIST'S INTERPERSONAL SKILLS

We would like to examine more closely the interpersonal skills that have been related to client outcome. Part of the discussion is based on "hard" data, but a significant portion is based on clinical intuitions. As researchers, we do not often have the opportunity to let our clinical experience and intuitions dominate our writing. We hope the reader will enjoy the opportunity with us.

It is often difficult to separate qualities of a therapist that can be most accurately described as personality characteristics from other qualities that can best be conceptualized as interpersonal skills. It is not even clear that there is such a thing as "personality" that transcends roles and social contacts. Some theorists have considered therapist warmth, genuineness, and empathy as personality characteristics, while others have considered them attitudes. Here, in addition, they are considered to be interpersonal skills that can be learned and sharpened with practice. If we consider warmth and empathy, for example, as *responses* that can be modified through feedback and as *responses* that are teachable, then, for training purposes, it is most useful to conceptualize them as skills as well as personality characteristics. Other research, dealing with the "inherently helpful person," which will be discussed later, emphasizes these facilitative conditions as fairly permanent characteristics, acquired naturally and operative in situations other than psychotherapy.

That an accurate and sensitive awareness of another person's feelings, aspirations, values, beliefs, and perceptions, that a deep concern for the other person's welfare, without attempts to dominate him, and that an open, nondefensive, nonphony being (genuineness) proves beneficial to any human interaction has long been recognized by philosophers and novelists as well as by theoreticians in psychotherapy and counseling, and indeed by others who study the broad areas of human relationships. The first systematic theoretical view focusing upon these central characteristics was proposed by Shoben (1953) from the learning-theory orientation. The next major comprehensive theoretical statement about these characteristics was made by Bordin (1955), a counseling theorist. The more specific and organized theoretical writings of Rogers (1957) marked a point of theoretical convergence for virtually all theorists within the mainstream of thinking about therapeutic interpersonal relationships. They all heavily underscored empathy, warmth, and genuineness. Freud, Fromm-Reichmann, Otto Rank, Alfred Adler, and virtually all of the phenomenologically oriented psychoanalysts as well as current behavioristically oriented theorists and therapists have agreed to the theoretic and clinical importance of these skills (reviewed in Truax and Carkhuff, 1967).

That these qualities are essential not just for the therapeutic relationship, but more generally for the self-growth of the individual, is emphasized not only by therapists, but also by philosophers such as Martin Buber (1953). He has said, ". . . the inmost growth of the self is not accomplished, as people like to suppose today, in man's relation to himself, but in the relations between the one and the other . . . in the making present of another self and in the knowledge that one is made present in his own self by the other . . . (p. 249)."

Clearly, the essential aspects of accurate empathic understanding, nonpossessive warmth, and genuineness are the common property and knowledge of all humanity. We do not have complicated research scales at our finger tips when in our everyday life we respond positively to the very human, nonpossessive warmth and caring experienced from one and respond negatively and perhaps defensively to the ungenuine, phony, defensive qualities displayed by another person. What goes into our perception and response of being understood as ourselves rather than as an object by fellow human beings? It is significant that we are able to recognize these qualities in others when we encounter them. While the complicated research scales are useful both in research and in training, a recent study initiated by Shapiro (1968a) compared estimations of degrees of these interpersonal skills exhibited in tape-recorded conversations when they were evaluated by

carefully trained raters using the scales and when they were evaluated within a ten-second period by untrained people. The findings indicated relatively close agreement—over half of the variability in the actual evaluations was in agreement (correlations of about .70). Perhaps it is simply because empathy, warmth, and genuineness are human qualities and cannot be "professionalized" in any rigid manner. When they become *professional* manipulations rather than human qualities, they are not effective in producing positive human behavior and personality change.

Although our current research evidence suggests that for effective interpersonal impact one must not be decidedly low on any of the three qualities, and be moderately high on at least any two of them, the order in which we discuss them does have some special significance.

Therapist Genuineness

To be therapeutically facilitative toward another human being requires that we be deeply sensitive to his moment-to-moment experiencing —grasping both the content and the meaning of his experiencing, feelings, beliefs, and values. But such a deep and receptive empathic understanding requires that we at least experience a minimal degree of warmth and respect for him without attempts to dictate to him or dominate him. Thus, deep understanding seems impossible in the face of hostile rejecting or unreceptive attitudes. It is as difficult for individual persons as it is for nations to understand in an empathic manner those they dislike and those who are enemies. In turn, and most basically, empathy and warmth could not be constructively meaningful unless they were given by a person who was at least minimally "real." Even if it were possible to be experiencing warmth and understanding from an unpredictable phony or a strongly defensive individual (including a potential enemy), it would seem likely to be more threatening than facilitative. In this sense, genuineness or nondefensiveness or nonphoniness is most basic to a human relationship. This makes a trusting and open relationship possible. Once this is established, then nonpossessive warmth provides the nonthreatening context and the positively motivating context of a relationship. Finally, the moment-by-moment empathic grasp of the meaning and significance of the other's word can lead to the "work" of changing another person by any dialogue or manner. We communicate our understanding and stimulate him to openly understand and accept himself—both his current behavior, his pride and shame of past behavior, and his hopes and fears for his future behavior.

Although we believe on the basis of current evidence that the effectiveness of accurate empathic understanding in producing or eliciting positive human behavior change depends on a warm and nondefensive or genuine relationship, this in no way implies that the helper will first be genuine, then develop a feeling of warmth, and finally be better able to be empathic. It seems that in practice quite the reverse is true. Most often we come to warmly value, prize, respect or like another person as we listen to him and discover the nature of his phenomenological world. As we understand his private world and hence the meaning of certain events for him, we increasingly are able to more easily and freely be ourselves in the relationship.

As we come to know some of *his* wants, some of *his* needs, some of *his* achievements, and some of *his* failures, and some of *his* values, we find ourselves living with the other person as much as we do with the hero or heroine of a novel. It is in this crucial sense that the psychoanalytical view of empathy as a process of "trial identification" has great meaning for effective interpersonal skills. Just as with the character in the novel, we come to know the person from his own internal viewpoint and thus gain some understanding and flavor of his moment-by-moment experiences. We come to see events and significant people in his life as they appear to him—not just as they are to us, but instead as he experiences them. As we come to know him from his own personal vantage point, we seem automatically to sympathize with his mode of existence and come to value and like him. Perhaps precisely because we are concentrating on his experience, we are much freer from our own threat and insecurity, and so in those moments can become more authentic and more genuinely ourselves. Thus, it seems that as we begin to receive and understand the events, experiences, and feelings of another person's existence "as if" they were parts of our own

life, we come to feel warmth, respect, and liking for a person who, in an objective sense, may be weak, cowardly, treacherous, vile, or despicable. Indeed, few modern novels choose as central characters impeccable paragons of virtue—most often they are even more weak, cowardly and despicable than ourselves.

Thus, as with the hero of novels, we come to know, and value, and warmly respect another not simply because he is good, exemplary, or what we ourselves would like to be, but instead because we understand him and his life experiences from the internal vantage point rather than from an external objective viewpoint.

What do we mean when we say that a person is acting himself, is integrated, authentic, nondefensive, or genuine? We mean that he is a real person in an encounter presenting himself without defensive phoniness, without hiding behind a professional facade or other role. The helping person is himself, but this does not mean that he will act or behave as he does at home with his family or as he does in many other situations. In an attempt to describe the clinical meaning of genuineness in the practice of counseling or therapy, Rogers and Truax (1967) say:

... so if I sense that I am feeling bored by my contacts with this client and this feeling persists, I think I owe it to him and to our relationship to share this feeling with him. The same would hold if my feeling is one of being afraid of this client, or if my attention is so focused on my own problems that I can scarcely listen to him. But as I attempt to share these feelings I also want to be constantly in touch with what is going on in me. If I am I will recognize that it is my feeling of being bored which I am expressing, and not some supposed fact about him as a boring person. If I voice it as my *own* reaction, it has the potentiality of leading to a deep relationship. But this feeling exists in the context of a complex and changing flow, and this needs to be communicated, too. I would like to share with him my distress at feeling bored and the discomfort I feel in expressing this aspect of me. As I share these attitudes I find that my feeling of boredom arises from my sense of remoteness from him and that I would like to be more in touch with him and even as I try to express these feelings they change. I am certainly not bored as I wait with eagerness and perhaps a bit of apprehension for his response. I also feel a new sensitivity to him now that I have shared this feeling which has been a barrier between us. I am very much more able to hear the surprise or perhaps the hurt in his voice as he now finds himself speaking more genuinely because I have dared be real to him. I have let myself be a person—real, imperfect—in my relationship with him. (p. 57)."

The measurement (Truax, 1962b) of therapist genuineness from recorded psychotherapy sessions used a scale descriptively specifying stages along a continuum. At its lowest level the scale includes such descriptions as ". . . there is explicit evidence of a very considerable discrepancy between his experiencing and his current verbalizations", and ". . . the therapist or counselor makes striking contradiction in his statements . . . or, the therapist may contradict the content . . . with voice qualities. . . ." At intermediate stages on the continuum "the counselor or therapist responds . . . in a professional rather than a personal manner . . . there is a somewhat contrived or rehearsed quality. . . ." At higher values on the continuum "there is neither implicit nor explicit evidence of defensiveness or the presence of a facade," and at the highest level "there is an openness to experiences and feeling by the therapist of all types—both pleasant and hurtful—without traces of defensiveness or retreat into professionalism. . . ."

From the research evidence and an examination of the raw data itself relating genuineness to outcome, as well as collateral evidence, it is clear that what is effective is an absence of defensiveness and phoniness—a lack of evidence that the therapist is not genuine. In other words, it is not the positive end of the genuineness scale that contributes to therapeutic outcome. Instead it is a lack of genuineness that mitigates against positive client change. The highest levels of the genuineness scale do not discriminate between differential outcomes. The scale itself and the evidence concerning the role of therapist genuineness would be more precise if we dropped the term genuineness and call it instead by some negative term that would include both defensiveness and being phony.

In daily life each of us can think of persons who are transparent and genuine, who are what they seem. This is the quality of genuineness.

Perhaps a large part of the reason for the effectiveness and central importance of genuine-ness lies in the fact that our own openness and personal freedom from defensiveness in a therapeutic encounter provides a model for the other person to follow in moving towards openness and freedom to be *himself*. Stating this negatively, we might ask "can we expect openness, self-acceptance, and personal freedom from defensiveness in another person when we ourselves lack these qualities in a relationship?"

Therapist Nonpossessive Warmth

Nonpossessive warmth, or a warmly receptive nondominating attitude, though separable from the other central skills in effective interpersonal relationships, inevitably overlaps and intertwines with the communication of accurate empathy and genuineness. Thus, Raush and Bordin (1957), in an excellent theoretical analysis of the components of warmth, specify the commitment of the person, his effort to understand, and his spontaneity. Our own research has also indicated that the intensity and the intimacy of a relationship is strongly related and overlaps with warmth. Another overlapping aspect of warmth involves the concept of psychological distance; the more distant the relationship, or the more aloof we are in a relationship, the less warmth we communicate. Warmth does not imply passivity or unresponsivity; nonpossessive warmth is an outgoing positive action involving active personal participation.

A careful cataloguing of the kinds of behavior and verbalizations that people use to communicate a nonpossessive warmth could easily fill a number of books. Warmth and respect can be communicated or not communicated in a variety of ways. It does involve an acceptance of *what is*, rather than a demand for *what ought to be*. To return to the analogy of the reader who identifies with the hero of a novel, as readers will become engrossed in following the actions and feelings of the hero without having to personally agree or disagree, approve or disapprove of his feelings and actions, in much the same way when we are engrossed in reading or understanding another person, we would have to stop and disengage ourselves from the relationship to feel or voice our agreements or disagreements, approvals or disapprovals of what lies in him. This does not mean a namby-pamby or sentimental acceptance of undesirable behavior, since the other person himself does not value all of his actions. Thus, in working with college underachievers, a good counselor can communicate very high levels of warmth and at the same time be able to confront the underachiever with the fact of his own laziness—not as a socially desirable or socially undesirable trait, but simply as what *is*.

From another point of view, it may be that our ability to experience warm positive feelings for another person depends basically on our ability to feel a receptivity and warmth for our own self—an openness to both the good and bad that lives with us. Both clinically and from research evidence there appears to be a fairly direct relationship between one's own self-regard and the regard felt for others (Fey, 1955; Kanfer and Marston, 1963).

The measurement of nonpossessive warmth (Truax, 1962a) specifies a continuum involving at the lower range such helping behaviors as "[he] acts in such a way as to make himself the locus of evaluation . . . [he] may be telling the patient what would be 'best' for him, or may be in other ways actively trying to control his behavior," or the therapist "responds mechanically to the client and thus indicates little positive warmth . . . or . . . ignores the patient where an unconditionally warm response would be expected—complete passivity that communicates a lack of warmth." At very high values "[he] clearly communicates a very deep interest and concern for the welfare of the patient. Attempts to dominate or control the patient are for the most part absent . . . except that it is important that he [the patient] be more mature . . . or that the therapeutic person himself is accepted and liked," or at the highest level ". . . the patient is free to be himself even if this means that he is temporarily regressing, being defensive, or even disliking or rejecting the therapist himself."

Therapist Accurate Empathy

Accurate empathic understanding involves the ability to *perceive* and *communicate* accurately and with sensitivity both the feelings and experiences of another person and their meaning and significance. Through a process of trial identification, we step into the other person's shoes and view his world from his emotional and perceptual vantage point. Because we cannot truly be another person, we can be both "inside" another person and yet also remain "outside," which allows us to sense the meaning of another person's anger, fear, or joy, its antecedents and its consequences, without ourselves being overwhelmed by the experiencing. This allows us to contribute to the expansion and clarification of the other person's own awareness of his experiences and feelings. This is the essence of the fine balance between identification with the other person and objectivity that is the hallmark of an accurately empathic person. Being empathic, we assume the role of the other person, and in that role initiate ourselves the process of self-exploration as if we were the other person himself. In dealing with the disturbed person, it is as if we were providing a model for him to follow, as if we were saying by our example "even fearful or terrifying experiences or feelings are not so terrible that they cannot be touched and looked at."

Intense focusing on the other person, of course, is central to the perceptive aspect of deep empathic understanding, since it allows us to note subtle nonverbal communications—the minute facial, postural, and gestural clues that often contradict or multiply the meaning of another person's verbal communications. This intense focusing on the other person also tends to ensure that errors in either our own perception or communication of understanding will be quickly recognized. We will be able to sense from his often subtle responses when our own communications do not fit exactly and, sometimes in midsentence, we can shift to correct for errors of language or content. In short, our intense and intimate focus on the other person makes possible the moment-to-moment contact necessary for accurate empathic understanding.

As we have all learned in life, people are not always what they seem. All of us have been conditioned from childhood to present social façades so that we often say in a polite manner when we are insulted or hurt and are asked about it, "Oh no, that doesn't matter." Even with a minimal empathic grasp, the other person should be able to see that it does indeed bother us a great deal. Thus, to be empathic we must separate the meaningful communications from another person from those arising from a defensive screen or social facade.

As the term empathy implies, many of the cues used for deciding what is true, or is false, and what is meaningful in things we hear from another person come from the root ground of our own experience and existence. We can often recognize from our own awareness of ourselves the outward signs that relate to inner feelings and experiences. Beyond this, we learn about the human condition from our success and our failure in understanding others, as well as from our reading of outstanding novelists and theoreticians of human behavior. Most basically, of course, we rely upon the moment-by-moment changes in the other person as a sign of what is most meaningful. The moment-by-moment changes in the other person alert us to our own deprivations. Thus, hurried and empty laughter can communicate as deeply and as clearly as moistened eyes; the overly strong denial tells us as much as the halting and strained confrontation. Often a blush, a stammer, a flood of words, a change in breathing, a tensing of posture, or the lack of socially appropriate feeling, may be much more important than what the other person at that moment is saying in words.

In one sense we help clarify another person's understanding of himself by serving as a mirror to his emotional and phenomenological self. Just as he learns about his physical self by seeing his image reflected in a mirror, he learns about his emotional and phenomenological self by hearing these aspects of him reflected by us.

The accurately empathic, therapeutic person not only indicates a sensitive understanding of the patient's *apparent* feelings, but goes further to clarify and expand what is hinted by voice, posture, and content cues. The Accurate Empathy Scale (Truax, 1961a) defines a continuum that specifies at its lower values such behaviors as "[he] seems completely unaware of even the most conspicuous of the patient's feelings. His responses are not appropriate to the mood and content of the client's statement and there is no determinable quality of empathy, hence no accuracy whatsoever"; whereas, at intermediate levels of the continuum, "he often responds accurately to more exposed feelings. He also displays concern for more hidden feelings which he seems to sense must be present, though he does not understand their nature" or "he shows awareness of many feelings and experiences which are not so evident . . . but in these he tends to be somewhat inaccurate in his understanding." At the higher levels of the continuum of accurate empathy, the therapist "shows awareness of the precise intensity of most underlying emotions . . . his responses move only slightly beyond the area of the client's own awareness, so that feelings may be present which are not recognized by the client or therapist," or, "accurately interprets all of the client's present, acknowledged feelings. He moves into feelings and experiences that are only hinted at . . . and does so with sensitivity and accuracy. [He] offers additions to the patient's understanding so that not only are underlying emotions pointed to, but they are specifically talked about." To both accurately predict and effectively communicate what the client or patient is currently experiencing and feeling, and therefore, of "what the patient *might well say*, were he more open and less defensive," is the quality of accurate empathic understanding.

A sharp distinction should be made between a therapist's *understanding* and the frequency, accuracy, extent, and depth of empathic *responses* that are communicated to the client. A therapist's understanding of his client can be defined and measured in a variety of ways that have to do with his diagnostic accuracy and his ability to predict future client behaviors and feelings. Such understanding relies to some extent upon the therapist's intellectual ability and expert knowledge.

While such understanding is a precondition to the therapist's making accurately empathic responses, it may or may not be related to actually making responses. Accurate empathic responses have been defined operationally in terms of the accurate empathy scale (Truax, 1961a). There, accurate empathy is defined as ". . . sensitivity to moment to moment feelings during the therapy session and the verbal facility to communicate this understanding in a language attuned to the client's current feelings." When empathy is defined in terms of operational scales measuring the therapist's responses to the client, it becomes clear that what is being measured is an interpersonal skill rather than simply an attitude or a personality attribute, since a person can have an understanding or empathic attitude, and even actually be sensitive and accurately understand, without making an accurately empathic response. In short, you have to understand to be able to make an accurately empathic response, but the absence of an accurately empathic response tells us nothing about the depth, extent, or accuracy of the understanding.

In summary, then, the essence of nonpossessive warmth is to preserve the client's self-respect as a person and a human being and to provide a trusting, safe atmosphere; the purpose of genuineness is to provide an honest, nondefensive relationship that allows us to point to unpleasant truths about the relationship and about the client rather than to hide behind a facade; accurate empathic understanding serves as the work of the therapeutic relationship.

THE MEASUREMENT OF ACCURATE EMPATHY, NONPOSSESSIVE WARMTH, AND GENUINENESS

For traditional psychotherapists, and indeed for many behavior therapists, the heart of psychotherapeutic behavior change is the interpersonal relationship itself. The majority of the theorists who have dealt with the therapeutic relationship have emphasized the importance of the therapist's understanding of the client, or his empathy (reviewed in Truax and Carkhuff, 1967). No theorist or therapist of any school, whether psychoanalytic, behavioristic, client-centered, rational-emotive, and the like, has suggested that his approach to helping a client would work in the hands of a therapist who consistently *misunderstood* the client—his feelings, his experiences, his problems. While a high level of human nonpossessive warmth from a mentally retarded therapist might have positive effects on his clients, we would expect them to be minimal. In this same way, a behavior therapist would not expect desensitization to be particularly helpful if the therapist misunderstood the client's problem (such as by desensitizing the client to snake fears when the client's problem was agoraphobia).

The accurate empathy scale differed from prior attempts to measure the level of therapist empathy by focusing not only on the understanding, but upon its communication; it focused on the therapist's responses rather than upon his attitude or intention, although we feel that responses represent relatively permanent attitudes and intentions modified by situational factors.

To date, the evidence is convincing that the depth and accuracy of therapist empathic responses, his warm nonpossessive responses, and his nondefensive or nonphony responses, do indeed play an important role in the process and outcome of psychotherapy. Before citing the more recent evidence, it might be well to look at the methodology typically employed in this type of research. In doing this we shall use accurate empathy as the example.

To estimate the accuracy and depth of empathic responses made by therapists during the psychotherapeutic transactions, trained raters or judges have applied the accurate-empathy scale to samples of psychotherapy. Most typically, brief samples of three minutes' duration are excerpted from audio tape recordings of psychotherapy, usually one sample from the middle third of the interview and one sample from the middle of the final third of the session. There is some variability from study to study, and it is apparent that the accurate-empathy scale can be applied to samples as long as 16 minutes or one-half hour, or can be applied to therapist-patient-therapist interaction units that may last less than a minute. While the scale is usually applied to audio tape recordings, it has also been applied to video tape recordings, and could be readily applied to live observations. Most often, samples have been taken from the middle and final third of the sessions because pilot studies in which consecutive samples have been taken of total interviews suggested that these parts of a therapeutic session normally involve the least nontherapy oriented conversation (such as polite small talk, arranging of future appointments, hellos, and good-byes). In most cases the person taking the sample for rating from a tape selects a sample by starting a tape recorder at the middle third of the session, listening until a new person talks, and continuing for the time duration specified, but with the

TABLE 9.5   Reliabilities of Rating Scales for Accurate Empathy,

Study	N Samples	N Patients	N Therapists	Group or Individual
Truax (1961b)	384	8	7	Individual
Truax and Carkhuff (1963)	297	14	10	Individual
Truax and Carkhuff (1963)	112	28	24	Individual
Truax (1962d)	448	14	10	Individual
Bergin and Solomon (1963)	28	28	18	Individual
Melloh (1964)	56	28	28	Individual
Truax, Wargo, Frank, Imber, Battle, Hoehn-Saric, Nash, and Stone (1966a)	182	40	4	Individual
Truax, Carkhuff, and Kodman (1965)	192	40	4	Group
Truax and Wargo (1967b)	698	160	15	Group
Truax and Wargo (1967a)	366	80	6	Group
Truax and Wargo (1969)	89	80	8	Group
Wargo (1962)	297	14	10	Individual
Dickenson and Truax (1966)	72	48	1	Group
Truax, Wargo, and Silber (1966)	192	40	2	Group
Truax and Carkhuff (1963)	64	8	8	Individual
Truax (1962e)	104	26	1	Individual
Truax, et al. (1966b) (screening interviews)	80	40	2	Individual (screening interviews)
Truax (1966b) (Edited)	50	5	5	Individual (edited)
(Nonedited)	50			(nonedited)
Truax (1966a) (TPT)	283	63		(TPT)
(PTP)	305	65	8	Group (PTP)
(Time)	384	80		(Time)
Truax and Carkhuff (1965)	45	3	1	Individual
Carkhuff and Truax (1965a)	151	70	28	Individual
Truax & Silber (1966)	144	48	16	Individual
Truax, Silber and Carkhuff (1965)	342	80	5	Group
Truax (1968c)	161	30	4	Group
Truax (1968b)	788	385	9	Group
Martin (1968)	256	4	4	Individual
Shapiro (1968a) (Role play)	25	2	2	Individual
Shapiro (1968b) Training/Quasi-group/role play)				
Audio video	39	6	6	Mixed
Audio audio-video	39	6	6	Mixed
Audio-video video	39	6	6	Mixed
Shapiro, Foster and Powell (1968)				
Photographs (Role play)	67	6	6	Individual
Truax (1968a) (Role play)	90	6	6	Individual
Truax (1969a)	306	16	11	Individual
Sander, Tausch, Bastine, and Nagel (1968)	36	12	4	Individual
Stoffer (1968)	210	35	35	Individual
Bozarth and Renzaglia (1968)	80	40	5	Individual
Bergin and Jasper (1969)	72	48	36	Individual
Wright & Truax (1969) (Video)	36	25	25	Individual

[a] Average Pearson correlations. All others are Ebel intraclass reliabilities for the pooled data used in analysis of findings.

Nonpossessive Warmth, and Genuineness from Specific Studies

Accurate Empathy	Nonpossessive Warmth	Genuineness
.87		
.89	.50[a]	.40[a]
.69[a]	.55[a]	
.69[a]		
.79[a]		
.62[a]		
.63	.59	.60
.87	.91	.72
.81	.76	.80
.95	.90	.95
.88	.77	.41
.89	.50[a]	
.83	.75	.25
.93	.81	.56
.57[a]	.62[a]	.45[a]
.69[a]	.55[a]	.40[a]
.75[a]	.57[a]	.55[a]
.66[a]	.84[a]	
.76[a]	.81[a]	
.84	.86	.81
.89	.85	.73
.92	.95	.95
.78	.70	.83
.43[a]	.48[a]	.62[a]
.54	.52	.46
.50	.71	.48
.59	.84	.85
.74	.66	.37
.88	.89	.86
.67	.89	.78
.42[a]	.23[a]	.35[a]
.70[a]	.52[a]	.59[a]
.54[a]	.51[a]	.60[a]
.63	.42	.69
.71	.50	.33[a]
.89	.50[a]	.40[a]
.89		
.74[a]	.75[a]	.20[a]
.95	.93	.95
.88		
.72	.53	.34

provision that the sample contain at least one therapist statement and one patient statement. In some studies the samples have been selected so as to include two therapist statements. The samples are then coded for later identification by use of a table of random numbers. Samples are then put together in random order and given to trained raters. The rating procedures themselves are, of course, the most crucial part of the research.

If the raters themselves have knowledge of psychotherapy, and particularly if they have knowledge of the patient or the therapist or the hypothesis under study, the results may be impossible to replicate and may have little to do with the actual scale being rated. When the investigator himself is the rater, any findings must remain suspect until replicated by independent investigators using more objective procedures.

Table 9.5 gives reliabilities obtained for the three scales measuring interpersonal skills in various early studies. Reliability estimates are important, of course, but in practice they are not closely tied to predictive validity in the sense that they reflect whether the scale is able to discriminate differential client process or outcomes. What is of most importance, once reasonably objective outcomes are measured, is that the group of therapists involved show a good spread between high and low levels of, say, empathy. Before attempting to relate levels of therapist interpersonal skills to measures of client process or outcome, it first must be shown that, in a given study, the therapist rated high in, say, empathy differs in empathy from those rated low. This is an important point that is sometimes overlooked by investigators. If there is no difference in levels of empathy, then we could not expect any consequent differences in process or outcome.

THERAPEUTIC INTERPERSONAL SKILLS AS REINFORCERS

Pioneering attempts aimed at interpreting the process of psychotherapy from a learning viewpoint stress the role of the therapist himself as a reinforcer. It should be clear that there is still considerable variation in the degree of client

outcome among "very-high-conditions" therapists and among "very-low-conditions" therapists. It seems probable that this variability would in part be accounted for by the particular patterns of reward or reinforcement, modeling, and the like, provided by the therapist *within the context of his level of "therapist-offered conditions."* It is tentatively theorized that accurate empathy, nonpossessive warmth, genuineness and other therapeutic interpersonal skills have indirect effects upon patient change in four modalities: (1) they serve to reinforce positive aspects of the patient self-concept, modifying the existing self-concepts and thereby leading to changes in the patient's own self-reinforcement system; (2) they serve to reinforce self-exploratory behavior and thereby elicit self-concepts and anxiety-laden material that can be then modified by selective reinforcement; (3) they serve to extinguish anxiety or fear responses associated with specific cues, both those elicited by the relationship with the therapist and those elicited by patient self-exploration; and (4) they serve to reinforce human relating, encountering, or interacting, and serve to extinguish fear or avoidance responses associated with human relating.

Accurate empathy, nonpossessive warmth, and genuineness are conceived of as having both direct and indirect effects in these four modalities: a direct effect through their introduction into the relationship by the therapist, and an indirect effect through the elicitation of positive affect (warmth, "comfort responses," "positive feelings," and the like) through the principle of reciprocal affect. Briefly, the principle of reciprocal affect simply states that in any interpersonal situation the affect elicited in one person is in kind and in proportion to the affect communicated by the other. In S–R terminology an affective stimulus serves as an unconditioned stimulus in automatically eliciting an affect response, which is in kind and proportion to the stimulus. In the therapy situation, when the therapist communicates warmth he thereby tends to elicit warmth in response from the patient. In contrast, if the therapist communicates negative feeling or negative affect, then negative feeling or affect is elicited in the patient. Assuming the presence of the core conditions to a high degree, then the stimulus is positive affect and the consequent patient response is positive affect.

The evidence on anxiety extinction suggests that extinction of anxiety in the therapy setting generalizes to extra-therapy contexts. A question has been raised, however, about the generalization to extra-therapy behavior of other changes in verbal behavior occurring in the therapy situation. That such verbal reinforcement in therapy does generalize to real life behavior is indicated by Krumboltz's (1963) study, in which he consciously gave verbal approval statements to vocational counselees whenever they indicated a verbal intention to seek information. Compared to a contrast group, the patients who had been verbally reinforced actually engaged in significantly greater information-seeking behavior in real life. Thus reinforcement of verbal behavior was shown to directly affect real life behavior.

The principle of "reciprocal affect" and the feasibility of the application of conditioning or reinforcement to traditional psychotherapy loom as central to the present viewpoint.

Reciprocal affect has been noted in clinical writings (Rogers, 1951) and in research (Fey, 1955) in terms of a strong relationship between acceptance of self and acceptance of others. It has also been observed in laboratory analogue studies (Kanfer and Marston, 1963), in terms of the correlation between externally induced changes in the rate of self-reinforcement and the consequent change in the rate of reinforcement given to others. A recent study by Heller, Myers and Kline (1963) demonstrates the operation of reciprocal affect in psychotherapy. Using actors to simulate patients for unsuspecting real therapists, they studied the effects upon the therapists of "patients" who were essentially friendly versus "patients" who were essentially hostile. Their results indicated that reciprocal affect was generated in the real therapists; therapists responded in a more friendly fashion to friendly "patients" and in a more hostile manner to hostile "patients." Converging evidence is also available from the Wisconsin Schizophrenic Research Project using real patients and real therapists (Truax, 1962).

The very notion of selective responding or the selective offering of high intensities or frequencies of such human qualities as empathy and warmth has been frequently decried by many dynamically-oriented traditional therapists. Rogers (1951, 1957) has consistently been a strong exponent of the view that selective responding would be damaging rather than helpful. In particular, Rogers has argued that empathy and warmth are primarily attitudinal in nature and that to be effective, they must be offered in a nonselective fashion to the patient; he specifies that they are not to be contingent upon the patient's in-therapy verbalizations or behaviors.

A recent report (Truax, 1965) deals specifically with the feasibility of the reinforcement aspect of the present viewpoint. A single, long-term, successful case handled by Carl Rogers was used as the basic raw data. Therapist-patient-therapist interaction units were selected randomly from the middle third of therapy hours throughout the 85 interviews.

To analyze these data, some nine separate classes of patient behavior that might theoretically be expected to be significant for behavioral change were separately rated by five experienced psychotherapists. Additionally, three "reinforcers" were also measured: (1) empathy, (2) nonpossessive warmth or acceptance, and (3) directiveness. The expectation was simply that the therapist, in this case Rogers, would systematically or nonrandomly vary the level of his "reinforcers" with levels of patient verbal behavior.

If there were no systematic selective use of empathy, warmth, or directiveness, then correlations between these variables and the patient categories would approach zero. The data, however, indicated strong relationships with certain patient behavior classes. The therapist significantly tended to respond selectively with differential levels of empathy, warmth, or directiveness to high and low levels of five of the nine classes of patient behavior. He did not systematically vary his level of empathy and the like with four classes of patient behavior. Thus a clear and significant pattern of selective responding was indicated by the data.

Now, since the basic property of a "reinforcer" is that it leads to change in behaviors, it was predicted that, other things being equal, the five classes of patient behavior that were selectively "reinforced" would show increases over time in therapy, while the four classes of patient behavior not "reinforced" would show no such increase over time. Of the classes of patient behavior to which the therapist selectively responded or "reinforced," four out of five, showed significant changes over time in therapy in the predicted direction. By contrast, of the classes of patient behavior to which the therapist did not selectively respond (those not selectively "reinforced"), three out of four did not show increase or decrease over time in therapy. Thus the data were consistent with the predictions from a reinforcement view in seven out of the nine classes of patient behavior (78 percent correct prediction).

Considering the likelihood that the therapist also used other types of reinforcers, and also reinforced in unknown intensities and frequencies other related patient behavior classes, considering the unknown differential difficulty level of the discriminanda of patient response classes, and considering the crudity of measurement, the findings strongly suggest the appropriateness of a "reinforcement" interpretation as an explanation of at least a part of the process of psychotherapy.

In a more recent study (Truax, 1968c), direct evidence was presented that the therapists' differential interpersonal reinforcement of client self-exploration led to an increase of self-exploration and greater therapeutic improvement in outcome measures. Excerpts from tape recordings of 30 clients participating in group therapy with four different therapists were analyzed in relation to pre-, post-, and one-year follow-up measures of outcome. Patients receiving high levels of therapist-offered differential reinforcement for self-exploration (using momentary differential levels of accurate empathy, nonpossessive warmth, and genuineness as reinforcers) showed greater overall self-exploration after three months and also greater therapeutic improvement than did patients receiving low or negative levels of differential reinforcement. Quite surprisingly, the counselor or therapist's use of the therapeutic triad as reinforcers was *unrelated* to his mean level of these conditions offered during therapy.

The general behavioristic view of the importance of differential reinforcement for therapeutic outcome and the more specific view that accurate empathy, nonpossessive warmth, and genuineness are effective differential reinforcers are both strongly supported by the present data. Since none of the therapists in the study just cited were oriented toward behavior therapy, it seems that future research using behavioristic models may contribute greatly to the understanding of therapist-patient transactions in traditional psychotherapy and counseling.

The findings that the levels of therapeutic conditions (accurate empathy, nonpossessive warmth, and genuineness) *did not* covary with their use as differential reinforcers in influencing patient depth of self-exploration, but still had significant effects on patient therapeutic improvement, adds a new dimension to the understanding of the role of these therapeutic conditions. The findings suggest that the moment-by-moment variation in levels of therapeutic conditions significantly affects the patients in therapy and extra-therapy behavior; the rewarding or reinforcing properties of the conditions effect outcome, depending upon how they are used. Most surprising in that study, in view of the client-centered and psychoanalytically oriented training of the therapists involved, was the finding that a great many patients received strong negative differential reinforcement for self-exploration. In fact, the Pearson correlations measuring degree of reinforcement varied from $+.94$ to $-.90$. Apparently therapists responded in therapy in terms of their prior habits of relating rather than in terms of their adherence to theory. They were clearly shutting off self-exploration in some patients, and quite systematically so.

While more research is needed and is underway to cross-validate, extend, and refine the findings dealing with interpersonal skills as reinforcers, the present data would suggest that major revisions are in order for the current client-centered, psychoanalytic, and eclectic views of the therapeutic role of interpersonal skills. Wittingly or unwittingly, these humanistic qualities, for the traditional therapist, appear to be used as rewards or reinforcers that change the patient's in-therapy and extra-therapy behavior. These findings suggest that both the therapist's general level of conditions (as proposed by traditional therapists) and his selective differential use of empathy, warmth, and genuineness (as proposed by learning theorists) have separate effects on patient therapeutic outcome.

TOWARD RESOLVING THE QUESTION OF CAUSATION

In general, the findings relating the therapist interpersonal conditions of accurate empathic understanding, warmth, and genuineness, and positive client outcome lead to an important question concerning causation. Is it the therapist or the client who determines the level of a particular condition that will occur in the given psychotherapy relationship? The question of causation was reviewed earlier (Truax and Mitchell, 1968) but a number of more recent studies conducted under the supervision of Dr. Robert Carkhuff at the State University of New York at Buffalo caused us to question our earlier conclusions.

Before reporting these new studies, perhaps it would be helpful to describe briefly the research strategy that has been employed in the past. One study (Truax, 1963), which is representative of the approach and the findings, was aimed at clarifying the question of causation for accurate empathy. Data were collected from 24 patients and 8 different therapists, who offered psychotherapy to all of these patients on a demand basis. Analysis of the therapist-offered condition indicated that different therapists produced different levels of accurate empathy, even when interacting with the same set of patients. In sharp contrast, different patients did not receive significantly different levels of conditions when interacting with the same therapists.

Another approach (Truax, 1962c) was to provide a single standard interviewer throughout the course of therapy who saw each patient periodically, in an attempt to provide a sampling of the in-therapy patient behavior of each patient. The findings indicated no significant correlation between a level of accurate empathy and genuineness offered throughout therapy and the levels occurring in this sampling interview, thus indicating that both accurate empathy and genuineness were not significantly affected by the patients. On the measures of nonpossessive warmth, however, there was a positive relationship ($p < .05$) suggesting that to some extent patients did indeed affect the level of nonpossessive warmth offered by the therapists and the standard sampling interviewer.

Very similar findings were obtained in a study by Truax, Wargo, Frank, Imber, Battle, Hoehn-Saric, Nash, and Stone (1966b), in which 40 patients were randomly assigned first to one of the senior psychiatrists for a screening interview and then to one of the four residents for psychotherapy. The data indicated that the two interviewers differed significantly from each other on both accurate empathy and therapist genuineness but not on non possessive warmth, while the therapists offered significantly different levels of all three conditions. The non-significant findings with interviewer warmth may mean either that the patients as well as the interviewers affected the level of warmth, or that the two interviewers provided equal levels of warmth.

Putting together these several studies focusing upon the question of who is causing the levels of conditions in interviewing, counseling, or psychotherapy, the evidence is both uniform and strong in indicating that in both therapeutic and informational interviewers it is the interviewer, not the patient, who determines what the level of accurate empathy and genuineness shall be. Furthermore, considering nonpossessive warmth, the findings from therapy interviews indicate that the different therapists offer different levels of warmth, and that patients in general have little affect on the level of warmth offered. However, the data from nontherapy interviews (that is, both the standard sampling interviews in the one study and the screening interviews in the other study) suggest that patients do indeed have a significant affect upon the level of nonpossessive warmth offered by the interviewer.

Anderson (1968) found that therapists in a counseling center offered very similar conditions of empathic understanding, warmth, and genuineness to student clients with declared educational, vocational, or personal-social problems. In other words, therapists offered similar levels of the conditions across different presenting problems, just as they did across different clients. If the therapist conditions were simply learned techniques or interpersonal skills, one might have expected differential levels offered as a function of the presenting problem. To the extent that this was not the case, it appears that empathy, warmth, and genuineness are relatively permanent personality characteristics and/or attitudes as well as specific interpersonal skills. By the same token, then, the study adds further support to the proposition that the therapist is the main contributor to the levels of accurate empathy, warmth, and genuineness.

A number of studies have focused on the experimental manipulation of client characteristics and their effect on therapist conditions. Alexik and Carkhuff (1967) conducted a pilot study in which one "client" was instructed to deliberately manipulate his levels of self-exploration with one therapist who had been rated high on accurate empathy, warmth, and genuineness, and one therapist who had been rated low on these conditions. The "client" was instructed to manipulate his depth of self-exploration in such a manner that he explored himself as deeply as he could during the first and last third of each hour but offered lower levels of self-exploration during the middle portion of the hour. It was found that the conditions offered by the high-functioning therapist were not altered during the hour, but that those offered by the low-functioning therapist were significantly altered. In a later study, using a larger sample of therapists, Carkhuff and Alexik (1967) obtained similar results. In the latter study, in addition, there was some tendency for therapists offering high facilitative conditions to increase these conditions during periods of low client depth of self-exploration. On the other hand, therapists low on the three conditions not only were manipulated by deliberately lowered client depth of self-exploration to offer even lower conditions of accurate empathy, warmth, and genuineness during the middle portion of the hour, but they also failed to reestablish, during the last portion of the hour, the levels of conditions they had offered during the initial phase of therapy.

In a more sophisticated study, Friel, Kratochvil, and Carkhuff (1968) studied the effect of client manipulation of depth of self-exploration on therapists as a function of type of training and level of experience. Although neither of these variables were related to the effect of client manipulation, findings indicated that therapists low on the core conditions were open to manipulation, while therapists functioning high on these conditions were not.

It may be that the findings just cited are not relevant to accurate empathy, nonpossessive warmth, and genuineness, since the investigators used an abbreviated version of the scales. Moreover, the abbreviated scales by Carkhuff have yet to be confirmed as predictive of patient outcome. Finally, raters were usually members of the research team who may have known the general purpose of the studies.

The question of the relative contribution of client and therapist to the core facilitative interpersonal skills is still not completely resolved. In general, the data offered by Carkhuff and his co-workers, if valid, indicate that when an experimental "client" is instructed to do so, he can manipulate the offerings of both high- and low-functioning therapists. The fact that these findings were demonstrated experimentally is also their major drawback. Although it has been demonstrated that a "client" *can* manipulate a therapist's offering of these conditions, the earlier research evidence seems to indicate that, in practice, clients do not. The demonstration that clients *can* manipulate therapists' levels is important since it leads us to expect that, under certain therapy conditions, the client may be motivated to do so and that if he is, he can. In other words, although the client may not consciously withhold deep self-exploration, he may do so unconsciously, and thereby alter his therapist's offerings of accurate empathy, warmth, and genuineness. Generally, however, despite the experimental demonstrations that "clients" so instructed can affect the therapist's offerings of empathy, warmth, and genuineness, the earlier research indicated that, in practice, the therapist is the primary contributor to the levels that he offers his clients.

THE INHERENTLY HELPFUL PERSON

The problem of causation is also related to the question of etiology. How do persons become empathic, warm, and genuine? There is ample evidence that these therapeutic skills can be taught (Carkhuff and Truax, 1965b; Truax and Carkhuff, 1967; and Truax and Mitchell, 1968). Within merely 100 hours of training (described in detail by Truax and Carkhuff, 1967), lay personnel such as hosptial aides can be brought to levels of accurate empathy, warmth, and genuineness usually offered by professional psychotherapists. The finding that these interpersonal skills can be learned in such a short amount of time leads to either of two inferences. Perhaps these skills are relatively superficial and thus can be learned quickly. Since the skills have been related to significant client growth and student achievement, however, it does not appear likely that they are superficial.

The second inference is that these skills are learned, either overtly or covertly, in early, formative interpersonal situations other than psychotherapy, and that focused training capitalizes on what may often have been past incidental learning. Such as inference brings us to the notion of the "inherently helpful person." To the degree that some persons are inherently helpful, and by that we mean that they have been rewarded for being helpful from their early, formative years onward, we would expect that these skills have been built upon and reflect fairly permanent personality characteristics. If such is the case, these skills will clearly continue to be more a function of the therapist-as-a-person than a function of client behavior.

Bergin (1966) has suggested that what is usually called "spontaneous improvement" in therapeutic research may well be caused by clients using some other person (usually a non-professional) as he would a counselor. Indeed, the available research evidence does not indicate that trained professional workers such as psychologists, psychiatrists, or social workers, have, on the average, more positive effects on clients or patients than do either control (no treatment) or untrained or briefly trained nonprofessionals (Truax and Carkhuff, 1967; Truax, 1968a). If the untrained or minimally trained individual has a naturally high level of accurate empathy, nonpossessive warmth, genuineness, and other interpersonal skills, then it seems likely, from the present vantage point, that individuals who spend time with him will be as helped, if not more helped, than if they

were receiving formal counseling or psychotherapy from the socially sanctioned professional. In fact, we might expect that clients themselves would be more discriminating if they were not led to believe that the professional psychotherapist or counselor was necessarily helpful. There is research evidence (Shapiro, Krauss and Truax, 1969) which indicates that people disclose themselves more deeply to those persons among their family and aquaintances who offer the highest levels of conditions, and in contrast, disclose themselves minimally to those who offer the lowest levels of conditions. Those data not only indicate that similar therapeutic conditions or interpersonal skills seem to work to bring about a more open and full relationship both in and out of psychotherapy, but also suggest that if the client or patient were left to his own devices, he would seek out therapists with the highest level of understanding, warmth, and genuineness. Of course, if that were the case for clients seeing professionals, then one could expect overall average positive effects of psychotherapy and counseling (by a simple process of elimination of counselors or therapists low in such interpersonal skills).

Indeed, that the inherently helpful person does influence others is shown by a recent study by Shapiro and Voog (1969). In that study, it was found that normal college students' levels of understanding, warmth, and genuineness was predictive of their roommates' grade-point averages. The level of understanding, warmth, and genuineness provided by one's roommate had significant effects on one's grade point average, and this effect even overshadowed the effects of aptitude as measured by the Cooperative School and College Ability Tests (SCAT). That is, although the students in the study had no idea that they were either the providers or recipients of interpersonal skills (positive *or* negative), the differential grade-point averages actually obtained indicate the power of such interpersonal skills. In this respect, it should be noted that there were both positive and negative, or hindering, effects. A quite similar viewpoint is offered by Jourard's (1964) concept of "healers" and "witches" as those who habitually help and hurt the people they interact with. The estimate from the Shapiro and Voog data suggests that between 10 and

14 percent of the variability in freshmen grade point averages is attributable to the level of understanding, warmth, and genuineness provided by one's roommate. Clearly, no man is an island, and many more people beyond a roommate influence a college student.

Much more direct evidence that inherently helpful people can be therapeutic without training is indicated in a recent study by Stoffer (1968). He studied adult female volunteers serving as community helpers, who each met with a single child twice each week for approximately three months. Thus, the number of interviews varied from 14 to 25. In the study there were 35 students and 35 community helpers. Because the purpose of the program was to determine the value of utilizing untrained personnel with minimal supervision, helpers were instructed to establish good relations, but were given no further specific directions on how this might be done. All 35 of the helpers were married women in the process of raising their own children, who averaged 38 years in age, with a mean level of educational attainment of 13.3 years. Problem children referred by school psychologists in the community around Ohio State University were those participating in the program. The children selected were those who had clear behavioral problems and IQs above 80, and who were educationally retarded. Thirty-five boys and girls ranging in age from 7 to 12 were drawn from some 15 elementary schools. When ratings were made of tape-recorded samples of the actual interaction between the untrained community workers and the child's behavior and achievement, it was found that high levels of nonpossessive warmth were significantly related to gains in achievement, reductions in teacher rated behavior problems, and gains reflected by the total outcome index (achievement plus behavioral ratings). Similarly, high ratings of accurate empathy in the late interview were significantly related to gains in achievement and gains reflected by the combined outcome index.

CURRENT RESEARCH

Now we turn to current research on the three therapist interpersonal skills, or conditions, of accurate empathy, warmth, and genuineness. The first is a study of a nine-year follow-up of the 16 schizophrenic patients from the original Wisconsin Schizophrenic Project. Then we shall present further validating evidence with respect to the level of therapeutic conditions, as well as a series of studies that have delineated therapist behaviors, perhaps more specific to the psychotherapy process, that are related to the conditions and to client outcome. Finally, we shall present evidence pointing toward the importance of the facilitative conditions in teaching and student personnel work, and the effectiveness of nonprofessional counselor aides.

Long-Term Follow-Up

A quite recent study (Truax, 1969a) provides evidence of the long-term effects of higher and lower levels of empathy, warmth, and genuineness.

A number of articles, and a massive and complex book (Rogers, Gendlin, Kiesler, and Truax, 1967) have been written about the attempt to apply client-centered therapy to a small group of hospitalized patients in Wisconsin. One of the central questions, if not *the* central question, to be asked about this attempt is "What were the effects on the normal process of hospitalization?" The hospital records of the Mendota State Hospital were examined, and other hospitals were checked for records, over nine years preceding therapy and nine years after the initiation of therapy for the therapy and control patients. When the patients were divided into those seen by therapists with higher conditions and those seen by therapists with relatively lower conditions, it was found that there was a significant difference in the linear trend of getting out of the hospital across time between patients exposed to control conditions versus those exposed to high therapeutic conditions from their therapists. Separately, patients exposed to high conditions from their therapists showed a significantly greater linear trend of getting out of the hospital than those exposed to low conditions. There was also a difference in the quadratic trend for patients exposed to high conditions opposed to those exposed only to control conditions. That is, they tended to get out of the hospital quicker at the outset. The general findings are presented in

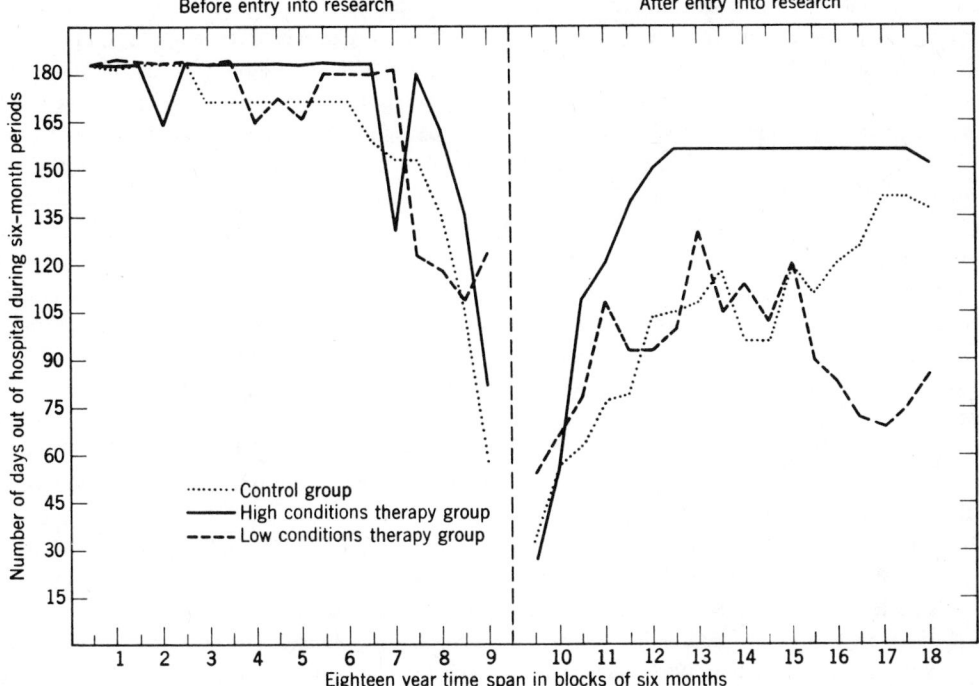

Figure 9.5

Figure 9.5, where it can be seen that there is no difference in the three groups in the nine years preceding treatment, but sizable differences after the initiation of treatment. What is perhaps most striking is the negative effects exerted over a nine-year period by therapists low in understanding, warmth, and genuineness. Their patients tended not to get out of the hospital, and if they did get out, they tended to come back. The data presented in Figure 9.5, reflecting an 18-year period in the lives of the patients, clearly indicates that the three groups differ much more after therapy than prior to therapy, and that this is most striking for patients seen by therapists low in empathy, warmth, and genuineness. Thus the power of the relationship is such that its influence is felt over a nine-year period.

Measuring Nonpossessiveness

Some controversy has developed about the emphasis placed on *nonpossessive* warmth. It has been argued that the therapist, if he is to be a real person in the hour, must be concerned both with the client and with his own needs to at least some degree and, consequently, cannot be truly nonpossessive. Indeed, it has been suggested that if the therapist were completely nonpossessive, he would be ungenuine. Much of this kind of debate is philosophical in nature in that it deals with one's image of how man should be. Granted that it has been difficult to crystalize all the aspects of nonpossessive warmth, there have been attempts to operationally define certain clearly defined parameters of nonpossessiveness. One such attempt involved therapist evaluative statements (Truax, 1969).

When the tapes from the Wisconsin Schizophrenic Project were further analyzed in terms of high versus low levels of therapist evaluation, there was considerable evidence to suggest that therapists who tended to make evaluative statements during therapy had patients who showed marked deterioration. Thus, in terms of the final outcome criterion, patients seen by therapists showing high frequencies of evaluative statements showed absolute average deterioration, in contrast to both the control group and patients seen by therapists who make relatively infrequent evaluative statements. More specifically, similar findings showing statistical significance were obtained using the Q sort and the

Pd and *Mf* scales of the MMPI. When analyses were conducted on data from 40 outpatients seen at Johns Hopkins, similar findings were obtained. More specifically, there was a statistically significant relationship indicating better patient improvement with less frequent therapist evaluative statements. In fact, the findings on all measures indicated that the less the therapists made evaluative statements, the greater the patient improvement. These findings seem to reflect one aspect of nonpossessive warmth: when the therapists are possessive in the sense of making frequent evaluative statements, they are destructive in their effects on their patients.

Further Validating Evidence

There are two series of quite recent cross-validations that are of major importance. First, there are two studies carried out by Tausch and his associates at the University of Hamburg, West Germany. In their first study (Sander, Tausch, Bastine, and Nagel, 1968) they translated both the accurate empathy and the depth of self-exploration scales. In applying these scales to a replication of an earlier experimental manipulation study (Truax and Carkhuff, 1965), they found a similar causal relationship: when therapist accurate empathy was lowered, it caused a lowering of patient self-exploration, and when the therapist level of accurate empathy was raised, it caused a rise in patient self-exploration.

More significantly, the recently completed study (Tausch, Eppel, Fittkau, and Minsel, 1969), related the therapist's level of accurate empathy to both client self-exploration and client improvement: the higher the therapist's level of accurate empathy, the higher the patient's level of self-exploration, and the greater the patient's degree of improvement.

In short, the early findings (Truax, 1963; Truax and Wargo, 1967; Truax and Carkhuff, 1967; and Truax and Mitchell, 1968) have been replicated, not only in several American studies, but also cross-culturally. Clearly, these findings are true of all human relationships, regardless of age, sex, degree of disturbance, or even cultural and language contexts.

The second study provided other important data. *S*s were 14 neurotic clients of *one* therapist. Naive raters rated typewritten transcripts of a number of early psychotherapy sessions on both therapist accurate empathy and client depth of self-exploration. First of all, in support of our contention that the levels of accurate empathy are a function of the therapist, it was found that therapist behavior did not differ significantly across clients. Secondly, in addition to establishing a strong relationship between objective ratings of accurate empathy and depth of self-exploration, there was also a significant relationship between the client's perception of the therapist's empathic behavior and constructive change in the client.

Even more striking, it was found that client statements following high accurate empathy showed higher levels of depth of self-exploration in the initial sentence than over the entire client response. In other words, high levels of accurate empathic understanding elicited *faster* as well as higher levels of client depth of self-exploration. This finding has clear and important implications for brief and time-limited psychotherapy, and should be replicated.

Horowitz (1969), in a recent report of some of the findings from the Psychotherapy Research Project of the Menninger Foundation, offered impressionistic validation of the importance of therapist warmth, and added to our conceptualization of accurate empathy. This is a particularly important paper, since it represents a psychoanalytical affirmation of our earlier findings. In this report, Horowitz was concerned with the "skill of the therapist" as measured by a rank ordering, by a research team, of the therapist's skill in a particular case and the degree to which it was felt that the personality of the therapist inhibited the treatment. Therapists were 26 psychiatrists and psychologists who had seen 42 patients in long-term psychoanalysis or psychotherapy. In almost every case the therapists had a minimum of five years' experience, and many of them had 10 to 15 years. The research team had access to psychological test data, family interviews, and process notes to measure patient improvement, as well as interviews with the therapists and superiors to measure therapist skill. An interesting finding was that, when the 26 therapists were rank-ordered in terms of skill, the distribution was decidedly bi-modal, with six therapists falling in the low and seven in the high category.

The report was concerned with these 13 therapists.

The first finding was that the "highs" were better able to convey warmth to their patients than the therapists ranked lowest on therapist skill. The research team characterized the high therapists as providing a "warm climate," as being "direct, spontaneous and warm," and as being "friendly, consistent, and firm." Thus, from a psychoanalytical point of view, impressionistic evidence suggested that therapist warmth was very much related to the research team's evaluation of positive patient outcome and high levels of therapist skills.

In discussing therapists who were ranked low on skill, Horowitz noted that they often were unable to recognize the seriousness of a patient's condition. He suggested that high levels of therapist empathy included the capacity to tolerate some patient deterioration and, the resultant therapist anxiety. In other words understanding a patient effectively includes both the recognition of patient strengths and weaknesses and the ability to tolerate the anxiety associated with patients' crises in therapy. Although he does not suggest it, an important study would relate therapist levels of empathy to independent measures of therapist anxiety. Clearly, however, it appears intuitively correct that high levels of empathy should be related to the therapist's general anxiety level and to his tolerance for situation-specific anxiety.

In summary, then, impressionistic reports from researchers reflecting a distinctly psychoanalytic orientation, offers further support for the importance of both therapist warmth and accurate empathy.

Other Therapist Characteristics in Process and Outcome Studies

More recent research indicates that several other dimensions of the therapeutic transaction have proven of therapeutic relevance. And other dimensions have shed new light on older findings.

A series of process studies have examined therapist-initiated confrontation in the first therapy interview (Berenson, Mitchell, and Laney, 1968; and Berenson, Mitchell and Moravec, 1968). In these studies, five confrontation categories were delineated: experiential, didactic, strength, weakness, and encouragement to action. Raters were two first-year graduate students in clinical psychology trained to identify appropriate types of confrontation. Experiential confrontation was defined as the therapist's specific response to any discrepancy between the patient and therapist's experiencing of the patient; or to any discrepancy between the patient's statement about himself and the patient's inner experience of himself; or to any discrepancy between the patient and therapist's experience of the therapist. A didactic confrontation was defined as the therapist's direct clarification of the patient's misinformation or lack of information. This type of confrontation may include the therapist's efforts to offer the patient information based on test data, behavior, or data about some aspect of the world, as well as details about the therapist or the structure and function of the therapy process. Confrontation of strength referred to an experiential confrontation that focused on the patient's resources. Weakness referred to an experiential confrontation that focused on the patient's liabilities or pathology. Finally, encouragement to action involved the therapist pressing the patient to act on his world in some constructive manner and discouraging a passive stance toward life. Frequency and type of confrontation were accepted only when the two independent judges agreed upon both presence and type of confrontation.

Briefly, it was found that therapists high on empathy, positive regard, genuineness, and concreteness confronted their clients significantly more often than therapists low on these conditions. Furthermore, high- and low-functioning therapists used confrontations differently. Those high on the three conditions offered significantly more Experiential, Didactic, Strength, and total number of confrontations, while the low functioning therapists offered significantly more Weakness confrontations.

Other pilot process studies have examined therapist reference to the client's significant others (Mitchell and Mitchell, 1968) and therapist immediacy (Mitchell and Mitchell, 1968). Although they are only pilot studies, an important finding is that when therapists are divided into high- and low-functioning types on the basis of empathy, warmth, and genuineness, significant differences in therapist *behaviors*, perhaps more specific to psychotherapy, occur. In these studies, high-functioning therapists, significantly more often than low-functioning therapists, focused their client's exploration on persons who at least theoretically would seem to be more important to the etiology and/or maintenance of their disordered behavior. In the second study, high-functioning therapists were significantly more likely to refer client statements to themselves, perhaps in order to heighten the transference effect and to explore the "here-and-now" therapist-client relationship.

Separate studies dealing with individual and group therapy and with client populations of neurotics, psychotics, juvenile delinquents, and the physically and mentally disabled, have all converged in demonstrating that therapists high in persuasive potency produce better client personality and behavioral improvement than equally trained therapists who are lower in persuasive potency or personal social influence value (Truax, Fine, Moravec, and Millis, 1968; Truax, 1969b).

Other studies have recently shown that therapists who focus greatly on defense mechanisms during the client-therapist transactions have better outcomes than those showing little or no attention to the client's defense mechanisms. However, and very importantly, therapists who are generally low in empathy, warmth, and genuineness but who do focus on client defense mechanisms do get moderately good client outcomes. Those therapists who are low on accurate empathy, nonpossessive warmth, and genuineness and also do not focus on client defense mechanisms account for the bulk of therapeutic failures (Truax, 1969c).

Several other studies on individual therapy show that the extent to which the therapist focuses on the sources of threat and anxiety in the client yields significant results almost identical to those obtained on accurate empathy. The interaction of accurate empathy and focus on threat source were studied and also proved significant. Those therapists high on accurate empathy and also high on threat or anxiety source produced the very best global patient improvement (Truax, 1969d).

A study of client behavior that may be related

to therapist focus on sources of threat and anxiety (Truax, Moravec, and Stephenson, 1969) found that those juvenile delinquents significantly higher on ratings of negative transference showed significantly greater improvement on outcome measures, including an overall outcome measure that included Q-sort measures, the Palo Alto Scale, and time out of institution after treatment. Although the findings indicated strong differences favoring high negative-transfer delinquents, further research is certainly warranted. Our guess is that delinquents are the most likely clients to profit from negative transference, and that perhaps such feelings can be heightened by therapist focus on client sources of threat and anxiety.

Extension of Findings to Student Personnel and College Instruction

Two studies (Wyrick and Mitchell, 1969 and Wagner and Mitchell, 1969) extended the findings from the psychotherapy process to the effectiveness of undergraduate dormitory "counselors" and college instructors, respectively.

Wyrick and Mitchell (1969) studied forty undergraduate dormitory counselors (18 males and 22 females randomly chosen from the population of 90 such counselors at the University of Arkansas). One male and one female actor were trained to play the part of a resident-hall student who had come to the counselor with a "serious" problem. Half of the male and female counselors saw the male actor and half saw the female actor. Analyses of the data indicated that there were no differences between the two actors on depth of self-exploration regardless of the sex of the counselor, and that the counselors did not differ in terms of the levels of accurate empathy, warmth, or genuineness offered the actors as a function of sex. The dormitory counselors were instructed to be as helpful as they could within the limits of their usual responsibilities as counselors.

Ratings of the tape recordings were made by a clinical psychologist with five years of psychotherapy experience, and half the tapes were also rated by an advanced graduate student in education administration who had no prior therapy or counseling experience. Interrater reliabilities were: accurate empathy, .58; warmth, .67; and genuineness, .14. Interrater agreement on genuineness was almost impossible to obtain even when a second effort was made with the second half of the tapes, after some discussion between the two raters. Consequently, findings were reported only for accurate empathy and warmth.

In addition to the objective ratings of empathy and warmth, the Duncan Residence Hall Counselor Evaluation Scale was completed by each dormitory counselor's Head Resident, and from 10 to 15 of his student residents.

The overall findings indicated a product-moment correlation of .30 ($p < .10$) between counselor accurate empathy and the student resident's perception of counselor effectiveness, and a significant correlation of .40 ($p < .05$) between counselor warmth and the students' perception of counselor effectiveness. There was no relationship between head residents' evaluations of the dormitory counselors and any of the core conditions.

Sex differences were extremely important. When male and female counselors were looked at separately, there were no significant correlations between the core conditions and either male resident students or Head Residents' evaluations of perceived male dormitory counselor effectiveness. For *females*, however, there were significant correlations between accurate empathy and female resident students' perceptions of female counselor effectiveness ($r = .52, p < .05$), and between these same evaluations and warmth ($r = .69, p < .01$). Interestingly, the ratings of accurate empathy and warmth were not related to the Head Residents' evaluations of counselor effectiveness.

In summary, while objective ratings of accurate empathy, warmth, and genuineness did not predict perceived dormitory counselor effectiveness among *males*, they did for *female* counselors, at least as far as the resident students were concerned. Our guess is that, as far as males are concerned, perhaps other variables such as masculinity and potency would be better predictors of perceived effectiveness, although further research is needed to test this hypothesis.

Wagner and Mitchell (1969) explored the relationship between instructors' and students' perceptions of the instructors' level of accurate empathy, warmth, and genuineness, and the students' final examination scores. *S*s included 29 instructors and 316 students at the University of Arkansas who taught and took five sections of Introductory Business; five sections of English Grammar and Sentence Structure; five sections of English Composition; and 14 sections of College Algebra. The college algebra sections were divided into two parts: those with freshmen only, and those with at least 25 percent upperclassmen.

The particular courses chosen were those in which each section was made up exclusively of freshmen (with the exception of college algebra) and in which each section took the same departmental final examination. The common departmental examination was necessary to insure that the criterion or outcome measure was the same for all students enrolled in a particular course regardless of their section and instructor.

Briefly, each student in each section and his instructor completed the Relationship Questionnaire as a measure of their perceived levels of the instructor's accurate empathy, warmth, and genuineness. The questionnaire was given approximately four weeks after the term began, before any exam had been given, late enough for the students to have had time to become acquainted with the instructor, but early enough to preclude student response to feedback from examinations.

The effect of the students' perception of the instructors' core conditions was studied by a multiple regression analysis for each course where empathy, warmth, and genuineness were treated as separate predictor variables, and students' SCAT scores were covaried in order to control for overall student academic aptitude. Students' perceptions of their instructors' accurate empathy was significantly related to final examination scores in the freshman section of college algebra ($p < .01$), and approached significance in the English grammar and the second algebra section ($p < .07$; and $p < .10$) respectively. Freshman algebra students' perceptions of their instructors' warmth and genuineness also approached a significant relationship with final exam scores ($p < .07$).

The relationship between the instructors' perceptions of their classroom level of empathy, warmth, and genuineness and students' final examination scores were examined by means of rank-order correlations, since the instructor n's in each course were fairly small. In Introductory Business, the correlations for accurate empathy, warmth, and genuineness were .69, .80, and 1.00, respectively. Since only five instructors were involved in this analysis, only the last correlation was significant ($p < .01$), but all correlations were quite high, and suggest a striking relationship between Introductory Business instructors' perception of their own classroom levels of their facilitative conditions and their students' final examination scores. The only other significant correlation was between the algebra instructors' (both sections) perceptions of genuineness and final scores ($r = .57$, $p < .05$).

These findings are somewhat difficult to integrate. Clearly, however, for freshmen taking college algebra, their perceptions of their instructors' empathy, warmth, and genuineness are related to their final examination scores. That the importance of this perception is related to their being freshmen is also clear, and probably reflects the fact that freshmen, perhaps being more anxious than upperclassmen about success, particularly in algebra, respond more overtly to perceived instructor qualities. It also seems that students' perceptions of accurate empathy are more important than their perceptions of instructors' warmth and genuineness, but that their instructors' perceptions of genuineness is more strongly related to their students' final examination scores than either empathy or warmth. We view these findings as somewhat tentative, but provocative motivations for further research in the general area of education.

Earlier studies with younger students indicate that the importance of accurate empathy, warmth, and genuineness, first demonstrated in the therapist-client relationship, are equally effective among young children. In a study of reading achievement in fourth-graders (Aspy, 1965) the effects of the teacher's level of empathy, warmth, and genuineness in the normal classroom was every bit as important a determinant of reading achievement as was the pupil's IQ. In a further study (Aspy and Hadlock, 1966), students taught by teachers high in accurate empathy, warmth, and genuineness showed an absolute reading achievement gain of over twice that obtained for pupils taught by teachers showing relatively lower levels of empathy, warmth, and genuineness—and the truancy rate in classes with low conditions was twice that occurring in high-condition classrooms.

An interesting hypothesis is that interpersonal characteristics of teachers have important effects upon young children but that, by the time students reach college, the interpersonal skills of teachers become relatively less important. One study (Lewis, Lovell, and Jessee, 1965) suggests that a shift in impact may take place as early as the ninth grade, or as the student leaves elementary school. We suspect that, in graduate school, teacher interpersonal skills may increase in importance, although no study we know of has made this comparison directly. Essentially, then, in the field of education, we are suggesting that there is a curvilinear relationship between the importance of teacher personality characteristics and interpersonal skills and student status as the student progresses from grade through graduate school.

Studies with Supportive Personnel

In this study counselor aides were recruited as secretaries and, without training, assumed varying degrees of responsibility in the rehabilitation counselor role. The design of this study was quite simple: clients in the Hot Springs Rehabilitation Center (they are called students there) were randomly assigned to counselors or counselor aides in one of three experimental conditions: (1) a counselor working alone in the traditional manner; (2) a counselor assisted by a counselor aide being utilized under maximal supervision; and (3) a counselor aide who, under daily supervision, functioned in the complete role of a counselor. Additionally, under each of these three conditions, counselors and counselor aides were randomly assigned to having high and low case loads; the high case-load condition handled twice as many clients as the low case-load condition. With random assignment, clients of equal difficulty or severity were seen under each condition.

Additionally, counselors, counselors plus aides, and aides alone, after an initial period of adjustment and on-the-job training, held regular weekly group counseling sessions with all of their assigned clients. Since the inception of this study, records of the client's vocational rehabilitation progress were kept and, to provide further information, counselors and counselor aides also kept daily diaries indicating the actual client contacts, length of contacts, and reason for contacts. Finally, all group counseling sessions were tape-recorded and were analyzed to evaluate the level of accurate empathy, non-possessive warmth, and genuineness offered to clients by both professional counselors, counselors and aides seeing the same cases, and aides functioning in the counselor role with daily supervision.

The measurement of client progress in vocational rehabilitation was obtained from the evaluation records of the Hot Springs Rehabilitation Center. These records included for each client evaluations of (1) client work quantity or work production; (2) client cooperativeness; (3) client work attitude; (4) quality of client work; (5) client dependability; (6) client ability to learn; (7) client progress in course during last month; and (8) overall progress in course of training.

In spite of the fact that twice as many clients were being handled under the high case-load conditions as under the low case-load conditions, the level of case load had no significant effect on the client's performance or progress.

Significant differential effects of utilizing counselors alone in the traditional fashion, utilizing counselors and aides on the same cases, and utilizing aides under supervision on their own case loads occurred on the client's progress as measured by his *work quantity or work production*, his *work attitude*, and his *dependability*. In each case, the best results were obtained by the aides working alone under the daily supervision of professional counselors. The professional counselors working alone had the second best results, while the counselor plus the aide working with the same individual cases had the poorest effects on clients.

Indeed, on the other measures where no differential significant effect was observed, the differences that did exist were in the same direction. That is, from this evidence there was a slight tendency for the aides, when functioning as counselors under the supervision of professional counselors but with their own separate

case loads, to have the most beneficial effects on clients. When an aide and a counselor jointly handled cases, the effects were somewhat worse than when either the aide or the counselor had their own individual case loads. It may be that too many cooks spoil the broth.

Another set of findings suggested that, in terms of the measures of client dependability, client ability to learn, client progress in course during last month, and client overall progress in course, the professional counselor had better effects under low case-load management, while the aide had better effects with clients when under high case loads. Surprisingly, there was no tendency for different individual professional counselors or different individual aides to respond more favorably to one condition than to another.

Another way of evaluating the effectiveness of the rehabilitation counseling process under high and low case load and conducted by the counselor, the counselor plus the aide, and the aide alone, was to obtain seven-point ratings by the referring field counselor on the quality of counseling and case management for the clients he had himself referred to the Hot Springs Rehabilitation Center. On this measure, the counselors and counselor aides having low case loads were evaluated as providing significantly greater understanding of the client, ability to influence the client, ability to predict problems, effectiveness in helping the client work out problems and arrive at decisions, effectiveness in helping clients with personal problems, effectiveness in helping the client choose alternative programs, and overall management of the case, than those with high case loads. Thus, referring field counselors felt their clients were helped significantly more when seen by counselors and counselor aides having low case loads than high case loads. By contrast, when these same evaluations were analyzed in terms of whether the client himself was seen by a counselor alone, a counselor plus an aide, or an aide alone under supervision, there were no significant differences. If anything, the non-significant differences again favored the aide working alone under daily supervision.

When the tape recorded sessions with clients were analyzed, a clue to the explanation for these disturbing and somewhat puzzling findings emerged. On the average, the aides working alone under daily supervision provided significantly higher levels of nonpossessive warmth to their clients, and showed a tendency to provide a higher level of empathy. As with the measures of outcome, when the counselor utilized an aide to assist him with his own case load, generally less warmth and empathy were communicated to the client.

For the professional rehabilitation counselor, only one positive finding emerged. The differences that did occur also demonstrated that counseling itself, even in the midst of the milieu effects of a comprehensive rehabilitation center, had significant effects on client learning and the vocational rehabilitation progress. When we consider that most clients are seen by a counselor or counselor aide for brief and infrequent sessions, it is perhaps surprising that even in the currently crude state of research, significant effects of counseling can be detected beyond the effects produced by the rest of the comprehensive rehabilitiation center staff combined. The client-counselor relationship in the rehabilitiation facility indeed is a significant aspect of the total vocational rehabilitiation process.

As another important aspect of the data collection, daily diaries were kept by all counselors and counselor aides. On this diary for the rehabilitation counseling project was recorded the daily contact with students and the actual contacts between the counselor aides and the counselor for supervisory or communication purposes. Thus, we have available for each day the names of the students seen by counselors or counselor aides, the reason, the number of minutes spent with each client, and whether this actually constituted "rehabilitation counseling." From a series of complex analyses (Truax, 1968a), some possible explanations of the differential effects of counselors, counselor plus aides, and aides alone under supervision emerged. Thus, we found that, in analysis of 6 months of rehabilitation counseling covering 109 counseling days, the average counselor spent 2150 minutes in contact with clients; the counselor plus aide working together spent an average of 2825 minutes in contact with clients; while the aide working alone under supervision spent on the average 4518 minutes. Thus, the aide working alone

spent over twice the amount of time with clients as did the counselor working alone. It seems likely that this striking finding (significant well beyond the .001 level) was due to the enthusiasm of the aides and their motivation to spend time with clients.

When we looked more closely at the time spent in various kinds of counseling activities, the same general pattern emerged. Thus, in the time spent seeing clients for reason of personal adjustment problems or relations with other students or staff, the same pattern emerged. However, there was also a striking tendency for the counselors to spend fewer actual minutes in contact with clients when their case load was high rather than low, while the aides spent over four times as many actual minutes in contact with clients when they had a high case load, than when they had a low case load ($p < .001$). Thus, it appears that under high case-load conditions, the aides were unusually motivated to see their clients, as if they were saying "I have so many clients to see I had better get busy," while the counselors acted as if they felt under high case loads, "there are just too many clients to see, what's the use?"

When the total number of minutes of actual "counseling" was analyzed, the same pattern emerged, with the aides alone spending almost twice as many minutes in "rehabilitation counseling" as the professional counselors alone ($p < .001$). Again, the aides working with their own case loads spent considerably more time counseling clients under high case-load conditions than low, while the professional counselors working with their own case loads spent considerably more minutes in counseling with their low case-load clients than with their high case-load clients.

In a large rehabilitation facility setting, counselors do not, of course, spend the same amount of time with each client, nor do they see different clients with the same frequency. It therefore became of interest to analyze the data in terms of the number of student contacts occurring under the conditions of counselor alone with his own case load, counselor plus aide with the same case load, and the aide alone with his own case load. There were, during the 109 working days, 143 student contacts by the counselor working alone, 176 contacts by the counselor plus aide working together, and 213 contacts by the aid alone ($p < .05$).

These findings just reviewed occurred in spite of the fact that there was no significant difference under the three conditions in the average number of actual students counseled (as indeed was expected since under random assignment, the case loads were equivalent).

That the effects on clients of the counselors working alone with their own case load, the counselor plus aide working on the same case load, and the aide under supervision working on his own case load, was not simply due to the frequency of contacts, was indicated by further analyses looking specifically at the effects of frequency of student contacts upon the measure of client progress in rehabilitation. There was no tendency or frequency of student contacts to be associated with client outcome.

Thus, it would seem that the somewhat more positive effects on client rehabilitiation when seen by aides under supervision working with their own case load was due both to the somewhat higher levels of warmth and empathy communicated to clients, and the greater motivation and enthusiasm of the counselor aides (as indicated by their spending more time with clients).

The findings concerning the effective use of supportive personnel in rehabilitation counseling are understandable. The counselor aides, of course, were chosen for their ability to relate, and it turned out that they provided significantly higher levels of empathy to their clients than did professional counselors, who were selected primarily on the basis of academic professional credentials. As evidence accumulates, it is becoming clear that the human interpersonal relationship is central to the therapeutic process. It is perhaps time that university training programs focus more closely on this aspect of professional development.

IMPLICATIONS OF THE FINDINGS TO DATE

Implications for Selection and Training

From existing data it would appear that only one out of three people entering professional training have the requisite interpersonal skills to prove helpful to patients. Further, there is no evidence that the usual traditional graduate training program has any positive value in producing therapists who are more helpful than nonprofessionals. In short, current procedures for selection and training are indefensible. Out of habit we still cling to them and perpetuate them even when the evidence is clear. Moreover, the chances that a trainee will be taught by a therapist who is himself either ineffective or harmful are two out of three. In this light it is not surprising that nonprofessionals in all studies to date apppear to be as effective or more effective than the average trained professional. What would be a sensible approach to selection and training and employment?

We would like to outline the selection and training procedures we used in the counselor-aide study just discussed, since we feel that the selection and training of helping personnel, whether they are professionals or not, have a number of commonalities. One implication, which we intend is that selection based on professional credentials, per se, is relatively worthless.

First, the candidate must meet existing qualifications for employment by the agency or facility. Primarily, these have been judgments by persons responsible for employment of the candidates—general abilities, dependability, sense of responsibility, ethics, appearance, and other such usual considerations that are applicable to any employee so as to minimally insure that he will be able to function within the setting that he is employed. These will vary from setting to setting, so that somewhat different standards would be used for the employment of a so-called "indigenous" person in a ghetto setting than in a middle-class school.

The second aspect of selection has involved drawing upon past research data (Truax, 1968b), and the summary of research studies published since 1963 showing personality correlates of such interpersonal scales as Accurate Empathy. We have been using the MMPI and the EPPS as selection devices. Specifically, we have looked for candidates who on the MMPI (using k-converted raw scores) scored less than 27 on Pt, less than 20 on D, less than 30 on Mf, less than 21 on Si, less than 30 on the Welsh Anxiety Index from the MMPI, and less than 0.92 on the Welsh Internalization Ratio, while we have looked for candidates whose score is higher than 19 on Ma and higher than 142 on the Constructive Personality Change Index of the MMPI. In using the Edwards Personal Preference Schedule for selection, we have looked for candidates who scored less than 10 on *N* Deference, less than 8 on *N* Order, less than 21 on *N* Intraception, less than 7 on *N* Abasement, less than 11 on *N* Consistency, more than 14 on *N* Dominance, more than 17 on *N* Change and more than 14 on *N* Autonomy. In an interpretive sense, the research evidence suggests that we will get candidates with more natural therapeutic or interpersonal skill if we look for people low in anxiety, depression, and introversion, who are at the same time themselves striving, strong, dominant, active, and autonomous individuals. As one can tell from looking over the selection scores, we are looking for stable "nice guys" with high ego-strength, who are strong rather than passive.

At the final, and most critical stage of selection, those candidates who have passed the first two aspects of selection are asked to do one or more group interviews (or group therapy, if that term is preferred) with real clients. They are told that their task is to get to know these particular clients, their feelings, their problems, their strengths, and their weaknesses. With these instructions, they are placed in the role of a group leader and asked to conduct a session that is itself tape-recorded. Thus far, we have simply tried to present the candidate with a more or less randomly selected group of the kinds of clients that we would expect him to work with. The tape recordings themselves, as they reflect his adequacy in interpersonal skills, constitutes the critical selection factor. These tapes are then rated on accurate empathy, nonpossessive warmth, and genuineness of the candidate in interacting with real clients, and the degree of self-exploration that he is able to elicit from the group. These scales are available on request from the Arkansas Rehabilitation Research and Training Center, University of Arkansas.

More specifically, candidates selected to become Trained Practical Counselors, or for employment as professional counselors, were those who averaged 4.0 or above on the non-possessive warmth scale, 4.0 or above on the genuineness scale, and 5.0 or above on the accurate empathy scale. In other words, we went about selecting people who were unusually naturally highly skilled in interpersonal relations and who could provide adequate levels of therapeutic conditions.

It is of considerable interest to note that postinternship and postpracticum students in Clinical Psychology and Counseling Psychology have been reported to score an average of 2.50 on the accurate empathy scale. In fact, it has been our experience over the past 9 years, that only a small percentage of professional counselors and psychotherapists achieve average scores of 5.0 or above. To give some indication of the degree of selection, in filling 7 Trained Practical Counselor positions, out of 34 individuals who passed stages 1 and 2, only 7 were able to achieve these minimally higher levels of interpersonal skills and were accepted. It is probable that in some areas even more rigid selection procedures along these lines would be possible where the potential pool of candidates is quite large. Where such a potentially large pool exists, it might be useful and economical to first preselect people on the basis of Relationship Questionnaires filled out on candidates by clients after relatively brief interactions. (The relationship questionnaire, also available from the Arkansas Rehabilitation Research and Training Center, is a rough paper-and-pencil test measuring such interpersonal skills as accurate empathy, warmth, and genuineness.)

In our own continuing effort at selection, we are beginning to incorporate recent research findings which show that such additional therapist characteristics as degree of persuasive potency and type and extent of constructive confrontations with the clients are also separate and significant contributions to client benefit.

After selecting on this basis, we have candidates who, according to available research evidence, are "inherently helpful" people—the kind of people whose neighbors and friends seek out in time of need and distress, and the kind of person who we all might wish were the only kind of person to enter graduate training in psychotherapy. The question becomes now, "What can we do to make him more helpful and how can we best utilize his abilities?"

The basic aspect of effective training, indeed the basis of the phenomena of learning itself, is structured *feedback*. Feedback telling the trainee of his own behavior and its consequences on the setting and personnel where he works, and most centrally of the consequences upon the client himself, is the central aspect of training and indeed of ongoing *quality control* throughout the tenure of his later employment. If he gets such feedback, he will continue to learn how to become more effective.

It is perhaps the most glaring deficit in the helping relationships that professional counselors, clinical psychologists, psychiatrists, social workers and others rarely, if ever, are given any systematic feedback of their effects on clients. It is the general case that the professional in the helping relationships can conclude all his training at a university and even receive a doctorate, can be employed, promoted, pass licensing examinations where they exist, and become a Diplomate of a Board of Examiners in his profession (where they exist) *without anyone, at any point, attempting to systematically evaluate the effects he has on his human clients.*

In the normal process of on-the-job-training, the professional and nonprofessional will receive very specific and concrete feedback about their performance in filling out forms, adhering to employer regulations and requirements, and ability to follow standard operating procedures. They will also normally obtain quite specific feedback, during on-the-job training, of any negative impact they have on other employees of the agency or facility. This is standard and predictable for any kind of employment in any kind of setting.

To insure that he will be able to provide maximum benefit *for clients*, however, the trainee must also get relatively specific and systematic feedback in terms of (1) the level of interpersonal skills with which he relates to clients and (2) the average level of client benefits obtained by his clients in comparison to the clients seen by other professional or non-professional counselors. This is basic to any counselor education program that is at all interested in producing effective counselors.

The majority of the research studies assessed the levels of empathy, warmth, and genuineness

by the use of these research scales developed for use with tape recordings of actual counseling or psychotherapy. As was suggested six years ago (Truax, 1963) the rating scales themselves can be used in a didactic manner for training beginning therapists. An approach to training, using the research scales in an integrated didactic and experiential program, has been described (Truax, Carkhuff, and Douds, 1964; Truax and Carkhuff, 1967). This training program has been applied to several training groups, both at professional and nonprofessional personnel levels.

The three central elements in the training approach can be summarized as (1) a therapeutic context in which the supervisor communicates high levels of accurate empathy, nonpossessive warmth, and genuineness to the trainees themselves; (2) a highly specific didactic training using the research scales for "shaping" the trainees' responses toward high levels of empathy, warmth, and genuineness; and (3) a focused group-therapy experience that allows the emergence of the trainee's own idiosyncratic therapeutic self through self-exploration and consequent integration of his didactic training with his personal values, goals, and life style.

While a complete description of the training program is contained in a book developed specifically for use in training and practice (Truax and Carkhuff, 1967), a few brief comments about the use of the research scales should help to clarify the didactic nature of the training. The scales are used to identify tape-recorded samples of experienced therapists who are, in fact, offering very high levels of therapeutic conditions, thus providing models for imitation. It should be remembered that even the best recordings of total sessions usually provide a number of examples of precisely what not to do. Secondly, the trainees are taught the use of the scales so that they will learn to identify high and low levels of empathy, warmth, and genuineness in their own therapy and in that of others. Thirdly, "empathy training," "warmth training," or "genuineness training" is provided by placing a tape recording of patient talk and then requiring trainees to make immediate "therapeutic responses" that are immediately rated on the research scales to provide prompt feedback. As they "shape" their responses toward higher levels of empathy, warmth, and genuineness, they begin role-playing; this, in turn, is recorded, brought to class, and rated by a group of trainees on the research scales. Thus, they compete among themselves in ability to communicate these therapeutic conditions. Finally, they begin one-shot interviews with real clients, which again are tape-recorded and brought to class session for rating.

In all, *the complete basic training program involves less than 100 hours of training.*

There now exist a number of studies (reviewed in Truax and Carkhuff, 1967) which indicate that trainees (both professional and non-professional counselors) can be brought to a level of interpersonal skill that is (1) nearly commensurate with that of highly experienced and effective counselors; (2) significantly above that of postpracticum and postinternship trainees in counseling and psychotherapy at major universities involved in doctoral training; and (3) effective in producing significant positive changes in mildly and severely disturbed clients. Taken together, the available evidence strongly suggests positive benefit for this approach to training.

More recently, our experience suggests that more permanent and lasting effects on therapist behavior can be produced by periodic workshops or "seminars" for those who have completed a basic short-term training program: the effect is to reinforce the habit of relating to clients with high levels of interpersonal skills and to discourage the counselor's tendency to fall back on his lifelong style of relating to others when dealing in a professional role with clients.

Recent research by Martin (1968) has demonstrated that trainees in professional counseling show gains in accurate empathy, nonpossessive warmth, and genuineness, by specific feedback from *self*-evaluations. It seems reasonable, and we are currently pursuing this in research, that minimally high levels of counseling skill can be maintained and enhanced by simply having groups of counselors periodically tape-record their own contacts with clients, and, in group meetings, obtain feedback from group ratings of their ability to provide high levels of therapeutic conditions or interpersonal skills (such as empathy).

Even more importantly, *feedback from measurement of client benefits* is central to maintaining and enchancing the effective qualities of counseling services. While no single criterion exists (and probably never will exist) for the measurement of client benefits, it is the clear and immediate responsibility of every counseling unit providing services to at least minimally state its goals for client benefits and then measure these benefits per client. This would provide *feedback* of the averages of such benefits per professional counselor or per non-professional counselor. This gives the counseling unit *quality control*, and provides individual feedback to counselors, on the basis of which they can more adequately judge what they should and should not be doing, and what does and what does not lead to successful counseling outcomes.

Implications for the Practicing Therapist

The implications for the practitioner are relatively straightforward.

First, the odds are two out of three that he is spending his energy, commitment, and care for mankind wastefully; he is either ineffective or harmful. Two out of three of his colleagues, he can be quite certain, are ineffective or harmful. In order to insure his own effectiveness he must himself have feedback as to his levels of interpersonal skills and, more importantly, about his short-term and long-term effects on patients. This means that some kind of evaluation of patient functioning should be carried out with each patient seen in private or public practice.

As to the practice of psychotherapy itself, a number of "rules" seem clearly valid. Therapists need feedback regarding patient behavior and improvement during and after psychotherapy. They also need on-going feedback of their own in-therapy behaviors over time and for different classes of patients. Thus, therapists can profit from feedback regarding changes in their own behavior, which may change in systematic ways as a function of time and patients.

Generally, therapists would be wise to learn what makes them effective and ineffective in situations other than psychotherapy, and apply these learnings to their in-therapy behavior. For too long we have viewed psychotherapy as an isolated, highly unique situation. Clearly, it is not. Any situation that involves change, persuasion, and helping can provide models for psychotherapy behavior. We are not saying that psychotherapy is nothing more than being a friend, a husband, or a father, but that these roles have some basic similarities to the role of the psychotherapist.

Basically, the personality of the therapist is more important than his techniques. Conversely, however, techniques that are specific to certain kinds of patients and psychotherapy goals can be quite potent in the hands of a therapist who is inherently helpful, and who offers high levels of empathic understanding, warmth, genuineness, potency, immediacy, and who can confront his clients in a constructive manner.

It would be too simple to take a relatively "know-nothing" attitude and state categorically that therapists should offer the highest possible levels of any of the interpersonal skills we have discussed. Time, however, is a most important factor. High levels of accurate empathy may be quite threatening to a psychotic if they are offered at the beginning of therapy. By the same token, high levels of warmth later in therapy may decrease a patient's motivation to change by reducing his anxiety below a level necessary for change. Knowledge of patient pathology and strengths, a clear and precise conceptualization of the knowledge we have gathered from psychoanalytic, client-centered, existential, and eclectic sources, should not be cast aside. We see our findings as adding to, not undoing, efforts of the past. We do, however, want to change the priorities. We want to emphasize the therapist-as-person before the therapist-as-expert or therapist-as-technician. We want to emphasize the commonality that psychotherapy has with other aspects of life. We want to emphasize the therapist as a viable human being engaged in a terribly human endeavor.

REFERENCES

Alexik, M. and Carkhuff, R. R. The effects of the manipulation of client depth of self-exploration upon high and low functioning counselors. *Journal of Clinical Psychology*, 1967, **23**, 212–215.

Anderson, D. L. A study of selected dimensions of the counselor-client relationship. Unpublished doctoral dissertation, University of North Dakota, 1968.

Aspy, D. N. A study of three facilitative conditions and their relationships to the achievement of third grade students. Unpublished doctoral dissertation, University of Kentucky, 1965.

Aspy, D. N., and Hadlock, W. The effects of high and low functioning teachers upon student performance. Unpublished thesis, University of Florida, 1966.

Berenson, B. G., Mitchell, K. M., and Laney, R. Level of therapist functioning, types of confrontation, and type of patient. *Journal of Clinical Psychology*, 1968, **24**, 111–113.

Berenson, B. G., Mitchell, K. M., and Moravec, J. A. Level of therapist functioning, type of confrontation, and patient depth of self-exploration. *Journal of Counseling Psychology*, 1968, **15**, 136–139.

Bergin, A. E. Some implications of psychotherapy research for therapeutic practice. *Journal of Abnormal Psychology*, 1966, **71**, 235–246.

Bergin, A. E., and Jasper, L. G. Correlates of empathy in psychotherapy: A replication. *Journal of Abnormal Psychology*, 1969, **74**, 447–481.

Bergin, A. E., and Solomon, S. Personality and performance correlates of empathic understanding in psychotherapy. In T. Tomlinson and J. Hart (Eds.), *New directions in client-centered therapy*. Boston: Houghton-Mifflin, 1970.

Betz, B. Bases of therapeutic leadership in psychotherapy with the schizophrenic patient. *American Journal of Psychotherapy*, 1963, **11**, 1090–1091.

Bordin, E. S. *Psychological counseling*. New York: Appleton-Century-Crofts, 1955.

Bozarth, J. D., and Renzaglia, G. A. Therapeutic counseling conditions with institutionalized mentally retarded. *Studies in mental retardation*, Study No. 2. Carbondale, Illinois: Southern Illinois University Press, 1968.

Buber, M. Distance and relation. *Psychiatry*, 1953, **16**, 104.

Carkhuff, R. R., and Alexik, M. Effect of client depth of self-exploration upon high and low functioning counselors. *Journal of Counseling Psychology*, 1967, **14**, 350–355.

Carkhuff, R. R., and Berenson, B. G. *Beyond counseling and therapy*. New York: Holt, Rinehart, and Winston, 1967.

Carkhuff, R. R., and Truax, C. B. Training in counseling and psychotherapy: An evaluation of an integrated didactic and experiential approach. *Journal of Consulting Psychology*, 1965, **29**, 333–336. (a)

Carkhuff, R. R., and Truax, C. B. Lay mental health counseling: The effects of lay group counseling. *Journal of Consulting Psychology*, 1965, **29**, 426–431. (b)

Dickenson, W. A., and Truax, C. B. Group counseling with college underachievers: Comparisons with a control group and relationship to empathy, warmth, and genuineness. *Personnel and Guidance Journal*, 1966, **45**, 243–247.

Eysenck, H. J. The effects of psychotherapy: An evaluation. *Journal of Consulting Psychology*, 1952, **16**, 319–324.

Fey, W. F. Acceptance by others and its relation to acceptance of self and others: A reevaluation. *Journal of Abnormal and Social Psychology*, 1955, **50**, 274–276.

Frank, J. D. *Persuasion and healing*. Baltimore: Johns Hopkins Press, 1961.

Friel, T., Kratochvil, D., and Carkhuff, R. R. Effect of client depth of self-exploration on therapists categorized by level of experience and type of training. Unpublished manuscript, State University of New York at Buffalo, 1968.

Halkides, G. An investigation of therapeutic success as a function of four variables. Unpublished doctoral dissertation, University of Chicago, 1958.

Hart, J. T. A replication of the Halkides study. Unpublished manuscript, University of Wisconsin, 1960.

Heller, K., Myers, R. A., and Kline, L. V. Interviewer behavior as a function of standardized client roles. *Journal of Consulting Psychology*, 1963, **27**, 117–122.

Horowitz, L. Therapist's personality and levels of competence. Paper read at American Psychiatric Association meeting, New York, 1969.

Jourard, S. M. *The transparent self*. Princeton: Van Nostrand, 1964.

Kanfer, F. H., and Marston, A. R. Conditioning of self-reinforcement responses: An analogue to self-confidence training. *Psychological Reports*, 1963, **13**, 63–70.

Kiesler, D. V. Some myths of psychotherapy research and the search for a paradigm. *Psychological Bulletin*, 1966, **65**, 110–136.

Krumboltz, J. D. Counseling for behavior change. Paper read at American Personnel and Guidance Association meeting, Boston, 1963.

Levitt, B. E. The results of psychotherapy with children: An evaluation. *Journal of Consulting Psychology*, 1957, **21**, 189–196.

Lewis, W. A., Lovell, J. T., and Jessee, B. E. Interpersonal relationships and pupil progress. *Personnel and Guidance Journal*, 1965, **44**, 396–401.

Martin, D. B. A method of self-evaluation for counselor education. Bureau of Research, Office of Education, Department of Health, Education, and Welfare, 1968.

Matz, P. B. Outcome of hospital treatment of ex-service patients with nervous and mental disease in the U. S. Veterans Bureau. *U. S. Veterans Medical Bulletin*, 1929, **5**, 829–842.

Melloh, R. A. Accurate empathy and counselor effectiveness. Unpublished doctoral dissertation, University of Florida, 1964.

Mitchell, K. M., and Mitchell, R. M. The significant other scale: A measure of content in psychotherapy. Paper read at South-western Psychological Association meeting, New Orleans, 1968.

Mitchell, R. M., and Mitchell, K. M. A measure of therapist immediacy. Unpublished manuscript, Arkansas Rehabilitation Research and Training Center, University of Arkansas, 1968.

Raush, H. L., and Bordin, E. S. Warmth in personality development and in psychotherapy. *Psychiatry*, 1957, **20**, 351–363.

Rogers, C. R. *Client-centered therapy*. Cambridge, Mass.: Riverside Press, 1951.

Rogers, C. R. The necessary and sufficient conditions of therapeutic personality change. *Journal of Consulting Psychology*, 1957, **22**, 95–103.

Rogers, C. R. The interpersonal relationship: The core of guidance. *Harvard Educational Review*, 1962, **32**, 416–429.

Rogers, C. R., Gendlin, G. T., Kiesler, D. V., and Truax, C. B. *The therapeutic relationship and its impact: A study of psychotherapy with schizophrenics*. Madison: University of Wisconsin Press, 1967.

Rogers, C. R., and Truax, C. B. The therapeutic conditions antecedent to change: A theoretic view. In Rogers, C. R., Gendlin, G. T., Kiesler, D. V., and Truax, C. B. *The therapeutic relationship and its impact: A study of psychotherapy with schizophrenics*. Madison: University of Wisconsin Press, 1967.

Ross, T. Z. *An enquiry into prognosis in the neuroses*. London: Cambridge University Press, 1936.

Sander, K., Tausch, R., Bastine, R., and Nagel, K. Die auswirkung experimenteller anderungen des psychotherapeutenverhaltens auf klienten in psychotherapeutischen gesprachen. Im manuskript 1968.

Shapiro, J. G. Relationships between expert and neophyte ratings of therapeutic conditions. *Journal of Consulting and Clinical Psychology*, 1968, **32**, 87–89. (a)

Shapiro, J. G. Relationship between visual and auditory cues of therapeutic effectiveness. Unpublished manuscript, Arkansas Rehabilitation Research and Training Center, University of Arkansas, 1968. (b)

Shapiro, J. G., Foster, C. P., and Powell, T. Facial and bodily cues of genuineness, empathy, and warmth. *Journal of Clinical Psychology*, 1968, **24**, 233–236.

Shapiro, J. G., Krauss, H. H., and Truax, C. B. Therapeutic conditions and disclosure beyond the therapeutic encounter. *Journal of Counseling Psychology*, 1969, **16**, 290–294.

Shapiro, J. G., and Voog, T. Effect of the inherently helpful person on student academic achievement. *Journal of Counseling Psychology*, 1969, **16** (in press).

Stoffer, D. L. An investigation of positive behavioral change as a function of genuineness, non-possessive warmth, and empathic understanding. Unpublished doctoral dissertation, Ohio State University, 1968.

Strupp, H. H. *Psychotherapists in action.* New York: Grune and Stratton, 1960.

Tausch, R., Eppel, H., Fittkau, B., and Minsel, R. Variablen and zusammenhange in der gesprachspsychotherapie. *Zeitschrift Fur Psychologie*, 1969, **176**, 93–102.

Truax, C. B. A scale for the measurement of accurate empathy. *Psychiatric Institute Bulletin*, Wisconsin Psychiatric Institute, University of Wisconsin, 1961, **1**, 12. (a)

Truax, C. B. Therapeutic conditions. *Psychiatric Institute Bulletin*, Wisconsin Psychiatric Institute, University of Wisconsin, 1961, **1**, 10. (b)

Truax, C. B. A tentative scale for the measurement of unconditional positive regard. *Psychiatric Institute Bulletin*, Wisconsin Psychiatric Institute, University of Wisconsin, 1962, **2**, 1. (a)

Truax, C. B. A tentative scale for the measurement of therapist genuineness of self-congruence. *Discussion Papers*, Wisconsin Psychiatric Institute, University of Wisconsin, 1962, **35**, (b)

Truax, C. B. Comparisons between control patients, therapy patients perceiving high conditions, and therapy patients perceiving low conditions on measures of constructive personality change. *Brief Research Reports*, Wisconsin Psychiatric Institute, University of Wisconsin, 1962, **31**, (c)

Truax, C. B. Variations in levels of accurate empathy offered in the psychotherapy relationship and case outcome. *Brief Research Reports*, Wisconsin Psychiatric Institute, University of Wisconsin, 1962, **38**, (d)

Truax, C. B. Effective ingredients in psychotherapy: An approach to unraveling the patient-therapist interaction. *Journal of Counseling Psychology*, 1963, **10**, 256–263.

Truax, C. B. Therapist empathy, warmth, and genuineness and patient personality change in group psychotherapy: A comparison between interaction unit measures, time sample measures, and patient perception measures. *Journal of Clinical Psychology*, 1966, **22**, 225–229. (a)

Truax, C. B. Influence of patient statements on judgments of therapist statements during psychotherapy. *Journal of Clinical Psychology*, 1966, **22**, 335–337. (b)

Truax, C. B. The evolving understanding of counseling and psychotherapy and the use of trained practical counselors or therapists. Paper read at the International Congress of Applied Psychology, Amsterdam, 1968. (a)

Truax, C. B. The use of practical counselors or therapists and the evolving understanding of counseling and psychotherapy. *Discussion Papers*, Arkansas Rehabilitation Research and Training Center, University of Arkansas, 1968, **12**. (b)

Truax, C. B. Therapist interpersonal reinforcement of client self-exploration and therapeutic outcome in group psychotherapy. *Journal of Counseling Psychology*, 1968, **15**, 225–231. (c)

Truax, C. B. Effects of client-centered psychotherapy upon schizophrenic patients: Nine years pre and post therapy hospitalization. Unpublished manuscript, University of Florida, 1969. (a)

Truax, C. B. Therapist persuasive potency and client outcome. Unpublished manuscript, University of Florida, 1969. (b)

Truax, C. B. Therapist focus on client defense mechanisms and client outcome. Unpublished manuscript, University of Florida, 1969. (c)

Truax, C. B. Therapist focus on source of client anxiety and client outcome. Unpublished manuscript, University of Florida, 1969. (d)

Truax, C. B., and Carkhuff, R. R. For better or for worse: The process of psychotherapeutic personality change. Paper read at Academic Assembly on Clinical Psychology, McGill University, Montreal, Canada, 1963.

Truax, C. B., and Carkhuff, R. R. The experimental manipulation of therapeutic conditions. *Journal of Consulting Psychology*, 1965, **29**, 119–124.

Truax, C. B., and Carkhuff, R. R. *Toward effective counseling and psychotherapy: Training and practice.* Chicago: Aldine, 1967.

Truax, C. B., Carkhuff, R. R., and Douds, J. Toward an integration of the didactic and experiential approaches to training in counseling and psychotherapy. *Journal of Counseling Psychology*, 1964, **11**, 240–247.

Truax, C. B., Carkhuff, R. R., and Kodman, F., Jr. Relationships between therapist-offered conditions and patient change in group psychotherapy. *Journal of Clinical Psychology*, 1965, **21**, 327–329.

Truax, C. B., Silber, L. D., and Carkhuff, R. R. Accurate empathy, non-possessive warmth, genuineness and therapeutic outcome in lay group counseling. Unpublished manuscript, Arkansas Rehabilitation Research and Training Center, University of Arkansas, 1966.

Truax, C. B., Fine, H., Moravec, H. A., and Millis, W. Effects of therapist persuasive potency in individual psychotherapy. *Journal of Clinical Psychology*, 1968, **24**, 359–362.

Truax, C. B., and Mitchell, K. M. The psychotherapeutic and the psychonoxious: Human encounters that change behavior. In Feldman, M. (Ed.), *Studies in psychotherapy and behavioral change.* Vol. 1. *Research in individual psychotherapy.* Buffalo: State University of New York Press, 1968. 55–92.

Truax, C. B., Moravec, J. A., and Stevenson, T. Role of negative transference in psychotherapy with institutionalized juvenile delinquents Unpublished manuscript, University of Florida, 1969.

Truax, C. B., and Silber, L. D. Personality and psychotherapeutic skill. Unpublished manuscript, Arkansas Rehabilitation Research and Training Center, University of Arkansas, 1966.

Truax, C. B., and Wargo, D. G. Psychotherapeutic encounters that change behavior for better or for worse. *American Journal of Psychotherapy*, 1966, **20**, 499–520.

Truax, C. B., and Wargo, D. G. Antecedents to outcome in group psychotherapy with juvenile delinquents: Effects of therapeutic conditions, alternate sessions, vicarious therapy pre-training and client self-exploration. Unpublished manuscript, Arkansas Rehabilitation Research and Training Center, University of Arkansas, 1967. (a)

Truax, C. B., and Wargo, D. G. Antecedents to outcome in group psychotherapy with hospitalized mental patients: Effects of therapeutic conditions, alternate sessions, vicarious therapy pre-training and patient self-exploration. Unpublished manuscript, Arkansas Rehabilitation Research and Training Center, University of Arkansas, 1967. (b)

Truax, C. B., and Wargo, D. G. Antecedents to outcome in group psychotherapy with outpatients: Effects of therapeutic conditions, alternate sessions, vicarious therapy pre-training and patient self-exploration. *Journal of Consulting and Clinical Psychology*, 1969, **33**, (in press).

Truax, C. B., Wargo, D. G., Frank, J. D., Imber, S. D., Battle, C. C., Hoehn-Saric, R., Nash, E. H., and Stone, A. R. Therapist empathy, genuineness and warmth and patient therapeutic outcome. *Journal of Consulting Psychology*, 1966, **30**, 395–401. (a)

Truax, C. B., Wargo, D. G., Frank, J. D., Imber, S. D., Battle, C. C., Hoehn-Saric, R., Nash, E. H., and Stone, A. R. Therapists' contribution to accurate empathy, non-possessive warmth and genuineness in psychotherapy. *Journal of Clinical Psychology*, 1966, **22**, 331–334.

Truax, C. B., Wargo, D. G., and Silber, L. Effects of high accurate empathy and non-possessive warmth during group psychotherapy upon female institutionalized delinquents. *Journal of Abnormal Psychology*, 1966, **71**, 267–274.

Wagner, H. M., and Mitchell, K. M. Relationship between perceived instructors' accurate empathy, warmth, and genuineness and college achievement. *Discussion Papers*, Arkansas Rehabilitation Research and Training Center, University of Arkansas, 1969, **13**.

Wargo, D. G. The Barron ego-strength and LH[4] scales as predictors and indicators of change in psychotherapy. *Brief Research Reports*, Wisconsin Psychiatric Institute, University of Wisconsin, 1962, **21**.

Whitehorn, J. C. Human factors in psychiatry. *Bulletin of New York Academy of Medicine*, 1964, **40**, 451–466.

Whitehorn, J. C., and Betz, B. A study of psychotherapeutic relationships between physicians and schizophrenic patients. *American Journal of Psychiatry*, 1954, **3**, 321–331.

Wright, L., and Truax, C. B. Interjudge agreement for therapeutic conditions offered in child therapy from video tape segments. Unpublished manuscript, University of Oklahoma Medical Center, Oklahoma City, 1969.

Wyrick, T. J., and Mitchell, K. M. Relationship between accurate empathy, warmth, and genuineness and perceived resident assistant effectiveness. *Discussion Papers*, Arkansas Rehabilitation Research and Training Center, University of Arkansas, 1969, **12**.

10

CONTENT-ANALYSIS STUDIES OF PSYCHOTHERAPY: 1954 THROUGH 1968[1]

GERALD MARSDEN

UNIVERSITY OF MICHIGAN

Content analysis is a venerable technique of naturalistic documentary research—one that has excited great enthusiasm for its promise of providing objectivity with substance, but one that has also been disparaged for defaulting on this very promise. The initial momentum in its development came from the fields of journalism, literature, and political science, but in recent years many sophisticated developments in content analysis, developments that served to renew its promise, have occurred in psychotherapy research. The purpose of this review is to discuss applications of content analysis to psychotherapy in the period from 1954, when they were reviewed by Auld and Murray (1955),[2] through 1968, to summarize the salient findings, and to discuss problems of method.

Content analysis denotes a research technique for the systematic ordering of the content of communication processes. Typically, it involves procedures for division of content into units, for assignment of each unit to a category or to a position on a metric, and for summarizing or otherwise manipulating coded units to provide a

---

[1] This chapter represents a considerable elaboration of a previously published article (Marsden, 1965).

[2] Auld and Murray's article reviewed some papers published during and after 1954, but their coverage is far more complete through 1953. In this chapter, studies involving comparison of interview content variables with physiological variables, and studies using content-analysis procedures to evaluate operant conditioning studies, are not treated systematically because they are beyond its scope and because they have been recently and well reviewed elsewhere, including some of the chapters of this volume.

basis for inference concerning their significance. The basic contribution of content analysis is that it makes public the grounds on which an investigator makes inferences about the significance of a body of communication. The varieties of content analysis applied to psychotherapy data fall into three broad procedure families which I have called models: the classical, the pragmatic, and the nonquantitative.

MODELS OF CONTENT ANALYSIS

The classical model was exhaustively described by Berelson (1952), who offered the following definition: "Content analysis is a research technique for the objective, systematic, and quantitative description of the manifest content of communication" (p. 18). Berelson discussed in detail several important assumptions underlying this definition.[3] Two of these are of particular interest here because their necessity is challenged by the nonclassical models discussed below. These are the assumptions regarding the limitation to manifest content and the use of quantitative methods.

The aim of those who developed the classical model was to achieve objective (for instance, reliable) and systematic results. They felt this could best be done through the use of quantitative methods. Berelson explicitly assumed the usefulness of quantifying communication content and also assumed that the frequency of content characteristics is an important dimension of the communication process. Quantification was, for him, an essential part of content analysis.

Berelson's restriction to manifest content derived from his desire to assure a common meeting ground for the communicator, the person with whom he communicates, and the content analyst. Yet the implications of the phrase "manifest content" have not always been understood as Berelson intended. He stated

explicitly that he considered musical, pictorial, plastic, and gestural systems of communication, as well as lexical systems, appropriate for content-analysis investigation (p. 13). The common distinction between formal characteristics of communication and a narrow definition of its content (for example, lexical content), though useful in some situations, seems unsatisfactory in any generic definition of content analysis. But more important is Berelson's use of the word "manifest," by which he intended to limit content analysis to the semantic and syntactic aspects of communication, in which meanings are relatively public, and to prevent its extension to the pragmatic aspect—to the relationship between the communication symbol and its user. The restriction was not intended to rule out the use of inference in coding relevant syntactic and semantic content units to the categories of the content-analysis system, but merely to define the realm within which inference was legitimate.

The pragmatic model challenges this requirement that content analysis be restricted from the pragmatic aspect of communication. While in the classical model units are coded to categories descriptive of the content itself, in the pragmatic model units are coded to categories that describe some condition of the communicator or the relation between him and his communication. In the classical model, once the units are coded, the analyst may make further inferences about the internal state of the communicator, and these inferences are the point at issue, subject to validation only by other procedures. In the pragmatic model, this kind of inference is made initially, at the time of coding, and is the basis of the coding. This procedure is usually chosen when the behavioral cue for the internal condition in question (on which the classical model depends) cannot be specified satisfactorily.[4]

This difference in research strategy provides one focus for argument of the more generic controversy of clinical versus statistical pre-

---

[3] A more recent discussion of definitions of content analysis and their underlying assumptions can be found in Holsti (1969, Ch. 1).

[4] The distinction between the classical and pragmatic models is related to, but not identical with, the distinction made in several places in Pool (1959a) between the representational and instru-

mental models of language behavior as bases for content analysis studies (for instance, Mahl, 1959a). Pragmatic model studies would be grouped among those based on an instrumental view of language, as would some but not all studies reviewed in the section on classical model studies of internal states.

diction (Gough, 1962). The classical model places a premium on objectivity and is designed so that a worker with minimal special training can reliably perform the analysis, maximizing his (and his reader's) ability to specify just what configuration of data led to the investigator's inference. The price paid for this precision is often superficial results. The pragmatic model attempts to realize psychological meaningfulness by working directly with complex clinical constructs. Admittedly, the pragmatic model involves assumptions not required by the classical model, and these constitute a weakness in the logic of the method, but a weakness tolerated in the interest of utilizing the skills and understanding of the clinician while formalizing the conditions under which they are used, to insure the procedural rigor suitable to a scientific undertaking. Those who place little stock in the power of clinical skills as instruments of science consider the compromise with objectivity unwarranted (Leary, 1960), while clinicians who deny the identity of predictive ability with the understanding of human behavior disparage what they consider the empty formalism of their detractors. The strategy selected often appears to hinge on which compromise implies a greater sacrifice to a given worker and is determined by his personality, his data, and the questions he seeks to answer.

Unlike the classical and pragmatic models, *the nonquantitative model* lacks methodological homogeneity. The studies representing it share the purpose of attempting to develop nonquantitative alternatives to the frequency approach of measuring intensity in communication materials. The classical model and many pragmatic model systems measure intensity in terms of the frequency of occurrence in accord with Berelson's and others' assumption that the frequency of occurrence of units in a category is highly correlated with the intensity of that category in the communication. This assumption has been a major target of criticism. Advocates and antagonists alike have asked how much of the variance this correlation could be expected to explain. They have wanted to know what factors other than frequency of occurrence are significant carriers of intensity, and in what situations they become important. Above all, they have asked how they might be measured

(Mahl, 1959a, p. 90; Salzinger, 1962; Strupp, 1962a, pp. 590-591; Strupp and Luborsky, 1962, pp. 292-298).

Viable answers to these questions have not yet appeared, but some promising beginnings have been made. Some investigators have attempted to measure both frequency and non-frequency aspects of intensity by using rating scales within categories, weighted units, and other measurement innovations (Lynch and Merrill, 1968; North, Holsti, Saninovich, and Zinnes, 1963, Ch. 4 and 5). Others have elected to work with systems designed to reveal the patterning of units. Rigorously formulated nonquantitative approaches not yet applied to psychotherapy research include George's (1959a, 1959b) "nonfrequency analysis" and Osgood's (1959) work on evaluative assertions. Methods that have already been applied and that are reviewed below include certain acoustical techniques, and linguistic and kinesic analysis.

CLASSICAL MODEL STUDIES

The lion's share of content-analysis studies of therapeutic interviews have been conducted within the classical model. Because of the great number of these studies, they are arranged here so as to bring together studies bearing on similar research problems. There are six such groups: characteristics of patients, therapist characteristics and therapy process, patient-therapist interactional systems, internal states, body movement research, and studies of contingent relationships.

Patient Characteristics

One focus of content-analysis research on patient characteristics has been the assessment of change or movement toward greater psychological health as a result of treatment (Auld and Murray, 1955; Dittes, 1959). Vargas (1954) reported a study in this tradition designed to test the hypothesis that judged success of client-centered therapy is positively correlated with changes in self-awareness reflected in client verbal behavior. A content-analysis system was used to measure various aspects of self-awareness. Unfortunately, the method was poorly reported; the scoring unit[5] was not even described. A strong positive correlation between self-awareness and success in therapy was found when the criterion of success was the therapist's rating. However, three other success criteria yielded low positive, near zero, and negative correlations with increasing self-awareness. Braaten (1961) achieved similar results using a related but more sophisticated content-analysis system to test the hypothesis that success in client-centered therapy is correlated with increasing expression of feelings referent to self as opposed to nonself material. Again, therapists' rating of success was the criterion best related to the measure.

Rice and Wagstaff (1967) also sought to delineate client process variables that could be related to outcome criteria. They argued that variables likely to prove useful would capture stylistic aspects of clients' attempts to be self-expressive, that they would lend themselves to moment-by-moment assessments with a minimum of inference about meanings, and that they would be quantifiable. They chose variables reflecting two quite different aspects of client communications. One of these was voice quality: they attempted to identify a limited number of voice patterns that varied among clients and over sessions, and that appeared to differentiate sessions previously characterized as good or poor hours. Four such patterns emerged and were described in terms of energy, pitch, range, tempo, and stress. The second group of four categories focused on lexical aspects of the stance the client took in relation to whatever he was discussing. The scoring unit was all client speech between two therapist statements, and each unit was coded to one of the four categories of each type by judges who listened to tape recordings. Three interviews (the first, second, and eleventh) from each of 53 clients were studied, and separate analyses were made

for each of the three interviews by means of a method analogous to factor analysis devised by the authors (Butler, Rice, and Wagstaff, 1963).

Four factors or interview types resulted for each of the three interviews, and were found to be meaningfully related to various outcome groups among the clients in a manner predicted in part by previous research (Butler, Rice, and Wagstaff, 1962). For example, one interview type distinguishable as early as the first interview and ultimately linked to treatment success was characterized "by a focused voice quality and an expressive stance about equally divided between objective analysis and subjective reaction. . . . the voice quality used suggests energy turned inward toward inner exploration." A related study of therapist behavior (Rice, 1965) is discussed below.

Smith, Bassin, and Froehlich (1960) examined the relation between verbal productivity and improvement in two groups of adult probationers. They found no statistically significant relationships. Shellhase (1960) examined relations between improvement in group psychotherapy, role acceptance, and activity in treatment, however, his study lacks adequate statistical analysis.

Rogers and his associates have produced a series of outcome studies. Based on his own formulation of the process of personality change, Rogers et al. developed a content-analysis system, known as the Process Scale, for measuring the degree of change during treatment (Rogers, 1959, 1961; Walker, Rablen, and Rogers, 1960). Rogers viewed personality on a continuum, with one end representing stasis, fixity, and rigidity, and the other looseness and flexibility. This continuum was comprised of seven aspects of psychological functioning that Rogers called "strands," conceptualized as discrete and separate at the rigid end, but merging and only artificially separable at the other.

---

[5] Dollard and Auld (1959, pp. 10–12) are the only analysts working in the period covered by this paper, to the writer's knowledge, who made a formal distinction between scoring, contextual, and summarizing units. The scoring unit is the entity that is actually coded and counted. The contextual unit is the communication material surrounding the scoring unit that is considered before the latter is assigned to a category. The summarizing unit is the group of scoring units about which some statement is made. For example, the number of nouns in two-minute segments of an interview are counted, and judgments as to whether a word is a noun is based on its use in the sentence in which it occurs. The two-minute segments represent summarizing units. The nouns themselves are the scoring units and the sentences in which the nouns appear are the contextual units. These distinctions, made by Berelson in 1952, are necessary and important; the failure of content analysts working with therapeutic interview material to make them has, at times, led to conceptual confusion and ambiguous results.

Each of these strands represented one category in the content-analysis system. Within each, a system of subcategories in the form of a 7-point rating scale was used to locate the patient on the continuum, with respect to that category. The system was not wholly faithful to its theoretical model in that the categories did not merge in the upper range. Scores for each of the categories were combined in early studies to produce a single index of the patient's overall position on the continuum, though theory-based procedures for this combination were not specified. Since 1960, Rogers and his associates have made numerous revisions of the scales and, in the process of this work, came to question that portion of the theoretical model calling for convergence of the strands. Thus, in later studies, scores for individual scales have been used rather than a combination score. They have also largely discarded three of the seven strands, and most recent work has involved the scale pertaining to client "experiencing," and occasionally the "personal constructs," "problem expression," and "manner of relating" scales (Gendlin and Tomlinson, 1967; Rogers, Gendlin, Kiesler, and Truax, 1967; van der Veen and Stoler, 1965; van der Veen, 1965). Scoring units were not implicit in the original conception, but considerable empirical investigation of various facets of this issue have been reported in connection with the experiencing scale (Kiesler, Mathieu, and Klein, 1964; Kiesler, Klein, and Mathieu, 1965; Schoeninger, Klein, and Mathieu, 1967; Kiesler, 1966; Schoeninger, Klein, and Mathieu, 1968).

Stoler (1963) found that ratings of client likability were significantly related to Process Scale ratings, and that both differentiated between more and less successful therapy cases, thus raising the question of process-rating contamination by rater's affective response to clients. This problem was the focus of a study by Tomlinson and Stoler (1967), who found that, while Process Scale ratings showed significant changes from early to late interviews, and differentiated between more and less successful cases, likability ratings remained essentially constant over the same time span, with a slight trend toward decreasing likability in more successful cases. Kiesler, Mathieu, and Klein (1967b) examined the possibility that the ex-

periencing scale might measure formal aspects of patients' speech, such as verbal productivity, rather than the more qualitative features it was intended to measure. Their findings provided support for the original conception.

Early studies, based on therapy with neurotic, university counseling-clinic outpatients, demonstrated the power of Process Scale ratings to differentiate between cases judged more and less successful by a variety of clinical criteria of success at a high level of statistical significance. Findings indicated that successful cases began and terminated at a significantly higher level on the scale than did less successful ones, and that successful cases showed greater movement along the scale during therapy (Rogers, 1961; Tomlinson and Hart, 1962). In a study of neurotic outpatients and hospitalized schizophrenics (each group evenly divided with respect to outcome), analyses of variance for four scales considered individually showed no general differences between early and later interviews. Significant interaction effects indicated that positive movement may be restricted to successful cases and that patterns of process change may differ in neurotics and schizophrenics (Tomlinson, 1962, discussed in Kiesler, Mathieu, and Klein, 1967c).

More recently, Rogers and his associates completed a large-scale investigation of psychotherapy with hospitalized schizophrenics, in which relations among therapist characteristics, patient process, and therapy outcome were examined and compared with similar characteristics of control and normal subjects. Briefly, the design called for three groups of 16 individuals each: relatively chronic schizophrenics, relatively acute schizophrenics, and normals. Subjects were selected in pairs matched for sex, age, and socioeconomic status, and schizophrenic subjects were also matched for degree of psychological disturbance. One member of each pair was randomly assigned to therapy, while the other functioned as a control subject. Eight therapists each treated a randomized triad composed of one member of each group. Research data consisted of recorded therapy interviews, recorded "sampling interviews" conducted by an independent interviewer at six-month intervals with all subjects (providing comparable verbal material for subjects whether or not assigned to the therapy condition), and a variety of instruments used to assess change in psychological status and treatment outcome (Gendlin and Rogers, 1967). The implementation of this design has provided a data bank on which several published studies have already drawn. The most extensive of these is, of course, the study that gave rise to the design (Rogers et al., 1967). Certain portions of this study will be discussed in the next section on therapist characteristics, while portions primarily dealing with the Process Scale are being considered here.

Because the experiencing scale was highly correlated with other Process Scale strands, it alone was used to assess process characteristics of these subjects (Gendlin, Beebe, Cassens, Klein, and Oberlander, 1968, p. 224). The experiencing scale yields a measure of the patient's manner of self-experiencing and his mode of dealing with and examining his feelings in therapy. It was applied by trained undergraduates, who listened to four-minute segments of therapy dialogue selected at random from the second half of each interview between the second and fifty-second, from every fifth interview beyond that point, and from the last five interviews in each case. Experiencing ratings were reliable and fairly well distributed over a relatively narrow range low on the scale, as one would expect with hospitalized schizophrenics (Kiesler, Mathieu, and Klein, 1967a).

Experiencing ratings for 14 schizophrenics showed a linear trend toward higher experiencing levels over successive thirds of therapy when peak (as distinct from modal) experiencing ratings were used. When the data was examined microscopically, complex, nonlinear patterns of process change emerged. When patient experiencing was considered in terms of treatment outcome, the earlier finding of a relation between Process Scale level and case outcome was confirmed, as was the relation between favorable outcome and long-term process movement. While these findings were complex and difficult to interpret, they suggest that more successful cases are distinguished from less successful ones more by the pattern and timing of process movement than by the amount of movement (Kiesler, Mathieu, and Klein, 1967c).

In an independent study using different data from the same project, Tomlinson (1967) used four process measures to explore the hypotheses that greater process movement would occur in more successful than in less successful cases, and that more successful cases would have higher initial process ratings. Cases were assigned to an outcome group when a substantial majority of seven outcome measures indicated a clear consensus of greater or lesser success. Twelve of 14 cases met this criterion. Process ratings were made by four judges (two experienced and two inexperienced) on each of the four process strands, using both tapes and typescripts of two four-minute samples from the first and last third of each of three interviews per case chosen from early, intermediate, and late points in the therapy. Interjudge reliabilities were high, indicating that judge experience was not important in applying these scales. Three of the four strands considered individually, and all four in combination, showed significant differences between more and less successful cases in process movement over therapy. More successful cases revealed a marked upward trend over the course of therapy, while less successful cases showed a moderate downward trend. More successful cases did not begin therapy at a higher process level as predicted, but at a nonsignificantly lower level. Product-moment correlations among the process strands ranged from 0.57 to 0.85, and the combined process score was not more discriminating than individual strand scores. But in still another study based on this project, van der Veen (1967) found that patient process movement was not significantly related to case outcome, though the previously found relation between outcome and process level appeared for two of the three process strands involved. Gendlin et al. (1968, pp. 225–230) reported a reanalysis of data from the schizophrenia project and earlier studies of neurotic patients, focused on a careful examination of the process level versus movement issue. They concluded that both are related to outcome, perhaps suggesting two patterns of achieving good outcome status. Other studies containing findings pertinent to patient Process Scale behavior are van der Veen and Stoler (1965), van der Veen (1965), Gross and DeRidder (1966), and Culbert, Clark, and Bobele (1968).

Studies relating patient behavior to treatment outcome have been a traditional focus of psychotherapy research. Yet the paucity of recent studies in this area attests to its declining favor. In part this must reflect the continuing problem of defining adequate and independent criteria of success (Auld and Murray, 1955; Marsden, 1965). Rogers and his associates' massive effort may well have been the last significant gasp in this area until some new approach to outcome research is devised. The Rogers et al. work is at once exciting and discouraging. Its excitement lies in its imaginative and innovative approach to the rigorous exploration of psychotherapy process and outcome with schizophrenic patients; but the herculean effort required to produce the modest change achieved is discouraging. Discouraging, too, is the thread of contradiction running through the Rogers et al. work concerning the relation between outcome measures and various indices of patient change. To some degree, of course, it is attributable to the use of different patient groups, and to the restricted variance of the change scores in the schizophrenia project. But one is left with the impression that the use, in that project, of a single Process Scale dimension on the grounds of its high correlation with the other dimensions was a strategic error (though possibly an economic necessity)—that the whole enterprise suffered from the lack of sufficient pilot exploration, refinement, and reconceptualization with the patient population in question prior to undertaking the expensive, large-scale project.

Other investigators have explored patient characteristics unrelated to treatment outcome. Matarazzo, Saslow, and their associates have conducted a series of studies using a content-analysis system based on the work of Chapple, who believed that a scientific theory of personality should be based on the time relationships in observable human interaction. He developed the Interaction Chronograph, a recording and computing instrument operated by an observer, to facilitate measurement of various behaviors and their time relationships. These procedures represent a sophisticated content-analysis system, in which both units and categories are derived from theoretical notions about personality and human interaction. An overview of his theoretical position, and a detailed discussion of the Interaction Chronograph, is presented in Matarazzo, Saslow, and Matarazzo (1956).

Recently they have used a more efficient, computer-mediated device that reliably generated the same data (Wiens, Matarazzo, and Saslow, 1965), have demonstrated that these data can be obtained from tape recordings as readily as from observations of live interviews (Wiens, Molde, Holman, and Matarazzo, 1966), and have shown that word counts yield data virtually identical with their more difficult to measure speech-duration variable (Matarazzo, Holman, and Wiens, 1967; see also, Mahl, 1959a, p. 115).

In most of their work, Matarazzo and associates have used a structured interview that has the effect of standardizing interviewer behavior along certain formal, nonlexical dimensions, and sharply varying other dimensions during different phases of the interview, thus treating the interviewer as an independent variable. In a series of five studies, this group demonstrated high levels of reliability in the interviewer's behavior (Matarazzo, Saslow, and Guze, 1956; Saslow, Matarazzo, and Guze, 1955), in the observers' recording (Phillips, Matarazzo, Matarazzo, and Saslow, 1957), in scoring the final chronograph record (Saslow et al., 1955), and in the interaction patterns of the interviewee from one interview to another over varying periods of time (Saslow, Matarazzo, Phillips, and Matarazzo, 1957; Saslow and Matarazzo, 1959; Tauson, Guze, McClure, and Beguelin, 1961). They have examined various aspects of the system's validity in cross-validation and replication studies (R. G. Matarazzo, Matarazzo, Saslow, and Phillips, 1958; Saslow and Matarazzo, 1959); in correlational studies with variables measured by other content-analysis systems (Hare, Waxler, Saslow, and Matarazzo, 1960; Phillips, Matarazzo, Matarazzo, Saslow, and Kanfer, 1961) and psychosociological variables (R. G. Matarazzo et al., 1958; Saslow and Matarazzo, 1959); in a factor-analytic study (Matarazzo, Saslow, and Hare, 1958); and in studies testing the system's capacity to differentiate between nosological groups and normal subjects (Matarazzo, 1962, pp. 479–490; Matarazzo and Saslow, 1961). They also generated normative data on the action and silence behavior of subjects (Matarazzo, Hess, and Saslow, 1962).

Matarazzo and his associates found re-peatedly that, while interviewee behavior was stable from one interview to another, there were significant changes in the behavior of the inter-viewee from one period to another within the same interview. These changes correspond to the planned changes in the behavior of the interviewer. They found, further, that this stability and modifiability in individuals and groups across interviews was maintained even with different interviewers so long as they oper-ated within the rules of the standardized inter-view (Matarazzo et al., 1956; Matarazzo, Saslow, Matarazzo, and Phillips, 1958; Mata-razzo, Weitman, Saslow, and Wiens, 1963; Saslow et al., 1955, 1957; Saslow and Matarazzo, 1959). Interviewee response duration appears to be independent of the lexical content of the interview (Matarazzo, Weitman, and Saslow, 1963), but varies with the nature of the inter-viewer's statement. For example, they found that interpretive interviewer statements could be differentiated from exploratory or information-seeking statements in terms of interviewee response duration (Kanfer, Phillips, Matarazzo, and Saslow, 1960). Interviewee speech durations were found to increase with increases in duration of interviewer speech, and with increases in frequency of interviewer head-nodding and mm-hmming (Matarazzo et al., 1963; Matarazzo, Wiens, and Saslow, 1965; Matarazzo, Saslow, Wiens, Weitman, and Allen, 1964; Matarazzo, Wiens, Saslow, Allen, and Weitman, 1964). Interviewee response latencies increase as inter-viewer response latencies increase, and can be influenced by the preinterview set of the inter-viewee (Matarazzo and Wiens, 1967; Allen, Wiens, Weitman, and Saslow, 1965). Interviewee interruption behavior was found to have con-siderable intra- and interinterview stability within individuals, and to be strikingly re-sponsive to interviewer behavior (Wiens, Saslow, and Matarazzo, 1966).

This body of research represents a vast ex-penditure of effort and has produced findings of general interest in social psychology, but its contribution to our understanding of psycho-therapy per se has been negligible, and its po-tential in this area is uncertain. However, Matarazzo and his associates appear, now, to be focusing more directly on psychotherapy.

The system has been applied to the assessment of psychotherapy training (Matarazzo, Wiens, and Saslow, 1966), and to research on the patient-therapist dyad (Matarazzo, Wiens, Matarazzo, and Saslow, 1968) discussed below.

Timmons, Rickard, and Taylor (1960) tested the hypothesis that the interviewer can be treated as an independent variable in a group therapy situation. They used a structured interview suggestive of Matarazzo and associates, and similar, though less elegant, measures of frequency and duration of verbal behavior derived from tape recordings. Initial findings supported their hypothesis, but a replication confounded these results. Taking their lead from this, Dinoff, Kew, Rickard, and Timmons (1962) next examined the stability of individual verbal behavior in a group setting. The findings indicated that as a function of group interaction, group members tend to establish a persistent hierarchy of verbal response behavior analogous to the pecking-order phenomena in chickens. Goldstein (1967) used frequency and duration of patient utterances as measures of the effective-ness of the psychodrama technique of "doubling" in eliciting the involvement of severely withdrawn hospitalized young adults in group therapy.

Grosz and Stern have examined various aspects of group psychotherapy, using the verbal response frequency as the content-analysis measure. They defined a verbal response as an uninterrupted segment of speech, regard-less of length. Sums of individual verbal re-sponses have been used as measures of patient-to-patient, patient-to-therapist, and therapist-to-patient verbal response frequencies. In their initial study (Grosz, Stern, and Wright, 1965), these measures were used to explore differences in patient and therapist interaction among groups, and the effects of group size on inter-actions between patients and therapists. They found that groups headed by different therapists differed significantly on all three measures. While differences in group size tended to be associated with a distinct trend in the number of patient-to-patient responses, the effect was not consistent within groups. They concluded that each group developed a unique pattern of verbal interaction despite similarity in therapist goals. In a second study (Stern and Grosz, 1966a) of personality correlates of patient interactions, low positive correlations were found between patient-to-patient interactions and extraversion, and between patient-to-therapist interactions and neuroticism and external control. In still another study (Stern and Grosz, 1966b), low scorers on neuroticism and extraversion were found to interact more with other low scorers, and high scorers more with other high scorers. An opposite trend was found on the external control dimension. Holmes (1967) found no significant relations between a paper and pencil measure of depression, and patient interaction frequency or utterance duration in group therapy. Dorfman (1968) studied two four-couple marital counseling groups over 25 and 30 sessions respectively, and found significantly greater similarity between spouses than between unmarried opposite-sex pairs or same-sex pairs on the number of statements both made and received.

Clark and Culbert (1965) hypothesized that T Group members would differ in their process movement patterns (problem expression scale, discussed above), and that those who showed the greatest positive movement would have entered into a greater number of intragroup relationships that they perceived as mutually therapeutic. Mutual perception of therapeutic qualities was assessed by means of a questionnaire designed to measure attitudinal characteristics of therapists (Barrett-Lennard, 1962). The group was composed of the trainer and nine upper-division UCLA students. Five members showed significant changes in process level between the first two sessions and sessions 30 and 31. Four of these were positive. Further, a significant positive relation obtained between positive process change ratings and the number of dyadic relationships in which both members perceived each other as therapeutic. A second study explored the effect of differences in trainer self-disclosure on both process change and the development of mutually perceived therapeutic relationships (Culbert, 1968).

Block (1964) developed a content-analysis system to investigate the relationship between patient affect, motivation, and expectations regarding psychotherapy. His purpose was to perform a critical test of two formulations of the discrepancy hypothesis in achievement-motivation theory. This hypothesis states that there is "a primary affective reaction attending the patient's evaluation of a discrepancy between past expectations (as governed by the adaptation level . . . of prior expectations) and the given therapeutic event such that an appropriate motive is redintegrated" (p. 268). His findings support the formulation that holds that the direction, rather than the size, of the discrepancy from the prevailing expectancy level determines primary affect and secondary motive. He concluded that his findings support the applicability of adaptation-level theory to psychotherapy research.

Rosenman (1955) explored the theoretical divergence between Freudian libido theory, which asserts that ego cathexis occurs in inverse proportion to cathexis of objects, and the views of Fromm, Sullivan, and some client-centered theorists that one's hatred or love for others is in direct proportion to one's hatred or love for oneself. He compared successful with unsuccessful client-centered counseling cases at the beginning and end of treatment in a content analysis of client verbal behavior. His system contained 48 categories designed to facilitate analysis of the representation of self- and other-directed action and evaluation in such a way that these categories were not contaminated by the effects of the representation of the self-other interaction. He found that positive evaluation of others decreased, while positive self-evaluation, self-to-self actions, and actions directed toward others increased in successful cases, but the magnitude of change was not as great. Unfortunately, Rosenman did not provide data pertaining to the statistical significance of these changes.

Luborsky (1967) made imaginative use of content analysis in his study of momentary forgetting during psychotherapy. In the treatment of 19 patients (2085 sessions), he noted 69 instances of momentarily forgotten and, in most cases, subsequently recovered thoughts. These included only those instances in which the entire session had been dictated, and the forgotten content and its immediate context were recorded verbatim. The following example is from the third session of a 19-year-old male patient in psychotherapy:

P: I realize that when I want something from a person, I get angry if I don't get it, or if I *do* get it. I was reading a book by a guy named Menninger,

"Love Against Hate." (Short pause.) I just forgot what I was going to say. (Pause, 25 sec.) Oh, yes. *There's a pleasure for me in achieving.* When I was home this weekend, I, for the first time, let my sister embrace me, and I embraced her. I never show affection that way. It embarrasses me a great deal, but what is wrong with that?—nothing. There's a girl I know. I wanted to go out with her, but she had been going out with someone else, and the fraternity wouldn't let me date her. I spoke to the girl, and now she's willing. The thing that intrigues me is that she seems to be *only* good. She *only* has good opinions of people, and I thought I would talk to her and give her some idea of the fact that there is evil in the world—at least make her see if she realizes that" (p. 181; Luborsky's italics).

Each instance of such forgetting and its context was extracted and paired, for control purposes, with an extract taken from another session with the same patient, in which there had been no momentary forgetting. Within each of the latter extracts, a thought was selected according to certain criteria to serve as a "pseudorecovered thought." Both the recovered thought and thought context of each pair were rated on 12 five-point scales developed after more casual study of the material.

Comparison of the "experimental" and control data across all patients revealed that both the recovered thoughts and the surrounding contexts differed significantly from the control data on nine of the rating scales. For example, momentary forgetting appeared to occur when the patient was on the brink of expressing a new attitude or belief, one which he had wished for but been unable to achieve previously, and such forgetting was often preceded by a state of distraction or attentional difficulty. Marked similarity between the mean ratings of the recovered thoughts and their contexts suggested that recovered thoughts were variations on themes already expressed. Indeed, they were rated significantly more abstract than the pseudorecovered thoughts, suggesting that they may have been derivatives of more concrete ideas that were forgotten and not recovered. The themes of recovered thoughts had considerable intrapersonal consistency. About half the patients' lost thoughts had to do with the issue of exercising control (self-mastery, strength, independence) or their lack of control. The rest were divided between concern with showing

affection and love, and with showing or receiving anger from a parent or other authority figure. These and other findings provided a basis for Luborsky's discussion of the implications of momentary forgetting for our understanding of memory functioning and repression, and their technical significance in psychotherapy.

Berg (1958) investigated lexical-grammatical characteristics of patients' verbal behavior and found that self-references, negative words, and words with expletive and explosive initial sounds decreased in frequency over therapy, while empathetic words increased. He failed, however, to test for the significance of these changes. Weintraub and Aronson (1962, 1964, 1965, 1967; Aronson and Weintraub, 1967a, 1967b) and Eichler (1966) used a method, based largely on word-count procedures, for analyzing aspects of patient speech for evidence from which clinical status or the use of specific defense mechanisms can be inferred. Lorenz and Cobb (1954) and Lorenz (1955) also used word-count procedures, and found that major diagnostic groups and normal subjects could be differentiated on the basis of intergroup differences in patterns of usage of various parts of speech and the number of different words. Conrad and Conrad (1956) applied similar techniques to a study of group therapy. Kohn and Sherwood (1964) attempted to differentiate various types of psychiatric patients on the basis of several measures derived from frequency of word usage with generally unpromising results.

Wigell and Ohlsen (1962) failed to support a series of hypotheses regarding changes during group therapy in the number of topics discussed and their treatment-relevance, in affect expression or in self-references. They did, however, find certain unpredicted shifts in topical focus. In another study, Ohlsen and Oelke (1962) found no relation between ratings of client growth during group therapy and content analysis findings pertaining to topic, affect, self-references, and total verbal activity. Colby (1960) investigated aspects of the effect of the psychoanalyst's presence on the free associations of the analysand, and (1961) the relative power of two types of therapist comments in amplifying free associations in a psychoanalytic analogue situation. Jackson, Riskin, and Satir (1961) used family interview material to demonstrate the use of categories derived from the work of Bateson, Jackson, and Haley on communication in families containing a schizophrenic member. Chance (1966) developed a system for studying qualitative features of patient's interpersonal experiences in terms of two orthogonal dimensions: positive-negative and active-passive. Leary and Gill (1959) produced an omnibus system containing what is probably the most complex category structure offered to date, but it has not been used since their initial demonstration.

Therapist Characteristics and Therapy Process

Bandura, Lipsher, and Miller (1960) explored therapist behavior in the face of patient hostility, and the effect on the patient of the therapist's reaction. A patient statement, the therapist response, and the next patient statement were studied. The first patient statement in this sequence (first scoring unit) was judged as being hostile or nonhostile. If nonhostile, the total segment was not considered further. If judged hostile, this scoring unit was further categorized as to the object of hostility. Next, the therapist response (second scoring unit) was judged as being one of avoidance or approach. Each of these categories had several subcategories facilitating the analysis of avoidance and approach techniques. Finally, the second patient statement (third scoring unit) was judged hostile or nonhostile in the same way as the first.

They found no differences among therapists when patient hostility was directed toward the therapist himself. In this situation therapists were more likely to avoid dealing with the hostility than they were when it was directed elsewhere. However, therapists rated by their colleagues as expressing hostility directly and rated low in need for approval were found more likely to deal actively with patient hostility directed toward objects having little to do with therapy than were therapists rated high on approval-seeking behavior or low on direct expression of hostility. When patient hostility was approached by the therapist, there was a high probability that the hostile expression would continue in the next patient statement. But when the therapist reacted with avoidance,

the patient was likely to change the object of his hostility or drop the hostile expression altogether. Bandura et al. limited their study to early interviews. Varble (1968) extended study of this problem to the entire course of treatment, using the Bandura et al. method, with minor modifications. He replicated the finding that therapists' approach to hostility expressions elicits further expressions, while therapists' avoidance discourages it. He did not find that therapists' approach to hostile statements had a reinforcing effect on client hostility expression as predicted. No experience effect was found with respect to approach to hostility when its focus was not considered, but inexperienced therapists (interns) approached hostility directed at themselves significantly more than did experienced therapists (staff). Counselor response to client hostility has also been studied by Gamsky and Farwell (1966, 1967) using a modification of Bales' Interaction Process Analysis.

Winder, Ahmad, Bandura, and Rau (1962) used the same general method employed by Bandura et al. to examine the effect of therapists' approach or avoidance of patients' dependency expressions on continuation versus termination of therapy. The correspondence between dependency expressions primarily avoided and termination, and dependency expression primarily approached and continuation, was striking, particularly when the therapist was the object of dependency. There was a clear tendency for approached dependency expressions to be followed by continuation of such expression, and for avoided dependency expression to be discontinued. Both Caracena (1965) and Schuldt (1966) used a similar method, and both replicated the finding that therapist approach elicits dependency expression, while therapist avoidance discourages it. Schuldt's work, however, pertained to the whole course of therapy, while Winder et al. and Caracena's work was based on early interviews. Caracena failed to replicate Winder et al's. finding regarding the relation between dependency and termination, nor did he find evidence that therapist approach or avoidance of patient dependency had a reinforcing effect. He did find that experienced therapists approached dependency expression more than inexperienced therapists. Schuldt did not find therapist experience to be a factor, but his inexperienced therapists were more experienced than Caracena's. Schuldt also found that therapists maintain a relatively consistent rate of approach over the course of therapy, and tend to approach dependency directed at themselves more than dependency directed at others. Clients in his study initiated significantly more dependency responses during early interviews.

Alexander and Abeles (1968) also used this content-analysis system, but with the addition of categories intended to bring into view possible variations in the course of dependency expression referent to different interpersonal domains. Data were obtained from the first, middle, and next-to-last interviews of each of 20 clients, whose treatment ranged from 6 to 22 sessions. They found different patterns over therapy in the frequency of dependency expression when it was focused on the therapy situation, the therapist, the client's family, or less central social relationships. Mills and Abeles (1965) also used this method to obtain percentages of therapist approach to client dependency and hostility, and found approached hostility positively related to an (Edwards Personal Preference Schedule) assessment of counselor needs for nurturance and affiliation. Approached dependency was not so related. Rottschafer and Renzaglia (1962) found that clients made more dependent statements in initial interviews when paired with counselors whose statements in those interviews were relatively leading as opposed to reflective. Clients' precounseling expectations also appeared related to their dependent statements, independent of counselor style. Snyder (1963) has also examined client dependency.

Salzberg and associates explored the effect of therapist verbal behavior on interaction in group therapy. In one study (Salzberg, 1961), he attempted to ascertain what type of therapist verbalization elicits general group interaction as opposed to responses directed to the therapist. The findings showed that group-member interaction varied inversely with the frequency of therapist verbalizations, particularly when the therapist responded directly to a patient rather than directing him to another member of the group. These results were elaborated in a second study (Heckel, Froelich, and Salzberg, 1962).

Salzberg (1962) next turned to the question of whether therapist silence or redirection most facilitated group interaction, and their effect on patient responses in group psychotherapy. The study's design called for a structured interview in which the therapist varied his verbal behavior through four conditions. The results suggested that, while silence appeared to facilitate interaction, it also facilitated verbalization by patients about nontherapeutic aspects of their environment. Redirection, on the other hand, while not leading to significantly more interaction, did lead to more group-directed patient response. Salzberg, Brokaw, and Strahley (1964) employed these silence-redirection strategies to investigate the development of spontaneity and problem-relevant discussion in a new psychotherapy group that lacked membership stability, and to compare this group with an older, more stable group. In still another study of a group having unstable membership, therapist absence in some sessions was related to greater spontaneity and decreased relevance of group activity in those sessions. Efforts by the therapist to direct the focus of group activity when he was present appeared related to a decrease in personally relevant statements and to an increase in comments about other group members during sessions when he was absent (Salzberg, 1967). Other content-analysis studies in this series are Heckel, Wiggins, and Salzberg (1963a, 1963b), and Heckel and Salzberg, (1967); see also Smith and Young (1968).

Harrow et al. have investigated the therapist's impact on group therapy and other aspects of the therapy process. They studied three therapy groups, each composed of five to seven hospitalized adult mental patients. Each group met six times per week for one hour over a four and a half month period under three different conditions: in two sessions per week the groups met with their psychiatric-resident leaders, in two other sessions the patient members met alone, and in the final two sessions the groups met with the therapist, with members' relatives and family present. This design facilitated study of differences between the three groups across session conditions, as well as condition effects across the three groups. A pilot study resulted in the isolation of 39 variables, and development of 9-point rating scales for each. Ratings were based on four-minute segments chosen from each third of each group session—thus providing an additional vantage point from which changes within therapy hours could be assessed. One study (Astrachan, Schwartz, Becker, and Harrow, 1967) sought to determine which variables were influenced by either or both the specific therapist-patient groups or the type of group session. Overall analyses of variance revealed that five variables were significantly influenced by particular therapist-patient groups, while four (including two of the five) were related to type of session. These findings were interpreted in terms of adjustive mechanisms evolved by the groups for dealing with problems of getting along together, and in terms of therapist stylistic differences. Other analyses of data derived from this project showed that unled, as opposed to therapist-led, sessions were significantly more active and less depressed in tone, and tended (nonsignificantly) to be warmer, more supportive, and less tense, but also more deflating of others. Family sessions differed significantly from conventional sessions in having more verbal interaction, more discussion of family issues and past events, more attempts at clarification of others' feelings and behavior, and less inhibition and depressed tone (Becker, Harrow, Astrachan, Detre, and Miller, 1968; Harrow, Astrachan, Becker, Detre, and Schwartz, 1967; Harrow, Astrachan, Becker, Miller, and Schwartz, 1967).

A comprehensive content-analysis investigation of therapist characteristics and behavior was undertaken by Strupp. After three initial studies (Strupp, 1955a, 1955b, 1955c) using Bales' Interaction Process Analysis system, he developed one of his own based on an explicitly stated theoretical rationale (Strupp, 1957c). This system was intended to be sufficiently general to make possible valid comparisons across theoretical orientations, and to be relevant to psychotherapy as a special kind of communication (Strupp, 1960). Strupp's system employed five major dimensions, each of which contained a category structure or rating scale. These tapped the gross behavior of the therapist, the degree of inference and warmth implicit in his communication, the degree to which he channeled the patient's communication, and whether he worked from within the patient's frame of reference or his own. The somewhat arbitrary

scoring unit consisted of all therapist communication occurring between two patient statements. Strupp noted that it was sometimes necessary to divide a therapist communication into two or three units, but offered no criteria for this division. All units were coded to each of the five dimensions. The contextual unit was all prior material in the interview series.

Strupp published two papers demonstrating this system. One (Strupp, 1957a) reported the analysis of interviews from a published case of brief psychotherapy by Wolberg. A second (Strupp, 1957b) compared the results of the first with a similar analysis of a published case by Rogers. The findings showed that Rogers' behavior was fairly consistent over the course of his interviews, while Wolberg's varied systematically. Wolberg was more inferential, and he exerted stronger guidance in the middle and terminal interviews. In three papers, Strupp (1958a, 1958b, 1958c) presented the findings of a study in which his system of content analysis was part of a larger design. The study attempted an exploration of the therapist's perceptions and evaluations of therapeutic problems, the relation of these to his treatment plans, and the relation of both to his actual behavior in the therapy sessions. The major finding was a clear interaction between the therapist's clinical observations, his treatment recommendation, his attitude toward the patient, and the nature of his communication to the patient. This interaction was patterned in some respects according to the training and experience of the therapist. A critical discussion of this study pertinent to the content analysis aspect appears in Jenkins, Wallach, and Strupp (1962). Other applications of this system are Strupp (1961) and Auerbach (1963).

The same design was used in a replicative study (Strupp and Wallach, 1965) employing a revised version of the content-analysis system. This version contained seven categories for therapist statements: facilitating communication, exploratory operations, clarification, interpretive operations (containing a three-category intensity scale), direct guidance, activity not relevant to therapy, and unclassifiable. The unit was again the total therapist statement, and each unit was typically (exceptions not specified) coded to a single category. In addition, the number of words and the number of seconds of latency for each statement were recorded. These data were gathered from 59 psychiatrists who viewed two therapy-interview films, during which they were given opportunities to record the response they would have made at certain points had they been the actual therapist. The content-analysis data were related to ratings of therapist empathy and to the results of a factor-analytic study of therapists' responses to a questionnaire completed following the viewing. Findings of the earlier study were, in general, replicated. Therapists communicated more empathically with patients they found suitable for treatment than with those they did not wish to treat. With the latter, they used communications that facilitated maintenance of distance between therapist and patient.

Cartwright (1966) took another tack in comparing therapists of differing orientations. Her purpose was to assess the effect of differences in therapeutic technique on patient verbal behavior, and the effect on the assessment of the latter resulting from use of evaluation methods rooted in different philosophies of treatment. She employed three content-analysis systems: Rogers' Process Scale reflecting client-centered theory, her own Self-Observation Scale based on psychoanalytic thinking concerning the importance of the observing function of the ego in psychotherapy, and Noble, Ohlsen, and Proff's (1961) version of Bales' Interaction Process Analysis categories, a theoretically neutral system. Two client-centered therapists and two psychoanalysts participated. Each client-centered therapist was paired with an analyst so that the members of each pair were similar with respect to sex and treatment experience, and treated patients matched on age, sex, general presenting complaint, and number of interviews. The content analyses were performed on the first and every fifth subsequent interview, and on the last interview in each series. Only the patient statements, in three typescript-page units, were considered for the Process Scale analysis, while all patient and therapist statements were coded for the other two systems. In all cases, the interview was used as the summarizing unit. The Process Scale showed positive movement for all cases, but greater movement in the two client-centered cases. However, the magnitudes in

question were small, movement was not linear, and no tests of significance were employed. Neither of the other two systems provided data on patient change over therapy, but both indicated that therapists of the same orientation were more similar in their responses than the cross-orientation pairs who treated similar patients. These patients responded similarly to the differing techniques of their therapists, though some differences in technique appeared related to differences in patient behavior. Again, there were no tests of the significance of these relationships.

But the most extensive body of content-analysis research on the characteristics and functioning of therapists stems from the work of Rogers. His thinking concerning the nature of the therapeutic process (discussed above) was based on an earlier theoretical statement, in which he specified the essential contributions of the therapist. He argued that, given minimal assumptions about the client's discomfort and the existence of psychological contact between client and therapist, the process of psychotherapy will be successfully set in motion to the degree that the therapist communicates three attitudinal conditions. These are congruence or genuineness within the therapeutic relationship, unconditional positive regard of client by therapist, and empathic understanding of the client's experiences and feelings and their meaning to him on a moment-by-moment basis within the therapy (Rogers, 1957; Rogers and Truax, 1967).

The first published content-analysis test of the relation of these qualities to measures of patient process movement occurred in a study of group therapy by Truax (1961). His purpose was to explore sources of variation on the Process Scale (supplemented by two other measures) in terms of three groups of prior variables: therapist conditions, group conditions directly influenced by the therapist, and group conditions indirectly influenced by the therapist. He used seven therapist-condition variables: congruence, unconditional positive regard, empathic understanding, accurate empathy, assumed similarity (of therapist and patient), responsivity, and leadership. The two sets of group conditions contained six and three variables respectively. The data were typescripts of 3-minute segments of group interaction from each of 42 successive therapy hours for each of three group-therapy groups composed of hospitalized mental patients. Each segment was coded to a 9-point rating scale for each of these variables (except responsibility, a frequency measure).

In general, the findings were that 7 of the 15 specific variables, at least 2 from each of the three clusters, accounted for independent and significant amounts of Process Scale variance. More directly relevant to this discussion, all therapist variables except empathic understanding and responsivity were significantly related to the Process Scale scores. The accurate empathy variable was included to test whether the critical aspect of therapist empathic behavior was empathic sharing (empathic understanding) or sensitivity (accurate empathy). And in subsequent research, accurate empathy has represented this domain. Truax also found that the relation of the therapist-condition variables to Process Scale scores was linear, except in the case of congruence. While low levels of therapist congruence occurred in the context of low process scores, there was no relation between intermediate and high congruence and Process Scale scores, suggesting that the presence or absence of therapist congruence may be the important factor. An analysis of the independence of the three therapist conditions indicated that only accurate empathy and congruence explained independent portions of the variance in Process Scale values.

These three therapist conditions occupied a central position in a subsequent program of research on psychotherapy with hospitalized schizophrenics, carried out by Rogers and his associates (Rogers et al., 1967) and discussed at length above. The reader is referred to that discussion for an overview of the design and a general description of the research. Therapist conditions were assessed by judges' ratings of therapy-interview excerpts, as well as by rating scales filled out periodically by both therapists and patients. These three types of data were used in testing hypotheses derived from the client-centered theory of psychotherapy pertaining both to process level and movement and to outcome criteria.

The therapist-condition ratings derived from interviews were beset by numerous measurement problems. Ratings of unconditional positive regard were unreliable, and when reliably rated segments for this variable were isolated and combined to provide an overall measure, it reflected an uneven representation of interviews over the course of therapy. Congruence ratings were confounded by certain types of patient behavior (Kiesler et al., 1967a). Accurate-empathy ratings were correlated with a combination of patient sex, socioeconomic status, and chronicity status, despite attempts to control on these variables, and with a number of other initial patient variables. While these relationships may, in themselves, represent important findings, they tended to confound tests of the hypotheses at issue (Kiesler, Klein, Mathieu, and Schoeninger, 1967). There is also the possibility that the accurate-empathy variable may not have been independent of the experiencing scale used to assess patient process characteristics, thus making their correlation artifactual (Kiesler, Mathieu, and Klein, 1967d).

Taking these difficulties into account insofar as possible, Rogers et al. concluded that therapist attitudes tended to stabilize fairly early in therapy, and while the three dimensions of therapist conditions were correlated, the correlations did not account for sufficient amounts of variance to suggest that they all tap some single dimension. Judges' ratings of therapy excerpts and patients' assessments of therapist conditions were positively correlated, while therapists' assessments of the conditions they offered were negatively correlated with ratings of both patients and judges. Different levels of therapist conditions were not associated with differential amounts of process movement in therapy, but high therapist conditions were associated with higher process levels. Patients receiving high levels of therapist accurate empathy showed the greatest shift away from schizophrenic pathology on the MMPI Sc Scale, while patients receiving low levels tended to increase their schizophrenic pathology on the same measure. Control subjects who received no therapy, were intermediate. Several other indices of change or outcome were positively but nonsignificantly correlated with high therapist conditions. Thus, as predicted, some measures of therapist conditions were related directly to outcome measures and to measures of process which, themselves, were related to measures of outcome.

But the authors also concluded that characteristics of the patient influenced the nature of the relationship between him and the therapist, and in some measure helped determine the therapist conditions available to him (Rogers, 1967; Kiesler et al., 1967d). Some of these findings also occurred in a separate study by van der Veen (1967) based on other data from this same project.

A plethora of studies dealing with these therapist conditions have appeared in the last few years, though they have at times been called by different names. For example, congruence has been termed genuineness, and unconditional positive regard has been called nonpossessive warmth, unconditionality and, more recently, respect. In work in which Truax participated, therapist conditions have been assessed on the same scales used in the Rogers et al. project (Truax and Carkhuff, 1967, p. 43). In more recent work by Carkhuff and his students, the scales have been revised, and while they presumably measure the same variables, this has not been demonstrated empirically. Additional therapist variables have also been introduced from time to time, for example, concreteness—the specificity with which the therapist focuses on particularized affects and events (Truax and Carkhuff, 1964). When actual indices of outcome were not used, the criterion of patient responsiveness to therapist conditions has most frequently been a scale of depth of self-exploration devised by Truax and based on the Process Scale used in the Rogers et al. project (Truax and Carkhuff, 1967, pp. 194–208). In some studies, this scale has been called self-disclosure (for example, Truax and Carkhuff, 1965a).

There have been no innovations in the use of content analysis per se in these subsequent studies: trained raters made judgments in terms of the categories embedded in the scales on the basis of taped segments from interviews. But there have been methodological innovations of other kinds. "Standard" clients have been asked to function as therapists prior to being placed in the patient role, in order to assess their own interpersonal functioning under optimal conditions. And some problems of method have been addressed. In the context of group psychotherapy, Truax (1966a) studied the

relative value of the traditional selection of interview segments by time-sampling methods, as opposed to segments selected for each patient, consisting of two patient statements with an intervening therapist statement on one hand, and two therapist statements with one intervening patient statement on the other. All three methods were about equally reliable and intercorrelated, and yielded nearly equivalent predictions of patient outcome for therapist accurate empathy, unconditional positive regard, and genuineness. Truax (1966b) also examined the possibility that ratings of therapist accurate empathy and unconditional positive regard might be contaminated by the presence of patient speech on tape segments, but found no meaningful evidence of contamination. Waskow and Bergman (1962) compared warmth-acceptance ratings by persons of different theoretical orientations, and found no meaningful differences. Shapiro, Foster, and Powell (1968) found that judges could rate therapist empathy, genuineness, and warmth from still photographs of therapists' faces with moderate reliability, and Shapiro (1968) found that ratings on these dimensions, and on client self-exploration, made from information presented through either the aural or visual channel were equivalent to ratings made on the basis of both channels. Zimmer and Anderson (1968) factor-analyzed the empathy and unconditional positive regard ratings of 100 counselor responses from a single interview to test the unidimensionality of those therapist conditions. They found eight presumably meaningful, orthogonal factors for each condition, and in several instances the same factor appeared on both. This initial study did not take into account the general condition level offered by the therapist. It seems likely that attention to this variable might be rewarding in light of its importance in the Rogers et al. project and in the research to be discussed below.

A series of studies was undertaken to seek additional support for the hypothesis that therapists offering a high level of therapist conditions tend to be associated with successful cases (Truax and Carkhuff, 1965a). These have involved applications to group therapy (Truax and Carkhuff, 1964b; Truax, Carkhuff, and Kodman, 1965; Truax, Wargo, and Silber, 1966; Dickenson and Truax, 1966), and to psychiatric residents as therapists instead of client-centered psychologists (Truax, Wargo, Frank, Imber, Battle, Hoehn-Saric, Nash, and Stone, 1966a). Others examined the degree of patient change during therapy relative to the discrepancy between therapist and patient (acting as therapist in a therapylike situation) on therapist conditions prior to therapy (Pagell, Carkhuff, and Berenson, 1967), and the degree of patient change associated with therapist change on the therapist-condition scales during therapy (Kratochvil, Aspy, and Carkhuff, 1967). Each of these studies lent support to the hypothesis of a positive relation between high level therapist conditions and successful treatment, though this statement requires qualification with respect to certain therapist-condition variables in certain studies. Other studies dealt with the relation of judges' ratings of therapist conditions to the perceptions of patients and therapists themselves, and the relation of these three sets of data to pre- and posttest indices of personality change. Little relation was found between the three types of ratings, and while judges' ratings were significantly related to change indices, patient perceptions were not (Truax, 1966a; Hansen, Moore, and Carkhuff, 1968; Burstein and Carkhuff, 1968).

Truax has begun to examine alternative propositions concerning the mechanisms through which therapist conditions may be associated with alterations in patient status. Rogers and other client-centered theorists have argued that the therapist conditions are attitudinal and are offered nonselectively within the limits of the therapist's capacity. Behaviorists have insisted that if therapy is effective, it is because the therapist sets out to change the patient's behavior, and that one means of doing so is through reinforcement techniques used consciously or otherwise. In an analysis of a long-term, successful case in which Rogers was the therapist, Truax (1966c) demonstrated that the therapist responded selectively to five of nine classes of patient behavior with statements judged high on empathy and unconditional positive regard or directiveness, and, moreover, that the incidence of four of these five patient behavior classes increased over the course of the therapy. In a second study, Truax (1968) showed that four therapists differentially reinforced 30

severely disturbed, hospitalized mental patients within group-therapy groups for greater depth of self-exploratory behavior, using as reinforcers the now familiar triad of therapist conditions: accurate empathy, unconditional positive regard, and congruence. Furthermore, reinforcement was positively related to a composite outcome measure, and was unrelated to therapists' average level of offered conditions!

Perhaps the most pregnant findings of the Rogers et al. research on hospitalized schizophrenics was that the patient in some degree determined the therapist conditions available to him (Rogers, 1967; Kiesler et al., 1967d). A prior study conducted within this project, but based on different data, had already reached the same conclusion (van der Veen, 1965). This issue goes to the heart of Rogers' theory of the therapy process, and has enormous consequences for any theory of psychotherapy. It has, therefore, become the focus of considerable research effort. An unpublished reanalysis of van der Veen's data led Truax and Wargo (reported in Truax and Carkhuff, 1967, p. 101) to the conclusion that van der Veen was in error. In another attack on this question, the design of which is too complex to detail here, the authors (Truax, Wargo, Frank, Imber, Battle, Hoehn-Saric, Nash, and Stone, 1966b) found that accurate empathy, unconditional positive regard, and congruence were primarily a function of the therapist, though the second of these is affected by the patient in early interviews. More recently, this question has been studied experimentally. In several studies, the level of conditions offered by the therapist has been experimentally manipulated so that therapists were offering high therapist conditions in the first and last thirds of the interview and low (Truax and Carkhuff, 1965b; Holder, Carkhuff, and Berenson, 1967) or intermediate (Piaget, Berenson, and Carkhuff, 1967) conditions in the middle third. A final study in this group (Cannon and Pierce, 1968) explored order effects in the manipulation of therapist conditions. The patient's level of functioning was also subject to experimental manipulation in one or more of these studies. In brief, the results indicate that patients functioning at both high and low levels of interpersonal skillfulness deteriorate in depth of intrapersonal exploration when their therapists function at low or intermediate levels of therapeutic conditions. The depth of intrapersonal exploration of patients generally functioning at low levels of interpersonal skillfulness is a function of the level of therapeutic conditions offered by high-level therapists, while high-level-functioning patients continue to explore themselves independently of the experimental manipulation of conditions by a high-level therapist. These findings were not subject to order effects.

In other studies, patients' depth of intrapersonal exploration was manipulated in the same fashion as were therapist conditions in the studies just discussed. Findings were that the levels of therapeutic conditions offered by therapists functioning at low levels generally corresponded to the level of patient intrapersonal exploration, while therapists functioning at high levels continued to offer high levels of therapeutic conditions independent of patient depth of intrapersonal exploration. Amount of therapeutic experience was found not to be a source of effect, though clinical trainees offered a higher level of therapeutic conditions than nonclinical trainees in one study (Alexik and Carkhuff, 1967; Carkhuff and Alexik, 1967; Friel, Kratochvil and Carkhuff, 1968).

Other research involving these therapist conditions has included their relation to lexical aspects of therapist behavior (Berenson, Mitchell, and Moravec, 1968; Berenson, Mitchell, and Laney, 1968; Berenson and Mitchell, 1968; Anderson, 1968; Holder, 1968), the relative efficacy of discussions with a "best friend" as opposed to interviews with a professional counselor (Martin, Carkhuff, and Berenson, 1966), the effects of racial differences within patient-therapist dyads (Carkhuff and Pierce, 1967; Banks, Berenson, and Carkhuff, 1967), and the training of therapists and its assessment (Carkhuff and Truax, 1965; Pierce, Carkhuff, and Berenson, 1967; Banks et al., 1967; Martin and Carkhuff, 1968; Carkhuff, Kratochvil, and Friel, 1968; Friel et al., 1968; Rosen, 1967).

In reviewing this extensive body of research, one is struck by the tidy coherence of the early studies—apparently a function of their intimate relation to client-centered theory. Therapist conditions represent constructs drawn from that

theory, and they were employed to systematically examine its usefulness in understanding the nature of the psychotherapy process. In sharp contrast, the more recent studies, while demonstrating greater methodological imagination, have largely lost this coherence. For the most part, they were not attempts to explore the implications of a theoretical position. Instead, they attacked a variety of sometimes trivial problems in scattergun fashion; the conditions constructs themselves were not considered in relation to theory, but appear to have been used as atheoretical, common-sense tools for looking at therapist behavior. Certainly the peculiar predilection of each successive generation of workers in this area to redefine or rename the constructs has contributed to this loss of coherence, and may well be symptomatic of an approaching disintegration of the client-centered orientation as a potent force in psychotherapy theory and research. Such a development would be regretable indeed, for whatever its conceptual limitations, the client-centered approach has played an inestimably important role in sparking critical thought about therapy process, and has been a pacesetter in psychotherapy research.

Holzman and Forman (1966) have reported development of a content-analysis system for use in the study of psychotherapy with schizophrenics, but one of sufficient generality and freedom from theoretical bias to make it appropriate for use in many situations. The category structure covers five dimensions of lexical content that can be coded without inference. These include grammatical structure (15 categories), patient objects (12 categories), locus of patient's difficulty (5 categories), and approval/disapproval (3 categories). Categories within the first two of these dimensions can be combined in various ways to produce more complex characterizations of the material. The unit is the simple or complex sentence as defined in English grammar, and each unit is coded to all appropriate dimensions. By way of demonstration, the authors presented findings from two studies of therapist behavior. The basic data were the analyses of 176 interviews, 16 selected systematically from each of 11 long-term treatments of schizophrenic patients conducted by psychoanalytically-oriented therapists. In addition, for purposes of comparison, they studied interviews with a schizophrenic patient conducted by Rogers and by Felder, who used the Whitaker-Malone method.

The findings revealed a high degree of intra- and intertherapist consistency among the 11 therapists in their use of the grammatical structure categories. The comparison with Rogers was based on a scale of "directiveness" that involved ranking therapist interventions from most to least directive as follows: questions having content, statements having content, questions without content, and statements without content. The distinction between units having or lacking content lay in whether the unit introduced content into the therapy. Ten of the 11 therapists relied most heavily on interventions coded to the two categories introducing content, whereas Rogers' interventions fell most frequently in the two statement categories. Thus, as expected, he was found markedly less directive than all but one of the psychoanalytically-oriented therapists. Felder, too, differed from the 11 therapists in theoretically predictable ways. He relied most heavily on interventions that emphasized the therapist's feelings, while this emphasis was least employed among the therapists under study. In a complex analysis of data pertaining to therapists' treatment of patients' objects, the authors found that two groups could be distinguished among the 11 therapists and that these groups were differently related to an outcome variable.

Comparisons between schizophrenic- and neurotic-patient behaviors in relation to therapist behaviors have been reported in a study by Tourney, Bloom, Lowinger, Schorer, Auld, and Grisell (1966). They employed a content-analysis system in which each of 10 patient variables (such as, thinking disturbance, verbal productivity, hostility to therapist, and depression) and 18 therapist variables (such as resistance interpretation, reassurance and reward, drive and motivation, errors of omission, anxiety, and silence) were rated on 9-point Likert-type scales once for each 5-minute period of the interview. Interrater reliability is reported as adequate (though in another report on the same project [Auld, 1968], in which reliability data is provided on 23 of the 28 variables, 11 have intraclass correlation coefficients of less than 0.50 and an

additional 5 have values between 0.51 and 0.60). The study was based on three consecutive therapy sessions of 10 schizophrenic and 7 neurotic patients who were treated by 10 therapists. Scores for each of the 28 variables were collapsed across time periods and intercorrelated. The authors report and discuss those patient and therapist variables that were significantly correlated with certain therapist variables in either patient group. They found, for example, that scores of schizophrenics more than of neurotics were significantly correlated with the therapist affect variables. Therapist errors of commission were significantly correlated with decrements in verbal productivity and positive feeling, and heightened anxiety, in the schizophrenics; with heightened resistance and hostility to the therapist in the neurotics; and with anxiety and hostility in the therapists themselves. Unfortunately, the results were frequently interpreted as if these correlations revealed causal relations, though Auld (1968) later explicitly warned against such interpretation. Moreover, the reader cannot be certain that some of the correlations were not artifacts and that other meaningful relations were not masked by the distribution of the 10 therapists over the 17 patients, since data on this distribution were not provided.

Rice (1965) sought to relate expressive facets of therapist behavior to case outcome. By expressiveness, she meant the degree to which the therapist's behavioral style functions as a stimulus tending to expand or contract the range of new experience that the client is able to generate. Her 9-category system was constructed around three aspects of therapist lexical and vocal behavior: freshness of words and word combinations, voice quality, and functional level (inner exploring, observing, and outside focus). The unit was all therapist speech between two patient statements, and the preceding patient statement was used as a contextual unit when necessary to clarify meaning. Ten such units were sampled from each third of the second and next-to-last interviews in each of 20 cases selected so that long and short cases were balanced for success and failure. The coded data were subjected to a factor-analysis-like procedure (Butler et al., 1963) that yielded three factors representing interview types defined by the combinations of therapist behaviors studied. One of these, marked by a distortion of voice quality suggesting artificiality and by a focus on the client as an object, was characteristic of failure cases and of relatively inexperienced therapists. Another, involving fresh, connotative language, expressive voice quality, and a focus on the client's immediate inner experience, appeared to be a correlate but not a predictor of therapeutic success by several outcome criteria, and was employed significantly more frequently by experienced therapists.

Several other studies have attempted to delineate correlates and effects of therapist behavior. Cutler (1958) found support for psychoanalytic propositions concerning the effects of counter-transference phenomena on the treatment process. Swensen (1967) found support in three therapy cases for the hypothesis that in successful therapy the patient and therapist should complement each other on the dimensions of love-hate and dominance-submission. Parker (1967) found that therapists who scored high on a paper and pencil measure of dominance were directive in their statements to clients, and that therapists responded non-directively to female clients more frequently than to male clients. Zimmer and Park (1967) studied the factor structure of counselor utterances rated on a coldness-warmth continuum. Ornston, Cicchetti, Levine, and Fierman (1968) found that experienced therapists used more nonquestioning statements and averaged more words per statement than novices in a therapy-analogue situation in which an actor played the part of an apparently psychotic patient. Truax, Fine, Moravec, and Millis (1968) found therapists rated high in persuasive potency associated with positive therapeutic outcomes, and this relation was independent of the relation between outcome and therapist warmth and accurate empathy.

Isaacs and Haggard (1966) reported a series of content–analysis studies of patient behavior following therapist attention to patient affect verbalization. They found that when the therapist responded to patient affect verbalizations, subsequent patient responses were more psychologically meaningful, more affectively oriented, and longer, if less frequent. The patient also more frequently returned spontaneously after a lapse of interview time to the content in connection with which the therapist dealt with affect. Moos and Clemes (1967) examined the relative influence of therapist and patient on each other, taking advantage of a situation in which each of four patients were assigned in counterbalanced order to each of four therapists for a single 20-minute therapeutic interview. Five variables assessed for both therapists and patients during successive 5-minute periods were total number of words, percent of feeling words, percent of action words, number of questions, and number of "mm-hmms." Their analysis showed that both patient and therapist behavior was determined by the patient, the therapist, and particular patient-therapist combinations. Other studies relevant to this issue are van der Veen, (1965); Truax and Carkhuff, (1967, p. 101); and Waxenberg, Strachstein, Leff, Laufer, and Bamberger, (1965).

Dipboye (1954) showed that counselor style varied with topics of discussion, and that within each topic, counselors tended to resemble each other in style. Danskin and Robinson (1954) investigated the degree of lead used by counselors at five universities. Danskin (1955) then attempted to ascertain whether the roles played by a counselor during a series of interviews could be inferred reliably from typescripts, and whether these roles were related to certain other interview variables. Raters unitized the contents of 30 interviews in terms of transitions from one role to another. Scoring units corresponded to the material between role-transition points. These units were then coded to 11 role categories. All the material in an interview representing a role was subsequently considered a "role unit," and rated on a scale of working relationship. In addition, each counselor remark within each role unit was used as a scoring unit and rated on degree of lead. Counselor remarks within role units were also coded to four categories of discussion topics. Danskin was able to show, among other things, that 71 percent of the transition points between role units occurred with a change in topic, that the amount of counselor lead was related to the counselor's role (and by implication, to the topic being discussed), and that the quality of the working relationship between client and counselor was similar across roles. Hoffman (1959) used a similar method of analysis to examine the frequency with which various roles were employed by experienced counselors, and the similarities of role patterning and range of roles used by counselors with different clients and from different counseling centers. Campbell (1962) applied Hoffman's procedures to protocols of interviews conducted by inexperienced counselors to compare their role behavior with Hoffman's experienced counselors, and to examine personality and background correlates of counselor role behavior. In a study of a single therapy group, Rabow (1965) found support for predictions concerning changes in the therapist's role over the life of the group. His major findings were that the therapist intervened less frequently but with longer statements in later sessions. Other studies of client and counselor role behavior in the context of group counseling are Cohn, Ohlsen, and Proff (1960) and Ohlsen and Pearson (1965).

Pallone and Grande (1965) used a counterbalanced design in a study of 80 initial counseling interviews in which at least 70 percent of counselor utterances fell in one of four categories (reflection, interrogation, interpretation, or confrontation), with clients whose problems were limited to one of four areas (education, vocational, personal, or social) to determine whether counselor verbal mode and/or problem focus were related to client problem-relevant communication. The latter variable was assessed by means of the proportion of each client's utterances meeting certain criteria of pertinence to that client's problem area. Both counselor verbal mode and the interaction of verbal mode and problem focus were found to be related to problem-relevant communication. Neither was related to postinterview client ratings of rapport. In a second, more naturalistic, study involving only five clients with educational-vocational problems, no significant relations were found between interview sequence (first through fifth) and counselor verbal mode, client problem-relevant communication, or client ratings of rapport (Pallone and DiBennardo, 1967).

Few variables used in content-analysis studies of therapeutic interviews have been subject to prior examination of their conceptual purity or the impact of changes in the conditions of their use. Perhaps as a testament to therapists' concern with their own role, only variables descriptive of therapist behavior have been so singled out (Bordin, Cutler, Dittman, Harway, Raush, and Rigler, 1954; Bordin, 1955). The concept of "depth of interpretation" is a case in point. Scales for its measurement have been developed, sometimes empirically (Harway, Dittman, Raush, Bordin, and Rigler, 1955), and examined regarding use with different methods of presentation to judges (Cutler, Bordin, Williams, and Rigler, 1958; Harway et al., 1955). Their unidimensionality (Raush, Sperber, Rigler, Williams, Harway, Bordin, Dittman, and Hays, 1956) and semantic structure characteristics (Howe, 1962b) have been explored and used to investigate other therapeutic process correlates of depth (Fisher, 1956; Howe, 1962a).

Speisman (1959) used the depth of interpretation scale developed and investigated by Harway et al. (1955) to test the hypothesis that deep interpretations lead to more resistance than superficial interpretations. Resistant behavior was coded to a system of categories, using the patient response as the scoring unit. In the depth of interpretation scale, the therapist's statement was used as the scoring unit, and the preceding patient response as the contextual unit. Ratings on each scale were made independently by different groups of judges. The results supported Speisman's hypothesis and indicated that the level of resistance suggested by a patient's response does not significantly influence the depth of the immediately following therapist interpretation. Frank and Sweetland (1962) and Frank (1964) obtained similar results with respect to the selective influence of therapist statements on patient responses.

Howe and Pope (1961b) developed scales for measuring therapist activity level, and investigated their unidimensionality characteristics (Howe, 1964, 1965; Howe and Pope, 1961a). In an application of their scale (Howe and Pope, 1962), they failed to support the hypothesis that the activity level of therapist responses was inversely related to the diagnostic utility of the following patient response. When the covariance contributed by verbal productivity was partialed out, the net correlations between activity level and diagnostic utility ratings failed to reach significance.

Pope and Siegman (1962) examined the relationship between activity level and specificity in therapist behavior on the one hand, and productivity and speech disturbance in patient behavior on the other. The specificity scale, developed by Lennard and Bernstein (1960), consisted of eight categories concerning the extent to which the therapist's statement "tends to place limits upon the array of verbal responses from which the patient may choose a reply" (p. 43). Subsequently, Siegman and Pope (1962) developed an empirical scale for measuring therapist specificity in initial therapeutic interviews. Specificity is the reverse of ambiguity, and ambiguity is one of the three attributes of the activity-level scale, along with lead and inference. The two scales should, therefore, correlate highly and yield similar results when compared with patient productivity and speech disturbance. Patient productivity was measured by counting the number of clauses in patient responses, while speech disturbance was measured by the Speech-Disturbance Ratio developed by Mahl (1956). Pope and Siegman hypothesized negative relationships between the therapist scales and patient measures. No support was found for their hypothesis with the activity-level scale, but the specificity scale was significantly negatively related to both patient productivity and speech disturbance. Further analysis indicated that the variance shared by both scales was only moderate.

In more recent work Pope and Siegman have used experimental analogues of initial interviews. Interviewer specificity, warmth, and anxiety-arousing topical focus, have served as independent variables, and the effect of their manipulation has been assessed in terms of such interviewee behavior as productivity, vocabulary diversity (TTR, see below), speech predictability, resistiveness, superficiality, and several measures of verbal fluency. Briefly, they found that low specificity was related to high interviewee productivity and superficiality, greater vocabulary diversity, and certain speech characteristics suggestive of hesitancy or caution. These findings appear consistent with Pope and Siegman's view that low interviewer specificity creates a condition of informational uncertainty

for the interviewee. Interviewer focus on anxiety-arousing topics was associated with greater interviewee productivity, vocabulary diversity, speech predictability, and speech disruption phenomena suggestive of anxiety. Interviewer warmth was positively related to productivity, but subject to an order effect in the presentation of the warm-cold condition (Pope and Siegman, 1965, 1967, 1968; Siegman and Pope, 1965a, 1966a, 1966b). In other studies they have examined relations between interviewee productivity and verbal fluency, and certain personality variables (Siegman and Pope, 1965b) and change in the interviewer's attractiveness to the interviewee from pre- to post-interview (Pope and Siegman, 1966). No relation was found between change scores and productivity, but interviewees who found the interviewer more attractive than they had expected had less silence and fewer speech hesitations.

Heller, Davis, and Myers (1966) used a therapy analogue situation to assess the interaction of therapist activity-passivity and friendliness-hostility on client reactions to the interview, their utilization of time available for speaking, proportions of words dealing with family, sex, and problems, and certain personality characteristics. Content analysis was employed both to provide a check on interviewer role maintenance and to assess several of the client variables. Friendly interviewers were best liked, and clients with active interviewers were more verbal. Findings concerning client use of family, sex, and problem words were difficult to interpret. Psathas and Arp (1966) performed an exploratory content analysis on thematic aspects of interviewer behavior in these same interviews, using the General Inquirer system.

The General Inquirer is a set of computer programs that systematically identifies words and phrases belonging to categories specified by the investigator, counts occurrences and specified co-occurrences of units in these categories, prints and graphs tabulations, performs statistical tests, and sorts and regroups sentences of text according to whether they contain instances of a particular category or combination of categories. These operations are performed on textual material punched on IBM cards in edited form. The category structure is embedded in a dictionary or word list constituting categories against which the computer compares each word of text. When a match occurs, the sentence within which the word appears is, in effect, coded to that category. A number of dictionaries have already been developed for various projects and are available for general use, or the user can devise his own to meet his special needs. (See Stone, Dunphy, Smith, and Ogilvie, 1966, for a general description.)

Psathas and Arp used a standard dictionary organized around psychosociological concepts in their initial analyses, but because of certain limitations they proceeded to develop one more tailored to their needs. Its eight categories accounted for an average of 82 percent of all interviewer statements, and, in various combinations, differentiated between the several interviewer styles under study. In terms of four of these categories, passive-hostile interviewers were found to be polar opposites of the active-friendly ones. Such polar opposition was not found between passive-hostile and active-hostile or passive-friendly and active-friendly interviewers. Thus, the analysis delineated certain classes of lexical interviewer behavior, by means of which the specified experimental conditions of the Heller et al. study were achieved. A further analysis focused on co-occurrences of these categories and on alterations in meaning accompanying them.

Interactional Systems

A number of classical content-analysis systems have been developed to facilitate investigation of patient-therapist interaction, applying the same categories to both participants in an effort to investigate their characteristics as a communication system, and to avoid the information loss inherent in conceptualizing them as independent organisms whose behavior is determined primarily by factors external to their interaction (Gottschalk, 1961, p. 163; Scheflen, 1963a). While the relatively few studies of this type vary in the degree to which they have explicitly articulated and achieved this goal, they have already demonstrated their fruitfulness in both the substantive and methodological realms.

A general-purpose content-analysis system, called Interaction Process Analysis, was developed by Bales (1950). It was based on a theory of small group behavior that conceived of interaction as problem-solving activity distributed across members and over time. Its 12 categories represented the dimensions of instrumental-adaptive and social-emotional behavior. The scoring unit was the act, defined as the smallest discriminable segment of verbal or nonverbal behavior that can be coded. Coding was done by trained workers observing the interaction, though alternative coding procedures have been suggested (Psathas, 1961). Each act was coded to a single category, and judgments were based on the context surrounding the act in question.

Bales and his associates found a marked phasing tendency over the course of experimental group sessions, from a relative emphasis on acts of orientation, to acts of evaluation, to acts of control. Group discussion was also found to progress in cycles, beginning with the introduction of a disturbance and ending with its resolution, thus achieving successive states of equilibrium (Bales, 1950, 1953; Bales and Strodtbeck, 1951). Talland (1955) reasoned that groups engaged in group psychotherapy differed from Bales' experimental groups in several important respects affecting these phase and equilibrium characteristics. With some deviations in procedure, and using a different statistical technique than the one used by Bales and Strodtbeck (1951), Talland found no evidence suggesting the operation of either the control-oriented phase sequence or the cyclical tendency to equilibrium. Smith, Bassin, and Froelich (1962) reached the same conclusions in a study essentially duplicating Talland's. These results were confounded by Psathas (1960b), who followed the Bales and Strodtbeck coding and statistical procedures. His findings clearly support Bales' formulations. Psathas and Igersheimer (1966) have applied this system to a delineation of differences in the functioning of the same therapist in two group-therapy groups, and to differences between the behavior of the patients and therapist in each group. Bales and Hare (1965) have published a reference population of interaction profiles that may be of use to persons using this system. Other more or less related studies are Fine and Zimet (1956), Noble et al. (1961), Psathas (1960a), Mills (1964), Dunphy (1966, 1968), and Munzer and Greenwald (1957).

Heckel, Holmes, and Salzberg (1967) attempted to obtain empirical evidence of distinct verbal phases occurring in group psychotherapy, and to determine whether phases are detectable for individual group members. Each of the 17 subjects attended at least 18 group therapy sessions in one of four groups that met two or three times per week during the period of the study. Patient responses in four pairs of successive sessions evenly spaced over the 18 sessions were coded to the categories of the content analysis system these investigators used in the studies discussed above. Four of six categories showed significant change over the sessions. Unfortunately, the categories appear to have little relevance for the theories of group therapy phasing discussed in the introduction to the paper. Moreover, the implications of the findings are obscure, particularly when it is kept in mind that the subjects came from different therapy groups that may have been in different stages of the therapy group "life cycle," if one exists. Levy (1967) found in 24 first psychotherapy interviews that those segments in which psychotherapist judges agreed psychotherapy was taking place, as opposed to those in which they agreed it was not, contained a significantly larger number of instances of both therapist and patient using affect words belonging to the same category. That such paired affect words are not simply another definition of "psychotherapy taking place" is indicated by the fact that pairing occurred in only 10 percent of the segments in which therapy was judged as occurring.

Lennard and Bernstein (1960) and their associates sought to delineate in quantitative terms the expectation- and communication-interactional systems of patient and therapist (Lennard, 1962; Lennard, Calogeras, and Hendin, 1957; Palmore, Lennard, and Hendin, 1959). Drawing on Bales' formulations concerning phase movement and equilibrium in problem-solving groups and on other social-science concepts, they developed a complex and sophisticated program of research anchored in theoretical notions of small-group behavior. Their method was two-pronged, involving the use of questionnaires administered to both patient and therapist at several points prior to and during treatment, and a multidimensional, multilevel classical content analysis of therapist and patient verbal behavior. The content-analysis system involved three sizes of scoring units, each one appropriate to one or more of five groups of categories.

The findings were complex. In brief, they discovered a great and increasing similarity between patient-therapist pairs in the longitudinal development of the interaction, despite major differences in behavior and expectations. They also found that the therapist-patient interactional system contained built-in mechanisms for maintaining system equilibrium. For example, sessions exhibiting more than the usual amounts of silence tended to be followed by those in which the therapist emitted more evaluative behavior, and behavior of greater informational specificity. This provocative research is marred by inadequate statistical analysis of data; tests of significance are either lacking or of questionable appropriateness. Its usefulness is further limited by the authors' apparent unfamiliarity with research already conducted on therapeutic interviews that employ the same or similar concepts to those the authors believe they are introducing *de novo*.

Jaffe (1961b), too, has insisted that the therapist and patient coming together in therapeutic sessions are appropriately regarded as a single interpersonal system. He called this system the dyad and developed a procedure for investigating its verbal behavior within the framework of the classical model of content analysis. His approach was simply to regard the speech of patient and therapist as if it emanated from one person, that is, to subject it to content analysis without regard to change of speaker.

Gottschalk (1961, pp. 205–206) has expressed skepticism about the utility of the dyad for many questions, in part because it masks the degree to which the two participants share the time of the interview. This information only becomes available if some other system of analysis is used in conjunction with dyadic analysis. In fact, most of Jaffe's applications of this technique were accompanied by additional analyses providing this information. The approach is also open to criticism precisely on grounds that data on the individual is lost in dyadic analysis. Jaffe (1961b) argued that these data are recoverable, since the speech samples in which one of the participants talked maximally or minimally can be analyzed separately. However, this manner of breaking the dyad into its components rests on the assumption that speech samples dominated by one of the speakers are equivalent to those in which there is more nearly equal interaction.

Most of Jaffe's work employed a content-analysis system known as the Type-Token Ratio (TTR). (See Mowrer, 1953, for a review of earlier studies applying the TTR to the speech of individuals.) This scheme uses the word as the scoring unit, and consists of the ratio of different words occurring in a summarizing unit (types) to the total number of words in that unit (tokens). Any size summarizing unit may be used, although its size determines the natural arithmetic limits of the ratio. TTR values of given speech samples are determined, in part, by the syntactic patterns of the language, but also by factors idiosyncratic to the speaker, or in this case, the dyad (Jaffe, 1961b). The TTR is thus an indicator of redundant word usage. Jaffe's pilot research (1958) showed a normal frequency distribution of dyadic TTR values in integrated conversation. Departures from the normal pattern or central tendency of TTR values for a given dyad can be considered indicative of changes in the pattern of communication taking place.

Dyadic analysis of pre- and posttreatment interviews, and of a third interview at time of discharge of a successfully treated psychotic patient, showed TTR changes at critical points both within interviews and over a series of interviews (Jaffe, 1957). Within the interviews, dramatic shifts in mean TTR levels or variation about these means appeared to mark the natural phasing of the interviews (Jaffe, 1961b). Jaffe speculated that these shifts may correlate with such clinical constructs as defensive maneuvering and stressful disorganization. The trend over the interview was toward diminished variability accompanied by a general rise in mean values. Thus, the communication of the dyad became more succinct, with clinically judged recovery from psychosis. Other aspects of TTR validity have been examined in two experimental studies (Fink, Jaffe, and Kahn, 1960; Jaffe, Fink, and Kahn, 1960).

More recently, Jaffe and his associates have explored the language behavior of the dyad and its members through a variety of computer-mediated techniques of lexical and nonlexical content analysis (Cassotta, Feldstein, and Jaffe, 1964; Jaffe, 1963). In a provocative paper intended to illustrate this approach, Jaffe (1964) reported several different analyses of a course of therapy completed in nine interviews. He found a convergence in word usage between therapist and patient, and four other indices—sentence length, utterance length, interpersonal orientation (ratio of usage of "I" to "you" for each speaker), and specificity (use of "a" versus "the")—each revealed a pattern of stabilization, most notably a "tracking" phenomenon not wholly attributable to either member of the dyad. The fifth interview in this series marked a pivotal point in the development of several of these variables. The tracking characteristics may well represent an independent manifestation of the equilibrium mechanisms found by Lennard and Bernstein (1960). Another of these content-analysis systems has been used to explore the appropriateness of various stochastic models to dyadic speech and silence behavior in non-therapy interviews (summarized in Jaffe, 1968), and to examine nonlexical characteristics of emotional expression (Feldstein, 1964).

Data suggestive of a tracking phenomenon in patient-therapist dyads has also been reported by Matarazzo, Wiens, Matarazzo, and Saslow (1968). After more than a decade of research (discussed above) devoted to exploring temporal relations in interviewee responses to variations in interviewer behavior, Matarazzo et al. have begun to explore these same variables in therapeutic dyads. In this report on three therapists working with seven patients, they found striking evidence of synchrony or tracking between patient and therapist in interruption and response latency behavior, and of relations between these two variables. Other findings, in particular those relating to the utterance-duration variable, are too complex to discuss here.

The convergent discovery of these "tracking" phenomena by three investigators—Lennard and Bernstein, Jaffe et al., and Matarazzo et al., each working with different methods and patient-therapist dyads—is a rare and exciting event in psychotherapy research. While it confirms the value of a systems approach to the study of psychotherapy, it also makes a strong claim for a high research priority, since questions concerning the relation between these independent discoveries and their implications for our theoretical understanding of the therapy process have not yet been addressed.

Analysis of Contingent Relationships

Some analysts working within the classical model have begun to focus on the contingent relationships between categories within summarizing units. Such a procedure enables one to make a different inference when category A is associated with category B than when it is associated with category C. Used with appropriate summarizing units, this method yields information concerning the associational structure of the communicator (Osgood, 1959; Pool, 1959b; Woodward, 1966).

This important advance largely overcomes a long-standing criticism of classical content analysis—that in ignoring transitional in favor of simple probabilities, content analysts fail to account systematically for the context in which the scoring unit occurs, and consequently each unit is assigned an inappropriately invariant meaning (Carroll, Agard, Dulany, Newman, Newmark, Osgood, Sebeok, and Solomon, 1951, p. 27; McQuown, 1954a; Pool, 1959b, pp. 196–197). A related argument holds that scoring units are coded traditionally on the basis of their representational meanings rather than their instrumental meanings when, in fact, information bearing on the instrumental characteristics of verbal behavior is required for the kind of inference the analyst wishes to make. Analysis of contingent relationships is one approach to dealing more directly with instrumental meanings in verbal behavior (Mahl, 1959b; Pool, 1959b, pp. 206–212).

One such method, called "contingency analysis," was developed by Osgood (1959) but, to the writer's knowledge, it has not been applied to therapeutic interview material. Rosenberg (1962) used a similar method in an analysis of the contingencies of topics discussed in group therapy. A study of contingent relationships by Auld and White (1959) is discussed below, among studies based on another content-analysis model.

Laffal developed a method called Analysis of Contextual Associates, rooted in word-association research showing, in part, that word associations appear in clusters corresponding to semantic superordinate structures or categories, and that common factors underlie single and continuous word associations, and free speech (Laffal, 1964; Laffal and Feldman, 1962, 1963). Using the word as the scoring unit, Laffal developed a category system representing possible superordinates for most words appearing in English language samples. Words were coded to categories on the basis of synonymity or denotative closeness. This procedure reduces the diversity of meaning in a speech sample, thereby facilitating comparison of categories across summarizing units (Laffal, 1961, 1963, 1964). The current category system is outlined, and coding definitions and rules are discussed, in Laffal (1965a, Appendix I).

This system was first applied to the examination of certain key words in the autobiography of a psychotic patient, Daniel Schreber, in an effort to throw light on the symbolic meaning of the sun and God in his delusional system (Laffal, 1960). In a second study (Laffal, 1961), the verbal behavior of a schizophrenic patient was analyzed and compared with the results of a similar analysis of a second psychotic patient and with the language of Schreber's autobiography. The results showed that coding reliability was high, that the method clearly discriminated the spoken and written language of different individuals, and that the language of a patient in one psychological state (unimproved) could be sharply differentiated from his language in another (markedly improved). A further analysis of certain features of this patient's language in psychotherapy appears in Laffal (1965a, pp. 127–148). In still another analysis concerning this patient's speech in psychotherapy, Laffal (1965b) showed that paralleling the improvement in psychological status and the increasing integration and organization of his language over therapy interviews, there occurred a significant decrease in silent pauses of 0.5 to 3.0 seconds. This finding was interpreted as supporting the belief that such pauses are related to motivational states as reflected in changes in social adjustment, and, of course, it suggests one kind of continuity between lexical and nonlexical aspects of speech. Pauses of less than 0.5 seconds were associated with less frequently occurring words, suggesting that short pauses may be associated with word-choice uncertainty.

Watson and Laffal (1963) have also explored the coherence of therapists' verbal behavior with different patients. The language categories used by patients were uncorrelated, while those used by therapists in describing one patient were significantly correlated with their language in describing another. The speech of therapists in describing a given patient was also significantly correlated with the therapy language of that patient. A related finding from experimental investigations of two- and three-person free-speech situations was that the topic of conversation was a more important determiner of language category usage than were individual consistencies in language usage across topics (Laffal and Feldman, 1963; Laffal, 1967).

A remarkably similar, computerized system has been developed by Harway and Iker (1964, 1966; Iker and Harway, 1965). Words occurring within interview time segments were correlated, yielding a measure of contingent associations over successive segments, and the resulting matrix was factor-analyzed. The General Inquirer system (discussed above) is a general-purpose, computer-based, content-analysis system designed to perform contingency studies as well as more traditional analyses (Stone et al., 1966). The paper by Psathas and Arp (1966), also discussed above, contains examples of this application of the General Inquirer.

These systems constitute one of the more exciting recent methodological developments in content analysis. Not only do they provide us with a new and useful tool for naturalistic studies of language behavior, but they should also prove useful in the examination of problems more directly pertinent to research in psychotherapy and psychopathology. These include such problems as possible continuities in the thinking of certain carefully selected patient groups, the nature and correlates of alterations in associational patterns with psychotherapy and other forms of treatment, and various issues in the area of therapist characteristics and patient-therapist interdependence.

Investigation of Internal States

A number of workers have used classical content analysis to study the emotional and other internal states of participants in therapeutic interviews. In such studies certain manifest behaviors are assumed to indicate the existence of these states, and these behaviors are the focus of the content analysis. The investigation of internal states was one of the earliest applications of content analysis to therapeutic interview research (Auld and Murray, 1955; Lasswell, 1935). Many early studies sought to establish, for a given individual, a more or less permanent level of the state in question. In the period covered by this paper, this aim has largely given way to the investigation of momentary changes. One focus of these efforts has been to specify changes in both lexical and nonlexical communication content. Such changes are then interpreted as indicative of changes in internal states.

The Discomfort-Relief Quotient (DRQ) is a lexical measure introduced by Dollard and Mowrer (1947) and assumed to tap drive-tension levels. It is computed by dividing the number of discomfort expressions (pain and unhappiness) by the number of discomfort plus relief expressions (happiness, pleasure, and satisfaction). A series of such quotients, calculated periodically, yields a record of change in relative frequencies of discomfort and relief expressions, presumably reflecting differential handling of drive tension, and thus indicating movement in treatment. Research prior to 1954 investigating the relation of the DRQ to therapy movement and success yielded mixed results (Auld and Murray, 1955; Mowrer, Light, Luria, and Zeleny, 1953). More recently, Murray, Auld, and White (1954) compared DRQ ratings with the results of a content analysis in which patient material was coded in terms of motivation and conflict. While the DRQ showed no decrease in discomfort levels over the course of treatment, the other content analysis showed very real movement. The authors concluded that the DRQ is not as useful as other content measures for assessing therapeutic progress. However, a study by Proff (1952), and discussion of his findings by Callis, Polmantier, and Roeber (1957), suggested that the DRQ may reflect movement toward problem solution if it is computed on the basis of patient discussion of feeling-laden material rather than cognitive material.

Lebo and Applegate (1958) and Callis et al. (1957) found that DRQ ratings depended in part on the topic of discussion. The former concluded that, to the extent that therapists influence topics of discussion, DRQ ratings reflect an interaction effect between therapist and patient rather than a purely internal state of the patient. Auld and Mahl (1956) compared DRQ ratings with the results of another content-analysis scheme designed to yield a measure of drive tension as manifested in the variables anxiety, hostility, and dependency. Correlations between the DRQ and global ratings of these three variables, taken separately and together, were positive but small. The authors concluded that if the combined criterion variables are measures of drive tension, the DRQ is not a very good measure of individual differences in drive tension. With these critical findings and conclusions, the death knell of the DRQ in psychotherapy research appears to have sounded, for it has not figured in reports published in recent years.

Platz and Honigfeld (1965) tested the hypothesis that tension decreases the intelligibility of verbal communication. They selected long patient passages from two published therapy cases, and from these selected the three having the most and fewest tension words. Every fifth word was deleted from these six passages, and 30 college students were asked to guess the missing words. High-tension passages were significantly more difficult, though students' anxiety level alone or in interaction with patient passages was not a factor.

Mahl developed a nonlexical method of investigating momentary anxiety in patients. He examined two general aspects of patients' speech: hesitancies and longer silences, and disturbances in speech. These phenomena, Mahl argued, can be considered either defensive behaviors designed to ward off or delay anxiety-provoking material, or as the disruptive, non-defensive effects of anxiety on complex forms of behavior such as language production (Mahl, 1956, 1959a). Silence was measured in terms of a quotient yielded by dividing the number of seconds of silence during two-minute segments

of interview time by the number of those seconds during which the patient might have spoken (that is, seconds not filled by therapist talk). Relatively little research using this measure has been reported, and Mahl (1956, 1961; Kasl and Mahl, 1956) has discussed complications in its use.

Far more work has been reported with Mahl's measure of speech disturbance. He identified eight types of speech disruption in interview protocols, among them the "ah" sound, repetitions, stuttering, tongue slips, and omissions. Analysis of a variety of speech materials indicated that such disturbances are ubiquitous in spoken English, though they pass largely unnoticed. The occurrence of these, as identified from tape recordings and typescripts, was used to calculate a Speech-Disturbance Ratio for two-minute summarizing units of patient speech. The ratio represents the number of speech disturbances divided by the number of words spoken by the patient. Subsequently, Mahl found that the "ah" sound, unlike other disruptions, did not vary with other measures of anxiety, and he has excluded it from the ratio, now called the Non-Ah Ratio (Kasl and Mahl, 1958; Mahl, 1958, 1959a, 1959b). This finding has been disputed by Panek and Martin (1959) and by Boomer. Boomer (1963) found that when Mahl's original Speech-Disturbance Ratio was divided into three types of speech-disruption phenomena, and their occurrence correlated with simultaneous nonpurposeful body movements (considered an independent indicator of anxiety), the resulting positive correlations differed markedly in magnitude and statistical significance. The "ah" and repetitions type were most highly correlated (0.42, p. < 01).

Still, Mahl (1959a, 1959b) has summarized several investigations, providing evidence for the validity of the Non-Ah Ratio as a measure of anxiety. An attempt by Boomer and Goodrich (1961) to replicate and extend one of these studies yielded inconclusive results. In an experimental study, Kasl and Mahl (1965) found that the Non-Ah Ratio, and each of the seven types of speech disturbance it summarizes, increased significantly during an anxiety interview in a two-interview sequence. That the anxiety interview did in fact evoke anxiety in the experimental subjects was supported by independent judgments of randomized segments of subjects' speech and by repeated measurements of palmar sweat (assumed to indicate anxiety) over both interviews. The Non-Ah Ratio was significantly and positively related to palmar sweat, and further analysis suggested that palmar sweat and speech disruption may be, in part, alternate ways of expressing anxiety. The Ah Ratio showed no significant changes with the evocation of anxiety, but did increase when the experimenter left the room during certain periods of the interview sequence. This finding was interpreted as consistent with the view that the Ah Ratio is a measure of uncertainty.

Schafer has argued (Knapp, 1963, p. 116) that the interpretation of the Non-Ah Ratio as an anxiety measure is too narrow. He believes it is more centrally correlated with those states or conditions that impair automatized ego functioning, such as a depletion of ego energies as in fatigue and emotional excitement, or the concentration of ego energies involved in heightened defense in response to intensified conflict. Anxiety is one by-product of some of these energic shifts. Tests of this hypothesis have not yet been reported, but Feldstein (1964) has examined the Non-Ah Ratio characteristics of seven common affective states. He had 30 actors and actresses read a standard passage to express sadness, hate, fear, anger, depression, nervousness, and joy. Tape recordings of these readings were analyzed in terms of the Non-Ah Ratio, breath intake, vocal intensity, and pause time. The Non-Ah Ratio differentiated the fear and nervousness condition from each other and from the other affect states. Other findings included a sex difference, actors' speech being more disrupted. Patterns for individual affective states across the four measures of vocal behavior were significantly different from each other. The finding of a sex difference on the Non-Ah Ratio is at odds with the findings of a study by Feldstein, Brenner, and Jaffe (1963), which examined the relation of the Ah and Non-Ah ratios to sex, topic, and interviewer verbal activity level in an experimental situation. Feldstein and Jaffe (1962b) found that neither the occurrence of "ahs" or the Non-Ah Ratio was related to experimentally induced anger. These authors have also reported a computer program that produces Ah and Non-Ah ratios from keypunched interview material (Feldstein and Jaffe, 1963).

In two investigations, Jaffe (1961a) and Feldstein and Jaffe (1962a) attempted to relate the Non-Ah Ratio, as an indicator of anxiety, to the TTR, as a measure of vocabulary diversity indicating general affective arousal including anxiety. In the first, a significant negative relationship obtained, but the data were derived from only two interviews with a single patient. In the second, 30 nonpsychiatric patients were compared with 30 schizophrenics on their responses to stimulus pictures. In this study, a significant inverse relationship resulted for the nonpsychiatric patients, but the relationship, while negative, was not significant for the schizophrenic patients (who were, however, on tranquilizing drugs). Siegman and Pope (1966a) found nonsignificant correlations between TTRs and both the Ah and Non-Ah ratios.

As part of a larger study, Pope and Siegman (1962) tested the hypothesis that patient speech disruption (anxiety) is negatively related to their measure of therapist activity level and to Lennard and Bernstein's measure of therapist specificity in the preceding therapist utterances. Using the original Speech-Disturbance Ratio, they found that the hypothesis with respect to therapist activity level was not confirmed, but that as therapist specificity increased, patient speech disturbances decreased in the following patient response. In subsequent work (also discussed above), they used the Ah and Non-Ah ratios and found repeated relationships between the Ah Ratio (viewed as a measure of caution or hesitancy) and low interviewer specificity, and the Non-Ah Ratio and anxiety-arousing topical focus (for example, Siegman and Pope, 1965a and Pope and Siegman, 1965b; see also Pope and Siegman, 1964).

In several studies, Mahl found evidence to confirm his judgment that nonlexical content-analysis systems provide a better route to the study of emotional states than systems based on lexical content only (Mahl, 1959a, 1963; Schulze, Mahl, and Murray, 1960). And he demonstrated his point (Mahl, 1963) by analyzing speech-disturbance findings in relation to the lexical behavior of the patient to highlight the idiosyncratic manner in which defensive and anxious behavior manifests itself in lexical content. Low correlations between his speech disturbance and silence measures and Gottschalk's anxiety scale based on the same two interviews (Mahl, 1961) provided fuel for a spirited methodological debate in the volume in which this study appeared.

Nevertheless, Gottschalk and his associates have worked diligently to find lexical indicators of internal states. Following early work on psychogrammatical categories of word types (Gottschalk, Gleser, and Hambridge, 1957; Gottschalk and Hambridge, 1955; Gottschalk, Kaplan, Gleser, and Winget, 1962), their attention turned to psychodynamic trends in thematic material (Gottschalk, Gleser, Daniels, and Block, 1958; Gottschalk and Kaplan, 1958; Kaplan and Gottschalk, 1958), resulting most notably in the development of scales considered sensitive to both conscious and unconscious material indicative of anxiety (Gleser, Gottschalk, and Springer, 1961), hostility (Gottschalk, Gleser, and Springer, 1963; Kaplan, Gottschalk, Magliocco, Rohovit, and Ross, 1961), social alienation–personal disorganization (Gottschalk et al., 1958; Gottschalk, Gleser, Magliocco, and D'Zmura, 1961), and capacity for human relatedness or object relations (Gottschalk, 1968). All but the last of these scales have been applied to a variety of drug effect and psychosomatic problems (Gottschalk, Gleser, Springer, Kaplan, Shanon, and Ross, 1960; Gottschalk et al., 1962; Gottschalk, Gleser, D'Zmura, and Hanenson, 1964; Gottschalk, Cleghorn, Gleser, and Iacono, 1965; Gottschalk, Gleser, Wylie, and Kaplan, 1965; Gleser, Gottschalk, Fox and Lippert, 1965), and to the investigation of patient-therapist behavior in psychotherapeutic and psychoanalytic interviews (Gottschalk, Springer, and Gleser, 1961; Gottschalk et al., 1963; Gottschalk, Winget, Gleser, and Springer, 1966).

The fundamental assumptions underlying these scales were derived from the psychoanalytic theories of defense mechanisms, affects, primary and secondary process thought, and object relations. The category structures consist of empirically determined weights applied to specified themes found in the verbal content. Over the years some scales have been somewhat revised with respect to the weights corresponding to certain themes (Gottschalk et al., 1966). The scoring unit is the grammatical clause. In some scales each unit is coded to all relevant categories, while in others it is only coded once. Validity studies of the hostility and anxiety scales are summarized in Gottschalk et al. (1962, 1963, 1966; Gottschalk and Frank, 1967), while validity data on the Social Alienation–Personal Disorganization Scale can be found in Gottschalk and Gleser (1964) and Gottschalk et al. (1958; Gottschalk, Gleser, Magliocco, and D'Zmura, 1961). Preliminary validity data on the Human Relations Scale appear in Gottschalk (1968).

The hostility and anxiety scales were employed, among other measures, in a study by Witkin, Lewis, and Weil (1968) to test the hypothesis, derived from Witkin's researches on the concept of psychological differentiation, that in their therapy sessions (apparently only the first two sessions were studied), less-differentiated patients would be more prone to shame than to guilt, to self-directed hostility than to other-directed hostility, and to both separation anxiety and diffuse anxiety. The opposite predictions were made for more-differentiated patients. The study involved eight patients: four more and four less differentiated according to Witkin's usual criteria. The hypotheses were, in general, supported, except that pertaining to separation anxiety. Still another hypothesis which linked differentiation to the tempo and duration of speech behavior was also supported.

Other internal-state studies include Dibner (1956, 1958), Eldred, Hamburg, Inwood, Salzman, Meyersburg, and Goodrich (1954), Kanfer (1959, 1960), Krause (1961), Krause and Pilisuk (1961), Berman (1967), and Laffal (1965b). General reviews of research in this area are Davitz (1964), Kramer (1963), and Mahl and Schulze (1964).

Body Movement Research

Only recently and in relatively few studies have body movements been examined as a source of information about psychotherapy by means of classical model systems. These investigations have focused on relations between body movements and internal states, more general patient and therapist characteristics, and the lexical content of therapy sessions. They might, therefore, easily have been included in other sections of this chapter, but because so few have been reported and because of the promise of this line of investigation, it seemed most appropriate to discuss them in a single section.

Indeed, one study has already been mentioned: Shapiro (1968) examined the relation between judges' ratings of therapist genuineness, empathy, and warmth, and patient self-exploration, when the information on which judgments were based was presented visually, aurally, or through both channels simultaneously. Judges rated 39 three-minute segments of interview interaction on each variable in all presentation conditions. Correlations between visual and aural channels for each variable were intermediate in magnitude, and significant except for the therapist-warmth variable. Correlations between both channels simultaneously, and the visual alone or the aural alone, were of equal magnitude, except in the case of therapist empathy, where the aural two-channel correlation was significantly larger.

Fretz (1966a, 1966b) related specific body movements to some of these same variables. He had 13 observers watch (through one-way mirrors) the first, third, and sixth interviews of 17 seven-interview counseling treatments, and describe on tape all observable movements of clients and counselors. Movements were described in terms of the grossest descriptive concept applicable to a change in position and to uninterrupted movement repetitions. They described 131 separate movements, 60 of which were used by three or more subjects. These 60 movements were used as the basis of study and were coded as occurring or not occurring during the first five-minute segments of the three interviews in each case. These data were then factor-analyzed, yielding 41 unrotated factors, 10 of which were common to both clients and counselors. Only one of these 10 factors showed a significant change in frequency of occurrence from first to sixth interview (for clients only), and five differentiated between client and counselor behaviors. A host of significant relationships were found when movement frequencies pertaining to the 10 common factors were correlated with scores on an inventory measure of unconditional positive regard, empathy, level of regard, congruence, and total relationship (Barrett-Lennard, 1962), and with scores from a

satisfaction and a charisma questionnaire, all of which were completed by both clients and counselors after the third and sixth interviews. For example, vertical hand movements were the best indicator of satisfaction for both clients and counselors, while movements associated with hand clasping best indicated unconditionality for both groups. Leaning forward and back was the best indicator of clients' relationship inventory variables. On the other hand, when the 10 movement factors were related to data on paper and pencil assessment of eight personality characteristics of both clients and counselors, fewer significant correlations were found than one would expect on a chance basis.

Mahl (1968, pp. 300–321) has reported an exploratory study first described in 1959 (Mahl, Danet, and Norton, 1959) of individual differences and intraindividual variation in gestures and (nonfacial) body movements during psychiatric intake interviews, and the relation of these to personality characteristics. Subjects were 18 adult, white, neurotic and character-disordered patients equally divided as to sex and varying considerably in religious and ethnic background and in socioeconomic status. Interviews were tape recorded and observed from behind a one-way mirror, the observer having no access to the verbal dialogue. A running account of patients' nonverbal behavior was recorded on a second tape, and a common signal was recorded on both tapes to facilitate their later collation. Data contained on the gesture record was then coded to 15 movement categories representing three general classes: general postural changes, communicative gestures (head shaking, pointing, fist pounding), and autistic actions (scratching, rubbing, and playing with rings or clothing). Summarizing units were one- or two-minute intervals, and for some movement categories the whole interview (that is, total frequency counts) as well. Based on these data, inferences were made concerning the individual patient's diagnosis, conflict areas, defensive patterning, and so on, and the behavioral bases for them were specified. These inferences were tested against various kinds of documentary data and the verbal content of the intake interviews.

Mahl found large individual differences in characteristic movements, some of which appeared related to sex-role patterning. Data on intraindividual variability in the frequency of certain movements across the one- and two-minute summarizing units were presented in graphic form for five patients, and demonstrated the lawfulness of these movement bursts when the patient's verbal behavior and the inferences made from the gesture record were considered. Of 43 such inferences, 36 were strikingly confirmed on the basis of the case record and interview verbal content. For example, Mrs. B played a great deal with the rings she wore, and Mahl inferred that she was experiencing marital conflict. The clinic summary contained the information that her major concerns were that too many "demands are placed on her by marriage and children, and that she must 'bottle-up' her anger and retaliatory impulses felt toward her husband. Complains that husband doesn't help with care of house and children, and never takes her out." Mrs. B was also frequently observed to inspect her fingernails and to scratch herself. Mahl inferred that she was conflicted over the expression of hostility and had turned aggressive impulses against herself. Evidence from the record indicated that Mrs. B's symptomatology included "depression, feelings of inferiority, and 'bottling-up' of aggression."

Students of psychotherapy have long been told that just such observations as these are utilized by any sensitive therapist. Mahl's rich and stimulating study serves to systematically isolate the movement data from the welter of simultaneously available information, begins the process of teasing out aspects of their communicative value with reference to clinical work, and proposes a classification of these. Four types of relations were found between the gestural and verbal records. Some movement patterns conveyed the same information carried by the verbal content, while others suggested contrary meanings. Movements sometimes anticipated verbal content, and some appeared to be related to aspects of the interaction with the interview. Other sections of this long paper dealt with noncontent-analysis aspects of Mahl's work on body movement data (some of which also appears in Mahl, 1967).

Freedman and Hoffman (1967) studied the hand and arm movements of two paranoid patients during two 10-minute segments of video and sound tapes selected from filmed psycho-therapy sessions. In both segments the patient discussed his symptom experience, once while in an acute phase and again in a clinically altered state. The scoring units were the visibly discriminable movement act, and the number of seconds of its duration. Each unit was coded as being body-focused or nonbody-focused, and related or unrelated to the verbal content. These two dichotomous categories were found to be intimately related: 95 percent of nonbody-focused acts were also coded speech-related, while 85 percent of body-focused acts were coded as nonspeech-related, and the four categories were therefore collapsed into object-focused acts and body-focused acts. The reader will have noted the parallel between this classification and Mahl's categories of communicative and autistic movements. Freedman and Hoffman further divided object-focused acts into five categories in terms of their degree of integration with verbal content. While not subjected to statistical tests, these categories appeared to differentiate the two patients in their acute stage, and to parallel their clinical course as assessed from the verbal content of their interviews.

Ekman and Friesen (1968) provide a lengthy and valuable discussion of issues connected with research on body movements, particularly concerning unit definition and meaning attribution, and they have described several methods (and their integration) employed in their own attack on these problems. One of these was content analysis. Their units were similar to those used by Freedman and Hoffman—the movement act and the number of seconds of its duration. They reported an illustrative analysis of the foot and hand acts of a single female patient during filmed admission and discharge interviews. Both hand and foot acts differed markedly in kind from one interview to the other, and the variety of acts emitted at discharge was greater and less stereotypic. Hand acts were also studied in terms of the accompanying verbal material. With but one exception, the several occurrences of each of eight hand acts selected for discussion was associated with a specific verbal theme. When all instances of certain of these acts were shown to judges out of context, they were judged (by means of an adjective check list) as conveying consistent and rather specific messages. Ekman and Friesen have also expanded Mahl's list of ways in which body movements may be related to the verbal content of the interview.

Haggard and Isaacs (1966) studied fleeting facial expressions that are not observable in real life interaction, or more accurately, in films run at normal speeds, but which can be discerned when films are run at about 1/6 normal speed (that is, 4 frames/sec.). The unit in this analysis was the expression change, and the summarizing unit was 24 frames at slow speed, and 120 frames at normal speed (24 frames/sec.) or, in both cases, five to six seconds of viewing time. An expression change was defined as a shift from an identifiable expression to a qualitatively different one involving some motion of facial muscles but excluding eye movements, and the mouth, tongue, and jaw movements involved in speech. Individual expression changes were later collated with the verbal transcript. These micromomentary facial expressions were extremely variable both within patients over interview time, and between patients. They appeared to occur most frequently during discussion of affective states or content when the patient was highly expressive in other ways as well (speech, gesture, general body movement). But this was less often true during periods when the patient was judged as being in active conflict, in contrast to periods when controls were functioning effectively. These expressions also tended to be inconsistent with the concurrent verbal content and adjacent expressions. In an analysis of one therapy hour, these expression changes were associated with denial statements and blocking, and (this may refer to a different hour) particular persons or conflict areas discussed by the patient.

Other studies have focused more specifically on internal states. Sainsbury (1955) tested the hypothesis that patients' gestural activity will increase if they are affectively disturbed during interviews. There were 12 subjects of varying diagnoses, 4 of whom were interviewed twice. Sainsbury used an electromyograph to count the number of movements in patients' shoulders, arms, and hands in such a way that the movement record could be coordinated with the verbal content. Interviews were semistructured, containing neutral initial and concluding topics, and intervening topics determined by the patient's problems and thus believed to be emotionally loaded. Heightened heart rate

(EKG) during these portions of the interview supported this belief. When the verbal content was unitized in half-minute segments and each segment was coded as stressful or nonstressful, the number of movements associated with stressful units was greater for each interview, and significantly larger in 14 of the 16 interviews. Other analyses supported this finding.

Dittmann (1962; Dittmann and Renneker, 1963) selected filmed interview excerpts from a single case representing five recurring mood states which the patient both recognized as such and named (angry, calm, gloomy, hurt, jittery). The frequency of nonpurposeful head, hand, and leg movements differentiated the five states, though the best combination of mood and movement data accounted for only about 25 percent of the movement variance. Boomer (1963) found these same movement data significantly related to Mahl's Non-Ah Ratio and to filled pauses (ahs and word repetitions). In an earlier study, Dittmann (Dittmann and Renneker, 1963) found no relation between speech disturbance (presumably the Non-Ah Ratio) and foot movements. Boomer and Dittmann (1964) examined some alternate theoretical explanations of relationships between speech rate, filled pauses, and body movements in an experimental study. Their results did not show body movements related to either speech rate or filled pauses.

Other noncontent-analysis studies relevant to work in this area include Dittmann, Parloff, and Boomer (1965), Ekman (1964, 1965), Ekman and Friesen (1967), and Kramer's review (1963). Still other body-movement studies are discussed below in connection with nonquantitative model studies.

PRAGMATIC MODEL STUDIES

The internal-state investigations discussed in the two preceding sections represent a variety of traditional approaches to discerning underlying conditions which contribute to the overt behavior seen in therapeutic interviews. Many writers, but perhaps most pointedly Mahl (1959a), Strupp (1962a, pp. 590–591; 1962b, pp. 35–36), Gottschalk (1961, p. 161) and Colby (1963), have discussed the fundamental philosophical and methodological problems facing those who investigate emotional and other internal states through classical content analysis. Mahl and others attempted to resolve these issues by remaining within the fold, forswearing work with lexical aspects in favor of the nonlexical, expressive dimensions of verbal behavior and body movements. Others have deserted the classical model in favor of the pragmatic model of content analysis.

Murray (1954, 1956; Murray et al., 1954) developed such a system, rooted in psycho-analytic and learning theory, which focused on internal emotional processes. Recognizing the complexity of the relationship between verbal behavior and underlying drive structure, his strategy was to infer the patient's needs, moti-vations, and conflicts from conscious or face-value meanings of the patient's speech. The scoring unit in this system was the grammatical clause or simple sentence. There were four major patient drive categories: sex, affection, dependence, and independence. Each of these contained three subcategories of drive com-ponents: approach, anxiety, and frustration. In addition, there were special categories for residual patient units. Therapist categories facilitated coding active and passive remarks and certain other aspects of therapist behavior. Murray applied this system to a published case of client-centered therapy. His hypotheses were that patient categories containing statements followed by therapist remarks having mild approval value would increase in frequency in the course of therapy, and that patient categories containing statements followed by therapist remarks having mild disapproval value would diminish in frequency over the course of therapy. Both hypotheses were supported. In another study (Schulze et al., 1960), Mahl's Speech-Disturbance Ratio was negatively related to Murray's measure of anxiety in one case and showed no relationship in several others. Speech disturbance was related to some of Murray's other categories, however, in ways specific to the individual patients. Application of a modified version of Murray's system to two cases of Rosen's direct analysis has also been reported (Murray, 1962).

Stimulated by Murray's work, Dollard and Auld (1959) developed a complex content-analysis system that has been the most extensive-ly used example of the pragmatic model. Developed empirically out of the mix of their psychoanalytic and learning-theory orientation, their clinical sensitivity, and their data, the category system ranged across the areas of overt behavior, symptoms, and aspects of the thera-peutic process. But its essential focus was on the dynamic motive states of the patient. These could be either conscious or unconscious. Motives were considered conscious if the patient could name them as his own. Unconscious motives were those that the patient never learned to label appropriately. They are nonetheless recognizable, the authors assert, and can be coded (Dollard and Auld, 1959, pp. 2–3, 4). There were also categories for processes associ-ated with motives and for motive referents. In contrast to the complexity of the 78 patient categories, there were only 6 broad therapist categories. For both patient and therapist categories, the scoring unit was the statement or simple sentence used by Murray, but more adequately discussed and defined (Auld and White, 1956). In addition, in those patient categories depending on overt nonverbal be-havior, temporal scoring units of five seconds were used. The contextual unit for both sets of categories was the material in the case preceding the unit in question.

Dollard and Auld discussed at length the reliability of their coding system, together with the rationale for the study of reliability of content-analysis data. They presented their own reliability data, broken down by categories to make possible the study of a case profile over a series of interviews. Some of their categories were found to be quite reliable, and others were not. They provided a useful discussion of the possible reasons for these problems and their implications.

Auld (1961) has presented an argument for the system's construct validity, and it has now been used in a variety of studies. The initial studies (Dollard and Auld, 1959) suggested that certain categories may differentiate neurotic from psychotic patients. Theory-based pre-dictions about relationships between certain categories were significantly supported in four cases, and were in the predicted direction in several others. Auld and White (1959) applied the system to four cases of psychoanalytically oriented psychotherapy. Using a sequential dependency analysis modification, they found that patients' speech was likely to persist in the same category to which the previous unit was coded, that psychoanalytically oriented therapists were more likely to intervene after resistances than at other times, that interpretations were not followed by heightened resistance in the following patient units, and that silence and speech judged resistant tended to occur in units that followed one another, thus providing a basis for the authors' conclusion that these are equivalent forms of resistance. To check on the possibility of bias in the classification of resistant speech, Goldenberg and Auld (1964) repeated this portion of the Auld and White study with methodological improvements. The initial results were strongly confirmed. But White, Fichtenbaum, and Dollard (1964a), using the Dollard and Auld system, showed that silences in initial therapy interviews were significantly related to patient's socio-economic status, thus qualifying the equation of silence with resistance. White, Fichtenbaum, and Dollard (1964b) successfully used a modification of the system to predict continuation in treatment of psychiatric outpatients from an analysis of initial interviews. These same interviews were reexamined to determine the degree to which socioeconomic status was related to patients' preoccupation with physiological complaints in initial interviews (White, Fichtenbaum, Cooper, and Dollard, 1966). Physiological concerns were not clearly patterned in a social class hierarchy. The amount of patient talk devoted to current physiological conditions varied inversely with the extent to which patients saw their presenting problems as originating in intimate interpersonal relations.

The method, with modifications, has also been applied in three studies investigating change during short term psychotherapy. In one (White, Fichtenbaum, and Dollard, 1966b), verbal and nonverbal changes in patient speech from the first to last quarter of a 13-week course of therapy were considered and compared with the intake worker's initial report and the therapist's posttreatment report in the case of a young lady who made only moderate gains and later returned to treatment. A second study (White,

Fichtenbaum, and Dollard, 1966a) explored whether changes occurred in the areas where the therapist intended to work for change, in the case of a young man with the symptom of nausea related to a woman he was dating. The therapist's goals were identified from the areas (in terms of the content categories studied) in which the therapist focused his comments during the last three quarters of the 13-week series of interviews. The therapist also provided weekly statements concerning his intention to work for change in the patient's motives in the various areas under study. A follow-up interview was conducted by the therapist 9 months after termination. The results showed that in the two areas in which the therapist had focused his efforts, the patient made changes judged adaptive between the first and last quarter of treatment, and that even greater adaptive change had occurred by the time of the follow-up interview. The third study (White, Fichtenbaum, and Dollard, 1968) was designed to test the hypothesis that neurotic patients considered changed by short-term therapy will have more interactive behavior in the last four hours than in the first four hours, while patients classified as unchanged will not show such an increase. Subjects were 10 students between the ages of 19 and 25 who received from 10 to 20 hours of therapy. Three criteria of change were used, one based on certain content-analyzed aspects of patients' verbalized concerns, while the others were derived from a follow-up interview 10 months after termination and from information concerning subsequent seeking of additional treatment. These criteria were in essential agreement in indicating that five cases showed change, while five did not. Three indices of interactive behavior were devised: interruptive dominance, initiation of talk after long silences, and shared laughter and humor. Finally, these were combined in a single measure. All three of these indices, as well as the combined measure, differentiated the changed cases from those that did not change.

Unfortunately, the credibility of these three studies is marred. The reader will recall that two of them dealt with analyses of individual therapy cases. The authors report precisely 4210 scoring units coded for each of the two patients. Moreover, in the third study, which reported results for 10 therapy cases, including one of those also reported on individually, we again find precisely 4210 patient scoring units, and, in addition, 1620 therapist scoring units—the exact number reported in the one single-case study that examined therapist speech. To further heighten the already remarkable coincidence, all three papers report virtually identical levels of inter-coder reliability based on these data.

These several studies have demonstrated that Dollard and Auld's system constitutes a sensitive tool of analysis pertinent to a variety of disparate problems, ranging from the effects of inter-pretation on subsequent patient behavior to prediction of treatment continuation and out-come. Yet, like most other content-analysis systems used in psychotherapy research, it has not found favor among other workers. One exception is Snyder (1963, pp. 13–39), who used certain patient categories from this system, together with elements of other systems, to study aspects of therapist technique and the therapeutic relationship in two cases in which client dependency was a central issue.

Sklansky, Isaacs, and Haggard (1960) devised a pragmatic model system (based on psycho-analytic concepts), designed to clarify the verbal interaction in psychotherapy, and its therapeutic effects, by studying the manifest and latent meanings of the patient's communication in relation to certain aspects of the therapist's responses. The scoring unit for the patient was the topical segment, defined as the conversation occurring between two successive points at which the patient changes the subject. The scoring unit for the therapist was each therapist response within each topical segment. The con-textual unit for both patient and therapist scoring units was the preceding therapy sessions. Patient units were judged by experienced psychotherapists who interpreted them at as many levels as seemed useful, ranging from the manifest to the deeply unconscious. Three or four levels were usual. Each patient unit was stated as if the patient had uttered it explicitly in the language of the level to which it had been assigned. Then each therapist response within the topical segment in question was coded as being either ego-syntonic or ego-dystonic for the patient, and either a direct, indirect, or irrelevant response to the patient at each of these meaning levels. The authors carefully pointed out the methodological difficulties concerning the re-liability of the operations performed on the patient units; meaning levels are a function of rater sensitivity and theoretical orientation, and agreements on unconscious meanings are noted for their unreliability. The authors' best solution to this problem was to work for consensual validation among several experienced judges of similar theoretical persuasion.

The method was found to differentiate among patients in terms of their manner of response and among therapists in terms of their therapeutic style. It also differentiated early and late sessions for a given patient-therapist pair. They found that when the therapist's response was direct at the manifest level and irrelevant at deeper levels, the topic was often dropped by the patient at all levels. When the therapist's responses were direct at the manifest level and indirect at latent levels, discussion of the topic continued even if the therapist made occasional responses irrele-vant at all levels. When the therapist responded directly at the manifest and at some latent levels, therapeutic activity seemed to be facilitated, but when the therapist's responses were directly pitched to latent-meaning levels and only in-directly dealt with the manifest level, there was a tendency for the patient to change the topic after a short time. Ego-syntonic responses facilitated therapeutic work, while ego-dystonic responses impeded it, though direct but ego-dystonic responses sometimes had the effect of shocking the patient into more intensive therapeutic work. Many of these findings were supported and elaborated in a second paper (Sklansky, Isaacs, Levitov, and Haggard, 1966).

Mann (1966, 1967) sought to delineate the feelings experienced by group members vis-à-vis the leader in therapy and training groups. Precisely because the greater portion of such feelings are not expressed or even experienced directly and explicitly, and because he wanted to work with categories that were conceptually related to the clinical and theoretical literature on group process and to the kind of inferences and conclusions he hoped to draw, Mann elected to work within the pragmatic model. His system consisted of 20 categories. Four of these specified the degree and form of symbolization that cloaked leader-related feelings. The remaining

16 specified the character of the feelings themselves, and were divided into five groups. Two of these, hostility and affection, each contained 4 categories describing feelings directed toward the leader; another group, authority relations, contained 3 categories descriptive of feelings evoked by the leader's authority status; the fourth and fifth groups consisted of the remaining 5 categories, which referred to feelings group members have about themselves in relation to the leader. The leader's utterances were coded to these same 16 categories, but in terms of the feelings he attributed to group members, and these units were also coded for the leader's approval, disapproval, or neutral orientation to the feelings he attributed.

The scoring unit was that portion of a single utterance, ranging from a single word to several sentences, within which the codable feelings were uniform and could be coded to the same categories. Mann's discussion clearly indicated that coders' decisions often depended on the context within which a unit occurred, but no formal contextual unit was specified. Units were coded to all appropriate categories, but to only one category in a given group. Thus, unitizing was dependent on the coding to an unusually heavy degree, and the whole enterprise clearly required the application of sensitive clinical skills and judgments, which are the hallmark of pragmatic-model systems. Unfortunately, reliability data are inadequately reported.

In both studies this system was applied to the protocols of self-analytic groups that met for 32 sessions in an academic setting. The earlier study (Mann, 1966) dealt with two such groups, and the data were analyzed for each group separately by means of a runs analysis for each of the 16 affect categories across all 32 sessions. This procedure led to a description and analysis of certain phases each of the groups appeared to encounter, to a discussion of differences between the groups, and to the presentation of a developmental scheme consisting of five stages in the growth of the member-trainer relationship that appeared to account for some of the phenomena highlighted by the study. The second, more exhaustive study (Mann, 1967) involved four groups. The data for all 20 categories for all sessions and all groups were factor-analyzed, resulting in six bipolar factors defined in terms

of the categories most heavily loaded on them and discussed at length in terms of individual sessions having high factor scores for each factor. Mann next presented a view of the process of group development in terms of these factors, pointing up regularities across groups and explaining changes over time in terms of the shifting nature, power, and composition of various competing subgroups within each group. Finally, certain functional role positions filled by individuals in each group and constituting focal points for subgroup activity were described, again on the basis of factor scores. The study is rich and provocative, but marred by superficial reporting of its statistical underpinnings.

Others have used the pragmatic model in whole or in part. Ashby, Ford, Guerney, and Guerney (1957) used several pragmatic variables as part of a larger study, as did Glad and Glad (1964; Glad, Hayne, Glad, and Ferguson, 1963) in their study of the relation between patient behavior in group psychotherapy, and therapist behavior and certain patient personality variables. Zimpfer (1967) attempted to relate feelings underlying counselees' group-therapy behavior to pre- and postcounseling self and peer evaluations. Frostig and Horne (1963) used a pragmatic model system to evaluate the treatment of psychotic children. Several other studies discussed elsewhere in this paper employed pragmatic-model elements (Bandura et al., 1960; Cutler, 1958; Eldred et al., 1954; Speisman, 1959; Strupp, 1960; Winder et al., 1962; Jackson et al., 1961).

In the writer's opinion, pragmatic-model systems have an importance out of all proportion to their use to date. Content analysis in psychotherapy research has frequently been superficial and mechanistic, precisely because the epistemological strictures implicit in the dominant classical model exert pressure on investigators to attend to the immediately observable and obvious facets of the therapeutic process, facets that have little relevance to our most richly heuristic theories of personality and psychopathology. Of course, some classical-model studies surmount these strictures by dint of imaginative application, but the pragmatic model promises to provide a conceptual vehicle by means of which psychotherapy data can be brought to bear with reasonable rigor on the theories with which therapists work.

NONQUANTITATIVE MODEL STUDIES

Linguistic-Kinesic Analyses

If pragmatic model systems facilitate work with dynamic constructs for which behavioral cues cannot be specified, linguistic analysis holds forth hope of making possible identification of these cues through a basically nonquantitative approach, or through its combination with appropriate statistical techniques. Many studies treated elsewhere in this paper have been enriched by the work of linguists, particularly those involving various forms of speech disruption which the linguist knows as paralinguistic phenomena. The studies treated in this section, however, are those utilizing or critically exploring linguistics, particularly microlinguistics, as the basis of analysis.

Linguists, and many content analysts as well, may be distinctly uneasy at the characterization of linguistic analysis as a type of content analysis. But it seems appropriate in terms of the applications of linguistic analysis in therapeutic interview research reviewed here. Like other types of content analysis, the goal of these studies is the systematic ordering of the communication content to provide a public basis for inference.

Linguistics has been put on a scientific footing within the present century, and is methodologically far in advance of other content-analysis techniques (Firth, 1956; McQuown, 1954b, 1957; Saporta and Sebeok, 1959). It commands rigorous, valid, and highly reliable[6] procedures for explicating the total structure of language, making accessible to the observer all the functioning parts and their mutual dependencies (Carroll, 1955; McQuown, 1954a, 1954b, 1957). These methods are traditionally nonquantitative, that is, they have been used to indicate the presence or absence and patterning of linguistic phenomena rather than their frequency of occurrence, but some linguists have applied statistical techniques to linguistic data (Carroll

et al., 1951; Pool, 1959b, pp. 224–225; Saporta and Sebeok, 1959, p. 139).

Writers discussing the relation of content analysis and linguistics have stated that they are different precisely in that content analysis is primarily concerned with meanings, while linguistic analysis is concerned with the properties of language as a code for the transmission of communication (Pool, 1959b, pp. 224–225; Saporta and Sebeok, 1959, p. 135). But if linguists have pursued a strategy of emphasizing structural considerations, linguistics is nonetheless ultimately concerned with meaning (Carroll, 1955, pp. 23–29). Moreover, it is entering a phase of development in which its methods are being applied to extralinguistic problems in cooperation with specialists in other disciplines, one result of which is a more immediate concern with the problems of meaning (Carroll et al., 1951, pp. 27–29; Firth, 1956, p. 133; Hoijer, 1954; McQuown, 1957; Pittenger and Smith, 1957). Recent applications of linguistic analysis to therapeutic interview material is one manifestation of this development.

The conventions and rationale of linguistic analysis were presented to psychotherapy researchers after 1957 in papers by Pittenger and Smith (1957) and Pittenger (1958). The first of these discussed several interview-research applications of linguistic analysis. Among them were identification of the specific linguistic cues that are the source of hunches and impressions achieved in traditional clinical work, development of more useful descriptive analyses of interaction patterns, and more precise understanding of differences in communication patterns believed to have diagnostic significance, such as flattened affect in schizophrenia. Such questions were explored by Pittenger, Hockett, and Danehy (1960) in an exciting and incredibly rich examination of the first five minutes of an initial psychiatric interview. This study combined the tools of linguistic and paralinguistic analysis and clinical inference in an effort to generate as much data as possible about this brief interlude in the lives of two people. Their skillful weaving together of these various kinds and levels of analysis demonstrated clearly that linguistic techniques applied to interview

---

[6] For a dissent regarding reliability, see Boomer (1964).

materials can produce insights quite impossible without them.

McQuown (1957) performed a classical content analysis on the data resulting from a linguistic analysis of the first half hour of an interview. His categories were designed to distinguish the cultural background norm of linguistic and paralinguistic behavior from the personality-defining departures from this norm. From the frequencies of linguistic phenomena in these categories, he developed personality profiles of both the psychoanalyst and the patient.

Eldred and Price (1958) attempted to explore the relation between four dimensions of the paralinguistic phenomena called "vocalization" and the clinical impression of certain affect states in the patient. They characterized each passage judged as expressing one of five affective states in terms of the vocalization pattern it reflected. They also characterized the patient's normal speaking voice in each interview. The findings showed alterations in the relatively stable patterns of normal voice over the period of 12 months from which the interviews were drawn. Affect states were characterized differently than the normal voice material in the rest of the interview in which an affect passage occurred. Furthermore, each of the affect states, except anxiety, was characterized by a different vocalization pattern.

An unfortunate weakness in this provocative study is the absence of any reliability measures of the various judgments made, or of the significance of results. This is particularly regrettable in light of a study by Dittman and Wynne (1961) investigating the relationship between linguistic phenomena and the clinical impression of affect. This study was broader in scope, including both linguistic and paralinguistic features, and applied appropriate statistical tests. The results indicated that the paralinguistic features could not meet conventional reliability standards. The linguistic features could be identified reliably, but were unrelated to affect. More recently, Markel (1965) demonstrated that certain paralinguistic features can be coded with high interrater and test-retest reliability, and Duncan (1966), too, reports adequate reliability. Duncan performed a factor-analysis-like study of six varieties of para-

linguistic phenomena on samples of both patient and therapist speech. Two therapy hours—a "peak" and a poor session—from each of 18 cases were included. The analysis yielded nine patient and six therapist factors (that is, clusters of related paralinguistic phenomena). Of these, one patient and one therapist factor were significantly associated with "peak" hours, while one patient and two therapist factors were related to the poor sessions. The portion of this study pertaining to therapist behavior is more extensively reported in Duncan, Rice, and Butler (1968; see also Rice, 1965 and Rice and Wagstaff, 1967).

Brosin (discussion in Birdwhistell, 1959) has appropriately criticized attempts such as those of Eldred and Price (1958) and Dittmann and Wynne (1961) to correlate specific classes of linguistic phenomena with other aspects of behavior as a misunderstanding of the function of linguistic analysis; meaning lies, he insists, in the patterning of linguistic features, and not in their frequency. Scheflen (for example, 1963b, 1966) has broadened the argument, decrying the isolation-of-variables approach on one hand, and the pooling-of-intuitive-judgments approach on the other, as being sterile and beside the point in most psychotherapy research. And he has demonstrated the potential of a naturalistic but rigorous alternative called context analysis.

Context analysis is a truly nonquantitative content-analysis method involving the integration of all media of communication, though applications to date have emphasized linguistic and kinesic data. (Kinesics is the study of patterned and learned aspects of body motion having communicational value.) Birdwhistell is the major figure in this work, and he has developed a conceptual apparatus analogous to that of linguistics, and a system of notation for accurate description of minute alterations in position. The best generally available accounts of this work appear in Birdwhistell (1961, 1963) and Hayes (1964), and in the discussion following Hayes' paper.

Context analysis was most fully explicated by Scheflen (1965c). Briefly, the method assumes that communication behavior (that is, behavior having transactional meaning for the participants) has a patterned structure consisting of a hierarchy of increasingly inclusive units ordered in particular ways. The objective of context analysis is to delineate basic or structural units by specifying their necessary and sufficient components, establishing the larger units of which they are a part, and determining the contexts in which they occur. Once these steps have been completed, inferences can be made regarding function or meaning. Structural units are defined as regular organizations of components occurring in specific contexts. That a set of possible components do constitute a structural unit can be tested by ascertaining whether they invariably occur together, and studying the context(s) or shifts in context regularly accompanying the occurrence of a tentative unit. Once a series of structural units is identified, the analysis can proceed to the next level in the hierarchy, focusing on how the structural units fit together and function in larger contexts. Many structural units regularly employed by Americans are already well known, making possible short-cuts in the analysis.

A less complete exposition of this method (Scheflen, 1966) is built around an example from a therapy case. Two structural units—cigarette lighting and smoking by the therapist—are shown to constitute a single more inclusive unit called refraining from conversation. Three other structural units—shifting the cigarette to the left hand and shifting posture, followed by instructing the patient on what to talk about—constitute another more inclusive unit called tactical shifting, and signals that the therapist will shortly engage in two more structural units—looking up, followed by an interpretation —which again constitute a more inclusive unit called interpreting. These three relatively inclusive units, together with others, constitute a still more inclusive unit that Scheflen calls structuring therapist-patient reciprocals. The example neatly illustrates the interdependence of lexical and kinesic behavior, as does another analysis in which the function of a particular hand gesture in the multiple therapy of Whitaker and Malone is explored (Scheflen, 1965a). Other less programmatic analyses appear in Scheflen (1963a, 1964, 1965b), and more theoretical aspects of human communication are discussed in Scheflen (1967, 1968). Another long-heralded, but still unpublished application of this method

is McQuown (in press). Condon and Ogston (1967, 1966) have used a related method, which revealed a synchronous "dancing" of the bodies of both the speaker and the listener to the "tune" of the articulatory segmentation of the speaker's voice.

Acoustical Analyses

A very different approach to the nonquantitative analyses of patient speech involves the study of its acoustical properties, primarily through the use of sound spectroscopy. Ostwald (1960, 1961, 1963, 1964, 1965) has employed these techniques to study the acoustical properties of sound patterns which are specific to various clinical states, and which form the basis for certain clinical judgments concerning affect expression. Starkweather (1962, pp. 436–445) and Rubenstein and Cameron (1968) have also worked in this area. Rubenstein and Cameron applied these methods in determining the characteristics of nonverbal communication that therapists can and cannot detect, and the voice components that carry affective information. Therapists selected recorded passages, from their own cases, which they felt were important for the nonverbal communication they contained, as well as control passages in which they detected no such communication. These passages were later read several times by the patients who originally uttered them, and both the spontaneous statements and the repetitions were analyzed. Loaded passages were shown to differ from unloaded passages in their acoustical properties, and changes in vocal frequency and amplitude were identified as carriers of emotional meaning. A general survey of acoustical properties of speech can be found in Flanagan (1965).

DISCUSSION: TRENDS, ASSESSMENTS, AND OTHER MATTERS

Having come at last to the end of this review, the reader cannot but be struck by the sheer bulk of the content-analysis literature in psychotherapy research. Figure 10.1 attests to the acceleration of effort in this field during the period reviewed. A few words are in order concerning the construction of Figure 10.1. It represents a tabulation of publication dates of references to this chapter, excluding book reviews, volumes bringing together or summarizing previously published papers, theoretical or methodological papers not concerned with content analysis per se, and papers only tangentially related to content analysis in therapy research. Its most likely systematic bias is the understatement of publications occurring in more recent years, since these are less frequently cited by other workers and thus hardest to locate. The figure is presented in the form of a frequency curve based on a three-year sliding average, in order to present the general trend and to minimize year-to-year fluctuations which, in themselves, have little meaning, given problems of publication lag and the like. The curve was not extended beyond 1967 because that is the last year for which three years can be averaged; the point for 1968 would show a sharp dip, primarily as an artifact of the method of presenting the information. The point representing 1954 is similarly artifactual.

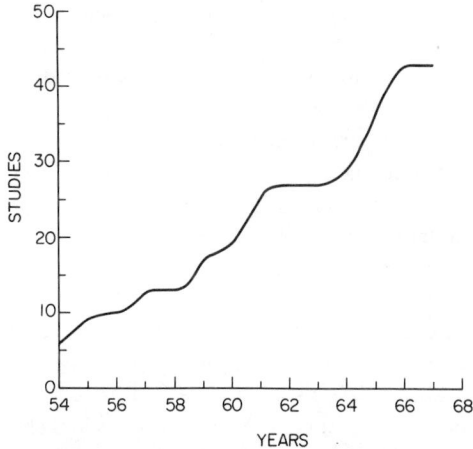

Figure 10.1 Frequency curve of content-analysis studies relevant to psychotherapy research published between 1954 and 1968.

Figure 10.1 allows only limited conclusions. It does not sanction statements concerning shifts in the popularity of various methods in psychotherapy research. Nor can we tell whether the increase in content-analysis work in this area parallels, exceeds, or falls behind the publication rate in psychotherapy research in general. Data needed for these more interesting analyses are not available, so far as the writer has been able to determine. But Figure 10.1

clearly indicates that, relative to previous content-analysis research in this field, the method is flourishing. Of studies included in Figure 10.1, 53 percent appeared in the last third of the 15-year period.

The writer's earlier review concluded by noting that what was even then perceived as a burgeoning of content-analysis studies of therapeutic interviews in the two preceding decades, reflected a tendency to create new systems rather than to make extensive use of those already developed:

System after system has been developed and presented in one or two demonstration studies, only to lie buried in the literature, unused even by its author. Moreover, few variables or notions about therapeutic interviews have received anything approaching programmatic or extensive content-analysis investigation. This has resulted in redundancy; systems were developed with apparent unawareness that other approaches to the same problem, or efforts to apply the same approach to other problems, had already been reported. (Marsden, 1965, p. 315.)

With the increased perspective of an additional five years, these conclusions ought to be reassessed. When they were formulated in 1964, only about 38 percent of the content-analysis systems under consideration had had so much as a second application. In the last five years, roughly another 20 percent of these have been used again. And of the systems published for the first time within the past five years, about 25 percent have already been applied in subsequent studies. Thus, content-analysis systems seem to be more frequently reapplied than appeared to be the case earlier. What amount of reuse constitutes an appropriate level is, of course, a matter of opinion.

But studies published in the last five years provide less need for modification of other elements of the earlier pessimism. The extent to which researchers have studied previously investigated variables without reference to the prior work remains striking. While several variables have been studied frequently, few indeed have received programmatic investigation. Some studies applying previously developed content-analysis systems appear misguided in that the systems were not well suited to the requirements of the new investigations. While some workers have studied a body of data by means of two or more systems, either to assess the relative validity of the systems or to throw a brighter, more penetrating light on the behaviors under study, this laudable practice has occurred far less frequently than one would expect, given the effort expended in this type of therapy research.

Some aspects of this state of affairs are a predictable consequence of the chaos at large in psychotherapy research. In the absence of a universally accepted theoretical basis for our therapeutic practices, lacking consensus on which are the important facets of therapeutic encounters, and in the face of competing conceptualizations of our theories and rival ways of making operational the concepts they encompass, it is not surprising, and not altogether unfortunate, that researchers have developed their own content-analysis systems which reflect their definition of importance and their formulations of theory. The disappointment occasionally expressed by some content analysts at our failure to have produced a few standard systems sufficient for the bulk of our research needs is shortsighted, neglecting as it does these more general deficiencies of the field.

These deficiencies and the resulting spirit of individualism in research contribute to the perception of a considerable range in the quality of these studies. For in addition to the more usual issues bearing on quality—the internal logic of the system, its relevance to the problem under study, the care with which it is applied, the attention paid during design and analysis phases to possible alternative explanations of findings, and so on—there are such matters as the relevance of the problem itself, and the adequacy of its formulation and of the theory in terms of which it was formulated. Charges that a given study is trivial often involve disagreement of the latter sort, reflecting problems of the general field more than of the specific study. But even when these considerations are set aside, wide variations in quality remain. Researchers have often simply documented the obvious, or have employed variables selected more for the ease with which they could be counted than for their intrinsic importance or relevance, even within their own theoretical systems. And an appalling number of studies have attempted to evaluate the effectiveness of

treatment or to compare types of treatment with respect to effectiveness, using only the work of neophyte therapists or trainees. At the other extreme are a few, but an increasing number, of truly imaginative and clearly significant studies which equal in sensitivity the clinical and theoretical writings from which they ultimately derive, and at the same time validate content analysis as a research technique in psychotherapy research.

Like psychotherapy research in general, content-analysis work in the period under review has begun to reflect a greater intimacy and integration with research conducted in areas quite removed from psychotherapy per se. If in some ways this development tends to reduce therapy research to a special case of a broader range of problems, the resulting cross-fertilization and stimulation can be expected to have a salutory effect. One manifestation of this trend is the now frequently encountered therapy-analogue situation, dealt with at length elsewhere in this volume. While some content analysts have always preferred to work with analogues rather than with actual therapy situations, there appears to be an increasing tendency for researchers to begin with the investigation of therapy, and, as particular problems are brought into sharper focus, to move to the more easily controlled analogue. This has resulted in some instances of programmatic investigation, the general absence of which was decried above, and, when well done, promises to produce appropriately controlled experimental studies that serve to neatly undergird or to discredit the findings of the original research. These studies have also increased the range of content-analysis applications in therapy research. Content analysis has traditionally been used as a tool of naturalistic investigation, both in purely descriptive work and in hypothesis-testing studies. But with the increasing popularity and sophistication of the therapy-analogue situation, it is also being used to assess the effects of attempts to manipulate the therapy variables under study.

Some Comments on Method

All too often in the studies reviewed, and even in methodological discussions, the problems of unit and category selection are treated as issues unrelated to each other, to the theory underlying the study, or to the types of analysis to be applied to the coded data. Any system of categories implies a theory of some sort. Categories, after all, represent the variables in terms of which questions under study are to be answered, usually by means of further analysis. And these questions, presumably, are derived from or have relevance for theory. The clarity of that theory and the precision with which the questions are stated largely determine the character of the categories and the appropriate techniques of analysis.

Scoring units, too, reflect the questions and underlying theory. Selection of a unit implies that it is meaningful to address the questions via the categories by means of that unit rather than some other—that it bears some important relation to the questions, either directly or by way of the category structure. But the choice of units has often reflected only the need to divide therapy dialogue into segments in systematic fashion. Despite some obvious exceptions to this criticism—the act as Mann defined it (1967), Scheflen's use of patterned linguistic and kinesic features (1965a), Luborsky's (1967) use of momentary memory lapses and subsequently recalled thoughts, Haggard and Isaacs' use of expression changes (1966), the discussion topic (Robinson, 1949), role behavior (Danskin, 1955; Hoffman, 1959; Campbell, 1962), and even the randomly selected four-minute segments of dialogue used by Rogers, et al. (Kiesler, 1966)—despite such exceptions, investigators have not generally argued for their choice of a unit in terms of its logical or psychological relation to either the category structure or the questions under investigation. While this is often the result of a casual regard for the logic of content analysis, it also reflects the very real difficulty of justifying units rigorously, not only in content analysis but in psychology generally (Salzinger, 1962).[7] When investigators have provided a rationale for their unit, it was often cast in terms of face-validity arguments. At present we have little more than common sense to go on. Hopefully, current research in psycho-

linguistics will help provide a sound psychological basis for unit selection in at least some areas of investigation (See Johnson, 1965; Dittmann and Llewellyn, 1967, 1968; Suci, 1967; Fodor and Bever, 1965).

This line of argument applies as well to other content-analysis units. Take the contextual unit in contingency analyses, for example. Contingency analyses have been used to delineate associational structures embedded in a patient's speech. The extensiveness of the contextual unit determines the amount of the dialogue within which concepts will be considered associated with a specific key concept. In common sense terms, restricting the contextual unit to, say, the simple sentence within which the key concept occurs, seems somewhat narrow, while on the other hand, use of the whole therapy hour seems much too broad. The point is that any decision in this matter clearly implies a theory of thinking, and should be based, insofar as possible on theoretical considerations.

Principles and problems pertaining to the formulation and application of category systems, in contrast to unit selection, have received considerable discussion in the methodological literature, and little would be gained by repeating that discussion here. The preceding review provides a view of the range of possible category structures in use. Berelson's book (1952) is an excellent general, if somewhat old, guide to the relevant technical considerations, but it focuses, of course, on frequency measures. Schutz (1958) also provides a useful treatment. While analyses based on frequency still dominate the field and will undoubtedly continue to do so, a number of innovations have been devised for use in conjunction with more traditional practices. They are nowhere treated exhaustively, but brief discussions can be found in Holsti's broad treatment of category development (1969, Ch. 5), in Pool (1959a), in North et al. (1963), and in Stone et al. (1966, Chs. 2, 4 and 6). The latter, while written largely in terms of the General Inquirer computer system, is nonetheless well worth the effort at translation occasionally required to bring its arguments to

---

[7] Studies in which the whole therapy hour served as the unit were excluded from this review, perhaps arbitrarily in terms of their obvious logical relation to other content-analysis studies, because these

studies seemed primarily to reflect the use of other research methods. See, for example, Bellak and Smith (1965); Strupp, Chassan, and Ewing (1966); Auerbach and Luborsky (1968).

bear on content analysis in general. Examples of how such innovations may be used can be found in Stone et al. (1966, Part II).

The best general discussion of research designs used in content-analysis studies, and of statistical analyses appropriate to them, is Stone et al. (1966, Ch. 7). Chassan (1967, Chs. 7 and 8) provides an excellent and detailed discussion of designs, based on the intensive statistical analysis of the single case. While designs of this type are particularly suited to many content-analysis investigations of psychotherapy, surprisingly few of the studies reviewed employed this strategy, and none approached realization of its full potential. Another useful paper dealing with techniques for quantification of interview material, which might be applicable to some content analyses, is Sargent, Coyne, Wallerstein, and Holtzman (1967).

The methodological innovations just discussed have come largely from outside the field of psychotherapy research. Content analysts working within this field have displayed considerable ingenuity in devising systems tailored to the special problems they face, and have applied sophisticated techniques in examining the measurability of certain concepts. But aside from these, they have conducted few specifically methodological studies, though certain problems of method are considered in several of the studies reviewed. Almost all the specifically methodological studies emanated from the work of Rogers and his students, with primary emphasis on problems inherent in sampling from therapy protocols as a means of reducing the total amount of material to be coded. They investigated the effects on ratings of patient speech, of using interview segments of different lengths (Kiesler et al., 1964), of selecting segments from different locations within a single hour (Kiesler et al., 1965), and of including the contiguous therapist speech in the material available to judges (Schoeninger et al., 1967). Truax, on the other hand, studied the effect on ratings of therapist conditions, of making the contiguous patient speech available to judges, and of combining patient and therapist statements in various ways (Truax, 1966a). Schoeninger et al. (1968) have compared methods of training judges to rate therapy materials. Metz (1965), working with a different content-analysis system, compared the use of tape-recorded speech with typescripts. None of these studies was designed to make possible generalization of findings to other content-analysis systems, but even within these studies there is clear evidence that the results were partially determined by specific factors, such as the forms of pathology in the patient groups involved. One implication is that one cannot safely act on the findings of these studies in different situations, and that similar studies should be carried out in pilot phases of research.

The reliability with which units were coded to categories was treated cavalierly in many of the studies reviewed. Indeed, standards of respectability current in the field appear quite low. Overall percentage-of-agreement figures and correlation coefficients can, and often do, one suspects, mask considerable disagreement on individual categories. Moreover, even when percentage of agreement is computed for individual categories, rarely is the baseline of agreement attributable to chance, or the effect of the number of categories, considered. And category structures frequently fail to meet the assumptions underlying the product-moment correlation, or even rank-order correlation statistics. Holsti (1969, Ch. 6) provides a useful discussion of these issues. Schutz (1952) introduced a percentage-of-agreement statistic that gives the probability that judges are using the criterion intended rather than chance factors, and provides tables of confidence limits from which the percentage of agreement needed to achieve the 0.05 level can be determined if one knows the number of judges and the number of judgments they must make. Scott (1955) suggested a percentage-of-agreement reliability formula which corrected both for the number of categories and for chance coder agreement. Funkhouser and Parker (1968) described a procedure to facilitate determination of the source of low reliability. Exline and Long (1965) employed scaling techniques to improve intercoder reliability in content analyses using rating scales.

If the problems of intercoder and category reliability have been handled casually, another reliability issue has been largely ignored. A considerable number of the studies reviewed involved coding from transcribed tape recordings. Yet almost all of these neglected to report on the reliability of the transcription process itself. The tedious job of transcription usually falls to a secretary, whose motivation is likely of a different order than the investigator's. But whatever her motivational state, there are certain inherent problems. Tape-recorded therapy dialogue is often obscure, and must be interpreted as well as transcribed. This is done by listening and relistening until the words "become clear." But the clarity they achieve has a projective quality; the secretary and the tape recording both contribute to the outcome. Add to this the more active processes of distortion of that content which arouses emotion in the transcriber, distortions that are often painfully visible if one looks for them, and the need for careful attention to transcription reliability becomes apparent. Scheflen (1965c, p. 24) reports that unskilled transcribers make about 20 percent errors.

Computers

Computer-performed content analyses are a product of the period covered by this review. To date, their development has had relatively little impact on psychotherapy research. Only a handful of the studies reviewed were computer-mediated. Yet, those few involved six computer content-analysis systems. Others already available might well be applied to therapy research, and still others are under development specifically for that purpose. There can be little doubt that by the time a new review in this field is warranted, computerized content analysis will have played a substantial role.

Considered in terms of the scoring unit with which they work, four types of computer content-analysis systems are now available. One group is comprised of systems designed to record patterns of speech and silence and their durations (Wiens et al., 1965; Cassota et al., 1964). These focus on the binary question of whether someone is speaking at a point in time. Another type computes Mahl's Ah- and Non-ah ratios, though just how this is done has not been specified (Feldstein and Jaffe, 1963). A third group, the largest, uses the word as the scoring unit, and performs a variety of analyses, including word counts, TTRs, vocabulary diversity studies, contingency analyses, and others

(Stone et al., 1966; Iker and Harway, 1965; Jaffe, 1964; Starkweather and Decker, 1964; Carlson, 1967). Lastly, one system is based on the "event," defined to take into account both psychological and real-life occurrences (Eiduson, Brooks, Motto, Platz, and Carmichael, 1967). This system, though not yet applied to psychotherapy research, is the only one known to the writer that has the capability of working with relatively large, thematic units.

Other distinctions roughly parallel this classification. These groups of content-analysis systems differ in the degree to which they require human handling of data prior to content analysis, and in the variety of analyses they are capable of producing. The first group requires no human intervention. Dialogue is fed directly from a microphone to an electronic device that transforms speech and silence into computer-readable signals and passes it on to a card punch or tape producing unit. Of course, these systems only yield analyses of speech and silence variables. The word-count systems vary somewhat in the amount of data preparation necessary. All require that the tape-recorded dialogue be keypunched (typed on IBM cards, in effect), and some require considerable additional editing. As noted above, they yield several types of analyses. The last system discussed above requires not only transcription, but translation into a language that has meaning for the computer programs constituting the system. Its capacity to deal with thematic units appears to provide a base on which a large variety of category structures could be built.

That computers do only what they are told to do, and that they have no tolerance for ambiguity, are by now commonplace observations—Stone et al. (1966) have called them extraordinarily accurate but stupid clerks. Because computers can be used in content analysis only when they can be told specifically what to do, certain kinds of problems and approaches appear to be beyond their reach, at least for the present. These include the pragmatic-model systems in which ambiguity is maximal, and considerable judgment must be exercised in the coding process. Similarly, classical systems heavily dependent on inference, such as the rating of therapist conditions (Rogers et al.), do not now seem amenable to computer content analysis. On the other hand, when the cues on which coding is based are explicit in the text (or can be made so without essentially doing the content analysis in the process of preparing data for submission to the computer), then the computer's clerical accuracy can be harnessed to perform analyses on a far larger number of variables than could easily and accurately be handled manually, or to perform far more complex analyses—involving multiple scoring units, for example—than can accurately be done by hand. Moreover, these more extensive and complex analyses can be carried out with astonishing rapidity. Relieved of the tedium of coding, the investigator is free to invest his time in the more meaningful and challenging problems of developing content-analysis systems of greater heuristic potential. And given the rapidity with which computers work, he is free to reanalyze old data, after making modifications in his content-analysis system on the basis of insights and hunches born of initial findings (for example, Psathas and Arp, 1966), or after devising wholly new systems.

There are limitations to these systems, too. Several of these have more to do with deficiencies of common sense and with magical fantasies of computer omnipotence than with problems intrinsic to computers. Overhead costs involved in developing such systems and of data preparation are high, and it makes little sense to devise one for a single study or for studies based on a few easily assessed variables occurring infrequently in large volumes of data. Existing computer systems do not take context into account (without the addition of edited-in cues), and therefore, for example, do not distinguish homographs. This and similar results of computer simple-mindedness mean that the task of specifying just what is relevant to the analysis and taking precautions against unfortunate surprises is considerably more arduous than is the case with many manual systems. Viewed more positively, this situation forces the rigorous explication of assumptions that might otherwise confound the analysis. A central attraction of computer content-analysis systems is the fact that they eliminate the problem of intercoder reliability. Indeed, the computer itself is nearly faultlessly accurate (and sometimes accurate to a fault), but to the degree that the data have to be prepared for computer use, reliability problems may still exist. Potential sources of unreliability lie in keypunching, in transcription from recording tape to paper prior to keypunching, and in editing, which may involve anything from identification of pronoun referents to providing the computer with information about syntactical structure (Stone et al., 1966) or translation into machine-usable language (Eiduson et al., 1967).

Useful discussions of computer content-analysis systems can be found in Stone et al. (1966) and Holsti (1969 Ch. 7), while Starkweather (1967) treats other computer applications to interview data as well.

Therapy Recording

The research reviewed in this chapter is both a cause and result of the development of techniques for making a permanent and more or less objective record of the therapeutic encounter. Paralleling the research literature is another concerned with various aspects of making such a record (by means of one-way screens, tape recorders, or sound films). In the years prior to 1954, and to a lesser degree since, that literature was largely polemical, philosophical, or descriptive, revealing little inclination to view the problems of record-making as a focus of research in its own right. This discussion will deal with reports appearing after 1954, and primarily with attempts to systematically gather and evaluate data pertinent to some of these problems. References to earlier work in this area can be found in the articles cited below.

Recent nonresearch discussions have focused on technical matters, on the ethical implications of recording, on adaptive and maladaptive modes of response by both patient and therapist, and on the danger that recording will alter the therapeutic process—either minimally and manageably, as do a variety of other conditions external to the treatment itself, or in ways that transform the treatment into an enterprise so artificial that the findings have little relevance to treatment as typically undertaken (Mahl, Dollard, and Redlich, 1954; Fleischmann, 1955; Carmichael, 1956; Roose, 1960; Shakow, 1960; Dittmann and Stein, 1966; van Vlack, 1966; Bergman, 1966; Jackson, 1966; Erickson, 1966;

English, 1966; Mackie and Wood, 1968; Gill, Simon, Fink, Endicott, and Paul, 1968).

Some of these issues have also been subjected to more systematic investigation. Watson and Kanter (1956) and Sutherland and Gill (1964) presented case analyses of reactions to the recording of therapy interviews. Sternberg, Chapman, and Shakow (1958) brought together a variety of data more or less directly related to the effects recording may have on treatment. Among other findings, they noted that filming a single hour in the middle of psychoanalysis appeared to mobilize additional transference and countertransference, and led the patient to explore new, transference-relevant content areas. Jaffe (1961c) explored differences in certain demographic and personality variables associated with reactions to learning that an initial interview was being recorded. Thirty-one patients were divided into two groups on the basis of their discussion of, or failure to mention, the obvious fact that a tape recorder was running. The no-mention group was older, less educated, more authoritarian (F-Scale), more often foreign-born, less frequently held professional or student status, and received shorter interviews. Lamb and Mahl (1956) studied the reactions to information that the interview was being recorded, of 35 patients, none of whom had had interviews recorded previously. Each patient was rated on his degree of manifest disturbance concerning recording and each reference to the recording procedure was judged as hostile or nonhostile. Ratings of general anxiety and hostility independent of references to recording were also available. They found that 80 percent of these patients showed no overt disturbance concerning recording after the first few minutes of the interview. Of the 34 patients who allowed recording, only 15 percent expressed overt hostility in reference to recording. The general hostility and anxiety ratings were not significantly related to degree of disturbance about recording.

Lamb and Mahl also reported questionnaire data concerning attitudes toward recording from 40 therapists who had used recording procedures. Among their findings was the positive correlation between the degree of disturbance felt by therapists while recording, and both the belief that they conducted therapy differently when recording and the feeling that patients were adversely affected. The authors suggested that this finding may reflect the therapists' projection of their concern about recording.

Haggard, Hiken, and Isaacs (1965) studied both direct and indirect interview references to the recording and/or filming of therapy sessions. Their data were the transcripts or recordings of the first 40 hours of three cases. Recorded therapist supervisory sessions were also available for one case. Another case served as a control in that it was neither filmed nor recorded, but the therapist took full notes during each session. The authors found large individual differences in both direct and indirect references to being recorded, with the nonrecorded, control patient falling above the median in the use of indirect references. Patients also differed as to where within the sessions their references tended to cluster, and in their use of the direct and indirect modes of reference. Analysis of the control case relative to the others led to the conclusion that patients treated in a research setting may be pushed to deal with their concerns about self-exposure earlier than patients treated in more traditional settings. When references to recording were initiated relatively frequently by therapists, patients tended to initiate fewer references, and vice versa. Study of the recorded therapist supervisory sessions revealed that the therapist employed both direct and indirect references, though he tended to use more direct references than did patients. He also spent considerably more time than the patients in discussing his reaction to recording but, like them, his discussion tended to cluster in certain hours. Haggard et al. concluded that the research context inevitably influences the process of treatment, as, for example, in the phenomenon of inclusion in the transference of research equipment and personnel, a phenomenon also noted by Roose (1960), Sutherland and Gill (1964), Watson and Kanter (1956), and Mackie and Wood (1968). But whether such phenomena facilitate or impede treatment appears to depend on factors specific to the case in question.

Roberts and Renzaglia (1965) compared interview behavior of counselors and clients when the recorder was in plain view, when only the microphone was in sight, and when recording was done secretly, with both counselors and clients believing that no recording was being done. They found that clients made more favorable self-references, and that counselors, working in a client-centered setting, were less client-centered in style, when they knew they were being recorded. The ethical and other implications of the deception practiced in this study were clearly underscored in a critical comment by Tyler (1965).

Perhaps the most striking observation concerning research in this area is that despite repeated discussion of the apparent fact that therapists more than patients are concerned about recording, and employ all manner of stratagems to avoid being recorded (Ward, 1964; Haggard et al., 1965), the largest volume and the best research has been devoted to exploring patient reactions to therapy recording. In part this must reflect the difficulties inherent in researching the professional behavior of one's colleagues. But one wonders if it does not also reflect a hands-off policy born of the same dynamics that prompt therapists to flee the tape recorder.

*   *   *

In conclusion, content analysis has proved itself a tool particularly well suited to the study of psychotherapy. Studies reviewed in this chapter demonstrate that when used with imagination and enterprise, it is capable of producing fruitful and exciting results. In the 15 years under review, content analysis has been applied to a vast range of problems in psychotherapy research, and in the process has undergone methodological elaboration and refinement. We now find ourselves possessed of a legion of findings badly in need of consolidation and integration, and with several promising lines of investigation to pursue.

REFERENCES

Alexander, J. F., and Abeles, N. Dependency changes in psychotherapy as related to interpersonal relations. *Journal of Consulting and Clinical Psychology*, 1968, **32**, 685–689.

Alexik, M., and Carkhuff, R. R. The effects of the manipulation of client depth of self exploration upon high and low functioning counselors. *Journal of Clinical Psychology*, 1967, **23**, 210–212.

Allen, B. V., Wiens, A. N., Weitman, M., and Saslow, G. Effects of warm-cold set on interviewee speech. *Journal of Consulting Psychology*, 1965, **29**, 480–482.

Anderson, S. C. Effects of confrontation by high- and low-functioning therapists. *Journal of Counseling Psychology*, 1968, **15**, 411–416.

Aronson, H., and Weintraub, W. Sex differences in verbal behavior related to adjustive mechanisms. *Psychological Reports*, 1967, **21**, 965–971. (a)

Aronson, H., and Weintraub, W. Verbal productivity as a measure of change in affective status. *Psychological Reports*, 1967, **20**, 483–487. (b)

Ashby, J. D., Ford, D. H., Guerney, B. G., Jr., and Guerney, L. F. Effects on clients of a reflective and a leading type of psychotherapy. *Psychological Monographs*, 1957, **71** (24, Whole No. 453).

Astrachan, B. M., Schwartz, A. H., Becker, R., and Harrow, M. The psychiatrist's effect on the behavior and interaction of therapy groups. *American Journal of Psychiatry*, 1967, **123**, 1379–1387.

Auerbach, A. H. An application of Strupp's method of content analysis to psychotherapy. *Psychiatry*, 1963, **26**, 137–148.

Auerbach, A. H., and Luborsky, L. Accuracy of judgments of psychotherapy and the nature of the "good hour." In J. M. Shlien, (Ed.), *Research in psychotherapy*. Vol. 3. Washington, D. C.: American Psychological Association, 1968. Pp. 155–168.

Auld, F., Jr. Emotions in the interview: Can they be measured? *Psychological Reports*, 1961, **8**, 239–242.

Auld, F., Jr. Vicissitudes of communication in psychotherapy. In J. M. Shlien, (Ed.), *Research in psychotherapy*. Vol. 3. Washington, D. C.: American Psychological Association, 1968. Pp. 169–178.

Auld, F., Jr., and Mahl, G. F. A comparison of the DRQ with ratings of emotion. *Journal of Abnormal and Social Psychology*, 1956, **53**, 386–388.

Auld, F., Jr., and Murray, E. J. Content-analysis studies of psychotherapy. *Psychological Bulletin*, 1955, **52**, 377–395.

Auld, F., Jr., and White, A. M. Rules for dividing interviews into sentences. *Journal of Psychology*, 1956, **42**, 273–281.

Auld, F., Jr., and White, A. M. Sequential dependencies in psychotherapy. *Journal of Abnormal and Social Psychology*, 1959, **58**, 100–104.

Bales, R. F. *Interaction process analysis*. Cambridge: Addison-Wesley Press, 1950.

Bales, R. F. The equilibrium problem in small groups. In T. Parsons, R. F. Bales, and E. A. Shils, *Working papers in the theory of action*. Glencoe, Ill.: Free Press, 1953.

Bales, R. F., and Hare, A. P. Diagnostic use of the interaction profile. *Journal of Social Psychology*, 1965, **67**, 239–258.

Bales, R. F., and Strodtbeck, F. L. Phases in group problem solving. *Journal of Abnormal and Social Psychology*, 1951, **46**, 485–495.

Bandura, A., Lipsher, D. H., and Miller, P. E. Psychotherapists' approach-avoidance reactions to patients' expressions of hostility. *Journal of Consulting Psychology*, 1960, **24**, 1–8.

Banks, G., Berenson, B. G., and Carkhuff, R. R. The effects of counselor race and training upon counseling process with Negro clients in initial interviews. *Journal of Clinical Psychology*, 1967, **23**, 70–72.

Barrett-Lennard, G. Dimensions of therapist response as causal factors in therapeutic change. *Psychological Monographs*, 1962, **76** (43, Whole No. 562).

Becker, R. E., Harrow, M., Astrachan, B. M., Detre, T., and Miller, J. C. Influence of the leader on the activity level of therapy groups. *Journal of Social Psychology*, 1968, **74**, 39–51.

Bellak, L., and Smith, M. B. An experimental exploration of the psychoanalytic process. Exemplification of a method. *Psychoanalytic Quarterly*, 1956, **25**, 385–414.

Berelson, B. *Content analysis in communications research*. Glencoe, Ill.: Free Press, 1952.

Berenson, B. G., and Mitchell, K. M. Therapeutic conditions after therapist-initiated confrontation. *Journal of Clinical Psychology*, 1968, **24**, 363–364.

Berenson, B. G., Mitchell, K. M., and Laney, R. C. Level of therapist functioning, types of confrontation and type of patient. *Journal of Clinical Psychology*, 1968, **24**, 111–113.

Berenson, B. G., Mitchell, K. M., and Moravec, J. A. Level of therapist functioning, patient depth of self-exploration, and type of confrontation. *Journal of Counseling Psychology*, 1968, **15**, 136–139.

Berg, I. A. Word choice in the interview and personal adjustment. *Journal of Counseling Psychology*, 1958, **5**, 130–135.

Bergman, P. An experiment in filmed psychotherapy. In L. A. Gottschalk and A. H. Auerbach (Eds.), *Methods of research in psychotherapy*. New York: Appleton-Century-Crofts, 1966. Ch. 4.

Berman, G. Communication of affect in family therapy. *Archives of General Psychiatry*, 1967, **17**, 154–158.

Birdwhistell, R. L. Contribution of linguistic-kinesic studies to the understanding of schizophrenia. In A. Auerbach (Ed.), *Schizophrenia: An integrated approach*. New York: Ronald Press, 1959. Ch. 5.

Birdwhistell, R. L. Paralanguage 25 years after Sapir. In H. W. Brosin (Ed.), *Lectures on experimental psychiatry*. Pittsburgh: Univ. of Pittsburgh, 1961. Pp. 43–63.

Birdwhistell, R. L. The kinesic level in the investigation of the emotions. In P. H. Knapp (Ed.), *Expression of the emotions in man*. New York: International Universities Press, 1963. Ch. 7.

Block, W. E. A preliminary study of achievement motive theory as a basis of patient expectations in psychotherapy. *Journal of Clinical Psychology*, 1964, **20**, 268–271.

Boomer, D. S. Speech disturbance and body movement in interviews. *Journal of Nervous and Mental Disease*, 1963, **136**, 263–266.

Boomer, D. S. Linguistics and speech behavior. In *Monograph series on language and linguistics* (No. 17). Washington, D. C.: Georgetown Univ. Press, 1964. Pp. 149–154.

Boomer, D. S., and Dittmann, A. T. Speech rate, filled pause, and body movement in interviews. *Journal of Nervous and Mental Disease*, 1964, **139**, 324–327.

Boomer, D. S., and Goodrich, D. W. Speech disturbance and judged anxiety. *Journal of Consulting Psychology*, 1961, **25**, 160–164.

Bordin, E. S. Ambiguity as a therapeutic variable. *Journal of Consulting Psychology*, 1955, **19**, 9–15.

Bordin, E. S., Cutler, R. L., Dittmann, A. T., Harway, N. I., Raush, H. L., and Rigler, D. Measurement problems in process research on psychotherapy. *Journal of Consulting Psychology*, 1954, **18**, 79–82.

Braaten, L. J. The movement from non-self to self in client-centered psychotherapy. *Journal of Counseling Psychology*, 1961, **8**, 20–24.

Burstein, J. W., and Carkhuff, R. R. Objective, therapist and client ratings of therapist-offered facilitative conditions of moderate to low functioning therapists. *Journal of Clinical Psychology*, 1968, **24**, 240–241.

Butler, J. M., Rice, L. N., and Wagstaff, A. K. On the naturalistic definition of variables: An analogue of clinical analysis. In H. H. Strupp and L. Luborsky, (Eds.), *Research in psychotherapy*. Vol. 2. Washington, D. C.: American Psychological Association, 1962, Pp. 178–205.

Butler, J. M., Rice, L. N., and Wagstaff, A. K. *Quantitative naturalistic research*. Englewood Cliffs, N. J.: Prentice-Hall, 1963.

Callis, R., Polmantier, P. C., and Roeber, E. C. Five years of research on counseling. *Journal of Counseling Psychology*, 1957, **4**, 119–123.

Campbell, R. E. Counselor personality and background and his interview subrole behavior. *Journal of Counseling Psychology*, 1962, **9**, 329–334.

Cannon, J. R., and Pierce, R. M. Order effects in the experimental manipulation of therapeutic conditions. *Journal of Clinical Psychology*, 1968, **24**, 242–244.

Caracena, P. F. Elicitation of dependency expressions in the initial stage of psychotherapy. *Journal of Counseling Psychology*, 1965, **12**, 268–274.

Carkhuff, R. R., and Alexik, M. Effect of client depth of self-exploration upon high- and low-functioning counselors. *Journal of Counseling Psychology*, 1967, **14**, 350–355.

Carkhuff, R. R., Kratochvil, D., and Friel, T. Effects of professional training: Communication and discrimination of facilitative conditions. *Journal of Counseling Psychology*, 1968, **15**, 68–74.

Carkhuff, R. R., and Pierce, R. Differential effects of therapist race and social class upon patient depth of self-exploration in the initial clinical interview. *Journal of Consulting Psychology*, 1967, **31**, 632–634.

Carkhuff, R. R., and Truax, C. B. Training in counseling and psychotherapy: An evaluation of an integrated didactic and experimental approach. *Journal of Consulting Psychology*, 1965, **29**, 333–336.

Carlson, A. R. Concept frequency in political text: An application of a total indexing method of automated content analysis. *Behavioral Science*, 1967, **12**, 68–72.

Carmichael, H. T. Sound film recording of psychoanalytic therapy. A therapist's experiences and reactions. *Journal of Iowa Medical Society*, 1956, **46**, 590–595. Also in L. A. Gottschalk and A. H. Auerbach (Eds.), *Methods of research in psychotherapy*. New York: Appleton-Century-Crofts, 1966. Ch. 5.

Carroll, J. B. *The study of language*. Cambridge: Harvard Univ. Press, 1955.

Carroll, J. B., Agard, F. B., Dulany, D. E., Newman, S. S., Newmark, L. D., Osgood, C. E., Sebeok, T. A., and Solomon, R. L. Report and recommendations of the interdisciplinary summer seminar in psychology and linguistics. Unpublished manuscript, Harvard Graduate School of Education Library, 1951.

Cartwright, R. D. A comparison of the response of psychoanalytic and client-centered psychotherapy. In L. A. Gottschalk and A. H. Auerbach (Eds.), *Methods of research in psychotherapy*. New York: Appleton-Century-Crofts, 1966. Ch. 30.

Cassotta, L., Feldstein, S., and Jaffe, J. AVTA: A device for automatic vocal transaction analysis. *Journal of the Experimental Analysis of Behavior*, 1964, **7**, 99–104.

Chance, E. Content analysis of verbalizations about interpersonal experience. In L. A. Gottschalk and A. H. Auerbach (Eds.), *Methods of research in psychotherapy*. New York: Appleton-Century-Crofts, 1966. Ch. 12.

Chassan, J. B. *Research design in clinical psychology and psychiatry*. New York: Appleton-Century-Crofts, 1967.

Clark, J. V., and Culbert, S. A. Mutually therapeutic perception and selfawareness in a T group. *Journal of Applied Behavioral Science*, 1965, **2**, 180–194.

Cohn, B., Ohlsen, M., and Proff, F. Roles played by adolescents in an unproductive counseling group. *Personnel and Guidance Journal*, 1960, **38**, 724–731.

Colby, K. M. Experiment on the effects of an observer's presence on the imago system during psychoanalytic free-association. *Behavioral Science*, 1960, **5**, 216–232.

Colby, K. M. On the greater amplifying power of causal-correlative over interrogative inputs on free association in an experimental psychoanalytic situation. *Journal of Nervous and Mental Disease*, 1961, **133**, 233–239.

Colby, K. M. A psychoanalyst's view of methods for studying emotions. In P. H. Knapp (Ed.), *Expression of the emotions in man*. New York: International Universities Press, 1963. Ch. 13.

Condon, W. S., and Ogston, W. D. Sound film analysis of normal and pathological behavior patterns. *Journal of Nervous and Mental Disease*, 1966, **143**, 338–347.

Condon, W. S., and Ogston, W. D. A segmentation of behavior. *Journal of Psychiatric Research*, 1967, **5**, 221–235.

Conrad, D. C., and Conrad, R. The use of personal pronouns as categories for studying small group interaction. *Journal of Abnormal and Social Psychology*, 1956, **52**, 277–279.

Culbert, S. A. Trainer self-disclosure and member growth in two T groups. *Journal of Applied Behavioral Science*, 1968, **4**, 47–73.

Culbert, S. A., Clark, J. V., and Bobele, H. K. Measures of change toward self-actualization in two sensitivity training groups. *Journal of Counseling Psychology*, 1968, **15**, 53–57.

Cutler, R. L. Countertransference effects in psychotherapy. *Journal of Consulting Psychology*, 1958, **22**, 249–256.

Cutler, R. L., Bordin, E. S., Williams, J., and Rigler, D. Psychoanalysts as expert observers of the therapy process. *Journal of Consulting Psychology*, 1958, **22**, 335–340.

Danskin, D. G. Roles played by counselors in their interviews. *Journal of Counseling Psychology*, 1955, **2**, 22–27.

Danskin, D. G., and Robinson, F. P. Differences in "degree of lead" among experienced counselors. *Journal of Counseling Psychology*, 1954, **1**, 78–83.

Davitz, J. R. *The communication of emotional meaning*. New York: McGraw-Hill, 1964.

Dickenson, W. A., and Truax, C. B. Group counseling with college underachievers. *Personnel and Guidance Journal*, 1966, **45**, 243–247.

Dibner, A. S. Cue-counting: A measure of anxiety in interviews. *Journal of Consulting Psychology*, 1956, **20**, 475–478.

Dibner, A. S. Ambiguity and anxiety. *Journal of Abnormal and Social Psychology*, 1958, **56**, 165–174.

Dinoff, M., Kew, J. K., Rickard, H. C., and Timmons, E. O. The stability of group verbal behavior. *Psychological Record*, 1962, **12**, 323–325.

Dipboye, W. J. Analysis of counselor style by discussion units. *Journal of Counseling Psychology*, 1954, **1**, 21–26.

Dittes, J. E. Previous studies bearing on content analysis of psychotherapy. In J. Dollard and F. Auld, Jr., *Scoring human motives: A manual*. New Haven: Yale Univ. Press, 1959. Appendix A.

Dittmann, A. T. The relationship between body movements and moods in interviews. *Journal of Consulting Psychology*, 1962, **26**, 480.

Dittmann, A. T., and Llewellyn, L. G. The phonemic clause as a unit of speech decoding. *Journal of Personality and Social Psychology*, 1967, **6**, 341–349.

Dittmann, A. T., and Llewellyn, L. G. Relationships between vocalization and head nods as listener responses. *Journal of Personality and Social Psychology*, 1968, **9**, 79–84.

Dittmann, A. T., Parloff, M. B., and Boomer, D. S. Facial and bodily expression: A study of receptivity of emotional cues. *Psychiatry*, 1965, **28**, 239–244.

Dittmann, A. T., and Renneker, R. Kinesic research and therapeutic process: Further discussion. In P. H. Knapp (Ed.), *Expression of the emotions in man*. New York: International Universities Press, 1963, Ch. 8.

Dittmann, A. T., and Stein, N. Sound motion picture facilities for research in communication. In L. A. Gottschalk and A. H. Auerbach (Eds.), *Methods of research in psychotherapy*. New York: Appleton-Century-Crofts, 1966. Ch. 3.

Dittmann, A. T., and Wynne, L. C. Linguistic techniques and the analysis of emotionality in interviews. *Journal of Abnormal and Social Psychology*, 1961, **63**, 201–204.

Dollard, J., and Auld, F., Jr. *Scoring human motives: A manual*. New Haven: Yale Univ. Press, 1959.

Dollard, J., and Mowrer, O. H. A method of measuring tension in written documents. *Journal of Abnormal and Social Psychology*, 1947, **42**, 3–32.

Dorfman, E. Content-free study of marital resemblances in group therapy. *Journal of Abnormal Psychology*, 1968, **73**, 78–80.

Duncan, S., Jr. Paralinguistic analysis of psychotherapy interviews. *Proceedings of the 74th annual convention of the American Psychological Association*. Washington, D. C.: American Psychological Association, 1966. Pp. 191–192.

Duncan, S., Jr., Rice, L. N., and Butler, J. M. Therapists' paralanguage in peak and poor psychotherapy hours. *Journal of Abnormal Psychology*, 1968, **73**, 566–570.

Dunphy, D. C. Social change in self-analytic groups. In P. J. Stone, D. C. Dunphy, M. S. Smith, and D. M. Ogilvie (Eds.), *The general inquirer: A computer approach to content analysis*. Cambridge: M.I.T. Press, 1966. Ch. 8.

Dunphy, D. C. Phases, roles, and myths in self-analytic groups. *Journal of Applied Behavioral Science*, 1968, **4**, 195–225.

Eichler, M. The application of verbal behavior analysis to the study of psychological defense mechanisms: Speech patterns associated with sociopathic behavior. *Journal of Nervous and Mental Disease*, 1966, **141**, 658–663.

Eiduson, B. T., Brooks, S. H., Motto, R. L., Platz, A., and Carmichael, R. Recent developments in the psychiatric case history event system. *Behavioral Science*, 1967, **12**, 254–267.

Ekman, P. Body position, facial expression, and verbal behavior during interviews. *Journal of Abnormal and Social Psychology*, 1964, **68**, 295–301.

Ekman, P. Differential communication of affect by head and body cues. *Journal of Personality and Social Psychology*, 1965, **2**, 726–735.

Ekman, P., and Friesen, W. V. Head and body cues in the judgment of emotion: A reformulation. *Perceptual and Motor Skills*, 1967, **24**, 711–724.

Ekman, P., and Friesen, W. V. Nonverbal behavior in psychotherapy research. In J. M. Shlien (Ed.), *Research in psychotherapy*. Vol. 3. Washington, D. C.: American Psychological Association, 1968. Pp. 179–216.

Eldred, S. H., Hamburg, D. A., Inwood, E. R., Salzman, L., Meyersburg, H. A., and Goodrich, G. A procedure for the systematic analysis of psychotherapeutic interviews. *Psychiatry*, 1954, **17**, 337–345.

Eldred, S. H., and Price, D. B. A linguistic evaluation of feeling states in psychotherapy. *Psychiatry*, 1958, **21**, 115–121.

English, O. S. Subjective reactions to being filmed. In L. A. Gottschalk and A. H. Auerbach (Eds.), *Methods of research in psychotherapy*. New York: Appleton-Century-Crofts, 1966. Ch. 6.

Erickson, M. H. The experience of interviewing in the presence of observers. In L. A. Gottschalk and A. H. Auerbach (Eds.), *Methods of research in psychotherapy*. New York: Appleton-Century-Crofts, 1966. Ch. 7.

Exline, R. V., and Long, B. H. An application of psychological scaling methods to content analysis: The use of empirically derived criterion weights to improve intercoder reliability. *Journal of Applied Psychology*, 1965, **49**, 142–149.

Feldstein, S. Vocal patterning of emotional expression. In J. Masserman (Ed.), *Development and Research*, Vol. 7. *Science and Psychoanalysis*. New York: Grune and Stratton, 1964. Pp. 193–210.

Feldstein, S., Brenner, M. S., and Jaffe, J. The effect of subject sex, verbal interaction and topical focus on speech disruption. *Language and Speech*, 1963, **6**, 229–239.

Feldstein, S., and Jaffe, J. A note about speech disturbances and vocabulary diversity. *Journal of Communication*, 1962, **12**, 166–170. (a)

Feldstein, S., and Jaffe, J. The relationship of speech disruption to the experience of anger. *Journal of Consulting Psychology*, 1962, **26**, 505–509. (b)

Feldstein, S., and Jaffe, J. An IBM 650 program written in SOAP for the computation of speech disturbances per time, speaker, and group. *Behavioral Science*, 1963, **8**, 86. (Abstract)

Fine, H. J., and Zimet, C. N. A quantitative method of scaling communication and interaction process. *Journal of Clinical Psychology*, 1956, **12**, 268–271.

Fink, M., Jaffe, J., and Kahn, R. L. Drug induced changes in interview patterns: Linguistic and neurophysiologic indices. In G. J. Sarwer-Foner (Ed.), *The dynamics of psychiatric drug therapy.* Springfield, Ill.: C. C. Thomas, 1960. Pp. 29–37.

Firth, J. R. Linguistic analysis and translation. In *For Roman Jakobson: Essays on the occasion of his sixtieth birthday.* The Hague: Mouton, 1956. Pp. 133–139.

Fisher, S. Plausibility and depth of interpretation. *Journal of Consulting Psychology*, 1956, **20**, 249–256.

Flanagan, J. C. *Speech analysis, synthesis and perception.* New York: Academic Press, 1965.

Fleischmann, O. A method of teaching psychotherapy. One-way-vision room technique. *Bulletin of the Menninger Clinic*, 1955, **19**, 160–172.

Fodor, J. A., and Bever, T. G. The psychological reality of linguistic segments. *Journal of Verbal Learning and Verbal Behavior*, 1965, **4**, 414–420.

Frank, G. H. The effect of directive and nondirective statements by therapists on the content of patient verbalizations. *Journal of General Psychology*, 1964, **71**, 323–328.

Frank, G. H., and Sweetland, A. A study of the process of psychotherapy: The verbal interaction. *Journal of Consulting Psychology*, 1962, **26**, 135–138.

Freedman, N., and Hoffman, S. P. Kinetic behavior in altered clinical states: Approach to objective analysis of motor behavior during clinical interviews. *Perceptual and Motor Skills*, 1967, **24**, 527–539.

Fretz, B. R. Personality correlates of postural movements. *Journal of Counseling Psychology*, 1966, **13**, 344–347. (a)

Fretz, B. R. Postural movements in a counseling dyad. *Journal of Counseling Psychology*, 1966, **13**, 335–343. (b)

Friel, T., Kratochvil, D., and Carkhuff, R. R. The effects of the manipulation of client depth of self-exploration upon helpers of different training and experience. *Journal of Clinical Psychology*, 1968, **24**, 247–249.

Frostig, M., and Horne, D. Changes in language and behavior in psychotic children during successful therapy: Method of evaluation and findings. *American Journal of Orthopsychiatry*, 1963, **33**, 734–737.

Funkhouser, G. R., and Parker, E. B. Analyzing coding reliability: The random-systematic-error coefficient. *Public Opinion Quarterly*, 1968, **32**, 122–128.

Gamsky, N. R., and Farwell, G. F. Counselor verbal behavior as a function of client hostility. *Journal of Counseling Psychology.* 1966, **13**, 184–190.

Gamsky, N. R., and Farwell, G. F. The effect of client demeanor upon the verbal responses of school counselors. *Personnel and Guidance Journal*, 1967, **45**, 477–481.

Gendlin, E. T., Beebe, J., Cassens, J., Klein, M., and Oberlander, M. Focusing ability in psychotherapy, personality, and creativity. In J. M. Shlien (Ed.), *Research in psychotherapy.* Vol. 3. Washington, D. C.: American Psychological Association, 1968. Pp. 217–241.

Gendlin, E. T., and Rogers, C. R. The design of the research. In C. R. Rogers et al. (Eds.), *The therapeutic relationship and its impact. A study of psychotherapy with schizophrenics.* Madison: Univ. of Wisconsin Press, 1967. Ch. 2.

Gendlin, E. T., and Tomlinson, T. M. The process conception and its measurement. In C. R. Rogers et al. (Eds.), *The therapeutic relationship and its impact. A study of psychotherapy with schizophrenics.* Madison: Univ. of Wisconsin Press, 1967. Ch. 7.

George, A. L. *Propaganda analysis: A study of inference made from Nazi propaganda in World War II.* Evanston, Ill.: Row, Peterson, 1959. (a)

George, A. L. Quantitative and qualitative approaches to content analysis. In I. Pool (Ed.), *Trends in content analysis.* Urbana: Univ. of Illinois Press, 1959. Pp. 7–32. (b)

Gill, M. M., Simon, J., Fink, G., Endicott, N. A., and Paul, I. H. Studies in audio-recorded psychoanalysis: I. General considerations. *Journal of the American Psychoanalytic Association*, 1968, **16**, 230–244.

Glad, D. D., and Glad, V. B. *Interpersonality synopsis.* New York: Libra, 1964.

Glad, D. D., Hayne, M. L., Glad, V. B., and Ferguson, R. E. Schizophrenic factor reactions to four group psychotherapy methods. *International Journal of Group Psychotherapy*, 1963, **13**, 196–210.

Gleser, G. C., Gottschalk, L. A., Fox, R., and Lippert, W. Immediate changes in affect with chlordiazepoxide. *Archives of General Psychiatry*, 1965, **13**, 291–295.

Gleser, G. C., Gottschalk, L. A., and Springer, K. J. An anxiety scale applicable to verbal samples. *Archives of General Psychiatry*, 1961, **5**, 593–605.

Goldenberg, G. M., and Auld, F. Equivalence of silence to resistance. *Journal of Consulting Psychology*, 1964, **28**, 476.

Goldstein, S. G. The effects of "doubling" on involvement in group psychotherapy as measured by number and duration of patient utterances. *Psychotherapy: Theory, Research and Practice*, 1967, **4**, 57–60.

Gottschalk, L. A. (Ed.) *Comparative psycholinguistic analysis of two psychotherapeutic interviews.* New York: International Universities Press, 1961.

Gottschalk, L. A. Some applications of the psychoanalytic concept of object relatedness: Preliminary studies on a human relations content analysis scale applicable to verbal samples. *Comprehensive Psychiatry*, 1968, **9**, 608–620.

Gottschalk, L. A., Cleghorn, J. M., Gleser, G. C., and Iacono, J. M. Studies of relationships of emotions to plasma lipids. *Psychosomatic Medicine*, 1965, **27**, 102–111.

Gottschalk, L. A., and Frank, E. C. Estimating the magnitude of anxiety from speech. *Behavioral Science*, 1967, **12**, 289–295.

Gottschalk, L. A., and Gleser, G. C. Distinguishing characteristics of the verbal communications of schizophrenic patients. In D. McK. Rioch and E. A. Weinstein (Eds.), *Disorders of communication.* Vol. 42. Baltimore: Williams & Wilkins, 1964. Ch. 28.

Gottschalk, L. A., Gleser, G. C., Daniels, R. S., and Block, S. The speech patterns of schizophrenic patients: A method of assessing relative degree of personal disorganization and social alienation. *Journal of Nervous and Mental Disease*, 1958, **127**, 153–166.

Gottschalk, L. A., Gleser, G. C., D'Zmura, T., and Hanenson, I. B. Some psychophysiologic relations in hypertensive women. *Psychosomatic Medicine*, 1964, **26**, 610–617.

Gottschalk, L. A., Gleser, G. C., and Hambridge, G., Jr. Verbal behavior analysis. *Archives of Neurology and Psychiatry*, 1957, **77**, 300–311.

Gottschalk, L. A., Gleser, G. C., Magliocco, E. B., and D'Zmura, T. L. Further studies on the speech pattern of schizophrenic patients. *Journal of Nervous and Mental Disease*, 1961, **132**, 101–113.

Gottschalk, L. A., Gleser, G. C., and Springer, K. J. Three hostility scales applicable to verbal samples. *Archives of General Psychiatry*, 1963, **9**, 254–279.

Gottschalk, L. A., Gleser, G. C., Springer, K. J., Kaplan, S. M., Shanon, J., and Ross, W. D. Effects of perphenazine on verbal behavior patterns. *Archives of General Psychiatry*, 1960, **2**, 632–639.

Gottschalk, L. A., Gleser, G. C., Wylie, H. W., and Kaplan, S. M. Effects of imipramine on anxiety and hostility levels. *Psychopharmacologia*, 1965, **7**, 303–310.

Gottschalk, L. A., and Hambridge, G., Jr. Verbal behavior analysis: A systematic approach to the problem of quantifying psychologic processes. *Journal of Projective Techniques*, 1955, **19**, 387–409.

Gottschalk, L. A., and Kaplan, S. A quantitative method of estimating variations in intensity of a psychologic conflict or state. *Archives of Neurology and Psychiatry*, 1958, **79**, 688–696.

Gottschalk, L. A., Kaplan, S. M., Gleser, G. C., and Winget, C. M. Variations in magnitude of emotion: A method applied to anxiety and hostility during phases of the menstrual cycle. *Psychosomatic Medicine*, 1962, **24**, 300–311.

Gottschalk, L. A., Springer, K. J., and Gleser, G. C. Experiments with a method of assessing the variations in intensity of certain psychologic states occurring during two psychotherapeutic interviews. In L. A. Gottschalk (Ed.), *Comparative psycholinguistic analysis of two psychotherapeutic interviews.* New York: International Universities Press, 1961, Ch. 7.

Gottschalk, L. A., Winget, C. M., Gleser, G. C., and Springer, K. J. The measurement of emotional changes during a psychiatric interview: A working model toward quantifying the psychoanalytic concept of affect. In L. A. Gottschalk and A. H. Auerbach (Eds.), *Methods of research in psychotherapy.* New York: Appleton-Century-Crofts, 1966. Ch. 11.

Gough, H. G. Clinical versus statistical prediction in psychology. In L. Postman (Ed.), *Psychology in the making.* New York: Knopf, 1962. Ch. 9.

Gross, W. F., and DeRidder, L. M. Significant movement in comparatively short-term counseling. *Journal of Counseling Psychology*, 1966, **13**, 98–99.

Grosz, H. J., Stern, H., and Wright, C. S. Interactions in therapy groups as a function of differences among therapists and group size. *Psychological Reports*, 1965, **17**, 827–834.

Haggard, E. A., Hiken, J. R., and Isaacs, K. S. Some effects of recording and filming on the psychotherapeutic process. *Psychiatry*, 1965, **28**, 169–191.

Haggard, E. A., and Isaacs, K. S. Micromomentary facial expressions as indicators of ego mechanisms in psychotherapy. In L. A. Gottschalk and A. H. Auerbach (Eds.), *Methods of research in psychotherapy.* New York: Appleton-Century-Crofts, 1966. Ch. 14.

Hansen, J. C., Moore, G. D., and Carkhuff, R. R. The differential relationships of objective and client perceptions of counseling. *Journal of Clinical Psychology*, 1968, **24**, 244–246.

Hare, A. P., Waxler, N., Saslow, G., and Matarazzo, J. D. Simultaneous recording of Bales and Chapple interaction measures during initial psychiatric interviews. *Journal of Consulting Psychology*, 1960, **24**, 193.

Harrow, M., Astrachan, B. M., Becker, R. E., Detre, T., and Schwartz, A. H. An investigation into the nature of the patient-family therapy group. *American Journal of Orthopsychiatry*, 1967, **37**, 888–899.

Harrow, M., Astrachan, B. M., Becker, R. E., Miller, J. C., and Schwartz, A. H. Influence of the psychotherapist on the emotional climate in group therapy. *Human Relations*, 1967, **20**, 49–64.

Harway, N. I., Dittmann, A. T., Raush, H. L., Bordin, E. S., and Rigler, D. The measurement of depth of interpretation. *Journal of Consulting Psychology*, 1955, **19**, 247–253.

Harway, N. I., and Iker, H. P. Computer analysis of content in psychotherapy. *Psychological Reports*, 1964, **14**, 720–722.

Harway, N. I., and Iker, H. P. Objective content analysis of psychotherapy by computer. In K. Enslein (Ed.), *Data acquisition and processing in biology and medicine.* New York: Pergamon, 1966. Pp. 139–151.

Hayes, A. S. Paralinguistics and kinesics: Pedagogical perspectives. In A. Sebeok, A. S. Hayes, and M. C. Bateson (Eds.), *Approaches to semiotics.* The Hague: Mouton, 1964. Pp. 145–172.

Heckel, R. V., Froelich, R. E., and Salzberg, H. C. Interaction and redirection in group therapy. *Psychological Reports*, 1962, **10**, 14.

Heckel, R. V., Holmes, G. R., and Salzberg, H. C. Emergence of distinct verbal phases in group therapy. *Psychological Reports*, 1967, **21**, 630–632.

Heckel, R. V., and Salzberg, H. C. Predicting verbal behavior change in group therapy using a screening scale. *Psychological Reports*, 1967, **20**, 403–406.

Heckel, R. V., Wiggins, S. L., and Salzberg, H. C. The effect of musical tempo in varying operant speech levels in group therapy. *Journal of Clinical Psychology*, 1963, **19**, 129. (a)

Heckel, R. V., Wiggins, S. L., and Salzberg, H. C. Joining, encouraging, and intervention as means of extinguishing a delusional system. *Journal of Clinical Psychology*, 1963, **19**, 344–346. (b)

Heller, K., Davis, J. D., and Myers, R. A. The effects of interviewer style in a standardized interview. *Journal of Consulting Psychology*, 1966, **30**, 501–508.

Hoffman, A. E. An analysis of counselor sub-roles. *Journal of Counseling Psychology*, 1959, **6**, 61–67.

Hoijer, H. (Ed.) *Language in culture.* Chicago: Univ. of Chicago Press, 1954.

Holder, T. Length of encounter as a therapist variable. *Journal of Clinical Psychology*, 1968, **24**, 249–250.

Holder, T., Carkhuff, R. R., and Berenson, B. G. Differential effects of the manipulation of therapeutic conditions upon high- and low-functioning clients. *Journal of Counseling Psychology*, 1967, **14**, 63–66.

Holmes, J. S. Relation of depression and verbal interaction in group therapy. *Psychological Reports*, 1967, **20**, 1039–1042.

Holsti, O. R. *Content analysis for the social sciences and the humanities.* Reading, Mass.: Addison-Wesley, 1969.

Holzman, M., and Forman, V. P. A multidimensional content-analysis of therapeutic technique in psychotherapy with schizophrenic patients. *Psychological Bulletin*, 1966, **66**, 263–281.

Howe, E. S. Anxiety-arousal and specificity: Rated correlates of the depth of interpretive statements. *Journal of Consulting Psychology*, 1962, **26**, 178–184. (a)

Howe, E. S. A study of the semantic structure of ratings of interpretive responses. *Journal of Consulting Psychology*, 1962, **26**, 285. (b)

Howe, E. S. Three-dimensional structure of ratings of exploratory responses shown by a semantic differential. *Psychological Reports*, 1964, **14**, 187–196.

Howe, E. S. Further data concerning the dimensionality of ratings of the therapist's verbal exploratory behavior. *Journal of Consulting Psychology*, 1965, **29**, 73–76.

Howe, E. S., and Pope, B. The dimensionality of ratings of therapist verbal responses. *Journal of Consulting Psychology*, 1961, **25**, 296–303. (a)

Howe, E. S., and Pope, B. An empirical scale of therapist verbal activity level in the initial interview. *Journal of Consulting Psychology*, 1961, **25**, 510–520. (b)

Howe, E. S., and Pope, B. Therapist verbal activity level and diagnostic utility of patient verbal responses. *Journal of Consulting Psychology*, 1962, **26**, 149–155.

Iker, H. P., and Harway, N. I. A computer approach towards the analysis of content. *Behavioral Science*, 1965, **10**, 173–182.

Isaacs, K. S., and Haggard, E. A. Some methods used in the study of affect in psychotherapy. In L. A. Gottschalk and A. H. Auerbach (Eds.), *Methods of research in psychotherapy.* New York: Appleton-Century-Crofts, 1966, Ch. 18.

Jackson, D. D. Filming of psychotherapeutic sessions as a personal experience. In L. A. Gottschalk and A. H. Auerbach (Eds.), *Methods of research in psychotherapy.* New York: Appleton-Century-Crofts, 1966. Ch. 8.

Jackson, D. D., Riskin, J., and Satir, V. A method of analysis of a family interview. *Archives of General Psychiatry*, 1961, **5**, 321–339.

Jaffe, J. An objective study of communication in psychiatric interviews. *Journal of the Hillside Hospital*, 1957, **6**, 207–215.

Jaffe, J. Language of the dyad: A method of interaction analysis in psychiatric interviews. *Psychiatry*, 1958, **21**, 249–258.

Jaffe, J. Discussion. In L. A. Gottschalk (Ed.), *Comparative psycholinguistic analysis of two psychotherapy interviews.* New York: International Universities Press, 1961. Pp. 162–173. (a)

Jaffe, J. Dyadic analysis of two psychotherapeutic interviews. In L. A. Gottschalk (Ed.), *Comparative psycholinguistic analysis of two psychotherapeutic interviews.* New York: International Universities Press, 1961. Ch. 5. (b)

Jaffe, J. Social factors in the doctor-patient relationship. In J. Masserman (Ed.), *Psychoanalysis and social process.* Vol. 4. *Science and psychoanalysis.* New York: Grune and Stratton, 1961. Pp. 81–88. (c)

Jaffe, J. Electronic computers in psychoanalytic research. In J. H. Masserman (Ed.), *Violence and War with Clinical Studies. Science and psychoanalysis.* New York: Grune and Stratton, 1963. Pp. 160–170.

Jaffe, J. Verbal behavior analysis in psychiatric interviews with the aid of digital computers. In D. McK. Rioch and E. A. Weinstein (Eds.), *Disorders of communication.* Vol. 42. Baltimore: Williams & Wilkins, 1964. Ch. 27.

Jaffe, J. Computer assessment of dyadic interaction rules from chronographic data. In J. M. Shlien (Ed.), *Research in psychotherapy.* Vol. 3. Washington, D. C.: American Psychological Association, 1968. Pp. 260–276.

Jaffe, J., Fink, M., and Kahn, R. L. Changes in verbal transactions with induced altered brain function. *Journal of Nervous and Mental Disease*, 1960, **130**, 235–239.

Jenkins, J. W., Wallach, M. S., and Strupp, H. H. Effects of two methods of response in a quasi-therapeutic situation. *Journal of Clinical Psychology*, 1962, **18**, 220–223.

Johnson, N. F. The psychological reality of phrase-structure rules. *Journal of Verbal Learning and Verbal Behavior*, 1965, **4**, 469–475.

Kanfer, F. H. Verbal rate, content, and adjustment ratings in experimentally structured interviews. *Journal of Abnormal and Social Psychology*, 1959, **58**, 305–311.

Kanfer, F. H. Verbal rate, eyeblink, and content in structured psychiatric interviews. *Journal of Abnormal and Social Psychology*, 1960, **61**, 341–347.

Kanfer, F. H., Phillips, J. S., Matarazzo, J. D., and Saslow, G. Experimental modification of interviewer content in standarized interviews. *Journal of Consulting Psychology*, 1960, **24**, 528–536.

Kaplan, S. M., and Gottschalk, L. A. Modifications of oropharyngeal bacteria with changes in psychodynamic state. II. A validation study. *Psychosomatic Medicine*, 1958, **20**, 314–320.

Kaplan, S. M., Gottschalk, L. A., Magliocco, E. B., Rohovit, D. D., and Ross, W. D. Hostility in verbal productions and hypnotic "dreams" of hypertensive patients: Studies of groups and individuals. *Psychosomatic Medicine*, 1961, **23**, 311–322.

Kasl, S. V., and Mahl, G. F. A simple device for obtaining certain verbal activity measures during interviews. *Journal of Abnormal and Social Psychology*, 1956, **53**, 388–390.

Kasl, S. V., and Mahl, G. F. Experimentally induced anxiety and speech disturbance. *American Psychologist*, 1958, **13**, 349. (Abstract)

Kasl, S. V., and Mahl, G. F. The relationship of disturbances and hesitations in spontaneous speech to anxiety. *Journal of Personality and Social Psychology*, 1965, **1**, 425–433.

Kiesler, D. J. Basic methodologic issues implicit in psychotherapy process research. *American Journal of Psychotherapy*, 1966, **20**, 135–155.

Kiesler, D. J., Klein, M. H., and Mathieu, P. L. Sampling from the recorded therapy interview: The problem of segment location. *Journal of Consulting Psychology*, 1965, **29**, 337–344.

Kiesler, D. J., Klein, M. H., Mathieu, P., and Schoeninger, D. Constructive personality change for therapy and control patients. In C. R. Rogers et al. (Eds.), *The therapeutic relationship and its impact. A study of psychotherapy with schizophrenics*. Madison: Univ. of Wisconsin Press, 1967. Ch. 11.

Kiesler, D. J., Mathieu, P., and Klein, M. H. Sampling from the recorded therapy interview: A comparative study of different segment lengths. *Journal of Consulting Psychology*, 1964, **28**, 349–357.

Kiesler, D. J., Mathieu, P., and Klein, M. H. Measurement of conditions and process variables. In C. R. Rogers et al. (Eds.), *The therapeutic relationship and its impact. A study of psychotherapy with schizophrenics*. Madison: Univ. of Wisconsin Press, 1967. Ch. 8. (a)

Kiesler, D. J., Mathieu, P. L., and Klein, M. H. Patient experiencing level and interaction-chronograph variables in therapy interview segments. *Journal of Consulting Psychology*, 1967, **31**, 224. (b)

Kiesler, D. J., Mathieu, P., and Klein, M. H. Process movement in therapy and sampling interviews. In C. R. Rogers et al. (Eds.), *The therapeutic relationship and its impact. A study of psychotherapy with schizophrenics*. Madison: Univ. of Wisconsin Press, 1967. Ch. 10. (c)

Kiesler, D. J., Mathieu, P., and Klein, M. H. A summary of the issues and conclusions. In C. R. Rogers et al. (Eds.), *The therapeutic relationship and its impact. A study of psychotherapy with schizophrenia*. Madison: Univ. of Wisconsin Press, 1967. Ch. 12. (d)

Knapp, P. H. (Ed.), *Expression of the emotions in man*. New York: International Universities Press, 1963.

Kohn, H., and Sherwood, S. L. Content-free analysis of psychiatric patients' language. A preliminary study. In K. Enslein (Ed.), *Data acquisition and processing in biology and medicine*. Vol. 3. New York: Macmillan, 1964, Pp. 125–141.

Kramer, E. Judgment of personal characteristics and emotions from nonverbal properties of speech. *Psychological Bulletin*, 1963, **60**, 408–420.

Kratochvil, D., Aspy, D., and Carkhuff, R. R. The differential effects of absolute level and direction of growth in counselor functioning upon client level of functioning. *Journal of Clinical Psychology*, 1967, **23**, 216–217.

Krause, M. S. Anxiety in verbal behavior: An intercorrelational study. *Journal of Consulting Psychology*, 1961, **25**, 272.

Krause, M. S., and Pilisuk, M. Anxiety in verbal behavior: A validation study. *Journal of Consulting Psychology*, 1961, **25**, 414–419.

Laffal, J. The contextual associates of sun and God in Schreber's autobiography. *Journal of Abnormal and Social Psychology*, 1960, **61**, 474–479.

Laffal, J. Changes in the language of a schizophrenic patient during psychotherapy. *Journal of Abnormal and Social Psychology*, 1961, **63**, 422–427.

Laffal, J. The use of contextual associates in the analysis of free speech. *Journal of General Psychology*, 1963, **69**, 51–64.

Laffal, J. Linguistic field theory and studies of word association. *Journal of General Psychology*, 1964, **71**, 145–155.

Laffal, J. *Pathological and normal language*. New York: Atherton Press, 1965. (a)

Laffal, J. Pauses in the speech of a schizophrenic patient. *Journal of General Psychology*, 1965, **73**, 299–305. (b)

Laffal, J. Characteristics of the three-person conversation. *Journal of Verbal Learning and Verbal Behavior*, 1967, **6**, 555–559.

Laffal, J., and Feldman, S. The structure of single word and continuous word associations. *Journal of Verbal Learning and Verbal Behavior*, 1962, **1**, 54–61.

Laffal, J., and Feldman, S. The structure of free speech. *Journal of Verbal Learning and Verbal Behavior*, 1963, **2**, 498–503.

Lamb, R., and Mahl, G. F. Manifest reactions of patients and interviewers to the use of sound recording in the psychiatric interview. *American Journal of Psychiatry*, 1956, **112**, 731–737.

Lasswell, H. D. Verbal references and physiological changes during the psychoanalytic interview: A preliminary communication. *Psychoanalytic Review*, 1935, **22**, 10–24.

Leary, T. Huck and Jim in their interpretive balloon. *Contemporary Psychology*, 1960, **5**, 337–338.

Leary, T., and Gill, M. The dimensions and a measure of the process of psychotherapy: A system for the analysis of the content of clinical evaluations and patient-therapist verbalizations. In E. A. Rubinstein and M. B. Parloff (Eds.), *Research in psychotherapy*. Washington, D. C.: American Psychological Association, 1959. Pp. 62–95.

Lebo, D., and Applegate, W. The influence of instructional set upon the discomfort-relief quotient. *Journal of Clinical Psychology*, 1958, **14**, 280–282.

Lennard, H. L. Some aspects of the psychotherapeutic system. In H. H. Strupp and L. Luborsky (Eds.), *Research in psychotherapy*. Vol. 2. Washington, D. C.: American Psychological Association, 1962. Pp. 218–236.

Lennard, H. L., and Bernstein, A. *The anatomy of psychotherapy*. New York: Columbia Univ. Press, 1960.

Lennard, H. L., Calogeras, R., and Hendin, H. Some relationships between verbal behavior of therapist and patient in psychotherapy. *Journal of Psychology*, 1957, **43**, 181–186.

Levy, W. H. The communication of affect in psychotherapy. *Archives of General Psychiatry*, 1967, **16**, 102–106.

Lorenz, M. Expressive behavior and language patterns. *Psychiatry*, 1955, **18**, 353–366.

Lorenz, M., and Cobb, S. Language patterns in psychotic and psychoneurotic subjects. *Archives of Neurology and Psychiatry*, 1954, **72**, 665–673.

Luborsky, L. Momentary forgetting during psychotherapy and psychoanalysis: A theory and research method. In R. R. Holt (Ed.), *Motives and thought. Psychoanalytic essays in honor of David Rapaport. Psychological Issues*. New York: International Universities Press, 1967, Vol. 5. No. 2–3. Ch. 4.

Lynch, M. D., and Merrill, J. C. Content analysis—a probabilistic approach. *Journal of Communication*, 1968, **18**, 151–159.

McQuown, N. A. Analysis of the cultural content of language materials. In H. Hoijer (Ed.), *Language in culture*. Chicago: Univ. of Chicago Press, 1954. Pp. 20–31. (a)

McQuown, N. A. Cultural implications of linguistic science. *Monograph series on language and linguistics*. Washington, D. C.: Georgetown Univ. Press, 1954, No. 7, Pp. 57–61. (b)

McQuown, N. A. Linguistic transcription and specification of psychiatric interview materials. *Psychiatry*, 1957, **20**, 79–86.

McQuown, N. A. (Ed.), *The natural history of an interview*. New York: Grune and Stratton, in press.

Mackie, R., and Wood, J. Observations on two sides of a one-way screen. *International Journal of Group Psychotherapy*, 1968, **18**, 177–185.

Mahl, G. F. Disturbances and silences in the patient's speech in psychotherapy. *Journal of Abnormal and Social Psychology*, 1956, **53**, 1–15.

Mahl, G. F. On the use of "ah" in spontaneous speech: Quantitative, developmental, characterological, situational, and linguistic aspects. *American Psychologist*, 1958, **13**, 349. (Abstract)

Mahl, G. F. Exploring emotional states by content analysis. In I. Pool (Ed.), *Trends in content analysis*. Urbana: Univ. of Illinois Press, 1959. Ch. 3. (a)

Mahl, G. F. Measuring the patient's anxiety during interviews from "expressive" aspects of his speech. *Transactions of the New York Academy of Sciences*, 1959, **21** (Ser. 2), 249–257. (b)

Mahl, G. F. Measures of two expressive aspects of a patient's speech in two psychotherapeutic interviews. In L. A. Gottschalk (Ed.), *Comparative psycholinguistic analysis of two psychotherapeutic interviews*. New York: International Universities Press, 1961. Ch. 6.

Mahl, G. F. The lexical and linguistic levels in the expression of the emotions. In P. H. Knapp (Ed.), *Expression of the emotions in man*. New York: International Universities Press, 1963. Ch. 5.

Mahl, G. F. Some clinical observations on nonverbal behavior in interviews. *Journal of Nervous and Mental Disease*, 1967, **144**, 492–505.

Mahl, G. F. Gestures and body movements in interviews. In J. M. Shlien (Ed.), *Research in psychotherapy*. Vol. 3. Washington, D. C.: American Psychological Association, 1968. Pp. 295–346.

Mahl, G. F., Danet, B., and Norton, N. Reflection of major personality characteristics in gestures and body movements. *American Psychologist*, 1959, **14**, 357. (Abstract)

Mahl, G. F., Dollard, J., and Redlich, F. C. Facilities for the sound recording and observation of interviews. *Science*, 1954, **120**, 235–239.

Mahl, G. F. and Schulze, G. Psychological research in the extralinguistic area. In A. Sebeok, A. S. Hayes, and M. C. Bateson (Eds.), *Approaches to semiotics*. The Hague: Mouton, 1964. Pp. 51–125.

Mann, R. D. The development of the member-trainer relationship in self-analytic groups. *Human Relations*, 1966, **19**, 85–115.

Mann, R. D. *Interpersonal styles and group development. An analysis of the member-leader relationship*. New York: Wiley, 1967.

Markel, N. N. The reliability of coding paralanguage: Pitch, loudness, and tempo. *Journal of Verbal Learning and Verbal Behavior*, 1965, **4**, 306–308.

Marsden, G. Content-analysis studies of therapeutic interviews: 1954 to 1964. *Psychological Bulletin*, 1965, **63**, 298–321.

Martin, J. C., Carkhuff, R. R., and Berenson, B. G. Process variables in counseling and psychotherapy: A study of counseling and friendship. *Journal of Counseling Psychology*, 1966, **13**, 356–359.

Martin, J. C., and Carkhuff, R. R. Changes in personality and interpersonal functioning of counselors-in-training. *Journal of Clinical Psychology*, 1968, **24**, 109–110.

Matarazzo, J. D. Prescribed behavior therapy: Suggestions from interview research. In A. J. Bachrach (Ed.), *Experimental foundations of clinical psychology*. New York: Basic Books, 1962. Ch. 14.

Matarazzo, J. D., Hess, H. F., and Saslow, G. Frequency and duration characteristics of speech and silence behavior during interviews. *Journal of Clinical Psychology*, 1962, **18**, 416–426.

Matarazzo, J. D., Holman, D. C., and Wiens, A. N. A simple measure of interviewer and interviewee speech durations. *Journal of Psychology*, 1967, **66**, 7–14.

Matarazzo, J. D., and Saslow, G. Differences in interview interaction behavior among normal and deviant groups. In I. A. Berg and B. M. Bass (Eds.), *Conformity and deviation*. New York: Harper, 1961. Ch. 9.

Matarazzo, J. D., Saslow, G., and Guze, S. B. Stability of interaction patterns during interviews: A replication. *Journal of Consulting Psychology*, 1956, **20**, 267–274.

Matarazzo, J. D., Saslow, G., and Hare, A. P. Factor analysis of interview interaction behavior. *Journal of Consulting Psychology*, 1958, **22**, 419–429.

Matarazzo, J. D., Saslow, G., and Matarazzo, R. G. The interaction chronograph as an instrument for objective measurement of interaction patterns during interviews. *Journal of Psychology*, 1956, **41**, 347–367.

Matarazzo, J. D., Saslow, G., Matarazzo, R. G., and Phillips, J. S. Stability and modifiability of personality patterns manifested during a standardized interview. In P. H. Hoch and J. Zubin (Eds.), *Psychopathology of communication*. New York: Grune and Stratton, 1958. Ch. 8.

Matarazzo, J. D., Saslow, G., Wiens, A. N., Weitman, M., and Allen, B. V. Interviewer head nodding and interviewee speech durations. *Psychotherapy: Theory, Research and Practice*, 1964, **1**, 54–63.

Matarazzo, J. D., Weitman, M., and Saslow, G. Interview content and interviewee speech durations. *Journal of Clinical Psychology*, 1963, **19**, 463–472.

Matarazzo, J. D., Weitman, M., Saslow, G., and Wiens, A. N. Interviewer influence on duration of interview speech. *Journal of Verbal Learning and Verbal Behavior*, 1963, **1**, 451–458.

Matarazzo, J. D., and Wiens, A. N. Interviewer influence on durations of interviewee silence. *Journal of Experimental Research in Personality*, 1967, **2**, 56–69.

Matarazzo, J. D., Wiens, A. N., Matarazzo, R. G., and Saslow, G. Speech and silence behavior in clinical psychotherapy and its laboratory correlates. In J. M. Shlien (Ed.), *Research in psychotherapy*. Vol. 3. Washington, D. C.: American Psychological Association, 1968. Pp. 347–394.

Matarazzo, J. D., Wiens, A. N., and Saslow, G. Studies in interview speech behavior. In L. Krasner and L. P. Ullmann (Eds.), *Research in behavior modification*. New York: Holt, Rinehart and Winston, 1965. Ch. 8.

Matarazzo, J. D., Wiens, A. N., Saslow, G., Allen, B. V., and Weitman, M. Interviewer mm-hmm and interviewee speech durations. *Psychotherapy: Theory, Research and Practice*, 1964, **1**, 109–114.

Matarazzo, R. G., Matarazzo, J. D., Saslow, G., and Phillips, J. S. Psychological test and organismic correlates of interview interaction patterns. *Journal of Abnormal and Social Psychology*, 1958, **56**, 329–338.

Matarazzo, R. G., Wiens, A. N., and Saslow, G. Experimentation in the teaching and learning of psychotherapy skills. In L. A. Gottschalk and A. H. Auerbach (Eds.), *Methods of research in psychotherapy*. New York: Appleton-Century-Crofts, 1966. Ch. 34.

Metz, A. S. A comparison of the use of the sound recording and the written transcript in the coding of verbal interaction. *Journal of Social Psychology*, 1965, **65**, 325–335.

Mills, D. H., and Abeles, N. Counselor needs for affiliation and nurturance as related to liking for clients and counseling process. *Journal of Counseling Psychology*, 1965, **12**, 353–358.

Mills, T. M. *Group transformation: An analysis of a learning group*. Englewood Cliffs, N. J.: Prentice-Hall, 1964.

Moos, R. H., and Clemes, S. R. Multivariate study of the patient-therapist system. *Journal of Consulting Psychology*, 1967, **31**, 119–130.

Mowrer, O. H. Changes in verbal behavior during psychotherapy. In O. H. Mowrer (Ed.), *Psychotherapy theory and research*. New York: Ronald Press, 1953. Ch. 17.

Mowrer, O. H., Light, B. H., Luria, Z., and Zeleny, M. Tension changes during psychotherapy, with special reference to resistance. In O. H. Mowrer (Ed.), *Psychotherapy theory and research*. New York: Ronald Press, 1953. Ch. 18.

Munzer, J., and Greenwald, H. Interaction process analysis of a therapy group. *International Journal of Group Psychotherapy*, 1957, **7**, 175–190.

Murray, E. J. A case study in a behavioral analysis of psychotherapy. *Journal of Abnormal and Social Psychology*, 1954, **49**, 305–310.

Murray, E. J. A content-analysis method for studying psychotherapy. *Psychological Monographs*, 1956, **70** (13, Whole No. 420).

Murray, E. J. Direct analysis from the viewpoint of learning theory. *Journal of Consulting Psychology*, 1962, **26**, 226–231.

Murray, E. J., Auld, F., Jr., and White, A. M. A psychotherapy case showing progress but no decrease in the discomfort-relief quotient. *Journal of Consulting Psychology*, 1954, **18**, 349–353.

Noble, F., Ohlsen, M., and Proff, F. A method for the quantification of psychotherapeutic interaction in counseling groups. *Journal of Counseling Psychology*, 1961, **8**, 54–60.

North, R. C., Holsti, O. R., Saninovich, M. G., and Zinnes, D. A. *Content analysis. A handbook with applications for the study of international crisis.* Evanston, Ill.: Northwestern Univ. Press, 1963.

Ohlsen, M. M., and Oelke, M. C. An evaluation of discussion topics in group counseling. *Journal of Clinical Psychology*, 1962, **18**, 317–322.

Ohlsen, M. M., and Pearson, R. E. A method for the classification of group interaction and its uses to explore the influence of individual and role factors in group counseling. *Journal of Clinical Psychology*, 1965, **21**, 436–441.

Ornston, P. S., Cicchetti, D. V., Levine, J., and Fierman, L. B. Some parameters of verbal behavior that reliably differentiate novice from experienced psychotherapists. *Journal of Abnormal Psychology*, 1968, **73**, 240–244.

Osgood, C. E. The representational model and relevant research methods. In I. Pool (Ed.), *Trends in content analysis.* Urbana: Univ. of Illinois Press, 1959. Ch. 2.

Ostwald, P. F. Visual denotation of human sounds. Preliminary report of an acoustic method. *Archives of General Psychiatry*, 1960, **3**, 117–121.

Ostwald, P. F. The sounds of emotional disturbance. *Archives of General Psychiatry*, 1961, **5**, 587–592.

Ostwald, P. F. *Soundmaking. The acoustic communication of emotion.* Springfield, Ill.: C. C. Thomas, 1963.

Ostwald, P. F. Acoustic manifestations of emotional disturbance. In D. McK. Rioch and E. A. Weinstein (Eds.), *Disorders in communication.* Vol. 42. Baltimore: Williams & Wilkins, 1964. Ch. 31.

Ostwald, P. F. Acoustic methods in psychiatry. *Scientific American*, 1965, **212**/3, 82–91.

Pagell, W. A., Carkhuff, R. R., and Berenson, B. G. The predicted differential effects of the level of counselor functioning upon the level of functioning of outpatients. *Journal of Clinical Psychology*, 1967, **23**, 510–512.

Pallone, N. J., and DiBennardo, F. R. Interview sequence in relation to counselor verbal mode, client problem-related content, and rapport. *Journal of Counseling Psychology*, 1967, **14**, 523–525.

Pallone, N. J., and Grande, P. P. Counselor verbal mode, problem relevant communication, and client rapport. *Journal of Counseling Psychology*, 1965, **12**, 359–365.

Palmore, E., Lennard, H. L., and Hendin, H. Similarities of therapist and patient verbal behavior in psychotherapy. *Sociometry*, 1959, **22**, 12–22.

Panek, D. M., and Martin, B. The relationship between GSR and speech disturbances in psychotherapy. *Journal of Abnormal and Social Psychology*, 1959, **58**, 402–405.

Parker, G. V. C. Some concomitants of therapist dominance in the psychotherapy interview. *Journal of Consulting Psychology*, 1967, **31**, 313–318.

Phillips, J. S., Matarazzo, J. D., Matarazzo, R. G., and Saslow, G. Observer reliability of interaction patterns during interviews. *Journal of Consulting Psychology*, 1957, **21**, 269–275.

Phillips, J. S., Matarazzo, R. G., Matarazzo, J. D., Saslow, G., and Kanfer, F. H. Relationships between descriptive content and interaction behavior in interviews. *Journal of Consulting Psychology*, 1961, **25**, 260–266.

Piaget, G. W., Berenson, B. G., and Carkhuff, R. R. Differential effects of the manipulation of therapeutic conditions by high and moderate functioning therapists upon high and low functioning clients. *Journal of Consulting Psychology*, 1967, **31**, 481–486.

Pierce, R., Carkhuff, R. R., and Berenson, B. G. The differential effects of high and low functioning counselors upon counselors-in-training. *Journal of Clinical Psychology*, 1967, **23**, 212–215.

Pittenger, R. E. Linguistic analysis of tone of voice in communication of affect. *Psychiatric Research Reports*, 1958, **8**, 41–54.

Pittenger, R. E., Hockett, C. F., and Danehy, J. J. *The first five minutes: A sample of microscopic interview analysis.* Ithaca, N. Y.: Paul Martineau, 1960.

Pittenger, R. E., and Smith, H. L., Jr. A basis for some contributions of linguistics to psychiatry. *Psychiatry*, 1957, **20**, 61–78.

Platz, A., and Honigfeld, G. Some effects of anxiety on the intelligibility of verbal communication in psychotherapy. *Journal of Personality and Social Psychology*, 1965, **2**, 122–125.

Pool, I. (Ed.) *Trends in Content Analysis.* Urbana: Univ. of Illinois Press, 1959. (a)

Pool, I. Trends in content analysis today: A summary. In I. Pool (Ed.), *Trends in content analysis.* Urbana: Univ. of Illinois Press, 1959. Ch. 7. (b)

Pope, B., and Siegman, A. W. The effect of therapist verbal activity level and specificity on patient productivity and speech disturbance in the initial interview. *Journal of Consulting Psychology*, 1962, **26**, 489.

Pope, B., and Siegman, A. W. An intercorrelational study of some indices of verbal fluency. *Psychological Reports*, 1964, **15**, 303–310.

Pope, B., and Siegman, A. W. Interviewer specificity and topical focus in relation to interviewee productivity. *Journal of Verbal Learning and Verbal Behavior*, 1965, **4**, 188–192.

Pope, B., and Siegman, A. W. Interviewer-interviewee relationship and verbal behavior of interviewee in the initial interview. *Psychotherapy: Theory, Research and Practice*, 1966, **3**, 149–152.

Pope, B., and Siegman, A. W. Interviewer warmth and verbal communication in the initial interview. *Proceedings of the 75th annual convention of the American Psychological Association.* Washington, D. C.: American Psychological Association, 1967. Pp. 245–246.

Pope, B., and Siegman, A. W. Interviewer warmth in relation to interviewee verbal behavior. *Journal of Consulting and Clinical Psychology*, 1968, **32**, 588–595.

Proff, F. C. A validity study of the distress-relief quotient as a measure of movement within the topical discussion unit. Unpublished doctoral dissertation, University of Missouri, 1952.

Psathas, G. Interaction process analysis of two psychotherapy groups. *International Journal of Group Psychotherapy*, 1960, **10**, 430–445. (a)

Psathas, G. Phase movement and equilibrium tendencies in interaction process in psychotherapy groups. *Sociometry*, 1960, **23**, 177–194. (b)

Psathas, G. Alternative methods for scoring interaction process analysis. *Journal of Social Psychology*, 1961, **53**, 97–103.

Psathas, G., and Arp, D. J. A thematic analysis of interviewer's statements in therapy-analogue interviews. In P. J. Stone, D. C. Dunphy, M. S. Smith, and D. M. Ogilvie, *The general inquirer: A computer approach to content analysis*. Cambridge: M.I.T. Press, 1966. Ch. 15.

Psathas, G., and Igersheimer, W. Interaction processes in two psychotherapy groups: Therapist and patient differences. *Journal of Nervous and Mental Disease*, 1966, **142**, 340–354.

Rabow, J. Quantitative aspects of the group-psychotherapist's role behavior: A methodological note. *Journal of Social Psychology*, 1965, **67**, 31–37.

Raush, H. L., Sperber, Z., Rigler, D., Williams, J., Harway, N. I., Bordin, E. S., Dittmann, A. T., and Hays, W. L. A dimensional analysis of depth of interpretation. *Journal of Consulting Psychology*, 1956, **20**, 43–48.

Rice, L. N. Therapist's style of participation and case outcome. *Journal of Consulting Psychology*, 1965, **29**, 155–160.

Rice, L. N., and Wagstaff, A. K. Client voice quality and expressive style as indexes of productive psychotherapy. *Journal of Consulting Psychology*, 1967, **31**, 557–563.

Roberts, R. B., Jr., and Renzaglia, G. A. The influence of tape recording on counseling. *Journal of Counseling Psychology*, 1965, **12**, 10–16.

Robinson, F. P. The unit in interview analysis. *Educational and Psychological Measurement*, 1949, **9**, 709–716.

Rogers, C. R. The necessary and sufficient conditions of therapeutic personality change. *Journal of Consulting Psychology*, 1957, **21**, 95–103.

Rogers, C. R. A tentative scale for the measurement of process in psychotherapy. In E. A. Rubinstein and M. B. Parloff (Eds.), *Research in psychotherapy*. Washington, D. C.: American Psychological Association, 1959. Pp. 96–107.

Rogers, C. R. A process conception of psychotherapy. In C. R. Rogers, *On becoming a person*. Boston: Houghton Mifflin, 1961. Ch. 7.

Rogers, C. R., Gendlin, E. T., Kiesler, D. J., and Truax, C. B. (Eds.) *The therapeutic relationship and its impact. A study of psychotherapy with schizophrenics*. Madison: Univ. of Wisconsin Press, 1967.

Rogers, C. R. The findings in brief. In C. R. Rogers et al. (Eds.), *The therapeutic relationship and its impact. A study of psychotherapy with schizophrenics*. Madison: Univ. of Wisconsin Press, 1967. Ch. 5.

Rogers, C. R., and Truax, C. B. The therapeutic conditions antecedent to change: A theoretical view. In C. R. Rogers et al. (Eds.), *The therapeutic relationship and its impact. A study of psychotherapy with schizophrenics*. Madison: Univ. of Wisconsin Press, 1967. Ch. 6.

Roose, L. J. The influence of psychosomatic research on the psychoanalytic process. *Journal of the American Psychoanalytic Association*, 1960, **8**, 317–334.

Rosen, J. Multiple-regression analysis of counselor characteristics and competencies. *Psychological Reports*, 1967, **20**, 1003–1008.

Rosenberg, P. P. Methodology for an objective analysis of the content of a group protocol. *International Journal of Group Psychotherapy*, 1962, **12**, 467–475.

Rosenman, S. Changes in the representations of self, other, and interrelationship in client-centered therapy. *Journal of Counseling Psychology*, 1955, **2**, 271–277.

Rottschafer, R. H., and Renzaglia, G. A. The relationship of dependent-like verbal behavior to counselor style and induced set. *Journal of Consulting Psychology*, 1962, **26**, 172–177.

Rubenstein, L., and Cameron, D. E. Electronic analysis of nonverbal communication. *Comprehensive Psychiatry*, 1968, **9**, 200–208.

Salzberg, H. C. Manipulation of verbal behavior in a group psychotherapeutic setting. *Psychological Reports*, 1961, **9**, 183–186.

Salzberg, H. C. Effects of silence and redirection on verbal responses in group psychotherapy. *Psychological Reports*, 1962, **11**, 455–461.

Salzberg, H. C. Verbal behavior in group psychotherapy with and without a therapist. *Journal of Counseling Psychology*, 1967, **14**, 24–27.

Salzberg, H. C., Brokaw, J. R., and Strahley, D. F. Effects of group stability on spontaneity and problem-relevant verbal behavior in group psychotherapy. *Psychological Reports*, 1964, **14**, 687–694.

Sainsbury, P. Gestural movement during psychiatric interview. *Psychosomatic Medicine*, 1955, **17**, 458–469.

Salzinger, K. Some problems of response measurement in verbal behavior: The response unit and intraresponse relations. Paper read at Conference on Methods of Measurement of Change in Human Behavior, Montreal, September 1962.

Saporta, S., and Sebeok, T. A. Linguistics and content analysis. In I. Pool (Ed.), *Trends in content analysis*. Urbana: Univ. of Illinois Press, 1959. Ch. 4.

Sargent, H. D., Coyne, L., Wallerstein, R. S., and Holtzman, W. H. An approach to the quantitative problems of psychoanalytic research. *Journal of Clinical Psychology*, 1967, **23**, 243–291.

Saslow, G., and Matarazzo, J. D. A technique for studying changes in interview behavior. In E. A. Rubinstein and M. B. Parloff (Eds.), *Research in psychotherapy*. Washington, D. C.: American Psychological Association, 1959. Pp. 125–159.

Saslow, G., Matarazzo, J. D., and Guze, S. B. The stability of interaction chronograph patterns in psychiatric interviews. *Journal of Consulting Psychology*, 1955, **19**, 417–430.

Saslow, G., Matarazzo, J. D., Phillips, J. S., and Matarazzo, R. G. Test-retest stability of interaction patterns during interviews conducted one week apart. *Journal of Abnormal and Social Psychology*, 1957, **54**, 295–302.

Scheflen, A. E. Communication and regulation in psychotherapy. *Psychiatry*, 1963, **26**, 126–136. (a)

Scheflen, A. E. Research in psychotherapy. In J. Masserman (Ed.), *Current psychiatric therapies*. Vol. 3. New York: Grune and Stratton, 1963. Pp. 33–46. (b)

Scheflen, A. E. The significance of posture in communication systems. *Psychiatry*, 1964, **27**, 316–331.

Scheflen, A. E. Context analysis. In O. S. English (Ed.), *Strategy and structure in psychotherapy. Three research studies of the Whitaker-Malone multiple therapy*. Behavioral Studies Monograph No. 2. Commonwealth of Penn.: Eastern Pennsylvania Psychiatric Institute, 1965. (a)

Scheflen, A. E. Quasi-courtship behavior in psychotherapy. *Psychiatry*, 1965, **28**, 245–257. (b)

Scheflen, A. E. *Stream and structure of communicational behavior*. Behavioral Studies Monograph No. 1. Commonwealth of Penn.: Eastern Pennsylvania Psychiatric Institute, 1965. (c)

Scheflen, A. E. Natural history method in psychotherapy: Communicational research. In L. A. Gottschalk and A. H. Auerbach (Eds.), *Methods of research in psychotherapy*. New York: Appleton-Century-Crofts, 1966. Ch. 20.

Scheflen, A. E. On the structuring of human communication. *American Behavioral Scientist*, 1967, **10/8**, 8–12.

Scheflen, A. E. Human communication: Behavioral programs and their integration in interaction. *Behavioral Science*, 1968, **13**, 44–55.

Schoeninger, D. W., Klein, M. H., and Mathieu, P. L. Sampling from recorded therapy interview: Patient experiencing ratings made with and without therapist speech cues. *Psychological Reports*, 1967, **20**, 250.

Schoeninger, D. W., Klein, M. H., and Mathieu, P. L. Comparison of two methods for training judges to rate psychotherapy recordings. *Journal of Consulting and Clinical Psychology*, 1968, **32**, 499.

Schuldt, W. J. Psychotherapists' approach-avoidance responses and clients' expressions of dependency. *Journal of Counseling Psychology*, 1966, **13**, 178–183.

Schulze, G., Mahl, G. F., and Murray, E. J. Speech disturbances and content analysis categories as indices of underlying emotional states of patients in psychotherapy. *American Psychologist*, 1960, **15**, 405. (Abstract)

Schutz, W. C. Reliability, ambiguity and content analysis. *Psychological Review*, 1952, **59**, 119–129.

Schutz, W. C. On categorizing qualitative data in content analysis. *Public Opinion Quarterly*, 1958, **22**, 503–515.

Scott, W. A. Reliability of content analysis: The case of nominal scale coding. *Public Opinion Quarterly*, 1955, **19**, 321–325.

Shakow, D. The recorded psychoanalytic interview as an objective approach to research in psychoanalysis. *Psychoanalytic Quarterly*, 1960, **29**, 82–97.

Shapiro, J. G. Relationships between visual and auditory cues of therapeutic effectiveness. *Journal of Clinical Psychology*, 1968, **24**, 236–329.

Shapiro, J. G., Foster, C. P., and Powell, T. Facial and bodily cues of genuineness, empathy and warmth. *Journal of Clinical Psychology*, 1968, **24**, 233–236.

Shellhase, L. J. Acceptance of role and resultant interaction in the group psychotherapy of schizophrenia. *Group Psychotherapy*, 1960, **13**, 208–229.

Siegman, A. W., and Pope, B. An empirical scale for the measurement of therapist specificity in the initial psychiatric interview. *Psychological Record*, 1962, **11**, 515–520.

Siegman, A. W., and Pope, B. Effects of question specificity and anxiety-producing messages on verbal fluency in the initial interview. *Journal of Personality and Social Psychology*, 1965, **2**, 522–530. (a)

Siegman, A. W., and Pope, B. Personality variables associated with productivity and verbal fluency in the initial interview. *Proceedings of the 73rd annual convention of the American Psychological Association*. Washington, D. C.: American Psychological Association, 1965. Pp. 273–274. (b)

Siegman, A. W., and Pope, B. The effect of interviewer ambiguity-specificity and topical focus on interviewee vocabulary diversity. *Language and Speech*, 1966, **9**, 242–249. (a)

Siegman, A. W., and Pope, B. Effect of interviewer specificity and topical focus on the predictability of interviewee's responses. *Proceedings of the 74th annual convention of the American Psychological Association*. Washington, D. C.: American Psychological Association, 1966. Pp. 195–196. (b)

Sklansky, M. A., Isaacs, K. S., and Haggard, E. A. A method for the study of verbal interaction and levels of meaning in psychotherapy. In J. S. Gottlieb and G. Tourney (Eds.), *Scientific papers and discussions, divisional meeting, Mid-West Area District Branches*. Detroit: American Psychiatric Association, 1960. Pp. 133–148.

Sklansky, M. A., Isaacs, K. S., Levitov, E. S., and Haggard, E. A. Verbal interaction and levels of meaning in psychotherapy. *Archives of General Psychiatry*, 1966, **14**, 158–170.

Smith, A. B., Bassin, A., and Froehlich, A. Changes in attitudes and degree of verbal participation in group therapy with adult offenders. *Journal of Consulting Psychology*, 1960, **24**, 247–249.

Smith, A. B., Bassin, A., and Froehlich, A. Interaction process and equilibrium in a therapy group of adult offenders. *Journal of Social Psychology*, 1962, **56**, 141–147.

Smith, R. W., and Young, H. H. Re-enforcement and changes in loquacity in group psychotherapy. *Psychological Reports*, 1968, **23**, 230.

Snyder, W. U. *Dependency in psychotherapy*. New York: Macmillan, 1963.

Speisman, J. C. Depth of interpretation and verbal resistance in psychotherapy. *Journal of Consulting Psychology*, 1959, **23**, 93–99.

Starkweather, J. A. Variations in vocal behavior. In D. McK. Rioch and E. A. Weinstein (Eds.), *Disorders of communication*. Vol. 42. Baltimore: Williams & Wilkins, 1962. Pp. 424–449.

Starkweather, J. A. Computer methods for the study of psychiatric interviews. *Comprehensive Psychiatry*, 1967, **8**, 509–520.

Starkweather, J. A., and Decker, J. B. Computer analysis of interview content. *Psychological Reports*, 1964, **15**, 875–882.

Stern, H., and Grosz, H. J. Personality correlates of patient interactions in group psychotherapy. *Psychological Reports*, 1966, **18**, 411–414. (a)

Stern, H., and Grosz, H. J. Verbal interactions in group psychotherapy between patients with similar and with dissimilar personalities. *Psychological Reports*, 1966, **19**, 1111–1114. (b)

Sternberg, R. S., Chapman, J., and Shakow, D. Psychotherapy research and the problem of intrusions of privacy. *Psychiatry*, 1958, **21**, 195–203.

Stoler, N. Client likability: A variable in the study of psychotherapy. *Journal of Consulting Psychology*, 1963, **27**, 175–178.

Stone, P. J., Dunphy, D. C., Smith, M. S., and Ogilvie, D. M. *The general inquirer: A computer approach to content analysis*. Cambridge: M.I.T. Press, 1966.

Strupp, H. H. The effect of the psychotherapist's personal analysis upon his techniques. *Journal of Consulting Psychology*, 1955, **19**, 197–204. (a)

Strupp, H. H. An objective comparison of Rogerian and psychoanalytic techniques. *Journal of Consulting Psychology*, 1955, **19**, 1–7. (b)

Strupp, H. H. Psychotherapeutic technique, professional affiliation, and experience level. *Journal of Consulting Psychology*, 1955, **19**, 97–102. (c)

Strupp, H. H. A multidimensional analysis of technique in brief psychotherapy. *Psychiatry*, 1957, **20**, 387–397. (a)

Strupp, H. H. A multidimensional analysis of therapist activity in analytic and client-centered therapy. *Journal of Consulting Psychology*, 1957, **21**, 301–308. (b)

Strupp, H. H. A multidimensional system for analyzing psychotherapeutic techniques. *Psychiatry*, 1957, **20**, 293–306. (c)

Strupp, H. H. The performance of psychiatrists and psychologists in a therapeutic interview. *Journal of Clinical Psychology*, 1958, **14**, 219–226. (a)

Strupp, H. H. The performance of psychoanalytic and client-centered therapists in an initial interview. *Journal of Consulting Psychology*, 1958, **22**, 265–274. (b)

Strupp, H. H. The psychotherapist's contribution to the treatment process. *Behavioral Science*, 1958, **3**, 34–67. (c)

Strupp, H. H. *Psychotherapists in action*. New York: Grune and Stratton, 1960.

Strupp, H. H. An analysis of therapist activity in two psychotherapeutic interviews. In L. A. Gottschalk (Ed.), *Comparative psycholinguistic analysis of two psychotherapeutic interviews*. New York: International Universities Press, 1961. Ch. 4.

Strupp, H. H. Patient-doctor relationships: The psychotherapist in the therapeutic process. In A. J. Bachrach (Ed.), *Experimental foundations of clinical psychology*. New York: Basic Books, 1962. Ch. 17. (a)

Strupp, H. H. The therapist's contribution to the treatment process: Beginnings and vagaries of a research program. In H. H. Strupp and L. Luborsky (Eds.), *Research in psychotherapy*. Vol. 2. Washington, D. C.: American Psychological Association, 1962. Pp. 25–40. (b)

Strupp, H. H., Chassan, J. B., and Ewing, J. A. Toward the longitudinal study of the psychotherapeutic process. In L. A. Gottschalk and A. H. Auerbach (Eds.), *Methods of research in psychotherapy*. New York: Appleton-Century-Crofts, 1966. Ch. 24.

Strupp, H. H., and Luborsky, L. (Eds.) *Research in psychotherapy*. Vol. 2. Washington, D. C.: American Psychological Association, 1962.

Strupp, H. H., and Wallach, M. S. A further study of psychiatrists' responses in quasi-therapy situations. *Behavioral Science*, 1965, **10**, 113–134.

Suci, G. J. The validity of pause as an index of units of language. *Journal of Verbal Learning and Verbal Behavior*, 1967, **6**, 26–32.

Sutherland, J. D., and Gill, H. S. The significance of the one-way vision screen in analytic group psychotherapy. *British Journal of Medical Psychology*, 1964, **37**, 185–202.

Swensen, C. H. Psychotherapy as a special case of dyadic interaction: Some suggestions for theory and research. *Psychotherapy: Theory, Research and Practice*, 1967, **4**, 7–13.

Talland, G. A. Task and interaction process: Some characteristics of therapeutic group discussions. *Journal of Abnormal and Social Psychology*, 1955, **50**, 105–109.

Tauson, V. B., Guze, S. B., McClure, J., and Beguelin, J. A further study of some features of the interview with the Interaction Chronograph. *American Journal of Psychiatry*, 1961, **118**, 438–446.

Timmons, E. O., Rickard, H. C., and Taylor, R. E. Reliability of content-free group verbal behavior. *Psychological Record*, 1960, **10**, 297–305.

Tomlinson, T. M. Three approaches to the study of psychotherapy: Process, outcome, and change. Unpublished Ph.D. dissertation, University of Wisconsin, 1962.

Tomlinson, T. M. The therapeutic process as related to outcome. In C. R. Rogers et al. (Eds.), *The therapeutic relationship and its impact. A study of psychotherapy with schizophrenics.* Madison: Univ. of Wisconsin Press, 1967. Ch. 13.

Tomlinson, T. M., and Hart, J. T., Jr. A validation study of the process scale. *Journal of Consulting Psychology*, 1962, **26**, 74–78.

Tomlinson, T. M., and Stoler, N. The relationship between affective evaluation and ratings of therapy process and outcome with schizophrenics. *Psychotherapy: Theory, Research and Practice*, 1967, **4**, 14–18.

Tourney, G., Bloom, V., Lowinger, P. L., Schorer, C., Auld, F., and Grisell, J. A study of psychotherapeutic process variables in psychoneurotic and schizophrenic patients. *American Journal of Psychotherapy*, 1966, **20**, 112–124.

Truax, C. B. The process of group psychotherapy: Relationships between hypothesized therapeutic conditions and intrapersonal exploration. *Psychological Monographs*, 1961, **75** (7, Whole No. 511).

Truax, C. B. Therapist empathy, warmth, and genuineness and patient personality change in group psychotherapy: A comparison between interaction unit measure, time sample measures, patient perception measures. *Journal of Clinical Psychology*, 1966, **22**, 225–229. (a)

Truax, C. B. Influence of patient statements of judgments on therapist statements during psychotherapy. *Journal of Clinical Psychology*, 1966, **22**, 335–337. (b)

Truax, C. B. Reinforcement and nonreinforcement in Rogerian psychotherapy. *Journal of Abnormal Psychology*, 1966, **71**, 1–9. (c)

Truax, C. B. Therapist interpersonal reinforcement of client self-exploration and therapeutic outcome in group psychotherapy. *Journal of Counseling Psychology*, 1968, **15**, 225–231.

Truax, C. B., and Carkhuff, R. R. Concreteness: A neglected variable in research in psychotherapy. *Journal of Clinical Psychology*, 1964, **20**, 264–267.

Truax, C. B., and Carkhuff, R. R. Client and therapist transparency in the psychotherapeutic encounter. *Journal of Counseling Psychology*, 1965, **12**, 3–9. (a)

Truax, C. B., and Carkhuff, R. R. Experimental manipulation of therapeutic conditions. *Journal of Consulting Psychology*, 1965, **29**, 119–124. (b)

Truax, C. B., and Carkhuff, R. R. *Toward effective counseling and psychotherapy: Training and practice.* Chicago: Aldine, 1967.

Truax, C. B., Carkhuff, R. R., and Kodman, F. Relationships between therapist-offered conditions and patient change in group psychotherapy. *Journal of Clinical Psychology*, 1965, **21**, 327–329.

Truax, C. B., Fine, H., Moravec, J., and Millis, W. Effects of therapist persuasive potency in individual psychotherapy. *Journal of Clinical Psychology*, 1968, **24**, 359–362.

Truax, C. B., Wargo, D. G., Frank, J. D., Imber, S. D., Battle, C. C., Hoehn-Saric, R., Nash, E. H., and Stone, A. R. Therapist empathy, genuineness, and warmth and patient therapeutic outcome. *Journal of Consulting Psychology*, 1966, **30**, 395–401. (a)

Truax, C. B., Wargo, D. G., Frank, J. D., Imber, S. D., Battle, C. C., Hoehn-Saric, R., Nash, E. H., and Stone, A. R. The therapist's contribution to accurate empathy, non-possessive warmth, and genuineness in psychotherapy. *Journal of Clinical Psychology*, 1966, **22**, 331–334. (b)

Truax, C. B., Wargo, D. G., and Silber, L. D. Effects of group psychotherapy with high accurate empathy and nonpossessive warmth upon female institutionalized delinquents. *Journal of Abnormal Psychology*, 1966, **71**, 267–274.

Tyler, L. E. Comment. *Journal of Counseling Psychology*, 1965, **12**, 16.

Varble, D. L. Relationship between the therapists' approach-avoidance reactions to hostility and client behavior in therapy. *Journal of Consulting and Clinical Psychology*, 1968, **32**, 237–242.

Vargas, M. J. Changes in self-awareness during client-centered therapy. In C. R. Rogers and R. F. Dymond (Eds.), *Psychotherapy and Personality Change.* Chicago: Univ. of Chicago Press, 1954. Ch. 10.

Veen, F. van der. Effects of the therapist and the patient on each other's therapeutic behavior. *Journal of Consulting Psychology*, 1965, **29**, 19–26.

Veen, F. van der. Basic elements in the process of psychotherapy. *Journal of Consulting Psychology*, 1967, **31**, 295–303.

Veen, F. van der, and Stoler, N. Therapist judgments, interview behavior and case outcome. *Psychotherapy: Theory, Research and Practice*, 1965, **2**, 158–163.

Vlack, J. van. Filming psychotherapy from the viewpoint of a research cinematographer. In L. A. Gottschalk and A. H. Auerbach (Eds.), *Methods of research in psychotherapy.* New York: Appleton-Century-Crofts, 1966. Ch. 2.

Walker, A. M., Rablen, R. A., and Rogers, C. R. Development of a scale to measure process changes in psychotherapy. *Journal of Clinical Psychology*, 1960, **16**, 79–85.

Ward, C. H. Psychotherapy research: Dilemmas and directions. *Archives of General Psychiatry*, 1964, **10**, 596–622.

Waskow, I., and Bergman, P. Does "theoretical orientation" influence ratings of "warmth-acceptance"? *Journal of Consulting Psychology*, 1962, **26**, 484.

Watson, D. L., and Laffal, J. Sources of verbalizations of psychotherapists about patients. *Journal of General Psychology*, 1963, **68**, 89–98.

Watson, P. D., and Kanter, S. S. Some influences of an experimental situation on the psychotherapeutic process. *Psychosomatic Medicine*, 1956, **18**, 457–470.

Waxenberg, S. E., Strachstein, H., Leff, J., Laufer, L. G., and Bamberger, H. Leadership style: Interaction and group climate. *Psychotherapy: Theory, Research and Practice*, 1965, **2**, 164–168.

Weintraub, W., and Aronson, H. The application of verbal behavior analysis to the study of psychological defense mechanisms. I. Methodology and preliminary report. *Journal of Nervous and Mental Disease*, 1962, **134**, 169–181.

Weintraub, W., and Aronson, H. The application of verbal behavior analysis to the study of psychological defense mechanisms: II. Speech pattern associated with impulsive behavior. *Journal of Nervous and Mental Disease*, 1964, **139**, 75–82.

Weintraub, W., and Aronson, H. The application of verbal behavior analysis to the study of psychological defense mechanisms III. Speech pattern associated with delusional behavior. *Journal of Nervous and Mental Disease*, 1965, **141**, 172–179.

Weintraub, W., and Aronson, H. The application of verbal behavior analysis to the study of psychological defense mechanisms: IV. Speech pattern associated with depressive behavior. *Journal of Nervous and Mental Disease*, 1967, **144**, 22–28.

White, A. M., Fichtenbaum, L., Cooper, L., and Dollard, J. Physiological focus in psychiatric interviews. *Journal of Consulting Psychology*, 1966, **30**, 363.

White, A. M., Fichtenbaum L., and Dollard, J. Evaluation of silence in initial interviews with psychiatric clinic patients. *Journal of Nervous and Mental Disease*, 1964, **139**, 550–557. (a)

White, A. M., Fichtenbaum, L., and Dollard, J. Measure for predicting dropping out of psychotherapy. *Journal of Consulting Psychology*, 1964, **28**, 326–332. (b)

White, A. M., Fichtenbaum, L., and Dollard, J. A content measure of changes attributable to psychotherapy. *American Journal of Orthopsychiatry*, 1966, **36**, 41–49. (a)

White, A. M., Fichtenbaum, L., and Dollard, J. Measuring change: A verbal and nonverbal content analysis method. *Psychotherapy: Theory, Research and Practice*, 1966, **3**, 107–113. (b)

White, A. M., Fichtenbaum, L., and Dollard, J. An interactive behavior index and verbal content analysis. *Journal of Nervous and Mental Disease*, 1968, **146**, 457–464.

Wiens, A. N., Matarazzo, J. D., and Saslow, G. The interaction recorder: An electronic punched paper tape unit for recording speech behavior during interviews. *Journal of Clinical Psychology*, 1965, **21**, 142–145.

Wiens, A. N., Molde, D. A., Holman, D. C., and Matarazzo, J. D. Can interview interaction measures be taken from tape recordings? *Journal of Psychology*, 1966, **63**, 249–260.

Wiens, A. N., Saslow, G., and Matarazzo, J. D. Speech interruption behavior during interviews. *Psychotherapy: Theory, Research and Practice*, 1966, **3**, 153–158.

Wigell, W. W., and Ohlsen, M. M. To what extent is affect a function of topic and referent in group counseling? *American Journal of Orthopsychiatry*, 1962, **32**, 728–735.

Winder, C. L., Ahmad, F. Z., Bandura, A., and Rau, L. C. Dependency of patients, psychotherapists' responses, and aspects of psychotherapy. *Journal of Consulting Psychology*, 1962, **26**, 129–134.

Witkin, H. A., Lewis, H. B., and Weil, E. Affective reactions and patient-therapist interactions among more differentiated and less differentiated patients early in therapy. *Journal of Nervous and Mental Disease*, 1968, **146**, 193–208.

Woodward, J. K. Contextual structure analysis. In K. Enslein (Ed.), *Data acquisition and processing in biology and medicine*. Vol. 1. New York: Pergamon, 1966. Pp. 45–50.

Zimmer, J. M., and Anderson, S. Dimensions of positive regard and empathy. *Journal of Counseling Psychology*, 1968, **15**, 417–426.

Zimmer, J. M., and Park, P. Factor analysis of counselor communications. *Journal of Counseling Psychology*, 1967, **14**, 198–203.

Zimpfer, D. G. Expression of feeling in group counseling. *Personnel and Guidance Journal*, 1967, **45**, 703–708.

11

QUANTITATIVE RESEARCH ON PSYCHOANALYTIC THERAPY[1]

LESTER LUBORSKY
UNIVERSITY OF PENNSYLVANIA

DONALD P. SPENCE
NEW YORK UNIVERSITY

Quantitative research on psychoanalytic therapy is a stepchild of the psychoanalytic profession. Rare is the therapist who knows of even two quantitative studies in this area, and still rarer (if any exist at all) is the therapist whose practice has changed as a result. A common and probably justified response to quantitative research is, "Does this finding agree with clinical knowledge?"

In part, the attitude of the profession seems to be modeled on two statements by Freud—one widely known and the other relatively obscure.

The first was addressed to Saul Rosenzweig in the early thirties. Asked to comment on Rosenzweig's analogue study of repression, Freud replied, "I have examined your experimental studies for the verification of the psychoanalytic assertions with interest. I cannot put much value on these confirmations because the wealth of reliable observations on which these assertions rest make them independent of experimental verification. Still, it can do no harm" (quoted in MacKinnon and Dukes, 1962). In effect, Freud was saying that his method yielded sufficiently

[1] This investigation was supported by Public Health Service, National Institute of Mental Health Grants MH-15442 and Research Scientist Award MH-40710 (to Dr. Luborsky); and MH-13615 and Research Scientist Award MH-14120 (to Dr. Spence). The senior author profited from discussions with his comembers of the Analytic Research Group of the Institute of the Pennsylvania Hospital. We wish to thank Drs. Merton M. Gill, Arthur H. Auerbach, and Robert R. Holt, who read and offered valuable suggestions on the content of the manuscript; and Freda Greene and Suzette Annin, who assisted in the preparation of the manuscript, and to whom we owe a special debt of thanks.

reliable observations to fit the definition of science.

The second statement comes from a somewhat earlier period, 1917, and indicates a more positive view of research. "Even if psychoanalysis should show itself as unsuccessful with other forms of nervous and mental diseases, it would still remain justified as an instrument of scientific research" (quoted in Eissler, 1965). Freud amplified this position in 1923, indicating that among the three main uses of psychoanalysis was the collection of psychological information leading to a new scientific discipline.

Taken together, these two statements support the position that research is justified *so long as it remains within the treatment setting.* By extension, then, any analogue—any attempt to *simulate* treatment conditions, or to single out one variable at the expense of others—is misleading and suspect. These conditions are not only restrictive, but circular. There is no agreed-upon unit, scale, or set of variables with which we can analyze the wide range of clinical phenomena we are continually confronting. Nor are there any specimen sets of clinical interviews as agreed-upon objects of study that can be investigated by all workers. But attempts to quantify and systematize necessarily segment the complex clinical situation and usually unduly simplify it. Thus there is no way out. Attempts to understand treatment are discouraged by its very richness.

It goes without saying that this position polarizes the situation prematurely. Some systematic observations are possible within the treatment setting without interference in its clinical purpose. (The battle for tape-recording analytic sessions without doing therapeutic harm is almost won at this writing.) Our review takes as its domain the attempts at quantitative research that rest on at least two articles of faith: (1) respect for the clinical theory of psychoanalysis and for the conditions of psychoanalytic treatment; and (2) an appreciation of the twin needs of science: to reduce diversity to simplicity and to state observations in objective language (see Rapoport, 1968). In this chapter, *we will use the word "quantitative" as a general term to refer to any use of controlled observation beyond the usual form of clinical observation.*

OBSTACLES TO QUANTITATIVE RESEARCH

What was essentially a restrictive attitude toward research would never have survived without the brilliant successes of early clinical research, which made the rejection of any need for controlled studies seem self-evident, as too obvious to need defense. In the clinical tradition, the model has been the naturalist who perches himself in a position to observe, refraining from intentional manipulation while trying to take into account his own impact on the observed scene. The research clinician tries to be a sensitive observer attuned to listening to his patients' free associations. He tries to combine three functions simultaneously: therapist, recorder of data, and investigator. After such a fruitful clinical research tradition, it is hard to convince clinicians of the value of adding certain controls to their approach. They might well respond: "Were not the contributions of our field made without these innovations?" We share this feeling, yet we believe the two approaches need not be antagonistic; they can, in fact, be confluent. (The compatibility of the two approaches has been advocated by the Committee on Therapy of the Group for Advancement of Psychiatry [GAP] [1970] in their recent report, "Psychotherapy and the Dual Research Tradition.")

Quantification has been inimical to psychoanalytic research since quite early in Freud's career. Holt (1962) has pointed out that even in the limited sense of the use of numbers of cases, there was an abrupt halt in such quantification when Freud broke off with his former friend and mentor, Wilhelm Fliess—who was inclined toward numerology. When Fliess went out, so did any reliance upon numbers.

The traditional form of training of psychoanalysts is also responsible for the cleavage. Psychoanalytic training is entirely clinical—clinical practice and occasionally clinical research. This is in contrast to such a field as client-centered psychotherapy, whose practitioners are trained in research as well as in practice, although their clinical training is less intensive than that given analysts. Research means to them quantitative research, since most are Ph.D. candidates at the time of their dual training. With a few exceptions, psychoanalysis has traditionally been separate from academic settings. The nonacademic settings usually make sophisticated quantitative research more difficult.

The length of psychoanalytic treatment is another obstacle to quantitative research. With psychoanalytic treatment usually lasting three to five years, planning an outcome study is a major life commitment on the part of the researcher. In these circumstances, sophisticated outcome research in which complex clinical evaluations are required from the therapist is extremely difficult, as well as time consuming (for example, the Menninger Foundation Psychotherapy Research Project [Wallerstein et al., 1956] has been in progress 16 years).

THE FOCUS OF THE REVIEW

The present chapter describes studies that are developing or applying the tools from which discoveries are coming. Little of what is usually considered to be clinical wisdom is included here, not because it is not significant, but because we will concentrate on methods now being developed that attempt to provide a more controlled and supported body of knowledge.

The focus of our review will be upon research on psychoanalytic treatment itself, not upon psychoanalytically oriented *psychotherapy*. Even though psychoanalytically oriented psychotherapy is probably the most commonly practiced form of psychotherapy in the United States (and may deserve a review in its own right), it includes a much wider range of techniques than does psychoanalytic treatment. Psychoanalytic treatment is a relatively clearly defined—if not widely practiced—treatment modality. It usually means an intensive treatment—three to five years of four or five sessions a week, in which the patient reclines and tries to say whatever comes to mind (*free association*), while the analyst responds interpretively with particular emphasis on the concepts of transference and defense.

No one has felt impelled to survey this tiny sidestream *in toto*. Schlessinger et al. (1966) have dealt with psychoanalytic contributions to psychotherapy research, but most of these are nonquantitative—of the 29 references, only two report quantitative studies (Alexander, French, & Pollock, 1968; Knapp, 1963). A survey by Hilgard (1952) of experimental approaches to psychoanalysis describes several that are pertinent to psychoanalytic treatment, most notable the series by Keet (1948) (see the Psychoanalytic Treatment Analogues section of this chapter), but none deal directly with psychoanalytic treatment. The best recent general review of psychoanalytic research on psychoanalytic treatment is by Strupp (1968). However, his focus is on technical developments that have occurred in the last few decades; he deals in large part with clinical research, rather than with quantitative psychoanalytic research. During the past 15 years, the articles appearing in the *Journal of the American Psychoanalytic Association* have become more diversified in their research style—no longer are all of them purely clinical research. Of all the psychological journals, *Psychological Issues* has had by far the best balance of clinical and quantitative psychoanalytic contributions. A popular topic among those interested in psychoanalytic research has been the broad issue of the *problems* of conducting research in psychoanalysis (sometimes listed under problems in clinical research or in personality research). These papers, written by outstanding theoreticians and researchers (including Freud), occasionally contain some references to quantitative studies of psychoanalytic treatment (such as Benjamin, 1950; Brenman et al., 1947; Engel, 1968; Escalona, 1952; Frenkel-Brunswik, 1954; Freud, 1913; Glover, 1952, 1955; Hartmann, 1958, 1959; Hartmann et al., 1953; G. Klein, 1949; Kris, 1947; Kubie, 1952; Lustman, 1963; Pfeffer, 1961; Pumpian-Mindlin, 1952; Ramzy, 1963; Rapaport, 1959; Rapoport, 1968; Shakow, 1960; Waelder, 1962; Wallerstein, 1966).

The studies to be reviewed are scattered in the literature, and we cannot claim to have achieved our aim of an exhaustive review; some articles may have been missed because of the contexts in which they have appeared, or because the psychoanalytic inspiration is not explicitly acknowledged.

Our review is organized around the main questions asked about psychoanalytic treatment. These turn out to be similar to those asked about any form of psychotherapy: (1) the kinds of patients who are most suited to it; (2) the kinds of therapists who are most suited to perform it; (3) the types of changes (outcomes) that are accomplished by it; and (4) the nature of the process the patient and therapist go through during it. We will also inspect the obstacles to further growth of quantitative psychoanalytic concepts and the movement from "protoscience" to mature science. Finally, we will offer some conclusions about the main implications of this literature for psychoanalytic practice.

RESEARCH ON QUALITIES OF MOST SUITABLE PATIENTS FOR PSYCHOANALYSIS

A large research literature concerns the type of patient who is most suitable for psychoanalytic treatment. It largely supports the common working assumption that patients for psychoanalysis should be in the neurotic range. They should start with symptoms that cause them considerable suffering, but should have considerable psychological-mindedness and capacity for insight.

In general, the analytic patient ought to have more assets than the patient for other forms of psychotherapy. This conclusion has been verified in a general way by a study done in 1952 of all patients in psychotherapy in the Department of Adult Psychiatry of the Menninger Foundation (Luborsky, 1962a). Obvious differences were found in the initial states of patients who were receiving different forms of psychotherapy. On the 100-point "Health–Sickness Rating Scale" (see Luborsky, 1962a), the patients receiving psychoanalysis began significantly higher (51.4) than the patients receiving expressive psychotherapy (38.2) or supportive psychotherapy (36.7). (These treatment modalities have been briefly defined by Wallerstein et al., 1956). The differences between these scores merely confirm that patients are, in fact, referred for treatment differentially on the basis of their degree of health or sickness, among other considerations. Findings are reported by Aronson and Weintraub (1968b) and Weintraub and Aronson (1968) on the social background

and vital statistics of patients who go into analysis.

Only four quantitative studies have been made of psychoanalytic patients in which an aspect of the patient's initial state was related to the outcome of the treatment. Three of these four dealt with small groups of patients. These are: H. Klein (1960; 30 patients); Knapp et al. (1960; 27 patients); the Menninger study (Wallerstein et al., 1956; 20 patients in psychoanalytic treatment and 20 in psychoanalytically-oriented psychotherapies). The fourth—a large mail survey (Hamburg et al., 1967)—covered approximately 3000 patients on whom therapists filled out initial and final questionnaires.

Findings from these four studies are similar to those of approximately 150 studies relating initial factors to outcome of treatment by any form of psychotherapy (see the review of Luborsky et al., 1970). In the psychotherapy studies, patients with the best initial personality functioning tended to show the best results from treatment in 13 studies; in 13 other studies, the relationship did not reach significance. None of the studies showed a significant negative relationship between initial level and treatment outcome. It is hard to discern why the relationship reached significance in some studies and not in others. In some cases (such as H. Klein, 1960), the range of dysfunction is relatively small (they were all analytic patients), which would limit the possibility of a significant relationship. Yet other samples (like Knapp et al., 1960) also included analytic patients, but showed a significant relationship. In the large survey (Hamburg et al., 1967), the patients were much more diverse; those with the poorest general personality functioning tended to do most poorly in treatment. Of those patients who were initially diagnosed as "schizophrenic," fewer were judged to be improved at the end of those treatments judged by the analyst to have been completed.

In the Hamburg et al. study, the patients who were initially diagnosed as anxious improved more than the patients without initial anxiety. This is consistent with the Menninger Study finding (Luborsky, 1962a) that patients with higher initial anxiety made more gains in treatment, a finding that applied to those patients who started treatment above 50 on the Health–Sickness Rating Scale—which is almost the same as saying that the finding pertained to *the patients who were in psychoanalytic treatment.* Knapp et al. (1960) found, however, that obsessional patients did better (p < .02) than other diagnostic groups. Hysterics did very well, or very badly, depending on the experience level of the therapist.

Hamburg et al. found that younger patients did better than older patients, and that the 46-and-older age group had a lower improvement rate than expected by chance. Knapp et al. also found that younger patients did better, even though the age range was only 20–40.

In the psychotherapy research studies (Luborsky et al., 1970) higher educational level was a good prognostic sign. Hamburg et al. (1967) found the same, but Knapp et al. (1960) found no relationship—possibly because the educational level of the whole sample was high.

In the psychotherapy research (Luborsky et al., 1970), similarity between patient and psychotherapist (such as on values or social class) tended to be prognostically favorable. That may be the meaning of the finding of Hamburg et al. (1967) that patients in the professional ranks or patients who are psychiatrists or analytic candidates are more likely to complete psychoanalytic treatment than the general population. (There are, of course, some obvious other factors that contribute to the completion behavior of candidates.)

Hamburg et al. (1967) and H. Klein (1960) found no relationship between having had previous treatment and the outcome of the present treatment. Hamburg et al. (1967) and Knapp et al. (1960) did not find that the patient's sex made any difference in the outcome of treatment.[2]

A very promising prognostic scale might be mentioned here, although it was developed as part of a study of short-term treatment (Gottschalk et al., 1967). It was based upon a prediction derived from psychoanalytic theory that patients with initially better "object relationships" should fare better in psychoanalysis. It requires a simple but sophisticated procedure: the patient talks freely for five minutes about a dramatic experience he has been through; scoring is based on a list of variables revealed by the description of the patient's relationships with people. The test of the scale in short-term treatment emerged with positive results; it has not yet been tried with psychoanalytic patients.

Isaacs and Haggard (1966) offer the similar concept of *relatability*, which in client-centered as well as psychoanalytically oriented settings proved to be a way to predict improvement. Relatability refers to a hierarchy of levels in a person's potential capacity for object relations. Relatability is determined from a measure of the object relations depicted in the patient's TAT. So far, however, it has not been used to predict the patient's future course in psychoanalytic treatment itself, but only in psychoanalytically oriented psychotherapy and client-centered psychotherapy.

Conclusion 1. Some quantitative research has been conducted on the relation of the initial qualities of the patient to the outcome of the treatment. If we take significant results in at least two studies as a basic requirement, we emerge with four positive initial qualities: (*a*) better general personality functioning (or

---

[2] Another questionnaire study (Aronson and Weintraub, 1968a) has been made of 127 patients seen in classical analysis by 28 analysts, but the information represents patients at any point in analysis, rather than at the beginning and end of analysis. Findings were: (*a*) the initial diagnostic state showed no significant relationship to gains from the treatment, although there was a nonsignificant tendency for the borderline patients, more often than patients with other diagnostic classifications, to become worse with analysis; (*b*) a steady increase in improvement occurred the longer the patients remained in analysis. (Luborsky et al., 1970, report the same finding for psychotherapy in 20 studies.) They checked the possibility that this increase in improvement with duration of therapy might be due to the quitting of patients who do not improve. When the data were divided into patients who remained in analysis up to and including completion versus an "attrition" group of patients who ended their treatment short of completion, it was found that those in the attrition group were not usually early dropouts who had not improved; in fact, the patients who stopped treatment before completion showed greater symptomatic improvement than other patients of the same treatment duration.

absence of severe psychopathology such as schizophrenia); (*b*) younger age; (*c*) stronger anxiety; and (*d*) higher educational level. Strong anxiety is an especially positive predictor in patients with good general personality functioning; that is, patients with intact egos.

Conclusion 2. These positive findings are similar to those based upon other forms of psychotherapy (as established in the studies reviewed by Luborsky et al., 1970).

RESEARCH ON DESIRABLE QUALITIES FOR PSYCHOANALYTIC THERAPISTS

More is demanded of psychoanalysts than of therapists who perform other types of psychotherapy, according to a survey of the clinical lore (see Holt and Luborsky, 1958, Vol. 2, Table 15.2). Opinions were elicited by interview from 55 training analysts. Although the list of qualities mentioned was long—approximately 90—there was much agreement about the more important ones. A number of other sources were also included in the survey: published references on requisites for psychiatry, psychoanalysis, psychotherapy, and clinical psychology (p. 369, Vol. 2), and another collection of expert opinion (Ellis, 1955a, 1955b). A summary was provided (Holt & Luborsky, 1958, Vol. 2, p. 392 ff.) on the agreement among various sources of *opinion* about personality requisites for psychiatric residents, psychiatrists, psychotherapists, and psychoanalysts; and, in the same table, of *research findings* about psychiatric residents. One way to extract the essence of a very long list in the table is to single out those qualities that are, in the opinions of the experts, requisite for psychoanalysis, *and* are also shown to be valuable in the research findings on psychiatric residents. *By this dual criterion, the following requisites emerge: intelligence; empathy; verbal facility; objectivity; capacity for growth; flexibility; self-objectivity; interest in psychiatry; and self-confidence and security.* One general conclusion from this huge survey is, as we have said, that more is demanded of the psychoanalyst than of other therapists. Nevertheless, the degree of overlap between the requisites for different types of therapists (psychiatric residents, psychiatrists, psychotherapists, and psychoanalysts) is impressive.

Quantitative research on qualities of psychoanalysts is, however, almost nonexistent, nor is there very much about the qualities of other kinds of psychotherapists. Relatively less is known about requisite qualities of therapists than about requisite qualities of patients (Luborsky, et al., 1970). The only qualities of the therapist on which quantitative research studies agree are the experience level of the therapist and certain major similarities between therapist and patient (for example, in values and orientation to people).

Available quantitative research tends to focus on psychiatric residents in training or psychoanalytic candidates in training—not finished practitioners. It has been found that supervisors' judgments of "competence as a therapist" correlate highly with their judgments of "competence as a future analyst" (Holt and Luborsky, 1958). The same correlation appears in the judgments of psychiatric residents by their peers—residents who are considered "good psychotherapists" are also considered to be "good potential psychoanalysts." Psychoanalysts who were retrospectively described as having superior skills as analysts (by their analysts) were considered to have been healthier to begin with, to have changed more in the course of their analysis, and to have had a more successful analysis.

H. Klein (1965, p. 82 ff.) has made the only study in which estimates of a psychoanalyst's competence by his supervisors were related to the success of his treatment of actual patients. She reports that for three groups of psychoanalysts in training—judged by supervisors as "superior," "above average," or "below average"—differences were found on a global score for therapeutic change in their patients; 63 percent of the patients treated by students of superior skills showed substantial improvement, but only 39 percent of the patients treated by below-average students showed comparable improvement. The limitation here is that the supervisor's estimate of the patient's improvement is necessarily colored by his view of the student analyst's ability. However, an independently applied scale estimating dependency was applied to the content of the patient's record at the beginning and end of treatment: for 40 percent of the superior "students" (psychoanalysts-in-training), more than one-half of their patients improved on the dependency scale, while for only 20 percent of the "below-average" students was there comparable improvement in their patients.

Conclusion 1. Almost no quantitative studies have been made of the personality qualities of the analyst.

Conclusion 2. What little research of this type exists concerns supervisors' opinions of analytic candidates. These results indicate considerable similarity between the qualities that are requisite for analysts and those that are requisite for psychotherapists of a psychoanalytically oriented, insight-giving type. The implication is that "healthier" analysts (in the sense of objectivity, self-confidence, and the like) will be of more help to their patients.

Conclusion 3. One study (H. Klein, 1965) does imply that the supervisor's estimate of skill of the student psychoanalyst is related to the benefits derived by the patient.

RESEARCH ON THE OUTCOME OF PSYCHOANALYTIC TREATMENT

Most of the studies fall into one of two main groups: simple studies in which the critical conditions are unspecified, and complex studies with more explicit conditions.

1. The simple outcome studies are a large, familiar group that have been with us for a long time. They typically report that a relatively unspecified kind of treatment has produced such-and-such a percentage of cures, another percentage of partially improved patients, and another percentage of patients who are unchanged or got worse.

The Berlin Psychoanalytic Institute outcome data of 1920–1930 are probably the earliest of such reports (Fenichel, 1930). A host of other such outcome reports have appeared, such as Alexander (1937); Duhrssen and Jorswieck (1965); Glover et al. (1937); Graham (1958,

1960); Knight (1941); Lorand and Console (1958); Nunberg (1954); Oberndorf (1950, 1953); and Schjelderup (1955). One of the latest is an analysis of clinical cases over 11 years at the Clinic of the Southern California Psychoanalytic Institute (Feldman, 1968). Ninety-nine patients were accepted during that period. According to a simple improvement scale rated by the therapist, about two-thirds of the patients treated by psychoanalysis seemed to improve. This figure is unsurprisingly similar to the results of other studies of treatment by psychoanalysis or any other form of psychotherapy. *Two-thirds* has long been thought to be the magical improvement figure, although the range is wider than has been assumed.

The best-known summary of this type of outcome study is by Eysenck (1952, 1961). His main conclusion, which is easy to miss (and most readers do miss it), is that *there is no good evidence* that any type of psychotherapy—psychoanalysis or any such form of treatment—does any good. The emphasis in the written conclusion to the 1952 paper is that *there is no good evidence*. What most readers conclude, however, is that he shows that psychotherapy does no good. Not much light and a lot of heat have come from Eysenck's review. Those who are inclined to feel that treatment does no good quote it without qualifying it; those who feel treatment does good tend to quote the rebuttals that clearly show major defects in Eysenck's summarization of data (Duhrssen and Jorswieck, 1962, 1965; Luborsky, 1954; Rosenzweig, 1954; Strupp, 1963).

2. As already noted, several complex outcome studies exist (Hamburg et al., 1967; H. Klein, 1960; Knapp et al., 1960; the Menninger Study by Wallerstein et al., 1956). These deal mainly with types of change that presumably occur as a result of psychoanalytic treatment. They do not report percentages of "cure," because such data are difficult to interpret in the absence of reasonable comparison groups.

The Menninger Foundation Psychotherapy Research Study is undoubtedly the most intensive study to date of the changes that occur during long-term psychotherapy and psychoanalysis. Psychological tests and interviews were done at three points in time: initially, at termination, and two years after treatment was completed. At each of those times not only was the *patient* studied, but near-relatives and occasionally the patient's employer were interviewed. Not only was the therapist interviewed, but also the therapist's supervisor, if one was available. Since long-term treatment was under scrutiny, the study, which began in 1954, is only just now nearing completion (as of early 1970).

The report by Hamburg et al. (1967) is certainly the most ambitious *survey* study of psychoanalysis. The final report contains results on 3019 patients on whom the treating therapist reported initially and at termination. As mentioned earlier, this study contains interesting results on the sample characteristics, and information about the relationship of the patient's initial state to whether he completed treatment (see above, *Research on Qualities of Most Suitable Patients for Psychoanalysis*). Very little in the final report, however, deals with the nature of the changes that occurred in psychoanalysis, because of uncertainty about the adequacy of the questionnaire method.

3. Comparative studies of the outcome of psychoanalysis versus other psychotherapies would be very desirable, but at present hardly any reasonably controlled ones exist. Eysenck (1952, 1961) tried to make some comparison of treatment results by combining the percentages of many outcome studies, but his figures were derived from the simple or unspecified type of outcome studies. Eysenck offered this result: psychoanalytically treated patients improved to the extent of 44 percent; eclectically treated, 64 percent; and those treated only custodially or by general practitioners, 72 percent. Since only *outcome* percentages—and nothing about initial level—are given, conclusions are hard to draw. The outcome figures may have much to do with the level of the patient's expectation from treatment or different standards and criteria of improvement, or they may have to do with the obvious differences in the initial state of the patients who received the different forms of treatment. As we noted earlier, patients who have received different forms of treatment tend to have started out with very different levels of mental health versus sickness.

Cartwright (1966) has contributed the only reasonably controlled comparative study in the entire literature, comparing psychoanalysis and client-centered therapy for the kinds of changes that take place.[3] She used two pairs of matched patients—two compulsive males and two anxious-hysteric females (a very small sample, needless to say)—and four therapists, two of them client-centered and two psychoanalysts. One male and one female patient received psychoanalytic therapy, and one male and one female patient received client-centered therapy. The segment of the treatment used was 40 sessions (very short, for psychoanalytic treatment). Measures used were the Rogers and Rablen process scale (scored for the patient), the R. D. Cartwright self-observation scale, and the Bales interaction process scale (both scored for the patient and the therapist). Cartwright found that the degree of experiencing and level of self-observation reached by matched patients were independent of professed style of therapy (that is, they were similar in the two types of treatment). There are, of course, limits to this study, possibly severe ones. The number of sessions was hardly adequate. The sample of patients was small, and the matching was done on the basis of "number of therapeutic contacts." For example, one patient seen on a 5-times-a-week basis for an 8-week period was compared with a patient seen on a 2-times-a-week basis for a 20-week period. Finally, the measures used refer more particularly to client-centered treatment than they do to psychoanalysis. Still, the results point to a degree of similarity in types of change.

It would be interesting to see what similarities would appear if measures that are supposed to be unique to psychoanalysis were applied to both the client-centered and psychoanalytic treatment samples. Some dimensions of change are crucial for psychoanalysis in terms of the emphasis of its theory of change, and therefore ought to receive a great deal of attention in outcome studies of psychoanalysis or in comparative studies. These are (according to Luborsky and Schimek, 1964): (*a*) anxiety level and anxiety tolerance; (*b*) insight; (*c*) transference resolution;

---

[3] One more limited study exists (Shlien et al., 1960) that compares the effects of time limits on client-centered versus Adlerian psychotherapy.

(*d*) regression in the service of the ego; and (*e*) neutralization of thinking.

Conclusion 1. Simple, unspecified outcome studies of psychoanalysis have been of no help, even toward their main aim of showing the efficacy of the treatment.

Conclusion 2. As compared with the simple outcome studies, the better-specified ones have more to say about the nature of the treatment and what changes occur in the course of psychoanalysis. Patients are found to increase their level of experiencing and self-observation (Cartwright, 1966). We must still *assume* that psychoanalysis is especially beneficial in achieving its stated aim of characterological change, in addition to a lessening of symptoms. Much more needs to be done to see whether, in fact, resolution of the transference occurs in successful treatment.

Conclusion 3. Controlled comparisons of psychoanalytic with other forms of treatment do not exist, except for Cartwright's (1966) comparison of psychoanalytic and client-centered treatment. The implication of this conclusion is obvious: it is impossible to say that one type of psychotherapy is better than another, or even that one type produces changes different from those produced by another type. The review by Luborsky et al. (1970) of *all* comparative studies of psychotherapies shows that there are relatively few comparative studies, and not enough of any one type of comparison to clearly establish one form as superior to another. As Parloff (1968) says: "Unfortunately, objective standards and techniques for assessing the outcome of any form of therapy— group or individual—are not yet available. Like beauty, therapeutic effectiveness is in the eye of the beholder. No form of psychotherapy has ever been initiated without a claim that it has unique therapeutic advantages, and no form of psychotherapy has ever been abandoned because of its failure to live up to these claims." Engel (1968) makes the same point: "No one has yet devised a scientifically valid means of testing the results of any form of psychotherapy" (p. 203). Actually, some guidelines are available, formulated by a committee of a clinical section of the

National Institute of Mental Health (Fiske et al., 1970); for example, necessity for multiple criteria, control over case assignments to each therapist, and establishment of the expectation level of the patient and therapist at the initiation of the treatment.

RESEARCH ON THE PROCESS OF PSYCHOANALYTIC TREATMENT

Concepts Dealing with Patient's Adequacy of Productions during Psychoanalysis

Meaningfulness. Isaacs and Haggard (1966) have carried out a series of studies on the meaningfulness of the patient's statements, and have shown that psychologists, psychoanalysts, and social workers can substantially agree on meaningfulness. Furthermore, when 20 therapist-judges were asked independently to rate each of 50 patient-statements for 9 characteristics, and a factor analysis of their ratings was performed, the following three factors were mainly correlated with meaningfulness: (*a*) the extent of the patient's concern with himself and his problems; (*b*) the patient's concern with his ability to relate to others; and (*c*) his current motivational state. In further studies, the authors explored the relationship of meaningfulness of patients' statements to interventions by the therapist. They concluded that patients were more likely to give meaningful material when the therapist's intervention contained affective words—that is, when the therapist deals with affective material, the patient follows suit. These results hold, whatever the therapist's therapeutic orientation. They suggest that when the therapist, regardless of his orientation, responds to the patient's affect, he is likely to elicit a more meaningful response containing affective verbalization, fewer and longer responses, and a greater number of spontaneous returns to the content of his intervention after a time interval.

Productivity of the Patient During the Sessions. Justin Simon (Brookdale Hospital) has been working with the concept of analytic productivity. This is one of a number of concepts that have been explored by means of tape recordings of a psychoanalytic patient. Clinicians were asked to judge which of a number of sessions were ones in which the patient was most productive. At that stage the clinicians were using whatever standards they would use ordinarily in judging patients' productivity. From these judgments was developed the Patient Productivity Rating Scale (PPRS), consisting of five main levels of analytic productivity. For example, minimal productivity was characterized by a fair amount of silence, an absence of reflectiveness, an absence of psychological-mindedness, and few, if any connecting links between different segments of material. In samples of high productivity, the patient attempted to link past and present, attempted to understand painful material, and maintained the dual position of reporting associations while observing himself associate. Simon and his group have carried out four studies using this scale; intrajudge reliabilities have ranged in significance from $P < .01$ to $P < .001$, which suggests that the rating scale can be consistently applied to short (3–6 min.) therapy segments.

In a further study, Spence (1969b) took 15 segments that had been clinically rated and submitted them to a computer-based analysis of variables including type-token ratio, ratio of long words to total words, ratio of qualifiers to total words, and ratio of reflectors to total words. Qualifiers included such words as "but," "perhaps," "probably," and the like; reflectors included such words as "because," "as," "if," "make sense," and the like. The best predictor, by a wide margin, proved to be reflectors/total words—it correlated .80 with the ratings of the judges ($P < .001$). In a further step, Spence selected 12 additional samples, rated them on the reflector ratio, and had them rated by two sets of judges. On the new sample, the correlations between reflector ratio and clinical rating (using the PPRS) were .59 in one set of judges ($P < .05$) and .71 in the other set ($P < .01$). These new values are encouragingly high, and point to a further refinement of the predictors that is now under way. Whether the same predictor will work with another patient remains to be seen; at the least, the reflectors *seem* to overlap with the dimensions of meaningfulness (see above) and experiencing (see below).

Experiencing. This variable describes a quality of the patient's verbal behavior in the course of treatment; more work has probably been devoted to it than to any other process variable. Experiencing has been shown by Rogers and others to predict the outcome of treatment, even when based upon only a 4-minute segment of the patient's speech (Kirtner et al., 1961; Rogers, 1959; Tomlinson, 1967; Tomlinson and Hart, 1962; Walker, Rablen, and Rogers, 1966). It is being tried by Marjorie Klein on some of the data of the original Gill project (see p.427, Brookdale Hospital Group). It can be rated reliably (Gendlin et al., 1968), although occasionally the reliabilities are only moderate; for example, in Auerbach and Luborsky (1968, the only study in which an entire session was used as the basis for rating "experiencing") the agreement between judges was .42, significant at the .01 level but low in terms of one's hopes for a reliability measure.

What is meant by *experiencing?* It seems to mean the patient's capacity to feel deeply and immediately, and to be aware of and reflective about this feeling. The patient would get a low score if he were remote from his feelings and unable to understand their implicit meanings. Defined this way, the concept begins to sound very similar to one frequently described in the psychoanalytic literature as essential for good patient performance in psychoanalytic treatment; that is, "the split in the ego," in which the patient's attention is alternately involved in his experience and reporting his experience, and in reflection on it.

Meaningfulness, productivity, experiencing (and also the quality to be described next, associative freedom) sound as if they have much in common. If they were all scored on the same sessions, very high correlations would probably be found among them. Very little information exists about the relationship among process variables. The only such study in which experiencing is included and in which entire sessions have been judged is that by Mintz, Luborsky, and Auerbach (1970). In that study of 60 sessions, 110 variables were rated, a high percentage of which were therapist variables. Factor analysis yielded four main variables, one of which—the intensive-interpretive mode factor—included the three intercorrelated variables of experiencing, receptiveness, and empathy for therapist. Apparently, experiencing is achieved in the context of the therapist's use of interpretation. One way of viewing the concomitance of experiencing and interpretation is to think of patient and therapist as being more reflective and interpretive at the same time. It is hard to know what, if any, cause-and-effect relationship is involved—whether a high level of experiencing, receptivity, and empathy for the therapist in the patient encourages the therapist to be more interpretive, or conversely, whether more interpretiveness in the therapist leads the patient to become more receptive and experiencing.

Associative Freedom. Free association—the freedom of flow of the patient's associations and his ability both to know and to say fairly freely the thoughts he is thinking—is the most common mental set suggested to patients in psychoanalysis at the beginning of treatment. The ability of patients to follow this instruction must vary widely. Some analysts believe that a patient cannot genuinely free-associate until the treatment nears its end. One would assume that the ability of the patient to free-associate could be assessed by clinical judges. This does not happen to be known and would, in itself, make an interesting study. It has not been demonstrated to what extent the mental set of free association can be taught, and to what extent it changes from the beginning to the end of treatment.

Even though free association has a central place in psychoanalytic treatment, psychotherapy researchers and personality researchers of all kinds have largely neglected it as a medium of and object of research (Janis, 1958), although a few beginnings at quantitative investigation have recently been made. Colby (1960) systematically varied some external conditions that might influence the content and quality of free associations. He found, for example, that when a (male) observer was present, as compared to a condition in which subjects talked to a tape recorder, the number of personyms (references to people) increased, and the drift was toward male personyms. He also found that "causal correlatives inputs" (that is, interpretations) resulted in significantly greater amounts of free association and a greater percentage of references to relevant people and topics (Colby,

1961). Strupp (1968) and Bordin (1966) have also investigated some factors that influence free association, and Bellak (in Spence, 1967) has developed an impressive conceptual model.

Associative freedom might also be related to other aspects of free association conceived of as a state of consciousness. A large literature has grown up over the years on free association as a state of consciousness, compared with dreaming, hypnosis, reverie, and other states. Some of this material is summarized in Gill and Brenman (1959).

Several steps might be taken to further the study of associative freedom: (1) the rating by clinicians of associative freedom in a sample of sessions, and examination of the sessions to determine the kinds of qualities that seem to go along with the clinical judgment; (2) a comparison of qualities of free-association sessions at the beginning and end of psychoanalytic treatment; (3) an intercorrelation, in a multivariate analysis, of associative freedom with such other concepts as experiencing and productivity; and (4) a rating of dimensions of states of consciousness in a sample of psychoanalytic sessions to see how these dimensions correspond to clinical judgments of associative freedom.

Conclusion. Quantitative studies have been made of four main concepts that conceptualize the patient's adequacy of production during psychoanalytic treatment: meaningfulness, productivity, experiencing, and associative freedom. Of these, productivity and meaningfulness have figured in most of the quantitative research. Productivity has been explored by means of computer systems. One of its core aspects, "reflective statements," suggests that it has much in common with experiencing. There is much need now for a multivariate study in which the same data are judged according to each of the four concepts, to determine the extent of overlap.

Therapeutic Techniques

Variety Versus Uniformity in Therapeutic Techniques. Even though the underlying therapeutic technique of psychoanalytic treatment is clearly stated (for example, Bibring, 1954), there is undoubtedly much variety in the ways the "basic rules" are applied by different analysts. To many analysts, the technique appeared to be so well specified that it came as something of a surprise to find that techniques differed and that the content they chose to focus upon differed, even when they were discussing the same patients and had available the same data about the patients (see Anna Freud's [1954] description of her experience with the old Vienna Seminar.) Considerable variations in technique exist from analyst to analyst, even though psychoanalysis is probably a more uniform mode than other psychotherapies. Glover was apparently the first to investigate the problem systematically; in 1940 he sent out questionnaires to the members of the British Psychoanalytic Association. The questionnaires (reported in Glover, 1955) revealed marked differences in technique. The differences, of course, were revealed by analysts' written responses to a questionnaire; much less is known about what was actually done. When the question is one of subscribing to views about preferred treatment techniques, agreement is probably higher than it would be if actual sessions were examined and classified in terms of technique, but the latter study has not been done. A well-known set of studies by Fiedler (1950a, 1950b, 1951) *implies* that experienced therapists, regardless of the kind of psychotherapy they perform, are in considerable agreement about ideal therapeutic relationships, and are in more agreement than are beginners.

On the other hand, inexperienced therapists of any particular school probably adhere more than experienced therapists to what they consider to be the techniques of their school and, within any one school, they would be more similar to one another than would be experienced therapists. A few quantitative studies support this view (Fey, 1958; Strupp, 1955, 1960).

Conclusion. There is likely to be much variation in technique from analyst to analyst, and this variation probably increases with experience.

Accuracy of Interpretations and Empathy. According to many writers on the technique of psychoanalysis, the crucial technique is interpretation. The other techniques, listed (for example, by Bibring [1954]) as suggestive, abreactive, manipulative, and clarifying, are to

some extent preparation for interpretation. Bibring classifies a psychotherapeutic technique as "any purposive, more or less typified, verbal or nonverbal behavior on the part of the therapist, which intends to affect the patient in the direction of the (intermediary or final) goals of the treatment." Psychoanalysis is thought to be distinguished from other psychotherapies in the proportion of these techniques, especially in its emphasis upon interpretation. As Bibring says, "Insight through *interpretation* is the supreme agent in the hierarchy of therapeutic principles characteristic of analysis." Kubie (1952) places the same stress upon interpretation: "Analysis stands or falls by the validity of its specific interpretations in specific instances." Kubie discusses the validity of interpretations and the inherent difficulties of demonstrating the probable truth of an interpretation: "Sometimes it is possible to show that presenting the patient with the hypothesis which is called technically an 'interpretation' may produce profound psychological changes, from which, in turn, we can deduce fresh hypotheses. None of this, however, has that directness as evidence which science requires." Kubie would look for evidence of the accuracy of interpretations mainly in the patient's further free associations. In essence, he suggests that our only tests of an interpretation's validity come "(1) from the patient's associations to it, which may confirm, correct, or reject; (2) from alterations of symptoms; and finally but only rarely, (3) through our ability to predict future behavior." A philosopher has recently clarified the difficulty in judging the truth of interpretations (Farrell, 1964). He presents a sample from a session with a 16-year-old boy and then takes certain statements of the therapist, examines them for their truth or falsity, and considers the criteria for acceptance of their truth (1) whether the patient accepts the statement; (2) whether it fits with the rest of what he says; and (3) whether the implied meaning is the usual implied meaning for other patients. He concludes with an obvious but frequently overlooked point: that one reason why our search for criteria of the truth of an interpretation is so difficult and frustrating is that such interpretations are not primarily declarative or hypothesis-stating in character. Their chief function seems to be instrumental; that is, many of the therapist's statements are intended to get the patient to recognize and talk about his feelings and to make him more relaxed and outgoing.

In view of the centrality of interpretation to analytic technique, quantitative research on this topic would be welcome. Some studies have been done on depth of interpretation in psychotherapy (such as Speisman, 1959). So far, the only quantitative research done on analytic interpretation in psychoanalysis is by Paul et al. (in preparation). They deal with the obvious first question: Can accuracy of interpretation be recognized by independent judges? The answer is that it can, with a remarkable degree of agreement. Judges listened to tape recordings of short segments of the patient's production followed by statements by the analyst, and then rated the "goodness" of each interpretation. An unexpected puzzle came to light when it was found that agreement among judges on the goodness of an interpretation was virtually as great when the patient's prior statement was not included! Obviously, the judges were basing their judgments of "goodness" on what the analyst said, *not* on what the patient said. Apparently, there exists a conception of good interpretations, so that judges can agree upon them. This is not an isolated finding. Those who have worked on an allied concept, the therapist's empathy, turned up something that seems to be identical: judges' ratings of empathy in a therapist statement are also not influenced by what the patient has just said (Truax, 1966). He concludes that "the findings support the original hypothesis suggesting that there is no significant degree of contamination of the measurement of therapist behavior (on accurate empathy and nonpossessive warmth) by knowledge of the patient behavior." Thus, the puzzle remains.

The difference between the therapist's "capacity to make accurate interpretations" and his "empathy" may be merely one of language. Analysts tend to use the former term, but all therapists (including analysts) use the concept of empathy. It is the client-centered therapists who are best known for their research on empathy. Within the past 10 years there has been a proliferation of empathy scales, the best known of which is *accurate empathy* (Truax, 1961). This scale is reproduced in Rogers et al.

(1967). The similar but simpler and less specifically defined scale by Raskin (1965) has also been widely used. Another slight revision of the Truax Accurate Empathy scale is the Bergin-Solomon revision (Truax and Carkhuff, 1967, p. 59). The last three originate mainly in research on client-centered psychotherapy. Bachrach's (1965, 1968) scale entitled *conjunctive empathy* is more influenced by psychoanalytic thinking in the form of similarity to Schafer's (1959) concept of *generative empathy*, although it is also similar to Truax's concept of *accurate empathy*. Conjunctive empathy refers to "the therapist's ability to flexibly communicate his understanding of the patient's responses in ways which show appropriate timing, tact, and evocative language attuned to the patient's momentary psychological states, *such that* the patient will confirm the therapist's responses with meaningful elaboration . . ." These scales are essentially similar, and if all of them had been used on the same sample simultaneously, the chances are good that they would correlate highly. Such a study will soon appear (Mechanick and Luborsky, in preparation), but not in time for this review.

Most of these empathy scales show moderate reliability when applied to 4-minute segments (for example, for "accurate empathy" for three judges, .63 interclass; .36 average correlation; Rogers et al., 1967, p. 149). In applying the Raskin version of the empathy scale to entire psychotherapy sessions rather than to 4-minute segments, Auerbach and Luborsky (1968) found that agreement between two professional judges was only .51 (but still significant at less than the .01 level).

Empathy is a promising variable for predicting the outcome of psychotherapy, and has been so used in several studies. The Truax Accurate Empathy scale significantly predicted the outcome in two studies (Truax, 1963; Truax et al., 1966). However, a recent study by Bergin and Jasper (1969) did not achieve significant results.

The empathy measures listed above are all derived from ratings of a taped transcript of a session. Therapist's empathy might instead be rated by the patient as in the Barrett-Lennard inventory (1959); such measures of empathy correlate significantly with outcome in three out of four studies (Luborsky et al., 1970).

A number of researchers (e.g., Bachrach, 1968) have started to investigate the factors that seem to be associated with empathy. Bachrach achieved a surprisingly high correlation between adaptive regression (regression in the service of the ego as estimated from the Holt Primary Process Manual for the Rorschach, 1964) and empathy as scored by his own Conjunctive Empathy Scale, a finding that suggests that the therapists who are capable of adaptive regression are also the ones who are capable of empathy. Some evidence indicates that the therapist's personality, training, and experience, and qualities of the patient, all influence the level of the therapist's empathy (Truax and Carkhuff, 1967; Bergin and Solomon, 1969). Bergin and Jasper (1969) similarly found that therapists' depression and anxiety, as scored on the D and Pt scales of the MMPI, correlate negatively with their empathy in actual psychotherapy. This is clearly consistent with the common supposition that the more healthy and integrated the therapist, the greater his therapeutic effectiveness; specifically, the less his depression and anxiety, the more the therapist can accurately hear what the patient is saying.

A systematic series of experiments on psychological and psychophysiological correlates of empathy is being carried out by Spence and his group. These studies suggest that Freud's assumption that free-floating attention facilitates empathy fits the data; for example, mild distraction can facilitate the taking in of certain kinds of information.

In one study (Spence and Greif, 1970) *S*'s attention was monitored as they listened to a passage of *double-entendres*. Depending on whether *S* attended to the manifest or the latent content, parts of the passage (e.g. "and so they went back and forth") could be heard either as an argument or as a seduction. Hearing the passage in a sexual way (i.e., hearing latent content) was correlated with paying less attention to the passage and more attention to a secondary task. It seems that sensitivity to latent content was increased by "listening away"— not paying full attention to the stimulus material. In a second study (Spence and Lugo, 1970), *S*s listened to excerpts from a therapy protocol and attempted to predict when a stomach pain would be reported. (The patient

was the one described in Luborsky, 1953; see p.423, "Symptom Context Methods.") Two groups of *S*s, as they listened, were distracted by two types of pacing task. A third group was not distracted. *S*s in the slow/fast distraction condition made more correct predictions of the stomach symptom than *S*s in the no-distraction and *S*s in the fast/slow distraction condition. A certain degree and kind of distraction appears to facilitate clinical sensitivity.

Conclusion 1: The kinds of findings reported for empathy will probably eventually be shown for accuracy of interpretation. It is for this reason that so much space has been devoted to a review of the findings on empathy. For the same reason, empathy and accuracy of interpretation will be treated as one variable in our conclusions.

Conclusion 2: Judges can agree quite well on the accuracy of the therapist's interpretations, or his empathy.

Conclusion 3: Accurate interpretations or empathy probably will continue to be shown to be good predictors of the outcome of treatment.

Conclusion 4: Accurate interpretations or empathy are probably shown most by the therapists who are most "healthy" and least disturbed by anxiety or depression during the session.

Conclusion 5: The fact that judgments of the goodness of interpretation or empathy can be made without knowledge of the patient's statements implies that the concept itself needs further clarification.

Research on Transference

Quantitative research on the patient's transference response to the analyst is almost nonexistent, even though clinicians have placed transference at the core of what needs to change in effective psychoanalytic treatment. What little research exists is seriously qualified by its apparently tenuous relation to the technical concept. Three out of four such studies illustrate the difficulty.

1. Transference in group therapy was investigated by Chance (1952). Transference was defined in terms of the similarity between the patient's description of his "significant parent" and his description of his psychotherapist. It is known that a classical transference reaction may take place quite outside of awareness, and may not be tapped by the patient's description of his therapist. Positive results in this study would be informative, but negative findings would be inconclusive.

2. In some of Fiedler's experiments (such as Fiedler and Senior, 1952), transference was supposed to have been measured by a comparison of the patient's description of his ideal person and his prediction of his psychotherapist's self-description, with similar measures filled out by the therapist. The same criticism would apply: transference refers to much more than a descriptive profile.

3. In another quantitative study of transference (Apfelbaum, 1958), the patient was required to fill out a special Q sort, in terms of his expectations about the therapist he would have (although he had not yet met the therapist). In effect, the patient was asked to describe his fantasy. The Q sort was readministered at the end of treatment. The types of transference were found by an inverse cluster analysis of the pretherapy Q sorts. The patients were grouped according to the kinds of expectations described in their Q sorts. Three clusters were found: *Cluster A* (therapist will give *nurturance*) characteristically subscribed to such items as "the patient is likely to get advice and guidance"; *Cluster B* (therapist will be a *model*) subscribed to such items as "the therapist is well adjusted and gets along well with the world"; and *Cluster C* (therapist will be a *critic*) subscribed to such items as "therapist expects the individual to shoulder his own responsibilities." It is interesting that each of these "transference" expectations tended to be maintained to the end of treatment—there is a substantial test-retest reliability of the Q sort, despite psychotherapy as an intervening condition. *Cluster B* patients achieved a larger test-retest correlation than patients in the other two clusters. The fact that "transference" expectations about the therapist tended to remain constant indicates that some

stable attitude was being measured. Whether it was an aspect of transference remains to be seen.

A major problem in all three studies is that transference is reduced to a linguistic formula—a set of descriptors. Words are only the tip of the clinical iceberg. To refine the concept further, samples of each patient's therapy might be extracted to clinically determine the transference pattern and relate it to the three clusters. Unfortunately, none of these studies was concerned with psychoanalytic treatment—a further qualification.

4. The Menninger Foundation study of psychotherapy (Wallerstein et al., 1956) included an estimate of transference, made initially by two clinicians working together and at termination by several other clinicians working together. The estimate of transference was a discursive, free description. A large and detailed file of interviews and test reports was available at both points from which to make the estimates, but the manner of conceptualizing the transference was left up to the judges. These descriptions might be the beginning of some worthwhile attempts at classification. At this point they have not yet been subjected to careful scrutiny, nor have they been related to other aspects of the treatment.

Conclusion 1. Several potentially valuable quantitative research methods have been used with the aim of capturing behavior that might be labeled *transference*, but so far no quantitative studies have been related to clinical conceptions of transference, or vice versa. It is therefore difficult to know whether the clinical and quantitative measures are estimating the same thing.

Conclusion 2. Clinical conceptions of transference are much in need of classifications that will lend themselves to quantification and these, in turn, may be worth relating to the quantitative methods described.

Countertransference Attitudes

As classically defined, countertransference is a subtle source of interference in treatment (see for example, Greenson, 1967, p. 348). Several attempts have been made to study therapist countertransference systematically.

1. One of the most systematic attempts was part of the Menninger Foundation's Psychotherapy Project. At termination of treatment, the evaluation group tried to discern the degree to which the therapist's countertransference attitudes had interfered with the treatment (according to a schedule of questions described in Luborsky et al., 1958). The evaluation group found that it was difficult to discern countertransference, even from the large amount of information available; that is, after two posttreatment interviews with the therapist, after reading the therapist's process notes for the entire treatment, after interviewing the patient, and even after interviewing the supervisor of the treatment. The supervisor most often had some clues about countertransference, but only when it obtruded in a form detrimental to the treatment.

2. Alexander (unpublished research) introduced a useful methodological variation; he provided the therapist with a key that could be pressed the moment he wanted to record the time of a personal reaction to be described at the end of the session. By this means, he could prevent some reactions from being forgotten, but could do nothing about reactions that took place outside of awareness—the bulk of countertransference responses.

3. Paul Bergman, as a member of the NIMH Psychotherapy Research Project, recorded his introspections after therapeutic sessions. Some of these data are available in Bergman (1966); the remainder have yet to be processed. From the methods of Alexander and Bergman, a design could be worked out in which the therapist notes when, in a session, he has some introspections about his mental operations, including countertransference attitudes. If he is taking notes, he can record these introspections briefly. A danger is of distraction in the conduct of the treatment. A further drawback is that the actual countertransference reaction often needs to be pointed out by a third person.

4. When the *therapist's* view of the transaction in a psychotherapy session differs markedly from the view of the *patient* or of *outside observers*, one might find countertransference activity to be the responsible agent. This possibility is being considered in the "triple-view" study of Auerbach et al. (in preparation).

The same difficulty arises here also: even when large differences in perception of the psychotherapy occur, it is hard to discover from the therapist the nature of the countertransference problem that *may* be responsible.

5. Similarly, the study of Fiedler and Senior (1952) might be connected with countertransference, but it is difficult to establish the relationships. In their study, both patients and therapists answered questions concerned with self-description and ideal description of one another. Certain differences in their answers might reveal countertransference attitudes.

Conclusion. Some beginning efforts have been made to deal systematically and quantitatively with the concept of countertransference in psychoanalysis, but in none of these attempts has the clinical sense of the concept been approximated. This area awaits the completion of ongoing research, as well as more ingenious designs. Methodological innovations, improving on Alexander's initial idea, are particularly needed.

Research on Therapist's Attitudes

Under this heading we should like to consider such attitudes as warmth, acceptance, neutrality, objectivity, affective distance, and the therapist's conveying the impression that he can help the patient. These may well be crucial attitudes. However, nothing systematic or quantitative has appeared in the psychoanalytic research literature, although there is much related literature from client-centered psychotherapy.

Other Process Studies

Symptom Context Methods. A different kind of process research has developed in recent years, aimed at overcoming the fact that each case and each session is a unique specimen. One method has been to isolate certain segments of the therapy process in which a critical event occurred. These segments are then matched with segments of therapy from the same patient in which the critical event did *not* occur. The two sets of events—critical and control—are then (a) rated on scales to see on which variables they differ; (b) rated by clinicians asked to discriminate critical from control segments; and/or (c) subjected to computer-based content analysis to determine which words distinguish critical from control.

The matching procedure owes a heavy debt to a study of changes in state of consciousness by Brenman, Gill, and Knight (1952). A landmark in quantitative naturalistic research, it was one of the first studies to organize the raw material of therapeutic sessions (in this case, hypnotherapy) according to a clearly defined behavioral "benchmark"—in this case, the spontaneous statement by the patient that he was "going deeper" (into hypnosis). Critical segments containing this statement were matched with control segments from the same patient. The main finding was a shift in the impulse-defense balance just before the experience. The method clearly facilitates systematic studies of the conditions that lead to the formation of symptoms (Freud, 1926).

More recently, Luborsky and Auerbach (1969) used this pairing method with three new symptomatic behaviors: stomach pain, headache, and momentary forgetting. In the case of the first two, the patient reported that his stomach was bothering him, or that he was having a headache; critical segments were matched with control segments from the same patient. One set of findings will illustrate the fruits of the method on the stomach-pain data. Luborsky and another judge rated the critical and control stomach segments on 18 categories and found significant discrimination for *both* independent judges on three: concern over loss of supplies, anxiety, and helplessness (all present to a greater extent in the critical segments). These findings were used in a subsequent study in which three judges rated 24 matched pairs of sentences first by "intuition" and then with the clue that the critical member of each pair was higher in "concern about supplies with a helpless feeling about being able to obtain them." With no clues, the rating outcome was only chance; rating with the additional clues, two of the three judges did significantly better than chance.

In a further study, Spence (1968) used categories from the Harvard Need Affiliation dictionary (Stone et al., 1966, p. 191 ff.) together with three categories based on Luborsky's three discriminating clues and the two words "down" and "up," chosen by another independent clinical rater as potentially differentiating labels.

A computer-based content analysis scanned the critical and control segments for frequencies of all categories; the resulting tabs were then inserted into a multiple-regression program with symptom or no symptom as the criterion. The words "up" and "down" were the best predictors, and accounted for about 25 percent of the variance; three categories from the Need Affiliation dictionary accounted for another 25 percent. The two words plus the three categories correlated .70 with the criterion of symptom or no symptom. It should be noted that Luborsky's rated categories (as translated into the word categories by Spence) did not appear among the best five predictors.

Clearly, some rationale is needed for the selection of categories in this kind of study. Luborsky, starting with a set of 18 variables, settled on three that seemed reasonably discriminating; the addition of categories from the Need Affiliation dictionary displaced Luborsky's; and the additional clinical rater, adding the two words "up" and "down," displaced all the rest. (Note that the final clinician, working only on hunch, wins this round.) A further set of categories might conceivably displace the two magic words; the process has, in theory, no limits, because we have not agreed on a minimal set of categories to use in this kind of rating.

Similar work has been done on samples matched according to momentary forgetting. In this case, the patient has a thought in mind and then loses it. The typical comment runs as follows: "I just had a thought (pause) but I forgot what I was going to say . . . Oh, this was it!" The target thought may or may not be permanently forgotten. Luborsky rated 37 pairs of critical and control segments on 12 categories (overlapping in some degree with the 18 categories used in the stomach-symptom research; see above). Some categories that discriminated critical from control segments were: new attitude or behavior; difficulty with attention; guilt; and lack of control or competence. A computer analysis using the Need Affiliation dictionary is planned for the near future.

The benchmark of momentary forgetting is a particularly good choice for this kind of research, because it occurs naturally in the course of treatment (although not frequently; Luborsky

[1964, 1967] noted 69 instances in 2079 sessions), and it is likely to be reported. In contrast, stomach pain and headache are not necessarily part of the flow of ideas, and hence the reporting of them is confounded by the state of the transference. If the patient is in a state of high resistance, for example, he may not wish to comply with the basic rule that he say everything that comes to mind, and a symptom, if it occurs, may not be reported. Thus we may have two sets of negative instances—one in which the symptom was indeed not present, and a second in which it was in awareness but not reported because of conditions in the transference. Presumably, the contexts would differ according to which set was chosen, but since they cannot be independently separated, no further analysis is possible.

Trend Analysis. Another approach that starts with the raw clinical material might be called *trend analysis* and can be illustrated by a recent study by Spence (in preparation). He used material from the Gill–Simon research analyses (see p.427). The patient investigated in this single-case study had been in analysis for seven months when treatment was unexpectedly terminated; five months later treatment was resumed with another analyst who, as it turned out, was five months pregnant. The pregnancy may have signaled the danger of another interruption; the patient, alerted by the first interruption and by related occurrences in her life history, was understandably sensitive to something similar happening again. In the fifth hour with the second analyst, the patient asked her if she were pregnant. Taking this segment as the target segment, Spence investigated the preceding four hours to determine whether the target segment had been anticipated in earlier hours and, if a trend did exist, what form it took. The trend analysis made use of specially developed categories of words and phrases that were related to pregnancy—motherhood, separation, childbirth, hospitalization, and the like. Added to the content categories was a set of formal categories related to patient productivity, described above in relation to Simon's work. Frequencies of each category were plotted over time (after dividing each hour into quarters to enlarge the data base) and fitted to a number of different curves. The

data analysis relied heavily on the work of Stone et al. (1966); the modified computer programs are described in Spence (1969a).

Early findings show that there was a trend over time, but not a simple monotonic increase. The strongest trend occurred within each hour, starting low and reaching a peak when the hour ended. This trend was repeated in each of the five hours. Apparently the therapeutic process had to be re-established anew at the start of each session, perhaps because of the early stage of treatment.

More generally, the trends themselves—and the critical units—may change as the stage of treatment changes. In the early phases, we might concentrate on the single hour; later in therapy, when we can assume a certain continuity, we can look for trends over larger blocks of time. An interesting question arises here: At what point in the course of treatment will a trend run over a weekend? . . over a week's holiday? . . over a summer vacation?

The initial question—Was there a progressive increase over time in pregnancy associates?—must be answered in the negative. What linear change there was, took place within each hour. But a larger change did occur across hours, although it was quite irregular. Associations about pregnancy started high, began to fall, recovered, and then fell again. The moment of confrontation (asking the therapist if she were pregnant) occurred just after the second peak. The shape of the function suggests that the patient may have been aware at the start that the therapist was pregnant, but was unable to ask the question until the relationship had stabilized, until her anxiety had diminished, until her ambivalence about resuming treatment had been clarified—there are any number of possibilities that can be resolved only by further analysis. The irregular function may also reflect the early state of treatment; five hours taken during a later period might show more continuity over time and support the clinical opinion that when the treatment situation is well established, it takes on a momentum of its own.

A final word about the method. It lends itself to computer-based content analysis, an obvious boon to reliability. On the other hand, it is restricted by the categories used. Urgently needed is a standard set of analytic categories that can be applied to a wide variety of clinical samples; the work of Dahl (see p.427) may help fill this gap.

Psychoanalytic Treatment Analogues

In terms of present knowledge, the treatment situation is too complex to be understood in analogue form; each case and each session differ along a number of dimensions hard to specify in advance. For this reason, Freud was probably right in his pessimistic evaluation of one of the early analogue studies (see p.408). The laboratory experimenter must show that he is dealing with the same phenomenon that has been observed clinically, and this is an all-but-impossible requirement. Nevertheless, despite flaws, a number of analogue studies deserve mention at this point.

Sears (1943a, 1943b) presented a most comprehensive review of what had been done up to that time on what is called "objective studies of psychoanalytic concepts." These were mainly experiments on supposed memory analogues to repression, or studies of later effects of early childhood experiences. These studies have had almost no influence on clinicians, mainly because they are usually thought to be not close enough to the clinical phenomena to represent a test of them. Madison later (1956) also reviewed objective studies of repression.

Analogues to phenomena that occur in psychoanalysis—such as free-association sessions—have been investigated by a number of researchers, including Colby (1960, 1961), Bordin (1966), and Keet (1948). The last study has been reviewed by Hilgard (1952). The Keet approach entails the induction and cure of so-called mild neuroses in the laboratory. These "artificial" neuroses can then be studied in terms of resolvability by various methods of treatment—for example, an expressive or nondirective technique versus an interpretive technique in the recovery of a forgotten word. It seems like a good approach, but there has been difficulty in replicating the finding that the interpretive technique was superior in recovering the word. Several attempts to replicate it have failed because of difficulty in establishing the artificial neurotic illness (see Merrill, 1952, for one unsuccessful attempt).

THE PRIMARY DATA BANK OF PSYCHOANALYTIC TREATMENT RECORDS

The problems of psychoanalytic research are aggravated by the paucity of primary data—data accumulated during actual analytic sessions. Ideally, two conditions should be met: the case should be clearly defined as analytic, meeting whatever criteria of process and outcome a panel of judges might determine; and the data should be recorded, transcribed, and indexed so as to maximize accessibility and visibility.

To date, no set of data exists that meets these conditions. The style of research in psychoanalysis has been based largely on the individual analyst's observation of his own cases and sharing of his experience with his colleagues. After 70 years of clinical psychoanalysis, no primary data bank exists. About 20 years ago Georg Zinn made the first recorded psychoanalytic case of any kind, but its many inconsistencies of technique made it atypical. The same criticism can be made of the Bergman case (p.423) and the Gill-Simon case (p.427). Nevertheless, the advantage of completeness of data sometimes outweighs clinical shortcomings, and we list below the best current sources.

Columbia Psychoanalytic Clinic

What must be by far the largest number of *written* records of psychoanalytic treatment has been gathered since 1959 at the Columbia University Psychoanalytic Clinic for Training and Research. The records include both psychoanalysis and psychoanalytically oriented psychotherapy of low-fee patients by psychiatrists in psychoanalytic training. Weber et al. (1966) have recently reported some results of the treatment of 1348 of these patients, 588 of whom were in psychoanalysis and 760 in psychotherapy. Within the limits imposed by basing their conclusions on written records rather than electrically recorded ones, the group does careful and sophisticated research; they are aided by computer analyses of the many types of information comparing the patient at the beginning and the end of treatment. An example of this sophistication is their way of dealing with the fact that patients are assigned to the two types of treatment on a nonrandom basis, and it is necessary to distinguish between the effects of selection and the effects of the type of treatment. One of their solutions was to compare groups of patients of the same diagnosis and same initial severity of discomfort. They found, for example, that in the group with "more severe" dysfunction at the beginning of treatment, patients diagnosed as "neurotic personality" showed a higher proportion of improvement in analysis than in psychotherapy. Although there was a net improvement in both forms of treatment of borderline and psychotic patients, this group got worse more often in analysis. Psychoanalysis, therefore, appears to be the treatment of choice for the neurotic personality but *not* for the borderline or psychotic patient. (Compare the discussion of "Most Suitable Patient Qualities," p.411.)

Gill and Simon—Brookdale Hospital Group

In 1964 Gill and his colleagues started a highly productive recording of an analytic case (Gill et al., 1968). Some clinical features of the case have been described above. The treatment is now ended, and an uninterrupted series of tape recordings is available on which a number of analytic questions may be applied. To increase accessibility to the raw taped data, two kinds of data reduction have been carried out: (a) typed summaries that reduce length by a factor of 3 have been made of each hour; and (b) these typed summaries have been coded on a set of categories (the Topic Index) by the analyst and sometimes one additional judge. The transcripts have been used to develop the Patient Productivity Rating Scale (see p.417). They have contributed to a number of other studies (such as Simon et al., 1967), and five hours from the treatment have been subjected to an intensive process analysis by Spence (see p.425). Dahl has taken the ratings from the Topic Index and reduced them (by factor analysis) to six main factors that account for 80 percent of the variance, and promise to provide a systematic overview of the treatment.

Rochester Project on the Computer Analysis of Content

A group at the University of Rochester has focused upon devising methods for efficient data

reduction of psychoanalytic sessions. Segments of a complete, successful tape-recorded analysis (carried out by Dr. Gordon Pleune) have been analyzed by a special computer-based factor-analytic method. Successive 5-minute segments of the treatment are scored for the frequency of individual words; intercorrelations among a selected set of words are obtained and factored. The factors appear to represent meaning clusters that are central for the patient. These meaning clusters seem to be largely independent of which words are selected—beginning with a different set of the patient's words tends to yield similar meaning clusters. These clusters seem to make clinical sense; that is, they correspond to the central themes of the protocol. The method is distinctive in that it does not depend on a set of external categories, but proceeds from within; this feature has been playfully labeled UHH, or *untouched by human hands* (Harway and Iker, 1964, 1966; Iker and Harway, 1965).

Dahl—Research Center for Mental Health of N.Y.U.

Late in 1968, Dahl began recording an analytic case, systematically transcribing his daily process notes, and then key punching the final product. The raw material is reduced by a factor of 3; more important, the summaries are in a form that can be processed by a computer-based content-analysis system such as the ones developed by Stone et al. (1966), Iker and Harway (1965), and Spence (1969a). Dahl is currently working on a dictionary of high-frequency words organized around such basic psychoanalytic concepts as positive transference, resistance, childhood memories, and the like. The words are the same as those used in the Harvard Psychosociological Dictionary, and represent the 3000 most frequent from the Thorndike-Lorge list. By applying the special analytic dictionary to the key-punched process notes, it will be possible to summarize the material in terms of critical psychoanalytic concepts, and in this way to maintain an up-to-date log of the key themes in the case. The log can also be used to index the raw taped protocols, and thus facilitate access to the primary data. Dahl also plans to summarize the process notes according to the categories contained in other standard dictionaries, such as the Need-Affiliation and Need-Achievement dictionaries (Stone et al., 1966). Given sufficient funds, Dahl also has plans to computer-process the raw text of the analysis.

Analytic Research Group of the Institute of the Pennsylvania Hospital

This group is composed of 10 experienced psychoanalysts who also have a research background. (Dr. Harold Graff is chairman; Dr. Sydney Pulver is secretary.) It has been meeting regularly since June 1968, in an effort to plan basic research in the process and outcome of the psychoanalytic method. The focus is on process hypotheses, although information will be available about the initial state of the patient and the outcome of the treatment. The target sample is a set of tape recordings of 30 psychoanalytic patients who have been in treatment for 50 sessions or more, and another set of 30 patients who terminated before the 50th session. All patients are given a battery of diagnostic tests and a tape-recorded clinical interview; the battery is the same as the one used in the on-going study by Luborsky and Auerbach of 80 patients in long-term psychotherapy.

The process research will consist of two parts. In *phase 1*, two patients not in the target sample will be studied in an attempt to formulate promising hypotheses. In *phase 2*, the hypotheses will be applied to the target sample after sufficient primary data have been accumulated. The following areas are being examined for further study: (*a*) quality of interpretation; (*b*) changes in specified aspects of the transference in the course of treatment; (*c*) changes in the form of defenses in the course of treatment; and (*d*) factors that trigger the onset of specific symptoms such as momentary forgetting, stomach pain, and headache (see p.424).

The Therapeutic Process Study (Mt. Zion Hospital and San Francisco Psychoanalytic Institute)

Drs. Emanuel Windholz, Joseph Weiss, and Harold Sampson head a group trying to create methods that are especially suited to the study of the process of psychoanalysis. Their methods permit the clinician access to sufficient data to allow free play to his clinical wisdom. They will

study complex psychoanalytic explanatory concepts and then cast them in the form of rigorously testable hypotheses. At present they are rating 100 sessions of the process notes of a completed analysis to investigate two related aspects of the process: what changes take place in defenses as they are successfully analyzed, and how certain modifications of defenses permit the emergence of formerly warded-off affects, impulses, ideas, memories, and behavior. They are also tape-recording a second patient's analysis.

University of Illinois School of Medicine Psychotherapy Film Laboratory

David Shakow started one of the earliest film laboratories for psychotherapy and psychoanalysis at the University of Illinois, originally with Ray Sternberg and Hugh Carmichael, and continued by Elizabeth Tower, Morris Sklansky, Arthur Miller, Kenneth Isaacs, and Ernest Haggard. Some of their recent work is referred to above under "*Relatability and Meaningfulness*": other work includes a systematic study of levels of meaning in the patient's and therapist's statements (Sklansky et al., 1966).

National Institute of Mental Health Filmed Therapy Project

Although the NIMH project started by David Shakow concerns psychotherapy and not psychoanalytic treatment, it deserves mention here because it is one of the few available samples of film and sound recording; the quality of the sound is exceptionally good (Bergman, 1966). The patient, a woman in her early 40's, was seen by an experienced psychoanalyst, Dr. Paul Bergman, for four years and three months—a total of 632 sessions. The patient initially sought treatment for her anxieties and nearly crippling phobias. Throughout treatment, the patient was more interested in symptomatic relief than in long-range goals, and in this respect alone the case is unlike an ideal analytic relationship.

The therapy was terminated by a change in the husband's job, which necessitated a family move. At the time of termination, the phobias had markedly diminished in number and severity. Hypochondriacal features had also diminished. A character trait described by Bergman as "unreasonableness" had almost disappeared. In other respects she was unchanged—she still disliked introspection and still feared the treatment process. The treatment was originally analytic, but for various reasons was changed to psychotherapy soon after it started. For this reason and because the treatment was terminated prematurely, it does not constitute an ideal case. But even though it is not an analytic case, it would be premature to say that it does not include some analytic material. Possibly, selected segments of this case would be undistinguishable from certain segments of the analytic cases mentioned elsewhere; at any rate, such a comparison would throw light on features that differentiate the two kinds of treatment. This kind of comparison might also be carried out by means of a computer-based category-listing procedure.

Some initial research and some preliminary observations on this case are described by Cohen and Cohen (1961); some studies of body movement in this case have been described by Dittmann (1962).

The Hampstead Index (The Hampstead Clinic)

In the Hampstead Index, aspects of psychoanalytic treatment are classified according to a long list of rubrics and in the form of a card index that can be used for research in psychoanalysis. Each typed card contains a piece of "material"—a so-called "unit of observation" and a reference to the pages in the patient's casenotes from which it was extracted, or which it summarizes. It also contains the name of the patient and related data (Sandler, 1962).

The method might be called a form of concept development that stands, in its degree of rigor, somewhere between unaided clinical research and quantitative research. It has much in common with the method used by Freud, but is more systematic and organized. It has advantages over the usual clinical research, in that (a) it is easier to find patients who fit a certain category, and (b) it is easier to refine psychoanalytic terms because the terms refer to specific patients. The Index differs from some other collections of data described in this section in that its contents are not primary data, but the therapist's observations of the therapy process. In this sense, it has much in common with Dahl's collection of process notes (see p.427).

One of the major defects of the Index also characterizes some aspects of the Menninger Foundation's Psychotherapy Research Project (Wallerstein et al., 1956): when a therapist is interviewed about his experience with a patient, the data are transmitted from the therapist to the research interviewer; the research interviewer does not have access to the actual way in which the patient and therapist interacted. It is obviously better to have the research interviewer *also* witness some of the patient-therapist interaction. Furthermore, the Index is especially vulnerable to varieties of usage of the same terms. Each therapist classifies the material from his patients under each rubric, but there is no adequate way of checking for similarity in the usage of terms because there is no reliability estimate.

Menninger Foundation Psychotherapy Research Project

By far the largest and oldest of the quantitative therapy projects is the Menninger Project, which began in its present form in 1954. (A smaller committee had been working since 1949.) Although not a source of raw data from treatment, it deserves mention here as a source of significant research methods. Particularly important was a procedure developed by Sargent (see Sargent, 1961; Sargent et al., 1968) for making predictions about the course and outcome of treatment. Her method calls for specifying three items for each prediction: the *if*-clause, the *then*-clause, and the *because*-assumption. A second useful method suggested by Sargent is the paired comparison procedure for the comparison of one treatment with another. Also noteworthy is the project's collection of intensive assessments of the patient before, just after, and two years after termination of treatment.

Problem of Recording Primary Data

Haggard et al. (1965) have reviewed the effects of recording and filming on the psychotherapeutic process, as have a number of other researchers recently (Bergman, 1966; Carmichael, 1966; English, 1966; Erickson, 1966; Jackson, 1966). These reviews indicate that one records or films at one's peril if one is not aware of the variety of meanings attributed by the patient to the act of recording or filming. One must deal with them as with any other aspect of the relationship that is introduced by the therapist. The peril comes from trying to ignore the meanings of this aspect of the relationship. With an awareness of the possible meanings and impact of the research, it is possible to maintain a viable treatment relationship, and the paraphernalia of the research and the very existence of the research become another problem in the treatment, to be dealt with along with such issues as the therapist's treatment technique, his style of setting fees, etc.

In all of these tape-recorded treatments, special care is taken to insure confidentiality—by using only numbers or initials on the tape box, filing tapes in locked cabinets with keys kept only by the experimenters, and the like. It is also helpful to both patient and therapist that any research using the tapes be done *after* the treatment is completed, rather than concurrently.

Problems of Agreement in Evaluating Primary Data

Mintz et al. (1970) have factor-analyzed the ratings on 60 sessions by three judges and have identified four groupings (factors) that seem to be the main dimensions that a judge tends to listen to when he hears psychotherapy sessions. These are (*a*) optimal therapeutic behavior; (*b*) therapist directiveness; (*c*) patient health versus sickness; and (*d*) therapist interpretiveness. It seems probable that the problem of agreement of judges is directly tied to the problem of the category being judged. If a judge is asked to attend to one of the four "natural" categories listed above, his reliability with the next judge will probably be much higher than if he is asked to listen to an "unnatural category." Bellak and Smith (1956), for example, found only moderate agreement among judges listening to psychoanalytic sessions; possibly they were being asked to focus on "unnatural" categories. Similarly, Auerbach and Luborsky (1968) found only moderate agreement among three judges using many variables to rate psychotherapy and psychoanalytic sessions; inspection of the variables might show that when "natural" factors were represented, agreement tended to be higher.

Other scoring procedures have been developed (for example, Leary and Gill, 1959;

Seitz, 1966), but reliabilities for those are not available, probably because of their complexity.

SUMMARY AND IMPLICATIONS FOR PSYCHOANALYTIC PRACTICE

The summary is provided by the conclusions about each topic listed at the end of each section above. Some broader generalizations from these form the general conclusions given below.

General Conclusions

1. We began the review with the main question: Does quantitative psychoanalytic therapy research deserve the limbo in which it is placed in relation to clinical practice? The answer is *mostly yes*. At times, in reviewing the literature, we were reminded of an experimenter who put an ad in a paper for a "reliable, vigorous young man for an important, decision-making job." Among the applicants was a spry, superannuated man who was obviously not qualified for the job. The interviewer asked him why he had applied. The old man answered, "Young man, I just came here to let you know that on *me*, you *can't* rely." *Quantitative research on psychoanalytic therapy presents itself, so far, as an unreliable support to clinical practice. At this point, what can be known through clinical wisdom is far more than what can be known through quantitative, objective means.* Much of what is contributed by the quantitative literature represents a cumbersome, roundabout way of showing the clinician what he already knows—for example Waelder (1962). (Quantitative research on psychoanalytic treatment is not, however, in a position different from quantitative research on other therapies with respect to the lack of impact upon practice; see Luborsky, 1969).

Still, some general conclusions can be drawn. Most of the present chapter describes studies that are developing and refining the tools from which may come later discoveries. Some of these later discoveries will, hopefully, add to our store of clinical wisdom. But as this review shows, *areas exist in which guidance could be given to practice, and the prospects for further guidance are definitely present.* (*a*) Some studies confirm clinical impressions about the selection of patients who are most suitable for psychoanalytic treatment; (b) in the selection of psychoanalysts, certain healthy qualities might be worth seeking, such as objectivity, self-confidence, and security; and (c) process research is the area in which the most rapid progress is now being made and it has, therefore, been given disproportionate space in the present review. Some of the findings about the qualities of the patient's productions (whether labeled *productivity*, *meaningfulness*, *experiencing*, or *associative freedom*) have been explored. One of the core aspects of productivity was found to be *the patient's reflective statements*. For the therapist's interpretive behavior, some of the studies of the psychoanalytic process (such as Spence and Greif, 1970) stress *the efficacy of the clinical concept of "listening away" as a way to sharpen one's hearing of what the patient is saying*. Specific methods for training therapists to develop this ability ought to be tried.

2. *In all scientific fields, the style has become more quantitative and controlled. We have listed some evidence that psychoanalysis, too, is beginning to follow the trend (despite its present small impact on practice).* Psychoanalysis is now showing signs of setting up a base of quantitative research to support it—note especially (under section *The Primary Data Bank*) the number of process studies under way.

In this review we have restricted ourselves to *quantitative* psychoanalytic research on psychoanalytic treatment, not because that is the only useful type of research, but because psychoanalysis needs a better balance between clinical wisdom alone and clinical wisdom combined with more controlled methods. From its inception, psychoanalysis has elicited strong responses—either favorable or unfavorable—rather than neutral ones. Today is no exception, although the main basis for the attack has shifted. Formerly it was aimed at the existence of unconscious contents; now insufficiently controlled research is more often the stated basis for the criticism. Occasionally criticism is in terms of preference for a simpler theory of the operation of psychotherapy; for example, the one put forward by the exponents of behavior therapy with their emphasis on the *sufficiency* of learning-theory explanations.

3. The same main questions are being asked about psychoanalytic treatment that have been asked about other forms of treatment: What kinds of patients are most suited to it? What kinds of therapists are most suited to perform it? What types of outcomes are accomplished by it? What process do patient and therapist go through in doing it? It will be interesting to see what convergence develops among the findings from psychoanalysis and from other forms of treatment (such as client-centered).

4. *The research with analogues of psychoanalytic concepts, which was so common in the past few decades, has not been useful*—mainly because it has not been possible to create real analogues to the clinically based concepts. This failure may in part be because many concepts need clarification to be useful in quantitative studies, but it may also be because until recently—and even now—a substantial part of quantitative psychoanalytic treatment research has been carried out by nonanalysts. This failure may have been what Rapaport (1959) was responding to when he said, "Psychoanalysis will use methods and concepts from other sciences, but results will be achieved by the sweat of our own brow." Rapaport apparently meant that few nonanalysts have the motivation or know-how to carry out the research properly. Our review shows that many nonanalysts have sweated over these issues, especially by trying to create experimental analogues of concepts, but too often have missed their essence.

5. *Researchers on psychoanalytic treatment have begun to conquer the difficulties of amassing sufficient primary data for proper research, and the prospects are good for much more becoming available.* Several recorded analyses and symptom context protocols are now available as specimens for examination by researchers of various viewpoints.

6. *More is known now about concepts, referring to the behavior of both patient and therapist, that can be judged from the psychoanalytic sessions or can be coded for computer manipulation.* Much more needs to be done in this area, but a start has been made. Some specific evidence for the revitalization of psychoanalytic concepts is to be found in the creation of reliable rating scales for certain concepts applicable to psychoanalytic and psychoanalytically oriented psychotherapy (Auerbach & Luborsky,

1968; Mintz et al., 1970; Mintz & Luborsky, 1970). Computer programs are being created for many analytic concepts (Spence, 1969a; Spence, 1969b).

There has also been a trend among analytic theoreticians toward a theoretical sharpening of psychoanalytic concepts by analysis of them into main components for which measures might more readily be developed. Such refined concepts might be more amenable than earlier formulations to use in controlled studies where agreement between judges must be shown. Holt's work on bound versus free cathexis (1962) and on energy concepts (1967) is an example of this development. Other reformulations have been attempted that bring together psychoanalysis and information and learning theory— see, for example, the work of Peterfreund (1969). Many of Rapaport's (1959) contributions were attempts to simplify and clarify psychoanalytic concepts with a view toward using them in quantitative research, as he had begun to do a few years before his untimely death.

CODA

It is fitting to end the chapter by putting the problem of quantitative research in historical perspective.

The main fruits of quantitative psychoanalytic research have been advances in method. Little has been "discovered" that has added to the store of clinical wisdom; few, if any, quantitative research findings have changed the style or outcome of psychoanalytic practice. In this respect, psychoanalysis is in the position of any new science. Changes in method must, of necessity, precede changes in content; much more work needs to be done simply to understand in some systematic way what the analyst does, how interpretations work, how transference can manifest itself, and how insight is acquired. These are all conventional clinical questions to which there are conventional clinical answers. What is needed are new answers that might provide more satisfactory explanations.

Psychoanalysts, like other psychotherapists, literally *do not know* how they achieve their results, although they have searched longer and deeper than others, and possess a unique store of clinical wisdom. They have learned their craft from a long line of practitioners schooled in a master-apprentice relationship; the rules are taught more by example than by explanation. Much work must be done in a naturalistic way (and here is where recordings are valuable) to understand what makes a good therapist good. Observation by means of video tape is particularly important because certain aspects of the therapeutic process operate outside of awareness, and therefore one cannot simply ask the therapist what he does. We cannot even tell the therapist that we are studying him, because if we do he may try to become aware of skills that are ordinarily autonomous; as they become more focal, they may become less effective. Some therapists may sense this problem and, for this among other reasons, refuse to participate in the needed research. It is too simple merely to dismiss this opposition as resistance; much careful thought must go into how to study the therapeutic process without changing it for the worse, and how to devise research methods that really capture the essence of psychoanalytic data.

Despite its rather prosaic nature, a systematic naturalistic inventory of the analytic process is long overdue. The field has skipped from the initial insights of Freud to high-flown metapsychological formulations; now it must step back and fill in the middle ground before any substantial progress can be made.

Because of the lack of fundamental tested knowledge, we are not able to make effective changes in treatment method and thereby increase its therapeutic effect. We can make no sensible revisions in our training procedure (which is probably too expensive, too long, and inefficient in relation to what it can produce) because we do not clearly understand the process by which analysts become skilled and how sensitivity is increased. We are bequeathed a workable treatment method that is poorly understood (in any systematic sense), and lack of basic knowledge fosters faith in tradition. We dare not make changes so we stay with the old model, not because it is necessarily the best, but because we have poor rules for testing it.

REFERENCES

Alexander, F. *Five-year report of the Chicago Institute for Psychoanalysis—1932–1937*. Chicago: Institute for Psychoanalysis, 1937.

Alexander, F., French, T., and Pollock, G. *Psychosomatic specificity*. Vol. 1. Chicago: University of Chicago Press, 1968.

Apfelbaum, B. *Dimensions of transference in psychotherapy*. Berkeley: University of California Press, 1958.

Aronson, H., and Weintraub, W. Patient changes during classical psychoanalysis as a function of initial status and duration of treatment. *Psychiatry*, 1968, **31**, 369–379 (a).

Aronson, H., and Weintraub, W. Social background of the patient in classical psychoanalysis. *Journal of Nervous and Mental Disease*, 1968, **146**, 91–97 (b).

Auerbach, A. H., and Luborsky, L. Accuracy of judgments of psychotherapy and the nature of the "good hour." In Shlien, J., Hunt, H. F., Matarazzo, J. P., and Savage, C. (Eds.), *Research in psychotherapy, Vol. 3*. Washington, D. C.: American Psychological Association, 1968. Pp. 155–168.

Auerbach, A. H., Luborsky, L., and Johnson, Marilyn. Assessments of psychotherapy sessions by patient, therapist, and external judges. (In preparation, 1970).

Bachrach, H. A scale for rating the quality of conjunctive empathy. Unpublished manuscript, University of Chicago, 1965.

Bachrach, H. Adaptive regression, empathy, and psychotherapy. *Psychotherapy: Theory, Research and Practice*, Dec. 1968, **5**, 203–209.

Barrett-Lennard, G. T. Dimensions of the client's experience of his therapist associated with personality change. Unpublished Ph.D. thesis, University of Chicago, 1959.

Bellak, L., and Smith, M. B. An experimental exploration of the psychoanalytic process. *Psychoanalytic Quarterly*, 1956, **25**, 385–414.

Benjamin, J. Methodological considerations in the validation and elaboration of psychoanalytical personality theory. (Approaches to a dynamic theory of development.) *American Journal of Orthopsychiatry*, 1950, **20**, 139–156.

Bergin, A. E., and Jasper, L. G. Correlates of empathy in psychotherapy: A replication. *Journal of Abnormal Psychology*, 1969, **74** (4), 447–481.

Bergin, A. E., and Solomon, Sandra. Personality and performance correlates of empathic understanding in psychotherapy. In, Tomlinson, T., and Hart, J. (Eds.), *New directions in client-centered therapy*. Boston: Houghton-Mifflin, 1969.

Bergman, P. An experiment in filmed psychotherapy. In Gottschalk, L. A., and Auerbach, A. H. (Eds.), *Methods of research in psychotherapy*. New York: Appleton-Century-Crofts, 1966. Pp. 35–49.

Bibring, E. Psychoanalysis and the dynamic psychotherapies. *Journal of the American Psychoanalytic Association*, 1954, **2**, 745–770.

Bordin, E. S. Free association: An experimental analogue of the psychoanalytic situation. In Gottschalk, L. A., and Auerbach, A. H. (Eds.), *Methods of research in psychotherapy*. New York: Appleton-Century-Crofts, 1966. Pp. 189–208.

Brenman, Margaret, Gill. M., and Knight, R. P. Spontaneous fluctuations in depth of hypnosis and their implication for ego function. *International Journal of Psychoanalysis*, 1952, **33**, 22–23.

Brenman, Margaret, Kubie, L., Murray, H. A., Kris, E., and Gill, M. Problems in clinical research. *American Journal of Orthopsychiatry*, 1947, **17**, 196–230.

Carmichael, H. Sound-film recording of psychoanalytic therapy: A therapist's experiences and reactions. In Gottschalk, L. A., and Auerbach, A. H. (Eds.), *Methods of research in psychotherapy*. New York: Appleton-Century-Crofts, 1966. Pp. 50–59.

Cartwright, Rosalind. A comparison of the response to psychoanalytic and client-centered psychotherapy. In Gottschalk, L. A., and Auerbach, A. H. (Eds.), *Methods of research in psychotherapy*. New York: Appleton-Century-Crofts, 1966. Pp. 517–529.

Change, Erika. The study of transference in group therapy. *International Journal of Group Psychotherapy*, 1952, **2**, 40–53.

Cohen, R. A., and Cohen, Mabel B. Research in psychotherapy: A preliminary report. *Psychiatry*, 1961, **24**, 46–61.

Colby, K. M. Experiment on the effects of an observer's presence on the imago system during psychoanalytic free association. *Behavioral Science*, 1960, **5**, 216–232.

Colby, K. M. On the greater amplifying power of causal-correlative over interrogative inputs on free association in an experimental analytic situation. *Journal of Nervous and Mental Disease*, 1961, **133**, 233–239.

Dittmann, A. T. The relationship between body movements and moods in interviews. *Journal of Consulting Psychology*, 1962, **26**, 480.

Duhrssen, A., and Jorswieck, E. Zur korrektur von Eysenck's Berichterstattung uber psychoanalitische behandlungsergebnisse. *Acta Psychotherapy*, 1962. **19**, 329–342.

Duhrssen, A., and Jorswieck, E. Ein Empirischstatistische Untersuchung zur Leistungsfahigkeit psychoanalytischer behandlung. (An empirical-statistical investigation into the efficacy of psychoanalytic therapy.) *Nervenarzt*, 1965, **36/4**, 166–169.

Eissler, K. *Medical orthodoxy and the future of psychoanalysis*. New York: International Universities Press, 1965.

Ellis, A. Psychotherapy techniques for use with psychotics. *American Journal of Psychotherapy*, 1955, **9**, 452–476 (a).

Ellis, A. New approaches to psychotherapy techniques. *Journal of Clinical Psychology, Monograph Supplement II*, 1955, 208–260 (b).

Engel, G. L. Some obstacles to the development of research in psychoanalysis. (With discussions and closing comments by David Beres, Mark Kanzer, Robert S. Wallerstein, and Elizabeth R. Zetzel, pp. 205–229.) *Journal of the American Psychoanalytic Association*, 1968, **16**, 195–204.

English, O. S. Subjective reactions to being filmed. In Gottschalk, L. A., and Auerbach, A. H. (Eds.), *Methods of research in psychotherapy*. New York: Appleton-Century-Crofts, 1966. P. 60.

Erickson, M. The experience of interviewing in the presence of observers. In Gottschalk, L. A., and Auerbach, A. H. (Eds.), *Methods of research in psychotherapy*. New York: Appleton-Century-Crofts, 1966. Pp. 61–63.

Escalona, Sibylle. Problems in psychoanalytic research. *International Journal of Psychoanalysis*, 1952, **33**, 11–21.

Eysenck, H. The effects of psychotherapy: An evaluation. *Journal of Consulting Psychology*, 1952, **16**, 319–324.

Eysenck, H. The effects of psychotherapy. In Eysenck, H., (Ed.), *Handbook of abnormal psychology*. New York: Basic Books, 1961, Pp. 697–725.

Farrell, B. The criteria for a psychoanalytic interpretation. In Gustafson, D. F. (Ed.), *Essays in philosophical psychology*. Garden City: Doubleday, 1964. Pp. 299–323.

Feldman, F. Results of psychoanalysis in clinic case assignments. *Journal of the American Psychoanalytic Association*, 1968, **16**, 274–300.

Fenichel, O. Statisticher bericht uber die therapeutische tatigkeit, 1920–1930. In *Zehn Jahre Berliner Psychoanalytisches Institut*. Vienna: Internationale Psychoanalytischer Verlag, 1930. Pp. 13–19.

Fey, W. F. Doctrine and experience: their influence upon the psychotherapist. *Journal of Consulting Psychology*, 1958, **22**, 403–409.

Fiedler, F. The concept of an ideal relationship. *Journal of Consulting Psychology*, 1950, **14**, 239–245 (a).

Fiedler, F. A comparison of therapeutic relationships in psychoanalytic, nondirective and Adlerian therapy. *Journal of Consulting Psychology*, 1950, **14**, 436–445 (b).

Fiedler, F. Factor analyses of psychoanalytic, nondirective, and Adlerian therapeutic relationships. *Journal of Consulting Psychology*, 1951, **15**, 32–38.

Fiedler, F., and Senior, Kate. An exploratory study of unconscious feeling reactions in 15 patient-therapist pairs. *Journal of Abnormal and Social Psychology*, 1952, **47**, 446–453.

Fiske, D. W., Hunt, H. F., Luborsky, L., Orne, M. T., Parloff, M. B., Reiser, M. F., and Tuma, H. Planning of research on effectiveness of psychotherapy. (Report of a workshop sponsored by the Clinical Projects Research Review Committee, National Institute of Mental Health, November 1968.) *Archives of General Psychiatry*, 1970, **22**, 22–32. Also in *American Psychologist*. (In Press, 1970).

Frenkel-Brunswik, E. Psychoanalysis and the unity of science. *Proceedings of the American Academy of Arts and Sciences*, 1954, **80**.

Freud, Anna. The widening scope of indications for psychoanalysis: Discussion. *Journal of the American Psychoanalytic Association*, 1954, **2**, 607–620.

Freud, S. (1913). The claims of psychoanalysis to the interest of the non-psychological sciences (standard edition). Vol. 13. London: Hogarth Press, 1955.

Freud, S. (1926). Inhibitions, symptoms, and anxiety (standard edition). Vol. 20. London: Hogarth Press, 1959.

Gendlin, E. T., Beebe, J., Cassens, J., and Oberlander, M. Focusing ability in psychotherapy, personality, and creativity. Pp. 217–241. In Shlien, J. et al. (Eds.), *Research in psychotherapy*. Vol. 3. Washington, D. C.: American Psychological Association, 1968.

Gill, M., and Brenman, Margaret. *Hypnosis and related states: Psychoanalytic studies in regression*. New York: International Universities Press, 1959.

Gill, M., Simon, J., Fink, Geraldine, Endicott, N. A., and Paul, I. H. Studies in audio-recorded psychoanalysis. I. General considerations. *Journal of the American Psychoanalytic Association*, 1968, **16**, 230–244.

Glover, E. Research methods in psychoanalysis. *International Journal of Psychoanalysis*, 1952, **33**, 403–409.

Glover, E. Common technical practices: A questionnaire research (1940). In Glover, E. *The technique of psychoanalysis*. New York: International Universities Press, 1955. Pp. 261–350.

Glover, E., Fenichel, O., Strachey, J., Bergler, E., Nunberg, N., and Bibring, E. Symposium on the theory of the therapeutic results of psychoanalysis. *International Journal of Psychoanalysis*, 1937, **18**, 125–189.

Gottschalk, L., Mayerson, P., and Gottlieb, A. Prediction and evaluation of outcome in an emergency brief psychotherapy clinic. *Journal of Nervous and Mental Disease*, 1967, **144**, 77–96.

Graham, S. R. Patient evaluation of the effectiveness of limited psychoanalytically-oriented psychotherapy. *Psychological Reports*, 1958, **4**, 231–234.

Graham, S. R. The effects of psychoanalytically oriented psychotherapy on levels of frequency and satisfaction in sexual activity. *Journal of Clinical Psychology*, 1960, **16**, 94–95.

Greenson, R. R. *The technique and practice of psychoanalysis*. Vol. 1. New York: International Universities Press, 1967.

Group for Advancement of Psychiatry (GAP) Committee Report: Knapp, P. (Chrmn.); Brosin, H., Meyer, E., Offenkrantz, W., Robbins, L., Scheflen, A., Shands, H., Tower, L., and Luborsky, L. (Consultant). *Psychotherapy and the dual research tradition. American Psychiatric Association,* in press, 1970.

Haggard, E. A., Hiken, Julia R., and Isaacs, K. S. Some effects of recording and filming on the psychotherapeutic process. *Psychiatry,* 1965, **28,** 169–191.

Hamburg, D., Bibring, Grete, Fisher, C., Stanton, A., Wallerstein, R., Weinstock, H., and Haggard, E. Report of *ad hoc* committee on central fact-gathering data of the American Psychoanalytic Association. *Journal of the American Psychoanalytic Association,* 1967, **15,** 841–861.

Hartmann, H. Comments on the scientific aspects of psychoanalysis. *The Psychoanalytic Study of the Child,* 1958, **13.**

Hartmann, H. Psychoanalysis as a scientific theory. In, Hook, S. (Ed.), *Psychoanalysis, scientific method, and philosophy.* New York: New York University Press, 1959.

Hartmann, H., Kris, E., and Loewenstein, R. The function of theory in psychoanalysis, In, Loewenstein, R. (Ed.), *Drives, affects, and behavior.* New York: International Universities Press, 1953.

Harway, N. I., and Iker, H. P. Computer analysis of content in psychotherapy. *Psychological Reports,* 1964, **14,** 720–722.

Harway, N. I., and Iker, H. P. Objective content analysis of psychotherapy by computer. In Enslein, K. (Ed.), *Data acquisition and processing in biology and medicine.* Vol. 4. New York, Pergamon Press, 1966.

Hilgard, E. Experimental approaches to psychoanalysis. In Pumpian-Mindlin, E. (Ed.), *Psychoanalysis as science.* Stanford: Stanford University Press, 1952. Pp. 3–45.

Holt, R. R. A critical examination of Freud's concept of bound versus free cathexis. *Journal of the American Psychoanalytic Association,* 1962, **10,** 475–525.

Holt, R. R. A manual for scoring primary process manifestations in Rorschach test responses. Unpublished manuscript (ninth draft), N. Y. U., 1964.

Holt, R. R. Beyond vitalism and mechanism: Freud's concept of psychic energy. In Wolman, B. (Ed.), *Historical roots.* New York: Harper & Row, 1967.

Holt, R. R., and Luborsky, L. *Personality patterns of psychiatrists: A study in selection techniques.* Vol. I. New York: Basic Books, 1958. (*Ibid.*) Vol. II. Topeka, The Menninger Foundation, 1958.

Iker, H. P., and Harway, N. I. A computer approach towards the analysis of content. *Behavioral Science,* 1965, **10,** 173–183.

Isaacs, K., and Haggard, E. Some methods used in the study of affect in psychotherapy. In Gottschalk, L. A., and Auerbach, A. H. (Eds.), *Methods of research in psychotherapy.* New York: Appleton-Century-Crofts, 1966. P. 226.

Jackson, D. Filming of psychotherapeutic sessions as a personal experience. In Gottschalk, L. A., and Auerbach, A. H. (Eds.), *Methods of research in psychotherapy.* New York: Appleton-Century-Crofts, 1966. Pp. 64–65.

Janis, I. L. The psychoanalytic interview as an observational method. In Lindzey, G. (Ed.), *Assessment of human motives.* New York: Rinehart, 1958. Pp. 149–182.

Keet, C. D. Two verbal techniques in a miniature counseling situation. *Psychological Monographs,* 1948, **62,** (Whole No. 294).

Kirtner, W. L., Cartwright. D. S., Robertson, R. J., and Fiske, D. W. Length of therapy in relation to outcome and change in personal integration. *Journal of Consulting Psychology,* 1961, **25,** 84–88.

Klein, G. A clinical perspective for personality research. *Journal of Abnormal and Social Psychology,* 1949, **44,** 42–50.

Klein, Henriette. A study of changes occurring in patients during and after psychoanalytic treatment. In Hoch, P. H., and Zubin, J. (Eds.), Current approaches to psychoanalysis. Proceedings of the 48th annual meeting of the American Psychopathological Association. New York: Grune & Stratton, 1960. Pp. 151–175.

Klein, Henriette. Psychoanalysts in training: Selection and evaluation. New York: Columbia University College of Physicians and Surgeons, 1965. P. 83, ff.

Knapp, P. H. Short-term psychoanalytic and psychosomatic predictions. *Journal of the American Psychoanalytic Association,* 1963, **11.** 245–280.

Knapp, P. H., Levin, S., McCarter, R. H., Wermer, H., and Zetzel, Elizabeth. Suitability for psychoanalysis: A review of 100 supervised analytic cases. *Psychoanalytic Quarterly,* 1960, **29,** 459–477.

Knight, R. P. Evaluation of the results of psychoanalytic therapy. *American Journal of Psychiatry,* 1941, **98,** 434–446.

Kris, E. The nature of psychoanalytic propositions and their validation. In Hook, S., and Konwitz, M. (Eds.), *Freedom and experience.* Ithaca: Cornell University Press, 1947.

Kubie, L. Problems and techniques of psychoanalytic validation and progress. In Pumpian-Mindlin, E. (Ed.), *Psychoanalysis as science.* Stanford: Stanford University Press, 1952. Pp. 74–89.

Leary, T., and Gill, M. The dimensions and a measure of the process of psychotherapy: A system for the analysis of the content of clinical evaluations and patient–therapist verbalizations. In Rubinstein, E., and Parloff, M. (Eds.), *Research in psychotherapy.* Vol. 1. Washington, D. C.: American Psychological Association, 1959.

Lorand, S., and Console, W. A. Therapeutic results in psychoanalytic treatment without fee. *International Journal of Psychoanalysis,* 1958, **39,** 59–64.

Luborsky, L. Repeated intra-individual measurements (*P technique*) in understanding symptom structure and psychotherapeutic change. In Mowrer, O. H. (Ed.), *Psychotherapy: theory and research*. New York: Ronald Press, 1953. Chapter 14.

Luborsky, L. A note on Eysenck's article, "The effects of psychotherapy: An evaluation." *British Journal of Psychology*, May 1954, **45**, 129–131.

Luborsky, L. Clinicians' judgments of mental health: A proposed scale. *Archives of General Psychiatry*, 1962. **7**, 407–417 (a).

Luborsky, L. The patient's personality and psychotherapeutic change. In Strupp, H., and Luborsky, L. (Eds.), *Research in psychotherapy*. Vol. 2. Washington, D. C.: American Psychological Association, 1962. Pp. 115–133 (b).

Luborsky, L. A psychoanalytic research on momentary forgetting during free association. *Bulletin of the Philadelphia Association for Psychoanalysis*, 1964, **14**, 119–137.

Luborsky, L. Momentary forgetting during psychotherapy and psychoanalysis: A theory and research method. In Holt, R. R. (Ed.), Motives and thought: Psychoanalytic essays in honor of David Rapaport. *Psychological Issues*, **5**, No. 2–3, Monograph 18/19, New York: International Universities Press, 1967. Pp. 177–217.

Luborsky, L. Research cannot yet influence clinical practice. (An evaluation of Strupp and Bergin's "Some empirical and conceptual bases for coordinated research in psychotherapy: A critical review of issues, trends, and evidence.") *International Journal of Psychiatry*, 1969, **7** (3), 135–140.

Luborsky, L., and Auerbach, A. H. The symptom-context method: Quantitative studies of symptom formation in psychotherapy. *Journal of the American Psychoanalytic ssociation*, January 1969, **17** (1), 68–99.

Luborsky, L., Chandler, M., Auerbach, A. H., Bachrach, H., and Cohen, J. Factors influencing the outcome of psychotherapy: A review of the quantitative research. *Psychological Bulletin*, in press, 1970.

Luborsky, L., Fabian, Michalina, Hall, B. H., Ticho, E., and Ticho, Gertrude. Treatment variables. *Bulletin of the Menninger Clinic*, 1958, **22**, 126–147.

Luborsky, L., and Schimek, J. Psychoanalytic theories of therapeutic and developmental change: Implications for assessment. In Worchel, P., and Byrne, D. (Eds.), *Personality change*. New York: Wiley, 1964. Pp. 73–99.

Lustman, S. L. Some issues in contemporary psychoanalytic research. *The psychoanalytic study of the child*, 1963, **18**, 51–74.

MacKinnon, D., and Dukes, W. F. Repression. In, Postman, L. (Ed.), *Psychology in the making*. New York: Knopf, 1962. Pp. 662–744.

Madison, P. Freud's repression concept. *International Journal of Psychoanalysis*, 1956, **37**, 75–81.

Mechanick, P. G., and Luborsky, L. Components of psychotherapeutic sensitivity: Relationships among five measures. (In preparation, 1970.)

Merrill, R. M. On Keet's study, "Two verbal techniques in a miniature counseling situation." *Journal of Abnormal and Social Psychology*, 1952, **47**, 722.

Mintz, J., and Luborsky, L. *P-technique* factor analysis in psychotherapy research: An illustration of a method. *Psychotherapy*, 1970, **7** (1), 13–18.

Mintz, J., Luborsky, L., and Auerbach, A. H. Dimensions of psychotherapy: A factor-analytic study of ratings of psychotherapy sessions. *Journal of Consulting Psychology*. (In Press, 1970).

Nunberg, H. Evaluation of the results of psychoanalytic treatment. *International Journal of Psychoanalysis*, 1954, **35**, 2–7.

Oberndorf, C. P. Unsatisfactory results of psychoanalytic therapy. *Psychoanalytic Quarterly*, 1950, **19**, 393–407.

Oberndorf, C. P. Results to be effected with psychoanalysis. *AMA Archives of Neurology and Psychiatry*, 1953, **69**, 655. (Society Transactions.)

Parloff, M. Analytic group psychotherapy. In Marmor, J. (Ed.), *Modern psychoanalysis*. New York: Basic Books, 1968. Pp. 492–531.

Paul, I. H., Gill, M. M., Simon, J., Fink, G., and Endicott, N. A. The differential effect of different interventions. (In preparation, 1969.)

Peterfreund, E. Psychoanalysis—an evolutionary biological approach. *Psychological Issues* (In press, 1970).

Pfeffer, A. Panel report: Research in psychoanalysis. *Journal of the American Psychoanalytic Association*, 1961, **9**, 562–570.

Pumpian-Mindlin, E. The position of psychoanalysis in relation to the biological and social sciences. In *Psychoanalysis as science*. Stanford: Stanford University Press, 1952. Pp. 125–158.

Ramzy, I. Research aspects of psychoanalysis. *Psychoanalytic Quarterly*, **32**, 1963.

Rapaport, D. The structure of psychoanalytic theory—A systematizing attempt. In Koch, S. (Ed.), *Psychology: A study of a science*. Vol. 3. New York: McGraw-Hill, 1959. Pp. 55–183. (Republished in *Psychological Issues*, No. 6. New York: International Universities Press, 1960.)

Rapoport, A. Psychoanalysis as science. *Bulletin of the Menninger Clinic*, 1968, **32**, 1–20.

Raskin, N. J. The psychotherapy research project of the American Academy of Psychotherapists. *American Psychologist*, 1965, **20**, 547. (Abstract.)

Rogers, C. R. A tentative scale for the measurement of process in psychotherapy. In Rubinstein, L., and Parloff, M. (Eds.), *Research in psychotherapy*. Vol. 1. Washington, D. C.: American Psychological Association, 1959. Pp. 96–107.

Rogers, C. R. Gendlin, E. T., Kiesler, D. J., and Truax, C. B. *The therapeutic relationship and its impact: A study of psychotherapy with schizophrenics*. Madison: University of Wisconsin Press, 1967. P. 555 ff.

Rosenzweig, S. A transvaluation of psychotherapy—a reply to Hans Eysenck. *Journal of Abnormal and Social Psychology*, 1954, **49**, 298–304.

Sandler, J. Research in psychoanalysis. The Hampstead Clinic as an instrument of psychoanalytic research. *International Journal of Psychoanalysis*, 1962, **43**, 287–291.

Sargent, Helen D. Intrapsychic change: Methodological problems in psychotherapy research. *Psychiatry*, 1961, **24**, 93–108.

Sargent, Helen D., Horwitz, L., Wallerstein, R., and Appelbaum, Ann. Prediction in psychotherapy research: A method for the transformation of clinical judgments into testable hypotheses. *Psychological Issues*, 1968.

Schafer, R. Generative empathy in the treatment situation. *Psychoanalytic Quarterly*, 1959, **28**, 342–373.

Schjelderup, H. Lasting effects of psychoanalytic treatment. *Psychiatry*, 1955, **18**, 109–133.

Schlessinger, N., Pollock, G. H., Sabshin, M., Sadow, L., and Gedo, J. E. Psychoanalytic contributions to psychotherapy research. In Gottschalk, L. A., and Auerbach, A. H. (Eds.), *Methods of research in psychotherapy*. New York: Appleton-Century-Crofts, 1966. Pp. 334–360.

Sears, R. R. *Survey of objective studies of psychoanalytic concepts*. New York: Social Science Research Council, 1943 (a).

Sears, R. R. Experimental analyses of psychoanalytic phenomena. In Hunt, J. McV. (Ed.), *Fundamentals of personality and behavior disorders*. New York: Ronald Press, 1943 (b).

Seitz, P. F. D. The consensus problem in psychoanalytic research. In Gottschalk, L. A., and Auerbach, A. H. (Eds.), *Methods of research in psychotherapy*. New York: Appleton-Century-Crofts, 1966. Pp. 209–225.

Shakow, D. The recorded psychoanalytic interview as an objective approach in reasearch psychoanalysis. *Psychoanalytic Quarterly*, 1960, **29**, 82–97.

Shlien, J., Mosak, H., and Dreikurs, R. Effective time limits: A comparison of client-centered and Adlerian psychotherapy. *American Psychologist*, 1960, **15**, 415. (Abstract).

Simon, J., Fink, G., and Endicott, N. A. *Journal of the Hillside Hospital*, July–Oct. 1967, **16**, Nos. 3 and 4.

Sklansky, M. A., Isaacs, K. S., Levitov, Edith S., and Haggard, E. A. Verbal interaction and levels of meaning in psychotherapy. *Archives of General Psychiatry*, 1966, **14**, 158–170.

Speisman, J. Depth of interpretation and verbal resistance in psychotherapy. *Journal of Consulting Psychology*, 1959, **23**, 93–99.

Spence, D. P. (Ed.). *The broad scope of psychoanalysis—selected papers of Leopold Bellak*. New York: Grune & Stratton, 1967.

Spence, D. P. Computer analysis of symptom contexts. Presented at a midwinter workshop in psychoanalysis research. American Psychoanalytic Association, New York, 1968.

Spence, D. P. Short-term prediction in psychoanalysis: A quantitative study of over-determination. (In preparation, 1970.)

Spence, D. P. PL/1 programs for content analysis. *Behavioral Science*, 1969, **14**, 432–433 (a).

Spence, D. P. Computer measurement of process and content in psychoanalysis. *Transactions of the N. Y. Academy of Science*. 1969, **31**, 828–841. (b).

Spence, D. P. and Lugo, M. The role of verbal cues in clinical listening. *Psychoanalysis and Contemporary Science*. (In Press, 1970).

Spence, D. P., and Greif, B. An experimental study of listening between the lines. *Journal of Nervous and Mental Disease*. (In Press, 1970).

Stone, P. J., Dunphy, D. C., Smith, M. S., and Ogilvie, D. M. *The general inquirer*. Cambridge: M.I.T. Press, 1966.

Strupp, H. H. Psychotherapeutic technique, professional affiliation, and experience level. *Journal of Consulting Psychology*, 1955, **19**, 97–102.

Strupp, H. H. *Psychotherapists in action: Explorations of the therapist's contribution to the treatment process*. New York: Grune & Stratton, 1960.

Strupp, H. H. Psychotherapy revisited: The problem of outcome. *Psychotherapy*, 1963, **1**, 1–13.

Strupp, H. H. Psychoanalytic therapy of the individual. In Marmor, J. (Ed.), *Modern psychoanalysis: New directions and perspectives*. New York: Basic Books, 1968. Pp. 293–342.

Tomlinson, T. M. The therapeutic process as related to outcome. In Rogers, C. R. (Ed.), *The therapeutic relationship and its impact*. Madison: University of Wisconsin Press, 1967.

Tomlinson, T. M., and Hart, J. T. A validation of the process scale. *Journal of Consulting Psychology*, 1962, **26**, 74–78.

Truax, C. B. A scale for the measurement of accurate empathy. *Psychiatric Institute Bulletin, Wisconsin Psychiatric Institute, University of Wisconsin*, **1**, No. 12, 1961.

Truax, C. B. Effective ingredients in psychotherapy: An approach to unraveling the patient–therapist interaction. *Journal of Counseling Psychology*, 1963, **3**, 256–263.

Truax, C. B. Influence of patient-statements on judgments of therapist-statements during psychotherapy. *Journal of Clinical Psychology*, 1966, **22**, 335–337.

Truax, C. B., and Carkhuff, R. R. *Toward effective counseling in psychotherapy*. Chicago: Aldine, 1967.

Truax, C. B., Wargo, D. G., Frank, J. D., Imber, S. D., Battle, Carolyne C., Hoehn-Saric, R., Nash, E., and Stone, A. Therapist empathy, genuineness, and warmth and patient therapeutic outcome. *Journal of Consulting Psychology*, 1966, **30**, 394–401

Waelder, R. Psychoanalysis, scientific method and philosophy. *Journal of the American Psychoanalytic Association*, 1962, **10**, 617–637.

Walker, A., Rablen, R. A., and Rogers, C. R. Development of a scale to measure process change in psychotherapy. *Journal of Clinical Psychology*, 1966, **16**, 183–225.

Wallerstein, R. The current state of psychotherapy: Theory, practice, and research. *Journal of the American Psychoanalytic Association*, 1966, **14**, 183–225.

Wallerstein, R., Robbins, L., Sargent, Helen, and Luborsky, L. The psychotherapy research project of the Menninger Foundation. *Bulletin of the Menninger Clinic*, 1956, **20**, 221–280.

Weber, J., Elinson, J., and Moss, L. M. The application of electronic machine techniques to psychoanalytic clinic records. Reprinted from *Excerpta Medica, International Congress Series #150: Proceedings of the World Congress of Psychiatry*, Madrid, Sept. 1966. Pp. 2317–2320.

Weintraub, W., and Aronson, H. A survey of patients in classical psychoanalysis: Some vital statistics. *Journal of Nervous and Mental Disease*, 1968, **146**, 98–102.

12

PLACEBO EFFECTS IN MEDICINE, PSYCHOTHERAPY, AND PSYCHOANALYSIS

ARTHUR K. SHAPIRO

CORNELL UNIVERSITY

INTRODUCTION

Study of the placebo effect provides an approach to the question of what is specific and non-specific in psychotherapy. This concept is not popular because psychotherapy is frequently believed to be a modern treatment based on scientific principles, while the placebo effect is viewed as a superstitious response to a drug. These attitudes result in excluding the placebo effect as a factor, or even the entire basis, for the existence, popularity, and effectiveness of any or all of the numerous methods of psychotherapy now in use.

The thesis of this paper is that much can be learned about a treatment if it is examined in relation to basic principles applicable to all treatment; in other words, much can be learned about psychotherapy by considering its relationship to the placebo effect.

If this sounds far-fetched, let us remember that both psychotherapy and the placebo effect function solely through a psychological mechanism. Adamant claims that psychotherapy is not susceptible to placebo effects conform to the principle that every placebo once accepted was vigorously defended as a nonplacebo. Medical history clearly demonstrates that despite the sensitivity of many practitioners to the non-specific or placebo effects of others, they were usually insensitive to their own. In fact, this insensitivity increases the potency of the placebo effect, which once begun is a self-fulfilling prophecy.

The importance of the placebo effect is always underestimated because it is easier to recognize the shortcomings of others than our own (Shapiro, 1960a, 1960b). For example, Hofling (1955), in a questionnaire about the use of placebos, found that physicians attributed their

439

use to other physicians three times more often than they attributed their use to themselves.

The tendency of physicians to impute the use of placebos to other physicians was confirmed in a study by the author. In addition, in a series of questions on what should be included in a definition of placebo, physicians tended to exclude their therapies from the definition. Surgeons excluded surgery, internists excluded active medication, and psychotherapists and psychoanalysts excluded psychotherapy and psychoanalysis.[1] These defensive attitudes about placebo effects are also reflected in the history and definition of the word *Placebo* (Shapiro, 1960b, 1964c, 1964d, in press a).

DEFINITION OF PLACEBO

The history of the placebo begins with the Hebrew Bible. The first word of Psalm 166:9 is "Ethalech," which was translated into the Latin Bible as "placebo," derived from the verb "placere," meaning "to please" (Murray, 1933). "Placebo" was the initial word of the first antiphon, and entered English in the twelfth century by becoming the name commonly given to the vespers for the dead, a custom which is no longer followed and whose meaning is now obscure (The Catholic Encyclopedia, 1911).

"Placebo" took on a secular meaning in the fourteenth century, and its connotations gradually became derisive during the next several centuries. The word was used to describe a servile flatterer, sycophant, toady, and parasite. This usage derives from disparagement of the professional mourners who were paid to "sing placebos" at the bier of the deceased, a role originally assigned to the family.

Before proceeding, errors in the etymology of the placebo must be clarified, because they have influenced all later histories. Few people realize that medical dictionaries have limited their definitions of the placebo to inert or inactive drugs only during the last 19 years (Blakiston's New Gould Medical Dictionary, 1949). In recent medical dictionaries, definitions have expanded, so that they are now closer to the original that appeared in the 1785 edition of *Motherby's New Medical Dictionary* (1795): "A commonplace

method or medicine." It is interesting that this original definition is either overlooked or misquoted as a "commonplace method *of* medicine." The distinction between "of" and "or" is important, since the former limits the definition to medicine, whereas the latter includes methods *and* medicine. Although the original definition included all therapies, as drugs became more important in medical theory and practice in the nineteenth century, the term became limited to medicine. This continued until 19 years ago when medical dictionaries, partly owing to perpetuation of early errors, began to limit the definition to inert substances. Such interpretation has influenced the thinking of many physicians and nonphysicians, who conceive of the placebo only as inert or limited to medicine. But recently, as treatment changed, and as psychotherapy became a prominent therapy, definitions in papers and dictionaries expanded and are now more like the original definition of 1785. My proposed definition, which I believe fulfills historic and heuristic criteria, follows:

A *placebo* is defined as any therapy, or that component of any therapy, that is deliberately used for its nonspecific, psychologic, or psychophysiologic effect, or that is used for its presumed specific effect on a patient, symptom, or illness, but which, unknown to patient and therapist, is without specific activity for the condition being treated.

A *placebo*, when used as a control in experimental studies, is defined as a substance or procedure that is without specific activity for the condition being evaluated.

The *placebo effect* is defined as the nonspecific, psychologic, or psychophysiologic effect produced by placebos.

In other words, any therapy may be used with or without knowledge that it is a placebo, including treatments given in the belief that they are not placebos but which actually are by *objective* evaluation. The placebo may be inert or active and may include, therefore, all medical treatment, no matter how specific or how administered. It may take the form of oral and parenteral medication, topical preparations, inhalants, and all mechanical, surgical, psychotherapeutic, and other therapeutic techniques. It

---

[1] Shapiro, in preparation a, b, c.

would include a treatment that produced symptoms or side effects which were not specific for it. A placebo may or may not result in a placebo effect, and the effect may be favorable or unfavorable—that is, positive or negative.

This definition makes no assumption about which treatments are placebos, or about the mechanism of placebo action. These issues are left open because the placebo effect is a multi-determined phenomenon that is not yet understood (Shapiro, 1960a, 1963, 1964, a, b, d, in press a). The definition is a phenomenological statement that avoids becoming tautological. It provides a good model for research and a structure into which variables can be placed for testing, and it makes possible an independent assessment about which everyone can agree.

The placebo was used originally as a pejorative and derisive epithet to describe treatment of other practitioners, and not knowingly or deliberately prescribed by physicians. Today, the criterion for placebo treatment is based on more than opinion about what is effective treatment. It is, or should be, based on scientific methodology and principles of controlled evaluation. This criterion is justified historically, linguistically, dynamically, and heuristically. Other alternatives result in many difficulties (Shapiro, 1964a, 1964b, in press a).

Although the definition may prove to be too inclusive, for heuristic reasons it would presently be premature to make specific exclusions. It is likely that various placebogenic factors will be reliably isolated in the future. When everything is known about the placebo and placebo effect, the definition will probably no longer be needed, except in lexicons of obsolete terms, but this is yet a desideratum for the future.

These considerations led to my attempt to seek generalizations and hypotheses about all methods of therapy, and resulted in the conclusion that it was important to include psychotherapy within the scope of the placebo effect, and to study the interaction of placebo effects and psychotherapy. Thus, hypotheses and conclusions about psychotherapy and the placebo effect will be derived from review of pre-scientific and modern treatment, and the placebogenic factors contributed by the physician-patient relationship, the patient, and the physician.

PRESCIENTIFIC MEDICINE

Psychological factors, always important in medicine, were recognized as early as the period of Hippocrates. Galen estimated that sixty percent of patients had symptoms of emotional rather than physical origin. This figure is close to the contemporary estimate of fifty to eighty percent. Despite Galen's and Hippocrates' acumen, none of the drugs they used were of any use. Treatment was primitive, unscientific, largely ineffective, and often shocking and dangerous (Shapiro, 1959, 1960a).

Patients took almost every known organic and inorganic substance—crocodile dung, teeth of swine, hooves of asses, spermatic fluid of frogs, eunuch fat, fly specks, lozenges of dried vipers, powder of precious stones, bricks, furs, feathers, hair, human perspiration, oil of ants, earthworms, wolves, and spiders, moss scraped from the skull of a victim of violent death, and so on. Blood from every animal was prepared and administered in every way, and was used to treat every conceivable symptom and disease. Almost all human and animal excretions were used.

Some famous treatments used for centuries included the Royal Touch, Egyptian mummy, unicorn horn, bezoar stone, and mandrake. Theriac contained 37 to 63 ingredients; mattioli contained 230 and required several months to concoct. Galen's elaborate pharmacopoeia, all worthless, contained 820 substances. Medical reasoning was primitive: Lung of fox, a long-winded animal, was given to consumptives. Fat of bear, a hirsute animal, was prescribed for baldness. Mistletoe, a plant that grows on the oak which cannot fall, was specific for the falling sickness (Lehmann & Knight, 1960). A wound was treated by sympathetic powder which was applied to the inflicting implement. Throughout medical history patients were purged, puked, poisoned, punctured, cut, cupped, blistered, bled, leached, heated, frozen, sweated, and shocked (Garrison, 1921; Haggard, 1929, 1933, 1934; Major, 1955; Shapiro, 1959, 1960a).

Though medicine held a place in the finest scientific, religious, cultural, and ethical traditions throughout history, one may wonder how physicians maintained their position of honor and respect. Useful drugs or procedures were applied infrequently and were usually forgotten by succeeding generations. For thousands of years physicians prescribed what we now know were useless and often dangerous medications. This would have been impossible were it not for the fact that physicians did help their patients.

Today we know that the effectiveness of these procedures and medications was due to psychological factors often referred to as the placebo effect. Since almost all medications until recently were placebos, the history of medical treatment can be characterized largely as the history of the placebo effect.

The first major contribution to the end of Galenism and to the beginning of scientific medical treatment is often attributed to Sydenham in the seventeenth century. He is erroneously credited with demonstrating that cinchoma bark (which contains quinine) was specific only for fevers of malarial origin, and not for all febrile infections (Duran-Reynals, 1946; Forrer, 1964a). Cinchoma bark often has been thought of as the first drug that was not a placebo, because previously there had been no way to distinguish between placebo and nonplacebo. But the placebo effect flourished as the norm of medical treatment even after the beginning of modern scientific medicine seven or eight decades ago (Shapiro, 1959, 1960a).

These considerations have led to the famous admonition: *Treat as many patients with the new remedies while they still have the power to heal.*

MODERN MEDICINE

Modern medicine no longer relies chiefly upon psychological factors, placebo effects, or the doctor-patient relationship. Today there are an increasing number of specific and predictable drugs and medical procedures. Although psychological factors may be minimized, they can never be excluded. Of course, if the dosage of a drug is high enough, all patients will react with toxicity or even death, regardless of psychological factors. But such predictability is of little consequence, because the majority of clinically useful drugs are prescribed in dosages that are far below the toxic level, and thus in a range in which psychological factors or placebo effects are important (Shapiro, 1963, in press a).

Despite these advances, the placebo effect is an important component of modern medicine, and many papers have demonstrated its importance and magnitude in every therapeutic area.[2]

Placebos can be more powerful than, and reverse the action of, potent active drugs (Wolf, 1959a). The incidence of placebo reactions approaches one hundred per cent in some studies Placebos can have profound effects on organic illnesses, and possibly even on malignancies (Shapiro, 1963). Placebos can often mimic the effects of active drugs (Lasagna, Laties, and Dohan, 1958). Uncontrolled studies report that drugs are effective four to five times more frequently than do controlled studies (Foulds, 1958; Fox, 1961). Placebo effects are so omnipresent that if they are not reported in controlled studies, these are commonly considered unreliable. Increased appreciation of placebo effects is reflected in the speculation that future historians will record the major medical achievement of the last decade as the development of methodology and controlled experimentation to test the efficacy of treatment.

RECENT INTEREST IN PLACEBO EFFECT

Physicians in internal medicine stimulated renewed interest in the placebo effect between the years of 1946 and 1953. Psychiatrists became interested shortly thereafter, following the introduction of tranquilizers in 1953. Although psychologists were the last group to become interested in the placebo effect, they have contributed more extensively than any other group.

---

[2] Beecher, 1955, 1959; Bull, 1959; Duran-Reynals, 1946; Foulds, 1958; Frank, 1958, 1961; Garrison, 1921; Hofling, 1955; Klopfer, 1957; Lasagna, Laties, and Dohan, 1958; Modell, 1955; Shapiro, 1959, 1960a, 1960b, 1964a, 1964d; Shapiro, Wilensky, and Struening, 1968; Uhlenhuth, Cantor, Neustadt, and Payson, 1959; Wolf, 1959.

The number of papers on the placebo effect has increased each year since 1946; more papers have been published since 1960 than in all previous years combined. This development is reflected in the increase of carefully controlled studies that use statistics, placebos, double-blind procedures, and other controls.

THE PLACEBO AS AN ADAPTIVE MECHANISM

The tendency to react with placebo effects is probably a built-in form of an adaptive mechanism that has helped mankind survive. Man's drive for survival and development would have been impaired by realistic reactions to the many unpredictable, overwhelming forces and phenomena to which he was exposed. Man's capacity, need, and ability to explain the unknown by projection of internal fantasy onto his environment provided adaptive psychological outlets in the form of externalization of fantasy, catharsis, control over internal and external environment, and other psychological mechanisms. This process would decrease anxiety, depression, despair, and hopelessness, and liberate energies for adaptation to realistic problems.

Man has always reacted to unknowable stressful stimuli with unrealistic fantasies of optimism, pessimism, and a combination of both. This was reflected in primitive periods by elaborate mythologies and magic. The world was populated by benevolent and malevolent forces—gods, devils, witches, incubi, dybbucks, miasmas, and so on. An optimistic fantasy might provide an adaptive denial of an otherwise unmanageable world. A pessimistic fantasy would be a useful preparation for adversity. A capacity for reality testing would be an important modifier of unrealistic fantasy. A propitious combination of these factors would be useful for survival, adaptation, and increased control of the environment.

As the world became more known and manageable, diffuse fantasy and projections were less necessary, and the witch doctor-priest-scientist differentiated into specialties. Today the scientist has a methodology and a philosophy to deal with the unknown. Religion has become institutionalized and increasingly restricted to vague spiritual aspects of man's existence. Although medicine has made great advances in its understanding and treatment of disease, illness still can provoke fantasy because of the importance of its unknown consequences and resolution.

Man's greater success in conquering his physical environment than in furthering his psychological understanding has increasingly led to a preoccupation with psychological problems. Previously, the physical environment was inexplicably intertwined with psychological problems and resolutions. With increasing control of the physical environment, somatic displacement and projection of psychological problems became a less adequate and necessary outlet. Psychological problems can be approached directly. But man's understanding of his impulses, conflicts, and relationship with others, and psychological insight into himself, is inadequately comprehended. With failure of traditional religious and other explanations, man's capacity for fantasy and projection has focused increasingly on self-understanding. Psychotherapy has become the institutionalized outlet for the expression and resolution of conflict. Placebo effects, formerly associated with physical illness and treatment, can now be expressed and experienced through psychological treatment.

This rationale, and the etymology and semantics of the word *placebo*, historically and heuristically justify an examination of psychotherapy as a placebo effect.

PLACEBOGENESIS

Patient-Therapist Relationship

The physician's role in society is unique. He performs and combines functions that have always been important to mankind—those of healer, priest, and scientist (Jaspers, 1965). These attributes facilitate the tendency of patients to relate unrealistically to physicians. This tendency has been referred to as *transference*, which is usually considered a process whereby such feelings as love, hatred, trust, and distrust, which the patient attached to significant persons in the past (usually parents or parent surrogates), are displaced onto the physician in the present.

The readiness of most patients for a positive transference or relationship to the physician is probably related to satisfactory early experiences with parents and parent surrogates that establish future patterns of adult behavior. Individuals who expect succor and comfort despite hunger, fright, and discomfort are probably one group of positive placebo reactors. Hope and optimism reflected in positive placebo reactions probably indicate a potential for health in the patient.

The patient's transference potential may be apparent in the initial interview, when he may be hostile, servile, compliant, rebellious, co-operative, or suspicious. He may not take the medication that is prescribed, or he may distort the instructions. He may report dramatic relief of symptoms or describe alarming side-effects, that is, positive and negative placebo effect.

The patient's transference relationship with the doctor, and the doctor's countertransference relationship with the patient, are important elements in placebo reactions and their direction (positive, negative, or absent), and they influence the outcome of all treatment. Although the concept of transference is difficult to demon-strate experimentally, it is frequently referred to as being important in the placebo effect. It may be referred to as the doctor-patient relationship, rapport, warmth, trust, faith, empathy, and so on.[3] Further understanding requires experi-mental study of the details that contribute to this gross phenomenon. An analysis of the elements in the patient and physician that contribute to placebo effects might contribute some of these details.

Patient Variables

Suggestibility. The most extensively investi-gated factor in studying the placebo effect has been the concept of suggestion. This approach is important because of presumed common components in tests of suggestibility and placebo effects. The concept is important in theories of hypnosis, and tests of suggestibility can be devised, discrete experiments designed, factors manipulated, and data analyzed. Over the years,

the meaning of the term has expanded to include many diverse phenomena, including the placebo effect. But the plausible expectation that tests of suggestibility would correlate with each other,[4] with the placebo effect, (Bentler, O'Hara and Krasner, 1963; Duke, 1962; Evans, 1967; Frank, Gliedman, Imber, Nash and Stone, 1957; Gliedman, Nash, Imber, Stone and Frank, 1958; Stukat, 1958; Whitman, 1961) and with clinical course (Gliedman et al., 1958; Hankoff, Freedman, and Engelhardt, 1960; Lehmann, 1964; Steinbook, Jones, and Ainslie, 1966; Whitehorn, 1958) has not been substantiated. What is the explanation?

Stimulus Variable. One possible explanation is that a placebo stimulus is not the same stimulus as a test of suggestibility. Because the latter is associated with laboratory experiments and the former with clinical situations, potent psychological factors in therapy are minimized or absent in the experiment. A test of suggesti-bility involves an experimenter rather than a therapist, a subject rather than a patient, and a laboratory rather than a clinical setting (Shapiro, 1960a, 1964d, 1968a). These differences may explain the poor correlation and different effects of these stimuli.

Despite these differences, potential factors held in common among clinical and experi-mental situations, hypnosis, placebo effects, suggestion, persuasion, and so forth, warrant further investigation.

Subject Variable. Another possible expla-nation is that the placebo effect may be unstable because it is sensitive to changes in the subject, clinical condition, physician-patient relation-ship, expectations of the patient, and so on (Hankoff, Freedman, and Engelhardt, 1958; Rashkis and Smarr, 1957; Shapiro, 1960a, 1964a, 1964b, 1968, in press a; Wolf, Doering, Clark, and Hagans, 1957). This idea is based on reports that inconstant placebo reactions are more common than constant positive or negative ones (Shapiro, 1968). But it is difficult to evalu-

---

[3] Frank, 1958, 1961; Hofling, 1955; Modell, 1955; Rashkis and Smarr, 1957, Shapiro, 1959, 1960a, in press b; Uhlenruth, Cantor, Neustadt, and Payson, 1959; Wolf, 1959.

[4] Bentler, O'Hara, and Kramer, 1963; Duke, 1962; Evans, 1967; Grimes, 1948a; Lehmann and Knight, 1960a, 1960b; Lehmann, 1964; Rashkis and Smarr, 1957; Stukat, 1958; Thorn, 1962; Whitman, 1961.

ate what is being measured because there are so many variables in repeated measures of the placebo effect. Certain aspects of initial and subsequent placebo reaction may be related; other aspects may be independent. The condition of the subject and the meaningfulness of the placebo stimulus to him may change with time. For example, the initial injection of pencillin may evoke a marked clinical response in a patient with a bacterial infection, but later injections may have little measurable clinical effect after he is well. A placebo may have a marked effect on a patient who is anxious and depressed, (Shapiro, 1968) but little effect on one without symptoms. Similar analogies apply to most medical procedures.

In addition, the initial reaction of a clinically stressed patient to a placebo may be the most important and clinically relevant prognostic parameter. Personality and other characteristics may be different in patients who react initially one way and subsequently another way, or constantly positive or negative. All types of placebo reaction patterns should be studied, including initial reaction, even though most subjects react inconsistently.

A similar problem is the tendency of most studies to compare groups of positive reactors with groups of combined nonreactors (absence of reaction) and negative reactors (placebo side effects). This has led to less information about negative reactors, blurring the distinction between them and nonreactors, and obscuring some of the important differences between positive and other types of reactors (Shapiro et al., 1968). The importance of distinguishing among these types of reaction was illustrated in a study by the author. Positive and negative placebo reactors shared more variance on many demographic and personality variables than they did with nonreactors. In other words, the two former groups were more alike and clearly differentiated from the latter.

Personality. Various investigators have attempted to relate placebo effects to the patient's personality. Placebo reactors have been charac-

terized as compliant, religious, hypochondriac, anxious, less educated, and frequently using cathartics (Lasagna, Mosteller, von Felsinger, and Beecher, 1954); disturbed and likely to react to drugs with atypical reactions (von Felsinger, Lasagna and Beecher, 1955); anxious (Beecher, 1959; Fisher and Olin, 1956; Gliedman et al., 1958; Kornetsky and Humphries, 1957; Roberts and Hamilton, 1958; Frank, 1961); depressed (Frank, 1961; Gliedman et al., 1958); dependent (Kornetsky and Humphries, 1957; Lasagna et al., 1954); ideational (Abramson, Jarvik, Levine, Kaufman, and Hirsch, 1955); neurotic (Fisher and Olin, 1956); extroverted (Black, 1966) and so on.[5]

The attempt to relate placebo effects to the patient's personality has failed. Traits found in one study have not been confirmed in others done under different conditions. It is possible that no definitive traits exist. If they do exist, sundry contaminating variables will have to be isolated before they become apparent.

Interaction Between Stimulus and Subject Variables. Of these variables, the problem of the placebo stimulus has not yet been considered. Some personality variables appear to describe patients for whom a placebo in the form of a drug would be culturally appropriate; for example, those of lower social class. A psychotherapeutic placebo stimulus might be more appropriate for higher social classes. Patients expecting psychotherapy might react negatively to a placebo stimulus that symbolizes and suggests treatment with drugs, while those expecting drug treatment might react negatively to a psychotherapy placebo stimulus, such as free association for an hour in a sensory-deprivation setting. This factor must be recognized before any attempt is made to understand the role of personality in the patient's reaction to placebos. The poor correlation among various studies offers some support for this hypothesis.

Clinical Prognosis From Placebo Effects. These ideas suggest that an initial placebo reaction in a clinically relevant context is a better

[5] Gartner, 1961; Hankoff, Engelhardt, Freedman, Mann, and Margolis, 1960; Honigfeld, 1964b; Knowles and Lucas, 1960; Morison, Woodmansey, and Young, 1961; Kurland, 1958; Liberman, 1962;

Linton and Langs, 1962; Muller, 1965; Roberts and Hamilton, 1958; Samuels and Edison, 1961; Shapiro, Wilensky, and Struening, 1968; Tibbets and Hawkins, 1956; Trouton, 1957.

predictor of clinical outcome than a laboratory test of suggestibility. This inference is supported by the failure of studies using tests of suggestibility to predict clinical course (Frank et al., 1957; Gliedman et al., 1957; Imber and Nash, 1955; Steinbook et al., 1966; Whitman, 1961) and by the association of the placebo effect with clinical course in six of seven studies (Bishop and Gallant, 1966; Gliedman et al., 1958; Hankoff et al., 1959, 1960; Lasagna et al., 1954; Glick, 1967; Shapiro et al., 1968). In other words, a test of suggestibility might have high reliability but low predictive validity; response to an initial placebo stimulus should have high reliability and possibly high validity.

These considerations led the author to develop a systematic method of measuring placebo reactions. This method was then used to test several hypotheses about the placebo effect (Shapiro et al., 1968). Several studies are now in progress.

Sex, Age, and Intelligence. Conclusions about the relationship between placebo effects and sex, age, and intelligence are not presently possible because the results of several studies are contradictory (Beecher, 1959; Shapiro, 1968a; Shapiro et al., 1968).

Some studies report that females have more placebo effects than males (Beecher, 1952; Gliedman et al., 1958; O'Brien, 1954; Abramson et al., 1955); others report that there is no difference between the sexes (Black, 1966; Lasagna et al., 1954; Roberts and Hamilton, 1958; Samuels and Edison, 1961; Tibbets and Hawkins, 1956). In some studies, young age correlated positively with placebo effects (Tibbetts and Hawkins, 1956; Gliedman et al., 1958; Kurland, 1958; Shapiro et al., 1968); in others, it correlated negatively (Lasagna et al., 1954; O'Brien, 1954), or did not correlate either negatively or positively (Abramson et al., 1955; Black, 1966; Fisher and Olin, 1956; Hankoff et al., 1960; Knowles and Lucas, 1960; Kornetsky and Humphries, 1957; Roberts and Hamilton, 1958; Stukat, 1958).

Projective Tests. The results of Rorschach and other psychological tests were inconclusive or contradictory in several studies.[6]

Psychiatric Diagnosis. Placebo reactions are not related to whether patients are neurotic or psychotic (Hankoff et al., 1960; Kurland, 1957, 1958; Samuels and Edison, 1961), although the intensity and range of such reactions may be greater in those who are psychotic. Shapiro et al. (1968a) reported placebo effects range between 18 and 67 percent for various diagnostic categories. Placebo effects are reported more frequently in patients with symptoms of anxiety and depression (Shapiro, 1959, 1960a, 1968).

Constancy of Placebo Effects. Severe illness and chronic symptoms do not preclude response to placebos (Beecher, 1959; Fisher and Olin, 1956; Hargreaves, Hamilton, and Roberts, 1958; Rashkis and Smarr, 1957; Roberts and Hamilton, 1958; Samuels and Edison, 1961; Tibbets and Hawkins, 1956; Shapiro et al., 1968), although brief illness has been related to positive placebo effects (Black, 1966; Tibbets and Hawkins, 1956). The response is believed to be ephemeral by some investigators and enduring by others (Beecher, 1959; Frank, 1961). Favorable prognoses may characterize patients with positive placebo response (Frank, 1961; Hankoff, Engelhardt, and Freedman, 1960; Hankoff et al., 1958; Shapiro et al., 1968b; Steinbook et al., 1966; Whitehorn, 1958). Inconstant placebo reactors are usually more frequent than constant positive or negative placebo reactors. Studies usually report a greater incidence of positive than negative placebo reactions (Gliedman et al., 1958; Hankoff et al., 1960; Lasagna et al., 1954; von Felsinger, Lasagna, and Beecher, 1955). Patients who fail to respond to a placebo in one study may respond in another (Rashkis and Smarr, 1957; Wolf et al., 1957). Reactions to placebos are generally not uniform, constant, or predictable (Hagans, Doering, Ashley, and Wolf, 1957; Kurland, 1957, 1958; Wolf et al., 1957). Despite this inconsistency, measurement of placebo reactions, as described earlier, and similar to the measurement of temperature in a feverish

---

[6] Abramson et al., 1955; Gliedman et al., 1958; Grimes, 1948b; Hankoff et al., 1960; Hull, 1933; Knowles and Lucas, 1960; Kornetsky and Humphries, 1957; Lasagna et al., 1954; Lehmann and Knight, 1960; Roberts and Hamilton, 1958; Linton and Langs, 1962; Uhlenhuth et al., 1959.

patient, might be reliable and valid if performed at the appropriate time in a patient's life, such as during acute anxiety.

Anxiety. The factor most frequently reported to be characteristic of placebo reactors is that of manifest, unelaborated, free-floating anxiety.[7] Beecher in anesthesiology, Castiglioni in history, Malinowski in anthropology, and Parsons in sociology believe that suggestibility increases with stress. Hysterical patients with *la belle indifférence*, or without manifest anxiety, are reported to react poorly to placebos, despite the fact that they have been traditionally considered the most suggestible of all patients. This surprising finding, especially if replicated, tends to confirm the importance of anxiety in placebo reactions. Patients without anxiety, such as sociopaths and obsessive compulsives, generally have poor prognoses and would be expected to be poor placebo reactors. Anxiety, agitation, and panic are generally considered favorable prognostic signs. Schizophrenic patients with marked anxiety, in homosexual panic or with schizoaffective features, other patients with agitated depression, and neurotics with manifest anxiety are among such patients. Anxiety is a favorable prognostic sign in psychotherapy, psychochemotherapy, insulin treatment, and lobotomy. In appropriate amounts, anxiety also facilitates learning and conditioning.

Many psychoanalysts believe that insight, the *ne plus ultra* of psychotherapy, occurs when interpretations of unconscious conflicts are associated with anxiety. Since anxiety is so important in placebo effects, the improvement of patients may be more a consequence of placebo effects than of insights and the correctness of interpretations. A review of the literature leaves no doubt that anxiety is an important element associated with placebo effects.

Negative and Nonplacebo Reactions. The negative and nonplacebo reactors have not been well characterized. Some researchers report that

psychotic patients have negative placebo reactions more frequently than neurotic patients (Fisher and Olin, 1956), but this claim is disputed by others, who report little difference in the reactivity of psychotics and nonpsychotics (Kurland, 1958; Shapiro et al., 1968). Negative reactors are described as vague, nonspecific, hard to pin down about their history, unresponsive to treatment (Fisher and Olin, 1956), and as more rigid and controlled, but with less personality deviation, than reactors (von Felsinger et al., 1955). One author questions individual adjustment as an important attribute of the placebo reactor (Kurland, 1958).

The results of a recent preliminary study by the author indicate that nonreactors are rigid, authoritarian, and stereotypic, tend to use the mechanism of denial, and are not psychologically oriented. More reactive patients respond to the placebo. Positive reactors rely more on outer stimuli; negative reactors rely more on inner stimuli, and tend to have more paranoid and masochistic traits (Shapiro et al., 1968).

Faith and Hope. The importance of faith is reflected in the fact that one of the major, best educated religious groups in the United States denies the rational efficacy of any treatment or medicine, and attributes all therapeutic benefits to faith. Faith is frequently mentioned in vague terms such as trust and faith in the doctor, confidence in the treatment, expectation and anticipation of relief, previous experience with treatment and doctors, fame and popularity of a treatment, and so on. When coupled with the patient's magic expectation, we get back to important elements in the doctor-patient relationship and transference.[8]

The arousal of hope in the patient by the therapist has been persuasively described by Frank as the major factor in psychotherapy and placebo effects. When hope is aroused, anxiety, depression and other symptoms decrease, the patient feels better, functions better, and may develop ego capacity (Frank, 1961).

---

[7] Beecher, 1959; Fisher and Olin, 1956; Frank, 1961; Gliedman et al., 1958; Goldstein, 1962; Kornetsky and Humphries, 1957; Lasagna et al., 1954; Roberts and Hamilton, 1958; Shapiro, A. P., 1955; Shapiro, 1960a, in press b; von Felsinger et al., 1955.

[8] Fisher and Olin, 1956; Frank, 1958, 1961; Gliedman et al., 1957; Gliedman et al., 1958; Goldstein, 1962; Hofling, 1955; Klopfer, 1957; Kurland, 1957, 1958; Modell, 1955; Parsons, 1951; Rosenthal and Frank, 1956; Shapiro, 1960a; Tibbets and Hawkins, 1956; Whitehorn, 1958.

Catharsis. Catharsis can occur in every therapy; in nonverbal medical treatment through symbolism and displacement, and in psychotherapy because the patient talks. Catharsis leading to guilt reduction is one of the constants in the history of medical treatment (La Barre, 1964; Murphy, 1964; Kiev, 1964; Rivers, 1924; Shapiro, 1963, 1964d, 1964f, 1964c, 1968) which, as pointed out previously, is largely the history of placebo effects (Shapiro, 1959, 1960a.)

The history of medicine is filled with procedures or substances that have important symbolic meaning. In every era methods of depletion were widely used: emetics, enemas, purges, stomachics, sweating, salivating, bleeding, leeching, cupping, lancing, trephination, starvation, and dehydration. Methods of depletion and expulsion, and manipulation of internal body wastes and vital fluids, may relieve symptoms by symbolically expelling bad thoughts and ego-alien impulses (Glover, 1931). The discomfort of submitting to these procedures and the ingestion of many vile substances may assuage and expiate considerable guilt (Fenichel, 1954; La Barre, 1964; Rivers, 1924). Today, in our edified and verbal culture, these primitive methods are on the wane. The same expression and relief of symptoms may occur when patients verbally express conflictual and guilt-ridden thoughts and feelings in the free, nonjudging, and accepting atmosphere of the doctor's office. The alimentary and other primitive methods of catharsis have been superceded by a more intellectual and appropriate verbal catharsis. The fundamental mechanism, however, may be similar (Frank, 1961; Meerloo, 1963; Kiev, 1964; De Grazia, 1952; Haley, 1963; Murphy, 1964; Gumpert, 1963).

Defense Mechanism. Placebo effects can be discussed as defense mechanisms such as repression, regression, displacement, substitute symptom formation, obsessions, compulsions, denial, distortion, projection, flight into health, and so on.[9]

Uncontrolled and nonspecific factors in medical, psychiatric, or psychoanalytic treatment can produce placebo effects by reassuring patients about their idiosyncracies, fantasies, fear of loss of control and potential insanity, guilt, and so on. The mechanism includes inexact and incomplete interpretation and other nonspecific factors that are a part of all treatment. The physician aids the patient to displace conflicts by suggesting such things as a carefree vacation, thus gratifying impulses but decreasing anxiety and guilt. (Glover, 1931). Countertransference is another factor. (Barchilon, 1958; Kolb and Montgomery, 1958).

Medicine may provide the same outlet for anxiety as do drinking, eating, and smoking. A patient may express his need for care by a physician by requesting medication or reporting hypochondriacal symptoms because he feels unworthy of love for himself as a person because of guilt. Some patients cannot express needs for dependency except by requesting and taking medicine.

The ritual of taking medicine, like the conventional ten drops in one half glass of water, one half hour before meals and at bedtime, can decrease symptoms because of the effects of obsessive-compulsive activity in reducing anxiety. Medicine may provide the patient with repetitive reminders of other reassuring aspects of the physician-patient relationship. The response of patients to medicine or placebo, whether positive, negative, or absent, may communicate important nonverbal responses to treatment (Shapiro, 1964d, 1964f).

The use and effectiveness of any defense depends on the character of the patient, the abilities and character of the physician, and the situation in which treatment occurs.

Motivation, Learning, Conditioning and Expectations. Motivation, learning, and conditioning, to the extent that they are independent of transference and other factors mentioned in this chapter, contribute to placebo effects. This is a new area for research and investigation.[10] The

---

[9] Forrer, 1964a, 1964b; Frank, 1961; Glover, 1931, 1952; Hankoff et al., 1960; Hofling, 1955; Linton and Langs, 1962; Schmideberg, 1939, 1958; Shapiro, 1960a, 1964f, in press b.

[10] Frank, 1958, 1961; Gliedman, Gantt, and Teitelbaum, 1957; Gliedman et al., 1958; Goldstein, 1962; Knoles, 1963; Knowles and Lucas, 1960; Krasner, 1962; Kurland, 1957, 1958; Lasagna et al., 1954; Trouton, 1957; Wolf, 1950, 1959.

expectations of the patient have been demonstrated by Goldstein (1962) and others to be an important determinant of the outcome of treatment and a determinant of the placebo effect.

Other Factors. Other important placebogenic factors are expectation and anticipation of relief (Glover, 1931), knowledge of an experience with the treatment (Abramson et al., 1955), previous experience with doctors, fame and popularity of the treatment (Shapiro, 1964b), possibilities of spontaneous remission or cure (Shapiro, 1963), and so on.

Situation Variables

Placebo effects are produced and influenced not only by patient and physician but also by the treatment situation. Here, the variables include staff attitudes, subject and patient population, treatment procedure, and miscellaneous factors.

Staff. Staff attitudes, expectations, biases, conflicts, and harmony can influence placebo effects.[11] The effect of a placebo can be reduced from 70 to 25 percent if the nurse's negative attitude toward the placebo injections is communicated to the patient (Volgyesi, 1954). In another study, patients treated with placebos improved more than those on tranquilizers, a result the authors attributed to the bias of the nurses against psychochemotherapy and for habit-training psychotherapy (Baker and Thorpe, 1957). The authors observed that nurses crushed, dissolved, and tasted the tablets in order to distinguish between placebo and active agent. Such attempts to identify the drugs used in controlled research have been reported in other studies (Fisher and Olin, 1956).

Staff behavior, such as interest and optimism, can influence patient behavior; for example, disturbed patient behavior has been attributed to staff conflict (Rathod, 1958; Linn, 1959; Shottstaedt et al., 1959; Stanton and Schwartz, 1954).

Changes associated with research activity can produce improvement in 80 percent of patients (Rashkis and Smarr, 1957). The bias of investigators has been noted previously to influence clinical and experimental results (Beecher, 1952, 1959; Eissen et al., 1959; Feldman, 1956; Foulds, 1958; Houston, 1938; Modell, 1955; Shapiro, 1960a). Research, while attempting to control variables, often introduces other variables (Ekman, 1961; Glaser and Whitlow, 1954; Knowles and Lucas, 1960; Rashkis, 1960; Rashkis and Smarr, 1957). The changes caused by the research are difficult to evaluate. It is not easy for researchers to observe objectively when they are involved in the process of being observed (Houston, 1938; Mezaros and Galigher, 1958; Rashkis and Smarr, 1957).

Subject and Patient Population. Subjects used for clinical and experimental drug studies are often volunteers who are assumed to be a normal control group. Several studies have demonstrated that this assumption is invalid, because volunteer subjects may have a high incidence of pathology. (Lasagna and von Felsinger, 1954; Perlin, Pollin and Butler, 1958; Pollin and Perlin, 1958). The converse was found in another study, which concluded that volunteer subjects were less ill or as normal as control nonvolunteer subjects (Richards, 1960). The degree of normality or abnormality appears to depend on the population studied. (Esecover, Malitz, and Wilkins, 1961; Perlin et al., 1958; Pollin and Perlin, 1958; Richards, 1960).

Treatment Procedure. Patients do not react uniformly to different treatment procedures (Wolf, 1959). Reaction to size, color, and shape of tablets or capsules varies (J.A.M.A., 1955; Leslie, 1954). Patients may dissolve and taste tablets if they suspect that they are a placebo (Fisher and Olin, 1956). Several investigators have reported that up to 50 percent of patients do not take their medication or follow instructions about dosage (Garetz, 1962). In another study, improvement with placebos was partially attributed to the fact that the placebo given to one group of patients was a sweet tablet, while the active drug given to another group was

---

[11] Baker and Thorpe, 1957; Eissen, Sabshin, and Heath, 1959; Golstein, 1962; Hofling, 1955; Linn, 1959; Mezaros and Galigher, 1958; Rathod, 1958; Shapiro 1960a; Shottstaedt, Pinsky, Mackler and Wolf, 1959; Stanton and Schwartz, 1954; Volgyesi, 1954; Von Mehring and King, 1957.

a bitter tablet (Baker and Thorpe, 1957). It is possible that a prescription of *exactly* nine drops of liquid medication would be more effective than the conventional and casually prescribed 10 drops. Even greater psychologic response, and placebo effects, would be expected with injections, various complicated procedures, and impressive machines.

Miscellaneous Factors. Spontaneous remission, transient everyday symptoms, new social group formation, change of environment, and many changes due to environmental factors can be attributed to placebos or treatment (Lasagna et al., 1954; Knowles and Lucas, 1960; Lehmann and Knight, 1960; Rashkis and Smarr, 1957; Rathod, 1958; Sabshin and Ramet, 1956; Shottstaedt et al., 1959; Wolf, 1959; Goldstein, 1962). Sometimes placebos and the general environment are as effective as, if not more so than, tranquilizing drugs in improving chronically hospitalized patients (Rathod, 1958). Psychologic factors interacting with social forces within the environment influence response to treatment on a metabolic ward (Rashkis and Smarr, 1957; Shottstaedt, et al., 1959). The transfer of psychotic patients from a state hospital to an intensive treatment hospital for lobotomies can result in considerable improvement in the behavior of patients prior to the surgery. The mood of a group, influenced by many factors, affects placebo responsivity (Knowles and Lucas, 1960). Placebo effects are increased in some subjects when they are tested as a group rather than as individuals. (Knowles and Lucas, 1960). Placebo reactivity is related to type of referral (Hankoff et al, 1960). Untreated patients may be influenced favorably by treated patients (Mezaros and Galigher, 1958). Merely filling out questionnaires can increase the number of responses, which can then be erroneously attributed to placebos (Glaser and Whitlow, 1954).

Patients may react differentially to private or clinic treatment or to treatment at a famous university center rather than at an informal private clinic. It is not known how patients differ in their response to physicians and personnel who are intimate or informal, busy or unhurried, matter-of-fact or involved, or supporting or rejecting. Studies of the psycho-social influences on psychiatric treatment have appeared recently in medical literature. The relationship between placebo effects and these important factors have not yet been explored.

Physician Variables

Although the relationship between physician and patient has been recognized throughout history as an important determinant of response to medical treatment, the responsibility of the patient for these effects has always been emphasized. Nevertheless, recent study of the physician's contribution to placebo and therapeutic effects has resulted in general agreement that his psychosociologic characteristics constitute a crucial variable in therapy.

The study of the mechanism whereby physicians contribute to placebo and therapeutic effects will be referred to as iatroplacebogenics—the study of placebo effects produced by physicians. Iatroplacebogenesis can be direct or indirect. The former refers to placebo effects directly produced by the physician's attitude to the patient as well as to the treatment and its results. Evidence supporting the concept of indirect iatroplacebogenesis, a subtle mechanism that has not been considered adequately in the literature, will be derived from the history of medicine, clinical and experimental studies, and case histories.

Direct Iatroplacebogenesis

Attitude to Patient. Attitude to patient refers to the therapist's interest, warmth, friendliness, liking, sympathy, empathy, neutrality, lack of interest, rejection, and hostility. Its general importance is indicated by a survey that cited the physician's personal interest—not his competence—as the main determinant of whether patients like their doctors (Polansky and Kounin, 1956).

PSYCHOTHERAPY. Studies have reported that the psychotherapist's interest in the patient is associated with likelihood of acceptance for treatment (Brill and Storrow, 1963; Lowinger and Dobie, 1963, 1964), fewer dropouts (Lowinger and Dobie, 1964, 1966; Nash, Frank, Gliedman, Imber, and Stone, 1957; Hiller, 1958; Freedman, Engelhardt, Hankoff, Blick, Kay, Buchwald, and Stark, 1958; McNair, Lorr, and Callahan, 1963), fewer complaints by patients

(Nash, Frank, Imber, and Stone, 1964), and successful outcome of treatment.[12]

Extensive research by Goldstein on the importance of patient-physician expectations in therapy indicates that the therapist's favorable feelings to the patient are related to the therapist's expectation of improvement and the patient's attraction to the therapist (Heller and Goldstein, 1961), and influence the obtained improvement (Garfield and Affleck, 1960; Goldstein, 1962).

Strupp has demonstrated in many studies that the therapist's liking or disliking of the patient is associated with the therapist's evaluation of the patient's personality, motivation, maturity, insight, anxiety, clinical status, diagnosis, treatment goals, proposed techniques, improvement expected, and mutual beliefs of patient and therapist.[13]

Interest in the patient is related to the amount of introspection (Truax and Wargo, 1966) and feeling expressed in therapy by the patient (Snyder, 1964; Fiedler, 1953); the therapist's understanding of the patient's behavior (Kahn, 1957); and factors common to both experienced and inexperienced therapists (Truax and Wargo, 1966; Fiedler, 1950, 1951).

The frequent observation, although inadequately studied, that therapists are often more successful when they begin their careers than when they have become experienced, may be related to greater interest of the novice in the patient.[14] Liking or not liking of patients may be a better explanation for reported cases of

countertransference cures (Barchilon, 1958; Kolb, 1958), for failures in therapy (Ends, 1957), and for the suggestibility of patients in psychoanalysis (Fisher, 1953).

PSYCHOCHEMOTHERAPY. Interest in the patient is related to successful treatment with antidepressants (Sheard, 1963) and minor tranquilizers (Unlenhuth et al., 1959, Rickels, Baum, Taylor, and Raab, 1964), as well as to the type of LSD response (Malitz, 1963) and drug acceptance by patients (Raskin, 1961).

PSYCHOLOGY. Psychologists who are warm and interested in their patients or experimental subjects are more persuasive (Sampson and French, 1960; Rosenthal, 1963b) and elicit better conditioning and learning,[15] higher intelligence scores (Masling, 1959; Gordon and Durea, 1948), and better Rorschach records (Luft, 1953; Lord, 1950).

GENERAL. The interest of the investigator affects surgery in dogs (Wolf, 1962), gastric acid secretion (Engel, Reichman, and Segal, 1956), metabolic changes (Schottstaedt, Pinsky, Mackler, and Wolf, 1956), laboratory procedures (Kaplan, 1956), and the galvanic skin response (Dittes, 1957). It has been described as a crucial variable for successful psychotherapy in summaries reported at national research conferences on psychotherapy (Parloff and Rubinstein, 1958; Strupp and Luborsky, 1958); as the cornerstone of Rogerian client-centered therapy (Rogers, 1951, 1957a, b, 1961); and as important in behavior therapy, psychotherapy and psychoanalysis,[16] psychochemotherapy (Rickels et al.,

---

[12] Heine, 1950; Seeman, 1954; Blaine and McArthur, 1958; Halkides, 1958; Board, 1959; Snyder and Snyder, 1961; Parloff, 1961; Cartwright and Lerner, 1963; Stoler, 1963; Strupp et al, 1964; Battle, Imber, Hoehn-Sarac, Stone, Nash and Frank, 1966; Gendlin, 1966. Truax and Wargo (1966) recently summarized 14 additional studies that attributed successful treatment of patients largely to the warmth or empathy of the therapist.

[13] Strupp, Wallach and Wogan, 1964; Strupp, 1958a, 1958b, 1958c, 1959, 1960a, 1960b; Strupp and Williams, 1960; Wallach and Strupp, 1960; Strupp and Wallach, 1965.

[14] Lowinger and Dobie, 1966; Truax and Wargo, 1966; Strupp, 1958c; Strupp and Williams, 1960; Ginsburg and Arrington, 1948; Brill, Koegler, Epstein, and Forgy, 1964; Berman, 1949; Kubie, 1956; Glover, cited by Kubie, 1956; Grinker, 1958; Barchilon, 1958; Frank, 1961; Cole, Branch, and Allison, 1962; Karno, 1965.

[15] Goldstein, 1962; Rosenthal, 1963a, 1963b; Ullman and McFarland, 1957; Masling, 1959, 1960; Sapolsky, 1960; Weiss, Krasner and Ullman, 1960; Krasner, 1962; Krasner, Ullman and Fisher, 1964; Rosenthal and Fode, 1963a; Rosenthal and Lawson, 1963c; Friedman, Kurland, Rosenthal, 1965.

[16] Parloff, 1961; Strupp, 1960a, 1960b; Strupp and Williams, 1960; Snyder, 1946; Fiedler, 1950; Ginsburg and Arrington, 1948; Barchilon, 1958; Frank, 1961; Cole, Branch, and Allison, 1962; Karno, 1965; Krasner, Ullman and Fisher, 1964; Snyder, 1958; Greenachre, 1953; Ferenczi, cited by Greenachre, 1953; Ferenczi, 1954; Fenichel, 1954; Braaty, 1954; Ellis, 1955; Breuer and Freud, 1957; Frank, Gliedman, Imber, Nash and Stone, 1957; Frank, 1958, Frank, cited in Rubenstein and Parloff, 1959; Messerman, 1957, 1963; Meerloo, 1963; Berman, 1949; Heine and Trossman, 1960; White, 1961; Hobbs, 1962; Lesse, 1962, 1964a, b; Voth, Herbert and Orth, 1962; Luborsky, 1962; Hammett, 1965; Paul, 1963; Jaspers, 1965.

1964; Rothman and Sward, 1956, 1957; Rothman, 1960; Sherman, 1959; Sarwer-Foner and Korayi, 1960, 1961; Weatherall, 1962), the placebo effect,[17] hypnosis (Barber, 1962), the success of Shamans (Frank, 1961; Kiev, 1964) and quacks, (Masserman, 1963), and the saving of derelicts by the Salvation Army (Feldman, 1956).

Attitude to Treatment. Recent research has established that the physician's attitude toward his treatment—such as faith, belief, enthusiasm, conviction, commitment, optimism, positive and negative expectations, skepticism, disbelief, and pessimism—is a nonspecific factor in most therapies.

PSYCHOCHEMOTHERAPY. Feldman (1956) was the first to present data supporting the idea that the success of drug therapy varied with the enthusiasm of the doctor. He reported similar findings in a follow-up study, and observed that unsuccessful therapists had a greater commitment to psychoanalysis than to psychochemotherapy (Feldman, 1963).

These results were confirmed in an important double-blind study by Uhlenhuth (Uhlenhuth et al., 1959), which showed that only the interested and enthusiastic physician obtained significant improvement with active drugs compared with placebos, while the uninterested and unenthusiastic physician showed no differences in improvement, whether active or inactive drugs were used. An important implication of this study is that the therapist's interest may be a necessary prerequisite for the success of some treatments. These results have been confirmed in subsequent studies (Rickels, Boren, and Stuart, 1964; Rickels, Baum, Taylor, and Raab, 1964b; Rickels et al., 1964a; Fisher, Cole, Rickels, and Uhlenhuth, 1964; Uhlenhuth, Rickels, Fisher, Park, Libman, and Mock, 1966).

Interest in drug treatment has been associated with successful treatment of depressed patients (Sheard, 1963; Haefner, Sacks, and Mason, 1960), schizophrenics and hospitalized patients (Honigfeld, 1962; Pearlin, 1962), and depressed patients on placebo (Honigfeld, 1963). Negative

attitudes toward drug treatment are associated with less favorable results.[18] Similar findings have been reported in the treatment of patients with bleeding ulcers (Volgyesi, 1954) and hypertension (Shapiro, A. P., 1954, 1955), as well as those treated by hypnosis (Orne, 1959; Troffer and Tart, 1964).

PSYCHOTHERAPY. A relationship between the psychotherapists' interest in treatment and successful outcome has been described in studies of brief psychotherapy (Frank, 1965) and in studies of psychotherapy given by psychiatrists (Board, 1959; Frank, 1965) or medical students (Ginsburg and Arrington, 1948; Frank, 1961; Goldstein and Shipman, 1961). The psychotherapists' interest in the treatment has also been associated with the likelihood of patients remaining in psychotherapy (McNair et al., 1963; Heine and Trossman, 1960) and was cited as important in the summary report of the first Research Conference on Psychotherapy (Rubenstein and Parloff, 1959). Optimistic therapists rate their patients more improved than do pessimistic therapists (Rickels et al., 1964; Rubenstein and Parloff, 1959).

Indirect evidence of a relationship between the therapist's interest in psychotherapy and success of treatment appears in the work of Strupp and Goldstein. Their work indicates that the therapist's evaluation of the patient's suitability for psychotherapy determines the therapist's interest in treatment (Strupp, 1960a), which, in turn, correlates with the mutual attraction of therapist and patient and evaluation of the patient's motivation, nondefensiveness, and capacity for insight, prognosis, and success in therapy (Strupp, Wallach, and Wogan, 1964; Goldstein, 1962; Strupp, 1960a, 1960b; Wallach and Strupp, 1960).

But in all of the cited studies it is difficult to differentiate between the therapist's interest in the patient and treatment. Several studies suggest, however, that the therapist's interest in treatment is primary and leads to a secondary interest in the patient. For example: A patient's motivation for therapy influences the therapist's

---

[17] Rickels et al., 1964a; Wolf, 1962; Lesse, 1964a, 1964b; Shapiro, A. P., 1959; Shapiro, A. K., 1959, 1960a, 1960b, 1963, 1964c, 1964d, 1964f, 1968; Honigfeld, 1963.

[18] Uhlenhuth et al., 1959; Feldman, 1963; Honigfeld, 1962; Rickels et al., 1964b; Fisher et al., 1964; Uhlenhuth et al., 1966; Haefner et al., 1960; Pearlin, 1962; Sabshin and Ramot, 1956; Baker and Thorpe, 1957; Eisen, Sobshin, and Heath, 1959.

estimation of prognosis and capacity to like the patient (Strupp, 1960a, 1960b; Strupp and Williams, 1960c; Strupp and Wallach, 1965). Some therapists dislike patients solely on technical grounds (Strupp, 1960b) or because they are severely disturbed (Wallach and Strupp, 1960). Patients who complete studies are liked more than dropouts (Rickels et al., 1964). The therapist's prognostic expectations relate to the patient's attraction to the therapist (Heller and Goldstein, 1961). The therapist's evaluation of prognosis, capacity for insight, liking, empathizing, and eagerness to accept the patient vary with the experimental manipulation of the patient's motivation for therapy (Wallach and Strupp, 1960). The likelihood of being accepted for therapy is related to the patient's motivation for therapy, diagnosis of psychoneurosis, and liking of the patient by the therapist (Brill and Storrow, 1963). The therapist's interest in the treatment is more important than his interest in the patient in retaining patients in psychotherapy (McNair et al., 1963). Experimenters may become more likeable, personal, and interested in the subject if early data returns are favorable (Rosenthal, 1963; Rosenthal, Kohn, Marks, and Carota. In press).

The observation about the success of younger therapists was previously related to their having more positive feelings toward patients than older therapists. The neophytes may also be excessively enthusiastic (Frank, 1961), and optimistic (Strupp, 1960b) about the effectiveness of treatment because of their inexperience, and more interested in the results of treatment because of their need for reassurance (Strupp, 1960b; Frank, 1961; Lesse, 1964b), whereas the needs of experienced therapists shift from curing to understanding (Barchilon, 1958) and other interests (Kubie, 1956). The observation that

some therapists are more successful with certain patients may be related to the therapist's interest in particular problems or types of patients.[19]

The profit motive has been conspicuously unexplored and may be a significant determinant of the therapist's interest in the treatment, patient, and results (Lesse, 1962; Kubie, 1964; Mowrer, 1963; Davids, 1964; Chodoff, 1964; Ubell, 1964; Foreman, 1964).

GENERAL. Finally, the therapist's interest in treatment is frequently cited as important in placebogenesis,[20] general medical treatment (Lord, 1950; Shapiro, A. P., 1955, 1959; Shapiro, A. P. et al., 1954; Janet, 1924; Honigfeld, 1964b; Houston, 1937–1938), insulin coma treatment (Shapiro, 1960a), psychochemotherapy (Sarwer-Foner and Koray; 1960, 1961; Weatherall, 1962; Pearlin, 1962; Sabshin and Ramot, 1956; Eisen et al., 1959; Wolf, 1959a; Honigfeld, 1964b), hypnosis (Orne, 1959, 1962; Troffer and Tart, 1964), brief psychotherapy (Fenichel, 1954), psychotherapy,[21] psychoanalysis,[22] and the success of Shamans (Kiev, 1962, 1964; Ellenberger, 1956; Eliode, 1964).

Attitude Toward Results. Attitude toward results refers to data distortion caused by random observer effects and by intentional or unintentional nonrandom observer bias (Rosenthal, 1966; Rosenthal and Halas, 1962).

Because they are not suspected (Rosenthal, 1966; Humphrey, 1963), data distortion or observer bias of the unintended type are probably more extensive and serious than frauds and other effects.

Rosenthal's technique of demonstrating that "experimenters obtain the results they want or expect" is illustrated in a study of rat learning (Rosenthal and Fode, 1963a; Rosenthal, 1966). Experimenters were told that their rats had been specially bred for either brightness or dullness,

---

[19] McNair et al., 1963; Snyder and Snyder, 1961; Goldstein, 1962; Strupp, 1960b; Heine and Trossman, 1960; Jaspers, 1965, Fenichel, 1945; Karpman, 1949; Oberndorf, Greenachre, and Kubie, 1953; Wolberg, 1954; Thompson, 1956; Alexander, 1958; Frank, 1959; Engel et al., 1956; Kubie, 1964.

[20] Frank, 1961; Lesse, 1962, 1964a, 1964b; Weatherall, 1962; Shapiro, 1959, 1960a, 1960b, 1963, 1964c, 1964d, 1964f, 1968; Baker and Thorpe, 1957; Frank, 1959; Janet, 1924, 1925; Tibbetts and Hawkins, 1956; Wolf, 1959, 1959b; British Medical Journal, 1961; Kelly, 1962; Liberman, 1962; Honigfeld, 1964b.

[21] Goldstein, 1962; Strupp, 1960b; Snyder, 1964; Ginsburg and Arrington, 1948; Frank, 1961; Cole et al., 1962; Krasner, 1962; Rogers, 1957b; Frank et al., 1957; Lesse, 1964a, 1964b; Jaspers, 1965; Kiev, 1964; Rubenstein and Parloff, 1959; Frank, 1959; Ward, 1964.

[22] Strupp, 1959, 1960a; Strupp and Williams, 1960; Berman, 1949; Barchilon, 1958; Frank, 1961; Krasner, 1962; Fenichel, 1954; Meerloo, 1963; Hemmett, 1965; Paul, 1963; Shapiro, 1968; Ward, 1964; Brown, 1929; Schmideberg, 1939; Greenachre, 1953; Bergman, 1958; Reznikoff and Toomey, 1959.

although rats in both groups were genetically pure strains. The results were that experimenters obtained significantly better learning from rats they considered bright than did experimenters who believed that their rats were dull.

This is not an isolated study. Similar results have been obtained in more than twenty different experiments involving several thousand rats, planaria, and human subjects and experimenters (Rosenthal, 1963b, 1964b, 1966; Rosenthal and Halas, 1962; Rosenthal, Persinger, Mulry, Vikan-Kline and Grothe, 1964; Rosenthal et al., 1963a).

Rosenthal has presented data relating the sources of experimenter bias to the experimenter's hypotheses (Rosenthal, 1963b), expectations (Rosenthal, 1964b), motivation (Rosenthal et al., 1964; Rosenthal, Friedman, Johnson, Fode, Schill, White and Viken, 1964c), and prestige (Rosenthal et al., 1963a; Rosenthal et al., 1964). Other factors are instances of cheating (Rosenthal, 1966; Rosenthal et al., 1964c), early data returns (Rosenthal, Persinger, Vikan-Kline, and Fode, 1963b; Rosenthal, Kohn, Marks, and Carota, 1965), nonspecific factors in the pre-data-gathering interaction (greeting, seating, and instructing) (Rosenthal, Fode, Vikan-Kline, and Persinger, 1964), verbal conditioning (Rosenthal et al., 1963a; Rosenthal et al., 1964), visual and verbal cues (Rosenthal et al., 1964c), several similar personality characteristics of experimenter and subject, the experimenter's sex (Rosenthal et al., 1963a, 1964), religion, race, likeability, personality, warmth, and interest in the subject (Rosenthal and Fode, 1963a; Rosenthal and Lawson, 1963c), and so on (Rosenthal, 1963c).

The behavior and personality of the unsuccessful biaser were strikingly similar to those of the unsuccessful psychotherapist. Possibly relevant to supervision in psychotherapy was the finding that the biasing phenomenon was successfully communicated by a senior experimenter to an assistant experimenter who was employed as data collector and actually performed the experiment, without the senior experimenter telling the assistant about the nature of the experiment (Rosenthal, Persinger, Vikan-Kline, and Mulry, 1963d).

Rosenthal's conclusion is "that human beings can engage in highly effective and influential unprogrammed and unintended communication with one another. This communication is so subtle that casual observation of human dyads is unlikely to reveal the nature of the process (Heine, 1960; Rosenthal, 1963b, 1966; Rosenthal et al, 1964).

Similar findings have been reported in clinical (Masling, 1959, 1960, 1965; Rosenthal, 1964) and experimental (Krasner et al., 1964; Orne, 1962; Rosenthal, 1966; McGuigan, 1963; Friedlander, 1964; Krasner, Knowles, and Ullman, 1965) psychology; the placebo effect;[23] psychochemotherapy;[24]   psychotherapy;[25] psychoanalysis;[26] clinical and experimental hypnosis (Barber, 1962, 1964a, 1965a, 1965b; Orne, 1959, 1962; Troffer and Tart, 1964); and clinical medicine (Friedman, Kurland and Rosenthal, 1965; Shapiro, A. P., 1959, Shapiro, A. P., 1954; Williams and McGee, 1962; Garland, 1960). Finally, the prestige of the investigator, physician, or healer influences clinical and experimental results,[27] and has always been one of the common denominators in "bandwagon effects" in science (Kety, 1961), the success of quacks (Frank, 1961) and Shamans (Shapiro, 1964d; Kiev, 1962; Eliode, 1964), the placebo effect (Lesse, 1962; Shapiro, 1959,

---

[23] Shapiro, 1959, 1960a, 1960b, 1963, 1964d, 1964f, 1964c, 1968; Baker and Thorpe, 1957; Kelly, 1962; Letermendia and Harris, 1959; Wilson and Huby, 1961; Wilson, 1962a, 1962b; Joyce, 1962.

[24] Shapiro, 1959, 1964d, 1964f; Feldman, 1956, 1963; Sabshin and Ramot, 1956; Baker and Thorpe, 1957, Eisen et al., 1959; Letermendia and Harris, 1959; Wilson and Huby, 1961; Wilson, 1962a, 1962b; Uhr and Miller, 1960; Foreman, 1964.

[25] Garfield and Affleck, 1960; Strupp, 1960b; Wallach and Strupp, 1960; Shapiro, 1964c, 1968; Ward, 1964, Reznikoff and Toomey, 1959, Cutler, 1958; Endicott, 1962; Grosz and Grossman, 1964; Gill and Brenman, 1948.

[26] Krasner, 1962; Greenachre, 1953; Ward, 1964; Rosenthal, 1963b; Gill and Brenman, 1948; Burrow, 1927; Schmideberg, 1958; Glover, 1952; Kubie, 1953; Ehrenwald, 1958; Marmor, 1962; Sullivan, 1936–37.

[27] Kahn, 1957; Karno, 1965; Ullman and McFarland, 1957; Friedman, Kurland, and Rosenthal, 1965; Masserman, 1957; Meerloo, 1963; Rosenthal, in press b; Rosenthal, Persinger, Mulry, Vikan-Kline, and Grothe, 1964; Krasner, Knowles, and Ullmann, 1965; Reiser, Reeves, and Armington, 1955.

1960a, 1960b, 1963, 1964c, 1964d, 1964f; Liberman, 1962), and other healing techniques (Greenachre, 1953; Jaspers, 1965).

During the last decade, physicians and investigators have become increasingly aware of their bias. Bias explains why uncontrolled studies report success more frequently than controlled studies (Foulds, 1958; Fox, 1961). Attempts to minimize bias have led to increased use of statistics, placebos, double-blind procedures, and other controls in recent studies. Whereas controlled studies appeared infrequently in medical literature before 1950, today they are the norm (Waife and Shapiro, A. P., 1959; Shapiro, 1960a, 1963, 1968).

Recognition of the subtlety and omnipresence of these effects has led some investigators to believe that objective experiments are illusory (Feldman, 1963; Kelly, 1962; Rosenthal, 1966; Rosenthal et al., 1964; Greiner, 1962; Kety, 1961). It has prompted suggestions that every experiment be done by an enthusiast and skeptic and that the investigator's bias about expected results be specified in the paper, and various suggestions about how to make methodology more rigorous and fool-proof.[28]

Discussion. An inescapable conclusion is that the therapist's interest in the patient, treatment, and results is related to success in treatment and placebo effects. The evidence is no longer isolated, fragmentary, or quantitative, and has reached a qualitative stage that has established the generality of the phenomena. The evidence includes many clinical studies of many patients with varying diagnoses and backgrounds, and treated with different methods by many therapists with diverse orientations and experience. The generality of the evidence is supported by similar findings in clinical and experimental psychology, and by the observations and conclusions of many physicians, psychotherapists, psychologists, and other investigators.

A second conclusion is that there is a complex interaction among the therapist's interest in the patient; the treatment; and the ultimate results. The explanation of how those factors influence results is not clear. It is also not clear which factors are primary or secondary, or how these factors are related to each other as cause and effect. For example, a therapist may be interested in the treatment of a patient, expect success, and then like the patient. The patient may react to the therapist with similar feelings and, in turn, stimulate the therapist with more interest in the patient, greater enthusiasm for the treatment, and increased expectation of favorable results. All of these factors may contribute to the final success of therapy.

A final conclusion is that understanding of the complex interactions of the therapist's interest in the patient, treatment, and results requires more than retrospective speculation. Careful prospective studies will be necessary to determine the relevance and primacy of these factors for placebogenesis and therapeutic effects.

If these conclusions can be accepted, what are the possible iatroplacebogenic mechanisms?

MECHANISM OF INTEREST IN THE PATIENT. The primary and direct effect of the therapist's interest in the patient is on guilt. Guilt is universal, and has been an important part of religion, philosophy, literature, and psychology throughout recorded history (Black, 1966; London, Schulman, and Black, 1966). It is involved in every system of psychopathology, clinically apparent in all patients with psychological and physical illness, and detected in nonpatients as well.[29] Guilt is manifested by or associated with many common feelings such as worthlessness, inadequacy, inferiority, impotence, depression, conflict between inner and outer behavior, and shame about inner impulses and past behavior. Fantasies are often perceived as ego-alien experiences, not shared by other people. Inner sensitivity to irrationality stimulates fear and defense against insanity and loss

[28] Goldstein, 1962; Rosenthal, 1963b, 1964a, in press b; Rosenthal, Persinger, Mulry, Vikan-Kline, and Grothe, 1964; Masling, 1959, 1960; Friedman, Kurland, and Rosenthal, in press; Masserman, 1957; Barber, 1962, 1965b; Feldman, 1963; Troffer and Tart, 1964; Orne, 1962; Ward, 1964; Reznikoff and Toomey, 1959; McGuigan, 1963; Greiner, 1962; Endicott, 1962; Barber and Calverley, 1964a, 1964b,

1964c; Kety, 1961; Shapiro, 1960a, 1961, 1963, 1964b, 1964a, 1968.

[29] Strupp, 1960b; Kahn, 1957; Fenichel, 1954; Hobbs, 1962; Kiev, 1962, 1964; Mowrer, 1963; Elliode, 1964; De Grazia, 1952; Rogers, 1956; Ripley and Jackson, 1959; Jersild and Lazar, 1962; Haley, 1963; Sargant, 1957; Mowrer, 1961; Murphy, 1964; La Barre, 1964.

of control, which cannot be fully examined without help from another person.

The prestigious heritage of the priest, scientist, and physician is represented in our culture by the psychotherapist (Frank, 1961; Jaspers, 1965; Kiev, 1964; Frank, 1959). To him are attributed omniscience, omnipotence, integrity, dedication, and esoteric knowledge (Schmidenberg, 1939). Society's sanction of this role makes him an even more prestigious figure.[30]

Illness is usually stressful (Kiev, 1964). Familiar cues for integration decrease; ambiguity and stimulus hunger increase (Heine, 1950; Frank, 1959, 1961; Krasner, 1962; Kiev, 1964; Ward, 1964; Schmideberg, 1939); and regressive fantasies (Fisher, 1953), guilt (Frank, 1961; Glover,1931), anxiety,[31]depression (Frank, 1961; Shapiro, 1963, 1964d, 1964f, 1964c, 1968), and dependency (Frank, 1961; Zukerman and Grosz, 1958; Jakubszak and Walters, 1959) are stimulated—all factors that have been cited as correlates of suggestibility and the placebo effect.[32]

The favorable feelings of the therapist have been associated with the increased expression of affect by patients (Fiedler, 1953; Frank, 1961), which may further decrease guilt through catharsis. It is also related to increased suggestibility, conditioning, and learning in patients. Patients become suggestible, and are inordinately reassured by the interest of the prestigious therapist (Strupp et al., 1964; Frank, 1961; Brown, 1929; Schmideberg, 1939; Sargant, 1957; Estes, 1948; Sherif and Haney, 1952). Powerful therapeutic forces have now been set into motion. Guilt, anxiety, and discomfort are reduced, hope is mobilized, and previously impaired assets can better be utilized (Frank, 1961; Estes, 1948). Spontaneous remission, as well as favorable environmental and other

changes, have a greater chance of occurring, and are more easily stimulated, integrated, and utilized because of the favorable psychological state of the patient. These changes may be attributed to therapy, increasing the suggestibility of therapist and patient. At the same time, the therapist's interest is associated with increased understanding of the patient's behavior. These nonspecific therapeutic factors may now intereact with the specific effects of various therapies.

Another possible mechanism is that interest in the patient leads to or coexists with an interest in the treatment and results.

MECHANISM OF INTEREST IN RESULTS. The credulity of patients toward materia medica is well-known, that of physicians less so.[33] Although fraudulent claims have been frequently associated with an intense interest in results, observer bias is a more complicated, subtle, and widespread determinant of spurious results.

Observer bias may be related to the therapist's need for results. Therapeutic failure would be cognitively dissonant (Board, 1959; Lesse, 1962, 1964b; Davids, 1964; Ubell, 1964; Wolens, 1962; Sullivan, 1936–37). For example, successful cases are remembered and failures are forgotten. Patients who are expected to be failures are disliked and their treatment potentials are evaluated negatively.

Therapists subtly and unknowingly communicate various data to patients, such as hypotheses, expectations, attitudes, cultural values, interpretations, and so on.[34] The returned communication is then regarded as an independent confirmation of the theory (Frank, 1961; Gendlin, 1966). This increases the credulity and suggestibility of both. Bias influences the selection of patients, prognostic

---

[30] Heine, 1950; Frank, 1961; Fenichel, 1954; Lesse, 1964a, 1964b; Jaspers, 1965; Kiev, 1962, 1964; Ellenberger, 1956; Gumpert, 1963; Scharaf and Lerivson, 1964.

[31] Goldstein, 1962; Krasner, 1962; Kiev, 1962, 1964; Ellenberger, 1956; Estes, 1948; Sherif and Haney, 1952; Dibner, 1958; Walters, Marshall, and Shooter, 1960; Walters and Ray, 1960c; Walters and Quinn, 1960; Walters and Parke, 1964.

[32] Strupp, Wallach, and Wogan, 1964; Goldstein, 1962; Barchilon, 1958; Frank, 1959, 1961; Krasner, 1962; Brown, 1929; Schmideberg, 1939; Kiev, 1962; Eliode, 1964; Sargant, 1957; Dibner, 1958; Walters,

Marshall, and Shooter, 1960; Walters and Ray, 1960; Walters and Quinn, 1960; Borodin, 1955.

[33] Kubie, 1956; Shapiro, 1960a, 1960b, 1963, 1964a, 1964b, 1964c, 1964d, 1964f, 1966, 1968, in preparation a; Wolff, 1954.

[34] Strupp, 1959, 1960b; Strupp and Wallach, 1965; Strupp, Wallach, and Wogan, 1964; Goldstein, 1962; Snyder, 1946; Karno, 1965; Rosenthal, 1963b; Rosenthal, Persinger, Mulry, Vikan-Kline, and Grothe, 1964; Krasner, 1962; Lesse, 1964a; Alexander, 1958, 1963; Gill and Brenman, 1948; Marmor, 1962; Sheard, 1962; Snow and Rickels, 1965; Frank, 1961; Rosenthal, 1966.

expectations, evaluation of insight potentiality, likeability, warmth, raw data obtained, perceived, and remembered, and the interpretation and presentation of results.

Interest in results stimulates need and activity to achieve them. It changes the therapist's behavior and interacts with his interest in the treatment and patient (Goldstein, 1966). The therapist is more interested in the treatment and the patient, gives more time and help, and shows more warmth and concern. The patient responds to the therapist with warmth and improvement. This relationship is reinforcing and circular.

All of these factors, and various interactions and secondary effects, result in real or imagined treatment success.

MECHANISM OF INTEREST IN TREATMENT. An intense interest in treatment by a prestigious therapist mobilizes the patient's hope and optimism. The patient can depend on the therapist's integrity and competence, and be supported by the belief that he will be helped. The more intense the belief of the therapist in his treatment, the more impressed will be the patient and the greater his belief. The patient may translate the therapist's belief: If the doctor is sure he can help me, I can rely on him to be helped (Frank, 1961; Kiev, 1964; Bergman, 1958; Menninger, 1959).

The therapist's interest in his treatment also has an effect on guilt. A patient is reassured when problems are treated as symptoms of illness and not shameful character traits (Strupp et al., 1964; Snyder, 1946; Frank, 1961), or when he learns that fears of losing control, insanity and pathological uniqueness are unrealistic fantasies. Reassurance can occur through symbolic displacement by the patient, omission or commission by the therapist, and in other subtle ways. It may occur in treatment with drugs and psychotherapy, in uncovering and repressive therapies, and whether or not direct reassurance is given.

The patient is in a highly suggestible state, as previously described, and may react to the therapist's interest with more hope and optimism than is warranted or realistic. Guilt and anxiety decrease, and may interact with other therapeutic factors such as spontaneous remission, environmental changes, better utilization of

resources, and other previously described factors. Finally, the therapist's interest in treatment may interact with his interest in the patient and results, and all of these factors may now interact with the potential specific effect of many therapies.

Indirect Iatroplacebogenesis

The physician's interest in his treatment and patient is a necessary component of almost every specific therapy, has a synergistic effect with most therapies, and often produces psychological or placebo effect in and of itself. Although the concept of direct iatroplacebogenesis has been demonstrated in many studies, another mechanism, indirect iatroplacebogenesis, perhaps the most subtle and extensively used mechanism, has not been considered adequately in the literature (Board, 1959; Berman, 1949; Frank, 1961; Greenachre, 1953; Honigfeld, 1964b; Rosenthal, 1963c; Glover, 1931). This concept may help explain the complex interaction described previously.

Medical History. Medical history is characterized by a succession of pretigious physicians with strong intellectual and emotional investments in various therapeutic theories and practices. These are frequently elaborate, detailed, expensive, time-consuming, fashionable, esoteric, and dangerous. The majority were later judged to be ineffective (Shapiro, 1959, 1960a). A common factor in these therapies is the interest of the physician.

The greater a physician's interest in a theory of therapy, particularly if he has innovated it, or if he is a recent convert, the more effective that therapy will be. This occurs when the patient displaces the interest from the therapy to himself and experiences the physician's interest in his treatment as a personal one. Many psychological factors arise in the patient-physician relationship. Hopes, expectations, fantasies, fears, feelings of guilt and inadequacy, and so on, become involved in the relationship and treatment. For example, if a patient has ego-alien impulses and fantasies, an interest on the part of the physician, to whom transference has developed, can decrease superego pressures, conflicts, and eventually symptoms. The patient may simply feel that if a physician is interested in him, then he is not so worthless.

The physician may be neutral, minimally interested, or uninterested in the patient, but because of a deep commitment to a treatment modality, the patient may experience the interest as an interest in himself. In addition, the physician's interest in his treatment procedure may enable him to tolerate or be unaffected by the personal idiosyncracies of the patient. The patient may expect criticism or rejection and be surprised or reassured when the physician responds with interest. In other words, some treatments, although ostensibly directed at the patient, but unknowingly having effects on the physician, which then mediate psychological change in the patient, would be classified as *indirect iatroplacebogenesis.*

Pharmacotherapy. Insulin coma treatment is increasingly thought of as a complex placebo treatment (Shapiro, 1960a). The interest of the staff, necessitated by the dangers during treatment, may provide part of the explanation for its effectiveness. Patients were selectively chosen for this treatment and were a therapeutic elite. The treatment was expensive, fashionable, elaborate, detailed, time-consuming, esoteric, and dangerous, and patients required considerable attention during and after treatment.

A physician with an interest in psycho-chemotherapy usually has considerable knowledge about such treatment. He will be interested in the symptoms and the differential response of the patient to various drugs and will be careful to observe side effects, especially those that may be dangerous. He may encourage the patient to call at any time if side effects develop. A new drug with inadequately evaluated indications, contraindications, and side effects will elicit even more interest, and promote in the physician using it a greater intellectual and emotional investment. This may explain, in part, the reports of almost universal effectiveness accompanying the introduction of new therapies (Shapiro, 1959, 1960a, 1960b, 1963, 1964c, 1964d, 1964f, 1968).

Indirect iatroplacebogenesis, can be illustrated by the following clinical case:

A 31-year-old married woman with a chronic borderline condition was referred for psycho-chemotherapy because of her inability to awaken in time for psychotherapy sessions. The under-lying reason was probably that she could not be tolerated by her therapist. She was a source of constant irritation, with excessive oral and dependent needs, and her behavior caused everyone to reject her. She had almost always reacted adversely to medication. The physician knew that he would have no greater success than others in changing the patient's masochistic pattern of thwarting attempts to help her. She was a severe and chronic negative placebo reactor. The psychiatrist decided to use a treatment method he had never dared try before, since there was no alternative. In addition, he wanted first to reassure himself that she was not highly sensitive to the effects of medicine.

She was put on an elaborate schedule of three different placebos totalling twelve tablets. Two hours after the patient left, she called; she said that all the tablets had fallen out of their boxes and were mixed up in her handbag.

She returned the following week, and in a rash of words described her horrendous experience: she cautiously took only half the dosage at bedtime and on awakening. Immediately after the morning dosage she was nauseated, dizzy, groggy, experienced feelings of unreality, became markedly depressed, sleepy, and began to cry. This lasted six days. Needless to say, the patient discontinued the medication. The doctor followed her associations carefully, recorded much of the interview, and at an appropriate moment told her that she had taken placebos. At first, she had no idea what a placebo was. Then she insisted that it was impossible for placebos to have caused her symptoms. Only after the doctor offered to swallow the remaining tablets, was she convinced.

Somewhat anxious about using this procedure, the physician became even more so when the patient exclaimed that if medicine didn't work, she had no alternative but to kill herself. Reassuring her that this was not necessary, the therapist told the patient that the procedure was used to demonstrate that her symptoms were caused by powerful psychological factors and not by the medication. The doctor acknowledged that the side-effects were not imaginary, but insisted that they could not be serious. It was emphasized that the subtle beneficial effects of the medication could not possibly compete with her overwhelming psychological reaction.

For treatment to be successful she must take the prescribed dosage of medication despite the development of side effects. If these did occur she could always call the doctor. Although serious side effects were unlikely, should any develop, he would be able to differentiate between serious and nonserious.

The patient seemed to accept the explanation, but needed time to get over the effects of the previous week.

Several months later, she called for an appointment. Treatment was begun with imipramine (Tofranil), 25 mgm tid. No calls were received during that week. At the next session the patient was improved, reporting only reliable side effects of medication. One week later she said that she didn't know if she had received placebos or not, but had had no side effects. The nurse checked and found that the patient had been given placebo tablets by mistake. Imipramine was then resumed. She was no longer a negative placebo reactor.

Many explanations for the patient's remarkable response are possible: the psychiatrist was strong, authoritative, and could not be manipulated; the patient felt safe, with less need to discharge anxiety through masochistic development of side effects; the confrontation improved reality-testing; and so on.

Although many explanations are possible, indirect iatroplacebogenesis is probably the best explanation. The psychiatrist was intellectually and emotionally interested in the placebo phenomenon, negative placebo responses, and the innovation of a treatment procedure. Management was elaborate, detailed, time-consuming, esoteric, dangerous, possibly fashionable, and potentially expensive.

In other words, interest in the phenomenon was responsible for the doctor's not reacting to the patient's masochism with distance, lack of interest, hopelessness, and rejection—exactly as she expected. The doctor's interest was experienced as an interest in her—an experience that was unique for this patient, who was a specialist in courting rejection. Under the usual circumstances of the patient-physician relationship, the doctor might have reacted to the patient's masochism with anxiety, guilt, distance, lack of interest, hopelessness, and possible rejection.

To view the method that was used as having an effect only on the patient would be misleading. Its effect on the doctor probably had an effect on the patient. Some treatment, then, although ostensibly directed at the patient, may actually function as a treatment for the doctor. The underlying mechanism is the indirect interest of the physician in the patient. The mechanism of indirect iatroplacebogenesis is formulated as treatment directed at the patient, but unknowingly having effects on the physician which, in turn, then mediates psychological change in the patient.

This formulation was confirmed in a tape-recorded interview three years later. The patient, markedly improved, was asked about the effect of the placebo procedure and what helped her get well. She said that the effect of those "clever" placebos made her feel that the doctor was really "trying to help . . . really interested and concerned," whereas physicians previously "were too busy," "uninterested" and "would only give her boxes of pills," and that she was then "able to have faith in the clinic and the doctors" which enabled her to take medication and finally improve.

Psychotherapy and Psychoanalysis. How would this formulation apply to intensive psychotherapy? Psychotherapy shares with other therapies many placebogenic factors (Shapiro, 1964a, 1964b, 1968). It is a new method with considerable emotional, intellectual, and financial investment by prestigious practitioners. It is elaborate, detailed, expensive, time-consuming, fashionable, esoteric, and sometimes dangerous.

Many clinicians would agree with this formulation, but might limit its applicability to therapies other than their own. For example, insight-oriented psychotherapists might say that the goal of other therapies was limited to reduction of symptoms achieved through non-specific factors or unresolved transference. The goal in psychotherapy is a reorganization of character; it is achieved through insight into unconscious processes, defense mechanisms, character traits, and a resolution of the transference neurosis. The therapist is characterized as a mirrorlike, objective, uninvolved technician with minimum direct interest in the patient and results (Strupp, 1959, 1960b; Hammet, 1965;

Murphy, 1958; Loenwald, 1960). Although the concept of the mirrorlike therapist is a formulation of the naive past and increasingly regarded as fiction rather than fact,[35] nevertheless the insight-oriented psychotherapist communicates less old-fashioned, naive, and simple interest in the patient than does the noninsight-oriented therapist. Direct interest in the treatment or technique, however, may be greater than in other therapies and lead to indirect iatroplacebogenesis. Classical psychoanalysis is a good example of a therapy with minimal direct interest in the patient and a maximal interest in the treatment. Examination of such therapy would be a crucial test of the hypothesis, and may clarify the problem of suggestion in psychoanalysis, which was referred to by Freud as inadequately understood forty years ago (Freud, 1948).

SELECTION OF PATIENTS. Acceptance for treatment by a prestigious physician has long been regarded as reassuring to patients. Because of the technical emphasis on suitability for psychoanalysis, many patients interpret acceptance for such treatment as evidence of intellectual capacity, insight potentiality, favorable prognosis, and not being seriously ill (Bergman, 1958; Schmideberg, 1958; Boring, 1964; Scharaf and Levinson, 1964).

The careful selection of patients for psychoanalysis involves many criteria that maximize response to therapy (Glover, 1952; Eysenck, 1965; Hatterer, 1965). The criteria for selection have changed since Freud first treated patients who were diagnosed as hysteric, and recently rediagnosed as psychotic or having severe character disorders (Zetzel, 1965). Patients are now the least ill of any group, and have comparatively favorable prognoses even without therapy. The criteria for selection may have evolved during the past sixty years into an empirical recognition of those patients most likely to respond to psychoanalytic treatment and perhaps to any appropriate treatment (Frank et al., 1957; Hobbs, 1962; Luborsky, 1962; Burrow, 1927; Eysenck, 1965; Hatterer, 1965; Zetzel, 1965; Meehl, 1955).

Patients who meet the criteria for psychotherapy or psychoanalysis frequently have sociocultural expectations, backgrounds, and interests that are similar to their therapists.[36] Cultural mutuality, as noted previously, is related to the therapist's interest in the patient; treatment, results, and the success of treatment (Goldstein, 1962; Frank, 1961; Cole, Branch and Allison, 1962; Heine and Trossman, 1960; Lesse, 1964; Gumpert, 1963). The patient's ability to pay a large fee for a long time is a prerequisite for treatment and the therapist's interest (Kubie, 1964; Mowrer, 1963; Chodoff, 1964; Hatterer, 1965).

Patients may be more educated, cultured, creative, intelligent, informed, accomplished, successful, and wealthier than the treating psychiatrist. Such patients would reject simple reassurance, persuasion, reeducation, support, and other culturally inappropriate placebo techniques. Only an unapproachable and prestigious physician, who was a master of esoteric dynamic theory, which is not easily understood by the uninitiated, would be able to engender the magic and mystery (oneupmanship) (Haley, 1963) necessary for suggestive responses. As Schmideberg, (1939) put it, drugs are a placebo for some patients; psychoanalysis for others, (Fenichel, 1954; Jaspers, 1965; Kiev, 1962; Levenson, 1962).

Many of the aforementioned place bogenic and iatroplacebogenic effects are illustrated by the following clinical case report. A 35-year-old physician with a character disorder began

---

[35] Lowinger and Dobie, 1963, 1964; Snyder and Snyder, 1961; Strupp, 1958c, 1959, 1960b; Strupp and Williams, 1960; Wallach and Strupp, 1960; Berman, 1949; Frank, 1961; Krasner, 1962; Meerloo, 1963; Hobbs, 1962; Hammett, 1965; Karpman, 1949; Oberndorf, Greenachre, and Kubie, 1953; Wolberg, 1945; Alexander, 1958; Schmideberg, 1939; Gill and Brenman, 1948; Hatterer, 1965; Glover, 1955; Wolff, 1956; Miller, 1949; Szasz and Nemiroff, 1963; Alexander, 1963; Jackson and Haley, 1963; Stein, 1966; Alexander, 1964.

[36] Lowinger and Dobie, 1963, 1964, 1966; Snyder and Snyder, 1961; Strupp, 1960a; Frank, 1961; Cole, Branch, and Allison, 1962; Rickels, Baum, Taylor, and Raab, 1964; Frank, Gliedman, Imber, Nash, and Stone, 1957; Heine and Trossman, 1960; Hobbs, 1962; Lesse, 1962; Luborsky, 1962; Burrow, 1927; Goldstein, 1966; Eysenck, 1965; Hatterer, 1965; Zetzel, 1965; Meehl, 1955; Schaffer and Myers, 1954; Hollingshead and Redlich, 1958; Levenson, 1962; Wood, Rokusin and Morse, 1965.

psychoanalytic treatment with a classically oriented training analyst.

REASSURANCE ABOUT GUILT. The analyst became less and less talkative during the initial six months of therapy, until he uttered not a word for three weeks, The patient wondered what had gone wrong and where he had gone astray, and became increasingly anxious. He tried to elicit guidance, looked for subtle cues about what he thought the analyst wanted him to say, and spoke about many things in an attempt to find something relevant and meaningful to which the analyst might respond. He tried logic and honesty, detailed shameful experiences and thoughts, expressed emotions, associations, and fantasies more freely, and repeated many of the analyst's interpretations—all to no avail; the analyst did not respond.

His fantasies and associations became less coherent and his defenses more primitive. He tried to seduce the therapist with warmth, provoke him with anger, and elicit compassion. He became increasingly anxious, resentful, and guilty. The analyst was unresponsive, he thought, because he was defensive and illogical and his associations irrelevant and worthless; that, in effect, he was worthless.

The situation became increasingly unreal, as if he were in a sensory isolation experiment. His one wish was simply that the analyst say something, anything; nothing was worse than the silence. The patient became disgusted and depressed, and his behavior outside of therapy was affected.

The patient was now in a highly suggestible state. The technique had unknowingly stimulated many factors known to be correlates of suggestibility and the placebo effect—sensory isolation, situational ambiguity, stimulus hunger, regression, primitive fantasy, marked anxiety, guilt, dependency, and depression.[37]

Finally the analyst spoke. The interpretation included observations about unconscious associations made by the patient during the past three weeks and preceding six months. The patient's reaction was immediate: he was listening, what I said was worthwhile, I am worthwhile. The depression vanished and the patient improved symptomatically. The interpretation, although

relevant, was less important than the reassurance that the analyst was listening and that the patient was worthwhile. Guilt in general, as well as that engendered during the previous weeks, was assuaged. Similar episodes recurred, and the effect was reinforced (Frank, 1961; Schmideberg, 1939; Haley, 1963).

REASSURANCE ABOUT FUNDAMENTAL FEARS. During these and other episodes, stimulated by the desperate need to end the analyst's silence and to uncover something relevant to which the analyst would respond, and supported by the analyst's permission, encouragement, and reassurance, the patient spoke openly about previously guarded and suppressed experiences and fantasies (Fenichel, 1954). Old fantasies were elaborated, new ones appeared, and associations were freely expressed (Frank, 1961). When they became inexplicable, irrational, and bizarre, the patient wondered about possible loss of control and of psychosis, beneath his facade of adjustment. The analysis was such a test which the patient felt he had passed when they did not occur. Thus, analytic technique, by encouraging extensive exploration of fantasies, anxieties, and guilt, is a reassuring test of fundamental fears.

REASSURANCE ABOUT UNIQUENES;. The patient was also reassured when he realized that his behavior was realistic despite unconscious manifestations, that he was not unique in having an unconscious, and that even the prestigious therapist had one, which was revealed by occasional slips, distortions, errors of omission and commission, and so forth (Frank, 1961; Kennedy, 1960).

CATHARSIS. Many of these factors contribute to the mechanism of catharsis, which also reduces guilt (see page 448).

INEXACT AND INCOMPLETE INTERPRETATIONS. Interpretations were accepted by the patient because of their apparent validity and heuristic value, and because of many extralogical pressures that were produced by the technique. Acceptance, however, was always conditional, because insights and interpretations were never experienced as exact or complete. Since real life is too complicated to be fully explained, all interpretation by a therapist, and

---

[37] See references in section, "Mechanism of interest in the patient."

all insights of a patient, as described elsewhere, are incomplete and inexact (Schmideberg, 1939; Glover, 1931). Partially correct insights and interpretations increase repression, reduce guilt, and may be reassuring (Fenichel, 1954; Hobbs, 1962; Glover, 1931; Kennedy, 1960). Since the achievement of insight through interpretation is important in analysis, many of the previously mentioned direct and indirect iatroplacebogenic effects may be inevitable consequences of the technique (Frank, 1961; Schmideberg, 1939).

VALIDITY OF INTERPRETATION. In addition, the patient frequently was unsure whether interpretations were based on data uninfluenced by the analyst, or whether he provided the data for the interpretations because of the pressure for him to say what he thought the analyst wanted him to say (Heine, 1950; Frank, 1961; Krasner, 1962; Marmor, 1962). This may reflect the frequent observation, now experimentally verified, that therapists communicate their expectations, attitudes, and feelings, and influence the data they obtain.[38] If it is believed that the theory is scientific, objective, and based on understanding without suggestive taint, the validity of the theory, data, and results is convincing to both therapist and patient. Increased conviction of therapist and patient are elements in placebogenesis (Frank, 1961; Schmideberg, 1939).

BREAKS IN TECHNIQUE. Breaks in the classical technique of psychoanalysis occurred on several occasions. The analyst subtly approved of the patient's positions in disputations with senior colleagues on several occasions, was interested in his research and published papers, and wrote important letters on his behalf. These breaks occur in every analysis (Frank, 1961; Obendorf, Greenachre and Kubie, 1953, Snow, Rickels, 1965; Glover, 1955; Wolff, 1956; Szasz and Nemiroff, 1963); they include referral of patients to the analysand, the analyst asking for advice about a problem about which the patient is expert, thanking the patient for talking about interesting material, shaking hands before and after each session, and so forth. On one occasion an analyst asked his patient, a

dental specialist, to treat a complicated dental problem. These incidents are more frequent than realized. They are often an important part of many less classical analytic techniques, and include exchange of gifts, socializing, and the therapist talking about himself and his feelings, sometimes expressing sexual attraction to the patient. In classical analysis, owing to the dearth of such interest, the rarity of such breaks, and the conflict with theory, the impact is greater than in other therapies (Frank, 1961). It is doubtful that they can be dismissed as an interesting experiment, or that they are without effect because of their supposed ultimate analysis. The technique imposes a deprived atmosphere which paradoxically produces a powerful iatroplacebogenic effect when the break in technique occurs.

DOMINANCE-SUBMISSION RATIO. Along with occasional breaks in technique, the therapeutic atmosphere changed as the analysis progressed: the analyst was perceived as less dominant and the patient as more dominant than when the therapy began. The analyst made more offhand observations, told jokes, and was less formal. The sessions became more relaxed, and the analysand was treated more as a colleague than a patient. The change in the dominance-submission ratio between the patient and the physician has been reported in several studies of psychotherapy and may be an important observation (Heine, 1950; Parloff, 1961; Lesse, 1964a; Sherif and Haney, 1952; Storrow and Spanner, 1962). It might be inherent in psychotherapeutic technique, stimulated by increased mutual knowledge, understanding, respect, interpersonal comfort, and so on (Palmore, Lennard and Hendin, 1959). Or the patient may be less anxious and more comfortable so that he can become more independent. Guilt reduction may be increasingly reinforced. It is a penultimate acknowledgement of the patient's acceptance and adequacy. Ultimate acknowledgement occurs when the patient is discharged from treatment as cured. Again, direct and indirect iatroplacebogenesis are likely mechanisms.

---

[38] Strupp, Wallach and Wogan, 1964; Goldstein, 1962; Strupp, 1959, 1960b; Strupp and Wallach, 1965; Snyder, 1946; Frank, 1961; Karno, 1965; Rosenthal, 1963b, 1966; Krasner, 1962; Lesse, 1964a; Alexander, 1958, 1963; Rosenthal, Persinger, Milry, Vikan-Kline, and Grothe, 1964; Gill and Brenman, 1948; Marmor, 1962; Sheard, 1962; Snow and Rickels, 1965.

DISCHARGE FROM TREATMENT. The most powerful reassurance and final *coup de grace* to guilt occur when treatment has been completed and the therapist certifies that the patient is cured. The technique imposes an expensive, time-consuming, painful, detailed, elaborate, and esoteric therapy on the patient. Therapists are dedicated to the correctness of their theory and convinced about the efficacy of the treatment. If we add the elite status that is bestowed on the patient by the prestigious therapist, who has been sanctioned as society's representative, we have all of the essentials that have produced placebo effects throughout history. The placebogenic effect of discharge from treatment has not been studied and may be an important factor in placebogenesis (Bergman, 1958; Burrow, 1927; Schmideberg, 1958; Gumpert, 1963; Hatterer, 1965).

Many psychoanalysts believe that analytic treatment is differentiated from other therapies because it has specific, nonplacebo, and nonsuggestive effects. This review suggests the contrary proposition; that it may have extensive, potent, and subtle suggestive (nonspecific or placebo) effects on patients for whom the treatment is appropriate (Frank, 1961; Kiev, 1964; Schmideberg, 1939; Goldstein, 1966; Hatterer, 1965; Glover, 1955; Bailey, 1965; Rachman, 1963).

Conclusions and Implications

The concept of iatroplacebogenesis is supported by its general applicability to many therapies. Contrary to many beliefs, psychoanalysis shares many direct and indirect iatroplacebogenic effects with other therapies. Iatroplacebogenesis is more important in some forms of therapy than others. It does not preclude concomitant specific effects, however, such as insights in psychotherapy, or chemical effects in psychochemotherapy. It may function as a prerequisite or catalyst for therapies that involve psychological factors or interpersonal relationships; see, for example, the evidence that specific effects occur in psychochemotherapy when the iatroplacebogenic atmosphere is favorable.

Therapy will be impaired if physicians are unaware of placebo effects. Therapeutic effects will be attributed to specific procedures which, unknown to the physician, are caused by nonspecific or placebo effects. The therapist's credulity about the efficacy and specificity of the procedure will be exaggerated, and it will encourage the use of one procedure or technique for all patients. Therapists who rely on one technique will be unable to treat many patients; some may be hurt because of inappropriate treatment (Jaspers, 1965; Ward, 1964), and specific indications for a therapeutic procedure will be obfuscated. Awareness of placebo effects will enable clinicians better to evaluate the effects of therapy, contribute to the development of more flexible and appropriate procedures, and make therapy more comprehensive, resourceful, and effective.

The recognition that these factors contribute to the treatment process will improve studies by investigators, and may help clarify unsolved problems of specificity in many therapies.

It is important to remember that, despite the massive evidence in support of the concepts of placebogenesis and iatroplacebogenesis, the evidence is based primarily on retrospective data. Careful prospective studies will be necessary for clarification of the primary, relevancy, and validity of these concepts.

The history of both physiologic and psychologic treatment is largely the history of the placebo effect; *those who forget it are destined to repeat it.* Garrison observed that "whenever many different remedies are used for a disease, it usually means that we know very little about treating the disease, which is also true of a remedy when it is vaunted as a panacea or cure-all for many diseases" (Garrison, 1921).

If we keep those thoughts in mind, we may avoid the problem that the complier of the Paris Pharmacologia insightfully observed a century ago: "What pledge can be afforded that the boasted remedies of the present day will not like their predecessors, fall into disrepute, and in their turn serve only as a humiliating memorial of the credulity and infatuation of the physicians who recommended and prescribed them" (Haggard, 1934).

REFERENCES

Abramson, H. A., Jarvik, M. E., Levine, A., Kaufman, M. R., and Hirsch, M. W. Lysergic acid diethylamide (LSD-25). XV. The effects produced by substitution of a tap water placebo. *J. Psychol.*, 1955, **40**, 367.

Alexander, F. Unexplored areas in psychoanalytic theory and treatment. *Behav. Sci.*, 1958, **3**, 293–316.

Alexander, F. The dynamics of psychotherapy in the light of learning theory. *Am. J. Psychiat.*, 1963, **120**, 441–449.

Alexander, F. An evaluation of the role of psychiatrist's personality in the interview. In *Science and Psychoanalysis*. New York: Grune & Stratton, 1964.

Bailey, P. *Sigmund the unserene.* Illinois: Charles C. Thomas, 1965.

Baker, A. A., and Thorpe, J. G. Placebo response. *A. M. A. Arch. Neurol. Psychiat.*, 1957, **78**, 57.

Barber, T. Experimental controls and the phenomena of "hypnosis." A critique of hypnotic research methodology. *J. Nerv. Ment. Dis.*, 1962, **134**, 493–505.

Barber, T. X. Physiological effects of "hypnotic suggestions." A critical review of recent research. *Psychol. Bul.*, 1965, **63**, 201–222.

Barber, T. X. Experimental analysis of "hypnotic" behaviour. A review of recent empirical findings. *J. Abnorm. Psychol.*, 1965, **70**, 132–154.

Barber, T. X., and Calverley, D. S. Effect of E's tone of voice on hypnotic-like suggestibility. *Psychol. Rep.*, 1964, **15**, 139–144.

Barber, T. X., and Calverley, D. S. Toward a theory of hypnotic behavior: Enhancement of strength and endurance. *Canad. J. Psychol.*, 1964, **18**, 156–167.

Barber, T. X., and Calverley, D. S. Toward a theory of hypnotic behavior: Effects on suggestibility of defining the situation as hypnosis and defining response to suggestions as easy. *J. Abnor. Soc. Psychol.*, 1964, **68**, 585–592.

Barchilon, J. On countertransference "cures." *J. Am. Psychoanal. Ass.*, 1958, **VI**, 222.

Battle, C. C., Imber, S. D., Hoehn-Saric, R., Stone, A. R., Nash, E. R., and Frank, J. D. Target complaints as criteria of improvement. *Am. J. Psychother.*, 1966, **20**, 184–192.

Beecher, H. K. Experimental pharmacology and measurement of the subjective response. *Science*, 1952, **116**, 157.

Beecher, H. K. The powerful placebo. *J. A. M. A.*, 1955, **159**, 1602.

Beecher, H. K. *Measurement of the subjective response.* New York: Oxford Univ. Press, 1959.

Bergman, P. The role of faith in psychotherapy. *Bul. Menninger Clinic*, 1958, **22**, 92–103.

Berman, L. Countertransferences and attitudes of the analyst in the therapeutic process. *Psychiatry*, 1949, **12**, 159–166.

Bernheim, H. *Suggestive therapeutics.* New York: G. P. Putnam's Sons, 1889.

Bishop, M. B., and Gallant, D. M. Observations of placebo response in chronic schizophrenic patients. *Arch. Gen. Psychiat.*, 1966, **14**, 497.

Blakiston's New Gould Medical Dictionary (1st edition). Philadelphia: Blakiston, 1949.

Black, S. M., and London, P. The dimensions of guilt, religion, and personal ethics. *J. Soc. Psychol.*, 1966, **69**, 39–54.

Blaine, G. B., and McArthur, C. C. What happened in therapy as seen by the patient and his psychiatry. *J. Nerv. Ment. Dis.*, 1958, **127**, 678–681.

Board, F. A. Patients' and physicians' judgments of outcome of psychotherapy in an outpatient clinic. *AMA Arch. Gen. Psychiat.*, 1959, **1**, 185–196.

Borodin, E. S. Ambiguity as a therapeutic variable. *J. Consult. Psychol.*, 1955, **19**, 9–15.

Boring, E. G. Cognitive dissonance: Its use in science. *Science*, 1964, **145**, 680–685.

Braaty, T. *Fundamentals of psychoanalytic technique.* New York: Wiley, 1954.

Breuer, J., and Freud, S. *Studies on hysteria.* New York: Basic Books Inc., 1957.

Brill, N. Q., Koegler, R. R., Epstein, L. J., and Forgy, E. W. Controlled study of psychiatric outpatient treatment. *Arch. Gen. Psychiat.*, 1964, **10**, 581–595.

Brill, N. Q., and Storrow, H. W. Prognostic factors in psychotherapy, *J.A.M.A.*, 1963, **183**, 913.

British Medical Journal, Placebos, (ed.) *B. M. J.*, 1961, **1**, 43–44.

Brown, W. *Science and personality.* New Haven: Yale Univ. Press, 1929.

Bull, J. P. The historical development of clinical therapeutic trials. *J. Chron. Dis.*, 1959, **10**, 218.

Burrow, T. *The social basis of consciousness.* New York: Harcourt, Brace & Co., 1927.

Cartwright, R. D., and Lerner, B. Empathy, need to change, and improvement with psychotherapy. *J. Consult. Psychol.*, 1963, **27** (2), 138–144.

The Catholic Encyclopedia. New York: Gilmary Society, **2**, **7**, **8**, 1911.

Chodoff, P. Psychoanalysis and fees. *Comprehens. Psych.*, 1964, **5**, 137–145.

Cole, N., Branch, C., and Allison, R. Some relationships between social class and the practice of dynamic psychotherapy. *Am. J. Psychiat.*, 1962, **118**, 1004–1012.

Cutler, R. Countertransference effects in psychotherapy. *J. Consult. Psych.*, 1958, **22**, 349–356.

Davids, A. The relation of cognitive-dissonance theory to an aspect of psychotherapeutic practice. *Amer. Psychol.*, 1964, **19**, 329.

De Grazia, S. *Errors of psychotherapy.* New York: Doubleday and Co., 1952.

Dibner, A. S. Ambiguity and anxiety. *J. Abn. Soc. Psychol.*, 1958, **56**, 165–174.

Dittes, J. E. GSR as a measure of patient's reaction to therapists' permissiveness. *J. Abn. Soc. Psych.*, 1957, **18**, 263–277.

Duke, J. D. *A study of the relationships between primary suggestibility, secondary suggestibility and placebo.* Doctoral dissertation, University of North Carolina, 1962.

Duran-Reynals, M. L. *The fever bark tree.* New York: Doubleday & Co., 1946.

Ehrenwald, K. J. Doctrinal compliance in psychotherapy and problems of scientific methodology. In Masserman, H. H., and Moreno, J. I. (Eds.), *Progress in psychotherapy.* New York: Grune & Stratton, 1958.

Eissen, S. B., Abshin, M., and Heath, H. A comparison of the effects of investigators' and therapists' attitudes in the evaluation of tranquilizers prescribed to hospital patients. *J. Nerv. Ment. Dis.*, 1959, **128**, 256.

Ekman, P. Research therapy. *J. Nerv. Ment. Dis.*, 1961, **133**, 229.

Eliode, M. *Shamanism.* New York: Random House, 1964.

Ellenberger, H. The ancestry of dynamics of psychotherapy, *Bul. Menninger Clinic*, 1956, **20**, 288–299.

Ellis, A. Psychotherapy techniques for use with psychotics, *Am. J. Psychother.*, 1955, **IX**, 452–476.

Endicott, N. A. The problems of controls in the evaluation of psychotherapy. *Comp. Psychiat.*, 1962, **3**, 37–46.

Ends, E. J., and Page, C. W. A study of three types of group psychotherapy with hospitalized male inebriates. *Am. J. Stud. Alc.*, 1957, **18**, 263–377.

Engel, G. L., Reichsman, F., and Segal, H. L. A study of an infant with a gastric fistula. *Psychosom Med.*, 1956, **XVIII**, 374–398.

Esecover, H., Malitz, S., and Wilkens, B. Clinical profiles of paid normal subjects volunteering for hallucinogenic drug studies. *Am. J. Psychiat.*, 1961, **117**, 910.

Estes, S. G. Concerning the therapeutic relationship in the dynamics of cure. *J. Consult. Psychol.*, 1948, **12**, 76–81.

Evans, Frederick J. Suggestibility in the normal waking state. *Psychol. Bull.*, 1967, **67**, 114.

Eysenck, H. J. The effects of psychotherapy. *Int. J. Psychiat.*, 1965, **1**, 97–142.

Feldman, P. E. The personal element in psychiatric research. *Am. J. Psych.*, 1956, **113**, 52.

Feldman, P. E. Non-drug parameters of psychopharmacotherapy. The role of the physician. In Rinkel, M. (Ed.), *Specific and non-specific factors in psychopharmacology.* New York: Philosophical Library, 1963.

Fenichel, O. *The psychoanalytic theory of neurosis.* New York: W. W. Norton & Co., 1945.

Fenichel, O. *Brief psychotherapy in the collected papers of Otto Fenichel.* New York: W. W. Norton & Co., 1954.

Fiedler, F. E. A comparison of therapeutic relationships in psychoanalytic non-directive and Adlerian therapy. *J. Consult. Psychol.*, 1950, **14**, 436–445.

Fiedler, F. E. Factor analyses of psychoanalytic, non-directive and Adlerian therapeutic relationships. *J. Consult. Psychol.*, 1951, **13**, 32–38.

Fiedler, F. E. Quantitative studies on the role of therapists' feelings toward their patients. In Mowrer, O. H., *Psychotherapy theory and research.* New York: Ronald Press, 1953. Pp. 269–315.

Fisher, C. The transference meaning of giving suggestions. *J.A.P.A.*, 1953, **1**, 406–437.

Fisher, H. K., and Dlin, B. M. The dynamics of placebo therapy: A clinical study. *Am. J. Med. Sci.*, 1956, **232**, 504–512.

Fisher, S., Cole, J. O., Rickels, K., and Uhlenhuth, E. G. Drug-set interaction: The effect of expectations on drug response in outpatients. In Bradley, P. B., Flugel, F., and Hock, P. (Ed.), *Neuropsychopharmacology.* New York: Elsevier Publishing Co., 1964.

Foreman, M. E. On cognitive dissonance as motivation toward successful therapy. *Am. Psychol.*, 1964, **19**, 777.

Forest, I. de. *The heaven of love. A development of the psychoanalytic theory and technique of Sandor Ferenczi.* New York: Harper Bros., 1954.

Forrer, G. R. The therapeutic use of placebo. *Mich. Med.*, 1964, **63**, 558 (a).

Forrer, G. R. Psychoanalytic theory of placebo. *Dis. Nerv. Syst.*, 1964, **25**, 655 (b).

Foulds, G. Clinical research in psychiatry. *J. Ment. Sc.*, 1958, **104**, 259.

Fox, B. The investigation of the effects of psychiatric treatment. *J. Ment. Sci.*, 1961, **107**, 493.

Frank, J. D. Some effects of expectancy and influence in psychotherapy. In Masserman, J. H., and Moreno, J. I. (Eds.), *Progress in psychotherapy.* Vol. III. New York: Grune & Stratton, 1958.

Frank, J. D. The dynamics of the psychotherapeutic relationship, determinants and effects of the therapist's influence. *J. Study Interpersonal Process*, 1959, **22**, 17–39.

Frank, J. D. *Persuasion and healing.* Baltimore: The Johns Hopkins Press, 1961.

Frank, J. D. Discussion of paper by H. J. Eysenck, "The effects of psychotherapy." *Int. J. Psychiat.*, 1965, **1**, 150–152.

Frank, J. D. In Rubinstein, E. A., and Parloff, M. B. (Eds.), *Research in Psychotherapy.* Washington, D. C.: American Psychological Association, 1959.

Frank, J. D., Gliedman, L. H., Imber, S. D., Nash, E. J., and Stone, A. R. Why patients leave psychotherapy. *J.A.M.A. Arch. Neurol. & Psychiat.*, 1957, **77**, 283.

Frank, J. D., Gliedman, L. H., Imber, S. D., Stone, A. R., and Nash, E. H. Patient's expectancies and relearning as factors determining improvement in psychotherapy. *Am. J. Psychiat.*, 1959, **115**, 961.

Friedlander, F. Type I and type II bias. Comment. *Amer. Psychol.*, 1964, **19**, 198–199.

Freedman, N., Engelhardt, D. M., Hankoff, L. D., Blick, B. S., Kay, H., Buchwald, J., and Stark, P. Drop-out from outpatient psychiatric treatment. *A.M.A. Arch. Neurol. & Psychiat.*, 1958, **80**, 657.

Friedman, N., Kurland, D., and Rosenthal, R. Experimenter behavior as an unintended determinant of experimental results. *J. Proj. Techn. & Pers. Asses.*, 1965, **29**, 479–490.

Freud, S. *Group psychotherapy and the analysis of the ego.* London, England: Hogarth Press, 1948.

Garetz, F. K. A comparison of urine pheothiazine test results with prescribed medication dosage. *Am. J. Psychiat.*, 1962, **118**, 1133.

Garfield, S. L., and Affleck, D. C. Therapists' judgments concerning patients considered for psychotherapy. *Am. Psychol.*, 1960, **13**, 414. (Abstract.)

Garland, L. H. The problem of observer error. *Bull. N. Y. Acad. Med.*, 1960, **36**, 569–584.

Garrison, F. H. *An introduction to the history of medicine.* Philadelphia, Pa.: W. B. Saunders, 1921.

Gartner, M. A., Jr. Selected personality differences between placebo reactors and non-reactors. *J. Am. Osteopath. Assoc.*, 1961, **60**, 377.

Gendlin, E. T. Research in psychotherapy with schizophrenic patients and the nature of that "illness." *Am. J. Psychother.*, 1966, **20** (1), 4–16.

Gill, M. G., and Brenman, M. Research in psychotherapy. *Amer. J. Orthopsychiat.*, 1948, **18**, 100–110.

Ginsburg, S. W., and Arrington, W. Aspects of psychiatric clinic practice. *Am. J. Orthopsychiat.*, 1948, **18**, 322–333.

Glaser, E. M., and Whitlow, G. C. Experimental errors in clinical trials. *Clin. Sci.*, 1954, **13**, 199.

Gliedman, L. H., Gantt, H., and Teitelbaum, H. A. Some implications of conditional reflex studies for placebo research. *Am. J. Psychiat.*, 1957, **113**, 1103.

Gliedman, L. H., Nash, E. H., Imber, S. D., Stone, A. R., and Frank, J. B. Reduction of symptoms by pharmacologically inert substances and by short-term psychotherapy. *A.M.A.J. Neurol. & Psychiat.*, 1958, **79**, 345.

Glover, E. The therapeutic effect of inexact interpretation: A contribution to theory of suggestion. *Int'l J. Psychoanal.*, 1931, **12**, 397.

Glover, E. Research methods in psychoanalysis. *Internat. J. Psychoanal.*, 1952, **23**, 403.

Glover, E. *The technique of psychoanalysis.* New York: Internat. Universities Press, 1955.

Goldstein, A. P. *Therapist–patient expectancies in psychotherapy.* New York: Pergamon Press, 1962.

Goldstein. A. P. Prognostic and role expectancies in psychotherapy. *Amer. J. Psychoth.*, 1966, **20**, 35–44.

Goldstein, A. P. Psychotherapy research by extrapolation from social psychology. *J. Counsel. Psychol.*, 1966, **13**, 38.

Goldstein, A. P., and Shipman, W. G. Patient expectancies, symptom reduction and aspects of the initial psychotherapeutic interview. *J. Clin. Psychol.*, 1961, **XVII**, 129, 133.

Gordon, L. V., and Durea, M. A. The effect of discouragement on the revised Stanford–Binet scale. *J. Genet. Psychol.*, 1948, **73**, 201–207.

Greenachre, P. In Obendorf, C. P., Greenachre, P., and Kubie, L., Symposium on the evaluation of therapeutic results. *Int. J. Psychoanal.*, 1953, **XXIX**, 8–32.

Greiner, T. Subjective bias of the clinical pharmacologist. *J.A.M.A.*, 1962, **181**, 120.

Grimes, F. Z. An experimental analysis of the nature of suggestibility with relation to other psychological factors. *Stud. Psychol. Psychiat.*, 1948, **7**, 44.

Grimes, F. Z. The nature of suggestibility. In Stafford, J. W. (Ed.), *Studies in psychology and psychiatry.* Washington: Catholic University, 1948.

Grinker, R. R. Discussion of article by W. Bromberg, "An analysis of therapeutic artfulness." *Am. J. Psychiat.*, 1958, **114**, 725.

Grosz, H. J., and Grossman, K. G. The sources of observer variation and bias in clinical judgments, *J. Nerv. Ment. Dis.*, 1964, **138**, 105.

Gumpert, G. Witch-doctor "psychiatrists." *SK&F Psych. Report*, 1963, **9**, 2.

Haefner, D. P., Sacks, J. M., and Mason, A. S. Physicians' attitudes toward chemotherapy as a factor in psychiatric patients' responses to medication. *J. Nerv. Ment. Dis.*, 1960, **131**, 64–69.

Hagans, J. A., Doering, C. R., Ashley, F. W., and Wolf, S. The therapeutic experiment. *J. Lab. Clin. Med.*, 1957, **9**, 282.

Haggard. H. W. *Mystery, magic and medicine.* New York: Doubleday, Doran & Co., Inc., 1933.

Haggard, H. W. *The doctor in history.* New Haven: Yale Univ. Press, 1934.

Haggard, H. W. *Devils, drugs, and doctors.* New York: Harper & Bros., 1929.

Haley, J. *Strategics of psychotherapy.* New York: Grune & Stratton, 1963.

Halkides, G. *An experimental study of four conditions necessary for therapeutic change.* Unpublished doctoral dissertation, University of Chicago, 1958.

Hammett V. B. P. A consideration of psychoanalysis in relation to psychiatry generally circa 1965. *Am. J. Psychiat.* 1965, **122**, 42–54.

Hankoff, L. D., Engelhardt, D. M., Freedman, N., Mann, D., and Margolis, R. Denial of illness. *A.M.A. Arch. Gen. Psychiat.*, 1960, **3**, 657.

Hankoff, L. D., Freedman, N., and Engelhardt, D. M. Placebo response in schizophrenic out-patients. *Arch. Gen. Psychiat.*, 1960, **2**, 33.

Hankoff L. D. Freedman, N., and Engelhardt, D. M. The prognostic value of placebo response. *Amer. J. Psychiat.*, 1958, **115**, 549.

Hargreaves, G. R., Hamilton, M., and Roberts, J. M. Treatment of anxiety states. II. Clinical trial of benactyzine in anxiety states. *J. Ment. Sci.*, 1958, **104**, 1056.

Hatterer, L. J. *The artist in society*. New York: Grove Press, 1965.

Heine, R. W. *A comparison of patients' reports on psychotherapy experience with psychoanalytic, nondirective, and Adlerian? therapists*, Unpublished doctoral dissertation, University of Chicago, 1950.

Heine, R. W., and Trossman, H. Initial expectations of the doctor–patient interaction as a factor in continuance in psychotherapy. *Psych. J. Study Interperson. Processes*, 1960, **23**, 275–278.

Heller, K., and Goldstein, A. P. Client dependency and therapist expectancy as relationship maintaining variables in psychotherapy. *J. Consul. Psychol.*, 1961, **25**, 371–375.

Hiller, E. W. An analysis of patient–therapist compatibility. *J. Consult. Psychol.*, 1958, **22**, 341.

Hobbs, N. Sources of gain in psychotherapy. *Am. Psychol.*, 1962, **17**, 741–747.

Hofling, C. K. The place of placebos in medical practice. *G.P.*, 1955, **XI**, 103.

Hollingshead, A. B., and Redlich, F. C. *Social class and mental illness*. New York: Wiley, 1958.

Honigfeld, G. Relationships among physicians' attitudes and response to drugs. *Psychol. Rep.*, 1962, **II**, 683–690.

Honigfeld, G. Physician and patient attitudes as factors influencing the placebo response in depression. *Dis. Nerv. System*, 1963, **124**, 1–4.

Honigfeld, G. Non-specific factors in treatment. *Dis. Nerv. Syst.*, 1964, **25**, 145–225 (a).

Honigfeld, G. Non-specific factors in treatment: Review of social-psychological factors. *Dis. Nerv. Syst.*, 1964, **25**, 225–239 (b).

Houston, W. R. Doctor himself as therapeutic agent. *Ann. Int. Med.*, 1938, **11**, 1416.

Hull, C. L. *Hypnosis and suggestibility*. New York: Appleton-Century, 1933.

Humphrey, H. H. Interagency coordination in drug research and regulation. Hearing before the Subcommittee on Reorganization and International Organizations of the Committee on Government Operations, United States Senate, Bureau of Medicine, in the Food and Drug Administration, 1963.

Imber, S. D., and Nash, E. J. Social class and duration of psychotherapy. *J. Clin. Psychol.*, 1955, **11**, 281.

Jackson, C. W., and Kelly, L. E. Influence of suggestion and subjects' prior knowledge in research on sensory deprivation. *Science*, 1962, **132**, 211–212.

Jackson, C. W., and Pollard, J. C. Sensory deprivation and suggestion: A theoretical approach. *Behav. Sci.*, 1962, **7**, 332–342.

Jackson, C. W., Pollard, J. C., and Kansky, E. W. The application of findings from experimental sensory deprivation to cases of clinical sensory deprivation. *Am. J. Med. Sciences*, 1962, **243**, 558–563.

Jackson, D. D., and Haley, J. Transference revisited. *J. Nerv. & Ment. Dis.*, 1963, **137**, 363–371.

Jakubszak, L. F., and Walters, R. H. Suggestibility as dependency behavior. *J. Abn. Soc. Psychol.*, 1959, **59**, 102–107.

James, W. *The varieties of religious experience*. New York: Modern Library, 1936.

Janet, P. *Principles of psychotherapy*. New York: The Macmillan Co., 1924.

Janet, P. *Phychological healing*. London: George Allen, Ltd., 1925.

Jaspers, K. *The nature of psychotherapy*. Chicago: The University of Chicago Press, 1965.

Jersild, A. T., and Lazar, E. A. *The meaning of psychotherapy in the teacher's life and work*. New York: Bureau of Publications, Teachers College, Columbia Univ., 1962.

J.A.M.A. Placebos (Editorial), 1955, **159**, 780.

Joyce, C. R. B. Difference between physicians as revealed by clinical trials. *Proc. Roy. Soc. Med.*, 1962, **55**, 776–778.

Kahn, R. K. *Therapist discomfort in two psychotherapies*. Unpublished doctoral dissertation. Pennsylvania State University, 1957.

Kaplan, S. M. Laboratory procedures as an emotional stress. *J.A.M.A.*, 1956, **161**, 677–688.

Karno, M. Communication reinforcement and "insight"—the problem of psychotherapeutic effect. *Am. J. Psychoth.*, 1965, **XIX**, 467–479.

Karpman, B. Objective psychotherapy. *J. Clin. Psychol.*, 1949, **V**, 1–154.

Kelly, M. The tempestuous winds of fashion in medicine. *Arch. Int. Med.*, 1962, **110**, 287.

Kennedy, A. Chance and design in psychotherapy. *J. Ment. Sci.*, 1960, **106**, 2–16.

Kety, S. The academic lecture, the heuristic aspect of psychiatry. *Amer. J. Psych.*, 1961, **118**, 365–397.

Kiev, A. The psychotherapeutic aspects of primitive medicine. *Hum. Org.*, 1962, **21**, 25–29.

Kiev, A. The study of folk psychiatry. In Kiev, A. (Ed.), *Magic, faith, and healing*. London: Collier-Macmillan, Ltd., 1964.

Klopfer, B. Psychological variables in human cancer. *J. Proj. Tech.*, 1957, **21**, 331.

Kolb, L. C., and Montgomery, J. An explanation for transference cure: Its occurrence in psychoanalysis and psychotherapy. *Am. J. Psychiat.*, 1958, **115**, 414–420.

Knowles, J. B., and Lucas, C. J. Experimental studies of the placebo response. *J. Mont. Sci.*, 1960, **106**, 231.

Knowles, J. B. Conditioning and the placebo effect. *Behav. Res.*, 1963, **1**, 151–157.

Kornetsky, C., and Humphries, O. Relationship between effects of a number of centrally acting drugs and personality. *A.M.A. Arch. Neurol. Psychiat.*, 1957, **77**, 325.

Krasner, L. Therapist as social reinforcement machine. In Strupp, H. H., and Luborsky, L. (Eds.), *Research in psychotherapy*. Washington: American Psychological Assoc., 1962.

Krasner, L., Ullmann, L. P., and Fisher, D. Changes in performance as related to verbal conditioning of attitudes toward the examiner. *Percept. & Mot. Skills*, 1964, **19**, 811–816.

Krasner, L., Knowles, J. B., and Ullmann, L. P. Effect of verbal conditioning of attitudes on subsequent motor performance. *J. Person. & Soc. Psychol.*, 1965, **1** (5), 407–412.

Kubie, L. Symposium on the evaluation of therapeutic results. *Int. J. Psychoanal.*, 1953, **XXIX**, 33.

Kubie, L. Some unsolved problems of psychoanalytic therapy. In F. Fromm-Reichmann and J. Moreon (Eds.), *Progress in psychotherapy*. New York: Grune & Stratton, 1956.

Kubie, L. The changing economics of psychotherapeutic practice. *J. Nerv. & Ment. Dis.*, 1964, **139**, 311–312.

Kurland, A. A. The drug placebo—its psychodynamic and conditional reflex action. *Behav. Sci.*, 1957, **2**, 101.

Kurland, A. A. The placebo. In Masserman, J. H., and Moreno, J. I. (Eds.), *Progress in Psychotherapy*. Vol. III. New York: Grune & Stratton, 1958.

LaBarre, W. Confession as cathartic therapy in American Indian tribes. In Kiev, A. (Ed.), *Magic, faith, and healing*. London: Collier-Macmillan, 1964.

Lasagna, L., Laties, V. G., and Dohan, L. J. Further studies on the "pharmacology" of placebo administration. *J. Clin. Invest.*, 1958, **37**, 533.

Lasagna, L., Mosteller, F., von Felsinger, J. M., and Beecher, H. K. A study of placebo response. *Am. J. Med.*, 1954, **16**, 770.

Lasagna, L., and von Felsinger, J. M. The volunteer subject in research. *Science*, 1954, **120**, 359.

Lehmann, H. E., and Knight, M. A. Measurement of changes in human behavior under effects of psychotropic drugs. In Rothlin, E. (Ed.), *Neuropsychopharmacology*. Basle, Switzerland: 1960.

Lehmann, H. E., and Knight, M. A. Placebo-proneness and placebo-resistance of different psychological functions. *Psychiat. Quart.*, 1960, **34**, 505.

Lehmann, H. E. The placebo response and the double-blind study. In Hoch, P., and Zubin. J. (Eds.), *Evaluation of psychiatric treatment*. New York: Grune & Stratton, 1964.

Leslie, A. Ethics and practice of placebo therapy. *Am. J. Med.*, 1954, **16**, 854.

Lesse, S. Placebo reactions in psychotherapy. *Dis. Nerv. System*, 1962, **23**, 1–7.

Lesse, S. Placebo reactions and spontaneous rhythms. *Arch. Gen. Psychiat.*, 1964, **10**, 497–505 (a).

Lesse, S. Placebo reactions and spontaneous rhythms: Their effects on the results of psychotherapy. *Am. J. Psychoth.*, 1964, **XVIII**, 99–115 (b).

Letermendia, F. J. J., and Harris, A. D. The influence of side-effects on the reporting of symptoms. *Psychopharmacologia*, 1959, **1**, 39.

Levenson, D. J. The psychotherapist's contribution to the patient's treatment career. In Strupp, H. H., and Luborsky, L. (Eds.), *Research in psychotherapy*. Washington, D.C.: American Psychological Assoc., 1958.

Liberman, R. An analysis of the placebo phenomenon. *J. Chron. Dis.*, 1962, **15**, 761–783.

Linn, E. L. Sources of uncertainty in studies of drugs affecting mood, mentation or activity. *Am. J. Psychiat.*, 1959, **116**, 97.

Linton, H. B., and Langs, R. J. Placebo reactions in a study of LSD-25. *Arch. Gen. Psychiat.*, 1962, **6**, 369.

Loenwald, H. W. On the therapeutic action of psychoanal. *Int. J. Psychoanal.*, 1960, **XLI**, 1–18.

London, P., Schulman, R., and Black, M. Religious guilt and ethical standards. *J. Soc. Psychol.*, 1966, **63**, 145–159.

Lord, E. Experimentally induced variations in Rorschach performance. *Psychol. Mono.*, 1950, **64** (10, Whole No. 316).

Lowinger, P., and Dobie, S. The attitudes and emotions of the psychiatrist in the initial interview. Paper presented at annual meeting of the Assoc. for the Advancement of Psychotherapy. St. Louis, May, 1963.

Lowinger, P., and Dobie, S. Psychiatrist as a variable in the process of interview and treatment. *Nature*, 1964, **201**, 1246.

Luborsky, L. In Strupp, H. H., and Luborsky, L. *Research in psychotherapy*. Washington, D. C.: Amer. Psychol. Assoc., 1962.

Luft, J. Interaction and projection. *J. Proj. Tech.*, 1953, **17**, 489–492.

McGuigan, J. F. The experimenter: A neglected stimulus object. *Psychol. Bul.*, 1963. **60**. 421–428.

McNair, D. M., Lorr, M., and Callahan, D. M. Patient and therapist influences on quitting psychotherapy. *J. Consult. Psychol.*, 1963, **27**, 10.

Malitz, S. Variables and drug effectiveness. In Rinkel, M. (Ed.), *Specific and non-specific factors in psychopharmacology*. New York: Philosophical Library, 1963.

Marmor, J. Psychoanalytic therapy as an educational process: Common denominators in the therapeutic approaches of different psychoanalytic "schools." In Masserman, J. H. (Ed.), *Science and psychoanalysis*. Vol. 5. New York: Grune & Stratton, 1962.

Masling, J. The effects of warm and cold interaction on the administration and scoring of an intelligence test. *J. Consult. Psychol.*, 1959, **23**, 336–341.

Masling, J. The influence of situational and interpersonal variables in projective testing. *Psych. Bul.*, 1960, **57**, 66–85.

Masling, J. Differential indoctrination of examiners and Rorschach responses. *J. Consult. Psychol.*, 1965, **29**, 198–201.

Masserman, J. H. Evolution vs. "revolution" in psychotherapy: A biodynamic integration. *Behav. Sci.*, 1957, **2**, 89–100.

Masserman, J. H. Humanitarian psychiatry. *Bull. N. Y. Acad. Med.*, 1963, **39**, 533–544.

Major, R. H. *Classic descriptions of disease*. Springfield: C. C. Thomas, 1955.

Meehl, P. E. Psychotherapy. *Ann. Rev. Psychol.*, 1955, **6**, 357–378.

Meerloo, J. A. M. The essence of mental cure. *Am. J. Psychoth.*, 1958, **XII**, 42.

Meerloo, J. A. M. The essence of mental cure. *Am. J. Psychoth.*, 1963, **XII**, 42–63.

Menninger, K. The academic lecture, hope. *Am. J. Psychiat.*, 1959, **115**, 481–491.

Mezaros, A. F., and Galigher, D. L. Measuring indirect effects of treatment on chronic wards. *Dis. Nerv. Syst.*, 1958, **19**, 1.

Miller, H. E. "Acceptance" and related attributes as demonstrated in psychotherapeutic interviews. *J. Clin. Psychol.*, 1949, **5**, 83–87.

Modell, W. *The relief of symptoms.* Philadelphia: W. B. Saunders, 1955.

Modell, W., and Houde, R. W. Factors influencing clinical evaluation of drugs. *J.A.M.A.*, 1958, **30**, 2190.

Morison, R. A. H., Woodmansey, A., and Young, A. J. Placebo response in an arthritis trial. *Ann. Rheum. Dis.*, 1961, **20**, 179.

Motherby, G. *A new medical dictionary or general repository of physics.* (4th Ed.) London: J. Johnson, 1795.

Mowrer, O. *The crisis in psychiatry and religion.* New York: Van Nostrand, 1961.

Mowrer, O. Payment or repayment? The problem of private practice. *Am. Psychol.*, 1963, **18**, 577–580.

Muller, B. P. Personality of placebo reactors and nonreactors. *Dis. Nerv. Syst.*, 1965, **26**, 58.

Murphy, W. R. A comparison of psychoanalysis with the dynamic psychotherapies. *J. Nerv. & Ment. Dis.*, 1958, **126**, 441–450.

Murphy, J. M. Psychotherapeutic aspects of shamanism on St. Lawrence Island, Alaska. In Kiev, A. (Ed.), *Magic, Faith, and Healing.* London: Collier-Macmillan, 1964.

Murray, J. H. *A new English dictionary on historical principles.* Oxford: Clarendon Press, 1933.

Nash, E. H., Frank, J. D., Gliedman, L. D., Imber, S. D., and Stone, A. R. Some factors related to patients remaining in group therapy. *Int. J. Grp. Psychoth.*, 1957, **7**, 264.

Nash, E. H., Frank, J. D., Imber, S. D., and Stone, A. R. Selected effects of inert medication on psychiatric outpatients. *Am. J. Psychoth.*, 1963, **XVIII**, 33–48.

Oberndorf, C. P., Greenachre, P., and Kubie, L. Symposium on the evaluation of therapeutic results. *Int. J. Psychoanal.*, 1953, **XXIX**, 13.

O'Brien, J. R. Is liver a "tonic"? A short study of injecting placebos. *Brit. Med. J.*, 1954, **11**, 136.

Orne, M. The nature of hypnosis: Artifact and essence, *J. Abnorm. Soc. Psychol.*, 1959, **58**, 277–299.

Orne, M. T. On the social psychology of the psychological experiment: With particular reference to demand characteristics and their implications. *Am. Psychol.*, 1962, **17**, 776–783.

Palmore, E., Lennard, H. L., and Hendin, H. Similarities of therapist and patient verbal behavior in psychotherapy. *Sociometry*, 1959, **22**, 12–22.

Parloff, M. B. Therapist–patient relationships and outcome of psychotherapy. *J. Consult. Psych.*, 1961, **25**, 29–38.

Parloff, M. B., and Rubinstein, E. A. Summary of research problems in psychotherapy conference, 1958. In Rubinstein, E. A., and Parloff, M. B. (Eds.), *Research in psychotherapy.* Washington: Amer. Psychol. Assoc., 1958.

Parsons, T. *The social system.* Glencoe, Ill.: The Free Press, 1951.

Paul, L. The operations of psychotherapy. *Comprehens. Psychiat.*, 1963, **4** (4), 281–290.

Pearlin, L. J. The values and enthusiasm for drugs in a mental hospital. *J. Interpersonal Proc.*, 1962, **25**, 170–179.

Perlin, S., Pollin, W., and Butler, R. N. The experimental subject. *A.M.A. Arch. Neurol. Psychiat.*, 1958, **80**, 65.

Polansky, N., and Kounin, J. Client's reactions to initial interviews. *Hum. Relat.*, 1956, **9**, 237.

Pollin, W., and Perlin, S. Psychiatric evaluation of "normal control" volunteers. *Am. J. Psychiat.*, 1958, **115**, 129.

Prange, A. J., Jr., Cochrane, C. M., and Abse, D. W. Changing psychiatric treatment patterns and their relationship to a double blind tranquilizer study in a teaching hospital. *J. New Drugs*, 1963, **3**, 85–84 (a).

Prange, A. J., Jr., Cochrane, C. M., Abse, D. W., and Boswell, J. I. A double blind clinical trial of chlorpromazine and reserpine in acute mental disturbance. *J. New Drugs*, 1963, **3**, 85–95 (b).

Rachman, S. *Critical essays on psychoanalysis.* New York: The Macmillan Co., 1963.

Rashkis, H. A. Cognitive restructing: Why research is therapy. *A.M.A. Arch. Gen. Psychiat.*, 1960, **2**, 612.

Rashkis, H. A., and Smarr, E. R. Drug and milieu effect with chronic schizophrenics. *A.M.A. Arch. Neur. Psychiat.*, 1957, **77**, 202.

Raskin, A. A comparison of acceptors and resistors of drug treatment as an adjunct to psychotherapy. *J. Consult. Psychol.*, 1961, **25**, 366.

Rathod, N. H. Tranquilizers and patients' environment. *Lancet*, 1958, **1**, 611.

Reiser, M. F., Reeves, R. B., and Armington, J. Effects of variations in laboratory procedure and experimenter upon ballistocardiogram, blood pressure, and heart rate in healthy young men. *Psychosom. Med.*, 1955, **XVII**, 185–199.

Reznikoff, M., and Toomey, L. C. *Evaluation of changes associated with psychiatric treatment.* Springfield, Ill.: Charles C. Thomas, 1959.

Richards, T. W. Personality of subjects who volunteer for research on a drug (mescaline). *J. Proj. Tech.*, 1960, **24**, 424.

Rickels, K., Boren, R., and Stuart, H. M. Controlled psychopharmacological research in general practice. *J. New Drugs*, 1964, **4**, 138(a).

Rickels, K., Baum, N. C., Taylor, W., and Raab, E. Humanism in clinical research. *Psychosomat.*, 1964, **V**, 315–316 (b).

Ripley, H. S., and Jackson, J. K. Therapeutic factors in Alcoholics Anonymous. *Am. J. Psych.*, 1959, **116**, 44–50.

Rivers, W. H. R. *The influence of alcohol and other drugs on fatigue.* London: Edw. Arnold, 1908.

Rivers, W. H. R. *Medicine, magic, and religion.* London: Macmillan & Co., 1924.

Roberts, J. M., and Hamilton, M. Treatment of anxiety states. *J. Ment. Sci.* 1958, **104**, 1052.

Rogers, C. R. *Client-centered therapy.* Boston: Houghton Mifflin, 1951.

Rogers, C. R. *Client-centered therapy: a current view.* In Fromm-Reichman, Frieda, and Moreno, J. L. (Eds.), *Progress in psychotherapy.* New York: Grune & Stratton, 1956.

Rogers, C. R. The necessary and sufficient conditions of therapeutic personality change. *J. Consul. Psychol.*, 1957, **21**, 95–103 (a).

Rogers, C. R. A therapist's view of the good life. *Humanist*, 1957, **17**, 291–300 (b).

Rogers, C. R. *On becoming a person.* Boston: Houghton Mifflin, 1961.

Rosenthal, D., and Frank, J. D. Psychotherapy and the placebo effect. *Psychol. Bull.*, 1956, **55**, 294.

Rosenthal, R. Experimenter attributes as determinants of subjects' responses. *J. Proj. Tech. Pers. Asses.*, 1963, **27**, 324–331 (a).

Rosenthal, R. On the social psychology of the psychological experiment: The experimenter's hypothesis as unintended determinant of experimental results. *Am. Sci.*, 1963, **51**, 268–283 (b).

Rosenthal, R. Experimental modeling effects as determinants of subjects' responses. *J. Proj. & Pers. Asses.*, 1963, **27**, 467–471 (c).

Rosenthal, R. Letter to the editor. *Behav. Sci.*, 1964, **9** (a).

Rosenthal, R. Experimenter outcome-orientation and the results of the psychological experiment. *Psychol. Bul.*, 1964, **61**, 405–412 (b).

Rosenthal, R. *Experimenter effects in behavioral research.* New York: Appleton-Century-Crofts, 1966.

Rosenthal, R., and Fode, K. L. The effect of experimenter bias on the performance of the albino rat. *Behav. Sci.*, 1963, **8**, 183–189 (a).

Rosenthal, R., Fode, K. L., Vikan-Kline, L., L. and Persinger, G. W. Verbal conditioning: mediator of experiment, expectancy effects. *Psychol. Rep.*, 1964, **114**, 71–74.

Rosenthal, R., Friedman, C. J., Johnson, C. A., Fode, K., Schill, T., White, R. C., and Viken, L. L. Variables affecting experimenter bias in a group situation. *Genet. Psychol. Monogr.*, 1964, **70**, 271–296 (c).

Rosenthal, R., and Halas, E. S. Experimenter effect in the study of invertebrate behavior. *Psychol. Rep.*, 1962, **11**, 251–256.

Rosenthal, R., Kohn, P., and Carota, N. Experimenters' hypothesis—confirmation and mood as determinants of experimental results. *Percept. & Mot. Skills*, 1965, **20**, 1237–1252.

Rosenthal, R., and Lawson, F. A longitudinal study of the effects of experimenter bias on the operant learning of laboratory rats. *J. Psychiat. Res.*, 1963, **2**, 61–72.

Rosenthal, R., Persinger, G. W., Mulry, R. C., Grothe, M., and Vikan-Kline, L. Changes in experimental hypotheses as determinants of experimental results. *J. Prog. Tech.*, 1964, **28**, 465–469.

Rosenthal, R., Persinger, G. W., Mulry, R. G., Vikan-Kline, L., and Grothe, M. Emphasis on experimental procedure, sex of subjects and the biasing effects of experimental hypotheses. *J. Prog. Tech.*, 1964, **28**, 470–473.

Rosenthal, R., Persinger, G. W., Vikan-Kline, L., and Fode, K. L. The effect of experimenter outcome-bias and subject set on awareness in verbal conditioning experiments. *J. Ver. Learn. Beh.*, 1963, **2**, 275–283 (a).

Rosenthal, R., Persinger, G. W., Vikan-Kline, L., and Fode, K. L. The effect of early data returns on data subsequently obtained by outcome-biased experimenters. *Sociometry*, 1963, **26**, 487–498 (b).

Rosenthal, R., Persinger, G. W., Vikan-Kline, L., and Mulry, R. C. The role of the research assistant in the mediation of experimenter bias. *J. Personal.*, 1963, **31**, 313–335.

Rothman, T. Disturbed communication and optimal psychotherapy. *J. Neuropsychopharm.*, 1960, **2**, 1.

Rothman, T., and Sward, K. Studies in pharmacological psychotherapy. *A.M.A. Arch. Neur. & Psych.*, 1956, **78**, 95–105.

Rothman, T., and Sward, K. Studies in pharmacological psychotherapy. *A.M.A. Arch. Neur. & Psych.*, 1957, **78**, 628–642.

Rubinstein, E. A., and Parloff, M. B. (Ed.). *Research in psychotherapy.* Washington, D. C.: American Psychological Association, 1959.

Sabshin, M., and Ramet, J. Pharmacotherapeutic evaluation and the psychiatric setting. *A.M.A. Arch. Neurol. & Psych.*, 1956, **75**, 362–370.

Sampsom, E. E., and French, Jr., J. R. P. An experiment on active and passive resistance to social power. *Am. Psychol.*, 1960, **13**, 396.

Samuels, A. S., and Edisen, C. B. A study of the psychiatric effects of placebo. *J. Louisiana Med. Soc.*, 1961, **113**, 114.

Sapolsky, A. Effect of interpersonal relationships upon verbal conditioning. *J. Abn. Soc. Psychol.*, 1960, **60**, 241–246.

Sargant, W. *Battle for the mind.* New York: Doubleday & Co., 1957.

Sarwer-Foner, G. J., and Korenyi, A. B. Accumulated experience with transference and counter-transference aspects of the psychotropic drugs. *Neuro-psychopharmacology*, 1961, **1**, 385–391.

Sarwer-Foner, G. H., and Korayi, E. K. Transference effects, the attitude of treating physician and counter-transference in the use of neuroleptic drugs in psychiatry. In Sarwer-Foner, G. L. *The dynamics of psychiatric drug therapy*. Springfield, Ill.: Charles C. Thomas, 1960.

Schaffer, L., and Myers, J. K. Psychotherapy and social stratification. *Psychiatry*, 1954, **17**, 83–93.

Scharaf, M. R., and Lerivson, D. J. The quest for omnipotence in professional training. *Psychiatry*, 1964, **27**, 135.

Schmidenberg, M. The role of suggestion in analytic therapy. *Psychoanal. Rev.*, 1939, **XXVI**, 223.

Schmidberg, M. Values and goals in psychotherapy. *The Psychiat. Quart.*, 1958, **32**, 333–365.

Schottstaedt, W. W., Pinsky, R. H., Mackler, D., and Wolf, S. Metabolic response to a group stress on a metabolic ward. *Clin. Res. Proceed.*, 1965, **IV**, 126.

Schottstaedt, W. W., Pinsky, R. H., Mackler, D., and Wolf, S. Prestige and social interactions on a metabolic ward. *Psychosom. Med.*, 1959, **21**, 132.

Seeman, J. *Psychotherapy and personality change*. In Rogers, C. R., and Symond, R. F. (Eds.), Chicago: University of Chicago Press, 1954.

Shapiro, A. K. The placebo effect in the history of medical treatment—implications for psychiatry. *Am. J. Psychiat.*, 1959, **116**, 298–304.

Shapiro, A. K. A contribution to a history of the placebo effect. *Behav. Sc.*, 1960, **V**, 109–135 (a).

Shapiro, A. K. Attitudes toward the use of placebos in treatment. *J. Nerv. & Ment. Dis.*, 1960, **130**, 200–211 (b).

Shapiro, A. K. A browsing double-blind study of ioniazid in geriatric patients. *Dis. Nerv. Syst.*, 1960, **21** (c).

Shapiro, A. K. Feasibility of "browsing" double blind studies. *Dis. Nerv. Syst.*, 1961, **XXXII**.

Shapiro, A. K. The psychological use of medication. In Lief, H. I., Lief, V. F., and Lief, N. R. (Eds.), *The psychological basis of medical practice*. New York: Harper Bros., 1963.

Shapiro, A. K. A historic and heuristic definition of the placebo. *Psychiatry*, 1964, **27**, 52 (a).

Shapiro, A. K. Rejoinder. *Psychiatry*, 1964, **27**, 178 (b).

Shapiro, A. K. Factors contributing to the placebo effect: Implications for psychotherapy. *Am. J. Psychother.*, 1964, **XVIII**, 73–88 (c).

Shapiro, A. K. Etiological factors in placebo effect. *J.A.M.A.*, 1964, **187**, 712. (d).

Shapiro, A. K. Rational use of psychopharmaceutic agents. *N. Y. State J. Med.*, 1964, **64**, 1084 (e).

Shapiro, A. K. Placebogenics and iatroplacebogenics. *Med. Times*, 1964, **92**, 1037–????. (f)

Shapiro, A. K. The curative waters and warm poultices of psychotherapy. *Psychosom. Med.*, 1966, **VII**, 21–23.

Shapiro, A. K. The placebo response. In *Modern perspectives in world psychiatry*. Howels, J. G. (Ed.), Edinburgh: Oliver and Boyd, 1968.

Shapiro, A. K., Wilensky, H., and Struening, E. L. Study of the placebo effect with a placebo test. *Compreh. Psychiatr.*, 1968, **9**, 118.

Shapiro, A. K. Semantics of the placebo. *Psych. Qtly.*, in press. (a)

Shapiro, A. K. Iatroplacebogenics. *Int'l. Pharmacopsychiat.*, in press. (b)

Shapiro, A. K. Defensiveness of physicians toward treatment, in preparation. (a)

Shapiro, A. K. Attitudes toward the use of placebos, in preparation. (b)

Shapiro, A. K. Questionnaire survey of the attitudes toward a definition of placebo, in preparation. (c)

Shapiro, A. P., Myers, T., Reiser, M. F., and Ferris, E. B. Comparison of blood pressure response to veriloid and to the doctor. *Psychosom. Med.*, 1954, **XVI**, 478–488.

Shapiro, A. P. Influence of emotional variables in evaluation of hypotensive agents. *Psychosom. Med.*, 1955, **17**, 291–305.

Shapiro, A. P. Psychological factors in evaluation of hypertensive drugs. *Psychosom. Med.*, 1955, **17**, 291.

Shapiro, A. P. *The investigator himself in the clinical evaluation of new drugs*. Waife, S. O., and Shapiro, A. P. (Eds.). New York: Harper & Bros., 1959.

Sheard, M. B. The influence of doctor's attitude on the patient's response to antidepressant medication. *J. Nerv. Ment. Dis.*, 1963, **136**, 555.

Sherif, M., and Haney, O. J. A study in eye functioning, elimination of stable audiorages in individuals with group silentness. *Sociometry*, 1952, **16**, 272–305.

Sherman, L. J. The significant variables in psychopharmaceuticals. *Am. J. Psychiat.*. 1959, **116**, 208–214.

Snow, L. H., and Rickels, K. Use of direct observation in the teaching and learning of psychotherapy. *Am. J. Psychoth.*, 1965, **XIX**, 487–491.

Snyder, W. U. *Research in psychotherapy*. In Rubinstein, E. A., and Parloff, M. B. (Eds.). Washington, D.C.: American Psychological Association, 1958.

Snyder, W. U. "Warmth" in non-directive counseling. *J. Abnorm. Soc. Psychol.*, 1946, **41**, 491–495.

Snyder, W. U., and Snyder, B. J. *The psychotherapy relationship*. New York: The Macmillan Co., 1961.

Stanton, A. H., and Schwartz, M. S. *The mental hospital*. New York: Basic Books, 1954.

Stein, M. H. A consideration of psychoanalysis in relation to psychiatry. *Am. J. Psychiat.*, 1966, **122**, 830–833.

Steinbook, R. M., Jones, M. B., and Ainslie, J. D. Suggestibility in the placebo effect. *J. Nerv. Ment. Dis.*, 1966, **140**, 87.

Sternback, R. A. The effects of instructional sets on autonomic responsivity. *Psychophysiol.*, 1964, **1**, 67–72.

Stoler, N. Client likeability: A variable in the study of psychotherapy. *J. Consult. Psychol.*, 1963, **27**, 175–178.

Storrow, H. A., and Spanner, M. Does psychotherapy change patients' behavior? *J. Nerv. Ment. Dis.*, 1962, **134**, 440.

Strupp, H. H. Nature of psychotherapist's contribution to treatment process. *A.M.A. Arch. Gen. Psychiat.*, 1960, **3**, 219–231. (a)

Strupp H. H. *Psychotherapists in action.* New York: Grune & Stratton, 1960. (b)

Strupp, H. H., and Williams, J. V. Some determinants of clinical evaluations of different psychiatrists. *A.M.A. Arch. Gen. Psychiat.*, 1960, **2**, 434–440.

Strupp, H. H., Wallach, M. S., and Wogan, M. The psychotherapy experience in retrospect: A questionnaire survey of former patients and their therapists. *Psychol. Monogr.*, 1964, **78**, 1–45.

Strupp, H. H., and Wallach, M. S. A further study of psychiatrists' responses in quasi-therapy situations. *Behav. Sci.*, 1965, **10**, 113.

Strupp, H. H. The performance of psychiatrists and psychologists in a therapeutic interview. *J. Clinic. Psychol.*, 1958, **XIV**, 219–226. (a)

Strupp, H. H. The performance of psychoanalytic and client-centered therapists in an initial interview. *J. Consul. Psychol.*, 1958, **22**, 265–274. (b)

Strupp, H. H. The psychotherapist's contribution to the treatment process. *Behav. Sci.*, 1958, **3**, 34–67. (c)

Strupp, H. H., and Luborsky, L. (Eds.), *Research in psychotherapy.* Washington, D.C.: American Psychological Assoc., 1958.

Strupp, H. H. The psychotherapist's contribution to the treatment process. *Psychiat.*, 1959, **22**, 349–362.

Stukat, K. Suggestibility: *A factorial and experimental analysis.* Stockholm: Almqvist and Wiksell, 1958.

Sullivan, H. S. A note on the implications of psychiatry, the study of interpersonal relations, for investigations in the social sciences. *Am. J. Sociol.*, 1936–37, **42**, 848–861.

Szasz, T. S., and Nemiroff, R. A. A questionnaire study of psychoanalytic practices and opinions. *J. Nerv. & Ment. Dis.*, 1963, **137**, 209–221.

Thompson, C. The role of the analyst and personality in therapy. *Am. J. Psychother.*, 1956, **10**, 347–359.

Thorn, W. F. The placebo reactor. *Australasian J. Pharm.*, 1962, **43**, 1035.

Tibbets, R. W., and Hawkins, J. R. The placebo response. *J. Ment. Sci.*, 1956, **102**, 60.

Troffer, S. A., and Tart, C. T. Experimenter bias in hypnotist performance. Laboratory of Human Development, Stanford University, California, 1964. (Abstract.)

Trouton, D. S. Placebos and their psychological effects. *J. Ment. Sci.*, 1957, **103**, 344.

Truax, C. B., and Wargo, D. G. Psychotherapeutic encounters that change behavior for better or for worse. *Am. J. Psychother.*, 1966, **XX**, 499.

Ubell, E. Efforts to measure psychotherapy success. *New York Herald Tribune*, Oct. 4, 1964.

Uhlenhuth, E. H., Cantor, A., Neustadt, J. O., and Payson, G. E. The symptomatic relief of anxiety with meprobamate, phenobarbital and placebo. *Am. J. Psychiat.*, 1959, **115**, 905–910.

Uhlenhuth, E. H., Rickels, K., Fisher, S., Park, L. C., Libman, R. S., and Mock, J. Drug, doctor's verbal attitude and clinic setting in the symptomatic response to pharmacotherapy. *Psychopharmacologia*, 1966, **9**, 392–418.

Uhr, L., and Miller, J. G. *Drugs and behavior.* New York: Wiley, 1960.

Ullman, L. P., and McFarland, R. L. Productivity as a variable in TAT protocols: A methodological study. *J. Proj. Tech.*, 1957, **21**, 80–87.

Volgyesi, F. A. "School for patients" hypnosis-therapy and psychoprophylaxis. *Brit. J. Med. Hypnotism*, 1954, **5**, 8.

Von Felsinger, J. M., Lasagna, L., and Beecher, H. K. Drug-induced mood changes in man. 2. Personality and reactions to drugs. *J.A.M.A.*, 1955, **157**, 1113.

Von Mehring, O., and King, S. R. *Renovating the mental patient.* New York: Russell Sage Foundation, 1957.

Voth, V. M., Herbert, M. C., and Orth, M. H. Situational variables in the assessment of psychotherapeutic results. *Bul. Menninger Clinic*, 1962, **26**, 73–81.

Waife, S. O., and Shapiro, A. P. *The clinical evaluation of new drugs.* New York: Hoeber, 1959.

Wallach, M. S., and Strupp, H. H. Psychotherapists' clinical judgments and attitudes towards patients. *J. Consult. Psychol.*, 1960, **24**, 316–323.

Walters, R. H., and Parke, R. D. Emotional arousal, isolation, and discrimination learning in children. *J. Exp. Child. Psychol.*, 1964, **1**, 163–173.

Walters, R. H., and Quinn, M. J. The effects of social and sensory deprivation on autokinetic judgments. *J. Pers.*, 1960, **28**, 210–219.

Walters, R. H., Marshall, W. E., and Shooter, J. R. Anxiety, isolation and susceptibility to social influence. *J. Pers.*, 1960, **28**, 518–529.

Walters, R. H., and Ray, E. Anxiety, isolation and reinforcer effectiveness. *J. Pers.*, 1960, **28**, 358–367.

Ward, C. H. Psychotherapy research: Dilemmas and directions. *Arch. Gen. Psychiat.*, 1964, **10**, 596–622.

Weatherall, M. Tranquilizers. *Brit. Med. J.*, 1962, **I**, 1219–1224.

Weiss, R. L., Krasner, L., and Ullmann, L. F. Responsivity to verbal conditioning as a function of emotional atmosphere and pattern of reinforcement. *Psychol. Rep.*, 1960, **6**, 415–426.

White, R. B. Recent developments in psychoanalytic research. *Dis. Nerv. System*, 1961, **XXII**, 2–15.

Whitehorn, J. C. Psychiatric implications of the placebo effect. *Am. J. Psychiat.*, 1958, **114**, 662.

Whitman, J. H. Suggestibility in schizophrenia. *J. Clin. Psychol.*, 1961, **XVII**, 203.

Williams, M., and McGee, T. F. The bias of the drug administrant in judgments of the effects of psychopharmacological agents. *J. Nerv. & Ment. Dis.*, 1692, **135**, 569–573.

Wilson, C. W. M., and Huby, P. M. An assessment of the responses to drugs acting on the central nervous system. *Clin. Pharm. & Ther.*, 1961, **2**, 587.

Wilson, C. W. M. Suggestion and the placebo: An analysis of bias in clinical trials. In Keels, C. A., and Smith, F. (Eds.), *The assessment of pain in man and animals*. London: E. & S. Livingston, Ltd., 1962. (a)

Wilson, C. W. M. An analysis of factors contributing to placebo responses. *Proc. Roy. Soc. Med.*, 1962, **55** 16. (b)

Wolberg, L. R. *The technique of psychotherapy*. New York: Grune & Stratton, 1954.

Wolens, E. Responsibility for raw data. *Amer. Psychol.*, 1962, **17**, 657–658.

Wolf, S., Doering, C. R., Clark, M. L., and Hagans, J. A. Chance distribution and the placebo reactor. *J. Lab. Clin. Med.*, 1957, **49**, 37.

Wolf, S. The pharmacology of placebos. *Pharm. Rev.*, 1959, **11**, 689–704. (a)

Wolf, S. Placebos. *Proceedings of the association for research in nervous and mental disease*. Baltimore: Williams & Williams Co., **XXXVII**, 1959, **147**, 161. (b)

Wolf, S. Placebos: Problems and pitfalls. Part IV. *Clin. Pharmacol. Therapeut.*, 1962, **3**, 254–257.

Wolf, W. Effects of suggestion and conditioning on the action of chemical agents in human subjects—the pharmacology of placebos. *J. Lab. Clin. Med.*, 1950, **29**, 100.

Wolff, W. Fact and value in psychotherapy. *Amer. J. Psychother.*, 1954, **8**, 466–486.

Wolff, W. *Contemporary psychotherapists examine themselves*. Illinois: Charles C. Thomas, 1956.

Wood, E. C., Rokusin, J. M., and Morse, E. Resident psychiatrist in the admitting office. *Arch. Gen. Psychiat.*, 1965, **13**, 54–61.

Zetzel, E. R. The effects of psychotherapy. *Int. J. Psychiat.*, 1965, **1**. 144–150.

Zuckerman, M., and Grosz, H. J. Suggestibility and dependency. *J. Consult. Psych.*, 1958, **22**, 328.

13

RESEARCH ON PSYCHOTHERAPY WITH CHILDREN[1]

EUGENE E. LEVITT

INDIANA UNIVERSITY SCHOOL OF MEDICINE

The entire child guidance movement in this country in 1909 comprised one psychiatrist, one psychologist, a secretary, and three small rooms on the ground floor of the juvenile detention home in Chicago. From this tiny inception, The Idea, as Healy (1948) once called it, was to grow in three score years to an established community force, operating with a corps of twelve hundred clinics, replete with "training centers and professorships in leading universities, specialized periodicals, national and international societies and conventions . . . and intensive research activities" (Kanner, 1967).

This spectacular burgeoning reflected a reasonable hope that dealing with the young was the ultimate solution to all of the nation's mental health problems. The rationale was invitingly simple and seemed unchallengeable.

The untreated, emotionally disturbed child is expected to become, eventually, an emotionally disturbed adult, an axis that Lewis (1965) has called "the continuity hypothesis." Effective intervention at the child level should not only improve the child's immediately subsequent adjustment, but ought also to effect a noticeable reduction in the future incidence of adult disorders. Lewis (1965) refers to this prediction as the "intervention hypothesis."

The value of child guidance, or more fashionably, child psychotherapy, is now being seriously questioned from within the movement for the first time (for example, Simmons, 1963; Hersh, 1968; Sonis, 1968) on the grounds that after 60 years, the intervention hypothesis is not yet conclusively demonstrated. Evaluation research fails to show unequivocally that child psychotherapy is effective. Six decades of child guidance do not seem to have reduced either the demand for mental health services to children, or the incidence of emotional illness among adults. As

[1] The author is grateful to the editors and to Dr. Gerald D. Alpern for their helpful criticisms.

Hunt (1958) remarked sadly, "Our hopes of preventing mental illness by mental health education and child guidance clinics have been disappointed, and there is no convincing evidence that anyone has ever been kept out of the state hospital by such measures."

The failure to demonstrate the effectiveness of child psychotherapy is reflected in the data of Table 13.1. These have been aggregated from two reviews (Levitt, 1957a, 1963), and represent 47 reports of the outcome of child psychotherapy spanning a 35-year period up to around 1960. Nine-thousand, three-hundred and fifty-nine cases are involved, including 5,140 cases evaluated at the close of treatment and 4,219 evaluated at follow-up. The findings may be summarized as follows:

1. About two-thirds of all cases are seen as improved to a noticeable extent at close of treatment.

2. This figure holds, approximately, for children classified as psychotic as well as those who are seen as having "neurotic" disorders.[2]

3. Children with acting-out symptoms have an improvement rate of only 55 percent.

4. At follow-up, nearly 80 percent of all cases are regarded as improved.

The improvement rate reported in Table 13.1 is approximately the same as that found in groups of treatment "defectors" or "terminators," that is, emotionally disturbed children who were offered formal clinic treatment but failed to take advantage of the opportunity

TABLE 13.1 Summary of Reports of Outcome of Psychotherapy with Children[a]

Diagnostic Group	N	Per cent Improved
Neurotic at close	4539	67.4
Psychotic at close	252	65.1
Acting-out at close	349	55.0
Total at close	5140	66.4
Neurotic at follow-up[b]	4219	78.2

[a] Data from Levitt (1957a, 1963).

[b] Estimated median interval of 4.8 years after close.

(Levitt, 1957a; Levitt, et al., 1959). Defectors appear to be the most appropriate medium for estimating the so-called spontaneous remission rate, provided that the group is properly selected. It should consist of cases which (a) have been subjected to the same diagnostic procedures as the treated cases; (b) have been accepted for treatment, and; (c) have never had any formal therapy sessions.

The use of defectors as a base line control is the salient hypostasis of the case for the unproven efficacy of child psychotherapy. The defector control has been sharply criticized, primarily on the grounds that defectors and treated cases are originally dissimilar on certain dimensions, such as intensity of disturbance,

which render the defectors a biased control group (Hood-Williams, 1960; Heinicke and Goldman, 1960; Eisenberg and Gruenberg, 1961). However, when the defector sample conforms to the description in the previous paragraph, objective comparisons reveal no meaningful differences between treated and defector children (Levitt, 1957c, 1958; Williams and Pollack, 1964).

Requirements of methodology demand that a treated group and its control group should be selected from the same population. With few exceptions, outcome studies are carried out by the staff of an agency or institution, which ordinarily has access only to those persons who have voluntarily sought services at that agency

[2] Diagnostic categories based on adult patients do not hold clearly for children and adolescents. For purposes of rough communication, "neurotic" refers to a child who has not been diagnosed as psychotic, or as having a primary behavior disorder or a special symptom.

or institution. The investigators are thus restricted to a particular population, within which the defector control group appears to be the most reasonable method of estimating spontaneous remission rate.

One of the rare outcome studies that employed a different sampling method was done as part of the Buckinghamshire Child Survey in England between 1961 and 1964 (Shepherd et al., 1966). The treated sample consisted of 50 randomly chosen "neurotic" children between the ages of 5 and 15, seen at child guidance clinics in the county for the first time in 1962 (27 percent of the total clinic population at that time). A control sample matched for age, sex, and symptoms was selected from a random sample of more than 6,000 children who had never obtained or sought psychiatric assistance.

Outcome ratings were made by clinicians based on interviews with parents in 1962 and again in 1964. Sixty-five percent of the treated sample was rated as improved, compared to 61 percent of the controls. Sixteen percent of the treated children and 9 percent of the controls was rated as worse, and the rest of both groups was rated as unchanged. The percentages of improvement, which do not differ significantly, are strikingly similar to those in Table 13.1.

The Buckinghamshire investigation is impressive, despite the relatively small samples, as a rare instance of true random sampling. Its results suggest strongly that the so-called spontaneous recovery rate lies somewhere between 60 and 70 percent, no matter how it is estimated.

A comparison of improvement rate with treatment against spontaneous remission rate assumes a condition suitable for a one-tailed test. It is presumed in physical medicine that, though a treatment may not result in symptomatic improvement, it will certainly not harm the patient. *Primum non nocere*; chemical therapies undergo exhaustive experimentation with infrahuman mammals to insure that there are no noxious side effects before administration to humans.

The assumption of no harm was also made for many years by psychotherapists and psycho-

therapy researchers, despite the absence of an animal research analog. Until very recently, rating scales used to evaluate treatment outcome did not include a category labelled Worse. A therapist, no matter how bumbling or webfooted he might be, could not possibly be inferior to no therapist at all. Currently, however, the concept of the "psychonoxious" therapist (Truax, 1963) or what Bergin (1967) calls "the deterioration effect," is now readily accepted by most psychotherapy researchers as the most probable explanation for the apparent failure of psychotherapy.[3]

Truax and Wargo (1966) suggest that there are individual differences in therapy effectiveness among clinics and treatment institutions as well as among therapists. Apparent support for this position is reflected in 18 reports of outcome of psychotherapy with children from various treatment sources (Levitt, 1957a). Improvement rates at close showed a statistically significant variation from 43 percent to 86 percent. The standard deviation of the distribution is 11.4, and the range is 1.6 standard deviation units above and 2.2 standard deviation units below the mean. These characteristics strikingly resemble those of a distribution of scores from any small sample drawn from a normal population. This is exactly what would be expected according to the hypothesis of effective-ineffective treatment agencies.

A survey of play-therapy practices (Ginott and Lebo, 1961, 1963) suggests that there is considerable variation in the specific behaviors of child therapists in the therapy situation, and that these differences may be unrelated to theoretical orientation. This type of finding has been reported in a number of studies of adult patients. It underscores the possibility that there is a broad variation in effectiveness among therapists.

The concepts of the psychonoxious therapist and the deterioration effect have turned the attention of psychotherapy researchers from unadorned outcome studies to investigations that seek to discover "what specific therapeutic interventions produce specific changes in specific patients under specific conditions" (Strupp and

---

[3] "In fact, four children viewed their psychotherapeutic experiences negatively, voiced some dislike of their therapist (3 of the 4 had the same therapist)" (Weiss and Burke, 1967).

Bergin, 1969), that is, the conditions under which the intervention hypothesis may be valid or invalid. This quest has instigated much therapist-patient-process research in the adult psychotherapy field in recent years. Unfortunately, it has stimulated little additional research in child psychotherapy, where the volume of objective investigations has always been much smaller than in the adult field. Only six of the reviewers of psychotherapy research in the *Annual Review of Psychology*, since its inception in 1950, found it necessary to employ a subheading for research with child patients. These six groupings encompassed only 2.2 percent of the pages in the 19 chapters. One explanation of this neglect is the extra methodological difficulties involved in child psychotherapy research (see below). Another is the general reluctance of administrators, parents, and other concerned adults to sanction experimentation with disturbed children. The prepotent reason, however, is that child guidance is perennially dominated by two notoriously anti-research forces: psychoanalysis and social work. Their exclusive emphasis on service and training has effectively kept research out of the country's child guidance clinics.

Hopefully, the reader, now forewarned, will not be disappointed by the sparseness of references in this chapter and by its repeated substantive gaps.

SPECIAL PROBLEMS OF PSYCHOTHERAPY RESEARCH WITH CHILDREN

The multitude of slippery methodological problems that plague the psychotherapy researcher have been detailed in a number of thoughtful articles during the past 15 years. Child therapy research faces several unique problems, though they may have analogs in the adult field. These problems and their implications for findings are often entirely ignored by investigators. They are presented here briefly for identification only; no solutions are proposed.

1. Because the child is a developing organism:
(a) *The many symptomatic manifestations in* *children who are basically normal tend to disappear in time as a function of development*, that is, are subject to so-called spontaneous remission. There is a substantial incidence among normal children of behaviors usually considered to be symptoms of emotional disturbance—temper tantrums, sleep disturbances, enuresis, hyperactivity, specific fears, and the like (Macfarlane, et al., 1954; Lapouse and Monk, 1959). Apparently, there is some reality in the common-sense notion that children "grow out" of symptomatic behavior, that is, learn to cope with the stresses that cause them as their capacities to adjust improve with maturation. But an alarmed mother may bring a symptomatic child to the guidance clinic, where developmental remission may be recorded as therapeutic success.[4] Identical remission is likely to occur in the comparable child who remained untreated, which will then suggest that treatment was not effective. A more significant inference would be that *treatment may have been unnecessary*, a conclusion advanced by Shepherd and his associates (1966). They found that

... referral to a child-guidance clinic is related chiefly to parental reactions. The mothers of clinic-children were more apt to be anxious, depressed and easily upset by stress; they were less able to cope with their children, more apt to discuss their problems and to seek advice.

The clinic children themselves were not more disturbed than non-referred children.

(b) *Symptoms that are pathognomic of an underlying emotional illness may also disappear as a function of development, but will then be replaced by other symptoms.* This *developmental symptom substitution* is not really a spontaneous remission. It simply reflects the finding that certain symptoms are more likely to occur at particular ages. School phobia is most common in the elementary school years, while the behaviors usually categorized as delinquent occur most frequently in adolescence. An emotionally disturbed child may "grow out" of one symptom and grow into another. Developmental symptom substitution seems to be fairly common. A follow-up of treated children (Levitt, 1957b) disclosed that 22 percent had developed new

[4] The improvement rate with treatment for various compartmentalized symptoms is reported as higher than for diffuse psychopathologies (Levitt, 1963).

symptoms since the close of treatment. The phenomenon is suggested by Gardner's (1967) investigation of child guidance patients who were later hospitalized with a diagnosis of schizophrenia.

Consider the methodological problem. An eight-year old child is treated for enuresis and nightmares with subsequent remission of these symptoms. Therapy, evaluated at close, evidently has been effective. Later on, the child is found to be manifesting severe obsessive-compulsive behavior, or aggressive acting-out. Can the researcher still be confident that treatment was effective, that the disappearance of the original symptoms was due to intervention and not to developmental factors?

2. *Persons other than the child patient may be a direct focus of treatment.* In most child clinics, an effort is made to involve at least the mother in treatment. Some clinics give priority to cases in which both mother and father are willing to be seen in treatment. Treatment focus is thus a variable, one not found in adult therapy. The research problem is to separate effects. For example, a successful treatment effort involves mother and child with separate therapists. Is success due to the child's therapist, the mother's therapist, to both therapists, equally or in what proportions, or is it possible to separate effects or to determine relative weights?

A VARIETY OF THERAPEUTIC APPROACHES

Inpatient Milieu

Segregated inpatient services for younger age groups are still comparatively rare, and inpatients under the age of 18—mostly adolescents —are commonly hospitalized on adult wards. The adolescent on the adult ward ordinarily has access to appropriate educational and recreational stimulation, so that the only important difference from the segregated ward is segregation itself.

Clinicians disagree about which milieu is more therapeutically effective. Beskind (1962), in a review of the earlier literature, refers to some of the advantages and disadvantages of each environment. On adult wards, adolescents are faced by poor adult models, lack proper social relationships, and may be poorly tolerated by patients and staff.[5] On the other hand, severely disturbed adolescents, especially those manifesting aggressive and destructive behavior, tend to disrupt segregated wards, are more easily managed on adult wards, and may receive more attention from doctors and from adult patients. Adolescents normally live surrounded by adults; this situation is desirably approximated by the adult-adolescent ward.

Two recent investigations (Hartman et al., 1968; Warren, 1965a, 1965b) furnish a somewhat labored comparison of outcome as a function of milieu. The studies are fairly comparable in terms of samples (institutionalized adolescents averaging about 15 years of age) and method of evaluating outcome (ratings based on interviews by psychiatrist and social workers). The data, in percentage of patients improved compared with status at admission, are summarized in Table 13.2. The Hartmann sample of adolescents treated on adult wards was evaluated at close, a half to one year later, and again one to two years later. The Warren sample, which was treated on a special ward for adolescents, was evaluated six years after discharge.

The Hartmann sample does well at the time of discharge; three out of four were rated as improved. Backsliding must begin almost immediately. Within a year after discharge, more than 15 percent of those rated as improved at close are now no better off or worse than they were on admission. At the end of the second year, more than 10 percent more have regressed, a total loss of 27 percent in the improvement rate in a relatively short time after discharge.

In contrast, the Warren sample reports an improvement rate of 54 percent after six years. This, too, represents a regression, since at least 65 percent of the cases were reported improved at close. (Unfortunately, the data are not presented in a form that permits a precise statement of outcome at close.)

Both samples were worse at follow-up than at close, but more of the patients treated on a

[5] In a follow-up of a small group of institutionalized children (Weiss and Burke, 1967), half the

expatients stated that the "most help in the hospital" had been provided by "living with other children."

TABLE 13.2 Percentage of Improved Cases Among Adolescents
Treated on Adult and Separate Wards

| | Treated on Adult Wards[a] | | Treated on a Separate Ward[b] | |
	At close	$\frac{1}{2}$–1 year later	1–2 years later	6 years later
Improved	75	59	48	54[c]
No change	25	20	42	18
Worse	—	22	10	28

[a] Data from Hartmann et al. (1968).
[b] Data from Warren (1965b).
[c] Percent improved at close was at least 65.

separate ward maintained improvement for a longer period of time. At the same time, however, there were more cases who were worse at the longer follow-up of the separate ward group.

Peculiarly, in both studies, status at discharge did not predict status at follow-up. This absence of correlation may be the result of a subgroup of patients who improve symptomatically upon institutionalization but regress upon discharge, and another subgroup that does not manifest favorable effects of treatment until some time after discharge. Or it may merely reflect the accidental circumstance that most of the evaluations at close were performed by psychiatry residents, and most of the follow-up evaluations were done by social workers.

Beckett et al. (1968) contrast the effects of a conventional inpatient adolescent service with a permissive milieu in which patient behavior was partly controlled by self-government. A one-year follow-up showed no differences between the effects of the two milieus on six of seven variables, including rehospitalization, contact with an outpatient facility, and overall adjustment rating. The patients who had been subjected to the more permissive milieu did, however, manifest considerably fewer aggressive and antisocial behaviors. The authors suggest that this may be due to the fact that the permissive milieu tended to be selectively more effective with patients whose antisocial symptoms had a neurotic rather than a sociopathic basis.

The Day Treatment Center

The day treatment center is a relatively new conception in the structure of psychological care. Temporally, it stands midway between the residential treatment center where the child patient spends the 24-hour day, and the conventional child guidance clinic with its weekly one-hour visit. The patient of the day treatment center is considered to be living at home. He is brought to the center in the morning by his parents and returns home each evening.

The day treatment center lies between the clinic and residential center on a structural dimension, but may not differ from the residential center along other dimensions. For example, there does not appear to be a high correlation between structure and degree of disturbance of the children admitted to the three types of treatment units. The children treated at the Children's Day Treatment Center and School in New York City (La Vietes, et al., 1960) seem no less disturbed, either in degree or intensity, than Project Re-ED children (Hobbs, 1966) or those of any other residential treatment center. In effect, the day treatment center is probably a less expensive substitute for the scarce residential treatment center.

The day treatment center therapy program of the La Vietes group includes a required treatment of both parents for a minimum of one session per week, group counseling of all mothers, and therapy sessions with the individual child from one to three times weekly. This "comprehensive family treatment program" has "a dynamic psychoanalytic orientation," and is considered essential because the child is still regarded as living at home.

The La Vietes group attempted an evaluation of 38 children treated during the first seven years of the existence of the Children's Day Treatment Center and School (La Vietes et al., 1965). The evaluation is incompletely reported. It indicates that about three-quarters of the treated children were considered at least moderately improved, whether the criterion is ability to function outside of center, clinical impression, or psychological tests. Interestingly enough, intellectual measures did not reveal statistically significant improvement (Reens, 1965). The finding is strikingly similar to that reported by Project Re-ED (Weinstein, 1969), Despite the marked attention paid to formal education by the treatment agency, improvement occurs along behavior-emotional dimensions, but not in the academic sphere. Is this paradoxical outcome a function of program emphasis, or a reflection of an unequitable investment or preparation of teachers, or selection of patients, or is there some other explanation? Again, the objective research, because of its paucity, raises more questions than it answers.

The Special Class

The school room, where a child spends about as much time during the week as he does in his own home, is a stressful environment for many emotionally disturbed children. Psychopathological manifestations seem more prone to erupt in the school than in the home. Acting-out behaviors such as destructiveness, assaultiveness, and hyperactivity disrupt the class, interfere with teaching, and threaten the teacher's control. The child whose pathology is expressed through such symptoms is seldom tolerated in the classroom for very long. His withdrawal is likely to be enforced by school authorities, a certain indication to parents that special measures must be taken in order to continue the child's education. Institutionalization is, of course, one possibility. Another is the special class for emotionally disturbed children, a service provided by some school systems.

There must be a sizeable number of such special classes around the country, but a study by Haring and Phillips (1962) is a rare instance of an attempt to objectively evaluate the effect of this type of facility. They set up three groups of elementary school children rated as emotionally disturbed, with specific symptoms of the type that usually necessitates removal of the child from a regular class. Group I had a highly structured atmosphere characterized by rigid limits on behavior and by isolation as a disciplinary technique. Group II children were simply left in their regular classrooms with regular teachers receiving extensive professional consultation about the disturbed children. Group II may be regarded essentially as a control. Group III was relatively permissive, especially compared to Group I, with the intent of encouraging freedom to express feelings.

Evaluation at the end of a school year was based on before-and-after scores on The California Achievement Test and the Behavior Rating Scale, an ad hoc instrument developed by the authors, which uses the class teachers as raters. On the CAT, Group I showed a mean gain of 1.97, compared to 1.02 for Group II and 0.70 for Group III. Unfortunately, these difference scores are perfectly negatively correlated with the pretreatment scores, apparently due to nonrandom assignment of subjects to groups. It is plausible that the Law of Initial Values prevented Group III (pretreatment mean 5.36) from advancing as far in the school year as Group I (pretreatment mean 2.19). The only safe conclusion is that Group I caught up with Group II by the end of the year, but both were still functioning at an academic level considerably below that of Group III.

The BRS data shows an identical situation with respect to pre-treatment scores. The difference scores, however, are not perfectly correlated. Group I again achieved the largest gain, but Group II made almost no improvement, while Group III progressed moderately.

If we overlook the highly questionable use of class teachers as raters and the absence of any independent ratings on the BRS, the findings of the Haring-Phillips study suggest that any type of segregated class with a specially trained teacher is likely to be more therapeutic than the regular class. A highly structured environment in which aberrant behavior is systematically negatively reinforced appears to be more therapeutic than a permissive milieu that emphasizes expression of affect. The latter comparison should delight the behavior therapists and dismay the traditionalists.

Foster Home Care

The vast majority of children who do not live with their natural parents are the victims of illegitimacy, broken homes, and absent parents. They are drawn largely from among the underprivileged, are below average in intelligence, and will probably have had more than one foster home placement before reaching adulthood (for example, Eisenberg, et al., 1958; Maas and Engler, 1959). They are, in Eisenberg's (1962) bitterly concise words, "children of the lower depths, children mistreated before they came into care and treated not too well afterward."

In many cases, there is an implicit assumption that placement has psychological implications, either therapeutic or preventive. In an unknown, but probably quite small, number of cases, the child is placed in a foster home for explicit psychotherapeutic reasons. It has been clinically determined by a public agency that the home atmosphere is so malignantly psychopathogenic that the prognosis for the child is zero unless he is transferred to a healthier environment. This judgment is made with extreme reluctance; placement is usually viewed by the agency as a desperate measure. It seems to follow that placed children will be severely emotionally disturbed, and that there will be a minimum of concern with the psychotherapeutic effectiveness of the foster home, such as led to the project reported by DeFries et al. (1964, 1965).

Fifty-two emotionally disturbed children in foster home placements were evaluated over a three-year period by means of psychiatric interviews. Half of the children had been subjected to concurrent, intensive, weekly psychotherapy. At the end of the treatment phase, 40 percent of the placed children were labeled as improved, 33 percent as worse, and the remainder as unchanged. Outcome was not materially affected by psychotherapy. Evidently, the effectiveness of foster home care in conventional terms is less than that of other forms of treatment. Its average effectiveness is practically nil. DeFries et al. (1965) conclude:

The foster family care concept carries with it the sentimental view that there is the need to simulate family life for the dislocated, neglected, and abused child. This view had been propounded partly in order to counteract the widely proclaimed ill effects of institutionalization on children, often discussed in the psychoanalytic literature. That it is possible to simulate a family for the disturbed foster child is an unrealistic and outdated concept, however, that must be critically examined before further progress can be made.

Foster home care appears most clearly to be a psychotherapeutic failure, on the average. The data also clearly suggest that there are psychotherapeutic foster homes and psychonoxious ones. Some of the potentially relevant "therapist" variables are indicated by DeFries et al. (1965). A majority of their foster parents were middle-aged, below average in intelligence and educational level, from lower income brackets, and had an average of three other children in the home. It would be prudent to investigate the "therapist" factor before concluding finally that foster home care is unrealistic and outdated.

Mother as the Therapist

There are divergent ideas as to how to come to grips with the national shortage of therapists, such as the training of nonprofessional therapists (Rioch et al., 1965; Truax, 1968) and Schofield's (1964) conception of the friend as a therapist. In the child area, recent attention has been paid to the possibility of the mother—a logical candidate—as a therapist. Thinking comes from two disparate sources: the behavior therapists, and the Rogerians, represented by the pioneer work of Guerney (1964).

The theoretical considerations underlying these two approaches appear, at first glance, to be entirely different. Guerney's technique consists primarily of training the mother to develop an empathic relationship with the child. The behavior therapy method places emphasis on determining the factors of parent behavior that maintain deviant child behavior. There is some overlap, however, in that Guerney allows that the behavior to be modified was "*learned* in the presence of, or by the influence of, parental attitude," and can therefore be "more effectively *unlearned*, or *extinguished* [my italics], under similar conditions . . . "(Stover and Guerney, 1967). Perhaps, as Truax (1966) suggested, client-centered therapy and behavior modification do have common elements.

Stover and Guerney (1967) present some evidence that suggests effectiveness of the latter's technique. Among the behavior therapists,

Wahler et al. (1965) were apparently successful in altering deviant behavior in two of three children using the mother as a behavior therapist, and single-case successes are reported by Zeilberger et al. (1968) and Hawkins et al. (1966). (See also Chapter 19.)

There is, perhaps, a question of how training a mother-therapist differs from parent counseling in the conventional child guidance or family service setting. Both share a common basic ingredient: a professional person evaluates the home situation and instructs the mother how to behave toward her child. The professional does not have direct contact with the child. The important difference is a diagnostic rather than a therapeutic one. The mother-therapist trainers observe the home situation *directly* and make an effort to record *systematically* the interaction of child and parent behaviors. The prescriptions that change the mother from erring parent to behavior therapist are thus based on much sounder evidence than is customarily available in the conventional clinic.

Child development theory indicates that the mother-therapist will be maximally effective with the preschool child. The handful of reports cited here suggest that the psychologists involved in training mother-therapists agree.

Presumably, a mother becomes a therapist for her own child only, whether the technique is Rogerian or learning-theory oriented. Unlike other approaches to training nonprofessional therapists, "filial" therapy does not seem to save much time for the professionals involved, and may, in fact, be more time-consuming than traditional techniques. Its practicality in a world of professional scarcity, as well as its efficacy, remain to be demonstrated.

NEWER THERAPEUTIC TECHNIQUES

Outcome studies like those in Table 13.1 have been repeatedly criticized on methodological grounds. Defector or other kinds of untreated control groups are actually individuals undergoing minimal treatment or are otherwise inappropriate; measuring instruments are insufficiently sensitive to detect changes in treated cases; percentage of cases improved is a misleading index because it can conceal more rapid improvement by treated cases; etc. These criticisms, like the concepts of the psychonoxious therapist and the deterioration effect, are essentially alternative hypotheses that seek to explain why the aggregated outcome reports fail to demonstrate that psychotherapy is effective. The primary purpose of process research is to validate these alternative hypotheses by pinning down conclusively the conditions under which psychotherapy is effective. For the moment, there is sufficient equivocality so that the choice of an hypothesis to support remains a matter of personal conviction. As Hersch (1968) points out, there is still no *convincing* proof that psychotherapy is effective, and in the meantime, "what we know with *certainty* about the effects of therapy is not heartwarming to the conscientious practitioner [italics mine]."

Despite the alternative hypotheses, there has been a noticeable dampening of enthusiasm for traditional psychotherapy in recent years. This has been manifested not so much by rejection of established techniques as by a willingness to consider new ones. Several recently developed approaches are currently receiving favorable consideration by the mental health professions. These newer techniques share certain common characteristics. Each places emphasis on current behavior patterns. Anamnestic appraisal is deemphasized. Conceptions like insight and the unconscious are unnecessary. Diagnostic categories are considered to have scant practical significance; little or no time is spent in formulating diagnoses. The significance of learning in the patient's life, rather than motivation, is stressed. It is anticipated that the duration of treatment will be measured in months, or even weeks, rather than years. Finally, there is a tendency toward the use of nonprofessional therapists, individuals other than the psychiatrist, clinical psychologist, and psychiatric social worker.

The emphases in these methods appear to render them most appropriate for the young and, indeed, we find that they have been used primarily with child and adolescent patients. They seem also to be most suited for dealing with behavioral symptoms rather than emotional states and thinking disorders. Again, the available reports suggest that those therapists who are using the techniques would agree.

Behavior Therapy

The technique that most clearly fits the descriptions in the previous paragraphs is called behavior modification or behavior therapy. In essence, it is a translation of learning theory, beginning with the Law of Effect, directly into therapy procedures. The symptom or "critical target behavior" is conceptualized as the consequence of disordered or maladaptive learning. The purpose of the therapy is to extinguish this behavior according to learning principles and, in some instances, to substitute a new, adaptive behavior.

Behavior therapy is actually a series of techniques using either operant or classical conditioning or desensitization, and varying along such dimensions as requisite skill of the therapist, requisite characteristics of the patient, and degree of control over reinforcements by the therapist, as well as the learning model (Kanfer and Phillips, 1966).

Since behavior therapy is extensively treated in other chapters of this volume, it will not be accorded any further consideration here. It is included only because it could not conceivably be omitted from any discussion of the newer approaches to psychological treatment.

Project Re-ED

The rationale and structure of this inpatient agency for children in the elementary school age range are described in two recent publications (Hobbs, 1966; Project Re-ED, 1967). The approach is clearly educative. The institutional setting itself is like a combination school and camp rather than a hospital or other conventional treatment center. The primary "therapist" is the *educateur* or teacher-counselor. As Hobbs (1966) notes, the teacher-counselors are the core of Re-ED, and a great deal of attention is devoted to selecting and training them. The training course requires nine months and covers a wide variety of subjects ranging from specialized teaching methods and use of professional consultants to arts, crafts, and games.

An evaluation of the effects of Re-ED on its first 250 inmates included such variables as social maturity and behavioral-emotional adjustment (Weinstein, in press). Surprisingly, all of the personality and emotional status variables reveal significant differences between pre-

admission and discharge or follow-up ratings, while changes in "academic adequacy" were statistically significant only for one of the two Re-ED schools. Six months after discharge, about 50 percent of all the cases were reported as substantially improved on behavioral-emotional ratings made by the Re-ED staff, using information provided by the child's regular school teacher. Parents and referring agencies were somewhat more impressed. Eighty-two percent of the mothers, 78 percent of the fathers, and 81 percent of the referring agencies viewed the ex-patients as moderately or greatly improved. The correlation between parent ratings was .67. Mothers and fathers are obviously not independent judges, and the coefficient cannot be used as a reliability estimate. Nonetheless, it can at least be stated that the parents are relatively in agreement, a circumstance which would exist if their respective ratings were indeed reliable.

Evidently, Re-ED has had a more pronounced effect on the child's behavior in the home than in the school. Perhaps it should be inferred that the teacher-counselors were more effective as counselors than as teachers, but it is nevertheless probable that they have succeeded in both roles to an unknown extent beyond the traditional residential treatment center. A best guess is that Re-ED's effectiveness is primarily a function of the careful selection and special training of the teacher-counselors, and secondarily of the school-camp, "unhospital" milieu.

Reality Therapy

Reality Therapy (Glasser, 1965) departs from traditional one-to-one and group treatment techniques along two theoretical lines. First, it places an announced premium on conventionally moral and responsible behavior on the part of the patient. The therapist is thus in the definite position of an advocate of social norms and mores, a purveyor of middle-class values. The assumption of this Mowrerian thinking is that the individual is capable of controlling his own behavior, analogous in a fashion to the Re-ED principle that "cognitive control can be taught" (Hobbs, 1966).

Second, the therapist seeks to exercise his influence on behalf of the moral and responsible by stepping out of the traditional, impersonal doctor role and deliberately seeking to involve himself with the patient. One is reminded of humanistic psychotherapy as espoused by Steinzor (1967) and the practical counselor-friend of Massimo and Shore (1967).

These two features of Reality Therapy suggest that it was tailored for use with adolescent delinquents and, in fact, the only published evaluation of its use to date reports on group therapy with institutionalized delinquent girls (Glasser, 1965). The outcome data are sketchy. Only 43 of a total of 370 treated inmates have been returned to the institution. Glasser states that his approach has been successful with 80 percent of the girls, but the basis of this contention is unclear.

SOME DIAGNOSTIC CLASSIFI-CATIONS: JUVENILE DELINQUENCY AND SCHOOL PHOBIA

Juvenile delinquency and school phobia are singled out for special attention in this chapter for several reasons. Both are characterized by clearly identifiable, manifest behavior and are thus diagnosed with relative facility. Both are viewed as a social problem by the community at large, and each has legal ramifications.

The differences between them are also striking. Delinquency has a comparatively high incidence, and a relatively low remission rate with treatment. School phobia has a low incidence and a high treatment remission rate. Perhaps the difference in remission rates accounts for the fact that there have been relatively few published, objective reports of evaluation of treatment of delinquency—especially considering the abundance of treatment programs—while evaluations of outcome with school phobia are relatively common, especially in light of the low incidence.

Delinquency

The diagnostic label "juvenile delinquent" is traditionally pinned to the nonadult whose primary symptoms include aggressive, hostile, destructive, or antisocial acting-out behaviors. The prevalence of delinquency is at an all-time high; nearly 700,000 cases were processed

through the country's juvenile courts in 1965 (Task Force Report, 1967).

Delinquency is a special challenge for child guidance, not only because of its growing prevalence, but also because it carries over into adult life with a much greater frequency than other emotional disorders of childhood. Robins (1966), summarizing the findings of a 30-year follow-up of child guidance clinic patients, remarks:

The neurotic children as adults resembled the control subjects. But the antisocial children produced a high proportion with arrests, alcoholism, divorce, poor job histories, child neglect, dependency on social agencies, and psychiatric hospitalization (p. v).

The report of the Task Force on Juvenile Delinquency and Crime of the President's Commission on Law Enforcement and Administration of Justice (1967) literally constitutes a volume in which sociological knowledge in these areas is summarized and synthesized.[6] Among more than 400 pages of text, only a single page is devoted to treatment. The authors of the relevant chapter (Rodman and Grams, 1967) explain as follows:

A tremendous amount of effort and expenditure is going into a variety of delinquency prevention and rehabilitation programs involving psychotherapy and environmental therapy. As yet there is but a molehill of evaluation to confront the mountain of services that has developed ... moreover, the few careful evaluative studies carried out have shown treatment efforts to be largely unsuccessful. The only projects that seem able to report success are those that have not been independently evaluated (p. 212).

Conventional psychotherapy methods appear to be least effective with delinquents. The reported improvement rate is more than a standard deviation below the mean for all treated cases (Table 13.1). Hersh (1968) suggests that failure to respond to conventional psychotherapy is characteristic of patients from lower socio-economic class milieus, which includes the bulk of delinquents. This may be the result of greater conflict between professional practice and expectations of the nature and structure of the therapy situation by lower-class patients. It has been

---

[6] For some unknown reason, the research staff and professional consultants of the Task Force seem to have been unaware of the recent work on treat-ment of delinquents which has appeared in the psychological literature.

hypothesized that such disharmony leads to poor therapy outcome (Levitt, 1966).

Gottesfeld's (1965) questionnaire survey of therapy concepts of professional workers and of male delinquents furnishes an objective account of the conflict. The traditional talking-listening-reflecting-nonjudgmental-impersonal role of the clinician is rejected by the delinquents in favor of an active, father-educator-counselor figure with heavy emphasis on the pragmatics of living. These discrepancies, Gottesfeld contends, suggest a need for new therapeutic strategies.

An innovative approach along the lines suggested by the Gottesfeld survey was carried out by Massimo and Shore with lower-class delinquent, adolescent boys. The therapist served as vocational counselor, remedial educator, and consultant on personal affairs, as well as psychotherapist in the usual sense (Massimo and Shore, 1967). Emphasis was placed on learning practical skills and dealing with various ordinary situations. The therapist went on shopping trips with his patient, helped him to get a driver's license, accompanied him when he went for an initial job interview, and so on. Place and time of session were informal.

The program ran for ten months and was effective in bringing about significant changes in a group of ten patients (Massimo and Shore, 1963). A two- to three-year follow-up (Shore and Massimo, 1966) indicated that the gains in therapy had been translated into successful community adjustment. Nine of the ten treated boys were employed, five had had additional education, five were married, and no one in the group had been arrested for a felony. In contrast, only six of the control patients were employed at the time of follow-up, and six had been convicted of felonies. These concrete, highly meaningful outcome measures make the Massimo–Shore study impressive even though the sample is small.

A report by Levinson and Kitchener (1966) from the National Training School for Boys suggests an analog in the treatment of delinquents with the Johns Hopkins findings concerning the relationship between personalities of patient and therapist (Whitehorn and Betz, 1954, 1960). Inmates at NTS live in cottages each having three counselors. The report concerns the method of assigning inmates to counselors within each cottage. In one cottage, the assignment was random. In another, the counselors selected the inmates whom they wanted, and in the third, selection was indirectly controlled by inmates themselves. The fourth type was a matching of counselor and inmate based on a Q sort of statements from the Edwards Personal Preference Schedule. The best-adjusted inmates in this cottage were assigned to a counselor to whom they were most similar in personality, while the poorly adjusted boys in this cottage were assigned to counselors who were dissimilar in personality. Over a period of five months, the matched counselor-inmate cottage ranked highest on six of eight objective indices of desirable behavior, and had a mean rank of 1.5 on all eight indices.

The conventional approach to therapy is represented by the studies of Persons (1966, 1967) and Truax et al. (1966). The former is a straightforward outcome evaluation of the effects of 80 hours of individual and group therapy on a group of institutionalized delinquent boys over a 20-week period. A one-year follow-up after discharge (Persons, 1967) disclosed that more of the treated boys, compared to a control group, were successfully employed, and fewer of them had committed parole violations or had had to be recommitted. Evidently, traditional methods can be effective, perhaps as a function of differences among therapists.

The concept of the "good therapist" personality (Truax and Carkhuff, 1967) led to a study of the effect of group therapy on institutionalized female delinquents (Truax et al., 1966). Moderately positive findings in favor of the treated group as compared to an untreated control were obtained on the Conformity Scale of the Minnesota Counseling Inventory and on a (more significant) objective index, the amount of time spent out of the institution during a one year follow-up period. However, since appropriate controls were not used, it cannot be inferred that these effects were due to the high levels of "accurate empathic understanding" and "nonpossessive warmth" of the two therapists rather than to group therapy itself.

School Phobia

The child who refuses to attend school is analogous to an adult who prefers not to be gainfully employed, and to whom the community applies terms of opprobrium like vagrant, tramp, bum, and idler. Each declines to carry out the primary function assigned to him by society and is therefore viewed with alarm by those forces responsible for maintaining social order.

Parents rarely fail to perceive school refusal as a problem that must be dealt with immediately by an agency outside the home. The decision to select a treatment or a correctional agency appears to depend upon whether anxiety is involved as a motivation for the child's behavior. When anxiety is not involved in school refusal, we ordinarily speak of *truancy*. When anxiety is a motivation, we refer to *school phobia*.[7]

Most comparisons of truants and school phobics (such as Leventhal and Sills, 1964; Hersov, 1960b) show clearly that unlike truants,

the school phobic is of above average intelligence, doing at least fairly well in school, comes from an intact home, and manifests psychosomatic but not sociopathic symptoms. School phobia may appear at any age during the school years, but is most common in the 9- to 12-year-old group. Most studies report no sex difference in incidence.

Truants are seldom referred for psychotherapy, but referral for school phobia is not rare. School phobics constitute between one and two percent of child guidance clinic cases (Eisenberg, 1958), and as much as 14 percent of cases viewed as psychiatric emergencies (Morrison and Smith, 1967). Only suicide attempts or threats have a greater incidence among the emergency cases seen in clinics.

Table 13.3 summarizes findings of eight recent reports of the treatment of school phobia. The standard of success is invariably a complete

TABLE 13.3   Treatment of School Phobia

Report	N	x̄ Age	x̄ IQ	Percentage Remission at	
				Close	Follow-up
Weiss and Burke (1967)	14	13	—	—	79
Adams (1966)	21	10.2	above average	90	—
Kennedy (1965)	50	9.5	—	100	100
Coolidge et al. (1964)	49	7	113	—	96
Chazan (1962)	33	10.5	106	88	88
Davidson (1961)	27	11	hi average	93	—
Hersov (1960[a])	50	11.8	106	68	100
Eisenberg (1959)	67	9.4[a]	110[a]	72	71[a]
Composite	311	9.9	108.9[b]	82.7	88.8

[a] Data from Rodriguez et al. (1959). The age and IQ data describe the 41 cases located on follow-up.
[b] Mean IQ is based on 173 cases for whom a numerical estimate was available.

remission of the symptom, that is, return to school. The outcome data in Table 13.3 indicate that school phobia is more amenable to therapy than the general run of emotional illnesses. Almost 83 percent of the cases were successfully treated. If the reports that include hospitalized cases (Weis, 1967; Hersov, 1960a) are removed,

the rate of cure is more than 86 percent. Follow-ups indicate that almost 89 percent of those cases that could be located showed no recurrence of symptoms.

A variety of different treatment approaches has been reported. Multidisciplinary, many-faceted approaches are not uncommon (Kahn

[7] Adelaide Johnson is usually regarded as the originator of the term "school phobia" (Johnson, et al., 1941). It has been used consistently ever since, at least in this country, though it has become plain

that in a number of instances, school phobia may not be a fear of school at all. The British seem to prefer the more behavioral, less dynamic expression, "school refusal."

and Nursten, 1964; Davidson, 1961), but intensity and scope of treatment does not seem to be related to outcome. One of the most successful reports (Kennedy, 1965) had a maximum treatment course of only three days.

A factor that appears to be related to outcome is type of school phobia, a distinction first suggested by Coolidge et al. (1957) and exploited most clearly by Kennedy (1965). According to Coolidge, there are two primary types of school phobic. The "neurotic-crisis" phobic, called Type 1 by Kennedy, is essentially an overprotected, anxiety-prone child. The "way-of-life," or Type 2, phobic is a severely disturbed, possibly psychotic or incipiently psychotic child whose school refusal is only one facet of a deeply-seated disorder.

Using return to school as the sole criterion of outcome—the usual procedure—the prognosis for the "neurotic," Type 1 child is excellent with any form of therapy, but is poor for the more disturbed, Type 2 child. Some of the outcome reports in Table 13.3 note that a proportion of the sample was discarded because the cases were not true school phobics, that is, showed evidence of more extensive disorder (for example, Coolidge et al., 1964; Weiss and Burke, 1967). The discards were very probably Type 2 cases. Kennedy (1965) deliberately discarded six cases diagnosed as Type 2 so that he could report on a homogeneous sample. Hersov's (1960a) outcome report is the poorest listed in Table 13.3. Notably, his sample included 29 inpatients, many of whom were probably Type 2 phobics.

It is possible that Type 2 cases are customarily discarded, or perhaps not diagnosed as school phobias even though school refusal is the paramount, manifest symptom. This would be one factor accounting for the high success rate in the treatment of school phobia.

One might argue that school refusal in the Type 2 case is only one symptom—perhaps even a minor one—among many, that it is incidental to more serious problems, and that, thus, the Type 2 case is rightfully excluded from the category of school phobia. The cogency of the contention is questionable. School phobia is, in *every* instance, a symptom rather than a diagnosis in the usual sense. Most school phobics,

regardless of type, have other psychological symptoms.

Another factor that seems to be related to treatment success is age. Most clinicians believe that therapy is more successful with younger school phobics. Eisenberg (1959) reports a 90 percent remission rate with children under 11 years old, compared to only 45 percent success with children older than 11 years.

A relationship between age and outcome can be crudely estimated from the reports in Table 13.3. The rank-order correlation between mean age of the sample and percentage of remitted cases at close (or follow-up if data at close are not given) is − .48. This coefficient falls short of conventional statistical significance, but is at least suggestive.

Age and type of phobia may be correlated, thus confounding the relationship between age and outcome. It is generally believed by clinicians that Type 2 cases tend to be older. It is notable that among the reports in Table 13.3, those that include inpatients have the highest mean ages (Hersov, 1960a; Weiss and Burke, 1967). A cautious, tentative inference would be that phobia type, rather than age per se, is the correlative factor.

School phobia as a symptom responds more frequently to therapy than other forms of maladjustment in children, often quickly and easily. Symptomatic treatment, though its usefulness is acknowledged, may very well leave an etiological core untouched. Some of the follow-ups of treated cases show little or no recurrence of the phobia among treated cases over periods of time ranging up to ten years (Chazan, 1962; Coolidge et al., 1964). Others report less favorable findings. The recurrence rate in the follow-up by Rodriguez et al. (1959) could be as high as 25 percent (the method of presentation of results does not permit a definite statement). Levenson (1961) reports on his treatment of ten school phobics in the 16- to 20-year-old range, all of whom had a history of the symptom in early childhood. Later behavior may suggest a continuing, underlying, causal factor, even though actual school refusal is not manifested. Coolidge et al. (1964) conducted one of the more careful, painstaking follow-up studies with a mean interval of nine years after close.

In our study, 47 of the 49 subjects have returned to school and have either graduated or are still attending high school. . . . Fifty per cent of our subjects are, however, manifesting symptoms which, on investigation, can be traced back to the original phobia. This may be a continued chronic apprehension in relation to attending school, or an exaggerated and unwarranted concern regarding studies and exams. It may be expressed as Monday morning anergia, vague aches or pains or absences due to feigned illnesses. . . . Even the children who appear to be doing quite well and would be considered "normal adolescents" express more than the ordinary concerns about leaving home and in general show a cautious approach to new situations (Coolidge et al., 1964, pp. 676–677).

Do the encouraging reports of the treatment of school phobia reflect simply symptomatic improvement in many cases, without a true curative action? Are we being deceived by developmental symptom substitution? Is school phobia easily driven underground only to emerge later as test anxiety? As usual, there is a healthy suspicion, but no conclusive answer.

SOME MISCELLANEOUS PROCESS REPORTS

Focus of Treatment

As previously noted, a unique aspect of child psychotherapy is that it is common for persons other than the child patient himself to enter into treatment. The argument holds that the therapist's influence on the child will be vitiated or negated unless therapeutic influence is exerted on the influential adults whose impacts have brought about psychopathology in the child. The mother, presumably the primary influence on the child, has always been a treatment focus. Some child guidance clinics insist on seeing every mother of every child in therapy. When the child is very young, sometimes only the mother will be treated. The father, as his influence is gradually being recognized, is also becoming a focus. In some cases, the entire family constellation will be involved in treatment.

The argument has rarely been subjected to objective examination, possibly because its logic appears to be overwhelming. Matarazzo's review (1965) of familial therapy does not include a single study directly relevant to assessment of effectiveness of treatment as a function of focus.

Several recent outpatient studies shed some provocative, though hardly definitive, light on the question. The patients came from a clinic in suburban Pittsburgh (Gluck et al., 1964), a large clinic in metropolitan Chicago (Lessing and Schilling, 1966), and from the Negro poverty community in New York City (D'Angelo and Walsh, 1967). The latter reports data in terms of mean change scores rather than percent of improvement as in the other two studies.

The pertinent data are summarized in Table 13.4. With a single exception, the three studies are in agreement that the order of effectiveness of treatment in terms of focus, from least to most, is (1) child alone, (2) mother alone, (3) mother and child, and (4) mother and father, or mother, father, and child.

TABLE 13.4   Outcome as a Function of Treatment Focus

	Study		
	Gluck et al. (1964)[a]	Lessing and Schilling (1966)[a]	D'Angelo and Walsh (1967)
Focus			
Child only	—	—	Worse
Mother only	55	62	—
Mother and child	67	71	No change
Mother and father	85	—	Improvement
Mother, father, and child	85	—	No change

[a] Data in percentage of improved cases.

The algebra of the Gluck study is clear; the critical factor in treatment success is a participating father. The D'Angelo and Walsh data suggest that there are two critical factors: a participating father and a nonparticipating child.

The hypothesis that treating parents has greater impact on the child than treating the child himself is regarded favorably by the child guidance movement. Acceptance by the mother of her responsibility for the child's symptoms is usually regarded as a positive prognostic sign. Frequently, treatment is not offered to children whose mothers do not verbalize such acceptance. It is tempting to conclude that the data in Table 13.4 support this position. There are several reasons why this conclusion would be premature.

First, there are alternative explanations for the data. It is conceivable that the improved prognosis when the father participates is due to the presence of a father interested and concerned enough to involve himself in the therapy process, not to the impact of the father's therapist.

Second, results from agencies other than conventional outpatient clinics are not necessarily in accord. For example, Hartmann et al. (1968) found that conjunctive parental treatment, either by a social worker or in group therapy, was unrelated to outcome with hospitalized adolescents. Seeman et al. (1964) report on a successful play therapy program with a group of second and third graders. Only the children were treated. Contact with the parents was deliberately kept to a bare minimum. Patients and controls were selected as the most poorly adjusted children after a screening of all second and third grades using peer and teacher ratings. This atypical procedure—actually an exercise in prevention—did not *require* participation of the parent. It would be impossible in the conventional outpatient setting, in which it is necessary for a parent to bring the child and usually to be involved in the diagnostic process.

It is conceivable that in some way, the importance of therapy for parents is a consequence of the child's awareness of parental responsibility for initiating the therapeutic contact. When the child does not perceive this responsibility, for whatever reason, the significance of parental involvement in therapy is diminished.

A study of remainers and terminators in child treatment by Cole and Magnussen (1967) suggests that terminating cases were more often ones in which only the mother participated, while the remainers more often included both mother and father. The authors infer support for the position that it is important to involve both parents in treatment. However, the data also suggest that whether the father becomes actively involved may depend partly upon the severity of the child's symptoms rather than on paternal motivation. Unfortunately, the data are not reported in sufficient detail to make a definitive inference concerning remaining in treatment and father participation.

The IJR Study

An attempt to relate treatment outcome to a number of patient, therapist, and process variables was carried out on cases treated at the Institute of Juvenile Research in Chicago during the period 1951–1960 (Lessing and Schilling, 1966). In 505 cases, only the child had been treated; in 332 other cases, both mother and child had been seen. Outcome was rated by therapists at close on a scale essentially corresponding to Improved, Partly Improved, and Unimproved or Worse.

Relationships with 29 variables were computed. Among those that were *not* related to outcome in either group were frequency and number of treatment interviews and total time in treatment; profession and experience of therapist; and similarity of sex, race, and religion of therapist to that of the patient. These findings are parallel to those of Hartmann et al. (1968) in that five measures of treatment, including number of hours, length of sessions, and therapy for parents, were unrelated to outcome in institutionalized adolescents. Similar findings of a lack of correlation between outcome and number of treatment hours have been reported by Phillips (1960) and Shepherd et al., (1966), and are reflected in the reports of treatment of school phobia in Table 13.3. Parallel results have been found by investigators of psychotherapy with adults.

If psychotherapy were a generally effective treatment method, some positive correlation between outcome and number of treatment interviews would be expected. The absence of a relationship supports the conclusions derived from Table 13.1, and underscores the need for fresh conceptualizations of the psychotherapy process.

Six variables in the IJR study were found to differentiate the outcome groups for cases in which the mother alone had been treated. Three of the relationships are clear. Improvement is more likely to occur if the patient's siblings are of the same sex, and if the mother accepts her involvement in the patient's problems and does not unconsciously encourage the child's pathology. Relationships for the remaining three variables are not linear, and thus not subject to a clear interpretation. (The percentage of cases in the Unimproved category falls between those of the two categories of improvement.)

Only three variables differentiated the outcome groups for cases in which mother and child were treated. Improvement tended to be inversely related to degree of disturbance, which was more often rated as moderate in the Improved categories and less often as severe. Relationships for the other two variables—presence of a learning problem or of a somatic problem—were not linear.

The IJR study attempts to utilize routinely gathered clinical data in psychotherapy research. The effort is praiseworthy, but like all "fishing expeditions," runs afoul of an unfortunate mathematical contingency. Whenever a large number of nonindependent statistical analyses are computed in a single study, there is no known method of estimating the number of analyses that are statistically significant by chance alone. An appeal to the binomial theorem is futile; it applies only to independent events. The best solution lies in the use of a model or closed theoretical structure that predicts expected correlations. Unfortunately, such systems are not yet available.

Another problem with the fishing expedition approach is that the predictor variables are not always independent of the criterion variables. Some of the predictor variables will be employed, wittingly or unwittingly, in assessing severity of illness, outcome, or prognosis. In the Hartmann et al. (1968) study, a predictor variable like "discharged to hospital or home" is likely to be related to status at close. The presence of regression as a primary defense suggests a more serious illness, while "normal" handling of aggression indicates a milder one. It is not surprising to find that these two factors were related to outcome in the Hartmann study.

When a predictor and a criterion variable are nonindependent, a statistically significant correlation is an unavoidable artifact. It merely testifies to the successful employment of a predictor variable in measuring the criterion. No further inference is warranted.

Race

College and urban crises in recent years have, for the first time, brought some attention to the question of race as a factor in psychotherapy with children. There has as yet been no quantitative investigation of this variable, and empirical data are not available. Two impressive clinical papers are noteworthy. Chethik et al., (1967) report on the first two Negro adolescents to be admitted to an inpatient treatment center that happens to have a high proportion of Negro workers. Lawrence (1968) forthrightly discusses his personal experiences as a Negro therapist working primarily with white children.

SOME INDICATIONS FOR THE PRACTICING CHILD PSYCHOTHERAPIST

Child guidance has its full share of standard rules of procedure, few of which have ever rested on a firm empirical basis. Many are now being directly challenged by recent research. These include such well-worn inheritances from psychoanalysis as:

1. The mother must invariably be a treatment focus if a school-aged child is to be treated successfully.

2. Involvement of the father is less significant in treating the child than is involvement of the mother.

3. Treatment outcome is positively related to intensity of treatment.

4. Permissiveness and encouragement to express negative feelings invariably constitute a desirable treatment procedure; punishment of undesirable behavior is never a desirable procedure.

5. Any home or family existence is likely to be more therapeutic than institutionalization.

6. Successful therapists are drawn exclusively from the ranks of psychiatry, clinical psychology, and psychiatric social work.

About a third of the children referred to child guidance clinics receive any kind of formal treatment.[8] There is an enormous investment of clinic time in the process—sometimes very elaborate—of identifying the fortunate third. Favorable prognosis is usually the paramount, determining factor. In turn, it is based on such variables as motivation of the mother for treatment, willingness of the parents to accept their responsibility for the child's symptoms, ego strength of the child, and the like. The outcome data suggest that we may have been treating the wrong children, that the establishment of a favorable prognosis means that the child will improve *with or without* formal intervention. It may be time for child guidance to give serious consideration to the possibility of revising prognostic criteria. For example, a high anxiety level in the mother may be an indication that developmental remission of symptoms is likely to occur and that formal treatment of the child is unnecessary.

Few conditions have been definitely established as requisite or even advisable for the treatment of the child patient. Innovation in therapy is the order of the day; rigid orthodoxies find scant empirical support. Finally, there seems to be no substitute for the *long-range*, follow-up study as the procedure for investigating either therapy outcome or therapy process when the patients are children.

[8] Twenty-eight percent of the cases seen at the St. Louis Municipal Psychiatric Clinic between 1922 and 1944, and 21 percent of admissions to Maryland child clinics in 1958–59, were offered treatment (Robins, 1966). Nationally, the treatment rate was 34·9 percent for cases closed during 1966 (OPC Report, 1966).

REFERENCES

Adams, P. L., McDonald, N. F., and Huey, W. P. School phobia and bisexual conflict: A report of 21 cases. *Amer. J. Psychiat.*, 1966, **123**, 541–547.

Beckett, P. G. S., Lennox, K., and Grisell, J. L. Responsibility and reward in treatment. *J. Nerv. & Ment. Dis.*, 1968, **146**, 257–263.

Bergin, A. E. Some implications of psychotherapy research for therapeutic practice. *Inter. J. Psychiat.*, 1967, **3**, 136–153.

Beskind, H. Psychiatric inpatient treatment of adolescents: A review of the clinical experience. *Comprehen. Psychiat.*, 1962, **3**, 354–369.

Betz, B. J., and Whitehorn, J. C. Relationship of the therapist to the outcome of therapy in schizophrenia. *Psychiatric Research Reports*, 1956, **5**, 89–140.

Chazan, M. School phobia. *Brit. J. Educ. Psychol.*, 1962, **32**, 209–217.

Chethik, M., Fleming, E., and Mayer, M. F. A quest for identity: Treatment of disturbed Negro children in a predominantly white treatment center. *Amer. J. Orthopsychiat.*, 1967, **37**, 71–77.

Cole, J. K., and Magnussen, M. G. Family situation factors related to remainers and terminators of treatment. *Psychother.*, 1967, **4**, 107–109.

Coolidge, J. C., Brodie, R. D., and Feeney, B. A ten-year follow-up study of sixty-six school-phobic children. *Amer. J. Orthopsychiat.*, 1964, **34**, 675–684.

Coolidge, J. C., Hahn, P. B., and Peck, A. L. School phobia: Neurotic crisis or way of life. *Amer. J. Orthopsychiat.*, 1957, **27**, 296–306.

D'Angelo, R., and Walsh, J. F. An evaluation of various therapy approaches with lower socio-economic group children. *J. Psychol.*, 1967, **67**, 59–64.

Davidson, S. School phobia as a manifestation of family disturbance: Its structure and treatment. *J. Ch. Psychol. & Psychiat.*, 1961, **1**, 270–287.

DeFries, Z., Jenkins, S., and Williams, E. C. Foster family care—a non-sentimental view. *Child Welfare*, 1965, **44**, 73–84.

DeFries, Z., Jenkins, S., and Williams, E. C. Treatment of disturbed children in foster care. *Amer. J. Orthopsychiat.*, 1964, **34**, 615–624.

Eisenberg, L. The pediatric management of school phobia. *J. Pediat.*, 1959, **55**, 758–766.

Eisenberg, L. School phobia: A study in the communication of anxiety. *Amer. J. Psychiat.*, 1958, **114**, 712–718.

Eisenberg, L. The sins of the fathers: Urban decay and social pathology. *Amer. J. Orthopsychiat.*, 1962, **32**, 5–17.

Eisenberg, L., and Gruenberg, E. M. The current status of secondary prevention in child psychiatry. *Amer. J. Orthopsychiat.*, 1961, **31**, 355–367.

Eisenberg, L., Marlowe, B., and Hastings, M. Diagnostic services for maladjusted foster children: An orientation toward an acute need. *Amer. J. Orthopsychiat.*, 1958, **28**, 750–763.

Gardner, G. G. The relationship between childhood neurotic symptomatology and later schizophrenia in males and females. *J. Nerv. & Ment. Dis.*, 1967, **144**, 97–100.

Ginott, H. G., and Lebo, D. Most and least used play therapy limits. *J. Genet. Psychol.*, 1963, **103**, 153–159.

Ginott, H. G., and Lebo, D. Play therapy limits and theoretical orientation. *J. Consult. Psychol.*, 1961, **26**, 337–340.

Glasser, W. *Reality Therapy: A new approach to psychiatry.* New York: Harper & Row, 1965.

Gluck, M. R., Tanner, M. M., Sullivan, D. F., and Erickson, P. A. Follow-up evaluation of 55 child guidance cases. *Behav. Res. & Ther.*, 1964, **2**, 131–134.

Gottesfeld, H. Professionals and delinquents evaluate professional methods with delinquents. *Soc. Probs.*, 1965, **13**, 45–59.

Guerney, B. J., Jr. Filial therapy: Description and rationale. *J. Consult. Psychol.*, 1964, **28**, 304–310.

Haring, N. G., and Phillips, E. L. *Educating emotionally disturbed children.* New York: McGraw-Hill, 1962.

Hartmann, E., Glasser, B. A., Greenblatt, M., Solomon, M. H., and Levinson, D. J. *Adolescents in a mental hospital.* New York: Grune & Stratton, 1968.

Hawkins, R. P., Peterson, R. F., Schweid, E., and Bijou, S. W. Behavior therapy in the home: Amelioration of problem parent–child relations with the parent in a therapeutic role. *J. Exp. Ch. Psychol.*, 1966, **4**, 99–107.

Healy, W., and Bronner, A. F. The child guidance clinic: Birth and growth of an idea. In Lowrey, L. G., and Sloane, V. (Eds.), *Orthopsychiatry, 1923–1948: Retrospect and prospect.* American Orthopsychiatric Assoc., 1948.

Heinicke, C. M., and Goldman, A. Research on psychotherapy with children: A review and suggestions for further study. *Amer. J. Orthopsychiat.*, 1960, **30**, 483–493.

Hersch, C. The discontent explosion in mental health. *Amer. Psychol.*, 1968, **23**, 497–506.

Hersov, L. A. Refusal to go to school. *J. Ch. Psychol. & Psychiat.*, 1960, **1**, 137–145. (a)

Hersov, L. A. Persistent non-attendance at school. *J. Ch. Psychol. & Psychiat.*, 1960, **1**, 130–136. (b)

Hobbs, N. Helping disturbed children: Psychological and ecological strategies. *Amer. Psychol.*, 1966, **21**, 1105–1115.

Hood-williams, J. The results of psychotherapy with children: A revaluation. *J. Consult. Psychol.*, 1960, **24**, 84–88.

Hunt, R. C. Ingredients of a rehabilitation program. *Proc. Ann. Conf. Milbank Memorial Fund, 1957.* 1958.

Johnson, A. M., Falstein, E. I., Szurek, S. A., and Svendsen, M. School phobia. *Amer. J. Orthopsychiat.*, 1941, **11**, 702–711.

Kahn, J. H., and Nursten, J. P. *Unwillingly to school.* New York: Macmillan, 1964.

Kanfer, F. H., and Phillips, J. S. Behavior therapy: A panacea for all ills or a passing fancy? *Arch. Gen. Psychiat.*, 1966, **15**, 114–128.

Kanner, L. History of child psychiatry. In Freedman, A. M., and Kaplan, H. I. (Eds.), *Comprehensive textbook of psychiatry.* Baltimore: Williams & Wilkins, 1967.

Kennedy, W. A. School phobia: Rapid treatment of fifty cases. *J. Abnorm. Psychol.*, 1965, **70**, 285–289.

Lapouse, R., and Monk, M. A. Fears and worries in a representative sample of children. *Amer. J. Orthopsychiat.*, 1959, **29**, 803–818.

La Vietes, R., Cohen, R., Reens, R., and Ronall, R. Day treatment center and school: Seven years experience. *Amer. J. Orthopsychiat.*, 1965, **35**, 160–169.

La Vietes, R., Hulse, W. C., and Blau, A. A psychiatric day treatment center and school for young children and their parents. *Amer. J. Orthopsychiat.*, 1960, **30**, 468–482.

Lawrence, L. E. The necessity for early confrontation concerning obvious racial characteristics. Paper read at the annual meeting of the American Association of Psychiatric Clinics for Children, 1968.

Lessing, E. E., and Schilling, F. H. Relationship between treatment selection variables and treatment outcome in a child guidance clinic: An application of data-processing methods. *J. Amer. Acad. Child Psychiat.*, 1966, **5**, 313–348.

Levenson, E. A. The treatment of school phobias in the young adult. *Amer. J. Psychother.*, 1961, **15**, 539–552.

Leventhal, T., and Sills, M. Self-image in school phobia. *Amer. J. Orthopsychiat.*, 1964, **34**, 685–695.

Levinson, R. B., and Kitchener, H. L. Treatment of delinquents: Comparison of four methods for assigning inmates to counselors. *J. Consult. Psychol.*, 1966, **30**, 364.

Levitt, E. E. The results of psychotherapy with children: An evaluation. *J. Consult. Psychol.*, 1957, **21**, 189–196. (a)

Levitt, E. E. A follow-up study of cases treated at the Illinois Institute for Juvenile Research: An evaluation of psychotherapy with children. Report of Mental Health Project No. 5503, Dept. of Public Welfare, State of Illinois, 1957. (b)

Levitt, E. E. A comparison of "remainers" and "defectors" among child clinic patients. *J. Consult. Psychol.*, 1957, **21**, 316. (c)

Levitt, E. E. A comparative judgmental study of "defection" from treatment at a child guidance clinic. *J. Clin. Psychol.*, 1958, **14**, 429–432.

Levitt, E. E. Psychotherapy with children: A further evaluation. *Behav. Res. & Ther.*, 1963, **60**, 326–329.

Levitt, E. E. Psychotherapy research and the expectation-reality discrepancy. *Psychother.*, 1966, **3**, 163–166.

Levitt, E. E., Beiser, H. R., and Robertson, R. E. A follow-up evaluation of cases treated at a community child guidance clinic. *Amer. J. Orthopsychiat.*, 1959, **29**, 337–347.

Lewis, W. W. Continuity and intervention in emotional disturbance: A review. *Exceptional Children*, 1965, **31**, 465–475.

Maas, H. S., and Engler, R. E. *Children in need of parents.* New York: Columbia Univ. Press, 1959.

Macfarlane, J. W., Allen, L., and Honzik, M. *A developmental study of the behavior problems of normal children between 21 months and 14 years.* Berkeley, Calif.: Univ. of California Press, 1954.

Massimo, J. L., and Shore, M. F. Comprehensive vocationally oriented psychotherapy: A new treatment technique for lower class adolescent delinquent boys. *Psychiat.*, 1967, **30**, 229–236.

Massimo, J. L., and Shore, M. F. The effectiveness of a comprehensive vocationally oriented psychotherapeutic program for adolescent delinquent boys. *Amer. J. Orthopsychiat.*, 1963, **33**, 634–642.

Matarazzo, J. D. Psychotherapeutic processes. In *Ann. Rev. Psychol.* Palo Alto, Calif.: Annual Reviews, Inc. 1965.

Morrison, G. C., and Smith, W. R. Emergencies in child psychiatry: A definition and comparison of two groups. Paper read at American Orthopsychiatric Assoc. meeting, 1967.

Persons, R. W. Psychological and behavioral change in delinquents following psychotherapy. *J. Clin. Psychol.*, 1966, **22**, 337–340.

Persons, R. W. Relationship between psychotherapy with institutionalized delinquent boys and subsequent community adjustment. *J. Consult. Psychol.*, 1967, **31**, 137–141.

Phillips, E. L. Parent-child psychotherapy: A follow-up study comparing two techniques. *J. Psychol.*, 1960, **49**, 195–202.

Reens, R. Intelligence quotients of children before and after intensive psychotherapeutic intervention. Unpublished paper, 1965.

Rioch, M. J., Elkes, C., Flint, A. A., et al. Pilot project in training mental health counselors. *U.S.P.H.S. Publ. No. 1254*, 1965.

Robins, L. N. *Deviant children grown up.* Baltimore: Williams & Wilkins, 1966.

Rodman, H., and Grams, P. Juvenile delinquency and the family: A review and discussion. In *Report of the Task Force on Juvenile Delinquency and Youth Crime of the President's Commission on Law Enforcement and Administration of Justice.* Washington, D.C.: U.S. Government Printing Office, 1967. Pp. 188–221.

Rodriguez, A., Rodriguez, M., and Eisenberg, L. The outcome of school phobia: A follow-up study based on 41 cases. *Amer. J. Psychiat.*, 1959, **116**, 540–544.

Schofield, W. *Psychotherapy: The purchase of friendship.* Englewood Cliffs, N.J.: Prentice-Hall, 1964.

Seeman, J., Barry, E., and Ellinwood, C. Interpersonal assessment of play therapy outcome. *Psychother.*, 1964, **1**, 64–66.

Shepherd, M., Oppenheim, A. N., and Mitchell, S. Childhood behavior disorders and the child guidance clinic: An epidemiological study. *J. Ch. Psychol. & Psychiat.*, 1966, **7**, 39–52.

Shore, M. F., Massimo, J. L., Kisielewski, B. A., and Moran, J. K. Object relations changes resulting from successful psychotherapy with adolescent delinquents and their relationship to academic performance. *J. Amer. Acad. Child Psychiat.*, 1966, **5**, 93–104.

Simmons, J. E. Are child guidance clinics becoming outmoded? Paper read at the Mideastern Regional meeting of the American Association of Psychiatric Clinics for Children, 1963.

Sonis, M. Implications for the child guidance clinic of current trends in mental health planning. *Amer. J. Orthopsychiat.*, 1968, **38**, 515–526.

Steinzor, B. *The healing partnership.* New York: Harper & Row, 1967.

Stover, L., and Guerney, B. G., Jr. The efficacy of training procedures for mothers in filial therapy. *Psychother.*, 1967, **4**, 110–115.

Strupp, H. H., and Bergin, A. E. Some empirical and conceptual bases for coordinated research in psychotherapy: A critical review of issues, trends, and evidence. *Inter. J. Psychiat.*, 1969, **5**, No. 2.

Truax, C. B. Effective ingredients in psychotherapy: An approach to unraveling the patient-therapist interaction. *J. Counsel. Psychol.*, 1963, **10**, 256–263.

Truax, C. B. Reinforcement and non-reinforcement in Rogerian psychotherapy. *J. Abnorm. Soc. Psychol.*, 1966, **71**, 1–9.

Truax, C. B. The use of trained practical counselors or therapists and the evolving understanding of counseling and psychotherapy. *Discussion Papers, Ark. Rehab. Res. & Trng. Ctr.*, 1968, **1**, No. 12.

Truax, C. B., and Carkhuff, R. R. *Toward effective counseling and psychotherapy: Training and practice.* Chicago: Aldine, 1967.

Truax, C. B., Wargo, D. G., and Silber, L. D. Effects of group psychotherapy with high accurate empathy and nonpossessive warmth upon female institutionalized delinquents. *J. Abnorm. Psychol.*, 1966, **71**, 267–274.

Wahler, R. G., Winkel, G. H., Peterson, R. F., and Morrison, D. C. Mothers as behavior therapists for their own children. *Behav. Res. & Ther.*, 1965, **3**, 113–124.

Warren, W. A study of adolescent psychiatric in-patients and the outcome six or more years later. I. Clinical histories and hospital findings. *J. Child Psychol. Psychiat.*, 1965, **6**, 1–17. (a)

Warren, W. A study of adolescent psychiatric in-patients and the outcome six or more years later. II. The follow-up study. *J. Child Psychol. Psychiat.*, 1965, **6**, 141–160. (b)

Weinstein, L. The Project Re-ED Schools for emotionally disturbed children: Effectiveness as viewed by referring agencies, parents and teachers. *Exceptional Children*, 1969, **35**, 703–711.

Weiss, M., and Burke, A. A five to ten-year follow-up study of hospitalized school phobic children and adolescents. Paper read at the annual meeting of the American Orthopsychiatric Association, 1967.

Whitehorn, J. C., and Betz, B. J. A study of psychotherapeutic relationships between physicians and schizophrenic patients. *American Journal of Psychiatry*, 1954, **111**, 321–331.

Whitehorn, J. C., and Betz, B. J. Further studies of the doctor as a crucial variable in the outcome of treatment with schizophrenic patients. *American Journal of Psychiatry*, 1960, **117**, 215–223.

Williams, R., and Pollack, R. H. Some non-psychological variables in therapy defection in a child-guidance clinic. *J. Psychol.*, 1964, **58**, 145–155.

Zeilberger, J., Sampen, S. E., and Sloane, H. N. Modification of a child's problem behaviors in the home with the mother as therapist. *J. Appl. Behav. Anal.*, 1968, **1**, 47–53.

Outpatient Psychiatric Clinics Annual Statistical Report, 1966. Biometry Branch, National Institute of Mental Health, 1966, PHS Publication 1854.

Project Re-ED: A demonstration project for the reeducation of emotionally disturbed children (revised). Nashville: George Peabody College for Teachers, 1967.

Report of the Task Force on Juvenile Delinquency and Youth Crime of the President's Commission on Law Enforcement and Administration of Justice. Washington, D.C.: U.S. Government Printing Office, 1967.

14

PSYCHOTHERAPY AND ATARAXIC DRUGS[1]

PHILIP R. A. MAY

CALIFORNIA STATE DEPARTMENT OF MENTAL HYGIENE AND UNIVERSITY OF CALIFORNIA AT LOS ANGELES

INTRODUCTION

The purpose of this chapter is to review the current position of ataraxic drugs[2] in relation to formal psychotherapy, considered in terms of a comparison of the effectiveness of these two manifestly different forms of intervention, and what is known of their usefulness in combination. A presentation of the findings from our own research study in the treatment of schizophrenia is followed by a discussion of theoretical issues, the contributions of the basic sciences to our knowledge in this area, the implications for treatment and treatment programs, and possible directions for future research and development.

The term *ataraxic drugs* is a convenient umbrella label for a number of compounds which, when administered in sustained dosage over a period of time (measured usually in weeks, months, or years), have been shown to be effective to some degree in the treatment of psychiatric disorders. Their introduction in the

[1] This paper originates from the Schizophrenia Research Project, supported by the Psychopharmacology Research Branch, National Institute of Mental Health, United States Public Health Service, Contract #PH-43-66-49 and Research Grants NIMH-02719 and NIMH-04589; and by research grants from the California State Department of Mental Hygiene, with the generous participation of Camarillo State Hospital, Camarillo, California (Vernon G. Bugh, M. D., Superintendent and Medical Director). The author is indebted to the many members of the Schizophrenia Research Project for their part in this study and to Wilfrid J. Dixon, Ph.D., Professor of Biomathematics at the University of California, Los Angeles, for his major contributions in statistics and design. Computing assistance was provided by the Health Sciences Computing Facility, University of California, Los Angeles, California (sponsored by NIH Grant FR-3). Daniel N. Frumkes, B.A. coordinated much of the major task of data processing.

[2] In this chapter the terms drugs and ataraxic drugs are used interchangeably.

1950's represented a breakthrough of the same order as the introduction of chemotherapy for bacterial infection a decade previously.

Two types are commonly distinguished. The *major ataraxics*, such as the phenothiazines and the butyrophenones, are commonly employed in the treatment of schizophrenia. They are distinguished from the *antidepressants*, which are used in the treatment of depressions of various sorts, psychotic and otherwise; and from the so-called *minor tranquilizers*, such as chlordiazepoxide and meprobamate, which seem to have little or no value in the treatment of schizophrenia but are widely used for psychoneurotic patients.[3] The major ataraxics are often—and I believe properly—referred to as *antipsychotic* drugs, and this usage seems reasonable, since schizophrenia is the commonest form of psychosis. The terms schizophrenia and psychosis are often used almost interchangeably, and one could hardly take a drug seriously as an antipsychotic agent unless it had some effectiveness in this particular class of disorders. Indeed, Hamilton (1965) believing that the label antipsychotic should be reserved for substances that act on a biochemical system rather than on a clinical state, has suggested that they should be renamed the *antischizophrenic* drugs.

I would hesitate to go quite that far, as the antipsychotic drugs are generally considered to have some place in the treatment of other psychoses, both functional and organic. Nevertheless, the discussion of psychoses in the present paper will center on schizophrenia with, at the most, marginal or passing reference to other types of psychoses.

It would be a Gargantuan task to attempt a comprehensive review of research on all the various types of drugs in the pharmacopeia and all the different forms of psychological intervention. For this reason, the present review is deliberately restricted to *ataraxic* drugs and to what may be defined as *formal* psychotherapy. The reader must recognize, however, that ataraxics are not the only drugs that have been used in the treatment of psychiatric disorders, either alone or in combination with psychotherapy.

For example, sedative drugs (usually barbiturates) or stimulant drugs such as amphetamine, methylamphetamine, pipradrol, and methylphenidate are sometimes given intravenously to facilitate abreaction—the admission of conflict-laden material into consciousness for diagnostic or for therapeutic purposes. Ether and nitrous oxide have been used for the same purpose—and so has hypnosis. Similar techniques are used occasionally to get mute catatonic schizophrenics to talk or to eat; or to produce dramatic relief of a major hysterical symptom; or (using smaller doses by mouth) to facilitate the process of group therapy.

There is, however, no such thing as a "truth serum" that can force a subject to reveal all the information he has in his mind; experimental and clinical evidence indicates that psychopaths may lie and distort under the influence of a drug, and that even the relatively honest individual can successfully disguise the facts. Others, plagued by guilt and depression or overly compliant, are more likely to reveal information, but even they may at times unconsciously distort and present fantasies as facts. It may therefore, be difficult to tell whether a subject is deliberately falsifying, turning to fantasy, or presenting fact (Gottschalk, 1960b).

Sedatives and hypnotics, such as bromides, barbiturates, chloral hydrate, and paraldehyde, are given to reduce anxiety and tension and to relieve insomnia; in larger doses they have been used to induce a state of continuous narcosis. This type of "sleep" treatment may be continued for days or even weeks in an effort to interrupt the course of the patient's illness.[4] Subcoma doses of insulin (not to be confused with the deep-coma therapy used in the treatment of schizophrenia) have also been used for anxiety-tension states.

The psychoanaleptic drugs (stimulant or energizer) that are used to counteract depression

---

[3] Reserpine and the rauwolfia alkaloids, now seldom used as ataraxic agents because of their uncertain effectiveness and occasional alarming side effects, occupy perhaps an intermediate position between the major and the minor ataraxics.

[4] It is of interest that chlorpromazine, the original major antipsychotic agent, was used at first in the induction of a state of artificial hibernation. Its special ataraxic effects were an incidental discovery.

include the monoamine oxidase inhibitors, imipramine, amphetamine, and related drugs. Despite their wide usage, there has been little systematic study of the combination of drugs and psychotherapy in the treatment of depressive illness, and the material available consists entirely of opinions in favor of a combined approach, and description of techniques based on the author's clinical experience (such as Lesse, 1966a; Ostow, 1960, 1961, 1966a).

More recently, research effort has been directed toward the use of lithium in manic-depressive illness, again without systematic study of its relationship to psychotherapy. There has also been great interest in the use of mescaline, LSD and other psychotomimetic drugs, either, as abreactive agents, to promote the discussion of conflict material; or to induce a consciousness-expanding or spiritual experience as an aid to psychotherapy or even as a substitute for it. In this latter case, the experience has been hypothesized as containing elements that lead to an insightful reordering of personality functioning. Published research in this area has been conspicuously lacking in acceptable controls, so the use of the psychotomimetic drugs as a form of therapy must, for the present, be regarded as purely speculative and experimental.

High-dosage insulin coma was widely used in the past for the treatment of schizophrenia, either alone or in combination with informal or formal psychotherapy; it is now virtually obsolete. The same applies to convulsive therapy induced by the injection of metrazol, now replaced by electroconvulsive therapy (ECT).

Indoklon (hexafluro-diethyl-ether), administered intravenously or by inhalation, has recently been introduced as a substitute for ECT. To judge by the preliminary uncontrolled reports, indoklon has no particular advantage over ECT, though it does have the potential for being a reasonably safe alternative.

Thus a wide variety of drugs have been and are being used in clinical practice, in combination with psychotherapy or as an alternative treatment. No doubt new substances will be introduced in the future—it is even possible that some of the substances developed for chemical and psychological warfare may have more peaceful uses.

This review, however, will be limited strictly to the *ataraxic drugs*, which at this time occupy a major center of attention and controlled research effort in psychopharmacology. The reader who wishes to pursue the subject of other types of drugs will find an excellent starting point in the elegant review by Elkes (1967) of behavioral pharmacology in relation to psychiatry, and in standard clinical texts such as Sargent and Slater (1964) or Kalinowsky and Hoch (1961).

This review is also restricted to *formal* psychotherapy, which I have defined elsewhere as a specific personal individualized intervention over and above the management and administrative therapeutic contact that is necessary for the treatment of all psychiatric patients. The basic ingredient is a deliberate attempt by the therapist to do psychotherapy, that is, to focus in a personal, individual way on the patient's sensitivities to life situations and his personal reactions to life experiences; on gaining insight into these susceptibilities in an effort to strengthen his ability to deal with himself and his reactions; and on gaining mastery of his life situation (May, 1968b). Group approaches will be included in this review only if the focus is on providing psychotherapy for the individual in the group, rather than promoting social interaction and structure.

Special mention must be made of what has been variously called counter-conditioning, operant conditioning, behavioral conditioning, conditioned reflex treatment, or reinforcement therapy. These methods are specifically excluded from this review, for two reasons. First, I have not found satisfactory comparison with drug therapy or reports of the effects of the two forms of treatment combined. (Comparisons will likely be made in the near future, and interaction between drugs and conditioning may become an important subject for investigation, as "conditioning" is now being used quite extensively in the treatment of psychiatric disorders.)

Second, conditioning does not fall within the boundaries of psychotherapy as defined above —indeed, as defined by most of those who consider themselves psychotherapists. If it is labeled as "psychotherapy," this will merely add further to the terminological confusion that is created by failure to distinguish between *psychotherapy*, *psychotherapeutic management*, and *that which is therapeutic for the psyche* (May, 1968b).

Although individual contacts and life experiences of many kinds may be therapeutic (in the sense of "beneficial"), accidentally or by design, they should not all be called "psychotherapy." If formal "psychotherapy" is taken as defined above, then other psychological approaches to treatment such as social service casework; pastoral counseling; vocational counseling; therapeutic community techniques; psychiatric nursing; occupational therapy; and recreational therapy should be included under psychotherapeutic management (May, 1968b).

These distinctions are necessary to stay on the right track when it comes to the subject of controls, as discussed in greater detail in a later section. For the moment it will suffice to say that psychotherapy, as defined above[5], is in these days of a shortage of trained professionals a highly priced and relatively scarce commodity. Furthermore, it may readily be observed that even those who in theory perceive psychotherapeutic elements in almost any kind of human contact, usually refer "psychotherapy" patients to a trained professional rather than to some kind of incidental and informal contact. It is therefore important to answer questions such as whether, for example, drugs and a deliberate professional attempt to give psychotherapy potentiate each other or interfere with each other when they are given together. Which gets better results, drugs or psychotherapy, or some combination? In which kind of case?

GENERAL STATUS

Defining the Issues

It may be taken as solidly established by well-controlled studies that the major ataraxic drugs are more effective in the treatment of

schizophrenia (and perhaps of some other types of psychoses) than ordinary routine hospital care, with or without placebo (Cole, Klerman, and Jones, 1960; Davis, 1965; Gilligan, 1965; Tuma, 1966, 1968). Their effectiveness in psychoneurotic disorders is less firmly established, but on the whole the bulk of the evidence points to a positive therapeutic effect. The important question is how these agents compare with and relate to psychological methods of treatment, in particular, psychotherapy.

Discussion will focus on these issues, taking as a point of departure recent reviews by Cole, Klerman, and Jones (1960); Davis (1965); Gilligan (1965); Gottschalk (1968); Grinspoon and Greenblatt (1963); May (1968a, 1968c); Tuma (1966, 1968); and Uhlenhuth, Lipman, and Covi (1969). The reader who wishes to read more deeply is referred to these articles as a basis for further references to supplement the specific illustrations and additional material reviewed in this chapter.

The Main Trend of Opinion

In general, the subject of psychotherapy and drugs has been sadly troubled by dogmatic expressions of opinion, a paucity of systematic observations, and—with a few prominent exceptions—an almost complete absence of controlled experimental evidence, a state of affairs typified by Solomon (1966) in his closing remarks at the end of a major conference on this topic: "It was the end of the afternoon. Since neither *** nor *** had presented much in the way of data, and ***, ***, and ***[6] had presented none at all, the audience had been treated to an interesting display of speculative opinion" (1966).

Since this reviewer has a preference for opinions that seem to be based on at least some systematic observation, it is inevitable that this chapter will refer at length only to the work of a few authors.

Indications. Much of the literature relates to psychoanalysis or psychotherapy of the neurotic

---

[5] The reader should assume that whenever the term "psychotherapy" appears in the remainder of this chapter, it refers only to psychotherapy as defined above.

[6] Asterisks refer to the five major participants.

patient and to the "minor tranquilizers." For this type of case and for this kind of drug, the main trend of opinion is that although drugs may perhaps be helpful as an adjunct in certain situations, it is generally preferable to use psychotherapy alone to help the patient to identify and to solve his problems.

However, the trend is also to believe that there is not necessarily any antagonism between the judicious use of drugs and a psychothera-peutic approach; and that in certain cases drugs may be helpful, not as an end in themselves but as an adjunct, as a temporary measure to facilitate psychotherapy—by controlling agres-sion and anxiety; by diminishing symptoms at the beginning of therapy to establish a more constructive, positive, and problem-exploring relationship; or by helping in crises or acute psychotic episodes that might supervene during the course of therapy (see references in May, 1968c).

Occasional dissenting voices suggest that drug treatment of the neurotic has been underrated (Koegler and Brill, 1967; Sargant, 1965), but they are probably counterbalanced by those who, as Davis (1965) comments, feel that "tranquilizers are just fancy sedatives" and by more who, without expressing their opinions in the literature, remain firmly unconvinced that drug therapy has any place in the treatment of this type of disorder and that drugs are incom-patible with dynamically-oriented psycho-therapy.

The treatment of psychosis is, however, a different matter, and it would be unwise to assume too hastily that experience with neuro-tics and the minor tranquilizers can be applied directly to the treatment of schizophrenics with major antipsychotic drugs. In fact, there is a substantial and steadily growing middle ground of opinion that drugs should play a greater role in the treatment of schizophrenia than they do in the treatment of neurosis; and that drugs and psychotherapy should play supplemental, rather than competing roles (see references in May, 1968c).

Admittedly, this middle ground ranges from those who see drugs as useful adjuncts to psychotherapy to those who see it the other way around, but either way, the general opinion is that drugs have their greatest use in estab-lishing a therapeutic contact in the stage of flagrant psychosis. Once symptoms have been reduced and a relationship has been formed, then psychotherapy can lead towards mastery of personality problems and behavior.

To illustrate this general opinion, Deniker (1964) writes that it is highly desirable to com-bine chemotherapy, psychotherapy, and socio-therapy in the treatment of the major psychoses; but for other disorders, the integration of the three methods remains a problem. Goldman (1962) and Rickels (1962a) observe that un-questionably many patients respond well to psychotherapy alone—and also, unquestion-ably, others respond to drug therapy alone, leaving a group for whom neither treatment alone is sufficient. Moreover, according to Blood (1962), emphasis in the psychoses will be on medication with psychotherapeutic sessions secondary; in psychoneurosis the reverse; and in borderline states the emphasis might be equal.

In treating children, Eisenberg (1965) does not assume that psychotherapy is any more specific than drug therapy, commenting that skill in using drugs requires both knowledge of their pharmacology and sensitivity to their psychologic significance; using drugs does not relieve the therapist of responsibility for seeking to identify and eliminate factors causing or aggravating the disorder.

Freud and the Psychoanalytic Viewpoint. Zetzel (1966) states that uncritical belief in the total applicability of psychotherapy is equalled only by its diametric opposite—total rejection. Her attitude is that drugs give us the oppor-tunity and the responsibility to utilize psycho-therapy more effectively toward mastery of the problems that predispose the individual illness. Even if regression is reversed by drugs, the patient may be left at an arrested stage of development; rehabilitation should not rest content with a recovery that includes substan-tial inhibitions, but should aim beyond imme-diate improvement to adaptability and self-realization. She points out that Freud (1933) took the position that psychoanalysis does not stand in opposition to other methods used in psychiatry, nor does it diminish their value or exclude them.

Freud's flexibility and tolerance is of great importance. He concludes a chapter on psychoanalytic technique with the following words:

But here we are concerned with therapy only in so far as it works by psychological means, and for the time being we have no other. The future may teach us to exercise a direct influence, by means of particular chemical substances, on the amounts of energy and their distribution in the neural apparatus. It may be that there are other undreamt-of possibilities of therapy. But for the moment we have nothing better at our disposal than the techniques of psychoanalysis. . . . (1938).

Freud also expressed the hope that hormones might eventually provide us with a means of coping successfully with the maldistribution of energy in the psychoses (1933). Elsewhere he wrote, "The hope of the future here lies in organic chemistry or access to it through endocrinology. This future is still far distant but one should study analytically every case of psychosis because this knowledge will one day guide the chemical therapy" (1930).

And, in another context:

. . . we must recollect that all other provisional ideas in psychology will presumably some day be based on an organic substructure. This makes it probable that it is special substances and chemical processes which perform the operations of sexuality and provide for the extension of individual life into that of the species. We are taking this probability into account in replacing the special chemical substances by special psychical forces (1914).

Ostow, credited by Sarwer-Foner (1963) with being the first to use neuroleptic drugs in psychoanalysis, records that Freud had discussed with Nunberg his anticipation of a time when it would be possible to use chemical substances to direct a therapeutic analysis into the most fruitful channels (1962).

Ostow has devoted a great deal of thought to this subject, for example, 1960, 1961, 1962, 1965, 1966a, 1966b, and 1967, his major contribution to the literature (1962) being based on intensive clinical observation of 13 patients treated by drugs and psychoanalysis; 5 patients treated by drugs and psychotherapy; and 39 patients treated primarily by drugs alone.[7]

His general position is that drug therapy lends itself to combination with psychoanalysis and psychotherapy for three main reasons: it does not disrupt ego function and therefore does not impede psychologic investigation and interpretation or the transference reaction; when properly employed, it actually facilitates psychotherapeutic work; and it can achieve quickly (though temporarily) the same ultimate therapeutic influence that can be achieved more lastingly (though slowly and painstakingly) by psychologic means.

By combining both modalities, we achieve a much greater degree of control of the patient's symptoms and behavior than by either alone. Psychoanalysis alone, he says, cannot undo or even locate disturbances in family relationships and self esteem—although it may place the patient in a better position to deal with these. A similar point was made by Lesse (1966a, 1968)—drugs are not an end in themselves. They do not enlighten the patient as to the source of his problem, nor inform him how to adapt or to whom, or how to take advantage of

---

[7] Ostow's work will be discussed in some detail, for it commands respect as a comprehensive and pioneering attempt to use systematic objective observation to clarify the relationship between psychoanalytic therapy and drug therapy. At the same time, this reviewer would himself be lacking in objectivity if he failed to point out that Ostow's contributions are not entirely free from mutually contradictory statements. For instance, he says "I have found that diagnostic classification furnishes no clue at all to the selection or dosage of a drug" (1965, page 6) and "All of these [major tranquilizers] have specific antipsychotic actions in certain phases of schizophrenia" (1965, page 7).

Nor are experimentally-minded research investigators likely to take kindly to his rather naive comments on scale reliability: "I have not actually checked this with any other individual, but I would find it difficult to see how two observers could differ by more than two scale positions. . . . Further, this problem does not arise when an individual analyst employs the scale to follow the vicissitudes of his patients' illness" (1962).

Nor are they likely to agree with Ostow that under the conditions of intensive case study "the observer is not likely to be misled into seeing things that are not there" (1962). On the contrary, they would be likely to maintain that it is in precisely this type of situation that objective verification is most acutely needed. The demurrer that psychoanalytic training is directed specially towards the attainment of objectivity in such a situation may or may not be accepted, but this reviewer would emphasize the need for a combination of objective methods and intensive case study.

opportunities. They do not make him realize his limitations and capacities, or that he needs to avoid certain stresses; they do not repair self-esteem or bad object-relationships.

There will no doubt be a number who will question Ostow's assertion that pathogenic tendencies arising from constitutional roots and early childhood experience can be influenced only by psychoanalysis—not by any chemical agent. Even if it is assumed that the pathologic process is one of conflict, it has yet to be demonstrated by objective criteria that interpretation and insight have any permanent corrective effect.

Is there any reason to advise analysis, if drugs alone can prevent an overt psychotic episode? Ostow's answer is a qualified "yes." Yes . . . if drugs bring the patient to the point where he can work on correcting his disturbed relationships. We must consider how long drug-induced "recovery" will persist. His criteria for the prediction of prolonged remission after drug therapy seem to be exactly those that are used by some psychotherapists to select patients for psychotherapy. There may be persistent remission when the precipitating cause no longer exists (a narcissistic blow, a temporary temptation or frustration, disappointment by some act of the love object, an ordeal, a marriage, or childbirth); when this is the first episode; when the patient is young, honestly desires to recover, can mobilize ingenuity in solving his problems, and disclaims a helpless position; and when there is no constitutional ego defect. If the opposite applies, the patient is likely to relapse unless kept on medication for a long period.

In Ostow's opinion, drugs should not be used when self-control, reality-testing, and capacity for self-observation are sufficient to permit the psychoanalytic process to meet the requirements of daily living. Nor should they be used simply to overcome resistances that can properly be handled by interpretation.

Gottschalk summarizes (1968) his views on the main uses for drugs in psychotherapy of nonpsychotic disorders: to suppress symptoms so that the patient can function domestically and vocationally, try out neurotically feared activity, and collaborate with the therapist; and to stimulate psychomotor activity and creativity, induce rapport, and reduce irrational affects so

that the patient's observing ego, his more rational self, can function adequately enough to gain understanding of his conflicts.

Drugs assist in establishing a working alliance and may prevent its dissolution when emotionally laden insight precipitates marked anxiety or even panic (Lesse, 1956a). Drugs can also diminish the danger of suicide, in Ostow's opinion. But it would be well to keep in mind that although many agitated depressed patients do well on chlorpromazine, there is a definite danger of suicide as the patient recovers; and that, therefore, severely agitated depressed patients with suicidal trends should not be treated on an outpatient basis (Lesse, 1956a).

Thus a main use of drug therapy is to hold otherwise inaccessible patients in psychotherapy. In this way, Ostow observes, it may actually do much to increase interest in psychotherapy and improve its practice. Moreover, since observable ego function can be used to monitor drug effect and regulate medication, the attempt to offer sound pharmacotherapy will automatically involve the therapist in simultaneous psychotherapy, for interviews that relate to ego functioning will naturally be occupied with a review of the patient's relationships with people.

One would hope that at least some of the patients who relapse when drugs are withdrawn might be freed from the need for medication by psychoanalysis or psychotherapy. "Whether this expectation will be fulfilled remains to be ascertained"—a statement by Ostow (1962) that serves to introduce the fact that, like drug therapy, psychotherapy also has its limitations.

Limitations of Psychotherapy. Hoch (1955) points out that, regardless of how skillfully applied, psychotherapy is often unable to overcome opposing influences in the environment; it is also of limited value in chronic cases. Lehrman (1961), Bergin (1966), and Truax and Carkhuff (1967) have presented evidence that psychotherapy seems to make some patients worse. Lehrman (1961) and Wheelis (1956) suggest that unresolved negative transferences may be one mechanism through which this harmful effect is mediated; for example, when the analyst attacks all a person values as nothing but reaction formation; his conscious reasoning as rationalization; and his will as magical thinking. The interpretations may be correct in content, but the manner of making them amounts to systematic tyrannization, so that as static insight increases, the patient's confidence steadily diminishes.

There are practical limitations of cost, duration, and shortage of therapists. Some illnesses, particularly the psychoses, are relatively impervious. One cannot always prevent destructive acting-out when interpretation and reconstruction act to remove inhibitions. Effectiveness is limited whenever there is a rigid ego. And finally, there is the matter of protracted dependence. Some patients successfully incorporate the treatment situation into their neurosis so that they protract it indefinitely in order to cling to transference gratifications (Ostow, 1961).

Dependency. Patients may also come to depend on drugs, a situation that gives rise to concern unless this is seen as replacement therapy, analogous to the use of insulin in diabetes. The minor tranquilizers may produce a genuine physical dependency, with severe physical withdrawal symptoms, especially when given in large doses over prolonged periods of time. The major ataraxics, however, do not induce physical dependence, and are not perceived as pleasure producing; also, there have been no reports of addiction. There is a potential for psychological dependence, but as Ostow points out, this may even, to some degree, be desirable, for the dependency on the therapist will make the patient wish to continue in psychotherapy even after recovery from the psychosis. On the other hand, if persons whose neurotic symptoms are relieved by drugs feel dependent on the effect, they may wish to continue for longer than necessary. It is hard to disagree with Hirsh (1962) that the aim of drug therapy should be to eliminate the need for itself. But one would hope that this would be the aim of every therapy—including psychotherapy.

It should also be pointed out that dependency is not necessarily a reaction to a pill. Psychotherapy and the physician-patient relationship may also have "toxic" effects. The patient reacts not only to the pill, but also to the

physician prescribing it and to the setting and manner in which it is administered. It is hard to distinguish dependency on *drugs* from dependence on the *therapist* and on *psychotherapy*—perhaps, indeed, they are all facets of dependence on the *patient-therapist relationship*.

Related to dependence is the syndrome of "narcissistic tranquility" (Ostow, 1967), characterized by detachment and remoteness, inability to tolerate object relationships, weight gain, and afternoon torpor. The patients are relatively content as long as their tranquility is not threatened, but vigorous clinging or explosive anger occurs at the prospect of separation or disappointment. Suggestions that the patient resume object relations are resisted, or obeyed perfunctorily and then abandoned. Analysis becomes an anaclitic relationship, and the patient complies with its rules only sufficiently to avoid being abandoned by the analyst.

This syndrome may develop during the administration of drugs to disturbed patients, but it also occurs commonly without drug therapy, characterizing a considerable number of so-called "simple," "ambulatory," or "partially remitted" schizophrenics. Ostow believes that it is not a direct consequence of medication, but rather a manifestation of an underlying retreat.

Transference. Psychoanalysts may fear that drugs may distort the transference. Ostow replies that alternatives such as hospitalization, electroshock, or abandoning therapy altogether, create an even more serious distortion; and that in any case, the essential point is to confront fantasy with reality—and this can still be done when drugs are given. One can analyze the unconscious meanings of medication just as readily as the unconscious meanings of other features of the therapeutic contract such as the disposition of the office furniture, arrangements for payment, and the like. Moreover, he adds, drugs often powerfully reinforce positive transference. In particular, drug-induced relief from the psychotic process allows a positive anaclitic transference to develop and, at the same time, assists the patient to develop reality-testing.

Lesse (1956a, 1968) also emphasizes the rapid development of intensive positive transference, while negative transferences are unusual. As happens in a surgical procedure, the physician who affords rapid relief from pain is likely to be aggrandized, and the therapist must take active steps to deal with denial, magical expectations, and childlike dependency, lest they block the treatment process. Importantly, when ataraxics have been administered during the course of therapy, rather than at its inception, there has been no striking change in the transference relationship. The patients maintained a realistic attitude towards the drug, and merely credited the therapist with good judgment for having employed medication. There was no stumbling block to the continuation of psychotherapy.

Interestingly, many patients report a striking increase in dreams during the first few weeks of drug therapy, and are eager to relate them to the therapist (Lesse, 1959, 1968; Azima, Cramer-Azima, and DeVerteuil, 1959). This corresponds to a period of rapid amelioration of anxiety and other symptoms; as reintegration occurs, it decreases.

Resistance. Therapists have expressed the fear that drugs will be used as a form of resistance to subsequent psychotherapy. In Ostow's experience (1962) this is not a major problem:

The patient who does disparage the value of psychotherapy or analysis following success with medication is giving vent to a resistance that must be analyzed. I have found this to be an infrequent occurrence, and one that is easily handled by analytic work.

This reviewer is impelled to add that most psychotic patients restitute without a great degree of insight, and are likely to be resistant to *any* kind of subsequent therapy, whether it be drugs, psychotherapy, or anything else. At the time he leaves hospital, the average schizophrenic patient recognizes little more than that he acts peculiarly or suffers symptoms, rationalizing these as inevitable or normal reactions to the environment which, in his conviction, has caused his disorder. Less than one percent attain even a slight degree of awareness of the genetic role of inner conflicts generated by past family relationships (May, 1968b).

Passing from resistance to psychotherapy, to resistance to taking medication, in Ostow's experience this occurs in three situations: first,

when self esteem is crucial and medication threatens the patient's omnipotence (he needs to deny the severity of his illness, and acceptance of help is a blow); second, when treatment is seen (perhaps correctly so) as an attempt by the love object to disengage himself; and third, when the patient is in a severe state of narcissistic withdrawal he may resent the object relationship that is implied by taking medication.

Other apprehensions. Nevertheless, despite the experience of those who have taken the trouble to make some systematic observation of the matter, many psychotherapists are not altogether comfortable about the concurrent use of drugs and psychotherapy, fearing that when anxiety is reduced, patients may stop working in therapy and become complacent (Grinspoon and Greenblatt, 1963). Throughout the literature there are recurrent warnings that drugs may impede the process of therapy.

Klerman (1963) observes that in recent years, now that it is almost universally agreed that the effect of drugs is not due to suggestion and enthusiasm alone, much of the controversy has subsided with the emphasis shifted to more reasoned elucidation of the interaction between drugs and other forms of treatment. Originally, it was feared that drug therapy would increase magical reliance upon medical treatment, foster dependency upon the physician, and blunt capacity for insight. Drugs were also regarded as having harmful effects upon the psychiatrist, limiting his psychotherapeutic skill by increasing latent tendencies to seek an easy way out. Others suggested that in prescribing drugs, the therapist was inappropriately applying a traditional medical role-model; and irrational feelings, motives, and authoritarian trends were ascribed to those who did. While interpretations of this kind had been originally applied to psychiatrists advocating psychosurgery and shock therapy, they were carried over to psychopharmacology. Alarm was even expressed over the moral consequences, for the nation as a whole, of the widespread use of these agents.

Most of the skepticism about ataraxic drugs emanated from centers that had already developed active treatment programs, either those intensely psychotherapeutic (especially in the U.S.A.) or those concentrating on environmental and milieu care (especially in Great Britain). In either setting, there was less enthusiasm for drugs, and when they were used, they tended to be given with less discretion and in smaller doses (Hordern, 1961) and with less understanding of their side effects.

There is no doubt that drugs, especially in large doses, may produce troublesome side effects that certainly complicate transactions between the patient and the therapist. When assaultive patients are "snowed" with drugs almost to unconsciousness, obviously they can receive no social or psychological treatment, and the staff attitude becomes custodial (Appleton, 1965). This, however, does not apply to the usual case; it represents a *misuse* of drugs rather than a *skillful* use; and no one who has any experience with drug therapy would seriously maintain that drugs should be given in massive doses except in most unusual situations.

Counter-Transference and Therapist Resistances. On occasion, drugs may be used for nonrational countertransference reasons—for example, to keep distance from a patient (Sarwer-Foner, 1960b) or because the therapist feels inadequate (Lesse, 1956b, 1960b). There may also be equally irrational reasons for not giving drugs, such as the narcissism of the therapist (Rickels, 1962b). Stone (1966) mentions the rescue fantasies of those who want to do it all by themselves without drugs and who cannot bear to share the patient's gratitude. Some of us have a prejudice against reliance on drugs to obtain relief (Ostow, 1966a). We do not regard the use of drugs in physical illness to be undesirable; for instance, the use of insulin in diabetes, digitalis in heart failure, or penicillin in pneumonia. Yet we seem to subscribe to the moralistic idea that a person should *work* his way out of psychological suffering and not get relief too easily. Such moralistic considerations should play no part in determining treatment (Ostow, 1966b).

Divergent attitudes toward drugs and psychotherapy may also appear as a manifestation of other, deeper, conflicts between different disciplines and professional groups (Klerman 1960). Lesse remarks that the intolerance of some psychotherapists to the use of drugs is reminiscent of the intolerance to psychoanalysis that existed a generation ago. Psychologists and social workers whose prestige and challenge to the traditional medical role depends on psychotherapy may tend to see drugs as a threat to their professional status (Klerman, 1960).

A common failing is to polarize around some organic-psychological dichotomy with the implication that only organic conditions can be treated with physical remedies. "It is not surprising that we find many psychoanalytically oriented psychotherapists reluctant to use psychoactive drugs. Implicit in the use of drugs to influence behavior is the admission that a narrowly psychodynamic framework is insufficient" (Pollard and Bakker, 1960). Lourie (1959) pricks this bubble by asking four salient questions: (1) If a person responds to anxiety with disorganization, what is wrong with giving the ego a lift to overcome the intensity of the anxiety? (2) If an individual has, as a part of his constitution, intense, sometimes overwhelming, instinctual drives, what is wrong with giving the ego a lift to overcome the intensity? (3) If the instinctual and other pressures on the developing ego have resulted in a fragile unorganized ego, what is wrong with giving a drug that may strengthen the ego's ability to organize? (4) In individuals with relatively good ego capacity, what is wrong with using drugs to deal with a level of impulse or anxiety that on an acute situational basis temporarily floods the ego and threatens to disorganize it?

In this connection, Hoch (1955) made the penetrating observation that psychotherapy itself is a procedure as organic as the introduction of a drug, the difference being that it is not applied directly to the nervous system. It has to pass through all the filtering and defense mechanisms that shield the organism against external stimulation, whereas drugs are introduced directly into the organism. It must be added that there are a number of bodily defenses against drugs also, and that psychotherapy can be seen as a series of stimuli that the psychotherapist hopes will be internalized and have a permanent effect—just as the drug therapist hopes that the drug stimulus will be internalized and have a permanent effect.

Pollard and Bakker (1960) discuss other irrational determinants of prescribing (and of not prescribing) drugs—unconscious magical, erotic, guilty, or retaliatory fantasies on the part of the giver and the receiver.

Factors in the Patient. Patients have pre-formed ideas of what treatment to expect, with multiple determinants, including social class and occupation as well as the individual's view of his own needs. The judicious use of drugs must take account of the significance that drug prescribing and taking has to the particular patient—". . . the capsule of love without understanding can become the bitter pill of rejection."

With this in mind, we pass from the problems of the therapist to focus on the patient's subjective experience. Sarwer-Foner, a pioneer in the psychodynamics of neuroleptic drug action,[8] emphasizes that the implications of using a drug must be worked through, for the patient always feels that this is an attempt to influence or to change him. Drug effects are integrated by the patient into a total situation that includes the milieu, his doctor, his family, the problems he is struggling with, and the like.

The therapeutic effect, as contrasted with the pharmacologic effect, depends on the meaning, to the patient, of the pharmacologic action in terms of his total situation and the motives he ascribes to whoever gives the drug.

If (Sarwer-Foner speculates from his clinical observations), the effect of the drug controls a target symptom, for example, aggressive or sexual impulses or feelings of inadequacy; and if this is interpreted as beneficial rather than detrimental; then the stage is set for ego growth. Control of symptoms that signify to the patient the core of his own impulsivity and former ego weakness has an immediate ego-fortifying effect. This can only occur when he is convinced of the physician's benevolent interest, and takes the drug effects as a "good" power to help him control himself and "drive out the badness." The "good" effects are incorporated and the patient feels a capacity for new ego growth. He is now, in his own eyes, a less fearsome, less

worthless, less perverse, stronger person. He tests out whether others see him as changed and therefore different, and at this point psychotherapy becomes more meaningful and perhaps of more benefit in reality-testing. The acceptance or rejection by significant others of this new visualization of himself is (he speculates) the cardinal point in determining whether successful ego integration continues.

Less favorable results occur if the patient interprets drug effect as not helping what he wants to have controlled—or even as threatening his controls (such as an aggressive or sexual assault, manipulation, or rejection); if he is struggling to repress passive feminine impulses and finds that this repression is challenged by drug-induced lassitude and restriction of motility; if side effects are seen as a brutal hostile attack rather than unpleasant temporary inconveniences or (by a hypochondriacal patient) as a threat to his somatic integrity; or if relationships with the family or among the treatment staff interfere with the process of recathexis[9].

Social Class. Physicians have special problems in selecting the appropriate treatment for a lower-class psychotic patient (Carlson, 1965). If he denies having problems and shows no interest in therapy the therapist withdraws, readily accepts the denial, rebuffs his need for medication, or remains distant and does not press for discussion of his life problems. Even in a clinic that is set up to serve patients without regard to socioeconomic standing, therapists are biased towards the somatic therapies in treating the lower classes (Shader and Rinstock, 1968).

Certainly patients from a lower social class are often relatively uninterested in psychotherapy, and regard it as less important in their treatment than physical recreation, manual work, and rehabilitation (Stotsky, 1956). However, it would be unwise to assume that

---

[8] I doubt that research methodologists will agree with Sarwer-Foner's reasons for not using double-blind technique—"They introduce far more variables . . . than they would solve" and "above all . . . such a 'trick' is a breach of faith with the patient."

[9] The following references are relevant to the

preceding discussion of the work of Sarwer-Foner and his associates: Sarwer-Foner, 1955, 1957a, 1957b, 1959a, 1959b, 1960a, 1960b, 1961 and 1963; Sarwer-Foner and Ogle, 1956a, 1956b; Sarwer-Foner and Koranyi, 1957, 1960; Sarwer-Foner, Koranyi, Mackay, and Grauer, 1959; and Sarwer-Foner and Korenyi, 1961.

drug therapy is more appropriate for lower-class patients than psychotherapy, since they also tend to depreciate and fail to cooperate with chemotherapy (see page 518).

CONTROLLED STUDIES OF OUTCOME

So much for theorizing and opinion based on uncontrolled observations. What is the experimental evidence?

It is generally agreed that there is a serious lack of adequately controlled studies, especially of the critical comparison between drug alone and drug plus psychotherapy, and of the interaction between drugs and psychotherapy (Tuma, 1966, 1968; Gilligan, 1965; Davis, 1965; Uhlenhuth, Lipman and Covi, 1969; May, 1968a, 1968c). "The combination of a tranquilizer with psychotherapy enjoys widespread popularity . . . as a method of treatment and as the subject of essays in the literature. There is, however, a surprising scarcity of formal studies to support this enthusiasm" (Uhlenhuth, Lipman, and Covi, 1969).

The most recent reviews are Uhlenhuth, Lipman, and Covi (1969) and May (1968a, 1968c). The former is a particularly critical analysis of controlled studies, with a few uncontrolled ones as well, including the Whitehorn and Betz study of A-B type and insulin therapy (1957), a virtually obsolete form of treatment. One wishes that the authors had been equally critical of studies relating to the effect on outcome of therapist experience and A-B type.

The controlled studies will now be reviewed under four main headings, followed by a summary.

Psychotherapy Alone Versus Drug Alone

Psychotic Inpatients. In a well-designed nine-hospital study with approximately 50 patients in each treatment group, Gorham, Pokorny, Mosely, McReynolds, and Kogan (1964) found that phenothiazine alone (in modest dosage) was significantly better than group psychotherapy alone (three sessions a week for 12 weeks), as measured by three independent global measures from different sources; by ratings of ten symptom areas (withdrawal, conceptual disorganization, mannerisms, grandiosity, lability, suspicion, hallucinations, uncooperativeness, unusual thought, and blunted affect); and by psychological test measures (reduction of rebellious, distrustful feelings, and better Rorschach responses). Psychotherapy was superior to drug therapy on ratings of somatization and tension, but there was no difference betwen the two on guilt, depression, anxiety, and motor retardation, nor on a test of subjective anxiety.

Results for the first twenty patients in each treatment group of our own Schizophrenia Research Project (May and Tuma, 1964, 1965a) indicated that drug therapy alone was significantly superior to individual psychotherapy alone in terms of release rate; length of hospital stay; amount of sedatives and hydrotherapy required; change in overall clinical status as judged by psychoanalysts; and final ratings of clinical status by nurses. There was no significant difference in readmission rates. The finding that the short-term[10] outcome of drug therapy alone is superior to that of psychotherapy is now supported by more detailed analyses covering a large number of clinical, administrative, and psychometric criteria on 228 patients, which showed a powerful drug effect but no significant effect from psychotherapy (May, 1968b).

Cowden, Zax and Sproles (1955, 1956) compared reserpine alone (seven patients); group psychotherapy plus placebo (eight patients); and no-treatment control (eight patients), over six months. Since reserpine is now not considered to be a major antipsychotic drug, this study is not included in the summary (page 514). They found no significant differences among the groups by ward behavioral rating scales or by psychological test measures. By number of packs, fights, seclusions, and disturbance reports, the control group showed the least improvement, but there was no particular difference between psychotherapy plus a placebo and reserpine alone.

Uhlenhuth, Lipman, and Covi (1969) comment that the control group did not get a placebo, so the

---

[10] i.e. Over the period from admission to release from hospital.

better results in the psychotherapy and reserpine groups could be due partly or wholly to the act of taking pills, irrespective of their contents. Technically, they are correct, but I would take this as a minor point, since it is well established that chronic schizophrenic patients are not particularly strong responders to placebo.

Honigfeld, Blumenthal, Lambert, and Roberts (1965) have also not been included in the summary. Their group meetings were intended to be "social therapy" rather than psychotherapy, and no data are presented on separate results for phenothiazines alone, and phenothiazines combined with group sessions.

Mixed Inpatients. A study by Evangelakis (1961) of a mixed group of inpatients (mainly psychotic) compared twenty patients treated by phenothiazine alone with twenty patients treated by placebo plus group psychotherapy twice a week, plus an intensive milieu program. The phenothiazine group did better in terms of improvement, release rate, and transfer to better wards.

Mixed Outpatients. Lorr, McNair, and Weinstein (1962) studied 150 outpatients selected as suitable for individual psychotherapy once a week—18 percent psychotic, 42 percent neurotic, 26 percent with personality disorders, and 15 percent with psychophysiologic disorders. The drug used was a minor ataraxic (chlordiazepoxide); the treatment period (four weeks) is unlikely to be accepted as a fair trial; and results were not analyzed separately by diagnosis. According to the therapists, there was a significantly positive drug effect on the overall severity of illness and on expression of affection and rapport. There was also a significant "capsule effect"—those receiving *either* drug *or* placebo therapy improved significantly more than those receiving individual psychotherapy alone, overall and in terms of anxiety, self-blame, and physical complaints. According to the patients, there was no significant effect from either psychotherapy or from drug therapy. There was, however, a significant "capsule effect". Both placebo and drugs were equally effective and superior to psychotherapy alone by the patient's own reports of psychological and social change, anxiety, and depression.

Attrition was so high (48 percent) as to cause serious question, and the drop-out rate was higher for groups receiving psychotherapy (25 percent) than for those not receiving psychotherapy (17 percent). Unlenhuth, Lipman, and Covi (1969) comment that differences and interaction patterns may have been attenuated by the attrition. This is true, but the reader should avoid drawing the implication that results might have been better for psychotherapy. Attrition biases results *in favor* of the group with the highest attrition rate if the dropouts tend to be those who feel that they have not benefited. In this case the implication is that, if anything. the results would have been *less favorable* for psychotherapy if there had been a correction for attrition.

Neurotic Outpatients. Perhaps the most comprehensive study is Koegler and Brill (1967), in which 299 patients were assigned to six groups: prochlorperazine (a major ataraxic, now seldom used for non-psychotic outpatients); meprobamate (a minor ataraxic); phenobarbital; placebo; psychotherapy; and no-treatment control.

According to ratings by the therapists (who were in general highly antagonistic to drug therapy), there were two trends (not statistically significant)—meprobamate and psychotherapy were the most improved, and phenobarbital and prochlorperazine, the least. Psychotherapy was rated significantly more effective in terms of ability to work effectively and understand the self.

By the patients ratings, however, meprobamate was better (statistically significant in five out of twelve ratings), and by ratings of overall condition, both meprobamate and psychotherapy were significantly better than the other groups. Psychotherapy patients more often felt they were helped by treatment.

No significant differences were reported by the relatives' evaluation or by psychological tests. Meprobamate and psychotherapy were found significantly better by social work ratings of social adjustment.

At follow-up, the control-group patients had improved considerably, and there were no significant differences.

All considered, one must agree with the authors' conclusion that brief contact therapy with drugs obtains substantially as good results as conventional psychotherapy averaging five months in duration. Considering the overt antagonism of many of the therapists to drug therapy, this is a remarkable finding.

Psychotherapy Alone Versus Psychotherapy Plus Drug

Psychotic inpatients. Analysis of results for the first twenty patients in each treatment group of our Schizophrenia Research Project (May and Tuma, 1964, 1965a) showed that psychotherapy plus drug therapy was significantly superior to psychotherapy alone in terms of release rate; length of hospital stay; amount of sedatives and hydrotherapy required; change in overall clinical status as judged by psychoanalysts; and ratings of final clinical status by nurses. There was no significant difference in readmission rates. These findings are now supported by more detailed analyses covering a large number of clinical, administrative, and psychometric criteria on 228 patients (May, 1968b).

Grinspoon, Ewalt, and Shader (1967, 1968) found that chronic schizophrenic patients did not appear to change with intensive individual psychotherapy alone by highly qualified therapists for two years—as judged by the patients' daily diaries and by two scales of manifest psychopathology and ward adjustment. By comparison, there was a statistically significant improvement in patients treated with the combination of drug and psychotherapy, in terms of symptom reduction; and making the patient more reachable, and more receptive to communication and open expression of pleasure or distress rather than masking or avoiding feelings. In patients treated without drugs there was, in most instances, little to suggest that any working alliance had ever been established—in fact, there was no significant difference before, during, or after the therapist's vacation. Much the same could be said of the drug-treated patients, except that in this case there was a suggestion that a few had developed the capacity to exhibit some sensitivity in responding to object-loss, and that for them the therapist may have had some importance.

Although there was no question that the patients on phenothiazines changed dramati-cally in relation to the on-off drug condition, the changes observed did not suggest—to the authors—that the patients were any less schizophrenic; merely that they exhibited fewer symptoms. With this, the reviewer disagrees. If withdrawal is taken as a fundamental schizophrenic process, then improved communication and expression of feelings and some indication of closer contact with the therapist suggests that there was some—admittedly not very much—recession. And reduction in symptoms must mean *something*. The comparison with a control group receiving the same psychotherapy and the same milieu program makes it unlikely that it was due to some environmental change.

A comment is indicated on the remark by Uhlenhuth, Lipman, and Covi (1969) that in this study, "Although the interpersonal therapies produced no noticeable effects over time, definite conclusions on this point could not be drawn, since suitable controls were not included." The reader should not be misled. It was very, very, clear that intensive individual psychotherapy by experts did little or nothing for these patients in two years time, and that it was less effective than psychotherapy combined with drug therapy. The controls in this respect were impressively adequate. Uhlenhuth, Lipman, and Covi do not specify just what they are asking for in the way of controls; but perhaps they mean to say that, even so, psychotherapy and milieu therapy may still have been having *some* effect. Unfortunately for this speculation, there was little or no change in the ten patients treated with psychotherapy alone. Perhaps they might have gotten worse without psychotherapy —but this would hardly be much of an achievement compared with the striking improvement that occurred when phenothiazine was added.

In a subsequent study of treatment by carefully supervised first year residents, Shader, Grinspoon, Ewalt, and Zahn found that psychotherapy combined with a phenothiazine was significantly better for young acute schizophrenic patients than psychotherapy combined with butytrophenone or a placebo on seven scales—hospital adjustment; behavioral disturbance; mental status; schizophrenic disorganization; total morbidity; motor disturbances; and excitement. Borderline significance was obtained on three additional scales—perceptual distortion, retardation and apathy, and conceptual disorganization (1969).

Gorham, Pokorny, Moseley, McReynolds, and Kogan (1964) found that for schizophrenic patients, group psychotherapy alone was significantly inferior to group psychotherapy combined with a phenothiazine, by five global measures of change (provided by a rating team of the patients' physician, nurses, the therapist, and a nonparticipant observer in the psychotherapy sessions); by fourteen of sixteen symptom areas rated; and by psychological test responses (rebellious-distrustful feelings and Rorshcach).

Cowden, Zax and Sproles (1956, 1955) found that group psychotherapy plus reserpine was better, although not significantly so, than psychotherapy alone. This study and Honigfeld, Rosenblum, Blumenthal, Lambert, and Roberts (1965) are excluded from the summary (page 514) for reasons previously given.

Mixed Inpatients. Evangelakis (1961) compared two groups of twenty patients, mainly psychotic, treated by group psychotherapy (plus an intensive milieu program) and group psychotherapy plus a phenothiazine. The group that received drugs plus psychotherapy did substantially better, in terms of release rate and transfer to better wards, than the group that received psychotherapy without drugs.

Mixed Outpatients and Inpatients. Gibbs, Wilkens, and Lauterbach (1957) studied a mixed group of neurotic and psychotic patients, finding no consistent significant difference between drug plus individual psychotherapy (once a week for six weeks) and placebo plus psychotherapy. Uhlenhuth, Lipman, and Covi (1969) comment correctly that there was bias in assignment of psychotic patients to the treatment and that the psychological test criteria tend to be insensitive to treatment differences.

Mixed Outpatients. Lorr, McNair, Weinstein, Michaux, and Raskin (1961) is an eight-week comparison of individual psychotherapy and psychotherapy plus meprobamate, chlorpromazine (in small doses), phenobarbital, or placebo. The attrition rate (41 percent) was so high as to cause serious question. Results were not analyzed separately according to diagnosis (16 percent psychotic, 57 percent psychoneurotic, and 27 percent psychosomatic and personality disorders), so the application of their findings—that the addition of ataraxics did not improve the outcome over psychotherapy alone from the viewpoint of either the patient or the therapist—is uncertain.

The same caveats apply to a subsequent four-week study of chlordiazepoxide (Lorr, McNair, and Weinstein, 1962). According to their therapists, patients who received drugs as well as psychotherapy became (by comparison with psychotherapy alone) significantly less ill after four weeks, with more overall improvement, better rapport, and greater ability to express affection. The patients, however, reported no significant difference except that somatic discomfort was reduced by the addition of the drug. The therapists judged medication to have facilitated psychotherapy in 32 percent, producing no particular effect in sixty-four percent. Thus medication did not impede the therapeutic relationship.

Roth, Rhudick, Shaskan, Slobin, Wilkinson, and Young (1964) followed up half the patients from the preceeding study for a further six months of psychotherapy. Medication was not controlled (45·8 percent of the drug group did not receive drugs, while 44·5 percent of the psychotherapy group did). Accordingly their data are not an experimental comparison of drugs and psychotherapy, but rather an uncontrolled description of what happened subsequently in their clinic. It is therefore not included in the summary on page 514. Their main observation was that patients who had previously received a placebo or no treatment did poorly by comparison with the others.

The authors ignore the possible role of drugs and focus on the role of psychotherapy in determining outcome—even though half the patients were receiving drugs. A restatement of one of their conclusions would seem to be in order. When the start of treatment—not just psychotherapy—is delayed by giving no help or ineffective help (such as a placebo or no treatment) there is a deleterious effect on outcome. On the other hand, quickly communicating recognition and acceptance of the patient's need for help, either through interpersonal techniques or effective medication, puts treatment—not just psychotherapy—on a solid basis.

Neurotic Outpatients. Rickels, Cattell, Weise, Gray, Yee, Mallin, and Aaronson (1966) compared the effects of individual psychotherapy (one interview a week) plus placebo, with psychotherapy plus meprobamate in 114 outpatients. Psychotherapy plus meprobamate was significantly more effective than psychotherapy plus a placebo, by global measures from patient and therapist, total questionnaire scores and individual items, two subscales of the Clyde Mood Scale, and the Ego Scale of the IPAT Verbal battery. There were no differences as the IPAT O-A Anxiety and Regression battery.

Drug Alone Versus Psychotherapy Plus Drug

Psychotic Inpatients. King (1963) found no significant difference in release rate between twenty chronic schizophrenic patients receiving chlorpromazine alone for one year in low dosage, and a matched group receiving chlorpromazine plus group therapy once a week.

Another study compared nineteen chronic schizophrenic patients receiving chlorpromazine alone for six months with another group receiving chlorpromazine plus group therapy. There was no significant difference in outcome between the two groups in terms of psychotic symptomatology (King, 1958).

Gorham, Pokorny, Moseley, McReynolds, and Kogan (1964) found no statistically significant differences between drug alone and psychotherapy plus drug, by three independent global measures from different sources; nor by ratings of guilt, depression, and ten symptom areas; nor by psychological test measures.[11] Psychotherapy plus drug therapy was, however, superior, by ratings of somatization, tension, anxiety, and motor retardation.

Cowden, Zax, Hague, and Finney (1956) compared four months of treatment in two groups of eight chronic schizophrenic patients each—chlorpromazine plus group psychotherapy, and chlorpromazine alone. Psychotherapy plus drug was somewhat better than drug alone, but the differences were not statistically significant. Unfortunately, comparison is contaminated by the fact that ECT was also given to both groups, but to a lesser extent in the combined treatment group. Thus one cannot

be confident that the observed differences might not have been due to differences in the amount of ECT.

Analysis of the first twenty patients in each treatment group of our own Schizophrenia Research Project indicated that there was no significant difference beween drug alone and psychotherapy plus drug in terms of release rate; length of hospital stay and amount of time in the hospital during the first three years after admission; amount of sedatives and hydrotherapy required; change in overall status as judged by psychoanalysts; and ratings of final status by nurses and psychoanalysts. Nor was there any difference in readmission rates (May and Tuma, 1964, 1965a). The findings up to the time of first release are now supported by more detailed analyses covering a large number of criteria on 228 patients (May, 1968b), which indicate that the differences between the two were mainly small and insubstantial.

Cowden, Zax, and Sproles (1954, 1955) found that reserpine combined with psychotherapy was not significantly better than reserpine alone. This study and Honigfeld, Rosenblum, Blumenthal, Lambert, and Roberts (1965) are excluded from the summary (page 514) for reasons previously given.

Mixed Inpatients. Evangelakis (1961) compared groups of twenty patients, mainly psychotic, treated by (1) drug plus in-ward adjunctive therapy; (2) drug plus off-ward adjunctive therapy and (3) drug plus both adjunctive therapies and group psychotherapy twice a week. In terms of improvement and release to their own home or to boarding homes, or transfer to better wards, there was essentially no difference between groups (2) or (3), but both were better (no significance tests given) than group (1). Thus the implication is that off-ward adjunctive therapy adds to the effect of drug therapy plus an on-ward program—but the further addition of group therapy does not.

Mixed Outpatients. In their study of chlordiazepoxide, Lorr, McNair, and Weinstein (1962) found no major difference between psychotherapy plus drug and drug alone. This study has serious limitations (see page 507).

[11] For details of the criteria, see page 509.

Drug-Psychotherapy Interaction

Controlled experimental studies of drug-psychotherapy interaction have been conspicuously lacking, probably because adequate statistical analysis requires a factorial design with four experimental groups: drug alone; psychotherapy alone; drug combined with psychotherapy; and a control group that receive neither of the two treatments.

Other Studies. It appears that only two other studies besides our own have performed an analysis of variance to distinguish between the separate effects of psychotherapy and drugs, and their interaction.

Lorr, McNair, and Weinstein (1962) report only one significant interaction effect in their study of chlordiazepoxide in neurotics. No statistics are given, but psychotherapy plus drug therapy was more effective than either psychotherapy alone or drug therapy alone in relieving somatic discomfort. Since they present data on a large number of outcome criteria, such a finding is compatible with chance alone.

Honigfeld, Rosenblum, Blumenthal, Lambert, and Roberts (1965) state that there was no evidence of joint or additive effect of group sessions and drugs in older schizophrenic patients without presenting relevant statistics.

The following section will present some relevant results from our own study.

Schizophrenia Research Project. 228 schizophrenic patients, age 16 to 45, without significant prior treatment, and chosen by a clinical estimate to be in the middle third of the prognostic range, were assigned by a random method to five treatment groups—psychotherapy alone; drug[12] alone; psychotherapy plus drug[12]; ECT; and a control group who received none of these treatments. The patients were treated by physicians with six years or less of psychiatric experience, who were either in residency training or had completed it. They were closely supervised by experienced clinicians in a good realistic trial—for at least six months and even as long as one year, unless the patient left the hospital earlier. A comprehensive multi-disciplinary evaluation was performed before and after treatment. (Details of the design, patient sample, and statistical procedures are given elsewhere [May, 1968b]; the reader will not be burdened with them here.)

CRITERIA. For this analysis, a wide variety of criterion measures were chosen.

1. Release rate.

2. Nurses' ratings on the four subscales and total score of the MACC and Menninger Health-Sickness Scales.

3. Therapists' ratings (total score) on the Jenkins Symptom Rating Scale and the six subscales of the Clyde Mood Scale.

4. The ratings of an independent team of psychoanalysts on the Menninger Health-Sickness Scale and CDAS Insight and Anxiety Scales.

5. The fourteen clinical and validity scales of the MMPI.

6. The total of the Similarities-Proverbs subscales of the WAIS.

7. The Shipley V.I.Q. and A.I.Q.

A three-way analysis of variance (excluding patients in the ECT group) was performed for release rate, and for the final, change, and covaried scores[13] on the other measures. This provides a separation of the variation of all the observations into three main parts, attributable to sex, drug, and psychotherapy, as well as an estimate of the various interactions. In particular, an interaction between psychotherapy and drug would indicate that the effect of psychotherapy was different, depending on whether the drug were given as well (or vice versa).

RESULTS. In general, there was very little to indicate that drugs interferred with or potentiated psychotherapy, or vice versa. For all except 7 of the 34 measures, the interactions were clearly of no statistical significance ($p > .25$), both for *final* and for *change* scores. Even for the other 7, the evidence of interaction is unimpressive. In fact, if there were indeed no true interaction, we might reasonably except findings of this order by sheer chance in this number of measures and variables. Nevertheless,

---

[12] Trifluoperazine (Stelazine).

[13] Final level adjusted by covariance for sex and initial level.

TABLE 14.1 Psychotherapy-Drug Interaction[a]

	Change	Final	Covaried
CDAS (Insight)	+.622	+.128	+.20–.30
(Nurses') Menninger Scale	+.147	+.147	+.10–.20
Clyde Scale (Aggressive)	+.145	+.145	N.A.
Clyde Scale (Clear Thinking)	−.970	−.103	−.30
MMPI *F* (Validity)	+.086	−.379	N.A.
MMPI *D* (Depression)	−.498	−.021	N.A.
Shipley Abstract I.Q.	+.008	+.391	+.01–.005

[a] Significance levels (p) for psychotherapy-drug interaction from three-way analyses of variance (sex × drug × psychotherapy) of *final* and *change* scores. Covaried levels are also given if the regression slopes were sufficiently equal among the treatments to make this procedure appropriate. (+) indicates potentiation, (−) interference between the two treatments.

it is advisable to consider their possible clinical significance if it is assumed that they may represent a true, rather than a chance, interaction effect.

Table 14.1 gives the relevant significance levels for interaction from the three-way analysis of variance for *change*; *final*; and *covaried* scores,

In general, the balance of the evidence (five of the seven measures) is towards a positive interaction, that is, a potentiation of effect when drugs and psychotherapy are combined[14]. Three clinical measures indicate weak positive interaction. By *final* and *change* scores for nurses. "Menninger" ratings and therapists' ratings of "Aggressive", psychotherapy plus drug was better than either treatment separately, and the interaction tends consistently towards significance (p = +.147 and +.145, respectively). The interaction was also consistently positive for psychoanalysts' ratings of "Insight," but tended towards significance only by the criterion of *final* scores (p = +.128), and perhaps by the criterion of covaried-scores (p = +.20 −.30).

On one clinical measure, therapists' ratings of "Clear Thinking," there was some (flimsy) evidence of interference between the two treatments. This was clearly not significant by change scores (p = −.970); it tended toward significance for *final* scores (p = −.103), and was not significant (p = −.30) for *covaried*

scores. On this measure, the final mean score for drug alone was somewhat higher than for psychotherapy plus drug, and considerably higher than psychotherapy alone. Thus, if anything, in this case the addition of psychotherapy interferred with a positive drug effect rather than vice versa.

On two of the fourteen MMPI scales there was some tendency to interaction. For *change* scores on the *F* (Validity) scale, the interaction was positive and approached significance (p = +.086). The drug alone group had higher (better) *change* scores than psychotherapy alone, but not significantly so; while the combination was better than either treatment alone. However, the balance of evidence for interaction on the *F* scale is not impressive. By the criterion of *final* scores, the interaction was nonsignificant and in the opposite direction (p = −.379): the mean *final* score for drug alone was actually (slightly) better than for psychotherapy plus drug, both being better than psychotherapy alone.

The evidence on the *D* (Depression) scale was also inconsistent and unimpressive. Interaction was negative and significant for *final* scores (p = −.021), but not for *change* scores (p. = −.498). The *final* mean score for psychotherapy alone was somewhat better than for drug alone, but both were better than psychotherapy plus drug. However, by the criterion of *change* scores, psychotherapy plus drug was slightly better than either treatment alone.

[14] *Negative* interaction indicates interference between the two.

In the case of the Shipley Abstract I.Q., the evidence for interaction was perhaps a little stronger, although still not sufficiently consistent to be entirely comfortable. By the criterion of change scores, interaction was positive and significant (p. = +.008), psychotherapy plus drug showing more improvement than either treatment separately. Interaction was not significant by the criterion of final scores (p = +.391) but by covaried scores, which are applicable in this case, it was significant (p = +.005 −.01).

DISCUSSION. The overall weight of evidence indicates that there was no significant interaction, positive or negative, between the effects of antipsychotic drugs and individual psychotherapy in our schizophrenic patients. From a large number of measures, only four indicated even as much as a consistent trend towards significant potentiation (nurses' "Menninger" ratings; therapists' ratings of "Aggressive"; psychoanalysts' ratings of "Insight"; and "Shipley Abstract I.Q."); with flimsy support from one additional measure (MMPI *F* scale). Two measures provided dubious evidence of interference (therapists' ratings of "Clear Thinking" and the MMPI *D* scale). Thus there was no support for the notion that antipsychotic drugs and psychotherapy interfere with each other when used concurrently in the hospital treatment of the schizophrenic patient. In fact, the opposite would seem to be the case with the evidence suggesting that, if anything, psychotherapy may potentiate the effect of antipsychotic drugs. If there are indeed interferences between these two forms of treatment that were not detected in this study, our results would indicate that they are unlikely to play a major role in determining the outcome of treatment while the patient is in the hospital.

Summary and Conclusions. The controlled studies reviewed above indicate that in general there is little difference between psychotherapy plus drug and drug therapy alone for hospitalized psychotic patients (but not for neurotic outpatients). The combination is, however, quite clearly superior to psychotherapy alone. Table 14.2 summarizes these findings in tabular form.

Drug therapy alone was better than psycho-therapy alone in four out of five studies; in one study of neurotic outpatients, there was no difference.

Combined treatment was better than psychotherapy alone in six out of eight studies. In two studies of mixed outpatients, there was no difference.

There was questionable evidence that combined therapy was superior to drug alone in five out of seven studies. In two inpatient studies, there was no difference.[15]

Uhlenhuth, Lipman, and Covi (1969) present an excellent summary of the different theoretical models for interaction effect and come to much the same conclusion—that, surprisingly consistent across different types of patients, drugs, and psychotherapies, *combined treatment usually offers no greater benefit than pharmacotherapy alone, but is consistently superior to psychotherapy alone.* They add that none of the studies provide evidence for inhibition between treatments, and that the results are mainly compatible with the "reciprocal" concept of interaction; that is, the effect of combined treatments is equivalent to the effect of the "more adequate" treatment alone. By this "reciprocal" model, two "fully adequate" treatments combined produce no greater benefit than each treatment alone; each treatment mobilizes the patient's recovery potential to its very limit.

As far as their formulation applies to the treatment of hospitalized psychotic patients with major ataraxic agents, the evidence is pretty conclusive. I would add only that in these patients, psychotherapy alone seems to have little effect; and that there is some uncertain evidence that in certain areas there may perhaps be some slight advantage to adding psychotherapy to drug therapy—but not enough to justify the addition unless cost and length of stay are of no concern (May, 1968b). However, the evidence in the case of neurotic patients and borderline or outpatient psychotics is much less strong, and perhaps a verdict should be deferred. So far there is nothing to show that drug treatment potentiates or interferes with psychotherapy in these cases—or vice versa—but more research is needed, particularly to study interaction among groups of patients with different severity and duration of neurotic illness.

[15] The adequacy of various types of outcome criteria will be discussed later (page 520).

TABLE 14.2 Summary of Controlled Comparisons of Psychotherapy and Drugs[a]

	Combined Treatment Vs. Drug Alone		Combined Treatment Vs. Psychotherapy Alone		Drug Alone Vs. Psychotherapy Alone	
	??? Better	Same	Better	Same	Better	Same
Schizophrenic In-patients	Cowden, Zax, Hague, and Finney (1956); King (1958); Gorham, Pokorny, Moseley, McReynolds, and Kogan (1964); May and Tuma (1964, 1965a), May (1968).	King (1963)	May and Tuma (1964, 1965a), May (1968); Grinspoon, Ewalt, and Shader (1967, 1968); Shader, Grinspoon, Ewalt, and Zahn (1969); Gorham, Pokorny, Moseley, McReynolds, and Kogan (1964).	Gibbs, Wilkens and Lauterbach (1967); Lorr, McNair, Weinstein, Michaux and Raskin (1961).	Gorham, Pokorny, Moseley, McReynolds, and Kogan (1964); May and Tuma (1964, 1965a); May (1968).	
Mixed In-patients, mainly psychotic		Evangelakis (1961)	Evangelakis (1961)		Evangelakis (1961)	
Mixed Out-patients	Lorr, McNair and Weinstein (1962)				Lorr, McNair, and Weinstein (1962)	
Neurotic Out-patients			Rickels, Catell, Weise, Gray, Yee, Mallin, and Aaronson (1966).			Koegler and Brill (1967)

[a] The entries are tabulated for each type of patient for the results of each of the three possible comparisons among treatments. A semicolon separates each separate study, for which there may be more than one report.

THE NATURE OF DRUG EFFECT

So far the relationship between drugs and psychotherapy has been considered purely in pragmatic clinical terms. To what extent can a conceptual framework be devised that will serve as a guide for practice and research?

Limitations of Experimental Laboratory Studies

Although such experimental effort has been directed to studies of ataraxic drugs in animals, and to laboratory studies of normal human subjects, it is far from clear whether these have any direct application to the clinical situation.

As Cole (1960) makes plain, the controls in experimental laboratory studies may be excellent but, however statistically significant the results, their practical significance remains in doubt. The problems in generalizing from the laboratory to real life are impressive, particularly when one takes into account the probability that disturbed psychiatric patients may respond to drugs differently than normal college students and the fact that almost all laboratory studies of normal subjects deal with single doses of the drug in question.

As Freedman (1959) observes, an investigator who studied the effect of aspirin in children without fever would never have discovered its antipyretic effect. Thus, although clinical observations may often be hard to interpret because of the lack of controls and because it is difficult to disentangle the effect of the drug from the effect of the psychiatric condition for which it is given, the results of clinical observation are likely to be much more relevant. For this reason, the discussion in this section will be largely in the "clinical" frame of reference.

Psychoanalytic Theory

Psychoanalytic theory, with a few outstanding exceptions, has paid little attention to drug effect. In 1961, Azima and Sarwer-Foner discussed two basic conceptual explanations of psychopharmacological events. Drugs, by altering inter- or intraneuronal relationships, may alter the memory traces of internal object relations. This concept, which does not seem to have been taken up by other authors, can be applied particularly when conflicts seem to center around super-ego components, which can be conceptualized as memory traces of actual or fantasied parental relations.

An alternative and more popular view is that drugs affect drives and psychic energy, following in the footsteps of Freud's hope that drugs would be discovered that could alter psychic energy. Ostow (1962) speculates that ataraxic drugs achieve their principal effect by redistributing psychic energies within the psychic

apparatus, and by influencing the amount of psychic energy (erotic and aggressive) available to the ego. Ataraxics, he believes, decrease the amount of instinctual energy available to the ego, by decreasing the rate of energy generation in the id. Since the pathogenic potential of an instinctual impulse is ultimately its strength relative to the hitherto adequate ego control, the major ataraxics offer more than mere relief of symptoms—they actually attenuate the pathogenic conflict by artificial depletion of ego libido. This, Ostow says, is similar to the effect that we strive to achieve by insight psychotherapy, in which, by making the unconscious conscious, we expect to drain off excessive libido.

Kubie (1960) speculates in neurophysiological terms, suggesting that drugs may strengthen controls by altering the level of activity of the nervous system, the threshold or intensity of response to stimulus, emotional modulation, or reverberating circuits.

Winkelman (1957, 1959, 1960) believes that drugs influence all aspects of psychic functioning: they may decrease id impulses, improve ego function and reality testing, and strengthen defenses. Azima, a pioneer in this field[16], (1959) hypothesized a shift in ego organization from paranoid to manic-depressive position; a change in cathexis, particularly of aggressive impulses towards external objects, with investment of the internal objects system of control, improved response to reality and object relationships, a partial abandonment of schizophrenic defenses of withdrawal and splitting; a change in mood toward elation; and a shift from an experiential state of being in bits to wholeness. Sarwer-Foner (1963) points out that although Azima speaks of instinctual drives, he is describing in Kleinian terms shifts in the continuum of ego defenses, and postulating a *redistribution* of psychic energy rather than the *decrease* hypothesized by Ostow.

Sarwer-Foner (1961, 1963) says that the instincts remain unchanged, but the methods of discharge and expression are modified. The

[16] To Azima and his group belongs the credit for being the first investigators to use a double-blind controlled experiment to investigate a psychoanalytically oriented hypothesis about drug action. Their publications, arrested by Azima's untimely death, are basic readings in this field—Azima, 1959; Azima and Sarwer-Foner, 1961; Azima, Cramer-Azima, and DeVerteuil, 1956, 1959; Azima, Azima, and Cleghorn, 1959; Azima, Azima, and Durost, 1959a, 1959b; and Azima, Sangowicz, Spindler, and Azima, 1959.

pharmacological effects as perceived by the patient, cause him to change his own perceptions of himself and of the nature of his ability to control his conflicts. Sarwer-Foner's explanation is therefore ego oriented—the effect on libidinal and aggressive energies is indirect.

Behavioral Toxicity

A fundamental question is whether ataraxic drugs cause adverse effects that interfere with psychotherapy.[17] Cole has sponsored the clinical application of the concept of behavioral toxicity, a term first used by Brady (1959) to describe the objective adverse effects of drugs on animal response in the operant situation. However, any broad consideration of behavioral toxicity in man must take into account the wider subjective and objective changes outlined in Cole's review (1960), and that of DiMascio and Shader (1968), which form the basis for the ensuing discussion.

Almost any drug, if given in great quantity, will produce adverse effects of some type, usually even death. Such effects are to be distinguished from behavioral toxicity, a term applied to unpleasant effects that appear when a drug is given in its usual therapeutic dosage; or in almost any patient if moderately large doses are used.

It is always a value judgement whether effects are to be labeled "therapeutic" (*good*) or "toxic" (*bad*). Behavioral toxicity, Cole remarks, like beauty, may on occasion be chiefly in the observer's eye: increased aggression may be improvement to the therapist, and an intolerable nuisance to the nurse. Stimulation or slowing of mental processes, or mood suppression, may be considered adverse for one patient and desirable for another; they may help a patient at one stage of his illness but hinder in another.

Excessive sedation, or paradoxical depression, agitation, hyperactivity, confusion, or delirium, are gross examples of behavioral toxicity. But are there more subtle adverse effects? In the absence of controlled studies of neurotic outpatients, there is no evidence to confirm or deny the possibility that drugs may cause adverse

effects by suppressing "good" anxiety. It is entirely possible that they may merely affect pathological anxiety. Concern has also been expressed about the effect of drugs on learning in children. However, as Cole points out, the only relevant controlled study showed that chlorpromazine improved reading skill in children with learning disability.

A similar problem is the effect of drugs on driving. DiMascio and Shader (1968) comment that despite the fact that it is widely concluded that this must be a serious problem, there is very little documented evidence. "Either the patients take extreme heed of the warnings, or our fears, based on extrapolation from clinical impressions and laboratory tests are groundless."

Individual Differences in Response

A central issue is that of individual differences in response. In general, the findings are that, although in some cases drugs improve functioning to facilitate psychotherapy or sociotherapy, in other cases there may be difficulty in stimulating interest and motivation, particularly in those whose initial level is more "normal," or with too high a dose. However, the impairment that occurs as a side effect may well be selective rather than generalized, and may be correctable by suitable psychologic means, such as reinforcement (Latz, 1963) or by giving a second supplemental medication, so that side effects are not necessarily insuperable.

In his review, Uhr (1960) concludes that although in normals drugs impair speed and coordinated psychomotor and simple perceptual skills, they consistently improve performance under stress and, apparently by lowering anxiety level, definitely affect motivation. This effect does not lead to improved performance in normal subjects who work at simple, straightforward tasks. But when tests are chosen because they are sensitive to and disrupted by anxiety, or when high anxiety levels are induced by stressors, performance tends to be improved. He comments that most studies of patients show an increase in intelligence level after drug therapy, but it seems reasonable to hypothesize that this represents a lessening of disruption

---

[17] Investigators never seem to ask the opposite question—whether psychotherapy might interfere with drug effect. This reviewer has not come across any experimental laboratory study to test this particular hypothesis.

rather than any direct effect of drug upon performance. (For additional material and references see May, 1968c).

Variables have been identified that determine whether the response of a particular individual will be favorable or not. Shimkunas, Gynther, and Smith (1966) found that the abstracting ability of high IQ patients increased markedly with phenothiazines, while low IQ patients did not change; and Fish, Shapiro, and Campbell (1966) found that speech-impaired schizophrenic children were significantly more responsive to drug than to nondrug therapy. This did not apply if speech impairment was mild; in fact, some of these patients became retarded and lethargic on the drug.

An interesting finding by Goldstein, Judd, Rodnick, and LaPolla (in press, 1969) is that phenothiazine medication elaborates *different* patterns of behavioral change in schizophrenics with good and poor premorbid adjustments. In the good premorbids, reduced arousal is associated with greater responsivity to changes in the environment and with avoidance behavior to threat; in the poor premorbids, with lessened responsivity to the environment and vigilance for threat. If we consider that good and poor premorbid patients were probably differentially responsive to their environments prior to their psychotic episodes, it may be that phenothiazine medication returns each type of patient to his premorbid style of coping, permitting relatively more appropriate behavior to reappear (Goldstein et al., in press, 1969).

Popular Misconceptions

Hamilton (1964) states forcibly that the nature of the ataraxic drug effect has been the subject of popular misconceptions:

Never has a group of drugs been more remarkably misnamed. Judging by their action on anxiety states and on agitated depressions, they have almost no tranquilizing effect at all. On the contrary, severe anxiety may develop in patients who have been loaded with toxic doses and it improves on stopping the drug.

Dews (1966) feels the same way:

There is no support for the unduly assumed specific effect of chlorpromazine on anxiety. Perusal of the literature inclines one to the view that a specific effect of chlorpromazine on anxiety is something that is accepted by the clinicians because they believe that it has been proved experimentally and by laboratory workers because they believe it to be a clinical fact.

He also casts doubt on the traditional notion that motivation, emotion, and learning are the selective targets of drug action (1965, 1966), questioning the validity of previous conditioning experiments.

Freyhan (1959) comments similarly ". . . the name assigned to them: tranquilizers . . . is morphologically too seductive, pharmacologically too unspecific, and in terms of results not infrequently untrue."

The findings of Klein (1962), Azima (1959), and Lorr, McNair, Weinstein, Michaux, and Raskin (1961) that there was no uniform effect on agitation or anxiety and that patients on active drugs verbalized more hostility than psychotherapy patients fit in with these comments. Klerman, DiMascio, Havens, and Snell (1960) point out that "tranquilizer," the term most popular in North America, was not used by the original French investigators of chlorpromazine. Laborit, the first to use chlorpromazine in psychiatric patients, employed the term *stabilisateur végétatif*, while Delay and Deniker introduced the concept of *neuroleptic* action.

Freyhan (1955) criticizes the "chemical lobotomy" theory. Whereas psychosurgery produces an ego-identical loss of affective tension, ego identity persists with drugs; the patient is aware of change and of its relativity.

In our own controlled study, drugs had little effect on the overt manifestations of anxiety, agitated overactivity, or aggression; but they did produce considerable improvement in terms of ego functioning. It is of particular interest that for the hospitalized schizophrenic patient, psychotherapy alone did not lead to any greater level of insight than milieu therapy. Drugs alone, however, had a significant beneficial effect. The point is, of course, that the insight of the restituted schizophrenic patient has to do more with reality testing than with a real understanding of internal dynamics (see page 520). The findings suggest that, at this stage of the illness, insight is a secondary development in the process of recovery. As ego-functioning is restored, so reality testing improves, and the patient develops the capacity to see himself and his illness in a more realistic way. Deeper psychological understanding may come later, if at all, after restitution has been achieved and consolidated.

Aronson (1968) comments that the insight gained by drugs is the increased awareness of some of those aspects of reality that had been blotted out as a blanket defensive operation. Drugs enable the blotting out to be selective rather than total, thus leading to some return to awareness of elements of the psychological situation. This "insight," however, may only be maintained if the selective blotting out is buttressed by drugs, alteration in the family situation, supportive relationship with the therapist, and the like.

It is my impression that the balance of the evidence is in favor of the hypothesis that drug-induced restitution is primarily a matter of improving ego-functioning, and that affective change is secondary or of secondary importance (May, 1968b). If accepted, this would support very strongly the integrated use of drugs and psychotherapy, the latter becoming more relevant as ego-functioning improves.

Nonspecific Factors in Drug Response

The introduction of drug therapy stimulated a wave of research that concentrated first on the factors involved in the placebo effect, and then subsequently on the more fundamental concept of the nonspecific factors involved in response to drug therapy—and, one might add, to any form of therapy including psychotherapy.

A fundamental distinction is made by Freedman (1966), who distinguishes between *drug action* expressed in biochemical language and *drug effect* determined by multiple factors and surrounding conditions. Along the same line, Von Baeyer (1964) distinguishes *eigenwirkung*—phenomena produced directly by the treatment method itself rather than the individual reaction of the patient.

Sarwer-Foner (see references in footnote, page 505) explains that outcome is not due to pharmacological action alone, but also to the interaction between the pharmacological effect as perceived by the patient, the patient's defenses, and the total situation (including the social setting, transference, and counter-

transference factors). Why, how, by whom, and in what context and with what intention, he is given a drug becomes important.

A superb summary statement of this field is the group of papers edited by Rickels (1968), which will bring the reader thoroughly up to date on work in this important area. Rickels enumerates as major nonspecific factors affecting the outcome of drug therapy, the patient's heredity, personality and social class; his attitudes and expectations; his feelings toward the physician; treatment milieu influences such as the physician's personality and attitude; his expectations, needs and countertransference feelings; and the attitudes and expectations of the family and others outside the direct treatment milieu (1964, 1965, 1966, 1968). He penetrates the mythology and clinical superstition that surround the placebo effect to make three important points: (1) nonspecific factors influence improvement on active drugs differently from improvement on placebo therapy. (2) they influence not only improvement, but also attention and reporting of side reactions; and (3) in many respects, patients who respond well to an active drug resemble those who are commonly believed to be suitable only for psychotherapy.

For example, patients low in intelligence and low on anxiety improve more on placebo but not on drug therapy than anxious intelligent patients. By contrast, patients with an IQ above the median had a higher percentage of improvement on drug therapy, and the outcome with drug therapy is better when the patient has favorable attitudes to the hospital, clinic and physician; is more emotionally minded and less hypochondriacal; and is from a higher social class. Agreeing with Winkleman (1964), Rickels finds that patients from a lower social class drop out more frequently from therapy than higher social-class patients, both on drug and placebo therapy. Lower-class patients also deviate more from prescribed dosage and report more side reactions—except that higher-class patients are more troubled by sedative side effects.

"Acquiescers", that is, people who tend to agree uncritically with authoritatively stated generalizations and cliches, pose a special problem. Contrary to what might be expected from current mythology, nonacquiescers respond better to active drug than to placebo therapy, and acquiescers do poorly. This has been formulated by McNair, Kahn, Droppleman, and Fisher (1968) as the problem of "the inexpert witness." Perhaps acquiescers are thoughtless and nondiscriminating rather than compliant conformers. Their adverse response to active drug may reflect a combination of unreliable reporting, with an exaggerated, diffuse, nondiscriminating, concerned response to somatic cues produced by the drug.

Cole, Bonato, and Goldberg (1968), Hamilton (1968), and Rickels (1968) point out that nonspecific effects are more important in neurotic patients than in psychotics; and in determining response to a placebo, minor ataraxics, and psychotherapy than to major ataraxics. Another important observation is that drugs affect both the primary and secondary symptoms of schizophrenia, and placebos only the secondary symptoms—and then less than drugs.

Paradoxical Response

The concept of nonspecific effects has been fruitfully extended to the occasional occurrence of a paradoxical response to drugs (excitement, agitation). Adherents of a *specific* explanation maintain that these are entirely physiologically determined, a toxicity akin to the extrapyramidal reactions. Adherents of a *nonspecific* explanation suggest that they are primarily psychological defensive reactions determined by basic personality characteristics.

Sarwer-Foner (see references in footnote, page 505) was the first to suggest that personality organization centered around physical activity or preoccupation with body image and body integrity might be a critical factor, basing this on his observation that certain pychotic patients disintegrated further and became more anxious on reserpine and chlorpromazine. This hypothesis has been substantially supported by the experiments of Klerman, DiMascio, Greenblatt, and Rinkel (1959); Henninger, DiMascio, and Klerman (1965); and DiMascio (1968). In their early work they identified two clusters of individuals designated as *Type A's* (extroverted,

assertive, nonanxious, athletic, aggressive and mesomorphic individuals organized about psychomotor activity, conscious mastery of inner impulses, and action) and *Type B's* (aesthetic, inhibited, endomorphic, introverted, passive, anxious intellectuals). These contrasting personality types differed in their responses to phenyltolaxamine, reserpine, and a placebo.

Phenyltolaxamine's sedative action elicited negative feelings in *Type A* subjects, who regarded restriction of their muscular activity as threatening, even though they performed better on psychomotor and arithmetic tests than the *Type B's*. Reserpine elicited negative attitudes from *Type B* patients, who found its visceral effects a source of concern.

In later work, it was found that the *Type A's* reacted negatively to chlorpromazine and secobarbital, becoming negative, irritable, unhappy, and apprehensive. They felt less rapport with the psychiatrist, and showed confusion and impaired learning. *Type B's*, on the other hand, were tranquil and indifferent. They felt more rapport with the psychiatrist,[18] improved on tests of intellectual functioning, and reported no negative feelings towards the drug. Trifluoperazine made both *A's* and *B's* more clumsy, slower, and less in control—but there were no differences between the personality types.

It was hypothesized that persons who worry about their bodies will react negatively to drugs with perceptible effects on autonomic and visceral functioning. For persons with a deep fear of passivity, who use activity as a defense against repressed and unacceptable passive-feminine identifications, sedation and psychomotor retardation are threats to their self-image and ego-identity—and drugs that produce these effects will generate behavioral disorganization.

In further work, DiMascio (1968) has delimited another type of paradoxical reaction. Anxious normals (many of whom had had prior psychiatric treatment) responded to minor tranquilizers (diazepam, chlordiazepoxide, oxazepam) with a lowered anxiety level, while a

---

[18] The psychiatrist rated *both* types as having less rapport—a commentary on the fallibility of such ratings. It is perhaps relevant that the Carl Rogers group (1967) found that with schizophrenic patients,

therapists tended to make considerably more favorable evaluations of the therapist-patient relationship than did their patients.

paradoxical reaction (increased anxiety) was noted in the nonanxious subjects[19].

Paradoxical responses may occur more frequently in children, who, as is well-known for morphine and sedative-hypnotics, do not respond to medication in the same way as adults.

Persistence of Drug Effect

There is solid evidence that taking a patient off drugs poses important problems relevant to combined treatment with psychotherapy.

There is no stable relationship between the length of time that a drug is excreted after it has been discontinued, and the patient's behavior (Kurland, 1965; Kurland, Huang, Hallam, and Hanlon, 1965); and therefore it is necessary to be flexible rather than arbitrary in the management of this phase of treatment. Gradual and carefully supervised withdrawal is indicated by the findings that withdrawal from higher doses produced greater decrements in adaptive behavior, and smaller changes in the stimulus situation produce smaller decrements (Miller, 1966). Elkes's (1966) statement that ". . . behavior can be an exquisitely sensitive instrument in monitoring biochemical change" should support the clinician in relying on his observations of the patient, rather than on chemical tests.

Miller (1966) and Otis (1964) have demonstrated that therapeutic gains on drugs may be tied to the drug condition. A practical conclusion is to select the dose that causes the least blocking of the patient's receptiveness to new learning and the least deviation from the nondrugged condition. Keeping a patient on higher doses than necessary to control symptoms may work against final therapeutic gains, for not only is he likely to be at a disadvantage in new learning, but whatever is learned may be so conditioned to the drug state that it may not survive when he is taken off.

Ray, Ragland, and Clark (1964), in a double-blind placebo-controlled study, found that carry-over effect from drug to nondrug condition was selective—patients retained their gains on some variables but not on others. They comment that an active training or special psychotherapeutic program during drug therapy might produce enduring gain, whereas the mere passive administration of drugs would not.

RESEARCH IMPLICATIONS

Outcome Criteria

This section will focus on a number of outcome criterion problems that have been discussed in the literature on controlled studies of drugs and psychotherapy. To avoid needless repetition, it will be assumed that the reader recognizes that the questions raised are equally pertinent to both forms of treatment; that double standards of evaluation have no place in science; that there is considerable room for methodological progress in outcome research in general; and that, in terms of controlled studies and methodological sophistication, pharmacotherapy must be considered to be the most intensively and soberly studied method of treatment at the present time. By comparison, there has been little published systematic evaluation of psychotherapy—a situation by no means independent of the relatively meager and rather confused state of psychotherapy research in general (Tuma, 1968).

Controlled studies that use symptomatic and behavioral criteria of change are often challenged on the grounds that disappearance of symptoms may be the result of changes in the patient's life circumstances without any "real" improvement in the underlying disease process, and that evaluation is impossible because so many factors play a role in an individual's emotional life that we cannot adequately evaluate all of them. This is, in fact, a powerful argument for the kind of randomized assignment to control and experimental groups that is customarily employed in such studies.

It is also maintained that it is important to measure effects at deeper and more abstract levels. This is surely no reason for ignoring the

---

[19] In this area, the research methodologist may wish to concern himself with what I will call the problem of "bounded variation." Those who score at the top or at the bottom of a scale can only move in one direction; patients who are absolutely healthy can only get worse, and those who are maximally sick can only move in the direction of health. (This phenomenon has also been referred to as regression toward the mean).

manifestations of change, whatever they may be, and it is perhaps a little presumptuous to derogate symptomatic improvement. After all, many of the remedies that are most effective in the practice of medicine act "symptomatically" rather than "curatively." Insulin revolutionized the treatment of diabetes, yet its action is corrective and not curative. Digitalis does not cure the diseased heart, yet it facilitates the all-important transformation from functional breakdown to compensation. The effect of drugs on restoration of function may call for similar therapeutic goals (Freyhan, 1959). Symptom relief is not the only goal of therapy, but it is a legitimate goal and so is restoration of function which is closely related. Gliedman, Nash, Imber, Stone, and Frank (1958) point out that when symptoms prevent the healthy part of the personality from functioning adequately, relief from symptoms may well liberate a person's capacities and so lead to a more general restoration of function.

In this respect, Alexander (1966) has emphasized that healing is possible only because of the regenerative faculties of the organism. Nature, not the physician, heals. The surfaces of a wound grow together because of the regenerative powers of the organism. The surgeon can favor this healing process but he cannot initiate it. The same is true for psychotherapy and psychoanalysis.

At one time it was assumed that insight was necessary for "genuine" improvement, whereas improvements without insight would be spurious or temporary. It is now well known that rapid "transference cures" often persist without further treatment, and that marked personality change may take place in following years, with further ego maturation. On the other hand, a considerable number of patients have a great deal of insight into their psychodynamic mechanisms without being able to change. The differentiation between intellectual and emotional insight expresses an awareness of this problem, and a cynic might observe that it is apparently only symptoms and behavior that are truly important, since "intellectual" insight

is insight *without* symptomatic and behavioral improvement, whereas "emotional" insight is insight *with* such change.

Moreover the fundamentals" proposed by the critics are, in fact, abstractions and interpretations based on lower-order observations. Thus, in the end, they are completely dependent on observation of behavior and symptoms. The as-yet unanswered question is whether any particular system and higher-order factor offers more valid predictions than others—or than the basic observations themselves.

As Guze and Murphy (1963) comment, assertions that drug therapy is "superficial" or "only supportive" are incompatible with a scholarly and scientific approach. It would seem perfectly proper to assume that patterns of adjustment developed over a life span are not likely to be modified easily, and to suspect the idea that short-term—or even long-term—treatment of any kind can promote radical change. But there is little information about the possible occurrence of change at deeper or more abstract levels or over a prolonged period of follow-up during either drug therapy or psychotherapy, and certainly no experimental support whatsoever for the notion that more such change occurs during psychotherapy than during an equivalent period of drug therapy.

The admonition to consider long-term outcome is a well-established custom of the pundits —yet there is considerable doubt whether a follow-up study has any value except as a piece of history (May, 1965b).

Elkes (1967) has drawn attention eloquently to the fact that a great measure of our ignorance of the nature of psychotropic drug effects in man may be attributed to neglect of their essentially personal and subjective nature. Overt behavior, including the ordinary tools of language, can be but a segment of the evidence; the larger portion lies within and will require special new, and in many ways novel, techniques for its adequate description, let alone understanding. A number of possibilities will be mentioned briefly.

Gottschalk and his associates[20] used introspection and free association. In one study,

---

[20] The following references are relevant: Gottschalk, 1960a, 1960b; Gottschalk and Gleser, 1960; Gottschalk and Hambidge, 1955; Gottschalk and Kaplan, 1958; Gottschalk, Gleser, and Hambidge, 1957; Gottschalk, Gleser, Springer, Kaplan, Shanon, and Ross, 1960; Gottschalk, Kapp, Ross, Kaplan, Silver, Macleod, Kahn, Van Maanen, and Acheson, 1956; Kaplan, Gottschalk, and Fleming, 1957.

trained subjects discriminated reliably by introspective self-observation between the psychologic affects of pipradrol and a placebo. In other
studies, a modified free-association technique
was used with verbal analysis from tape recordings of word types and psychodynamic themes
to provide indices of masochistic trends, social
alienation, and disorganization; to differentiate
between genuine and false suicide notes; and to
distinguish between pipradrol and a placebo and
between perphenazine and a placebo.

In the past, investigations of dreams have
been limited to the capriciousness or defensiveness of memory. The discovery that dreams are
associated with characteristic rapid eyemove-
ments and EEG patterns has made it possible to
awaken the dreamer immediately during or after
a dream. This insures recall and bypasses a
substantial amount of secondary elaboration
and distortion, a technique that has been used
(to study the effects of drugs) by Whitman,
Pierce, and Maas (1960); Whitman, Pierce,
Maas and Baldridge (1961); Whitman (1963);
and Kramer, Whitman, Baldridge, and Ornstein (1966).

It seems to be generally agreed that objective
assessment of ego functions is in order. The first
steps in this direction appear in the Menninger
Foundation Psychotherapy Research Project
(Wallerstein, Robbins, Sargent, and Luborsky,
1956; Wallerstein, Robbins, Sargent, Luborsky,
Fabian, Hale, Ticho, Ticho, Modlin, Faris, and
Voth, 1958; Wallerstein, Robbins, and Hall,
1960.) More recently, other investigators have
made further contributions towards progress in
this area, such as Prelinger and Zimet (1964);
Karush, Easser, Cooper, and Swerdloff (1964);
Cooper, Karush, Easser, and Swerdloff (1965);
Bellak and Hurvich (1967); and Bellak, Hur-
vich, Silvan, and Jacobs (1968).

Nowlis (1960) reviews methods that might be
used to study drug effects on group functioning. Elkes (1966) has observed that the study of
verbal behavior and linguistics holds great
promise. Of particular interest in this respect are
the computer-based anthropologic-linguistic
matrix techniques applied to analyzing the
patterns of schizophrenic language (Tokar and
Stefflre, 1969; Tokar, Stefflre, and Harding,
1969). These offer exciting possibilities for
identifying basic dimensions in thought disorder and in psychotherapy and drug effects,
and are now being applied to studies of the
effects of marihuana and ataraxic drugs (Tokar,
1969).

Intensive Versus Extensive Design

In the psychotherapy literature there is much
emphasis on the advantage of the intensive
longitudinal study of the individual, often
referred to as an "intensive" research design
(Chassan, 1967).

The work of Azima, one of the pioneers in
the psychoanalytic study of the nature of
ataraxic drug effect, is an outstanding model of
a careful and rigorous approach using an intensive design. To take an example, Azima, Azima,
and Durost (1959b) studied ten schizophrenic
patients in a double-blind intensive design,
using the patient as his own control under four
experimental conditions—no drug; phenobarbital; reserpine; and no drug. During the
second and third periods patients received
reserpine or phenobarbital in random fashion,
not all patients receiving the same drug at one
time. The experimenters studied three dimensions of psychic structure (ego; instinctual
drives; and object relations), using three sectors
of observation (behavior, mood, and thought)
from which to infer these dimensions. For interview material, which was obtained twice weekly,
they used two independent observers, one of
whom did the interviewing. The psychologist
tested the patients independently and did a
blind analysis of the data.

Bellak and his associates have performed a
number of intensive studies along these lines,
such as a study of the effects of an antidepressant combination on depressive symptoms, in
which clinical ratings were used to tap conscious
material; projective techniques were used for
pre-conscious and unconscious indicators, and
dreams were collected to evaluate unconscious
elements (Bellak, Salk and Rosenhan, 1961).
This particular study did not show any statistically reliable differences between drug and
placebo, but a similar appraisal in a subsequent
study (Bellak and Rosenberg, 1966) supported
the hypothesis that the imipraminelike non-
MAO[21] inhibitor antidepressants strengthen

---

[21] Monoamine oxidase inhibition is a biochemical characteristic of certain antidepressant drugs.

controlling functions, whereas the MAO inhibitors produce affective arousal.

Bellak, Hurvich, Silvan, and Jacobs (1968) point out (correctly) that with the usual controlled study model (which they refer to as *extensive* design) there may be inequality in the treatment groups, which results in a lack of sensitivity, due to the "noise" effects of background factors. They go on to assert that it is difficult, with an extensive design, to determine which patient characteristics are related to treatment effects, because of the large number of relevant variables in relation to the number of patients. It would seem to me that this particular point applies with even greater force to *intensive* design. No matter how deep and sophisticated, an analysis of *one* patient will only tell you what happened in *one* instance; what may happen to *other* patients or to *other types* of patients is purely a matter of speculation until the experiment has been repeated with a sufficient number of different patients. Thus in the end the *extensive* model has to apply. It would seem that *intensive* design has its main application in exploratory hypothesis-seeking, and that the eventual solution may lie in attempting to reap the advantages of both models. Bellak, Hurvich, Silvan, and Jacobs (1968) suggest combining an extensive design with an intensive design study of a limited number of the subjects. This might be an acceptable compromise if resources are limited and the statistical problems of intensive design can be worked through.

Gottschalk (1968) comments on the advantages of intensive design with repeated giving of a drug and its withdrawal from the same person over a relatively long period of time. He points out, however, that there are special not-to-be ignored—and as yet unresolved—statistical problems created by the use of repeated measures of change. It is not generally recognized that intensive design poses formidable problems in data collection and analysis. Moreover, repeated administration and withdrawal of a treatment (drug) confounds the effect of the treatment (drug) with the effect of the conditioned response to the circumstances surrounding earlier administrations and withdrawals. (cf. the literature on nonspecific factors in drug response, reviewed on pages 518 to 519).

Uhlenhuth, Lipman, and Covi (1969) refer to this particular defect. They make plain that unrecognized carry-over effects from one medication period to another may confound the results; and that studies based on intensive design cannot demonstrate true interaction between drugs and psychotherapy, since it is assumed that any effects must be additive, and the psychotherapeutic factor is usually treated as constant—a questionable assumption, since clinical experience suggests that psychotherapeutic gain is uneven and occurs in spurts.

A possible solution to some of the particular statistical problems created by the collection of data at repeated points in time may lie in the concept of process analysis, presented by Dixon and May (1969). In this article, a number of preliminary ideas on appropriate mathematical models for the analysis of process (as dynamic change over time) are examined and contrasted with orthodox conventional static analysis (of status at any one point in time).

An important defect of the usual statistical analysis in an *extensive* design experiment is that a "statistically significant" effect may actually reflect a true effect in a very few patients or even in a single patient (Chassan, 1967). This problem of extreme or unusual cases (so-called "outliers") is likely to become a focus of increasing research attention. One possible solution is "Winsorising," successfully applied to psychiatric data by Dixon and May (1968) as a method of investigating the applicability of observed rules to "the usual case." This procedure removes the major distorting effect of "outliers" by replacing extreme values with less extreme ones.

The reverse side of the coin is the possibility that the effect of a particular (treatment) drug—or of a particular patient characteristic—may appear only in extreme or unusual cases. A possible approach here is the "Advantage Score," (May, and Forsythe 1969; Forsythe, May, and Engleman, 1969). By computing the advantage of one treatment (or characteristic) over another, attention can be focused on any particular group of deviant cases—for instance, those with an unusually good or bad response.

Controls

Likely avenues for future development are,

on the one hand, a study of ways to resolve the difficulties and problems that are created by attempting to combine drug therapy with psychotherapy and, on the other hand, an attempt to identify predictive factors that will assist in the more appropriate selection of the best treatment or combination for the individual patient. Uhlenhuth, Lipman, and Covi (1968) suggest that the role of psychotherapy may be clarified by including assessments of the effect of psychotherapy alone and pharmacotherapy alone in the designs of future studies. One should be careful, however, to keep in mind Cole's observation (1968) that the currently available evidence would make most clinical investigators reluctant to place acutely ill schizophrenics on psychotherapy without drugs for any prolonged period. In short, the ethics of the matter would dictate that such a design could be considered only for nonschizophrenic patients.

It should be noted that, in the past, even experienced and prominent investigators have often failed entirely to control administration of ataraxic drugs in studies that examined the outcome of psychotherapy in schizophrenic patients; for example, Rogers, Gendlin, Keiser, and Truax, (1967); and Fairweather, Simon, Gebhard, Weingarten, Holland, Sanders, Stone, and Reahl (1960). Considering what we now know of the existence of powerful drug effects, the results of these studies must be considered inadmissible as a measure of the efficacy of psychotherapy alone, and of dubious value as a measure of the efficacy of psychotherapy combined with drugs. Psychotherapy research investigators must realize that we have now reached the point of knowledge when confounding of drug and psychotherapy effects is totally unacceptable.

Heterogeneity of Psychotherapy

Controlled comparisons of psychotherapy with drugs (or a control group) have sometimes been depreciated on the grounds that "psychotherapy" is a relatively heterogeneous set of interventions, some quite powerful and some quite weak, whereas drugs are relatively homogeneous. Thus, the story goes, the controls are inappropriate and the research is asking the wrong question; it may be of practical value to

know that average heterogeneous psychotherapy is relatively ineffective, but this does not advance the field much.

Unfortunately for this argument, we have not arrived at the point where we are no longer concerned with the average state of affairs. Indeed, I would hope that one of the primary concerns would be to establish, define, or develop techniques for use by the average therapist—otherwise, investigation may become increasingly detached from reality and preoccupied with tiny details or with methods that have little practical value or are only of heuristic worth. Some of us, studying the results of controlled "average" research, may think that some practices *should* (for the usual therapist, at any rate) be on their death bed for the treatment of certain closely defined groups (such as hospitalized schizophrenics). But the evidence for other groups of patients is so meager and so poorly controlled that a confident verdict cannot be given; it is certainly not of sufficient quality to support a conclusion that effectiveness is confined to a therapeutic aristocracy or to a particular technique.

It is, of course, true that the ultimate goal is to pick the right treatment for the right patient. But this is no justification for neglecting the average. Sophisticated outcome research in this day and age is well aware that the question, "What kind of treatment produces what kind of change in what kind of patient, and under what conditions?" contains two components—an average and deviations from the average.

We must be careful not to allow narcissism to masquerade as a problem in research methodology. The heterogeneity platform is a variant of "If only I had done the therapy. . . ." or "If only you had done it my way. . . ."—an a priori assumption of effectiveness that cannot be accepted as a defense against controls, to bypass the question of the effectiveness of psychotherapy. Overlooked is the fact that in these controlled studies the psychotherapists believed that what they were doing was effective for the kind of patient they were treating. In this respect it may be salutary to recall the experience of Teuber and Powers (1953). The control group and insistence on objective description seemed slightly blasphemous to some of their counselors, like a statistical test of the efficacy of prayer. They insisted that relationships had a value in themselves, irrespective of their possible effect on behavior, and they were not perturbed when the seemingly negative results became known. Other counselors felt that research was superflous, since all the necessary rules of therapy were already known. When informed of the outcome, they reacted in a characteristic fashion: those who were analytically trained and oriented asserted that the results would have been positive had analytic principles been applied by all staff members. Conversely, those who were followers of Carl Rogers' approach averred that a systematic use of non-directive methods would have produced more definite success.

Undoubtedly a wide number of different approaches (each with varying numbers of advocates and detractors) may be subsumed under the rubric of "psychotherapy." But this has no validity whatsoever as an argument against comparison with a control group. Rather, it is a powerful plea to specify the nature and amount of psychotherapy that is believed to be effective as carefully as the psychopharmacologist does for drug therapy— and then put it to the test of a control group. If the psychotherapist maintains that psychotherapy is good for all types of patients, then the comparison will be for all patients. If, like Meehl (1965), he believes that it is suitable for only a small percentage, then he should specify the criteria for selection and submit them to the test of controlled comparison. He should do likewise if he believes that only a few therapists are effective. Bergin (1967), commenting on the deplorable lack of commitment to scientific inquiry in the field of psychotherapy and the unwillingness of many therapists to open their practice to objective scrutiny, remarks that it has been conservatively estimated that there are at least thirty-six identifiable systems of therapy. If, he says, proper attention were paid by the originators of these systems to empirically evaluating their approaches, there would probably be fewer systems, less dogmatism, and more people getting better.

Meehl (1965) has the opinion that the negative results of control group comparisons can be attributed to the fact that psychotherapy is actually appropriate for only 25 percent of the clients currently in treatment, and that only 25 percent of practicing therapists are competent in the art, yielding only a 6 percent chance that the psychotherapy being studied meets the criterion of decent practice. This is hardly an argument against a control group—in fact, Meehl recommends that patients be selected as suitable for psychotherapy and then assigned at random to treatment and control groups treated by selected experts. And I would disagree profoundly with the statement that we should not be interested in outcome studies that fail to meet this narrow design. Evidence that shows the kind of results that are obtained *in general by most psychotherapists* would be very welcome—to the patient and to the taxpayer, if to no one else. And comparison with the results of drug therapy given by the same therapists may contribute substantially to our basic understanding of the nature of psychotherapy effect and so to a clearer definition of "who, when, why, and for whom?"

Length of Treatment

Grinspoon, Ewalt, and Shader comment (1968) that in discussing comparisons of psychotherapy with drugs there are those who would argue that even nearly two years of psychotherapy with exceptionally well-qualified therapists is not enough time to draw any meaningful conclusions about its usefulness in chronic schizophrenic patients—that it takes five or even ten years of psychotherapy with sick patients to accomplish anything substantial, let alone to effect a cure. They point out that, if this were the case, then intensive psychotherapy as a treatment for chronic schizophrenic patients would have merely heuristic worth, since it would be available for only an infinitesimally small number. Moreover, since after almost two years of psychotherapy little or no change occurred in their patients, by extrapolation one might question whether any number of years would affect a fundamental alteration.

Therapist Characteristics

It may be important in studies of drugs and psychotherapy to control or assess certain covarying therapist characteristics. Uhlenhuth, Lipman, and Covi (1969) recommend comparing results at different levels of experience;

empathy, warmth, and genuineness; A-B scale scores; and Strong Vocational Interest Scale scores.

These recommendations are based on the fact that it is possible to criticize a number of the controlled studies that compare psychotherapy unfavorably with drug therapy—or that obtained unfavorable results with psychotherapy alone—on the grounds that it is difficult to evaluate whether the psychotherapy was effectively given. It must be pointed out, however, that it is necessary to avoid the trap of circular reasoning. If psychotherapy is deemed *effective* only if it is *successful*, then obviously this will lead to a circular conclusion that psychotherapy is 100 percent *successful*, when given effectively!! A possible solution is to obtain a rating of the therapist that is independent of success with the cases under study. This was obtained in our own study (May, 1968b), but the results of the relevant analysis are not yet available. The only analysis of this type reported in the literature is Koegler and Brill (1967), who, in their study of outpatient neurotics, found no relationship between outcome and rankings of therapist effectiveness (by the therapists themselves and by peers).

A number of reviewers and investigators, making the plausible (but questionable) assumption that experience relates directly to effectiveness, express the view that studies should include only highly experienced therapists. Quite apart from the corollary of this assumption—that psychotherapy can have only limited value and application if this is true—there is unfortunately very little satisfactory evidence that experienced therapists get any better results than inexperienced therapists, except for comparisons with beginners who have had virtually no previous experience in a therapist-patient (or physician-patient) relationship. In fact, there are a number of studies in which experienced therapists did not obtain any better results than a control group; for example, Teuber and Powers, 1953; Barron and Leary, 1955; Horwitz, Polatin, Kolb, and Hoch, 1958; Bookhammer, Meyers, Schober, and Piotrowski, 1966; Rogers, Gendlin, Keiser, and Truax, 1967; Grinspoon, Ewalt, and Shader, 1967.

Lichtenberg (1958) and Betz and Whitehorn (1956) report that there was no difference in the results of residents, whatever the length of their experience, and Lehrman (1961) and Wheelis (1956) have discussed the mechanism by which some experienced therapists may make psychotherapy patients worse. It is also necessary to point out that if it is reasonable to assume that experienced therapists get better results with psychotherapy, they may also give drug therapy more effectively and get better results with that form of treatment too.

A major discussion of "A" and "B" Type therapists, and of scores on the Strong Vocational Interest Blank, would take us too far afield at this junction, but it is appropriate to point out that the A-B literature is in some respects (such as overlapping samples and a number of different A-B scales) confusing; and that cross-validation of the A-B concept leaves much to be desired. Stephens and Astrup (1965) found no correlation between patients' condition at discharge or follow-up and their therapist's A-B type; and in a study of four A-B scale methods, only 27 of 63 physicians were classified in the same way by all four scales.

Koegler and Brill (1967) found no correlation between A-B type and outcome, and—interestingly—they found no evidence that those therapists who were more positive in their attitude towards psychotherapy were any more successful than those who were less positive.

Nonprofessional Help

Truax and Carkhuff (1967) observe that it is commonly argued that in controlled studies the therapeutic effect of professional help is obscured by the fact that the normally existing nonprofessional help of friends, acquaintances, clergymen, bartenders, and the like is also (equally) effective. Such an argument is, he says, no argument at all; it implicitly concedes that the professional counselor or therapist is no more effective than the nonprofessional help a client would ordinarily seek.

I would add that it is important to learn whether (or in what kind of patient) *a deliberate formal attempt to give psychotherapy by our current methods* adds anything to the results of drug treatment; to the results of ordinary nursing care; or to the experience of merely coming to a clinic. If it doesn't, then surely we should stop wasting our time and the patient's time and start looking for something better.

Children

Eisenberg (1959) has some stimulating observations on the special opportunities for the study of drug effect in children. He suggests that studies at various stages of maturation may succeed in dissecting out the determinants of behavior and of learning, and also that there may be much to be gained by investigation of particular constitutional types. If there are infants with unusual sensitivity to sensory stimulation, and if this is related to illness, then drugs that might insulate the organism from the environment by damping input curves could conceivably confer stability. Contrariwise, the autistic child who is remarkably unresponsive to at least some aspects of his environment might be impelled to attend to them by drugs that amplify inner excitation.

As a closing practical point, Fish, Shapiro, and Campbell (1966) have shown that in research with autistic retarded children it is necessary to stratify the sample according to the degree of language impairment. Significant drug-placebo differences were found in those with severe language impairment, but not where impairment was less severe.

The Investigator

Elkes (1967) recommends that thought be given to the type of investigator who is likely to contribute maximally to research on combining pharmacotherapy and psychotherapy. It is his impression that only rarely can observers with a purely academic training in one of the social or behavioral sciences be taught the relevant action cues to a therapeutic transaction (be it individual or social) unless they have worked in a mental hospital themselves. He suggests collaboration between professional personnel at an operational level, and investigators of more formal training. With this I would heartily agree. There is nothing more tiresome than ivory-tower technicians who think that, alone and unaided, they can obtain valid data from the rough and tumble of a psychiatric hospital—unless it be those who, having failed miserably in their hospital experiment, retreat back to their ivory tower to author a peevish harangue depicting what seemed to them to be the inadequacies of the hospital and its staff.

Areas for Future Research

General Questions. Gottschalk (1968) considers as the most important points of attack for nonpsychotic disorders the following:

1. What is the site and mechanism of action of psychoactive drugs and the relationship of these facts to psychological and behavioral change?

2. Can we differentiate the effects of *nonspecific* factors from the *specific* effects of psychotherapy and drug therapy?

3. How may the processes of learning and memory be enhanced or inhibited through pharmacologic agents?

Clinical Questions. Elsewhere (May, 1968b) I have identified practical clinical research goals for schizophrenia that could probably be applied also to the nonpsychotic disorders:

1. Is it possible to predict which patients will respond or not respond to a particular treatment method? In the final analysis, it is the treatment of the individual patient that counts, and not just the mass average. What is the right treatment for most, or even almost everyone, is not necessarily right for all.

When we started our own project I was convinced that we would probably find substantial numbers of schizophrenic patients who would respond more or less specifically to each of the five treatment methods. However, the findings from Winsorized data seem to indicate that ataraxic drugs had a substantial effect on the majority of patients. Accordingly, if I were forced to speculate from the facts available at the moment, I would say that there are likely to be few, if any, schizophrenic patients who respond specifically to individual psychotherapy. There is perhaps more to be gained by attempting to identify the occasional patient who may do better with psychotherapy plus drug than with drug alone, but here I have some reservations about our chances of success. I hope I am wrong, as I find it very hard to give up the idea of "the right treatment for the right patient."

On the other hand, drugs seem to be less effective in nonpsychotic patients, and I would therefore be much more sanguine about the prospect of identifying the kinds of neurotic patients who respond specifically to psychotherapy rather than to drugs.

2. Do ataraxic drugs or individual psychotherapy have any merit at all for the kind of good-prognosis patients who restitute rapidly? Are the results perhaps just as good without pushing the patient with unnecessary intrusive interventions?

3. Study of the influence of therapist experience on treatment outcome is another obvious focus for future research. The crucial information that is needed could be obtained in a fairly simple experiment—a comparison of the results of drugs alone with the results of individual psychotherapy plus drugs, when the patients are treated by gifted specialists and by the usual therapist.

4. There are certain problems relating to drug effect that deserve special and serious study. There are not enough adequate studies of the fundamental nature of drug effect in *patients*; and many of the studies that do deal with patients suffer from the same defects of design that frequently appear in clinical treatment outcome studies—controls poor or completely lacking; contamination by the effects of treatments other than drugs; nonrandom assignment to the drugs under study; failure to distinguish between acute and chronic dosage; and deficient statistical presentation. Zubin and Katz (1966) point out in their review that there is a lack of adequate methodology in this area, and question the usefulness of the usual psychometric methods. Perhaps the point should be made that studies of the fundamental nature of drug effect *in patients* will require the same attention to details of design and controls that is now lavished on drug-placebo or drug-comparison treatment-outcome experiments—indeed, these two aspects of research might often be productively combined.

One also has the impression that *patient* studies have tended to continue to look repeatedly in the wrong place for the nature of drug effect, like the drunk looking under the street light for his keys "because that's where the light is." This results in formulations that may strike the clinician as "how drugs don't work" (rather than how they do). As Hamilton (1965) observed caustically, investigations based on psychological tests have tended to use types of tests that appear irrelevant to clinical phenomena and, not surprisingly, the general outcome of these experiments has been to show that the drugged subjects do worse than nondrugged ones.

Similarly, Lloyd and Newbrough (1964) comment that the fact that phenothiazines produce central nervous system dysfunction has been repeatedly demonstrated by numerous studies. Yet the emphasis in research has been repeatedly and almost exclusively on motor signs of dysfunction or on studies in which perception and motor responses were inextricably tied together in the test performance. Powerful drugs such as chlorpromazine do indeed have obvious side effects, but we should not be misled into thinking that these are necessarily responsible for the longer-term improvement in the manifestations of psychosis.

5. Can teachable techniques be devised that will integrate ataraxic drug therapy with individual psychotherapy or psychotherapeutic management? What are the best ways of lessening the potential psychological hazards of ataraxic drugs, such as passivity, undue dependence on the therapist and on pills, or resistance to self-examination?

TREATMENT IMPLICATIONS

The Individual Patient

There seems to be no reasonable doubt that ataraxic drugs are here to stay as effective agents in the management of psychiatric disorders, particularly in the treatment of psychotics, and in the treatment of nonpsychotic disorders when psychotherapy is not available, not practical, not acceptable, or not likely, unaided, to achieve the optimum goals that might reasonably be set for a particular patient.

The situation need not be perceived in oppositional terms of either *drugs* or *psychotherapy*. We have no panacea in the treatment of psychiatric patients, nor can we at present afford to give up any form of treatment that offers promise of helping a person who might not be helped otherwise. The problem, therefore, is to combine and integrate drug therapy with other forms of treatment, and to adapt the overall treatment plan to the individual patient. First, let us deal with the treatment of psychosis, in which the role of drugs seems to be more clearly defined. From the evidence, we can dismiss the story that ataraxic drugs should be avoided because they interfere with the psychotherapy of the hospitalized schizophrenic patient—provided, of course, that they are properly given. In the hospital stage of the illness, individual psychotherapy alone without ataraxic drugs is an expensive and ineffective form of treatment that apparently adds little or nothing to conservative milieu therapy.

Although it should be clear beyond reasonable doubt that, on the whole, major ataraxic drugs are likely to give better results at less cost than individual psychotherapy alone, this does not mean that all hospitalized patients should be given drugs indiscriminately. Obviously, patients who are already on the way to restitution during the initial evaluation period should not receive any "specific" treatment, unless it can be established that there is a good probability that this will either improve their final condition or lessen their financial burden. Just as obviously, at the other extreme, ataraxic drugs should not be given to those chronic cases who have failed to respond to previous drug therapy in adequate doses.

These cautionary remarks about drug therapy should be accompanied by a similar admonition that we should use psychotherapy with equal discrimination. Judging by the results of controlled research, the value of individual psychotherapy alone for the hospitalized schizophrenic patient has been greatly exaggerated. Evidently a thoughtful reappraisal of our whole thinking about the psychotherapy of the schizophrenic is in order. Perhaps we need to give up some of our artificial concepts as to what is beneficial—but we must be careful not to throw the baby out with the bath water. Individual psychotherapy may be of no great help in achieving restitution in the earlier stages of the schizophrenic illness, but this does not mean that it should never be used at all.

In certain rare situations where cost and length of hospital stay are of no concern, it may

be justifiable to add psychotherapy to drug therapy for the hospitalized schizophrenic patient as long as it is understood that, as far as one can tell, the gains are likely to be relatively small and confined to a few areas of functioning. For a few patients such a gamble is well worth taking. Generally, however, there may be more prudent ways of spending money for the schizophrenic patient than on giving formal orthodox psychotherapy during the hospital restitution phase. For instance, there might be more to be gained by working with other members of the family; or by saving the money to be spent later to provide a better level of after care after the patient has left the hospital—in particular, to provide satisfactory psychotherapeutic management and psychotherapy.

It may also be that individual psychotherapy is indicated for the patient who fails to respond to a reasonable trial of drug therapy combined with proper psychotherapeutic management. Radical and even paradoxical as this proposal may seem, it makes more common sense than the prevalent custom of applying orthodox individual psychotherapy indiscriminately to all cases or reserving it for patients with a good prognosis who may do perfectly well without it. Furthermore, if there are indeed psychotic patients who respond better to psychotherapy alone or to psychotherapy plus drug therapy than to ataraxic drug therapy alone, they are likely to be concentrated in this particular group of patients.

These remarks should not be interpreted as meaning that we should pay no attention to the schizophrenic patient's psychologic needs while he is in the hospital. In fact, it is in precisely this area of treatment that our techniques may need the most reappraisal. A distinction needs to be made between *psychotherapy* and *what is therapeutic for the psyche*. Instead of formal psychotherapy, particularly the kind of orthodox psychotherapy that is commonly used with psychoneurotic outpatients and which is seemingly not very helpful in the process of schizophrenic restitution, we should concentrate on improving what I shall call psychotherapeutic management. By this I mean the application of understanding of psychopathology and psychodynamics to the remedial management of the individual patient—including work with other family members and in the community; appropriate techniques of milieu therapy and social casework; and, once restitution has been achieved, an attempt to help the patient identify and deal with his current life problems.

Thus, in general, the *hospital* treatment of the schizophrenic patient should concentrate on psychiatric first aid and restitution; while for the *outpatient* phase, stabilization of the personality is the ultimate goal. It is in the stabilization phase (and not in the hospital phase) that psychotherapy is likely to be of most help. Our overall treatment strategy for the psychotic patient should therefore center around the careful integration of hospital and outpatient care. There should be a vigorous effort to provide continuity of follow-up and after-care, and to integrate drug therapy, psychotherapy, and psychotherapeutic management into a constructive and efficient treatment approach, rather than thinking of them in terms of some rigid organic-functional dialectic, as mutually exclusive competitors. We must learn to integrate the psychodynamic and somatic approaches with discretion and finesse, and to develop a science of timing that uses them both appropriately and in harmony.

By contrast, in the treatment of the neurotic outpatient, the major ataraxic agents are seldom indicated. The minor ataraxic agents should generally be used only when psychotherapy is not available, not practical, not acceptable, or not likely, unaided, to achieve the optimum goals that might reasonably be set for the patient. Thus in neurotics, drug therapy will be given less frequently and for shorter periods of time.

In actual practice, the combination of drug therapy and psychotherapy is not entirely a simple matter. A therapist must have adequate experience in both drug therapy and in psychotherapy before he can realistically utilize combined treatment. Considerable skill and experience is needed to find the right drug and the correct dose, and to deal with subtle factors (Lesse, 1966a, 1968; Sarwer-Foner and Koranyi, 1960). Neglect of medication, due to lack of information about psychopharmacology, and the unnecessary use of drugs, due to lack of reasonable psychotherapeutic skill, are equally inexcusable (Blood, 1962). Yet this lack of broad training has led to the formation of mutually hostile schools of thought, in which the proponents have extolled their own specific techniques and have been scotomatized to the benefits of others.

Rickels (1962a) remarks that one of the most important factors in the successful adjunctive use of drugs in psychotherapy is the therapist's ease and understanding in using these agents. If his use of drugs is based on constructive understanding and he feels relaxed about using them; if he understands the dynamics of his patient; if he prescribes drugs constructively for well-founded reasons; if he does not attribute magic to drugs, but uses them because of effects that might help the patient to handle his problems more maturely; then he will usually see rewarding results. If, on the other hand, he prescribes drugs against his better judgment, or because of conscious or unconscious feelings that cloud his judgment; if he uses a drug to put distance between himself and the patient, because the patient makes him feel anxious, angry or frustrated; if he does not believe in drug therapy and consequently often does not know how to use drugs properly; then he is likely to get poor results.

It would seem to this reviewer that the therapist who gives attention to the development of skill and sophistication in both pharmacotherapy and psychotherapy will optimize his treatment results in comparison with the therapist who gives either one or the other ineptly or ignorantly.

It is important to define one's goals carefully, both long- and short-term, and then to consider which, if any, drug may have an effect in the desired direction. A psychotherapeutic program that has as its major aim to increase the affect experienced by an obsessive compulsive will obviously require a different drug as an accompaniment to psychotherapy than when the goal is to decrease affect or arousal capacity (Gottschalk, 1968).

If a psychotherapist is to deal adequately with patients on drug therapy, it is essential that he familiarize himself with the various side effects of the different drugs—relatively minor aggravations, such as weight gain, blurred vision due to poor accommodation, stuffiness of the nose, dryness of the mouth, and hypotension; the sometimes frightening and distressing dystonias, tremor, and other extrapyramidal symptoms; and major complications such as agranulocytosis, retinitis, and hepatitis.

Extrapyramidal symptoms such as stiffness, tremor, rigidity, and restless shuffling (akathisia) generally respond to antiparkinson medication; in the case of the acute dystonias, this may need to be given parenterally.

Excessive sedation is mentioned as a side effect of almost every drug. Although this is usually only a passing phase early in treatment, and tolerance generally develops rapidly, it must be taken into account in judging whether a patient should drive a car or resume work in a hazardous occupation. In some cases—for instance, in excited patients—the sedative side effect of a drug may be exploited to quiet a patient until the main antipsychotic effect takes hold. Along the same lines, when there is insomnia, it may help to give medication in a single dose at night.

While on the subject of dosage, it is not necessary to follow the hallowed medical prescription "Three times a day after meals and once at night." One dose in 24 hours is usually adequate, certainly no more than two. The timing is usually unimportant, unless a drug with a sedative side effect is being used, in which case it is generally best to give it at bedtime.

Patients on drugs should be seen frequently, since the more that is known about the psychic state and interpersonal relationships, the more precisely can drug dosage be adjusted to meet particular individual needs. Adequate time should be allowed at the beginning to discuss medication at some length and to establish as positive a relationship with the patient as is possible under the circumstances. Some patients will be positive and expectant, others negative and apprehensive—an understanding discussion of reality and fantasy will optimize the patient-therapist-drug relationship. Only in this way can one arrive at an informed estimate as to how the pharmacological actions of a drug will interact with the patient's past history; his initial state at the time of administration; his motivation; and the symbolic value of the drug as a helping agent. One interview may be all that can be managed in an acute crisis, but there is no emergency so grave nor patient so disturbed

that the therapist can afford to dispense with this vital prerequisite; in the usual non-emergency case, it is advisable to work through the significance of this step over several days before actually giving the drug.

In particular, it is absolutely essential to review, in as much detail as possible, the patient's (and the family's) precise experience with and response to drugs, and to achieve some knowledge of prior type and dosage. It may readily be observed that therapists often provoke needless battles with their patients and reinforce their paranoia by thoughtless administration of particular drugs to which the patient is antagonistic. If it is indeed advisable to prescribe a specific drug to which the patient objects, it is surely worthwhile to take the trouble to establish with the patient a reasonably firm basis for so doing.

It is not unusual for psychotherapists to see patients for whom ataraxic drugs have been prescribed by other physicians. In these instances, psychotherapists should not impulsively discontinue drug therapy without careful evaluation of its effect—and then only after consultation with the physician who originally instituted it (Lesse, 1968). If it is decided to discontinue medication, this should be done gradually—abrupt withdrawal may precipitate an acute worsening of the patient's condition.

Particular attention should be paid to evaluation of a patient's tendencies to uncritical agreement with authority and thoughtless lack of discrimination, which will have to be suitably handled if an active drug is to be prescribed; also, to determining to what extent the patient's defenses are organized around the use of physical activity and acting out, since this may imply an unfavorable response to chlorpromazine in particular and perhaps to other drugs that have pronounced sedative side effects.

It is also important that the therapist translate his intellectual insight into the role of non-specific factors in drug response, and the importance of his own countertransferences into some real action to potentiate drug effect by suitably influencing the patient's attitudes and expectation. The common practice of giving drugs without establishing a suitable relationship for giving them, sometimes without even telling the patient what to expect, can only be vigorously condemned. There is good experimental evidence to indicate that the physician prescribing *active* drugs (not just a placebo) will get better results if he expresses a positively expectant attitude to drug therapy; if he tells the patient that he may expect relief and in general indicates the areas in which this may occur; if he tells the patient that he may experience common side effects such as drowsiness or dry mouth, but interprets these ahead of time in a positive manner, that is, as perhaps irritating, but readily managed and a good sign because they indicate that the drug is working (Fisher, Cole, Rickels, and Uhlenhuth, 1964). This induction of a positive attitude to drug therapy as a prerequisite to success is closely paralleled in psychotherapy, where Frank and his co-workers had shown that outcome can be greatly influenced by suitable preparatory interviews (Gliedman, Nash, Imber, Stone, and Frank, 1958; Frank, Nash, Stone and Imber, 1963; Hoehn-Saric, Frank, Imber, Nash, Stone, and Battle, 1964; Nash, Frank, Imber, and Stone, 1964; Nash, Hoehn-Saric, Battle, Stone, Imber, and Frank, 1965).

According to the patient's current level of understanding, he should be provided with some rationale for drug treatment, as well as a discussion of the name and dosage, size, shape, and color of his medication. To one patient a small pill may signify immense potency and danger; to another it may mean impotence and ineffectiveness. Different colors mean different things to different people, and it may be fruitful to ask the patient whether he would prefer to take the medication in liquid or in tablet form—and to inquire about associated fantasies.

In general, the patient will distort the prescription transaction according to his own defensive structure—and this should eventually be interpreted to him (Blood, 1962). Hirsh (1962) emphasizes the importance of understanding the symbolic meaning of giving a drug. It may be the magic which the patient must find to dilute the omnipotence of the therapist in order to move from his isolation; or something for the hostile patient to vent his wrath on while maintaining a tenuous relationship with his therapist; it may be an anxiety-relieving ritual, or the giving of love, care, and protection.

The work of Davison and Valins (1968, 1969) would indicate that behavior changes that are believed to be brought about actively by oneself will be maintained to a greater degree than behavior changes that are believed to be due to external forces or agents such as a drug. (Note that it is not necessary that the subject *actually* be responsible for his changed behavior, rather that he *believe* that he is.) Although this work was in the context of single drug doses in behavioral conditioning, it is appealing to generalize to the context of longer-term dosage and psychotherapy. I would deduce that it may be important to structure drug therapy in such a way that the patient believes that he himself is taking the responsibility for controlling his behavior—at the beginning, for example, by making the decision to take the drug; later on, perhaps by participating in decisions on dosage; still later on, by deciding when it should be discontinued; and, hopefully, in the end, by feeling that he is controlling himself without any drug at all. Adequate psychotherapeutic support is essential to insure a psychotic patient's cooperation with drug therapy and, indeed, his participation in medication decisions can serve as a valuable therapeutic experience in mastery and control.

A similar point is made by Sarwer-Foner (1960b), who comments that drugs may compromise the patient's personal responsibility in his own improvement and may lessen his confidence in his own controls. He recommends that when drugs are being used in the treatment of neurosis, patients should be told that they are a temporary measure for a short period of time.

In regulating dosage, it is wise to keep the dosage level below that at which there is toxic impairment of ego functioning. One should avoid "snowing" the patient—and it may need some special effort in education and supervision to help psychiatrists to avoid doing this to assaultive patients (Appleton, 1965). Janecek and Mandel (1965) found that in patients who do poorly in therapy and who rely only on medication, it may be possible to get better results by making attendance at group sessions mandatory if they wish to secure medication. This will make it easier to change, adjust, or regulate medication and to make the use of medication more appropriate or to reduce it. Probably it would be easier to make attendance mandatory if the group sessions are presented, in the first instance at any rate, not as psychotherapy per se but as a session to discuss medication—and perhaps other problems that come up.

It is generally agreed that in the treatment of hospitalized psychotic patients after the phase of restitution, once the patient has returned to the community, rehabilitation and stabilization of the personality usually requires an extended therapeutic effort. In fact, now that, with the use of drugs, many patients can move rapidly to being well enough for outpatient aftercare, or even avoid hospital care altogether, the main effort in psychotherapy and sociotherapy may shift from the hospital to the outpatient phase of treatment. The transition from hospital to community must necessarily involve a profound readjustment. Since changes in drugs dosage are likely to be made around this time, creating problems in shift from drug to nondrug state, there is double reason for extra caution and a concerted therapeutic effort in this transition. Sensitive adjustment of drug dosage to optimum levels must be combined with continuity between hospital and aftercare to provide a stable therapeutic contact. Hopefully, this will assist the patient to work towards the eventual goal of stabilization of his personality and mastery of his illness.

To the extent that the patient's illness permits, drugs should be reduced in the final stages of hospital care, not too abruptly, and with special psychotherapeutic effort to facilitate the reduction and to promote transfer of learning and restitution from the "drug" to the "nondrug" condition. Further reduction of drug dosage should be accomplished in the outpatient stage so that, hopefully, treatment may continue with psychotherapy alone.

Treatment Programs

In occasional (!) instances, research investigators have made recommendations that might be helpful to those responsible for the design and operation of institutional treatment programs. Koegler and Brill (1967), for example, present an extended discussion of the social and treatment implications of their outpatient study, stressing the need to apply new techniques, particularly if the psychiatrist is going to work with the patients whose backgrounds are dissimilar to his own or with larger numbers. They believe that the time has come for a reevaluation of conventional psychotherapeutic approaches; that we should feel some sense of social urgency to find less time-consuming and less expensive treatment methods and focus attention on the quantity and quality of care received by lower socioeconomic classes. In this respect they suggest that short-term brief-contact therapy combined with drugs may have a lot to offer in extending effective treatment to larger numbers.

Cole (1959) indicates that the use of drugs has organizational implications for child guidance and mental health clinics. Does the need for optimal coordination of drug therapy and psychotherapy justify the clinic's taking over the administration of drugs—something clinics have been reluctant to do in the past? This reviewer would ask the question another way. Can the interprofessional relationships among the various disciplines of a community clinic be amicably structured and defined in such a way as to ensure that each patient receives his particular optimum blend of psychotherapy and drug therapy—rather than a program rigidly structured along doctrinaire lines?

In applying the results of the Schizophrenia Research Project to hospital programs for first-admission schizophrenic patients, I have recommended (May, 1968b) that provision be made for the early identification of those patients for whom no "specific" treatment is indicated, and who might well be treated with psychotherapeutic management plus milieu therapy without formal psychotherapy or ataraxic drugs. It would be well, however, to organize a program that orients them to the possibility of psychotherapy and that encourages them to consider it seriously after they leave the hospital. Such patients should be discharged at the earliest reasonable moment, to be followed in an aftercare unit that can continue adequate psychotherapeutic management and drug therapy or psychotherapy if indicated. The ideal program would be one in which the hospital therapist continues his treatment relationship in the outpatient clinic. There is no valid excuse for the prevalent public and university hospital practice of making an artificial separation between inpatient and outpatient therapists; inertia and administrative convenience should not be permitted to interfere with effective treatment.

The remainder of the patients, that is, all those who are unlikely to restitute without "specific" treatment, should be treated with ataraxic drugs and psychotherapeutic management. Formal psychotherapy is not likely to be of advantage while they are in the hospital but, as with the better-prognosis patients, an attempt should be made to encourage psychotherapy after release from the hospital to stabilize restitution. Again, the general goal should be discharge to aftercare at the earliest reasonable moment.

Traditionally, hospital programs focus staff attention and treatment resources on the newly admitted patient. By contrast, the approach suggested above would free a substantial proportion of staff time for the treatment of the more chronic patient. Avoiding unnecessary treatment for those who do not need it and the vigorous application of drug therapy (plus psychotherapeutic management) to those who do, should make it possible to redistribute the treatment staff in such a way as to provide a higher level of care for the nonresponders. I have suggested (May, 1968b) that it is the non-responders who should receive the highest level of care—not the newly admitted patient—and that patients who develop toxic reactions on ataraxic drugs, or who do not show any improvement after an adequate trial, should be transferred to a special intensive treatment and research unit able to provide (as necessary and desirable) any form of treatment.

In general, the development of an integrated institutional program of drug therapy and psychotherapy requires imagination and administrative skill, and a great deal of careful and sophisticated thought directed towards the management of the prejudices and biases that bedevil the therapists of various professions that compose the institution.

Epilogue

It seems fitting to conclude this chapter by joining in the hope expressed by Ostow (1962) that the new generation of therapists will understand that sound treatment must be securely based upon a sound psychology; but will not on that account neglect the study of the physiology of the brain, nor disdain to exploit it for the benefit of their patients and their science.

REFERENCES

Alexander, L. Contribution of physical treatment to the processes and goals of psychotherapy. *American Journal of Psychiatry*, 1966, **123**, 87–91.

Appleton, W. S. The snow phenomenon—tranquilizing the assaultive. *Psychiatry*, 1965, **28**, 88–93.

Aronson, G. J. A human therapist must decide when a chemical must replace him, supplement or be discarded by him. In P. R. A. May, *Treatment of schizophrenia*. New York: Science House, 1968. Pp. 294–296.

Azima, H. Changes in organization of mood as a therapeutic and research problem in pharmacotherapy. *Neuro-psychopharmacology*. Amsterdam: Elsevier, 1959, 491.

Azima, H., Azima, F., and Cleghorn, R. A. Psychodynamic action of Rauwolfia derivatives. *Psychopharmacology Frontiers*. Boston: Little, Brown, 1959.

Azima, H., Azima, F., and Durost, H. B. Psychoanalytic formulations of effects of Reserpine on schizophrenic organization. *Arch. Gen. Psychiatry*, 1959, **1**, 662–670.

Azima, H., Cramer-Azima, F., and DeVerteuil, R. A comparative behavioral and psychodynamic study of the effect of Reserpine and Raudixin in schizophrenia. *Monographs on Therapy*, 1956, **2**, 10–13.

Azima, H., Cramer-Azima, F., and DeVerteuil, R. Effects of Rauwolfia derivatives on psychodynamic structure. *Psychiat. Quart.*, 1959, **33**, 623–635.

Azima, H., Sangowicz, J., Spindler, J., and Azima, F. Psychodynamic alterations concomitant with intensive Meprobamate administration. *Dis. Nerv. Syst.*, 1959, **20**, 5.

Azima, H., and Sarwer-Foner, G. Psychoanalytic formulations of the effect of drugs in pharmacotherapy. *Rev. Canad. Biol.*, 1961, **20**, 507–518.

Barron, F., and Leary, T. F. Changes in psychoneurotic patients with and without psychotherapy. *J. Consult. Psychology*, 1955, **19**, 239–245.

Bellak, L., and Hurvich, M. A systematic study of ego functions. Paper read at the annual meeting of the American Psychoanalytic Assoication, Detroit, Michigan, May, 1967.

Bellak, L., Hurvick, M., Silvan, M., and Jacobs, D. Towards an ego-psychological appraisal of drug effects. *Amer. J. Psychiat.*, 1968, **125**, 593–604.

Bellak, L., and Rosenberg, S. Effects of anti-depressant drugs on psychodynamics. *Psychosomatics*, 1966, **7** 106–114.

Bellak, L., Salk, L., and Rosenhan, D. A process study of the effects of Deprol on depression. *J. Ner. Ment. Dis.*, 1961, **132**, 531–538.

Bergin, A. E. Some implications of psychotherapy research for therapeutic practice. *J. Abnormal Psychology*, 1966, **71**, 235–246.

Bergin, A. E. Further comments on psychotherapy research and therapeutic practice. *Int. J. Psychiat.*, 1967, **3**, 317–323.

Betz, B. J., and Whitehorn, J. C. The relationship of the therapist to the outcome of therapy in schizophrenia. *Psychiat. Research Reports*, 1956, **5**, 89–117..

Blood, A. M. Considerations other than pharmacological effects in psychiatric drug prescriptions. *Dis. Nerv. System*, 1962, **23**, 216–218.

Bookhammer, R. S., Meyers, R. W., Schober, C. C., and Piotrowski, Z. A. A five year clinical follow-up study of schizophrenics treated by Rosen's "Direct Analysis," compared with controls. *Amer. J. Psychiat.*, 1966, **123**, 602–604.

Brady, J. V. Procedures, problems and perspectives in animal behavioral studies of drug activity. In J. O. Cole and R. W. Gerard (Eds.), *Psychopharmacology: Problems in evaluation*. Washington, D. C.: N.A.S.—N.R.C., 1959, 255–264. Publication #583.

Carlson, D. A., Coleman, J. V., Herrara, P., and Harrison, R. Problems in treating the lower-class psychotic. *Arch. Gen. Psychiat.*, 1965, **13**, 269–274.

Chassan, J. *Research design in clinical psychology and psychiatry*. New York: Appleton-Century-Crofts, 1967.

Cole, J. O. Behavioral toxicity. In L. Uhr and J. G. Miller (Eds.), *Drugs and behavior*. New York: Wiley, 1960, 160–181.

Cole, J. O. A unique study which may never be repeated. In P. R. A. May, *Treatment of schizophrenia*. New York: Science House, 1968. Pp. 309–310.

Cole, J. O., Bonato, R., and Goldberg, S. C. Non-specific factors in the drug therapy of schizophrenic patients. In K. Rickels (Ed.), *Non-specific factors in drug therapy*. Springfield, Illinois: Charles C. Thomas, 1968, 115–127.

Cole, J. O., Klerman, G. L., and Jones, R. T. Drug therapy—1959. In E. J. Spiegel (Ed.), *Progress in neurology and psychiatry*. Vol. 15. New York: Grune & Stratton, 1960. Pp. 540–576.

Cole, K. G. Discussion of paper, "Populations, behaviors and situations; some ecological considerations in child drug research," by L. J. Borstelman. In S. Fisher (Ed.), *Child research in psychopharmacology*. Springfield, Illinois: Charles C. Thomas, 1959. Pp. 76–81.

Cooper, A. M., Karush, A., Easser, B. R., and Swerdloff, B. The adaptive balance profile and prediction of early treatment behavior. In G. S. Goldman and D. Shapiro (Eds.), *Developments in psychoanalysis at Columbia University. Proceedings of the 20th anniversary conference, Columbia Psychoanalytic Clinic for Training & Research*, October, 1965. Pp. 183–214.

Cowden, R. C., Zax, M., and Sproles, J. A. Reserpine alone and as an adjunct to psychotherapy in the treatment of schizophrenia. *Arch. Neurol. Psychiat.*, 1955, **74**, 518–522.

Cowden, R. C., Zax, M., and Sproles, J. A. Group psychotherapy in conjunction with a physical treatment. *J. Clin. Psychol.*, 1956, **12**, 53–56.

Cowden, R. C., Zax, M., Hague, J. R., and Finney, R. C. Chlorpromazine, alone and as an adjunct to group psychotherapy in the treatment of psychiatric patients. *Am. J. Psychiat.*, 1956, **112**, 898–902.

Davis, J. M. Efficacy of tranquilizing and anti-depressant drugs. *Arch. Gen. Psychiat.*, 1965, **13**, 552–572.

Davison, G. C., and Valins, S. Drugs, cognition and behavior therapy. Paper presented at the annual meeting of the American Psychological Association, San Francisco, California, 1968.

Davison, G. C., and Valins, S. Maintenance of self-attributed and drug-attributed behavior change. *Jour. Personality & Social Psychology*, 1969, in press.

Deniker, P. Efficacy of chemotherapy in comparison to psychological and social methods of treatment. In P. B. Bradley, F. Flugel, and P. H. Hoch (Eds.), *Neuro-psychopharmacology*. Proceedings of the Third meeting of the Collegium Internationale Neuropsychopharmacologicum. New York: Elsevier, 1964. Pp. 127–133.

Dews, P. B. Pharmacology of positive reinforcement and discrimination. In M. Y. Mikhelson and V. G. Longo (Eds.), *Pharmacology of conditioning, learning and retention*. Vol. 1. Proceedings of the Second International Pharmacological Meeting, August, 1963. New York: Macmillan, 1965. Pp. 91–98.

Dews, P. B. Conditioned behavior as a substitution for behavioral effects of drugs. In P. Solomon (Ed.), *Psychiatric drugs*. New York: Grune and Stratton, 1966. Pp. 22–31.

DiMascio, A. Personality and variability of response to psychotropic drugs. Relationship to paradoxical effects. In K. Rickels, *Non-specific factors in drug therapy*. Springfield, Illinois: Charles C. Thomas, 1968. Pp. 40–49.

DiMascio, A., and Shader, R. I. Behavioral toxicity. In D. H. Efron, J. O. Cole, J. Levine, and J. R. Wittenborn (Eds.), *Psychopharmacology—a review of progress, 1957–1967.* Public Health Service Publication, No. 1836. Washington, D. C.: U. S. Government Printing Office, 1968. Pp. 551–560.

Dixon, W. J., and May, P. R. A. Methods of statistical analysis. In P. R. A. May, *Treatment of schizophrenia.* New York: Science House, 1968.

Dixon, W. J., and May, P. R. A. Process analysis in the assessment and prediction of psychiatric outcome. In P. R. A. May, and J. R. Wittenborn (Eds.), *Psychotropic, recent advances in Drug Response prediction.* Springfield, Illinois: Charles C. Thomas, 1969.

Eisenberg, L. Basic issues in drug research with children—opportunities and limitations of a pediatric age group. In S. Fisher (Ed.), *Child research in psychopharmacology.* Springfield, Illinois: Charles C. Thomas, 1959. Pp. 21–42.

Eisenberg, L. Role of drugs in treating disturbed children. *Children,* 1965, **2,** 167–173.

Elkes, J. Psychoactive drugs—some problems and approaches. In P. Solomon (Ed.), *Psychiatric drugs.* New York: Grune & Stratton, 1966. Pp. 4–21.

Elkes, J. Behavioral pharmacology in relation to psychiatry. Psychiatric der Gegenwart, Forschung und Praxis. Grundalagen forschung zur psychiatrie. In Teil, A., Gruhle, H. W., Jung, R., Mayer-Gross, W. and Muller, M. (Eds.), Springer-Verlag (Berlin, Heidelberg, New York), 1967, 929–1038.

Evangelakis, M. G. De-institutionalization of patients (the triad of trifluoperazine-group psychotherapy-adjunctive therapy). *Dis. Nerv. Syst.,* 1961, **22,** 26–32.

Fairweather, G. W., Simon, R., Gebhard, M. E., Weingarten, E., Holland, J. L., Sanders, R., Stone, G. B., and Reahl, J. E. Relative effectiveness of psychotherapeutic programs—a multicriteria comparison of four programs for three different patient groups. Psychological Monographs (74, Whole No. 492), 1960, 1–26.

Fish, B., Shapiro, T., and Campbell, M. Long-term prognosis and the response of schizophrenic children to drug therapy—a controlled study of trifluoperazine. *Amer. J. Psychiatry,* 1966, **123,** 32–39.

Fisher, S., Cole, J. O., Rickels, K., and Uhlenhuth, E. H. Drug-set interaction—the effect of expectations on drug response in outpatients. In P. B. Bradley, F. Flugel, and P. Hoch (Eds.), *Neuropsychopharmacology.* Vol. 3. Amsterdam: Elsevier, 1964. Pp. 149–156.

Forsythe, A. B., May, P. R. A., and Engleman, L. Computing advantage scores by multiple regression. In Wittenborn, J. R., and Goldberg, S. C. (Eds.), *Psychopharmacology and the Individual Patient.* New York: Raven Press. In Press.

Frank, J. D., Nash, E. H., Stone, A. R., and Imber, S. D. Immediate and long term symptomatic course of psychiatric outpatients. *Amer. J. Psychiat.,* 1963, **120,** 429–439.

Freedman, A. M. Discussion. In S. Fisher (Ed.), *Child research in psychopharmacology.* Springfield, Illinois: Charles C. Thomas, 1959. Pp. 42–47.

Freud, S. Letter to Marie Bonaparte, January 15th, 1930. Cited by E. Jones in *The life and work of Sigmund Freud.* Vol. 3. New York: Basic Books, Inc., 1957. Pp. 449.

Freud, S. *On narcissism—an introduction* (1914). J. Strachey Trans. London: Hogarth Press, 1962. Pp. 73–102.

Freud, S. *New introductory lectures on psychoanalysis* (1933). J. Strachey Trans. London: Hogarth Press, 1964. Pp. 136–157.

Freud, S. *An outline of psychoanalysis* (1938). J. Strachey Trans. London: Hogarth Press, 1964. Pp. 172–182.

Freyhan, F. A. Immediate and long range effects of chlorpromazine on mental hospitals. In *Chlorpromazine & mental health.* Philadelphia: Lea & Febiger, 1955. Pp. 71–84.

Freyhan, F. A. Therapeutic implications of different effects of new phenothiazine compounds. *Amer. J. Psychiat.,* 1959, **115,** 577–585.

Gibbs, J. J., Wilkens, B., and Lauterbach, C. G. A controlled clinical psychiatric study of chlorpromazine. *Jour. Clin. Exp. Psychopathology,* 1957, **18,** 269–283.

Gilligan, J. Review of literature. In M. Greenblatt, M. H. Solomon, A. S. Evans, and G. W. Brooks (Eds.), *Drug and social therapy in chronic schizophrenia.* Springfield, Illinois: Charles C. Thomas, 1965. Pp. 24–76.

Gliedman, L. H. Nash, E. H., Imber, S. D., Stone, A. R., and Frank, J. D. Reduction of symptoms by pharmacologically inert substances and by short term psychotherapy. *A.M.A. Arch. Neurol. Psychiat.,* 1958, **79,** 345–351.

Goldman, D. Psychotherapy and drugs in private practice. In *Psychosomatic medicine.* Philadelphia: Lea & Febiger, 1962. Pp. 793–799.

Goldstein, M. J., Judd, L. L., Rodnick, E. H., and La Polla, A. Psychophysiological and behavioral effects of phenothiazine administration in acute schizophrenics as a function of premorbid status. *J. Psychiatric Research,* 1969, in press.

Gorham, D. R., Pokorny, A. D., Moseley, E. C., McReynolds, P., and Kogan, W. S. Effects of a phenothiazine and/or group psychotherapy with schizophrenics. *Dis. Nerv. Syst.,* 1964, **25,** 77–86.

Gottschalk, L. A. Introspection and free association as experimental approaches to assessing subjective and behavioral effects of psychoactive drugs. *Drugs & behavior.* New York: Wiley, 1960. (a)

Gottschalk, L. A. The use of drugs in information seeking interviews. *Drugs & behavior.* New York: Wiley, 1960. (b)

Gottschalk, L. A. Some problems in the evaluation of the use of psychoactive drugs, with or without psychotherapy, in the treatment of non-psychotic personality disorders. *Psychopharmacology—a review of progress, 1957–1967.* Public Health publication No. 1836. Washington, D. C. U. S. Government Printing Office, 1968.

Gottschalk, L. A., and Gleser, G. C. An analysis of the verbal content of suicide notes. *Brit. J. Med. Psychol.*, 1960, **33**, 195–204.

Gottschalk, L. A., Gleser, G. C., and Hambidge, G. Verbal behavior analysis: Some content and form variables in speech relevant to personality adjustment. *Arch. Neurol. Psychiat.*, 1957, **77**, 300–311.

Gottschalk, L. A., Gleser, G. C., Springer, K. J., Kaplan, S. M., Shanon, J., and Ross, W. D. Effects of perphenazine on verbal behavior patterns: A contribution to the problem of measuring the psychologic effects of psychoactive drugs. *Arch. Gen. Psychiat.*, 1960, **2**, 632–639.

Gottschalk, L. A., and Hambidge, G. Verbal behavior analysis: A systematic approach to the problem of qualifying psychologic processes. *J. Proj. Tech.*, 1955, **19**, 387–409.

Gottschalk, L. A., and Kaplan, S. M. A quantitative method of estimating variations in intensity of a psychologic conflict or state. *Arch. Neurol. Psychiat.*, 1958, **79**, 688–696.

Gottschalk, L. A., Kapp, F. T., Ross, W. D., Kaplan, S. M., Silver, H., Macleod, J. A., Kahn, J. B., Van Maanen, E. F., and Acheson, G. H. Explorations in testing drugs affecting physical and menial activity. *J. Amer. Med. Assn.*, 1956, **161**, 1054–1058.

Grinspoon, L., Ewalt, J. R., and Shader, R. Long term treatment of chronic schizophrenia: A preliminary report. *International J. Psychiat.*, 1967, **4**, 116–128.

Grinspoon, L., Ewalt, J. R., and Shader, R. Psychotherapy and pharmacotherapy in chronic schizophrenia. *Amer. J. Psychiat.*, 1968, **124**, 1645–1652.

Grinspoon, L., and Greenblatt, M. Pharmacotherapy combined with other treatment methods. *Comp. Psychiat.*, 1963, **4**, 256–262.

Guze, S. B., and Murphy, G. E. An empirical approach to psychotherapy: The agnostic position. *Amer. J. Psychiat.*, 1963, **120**, 53–57.

Hamilton, M. Prediction of clinical response from animal data—a need for theoretical models. In H. Steinberg, A. V. S. De Reuck, and J. Knight (Eds.), *Animal behavior and drug action.* Boston: Little, Brown, 1964. Pp. 299–307.

Hamilton, M. Psychological effects of anti-psychotic drugs in man. In D. Bente, and P. B. Bradley (Eds.), *Neuropsychopharmacology.* Vol. 4. Amsterdam: Elsevier, 1965. Pp. 100–102.

Hamilton, M. Discussion. In K. Rickels, *Non-specific factors in drug therapy.* Springfield, Illinois: Charles C. Thomas, 1968. Pp. 133–135.

Heninger, G., DiMascio, A., and Klerman, G. L. Personality factors in variability of response to phenothiazines. *Am. J. Psychiat.*, 1965, **121**, 1091–1094.

Hirsh, H. Selection of patients for combined drug and psychotherapy. In *Psychosomatic Medicine.* Philadelphia: Lea & Febiger, 1962. Pp. 771–775.

Hoch, P. H. Aims and limitations of psychotherapy. *Amer. J. Psychiat.*, 1955, **112**, 321–326.

Hoehn-Saric, R., Frank, J. D., Imber, S. D., Nash, E. H., Stone, A. R., and Battle, C. C. Systematic preparation of patients for psychotherapy. 1. Effects on therapy behavior and outcome. *Jour. Psychiat. Research*, 1964, **2**, 267–281.

Honigfeld, G., Rosenblum, M. P., Blumenthal, I. J., Lambert, H. L., and Roberts, A. J. Behavioral improvement in the older schizophrenic patient: Drug and social therapies. *J. Amer. Geriatrics Society*, 1965, **13**, 57–72.

Hordern, A. Psychiatry and the tranquilizers. *New Eng. J. Med.*, 1961, **265**, 584–587; 634–688.

Horwitz, W. A., Polatin, P., Kolb, L. C., and Hoch, P. H. A study of cases of schizophrenia treated by direct analysis. *Amer. J. Psychiat.*, 1958, **114**, 780–783.

Janecek, J., and Mandel, A. The combined use of group and pharmacotherapy by collaborative therapists. *Comprehensive Psychiatry*, 1965, **6**, 35–40.

Kalinowsky, L. B. Somatic treatments in psychiatry. *Amer. J. Psychiat.*, 1966, **123**, 338–340.

Kalinowsky, L. B., and Hoch, P. H. *Somatic treatment in psychiatry.* New York: Grune & Stratton, 1961.

Kaplan, S. M., Gottschalk, L. A., and Fleming, D. E. Modifications of the oropharyngeal bacteria and changes in the psychodynamic state. *Arch. Neurol. Psychiat.*, 1957, **78**, 656–664.

Karush, A., Easser, B. R., Cooper, A., and Swerdloff, B. The evaluation of ego-strength. I. A profile of adaptive balance. *J. Nerv. Ment. Dis.*, 1964, **139**, 332–349.

King, P. D. Regressive ECT, chlorpromazine and group therapy in treatment of hospitalized chronic schizophrenics. *Amer. J. Psychiat.*, 1958, **115**, 354–357.

King, P. D. Controlled study of group psychotherapy in schizophrenics receiving chlorpromazine. *Psychiatry Digest,* 1963, **24** 21–26.

Klein, D. F., and Fink, M. Behavioral reaction patterns with phenothiazines. *Arch. Gen. Psychiat.*, 1962, **7**, 449–459.

Klerman, G. L. Staff attitudes, decision making and the use of drug therapy in the mental hospital. In H. C. B. Denber (Ed.), *Research Conference on Therapeutic Community.* Springfield, Illinois: Charles C. Thomas, 1960. Pp. 191–214.

Klerman, G. L. Assessing the influence of the hospital milieu upon the effectiveness of psychiatric drug therapy: Problems of conceptualization and of research methodology. *J. Nerv. Ment. Dis.*, 1963, **137**, 143–154.

Klerman, G. L., DiMascio, A., Greenblatt, M., and Rinkel, M. The influence of specific personality patterns on the reactions to phrenotropic agents. In J. Masserman (Ed.), *Biological psychiatry.* New York: Grune & Stratton, 1959. Pp. 224–242.

Klerman, G. L., DiMascio, A., Havens, L. L., and Snell, J. E. Sedation and tranquilization. *Arch. Gen. Psychiat.*, 1960, **3**, 4–13.

Koegler, R. R., and Brill, N. Q. *Treatment of psychiatric outpatients*. New York: Appleton-Century-Crofts, 1967.

Kramer, M., Whitman, R. M., Baldridge, B. J., and Ornstein, P. H. The pharmacology of dreaming. In G. J. Martin, and B. Kisch (Eds.), *Enzymes in mental health*. Philadelphia: J. B. Lippincott, 1966. Pp. 102–116.

Kubie, L. S. A psychoanalytic approach to the pharmacology of psychological processes. In L. Uhr and J. G. Miller (Eds.), *Drug and behavior*. New York: Wiley, 1960. Pp. 209–224.

Kurland, A. A. Chlorpromazine—its metabolism and the schizophrenic patient. In D. D. Bente, and P. B. Bradley (Eds.), *Neuropsychopharmacology*. Vol. 4. Amsterdam: Elsevier, 1965. Pp. 283–286.

Kurland, A. A., Huang, C. L., Hallam, K. J., and Hanlon, T. E. Further studies of chlorpromazine metabolism and relapse rate. *J. Psychiatric Research*, 1965, **3**, 27–35.

Latz, A. The differential effects of chlorpromazine and secobarbital on sustained attention in chronic schizophrenics. *Federation Proceedings*, 1963, **22**, 509.

Lehrman, N. S. The potency of psychotherapy. *J. Clin. Experimental Psychopath.*, 1961, **22**, 106–111.

Lesse, S. Combined use of psychotherapy with ataraxic drugs. *Dis. Ner. Syst.*, 1956, **18**, 1–5. (a)

Lesse, S. Psychotherapy and ataraxics. *Amer. J. Psychotherapy*, 1956, **10**, 448–459. (b)

Lesse, S. Experimental studies on the relationship between anxiety, dreams and dream-like states. *Amer. J. Psychotherapy*, 1959, **13**, 440–455.

Lesse, S. Combined drug and psychotherapy of severely depressed ambulatory patients. *Canadian Psychiatric Assn. Jour.*, 1966, **11**, 5123–5130. (a)

Lesse, S. Drugs in the treatment of neurotic anxiety and tension—clinical studies. In P. Solomon (Ed.), *Psychiatric drugs*. New York: Grune & Stratton, 1966, 211–224. (b)

Lesse, S. Indications for the use of psychotherapy in combination with psychotropic drugs in ambulatory patients. *Psychosomatics*. 1968, **9**, 84–88.

Lichtenberg, J. D. A statistical analysis of patients' care at the Sheppard & Enoch Pratt hospital. *Psychiatric Quarterly*, 1958, **32**, 13–40.

Lloyd, E. N., and Newbrough, J. R. Sensory changes with phenothiazine medication in schizophrenic patients. *J. Nerv. Mental Dis.*, 1964, **139**, 169–175.

Lorr, M., McNair, D. M., Weinstein, G. J., Michaux, W. W., and Raskin, A. Meprobamate and chlorpromazine in psychotherapy: Some effects on hostility in out-patients. *Arch. Gen. Psychiatry*, 1961, **4**, 381–389.

Lorr, M. McNair, D. M., and Weinstein, G. J. Early effects of chlordiazepoxide used with psychotherapy. *J. Psychiatric Research*, 1962, **1**, 257–270.

Lourie, R. S. Basic problems involved in the use of the newer neuropharmacologic drugs in childhood. In S. Fisher (Ed.), *Child research in psychopharmacology*. Springfield, Illinois: Charles C. Thomas, 1959. Pp. 48–55.

May, P. R. A. Psychotherapy and anti-psychotic drugs in schizophrenia. Paper presented at the annual meeting of the American Psychiatric Assn., Boston, May, 1968. (a)

May, P. R. A. Treatment of schizophrenia. New York: Science House, 1968. (b)

May, P. R. A. Anti-psychotic drugs and other forms of therapy. In D. H. Efron, J. O. Cole, J. Levine, and J. R. Wittenborn (Eds.), *Psychopharmacology—review of progress, 1957–1967*. Public Health Service Publication No. 1836. Washington, D. C.: U. S. Government Printing Office, 1968. Pp. 1155–1176.(c)

May, P. R. A., and Forsythe, A. B. A contribution to the methodology of prediction-advantage score technique. In Wittenborn, J. R., and Goldberg, S. C. (Eds.), *Psychopharmacology and the Individual Patient*. New York: Raven Press. In Press.

May, P. R. A., and Tuma, A. H. Ataraxic drugs and psychotherapy: The effect of psychotherapy and stelazine on length of hospital stay, release rate and supplemental treatment of schizophrenic patients. *Jour. Nerv. Ment. Dis.*. 1964, **139**, 362–369.

May, P. R. A., and Tuma, A. H. Treatment of schizophrenia. *Brit. J. Psychiat.*, 1965, **3**, 503–510. (a)

May, P. R. A., Tuma, A. H., and Kraude, W. Community follow-up of treatment of schizophrenia—issues and problems. *Amer. J. Orthopsychiatry*, 1965, **35**, 754–673. (b)

McNair, D. M., Kahn, R. J., Droppleman, L. F., and Fisher, S. Patient acquiescence and drug effects. In K. Rickels (Ed.), *Non-specific factors in drug therapy*. Springfield, Illinois: Charles C. Thomas, 1968. Pp. 59–72.

Meehl, P. E. Discussion of H. J. Eysenck. The effect of psychotherapy. *Int. J. Psychiatry*, 1965, **1**, 156–157.

Miller, N. E. Some animal experiments pertinent to the problem of combining psychotherapy with drug therapy. *Comprehensive Psychiatry*, 1966, **7**, 1–12.

Nash, E. H., Frank, J. D., Imber, S. D., and Stone, A. R. Selected effects of inert medication on psychiatric outpatients. *Amer. J. Psychotherapy*, 1964, **18**, 33–48.

Nash, E. H., Hoehn-Saric, R., Battle, C. C.. Stone, A. R., Imber, S. D., and Frank, J. D. Systematic preparation of patients for short term psychotherapy. 2. Relation to characteristics of patient, therapist and the psychotherapeutic process. *Jour. Nerv. Ment. Dis.*, 1965, **140**, 374–383.

Nowlis, V. Methods for the objective study of drug effects on group functioning. In L. Uhr and J. G. Miller (Eds.), *Drugs and behavior*. New York: Wiley, 1960. Pp. 563–581.

Ostow, M. The effects of the newer neuroleptic and stimulating drugs on psychic function. In G. J. Sarwer-Foner (Ed.), *The dynamics of psychiatric drug therapy*. Springfield, Illinois: Charles C. Thomas, 1960. Pp. 172–191.

Ostow, M. The advantages and limitations of combined therapy. *Psychosomatics*, 1961, **11**, 11–15.

Ostow, M. *Drugs in psychoanalysis and psychotherapy*. New York: Basic Books, Inc., 1962.

Ostow, M. Method and madness: A critique of current methodology in psychiatric drug research. *Jour. New Drugs*, 1965, **5**, 3–8.

Ostow, M. The complementary roles of psychoanalysis and drug therapy. In P. Solomon (Ed.), *Psychiatric drugs*. New York: Grune & Stratton, 1966. Pp. 91–111. (a)

Ostow, M. Continuing drug needs in mental illness and its pathogenetic basis. In *Non-narcotic drug dependency and addiction*. Washington, D. C.: Amer. Psych. Assoc., 1966. Pp. 33–38. (b)

Ostow, M. The syndrome of narcissistic tranquility. *Int. J. Psycho-anal.*, 1967, **48**, 573–583.

Otis, L. S. Dissociation and recovery of a response learned under the influence of chlorpromazine or saline. *Science*, 1964, **143**, 1347–1348.

Pollard, J. C., and Bakker, C. What does the clinician want to know about psychoactive drugs? In L. Uhr and J. G. Miller (Eds.), *Drugs and behavior*. New York: Wiley, 1960. Pp. 199–208.

Prelinger, E., and Zimet, C. N. *An ego psychological approach to character assessment*. London: Free Press of Glencoe, 1964.

Ray, S., Ragland, R. E., and Clark, M. L. Chlorpromazine in chronic schizophrenic women—comparison of differential effects during and after treatment. *Jour. Nerv. Ment. Dis.*, 1964, **138**, 348–353.

Rickels, K. Indications for tranquilizers in psychotherapy. In L. H. Nodine and J. H. Moyer (Eds.), *Psychosomatic medicine*. Philadelphia: Lea & Febiner, 1962. Pp. 776–779. (a)

Rickels, K. Discussion of psychotherapy and drugs in private practice. In J. H. Nodine and J. H. Moyer (Eds.), *Psychosomatic medicine*. Philadelphia: Lea & Febiger, 1962. (b)

Rickels, K. The use of psychotherapy with drugs in the treatment of anxiety. *Psychosomatics*, 1964, **5**, 111–115.

Rickels, K. *Non-specific factors in drug therapy*. Springfield, Illinois: Charles C. Thomas, 1968. Pp. 3–26.

Rickels, K., Cattell, R. S., Weise, C., Gray, B., Yee, R., Mallin, A., and Aaronson, H. G. Controlled psychopharmacological research in private psychiatric practice. *Psychopharmacologia*, 1966, **9**, 228–306.

Rickels, K., and Downing, R. Verbal ability (intelligence) and improvement in drug therapy of neurotic patients. *J. New Drugs*, 1965, **5**, 303–307.

Rogers, C. R., Gendlin, E. T., Keiser, D. J., and Truax, C. B. *The therapeutic relationship and its impact: A study of psychotherapy with schizophrenics*. Milwaukee, Wisconsin: University of Wisconsin Press, 1967.

Roth, I., Rhudick, P. J., Shaskan, D. A., Slobin, M. S., Wilkinson, A. E., and Young, H. H. Long term effects on psychotherapy of initial treatment conditions. *J. Psychiat. Res.*, 1964, **2**, 283–297.

Sargant, W. Drugs or psychotherapy. *Annales Medico-Psychologiques*, 1965, **121**, 26–29.

Sargant, W., and Slater, E. *An introduction to physical methods of treatment in psychiatry*. (4th ed.) Baltimore, Maryland: Williams & Wilkins, 1964. Pp. 197–221.

Sarwer-Foner, G. J. The use of reserpine with neurotic patients. Paper presented at the First Conference on Psychopharmacology, Montreal, Canada, March 1955.

Sarwer-Foner, G. J. Psychoanalytic theories of activity-passivity conflicts. Experimental verification with reserpine and chlorpromazine. *A.M.A. Arch. Neurol. Psychiat.*, 1957, **78**, 413. (a)

Sarwer-Foner, G. J. The transference and non-specific drug effects in the use of the tranquilizing drugs and their influence on affect. *A.P.A. Psychiat. Research Report No. 8*, 1957, 153. (b)

Sarwer-Foner, G. J. Some psychodynamic and neurological aspects of "paradoxical" behavioral reactions. In P. B. Bradley, P. Deniker, and C. Radouco-Thomas (Eds.), *Neuro-psychopharmacology*. Amsterdam: Elsevier, 1959. Pp. 680–682. (a)

Sarwer-Foner, G. J. Theoretical aspects of the modes of action of the neuroleptic drugs in schizophrenia. In N. S. Kline (Ed.), *Psychopharmacology frontiers*. Boston: Little, Brown, 1959. Pp. 295–303; **438**, 445–476. (b)

Sarwer-Foner, G. J. The dynamics of psychiatric drug therapy. Springfield, Illinois: Charles C. Thomas, 1960. Pp. 624. (a)

Sarwer-Foner, G. J. The role of neuroleptic medication in psychotherapeutic interaction. *Comprehensive Psychiatry*, 1960, **1**, 291–300. (b)

Sarwer-Foner, G. J. Some comments on the psychodynamic aspects of the extrapyramidal reactions. *Rev. Can. Biol. Extrapyramidal System & Neuroleptics*, 1961, **20**, 527–533.

Sarwer-Foner, G. J. On the mechanisms of action of neuroleptic drugs: A theoretical psychodynamic explanation. *Recent Advances in Biological Psychiatry*, 1963, **6**, 217–232.

Sarwer-Foner, G. J., and Kerenyi, A. B. Accumulated experience with transference and counter-transference aspects of the psychotropic drugs, 1953–1960. In E. Rothlin (Ed.), *Neuropsychopharmacology*. Amsterdam: Elsevier, 1961. Pp. 385–391.

Sarwer-Foner, G. J., and Koranyi, E. K. The clinical investigation of pacatal in open psychiatric settings. *Can. Med. Assoc. J.*, 1957, **77**, 450.

Sarwer-Foner, G. J., Koranyi, E. K., Mackay, J., and Grauer, H. Clinical investigation of trifluoperazine (Stelazine) in open psychiatric settings. *Can. Med. Assoc. Jour.*, 1959, **81**, 717.

Sarwer-Foner, G. J., and Koranyi, E. K. Transference effects, the attitude of the treating physician and counter-transference in the use of the neuroleptic drugs in psychiatry. In G. J. Sarwer-Foner, (Ed.), *The dynamics of psychiatric drug therapy*. Springfield, Illinois: Charles C. Thomas, 1960. Pp. 302–402.

Sarwer-Foner, G. J., and Ogle, W. Psychodynamic aspects of reserpine. *Can. Psychiat. Assoc. J.*, 1956, **1**, 11.

Sarwer-Foner, G. J., and Ogle, W. Psychosis and enhanced anxiety produced by reserpine and chlorpromazine. *Can. Med. Assoc. J.*, 1956, **74**, 526.

Shader, R. I., and Rinstock, W. A. Subjective determinants of drug prescription. A study of therapist's attitudes. *Hospital and Community Psychiatry*, 1968, **19**, 384–387.

Shader, R. I., Grinspoon, L., Ewalt, J. R., and Zahn, D. A. Drug responses in acute schizophrenia. In *Schizophrenia—an appraisal*. Hicksville, N.Y.: P.J.D. Publishers, in press, 1969.

Shimkunas, A. M., Gynther, M. D., and Smith, K. Abstracting ability of schizophrenics before and during phenothiazine therapy. *Arch. Gen. Psychiat.*, 1966, **14**, 79–83.

Solomon, P. (Ed.), *Psychiatric drugs: Proceedings of a research conference of the American Psychiatric Association, 1965*. New York: Grune & Stratton, 1966.

Stephens, J. H., and Astrup, C. Treatment outcome in process and non-process schizophrenics treated by A & B types of therapists. *J. Nerv. Ment. Dis.*, 1965, **140**, 449–456.

Stone, A. A. Discussion. In *Psychiatric drugs: Proceedings of a research conference of the American Psychiatric Association, 1965*. New York: Grune & Stratton, 1966. Pp. 66–67.

Stotsky, B. How important is psychotherapy to the hospitalized psychiatric patient? *J. Clin. Psychol.*, 1956, **12**, 32–36.

Teuber, H. L., and Powers, E. Evaluating therapy in a delinquency prevention program. *Proceedings of the Assoc. for Research in Nervous & Mental Disease*, 1953, **31**, 138–147.

Tokar, J. Personal communication, 1969.

Tokar, J. T., and Stefflre, V. A technique for studying an individual and his language. Part I. Techniques for eliciting patterns of use of an individual's key words. *Psychotherapy, theory, research & practice*, in press, 1969.

Tokar, J. T., Stefflre, V., and Harding, J. Some techniques for comparison of normal and schizophrenic language. *Language and thought in schizophrenia*, in press, 1969.

Truax, C. B., and Carkhuff, R. R. Toward effective counseling and psychotherapy. *Training & practice*. Chicago: Aldine, 1967.

Tuma, A. H. The prediction of response to pharmacotherapy among schizophrenics: An historical perspective. In J. R. Wittenborn and P. R. A. May (Eds.), *Prediction of response to pharmacotherapy*. Springfield, Illinois: Charles C. Thomas, 1966. Pp. 43–68.

Tuma, A. H. An historical perspective of research into the comparative outcome of treatment in schizophrenia. In P. R. A. May, *Treatment of schizophrenia*. New York: Science House, 1968.

Uhlenhuth, E. H., Lipman, R. S., and Covi, L. Combined pharmacotherapy and psychotherapy: Controlled studies. *J. Nerv. Ment. Dis.*, 1969, **148**, 52–64.

Uhr, L. Objectively measured behavioral effects of psychoactive drugs. In L. Uhr and J. G. Miller (Eds.), Drugs & behavior. New York: Wiley, 1960. Pp. 610–633.

Van Baeyer, W. The clinical and psychopathological mode of action of somatic therapies. *Comprehensive Psychiatry*, 1964, **5**, 146–154.

Wallerstein, R. S., Robbins, L. L., Sargent, H. D., and Luborsky, L. The psychotherapy research project of the Menninger Foundation: Rationale, method and sample use. *Bull. Menninger Clinic*, 1956, **20**, 221–278.

Wallerstein, R. S., Robbins, L. L., Sargent, H. D., Luborsky, L., Fabian, M., Hale, B. H., Ticho, E., Ticho, G. R., Modlin, H. C., Faris, M. T., and Voth, H. M. The psychotherapy research project of the Menninger Foundation—second Report. *Bull. Menninger Clinic*, 1958, **22**, 115–166.

Wallerstein, R. S., Robbins, L. L., and Hall, B. H. The psychotherapy research project of the Menninger Foundation—third Report. *Bull. Menninger Clinic*, 1960, **24**, 157–216.

Wechsler, D. *The Wechsler adult intelligence scale*. New York: Psychological Corp., 1955.

Wheelis, A. Will and Psychoanalysis. *J. Amer. Psychoanalytic Assoc.*, 1956, **4**, 285–303.

Whitehorn, J. C., and Betz, B. J. A comparison of psychotherapeutic relationships between physicians and schizophrenic patients when insulin is combined with psychotherapy and when psychotherapy is used alone. *Amer. J. Psychiatry*, 1957, **113**, 901–910.

Whitman, R. M. Drugs, dreams and the experimental subject. *J. Can. Psychiat. Assoc.*, 1963, **8**, 395–399.

Whitman, R. M., Pierce, C. M., and Maas, J. Drugs and dreams. In Uhr and Miller (Eds.), *Drugs and behavior*. New York: Wiley, 1960. Pp. 591–595.

Whitman, R. M., Pierce, C. M., Maas, J. W., and Baldridge, B. Drugs and dreams. II. Imipramine and prochlorperazine. *Comprehensive Psychiatry*, 1961, **2**, 219–226.

Winkelman, N. W. An appraisal of chlorpromazine. *Amer. Jour. Psychiat.*, 1957, **113**, 961–971.

Winkelman, N. W. A psychoanalytic study of phenothiazine action. In N. S. Kline (Ed.), *Psychopharmacology frontiers*. Boston, Mass.: Little, Brown, 1959. Pp. 305–315.

Winkelman, N. W. The use of chlorpromazine and prochlorperazine as adjuncts to psychoanalytic psychotherapy—general principles for combined therapy. In Sarwer-Foner, J. E. (Ed.), *The dynamics of psychiatric drug therapy*. Springfield, Illinois: Charles C. Thomas, 1960.

Winkelman, N. W. A clinical and socio-cultural study of 200 patients started on chlorpromazine ten and one half years ago. *Amer. J. Psychiatry*, 1964, **120**, 861–849.

Zetzel, E. R. Discussion in *Psychiatric drugs*. New York: Grune & Stratton, 1966. Pp. 75–85.

Zubin, J., and Katz, M. M. Psychopharmacology and personality. *Inter. J. Psychiat.*, 1966, **2**, 640–675.

PART III

ANALYSIS OF BEHAVIORAL THERAPIES

15

COUNTER CONDITIONING AND RELATED METHODS

H. J. EYSENCK
H. R. BEECH

UNIVERSITY OF LONDON

THE ORIGIN OF COUNTER-CONDITIONING METHODS

The notion that psychological disorders can be acquired is certainly not a new one for, in this particular sense, behavior therapy and psychoanalytic theories cannot be distinguished. For behavior therapy, however, with its emphasis upon the mechanisms of learning, rather than the content of what has been learned, the acquisition of psychological disturbance takes on a quite different and unique significance.

To call attention to one study as being a starting point has obvious dangers, but Watson and Rayner's (1920) study of Little Albert, probably more than any other, could be said to be a point of origin for behavior therapy. In this paper, these writers not only grasped and demonstrated the possibilities of establishing emotional reactions by conditioning, but also put forward therapeutic ideas that have become a central part of modern behavior therapy. Watson's procedure for producing emotional reactions in Albert, a stolid 11-month-old infant, was simple but effective. A white rat was offered to the child and a loud noise was made just at the moment when Albert reached out to touch the animal. Repetition of this association between a frightening sound and the white rat soon led to an emotional reaction to the animal alone. This, in Watson's view, paralleled the conditioning phenomena to be observed in Pavlov's laboratories. It was also possible to show that the emotional reaction to the rat had transferred or generalized to other stimuli that were similar to the rat, but not to others that had no obvious connection with that stimulus. Furthermore, both the directly conditioned emotional response and as those conditioned by transfer tended to persist over a period of time. One simple experiment, therefore, effectively demonstrated that by association fears may be acquired that may be generalized and persistent. (Replication of the experiment has not always proved easy or successful.)

Little Albert's ultimate fate is not known, although it was Watson's belief that the newly acquired emotional responses would continue and would "modify personality throughout life." Indeed, Watson envisaged a situation in which Albert might be confronted by a psychoanalyst who would elicit the memory of Albert's attempt to play with his mother's pubic hair as the source of the phobia.

Perhaps most important from the viewpoint of contemporary therapeutic procedures were Watson's ideas concerning the removal of conditioned emotional reactions. He notes that Albert's thumb-sucking appeared to be ". . . a compensatory device for blocking fear . . .," and this observation seemed to be directly related to his therapeutic method involving presentation of fear stimuli while at the same time calling forth alternative responses by stimulating the erogenous zones or by feeding. This was called an attempt to "recondition," and is quite clearly a description of what is now called reciprocal inhibition therapy.

Watson's therapeutic ideas, were taken up by Mary Cover Jones (1924) in her study of methods of removing existing fears of young children. Apparently the most successful method was found to be that of "direct conditioning," where attempts were made to associate the stimulus to fear with some other stimulus evoking a "positive (pleasant) reaction," as Watson had suggested. But to do this, it was found necessary to introduce the feared object by degrees, while simultaneously evoking some alternative response to fear, such as feeding. Certainly this method seemed to work very well in Jones' most celebrated case of Peter who, prior to treatment, showed great anxiety in the presence of a rabbit, a rat, and various other objects, although Jones points out that careful attention must be given to a situation in which

two response systems are being manipulated, in case the fear should transfer to the positive stimulus instead of in the expected direction. It is also significant that other methods, such as attempts to connect pleasant reactions with the fear object by verbal means, by repeated presentation of the stimulus to fear, and by applying mild punishment, were far less effective than "direct conditioning." These findings have been repeatedly confirmed by later experiment.[1]

It might be argued that, while the contributions made by Watson and Jones were not full and detailed, and the theoretical propositions were not well developed, nevertheless their findings, therapeutic procedure, and general model were not fundamentally different from those put forward today.[2] The surprising aspect of this piece of history is that the importance of conditioning in the acquisition and removal of fears was briefly recorded and then, apparently, forgotten, although the basic idea of gradual presentation of the stimuli to anxiety was revived for a time by Herzberg (1945), who reported significant success for the method, in terms of both the speed and the effectiveness of therapeutic outcome.

There was, however, another strand of research that seemed to generate a more durable and sustained interest among investigators. This involved the study of what came to be known as Experimental Neuroses. In fact, numerous rather different methods were employed to produce, in the laboratory, a variety of behavior disturbances (Krasnogorski, 1925; Pavlov, 1927; Liddell, 1944; Anderson and Liddell, 1935; Karn, 1938; Dimmick, Ludlow, and Whiteman, 1939; Masserman, 1943; Gantt, 1944; Maier, 1949; and many others).

It is certainly the case that much of this work on experimental neurosis seemed to indicate that conflict of needs and drives was strongly implicated in producing breakdown. However, it is by no means true, as Wolpe suggests (1958), that all workers in this area argued for the necessity of conflict in order to produce abnormal behavior. Indeed, Pavlov's anecdotal account of the effect upon one of his dogs of

---

[1] The Implosive Therapy treatment propounded by Stampfl is a notable exception to this rule.

[2] The work of Jones (1924), and the later but equally important studies of Jersild and Holmes

(1935), were done at Teachers College, Columbia, under the guidance of E. L. Thorndike, whose influence on behavior therapy has not been sufficiently recognized.

flooding of his laboratory in 1912 is only one example of the general point that "overstrain of excitatory processes" alone was capable of producing abberant be-havior. (See also, for example, Miller, 1948).

Perhaps the most striking aspects of this work were the repeated confirmations that disturbances in behavior could be induced by the systematic application of certain conditions, and that these effects could persist over a lengthy period of time and could show generalization. A further important aspect of this work concerned the individual differences in responsiveness to particular conditions, perhaps most clearly seen in Pavlov's own work. This evidence suggested that not only may some animals remain unresponsive to the kinds of stress imposed, but also that when animals with *different types of nervous systems* were exposed to similar stresses, they tended to develop different kinds of reactions. The clear implication of this latter point is that a theory of psychological disorder based exclusively upon the presence or absence of traumatic environmental circumstances would be quite inadequate.

However, while much has been made, by behavior theorists, of the finding that persistent abnormal patterns of behavior can be created under laboratory conditions (Wolpe, 1958), relatively little attention has been paid to the differential responsiveness of organisms, although a beginning has been made. (Eysenck, 1957, 1967).

Prior to Masserman's experimental work, the therapeutic aspects of experimentally induced disorders were relatively neglected, and it was these studies that probably provided greatest impetus to Wolpe's development of reciprocal inhibition therapy. Masserman's experiments (1943) were unexceptional in the manner in which behavior disturbances were created, but his attempts to restore adaptive and "stable" responses did excite some attention. One of the treatments he employed successfully seemed not to be different from that which Watson had suggested and Jones had implemented in their

studies, namely to present some elements of the stimulus to fear under conditions where an alternative response to fear is being evoked. This method was referred to by Masserman as "reassurance and suggestion," and seemed to him to be related to "transference" mechanisms.

However, it is of considerable interest to note that, in all, six therapeutic methods produced some measure of success, but that the most valuable appeared to be those involving a "forced solution of the motivational impasse through environmental manipulation," and affording "partial control of the experimental situation by the animal subject," with the latter producing the better results. Wolpe (1958) mentions Masserman's "forced solution" technique, noting that he himself obtained similar results; however, he omits mention of Masserman's most successful method. One might speculate upon the direction that behavior therapy could have taken had Masserman's "partial control" method been investigated and confirmed as superior by Wolpe. As it was, one of the less successful of Masserman's treatments, "reassurance and pursuasion" by coaxing, petting, and feeding by hand, was confirmed by Wolpe's own findings and led to the development of the reciprocal inhibition model.

In yet another way, the situation following Masserman's experiments might well have led to a different pattern of development, or at least a different emphasis, in behavior therapy.[3] Both Jones and Masserman had found that "social imitation" (Jones) or "social interaction" (Masserman) could exercise some degree of beneficial influence upon aberrant behavior and, at this stage, perhaps this type of "treatment" appeared to be just as promising as any of the alternatives. Wolpe's studies, not only of animals but of the human neurotic condition, may well have decided the direction in which the major therapeutic emphasis would be directed. It is of some interest, however, to note that Bandura (1962) adopted the alternative therapeutic possibility, and has succeeded in directing a good deal of the attention given to his social

[3] The term "behavior therapy," with the meaning it now carries, was introduced by Eysenck (1959), although it had been used independently by Skinner (1953) and Lazarus (1958) in a much more restricted sense at an earlier date. For Eysenck, behavior therapy includes all methods of behavior modification based on modern learning theory and laboratory practice; Skinner and Lazarus were clearly concerned only with operant conditioning and desensitization, respectively.

imitation and modelling approach to effecting changes in behavior.

Wolpe's (1958) contribution to the development and refinement of the treatment now known as desensitization proved crucial. It is in this respect, rather than as the discoverer of this form of therapy, that he has made his mark in the field. Nevertheless, so far as one can determine, his particular emphasis upon one aspect of the neurotic condition also gave a particular direction and focus to later work. The special bias he imparted can be seen quite clearly in his evaluation of the literature on experimental neurosis, the definition of neurotic behavior he accepts, and the role of anxiety in the total complex of behavioral abnormality.

There is no doubt at all, judging by the descriptions of behavior under experimental neurosis conditions, that fear (which Wolpe [1958] equates with anxiety—the word "anxiety" is used throughout this chapter synonymously with "fear") is only one of the numerous possible reactions. There is reason to suppose that it is a major component, in that it is perhaps the most frequent and obtrusive outcome of noxious stimulation, but not that it is the only one. Aggression, inactivity and stupor, stereotypy of movements, eczema, disappearance of existing conditioned responses, and many other effects have been noted. While certain of these reactions may be explicable in terms of "anxiety" or "fear," we cannot be sure about this, and we would need to be circumspect in our interpretations and evaluations of behavior ensuing from the application of stressful stimulation.

Wolpe, while adopting an extremely broad-based definition of neurotic behavior (". . . any persistent maladaptive behavior acquired by learning in a physiologically normal organism"), regards anxiety as the central and most important aspect of such disturbances. Of course there is no reason to suppose that this need be the case, either from the descriptions of experimental neurosis behavior, or from Wolpe's definition of the neurosis. There, is, however no doubt at all that Wolpe's great emphasis in treatment is upon the control of anxiety, almost to the complete exclusion of other considerations, and his theory and therapeutic method are obviously colored by this emphasis. Again, it is interesting to speculate as to what the current

status and practice of behavior therapy would be, had Wolpe's special emphasis been absent.

In respect to allocating a central role to anxiety in psychological disturbance, Wolpe has aligned himself with the traditional psychoanalytic viewpoint. The crucial difference, which comes out particularly clearly in contrasting Wolpe's experimental animal work with that of Masserman (1943), lies in the importance that the latter, following psychoanalytic practice, attaches to *conflict*. Wolpe argued in favor of a simple aversive conditioning paradigm, while Masserman postulated the necessity of "motivational conflicts." The work of Smart (1965), specially designed to throw light on this controversy, unambiguously supports Wolpe; "the present study clearly indicates that conflict does not facilitate [the production of experimental neuroses]" (page 218). Theoretically this is a very important point that clearly demarcates the two rival theories, and Smart's conclusion should be borne in mind by those who believe that Freud's and Wolpe's theories are similar, differing only in the kind of language in which they are expressed. A general review of work on experimental neuroses can be found in Cosnier (1966).

One other strand in the history of behavior therapy should receive mention, namely the attempts, notably by Mowrer and by Dollard and Miller, to relate learning theory to existing therapeutic theories and techniques. Mowrer's views have, of course, undergone a great change (1965), but it is not without significance that he, like Dollard and Miller, apparently began with the assumption that psychoanalytic postulates and principles had a certain value, and for this reason it would be advantageous to express them, and the mechanisms that were presumed to subserve them, in learning-theory terms. In Mowrer's discussion of identification (1950), for example, doubts concerning the acceptability of Freudian concepts appear to be few, and the expression of such concepts in learning-theory terms (as in his two-factor analysis of imitative learning, and the relation between imitation and the Freudian concept of identification) is perceived to be a fruitful approach. In his more recent writings, of course, Mowrer castigates psychoanalysis as theoretically false and practically useless, if not actively pernicious.

The most systematic and comprehensive attempt to relate learning theory to psychoanalytic principles was, however, that by Dollard and Miller (1950). Their goal was that of a systematic analysis of psychotherapy in terms of the laws of learning. Their basic assumption was not at all different from that of contemporary behavior therapists—if a neurosis is learned, then it must be learned "according to known and experimentally verified laws of learning . . .," although accompanied by the reservation that quite new laws might eventually be found to be necessary. Their strategy involved a straightforward and direct substitution of learning for psychoanalytic principles, so that reinforcement is substituted for Freud's pleasure principle, "repression" becomes the inhibition of cue-producing responses, transference is seen as a special case of generalization, and so on.

Their account of how symptoms are acquired is similarly not at all at variance with that offered by contemporary behavior therapists (although there is an interesting difference in focus upon the *context* in which acquisition occurs). The important point of departure, however, occurs when the theoretical accounts are translated into therapeutic terms, for it seems clear that Dollard and Miller provide only endorsement and justification in "scientific" terms for existing treatment methods. Free association, for example, becomes the means by which the anxiety generated by a repressed idea can be weakened by extinction, and interpretation is the means by which new responses (new verbal units) are acquired and become attached to the "correct" cues. However, Miller, like Mowrer, has changed his mind on traditional methods and theories, and would not now advocate these ideas (personal communication).

It seems at least possible that, while Dollard and Miller provide no new system of therapy based upon learning-theory principles, the mere fact that such principles *could* be applied to the development and treatment of neurotic conditions must have helped to create an atmosphere and climate of opinion in which behavior therapy could develop. However, Wolpe's published work (1958) concerning the exposition of the principle of reciprocal inhibition, and his large-scale application of the therapeutic method, undoubtedly gave great impetus to the growth of behavior therapy, although, as will be pointed out in a later section of this chapter, treatment by the application of aversive stimuli had by this time become quite widespread.

The situation, with respect to treatment derived from learning theory, was further developed by the publication of *Behavior Therapy and the Neuroses* (Eysenck, 1960b). This book brought together a number of previously separate forms of treatment and emphasized their dependence upon a general learning-theory framework, as well as making clear that, in the field of abnormality, we may usefully regard treatment as being directed toward two main classes of abnormal phenomena; superfluous learning and deficiencies in learning.

Subsequent to this publication, several trends have become apparent. One of these is made clear by reference to section headings in *Behavior Therapy and the Neuroses* and comparing them with later works, for it will be seen that while the position of reciprocal inhibition and aversion therapies has strengthened and developed, that of "negative practice" and "feedback control" have, if anything, weakened. These trends are more probably attributable to the limitations of applicability of the latter to psychological conditions rather than to any fundamental theoretical flaws. Perhaps most significant, however, has been the emergence of operant procedures as a major therapeutic tool, the importance of which is dealt with in a separate chapter of this book.

Other trends, as will be made clear in succeeding sections, have been the proliferation of special techniques and procedures (such as covert sensitization), and the more sophisticated use of refinements of laboratory experimentation (such as employment of intermittent reinforcement). In these ways behavior therapy has strengthened its early tenuous relationship with its putative origins.

So far these developments represent the implementation and extrapolation of basic principles and assumptions, although it might be anticipated that at some stage the relationship between learning theory and behavior therapy will be of a different kind. One might hope, for example, that the findings from behavior therapy might in some measure shape and modify the development of learning theories themselves, and will feed back into those theories something of value.

THE CONDITIONING THEORY OF NEUROSIS

It is possible to specify methods of treatment for neurotic disorders, and to test their efficacy, without postulating a theory of neurosis, or even defining precisely what is meant by the term "neurosis." Like the proverbial elephant, neurotic disorders are easier to recognize than to describe or define; most dictionary and textbook definitions are uninformative and circular. We hold the view that the methods of treatment here discussed are associated so closely with a particular definition and theory of neurosis that a brief discussion of that theory seems called for; it should be said, however, that not all behavior therapists may agree with the particular form of the theory here presented, and that in addition, the correctness or incorrectness of the theory does not affect the empirical effectiveness of the desensitization or aversion-therapy methods. Our theory may be erroneous, in part or *in toto*, yet the methods of behavior therapy may work perfectly well; just as our theory may be along the right lines, while the methods of treatment under discussion may fail for a variety of reasons.

The most interesting discussions of the definition of neurosis have taken place among animal psychologists concerned with "animal neurosis," simply because for them the problem of creating an animal analogue of human neurosis in the absence of verbal complaints necessitated a consideration of the criteria by which neurosis could be objectively recognised (Hamilton, 1927; Foley, 1935; Lubin, 1943; Davis, 1954; Broadhurst, 1960). Hebb's (1947, p. 11) definition is regarded as the most authoritative: "Neurosis is in practice an undesirable emotional condition which is generalized and persistent; it occurs in a minority of the population and has no origin in a gross neural lesion."

In addition to the six elements contained in this definition, Hebb considers and dismisses three others—lack of a known physiological basis, marked behavioral change from an earlier base line, and sequel to some "traumatic" experience.

Our own description and definition agree with Hebb's main points, but are sufficiently different to require discussion; some of these differences arise from the fact that we are concerned with human neurosis pure and simple, without attempting to formulate a definition that could be applied directly to animal experimentation. In the first place, then, we would define neurosis in terms of *behavior*, rather than in terms of *emotion*; the formidable difficulties raised by the concept of emotion, and the additional ones of measuring it, make a definition in these terms awkward. Neurotic behavior is *maladapted* to the enduring needs of the organism and of society, and this lack of adaptation will usually be cognitively clear to the neurotic himself; in other words, it is not due to lack of intelligence or education and knowledge. This maladaptive behavior is not due to gross neural lesions, but occurs either (1) as a consequence of maladaptive conditioning, or (2) as a consequence of the failure of adaptive conditioning to take effect. Such behavior shows persistence; that is, it is chronic to some degree, continuing after the cessation of the specific unconditioned stimulus, and it is generalized to stimuli other than the specific unconditioned stimulus. In terms of a definition, then, *neurosis is persistent, generalized, maladaptive behavior due to faulty conditioning*. We will discuss in some detail the particular faults in conditioning that are likely, in our view, to produce neurotic behavior; for the moment, let us consider some consequences of our definition.

In the first place, the very term "neurosis" is seen to be nothing but an erroneous reification of a misplaced medical disease concept; there is no such thing as a neurosis, but only maladaptive behavior of the kind described.[4] Such behavior lies along a continuum; there are many

---

[4] This somewhat inconoclastic proposal might suggest the abandonment of the term "neuroticism," which has traditionally been used to designate one of the two major dimensions of personality, and which Eysenck has identified tentatively as an inherited autonomic imbalance predisposing a person to the development of neurotic symptoms, particularly when coupled with an introverted personality. The alternative term "emotionality" might seem preferable, and indeed the two terms are often used interchangeably. The importance of strong emotional arousal in mediating maladaptive behavior will be discussed later.

degrees of maladaptation, of persistence, of generalization. Some of these continua are properly associated with the individual, as we shall see later—different people form conditioned responses with different speed and vigor, show stimulus and response generalization to different degrees, and the like. Other continua are properly associated with environmental conditions that are largely accidental, such as traumatic events of one kind or another, or a series of subtraumatic situations to which the subject is exposed. Still other continua are related to the particular society in which the subject lives—homosexuality was not maladaptive in ancient Greece, was a punishable offence in Great Britain until recently, and may be adaptive in certain artistic and theatrical circles. The term "neurosis" consequently has no scientific meaning or value; it is multidimensional and does not refer to a particular, recognizable state—hence, the ease with which extreme degrees of neurotic behavior can be recognized and diagnosed, and the notorious difficulties of doing the same when less extreme degrees are involved. Terms such as "tall" and "short" or "high" and "low" are not useful scientifically; they are descriptive of extremes along a continuum, and scientists prefer to quantify stages along the continua in question. In the case of a multidimensional concept, these difficulties are compounded, and it becomes essential to sort out the dimensions involved, and quantify each in turn. It scarcely needs to be said that this task has hardly even been attempted in the field of neurotic behavior. ("Neurotic behavior" is acceptable where "neurosis" is not; it does not reify a nonexistent state or disease, and carries no more implications than the definition given above.)

In the second place, the traditional distinction between "neurosis" and "neurotic symptoms" breaks down; if there is no such thing as a neurosis, then all we are left with are the so-called "symptoms," that is, the very items of neurotic behavior that we have regarded as the essence of the disorder we are dealing with. (Behavior is here used in its most all-embracing sense; that is, it includes observable autonomic changes, hormonal discharges, neural innervations, and the like). The distinction between "disease" and "symptom" in the case of neurotic disorders is a carry-over from inappropriate medical terminology, adopted by the psychoanalytic school and popularized by them. Such a theory undervalues the observable and measurable "symptoms" and overvalues the hypothetical and possibly nonexistent "disease," that is, the various unconscious and repressed "complexes" postulated by Freud and his followers. Behavior therapists, in turn, have no place for these hypothetical disease concepts, and deal entirely with the observable maladaptive behavioral consequences of past faulty conditioning. In this sense, the symptom *is* the disease; the medium is the message, to adapt an absurd phrase to a meaningful context. *Cure the symptom (or rather the totality of the symptoms, as there will usually, of course, be more than one, due to the process of generalization) and you have cured the disease. The old-fashioned and inappropriate terminology lends this statement an aura of paradox; rephrase it to read "Reconditioning of maladaptive behavior makes it adaptive," and the paradox vanishes.*

In the third place, it will be obvious that most neurotic behaviors will be minor ones, and occur in persons not normally diagnosed as "neurotic." Exaggerated fears of spiders, harmless snakes, or rodents are neurotic in our sense, particularly when they are generalized, as they often are; fear of spiders often generalizes to daddy longlegs, and the like. Such fears are maladaptive, but only to a minimal degree; few sufferers would complain about them to a psychiatrist, or seek special advice on how to get rid of them. This makes them ideal testing beds for deconditioning therapies; they partake of the nature of the behavior we are interested in, but they are not so severe that ethical considerations make us hesitate to use the experimental method in its strictest form in their study. A seriously neurotic person who is assigned to a control group might have to be transferred to a treatment group if he is getting worse, and threatens suicide; this is not likely to happen in minor behavioral disorders.

In the fourth place, our definition admits types of behavior which many people would regard as neurotic, but which under Hebb's definition might be difficult to include. Examples are psychopathic or sociopathic behavior, various types of criminal behavior, and certain hysterical disorders; all of these frequently fail to show the typical "undesirable emotional conditions" demanded by Hebb which are more characteristic of dysthymic neurotics. The distinction here made follows that made by Eysenck and Rachman (1965) between disorders of the first kind and disorders of the second kind. Disorders of the first kind (phobic reactions, anxiety states, obsessional and compulsive disorders, and other dysthymic reactions), in our theory, "are caused by conditioned autonomic fear responses and the reactions, skeletal, muscular and hormonal, of the organism to these conditioned responses" (p. 6.) In disorders of the second kind, "we postulate not the occurrence of a conditioning process leading to maladaptive habits, but rather the failure of a conditioning process to occur which would produce socially desirable habits" (p. 7.) The theories underlying disorders of the second kind have been discussed at some length elsewhere (Eysenck, 1964a); we shall revert to this distinction in the next section in relation to personality correlates of neurotic behavior.

We must now trace in some more detail the theoretical course of neurotic behavior, particularly of the first kind. Eysenck (1960b, 1964b) has proposed a three-stage theory which, in brief, holds that in the first instance we have a single traumatic event, or else a series of subtraumatic events producing unconditioned but strong autonomic (emotional) reactions, mainly of the sympathetic nervous system. These strong emotional reactions may themselves serve to disorganize behavior and make it maladaptive, but such reactions are too widespread and "normal" to be properly regarded as neurotic; furthermore, they are neither persistent nor generalized. At the second stage, we find that in a certain number of cases, conditioning takes place, in the sense that a previously neutral stimulus, through association, becomes connected with the unconditioned stimulus that gives rise to the traumatic emotional reaction. From now on it will be found that the conditioned stimulus, as well as the unconditioned stimulus, produces the original, maladaptive, emotional behavior; that stimulus and response generalization take place; and that the complex of maladaptive reactions becomes persistent.

A third step, however, is still required. Conditioned responses that are not reinforced begin to extinguish, and as the CS for neurotic behavior is unlikely in most situations to be followed by the UCS, extinction should take place. Eysenck (1963b) has suggested that the frequently reported phenomenon of "spontaneous remission" represents the effect of such extinction; Figure 15.1 shows how marked this phenomenon is in relation to serious neurotic-type behaviors when no psychiatric treatment is in fact attempted. Other hypotheses may be

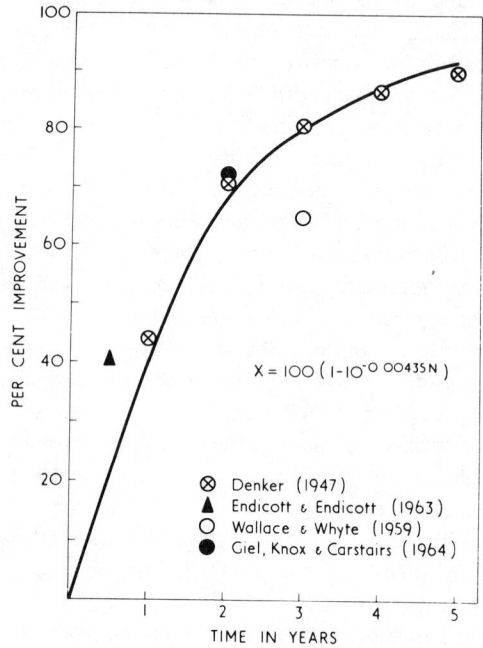

$$X = 100\,(1 - 10^{-0.00435N})$$

⊗ Denker (1947)
▲ Endicott & Endicott (1963)
○ Wallace & Whyte (1959)
● Giel, Knox & Carstairs (1964)

TIME IN YEARS

Figure 15.1 Proportion of patients with severe neurotic disorders cured or very much improved after varying period without psychiatric treatment. The formula shows the rate of spontaneous remission (*X*) as a function of time (*N*) in weeks since the beginning of the experiment. Results from four studies are combined as shown.

advanced to explain spontaneous remission, at least in certain cases; sufferers from neurotic disorders frequently consult priests, relatives, or sympathetic friends and acquaintances, and by discussing with them their troubles create conditions similar to, although probably less effective than, those produced in behavior therapy (desensitization). (In a similar way it has been suggested that whatever effect psychotherapy may have is due to certain elements of desensitization unwittingly incorporated in it;

the demonstration that certain personality qualities in therapists determine whether psychotherapy—of whatever persuasion—will be helpful or harmful for the patient [Truax and Carkhuff, 1967] lends credibility to this view, particularly as the required personality traits are very like those posited in the sympathetic lay listener mentioned above.) It is unfortunate that no detailed studies of spontaneous remission seem to be available; as Eysenck (1964b) has pointed out, time by itself cannot cure neurotic disorders. We must postulate certain events that take place in time, and evidence is lacking concerning these events.

Why do conditioned maladaptive responses often not extinguish, in spite of lack of positive reinforcement, and why do they frequently persist in the face of persistent negative reinforcement? This "neurotic paradox," as Mowrer (1950) has called it, may have more than one answer. Whichever may be the correct one (and it is possible that all those suggested below may be active), we must postulate a third stage in the development of persistent maladaptive responses. Eysenck (1960b), following Mowrer's animal model (1950), has suggested that in many cases the Pavlovian conditioning of anxiety/fear postulated as our second step is followed by a process of instrumental conditioning. It was suggested that when the CS occurs without positive reinforcement, then it should extinguish; this is certainly so in the laboratory situation. But human beings are not restrained in a harness, having to submit to the occurrence of the CS; they have the alternative of withdrawing from the CS, or of avoiding it altogether. Approaching the CS is postulated to give rise to conditioned fear and anxiety responses; withdrawing would be positively reinforced by an offsetting of these CSs, and hence the subject would become conditioned to avoid CS in the future, thus making extinction impossible because no further CS could occur. Exposure to CS corresponds in some ways to the concept of "reality testing" employed by psychiatrists; this process of instrumental conditioning protects the Pavlovian conditional response (CR) from extinction. Illustrations of this process are given in Eysenck and Rachman (1965). Escape-avoidance learning of this type is of course well known in the

experimental literature; Bolles (1967) gives an excellent theoretical account and highlights some of the experimental problems encountered.

An alternative (or additional) explanation of the persistence of neurotic responses in spite of failure of reinforcement to occur may be found in the phenomenon of *incubation*. Traditionally, this term has been used to refer to "a growth of fear over a time interval which follows some aversive stimulation. The increase in fear is assumed to be spontaneous in the sense that the time interval is free of further exposure to the aversive stimulus" (McAllister and McAllister, 1967, p. 180). This notion was introduced into the experimental literature by Diven (1937), and has since found support in the work of Bindra and Cameron (1953); Breznitz (1967); Brush and Levine (1966); Desiderato et al. (1966, 1967); Golin and Golin (1966); Kamin (1957, 1963); McMichael (1966); Tarpy (1966); and others. McAllister and McAllister (1967) conclude a review of this field by saying that "although the incubation-of-fear hypothesis has been tested in a wide variety of situations, the phenomenon has yet to be convincingly demonstrated" (p. 189). Eysenck (1968) takes the view that incubation so defined is akin to reminiscence in ordinary learning data, mediated by consolidation of the memory trace (Eysenck, 1965), as much a "now-you-see-it-now-you-don't" phenomenon as reminiscence (particularly in verbal learning) has always been known to be. As such it does not deserve a special name, and is of limited interest in behavior therapy and learning theory generally.

Eysenck (1968) suggests that the term "incubation" be reserved, instead, for a somewhat different phenomenon, namely the incrementation of CRs during a period when only unreinforced CSs (symbolized as $\overline{CS}$) are administered. (Because of the striking nature of the data presented in this connection by Napalkov, 1963, Eysenck, 1967a, suggested the name "Napalkov phenomenon" as an alternative to the term "incubation"). Napalkov, working with dogs, found that various nocive stimuli produced increases in blood pressure of less than 50 mm, complete adaptation occurring after some 25 applications. A single conditioning trial, however, followed by repeated administrations of the $\overline{CS}$ (never the UCS) brought about increases in blood pressure of 30 to 40 mm at first, rising to 190 to 230 mm; the hypertensive state produced lasted over a year in some cases. In the field of human conditioning, Sanderson et al. (1964) gave a single-trial temporary interruptions of respiration lasting for about 100 sec., an extremely harrowing experience. (Injections of succinylcholine chloride dihydrate provided the UCS). One hundred extinction trials were given over a period of three weeks, and autonomic responses recorded. Instead of extinction, there appeared an increase in size of the CER, together with stimulus generalization. Dykman, Mack and Ackerman (1965), working with dogs, found that "apparently to some dogs the threat is more traumatic than the presence of shock," i.e. CR is stronger than UCR; in several other studies Dykman and Gantt (1958, 1960a, 1960b) have found that "the threat of trauma continues to operate in extinction." Lichtenstein (1950) came to similar conclusions. Bridger and Mandel (1964) have demonstrated in the human field the strength of threats ($\overline{CS}$s) as compared with shocks (UCSs). Studies of "partial irreversibility" (Solomon et al., 1953; Solomon and Wynne, 1953, 1954) are also relevant, although they use the escape-avoidance paradigm. Other minor studies are mentioned in Eysenck (1968), but on the whole there seems to be little doubt that under certain circumstances $\overline{CS}$ can produce incrementation of CR, instead of decrementation (extinction) as is usual. It seems likely that both incubation and extinction always take place when unreinforced CSs are presented, and that the outcome of the experiment depends upon the strength of the two responses.

The theory advanced to explain this phenomenon, put baldly, briefly, and perhaps implausibly, is that the CR (or rather, response-produced stimuli depending for their evocation on the CS) can itself act as a reinforcer for unreinforced CSs (Eysenck, 1968). It is postulated that the UCS (for example, shock) produces a complex of UCRs containing elements of pain, fear, avoidance reactions, resentment, and the like; these are all nocive and may be jointly referred to as NR (nocive response). When shock is paired with CS, then CS acts as a signal for the evocation of NR and, by virtue of classical conditioning, evokes all or

part of NR. But the evocation of NR, in whole or part, reinforces the CS–NR connection; the signal ($\overline{CS}$), even though not reinforced by UCR, still signals some nocive reactions, and it is to that extent seen to be justified. The organism expects an aversive response and it does, in fact, get one. And if threat, as we have seen, can be more aversive than shock itself, then the CR may in fact be more reinforcing than the UCR. The details of this process need not detain us here, but we may note that Hull (1929), in a very early anticipation of the model of neurosis here presented, suggested that with weak UCSs, extinction would gradually weaken defense reactions to the point where the noxious stimulus occurred again, thus initiating a stop-and-go series of reactions. However, where avoidance reactions to strong stimuli were concerned, he thought that experimental extinction might be held "progressively in abeyance as the gravity of the injury increased" (p. 510). Eysenck (1968) has in fact suggested that the strength of the UCR (rather than the UCS; the two are related, but may not be identical) is one of the parameters controlling whether extinction or incubation should be found in an experimental situation; the other variable he suggested was personality, which will be dealt with in the next section.

The same mechanism discussed above must be assumed to be present when CS, rather than $\overline{CS}$, is administered; we would postulate that to the NR produced by the UCS there is added an increment of NR produced by the CS. In this way it becomes possible to account for the very strong NRs achieved on the basis of rather weak UCRs (for example, Anderson and Parmenter, 1941; Liddell, 1944). UCRs tend to decrement, due to habituation and adaptation, just as unreinforced CRs tend to extinguish; these trends are opposed, sometimes successfully, sometimes not, by the CS/NR mechanism. To put the matter less technically, but perhaps more intelligibly: Shock is followed by pain, and $\overline{CS}$ is followed by fear. Shock + CS is followed by pain + fear; this combined NR is more potent (more disagreeable, more nocive, and more aversive) than either alone, and hence has greater reinforcing properties. $\overline{CS}$ is followed by fear as the CR, which is less reinforcing than pain + fear, but may be sufficiently reinforcing to more than counteract the decremental effects of extinction. When this occurs, incubation can be seen to have taken place. When shock is experienced a number of times, habituation/adaptation occurs. When shock is accompanied by CS, the addition of fear to pain may delay habituation/adaptation, or even become stronger in the balance and lead to the occurrence of NRs that are stronger than the original UCR. Thus there is a dynamic interplay between the components of the NR (UCR and CR), and the forces of habituation/adaptation and extinction that work against an incrementing and towards a decrementing of the CS-NR association.

Incubation has been discussed at some length, partly because the concept is relatively novel, but mainly because it seems indispensable in properly accounting for certain properties of neurotic disorders that previously remained somewhat mysterious. (In addition, as we shall see later, the concept is required in order to explain certain phenomena in desensitization and aversion therapies which, without it, would remain puzzling.) As regards the development of neurotic disorders, the account given above, leaning heavily on the theoretical and experimental work of Hull (1929), Mowrer (1950), Solomon and Wynne (1954), May (1948), and Miller (1948), describes well enough certain types of disorder, but fails to do justice to others. It has often been observed in the development of neurotic disorders resulting from traumatic conditioning that while the first stage (classical fear conditioning) seems to occur, there is a long delay before any evidence can be found for the occurrence of the second stage (instrumental conditioning). One would have expected extinction to have occurred in the interim, and while it is possible to bridge the gap by postulating changing levels of general excitement and sensitivity, nevertheless an incubation process would seem to be a more promising concept to mediate the final strong anxiety responses that are observed.

Most neurotic disorders, however, are probably not built upon traumatic events at all, whether single-trial or not, but rather upon repeated subtraumatic events in work or family situations. The problem here is that the UCR is usually not particularly strong; why then does the CR finally reach degrees of strength that

seem out of proportion to the situation? In the animal field, this problem has been encountered, as mentioned above, by Anderson and Parmenter, and by Liddell; the incubation effect, by having CR added to UCR, would account for a build-up of reaction potential vastly in excess of UCR strength. This may of course not be the mechanism responsible for the observed facts, but at the moment it would seem to be the only suggestion that learning theory has to offer. Without some sort of incubation effect, the learning-theory model of the genesis of neurotic behavior would seem to be decidedly lacking in several respects, and to offer no explanation for certain well-documented phenomena.

Our discussion so far has been in terms of classical conditioning, which is traditionally contrasted with instrumental learning. However, Miller (1951, 1959) has argued that those visceral responses that are subject to classical conditioning should also be subject to instrumental learning, and this possibility was (weakly) supported by some experimental studies (Miller, 1966). More recently (Miller, 1967), the same author has reported a series of experiments, mostly done with curarized rats, that seem to establish this principle beyond doubt in animals (Carmona, 1967; Miller and Bannazizi, 1968; Miller and Carmona, 1967; Miller and DiCara, 1967; Trowill, 1967), and Kimmel (1967) has summarized the literature as far a humans subjects are concerned, also with positive findings. These important discoveries have not yet been incorporated properly into behavior therapy, but, as Miller (1967) points out, "the instrumental learning of visceral responses . . . opens up interesting new therapeutic possibilities. By recording such responses and immediately rewarding first small and then larger changes, it should be possible to teach a well-motivated patient to change undesirable responses to more desirable ones." In a similar way, the possibilities should be investigated of acquiring undesirable (neurotic) behavior patterns through inadvertent reinforcement schedules imposed by their environment. The imbrication of classical and instrumental conditioning makes the whole scheme here proposed much less rigid and perhaps more lifelike than it would otherwise be.

The theory of neurotic disorders and their genesis here adumbrated is of course subject to experimental verification, and it seems odd and indeed unfortunate that so little effort has gone into attempts to produce experimental "mini-neuroses" in human subjects. (Much more work has been done with animals, but the relevance of most of the studies has been questioned—for example, by Broadhurst, 1960). The famous Watson and Rayner study (1920), in which an experimental phobia for rats was produced in an eleven-month-old infant, Albert, by pairing the sight and touch of these animals with a loud, fear-producing noise, is of course well known; in spite of its tremendous potential usefulness in leading to an understanding of the nature of neurotic disorders, little seems to have been done to replicate this work. Rachman (1966a), in an interesting experimental design deriving from Watson and Rayner, attempted to show that fetishistic rituals can be produced by conditioning. He used a penile plethysmograph to measure sexual reactions, and showed that pictures of nude women produced such reactions, while pictures of shoes did not. By pairing the CS (boot) with the UCS (nude women), he managed to obtain penile reflexes to the CS; furthermore, these CRs generalized to shoes and other types of footwear. He ruled out the possibility of pseudoconditioning and sensitization by showing that when the stimuli were presented in reverse order (UCS preceding CS), no conditioning took place. (See also Rachman and Hodgson, 1968) These imaginative experiments will, it is hoped, lead to further investigations of the conditioning paradigm for neurotic disorders; only in this way can we hope to put our theories on a firm factual basis.

Our discussion of the genesis of neurotic disorders, which has leaned very much on conditioned emotional responses and secondary reinforcement through avoidance of anxiety responses, may seem to be in contradiction to our definition of neurosis, and our disagreement with Hebb, who makes "an undesirable emotional condition" the main point of his definition of neurosis. The contradiction is only apparent; a definition, such as ours, in terms of unadaptive behavior does not imply the absence of strong emotions. We simply wish to stress

immediately observable aspects of the hypothetical concept with which we are dealing; to include in a definition unobservable aspects involving concepts whose very reality is doubted by many recent authors (Duffy, 1962), would seem to pose unnecessary complications. Thus our stress on *behavior* in the definition does not contradict our stress on *emotion* in our theoretical account; definitions should only include universally agreed observables, while a theory may lean on less universally agreed hypothetical constructs and intervening variables. Even so, our account clearly leaves many questions unanswered, and the remainder of this section is devoted to a brief discussion of some of these. The first question relates to the problem of disorders of the second kind; our theory would appear to apply primarily to disorders of the first kind (dysthymic disorders), and to leave disorders of the second kind (antisocial disorders) out of account. This omission will be made good later on, where we deal with personality differences in relation to neurotic disorders; without a detailed consideration of these, it would be difficult to present our theory of disorders of the second kind in an appropriate manner.

The second point to be raised concerns the propriety of defining neurotic disorders in what may appear to be an arbitrary fashion, particularly as this definition would seem to leave out many of the central concepts that have in the past been considered to be essential in such a definition—concepts such as complex, unconscious repression and uncovering. We do not wish to enter into any lengthy argument on this point. What we have attempted to do has simply been to try to account for certain observed phenomena in terms of concepts and theories widely accepted in modern learning theory, and supported by laboratory experiments on both human and animal subjects.[5] (Conversely, of course, we also believe that the observed phenomena of neurotic disorder pose an unavoidable problem to the learning theorist, and provide him with an opportunity for studying *in vivo* the effects of certain strong emotional experiences that he would not be able to create artificially in the laboratory. The relationship between learning theory of the laboratory kind, and abnormal psychology, is conceived by us as akin to the relationship between experimental physics and astronomy; the latter is essentially observational rather than experimental, but it provides us with phenomena that the physicist cannot reproduce in the laboratory, and thus permits him to check on theories originally derived from experimental data).[6]

The attempt to carry out such a program is not obviously absurd even though, to many clinical psychologists, it may seem doomed to failure. Several outcomes are possible: (1) failure; it may prove impossible to account for the phenomena in question in terms of learning

theory; (2) success; a nomological network can be constructed linking laboratory phenomena, theoretical concepts and neurotic disorders; or (3) partial success; certain phenomena in the abnormal field can be accounted for on the basis of well-reputed theories and mechanisms in learning theory, while others resist such integration and explanation. We believe that outcome (3) represents the present situation most accurately, and we would like to add that the problems thrown up by the failure of isomorphism may prove of great value in directing the attention of learning theorists towards aspects of their material previously not sufficiently

---

[5] Critics have on occasion objected that there is less consensus among learning theorists than is implied in this sentence. This criticism is discussed in detail in a later section. Here let us only note that such a view seems to take as its ideal the Newtonian, monolithic type of theory that prevailed for over a century in physics. Nothing of the kind exists in psychology, but likewise, nothing of the kind exists in modern physics either; theories like Newton's have never been typical of scientific theories, and Hull's explicit aim to create a theory similar in kind to Newton's has produced sad confusion rather than clarification. The reader who doubts our statement of the position in modern physics may like to deduce the facts of superconductivity from general physical theory, and account for all the known facts in this field by any means whatever! In psychology, even quite gross apparent divergencies in theory can be reconciled by paying attention to previously neglected parameters; thus the ancient battle between Tolman's cognitive type of theory and the Hull-Spence type may be resolved by noting that the protagonists used quite different strains of experimental animals. Tolman's rats did not pause in their maze-running to consult cognitive maps; they were simply reacting to particularly strong types of S_D, having been bred for high emotionality, and showing appropriate fear responses. The case has been argued by Eysenck (1967) and extended to typological differences between humans; neglect of individual and strain differences is undoubtedly responsible for many apparent failures to replicate experimental results, and for many pseudotheoretical differences.

Theoretical failures in psychology are very much less serious than the recent collapse of the so-called "conservation laws" governing the reactions of subatomic particles in physics. Since the parity principle went in 1957, there has been a progressive collapse of what were reckoned to be the most fundamental principles in physics, leading to the breakdown for some particles of the combined CP preservation laws in 1964, until now even CPT symmetry is threatened. But all this revolutionary upheaval has had no effect at all on the applications of physics and technology in general.

[6] We have concentrated on conditioned fear responses in this discussion because we believe that

most neurotic "symptoms" do in fact arise through a conditioning process, but we would not insist that innate fears might not play an important part in the development of certain phobias; animal work, as Hebb was one of the first to point out, contains ample evidence on this point, and modern ethologists have added greatly to the literature. It is perhaps unlikely that what is innate is a specific fear for a specific animal (snake, bird, spider, mouse, and the like); what is more likely is that there are innate fears for specific *types* of stimuli, such as sudden movements, incongruous appearance, and unexpectedness, and that animals incorporating some of these, or accidentally linked with others, become fear objects through a process of conditioning—rather like Watson's rats became feared through association with fear-producing noise. This view would simply extend the range of innately fear-producing stimuli beyond Watson's trinity. Other people's fear reactions may also be innately fear-producing; fear certainly is infectious in primates and other animals. Eye-blink conditioning data (Irene Martin et al., 1969) on animal phobics, social phobics, and agoraphobics certainly leave little doubt that these groups differ on the experimental variable; animal phobics showed the highest acquisition rate and also the slowest extinction rate. "When anxiety is equated across groups, there is a large and statistically significant difference among groups in extinction rates, showing that specific phobics extinguish more slowly." However, "when acquisition CRs are equated across groups, there is no difference in extinction rates." These data may suggest, but certainly do not prove, that specific animal phobias may be largely inherited, and persist in people who are slow to extinguish fear responses. Much more evidence will be required to make this suggestion acceptable. Martin's data do, however, provide us with one very important bit of information that fits in well with the conditioning paradigm of treatment to be discussed presently; over all groups, eye-blink conditioning acquisition scores correlate very significantly with improvement in therapy—0.46 in all patients, and 0.53 in those patients treated with behavior therapy only. These correlations are high enough to suggest that research designs (and clinical studies also) should include eye-blink conditioning as a major predictive variable.

considered, thus perhaps leading to an improvement in learning theory itself. In chemistry, the phlogiston theory of heat led to the very important step of measuring the substances subjected to burning, both before and after; this in turn led to the improvement and finally the abandonment of the theory of phlogiston. This is the kind of interplay we envisage between learning theory and abnormal psychology.

The objection may remain that we have arbitrarily selected certain phenomena for investigation, and have rejected others, such as transference. Two answers are possible. In the first place, the phenomenon which we have left out of account may not in fact be directly observable phenomena at all, but rather be hypotheses built upon imperfect observations. A "complex" is not observable in the same sense that a phobia for snakes is observable (and measurable); it is part of a theory, rather than part of the data to be explained. Much the same is true of "transference." Eysenck (1963b) has elsewhere tried to show to what extent this concept is a theoretical one, deriving from a more general theory of neurosis and personality, and to what extent it is descriptive of observable behavior. The outcome of this discussion was that insofar as we are dealing with observable behavior, we can account for the facts in terms of concepts derived from learning theory. This type of conclusion may be applicable to other "dynamic" concepts in equal measure.

Our second answer would be that a theory is not required to embrace all observations without careful selection. One of the main attributes of a good theorist is that he does not try to bring under one umbrella discordant and unrelated phenomena; his acumen is shown precisely by his skill in selecting those phenomena that can be brought together under one set of rules or laws. Mendel was preceded by many geneticists who studied the obvious similarities between related plants, but they did so without selecting specific aspects for study, and thus failed to produce any meaningful generalizations. By insisting on careful study of just two aspects of *pisum* (tall versus short and smooth versus wrinkled) Mendel succeeded in laying the foundations of modern genetics. If our theory should prove to apply to a certain range of phenomena, then we would be quite content; to

attempt at this stage to account also for what may be irrelevant phenomena would be to court certain failure. The sprawling vagueness of overinclusive theories may be in part responsible for the premature crystallization of spurious orthodoxies so characteristic of this field; restriction to testable hypotheses and observable phenomena does not guarantee success, but makes it easier to assess success or failure. If additional concepts and hypotheses are found to be required, then a restricted theory can be easily expanded; it is much more difficult to sort out the positive from the negative features of an overinclusive theory.

These points are made here, in connection with the genesis of neurotic disorders, but they apply equally to our treatment of desensitization and aversion therapies. Our explicit intention to restrict ourselves to the extinction and deconditioning of maladaptive conditioned responses, and to the conditioning of adaptive responses, has often been criticized as being too narrow, and as leaving out many other desirable and important changes in the patient that might be attempted. Undoubtedly there are many other changes that could be made, or at least attempted, but these are outside our theory and methodology; we do not wish to solve all the problems of human beings, but purposely restrict ourselves to a particular kind of problem, carefully defined and explicitly stated. This has always been the methodology of science, and we can see no reason for departing from it on this occasion.

A last point to be considered is the view, sometimes voiced, that conditioning and learning theories such as the one here advanced are in principle similar to (and in practice, little but) rewordings, in slightly different terminology, of dynamic theories and formulations. This view we find not so much difficult to answer, but difficult to understand. The two domains of discourse are so disparate that it is not easy to see what could be meant by suggestions of "similarity." It may be possible to translate some portions of psychoanalytic teaching into the language of learning theory; Dollard and Miller's (1950) valiant attempt to do so has not on the whole found much favor with psychoanalysts, nor has it inspired any large body of research on the psychological side. On the simple level of common sense, consider the psychoanalytic and the learning theory explanations of enuresis, to take but one concrete example. Mowrer (1938), Lovibond (1964), and other learning theorists regard enuresis as a simple habit deficiency, the effects of which may lead to anxiety through the socially undesirable consequences of the act. Psychoanalysts, as Mowrer has pointed out (1950), view enuresis as a form of sexual gratification; enuresis may be regarded as a substitute form of gratification of repressed genital sexuality, a direct manifestation of deep-seated anxieties and fears, or a disguised form of hostility towards parents or parent-substitutes, or even several of these in combination. In any case, enuresis is viewed as a *regressive phenomenon, produced by intense anxiety following repression.* This anxiety has its source in tabooed impulses of a sexual or aggressive and hostile character. The similarity of this theory to that of a simple habit deficiency —that is, a failure to acquire a conditioned response—is not obvious to us. Here as elsewhere, it is not sufficient simply to say that psychoanalytic and learning theory views are similar or identical; what is required is a thorough, well-argued and clearly documented theoretical account stating precisely what is being suggested, and how the postulated similarities and differences can be operationally defined and tested. The existence of a large number of clearly demarcated areas of disagreement between the two accounts makes it unlikely that such an effort would succeed very easily.

The outstanding difference between the two theories relates, of course, to the postulation of a causal factor ("complex") behind the set of symptoms by the psychoanalysts, and the explicit disavowal of such a factor by behavior therapists. There is no parallel in behavior therapy to the concepts of unconsciousness, repression, transference, resistance, complex, libido, and the like, just as there is no obvious parallel in psychoanalysis to the concepts of conditioned response, stimulus generalization, extinction, UCS, and the like. To allege similarity, or even identity, without extensive argumentation and explanation, and explicit identification, seems only likely to mislead and confuse. The same must be said of suggestions that in psychiatric practice both theories should

be amalgamated in some fashion, and treatment be based on a combination of psychotherapy and behavior therapy. Theories that are explicitly in contradiction to each other cannot so easily be reconciled, and little service is done to the understanding of neurotic disorders, or the improvement of treatment, by a vague throwing together of disparate and dissimilar theories and methods. Until the contrary has been demonstrated we shall continue to treat the theory here espoused as entirely different to standard psychoanalytic theories, and as in essence alternative to them. We furthermore believe that the interest of both theories are best served by elaborating experimentally the differences between them, and seeking for crucial evidence regarding the truth or falsity of either.

We must now turn to a consideration of individual differences. Our discussion will be brief and consequently more dogmatic than might be desirable; however, the issues involved are too complex to be treated in sufficient detail in a presentation such as this, and the relevance of the points to be considered may not be as obvious to others as they are to us. For detailed consideration of the evidence and of possible criticisms the reader may consult *The Biological Basis of Personality* (Eysenck, 1967) and *The Structure and Measurement of Personality* (Eysenck and Eysenck, 1969); here we will simply state the main conclusions from these two surveys.

Why is personality theory relevant to a theory of neurotic disorders and a discussion of conditioning methods of treatment? A systematic answer has been given by Savage and Eysenck (1964), whose treatment we will follow here. Consider stimulus generalization; this clearly plays an important role in our theory of neurosis, and is one of the cardinal points mentioned by Hebb in his definition of neurosis. Now it is well known that "increased drive broadens the generalization gradient, both in the classical and instrumental conditioning situation" (Kimble, 1961, p. 340); the work of Bersh et al. (1950), Jenkins et al. (1958), and Rosenbaum (1953) may be considered in this connection. The latter found that the threat of a strong shock led to greater generalization than did the threat of a weak shock; he also found (Rosenbaum, 1956)

that identical threats produced broader generalization gradients in highly anxious subjects than
in nonanxious subjects. In other words, we can
alter generalization gradients by *either* altering
stimulus conditions *or* by using subjects of a
different personality type; generalization is
determined by the product of the strength of the
UCS and the constitutional anxiety-proneness
of the subject. Savage and Eysenck (1964) make
an analogy to Hooke's law of elasticity; Stress
$= k \times$ Strain, where k is constant (the modulus
of elasticity, which depends upon the nature of
the material and the type of stress used to
produce the strain). This constant k (that is, the
ratio Stress/Strain) is called Young's modulus,
and is illustrated (with certain simplifications) in
Fig. 15.2a. A and B are two metals differing in
elasticity; they are stressed by increasing loads,
the elongation corresponding to each load
plotted on the abscissa. It will be seen that
identical loads give rise to quite divergent
elongations, α and β. Fig. 15.2b illustrates a
similar analysis of human behavior in an experimental situation productive of emotion. Again
the stress (for example, threat of shock) is
plotted on the ordinate, and the strain (for
example, generalization) on the abscissa; A and
B represent the nonanxious and the anxious
groups respectively. Identical stress θ_1 gives rise
to quite different strains α and β. It would
require stress θ_2 to make the strain in nonanxious subjects equal to that produced by θ_1
in anxious subjects. Differences between θ_1 and
θ_2 are the kinds of differences traditionally
studied by experimental psychologists; differences between A and B are the kinds of differences traditionally studied by personality
psychologists. Physicists have never attempted
to make a choice between these two sets of
variables, or to study them in isolation; it seems
equally futile for psychologists to do so.
Provided the modulus employed is even moderately correct, and more than a mere analogy, the
experimental possibilities suggested by this
method of approach seem promising.

What measures of personality are relevant to
our theory? It is suggested that modern research
overwhelmingly converges on two personality
factors that emerge again and again from researches in many countries; these are variously
called neuroticism, emotionality or instability,

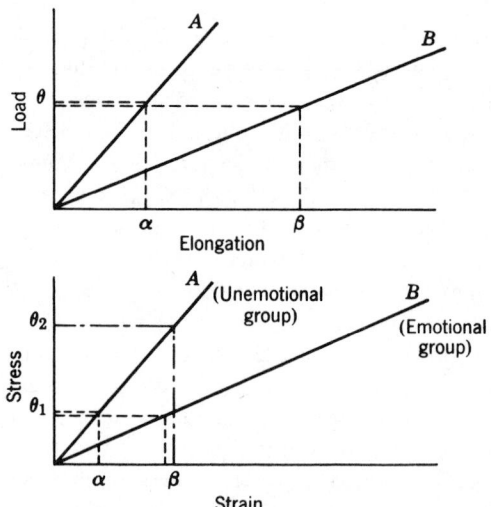

Figure 15.2 Emotional stress and strain
shown as interacting with personality-
variable "emotionality." Upper diagram
shows similar interaction in metals (Hooke's
Law). For explanation see text. From Savage
and Eysenck, 1964.

as contrasted with stability and extroversion-
introversion (Eysenck, 1960a). Both, in the
language of factor analysis, are second-order
factors, empirically derived from the intercorrelations of first-order factors like im-
pulsiveness, sociability, carefreeness, optimism,
and responsiveness (extroversion), or depression,
aggressiveness, sleeplessness, moodiness, and
rigidity (neuroticism). These factors appear
equally strongly in the inventories of Cattell,
Guilford, and Eysenck (Eysenck and Eysenck,
1969); they are uncorrelated with each other.
(Anxiety, as measured for instance by the Taylor
MAS, is a compound of neuroticism and introversion correlating significantly with both, but
more strongly with N.) The nature of these
factors is empirically determined; the theories
associated with Jung play little part in the
interpretation of the extroversion-introversion
factor. It should also be pointed out that
neuroticism denotes a predisposition to neurotic
breakdown, but is not identical with it; stress is
required to translate predisposition into maladaptive behavior. (A third personality factor,
entitled psychoticism or predisposition to
psychotic disorder, is also postulated by
Eysenck on the basis of factorial studies; here
we are not concerned with this elaboration of
the dimensional model of psychiatric disorders
[Eysenck] 1968b.).

The E and N factors relate to psychiatric classification in the following way. Dysthymic disorders tend to be characterized by high N scores and low E scores (neurotic introverts); psychopaths and certain types of criminals tend to be characterized by high N scores and high E scores (neurotic extroverts). Hysterics are high on N and intermediate on E, between dysthymics and psychopaths. These relations are based on constitutional differences (a lengthy review of the importance of heredity for the determination of individual differences in both E and N is given by Eysenck, 1967), and consequently both E and N are regarded as being semipermanent characteristics of the individual. A follow-up study by Burt (1965) may illustrate the relations indicated. Seven hundred and sixty-three children, of whom 15 percent and 18 percent later became habitual offenders or neurotics respectively, were rated by their teachers for N and E. Follow-up of the children disclosed that over thirty years later, of those who became habitual offenders, 63 percent had been rated as high on N, 54 percent as high on E, but only 3 percent as high on I (introversion). Of those who became neurotics, 59 percent had been rated as high on N, 44 percent as high in I, but only 1 percent as high on E. (For a more detailed review on this evidence of criminality, see Eysenck, 1964a; on dysthymic neurosis, see Eysenck and Rachman, 1965).

Both N and E are based on physiological structures that can be specified; neurotic and extroverted behavior are the outcome of an interaction between experience and individual reactions mediated by these structures. According to Eysenck's theory (1967), individual differences in the thresholds to stimulation of the visceral brain are responsible for differences in Neuroticism-Emotionality, and high N-scorers have a more labile, more easily aroused autonomic system, with a tendency for arousal to die down less readily. Individual differences in E are mediated by differential thresholds to stimulation of the ascending reticular activating system, in the sense that introverts are characterised by a higher state of cortical arousal and extroverts by a lower state of cortical arousal. These states of high or low arousal mediate excitatory and inhibitory states (Eysenck, 1957), leading to high excitatory-low inhibitory states in introverts, and low excitatory-high inhibitory

states in extroverts. (Note that the terms inhibition and excitation here refer to states of the cortex; if the cortex is in a state of excitation/arousal, it inhibits the activities of the lower centers, thus producing inhibited behavior, while a state of inhibition in the cortex frees the lower centers from cortical control, thus leading to uninhibited behavior. (Alcohol *depresses* cortical activity, but *disinhibits* behavior).

A few experimentally verified consequences of these theoretical postulates may be mentioned, as they are important for our theory of neurosis. High-N scorers tend to react more strongly to emotion-arousing stimuli, and their autonomic reactions tend to last much longer. High-E scorers tend to have high sensory thresholds, which leads to stimulus-hunger and relative disregard of painful stimuli; low-E scorers tend to have low sensory thresholds, which leads to stimulus-avoidance and relative disregard of sensory deprivation. Introverts learn and condition better, particularly when conditions are suboptimal, than do extroverts; high cortical arousal produces better consolidation of the memory trace, as well as making the strength of the UCS subjectively greater. (Under certain conditions, specifiable according to derivations from the theory, extroverts may condition better; very strong UCSs, long CS/UCS interval, and 100 percent reinforcement constitute a set of conditions that favor formation of CRs by extroverts; see Eysenck and Levey, 1967). Many perceptual and motor behavior differences have also been demonstrated between extroverts and introverts; they are also differentiated with respect to social behavior patterns and physiological measures, such as EEG.

Individuals high on N and low on E would appear predisposed to dysthymic disorders. If such disorders are conceived of as conditioned reactions following upon aversive stimuli, then (1) high-N subjects would be expected to experience identical stimuli (UCSs) as more aversive than low-N subjects, due to greater emotional reactions (cf. Figure 15.2); (2) low-E subjects would, by virtue of their low sensory thresholds, also experience certain painful stimuli (both exteroceptive and interoceptive) as more painful than would high-E subjects; (3) low-E subjects would, in most instances, form conditioned responses more readily, more strongly, and more lastingly than would high-E subjects; (4) stimulus generalization would be greater in high-N—low-E subjects, as mentioned before; and (5) incubation would be expected to be stronger in high-N—low-E subjects, on theoretical grounds. The observed relationship between dysthymic disorders and high-N—low-E personality does not, therefore, come as a surprise; it is exactly what would have been expected from theoretical considerations.

Individuals high on N and also high on E would appear predisposed to psychopathic disorders (Instead of psychopathic we might perhaps write "asocial" or even "antisocial"; individuals in this quadrant have been found to manifest such "symptoms" as V.D., traffic law violations and accidents, having babies out of wedlock, and the like. Psychopaths clinically diagnosed constitute only a portion of the individuals in this group; as noted before, criminals probably take up a much larger proportion—they might, of course, be diagnosed as psychopaths if psychiatrically investigated, but the great majority are in fact never seen by a psychiatrist). Theoretically, Eysenck (1964a) has argued that "conscience", which causes people to act in a socially desirable manner, is a result of a long-continued conditioning procedure, extending through infancy and even into adolescence; if, as we have argued, extroverts are slower to condition, then under identical conditions of upbringing they would acquire less "conscience" than introverts, and hence behave in a more antisocial or asocial manner. In addition, their stimulus-hunger would lead them into situations intrinsically dangerous and tempting, and their impulsive, risk-taking propensities would lead them on into the kind of activities disapproved by society. In addition to E, we must also emphasize the importance of high N; according to the Spence-Taylor (Spence, 1956) theory, this is conceived of as a drive variable, multiplying with the habits just described, and hence acting as an amplifying device, making it more difficult for the individual to change his habits and act in conformity with normal rewards and punishments. It is noteworthy that criminals tend to have N scores as high as neurotics in treatment; criminality is not usually regarded as a "neurotic" pattern of behavior, but it fits our definition, as well as Hebb's, and should not be left out of consideration.

As an illustrative paradigm of his general theory, Eysenck (1963d) has reported a rat experiment in which two groups of animals (genetic strains high and low on emotionality, respectively, as measured by the open field test) were submitted to a "conscience"-producing conditioning procedure. A signal preceded the dropping of food into a cup; the approved response was for the rat to wait three seconds before beginning to eat. If it started to eat too early, it received an electric shock. Three responses were observed: (1) integrated behavior—rat waits three seconds and then eats. (2) psychopathic behavior—rat doesn't wait and eats; and (3) dysthymic behavior—rat retreats from the food hopper and doesn't eat at all, even when permitted to do so. On the basis of the argument just presented, that is, that emotionality acts as an amplifying valve, augmenting habits already present in the organism, it would be expected that integrated behavior would be more frequent in the lowly emotional rats, and psychopathic and dysthymic behavior in the highly emotional rats. This was in fact found to be so, at an acceptable level of statistical significance. (The difference between the two nonintegrative reactions are assumed to be due to high and low conditionability respectively; it might be possible to use this experiment as an animal analogue of "extroversion" and "introversion"). It will be seen that the two nonintegrative patterns of behavior are in fact maladaptive—the rat foregoes the food, or it receives a shock unnecessarily. Persistence and generalization of behavior were not studied; if these were found to be present, even if only in a rudimentary form, we might regard this experiment as a paradigm of animal neurosis.

The position of hysterics, and the theory regarding the causation of their "symptoms," is less clear. Jung originally suggested that hysteria was a typical neurotic disorder of the extrovert, but the evidence suggests that while hysterics are more extroverted than dysthymics, they are less so than psychopaths, and no more so than normals. It seems possible that our characterization of extroverts as low on arousal and high on inhibition may be oversimplified; it is plausible to argue that while correlated overall, these two activities of the reticular formation may in some people be somewhat dissociated. Psychopaths on this view would be characterized by low arousal, but average inhibition; hysterics by average arousal, but high inhibition. It is notable that most of the classical hysterical symptoms are inhibitory in nature; paralyses, fugues, anesthesias, and the like may all be accounted for theoretically in terms of some strong inhibitory forces possibly associated with the synchronizing part of the reticular formation. This view is highly speculative, but it is not incapable of being refuted experimentally; certainly some causal hypothesis is required to account for the obvious differences in symptomatology shown by hysterics and psychopaths.

Does this division of neurotic behavior patterns into introverted-dysthymic and extroverted-psychopathic coincide with the division between disorders of the first kind and disorders of the second kind that we made earlier in this section? The answer must be partly yes; for most disorders, agreement is fairly close. We may say in general that disorders of the first kind tend to cause pain and trouble to the patient, who will tend to seek psychiatric help— hence the prevalence of these disorders in the psychiatric clinic. Disorders of the second kind tend to cause trouble to society (crime, V.D., traffic offences, psychopathic behavior), and only indirectly to the individual, that is, through society's efforts to wreak vengeance; consequently, disorders of the second kind tend to be rare in the psychiatric clinic, and to be found more frequently in prisons and other correctional institutions. But the association is not perfect. Some criminals (particularly many older recidivists) are introverts rather than extroverts; they tend to go into crime as a last resort, having failed (through dullness, inactivity, and other causes) at other attempts to earn a living. Such individuals are perhaps characterized as coming into crime relatively late in life; the typical psychopathic, extroverted criminal enters early (Gibbens, 1966). Criminality is such a heterogeneous classification altogether that generalizations should refer to subgroups rather than to "all criminals." Furthermore, we must of course bear in mind

that even though extraverts may condition less well than introverts under certain circumstances, and have other debilities, yet circumstances of upbringing and the like are seldom equal, and may tilt the balance; the neglect of constitutional factors in this field on the psychoanalytic side should not be equalled by the neglect of the environmental factors that undoubtedly played an important part. But with this and other possible exceptions in mind (Eysenck and Rachman, 1965) we may yet say that, on the whole, disorders of the first kind tend to result from *over*conditioning, and disorders of the second kind from *under*conditioning; that the former occur more frequently in introverts, and the latter more frequently in extroverts; and that in both cases, high N (emotionality) plays an important part.

These generalizations suggest that two quite distinct types of therapy would be appropriate for disorders of the first and second kind Introvertive disorders would seem to require some form of deconditioning or *desensitization*; extrovertive disorders would seem to require some form of reconditioning or *aversive therapy*. This argument will be presented in more detail when we come to our discussion of these two methods of therapy; here let us merely note this bifurcation as being rather fundamental for any consideration of behavior therapy. The connection between personality and type of disorder here presented may not be acceptable to all behavior therapists, and in one sense it might be said that it is not crucial to an evaluation of behavior therapy; this particular theory could be erroneous, while the methods of desensitization and aversion therapy might still work successfully (and vice versa!) Nevertheless, we feel that a better understanding of the causes of disorders must help in the improvement of methods of therapy, and we also feel that the evidence for some interaction between personality and neurotic disorder is now so strong that it cannot be entirely disregarded. We will also argue, in later sections, that, diagnostically, knowledge of the patient's personality (N, E, conditionability, aptitude for stimulus generalization, and the like) must be of importance in designing a suitable form of therapy; indeed, here too there is evidence that should not be overlooked.[7] The very fact that different individuals react differently to stress, or to therapy, suggests that elimination of the personal constant in theories of neurotic disorder or of treatment must lead to oversimplification and ultimately to unnecessary failure in many instances. The theory here adopted may of course be incorrect in many details, or even erroneous in toto; however, there does not seem to be any alternative theory within the universe of discourse we have chosen, that is, that of experimental determination and laboratory evidence. Pending the arrival of a better theory, therefore, we shall continue to use the one presented so briefly above, subject of course, to further factual support or rejection.

DESENSITIZATION THERAPY

The modern phase of development in behavior therapy has been largely concerned with two important problems. The first of these, and in many ways the most crucial, has been the devotion to testing the therapeutic value of the techniques under controlled experimental conditions; accounts of the empirical tests of desensitization and aversion therapy are given in a later section. The second problem has been that of establishing a firmer theoretical basis for the procedures, and it is this problem which we shall now examine.

Wolpe's finding concerning the successful use of "counter-conditioning" treatment for experimental neuroses was, as we have shown, not at all a new discovery. Jones (1924), for example, had found the method valuable in removing the specific and unadaptive fears of children, while Watson (1920) had called attention to this possibility in his earlier study of little Albert.

Neither Jones nor Watson, however, offered a satisfactory or detailed theoretical account for their method. Watson, for example, called the process "reconditioning," by which he simply meant the forming of a new association between the feared stimuli and a pleasurable (positive) response. Nevertheless, he did point out, in his incidental observations, that fear and rage in infants could be observed to be blocked by thumbsucking, and the implication of reciprocally inhibiting forces is apparent in such statements.

Jones' account is hardly more detailed. She called the method one of "direct conditioning," and used this term to cover all situations in which an attempt is made to associate a fear object with some stimulus arousing a positive (pleasant) reaction. Her method of using the "hunger motive" was simply a matter of convenience, and the means of application is made clear by the following account.

The fear-object is brought in, starting a negative response. It is then moved away gradually until it is at a sufficient distance not to interfere with the child's eating. The relative strength of the fear impulse and the hunger impulse may be gauged by the distance to which it is necessary to remove the fear-object. While the child is eating, the object is slowly brought nearer the table, then placed upon the table, and finally as the tolerance increases it is brought close enough to be touched.

Thus the elements of the situation are such as to allow the presence of the fear stimulus under conditions where an alternative response to the fear has been induced. We are left to assume that repeated presentations in this manner lead to the progressive strengthening of a new bond between the fear stimulus and the positive (pleasant) response.

This process, at first sight, does not seem to be

---

[7] The term "conditionability" may be objected to, as evidence of generality between different types of conditioning in humans (eye blink, G.S.R., cardiac, and the like) is lacking; correlations tend to be low or nonexistent. Eysenck (1960c) has discussed some of the reasons for this experimental failure to find consistency in some detail; he has also drawn attention to the fact that far more attention has to be paid to experimental parameters, such as strength of UCS and length of CS-UCS interval, before proper comparisons can be made. Experimental studies have supported this view of a close relation between changes in parameter values and

changes in correlations with personality, and have shown that these changes are in fact predictable from theoretical considerations (Eysenck, 1967b). Furthermore, Martin et al. (1969) have demonstrated quite high correlations between eye-blink conditioning and improvement of neurotic patients after therapy; if such correlations of $+0.5$ can be achieved with one single type of conditioning measure, and without correction for attenuation in the (inevitably somewhat unrealiable) psychiatric criterion, then our proposal does seem to acquire some cogency.

very different from that which Dollard and Miller believed characterized the more usual psychotherapeutic process. They say, for example, that in his revelations to the therapist the patient proceeds from statements to which weak anxiety attaches, to those characterized by stronger emotion. In the permissive environment provided by the therapist the weak anxiety becomes extinguished (apparently because the statements are not followed by punishment), and these extinction effects then generalize to other anxiety-producing cues, thus enabling the patient to verbalize those sentences that would ordinarily have evoked strong anxiety. The cycle of fear, extinction of fear, and generalization of extinction is repeated again and again in therapy.

This particular approach, however, appears to emphasize extinction as the main therapeutic agent which, at best, seems to be an uneconomical procedure (Miller, 1951). While it is the case that Dollard and Miller advise a "little-by-little" extinction process, quite unlike the "maximum confrontation" approach characteristic of experiments aimed at the extinction of fear-motivated avoidance behavior, nevertheless it seems that an unaided extinction program is being suggested.

In this connection it is of some interest to note that Stampfl (1967) apparently takes the view that the *essential* ingredient for securing extinction is that the reaction (fear, anxiety) to the stimulus should be as strong as possible. He derives support for this view from Miller (1951) and Solomon, Kamin, and Wynne (1953), among others. It will be clear that such ideas are diametrically opposed to the graded approach advocated by Wolpe, as well as to those put forward by Lader and Wing (see below).

Wolpe bases his theoretical position upon the Mowrer–Miller hypothesis concerning the inhibitory effects of response elicitation which, under certain circumstances, produces the conditioned inhibition of a response. In particular, it is argued that conditioned inhibition is built up during extinction because traces of the conditioned stimulus appear in conjunction with the reactive inhibition of the conditioned response. Wolpe argues that if this is the case, then any other means of inhibiting the conditioned response will similarly lead to the conditioned inhibition of that response; it would only be necessary to provide some form of drive reduction (reinforcement) in the presence of response inhibition, The response inhibition can be easily achieved by selecting some reaction for evocation that is incompatible with the response.

Wolpe thus adopts a Hullian account of extinction as opposed to Guthrie's (1952) model of interfering responses. This of course involves the acceptance of one of two possible theories, both of which are less than satisfactory. Furthermore, it involves the extrapolation of the theory to include situations in which the response inhibition has not been achieved by building up reactive inhibition of that response, but rather by deliberate exclusion occasioned by evoking an incompatible reaction.

Wolpe points out that this model for dealing with defense reactions is applicable to an early experiment by Pavlov (1927), although the response to be inhibited in this case was an unconditioned one. The procedure was to make a weak electrical current the conditioned stimulus for food in a dog, the current being strengthened over a period of time, but by stages, so that no defense reaction to severe shocks was produced. The argument here is that the procedure had enabled the progressive inhibition of defense reactions to electric shock to take place.

However, it will be appreciated that the results of the kind of experiments considered by Wolpe and others lend themselves just as readily to interpretation in terms of an "interference" model; that is, extinction has occurred as the outcome of acquiring interfering responses. Kimble (1961), in his discussion of the extinction of avoidance behavior, raises this possibility when referring to the results of Page's (1955) experiments. Two methods of extinction of avoidance behavior were tested in this experiment, the first being the usual method employed, while the second afforded the animal an opportunity to learn an interfering response in addition. Extinction was far more rapid for the second group, but the question was that of whether the extinction consisted of the reduction of fear or of the learning of an interfering response. It was argued that if the latter were the case, then the reversed training—learning to take food from the compartment where shock had been given previously—would be productive of longer latencies for the "interfering-response" than the "normal-extinction" group. This was indeed the case, suggesting that fear had not extinguished in the "interfering-response" condition, although the avoidant response had disappeared. Thus fear, presumably, remains, as Kimble points out, to possibly instigate other habits.

Of course it may reasonably be held that the "interfering-response" model is less likely to be the appropriate account of extinction by means of reciprocal inhibition for several reasons. First, it could be argued that it is the *fear itself* upon which the patient reports during reciprocal inhibition therapy, and which apparently shows diminution in time. (However, it may be countered that questions about fear usually involve asking about the presence or absence of avoidant behavior, and any persistence of fear itself may be overlooked). Secondly, it could be said that the outcome of applying reciprocal inhibition therapy is not that of preserving a set of strong counter anxiety behaviors in the presence of former fear objects; we do not see, for example, patients who become completely relaxed at the sight of some former phobic object. This seems to cast a little doubt upon the "interfering-response" explanation. Thirdly, the conclusions drawn from Page's experiment might well lead us to expect symptom substitution on a substantial scale—assuming that fear remains, even though the avoidant response has been extinguished. This seems to be a rare rather than a frequent occurrence (Gelder, Marks, and Wolff, 1967), and this fact might weaken the case for an "interfering response" explanation.

Baum (1969), in his studies of extinction of avoidance response extinction following response prevention, came to the conclusion that

... the argument advanced by Page (1955) that response prevention eliminates the avoidance response but that fear remains and motivates a new, competing response, does not appear to apply to the present findings. When response prevention was successful, no competing response was observed. Rather, undifferentiated exploratory activity and grooming seemed to replace the avoidance response. (Page 9).

Baum also found that

... several factors influence the efficacy of response prevention in facilitating the extinction of an avoidance response. These factors include the amount of response prevention given, the intensity of the shock used to motivate learning of the avoidance response, and whether or not the response has been overtrained." (Ibid.; see also Baum, 1968, and Oler and Baum, 1968).

Much of what Baum found is also relevant to the second stage of our neurosis model, and to the discussion of Stampfl's "implosion" theory.

Yet another model to account for the results of "reciprocal inhibition" treatment has been put forward by Lader and Wing (1966) and Lader (1967), and elaborated by Lader and Matthews (1968). It is pointed out that work on "arousal" among a variety of clinical conditions and normal subjects indicates substantial individual differences in the number of spontaneous fluctuations in palmar skin conductance, as well as habituation (on the same measure) to repeated presentations of an auditory stimulus. Of particular importance are the observations that agoraphobic and socially phobic patients, as well as patients classified as suffering from "anxiety states," show more spontaneous fluctuations of PSC than patients with specific phobias, and also that GSR habituation is inversely related to spontaneous fluctuations ("arousal"). It was then postulated that when the "arousal" level is low, a repeated or continuing stimulus would only succeed in raising the "arousal" level briefly, and habituation would therefore take place rapidly. Conversely, for an existing high level of arousal, habituation would be slow or nonexistent, or responsiveness might even be increased (see the discussion of the Napalkov phenomenon in an earlier section). In other words, a critical level of arousal is postulated, which would determine whether habituation would take place. In effect this would mean that a patient suffering from, say, an anxiety state, could maintain or even elevate his level of arousal (experienced as anxiety) to minimal stimulation.

This model would lead one to suggest that desensitization would be relatively ineffective for social phobias, agoraphobias, and anxiety states, as no permanent decrease from existing high arousal levels would be possible. To some extent the experimental evidence appears to confirm this expectation, at least insofar as agoraphobias are concerned (see later section).

Bearing in mind the necessary assumptions that the above model makes, it is possible to put forward an alternative account of desensitization to that proposed by Wolpe. Central to this alternative is the idea that desensitization is simply a case of habituation under optimal conditions; that is, where the level of arousal is kept as low as possible, consistent with maintaining consciousness. The total relaxation situation, as an element in the desensitization therapy, serves the vital function of producing a low arousal level.

Lader and Mathews (1968) suggest that for a variety of reasons this model is superior to Wolpe's, and that, in general, it accounts for more of the available evidence, as well as generating its own predictions concerning new facts. There is, as yet, too little evidence to be categorical about their model, but at this stage it appears to hold considerable promise. There is, however, one important reservation that one might hold concerning this theory. It has generally been assumed that the use of *in vivo desensitization*[8] produces similar results to those of *imaginal desensitization with relaxation*; while no critical comparisons can be made at this stage, should this assumption hold true, then it would present a serious problem for a model arguing that therapeutic effects depend upon the creation of low-arousal conditions. In this connection it is of interest to note the results of a small-scale experiment by Cooke (1966). He found no overall differences between the two forms of desensitization treatment, although some tendency was noted for highly anxious individuals to do better under imaginal desensitization conditions.

A further possible explanation of the mechanisms involved in desensitization therapy has been suggested by Wagner and Cauthen (1968). They argue that during preliminary relaxation training, it is possible that the presence of the therapist, in association with the elicitation of a counteranxiety response (relaxation), is positively reinforcing. It may be, therefore, that the therapist becomes an extremely powerful source of positive reinforcement to counteranxiety responses. In other words, desensitization could be viewed as a special case of operant conditioning, in which certain behaviors are strengthened by virtue of their positively reinforcing consequences.

These authors offer the results of a brief experiment in support of their theory, employing five subjects suffering from snake phobia. Three of these individuals were given a number of "positive reinforcement" trials in which the therapist, by making liberal compliments about the subject, endeavored to become a source of positive reinforcement. Following this the therapist arranged to provide verbal reinforcement ("good" or "excellent") each time the subject made an approach to the fear object. The results of this training were then compared with those obtained using an orthodox desensitization approach.

The small numbers involved make sensible comparisons difficult but, at least superficially, no obvious advantage accrued to either form of therapy. It would be of obvious interest to replicate this experiment using larger numbers and perhaps a more sophisticated design, but at least the operant conditioning explanation is seen as a tenable hypothesis on the basis of results to date. Eysenck (1963b) had already suggested a similar reinforcement theory to explain the alleged phenomena of "transference."

Other experiments with a more theoretical orientation have been conducted with a view to obtaining a clearer understanding of the elements involved in desensitization treatment. Certain of these studies have concentrated attention upon the role of relaxation.

Wolpe regards the presence of anxiety and relaxation as being incompatible states of the organism, quoting various findings as being consistent with this assumption (Jacobson, 1939, 1940; Drovta, 1962; Clark, 1963; Wolpe, 1964). Indeed, Jacobson (1964) has argued that not only do states of muscular tension accompany emotional reactions, but that the latter are dependent upon the former. Thus relaxation, by diminishing proprioceptive impulses, prevents the development of emotional states. The

---

[8] In vivo ("live") desensitization refers to the situation in which the actual stimulus to anxiety is presented to the subject; imaginal desensitization, on the other hand, refers to the presentation of mental pictures of events, objects, and situations of which the subject is afraid.

evidence is, however, equivocal. Lader and Mathews (1968), for example, find that in several patients seen by them, the amount of muscle tension may be extremely low while the patient reports experiencing anxiety, whereas increases in muscle tension have sometimes been accompanied by diminished experience of anxiety. Furthermore, they point out that muscle-relaxant drugs, such as mephenesin, seem not to control anxiety effectively. Is relaxation, therefore, a necessary part of the desensitization procedure and, if so, what part does it play?

The first question has received a reasonable amount of attention from experimental investigators. Davison (1968), for example, investigated the effects of various procedures on the reduction of snake phobia in nonpsychiatric subjects. One group received formal desensitization (that is, presentation of images in hierarchical order) under relaxation; another group was given irrelevant images under relaxation conditions; a third group received desensitization alone, without any relaxation; and the fourth group, which received no treatment, served as control for evaluating the results. Only those receiving desensitization together with relaxation showed improvement, while no differences were observed between any other group over and above changes found among the untreated controls. In other words, this outcome suggests that only the combination of appropriate images under relaxation conditions is effective; neither relaxation nor desensitization alone seem to be therapeutic.

Similar results were obtained by Rachman (1965c) in his investigation of spider phobia in nonpsychiatric cases. Here again, the combination of relaxation and desensitization proved to be effective, while neither element used alone produced the desired results. Lang, Lazovik, and Reynolds (1966) have also reported that relaxation given in combination with a "pseudo-

therapy" (which, it was hoped, subjects would assume to be a relevant form of interpretive psychotherapy) was inferior to the more usual form of systematic desensitization, again suggesting that relaxation alone is ineffective. Kondas (1967) has drawn similar conclusions in his study of examination anxiety, after comparing relaxation alone, desensitization alone, and a combination of both conditions. These studies, together with others, argue strongly for both elements (desensitization *and* relaxation) being necessary to obtaining effective changes.

However, the observations made by Lader and Mathews seem to be at variance with such a conclusion, at least insofar as the idea of relaxation being incompatible with the presence of anxiety is concerned. What these authors point out is that rather than muscle relaxation itself being the important factor in desensitization, it is the *relaxed environment* (perhaps created by the instructions, the warm, sympathetic therapist, and the like) which induces a state of *mental* calm, and it is this latter which is important to achieve (See also Rachman, 1968).

The role of muscle relaxation is made even less clear by the results of an experiment by Wolpin and Raines (1966). Here relaxation with desensitization seemed to produce essentially the same outcome as desensitization accompanied by *deliberate tensing* of the muscles in the treatment of snake phobia. Of special interest is the observation that a patient could feel more relaxed even though maintaining a "tensed-up posture." This finding accords with that of Lazarus and Abramovitz (1962), in that the use of counteranxiety imagery (imagining driving a sports car) which produced a state of excitement was effective in reducing a fear of dogs. Again, to the extent that in vivo desensitization is successful (Cooke, 1966; Garfield, 1967; Ritter, 1968), the necessity for relaxation as a counter anxiety state is rendered more doubtful.[9]

---

[9] Relaxation is usually produced by voluntary effort on the patient's part, normally instructed in the art by the therapist. Drugs have only rarely been used, although Friedman (1966) and others have reported excellent clinical results with methohexitone as a muscle relaxant, used in conjunction with desensitization. Yorkston, Sergeant, and Rachman (1968) failed to demonstrate any superiority in this procedure when comparing it with three control procedures in the treatment of severely aporaphobic patients. In spite of the excellence of their research

design, the choice of patients may not have been such as to bring out the possibilities inherent in this type of therapy; severe agoraphobics have proved resistant to most types of therapy. Active research into the possibilities of drug-controlled relaxation is urgently needed—if successful, this very much increases the number of patients that can be accommodated by a given therapist, and it also decreases dramatically the number of sessions required. Theoretical questions are also raised by this procedure which the existing literature does little to answer.

A further problem of theoretical significance, that of the effects of massed and spaced practice, has received attention from Ramsay, Barends, Breuker, and Kruseman (1966). Contrary to what might have been expected from an "extinction" model, these investigators report that spaced practice produced superior results. However, in this study "spacing" comprised four treatment sessions each dealing with four hierarchy items, while "massing" comprised two sessions with eight anxiety items in each. While it is true that there were actually more trials in each session under "massed" conditions, the intervals *between hierarchy items* were the same for both "massed" and "spaced" treatments. It may well be that the critical condition would be that of manipulating the interitem presentation time, rather than the total number of extinction trials given on any one occasion.

The differential effects of spaced and massed practice in relation to desensitization have also been examined in a study by Lanyon, Manosevitz, and Imber (1968). The group receiving "spaced" training were given two to three treatment sessions each week, while those receiving "massed" training had sessions several times each day. No difference between the amount of fear reduction in the two groups for the specific phobia (for spiders) was observed, but the "spaced" schedule seemed to produce a definite reduction in general anxiety, while "massed" treatment did not.

The study is open to the same criticism as that mentioned in connection with Ramsay's, but it is of some interest to note that neither finding offers support for an extinction-based model.

Rachman (1966b) has also considered a problem of theoretical significance to desensitization, namely the speed at which generalization occurs. In particular, this investigation was concerned with the rate at which generalization occurred from the imagined event (in imaginal systematic desensitization) to the real-life situation. The main finding was that in more than 82 percent of observations made (on only three subjects, however), generalization to the real-life situation (*real* spider stimuli) was immediate. Equally important from a theoretical viewpoint was Rachman's finding that recurrence of anxiety following a treatment session was noted on 50 percent of occasions. Spontane-

ous recovery would in fact be an expected outcome of an extinction procedure and, as Rachman reports, its appearance may depend upon the number of desensitization presentations given.

It is abundantly clear that the theory of reciprocal inhibition as formulated by Wolpe is only one of several possible theoretical accounts of desensitization procedures, and it could well be that other alternatives will be forthcoming. This is, of course, the hallmark of a developing field and a cause for optimism rather than dismay.

Clearly many such direct experimental attacks on the problems raised, like those of Grings and Uno (1968) or Millenson and Hendry (1967), are required before we can feel that we have a general theory of desensitization that is reasonably acceptable. On the other hand, it is equally true that the theoretical ramifications and implications of desensitization theories have been of less concern to many behavior therapists than the therapeutic aspects; such a situation does seem to present an unfortunate imbalance that future investigators must correct. What, in fact, are the therapeutic results?

Even the most cursory examination of the literature on desensitization therapy reveals serious deficiencies in the character of the early evidence. A good deal of this evidence consisted of anecdotal accounts of the successful application of the treatment to one or two cases, without the refinements of either proper controls or sound techniques of assessment. The situation was such as to invite the comment that the evidence for the efficacy of behavior therapy was no better than that advanced in support of psychotherapy (see Beech, 1963). More recently, these early deficiencies have received a certain amount of attention, and the picture respecting desensitization therapy is becoming clearer.

The research literature can be conveniently divided into two parts, one dealing with nonpsychiatric subjects, and the other with psychiatrically disturbed individuals. We may begin by considering the former.

The study by Lang and Lazovik (1963) has already received brief mention in a previous section, and is especially noteworthy as representing perhaps the first well-controlled study of any form of psychological treatment. These investigators conducted a carefully controlled study of snake phobia in 24 volunteer college students, in which systematic desensitization therapy was compared with repeated exposure to phobic stimuli. The results of this experiment indicated that the former treatment was extremely effective in dealing with the phobia, for although only 11 treatment sessions were given, both the subjective ratings of fear and overt avoidance behavior were significantly modified. Furthermore, the benefit derived was maintained or had even increased at a follow-up check six months later, and no evidence of symptom-substitution could be discovered.

The presence of an isolated snake phobia also received experimental attention from Lang, Lazovik, and Reynolds (1966), this time a comparison being made between systematic desensitization and two "control" groups, one of which received no treatment, while the other was given "pseudotherapy" (a series of interviews not comforming to any recognized effective treatment). Modification of this phobia, in the nonpsychiatric subjects employed, was once again noted to occur in connection with desensitization therapy, while the "controls" did not show improvement. While it can be argued that the comparison treatment in this study was essentially weak, the outcome does indicate that desensitization is an effective method for dealing with, and removing, fear of snakes in otherwise "normal" individuals.

In some ways a more convincing study was that conducted by Paul (1966, 1967), who investigated the possibility of modifying a fear of public speaking among college students. Subjects in this experiment were allocated to one or another of three treatment groups; systematic desensitization; a presumably ineffective "pseudotherapy;" and "insight" therapy, which appeared to have the usual characteristics of psychotherapy. A comparison between the first and last of these treatments would, of course, be of special interest, as we should not only ask questions concerning the effectiveness of desensitization over and above "no treatment" or other control conditions, but also about the *comparative* efficiency of this form of therapy. In this respect, the design of the study contained a most interesting facet; those involved, whichever form of treatment was to be given, were skilled and experienced insight therapists. Clearly, any bias in outcome might be expected to favor the type of treatment in which the therapists were expert.

The results indicated a very decided superiority for desensitization over and above those obtained for "insight" and "pseudotherapy"—both of which met with a 50 percent success rate—while a "no-treatment" control group showed a 17 percent recovery rate. Perhaps just as compelling was the impact of the desensitization program upon the therapists who expressed their intention to recommend this form of treatment, and to demonstrate it in the course of their training and consulting work. This latter point, of course, may be regarded as a somewhat hasty and possibly ill-judged reaction by these insight therapists. After all, the subjects were not psychiatrically disturbed, and perhaps "insight" therapy requires a rather longer time before benefits to the patient can be expected to accrue. Furthermore, it might well be argued that the "psychotherapies" have a much broader aim than that of simple symptomatic relief, so that the criteria of recovery and improvement would need to be scrutinized most carefully before drawing firm conclusions. Further light upon these possibilities is shed by studies quoted later in this section.

Davison's (1968) study, already mentioned in the previous part of this chapter, also adds to the weight of evidence that desensitization is an effective treatment for the simple phobias of nonpsychiatric populations. This study of snake phobia among female subjects not only threw some light upon the active ingredients of desensitization therapy (suggesting that *both* relaxation *and* relevant imagery were necessary), but also showed that this form of treatment produces results significantly better than for a "no-treatment" control. This finding was consistent with Rachman's (1965) study of spider phobia, showing that effective modification of the phobia certainly occurs with desensitization, but this requires the combination of both relaxation and graded presentation of fear stimuli (Fig. 15.3). The main limitation of this study was, however, the same as that which characterized Davison's, namely that one is only dealing with a simple, circumscribed problem in a relatively stable population.

Other controlled experimental investigations of desensitization employing nonpsychiatric

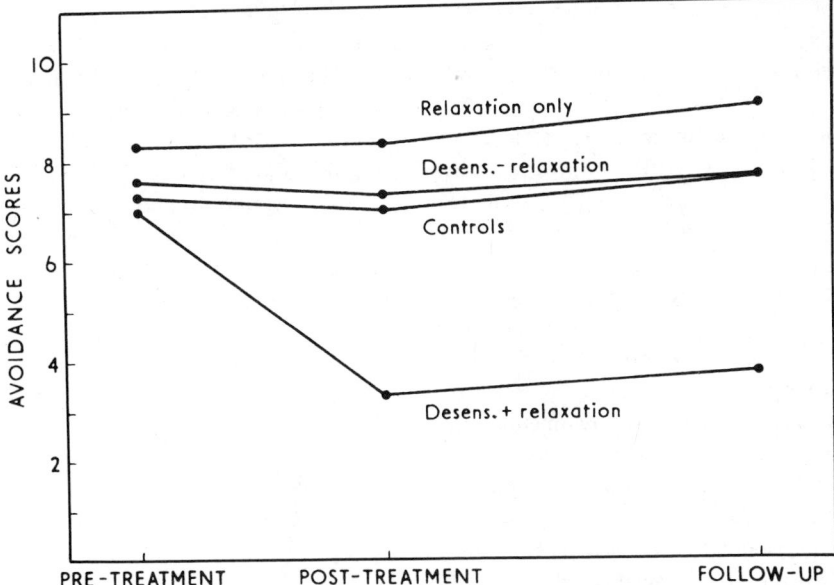

Figure 15.3 Comparisons of four different techniques of therapy used on spider phobics. Behavior therapy (desensitization+relaxation) is clearly superior to either desensitization or relaxation alone, or to no treatment (control). From Rachman (1965). Used with permission.

subjects, have produced essentially similar results to those already mentioned. Among them are Cooke's (1966) study of individuals declaring themselves to be afraid of laboratory rats, Paul and Shannon's (1966) treatment of "chronically anxious" students, and Kondas's (1967) investigation of students with examination anxiety. There is little room for doubt that these, together with other experiments, indicate that systematic desensitization under relaxation conditions is successful in reducing or eliminating the monosymptomatic phobias of nonpsychiatric cases. Further work along these lines only serves to extend the variety of phobias treated, for no negative results have appeared that might occasion any reservations concerning the above conclusions. While further investigations of the precise mechanisms involved in desensitization treatment are clearly important and are most easily conducted using "normal" individuals, there is an obvious need for studies of the more pressing, severe, and incapacitating disorders found among psychiatric patients.

It would, of course, be erroneous to consider that psychiatric attention is devoted solely to the more seriously disturbed patients; it may well be that many severely psychologically handicapped individuals do not come into psychiatric

care and, conversely, perhaps the psychiatrist often becomes involved with cases which, in other contexts, would be regarded as essentially "normal." However, two studies that might be regarded as dealing with the more serious disturbances of a "normal" population might be considered before passing to a review of desensitization studies among formal "psychiatric" groups. These are the studies of Lazarus (1961) and Moore (1965).

Lazarus' study was important in two respects. First, while subjects were not drawn from a psychiatric population, nevertheless they were all said to be severely handicapped in terms of both their social relationships and general adjustment. Secondly, the possibility of group desensitization was explored for the first time.

A comparison was made in this study between "interpretive" therapy and desensitization, and the outcome was strongly in favor of the latter as the more successful treatment. Indeed, while 13 out of 18 patients in the desensitization group recovered (with 3 later relapses), only two patients receiving interpretive therapy—with or without relaxation as an adjunct—reached the same criterion, of whom one later relapsed. Perhaps of even greater significance was the finding that when those failing to benefit from interpretive therapy were given desensitization, the recovery figures were much the same as when desensitization had been offered as a first treatment.

These findings certainly appear to confirm not only the success of desensitization treatment in dealing with severe problems of a more "neurotic" kind, but also the fact that this treatment has decided advantage over "interpretive" therapy. However, certain major reservations concerning this experiment might be expressed, two of which could be said to be crucial. In the first place, Lazarus himself was responsible for the selection, treatment, and evaluation of all subjects and, as he was a practicing behavior therapist, the possibilities of bias could not reasonably be excluded. Secondly, while Lazarus is an acknowledged expert in the methods of behavior therapy, it could be argued that his administration of interpretive therapy was possibly less skilled.

Moore's study (1956) also seems to indicate that what one could reasonably argue were more serious psychological complaints than those afflicting phobic "normals" can be responsive to desensitization treatment. In this investigation, 12 asthmatic patients were offered three types of treatment (relaxation alone, relaxation accompanied by powerful suggestion concerning improvement, and desensitization under relaxation), the order in which each patient received the treatments being varied. The outcome indicated that while all three "therapies" produced a measure of subjective improvement, only desensitization with relaxation was accompanied by objective evidence of recovery from the asthmatic condition.

Studies concerning the use of systematic desensitization therapy with individuals formally categorized as "psychiatric patients" have been marked, as mentioned earlier, by an emphasis upon the single case report. This tendency, while understandable, has contributed little to the evaluation of behavior-therapy treatments unless, as in some cases (Yates, 1958; Beech, 1960; Flanagan et al., 1958) it can be clearly demonstrated that the outcome is predictable in terms of existing theory, and that the abnormal phenomenon has been brought under some form of experimental control. In effect, this means that the experimenter must demonstrate that

variations in the phenomenon concerned are related to certain identifiable conditions and, preferably, that these conditions can be specified precisely from certain theoretical propositions.

For example Beech (1960) was able to show the differential effect upon the various symptoms of writer's cramp according to whether treatment was given or withheld, and that certain effects, such as spontaneous recovery with some apparent permanent decrement in habit strength, followed the massed practice of a cramping movement (see Figure 15.4).

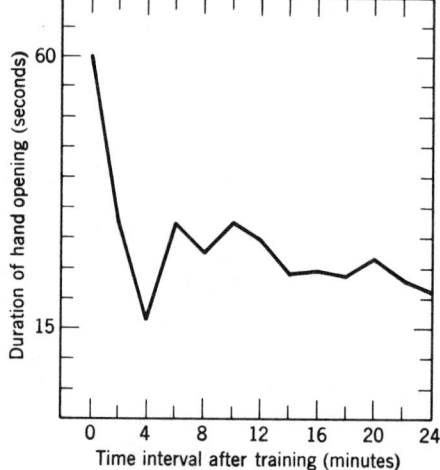

Figure 15.4 Spontaneous recovery of "hand closing" habit in patient suffering from writer's cramp at varying intervals after dynamometer practice (extinction trials). From Beech, 1960.

Similarly, Yates (1958) in a series of excellent experimental investigations of a tiqueur, demonstrated that the observed abnormalities could be brought under experimental control in accordance with certain theoretical expectations. Such studies are a relatively rare occurrence; behavior therapy of the single case has most frequently involved the observation that the patient has improved during the treatment, without establishing that what was done was related to changes in behavior.

In some ways more convincing, but still less than fully satisfactory, are the larger-scale uncontrolled studies. The greater confidence engendered by such studies derives from the seemingly unlikely probability that large numbers of persons could, after variable periods of handicap from psychological causes, show spontaneous recovery coincident with treatment.

In one such study Wolpe (1958) presents data obtained on 210 patients treated by his methods, using Knight's (1941) criteria to evaluate the outcome of therapy. He regarded almost 90 percent of his cases as being "apparently cured" or "much improved," while only 12 percent could be said to be "slightly to moderately improved" or "unimproved". These are remarkable statistics by any standard, especially in view of the relatively short periods of treatment involved (an average of approximately 11 months and 46 interviews), and are enhanced by Wolpe's comparison with results obtained at two psychoanalytic institutes, where the appropriate improvement figures apparently varied between 38 percent and 60 percent. Obviously, the substantial discrepancy could possibly be explained in terms other than a difference in the forms of treatment, such as the type of cases, strictness of rating methods, criteria considered, and so on, and no categorical conclusions can be drawn on the basis of this type of study.

Weight was added to the general case for the relative efficiency of desensitization by Lazarus' (1963) publication of the results of treating 408 neurotic patients. Here the percentage of patients classified as "apparently cured" or "much improved" was 78, which presents a picture only a little less satisfactory than that provided by Wolpe's figure of 90 percent. An interesting feature of Lazarus' report was the outcome of treatment of 126 cases of particularly *severe* neurotic condition, this sample being extracted from the main body of 408 patients. For this smaller sample a successful outcome was observed in only 62 percent of cases, suggesting that severe disturbances are less likely to succumb to behavior therapy by desensitization.

An early attempt to introduce more adequate controls was made by Cooper (1963). The study was concerned with a comparison of several forms of behavior therapy on the one hand, and alternative treatments, such as psychotherapy and drugs, on the other, In effect, Cooper attempted to match, on relevant variables, patients who had received one or other of these two alternatives, although the difficulty here was to achieve adequate matching and evaluation, on a retrospective basis, from case-note material. The outcome at the end of treatment was judged to be more favorable to behavior therapy although, in the follow-up, differences in improvement rate were similar.

The situation was made a little clearer when the patients in the above study were augmented by others (Cooper et al., 1965), giving a total of 77 cases categorized as agoraphobias, "other phobias," obsessionals, writer's cramp, and "miscellaneous complaints." Retrospective analysis showed that the overall improvement rate for behavior therapy was 61 percent, while that for other treatments was only 44 percent, but of possibly greatest interest was the finding that *all* phobic patients were initially successfully treated by behavior therapy. Once again, however, the relapse rate was disquieting, much of the initial improvement made by phobic patients being lost over a period of time.

It would be difficult to draw firm conclusions on the basis of this study, partly because of the matching problems mentioned earlier, and partly for other reasons, such as the limited experience of the therapists in administering these new techniques. Nevertheless, one might make three generalizations to be scrutinized in the light of further investigations. The first would be that, given similar patients, behavior therapy—and especially desensitization for phobias—is more effective than the conventional alternative treatments, at least in the short term. The second would be that the overall success rate (that is, including all types of patients and a variety of behavior therapy methods) is lower than that quoted in studies of nonpsychiatric subjects. Third, one could say that while the improvement rates at the end of treatment for phobic patients appear to be similar to those quoted by Wolpe, the figures subsequently obtained are less encouraging.

A study with more circumscribed aims, although once again retrospective, was conducted by Marks and Gelder (1965), the project being restricted to phobic cases subdivided into "agoraphobias" and "other phobias." Two main treatments were considered, behavior therapy by desensitization and psychotherapy, although it should be noted that other forms of treatment, such as ECT and drugs, were frequent adjuncts to the main therapies. The success of behavior therapy, respecting the main phobic symptom, seemed to be rather greater than for psychotherapy, where agoraphobic patients were concerned; at the end of the treatment period, nine agoraphobics were "much improved" and eight had shown "no change" following desensitization, while the corresponding figures for psychotherapy were five patients "much improved" and nine showing "no change." The same conclusion could be drawn at assessment one year later. Respecting changes other than in the main phobic symptom, little progress seemed to be made with either form of treatment, only a small proportion of patients showing evidence of modification.

Where the group of "other phobias" were concerned, however, quite a different picture emerged. By the end of treatment all 11 phobics treated by desensitization had shown evidence of improvement, while only 3 of the 10 psychotherapy patients could be similarly classified; although evaluation one year later revealed that the gap between psychotherapy and behavior therapy had narrowed a little, but still remained in favor of the latter.

The main generalization that could be made on the basis of this study was that desensitization seemed to produce greater benefit than psychotherapy, at least in the short term, and probably still after one year. A second conclusion would be that while desensitization was attended by highly efficient results with some patients, the agoraphobics failed to respond so well to this kind of treatment. Indeed, the oustanding problem emerging from these results was the failure to achieve effective modification among many agoraphobic patients, particularly where symptoms other than the main phobia itself were concerned. This differential responsiveness is, of course, quite consistent with both the Lader and Wing hypothesis discussed earlier and the incubation theory described in this chapter.

The degree of confidence in these conclusions is, of course, necessarily limited by the defects of the study itself, among which are the retrospective nature of the investigation with all the attendant problems this involves, the contamination of the main therapies by treatment adjuncts, and the fact that most desensitization patients had been treated "in vivo," a method that may well prove to be inferior to imaginal desensitization.

A more satisfactory prospective study was carried out by Gelder and Marks (1966), to examine once again the problem of the agoraphobic patient in the context of a comparison between desensitization and psychotherapy. The procedure was to accept 20 agoraphobic patients, and to allocate them in an unbiased way either to treatment by behavior therapy (desensitization) or by psychotherapy. The aim was to match the groups carefully for a number of possibly important variables, such as age, duration and type of symptom, and severity of phobia.

The main finding was that both treatments appeared to obtain the same degree of success respecting the main complaint of agoraphobia; 7 out of 10 patients in each group showed some improvement. However, when treatment was finally terminated, all patients were left with some residual difficulty in terms of their agoraphobia, and part of the progress made tended to be lost some time after treatment had been concluded. Furthermore, neither type of therapy appeared to have much impact upon the various complaints (anxiety, depression, other phobias, and obsessions), other than agoraphobia, found among the patients.

However, in this connection it is pertinent to observe that these other symptoms were not especially troublesome to patients, being present to only a mild degree and therefore having little scope for improvement. On the other hand, phobias, especially the main phobic symptom, were severe and incapacitating, and an opportunity for modification was more clearly apparent.

In spite of the several flaws in this study (such as inexperienced therapists and the contamination of the main treatment with a variety of adjuncts), the results must be viewed as somewhat disappointing. It is true that some individual patients fared better than others, the tendency to respond well being a function of several factors (such as less severe symptoms at the onset of treatment, a better history of work adjustment, and the patient's lesser dissatisfaction with himself as a person). However, it seems clear that, in general, these results are much less satisfactory than those obtained with non-psychiatric subjects.

A more ambitious study, this time comparing three different forms of treatment for agoraphobia—desensitization, group psychotherapy, and individual psychotherapy—has also been conducted by Gelder, Marks, and Wolff (1967). The outcome was favorable to behavior therapy in two main ways. First, this form of treatment appeared to be more economical, being administered once weekly for one hour over an average period of 9 months. By comparison, individual psychotherapy was given with a similar frequency over an average of 12 months, and group psychotherapy for 18 months. Secondly, behavior therapy by systematic desensitization seemed to produce generally more favorable results than either of the alternatives, although this superiority was not always significant and was more marked early in treatment than on later follow-up. Some 7 months following the final rating (made 18 months after commencement of treatment), an independent evaluation of status was made by a psychiatric social worker. This inquiry revealed that $\frac{6}{10}$ of the desensitization group could still be regarded as "much improved," while only $\frac{3}{10}$ of the individual psychotherapy and $\frac{2}{10}$ of the group psychotherapy patients could be similarly categorized.

Generally speaking, the changes, while only occasionally reaching an acceptable level of statistical significance, reflected larger and more consistent changes for desensitization than for either alternative therapy. As Gelder and his colleagues comment, "All raters agreed that, of the three treatments, desensitization produced more patients whose symptoms improved at the end of treatment and follow-up," and that "symptoms . . . improved faster with desensitization." This general superiority of behavior therapy was also noted in areas of difficulty other than those involved in the symptom itself; for example, in work and leisure adjustment.

This is a surprising outcome for one particular reason. While all therapists taking part had received at least 18 months of training and experience in psychotherapy, all but one of those administering behavior therapy were applying these techniques for the first time, albeit under the supervision of a psychiatrist with some experience of desensitization. Such inexperience might well have affected both the efficiency with which the method was applied and the ratings made.

The study has a variety of limitations, both in terms of conception and design, but the main outcome does seem to bear out certain generalizations that could be put forward as the basis of previous studies. The first of these generalizations would be that desensitization may be more efficient, in terms of both the amount and speed of changes induced, than the more usual alternatives offered in the treatment of psychological abnormalities mediated by anxiety. The second would be that the results of applying these methods to psychiatrically disturbed patients are less successful than for "normals" with isolated phobias. Indeed, respecting this latter point, Gelder and his colleagues have pointed out (1967) that the degree of abnormality seems to be implicated in the prognosis for recovery. Third, it is apparent, as the above point suggests, that there are individual differences in responsiveness to desensitization such that greater anxiety and an agoraphobic condition militate against successful outcome. Finally, in no study has there been any evidence of symptom substitution; indeed, if anything, specific symptomatic treatment by desensitization has led to greater all-round improvement than other forms of therapy. This last point has, of course, very considerable theoretical implications in that it strongly suggests that a neurosis is likely to comprise the "symptoms" and other behavioral disturbance, rather than some hidden and deep-seated complex (Cahoon, 1968).

Before leaving this study by Gelder, Marks, and Wolff, it is perhaps of interest to draw attention to a conclusion drawn by these authors. They reason that while ". . . psychotherapy need not be given routinely . . . it can be . . . offered to all patients . . . left with other troublesome symptoms or personality disturbances," and that "desensitization and psychotherapy can each contribute in different ways to the treatment of phobic patients . . . and some patients may need both." The evidence from studies reported to date would seem to cast doubt upon the above conclusions. Indeed, the results of the Gelder, Marks, and Wolff study strongly suggest that individual psychotherapy, group psychotherapy, and desensitization seem to help the same kind of patients in the same ways, with desensitization doing so rather more efficiently, and there is no evidence for any specific type of effectiveness related to the form of therapy. Should this conclusion be borne out in yet other studies, then the problem would be one of improving the success rate attending behavior therapy, to increase the volume of training in these methods, and to discontinue the allocation of patients to psychotherapy.

Attention should also be drawn to the most recent study by Gelder and Marks (1968), in which desensitization has been compared with a form of psychotherapy. The patients in this inquiry were seven phobics (five of whom were agoraphobic) who had failed to show improvement following 18 months of group psychotherapy; the idea behind the study was to transfer these patients to desensitization treatment and to evaluate any changes that were then produced. On the average, the phobias of these seven patients showed three times as much improvement under desensitization as had occurred in the previous two years, as well as showing a reduction in other symptoms, such as anxiety and depression.

It could be argued that the modification of symptoms noted under desensitization treatment was simply the delayed outcome of psychotherapy. This explanation does not carry much conviction, however, for not only was the change a sudden and dramatic one, but no spontaneous recovery had been noted in the six-month interval between the termination of psychotherapy and the beginning of desensitization. The most reasonable conclusion seems to be that, with phobic patients at least, desensitization is producing benefits over and above any attributable to group psychotherapy, and is capable of doing so in a relatively brief space of time. A good review of controlled studies in behavior therapy is given by Marks and Gelder (1968).

An unpublished (and unfinished) study by P. Gillan and S. Rachman may also be quoted as indicating the sort of research design which the writers consider acceptable. Phobic patients were distributed in a random manner over four types of treatment—psychotherapy (carried out by a professional therapist of good standing), behavior therapy, relaxation alone, and desensitization without relaxation (carried out by a behavior therapist). Pre- and posttreatment assessments were made by an independent psychiatrist, uncommitted to either method, and acting blind, that is, in ignorance of the type of treatment planned or given. Self-assessments were also obtained from patients, behavioral avoidance tests were constructed pre- and post-therapy, and physiological recordings were made of patients' reactions to the image of the feared object, at various stages of treatment. A follow-up was instituted, and the same data were again obtained. Data obtained so far on six patients in each group (a total of ten in each group is planned) show (1) an overall lead on all criteria of behavior therapy, suggesting a very strong superiority over the other three methods; (2) a tendency for the psychotherapist to over-rate his success, when compared with outside criteria, the fellow psychiatrist's judgment, and the patient's own rating; and (3) a continuation of improvement over the follow-up period. Studies of this type will undoubtedly contribute to a better understanding of the nature and effects of behavior therapy; the criteria used, and the randomization process employed, give a minimum design from which nothing should be dropped in future replications if satisfactory conclusions are to be drawn from the results. However, it may be permissible to drop the two control groups using relaxation only and desensitization without relaxation; the evidence is now reasonably strong that by themselves these two methods achieve very little, as compared with the combined method.

Finally, in this section, some brief mention may be made of the specific use of desensitization procedures in the treatment of children. The early study by Jones (1924), as well as the later survey by Jersild and Homes (1935), had already indicated the potential value of such methods in dealing with children's fears, but the more recent reports have been almost exclusively concerned with the applications of desensitization to adults.

Anecdotal reports of the employment of desensitization to child phobics have appeared from time to time, but these have done little or nothing to either increase or to undermine our confidence in this form of treatment. On the other hand, two controlled studies appear to offer rather more tangible evidence for the efficacy of desensitization in modifying specific abnormal fears in young people.

The first of these, by Humphrey (1966), compared the results obtained using desensitization (as well as other behavior-therapy techniques) with those accompanying psychotherapy, and with any changes occurring without any form of treatment being administered. While this investigation contained several important faults, the outcome strongly suggested that the improvements obtained following desensitization were much superior to those found in either of the control groups. Furthermore, as has been found in other studies reported here, desensitization proved to be the more economic procedure, taking an average of 9 treatment sessions as opposed to the 21 required in the case of psychotherapy (outcome ratings were made by independent psychiatrists acting "blind," and patients were allocated to treatments on a random basis).

The second study, by Ritter (1968) compared "vicarious desensitization" (where the children concerned observed the therapist and others fearlessly dealing with the object of their fear) with "contact desensitization," which latter treatment corresponded to orthodox in vivo treatment. In this study, 44 children with some degree of snake phobia were included, fourteen of whom were nontreated controls. The outcome indicated a significant superiority in effectiveness for "contact desensitization" over the "vicarious" procedure, with the latter producing better results than no treatment at all.

The emphasis generally, whether in enlarged studies or in single-case inquiries, has been upon "real-life" situations, rather than upon the imaginative recreation of such events. This is of course probably necessary in the treatment of the young, for obvious reasons. However, in spite of the somewhat different emphasis respecting *in vivo* and *imaginal* desensitization in children and adults, the outcome has been much the same in demonstrating important advantages of such treatment over alternative forms of therapy.

AVERSION THERAPY

Aversion therapy, as explained earlier in this chapter, is aimed specifically at disorders of the second kind, that is, at behaviors which are socially undesirable, or undesirable in the patient's own long-term interests, but which he finds reinforcing, at least in part. Alcoholism, drug addiction, homosexuality, fetishism, transvestism, obesity, and psychopathic and criminal behavior patterns all clearly fall into this field. Some disorders must also be included, although they are not in fact reinforcing —enuresis is an example. (It might be argued that the release of bladder control in the warmth of one's bed, thus avoiding having to get up and go to the toilet in the cold, is reinforcing, but this is a doubtful argument). For most of these disorders we may perhaps argue that there has been a failure of proper conditioning to occur; enuresis, psychopathic behavior, and criminality are obvious examples, and some discussion has already been given of this point. However, not all disorders of the second kind are due to failure of conditioning to occur. Homosexuality is probably in many cases a strongly constitutional form of behavior; in other cases there would appear to have occurred a clear form of conditioning and generalization (for example, in residential schools, prisons, navy and army units, and the like). It would be naive to suggest that this behavior developed because of a failure of normal heterosexual patterns to be conditioned, although it might be suggested that homosexual behavior (and this may also be true of other sexual deviations mentioned above) can develop only if the restraints of "conscience" (that is, a set of early conditioned responses) are weak or absent; in this sense it might be said that these disorders, too, incorporate some form of lack of conditioning. However, we shall not insist on this, and the point is probably irrelevant to the actual operation of aversive conditioning. Alcoholism, too, may involve some failure to condition appropriate behavior patterns for dealing with the intake of drugs. The disorders of the second kind may also include behavior patterns that are self-reinforcing and pleasurable but that turn out to be maladaptive for reasons essentially outside the control of the patient— homosexuality may be made illegal in the country he inhabits, or alcohol may have certain specific effects of an addicting kind on his metabolism.

When faced with conduct that is itself re-inforcing, but that for some reason the patient wishes to stop, the obvious procedure would seem to be some form of punishment; society has for thousands of years tried this method in cases of criminality and of sexual deviation, without much success. The main reason for this failure, of course, is the noncontingent nature of the punishment (that is, its failure to occur in the majority of cases), and the length of time elapsing from the commission of the crime to trial, sentence, and punishment (Vogel, Sprott and Burrows, 1969). There are other reasons for viewing punishment with disfavor; we shall return to this point in our theoretical analysis of aversion therapy. The alternative favored by behavior therapists is an inverted form of de-sensitization therapy; aversion therapy might also be called "sensitization therapy," in the sense that the reciprocal inhibition principle is evoked in reverse. Instead of invoking the CR in its full strength, the therapist using de-sensitization techniques invokes it at some low level, to the accompaniment of relaxation and other behaviors antagonistic to anxiety. Con-versely, in aversion therapy, the therapist in-vokes the pleasurable to-be-deconditioned be-havior (the CS, in this case) and follows it with a strong aversive UCS-UCR combination. In this way it is hoped that, after a number of pairings, the $\overline{\text{CS}}$ will now evoke not pleasure, but pain and anxiety, so that the patient ceases to seek this particular form of gratification.[10] The difference of this form of conditioning from ordinary punishment procedures will be elabor-ated later.

In discussing aversion therapy, as compared with desensitization therapy, the theorist is beset by a number of difficulties. In the first place, the number of studies reported in the literature is relatively small; for every 100 patients treated by desensitization therapy, there is only one treated by aversion therapy. In the second place, where we have several excellent experimental studies of desensitization therapy, there are practically none for aversion therapy. And in the third

place, while the theory underlying desensiti-zation therapy is relatively well worked out, this is by no means so in the case of aversion therapy. Add the very cogent point that most of the work done on aversion therapy has been amateurish to a degree, often with total disregard for quite elementary rules of conditioning, and it will be apparent why this section will inevitably be less satisfactory than the last.

Why has aversion therapy been used less frequently than desensitization? The use of punishment or aversive stimuli in any form is ethically dubious, even when it is used in the interests of the patient; it must not only be used for the benefit of the patient, but it must be seen to be for the benefit of the patient. This demand inevitably produces difficulties that do not occur with desensitization treatment, where the patient is the obvious sufferer, and demands succor. In most disorders where aversion therapy is appropriate, it is society that suffers, rather than the patient; his sufferings occur only because of some action taken by society. Thus social dis-approval of homosexuality may cause the patient to ask for a cure, rather than his own internal suffering. Threat of prison may cause the psychopath to wish for treatment, rather than his own feelings of anxiety and depression. The fetishist and the transvestite may be driven by their wives to seek help, without having any really strong desire, based on suffering, to give up their deviant practices. The fear may be expressed that aversion therapy serves only to make people conform to the mores of society, and that it thus fulfils the role of policeman, rather than that of the physician. Often, indeed, patients are in fact referred by courts for treat-ment (and this is equally true of psychotherapy or psychoanalysis as of behavior therapy), on pain of going to prison if treatment is not accepted. Conditions such as these do not pro-vide a very strong drive for a "cure."

These points cannot be dismissed; there are many cases in which it would be ethically in-admissible for aversion therapy to be under-taken. However, there are also many cases in

---

[10] The originator of aversion therapy, according to Plutarch, was the Athenian orator Demonsthenes, who suffered from a severe shoulder tic that caused him to throw up his right shoulder spasmodically. He suspended a very sharp sword just above his right shoulder, so that every time the spasm occurred and his shoulder was thrown up, the skin was punctured by the tip of the sword. The patient, we are told, was cured in a matter of days!

which the interests of the patient himself suggest that intervention, if successful, would be to his advantage. A well-known Queen's Counsel consulted one of us a few years ago about the possibility of having his homosexual tendencies, which caused him great internal conflict and suffering, relieved by aversion therapy; in view of the early stage of development of these methods, and the nonavailability of suitable apparatus, he had to be declined. A few weeks later he committed suicide. Would it have been unethical to have helped him, provided that this had been possible? His conflicts and suffering probably arose from early religious conditioning in childhood, later reinforced by our general system of social mores; in this sense, it might be said that social pressure drove him to seek help, and later to suicide. Would therapy then have been merely the handmaiden of conformity, seeking to mold him in the fashion of society? Is the fact that he wanted desperately to conform irrelevant? These are difficult ethical points which we are not qualified to judge. In our submission, the therapist must differentiate between cases in which pressure is clearly exerted from outside, and others in which the patient himself clearly seeks help; the former, we believe, are not suitable for therapy, and the latter ones are. There will inevitably remain some cases in which any decision must be doubtful; ethical conundrums are not easily solved by formula. However, what is said here applies not only to aversion therapy, but also to all forms of therapy; arguments are more likely to be raised in connection with aversion therapy because it holds out greater promise of success, and because it involves some form, however mild, of aversive stimulation or "punishment". However, psychoanalysis also involves "punishment"; the patient is incarcerated for many hours each week with his analyst, he has to pay heavy "fines" in the form of fees, and many patients find the treatment actually painful and distasteful (York, 1966). *We have had patients express their considered judgment when they said that they preferred a number of relatively weak electric shocks to the eternal probing of their analysts!* Certainly the notion that aversion therapists are "sadistic" must be rejected as unlikely; dentists and surgeons also inflict pain, but as long as the procedure is clearly for the benefit of the patient, and carried out with his express approval, they are not held to go outside the Hippocratic province.

With respect to criminals, certain further problems arise. The notion of criminality as a disorder was mooted in Samuel Butler's *Erewhon*, but it makes some scientific sense nowadays (Eysenck, 1964a); if it is a disorder, akin to dysthymic neurosis, should treatment be withheld? We have been approached at times by criminals who had heard about behavior therapy and desperately wished to have this applied to themselves; as one of them put it: "I don't know what makes me do crimes, but I want it removed!" This may not be typical of criminals, but many have in fact expressed interest in the possibilities opened up by behavior therapy; why should they be denied treatment on pseudoethical grounds? A further point, often neglected, is, of course, that society also has certain rights; is it ethically superior to punish criminals, or try to reclaim them, as by behavior therapy? We have no wish to settle these problems by fiat, nor are we competent to solve them by argument; they must be left as questions, the answers to which will no doubt be long debated. We would not in fact have raised these points, except for the fact that many critics of behavior therapy have fastened upon them; a brief discussion therefore seemed apposite.

Apart from the considerations advanced so far, there are good psychological reasons for believing that aversion therapy should be less successful, and more prone to relapse, than desensitization therapy. The matter of motivation has already been touched upon; there seems ample justification for believing that intrinsic motivation for undergoing treatment to eliminate self-rewarding patterns of behavior must be weaker than motivation for undergoing treatment to eliminate self-punishing patterns of behavior. The role of motivation, drive, and incentive in behavior generally is not too well understood (Bolles, 1967), but there seems little doubt from the experimental side that they play an important part in mediating both learning and performance. Even in patients genuinely motivated one must always suspect covert contrary motivations working to prolong the enjoyment of the rewards of the behavior to be eliminated. This must restrict severely the possibilities of treatment.

Relapses are much more likely in aversion therapy than in desensitization therapy, as Eysenck (1963c) pointed out, In desensitization, we are merely helping natural forces to produce extinction; as pointed out earlier, extinction is the natural fate of neurotic disorders, and special circumstances and mechanisms are required in order to avoid this in a small number of recalcitrant cases. Hence the therapist is batting on a good wicket, and his efforts are unlikely, if successful, to be frustrated by a relapse; he is working in the direction of producing an increase in entropy, so to speak.[11] The aversion therapist is in exactly the opposite position; he is seeking to *establish* a conditioned response that goes counter to the reward system under which the organism operates, and that is subject to extinction. Hence he is trying to produce a decrease in entropy, which in the long run may seem self-defeating effort. He is further hampered in his efforts by several facts. In the first place he is bound by ethics and law to use only relatively mild aversive stimuli; hence conditioning, whose effectiveness depends in part on the strength of the UCR, must be suboptimal. He is restricted further in the number of paired administrations of CS and UCS that he can give; these restrictions derive from limitations of time (both his and the patient's) and from the desire to administer only a bare minimum of aversive stimuli, a desire probably shared by both patient and therapist. But it is well known

that number of reinforcements is the most important variable in producing $_SH_R$; consequently, habit strength will inevitably be weak. In the third place, unreinforecd CS presentations will inevitably occur with considerable frequency, due in part to the habits previously formed (leading to the ex-alcoholic passing pubs and bars, being offered drinks, and the like; or to the ex-homosexual being accosted by former associates), and in part to the almost universal distribution of these stimuli. In desensitization treatment such encounters help extinction along; here they go counter to the maintenance of the therapeutically conditioned aversive response, and lead to extinction and hence to relapse. And in the fourth place there can be no doubt that aversion therapy, by removing a rewarding type of behavior with a long history of positive reinforcement, frequently leaves a conspicuous gap that itself has aversive properties; by removing a person's homosexual feelings, the therapist does not automatically endow that patient with heterosexual ones, and even if he did, the patient would still lack skills and experiences required for a successful heterosexual adaptation. Similarly, the alcoholic who has spent a large part of his leisure time with his cronies in pubs and bars is now "cured," but is also left with no friends and nothing to do; unless this void is filled he may easily drift back —not because the "cure" did not work, but because the change in behavior pattern set in motion other forces that push him back towards the old life.

[11] This view may be too sanguine. Cremerius (1962), in a 10-year follow-up study of many different types of neurotics treated by many different procedures including psychoanalysis, autogenic training, hypnosis, and the like, found that while 73 percent of his cases were rated as cured or improved at termination of treatment, 75 percent were rated as unimproved at follow-up. The large number of cases used (over 600) and the exceptional care taken over the investigation, as well as the exemplary success of tracing patients for the follow-up, make this study a very important source for the study of the time-course of neurotic disorder. It is interesting to consider in particular the long-term effects of psychoanalytic therapy; analysts often seem to suggest that almost by definition their method of treatment is immune to relapse or symptom substitution, while all other methods of treatment cannot fail to lead to one or the other. Among patients so treated (and it should be noted that they were specially selected for "suitability," and hence had the best prospects in any case),

12 percent showed symptom substitution, 6 percent showed a relapse that made them worse than before the treatment, and 30 percent showed unchanged symptomatology. Thus, only 52 percent demonstrated continued improvement. This figure was higher than that for any other method of treatment (behavior therapy was not used in this study), but this appears to have been a consequence of the special selection process; as the author puts it, "*auf Grund meiner eigenen Untersuchung scheint das entscheidende prognostische Moment in der prämorbiden Persönlichkeit des Kranken zu liegen . . . (Sie) bestimmt die Wahl des Behandlungsverfahrens, die Dauer der Behandlung und die Tiefe, bis zu welcher die Probleme durchgearbeitet werden können. Alles weitere ist vor allem Folge dieser Wahl.*" (page 57). This stress on the overwhelming importance of the premorbid personality of the patient is in good accord with the arguments put forward earlier, although it doubtful if Cremerius would agree with our specific analysis of personality.

None of these objections are fatal. Once the need for overlearning, that is, for a large number of reinforcements *beyond* the point where the CR first appears, is realized, there is no real obstacle to producing very strong CS-UCS bonds; habit strength can be increased well beyond what is customary without using overly punishing UCRs. Extinction can be counteracted in a number of ways, apart from overlearning; partial reinforcement is one obvious technique (Lovibond, 1964), and booster treatments given regularly every year or two is another. (Booster treatments are quite usual in many types of medical work, as in connection with desensitization treatment of allergies). The fourth point raised presents more difficulties, but is also not insuperable. Behavior therapists have begun to try following aversion treatment (for example, of homosexuality) by the production of positive conditioned responses to alternative stimuli. Thus pictures of nude males may be the UCS followed by onset of shock (CS), while the cessation of shock is preceded by the appearance of pictures of nude women; in this way it is hoped to condition the pleasant experiences associated with cessation of shock to females, while the unpleasant experiences associated with onset of shock are conditioned to males (Feldman and MacCulloch, 1965). Or patients may be instructed to masturbate to imaginary scenes involving females; again it is hoped that the pleasant feelings associated with masturbation and orgasm will condition to the CS, here the imagined scenes and actions involving women (see McGuire et al. [1965] and Evans [1968] for masturbation as reinforcement.).

Other workers have provided posttreatment support for alcoholics and other patients, through regular social meetings with fellow-patients, and in other similar ways. These are all problems of patient management that are set in a wider context than behavior therapy, and their discussion would not be appropriate here.

Of particular concern is another difficulty that lies at the very root of our attempt to produce an aversive conditioned response in the laboratory situation that is intended to generalize to conditions outside the laboratory. As Mowrer (1938) pointed out, autonomic CRs tend to be fragile, and to be very much under cortical control; thus he reports that GSR responses were eliminated completely when the shock electrodes were removed. Similarly, Wilson (1968) has shown that CRs are in fact reversible, depending on cognitive appraisal; having conditioned shock to blue stimuli (CS+) and no-shock to yellow stimuli (CS−), he told Ss that shock would now follow yellow, rather than blue. (In fact, no further shocks were administered). Nevertheless, GSRs for blue disappeared, and GSRs for yellow incremented, showing that autonomic responses were very much dependent on cognitive factors. How, then, can we hope that aversive stimuli associated with undesirable practices, or the imaginary revival of such practices, or pictures of stimuli associated with them, can transfer from the limited laboratory environment to the outside world, where cognitive discrimination between the laboratory and the outside (that is, between the possibility of receiving aversive stimuli and the lack of possibility of receiving aversive stimuli) is so easy? Several considerations relevant to this point will be mentioned later on; here, let us merely note that such generalization has in fact been shown to occur, and that we must bear in mind such factors as strength of UCR, number of reinforcements received, and multiplicity of autonomic reactions conditioned. The work of Mowrer, Wilson, and others who have stressed the cognitive modifiability of autonomic responses has usually been concerned with weak stimuli, few reinforcements, and isolated autonomic responses; we cannot necessarily generalize from these conditions to those obtaining in aversive therapy.

One further point may repay discussion. The frequent relapses of patients showing behavior patterns of the second kind and requiring aversion therapy have, at times, been used as arguments against behavior therapy and the theory underlying it. Both on the theoretical and the applied sides this argument seems to us to be misconceived. All methods of treatment have encountered this problem in connection with alcoholism, homosexuality, enuresis, and the like; from the applied point of view, the important question is whether behavior therapy, under optimal conditions (that is, using partial reinforcement, booster treatments, and the like) shows a smaller number of "cures" and a greater number of relapses than other treatments, or whether the boot is on the other foot. We will turn to this question later. From the theoretical point of view, we must note that the much greater liability to relapse of these patients, as compared with patients exposed to desensitization therapy, is predictable from learning theory, and from our theory of neurotic disorder; it surely cannot be argued seriously that because certain events are predictable from theory, therefore the fact that these events happen is an argument against the very theory that has predicted them. The psychologist is concerned with lawful sequences of events, and the events following aversion therapy are certainly lawful; insofar as this is true, insofar we may regard our theory as supported. Psychiatrically, the frequency of relapse is lamentable, but the very lawfulness of the phenomenon suggests that we have achieved some understanding of its causes, and the suggestions made for reducing drastically the number of relapses (overlearning, partial reinforcement, and the like) have already in some instances shown that practical effects can be achieved in cutting down the rate of relapses (Eysenck, 1963c).

Aversion therapy involves a CS—that is, a stimulus that provokes the undesirable reaction (such as drinking, homosexual conduct, and enuresis), and that can either be manipulated experimentally (drinking) or that happens in the ordinary course of events, and must be awaited (enuresis). A great variety of stimuli have in fact been used, ranging from actual behavior patterns identical with those to be eliminated, to all sorts of replicas—pictures, verbal descriptions, imaginary scenes, and so forth. There is little evidence regarding the relative success of different CSs; experimenters tend to make decisions on the basis of ethical, legal, and other extraneous considerations. Transvestites receive aversive stimuli while actually cross-dressing, which is legal (Marks and Gelder, 1967); homosexuals are not encouraged to indulge in actual homosexual behavior, but have to look at pictures of nude males, or imagine scenes (Feldman and MacCulloch, 1965). This may be one factor responsible for the greater success of treatment with transvestites compared with homosexuals. Enuresis is always treated in situ; that is, the

aversive stimulus that wakes the patient is activated by the act of urinating; it would be interesting to know if imaginary evocation of the scene could be used to advantage. Therapists have been rather unimaginative and hidebound in their efforts; it is not surprising that we have no idea at present of the relative success of different methods of presenting UCS, or of the interaction effects of these methods with personality. (It seems very likely that different methods achieve different degrees of success with different types of people—extroverts and introverts, patients high in neuroticism versus patients low in neuroticsm, and the like).

The CS (drinking, urinating, looking at pictures of nude males, cross-dressing, or what not) leads to a CR that is in effect emotional in nature—as Thorndike would have put it, the CR is the experience attending a satisfactory state of affairs. (Strictly speaking, of course, it is not these activities which constitute the CS, but the response-produced stimuli associated with them. The point is probably not important). In order to effect proper forward conditioning, the CS must just precede the UCS, or, more important, the UCR. (Eysenck, 1968b, has discussed this point in some detail. The traditional statement that CS must precede UCS is in fact wrong; the important relation is between CS and UCR. The orthodox statement only makes sense when applied to the usually employed types of stimuli where UCS and UCR are almost simultaneous, so that sequential statements made of one also apply to the other.) Three main types of UCS have been used: (1) chemical, usually some drug like apomorphine, which leads to nausea (UCR) and vomiting; succinylcholine chloride dihydrate, which leads to paralysis of the skeletal musculature, including those muscles associated with respiration (UCR), is another example; (2) electrical, that is, shock produced by current from a battery; and (3) imagery; the patient is asked to *imagine* some fear-producing or nauseating experience, and this UCS often leads to actual nausea and/or anxiety as the UCR (Gold and Neufeld, 1965; Cautela, 1967; Anant, 1967; Ashem and Donner, 1968). A possible fourth variety is a loud noise to waken the sleeping patient, as in the treatment of enuresis (Lovibond, 1964); it is not certain that this treatment should in fact be considered aversive, and we will in our discussion concentrate on the other three.

Rachman and Teasdale (1969) have discussed in detail the advantages and disadvantages of chemical and electrical stimuli, and Azrin and Holz (1966) have discussed the properties considered desirable in an aversive stimulus, from the experimental point of view. It seems clear that electrical stimulation has many important advantages: (1) chemical methods are arduous, complicated, and unpleasant, and they tend to bring about aggressiveness and hostility on the part of the patient (Morgenstern, Pearce, and Davies, 1963); (2) drugs have unpleasant side effects, and can be dangerous; they are medically contraindicated in certain conditions; (3) electrical stimulation, unlike chemical stimulation, can be precisely controlled (in quantity, effect, and timing); this is all-important in connection with a conditioning paradigm, where exact timing can be crucial; (4) unlike chemical treatment, electrical stimulation permits frequent repetition of the association between CS and UCR; this makes possible much greater frequency of conditioning trials; (5) portable apparatus can be used for electrical stimulation (McGuire and Vallance, 1964), and treatment can even be made self-administered (Wolpe, 1965); and (6) electrical stimulation, because of the more precise therapeutic control it makes possible, enables the therapist to make accurate measurements of the progress of the treatment (Rachman, 1961; McGuire and Vallance, 1964; Feldman and MacCulloch, 1964; Marks and Gelder, 1967). All these considerations favor electrical treatment, which appears to have been first used for therapeutic purposes by Max (1935) in a pioneering paper on the treatment of a homosexual; it has been widely used only quite recently. Chemical treatments seem to have been used quite extensively, mainly in connection with alcoholism; Miller et al. (1964) have traced 169 references to conditioning procedures in the treatment of alcoholics alone. No doubt, disadvantages in the use of electrical stimulation will emerge as this method is more widely used (Rachman and Teasdale, 1969); for the time being, it emerges as undoubtedly superior to chemical methods.

The third type of aversive stimulation, curiously named "covert sensitization" (Cautela, 1966, 1967), or "verbal aversion" (Anant, 1967), has been used so rarely (Ashem and Donner, 1968; Gold and Neufeld, 1965; Davison, 1968; Kolvin, 1967; Stuart, 1965), and is of so recent origin, that little can be said about it. In essence, this procedure relies on the aversive concomitants of *imagining* nausea and other disagreeable feelings and sensations in connection with the activity, or some simulacrum of the activity, to be deconditioned. The studies quoted report significant success with alcoholism and sexual deviation, and although long-term follow-ups are not available, the fact that some success has been achieved makes this method interesting and possibly important. It derives, of course, from Wolpe's desensitization procedure where, when too high an item on the habit hierarchy is attempted, strong anxiety and aversive emotions supervene and interrupt the treatment. Here this aversive effect of imaginative evocation is used to good purpose instead of being an undesirable disturbing influence.

It may be possible to regard the procedure of aversion therapy as a method for producing neurosis-like conditioned behavior patterns (except that, of course, they are not maladaptive). Consider the following case history, in which one of several patients suffering from alcoholism had been treated by single-trial aversive conditioning, using succinylcholine chloride dihydrate as the UCS, and producing apnoeic paralysis just after the presentation of a drink (the CS). This subject "reported broad generalization of his aversion. He reportedly has become extremely anxious about anything to do with alcohol and claims to have violent reactions to such relatively innocuous things as mouth wash and hair spray" (Farrar, Powell and Martin, 1968). Note the persistence (this is a 12-month follow-up) and the degree of generalization; one might also argue that some of the generalizations are in fact maladaptive, so that this could serve as a proper example of a genuine neurotic disorder. Unfortunately the authors do not seem to have investigated this case in any detail, but to have been preoccupied with the effects of the aversive treatment as such. Scientifically, many important questions arise, all of them relevant to a theory of neurotic disorder. Why did only two out of their nine subjects remain totally abstinent, that is, present a typical "neurotic" effect? How did they differ from the other subjects in personality, circumstances, and temptations? How is extinction related to the strength of the CR shortly after conditioning has taken place? We would seriously suggest that one of the most important aspects of aversion therapy from the scientific point of view is the light that it can throw on the origins of neurotic disorder; the ethical justification for producing such a "minineurosis" lies in the effective cure of a much more serious disorder, and this justification would be absent in other attempts to imitate the example of Watson and Rayner.

One possible reason for the disappointing overall results of the Farrar, Powell, and Martin experiment may be the difficulty of accurate timing, and their failure to pay much attention to this crucial variable in conditioning. In some recent work, Thomson and Rathod (1968) have tried the same method of aversive conditioning with 10 patients with heroin addiction, a condition well known for the difficulties of achieving lasting success (they also had a control group of nine Ss). By paying considerable attention to the timing of the injection of the paralyzing drug, they managed to obtain paralysis within 1 second of the heroin injection; this was repeated in all 5 or 6 times. After the treatment, a full heroin syringe was left with the patient for 24 hours; none of the patients made use of it. A reasonable follow-up period has failed to show any evidence of relapse in any of the 10 cases. In all cases the fear that developed was attached to the CS, that is, the syringe; one patient required to have a medical operation (unconnected with his addition) refused to have an injection, and had to be anesthetized by gas. It seems likely that the success of Thomson and Rathod, compared with the relative failure of the other authors, is due in large part to close attention to the laws of conditioning; when these are disregarded, little in the way of success can be expected. At the same time, such failure cannot discredit the laws so flagrantly flouted.

Postponing the question of just how well aversion therapy works in clinical practice, we must now turn to the theoretical problems involved. There are three main paradigms for the

effectiveness of punishment: habit weakening, "escape" conditioning, and classical "avoidance" conditioning. Before discussing these in any detail, we wish to point out that aversion therapy may be altogether inappropriate in many cases where at first sight it would appear clearly indicated; that is, where some response that is maladaptive is produced frequently and apparently without conscious possibility of control on the part of the patient. *Beech* (1960) *found that the association of shock with writer's cramp had an adverse rather than a beneficial effect on anxious patients; in a later case of writer's cramp and stuttering, Beech* (1963) *showed that the undesirable behavior appeared to be motivated by anxiety attached to authoritarian figures. By eliminating this anxiety through desensitization, he also eliminated the writer's cramp and the stuttering, without resorting to aversion techniques which, by increasing the anxiety, would also have increased the severity of the symptoms.* Solomon and Wynne's (1953) experiment on training dogs to make an avoidance response (jumping a hurdle to avoid traumatic shock) presents an analogue; when they tried to eliminate the jumping response by aversive treatment (shocking the dogs for jumping), they found that this actually enhanced the jumping response—presumably through increasing the anxiety that motivated the performance in the first place. *This example shows that a clear theoretical understanding of the dynamics of each particular situation is essential if the proper therapeutic course is to be followed; rule-of-thumb application of principles not geared to the particular case in question may be worse than no treatment at all.* The example also indicates the importance of personality differences; less-emotional patients suffering from writer's cramp have been treated with considerable success by aversion therapy, while Beech's more emotional patients were made worse (Liversedge and Sylvester, 1955).

Evidence from the animal literature certainly suggests that strength of drive is very relevant to the effectiveness of punishment; reduction of motivation to emit the punished response enhances the suppressive effect of punishment on that response. Dinsmoor (1952), Azrin, Holz, and Hake (1963), Masserman (1946) and Storms, and Boroczi and Broeu (1962) are among the authors who have shown this dependence of the effectiveness of punishment on drive level. If the relevant drive in aversion therapy is anxiety, and if anxiety is very high at the beginning of the experiment, then clearly some form of desensitization is indicated in order to lower this level to manageable proportions (Eysenck, 1960b). Blake (1965), whose work will be considered later on, has demonstrated the wisdom of this procedure, although of course much further work will be needed to establish this generalization as a valid principle in behavior therapy.

There has been much doubt about the efficacy of punishment in the reduction of behavior since Thorndike (1932) repealed the punishment part of the "law of effect," and Stone (1953) reported what seems a rather conclusive experiment supporting Thorndike's position. Skinner's views are well known, both that punishment is probably the most common means of controlling human behavior (1953), and that it is a most ineffective and morally indefensible one (1948). More recently, Solomon (1964) and Church (1963) have castigated the "myth" that punishment is ineffective in producing lasting suppression of the punished response—a myth that seems to have originated with a paper by Estes (1944). Nevertheless, there seems to be no doubt that the effects of punishment (defined by Bolles, 1967, as "the presentation of an aversive stimulus after a response has occurred") may be inconsistent, leading sometimes to the cessation of the punished response, sometimes to no change, and sometimes even to the enhancement of the punished response (Martin, 1963; Sandler, 1964). The important fact to grasp is that punishment does not weaken existing habits; it leads, rather, to the acquisition of an alternative response to the punished one. "Not since Thorndike abandoned the idea that punishment weakens S-R connections has a major systematist defended it" (Bolles, 1967). The notion of punishment "stamping out" behavior still lingers on among psychiatrists, penologists, and the general public, and it still informs many attempts to design aversion therapies. We will not enter into a prolonged discussion of the issue, or a detailed criticism of such studies; let us merely note that the failure of therapeutic efforts based on paradigms taken from an outmoded and superseded theory in no way implicates the more recent and better supported theories. Punishment, therefore, understood as producing extinction of existing habits through pairing a response with an aversive stimulus, cannot account for aversion therapy; we are left with two alternative hypotheses.

The first of these was introduced by Miller and Dollard (1941), as the elaboration of an escape paradigm: the animal learns on the basis of reinforcement that occurs when the punishment is terminated. Consider a rat that is shocked a few seconds after eating; the animal quickly withdraws, crouches, and so on. Single-trial learning may take place (Hudson, 1950; Maatsch, 1959; Heriot and Coleman, 1962; Essman and Alpern, 1964) or several repetitions may be required. In any case,

... what the animal learns, according to this position, is to withdraw from food when near it. Withdrawal occurs, by generalization, to stimuli similar to those to which withdrawal is conditioned ... What is proposed here is that the stimuli which initially control approach responses come to elicit withdrawal because of the very rapid learning (escape learning) of withdrawal in the presence of stimuli like those that initially controlled the approach. (Bolles, 1967).

The assumption is made that punishment leads to the acquisition of behavior that *interferes* with the punished response; it does not weaken it directly. This conception links up the hypothesis with Miller's approach-avoidance conflict situation.

The escape hypothesis has led to many studies of the factors that govern the strengths of the old approach response and the newly acquired withdrawal response. Kaufman and Miller (1949) have shown the quantitative importance of the number of times that approach has been reinforced, and punished; shock intensity (Karsh, 1964; Appel, 1963), proximity to the point of shock (Brown, 1948; Karsh, 1962), previous strength of response (Karsh, 1962; Miller, 1960), and delay in shock administration (Warden and Diamond, 1931) have all been found related to the effect of punishment in rats, and Azrin and his colleagues (see the review by Bolles, 1967) have found similar results in pigeons. We will return to a consideration of the optimum conditions for successful punishment procedures later.

The simple escape paradigm runs into two difficulties, as Bolles points out.

The punishments used are typically of very short duration, frequently only ·1 sec. It would seem to be impossible for the subject to make (or even begin) an escape response in so short an interval. Moreover, Leitenberg (1965) and Bolles and Warren (1966) have found that delaying the termination of the punishing stimulus does not reduce its punishing efficacy. It appears to be the onset of the punisher rather than its termination which counts. The second problem is that the subjects in these studies were quite evidently frightened, and the escape paradigm, at least in the simple form we have stated it, makes no provision for possible effects of fear. (1967, p. 422)

It is possible to overcome both difficulties by making use of an avoidance paradigm in which fear is conceived of as a classically conditioned response in the kind of situation considered above; the aversive properties of fear account for the animal's withdrawal, and also for the fact that the animal is reinforced for withdrawing. Stimulus generalization is of course posited to occur, thus providing a spatial gradient of avoidance.

A crucial difference between the avoidance and the escape paradigm is that according to the former the subject should show increased sensitization because repeated fear reduction should reinforce progressively further withdrawal; whereas according to the latter, withdrawal should rapidly extinguish because of the fact that it prevents further reinforcement (Bolles, 1967, p. 423).

This avoidance hypothesis was developed particularly by Estes and Skinner (1941) and Estes (1944), and much support was given to it in studies showing that the hypothetical CER (conditioned emotional response) behaved very much like other classically conditioned responses.

All these studies are as relevant to a consideration of aversion therapy as they are to a consideration of our theory of the genesis of neurotic disorders of the first kind; as pointed out before, aversion therapy in fact amounts to nothing more or less than the creation of a kind of limited neurotic (dysthymic) symptom that acts in a direction contrary to that of the original to-be-deconditioned habit. Hence the detailed discussion given of these theoretical points

above; they are important for the general theory of neurosis, not only for aversion therapy.

Bolles (1967, p. 429) summarizes his discussion in the following words: "*When punishment leads to learning, what is learned are the responses which the punisher elicits, including fear.*" This elicitation hypothesis is strongly supported by specially designed experiments (Fowler and Miller, 1963; Adelman and Maatsch, 1955; Bolles and Seelbach, 1964), and pending the uncovering of new evidence disproving this hypothesis, we will use it provisionally in our discussion of the effects of aversion therapy. As pointed out above, the studies related to this hypothesis have given rise to a number of parametric investigations that suggest optimal ways of setting up experiments in aversion therapy; we will quote the summary given by Azrin and Holz (1966). They say:

We have seen above that punishment can be quite effective in eliminating behavior. Let us imagine that we are given an assignment to eliminate behavior by punishment. Let us summarize briefly some of the circumstances which have been found to maximize its effectiveness: (1) The punishing stimulus should be arranged in such a manner that no unauthorized escape is possible. (2) The punishing stimulus should be as intense as possible. (3) The frequency of punishment should be as high as possible; ideally the punishing stimulus should be given for every response. (4) The punishing stimulus should be delivered immediately after the response. (5) The punishing stimulus should not be increased gradually but introduced at maximum intensity. (6) Extended periods of punishment should be avoided, especially where low intensities of punishment are concerned, since the recovery effect may thereby occur. Where mild intensities of punishment are used, it is best to use them for only a brief period of time. (7) Great care should be taken to see that the delivery of the punishing stimulus is not differentially associated with the delivery of the reinforcement. Otherwise the punishing stimulus should be made a signal or discriminative stimulus that a period of extinction is in progress. (8) The degree of motivation to emit the punished response should be reduced. (9) The frequency of positive reinforcement for the punished response should similarly be reduced. (10) An alternative response should be available which will not be punished but which will produce the same or greater reinforcement as the punished response. For example, punishment of criminal behavior can be expected to be more effective if non-criminal behavior, which will result in the same advantages as the criminal behavior, is available. (11) If no alternative response is available, the subject should have access to a different situation in which he obtains the same reinforcement without being punished. (12) If it is not possible to deliver the punishing stimulus itself after a response, then an effective method of punishment is still available. A conditioned stimulus may be associated with the aversive stimulus and this conditioned stimulus may be delivered following a response to achieve conditioned punishment. (13) A reduction of positive reinforcement may be used as punishment when the use of physical punishment is not possible for practical, legal or moral reasons. Punishment by withdrawal of positive reinforcement may be accomplished in such situations by arranging a period of reduced reinforcement frequency (time-out) or by arranging a decrease of conditioned reinforcement (response cost). Both methods require that the subject have a high level of reinforcement to begin with; otherwise, no withdrawal of reinforcement is possible. If non-physical punishment is to be used, it appears desirable to provide the subject with a substantial history of reinforcement in order to provide the opportunity for withdrawing the reinforcement as punishment for the undesired responses.

Granted that these general rules provide us with a framework for applying aversion therapy to human subjects, there still remains an important stumbling block, at least in the theoretical field. This problem is that of the generalization of the suppression of the punished response; if rats are provided with a stimulus to indicate when they can make the otherwise punished response without actually receiving punishment, the animals are known to make the discrimination and perform the response in the presence of the safety signal, while refraining from doing so in the absence of the safety signal (Azrin, 1956; Brethower and Reynolds, 1962; Dinsmoor, 1952; Hunt and Brady, 1955). Humans are not inferior to rats in ability to make use of the cognitive factors of this kind, and we have already quoted the work of Mowrer (1938) and Wilson (1968) to show that experimental work with human subjects reinforces our disquiet. (See also Cook and Harris, 1937; Bridger and Mandel, 1965; Grings and Lockland, 1963; Silverman, 1960; Spence and Goldstein, 1961; Chatterjee and Eriksen, 1962; and Collier, 1965). Rachman and

Teasdale (1969) suggest the importance of interoceptive conditioning. (Razran, 1961), that is, "classical conditioning in which either the conditioned stimulus (CS) or the unconditioned stimulus (US) or both are delivered directly to the mucosa of some specified viscus."

Selected quotations from Razran's summary and conclusions will indicate the direct relevance of the phenomenon of interoceptive conditioning to the problem of obtaining classically conditioned responses that are resistant to extinction and independent of the subject's voluntary control:

(1) Unlike the continuum of exteroceptive stimulation which is the body material of all our conscious experience, the continuum of interoceptive stimulation leads largely to unconscious reactions.

(2) Interoceptive conditioning, whether involving conditioned or unconditioned interoceptive stimuli, is readily obtainable and is by its very nature largely unconscious in character.

(3) Interoceptive conditioning is somewhat slower in formation than is exteroceptive but, once conditioned, it is more fixed and irreversible (less readily extinguished).

(4) When equal but opposing interoceptively produced and exteroceptively produced reactions are juxtaposed, the interoceptive reactions dominate the exteroceptive ones, with the final result that preceding exteroceptive stimuli become conditioned stimuli for succeeding interoceptive reactions whereas preceding interoceptive reactions become strengthened by exteroceptive reactions succeeding them.

(5) The juxtaposition of conditioned interoceptive and exteroceptive stimuli of the same conditioned reaction, unlike similar juxtapositions of exteroceptive stimuli of different modalities, produces a certain amount of conflict and decrementation of conditioning.

Interoceptive conditioning is thus one possible way out of the dilemma posed by the existence of cognitive control factors; another is the incubation effect already mentioned in some detail in a previous section of this paper—that is, the incrementation of CR with presentation of the unreinforced CS ($\overline{CS}$) (Eysenck, 1968d). Possibly these two hypotheses are not unconnected; it is likely that incubation occurs most frequently in cases in which one would expect interoceptive conditioning to play a part. However that may be, the evidence is not sufficient to make dogmatic assertion possible at this point; we can only suggest that these factors may play some part in the undoubted efficacy of aversion therapy under certain conditions.

Just how effective, then, is aversion therapy? It must be admitted that in this field, even more than in that of desensitization therapy, proper clinical trials involving control groups are almost entirely lacking; however, this is not as severe a handicap as it might appear. Due to the fact that we are here dealing with disorders of the second kind, spontaneous remission is theoretically expected to be almost entirely absent, and clinical experience certainly suggests that lack of treatment would almost always mean absence of improvement.

Aversion therapy was first seriously undertaken in connection with alcoholism, and in the minds of most psychiatrists it is still connected with this addictive neurosis. Aversion therapy is also often dismissed by psychiatrists because of its alleged failure in curing alcoholism. This is unjust; Franks (1960, 1963, 1966) has drawn attention to the poor quality of much of the early work on aversion treatment for alcoholics:

Unfortunately, not all modern practice is sound. . . . For example, some clinicians advocate giving the alchohol after the patient reaches the height of nausea. This, of course, is backward conditioning (since the unconditioned stimulus of the apomorphine or the emetine is preceding the conditioned stimulus of the alchohol) and backward conditioning, if it occurs at all, is at best very tenuous.[12] (Franks, 1963).

(Actually, as Eysenck, 1968a, has argued, the UCS is not the important variable here, as it has to precede the CS in any practicable arrangement; the important thing is that the CS should precede the UCR; that is, the alcohol should be administered just before the onset of nausea. This, is, in effect, the procedure of Voegtlin and his colleagues, whose work has been the most successful to date). Further, in any conditioning situation, the time intervals that elapse between the presentation of the various stimuli and the response are of considerable importance and, as Franks has pointed out, aversion therapists were

either ignorant of this fact, or chose to ignore it. "Under such circumstances, it is hardly surprising that reports of evaluation studies range from virtually zero success to virtually one hundred per cent success." Furthermore, as Eysenck and Rachman (1965) point out, "some of the drugs which have been used to induce nausea also act as central depressants. The effect of this type of drug would be to interfere with the acquisition of the conditioned response." (Cf. Eysenck, 1963a).

Adequate surveys of the early work have been given by the authors cited, particularly Franks (1960, 1963) and Eysenck and Rachman (1965); here we will only mention the studies reported by Voegtlin and his colleagues (Voegtlin and Lemere, 1942; Lemere and Voegtlin, 1950). These authors, using a more adequate methodology than most of their successors, treated and followed up over 4000 patients, of whom the following percentages succeeded in reachings the criterion of complete abstinence:

Abstinent for one to two years after treatment
60 percent
Abstinent for two to five years after treatment
51 percent
Abstinent for five to ten years after treatment
38 percent
Abstinent for ten to thirteen years after treatment
23 percent

Twenty-nine percent of the original patients relapsed and were treated a second time. Of these, 39 percent remained abstinent subsequently. At the time of writing, Lemere and Voegtlin (1950) quoted an overall abstinence rate of 51 percent for all their patients. As Eysenck and Rachman (1965) comment, "considering the probability of relapse in aversion therapy, this is an extremely encouraging figures, particularly as the procedure itself leaves much to be desired." Unfortunately, psychiatrists who claimed to have replicated their methods made such serious changes in the procedure, changes that go directly counter to the laws of learning theory, that positive results would have been astonishing (for example,

---

[12] This generalization may require rephrasing in view of the very impressive data published by Dostalek (1964) in which he apparently obtained "rückläufige bedingte Verbindungen." While of great systematic importance, his work does not suggest that Frank's criticisms in this particular case were mistaken.

Edlin, 1945; Wallerstein et al., 1957); miracles did not occur, and results were disappointing. This outcome, which was in complete agreement with prediction from learning theory, has since been used to discredit learning theory, and aversion therapy in particular; we find these vagaries of psychiatric reasoning hard to follow.[13]

Following Eysenck's (1960b, 1964b) suggestion that electrical stimulation should be used in aversion therapy instead of chemical methods, for reasons already stated, several articles appeared describing various methods of using shock. McGuire and Vallance (1964) appear to have been the first in the field, followed a year later by Hsu (1965); the former reported encouraging results, and the latter used 30-second shocks to the head, a procedure too harrowing to be recommended, and also one that caused most of his volunteer subjects to discontinue treatment. MacCulloch et al. (1960) reported failure with four patients, using an "anticipatory avoidance learning" technique that does not look promising theoretically, for reasons given by Rachman and Teasdale (1969). We will concentrate here on the work of Blake (1965), which seems to us the most promising. This author compared the effects of electrical aversion therapy, used by itself, and electrical aversion therapy combined with relaxation training, with the latter introduced as a preparatory step in the proceedings.

The 37 patients who received aversion therapy combined with relaxation underwent a three-part program, whose three phases are relaxation training, motivation arousal, and aversion conditioning proper. After the patient had acquired the ability to relax successfully, he was given a few sessions of what appears to be counselling and, during these periods, he was forcibly reminded of the undesirable consequence of his alcoholism. Attempts were also made to increase his desire to participate in the treatment and to rid himself of the disorder. The final phase of the treatment consisted of the aversion conditioning procedure. The treatment was carried out with the subject and therapist in separate rooms. Each subject was supplied with a glass, water, and alcohol of his choice and was instructed to mix his drink according to his taste. The method is described by Blake as follows.

"He is told to sip his drink but not to swallow. A shock of increasing intensity randomly starting above the threshold reported by him in a preaversion test to be unpleasant, is delivered contiguously with his sip on reinforced trials. He is instructed to spit out the alcohol (into a bowl provided) as a means of having the shock terminated." The conditioning treatment extended over 4 to 8 days and the whole program took an average of 4.93 hours per subject. This aversion treatment procedure was also used in treating the patients in the "aversion-therapy-only" group. Attempts were made to see each subject at intervals of 1, 3, 6, 9, and 12 months. The success of the treatment was assessed in terms of 5 criteria proposed by Knight where these were applicable. In addition, follow-up information was obtained wherever possible from at least one independent person. The abstinent category included those individuals who were known to be abstinent during the one-year follow-up period. The improved category included "those people whose drinking was now of a social order . . . and appeared to be in no danger of pathological escalation . . ."

Blake (1967) reported follow-up results after one year. Of the 37 patients treated by the combined procedure, 46 percent were abstinent, 13 percent were improved, 30 percent had relapsed, and 11 percent were unaccounted for. The 22 patients who had been treated by electrical aversion therapy alone showed a somewhat less

---

[13] In respect to aversion therapy as applied to alcoholism in particular, Garcia et al. (1967, 1968) have reported experiments that suggest that the position is not as simple as it originally appeared. They found that "gustatory stimuli are specifically and rapidly associated with visceral states, while auditory and visual stimuli are specifically and rapidly associated with cutaneous stimuli such as peripheral pain" (page 717; see also Garcia et al., 1966). They also refer to anatomical divisions which, they say, "could provide the structural basis for the specificity and appropriateness of stimuli observed in behaviour" (Page 718). If research confirms the existence of such stimulus-response contingency specificity, and also the fact that where certain such bonds are involved, much longer CS-UCS intervals can be tolerated than is usual, then new and improved methods of aversion therapy with alcoholic patients may be possible.

promising picture: 23 percent were abstinent, 27 percent were improved, 27 percent had relapsed, and 23 percent were unaccounted for. The differences between the groups were not statistically significant in terms of the abstinent and improved categories, but it would appear that the relaxation procedure combined with aversion treatment produced somewhat greater success, at least over a one-year period. The results, as Blake pointed out, give no ground for complacency, but they are encouraging. An interesting feature of his procedure is that he recorded GSR changes during the conduct of the therapy; no detailed report of his findings has yet appeared, but it seems that the great majority of his patients did in fact develop conditioned reactions during the course of treatment. Such recording of autonomic reactions should be standard practice in scientifically oriented behavior therapy.

In summary, it seems quite possible to "cure" half the patients suffering from alcoholism, either by chemical or by electrical methods; motivation needs attention, and booster doses may have to be given. However, improvements in the methods used (such as the employment of partial reinforcement schedules, or the use of CNS stimulant drugs to improve speed of conditioning) may raise this tentative figure to more impressive heights—although it is only fair to point out that even a 50 percent success rate is considerably above that achieved by any other technique. Considering the theoretical difficulties of aversion therapy mentioned earlier, the results are promising; they certainly encourage further experimentation, hopefully leading both to better understanding of the processes underlying improvement, and to more certain and more numerous cures.

Apart from alcoholism, the greatest area of usefulness (and research) for aversion therapy has lain in the field of sexual disorders (that is, homosexuality, fetishism, transvestism, and the like; this may not be unconnected with the well-known fact that sexual responses are among the easiest to modify by conditioning procedures (Ford and Beach, 1952). Many of the reports, following upon the pioneering effort of Max (1935), who claimed success in treating a homosexual with the use of faradic aversive conditioning, have been of single cases, or small groups of cases (Raymond, 1956; James, 1962; Thorpe, Schmidt and Castell, 1964; Eysenck and Rachman, 1965; McGuire and Vallance, 1964; Clark, 1963a, 1963b; Morgenstern, Pearce and Davies, 1963; Barker et al., 1961; Glynn and Harper, 1961; Blakemore et al., 1963; Bancroft, 1966; Kushner and Scundle, 1966.) This practice has sometimes been criticized as not providing clear-cut evidence for the superiority of the procedures used; such criticism is correct, but irrelevant. Most of these studies were undertaken in an effort to work out suitable procedures, to study details of patients' responding, and to verify the *possibility* of success; none claimed to have proved the superiority of aversion techniques to all alternative methods of treatment. In any case, many of the patients had in fact already been treated by alternative methods, sometimes for many years, without success, and probability suggested that spontaneous recovery was unlikely; indeed, aversion therapy is seldom tried in any but the most recalcitrant and unpromising cases, so that success, particularly quick and lasting success, produces evidence not entirely without value, This is not to deny the need for control groups. and long-continued follow-up; what is suggested is merely that a new method must show some justification for undertaking such difficult and, costly investigations, and preliminary, small-scale "feasibility" studies are obviously called for. It might even be said that some of the early studies conducted on a large scale (such as Freund, 1960) might have benefitted from a series of earlier, small-scale "feasibility" experiments; success might hang on quite small changes in parameter values, which our theories are not quantitative enough to allow us to predict. No attempt will here be made to discuss these many studies in detail (Rachman and Teasdale, 1969, have performed that service for us); they have contributed considerably to our knowledge of what can and what cannot be done along those lines, and also they have shown (or perhaps "suggested" is a more appropriate term) just what are the best methods to use. We will rather concentrate on two quite recent studies which, in our opinion, combine the best available methodology with the most detailed quantitative assessment and the most objective response-recording technique. (Our choice has not been influenced by the fact that both studies were carried out by present or former associates at the Maudsley!).

We shall first consider the work of Feldman and MacCulloch (1965), MacCulloch, Feldman, and Pinschof (1965), and Feldman (1966) on homosexuality. Using an anticipatory avoidance paradigm for their therapy procedures, they carefully designed the following procedure. After undergoing fairly extensive psychological investigations, the patient was asked to assess a large series of slides depicting males both clothed and unclothed and then to arrange them in a hierarchy of attractiveness. The hierarchy usually comprised about eight slides, and treatment was commenced with the slide that was only mildly attractive. The patient was then worked up through a hierarchy in ascending order. The patient was also asked to compile a hierarchy of female slides and in this case the highest slide, that is, the most attractive, was presented first, and the patient then worked down the hierarchy in descending order. Feldman and MacCulloch then established a level of shock that was described by the patient as being very unpleasant. The treatment was carried out in a dark and quiet room at the hospital.

. . . The patient is told that he will see a male picture and that several seconds later he might receive a shock. He is also told that he can turn off the slide by pressing a switch, with which he is provided, whenever he wishes to do so, and that the moment the slide leaves the screen, the shock will also be turned off. Finally, he is told that he will never be shocked when the screen is blank. It is made clear to him that he should leave the slide on the screen for as long as he finds it sexually attractive. The first slide is then presented. The patient has the choice of switching it off or leaving it on the screen. Should he switch it off within eight seconds, he is not shocked, and this is termed an avoidance response. Should he fail to turn it off within eight seconds, he receives a shock. If the shock strength is not sufficiently high to cause him to switch it off immediately, it is increased until he does so. In practice, this had hardly ever been necessary. The moment a patient performs the switching-off response, the slide is removed and the shock is terminated. This is termed an escape trial. In addition to switching off, the patient is told to say "no" as soon as he wishes the slide to be removed. It is hoped that a further

increment of habit strength will accrue to the avoidance habit by means of this further avoidance response. The usual course of events is several trials, in all of which escape responses are made; a sequence of trials, some of which the patient escapes, and some of which he avoids; and a sequence of trials in which the patient avoids every time.

After the patient has successfully avoided on three successive trials, he is placed on a predetermined schedule of reinforcement. In addition to the attempt at suppressing sexual responses to nude males, Feldman and MacCulloch tried to make the patients more responsive to female photographs. This was attempted by introducing a female slide contiguous with the removal of the male slide. "That is, we attempt to associate the relief of anxiety with the introduction of the female." They go on to say that the female slide was always removed by the therapist and never by the patient, "so that his habit of avoiding females is not strengthened in the training situation."

There is no doubt about the success of the treatment; detailed figures will be found in the original papers. There is considerable doubt about the theoretical rationale underlying the procedure, as Rachman and Teasdale (1969) point out in detail; they suggest

. . . that the effective process operating in the Feldman and MacCulloch procedure is not the development of a motor avoidance response, but the classical conditioning of anxiety to the homosexual stimuli, "devaluing" them of their sexual arousal properties.

The same writers suggest:

. . . that more effective results might be obtained by the use of imaginal stimulation in which the patient could be asked to produce phantasies concerning the *sexual behavior in which he indulges*—in the manner of Marks and Gelder (1967).

Even as they stand, however, the results are not discouraging; of 43 patients treated, 7 defected from treatment, 25 were improved, and 11 were unsuccessful. This is a quite unusually high success rate, and suggests that with further theoretical and practical improvement, this method may lead to a generally workable treatment of homosexuality. It should be noted that MacCulloch, Feldman, and Pinschof (1965) have published some additional information on physiological changes occurring during treatment; these are interesting, but insufficient to enable firm conclusions to be drawn.

The above-mentioned paper by Marks and Gelder (1967) deals with five patients suffering from fetishism and/or transvestism, and submitted to a concentrated course of aversion therapy. The importance of the paper lies in the careful quantitative and qualitative assessments of the behavior, physiological reactions, and attitudes of the patients before, during, and after treatment. All the patients were assessed on the semantic differential test, and their penile reactions to appropriate and deviant sexual stimuli gauged with an adaptation of the Freund (1958, 1967) penis plethysmograph. The patients were treated on an inpatient basis for two weeks; they received two aversion therapy sessions per day, each lasting for about one hour. After discharge they were given booster treatments at first weekly, and then monthly, for several months.

In the initial stages of treatment, the shock was delivered when the patient imagined himself in a sexually provocative and arousing situation that incorporated some features of his sexually deviant behavior. In the second stage of treatment, which usually commenced on about the third or fourth day of treatment, the patients were shocked when they actually carried out the deviant behavior in reality. The shock was delivered on an intermittent schedule, and approximately one quarter of all trials were not shocked. The effects of the treatment were assessed by reported changes in the patients' behavior, plethysmographic recordings, concept changes, and reports obtained from the members of the patients' families (especially their wives). All five patients masturbated while cross-dressing or while in contact with the fetishistic object, and all of them had commenced this deviant sexual behavior in childhood or early adolescence. All but one of them had engaged in deviant sexual behavior for at least 20 years.

One of the first observations to emerge from this study was that, with increasing exposure to the electrical aversion treatment, the patients experienced increasing difficulty in conjuring up the required images. The time taken to obtain the image increased, and in numerous instances the patient eventually reached the point where

he was unable to obtain images at all. This increase in latency is clearly illustrated in Figures 15.5 and 15.6.

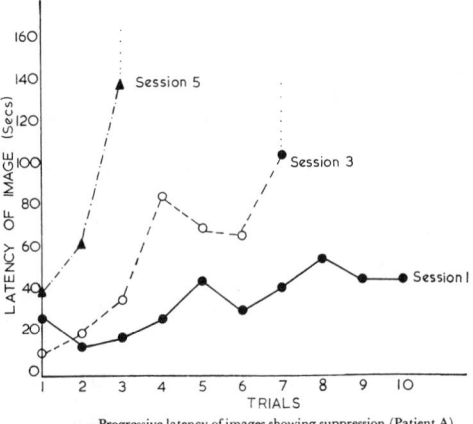

—Progressive latency of images showing suppression (Patient A).

Figure 15.5 Progressive increase in latency of images during aversion therapy for one patient. From Marks and Gelder, 1967. Used with permission.

Marks and Gelder checked the effect of simple repetition of the image and found that no change in latency occurred *except* when the image was followed by the delivery of the electric shock. In other words, the change in ability to obtain the abnormal sexual image can probably be attributed to the effects of aversive stimulation, and is not a simple habituation effect. The increase in latency observed was paralleled by an increase in the time that elapsed before the abnormal stimulus produced an erection in the patient. In the early stages of treatment (and certainly before treatment commenced), patients generally produced fairly rapid and substantial erections when presented with the abnormal sexual stimuli. As the treatment progressed, however, the erectile response was increasingly delayed until, in many cases, the stimulus failed to produce any reaction. Figure 15.7 illustrates the increasing erection latency observed in one of their patients (a transvestite).

Another interesting aspect that is illustrated in this figure is the remarkable specificity of the erectile changes that occurred during treatment. It can be seen that the erection latency observed in response to a particular stimulus was fairly strictly related to the type of aversion treatment that had been administered. The first item that was treated in the case of this patient was the

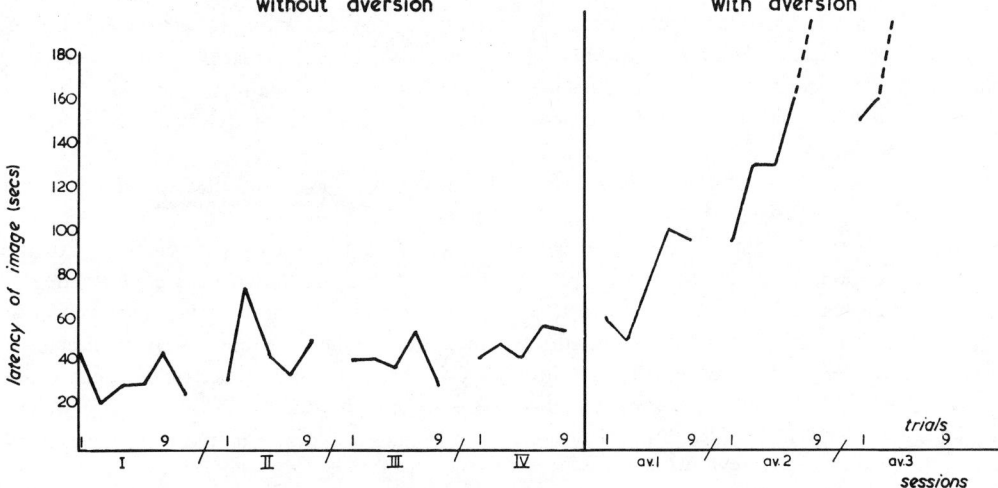

Figure 15.6 Change in latency of images, with and without aversion treatment, in one patient. From Marks and Gelder, 1967. Used with permission.

panties, and it will be observed from the figure that erections in the presence of panties were totally eliminated after a few sessions of treatment. Notice, however, that the other sexual stimuli (skirt, slip, and pyjamas) remain unaffected until they in turn were subjected to the treatment. *The patient continued to show erectile responses to the stimuli until they had 'been associated with electrical stimulation.* The second item that the therapist knocked out was "pyjamas," and again by referring to the figure, one can see that the effects of treating this item was highly specific. The next items to be eliminated were "skirt" and "blouse," and then the

therapist had to deal with the last item—a woman's slip. These effects spread from the clinic to the external world and from a few selected sexual items to a very wide range of stimulating conditions.

Marks and Gelder also observed that the patient's sexual and other concepts changed in a way that paralleled these physiological alterations and imaginary productions. The patient's attitudes, erectile reactions, and images all changed in the same direction but "at rather different speeds." The main attitudinal changes observed in this group of patients was that the abnormal sexual stimuli became "devalued"

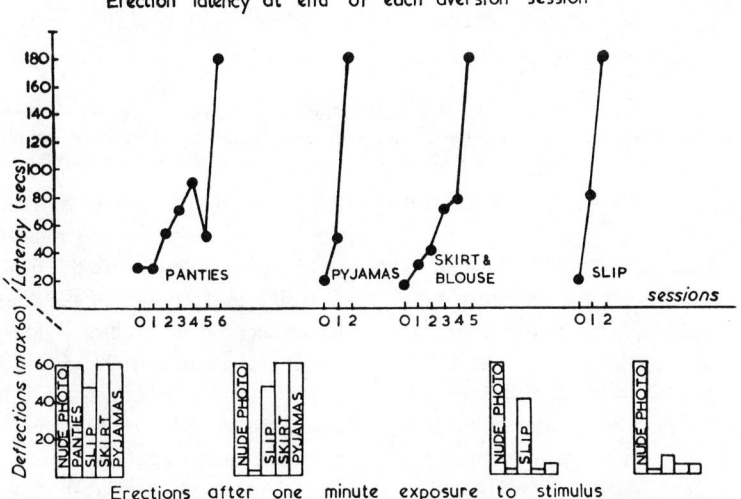

Figure 15.7 Specificity of autonomic changes after aversion therapy in one patient. From Marks and Gelder, 1967. Used with permission.

or "neutralized" as the treatment progressed. For example, the attitudes of transvestites to items like panties, corsets, and so on, changed from "favorable" at the beginning of treatment to "not favorable" at the end of treatment. It should be noted, however, that in the main the patients' attitudes changed from favorable to neutral rather than, as might have been expected, to intensely unfavorable. Contrary to expectation, the patients did *not* develop aversive attitudes towards the previously stimulating objects. In this sense, the aversion therapy did not produce aversion—but rather a neutralization of sexual affect. It was also noted that the patients' changed attitudes were also, like the plethysmographic changes, highly specific to each phase in the treatment. The selective attitudinal changes are neatly illustrated in Figure 15.8.

In general, the therapeutic outcome in these cases was encouraging. In all five cases the abnormal sexual behavior was eliminated by the end of the concentrated course of treatment. Unfortunately, two of the patients showed some measure of relapse within a year of discharge. Of all the techniques of electrical aversion that are currently in use, the one described by Marks and Gelder appears to be the most satisfactory

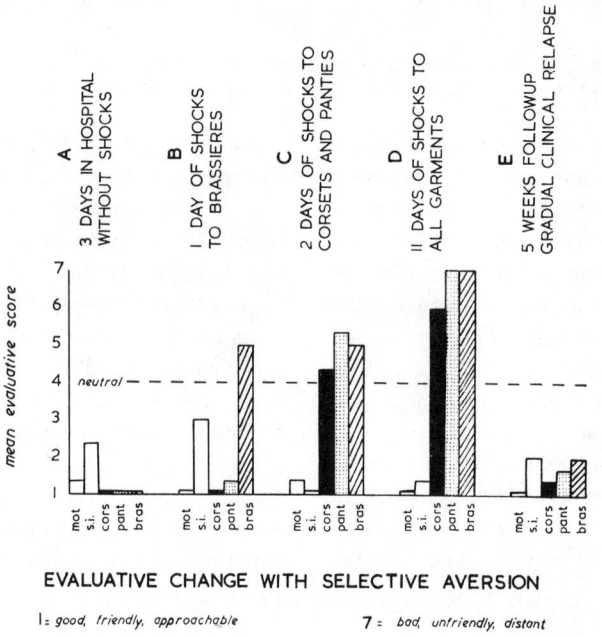

EVALUATIVE CHANGE WITH SELECTIVE AVERSION

1 = good, friendly, approachable   7 = bad, unfriendly, distant

mot = mother / si. = sexual intercourse / cors = corsets / pant = panties / bras = brassieres

Figure 15.8 Specificity of attitude change after aversion therapy in one patient. Shown are mean scores from three evaluative scales: good-bad; friendly-unfriendly; and approachable-distant. From Marks and Gelder, 1967. Used with permission.

in bringing about a termination of deviant behavior.

Rachman and Teasdale (1969) make one or two criticisms of the procedure; thus they question the use of the image as the signal for the administration of the UCS, and suggest that one should administer the shock when a plethysmographic reaction to the abnormal stimulus occurs. However, they agree that this is the best and most useful form of aversion therapy developed to date for sexual deviations of this kind, and the very fact that detailed,

factual questions about procedure can be raised, and experiments suggested to settle them, is a tremendous advance in this field. Altogether, we would suggest that while the Marks and Gelder technique is optimal for sexual deviations, Feldman and MacCulloch's is more appropriate for homosexual disorders, and Blake's for alcoholism. All three are of course still in the early stages of development, but the results reviewed are distinctly promising, particularly when the generally poor outlook for disorders of this kind is borne in mind.

One further area in which aversion therapy has been applied, with some promise, is that of drug addiction. (Alcoholism may of course be considered as a kind of drug addiction, but the problem of these two types of disorder are so different that they are best kept apart). Raymond (1962), Wolpe (1965), and Liberman (1968) have reported on a small number of cases (the first two used single subjects, the last-named used two); two patients responded well, abstaining after follow-ups of over a year ($2\frac{1}{2}$ years in the case of Raymond). No firm generalizations or conclusions are of course possible at this early stage, but we may note Liberman's conclusions:

The exploratory experiments with aversive conditioning in drug addiction ... indicate that the method has some promise. Aversive conditioning to narcotic-taking does occur, is generalized outside the treatment situation, and seems to be a tangible help to the patients in their attempts to deal with their craving for drugs.

In view of the growing size of the problem, and the failure of most other psychiatric methods, it seems likely that aversion therapy will be increasingly used in this connection; it seems an urgent task for psychologists to work out optimal methods of procedure, and for psychiatrists to study the effectiveness of these methods in well-controlled clinical trials. The promise held out by aversion therapy in heroin addiction, as used by Thomson and Rathod, has already been quoted.

Specific references to the use of aversion therapy in children are almost entirely absent from the literature, and nearly all studies in which noxious stimulation has been applied to young people have been described in the literature as examples of operant conditioning with negative reinforcement. The methods referred to in these studies could perhaps be analyzed in the same theoretical terms as aversion therapy (that is, an account could be given in which the classical conditioning of autonomic reactions is implied), and for this reason it would be of interest to ask why the term "aversion" appears almost exclusively in the context of adult therapy. One immediately apparent possibility is that the term "aversion" has an unwelcome primitive connotation that is inappropriate in connection with child therapy. However this may be, a more detailed discussion of the application of noxious stimulation in the treatment of children may be found in the accounts of operant conditioning elsewhere in this book.

In summary of this section, we agree with Rachman and Teasdale (1969) that "there is sufficient evidence to support the further exploration of aversion therapy. In particular, we may be approaching the establishment of a viable method for the treatment of sexual disorders and possibly alcoholism. The range of effectiveness of aversion therapy now has to be demonstrated by properly controlled clinical trials." In addition to clinical trials of a well-controlled kind, we obviously need more detailed physiological recordings of the effects of aversive stimulation, coupled with equally detailed assessment of other behavioral and "mental" effects; the Marks and Gelder (1967) study might well be followed in this respect. But above all, in our opinion, we need careful comparative studies into the different parameters of the aversion process, along the lines discussed in the body of this section; such studies should always be undertaken with the importance of personality differences clearly in mind. Optimal conditions for establishing conditioned response differ for extroverts and introverts (Eysenck 1967b), and probably for subjects high and low on N respectively (Spence, 1964); it is idle to establish optimal values for imaginary standard (average) persons that do not in fact apply to particular patients. Altogether we believe that stress has been too much on aversion therapy as a *therapy*, that is, as a method of curing neurotic patients; we would at this stage prefer to stress aversion therapy as a research technique, that is, as part of experimental psychology, rather than of psychiatry. We believe that only by gaining more knowledge of the experimental properties of the procedure will we be able to make it into a successful and useful curative process.

CRITICISMS AND OBJECTIONS

In the past few years several critiques of behavior therapy have appeared in print (for example, Breger & McGaugh, 1965; Weitzman, 1967; Freeman, 1968; Gelder, 1968), and many incidental criticisms have been voiced in articles ostensibly devoted to other purposes. We shall here list representative criticisms under three main headings, subdivided into different categories. We shall then deal with these criticisms, not by going through the lists individually, but by way of a general discussion; this seems advisable, as sometimes a general answer suffices to reply to several particular and apparently quite dissimilar criticisms. It will be obvious that the various criticisms are of quite unequal importance; some are serious, others are merely notional. All, however, deserve an answer, even though this answer may be very short in some cases. Answers to specific points are followed by number-and-letter reference to the criticism in question. Finally we shall end by considering an important point that is not essentially a criticism, but which has given rise to a considerable amount of controversy, viz. the degree of oversimplification of which behavior therapists are guilty. Some of the points raised have already been dealt with more or less adequately in the preceding chapters, and will therefore be commented on very briefly.

Critics have seized upon three main points. They have maintained (1) that learning theory itself is not sufficiently advanced to serve as a basis for specific therapies, that (2) there is in any case little connection between learning theory and the practices of behavior therapists, and that (3) the evidence for the efficacy of behavior therapy is insufficient. There is of course much in all three points; it will be our task not so much to contradict the critics, but rather to see in what precise manner, and to what precise degree, their views are justified, and how much they may be said to devalue the contribution of behavior therapy.

1. *Learning theory provides an unsatisfactory basis for any form of therapy because the foundations of learning theory are themselves insecure.*

(a) There is not just one theory but several, with conflicting points of view; thus, different predictions may be made according to which theory one uses.

(b) Existing theories have considerable difficulty in dealing with the problems of simple learning situations—how can we hope that such theories may be usefully extended to cover the complex phenomena of neurosis?

(c) Learning theory deals very largely with observable, overt behavior, and is mainly concerned with the explanation of this aspect of human activity; in neurotic disorders we are primarily concerned with internal events— thinking processes, attitudinal phenomena, judgments, values, and the like. We can often see (as in the Wolpe case quoted by Breger and McGaugh) that the symptoms are subserved by very complex internal processes. This situation forces the behavior therapist to resort to all manner of purely verbal solutions, such as calling imagined and other cognitive events "responses."

(d) Various learning theories offer different and opposing accounts of the same phenomenon. This leads to uncertainty respecting the theoretical basis of behavior therapy techniques; for example, we have seen in an earlier section that at least four different models can be applied to account for desensitization effects.

(e) Learning theorists themselves are becoming more "cognitive." The theories currently utilized by behavior therapists are, in fact, old-fashioned and redundant. Experiments in "constancy" and "transposition" seem to imply the importance of "mediational" processes.

Underlying most of these criticisms is a misunderstanding of the nature of theory in science, and in particular a failure to understand the difference in science between "weak" and "strong" theories (Eysenck, 1960c). Psychologists seldom know enough physics to realize that such theories as the Newtonian theory of gravitation, which is an example of a "strong" theory, are quite unrepresentative of theories at the forefront of advance; these are invariably "weak," and often do not last longer than a year or two before they are thrown overboard for something better—which in turn will not outlive its usefulness. Furthermore, there are usually several alternative theories current at the same time, and much experimental work is directed at finding experiments to decide between them. Consider, for instance, the position in cryogenics during the fifty years of its development; Mendelssohn (1966) makes it quite clear that the search for lower and lower temperatures was informed by theories that were in fact sent packing every six months, and none of which was held very firmly, even by its originator. The same is true of subatomic physics; the original Bohr model of the atom was known to be incompatible with many facets of reality even when it began its extremely important and fruitful career. Scientific theories are not (with notable exceptions) statements of immutable laws; as J. J. Thomson put it, "a theory in science is a policy, not a creed." We do not regard learning theory as a statement of laws from which we can directly derive methods for treatment; we regard it, rather, as a set of more or less firmly based hypotheses linking more or less well-established experimental facts. In the present state of development we would not expect a single, monolithic learning theory, without rivals or alternatives; the early stages of any developing science inevitably lack such a theory, and it would be grossly unrealistic to expect to find it in psychology. If there are different theories, leading to different outcomes, then we must simply test these outcomes; such is the way of progress (1(a); 1(d)).

Nor is it necessarily true that laboratory learning situations are simpler to study and understand than life phenomena such as neurosis; the opposite may be true. Gravitation was first studied on the astronomical scale; it is in fact extremely difficult to study and experiment upon in the laboratory. Emotions may be easier to study when they are very strong (as in neurotics) than when they are very weak (as in the laboratory situation). Such matters cannot be decided on an a priori basis, but must be looked into empirically. In any case, we have no alternative; existing learning theories are the best we have, being the only ones we have, and must be regarded as better than nothing. If they are inadequate, we may hope that the facts that emerge from careful experimental work with neurotics will suggest better theories (1(b)). Nor need we worry that our theories deal largely with behavior; they do, after all, accommodate physiological processes, cortical arousal, and many other events that to some people may appear "internal." We would agree that as large a slice of behavior as possible should always be studied, but we cannot agree that anything that is not behaviorally observable is or even can be

the subject matter of science (1(c)). We will return to this point later. (See also Rachman and Eysenck, 1960.)

The importance of "mediational" processes is not necessarily overlooked by behavior therapists; after all there are fractional antedating reactions and $(r_g — s_g)$ conceptions and other mechanisms that may serve this function. We do not wish to suggest here whether Osgood's or some other theorist's explanation of the mediation phenomenon is better grounded, nor do we in fact wish to argue that such processes are or are not required to account for all the facts. Any changes in learning theory that are enforced by the facts will, or so we would hope, be reflected in the practice of behavior therapy; we have no wish to lay down the law in this respect and decide here and now what path learning theory must follow. This would be both absurd and unrealistic. We merely wish to state that in making learning theory the foundation of advances in behavior therapy, we have no wish to specify any particular branch or type of learning theory; this must be and remain an empirical matter (1(e)). We would, however, like to turn the argument around and say that behavior therapy is not only a consumer of theories, so to speak, but, reciprocally, is likely to supply to the theorist many empirical research data of outstanding importance, data that in turn may have theoretical repercussions. Thus the behavior therapist may return his debt to the laboratory with interest. Indeed, we believe that some at least of the data referred to in this chapter already throw some light on learning theory as such, so that this interactive process may be said to have already begun. As we shall see later on, it is precisely this give and take between fundamental theory and applied practice that has characterized so much of scientific advance, and we believe that behavior therapy will be no exception. After all, the objections listed above are all a priori; they can only be properly evaluated in relation to actual attempts to apply such portions of learning theory as are found useful.

2. *Behavior therapy does not derive from learning theory, but has merely some superficial "associationist" elements in common with such theory.*

(a) The putative affinity with learning theory affords status and scientific respectability to behavior therapy, but is too loose to allow of genuine deduction.

(b) Behavior therapists appeal to "learning theory experiments" in order to support their pretensions to possessing a valid body of knowledge and theory.

(c) Little use has in fact been made of learning theory concepts, except in the most general way.

(d) Desensitization theory itself is an extrapolation of an existing theory, and not the implementation of existing carefully tested ideas.

(e) Examples exist of quite astonishingly primitive notions concerning the application of learning theory concepts by behavior therapists.

(f) The terms "stimulus" and "response" become meaningless in the behavior-therapy situation ("remotely allegorical," to use Breger and McGaugh's term).

(g) The statement that the symptoms "are" the neurosis is erroneous; neurosis is in fact a complex structure involving not only "habits" but also values, attitudes, false beliefs, personal constructs, and the like.

(h) Behavior therapists may find difficulty in dealing with the successful outcome of dubious applications of learning theory, such as cases of apparent backward conditioning in alcoholics by aversion therapy.

(i) It is probably misleading to formulate analogies from animal conditioning to human conditioning; many new and special considerations arise that probably demand new laws, such as language, cooperation, influence of verbal instructions and the like.

It is well known in science that the application of laboratory-based findings and principles always involves considerable difficulty and may require much additional research. From Faraday's fundamental research to Edison's application of the laws of electricity, fifty years of unremitting research had to elapse; we would be failing in historical perspective if we assumed that, in the application of learning theory to neurotic behavior, an immediate transfer could be achieved. There will be many false steps, many disappointments, and many apparently inexplicable phenomena; all this does not argue against making the attempt, however.

It is possible that some behavior therapists only pay lip service to the principles of learning theory (2(a); 2(b)), and some of them undoubtedly manifest ignorance and produce primitive ideas (2 (e)); readers of this chapter will not need reminding that this is not universally true, and it would not seem reasonable to condemn a whole movement because of the actions or words of a few unrepresentative hangers-on. Can it in fact be said that behavior therapists make little use of learning theory concepts (2 (c))? Again we may with advantage refer to the preceding sections, which give many illustrations of such applications. Of course, behavior-therapy practices have precursors that may antedate the growth of modern learning theory, such as Watson's famous experiment with little Albert; the same can be said for almost every scientific advance—the precursors of Darwin in the elaboration of the theory of evolution fill whole books! However true, this is not a real criticism; it is only since these practices became associated with learning theory that they have achieved any sort of widely recognized status and efficacy (2 (d)).

Objections relating to the statement that the symptoms "are" the neurosis, on the grounds that a neurosis is a much more complex sort of thing involving not only habits, but also values, attitudes, and the like, seems misleading because in learning theory such values, attitudes, and the like are also classed as habits (Eysenck, 1953), and may thus form part of the set of "symptoms" that constitutes the neurosis (2 (g)). Indeed, an important part of the work on aversion therapy has dealt with the "devaluing" of concepts and attitudes held before the therapy began, and semantic differentials and other methods of evaluation have been used, in addition to such more physiological devices as the penis plethysmograph. Much interesting work promises to be done on the interrelations between these different types of "symptoms"; the evidence suggests that verbal, behavioral, and physiological responses are not changed *pari passu*, but obey somewhat different rules, and change at different rates. This is not, in our view, a criticism of behavior therapy; the fact would probably never have been unearthed had it not been for behavior therapy. Admittedly the fact was not predicted by learning theory, but how many facts of this kind are normally predicted by an existing scientific theory in an early stage of development? The reader familiar with the development of cryogenics will find again and again that theory and practice interacted precisely in this manner—theory predicting one thing, practice turning up something quite different, and often quite unexpected. To anticipate anything else, such as, for instance, the completely accurate prediction of observations and facts in such a novel area from existing theories, would be to fly in the face of all experience of scientists in the most varied fields.

No doubt other observations made by behavior therapists will equally tax our theoretical underpinnings (2(h)); some efforts to do this have of course already been made (Eysenck, 1968a). But again, this can hardly be regarded as a criticism of behavior therapy; it would be more realistic to regard it as part of that process of reciprocal enrichment between theory and practice that we have already mentioned before. If work on behavior therapy throws up new facts and discoveries that pose problems for existing theories, then we would consider this all to the good. The more widespread the network of known facts, the more testing it will prove for any theory; if all theories fail, it will be all the more obvious that something new and radically different is required. It is only if one were to maintain that existing theories are all-inclusive and complete in themselves that such criticisms would have any value; we know of no psychologist, and certainly of no behavior therapist, who would have such an exaggerated view of modern learning theory. Scientific theories are never like that, even the most firmly established ones; "weak" theories, like all psychological ones, are even more clearly expendable than most, and should only be accepted from a strictly heuristic point of view. They should not, however, be rejected because they do not measure up to impossibly idealized notions of what scientific theories can and cannot do. The same point applies to another criticism, viz. that suggesting that no proper analogies are possible from animal conditioning to human conditioning (2(i)). Unless we test the hypothesis that some general statements can be made to cover both animal conditioning and human conditioning, we will never know just how far

this can be done, and to what extent other concepts are needed; after all, behavior therapists advance this notion as a hypothesis, not as a covenant of the Ark. If the facts disprove it, another hypothesis will have to be put forward and tested. The critics may well be right, but if we do not put their view to the test, how shall we ever know whether, and to what extent, valuable analogies can in fact be drawn? The fact that there is spontaneous recovery of extinguished responses suggested to Rachman (1966b) that after a session of behavior therapy the extinguished anxiety responses should build up again and show recovery; his demonstration that this did in fact happen constitutes an important new contribution to the practice and theory of behavior therapy. Here the analogy seems to have worked; should he have forborne to carry out the experiment because it might not have done so? Eysenck (1963) argued that animal and laboratory experiments suggested relapse after behavior therapy for disorders of the second kind, but not for disorders of the first kind, and the facts seem to bear out this distinction. Should it not have been made because the facts might have disproved it?

The objection that the terms "stimulus" and "response" do not apply properly to what goes on in behavior therapy under those names is often made (2(f)); it certainly requires a proper answer, because at first sight it may seem to be stretching the meaning of such a term as "stimulus" a little if we include imagery under that title. Even if we use the more appropriate terminology of response-produced stimuli, the reader may still feel that a very complex chain of events is being smuggled into a conditioning paradigm under some verbal guise. Certainly it is true that such an order as: "Imagine that you are being beaten on the buttocks" is less specific than a precisely specified auditory stimulus, and that there are a number of intervening steps that ought to be spelled out in detail. However, we can without much difficulty anchor this set of intervening variables on the response side as well as on the stimulus side; thus, we might ask S to imagine sexual intercourse (stimulus) and measure the penile response with a plethysmograph. Alternatively, or concurrently, image latency may be measured. As an example of what can (and should) be done, consider the following experiment reported by Marks (1968). A sado-masochist was being treated by shock aversion therapy and the results are shown in Figure 9.

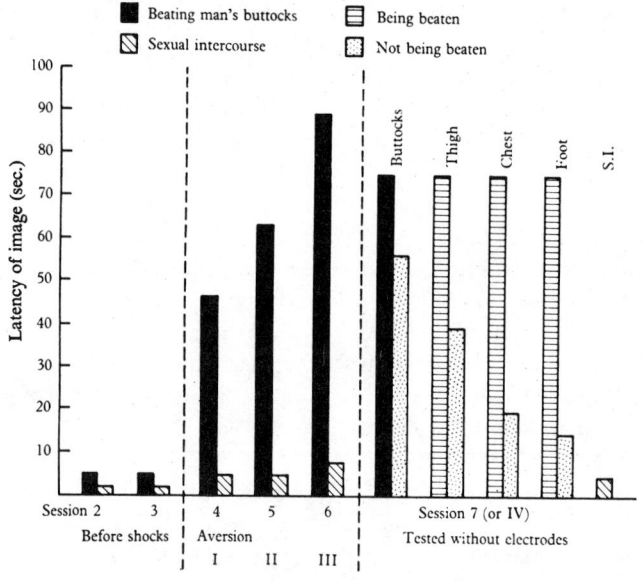

Figure 15.9 Generalization gradient in latency of image after aversion therapy. From Marks, 1968. Used with permission.

Before the shocks were given, the patient . . . could imagine quickly a scene in which he was beating a man's buttocks. Sexual intercourse could also be imagined quickly. Simple repetition for three sessions did not change the time taken to imagine the fantasy (the "latency"). In the next three sessions, aversion treatment was applied to the fantasy of beating, no shocks were given when normal intercourse was imagined. The latency of the shocked fantasies increased markedly, that of the normal fantasy changed little. At the next session the patient was tested without electrodes on his arm. When he imagined beating any part of the body the latency was long. When he imagined the part, without thinking of beating, then a gradient of response latency was found—the farther from the original part, the shorter the latency. Sexual intercourse was still imagined promptly. Similarly, further tests showed a gradient when different degrees of sadistic behaviour were imagined—the least sadistic having the shortest latency. Generalization gradients of this kind lend support to the idea that a form of internal avoidance conditioning is taking place. This generalization gradient in repressed material persisted over the next four months. It would be difficult even for a sophisticated observer to fake this result, as the fantasies were produced in random order on each occasion and patients were very inaccurate on those rare occasions

when they were asked to estimate how long it took them to produce a fantasy. (Twenty patients, in all, took part in these experiments)

Direct physiological recording of the GSR effects of imagery before and after treatment is reported by White et al. (1968); one example of their work is shown in Figures 10 and 11; where intervening constructs can be thus clearly anchored in an objective manner both preceding and following the hypothesized event, even strict Hullian canons permit us to use such constructs. From the point of view of size and specificity of response there is little to choose between imagery (as in the studies cited) and, say, slide presentation of pictures of the feared object (for example, Wilson, 1967). Figure 12 illustrates Wilson's results.

These experiments (as well as others by Marks and Gelder already mentioned in an earlier section) demonstrate that imagery behaves in a lawful manner, and that predictable responses can be evoked with considerable reliability. To suggest that relationships with orthodox stimulus-response learning theory are "remotely allegorical" does not seem to us to represent the facts correctly; quite specific expectations,

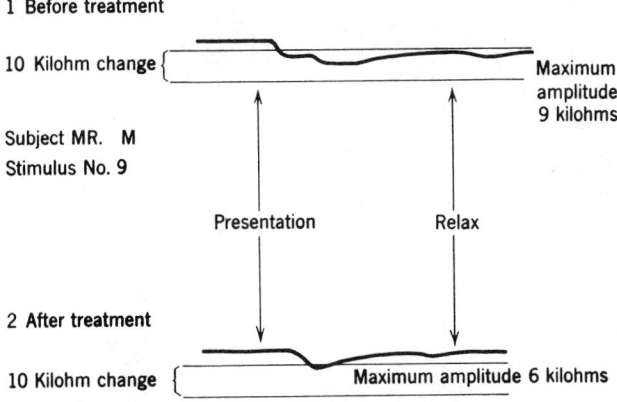

Figure 15.10 GSR to neutral stimulus, before and after desensitization treatment. From White et al., 1968. Used with permission.

deriving from animal experiments and laboratory explorations with human subjects under "simple" conditions, lead us to expect precisely the kind of generalization gradient here observed. Admittedly, this is only one example, but others can be given; critics would be well advised not to advance their views in the abstract, but rather in relation to experimental demonstrations such as this. Undoubtedly it would be correct to say that the careful experimental work of Marks, Gelder, and other workers from the Maudsley is not typical of many behavior therapists whose main interest lies in the practical application, rather than the theoretical underpinning of these new methods; however, this is not perhaps unusual in the therapeutic field, and general comments about theoretical issues should deal with such evidence as is available. Imagery, although it presents some difficulties to stimulus-response interpretation, cannot be said to obey entirely different laws to the stimuli more frequently used in the laboratory.[14] And the extension of laboratory measurements to this field presents

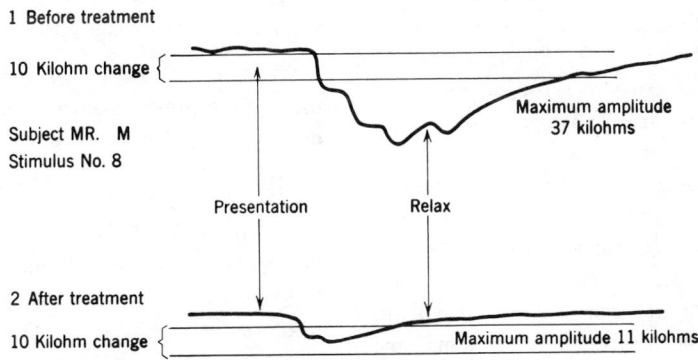

Figure 15.11 GSR to anxiety stimulus, before and after desensitization treatment. From White et al., 1968. Used with permission.

[14] Critics sometimes overlook the fact that imagery has been firmly placed into a behavioristic framework, both experimentally and theoretically, by such investigations as those of Ellson (1941) and Leuba (1940), leading to the theoretical statements of Staats (1968) and others. Craig (1968) has investigated experimentally similarities and differences in physiological reactions to imagined, vicarious, and direct-stress experiences; he found that in all conditions there were increases in skin conductance and in the frequency of nonspecific GSRs, but that heart rate and respiration rate operated in opposite directions in different conditions. Other workers to provide evidence of physiological arousal to imagined aversive stimuli, under experimental conditions, are Barber and Hahn (1964) and Grossberg (1967). Rimm and Battrell (1969) have compared different measures of visual imagination in a meaningful way.

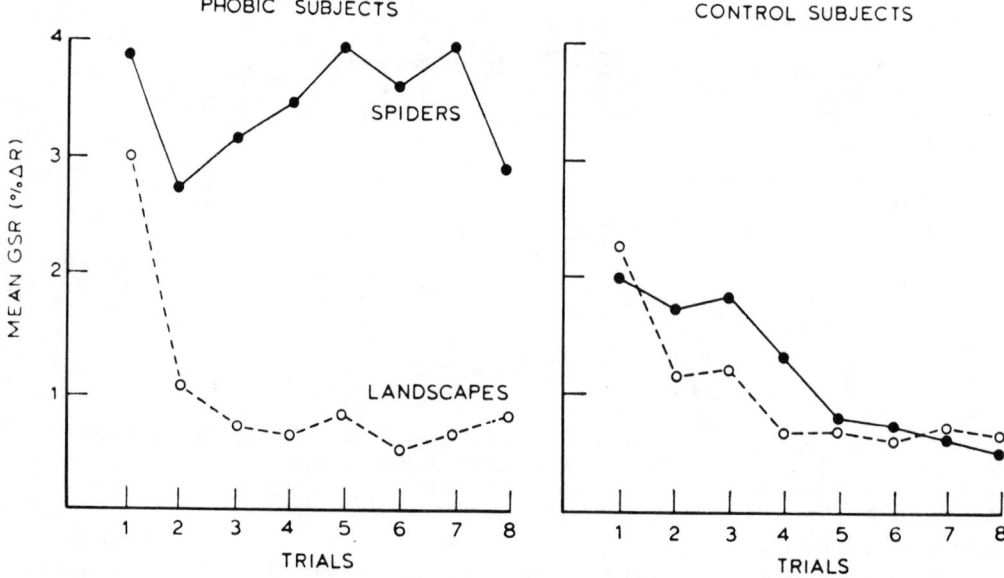

Figure 15.12 GSRs of phobic and control subjects to fear-related and neutral stimuli. From Wilson, 1967. Used with permission.

us with a distinct gain in knowledge, insofar as it extends the area of applicability of certain general laws, such as response generalization.

3. *The evidence for the efficacy of behavior therapy is in a very unsatisfactory state.*

(a) There do not exist any satisfactory studies of behavior therapy using adequate numbers (more than 20 Ss in each group), proper controls (for example, the treatment of "insight-therapy" is too short to provide a proper test), and methods of evaluation (which are almost always very crude).

(b) Comparisons with other forms of treatment (such as Wolpe's comparison of his results with those of psychoanalytic institutes) are partly meaningless, because of the possible lack of comparability in terms of types of patients treated, outcome criteria, different aims, and the like.

(c) Many, if not most, papers dealing with behavior therapy contain single case histories; these are anecdotal and prove nothing, however successful the outcome.

(d) There is little evidence concerning the types of disturbances and individual patient characteristics that would suggest behavior therapy treatment in preference to other types of treatment.

(e) More goes on in behavior therapy (reassurance, suggestion, and directives) than is contained in the programmatic presentations of the theory, and these features may be the important elements in the "cures."

(f) The patient-therapist relationship is the crucial active agent—perhaps along psychodynamic lines (transference), or in the operant conditioning sense as a positive reinforcer.

We have both expressed dissatisfaction with the existing clinical evidence presented in favor of behavior therapy (Beech, 1969; Eysenck and Rachman, 1965), and consequently we would not dispute points 3(a) and 3(b) very seriously, although we would like to draw attention to the excellent studies carried out by Marks and Gelder on clinical material. But on the whole we would agree that behavior therapists have not done conspicuously better than psychotherapists and psychoanalysts in demonstrating the clinical effectiveness of their methods as compared to other methods, or even to spontaneous remission. There are, however, certain ameliorating circumstances that are not always given full weight. Thus behavior therapists in our experience are frequently given patients who are exceptionally difficult, whose disorders are particularly long-standing, and on whom other methods of therapy have been tried and failed. This consideration is also relevant to point 3(c); a single case history acquires some importance when a very seriously incapacitated patient of some 20 years' standing, who has been treated by psychoanalysis, drugs, and various other methods without success, is completely cured by behavior therapy in a relatively short time, and without any adventitious change in external circumstances relevant to the case. We are not complaining that behavior therapists should be given such difficult cases; in the present stage of development this is perhaps only natural. We would like to enter a mild complaint, however, when critics neglect this fact in comparing psychoanalysis (where only the most promising and spontaneous-remission-ripe patients are chosen from a large number) with behavior therapy!

A second point relates to the length of treatment. Spontaneous remission is a serious counterhypothesis when patients get better under psychoanalysis; the treatment lasts so long that spontaneous remission has much room to play a part. Behavior therapy is much quicker, and if it works at all usually does so in such a short time that spontaneous remission does not seem to be a reasonable counterhypothesis. Furthermore, behavior therapy often attacks different systems sequentially, and it can be demonstrated (even in single cases) that recovery is usually linked with this sequence,—that is, when symptom 1 is being treated, symptom 1 shows improvement; when treatment shifts to symptom 2, this improves; and the like. This clear temporal relation between treatment and improvement, as Glover (1952) has admitted, is absent in psychoanalysis; its presence must be regarded as an important if partial proof of efficacy. And as a last point in connection with the "clinical proof," we would like to state that point 3(c) is not well taken when it is suggested that single-case studies are presented to *prove* the efficacy of behavior therapy; as mentioned previously, they are often used either to *illustrate* it (for didactic purposes), or to demonstrate new ways of linking theory with practice. Both illustration and demonstration have a role to play in the development of a new set of techniques; not every study is meant to prove the superiority of the methods used over other

methods. But our main contention would be rather different. Kuhn (1962) has suggested that science advances by revolutions; a particular paradigm or set of paradigms is given up, and another set adopted. We see behavior therapy as such a revolution; the paradigm(s) of psychoanalysis construed for some 50 years a field of inquiry within which most theories and methods of treatment were content to dwell, and from which they took their problems. Behavior therapists completely reject this set of paradigms, and put another in its place; under such circumstances direct comparison, as Kuhn points out, becomes difficult or indeed impossible.

The arguments regarding criteria between psychoanalysts and behavior therapists are an instance of what we mean; if the former wish to make the patient into a "better person," while not caring for his symptoms very much, whereas the latter wish to eliminate his symptoms, but don't wish to change his whole personality, then any clinical trial between the two sets of doctrines will become a caucus race—there is no unambiguous verdict because there is no agreement on outcome criteria. This must limit severely the value of clinical studies, and while we still believe that outcome studies are of the utmost importance, particularly when accompanied by lengthy follow-ups, we are under no illusion as far as their value in converting opponents of the behavioristic outlook is concerned. Competing paradigms do not meet, and the loser is likely to simply fade away, as old soldiers are reputed to do, rather than die a hero's death on the battlefield. In terms of behavior therapy, psychoanalytic criteria and practices are meaningless, and cannot be assessed or compared with those suggested by learning theory; their fate will be determined by the fact that increasing numbers of psychologists and psychiatrists actually see them as meaningless.

Comment 3(d) is not so much a criticism as a statement of fact. Eysenck and Rachman (1965) have pointed out the great importance of personality differences for treatment by behavior therapy, and have suggested ways of approaching this area; unfortunately, very little has in fact been done along these lines. We can only reiterate that in our opinion the operation of psychological laws is complicated by inter-action with the personality variables that are relevant to treatment (for example, neuroticism and extroversion-introversion); we believe that behavior therapists could profitably devote much of their endeavor to such problems, especially where there are already well-researched personality dimensions of obvious relevance to which reference can be made.

Points 3(e) and 3(f) are difficult to deal with because they assume that which is to be proved. It is of course possible that behavior therapy "works" (assuming that it does) for reasons other than those theoretically advanced by its proponents. Much work has been done, as reported in earlier sections, to test alternative hypotheses, and such work will of course be continued in the future, and presumably improved in its sophistication. But the criticism that *something* other than the conditioning measures involved may be responsible for improvement is too broad and vague ever to be refuted; we cannot hope to prove a negative. All that can be said is that the evidence, such as it is, is in broad agreement with the hypotheses being tested, and that possible alternatives have been eliminated. We do not consider it useful to suggest further vague alternatives that cannot be pinned down experimentally; critics would do behavior therapy a much better service if instead they worked out specific alternative hypotheses, incorporated these in actual clinical methods and procedures, and tested them against orthodox behavior therapy treatment. Only in this way will progress be made. We may, how-ever, even now exclude the hypothesis that the patient-therapist relationship is the vital point; differences in effectiveness observed between different methods, all of which included such relationships (Paul, 1966; Lang and Lazovik, 1963; Rachman, 1965; Davison, 1965; Marks and Gelder, 1967) in equal amount, or even disfavored behavior therapy, demonstrate con-clusively that this argument is not any longer viable.

Perhaps the added demonstrations that when therapist contact is controlled and experi-mentally varied, no differences in effectiveness of behavior therapy became evident (Kahn and Baker, 1968), or that desensitization therapy can be automated without loss of effectiveness

(Melamed and Lang, 1967; Donner and Guerney, 1969), will persuade even the most critical.

Even when the purely speculative notion of "transference" is translated into that of positive reinforcement (Eysenck, 1963), the causal determination is seen to go the wrong way—because the patient gets better, therefore he regards the therapist as a positive reinforcer, not vice versa! (See also Wilson et al., 1968).

In summarizing our position with respect to the effects of behavior therapy, we would like to make a general comment that we believe also affects many of the other points and criticisms that we have discussed. Many behavior thera-pists are therapists first and foremost; they have sought new and better methods of treatment than the orthodox "dynamic" ones, and feel that they have found what they looked for in behaviour therapy—often in just one of the methods of behavior therapy, such as desensiti-zation. For them, simple clinical experience, perhaps bolstered by summaries of other people's successes and statistics, is sufficient—as similar experiences have been sufficient for psychoanalysts and many other types of psycho-therapists. They are quite content on this basis to incorporate behavior therapy methods in their armamentarium, and to use them, either alone or in conjunction with other, theoretically quite incompatible methods, in their actual practice. Their argument would be that when faced with clinical realities, the practitioner has to use anything that comes to hand—without paying too much attention to theoretical refine-ment or empirical validation. We deplore this attitude in behavior therapists as we deplore it in psychotherapists; we believe that it results in a gigantic mish-mash of theories, methods, and outcomes that is forever beyond the capacity of scientific research to resolve. Theoretical differ-ences should be recognized and their practical and applied consequences differentiated as clearly as possible; only in this way can the good and bad points of each theory be disentangled.

We do not feel that at the present moment treatment of severely disabled neurotics presents adequate possibilities for carrying out such a program, and that the experimental, controlled treatment of otherwise normal, monosympto-matic phobic conditions is an infinitely better test-bed for the investigation of therapeutic theories. Clearly we cannot necessarily transfer results completely from these conditions to those of severely neurotic patients, just as little as we can expect 100 percent transfer from animal experiments to human experiments; nevertheless, we believe that such extension is in principle possible, and that general laws discovered in the one field can with advantage be tried out in the other. Hence our claims for behavior therapy as a scientific discipline are based far more strongly on the discovery of lawful behavior in these well-controlled situations and experiments than on the findings, however encouraging and confirmatory they may be, based on the clinical treatment of severely incapacitated patients.

This argument, and our theoretical treatment in general, is often countered with the criticism, which is in fact basic to many of the detailed points we have already considered, that our views are grossly oversimplified. We would agree that the statement regarding oversimplification is correct, if by this is meant that our theories do not do full justice to the complexity of real life. We would not agree that this statement constitutes a criticism of what has been presented; all scientific theories by definition oversimplify in this fashion. Science is abstract by nature, and something is inevitably lost in the process of abstraction. Biologists before Mendel had considered overt similarities and differences between plants, but they did so in a wholesale fashion, taking in all the complexity of size, texture, color, and the like. Mendel succeeded in founding the new science of genetics by concentrating on two simple characteristics of the pea: tall versus short and smooth versus wrinkled. His contemporaries considered all this grossly oversimplified, and his great discovery was in fact forgotten for thirty years; nevertheless, only by thus oversimplifying was it possible to make a proper beginning, and to make it possible later on to overcome the shortcomings of these oversimplifications. If we begin by considering all the complexities involved in real-life events, we will never arrive at a scientific theory; if we are willing to oversimplify, we are at least enabled to make a beginning, and thus to correct our errors.

Consider the shape of the sun. For Newton it was sufficient to assume that it was perfectly spherical; his theory of gravitation made this explicit oversimplification, and even as late as 1965 this assumption was used to support certain deductions from Einstein's general theory of relativity. This theory predicted that the advance of the perihelion of Mercury should be 43 seconds of arc greater per century than that expected from a strict Newtonian theory. When the actual excess was found to be almost exactly 43 seconds of arc, relativity was thought to have been conclusively demonstrated. However, in 1966 Dicke and Goldenberg showed that the sun has an oblateness of one part in 20,000, implying that the central core of the sun is rotating very rapidly; such an oblateness would cause the perihelion of Mercury to advance 3.4 seconds of arc per century. On Einstein's simple tensor relativity, then, the total effect now becomes an excess of 46.4 seconds of arc, clearly at variance with the 43.0 seconds of arc measured value; this leaves Einstein's general relativity without a single definitive quantitative test. Newton's oversimplification was acceptable for his purposes, but requires correction for our purposes; however, no such correction could possibly be made (or required) had we not advanced along Newton's lines and assumed as correct what we now know to be slightly in error. *Science is self-correcting, and oversimplification endemic in its development; to accuse behavior therapy of oversimplification is therefore little more than to accuse it of following the usual scientific lines of advance.*

Even justified criticisms may not always be useful to scientific advance at certain periods of development of a theory. Consider Leibnitz' criticisms of Newton's theory of gravitation (in his letter to S. Clarke). Einstein (1950) has noted that Leibnitz' criticisms were in fact justified, but adds that "had they won out at the time, it hardly would have been a boon to physics, for the empirical and theoretical foundations necessary to follow up his idea were not available in the 17th century." We would by no means rule out the possibility that some of the criticisms made by psychoanalysts and others of behavior therapy may in due course be found to be justified, and to necessitate considerable changes in the theory; we would also maintain, however, that at present

*the empirical and theoretical foundations neces-
sary to follow up these views are not available.
We would conclude, therefore, that our present
theories and practices, however crude, oversimplified, and elementary, are at least capable of
improvement and perfection, and thus lay a
scientific basis for modern methods of treatment
for the neuroses.*

REFERENCES

Adelman, H. M., and Maatsch, J. L. Resistance to extinction as a function of the type of response elicited by frustration. *J. Exp. Psychol.*, 1955, **50**, 61–65.

Anant, S. A note on the treatment of alcoholics by a verbal aversion technique. *Canadian Psychologist*, 1967, **80**, 19–22.

Anderson, O. D., and Liddell, H. S. Observations on experimental neurosis in sheep. *Arch. Neurol. Psychiat.*, 1935, **34**, 330–354.

Anderson, O. D., and Parmenter, R. A long-term study of the experimental neurosis in the sheep and dog. *Psychosomatic Med. Monogr. Supplem.*, 1941.

Appel, J. B. Punishment and shock intensity. *Science*, 1962, **141**, 528–529.

Ashem, B., and Donner, L. Covert sensitization with alcoholics: A controlled replication. *Beh. Res. & Ther.*, 1968, **6**, 7–12.

Azrin, N. H. Effects of two intermittent schedules of immediate and non-immediate punishment. *J. Psychol.*, 1956, **42**, 3–21.

Azrin, N. H., and Holz, W. C. Punishment. In W. K. Honig (Ed.), *Operant Behavior*. New York: Appleton-Century-Crofts, 1966.

Azrin, N. H., Holz, W. C., and Hake, D. F. Fixed-ratio punishment. *J. Exp. Anal. Behav.*, 1963, **6**, 141–148.

Bancroft, J. Aversion Therapy. DPM Dissertation. University of London, 1966.

Bandura, A. Social learning through imitation. In Jones, M. R. (Ed.), *Nebraska Symposium on Motivation*. Lincoln: University of Nebraska Press, 1962.

Barber, T. X., and Hahn, K. W. Experimental studies in "hypnotic" behaviour: Physiologic and subjective effects of imagined pain. *J. Nerv. Ment. Dis.*, 1964, **139**, 416–425.

Barker, J. C., et al. Behaviour therapy in a case of transvestism. *Lancet*, 1961, **1**, 510.

Baum, M. Efficacy of response prevention (flooding) in facilitating the extinction of an avoidance response in rats; the effect of overtraining the response. *Beh. Res. & Ther.*, 1968, **6**, 197–203.

Baum, M. Extinction of an avoidance response following response prevention: Some parametric investigations. *Canad. J. Psychol.*, 1969, **23**, 1–10.

Beech, H. R. The symptomatic treatment of writer's cramp. In Eysenck, H. J. (Ed.), *Behaviour Therapy and the Neuroses*. London: Pergamon Press, 1960.

Beech, H. R. Some theoretical and technical difficulties in the application of behaviour therapy. *Bull. Brit. Psychol. Soc.*, 1963, **16**, 25–32.

Beech, H. R. *Changing man's behavior*. London: Penguin Books, 1969.

Bersh, P. J., Notterman, J. M., and Schoenfeld, W. N. Generalization to varying time frequencies as a function of itensity of unconditioned stimulus. *Air Univ., School of Aviation Med.*, U.S.A.F., Randolph A.F.B., Texas, 1956.

Bindra, D., and Cameron, L. Changes in experimentally produced anxiety with the passage of time: Incubation effect. *J. Exper. Psychol.*, 1953, **45**, 197–203.

Blake, B. G. The application of behaviour therapy to the treatment of alcoholism. *Behav. Res. Ther.*, 1965, **3**, 78–85.

Blake, B. G. A follow-up of alcoholics treated by behaviour therapy. *Behav. Res. Ther.*, 1967, **5**, 89–94.

Blakemore, C. B. et al. Application of faradic aversion conditioning to a case of transvestism. *Behav. Res. Ther.*, 1963, **1**, 26–35. (a)

Blakemore, C. B. et al. Follow-up note. *Behav. Res. Ther.*, 1963, **1**, 191. (b)

Bolles, R. C. *Theory of motivation*. New York: Harper, 1967.

Bolles, R. C., and Seelback, G. E. Punishing and reinforcing effects of noise onset and termination for different responses. *J. Comp. Physiol. Psychol.*, 1964, **58**, 127–131.

Bolles, R. C., and Warren, J. A. Effects of delay on the punishing and reinforcing effects of noise onset and termination. *J. Comp. Physiol. Pyschol.*, 1966, **61**, 475–477.

Breger, L., and McGaugh, J. Critique and reformulation of "learning theory" approaches to psychotherapy and neurosis. *Psychol. Bull.*, 1965, **63**, 338–358.

Brethower, D. M., and Reynolds, G. S. A facilitative effect of punishment on unpunished behaviour. *J. Ex. Anal. Behav.*, 1962, **5**, 191–199.

Breznitz, S. Incubation of threat: Duration of anticipation and false alarm as determinants of the fear reaction to an unavoidable frightening event. *J. Exper. Res. and Person.*, 1967, **2**, 173–179.

Bridger, W. H., and Mandel, I. J. A comparison of GSR fear responses produced by threat and electric shock. *J. Psychiat. Res.*, 1964, **2**, 31–40.

Bridger, W. H., and Mandel, I. J. Abolition of the PRE by instructions in GSR conditioning. *J. Exper. Psychol.*, 1965, **69**, 476–482.

Broadhurst, P. L. Abnormal animal behaviour. In H. J. Eysenck (Ed.), Handbook of Abnormal Psychology. New York: Basic Books, 1960. Pp. 726–763.

Brown, J. S. Gradients of approach and avoidance responses and their relation to level of motivation. *J. Comp. Physiol. Psychol.*, 1948, **41**, 450–465.

Brush, F. R., and Levine, S. Adrenocortical activity and avoidance learning as a function of time after fear conditioning. *Physiol. & Behav.*, 1966, **1**, 309–311.

Burt, C. Factorial studies of personality and their bearing on the work of the teacher. *Brit. J. Ed. Psychol.*, 1965, **35**, 368–378.

Cahoon, D. P. Symptom substitution and the behaviour therapies: A re-appraisal. *Psychol. Bull.*, 1968, **69**, 149–156.

Carmona, A. Trial-and-error learning of the voltage of the cortical EEG activity. Unpublished Ph.D. thesis, Yale University, 1967.

Cautela, J. Treatment of compulsive behaviour by covert sensitization. *Psychol. Record*, 1966, **16**, 33–42.

Cautela, J. Covert sensitization. *Psychol. Rep.*, 1967, **20**, 459–468.

Chatterjee, B., and Eriksen, C. Cognitive factors in heart rate conditioning. *J. Exp. Psychol.*, 1962, **64**, 272–279.

Church, R. M. The varied effects of punishment on behaviour. *Psychol. Rev.*, 1963, **70**, 369–402.

Clark, D. F. The treatment of monosymptomatic phobia by systematic desensitization. *Behav. Res. Ther.*, 1963, **1**, 63–68.

Clark, D. F. Fetishism treated by negative conditioning. *Brit. J. Psychiat.*, 1963, 109, 404–407. (a)

Clark, D. F. Letter. *Brit. J. Psychiat.*, 1963, **109**, 695–696. (b)

Collier, R. M. The effect of verbal exploration of the affective-curative content of a CR upon the rate of extinction. *J. Clin. Psychol.*, 1965, **21**, 136–141.

Cook, S. W., and Harris, R. E. The verbal conditioning of the GSR. *J. Exp. Psychol.*, 1937, **21**, 202–210.

Cooke, G. The efficacy of two desensitization procedures: An analogue study. *Behav. Res. Ther.*, 1966, **4**, 17–24.

Cooper, J. E. A study of behaviour therapy in 30 psychiatric patients. *The Lancet*, 1963, **1**, 411–415.

Cooper, J. E., Gelder, M. G., Marks, I. M. The results of behaviour therapy in 77 psychiatric patients. *Brit. Med. J.*, 1965, **1**, 1222–1225.

Cosnier, J. *Les néuroses experimentale*. Paris: Editions du Seuil, 1966.

Craig, K. D. Physiological arousal as a function of imagined vicarious, and direct stress experience. *J. Abnorm. Psychol.*, 1968, **73**, 513–520.

Cremerius, J. *Die Beurteilung des Behandlungserfolges in der Psychotherapie*. Berlin: Springer, 1962.

Davis, D. R. Some applications of behaviour therapy in psychopathology. *Brit. J. med. Psychol.*, 1954, **27**, 216–223.

Davison, G. C. Elimination of a sadistic fantasy by a client-controlled counter conditioning technique: A case study. *J. Abnorm. Psychol.*, 1968, **73**, 84–90.

Davison, G. C. Systematic desensitization as a counter-conditioning process. *J. Abnorm. Psychol.*, 1968, **73**, 91–99.

Denker, P. G. Results of treatment of psychoneuroses by the general practitioner: A follow-up study of 500 cases. *Arch. Neurol. Psychiat.*, 1947, **57**, 504–505.

Desiderato, O., Butler, B., and Meyer, C. Changes in fear generalisation gradients as a function of delayed testing. *J. Exper. Psychol.*, 1966, **72**, 678–682.

Desiderato, O., and Wassarman, M. E. Incubation of anxiety: Effect on generalisation gradients. *J. Exper. Psychol.*, 1967, **74**, 506–510.

Dinsmoor, J. A. A discrimination based on punishment. *Quart. J. Exp. Psychol.*, 1952, **4**, 27–45.

Dimmick, F. L., Ludlow, N., and Whiteman, A. A study of "experimental neurosis" in cats. *J. Comp. Psychol.*, 1939, **28**, 39–43.

Diven, K. Certain determinants in the conditioning of anxiety reactions. *J. Psychol.*, 1937, **3**, 291–308.

Dollard, J., and Miller, N. E. *Personality and psychotherapy*. New York: McGraw Hill, 1950.

Donner, L., and Guerney, B. A. Automated group desensitization for test anxiety. *Beha. Res. & Ther.*, 1969, **7**, 1–13.

Dostálek, Ctibor. *Rückläufige Bedingte Verbindungen*. Verlag der Tschechoslowakischen Akad. d. Wiss., Praha, 1964.

Drvota, S. In Wolpe, J., and Lazarus, A. A. *Behaviour therapy techniques*. London: Pergamon Press, 1966.

Duffy, G. *Activation and behaviour*. London: Wiley, 1962.

Dykman, R. A., and Gantt, W. H. Cardiovascular conditioning in dogs and humans. In Gantt, W. H. (Ed.), *Physiological basis of psychiatry*. Springfield: C. C. Thomas, 1958, 171–195.

Dykman, R. A., and Gantt, W. H. A case of experimental neurosis and recovery in relation to the orienting response. *J. Psychol.*, 1960, **50**, 105–110. (a)

Dykman, R. A., and Gantt, W. H. Experimental psychogenic hypertension: Blood pressure changes conditioned to painful stimuli (schizokinesis). *Bull. Johns Hopkins Hosp.*, 1960, 107, 72–89. (b)

Dykman, R. A., Mack, R. L., and Ackerman, P. J. The evaluation of autonomic and motor components of the nonavoidance conditioned response in the dog. *Psychophysiology*, 1965, **1**, 209–230.

Edlin, J. V. et al. Conditioned aversion treatment in chronic alcoholism. *Amer. J. Psychiat.*, 1945, **101**, 806–809.

Einstein, A. On the generalized theory of gravitation. *Scientific American*, April, 1950.

Ellson, D. Hallucinations produced by sensory conditioning. *J. Exper. Psychol.*, 1941, **28**, 1–20.

Endicott, G. A., and Endicott, J. "Improvement" in untreated psychiatric patients. *Arch. Gen. Psychiat.*, 1963, **9**, 575–585.

Essman, W. B., and Alpern, H. Single trial conditioning: Methodology and results with mice. *Psychol. Rep.*, 1964, **14**, 731–740.

Estes, W. K. An experimental study of punishment. *Psychol. Monographs*, 1944 (**47**, Whole No. 263).

Estes, W. K., and Skinner, D. F. Some quantitative properties of anxiety. *J. Exp. Psychol.*, 1941, **29**, 390–400.

Evans, D. R. Masturbatory fantasy and sexual deviation. *Beh. Res. Therapy*, 1968, **6**, 17–20.

Eysenck, H. J. *The psychology of politics*. London: Routledge & Kegan Paul, 1953.

Eysenck, H. J. *The dynamics of anxiety and hysteria*. London: Routledge & Kegan Paul, 1957.

Eysenck, H. J. Learning theory and behaviour therapy. *J. Ment. Sci.*, 1959, **105**, 61–75.

Eysenck, H. J. *The structure of human personality*. London: Methuen, 1960. (a)

Eysenck, H. J. (Ed.). *Behaviour therapy and the neuroses*. New York: Pergamon Press, 1960. (b)

Eysenck, H. J. The place of theory in psychology. In Eysenck, H. J. (Ed.), *Experiments in personality*. Vol. 2. London: Routledge & Kegan Paul, 1960. Pp. 303–315. (c)

Eysenck, H. J. *Experiments with drugs*. Oxford: Pergamon Press, 1963. (a)

Eysenck, H. J. Behaviour therapy, spontaneous remission and transference in neurotics. *Amer. J. Psychiat.*, 1963, **119**, 867–871. (b)

Eysenck, H. J. Behaviour therapy, extinction and relapse in neurosis. *Brit. J. Psychiat.*, 1963, **109**, 12–18. (c)

Eysenck, H. J. Emotion as a determinant of integrative learning: An experimental study. *Beh. Res. Ther.*, 1963, **1**, 197–212. (d)

Eysenck, H. J. *Crime and personality*. Boston: Houghton Mifflin, 1964. (a)

Eysenck, H. J. (Ed.). *Experiments in behaviour therapy*. New York: Pergamon Press, 1964. (b)

Eysenck, H. J. A three-factor theory of reminiscence. *Brit. J. Psychol.*, 1965, **56**, 163–181.

Eysenck, H. J. Single-trial conditioning, neurosis and the Napalkov phenomenon. *Beh. Res. Ther.*, 1967, **5**, 63–65. (a)

Eysenck, H. J. *The biological basis of personality*. Springfield: C. C. Thomas, 1967. (b)

Eysenck, H. J. A theory of the incubation of anxiety/fear responses. *Beh. Res. Ther.*, 1968, **6**, 309–322. (a)

Eysenck, H. J. A Dimensional system of psychodiagnostics. In A. R. Mahrer (Ed.), *New approaches to diagnostic systems*. New York: Aldine, 1968. (b)

Eysenck, H. J., and Eysenck, S. B. G. *The structure and measurement of personality*. San Diego: R. R. Knapp, 1969.

Eysenck, H. J., and Levey, A. Konditionierung, Introversion-Extraversion und die Starke des Nervensystems. *Ztschr. f. Psychologie*, 1967, **174**, 96–106.

Eysenck, H. J., and Rachman, S. *The causes and cures of neurosis*. San Diego: R. R. Knapp, 1965.

Farrar, C. H., Powell, B. J., and Martin, L. K. Punishment of alcohol consumption by apnoeic paralysis. *Beh. Res. Ther.*, 1968, **6**, 13–16.

Feldman, M. P. Aversion therapy for sexual deviations: A critical review. *Psychol. Bull.*, 1966, **65**, 65–79.

Feldman, M. P., and MacCulloch, M. J. The application of anticipatory avoidance learning to the treatment of homosexuality. I. Theory, technique and preliminary results. *Beh. Res. Ther.*, 1965, **2**, 165–183.

Flanagan, B., Goldiamond, I., and Azrin, N. Operant stuttering: The control of stuttering behaviour through response-contingent consequences. *J. Exp. Anal. Behav.*, 1958, **1**, 173–177.

Foley, J. P. The criterion of abnormality. *J. Abnorm. Soc. Psychol.*, 1935, **30**, 279–291.

Ford, C. S., and Beach, F. A. *Patterns of sexual behaviour*. London: Eyre & Spottiswoode, 1952.

Fowler, H., and Miller, N. E. Facilitation and inhibition of runway performance by hind- and forepaw shock of various intensities. *J. Comp. Physiol. Psychol.*, 1963, **56**, 801–805.

Franks, C. M. Alcohol, alcoholism and conditioning. In Eysenck, H. J. (Ed.), *Behaviour therapy and the neuroses*. Oxford: Pergamon Press, 1960.

Franks, C. M. Behaviour therapy, the principles of conditioning and the treatment of the alcoholic. *Quart. J. Stud. Alcohol.*, 1963, **24**, 511–529.

Franks, C. M. Conditioning and conditioned aversion therapies in the treatment of alcoholics. *The Int. J. of Addictions*, 1966, **1**, 61–98.

Freeman, T. A psychoanalytic critique of behaviour therapy. *Brit. J. Med. Psychol.*, 1968, **41**, 53–60.

Freund, K. Problems in the treatment of homosexuality. In H. J. Eysenck (Ed.), *Behaviour therapy and the neuroses*. Oxford: Pergamon Press, 1960.

Freund, K. Diagnosing homo- or heterosexuality and erotic age-preference by means of a psychophysiological test. *Beh. Res. Ther.*, 1967, **5**, 209–228.

Freund, K., Diamant, J., and Pinkava, V. On the validity and reliability of the haloplethysmiographic diagnosis of some sexual deviations. *Rev. Czech. Med.*, 1958, **4**, 145–151.

Friedman, D. A new technique for the systematic desensitization of phobic symptoms. *Beh. Res. Ther.*, 1966, **4**, 139–140.

Gantt, W. H. Experimental basis for neurotic behaviour. *Psychosom. Med. Monogr.*, 1944, **3**, Nos. 3 & 4.

Garcia, J., Ervine, F. R., Yorke, C. N., and Koelling, R. A. Conditioning with delayed vitamin injections. *Science*, 1967, **155**, 716–718.

Garcia, J., and Koelling, R. A. Relation of cue to consequence in avoidance learning. *Psychonom. Sci.*, 1966, **4**, 123–124.

Garcia, J., McGowan, B. K., Ervine, F. R., and Koelling, R. A. Cues: Their relative effectiveness as a function of the reinforcer. *Science*, 1968, **160**, 294–295.

Garfield, Z. H., Darwin, P. L., Barton, A. S., and McBrearty, J. F. Effect of "in vivo" training on experimental sensitization of a phobia. *Psychol. Rep.*, 1967, **20**, 515–519.

Gelder, M. G. Desensitization and psychotherapy research. *Brit. J. Med. Psychol.*, 1968, **41**, 39–46.

Gelder, M. G., and Marks, I. M. Severe agoraphobia: A controlled retrospective trial of behaviour therapy. *Brit. J. Psychiat.*, 1966, **112**, 309–320.

Gelder, M. G., and Marks, I. M. Desensitization and phobias: A cross-over study. *Brit. J. Psychiat.*, 1968, **114**, 323–328.

Gelder, M. G., and Marks, I. M. Aversion treatment in transvestism and transsexualism. In R. Green (Ed.), *Transsexualism and sex reassignment*. London: Hopkins Press, 1968.

Gelder, M. G., Marks, I. M., and Wolff, H. H. Desensitization and psychotherapy in the treatment of phobic states: A controlled inquiry. *Brit. J. Psychiat.*, 1967, **113**, 53–73.

Gibbens, T. C. N. Psychiatric research in delinquency behaviour. *Brit. Med. J.*, 1966, **2**, 695–698.

Giel, R., Knox, R. S., and Carstairs, G. M. A five-year follow-up of 100 neurotic outpatients. *Brit. Med. J.*, 1964, **2**, 160–163.

Glover, E. Research methods in psycho-analysis. *Int. J. Psycho-Anal.*, 1952, **33**, 403–409.

Glynn, J. D., and Harper, P. Behaviour therapy and transvestism. *Lancet*, 1961, **1**, 619.

Gold, S., and Neufeld, I. A learning theory approach to the treatment of homosexuality. *Beh. Res. Ther.*, 1965, **2**, 201–204.

Golin, S., and Golin, A. H. Incubation and inhibition. *J. Exper. Psychol.*, 1966, **71**, 208–211.

Grings, W., and Lockhart, R. Effects of "anxiety lessening" instructions and differential set development on the extinction of GSR. *J. Exp. Psychol.*, 1963, **66**, 292–299.

Grings, W. W., and Uno, T. Counterconditioning in fear and relaxation. *Psychophysiology*, 1968, **4**, 479–485.

Grossberg, J. M. Physiological changes accompanying imagined fear situations. Paper presented at the meeting of the Western Psychological Association, San Francisco, 1967.

Guthrie, E. R. *The psychology of learning*. New York: Harper, 1952.

Hamilton, G. V. Comparative psychology and psychopathology. *Amer. J. Psychol.*, 1927, **39**, 200–211.

Hebb, D. O. Spontaneous neurosis in chimpanzees: Theoretical relations with clinical and experimental phenomena. *Psychosom. Med.*, 1947, **9**, 3–16.

Heriat, J. T., and Coleman, P. D. The effect of electroconvulsive shock on retention of a modified "one-trial" conditioned avoidance. *J. Comp. Physiol.*, 1962, **55**, 1082–1084.

Herzberg, A. *Active psychotherapy*. New York: Grune & Stratton, 1945.

Hsu, J. Electroconditioning therapy of alcoholics: A preliminary report. *Quart. J. Stud. Alcohol.*, 1965, **26**, 449–459.

Hudson, B. G. One-trial learning and the domestic rat. *Genet. Psychol. Monogr.*, 1950, **41**, 99–145.

Hull, C. L. A functional interpretation of the conditioned reflex. *Psychol. Rev.*, 1929, **36**, 498–511.

Humphrey, J. Behaviour therapy with children: An experimental evaluation. Unpublished Ph.D. thesis, University of London, 1966.

Hunt, H. F., and Brady, J. V. Some effects of punishment and intercurrent anxiety on a simple operant. *J. Comp. Physiol. Psychol.*, 1955, **48**, 305–310.

Jacobson, E. Variation of blood pressure with skeletal muscle tension and relaxation. *Ann. Int. Med.*, 1939, **12**, 1194–1212.

Jacobson, E. Variation of pulse rate with skeletal muscle tension and relaxation. *Ann. Int. Med.*, 1940, **13**, 1619–1625.

Jacobson, E. *Anxiety and tension control*. Philadelphia: Lippincott, 1964.

James, B. Case of homosexuality treated by aversion therapy. *Brit. Med. J.*, 1962, **1**, 768–770.

Jenkins, W. O., Pascal, G. R., and Walker, R. W. Deprivation and generalisation. *J. Exper. Psychol.*, 1958, **56**, 274–277.

Jersild, A. T., and Holmes, F. B. Methods of overcoming children's fears. *J. Psychol.*, 1935, **1**, 25–104.

Jones, M. C. The elimination of children's fears. *J. Exper. Psychol.*, 1924, **7**, 383–390.

Kahn, M., and Baker, B. Desensitization with minimal therapist contact. *J. Abnorm. Psychol.*, 1968, **73**, 198–200.

Kamin, L. J. The retention of an incompletely learned avoidance response. *J. Comp. Physiol. Psychol.*, 1957, **50**, 457–460.

Kamin, L. J. Retention of an incompletely learned avoidance response: Some further analyses. *J. Comp. Physiol. Psychol.*, 1963, **56**, 713–718.

Karn, H. W. A case of experimentally induced neurosis in the cat. *J. Exper. Psychol.*, 1938, **22**, 589–593.

Karsh, E. B. Punishment: Trial spacing and shock intensity as determinants of behaviour in a discrete operant situation. *J. Comp. Physiol. Psychol.*, 1964, **58**, 299–302.

Karsh, E. B. Effects of number of rewarded trials and intensity of punishment on running speed. *J. Comp. Physiol. Psychol.*, 1962, **55**, 44–51.

Kaufman, E. L., and Miller, N. E. Effect of number of reinforcements on strength of approach in an approach-avoidance conflict. *J. Comp. Physiol. Psychol.*, 1949, **42**, 65–74.

Kimble, G. A. *Hilgard and Marquis' conditioning and learning.* New York: Appleton-Century-Crofts, 1961.

Kimmel, H. D. Instrumental conditioning of autonomically mediated behaviour. *Psychol. Bull.*, 1967, **67**, 337–345.

Knight, R. P. Evaluation of the results of psychoanalytic therapy. *Amer. J. Psychiat.*, 1941, **98**, 434–444.

Kolvin, I. Aversive imagery treatment in adolescents. *Beh. Res. Ther.*, 1967, **5**, 245–248.

Kondas, O. Reduction of examination anxiety and "stage-fright" by group desensitization and relaxation. *Beh. Res. Ther.*, 1967, **5**, 273–281.

Krasnogorski, N. I. The conditioned reflexes and children's neuroses. *Amer. J. Dis. Child.*, 1933, **45**, 355–370.

Kuhn, T. S. *The structure of scientific revolutions.* Chicago: Univ. Chicago Press, 1962.

Kushner, M., and Sandler, J. Aversion therapy and the concept of punishment. *Beh. Res. Ther.*, 1966, **4**, 179–186.

Lader, M. H. Palmar conductance measures in anxiety and phobic states. *J. Psychosom. Res.*, 1967, **11**, 271–281.

Lader, M. H., and Mathews, A. M. A physiological model of phobic anxiety and desensitization. *Beh. Res. Ther.*, 1968, in press.

Lader, M. H., and Wing, L. *Physiological measures, sedative drugs, and morbid anxiety.* London: Oxford University Press, 1966.

Lang, P. J., and Lazovik, A. D. The experimental desensitization of a phobia. *J. Abnorm. Soc. Psychol.*, 1963, **66**, 519–525.

Lang, P., Lazovik, A. D., and Reynolds, D. Desensitization ,suggestibility, and pseudo-therapy. *J. Abnorm. Soc. Psychol.*, 1965, **70**, 395–402.

Lanyon, R. I., Manosevitz, M., and Imber, R. R. Systematic desensitization: Distribution of practice and symptom substitution. *Beh. Res. Ther.*, 1968, **5**, in press.

Lazarus, A. A. New methods in psychotherapy: A case study. *S. Afr. Med. J.*, 1958, **33**, 660–663.

Lazarus, A. A. Group therapy of phobic disorders. *J. Abnorm. Soc. Psychol.*, 1961, **63**, 504–512.

Lazarus, A. A. The results of behaviour therapy in 126 cases of severe neurosis. *Beh. Res. Ther.*, 1963, **1**, 65–78.

Lazarus, A., and Abramovitz, A. The use of "emotive imagery" in the treatment of children's phobias. *J. Ment. Sci.*, 1962, **108**, 191–195.

Leitenberg, H. Response initiation and response termination: Analysis of effects of punishment and escape contingencies. *Psychol. Rep.*, 1965, **16**, 569–575.

Lemere, G., and Voegtlin, W. An evaluation of the aversion treatment of alcoholism. *Quart. J. Stud. Alcohol.*, 1950, **11**, 199–204.

Leuba, L. Images as conditioned sensations. *J. Exper. Psychol.*, 1940, **76**, 345–351.

Liberman, R. Aversive conditioning of drug addicts: A pilot study. *Beh. Res. Ther.*, 1968, **6**, in press.

Lichtenstein, F. E. Studies in anxiety. I. The production of a feeding inhibition in dogs. *J. Comp. Physiol. Psychol.*, 1950, **43**, 16–29.

Liddell, H. S. Conditioned reflex method and experimental neurosis. In J. McV. Hunt (Ed.), *Personality and the behaviour disorders.* New York: Ronald Press, 1944.

Liddell, H. S. *Emotional hazards in animals and man.* Springfield: C. C. Thomas, 1956.

Liversedge, L. G., and Sylvester, J. D. Conditioning techniques in the treatment of writer's cramp. *Lancet*, 1955, 1147–1149. Also in H. J. Eysenck (Ed.), *Behaviour therapy and the neuroses.* Oxford: Pergamon Press, 1960.

Lovibond, S. H. *Conditioning and enuresis.* New York: Pergamon Press, 1964.

Lubin, A. J. The experimental neurosis in animals and man. *Amer. J. Med. Sci.*, 1943, **205**, 269–277.

Maatsch, J. L. Learning and fixation after a single shock trial. *J. Comp. Physiol. Psychol.*, 1959, **52**, 408–410.

McAllister, D. E., and McAllister, W. R. Incubation of fear: An examination of the concept. *J. Exper. Res. in Person.*, 1967, **2**, 180–190.

Macculloch, M. J., Feldman, M. P., Orford, J. F., and Macculloch, M. L. Anticipatory avoidance learning in the treatment of alcoholism: A record of therapeutic failure. *Beh. Res. Ther.*, 1966, **4**, 187–196.

Macculloch, M. J., Feldman, M. P., and Pinschof, J. M. The application of anticipatory avoidance learning to the treatment of homosexuality. II. Avoidance response latencies and pulse rate changes. *Beh. Res. Ther.*, 1965, **3**, 21–44.

McGuire, R., and Vallance, M. Aversion therapy by electric shock, a simple technique. *Brit. Med. J.*, 1964, **1**, 151–152.

McGuire, R., Carlisle, J. M., and Young, B. G. Sexual deviations as conditioned behavior: A hypothesis. *Beh. Res. Ther.*, 1965, **2**, 185–190.

McMichael, J. S. Incubation of anxiety and instrumental behaviour. *J. Comp. Physiol. Psychol.*, 1966, **61**, 208–211.

Maier, N. R. F. *Frustration: The study of behaviour without a goal.* New York: McGraw Hill, 1949.

Marks, I. M. Aversion therapy. *Brit. J. Med. Psychol.*, 1968, **41**, 47–52.

Marks, I. M., and Gelder, M. G. A controlled retrospective study of behaviour therapy in phobic patients. *Brit. J. Psychiat.*, 1965, **111**, 561–573.

Marks, I., M. and Gelder, M. G. Transvestism and fetishism: Clinical and psychological changes during faradic aversion. *Brit. J. Psychiat.*, 1967, **119**, 711–730.

Marks, I. M., and Gelder, M. G. Controlled trials in behaviour therapy. In R. Porter (Ed.), *The role of learning in psychotherapy*. London: Churchill, 1968.

Martin, B. Reward and punishment associated with the same goal response: A factor in the learning of motives. *Psychol. Bull.*, 1963, **60**, 441–451.

Martin, I., Marks, I. M., and Gelder, M. G. Conditioned eyelid responses in phobic patients. *Beh. Res. & Ther.*, 1969, **7**, 115–124.

Masserman, J. M. *Behaviour and neurosis*. Chicago: Univ. Chicago Press, 1943.

Max, L. Breaking up a homosexual fixation by the conditioned reaction technique. *Psychol. Bull.*, 1935, **32**, 734.

May, M. L. Experimentally acquired drives. *J. Exper. Psychol.*, 1948, **38**, 66–77.

Melamed, B., and Lang, P. Study of the automated differentiation of fear. Paper read at the meeting of the Midwestern Psychol. Ass., Chicago, May 1967.

Mendelssohn, K. *The quest for absolute fear*. London: Weidenfeld & Nicholson, 1966.

Millenson, J. R., and Hendry, D. P. Quantification of response suppression in conditioned anxiety training. *Canad. J. Psychol.*, 1967, **21**, 242–252.

Miller, E., Dvorak, B., and Turner, D. A method of creating aversion to alcohol by reflex conditioning in a group setting. In C. M. Franks (Ed.), *Conditioning techniques in clinical practice & research*. New York: Springer, 1964.

Miller, N. E. Studies of fear as an acquired drive. I. Fear as motivation and fear-reduction as reinforcement in the learning of new responses. *J. Exper. Psychol.*, 1948, **38**, 89–101.

Miller, N. E. Comments on multiple process conceptions of learning. *Psychol. Rev.*, 1951, **58**, 375–381. (a)

Miller, N. E. Learnable drives and rewards. In S. S. Stevens (Ed.), *Handbook of experimental psychology*. New York: Wiley, 1951. (b) Pp. 435–472.

Miller, N. E. Liberalization of basic S-R concepts. In S. Koch (Ed.), *Psychology: A Study of a Science*. Study 1, Vol. 2. New York: McGraw Hill, 1959. Pp. 196–292.

Miller, N. E. Learning resistance to pain and fear: Effects of overlearning, exposure, and rewarded exposure in context. *J. Exp. Psychol.*, 1960, **60**, 137–145.

Miller, N. E. Psychosomatic effects of specific types of training. Paper read at conference on experimental approaches to the study of emotional behaviour, New York Acad. Sciences, 1967.

Miller, N. E., and Bannazizi, A. Instrumental learning by curarized rats of a specific visceral response, intestinal or cardiac. *J. Comp. Physiol. Psychol.*, 1968, **65**, 1–7.

Miller, N. E., and Carmona, A. Modification of a visceral response, salivation in thirty dogs, by instrumental training with water reward. *J. Comp. Physiol. Psychol.*, 1967, **63**, 1–6.

Miller, N. E., and Di Cara, L. V. Instrumental learning of heart-rate changes in curarized rats: Shaping and specificity to discriminative stimulus. *J. Comp. Physiol. Psychol.*, 1967, **63**, 12–19.

Miller, N. E., and Dollard, J. Social learning and imitation. New Haven: Yale University Press, 1941.

Moore, N. Behaviour therapy in bronchial asthma: A controlled study. *J. Psychosom. Res.*, 1965, **9**, 257–276.

Morgenstern, F., Pearce, J., and Davies, B. The application of aversion therapy to transvestism. Paper read at the Reading Conference of Brit. Psychol. Soc., 1963.

Mowrer, O. H. Preparatory set (expectancy)—a determinant in motivation and learning. *Psychol. Rev.*, 1938, **45**, 62–91.

Mowrer, O. H. Apparatus for the study and treatment of enuresis. *Amer. J. Psychol.*, 1938, **51**, 163–166.

Mowrer, O. H. *Learning theory and personality dynamics*. New York: Ronald Press, 1950.

Mowrer, O. H. Learning theory and behaviour therapy. In Wolman, B. B. (Ed.), *Handbook of clinical psychology*. New York: McGraw Hill, 1965.

Napalkov, A. V. Information process of the brain. In N. Wiener and J. C. Schadé (Eds.), *Progress in brain research*. Vol. 2. *Nerve, brain and memory models*. 1963. Pp. 59–69.

Oler, I. D., and Baum, M. Facilitated extinction of an avoidance response through shortening of the inter-trial interval. *Psychonom. Sci.*, 1968, **11**, 323–324.

Page, H. A. The facilitation of experimental extinction by response prevention as a function of the acquisition of a new response. *J. Comp. Physiol. Psychol.*, 1955, **48**, 14–16.

Paul, G. L. *Insight vs. desensitization in psychotherapy: An experimental in anxiety reduction*. Stanford: Stanford University Press, 1966.

Paul, G. L. Two-year follow-up of systematic desensitization in therapy groups. *J. Abnorm. Psychol.*, 1968, **73**, 119–130.

Paul, G. L., and Shannon, D. T. Treatment of anxiety through systematic desensitization in therapy groups. *J. Abnorm. Psychol.*, 1966, **71**, 124–135.

Pavlov, I. P. *Conditioned reflexes*. Oxford: Oxford University Press, 1927.

Rachman, S. Sexual disorders and behaviour therapy. *Amer. J. Psychiat.*, 1961, **118**, 235–240.

Rachman, S. Pain-elicited aggression and behaviour therapy. *Psychol. Record.*, 1965, **15**, 465–467. (a)

Rachman, S. Aversion therapy: Chemical or electrical? *Beh. Res. Ther.*, 1965, **2**, 289–300. (b)

Rachman, S. Studies in desensitization. I. The separate effects of relaxation and desensitization. *Beh. Res. Ther.*, 1965, **3**, 245–252. (c)

Rachman, S. Sexual fetishism: An experimental analogue. *Psychol. Record.*, 1966, **16**, 293–296. (a)

Rachman, S. Studies in desensitization. III. Speed of generalization. *Beh. Res. Ther.*, 1966, **4**, 7–15. (b)

Rachman, S. Systematic desensitization. *Psychol. Bull.*, 1967, **67**, 93–100. (a)

Rachman, S. The role of muscular relaxation in desensitization therapy. *Beh. Res. Ther.*, 1967, **5**, 1–8. (b)

Rachman, S. Aversion therapy. In C. Franks (Ed.), *Behavioural therapies*. New York: Wiley, 1968.

Rachman, S., and Eysenck, H. J. Reply to a "critique and reformulation" of behaviour therapy. *Psychol. Bull.*, 1966, **65**, 165–169.

Rachman, S., and Hodgson, R. J. Experimentally induced "sexual fetishism": Replication and development. *Psychol. Record.*, 1968, **18**, 25–27.

Rachman, S., and Teasdale, J. D. *Aversion therapy*. London: Routledge & Kegan Paul, 1969.

Ramsay, R., Barends, J., Breuker, J., and Kruseman, A. Massed versus spaced desensitization of fear. *Beh. Res. Ther.*, 1966, **4**, 205–207.

Raymond, M. Case of fetishism treated by aversion therapy. *Brit. Med. J.*, 1956, **2**, 854–857.

Raymond, J. J. The treatment of addiction by aversion conditioning with apomorphine. *Beh. Res. Ther.*, 1964, **1**, 287–291.

Razran, G. The observable unconscious and the inferable conscious in current Soviet psychophysiology. *Psychol. Rev.*, 1961, **68**, 81–147.

Rimm, D. C., and Bottrell, J. Four measures of visual imagination. *Beh. Res. & Ther.*, 1969, **7**, 63–69.

Ritter, B. The group desensitization of children's snake phobias using vicarious and contact desensitization procedures. *Beh. Res. Ther.*, 1968, **6**, 1–6.

Rosenbaum, G. Stimulus generalisation as a function of level of experimentally induced anxiety. *J. Exper. Psychol.*, 1953, **45**, 35–43.

Rosenbaum, G. Stimulus generalisation and a function of clinical anxiety. *J. Abnorm. Soc. Psychol.*, 1956, **53**, 281–285.

Sanderson, R., Campbell, D., and Laverty, S. An investigation of a new aversive conditioning technique for alcoholism. In C. M. Franks (Ed.), *Conditioning techniques in clinical practice and research*. New York: Springer, 1964.

Sandler, J. Masochism: An empirical analysis. *Psychol. Bull.*, 1964, **62**, 197–204.

Savage, R. D., and Eysenck, H. J. The definition and measurement of emotionality. In H. J. Eysenck (Ed.), *Experiments in motivation*. New York: Pergamon Press, 1964. Pp. 292–314.

Silverman, R. G. Elimination of a conditioned GSR by reduction of experimental anxiety. *J. Exp. Psychol.*, 1960, **59**, 122–125.

Skinner, B. F. *Walden two*. New York: Macmillan, 1948.

Skinner, B. F. *Science and human behaviour*. New York: Macmillan, 1953.

Skinner, B. F. Studies in behaviour therapy, Metropolitan State Hospital, Mass. Status Report I: Preliminary report on the study of psychotic behaviour. Office of Naval Research, U.S. Navy, 1953.

Smart, R. G. Conflict and conditioned aversive stimuli in the development of experimental neuroses. *Canad. J. Psychol.*, 1965, **19**, 208–223.

Solomon, R. L. Punishment. *Amer. Psychologist*, 1964, **19**, 239–253.

Solomon, R. L., Kamin, L. J., and Wynne, L. C. Traumatic avoidance learning: The outcomes of several extinction procedures with dogs. *J. Abnorm. Soc. Psychol.*, 1953, **48**, 291–302.

Solomon, R. L., and Wynne, L. C. Traumatic avoidance learning. *Psychol. Monogr.*, 1953, **67**, 4.

Solomon, R. L., and Wynne, L. C. Traumatic avoidance learning: The principles of anxiety conservation and partial irreversibility. *Psychol. Rev.*, 1954, **61**, 353–385.

Spence, K. W. *Behaviour therapy and conditioning*. New Haven: Yale University Press, 1956.

Spence, K. W. Anxiety (drive) level and performance in eyelid conditioning. *Psychol. Bull.*, 1964, **61**, 129–139.

Spence, K. W., and Goldstein, H. Eyelid conditioning performance as a function of emotion-producing instructions. *J. Exp. Psychol.*, 1961, **62**, 291–294.

Staats, A. W. *Learning, language and cognition*. New York: Holt, Rinehart and Winston, 1968.

Stampfl, T. G., and Levis, D. J. Essentials of implosive therapy: A learning-theory-based psychodynamic behavioural therapy. *J. Abnorm. Soc. Psychol.*, 1967, **72**, 496–503.

Stone, G. R. The effect of negative incentives in serial learning. VII. Theory of punishment. *J. Gen. Psychol.*, 1953, **48**, 133–161.

Storms, L. H., Boroczi, G., and Broen, W. E. Punishment inhibits an instrumental response in hooded rats. *Science*, 1962, **135**, 1133–1134.

Stuart, R. B. Behavioural control of overeating. *Beh. Res. Ther.*, 1967, **5**, 357–365.

Tarpy, R. M. Incubation of anxiety as measured by response suppression. *Psychonomic Sci.*, 1966, **4**, 189–190.

Thomson, I. G., and Rathod, N. H. Aversion therapy for heroin dependence. *Lancet*, Aug. 17, 1968, 382–384.

Thorndike, E. L. The fundamentals of learning. New York: Columbia Univ. Press, 1932.

Thorpe, J., Schmidt, E., and Castell, D. A comparison of positive and negative (aversive) conditioning in the treatment of homosexuality. *Beh. Res. Ther.*, 1964, **1**, 357–362.

Trowill, J. A. Instrumental conditioning of the heart rate in the curarized rat. *J. Comp. Physiol. Psychol.*, 1967, **63**, 7–11.

Truax, C. B., and Carkhuff, R. R. Toward effective counseling and psychotherapy. Chicago: Aldine, 1967.

Voegtlin, W., and Lemere, F. The treatment of alcohol addiction. *Quart. J. Stud. Alochol*, 1942, **2**, 717–803.

Vogel-Sprott, M., and Burrows, V. Response suppression in humans as a function of contingent and non-contingent punishment: Signal properties of stimuli. *Canad. J. Psychol.*, 1969, **23**, 66–74.

Wagner, M. K., and Cauthen, N. R. A comparison of reciprocal inhibition and operant conditioning in the systematic desensitization of a fear of snakes. *Beh. Res. Ther.*, 1968, **6**, 225–227.

Wallace, H. E. R., and Whyte, M. B. N. Natural history of the psychoneuroses. *Brit. Med. J.*, 1959, **1**, 144–148.

Wallerstein, R. S. et al. Hospital treatment of alcoholism. *Menninger Monograph Series No. 11.* London: Imago Press, 1957.

Warden, C. J., and Diamond, S. A. A preliminary study of the effect of delayed punishment on learning in the white rat. *J. Genet. Psychol.*, 1931, **39**, 455–462.

Watson, J. B., and Rayner, R. Conditioned emotional reactions. *J. exper. Psychol.*, 1920, **3**, 1–14.

Weitzman, B. Behaviour therapy and psychotherapy. *Psychol. Rev.*, 1967, **74**, 300–317.

Graham White, J., Caldbeck Meenan, J., and McAllister, N. The desensitization of phobic anxiety and its physiological concomitants. *Papers in Psychology, Queens Univ. Belfast*, 1968, **2**, 1–7.

Wilson, G. D. GSR response to fear-related stimuli. *Percept. & Motor Skills*, 1967, **24**, 401–402.

Wilson, G. D. Reversal of differential GSR conditioning by instructions. *J. Exper. Psychol.*, 1968, **76**, 491–493.

Wilson, G. I., Hannon, A. E., and Evans, W. I. M. Behaviour therapy and the therapist–patient relationship. *J. Consult. Clin. Psychol.*, 1968, **32**, 103–109.

Wolpe, J. *Psychotherapy by reciprocal inhibition.* Stanford: Stanford Univ. Press, 1958.

Wolpe, J. Behaviour therapy in complex neurotic states. *Brit. J. Psychiat.*, 1964, **110**, 28–34.

Wolpe, J. Conditioned inhibition of craving in drug addiction: A pilot experiment. *Beh. Res. Ther.*, 1965, **2**, 285–287.

Wolpin, M., and Raines, J. Visual imagery, expected roles and extinction. *Beh. Res. Ther.*, 1966, **4**, 25–38.

Yates, A. J. The application of learning theory to the treatment of tics. *J. Abnorm. Soc. Psychol.*, 1958, **56**, 175–182.

York, C. *If hopes were dupes.* London: Hutchinson, 1966.

Yorkston, N. J., Sergeant, H. G. S., and Rachman, S. Methohexitone relaxation for desensitizing agoraphobic patients. *Lancet*, Sept. 21, 1968, 651–653.

16

THE OPERANT APPROACH IN BEHAVIOR THERAPY[1]

LEONARD KRASNER

STATE UNIVERSITY OF NEW YORK AT STONY BROOK

THE OPERANT APPROACH

This chapter will present an overview and evaluation of an approach to the modification of human behavior to which the label of operant conditioning is now usually attached.

In each of the sections of the chapter, selective studies will be described. There will be no attempt to be exhaustive, since this is a field of research that has grown in recent years to the point where published reports of operant applications to "clinical" problems now run well over a thousand, and these are supplemented by a considerable additional number of as yet unpublished reports. This chapter will focus on those studies involving applications of operant procedures to specific behavior problems of adults and children as studied in the laboratory, clinic, hospital, and home. It will also discuss research procedures used in these studies and offer some speculation as to eventual implications of these studies for treatment procedures and for society. It is of course necessary to start with a definition of operant methods that will clearly differentiate them from other procedures described elsewhere in this book. This is not as easy as it should be despite the apparently clear-cut operational definition usually associated with operant conditioning.

Before going into detail as to operant methodology, it is necessary to differentiate two major intertwined approaches to human behavior. Skinner (1938) distinguished between two kinds of behavior, respondent and operant. Respondent behavior is learned by Pavlovian or classical conditioning, which means that a

[1] The preparation of this chapter was supported in part by United States Public Health Service Grant No. MH-11938.

stimulus elicits and precedes the response. Watson and Raynor (1920) offer the classic example of respondent conditioning in humans. A loud noise had elicited a fear reaction from a young boy, Albert. Observation indicated that a white rat did not elicit such a reaction. The investigators presented a white rat in front of Albert, immediately followed by a loud noise (the unconditioned stimulus). After repeating this several times, the rat, previously a neutral stimulus by itself, now elicited a fear response from Albert and hence became a conditioned stimulus. In contrast, in operant conditioning the sequence of stimulus and response is reversed. The individual first emits a response to a situation and then an environmental event occurs *subsequent* to the response. Operant behavior implies an active individual operating on his environment, and behavior that is determined by its consequence. It should be made clear that these two kinds of behavior are interrelated in that operant and respondent conditioning complement each other. For purposes of this chapter, the concentration will be on the methodology and applications that have derived from operant conditioning. Research in clinical applications of Pavlovian conditioning is covered elsewhere in this book.

There are now available a considerable number of reviews of the general field of operant methodology, approach, and theory (Catania, 1968; Ferster and Skinner, 1957; Honig, 1966; Keller and Schoenfeld, 1950; Reese, 1966; Reynolds, 1968; Skinner, 1938, 1953, 1957; Staats, 1964; Verhave, 1966). This approach has developed a highly technical set of terms and concepts that we will not try to duplicate here, since they are already well covered elsewhere. However, when these terms (such as shaping) occur in the descriptions of applied operant work we will define them.

Reynolds (1968) offers a useful introduction to the operant methodology approach:

Operant conditioning is an experimental science of behavior. Strictly speaking, the term operant conditioning refers to a process in which the frequency of occurrence of a bit of behavior is modified by the consequences of the behavior. Over the years, however, operant conditioning has come to refer to an entire approach to psychological science. This approach is characterized in general by a deterministic and experimental analysis of behavior. It is also charcterized by a concentration on the study of operant or instrumental behavior, although not to the exclusion of the study of instinctive and reflexive behavior.

As an approach to the study of behavior, operant conditioning consists of a series of assumptions about behavior and its environment; a set of definitions which can be used in the objective, scientific description of behavior and its environment, a group of techniques and procedures for the experimental study of behavior in the laboratory; and a large body of facts and principles which have been demonstrated by experiment.

Operant conditioning is concerned with the relationship between the behavior of organisms and their environment. Research in operant conditioning gathers knowledge about behavior from the experimental study of the effects on behavior of systematic changes in the surrounding environment. Operant conditioning attempts to understand behavior by gaining knowledge of the factors that modify behavior. As an objective science, it is restricted to the study of factors that can be observed, measured and reproduced. The psychologists who use this approach differ greatly in their degree of commitment to the principles of operant conditioning. At one extreme of commitment are those who accept only the experimental techniques because they are convenient methods for studying behavior. At the other extreme are those who accept, at present partly on faith, the beliefs and findings of operant conditioning as being truly descriptive of behavior and as guides to the conduct of their personal lives. (Reynolds,) 1968, pp.. 1–2).

This statement nicely summarizes the main features of operant methodology: the intensive study of individual subjects, the control of the experimental environment, the control of individual behavior, the emphasis on objective observation and recording of behavior, the importance of consequences of behavior, the empirical nature of the approach, and the intense involvement of most of its proponents.

Facets of these main characteristics of the operant approach will be manifested in the area of direct relevance to this chapter, that in which the operant methods focus on the modification of human behavior. For example, to refer to the fact that a bit of behavior is modified by the consequences of that behavior means, in practical terms, that this involves the systematic manipulation of rewards and punishments. An organism performs an act which is followed by an environmental event. If the individual is likely to repeat the act, then we may label the environmental event a reinforcing stimulus. If the bar-pressing of the rat is followed by a food pellet; if the verbalization of an emotional word is followed by an experimenter saying "good"; if shaving yourself is followed by a token; if the reporting of having looked up information on a particular vocation in the library is followed by a counselor's nod of approval; if fluent speech for thirty seconds in a stutterer is followed by a ticking of a clock indicating that he has earned 10¢; if sitting in a seat in a classroom for five minutes is followed by a piece of candy; then these behaviors are *likely* to be repeated. In that event, these environmental consequences can be called reinforcers.

Before these operant approaches are presented, they should be placed within a conceptual framework of how deviant human behavior is approached. In recent years there has emerged a variety of terms (such as behavior therapy and behavior modification) with a variety of meanings, not all of which are consistent with each other. A series of recent books has specifically reviewed the application of operant approaches to changing deviant human behavior. (Ferster and Perrot, 1968; Franks, 1965; Krasner and Ullmann, 1965; Ullmann and Krasner, 1965, 1969; Ulrich, Stachnick, and Mabry, 1966). The relationship between operant procedures and treatment procedures must be clarified. Operant conditioning as herein defined is one type of procedure used in the broader category of behavior therapy. We have elsewhere (Krasner, 1962; Krasner and Ullmann, 1965; Ullmann and Krasner, 1965, 1969) attempted to define a series of concepts that are basic and necessary in this field. These include behavior influence, behavior modification, and behavior therapy. *Behavior influence* situations are those in which one human being exerts some degree of control over another. This would include formal school education, studies of opinion change, and techniques of learning. The focus is upon the process and *not* upon evaluating the social desirability of the behavior being changed. *Behavior modification*, on the other hand, involves the changing of behavior that has been labeled socially deviant. The term may

be applied to different techniques used with a broad spectrum of educational and behavioral problems. These include such techniques as modeling, operant conditioning, reciprocal inhibition, hypnosis, and psychoanalysis.

There are two conceptually different approaches within behavior modification. *Behavior therapy* derives from a model that aims to alter a person's behavior *directly* through the application of general psychological principles. In contrast, *evocative psychotherapy* is treatment deducible from a medical, psychoanalytic, or psychodynamic model that aims to alter a person's behavior *indirectly* by first changing intrapsychic organization. To summarize, both evocative psychotherapy and behavior therapy are forms of behavior modification, which in turn is one type of behavior influence. Thus, the operant studies being reviewed in this chapter would fall within the category of behavior therapy.

It follows from these two models that the treatment procedures subsumed under each will have very different objectives and techniques. Behavior therapy, as contrasted with evocative psychotherapy, usually involves direct treatment of the problem behaviors, the deliberate use of social influence, reliance upon laboratory findings from basic human and animal experiments, a focus on training relevant people in the social environment, an emphasis on and manipulation of present environmental events, and an active therapist. The research efforts that derive from these two models and approaches are consequently very different in design, purpose, and the relationship between the laboratory and "real life."

Within behavior therapy, it is becoming increasingly difficult to differentiate the various techniques into discrete categories. At one point it was relatively simple to describe behavior therapy research in terms of operant conditioning, systematic desensitization, modeling, or extinction. Early reviews of the techniques and research involved used variation of these terms. Bandura (1961) organized his review of behavior therapy around the topics of extinction, discrimination learning, reward, punishment, and social imitation. Grossberg (1964) organized his review around the topics of aversion, negative practice, positive conditioning, reinforcement withdrawal, and desensitization. Kalish (1965) reduced the techniques to extinction and conditioning.

Only a relatively few years ago a chapter surveying research in the area of operant conditioning as applied to behavior modification would have been relatively simple. There were only a few studies, such as those of Lindsley and Skinner (1954), which clearly belonged in this area. Their research involved application of procedures developed in the psychology laboratory to human beings in a mental hospital. In a crude sense, it could be said that early results of operant work with adults demonstrated that when a psychotic patient was put in a large Skinner box, his performance was as lawful as that of a pigeon or a rat.

Currently it is impossible to limit the boundaries of the application of operant conditioning research to behavior problems, to the laboratory, or even to the clinic. It has been extended to the state hospital, mental retardation centers, the schoolroom, the home, and the community. Special areas such as the classroom and the home are covered elsewhere in this book, and these applications will only be mentioned in passing in this chapter.

THE OPERANT PARADIGM

At this point ground rules must be set as to what type of operant study should be included and what should be excluded in this review. In a simple sense, the operant paradigm may be expressed with the statement that behavior is determined by its consequences. If this is so, then any study that is designed to affect behavior by controlling and manipulating its consequences should belong within this category. The studies to be described in this paper, then, have two types of characteristics. First, there are the studies that concern the manipulation of consequences of behavior or reinforcement, so as to influence subsequent behavior of a human being. Second, there are studies in which the behavior to be influenced is such that it has been labeled undesirable or maladaptive by a person in a power position (that is, controls the source of reinforcement) vis-à-vis the individual. This includes studies done in a laboratory context,

since even in this situation, artificial as it may be, the decision has been made by the person in power, in this instance the experimenter, that a certain behavior should be changed, even though the focus is on the process of change itself.

An important point must be emphasized here. The studies under review, labeled as operant conditioning, verbal conditioning, token economy, and the others, were undertaken within a reinforcement framework. We will not deal with the question that many investigators in this field have raised, as to whether there are operant components to other behavior therapy procedures such as modeling or relaxation, although a good case could be made for the view that reinforcement in the form of examiner approval is implicit, for example, in the shaping of systematic desensitization. It would only represent operant jingoism, however, to claim "credit" for all behavioral successes. Nor is it a function of this chapter to do so. This point will be repeated later on in describing verbal conditioning techniques that can explain some of the verbal behavior shaping that occurs in evocative psychotherapy, but that clearly do *not* account for all behavior change that may take place. Conversely, a major emphasis in this chapter will be to point out that operant procedures when used as behavior therapy are frequently not "pure" in the sense that they make use *only* of reinforcement. In fact, it will be contended that the operant approach with human beings makes use of many of the techniques included in the broader rubric of behavior influence (such as, modeling, experimenter bias, and demand characteristics).

CONCEPTUALIZATION OF ABNORMAL BEHAVIOR

A definition of abnormal behavior that could serve as the framework into which an operant conditioning approach can be fitted should be presented. This approach must be clearly differentiated from the procedures that derive from a disease or psychopathology model. If you view the locus of a disorder as a basic malfunctioning within the organism, then evocative psychotherapy, which attempts to extirpate the pathology, makes sense. If, however, the locus of malfunctioning is external, then behavior therapy is the treatment of choice. The specific procedures the therapist is likely to use follows from the theoretical model of "abnormality" that he holds.

Ullmann and Krasner (1969) present a conceptualization of abnormal behavior that is compatible with and necessary for operant conditioning procedures. The following passage describes their viewpoint.

Behavior which is called abnormal must be studied as the interaction of three variables: the behavior itself, its social context, and an observer who is in a position of power. No specific behavior is abnormal in itself. Rather, an individual may do something (e.g. verbalize hallucinations, hit a person, collect rolls of toilet paper, refuse to eat, stutter, stare into space, or dress sloppily) under a set of circumstances (e.g. during a school class, while working at his desk, during a church service) which upsets, annoys, angers, or strongly disturbs somebody (e.g. employer, teacher, parent, or the individual himself) sufficiently that some action results (e.g. a policeman is called, seeing a psychiatrist is recommended, commitment proceedings are started) so that the society's professional labelers (e.g. physicians, psychiatrists, psychologists, judges, social workers) come into contact with the individual and determine which of the current sets of labels (e.g. schizophrenic reaction, sociopathic personality, anxiety reaction) is most appropriate. Finally, there follow attempts to change the emission of the offending behavior (e.g. institutionalization, psychotherapy, medication). The label applied is the result of the training of the labeler and reflects the society which he represents. The labeling itself leads others to react to the individual in terms of the stereotypes of that label (e.g., "Be careful, he's a dangerous schizophrenic"; "Poor girl, she's hysterical") (p. 21).

It is important to emphasize that operant procedures are usually applied within a framework that conceptualizes the behavior to be changed as deviant, not as psychopathological in the traditional disease sense. The implications of the latter view (the disease model) is that behavior cannot change basically unless underlying causes are eliminated, because other undesirable behavior will replace it (symptom substitution). It should be noted that a number of very diverse views are being lumped together under the "disease" model, including medical concepts of organic or biochemical origins of behavior and psychoanalytic concepts of "dynamic" origins of behavior. For purposes of the discussion in this chapter, they are being subsumed under the "disease" model because of their similarity in focusing treatment (drugs or "insight") on "underlying" internal variables that may indirectly affect behavior rather than focusing directly on behavior itself.

The implication of the alternative view expressed above (social labeling) is that deviant behavior is a *learned social phenomenon*, and hence changed behavior will represent "real" changes in the individual. Every behavioral change has social consequences that change the individual's environment by eliciting new responses from others and from the individual himself. Further, the behavior itself becomes the direct focus of the treatment process.

EARLY HISTORY OF OPERANT APPROACH

Fuller (1949) was probably the first investigator to present a report of the deliberate application of Skinnerian operant conditioning in a clinical setting. He worked with an 18-year-old "vegetative idiot," and was able to "shape" the movement of his right arm by successive approximations, using a syringe filled with a warm sugar-milk solution. Fuller's success had many of the characteristics of later operant studies, including the fact that the physicians in the institution thought it would be impossible for the boy to learn anything. However, Fuller demonstrated that in four sessions an appreciable addition had been added to the idiot's behavior repertoire.

A major step forward in the application of operant procedures was taken by Lindsley and Skinner in their studies at Metropolitan State Hospital. In fact, in one of their reports (Lindsley and Skinner, 1953), they use the term "behavior therapy" in the title of their report. Wolpe (1968) suggests that this was the first use of the term in the modern literature. However, their use of the term to describe operant conditioning procedures seems clearly differentiated from the later classical conditioning usage attributed to it (Eysenck, 1959).

In the Lindsley and Skinner study, fourteen male psychotic patients averaging 38 years of age and seventeen years of hospitalization were placed in a small experimental room that minimized extraneous variables. The response measured by the investigators was that of lever pulling on an apparatus comparable to a cigarette vending machine. Candy, cigarettes, and projected colored pictures were used as reinforcing stimuli (rewards). The patients were not reinforced for every response; instead, two schedules of intermittent reinforcement were used: a one-minute, "*variable-interval*" schedule (reinforcement occurred on the average of one every minute) and a "*fixed-ratio*" schedule (every twentieth response was reinforced). Responses were recorded on counters and cumulative response recorders. Sixteen hundred hours of psychotic behavior were recorded, an average of about 110 hours per patient.

The investigators found that the patients worked on the one minute variable-interval schedule at stable rates, ranging from 5,000 to 9,000 responses per individual per hour. There were considerable individual differences in performance. On the fixed-ratio schedule, clear-cut breaks in response rates followed each reinforcement. The authors found these pauses to be characteristic of the performance of lower organisms on this schedule under conditions of low motivation. The authors concluded that the behavior of the psychotic patient can be successfully investigated with operant conditioning techniques. The behavior generated was stable and predictable, and thus could provide a uniform baseline for investigating therapeutic, pharmacological, and physiological variables.

These reports of the performance of specific individuals foreshadowed much of the later operant work. The first formal reports of these early studies at Metropolitan State Hospital appear in papers by Lindsley and Skinner (1954) and Lindsley (1956, 1960). In his 1956 paper, Lindsley presents four general assumptions useful in analyzing behavior of psychotic patients. These are (a) the need to increase the precision of the measurement of behavior itself before determining the conditions under which behavior occurs; (b) the seeking of physical events in the patient's environment controlling his behavior; (c) the application of the experimental

method in its most rigorous and objective manner; and (d) the use of a behavioristic description of the patient.

Based on these assumptions, Lindsley offers five methodological advantages of the operant method. These are (a) high experimental control; (b) automatic recording and scheduling, which should eliminate experimenter bias; (c) high generality involving many situations, subjects, and species; (d) the free operant nature of the method based on the individual's "natural" performance, thus increasing sensitivity to individual behavior; and (e) the lack of instructions permitting the study of nonverbal behavior and of individuals who do not communicate. These assumptions and description of the methodology are still applicable to later studies.

It is of interest to note that even in these early studies, operant procedures were used in combination with other behavior influence methods, such as modeling. Lindsley describes what happens when the subject did not respond to the candy machine in front of which he had been placed. If the patient had not made a response within 15 minutes, the experimenter entered the room, pulled the knob, and ingested a reinforcement with obvious relish. He then left, saying nothing. If no response was made for 15 minutes after this demonstration, the experimenter again entered, placed the patient's hand on the knob, and helped him pull it. Then reinforcement was given to the patient.

Lindsley (1960) reported additional data on individual performance on tasks similar to that reported in the earlier paper. The emphasis in this paper again is on the observation of the behavior of the patients. "To a behaviorist, a psychotic is a person in a mental hospital. If psychosis is what makes, or has made, this person psychotic, then psychosis is the behavioral deviation that caused this person to be hospitalized or that is keeping him hospitalized. Looked at from this point of view, very few psychotics are at this moment behaving psychotically. Neither is there any assurance that they will behave psychotically when we wish to evaluate or to sample their behavior in a brief test conducted at irregular intervals. In fact, psychosis defined in terms of the behavior that hospitalizes a person is most often highly infrequent. Most patients are hospitalized because the time of occurrence of their infrequent psychotic episodes cannot be predicted." (Lindsley, 1960, p. 66). From this view it then follows that the emphasis is upon measuring behavior "long enough to capture a psychotic episode in one of our experimental observation sessions." The most striking characteristic of the free operant behavior of chronic psychotics is the extreme degree of "behavioral debilitation" found in most patients. In this respect Lindsley's analysis of psychotic behavior is similar to Schaefer and Martin's description of apathy, to be described later in the chapter. It was a *slow rate of response* that characterized the behavior of hospitalized patients. This was clearly evidenced by contrasting the cumulative response records of the hospitalized patients with that of normal adults on one-minute variable-interval schedules of intermittent reinforcement.

Lindsley used a variety of reinforcers in order to rule out the possibility of inappropriate reinforcement. Reinforcers included money, food, candy, cigarettes, male and female nude pictures, bursts of music, tokens, escape from loud noise, and escape from a dark room. "Although significant differences in rate of response for these different reinforcers were found in most of the patients, no patient was restored to a normal rate of responding by any of these reinforcers."

The impact of the early Lindsley and Skinner studies was primarily to demonstrate the feasibility of operant conditioning procedures with psychotic patients. In this sense, these studies were eventually to culminate in the token economy programs that broaden the base of both the behaviors to be reinforced and the variety of reinforcers available.

The early studies of Peters and Jenkins (1954) and King, Armitage, and Tilton (1960) are worthy of mention as preludes to later operant conditioning studies, although they were not specifically performed within the operant framework. However, their procedures were similar, in general principles, to the Lindsley and Skinner studies. In one instance, Peters and Jenkins introduced the unique notion of exposing the patients to deliberate deprivation (of sugar) to enhance the likelihood of responsivity to the reinforcement used (fudge candy).

These early studies served as the basis of the extension of the operant approach from the mental hospital where it first came to fruition to every other kind of social institution working with deviant behavior. Before picking up the threads of these developments, we will briefly mention two aspects of the operant approach, assessment and design.

ASSESSMENT PROCEDURES IN OPERANT APPROACH

Although the focus of this book is on modification procedures, the operant procedure calls for a very close liaison between assessment and modification; in fact, the two are inseparable. The operant assessment procedures are reviewed elsewhere (Weiss, 1968; Mischel, 1968). However, brief note of them should occur at this point to emphasize their importance.

The area of assessment is as complex as any other involving operant procedures. One group of investigators argues that the operant approach opens the way to use behavioral principles in *classification of deviant behaviors* (Sidman, 1962; Ferster, 1965; Kanfer and Saslow, 1965). A second linkage with assessment procedures is the utilisation of the responsiveness to social reinforcement, as in a verbal conditioning study as a means of *predicting responsiveness to* some other kind of behavior influence procedure (Krasner, 1965; Patterson, 1965). Another variation is the viewing of responsiveness to social reinforcement as *an indicator of a short-trial period* of responsiveness to operant treatment procedures. In any case, it is clear that there is a close interrelationship between assessment and modification. Whatever assessment procedures are developed must be related to the actual operations in the treatment procedure.

THE RESEARCH DESIGN IN OPERANT STUDIES

The variables involved in operant research are the same as those in any other types of behavior modification research (Krasner, 1962; Kiesler, 1966; Paul, 1969). Sometimes this point is lost sight of because of the belief that operant conditioning investigations impose a different set of standards. These variables may be subsumed under the categories of influencer, influencee, situation, and the interaction among the three. Even a uniquely operant characteristic such as the schedule of reinforcement may be included within the influencer variable, since it is the influencer who determines what schedule will be used at any given point in the study.

The therapist, or influencer, must be viewed as a social reinforcer to and educator or trainer of other people. Thus, anything that enhances his role is of importance, including "personality characteristics." Clear, specifiable variables that may affect the therapist's behavior include years of experience, prestige among peers, socioeconomic background, degree of self-confidence, value system, theoretical orientation, "expectancy" of success, and techniques used. The verbal operant conditioning studies to be described later in this chapter have investigated each of these variables. Comparable sets of variables can be attributed to the clients or influencees.

It is undesirable to divorce the concept of "reinforcement," so characteristic of operant technique, from the concept of "reinforcer." This means that it is necessary to include within the design of an operant study control of the characteristics of the dispenser of reinforcement. The "power" of reinforcement with human beings lies not in a token or food or a "very good" per se, but in these items *plus* the "giver" of the "good things," The operant studies have generally not given sufficient cognizance to this important element in the behavior influence process.

Since reinforcers are so crucial in the operant approach, what comprises a reinforcer and how does the investigator determine which of the multitude of possible stimuli may serve as a reinforcer? In some instances there is an attempt to determine the likelihood of an object's serving as a reinforcer before the study. Staats et al. (1964) had their children preselect toys that were then used as reinforcers. Barrett (1962) asked her patient in advance what music he liked. Hutchinson and Azrin (1961) ascertained that their subjects were heavy smokers

before using cigarettes as reinforcers. Cautela and Kastenbaum (1967) have developed a checklist of reinforcers which subjects fill out before starting to work.

It is important to note that a reinforcer is not a reinforcer forever. What may serve as a reinforcer in increasing behavior for one individual may serve to decrease the behavior of another person. There are strong reinforcers and there are weak reinforcers. Ayllon and Azrin (1968a) report on a technique of "reinforcer sampling" that can be used in situations in which the reinforcers are available, but have been rarely used by individuals.

There is clearly a very pragmatic approach to reinforcers; they can be anything that *works* to affect output of behavior. However, what will serve as a reinforcer for any given individual must be determined by observation and assessment of the individual's behavior in a natural setting.

Research in the general area of psychotherapy has alternated in a fadistic way between emphasis on outcome and on process. Outcome studies have generally been so difficult to do and so discouraging in results that they were almost wholly abandoned in the 1950s for the easier to do, but less meaningful, process studies. The current behavior therapy situation has been summarized by Paul (1969) as follows:

Historically, behavior modification research has been dichotomized into "process" and "outcome" investigations, depending upon whether questions were asked about the "ultimate" change in client's behavior after treatment termination (outcome), or about the way in which intratreatment phenomena transpired (process). On the other hand, "process" may refer to studies designed to answer questions related to determining *mechanisms* of change or testing competing explanatory hypotheses of *how* changes come about. While experimental operations and designs may focus on both sets of questions concurrently, it is possible and often desirable for behavior modification research to focus on outcome questions without including the necessary operations for identifying mechanisms of change.

It seems clear that if we had to dichotomize the operant studies described in this chapter as process or outcome, they would be primarily outcome studies. Yet, as Paul makes clear, this is no longer a meaningful distinction. The process is subsumed within the investigation of the outcome. This can be illustrated by the usual design of an operant study, frequently labeled as ABA (or ABAB).

The ABAB Design and its Variations

As an example of the ABAB design, Agras, Leitenberg, and Barlow (in press) report an investigation in which therapists' verbal behavior was varied so that the effect of selective positive contingent reinforcement (social praise) on agoraphobic behavior could be determined. They worked with three subjects who had been severely phobic for 1, 15, and 16 years, respectively. The authors isolated the behavior they wished to work with. They described it as the individual's difficulty in leaving a dependent situation. They designated *time* spent away from the clinic and *distance* walked from the clinic as the *target behavior* under measurement and treatment. A baseline period (the A of the ABA design) was set up in which the patient was asked to walk by himself as far as he could along a measured distance from the clinic. During the baseline period, "the therapist maintained a pleasant relationship with the patient but made no comment on the distance walked or time spent away. Reports of improvement made by the patient were also ignored." In the *reinforcement* phase (the B period), the first trial of every day, and all trials that met a slow, increasingly more difficult criterion of time spent away were reinforced by verbal phases such as "good", "you're doing well", and "excellent", given with appropriate enthusiasm. During the reinforcement phase, by verbal phases such as good, you're doing well, and excellent, given with appropriate enthusiasm." During the reinforcement phase, remarks made by the patient to the nursing staff about progress were also praised. The *nonreinforcement* period (the second A of the design) consisted of a return to baseline conditions, stopping selective praise but taking care to maintain a generally pleasant supportive attitude towards the patient. In this way a distinction between general support and selective social reinforcement could be made. A fourth phase would then constitute a return to the reinforcement period (B) to determine if the target behavior then returns to its previous strength.

Two variations of this design are the testing of an interaction between two variables (baseline, one experimental procedure introduced, and effects measured, then a second procedure introduced and the effects measured. This gives the effects of procedure A *plus* procedure B. Then procedure A can be withdrawn, procedure B withdrawn, and both can then be reintroduced); a comparison of a number of different procedures with the same subject (baseline, procedure A introduced, procedure A withdrawn, procedure B introduced, then withdrawn, etc.).

There are further possible variations of this design, depending upon the ingenuity of the experimenter. *In fact, it would seem that the clinical adaptation of this own-control design is a major contribution of the operant investigators to the current field of clinical psychology.* The interesting point here is that despite the animal origins of the early operant work and despite the rigid experimental genesis of operant conditioning, it has come full cycle to the basic tenets of the clinical approach, that of assessing change relative to the individual's own behavior. Changes in the individual client's behavior is the basic yardstick against which success in treatment procedures must be measured. The own control is not, however, the only design used, since the usual kinds of control groups are also used in some operant studies.

An important point to be made about the ABAB design is that it may raise some questions as to the relationship between scientific and therapeutic goals. That is, scientifically the design demonstrates that the behavior has been under the control of the original contingencies. But from a therapeutic viewpoint, to the extent that baseline level is returned to when the original conditions are restored, then no real change is effected by the treatment method. Further, is the therapist harming the individual by returning him to a situation that will elicit his previous undesirable behavior? There are several answers to these questions. First, the evidence of the operant studies thus far done within the ABAB concept indicate that the rate of responding during the second A period does not return to the level of the first A period. In fact, investigators have demonstrated that the ABAB design can be extended through an additional series of reversals, in which the desired behaviors occurring in the B periods decrease less and less as the contingencies are reversed, and as they are more and more being maintained by natural environmental reinforcement. An additional therapeutic goal can be achieved during the reversal procedure. This is a dramatic demonstration to the controller of the reinforcement, be it teacher, parent, nurse or peer, that he indeed is influencing the subject's behavior. This kind of feedback is in itself a reinforcer of eventual change of this key environmental figure.

Discussion and evaluation of the design of operant studies is implicit in the material to follow. At this point we return to a survey of operant studies as they have developed in various categories. First, we offer the operant studies as they can be conceptualized in one approach to changing deviant behavior.

OPERANT APPROACHES TO MODIFYING "DISEASE ENTITIES"

An important aspect of the operant approach as applied to modifying behavior is the reformulation of "disease entities" into component behaviors. The goal then becomes one of changing these behaviors by manipulating their consequences. Implicit in early operant studies of Lindsley and Skinner is a view of schizophrenia as a collection of undesirable behaviors. For example, Ullmann and Krasner (1969) point out that the key behavioral indicants for the *label* of schizophrenia are disorganization of thinking, apathy, social withdrawal, and verbalizations that are bizarre or aversive to listeners. Within this framework they cite a series of operant studies designed to change specific behaviors of schizophrenic patients in each of these categories. In effect, this is an approach to treating "schizophrenia" by changing its component behaviors. As such it is prototypical of the operant approach to any of the current mental diseases.

If we start with "disorganized thinking," subsumed under it would be tasks involving abstract thinking. An illustrative study is Meichenbaum's (1966a), in which he positively reinforced the abstract interpretation of proverbs in the first of four groups. A second group received noncontinegent positive reinforcement; they received social reinforcement regardless of the quality of their response. The third group received contingent negative reinforcement whenever a vague, false or absurd response was given (examples of negative reinforcement were "uh, uh"; "no"; and "poor.") In the control group the experimenter remained neutral throughout. The contingent positive group significantly increased the verbalization of abstract meanings as compared with the other three groups. Further, performance on a test of abstract thinking, the similarities test, significantly improved *only* in the contingent positive group.

Other studies using the verbal operant conditioning paradigm have directly manipulated measures of disorganized thinking in experimental situations. Ullmann, Krasner and Edinger (1964), working with schizophrenic patients whose total hospitalization averaged fifteen years, obtained significant changes in a *word association test* by verbal conditioning of common word associations. Panek (1967) also significantly influenced emission of common word associations by using tokens in a response contingent manner. In both of these studies the investigators viewed the behavior change in the ability to give common word associations as indicative of a change in the ability to do abstract thinking.

Wagner (1968) also worked within the same framework. He examined the effects of training schizophrenics to attend to stimuli and to respond correctly to abstract discriminative stimuli under conditions of contingent and noncontingent reinforcement. An elaborate training procedure using contingent reinforcement was devised to reinforce "abstract responses." By these contingent reinforcement procedures he was able to improve significantly the abstractibility of the schizophrenic patients. He concludes that his study demonstrated the modifiability of the schizophrenic's abstracting ability and carries "the implication that the extent to which corrective modification occurs is dependent upon the degree to which the training situation provides direct reinforcement for making abstracting responses."

A second set of schizophrenic behaviors that had been manipulated by operant conditioning procedures is that of *apathy*. It is generally agreed that schizophrenics are apathetic, but even that is too molar a concept to work with. How can apathy be broken into measurable and modifiable behaviors? It would be reasonable to include the inability to verbalize emotionally toned statements as one form of apathy. In a series of verbal operant conditioning studies (Weiss, Krasner, & Ullmann, 1963; Ullmann, Krasner, & Sherman, 1963), the number of *emotional* words used by schizophrenic patients was significantly increased by contingent social reinforcement. Salzinger and his co-workers (Salzinger & Pisoni, 1960; Salzinger, Portnoy, & Feldman, 1964) report similar results with conditioning positive self-reference statements.

One aspect of apathy, as above, involves verbal behavior. A second aspect deals with motor behavior. Schaefer and Martin (1966) analyzed the apathy of schizophrenic patients as a *lack* of the kind of behavior which will elicit reinforcement from others. They worked with forty schizophrenic patients whose medical records indicated apathy in the preobservation period. They concluded that the best measure of apathy was the *absence* of "concomitant" behavior—talking, singing, playing music, painting, reading, listening to others, listening to the radio, watching TV, and group activity. The target behavior for these patients was the enhancement of these concomitant behaviors. If these behaviors were changeable, "apathy" was modifiable. They used the token economy approach to be described in detail in a later section. The forty patients were divided into experimental and control groups of 20 each. Using token reinforcement with the experimental group, they were able to increase significantly the target concomitant behaviors. Here again the operant conditioning significantly changed a series of "schizophrenic" behaviors.

A third set of such behaviors can be labeled "*social withdrawal.*" One of the first studies applying operant procedures to schizophrenic behaviors (after the initial Lindsley-Skinner series) was that of King, Armitage, and Tilton (1960), who performed an early and by now classic study of modifying social withdrawal.

Their approach involved the "shaping" of patient behavior, starting with what behavior was available in the individual's repertoire and slowly moving it in the direction of more socially desirable behavior. King et al. worked with schizophrenic patients assigned to four experimental groups of twelve each. These were a recreation therapy group, a verbal therapy group, a no-treatment control group, and an operant-interpersonal (experimental) group. This was one of the first investigations to use control groups as bases of comparison for the effectiveness of operant procedures in a mental hospital. There were three phases in the operant-interpersonal approach. In the first, the therapist demonstrated the use of a machine with its lever which had to be pulled to obtain a reinforcement (similar to the machine used earlier by Lindsley and Skinner). The therapist modeled the procedure and then guided the participation of the patient to the point of putting a candy reinforcer in the patient's mouth, if necessary. In the second phase, the possible movements of the lever became more complex (for example, could be moved right and left, as well as toward and away). In the third phase, the therapist slowly introduced verbal behavior into the situation by giving directions toward the formulation of the problem. The therapist and patient began to work together as a team, first one doing something, then the other. Task-oriented verbal interactions were encouraged, such as "who does what next." Patients would also begin to work with each other. The therapist might even deliberately make a mistake so that the patient could point out the error. In effect, in the task-oriented situation, speech was highly relevant and reinforced. A basically simple situation became a complex, cooperative one. The investigators collected a series of measures of adjustment before and after therapy. All of the measures pointed to the operant-interpersonal technique as being more effective. The authors conclude:

The operant-interpersonal method was more effective than all the control methods in promoting clinical improvement, based on both ward observations and interview assessments. Comparisons on the following variables also yielded differences in favor of the operant-interpersonal method: level of verbalization, motivation to leave the ward, resistance to therapy, more interest in occupational therapy, decreased enuresis, and transfers to better wards. The patients undergoing verbal therapy became worse in some ways (e.g., verbal withdrawals) (p. 286).

The fourth area of deviant schizophrenic behavior is that of *bizarre verbalization*. Peculiar speech usually annoys other people who do not understand it and are often frightened by it. A variant of bizarre speech is no speech at all, which annoys and frightens others even more. Thus, the task of the therapist is to change the bizarreness of the individual's speech, to help him develop a verbal repertoire, or to modify the behavior of people who get upset by bizarre speech (including therapists).

Wilson and Walters (1966) used three groups of four subjects each who had a very low rate of speech. The task for all subjects was to tell what was happening on slides that depicted everyday scenes. During the first session, all subjects were treated alike. The experimenter remained silent save for standard prompts. During sessions two through seven, two groups of subjects were exposed to a verbalizing *model*, an experimenter who talked rapidly and continuously about each slide. One of these two groups was reinforced with pennies for the production of words, while the other was exposed to the model treatment only and did not receive the penny reinforcement. A third group received neither model nor response contingent reinforcement, but both this group and the model-only group received money at the end of each session, so that take-home pay was held constant. The eighth session was a nonreinforcement session similar to the first. During sessions 9 through 14, all groups received modeling plus reinforcement, and the final two sessions, number 15 and 16, were again nonreinforcement. The model-plus-reinforcement group experienced a significant increase in verbal productivity, while that of the model-only group approached but did not reach statistical significance. The actual production of words in the model-plus-reinforcement group quadrupled. To the extent that apathy involves a reduced output of words, this aspect of schizophrenia may be directly modified. The more effective combination of modeling plus reinforcement has been noted in other studies and will be emphasized in a later section on

token economy, where we will argue that most operant studies have implicit or explicit modeling components.

Another approach to the speech of the hospitalized schizophrenic patient deals with response-contingent reinforcement aimed towards developing a type of speech likely to lead to societal approval. Ullmann et al. (1965) performed an experiment in which each of five experimenters saw 12 patients, four each under three different conditions. The situation was a 20-minute semistructured clinical interview. After a base line period, during which the interviewer made no response save to ask questions, the experimental conditions were instituted. In one group, whenever the subject emitted "healthy talk", the examiner would smile, nod his head, and show approval. In the second group, the experimenter did the same thing whenever the patient emitted "sick talk." Healthy talk, in contrast to sick talk, was defined in terms of the verbalization of comfort rather than discomfort, liking or approach behavior as distinct from disliking and avoidance behavior, good physical and mental health as distinct from poor physical and mental health, personal assets rather than personal liabilities, presence rather than absence of motivation, realistic nonpathological statements as distinct from bizarre ideation, and optimism, well-being, self-esteem, contentment, enthusiasm, and favorable perceptions of others rather than negative self-references, discontent, upset, and anxiety. A third group served as a control. In order to approximate the number of experimenter-emitted reinforcing stimuli, without biasing the patient in either a sick-talk or healthy-talk direction, the experimenter emitted his approving behaviors whenever the patient used a plural noun. The results were that the group reinforced for healthy talk decreased in the percentage (sick talk divided by sick talk plus healthy talk) of sick talk, while the group reinforced for sick talk and the control group reinforced for plural nouns showed a tendency approaching statistical significance to increase the relative frequency with which they emitted sick talk. The differences among the groups were significant.

Two personality scales also had been administered before the induction of experimental conditions. One of these was significantly correlated with the percentage of sick talk emitted during the base line period, while one was not. There was a significant change when the tests were readministered after the interview period in the scale that had been correlated with the percentage of sick talk, while there was no significant postexperimental difference among the groups in the scale that had not been correlated with the target verbal class. In short, the relative rate of emission of aversive (grouch, gripe, and grotesque) talk could be directly manipulated, and an effect was obtained on an independent test measure.

Further work, with a more restricted definition of "sick talk" in the direction of bizarre verbalization, and with interviews on ten successive days, was carried out by Meichenbaum (1969). Meichenbaum worked with six experimental groups and two control groups. His goal was to investigate the relative effectiveness of prolonged training of schizophrenics with contingent social and token reinforcement on (a) the level of abstraction as measured on a proverbs task, and (b) the percentage of "sick talk" emitted in a structured interview. Prior to treatment, the schizophrenic subjects had been compared with nonpsychiatric hospitalized medical patients and were found to be significantly inferior on the proverbs test and had emitted five times more "sick talk" in a structured interview. The results indicated that the experimental treatments were effective in increasing abstraction to proverbs and in decreasing the percentage of "sick talk." The subjects who were trained with token reinforcement improved most. The effects of the experimental treatments generalized over time to a follow-up interview administered by the experimenter, to a posttest interview administreed by a patient confederate, and to other verbal tasks administered under neutral conditions.

Meichenbaum offers some acute observations about what took place during the operant training. He argues that the instructions given by the experimenter become discriminative stimuli for the subject and act as a general set for behavior emitted on other tasks. For example, patients who were trained only to emit "healthy talk" repeated aloud and spontaneously the experimental instruction "give healthy talk, be coherent and relevant" while being tested for proverb abstraction. This self-instruction aided the subject in his attending to the demands of the task, thus not permitting any internally generated stimuli to interfere with his language behavior. Meichenbaum points out that the operant conditioning makes the subject more attentive to the demands of the task by focusing the individual's attention on the feedback from the response he has just made and away from distracting stimuli. A key point in this study is the fact that whenever social or token reinforcement was given, the experimenter attempted to secure eye contact with the subject, "conveying to him the adequacy of his response." This is in contrast to the operant programs which may attempt to deliver a reinforcement completely mechanically. This point will again be emphasized in the review of the token programs.

This section has reviewed a series of operant conditioning studies that have illustrated an approach to a nosological category such as schizophrenia via a breakdown of the label and the component behaviors. It is important to note that although the individual specifiable behaviors were all clearly modifiable, this is not to imply that the individuals with the label were "cured." None of these studies had as a goal the improvement of individual behavior to the point of discharge from the hospital. At best, the studies illustrated the possible procedures and techniques that are used in the operant approach to modifying deviant behavior. The studies reviewed in this section used control groups in the fairly standard pattern of experimental psychology. However, there is considerable doubt as to the validity of using as a comparison point, people who do not receive a specific procedure or those who receive an alternative procedure. The most difficult aspect of utilizing comparable groups is to control for the therapist variable. Are you actually comparing techniques and procedures, or are you comparing effectiveness of examiners? As far as can be ascertained, the above studies controlled for this by using the same experimenter or team in each of the various conditions. *But it should be clear at this point that it is difficult and even undesirable to abstract the operant procedures from other behavior influence aspects of social control.* We see that most clearly in the comments on the Meichenbaum study and in the combination, implicit and explicit, of modeling procedures with contingent reinforcement in some of the other studies. These points might be summarized by saying that the type of study described in this section has kept rigidly within the design of experimental studies that might be more appropriate to animal work and laboratory work with humans, but less so to studies in natural environments such as those involving hospitalized schizophrenics. A further problem in these kinds of studies has been that the evidence for maintenance of change is weak. Either there is no followup, or the change has not been maintained over a period of time. Theoretically, this makes sense, because there is no reason for a new behavior to continue unless environmental circumstances are such that it is reinforced in the natural setting. This is particularly true of verbal conditioning studies, which are usually of a "laboratory" nature and are not designed to bring about changes in a ward setting outside the laboratory. It is because of some of these problems that the operant investigators developed alternative experimental methods particularly designed to modify individual behavior so as to bring to bear the findings of the more general group-comparison studies.

OPERANT APPROACHES TO MODIFYING THE BEHAVIOR OF CHILDREN AND ADOLESCENTS

Although this chapter has concentrated on the operant approach in working with adults, it is in the field of children's behavior problems that this approach has achieved its most important applications. In all of these programs, the general principles are the same as those described with adults. Chapter 19 in this book summarizes in detail much of this work. In this chapter we will cite several additional illustrations, insofar as they concern different problems.

The work of the Schwitzgebel brothers with the modification of delinquent behavior is a typical illustration. This group of investigators (Schwitzgebel, 1960, 1961, 1963, 1964, 1967;

Schwitzgebel, Schwitzgebel, Pahnke, and Hurd, 1964; Slack, 1960) developed a pioneering approach to delinquents involving a functional analysis of behavior. The subjects worked with adolescent delinquents. Their laboratory was a large store within the confines of a respectable business area. Thus the project became known as "Street Corner Research." The experimental group consisted of 30 white males employed by the project for six months or longer, 25 of whom had appeared in courts and 20 of whom had served at least six months or longer in some type of correctional institution. These subjects averaged 18 years of age and $9\frac{1}{2}$ years of schooling. A control group was initiated by matching each member of the experimental group with a male offender picked from police files. The techniques exercised with the initial group of experimental delinquents consisted of four sequences: (a) defining in measurable units the final, desired behavior as specifically as possible; (b) determining the available reinforcers that were most likely to be effective; (c) determining the subject's repertoire of present and previous behavior; and (d) applying the reinforcers according to an explicit theoretical model and modifying the application according to the feedback. The primary purpose of the project was to set up an experimental laboratory using adolescents. The experimenters accomplished this by approaching the community with an offer to hire people with delinquent records as subjects in a study of delinquency. In return for their participation, these people were paid for talking into a tape recorder relating their delinquent experiences. For those who failed to report to the laboratory, a gradual shaping procedure was used whereby the subjects were given cigarettes or food as they came closer to the laboratory. The subjects received sums of money depending upon how near they approximated the agreed-upon time of arrival at the laboratory. Once they were in the laboratory the boys were interviewed and were paid for specific chores such as soldering. After a time many obtained jobs beyond the laboratory in the community.

Three years after termination of employment in the program, a follow-up study of the first 20 subjects (Schwitzgebel, 1964) indicated that the number of arrests and time of incarceration of the employees was about *half* that of a matched control group. Within the overall program, Schwitzgebel (1967) reports the results of seven controlled studies that demonstrate the points made in this chapter about the effects of contingent response-reinforcement. Schwitzgebel matched two groups of his delinquent employees and treated them differentially during the course of 20 tape-recorded interviews on four classes of operants: hostile statements, positive statements, prompt arrival at work, and general employability. Hostile statements were followed by mild aversive consequences (inattention and mild verbal disagreement), while the other target operants were followed by a positive consequence (verbal praise or a small gift such as cigarettes, candy, or cash). The results in both a laboratory and a *natural setting* such as a restaurant indicated that there was a significant increase in the frequency of the three target behaviors that were followed by positive consequences. The hostile statements, however, which were followed by "punishment," did not significantly decrease.

The studies of Ferster and Lovaas and their collaborators illustrate the operant approach with children with very deviant behavior. Ferster and DeMyer (1961) pioneered the field of altering infantile autism. Their general approach first involved the selection of a simple response (pressing a key), and then sustaining the behavior with positive reinforcement. In one endeavor, three children, severely disturbed and diagnosed as schizophrenic reaction, childhood type with no obvious brain dysfunction, were placed in a room with various coin-operated machines dispensing candy and tiny toys. The subjects moved on from simply pressing a key to matching-to-sample. But instead of pressing the key for tokens, the children were first taught to respond to samples appearing in a center window of a display panel. Touching the sample drew the child's attention to it. The sample appeared in the center window, with a matching figure to either the left or the right and a nonmatching figure in the remaining position. When the child touched the matching figure he was rewarded with a token; when he touched the nonmatching figure, the machine turned off for a period of

time (reinforcement was denied for a time). After a period of simpler accomplishment in matching figures, the tasks became gradually more complicated until very high levels of accuracy were obtained.

At least one other investigator who has focused on work with children must at least be briefly mentioned. Lovaas and his collaborators have offered a series of applications of the operant approach to modifying the behavior of seriously disturbed children (Lovaas, 1961; Lovaas, Freitag, Nelson, and Whalen, 1967; Lovaas, Schaeffer, and Simmons, 1965; Lovaas, Freitag, Gold, and Kassorla, 1965).

The work of these investigators has had a major impact in the development of operant conditioning with autistic children. They have developed a methodology that has attracted considerable attention because of its promise of at least some success in modifying the behavior of children who have been considered almost completely unchangeable. They have concentrated on the development of social reinforcers for children who have rarely been responsive to other human beings. For example, in one such study (Lovaas et al., 1966) they present a methodology for the establishment and maintenance of social stimuli as reinforcers for certain behaviors of two schizophrenic children characterized as autistic. The first phase of the experiment was concerned with the establishment of a social stimulus (being patted on the back and having the experimenter saying, "good") as discriminative for food. The second phase involved the delivery of the social stimulus contingent upon a bar-pressing response, to test the reinforcing properties that may have been acquired during the first phase. The results indicated that the social stimulus acquired reinforcing properties for these children, since several thousand responses were made to it; and as long as the social stimulus was maintained as discriminative for food, it showed no signs of losing its acquired reinforcing properties.

In this section we have only briefly alluded to the operant work with children. The principles and procedures are similar to those of other kinds of studies described in this chapter. For a more complete review, see Ross (1970) and Chapter 26 in Ullmann and Krasner (1969).

THE CONDITIONING OF VERBAL BEHAVIOR

The verbal conditioning studies represent a major research technique in the application of operant conditioning to verbal behavior. Greenspoon (1954, based on a 1951 Ph.D. dissertation) is usually credited with originating this series of studies. His subjects were asked to ". . . say all the words that you can think of." The specific response class selected to be reinforced was that of plural nouns. Thus, when the subject would verbalize a plural noun, the experimenter would respond with an "mm-hum." This verbal response is theoretically interpreted as indicating that the examiner is paying attention, thus serving as a generalized reinforcer that strengthens the likelihood of repeating the target verbalization. The verbal conditioning studies have been extensively reviewed since their origin in the early 1950s (Holz and Azrin, 1966; Krasner, 1958, 1962, 1965; Salzinger, 1959; Greenspoon, 1962; Kanfer, 1968; Williams, 1966).

In his review of this field, Kanfer (1968) observed that research on verbal conditioning has undergone four stages: (a) demonstration; (b) reevaluation; (c) application; and (d) expansion. This is a useful way of summarizing these studies, particularly as they are related to behavior therapy research. The studies in the first stage demonstrated that verbal behavior could be brought under the control of environmental stimuli; verbal behavior followed the same principles as motor behavior, and these were similar to that of animal behavior. In that sense, the early verbal conditioning studies were similar to other early operant conditioning studies; they demonstrated that reinforcement, *under certain conditions*, can systematically influence verbal behavior. The second stage, that of reevaluation, demonstrated that what was being dealt with was a far more complex phenomenon than at first was evidenced by a simple operant explanation. Responsivity to verbal conditioning was affected by variables such as social setting; previous experience with examiner; subject and examiner expectancy; variations in the meaning of reinforcing stimuli; and other variables. It became clear that

these studies involve the full gamut of *behavior influence* variables.

In the third stage, that of application, verbal conditioning studies were used to specifically change verbal behavior with a therapeutic intent (for example, Isaac, Thomas, and Goldiamond, 1960; Williams and Blanton, 1968). The Williams and Blanton study was one of the few in which the verbal-conditioning technique was used with deliberate therapeutic intent. The subjects in the treatment groups were explicitly told that they had been referred for "psychotherapy." Eighteen nonpsychotic patients were assigned to three treatment groups. Two groups received conditioning by verbal reinforcement, one for emitting statements expressing *feeling*, the other for emitting statements without discriminable feeling content. The third group received psychotherapy as usually administered. After an initial operant-level session, treatment was administered for nine half-hour sessions, the same therapist being used for all sessions. Recordings of the sessions were scored for number of statements expressing feelings over sessions for all groups. The percentage of feeling statements increased for the group receiving reinforcement for that category, and for the group receiving ordinary psychotherapy. For the group receiving reinforcement for statements without feeling content, the percentage of feeling statements decreased slightly, but the percentage of non-feeling statements did not increase. The subjects did not express awareness of the reinforcement contingency. Thus, in this study, the verbal conditioning was at least as effective as traditional psychotherapy, at least by the limited criterion of being able to elicit feeling statements.

Ince (1968) offers a variation of the Williams and Blanton "verbal conditioning as psychotherapy" paradigm. It involves a return to the more "traditional" ABA single-case design rather than that of group comparisons. An experimental setting was designed to replicate a psychotherapist's office and subjects were seen daily. Variable-interval reinforcement was employed to modify the rate of emission of positive self-reference statements. The results demonstrated that the verbal reinforcement exerted a definite, marked effect on the verbal behavior of the subjects in that all subjects conditioned, that is, emitted more positive self-references. Ince concludes that serious consideration should be given to the use of verbal conditioning in "actual psychotherapy." He even reports the anecdotal evidence of subjects reporting that they felt "much better" after the sessions because of the help they received in "talking things over." It should be clear from this study that *results in verbal conditioning studies emphasize the importance of the most minute therapist behavioral cues in controlling the patient's behaviors.*

The fourth stage of development of these studies, which Kanfer labels the "expansion" stage, involves those studies investigating theoretical issues related to the capability of human beings for self-regulation. These include processes such as vicarious learning, (Kanfer, 1965) the role of awareness in learning, (Krasner, 1967; Matarrazo, Saslow, and Pareis, 1960; Spielberger, 1966) self-reinforcement and self-control (Kanfer and Marston, 1963), and the associative relationship of words.

In perspective, it is clear that verbal conditioning is a research technique that developed as a combination of operant conditioning and clinical interests in verbal behavior. Many of the early investigators were interested in the process of psychotherapy, which during the early 1950s was primarily of the evocative model. Here at last it seemed as if operant conditioning offered a technique for setting up an analogue of psychotherapy in a rigorously objective manner. It is clearer now that verbal conditioning and psychotherapy are not the *same* process, nor is one an analogue of the other. However, some verbal conditioning does take place in evocative psychotherapy, and some of the relationship variables of the latter cannot, and should not, be eliminated from the former.

In an earlier paper (Krasner, 1958), it was possible to cover the approximately 35 verbal conditioning studies then in the literature. Since then the number of verbal conditioning studies has increased to well over 1000, and almost every conceivable variable in the situation has been investigated, often with contradictory findings. As these studies multiplied, it became obvious that the variables involved were very complex, and have not always been adequately controlled. The major uncontrolled variable, in these studies, has been the examiner —his expectancies and biases, and the interactions of his "characteristics" with other variables of the situation. Studies investigating several variables at the same time have demonstrated complex interactional effects (Sarason and Minard, 1963). It has been this very sensitivity of verbal conditioning to the many variables of human interaction that has emphasized its usefulness as a research device.

Verbal Conditioning Tasks and Response Classes

Investigators of verbal conditioning have usually used one of two different task situations. There is, first, the task that offers the subject a limited choice of responses (Taffel, 1955). For example, a card may be presented with six pronouns, and the subject asked to make up a sentence using one of the pronouns. The reinforced response class, then, may be sentences starting with "I" or "we," or the similar task that involves making up sentences from a choice of verbs, or giving a "yes," "no," or "maybe" response to a paper-and-pencil personality inventory. This Taffel-type task has become the most popular verbal-conditioning technique, primarily because of the limited number of responses possible and the consequent ease of scoring. However, for purposes of interpretation and extrapolation to more general behavior influence situations, this type of task involves a far too limited response repertoire. Further, this taks has been criticized as not really representing a true operant conditioning situation, but rather a discrimination learning task.

One may speculate as to why this type of task persists in verbal conditioning studies if it has such little generality. There are several reasons: it is relatively easy to incorporate into a research design; it does not require training in identification of a complex response class; it results in lawful interactions (under these limited circumstances); and it allows for isolation of variables and a careful control of interactions. It also increases the likelihood of the emergence of a relationship between performance and verbalized awareness. Greenspoon (1962, p. 546), in a critique of this experimental paradigm, summarizes these critical points:

It appears to the writer that some questions may be raised concerning the inclusion of research using the Taffel-type situation with the operant conditioning paradigm. This writer has serious doubts about its conclusions because an essential element of operant conditioning is missing. Skinner (1935) emphasized the importance of the generic nature of the concept of response in that a single response is unique and it is necessary to conceive of a class of responses, the members of which have certain common characteristics. The Taffel-type situation in which a specific personal pronoun is reinforced certainly does not provide for generalization within a class of responses. The modification of the Taffel-type situation in which hostile verbs, bodily active verbs, etc. are reinforced does provide opportunity for generalization within the class of hostile or bodily active verbs. Some of the confusion in the results of research in verbal conditioning may be a product of apparatuses, materials and procedures that do not fit within the operant conditioning paradigm.

The other type of verbal conditioning task takes the form of an interview or story-telling situation (Salzinger & Pisoni, 1958; Krasner, 1958). The subject can respond to the task out of a broad behavior repertoire. Illustrations of this type of task include instructions such as "Say all the words you can think of" (Greenspoon, 1954); "Tell a story" (Krasner and Ullmann, 1958); or "What do you see in these inkblots?" (Fahmy, 1953).

The free-operant task is usually presented in somewhat disguised form. It should have a role- or face-validity to it; it must make sense as an experimental task as stated or the subject will attempt to hypothesize a real "meaning" to it. Thus, it sounds plausible to investigate "how people tell stories" or "use their imagination." Also, the task is usually one in which the subject can be fully preoccupied, for example an interview, a convesation, or making up a story. There is little time or energy left over to make up hypotheses about the nature of the task, and if it is done, the speculations are usually in relation to the given task, for example, "you were saying 'mm-hum' to hinder me, to interfere with my story telling."

The advantages to this type of task are that it more clearly approximates "real" life and other behavior influence situations such as evocative psychotherapy. Examples of verbal units reinforced include emotional words (Krasner, Ullmann, Weiss, and Collins, 1961), affect statements (Salzinger and Pisoni, 1961, 1960), a particular content area (Quay, 1959), or self-reference statements (Adams and Hoffman, 1960; Rogers, 1960). Further, the relationships between variables are more complex and thus there is less likelihood of the subject reporting awareness of the purpose of the study or the pattern of the examiner's reinforcing behavior. The clearer, less ambiguous a task, the more likely a well-motivated individual will perform it.

The point must be made that the operant approach involves focusing on the environmental cues that may serve as reinforcers (such as food, cigarettes, smiles, toys, tokens, head nods, "very good," and the like), as well as what kind of verbal behavior may serve as a response class. Salzinger (1967) reviews his considerable number of studies on defining the response class in verbal conditioning and offers several sets of "complexities" involved in determining what a response class is. Response complexity stems, first, from the fact that reinforcement always affects *classes* of response and not just individual responses. A second source of response complexity is the *unit size* of the response. Third, response complexity manifests itself in terms of the emission of one response producing a *change* in the situation, providing the subject with an opportunity for making a much larger number of different responses than before that response has been made. A fourth way in which response complexity is manifested is in terms of response *incompatibility*. The conditioning of one response may come to suppress another one merely because it has a greater response strength and because the two cannot be emitted at the same time or place. A fifth complexity stems from the fact that the same response may function *both* as an operant and as a respondent. An interesting research question is whether a response, such as a tic, known to be conditioned as a respondent (perhaps as a result of some traumatic incident) can be extinguished by means of a purely operant procedure.

Thus, just what constitutes a response class is an important and insufficiently investigated area of research. In our own research we have used the response class of emotional words (Ullmann and MacFarland, 1957) and reinforcers such as "mm-hmm" and "good" to investigate a number of the variables that influence verbal behavior. These have included the effects of examiner differences (Krasner, Ullmann, Weiss, and Collins, 1961); subject personality variables (Ullmann, Krasner, and Weiss, 1963); the relationship between awareness and performance (Krasner, Weiss, and Ullmann, 1961); the effects of instructional sets (Ekman, Krasner, and Ullmann, 1963); generalization effects (Ullmann, Krasner, and Collins, 1961); atmosphere effects (Weiss, Krasner, and Ullmann, 1960, 1963); changes in response class reinforced (Krasner and Ullmann, 1958); "placebo" effects (Gelfand, Ullmann, and Krasner, 1963); and relationship to other behavior inflence situations such as hypnosis (Bentler, O'Hara, and Krasner, 1963). These are cited to illustrate the range of variables and types of studies that may be investigated with verbal conditioning.

As we have seen, verbal conditioning lends itself to the study of interactions of variables. Two studies will be cited to illustrate this, both attempting to relate the verbal conditioning paradigm to psychotherapy. Sapolsky (1960) used the Schutz FIRO-B Scale of interpersonal "needs" to determine the relative "compatibility" of two given individuals. He hypothesized that the influence process in verbal conditioning would be most effective when the S's and the E's "needs" were compatible with each other. In one study, he assigned students as Ss and as Es on a basis of compatibility of personality "needs" for one group, and incompatibility of "needs" for another. Results were that during the acquisition period the compatible group conditioned, whereas incompatible Ss did not. During the extinction period (E out of room), compatible Ss did not extinguish in their use of reinforced pronouns, whereas incompatible Ss increased their use of the pronouns to the level obtained by the compatible Ss. A second Sapolsky study, similarly designed, used—instead of compatibility—an experimental "set" of high personal "attraction" on the part of the Ss. The resulting curves in this study were almost

identical with those in the first study. These two studies raise further testable implications for the influencing process: (a) the influencing process may be most effective when the "personality" of the S and the E are "compatible;" (b) the influencing process may be most effective when the S expects or has the "set" that he will like the E; (c) the influencing process, even with an incompatible E-S combination, may become effective when E is physically removed, and, most important, (d) the relationship between S and E can be experimentally manipulated.

Taylor (1968) replicated part of the Sapolsky findings by investigating the relationship between the *interpersonal orientation* of a subject as measured by the FIRO-B and his conditionability. The more "interpersonally" (positively) oriented the individual subject is, the more susceptible he is to verbal conditioning. Unfortunately, this latter study did not directly study the E-S interaction as such, but only the interpersonal orientation of the subject. The effects of the converse of a "positive" subject "attitude" has been also demonstrated; "hostile" examiners inhibit conditioning (Bryan and Lichtenstein, 1966; Weiss, Krasner, and Ullmann, 1960).

As we have emphasized, research in verbal conditioning, as with other operant approaches to human behavior, has offered an opportunity to explore the effects of manipulating and controlling relevant behavior influence variables (for example, is verbal reinforcement more effective in producing change when administered by, for instance, a "warm," prestigeful examiner to an "extroverted" subject?) The hypotheses of what may be relevant variables for these studies have come from current "personality" theories, and this has been a source of difficulty, because the findings of most studies using these traditional variables do not replicate. It is necessary to approach human behavior by focusing on observing with "operant eyes" just how people perform in interpersonal situations. This kind of approach can be illustrated by the work of Goldiamond and Dyrud (1968).

They have explicitly extended the operant investigation of verbal behavior into the area of behavioral analysis of psychotherapy. They point out that "although words can now control machine behavior and computer processes, the major function served by verbal behavior, that is, its major consequence, is the control of the behavior of other people and ourselves (p. 54)." They make the same kind of connection that many of the verbal conditioning experimenters have, namely, that there is a similarity between the operant conditioning strategy in research and that of the practitioner of psychotherapy.

Goldiamond and Dyrud argue that:

If the transactions of psychotherapy can be translated into the observational and procedural terms of the experimental analysis of behavior, a corollary task is to utilize that representational system to describe the functional relations between dependent and independent variables in an ongoing therapy session and establish them where advisable (p. 64).

The use of such language ties in with a literature of laboratory-derived procedures for the establishment, maintenance, and alteration of behavior.

Accordingly, we decided to observe therapy sessions further, to ascertain the relevant transactive units and procedures employed in the change ... An example of such analysis is provided by a discussion after a session, when the observer asked the therapist if he was trying to provide certain possibilities for the patient. The therapist agreed that the analysis was correct. "Well," asked the observer, "why not state these openly." "Because I want the patient to find out for herself," was the answer. Rather than argue this point, both observer and therapist then decided to observe what therapist procedures defined "having the patient find out for herself." It turned out that the procedures employed were almost identical with operant abstraction training, in which stimuli are used which are intentionally multidimensional, rather than clearly occasioning the appropriate response (p. 64). Much of the verbal conditioning research with nods and "uh-huhs" may be beside the point when it assumes that such reinforcers change behavior therapeutically. They may merely keep the patient talking and maintain the behaviors of going through the implicit program. The brunt of the therapy may be borne by the content of the transactions. We have discovered in our research that our "uh-huhs" and nods, and many questions and statements, as well, merely serve to maintain behavior. When reinforcements are given which *shape* behavior these are quite often noticeable and quite rare (p. 73).

The patient has the undivided attention of the therapist. The nods and "uh-huhs" of the therapist may be merely conditioned reinforcers or discriminative stimuli accompanying such attention. It may be that the therapy session, with its questions, restatements, and implicit approval, provides the patient with an opportunity to emit verbal behavior. Premack's investigations (1965), as well as extension by others, emphasize the reinforcing power of the opportunity merely to behave. In the therapy situation, it is the unlimited chance to verbalize. Goldiamond and Dyrud go on to argue that:

One of the questions we have addressed ourselves to is what behaviors this reinforcer, namely, the opportunity to talk at length, is contingent upon. One behavioral requirement involves using the language of the therapist. When the patient is speaking in one language, for example, is describing an experience in terms of his own feelings, a therapist with a different language, say, a behavioral one, may continually interrupt him and ask for a clarification which amounts to a redefinition in behavioral terms. The patient will soon come to talk in the behavioral language of the therapist (Goldiamond and Dyrud, pp. 73-74).

These investigators report on their study of traditional psychotherapy as carried on by a psychoanalytically oriented psychotherapist. The assessment and observation of the "traditional" psychotherapeutic interaction via operant eyes represents a major extension of the approach described in this chapter. Significant observations will result in research further developing the variables involved in behavior influence.

Operant Approach to Stammering

"Stammering" represents a deviant verbal behavior, the modification of which has been approached through operant procedures. For example, Russell, Clark, and van Sommers (1968) report a series of experimental studies with three stammerers. One of these studies may serve as an illustration of this technique. The subject was asked to read aloud words or phrases projected from slides on a 12×8 in. screen. He was intermittently rewarded for reading the material fluently; that is, reading without blocking, prolongation, interjected words or sounds, or repetitions of words or sounds. Where the subject read a word in this way a new slide was immediately projected on the screen. When the subject stammered, the slide was exposed for five seconds before a new slide was presented. Some correct (fluent) responses were rewarded not only by the immediate exposure of a new stimulus but also by the sounding of a buzzer and the flashing of a green light in the corner of the screen. At the same time a counter mounted on the screen counted backwards to zero.

These additional reinforcements were arranged on a variable ratio schedule of 1:5; that is, on the average there was one reward for every five correct responses. The experimenter controlled reinforcements by means of a hand switch that he pressed when the subject said a word correctly. This operated an apparatus that "decided" whether a preprogrammed sequence of reinforcements was either in the "reinforce" or the "not-reinforce" condition, and then delivered a reinforcement if appropriate. It also changed the slide, presenting a new word. In addition, it recorded presentations, correct responses, and reinforcements. A study was carried out with one subject with ABA design. With eleven sessions of this programmed series of reinforcements, there was a drop in stammering rate from 35 to 15 percent. The improvement was evidenced by a regular decline, except for a sharp drop to a 5 percent of errors in the sixth session. The program was discontinued in session 12. Error rate, over six sessions, returned to a level of errors comparable with the initial rate. With the reintroduction of the program for six sessions, errors again decreased sharply. Thus error rate rose and fell in response to the experimental manipulation. Similar results were obtained with two other subjects. The authors conclude that positive reinforcement is more effective in stammering than aversive therapy. However, the authors made no direct comparison between the two forms of treatment.

CASE REPORTS

Another series of operant studies are essentially case reports that involve own-control procedures. They are a prototype of one kind of operant research and they suggest areas of investigation to which more carefully controlled research studies may be applied. Such a study is that of Burgess (1968) on the application of contingency management to depressive behaviors. Depression may well be the last type of behavior to come within the behavior-therapy paradigm. It has only been briefly referred to in the behavior-therapy literature (Lazarus, 1968). Ferster (1965) viewed depression as a consequence of decreased reinforcement. Burgess, following the implication of Ferster's view, argued that a broad class of *active* task-oriented responses labeled as a "performing" response class can be differentiated from a "depressive" response class involving a retarded motor response rate, sad face and body appearances, and mournful verbalizations. As the frequency of performing behaviors begins to diminish, there is simply a greater absence of occasion for reinforcement. "Concurrent with the extinction of performing behaviors may be the conditioned acquisition of depressive behaviors." It would follow from this analysis that the treatment procedures should involve the *reversal* of all contingencies. Reinforcement should be made contingent upon performing behaviors, and depressive behaviors should not be responded to and hence should extinguish.

Following this paradigm, Burgess reports on the treatment of six clients seen in a university counseling center. The treatment methods ran as follows: If the history of the individual indicated the loss of a specific reinforcer that had been previously available, efforts to reinstate it were made. If reinforcement losses were more generalized or nonspecific, the client was immediately requested to emit a few performing behaviors that required minimal effort for completion. The client's attention was brought to the importance of successful completion rather than to the nature or value of the task. Gradually, task requirements were increased so that behaviors accelerated in frequency, duration, quality, and successively approximated former behaviors from the client's repertoire. If available, a mate was taught to augment treatment by providing reinforcement specified according to prescribed contingencies. Clients were seen daily for the first week to maximize therapist reinforcing power, and then seen with decreasing frequency as natural reinforcers began to become effective. Therapist attention and approval were used as reinforcers during the interviews, as the clients reported either orally or in writing about their activities. No attention was paid to depressive behaviors after the first interview. "It should be noted that techniques changed as a function of individual reinforcement histories, contingencies, and environmental components." Burgess concluded that:

... contingency management, which promotes reinforcement for the completion of performing behaviors and extinction of depressive behaviors seems to be effective for the treatment of depression when reinstatement of a reinforcer cannot be accomplished. All clients were able to perform in their life situation with at least passable facility within three weeks of treatment inauguration. Case reports, however, are not adequate to establish the efficacy of any treatment method. The need for controlled research is obvious.

A variation of the case report is represented by those studies that are avowedly *own-control* designed and that also derive from the earlier operant investigations. They combine a research approach with clinical applications (a "real-life" genuine problem); they use a base-line period that measures the target behavior before any attempt at modification is attempted as a comparison point from which to measure the effectiveness of the specific procedures; they stress quantification and measurement of behavior (sometimes with the individual involved trained to quantify his own behavior); the ABA, off-on-off design is usually used; social influence procedures are used in such a way as to maximize the likelihood of the operant procedures working; frequently there is a follow-up over a period of some time; there is an attempt to determine if there have been changes in other behaviors that may be related to the target behaviors; the investigator may move directly into the home as the locus for setting the conditions for change. As a prototype of these studies and as one of the most interesting and ingenious of them, the report by Stuart (1968) is cited. The design was an own-control one with a base-line period, a treatment period, and then a follow-up report. Stuart undertook the study within the framework of treating marital problems. He worked with four couples who sought treatment in a last effort to avoid a divorce. "The typical couple complain of a lack of communication,

which is a euphemism for a failure to reinforce each other." He offered certain assumptions about the character of marital interaction upon which his treatment procedure rests. These assumptions are important because they lay the basis for the extension of the operant approach into the ordinary everyday activities of individuals seeking help in an outpatient setting. Stuart assumes that:

... the exact pattern of interaction which takes place between a husband and his wife at any point in time is the most rewarding of all of the currently available alternatives. While the specifics may vary for each couple, most married adults expect to enjoy reciprocal relations with their partners. In order to modify an unsuccessful marital interaction, it is essential to develop the power of each partner to mediate rewards for the other.

Based upon this formulation, the "operant interpersonal approach" (a term which Stuart uses in a manner similar to that of King, Armitage, and Tilton, 1960) seeks to construct a situation in which the frequency and intensity of mutual positive reinforcement is increased. The treatment procedure then follows from this assumption in a logical manner.

The first step is to train the couple in the logic of his approach. He then requested both husband and wife to list the three behaviors that each would like to accelerate in the other. Even this phase comprises elements of *training*, that of training people in the ways of observing and conceptualizing a behavioral sequence. The third step is to train each individual in transferring the observed data onto a graph on which each person is to keep a record of the other's positive behavior. Step four consists of working out a series of exchanges of desired behaviors.

To carry out his program, Stuart introduced a token system into the home situation. He started with the one behavior that was much desired by each of the wives, that of having the husband converse with her more fully. Each wife was instructed to purchase a timer and to give her husband a token after each hour in which the husband talked for sufficient time with the wife to meet her criterion. However, an important part of the procedure was that the wife must feed back to the husband within the first 30 minutes of each hour cues as to his performance if it is unsatisfactory. If she fails to do this he must be given a token at the end of the hour even if he did not perform adequately. With each of the four couples, tokens were redeemable at the husband's request "from a menu stressing physical affection." A different "menu" was constructed for each couple, which took into account the base-line level of sexual activity, the desired level of activity, and the number of hours available for nonsexual (conversational) interchange. On this basis, husbands were charged three tokens for kissing and/or "light petting" with their wives, five tokens for "heavy petting," and 15 tokens for sexual intercourse. The results indicated that, as compared with base-line measures, the "rates of conversation and sex increased sharply after the start of treatment and continued through 24 and 48 week followups." The participants were asked to fill out inventories about their own satisfaction and their perception of their spouse's satisfaction in marriage. These reports also indicated a dramatic increase in their own self-satisfaction as well as satisfaction with their spouse. It should be noted that the actual sessions with the therapist (by each individual couple) numbered only seven, interspersed during the first, fourth, sixth, eighth, and tenth weeks of the treatment program.

This study emphasizes many of the points about the operant-case approach. The individual is trained to provide new stimuli to the key people in his life so as to elicit different behavior from them. "Each spouse was directed in specific modifications of his own behavior in an effort to modify the behavioral environment in which his partner's behavior occurred." Actually, the therapist did not introduce anything really new in terms of behavior. Stuart points out that he merely suggested behaviors that had doubtless been requested, cajoled, and demanded by each party many times in the past. In that sense they were of no different an order than the many items of behavior that pay off for a hospitalized patient in a token economy (in the one instance conversing more, in the other self-grooming). But in this instance the therapist clarified and spelled out the contingencies involved. He introduced the clear expectation of change in the partners and, most important of all, he removed the situation from that of a coercive context. In the home situation, when a request

is put in the form of a demand, which is what had been occurring in these families, then adherence to the request involves the reinforcing of "demands," something usually held to be undesirable by most people. Nor should the importance of the gamelike qualities that the therapist gave to the treatment be ignored. In fact, the game was termed "prostitution" because "all games must have names and prostitution appealed to the fantasies of all concerned." Whether it was the specific token program that resulted in the dramatic changes in behavior or whether the results could have been achieved by any other kind of forceful intervention is of course not adequately clarified in this study, a critique that can always be made about case studies. However, the more general issue of evaluating operant "programs" will be discussed in a later section.

OPERANT CONDITIONING IN REHABILITATION

The field of physical rehabilitation offers an excellent opportunity for the operant approach because of the types of motor behavior involved. Further, much of the behavior modification must be done "in the field," in the hospital or the home where the handicapped individual lives. The term "rehabilitation" of course has a wide range of meaning, covering as it does both the physically and socially handicapped. Several studies primarily using own-control methods will illustrate the range of operant applications in this field of problem behavior.

Ince (1968) reports the application of the standard operant conditioning procedures to modify the behavior of two disabled individuals "without the use of laboratory facilities or sophisticated equipment." In both instances the specific disabling behaviors were measured for base line, a reinforcement procedure was introduced, and change in performance was measured. In one instance, the target behavior was "ambulation" in a Parkinsonian patient (walking from 5 to 20 feet, and making various turns). The second behavior was "typing" by a young girl suffering from a disease involving loss of control of muscles and limbs. In both instances, the contingent reinforcements were verbal statements such as "very good." The performance of the target behavior in both cases significantly improved, and self-confidence increased, as manifested by other positive behavioral changes. Ince concludes cautiously that:

... there were probably variables other than the specific reinforcement at work in both cases which it was not possible to control for. Perhaps social reinforcement from family and friends played a role. Perhaps practice can account, at least in part, for the effects obtained. Further work obviously needs to be done along these lines. I would like to make one more point, namely that despite disabilities which at first appear beyond modification, either because of their apparent severity or because of the nature of the setting, there is much that can be done for the disabled person using behavior modification techniques.

Zimmerman et al. (1968) also report the application of operant approaches to a community sheltered workshop setting and to the problem of increasing productivity in multiply handicapped clients. Sixteen clients who were participating in a special prevocational training program for hard-core handicapped people served as the subjects of the investigation. Clients admitted to the prevocational training program had either been previously denied entrance into a workshop program because of poor prognosis for productive employment or had been exposed to previous workshop experiences and had failed to make satisfactory progress. The clients were exposed to a set of preliminary procedures designed to train them in receiving and exchanging tokens (point cards) for tangible goods and services. These clients were then exposed to a series of successive control and experimental conditions designed to assess the effects of token reinforcement on productivity. While the clients were treated as a group with respect to the introduction and removal of experimental conditions, each client served as his *own control* in the sense that he received token reinforcement programmed on the basis of his own recent work history. This meant that the reinforcements were individualized rather than being universal.

Throughout the investigation, the clients worked five days a week for six hours a day in a 500-square-foot area of the Industrial Services (subcontract) Department. This area contained six work tables, and two to four clients worked at a given table. A staff person monitored the number of work units (a Western Electric terminal board) completed throughout each day. After the training period, the clients were put on a contingent program that related work performance to receipt of tokens, alternating with a period of noncontingent reinforcement. The authors concluded that the results indicated.

(a) work contingent token reinforcement can significantly increase productivity, (b) the removal of token reinforcement can lead to a significant decrease in productivity, and (c) factors other than token reinforcement contingencies can also significantly increase productivity. The first two results systematically replicate results previously obtained by other investigators with other groups of handicapped people and in other settings. The third result suggests that factors other than token reinforcement contingencies can significantly contribute to results obtained in token reinforcement studies and, thus, investigators using such an approach should consider employing control conditions besides those which involve the removal of token reinforcement or token contingencies.

Henderson and his group at Spruce House (Henderson, 1968; Scoles and Henderson, 1968) report a token economy program that had many of the features of the Zimmerman program, as well as some unique ones.

The program was designed to differ from the state hospital in three ways: it is operated in a nonstigmatizing "house" rather than in a "mental hospital;" it undertakes to strengthen social and vocational coping behaviors which are frequently weakened or punished within the typical state hospital setting. The emphasis at Spruce House is on the modification of overt behavior (operants) through a system of rewards (reinforcements). Adaptive vocational behavior, adaptive social interaction, and counter-symptomatic behavior are reinforced. Symptomatic or maladaptive behavior is not reinforced. The social responses of staff members and other patients are made contingent on adaptive or desirable social behaviors by the patient. Behavior revealing delusions or hallucinations is ignored and social approach responses are socially reinforced.

For regressed patients, primary reinforcers such as candy and cigarettes were used. A patient would be given candy when he was working and not when he was standing about. A patient on a reading program was given a piece of candy for every so many words that he read successfully, with this rate of "payment" specified to him in advance. Another part of the system was based on secondary reinforcing tokens called "grickles," which were earned by patients for appropriate vocational or social behavior and were then exchanged for extra food at mealtime, candy, passes, phone calls, and special privileges.

A work habituation program was constructed hierarchially. Jobs that required the least initiative or interpersonal competence yielded the smallest token payments. With successive promotions in jobs requiring greater responsibility, independence, and interaction with others, the token pay was correspondingly higher. Promotion was ordinarily accomplished by earning the maximum available number of grickles for the job previously held. Consistent performance within a job was brought about by the awarding of bonuses at the end of each work period, at the end of each work day, and at the end of each work week. Token reinforcements were awarded for participation in the many social activities available. The least token reinforcement was attached to nonsocial participation in an activity. Superficial conversation with other persons, interpersonal transactions indicative of "social involvement," and occurrences of initiative or role modeling resulted in successively higher token payments. Residents engaging in interesting conversation with community persons were paid bonuses in order to foster transition of the resident into the community.

The results of these studies are similar to those of other operant studies. For example, Scoles and Henderson summarize one substudy as follows.

Seven subjects in a token behavioral environment participated in a study in which contingent token reinforcement was accorded for social interaction at three levels for six weeks; reinforcement was suspended during the seventh week and reinstituted during the eighth, ninth and tenth weeks. Under contingent token reinforcement, significant increases or increases approaching significance were found on most of the social variables. When reinforcement was suspended decrements resulted, most of which attained or approached statistical significance. When reinforcement was reinstituted, there were significant increases in social performance on all the variables studied. It was observed that the suspension and reinstitution of reinforcement had a general activating effect on performance within the token environment.

Based on the first 13 months of its operation, Henderson concludes that whereas state or general hospitals may return subjects to the community more rapidly than Spruce House, a larger proportion of Spruce House subjects are employed once they return to the community than those returned from other facilities, thus increasing the likelihood of their remaining in the community.

These several studies demonstrate the applicability of the operant approach to rehabilitation problems, the necessity for caution in attributing change solely to the specific operant procedures narrowly defined, and the need to conceptualize this approach within a broader behavior influence framework that will be discussed in the next section on token economy.

TOKEN-ECONOMY PROGRAMS

Token-economy programs are the most recent illustration of the broad application of the operant conditioning approach to modifying deviant behavior. The nature of these programs emphasizes the point made throughout this chapter that the operant techniques must be viewed as part of a general behavior influence approach. The critique and evaluation of these studies will differ if they are considered solely as operant conditioning or if they are put in a social influence context.

At the simplest level, a token-economy program involves the setting up of a contingent reinforcement program with three aspects. First, the institutional staff designates certain specific patient *behaviors* as good or desirable, hence reinforceable. Second, there is a *medium of exchange*, an object, the token, that "stands for" something else, a back-up reinforcer. The token may be plastic rectangles shaped like credit cards, small metallic coins, poker chips, marks on a piece of paper, or even green stamps. Third, there is a way for utilizing the tokens, the *back-up* reinforcers themselves. These are the good things in life, the desirable things for a given individual, and may range from food to being allowed to sit peacefully in a chair. The "economy" part of the term appropriately relates to the "supply and demand" aspects of the programs, which determine changing token values, and the relationship between prices and wages.

The goals of a token program are to develop behaviors that will lead to social reinforcement from others, to enhance the skills necessary for the individual to take a responsible social role in the institution and eventually, to live successfully outside the institution. Basically, the individual learns that he can control his own environment in such a way that he will elicit positive reinforcement from others.

However, a simple analogue from animal operant conditioning studies is not appropriate, since it is *human beings* who deliver the reinforcement and hence bring into the situation complex social influence variables. We will present a brief description of several token programs that will illustrate the complexities involved.

One of the first uses of *tokens* to replace primary reinforcers was that by Staats (1965) to train reading discrimination in children. The responses of the children in his study were reinforced with marbles, which were exchangeable for various back-up reinforcers. Staats reported that there were scheduling effects that depended upon the way in which tokens and back-up reinforcers were related, in addition to the schedules involving the manner in which tokens were made contingent upon the behavior of the individual.

Ayllon and his colleagues (Ayllon, 1963; Ayllon and Houghton, 1962, 1964; Ayllon and Michael, 1959) reported a series of applications of operant principles to a mental-hospital setting. These studies were, for the most part, dramatic examples of ABA design that opened the way for introduction of the more encompassing token-economy program.

Ayllon and Azrin (1965, 1968b) report the results of the first application of a token program to a psychiatric hospital ward. The behaviors selected for reinforcement included such things as serving meals, cleaning floors, sorting laundry, washing dishes, and self-grooming. Ayllon and Azrin made no a priori decisions about what might be an effective reinforcer for schizophrenic patients. Instead, their approach involved the observation of patients' behavior to discover what patients actually did. They applied the general principle, expressed by Premack (1955), that any behavior with a high frequency of occurrence can be used as a reinforcer. Reinforcement consisted of the opportunity to engage in activities that had a high level of occurrence when freely allowed. The reinforcers selected were part of the naturalistic environmental context. Thus, the reinforcers included such things as having a room available for rent; being able to select people with whom to dine; passes; a chance to speak to the ward physician, chaplain, or psychologist; opportunity to view T.V.; candy; cigarettes; and other amenities of life. Tokens serve as *acquired* reinforcers that bridge the delay between behavior and an ultimate reinforcement. The investigators placed particular emphasis on the objective definition and quantification of the responses and reinforcers, and upon programming and recording procedures.

Ayllon and Azrin (1965) report a series of six experiments, in each of which they demonstrated that target behavior *systematically* changed as a function of the token reinforcement. One experiment is typical of the procedures developed by these investigators. The response they were interested in consisted of off-ward work assignments. A patient would select the job he preferred from a list of available ones for which tokens would be given. After ten days he was told that he could continue working on his job, but there would be *no* tokens for the work. Of the eight patients involved, seven immediately selected another job that had previously been nonpreferred, but that would now pay tokens. The eighth patient switched a few days later. In the third phase of the experiment, the contingencies were reversed and the previously preferred jobs led to tokens. All eight patients immediately switched back to their previously preferred, original jobs.

The results of the six experiments demonstrated that the reinforcement procedure was effective in maintaining desired performance. In each experiment the performance fell to a near zero level when the established response-reinforcement relation was discontinued. On the other hand, reintroduction of the reinforcement procedure restored performance almost immediately and maintained it at a high level.

The Ayllon and Azrin token economy functioned on a ward in a midwestern state hospital with a population of long-term female patients. Another token-economy program (Atthowe and Krasner, 1968; Krasner, 1968) was set up in a Veterans Administration Hospital in California with male patients averaging 58 years of age and a median length of hospitalization of 24 years. Most of these patients had been labeled chronic schizophrenics, and the remainder had been labeled "organic". As a group, their behavior was apathetic and indifferent, manifested by inactivity, dependency, and social isolation. The procedures used were similar to those developed by Ayllon and Azrin. However, one of the major differences was in the amount of total control exerted by the experimenters. The Atthowe and Krasner program was designed to be an *open* ward on which patients could come and go, if, of course, they had the right number of tokens for the gate keeper. The token economy had to compete with the extra-ward economy, which used dollars and cents as their tokens. Many kinds of *economic* problems had to be faced. To cope with these problems, special procedures had to be developed such as a banking system to foster savings, a monthly discount rate to cut down hoarding, and yellow tokens to prevent stealing.

Prior to the introduction of tokens, most patients refused to go to any of the activities available to them and showed little interest in their environment. The patients sat or slept on the ward during the day. In effect, their behavior represented the end point of years of shaping of compliant and apathetic institutional behavior. The investigating team decided that there were better things in life for these people to do than to sit and waste away their lives. Among the valued things were enacting the role of responsible people who are adept at self-grooming, keeping their living facilities clean, dressing neatly, holding a job, and interacting with other people. Responsibility also involved their being responsive to normal social reinforcement. Thus, each time a token was given it was accompanied by social reinforcement such as "good," "I'm pleased," "fine job," and an explicit statement as to the contingencies involved, such as, "You received three tokens because you got a good rating from your job supervisor."

This token-economy program was a significant success, as measured by changes in specified behavior, observer's ratings, and reactions of the hospital staff. The changes in behavior, such as attendance at group activity, were a function of the number of tokens (value) given for the activity. Group attendance increased as more tokens were given for such an activity, and then decreased as the "payoff" returned to its previous value.

The greatest change was in the appearance and atmosphere of the ward and in the staff expectations concerning the patients' capabilities. The token program had a major effect on the attitudes of the staff, who now found that they could have a therapeutic effect on patient behavior by the kinds of acts they performed. Staff morale increased, and it became a matter of prestige to work on the token ward. Finally, while the Atthowe and Krasner program was underway, two additional wards in the same hospital adopted similar token economies as a *way of life* because of its apparent usefulness in changing patient behavior.

We have stressed that there are economic aspects of token programs that have barely begun to be explored. The term "economic" refers to the ever-growing complex relationship between prices and wages. An eventual complete operant analysis will refer to response chaining. However, to this point, the investigation that comes closest to directly studying the economic features of token programs is that of Winkler (1968a, 1968b).

Winkler (1968a) reports the results of a token economy program that has many of the same features as that of the earlier programs, with some additional novel features. This program was established in a closed female ward with patients averaging 49 years of age and twelve years of hospitalization in Gladesville Hospital, New South Wales, Australia. The patients' behavior was characterized by an excessive amount of violence and screaming, as well as apathy and general lack of response to the ward environment. In the token program introduced in this setting, Winkler gave particular emphasis to economic factors. For example, prices and wages were initially arranged so that the patients' average daily income tended to exceed their average daily expenditure. This basic economic fact of life, that income must equal or exceed outgo is a necessity for a viable economy. However, the economic aspects of a token economy may be in dispute, just as a Keynesian approach in our broader society may differ from a more standard conservative approach.

Winkler reports that, without exception, every type of behavior that was reinforced improved. In addition, behaviors not specifically in the program, such as violence and making loud noise, decreased. Winkler also carried out a number of experiments designed to determine whether the patients' behaviors were really under the control of the tokens. In one experiment, tokens for shoe cleaning were stopped for three weeks and then reintroduced. There was an immediate decrease of this behavior with a discontinuation of tokens and an immediate increase on their reintroduction. Similar results occurred with other behaviors.

Winkler also reported a significant improvement in staff morale, as indicated by a drop in absenteeism. Absenteeism in the four months after the program began was 24 percent below the absenteeism for the four months before the program, while in a comparable ward, absenteeism over the same periods dropped only 3 percent. This emphasizes, as is clear in every token study, that staff morale, as mediated by the training program and feedback as to the effectiveness of the procedures, is a necessary ingredient in an operant program.

In the next phase of his program, Winkler (1968, b) was concerned with the effect on behavior of the relationships between the number of tokens in the patients' possession, the system's economic balance, and the amount of reinforcement (wages). At any one time, a token system can be considered as having a certain economic balance that may be regarded as the discrepancy between total patient income (the total number of tokens given to the patients) and total patient expenditure (the total number of tokens spent). Under normal circumstances in a token system, the economic *balance* determines the speed with which patients accumulate tokens, and hence is involved in determining the number of tokens in the patients' possession at any one time. This

variable was called *savings*. If income consistently exceeds expenditure over a period of time, savings will automatically increase, and if expenditure exceeds income, savings will decrease. Both economic balance and savings are affected by many different factors in a token system, but they are perhaps most strongly affected by changes in wages and changes in prices.

Studies were designed to separate savings from economic balance, in order to examine whether savings did affect earning behavior. Savings and economic balance were manipulated independently. Savings were manipulated by abruptly changing the currency used in the system. For three weeks a new token was made the only legitimate currency, and the old tokens were useless until the three weeks ended. In effect, savings were abruptly reduced to zero for all patients. Simultaneously, all prices were dropped to one token; wages remaining unchanged. Expenditure was therefore lowered and economic disequilibrium, with income exceeding expenditure, occurred. Under the usual token system such a disequilibrium would not occur without high savings. But with the new tokens the disequilibrium coincided initially with low savings. If savings and not economic balance were affecting performance, token-earning behavior would improve rather than deteriorate. Hence, it was hoped that the disequilibrium created by reduced prices would be held as constant as possible during the three-week experimental period. This would automatically insure that savings would increase rapidly and steadily while the economic balance was constant, and thus provide a further test of the relationship between savings and token-earning behavior.

In six of the seven token-earnings behaviors that were investigated, the mean daily performance in the first week of the experiment was higher than the base-line performance. The percentage improvements ranged from 2 to 52 percent, indicating that despite the disequilibrium favoring income, the drop in savings coincided with improved performance. Tidy appearance was the only behavior not to improve. In six of the seven token-earning behaviors, mean daily performance in the first week of the experimental period was superior to mean daily performance in the third week of the experiment, when savings were high. In the third week, six of the seven behaviors had deteriorated 16 to 44 percent below the initial base line. Getting up was the only behavior not to increasingly deteriorate. If savings were the controlling behavior, then the behavioral deterioration to a level below the base line would indicate that savings in the third week of the experimental period exceeded savings prior to that period.

This first experiment then indicated a close relationship between savings and token earning behavior. Behavior under low savings was better than behavior under high savings, and reduction in savings improved behavior. The improvement in behavior when the economic balance was altered in favor of income and the change in behavior during the three weeks of disequilibrium suggest that the economic balance does not affect behavior directly, but rather indirectly through the way in which it affects savings.

Winkler concludes that these two analyses suggest that the process by which savings control behavior involves more than a simple fluctuation in primary deprivation level. The failure of savings to be affected by prices suggests that savings may operate to some extent independently of what they can buy, and the absence of a drop in purchasing with low savings suggests that the patients were working harder to avoid the loss of rewards rather than being motivated by an actual deprivation. Further analysis of the relationship between token deprivation and primary deprivation should clarify these issues. Winkler's approach, described here in some detail, represents a method of studying the natural process of reinforcement.

Another variation of experimental design in token programs has been reported by Lloyd and Garlington (1968). Seven types of behavior of 13 chronic schizophrenic female patients were rated during four experimental phases. During conditions 1 and 3, the patients were given a token allowance in the morning on a noncontingent basis. During conditions 2 and 4, tokens were paid on a contingent basis, that is, the patients received tokens commensurate with the ratings of their behavior (such as neatness, bed-making, and eating habits). These ratings, based on frequency of occurrence of desirable behavior, were higher during conditions 2 and 4 than during conditions 1 and 3. The authors concluded that *contingent* tokens were controlling the behavior of the patients.

Other successful token economy programs with adult psychiatric patients have been reported by Steffy et al. (1966), Garicke (1965), and others cited in this chapter. Token-economy programs have been extended to other groups of individuals including mental retardates, delinquents, adolescents, and classroom behavior problems. Krasner and Atthowe (1968) offer a bibliography of over fifty reports of token programs in various parts of the world.

However, the token economy, as do other operant procedures, must be approached critically in a research context for evaluation. The problems in doing token economy research are as complex as in any other area of investigation involving human behavior change, and perhaps more so. Institutional research is particularly difficult because of the difficulty in controlling relevant variables. Most evidence from mental-hospital research would point to the fact that some change in the behavior of patients can be brought about by almost any program involving some sort of "total push." The enthusiasm, positive expectation, increased and more focused attention and interest of the staff brought about by participation in a prestigeful research program all provide additional and massive amounts of social reinforcement, which is likely to bring about and maintain new and desirable patient behavior. The goals of the research investigator using a token economy are to demonstrate first, significant behavioral change, and second, that the change is a function of the specific techniques involved in the token program.

The token economy program, insofar as research techniques are concerned, may be divided into the following categories:

1. Those programs that are primarily demonstrational projects; no attempt is made to control variables. Although change may be observed, it is difficult to attribute it to the tokens, per se. Many of the programs reported belong in this category.

2. Those programs using base rate and own controls, essentially the ABA design. Measurement is taken of the operant rate of specified patient behaviors for a specific period of time.

The token program is introduced and the same behaviors are continued to be measured. The token contingencies may be removed, and again the behavior continues to be measured. Then the token contingencies are reintroduced. The previously described Ayllon and Azrin program is an illustration of this. In the Atthowe and Krasner study the value (number of tokens given) of various activities were changed and the rate of performance was measured. This was illustrated by the change in the rate of patient attendance in group activities as the rate of tokens increased from one to two and back again to one.

3. The effectiveness of the token economy procedure is tested by the use of control groups which receive either no specific treatment or a different treatment. A study by Marks, Shalock, and Sonoda (1967) illustrates this approach. They worked with twenty-two chronic schizophrenics males divided into eleven matched pairs based on rated hospital adjustment. One member of each pair was assigned to Group A, called "reinforcement therapy," and the other patient of the pair was assigned to Group B, called "relationship therapy." In Group A each patient received tokens (poker chips) for individual specified behaviors. The cost of meals was ten tokens per meal. Initially the reinforced behaviors were selected by the staff. Later the goals were frequently set by the patients themselves. Selected behaviors were tailored to the individual and his progress. One man might be rewarded for simply receiving and paying tokens, another for improving his appearance, another for discussing discharge plans with a social worker, and another for expressing feelings. The relationship therapy (Group B) was designed to enlarge and deepen the patient's self-understanding and self-acceptance by daily psychotherapy meetings. The nine therapists involved avoided giving social reinforcement at the appearance of specific behaviors. Each subject received both forms of treatment alternately, approximately ten weeks on each. To assess these therapies, 18 pre-post measures were taken. Most of these measures included work, social, and conceptual performance. The authors concluded that both therapies were effective in improving the behavior of chronic hospitalized patients. However, reinforcement therapy was more *economical* of staff time. They concluded also that "reinforcement can be used in a 'psychodynamic' way. It can be used to shape self-assertive, critical, and dominating behaviors as well as the more conforming ones. Under both therapies there are more evidences of changes in behavioral efficiency than of changes in self-regard or personality structure."

4. Performance in the token economy program is related to performance in another learning task. Panek (1967) worked with 32 chronic schizophrenics (from the Atthowe-Krasner ward). He conditioned common word associations (from the Kent–Rosanoff and Russell–Jenkins lists) with positive and negative contingencies of verbal and token reinforcement. The study then compared success in associate learning with total number of ward token transactions. This latter figure was taken as a measure of the responsiveness to reinforcement; that is, the patient who *earned* most tokens and *spent* most tokens was considered most *responsive* to the token program. The results showed a significant increase of common word associations under either positive (saying "right" and giving a fractional ward token) or negative (saying "wrong" and taking away a fractional ward token) reinforcement, but no significant differences between the two contingencies. Most important, learning-rate rankings were significantly correlated with rankings of total token usage. This is one of the few studies that has demonstrated that the individual who is responsive in one conditioning task such as a token economy is also responsive in an individual verbal-conditioning task. This suggests the possibility of utilizing a verbal-conditioning task as a predictor for response to token-type reinforcement programs. It also relates to a previous series of studies (Krasner, Ullmann, and Fisher, 1964; Krasner, Knowles and Ullmann, 1965), which demonstrated that verbal conditioning of "attitudes" in one task was significantly related to performance in another task requiring a motor performance.

THE USE OF APPARATUS IN THE OPERANT CONTROL OF BEHAVIOR

One of the interesting features of the application of operant procedures to real life settings is the development of various kinds of apparatuses to simplify and enhance the procedures. Usually such apparatuses are developed so that the stimuli that are needed for a prescribed behavioral change can be supplied. In effect, an operant conditioning device must be able to discriminate physically when a desired response occurs, and only then deliver the reinforcing stimuli. It is the use of such equipment that has given both a false and an accurate portrayal of operant methodology. It is false to the extent that it gives the impression of a mechanicalness that is *not* inherent in operant procedures. It is true to the extent that it gives the impression of attempted precision in these procedures.

As an example of the use of such devices, Azrin et al. (1968) selected as their target behavior poor posture or "slouching." This behavior was selected because it is socially undesirable, because medical authorities consider it to be unhealthy, and because it usually elicits an unfavorable reaction from others, particularly when it occurs, as it does so frequently, in individuals living in an institution. An apparatus was developed that provided a warning stimulus followed by an aversive tone for the duration of slouching. Slouching was thereby punished by the onset of the tone, and nonslouching was reinforced by tone termination and postponement. Twenty-five adults wore the apparatus during their normal working day during alternating periods in which the aversive tone was connected and disconnected experimentally. A miniature time meter recorded the duration of the slouching. The results showed that the slouching decreased for each subject during each period in which the slouching produced the aversive tone. The conclusion was that the substantial changes in posture indicated the procedure to be an effective treatment. There are similar examples of such devices throughout the operant research literature (Schwitzgebel, 1968).

OPERANT CONDITIONING OF AUTONOMIC FUNCTION

There is one group of operant studies that must be mentioned because of their implications for future research. They are of recent origin and

have not yet been extended to include specific treatment procedures but, as will be obvious, they soon will. These are the studies of instrumental conditioning of autonomic function. Among the autonomic functions that have been operantly conditioned in humans are brain waves, galvanic skin response, heart rate, and electrodermal fluctuations.

As an illustrative study Lang, Stroufe, and Hastings (1967) have demonstrated the remarkable control that an individual can attain over his heart rate when heartbeat is viewed as an operant response. They presented to their subjects elaborate equipment that was described as measuring heart rate. The task of the subject was to maintain his own heart rate within certain limits on the dial of the equipment, which he could clearly view. Lang and his associates found that when subjects received visual feedback on each trial as to how successful they were, they were literally able to maintain their heart response within the prescribed limits (in contrast to the inability to do so by a control group that did not receive feedback). Subjects were also able to control their heart rate on instruction. It was not clear to the investigators what mechanism was used to control heart rate except that it was clear that respiration, an obvious choice, was not the mechanism used. Similar results had been reported by Shearn (1962), where delay of shock was made contingent on accelerated heart rate.

Ascough and Sipprelle (1968) also demonstrated that spontaneous *increase* and *decrease* in heart rate can be brought under control of operant verbal conditioning. Their results showed significant conditioning effects with increasing differences from the original base line over a group of sessions, even when possible mediating responses were taken into account and controlled. As with the Lang study, the possibility of respiratory changes being responsible for changes in heart rate was ruled out. Similar reports of operant conditioning of spontaneous electrodermal fluctuations have been reported by Crider, Shapiro, and Tursky (1966) and Kimmel and Kimmel (1963).

These studies open many possibilities of application of operant procedures to problems involved in the area of psychosomatic disorders. The relationship between autonomic functioning and overt behavior will be a major field of operant investigation in the near future.

ON GENERALIZATION

One of the major questions that keep arising with operant research, as indeed with all behavior modification research, is that of "generalization." It is relatively easy to change a behavior in an institutional setting or in a clinic office. But what is the evidence that such changes carry over to a meaningful situation in the real world? The direction of research in this area should be to restructure the question of generalization so that it can be handled within an operant framework. The question should not be phrased as "Does this behavior carry over to another situation?" but rather, "What behavior is required in a new situation as a result of a functional analysis of the target situation?"

Although laboratory studies and individual case studies using operant procedures have to some extent attempted to approach problems of generalization (such as changing classroom behavior and measuring changes in behavior out of the classroom), most of the token-economy programs have not attempted such measures. The token programs approach behavior change in "outside" situations in a somewhat different manner. The goal of institutional change is usually to bring about behavior that will enable the individual to function adequately in a situation outside the institution. In order to do that it is necessary to first analyze the new extra-institutional situation to determine what behaviors are necessary in order that the individual may maximize social reinforcement for himself so that he may present himself to others as a social stimulus that elicits positive reinforcement from them.

Rather than a generalized attempt to change behavior within the institution with the *hope* of subsequent change on the outside, it must first be determined what behaviors will "pay off" for the individual in a foster home, in his own home, or living with other patients in a community setting. For example, if the patient is to move into a home, living with other ex-patients, then the important behaviors to develop include cooking, housecleaning, shopping, management

of money, and especially gardening and maintenance of appearance of the home. This latter is extremely important so as to elicit favorable response from neighbors who will perceive the ex-patient's efforts as enhancing property values rather than as a potential danger to the community.

OPERANT CONDITIONING AND BEHAVIOR CONTROL

It is undesirable to write a chapter on operant conditioning procedures and behavior modification without touching upon the issues of behavior control and social implications. Issues of the desirability and inevitability of behavior control have been extensively discussed elsewhere (Rogers and Skinner, 1956; Krasner, 1962; Kanfer, 1965; Goldiamond, 1965). In this chapter we will discuss only one aspect of this problem, that of the possible *misuse* of these procedures. These misuses arise primarily because of the apparent simplicity of the operant techniques. Bachrach and Quigley (1966) summarize this point in referring to operant procedures by saying, "It is, therefore, a field in danger of being ruined by amateurs (p. 510)."

An illustration of the relationship among the behavior modification programs, social planning, and ethical issues has occurred in several recent incidents in a midwestern state hospital and in a Vietnamese mental hospital. The moral principles involved in both incidents are similar. In the first incident a token program was introduced on a female ward and, to make the tokens more effective, traditional hospital *physical* restraints were reintroduced. Patients who could exhibit control of their behavior were given tokens with which they could eventually buy their way out of restraints. Not surprisingly, this set of procedures came to the attention of people outside the hospital, such as relatives and newspaper people. An uproar resulted in a hospital investigation, the stopping of the program, serious damage to all future behavior programs, and the resignation of several of the staff members involved.

This societal concern about the consequences of what the behavior planner is doing is certainly justified. The use of restraints to develop a situation from which one can use tokens to escape indicates a lack of awareness of the real purpose of token programs as outlined here, that is, the training of staff to respect the individual and to treat him as a responsible person who is learning to cope with and control his environment.

The other incident is reported in the American Journal of Psychiatry (1967) by an American psychiatrist in a paper entitled "Operant Conditioning in Vietnamese Mental Hospital." Cotter, the author, having read about some of the studies previously described, decided that shock was the essential ingredient in operant conditioning and brought this form of American treatment with him in a visit to a Vietnamese mental hospital. He instituted a program that he labeled as operant conditioning. He gave the 130 male patients a choice between ECT (electric shock therapy) three times a week and working for their living in the hospital. The rationale was that ECT "served as a negative reinforcement for the response of work for those patients who chose to work rather than to continue receiving ECT." This treatment worked well with the male patients, most of whom qickly volunteered for work. He then tried the procedure with a ward of 130 women patients with much less success, since at the end of the treatment period only 15 women were working. So he introduced another procedure—*work or no food.* This apparently was more effective with the women. Cotter pointed out that these were not cruel methods; rather, it was like giving an injection to a sick person, which may hurt a little, but is for his own benefit. Besides, he observed, the Vietnamese are smaller people than the Americans and thus never had bone fractures, a not uncommon concomitant of electric shock in this country. To cap off his achievements with operant conditioning, and as a contribution to our war effort in Vietnam, he worked out an arrangement with a team of American special forces, the Green Berets. He learned that the Green Berets were unsuccessful in utilizing Viet Cong prisoners to tend the crops in the Headquarters area. Apparently using the above techniques, Cotter was able to supply the Green Berets with his mental patients to tend the crops by discharging them from the hospital to the custody of the troops. This helped the war effort

and increased the "self-esteem" of the patients who were now part of the "team." Admittedly these ex-patients were now placed under the fire of the Viet Cong, but as Cotter concludes, a little stress such as a war situation (for example, the people in London bore up well under fire) is psychiatrically healthy. Thus we have another successful application of operant conditioning!

It is easy to mock this effort, but it seriously points up what must be considered to be a basic misunderstanding of operant procedures in behavior therapy. The aim of such programs is to arrange the environment in such a way that there is an increased likelihood of the individual leaning new behavior more likely to elicit positive reinforcement from others in the environment. The major technique in all forms of behavior therapy in institutional settings involves training people such as nurses, aides, psychologists, and psychiatrists so that they can react to the individual not as a sick patient but as a responsible individual who is acquiring new skills in learning to behave adequately in his environment. To introduce a procedure such as electric shock or physical restraints is to communicate denigration of the individual, and thus to defeat the purpose of the training program. You cannot shape responsible behavior in an individual while at the same time treating him inhumanely. You cannot build a new social environment with any chance of enhancing human dignity based on procedures inducing indignity. Here, clearly, the means will distort and destroy the ends. Further, it is not completely certain that all therapists would consider that the behavior of tilling soil to produce food for soldiers to kill Viet Cong is necessarily a desirable social goal, but that clearly is a value decision.

The program of Cotter's is not an operant-conditioning one, since it does not involve any of the principles of contingent reinforcement, nor is it any form of behavior therapy, since it demonstrates no respect for the integrity of the individual. It is a program of coercion, and as such demonstrates the dangers inherent in the misunderstanding and potential misuse of operant conditioning procedures.

ENVIRONMENTAL DESIGN

In terms of future research, it is increasingly

obvious that operant conditioning applied to behavior therapy will lead in the direction of a research area involving environmental design. If behavior is determined by environmental consequences, then the environment must be planned to maximize the availability of reinforcers. The concept of the environment would include architecture of living space, climate control, and planning for occupational and recreational behavior. The token economy programs have already moved in this direction (Cohen et al., 1968). It is no coincidence that Skinner foresaw the consequences of operant conditioning research extending into a utopian society by writing his science-fiction novel, *Walden Two* (1948). As a society, Walden Two is based upon operant conditioning principles, just as is a token economy. The extension of research in this direction will pose interesting theoretical and ethical issues (Krasner, 1969). Actually, many social and economic problems could be translated into terms allowing for systematic investigation by operant procedures. For example, what is the effect of a guaranteed annual wage upon human behavior? This important economic problem can be translated into a comparison of programs involving contingent versus noncontingent reinforcement. Some token programs already underway are testing such problems. It is a note of irony that what we are proposing is that mental hospitals become the testing grounds for utopian planning. Yet this is perfectly consistent with the view of deviant behavior being a socially learned phenomena. We are merely carrying this view out to its logical consequences.

FUTURE DIRECTIONS OF OPERANT RESEARCH

As in other areas of research, current studies and theories foreshadow at least the more immediate directions that operant research will take. The trouble with writing a section predicting things to come is that the most likely developments are probably in existence here already. For example, it is safe to make the prediction that operant research will not remain "pure," since it is questionable whether it ever has been pure.

One social-influence procedure that will be combined with operant techniques such as token economies, will be to change the theoretical model within which the token program operates. Until recently, residence in a hospital has been, ipso facto, an indication of sickness. As has been indicated earlier, the medical model of psychopathology is under continual attack. It is manifested by daring changes in hospital settings such as those (Jones, Kahn, and Wolcott, 1964) in which hospital personnel wear street clothes and patients are referred to as personnel. Rothaus et al. (1963) report a study utilizing role playing that demonstrated that patients make a better impression on prospective employees when they play a role stressing their difficulties as having been problem behavior rather than recovering from illness. Future studies should demonstrate that token programs are successful to the extent that they are set up in an atmosphere in which the patients are reacted to as responsible individuals and not as sick patients.

There will be continued efforts to demonstrate the operant aspects involved in other approaches to modifying behavior, including other behavioral methods. This is illustrated by Leitenberg et al. (1968), who demonstrated that "therapeutically oriented instructions and verbal positive reinforcement" were the significant element in the effectiveness of standard systematic desensitization procedure used with snake phobias. This study seemed to point in the direction of operant procedures as being a key element in what was believed to be primarily a classical conditioning procedure. Similar studies will likely follow in this direction.

CONCLUSIONS

One thing obvious from the current operant studies is the movement in the direction away from one-to-one treatment to milieu or environmental manipulation. Yet the focus in these approaches still remains upon bringing about changes in the individual, through the mechanism of the behavior of other people. The difference between the current operant-based approaches and previous dynamic-based ones is not a real change from one-to-one relationship, but in the nature, role, and function of the "one" in the therapeutic part of the relationship. It has shifted from an individual in the social role of a healer, therapist, physician, psychiatrist, or psychologist to that of a natural member of the environment—a nurse, aide, teacher, parent, peer, or research experimenter. The latter individual is now behaving "therapeutically" (with intent to change behavior in a socially desirable direction) towards the target individual. This behavior, programmed by the training procedures received, is taking place in a "natural" setting (such as hospital, school, or home) rather than in an artificial setting such as the therapist's office.

Further, the view that the behavior dealt with by operant procedures is too molecular or atomistic, hence inconsequential, simply does not hold up. As a change in behavior is brought about, even a small change, it is the "whole" individual to whom others react, not a part of a person.

One of the major controversies involving operant conditioning procedures involves the relationship between behavior and so-called cognitive functions. The controversy appears in different forms. For example, in the verbal conditioning area it is phrased in terms of the relationship between behavior change or conditioning and awareness (Krasner, 1967). In other operant conditioning studies this issue may be expressed in terms of relation between behavior change and the amount and kind of information given to the subject. For example, if a patient is told by a nurse the reason for his receiving a token, does this mean we have departed from the operant-conditioning paradigm?

There are a number of points that should be made about this issue. As the author has tried to make clear throughout the chapter, operant techniques, with their focus on manipulating consequences of behavior, have to be considered within a broader behavior influence framework. Eventually, crucial research studies will demonstrate that the operant technique significantly adds to the maximization of this behavior. In any given situation, be it labeled research or psychotherapy, the behavior required of the subject or patient is communicated implicitly or explicitly. This of course is a paraphrasing of

the concept of the effect of the demand characteristics of the situation (Orne, 1961). In effect, given a situation in which the experimenter or therapist maximizes the behavior influence variables as expressed by demand characteristics, subject and experimenter biases and expectancies, and experimenter prestige, then the specific operant techniques such as the contingent offering of a token or verbalizing "good" significantly add to the modification aspects of the situation.

The analogue at this point is the study by Paul (1966) using a desensitization technique. As a control group, Paul devised a situation that included the procedures that are likely to enhance placebo effects. This included offhand statements by the receptionist that the subject was lucky to see an excellent therapist; the spelling out in explicit terms to the subject of the rationale of the treatment; and communication of expectancies of being helped. Of the two experimental groups, one received systematic desensitization and the second received traditional psychotherapy. The results indicated that a placebo-control group was about as effective as the traditional psychotherapy procedure in bringing about change in the target behavior (anxiety in interpersonal situations). The very specific desensitization procedures *added* to the behavior influence procedures of the other two techniques, *significantly* augmenting their effectiveness in changing the target behavior. Thus far there has been no analogous study with the use of operant techniques. Investigators using operant techniques should concentrate on demonstrating that these procedures add to the behavior-influence variables rather than, as some have suggested, to the elimination of these aspects of the influence process. It makes no sense to attempt a study with a human being that approaches him as a stupid animal who cannot understand English.

This has been increasingly recognized in operant-conditioning studies. For example, early verbal-conditioning studies invariably used control groups that received no reinforcement. It eventually became obvious that this was an inadequate control. When a subject is in a situation in which another individual never responds to him, then that situation becomes aversive, and it certainly is not an adequate control. Even a random reinforcement group presents problems. Harmatz and Lapuc (1968) argue that the ideal control subject would receive the same number of reinforcements, spaced exactly the same way as his experimental counterpart, but delivered noncontingently. A yoked control paradigm would result in this ideal control, since the experimental subject and his yoked control receive exactly the same reinforcement, except that for the control subject, they are administered noncontingently. Thus, once again a growth and sophistication of design has to take into consideration the effects of the situation upon the human being. The progression of operant studies has been steadily in the direction of recognizing and incorporating the basic variables that control human behavior.

SUMMARY

This chapter has presented an overview of research in operant approaches to modifying human deviant behavior. The research investigations in this area are characterized by (a) working within a *social learning* framework of abnormality; (b) the extension of experimental *laboratory* studies of humans and animals to real-life problem behaviors; (c) a close linkage of experimental *attitudes* with clinical problems; (d) the development of new *assessment* procedures based on observation of behavior; (e) the necessity of conceptualizing operant research within a broader behavior influence framework; (f) the apparent effectiveness of operant approaches in modifying a wide category of behaviors; (g) the complexity of the three sets of variables involved in operant research—influencer, influencee, and situation; (h) the extension of training of key environmental figures in the community; (i) the clinical usefulness of operant research designed as own-control; (j) the broad social and ethical implications that are inherent in the extension of operant research to social planning; and (k) the final comment that no self-respecting research investigator can neglect—the need for more carefully controlled and ingenious variations of current operant research, which will move the field more clearly into recognition of its place within a psychology of behavior influence.

REFERENCES

Adams, J. S., and Hoffman, B. The frequency of self-reference statements as a function of generalized reinforcement. *Journal of Abnormal and Social Psychology*, 1960, **60**, 384–389.

Agras, W. S., Leitenberg, H., and Barlow, D. H. Social reinforcement in the modification of agoraphobia. *Archives of General Psychiatry*, in press.

Ascough, J. C., and Sipprelle, C. H. Operant verbal conditioning of autonomic responses. *Behaviour Research and Therapy*, 1968, **6**, 363–370.

Atthowe, J. M., Jr., and Krasner, L. A preliminary report on the application of contingent reinforcement procedures (token economy) on a "chronic" psychiatric ward. *Journal of Abnormal and Social Psychology*, 1968, **73**, 37–43.

Ayllon, T. Intensive treatment of psychotic behaviour by stimulus satiation and food reinforcement. *Behaviour Research and Therapy*, 1963, **1**, 53–61.

Ayllon, T., and Azrin, N. H. The measurement and reinforcement of behavior of psychotics. *Journal of Experimental Analysis of Behavior*, 1965, **8**, 357–383.

Ayllon, T., and Azrin, N. H. Reinforcer sampling: A technique for increasing the behavior of mental patients. *Journal of Applied Behavior Analysis*, 1968, **1**, 13–20a.

Ayllon, T., and Azrin, N. H. *The token economy: A motivational system for therapy and rehabilitation.* New York: Appleton–Century–Crofts, 1968b.

Ayllon, T., and Haughton, E. Control of the behavior of schizophrenic patients by food. *Journal of Experimental Analysis of Behavior*, 1962, **5**, 343–352.

Ayllon, T., and Haughton, E. Modification of symptomatic verbal behavior of mental patients. *Behaviour Research and Therapy*, 1964, **2**, 87–97.

Ayllon, T., and Michael, J. The psychiatric nurse as a behavioral engineer. *Journal of the Experimental Analysis of Behavior*, 1959, **2**, 323–334.

Azrin, N., et al. Behavioral engineering: Postural control by a portable operant apparatus. *Journal of Applied Behavior Analysis*, 1968, **1**, 99–108.

Bachrach, A. J., Erwin, W. J., and Mohr, P. J. The control of eating behavior in an anorexic by operant conditioning techniques. In L. P. Ullmann and L. Krasner (Eds.), *Case studies in behavior modification.* New York: Holt, Rinehart and Winston, 1965.

Bachrach, A. J., and Quigley, W. A. Direct methods of treatment. In I. A. Berg and L. A. Pennington (Eds.), *Introduction to clinical psychology.* (3rd ed.) New York: Ronald Press, 1966.

Bandura, A. Psychotherapy as a learning process. *Psychological Bulletin*, 1961, **58**, 143–159.

Barrett, B. H. Reduction in rate of multiple tics by free operant conditioning methods. *Journal of Nervous and Mental Disease*, 1962, **135**, 187–195.

Bentler, P. M., O'Hara, J. W., and Krasner, L. Hypnosis and placebo. *Psychological Reports*, 1963, **12**, 153–154.

Bryan, J. H., and Lichtenstein, E. Effects of subject and experimenter attitudes in verbal conditioning. *Journal of Personality and Social Psychology*, 1966, 182–189.

Burgess, E. P. The modification of depressive behaviors. Paper presented at the annual meeting of the Association for the Advancement of the Behavioral Therapies, San Francisco, California, September 1, 1968.

Catania, A. (Ed.). *Contemporary research in operant behavior.* Glenview, Illinois: Scott, Foresman & Co., 1968.

Cautela, J. R., and Kastenbaum, R. A reinforcement survey schedule for use in therapy, training, and research. *Psychological Reports*, 1967, **20**, 1115–1130.

Cohen, N. L., Goldiamond, I., Filipczak, J., and Pooley, R. Training professionals in procedures for the establishment of educational environments. *Educational Facility Press*, IBR, Md. 1968.

Cotter, L. H. Operant conditioning in a Vietnamese mental hospital. *American Journal of Psychiatry*, 1967, **124**, 23–28.

Crider, A., Shapiro, D., and Tursky, B. Reinforcement of spontaneous electrodermal activity. *Journal of comparative and physiological psychology*, 1966, **61**, 20–27.

Dinoff, M., et al. Conditioning verbal behavior of a psychiatric population in a group therapy-like situation. *Journal of Clinical Psychology*, 1960, **16**, 371–372.

Ekman, P., Krasner, L., and Ullmann, L. P. Interaction of set and awareness as determinants of response to verbal conditioning. *Journal of Abnormal and Social Psychology*, 1963, **66**, 387–389.

Eysenck, H. J. Learning theory and behaviour therapy. *Journal of Mental Science*, 1959 **105**, 61–75.

Fahmy, S. A. Conditioning and extinction of a referential verbal response class in a situation resembling a clinical diagnostic interview. *Dissertation Abstracts*, 1953, **13**, 873–874.

Ferster, C. B. Classification of behavioral pathology. In L. Krasner and L. P. Ullmann (Eds.), *Research in behavior modification*, New York: Holt, Rinehart and Winston, 1965.

Ferster, C. B. Animal behavior and mental illness. *The Psychological Record*, 1966, **16**, 345–356.

Ferster, C. B., and De Meyer, M. K. The development of performances in autistic children in an automatically controlled environment. *Journal of Chronic Diseases*, 1961, **13**, 312–345.

Ferster, C. B., and Perrott, M. C. *Behavior principles.* New York: Appleton–Century–Crofts, 1968.

Ferster, C. B., and Skinner, B. F. *Schedules of reinforcement.* New York: Appleton–Century–Crofts, 1957.

Franks, C. M. (Ed.). *Conditioning techniques in clinical practice and research.* New York: Springer Publishing Co., 1964.

Franks, C. M. Behavior therapy, psychology, and the psychiatrist. *American Journal of Orthopsychiatry*, 1965, **35**, 145–151.

Fuller, P. R. Operant conditioning of a vegetative human organism. *American Journal of Psychology*, 1949, **62**, 587–590.

Gelfand, S., Ullmann, L. P., and Krasner, L. The placebo response: An experimental approach. *Journal of Nervous and Mental Disease*, 1963, **136**, 379–387.

Gericke, O. L. Practical use of operant conditioning procedures in a mental hospital. *Psychiatric Studies and Projects*, 1965, **3**, 1–10.

Goldiamond, I. Justified and unjustified alarm over behavioral control. In O. Milton (Ed.), *Behavior disorders.* New York: Lippincott, 1965.

Goldiamond, I., and Dyrud, J. E. Some applications and implications of behavior analysis for psychotherapy. In J. M. Shlien et al. (Eds.), *Research in psychotherapy.* Vol. III. Washington, D.C.: American Psychological Association, 1968. Pp. 54–89.

Greenspoon, J. The effect of two nonverbal stimuli on the frequency of members of two verbal response classes. *American Psychologist*, 1954, **9**, 384.

Greenspoon, J. Verbal conditioning. In A. J. Bachrach (Ed.), *Experimental foundations of clinical psychology.* New York: Basic Books, 1962.

Grossberg, J. M. Behavior therapy: A review. *Psychological Bulletin*, 1964, **62**, 73–88.

Harmatz, M. G., and Lapuc, P. S. A technique for employing a yoked control in free operant verbal conditioning experiments. *Behavior Research and Therapy*, 1968, **6**, 483.

Henderson, J. D. Conditioning techniques in a community-based residential treatment facility for emotionally disturbed men. Unpublished manuscript, Spruce House, Horizon House, Inc., Philadelphia, Penna., 1968.

Holz, W. C., and Azrin, N. H. Conditioning human verbal behavior. In W. K. Honig (ed.) *Operant behavior.* New York: Appleton, 1966.

Honig, W. K. (Ed.). *Operant behavior: Areas of research and application*. New York: Appleton–Century–Crofts, 1966.

Hutchinson, R. R., and Azrin, N. H. Conditioning of mental-hospital patients to fixed-ratio schedules of reinforcement. *Journal of the Experimental Analysis of Behavior*, 1961, **4**, 87–95.

Ince, L. P. A behavioral approach to motivation in rehabilitation. *Psychological Record*, 1969, **19**, 105–111.

Isaacs, W., Thomas, J., and Goldiamond, I. Application of operant conditioning to reinstate verbal behavior in psychotics. *Journal of Speech and Hearing Disorders*, 1960, **25**, 8–12.

Jones, N., Kahn, M., and Wolcott, O. Wearing of street clothing by mental personnel. *International Journal of Social Psychiatry*, 1964, **10**, 216–222.

Kalish, H. I. Behavior therapy. In B. B. Wolman (Ed.), *Handbook of clinical psychology*. New York: McGraw–Hill, 1965.

Kanfer, F. H. Vicarious human reinforcement: A glimpse into the black box. In L. Krasner and L. P. Ullmann (Eds.), *Research in behavior modification*. New York: Holt, Rinehart and Winston, 1965. Pp. 244–267.

Kanfer, F. H. Issues and ethics in behavior manipulation. *Psychological Reports*, 1965, **16**, 187–196.

Kanfer, F. H. Verbal conditioning: A review of its current status. In T. R. Dixon and D. L. Horton (Eds.), *Verbal behavior and general behavior theory*. New York: Prentice–Hall, 1968.

Kanfer, F. H., and Marston, A. R. Determinants of self-reinforcement in human learning. *Journal of Experimental Psychology*, 1963, **66**, 245–254.

Kanfer, F. H., and Saslow, G. Behavioral analysis. *Archives of General Psychiatry*, 1965, **12**, 529–538.

Keller, F. S., and Schoenfeld, W. N. *Principles of psychology*. New York: Appleton–Century–Crofts, 1950.

Kiesler, D. J. Some myths of psychotherapy research and the search for a paradigm. *Psychological Bulletin*, 1966, **65** (2), 110–136.

Kimmel, E., and Kimmel, H. D. A replication of operant conditioning of the GSR. *Journal of Experimental Psychology*, 1963, **65**, 212–213.

King, G. F., Armitage, S. G., and Tilton, J. R. A therapeutic approach to schizophrenics of extreme pathology: An operant-interpersonal method. *Journal of Abnormal and Social Psychology*, 1960, **61**, 276–286.

Krasner, L. Studies of the conditioning of verbal behavior. *Psychological Bulletin*, 1958, **55**, 148–170.

Krasner, L. The therapist as a social reinforcement machine. In H. H. Strupp and L. Luborsky (Eds.), *Research in psychotherapy*. Vol. 2. Washington, D.C.: American Psychological Association, 1962.

Krasner, L. Behavior control and social responsibility. *American Psychologist*, 1962, **17**, 199–204.

Krasner, L. Verbal conditioning and psychotherapy. In L. Krasner and L. P. Ullmann (Eds.), *Research in behavior modification*. New York: Holt, Rinehart and Winston, 1965. Pp. 211–228.

Krasner, L. Verbal operant conditioning and awareness. In K. Salzinger and S. Salzinger (Eds.), *Research in verbal behavior and some neurophysiological implications*. New York: Academic Press, 1967. Pp. 57–77.

Krasner, L. Assessment of token economy programmes in psychiatric hospitals. In R. Porter (Ed.), *The role of learning in psychotherapy*. London: Churchill, 1968.

Krasner, L. Behaviour therapy: Ethics and training. In C. M. Franks (Ed.), *Behavior therapy: Appraisal and status*. New York: McGraw–Hill, 1969.

Krasner, L., and Atthowe, J. M., Jr. Token economy bibliography. New York: State University of New York, Stony Brook, 1968.

Krasner, L., Knowles, J. B., and Ullmann, L. P. Effect of verbal conditioning of attitudes on subsequent motor performance. *Journal of Personality and Social Psychology*, 1965, **1**, 407–412.

Krasner, L., and Ullmann, L. P. Variables in the verbal conditioning of schizophrenic subjects. *American Psychologist*, 1958, **13**, 358.

Krasner, L., and Ullmann, L. P. (Eds.). *Research in behavior modification*. New York: Holt, Rinehart and Winston, 1965.

Krasner, L., Ullmann, L. P., and Fisher, D. Changes in performance as related to verbal conditioning of attitudes toward the examiner. *Perceptual Motor Skills*, 1964, **19**, 811–816.

Krasner, L., Ullmann, L. P., Weiss, R. L., and Collins, B. J. Responsivity to verbal conditioning as a function of three different examiners. *Journal of Clinical Psychology*, 1961, **17**, 411–415.

Krasner, L., Weiss, R. L., and Ullmann, L. P. Responsivity to verbal conditioning as a function of "awareness." *Psychological Reports*, 1961, **8**, 523–538.

Lang, P. J., Stroufe, L. A., and Hastings, J. E. Effects of feed-back and instructional set on the control of cardiac-rate variability. *Journal of Experimental Psychology*, 1967, **75**, 425–431.

Lazarus, A. A. Learning theory and the treatment of depression. *Behaviour Research and Therapy*, 1968, **6**, 83–89.

Leitenberg, H., Agras, W. S., and Thomson, L. E. A sequential analysis of the effect of selective positive reinforcement in modifying anorexia nervosa. *Behaviour Research and Therapy*, 1968, **6**, 211–218.

Lindsley, O. R. Operant conditioning methods applied to research in chronic schizophrenia. *Psychiatric Research Reports*, 1956, **5**, 118–153.

Lindsley, O. R. Characteristics of the behavior of chronic psychotics as revealed by free-operant conditioning methods. *Diseases of the Nervous System*, 1960, **21** (monograph supplement), 66–78.

Lindsley, O. R., and Skinner, B. F. A method for the experimental analysis of the behavior of psychotic patients. *American Psychologist*, 1954, **9**, 419–420.

Lindsley, O. R., and Skinner, B. F., and Solomon, H. C. Studies in behavior therapy. Metropolitan State Hospital, Status Report I, May, 1953.

Lloyd, K. E., and Garlington, W. K. Weekly variations in performance on a token economy psychiatric ward. *Behaviour Research and Therapy*, 1968, **6**, 407–410.

Lovaas, O. I. Effect of exposure to symbolic aggression on agressive behavior. *Child Development*, 1961, **32**, 37–44.

Lovaas, O. I., Freitag, G., Gold, V. J., and Kassorla, I. C. Experimental studies in childhood schizophrenia: Analysis of self-destructive behavior. *Journal of Experimental Child Psychology*, 1965, **2**, 67–84.

Lovaas, O. I., Freitag, L., Nelson, K., and Wahlen, C. The establishment of imitation and its use for the development of complex behavior in schizophrenic children. *Behaviour Research and Therapy*, 1967, **5**, 171–181.

Lovaas, O. I., Schaeffer, B., and Simmons, J. Q. Building social behavior in autistic children by use of electric shock. Journal of Experimental Research in Personality, 1965, **1**, 99–109.

Marks, J., Shalock, R., and Sonoda, B. Reinforcement vs. relationship therapy for schizophrenics. *Proceedings of the 75th Annual Convention of the American Psychological Association*, 1967, 237–238.

Matarrazo, J. D., Saslow, G., and Pareis, E. N. Verbal conditioning of two response classes, some methodological considerations. *Journal of Abnormal and Social Psychology*, 1960, **61**, 190–206

Meichenbaum, D. H. Sequential strategies in two cases of hysteria. *Behaviour Research and Therapy*, 1966, **4**, 89–94(a).

Meichenbaum, D. H. Effects of social reinforcement on the level of abstraction in schizophrenics. *Journal of Abnormal and Social Psychology*, 1966, **71**, 354–362(b).

Meichenbaum, D. H. The effects of instructions and reinforcement on thinking and language behavior of schizophrenics. *Behaviour Research and Therapy*, 1969, **7**, 101–114.

Mischel, W. *Personality and assessment*. New York: Wiley, 1968.

Orne, M. T. On the social psychology of the psychological experiment: With particular reference to demand characteristics and their implications. *American Psychologist*, 1962, **17**, 776–783.

Panek, D. M. Word association learning by chronic schizophrenics under conditions of reward and punishment. Paper read at Western Psychological Association Convention, 1967.

Patterson, G. R. Responsiveness to social stimuli. In L. Krasner and L. P. Ullmann (Eds.), *Research in behavior modification*. New York: Holt, Rinehart and Winston, 1965. Pp. 157–178.

Paul, G. L. *Insight vs. desensitization in psychotherapy*. Stanford, California: Stanford University Press, 1966.

Paul, G. L. Behavior modification research: Design and tactics. In C. M. Franks (Ed.), *Behavior therapy: Appraisal and status*. New York: McGraw–Hill, 1969.

Peters, H. N., and Jenkins, R. L. Improvement of chronic schizophrenic patients with guided problem solving, motivated by hunger. *Psychiatric Quarterly Supplement*, 1954, **28**, 84–101.

Premack, D. Toward empirical behavior laws. I. Positive reinforcement. *Psychological Review*, 1959, **66**, 219–233.

Quay, H. The effect of verbal reinforcement on the recall of early memories. *Journal of Abnormal and Social Psychology*, 1959, **59**, 254–257.

Reese, E. P. *The analysis of human operant behavior*. Dubuque, Iowa: Wm. C. Brown, Publishers, 1966.

Reynolds, G. S. A primer of operant conditioning. Glenview, Illinois: Scott, Foresman and Co., 1968.

Rogers, J. M. Operant conditioning in a quasi-therapy setting. *Journal of Abnormal and Social Psychology*, 1960, **60**, 247–252.

Rogers, C. R., and Skinner, B. F. Some issues concerning the control of human behavior: A symposium. *Science*, 1956, **124**, 1057–1066.

Ross, A. O. Behavior therapy. In B. B. Wolman (Ed), *Manual of Child Psychopathology*, New York: McGraw–Hill, 1970.

Rothaus, P., Hanson, P. G., Cleveland, S. E., and Johnson, D. L. Describing psychiatric hospitalizations: A dilemma. *American Psychologist*, 1963, **18**, 85–89.

Russell, J. C., Clark, A. W., and Van Sommers, P. Treatment of stammering by reinforcement of fluent speech. *Behaviour Research and Therapy*, 1968, **6**, 447–454.

Salzinger, K. Experimental manipulation of verbal behavior: A review. *Journal of Genetic Psychology*, 1959, **61**, 65–94.

Salzinger, K. The problem of response class in verbal behavior. In K. Salzinger and S. Salzinger (Eds.) *Research in verbal behavior and some neurophysiological implications*. New York: Academic Press, 1967.

Salzinger, K., and Pisoni, S. Reinforcement of verbal affect responses of normal subjects during the interview. *Journal of Abnormal and Social Psychology*, 1960, **60**, 127–130.

Salzinger, K., and Pisoni, S. Some parameters of the conditioning of verbal affect responses in schizophrenic subjects. *Journal of Abnormal and Social Psychology*, 1961, **63**, 511–516.

Salzinger, K , Portnoy, S., and Feldman, R. S. Experimental manipulation of continuous speech in schizophnenic patients. *Journal of Abnormal and Social Psychology*, 1964, **68**, 508–516.

Sapolsky, A. Effect of interpersonal relationships upon verbal conditioning. *Journal of Abnormal and Social Psychology*, 1960, **60**, 241–246.

Sarason, I. G., and Minard, J. Interrelationships among subject, experimenter, and situational variables. *Journal of Abnormal and Social Psychology*, 1963, **67**, 87–91.

Schaefer, H. H., and Martin, P. L. Behavioral therapy for "apathy" of hospitalized schizophrenics. *Psychological reports*, 1966, **19**, 1147–1158.

Schwitzgebel, R. A new approach to reducing adolescent crime. *Federal Probation*, March 1960, 20–24.

Schwitzgebel, R. Reduction of adolescent crime by a research method. *Journal of Correctional Psychiatry and Social Therapy*, 1961, **7**, 212–215.

Schwitzgebel, R. Delinquents with tape recorders. *New Society*, January 1963, 14–16.

Schwitzgebel, R. *Street-corner research: An experimental approach to the juvenile delinquent*. Cambridge, Mass.: Harvard University Press, 1964.

Schwitzgebel, R. Short-term operant conditioning of adolescent offenders on socially relevant variables. *Journal of abnormal psychology*, 1967, **72**, 134–142.

Schwitzgebel, R., Schwitzgebel, R., Pahnke, W. N., and Hurd, W. S. A program of research in behavioral electronics. *Behavioral Science*, 1964, **9**, 233–238.

Schwitzgebel, R. L. A survey of electromechanical devices for behavior modification. *Psychological Bulletin*, 1968, **70**, 444–459.

Scoles, P. E., and Henderson, J. D. Effects of token reinforcement on the social performance of psychotic men. Unpublished manuscript, Spruce House, Horizon House, Inc., Philadelphia, 1968.

Shearn, D. W. Operant conditioning of heart rate. *Science*, 1962, **137**, 530–531.

Sidman, M. Operant techniques. In A. J. Bachrach (Ed.), *Experimental foundations of clinical psychology*. New York: Basic Books, 1962, 170–210.

Skinner, B. F. *The behavior of organisms*. New York: Appleton–Century–Crofts, Inc., 1938.

Skinner, B. F. *Walden two*. New York: Macmillan Co., 1948.

Skinner, B. F. *Science and human behavior*. New York: Macmillan Co., 1953.

Skinner, B. F. *Verbal behavior*. New York: Appleton–Century–Crofts, 1957.

Skinner, B. F., Solomon, H. C., Lindsley, O. R., and Richards, M. E. Studies in behavior therapy. Metropolitan State Hospital, Waltham, Mass. Status Report II. May 31, 1954.

Slack, C. W. Experimenter-subject psychotherapy: A new method of introducing intensive office treatment for unreachable cases. *Mental Hygiene*, 1960, **44**, 236–256.

Spielberger, C. D. The role of awareness in verbal conditioning. In C. W. Eriksen (Ed.), *Behavior and awareness*. Durham, N.C.: Duke University Press, 1962.

Staats, A. W. *Human learning*. New York: Holt, Rinehart and Winston, 1964.

Staats, A. W. A case in and a strategy for the extension of learning principles to problems of human behavior. In L. Krasner and L. P. Ullmann, (Eds.), *Research in behavior modification*. New York: Holt, Rinehart and Winston, 1965. Pp. 27–55.

Staats, A. W., Minke, K. A., Finley, J. R., Wolf, M., and Brooks, L. O. A reinforcer system and experimental procedure for the laboratory study of reading acquisition. *Child development*, 1964, **35**, 209–231.

Steffy, R. A., et al. An application of learning techniques to the management and rehabilitation of severely regressed, chronically ill patients: Preliminary findings. Paper presented at the meeting of the Ontario Psychological Association, Lakeshore Psychiatric Hospital, Ottawa, 1966.

Stuart, R. B. Prostitution as treatment of marital discord. Paper presented at the meeting of the American Psychological Association, Aug. 31, 1968, San Francisco, California.

Taffel, C. Anxiety and the conditioning of verbal behavior. *Journal of Abnormal and Social Psychology*, 1955, **51**, 496–501.

Taylor, E. W. Interpersonal orientation and verbal conditioning effects. Proceedings of the 76th Annual Convention, American Psychological Association, 1968.

Ullmann, L. P., Forsman, R. G., Kenny, J. W., McInnis, T. L., Jr., Unikel, I. P., and Zeisset, R. M. Selective reinforcement of schizophrenics' interview responses. *Behavior Research and Therapy*, 1965, **2**, 205–212.

Ullmann, L. P., and Krasner, L. *Case studies in behavior modification*. New York: Holt, Rinehart and Winston, 1965.

Ullmann, L. P., and Krasner, L. *A psychological approach to abnormal behavior*. Englewood Cliffs, New Jersey: Prentice–Hall, 1969.

Ullmann, L. P., Krasner, L., and Collins, B. S. Modification of behavior through verbal conditioning: Effects in group therapy. *Journal of Abnormal and Social Psychology*, 1961, **62**, 128–132.

Ullmann, L. P., Krasner, L., and Edinger, R. L. Verbal conditioning of common associations in long-term schizophrenic patients. *Behaviour Research and Therapy*, 1964, **2**, 15–18.

Ullmann, L. P., Krasner, L., and Sherman, M. MMPI items associated with pleasantness of emotional words used in thematic story-telling. Veterans' Administration, Palo Alto, Calif., *Research Reports*, **25**, 1963.

Ullmann, L. P., Krasner, L., and Weiss, R. L. Personality correlates of students and patients' response to to reinforcement of emotional words in an interpersonal situation. Paper presented at the meeting of the California State Psychological Association, San Francisco, California, December, 1963.

Ullmann, L. P., and McFarland, R. L. Productivity as a variable in TAT protocols, a methodological study. *Journal of Projective Techniques*, 1957, **21**, 80–87.

Ulrich, R., Stachnik, T., and Mabry, J. *Control of human behavior*. Glenview. Illinois: Scott, Foresman and Co., 1966.

Verhave, T. (Ed.). *The experimental analysis of behavior*. New York: Appleton–Century–Crofts, 1966.

Wagner, B. R. The training of attending and abstracting responses in chronic schizophrenics. *Journal of Experimental Research in Personality*, 1968, **3**, 77–88.

Watson, J. B., and Rayner, R. Conditioned emotional reactions. *Journal of Experimental Psychology*, 1920, **3**, 1–14.

Weiss, R. L. Operant conditioning techniques in psychological assessment. In P. McReynolds (Ed.), *Advances in psychological assessment*. Palo Alto, California: Science and Behavior Books, 1968. Pp. 169–190.

Weiss, R. L., Krasner, L., and Ullmann, L. P. Responsivity to verbal conditioning as a function of emotional atmosphere and pattern of reinforcement. *Psychological Reports*, 1960, **6**, 415–426.

Weiss, R. L., Krasner, L., and Ullmann, L. P. Responsivity of psychiatric patients to verbal conditioning: "Success" and "failure" conditions and pattern of reinforced trials. *Psychological Reports*, 1963, **12**, 423–426.

Williams, J. H. Conditioning of verbalization: A review. *Psychological Bulletin*, 1966, **62**, 383–393.

Williams, R. I., and Blanton, R. L. Verbal conditioning in a psychotherapeutic situation. *Behaviour Research and Therapy*, 1968, **6**, 97–103.

Wilson, F. S., and Walters, R. H. Modification of speech output of near-mute schizophrenics through social-learning procedures. *Behaviour Research and Therapy*, 1966, **4**, 59–67.

Winkler, R. Management of chronic psychiatric patients by a token reinforcement system. Paper presented at the annual meeting of the Australian Psychological Society, Brisbane, Australia, August, 1968 (a).

Winkler, R. Healthy and unhealthy economics. Paper presented at the annual meeting of the Australian Psychological Society, Brisbane, Australia, August, 1968 (b).

Wolpe, J. Outgoing presidential report. *Association for Advancement of Behavioral Therapy*, November, 1968, **3**, 1–2.

Zimmerman, J., et al. Effects of token reinforcement on productivity in multipally handicapped clients in a sheltered workshop. *Prepublication technical report*. Indiana University, School of Medicine and Indianapolis Goodwill Industries, Inc., 1968.

17

PSYCHOTHERAPY BASED UPON MODELING PRINCIPLES[1]

ALBERT BANDURA

STANFORD UNIVERSITY

Psychological approaches to the modification of human behavior have until recently relied heavily upon verbal influence procedures. Although the paramount role of corrective learning experiences was widely acknowledged in theoretical formulations of psychotherapy, use of the interview as the basic vehicle for producing changes placed severe restrictions on the quality, range, and intensity of experiences that could be created under the prescribed conditions. It would appear from the weak and inconsistent effects associated with conversational approaches that the popularity of interview methods is attributable more to their ease of application than to their demonstrated efficacy. Recent years have witnessed a vigorous growth of new treatment approaches that achieve psychological changes mainly through guided learning experiences (Bandura, 1969a).

Modification programs based upon social-learning principles differ from interview approaches, among other ways, in the *content*, the *locus*, and the *agents* of treatment. With regard to content, therapeutic procedures are mainly applied to the actual problem behaviors requiring modification instead of to their verbal substitutes. Therapists, therefore, devote the major portion of their time to altering the conditions governing deviant behaviors rather than conversing about them. To increase further transfer of changes to everyday life, treatment is typically carried out in the natural settings in

[1] Preparation of this chapter was facilitated by grants M-5162 and IF03 MH42658 from the National Institute of Mental Health, United States Public Health Service. The author also gratefully acknowledges the generous assistance of the staff of the Center for Advanced Study in the Behavioral Sciences. Some of the material contained in this review is drawn from A. Bandura, *Principles of Behavior Modification*. Holt, Rinehart, & Winston, 1969.

which the psychological problems arise. Moreover, treatment programs are generally implemented under close professional supervision by persons who have the most intensive contact with the client and can therefore serve as powerful therapeutic agents. The potential influence of such persons derives from the fact that, being closely associated with the clients, they exercise considerable control over the very conditions that regulate both deviant and desired behavior. For reasons given above, the therapeutic conditions created in social-learning approaches are ideally suited for producing enduring and generalized changes in psychological functioning.

It is often mistakenly assumed, from the fact that behaviorally oriented therapists achieve changes in behavior rather than in verbal contents, that such approaches are more concerned with manipulating behaviors than in removing their causes. Response patterns can be modified only by altering the conditions that regulate their occurrence. Hence, all forms of psychotherapy, regardless of their self-conferred honorific titles and noble aims, effect behavioral changes through either deliberate or unwitting manipulation of controlling variables. Psychodynamic and social-learning approaches to psychotherapy are, therefore, equally concerned with modifying the determinants of deviant behavior; however, these theories differ, often radically, in what they regard these "causes" to be. These differences in causal interpretations, in turn, influence the types of determinants that are singled out for consideration. *It would, therefore, be more accurate and advantageous to redefine the cause-symptom controversy as being primarily concerned with the question of whether a particular form of therapy chooses to modify conditions that, in reality, exercise strong, weak, or no significant control over the behavior in question.*

Although behavioral and psychodynamic approaches espouse somewhat different causal systems and treatment procedures, they do involve some common change processes, as do most other influence enterprises. Much spirited rhetoric has been devoted to disputes over the types of disorders for which the latter forms of treatment are most appropriate, and their comparative efficacy. Considering the difficulty

of achieving consensus on what the brand names represent, it seems unlikely that the controversies will ever be satisfactorily resolved. Greater progress would perhaps be achieved in developing powerful treatment procedures if these ill-defined partisan labels were retired from use. A more productive approach to the understanding of social influence processes is to focus on the basic mechanisms through which psychological changes are achieved. These mechanisms are undoubtedly enlisted to varying degrees by conditions created, either deliberately or unwittingly, by change agents in influence attempts arbitrarily designated behavior modification, psychotherapy, counseling, reeducation, or some other appellation. In each of the aforementioned endeavors, for example, change agents model certain attitudes and social behavior. One might, therefore, analyze these various activities in terms of the behavior the change agents are modeling, its functional value for the recipients, and the extent to which conditions that facilitate modeling are present. A major criticism of conventional interview treatments is that therapists mainly exemplify silence and interpretive behaviors that have limited functional value for clients. To the extent that clients emulate these behaviors in their everyday relationships they become pests or bores. Similarly, one might examine reinforcement influences, which are operative in all social interactions, to determine what behavior is being reinforced, with what frequency, and by what means, in different systems designed to alter psychological functioning. The major task is to discover the best means of implementing established principles of learning to ameliorate the psychological problems for which people seek help.

The fact that diverse approaches may involve some common processes does not mean that psychological changes achieved by the different methods are necessarily due to the common factor. This point is well illustrated in Weitzman's (1967) reinterpretation of the process through which systematic desensitization presumably achieves its effects. Weitzman reports that during the course of desensitization the aversive scenes presented by therapists for visualization are often transformed and elaborated by clients into imaginal content far removed from the intended stimulus. On the basis of these informal observations he concludes that the changes accompanying desensitization therapy derive primarily from the associative material that is aroused and eventually integrated into the "ego complex." It has been shown in several studies (Lazovik and Lang, 1960; Weinberg and Zaslove, 1963) that clients who modify presented scenes by either transforming them into less threatening events, or by introducing unintended anxiety-provoking elements, are least likely to benefit from desensitization. These findings thus suggest that the associative processes invoked by Weitzman can better account for the failures of desensitization therapy than for its successes. Some further support for this conclusion is provided by experiments (Strahley, 1966) showing that much better outcomes are attained by desensitization based on exposure to actual aversive stimuli that can be precisely controlled than that relying on self-produced imaginal contents.

A number of different treatment procedures have been derived from social-learning principles (Bandura, 1969a), each method being especially well suited to produce a particular type of psychological change. The present chapter is devoted to a discussion of modes of therapy based upon modeling principles. Research conducted within a social-learning framework demonstrates that virtually all learning phenomena that result from direct experiences can occur vicariously, as a function of observing other people's behavior and its consequences for them. Modeling procedures can, therefore, be employed to achieve diverse psychological changes.

Development of efficacious methods of treatment requires research at three different levels. First, investigations are needed into the basic mechanisms through which a given set of operations produces its effects. Knowledge of the underlying processes provides the basis for selecting optimal treatment strategies. Unfortunately, research at this theoretical level, which appears remote from clinical concerns, is often cavalierly dismissed by practitioners as essentially irrelevant. At the second level, the method that has been developed must be tested under controlled laboratory conditions to evaluate its effectiveness, and to determine whether the various components in the compound procedure are necessary, facilitative, irrelevant, or a hindrance to the achievement of desired outcomes. After the power of the method has been demonstrated, clinical applications are then warranted. In other words, the major purpose of research at the clinical level is not to ascertain whether a given procedure is capable of producing changes, because the outcomes are invariably confounded by the operation of countless uncontrolled extraneous variables. Rather, applied research should be concerned with the manner in which proven methods might be further extended, refined, and combined with other efficacious techniques to ensure a high degree of success with each individual case.

Perhaps because psychological interventions rarely have immediate and spectacular consequences, a casual attitude has developed toward using untested techniques. New approaches are promoted enthusiastically, and it is not until the methods have been applied clinically for some time by a coterie of advocates that objective tests of efficacy are conducted, if at all. Usually the methods are unceremoniously retired by subsequent controlled studies or informal evaluation. Workers in psychotherapy have, therefore, come to view any new therapeutic approach as a passing fad. Now that the behavioral consequences of social practices are being measured systematically, it is evident that some of the methods that are assumed to have therapeutic value, in fact, have deleterious effects (Ayllon and Michael, 1959; Harris, Wolf, and Baer, 1964; Lovaas, 1967). When laboratory tests of efficacy precede clinical applications, people are not only spared needless distress resulting from ineffectual or harmful procedures, but, since new methods are carefully evaluated at each stage of development, those that evolve are likely to produce outcomes sufficiently promising to weather the test of time. In accord with the three-phase strategy of experimentation, the present chapter reviews the mechanisms governing modeling phenomena, laboratory tests and component analyses of modeling procedures, and their various clinical applications.

Three Major Effects of Modeling Influences

Modeling influences can produce three differentiable types of effects in observers, each of which has an important therapeutic counterpart. First, observers may acquire new patterns of behavior that did not previously exist in integrated form within their behavioral repertoires. This *observational learning effect* is demonstrated most clearly when models exhibit novel responses which observers have not yet learned to make and which they later reproduce in a substantially identical form.

Complex patterns of behavior are developed by organizing response elements that are usually present as products either of maturation, or of prior observational learning and instrumental conditioning. Thus, for example, persons can produce a variety of elementary sounds as part of their natural endowment. By combining existing sounds, one can create a novel and exceedingly complex verbal response such as *supercalifragilisticexpialidocious*. Some writers (Aronfreed, 1969; Patterson, Littman and Bricker, 1967) have questioned whether behavior formed through unique combinations of available elements represents response learning, because the components already exist in subjects' repertoires. According to this line of reasoning, a pianist who has mastered a Beethoven piano concerto has learned nothing new, because all the intricate finger movements existed in his repertoire; and Beethoven cannot be credited with creating new symphonic music, as he simply rearranged a few pre-existing notes. Any behavior that has a very low or zero probability of occurrence under appropriate stimulus conditions qualifies as a novel response. Most new compound responses are composed of common behavioral elements.

Until recent years it was widely believed that new response patterns are acquired through a gradual shaping process involving selective reinforcement of trial-and-error performances. Fortunately, for reasons of survival and efficacy, most learning under natural conditions does not proceed in this manner. New patterns of behavior can be acquired observationally without proceeding through a laborious response-shaping process. In this nonresponse acquisition process, observers organize response elements into new patterns of behavior at a symbolic level on the basis of information conveyed by modeling stimuli. The conceptual scheme summarized later, and reviewed more fully elsewhere (Bandura, 1969a), illustrates the manner in which information transmitted through verbal, pictorial, and behavioral modeling stimuli are coded and stored, and serve as representational guides for subsequent response reproduction.

A second major function of modeling influences is to strengthen or to weaken inhibitions of responses that already exist in observers' repertoires (Bandura, 1970). The influence that modeling exerts on behavioral restraints is largely determined by observation of rewarding and punishing consequences accompanying models' responses. *Inhibitory effects* are indicated when observers show either decrements in the modeled class of behavior or a general reduction of responsiveness as a result of seeing the behavior of models produce negative consequences. On the other hand, *disinhibitory effects* are evident when observers display an increase in formerly inhibited behavior after observing models engage in threatening activities without experiencing any adverse consequences. Modeling influences are seldom deliberately employed to create inhibitions, but such procedures are being increasingly applied, with notable success, to eliminate disabling fears and inhibitions.

The behavior of others can also serve as discriminative stimuli for observers in facilitating the occurrence of existing responses in the same general class. *Response facilitation effects* can be distinguished from observational learning and disinhibition by the fact that no new responses are acquired, and disinhibitory processes are not involved because the behavior in question is socially sanctioned and, therefore, is unencumbered by restraints. Since the social activities that people engage in at any given moment are partly regulated by the behavior of others, the response-eliciting and cueing function of modeling influences is invariably operative in all social situations.

The remaining sections of this chapter discuss at length applications of modeling procedures to create new patterns of behavior, to eradicate intractable fears and inhibitions, and to facilitate performance of desired modes of response. In any given case, the psychological changes accompanying modeling treatments may result from one or more of the modeling influences mentioned above. Increased social behavior in withdrawn children, for example, may reflect, to varying degrees, acquisition of new social skills, reduction of inhibitions over social responses present in children's repertoires, and facilitation of uninhibited behavior that they are quite capable of performing. Similarly, a modeling treatment may enable phobic clients to interact with objects that they formerly avoided, because their fears have been vicariously extinguished and they have learned more effective means of coping with the dreaded events, thereby reducing their threat value. Although the three principal effects of modeling influences are separable, categorization of individual cases in terms of the type of modeling process involved may be somewhat arbitrary when changes are multiply determined.

DEVELOPMENT OF NEW PATTERNS OF BEHAVIOR THROUGH MODELING

Modeling phenomena involve four interrelated subprocesses that determine whether exposure to the behavior of others will produce new modes of response in observers. Before proceeding to a discussion of treatment applications, the four subsystems governing observational learning will be reviewed briefly, because they specify the conditions that must obtain for modeling procedures to achieve optimal results.

Attentional Processes

One of the main component functions in observational learning involves attentional processes. Simply exposing persons to modeled responses does not in itself guarantee that they will attend closely to them, and that they will necessarily select from the total stimulus complex the most relevant events, or that they will even perceive accurately the cues to which their attention has been directed. An observer will fail to acquire matching behavior, at the sensory registration level, if he does not attend to, recognize, or differentiate the distinctive features of the model's responses. Discrimina-

tive observation is therefore a requisite condition for observational learning.

A number of attention-controlling variables, some related to incentive conditions, others to observer characteristics, and still others to the properties of the modeling cues themselves, will be influential in determining which modeling stimuli will be observed and which will be ignored.

Retention Processes

Another basic component function involved in observational learning concerns the retention of modeled events. When a person observes a model's behavior without performing the responses, he can acquire the modeled responses while they are occurring only in representational form. In order to reproduce social behavior without the continued presence of external modeling cues, a person must also retain the original observational inputs in some symbolic form.

Observational learning involves two representational systems—an imaginal and a verbal one. During exposure, modeling stimuli produce, through a process of sensory conditioning, relatively enduring, retrievable images of modeled sequences of behavior. Indeed, under conditions where stimulus events are highly correlated, as when a name is consistently associated with a given person, it is virtually impossible to hear the name without experiencing imagery of the person's physical characteristics. Similarly, reference to activities (such as golfing and surfing), places (like San Francisco, New York, and Paris), and things (such as the Washington Monument or an airliner) that one has previously observed, immediately elicits vivid imaginal representations of the absent physical stimuli.

The second representational system, which probably accounts for the notable speed of observational learning and long-term retention of modeled contents by humans, involves verbal coding of observed events. Most of the cognitive processes that regulate behavior are primarily verbal rather than visual. To take a simple example, the route traversed by a model can be acquired, retained, and later reproduced more accurately by verbal coding of the visual information into a sequence of right-left turns (for example RRLRR) than by reliance upon visual imagery of the itinerary. Observational learning and retention are facilitated by such codes because they can carry a great deal of information in an easily stored form. After modeled responses have been transformed into images and readily utilizable verbal symbols, these memory codes serve as guides for subsequent reproduction of matching responses. The influential role of symbolic coding operations in observational learning is disclosed by studies (Bandura, Grusec, and Menlove, 1966; Gerst, 1969) demonstrating that subjects who actively code modeling stimuli into verbal and imaginal representations achieve higher acquisition and better retention of modeled responses than those who passively observe or engage in symbolic activities that impede stimulus transformation processes.

Modeling involves not only reproduction of specific responses exhibited by others, but also the abstract properties of modeled behavior. In the latter higher-order form of modeling, observers abstract common attributes exemplified in diverse modeled responses and formulate a principle for generating similar patterns of behavior. Responses that embody the observationally derived rule are likely to resemble the behavior that the model would be inclined to exhibit under similar circumstances.

Motoric Reproduction Processes

The third major component of modeling phenomena is concerned with motoric reproduction processes. This involves the utilization of symbolic representations of modeled patterns to guide overt performances. The process of representational guidance is essentially the same as response learning under conditions where a person behaviorally follows an externally depicted pattern, or is directed through a series of instructions to enact novel response sequences. The only difference is that, in the latter cases, performance is directed by external cues whereas, in delayed modeling, behavioral reproduction is monitored by symbolic counterparts of absent stimuli.

The rate and level of observational learning will be partly governed, at the motoric level, by the availability of essential component responses. Complex modes of behavior are produced by combinations of previously learned components that may, in themselves, represent relatively complicated compounds. In instances where observers lack some of the necessary components, first the constituent elements may be established through modeling and then, in a stepwise fashion, increasingly intricate compounds can be developed imitatively.

In many instances, modeled response patterns have been acquired and retained in representational forms, but they cannot be reproduced behaviorally because of physical limitations. Accurate behavioral enactment of demonstrated activities is also difficult to achieve under conditions where the model's performance is governed by subtle adjustment of internal responses that are unobservable and not easily communicable, as in the development of articulation skills.

The problem of behavioral reproduction is further complicated in the case of highly coordinated motor skills, in which a person cannot observe many of the responses that he is making, and must therefore rely primarily upon proprioceptive feedback cues. For these reasons, performances that contain many motor components usually require, in addition to the guidance of a proficient model, some overt practice.

Reinforcement and Motivational Processes

The final component function concerns motivational or reinforcement variables. A person may acquire, retain, and possess the capabilities for skillful execution of modeled behavior, but the learning may rarely be activated into overt performance if negative sanctions or unfavorable incentive conditions obtain. Under such circumstances, when positive incentives are introduced, observational learning is promptly translated into action (Bandura, 1965b). Reinforcement variables not only regulate the overt expression of matching behavior, but they also affect observational learning by exerting selective control over the types of modeling cues to which a person is most likely to attend. Further, they facilitate selective retention by activating deliberate coding and rehearsal of modeled responses that have high utilitarian value.

As long as therapists are able to produce

imitative behavior simply by modeling and reinforcing it, then some of the aforementioned subprocesses that govern the outcomes tend to be disregarded. A therapist who repeatedly demonstrates desired responses, instructs others to reproduce them, manually prompts the behavior when it fails to occur, and then administers powerful reinforcers, will eventually elicit matching responses in most clients. It may require 1, 10, or 100 demonstration trials, but if one persists, the desired behavior will eventually be evoked. As will be shown later, however, in the treatment of clients exhibiting profound deficits in psychological functions, repeated modeling under favorable reinforcement conditions either fails to produce matching performances or results in an exceedingly slow rate of progress. In order to increase the effectiveness of modeling procedures, one must identify the subsystems in which the dysfunction resides. In any given case, absence of appropriate matching behavior following exposure to modeling stimuli may result from either failures in the attentional system, inadequate coding of modeling stimuli for memory representation, retention decrements, motoric deficiencies, or inadequate reinforcement.

Modeling with Reinforced Guided Performance

Some of the most intractable behavior disorders are characterized by gross deficits not only in behavior but also in the basic psychological functions essential for learning. The more severe cases, such as autistic children and adult schizophrenics, generally manifest little or no functional speech; they lack social skills that are conducive to reciprocally rewarding relationships, and interpersonal stimuli, which ordinarily serve as the principal medium of social influence, often have relatively little impact on them. Since human behavior is largely acquired through modeling and regulated by verbal cues and symbolic reinforcers, profound deficiencies in functions of this nature create major obstacles to treatment. These issues are best exemplified by the treatment of autism.

The development of new competencies in autistic children is further complicated by the fact that they are generally engrossed in repetitive motoric activities and other forms of self-stimulatory behavior. Consequently, they remain oblivious much of the time to relevant environmental influences. The marked self-isolation is also generally coupled with strong resistance to situational demands, as evidenced by their unwillingness to perform appropriate responses that they are obviously capable of making (Cowan, Hoddinoth, and Wright, 1965). When behavioral demands within their capabilities are firmly applied, the children are inclined to avoid responding by evading the therapist, or resorting to tantrums and bizarre motoric activities (Lovaas, 1966; Colby, 1967). After such aversive behaviors lose their functional value for avoiding social demands through consistent nonreinforcement, autistic children typically respond with appropriate behavior (Risley and Wolf, 1967). However, the aversive countercontrol and lack of positive responsiveness eventually extinguish the concerted efforts of less durable therapists. Disappointing treatment outcomes, therefore, are frequently attributed to neurophysiological malfunction.

Although physiological variables are probably contributing factors in autism, it should be noted that even biologically deficient organisms are capable of learning, provided that appropriate conditions are arranged. Nor do capacity variables account for gross deficits in relatively simple motor, conceptual, and emotional responses that are clearly within the capabilities of autistic children. It is evident, however, from the adverse behavior characteristics of autism, that extraordinary interventions must be employed, particularly in initial phases, if any fundamental changes are to be effected in the in the psychological functioning of autistic children.

One of the most provocative behavioral approaches to the treatment of autism, in which modeling procedures figure prominently, has been developed by Lovaas and his colleagues (Lovaas, 1967). The therapeutic program is based on the view that the total rehabilitation of autistic and schizophrenic children can be best achieved through the establishment of stimulus functions that make one amenable to social influences. This process primarily involves developing children's responsiveness to modeling cues, increasing the discriminative value of stimulus events so that children attend and respond appropriately to aspects of their environment that they have previously ignored, and endowing social approval and other symbolic stimuli with reinforcing properties. After a strong modeling set has been created, and children have become adequately responsive to environmental influences, the major task of broadening their social and intellectual competencies can be effectively carried out by parents, teachers, and other agents. Since interpersonal communication and social learning are extensively mediated through language, the development of linguistic skills is also selected as a central objective of treatment.

As noted previously, discriminative attention is a requisite condition for observational learning. Autistic children generally show defective reception of external stimuli, a deficit that has been attributed by some researchers to neurophysiological impairment (Hutt, Hutt, Lee, and Ounsted, 1965; Rimland, 1964). It cannot be determined from the available data whether the weak registration of external stimulation results from the interfering effects of high central arousal, from insufficient activation, or from children's intense preoccupation with their own self-produced stimulation. Lovaas, Litrownick, and Mann (1969) found that autistic children are especially unresponsive during periods when they are engaged in self-stimulatory behavior. In the absence of neurophysiological measures, the question remains whether self-stimulation blocks sensory registration of external stimuli or interferes with instrumental responding to stimuli that have been registered. Whatever the reasons may be, it is evident that little headway can be made toward effecting behavioral change unless adequate control is gained over children's attending behavior.

In the method employed by Lovaas for developing language functions in autistic children, who display marked withdrawal and bizarre self-stimulatory behaviors most of the time, attentional control is achieved through several means. First, the therapist establishes close physical contact by sitting directly in front of the child so he cannot easily ignore the responses that are being modeled. Second, during the session the child is not permitted to

avoid the therapeutic task by withdrawal or resort to bizarre activities. If necessary, the therapist physically restrains the child from turning away, establishes eye-contact by asking the child to look at him, and may withhold positive attention, address the child sharply, or even slap him on the thigh to terminate stereotyped bizare behavior. Firm intervention of this type, if thoughtfully employed, may serve a therapeutic function when failure to respond appropriately to situational demands reflects unwillingness rather than inability. This is dramatically illustrated in a telling sequence from a film depicting the language-learning program (Lovaas, 1966). A therapist repeatedly asks a girl to name the color of a yellow crayon, to which she responds with increasingly bizarre arm-flapping and peculiar grimacing. Finally, the girl is slapped on the thigh, and instructed to name the color, whereupon she abruptly ceases the bizarre behavior and calmly answers "Yellow." As a further means of augmenting and sustaining the child's attentiveness to modeling cues, food rewards, expressions of affection, and social approval are made contingent upon imitation.

The rate and fidelity with which modeled responses are behaviorally reproduced is partly determined by the availability of component responses. Given an impoverished behavioral repertoire, children's reproductions may be deficient even though they attend closely to what is being modeled, because the requisite response elements are lacking. In such cases complex activities must be reduced to small subunits of behavior, each of which is established through modeling. Poorly designed learning sequences, which result in stressful failure experiences, tend to jeopardize attentional control by reducing the child's motivation to observe the modeled responses and by arousing disruptive escape behaviors. To obviate this problem, complex modeled responses are developed in incremental steps, each of which can be easily acquired.

In teaching autistic children communicative speech, a procedure combining modeling with reinforced guided performance is employed, in which the therapist displays progressively more complex forms of verbal behavior and rewards increasingly closer reproductions of the modeled responses. In teaching a mute child to talk, for example, the therapist first rewards any visual attentiveness and random sounds made by the child. When vocalization has been increased, the therapist utters a sound and the child is rewarded only if he produces a vocal response within a certain time limit. After the therapist's speech is established as an effective stimulus for the child's vocalizations, he is reinforced only for precise verbal reproduction of specific sounds, words, and phrases modeled by the therapist. By this method children are first taught phonetic sounds that have distinct visual components and can be manually prompted and then, in a stepwise fashion, more complicated utterances and combinations of words are added. Essentially similar methods for establishing verbal imitativeness are described in considerable detail by Risley and Wolf (1967) in the treatment of autistic children and by Sloane, Johnston, and Harris (1968) in remedial programs for speech-deficient young children.

As exemplified by an illustrative case in Figure 17.1, it may require several days for an autistic child to master the first word, but subsequent imitative word learning generally proceeds at a more rapid rate (Lovaas, Berberich, Perloff, and Schaeffer, 1966). The fact that the establishment of two sounds and one verbal response is accompanied by immediate production of many new words composed of elements that were never directly trained suggests that autistic children possess greater linguistic competencies and comprehension of grammatical features than is commonly believed. One would expect some language acquisition to occur through observational learning as a function of extensive exposure to grammatical speech in the course of daily social interactions. The absence of verbal behavior in autistic children may, therefore, partly represent a motivational rather than a behavioral deficit. It remains unclear whether the abrupt rise in verbal productivity results from children's acquisition of a modeling set, from realization that oppositional tactics have become nonfunctional, or from some other factors.

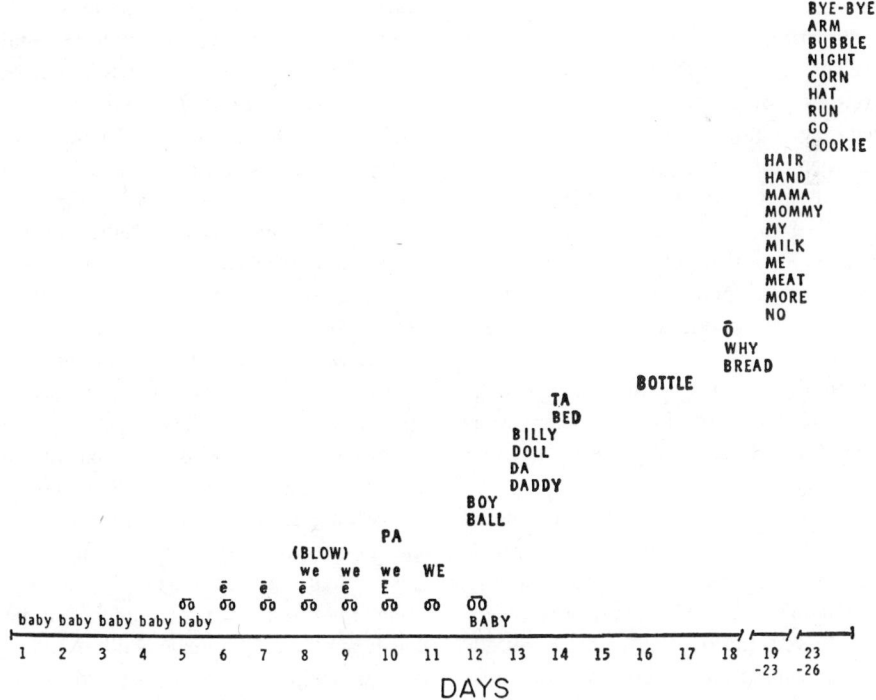

Figure 17.1 Rate of verbal imitation by a previously mute autistic child during the first 26 days of treatment. The words and sounds are printed in lower-case letters on the days they were introduced and trained, and in capital letters on the days they were successfully reproduced (Lovaas, Berberich, Perloff and Schaeffer, 1966).

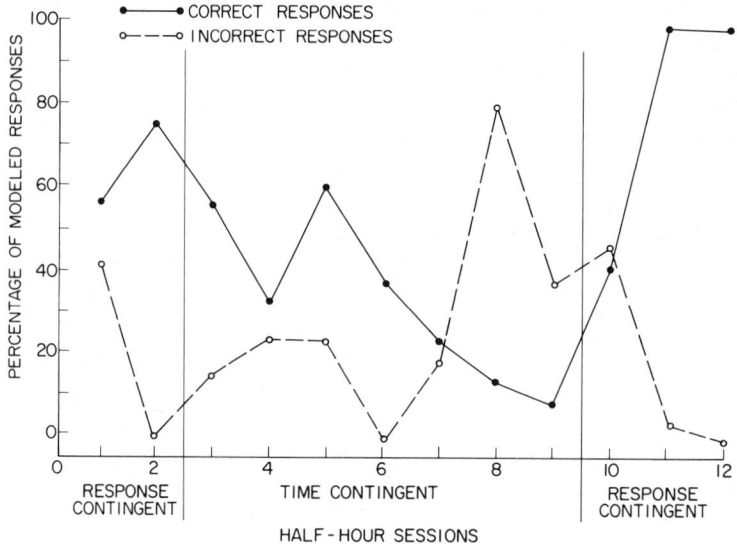

Figure 17.2 Percentage of modeled responses correctly and incorrectly reproduced by an autistic child during periods when rewards were made contingent upon matching perfectly the adult's speech (response contingent) or upon the elapsing of a certain amount of time (time contingent) (Lovaas, 1967).

Lovaas also provides some evidence to indicate that, during the initial phase of treatment, extrinsic incentives may be essential for accurate observation and reproduction of the therapist's performances. Children displayed a high level of accurate imitative responsiveness when rewards were made contingent upon matching the adult's speech perfectly; by contrast, when children were equally generously rewarded after a certain time had elapsed without regard to the quality of their verbalizations, their imitative behavior progressively deteriorated to the point where it bore little resemblance to the model's responses (Figure 17.2).

However, in later stages of treatment, similar shifts from response- to time-contingent reinforcement did not adversely affect modeling outcomes.

When children have advanced to the point where they learn new words imitatively with ease, they are taught a labeling vocabulary so that they understand what the words mean. This is achieved through a form of paired-associate learning in which the therapist presents an object (such as a glass of milk) or models an activity (for example, claps hands) and simultaneously provides the correct verbal label. On succeeding trials the adult's verbal

prompt is gradually withdrawn, until eventually the child gives correct verbal responses to the nonverbal events alone. In this way a wide variety of object-word associations are learned and discriminated. Reading skills are established in a similar manner, except that letter-picture and letter-word associations are presented to the children until they learn to make the appropriate verbal responses to printed words in the absence of pictorial or vocal prompts.

After children have been taught to speak and to correctly label common objects and activities, training in abstract functions is commenced. This program consists essentially of rewarding the child's discriminative responsiveness to verbally or behaviorally modeled events. Whenever the child fails to respond or responds incorrectly, he is aided by verbal and manual prompts that are gradually faded out on succeeding trials. Training in the use of prepositions will serve to illustrate the basic discriminations that are developed. Behavioral matching of a verbal stimulus can be more easily achieved by autistic children than can the verbal labelling of nonverbal events. Therefore, initially the adult gives a verbal instruction involving a preposition (such as "Put the ball inside the box"), and the child is rewarded for performing the motor response appropriate to the verbal stimulus. If the child fails to execute the response correctly, the therapist moves the child's hand with the ball to the box while verbalizing the action. In the second discrimination, objects are arranged in a particular way, and the child is asked to describe verbally the relationships between the objects, using the proper preposition. In the third step, which calls for grammatical conversation, the child responds verbally to a verbal stimulus (such as "What did you do yesterday?") without concomitant behavioral enactment of the events to which reference is made. As in other forms of rule learning, children are taught to generalize the linguistic rule by modeling a variety of objects in a variety of prepositional relationships. Essentially the same procedures have been successfully employed to establish increasingly complex forms of linguistic and conceptual behaviors (Lovaas, Berberich, Kassorla, Klynn, and Meisel, 1966; Lovaas, Dumont, Klynn, and Meisel, 1966).

Formal language training is well suited for establishing verbal skills, but it may result in speech that is lacking in spontaneity and overly dependent upon specific external cueing. Therefore, after the requisite skills for generative grammatical speech have been established, children are taught to use their language to initiate and to maintain social interactions, to express their feelings and desires, and to seek and to exchange information about their environment. Self-generated spontaneous speech is initially fostered in several ways. First, by the withholding of desired objects and activities until they verbalize their wants, children are taught to influence and to control their environment verbally; second, they are encouraged to develop comments and stories about activities depicted in magazines and books, and are rewarded for increasingly elaborate and novel verbalizations; third, they are asked to recount, in detail, past experiences; and finally, the concepts that they have learned in the formal tasks are extended into informal daily interactions, where verbal approval, affectional expressions, play activities, and a sense of accomplishment replace primary rewards as major reinforcing events.

Echolalic and mute autistic children differ substantially in the rate with which they acquire linguistic skills. Echolalic children are much less inclined to engage in impeding self-stimulation and, having already developed imitative speech, they start at a more advanced level and progress faster than children who are mute. In the language-learning program for echolalics, inappropriate imitative responses are extinguished through reinforcement withdrawal, but otherwise the procedures are similar to the ones previously described.

There is some evidence (Lovaas, Rehm, and Schreibman, 1969) to suggest that learning in autistic children may be impaired by attentional deficits. Normal, retarded, and autistic children were trained to respond discriminately for food rewards whenever a complex stimulus consisting of visual, auditory, tactual, and temporal cues was presented. Test trials, in which the elements were presented separately, showed that normals learned to respond to all stimulus elements, retardates generally responded to two modalities, while for autistics, only one feature of the compound stimulus acquired controlling properties. Thus, for example, children who came under auditory control behaved as though they had never encountered the stimulus when it was presented in visual, temporal, or tactual form.

Training procedures characteristically involve multiple stimulus influences. In fact, verbal and visual prompts that are likely to exercise strong control over desired behavior are frequently employed to accelerate behavioral changes, even though the behavior is ordinarily regulated by stimuli that take quite different forms. After the behavior has been evoked and firmly established, the artificial stimulus supports are gradually withdrawn as control is transferred to stimuli most likely to function as appropriate elicitors under naturalistic conditions. If autistic children encounter difficulties in processing information presented simultaneously in several different modalities, then some of the benefits of extraneous stimulus prompts in response acquisition may be lost in the transfer stage to the extent that only the prompt acquires functional control, and the concomitant stimuli are disregarded. With better understanding of attentional processes in autistic children, modeling procedures could be modified so as to further increase their effectiveness. Results of a study by

Wasserman (1969) provide some support for this assumption. Autistic children, whose rate of learning under reward conditions was much inferior to that of retardates, and even primates, achieved notable gains when their attention to relevant stimuli was better channeled, the discriminability of the stimuli was increased, and errors were negatively reinforced.

The preceding material illustrates how failures in matching performances aroused interest in the influential role of attentional processes in learning. If it should be found that autistic children often fail to retain what they have learned, then greater attention would have to be paid to retention processes. Long-term retention of modeled activities could be substantially increased by incorporating into the treatment procedures coding, rehearsal, and organizational activities.

Self-care skills, play patterns, appropriate sex-role behaviors, intellectual skills, and interpersonal modes of behavior can be established in autistic children more rapidly than linguistic behavior by modeling the appropriate activities and rewarding the children's matching performances (Lovaas, Freitag, Nelson, and Whalen, 1967). The training program in nonverbal behavior relies upon the same basic methods employed in language learning. The therapist first establishes control over children's attending behavior; complex response patterns are gradually elaborated by modeling activities in small steps of increasing difficulty; and children are physically guided in performing the behavior if they fail to respond. The physical prompts are gradually withdrawn, and reinforcement for prompted behavior is later withheld, to counteract passive responding. After imitative behavior is strongly developed, stimulus control is shifted from modeling cues to verbal stimuli and appropriate environmental events. Children may, for example, initially engage in painting activities only when they are modeled by an adult, but by reinforcing artistic efforts prompted by verbal suggestions and art materials, they eventually learn to pursue such activities without requiring performing models and other extraneous influences.

The encouraging results of the foregoing project suggest that approaches utilizing rein-forced modeling merit serious consideration in the treatment of gross deficit conditions. Since the beneficial outcomes are achieved with nurses, parents, and college students serving in the role of therapists, this treatment approach gains further social significance. However, evidence that children vary tremendously in the rate with which they acquire new skills, particularly in the early stages of training, indicates the need for comparative studies to evolve procedures that would permit even greater control over the change process. It is possible that language learning may be retarded in some autistic children due to deficiencies in speech perception. In such cases, a brief program of discrimination pretraining (Winitz and Preisler, 1965) may accelerate the modeling process and reduce variability in performance.

For children who do not know the meanings of modeled utterances, word reproduction is apt to be a dull and tiresome exercise. A preliminary program aimed at increasing word comprehension would make the situation more meaningful and perhaps facilitate productive word learning. A sequence similar to this type has been employed by Humphery (1966) in developing language functions in autistic children. As a way of ensuring necessary attentiveness, children are seated in a semi-darkened room and equipped with earphones. In the initial language comprehension phase of the program, children see pictures of objects projected on a screen and hear the corresponding verbal labels without having to reproduce them. After the word-object association has been repeated sufficiently to establish the meanings of the utterances, children are reinforced for correct production of modeled verbalizations. Generalization and discrimination are not left to chance; thus, for example, children may see a dog first presented as the focal object of a slide, but later as part of increasingly complex arrays of animals that will have to be accurately discriminated. By including pictures or demonstrations representing actions, qualifying attributes, and object interrelationships, the same procedure can be extended to develop increasingly complex linguistic skills. Humphery has also found it advantageous to include slides of the children themselves and their peers pursuing activities in their natural surroundings, because the immediacy of these stimuli make them especially vivid and compelling inputs. This approach is similar in many respects to language learning under naturalistic conditions, where children observe a considerable amount of verbal behavior before they are taught to produce words and grammatical sentences. However, the optimal sequences for word and meaning training remain to be demonstrated.

Except for a few minor applications (Sherman, 1965; Wilson and Walters, 1966), there has been no systematic use of modeling procedures in the treatment of adult psychotics. This is all the more surprising considering that a majority of the chronic cases suffer from debilitating behavioral deficits that must be overcome if they are to function effectively in community life. The relative neglect of this powerful approach probably results, in a large part, from therapists' strong allegiances solely to operant conditioning methods or to interview procedures in which a great deal of time is devoted to analyzing patients' ineffectual behaviors.

Sarason and Ganzer (1969) report preliminary studies that make use of modeling procedures with delinquents to develop social and other skills requisite for effective vocational and interpersonal functioning. Models demonstrate and then the boys rehearse proficient ways of handling common problem situations such as coping with authority figures, negative peer influences, vocational demands, situations requiring self-controlling behavior, and a variety of social predicaments. Delinquents who participate in this type of program achieve greater changes in attitudes and behavior than matched control boys.

Applications of modeling procedures are by no means confined to children or to grossly deviant conditions. Behavioral enactment methods are frequently utilized for a wide variety of purposes in which people who want to develop new competencies are provided with actual or symbolic models of desired behavior, and are given opportunities to perform these patterns initially under favorable conditions before being encouraged to apply them as they go about their everyday life. Since, in modeling approaches, a person observes and practices alternative ways of behaving under lifelike

conditions, transfer of learning to naturalistic situations is greatly facilitated.

Some treatment approaches, such as Kelly's (1955) fixed-role therapy, rely almost exclusively upon modeling procedures. In the initial phase, the therapist writes a personality sketch suitable for enactment by the client. He is then asked to perform the role behaviors continuously as if he were, in fact, the person portrayed in the sketch. For example, a passive nonassertive person may be assigned an active assertive role. The new behavioral patterns, which are usually in marked contrast to the client's customary modes of response, are consistently enacted for several weeks or some other preselected period. This phase of the program is structured to the client as representing brief experimentation with, rather than permanent adoption of, new characteristics. Moreover, the client is never told that he should be the new character, only that he should act like him on a trial basis. The emphasis on brief experimentation and simulation is considered essential for minimizing the initial threat of making sweeping changes in one's mode of life.

The provision of a role prescription alone will be of limited value unless a person knows how to translate it into concrete actions under a variety of circumstances. In Kelly's approach the treatment sessions, usually scheduled on alternate days, are mainly devoted to rehearsing the prescribed role as it might apply to everyday events involving vocational and social relationships, heterosexual interactions, parental relations, and life orientations. Therapist and client usually alternate in the role enactment. Through such role reversal, the client not only benefits from the therapist's demonstration of skillful ways of relating to others, but also experiences how people are likely to be affected by the behaviors being modeled.

After new forms of responsiveness to different types of interpersonal situations have been adequately rehearsed, and the client's actual experiences in implementing the role have been thoroughly discussed, the client decides whether he wishes to adopt the new role behaviors on a more lasting basis. If he has found the new role effective and wishes to go on with the program, the behavioral rehearsals are continued as long as necessary. With further experience, the client becomes increasingly skillful and comfortable in the new role behaviors, until eventually they are spontaneously performed.

Although there is every reason to expect, from evidence of modeling studies, that the type of approach advocated by Kelly should be highly efficacious, there have been no systematic attempts made to measure the degree of success associated with this particular method. Research is also needed to determine whether the recommended practices (such as selection of markedly contrasting behavior that is continuously enacted under a simulated set in all areas of social functioning) are, in fact, the optimal conditions for establishing new role behaviors. Desired outcomes might be more consistently attained by gradual role adoption in progressively more difficult social situations than by complete role enactment from the outset. Under a graduated procedure, the behavioral requirements would be adjusted to the client's capabilities at any given time and would hence reduce the possibility that his initial attempts at new ways of behaving would be poorly received by others. By careful selection of both the real-life situations in which the client enacts new modes of behavior and the manner in which they are expressed, the likely consequences of modeled behavior can be controlled to a considerable extent rather than left to fortuitous circumstances.

There are many other treatment approaches in which modeling techniques, variously labeled psychodramatic enactment (Moreno, 1958; Sturm, 1965), behavior rehearsal (Lazarus, 1966; Wolpe & Lazarus, 1966), and role playing (Corsini and Putzey, 1957) are employed to overcome specific response deficits or to transmit more extensive repertoires of social behavior. Modeling in the form of role practice has also been extensively adapted for training of industrial and managerial skills (Corsini, Shaw, and Blake, 1961). As is generally true of the psychotherapy literature, the strategies to be followed in implementing modeling principles are presented in strong prescriptive terms and the methods are credited with much success, but rigorously controlled studies of outcomes are virtually nonexistent.

The efficacy of modeling approaches will be largely determined by what is being enacted. If change agents mainly encourage clients to perform their customary ineffectual forms of behavior, to reconstruct past relationship experiences, and to revivify the emotional reactions engendered by their inadequacies, then these methods are unlikely to fare any better than interpretive interview approaches that similarly accentuate the negative. On the other hand, treatment approaches that employ modeling procedures to establish effective modes of behavior often lack an adequate transfer training program in which clients are provided with opportunities to test their newly acquired skills under conditions likely to produce rewarding consequences. If change agents themselves portray requisite interpersonal competencies, and arrange optimal conditions for their clients to learn and to practice more effective means of coping with potential problems, then this type of approach is almost certain to prove successful.

Before turning to other therapeutic issues, we should like to comment briefly on the nature of the effects produced through modeling. When people are deliberately instructed to observe and to reproduce either the behavior exemplified by others or an imaginatively reconstructed role, there may be a tendency to view the resultant changes as feigned and superficial. In fact, as will be shown later, behavioral enactment techniques have proved to be one of the most effective means of inducing stable affective and attitudinal changes. These findings provide support for the view that self-evaluative and cognitive events may be partly epiphenomena arising from one's competencies and the consequences of one's behavior. Modeling, even under simulated conditions, can have far-reaching effects.

Modification of Prepotent Response Patterns Through Symbolic Modeling

The discussion thus far has been concerned with the use of modeling procedures to overcome behavioral deficits. In many instances, a change agent is faced with the opposite problem —that of eliminating strongly established patterns of deviant or maladaptive behavior. One might attempt to accomplish this objective by a program of differential reinforcement, in which desirable behavior is positively reinforced and deviant response patterns are either non-rewarded or punished. Selective reinforcement is often a slow and inefficient process when a person displays a strong dominant response tendency and alternative modes of behavior are only weakly established or nonexistent in his behavioral repertoire. Under these circumstances, one may have to wait an unnecessarily long or indefinite period for the appearance of alternative responses. In such cases, the change process may be greatly facilitated by the use of modeling procedures designed to transmit, elicit, and support modes of response that are incompatible with the deviant behavior that a therapist is attempting to eliminate. This, in effect, was the strategy employed by Chittenden (1942) in modifying children's hyperaggressive and domineering responses to frustration.

It has been widely assumed on the basis of psychodynamic theories and other energy models of personality that either vicarious participation in, or the direct expression of, aggressive behavior serves to discharge "pent-up energies and affects" and thereby to reduce, at least temporarily, the incidence of aggressive behavior. Guided by this catharsis theory, many parents, educators, rehabilitation workers, and child psychotherapists subtly or openly instigate hyperaggressive children to express aggression in one form or another. The overall evidence from laboratory studies (Bandura, 1965a; Berkowitz, 1969) strongly indicates that psychotherapies employing these conventional cathartic or abreactive procedures may be unwittingly maintaining deviant behavior at its original strength, or, still more likely, increasing it rather than producing the expected reductions in aggressive tendencies. In contrast, therapy based upon social-learning principles would concentrate, from the outset, upon developing and strengthening constructive alternative modes of coping with interpersonal problems. Proceeding on this basis, Chittenden (1942) employed symbolic modeling procedures for altering children's aggressive reactions to frustration.

Children who were excessively domineering and hyperaggressive observed and discussed a series of eleven 15-minute plays, in each of which dolls, representing preschool children, exhibited alternatively an aggressive and a cooperative solution to interpersonal conflicts under circumstances that the children were likely to encounter in everyday interactions. In addition to modeling these two competing response patterns, the consequences of aggression were shown to be unpleasant and those of cooperativeness to be rewarding. In one of the modeled situations, for example, two boys engage in a fight over the possession of a wagon; during the struggle, the wagon is broken, and both boys end up unhappy. By contrast, the cooperative alternative presents the boys enjoying themselves as they take turns playing with the wagon.

Children for whom the different reactions and consequences were modeled showed a decrease in dominative aggressiveness (as measured by situational tests in which two children were placed in a room with a single attractive toy) compared with a group of similarly hyperaggressive children who received no treatment. Of even greater interest is the finding that children who had observed the discriminative modeling displayed a significant decrease in domination and an increase in cooperativeness as assessed from behavior observations in the nursery school made prior to treatment, immediately after treatment, and a month later (Figure 17.3). One cannot determine from these data the relative contribution of vicarious reinforcement and modeling to the obtained outcomes. The children's spontaneous comments and enactments during test trials, in which they were required to provide their own solutions to social conflicts involving the dolls, indicated that they had learned the cooperative strategies. Some, however, gave evidence of also being strongly affected by the consequences depicted: "Well, let's don't have them fight; I don't like to have them bump their faces together, that hurts. . . . Let's have them take turns; then they won't fight. Let them ask Darrell (subject's name) what to do. 'Ask me, Sandy and Mandy (dolls' names). I'll tell you to take turns; then you won't have a fight.' (pp. 53–54)"

In a preliminary report, Gittelman (1965) illustrates how modeling combined with behavioral enactment can be adapted for modifying aggressive behavior in older children. They

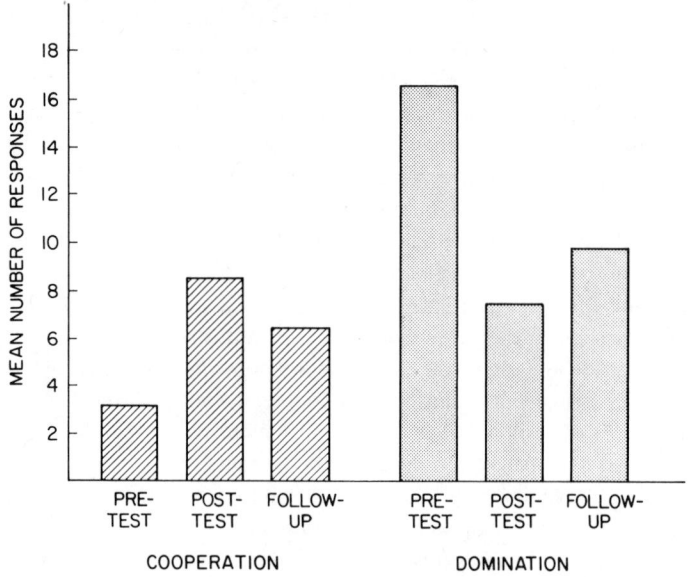

Figure 17.3 Amount of cooperative and domineering behavior exhibited by hyper-aggressive children in nursery school interactions before and after receiving symbolic modeling treatment (Drawn from the data of Chittenden, 1942).

are first asked to describe situations that typically provoke them to aggression and belligerence. A hierarchy of irritating situations is then constructed, ranging from those causing only mild annoyance to extremely instigatory ones. The child and other group members enact these progressively aggravating situations and practice effective nonviolent means of coping with them.

The treatment program devised by Chittenden primarily relied upon modeling techniques. After desired patterns of behavior have been established through some form of modeling, their maintenance will be largely controlled by the reinforcement practices existing within the naturalistic setting. Hence, it may be necessary to arrange favorable consequences to support newly acquired response patterns. This would apply particularly to behavior that is ordinarily associated with less optimal reinforcement conditions, as in the case of cooperativeness, which was more difficult to establish and to maintain. The combined use of modeling and reinforcement procedures is probably the most efficacious method of transmitting, eliciting, and maintaining social response patterns.

There is additional evidence that symbolic modeling approaches, in which desired response patterns are demonstrated concretely through play activities, may be especially well-suited for

modifying the behavior of young children. Marshall and Hahn (1967) showed that pre-school children, who participated in several doll-play sessions with an adult who enacted topics commonly used in children's play, subsequently increased their dramatic play with peers in daily interactions. The absence of any significant changes in the play behavior of control groups of children who either received the same amount of adult warmth and attention during the assembly of blocks and puzzles, or had no contact with the adult, indicates that modeling and support of social play behavior was the major determinant.

The foregoing studies illustrate the way in which the same method (that is, doll play) is utilized in radically different ways depending upon whether one views behavior from a psychodynamic or a social-learning perspective. In the former case, children are typically prompted to perform, in doll play, assaultive and other negative response tendencies toward parents, teachers, siblings, and peers, which, if transferred to real-life situations, would further exacerbate their problems. In contrast, the latter approach provides more satisfactory solutions to interpersonal conflicts and models beneficial modes of behavior that are likely to foster positive social experiences.

Results of a study by O'Connor (1969) involving positive symbolic modeling lend further empirical support to the above view. Preschool children were selected who showed extreme social withdrawal, a behavior problem that often reflects both deficits in social skills and fear of close interpersonal contact. Half these children were shown a control film, while a matched group of isolates observed a sound film depicting a variety of social interactions at a progressively more spirited activity level. Each filmed sequence portrayed a child initially watching the ongoing activities at a distance but eventually joining and interacting with the other children, with evident positive consequences. In a behavioral assessment conducted immediately after the treatment sessions, the controls remained markedly withdrawn, whereas children who received the symbolic modeling showed a substantial increase in social interaction to the base-line level displayed by nonwithdrawn children (Figure 17.4).

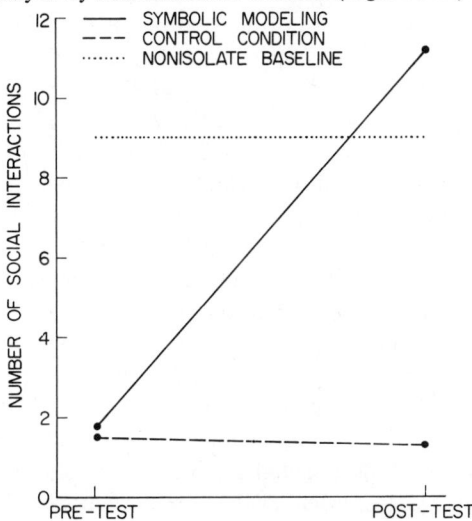

Figure 17.4 Amount of social interaction shown by withdrawn children in symbolic modeling and control conditions before and after the treatment session. The dotted line represents the amount of social interaction displayed by a group of nonisolate children whose behavior was observed at the pretest phase of the study (O'Connor, 1969).

This study was primarily designed to test the efficacy of modeling procedures for inducing desired patterns of behavior. By providing adequate practice and reinforcement of newly established social skills, such behavior would undoubtedly asume greater functional value and endure after special treatment conditions have been discontinued.

ELIMINATION OF ANXIETIES AND INHIBITIONS THROUGH MODELING

Controlling Conditions in Defensive Behavior

Most theories of psychopathology assume that defensive patterns of behavior are motivated by anxiety and reinforced by anxiety reduction. In these formulations, anxiety is typically defined in terms of peripheral autonomic reactivity. There is evidence that fear arousal serves a regulatory function in defensive behavior although, as will be shown later, theories postulating that avoidance responses are under autonomic control are seriously challenged by several lines of evidence.

Numerous tests have been conducted of the dual-process theory of learning, which assumes that classically conditioned fear arousal exercises mediating control over avoidance behavior. The relationship between fear conditioning and instrumental responding is most convincingly demonstrated by Solomon and his associates (Rescorla and Solomon, 1967; Solomon and Turner, 1962). These studies typically employ a three-stage paradigm in which animals first learn to make an avoidance response to a light stimulus. They are then skeletally immobilized by curare to prevent avoidance responses from being conditioned directly to external stimuli; during this period, one tone is repeatedly paired with shock to endow it with arousal potential, while a different tone is never associated with shock, in order to preserve its neutral properties. In subsequent tests conducted in a noncurarized state, animals display essentially the same degree of avoidance in response to the negatively valenced tone and the light, both of which evoke common arousal reactions, whereas avoidance responses rarely occur to the neutral tone. Considering that the light and the tones were never associated, and assuming that curare blocked all skeletal activity (Black, 1967), thus precluding any differential conditioning of avoidance responses to the tones, the controlling power of the negatively valenced tone must be mediated through an internal arousal mechanism.

Results of diverse studies refute the widely accepted view that autonomic arousal is the determinant of defensive behavior. Experiments in which autonomic and avoidance responses are measured concurrently reveal that these two sets of responses are partially correlated but not causally related. Black (1959), for example, found that avoidance responses during extinction persisted long after autonomic responses had been extinguished. The generality of the preceding results, and other studies (to be cited later) showing defensive responding in the absence of autonomic arousal, is limited, however, by the fact that only a single autonomic response was measured. In view of evidence (Lacey, 1950) that individuals vary in their characteristic modes of physiological reactivity to stress, and that different responses are not highly intercorrelated, no single measure of autonomic reactivity can be considered an adequate index of autonomic arousal.

Laboratory investigations of the acquisition and maintenance of avoidance responses in sympathectomized animals (Wynne and Solomon, 1955) provide the most critical test of the hypothesis that autonomic arousal serves a mediating function in avoidance behavior. These experiments disclose that removal of autonomic feedback by surgical section of the sympathetic segment of the autonomic nervous system or by vagus-drug parasympathetic blocking procedures has only a partial effect on the acquisition of avoidance behavior, with the differences occurring mainly in the initial phase of learning. All sympathectomized animals acquired stable avoidance responses, though they were a bit slower to do so than unoperated controls. However, speed of extinction in animals deprived of normal autonomic functioning after avoidance responses had been firmly established did not differ from that of normal controls. Moreover, no consistent relationship was obtained between the avoidance-learning pattern and the portion of the autonomic nervous system that was blocked or resected.

The above findings suggest that autonomic arousal may play a facilitative role, but is not required for the establishment of avoidance behavior; maintenance of previously learned avoidance responses is apparently even less dependent upon autonomic feedback stimulation. The overall evidence thus indicates that mechanisms other than autonomic arousal govern avoidance responding. Indeed, the latencies of autonomic reactions and their associated feedback are much longer than those of skeletal responses; consequently, avoidance behavior is typically executed before autonomic reactions could possibly be elicited. This factor alone precluded autonomic control of avoidance behavior.

In a comprehensive review of research bearing on the dual-process theory, Rescorla and Solomon (1967) propose the tenable view, principally on the basis of exclusion rather than direct corroborative evidence, that defensive behavior is mainly regulated by central mediators that can be established and eliminated through classical conditioning operations. Since central processes exert control over both autonomic and instrumental responding, these two response systems are, in general, partially correlated. Major obstacles to clarification of the role of central mediators in avoidance behavior are created by the failure to specify the locus and the nature of the mediating systems and the most valid indices of their activities.

Identification of the mechanisms governing defensive behavior is further complicated by suggestive evidence (Lacey, 1967) that the different arousal systems—electroencephalographic, autonomic, and behavioral—are functionally separable. Although they generally appear concomitantly, physiological and behavioral arousal can be markedly dissociated pharmacologically. Thus, organisms may be centrally aroused but behaviorally unresponsive, or conversely, they may be behaviorally excited in the absence of central activation as mesaured by standard electrocortical signs. These findings indicate that, under certain conditions, external stimuli may control avoidance responses independently of physiological arousal. Nevertheless, it is clear from studies reported earlier, in which stimuli are endowed with emotional arousal properties under curare, that the stimuli are not directly conditioned to avoidance responses, since these never occur.

According to social-learning theory, defensive behavior is governed by a variety of controlling conditions. During early stages of emotional conditioning, when stimulus events assume aversive properties through association with painful experiences, the conditioned aversive stimuli generate fear arousal, which motivates defensive behavior in accordance with dual-process theory. However, unlike conditioning explanations that attribute emotional arousal to external stimulus sources, the social-learning interpretation assigns a prominent role to symbolically mediated self-stimulation, both in the original conditioning of emotional arousal to external stimuli and in its subsequent activation.

The important function of self-generated arousal is best illustrated by experiments in which emotional conditioning is achieved by substituting symbolically produced arousal for aversive physical stimulation, like the unconditioned stimulus. Subjects are informed that a CS will sometimes be followed by shock; they are given a sample shock or a single confirmation trial during the acquisition series, but otherwise the CS is never paired with any externally administered aversive stimulation. Subjects develop conditioned autonomic responses in the absence of an external UCS by generating fear-arousing thoughts in conjunction with the occurrence of the CS (Dawson and Grings, 1969; Grings, 1965). Indeed, Bridger and Mandel (1964) found autonomic conditioning was similar regardless of whether the CS was associated with threat of shock alone, or with threat and actual shock stimulation. Some further evidence for the influential role of self-stimulation in symbolic emotional conditioning is provided by Dawson (1966), who found that the degree to which subjects believed that shock would follow a certain stimulus and the severity of shock they anticipated were positively correlated with the extent of fear conditioning.

Once avoidance behavior is established, it can be strongly reinforced by its success in preventing the occurrence of anticipated aversive experiences. In naturalistic situations individuals, of course, periodically encounter punishing experiences and often find themselves in fear-provoking situations. Defensive behavior is, therefore, reinforced not only by fear reduction accompanying forestallment of anticipated threats, but also by termination of distressing experiences through escape from actual aversive situations. In experiments designed to evaluate separately the various factors that might reinforce avoidance behavior, Kamin (1956, 1957) found that either termination of fear-arousing stimuli or avoidance of physically painful stimulation increased defensive behavior. As might be expected, avoidance behavior was most pronounced when it both removed fear-provoking stimuli and prevented painful stimulation.

After successful avoidance behavior has been developed, it can be controlled cognitively and by discriminative stimuli signifying potential threats without requiring emotional arousal. Notterman, Schoenfeld, and Bersh (1952) found that after subjects were provided with an effective means of coping with a potentially threatening situation, they continued to perform appropriate avoidance behavior, although their autonomic responsiveness was completely extinguished. The latter finding is further corroborated by Grings and Lockhart (1966), who report that subjects exhibit a sudden decrease in autonomic arousal after learning that they can successfully avert painful stimulation by performing a designated avoidance response.

Numerous investigations of symbolic control of emotional behavior reveal that persons who are informed that threatening stimuli will no longer be accompanied by painful stimulation display a precipitous decrement in both conditioned autonomic responses (Chatterjee and Eriksen, 1962; Grings & Lockhart, 1963; Notterman, Schoenfeld, and Bersh, 1952; Wickens, Allen, and Hill, 1963) and instrumental avoidance behavior (Lindley and Moyer, 1961; Moyer and Lindley, 1962), whereas uninformed subjects show a more gradual decline in responsiveness.

The powerful symbolic control over emotional responses observed under laboratory conditions contrasts sharply with the refractory quality of fears acquired through natural experiences. The difference may arise partly from the degree of control exercised by change agents over the feared events. By turning off the shock apparatus or removing shock electrodes, experimenters can completely remove any potential threats from the situation. By contrast, in real-life situations, where actual or imagined consequences of certain actions may be injurious, and where environmental events are not entirely predictable, verbal influences are relatively ineffectual. It is extremely unlikely, for example, that informing snake-phobic persons that a particular reptile is harmless will result in any appreciable decrease in snake avoidance behavior. Naturally feared objects that are ordinarily innocuous can occasionally produce hurtful effects despite assurances to the contrary. Even "harmless" snakes or dogs do bite. However, this explanation does not fully reconcile the divergent findings because snake phobics, for example, experience considerable emotional disturbance when shown pictures of reptiles, while acknowledging that the agitation is groundless because pictorial snakes cannot possibly inflict any injury. Here symbolic processes exercise weak control over emotional responsiveness.

The experimental and anecdotal evidence taken together support the view that emotional behavior is controlled by two different stimulus sources. One is the emotional arousal that is self-generated by symbolic activities. The second is the response evoked directly by conditioned aversive stimuli. A study by Bridger and Mandel (1964) suggests that the strength of symbolic control depends partly on the conditions under which emotional behavior was originally acquired. A neutral stimulus could be endowed with arousal potential to the same degree by being associated with the threat of shock, as with threat and shock stimulation. However, emotional responses established on the basis of actual painful experiences were less susceptible to cognitive control. Whereas threat-conditioned responses were promptly abolished by the information that shocks would be discontinued, emotional responses produced by painful experiences were much more resistant to extinction. It would follow from the latter findings that the fear component produced through the self-arousal mechanism is modifiable by reducing emotion-provoking cognitions. On the other hand, elimination of the nonmediated fear component requires repeated nonreinforced exposure to threatening events either directly or vicariously.

In accord with the theory outlined above, numerous laboratory studies (Bandura, 1969a; Black, 1958) have shown that neutralization of threatening stimuli alone can markedly facilitate extinction of avoidance responses. Modeling approaches to the modification of emotional disorders are likewise predicated on the assumption that extinction of fear arousal through observational experiences will reduce defensive behavior.

Vicarious Extinction Through Modeling Procedures

Vicarious extinction of fears, inhibitions, and other avoidance behaviors is achieved by exposing fearful observers to modeled events in which performers are shown engaging in threatening activities without experiencing any adverse response consequences. Repeated observations that feared performances engender no unfavorable outcomes would be expected to extinguish both fear-arousing cognitions and nonmediated emotional responses. In a study that will be discussed more fully later (Bandura, Blanchard, and Ritter, 1969), snake-phobic adults participated in a self-administered modeling treatment in which they observed a graduated film depicting others engaging in progressively more threatening interactions with a large snake. For one group of subjects, self-presentation of modeling stimuli was combined with relaxation, whereas a second group observed the modeled events without concurrent relaxation. Subjects rated the degree of fear arousal evoked by the modeled scenes initially and by each subsequent reexposure to the same scenes. As summarized in Figure 17.5, both groups of subjects showed a progressive decline in fear arousal with each successive exposure to modeled approach behavior. In a related study, Blanchard (1969) found that the more thoroughly fear arousal was vicariously extinguished, the greater was the reduction in avoidance behavior and the more generalized were the behavioral changes.

Graduated Modeling

Since nonoccurrence of anticipated aversive consequences is a requisite condition for fear

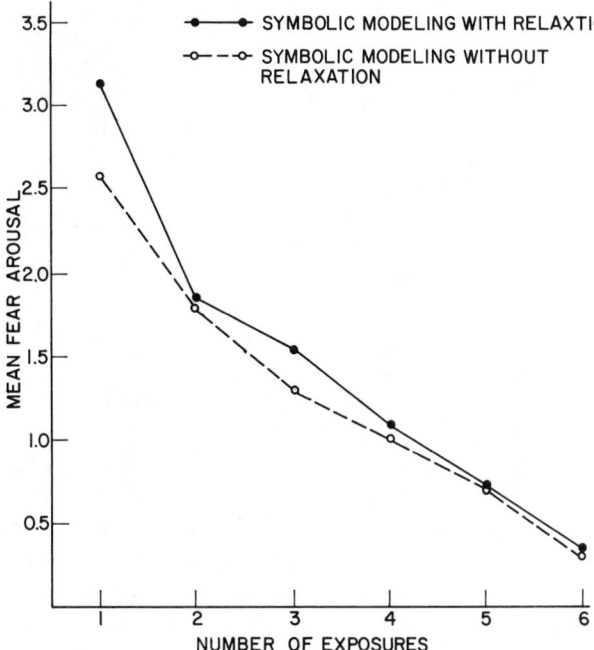

Figure 17.5 Mean level of fear arousal evoked by modeled events initially and by each subsequent exposure to the same filmed scenes in individuals receiving symbolic modeling with relaxation and symbolic modeling alone (Bandura, Blanchard, and Ritter, 1969).

extinction, the modeling displays most likely to have strong effects on fearful observers are ones in which performances that they regard as hazardous are repeatedly shown to be safe under a variety of threatening circumstances. However, if people are to be influenced by modeled behavior and its accompanying consequences, then the necessary observing responses must be elicited and maintained. Presentation of modeled approach responses toward the most threatening situation at the outset is likely to generate in observers high levels of emotional arousal. To the extent that such conditions activate avoidance responses designed to reduce vicariously instigated distress (such as withdrawing or looking away), they will impede vicarious extinction. Therefore, the efficacy of vicarious extinction procedures may depend partly on the manner in which modeled performances are presented.

Several investigators (Davis and Wagner, 1969; Kimble and Kendall, 1953; Poppen, 1968) have studied the rate of extinction in infrahuman subjects when aversive stimuli are presented either at a gradually increasing intensity or at a constant high intensity.

Incremental procedures characteristically produce superior results. In applying this stimulus-change principle to vicarious extinction (Bandura, 1968), persons initially oberve a model responding in a positive manner to situations that have low arousal value. After emotional responses to attenuated threats have been extinguished, progressively more aversive modeling stimuli, which are weakened by generalization of anxiety extinction from preceding displays, are gradually introduced and neutralized. Results of these studies disclose that graduated modeling reduces phobic behavior in virtually all subjects, with minimal distress.

Avoidance behavior can of course be eliminated, albeit at a slower rate, by repeated exposure only to highly feared situations. There is no reason to assume, therefore, that stimulus graduation is a necessary condition for vicarious extinction. In treatment applications other reasons exist, apart from the speed with which desired changes can be achieved, for utilizing graduated modeling. Such procedures permit greater control over the change process; they reduce to a minimum unnecessary anxiety elicitation that can impede participation in the treatment; and they obviate the risk of heightening fearfulness that can result from confrontation with modeled events having high threat value.

The author and his associates have conducted a program of research designed both to develop efficacious modeling treatments and to investigate theoretical issues pertaining to basic change processes. All of the studies in this series employ essentially the same experimental design. Subjects are first administered an objective test of avoidance behavior in which they are asked to perform progressively more threatening activities. Those who are sufficiently fearful to qualify for the project are then assigned, on the basis of the severity of their avoidance behavior, to various treatment conditions.

Evidence that deviant modes of response can be modified by a particular method is of limited therapeutic significance unless it can be demonstrated that newly established behaviors generalize to stimuli beyond those encountered in treatment, and that induced changes endure after the special therapeutic conditions have been discontinued. Therefore, to measure transfer effects, the behavior avoidance tests are administered with different phobic objects after subjects have completed the treatment program. The same assessment procedures are repeated after one month to determine how well the behavioral changes have been maintained.

The methodology outlined above was selected to provide measures of three separable processes essential for adequate evaluation of any method of treatment. As previously alluded to, the three major factors are concerned with whether a given method can *induce* desired changes in behavior, whether the established changes *generalize*, and whether the changes are *maintained* over time. Unless these three processes are distinguished, results of psychotherapy outcome studies are not only difficult to interpret, but also may lead to erroneous conclusions. If, for example, a given method produces changes that are no longer evident some time after the treatment has been discontinued, it does not necessarily mean that the method is inadequate. On the contrary, it may be exceedingly powerful for inducing changes,

but the gains are short-lived because necessary maintaining conditions have not been arranged. One would, therefore, supplement the method with a maintenance program rather than discard it. In other instances, enduring behavioral changes are achieved, but they do not generalize to extratherapeutic situations, thus requiring ancillary procedures to ensure optimal transfer.

Efficacy of Graduated Live Modeling

The first study in the series (Bandura, Grusec, and Menlove, 1967) involved a stringent test of the degree to which strong avoidance behavior of long standing can be extinguished vicariously. It also explored the possibility that induction of positive affective responses in observers during exposure to potentially threatening performances may expedite the vicarious extinction process.

Young children who exhibited marked avoidance of dogs were assigned to one of four treatment conditions. One group participated in eight brief sessions, during which they observed a fearless peer model exhibit progressively more fear-provoking interactions with a dog. For these children, the modeled approach behavior was presented within a highly positive party context designed to counteract fear arousal. The aversive properties of the modeled performances were gradually increased from session to session by varying simultaneously the physical restraints on the dog, the directness and intimacy of the modeled approach responses, and the duration of interaction between the model and his canine companion. A second group of children observed the same graduated modeled performances, but in a neutral context. In the two treatment conditions described, the stimulus complex contained both nonreinforced modeled behavior and repeated observation of the feared animal. Therefore, in order to measure the effects of exposure to the threatening object itself, a third group of children observed the dog in the positive context but with the model absent. A fourth group participated in the positive activities but was never exposed to either the dog or the modeled displays, in order to furnish a measure of the changes that might result from repeated behavioral assessments and positive relationship experiences.

Children were readministered tests for avoidance behavior toward different dogs following completion of the treatment program and again a month later. The graded series of tests included approaching and petting the dogs, releasing them from a playpen, removing their leashes, feeding them dog biscuits, and spending a fixed period of time alone in the room with each animal. The final and most difficult set of tasks required the children to climb into the playpen with each dog and, after having locked the gate, to pet it, and to remain alone with the animal under the confining conditions.

The modeling procedure produced highly stable and generalized vicarious extinction of avoidance responses (Figure 17.6). The two groups of children who had observed the peer model interact fearlessly with the dog displayed significantly greater approach behavior toward both the experimental and an unfamiliar animal than did children in both the dog-exposure and control conditions, which did not differ from each other. The positive context, however, did not contribute much to the favorable outcomes obtained. Further evidence for the effectiveness of this method is that

67 percent of the children receiving the modeling treatment were able to remain alone in the room confined with the dog in the playpen. In contrast, this demanding task was successfully completed by relatively few children in the two control conditions.

Vicarious Extinction as a Function of Multiple Modeling

One would expect, from knowledge of generalization processes, the degree of vicarious extinction to be partly determined by the variety of modeling stimuli that are neutralized. Exposure to diverse models who display fearless behavior toward variant forms of the feared object without adverse consequences should produce thorough extinction of fear arousal, and consequently extensive reduction in avoidance behavior. On the other hand, observers whose emotional responsiveness is extinguished to a limited set of modeled aversive elements may display weaker and less generalized extinction effects. Indeed, bold performances by a single model directed toward a single threatening object can be easily discounted by observers on the grounds that either the performer possesses special expertise that enables him to prevent injurious consequences, or that an

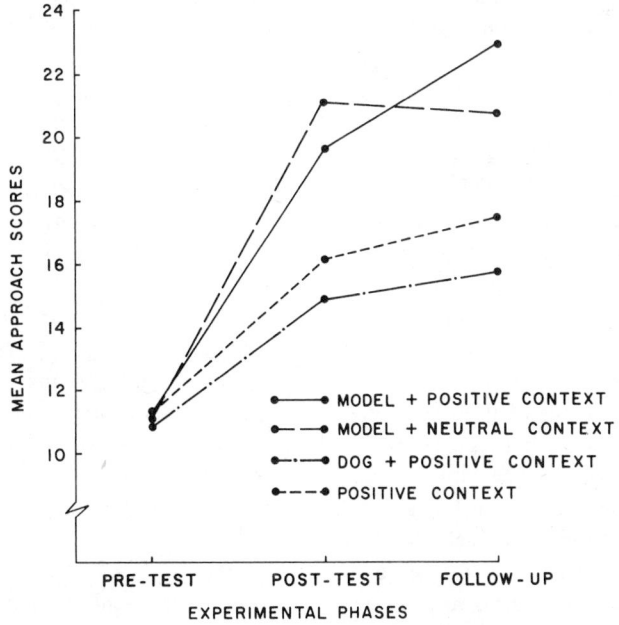

Figure 17.6 Mean dog-approach scores achieved by children in each of the treatment conditions on the three different periods of assessment (Bandura, Grusec, and Menlove, 1967).

atypical object was selected. Such verbal labeling of modeled performances could serve to protect inappropriate fears from extinction.

Under conditions where a set of aversive modeling stimuli is presented only once, certain observer characteristics might also influence the extent to which emotional responses undergo extinction. Observers who are highly susceptible to emotional arousal would most likely respond to threatening modeling displays with pronounced fear and might, therefore, show relatively strong resistance to vicarious extinction. Thus, emotional proneness might serve as an additional determinant of the rate at which avoidance behavior is reduced through modeling procedures.

The above propositions were tested in an experiment (Bandura & Menlove, 1968) employing the same assessment methodology with children who displayed severe dog-avoidance behavior. In this project, however, the modeled performances were presented in a series of brief movies, in order to test the efficacy of symbolic modeling techniques that lend themselves conveniently to psychotherapeutic applications. One group of children, who participated in a single-model treatment, observed the fearless male model display the same progressively more fear-provoking interactions with a dog as in the preceding experiment. The second group of children, receiving a multiple-model treatment, observed several different girls and boys of varying ages interacting positively with many dogs ranging from diminutive breeds to larger specimens. The size and fearsomeness of this canine aggregation were progressively increased from small dogs that were non-threatening in appearance to the more massive varieties. Children assigned to a control group were shown movies that had no canine characters.

The dog-approach scores obtained by children in each of the three conditions in the pretest, posttest, and follow-up phases of the experiment are shown graphically in Figure 17.7. Children who observed approach behavior modeled without any adverse consequences to the performer displayed enduring and generalized reductions in avoidance behavior, whereas the controls showed no changes in this regard. The overall pattern of changes reveals the

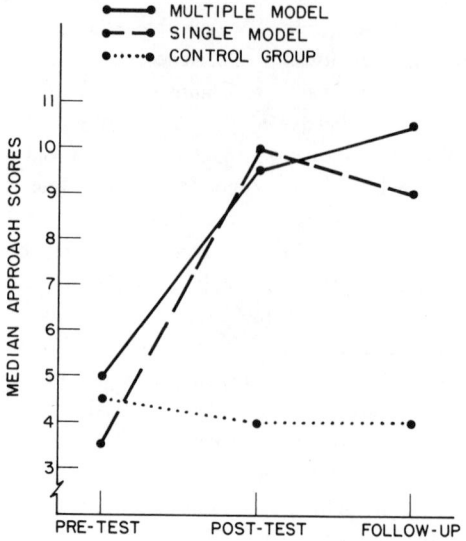

Figure 17.7 Median dog-approach scores achieved by children who received either single-model or multiple-model treatments, or who participated in a control condition (Bandura and Menlove, 1968).

multiple-modeling treatment to be superior to the single-modeling procedure for completely eliminating avoidance behavior. Although the two modeling approaches did not differ in their effects as measured immediately after treatment, children who received diverse modeling showed continued improvement and were twice as likely as their single-modeling counterparts to achieve terminal performances in the follow-up assessment. Interestingly, the modeling treatments were equally effective regardless of the severity of children's phobic behavior. However, those who manifested a wide variety of fears benefited somewhat less from a single exposure to multiple-modeling than children who had fewer fears.

As a further test of the therapeutic value of symbolic modeling, control children were administered the multiple-modeling treatment after the main experiment was completed. The control children, whose avoidance behavior remained unchanged in several tests conducted during the control period, displayed a sharp increase in dog approach behavior following treatment (Figure 17.8). The increased boldness of one of the control children who had been subsequently treated is portrayed in Figure 17.9. The top frames show the model's dauntless behavior; the lower frames depict the girl's

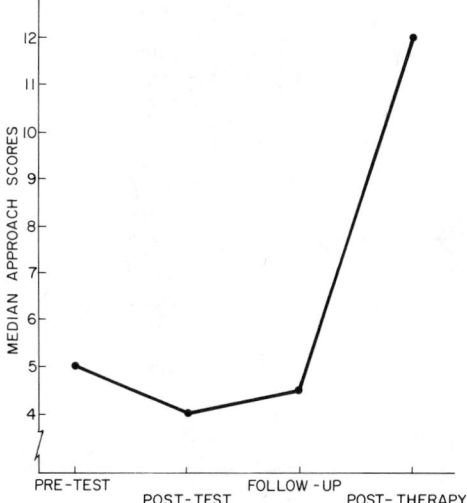

Figure 17.8 Median dog-approach scores achieved by control children during three test periods and after they had received the multiple-modeling treatment (Bandura and Menlove, 1968).

fearless intereaction with the animals, both of which she boldly corralled in the playpen after the formal test.

Comparative Efficacy of Live and Symbolic Modeling

Previous research (Bandura, Ross, and Ross, 1963) has established that pictorially presented models can be as effective as exposure to actual performances in modifying the actions of observers. The generality of the latter findings may be limited, however, because they are based on studies of aggressive behavior that can be readily transmitted and disinhibited by modeling stimuli regardless of the particular form in which they are presented.

Comparison of results of the preceding experiments suggests that in the case of refractory avoidance behavior, symbolic modeling may be somewhat less powerful than live demonstrations of essentially the same behavior. Subjects who observed the single symbolic model displayed less vicarious extinction than children who viewed live performances of analogous approach responses by the same model. There is some evidence, however, that the diminished efficacy of symbolic modeling can be offset by a wider sampling of models and aversive objects. This is shown by the fact that children who received multiple symbolic modeling successfully completed terminal approach tasks at rates comparable to those of equally avoidant children who observed fearless behavior performed by a single real-life model.

A later section describes a self-regulated symbolic modeling procedure, originally employed by Bandura, Blanchard, and Ritter (1969), that permits clients to conduct their own treatment. Hill, Liebert, and Mott (1968) and Spiegler, Liebert, McMains, and Fernandez (1969) have also successfully eliminated persistent avoidance behavior in children and adults through brief symbolic modeling. The latter studies, however, involve multielement procedures that combine modeling with persuasive narratives and other fear-mitigating techniques. A decided advantage of treatment programs based upon modeling principles is that they can be readily applied on a group basis. Moreover, evidence that film-mediated procedures can produce beneficial results indicates that therapeutic films could be developed for preventive programs to eliminate common fears before they become strongly established and widely generalized.

It is interesting to note that the influential role of modeling factors in the transmission of fears is widely acknowledged, but their therapeutic value has sometimes been questioned on the grounds that fears persist even though modeling frequently occurs under ordinary conditions of life. The effectiveness of any principle of learning depends not only on its validity but also on the manner in which it is implemented. Inconsistent, haphazard, and inadequately sequenced learning experiences will produce disappointing outcomes regardless of the cogency of the principle supposedly guiding the treatment.

In many instances weak fears are undoubtedly extinguished, or substantially reduced, through fortuitous naturalistic modeling. However, carefully planned modeling experiences are essential for the modification of more tenacious avoidance tendencies. There is some evidence (Bandura and Menlove, 1968) that parents of children who exhibit severe fearfulness make no attempts to overcome their children's fears because they suffer from similar apprehension. Consequently, they seldom model fearlessness

Figure 17.9 Photographs of a girl who was apprehensive about dogs engaging in fearless interactions with dogs after exposure to the series of films in which a peer model displays progressively more threatening interactions with dogs (Bandura and Menlove, 1968).

and, on the infrequent occasions when they do so, the modeling endeavors do not involve a carefully graded presentation of threatening stimuli, without which this method is not only likely to be ineffective, but may actually exacerbate anxiety reactions. A not uncommon domestic modeling scene, for example, is one in which a parent is busily petting a dog that is jumping about, while simultaneously bidding the child, who is clinging fearfully, to touch the bounding animal. By contrast, the modeling treatments, in addition to utilizing the principle of graduation to reduce fear arousal, involved concentrated exposures to modeling displays under protected observation conditions, and extensive variation of model characteristics, intimacy of approach behavior, and aversive properties of the feared object. Had modeling sequences in the treatment programs been presented in a widely dispersed and haphazard fashion and limited to less compelling demonstrations by adults (whom children are likely to discriminate as better able to protect themselves), the vicarious extinction outcomes might also have been relatively weak and unpredictable.

Diverse Changes Accompanying Modeling Treatments

Behaviorally oriented treatments are characteristically evaluated solely in terms of the response changes they produce. It is, therefore, commonly assumed that such methods may be appropriate for altering behavior, but other procedures, usually of a conversational type, must be employed to effect changes in attitudes, self-evaluations, and affective dispositions. Results of an experiment conducted by Bandura, Blanchard, and Ritter (1969), using multiple outcome measures, reveal that the changes accompanying social-learning approaches are by no means confined to motoric performances.

The aforementioned project employed an elaborate experimental design to assess the comparative efficacy of modeling and desensitization modes of treatment for producing behavioral, affective, and attitudinal changes. The participants were adolescents and adults who suffered from snake phobias that, in most cases, unnecessarily restricted their activities and adversely affected their psychological

functioning in various ways. Some of the people were unable to perform their jobs in situations in which there was any remote possibility that they might come into contact with snakes; others could not take part in recreational activities such as hunting, gardening, camping, or hiking, because of their dread of snakes; and still others avoided purchasing homes in rural areas, or experienced marked distress when they would be unexpectedly confronted with pet snakes in the course of their social or occupational activities.

In the initial phase of the experiment, the participants were administered a behavioral test that measured the strength of their avoidance of snakes. In addition, they completed a comprehensive fear inventory to determine whether elimination of fear of snakes is associated with concomitant changes in other areas of anxiety. Attitudinal ratings on several scales describing various encounters with snakes and on the evaluative dimensions of the semantic differential technique were also obtained.

One group of subjects participated in a self-administered symbolic modeling treatment in which they observed a graduated film depicting young children, adolescents, and adults engaging in progressively more threatening interactions with a large king snake (Figure 17.10). To increase even further the power of this method, two other features were added. First, subjects were taught to induce and to maintain anxiety-neutralizing relaxation throughout the period of exposure. A self-regulated modeling treatment should permit greater control over extinction outcomes than one in which persons are exposed to a sequence of aversive modeling stimuli without regard to their anxiety reactions. Therefore, the rate of presentation of modeling stimuli was regulated by subjects through a projector equipped with remote-control starting and reversing devices. They were instructed to stop the film whenever a particular modeled performance proved anxiety-provoking, to reverse the film to the beginning of the aversive sequence, and to reinduce deep relaxation. Subjects then reviewed the threatening scene repeatedly in this manner until it was completely neutralized before proceeding to the next item in the graduated sequence. They conducted their own treatment in this manner until their

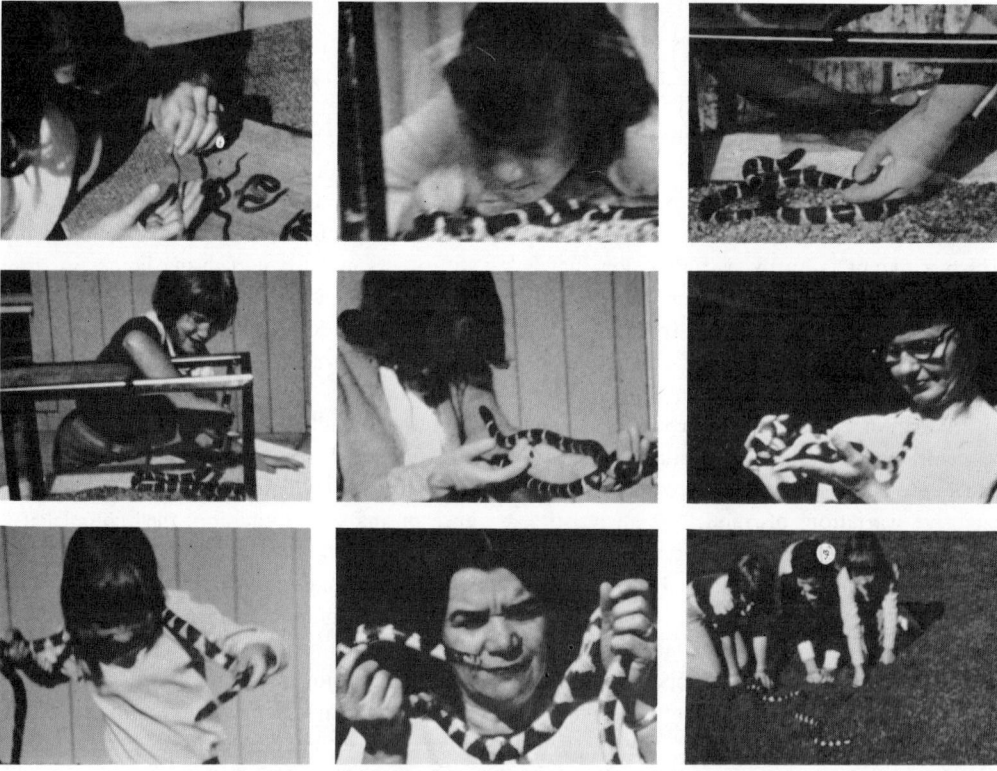

Figure 17.10 Children and adults modeling progressively more fear-arousing interactions with a king snake (Bandura, Blanchard, and Ritter, 1969).

anxieties to the modeled performances were thoroughly extinguished.

The second group of subjects received a form of treatment combining graduated live modeling with guided participation. The principal elements of this method were developed by Ritter (1968a; 1969a) as contact desensitization. In the procedure employed in the present study, the model initially demonstrated the desired behavior under secure observational conditions, after which subjects were aided through further demonstration and joint performance to execute progressively more difficult responses. Whenever subjects were unable to perform a given behavior upon demonstration alone, they were assisted physically by enacting the feared activities concurrently with the model. The physical guidance was then gradually reduced, until subjects were able to perform the behavior without assistance.

In applying the above method, the therapist himself performed the fearless behavior at each step and gradually led subjects into touching, stroking, and then holding the snake's body with gloved and bare hands while the experimenter held the snake securely by the head and tail. If a subject was unable to touch the snake following ample demonstration, she was asked to place her hand on the experimenter's and to move her hand down gradually until it touched the snake's body. After subjects no longer felt any apprehension about touching the snake under these secure conditions, anxieties about contact with the snake's head area and entwining tail were extinguished. The therapist again performed the tasks fearlessly, and then he and the subject performed the responses jointly; as subjects became less fearful, the experimenter gradually reduced his participation and control over the snake, until eventually subjects were able to hold the snake in their laps without assistance, to let the snake loose in the room and retrieve it, and to let it crawl freely over their bodies. Progress through the graded approach tasks was paced according to the subjects' apprehensiveness. When they reported being able to perform one activity with little or no fear, they were eased into a more difficult interaction.

Participant modeling includes several factors designed to facilitate elimination of defensive behavior. The modeling component both exemplifies how desired activities can be performed most effectively and helps to reduce fears and behavioral inhibitions. To further aid in eliciting potentially threatening performances, they are divided into a series of small graded steps, each of which is initially accomplished under circumstances affording ample protection against feared consequences. Whenever these favorable conditions fail to produce the desired behavior, clients are physically guided in performing the responses and their efforts are socially reinforced. As treatment progresses the amount of demonstration, protection, and guidance is progressively diminished.

A third group of subjects in the experiment received the standard form of desensitization treatment (Wolpe, 1958). In this procedure deep relaxation was successively paired with imaginal representations of snakes arranged in order of increasing aversiveness. Subjects assigned to the control condition participated in the behavioral and attitudinal assessments without receiving any intervening treatment.

Following completion of the treatment series the assessment procedures were readministered to all subjects. The behavioral test, which was conducted with snakes strikingly different in coloration, consisted of a series of tasks requiring the subjects to approach, look at, touch and hold a snake with bare and gloved hands; to remove the snake from its cage, let it loose in the room, and then replace it in the cage; to hold it within five inches of their faces; and finally, to tolerate the snake in their laps while they held their hands passively at their sides. Immediately prior to and during the performance of each task, subjects rated the intensity of their fear arousal on a 10-interval scale to measure extinction of affective arousal accompanying specific approach responses.

As shown in Figure 17.11, control subjects remained unchanged in avoidance behavior; symbolic modeling and desensitization produced substantial reductions in phobic behavior; while live modeling, combined with guided participation, proved to be an unusually powerful treatment that eliminated snake phobias in virtually all subjects (92 percent).

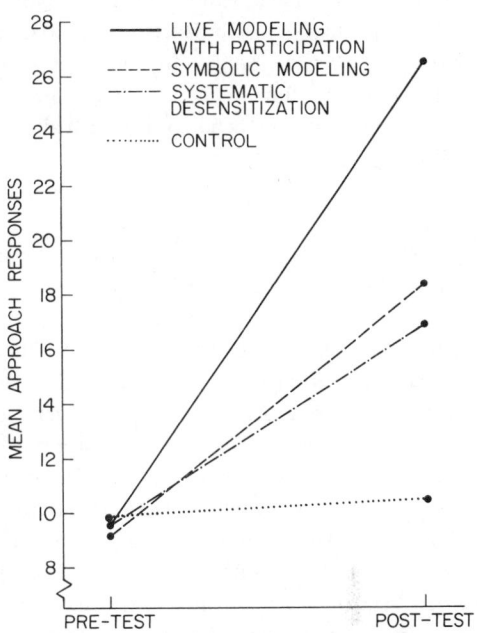

Figure 17.11 Mean number of snake approach responses performed by subjects before and after receiving different treatments (Bandura, Blanchard, and Ritter, 1969).

The modeling procedures not only extinguished avoidance responses of long standing, but they also neutralized the anxiety-arousing properties of the phobic stimuli. Both of the modeling treatments achieved marked decrements in anticipatory and performance anxiety. Although subjects who had received desensitization treatment also experienced less emotional arousal while performing snake-approach responses, the magnitude of their fear reduction was less than that shown by their counterparts in the modeling conditions.

Attitudinal Changes Accompanying Modeling Treatments

In discussions of treatment outcomes, the modification of attitudes is frequently considered an important objective. Selection of attitude change as a therapeutic goal is primarily based on the assumption that attitudes are determinants of overt actions. In fact, most change agents who strive to alter people's attitudes are not interested in attitudes per se. Rather, the attitude-change approach is resorted to as a means of influencing behavior when, for practical or other reasons, it cannot be directly elicited and reinforced. Although attitude change has been extensively studied, the research is based on a limited range of procedures and, surprisingly, the fundamental issue of whether attitudes control overt behavior has been almost totally ignored.

One can distinguish among three basic modes of attitude change. The *cognitive-oriented* approach attempts to modify persons' attitudes by altering their beliefs about the attitude object through various forms of persuasive communications. This method can produce changes in attitudes, but it often has little effect upon overt actions. A second general strategy involves an *affect-oriented* approach wherein both evaluations of, and behavior toward, particular attitude objects are modified by altering their emotion-arousing properties, usually through direct or vicarious conditioning procedures. The third approach, which is often used in social learning (Bandura, 1969a), and in experimental social psychology, relies upon a *behavior-oriented* strategy. Results of the latter procedure provide considerable evidence that attitudinal changes can be successfully achieved by getting a person to engage in new behavior in relation to the attitude object without untoward consequences. The relative superiority of the behavioral approach probably stems from the fact that a basic change in behavior and the resultant experiential feedback provide an objective and genuine basis for new evaluations.

Findings of the present experiment reveal that applications of social learning procedures have important attitudinal consequences. Both symbolic modeling and desensitization, which primarily involve extinction of negative affect aroused by aversive stimuli, produced favorable changes in attitudes toward snakes (Figure 17.12). Consistent with expectation, the participant modeling treatment that reduced the fear-arousing properties of snakes and enabled subjects to engage in intimate interactions with snakes effected the greatest attitudinal changes.

Previous research using mainly persuasive communications (Festinger, 1964) found changes in attitudes and actions to be essentially unrelated. In contrast to these findings, the modifications in attitudes and approach behavior produced by desensitization and modeling treatments were positively correlated to a moderately high degree. In a study employing similar procedures, Blanchard (1969) also found a high positive relationship between changes in attitudes and behavior as induced through modeling influences.

The correlated changes achieved by social-learning procedures in different response systems may be interpreted in several ways. According to most contemporary attitude theories (Abelson et al., 1968), there exists a strong drive for consistency among beliefs, feelings, and actions. A change in any one of the components will, therefore, engender congruous modification in the other constituents. In these consistency models, changes in attitudes or behavior are treated, not simply as consequent events, but as causal factors affecting other classes of behavior. An alternative interpretation is that social influences have similar but independent effects on attitudes, behavior, and emotional arousal. Thus, for example, if a child has been severely bitten by a dog, this aversive experience can simultaneously produce a dislike of dogs, endow dogs with fear-arousing properties, and establish dog-avoidance behavior. In this view, attitude-behavior consistencies represent correlated coeffects rather than outcomes of a process in which modification of one type of behavior forces changes in other forms of responding to eliminate cognitive disequilibrium. Indeed, when attitudes are inferred from nonverbal behavior, as is often the case, the issue of whether attitudes influence behavior reduces to the question of whether a particular response pattern determines itself.

Definitive tests of the parallel-effects and consistency explanations of change processes are precluded by the absence of a methodology that would permit simultaneous measurement of attitudes, affect, and actions. If incongruity creates an internal stimulus for psychological change, then a sequential testing procedure unavoidably confounds the effects of external influences and the consistency drive. Conversely, if environmental influences have analogous effects on different classes of response, without concurrent measurement, correlated changes would be erroneously attributed to the operation of a consistency drive. These alternative formulations perhaps should be regarded as complementary rather than competing. Under

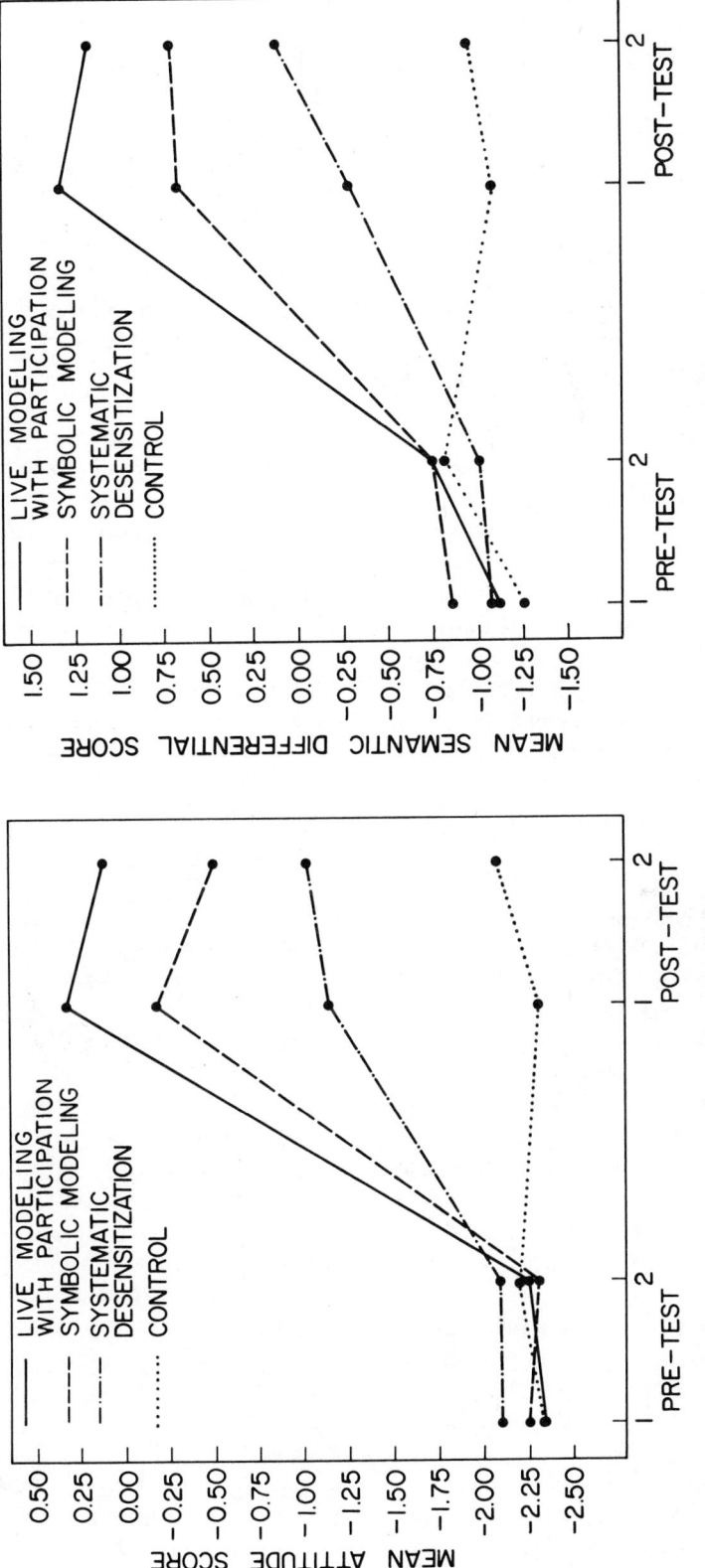

Figure 17.12 Attitudinal changes for persons who received either one of the treatment procedures or served as untreated controls. The numeral 1 indicates subjects' attitudes prior to the behavioral test, and the numeral 2 shows their attitudes immediately after the test of avoidance behavior (Bandura, Blanchard, and Ritter, 1969).

most conditions, powerful social influences produce corresponding changes in different modes of responding, and performance of new behavior is likely to have additional cognitive and emotional consequences.

Positive Transfer of Anxiety Decrements

One would ordinarily expect favorable changes induced in one area of behavior to set in motion beneficial changes in related areas of psychological functioning. Analysis of the fear inventory scores in the present study does indeed reveal some degree of anxiety reduction toward situations beyond the specifically treated phobia, the decrements being roughly proportional to the potency of the treatments employed. Nontreated controls showed no changes in either number or intensity of fears. Desensitization produced a decrease only in severity of fears toward other animals, whereas symbolic modeling was accompanied by a reduction in the number of animal fears and a general diminution in the intensity of anxiety in several other areas of functioning. Participant modeling, on the other hand, effected widespread fear reductions in relation to a variety of threats involving both interpersonal and nonsocial events.

The positive transfer obtained probably reflects the operation of at least two somewhat different processes. The first involves generalization of fear extinction effects from stimuli that are neutralized, by the treatment, to related anxiety sources. The second process entails positive reinforcement of a sense of capability through success, which mitigates emotional arousal to potentially threatening situations. Having successfully overcome a phobia that had plagued them for most of their lives, subjects reported increased confidence that they could cope effectively with other fear-provoking events.

Under conditions where a given treatment procedure exercises weak behavioral control, many other variables (such as the personality characteristics of therapists, attributes of clients, and minor technical variations) are often found to be influential determinants of change. A strong method should be able to override such influences. The goal of psychotherapy research, therefore, should be the development of treatment methods that are sufficiently powerful to produce consistent changes by different therapists, just as one would not be content with medical procedures whose effects depend heavily upon the personality characteristics of physicians and clients.

In order to determine, in cases that showed only partial improvement, whether the deficiencies reside in the treatment method or in the client, all persons who failed to achieve terminal performances were subsequently administered the participant modeling treatment. Phobic behavior was thoroughly extinguished in all of these subjects within a few brief sessions regardless of their age, sex, anxiety proneness, and severity of avoidance behavior (Figure 17.13). Moreover, this supplementary treatment produced further reductions in fearfulness toward both the phobic stimuli and other types of threats, and additional attitudinal changes. The follow-up assessment revealed that the beneficial changes produced in behavior, attitudes, and emotional responsiveness were effectively maintained. The clients also displayed evidence that the behavioral improvements had generalized from therapeutic to real-life situations.

Additional Tests and Therapeutic Applications of Modeling Procedures

Numerous experiments have been reported on results achieved by modeling procedures and their relative efficacy compared to other behavioral approaches. Ritter (1968a) obtained uniform success with group-modeling procedures administered to children who displayed fear of snakes. Groups of children participated in two 35-minute sessions in which they either merely observed several fearless children exhibit intimate interactions with a snake, or they received the participant modeling form of treatment, during which the therapist displayed positive responses toward the snake and then gradually eased the children into performing the feared behavior. Snake phobias were completely extinguished in 53 percent of the children by modeling alone, and in 80 percent of the children who received modeling combined with guided participation. None of the children in a control condition was able to perform the terminal approach behavior. In a related study

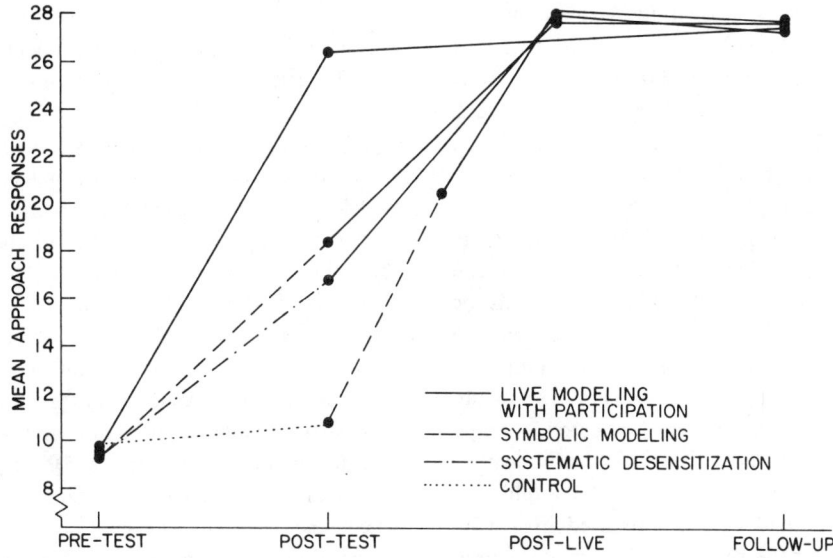

Figure 17.13 Mean number of snake-approach responses performed by individuals before and after (post-test) receiving different treatments. Control subjects were subsequently administered symbolic modeling treatment without relaxation. All individuals in the desensitization, symbolic modeling, and treated control conditions who failed to perform the terminal approach behavior then received the treatment combining live modeling with guided participation (post-live). Snake-approach behavior was measured again in a follow-up study conducted one month later (Bandura, Blanchard, and Ritter, 1969).

(Ritter, 1968b), the latter method administered individually completely extinguished snake-phobic behavior in 83 percent of adolescent subjects, whereas only 17 percent of nontreated controls achieved terminal performances.

The potency of participant modeling is further confirmed by Rimm and Mahoney (1969), who rapidly extinguished snake-avoidance behavior with this method in adults who were unable to achieve any behavioral improvement when offered increasing monetary rewards for performing a graduated series of approach responses. It was previously shown (Bandura, Blanchard, and Ritter, 1969) that modeling combined with guided participation was superior to symbolic desensitization in eliminating a circumscribed phobia. This finding is replicated in two other experiments. Litvak (1969) found that a single group session of participant modeling produced substantially greater reduction in phobic behavior than either group desensitization or no treatment.

Perloff (1970) examined the comparative effectiveness of participant modeling as part of a larger project assessing the influence of muscular relaxation and positive imagery on extinction of

avoidance behavior through systematic desensitization. The facilitative effects of relaxation procedures on desensitization outcomes may be attributable to the conditions produced by muscular relaxation, to the tranquilizing effects of positive imagery employed in the standard induction method, or to the mere fact that engaging in any competing activity terminates threatening stimuli before they reach aversive levels. In order to evaluate the relative contribution of these component influences, snake-phobic subjects received desensitization treatments in which fear-arousing scenes were contiguously associated with either muscular relaxation devoid of positive imagery, positive imagery without muscular relaxation, or neutral imagery. Treatments employing positive and neutral imagery, which proved equally effective, were superior to muscular relaxation. On the other hand, control subjects, who exhibited no significant change in avoidance behavior, matched or surpassed the desensitization treatments after a brief group program of live modeling with guided participation.

Modeling procedures can be effective in the treatment of other types of anxiety conditions as well. As noted earlier, interpersonal anxieties and animal phobias have been eliminated by modeling alone. Ritter has also successfully treated a variety of phobic conditions through modeling with guided participation, including a dissection phobia (Ritter, 1965), a street-crossing phobia (Ritter, 1969a), and numerous cases suffering from acrophobia (Ritter, 1969b, c). The traditional method of overcoming social inhibitions has been to provide a permissive atmosphere and wait for desired behavior to emerge. This approach is usually minimally effective and highly time-consuming. In an early publication of action-oriented therapy techniques, Levy (1939) provides many demonstrations of how severe behavioral inhibitions in children could be easily reduced by having them observe the therapist perform the feared activities himself.

Component Analysis of Modeling with Guided Participation

Most therapeutic procedures contain multiple elements, and it is therefore necessary to conduct component analyses to determine whether the constituent factors are necessary, facilitative, irrelevant, or serving as impediments to the outcomes produced by the composite procedure. Within the treatment combining modeling with guided participation, three major processes are operative that might contribute in varying degrees to psychological changes. These include observation of fearless behavior being repeatedly modeled without any unfavorable consequences; incidental information received about the feared objects; and guided direct contact with threatening objects that engender no adverse effects.

In an experiment aimed at isolating the relative influence of these component variables, Blanchard (1969) matched subjects in terms of their snake-avoidance behavior and assigned them to one of four conditions. One subject in each quartet received the standard procedure, which includes the benefits of modeling, information, and guided performance. A second subject simultaneously observed the modeling sessions and listened to the verbal interchanges, thus being exposed to both modeling and informational influences. The third subject received only the modeling component, while the fourth, who merely participated in the testing procedures, experienced none of the constituent influences. Figure 17.14 summarizes the behavioral, affective, and

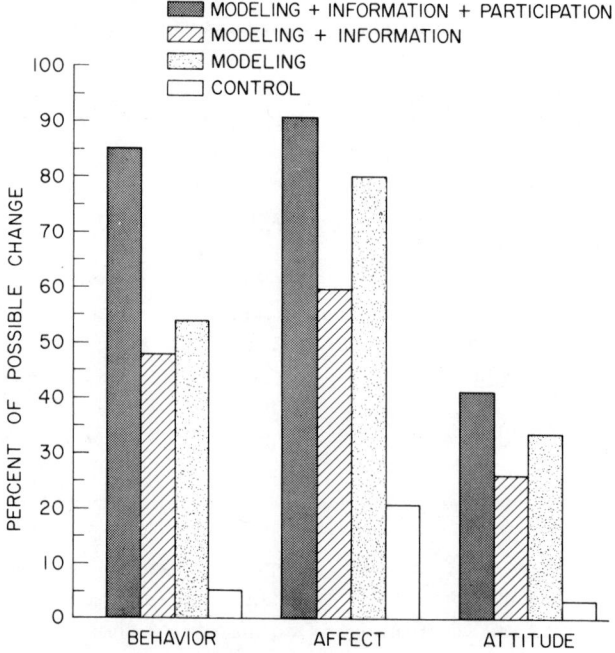

Figure 17.14 Percentage of change in approach behavior, fearfulness, and attitudes displayed by individuals who received different components of the treatment combining modeling with guided participation (Blanchard, 1969).

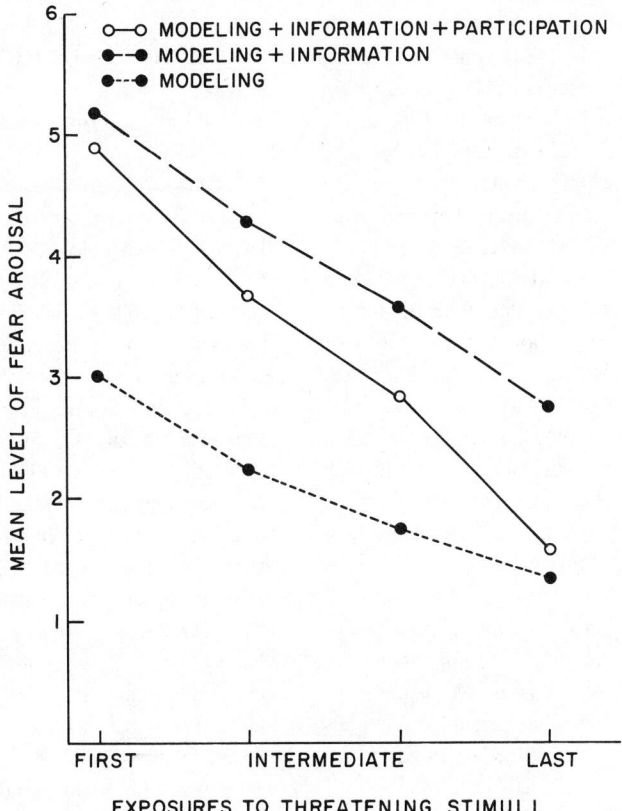

Figure 17.15 Mean level of fear arousal evoked by approach behavior initially and by subsequent repetitions of the same actions in persons who either participated directly in the treatment, or observed the approach performances with or without informational influences (Blanchard, 1969).

attitudinal changes associated with these various treatment conditions. Modeling accounted for approximately 60 percent of the behavior change, and 80 percent of the changes in attitudes and fear arousal; guided participation contributed the remaining increment. Informational influences, on the other hand, had no effect on any of the three response classes. In fact, the latter condition yielded the lowest scores on all the three sets of dependent measures. Apparently, giving information to severely phobic people may, if anything, increase their fearfulness. This is shown most clearly in subjects' ratings of their fear arousal while observing the participant member initially perform the graded set of approach responses, and on each subsequent repetition of the same behavior (Figure 17.15). Subjects who received modeling with information displayed the highest level of fear arousal throughout the modeling

trials. On the other hand, subjects in the participant modeling condition initially experienced high arousal, followed by a rapid rate of extinction, and at the final performance of each approach response they reported no more fear than the modeling group, despite the fact that they were confronted with direct threats rather than weaker observed ones.

The findings of the above study reveal the importance of including tests for generalization in evaluating the relative efficacy of different treatment approaches. Modeling with guided participation proved superior to live modeling alone in tests conducted with the snake that was originally employed in the treatment, but the two methods yielded essentially equivalent results on generalization tests with an unfamiliar reptile.

The guided-participation component of the modeling approach under discussion can be further analyzed into several elements. Participant observers enact progressively more difficult responses without the occurrence of feared consequences, and these repeated disconfirming experiences can, in themselves, produce direct extinction of fear arousal and avoidance behavior. In addition, whenever clients are physically assisted in performing the behavior required at each step in the graded sequence, their fears and inhibitions may be reduced to some degree by physical contact with the model and by the added protection that his behavior provides. For example, snake phobics are willing to attempt tentative approach responses that they would otherwise be unable to make, provided the model holds the snake securely by the head and tail; and acrophobics may be aided in climbing heights, given the security of the therapist's physical support. Ritter gives special emphasis to the possible anxiety-mitigating effects of physical contact. Consistent with this assumption, there is some suggestive evidence (Kissel, 1965; Mason, 1960) that even the mere presence of familiar persons diminishes emotional arousal in subjects in stressful situations.

In order to evaluate the independent influence of physical guidance and performance of approach responses, Ritter (1969c) administered to acrophobic subjects one of three treatments during a single 35-minute session. For one group of subjects, the therapist exhibited increasingly threatening climbing responses and physically assisted subjects in performing the same activities; in the second condition, the therapist demonstrated the behavior, but only verbally guided subjects in enacting matching performances; a third group simply observed the demonstrated activities. At the completion of the session all subjects were readministered a behavioral test requiring them to climb to a series of heights atop a seven-story building, where the treatment was originally conducted. Modeling accompanied by physically guided performance produced greater changes than modeling with verbally guided enactment, which, in turn, was superior to brief demonstration alone. A further experiment is needed to determine whether the facilitative effects of physical guidance derive from interpersonal contact, from protection against potential

injurious consequences, or, as seems most likely, from both factors. This would require a design in which extinction rates are compared when physical guidance is socially mediated or provided to the same degree through nonsocial means.

The research previously reviewed both with children (Bandura, Grusec, and Menlove, 1967; Bandura and Menlove, 1968; O'Connor, 1969; Ritter, 1968a) and adults (Bandura, Blanchard, and Ritter, 1969; Blanchard, 1969) demonstrates that virtually all subjects benefit from modeling alone, and that a substantial number of them achieve complete and generalized extinction of avoidance behavior. However, two studies reported by Ritter (1969b, 1969c) failed to obtain significant reductions in avoidance behavior solely through modeling. Ritter attributes the discrepant findings to the brevity of the treatment, and to the fact that in one of the experiments involving a group procedure, observations of the fearful performances of group members may have attenuated the facilitative effects of modeling. As was noted earlier, fear arousal is progressively diminished with repeated modeling trials. In order to obtain consistently favorable results, modeling treatments should be continued to the point where fear arousal is vicariously extinguished below the threshold for activating avoidance behavior.

The process of change associated with the powerful procedure involving modeling combined with guided participation may be conceptualized as follows. Repeated modeling of approach responses, mainly through its informative function, decreases the arousal potential of aversive stimuli below the threshold for activating avoidance responses, thus enabling persons to engage, albeit somewhat anxiously, in approach behavior. Whenever vicarious extinction alone does not restore desired behavior, physical guidance, through its reassuring and protective functions, serves as an additional means of reducing fear arousal and facilitating performance of previously inhibited responses. Direct contact with threats that are no longer objectively justified provides a variety of new experiences which, if favorable, further extinguish residual anxiety and avoidance tendencies. Without the benefit of prior vicarious extinction, the reinstatement of severely inhibited behavior generally requires a tedious and protracted program. After approach behavior toward formerly avoided objects has been fully restored, the resultant new experiences give rise to substantial reorganization of attitudes.

The overall findings of studies reviewed above indicate that a powerful form of treatment is one in which therapeutic agents themselves model the desired behavior and arrange optimal conditions for clients to engage in similar activities until they can perform the behavior skillfully and fearlessly. The therapeutic outcomes associated with this approach are sufficiently promising to warrant its further extension to other types of anxiety conditions. It is undoubtedly best suited for behavioral dysfunctions in which the feared consequences are inspectional.

The overall results suggest that in clinical practice, the optimal treatment strategy for achieving the most generalized changes with minimum distress would initially employ live or symbolic modeling to produce the principal changes, followed by a brief program of additional modeling with guided performance to extinguish any residual fears and defensive behavior. Approximately forty percent of clients will achieve complete extinction of avoidance tendencies on the basis of modeling alone, and the remainder will require a much shorter period of direct treatment than if they did not have the prior benefits of modeling. In the study by Bandura, Blanchard, and Ritter (1969), this treatment sequence achieved thorough extinction of avoidance behavior in 96 percent of the cases and complete generalization in 83 percent of the subjects.

Vicarious Extinction and Model Similarity

In devising treatment programs based on modeling principles, questions arise about the types of models that are likely to have greatest impact on observers. Among the various factors that are believed to facilitate modeling (Bandura, 1969b), the degree of similarity to the model is often assigned a prominent role. Stotland and his co-workers (Burnstein, Stotland, and Zander, 1961; Stotland and Hillmer, 1962; Stotland and Patchen, 1961; Stotland, Zander, and Natsoulas, 1961) report that persons who are told they have some qualities in common with an unfamiliar model are more inclined to imitate additional new responses portrayed by the model than subjects who initially share no common characteristics. The generalization of similarity is attributed by Stotland to a drive for cognitive consistency in self-concept. According to this view, when a person conceives of himself as having some characteristics in common with a model, he introjects other attributes of the model into his self-concept in order to maintain cognitive or perceptual consistency.

Close examination of research findings reveals that similarity has, at best, weak effects on modeling. The elusiveness of the phenomenon is most clearly shown in studies that include a control condition in which no attempt is made to induce social resemblance. Whereas in many comparisons subjects in high and low similarity conditions display differential matching behavior, the two groups usually do not differ significantly from controls. Considering that both the similarity induction and the model's behavior are typically presented in verbal form by the same researcher in the same situation, the relatively weak response-generalization effects may be a function of an experimentally induced set for agreement, rather than internal pressures for cognitive consistency.

On the occasions when similarity facilitates modeling, it may do so primarily through interpersonal attraction rather than as a consequence of striving for cognitive consistency. Byrne (1969) has shown in a series of experiments that perceived similarity between a given individual and a stranger increases attraction toward the stranger. Conversely, dissimilarity manipulations that portray the divergent model as espousing contrary interests may reduce matching behavior by arousing antipathy toward the model. Data from a condition in which the model is clearly dissimilar but possesses attributes that the subject admires and aspires to have would be particularly relevant to these alternative explanations. The cognitive consistency and the attraction hypotheses lead to opposite predictions regarding imitation of admired dissimilar models. In everyday life, of course, models who possess emulative qualities that can be attained with concerted effort serve as more important sources of desired patterns of behavior than persons who share similar behavioral deficits.

It would appear from the available evidence that similarity is unlikely to exert a sizeable influence on modeling outcomes. This conclusion must be accepted with reservation, however, because the aforementioned experiments are primarily concerned with inconsequential preferences or behaviors that observers could easily perform if they so wished. Moreover, model similarity may have differential effects on treatment outcomes, depending on whether the likeness is based on the class of behavior being modified, or on characteristics in some other domain. Let us first consider therapeutic procedures in which clients and models are similar on the response dimension selected for modification. It remains an open question whether observation of fearful models undergoing change is more or less effective than an equivalent amount of exposure to bold behavior by dauntless models.

There is reason to assume that model similarity can both facilitate and impede reduction of defensive behavior. Witnessing fearful models exhibiting progressively more daring performances without adverse consequences would serve to reinforce positive expectations in apprehensive observers that similar changes are readily attainable. Evident successes by similarly handicapped models should therefore increase client's performance efforts and sustain them in the face of occasional setbacks. On the other hand, daring performances of fearless models may be discounted by observers on the grounds that the models possess special expertise enabling them to prevent injurious consequences that might otherwise befall unskilled practitioners. According to this discrimination view of extinction, which receives considerable empirical support (Bandura, 1969a), a herpetologist would have weaker disinhibitory effects on snake-phobic observers than a less experienced model displaying the same approach responses. To the extent that such discriminations, even though objectively erroneous, are formed, observers would be reluctant to attempt matching behavior and easily dissuaded by any negative experiences.

The positive motivational effects of model similarity must be weighed against its fear-arousal potential. Studies of vicarious emotional processes, to be reviewed next, demonstrate that negative affective expressions by others elicit fear and avoidance behavior in observers. Fearful models may, therefore, retard the rate of vicarious extinction by generating high levels of fear arousal. It is interesting to note in this connection that experiments in which modeling alone proved of limited efficacy (Spiegler, Liebert, McMains, and Fernandez, 1968; Ritter, 1969b) included brief exposure to fearful performers.

It is possible to capitalize on response generalization due to similarity without exacerbating the condition that the treatment is intended to eliminate. This may be achieved by establishing model similarity on dimensions that differ from those undergoing change, or the similarity may be presented historically by depicting the model as a person who previously suffered similar fears that were successfully eliminated through treatment. However, the problem of the influence on avoidance extinction of similarity even in irrelevant characteristics is complicated by a number of factors. In the previously cited study of vicarious extinction in adults (Bandura, Blanchard, and Ritter, 1969), the treatment film contained not only fearless adult models but also several young children, on the assumption that their lack of fear while performing responses that adult observers regarded as hazardous would provide the most dramatic disconfirmation of anticipated aversive consequences. The foregoing discussion illustrates the need for systematic investigation of the degree to which model-subject similarity on a relevant dimension (that is, fearfulness) and also on irrelevant dimensions (that is, attitudes, interests, and general background) affects the rate of vicarious extinction of phobic behavior.

According to the theory of modeling presented by Bandura (1969b), response consequences to models generally outweigh their characteristics in producing matching behavior in observers. Thus, for example, witnessing a similar model bitten by a snake would in all likelihood increase snake-avoidance behavior, whereas seeing a dissimilar model handle a snake without any untoward consequences would weaken avoidance responses. Consistent with this view,

Miller and Dollard (1941) demonstrated that whether children imitated peers or dissimilar adult models depended on response outcomes rather than on likeness in attributes. Under conditions where modeled behavior has limited utilitarian value and response consequences are relatively weak, similarity may facilitate matching behavior (Rosekrans, 1967). Considering, however, that models' response outcomes can be easily controlled, therapeutic results would be more consistently achieved by arranging favorable consequences for modeled behavior than by relying on generalization on the basis of irrelevant characteristics that clients and models may share, or presume to share, in common.

Influence of Affective Modeling Cues on Vicarious Extinction

Findings derived from investigation of vicarious fear arousal suggest that the affective expressions accompanying a model's behavior may exercise some degree of control over vicarious extinction. In laboratory studies of this phenomenon, observers' autonomic reactivity, avoidance responding, and other indices of emotional arousal are measured during exposure to the emotional responses of others in fear-provoking situations. It has been demonstrated with both primates (Miller, 1967) and human subjects (Craig, 1968; Lazarus et al., 1962) that negative affective expressions by others can serve as powerful cues for arousing fear and avoidance in observers. In fact, Miller and his colleagues (Miller, Murphy, and Mirsky, 1959) have shown that exposure to a subject reacting in an apprehensive or fearful manner could reinstate avoidance responses in observers even after such responses had been completely extinguished.

It has been further shown (Bandura and Rosenthal, 1966; Craig and Weinstein, 1965; Berger, 1962) that if emotional responses are vicariously elicited in observers in conjunction with formerly neutral stimuli, the stimuli themselves gradually acquire emotion-arousing potential. Thus, fearful modeling not only arouses emotional responses in observers, but, if sufficiently intense, it can vicariously condition negative properties to stimulus events that repeatedly occur in temporal contiguity.

The foregoing research has important implications for therapeutic utilization of modeling principles. Fearful modeling is likely to generate in observers needless emotional arousal that prolongs the extinction process. Therefore, in the modeling procedures previously reported, several factors were included to maintain fear arousal at a minimum level. First, threatening modeling stimuli are initially presented in weak forms and gradually increased to their full threat value. Second, aversive modeling stimuli are usually presented in conjunction with fear-mitigating stimuli. And third, the models frequently display positive emotional reactions as they perform approach responses in a relaxed manner. It would follow from the above discussion that if modeled approach responses were accompanied by positive affective expressions, they would engender less fear arousal in observers and hence, faster vicarious extinction than if models manifested fearful reactions while performing the same approach behavior.

Contribution of Fear-Reducing Conditions to the Efficacy of Modeling Procedures

There is some evidence from laboratory studies (Poppen, 1968; Wilson, 1969) that the aversive properties of threatening stimuli can be extinguished more rapidly when administered in conjunction with fear-neutralizing events than when presented alone. The presence of positive events, in the form of deep relaxation, positive imagery, reassuring social stimuli, appetizing foods, and tranquilizing drugs, may facilitate elimination of defensive behavior in at least two different ways. According to one mode of operation, positive stimuli elicit responses that are incompatible with fear, and thereby attenuate the arousal capabilities of aversive stimuli. Support for this interpretation is profided by Grings and Uno (1968), who found that subjects displayed the strongest atonomic responses to a fear cue alone, the weakest responses when fear and relaxation cues were presented simultaneously as a compound stimulus, and emotional responses of intermediate magnitude to a compound stimulus containing the fear cue and a neutral stimulus. Paul (1969) likewise reports that relaxation decreased subjects' physiological responsiveness to imagined aversive stimuli.

The use of positive events in conjunction with threatening stimuli may hasten elimination of defensive behavior because the positive conditions enable the individual to expose himself to threats for a longer time, rather than because of their fear-mitigating effects. Nelson (1966) found that animals willingly entered a feared situation twice as frequently and remained there approximately three times as long when food was present in the situation than when it was absent. However, animals that were confined in the feared compartment for an equivalent period without food showed a similar amount of reduction in avoidance responses. The influential role of duration of exposure on extinction in humans is corroborated by Proctor (1968), who demonstrated that longer exposure produced greater reduction in avoidance behavior. Positive events can, therefore, facilitate the extinction process by serving both as incentives for self-exposure to threatening situations and as fear reducers.

Several studies have been conducted in which therapeutic outcomes are compared when modeling procedures are administered alone, and in conjunction with positive stimuli intended to counteract fear arousal. Bandura, Grusec, and Menlove (1967) found that modeling alone produced equivalent reduction in phobic behavior to modeling presented within a highly positive context. In a follow-up assessment, however, children in the latter treatment condition displayed additional significant improvement in approach behavior.

In the experiment previously discussed (Bandura, Blanchard, and Ritter, 1969), after the posttreatment assessment was completed, subjects in the control group received the symbolic modeling treatment, except that they did not utilize relaxation to counteract fear arousal. They simply reviewed threatening scenes repeatedly until these were completely neutralized, and recorded their level of fear arousal during each exposure. Symbolic modeling alone produced substantial increases in approach behavior. In fact, 45 percent of the phobic subjects exhibited complete and generalized extinction of snake-phobic behavior. This treatment also produced favorable attitudinal changes, and it reduced fear arousal to both snake-approach behavior and a variety of other potentially threatening situations measured by the fear inventory.

Comparisons were made of the changes achieved by control subjects through symbolic modeling alone and by experimental subjects who received symbolic modeling with relaxation. No differences were found between the groups either in amount of approach behavior or in the decrements they displayed in generalized anxiety. However, subjects who paired theatening modeling cues with relaxation subsequently experienced significantly less fear arousal while performing snake-approach responses, and they showed greater positive changes in their attitude toward snakes. Further results of this study reveal that relaxation can reduce the time required to neutralize fear-arousing modeling stimuli. Subjects who received modeling alone required approximately twice as many re-exposures as those who paired modeling with relaxation to achieve complete extinction of fear arousal to the filmed displays.

Rimm and Medeiros (1970) compared extinction of phobic behavior in subjects who received either participant modeling with relaxation, participant modeling alone, only relaxation, or no treatment. Participant modeling produced large generalized, and enduring reductions in avoidance behavior, but the addition of relaxation did not contribute significantly to the results obtained with this method. Since virtually all subjects achieved terminal performances through participant modeling alone, supplemental conditions cannot emerge as contributory factors unless the study is confined to markedly phobic subjects and exceedingly demanding performance tests are employed. At variance with the preceding findings, Spiegler et al. (1969) report that relaxation significantly enhanced the effectiveness of symbolic modeling in which snake-phobic subjects viewed a brief film depicting a fearful model gradually overcoming her fear of snakes with the aid of a bold demonstrator. Several factors might account for the divergent results, including differences in the form and length of modeling, in the fearfulness of the models, or in the latitude for behavioral change.

The overall evidence suggests that fear-reducing procedures are most likely to augment the efficacy of modeling treatments under conditions of brief massed presentation of modeling stimuli. On the other hand, when subjects are provided with multiple modeling trials distributed over several sessions, positive factors may serve as less influential contributors to change. Some support for this conclusion is provided by comparison of the rate with which fear arousal is extinguished in subjects who observe modeled performances with and without the benefit of relaxation (Bandura, Blanchard and Ritter, 1969). Subjects who combined modeling with relaxation experienced greater reduction in fear on the second exposure to the threatening scenes than their counterparts who received modeling alone; on subsequent reexposures, however, the rate of fear extinction was essentially the same.

It also seems plausible that fear reducers would assume a facilitative role in extinction primarily with cases involving marked behavioral inhibitions. Assuming a threshold notion, a person's fears must be reduced below a certain level before he will be willing to perform even tentative approach responses. A severe phobic would, therefore, require relatively powerful fear-mitigating procedures to achieve subthreshold reductions, whereas weaker methods could restore approach behavior in moderately inhibited clients. Findings of a study by Schubot (1966) (that relaxation in symbolic desensitization was essential for modifying extreme phobic behavior, but it did not facilitate extinction of avoidance responses of moderate strength) lend support to the above assumption.

Durability of Therapeutic Changes

Given that fearful behavior can be readily eliminated through modeling procedures, the question arises as to whether it is likely to be reinstated if, on later occasions, individuals should undergo aversive experiences or observe approach behavior in others meet with negative consequences. This issue, of course, is not unique to modeling treatments, and applies equally to psychological changes achieved through other methods.

There are several factors that favor persistence of disinhibited response patterns long after the formal treatment conditions have been discontinued. Removal of unwarranted fears alleviates subjective distress and enables people to participate in rewarding activities that they formerly avoided (Bandura, Blanchard, and Ritter, 1969). Consequently, newly established approach tendencies are generally strengthened and maintained by favorable conditions of reinforcement existing within the natural environment without requiring special maintenance procedures.

The second factor concerns the requisite conditions for instating fear and defensive behavior. Rescorla (1969) has shown in a variety of studies that fear conditioning depends on the degree of correlation that obtains between stimulus events. Therefore, an effective means of reducing a person's vulnerability to negative experiences is to have him interact extensively with formerly threatening objects under advantageous conditions after the treatment has been completed. Occasional hapless occurrences in the context of many neutral or rewarding experiences are generally ineffectual in reinstating fearful responding. Thus, for example, a dog-phobic child who, following treatment, has had many positive interactions with a variety of dogs, is unlikely to become unduly affected by a few unfortunate experiences. At most, such experiences will lead to the development of discriminative avoidance of realistic threats, which has adaptive value. On the other hand, for persons who have had limited contact after treatment with previously feared objects, a few unfavorable experiences may reestablish fearful behavior that is inappropriately overgeneralized.

If behavior that has been disinhibited is regularly correlated with punishing consequences in everyday life, then the therapeutic changes will be short-lived unless the environmental contingencies are modified. No psychological methods exist that can render an organism insensitive to the consequences of its actions. Nor would such an outcome be desirable, even if it were possible, because an organism that is not guided by response feedback would function in a grossly maladaptive way.

It should also be noted in passing that persons whose fears have been extinguished through modeling do not display indiscriminate approach behavior. Elimination of an automobile phobia, for example, does not dispose un-impeded clients to saunter heedlessly into onrushing traffic on busy thoroughfares. Rather, stereotyped avoidance is replaced by approach behavior that is cognitively controlled by judgments of probable consequences resulting from prospective actions. In the treatment of young children, whose discriminative capacities are less well developed, the conditions under which it is appropriate to perform the restored behavior are carefully labeled to ensure discriminative responsiveness.

SOCIAL FACILITATION OF ESTABLISHED BEHAVIOR THROUGH MODELING

The material presented so far illustrates how the behavior of others can be effectively em-ployed to transmit new response patterns, and to eliminate unwarranted fears, inhibitions, and defensive behaviors. In the present section we shall focus our attention on the use of modeling influences to facilitate expression of preexisting behavior that observers are able to perform, but fail to because of inadequate social supports rather than the presence of strong inhibitions.

Human behavior is extensively under model-ing stimulus control. The response-facilitating effects of modeling influences are well docu-mented in countless laboratory studies (Bandura, 1969b; Bandura and Walters, 1963; Campbell, 1961; Flanders, 1968), demonstrating that diverse response patterns, including prosocial and deviant behavior, emotional expressions, preferences, and cognitive activities, can be substantially increased as a function of witness-ing the behavior of real-life or symbolic models. However, observers differ in the extent to which their behavior is guided by the actions of others, and not all models are equally influen-tial in evoking the types of behavior that they themselves exemplify. Responsiveness to model-ing influences is largely governed by three sets of variables. These include, in order of importance, the reinforcement contingencies associated with matching behavior, the attributes of the models, and observer characteristics.

Reinforcement Control of Matching Behavior

It will be recalled that in the multiprocess theory of modeling presented earlier, the degree to which previously learned matching responses are overtly performed depends upon the rein-forcing consequences they produce. Studies in-vestigating reinforcement control of imitative behavior, indeed, reveal that matching responses are performed at a high level when they produce rewarding outcomes, whereas the behavior exemplified by models is seldom reproduced when it results in punishing consequences or goes unrewarded (Baer, Peterson, and Sherman, 1967; Bandura and Barab, 1969; Kanareff and Lanzetta, 1958, 1960; Miller and Dollard, 1941).

Performance of matching behavior is regula-ted by observation of rewarding and punishing consequences to the model as well as by directly experienced outcomes. Like the effects of direct reinforcement, matching behavior in observers is generally increased by observed reward and decreased by observed punishment. Observed consequences not only can play an influential role in regulating behavior, but they also provide observers with a reference standard that determines whether a particular reinforcer that is externally administered will function as a reward or as a punishment.

Vicarious reinforcement may operate through at least five different mechanisms to produce psychological changes in observers (Bandura, 1970). One explanation is in terms of the *informative function* of observed outcomes. Response consequences experienced by per-formers convey information to observers about the type of behavior that is likely to meet with approval or disapproval in similar situations. This knowledge can aid in facilitating or inhibiting analogous responding.

When the same behavior is differentially reinforced depending on the social circum-stances under which it is performed, as is often the case, vicarious reinforcement enables observers to identify more readily the situations in which the modeled activities are considered appropriate and reinforceable. The resultant *discrimination learning* tends to enhance per-formance of similar behavior in situations where the model previously responded with favorable consequences.

Observed reinforcement is not only informative, but it can also have *incentive motivational effects*. Witnessing others reinforced with valued incentives functions as a motivator by arousing in observers expectations that they will be similarly rewarded for engaging in imitative behavior. Anticipatory rewards determine the speed, intensity, and persistence with which matching responses are performed.

Models generally exhibit emotional reactions while undergoing rewarding or punishing experiences. As was previously shown, emotional responses evoked in observers by the affective expressions of others can become conditioned either to the modeled behavior itself or to environmental stimuli that are regularly associated with performers' distress reactions. As a consequence, later performance of matching responses by the observer or the presence of the negatively valenced stimuli are likely to evoke fear and response suppression. Fear arousal and behavioral inhibition can be extinguished as well as acquired on a vicarious basis. *Vicarious conditioning and extinction of emotional arousal* may, therefore, partially account for the behavioral suppression or facilitation that results from observing affective consequences accruing to models.

In addition to the aforementioned effects of vicarious reinforcement, social status can be conferred on performers by the manner in which their behavior is reinforced. Punishment tends to devalue the model and his behavior, whereas the same model assumes emulative qualities when his actions are praised and otherwise rewarded. *Modification of model status*, in turn, influences the degree to which observers pattern their own actions after the behavior exemplified by different models. Vicarious reinforcement, depending on its nature and context, may thus affect the level of imitative responding through any one or more of the five processes outlined above.

Human behavior is regulated not only by externally administered consequences and by vicarious reinforcement, but also by the control people exercise over their own actions through self-reinforcement (Bandura, 1970). In this process, individuals set themselves certain standards of conduct and respond to their own behavior in self-rewarding and self-punishing

ways in accordance with their self-imposed demands. Observers will, therefore, be disinclined to adopt modeled behavior that is personally devalued; conversely, they are apt to be highly responsive to the actions of others considered exemplary, because imitation of such performances results in positive self-evaluations.

Influence of Model Characteristics

Model characteristics are an additional factor that can influence the extent to which imitative behavior will be elicited from observers. It has been abundantly documented in social-psychological research (Bandura, 1969b; Blake, 1958; Campbell, 1961) that models who possess high status in prestige, power, and competence hierarchies are emulated to a considerably greater degree than models of subordinate standing. The influence of model status on matching behavior is generally explained in terms of differential reinforcement and generalization processes (Miller & Dollard, 1941). According to this interpretation, the behavior of high-status models is more likely to be successful in achieving favorable outcomes, and hence have greater utilitarian value for observers, than the behavior of models who possess relatively low vocational, intellectual, and social competencies. As a result of repeated differential reinforcement for matching models who possess diverse attributes, the identifying characteristics or status-conferring symbols assume informative value in signifying the probable consequences associated with behavior exemplified by different models. Moreover, the effect of a model's prestige tends to generalize from one area of behavior to another, and to unfamiliar persons to the extent that they share similar characteristics with past reward-producing models.

The preceding material illustrates how a model's power to influence the behavior of others is mediated through competence and superior status. Models also derive power through interpersonal attraction. Individuals who are warm and nurturant generally elicit more spontaneous imitative behavior than models who lack rewarding qualities (Bandura and Huston, 1961; Hetherington and Frankie, 1967; Mischel and Grusec, 1966; Mussen and

Parker, 1965). In fact, the latter model characteristic is singled out as a requisite condition in most traditional forms of psychotherapy.

Influence of Observer Characteristics

Not only are models differentially effective, but observers also differ in their susceptibility to modeling influences. Persons who have been frequently rewarded for imitative behavior (Masters and Morris, 1970; Miller and Dollard, 1941), and those who lack self-esteem (de Charms & Rosenbaum, 1960; Gelfand, 1962), who feel incompetent (Kanareff and Lanzetta, 1960), and who are highly dependent (Jakubczak and Walters, 1959; Ross, 1966), are especially prone to pattern their behavior after successful models. Similarity between observers and models in age (Hicks, 1965), sex (Bandura, Ross and Ross, 1963), socioeconomic and racial status (Beyer and May, 1968), and on other dimensions (Stotland, 1969) has likewise been shown to facilitate imitation.

In devising treatment programs, the widely reported observer correlates of modeling must be accepted with reservation for several reasons. The generality of the findings is open to question because the relationships are mainly based on data from ambiguous experimental situations in which unfamiliar models perform inconsequential responses that have little functional value for subjects. In such situations the main rewards for brighter and bolder subjects are derived from outwitting the experimenter by disregarding the modeling influences. On the other hand, there is a paucity of research studying the degree to which people differing in intelligence, perceptiveness, and confidence emulate idealized models and those whose behavior has high functional value for observers. When modeling influences are explicitly employed to teach people how to communicate effectively, how to conduct themselves in given interpersonal situations, and how to perform vocational activities competently, the more venturesome and talented are likely to derive the greater benefits from observation of examplary models.

A second reason for minimizing the role of both observer characteristics and model attributes as limiting conditions is that the long-term influence of these factors on modeling is relatively weak and can be readily obviated or even reversed (Bandura, 1965b; Miller & Dollard, 1941) by altering the reinforcing consequences that accompany matching behavior. Whatever controlling power observer and model characteristics exercise over imitation is largely derived from historical conditions of reinforcement. That is, people with certain characteristics are highly responsive to modeling influences because they have generally achieved better outcomes with minimal effort costs by following the examples of successful models than through their own independent trial-and-error behavior. Similarly, certain types of models are favored because their modes of behavior have proved most satisfactory for adopters. In new social situations, where the value of behavior exemplified by different models is undetermined, people generalize imitative responses in accordance with anticipatory consequences created by their past experiences. However, one would not expect matching performances that are primarily sustained by anticipatory outcomes to survive for long in the face of opposing contemporaneous reinforcement. A prestigeful or attractive model may induce a person to try a given course of action, but if the behavior should prove unsatisfactory, it will be discarded and the model's future influence diminished.

The preceding discussion has important implications for the social conditions that receive emphasis in the development and implementation of modeling procedures. In interview methods of treatment, a great deal of attention is devoted to client characteristics and to therapist attributes that might increase the therapitst's attraction power, but little effort is made to arrange favorable reinforcement contingencies to support desired behavior within either the therapeutic setting or the natural environment. It is confidently believed that after research deciphers the manner in which client and therapist variables interact to determine behavioral changes, it will be possible to arrange ideal interpersonal matches and thereby to enhance therapeutic outcomes. Findings of modeling studies, some of which are summarized above, would indicate that most interview practices involve a misplaced emphasis and, therefore, an unrealizable hope.

Social-learning approaches consider it essential that therapeutic agents model response patterns directly applicable to the goals selected by clients and will, therefore, have functional value for them in their everyday life. Professional personnel are not necessarily best suited to serve as models for the myriad behavioral changes required by different clients. Therapeutic goals can be achieved more consistently and more expeditiously by utilizing resource people who, by virtue of their specialized competencies and ability to develop intensive working relationships with clients, are most qualified to implement modeling procedures. Hence, in treatment programs given detailed consideration earlier, teachers, parents, nurses, college students, peers, and even formerly treated clients, served effectively under the guidance of professional personnel as models for desired psychological changes. More people would receive greater help than they do under current practices if professional personnel utilized their time and knowledge to develop efficacious treatment programs for able resource persons to implement in natural settings under their guidance and direction. Having professionals assume mainly supervisory rather than practitioner functions in no way minimizes relationship experiences, as is commonly claimed of behavioral treatment. A mother who has been helped to use reinforced modeling to develop linguistic and social competencies in her autistic child is ensuring more genuine and enduring relationship experiences than those derived from a purchased relationship provided by a busy professional therapist at brief weekly intervals.

In addition to underscoring the type of behavior that therapeutic agents are modeling, social-learning approaches assign importance to the development of reinforcement conditions necessary to maintain psychological changes produced by the treatment procedures. Demonstrations that personality characteristic of clients and therapists determine the degree to which desired changes are achieved indicate that the method itself is not sufficiently powerful to override the influence of extraneous factors. It is encouraging to note in this respect that modeling procedures (Bandura, Blanchard, and Ritter, 1969) and other behavioral approaches (Mann and Rosenthal, 1969; Paul, 1966) have proved equally effective when applied by therapists differing widely in personality characteristics.

Applications of Modeling Influences to Facilitate Psychological Changes

In psychotherapeutic practice, modeling influences vary considerably in terms of the behavior being modeled and in the degree to which conditions are explicitly arranged to aid clients in adopting exemplified patterns. At one extreme are interview approaches that advocate therapist ambiguity and partial concealment of feelings, opinions, and social behavior in order to foster inappropriate transference reactions. Under these conditions, modeling influences not only occur inadvertently, but the behavioral examples with which clients are provided are limited to therapists' customary interview responses; these may be of limited usefulness to clients in coping with their everyday problems.

Although the range of social behavior exhibited by therapists in interview approaches is restricted, their attitudes and personal preferences are inevitably revealed through their selective responsiveness and interpretive comments (Parloff, Iflund, and Goldstein, 1960). These attitudes are likely to be adopted by clients who remain in treatment for a long period even though therapists may strive to maintain a nonjudgmental orientation (Pentony, 1966; Rosenthal, 1955). It cannot be determined from correlational data, however, whether attitudinal similarities are attributable to modeling or to differential reinforcement of clients' verbalizations; undoubtedly both kinds of influence processes are operative. Preference changes alone are of limited significance unless it is also shown that the self-reported attitudes are accompanied by improved interpersonal functioning.

Several experiments have been reported demonstrating that classes of verbal responses that are considered of special interest in interview treatments can be modified through modeling influences. Wilder (1968) found that exposure to verbal modeling of self-referent affective statements significantly increased the frequency with which college students expressed self-referent verbalizations in a quasi-counseling interview. A closely related study by Brody (1968) further revealed that greater and more enduring increases in self-referent responding can be achieved by combining modeling procedures with social reinforcement of similar verbal behavior. Positive sanctions similarly operate to enhance modeling of personal self-disclosures in the presence of strangers, which people are reluctant to do on the basis of observation or instruction alone (Whalen, 1969).

The potency of modeling influences in facilitating behavioral changes can be augmented not only by direct reinforcement, but also through vicarious reinforcement procedures. Marlatt, Jacobsen, Johnson, and Morrice (1970) showed that interviewees were more inclined to reveal personal problems after witnessing a brief waiting-room conversation in which a model's self-disclosure was either accepted or socially rewarded by the interviewer than if the model's behavior was discouraged or subjects had no exposure to a problem-admitting model.

One of the obstacles to progress in interview therapy arises from the fact that clients are usually confused about what they are supposed to do in order to achieve beneficial effects, and verbal explanation inadequately conveys the requisite role behaviors. This ambiguity can be easily overcome by providing clients with concrete examples of appropriate therapeutic responsiveness (Marlatt, 1968a, 1968b). Truax and his colleagues (Truax & Carkhuff, 1967) demonstrated that clients who listened to tape-recorded excerpts exemplifying self-exploration (considered to be "good" therapy behavior) prior to undergoing treatment subsequently achieved greater positive changes on a variety of personality tests than clients who received the same type of treatment without benefit of the initial modeling experience.

The preceding studies indicate that modeling procedures can be successfully employed to induce changes in verbal behavior. However, considering the weak relationships that exist between alterations of verbal behavior—whether in the form of value preferences, verbal statements, or endorsements of personality test items—and nonverbal modes of response, it would seem that models could be used far more advantageously to promote effective interpersonal behaviors directly.

Results of an experiment by Schwartz and Hawkins (1965) are of special interest because they illustrate how modeling influences, depending on their nature, can impede as well as facilitate desired changes. Adult schizophrenics participated in a series of group therapy sessions during which affective verbalizations were socially reinforced. Two patient models, who expressed affect with ease, were added to one group; a second group was provided with two models who were equally talkative, but whose verbalizations lacked affect; while no special models were added to the control group. As shown in Figure 17.16, schizophrenics whose emotional statements were positively reinforced increased affective expressions when their group was provided with models who frequently verbalized their feelings; under the same reinforcement conditions, affective responsiveness was decreased when the added models displayed predominantly nonaffective verbalizations.

Evidence that substantially different group behavior can occur under the same reinforcement conditions, depending upon the behavior of influential models, has important implications for research in which reinforcement is administered in social situations. It has sometimes been assumed (Patterson, Littman, and Bricker, 1967; Patterson and Reid, 1970) that modeling influences play a minor role in the performance of social behavior, on the grounds that the relevant responses already exist in the organism's repertoire, and control of their expression resides in reinforcement contingencies.

Human behavior is regulated by a variety of discriminative stimuli, among which the behavior of others is the most influential and ubiquitous. Consequently, in social situations, behavior always remains partly under modeling stimulus control. The actions of persons who occupy prestigeful positions in a given social group usually serve as major determinants of the type of behavior that other group members are likely to engage in. The force of example is strikingly illustrated in a study of behavioral contagion conducted by Lippitt, Polansky, and Rosen (1952). Children residing in summer camps were rated by their peers for their social power to influence others. Observers then

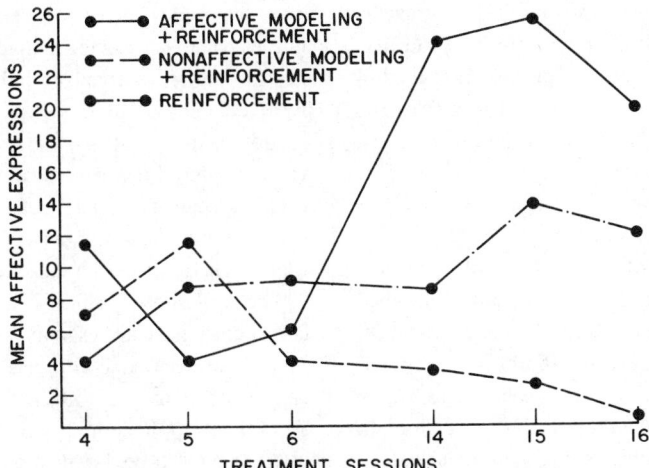

Figure 17.16 Mean frequency of affective responses expressed in early and late phases of treatment by schizophrenics who received either affective modeling with social reinforcement, nonaffective modeling with reinforcement, or reinforcement alone (Schwartz and Hawkins, 1965).

recorded the frequency of behavioral contagion, defined as spontaneous imitation of the actions of another person where the model displays no intent to get others to follow his example. Boys who were attributed high power served as the major sources of social behavior for other group members. These findings indicate that the behavior of entire groups can be effectively guided by altering the behavior of focal models, provided that changes are achieved in ways that do not reduce their status.

It would follow from the research cited above that variations in social behavior accompanying reinforcement of members of psychiatric wards (Ayllon and Azrin, 1968), of families (Patterson, Ray, and Shaw, 1968), or of other social groups cannot be attributed solely to the effects of the programmed consequences. To the extent that incentive conditions modify the behavior of prestigious models, other members are likely to adopt their behavior, apart from the influence of reinforcers administered by external change agents. When modeling influences covary with reinforcement conditions, but only the latter determinants are recognized, the resultant behavioral changes may be incorrectly ascribed to the reinforcement practices alone. On the other hand, reinforcement procedures may prove relatively ineffective if influential models either display alternative behaviors to those desired by change agents (Schwartz and

Hawkins, 1965), or actively counteract their influence attempts. Without knowledge of the opposing modeling influences operating in the situation, the adequacy of the reinforcers may be erroneously faulted. As illustrated in the study by Schwartz and Hawkins, a potentially powerful incentive system cannot exert much effect if a few influential models repeatedly divert the behavior of others in undesired directions.

In recent years modeling procedures have been increasingly employed, either singly or in combination with other methods, to promote behaviors of value to clients. A number of experiments that illustrate the different forms in which modeling influences may be applied and their relative efficacy are discussed next. Before proceeding to a detailed consideration of this research literature, I should like to comment on conceptual confusions that sometimes arise from assigning radically different labels to variations in the mode of model presentation. Modeling stimuli can be presented behaviorally, pictorially, or verbally. Thus, for example, one can acquire automobile-driving skills by observing live demonstrations, by following pictorial displays, or by reading verbal instructions that describe the correct responses and the correct order in which they should be performed. Under conditions where modeling stimuli produce changes mainly through their informational function, the different modes of model presentation may yield comparable results, provided that they convey the same amount of information and they are equally effective in controlling the attention of observers.

Sharp distinctions are often drawn between modeling and role playing in studies of response facilitation effects. Actually, role playing comprises a modeling component combined with behavioral enactment. In some instances people are instructed to reproduce response patterns that are described verbally, in which case the method relies on verbal modeling. In other instances, subjects are simply asked to perform a given social role without being furnished any concrete examples. Under minimal external cues, appropriate performances must be guided by representational examples that subjects supply themselves, derived from past observations of models occupying these particular roles. Thus, subjects could enact the role behavior of a teacher with ease, whereas they would be at a loss to role-play a zoognick, for which they have no symbolic model.

Modeling Supplemented with Guided Performance

Several lines of evidence were presented earlier that modeling procedures are most powerful when supplemented with guided performance of desired behavior. This conclusion receives further support from a study designed by Friedman (1968) to increase assertive behavior in passive college students. Subjects who responded nonassertively in interpersonal situations, as measured by self-reports and standardized behavioral tests, were assigned to one of five treatment conditions. One group received verbal modeling supplemented with behavioral rehearsal. These students were provided with a script describing appropriate assertive responses to provocations which they enacted several times with an associate who behaved obnoxiously. A second group participated in a treatment combining behavioral modeling with behavioral rehearsal in which, after observing a model demonstrate assertive responding, they performed the same behavior in relation to the irritating associate. Students assigned to a third group had to generate their own examples of assertiveness to serve as guides for the behavioral enactment. Still other groups either received verbal modeling alone, received behavioral modeling alone, or served as nontreated controls. All students were then readministered the behavioral test, during which their assertive verbal responses toward a provocateur who annoyingly interfered with their performance on a task were recorded.

The differential efficacy of the single and compound procedures may be seen in Figure 17.17. Nontreated controls showed no significant change in their assertiveness. Behavioral modeling supplemented with behavioral enactment proved to be the most powerful treatment, producing approximately a triple increase in assertive behavior. The remaining procedures, which at least doubled the students' level of assertive responding, were found to be equally effective.

The above study was principally designed to compare the potency of modeling alone and in combination with guided performance for inducing circumscribed changes in assertive behavior. To achieve generalized and enduring changes through these approaches would require modeling general strategies of assertiveness that are applicable to diverse situations commonly encountered in everyday life. Moreover, optimal transfer programs would be devised to ensure that clients' initial assertive ventures produce favorable consequences.

Modeling Supplemented with Reinforcement

A number of therapeutically oriented studies have been reported in which modeling procedures are supplemented with reinforcement to increase modes of response that are within individuals' behavioral repertoires. These experiments furnish evidence of the effectiveness of the compound procedure, but most of the designs employed do not permit one to evaluate fully the relative contribution of the separable elements.

Sherman (1965) successfully reinstated verbal behavior through reinforced modeling in mute psychotics for whom contingent reinforcement for vocalizations proved ineffective. In the procedure used, patients were rewarded with food for reproducing progressively more complex modeled behavior, from nonverbal

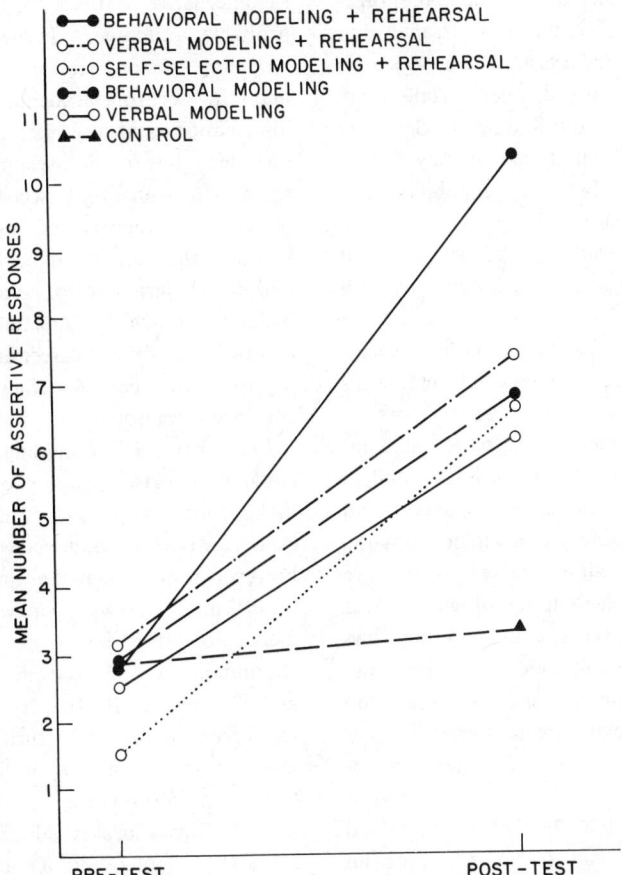

Figure 17.17 Mean number of assertive responses performed by individuals before and after receiving different forms of modeling treatments with or without behavioral rehearsal (Friedman, 1968).

responses, through vocalizations, and to appropriate verbalizations. An intrasubject replication design was utilized to demonstrate the influential role of contingent reinforcement in maintaining reinstated behavior. Patients showed continuous improvement under reinforced modeling; their verbal responding decreased markedly when they were equally reinforced, but never for appropriate verbalizations, and their verbal productivity rose again substantially when contingent reinforcement for verbalizations was reinstated.

The preceding findings are partially confirmed by Wilson and Walters (1966), who compared verbal productivity of near-mute schizophrenics after they received either reinforced modeling, modeling alone, or neither form of influence. Schizophrenics who were exposed to a verbalizing model, and those given modeling with

reward for verbal responsiveness, showed analogous increases in verbal output. However, when all three groups were subsequently administered reinforced modeling, patients who originally received this treatment displayed the largest additional increases in verbal productivity. A further study would be needed to determine whether the differential response to reinforced modeling is attributable to the effect of mere change in treatment conditions or to longer exposure to verbalizing models and contingent reinforcement. As might be expected, patients decreased their talkativeness when all supports for verbalization, including modeling, verbal prompts, and reinforcement, were withdrawn.

Research evidence is now accumulating on the effect of modeling with and without reinforcement. The occurrence of psychological changes under circumstances where reinforcement contingencies remain the same but modeling stimulus supports are either present or absent warrants equally detailed examination. It would follow from the findings of Schwartz and Hawkins (1965) that people may fail to exhibit behavior within their capability, due either to inadequate reinforcement or to lack of appropriate models. This is borne out by studies comparing reinforced modeling with reinforcement alone.

Hansen, Niland and Zani (1969) sociometrically measured changes in children's social status produced by different types of group counseling. One set of groups was composed of children low in popularity, as well as several peer models who exemplified successful social behavior. During the group sessions the therapist reinforced all references to effective social behavior. A second set of groups was similarly reinforced, but it contained only low-status children; control subjects met in group activities for an equivalent period. Children who had the benefit of exposure to successful peer models and reinforcement of behavioral intentions not only achieved a significant rise in sociometric status, but they also maintained their increased popularity in a follow-up assessment conducted two months later. On the other hand, control children and those who received only social reinforcement made negligible gains, and did not differ in this respect.

Krumboltz, Thoresen, and their associates have conducted numerous experiments on the relative efficacy of symbolic modeling for promoting educational and occupational planning in high school students. Career exploration was selected as a principal objective on the grounds that a career choice is a crucial decision that largely determines the course of one's furture life. Students must therefore be aided in seeking pertinent information, on the basis of which they can make provisional decisions about future pursuits.

The studies generally employ a paradigm in which one group of students receives symbolic modeling combined with direct social reinforcement. In this procedure, subjects first listen to a brief tape-recording of a student discussing with a counselor the way in which he has gone about obtaining information relevant to alternative courses of action and their probable outcomes. Immediately after the modeling session, students discuss their own plans for securing academic and occupational information, and any reference to previous or intended information-seeking activities are socially reinforced. A second group is reinforced for reports of information-seeking without the benefit of prior modeling. In addition, several control conditions are usually included, in which students either receive no counseling or discuss career exploration without exposure to peer modeling or information-contingent reinforcement.

Both forms of counseling tend to increase students' efforts to gain knowledge needed to make sound vocational and educational decisions. Modeling combined with reinforcement, however, produces greater amounts and variety of information-seeking behavior than reinforcement alone for males, but not for females (Krumboltz and Schroeder, 1965; Krumboltz and Thoresen, 1964). The effectiveness of reinforced modeling is further enhanced for males if the counseling utilizes male models (Thoresen, Krumboltz, & Varenhorst, 1967), and the procedure is administered in group form (Krumboltz and Thoresen, 1964). The differential efficacy of these counseling procedures as a function of sex of students does not reflect low responsiveness on the part of girls. Rather, they appear to be easily motivated even by weak influences to seek occupational information, and do not require the additional impetus provided by peer modeling. Boys, on the other hand, are most responsive when reinforcement of intentions is supplemented with the influence of example.

Other studies conducted within this series reveal that the degree to which reinforced modeling influences students' career exploration is partly determined by such factors as subject characteristics, model attributes, and the type of counselor who presides over the reinforcement phase of the compound procedure (Stilwell, 1969; Thoresen, Hosford, and Krumboltz, 1970; Thoresen & Krumboltz, 1968). These findings suggest that the basic method could be further increased in power to make it less vulnerable to a variety of extraneous variables. This might be achieved by using videotape presentations portraying models actually performing the desired information-seeking activities rather than describing them to a counselor. Since modeling combined with performance is generally superior to modeling alone, after each demonstration sequence, subjects might be urged to perform (during the modeling sessions) some preliminary exploratory behavior that will later serve as an effective directive for further inquiry. Multiple models and portrayal of favorable consequences accompanying exploratory behavior might also be employed to enhance the modeling component of the treatment. The potency of the reinforcement component, in turn, could be increased if, in addition to reinforcing behavioral intentions, rewarding activities were made contingent upon the actual amount of information-seeking behavior that students completed.

CONCLUDING COMMENTS

This chapter has been devoted to a review of modeling principles and treatment procedures as they apply to three broad and important areas of psychological functioning. These include the utilization of models to transmit new patterns of behavior, to eliminate unwarranted fears and inhibitions, and to facilitate expression of preexisting modes of response.

When inability to function effectively is due mainly to faulty or deficient behavior, modeling is not only the most appropriate, but often an essential, means of developing requisite skills and interpersonal competencies. With the provision of exemplary models, individuals are able to acquire through observation complex behaviors in large segments or in their entirety without having to undergo a laborious trial-and-error process. Vicarious extinction of fears and behavioral inhibitions can also be achieved by having persons observe models performing fear-provoking behavior without experiencing any adverse consequences. Modeling procedures have been employed with considerable success either singly or in conjunction with other methods to eliminate dysfunctions arising from conditioned emotionality. This approach is probably best suited to the treatment of anxiety conditions in which absence of anticipated aversive consequences can be repeatedly demonstrated with ease. Since human behavior is extensively under modeling stimulus control, the behavior of influential models can, furthermore, serve as one of the most effective means of eliciting and guiding the actions of others at any given time.

There are many different ways of implementing modeling principles, some of which are more effective than others. A method that has yielded the most impressive results with varied types of disorders contains three major components. First, desired behavior is repeatedly modeled, preferably by mutliple models who demonstrate progressively more difficult performances. Second, observers are provided with necessary guidance and ample opportunities to enact the modeled behaviors at each step in the graduated sequence of activities under favorable conditions. The latter procedures are ideally suited for inducing psychological changes, but they are unlikely to endure unless established behaviors produce rewarding consequences. Arrangement of favorable reinforcement contingencies to maintain matching behavior, therefore, constitutes the third component in the powerful compound method.

Behaviorally oriented therapists are generally intrigued with demonstrations that behavior can be controlled by its external consequences. However, in a comprehensive treatment program, after behavior has been brought under external reinforcement control, efforts should be made to establish self-reinforcing systems, so that a person's actions become increasingly governed by the intrinsic and self-evaluative consequences they engender. Recent studies have shown how desired behavior can be rendered partially independent of the vagaries of external consequences through development of self-regulatory functions (Bandura, 1969a).

The potency of modeling procedures, especially when supplemented with guided performance and appropriate reinforcement, derives largely from the fact that clients learn and practice effective modes of behavior under conditions that are similar to those they face in their regular environment. A further advantage of this form of treatment is that a broad range of resource people can be enlisted to aid in the attainment of diverse psychological goals.

REFERENCES

Abelson, R. P., Aronson, E., McGuire, W. J., Newcomb, T. M., Rosenberg, M. J., and Tannenbaum, P. H. *Theories of cognitive consistency: A sourcebook.* Chicago: Rand McNally, 1968.

Aronfreed, J. The concept of internalization. In D. A. Goslin (Ed.), *Handbook of socialization theory and research.* Chicago: Rand McNally, 1969.

Ayllon, T., and Azrin, N. H. *A motivating environment for therapy and rehabilitation.* New York: Appleton–Century–Crofts, 1968.

Ayllon, T., and Michael, J. The psychiatric nurse as a behavioral engineer. *Journal of the Experimental Analysis of Behavior,* 1959, **2**, 323–334.

Baer, D. M., Peterson, R. F., and Sherman, J. A. The development of imitation by reinforcing behavioral similarity to a model. *Journal of the Experimental Analysis of Behavior,* 1967, **10**, 405–416.

Bandura, A. Vicarious processes: A case of no-trial learning. In L. Berkowitz (Ed.), *Advances in experimental social psychology.* Vol. II. New York: Academic Press, 1965. Pp. 1–55(a).

Bandura, A. Influence of models' reinforcement contingencies on the acquisition of imitative responses. *Journal of Personality and Social Psychology,* 1965, **1**, 589–595. (b).

Bandura, A. Modelling approaches to the modification of phobic disorders. In R. Porter (Ed.), *Ciba Foundation Symposium. The role of learning in psychotherapy.* London: Churchill, 1968. Pp. 201–217.

Bandura, A. *Principles of behavior modification.* New York: Holt, Rinehart & Winston, 1969(a).

Bandura, A. Social-learning theory of identificatory processes. In D. A. Goslin (Ed.), *Handbook of socialization theory and research.* Chicago: Rand McNally, 1969. Pp. 213–262. (b).

Bandura, A. Vicarious and self-reinforcement processes. In R. Glaser (Ed.), *The nature of reinforcement.* Columbus: Merrill, 1970, in press.

Bandura, A., and Barab, P. G. Conditions governing "generalized imitation." Unpublished manuscript, Stanford University, 1969.

Bandura, A., Blanchard, E. B., and Ritter, B. The relative efficacy of desensitization and modeling approaches for inducing behavioral, affective, and attitudinal changes. *Journal of Personality and Social Psychology,* 1969, **13**, 173–199.

Bandura, A., Grusec, J. E., and Menlove, F. L. Observational learning as a function of symbolization and incentive set. *Child Development,* 1966, **37**, 499–506.

Bandura, A., Grusec, J. E., and Menlove, F. L. Vicarious extinction of avoidance behavior. *Journal of Personality and Social Psychology,* 1967, **5**, 16–23.

Bandura, A., and Huston, A. C. Identification as a process of incidental learning. *Journal of Abnormal and Social Psychology,* 1961, **63**, 311–318.

Bandura, A., and Menlove, F. L. Factors determining vicarious extinction of avoidance behavior through symbolic modeling. *Journal of Personality and Social Psychology,* 1968, **8**, 99–108.

Bandura, A., and Rosenthal, T. L. Vicarious classical conditioning as a function of arousal level. *Journal of Personality and Social Psychology,* 1966, **3**, 54–62.

Bandura, A., Ross, D., and Ross, S. A. Imitation of film-mediated aggressive models. *Journal of Abnormal and Social Psychology,* 1963, **66**, 3–11.

Bandura, A., and Walters, R. H. *Social learning and personality development.* New York: Holt, Rinehart & Winston, 1963.

Berger, S. M. Conditioning through vicarious instigation. *Psychological Review,* 1962, **69**, 450–466.

Berkowitz, L. Control of aggression. In B. M. Caldwell & H. Ricciuti (Eds.), *Review of child development research.* Vol. 3. New York: Russell Sage Foundation, 1969.

Beyer, N. L., and May, J. G., Jr. The effects of race and socioeconomic status on imitative behavior in children, using white male and female models. Unpublished manuscript, Florida State University, 1968.

Black, A. H. The extinction of avoidance responses under curare. *Journal of Comparative and Physiological Psychology,* 1958, **51**, 519–524.

Black, A. H. Heart rate changes during avoidance learning in dogs. *Canadian Journal of Psychology,* 1959, **13**, 229–242.

Black, A. H. Transfer following operant conditioning in the curarized dog. *Science,* 1967, **155**, 201–203.

Blake, R. R. The other person in the situation. In R. Tagiuri and L. Petrullo (Eds.), *Person perception and interpersonal behavior.* Stanford: Stanford University Press, 1958, Pp. 229–242.

Blanchard, E. B. The relative contributions of modeling, informational influences, and physical contact in the extinction of phobic behavior. Unpublished doctoral dissertation. Stanford University, 1969.

Bridger, W. H., and Mandel, I. J. A comparison of GSR fear responses produced by threat and electric shock. *Journal of Psychiatric Research,* 1964, **2**, 31–40.

Brody, H. A. The effect of three modeling procedures on the frequency of emission of self-referent affect statements. *Dissertation Abstracts,* 1968, **29**, 767B.

Burnstein, E., Stotland, E., and Zander, A. Similarity to a model and self-evaluation. *Journal of Abnormal and Social Psychology,* 1961, **62**, 257–264.

Byrne, D. Attitudes and attraction. In L. Berkowitz (Ed.), *Advances in experimental social psychology.* Vol. IV. New York: Academic Press, 1969. Pp. 36–89.

Campbell, D. T. Conformity in psychology's theories of acquired behavioral dispositions. In I. A. Berg and B. M. Bass (Eds.), *Conformity and deviation.* New York: Harper, 1961. Pp. 101–142.

Charms, R. de, and Rosenbaum, M. E. Status variables and matching behavior. *Journal of Personality*, 1960, **28**, 492–502.

Chatterjee, B. B., and Eriksen, C. W. Cognitive factors in heart rate conditioning. *Journal of Experimental Psychology*, 1962, **64**, 272–279.

Chittenden, G. E. An experimental study in measuring and modifying assertive behavior in young children. *Monographs of the Society for Research in Child Development*, 1942, **VII** (1, Serial No. 31).

Colby, K. M. Computer-aided language development in nonspeaking mentally disturbed children. Technical Report No. CS85, Stanford University, 1967.

Corsini, R. J., and Putzey, L. J. *Bibliography of group psychotherapy*. Beacon, N.Y.: Beacon House, 1957.

Corsini, R. J., Shaw, M. E., and Blake, R. R. *Roleplaying in business and industry*. New York: Free Press, 1961.

Cowan, P. A., Hoddinoth, B. A., and Wright, B. A. Compliance and resistance in the conditioning of autistic children: An exploratory study. *Child Development*, 1965, **36**, 913–923.

Craig, K. D. Physiological arousal as a function of imagined, vicarious, and direct stress experiences. *Journal of Abnormal Psychology*, 1968, **73**, 513–520.

Craig, K. D., and Weinstein, M. S. Conditioning vicarious affective arousal. *Psychological Reports*, 1965, **17**, 955–963.

Davis, M., and Wagner, A. R. Habituation of startle response under incremental sequence of stimulus intensities. *Journal of Comparative and Physiological Psychology*, 1969, **67**, 486–492.

Dawson, M. E. Comparison of classical conditioning and relational learning. Unpublished M.A. thesis, University of Southern California, 1966.

Dawson, M. E., and Grings, W. W. Comparison of classical conditioning and relational learning. *Journal of Experimental Psychology*, 1969, in press.

Festinger, L. Behavioral support for opinion change. *Public Opinion Quarterly*, 1964, **28**, 404–417.

Flanders, J. P. A review of research on imitative behavior. *Psychological Bulletin*, 1968, **69**, 316–337.

Friedman, P. H. The effects of modeling and role playing on assertive behavior. Unpublished doctoral dissertation, University of Wisconsin, 1968.

Gelfand, D. M. The influence of self-esteem on rate of verbal conditioning and social matching behavior. *Journal of Abnormal and Social Psychology*, 1962, **65**, 259–265.

Gerst, M. S. Symbolic coding operations in observational learning. Unpublished doctoral dissertation, Stanford University, 1969.

Gittelman, M. Behavior rehearsal as a technique in child treatment. *Journal of Child Psychology and Psychiatry*, 1965, **6**, 251–255.

Grings, W. W. Verbal-perceptual factors in the conditioning of autonomic responses. In W. F. Prokasy (Ed.), *Classical conditioning: A symposium*. New York: Appleton–Century–Crofts, 1965. Pp. 71–89.

Grings, W. W., and Lockhart, R. A. Effects of "anxiety-lessening" instructions and differential set development on the extinction of GSR. *Journal of Experimental Psychology*, 1963, **66**, 292–299.

Grings, W. W., and Lockhart, R. A. Galvanic skin response during avoidance learning. *Psychophysiology*, 1966, **3**, 29–34.

Grings, W. W., and Uno, T. Counterconditioning: Fear and relaxation. *Psychophysiology*, 1968, **4**, 479–485.

Hansen, J. C., Niland, T. M., and Zani, L. P. Model reinforcement in group counseling with elementary school children. *Personnel and Guidance Journal*, 1969, **47**, 741–744.

Harris, F. R., Wolf, M. M., and Baer, D. M. Effects of adult social reinforcement on child behavior. *Young Children*, 1964, **20**, 8–17.

Hetherington, E. M., and Frankie, G. Effects of parental dominance, warmth, and conflict on imitation in children. *Journal of Personality and Social Psychology*, 1967, **6**, 119–125.

Hicks, D. J. Imitation and retention of film-mediated aggressive peer and adult models. *Journal of Personality and Social Psychology*, 1965, **2**, 97–100.

Hill, J. H., Liebert, R. M., and Mott, D. E. W. Vicarious extinction of avoidance behavior through films: An initial test. *Psychological Reports*, 1968, **22**, 192.

Humphery, J. Personal communication, 1966.

Hutt, S. J., Hutt, C., Lee, D., and Ounsted, C. A behavioural and electroencephalographic study of autistic children. *Journal of Psychiatric Research*, 1965, **3**, 181–197.

Jakubczak, L. F., and Walters, R. H. Suggestibility as dependency behavior. *Journal of Abnormal and Social Psychology*, 1959, **59**, 102–107.

Kamin, L. J. The effects of termination of the CS and avoidance of the US on avoidance learning. *Journal of Comparative and Physiological Psychology*, 1956, **49**, 420–424.

Kamin, L. J. The effects of termination of the CS and avoidance of the US on avoidance learning: An extension. *Canadian Journal of Psychology*, 1957, **11**, 48–56.

Kanareff, V. T., and Lanzetta, J. T. The acquisition of imitative and opposition responses under two conditions of instruction-induced set. *Journal of Experimental Psychology*, 1958, **56**, 516–528.

Kanareff, V. T., and Lanzetta, J. T. Effects of task definition and probability of reinforcement upon the acquisition and extinction of imitative responses. *Journal of Experimental Psychology*, 1960, **60**, 340–348.

Kelly, G. A. *The psychology of personal constructs*. Vol. II. *Clinical diagnosis and psychotherapy*. New York: Norton, 1955.

Kimble, G. A., and Kendall, J. W., Jr. A comparison of two methods of producing experimental extinction. *Journal of Experimental Psychology*, 1953, **45**, 87–90.

Kissel, S. Stress-reducing properties of social stimuli. *Journal of Personality and Social Psychology*, 1965, **2**, 378–384.

Krumboltz, J. D., and Schroeder, W. W. Promoting career planning through reinforcement. *Personnel and Guidance Journal*, 1965, **44**, 19–26.

Krumboltz, J. D., and Thoresen, C. E. The effect of behavioral counseling in group and individual settings on information-seeking behavior. *Journal of Counseling Psychology*, 1964, **11**, 324–333.

Lacey, J. I. Individual differences in somatic response patterns. *Journal of Comparative and Physiological Psychology*, 1950, **43**, 338–350.

Lacey, J. I. Somatic response patterning and stress: Some revisions of activation theory. In M. H. Appley and R. Trumbell (Eds.), *Psychological stress: Issues in research*. New York: Appleton–Century–Crofts, 1967. Pp. 14–42.

Lazarus, A. A. Behaviour rehearsal vs. nondirective therapy vs. advice in effecting behaviour change. *Behaviour Research and Therapy*, 1966, **4**, 209–212.

Lazarus, R. S., Speisman, J. C., Mordkoff, A. M., and Davison, L. A. A laboratory study of psychological stress produced by a motion picture film. *Psychological Monographs*, 1962, **76** (34, Whole No. 553).

Lazovik, A. D., and Lang, P. J. A laboratory demonstration of systematic desensitization psychotherapy. *Journal of Psychological Studies*, 1960, **11**, 238–247.

Levy, D. M. Trends in therapy. III. Release therapy. *American Journal of Orthopsychiatry*, 1939, **9**, 713–737.

Lindley, R. H., and Moyer, K. E. Effects of instructions on the extinction of a conditioned finger-withdrawal response. *Journal of Experimental Psychology*, 1961, **61**, 82–88.

Lippitt, R., Polansky, N., and Rosen, S. The dynamics of power. *Human Relations*, 1952, **5**, 37–64.

Litvak, S. B. A comparison of two brief group behavior therapy techniques on the reduction of avoidance behavior. *Psychological Record*, 1969, **19**, 329–334.

Lovaas, O. I. *Reinforcement therapy* (16 mm. sound film). Philadelphia: Smith, Kline and French Laboratories, 1966.

Lovaas, O. I. A behavior therapy approach to the treatment of childhood schizophrenia. In J. P. Hill (Ed.), *Minnesota symposia on child psychology*. Vol. 1. Minneapolis: University of Minnesota Press, 1967. Pp. 108–159.

Lovaas, O. I., Berberich, J. P., Kassorla, I. C., Klynn, G. A., and Meisel, J. Establishment of a texting and labelling vocabulary in schizophrenic children. Unpublished manuscript, University of California, Los Angeles, 1966.

Lovaas, O. I., Berberich, J. P., Perloff, B. F., and Schaeffer, B. Acquisition of imitative speech by schizophrenic children. *Science*, 1966, **151**, 705–707.

Lovaas, O. I., Dumont, D., Klynn, G., and Meisel, J. Program for the establishment of appropriate speech and intellectual skills in schizophrenic children. Unpublished manuscript, University of California, Los Angeles, 1966.

Lovaas, O. I., Freitag, L., Nelson, K., and Whalen, C. The establishment of imitation and its use for the development of complex behavior in schizophrenic children. *Behaviour Research and Therapy*, 1967, **5**, 171–181.

Lovaas, O. I., Litrownick, A., and Mann, R. Response latencies to auditory stimuli in autistic children during self-stimulatory behavior. Unpublished manuscript, University of California, Los Angeles, 1969.

Lovaas, O. I., Rehm, R., and Schreibman, L. Attentional deficits in autistic children to multiple stimulus inputs. Unpublished manuscript, University of California, Los Angeles, 1969.

Mann, J., and Rosenthal, T. L. Vicarious and direct counterconditioning of test anxiety through individual and group desensitization. *Behaviour Research and Therapy*, 1969, **7**, 359–367.

Marlatt, G. A. Exposure to a model and task ambiguity as determinants of verbal behavior in an interview. Paper read at Western Psychological Association, San Diego, April, 1968(a).

Marlatt, G. A. Vicarious and direct reinforcement control of verbal behavior in an interview setting. Unpublished doctoral dissertation, Indiana University, 1968(b).

Marlatt, G. A., Jacobsen, E. A., Johnson, D. L., and Morrice, D. J. Effect of exposure to a model receiving evaluative feedback upon consequent behavior in an interview. *Journal of Clinical and Consulting Psychology*, 1970, **34**, 104–112.

Marshall, H. R., and Hahn, S. C. Experimental modification of dramatic play. *Journal of Personality and Social Psychology*, 1967, **5**, 119–122.

Mason, W. A. Socially mediated reduction in emotional responses of young rhesus monkeys. *Journal of Abnormal and Social Psychology*, 1960, **60**, 100–104.

Masters, J. C., and Morris, R. I. Effects of contingent and noncontingent reinforcement upon generalized imitation. *Child Development*, 1970, in press.

Miller, N. E., and Dollard, J. *Social learning and imitation*. New Haven: Yale University Press, 1941.

Miller, R. E. Experimental approaches to the physiological and behavioral concomitants of affective communication in rhesus monkeys. In S. A. Altmann (Ed.), *Social communication among primates*. Chicago: University of Chicago Press, 1967. Pp. 125–134.

Miller, R. E., Murphy, J. V., and Mirsky, I. A. Nonverbal communication of affect. *Journal of Clinical Psychology*, 1959, **15**, 155–158.

Mischel, W., and Grusec, J. Determinants of the rehearsal and transmission of neutral and aversive behaviors. *Journal of Personality and Social Psychology*, 1966, **3**, 197–205.

Moreno, J. L. Fundamental rules and techniques of psychodrama. In J. H. Masserman and J. L. Moreno (Eds.), *Progress in psychotherapy.* Vol. 3. *Techniques of Psychotherapy.* New York: Grune and Stratton, 1958. Pp. 86–131.

Moyer, K. E., and Lindley, R. H. Supplementary report: Effects of instructions on extinction and recovery of a conditioned avoidance response. *Journal of Experimental Psychology,* 1962, **64**, 95–96.

Mussen, P. H., and Parker, A. L. Mother nurturance and girls' incidental imitative learning. *Journal of Personality and Social Psychology,* 1965, **2**, 94–97.

Nelson, F. Effects of two counterconditioning procedures on the extinction of fear. *Journal of Comparative and Physiological Psychology,* 1966, **62**, 208–213.

Notterman, J. M., Schoenfeld, W. N., and Bersh, P. J. A comparison of three extinction procedures following heart rate conditioning. *Journal of Abnormal and Social Psychology,* 1952, **47**, 674–677.

O'Connor, R. D. Modification of social withdrawal through symbolic modeling. *Journal of Applied Behavior Analysis,* 1969, **2**, 15–22.

Parloff, M. B., Iflund, B., and Goldstein, N. Communication of "therapy values" between therapist and schizophrenic patients. *Journal of Nervous and Mental Disease,* 1960, **130**, 193–199.

Patterson, G. R., Littman, R. A., and Bricker, W. Assertive behavior in children: A step toward a theory of aggression. *Monographs of the Society for Research in Child Development,* 1967, **32** (No. 5, Serial No. 113).

Patterson, G. R., Ray, R., and Shaw, D. Direct intervention in families of deviant children. Unpublished manuscript, University of Oregon, 1968.

Paul, G. L. *Insight vs. desensitization in psychotherapy.* Stanford: Stanford University Press, 1966.

Paul, G. L. Inhibition of physiological response to stressful imagery by relaxation training and hypnotically suggested relaxation. *Behaviour Research and Therapy,* 1969, **7**, 249–256.

Pentony, P. Value change in psychotherapy. *Human Relations,* 1966, **19**, 39–46.

Perloff, B. Influence of muscular relaxation and positive imagery on extinction of avoidance behavior through systematic desensitization. Unpublished doctoral dissertation, Stanford University, 1970.

Poppen, R. L. Counterconditioning of conditioned suppression. Unpublished doctoral dissertation, Stanford University, 1968.

Proctor, S. Duration of exposure to items and pretreatment training as factors in systematic desensitization therapy. Unpublished manuscript, Indiana University, 1968.

Rescorla, R. H. Pavlovian conditioned inhibition. *Psychological Bulletin,* 1969, **72**, 77–94.

Rescorla, R. H., and Solomon, R. L. Two-process learning theory: Relationships between Pavlovian conditioning and instrumental learning. *Psychological Review* 1967, **74**, 151–182.

Rimland, B. *Infantile autism.* New York: Appleton–Century–Crofts, 1964.

Rimm, D. C., and Mahoney, M. J. The application of reinforcement and participant modeling procedures in the treatment of snake-phobic behavior. *Behaviour Research and Therapy,* 1969, **1**, 369–376.

Rimm, D. C., and Medeiros, D. C. The role of muscle relaxation in participant modeling. *Behaviour Research and Therapy,* 1970, **8**, 127–132.

Risley, T., and Wolf, M. Establishing functional speech in echolalic children. *Behaviour Research and Therapy,* 1967, **5**, 73–88.

Ritter, B. Treatment of a dissection phobia. Unpublished manuscript, Queens College, 1965.

Ritter, B. The group treatment of children's snake phobias, using vicarious and contact desensitization procedures. *Behaviour Research and Therapy,* 1968, **6**, 1–6. (a).

Ritter, B. The effect of contact desensitization on avoidance behavior, fear ratings, and self-evaluative statements. *Proceedings of the 76th Annual Convention of the American Psychological Association,* 1968, **3**, 527–528. (b).

Ritter, B. Eliminating excessive fears of the environment through contact desensitization. In J. B. Krumboltz and C. E. Thoreson (Eds.), *Behavioral counseling: Cases and techniques.* New York: Holt, Rinehart and Winston, 1969. Pp. 168–178. (a).

Ritter, B. Treatment of acrophobia with contact desensitization. *Behaviour Research and Therapy,* 1969, **7**, 41–45. (b).

Ritter, B. The use of contact desensitization, demonstration-plus-participation, and demonstration alone in the treatment of acrophobia. *Behaviour Research and Therapy,* 1969, **7**, 157–164. (c).

Rosekrans, M. A. Imitation in children as a function of perceived similarity to a social model and vicarious reinforcement. *Journal of Personality and Social Psychology,* 1967 **7**, 307–315.

Rosenthal, D. Changes in some moral values following psychotherapy. *Journal of Consulting Psychology,* 1955, **19**, 431–436.

Ross, D. Relationship between dependency, intentional learning, and incidental learning in preschool children. *Journal of Personality and Social Psychology,* 1966, **4**, 374–381.

Sarason, I. G., and Ganzer, V. J. Social influence techniques in clinical and community psychology. In C. D. Spielberger (Ed.). *Current topics in clinical and community psychology.* New York: Academic Press, 1969. Pp. 1–66.

Schubot, E. D. The influence of hypnotic and muscular relaxation in systematic desensitization of phobic behavior. Unpublished doctoral dissertation. Stanford University, 1966.

Schwartz, A. N., and Hawkins, H. L. Patient models and affect statements in group therapy. In *Proceedings of the 73rd Annual Convention of the American Psychological Association.* Washington, D.C.: American Psychological Association, 1965. Pp. 265–266.

Sherman, J. A. Use of reinforcement and imitation to reinstate verbal behavior in mute psychotics. *Journal of Abnormal Psychology*, 1965, **70**, 155–164.

Sloane, H. N., Jr., Johnston, M. K., and Harris, F. R. Remedial procedures for teaching verbal behavior to speech deficient or defective young children. In H. N. Sloane, Jr. and B. A. MacAulay (Eds.), *Operant procedures in remedial speech and language training*. Boston: Houghton Mifflin, 1968, Pp. 77–101.

Solomon, R. L., and Turner, L. H. Discriminative classical conditioning in dogs paralyzed by curare can later control discriminative avoidance responses in the normal state. *Psychological Review*, 1962, **69**, 202–219.

Spiegler, M. D., Liebert, R. M., McMains, M. J., and Fernandez, L. E. Experimental development of a modeling treatment to extinguish persistent avoidance behavior. In R. D. Rubin and C. M. Franks (Eds.), *Advances in behavior therapy, 1968*. New York: Academic Press, 1969. Pp. 45–51.

Stilwell, W. E. Effects of ethnic social modeling techniques on adolescent vocational opinions, interests, and information-seeking behaviors. Unpublished doctoral dissertation, Stanford University, 1969.

Stotland, E. Exploratory investigations of empathy. In L. Berkowitz (Ed.), *Advances in Experimental Social Psychology*. Vol. IV. New York: Academic Press, 1969. Pp. 271–314.

Stotland, E., and Hillmer, M. L., Jr. Identification, authoritarian defensiveness, and self-esteem. *Journal of Abnormal and Social Psychology*, 1962, **64**, 334–342.

Stotland, E., and Patchen, M. Identification and changes in prejudice and in authoritarianism. *Journal of Abnormal and Social Psychology*, 1961, **62**, 265–274.

Stotland, E., Zander, A., and Natsoulas, T. The generalization of interpersonal similarity. *Journal of Abnormal and Social Psychology*, 1961, **62**, 250–256.

Strahley, D. F. Systematic desensitization and counterphobic treatment of an irrational fear of snakes. *Dissertation Abstracts*, 1966, **27**, 973B.

Sturm, I. E. The behavioristic aspect of psychodrama. *Group Psychotherapy*, 1965, **18**, 50–64.

Thoresen, C. E., Hosford, R. E., and Krumboltz, J. D. Determining effective models for counseling clients of varying competencies. *Journal of Counseling Psychology*, 1970, in press.

Thoresen, C. E., and Krumboltz, J. D. Similarity of social models and clients in behavioral counseling: Two experimental studies. *Journal of Counseling Psychology*, 1968, **15**, 393–401.

Thoresen, C. E., Krumboltz, J. D., and Varenhorst, B. Sex of counselors and models: Effect on client career exploration. *Journal of Counseling Psychology*, 1967, **14**, 503–508.

Truax, C. B., and Carkhuff, R. R. *Toward effective counseling and psychotherapy*. Chicago: Aldine, 1967.

Wasserman, L. Discrimination learning and development of learning sets in autistic children. Unpublished doctoral dissertation, University of California, Los Angeles, 1968.

Weinberg, N. H., and Zaslove, M. "Resistance" to systematic desensitization of phobias. *Journal of Clinical Psychology*, 1963, **19**, 179–181.

Weitzman, B. Behavior therapy and psychotherapy. *Psychological Review*, 1967, **74**, 300–317.

Whalen, C. Effects of a model and instructions on group verbal behaviors. *Journal of Consulting and Clinical Psychology*, 1969, **33**, 509–521.

Wickens, D. D., Allen, C. K., and Hill, F. A. Effects of instruction and UCS strength on extinction of the conditioned GSR. *Journal of Experimental Psychology*, 1963, **66**, 235–240.

Wilder, S. N. The effect of verbal modeling and verbal reinforcement on the frequency of self-referred affect statements. *Dissertation Abstracts*, 1968, **28**, 4304–4305B.

Wilson, E. H. Facilitated extinction of avoidance behavior through inhibition of fear by feeding. Paper presented at the American Psychological Association, Washington, September, 1969.

Wilson, F. S., and Walters, R. H. Modification of speech output of near-mute schizophrenics through social-learning procedures. *Behaviour Research and Therapy*, 1966, **4**, 59–67.

Winitz, H., and Preisler, L. Discrimination pretraining and sound learning. *Perceptual and Motor Skills*, 1965, **20**, 905–916.

Wolpe, J. *Psychotherapy by reciprocal inhibition*. Stanford: Stanford University Press, 1958.

Wolpe, J., and Lazarus, A. A. *Behavior therapy techniques*. New York: Pergamon, 1966.

Wynne, L. C., and Solomon, R. L. Traumatic avoidance learning: Acquisition and extinction in dogs deprived of normal peripheral autonomic function. *Genetic Psychology Monographs*, 1955, **52**, 241–284.

18

THE NATURE OF LEARNING IN TRADITIONAL AND BEHAVIORAL PSYCHOTHERAPY[1]

EDWARD J. MURRAY
LEONARD I. JACOBSON

UNIVERSITY OF MIAMI

This chapter is an attempt to integrate conceptually the methods used in traditional and behavioral psychotherapy, within the context of a modern view of the learning process. In recent years there has been increasing agreement among many therapists and investigators that psychotherapy may be effectively viewed as a learning process. This has not always been the case.

Historically, the first comprehensive attempts to apply learning concepts to psychotherapy came in the decade following the second World War (Dollard and Miller, 1950; Mowrer, 1950; Murray, 1954; Rotter, 1954; Shoben, 1949). Dollard and Miller, for example, reinterpreted psychoanalytic psychotherapy in learning terms such as reinforcement, generalization, and extinction. A significant aspect of their effort was that they found it necessary to postulate many additional processes, such as mediated discrimination and generalization, verbal labels and cue-producing responses, and approach-avoidance conflict on the symbolic level, in order to account for the higher mental processes

[1] This research was supported in part by Grant MH-14716-01 from the United States Public Health Service, National Institute of Mental Health and in part by Grant NGL-10-007-010 from the National Aeronautics and Space Administration.

We would like to express our thanks to Stephen E. Berger, Jim Millham, and Diane Nuber for their assistance.

that were involved in the phenomena they were attempting to explain. In addition, they made a number of assumptions about learned social responses in order to account for the social aspects of the patient's difficulties and the transference relationship between the patient and therapist. In making these assumptions about the higher mental processes and social relationships, Dollard and Miller went far beyond the simplistic concepts of learning prevalent at the time, conceptions that were derived largely from the animal laboratory.

Initially, the application of learning concepts to psychotherapy received a cool reception from most dynamically oriented psychologists and clinicians. In reviewing Dollard and Miller's book, Rapaport (1953) took the position that most theories of learning had not really developed to the point where they could deal with many clinical problems. In spite of the fact that Dollard and Miller went beyond the theories of their day, Rapaport felt that they did not come to grips with ego functions or with social and cultural factors.

In later years, some dynamic theorists came to accept the idea that psychotherapy might best be viewed as a learning process. Franz Alexander (1963) took this position, but emphasized that the most significant learning occurs within the context of the interpersonal relationship of the therapist and the patient. In general, the main objection raised to the application of learning theory to psychotherapy was that it did not adequately account for the importance of cognitive, personality, and social variables.

Recently, a new era in the application of learning theories to psychotherapy has emerged (Eysenck, 1960; Krasner and Ullmann, 1965; Wolpe, 1958). The current era has been characterized by the development of new techniques and the application of learning principles in novel ways to a variety of clinical problems. Methods of counterconditioning, verbal reinforcement, and active behavioral control have been established.

In contrast to the earlier learning applications, the newer behavioral approaches tend to avoid consideration of cognitive and emotional processes, as well as interpersonal aspects of the therapeutic situation. As a result of this orientation, behavior therapy has been criticized for using a model that does not account adequately for the more complex and covert aspects of behavior change (Breger and McGaugh, 1965). This critique has led to a rather heated controversy concerning the adequacy of the theoretical basis of behavior therapy (Breger and McGaugh, 1965, 1966; Rachman and Eysenck, 1966; Wiest, 1967). However, as Murray (1963) has pointed out, a learning approach does not preclude a consideration of cognitive, emotional, and social variables.

At the same time that this controversy over the application of learning principles has been taking place, the field of learning, itself, has been undergoing a quiet revolution. Many changes have occurred in the psychology of learning in recent years, and quite a few of the once solidly established principles of behavior are not quite so solid any more. Although it is not easy to characterize the changes occurring in an area in a state of flux, it is accurate to state that the general direction of these changes has been towards an acceptance of cognitive, personality, and social interaction variables as fundamental parameters of the learning process. These factors, once thought of by many investigators as artifacts and error variance, have become increasingly recognized as legitimate and significant aspects of the learning situation.

Therefore, an interesting situation has emerged. Clinicians have in recent years shown considerable interest in applications of the psychology of learning. At the same time, learning researchers have become increasingly impressed with the importance of many of the variables that have been of traditional importance to clinicians. This convergence may result in the development of an increasingly powerful and exciting psychology, in which human behavior with all its ramifications can become an active area of scientific investigation.

In this chapter we shall discuss this developing convergence of clinical and learning psychology. We will begin by reviewing research indicating the increased emphasis on cognitive, personality, and social interaction variables as fundamental parameters of human learning. We will then proceed to view both traditional and behavioral psychotherapy in terms of these same factors, and conclude by applying our analysis directly to some of the problems and controversies in psychotherapy and behavior modification re-search and practice. We hope to demonstrate that all three areas—learning, traditional psychotherapy, and behavioral psychotherapy—are moving closer together because it is being increasingly recognized that they deal with many of the same problems and parameters.

COGNITIVE, PERSONALITY, AND SOCIAL INTERACTION VARIABLES AS FUNDAMENTAL PARAMETERS OF HUMAN LEARNING

The purpose of this section is to indicate some of the significant changes that have occurred in the psychology of learning in recent years. The increasing emphasis upon cognition, personality, and social psychology will be evaluated with regard to four major areas of human learning research that are of current importance: (a) classical conditioning; (b) operant conditioning; (c) vicarious learning; and (d) verbal learning and complex processes.

Classical Conditioning

In a recent symposium on classical con-ditioning (Prokasy, 1965), a substantial number of papers were concerned with problems of cognition, personality, and "complex factors." Some of the problems that were discussed were summarized by Grings (1965, p. 85):

The troublesome variables are, for the most part, subject variables (cognitions, perceptions, and stimulus interpretations) which are not completely definable in terms of stimulus manipulations. Efforts to response-infer the variables have not been entirely successful. The result is that cognitive and perceptual variables remain to complicate the human conditioning scene. It has been asserted here that the researcher in autonomic conditioning can at the present time neither handle these variables well conceptually nor can he control them ade-quately by such means as disguising his experimental situation.

The problem of self-instruction and hypo-thesis testing by subjects in classical conditioning experiments has also been found to be of importance:

In the absence of formal instructions, subjects often adopt self-instructions that may facilitate or interfere with the acquisition of CRs. . . . In the absence of objective criteria, subjects may provide self-instructions that tend to increase between-subject variability and that may or may not be consistent with the objectives of the experimenter. On the other hand, if the experimenter provides information feedback concerning the adequacy of the response under observation, the classical conditioning paradigm will be markedly altered (Gormezano, 1966, p. 387).

The role of cognitive factors in classical con-ditioning has been demonstrated by Spence (1966). He found that cognitive factors play an important role in the extinction of classically conditioned responses. One indication appears to be that while in animal studies the extinction rate approximates the acquisition rate, extinc-tion has been found to occur much more rapidly than acquisition in human subjects. Spence reports that in his investigations the frequency of occurrence of the conditioned re-sponse dropped to a random level after two to four nonreinforced responses.

In a study by Spence, Rutledge, and Talbott (1963), it was found also that most human subjects reported their discrimination of the shift from acquisition to extinction. Spence (1966) hypothesized that in extinction subjects "became aware (p. 452)" that their eyelid had been conditioned, and immediately adopted a set not to blink to the conditioned stimulus. Spence (1966, p. 445) has tersely summarized this new view of human extinction:

It is strongly suspected that complex processes, call them cognitive factors, sets, mediating processes, or what you will, have greatly affected the extinction data heretofore reported for human subjects.

Much attention has been given in recent years to the role of personality in classical con-ditioning. The importance of such factors seems to have surfaced for the first time in the early 1950s with discussion of the problem of "voluntary responders." These are subjects in an eyelid conditioning experiment who blink rapidly to a "ready" signal and keep their eyes shut until after the unconditioned stimulus (air puff) has been terminated. These subjects are sometimes said to be "cooperating" with the experimenter, and tend to demonstrate response curves similar to those who have been instructed to blink, and those who report blinking voluntarily in order to avoid the air puff. Since classical conditioning is supposed to be an automatic, reflexive process, voluntary responders are not viewed happily. Procedures have been devised for detecting and eliminating them from the group of subjects who demonstrate "true" conditioning (Spence and Ross, 1959; Spence and Taylor, 1951).

Ross (1965) has broadened the discussion of subjects who actively facilitate their responses by identifying a second group of subjects who do not play by the rules. These subjects might be called "voluntary inhibitors," since they actively seek to inhibit their responses. Ross states that athletes, in particular, seem to do this because they appear to believe that blinking to a little air puff may be a sign of weakness. It appears that the tendency to facilitate or inhibit responses is an important personality factor in classical conditioning, and influences the results of a substantial portion of the subjects. Ross (1965, pp. 259–260) has recognized the implications of this problem:

While we have carefully controlled the properties of, and time relations among, physical stimuli in the eyelid conditioning situation we have sadly neglected a large number of extremely important S variables. . . . A comparison of the personality characteristics of inhibiting and voluntary responding Ss would be of interest. It may be that one of the most significant contributions of eyelid conditioning will come about through our growing ability to classify different modes of responses on a dimension from nonvoluntary to voluntary, and these both to personality factors and traditional learning parameters.

Operant Conditioning

Much research has been performed in recent years in the area of human operant conditioning, particularly of verbal operant conditioning. Verbal conditioning has been referred to by researchers as a procedure by which it is possible to investigate the same kind of variables that have been investigated with the nonverbal behavior of humans and infrahumans (Greenspoon, 1962). At the same time, it has been described as an excellent method for studying

psychotherapy and personality development (Greenspoon, 1962; Krasner, 1962, 1965).

Much attention has been given to the role of cognitive factors in verbal conditioning. This research has centered around the problem of learning and consciousness. The specific question that has been asked is whether behavior may be modified by reinforcement in the absence of the subject's awareness of the relationship between the reinforcing stimulus and his behavior. The problem of the necessity of awareness of the correct response-reinforcement contingency is a controversial issue analogous to problems that clinicians have debated for years. Among these are the following: Is insight a necessary precondition for personality change and/or a "cure" to occur? Is unconscious learning possible? To what extent is behavior consciously determined?

An important question is the definition of awareness. In most studies, awareness is defined as a verbal report by the subject that he recognizes that presentation of the reinforcing stimulus is contingent upon the emission of specific responses by him. In the early verbal-conditioning studies, these reports were elicited frequently in response to a small number of ambiguous questions asked subsequent to conditioning (such as "What do you think the purpose of this experiment was?"). Most of these studies found evidence for learning without awareness and for the automatic effects of reinforcement on behavior (see Adams, 1957; Krasner, 1958; and Salzinger, 1959).

In recent years, methods of measuring awareness have become increasingly sophisticated. Investigators have used a variety of measures, including detailed postconditioning interviews that elicit the subject's hypotheses and motivation level (see Spielberger, 1962). It has been found that such interviews are an excellent means of assessing awareness and, despite their comprehensiveness, do not appear to suggest awareness to subjects who already have been conditioned (Jacobson, 1969; Spielberger and DeNike, 1966). Investigators have also used a note-taking method, in which subjects write down their "thoughts about the experiment" during conditioning (DeNike, 1964), a threshold recognition indicator (Klein and Wiener, 1966), and conversations with stooges (Weinstein and Lawson, 1963.)

Using these more comprehensive measures, *most of the recent studies have found that subjects who are aware of the correct response-reinforcement contingency demonstrate acquisition and extinction of verbal behavior; whereas, unaware subjects do not condition* (Dulany, 1962; Jacobson, 1969; Matarrazzo, Saslow, and Pareis, 1960; Spielberger and DeNike, 1966). Using the notetaking procedure, it has been found also that initial performance increments and awareness occur simultaneously (DeNike, 1964). It appears, then, that the earlier findings indicating learning without awareness resulted from the use of inadequate methods of assessing awareness.

The Jacobson study is representative of this newer research. Figure 18.1 indicates the re-

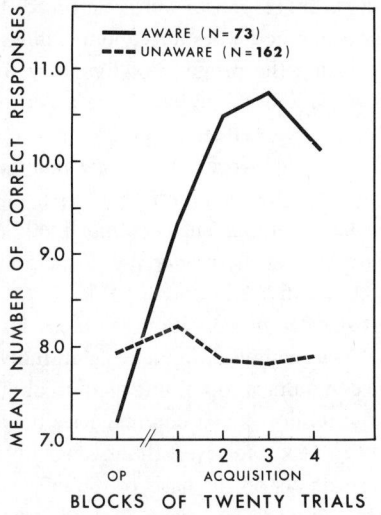

Figure 18.1 Response acquisition in verbal conditioning for aware and unaware subjects (after Jacobson, 1969).

lationship between awareness and verbal conditionality during acquisition. Acquisition is apparent for aware subjects only; unaware subjects remain at their operant level. Figure 18.2 indicates the change in performance between the last acquisition trial block and the extinction period. Extinction was found to occur within the first nonreinforced trial block. Further analysis indicated that aware subjects demonstrated this extinction within the first five nonreinforced trials. The finding of rapid extinction in verbal operant conditioning is consistent with Spence's

(1966) results in classical conditioning and provides further evidence of the role of cognitive factors in human extinction. As Jacobson has stated:

It may be hypothesized that when awareness and other cognitive variables are properly identified, the shape of the extinction curve in many areas of human research will be found to be quite different from those often published in animal studies. The remarkably similar findings of Spence and the present study raise serious theoretical questions concerning the interpretation of human extinction data within a traditional S-R framework. One question which may be asked is whether human and animal extinction are a function of the same or differing processes (Jacobson, 1969, pp. 211-212).

The role of awareness has been demonstrated also in the operant conditioning of nonverbal responses. Paul, Eriksen, and Humphreys (1962) placed subjects in a heat-humidity chamber in which the temperature was 105 degrees F. and the humidity was 85 percent. A 10-second draft of cool air was used as the reinforcer. The investigators then systematically reinforced

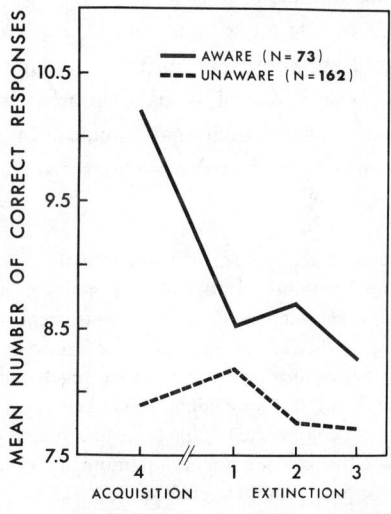

Figure 18.2 Extinction in verbal conditioning for aware and unaware subjects (after Jacobson, 1969).

various motor responses. Conditioning was found only for subjects who were able to verbalize the relationship between their responses and the reinforcer.

The case for the role of awareness in acquisition and extinction in human operant conditioning is strong enough to support these comments by Eriksen (1962, p. 11):

The tasks that have now been investigated do constitute a fair sampling of the learning situations for humans. The evidence includes concept formation, simple verbal habits, perceptual cue learning, and operant conditioning of nonverbal motor responses. In none of these situations is impressive or unequivocal evidence of learning without awareness obtained.

The awareness controversy has assumed great importance because it relates directly to fundamental assumptions concerning the learning process. Learning without awareness is consistent with a traditional model that assumes automatic conditioning as a result of reinforcement and/or contiguities between stimulus and response. Learning that requires awareness is more consistent with a model that stresses the importance of thought, affect, motivation, personality, social influence, and the more spontaneous aspects of human behavior. Thus, the awareness controversy involves a fundamental disagreement concerning the factors that are of importance in understanding human learning and behavior.

It is of interest to note that B. F. Skinner, while using somewhat different terminology, views what is called verbal reinforcement as primarily an informational stimulus. In commenting on the study by Matarazzo et al., Skinner said:

It seems to me quite reasonable that the so-called reinforcement in period two acts more as a discriminative stimulus than as a reinforcement. In talking to the lady on my right at a dinner party, I may try various subjects without much success. When I hit on something which gets a nod of interest, I continue along the same line, not so much because the response has been reinforced, as because the response plus the reinforcement act as an S^D indicating that this is the kind of audience which reinforces certain kinds of responses (quoted in Matarazzo et al., 1960, p. 205).

A similar point is made by Merbaum and Southwell (1965) about the control of verbal behavior in a laboratory setting. Affective statements of the subject were reinforced by exact repetition or paraphrase. The authors point out that the affective verbal responses of the subject had been acquired in the subject's previous life history, so that the response-frequency changes obtained represented compliance with audience cues rather than operant conditioning. Thus, the stimuli presented by the experimenter functioned more as discriminative than as reinforcing stimuli.

If the critical factor in many verbal conditioning experiments is the communication of information, it would appear that there are more efficient means of achieving this goal than the protracted processes of response shaping and extinction. One direct method is to provide information by means of instructions. The potency of instructions in a verbal conditioning setting was demonstrated by Merbaum and Lukens (1968). The subjects were required to construct imaginative stories and the experimenters attempted to increase the frequency of either positively or negatively toned emotional words by one of three methods. In the *reinforcement* method, correct verbal responses were reinforced. In the *elicitation* method, questions about feelings were asked during the progress of the story. In the *instruction* method, subjects were asked at the beginning to use either positively or negatively toned emotional words. The *instruction* method was significantly more effective than the *reinforcement* method. The *elicitation* method was also superior to the *reinforcement* method, but only for negative emotional words.

Verbal operant conditioning, then, may be viewed as a method of influencing an individual by the communication of information about the response-reinforcement contingencies operating in a given task. However, the manner in which the person acts on the basis of the information received depends on many factors, primarily motivational and personality factors. For example, a person might use the reactions of the lady on his right at dinner to find out not what would please but what would shock. It would seem reasonable to expect that the results of human operant conditioning depend on a number of personality and social factors.

The relationship between personality variables and verbal conditionability has been explored by a number of investigators. Greenspoon (1962) has noted the large variability in verbal conditioning performance that has been reported. Some subjects show much conditioning, others show little or none. A single subject's rate of responding may vary widely within the same experiment. In line with this, modest relationships have been found between response acquisition and such diverse personality characteristics as anxiety, hostility level, internal-external controls, suggestibility, neuroticism, and hypnotizability (see Greenspoon, 1962; Krasner, 1962).

The importance of personality factors in verbal conditioning was shown dramatically in a series of studies using the Blacky test to select groups of "oral" and "anal" subjects. According to Freudian theory, oral character types should be more compliant and anal types more negativistic. Timmons and Noblin (1963) found that orals verbally conditioned better than anals. Noblin, Timmons, and Kael (1966) found that oral subjects increased response frequency with positive verbal reinforcers, such as "good," and decreased response frequency with negative reinforcers, such as "no." The anal subjects showed an opposite and negativistic pattern; positive reinforcers depressed behavior and negative reinforcers increased it.

The verbal conditioning situation also has been found to reflect the effects of subject-experimenter interaction. Binder, McConnell, and Sjohelm (1957) used two experimenters who differed in both sex and personal appearance. They found that an attractive and petite female elicited greater conditioning than a big, husky male. The investigators employed a Taffel task in which the subject was reinforced for constructing sentences with hostile verbs. However, experimenter effects were not found when non-hostile verbs were reinforced (Krasner, Ullmann, Weiss, and Collins, 1961). The importance of experimenter-subject interaction is further demonstrated in a study by Sapolsky (1960), who found that level of conditioning depended significantly on the compatibility of subject and experimenter score patterns on FIRO-B.

Katkin, Risk, and Spielberger (1966) evaluated the effects of experimenter status on the verbal conditioning of college students. In the high-status condition, the subjects were conditioned by a member of the university faculty in an office that bore his name and title. The experimenter was highly formal, and a picture of Freud hung on the wall. In the low-status condition the experimenter was an unkempt male undergraduate who conditioned his subjects in the basement of the psychology building. The investigators found that the low-status experimenter elicited better conditioning than the high-status experimenter.

The general susceptibility of human and animal research to social interaction and social-influence variables may be seen clearly in the research of Rosenthal (1966) and his collaborators. In a study of the effects of experimenter expectancy in the operant conditioning of rats, it was found that experimenters who were told that they were conditioning "bright" rats actually found that their rats demonstrated more rapid acquisition than experimenters who were told that their rats were "dull" (Rosenthal and Lawson, 1964). Similar results have been found when the subjects were flatworms (Cordaro and Ison, 1963) and, of course, humans.

One of the most significant of these studies with human subjects is a recent investigation of teacher expectancy in a California school (Rosenthal and Jacobson, 1968). Teachers were told which of the children in their class would demonstrate intellectual "blooming" and "spurting." Actually, the children assigned to this experimental group were chosen randomly. Intelligence tests were administered prior to assignment to the experimental or control groups and one and two years after assignment. Considerable gains in IQ were found for children in the favorable-expectation group in comparison with children in the control group.

Vicarious Learning

We have described earlier some of the modifications which have taken place in the area of human conditioning. Even in these most simple, "reflexive," and automatic forms of learning it was found that cognitive, personality, and social interaction variables were of significance.

Perhaps the most important factor that retarded the acceptance by experimental psychologists of the importance of cognitive processes and personality variables was the belief that a stimulus-response approach would be sufficient for the formulation of a science of human behavior. One of the areas of investigation that played a significant role in demonstrating that such an approach was not sufficient was research on vicarious learning and extinction.

Bandura (1965) has pointed out that two of the assumptions of traditional stimulus-response psychology were that for learning to occur it was necessary that (a) the subject perform a response and (b) the response be promptly reinforced. Neither of these conditions is met in the training procedures sometimes referred to as vicarious learning, modeling, or imitation.

Bandura has described this research earlier in this volume, so there is little need to reiterate his findings. Briefly, modeling may be defined as a social learning procedure in which the behavior of an observer is influenced by the observation of a model. The observer is usually influenced in the direction of becoming more like the model. This procedure is sometimes referred to as *no-trial learning* because the subject learns by observation without being required to give an overt response. Perhaps a more accurate title would be *no-response learning*.

Modeling has been described by Bandura (1965) as a highly pervasive and efficient method of teaching humans new responses; whereas operant conditioning is viewed by him as an effective way of managing already learned behaviors. Bandura (1965, p. 312) has contrasted the two procedures in the following manner:

One does not employ trial-and-error or operant conditioning methods in training children to swim, adolescents to drive an automobile, or in getting adults to acquire vocational skills. Indeed, if training proceeded in this manner, very few persons would ever survive the process of socialization. It is evident from informal observation that the behavior of models is utilized extensively to accelerate the acquisition process, and to prevent one-trial extinction of the organism in situations where an error may produce fatal consequences.

Recently vicarious extinction, or no-trial extinction, has been demonstrated by the use of modeling techniques (Bandura, Grusec, and Menlove, 1967; Bandura and Menlove, 1968).

Although we have emphasized the role of no-trial learning in human behavior, such learning occurs in many species. Latent learning and extinction (Black, 1958; Clifford, 1964) are well-established procedures with animals. Perhaps the most dramatic case of latent extinction is Black's experiment (1958) in which paralyzed dogs under the influence of curare demonstrated powerful latent extinction.

Verbal Learning and Complex Processes

A great deal of traditional verbal-learning research involved "simple rote learning," a process in which verbal stimuli were supposed to become connected to verbal responses with or without the consent of the passive, relatively nonthinking organism in between. This view, dominant until the middle 1950s, is now totally rejected. As we have indicated elsewhere with regard to paired associate learning (Jacobson, Elenewski, and Lordahl, 1968), simple rote learning is neither simple (McGuire, 1961; Underwood and Schulz, 1960), nor rote (Battig, 1966; Dallett, 1964), and probably not even learning (see Mandler, 1967, pp. 9–11).

The new verbal-learning movement is formulating a model of a thinking, motivated person who actively seeks to deal with his world. The emphasis is upon organizational processes, hypothesis testing, information processing, mediation, and cognitive and behavioral strategies rather than on simple stimulus-response connections. As Mandler (p. 42) has described it:

The human organism does not passivley associate pairs of items but organizes, structures, and conceptualizes the task in a variety of ways. Programs are initiated in order to maximize output (p. 31). . . . organization rather than increasing strength of inter-item associative bonds determines recall.

The more recent emphases are apparent in investigations of computer-simulation models (Feldman, 1961, 1962; Hunt, Marin, and Stone, 1966; Newell and Simon, 1961, 1963; Simon and Feigenbaum, 1964); strategies of information processing (Bruner, Goodnow, and Austin, 1956; Hunt, 1962; Jacobson, Millham, and Berger, 1969; Millham, Jacobson, and Berger, 1969); organization processes, chunking, and rule learning (Battig, 1966; Mandler, 1967; Miller, 1956); abstraction and imagery (Paivio and Madigan, 1968; Paivio, Yuille, and Madigan, 1968); and individual differences in learning (Jacobson, Dickinson, Fleishman and Haraguchi, 1969; Jacobson, Elenewski, Lordahl, and Liroff, 1968; Osler and Fivel, 1961; Osler and Trautman, 1961).

Underwood (1964, p. 52) has expressed the new spirit in the following manner:

The image of a subject in a verbal-learning experiment as being a *tabula rasa* upon which the investigator chisels associations, and quite against the S's wishes, is archaic. The S is far from passive and the tablet has already impressed upon it an immense network of verbal habits. Some of these habits are simple and direct and some are conceptual in their inclusiveness. . . . A more accurate description of the verbal-learning experiment is one in which the S actively "calls upon" all the repertoire of habits and skills to outwit the investigator.

LEARNING IN TRADITIONAL PSYCHOTHERAPY

We turn now to an examination of traditional psychotherapy, particularly the psychoanalytic and client-centered forms of therapy. We will try to show that many of the changes occurring in psychotherapy that are ordinarily attributed to personal growth or personality reorganization can be more profitably viewed as resulting from cognitive, emotional, and social learning. We shall review data indicating that traditional therapy involves events such as the extinction of anxiety, changes in belief systems, social reinforcement, and social influence by the therapist. We will not try to oversimplify psychotherapy, but rather, we shall deal with some of the complex cognitive, emotional, and behavioral changes occurring within the interpersonal context.

The Role of Anxiety in Psychotherapy

The patient who seems to profit most from traditional interview therapy tends to be a member of the middle or upper socioeconomic classes and to possess the verbal skills and interests associated with education. Typically, such a person enters therapy more or less voluntarily because he is suffering emotional pain as a result of unsatisfactory human relationships (Murray, 1964).

These characteristics have important implications for the nature of the learning process in traditional psychotherapy. The social-class factor indicates that many patients enter therapy already holding values consistent with the expectations of both the therapist and society. The verbal skills which the patient brings are of great importance also, since traditional therapy is so heavily dependent upon verbal interaction.

Finally, the presence of personal anguish provides motivation for the patient and dictates that therapy must be oriented towards the alleviation of emotional distress, particularly the reduction of anxiety.

The anxiety that is important in psychotherapy is usually not simple physical pain, but the type of distress that grows out of inadequate human relationships. Anxiety appears to be reduced by the kinds of social interactions suggested by the contact comfort studies with monkeys and the maternal deprivation studies with infants (King, 1966).

Most forms of psychopathology may be viewed primarily as unsuccessful patterns of interaction with significant others that interfere with the continuity and stability of important relationships. These interactions may be regarded as unsatisfactory by the patient, or the significant others, or both. One of the results of these unsuccessful interactions for the patient is the development of acute emotional distress (Murray, 1964; Murray, 1968a).

These considerations about the importance of anxiety in the life of the typical psychotherapy patient, and its social basis, make more understandable one of the more dramatic effects associated with traditional psychotherapy and other forms of treatment. We are referring here to the frequently made observation that upon entering psychotherapy many patients experience a reduction of anxiety and related symptoms. For example, content-analysis measures show a rapid decline in uninterpreted intellectual defenses (Murray, 1954), physical complaints (Murray, 1956), and psychotic symptoms (Murray, 1962).

The explanation of the phenomenon of rapid anxiety and symptom reduction is made even more challenging by findings indicating that similar effects can be obtained by giving a patient a placebo or by putting him on a waiting list (Frank, 1961). Apparently, the patient's expectations of being helped by a socially designated helping agent result in a strong sense of hope, relief, and confidence, and these exert a powerful influence on his emotions, thoughts, and behavior. The basic reaction is reminiscent of the monkey clinging to his surrogate mother or the frightened child running to his mother for comfort.

Subsequent to the initial reduction of anxiety, resulting from the processes described above, traditional psychotherapy appears to move into a more complex phase. This new phase may involve an increase in anxiety and an intensification of symptoms. These events have been described as manifestations of an approach-avoidance conflict (Murray, 1964; Murray, 1968a).

In one case, for example, the patient appeared to be in conflict between anxiety and hostility (Murray, 1954). The anxiety-motivated defensive behavior consisted of intellectualization and somatic complaints. Content categories for defensiveness and hostility were used to provide quantitative measures of the events that occurred during the psychoanalytically oriented psychotherapy provided in this case. The results are shown in Figure 18.3. The initial decline in the anxiety-motivated defenses probably reflected the reduction of anxiety and increased self-confidence that resulted from entering therapy. Following this there was an increase in hostile expressions that represented an approach to the significant problems and feelings of the patient. Hours 4 to 8 show an alternation between approach and avoidance usually referred to as conflict oscillation. The anxiety appears to have undergone a gradual extinction, so that by the end of the therapy the problems associated with hostility were being discussed openly and consistently.

In a study of direct analysis (Murray, 1962), it was shown that comparable categories of psychotic symptoms and family conflicts also appeared to reflect an approach-avoidance conflict. There was an initial reduction in the psychotic-symptom category, and then an alternation of family conflicts and psychotic symptoms. An important implication of these findings is that the psychotic symptoms in this schizophrenic patient functioned in about the same way as neurotic defenses in the patient discussed above. Furthermore, the same learning principles appear to apply to these different therapeutic methods.

The reduction of anxiety over the course of psychotherapy in the cases described above has been attributed to extinction. A more direct demonstration of an extinction process in a patient treated with psychoanalytic psychotherapy was presented by Dittes (1957a). A continuous measure of galvanic skin response (GSR) was made during the therapy sessions. The content of the patient's speech was scored for Embarrassing Sexual Statements. Over the course of therapy the GSR reaction to Embarrassing Sexual Statements decreased in a manner very similar to anxiety extinction curves in other situations. In a related study, Dittes (1957b) showed that GSR measures for the hour as a whole were related to the judged permissiveness of the remarks and general attitudes of the therapist.

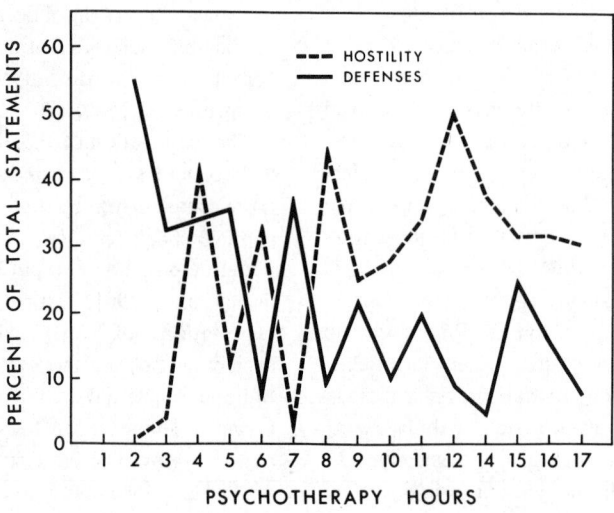

Figure 18.3 Hostility and defenses during traditional psychotherapy (after Murray, 1954).

It is important to note that although emotional responses to various stimuli may extinguish throughout the psychotherapeutic process, the overall level of tension does not necessarily decrease during psychotherapy. Murray, Auld, and White (1954) have shown that in a successful treatment case, the patient progressed into more and more significant areas. As anxiety about one area decreases, the patient may move into other areas also associated with anxiety. Therefore, the level of tension may remain high even though considerable progress is being made.

Cognitive Learning

Dollard and Miller (1950) suggest that an important consequence of the reduction of anxiety and the avoidance of significant conflict areas is an increase in the person's problem-solving capacities in those areas of social living. The person may be able to reevaluate his fears and beliefs. In short, anxiety reduction may lead to significant cognitive and behavioral changes.

There appears to be some reluctance to see cognitive changes as of central importance in traditional therapy and, indeed, in most forms of psychotherapy. This reluctance may be based on several misconceptions. Cognitive change may imply for many psychotherapists an emphasis on purely intellectual insight (Berenson and Carkhuff, 1967). However, we are referring here to cognitive processes closely tied to motivational, emotional, and behavioral variables. Secondly, many therapists associate cognition, and especially insight, with the classical Freudian theory of instincts and psychosexual development. However, we are referring to a more general view of cognitive processes that is not bound to any particular theory of motivation or development.

A good example of the kinds of cognitive variables that appear to be of importance in personality, psychopathology, and psychotherapy is found in Frank's theory of the "assumptive world" of the person (Frank, 1961.) For example, an individual may assume that he must be perfect in order for anyone to love him. Successful psychotherapy appears to involve a change in the assumptions a person has about himself and the world. Frank is referring to a complex set of images, values, and expectations that are closely related to emotional states. A realistic and internally consistent assumptive system may be an important factor in maintaining reliable and satisfactory relations with others, whereas an inaccurate and internally conflicted assumptive system may lead to frustration and failure.

Frank's assumptive world is related to what has sometimes been referred to as beliefs or belief systems. As employed in this chapter, the belief-system construct is an attempt to conceptualize some of the significant factors that result in an individual's daily behavior and interactions. A belief system may be viewed as a conceptualization of the organization of an individual's values, expectations, and beliefs about himself, the world, and the people with whom he interacts. Such a system is formed and integrated through learning in the course of the individual's social development.

An emphasis on beliefs and belief systems has characterized the approach of several cognitively oriented psychotherapists, who have developed techniques that are specifically designed to reveal hidden assumptions and to change key beliefs (Ellis, 1962; Kelly, 1955). However, our point here is a more general one. All successful psychotherapy may be viewed as involving procedures through which the patient's belief systems are clarified, evaluated, and modified. These cognitive changes must also be coordinated with emotional and behavioral changes.

Social Reinforcement and Social Influence in Traditional Psychotherapy

The reduction of anxiety, the increase in approach to significant topics, and the cognitive changes during psychotherapy described in the previous sections are influenced by the activities of the therapist. We have already seen that GSR extinction is related to the permissiveness of the therapist. According to Frank (1961), psychotherapy involves the use of the therapist's influence in changing the assumptions of the patient. We shall emphasize the role of social reinforcement and social influence in the acquisition and modification of the patient's belief systems.

It would appear that all therapists communicate information about their attitudes and beliefs to the patient. It does not seem possible to avoid such communication. In this sense a truly nondirective therapy, as originally described by Rogers (1942), does not seem possible. In order to test this hypothesis, Murray (1956) applied a content-analysis system to a verbatim nondirective case published by Rogers (1942). Inspection of the results showed that one group of categories (primarily "independence") was approved, and another group (including "dependence," "sexual material," and "defenses") was disapproved. It was predicted that verbal behavior related to the approved categories would increase and that verbal behavior related to the disapproved ones would decrease. Figure 18.4 indicates that these predictions were confirmed. These results suggest that therapist approval and disapproval function as positive and negative reinforcers. Furthermore, reinforcement may be applied systematically and differentially, even in Rogerian therapy.

Recently, Truax (1966) has essentially replicated Murray's findings. Rogers (1961) assumes that the client learns a great deal about himself and his relations with others in client-centered therapy. This learning is supposed to result from the creation by the therapist of certain general therapeutic conditions, such as empathic understanding and unconditional positive regard. In a case treated by Rogers, Truax showed that therapeutic conditions were not uniformly distributed, but were systematically related to certain client categories. Thus, for example, the

therapist was more empathic and positive when the client showed evidence of insight, discrimination learning, and expressive style similar to that of the therapist. Furthermore, these reinforced categories increased in frequency during the course of therapy.

The similarity between the verbal interactions in psychotherapy and the effects of verbal reinforcement in a laboratory setting was demonstrated in a recent study by Williams and Blanton (1968). These investigators found that nonpsychotic neuropsychiatric patients assigned to a verbal-conditioning group in which reinforcement was given for affective statements demonstrated a gradual increase in affective responding similar to that of a group of patients assigned to traditional psychotherapy. This increase in affective responding was not found for patients assigned to a verbal-conditioning group in which reinforcement was given for nonaffective statements.

Psychoanalytic therapies also appear to involve subtle directive communications transmitted through reinforcement effects. Approval and disapproval have been demonstrated in both cases mentioned in the previous section—one treated by psychoanalytically-oriented psychotherapy (Murray, 1954) and the other by direct analysis (Murray, 1962). Truax (1968) found that psychoanalytic and eclectic, as well as client-centered, group therapists used empathy,

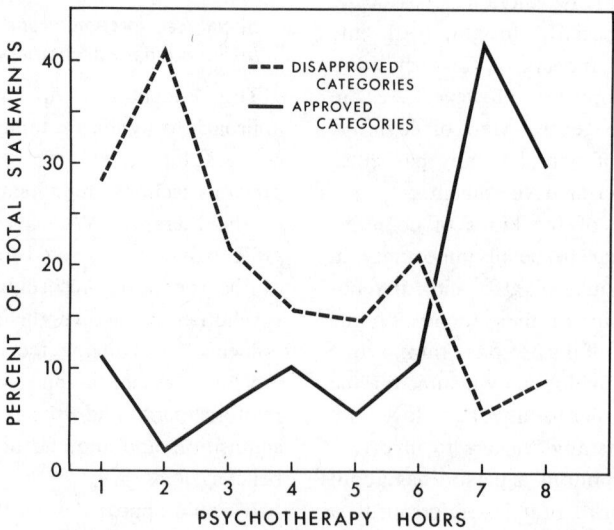

Figure 18.4 The effects of subtle approval and disapproval in nondirective psychotherapy (after Murray, 1956).

warmth, and genuineness as differential re-inforcers for self-exploration. In addition, it has been shown that psychoanalytic interpretations can function as positive reinforcers in a verbal-conditioning task (Timmons, Noblin, Adams, and Butler, 1967). Psychoanalytic interpretations, however, are more complex in their effects than simple verbal reinforcers. They may raise anxiety as well as indicate therapist interest. In fact, as interpretations get "deeper," they become more anxiety arousing (Howe, 1962). One psychoanalyst (Greenwald, 1967) suggests that many interpretations, such as calling homosexuality "infantile," function as aversive stimuli.

Several studies have shown that therapist responses in general eclectic psychotherapy may be divided into those approaching a given topic and those avoiding it. Approach is assumed to function as a positive reinforcer and avoidance as a negative one. Bandura, Lipsher, and Miller (1960) found that within a therapy hour, patients continued to express hostility following an approach response on the part of the therapist. However, a therapist avoidance response was likely to result in dropping the topic. Winder, Ahmad, Bandura, and Rau (1962) replicated this finding and found a similar effect for therapist approach and avoidance for a dependency category. Caracena (1965) also found evidence for this effect.

In a recent study, Varble (1968) has raised the question as to whether the short-term reinforcing effects of approach and avoidance produce a long-term conditioning effect. This might be demonstrated by showing that the positively reinforced response category increases in frequency from hour to hour. Varble showed the same immediate differential effect of therapist approach and avoidance that was found in the above studies. He did not, however, find an increase in the hostility category over the course of therapy. In fact, he found a decrease. This led Varble to question the adequacy of the operant conditioning framework as an explanation of events in psychotherapy.

In commenting on Varble's study, Murray (1968b) pointed out that the data did not permit a test of the reinforcement hypothesis. The therapists were both approaching and avoiding hostility in an inconsistent fashion—about 50 percent approach and 50 percent avoidance. A test of the reinforcement hypothesis requires separating approach and avoidance categories. However, Varble has raised some interesting points about the clarity and adequacy of operant conditioning concepts.

The nature of verbal reinforcement in psychotherapy is related to the question of awareness which, as indicated earlier in this chapter, appears to be essential in verbal conditioning experiments. Awareness in psychotherapy was studied by Murray (1956) in connection with the Rogerian case. Twenty naive students were asked to read Hour 6, the critical session just before the major increase in the approved categories. On a questionnaire, the students indicated, in their own words, that the patient was trying to choose between independence and dependence. Nearly all the students indicated that they thought that the therapist wanted the patient to choose independence. Furthermore, they felt that the therapist communicated his views in a subtle and indirect way. If these students were so clearly aware of what the objective content analysis showed the therapist to be doing, then it would seem logical to assume that the patient was aware also.

Recently, Murray (1968b) has pointed out that the effects of reinforcement have been found to be extremely complex in laboratory situations. The same verbal message may facilitate behavior in some people and inhibit it in others. So, too, the effect may vary for the same person, depending on his motivational state. Caracena (1965) has attempted to show that these approach and avoidance responses function more as eliciting than as reinforcing stimuli. This is similar to the previous point that much of what is called verbal reinforcement may be the presentation of discriminative stimuli or audience cues in order to influence the subject. (Skinner, in Matarazzo, et al., 1960; also Merbaum and Southwell, 1965).

As in the verbal conditioning studies discussed earlier, verbal reinforcement in psychotherapy may be viewed primarily as a method of transmitting information about the response-reinforcement contingencies operating in both the therapeutic encounter and the patient's daily life. This information may be greeted with a positive or negative reaction from the patient and frequently with both simultaneously. Thus, the verbal behavior of the therapist has complex informational and motivational significance for the patient, relating to his ability to maintain the therapeutic relationship and to solve his personal problems.

The Therapeutic Relationship

It is generally agreed that the relationship between the therapist and the patient is of central importance in psychotherapy. Patient improvement seems to depend on characteristics of the patient, the therapist, and the patient-therapist interaction. The therapeutic relationship seems to be particularly important in producing changes in belief systems. Alexander (1963) has suggested that "emotional insight" occurs in the context of the relationship between the therapist and the patient. He states that the therapeutic relationship leads to reduced conflict and greater harmony for the patient, first in his relationship with the therapist and, later, in his relationships with others.

There is considerable evidence now that the facilitative conditions originally described by Rogers—accurate empathy, nonpossessive warmth, and genuineness—predict positive outcome in several forms of psychotherapy (Truax and Carkhuff, 1964; Truax, Wargo, Frank, Imber, Battle, Hoehn-Saric, Nash, and Stone, 1966). Perhaps the most significant finding in this area was that therapists who provide low facilitative conditions may not only fail to help patients improve but may make them worse (Truax and Carkhuff, 1967).

A bridge between these studies on facilitative conditions and the reinforcement effects described earlier is the investigation by Truax (1966), which related the systematic application of facilitative conditions by Rogers to effects on selected response categories. If this reinforcement phenomenon can be shown to be a general one, it will go far in showing one way in which facilitative conditions function to promote therapeutic progress.

There is a possible connection between the categories of approach and avoidance and facilitative conditions. One approach category, for example, is reflection, and this might overlap with accurate empathy. So, too, approval seems related to nonpossessive warmth. Genuineness is

more complex, but could emerge in a number of approach categories. The avoidance categories could reflect low facilitative conditions. In any case, approach and avoidance categories can be related to material relevant to the therapeutic relationship.

Winder et al. (1962) demonstrated the importance of therapist approach-avoidance in the therapeutic relationship. Not only did approach and avoidance have short-term reinforcing effects, but these were related also to whether patients continued or terminated therapy. Those patients whose therapists reacted to patient dependency with approach more than with avoidance tended to remain in therapy; those patients whose therapists avoided dependency more than they approached it tended to terminate therapy. This effect was most marked when the dependency was directed towards the therapist himself. Although there are a number of interactions here, it would appear that some therapists foster a dependent relationship and thereby retain some patients whom they might otherwise lose.

What determines the use of approach or avoidance of important topics on the part of the therapist? At least two factors have been demonstrated. The first factor is the personality of the therapist, specifically his anxiety in various areas. Bandura (1956) has shown that therapeutic effectiveness is related to the therapist's anxiety in the areas of dependency, hostility, and sex. Subsequently, Bandura et al. (1960) showed that therapists' anxiety level in the hostility area predicted whether they would approach or avoid the expression of hostility by the patient. As Winder et al. (1962) point out, a similar prediction could be made also for dependency anxiety. The second variable is training. Bohn (1967) demonstrated that student therapists became less directive in their responses to tape recordings with increased training.

An important aspect of the behavior of the therapist in approaching or avoiding and in creating facilitative or nonfacilitative conditions is his emotional response. The feelings of the therapist may be only partly communicated verbally. Other aspects of his feeling may be expressed in his tone of voice and bodily movements. Evidence for this view is found in a study by Milmoe, Rosenthal, Blane, Chafetz, and Wolf (1967). Successful referral of alcoholics to a special clinic was related to physicians' feelings about this population. This was demonstrated by having the physicians discuss their experiences in an interview. The interview was taped, and high-frequency sounds were filtered out to eliminate meaningful content. Some of the feelings came through in the content, and other feelings when content was filtered out. The feelings predicted success in referral.

While the reinforcing effects of the therapists' approach and avoidance behavior are important, they are not the only significant aspects of the therapeutic relationship. Thus, for example, Truax (1968) found that the overall level of facilitative conditions in group therapy was independent of the degree to which these conditions were used as differential reinforcers. Since the overall level of facilitative conditions is related to outcome, these facilitative conditions may influence the client in other ways.

The facilitative conditions provided by the effective therapist may have a direct effect on the belief systems and emotions of the patient, particularly on his self-esteem. Facilitative conditions also resemble the kinds of variables found important in imitation, modeling, and identification (Kagan, 1964), as evidenced by the fact that successful patients change their values towards those of the therapist (Rosenthal, 1955).

In summary, the traditional therapeutic process now looks something like this: an anxious, conflicted patient enters therapy. The establishment of a dependent relationship provides an initial reduction in anxiety and an increase in hope and self-confidence. The therapist attempts to clarify, evaluate, and modify the patient's belief systems and to co-ordinate these cognitive changes with modifications in the patient's emotional and behavioral response systems. The primary method he has for doing this is the systematic use of his own personality—his warmth, interest, sensitivity, and the like. It is probably these spontaneous and genuine verbal and emotional communications of the therapist that provide the basic social reinforcement and social influence in therapy. The therapist's verbal responses serve also as discriminative cues that convey information about the kinds of responses the patient

can perform in order to maintain or elicit the emotional warmth and positive feelings of the therapist. Thus, the therapist uses an emotional lever in order to elicit anxiety-laden responses so that extinction, changes in belief systems, and emotional and behavioral changes can occur. Some of the most important of these changes occur within the context of the therapeutic relationship itself (Murray, 1964; Murray, 1968a).

LEARNING IN BEHAVIORAL PSYCHOTHERAPY

In this section we shall consider the nature of the learning processes involved in three of the better-known behavioral techniques—systematic desensitization, operant therapy, and aversion therapy. Although these behavioral techniques are explicitly based on learning theory, they tend to be derived from older and simplistic versions of learning theory that do not reflect the changes described in the first section of this chapter. Typically, the learning that occurs is attributed to classical conditioning or simple reinforcement effects. Nevertheless, as we shall try to show, research has begun to make it increasingly clear that the learning occurring in the behavioral therapies involves complex cognitive, emotional, and motivational changes operating within a social context.

Systematic Desensitization

Systematic desensitization is a procedure developed by Wolpe (1958) to treat anxiety responses, particularly the relatively focalized fears involved in phobias. Typically, the patient is taught deep muscular relaxation. Then he is asked to imagine a graded series of scenes relevant to the phobia. Progress along this hierarchy is halted whenever the patient experiences anxiety. The procedure has been used successfully in a wide variety of clinical and laboratory situations (Lang, Lazovik, and Reynolds, 1965; Paul, 1966, 1967, 1968; Rachman, 1967; Wolpe and Lazarus, 1966). It is a laudatory technique both for the rapidity with which therapists can be taught to use it and for its rapid and effective results as a method of treatment.

According to Wolpe (1958), systematic desensitization is based on the principle of counterconditioning. The fearful stimulus is presented while the patient is relaxed. Since muscular relaxation is incompatible with the autonomic responses involved in fear, the relaxation is conditioned to the imagined stimulus. The progressive hierarchy is important to insure that the imagined stimulus does not elicit the anxiety response in spite of the relaxation.

However, the procedure would appear to involve more complex processes. To begin with, imagining a scene implies a cognition; but in addition to the involvement of images, the significant question is whether the actual desensitization is contingent upon emotional changes, cognitive changes, or both. Davison (1968) addressed himself to this problem in a study designed to see whether counterconditioning is the critical factor in desensitization. Using coeds with snake phobias, Davison found that a traditional desensitization group in which both relaxation and imagery were employed was superior to a group trained with relaxation alone and a group trained with imagery alone.

In contrast with Davison's results, several studies strongly suggest that cognitive rehearsal alone is a sufficient condition for desensitization. It has been demonstrated that simple observation of a model approaching a phobic object, such as a snake, results in a marked reduction of avoidance in subsequent behavioral tasks (Bandura, in press; Bandura, Blanchard, and Ritter, 1969; Geer and Turtletaub, 1967; Ritter, 1968). The changes occurring as a result of such observation appear to involve vicarious extinction, but no systematic relaxation training or counterconditioning. The procedure is sometimes referred to as vicarious desensitization.

Further evidence is provided in a study by Folkins, Lawson, Opton, and Lazarus (1968). These investigators found that either cognitive rehearsal or relaxation was as effective in reducing subjective and physiological anxiety reactions to a traumatic movie film as they were when both were combined into a counterconditioning procedure. Actually, cognitive rehearsal seemed to be the most effective method. The treatments were all presented as means of preparation for the film, so that even the relaxation condition involved some expectation of being helped to deal with the film. The authors conclude that the importance of cognitive processes has been overlooked.

The possibility that relaxation alone is sufficient for desensitization was explored by Zeisset (1968). He found that relaxation combined with instructions on how to apply it to fearful situations was as effective as regular systematic desensitization. As in the Folkins et al. study just described, the subjects were led to believe that the relaxation would help them cope with the fearful situations.

An interpretation of the effects of muscular relaxation in terms of suggestion is supported by the study of Wolpin and Raines (1966), who reduced snake phobias while having subjects tense their muscles. After reviewing evidence from a variety of sources, Rachman (1968), formerly an advocate of the necessity of muscular relaxation, concluded that muscular relaxation is not necessary for desensitization. Nevertheless, Rachman still suggests that an absence of *anxiety* is important. The view that relaxation is not necessary for successful desensitization is supported by Cooke (1968). He found that systematic desensitization with and without relaxation was equally effective in reducing fears of laboratory rats. Both desensitization methods were superior to groups that had only relaxation or a period of hierarchy construction without the rest of the procedure.

It would appear, then, that a major aspect of successful desensitization therapy is some form of cognitive fantasy accompanied by little or no anxiety. This anxiety-free fantasy seems to be an important part of traditional desensitization, vicarious desensitization, and simple cognitive rehearsal. However, the limitations of such a view are clear when it is noted that there is another effective technique derived from learning theory that involves anything but a low, controlled level of anxiety. This is implosive therapy, which emphasizes a flooding of anxiety (Stampfl and Levis, 1967).

In one study (Hogan and Kirchner, 1967), a group of coeds with fears of rats—quite comparable to groups treated with desensitization—were induced to imagine the most horrifying things they could about rats. They were told to think of rats running over them, entering their bodies, and devouring their organs. In a later test, the treated subjects were able to pick up and pet rats, while untreated controls were not able to do this. Apparently, the extinction of anxiety had taken place. Similar results with implosive therapy have been reported for snake phobias (Hogan and Kirchner, 1968) and other types of clinical cases (Levis and Carrera, 1967).

The results of implosive therapy also raise questions about the need for a graded hierarchy. Wolpin and Raines (1966) reduced snake phobias even when they started at the top of the hierarchy. In a more systematic study, Cohen (1969) used group desensitization to reduce test anxiety in college students. Half the subjects were given the usual progressive hierarchy, while the other half imagined only the most anxiety-arousing items for the same number of trials. Both conditions resulted in about the same amount of test anxiety reduction. These results led Cohen to question the necessity of a progressive hierarchy in desensitization procedures.

In comparing desensitization and implosive therapy, London (1964) points out that both depend on imagery and may involve discriminations between fantasy and reality. Instead of reacting with intense emotional reactions such as panic, the person learns to respond cognitively. Actually, London is suggesting a new form of counterconditioning—cognitive rather than emotional, skeletal, or motor counterconditioning. London's analysis is useful but overly general. More specifically, the process seems to involve a direct change in beliefs about the self and one's ability to deal with fears.

Direct support for this view may be found in an ingenious experiment by Valins and Ray (1967). They led subjects to believe that they were listening to their own heart beats, but they were actually listening to bogus beats. They heard their "heart beats" increase appropriately when they anticipated shock, but there was no apparent increase when they saw slides of snakes or an actual snake. Thus, they were led to believe that they were not as afraid of snakes as they thought they were. Another group was used to control for cognitive rehearsal and extinction. It was found that the experimental subjects approached snakes more frequently than the controls. The authors conclude that the behavior of the subjects in the experimental group was modified by changing beliefs about the self by the use of false information.

Further support for the view that desensitization depends upon a change in beliefs is derived from a study by Marcia, Rubin, and Efran, (1969), in which systematic desensitization of animal phobias in college students was compared with a procedure called "T-scope therapy." Subjects were told that phobic stimuli would be presented on a tachistoscope at a speed too fast to be seen consciously. Subjects were told, however, that the stimuli would be perceived unconsciously and that this unconscious perception would be followed by a mild electric shock.

The procedure was presented as highly effective in reducing fear, and false GSR records were presented to document the improvement. Actually, only blank cards were shown in the tachistoscope. Nevertheless, this form of "T-scope therapy" was as effective as systematic desensitization in reducing phobic behavior.

Furthermore, another group was given "T-scope therapy," but subjects were told that the crucial element, the phobic picture, would be omitted so that no improvement could be expected. This "T-scope" group, as well as a no-treatment control group, did not show a reduction in phobic behavior. Thus, the results of both an experimental procedure and a control group, similar to those employed in systematic desensitization studies, were duplicated by a bogus procedure that manipulated expectancy of therapeutic change.

We now have a process that may help to explain the effects of these diverse methods of reducing fear. The critical change required appears to be that the person comes to believe that he can cope with the situation. Once this belief is attained, anxiety declines. Such cognitive changes can come about through a variety of methods. The direct presentation of information, if convincing enough, may be sufficient. Relaxation may be helpful if the person believes it will help him to cope with the situation. Other methods include observation of models, repeated imagining, and direct contact with the feared object (Cooke, 1966; Ritter, 1968).

The idea that desensitization involves changes in belief systems, specifically beliefs about the self, is supported by a phenomenon of considerable interest that has been emerging in the literature. Rather than the symptom substitution feared by dynamic therapists, published and unpublished reports by therapists indicate that when a symptom is removed it is often followed by a general, nonspecific improvement in the individual's daily life.

For example, Gelder et al. (1967) used systematic desensitization with a group of patients with severe phobias. The systematic desensitization not only decreased the main phobia and related fears more effectively than individual and group therapy, but also had generalized effects in areas that had little connection with the focus of treatment. Thus, the systematic-desensitization group showed greater improvements in adjustment to work and leisure-time activities than either of the other two treatments, and as much improvement in general social relationships as those patients in group therapy. As this effect occurred only after the main phobia was eliminated, it seems that the elimination of a phobic symptom may have a salutary effect on the person's general self-confidence.

If desensitization involves changes in beliefs about the self, then we would expect that interpersonal aspects of the situation would influence the effectiveness of the procedures. Such an influence was clearly demonstrated in the study by Cohen (1969). Subjects were placed in one of two types of groups. In one group, they were encouraged to interact with each other and discuss their test anxiety. In another group, the subjects were not allowed to interact, and the exchange of information among them was controlled by having subjects write out questions to be answered during a formal lecture. The results showed that the subjects allowed to interact reduced test anxiety significantly more than those not permitted to interact. Apparently, the emotional support of the group is helpful in reducing anxiety about tests.

In contrast to some of the more mechanistic behavior therapists, Wolpe and Lazarus (1966) point out the importance of establishing a good therapeutic relationship. Gelder, Marks, and Wolff (1967) observed that a transference relationship builds up, during desensitization treatment, although it is not encouraged or interpreted as in traditional therapy. They suggest that the positive aspect of the transference is useful as a means of engaging the cooperation of the patient. Negative transference may lead to dropping out of treatment, so Gelder et al. recommend interpretation of the negative transference as an adjunct to desensitization.

Wolpin and Raines (1966) go further and suggest that the subject must trust the helping person and be prepared to do what he requests. In addition, they observed that their most successful patients were those who were most compliant and cooperative. While Lang et al. (1965) reported no relationship between measures of hypnotic suggestibility and outcome in desensitization, there is some indication that other relevant personality variables may be involved. Wolpin and Raines (1966) found that high neuroticism and low extroversion are associated with favorable outcome. Rachman (1967) reviewed evidence showing that anxiety is related to outcome, but there are conflicting reports as to whether anxiety is facilitative. Zeisset (1968) found a complex relationship between therapeutic success and length of hospitalization. Thus, it appears that there are individual differences in responsiveness to desensitization and that social compliance is probably of particular importance.

The role of social reinforcement and social influence in systematic desensitization is just beginning to be recognized. Lang et al. (1965) point out that the feedback the subject gets from the therapist probably functions as a reinforcer. A positive-reinforcement paradigm was used in one study of desensitization (Wagner and Cauthen, 1968). The subject was reinforced verbally for allowing the experimenter to roll the chair closer to a snake. The authors point out that the effectiveness of the verbal reinforcement depends on the relationship between the subject and the experimenter. The fact that successful desensitization may occur with minimal therapist contact (Kahn and Baker, 1968) and can even be performed by a machine (Lang, 1968) does not necessarily reduce the importance of the social aspects of treatment, since a machine is man-made and exerts influence within the context of a helping relationship (Schwitzgebel and Traugott, 1968).

Although the evidence on the nature of systematic desensitization is incomplete, there is serious doubt as to whether it can be described adequately as a counterconditioning procedure. Neither muscular relaxation, nor a progressive hierarchy, nor imaginal rehearsal seems essential. A variety of techniques aimed at influencing beliefs seem to be of central importance in successful desensitization; furthermore, the procedure takes place within an interpersonal context. Thus, systematic desensitization may be viewed most adequately as a method of modifying beliefs and attitudes by the use of social influence.

Operant Therapy

The numerous case studies of operant methods (for example, Ullmann and Krasner, 1965) clearly demonstrate that it is possible, given enough control over the environment, to get a person to do nearly anything in order to get something he wants. Thus, a mentally retarded child can be taught to operate a machine to get candy; a psychotic patient can be gotten to speak and act sensibly in order to get social attention; and a variety of behavior problems can be eliminated by extinction or punishment. The most dramatic changes have been reported in institutions and situations where something approaching total control is available. In one case (Bachrach, Erwin, and Mohr, 1965), an anorexic patient was housed in a stark room with access to radio, television, or phonograph made contingent upon eating. Of course, this degree of experimental control is not always possible in therapeutic encounters.

In order to understand the effects of operant techniques, it is important to distinguish between behavioral control in therapy and the learning that results from treatment. Most of the examples described in the preceding paragraph involve the performance of previously well-learned responses, so that the individual can gain access to various sources of reinforcement. The events that occur involve problems primarily in motivation rather than in learning.

A good example of the motivational nature of these events is the token economies based on reinforcement principles that have been set up on a number of hospital wards (Liberman, 1968). Typically, there is relatively little difficulty in making the person aware of the new contingencies. However, once these contingencies are understood by the patients, or when criteria for reinforcement are increased, there is a sharp increase in "elopements" from the hospital. Female patients may foil the system by getting various reinforcers from male patients. Other patients hoard or steal tokens. These problems can be dealt with by tightening controls, but they illustrate the difference between learning and motivation.

However, the patient in operant therapy may *learn* a number of useful things about his situation. As we have seen, he may be learning about the contingencies in his immediate environment. Such learning may or may not generalize to other aspects of his life. The patient may also learn that some people care enough about him to help him and even to help save his life. Finally, he may learn something about himself, his capabilities, and the way he interacts with others. In this section we shall consider some of these broader aspects of learning during operant psychotherapy.

In the first section of this chapter, we reviewed evidence showing that human operant conditioning is dependent upon awareness. We indicated that the presumed reinforcer is often primarily an informational stimulus. Furthermore, it was demonstrated that direct instructions were superior to a verbal reinforcement procedure in changing behavior. It is likely that response shaping and chaining under conditions of positive and/or negative reinforcement are highly effective methods of teaching withdrawn, sometimes nonverbal, institutionalized patients (Spence, Goodstein, and Lair, 1965). However, with the greater majority of noninstitutionalized patients, we would expect that instructions and modeling are more efficient methods of conveying information and changing behavior.

Some therapists using operant techniques have added instructions as a means of speeding up behavior change. Thus, Bijou and Orlando (1965) gave verbal instructions and modeling demonstrations to mentally retarded children in order to get them to pull a lever to get candy. However, these authors do not view the instructions as providing information about contingencies but as "drive operations . . . which may affect *Ss*' rates and patterns of responding." This may be the reason why the use of instructions was somewhat limited.

On the other hand, several investigators have emphasized changes in beliefs and attitudes with encouraging results. Peterson and London (1965) cured a three-year-old who retained his feces for days on end, by a deliberate effort to change his cognitions. In three office visits, the child was told in a repetitive, hypnotic fashion that if he went potty it would not hurt; his parents would be very happy; and he would get lots of popsicles.

In another specifically cognitive approach, Giebink, Stover, and Fahl (1968) taught aggressive boys in a residential treatment center new and more adaptive responses to common frustrations. This was done by giving instructions in the form of a table game. In both of these studies the authors point out that it is necessary that the information provided to the subjects be accurate. The parents or the counselors also must provide reinforcement, in order to maintain the behavioral performance.

The role of cognitive processes in behavior modification becomes of even greater importance when we consider efforts to work with adult outpatients. In these situations, the therapist has limited environmental control. Therefore, the behaviorally oriented therapist may try to modify the behavior of the person by suggestions and instructions.

For instance, Sulzer (1965) suggested to a patient a method of studying, a change of job, and a way of dealing with his wife. Although there was some verbal approval in the interview, most of the reinforcement occurred in the patient's daily life. For example, the patient was directed not to respond with anger to his wife's criticisms. As a result, he found that her critical attacks decreased. It is clear that Sulzer was teaching the patient successful methods of social living, and that his effectiveness depended to a great extent upon the accuracy of his instruction. If the information was incorrect and the person ran into increased difficulties, the results might have been quite different.

In addition to transmitting information, operant types of therapy may do a good deal of teaching on the basis of modeling. One of the best-known examples of operant therapy is Lovaas' (1968) use of positive and negative reinforcement with schizophrenic children. Recently, however, Lovaas has found that,

after an initial period in which reinforcement is important, schizophrenic children show highly effective speech acquisition on the basis of imitation, which is not maintained by external reinforcement.

Support for Lovaas' current view concerning the usefulness of modeling is found in an investigation recently completed in our laboratory. Jacobson, Berger, Bergman, Millham, and Greeson (1969) investigated the acquisition of conceptual behavior and learning sets by preschool, predominantly black children from poverty backgrounds living in central-city slum areas. They compared the effectiveness of three procedures in the learning of a 20-hour conceptual development program devised by the investigators. The three procedures were (a) a reinforcement technique that employed both food and social reinforcers; (b) a reinforcement-plus-modeling procedure; and (c) a reinforcement-plus-information feedback procedure. The latter two methods provided instruction to the subject either before or after the learning trials, in addition to the information and incentive provided by the reinforcers.

All three of the experimental procedures were found to be equally effective in generating learning sets. However, the three conditions differed with regard to the related changes in intelligence obtained. The reinforcement procedure resulted in a mean increase in intelligence of 10.58 points as measured by the Stanford-Binet; the feedback condition resulted in a mean increase of 8.17 points on the Stanford-Binet. The increases in IQ scores were highly significant in both conditions. In contrast, no significant change in IQ scores was found in a control condition in which the Stanford-Binet was administered to subjects twice. However, the most striking changes obtained occurred in the modeling condition in which a mean increase of 21.08 points was found on the Stanford-Binet. This study indicates the remarkable effectiveness of modeling techniques in influencing learning and behavior.

In a recent review, Sarason and Ganzer (in press) described a wide variety of modeling procedures used to establish various kinds of operant responses, particularly in the teaching of behavioral control techniques to parents, teachers, and mental health professionals. The authors also describe their own program, based on modeling techniques with institutionalized juvenile delinquents. The delinquent boys were taught a variety of adaptive operant responses through a role-playing procedure in which clinical psychology graduate students acted out prepared scripts about problem situations. For example, the scripts suggested prosocial responses to police officers, job interviewers, and annoying employers. The boys also took various roles, thereby combining reinforcement and modeling procedures.

Operant therapy, then, may involve a good deal of teaching about reinforcement contingencies in the social environment. Much of the verbal responding on the part of the therapist has an informational as well as a motivating function. Information may be acquired effectively through instructions and modeling procedures. The ultimate source of reinforcement for the patient is outside of therapy, in his daily life and natural environment. However, it would be incorrect to conclude that the therapeutic situation itself is not reinforcing in an important way. Psychotherapy based on operant techniques involves human relationships, and human relationships are sources of reinforcement.

The importance of the patient-therapist relationship in treatment methods based on operant principles has been pointed out recently by Wilson, Hannon, and Evans (1968). Additionally, therapist and patient variables and their interactions are related to the effectiveness of a given therapist as a reinforcer. This has been demonstrated in therapeutic contexts as well as in the verbal conditioning studies reviewed earlier. The operant methods used with psychotic children, reviewed by Leff (1968), frequently involve an intense interpersonal relationship. For example, after the initial stages of training an autistic child, the child may develop an attachment to his teacher, even in the face of decreasing primary reinforcements. In some instances, the child is rewarded by close physical contact. These "love-oriented" techniques are used in the therapy by making love and affection contingent upon certain desired behaviors.

While the therapeutic relationship is less dramatic in behavioral-interview therapy, it is no less critical. According to Kanfer and Philips (1966), behavioral-interview therapy places the greatest demand on the therapist because he has no direct control over the environment of the patient. Therefore, the therapist can be effective in persuading and suggesting behavioral change to the patient only to the extent that a good relationship has been established.

Although the effects of contingent social reinforcement have been amply demonstrated in the clinic and laboratory, the possibility that noncontingent motivational effects may be of importance in operant therapies should not be ignored. For example, D'Zurilla (1966) compared the effectiveness of verbal reinforcement and antecedent persuasion in a small group on increasing verbal production in a larger class. A control group was seen also in the small-group situation, but received minimal praise or persuasion. Curiously, this group did as well as the experimental group. In a postexperimental questionnaire, the subjects in the control group indicated that being singled out of a large class and receiving personal attention was important to them. This attention was not contingent upon specific responses.

As with systematic desensitization, it does appear that operant behavior therapy often results in nonspecific adaptive effects in the patient's life that are difficult to attribute directly to the focalized treatment procedures used. Evidence for this view is provided in a study by King, Armitage, and Tilton (1960). These investigators used a reinforcement approach with extremely withdrawn chronic schizophrenics in order to increase motor, verbal, and cooperative behavior in a mechanical problem-solving task. In comparison with verbal-therapy, recreational-therapy, and no-therapy control groups, the reinforcement method had generalized effects. It not only resulted in increased verbalization and general clinical improvement as assessed by an interview technique, but also in better adjustment on the ward, increased interest in occupational therapy, and greater motivation to leave the ward, go to an open ward, and leave the hospital. It is difficult to see how such widespread effects can be attributed to the specific reinforcement procedure employed, unless one assumes that it resulted in some basic change in the patients' attitudes and conceptions about themselves and their interpersonal environment.

Leff (1968) has reviewed a number of studies of operant techniques used with psychotic children. In many of these studies there were nonspecific effects that neither the authors nor the reviewer could account for in terms of the reinforcement procedures used. Such changes are too complex to be attributed glibly to stimulus generalization. For example, in Lovaas' laboratory, children being reinforced for verbal responses also changed their walking gait, facial expression, and appetite. They increased contact with adults, learned to "cup" themselves into the contours of the adult's body, and developed social smiles—all without reinforcement directly contingent upon modification of these responses. The descriptions suggest the factor complex of primary importance to be the discovery, formation, and development of significant human relationships. It would be difficult to account for these events in terms of the strengthening of secondary reinforcers.

Leff suggests that several important processes are involved in these general changes. First, the child seems to be learning to orient himself and to attend to new aspects of the environment, especially the social environment. Thus, new sources of reinforcement became available to him. Secondly, successful completion of a task seems to be related to a feeling of mastery. This motivational change appears to help in the child's approach to quite different situations. Finally, the child appears to be acquiring learning sets or strategies that apply to many different tasks. This might include an imitative set or a strategy of seeking out other people when hurt in various ways.

Leff's analysis is supported in a recent study by Sabatasso and Jacobson (1970). These investigators employed modeling, shaping, and reinforcement in a behavioral-therapy program that attempted to reinstate verbal behavior in a 58-year-old psychotic with severe chronic brain damage, who had been mute for five years prior to the study. Within ten hours of therapy, the subject verbalized 307 words, 45 different words, and several simple sentences. The reinstated verbal behavior generalized to the subject's verbal behavior on the ward and had not extinguished one year after the therapy program was terminated.

This study indicates the striking effectiveness of behavioral therapy in producing rapid and significant behavior change. However, the point of interest here is that the investigators indicated that most of the reinstated words and sentences were neither shaped nor modeled directly, although they were reinforced once they occurred. Consequently, the investigators did not view the effects obtained as simple ones that resulted directly from the application of behavior shaping and modeling. Sabatasso and Jacobson concluded that the techniques employed provided conditions in which information was communicated to the subject, within an interpersonal situation, concerning what was desired and expected of him, and the subject's motivation to verbalize was increased.

In a recent article, Rehm and Marston (1968) have described a new therapeutic technique that illustrates and integrates many of the points made in this section. The technique employs reinforcement principles but is based also on the assumption that behavior can be modified through cognitive changes. Specifically, college men with social anxiety were taught a method of self-reinforcement for approaching girls. For example, they might get a point for calling up a girl for a date. In comparison with several control groups, the self-reinforcement subjects showed an increase in approach behavior and a decrease in self-reported anxiety.

Rehm and Marston assumed also that the anxiety reduction and increased approach behavior were dependent upon a positive change in self-concept. This assumption was supported by a significant increase in self-confidence reported by the self-reinforcement group. The experimental subjects indicated that they understood themselves better and could evaluate their behavior in social situations more adequately. Therefore, there were important cognitive changes associated with the behavioral and emotional ones.

In summary, then, many operant procedures are admirably simple to administer and highly effective in the management of certain patient groups, such as institutionalized schizophrenics and children. However, a theoretical understanding of the operation and effects of these techniques is complex and poorly understood. In addition to the control of behavior through contingent reinforcement that is emphasized by operant investigators, many other factors are important also. These involve complex cognitive, motivational, and emotional variables operating within an interpersonal relationship.

Operant investigators have knowingly or unknowingly used the strategy of conveying significant information through reinforcement contingencies. However, informational learning may be approached more directly through instructions, modeling, and self-evaluative techniques. The appropriate procedure to use would appear to be the one that works most effectively with a particular type of problem and population.

Successful operant psychotherapy seems to involve, also, an increase by the patient in feelings of mastery, greater self-confidence, and, generally, more positive beliefs about the self. Such beneficent changes can result at least partially from what the patient interprets to be successful experiences within the therapeutic context, such as gaining tokens or approval from the therapist. For example, the dispensation of a token may indicate to the patient, often correctly so, that the therapist is pleased and wants him to behave in such a way as to gain tokens. It is important to recognize that it is not necessary that the therapist actually give the token such meaning or even desire it to have such meaning. It is frequently a sufficient condition for behavior modification that the patient *believe* that certain conditions exist. Changes in beliefs about the self and others are probably also related to the positive, noncontingent changes that occur so frequently in the behavior therapies.

Although the variables and relationships that would constitute a theoretically satisfying account of this area are poorly understood, it is clear that a considerably broader theoretical framework is necessary than is now employed by most operant therapists and investigators.

Aversion Therapy

Although aversion therapy is among the oldest of the behavioral techniques it is still the most controversial and variable in outcome (Feldman, 1966; Kalish, 1965; Rachman, 1965).

Aversion therapy includes a variety of specific techniques based on both classical and instrumental conditioning paradigms, and is sometimes combined with other behavioral techniques. Typically, aversion therapy is used to eliminate various types of approach behavior, such as alcoholism and other addictions, various forms of sexual behavior, smoking and overeating, and some forms of obsessive-compulsive responding.

A historically important case described by Raymond (1956) illustrates the dramatic results that sometimes occur as well as the basis for the marked ambivalence towards aversion therapy on the part of many clinicians. The patient was a fetishist who had attacked baby carriages and handbags since the age of ten. Traditional therapy had failed and the patient had been arrested for a recent attack. The aversion treatment consisted of many pairings of handbags, baby carriages, and photographs of these objects with an injection of a drug that produced nausea and vomiting in a grueling week-long, day-and-night marathon. The treatment was repeated several times with excellent results.

There have been a number of changes in aversion therapy since the time of Raymond's study. There has been a gradual shift from the use of chemical aversive stimuli to the use of electrical (Feldman, 1966; Rachman, 1965) and purely imagined stimuli (Cautela, 1966; Gold and Neufeld, 1965). Similarly, there has been a shift in the type of conditioned stimulus employed, from the actual objects to pictures (Feldman and MacCulloch, 1965), printed and spoken words (Thorpe, Schmidt, Brown, and Castell, 1964), and imagined stimuli (Anant, 1968). There has been more recent emphasis also on instrumental avoidance learning than on simple classical conditioning (Feldman, 1966). Many of these recent developments emphasize voluntary and symbolic responses to a greater extent than the original procedures and formulations.

Some of the theoretical problems raised by aversion therapy can be illustrated by Cautela's (1966, 1967) covert sensitization technique. Cautela first trains a patient to relax, as Wolpe does, and then he relies entirely on imagination. The patient visualizes a relevant scene, such as bringing a glass of alcohol to his lips, and is instructed to imagine himself becoming sick to his stomach and then vomiting.

Although covert sensitization *increases* avoidance behavior, it is remarkably similar to systematic desensitization, which *decreases* avoidance behavior. (This similarity was first pointed out to us in a conversation with Janet Taylor Spence.) In systematic desensitization, the relaxed patient imagines a stimulus that ordinarily makes him fearful, but the relaxation inhibits the fear. In covert sensitization, the relaxed patient imagines a stimulus that ordinarily produces pleasure and relaxation, which is then followed by unpleasant feelings.

It may be asked why it is that relaxation predominates in one situation but not in the other? The critical factor does not appear to be the relative response strength of the patient's emotional reactions, but rather the instructional set accompanying each procedure. In systematic desensitization, the patient is led to believe that relaxation will predominate, while in covert sensitization, he is led to believe that he can eliminate his problem by associating the pleasurable stimulus with an unpleasant event.

Another problem in understanding the nature of aversion therapy is that similar effects are obtained from various groups thought to be controls. For example, in an evaluation study of covert sensitization, Ashem and Donner (1968) found that both forward- and backward-conditioning groups did better than a no-contact control group. The excellent results from the backward-conditioning "control" group were explained away by assuming that the imagined stimulus was associated with the nausea aroused on subsequent trials.

However, according to Franks (1963), it is this very failure to clearly differentiate between forward and backward conditioning that accounts for the poor outcome of many attempts to use aversion therapy with alcoholics. The situation is further complicated by the finding that quite different kinds of control groups sometimes show improvement similar to that found in aversion therapy. For example, Ober (1968) found that both positive reinforcement and self-punishment techniques were more helpful in getting people to stop smoking than a no-treatment control condition. However, as an additional control, Ober used a group treated

with a "game analysis" procedure that was not expected to produce behavioral change, but turned out to be as effective as the reward and punishment techniques.

These results suggest that aversion therapy may produce at least some of its effects through the arousal of an expectation or belief about being helped, usually described as the placebo effect (Frank, 1961), rather than through conditioning. Evidence supporting such a view includes a recent study in which a dramatic punishment technique used with alcoholics, involving a terrifying drug-induced stoppage of breathing, was found to produce no greater recovery than a placebo (Madill, Campbell, Laverty, Sanderson, and Vanderwater, 1966). In a study on smoking, Keutzer (1968) found that an attention-placebo control group did as well as operant, aversion, and negative practice groups.

The possibility that beliefs and expectancies are acquired through the use of social influence in aversion therapy and that this acquisition process is central to the results obtained was studied directly by Carlin and Armstrong (1968). Persons wishing to stop smoking were given classical conditioning that paired smoking with electric shock. Instead of a backward-conditioning control, the investigators used a pseudoconditioning group, in which largely irrelevant slides were paired with shock. Finally, a no-shock group was asked to smoke, and subjects were told that they would receive subliminal shock. Although the electrodes were placed on the subjects in this last group, they did not actually receive any shock. The results indicated that all groups did equally well in reducing smoking. The authors suggest that the effect in all groups resulted from the subjects' belief in the efficacy of the university medical center personnel and the expectancy of being helped.

Carlin and Armstrong suggest also that the therapeutic effect on smoking may have been a means of reducing cognitive disssonance. There is an inconsistency with aversive consequences about having taken the time and trouble to go to a respected medical center, submitting oneself to a stress procedure, and then continuing to smoke. In fact, Wilde (1964) suggests that some of his subjects may have given up smoking in order to avoid continuing in aversion therapy.

Although the role of cognitive dissonance is not demonstrated unequivocally by Carlin and Armstrong, they raise an interesting question as to why people submit themselves to aversion therapy at all. On a theoretical level, an aversive stimulus should produce avoidance behavior very quickly. Were it not for the confining cage, any self-respecting laboratory rat would get as far away from an electrically charged grid as he could. On the human level there are, of course, cases in which patients leave therapy as soon as its aversive nature becomes apparent—in one study, about a third of the cases reported dropped out (Morgenstern, Pearce, and Rees, 1965)—but in most instances patients do not show gross avoidance.

In all probability, patients stay in aversion therapy because they are in a conflict about their problematic approach behavior. For example, many of the patients with sexual problems who receive averson therapy may demonstrate one or more of the following: (a) trouble with the law at the time of referral (Gold and Neufeld, 1965; Kushner and Sandler, 1966; Morgenstern et al., 1965); (b) considerable guilt and anxiety about their behavior (McGuire, Carlisle, and Young, 1965; Thorpe, Schmidt, Brown, and Castell, 1964); and (c) avoidance conflict about normal heterosexual behavior (McGuire et al., 1965; Ramsay and Van Velzen, 1968). In short, the effect of aversion therapy should be viewed in the context of creating additional aversive consequences that intensify some aspects of an existing complex conflict (Murray, 1968). Thus, one of the patients treated by Thorpe et al. reported that aversion-relief therapy had given him the added "boost" he needed to help him in his own efforts to control his homosexual feelings.

The possibility that aversion therapy operates primarily by changing the individual's beliefs about himself has not received much direct attention, but numerous incidental observations in the aversion literature suggest that such changes are important. For example, McGuire et al. (1965) reported that the majority of their group of patients with sexual problems believed that it was not possible for them to have a normal sex life. Feldman (1966) reported that

it is the most personally insecure individuals with sexual problems who respond best to aversion therapy. At least some patients show signs of improving their self-concept as they change behaviorally (Thorpe et al., 1964). Cautela (1967) suggests that an important reason why aversion therapy is successful is that the individual develops feelings of self-mastery and a sense of being able to control his own life and behavior. As Ratliff and Stein's (1968) neuro-dermatitis patient put it, he "never thought that he had enough will power to resist an urge to scratch" (p. 398). Aversion therapy changed his belief about his will power.

If, indeed, aversion therapy involves a change in beliefs about the self, we would expect that personality characteristics of the patient and the therapist and their interaction would have some effect. Again, little research has been done in this area, but there are some indications that personality and social factors are of importance. Morgenstern et al. (1965) found that the transvestites who responded best to aversion therapy tended to be more intelligent and suggestible, as well as less introverted and anxious, than those who responded less success-fully. Feldman and MacCulloch (1965) reported in their study that a supportive relationship between doctor and patient developed, although they did not specifically encourage it, nor did they interpret it in a Freudian sense. Liberman (1968), in applying aversion therapy to drug addiction, commented on the importance of the confidence of the patient in the technique and the "alliance" between the patient and therapist.

In summary, there is growing evidence that aversion therapy involves considerably more than simple classical or instrumental avoidance conditioning. Aversion therapies involve, to a marked degree, changes in beliefs and expec-tancies, in particular what has been termed placebo effects. In some aversion procedures, the therapeutic intervention is attempted almost entirely on an imaginal level. Aversion therapies appear to gain much of their success by facilitat-ing the resolution of complex conflicts, such as approach-avoidance conflicts. The method of resolution involves interventions that result in changes in the patient's beliefs about himself, especially his ability to control his behavior.

The social and interactional context of aversion therapy seems to be of importance also, but has received little attention.

CONCLUSIONS AND IMPLICATIONS

In this chapter we have presented evidence for the usefulness of a sophisticated view of social learning in integrating and explaining a wide variety of traditional and behavioral therapeutic techniques. An attempt was made to show that recent developments in the area of learning have emphasized the role of cognitive, motivational, emotional, personality, and social interaction factors in human behavior.

We have indicated that the modern view of the learning process that is now emerging can provide the theoretical foundation for both traditional and behavioral psychotherapy. It has not been suggested that such a theory currently exists in a completed form, nor that the details of such a framework are being presented here. Rather, we have tried to call attention to these new developments, to indicate something of the form of this new social learning approach, and to suggest some lines for its future development.

This chapter has been concerned with a theoretical analysis of the therapeutic process rather than with an evaluation of therapy outcome. Nevertheless, we would like to note that some answers to Eysenck's (1953) challenge have been emerging slowly and have come almost exclusively from research-trained clinical psychologists. As critical variables have been specified, such as therapist-induced facilitative conditions, it has become possible to predict to some extent when various forms of dynamic, client-centered, and eclectic therapy will be effective. The behavioral therapies have been shown also to be effective with respect to carefully specified and measured outcome criteria. Thus, as the outcome crisis resolves itself, a new set of problems concerning the nature of psychotherapy has emerged. One question that may be asked is, how can approaches as divergent, theoretically and technically, as traditional and behavioral therapy all have some degree of success? A second question is, why are these therapies successful in some areas but not in others? It is apparent that some new theoretical formulations are needed.

In this chapter we have attempted to distinguish between methods of treatment and the theoretical explanations offered by their proponents. For example, in dynamic psychotherapy it is clear that interpretations have important effects. Psychoanalysts usually view this process as one of making the unconscious conscious. However, an interpretation may be viewed also as a complex communication between therapist and patient. This communication contains information about the attitudes and motives of the therapists and provides cues that the patient may interpret as indicating what is expected of him. Similarly, aversion therapy may be successful with a person with a compulsive habit, as a result of demonstrating clearly to the individual by avoidance conditioning that his behavior can be modified. Here again, the genuine controlling variables appear to be considerably different from those conceptualized by the behavioral therapist. The evidence presented in this chapter strongly suggests that both traditional and behavioral psychotherapy achieve their results as a function of critical parameters and processes for which there is little place in the theoretical systems of these therapies.

In general, we have found that the current state of theory in both traditional and behavioral therapy is inadequate. The explanation of traditional therapy in terms of personal growth and personality reorganization does not take sufficient account of social learning and social influence processes; the explanations of behavioral therapies do not adequately recognize the importance of cognitive and emotional response systems operating within interpersonal relationships.

It is necessary to begin to construct a new and integrative theoretical system that can account for both traditional and behavioral psychotherapy with the same set of principles. In this section we shall try to specify some of the relevant principles of such an analysis. Since the scientific study of psychotherapy is very recent, the concepts and principles discussed should be considered as tentative working hypotheses that might be useful in research and practice. The topics to be discussed are (a) expectations of help; (b) nonconfirming experiences; (c) informational learning; (d) changes in self-concept; (e) social reinforcement and social influence; and (f) the interpersonal meaning of behavior.

Expectations of Help

The importance of expectancy as a critical factor in behavior change has been discussed earlier. The most important expectations operating in all forms of psychotherapy appear to be expectations of help, particularly the well-known placebo effect.

In both psychoanalytic and client-centered therapy, content analysis measures indicate a dramatic decrease in symptomatology as soon as the patient enters psychotherapy. Evidence for a psychological placebo effect is shown also in various groups designed as controls for systematic desensitization, implosive, operant, and aversion therapies. Therefore, we may conclude that the client's expectations of help operate in all forms of psychotherapy. This finding has both practical and theoretical implications.

The client's expectations have practical implications for the evaluation of the effectiveness of specific therapeutic techniques. Although the outcome of a group treated with a specific technique may be compared with a no-contact control group, in order to rule out the effect of spontaneous changes over time, the use of a no-contact control does not rule out placebo effects. The contribution of the specific technique, over and above the nonspecific effects based on expectations of help, must be evaluated by comparison with an appropriate control group. Ideally, the placebo control group should involve the same degree of enthusiasm, attention, and sincere belief on the part of both the therapist and the patient.

At the same time, expectations of help in psychotherapy should not be viewed as artifacts to be eliminated. Rather, such expectations should be viewed as lawful factors of great importance in achieving the changes desired in all forms of psychotherapy. Real and dramatic anxiety reduction is involved in the placebo effect. Not only does this have a tonic effect on the physical health and psychological outlook of the patient, but it may be a necessary condition for the patient's continuing in therapy and complying with whatever social influence technique is being employed.

The patient's expectations of being helped have been capitalized on in psychotherapy in various beneficial ways. There is a definite need for a type of therapy in which the patient is given enough hope to carry him over a crisis situation. The use of a telephone contact in suicide prevention and the development of walk-in clinics are obvious examples. This is also the most appropriate use for the bulk of the drug therapies. The supportive social therapies involved in Alcoholics Anonymous and similar organizations depend in part on the knowledge that someone is available in a time of crisis. Severely disturbed patients might be helped by having a readily available hospital facility to which the patient could go for a few hours or days without red tape.

Although there is relatively little hard data on the long-range effects of receiving help, it does not seem logical to expect that most placebos will continue to be effective over long periods of time. Pharmacological placebos go out of style rather rapidly. Even the reassurance of a good physician tends to habituate after a while. The pathetic rounds of some patients who journey from doctor to doctor seeking some new panacea testify to the limitations of the placebo as a long-term, all-purpose cure for even the most suggestible. Therefore, we do not recommend exclusive reliance on placebos; instead, it is suggested that a patient's expectations of change be used as a powerful tool for introducing other procedures that will result in more general and permanent changes.

Nonconfirming Experiences

Most patients have many nonadaptive beliefs about the world. These beliefs often play a critical role in creating the problems that bring the individual into therapy. Since all forms of psychotherapy seem to involve changes in belief systems, a powerful tool in therapy is the provision of nonconfirming experiences, as a result of which nonadaptive beliefs can be replaced by more effective ones.

Many years ago, psychoanalysts discovered that simply telling a patient that a belief was not correct was a weak therapeutic technique.

Instead, it was found that such a belief could be more effectively and permanently changed by a succession of nonconfirming experiences in the therapeutic interaction. Such changes in beliefs can be seen in traditional psychotherapy in the reduction in anxiety about sexual matters that results from experiences with a permissive therapist. The patient evidently believes that people in general, or perhaps authority figures, will be punitive in their reactions to his sexual thoughts and desires. The permissiveness of the therapist is a nonconfirming experience, just as experimental extinction is to the laboratory subject.

Traditional psychotherapy relies heavily on passive nonconfirming experiences similar to experimental extinction. Some of the more existential therapies seem to rely on the active nonconfirming experiences involved in confrontations with the patient. Such a confrontation might involve a direct attack on beliefs or a comparison of patient and therapist beliefs. Techniques along this line seem to be involved in the more dramatic types of therapy, such as direct analysis and rational-emotive psychotherapy.

Behavioral techniques also involve changes in strongly held beliefs. Systematic desensitization, implosive therapy, vicarious desensitization, and similar techniques provide dramatic demonstrations that the feared stimuli need not necessarily have an overwhelming and disorganizing effect on the patient. Operant therapy provides an excellent way of changing many beliefs the person has about environmental contingencies. For example, the hospitalized patient may learn that certain contingencies will result in successful living on the ward; he may learn that sensible talk will get him attention. Finally, aversion therapy may change the patient's belief about the involuntary nature of his behavior. The very act of beginning therapy may indicate to the patient that some people believe that he can change and live more effectively.

Group therapy offers many opportunities for nonconfirming experiences. As discussion becomes more open, group therapy provides numerous experiences that are inconsistent with many of the patient's beliefs. Most individuals believe that their problems are unique. One of the most general and significant results of group therapy is the inevitable discovery of the commonality of human thoughts and feelings, problems, and aspirations. The group is also an excellent place for the patient to change his beliefs about the way other people view him. Every group therapist has seen the shocked reaction of a patient who thinks of himself as pitiful and inadequate, when he is told that he is envied by another member of the group who feels that his problems are worse.

Nearly all therapists make use of nonconfirming experiences that happen to the patient outside of therapy. Nonconfirming experiences may occur fortuitously; at other times, the therapist may suggest that the patient seek such experiences. This suggestive approach has its dangers—a supposedly nonconfirming experience may turn out to be a confirming one. The shy lad who is encouraged to call up a girl may get a rebuff. In fact, in order to avoid the occurrence of such confirming events, behavioral therapists originally recommended the construction of fear hierarchies in systematic desensitization. Therefore, we would suggest a conservative use of direct suggestion. Such a tactic is best employed when the patient and the situation are well-known to the therapist, and the outcome of the suggestion is not in great doubt.

Informational Learning

Too much significance seems to be attached to alleged critical incidents or events in psychotherapy at the same time that the more frequent and prosaic conversations between patient and therapist are neglected. Through these regular conversations, patient and therapist often gain many new experiences. The therapist learns about a variety of subcultures, occupations, and family interactions, and meets many interesting individuals with whom he would not otherwise have contact. The patient, in turn, is exposed to a sophisticated individual who may provide, among other things, a model of an effective person. An upwardly mobile lower-class patient may obtain his first genuine understanding of upper-middle-class mores from the therapist. Many patients, particularly in group therapy, learn as much about the behavior of others as they learn about themselves.

The process of transmitting information through communicative exchanges occurs in all forms of psychotherapy. As indicated earlier, the values of the successful patient tend to move closer to those of the therapist, even in client-centered therapy. Most therapists also take it upon themselves to provide information, ranging from sexual interpretations and instructions to existential philosophy. In behavioral therapy, specific assertive techniques are often taught in a direct fashion. However, it is likely that the relevance and usefulness of this process of information transmission can be improved greatly by recognizing its importance and creating techniques that directly facilitate the acquisition of significant knowledge.

It appears that the role of informational learning has not been adequately emphasized, particularly with regard to the study of interpersonal behavior. Informational learning can be achieved in a variety of ways—from directive, didactic lectures to group therapy. Even the quaint mental health movies have been found to be useful in orienting naive lower-class patients to psychotherapy and in training psychiatric aides. A more sophisticated approach might be even more useful.

There is a strong tradition in the mental health field of keeping diagnostic information away from patients. While there may be some instances in which the sharing of information with a patient could have negative consequences, it is possible that the general phobic reaction of diagnosticians to such sharing is as inappropriate as the fear of symptom substitution. On the other hand, quite positive effects might result from the use of diagnostic and related information in changing beliefs and attitudes of the patient.

A clinical colleague reported one incident in which the accidental sharing of information had a beneficial effect on a boy who had been failing in school. The pattern of failure had begun after the divorce of the parents, but by the time of referral the school considered the boy a problem, and he was convinced that he could not cope with his schoolwork. Through an administrative error, the psychologist's report to the school came into the hands of the boy. The psychologist had stated quite simply in the report that the boy had no genuine intellectual problem and that his emotional difficulties were easily traceable to the upset of the divorce. Furthermore, the report said that if everyone would relax a bit the boy's problems would very likely clear up. The boy was strongly moved by the report he received by mistake. He carried it in his pocket at all times, and showed it to his teachers and friends. Although the psychologist was initially disturbed by the loss of the report, he was deeply impressed by the subsequent positive change in the boy's feelings about himself and his schoolwork.

There are, of course, different kinds of diagnostic reports and different kinds of diagnosticians. Just as there are facilitative and nonfacilitative therapists, there are probably facilitative and nonfacilitative diagnosticians. Our diagnostician above showed evidence in his behavior and in his report of warmth, empathy, and sensitivity.

It might be useful to develop a program in which the diagnostic process would be viewed as a form of behavior modification. Such a program might involve the sharing of information from intelligence, aptitude, and interest tests. This is now frequently done in counseling psychology. The program might go further by sharing information about the individual's general functioning and interpersonal behavior, and providing suggestions for more effective living. Such a use of personality tests would quickly induce a trend towards more relevant instruments and evaluations.

In general, more direct feedback could be given the patient concerning his interpersonal relations. Many therapists now provide their patients with some feedback about the social meaning of their behavior. However, few do this systematically. Creative use could be made of tape recordings, motion pictures, and video tapes that allow instant replay. Behavioral ratings by staff and patients might be employed also. These measures could be repeated periodically in order to provide an indicator of whether the patient is adopting new patterns of behavior. A therapeutic program that included such techniques might be a powerful way of impressing the patient with the efficacy of new modes of living and of his ability to change his behavior.

It might be possible also to effect changes in

feelings about the self through exposure to relevant information. For example, a frank discussion between parents about their child could be replayed later for the child with the permission of the parents, and vice versa. Perceptions of the self might be altered also by having a patient listen to a staff conference about him, as we have seen ourselves. Viewing a sociogram of one's social or business group might be similarly enlightening. Of course, these procedures must be used judiciously and within a generally supportive context.

Changes in Self-Concept

Among the most important beliefs dealt with in psychotherapy are those concerned with the client himself. Most patients in psychotherapy have problems involving low self-esteem, and behavioral patterns that attempt to avoid feelings of low self-esteem. Patients frequently believe that they are not capable of dealing with their problems; that they are not able to love and are not worthy of being loved; and that they have fixed and unchangeable personality characteristics of an undesirable nature. Successful therapy of any kind seems to involve changes in such beliefs.

Among the traditional therapies, the client-centered approach has most explicitly emphasized the importance of positive changes in self-concept. In fact, members of this group have used such changes in self-concept as the chief criterion of successful outcome. According to client-centered theory, these changes come about more or less spontaneously when the therapist creates an atmosphere of trust and respect. The recent work on facilitative conditions and successful outcome in several types of traditional therapy is somewhat supportive of the client-centered approach. However, the client-centered theory appears to have considerable limitations. A more detailed analysis of the specific processes involved in changes in self-evaluation seems necessary.

To begin with, self-esteem may be enhanced simply by the acceptance of a client in therapy and the continued acceptance of him by the therapist as the client reveals what he believes are negative things about himself. Thus, changes in self-esteem may occur as a result of the placebo phenomenon and the nonconfirming

experiences mentioned earlier. The client comes to believe that he has some redeeming qualities, since the therapist continues to accept and respect him, in spite of his negative characteristics and many failures. Since nearly all therapists adopt this sort of accepting, supportive, and permissive stance, a general enhancement of self-esteem may be viewed as a common ingredient in all therapy.

However, our analysis has indicated that the client-centered therapist does more than create a general atmosphere. He uses his approval also and, more generally, his facilitating communications in a systematic and reinforcing way. Thus, he shapes the attitudes and behaviors shown by the client. As the client changes, he receives more and more positive communications from the therapist and, possibly, from other significant people, and this process results in greater self-esteem. Thus, as the client shows more personal independence he earns more respect and respects himself more.

There is another aspect to the problem of implicit therapist expectations. As mentioned previously, the perception by the client that the therapist expects change implies that the therapist believes that such change is possible. This nonconfirming experience may have a powerful effect on the client who believes that he is incapable of independent action, competence at work, or satisfactory sexual relations. In fact, successful therapy may not be possible without the therapist communicating some hopeful belief about the client's ability to modify his behavior.

This analysis of changes in beliefs about the self in client-centered therapy could be extended to all forms of traditional therapy. On the other hand, behavioral therapies do not deal specifically with phenomena of this sort. However, as we have seen, there is much evidence that changes in beliefs about the self are quite significant in behavioral therapy and possibly of critical importance.

Perhaps the clearest example of the effect of changes in beliefs about the self in behavioral psychotherapy is the study previously cited of Valins and Ray (1967), in which a decrease in overt phobic behavior occurred as a result of the presentation of falsified information about the subject's autonomic reactions to the phobic object. The subject was led to believe that he could cope with the phobic object. The results strongly suggest that the critical factor in systematic desensitization therapy is a change in beliefs about the self—similar to that occurring in traditional therapy—rather than the mechanics of relaxation, hierarchies, images, and so on. Patients who have been successfully desensitized often talk about their increased self-confidence. It is quite likely that such increased self-confidence is the primary factor accounting for patients' reports of decreases in unrelated fears and difficulties. The mastery of a long-term phobia, even a minor one, forces the individual to change his beliefs about what he can and cannot do.

Other forms of behavioral therapy also involve changes in self-concept. Operant techniques may produce changes that lead to increased feelings of competence. A particularly promising technique is training in self-reinforcement. The self-reinforcement procedure appears to teach the patient how to examine, evaluate, and modify his own behavior. This sort of procedure is particularly valuable because the patient, quite literally, can take it with him when he leaves therapy. There may be a great many other ways of training individuals to monitor their own behavior. Finally, we have seen that aversion therapy may involve a concrete demonstration that the person can control his behavior. In all of these behavioral techniques, as with traditional methods, the expectations and beliefs of the therapist about the person's ability to change have a powerful influence on the person's self-confidence.

Social Reinforcement and Social Influence

Reinforcement effects resulting from therapist interventions can be demonstrated in all forms of psychotherapy. We have already mentioned that verbal approval and facilitative communications are used selectively in client-centered, dynamic, and eclectic psychotherapy with predictable effects on the verbal behavior of the patient during therapy. Many interpretive remarks by the therapist function as positive or negative reinforcers. The theoretical significance of these research findings is that all therapy involves social influence through the contingent use of the therapist's verbal and nonverbal

reinforcing behavior. There has been a great amount of resistance to these findings and their implications. It seems likely that more progress could be made by accepting the role of social influence in psychotherapy, and systematically using such influence, than by attempting to purge psychotherapy of one of its central factors.

Behavioral therapy, of course, involves reinforcement. Reinforcement effects may be observed in systematic desensitization and in aversion therapy, as well as in operant therapy. We have shown that much of the progress made by a patient in systematic desensitization results from the use of social reinforcement and social influence by the therapist in modifying the patient's beliefs and emotional reactions.

Although reinforcement effects have been demonstrated in many treatment procedures, our analysis of laboratory and therapy research using operant techniques suggests that operant learning theory must be modified. It seems that much of the learning that occurs in human operant conditioning is cognitive learning involving the acquisition, modification, and elimination of beliefs by the use of social reinforcement and social influence procedures. Behavior is guided by such beliefs and belief changes. Operant conditioning can be viewed as a method for transmitting information as well as for providing motivational incentives for controlling behavior. The informational aspect of reinforcement is particularly clear in the case of verbal reinforcement.

Verbal reinforcement, viewed largely as a means of transmitting information, would seem to be particularly useful with noncommunicative patients. On the other hand, more direct methods appear to be better suited for dealing with other types of patients. These more direct methods include instructional sets and modeling. Both of these methods are promising means of teaching patients and of modifying behavior.

The results of our analysis have shown also that verbal reinforcement in psychotherapy occurs in the context of the therapeutic relationship. The important point seems to be that the therapist is communicating his views and expectations through his verbal responses. The patient uses these cues to modify his behavior. The patient seems to be motivated to maintain the respect, goodwill, and affection of the therapist. The basic emotional reinforcement involved in the relationship appears to be important so that the patient remains in therapy and makes progress. Ultimately, of course, the patient must seek basic emotional reinforcement in his own life situation outside of psychotherapy.

The therapeutic relationship appears to be important in behavioral as well as in traditional psychotherapy. This is most eloquently demonstrated in the social development of the autistic child in the context of the therapeutic relationship. The child seems to find a new kind of security in human relationships and, as a result, changes greatly. It seems that all therapeutic approaches might be most effectively viewed in terms of the nature of the therapeutic relationship involved. We would encourage experimentation with different types and grouping of human relationships. The various milieu therapies, sensitivity groups, and experimental communities sprouting throughout the nation are attempting very positive things along these lines. These efforts should be encouraged, but at the same time systematic scientific evaluation of these groups should be performed.

The Interpersonal Meaning of Behavior

We indicated earlier that we are attempting to present some of the significant factors of a modern social learning approach but are not presenting a finished system. We would like to emphasize this again. The understanding of complex social behavior is probably more in its infancy than any of us would care to admit. In considering our review of psychotherapy, we were surprised to discover how little investigation there has been of the social and interpersonal meaning of psychopathology and psychotherapy. As an illustration of the primitive state of knowledge in this area, let us consider how a communications analyst such as Haley (1963) would look at some of the behavior that has been considered.

Haley can be described as a radical social behaviorist. His basic unit of analysis is the way individuals communicate with each other within the framework of a social relationship. It is through such communication that a relationship is defined. Communicative messages may be transmitted in four modes or levels simul-

taneously: words, vocal and linguistic patterns, bodily movements, and the context in which these take place. Messages at different levels may be congruent or dissonant.

Haley has applied this communications model to psychopathology. A symptom is viewed as a tactic through which an individual attempts to control the definition of a relationship. The communication may be paradoxical in that the individual performs the response but denies responsibility for the action. Haley gives as an example the case of a woman who was dominated by her authoritarian husband. The wife was unable to oppose her husband on any issue except one, a hand-washing compulsion that she had developed. The husband forbade her to wash her hands. He also hid the soap and followed her around the house. He was unsuccessful, and the woman continued to protest that she could not help herself.

Haley's view of this series of events is quite different from that of the psychoanalyst who might view the situation in terms of guilt, repression, and so on, or the behavioral therapist who might view the problem as one of eliminating an operant. Haley points out that both of these interpretations miss the most important factor in the situation. The wife was able to foil her husband completely with this symptom. She could not clean the house as he wished; she could not wash the dishes; she could not go out. It is this understanding of the interpersonal meaning of behavior that is missing from most traditional and behavioral analyses.

Haley also applies this communications model to a wide variety of psychotherapeutic procedures, including hypnotism, directive therapy, nondirective therapy, psychoanalysis, group therapy, behavior therapy, marriage counseling, and family therapy. He describes the types of maneuvers that occur in therapy as attempts to define who is in control of the relationship. The therapist's goal is a behavioral change. However, he does not achieve this through insight, emotional counterconditioning, or any other internal process, but rather through exposing the patient to a series of paradoxical situations within the therapy encounter.

Thus, Haley suggests that the changes that occur in psychoanalysis are not due to self-exploration, as Freud and other analysts thought, but are byproducts of the interpersonal situation in which self-exploration occurs. Psychoanalysis is a basically paradoxical situation. As Haley sees it:

The patient comes to the nondirective psychoanalytic therapist, an authority who can tell him what to do to solve his problems, and is instructed to indicate everything that happens with the therapist. He is directed to communicate in other than his usual way by not using his symptomatic behavior and by communicating free associations and dreams. He must "voluntarily" change his type of maneuvering on the basis of minimal indications from the therapist, he is prevented from using the therapist's type of maneuvers by the structure of the situation, and usually his attempts to win control are anticipated in such a way that the therapist can label them as resistance to treatment (Haley, 1963, p. 80).

So, too, Haley views Wolpe's systematic desensitization as involving paradoxes. As was pointed out earlier, when a patient is advised to enter an anxiety-arousing situation voluntarily in order to decrease his anxiety, he has been given a paradoxical communication. The desensitization procedure is described as follows:

The problem posed the patient is a most paradoxical one. He enters treatment to recover from, and therefore to avoid, feeling anxious. He is asked to think about those situations which provoke him to feel anxious. . . . Yet he is not allowed to feel anxious. If he exhibits the least anxiety, the treatment session is stopped. When this occurs, he must return again, paying an additional fee, and again be faced with a situation which makes him anxious. Yet if he becomes anxious, he is again dismissed and must return. Faced with a benevolent therapist who is placing him through an anxiety arousal ordeal, the patient is forbidden to feel anxious, and the procedure will only be terminated when the symptoms cease (Haley, 1963, p. 62).

Haley's analysis of psychopathology and the various forms of psychotherapy may not turn out to be fully accurate upon closer experimental investigation. However, his novel approach clearly illustrates the limitations of our current conceptions. An adequate model of social learning in psychotherapy will have to deal directly with the interpersonal meaning of behavior.

Concluding Remarks

We have stressed the role of social influence in modifying the beliefs, emotions, and motivations of individuals. Psychotherapy has been viewed in this chapter primarily as a set of social influence techniques in which the individual's beliefs about himself and others are modified, resulting in behavioral and emotional changes.

We have called for a liberalization of current conceptions. However, it may be that current theories are so far from adequate that only a framework radically different from any now known will suffice. For example, the importance of social influence in psychotherapy implies that an adequate analysis of the rules and mores of society and the way society influences its members is essential in order to properly understand psychotherapy. How many current theories, no matter how liberally stretched, could integrate such an account into their conceptual frameworks?

It seems to us that, given the current state of theory in psychotherapy, it is undesirable to be overly committed to any single theoretical position. In our analysis, each theoretical framework has been found to be inadequate. It seems undesirable to maintain a fixed position by attempting to make the exciting and complex social learning laboratory called psychotherapy conform to any set of simplistic notions. We need many more investigations that explore experimentally and empirically the range of relevant cognitive, emotional, motivational, personality, and interpersonal variables that operate simultaneously in psychotherapy. Until these complexities are unraveled, it is doubtful that any theory can be adequate; however, out of such intensive long-range investigations, an adequate understanding of psychotherapy may some day emerge.

REFERENCES

Adams, J. K. Laboratory studies of behavior without awareness. *Psychological Bulletin*, 1957, **54**, 383–405.

Alexander, F. The dynamics of psychotherapy in the light of learning theory. *American Journal of Psychiatry*, 1963, **201**, 440–448.

Anant, S. S. Comment on "A follow-up of alcoholics treated by behavior therapy." *Behaviour Research and Therapy*, 1968, **6**, 133.

Ashem, B., and Donner, L. Covert sensitization with alcoholics: A controlled replication. *Behaviour Research and Therapy*, 1968, **6**, 7–12.

Bachrach, A. J., Erwin, W. J., and Mohr, J. P. The control of eating behavior in an anorexic by operant conditioning techniques. In L. P. Ullmann and L. Krasner (Eds.), *Case studies in behavior modification.* New York: Holt, Rinehart and Winston, 1965. Pp. 153–163.

Bandura, A. Psychotherapist's anxiety level, self-insight, and psychotherapeutic competence. *Journal of Abnormal and Social Psychology*, 1956, **52**, 333–337.

Bandura, A. Behavioral modification through modeling procedures. In L. Krasner and L. P. Ullmann (Eds.), *Research in behavior modification.* New York: Holt, Rinehart and Winston, 1965. Pp. 310–340.

Bandura, A. Modeling approaches to the modification of phobic disorders. In *CIBA foundation symposium: The role of learning in psychotherapy.* London: Churchill, in press.

Bandura, A., Blanchard, E. B., and Ritter, B. Relative efficacy of desensitization and modeling approaches for inducing behavioral affective, and attitudinal changes. *Journal of Personality and Social Psychology*, 1969, **13**, 173–199.

Bandura, A., Grusec, J. E., and Menlove, F. L. Vicarious extinction of avoidance behavior. *Journal of Personality and Social Psychology*, 1967, **5**, 16–23.

Bandura, A., Lipscher, D. H., and Miller, P. E. Psychotherapists' approach-avoidance reactions to patients' expressions of hostility. *Journal of Consulting Psychology*, 1960, **24**, 1–8.

Bandura, A., and Menlove, F. L. Factors determining vicarious extinction of avoidance behavior through symbolic modeling. *Journal of Personality and Social Psychology*, 1968, **8**, 99–108.

Battig, W. F. Evidence for coding processes in "rote" paired associate learning. *Journal of Verbal Learning and Verbal Behavior*, 1966, **5**, 177–181.

Berenson, B. G., and Carkhuff, R. R. *Sources of gain in counseling and psychotherapy.* New York: Holt, Rinehart and Winston, 1967.

Bijou, S. W., and Orlando, R. Rapid development of multiple-schedule performances with retarded children. In L. P. Ullmann and L. Krasner (Eds.), *Case studies in behavior modification.* New York: Holt, Rinehart and Winston, 1965. Pp. 339–347.

Binder, A., McConnell, D., and Sjoholm, N. A. Verbal conditioning as a function of experimenter characteristics. *Journal of Abnormal and Social Psychology*, 1957, **55**, 309–314.

Bohn, M. J. Therapist responses to hostility and dependency as a function of training. *Journal of Consulting Psychology*, 1967, **31**, 195–198.

Breger, L., and McGaugh, L. L. A critique and reformulation of "learning theory" approaches. *Psychological Bulletin*, 1965, **63**, 338–358.

Breger, L., and McGaugh, J. L. Learning theory and behavior therapy: A reply to Rachman and Eysenck. *Psychological Bulletin*, 1966, **65**, 170–173.

Bruner, J. S., Goodnow, J. J., and Austin, G. A. *A study of thinking.* New York: Wiley, 1956.

Caracena, P. F. Elicitation of dependency expressions in the initial stage of psychotherapy. *Journal of Counseling Psychology*, 1965, **12**, 268–274.

Carlin, A. S., and Armstrong, H. E. "Aversive conditioning": Learning or dissonance reduction. *Journal of Consulting and Clinical Psychology*, 1968, **32**, 674–678.

Cautela, J. R. Covert sensitization. *Psychological Reports*, 1967, **20**, 459–468.

Cautela, J. R. Treatment of compulsive behavior by covert sensitization. *Psychological Record*, 1966, **16**, 33–41.

Clifford, T. Extinction following continuous reward and latent extinction. *Journal of Experimental Psychology*, 1964, **68**, 456–465.

Cohen, R. The effects of group interaction and progressive hierarchy presentation on desensitization of text anxiety. *Behaviour Research and Therapy*, 1969, **7**, 15–26.

Cooke, G. The efficacy of two desensitization procedures: An analogue study. *Behaviour Research and Therapy*, 1966, **4**, 17–24.

Cooke, G. Evaluation of the efficacy of the components of reciprocal inhibition psychotherapy. *Journal of Abnormal Psychology*, 1968, **73**, 464–467.

Cordaro, L., and Ison, J. R. Observer bias in classical conditioning of the planarian. *Psychological Reports*, 1963, **13**, 787–789.

Dallett, K. M. Implicit mediators in paired-associate learning. *Journal of Verbal Learning and Verbal Behavior*, 1964, **3**, 209–214.

Davison, G. C. Systematic desensitization as a counterconditioning process. *Journal of Abnormal Psychology*, 1968, **73**, 91–99.

DeNike, L. D. The temporal relationship between awareness and performance in verbal conditioning. *Journal of Experimental Psychology*, 1964, **68**, 521–529.

Dittes, J. E. Extinction during psychotherapy of GSR accompanying "embarrassing" statements. *Journal of Abnormal and Social Psychology*, 1957, **54**, 187–191. (a).

Dittes, J. E. Galvanic skin response as a measure of patient's reaction to therapist's permissiveness. *Journal of Abnormal and Social Psychology*, 1957, **55**, 295–303. (b).

Dollard, J., and Miller, N. E. *Personality and psychotherapy.* New York: McGraw–Hill, 1950.

Dulany, D. E. The place of hypotheses and intentions: An analysis of verbal control in verbal conditioning. In C. W. Eriksen (Ed.), *Behavior and awareness.* Durham: Duke University Press, 1962. Pp. 102–139.

D'Zurilla, T. J. Persuasion and praise as techniques for modifying verbal behavior in a "real-life" group setting. *Journal of Abnormal Psychology*, 1966, **71**, 369–376.

Ellis, A. *Reason and emotion in psychotherapy.* New York: Lyle Stuart, 1962.

Eriksen, C. W. Figments, fantasies, and follies: A search for the subconscious mind. In C. W. Eriksen (Ed.), *Behavior and awareness.* Durham: Duke University Press, 1962. Pp. 3–26.

Eysenck, H. J. (Ed.). *Behavior therapy and the neuroses.* New York: Pergamon, 1960.

Eysenck, H. J. *Use and abuses of psychology.* Harmondsworth, Middlesex: Penguin Books, 1953.

Feldman, J. Simulation of behavior in the binary choice experiment. *Proceedings of the 1961 Western Joint Computer Conference.* New York: IRE, 1961. Pp. 133–144.

Feldman, J. Computer simulation of cognitive processes. In H. Borko (Ed.), *Computer applications in the behavioral sciences.* Englewood Cliffs: Prentice–Hall, 1962.

Feldman, M. P. Aversion therapy for sexual deviations: A critical review. *Psychological Bulletin*, 1966, **65**, 65–79.

Feldman, M. P., and MacCulloch, M. J. The application of anticipatory avoidance learning to the treatment of homosexuality. 1. Theory, technique, and preliminary results. *Behaviour Research and Therapy*, 1965, **2**, 165–183.

Folkins, C. H., Lawson, K. D., Opton, F. M., Jr., and Lazarus, R. S. Desensitization and the experimental reduction of threat. *Journal of Abnormal Psychology*, 1968, **73**, 100–113.

Frank, J. D. *Persuasion and healing.* Baltimore: Johns Hopkins, 1961.

Franks, C. M. Behavior therapy, the principles of conditioning and the treatment of the alcoholic. *Quarterly Journal of Studies of Alcohol*, 1963, **24**, 511–529.

Geer, J. H., and Turtletaub, A. Fear reduction following observation of a model. *Journal of Personality and Social Psychology*, 1967, **6**, 327–331.

Gelder, M. G., Marks, I. M., and Wolff, H. N. Desensitization and psychotherapy in the treatment of phobic states. A controlled inquiry. *British Journal of Psychiatry*, 1967, **113**, 53–73.

Giebink, W., Stover, D. O., and Fahl, M. A. Teaching adaptive responses to frustration to emotionally disturbed boys. *Journal of Consulting and Clinical Psychology*, 1968, **32**, 366–368.

Gold, S., and Neufeld, I. L. A learning approach to the treatment of homosexuality. *Behavior Research and Therapy*, 1965, **2**, 201–204.

Goldstein, A. P. *Therapist-patient expectancies in psychotherapy.* New York: Pergamon 1962.

Greenspoon, J. Verbal conditioning and clinical psychology. In A. J. Bachrach (Ed.), *Experimental foundations of clinical psychology.* New York: Basic Books, 1962. Pp. 510–553.

Greenwald, H. (Ed.), *Active Psychotherapy.* New York: Atherton, 1967.

Gregory, H. H. Applications of learning theory concepts in the management of stuttering. In H. H. Gregory (Ed.), *Learning theory and stuttering therapy.* Evanston: Northwestern University Press, 1968. Pp. 107–128.

Grings, W. W. Verbal-perceptual factors in the conditioning of autonomic responses. In W. F. Prokasy (Ed.), *Classical conditioning.* New York: Appleton–Century–Crofts, 1965. Pp. 71–89.

Gormezano, I. Classical conditioning. In J. B. Sidowski (Ed.), *Experimental methods and instrumentation in psychology.* New York: McGraw–Hill, 1966. Pp. 385–420.

Haley, J. *Strategies of psychotherapy.* New York: Grune and Stratton, 1963.

Hogan, R. A., and Krichner, J. H. Implosive, eclectic verbal, and bibliotherapy in the treatment of fears of snakes. *Behaviour Research and Therapy*, 1968, **6**, 167–171.

Hogan, R. A., and Kirchner, J. H. Preliminary report of the extinction of learned fears via short-term imposive therapy. *Journal of Abnormal Psychology*, 1967, **72**, 106–109.

Howe, E. S. Anxiety-arousal and specificity: Rated correlates of the depth of interpretive statements. *Journal of Consulting Psychology*, 1962, **26**, 178–184.

Hunt, E. B. *Concept learning: An information processing problem.* New York: Wiley, 1962.

Hunt, E. B., Marin, J., and Stone, P. *Experiments in induction.* New York: Academic Press, 1966.

Jacobson, L. I., The effects of awareness, problem solving ability, and task difficulty on the acquisition and extinction of verbal behavior. *Journal of Experimental Research in Personality*, 1969, 3, 206-213.

Jacobson, L. I., Berger, S. E., Bergman, R. L., Millham, J., and Greeson, L. E. Intelligence and the development of learning sets in preschool children from poverty backgrounds. In *NASA research reports.* No. 1. Miami: Cognitive and Language Development Laboratory, University of Miami, 1969.

Jacobson, L. I., Dickinson, T. C., Fleishman, J. M., and Haraguchi, R. S. The relationship of intelligence and mediating processes to concept learning. *Journal of Educational Psychology*, 1969, **60**, 109–112.

Jacobson, L. I., Elenewski, J. J., and Lordahl, D. S. The relationship between rote learning and mediated and nonmediated concept learning. *Psychonomic Science*, 1968, **10**, 347–348.

Jacobson, L. I., Elenewski, J. J., Lordahl, D. S., and Liroff, J. H. The role of creativity and intelligence in conceptualization. *Journal of Personality and Social Psychology*, 1968, **10**, 431–436.

Jacobson, L. I., Millham, J., and Berger, S. E. Individual differences in information processing during concept learning. *Psychonomic Science*, 1969, **14**, 287–289.

Kagan, J. Acquisition and significance of sex typing and sex role identity. In M. L. and L. W. Hoffman (Eds.), *Review of child development research*, New York: Russell Sage, 1964.

Kahn, M., and Baker, B. Desensitization with minimal therapist contact. *Journal of Abnormal Psychology*, 1968, **73**, 198–200.

Kalish, H. J. Behavior therapy. In B. B. Wolman (Ed.), *Handbook of clinical psychology*. New York: McGraw–Hill, 1965. Pp. 1230–1253.

Kanfer, F. H., and Phillips, J. S. Behavior therapy: A panacea for all ills or a passing fancy? *Archives of General Psychiatry*, 1966, **15**, 114–128.

Katkin, E. S., Risk, R. T., and Spielberger, C. D. The effects of experimenter status and subject awareness on verbal conditioning. *Journal of Experimental Research in Personality*, 1966, **1**, 153–160.

Kelly, G. A. *The psychology of personal constructs*. New York: Norton, 1955.

Keutzer, C. S. Behavior modification of smoking: The experimental investigation of diverse techniques. *Behaviour Research and Therapy*, 1968, **6**, 137–157.

King, D. L. A review and interpretation of some aspects of the infant-mother relationship in mammals and birds. *Psychological Bulletin*, 1966, **65**, 143–155.

King, G. F., Armitage, S. G., and Tilton, J. R. A therapeutic approach to schizophrenics of extreme pathology. *Journal of Abnormal and Social Psychology*, 1960, **61**, 276–286.

Klein, B., and Weiner, M. Awareness in the "learning without awareness" paradigm. *Journal of Experimental Research in Personality*, 1966, **1**, 145–152.

Krasner, L. Studies of the conditioning of verbal behavior. *Psychological Bulletin*, 1958, **55**, 148–170.

Krasner, L. The therapist as a social reinforcement machine. In H. H. Strupp and L. Luporsky (Eds.), *Research in psychotherapy*. Vol. II. Washington, D.C.: American Psychological Association, 1962. Pp. 61–94.

Krasner, L., and Ullmann, L. P. *Research in behavior modification*. New York: Holt, Rinehart and Winston, 1965.

Krasner, L., Ullmann, L. P., Weiss, R. L., and Collins, B. J. Responsivity to verbal conditioning as a function of three different examiners. *Journal of Clinical Psychology*, 1961, **17**, 411–415.

Kushner, M., and Sandler, J. Aversion therapy and the concept of punishment. *Behaviour Research and Therapy*, 1966, **4**, 179–186.

Lang, P. J., Lazovik, A. D., and Reynolds, D. J. Desensitization, suggestibility, and pseudotherapy. *Journal of Abnormal Psychology*, 1965, **70**, 395–402.

Lang, P. J. Fear reduction and fear behavior: Problems in treating a construct. In J. M. Shlien (Ed.), *Research in psychotherapy*. Vol. III. Washington, D.C.: American Psychological Association, 1968. Pp. 90–102.

Leff, R. Behavior modification and the psychoses of childhood: A review. *Psychological Bulletin*, 1968, **69**, 396–409.

Levis, D. J., and Carrera, R. N. Effects of ten hours of implosive therapy in the treatment of outpatients: A preliminary report. *Journal of Abnormal Psychology*, 1967, **72**, 504–508.

Liberman, R. A view of behavior modification projects in California. *Behaviour Research and Therapy*, 1968, **6**, 331–341.

Liberman, R. Aversive conditioning of drug addicts: A pilot study. *Behaviour Research and Therapy*, 1968, **6**, 229–231.

London, P. *The modes and morals of psychotherapy*. New York: Holt, Rinehart and Winston, 1964.

Lovaas, O. I. Some studies on the treatment of childhood schizophrenia. In J. Schlein (Ed.), *Research in psychotherapy*. Vol. III. Washington, D.C.: American Psychological Association, 1968, Pp. 103–121.

Madill, M. F., Campbell, D., Laverty, S. G., Sanderson, K. E., and Vanderwater, S. L. Aversion treatment of alcoholics by succinylcholine-induced apneic paralysis. *Quarterly Journal of Studies of Alcohol*, 1966, **27**, 483–509.

Mandler, G. Verbal learning. In G. Mandler *et al.*, *New directions in psychology III*. New York: Holt, Rinehart and Winston, 1967. Pp. 1–50.

Marcia, J. E., Rubin, B. M., and Efran, J. S. Systematic desensitization: Expectancy change or counterconditioning? *Journal of Abnormal Psychology*, 1969, **74**, 382–387.

Matarazzo, J. D., Saslow, G., and Pareis, E. N. Verbal conditioning of two response classes: Some methodological considerations. *Journal of Abnormal and Social Psychology*, 1960, **61**, 190–206.

McGuire, R. J., Carlisle, J. M., and Young, B. G. Sexual deviations as conditioned behavior: An hypothesis. *Behaviour Research and Therapy*, 1965, **2**, 185–190.

McGuire, W. J. A multiprocess model for paired-associate learning. *Journal of Experimental Psychology*, 1961, **62**, 335–347.

Merbaum, M., and Lukens, H. C. Effects of instructions, elicitations, and reinforcements in the manipulation of affective behavior. *Journal of Abnormal Psychology*, 1968, **73**, 376–380.

Merbaum, M., and Southwell, E. A. Conditioning of affective self-references as a function of the discriminative characteristics of experimenter intervention. *Journal of Abnormal Psychology*, 1965, **70**, 180–187.

Miller, G. A. The magical number seven, plus or minus two: Some limits on our capacity for processing information. *Psychological Review*, 1956, **63**, 81–96.

Millham, J., Jacobson, L. I., and Berger, S. E. Individual differences in strategies of information processing during concept learning. Paper presented at the meetings of the Eastern Psychological Association, Philadelphia, April, 1969.

Milmoe, S., Rosenthal, R., Blane, H. T., Chafetz, M. E., and Wolf, I. The doctor's voice: Postdictor of successful referral of alcoholic patients. *Journal of Abnormal Psychology*, 1967, **72**, 78–84.

Morgenstern, F. S., Pearce, J. F., and Rees, W. L. Predicting the outcome of behavior therapy by psychological tests. *Behaviour Research and Therapy*, 1965, **2**, 191–200.

Murray, E. J. A case study in a behavioral analysis of psychotherapy. *Journal of Abnormal and Social Psychology*, 1954, **29**, 305–310.

Murray, E. J. A content–analysis method for studying psychotherapy. *Psychological Monographs*, 1956, **70** (13, Whole No. 420).

Murray, E. J. Direct analysis from the viewpoint of learning theory. *Journal of Consulting Psychology*, 1962, **26**, 226–231.

Murray, E. J. Learning theory and psychotherapy: Biotropic versus sociotropic approaches. *Journal of Counseling Psychology*, 1963, **10**, 250–255.

Murray, E. J. Sociotropic-learning approach to psychotherapy. In P. Worchel and D. Byrne (Eds.), *Personality change*. New York: Wiley, 1964. Pp. 249–288.

Murray, E. J. Conflict: Psychological aspects. In *International encyclopedia of the social sciences*. New York: Crowell–Collier and Macmillan, 1968. Pp. 220–226.

Murray, E. J. Social learning, personality change, and psychotherapy. In H. H. Gregory (Ed.), *Learning theory and stuttering therapy*. Evanston: Northwestern University, 1968. Pp. 21–51. (a).

Murray, E. J. Verbal reinforcement in psychotherapy. *Journal of Consulting and Clinical Psychology*, 1968, **32**, 243–246. (b).

Murray, E. J., Auld, F., and White, A. M. A psychotherapy case showing progress by no decrease in the discomfort-relief quotient. *Journal of Consulting Psychology*, 1954, **18**, 349–353.

Newell, A., and Simon, H. A. The simulation of human thought. In W. Dennis (Ed.), *Current trends in psychological theory*. Pittsburgh: University of Pittsburgh Press, 1961.

Newell, A., and Simon, H. A. GPS, a program that simulates human thought. In E. A. Feigenbaum and J. Feldman (Eds.), *Computers and thought*. New York: McGraw-Hill, 1963.

Noblin, C. D., Timmons, E. P., and Kael, H. C. Differential effects of positive and negative verbal reinforcement on psychoanalytic character types. *Journal of Personality and Social Psychology*, 1966, **4**, 224–228.

Ober, D. C. Modification of smoking behavior. *Journal of Consulting and Clinical Psychology*, 1968, **32**, 543–549.

Osler, S. F., and Fivel, M. W. Concept attainment. I. The role of age and intelligence in concept attainment by induction. *Journal of Experimental Psychology*, 1961, **62**, 1–8.

Osler, S. F., and Trautman, G. E. Concept attainment. II. Effect of stimulus complexity upon concept attainment at two levels of intelligence. *Journal of Experimental Psychology*, 1961, **62**, 9–13.

Paivio, A., and Madigan, S. A. Imagery and association value in paired associate learning. *Journal of Experimental Psychology*, 1968, **76**, 35–39.

Paivio, A., Yuille, J. C., and Madigan, S. A. Concreteness, imagery, and meaningfulness values for 925 nouns. *Journal of Experimental Psychology* (Monog. Suppl.), 1968, **76**, 1–25.

Paul, G. L. *Insight versus desensitization in psychotherapy:* An experiment in anxiety-reduction. Stanford: Stanford University, 1966.

Paul, G. L. Insight versus desensitization in psychotherapy two years after termination. *Journal of Consulting Psychology*, 1967, **31**, 333–348.

Paul, G. L. Two-year follow-up of systematic desensitization in therapy groups. *Journal of Abnormal Psychology*, 1968, **73**, 119–130.

Paul, G., Eriksen, C. W., and Humphreys, L. G. Use of temperature stress with cool air reinforcement for human operant conditioning. *Journal of Experimental Psychology*, 1962, **64**, 329–335.

Peterson, D. R., and London, P. A role for cognition in the behavioral treatment of a child's eliminative disturbance. In L. P. Ullmann and L. Krasner (Eds.), *Case studies in behavior modification*. New York: Holt, Rinehart and Winston, 1965. Pp. 289–295.

Prokasy, W. F. (Ed.). *Classical conditioning*. New York: Appleton–Century–Crofts, 1965.

Rachman, S. Aversion therapy: Chemical or electrical? *Behaviour Research and Therapy*, 1965, **2**, 289–299.

Rachman, S. The role of muscular relaxation in desensitization therapy. *Behavior Research and Therapy*, 1968, **6**, 159–166.

Rachman, S. Systematic desensitization. *Psychological Bulletin*, 1967, **67**, 93–103.

Rachman, S., and Eysenck, H. J. Reply to a "critique and reformulation" of behavior therapy. *Psychological Bulletin*, 1966, **65**, 165–169.

Ramsay, R. W., and Van Velzen, V. Behavior therapy for sexual perversions. *Behaviour Research and Therapy*, 1968, **6**, 233.

Rapaport, D. A critique of Dollard and Miller's "Personality and Psychotherapy." *American Journal of Orthopsychiatry*, 1953, **23**, 204–208.

Ratliff, R. G., and Stein, N. H. Treatment of neurodermatitis by behavior therapy: A case study. *Behaviour Research and Therapy*, 1968, **6**, 397–399.

Raymond, M. J. Case of fetishism treated by aversion therapy. *British Medical Journal*, 1956, **2**, 854–856.

Rehm, L. P., and Marston, A. R. Reduction of social anxiety through modification of self-reinforcement: An instigation therapy technique. *Journal of Consulting and Clinical Psychology*, 1968, **32**, 565–574.

Ritter, B. The group desensitization of children's snake phobias using vicarious and contact desensitization procedures. *Behavionr Research and Therapy*, 1968, **6**, 1–6.

Rogers, C. R. *Counseling and psychotherapy*. Boston: Houghton Mifflin, 1942.

Rogers, C. R. The process equation in psychotherapy. *American Journal of Psychotherapy*, 1961, **15**, 27–45.

Rosenthal, D. Changes in some moral values following psychotherapy. *Journal of Consulting Psychology*, 1955, **19**, 431–436.

Rosenthal, R. *Experimenter effects in behavioral research*. New York: Appleton–Century–Crofts, 1966.

Rosenthal, R , and Jacobson, L. *Pygmalion in the classroom*. New York: Holt, Rinehart and Winston, 1968.

Rosenthal, R., and Lawson, R. A longitudinal study of the effects of experimenter bias on the operant learning of laboratory rats. *Journal of Psychiatric Research*, 1964, **2**, 61–72.

Ross, L. Eyelid conditioning as a tool in psychological research: Some problems and prospects. In W. F. Prokasy (Ed.), *Classical conditioning*. New York: Appleton–Century–Crofts, 1965. Pp. 249–268.

Rotter, J. B. *Social learning and clinical psychology*. Englewood Cliffs, New Jersey: Prentice–Hall, 1954.

Sabatasso, A. P., and Jacobson, L. I. Case report: Use of behavioral therapy in the reinstatement of verbal behavior in a mute psychotic with chronic brain syndrome. *Journal of Abnormal Psychology*, 1970, in press.

Salzinger, K. Experimental manipulation of verbal behavior: A review. *Journal of General Psychology*, 1959, **61**, 65–94.

Sapolsky, A. Effect of interpersonal relationships upon verbal conditioning. *Journal of Abnormal and Social Psychology*, 1960, **60**, 241–246.

Sarason, I. G., and Ganzer, V. J. Social influence techniques in clinical and community psychology. In C. D. Spielberger (Ed.), *Current topics in clinical and community psychology*. New York: Academic Press, in press.

Schwitzgebel, R. K., and Traugott, M. Initial note on the placebo effect of machines. *Behavioral Science*, 1968, **13**, 267–273.

Shoben, E. J. Psychotherapy as a problem in learning theory. *Psychological Bulletin*, 1949, **46**, 366–393.

Simon, H. A., and Feigenbaum, E. A. An information-processing theory of some effects of similarity, familiarization, and meaningfulness in verbal learning. *Journal of Verbal Learning and Verbal Behavior*, 1964, **3**, 385–396.

Spence, J. T., Goodstein, L. D., and Lair, C. V. Rote learning in schizophrenic and normal subjects under positive and negative reinforcement conditions. *Journal of Abnormal Psychology*, 1965, **70**, 251–261.

Spence, K. W. Cognitive and drive factors in the extinction of the conditioned eye blink in human subjects. *Psychological Review*, 1966, **73**, 445–458.

Spence, K. W., and Ross, L. E. A methodological study of the form and latency of eyelid responses in conditioning. *Journal of Experimental Psychology*, 1959, **58**, 376–381.

Spence, K. W., Rutledge, E. F., and Talbott, J. H. Effect of number of acquisition trials and the presence or absence of the UCS on extinction of the eyelid CR. *Journal of Experimental Psychology*, 1963, **66**, 286–291.

Spence, K. W., and Taylor, J. A. Anxiety and strength of the UCS as determiners of the amount of eyelid conditioning. *Journal of Experimental Psychology*, 1951, **42**, 183–188.

Spielberger, C. D. The role of awareness in verbal conditioning. In C. W. Eriksen (Ed.), *Behavior and awareness*. Durham: Duke University Press, 1962. Pp. 73–101.

Spielberger, C. D., and DeNike, L. D. Descriptive behaviorism versus cognitive theory in verbal operant conditioning. *Psychological Review*, 1966, **73**, 306–326.

Stampfl, T. G., and Levis, D. J. Essentials of implosive therapy: A learning-theory-based psychodynamic behavioral therapy. *Journal of Abnormal Psychology*, 1967, **72**, 496–503.

Sulzer, E. S. Behavior modification in adult psychiatric patients. In L. P. Ullmann and L. Krasner (Eds.), *Case studies in behavior modification*. New York: Holt, Rinehart and Winston, 1965. Pp. 196–200.

Thorpe, J. G., Schmidt, E., Brown, P. T., and Castell, D. Aversion-relief therapy: A new method for general application. *Behaviour Research and Therapy*, 1964, **2**, 71–82.

Timmons, E. O., and Noblin, C. D. The differential performance of orals and anals in a verbal conditioning paradigm. *Journal of Consulting Psychology*, 1963, **27**, 383–386.

Timmons, E. L., Noblin, C. D., Adams, H. E., and Butler, J. R. Operant conditioning with schizophrenics comparing verbal reinforcers versus psychoanalytic interpretations: Differential extinction effects. *Journal of Personality and Social Psychology*, 1965, **1**, 373–377.

Truax, C. B. Reinforcement and nonreinforcement in Rogerian psychotherapy. *Journal of Abnormal Psychology*, 1966, **71**, 1–9.

Truax, C. B. Therapist interpersonal reinforcement of client self-exploration and therapeutic outcome in group psychotherapy. *Journal of Counseling Psychology*, 1968, **15**, 225–231.

Truax, C. B., and Carkhuff, R. R. Significant developments in psychotherapy research. In L. E. Abt and B. F. Reiss (Eds.), *Progress in clinical psychology*. New York: Grune and Stratton, 1964.

Truax, C. B., and Carkhuff, R. R. *Toward effective counseling and psychotherapy: Training and practice*. Chicago: Aldine, 1967.

Truax, C. B., Wargo, D. G., Frank, J. D., Imber, S. D., Battle, C. C., Hoehn-Saric, R., Nash, E. H., and Stone, A. R. Therapist empathy, genuineness, and warmth and patient therapeutic outcome. *Journal of Consulting Psychology*, 1966, **30**, 395–401.

Ullmann, L. P., and Krasner, L. *Case studies in behavior modification.* New York: Holt, Rinehart and Winston, 1965.

Underwood, B. J. The representativeness of rote verbal learning. In A. W. Melton (Ed.), *Categories of human learning.* New York: Academic Press, 1964. Pp. 47–78.

Underwood, B. J., and Schulz, R. W. *Meaningfulness and verbal learning.* Philadelphia: Lippincott, 1960.

Valins, S., and Ray, A. A. Effects of cognitive desensitization on avoidance behavior. *Journal of Personality and Social Psychology,* 1967, **7,** 345–350.

Varble, D. L. Relationship between the therapists' approach-avoidance reactions to hostility and client behavior in therapy. *Journal of Consulting and Clinical Psychology,* 1968, **32,** 237–242.

Wagner, M. K., and Cauthen, N. R. A comparison of reciprocal inhibition and operant conditioning in the systematic desensitization of a fear of snakes. *Behaviour Research and Therapy,* 1968, **6,** 225–227.

Weinstein, W. K., and Lawson, R. The effect of experimentally-induced "awareness" upon performance in free-operant verbal conditioning and on subsequent tests of "awareness." *Journal of Psychology,* 1963, **56,** 203–211.

Wiest, W. M. Some recent criticisms of behaviorism and learning theory with special reference to Breger and McGaugh and to Chomsky. *Psychological Bulletin,* 1967, **67,** 214–225.

Wilde, G. J. S. Behavior therapy for addicted cigarette smokers: A preliminary investigation. *Behaviour Research and Therapy,* 1964, **2,** 107–109.

Williams, R. I., and Blanton, R. L. Verbal conditioning in a psychotherapeutic situation. *Behaviour Research and Therapy,* 1968, **6,** 97–103.

Wilson, G. T., Hannon, A. E., and Evans, W. I. M. Behavior therapy and the therapist-patient relationship. *Journal of Consulting and Clinical Psychology,* 1968, **32,** 103–109.

Winder, C. L., Ahmad, F. Z., Bandura, A., and Rau, L. C. Dependency of patients, psychotherapists' responses, and aspects of psychotherapy. *Journal of Consulting Psychology,* 1962, **26,** 129–134.

Wolpe, J. *Psychotherapy by reciprocal inhibition.* Stanford: Stanford University Press, 1958.

Wolpe, J., and Lazarus, A. A. *Behavior therapy techniques.* New York: Pergamon, 1966.

Wolpin, M., and Raines, J. Visual imagery, expected roles and extinction as possible factors in reducing fear and avoidance behavior. *Behaviour Research and Therapy,* 1966, **4,** 25–37.

Zeisset, R. M. Desensitization and relaxation in the modification of psychiatric patients' interview behavior. *Journal of Abnormal Psychology,* 1968. **73,** 18–24.

THERAPEUTIC APPROACHES TO THE HOME, FAMILY, SCHOOL, GROUP, ORGANIZATION, AND COMMUNITY

19

BEHAVIORAL INTERVENTION PROCEDURES IN THE CLASSROOM AND IN THE HOME[1]

G. R. PATTERSON

UNIVERSITY OF OREGON AND OREGON RESEARCH INSTITUTE

The behavior modifiers working within the settings of the classroom and the home operate on a set of implicit assumptions about behavior and social engineering that should probably be explicated at the outset. Most investigators working within the operant framework assume that the behavior of the child is primarily under the control of reinforcing contingencies supplied by the environment (Skinner, 1953). This is not to say that a child does not think, that he does not "feel," or that some of these "inner variables" do not control some of the child's behavior. While some investigators may indeed conceptualize the Law of Effect as being a necessary and sufficient condition for alterations in behavior, most investigators seem to believe

that reinforcement is neither necessary nor sufficient, but rather, that it is a significant variable. In fact, most of the variables held most dear by psychologists would belong in the same category; that is, motivational states and strategies are not necessary and sufficient conditions for behavior change, either.

At the level of social engineering, the question is, rather, how effectively reinforcement contingencies can be manipulated in altering the behavior of the child. As a research tactic, one may carry out these manipulations without, in any sense, assuming he possesses a complete theory of behavior.

The stress laid upon reinforcing contingencies leads in turn to a focus upon the parameters

[1] The preparation of this manuscript was partially financed by PHS 13330 and MH 15985.

that govern the dispensers of these reinforcers. These "dispensers" are the people who constitute the social environment for the deviant child. Presumably, it is they who shape and maintain his deviant behavior. This being the case, then it would follow that the focus for intervention should be that of attempting to *modify* the *dispensers* who provide these contingencies. One might, therefore, label the group of investigators who work in the classroom and in the home as "dispenser modifiers" in that they introduce procedures which alter the behavior of the peer, the teacher, the parent, and the sibling.

In its broad outlines such an approach constitutes an, as yet, inchoate rapprochement between reinforcement theory on the one hand, and social psychology on the other. There is as yet no articulated theory; rather, it is more the case that each investigator shares the implicit assumption that intervention should occur in the environment in which the child lives, and then sets about devising his own means of bringing this about. In its more sophisticated form this can constitute a "systems" approach to the behavior modification of at least two members of a family or a classroom. In such an approach it is necessary not only to arrange reinforcement schedules provided by the parent, teacher or peer group that will alter the deviant behavior but, in addition, to arrange reinforcing contingencies for simultaneously maintaining the behavior of these dispensers.

There are a set of consistent findings in the research literature that make such preoccupations with altering dyads or systems seem imperative. These are the findings that demonstrate that a wide range of social agents are busily engaged in the process of reinforcing an impressive spectrum of deviant child behaviors. These findings support one of the main assumptions underlying the social-learning approach. *This assumption states that the social environment provides positive social reinforcers contingent upon deviant child behaviors that are sufficient to maintain these behaviors.* The study by Hawkins, Peterson, Schweid, and Bijou (1966) showed

not only that parents provided social reinforcers contingent upon aggressive and negativistic child behaviors, but also that the rates of deviant behavior and positive reinforcers tended to covary over days (the correlation was .39). The report by Patterson, Ray, and Shaw (1968) provided data based upon ten hours of baseline study for each of seven homes that had produced deviant children. The data showed that the family members provided attention, interest, approval, or positive physical contact contingent upon the occurrence of such out-of-control behaviors as yelling, hitting, teasing, and noncompliance. The average proportion of such deviant responses reinforced by these families for the deviant child during the baseline period were .43, .44, .01, .36, .14, .22, and .22. With one exception, these are impressively rich schedules of positive reinforcement, and more than sufficient (apparently) to offset the schedules of aversive consequences also supplied for these same behaviors.[2] The aversive consequences were usually rather mild and consisted of such responses as nagging, scolding, or threats; it was seldom that the parents actually used high-intensity aversive consequences such as hitting. The proportion of deviant behaviors for which the family supplied aversive consequences were .20, .13, .10, .52, .43, .13, and .33. Similar findings were reported for autistic children and their mothers in an observation study by Ray (1965).

These data are suggestive in indicating that social reinforcers are probably being supplied by parents and siblings for an impressive variety of deviant child behaviors. These findings also suggest that something as prosaic as a smile, a nod, or "attending," while typically overlooked in man's search for explanations, may come to occupy the main focus in planning intervention programs. While at first blush we may seem to do little but "unearth the commonplace," if these commonplace contingencies are not altered, then the effects of intervention programs will likely be short-lived.

The sections that follow outline some procedures that have been developed, by and large

---

[2] It is interesting in this regard to note that the child receiving positive reinforcement for only 1 percent of his deviant behavior displayed the lowest rate of deviant behavior observed in any home thus far (less than .10 responses per minute). Although the child displayed high rates of out-of-control behaviors in the school, he did not do so in the home.

within the last decade, for altering the behavior of the significant "others" who interact with the deviant child. The first section describes procedures for training family members; the second outlines procedures for training teachers and members of the peer group.

TRAINING FAMILY MEMBERS

The emphasis upon working with the family, rather than just the deviant child, has of course been a traditional feature of both the case work and the traditional psychiatric approach as reflected in the American Orthopsychiatric Association. The approaches taken in working with the families have traditionally varied from psychoanalytic (Ackerman, 1958) to emphasis upon family roles (Bell, 1962) and, more recently, communication networks (Haley, 1963).

These approaches would assume that deviant child behavior is the outcome of some underlying neurotic conflict in one or more of the parents (Ackerman, 1958) or some disruptions in roles, with the accompanying disruptions in communications among family members (Haley, 1963). Within the traditional framework it would be assumed that long-term changes in deviant child behavior could be brought about only as a function of alterations in these underlying conflicts within the family.

Contemporary behaviorists would tend to question both of these assumptions. The research literature reviewed by Fontana (1966) supports the growing suspicion entertained by many investigators that "neuroses," or underlying conflicts, are neither necessary nor sufficient conditions for producing deviant child behavior. There are a number of conditions under which the family members might provide the reinforcing contingencies necessary to the acquisition and maintenance of deviant child behavior, but, as outlined by Patterson & Reid (1970), they are not necessary outcomes of underlying pathology. For this reason it is also assumed not only that is it possible to train family members to alter these reinforcement schedules, which will in turn reduce the rate of deviant behavior, but also that these alterations will not be accompanied by increases in other forms of pathology (symptom substitution). In

this sense, the issue of symptom substitution becomes a crucial assumption held by the traditional family therapies, for if the speculations about antecedents of deviant child behaviors are correct, then one would predict that failure to resolve the underlying conflicts would result in little or no change in the overall rate of deviant child behavior.

Other than the content of their speculations about the antecedents of deviant child behavior, probably one of the main differences between traditional family therapies and current behavior modification lies in their relative commitment, or lack of commitment, to behavioristic tenets. Perhaps the only enduring features of the activities of contemporary behavior modifiers will be the dual themes of "testability" and "data" that comprise such a large component of the standard litany. Most of the investigators make strenuous efforts to present variables that lend themselves to observation and to the production of data. It is of course these data that determine the behavior of the scientist in making decisions about the significance of a variable, or the success of a treatment outcome. Behavior modification is little more than a reasonable extrapolation of behaviorist tenets to investigations of clinical problems.

In the earlier published reports, behavior modifiers concerned themselves with training parents to handle relatively simple child behaviors, and most of the training was carried out in the clinician's office. Perhaps the classic example of this was the study by Williams (1959), in which the parents were trained to discontinue providing social reinforcers for the child's temper tantrums. The training was carried out in a brief series of interviews in the psychologist's office. The duration of tantrums each night decreased at very little investment of professional time. Shah (1967) also described procedures for training a mother to alter both her own assaultive behavior and the acting-out behavior of the child. Again, the training took place during interviews in the psychologist's office. The general trend has been to develop more powerful procedures than the interview for training the parent. For example, as a next stage of development, some investigators made provision for the parent to imitate the experimenter. The parents learned by observing the behaviors of the experimenters as they altered the behavior of the child in the playroom (Straughan, 1964).

Laboratory Training. While talking to parents in an interview or modelling appropriate interactions may indeed alter the reinforcement schedules used by some parents, it seems likely that more powerful procedures will be needed to control the behavior of many parents who come seeking assistance. Much closer supervision might be required, for example, for training procedures in which the parents produce responses that can then be shaped and supported. Such careful training could be carried out either in the home or in the laboratory attached to the clinic. This could include careful training in discriminating among various parent and child behaviors as was done by Martin (1967) and Kaswan, Love, and Rodnick (1968). Training the parent (in six sessions) to attend carefully to his own behavior as well as that of the child produced significant changes in the family interactions in the laboratory, and these alterations were accompanied by changes in child behaviors in the classroom as reflected in teachers' ratings (Martin, 1968). Such changes did not occur in the nontreated control families.

The larger-scale study by Kaswan et al. (1968) also showed alterations in family interaction as a function of fifteen hours of training in the laboratory setting. Observation data and teacher ratings collected in the classroom showed that improvements in both social behavior and grades for the training group were greater than the changes found in groups treated by traditional therapies. Data from nontreated control families were not analyzed in the preliminary report.

These two studies are of particular importance in that they represent a kind of precision teaching process that trains the parent to *attend* more carefully to his behavior and to that of the child. It suggests that one reason for some of the parents' difficulties in training the child is due to faulty tracking of the child's responses and the effect of their own reactions to this behavior. Presumably, the parent must be taught to observe, before he can retrain the child.

Training to observe. The Kansas Medical Center group (Lindsley, 1966) also places particular emphasis upon "pinpointing behavior" and "observing" in their training programs for both parents and teachers. The frame of reference adopted by this group is operant conditioning in contradistinction to the communications and role-theory framework espoused by Kaswan et al. and Martin, but the emphasis upon the importance of careful observation is similar. In the Kansas group, for example, the parent is taught not only to attend but also to graph the data as a means of summarizing the parental observations (Koenig, 1967). The data showed that the simple act of counting behavior served as a mildly aversive consequence for the child and produced significant decreases in rate for about 20 percent of the deviant behaviors investigated (Lindsley, 1966). Thorne, Tharp, and Wetzel (1966), Walder et al. (1967), and Patterson et al. (1968) also emphasized the training of the parent to observe and collect data as being an integral part of the intervention program.

In the example below, a 26-year-old mother of two children (Mrs. S) was referred because the school complained about her son being out of control; recently a friend had described him as being "evil." In the first group session, the necessity for observing and counting child behavior is being discussed with her.

DR. COBB: What you do is collect these data and bring them in, and we'll talk about them and try to find ways that we can change this. After you try these changes that we come up with, then the question is, does it go down to five times a day, once a day, or not at all? What we are collecting data on are very specific things that are giving you trouble.

MISS GULLION: Try to keep a count between now and Tuesday of how many times he bugs you. Count the number of times that he interrupts you when you are talking. . . .

On this data recording sheet you put the date and the time that you start. If it is something that you do not do all day, then you record here the time when the kids get up, or whenever it is that you began to observe. Write the beginning time down here; and then also write down when you stop. For example bed time. Write that down here. That way we can figure out total time in minutes. . . . And the number of whatever you count is over here, just a plain tally. You should have your piece of paper and pencil someplace where it is convenient for you to use it;

or you might use this golf counter so you won't have to worry about the paper and pencil.

MRS. S: OK, but what do I say to him about it?

MISS GULLION: Just tell him that you are keeping track of some things that are going on in the family and that later on he might help you with some of it.

MRS. S: But what if he asks me what I'm counting?

MISS GULLION: That is fine; just tell him that you are counting "bugging," and that each time he does it you make a mark. Sometimes you don't have to plan a program at all; just count it and they find it aversive and stop behaving that way.

MRS. S: Let's see now, I'll count bugging in the morning and then when he gets home from school.

MISS GULLION: Right, and I'll call you every day during this week to see how it is coming along. By the way, are we clear on what bugging is?

MRS. S: Well, it is stuff like when he interrupts other people when they are talking or like when he is calling his sister stupid and. . . .

In our own experience we have found that some parents have enormous difficulty in fulfilling the requirements of collecting observation data. For them, it requires daily telephone calls by the staff to prompt the behavior and to reinforce it if it has occurred. These latter parents are characteristically very diffuse individuals whose behavior demonstrates little stimulus control.

In retrospect, it is strange that the necessity for training parents to observe was not "discovered" earlier. Most parents are not careful observers of their own or their child's behavior; in addition, the language that they use to describe behavior is vague and diffuse. Given this double-layered confusion, it seems unlikely that the psychologists using even the best of all possible theories would have been able to teach parents to alter child behavior.

Training to Reinforce. The next step in the development of systematic programs for retraining parents can be found in the extensive investigations of C. Hanf (1968) with the mothers of physically handicapped children. Similar procedures were used by Bernal, Duryee, Pruett, and Burns (1968) in working with a preschool child. Although neither of these investigators as yet has adopted the technique of training the parent to observe and graph data, both observed parent-child interactions in the laboratory and used this information to teach the parents how to alter their reinforcement contingencies. In the detailed report by Bernal et al. (1968), the mother was trained to partially extinguish the temper tantrums, aggressiveness, and bizarre verbal behavior of her eight-year-old son:

. . . the first step in training was to teach the mother to reduce her verbal output and to selectively ignore all of Jeff's abusive behaviors, from sulking to direct physical assault. This plan was intended to help her make decisions about her own behavior as she and Jeff interacted, and to extinguish his abuse.

Step two was to establish certain maternal behaviors as conditioned negative reinforcers by associating them with physical punishment. The behaviors, or cues, consisted of ignoring abuse and if ignoring did not stop it, the mother was to express anger and order him to stop. Finally, if he did not stop, she was to spank him. Hopefully, these cues, ignoring, frowning, angry tone of voice, the word "don't" etc., if clearly presented and consistently paired with punishment when the boy did not obey, would take on properties of conditioned negative reinforcers. . . .

Preintervention interactions of mother and son were videotaped. These and later tapes were used to teach the mother specific aspects of her interaction that facilitated the output of deviant behavior. Following this instruction, she again interacted with her son. On those occasions that Jeff became abusive, a brief tone was sounded in the room, cueing the mother to produce an aversive consequence. Following each session, the mother was reinforced for those occasions on which she had responded appropriately. Nine training sessions were sufficient to produce dramatic changes in the child's behavior.

Patterson and Brodsky (1966) described a procedure for training the mother to reinforce behaviors, which would compete with the occurrence of fear responses. The mother counterconditioned the behaviors in both the laboratory and in the school. The data showed significant changes in the boy's behavior, which persisted over a follow-up period.

Training in Groups. Wahler (1965), Ray (1965), and Lindsley (1966) have presented brief reports describing attempts to train groups of parents. In Ray's approach, four mothers of atypical (some were autistic) children were observed interacting in their homes, over a series of twelve twenty-minute baseline sessions.

Following this, the mothers participated in a series of five group meetings. At termination, they were again observed for twelve sessions in the home. The group-training sessions made use of programmed materials outlining reinforcement theory and child management principles. The observation data showed several significant changes in the behavior of the mothers, including increases in the frequency of nonaversive initiations from the child and increased responsiveness to nonaversive initiations from the child. They also tended to respond nonaversively even when the child initiated an aversive interchange. The data showed the greatest changes for mothers of nonautistic children. These are very impressive changes in parent behaviors as a function of such a small investment of professional time.

A preliminary report by Lindsley (1966) described group training procedures for fathers of retarded children. Of an original group of 24 volunteers, nine were actually able to pinpoint a problem behavior and introduce contingencies for altering it. Although the data were not presented, the author claimed that 85 percent of the fathers who tried were successful in altering the problem behavior on the first attempt. In addition to these impressive claims for parental effectiveness, Lindsley indicated that three of these fathers went on to organize their own parent groups. The latter seems to be an extremely important innovation in view of the potential contribution to meeting current mental-hygiene needs. For this reason it is particularly unfortunate that adequate data are not presented that would make it possible to evaluate the procedure.

Group training of this kind is currently in extensive use in our University of Oregon laboratories; observation data are being collected in the homes and classrooms to determine its effectiveness. In these procedures, two weeks' baseline observation data are collected in the home, describing family interaction. Following this, the parents respond to a programmed textbook that outlines social learning theory (Patterson & Gullion, 1968). Contingent on their completing this assignment, the professional staff then spends one hour in helping them pinpoint one or two child behaviors and setting up a schedule for the parents to observe

their child's behavior. Daily telephone calls serve both to prompt continued cooperation and to reinforce it when it occurs. Several days of consistently good data earn for the parents the right to enter the group.

The group consists of three to five families, all of which contain at least one child whose behavior represents some extreme of antisocial behavior. Each parent is given thirty minutes in which to present his current data, describe the program used last week, and outline the current management problem. A timing device provides the necessary stimulus control; those parents who have no data (a rare occurrence) must wait until last. All of the group members participate in planning behavior-management programs for each other and in examining the data that are being passed around. Home observations are again made at four and at eight weeks. If at the four-week probe the data show that progress has been made, then arrangements are made for observers to go to the school and to begin collecting the baseline observations that will serve as a basis for classroom intervention programs. However, it is made clear to the parents that they must "earn" this additional involvement. After termination of all programs the families are followed up, systematically, for at least a six-month period. The data collected thus far indicate that these are promising procedures, but as yet no reports have been published that provide the details necessary to evaluate their effectiveness.

It seems likely that some families applying for outpatient assistance in handling their child will find that training in an interview, laboratory, or group situation will be ineffective, simply because the procedures are not systematic enough to control their behavior or because the relevant reinforcing contingencies (for parent and child) cannot be properly presented. The necessity for additional precision in training for such families is provided by having the behavior modifier go into the home and carry out the training program in that setting.

Training in the Home. There are at present seven published reports presenting extensive observation data showing the effects of training the parents in their homes (O'Leary, O'Leary,

& Becker, 1967; Hawkins et al., 1966; Hastings, 1967; Walder et al., 1967; Patterson, Hawkins, McNeal, & Phelps, 1967; Patterson et al., 1968; and Zeilberger, Sampen, & Sloane, 1968). All told, however, these efforts present the results for eighteen families and cover problems primarily concerned with autism (Walder et al., 1967) and conduct-disorder behaviors (O'Leary et al., 1966; Hawkins et al., 1966; Hastings, 1967; Zeilberger et al., 1968; Patterson et al., 1967; and Patterson et al., 1968). Most of the children were of preschool age and none were adolescents.[3] This suggests that the range of problems dealt with has been extremely limited. Of the investigators training parents in the home, Walder et al. (1967), Thorne et al. (1966), and Patterson et al. (1968) have made particular mention of the necessity for training parents to *observe* and to *collect data*.

Each of the investigators varies a good deal in terms of how much formal instruction the parents are given in reinforcement theory and in intervention techniques. In the procedures described by Walder et al. (1967), formal seminars were held with groups of parents who were then supervised in the home. In the procedures used by Ray (1965), Patterson et al. (1967), Hastings (1967), and Patterson et al. (1968), programmed materials that were constructed specifically for parents and teachers, outlined general reinforcement principles. In our experience, only a few parents have changed their behavior as a function of simply reading this material. The most likely function served by the text is that of a catalyst that may accelerate the effect of the supervision of the parent by the professional.

In training the parents, most of the investigators agree in their emphasis upon reducing the reinforcement for deviant behavior. The data showed that such reductions did occur in the reports by Hawkins et al. (1966) and

Patterson et al. (1968). In order to further reduce the strength of deviant behavior, some investigators emphasize the use of "time-out" procedures as a mildly aversive consequence that provides added control (Hawkins et al., 1966; Zeilberger et al., 1968; Patterson et al., 1968; and Wahler, 1968). In applying this technique, the child is placed in a nonreinforcing setting immediately following the occurrence of a deviant response. Typically, he is left there for only five or ten minutes. The parent is instructed to remain calm and to apply the consequence each time the behavior occurs. Wahler (1968) points out that some of the parents he has trained were ineffective in controlling the child with just social reinforcers, and that time out was a necessary adjunct to the program.

All of the investigators make some provision for training the parents to reinforce some set of socially adaptive behaviors that will presumably take the place of the deviant behaviors.[4] While some of the investigators rely solely upon social reinforcers dispensed by the parent, many supplement these consequences with token systems of various kinds. The reason for this is that many deviant children seem relatively nonresponsive to social reinforcers dispensed by adults (Levine & Simmons, 1962; Patterson 1965a; Perkins, 1967) or by parents (Patterson et al., 1967; Wahler, 1967). The rather weak control provided by such consequences would mean that the program would be nonreinforcing for some parents. Therefore, as a means of supporting the behavior of the parent as well as of the deviant child, it seems wise to introduce additional, and presumably more effective, consequences during the earlier phases of the training program. In such a program, the child is given points, as well as social reinforcers, for each occurrence of an adaptive behavior. These points earn such back-up reinforcers as candy,

---

[3] In a series of reports, Thorne et al. (1966, 1967) have outlined a set of procedures by which trained lay personnel go into homes of families who have produced predelinquent boys. The parents are trained to use token systems and social reinforcers to shape adaptive behaviors. They have intervened in 92 cases and have achieved changes in the majority of these families. However, at the time of this writing the data evaluating the program have not been available.

[4] It should be noted that none of the writers suggest that deviant behaviors are completely

extinguished by these training programs. It is implied that these behaviors are simply shifted on the response hierarchy, to be "replaced" (for the time being at least) by responses with much higher probabilities of occurrence. In effect, these behavior-modification procedures make use of an interference theory in which probabilities of occurrence of deviant and adaptive behaviors are shifted *slightly*. These slight shifts, however, are assumed to be sufficient to produce markedly altered reactions from the social environment.

pennies, toys, or trips with the parents. They are tailored to the individual child and altered every few days to minimize satiation.

It is interesting to note that such simple pairing of the behavior of the adult with these massive schedules of nonsocial reinforcers enhances his effectiveness as a social reinforcer, as shown in the carefully controlled studies by Patterson (1965a), Wahler (1967), Perkins (1967), and Patterson et al. (1967). These findings suggest that "responsiveness to social reinforcers" is more akin to a "state variable," and readily effected by relatively simple manipulation. Perhaps it is some aspect of the parents' pattern of aversive interaction with the child that temporarily reduces the effectiveness of social reinforcers dispensed by some parents. Terminating such aversive interactions, and instead establishing their behavior as a discriminative stimulus for massive quantities of nonsocial reinforcers, might then be sufficient to alter that status. The following case illustrates these concepts.

Mrs. W was the twenty-nine-year-old mother of five children. Living alone and supported by welfare, she found herself unable to manage her children. Following baseline observation in the home, it was decided to carry out direct family intervention in the home. The following excerpts are taken from a more detailed report of the program (Patterson et al., 1968).

While talking with Mrs. W about the enuresis program, we constantly were interrupted by the children. They stood quite near their mother simultaneously demanding her attention. They followed her about the house like miniature furies, while she frantically attempted to respond to all of their demands. We labeled the phenomenon the "gnat cloud," since the children were as thick, persistent, and annoying as the cloud of gnats which typically preceed a rainstorm in the tropics.

A series of programs were prepared which would serve both to train Mrs. W to use positive reinforcers to control child behaviors and at the same time to reduce the intensity of the "gnat cloud" phenomenon. As a first step the mother collected data on the frequency with which Walter stood within three feet of her. Two days of baseline data showed that the "proximity response" occurred about nine or ten times each day. The mother was then instructed to use such positive reinforcers as attending, touching, and smiling whenever the

response occurred. Under this conditioning there was a greater than two-fold increase in proximity. On the tenth day the mother was instructed to discontinue the reinforcement and the behavior returned to baseline level.

To the experimenters, these data were a convincing demonstration of the mother's prowess in shaping "proximity behaviors" and also indirect confirmation of her role in generating the "gnat cloud." However, the mother was little impressed with the demonstration and showed no change in her interactions with the children. The "gnat cloud" was omnipresent as was the full repertoire of aversive controlling techniques used by the mother.

... a "mother box" was constructed which contained a collection of inexpensive materials such as clay, crayons, construction paper, pipe cleaners, and blunt nosed scissors. While Mrs. W fixed supper, a chair was placed across the kitchen door, and the children were informed that mother was not to be disturbed. Walter was assigned the role of art instructor for the younger children. He distributed supplies and reinforcement to each child, under the tutelage of E. Walter and the children were told that if they were successful in not interrupting the mother for eight minutes they would earn a number of M & M candies. In each practice session the duration of the training period was increased up to thirty minutes. While the mother was pleased with this device and used it often as a means of turning off the "gnat cloud," the effects did not generalize to the extent of altering the "basic" patterns of interaction.

... To further accelerate the changes in her interaction patterns with the children a procedure was employed which was more expensive in terms of professional time but also one which ensured generalization. One of the staff would simply spend part of the morning following Mrs. W about the house as she interacted with the children. When a "gnat cloud" began to develop she was shown how to interact with, and reinforce, one child at a time. She was also shown how to attend more carefully to each of her children as they behaved reasonably or went about their chores. When she missed an opportunity to reinforce a child this was also pointed out to her. Four such training sessions were held, each consisting of one to two hours.

Figure 19.1 shows the effect of this series of programs in altering the mothering behaviors of Mrs. W. One set of data shows the changes in rate for such aversive consequences provided by the mother as yelling, physical punishment, humiliating, negativism, and ignoring. The second set of data indicates the changes in the rate of angry commands;

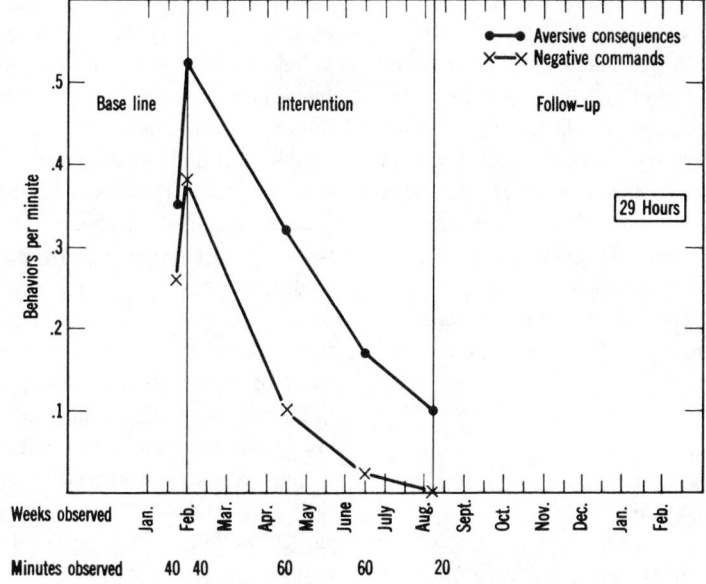

Figure 19.1 The "Xantippe" syndrome.

these are requests which are stated in the form of implied threats.

These data showed an impressive rate of aversive stimuli being dispensed by this mother. During the baseline period she dispensed an average of one such response every one or two minutes! The data for the last three months of intervention indicated approximately an 80 percent drop from this baseline level. This reduction in rate was achieved at a total cost of 29 hours of professional time. The data from the two month follow-up indicated that the results were holding well.

As the use of time out and nonsocial reinforcers bring the behavior under parental control, parents are encouraged to begin fading out these procedures until the child's behavior is being maintained by positive social consequences to be found within the family. In our experience, it is the latter step which has proven to be extremely difficult. Zeilberger et al. (1968) noted the same problem. The parent tends to take the adaptive behavior for granted and "forgets to reinforce it." For this reason, it has been necessary to develop a variety of procedures to emphasize this aspect of the training program. In our own procedures, the parents are called daily on the telephone and asked for descriptions of reinforcers given for adaptive behavior. In some instances the experimenter goes into the home and trains the mother with a "bug-in-the-

ear" radio device as she is interacting with her children. With others, a tape recorder is sent home with the parents and they collect several hours of family interaction, which is then brought into the laboratory, where they are given specific discrimination and modelling training in the use of positive social reinforcers, using the tape as a basis for the training.

Intervention procedures usually produce changes in behavior over a relatively short period. These changes in child behavior are often very reinforcing for the parents; however, the changes are *not reinforcing for all parents*. Some parents participate in the program only because they have been coerced by the court or the school, but they themselves may have little investment in producing behavior change. Other parents seem so little involved with the child that alterations in behavior are simply not effective reinforcers. For such parents, attempts have been made to make money, trips to the hair dresser, or driving lessons contingent upon the *parents'* reinforcement programs for their own deviant children (Patterson et al., 1968; Patterson & Reid, 1970). However, there is more than a reasonable doubt as to the long-term efficiency of such programs, because long-term effects would demand that changes in behavior be supported within the system. In these instances, it is not clear as to what these contingencies might be that will continue to support the agent of change when the formal program is withdrawn. One possibility would be to increase the "sending" status of the child. The child could be taught to be more reinforcing to the parent, on the assumption that this in turn would support the behavior of the parent in continuing the program. Several such attempts have been made; one was apparently successful (Patterson et al., 1968) and one unsuccessful (Patterson & Reid, 1970). This remains a difficult problem at both the conceptual and the engineering level.

CRITIQUE OF FAMILY INTERVENTION PROGRAMS

The studies reported constitute an impressive beginning. Each of the studies offered from ten to thirty hours of observation collected prior to and during intervention, and together they provide a solid basis upon which to build a new technology. The range of problem behaviors sampled by the eighteen families described thus far is too limited a sample to form a basis for comparing the relative efficiencies of behavior modification and traditional therapies. However, there are several features of the two technologies that merit discussion. The two points of comparison that will be considered in this section are "depth versus superficiality" and "traditional assessment versus observation."

Behavior Change as a "Surface" Phenomenon. Perhaps the most typical reaction to materials such as those presented in the preceding section goes something like, "That is just superficial manipulation. It is scientism in the garb of clinical psychology." In considering such reactions, there are several points to keep in mind. One concerns the possibility that the statement is based upon erroneous assumptions about causes of deviant child behavior, and the second concerns the possibility that, in point of fact, the statement may be false.

Our traditional theories about the determinants of social behavior have been such that the stress is almost invariably placed upon internal mediating processes (self, motivational states, conscience, constructs, insights, and the like).

This single-minded focus has lead theory development away from the possibility that the individual is much more responsive to his *immediate social environment*. While the two points of emphasis are not necessarily incompatible, it is unfortunately true that our present rather primitive theories of personality have not generally incorporated both points of view. This being the case, the psychologist conditioned by traditional courses in personality theory is likely to react in predictable fashion to speculations that do not stress the importance of traditional mediational processes. However, questions about determinants of social behavior are decided not by the amplitude of the reactions of piqued scientists but rather by data (in the long run, at least). The data reviewed in an earlier section of this report did support the notion that some deviant behaviors seemed to be supported by the immediate reactions provided by the social environment. While these findings do not constitute confirmation for the general assumption about determinants, they should constitute a sufficient basis for at least withholding judgment on this matter until additional data are obtained. It is possible that the traditional assumptions about social behaviors are oversimplified. There is, for example, the distinct possibility that man's behavior shows small but continuous alterations in the probability of occurrence of any given response. In this case, the concept of *change* becomes a key word in the new look in personality theory, and such variables as "settings" and "situations" become relevant puzzles for investigation (Patterson, & Bechtel 1970).

Whether or not alterations in such processes as "changes in self-concept" or "feelings and conflicts" are necessary antecedents for behavior change, it is conceivable that they are frequent accompaniments of such changes. It is possible, for example, that the traditional personality theories have oversimplified things by laying such stress upon the unilateral relations between internal states, such as "self-concept" and social behavior. It is usually implied that changes in self-concept will be followed by, or accompanied by, alterations in social behavior. However, it is equally reasonable to assume that alterations in social behavior will change the way in which other persons react to the child.

The altered reactions from the social environment may in turn change the way that the child describes himself; it may also change the feelings that he has about other people. As yet, we have no data that provide a rigorous check on this hypothesis, but the "clinical reports" that we obtain from many of these families suggest that it is certainly a reasonable one to investigate. For example, many of the mothers describe their intense negative feelings about these children who are so difficult for them to control. Each week they receive several complaints from the school, the neighbors, or relatives about their child. It is seldom that his behaviors produce reinforcing reactions from the community that would give the mother any satisfaction. As she states it, she literally hates the child. Some parents feel so strongly about this that they cannot use positive social reinforcers during early phases of the intervention program. It is only later, after they see that using such procedures as "time out" or "point systems" will control the child's behavior that they will even begin to use social reinforcers. It is later still that they report feeling differently about the child.

Several families have also noted that, once the programs are in effect, many members of the family seem to be more "giving" to each other. This suggests that, in some families, the effect of a "surface manipulation" may instigate a chain of reactions that results in alterations in family structure. A statistical analysis of several families following intervention indicated that such a possibility was indeed likely (Patterson & Reid, 1970).

Observation as an Alternative to Traditional Assessment. The main assumptions underlying the traditional assessment of personality are, first, that motivational states, defenses, and traits constitute a body of information relevant as explanations for deviant child behavior, and second, that the instruments used in the diagnostic studies are valid measures of these constructs.

The possibility has already been reviewed that not all deviant child behaviors are determined primarily by anxiety, conflicts, faulty defenses, or faulty self-concepts. Reviews of the current assessment literature reveal a growing consensus as to the low proportion of criterion variance accounted for by contemporary personality-measurement devices. Taken together, these trends suggest to the present writer that traditional assessment procedures may be characterized as weak measures of personality theories that are themselves inadequate explanations of deviant child behavior. If either the "weak-measurement" or "weak-theory" criticism is accurate, then it would seem that massive investments of professional time in such enterprises as the traditional diagnostic testing sequence might better be used to either collect more relevant assessment data, or to proceed directly with the matter of treating the child.

Aside from these alleged weaknesses in theory and technology, the traditional personality assessment procedures simply do not provide very much information that is relevant to a social-learning approach to treatment. From this latter viewpoint, the relevant questions are these: What are the rates of occurrence of the deviant child behaviors? What kind of reinforcers are being supplied and by whom? There is little in traditional personality assessment that provides information relevant to either of these questions. Observation procedures do provide information relevant to all three questions, and for this reason have quickly become the assessment procedures of choice to most behavior modifiers. Observed rates of deviant child behavior not only serve to establish the validity, or lack of it, of adult complaints about the child, but also serve as one built-in criterion for assessing the outcome of treatment. It is assumed that deviant child behaviors can be *observed* and *counted*.

While the reliability of observation data is almost invariably very high (Wright, 1960), there are methodological problems associated with its use that should be considered. Perhaps the first consideration is the amount of time involved. These procedures require 10 to 30 hours of observer time, in contrast to the traditional reliance upon rating devices, which require little or no staff time to obtain. For example, simply asking the teacher or parent for a global rating has been a traditional technique for evaluating child therapy. Unfortunately, such "cheap data" has some built-in liabilities. In the first place, there is a growing body of data that demonstrates the general un-reliability of parental reports (Radke-Yarrow, Campbell, & Burton, 1964; Haggard, Brekstad, & Skard, 1960). Not only do parents distort some areas of the report (Haggard et al., 1960), but there are also data that show that different interviewers elicit markedly different reactions (Ward, Beck, Mendelson, Mock, & Erbaugh, 1962). Even assuming that the interview did not produce parental distortions of data, there remains the possibility that parents are not accurate observers of child behavior. It seems likely that the parent report of child behavior provides a global summary that maximizes a few behavioral events rather than serving as an accurate summary of the rates of occurrence of various child behaviors. This may be a reason for findings from a number of studies that showed little relation between parents' reports and behaviors observed in the home (Smith, 1958; Crandal & Preston, 1961; Schalock, 1958; Sears, 1965).

It seems, too, that a parent's global summary of therapy outcomes can be influenced by his wish to please the therapist. For example, in a study by Collins (1966), parents were given to understand that their children were to be en-rolled in a "treatment program"; however, the intervention program was delayed for some weeks, and in the meantime, the parents were asked to provide a second set of ratings. The data showed that the untreated children were perceived by the parents as significantly im-proved! Similar findings were reported in a study by Clement & Milne (1966) which sug-gested that under similar conditions, mothers are likely to bias their statements in favor of improvement. In that study, shy, withdrawn children were assigned to either control or treatment experimental groups. Even though the observation of the behavior of the children assigned to the control group showed no changes, the mothers' reports were consistently biased towards "improvement." In fact, the data for all the groups suggested that the mother reported more changes than were observed.

Taken together, this series of studies would suggest that, while parents' perception of improvements may be easily obtained and even necessary accompaniments of sound clinical intervention, these data may have severe limi-tations as criteria of behavior change. With this in mind, it is perhaps feasible to develop training programs to produce technicians who will collect several hours of observation data in the home and school as part of an assessment program. A large number of studies reviewed by Wright (1960) have established the feasibility of training observers to high levels of reliability. However, a recent study by J. Reid (personal communication) showed that, following success-ful training to high levels of agreement, brief periods of field experience altered the behavior of the observers and produced abrupt decreases in reliability. This suggests the need for con-tinued calibration of the observers through all phases of the study.

In addition, there is the problem of observer bias, which has been noted by many and particularly emphasized by Rosenthal (1966). Such preliminary findings as those presented in well-controlled studies by Scott, Burton, & Radke-Yarrow (1967) and Rapp (cited by Rosenthal, 1966) leave little doubt that the assumptions and expectancies held by the observers lead to distortions in the data. Although the import of these studies is clear, very few investigators currently publishing within the behavior modification enterprise have taken the trouble to keep the observer uninformed (or misinformed) as to the hypo-theses being tested. The research by Ebner (1967), Scott et al. (1967), and Patterson & Brodsky (1966) are exceptions.

In addition to the problem of observer bias, there is the conjoint problem relating to the effect of the observers' presence. In a pilot study reported by Patterson and Reid (1970) a mother was trained to observe interaction in her own family. Following five hours of observation in the home, an "outside observer" collected the same type of data. The presence of the observer produced changes in the rates of positive and aversive consequences supplied by family members. A more recent study, based upon a sample of fifteen families (Patterson & Harris, 1968), also showed that the presence of the observer in the home produced some distortion in estimates of behavioral events. More to the point, the fact that many of the families habituated to the presence of the observer suggested that current behavior modification publications may be *underestimating* the magnitude of intervention effect; more methodological studies are in order before we can be sure of this.

It seems then that a social learning position offers some alternatives, in terms of both a set of eminently testable statements about the antecedents of deviant behavior and an alternative set of assessment procedures. The latter, however, may be a mixed blessing, in view of the methodological problems that have yet to be resolved in the application of observation procedures. The section that follows outlines the applications of social learning principles and observation techniques to yet another social setting, the classroom.

INTERVENTION IN THE CLASSROOM

While much has been written about the classroom milieu, there has been surprisingly little systematic observation of teacher-student interaction. For this reason, there has been little understanding of the process that produces such inefficient control over the social and academic behaviors of children in that setting. Within the context of behavior modification, such ineffective control would be examined in terms of the reinforcement schedules being provided for adaptive and deviant child behaviors by the teacher and by the peer group. For example, one observation study made in the classroom showed that positive social reinforcers dispensed by the teacher were in limited supply, and as likely to be dispensed for deviant as for adaptive child behavior (Hotchkiss, 1966). Reinforcement contingencies are apparently either poorly understood or their importance is not appreciated by teachers. In one study the data showed that the *majority* of teacher attention followed *non*study behavior! (Hall, Lund, & Jackson, 1968.) However, there are wide individual differences among teachers in their reinforcing reactions to both deviant and appropriate child behaviors. In the observation study of two elementary-school teachers by Madsen, Becker, and Thomas (1968), the baseline classroom data showed that one teacher reinforced appropriate

child behavior an average of 19.2 times per 20-minute session, while the comparable frequency for the other teacher was 1.2. These same teachers reinforced inappropriate behaviors an average of 1.9 and 8.7 times during the same time periods.

Observations made in a special classroom showed that a small group of disruptive children monopolized most of the teacher's attention. For these deviant children, the rates of deviant behavior covaried with the rate of teacher attention (Anderson, 1964). This, of course, is a very inefficient use of teacher time; but, as pointed out by Staats (1968), only the very deviant *or* the academically skilled child can consistently produce high rates of teacher attention and interest. *While the middle-class child may have been previously trained to respond under such lean schedules, the culturally deprived child and the "immature" child have not been trained for such skills and are thus unable to secure their share of an already limited supply of social reinforcers available in that setting.* The increasing discrepancy between the environmental demands and the child's repertoire leads to a situation in which the child is probably going to either develop escape and avoidance behaviors or learn some highly coercive methods of forcing the environment to respond. In such an inefficient social system, it is not surprising that it takes the first three or four school years to train many children in the simple skills of "attending" and "working."

Because of the high rates of nonattending behaviors, the deviant child simply does not have time to learn academic skills; most of his time is expended in talking to his neighbor (which *is* reinforcing), walking about the room (which *is* reinforcing), giggling, clowning, or fooling around in his seat (all of which are reinforcing). Presumably, the normal and deviant child differ from each other in the rates with which they emit these and other behaviors (the case of the psychotic or brain-damaged child is not being considered here). The data by Werry and Quay (1968) showed that the deviant child was out of his seat twice as much as the normal child; he made noise twenty times as often and talked out of turn twice as often. While the normal child attended to his task about 77 percent of the time, the deviant child was on task only 53 percent of the time. These data are in essential agreement with the figure of 39 percent provided by Walker, Mattson, and Buckley (1969) for a class of disturbed boys. Similarly, Hamerlynck, Martin, and Rolland (1968) showed that a special class of retarded children spent an average of only 45 percent of their classroom time "on task." Ebner's (1967) observation data also showed very high rates of nonattending behaviors in several classrooms of retarded children.[5]

These facts, taken in conjunction with the preceding point that the classroom provides only weak support for adaptive behaviors, would suggest the main outlines for classroom intervention programs. An effective program would provide some means of reducing the supply of social consequences provided for deviant behavior and increasing the support for adaptive behaviors. The sections that follow outline several different means of accomplishing this dual-purpose program.

Teacher Training

Probably the most parsimonious means of altering the classroom milieu would be to train the teachers, particularly those at the primary level, to apply reinforcement procedures in order to alter deviant behaviors in the children in the first few grades. However, until these principles are built into the teacher-training program, the immediate problem becomes that of constructing training programs that will alter the behavior of teachers who are already in the public school system. For such training programs, there are a series of questions to be considered. First, can the teacher alter deviant behavior in the classroom? Second, what are the reinforcers that will maintain her behavior as she is trained and carries out the program in the classroom? Third, what is the most efficient method of retraining the teacher? In this section, only techniques that rely upon social reinforcers and other natural consequences for controlling the behavior of the child will be considered. Programs in which the teacher is trained to use token systems to alter behavior will be considered in a later section.

As various investigators became involved in the problem of teacher training, "stylistic" differences appeared in their training programs. While most of the programs trained the teachers to use *positive* consequences to control behavior (Krumboltz & Goodwin, 1966; Hall et al., 1968; Thomas, Becker, & Armstrong, 1968), one group of investigators has trained them to use *aversive* consequences (Haughton, 1968; Koenig, 1967). The fact that the two training programs do stress different behavioral control techniques has some rather interesting implications; for this reason they will be considered separately.

There have been a number of procedures developed for the purpose of training teachers to use positive reinforcers. For example, Krumboltz and Goodwin (1966) devised a training film. Other investigators arranged to go into the classroom and provide signals to the teacher for various contingencies (Hall et al., 1968; Becker et al., 1967). Most of the programs make some provision for didactic training; most have used a seminar format (Barclay et al., 1967; Becker et al., 1967; Haughton, 1968; Hewett, Artuso, & Taylor, 1968). There seems to be no consensus as to which of these, singly or in combination, is most efficacious. However, it does seem to be important to actually get the teacher to practice the *behavior* in the classroom rather than just read about or talk about general principles.

Most of these programs train the teacher to use the natural consequences found in the social environment, which could be made contingent upon the child's adaptive classroom behavior. For example, the teacher will be encouraged to use glances, smiles, words denoting approval, or touch, contingent upon academic achievement behaviors or socially appropriate responses (Madsen et al., 1968; Hewett et al., 1968; Valett, 1966; Zimmerman & Zimmerman, 1965). In addition, their training might include the use of point systems that can earn any one of a variety of back-up reinforcers (Hewett, 1968; Valett, 1966).

---

[5] While differences in intellectual ability between normal and retarded children are undoubtedly related to differences in academic skills, these two studies would suggest that the two groups also differ in their rates of "attending" behaviors. This is of some interest, because the evidence suggests that skill in attending or working is not necessarily related to IQ.

With two exceptions, most investigators report successful outcomes for their teacher-training programs in that the programs seem effective in altering classroom behaviors for problem children (Becker, Madson, Arnold, & Thomas, 1967; Hall et al., 1968; Thomas et al., 1968; Madsen, 1968; Hewett et al., 1968). However, two of the earlier investigators reported equivocal success in such training programs (Barclay, 1967; Krumboltz & Goodwin, 1966). It seems that there are several difficulties; one of which is the difficulty that some adults have in using positive reinforcers. For example, Hall et al. (1968) noted that one of the teachers in their training program had particular difficulty in learning to reinforce adaptive behaviors. A study by Madsen et al. (1968) showed that one teacher reinforced adaptive behaviors ten times more than did a second teacher! However, the concomitant problem of providing social reinforcers that still *maintain* the behavior of *the teacher* is even more pressing. Most of the behavior changes reported by investigators in which teachers have been trained to use positive reinforcers showed rather slow changes in behavior. This means that the behavior of the teacher must be maintained for rather lengthy periods of time while these changes accrue. One might think of the combination of slow changes in child behavior, demand for many teacher responses (reinforcers), and the period of one or two week's effort required to produce the change, as constituting programs that are "high response cost" from the teacher's viewpoint.

The question is, "What maintains the behavior of the teacher while she alters the behavior of the child?" In most of the studies, it seems that the investigators supply a great deal of reinforcement for the cooperation of the teacher, including being present in the classroom and reinforcing the teacher for carrying out the program. The research by Brown, Montgomery, and Barclay (1968) suggests that without these reinforcement "props," the teacher's behavior may *not* be maintained. In their study, the teachers carried out a program designed to alter "out-of-seat behavior" for an educationally retarded nine-year-old boy. During a baseline period, the rate of positive reinforcement by the two teachers for in-seat

behavior was recorded, as well as the rate of deviant behavior for the boy. Following this, the teachers were instructed to reinforce him for being in his seat; this second phase was carried out over a period of six days. During this phase, the psychologist reinforced the teachers for *their* reinforcing behavior. During the third phase, the psychologist discontinued his social reinforcement of the teachers; in the fourth phase, he reinstated it again. The data in figure 19.2 show the changes in the contingent reinforcement supplied by the teachers for the child's in seat behavior.

The data show that the reinforcing behavior of the teacher was very clearly under the control of the reinforcing behavior of the psychologist. To those who wish to believe that the behavior of teachers (and parents) is controlled by such abstractions as "love of children" or "duty," these data should be rather disconcerting. Figure 19.3 indicates the impact of the changes in teachers' behavior upon the behavior of the deviant child.

These studies show that it is in fact possible to train teachers to use positive social reinforcers to alter the behavior of children. They also raise the question of how it is that the behavior of the teacher is to be maintained while she carries out the program.

The Kansas group (O. Lindsley) displays a particular genius in working out classroom contingencies that require little response cost and produce rapid changes in child behavior (Haughton, 1968; Koenig, 1967). In this operation, the teacher is first trained in a few hours of lectures and group participation to observe, count, and graph child behavior. Following this operation, the teacher is trained to arrange some mildly aversive natural consequences contingent upon the deviant behavior. For example, "out-of-seat" behaviors might lead the teacher to request that the child write ten spelling words, calculate several arithmetic problems, or wear a mask (Haughton, 1968). Aggressive behavior might lead to a request that the child call his parent and tell her what he has just done. The graphed data produced by a large number of teachers trained in this manner show impressive control over a wide variety of deviant child behaviors and at little response cost to themselves. However, as yet there are no systematic

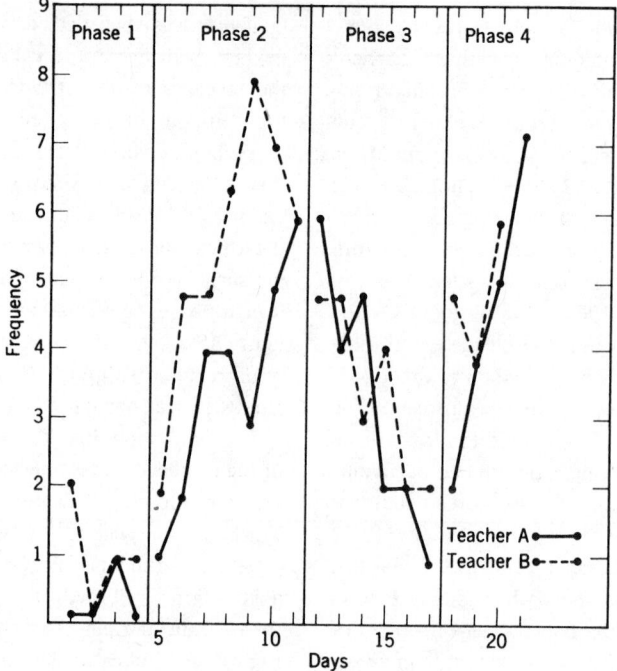

Figure 19.2 Frequency of social reinforcers emitted by teachers.

studies carried out that indicate *how many* teachers trained in this fashion *actually* do *carry out* the programs.

Positive and aversive reinforcement training programs differ along several important dimensions. Although the procedures involving mildly aversive consequences *may* produce more rapid control over the deviant child behavior, no provisions are made in such an approach for teaching the child an alternative mode of producing reinforcers from the environment. In this sense, the child's development of competencies is left to chance rather than being planned. Follow-up data would presumably show that shaping adaptive classroom behaviors would have more lasting effects than just

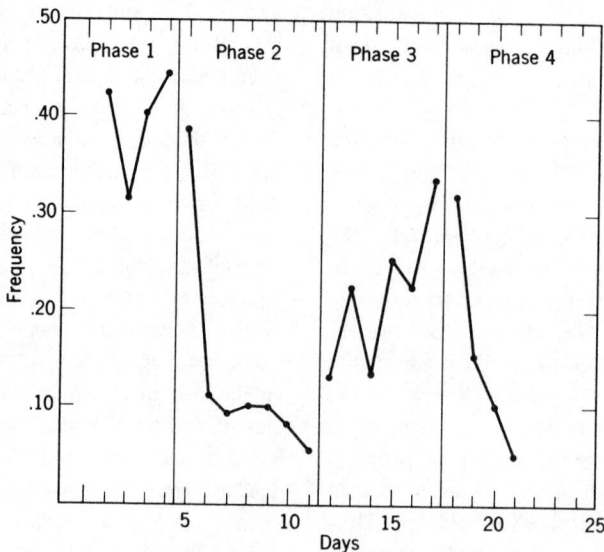

Figure 19.3 Billy's out-of-seat behavior.

decelerating deviant behavior with aversive consequences.

Whether the programs involve positive or aversive consequences, the major problem is to identify the reinforcers that *maintain* the *teacher's behavior during and after* the training program. Because of the high response cost to the teacher, the program utilizing positive consequences will have to pay even more careful attention to the problem than will those programs using aversive consequences. It is the writer's impression that for many teachers, even though either program "works," alterations in child behavior are simply not all that reinforcing for the teacher, and many will not continue to apply the contingencies six months after termination of the training. The long-term effects of such training would probably be more effective if the *teachers' salaries* were contingent partially upon their ability to alter such behavior. For example, the report by Koenig (1967) outlined a procedure for training student teachers in which the teachers' course grades were contingent upon the data showing the effectiveness of their behavior in accelerating academic behaviors of their pupils. Other than this study, the problem of teacher reinforcers has not really been considered; but there is little doubt that it constitutes a key problem in designing engineering programs for the classroom.

It seems likely that it will be possible to retrain some teachers in such a fashion that they can apply these techniques to alter the behavior of children who display moderately high rates of deviant behavior. However, in a situation where the child displays an array of high-rate deviant behaviors, it may be necessary to bring in a behavior modifier who first obtains control of the behavior and then turns the program over to the teacher and the peer group, who can then carry it on at very little response cost. Presumably the initial phases in training such a child may require high expenditure of time, which would be impractical for most teachers. The section that follows outlines some of these direct intervention procedures.

Direct Intervention in the Classroom

The general format for classroom intervention requires that the behavior modifier perform in the classroom rather than in his office, in order to maximize the likelihood that his efforts will be "taken over" by the teacher and peer group. It also requires some set of procedures for dispensing massive amounts of social reinforcers contingent upon socially adaptive behavior. The procedures require some technique for signalling the child, contingent upon the child's emitting adaptive classroom behavior. These signals must of course be presented in such a manner as to be minimally disruptive to the other children in the classroom. Typically the child receives these signals upon a variable interval schedule ranging from a few seconds for the extremely hyperactive child up to sixty seconds for the less deviant child. These signals are typically dispensed by a box placed on the child's desk (Anderson, 1964; Patterson, 1965b; Ebner, 1967; Grindee, 1964) or by radio signals (Patterson, Whittier, Wright, & Jones, 1965; Grindee, 1965; Nixon, 1966; Koenig, 1967). The signals denote that the child has earned a variety of back-up reinforcers ranging from M&M candies (Anderson, 1964; Ebner, 1967; Grindee, 1964; Nixon, 1966) to trinkets (Grindee, 1965) to points for a classroom party. In a number of these studies, the earned back-up reinforcers were divided among the members of the peer group (Anderson, 1964; Patterson et al., 1965; Evans, 1967; Hauck & Haring, 1968) on the assumption that this would produce reactions from the peer group that would accelerate the effects of the program. As yet this assumption has not been empirically tested.

When it is in use, the conditioning device produces very rapid control over the child's behavior. However, a series of ten or more 20-minute conditioning sessions are required to produce changes that *generalize* to occasions when the device is not present.

The results from the first five studies are summarized in the report by Patterson, Shaw, and Ebner (1969), which showed significant generalization for five out of six hyperactive deviant children, some of whom were brain-damaged and retarded. Data from several studies reviewed in that report also showed significant persistence in three out of four cases during follow-up. Observations were also reported for five hyperactive nontreated control subjects; the data showed no significant changes in their behavior.

As shown in the above studies, a range of three to ten hours of professional time produced an average decrease of 20 per cent in the rate of nonattending behaviors from baseline to intervention. However, it seems likely that even these modest reductions would not persist unless the changes in behavior produced sufficient positive social consequences from peers or teacher to maintain them during extended follow-up. There is some reason to believe that in special classes in which many of the children exhibit deviant behavior and presumably reinforce each other on rich schedules for these deviant behaviors, the effects of such a program will be short-lived (Quay, Sprague, Werry, and McQueen, 1967; Ebner, 1967). Perhaps in such a setting, once the behaviors are under control, it will be necessary for the teacher to maintain a token system in order to overcome the effects of the peer reinforcement schedules.

It does seem, however, that ten hours is an unreasonable amount of time to spend on a program that produces only a 20-percent reduction rate in deviant behavior for one child. Certainly, it is necessary to devise intervention procedures that require less investment of professional time and produce a greater magnitude of reduction in deviant behavior. The procedures were altered in such a manner as to produce 40 to 70 percent reductions in rate of deviant behavior at costs ranging from seven to thirty hours (Patterson et al., 1968b). These changes were brought about by the use of "lay" personnel at very early stages of the classroom intervention.

Probably the greatest untapped reservoir of aid for intervention programs lies in the peer group, teacher, and parent; however, only the beginnings have been made in actually involving these agents of change in the classroom setting. In the reports by Patterson (1969) and Patterson et al. (1968), parents were trained to collect observation data in the classroom and to function as reinforcing agents in that setting. This not only reduced the amount of professional time, but also gave the parent training in the application of reinforcement principles. The latter report also described procedures in which the peers functioned as reinforcing agents in using programmed materials to teach the deviant child basic academic skills.

Wahler (1967) demonstrated that preschool peers could shape social behaviors in free settings. Koenig (1967) demonstrated that peers could function in training a child in arithmetic skills. In one program for an isolated child (Patterson & Brodsky, 1966), both the deviant child and the members of the peer group received reinforcements contingent upon appropriate behaviors. The program produced highly significant changes in approach behaviors of both the deviant child and the members of the peer group.

Peers have also been trained to reinforce the child as he progresses through programmed materials in acquiring academic skills (Koenig, 1967; Patterson et al., 1968; Hauck & Haring, 1968). Staats Minke, Goodwin, and Landeen (1967) also described a procedure for training peers and lay adults to reinforce retarded children who were being trained to read. After some thirty hours of conditioning, the experimental group showed significantly greater increases in sight vocabulary than did the control group, which had been enrolled in a traditional training program. Only three or four hours of training were required to prepare the "coaches" for their roles as reinforcing agents.

A successful attempt was also made to train a peer member to use reinforcement and modelling techniques in training a deviant child in a set of social behaviors. As the coach and deviant child progressed in the acquisition of the skill, the whole class earned additional recess time; this latter insured massive support for both coach and deviant child (Patterson & Reid, 1970).

Under certain conditions, the most expedient method for altering the behaviors may be to focus upon an entire group of deviant children in a "token-culture classroom." These procedures and their concomitant data are described in the next section.

Token-Culture Classrooms

In many respects, the most dramatic application of behavior modification principles is to be found in the reports describing the token-culture classroom. Although innovated as recently as 1962–1963, procedures such as those described in the reports by Zimmerman and

Zimmerman (1962), Homme (1963), and Birnbrauer, Bijou, Wolf, and Kidder (1965) have lead to a series of attempts to extrapolate these procedures and to provide extensive data with which to evaluate their efficiency (Haring and Kunzelmann, 1966; Kounin, Friesen, and Norton, 1966; Valett, 1966; Quay, Werry, McQueen, and Sprague, 1966; Hotchkiss, 1966; Hewett, 1967; O'Leary and Becker, 1967; Walker et al., 1969; Clark, Lackowicz, and Wolf, 1967; Hewett, 1967). The sum of evidence from these studies supporting the effectiveness of token systems in altering deviant social behavior for groups of children is overwhelming. While the various programs have displayed some minor differences in terms of the kinds of contingencies being applied to behavior, they are similar enough to be considered as replications. A *series* of replications is, of course, a rare situation in contemporary psychology. These studies, many of which are of high quality, provide observation data that demonstrate significant, and often dramatic, decreases in the rates of deviant classroom behavior for samples of predelinquent boys (Walker et al., 1969), adolescent delinquent boys (Martin, Burkholder, Rosenthal, Tharp, and Thorne, 1968; Clark et al., 1967), emotionally disturbed boys Quay et al., 1966; Hotchkiss, 1966; Haring and Kunzelmann, 1966; O'Leary and Becker, 1967; Hewett, Artuso, and Taylor, 1968, and preschool children (Homme, 1963; Risley, 1968).

The general tactic in these studies has been first to decrease the rate of deviant behaviors and then to introduce contingencies that will strengthen academic skills such as reading, arithmetic, and spelling. These programs are usually carried out by a teacher who has been trained and supervised as a behavior modifier. The length of time that a child is enrolled in such a program is highly variable, and probably largely determined by the degree of control affected over the child's behavior and the practical arrangements necessary to transfer the child "back" to his normal classroom. The program described by Hotchkiss (1966) achieved marked alterations in behavior in something less than 22 days of class sessions. In the token classrooms with the Department of Special Education at the University of Oregon, the data showed that the program effected very rapid

control over deviant behavior (within a few days), but that approximately four weeks of enrollment in the class was necessary before it could be expected that these effects would reliably generalize to the public school classroom (Walker et al., 1969). Perhaps children with higher rates of deviant behavior or organic or autistic impairment would require somewhat longer periods of training.

The reinforcing signals are dispensed by a variety of means and earn a wide variety of "back-up reinforcers." In some of the procedures, the signal was dispensed via a box placed upon the desk of each student. If the student was attending or working at the time the experimenter observed him, he received a signal (Quay et al., 1967). Other children whose behavior does not occur at such high rates may be controlled by signals dispensed on a much leaner schedule, as for example a mark on a card placed on their desk at the *end* of a lesson (O'Leary et al., 1966). For others, each individual child may contribute to a cumulative counter for the entire group, and each individual's contribution to the group total is also recorded (Walker et al., 1969). Hotchkiss' (1966) procedure was similar in that the children received points contingent upon the entire group displaying only adaptive behaviors for a period of time.

As shown in the earlier work of Staats, Staats, Schutz, and Wolf (1962), *just* social reinforcers or just "knowledge of being right" prove to be weak consequences in maintaining the acquisition of reading skills. In working with the academically handicapped, the delinquent, or the emotionally disturbed child, it would seem of particular importance to provide maximum support during the early stages in the acquisition of academic skills. For this reason most classroom programs use both social and nonsocial reinforcing contingencies to support these behaviors. The back-up reinforcers actually used have been candies and pennies (Hotchkiss, 1966; Clark et al., 1967), prizes such as model cars or trinkets (O'Leary et al., 1966; Walker et al., 1968; Staats et al., 1962), and group field trips (Walker et al., 1968). One of the more interesting back-up reinforcers emphasized the natural consequences that can be found in the normal classroom. These would include such things as listening to the phonograph, playing with scientific laboratory equipment, coloring, or reading. Various investigators have displayed great ingenuity in setting up "reinforcement areas" within the classroom (Hewett et al., 1968; Valett, 1966). The child buys time in such areas according to the amount of points that he has earned (Walker et al., 1969; Haring and Kunzelmann, 1966). For some even more difficult cases, such as the adolescent delinquent, it has been necessary to construct special reinforcing contingencies that are tailored to the interests of each child (Martin et al., 1968).

The latter stages of the training program will typically provide for increasingly lean schedules of nonsocial reinforcers to the point where the child's behavior is maintained entirely by natural consequences found in the classroom. This latter stage of training has been followed carefully by only a few investigators as yet (Walker et al., 1969).

Several efforts have also been made not only to reduce the supply of social reinforcers provided for deviant classroom behaviors but also to further decrease their rate of occurrence by arranging for "time out" as a consequence. On each occasion that the child "yells" or "gets out of seat" or in any way disrupts the class, he is placed in a nonreinforcing situation (adjoining room) for ten minutes (Walker et al., 1969; Quay et al., 1966). In a careful analysis of the effects of this program by Walker et al. (1969), the class was first carefully programmed, using a combination of social reinforcers, token-point contingencies, and "time out" as consequences. Once the behavior of the class was characterized by very high rates of attending behavior, "time out" was discontinued as an aversive consequence. This resulted in a loss of control for four of the five deviant children. A comparable attempt that removed token points resulted in no loss in attending behaviors. This analysis suggests that for some high-rate deviant children, the use of "time out" might not only accelerate the obtaining of control of the behavior, but might also be necessary for some time even when the control seems to be relatively good. The reader will recall that Wahler (1968) has also noted that for the high-rate oppositional child, it is necessary for the parent to use *both*

"time out" and reinforcement schedules to control his behavior. It may well be that schools of the future will include plans for both "time out" and reinforcement areas as an integral part of school architecture.

While there are many reports demonstrating decreases in deviant behavior for token classrooms, the data showing increases in academic skills are in more limited supply. The report by Birnbrauer et al. (1965) provided data from one subject; Hotchkiss (1966) provided anecdotal evidence from the teachers and parents suggesting increased academic efficiency. The most recent report by Walker et al. (1969) showed increases in academic scores for five children in a token classroom. Staats et al. (1967) provided data on increases in sight vocabulary as a function of programmed reading instruction for a large group of "nonreaders," using individualized programs of reinforcement. The recent publication by Staats (1968), also described the output from several years of programmatic research, which includes data from working with individual subjects and small groups. This publication constitutes a major contribution in the development of procedures for work with academic skills; however, more data of this type are needed.

A step toward the direction of more controlled research in this area is to be found in the report by Hewett et al. (1968). They compared the relative efficiency of classrooms in which the teachers were trained to use social reinforcers with the efficiency of a classroom in which the teachers used both social reinforcers and "point systems" with back-up reinforcers. Pre- and postachievement testing for arithmetic skills showed a much greater gain for the classroom on the point system than for the classroom on social reinforcement. However, these differences were *not* found in reading achievement.

Critique

It is exciting to be a spectator to the development of techniques that are appropriate for the classroom setting. As more investigators become involved, the rate of publication of high-quality data is increasing, as are the listing of various techniques found to be effective in altering child behavior. The status of the literature in this section should not be described as "a promising beginning," but rather as a promise that has been partially confirmed. This body of research represents one of the few developments within psychology in which the data have the dual characteristics of being replicable and meaningful. Certainly, the fact that deviant behaviors may be altered with reasonable expenditures of professional time would have broad implications for many areas of education and child clinical psychology.

There are, however, several crucial areas that have been neglected in these first five years of investigation. Depending upon the outcome of investigations in these areas, it might be necessary to add qualifications to the enthusiastic statements made in the preceding paragraph.

At the present time the greatest immediate area of weakness lies in the inadequate follow-up data for studies carried out in the normal classroom and inadequate generalization data for studies carried out within the token-culture classroom. It is imperative that we know whether the teacher continues to apply her new-found technology to problem behaviors in her classroom. We also need to know how long the effects persist for the alterations in the child's behavior. For example, do the members of the peer group support the alterations once they have occurred or do they provide contingencies which result in reshaping deviant child behaviors? Some authors report that the changes in child behavior did in fact persist, but provided no data to substantiate these claims (Duncan, 1967; Hotchkiss, 1966). Patterson et al. (1968) provided data that showed that direct intervention in the classroom produced changes that persisted for six months for three out of four children. While such data are somewhat reassuring, they are not sufficient to evaluate the question. To the writer's knowledge, there are, as yet, no studies that demonstrate long-term changes in the behavior of the teacher.

When considering follow-up data for the token classroom, the problem is related also to generalization of intervention effects. The question concerns the persistence of intervention effects when the child is removed from the highly controlled environment of the token-culture classroom to the public school class-room. The report by Nolen, Kunzelmann, and Haring (1967) showed that behavior control was partially lost for three subjects when they were transferred back to the public school. Probably the best study of its kind is to be found in the report by Walker et al. (1969), in which the children spent most of the day in the token classroom and a limited amount of time each day in the public school classroom. Observation data collected in both settings were used to determine the point at which intervention effects generalized to the classroom setting. The teacher in the regular classroom was partially trained to maintain the program in order to maximize generalization. Three months following termination of the token-culture class, four of the subjects observed in the public school classroom remained at or above 72-percent efficiency when compared to their performance during training. The figure was based upon the proportion of the time the child spent "working or attending." The two remaining subjects did not fare so well, and fell far below this figure. These are impressive data, and demonstrate that with careful attention to procedures for maximizing generalization, it is possible to produce long-term effects for four out of six problem children. What is needed are more studies of this caliber and more innovations in attempts to retrain the setting to which the child will be returned.

Intervention studies in the classroom setting have come of age in the sense that we should now be ready to move beyond the "Whoopee-we-did-it" phase to more carefully designed studies that compare the relative efficiency of several different techniques. However, it is not clear as to just what the procedures are that merit inclusion in such comparative studies. For example, the review by Kranzler (1967) of a series of well-controlled studies showed that both group and individual counseling procedures for elementary children failed to produce significant differences between treated and nontreated problem children. Hundreds of cases were included in these studies, and careful attention was paid to utilizing sound criterion data. Similarly, the well-controlled study by Minde and Werry (1968) showed that 300 hours of psychiatric consultation, 1500 hours of tutorial time, and 200 hours of social worker time and investment in working with the teachers were not successful in altering the observed classroom behavior of the children in the "treated" group when compared to the control group.

Thus far, only a few studies have included nontreated control groups as part of their evaluation (Hotchkiss, 1966; Staats, 1967; Barclay, 1967; Clark et al., 1967). With the exception of the study by Barclay, the data showed that the intervention procedures were more effective than the passage of time in producing changes in behavior. However, the eventual status of behavior modification procedures in the classroom setting must rest upon more than statements about "better than." It will rest instead upon the increase in efficiency that they provide relative to other forms of intervention. Estimates of efficiency should include not only observation data showing changes in rates of deviant and adaptive behavior, but also estimates of the amount of

professional time required to bring about these changes. Finally, the comparative studies should also include follow-up data indicating how long these effects persist.

In this first rush of investigations, most of the focus has been upon the "easiest" target, that is, the alteration of social behaviors. In most of these studies, it has been safe to assume that the child possesses in his repertoire the requisite behaviors necessary for social interaction. Seldom is it the case that the target behavior is not available. Situations in which the problem occurs because of *omissions* in previous training represent more complex and time-consuming endeavors. The area of academic skills is of course such an area, and one that the behavior modifiers are only beginning to investigate. For this reason, it is to be expected that in the future we will have more studies of the kind carried out by Staats and his group, which investigate the problems involved in the acquisition of academic skills.

REFERENCES

Ackerman, N. W. *The psychodynamics of family life*. New York: Basic Books, 1958.

Anderson, D. Application of a behavior modification technique to the control of a hyperactive child. Unpublished master's thesis, University of Oregon, 1964.

Barclay, J. Effecting behavior change in the elementary classroom: An exploratory study. *Journal of Counseling Psychology*, 1967, **14**, 240–247.

Becker, W. C., Madsen, C. H., Jr., Arnold, C. R., and Thomas, D. R. The contingent use of teacher attention and praise in reducing classroom behavior problems. *Journal of Special Education*, 1967, **1**, 287–307.

Bell, J. E. Recent advances in family group therapy. *Journal of Child Psychology and Psychiatry*, 1962, **3**, 1–15.

Bernal, M., Duryee, J., Pruett, H., and Burns, B. Behavior modification and the "brat syndrome." *Journal of Consulting Psychology*, 1968, **32**, 447–455.

Birnbrauer, J. S., Bijou, S. W., Wolf, M. M., and Kidder, J. D. Programed instruction in the classroom. In L. Ullmann and L. Krasner (Eds.), *Case studies in behavior modification*. New York: Holt, Rinehart & Winston, 1965. Pp. 358–363.

Brown, J., Montgomery R., and Barclay, J. An example of psychologist management of teacher reinforcement procedures in the elementary classroom. *Psychology in the Schools*, 1969, **6**, 336–340.

Clark, M., Lackowicz, J., and Wolf, M. M. A pilot basic educational program for school dropouts incorporating a token reinforcement system. *Behavior Research and Therapy*, 1968, **6**, 183–188.

Clement, P. W., and Milne, D. C. Group play therapy and tangible reinforcers used to modify the behavior of eight-year-old boys. Unpublished manuscript, Harbor General Hospital, Torrance, California, 1966.

Collins, R. C. The treatment of disruptive behavior problems by employment of a partial-milieu consistency program. Unpublished doctoral dissertation, University of Oregon, 1966.

Crandall, V., and Preston, A. Verbally expressed needs and overt maternal behavior. *Child Development*, 1961, **32**, 261–270.

Duncan, A. D. Self-application of behavior modification by teenagers. Research training paper #11, Bureau of Child Research and School of Education, University of Kansas, 1967.

Ebner, M. An investigation of the role of the social environment in the generalization and persistence of the effect of a behavior modification program. Unpublished doctoral dissertation, University of Oregon, 1967.

Evans, G. W., and Oswalt, G. L. Acceleration of academic progress through the manipulation of peer influence. *Parsons Research Center Working Paper*, No. 155, 1967.

Fontana, A. F. Familial etiology of schizophrenia: Is a scientific methodology possible? *Psychological Bulletin*, 1966, **66**, 214–227.

Grindee, K, T. Operant conditioning of attending behavior in the classroom: A case study. Unpublished bachelor's thesis, Reed College, 1965.

Grindee, K. T. Operant conditioning of attending behaviors in the classroom for two hyperactive Negro children. Unpublished manuscript, Reed College, September 1964.

Haggard, E. A., Brekstad, A., and Skard, A. G. On the reliability of the anamnestic interview. *Journal of Abnormal and Social Psychology*, 1960, **61**, 311–318.

Haley, J. *Strategies of psychotherapy.* New York: Grune & Stratton, 1963.

Hall, R. V., Lund, D., and Jackson, D. Effects of teacher attention on study behavior. *Journal of Applied Behavior Analysis*, 1968, **1**, 1–12.

Hamerlynck, L. A., Martin, J. W., and Rolland, J. C. Systematic observation of behavior: A primary teacher skill. *Education and Training of the Mentally Retarded*, 1968, **3**, 39–42.

Hanf, C. Modification of mother-child controlling behaviors during mother-child interactions in standardized laboratory situations. Paper presented at the meeting of the Association for the Advancement of Behavior Therapies, Olympia, Washington, 1968.

Haring, N. G., and Kunzelmann, H. The finer focus of therapeutic behavioral management. *Educational Therapy*, **1**, Special Child Publications, Seattle, Washington, 1966.

Hastings, A. S. Operant conditioning with children in the home with the mother as the experimenter. Unpublished master's thesis, Washington State University, 1967.

Hauck, M. A., and Haring, N. G. Individualized reading program with continuous evaluation of progress. Paper presented at the Conference of the Washington Organization for Reading Development, Lynwood, Washington, April 1968.

Haughton, E. Training counselors as advisers of precision teaching. Paper presented at the meeting of the CEC Convention, New York, April 1968.

Hawkins, R. P., Peterson, R. F., Schweid, E., and Bijou, S. W. Behavior therapy in the home: Amelioration of problem parent-child relations with the parent in a therapeutic role. *Journal of Experimental Child Psychology*, 1966, **4**, 99–107.

Hewett, F. M. Educational engineering with emotionally disturbed children. *Exceptional Children*, 1967, **33**, 459–467.

Hewett, F. M., Taylor, F. D., and Artuso, A. A. The Santa Monica Project. Demonstration and evaluation of an engineered classroom design for emotionally disturbed children in the public schools. Project #62893, OEG 4-7-062893-0377, Office of Education, Bureau of Research, U.S. Department of Health, Education and Welfare, 1967.

Homme, L. D., de Baca, P. C., Devine, J. V., Steinhorst, R., and Rickert, E. J. Use of the Premack principle in controlling the behavior of nursery school children. *Journal of Experimental Analysis of Behavior*, 1963, **6**, 544.

Hotchkiss, J. M. The modification of maladaptive behavior of a class of educationally handicapped children by operant conditioning techniques. Unpublished doctoral dissertation, University of Southern California, 1966.

Kaswan, J. W., Love, L., and Rodnick, E. The effectiveness of information and consultation. Unpublished manuscript, Ohio State University, 1968.

Koenig, C. H. Precision teaching with emotionally disturbed pupils. Research Training Paper, No. 17, Special Education Research, Children's Rehabilitation Unit, University of Kansas Medical Center, 1967.

Kounin, J. S., Frisen, W. V., and Norton, E. A. Managing emotionally disturbed children in regular classrooms. *Journal of Educational Psychology*, 1966, **57**, 1–13.

Kranzler, G. D. Elementary school counseling: An evaluation. Paper presented at the meeting of the American Personnel Guidance Association, Dallas, Texas, 1967.

Krumboltz, J. D., and Goodwin, D. L. Increasing task oriented behavior: An experimental evaluation of training teachers in reinforcement techniques. Final Report, 1966, School of Education, Stanford University, Grant 5-85-95, Office of Education.

Levine, G. R., and Simmons, J. J. Response to praise by emotionally disturbed boys. *Psychological Reports*, 1962, **11**, 10.

Lindsley, O. R. An experiment with parents handling behavior at home. *Johnstone Bulletin*, 1966, **9**, 27–36.

Madsen, C. H., Jr., Becker, W. C., and Thomas, D. R. Rules, praise, and ignoring: Elements of elementary classroom control. *Journal of Applied Behavior Analysis*, 1968, **1**, 139–150.

Martin, B. Family interaction associated with child disturbance: Assessment and modification. *Psychotherapy: Theory, Research and Practice*, 1967, **4**, 30–35.

Martin, M., Burkholder, R,. Rosenthal, T. L., Tharp, R. G., and Thorne, G. L. Programming behavior change and reintegration into the school milieux of extreme adolescent deviates. *Behavior Research and Therapy*, 1968, **6**, 371–383.

Minde, K. K., and Werry, J. S. The response of school children in a low socio-economic area to extensive psychiatric counselling of their teachers: A controlled evaluation. Paper presented at the meeting of the American Psychiatric Association, Boston, 1968.

Nixon, S. B. Ways by which overly active students can be taught to concentrate on study activity. Cooperative Research Project No. S-379, School of Education, Stanford University, 1966.

Nolen, P., Kunzelmann, H., and Haring, N. Behavioral modification in a junior high learning disability classroom. *Exceptional Children*, 1967, **34**, 163–168.

O'Leary, K. D., and Becker, W. C. Behavior modification of an adjustment class: A token reinforcement program. Unpublished manuscript, University of Illinois, 1967.

O'Leary, K. D., O'Leary, S., and Becker, W. C. Modification of a deviant sibling interaction pattern in the home. *Behavior Research and Therapy*, 1967, **5**, 113–120.

Patterson, G. R. An application of conditioning techniques to the control of a hyperactive child. In L. Ullmann and L. Krasner (Eds.), *Case studies in behavior modification*. New York: Holt, Rinehart & Winston, 1965. Pp. 370–375. (b)

Patterson, G. R. A learning theory approach to the treatment of the school phobic child. In L. Ullmann and L. Krasner (Eds.), *Case studies in behavior modification*. Holt, Rinehart & Winston, 1965. Pp. 279–284. (a)

Patterson, G. R. Teaching parents to be behavior modifiers in the classroom. In J. D. Krumboltz and C. E. Thoresen (Eds.), *Behavioral counseling: Cases and techniques*. New York: Holt, Rinehart & Winston, 1969. Pp. 155–161.

Patterson, G. R., and Bechtel, G. G. Formulating the environment in relation to states and traits. In R. B. Cattell (Ed.), *Handbook of modern personality study*. Chicago: Aldine, 1970, In press.

Patterson, G. R., and Brodsky, G. D. A behaviour modification programme for a child with multiple problem behaviours. *Journal of Child Psychology and Psychiatry*, 1966, **7**, 277–295.

Patterson, G. R., Shaw, D. A. and Ebner, M. J., Teachers, peers and parents as agents of change in the classroom. In F. A. M. Benson (Ed.), *Modifying deviant social behaviors in various classroom settings*. Eugene, Oregon: University of Oregon, 1969, No. 1. Pp 13–47

Patterson, G. R., and Gullion, M. E. *Living with children: New methods for parents and teachers*. Champaign, Illinois: Research Press, 1968.

Patterson, G. R., and Harris, A. Some methodological considerations for observation procedures. Paper presented at the meeting of the American Psychological Association, San Francisco, 1968.

Patterson, G. R., McNeal, S., Hawkins, N., and Phelps, R. Reprogramming the social environment. *Journal of Child Psychology and Psychiatry*, 1967, **8**, 181–195.

Patterson, G. R., Jones, R., Whittier, J., and Wright, M. A. A behaviour modification technique for the hyperactive child. *Behaviour Research and Therapy*, 1965, **2**, 217–226.

Patterson, G. R., Ray, R. S., and Shaw, D. A. Direct intervention in families of deviant children. *Oregon Research Institute Research Bulletin*, 1968, **8** (9).

Patterson, G. R., and Reid, J. B. Reciprocity and coercion: Two facets of social systems. In C. Neuringer and J. Michael (Eds.), *Behavior modification in clinical psychology*. New York: Appleton-Century-Crofts, 1970. Pp. 133–177.

Perkins, M. J. Effects of play therapy and behavior modification approaches with conduct problem boys. Unpublished doctoral dissertation, University of Illinois, 1967.

Quay, H. C., Spraque, R. L., Werry, J. S., and McQueen, M. M. Conditioning visual orientation of conduct problem children in the classroom. *Journal of Experimental Child Psychology*, 1967, **5**, 512–517.

Quay, H. C., Werry, J. S., McQueen, M, M., and Spraque, R. L. Remediation of the conduct problem child in the special class setting. *Exceptional Children*, 1966, **32**, 509–515.

Radke-Yarrow, M., Campbell, J., and Burton, R. V. Reliability of maternal retrospection: A preliminary report. *Family Process*, 1964, **3**, 207–218.

Ray, R. S. The training of mothers of atypical children in the use of behavior modification techniques. Unpublished master's thesis, University of Oregon, 1965.

Risley, T. Learning and lollipops. *Psychology Today*, 1968, **1**, 28–31, 62–65.

Rosenthal, R. *Experimenter effects in behavioral research*. New York: Appleton-Century-Crofts, 1966.

Schalock, H. D. Observer influence on mother-child interaction in the home: A preliminary report. Paper presented at the meeting of the Western Psychological Association, Carmel, Calif., 1958.

Scott, P. M., Burton, R., and Radke–Yarrow, M. R. Social reinforcement under natural conditions. *Child Development*, 1967, **38**, 53–63.

Sears, R. R. Comparison of interviews with questionnaires for measuring mothers' attitudes toward sex and aggression. *Journal of Personality and Social Psychology*, 1965, **2**, 37–44.

Shah, S. A. Training and utilizing a mother as the therapist for her child. Unpublished manuscript, National Institute of Mental Health, Chevy Chase, Maryland, 1967.

Skinner, B. F. *Science and human behavior*. New York: Macmillan, 1953.

Smith, H., T. A comparison of interview and observation measures of mother behavior. *Journal of Abnormal and Social Psychology*, 1958, **57**, 278–282.

Staats, A. W. *Learning, language and cognition*. New York: Holt, Rinehart & Winston, 1968.

Staats, A. W., Minke, K. A., Goodwin, W., and Landeen, J. Cognitive behavior modification: "Motivated learning" reading treatment with subprofessional therapy-technicians. *Behaviour Research and Therapy*, 1967, **5**, 283–299.

Staats, A. W., Staats, C K., Schutz, R. E., and Wolf, M. M. The conditioning of textual responses. using "extrinsic" reinforcers. *Journal of the Experimental Analysis of Behavior*, 1962, **5**, 33–40.

Straughan, J. H. Treatment with child and mother in the playroom. *Behaviour Research and Therapy*, 1964, **2**, 37–41.

Thomas, D. R., Becker, W. C., and Armstrong, M. Production and elimination of disruptive classroom behavior by systematically varying teacher's behavior. *Journal of Applied Behavior Analysis*, 1968, **1**, 35–45.

Thorne, G. L., Tharp, R. G., and Wetzel, R. J. The behavioral research project: An interim report on the first 14 months of operation. HEW Grant 65023 and 66020, Office of Juvenile Delinquency and Youth Development, 1966.

Thorne, G. L., Tharp, R. G., and Wetzel, R. J. Behavior modification techniques: New tools for probation officers. *Federal Probation*, 1967, **31**, 21–26.

Valett, R. E. A social reinforcement technique for the classroom management of behavior disorders. *Exceptional Children*, 1966, **33**, 185–189.

Wahler, R. G. Behavior therapy for oppositional children: Love is not enough. Paper presented at the meeting of the Eastern Psychological Association, Washington, D.C., April 1968.

Wahler, R. G. Behavior therapy with oppositional children: Attempts to increase their parents' reinforcement value. Paper presented at the meeting of the Southeastern Psychological Association, Atlanta, April 1967. (a)

Wahler, R. G. Child-child interactions in free field settings: Some experimental analyses. *Journal of Experimental Child Psychology*, 1967, **5**, 278–293. (b)

Wahler, R. G., Winkel, G. H. Peterson, R. F., and Morrison, D. C. Mothers as behavior therapists for their own children. *Behaviour Research and Therapy*, 1965, **3**, 113–124.

Walder, L., Cohen, S., and Daston, P. Teaching parents and others principles of behavior control for modifying the behavior of children. Progress Report, 1967, 32-30-7515-5024, U.S. Office of Education.

Walker, H. M., Mattson, R. H., and Buckley, N. K. Special class placement as a treatment alternative for deviant behavior in children. In F. A. M. Benson (Ed.), *Modifying deviant social behaviors in various classroom settings.* Eugene, Oregon: University of Oregon, 1969, No. 1.

Ward, C. H., Beck, A. T., Mendelson, M., Mock, J. E., and Erbaugh, J. K. The psychiatric nomenclature. *Archives of General Psychiatry*, 1962, **7**, 198–205.

Werry, J. S., and Quay, H. C. Observing the classroom behavior of elementary school children. *Exceptional Children*, 1969, **35**, 461–470.

Whelan, R. F., and Haring, N. G. Modification and maintenance of behavior through systematic application of consequences. *Exceptional Children*, 1966, **32**, 281–289.

Williams, C. D. The elimination of tantrum behaviors by extinction procedures. *Journal of Abnormal and Social Psychology*, 1959, **59**, 269.

Wright, H. D. Observational child study. In P. Mussen (Ed.), *Handbook of research methods in child development.* New York: Wiley, 1960. Pp. 71–139.

Zeilberger, J., Sampen, S., and Sloane, H. Modification of a child's problem behaviors in the home with the mother as therapist. *Journal of Applied Behavior Analysis*, 1968, **1**, 47–53.

Zimmerman, E. H., and Zimmerman, J. The alteration of behavior in a special classroom situation. *Journal of Experimental Analysis of Behavior*, 1962, **5**, 59–60.

20

EVALUATIVE RESEARCH AND COMMUNITY MENTAL HEALTH

SHELDON R. ROEN

HUMAN SCIENCES, INC., NEW YORK

Community mental health is not yet well defined, and program evaluation as a scientific pursuit is only now beginning to emerge. This situation leaves the writing of this chapter without authoritative guidelines. The reader, then, should be advised that he is not necessarily obtaining a definitive statement, but a review that reflects, more than usual, one person's outlook on progress in evaluation of community mental health activities as gleaned from the publications of many people.

The developing field of community mental health is breaking new ground by attempting to meet needs that were previously dodged. Programs, methods, and techniques of inquiry are still emerging, and hard, definitive findings are understandably not readily obtainable. Nevertheless, a survey of reports that contain only "lip service" data would not be a contribution. Fortunately, there are readily available sources from which broader inquiry

into community mental health can be facilitated. For literature prior to 1960, the reader is referred to a reference guide prepared by a committee from the Massachusetts General Hospital (Harvard Medical School, 1962), and for literature thereafter, to a Coordinate Index Reference Guide prepared by Golann (1968). Also available is an annotated bibliography specific to program evaluation reports published between 1955 and 1964 (Bloom, 1965).

THE PROBLEM

The developments to be discussed were focused when President John F. Kennedy, on February 5, 1963, delivered a special message to Congress in which he proposed "a bold new approach" to mental illness. This marked the first occasion where a head of state addressed his country's representatives on the subject of mental health.

Congress responded in October by passing the Community Mental Health Centers Act of 1963 (Title II of Public Law 88–164), which provided up to two thirds of the funds necessary for construction of facilities for comprehensive coordinated mental health programs within communities, defined as sensibly delineated catchment areas containing 75,000 to 200,000 people. The community was to participate in planning the program according to guidelines specifying as essential such innovative elements as a 24-hour emergency service, partial hospitalization, and consultation and education services. The expectation was that 2000 programs would be in operation throughout the country by 1975. In order to qualify for matching funds, each state had to submit a long-range plan containing a thorough survey of its resources and needs, the delineation of catchment areas, and the setting of priorities for implementation. Federal funds were made available for planning purposes, and 53 states and territories submitted detailed plans. The planning represented the participation of some 25,000 individuals (Stretch, 1967). In 1965, President Lyndon B. Johnson requested and obtained additional funds from Congress to help pay the staffing costs of programs.

According to Glasscote, Sussex, Cumming, and Smith (1969), in the first four years of the program Congress authorized $200 million for construction, but appropriated only $180 million, of which $135 million became available in the apportionment of National Institute of Mental Health (NIMH) funds. Construction and staffing funds combined came to $232 million for the period 1964–1968. This is approximately the amount of money required to run the New York State Department of Mental Hygiene for five months. Nevertheless, NIMH reports (personal communication) that 351 centers have been funded by them as of December 31, 1968. This figure, of course, does not take into consideration the large number of mental health facilities that have independently included community mental health activity as part of their program.

Although these events formally ushered in what is now known as the community mental health movement, they are here to be considered as only one path for implementating the fresh ideas for fostering social well-being derived from the new specialties of social psychiatry, community psychology, psychiatric sociology, and human ecology.

Characterization of the Field

Our first task is to attempt to provide a frame of reference through a description of the field. It is a grand commentary on the creative energies of mental health professionals that once the momentum for change developed, a barrage of activity ensued which attempted to transcend professional territoriality, cross disciplinary barriers, and overcome narrowly delineated latitudes of concern. Although some might describe what has happened as diffusion, it can also be seen as the more typical expansiveness following an excitement generated by freedom from past constraints.

Community mental health is currently a conglomerate endeavor based on a pattern of conceptions and strategies generated, I think, by a shift in focus from studying the nature of man to concentrating on the nature of the problems faced by man. While many of the concepts are not new, they have in the past been generally ignored. The Federal emphasis has resuscitated them, and concrete projects for testing their value have been undertaken. The following is an outline of some of the more important notions underlying the field:

1. The environmental context is always relevant, and social realities are often prepotent, in determining and changing behavior.

2. Mental health professionals are accountable to the communities they serve.

3. Social approaches to amelioration can be effective.

4. Prevention is the most valued answer to the mass problem of mental disorder.

5. Help for a problem is best offered in close proximity to where the problem became visible, and through indigenous resources.

6. Optimal programming requires community participation, if not control.

7. The more urgent needs of local populations or groups should order program priorities and determine the characteristics of facilities.

8. Regaining or enhancing competence are important objectives of treatment.

9. Since milieu can be structured to facilitate mental health, intervening at the level of social system is a preferred strategy.

10. Services should reach out to recalcitrant high-risk groups and be rendered parsimoniously, efficiently, and equitably.

11. The accidental or developmental stresses and strains of life are strategic points of entry for preventive intervention.

12. Since the causative chain in mental disorder seems linked to the stresses of debilitating social problems, social reform is an important professional goal.

13. Professionals can be better deployed and the manpower pool effectively enhanced by training nonprofessionals to perform helping tasks.

14. Careful planning, innovative programming, and the formulation of new conceptual models are to be encouraged.

15. Since psychological disorder is practically legion, public education about mental health should be a high priority activity.

The conglomerate character of the activities associated with community mental health stems from these conceptions as selectively interpreted through the perspective of several interest groups. From the viewpoint of government committed to meeting public need, emphasis is placed on continuity of care, comprehensive coverage, and coordination of services connoting such programs as pre- and aftercare, partial hospitalization, and more effective communication among agencies. On the other hand, the mental health practitioner quite naturally concerns himself with perfecting new techniques for handling emergencies, shortening treatment time, serving as a consultant to community-care givers, enhancing group process, and helping clients cope better with their immediate problems. The mental health administrator has his major stake in such issues as recruitment, training, and deployment of manpower; thoroughly knowing the character and needs of his catchment area; better intake procedure; and the costs of alternative services. The innovator is most interested in creating and implementing new modes of rehabilitation (such as sheltered workshops and cooperative apartments); devising new intervention strategies (such as crisis theory and therapeutic milieus);

and inventing new service delivery systems (such as neighborhood storefront centers and walk-in clinics). The researcher spends time discovering new variables to correlate with the program outcome (such as professional mental health ideology), developing new information storage and retrieval systems (such as case registers), and applying findings from other fields (for example, the use of valued tokens as motivators for patients on hospital wards). And the public health worker, with his concern for the total community context, reaches out for those "high-risk" populations who were previously not included in the main stream of mental health concern (such as the poor, the aged, the retarded, and the addicted).

Challenges in Reviewing a Developing Field

Since community mental health is in the testing-of-limits stage of development, a tolerant approach is perhaps best, in order to not close off the options. While there are inherent dangers in too loose a stance for too long a time, there is also an advantage in not institutionalizing ideas or activities prematurely. Our position then will be that community mental health is an orientation to programming services for promoting the *general well-being* of population groups. Included in this position is Caplan's (1964, p. 16) definition of preventive psychiatry, the action elements of which he characterizes as planning and carrying out "programs for reducing (1) the incidence of mental disorders of all types in a community ('primary prevention'), (2) the duration of a significant number of those disorders which do occur ('secondary prevention'), and (3) the impairment which may result from those disorders ('tertiary prevention')."

Because our specific concern here is with evaluation, it seems appropriate to concentrate first on trends in methodology. From there the writer shall attempt to document some generalizations derived from careful studies, and shall conclude with a discussion of the problems encountered in conducting research in this field.

METHOD

There are special considerations for evaluative research in community mental health which require methods that will not so simplify the phenomenon studied as to take it out of context and render the findings unusable for practical programming. Although important knowledge in this field is certainly derivable from the tested methodological traditions of the behavioral sciences, the major assumptions of community mental health seem in some ways to be diametrically opposed to approaches that set special conditions, restrict the response repertoire of subjects, or screen out the influence of subsystems on each other. This section will discuss some research methods more congenial to the field, and will give examples of how these methods are translated into practice. Six methodological approaches are to be discussed, most of them new to the behavioral sciences and not yet incorporated into academic research training. Most have historical roots in the special needs of other disciplines. The three more abstract and elaborated approaches to be outlined are epidemiology, ecology, and systems analysis. The three more concrete and direct approaches are action research, repeatable demonstrations, and prescriptive contextual research.

Epidemiology

Epidemiologic method serves the public health mission of preventing or controlling disease through supplying clues to etiology and mode of spread by focusing on the natural history of the disease. Since public health is interested in generalizing to the population universe, epidemiology uses "population" as its unit of observation in contrast to the clinical approach which deals mainly with the individual case. In this sense epidemiology has been referred to as the science of mass phenomenon. Causation is seen pluralistically as a chain of linked variables related to a host and an environment. Intervening at any one point in this chain might make prevention possible. Clues about origins are obtained by *descriptive epidemiology* through surveying frequency of events among populations with distinguishing characteristics at different points in time. This is carefully accomplished with exacting definitions of, for example, annual incidence rate, in which the numerator is the number of new cases manifest-

ing a condition in a given year, and the denominator is the average number of persons at risk during that year. This index is particularly important in studying conditions historically, and is rather crucial in uncovering causes. A point-prevalence rate can be determined by placing the number of persons manifesting a condition at a stated point in time in the numerator, and having as denominator the number of such persons at risk at the time. Through these indices definitive information can be obtained about the distribution of a condition in relation to biographical, socioeconomic, or ethnic variables. Learning about the natural history of the disorder through this mass-phenomena technique can permit the uncovering of a correlational matrix of etiological interest. Hypotheses can thereby be generated, and plausible programs for prevention developed. Since it is often easier to uncover and cope with environmental causes, an important strategy becomes the removal or alteration of "community hazards."

Once hypotheses are generated, they can be tested with *analytic epidemiological methods* by controlled investigations of the interplay of host conditions (that is, whether the risk of becoming ill for groups with certain characteristics is greater than for groups with different attributes) and environmental variables (that is, whether exposure versus nonexposure, in groups with the same characteristics, adds to the risk of becoming ill). Analytic research designs can be retrospective in terms of case histories or prospective through cohorts followed for a period of time.

Public health has made impressive strides in the prevention of illness through the use of these methods. Although psychiatric epidemiology is relatively new, having been rarely spoken of before 1949, when the Milbank Fund began its efforts to bring psychiatry and public health together, a good deal of current public practice is based on its findings. Such findings have focused attention on links between mental disorder and social class, sex, age, relocation experiences, cultural patterns, conditions in the community, and the roles of gatekeeper to services.

Morris (1964) cites the example of duodenal (peptic) ulcer to point out the usefulness of the epidemiological strategy as complementary to other approaches. With the use of clinical methods, workers defined the existence of a duodenal ulcer in individual cases, and noticed that symptoms developed and relapsed in relation to tensions, work strains, and threats. They also took notice of reports of cure in concentration camps. Laboratory study, through analysis and experiment, uncovered high blood pepsinogen levels that correlated with physiological predisposition, found evidence in some cases of "organ inferiority," and experimentally proved that conscious and unconscious ideas can affect gastric functioning. The laboratory method was also able to produce the symptom in monkeys as a result of psychological stress. Studies in epidemiology revealed that duodenal ulcers were more common in urban people than in agricultural workers, who seemed relatively immune, and more common in class I and II men who hold positions of responsibility. Use of the epidemiological method further enabled workers to find that the condition has been recently declining without obvious explanation.

The Stirling County Study, a most ambitious and intensive effort spanning almost two decades, can serve as a good example of the epidemiological approach in all its ramifications, even though hindsight shows some of its methodology to be weak. According to Alexander H. Leighton, the project's director, the study was conceived in order "to discover the distribution of psychiatric disorders in communities in relation to social organization and cultural patterns and to see if, in this frame of reference, significant differences can be detected between pathological and normal individuals" (Leighton, 1950, p. 128). The central hypothesis of the study was that individuals from a disintegrated community would show the impact of disintegration by poor mental health. This was to be tested in the small towns and rural area of Nova Scotia, which appeared to the project members to represent in microcosm much of the diversity of modern American life. The populations were small enough to make it possible to map out the interconnections between individuals and environment, and to make comparisons between matched communities that varied in their degree of social disintegration.

Project members conceived of a community as a unit and a system, rather than a heterogeneous collection of people and institutions. Accordingly, the integrative capacity of the community organization depended on its ability to provide the following: a perpetuation of itself, subsistence, protection against dangers, promotion of harmony, control of hostility, division of labor, and the functioning of leaders and followers. A disintegrated community was defined by its failure to perform these functions effectively and by not being able to satisfy its residents' essential striving sentiments. The findings (Leighton, Leighton, and Armstrong, 1964) indicated that the level of integration of the community was more strongly related to mental health than was sex, age, or occupational position. There were more individuals rated as "cases," greater numbers of different kinds of symptoms, and greater impairment among people from the disintegrated area than was true of those who came from the integrated community. This difference was found to be significant at the .001 level, thereby confirming the basic hypothesis and suggesting the proposition that the whole tenor of community life is the important force in mental health, and not poverty or low socioeconomic status *per se.*

In addition to this conclusion, useful findings were obtained from their epidemiological study of prevalence. About half the people sampled from the general population exhibited psychiatric symptoms quite clearly, and only 17 percent were entirely free of them. About a third of the population showed noticeable impairment of functioning (20 percent to 30 percent interference) as a result of these symptoms, and about 20 percent seemed to require psychiatric help. Psychophysiologic and psychoneurotic symptoms were most common; the psychoses were detected in less than 2 percent. Women consistently manifested more symptoms, particularly of the neurotic variety, than men, across the full age range. Younger people were least likely to evidence nervous disturbance; but thereafter the symptom rate rose irregularly to age 70, after which it diminished. There were "peaks" for each sex between the ages of 60 and 69, one for men between 30 and 39, and one for women between 40 and 49.

One of the criticisms leveled at this monumental study was that it overlooked the differential meaning of symptoms to different groups of people and too readily equated the presence of symptoms with mental disorder. However, if one accepts the investigator's definitions and system of categorizing psychiatric disorder (which paid particular attention to symptoms designated as behavior patterns commonly but not exclusively seen in psychiatric disorders and to the degree to which an individual was impaired or disabled by these patterns) one can be sympathetic to Leighton's (1968, p. 7) most recently formulated overall conclusions: with regard to poverty, cultural change, and migration, these are conditions "of risk with respect to the development of social disintegrations; social disintegration in turn is a condition of risk with respect to the emergence of psychiatric disorder."

Ecology

Ecological methods are used to understand the mutual relations between organisms and their environments, especially in regard to research problems that cannot in principle be solved through laboratory experimentation. Approaches to human ecology take at least four directions. Following the biological model, geographers study the relationship of the physical environment in specific regions to the activities of people inhabiting these regions. For sociologists, the focus is on the setting, growth, and decline of human communities. Medical ecology (Dunham, 1968) emphasizes the relationships of environment to disease and health, viewed as the maintenance of a delicate balance between a disease agent, the organism, and the environment. Ecological psychology (Barker, 1965) is concerned with the psychology of peoples' environment, which includes all of their nonpsychological world. Although the sociological and medical directions are of considerable significance to the interests of this review, the psychological orientation will be the one used to illustrate the approach.

The ecological method of studying organisms in their natural environment without preselection or prearranging of variables is particularly suited to community mental health, especially its resolve to help people as they are in the setting to which they have become accustomed. The questions asked by the community researcher are not the same questions asked by the laboratory experimenter. The community researcher wants to uncover facts about how variables distribute themselves in life as it is lived in ordinary surroundings. He assumes that the environmental setting is very rarely the passive recipient of behavior but more often the instigator, if not the molder, of what is to happen. Since 1947, Barker and his colleagues at the Midwest Psychological Field Station in Kansas have studied people in natural settings with techniques developed to answer questions about "What exists?" and "What goes on here?" This contrasts sharply to the more traditional question of "What goes on here under conditions that have been prearranged?" In obtaining data as "traducers" rather than as "operators," they have been able to develop a taxonomy of environmental input that contributes significantly to explaining variance in human behavior.

The environment is seen to consist of highly structured, improbable arrangements of objects and events which coerce behavior in accordance with their own dynamic patterning. We found, in short, that we could predict some aspects of children's behavior more adequately from knowledge of the behavior characteristics of the drug stores, arithmetic classes, and basketball games they inhabited than from knowledge of the behavior tendencies of particular children (Barker, 1968, p. 4).

An example of particularly relevant research conducted from that perspective can be found in the work of Kelly (1967, 1968), who used the ecological analogy to develop theoretical propositions about how individuals become effective and survive in varied social environments. To study this phenomenon, he set about to try to measure such variables as coping styles, adaptive role functions, social settings, and the structural properties of the environment. His exploratory research was conducted in two Columbus, Ohio high schools, one of which he characterized as fluid, because 42 per cent of the entrants left within a calendar year, and the other as constant, since this figure came to less than 10 percent. Observation points were set up in hallways, cafeterias, and the principal's offices. Field notes by observers were supplemented by interview material gathered in small group sessions from a stratified sample of 120 students from each school. It was noted that in the fluid-environment high school, both boys and girls were dressed in a more varied fashion; there were fewer groups in the halls, but the median for them was seven; body and gestural movements were quite pronounced; noise level was very high; there was a range of 30 to 110 entrances to the principal's office per three-minute period; and informal welcoming committees operated to meet incoming students, to identify their interests and needs and impart to them information about school life, what teachers to avoid, and where to smoke. In the constant environment, it was observed that dress was so similar in the hallways as to be classified almost as uniforms; there was a minimum of body motion in the way students walked; there was no display of affect; groups had a median of two persons; the principal's office had a range of 1 to 15 entrances per three-minute period; and there was a nonresponsiveness to newcomers, which had the effect of a silent treatment until the new person in some way declared himself.

In relation to these naturalistic observations, Kelly hypothesized that students who have high preferences for exploration will have a high probability of emerging as adaptive members in a fluid environment, but will develop maladaptive roles in a constant environment. He designed a study that is being conducted in four high schools, two in a suburban area of Detroit and two others within the inner city of Detroit. One of each has a high exchange rate of students (fluidity), and the other a low exchange rate. He will be measuring exploratory behavior with a 30-item questionnaire tested for reliability, validity, and social desirability containing such items as "I like staying home and keeping friendships with people I've known a long time" and "I don't like it when a special TV program takes the place of the one I usually watch."

The ecological orientation to behavioral research is just in its infancy. Much more experience with it is necessary before its power can be adequately assessed. However, the vantage it offers seems reasonable assurance that it will be pursued, especially in relation to questions whose answers require contextual formulations.

The General Systems Approach and Computer Usage

The multisystem interests of community mental health requires a way of thinking that transcends the classical models of science. The approach embodied by general systems theory seems relevant to those interests. It looks at the multifactorial transactions among components of a particular system and between it and other systems with which it interacts. It expresses these multiple relationships as existing at a given point in time, and in so doing, responds to the increased complexity of relationships in contemporary society and man's greater striving to understand and coordinate them. Thinking in terms of general systems is particularly valuable for mental health, because its concerns involve the general environmental context that underlie the difficult issues plaguing the field. It also encourages necessary interdisciplinary thinking by countering the tendency to look at models of mental disorder pertinent only to single specialties.

Ludwig von Bertalanffy (1968), a theoretical biologist, is credited with being the creator of general systems theory. His motivating notion, back in 1937, was that since organisms were *organized* things, we should study this very quality. To lend scientific substance to this organismic view, he felt that something beyond the open system and steady-state theories of conventional science was necessary, and after World War II he made considerable progress in practically formulating a scientific approach to understanding a system. Through the following approaches, general systems theory has determined that systems have general properties that can be mapped out as pattern formulations:

Cybernetics—principle of feedback or circular causal chains from which goal-seeking and self-controlling forms of behavior emerge.

Information theory—related to cybernetics, but stressing the concept of information as a quantity that is measurable and that comprises the universal flux of systems.

Decision theory—analyzes rational choices within human organizations.

Game theory—related to decision theory, but utilizing mathematical analysis of rational competition between two or more antagonists for maximum gain and minimum loss; studies decisions made in the face of uncertainty and in the presence of other, perhaps opposed, decision makers.

Topology or relational mathematics—works with nonmetrical fields such as network and graph theory; considers human beings as literally one vector among many tending toward a "steady state" at one point in time.

Factor analysis—mathematical isolation of factors in multivariate problems.

Computer simulation—computer programming for the purpose of assuming or mimicking the appearance of a phenomenon.

Stochastic models—simulation through mathematical formulas reflecting the actual conditions in processes that develop in time according to probabilistic laws (Bartholomew, 1967).

Technical advances have been made by applying these approaches in terms of systems engineering (plan, design, evaluation, and construction of man-machine systems); operations research (control of existing systems of man, machines, materials, and money); and human engineering (adaptation of systems and machines to obtain maximum efficiency).

Workers in the field of mental health are only now beginning to learn to use the tools afforded by the general systems approach. Hutcheson and Krause (1969) point out in general terms how "mental health services are badly in need of a more rational approach to planning and . . . show how specific systems analysis techniques can be used to describe a mental health system and, at the same time, to evaluate consequences and costs of changing the system in different ways" (p. 29). Some examples of recent contributions of computer usage and systems analysis follow.

Eicker (1967), with the help of associates, has made a promising beginning in applying the techniques of systems analysis to the evaluation, design, and development of an optimal community mental health service system. He has looked at the Adolf Meyer Zone Center in Decatur, Illinois from the point of view of how it goes about its routines, including the gathering of information required to make some of the subsystems and networks operate. His flow charts reflect the primacy of conceptualizing the large operation as a necessarily dynamic configuration of interdependent components. An example of use to which the analysis was put can be found in the Community Transaction Audit (COMTA) designed to monitor the transactions of staff with individuals and agencies in the community. He hopes to utilize some of his procedures to simulate such possibilities as reassigning 25 percent of the police force in that community to the role of neighborhood social workers (no guns or badges), and the development of a mobile mental health unit travelling throughout high-risk population areas for the purpose of holding regular group-discussion meetings with housewives.

Computers are being used as a psychiatric aid and research tool in a particularly interesting way through the cooperation of the University of Minnesota and the Institute of Living at Hartford, Connecticut (Glueck, 1968). The Minnesota-Hartford Personality Assay and Automated Nursing Notes produce a daily print-out summarizing salient patient behavior for the days and hours just preceeding the input. Detailed observational information, free of jargon and capable of statistical handling, is the result. On the basis of information gathered in that way, nurses were put on alert for possible suicides in patients, not realizing that it was their own observations that made this possible. In a particular incident, violence on a male ward became predictable through a clear and specific early warning signal from the computer.

Localities in Maryland (Bahn, 1965) and New York (Gardner, 1966) have served as laboratories for the development of automated psychiatric case registers. These data systems have been useful in supplying base-line information against which new services could be evaluated, in providing longitudinal information about changes in diagnosis and outcome, and in offering a sampling frame for more intensive studies. This development, seen in relation to the generalized information-processing system for storing and analyzing the complete body of information contained in a case record (Eiduson, Brooks, and Motto, 1966) suggests that it will not be long before outputs from regional or national psychiatric data banks will be revitalizing behavioral theory building and changing many current conceptions regarding the mental health enterprise.

Based on an empirically derived content analysis of Reiss-Davis Child Study Center records, Eiduson (1966) describes a generalized information-processing system that permits computer processing of the entire body of information contained in psychiatric case records. Among the criteria met for developing the system are the following: (a) there should be no changes in the usual recordings of source information; (b) the diverse forms and sources must be easily incorporated into the system; (c) the system must answer almost all questions and provide almost any report; (d) it must deliver the requested report in a timely and efficient manner; (e) it must be able to handle facsimile images of source information; (f) it must protect the integrity and privacy inherent in confidential source information; and (g) it must be able to incorporate additions and improvements in hardware, concept, methodology, and scope. The system was developed through painstaking empirical analysis around the Event Concept, which stipulates that everything that occurs to a patient or to a significant person in his life is an event. Events are actual happenings, and also include psychological phenomena such as fears, fantasies, attitudes, opinions, and the like. Eiduson's publication prescribes the explicit procedures governing the transcriptions to the point of keypunch.

Further examples of innovative computer usage are contained in an entire supplement of the *American Journal of Psychiatry* (1969).

Action Research

Most closely associated with the work of Kurt Lewin (Chein, Cook, and Harding, 1948) at M.I.T., the action-research method provides a model for coping with hasty "in vivo" programming necessitated by institutional urgencies and no longer amenable to adequate research control. Careful description of what actually takes place, analysis of problems encountered, retrospective arranging of variables by matched cohorts, and follow-up information, can provide useful leads for answering some urgent, complex questions about the action. If the researcher is on his toes and makes himself available quickly, he may be able to participate early enough to

obtain before-and-after data in a research design adequate for more telling evaluation. Action research, although limited as a method, has some serendipitous advantages in that it is capable of influencing practice because the research often involves the participation of the perpetrators, and the action is typically of such moment as to maximize interest. The mere presence of the research effort and its inquiring stance may help the participants to better work through some of their own questions and doubts.

An example of action research, somewhat distantly related to mental health but of direct relevance to social well-being, can be seen in the work of Teele, Jackson, and Mayo (1967). They studied the motivations and experiences of Negro parents who joined together in busing their children from overcrowded, racially imbalanced schools near their homes in the Roxbury section of Boston to uncrowded, predominantly white schools in other areas of the city. Project Exodus, as this program got to be named, came to fruition swiftly, taking many by surprise. However, within a few weeks several social scientists managed to meet together to plan an evaluation. They saw value in feeding back information to the program as it was evolving, and in supplying information about the experiences in Boston to other cities facing similar problems. Being pinched for time and funds, they decided to have Exodus parents themselves do the data gathering. The investigators trained the parents on interview-schedule design, interviewing technique, and data processing, all of which the parents enthusiastically learned. Of the 126 mothers on whom interviews were attempted, 82 percent were successfully interviewed. Those not interviewed did not refuse; they were simply impossible to locate or failed to keep several appointments. The 103 mothers interviewed had a total of 221 children in Exodus. The following information was obtained: practically 70 percent of the parents learned about the project from a friend or had helped formulate it; 86 percent indicated they were motivated to join the program only by the desire for a better educational opportunity for their children; while 97.5 percent of the mothers indicated they had engaged in some prior educational activity, only

40 percent said they had participated in a civil rights activity; 77.7 percent said they were very satisfied with the Exodus program, and 94.8 percent responded that they would want to continue busing without reservation; 76.7 percent of the mothers said their children were very satisfied with the program; 58 percent thought their children were doing better work in the new school; about 76 percent of the parents said that their children did not encounter any prejudice or discrimination at the new school; and 75.5 percent said their children had benefitted greatly from the experience. Analysis of relationships between selected variables further added to the findings that helped the investigators spell out implications for action, and draw plans for further research.

Action research in the field of mental health is often too sketchy to be found in print. It has, however, undoubtedly found a place as a forerunner to more exacting efforts based on programs instituted without provision for evaluation, but where an observant researcher was nevertheless present. Even the "hard" sciences recognize that important leads can be derived from sound observation of spontaneous actions.

Repeatable Demonstrations

Demonstration projects are to community mental health what individual case studies are to psychotherapy. If a procedure is used in a definable way on a specified population, and positive outcomes are secured, there is a tendency to want to confirm its value by repetition. For a demonstration to be of importance and influence, it should be fully and carefully described, responsive to a general need or problem also encountered by other agencies, and an obvious advance over past practice. Although a demonstration is not research, the in-house researcher has the obligation to extract its full value by consulting to the demonstrators about pinpointing their objectives, ascertaining when and how they will know they have been successful, defining procedures, and keeping adequate records. In well-carried-out demonstrations, worthwhile hypotheses are often generated that can be tested later in a more exacting fashion. Described below are examples of some demonstrations that have had wide impact.

In what has historically come to be known as the Marlborough Experiment, Bierer (1964) fashioned ways of enabling "the patient to change his role from that of a passive object of treatment to an active participant and collaborator in the treatment process." He first established a therapeutic social club in 1938 and then went on to develop a day hospital, a night hospital, an aftercare rehabilitation center, a self-governed community hostel, neurotics nomine (encouraging the patients to help others who are in a worse state than they), and a weekend hospital. Over the years Bierer combined these complementary projects to form one comprehensive program. His innovative demonstrations have been accepted at face value, as it were, as procedural improvements over past insipid custodial practice, and adopted by many institutions and advocated in Federal community mental health guidelines. The mere demonstration that mental patients can be approached in a flexible, respectful manner proved to be a most influential finding.

Rendering adequate mental health services to underdeveloped rural regions is obviously difficult. In New Mexico, which in 1959 lacked professional facilities, Libo and Griffith (1966) helped devise a community consultant approach that has served as a model for other rural areas with similar problems. Conceptualizing the issue as one in which local resources would have to be developed, it was decided that qualified professionals (psychologists, social workers, or public health nurses) could be placed in locations from which they could serve an extended territory as leaders in community development and as consultants in mental health. The model followed was that which "had been thoroughly proved by the 'county agent' program of the nation's land-grant colleges [in which] locally based agricultural specialists had revolutionized American farming simply by demonstrating scientific methods to farmers and making the latest scientific data on food and fiber production available to them" (p. 164). One consultant, with a part-time travelling psychiatrist as backup, was assigned to one of four districts participating in the program (a district consisted of three or four counties), and given the responsibility for developing an indigenous program befitting local needs, customs, and resources.

Daily logs kept by the consultants indicated how the percent of time spent at various activities shifted during the succeeding stages of the program and how time spent varied from district to district. In one, a research and service project was aimed at curbing drinking problems among Navajo Indians who had come to the attention of law enforcement agencies. In another, a pilot psychiatric screening project was developed for second-grade students, accompanied by advisory and referral services for parents and school personnel. By the end of the demonstration-project period (1959–1963), "it was clear that an effective and economical way had been found to provide mental health services to the public in professionally under-developed areas" (p. 169). In only one district was success limited by a high level of opposition and the early resignation of the consultant.

Demonstrations do not necessarily have to end with success in order for them to be useful. For example, a much-heralded failure (Cumming and Cumming, 1957) has taught us a great deal about the pitfalls of an overly enthusiastic, but (seen with hindsight) naive, attempt to modify attitudes toward mental illness through an intensive educational program. In a remarkable critique of their own work, the Cummings detail the mistakes they made that led to "closed ranks" by a fairly stable, wealthy community of 1500 people in Prairie Province in Canada. Their "experiment in mental health education" emphasized three principles: (a) behavior is caused, and therefore understandable and subject to change; (b) there is a continuum between normality and abnormality; and (c) there is a wider variety of normal behavior than is generally realized. In their efforts to spread their teachings they made numerous individual local contacts, cultivated the community leaders, issued press releases and weekly news reports, spoke at PTAs, produced film festivals of mental health films, sponsored radio broadcasts, and brought off public debates. Working for them was the fact that they knew the community and did not therefore have to overcome the stigma of "foreignness."

They designed the program evaluation as a before-and-after study, with a matched community serving as a control. Data from pretested questionnaires in the form of Guttman scales, measuring what they called "social distance" and "social responsibility," were obtained by house-to-house canvassing. Although they concluded that "the six-month educational program, in its all-out attempt to improve attitudes toward mental illness, produced virtually no change in the general orientation of the population either toward the social problem of mental illness or toward the mentally ill themselves" (p. 88), they achieved a most important insight: "It is impossible to think too hard *before* such an experiment." Among the lessons learned were the need for paying more attention to the method of entering a community; the need for not assuming a prior knowledge of content of community attitude toward human behavior and its causes; the value of letting members of the community interpret to others after they were educated in small groups; and the fact that there is nothing so practical as a good theory.

Prescriptive Contextual Research

The methods discussed so far are not, of course, mutually exclusive. In practice they are often combined according to the requirements of the situation in a procedure that we shall call prescriptive contextual research. Most community mental health programs are devised to meet clinical contingencies that, even before research intervention, represent compromises stemming from such issues as deployment of scarce manpower, cooperation among agencies, the amount of funds available, and the different viewpoints of the program planners. Belief in the program's effectiveness has for the most part already been affirmed, and the need for evaluation, if it comes to the fore at all, is an afterthought. If it were not for the fact that the awarding of funds typically makes formal evaluation a prerequisite, most programmers would be content with subjective judgements about the program's value based on their experiences with it. For many, this procedure is steeped in honored historical precedent. It is therefore understandable that, more often than not, the researcher and his team are brought into the picture after the fact of program adoption.

From his viewpoint, the researcher has constraints of his own in terms of his obligations to the scientific community. His career and reputation will be enhanced if he can contribute meaningfully to the search for knowledge. This is not easy to do in a compromised setting, and not many good researchers are willing to expose themselves in this way. Or, for that matter, not many believe that what can be accomplished under these circumstances is worth the long-term commitment to the typically time-consuming, pressured, overly complex, and not very comfortable work atmosphere. However, those who do accept and carry through this type of assignment can find the challenge quite gratifying. Among the issues they will have to confront are the following:

1. Agencies with similar resources should be able to repeat the program, if they wanted to, on the basis of the description to emerge.

2. The measures defining inputs and characterizing outcomes should be sufficiently broad as not to require elaborate, expensive efforts which, if not carried out to perfection, could be an excuse for program failure. The taxonomies of the past are not necessarily relevant to the practicalities of the present.

3. Since singular modes of intervention will not be applicable to groups of people with different characteristics, general programs must be narrowed or parallel subprograms formulated.

4. Since conclusions from a study of this kind are necessarily tentative, seeding should be done early for follow-up projects that can better test the emerging hypotheses.

5. If suggestions for change in program design are to be accepted, they are best made in the context of the normal resources of the setting and the normal functions of existing community agencies.

6. While intellectual curiosity often follows tangential issues, which bring rewards in the academic world, esoteric findings will not be what is most valued by the agency. They will expect the evaluation to answer practical questions.

Each of the methods outlined has a role to play in conducting prescriptive contextual research. Before the effect of a program can be determined, some base line has to be established. It is rare to find a substitute for knowing in

some way how things were before an intervention. If an epidemiological type survey is required for base-line data, it should be broad enough to help categorize study populations and survey resources so that additional patterns of disposition can be found for comparative purposes. Simulation models can then be constructed and the program staff can be invited to participate in the evaluative action by helping to formulate questions to be asked of the program, pretesting procedures, and gathering the data required to answer the questions.

A personal experience by the author can serve as an example of prescriptive contextual research. The South Shore Mental Health Center in Quincy, Massachusetts had obtained funding for a project to demonstrate effective communication patterns in community aftercare. The project derived from a period in the late 1950s when the Center, in expanding its programs into the community, realized that hundreds of discharged psychiatric patients were not having their needs met. A concerned group from the community, representatives from the South Shore Mental Health Center, and staff from Medfield State Hospital, which served the district, met together to formulate a program that was put into operation on a limited basis almost immediately. After several years of sharing information, working out a referral system among agencies, and developing guidelines for delegating responsibilities, it was decided that sufficient experience had been gained to organize a comprehensive program that would take responsibility for all ex-patients residing in the community. Supporters of the funded project argued that a community oriented program of multiple aftercare services, planned for at the time of hospitalization, would significantly enhance the patient's chances for readaptation to the community and serve to minimize his need for rehospitalization.

At this point a research director was called in to monitor the demonstration. He began his work by (a) observing closely how the program was being carried out, (b) organizing the staff and interested community participants into task forces for solving logistical problems, and (c) gathering information on the patient population and the resources and demographic characteristics of the community. Among the jobs performed by the various task forces were the selecting and constructing of measuring instruments, the developing of data gathering forms, the clarifying of aftercare strategies, the structuring of a congenial milieu in the aftercare-clinic waiting room, the finding of a building to serve as a halfway house, the perfecting of interview techniques for understanding the realities faced by patients, and the resolving of issues related to coordination with other agencies. Instruments selected, and those specially developed, included a psychological test battery (projective, IQ, MMPI), a Social Appearance Schedule, symptom checklists, the Leary interpersonal scales, and standardized interview forms for relatives. A main feature of the program was a "community conference" on each patient held at Medfield State Hospital soon after hospitalization and again at the Quincy Aftercare Clinic soon after discharge. At these conferences, treatment plans were tailored to meet the needs of individual patients.

A study of decisions made at the community conferences, when related to published findings about schizophrenia, suggested that patients could be easily categorized into two groups: (a) the "process" group, who had a long history of chronic disability, and (b) the "reactive" group, whose breakdown had been acute and who currently had major sectors of their personalities free of debilitating influence. The quality of patients' immediate environmental resources seemed to be a second characteristic important in making dispositional decisions, and this cut across the first categorization. The various dispositions of choice discussed at these conferences, when filtered through the ability of the

agency to work out group programs for implementation, were also readily characterizable. It was further noted that those patients who possessed ego assets that were relatively conflict-free (the reactive type) would be approached with a stance of expectation, and the chronically weak would be approached with a stance of support. Accordingly, the model in Figure 20.1 was formulated.

To test the hypotheses implied by the model, about 180 discharged patients were randomly assigned to the six specified aftercare patterns: (a) the *psychotherapy pattern* was defined as a professional worker seeing a patient in a one-to-one relationship for 45 minutes once a week; (b) the *work pattern* had patients assigned to a vocational counselor who, after studying the patient's employment record, would help him either readjust to his old job or obtain new employment (for homemakers, this was translated as counseling them with their household responsibilities); (c) the *social pattern* was organized as "The Tuesday Evening Adult Social Group," which met weekly for recreation at the Quincy YMCA with friends, relatives, and community guests invited by the program; (d) the *relative pattern* consisted of seeing the relatives of patients in small discussion groups once a week in an effort to support their tolerance of patients; (e) the *nursing pattern* consisted of assigning public health nurses to visit the patient at home on a regular basis; and (f) the *aftercare clinic pattern* was the traditional 10- to 20-minute visit to a psychiatrist at about monthly intervals. Before patients were placed in one of the six aftercare programs, they saw a psychiatrist who prescribed medication and

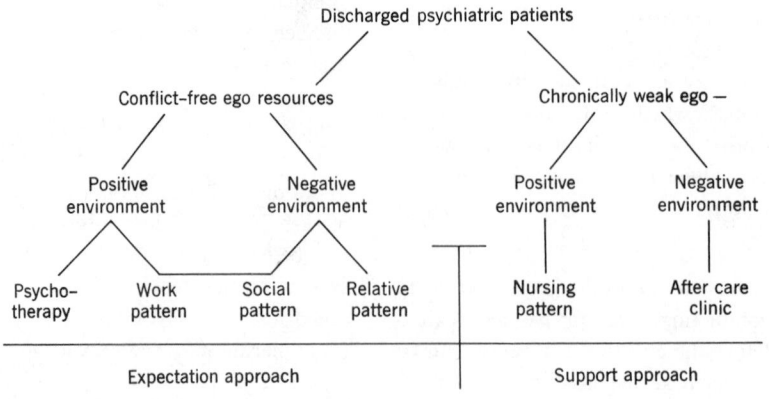

Figure 20.1

assured them of his availability if they needed him. It was hypothesized that patients with relatively conflict-free ego resources who had intact home environments would do well in either the psychotherapy or work pattern; and at the other extreme, patients who were chronically weak and had negative home environments would do best through visits to the aftercare clinic. Because these dispositions were fairly similar to what was being suggested previously, and since the clinicians making these dispositions admitted to not having an objective basis for making them, there was little opposition to these random assignments.

Over and above the pattern hypotheses was the requirement for evaluating the entire aftercare program. This was planned for through a design designating the patient cohort discharged from Medfield State Hospital to another community, not having comprehensive community mental health services, as a control group.

One of the major problems of the evaluation was to find an appropriate criterion of improvement. Although not being rehospitalized was to be considered one index, this was immediately seen as unsatisfactory, since in many instances going back to the hospital, especially for short periods, could not be considered failure, but more a part of the life cycle of patients so afflicted. By clarifying program objectives, it was agreed that the main goal of aftercare was to readjust people to their community by helping them reenter the mainstream and partake of its resources. A Community Adaptation Schedule (Roen and Burnes, 1968) was constructed, standardized, and validated for the South Shore community. This objective type of instrument was designed to tap 33 aspects of a person's relationship to his social environment, including work, family, volunteer activities, housing arrangements, friends, neighbors, recreational activities, financial habits, current events, and shopping.

As one might expect from so complex a before-and-after procedure, all was not carried forth as intended, and individual cells for statistical analysis were too small for definitive findings. However, sufficient data were generated to formulate the following conclusions: (a) significantly fewer patients were returned to the hospital from the Quincy area than from the control area; (b) in general, the successful outcome trends suggested by the abstracted model held true; and (c) effective communication patterns in community aftercare could be established among and between the psychiatric hospital, local agencies, and community-at-large. Considerable additional information was of course gathered that proved valuable in improving the program and helping others to formulate aftercare programs in their own communities (Roen, Cooper, Burnes, Rosenblum, and Ottenstein, 1966).

FINDINGS

Since it is not possible in this chapter to be exhaustive, the intent of this section is to specify some representative generalizations in community mental health for which carefully evaluated programs furnish evidence.

Hospitalization Can Be Avoided

In recent times it was thought that a serious mental breakdown could only be dealt with in a hospital or institution. The condition was perceived in terms so pessimistic or onerous as to be most practically disposed of in large, isolated custodial arrangements. Although there were concerned citizens who pointed out the mental hospital's need for reform (Deutsch, 1949), for the professional it was Goffman's (1961) poignant observations of the dehumanizing character of *asylums* and other "total institutions" that once read could never again be overlooked. Goffman observed how the mental patient's complete break from his former society through the relinquishment of the accoutrements of self, be they material goods or intangibles such as responsibility, leave him, in effect, a nonperson. The insistent split between roles of inmates and staff, stigmatization by the community, the feeling of betrayal by and alienation from those close to him who have typically initiated the process of having him committed, and the necessary "secondary adjustments" through unsanctioned channels that characterize the "underlife of a public institution," form the framework for the patient's judgment of himself and others, and mitigates against successful return to the out-side. This is too high a price to pay, and some (Querido, 1956) have advised the avoiding of hospitalization. The following investigations attest to the fact that this is now quite possible.

A classic study, known as the Worthing Experiment (Carse, 1958) was conceived as a response to serious overcrowding at Grayling-well, a 1210-bed psychiatric hospital serving a population of 412,000 in the county of West Sussex in England. On January 1, 1957, the hospital greatly expanded its outpatient treat-ment facilities in the Worthing region of the county to see if they could reduce the number of patients being admitted. It was specified that no patient living in the Worthing region would be admitted to Graylingwell until he had first been seen by a psychiatrist in the community and the situation had been fully assessed. During the first year, the number of admissions from the Worthing region was reduced by 56 percent, whereas it actually increased slightly for both Chichester and Horsham, the two other regions of the county served by the hospital. The impact of this finding led to the starting of a psychiatric service on January 1, 1958 in Chichester, a more rural setting, which had even more elaborate plans for participation by com-munity agencies and caregivers (Sainsbury and Grad, 1966). Admissions for the calendar year 1958 from the Chichester region declined 51 percent. Admissions from Worthing declined a little more during this year, and for Horsham, the control region, admissions actually went up. Patients not admitted were seen as outpatients, were visited in their homes, were given only day care, or, in the case of the senile, were referred to private nursing homes. The outpatient staff was aided by 73 general medical practitioners residing in the community. No data are reported concerning how much of a burden, if any, this program imposed on the community at large.

In the highly urban setting of Kings County Hospital in Brooklyn, N.Y., immediate psychi-atric treatment services were offered in the hospital admitting office in 1961. After a thorough case history was obtained with the aid of one of the patient's family members or friends, most patients were offered regularly scheduled outpatient appointments once or twice a week. The opportunity for daily or emergency appointments were also made available. During a six-month period, 392 patients were seen, of whom 60 percent were diagnosed as psychotic. Only 13 percent were admitted. About one third of the patients failed to keep subsequent appointments. Of the patients seen, it was judged that 38 percent had shown improvement, while 19 percent remained unchanged (Waltzer, Hankoff, Englehardt, and Kaufman, 1963).

In a study that represents the first comprehen-sive attempt to apply the experimental method to this problem, Pasamanick, Scarpitti, and Dinitz (1967) attempted to determine whether home care was a better or poorer method of treatment than hospitalization. Their study was conducted in Franklin County, Ohio, over a three-year period, with patients diagnosed as schizophrenic, whose family members indicated a willingness to take the patient back home. They randomly assigned 152 patients who came to the hospital for admission, and who met these criteria, to the following three groups: (a) a drug therapy group, which was sent back home; (b) a placebo therapy group, which was treated identically with the drug therapy group; and (c) a hospital control group. Those who were placed in home treatment were assigned a public health nurse who made weekly visits during the first three months. Extensive data on each patient was gathered through psychiatric evaluations, psychological tests, social histories, and nurses' reports. Over 77 percent of the drug home-care patients remained in the community throughout their participation in the project. However, only 34 percent of the placebo cases similarly remained. The mean hospitalization period for the control group was 83 days. The authors concluded that "the project demon-strated in the most conclusive way that home care under drug medication with systematic public health nursing care is quite feasible for newly hospitalized and ambulatory schizo-phrenic patients."

If current trends continue and mental health centers located in the community overcome the stigma of mental disorder, prevention of hos-pitalization will become ever easier. Already, measures of hospital proneness (Freedman, Rosen, Engelhardt, and Margolis, 1967) have been constructed that can significantly predict psychiatric hospitalization so as to make this particular outpatient population more amenable to study and targeted intervention.

Restructuring Institutional Milieu and Linking Programs with the Community Can Facilitate Patient Improvement

One of the fundamental tenets of community mental health is that the social environment has a significant influence on behavioral maladaptations and disorders. The practical usefulness of this principle was fashioned in a large part by sociologists and anthropologists who in the 1950s found mental hospitals fertile laboratories for their interests. The study of *The Mental Hospital* by Stanton, a psychiatrist, and Schwartz, a sociologist (1954), greatly increased our understanding of how communication and interpersonal relations at all levels within the hospital either facilitate or inhibit the therapeutic process. The work of Caudill (1958), a social anthropologist, who studied *The Psychiatric Hospital as a Small Society*, illustrated how "the operation of the hospital as a system was continually shaken by the effects of differences of opinion . . . [and how] a lack of complement between roles in a social system leads to disequilibrium and faulty functioning" (p. 226). The studies to be described below are seen as providing further evidence for the hypothesis that social factors have powerful effects on the therapeutic process.

Rapoport (1960), an anthropologist, spent four years studying, from a social science point of view, the characteristics of "one of the earliest and most vigorous pioneering attempts at the construction of a therapeutic community" (p. 10). In 1947, under the direction of Maxwell Jones, a Social Rehabilitation Unit was introduced to Belmont Hospital (now called Henderson Hospital) near London. The Unit served all of the United Kingdom and mainly admitted voluntary patients. Half of them were between the ages of 20 and 29, about two-thirds were single, and the majority were of middle-class status. The treatment "ideology" of the Unit specified that "socio-environmental influences are themselves capable of effectively changing individual patterns of social behavior" (p. 269). Among the programmatic elements were teas, meetings, workshops, and the involvement of the patient's family. A careful exploratory analysis was done on a sample of 168 patients, but, because of small sample size and crudity of available operational indices, the findings were considered suggestive only. Among the tentative conclusions drawn were the following: (a) improvement on the Unit increased steadily with length of stay; (b) demographic factors (age, sex, education, and class) were not important in distinguishing patients' responses; (c) the Unit was more successful with disturbed patients who had greater personality resources and ego strength than with others; and (d) varying periods of short-term treatment (two weeks versus six months) did not differentiate adjustment, but patients who had more than six months treatment did seem more rehabilitated.

In a project directed toward the reeducation of emotionally disturbed children (Hobbs, 1966), an alternative institutional model to the psychiatric hospital treatment unit was constructed. Whereas the prevailing approach depended heavily on psychotherapy as the means of affecting changes in behavior, the "Project Re-Ed" program was one of social intervention based on a 24-hour schedule of planned behaviors and contingent rewards formed around such concepts as life is to be lived now, competence makes a difference, symptoms can and should be controlled, the group is important to children, and a child should know joy. Two institutions were organized (Cumberland House Elementary School in Nashville, Tenn. and Wright School in Durham, N.C.) to service emotionally disturbed children who would otherwise have been hospitalized. The school program was organized around groups containing eight children, each led by a team of two carefully selected teacher-counselors, most of whom were graduates of a 9-month training program at Peabody College. The overall theoretical assumption of the program was that "the child is an inseparable part of a small social system, of an ecological unit made up of the child, his family, his school, his neighborhood and community . . . The effort is to get each component of the system above threshhold with respect to the requirement of the other components" (p. 1108). The brief Re-Ed school intervention was seen as an aid to making the system function effectively once more, and intervention sought the least practical disruption of normal patterns of living. Among the program's strategies were the use of parents as collaborators, having the children go home weekends, and the employment of a liaison teacher who was responsible for maintaining communications with the child's regular school. Procedures were couched in the idiom of competence and self-fulfillment rather than of illness and pathology. Several methods were devised for evaluating the program. A before-and-after design found that ratings of improvement from a 6-month follow-up ($N = 93$) gives a success rating of approximately 80 percent. The improvement index was a composite of the following: mothers and fathers independently reported a decrease in symptoms, a Vineland type check list showed an increase of social maturity, teachers rated social adjustment more favorably, and improvement was shown on a semantic differential measure of discrepancy between how the child is seen and parental standards for him. A panel of highly esteemed professional experts visited the schools regularly and indicated strong support for the program. Impressive public and state support was forthcoming for the retention and expansion of the programs. And, whereas the traditional hospital based program averaged about $60 per day per child to operate, the Re-Ed Schools, costs were from $20 to $25.

Donahue, Gottesman, and Coons (1968), at the Division of Gerontology of the University of Michigan, demonstrated that even chronic "back-ward" geriatric patients can be helped to resume a more independent life, to work, and in many cases to leave the hospital, if they experience milieu therapy oriented toward normal community life. This conclusion was generated after a series of studies were undertaken at Ypsilanti State Hospital, based on experiences the investigators had with pilot programs in private institutions for the aged. The first study hypothesized that rehabilitation was more likely to be accomplished in a setting offering psychosocial rehabilitation than in the usual hospital regimen. An experimental ward with a sheltered workshop and a stimulating "community"-oriented atmosphere was developed. Out of 170 geriatric patients, of whom 70

percent were diagnosed as chronic brain syndrome and 15 percent as schizophrenic, half were randomly assigned to the experimental ward and the rest to the regular hospital geriatric wards, where they were mixed with nonresearch patients. Study patients improved more than controls on measures of instrumental behavior, social behavior, cognitive/intellectual skills, and psychotic symptoms. To test the program's effect on long-term patients, a second study concentrated on patients who were hospitalized from 5 to 32 years (the first study eliminated patients who were admitted more than four years prior to the beginning of the study). Schizophrenia was the diagnosis for 70 percent of these patients. In this second study, a similar research design showed that experimental ward patients responded quickly to the therapeutic situation as reflected in the measures listed above. This result led to a third study designed to delineate the factors apparently operative in this kind of therapy. It was hypothesized that the milieu-therapy program, emphasizing the creation of a worker role through a sheltered workshop, would be more effective as a therapeutic agent than a milieu therapy emphasizing the traditional institutional role of passive participation in such diversional activities as recreational and occupational therapy. The hypothesis was reported as confirmed through a research design calling for four wards, two with an institutional focus and two with a community focus, one of each focus having only a nursing staff, and the other having a program staff as well. A subsidiary finding was that the usual hospital staff, after proper training, can sustain a high level of this type of therapy.

At the Hudson River State Hospital in New York State, a special Duchess County Unit was set up to provide a comprehensive and integrated service for the mentally ill of Duchess County (Gruenberg and Brandon, 1966). The unit provided decentralized, integrated, small, open, and community-centered services of flexible and continuous care. One emphasis for the Unit was to reduce the "enormous burden of disability associated with psychotic mental illnesses" described as the "social-breakdown syndrome." In order to know whether their objective would be achieved, the investigators chose the direct approach of determining the point prevalence of this syndrome in the entire population at risk. A register of all Duchess County residents who had sought psychiatric treatment after April 1, 1955 in the institutions, clinics, and agencies in the county was prepared. Representative samples from this group were then appraised at one point in time. Data gathered in this fashion showed an annual rate for the "social breakdown syndrome" in non-geriatric adult patients to be about 50 per 100,000 at the end of the experimental period, which was half as much as it was estimated to be for the two prior years. The investigators believe this reflects a true decline in incidence during the demonstration period.

The studies described are only representations from a growing body of literature, such as Sanders, Smith, and Weinman (1967), pointing to the effectiveness of socioenvironmental treatment for certain groups of patients. More exacting explanations of why these approaches work, embedded in a body of theory, may well follow the logic of Cumming and Cumming (1962), who bring together in their book, *Ego and Milieu*, the results of investigations on the social and interpersonal aspects of hospital treatments and relate them to developments in ego psychology. Their theoretical assumptions rely heavily on the sociological theories of Parsons and the psychoanalytic theories of Erikson.

The Use of Nonprofessionals Can Be Mutually Advantageous

Since the enormous demand for mental health services outstrips the availability of professionals, and since some of this need is directly attributable to groups in the population whose problems would be ameliorated by enhancing employment opportunities, programs attempting to meet both requirements with a single stroke are rather compelling. Some of the better evaluated projects attempting simultaneously to meet both needs are described below.

Margaret Rioch (1967), in relation to the problem of "second careers" for women, developed a project to determine whether, and to what extent, mature, intelligent women with no previous special preparation could, after two years of part-time training, become "mental health counselors" who would function effectively as psychotherapists in certain limited situations. Educated middle-class women were chosen carefully through such selection aids as written autobiographies and observations of participation in group procedures. The training program consisted of (a) practical work and supervision at agencies, (b) observations of individual, family, and group therapy, (c) case seminars and special lectures, and (d) courses on personality development, adolescence, family dynamics, and psychopathology. Although eleven people had some part in rendering instruction, their time spent on the project was only the equivalent of two full-time workers. The program was evaluated at midpoint by four outside raters knowing nothing of the program, who assessed sample tape-recorded interviews of students with clients. At the end of the second year, a panel of three highly qualified examiners were invited to read a case report, examine each student for about an hour, and listen to taped interviews. Both procedures had a positive outcome, with the final examiners commenting on the students' degree of commitment, lack of defensiveness, skill at practice, secure status, and good group identification. A follow-up four years after graduation showed all eight of the original students still employed and employers, supervisors, and co-workers pleased with them. The success of this project led to another (Lourie, 1968) of similar design, except that training this time was directed toward producing women who could counsel mothers about the problems of young children. Here it was found that the eight women who went through this second program could be trained to counsel effectively, but had difficulty in securing positions in agencies.

Socially deprived youth, who had experienced considerable "hard-core" problems, were trained for new professional roles in the human service fields at the Bakers Dozen Youth Center (MacLennan, Klein, Pearl, and Fishman, 1966; Fishman, 1968). The Institute for Youth Studies at Howard University helped formulate the program, which "screened-in" rather than "screened-out" applicants residing in an area of Washington, D.C. that had the highest levels of poverty, unemployment, and substandard housing. Applicants were considered with characteristics that ordinarily would have barred them from employment. The eight trainees selected were divided into high- and low-risk groups, four in each. High-risk youths were described as deprived youths who had a series of police and criminal involvements and some emotional or delinquency problems, and those who spent time in an institution for an offense. Also, their reading level was not above the fifth grade, they dropped out of school early, and they never worked longer than three months at any given job. The low-risk group was composed also of deprived youth who dropped out of school and were working at menial jobs, but they had no police record, dropped out of school for family reasons, and worked at jobs for longer periods of time. The goals of the training program were to develop in these youths necessary motivation, identity, and values, and to have them learn the basic personal, social, interpersonal, and mental health skills that would help them successfully cope with the clients they were to serve. Their future jobs were to include being leaders for groups of children, participating in program development with professionals, observing and recording individual and group behavior, conducting interviews, escorting groups on trips and tours, attending staff conferences, writing progress reports, and keeping records. Evaluation of the program was accomplished by collecting data in the form of self-reports, projective tests, and observations made on the aides in experimental and natural situations. From the information collected, the investigators concluded that young people such as these can be trained to do successful work as aides. Although personality traits did not appear to change significantly, their social adjustment improved markedly. Both the high- and low-risk groups performed well and, with the one exception of a boy who dropped out early owing to trouble with the police, no essential differences in outcome between the groups were found.

Volunteers are another source of nonprofessional manpower used in mental health activities. Programs enlisting college students are among those that have been most carefully evaluated. One such project, the Companion Program of the Connecticut Valley Hospital, has been in operation for almost a decade (Holzberg, Knapp, and Turner, 1967), starting with Wesleyan University undergraduates and spreading to several other Connecticut universities. Much of the initial inspiration came from the experience of Harvard students who functioned as helpers in recreational programs and case aides assigned to individual patients in a Massachusetts psychiatric hospital (Umbarger, Dalsimer, Morrison, and Breggin, 1962). The objectives of the Connecticut program were to give patients the experience of a gratifying social relationship, provide a rewarding intellectual and emotional experience for the students, and boost the morale of the often frustrated hospital personnel. Students, under the supervision of a mental health professional, were assigned to carefully selected patients as Companions. The range of activities in which the student and patient engaged was limited only by the interests of the patient and the good taste and judgment of the student. Some Companions took patients into town or on visits to the university. The design for program evaluation called for the comparative analysis of standard psychological tests administered to Companions and matched control students not participating in the program. The following conclusions, some of them based on replicated findings, were reached about Companions: (a) they were not unstable adventure seekers, but seemed rather to use the experience to satisfy impulses of "generosity and altruism," having few available outlets for this in the college environment at that time; (b) they showed more "stirring-up" of attitudes; (c) they shifted conspicuously toward greater self-acceptance, while the controls showed a slight trend toward less self-acceptance at the end of the year; and (d) in follow-up of alumni, it was found that the program had lasting value as remembered in retrospect. In comparison with students who had volunteered for other forms of social-service activities in the local community, Companions gained significantly in knowledge and positive attitudes toward mental illness, although there were no significant differences between groups at the outset. Thus two individuals who normally would have a rare or transient encounter were brought together, and the conclusion was reached that the Companion Program had made a significant contribution to the treatment of the patient population as measured by a significant decline on the depression scale of the MMPI as compared to non-Companion controls; to the morale of the hospital; and to the nonintellective education of college students.

Other sources of manpower have been described in the literature, one of the more intriguing of which is *The Indigenous Nonprofessional* (Reiff and Riessman, 1965). The indigenous worker, through such unique characteristics as having peer status with and a similar style of life as the client, adds a "bridge" dimension of great usefulness to the professional trying to be of help, especially to those of lower socioeconomic strata. They can function as "aides" in community action, housing, homemaking, child care, or parent education programs, or fulfill general roles as "expediters" and "ombudsmen." Another interesting manpower development, somewhat related, is the advocacy of *New Careers for the Poor* (Pearl and Riessman, 1965), especially as directed toward helping occupations. These and the other programs mentioned would seem to be appropriate responses to the now-recognized observation (Albee, 1959) that in the foreseeable future there is not likely to be a sufficient number of mental health professionals to meet the demands for services.

Mental Health Ideology Is a Measurable Influence on Program Development

In mental health practice, where so great a variety of procedures are used, it is unlikely that an approach will be effective unless there is belief in its underlying assumptions. Greenblatt, Levinson, and Williams (1957) report the findings of several studies which show that the way clinicians view personality and conceive of mental illness influences their professional role definitions. Hollingshead and Redlich (1958) were able to divide psychiatrists into categories of directive-organic and analytic-psychological on the basis of the psychiatrist's beliefs as to the causes of mental illness. Kotin and Sharaf (1967) studied the conceptual and ideological commitment of the Boston State Hospital staff and concluded that it was a highly significant factor in their work.

Armor and Klerman (1968) postulated at least three treatment orientations in psychiatry that qualify as professional ideologies: somatic, psychotherapeutic, and sociotherapeutic. They conducted a factor-analytic study of questionnaire responses of 365 psychiatrists at 15 different hospitals in the East and Midwest. Responses to the mailed questionnaire, which included 57 Likert-type attitude questions, represented an 80 percent return rate. The factor accounting for most of the variance could be labeled clearly "somatotherapeutic," since it had highest loadings on items stressing biological causes and somatic treatments of mental illness. The second factor had the highest loadings on items emphasizing psychotherapy, psychoanalysis, and the doctor-patient relationship. Although Factor 3 accounted for the least amount of variance, the items that loaded the highest on it stressed the milieu's importance in the improvement of psychiatric patients. This third factor, however, lacked both etiological content and strong comparative preference to the other forms of treatment.

In a study aimed directly at constructing a Community Mental Health Ideology Scale (CMHIS), Baker and Schulberg (1968) surveyed psychiatrists working in settings other than hospitals, as well as other mental health professionals, and showed the measure to be clearly differentiating. The item-analyzed scale consists of 38 declarative statements that elicit responses of agreement or disagreement on five conceptual categories: a population focus, primary prevention, social treatment goals, comprehensive continuity of care, and total community involvement. The scale was mailed to various criterion groups of mental health specialists, some of whom were known to be highly oriented to community mental health, and others who were not. The 484 responses represented a return rate of 61.7 percent. Three methods of determining reliability for the scale each produced coefficients above .90. The scale significantly discriminated groups known to have positive community mental health views from random samples of mental health professionals. Also, the scores related significantly to self-reported responses of identification with a community mental health orientation, interest in keeping up with new developments in community mental health, and preference for a symposium on recent advances in community mental health. As compared to low scores, those scoring high on community mental health ideology (a) spent a significantly greater portion of their time in administration, consulting with community agencies, and teaching; (b) worked in significantly greater numbers in universities, medical schools, general hospitals, community clinics, and schools systems; and (c) tended to be significantly younger and to have received their advanced training more recently.

Langston (in press) replicated the Baker-Schulberg study on employees of the first two community mental health centers established in Houston. His results were similar in that he found significant relationship between CMHIS scores and professional affiliation, years of liberal arts education, and length of time working in a mental health center. He concluded that the scale was reliable and that a medical education would appear to have a different effect on adherence to the ideology of the community mental health movement than would a liberal arts education. The rank order of mean scores from high community mental health ideology to low was found, among the professional groups, to be as follows: social work, psychology, occupational therapy, nursing, and psychiatry.

Suicide Prevention Centers Can Be Effective

In a recent international survey of suicide studies, the World Health Organization (1968) has estimated that an average of at least 1000 persons a day commit suicide in the world, the ratio of attempted suicide to suicide being about 8:1. Among the findings reported are the following: (a) a suicidal act is committed frequently as a "cry for help" rather than a clear desire to die; (b) a person who has made a previous attempt is more likely to die through suicide than one who has no history of suicide attempts, and if there have been two previous attempts, the subsequent risk is considerably increased; (c) the danger of a repetitive attempt depends on whether the act has brought about a change in the life situation and mental state; (d) a high percentage of persons committing or attempting suicide have given previous warning of their intent; and (e) a disruption of

close personal relations is one of the main precipitating factors in suicidal behavior. On a note of optimism, they report that "there is now some evidence that the recently instituted 24-hour telephone services, giving isolated, lonely, or desperate persons a possibility to communicate, may help to avert suicide acts" (p. 15).

Since this particular finding has often been corroborated, it will not be greatly elaborated upon here. Suicide-prevention centers (Farberow and Shneidman, 1961) vary in complexity from independent comprehensive service and research units to a simple around-the-clock telephone service in the emergency room of a general hospital. Data gathered from one such telephone service is illustrative. Waltzer and Hankoff (1965) report on a program sponsored by the emergency psychiatric treatment service of Kings County Hospital in Brooklyn. Daily papers, radio, and television carried the news of the initiation of the service, and its telephone number was listed under "Suicide Prevention Service" in the local telephone directories. Of the 1523 calls received during the year, 383 directly concerned suicide. The police were notified of 51 calls, which were viewed as emergencies. One third of the identifiable callers came to the hospital for help. A little more than half of these were referred for emergency outpatient psychiatric treatment, about a third were immediately hospitalized, and a few were referred to other facilities. Although control data was lacking, the investigators' conclusion that the service had value as an immediate deterrent to suicide seems warranted.

In a finding even more directly to the point, it was reported that at the University of Texas (Behavioral Science Newsletter, 1968), after the establishment of an Emotional Crisis Center, only one suicide occurred, whereas during a comparable period of time, between 5 and 10 would have been expected. "Since it began operation, the Center received 13,000 calls from students, thwarted 15 suicide attempts, and counseled 1200 students who indicated their emotional stress by calling" (p. 2). If, according to Ross (1969), suicide is second to automobile accidents as a cause of death among college students, programs like this would seem to have the potential for significantly changing the picture.

Workable preventive programs in the behavioral realm are not easy to come by. When one is developed it is worth serious study and consideration. McGee (1965) advocates its use as a model for community mental health programs, and details a design that "emphasizes immediate answers to all 'cries for help' as well as a wide range of research activities" (p. 162). What will have to be overcome, however, is the criticism (Hitchcock, 1969) that suicide-prevention services are focused on the symptomatic behavior of a highly select group in that there are few calls from persons over 65 or from blacks.

Symptoms of Mental Disorder Correlate with Demographic, Socioeconomic, and Cultural Variables

If factors reflecting social conditions are found to relate to mental illness, etiological theory would have to be extended beyond the previously dominant organic and psychodynamic hypotheses to include the possibility of a third force. This consideration would be seen as a major finding of wide significance to the behavioral sciences. It is then no wonder that the issue has been pursued in some depth from the perspective of each of the disciplines concerned and has become part of the foundation for such subspecialties as social psychiatry, psychiatric sociology, anthropological or cross-cultural (transcultural) psychiatry, and community psychology.

The now classical study by Faris and Dunham (1939) opened up the modern era of research into this phenomenon by reporting significant differences in rate patterns for different psychoses in separate regions of Chicago. Based on 28,763 admissions from Chicago to four state hospitals during the years 1922 to 1934, they found that most schizophrenic patients had resided near the center of the city or in other low socio-economic areas of high residential mobility where the foreign-born lived in slums amid ethnic groups. Manic-depressive and senile psychoses did not conform to any characteristic ecological pattern. This touched off the still active controversy of whether unsatisfactory social circumstances with multiple deprivation breed major kinds of mental disorder or whether people, because of their mental condition, "drift" into class and community positions. In other words, are theories of social causation or social selection more explanatory for this finding?

Although subsequent epidemiological surveys of mental illness, such as the series done by Lemkau (1943) and his associates in Baltimore, corroborated relationships between mental disorder and social variables, the large-scale, fairly exhaustive, long-term effort by Hollingshead and Redlich (1958) in New Haven brought matters to a head. Their study tried to answer the question not only of whether mental illness was related to social class, but also of whether a mentally ill patient's position in the status system influences his treatment. Their comprehensive survey of the community social structure, the psychiatric patients in treatment, the institutions where they were cared for, and the psychiatrists who were treating them, gave affirmative answers to both questions. In proportion to its size, the lowest class contributed 10 times more of the mentally ill than did the two highest classes combined; and although psychiatrists claimed that selection of treatment was based purely on psychiatric criteria, the higher the class, the more gentle and insightful were their methods, while the lower the class, the more direct, authoritative, compulsory and, at times, "coercively brutal," were the methods.

In a follow-up study, Myers and Bean (1968) asked whether social class was a determinant of the New Haven patient's experience in the 10 years following the original study. For the 1563 patients followed, they found that the higher the class, (a) the less likely the patients were to be hospitalized 10 years after the original study; (b) the greater the proportion of outpatient treatment; (c) the more likely the person was to be living in the community at the time of death, and (d) the greater the chances of hospital discharge following a readmission. In terms of type of hospital treatment received, the higher the class, the greater the proportion of patients receiving therapies associated with higher discharge rates, such as psychotherapy, and the lower the social status, the more likely they were to receive drug therapy and custodial care. Myers and Bean's inquiry into the former patient's adjustment in the community was accomplished by comparing them with a matched control group of never-treated individuals on both the psychobiological dimension (mental status impairment) and the social dimension (performance and participation). They arrived at the following conclusion (p. 206):

In brief, mental illness is apparently catastrophic for the lower class patient and his family. The social and economic problems which characterize this class level in our society are magnified for the former mental patient. If hospitalized, the chances are less than at higher social levels that he will return to the community. If the patient does return or is treated in outpatient facilities, the impact of his illness is maximal, resulting in serious employment and financial problems and a high degree of social isolation.

Clausen and Kohn (1959), however, could not replicate the finding of relationship between neighborhood characteristics or father's occupation and rates of schizophrenia. They studied all those persons who had been hospitalized from the Hagerstown community in any mental hospital in the state of Maryland during a given period with a diagnosis of schizophrenia, manic-depressive psychosis, involutional psychosis, or paranoia. The main interest of the investigation was to test the hypothesis that enforced social isolation was of etiological significance, and although they did find that roughly a third of their schizophrenics had been solitary or isolated from peers in childhood, as compared to the controls, there was little evidence that their social isolation was externally imposed, and the hypothesis had to be rejected.

Next, Srole, Langer, Michael, Opler, and Rennie (1962) attacked the issue by surveying untreated as well as treated disorders in midtown Manhattan, and found not only that there was a significant relationship between psychiatric symptoms and the socioeconomic status of their subjects, but also that the relationship was almost as high for the parent's socioeconomic status as well. This finding further weakened the "drift" hypothesis and focused interest on a "stress" formulation; that is, the more sources of stress, the higher the probability of mental disorder. However, the fact that the Midtown Study identified more than 80 percent of a socially functioning group of people as

being in some category of mental illness, seems to call for a reexamination of the criteria for mental disorder.

Meanwhile, the Stirling County Study (Leighton, Leighton, and Armstrong, 1964), which has already been described in some detail, also provided evidence of the relationship of psychiatric symptoms to social conditions, with focus on the hypothesis that community disintegration was a mediating factor.

A review by Dohrenwend and Dohrenwend (1965) of over 25 attempts to count untreated cases of psychological disorder in community populations in various parts of the world, in both urban and rural settings, brought into focus the problem of construct validity in the measures used. While they concluded that "the cumulative evidence . . . appears to establish the association of low socioeconomic status with a high rate of judged psychopathology" (p. 63), they find reason for entertaining the hypothesis that many of the symptoms that produced these judgments may represent transient responses by normal persons to objective stress-producing events in their immediate environment. Following this line of reasoning, Dohrenwend (1967) conducted a study that interviewed a probability sample of 1000 adults, ages 21 to 59, from the Washington Heights section of New York City and compared them to a group of about 1000 psychiatric outpatients attending various clinics in the area. The interview procedures used were similar to those of the Midtown and Stirling County studies. In both groups, he found strong ethnic and class differences in modes of expressing distress. For example, in the nonpatient samples, he found that Puerto Ricans scored higher than Jewish, Irish, or Negro subjects on an instrument that relied heavily on psychophysiological items such as headaches, cold sweats, and personal worries that get one down physically. There were also indications of ethnic-group differences in tendencies to "yea-say" (high for less-educated Negroes on some items) and "nay-say" (high for the Irish on some items); and there appeared to be a sharp difference in the way members of different ethnic groups rate the social desirability of many of the symptom items, suggesting that some of the items themselves may have different meanings and hence different implications in the different subcultures. Follow-up interviews on 150 of the nonpatients, about two years after the first interview, produced the finding that symptom scores tended to increase with negative intervening events, such as the serious physical illness of a spouse, and decrease with positive intervening events, such as a job promotion. These results appear to raise questions about the psychiatric meaning of the relationship between social class and psychological symptomology. Dohrenwend suggests that much of the untreated symptomotology reported in community studies may "consist actually of normal and reversible responses to stressors in the contemporary situations of the respondents." In a sense, this is an ecological conclusion that places psychological symptoms in the context of sociocultural adaptation.

Early Detection and Intervention May Reduce Prevalence

Secondary prevention is often approached through early detection, since change is usually easier to accomplish at the incipient stages of a disorder than it is after the problem has become ingrained with the passing of time. The schools have long been seen as attractive loci for preventive efforts because they are relatively approachable structured institutions in which practically the cross-section of an entire population spends considerable time. School surveys of pathogenic symptoms have varied in their estimates since Mangus and Seeley (1955) studied the mental health needs of a rural county in Ohio and concluded that "at least 18 percent of all third graders in all schools in the county were poorly adjusted and in need of some kind of mental health aid and an even higher proportion of the sixth-grade children showed evidences of poor mental health" (p. 205). But the variations in estimates found in other studies seem due to environmental and sociocultural settings rather than to discontinuous findings of need.

In what developed into one of the more ambitious undertakings in this realm, an active organization of educators and lay people undertook, in 1947 in the city of St. Louis, a group therapy project for parents of children with behavior problems in the public schools (Gildea, Glidewell, and Kantor, 1967). The

professional staff hired to perform this function saw as their first task the classifying of the mental health of children. They decided to approach this by considering the child's general state of emotional well-being from the points of view of his teacher, his mother, and his classmates (Glidewell, Mensh, Domke, Gildea, and Buchmueller, 1957). The assessments, made by professionals, were aided by a specially devised symptom checklist, a sociometric questionnaire, a semiprojective story-completion instrument called "Secret Stories," an adaptation of Roger's use of a "wishes" test, and a method of classroom observation called "The Bean Game" devised by Ronald Lippitt. In 80 percent of the cases, there was exact numerical agreement between the ratings of the teachers and the ratings of the professionals. Follow-up interviews in the earlier aspects of the study showed that 80 percent of the children whose parents participated in the group therapy were seen as improved in adjustment by the teachers, while about the same percent of "disturbed" children whose parents did not participate were seen as unimproved. However, subsequent controlled studies, repeated annually three times, did not result in significant changes. More positive conclusions were that as a screening tool, the mother's reports of symptoms can be used with about 70 percent efficiency, which is about as good as any medical screening device, and with the addition of a clinic team plus teachers, 90 percent selection can be attained. Also, teachers involved in the program became more sensitive to the emotional adjustment of their children, and involved mothers generally seemed to be accepting more responsibility for their children's behavior.

Bower and Lambert (1961) used screening instruments for kindergarten through third grade, which were partially validated on 650 children through teacher-, peer-, and self-ratings. Their scales ask for ratings on a 7-point continuum ranging from markedly disturbed psychotic children to those with normal problems of everyday living. They suggested the following criteria be used in large-scale school screening procedures: (a) it should be possible to complete the procedure with only such information as the teachers could obtain without outside technical or professional assistance; (b) the procedure should be simple enough for the teacher to undertake without long training or daily supervision; (c) it should result in tentative identification of problems followed by referral to specialists; (d) it should not encourage the teacher to label or diagnose children; (e) it should not threaten the children or violate privacy or good taste; and (f) it should be inexpensive to use.

Cowen and Zax (1968) reported a series of studies in which they clipped a "Red Tag" to the records of children who in an early school screening process were found to be emotionally disturbed. Although their early-intervention program has gone through certain meta-morphoses over the years, their "enduring component has been the utilization of professional staff in the schools as an educative, consultative, and resource team" (p. 52). Their target group consisted of third-grade youngsters who had been exposed to the program for three years. Two control schools, demographically comparable to the experimental school, provided a frame of reference for evaluation. From the data gathered they conclude that (a) there is a cluster of salutary consequences of the prevention program tapping adjustive, performance, achievement, and sociometric measures in children exposed to it for three years; and (b) children evidencing ineffective behavior in the first year (Red-Tag) are by the end of the third year performing less adequately in school, showing greater signs of maladjustment on both objective tests and behavior ratings, obtaining lower scores on standard achievement tests, being rated more negatively sociometrically, and manifesting more physical complaints in the school situation, all in comparison to their non Red-Tag peers. Follow-up studies of alumni of their first prevention program at seventh grade produced evidence indicating that the earlier-diagnosed "Red-Tag" child, if left untreated, continued to show poorer development throughout his entire elementary school career. In their current program (Zax and Cowen, 1967), a school social worker and school psychologist devote themselves to early detection among first graders. Their diagnostic battery is administered with the help of the classroom teachers shortly after the start of the school year to small groups of 10 to 15 children. It includes the California Test of Mental Maturity and the Goodenough Draw a Man Test. Behavioral observations and teacher's estimate of ability are additional inputs. The social worker then interviews the mother in a way that structures it as part of a routine procedure for getting better acquainted and as a reflection of the continuing interest of the school and the project team in the child and his family. Based upon the cumulative record, when emotional difficulties are already manifest or incipient difficulties are judged to be probable, the child's folder is clipped with a Red-Tag. The preventive features of the program include help for these children by teacher aides (typically middle-aged housewives), who undergo a five-week training program, and after-school programs staffed by undergraduate education-major volunteers from the University of Rochester who take on the role of "companion," supervised in groups of six by a fourth-year clinical graduate student. A third group of nonprofessionals trained to perform in the program were retired persons.

Early-detection procedures are not only applicable to beginning elementary school, but could also be used with effectiveness in other transitional phases of development. For example, Osborn (1968) reports a study done at Ohio State University of two groups of college students who had been identified as potential social and emotional "dysfunctioners" by administration of the Cornell Index during freshman orientation. The students in one group were seen for one or more screening interviews in the Mental Hygiene Clinic, while those in the other group were not. The comparison showed that the students who had received a screening interview stayed in college longer, were dismissed less frequently, received fewer notations of low academic achievement on their transcripts, made fewer changes from one college to another within the University, and paid fewer visits to the University Health Service for physical complaints.

The procedures and findings discussed in this section lead quite naturally to the next and last generalization to be elaborated upon here, perhaps the most crucial of all in that it concerns primary prevention through anticipation of turmoil.

Hazardous Situations Provide Opportunities for Preventive Intervention

Aside from making it easier to treat the patient in the context of his own community, the change wrought by community mental health has approached "revolutionary" proportions (*Time*, 1969) in the way mental health professionals have changed in their mode of public practice. The relatively long-term psychotherapy approach seems to be giving way in public practice to "crisis intervention," a technique that attempts to deal immediately and quickly with emotional turmoil precipitated by a clear and present hazard.

A short elaboration of crisis theory, a formulation (Caplan, 1964) that has given strong impetus to the entire community mental health movement, may be of interest here. Crisis theory relegates importance to the timing and mode of an intervention. A crisis is seen as a transition period for the individual in which is embedded not only opportunity for personal growth, but also potential for serious damage. The disequilibrium caused by accidental or developmental crises places people in a highly responsive state toward help. The briefest kinds of intervention at this time could forestall the fixating of symptoms and determine a more appropriate outcome, and might educate the individual to a problem-solving attitude that would be helpful in subsequent disruption. A rather useful implication of this conception is that a study of the crises commonly experienced in life—the birth of premature children, bereavement, divorce—may enable the practitioner to reach out to the normal institutions that serve people in crisis and educate them to the mental health issues involved.

Crisis theory developed in part from a study by Lindemann (1944) of bereavement reactions of family members of those who died in the Coconut Grove night club fire of 1942. He found that the duration of a grief reaction was dependent on the success with which a person did his "grief work," and described the stages in the normal course of grief, suggesting that individuals could be helped through these stages to prevent prolonged and serious alterations in social adjustment. He postulated that there are both adaptive and maladaptive ways of meeting a range of emotional hazards during the life cycle, each one of which may have significant consequences for later psychological soundness and ability to cope. To further explore the implications of his findings, in 1949, through the Harvard School of Public Health, he helped establish the Wellesley Human Relations Service, which proved to be a forerunner for ideas about the delivery of innovative community mental health services (Klein and Lindemann, 1961).

Crisis theory has been studied and extended in many ways. One example of how research is accomplished in this area is furnished by Caplan, Mason, and Kaplan (1965) who studied mothers of premature children at the time of birth by first doing exploratory studies followed by predictive research designs. In their first exploration, on the basis of ten cases (five judged to have had a healthy outcome and the other five an unhealthy outcome), they observed that those families of healthy outcome exhibited a continuous concern for their situation, gathered as much information as they could obtain about prematurity, showed continuous awareness of negative feelings, actively sought help from within the family or the community to accomplish the tasks associated with care of the premature baby, and tried to find assistance in dealing with their negative feelings. On the other hand, the unhealthy-outcome families did not exhibit this behavior. The investigators then randomly selected 28 mothers and made predictions in each case on the quality of the mother-child relationship to be found six weeks after the baby was home from the hospital. The prediction took the form of a global rating based on interviews conducted during the first five days following the birth of the baby. Predictions turned out to be highly accurate. In a second exploratory study, the investigators isolated four major psychological tasks that appeared to be essential both for successful mastery of the prematurity crisis situation and for providing a sound basis for a future healthy mother-child relationship. This was accomplished by inspecting the data gathered on mothers categorized in terms of the mental health outcome. After formulating what these tasks were, they then set about to verify them as hypotheses in relation to 30 mothers of premature babies. Measurements of the manner in which mothers accomplished tasks were derived from interview records and observations. Outcome was measured six weeks later by interviews and observations made by social workers, who were not told the outcome predictions and were given no information about the mother's statements or behavior during the period when the babies were in the hospital. Predictions were found to be 80 percent accurate. This series of studies involved 86 cases of premature birth in intact families, and although fraught with serious methodological problems of which the investigators were well aware, it was felt that the findings advanced their thinking about crisis theory in general, and handling situations of premature births in particular.

For example, out of the same laboratory (Baler and Golde, 1964) emerged the design of a study of conjugal bereavement which hypothesized that (a) the widowed, in comparison with the married, experience a significantly higher risk of mental disorders and psychosomatic illness; (b) there is a significant association between mental and physical health outcome, and patterns of coping behavior in response to intrapsychic and external reality tasks imposed by the loss of a spouse; and (c) the excess risk of mental disorders and psychosomatic illness among the widowed can be significantly reduced by preventive intervention techniques that specifically modify coping behavior.

Over the last two decades there has been ample documentation of the effects of environmental stress, social tensions, and residential dislocation on psychological as well as physical or medical adjustment (Ojemann, 1963). The following résumé is in the form of a sampling of publications from which the interested reader can obtain more of the details. Scotch (1960) carefully compared Zulus who moved into cities to those who remained on reservations in South Africa in terms of incidence of hypertension. He found the move to the city clearly stressful. Skipper and Leonard (1968) report data from a field experiment indicating that "independent of illness, the social environment of the hospital may produce stress for child surgical patients and their mothers . . . [and that] social inter-

action with hospital personnel, providing information and emotional support, . . . may reduce a child's stress and have indirect but profound effects on his social, psychological, and even physiological responses to hospitalization and surgery" (p. 275). Kantor (1965) edited a collection of research reports on *Mobility and Mental Health* that describes some of the conditions under which residential change affects psychological adjustment. Fried (1963) studied urban renewal in the West End of Boston and found dislocation to be so disruptive and disturbing as to characterize it as "a crisis with potential danger to mental health for many people." Of his sample, 46 percent showed symptoms of severe grief and fragmentation of their sense of spatial and group identity. The effect of social stress on cardiovascular disease is summarized in an edited volume by Syme and Reeder (1967), and issues in research on psychological stress are discussed in detail in an edited book by Appley and Trumbull (1967).

Definitive studies of the actual techniques used for intervening in hazardous situations have been slow to materialize. However, some inroads have been made. For example, Waldfogel and Gardner (1961), in a study of internal and external factors in school phobia crises, "discovered a striking and unexpected relationship between the remission of the acute symptom and the promptness with which treatment was begun" (p. 307). They concluded that recent antecedent events are important not only in the choice of symptom but also its severity. Arnold (1967) described and evaluated an effective Peace Corps field group-therapy program for culture shock which, he finds, "provides the focal point for nearly all overseas adjustment problems" (p. 53). The various types and purposes of the brief psychotherapies used in community mental health centers are reviewed by Barten (1969) in Volume 1 of a contemplated series entitled *Progress in Community Mental Health*, and Parad (1966) has brought together selected readings on the specific technique of crisis intervention.

Other Findings

There are, of course, other well-documented findings in community mental health for which generalizations could be attempted. If they were to be pursued, they would relate to such problems as the aftercare of ex-hospital patients (Freeman and Simmons, 1963; Morrissey, 1965), mental-health education (Nunnally, 1961), and helping "hard-core" families (Minuchin, Bontalvo, Buerney, Rosman and Schumer, 1967). On the other hand, there are crucial problems for which well-documented findings are not available. For example, the consultation process, one of the central activities in community mental health, has not been well researched. It is fraught with all the difficulties of psychotherapy research and then some. However, the positive subjective evaluations of those engaged in this activity have helped it become quite widespread as a mental health technique.

DISCUSSION

Many of the studies described have inelegancies. If space were taken for exacting critique (and some studies have been dissected in the literature), I believe we would be doing an injustice to the main point of community mental health. Mental health studies that are methodologically excellent are typically devoid of practical value. Since the field under discussion is characterized by urgencies that require action on the basis of plausible practicality, the problem is seen more as one of what to conclude on the basis of information obtained. This review has taken the stance that all serious and thoughtful study adds in some measure to knowledge or lays the groundwork necessary for further pursuit of that knowledge.

This is not to say it is unnecessary to judge the value of what is being done. Rather, under the present circumstances, where exacting answers to pointed questions cannot be obtained with complete confidence, it is not strategic in field studies to discard serious efforts out of hand or use lack of precision as a restriction as to where we search for evidence. The analogy suggested by Binner (1966) seems appropriate to this issue: "It is as though we are working on a light bulb, discovering the indandescent light. Early in the work it might be quite dim—in fact, it flickers. We would propose to use this instrument to light up the landscape and some-

one would say, 'No, no, let's not use it. It is very dim, it is flickering, it casts all kinds of shadows, it distorts, and we'll make all kinds of mistakes if we use this' . . ." (p. 352).

Structure of the Problem

In a community mental health setting, pressure for research and evaluation services are felt from several sources. How the research team spends its time depends upon whose needs are given priority or whose role at the agency dominates, or upon the particular perspective of the investigator, if he has achieved independent status. The following wide scatter of topics reported on in the literature reflects this situation. If the theme of the center becomes planning, efforts are expended in epidemiological-survey directions to uncover information relating to populations at risk, more fuller understanding of the community, or paths to the agency. If operations are at issue, research and evaluation become concerned with deployment and use of manpower, efficiency at intake, the problem of psychotherapeutic dropouts, or the conservation of treatment time. If agency administration comes to the fore, time can be spent on developing a computer system to give the executive immediate feedback of crucial data or on working out more efficient ways of keeping records in an up-to-date information storage and retrieval system. If broader participation in the program is of prime concern, one might study the roles of clinic boards and local mental health associations, or research the value of mental health education and the use of volunteers. If coordination among community agencies becomes salient, one can look into networks of communication or patterns of consultation. If the manifest need of patients is what becomes paramount, work might be carried forth on more effective ways of relieving symptoms or eradicating stigma. If the families of hospitalized patients are seen as a point of pressure, one can study the upgrading of tolerance levels or evaluate a program that pays immediate attention to the children of hospitalized mothers. If public concern over special social issues makes itself felt, one might study programs relating to aging, alcoholism, drug addiction, or a more relevant school curriculum. And if most commitment is toward agency growth, what seems current and opportune on the national scene and likely to bring funding and fame will probably take precedence.

All of the above can be subsumed under the goal-attainment model (Schulberg, Sheldon, and Baker, 1970) of program evaluation, which emphasizes measurement of the degree of success or failure encountered by the program in reaching predetermined objectives. The other conception of evaluation, the systems model, takes in the various levels of an organization's functioning simultaneously. The broader-gauge, multiple-social-system orientation implicit in the system model is, of course, the more intriguing approach to evaluation if community mental health is to be viewed as a coordinated, coherent movement. However, whether it is through an inductive, piecemeal process that we retain what works and discard what is ineffective, or through the deductive strategy of starting with the mission as a whole and molding the specific programs to fit, we still have to concern ourselves with the mutuality of involvement and feedback to make what emerges fit with the social reality rather than intellectualizations of what ought to be.

One needs also to distinguish between program evaluation and evaluative research. The former may be defined as the careful appraisal through sensible methods of the extent to which a particular program under study is meeting its stated goals, but the latter distinctly implies the use of the scientific method. Since, ultimately, our efforts will stand or fall under the telling lenses of the scientific method, it is an approach that should be used whenever conditions make it possible.

Techniques of Evaluative Research

Significant mental health research is typically a large-scale, long-term, high-energy, investment-type enterprise. The stakes are high and the commitment of time, manpower, and money cannot be approached lightly. Therefore, at the onset, a long hard look at the total undertaking could go a long way in helping to unearth as much of the buried treasure as exists. Although the hypothesis-control method normally would be the approach of choice, because it is often not possible to use in the total evaluation need not

mean that the uncovering of other worthwhile information and exploration of untrodden ground should be impeded. Methodological care, however, ought not to be neglected, since even if a formal scientific method is used only to illuminate one small aspect of the program, it can nourish the soul, if you will. What will be outlined below can be seen as a kind of checklist in methodology, specifically related to evaluation in community mental health. Its use might help avoid gross errors.

A. Planning Phase

1. The beginning of evaluation is working with a sincere program based in a dedicated center. The investigator should test the mutual commitments by thoroughly expressing himself on the program as a whole so he can feel comfortable in being part of the propriertorship and be accepting of both large and small purposes of the center.

2. Overall goals should be differentiated from specific objectives. The goals of a program may be specified in most inspiring terms—for example, reduce incidence and control prevalence of mental illness or improve a population's social adjustment to the community—but attainable objectives will need to be spelled out as benchmarks toward the pursuit of the larger end; for example, significantly shorten treatment time for the average patient or significantly reduce the overlap of services. In this vein, Kiresuk and Sherman (1968) propose a method for "goal-attainment scaling," by which each community mental health program can proceed to their goal with their own operational definitions and measures.

3. Conceptual access to the total mental health system in which the program is embedded is necessary. This implies some sort of charted analysis of the total system reflective of levels of inputs, programs, and outputs formulated as a composite of interlocking subsystems. Each of the subsystems should be described in relation to its actual contribution to services rendered specified as particular program objectives.

4. Several general evaluative designs should be thought through in terms of agency priorities as well as research necessities, and alternative options kept viable up to the point at which the

program solidifies. A good program is often kept flexible in its early stages so as to benefit from actual experience.

5. Explorations with research procedures should be made in the natural setting, preferably as dry runs, with a qualitative study of what transpires case by case. Such prior "tooling up" will be rewarded, since not all techniques are transferable from setting to setting.

B. Program Phase

6. When a particular researchable problem has been decided upon, a model of its dimensions should be made. If possible, simulation of what is to transpire can be accomplished. These precautions can go a long way in pointing out gaps, deficiencies, or other limitations that can still be rectified.

7. Now comes a most crucial step, asking the right questions. How questions are formulated will be the main determinant of the research design. Questions should be answerable, of interest to the agency power structure, and relevant enough so that answers could make a contribution to the overall program as well as to the extension of knowledge. Since, all too often, the wrong people ask the questions, one should not hesitate to bring in outside consultants at this crucial stage.

8. On the basis of the questions asked, it is now necessary to formulate specific research designs. Thinking should be focused on the possibility of answering some of the questions by controlled hypothesis testing, since the stronger the design, the richer will be the findings. It is obviously better to prethink the issue of proof than to explain away contaminating factors after the fact. The discipline involved in actually formulating the hypotheses should in itself clarify and enrich the ultimate study. Too often one is seduced by the current ease of feeding the computer with anything that could be counted or measured, only to find that the concluded research is left in the compromised state of not being able to explain findings. If using control populations is not feasible, strong research design can still be attained by the use of base-line data, before-and-after measures, or retrospective cohort analysis.

9. Instrumentation is the next important step. Findings have to be based on technically satisfactory indicators, which are accurate and refined enough to do the job required. One needs to develop the sophisticated awareness that sometimes what on the surface suggests exactness, as in recorded hospital admission and discharge rates, can be the product of extensive manipulation that serve purposes of its own but which will be disastrous for research.

10. Data have to be carefully collected. Each method of gathering data has its advantages and disadvantages, and serves a different purpose. Objective measurement, open-ended interviews, individual or group administration, mailed responses, and judgements of those in a position to know, all must be looked at carefully. The experiences of others should be taken into account. For example, studies that have attempted to obtain information about patients from relatives and friends through mailed questionnaires were capable of securing only about a 30 percent response rate, varying greatly in relation to race and social class (Berger, Rice, Sewall, and Lemkau, 1963). Provision for lost cases and problems to be encountered in follow-up need to be made.

11. The designation of a criterion is always a sticky problem in mental health. It can often help if the question of how one knows a program will be successful is approached in terms of what clinical indications suggest a particular intervention for a particular population. Whether one chooses adaptation to the community, fewer referrals, symptom reduction, or developing better staff cohesiveness as criteria, reliable and valid measures of outcome must be a central focus of concern.

C. Dissemination Phase

12. The analysis of data goes hand in hand with what kind of information about the program one wants to impart to others. The previous warning about capriciously plugging into the computer almost all of what one observes must be balanced against the hazard of building up masses of unanalyzed data that become so overwhelming as to leave no alternative but to set them aside for a future time that never comes. It is wise to plan to code information,

and even punch cards as data come in. If one's horizons are very broad, the data bank notion can be entertained as useful for other purposes, including base-line information for subsequent projects.

13. The correlational method of dealing with subsidiary information should not be ignored. Serendipitous findings are often the most revealing of all, and frequently serve as a rich source for additional research ideas.

14. Writing the final report is often a difficult task. For some the problem is in its intrinsic nature, and for others the issue is new commitments made. It is therefore often judicious to make provision at the beginning of a project for placing someone with writing skills in the role of historian. He would take responsibility for recording the step-by-step progress of the project and pay special attention to those elements to be included in a final report. Another strategy currently in vogue is to sustain writing satisfactions and efficiency by informational type publishing of interesting parts of the study as they emerge. Most large projects are reported in the journals in stages, capped off several years later by a definitive book which then coordinates the articles and places them in proper perspective.

15. Writing the report is not the last step. Attention should be paid to disseminating results in relation to particular purposes. Some use the rapid and efficient technique of mailing inexpensively duplicated reports to private mailing lists of interested colleagues; others, if the findings warrant, take to press releases. Not to be neglected is feedback, in some more meaningful way than print, to the staff and constituency of the agency. Halpert (1966) highlights the importance of communications in promoting the utilization of research findings by describing a study done in a mental hospital resulting in the finding that where Swedish modern furniture was used in day rooms (as compared with early American furniture), patients consistently favored these rooms. However, when the hospital studied needed new furniture, no attention was paid to these results, since the supplies-requisitioning staff ordered what they had always ordered, early American furniture.

Special Concerns

In doing large-scale mental health research, problems are encountered that require special consideration over and above those related to having the scholarly attributes of a good researcher. Many of these problems can be categorized under the headings of largeness and complexity, technical problems, and research accountability.

Largeness and Complexity. The search for the one all-encompassing explanation for disordered behavior, or its corollary, the single all-potent treatment intervention, has to be, at this stage of our mental health sophistication, passé. We have surely passed the stage of relatively easy "magic bullet" solutions. This is not to say that we should give up our search for appropriate analgesia, or intervention techniques that are applicable to the many rather than to the few; but it does mean that different classification categories (perhaps in relation to social realities and what we know of the contextual aspects of behavior rather than by symptoms or personality) should be used for differential solutions. Several matters can trip the call for help and several approaches can be selected for responding to that call. The task is to match the most effective response to the particular caller and his context.

We live in a world of separate but interconnected systems that cannot often be reduced one to the other. Wignall and Koppin (1967), for example, collected data on Mexican-American usage of state mental hospital facilities in Colorado that point to certain age-sex-diagnoses specific to social processes. They suggest that ethnicity as a system within a system must be looked at separately, especially when dealing with less acculturated groups. Similarly, the "social circle" phenomenon of friends and supporters of psychotherapy (Kadushin, 1969) must be appreciated if we are to understand and respond properly to the calls for help from the upper classes. Besides relevant sociocultural characteristics, one must look at such environmental variation (Forehand and Gilmer, 1964) as urban, rural, or suburban settings, the availability of supporting resources, transportation patterns, class or political ideologies, and the attitudes of community leadership. Willems and Raush (1969) have edited a book containing naturalistic viewpoints in psychological research relevant to these issues.

Another important dimension in the search for effective intervention is the variations among and the complexities within mental health organization delivering services. Orientations and commitments of staff, preferential working habits, professional boundaries and concerns, and the physical structure of the facility are some of the influential variants. Etzioni (1964) offers some handles by which complex organizations can be studied by emphasizing the "core variable" of compliance and two "essential" concepts of involvement and power.

Finally, there is the intrapsychic system, the analysis of which has made considerable headway. Of particular interest here is the work of Freeman and Simmons (1963), who documented the conclusion that discharged psychiatric patients have a rehabilitation prognosis dependent on at least two apparently independent dimensions, successful community tenure and instrumental performance. In other words, rehospitalization seems to bear little relationship to readjustment to former living patterns.

Technical Problems. There are several technical problems unique to large-scale mental health research which should be considered before embarking on a project. Among them are the predictable contingencies that will emerge to plague the investigator unless prior planning is effective. For example, it is the better side of sophistication not to take the easy way out and cry "foul" when it is belatedly learned that study patients were being discharged from hospitals prematurely because the aftercare program under investigation guaranteed their being followed, while control patients were being screened more carefully prior to discharge because their communities did not provide aftercare services. One must also take seriously the understanding we now have that programs to which we commit ourselves are more likely than not to have positive outcomes due to the Hawthorne effect, or experimenter bias arising from expectation (Rosenthal, 1963). Enthusiasm and hard work directed toward a particular goal can be catching on the part of the target populations. How to sustain the enthusiasm beyond the project period is an important key problem. It will hurt when, after years of successful demonstration, a program disintegrates because excitement has waned. The following are among some of the other technical issues that should be mentioned.

1. Staffing the research project with key personnel and keeping the team intact for the duration of the project is itself a problem especially when the tendency is to select young upwardly mobile professionals. It is said that the average professional changes jobs about every three years.

2. Assured findings in mental health are mainly obtained through replication. Since no two programs or styles at mental health centers can be exactly the same, care must be taken to conduct one's program in broad enough terms so as to make it amenable to replication. Over-particularized programs, regardless of original findings, will probably not be repeated.

3. Identifying the target population, especially if psychiatric diagnoses are the method, should be looked at carefully. Blum (1962) discusses at length the sources of error in psychiatric interviews and the limitations of symptom reporting.

4. Certain indicators change their meaning over time. Schwartz and Schwartz (1964) point out that the very fact of having more facilities available, educating the population to make better use of them, and sweetening the institutional or treatment process so as to meet specific needs can cause, and has in fact caused, more people to apply for services rather than less. Innovative mental health programs would then appear to promote rather than lessen disorder. Similarly, sensitizing teachers to pay closer attention to the emotional problems of children may result in more referrals or higher ratings of pathology and contradict the hypothesis in, for example, a school consultation program.

Research Accountability. In structuring the problem, the section above began with an enumeration of the pressures community mental health research units face from a variety of sources. Like the movement within which it operates, researchers are accountable to their constituency if they can determine just who that is. On the list of ten services expected in comprehensive community mental health centers, as specified by Federal guidelines, research and evaluation is last. The most recent review of these centers (Glasscote, Sussex, Cumming, and Smith, 1969) found very few of them to contain research units and very few to be carrying through evaluation of their programs.

Obtaining research support from the center's administrators is not easy. In the past, research and evaluation have not added measurably to the mission or work of mental health professionals. If research is conducted with the blessing of the agency, it is most often seen as an adjunctive, independent activity not strongly linked to the center's total program. It is frequently viewed as serving the collateral needs of advancing the center's prestige, bringing in supplemental money to carry out programs not otherwise likely to be funded, and adding a cosmetic dimension that will help in recruiting scarce staff. Therefore, when one does conduct research at a center, the implicit as well as the explicit objectives of a particular program should be determined. These may not be clear even to the administrators who will move the program along anyhow, but the distinction is crucial to the research-evaluator, who must be able to define the purposes of his study so that he can meet some of the practical needs of administrators while also furthering the pursuit of knowledge and the well-being of the community served. This tri-part requirement is obviously not easily met.

REFERENCES

Albee, G. W. *Mental health manpower trends.* N.Y.: Basic Books, 1959.

American Journal of Psychiatry *Computers in psychiatry.* 1969, **125** (7) (January, whole issue supplement).

Appley, M. H., and Trumbull, R. (Eds.) *Psychological stress.* N.Y.: Appleton-Century-Crofts, 1967.

Armor, D. J., and Klerman, G. L. Psychiatric treatment orientations and professional ideology. *Journal of Health and Social Behavior,* 1968, **9**, 243–255.

Arnold, C. B. Culture shock and a Peace Crops field mental health program. *Community Mental Health Journal,* 1967, **3**, 53–60.

Bahn, A. K. An outline for community mental health research. *Community Mental Health Journal,* 1965, **1**, 23–28.

Baker, F., and Schulberg, H. C. *Manual for the community mental health ideology scale.* N.Y.: Behavioral Publications, 1968.

Baler, L. A., and Golde, P. J. Conjugal bereavement. *Working Papers in Community Mental Health,* 1964, **2**, 1–18.

Barker, R. G. Explorations in ecological psychology. *American Psychologist,* 1965, **20**, 1–14.

Barker, R. G. *Ecological psychology: Concepts and methods for studying the environment of human behavior.* Stanford, California: Stanford University Press, 1968.

Barten, H. H. The coming of age of the brief psychotherapies. In L. Bellak and H. H. Barten (Eds.), *Progress in community mental health. Vol. 1.* N.Y.: Grune and Stratton, 1969. Pp. 93–122.

Bartholomew, D. J. *Stochastic models for social processes.* N.Y.: Wiley, 1967.

Berger, D. G., Rice, C. E., Sewall, L. G., and Lemkau, P. V. Factors affecting the adequacy of patient community adjustment information obtained from the community. *Mental Hygiene,* 1963, **47**, 452–460.

Bertalanffy, L. von. General systems theory—a critical review. In W. Buckley (Ed.), *Modern systems research for the behavioral scientist: A sourcebook.* Chicago: Aldine, 1968. Pp. 11–30.

Bierer, J. The Marlborough experiment. In L. Bellak (Ed.), *Handbook of community psychiatry and community mental health.* N.Y.: Grune and Stratton, 1964. Pp. 221–247.

Binner, P. R. Discussion. In E. M. Gruenberg (Ed.), Evaluating the effectiveness of mental health services. *Milbank Memorial Fund Quarterly,* 1966, **44** (No. 1, Part 2), 351–352.

Bloom, B. L. *Mental health program evaluation: A review of the literature and an annotated bibliography.* 1955–1964. Washington, D.C.: U.S. Public Health Service, 1965.

Blum, R. H. Case identification in psychiatric epidemiology: Methods and problems. *Milbank Memorial Fund Quarterly,* 1962, **40**, 253–288.

Bower, E. M., and Lambert, N. *A process for in-school screening of children with emotional handicaps: Technical report for school administrators and teachers.* Princeton: Education Testing Service, 1961.

Caplan, G. *Principles of preventive psychiatry.* N.Y.: Basic Books, 1964.

Caplan, G., Mason, E. A., and Kaplan, D. M. Four studies of crises in parents of prematures. *Community Mental Health Journal,* 1965, **2**, 149–161.

Carse, J. A district mental health service: The Worthing experiment. *Lancet,* 1958, **1**, 39–41.

Caudill, W. *The psychiatric hospital as a small society.* Cambridge, Mass: Harvard University Press, 1958.

Chein, I., Cook, S., and Harding, J. The field of action research. *American Psychologist,* 1948, **3**, 43–50.

Clausen, J. A., and Kohn, M. N. Relation of schizophrenia to the social structure of a small city. In B. Pasamanick (Ed.), *Epidemiology of mental disorder.* Washington, D.C.: American Association for the Advancement of Science, 1959. Pp. 64–94.

Cowen, E. L., and Zax, M. Early detection and prevention of emotional disorder. In J. W. Carter, Jr. (Ed.), *Research contributions from psychology to community mental health.* N.Y.: Behavioral Publications, 1968. Pp. 46–59.

Cowen, E. L., Zax, M., Izzo, L. D., and Trost, M. A. Prevention of emotional disorders in the school setting. *Journal of Consulting Psychology,* 1966, **30**, 381–387.

Cumming, E., and Cumming, J. *Closed ranks: An experiment in mental health education.* Cambridge, Mass.: Harvard University Press, 1957.

Cumming, J., and Cumming, E. *Ego and milieu.* N.Y.: Atherton, 1962.

Deutsch, A. *The mentally ill in America.* N.Y.: Columbia University Press, 1949.

Dohrenwend, B. Social status, stress, and psychological symptoms. *American Journal of Public Health,* 1967, **57**, 625–632.

Dohrenwend, B., and Dohrenwend, B. S. The problem of validity in field studies of psychological disorder. *Journal of Abnormal Psychology,* 1965, **70**, 52–69.

Donahue, W., Gottesman, L. E., and Coons, D. Milieu therapy and the long-term geriatric mental patient. In *Mental health program reports—2.* Washington, D.C.: U.S. Government Printing Office, 1968. Pp. 37–52. (PHS Publication No. 1743.)

Dunham, H. W. Epidemiology of psychiatric disorders as a contribution to medical ecology. *International Journal of Psychiatry,* 1968, **5**, 124–153.

Eicker, W. F., Bremmer, B., Burgess, J., and Jhangiani, A. *The application of systems technology to community mental health.* Decatur, Ill.: Adolf Meyer Zone Center, Department of Mental Health, 1967.

Eiduson, Bernice T. *Psychiatric case history event system: Transcription procedures with lexicons.* Los Angeles: Reiss-Davis Child Study Center, 1966.

Eiduson, B. T., Brooks, S., and Motto, R. L. A generalized psychiatric information processing system. *Behavioral Science,* 1966, **11**, 133–145.

Etzioni, A. *Modern organizations.* Englewood Cliffs, N.J.: Prentice-Hall, 1964.

Farberow, N. L., and Shneidman, E. S. (Eds.) *The cry for help.* N.Y.: McGraw-Hill, 1961.

Faris, R. E. L., and Dunham, H. W. *Mental disorders in urban areas: An ecological study of schizophrenia and other psychoses.* Chicago: University of Chicago Press, 1939.

Fishman, J. Baker's Dozen: A program of training young people as mental health aides. In *Mental health reports—2.* Washington, D.C.: U.S. Government Printing Office, 1968. Pp. 11–24. (PHS Publication No. 1743.)

Forehand, G. A., and Gilmer, B. von H. Environmental variation in studies of organizational behavior. *Psychological Bulletin,* 1964, **62**, 361–382.

Freedman, N., Rosen, B., Engelhardt, D. M., and Margolis, R. Prediction of psychiatric hospitalization. *Journal of Abnormal Psychology,* 1967, **72**, 468–477.

Freeman, H. E., and Simmons, O. G. *The mental patient comes home.* N.Y.: Wiley, 1963.

Fried, M. Grieving for a lost home. In L. J. Duhl (Ed.), *The urban condition.* N.Y.: Basic Books, 1963. Chapter 12.

Gardner, E. A., and Miles, H. C. A psychiatric case register. *Archives of General Psychiatry,* 1966, **14**, 571–580.

Gildea, M. C. L., Glidewell, J. C., and Kantor, M. B. The St. Louis school mental health project: History and evaluation. In E. L. Cowen, E. A. Gardner, and M. Zax, *Emergent approaches to mental health problems.* N.Y.: Appleton-Century-Crofts, 1967.

Glasscote, R. M., Sussex, J. N., Cumming, E., and Smith, L. *The community mental health center: An interim appraisal.* Washington, D.C.: American Psychiatric Association, 1969.

Glidewell, J. C., Mensh, I. N., Domke, H. R., Gildea, M. C. L., and Buchmueller, A. D. Methods for community mental health research. *American Journal of Orthopsychiatry,* 1957, **27**, 38–54.

Glueck, B. C. Jr. The computer as psychiatric aid and research tool. In *Mental health program reports—2.* Washington, D.C.: U.S. Government Printing Office, 1968. Pp. 353–372. (PHS Publication No. 1743.)

Goffman, E. *Asylums.* N.Y.: Doubleday, 1961.

Golann, S. E. *Coordinate index reference guide to community mental health.* N.Y.: Behavioral Publications, 1969.

Greenblatt, M., Levinson, D. J., and Williams, R. H. (Eds.) *The patient and the mental hospital.* Glencoe, Ill.: The Free Press, 1957.

Gruenberg, E. M., and Brandon, S. Identifying cases of social breakdown syndrome. In E. M. Gruenberg (Ed.), *Evaluating the effectiveness of mental health services.* N.Y.: Milbank Memorial Fund, 1966.

Halpert, H. P. Communications as a basic tool in promoting utilization of research findings. *Community Mental Health Journal*, 1966, **2**, 231–238.

Harvard Medical School, *Community mental health and social psychiatry: A reference guide.* Cambridge, Mass.: Harvard University Press, 1962.

Hitchcock, J. Paper read at the annual meeting of the American Psychiatric Association, 1969, Miami Beach.

Hobbs, N. Helping disturbed children: Psychological and ecological strategies. *American Psychologist*, 1966, **21**, 1105–1115.

Hollingshead, A. B., and Redlich, F. C. *Social class and mental illness.* N.Y.: Wiley, 1958.

Holzberg, J. D., Knapp, R. H., and Turner, J. L. College student as companions to the mentally ill. In E. L. Cowen, E. A. Gardner, and M. Zax (Eds.), *Emergent approaches to mental health problems*, N.Y.: Appleton-Century-Crofts, 1967. Pp. 91–109.

Hutcheson, B. R., and Krause, E. A. Systems analysis and mental health services. *Community Mental Health Journal*, 1969, **5**, 29–45.

Kadushin, C. *Why people go to psychiatrists.* N.Y.: Atherton Press, 1969.

Kantor, M. B. (Ed.) *Mobility and mental health.* Springfield, Ill.: Charles C. Thomas, 1965.

Kelly, J. G. Naturalistic observations and theory confirmation. *Human Development*, 1967, **10**, 212–222.

Kelly, J. G. Toward an ecological conception of preventive interventions. In J. W. Carter Jr. (Ed.), *Research contributions from psychology to community mental health*, N.Y.: Behavioral Publications, 1968. Pp. 75–99.

Kiresuk, T. J., and Sherman, R. E. Goal attainment scaling: A general method of evaluating comprehensive community mental health programs. *Community Mental Health Journal*, 1968, **4**, 443–453.

Klein, D. C., and Lindemann, E. Preventive intervention in individual and family crisis situations. In G. Caplan (Ed.), *Prevention of mental disorder in children.* N.Y.: Basic Books, 1961. Chapter 13.

Klein, D. C., and Ross, A. Kindergarten entry: A study of role transition. In M. Krugman (Ed.), *Orthopsychiatry and the school.* N.Y.: American Orthopsychiatric Association, 1958. Pp. 60–69.

Kotin, J., and Sharaf, M. Factors in programming. *Psychiatry*, 1967, **30**, 3–15.

Langston, R. D. Community mental health centers and community mental health ideology. *Community Mental Health Journal*, in press.

Leighton, A. H. A proposal for research in the epidemiology of psychiatric disorders. In *Epidemiology of mental disorder.* N.Y.: Milbank Memorial Fund, 1950. Pp. 128–135.

Leighton, A. H. Some propositions regarding the relationship of sociocultural integration and disintegration to mental health. In J. Zubin and F. Freyhan (Eds.), *Social psychiatry* N.Y.: Grune and Stratton, 1968.

Leighton, D. C., Leighton, A. H., and Armstrong, R. A. Community psychiatry in a rural area: A social psychiatric approach. In L. Bellak (Ed.), *Handbook of community psychiatry.* N.Y.: Grune and Stratton, 1964. Pp. 166–176.

Lemkau, P., Tietze, C., and Cooper, M. A summary of the statistical studies on the prevalence of mental disorder in sample populations. *Public Health Reports*, 1943, **5** (Whole No. 53).

Libo, L. M., and Griffith, C. R. Developing mental health programs in areas lacking professions facilities: The community consultant approach in New Mexico. *Community Mental Health Journal*, 1966, **2**, 163–169.

Lindemann, E. Symptomotology and management of acute grief. *American Journal of Psychiatry*, 1944, **101**, 141–148.

Lourie, R. S. Child development counselors: Lessons from their training and use. In *Mental health reports—2.* Washington, D.C.: U.S. Government Printing Office, 1968. Pp. 285–294. (PHS Publication No. 1743.)

Mangus, A. R., and Seeley, J. R. Mental health needs in a rural and semi-rural area in Ohio. In A. M. Rose (Ed.), *Mental health and mental disorder.* N.Y.: Norton, 1955.

MacLennan, B. W., Klein, W., Pearl, A., and Fishman, J. Training for new careers. *Community Mental Health Journal*, 1966, **2**, 135–143.

McGee, R. K. The suicide prevention center as a model for community mental health programs. *Community Mental Health Journal*, 1965, **1**, 162–170.

Minuchin, S., Bontalvo, B., Buerney, B., Jr., Rosman, B., and Schumer, F. *Families of the slums: An exploration of their structure and treatment.* N.Y.: Basic Books, 1967.

Morris, J. N. *Uses of epidemiology.* Baltimore: Williams and Wilkins, 1964.

Morrissey, J. R. *The case for family care of the mentally ill.* N.Y.: Behavioral Publications, 1967.

Myers, J. K., and Bean, L. L. *A decade later: A follow-up of "Social Class and Mental Illness."* N.Y.: Wiley, 1968.

Nunnally, J. C. *Popular conceptions of mental health.* N.Y.: Holt, Rinehart and Winston, 1961.

Ojemann, R. H. (Ed.) *Recent research on creative approaches to environmental stress.* Proceedings of the Fourth Institute on Preventive Psychiatry. Ames, Ohio: State University of Iowa, 1963.

Osborn, R. R. Pre-crisis intervention. *Journal of School Health*, 1968, **38**, 567–575.

Parad, H. J. (Ed.) *Crisis intervention: Selected readings.* N.Y.: Family Service Association of America, 1966.

Pasamanick, B., Scarpitti, F. R., and Dinitz, S. *Schizophrenics in the community: An experimental study in the prevention of hospitalization.* N.Y.: Appleton-Century-Crofts, 1967.

Pearl, A., and Riessman, F. *New careers for the poor.* N.Y.: Free Press, 1965.

Querido, A. Early diagnosis and treatment services. In *Elements of a community mental health program,* N.Y.: Milbank Memorial Fund, 1956.

Rapoport, R. N. *Community as doctor: New perspectives on a therapeutic community.* Springfield, Ill.: Charles C. Thomas, 1960.

Reiff, R., and Riessman, F. *The indigenous nonprofessional.* N.Y.: Behavioral Publications, 1965.

Rioch, M. J. Pilot projects in training mental health counselors. In E. L. Cowen, E. A. Gardner, M. Zax (Eds.) *Emergent approaches to mental health problems.* N.Y.: Appleton-Century-Crofts, 1967. Pp. 110–127.

Roen, S. R., and Burnes, A. J. *Community adaptation schedule: Test and manual.* N.Y.: Behavioral Publications, 1968.

Roen, S. R., Cooper, S., Burnes, A. J., Rosenblum, G., and Ottenstein, D. *Communication patterns in community aftercare.* Quincy, Mass.: South Shore Mental Health Center, 1966.

Rosenthal, R. On the social psychology of the psychological experiment: The experimenter's hypothesis as unintended determinant of experimental results. *American Scientist,* 1963, **51,** 268–283.

Ross, M. Paper presented to the annual meetings of the American College of Physicians, 1969, Chicago.

Sainsbury, P., and Grad, J. Evaluation of the Chichester and district psychiatric services. In E. M. Gruenberg (Ed.), *Evaluating the effectiveness of mental health services.* N.Y.: Milbank Memorial Fund, 1966. Pp. 231–278.

Sanders, R., Smith, R. S., and Weinman, B. S. *Chronic psychosis and recovery: An experiment in socio-environmental treatment.* San Francisco: Jossey-Bass, 1967.

Schulberg, H. C., Sheldon, A., and Baker, F. (Eds.) Program evaluation in the health fields. N.Y.: Behavioral Publications, 1970.

Schwartz, M. S., and Schwartz, C. G. *Social approaches to mental patient care.* N.Y.: Columbia University Press, 1964.

Scotch, N. A preliminary report on the relations of sociocultural factors to hypertension among the Zulu. *Annals of the New York Academy of Science,* 1960, **84,** 1000–1009.

Skipper, J. K., and Leonard, R. C. Children, stress and hospitalization: A field experiment. *Journal of Health and Social Behavior,* 1968, **9,** 275–287.

Srole, L., Langer, T. S., Michael, S. T., Opler, M. K., and Rennie, T. A. *Mental health in the metropolis.* N.Y.: McGraw-Hill, 1962.

Stanton, A., and Schwartz, M. *The mental hospital.* N.Y.: Basic Books, 1954.

Stretch, J. C. Community mental health: The evolution of a concept in social policy. *Community Mental Health Journal,* 1967, **3,** 5–12.

Syme, S. L., and Reeder, L. G. (Eds.) Social stress and cardiovascular disease. *Milbank Memorial Fund Quarterly,* 1967, **45** (No. 2, Part 2, whole issue).

Teele, J. E., Jackson, E., and Mayo, C. *Family experiences in Operation Exodus.* N.Y.: Behavioral Publications, 1967.

Time. Psychiatry's new approach: Crisis intervention. N.Y.: *Time,* May 9, 1969, p. 74.

Umbarger, D. D., Dalsimer, J. S., Morrison, A. P., and Breggin, P. R. *College students in a mental hospital.* N.Y.: Grune and Stratton, 1962.

Waldfogel, S., and Gardner, G. E. Intervention in crises as a method of primary prevention. In G. Caplan (Ed.), *Prevention of mental disorder in children.* N.Y.: Basic Books, 1961. Pp. 307–322.

Waltzer, H., and Hankoff, L. D. One year's experience with a suicide prevention telephone service. *Community Mental Health Journal,* 1965, **1,** 309–315.

Waltzer, H., Hankoff, L. D., Engelhardt, D. M., and Kaufman, I. C. Emergency psychiatric treatment in a receiving hospital. *Mental Hospitals,* 1963, **14,** 595–600.

Wignall, C. M., and Koppin, L. L. Mexican-American usage of state mental health facilities. *Community Mental Health Journal,* 1967, **3,** 137–148.

Willems, E. P., and Raush, H. L. (Eds.) *Naturalistic viewpoints in psychological research.* N.Y.: Holt, Rinehart and Winston, 1969.

Zax, M., and Cowen, E. L. Early identification and prevention of emotional disturbance in a public school. In E. L. Cowen, E. A. Gardner, and M. Zax. (Eds.), *Emergent approaches to mental health problems.* N.Y., Appleton-Century-Crofts, 1967.

21

EMPIRICAL RESEARCH IN GROUP PSYCHOTHERAPY

RICHARD L. BEDNAR, Ph.D.
G. FRANK LAWLIS, Ph.D.[1]

UNIVERSITY OF KENTUCKY

INTRODUCTION

As a new psychotherapist begins his first group-therapy session, he has the usual doubts and anxieties that accompany inexperience. Because research appears too bulky to disseminate systematically and too complex to answer practical questions, the new therapist usually learns by trial and error. Our purpose is to organize empirical research around basic issues of concern to the practitioner and stimulate future research efforts through examination and elaboration of existing research methodology. In reviewing the literature, the authors felt that three major considerations were important to researchers and practitioners. First, the practitioner should be alert to the limitations accompanying the use of various research designs. The sections on *Methodology* will discuss these considerations. Second, a synthesis of research information, in which results are brought together on the basis of common research elements and relevant professional issues, is necessary. The sections on *Results* will provide this synthesis of data. And third, implications for practice need to be identified, based on replicated experimental findings. These are discussed under the heading of *Implications*.

Many research designs have been used to investigate group psychotherapy. In an attempt to add order to the wide variety of research procedures employed, the authors have classified investigations together on the basis of simi-

---

[1] Development of this chapter was a cooperative effort with Dr. Lawlis responsible for the sections on methodological considerations and Dr. Bednar responsible for the sections dealing with results and implications.

larity in independent variables investigated and research methods. The first grouping contains outcome studies that help identify (1) the treatment effects of group therapy; (2) the kind of behavior changes that are attributable to group therapy; and (3) the type of patients and problems that are amenable to treatment by group therapy. Most of these investigations employ the pre-post method. The second grouping contains studies attempting to relate group process variables to client improvement. These investigations help identify (1) antecedent conditions to client improvement; (2) personality traits of therapists who have a positive influence on group procedures; and (3) group interaction patterns that appear to benefit those involved. The last group of studies examines pretherapy variables that are important in identifying methods of patient selection and preparation for group treatment.

OUTCOME STUDIES

Methodology

One of the most critical questions in evaluating therapeutic improvement is: What change can be attributable to group psychotherapy rather than spurious factors extraneous to the therapeutic situation? The obvious approach to answering this question would be to identify a measurable characteristic, such as a test score, and state the probability of specific changes resulting from therapy. Change on pre-post scores is the method most often used, and it allows a simple interpretation in terms of "improved" or "not improved." Such a design has the disadvantage of lack of control over what kinds of effects are actually occurring, and it is difficult to establish whether improvement or lack of improvement is the result of therapy. In many instances, attention and other non-specific influences may have effects that make it difficult to attribute observed changes to psychotherapy. Most researchers have, therefore, used no-therapy control groups with which to compare treatment groups.

If the criterion for change is based on a standardized instrument, even administering the instrument may have an effect on outcome. When the testing process focuses attention on a written or spoken description of personal dis-

comfort, the patient may incidentally learn a new vocabulary and possibly new ways of seeing his world, thus spuriously improving later self-descriptions. Also, experimental observations can be influenced by time and experience. As judgers or raters become more familiar with experimental objectives, personal biases may contaminate ratings, interrater reliabilities may deteriorate, and perceptual sets may change. In spite of these methodological criticisms, it is still possible to extract valuable information with regard to "change."

A good example of a study characterizing these problems was completed by Kraus (1959). He utilized the before-after design to demonstrate the effect of group psychotherapy with chronic psychotic patients. The subjects were two groups of eight, matched by age, sex, diagnosis, intelligence, and education. Both groups met separately and were tested. By the flip of a coin, one group was designated as the experimental group, which met twice a week in regular group therapy sessions for three months. The control group did not meet again until the end of the three-month period. Psychological group tests (MMPI and Zulliten Ink Blots) and evaluations made by ward psychologists and psychiatrists were used as measures of change. The experimental group did show significant changes on some scales of the MMPI; however, significant changes were not found in evaluations by psychologists and psychiatrists, or in the Zulliten Ink Blots. Because of the aforementioned disadvantages of the method, it is possible to question whether the therapy group improved on the MMPI purely because the persons involved received more attention, because they felt they should "appear" improved, or because experience with this kind of self-description tends to modify the self-description itself. Perhaps an alternative plan that would have made the results clearer would have been to use a control group getting equal attention, such as supervised activity-work. This would equate attention effects.

Results

Can Group Therapy Help? Evaluating the potency of group therapy in inducing behavior and personality change raises two basic questions. First, what research evidence is available suggesting that group psychotherapy procedures can elicit positive personality changes? Second, if group therapy does induce patient change, what are the dimensions of psychological functioning being affected?

Table 21.1 summarizes the results of research literature in which constructive changes in personality can reasonably be assumed to be a function of group therapy procedures. These investigations have been classified into three categories on the basis of outcome criteria employed: (1) self-adjustment; (2) environmental adjustment; and (3) mental functioning. Each grouping contains information depicting the experimental conditions for each study, the outcome measures, the population investigated, and significant findings.

The most frequent variable investigated was group therapy in its most generic form. Even though there are many group therapies and pronounced stylistic and theoretical differences among group therapists, these differences are largely unstudied in the research. Currently, group therapy is a very undifferentiated research variable. Treatment effects of group therapy have been most frequently investigated by comparing outcome measures between group therapy and a no-treatment control group; by adding group therapy to other treatment programs, such as Alcoholics Anonymous or drug regimes; and by comparing the outcome measures between group and individual therapy or combinations of the two. Relatively few investigations have studied differential treatment effects accompanying variations in group-therapy procedures.

There are approximately equal numbers of outcome measures reflecting self-adjustment and environmental adjustment, with significantly fewer investigations reflecting mental functioning. There is a conspicuous absence of significant findings when *projective tests* are used as the criterion of change. The populations investigated are basically psychiatric, with pscychoneurotic disorders predominating, followed by character disorders of varying types. A number of investigations have addressed themselves exclusively to group-treatment methods with schizophrenics and delinquents.

In the process of preparing the data in Table 21.1 for presentation, some information regarding treatment methods, characteristics of the population, and outcome measures have been omitted because of space limitations. In spite of these deletions, each summary does contain the essential information summarizing the investigation, and as such, these data provide a basis for inferring the treatment value of group psychotherapy based on a wide variety of group therapies and outcome measures.

The interpretation of these data depends on the standard of research employed. First reactions may suggest that there is an impressive amount of empirical information demonstrating the utility and value of group therapy. But the demanding critic can point out that few of the better experiments have been replicated. Furthermore, evidence (Fairweather, 1963) based on follow-up investigations suggests that positive treatment effects are short-lived and tend to dissipate with time. More important, other methodological limitations such as biased sampling, rater contamination, and spontaneous remissions lead to even less confidence in the meaning of these data.

On the other hand, it is encouraging that a large number of varied, independent investigations studying similar independent and dependent variables are reporting similar findings. As the number of independent supportive findings increases, it becomes less reasonable to believe that positive findings are simply a function of experimenter bias (Rosenthal, 1966) or experimental error. Using construct validity as a criterion, the converging evidence is consistent with the view held by many practitioners that group therapy is a valuable tool of the helping professions. What was once intuitive confirmation in the mind of many clinicians is now on the road to experimental verification.

Dimensions of Change. If it is reasonable to believe that group therapy is effective in facilitating constructive personality change, it then becomes essential to clarify the meaning of the illusive term "constructive personality change." To approach this question adequately, one must necessarily have a classification scheme that reflects dimensions of psychological functioning built around the treatment goals of group therapy. Unfortunately, such a multidimensional

TABLE 21.1   Literature Review Summarizing Group—Therapy Outcome Studies.

Author	Experimental Conditions	Outcome Measures	Population	Findings
		SELF-ADJUSTMENT		
Fairweather (1960)	Group therapy vs. individual therapy vs. group living vs. control	MMPI scores Q sort Follow-up	Psychiatric inpatients	Group therapy and group living associated with less time in therapy and global improvement.
Fairweather (1963)	18-month follow-up of Group therapy vs. individual therapy vs. group living vs. control	MMPI scores Q sort Follow-up	Psychiatric inpatients	The significantly greater percentage of patients from the therapy treatment groups working during the first six months disappears by 18 months. One treatment continued to correlate with remaining out of the hospital and being employed; group therapy.
Truax (1968)	Vicarious therapy pretraining (VTP) vs. no VTP	MMPI Q sort	Delinquents	VTP improved ideal self-concept; reduced MMPI.
Persons (1966)	Group therapy vs. control	MMPI Manifest Anxiety (MAS)	Juvenile delinquents	Reduced pathology and anxiety.
		RATE OF RETURN		
Cabeen (1961)	Effect of group therapy (pre-post)	MMPI Staff judgments	Sex offenders	Significant "improvement." Lower rate of return. Positive relation between amount of formal Group Therapy and improvement.
Ends (1959)	Alcoholics Anonymous vs. A. A. activity and group therapy	MMPI Q sort	Alcoholics	Improved A. A. treatment program.
Rashkis (1946)	Effect of group therapy (pre-post)	MMPI	Psychiatric Battle cases	Reduced MMPI.
Barron (1955)	Group vs. individual therapy vs. control	MMPI	Psychoneurotics	Reduced MMPI in both group and individual therapy.
Johnson (1964)	Spiritual growth group vs. controls	MMPI Q sort Edwards Personal Preference Schedule	Normals	Positive changes in self-concept; better interpersonal relations.
Kraus (1959)	Group therapy vs. control	MMPI	Psychiatric patients	Improved ratings by ward physician; reduced MMPI.
McGinnis (1963)	Alcoholics Anonymous activity vs. A. A. activity and group therapy	MMPI	Alcoholics	Increased ego strength.

Author	Experimental Conditions	Outcome Measures	Population	Findings
Feder (1962)	Group therapy vs. control	Q sort Monkey problem checklist	Delinquents	Increased therapeutic readiness.
Baehr (1954)	Group therapy vs. individual therapy vs. group therapy and individual therapy	Discontentment scale	Psychiatric patients	Greatest improvement when group therapy used in conjunction with individual therapy.
Luria (1959)	Group therapy vs. control	Semantic differential (self-perception)	College students	Improved self-concepts.
Feifel (1953)	Group therapy vs. control	Staff judgment "improvement"	Psychotics	Greater improvement following group therapy.
Zimet (1955)	Group involvement vs. group lecture	Participation Rating Scale Combs Desire List Picture Story Test	School administrators	Positive changes in perception of self and others.
Novick (1965)	Group vs. individual therapy for high and low ego strength	Behavior Problem Rating Scale	Mildly disturbed children	High Es showed more improvement whether group (therapy) or individual therapy.
Semon (1957)	Group therapy vs. control	Palo Alto Hospital Adjustment Scale	Schizophrenics	Improved ratings on Hospital Adjustment Scale.
Imber (1957)	Group vs. individual treatment and amount of therapeutic contact	Social Ineffectiveness Scale	Psychiatric patients	Group and individually treated patients showed equivalent greater therapeutic contact and greater therapeutic gain.
Anker (1961)	Group therapy vs. group therapy and special activity program	MACC Behavioral Adjustment Scale	Schizophrenics	Activity group showed significant changes on all four subscales: Motility, Adjustment, Cooperation and Communication. GP group showed significant positive changes only on motility.
Sacks (1954)	Group psychotherapy vs. control	Movement to more or less disturbed ward; discharge	Schizophrenics	Significantly greater movement to improved ward and significantly less maintenance of status quo.
Cadman (1954)	Experimental vs. control	Weschler-Bellevue Rorschach MAPS	Psychiatric patients	Improvement interpersonal functioning; reduced pathology and mental ailments.
Exener (1966)	Therapist attendance	Rating of improvement on 15-item rating scale	Schizophrenics	Improvement in therapist groups and deterioration in no-therapist groups.
Boe (1966)	Group therapy vs. control	Interpersonal checklist		Group members were less assertive and pompous.

Author	Experimental Conditions	Outcome Measures	Population	Findings
Williams (1962)	Group living program vs. conventional treatment with schizophrenics	Hospital Adjustment Scale; Psychopathological Ratings (MSRPP); Weschler-Bellevue; Rorschach; TAT; patient self-ratings; social adjustment ratings	Schizophrenics	Significant improvement over control on TAT.
Reiser (1961)	Therapy vs. Non-therapy work groups	WAIS; Semantic Differential; Minnesota Rate of Manipulation Test; Crawford Small Parts Dexterity Test	Vocational readjustment subjects	Therapy group showed gain in ego strength.
ENVIRONMENTAL ADJUSTMENT				
Wilcox (1957)	Group therapy vs. control	Hospital Adjustment Scale	Mental retardates	Improved institutional adjustment.
Cowden (1956)	Group therapy vs. chlorpromazine vs. group therapy and chlorpromazine	Behavioral measures	Psychiatric patients	Chlorpromazine plus group therapy more effective in reducing disruptive ward behavior.
Semon (1957)	Group-centered group vs. leader-centered group vs. control	Hospital Adjustment Scales I and II	Psychiatric patients	Improved interpersonal functioning in both groups.
Somers (1966)	Group vs. individual therapy	MacDonald Deep Test of Articulation	Children with speech problems	Both treatments improving speech articulation.
Tucker (1956)	Group therapy vs. control	Frequency of soiling	Psychiatric patients	Reduced soiling behavior.
Wilson (1967)	Short-term therapy vs. controls	Social adjustment		Improved social adjustment.
Snyder (1959)	Directive group therapy vs. placebo vs. no therapy	Institutional adjustment conduct violations	Dull-normal delinquents	Greatest improvement with group-therapy institutional adjustment.
McDavid (1964)	Post-therapy attitudes vs. pre-therapy controls	Social Reinforcement Interp. Test	Delinquents	Increased awareness of social approval and disapproval.
MENTAL FUNCTIONING				
Teahan (1966)	Therapy vs. no therapy	Academic grades	University students	Students of high ability improved with group psychotherapy.
Thoma (1964)	Group therapy pre-post	Grades	Underachievers	37 out of 43 showed improvement in grades.
Jones (1952)	Short-term therapy (pre-post evaluations)	Porteus Maze Gardener Behavior Chart Mirror Tracing	Psychiatric patients	Improved mental functioning and improved social adjustment.
Coons (1957)	Interaction vs. insight group Therapy	Weschler-Bellevue Rorschach	Psychiatric outpatients	Increased functioning; rated as improved.

scheme is not available. Drawing from psychological theory and principles of behavior change, however, one can furnish relevant dimensions. The outcome studies summarized in Table 21.1 were grouped into the following three categories on the basis of outcome criteria: (1) self-adjustment; (2) environmental adjustment; and (3) mental functioning. The three major classification dimensions can be viewed as representing rather broad, but basic, dimensions of psychological functioning. Unfortunately, the dimensions are so broad as to include a wide variety of heterogeneous measurements. More precise statements regarding the nature of improvement can be conjectured on the basis of "psychological sense" and empirical evidence.

A recent investigation (Truax, 1968) has produced evidence indicating that Q-sort measures and other measures of self-adjustment, including the MMPI, covary together with the status of client adjustment. That is, as client adjustment tends to improve or deteriorate, scores among the various measures of self-adjustment tend to covary together. It should be mentioned that the information for most of these measures was based on clients' self-reports, and that several of these instruments are psychometrically quite sophisticated. In the self-adjustment group, virtually all of the investigations employed the MMPI and/or Q-sort measures of self-concepts, as well as other measures assessing personal discomfort.

Among these studies, two independent investigations reported reductions on the neurotic triad of the MMPI of similar magnitude. Depression was the symptom most frequently reported as improved. Equally interesting is the observation that three investigations reported reductions on the psychasthenia scale of the MMPI, while no investigations reported reductions on the schizophrenia scale. These observations suggest that patients suffering from mood disorders, anxiety states, and somatic complaints experience relief from their distress. More severe thought disorders and marked interpersonal withdrawal do not appear to be as readily influenced by group therapy.

Improvement on Q-sort measures suggests reduced discrepancy between the ideal self and the perceived self, and by inference, more self-acceptance. These data suggest that group

therapy may contribute to feelings of relief from personal discomfort, to feelings of self-depreciation and inadequacy, and to a sense of improved psychological well-being and self-acceptance. In brief, group therapy contributes to improved self-adjustment.

The measures reflecting environmental adjustment most frequently are indicaters of improved ward behavior in hospital settings. It is significant that these measures often represent overt observable behavior rather than inferred hypothetical constructs. Many psychologists have been becoming increasingly critical over the preoccupation of many therapies with improving attitudes, feelings, and other covert dimensions of psychological functioning with relatively little attention directed toward observable behavior. The data on environmental adjustment suggest that group therapy can contribute to improving observable behavior patterns, at least in a hospital setting. Closer inspection of many of these outcome measures indicate that they represent patients' gaining control over disruptive behavior patterns. Examples of outcome measures depicting improved environmental adjustment are (1) rating scales reflecting ward interpersonal behavior; (2) institutional adjustment based on hospital adjustment scales and staff judgment; (3) movement to less versus more disturbed wards; and (4) psychometric measures of social adjustment.

While these data do not provide a firm basis for judging whether improved client adaptation is the result of a therapeutic milieu that develops on hospital wards, or of reduced patient tensions by periodic opportunities to ventilate pinned up feelings, or of improved patterns of interpersonal functioning learned within group-therapy sessions, the evidence does suggest that involvement in group therapy is related to improved environmental adjustment.

Three investigations used outcome measures reflecting improved intellectual functioning. In view of the literature available indicating that anxiety can have a restricting effect on attention and intellectual functioning, and that it generally inhibits and restricts complex mental ideation, it seems most reasonable to attribute these findings to reducing patient anxiety. In this sense, as well as in connection with the other indices of patient improvement employed, these studies might also be grouped with the self-adjustment investigations.

Can Group Therapy Hurt? The deterioration effect (Bergin, 1967; Truax et al., 1964), suggesting that individual psychotherapy can cause people to become better or worse adjusted, requires any therapeutic practice to be evaluated for negative as well as positive treatment effects.

The deterioration effect is based on the observation that the variability on criterion variables reflecting client change for treated groups is greater than for untreated groups, whereas the overall degree of change for both groups is similar. The interpretation of this phenomenon is that subjects receiving therapeutic treatment become better or worse adjusted, depending on the characteristics of the therapist, while the control-group subjects remain unchanged. In brief, *mean* improvement among treated subjects is masked because of a concellation effect between the patients who have improved and others who have deteriorated. The significant difference in *variability* between treatment and control groups has been used as a basis for inferring the potential value and harm of therapeutic treatments. Again, the interpretation of this phenomenon is that subjects receiving therapeutic treatment become better or worse adjusted, while the control subjects remain unchanged.

The obvious question is, do group psychotherapy procedures also contribute to a deterioration effect?

Three sets of independent data are pertinent to this issue. Fortunately, these data stem from more "solid" experimental procedures, thus adding credibility to the findings. Fairweather's (1960) analysis of data included pre-post comparisons in variability for subjects receiving treatment in individual psychotherapy, group therapy, or group living. These data indicated that all treatment groups showed greater variability on outcome measures after treatment than did no-treatment control subjects. Subjects involved in group treatment programs tended to show more change and variability in interpersonal behavior, while subjects receiving individual therapy tended to show more change and variability in perceptual spheres. These changes reflect parameters consistent with the goals of the different therapeutic treatments. These data suggest that group therapy did contribute to making patients better or worse along behavioral dimensions most reasonably affected by group or individual psychotherapy. In brief, some patients receiving therapy were getting better and others were getting an equal amount worse, whereas patients not receiving therapy tended to remain unchanged.

Barron's (1955) analysis of data did not include significant tests of the variability between treatment and control subjects. Inspection of the standard deviations representing posttherapy testing for the experimental and control subjects reveals suggestive findings, however. Five subscales from the MMPI showed standard deviations twenty percent or more larger for the subjects receiving treatment than for the no-treatment control group. These data are consistent with the rationale for inferring a deterioration effect, but should only be regarded as suggestive in the absence of appropriate statistical tests.

The last set of data bearing on this question is the most direct, impressive, and informative. On the basis of outcome data collected as part of a large-scale investigation of group therapy (Truax, 1966), it was possible to rank-order the sixteen different therapists on the basis of effectiveness in facilitating constructive personality changes. This was accomplished by converting each of the different outcome measures employed into standard scores and then averaging together all the scores per patient and per therapy group. This resulted in an index of average group benefit or deterioration based on a variety of different outcome measures. It must be recognized that there are obvious difficulties in averaging different measures together. Converting different measures into standard scores and averaging represents a process that *reduces* the effects of extreme scores and independent measures by the transformation of numbers and addition of essentially heterogeneous variables. Such a process, however, should make it more difficult, rather than easier, to detect differences between therapists. In view of this, these results are particularly interesting.

Table 21.2 summarizes the data reflecting the rank ordering of therapists and the range of

TABLE 21.2 Rank Order of Group-Therapist Effectiveness Based on Averaged Standard Scores of Patient Change

Therapist Number	Averaged Standard Scores of Patient Change
1	+.54
2	+.40
3	+.37
4	+.22
5	+.20
6	+.14
7	+.13
8	−.03
9	−.03
10	−.05
11	−.09
12	−.10
13	−.23
14	−.31
15	−.46
16	−.52

scores reflecting the average positive and negative change for each group. Notice that the scores range from +.54 to −.52. Considering the marked restriction in range that accompanies averaging standard scores, these data indicate that the treatment effects of some groups were clearly positive and constructive, while other groups showed an equally pronounced deterioration effect.

It would be unwarranted to attribute these findings solely to the differences in therapeutic styles of the therapists, inasmuch as the different experimental conditions for this study are completely confounded with therapeutic skills. For this reason, these data do not help identify sources of deterioration, but this does not change the essential interpretation of the data. Different parameters of group psychotherapy, including, perhaps, group therapists, clearly contribute to deterioration of the adjustment of some clients, just as other parameters of group psychotherapy contribute to improvement.

Implications

1. Like so many other forms of physical or mental treatment, group therapy should be viewed as a two-edged sword that can both help and hinder client adjustment. Group therapists doubtless play a major role in facilitating client adjustment and deterioration. Therefore, therapists ought to be able to identify their major behavioral assets and liabilities in terms of their impact on client adjustment, and guide their professional behavior accordingly. Appropriate evaluation procedures should be initiated to provide the individual therapist with feedback about his general effectiveness, the type of client with whom he is most and least successful, the composition of groups with whom he is most and least successful, and the type of clients and groups who should routinely be referred to colleagues. This is a first step in developing a system for correctly placing patients in specific types of groups with specific therapists.

2. Because group therapy can be a two-edged sword, certain events in such therapy are predictable and can be anticipated. First, not all patients will do well in group therapy. Therapists should be alert, especially during early sessions, for patients who do not possess the emotional, intellectual, or interpersonal resources to use a group for corrective emotional experiences. Once identified, these patients could receive "special training" that will help them understand the process of group therapy and clarify their roles in helping themselves within the group. Care should be taken to accommodate these needs without further

invalidating the patient's already inadequate self-system. This helping procedure should be seen by the patient or the staff not as a special case needing sympathy, but as a problem of preparing patients to use group therapy for their benefit. If such "special training" fails, then other treatment besides group psychotherapy should be used. It seems equally appropriate to inform patients during pretherapy orientation that there will be differences in patient improvement and that evaluation periods will be provided in which patients can participate in the task of evaluating group and client adjustment as well as their own progress.

3. Group therapy has been reported effective with neurotics, psychotics, and patients with character disorders, with the most positive results being reported on neurotic symptomology. Overt behavior patterns and adjustment to residential living have been reported improved by a number of independent investigations. The evidence is sufficiently clear to indicate the potential value of group therapy, irrespective of the treatment population, in any program involved with institutional living.

4. Follow-up investigations indicate that the first six months of community adjustment are critical, since much of the client's improvement will dissipate during this time. Follow-up treatment contacts on an increasingly intermittent schedule would probably help arrest the rate of relapse after treatment is terminated. These data further suggest that practitioners should focus on methods of strengthening, maintaining, stabilizing, and transferring newly acquired behavior patterns or attitudes from the treatment room to the community. Without a follow-up treatment contact that emphasizes transfer of treatment effects, there is considerable risk that the gains reported immediately after treatment will dissipate.

GROUP PROCESSES AND CLIENT IMPROVEMENT

Methodology

The main question to be considered at this point is: What kinds of therapeutic conditions produce change? The most frequent method of answering this question is one that relates group process variables to outcome measures. The process-outcome designs have the same problems measuring criterion variables as pre-post studies, in addition to difficulty in measuring process variables. For example, studies can be criticized for psychological testing with such instruments as the MMPI or Rorschach during actual treatment. As a result of this testing, outcome effects could be attributed to the psychological testing or attention effect instead of to the therapeutic treatment.

Group process variables are frequently observed by trained raters and judges. Many studies have used observation techniques similar to Bale's Interaction Categories or Hill's Interaction Matrix as a quantitative methods for describing overt behavior. Several cautions are in order when using these measurement techniques. Preformed behavioral rating systems run the risk of being invalid because the behavioral categories may be inappropriate. Even though behavioral rating systems are useful and efficient in classifying observable behavior, they do not discriminate between behaviors that are observably similar, but dynamically different. For example, two people in a group may express anger for clinically different reasons; one may be ventilating hostility, while the other is seeking attention.

Some researchers have used subjective criteria to measure both process variables and therapeutic outcome. Most of these measures include the individual's own assessment of his personal happiness, his observations of his behavior in the group, and the perceived growth resulting from group psychotherapy. Sechrest and Barger (1961) examined the relationship between group participation and perceived benefits by quantifying actual verbal participation (number of sentences spoken and speeches made). Each person filled out a questionnaire that purported to measure the benefit of each session. Results tend to confirm the hypothesis that patients will perceive as most beneficial those sessions in which they participated most. It can hardly be conceded that a patient's feelings of satisfaction with himself or with group psychotherapy can be considered either a major goal of the procedure or evidence of its success. People tend to be remarkably well satisfied with fortune tellers and tend to feel they have derived much from the association with them.

A major methodological problem in studying the relationship between group process variables and therapeutic outcome is presenting the independence between the two sets of measurements. That is, the measurement of group process variables cannot be allowed to contaminate or influence the measurement of patient improvement. For example, Truax (1961) studied the relationships that contributed to variation inpatient intrapersonal exploration. Three heterogeneous groups, involving a total of forty-five hospitalized mental patients led by therapists differing in their theoretical orientations to psychotherapy, were selected. Tape-recordings were then obtained on forty-two successive hours of psychotherapy from each of the three groups. From these recordings, transcriptions were made of 126 three-minute group interactions to provide basic data for analysis. The measures of empathic understanding, accurate empathy, unconditional positive regard, and self-congruence were devised to rate each therapist's responses. Additionally, the frequency of each therapist's responses was tabulated within the sample as a measure of his responsivity. Scales were also devised to quantify characteristics of group interaction. These were concreteness of group discussion, deindividuation of group interactions, empathic understanding of the group, unconditional positive regard to the group, spirit of cooperation, and sociability of the group.

There were statistically significant relationships between the therapeutic conditions and the criterion measure of intrapersonal exploration by the patient-members (Rogers and Rablen Process Scale). A number of correlations between the therapeutic conditions and self-exploration are spuriously inflated because the two variables were rated on the *same* verbal content, namely, the group's verbalizations. In this case, one might ask if each of the therapeutic variables and group process variables are orthogonal or correlational with patient verbal reports. It would be extremely interesting to reveal the relationships with partial correlations.

Another question related to this issue is: Are there developmental stages in the therapeutic process that can be identified? For example, Heckel's study (1967) attempted to find discrete stages in the therapeutic sequence. After each interview the subject answered a questionnaire describing environmental responses, personal responses, group responses, therapist directed responses, and group-building responses.

The main criticism is based on the fact that repeated measures include additive error variance due to day-to-day catastrophes and responsive fluctuations in the behavior being measured. For example, many therapists observed the effect of President Kennedy's assassination on the behaviors within their groups.

The main criticism of this procedure is the same as with any repeated measurement technique, instrument effects, and/or reliability deterioration. Even with the most reliable instruments, the test-retest reliabilities are about .90. With as many as four administrations, these reliabilities would be reduced to .73. Five administrations would reduce the reliability to .66. A possible remedy might be to rely more upon psychophysical criteria to determine change. These authors have yet to review a study in which different stages of group psychotherapy were related to physiological evidence, such as heart rate or galvanic skin response, although there is some evidence (Anderson, 1956) suggesting that psychophysiological measures are sensitive to psychological events during therapy.

Results

Group Cohesion. The identification of curative factors operating in group therapy are complex and problematic. Perhaps this accounts for the virtual absence of systematic investigations relating the group therapy process to therapeutic outcome. In spite of the lack of evidence, there is considerable clinical sentiment that group cohesion is an important curative agent in group therapy. In the eyes of many practitioners, the cohesive climate of the group has assumed the same stature as the patient-therapist relationship in individual psychotherapy. There is considerable literature on group dynamics (Yalom and Rand, 1966; Goldstein, Heller, and Sechrest, 1966) that adds indirect support to the belief in the value of group cohesion in group therapy. For example, it has been demonstrated that members of cohesive groups (1) are more productive; (2) are more open to influence by other group members; (3) experience more security; (4) are more able to express hostility and adhere more closely to group norms; (5) attempt to influence others more frequently; and (6) continue memberships in groups longer.

On the basis of both sentiment and related research, it appears that understanding the relationship between group processes and therapeutic outcome is fundamental to an adequate understanding of a subset of antecedent conditions for constructive personality change.

In order to approach this question on the basis of research data currently available, the authors have classified and subsumed the assorted independent variables representing group therapy processes into new categories on the basis of apparent common elements. The first category groups together those investigations that deal with feelings of personal involvement in the group, expressions of feeling, and the affective atmosphere of the group, all of which have as a prerequisite a group atmosphere of interpersonal trust and solidarity. In other words, these investigations have as a common element a cohesive bond between group members. The remaining investigations are most amenable to classification representing a mechanical dimension. The variables in this classification are not ego-involving for the subjects and represent, for the most part, manipulation of events that the subject has little apparent control over, involvement with, or commitment to. Table 21.3 summarizes the research literature representing these two classifications.

Inspection of Table 21.3 reveals some interesting findings. First, three major sets of affective dimensions have been investigated: (1) expressions of feeling; (2) meaningful participation; and (3) empathy, warmth, and genuineness emanating from both therapist and group. All of these dimensions have been related to constructive changes in personality. The outcome measures consist of more favorable responses from peers, perceived self-help, and improvement on the MMPI and Q-sort measures.

This indirect evidence is further strengthened by the findings of Yalom (1967), in which indicators of group cohesiveness measured at the sixth-therapy session were predictive of future therapeutic outcome. These data clearly suggest that feelings of personal involvement, a group atmosphere of warmth and unity, an experiencing of feelings of personal acceptance—in short, an atmosphere of group cohesion—play a prominent role in providing patients with the necessary conditions for the occurrence of a corrective emotional experience in their interpersonal relationships within a group-therapy setting. Two investigations of verbal participation epitomize the apparent meaning of this group of investigations. When verbal participation was measured in terms of length of speech and words spoken (Smith and Bassin, 1960), there was no relationship between the extent of participation and client improvement. However, when verbal participation included a measure that reflected participation that was at a meaningful level for the client, a positive relationship between the extent of participation and improvement was discovered (Sechrest and Barger, 1961).

Literature in related fields has identified some of the determinants of group cohesion. Contributing to group cohesion are variables such as its ability to meet the personal needs of group members, the degree of positive feelings the member has for the activities of the group, and the status position held in the group (Frank, 1959). More recent evidence growing directly out of the psychotherapy literature (Yalom, 1966) suggests that group compatibility may be the key variable in building cohesive groups.

The technical manipulations do not produce the same degree of consistency in findings, nor do clusters of similar independent variables emerge warranting special comment. It is interesting to notice in passing that increasing client exposure to therapy seems beneficial, while having the therapist absent on alternate sessions retards therapeutic progress.

Treatment of Choice: Group or Individual Psychotherapy. Currently, there is insufficient research evidence to clearly identify the conditions under which individual or group psychotherapy is the treatment of choice. The existing data do, however, provide valuable clues for developing guidelines for identifying the conditions under which it may be more appropriate to use individual or group psychotherapy.

TABLE 21.3 Literature Review Summarizing Group Process Variables Related to Therapeutic Outcome

Name	Independent Variables	Dependent Variables	Population	Findings
		COHESIVE		
Truax (1965)	Group levels of empathy, warmth, and genuineness Therapist-offered empathy, warmth, and genuineness	Q sort Anxiety reaction Palo Alto Scale MMPI; 1-year follow-up time out of institution	Psychiatric patients	Group atmosphere of empathy, warmth, and genuineness and therapist-offered empathy, warmth and genuineness equally predictive of positive outcome.
Kapp (1964)	Perceived group unity and feelings of personal inducement	Client-perceived improvement	Volunteers	Unity and group stability contributed to perceived improvement.
Zimet (1955)	Group lecture vs. group-centered	Picture Story Test Combs Desire Test Participation Rating	School administrators	Change in attitude, affect, and desires following group therapy.
Truax (1961)	Helpful characteristics of therapist and group: A. Empathy B. Warmth C. Genuineness	Self-exploration (process scale)	Psychiatric patients	Therapist empathy, warmth, genuineness, leadership and responsibility, as well as group genuineness, cohesion and ego involvement, were related to insightfulness.
Zimpfer (1967)	Expression of feelings	Peer approval and self-evaluation	High-school students	Peer approval increases with expression of warmth.
Sechrest (1961)	Meaningful verbal participation	Client-perceived improvement	Female psychiatric patients	Patients perceive as more beneficial those sessions in which they participated most.
Yalom (1966)	Popularity in therapy groups	Global improvement	Outpatients	Group popularity and group cohesiveness related to client improvement.
		MECHANICAL		
Bassin (1962)	Verbal participation	Personality change (TAT) and Human Relations Inventory	Law offenders	No relationship between verbal participation and improvement.
Truax (1968)	Therapist absent on alternate sessions	MMPI Q sort	Mental patients Delinquents	Alternate sessions resulted in less therapeutic gain than did regular sessions alone.
Cabeen (1961)	Amount of therapy	MMPI Rate of return Staff ratings	Sex offenders	Greater improvement with increased contact.
Coons (1957)	Amount of therapy	Rorschach Weschler-Bellevue	Psychiatric patients	Greater improvement with increased contact.

The studies generally consist of measuring personality and behavioral changes between patients receiving group psychotherapy and other similar patients receiving individual psychotherapy. For example, Novick (1965) employed a factorial arrangement of treatments to compare the effects of group and individual psychotherapy, using high and low ego-strength subjects. The results indicated that high ego-strength children were equally responsive to group and individual psychotherapy. Similarly, Somers (1966) employed a similar factorial arrangement of treatments to study the effects of group and individual psychotherapy, using subjects differing in the severity of the presenting speech problem. The criterion of improvement was speech articulation. Again, there were no significant differences between the treatment methods. Imber (1957) compared psychiatric patients assigned to group therapy and different types of individual therapy, but found that therapeutic contact was the most essential variable related to improvement. In brief, all of these investigations suggest that there was no treatment of choice.

On the other hand, Baehr (1954) compared group and individual psychotherapy and various combinations of each. He found that the combination of group and individual therapy was more effective than either treatment alone using client discontentment as a criterion variable. He also rank-ordered the various treatment combinations on the basis of their apparent value in the following order: (1) the combination of group and individual psychotherapy; (2) individual psychotherapy alone; and (3) group psychotherapy alone. It should be pointed out, however, that these conclusions were based on trends rather than on statistically significant findings.

Fairweather's (1963) study is perhaps the most significant. He treated four groups under one of the following conditions: (1) individual work assignments and individual psychotherapy; (2) individual work assignments and group psychotherapy; (3) group work assignment and group psychotherapy; and (4) a control group. The criteria of change were ward behavior, MMPI, Q-sort, Holland Vocational Preference Inventory, TAT, and a follow-up rating scale. The analysis of data revealed a number of interesting facts. First, patients receiving individual psychotherapy remained in treatment longer than the other three groups. Conversely, group therapy plus work assignments was the most economical in terms of time and efficiency of treatment. The data also indicated that grossly psychotic patients improved more with individual therapy, while nonpsychotic patients improved more in group psychotherapy.

Several tentative conclusions are suggested by these data. Unfortunately, care must be exercised to emphasize the tentative nature of these conclusions to guard against overgeneralizing. In brief, these data may be summarized as follows: (1) group psychotherapy produces good results when it is used to supplement other treatment methods; (2) group psychotherapy seems to have less power with psychotic patients, and conversely, more power with nonpsychotic patients; and (3) individual psychotherapy is more effective with grossly psychotic patients and less effective with nonpsychotic populations.

Group Therapy for Schizophrenics. Schizophrenia represents a marked disturbance characterized by pronounced interpersonal withdrawal, confused and bizarre thinking, and anhedonia. As a treatment problem, this disorder is surpassed by none. Group therapy treatment methods for schizophrenia have varied from highly structured didactic lectures to more traditional group-centered methods favoring expression of feelings and mutual understanding. Group-centered therapies are currently in vogue, but historically, more structured approaches have predominated. Therapists also vary in their approach to the treatment of schizophrenics. Some therapists favor doing therapy in a group, others favor doing therapy through a group, and still others feel that schizophrenia is a biological rather than a psychological problem.

In recent years there has been increasing evidence that group therapy can facilitate constructive personality changes in schizophrenics (Semon and Goldstein, 1957; Williams, McGhee, Kittleson, and Halperin, 1962; Sachs and Berger, 1954; Jones and Peters, 1952; Fiefel and Schwartz, 1953; Cowden, Zachs, and Sproles, 1956; and Cowden, Zachs, Hague, and

Finney, 1956). Optimism springs modestly from these data, since the results are far from clear. Again, most of these investigations have studied group therapy in its generic form and left untouched the more complex problems of specific treatment factors and antecedent conditions contributing to client improvement or deterioration.

Since the classic Lewin, Lippit, and White (1939) experiment demonstrating that democratic groups are more successful than authoritarian groups in creating a cohesive atmosphere, group leaders have tended to converge toward democratic group processes. There is another body of data, probably not so well known, suggesting that emotionally disturbed individuals respond more favorably to structured situations (Adorno et al., 1950). In view of these contradictory findings, the degree of structure involved in group procedures with schizophrenics emerges as a significant variable affecting group process and therapeutic outcome. Unfortunately, there are relatively few investigations that shed light on this issue. The grouping of investigations on the degree of apparent structure involved in the treatment procedures does produce suggestive findings.

Singer (1954) experimentally constrasted authoritarian (leader-centered) and democratic (group-centered) group-psychotherapy procedures with schizophrenics. These two approaches reflect the two basic social atmospheres most frequently employed with schizophrenics. The subjects assigned to the authoritarian group were exposed to highly structured treatment procedures. The therapy room was similar to a lecture hall, with a speaker's table and balanced rows of seats. The patients were brought to the therapy room by aides, roll was routinely taken, and patients were assigned seats. Discussion periods were provided at the close of each lecture. Patients assigned to the democratic group worked with a therapist who encouraged the expression of feelings, encouraged patients to discuss personal problems, frequently asked clarifying questions, and reflected feelings. The blackboard was removed from the room and seats were arranged in a circle with no fixed seating.

The results of this investigation indicated that the authoritarian group initially had a higher frequency of relevant comments by patients. This initial superiority in relevant comments declined sharply in later sessions. The democratic group, although initially less relevant and more disorganized in their communications, eventually surpassed the authoritarian group. In general, the democratic group gave evidence of higher morale and greater cohesiveness. It appears that the didactic group-therapy approach had relatively little long-term therapeutic value. Its primary contribution was affording the chronic schizophrenic with a structure that was useful in facilitating early communication. This very advantage appears in the long run to be self-defeating, however. On the basis of these data, it appears that structure is initially helpful in working with schizophrenics, but that its long-term effects are detrimental.

There is other suggestive evidence indicating that structure plays an important role in working with schizophrenics. Anker (1961) employed a $2 \times 2 \times 2$ factorial arrangement of treatments to investigate the role of traditional group therapy, a specially designed therapeutic activity, and group homogeneity. The special group activity consisted of patients producing plays for hospital patients and personnel. The activity was structured, but the group atmosphere was permissive and designed to promote a sense of belonging. Improvement was measured on the MACC rating scale depicting patient mobility, cooperation, communication, affect, and total adjustment. The results of this study indicate that the therapy program based on a more structured special activity program produced significant and consistent improvement on the rating scales. Group therapy produced relatively minor positive results. Spear (1960) reported data, although less direct, in which the primary variable associated with improvement among schizophrenics was a physical-treatment program. All of these data suggest that the degree of structure involved with the treatment of schizophrenics is a problem warranting serious consideration, and that structure and activity level should be used to initiate therapy groups with schizophrenic patients.

Implications

1. The cohesive atmosphere of the group is a primary antecedent to constructive personality

change. It is one of the few such variables that have been identified, and its helpful benefits should be fully exploited. This could be most easily accomplished by preserving well-developed groups so that the interpersonal honesty, personal feedback, warmth, and understanding would be available to members across the developmental phases of treatment and community readjustment. Often it would be feasible for groups to function as a unit from the beginning of hospitalization or community treatment through several years of critical problem-solving and personal adjustment. Group psychotherapy could take a developmental approach in which the first step would consist of attempts at mutual self-help and relief from personal discomfort. Most groups usually terminate at this point, because the press of immediate personal discomfort has been alleviated or key group members have been discharged. But it is entirely possible that groups could continue to function as units participating in such activities as (a) deciding a time for group discharge so that the group leaves the hospital rather than that individuals leave the group; (b) group vocational guidance, giving group members an opportunity to develop their vocational plans within the group and thus allowing more reality testing; and (c) community readjustment programs accommodating the special needs of group members. Gradually, the group would meet on a more intermittent basis until it was terminated. This approach simply lengthens the life of the group and makes the supportive elements of a cohesive group available on a longer, more intermittent schedule. This approach would also provide continued therapeutic contact during the first critical months of community readjustment.

In a similar vein, it could be equally promising to develop criteria for group membership selection that would increase the chances of patients within the group forming lasting personal friendships. Again, the focus is on developing enduring "helpful" relationships.

2. Group therapists need not express the degree of concern over the silent members as has historically been the case. The uninvolved group member, not the silent member, should command the attention of the therapist. The degree of emotional involvement in the group, as evidenced by body movements and facial expressions during critical hours of therapy, should be the therapist's guide to patient involvement, rather than the number of comments made. Involvement, not simple verbal participation, is the key variable to gaining in group therapy.

3. The data comparing the usefulness of group and individual psychotherapy suggests that there are a number of prerequisites for healthy involvement in group psychotherapy. The most basic variable seems to be a non-psychotic disorder. Group psychotherapy seems to have less power with severely psychotic patients, probably because of the difficulty in establishing interpersonal relationships. Because a severely psychotic person has difficulty relating to just one person, it is only reasonable to expect even greater difficulty if he has to cope with the threat of a group of people. On the basis of this observation, it seems reasonable to suggest that more severely disturbed patients need a "good therapeutic experience" with an individual therapist. In terms of a treatment sequence, it may be possible to gradually supplement individual treatment with group treatment. With increasing time, the patient would gradually become more involved in group therapy as he acquired greater skill and personal strength for coping with a group of people. When interpersonal activities are involved between ward members, schools, or other collective tasks, however, group therapy represents a good technique for facilitating desirable behavior change. It closely approximates a model of reality, and can provide a training laboratory for more effective living.

4. Therapeutic progress with schizophrenic groups may be optimal when the group is initially structured, with a gradual increase in group-centered activity as the group develops. Equally potent may be the activity level present in the group. Attempts to activate patient behavior through physical activity, task-oriented activity, or the use of drugs may be extremely useful for developing a group among schizophrenic patients. These procedures may alleviate some of the strain and accompanying anxiety as schizophrenics attempt to cope with the stress and ambiguity associated with developing interpersonal relationships in a group.

PRETHERAPY CONSIDERATIONS

Methodology

A major problem in group psychotherapy is how to initiate a group in order to achieve desired group activity. To provide solutions to this problem, most researchers usually select a group of individuals to be involved in group psychotherapy and submit them to various levels of pretherapy treatment conditions. Most criticisms of this procedure are based on the extent to which subjects are assigned to treatment in a genuinely *random* manner.

For example, Truax (1968) subjected patients to role-learning experiences via tape recordings to reveal whether they would influence therapeutic outcome.

The researcher assumed that group members react very much alike before measurements; therefore, it becomes difficult to generalize that differences are due to pretherapy variables rather than other causes. If the subjects differ, this difference could have resulted from biased selection or recruitment of the persons making up the groups. A second variable is that the group may differ, not because individual members have changed, but because the biased subset of members has dropped out. Generally speaking, such designs have the inherent disadvantage of failing to determine whether such pretherapy variables have effects on outcome. Since most researchers vary the pretherapy conditions in more than one way, it becomes important to utilize more than one group in any measurement.

Results

Pretherapy Training. It is becoming increasingly clear that the most formidable task facing a group therapist is cultivating a group of unhappy, interpersonally tense, and inept individuals into a cohesive unit characterized by warm interpersonal relationships and mutual attempts at self-help. The impact of early group meetings on subsequent group development and eventual behavior change is obviously tremendous. Laboratory and clinical research has demonstrated the importance of early group meetings in establishing norms for future group behavior (Jacobs, 1961). Similarly, patients who establish their popularity within groups early

and report satisfying experiences are more likely to show clinical improvement after 50 sessions (Yalom, 1967). And finally, recent investigations have demonstrated that early interaction patterns and eventual therapeutic outcome in individual psychotherapy can be influenced by pretherapy training (Goldstein and Shipman, 1961; Frank, 1959). All of these data lead to the conclusion that the initial therapeutic sessions are of prime importance.

The question then arises: Can pregroup psychotherapy training which clarifies client expectations, presents models of good patient behavior, and provides cognitive guidelines to help patients anticipate critical events in the development of an effective group contribute to the efficacy of group therapy?

Pretherapy training is a relatively new concept. Its therapeutic potency is yet to be clearly established; yet, using evaluation standards for the innovative needs of a growing enterprise, one can see that the future of pretherapy training is more than optimistic. Because of the enormous potential contribution of pretherapy training to many phases of group development and therapeutic improvement, as well as the more sophisticated research that has accompanied the development of this concept, two investigations warrant a more detailed presentation.

The first investigation (Yalom et al., 1967) randomly assigned sixty subjects from a waiting list for group therapy at an outpatient clinic to experimental and control group conditions. There were three experimental groups and three control groups. The experimental condition consisted of a 25-minute preparatory lecture clarifying and elaborating the following content areas related to participation in group psychotherapy: (1) all patients seeking group psychotherapy have the same basic difficulty of establishing and maintaining close, gratifying interpersonal relationships; (2) group therapy is a special microcosm where honest exploration of interpersonal relationships with group members is not only permitted but encouraged; and (3) the goal of group therapy is the development of relationships with other group members, even though this may create stress at times. In addition, a research investigation was reviewed, and it was pointed out that a high proportion of group therapy patients who remained in therapy for a year were significantly improved; and patients were advised that they could help themselves most by being honest and direct with their feelings at the time they experienced them. It was repeatedly pointed out that dealing with feelings at the time they occurred was the core condition for effective therapy, and large portions of the lecture were devoted to this point. The presentation may be summarized as an attempt to focus interpersonal behavior on the here and now, to increase the patient's faith in the efficacy of the group therapy process, and to provide cognitive information that would help patients anticipate critical events in the development of a cohesive group.

The findings of this study indicate that patients systematically prepared for group therapy engaged themselves in discussion of inter-member relationships in the group much more quickly than patients not so prepared. Also, patients were asked to estimate the percentage of patients helped by group therapy before the experiment started and again after the twelfth session. Experimental groups tended to be more optimistic than the control groups, suggesting that the patients' faith in the efficacy of group therapy had also been increased by the pre-therapy training. Even though this investigation did not employ measures of eventual thera-peutic outcome, these data suggest that pre-paring patients for involvement in group therapy has a positive influence on group therapy processes, which are probably important pre-decessors of behavior change.

Truax (1968) proposed that the value of patient self-exploration could be more vividly portrayed by having patients listen to tape recordings of portions of group therapy sessions illustrating "good" patient behavior at high levels of therapeutic conditions. The objective of this procedure was to help patients understand their role in the therapeutic process. Two populations, mental patients and juvenile delinquents, were used to investigate the value of this pretherapy training. Eight groups of ten patients each were investigated. Within each subpopulation, two groups had vicarious pre-therapy training that the others did not receive. Other treatment effects were also investigated in this study, but they will be reported in another section.

Using Q sort measures as outcome criteria, this investigation indicated that the vicarious pretherapy training groups made positive changes on all five self-concept measures, while the groups not receiving the pretherapy training regressed on four of the five measures and made a low positive change on the fifth measure. The statistical analysis of the data indicated that three of the five differences were statistically significant. The treatment effects remained constant for the mental patients and juvenile delinquents. These data clearly indicate that pretherapy training that clarifies patient role expectations and provides models of desirable therapeutic behavior has a positive effect on both the therapeutic process and eventual therapeutic improvement.

Group Composition. Experienced clinicians are now finding research support for their belief that about a third of the patients beginning group therapy drop out within the first dozen meetings unimproved (Yalom, 1966; Johnson, 1963). A recurring problem of this magnitude so disruptive to the development of effective groups calls for an awareness of the dimensions of group composition that have been related to desirable group interaction patterns and thera-peutic improvement. A number of writers have addressed themselves to the problem of group composition for more effective group therapy. Content areas cover group homogeneity and heterogeneity, premorbid history, current ad-justment, emotional and intellectual resources, and group compatibility. Sources of information vary from armchair speculation to empirical prediction studies. Considering the divergent sources of information, the bulk of writing arrives at a remarkably similar conclusion: the brighter, more capable, nonpsychotic patient tends to be more responsive to group-therapy treatment procedures than are other patients.

Giedt (1961) developed an index of suitability for group therapy by relating MMPI scales and ratings of work behavior based on the MACC (motility, affect, cooperation, and communi-cation) to the amount of participation, quality of communication, and personal development of group-therapy patients during the first sixteen sessions. Using these instruments, Giedt was able to predict with 84 percent accuracy subsequent group-therapy behavior. The variables that emerged as the best predictors were motility, cooperation, communication, and total adjustment from the MACC and the mid-range scores from Welsh's R factor. Even if future cross-validation of this instrument should produce considerable shrinkage, it appears that nurses' ratings of ward behavior can be a useful method for selecting patients for group therapy who possess the minimum prerequisite interpersonal skills to interact constructively with other group members.

In a similar vein, Fairweather's data (1960) demonstrated that neurotic and short-term psychotic patients showed improvement on Welsh's R factor, while long-term psychotics showed deterioration on the same measure in response to three types of treatment, which included group therapy and group living. Similarly, neurotics and short-term psychotics showed large positive changes on Q-sort measures in response to the same three sets of treatments, while long-term psychotics showed moderate negative change.

Using a brief factors scale composed of demographic and behavioral data, Heckel and Salzberg (1967) attempted to predict verbal response level and verbal exchanges in group therapy. Results suggested that the instrument was sensitive enough to identify those persons who could develop verbal interactions in group therapy and be responsive to persons other than the therapist. McFarland (1962) investigated the relationship between group-therapy participation as measured on the Finney interaction scale and intelligence test scores, verbal fluency, and a projective device. Results indicated that intelligence scores were the best predictors of subsequent desirable participation in therapy, and that a short, practical, screening battery to select patients for group therapy could easily be employed.

Moving away from specific patient characteristics to group composition, one notes that group therapy literature has frequently made reference to the homogeneity-heterogeneity problem. Powdermaker and Frank (1953) suggested that it was important to match patients to specific groups on the basis of compatible needs. Samuels (1964) also argued for group balance by having therapists attend to personality traits and psychodynamic factors in order to compose a group in such a way as to maximize therapeutic interaction.

A recent investigation by Yalom (1966) addressed itself directly to the relationship between interpersonal compatibility within group-therapy sessions and group cohesiveness. Five outpatient therapy groups provided the data for this investigation. Interpersonal compatibility was measured by the FIRO-B and related to group cohesiveness during the first twelve therapy sessions. The results indicated that highly compatible groups were significantly more cohesive than less compatible groups, and less compatible group members tended to report less satisfaction and to terminate prematurely. A major conclusion of this study was that interpersonal compatibility of the group members was more significant than the influence of the therapist in establishing a cohesive group. These findings have been further validated by converging evidence (Goldstein, Heller, Sechrest, 1966) indicating a close relationship between interpersonal attraction and attitudinal similarity. These data clearly suggest that there are identifiable behavioral and emotional prerequisites for effective involvement in group psychotherapy ranging on a dimension of severity of disturbance, intellectual and emotional resources, and group compatibility.

The Leaderless-Group Issue. In recent years, increasing attention has been directed toward the treatment value of leaderless therapeutic groups. Self-help groups have been organizing methods of treatment utilizing as helping persons lay men and women who have successfully overcome their own personal problems. Such organizations as Synanon (for character disorders, especially drug addicts), Alcoholics Anonymous, and the Seven Steps Foundation (for recently released convicts) have all reported success in facilitating positive personality changes in their populations.

Professional attention has also been focusing on the issue of leaderless therapeutic groups. Writers (Wolf, 1961; Wolf and Schwartz, 1962) have argued on theoretical grounds that the absence of the therapist from group-therapy sessions on alternate meetings would enhance the effectiveness of group treatment by not allowing the group to become dependent on the therapist for leadership. Others (Slavson, 1963) have raised objections to this position, predicting that the absence of the therapist on alternate sessions would be damaging rather than therapeutic. Unfortunately, the research data bearing on this question is unclear. Supporting evidence for each position can and should be cited.

Using subjects from a normal population, Berzon (1968) presented data indicating that self-directed groups were feasible and profitable as judged against the specific criteria of absenteeism, attrition, the ability of the group to function without a leader, and evaluations of the group by the subjects. It should be mentioned that professional leaders were available to the groups at request, and there is no indication of how frequently the leaders were used.

While Cadman (1954) did not use the control of a therapist-led group, his findings lend support to the value of leaderless therapy sessions. Using committed mental patients as subjects, he found that, in comparison to control subjects not receiving group therapy, patients in leaderless groups significantly improved their IQ scores on the Weschler-Bellvue, showed more normal responses on projective tests, and were rated improved on the basis of ward behavior, personal appearance, increased social awareness, and the development of group spirit. It is not possible to comment on the benefits that would have been derived had the patients been placed in groups with professional leaders. Nevertheless, these data demonstrate some benefits from leaderless group therapy.

Exner's (1966) investigation employed a design comparing the treatment effects of therapists' regular attendance, irregular attendance, and nonattendance. Thirty female patients, fourteen of whom were diagnosed as psychoneurotic and sixteen as having character disorders, were randomly selected from a treatment waiting list and assigned to five therapy groups with six patients in each group. Two of these groups were assigned to each of two therapists. The fifth group was not assigned a therapist and was the leaderless group. Each therapist attended the sessions of one of his groups regularly and the second irregularly. Irregular sessions were attended randomly, but scheduled so that the therapist was present at half the meetings. Prior to group-therapy assignments, the patients were rated on a 15-item scale concerning symptoms and prognosis, by staff members not involved in the study. The ratings were completed again after therapy. A number of interesting results emerged from this study. First, the ratings of client adjustment and prognosis showed improvement after treatment for all four groups in which a therapist was present, but a decrease in client adjustment ratings in the group where there was no therapist. It should be noted that 11 of the 12 patients in the irregularly attended groups were discharged by staff recommendation, while 7 of the 12 patients in the regularly attended groups and only one of the six patients in the no-therapist groups were similarly discharged. Appropriate significance tests indicate that these differences would arise by chance less than one time in a hundred. On the basis of these data, it was concluded that irregular attendance by the therapist was a variable more conducive to patient improvement than either regular attendance by a therapist or no attendance whatsoever. Regular attendance by the therapist, however, does appear to be more conducive to improvement than no therapist attendance whatsoever. On the basis of these data, the rank-order relationship between therapist presence and patient improvement would be as follows: (1) therapist attending irregularly; (2) therapist attending regularly; and (3) no therapist attendance whatsoever.

Contradictory findings do, however, exist. Using mental patients and juvenile delinquents, Truax (1968) investigated the effects of having the therapist absent from group therapy sessions on alternate meetings. Eight different therapy groups were investigated, four with juvenile delinquents and four with mental-hospital patients. Two groups of delinquents and two groups of mental-hospital patients took part in the 14 alternate sessions with the therapist absent. On three of the five Q-sort measures employed to measure patient improvement, patients in the alternate group sessions regressed, while the groups that had only regular sessions showed constructive change on all five measures. It is apparent that alternate sessions had a retarding effect upon the development of adequate self and ideal self-concepts in this study. More specifically, patients who engaged in alternate sessions described themselves after therapy as less similar to the way in which experts describe positive mental health characteristics than they had before therapy. The alternate sessions apparently influenced patients to see themselves in a more pathological fashion, and this fact certainly suggests that therapist absence during alternate sessions is detrimental to positive personality changes.

Investigations have also been reported describing the interaction patterns of leaderless groups. Becker (1968) reported less silence, more simultaneous attempts at initiating conversation, and a trend toward less anxiety with the therapist absent from the group. Salzberg (1967) reported less problem-relevant behavior and more spontaneity in leaderless groups. Patients also tended to place less emphasis on personal problems and become increasingly concerned with problems of other group members. Rothaus (1967) found that self-directed groups produced more play and had less need for personal attention than therapist-led groups. On the basis of these investigations, it appears that leaderless groups are less anxious, more spontaneous, and more play-oriented. Apparently, one of the primary jobs of a therapist is keeping the group focused on therapeutic tasks such as talking about interpersonal difficulties, and reducing the resistance to talking about anxiety-provoking topics.

It is unfortunate that the research data on such a vital issue is contradictory. Many variables could account for these differences. Different populations have been investigated, improvement has been defined and measured differently, and different therapists and therapies have been employed. On the basis of current data, it is not possible to separate the causal factors that would account for the contradictory findings and provide a basis for clear recommendations.

Implications

1. On the basis of accumulating evidence, it is apparent that the composition of a group is a powerful determinant of group behavior and group adjustment. The most skilled clinician could have the composition of the group stacked against him in such a way that even his most insightful, thoughtful, and helpful group

intervention could pass unnoticed. In a population with psychiatric disorders, there is probably a normal distribution of behavioral assets that are prime prerequisites for effective group therapy. Clinicians should capitalize on these assets by placing patients in groups so that sufficient group resources are available to facilitate (1) warm responsive interactions between some group members; (2) sufficient courage to discuss the unpleasant; (3) sufficient compatibility to increase personal attraction; and (4) sufficiently adequate adjustment to provide models for more effective ways of coping with stress. When patient pools are sufficiently large, selection procedures should be initiated so that the distribution of behavioral strength in the patient population is approximated equal in any particular group therapy session.

2. The selection of patients should be only the first step in preparing patients for involvement in group therapy. The current evidence is clear, consistent, and as sophisticated as any mental health literature is now producing; preparing patients for treatment pays off. Clarifying client role expectations, modeling desired client behavior patterns, and providing a framework that helps a patient anticipate and understand the group-therapy process should be regarded as prerequisites for treatment. By devoting more time to preparing patients for treatment and less time in actual treatment of patients, therapists could probably increase their general effectiveness.

3. Current data, in contrast to the group dynamic literature, suggest that leaderless groups with psychiatric patients are probably more potentially dangerous than professionally led groups. Group therapists play an important role in keeping the group focused on its therapeutic tasks and minimizing the accompanying anxiety. Therapists should be reluctant to sponsor leaderless groups with psychiatric patients, although there are probably conditions under which periodic absences can be beneficial. Unfortunately, in view of the contradictory research findings, this is currently a problem requiring clinical judgment.

Closing Comments on Research

In the preceding discussion, much has been

said about the lack of sophistication in group-psychotherapy research. Hopefully, research will advance to the stage of testing group member processes instead of treating the group as a unit. The area of group dynamics has served as a model for problem solving and communications, and it might be profitable to adopt similar models to evaluate interactions and reflections of personality changes. Also it is possible that there are other people in groups that effect positive change. In other words, group therapy may offer more degrees of freedom for a person to find the therapeutic personality than individual therapy.

With the availability of computers, more application of multivariate statistical analyses can be utilized. Matrix algebra and nonlinear mathematics may also be adopted to better characterize group processes. For example, one could study relationships between group members on several different kinds of measurable dimensions by plotting an interaction matrix. To illustrate this point, assume that the warmth transmitted from one person to another was plotted on a matrix. The horizontal dimension indicates a response from one individual to another, and the vertical dimension would reflect the response received from another individual. For example, in Figure 21.1, person B extends a warmth response to persons A and E, and person E then extends a response to B. If the final matrix is squared, the resulting matrix (Figure 21.2) indicates the number of second-order interactions each person entered into (the extent of indirect influence through another person.) For example, a response starting with person H has an indirect influence on persons B and G. The diagonal indicates the persons two-way interaction that exist from a person back to himself. In our illustration, persons B and C had mutual communications of warmth.

The cube of the matrix (Figure 21.3) indicates third-order interactions (indirect influence on other people.) In our illustration, person A influences B only through two other people. The diagonal now indicates the three-step connections from a person back to himself. Persons C and D each have two third-order interactions in our illustration. By observing the diagonal of the cube matrix, the core of partici-

pants in group psychotherapy soon becomes expressed by the high number of mutual interactions. If the number is composed of n members, the numbers appearing in the diagonal for each of the members will be equal to $(n-1)(n-2)$.

By analyzing interaction data in this manner, criteria can be compared between those persons participating in the main interaction and those participating on the periphery of the group-therapy situation. Developmental trends can be investigated over time to see if cohesion of the group actually influences less-participating subjects. This kind of analysis is only limited by the kinds of outcome criteria available and the imagination of the psychologist.

Matrix algebra can also be used to depict levels of interaction by adding the matrix of measured dimensions to its transpose (rows become columns and columns become the rows). The sum will result in the kind of therapeutic conditions each individual experiences. For example, assume that we measure agreeableness in a continuum of $+3$ to -3, and the resultant matrix is formed (Figure 21.4). As one can see in the summed matrix (Figure 21.5), there is friction between persons C and D (-4); however, persons C and B responded to one another with high agreement $(+3)$. In this example, one would be interested in outcome measures between the two subgroups and possible trends of future interactions in later sessions.

Few areas in psychology are characterized by as diffuse experimentation as group psychotherapy. This may be partly the result of a practical interest in specific areas, but mainly it represents the elementary satus of group psychotherapy as a scientific discipline. Most of the literature is not experimental in nature, but rather descriptive of therapists' experience or recommendations.

With the increasing need for psychotherapists and the apparent economy of group therapy, the major advances in the study of group-therapy techniques will have to be made within the next few decades. This immediacy, coupled with attempts to relate research more closely to important theoretical issues, will contribute to better and more precise research.

	A	B	C	D	E	F	G	H	I	J	K
A		1									
B					1						
C					1	1					1
D									1		1
E		1	1		1						
F		1			1			1			
G				1					1		
H											
I				1			1				
J											
K	1							1			

The "From" label spans the column headers.

Figure 21.1 Matrix of directionality.

	A	B	C	D	E	F	G	H	I	J	K
A					1						
B		1	1		1						
C	1	1	2		2			1			
D	1			1			1				
E		1	1		3	1					1
F		1	1		2	1					1
G				1			1		1		1
H											
I				1					2		1
J											
K		1									

Figure 21.2 Squared matrix.

	A	B	C	D	E	F	G	H	I	J	K
A		1	1		1						
B		1	1		3	1					1
C		3	2		5	2					2
D		1		1					2		1
E	1	3	4		6	1		1			1
F	1	2	3		5	1		1			1
G	1			2			1		2		1
H											
I	1			2			2		1		1
J											
K											

Figure 21.3 Cubed matrix.

	A	B	C	D	E
A		+3	+2	+1	1
B	−3		+1	−2	1
C	−3	+2		−3	−1
D	−3	+3			−1
E	1	1	−1	1	

Figure 21.4 Agreeableness coefficient matrix.

	A	B	C	D	E
A		0	−1	−2	2
B	0		3		
C	−1	3		−4	−2
D	−2	1	−4		0
E	2	2	−2	0	

Figure 21.5 Sum of matrix and transpose.

REFERENCES

Adorno, T. W., Frenkel-Brunswick, E., Levinson, D. J., and Sanford, R. N. *The authoritarian personality.* New York: Harper, 1950.

Anderson, R. P. Physiological and verbal behavior during client-centered counseling. *Journal of Counseling Psychology*, 1956, **III**, 174–184.

Anker, J. M. and Walsh, R. P. Group psychotherapy, a special activity program, and group structure in the treatment of chronic schizophrenics. *Journal of Consulting Psychology*, 1961, **25**, 476–81.

Baehr, G. O. The comparative effectiveness of individual psychotherapy, group psychotherapy, and a combination of these methods. *Journal of Consulting Psychology*, 1954, **13**, 179–183.

Barron, F., and Leary, T. F. Changes in psychometric patients with and without psychotherapy. *Journal of Consulting Psychology*, 1955, **19** (4), 239–245.

Bassin, A. Verbal participation and improvement in group therapy. *International Journal of Group Psychotherapy*, 1962, **12** (3), 369–373.

Becker, R. E., Harrow, M., Astrachan, B. M., Detre, T., and Miller, J. C. Influence of the leader on the activity level of therapy groups. *Journal of Social Psychotherapy*, 1968, **74**, 39–51.

Bergin, A. E. Some implications of psychotherapy research for therapeutic practice. *International Journal of Psychiatry*, 1967, **3**, 136–150.

Berzon, B. Self-directed small group programs: A new resource in rehabilitation. Final Narrative Report, Vocational Rehabilitation Administration, Project RD-1748, January, 1968.

Berzon, B., Pious, C., and Farson, R. E. The therapeutic event in group psychotherapy. A study of subjective reports by group members. *Journal of Individual Psychology*, 1963, **19** (2), 204–212.

Boe, Erling, E., Gocka, E. F., and Kogan, W. S. The effect of group psychotherapy on interpersonal perceptions of psychiatric patients. *Multivariate Behavioral Research*, 1966, **1** (2), 177–187.

Cabeen, C. W. Group therapy with sex offenders: Description and evaluation of group therapy program in an institutional setting. *Journal of Clinical Psychology*, 1961, **17** (2), 122–129.

Cadman, W. H., Misback, L., and Brown, D. V. An assessment of round-table psychotherapy. *Psychological Monographs*, 1954, **68** (13), 1–49.

Coons, W. H. Interaction and insight in group psychotherapy. *Canadian Journal of Psychology*, 1957, **11**, 1–8.

Cowden, R. C., Zax, M., Hague, J. R., and Finney, R. C. Chlorpromazine: Alone and as an adjunct to group psychotherapy in the treatment of psychiatric patients. *American Journal of Psychiatry*, 1956, **112**, 898–902.

Cowden, R. C., Zax, M., and Sproles, J. A. Group psychotherapy in conjunction with physical treatment. *Journal of Clinical Psychology*, 1956, **12**, 53–56.

Ends, E. J., and Page, C. W. Group psychotherapy and concomitant psychological change. *Psychological Monographs: General and applied.* 1959, **73** (10), 1–31.

Exener, J. E. Therapist attendance as a variable in group psychotherapy. In Stollak, G. E., Guerney, B., and Rothberg, M. (Eds.), *Research in Psychotherapy; Selected Readings.* Chicago: Rand McNally, 1966.

Fairweather, G. W., and Simon, R. A further follow-up comparison of psychotherapeutic programs. *Journal of Consulting Psychology*, 1963, **27** (3), 186.

Fairweather, G. W., Simon, R., Gebhard, M. E., Weingarten, E., Holland, J. L., Sanders, R., Stone, G. B., and Reahl, J. E. Relative effectiveness of psychotherapeutic programs: A multidimensional criteria comparison of four programs for three different patient groups. *Psychological Monographs*, 1960, **74** (5, Whole No. 492).

Feder, B. Limited goals in short-term group psychotherapy with institutionalized delinquent adolescent boys. *International Journal of Group Psychotherapy*, 1962, **12** (4), 503–507.

Feifel, H., and Schwartz, A. D. Group psychotherapy with acutely disturbed psychotic patients. *Journal of Consulting Psychology*, 1953, **17**, 113–121.

Frank, J. The dynamics of the psychotherapeutic relationship. *Psychiatry*, 1959, **22**, 17–39.

Giedt, F. H. Predicting suitability for group psychotherapy. *American Journal of Psychotherapy*, 1961, **15** (4), 582–591.

Goldstein, A. D., Heller, K., and Sechrest, L. *Psychotherapy and the psychology of behavior change.* New York: Wiley, 1966.

Goldstein, A. D., and Shipman, W. G. Patient expectancies, symptom reduction, and aspects of the initial psychotherapeutic interview. *Journal of Clinical Psychology*, 1961, **17**, 129–133.

Grosz, H., Stern, H., and Wright, C. S. Interactions in therapy groups as a function of differences among therapists and group size. *Psychological Reports*, 1965, **17**, 827–834.

Harrow, M., Astrachan, B. M., Becker, R. E., Miller, J. C., and Schwartz, A. H. Influence of the psychotherapist on the emotional climate in group therapy. *Human Relations*, 1967, **20** (1), 49–64.

Heckel, R. V., and Salzberg, H. C. Predicting verbal behavioral change in group therapy using a screening scale. *Psychological Reports*, 1967, **20**, 403–406.

Heller, K. Client dependency and therapist expectancy as relationship maintaining variables in psychotherapy. *Journal of Clinical Psychology*, 1963, **25** (5), 371–375.

Imber, S. D., Frank, J. D., Nash, E. H., Stone, A. R., and Gliedman, L. H. Improvement and amount of therapeutic contact: An alternative to the use of no-treatment controls in psychotherapy. *Journal of Consulting Psychology*, 1957, **21** (4), 309–315.

Jacobs, R. C., and Campbell, D. T. The perpetuation of an arbitrary tradition through several generations of a laboratory microculture. *Journal of Abnormal Social Psychology*, 1961, **62**, 649–658.

Johnson, J. A. *Group therapy: A practical approach.* New York: McGraw-Hill, 1963.

Johnson, K. E. Personal religious growth through small group participation: A psychological study of personality changes and shifts in religious attitudes which result from participation in a spiritual growth group. *Dissertation Abstracts*, 1964, **25** (1).

Jones, F. D., and Peters, H. H. An experimental evaluation of group psychotherapy. *Journal of Abnormal Social Psychology*, 1953, **47**, 345–353.

Kapp, F., Gleser, G., Brissenden, A., Emerson, R., Wingt, J., and Kashdan, B. Group participation and self-perceived personality change. *Journal of Nervous and Mental Disease*, 1964, **139** (3), 255–265.

Kraus, A. R. Experimental study of the effect of group psychotherapy with chronic psychotic patients. *International Journal of Group Psychotherapy*, 1959, **9**, 293–302.

Lewin, K., Lippitt, R. E., and White, R. K. Patterns of aggressive behavior in experimentally-created social climates. *Journal of Social Psychology*, 1939, **10**, 271–301.

Luria, Z. A semantic analysis of a normal and neurotic therapy group. *Journal of Abnormal Social Psychology*, 1959, **58**, 216–220.

McDavid, J. W. Immediate effects of group therapy upon response to social reinforcement among juvenile delinquents. *Journal of Consulting Psychology*, 1964, **28** (5), 409–412.

McFarland, R. L., Nelson, C. L., and Rossi, A. M. Prediction of participation in group psychotherapy from measures of intelligence and verbal behavior. *Psychological Reports*, 1962, **11**, 291–298.

McGinnis, C. A. The effects of group therapy on the ego-strength scale scores of alcoholic patients. *Journal of Clinical Psychology*, 1963, **19** (3), 346–347.

Novick, J. I. Comparison between short-term group and individual psychotherapy in effecting change in nondesirable behavior in children. *International Journal of Group Psychotherapy*, 1965, **15** (3), 366–373.

Persons, R. W. Psychological and behavioral change in delinquent following psychotherapy. *Journal of Clinical Psychology*, 1966, **22** (3), 337–340.

Powdermaker, F. B., and Frank, J. B. *Group psychotherapy: Studies in methodology of research and therapy.* Cambridge: Harvard University Press, 1953.

Rashkis, H. A., and Shaskon, D. A. The effects of group psychotherapy on personality inventory scores. *American Journal of Orthopsychiatry*, 1946, **16**, 345–349.

Reisper, M., and Waldman, M. Group therapy in a work adjustment center. *Journal of Jewish Communal Service*, 1961, **38**, 167–170.

Rosenthal, R. Experimenter effects in behavioral research. New York: Appleton-Century Crofts, 1966.

Rothaus, P., Johnson, D. L., Hanson, P. G., Brown, J. B., and Lyle, F. A. Sentence completion test prediction of autonomous and therapist-led group behavior. *Journal of Counseling Psychology*, 1967, **14**, 28–34.

Sacks, J. M., and Berger, S. Group therapy techniques with hospitalized chronic schizophrenic patients. *Journal of Consulting Psychology*, 1954, **18**, 297–307.

Salzberg, H. C. Effects of silence and redirection or verbal responses in group psychotherapy. *Psychological Reports*, 1962, **11**, 455–461.

Samuels, A. Use of group balance as a therapeutic technique. *Archives of General Psychiatry*, 1964, **2**, 411–420.

Sechrest, L. B., and Barger, B. Verbal participation and perceived benefit from group psychotherapy. *International Journal of Group Psychotherapy*, 1961, **11**, 49–59.

Semon, R. G., and Goldstein, W. The effectiveness of group psychotherapy with chronic schizophrenics and an evaluation of different therapeutic methods. *Journal of Consulting Psychology*, 1957, **21**, 317–322.

Singer, J. L., and Goldman, G. D. Experimentally contrasted social atmospheres in group psychotherapy with chronic schizophrenics. *Journal of Social Psychology*, 1954, **40**, 23–37.

Slavson, S. S. *Textbook in analytic group psychotherapy.* New York: International University Press, 1963.

Smith, A., Bassin, A., and Froehlich, A. Changes in attitudes and degree of verbal participation in group therapy with adult offenders. *Journal of Consulting Psychology*, 1960, **3**, 247–249.

Snyder, R. and Sechrest, L. An experimental study of directive group therapy with defective delinquents. *American Journal of Mental Deficiency*, 1959, **64**, 117–123.

Sommers, R. K., Schalffer, M. W., Leiss, R. H., Gerber, A. J., Bray, M. A., Fundrella, D., Olson, J. K., and Tomkins, E. R. The effectiveness of group and individual therapy. *Journal of Speech and Hearing Research*, 1966, **9**, 219–225.

Spear, F. G. Deterioration in schizophrenic control groups. *British Journal Medical Psychology*, 1960, **33**, 143–148.

Teahan, J. E. Effect of group psychotherapy on academic low achievers. *International Journal of Group Psychotherapy*, 1966, **16** (1), 78–85.

Thoma, E. Group psychotherapy with underachieving girls in a public high school. *Journal of Individual Psychology*, 1964, **20** (1), 96–100.

Truax, C. B. *Antecedents to Outcome in Group Counseling with Institutionalized Juvenile Delinquents: Effects of Therapeutic Conditions, Patient Self-Exploration, Alternate Sessions and Vicarious Therapy Pretraining.* Vol. 2, No. 14, Discussion Paper, Arkansas Rehabilitation Research and Training Center, #264, University of Arkansas.

Truax, C. B. Counseling and psychotherapy: Process and outcome. Unpublished final report, V.R.A. Research and Demonstration Grant, #906-P, 1966.

Truax, C. B. The process of group psychotherapy: Relationships between hypothesized therapeutic conditions and intrapersonal exploration. *Psychological Monographs*, 1961, **75** (7), 1–35.

Truax, C. B., and Carkhuff, R. R. For better or worse: The process of psychotherapeutic personality change. In *Recent advances in the study of behavior change*. Montreal, Canada: McGill University Press, 1964. Pp. 118–163.

Truax, C. B., Carkhuff, R. R., and Kodman, F., Jr. Relationships between therapist-offered conditions and patient change in group psychotherapy. *Journal of Clinical Psychology*, 1965, **21**, 327–329.

Truax, C. B., Schuldt, W. J., and Wargo, D. G. Self-ideal concept congruence and improvement in group psychotherapy. *Journal of Consulting and Clinical Psychology*, 1968, **32**, 47–53.

Truax, C. B., Shapiro, J. G., and Wargo, D. G. Effects of alternate sessions and vicarious therapy pretraining on group psychotherapy. *International Journal of Group Psychotherapy*, 1968, **18**, 186–198.

Tucker, J. E. Group psychotherapy with chronic psychotic soiling patients. *Journal of Consulting Psychology*, 1956, **20** (6), 430.

White, R., and Lippitt, R. Leader behavior and member reaction in three "social climates." In Cartwright, D., and Zander, A., *Group Dynamics, Research and Theory*. (2nd ed.) Evanston, Illinois: Row-Peterson, 1960, 527–553.

Wilcox, G. T., and Guthrie, G. M. Changes in adjustment of institutionalized female defectives following group psychotherapy. *Journal of Clinical Psychology*, 1957, **13**, 9–13.

Williams, M., McGee, T. F., Kittleson, S., and Halperin, L. An evaluation of intensive group living programs with schizophrenic patients. *Psychological Monographs*, 1962, **76** (24, Whole No. 543).

Wilson, D. L., Wilson, M. E., Jr., Sakata, R., and Frumkin, R. M. Effects of short-term group interaction on social adjustment on a group of mentally retarded clients. *Psychological Reports*, 1967, **21**, 7–16.

Wolf, A. Group psychotherapy with adults: The alternate meeting. Paper read at APGA Conference, New York, January 27, 1961.

Wolf, A., and Schwartz, E. K. *Psychoanalysis in groups*. New York: Grune & Stratton, 1962.

Yalom, I. D. A study of group therapy drop-outs. *Archives of General Psychiatry*, 1966, **14**, 393–414.

Yalom, I. D., Houts, P. S., Newell, G., and Rand, K. H. Preparation of patients for group therapy. *Archives of General Psychiatry*, 1967, **17**, 416–427.

Yalom, I. D., Peters, H. S., Sheldon, M. Z., and Rand, K. H. Prediction of success in group therapy. *Archives of General Psychiatry*, 1967, **17**, 159–168.

Yalom, I. D., and Rand, K. Compatibility and cohesiveness in therapy groups. *Archives of General Psychiatry*, 1966, **13**, 267–76.

Zimet, C. N., and Fine, H. J. Personality changes with a group therapeutic experience in human relations seminar. *Journal of Abnormal Social Psychology*, 1955, **51**, 68–73.

Zimpfer, D. G. Expression of feelings in group counseling. *Personnel and Guidance Journal*, 1967, **45** (7), 703–708.

22

THE EFFECTS OF HUMAN RELATIONS TRAINING

JACK R. GIBB

LA JOLLA, CALIFORNIA

A classification of the wide range of activities called "human relations training" in the literature and in practice is presented in Table 22.1. The table includes a statement of the primary aims of each individual method as practitioners phrase them, and a brief description of the identifying or definitive characteristic of the method. For each category a reference is cited where a reputable practitioner describes the method as it is currently used. A more rigorous or systematic taxonomy of method is not as yet possible in this lively field. No standard terminology is available. Invention of new technology and widespread experimentation with methods of intervention lead to increasingly greater differences in practice, even among group leaders who use identical terms to describe the method used. Complicating the picture is the fact that space limitations force such sketchy descriptions of group events that it is impossible to determine with precision what actually happened in a given training session. Such great diversity and rapid change will probably have enduring and felicitous effects upon the field, but bring obvious complications to the appraisal of the effects of such training.

In this chapter an attempt is made to analyze the published studies relevant to an evaluation of the effectiveness of the nine methods listed in Table 22.1. Human-relations training usually involves an intensive small-group experience of some kind. Although there is an increasing overlap among activities in "therapy groups" and "training groups", most practitioners make distinctions between the two (for example, Bradford, Gibb, and Benne, 1964; Schein and Bennis, 1965). Training is usually characterized by the following conditions:

1. The focus is more upon analysis of here-and-now data perceptually available in the group rather than upon historical data or upon organizational or family life.

2. The focus is more upon personal growth and increased human potential than upon remedial or corrective treatment.

3. The focus is more upon the available inter-personal data than upon analysis of unconscious or motivational material.

4. The focus is more upon group processes, the functioning of the group, and the inter-member interactions than upon leader-member relationships.

5. The focus is more upon trying out of new behavior in the training group than upon achieving new insight or new motivation.

6. The immediate and primary intent of the leader is to improve effectiveness or change behavior of normal people in the organizational or natural-group setting, rather than to relieve distress or to change personality or character structure.

7. Participants usually see themselves as normal people attempting to function more effectively at the interpersonal level, as group or organization members rather than as sick people seeking treatment to relieve suffering.

The methods in Table 22.1 are listed in rough sequence, from those at the top of the table, which most nearly approximate therapy, to those at the bottom, which most nearly approximate formal "education." Although great changes are occurring in both the

TABLE 22.1 Categorization of Human Relations Training Treatments

Treatment Designation	Central Aims	Definitive Activities or Characteristics	Description
1. Creativity-growth	Creativity Awareness Releasing human potential	Induced experiences designed to expand human awareness.	Otto & Mann (1968)
2. Marathon	Personal growth Greater capacity for being intimate	Uninterrupted interpersonal intimacy.	Stoller (1968)
3. Emergent	Personal growth Group growth	Absence of leader. Nonprogrammed, unpredictable, emergent activities.	Gibb & Gibb (1968b)
4. Authenticity	Openness Authentic encounter	Interventions and experiences focused on openness and consonance.	Bugental (1965)
5. Sensitivity	Personal competence Group effectiveness Organizational effectiveness	Focus on here-and-now experiences, and on group processes.	Bradford, Gibb, & Benne (1964)
6. Programmed	Personal growth and/or competence Group effectiveness Organizational effectiveness	Experiences initiated and/or directed by absent leaders.	Berzon & Solomon (1966)
7. Microexperience	Interpersonal skills Group effectiveness Organizational effectiveness	Limited time (2 to 20 hours; 1 to $2\frac{1}{2}$ days). Restricted depth.	Bradford, Gibb, & Lippitt (1956)
8. Inquiry	Skills of inquiry Group effectiveness System effectiveness	Data-gathering, quasi-structured experiences. Focus on explicit and predictable individual and group learnings.	Miles (1965)
9. Embedded	Team effectiveness Organizational effectiveness Problem-solving skills	Training experience embedded in sequential and continuous organization-based program of inputs, data-gathering, and experiences.	Argyris (1962) Friedlander (1968)

classroom and the training group, it is possible to make distinctions between activities usually thought of as having a "human relations training" focus and activities designated as "educational." Three distinctions are usually made in the literature:

1. Training has an explicit focus upon behavior change, whereas education usually emphasizes changes in knowledge and insight.

2. Training places a focus upon the "process" rather than upon the "content" of group interaction. The central activity of training groups is the analysis of persons *qua* persons and of process *qua* process. That is, groups focus upon the available interactions, leadership, feelings, structural patterns, perceptions, and other dynamics of the "here and now." When group methods are used in the classroom, the focus is usually upon content and the use of such participatory "activities" as field trips, case methods, group discussions, seminars, simulations, and visual aids.

3. In training, there is usually a greater concern with affective and conative processes than with ideational processes. While in each case leaders may speak of working with the "whole person," for instance, the trainer is more likely to concentrate upon feelings and interactions among group members and the educator upon ideas and cognitive problems.

Even if studies have evaluated programs that have been called human-relations training, if the activities were largely "educational" in the above sense, they have been omitted from the review. Discussion and instructional methods usually do not include an intensive group experience, have not been found to produce behavior change, and usually have expressed aims of giving information rather than of producing change in behavior or personality.

The chapter is divided into three sections. The first section contains a discussion of the general effects of the nine methods listed in Table 22.1, considered as one "treatment." The second section contains a discussion of each of the nine methods as technologies for behavior change, together with a review of the limited amount of research relating to the effectiveness of specific aspects of technology. The third section deals with implications for practice.

RESEARCH ON EFFECTS OF TRAINING

The research on training will be considered in terms of stated aims. The six most frequently recurring objectives in the training literature are related to those stated by professionals doing therapy, and are closely correlated with the listed characteristics of positive mental health (Jahoda, 1958). The conceptual and mensurational diversity in the studies makes it impossible to give crisp operational distinctions among the six variables described in the training literature:

1. Sensitivity. Training is aimed at inducing greater sensitivity to self, to the feelings and perceptions of other people, and to the general interpersonal environment. Sensitivity is seen as an input process involving greater awareness of the feelings and perceptions of others. It also has an output component, aspects of which are described variously as availability of self, transparency, openness, authenticity, or spontaneity.

2. Managing feelings. Trainers speak of such outcomes as awareness of one's own feelings, acceptance by oneself of the feeling component in one's own actions and speech ("owning" one's feelings), consonance between feelings and behavior, clarity of expression of feelings, and integration of emotionality into various life processes.

3. Managing motivations. The training literature refers to such hoped-for motivational outcomes as self-actualization, awareness of one's own motives, clear communication of one's own motives to others, self-determination, commitment, greater energy level, inner-directedness, and becoming.

4. Functional attitudes toward self. Practitioners mention acceptance of self, self-esteem, congruity of actual self and ideal self, and feelings of confidence as potential positive outcomes of training.

5. Functional attitudes toward others. Training is thought to produce such changes in attitudes as decreased authoritarianism, greater acceptance of others, reduced prejudice, reduced regard for structure and control, and attitudes commensurate with interdependence theories of management, such as "Theory Y" (McGregor, 1960) and "participative management" (Likert, 1967).

6. Interdependent behavior. Effective behavior is described variously as interpersonal competence, task effectiveness, teamwork, being a "good group member," democratic leadership, problem-solving effectiveness, or interdependence.

The bibliography at the end of this chapter contains 106 studies reporting quantitative data relevant to the effect of training on the above six outcome variables. The bibliography includes seven earlier reviews of the studies on training, each of which has a special emphasis and none of which attempts a comprehensive or complete survey of the effects of training on behavior change (Bradford, 1953; Buchanan, 1965; Bunker, 1965; Campbell and Dunnette, 1968; Hampden-Turner, 1966; House, 1967; Stock, 1964); and two annotated bibliographies (Durham and Gibb, 1960; Knowles, 1967).

When considered from the viewpoint of the frequent mention in the general psychological literature of the lack of research on training, the quantity and quality of available research is surprisingly high. When compared with the standards of research in the psychological laboratory and with the desirability of definitive statements about the effects of training, the methodological impurities of the studies loom large, and the results are disappointingly equivocal.

The barriers to precise and satisfying research on the effects of training are many. One problem relates to the inadequacy of theories of training and the lack of cross-fertilization between training and research. Too much of the research has a "bits and pieces" quality, seems opportunistically empirical, and lacks an integrating or programmatic directionality. Innovation and change in training methodology is largely clinical and intuitive in genesis. New methods go untested, and research has little influence upon the evolution of methods and theories of training. Recent developments are gradually changing this picture, however, and some research programs seem promising. For instance, French and his colleagues (French, Sherwood, and Bradford, 1966) have applied a self-identity and process-feedback model to training-group phenomena, and provide data relevant to the model (Sherwood, 1962, 1965). Clark and Culbert (1965; Culbert, 1966, 1968) have constructed a model centering around mutually therapeutic relationships and provide some data that suggest a basis for predicting training effectiveness. Hampden-Turner (1966) provides an existential learning model that has promise for integrating diverse empirical findings. Berlin (1964) has made a creative synthesis of phenomenological-therapeutic concepts and operant-conditioning concepts to provide a theory of training that is applied extensively to organizational settings. Gibb and Gibb (1968a; 1968b) have constructed a model of the training and group management processes around the constructs of fear and trust, and have applied the model to a wide variety of training environments. Miles (1960, 1965) integrates his data into a feedback model of training and suggests further hypotheses for research that emerge from his extensive studies.

Other barriers to training research have to do with design problems. Training is almost always done under field conditions in which the researcher is an unwelcome intruder. Training environments are determined, by and large, by training criteria rather than by research criteria. In most cases the researcher knowingly settles for the best of poor design alternatives or outcome measures that were permitted by such factors as expense, training conditions, participant resistance, and imprecise instruments. Researchers have been unable to resolve some thorny design issues. For instance, they have been unable to find or construct adequate "control" or "comparison" groups. One of the presumably key variables, degree of readiness or willingness to volunteer for depth training, is related to the amount of distrust and resistance in the training group. Matching groups that are equally "ready," and then delaying the training of one set of groups so that they will serve as controls for the training groups, brings into play some indeterminable effects of the delay.

One of the most effective practical solutions to the control-group problem was first used by Miles (1960), and later by others (Bunker, 1965; Valiquet, 1964). Each participant in the training group was asked to nominate a "control" person who was in a similar organizational role and who had not participated in training. It is difficult to determine what this constructed control group is like, particularly on such a critical variable as willingness to volunteer for training. A much more telling criticism of current training-research designs is their lack of "representativeness." That is, researchers often take great care in getting a random or representative sample of participants in the training group, but then reduce the generality of their results by studying one trainer, one organization, or one training environment.

Measurement is another persistent problem. The more reliable measures are often of trivial outcomes. Reliable measures are often not validated against acceptable indices of mental health, personal growth, or personal effectiveness in a natural setting. Measurement often affects the process itself in indeterminable ways. Researchers report an increasing resistance to multiple measurements in the training setting. Measurement is seen by the participant as irrelevant to his goals, tedious, manipulative, of doubtful value, and wasteful of "training time," as well as generally intrusive. The more promising of the methods of measurement that have been developed within the training-group settings are those developed by Bales (1950) for coding observer data on group member roles; by the Chicago group for determining group modalities and member predispositions for taking group roles (Ben-Zeev, Gradolph, Gradolph, Stock, and Thelen, 1954); by Hill (1965) for coding member interactions; by Horwitz and Cartwright (1953) for making projective tests of member behavior; by Stoller (1968b) for getting visual feedback upon member behavior; and by Miles, Cohen, and Whidman (1959) for measuring performance and sensitivity.

Sensitivity

Sensitivity training was the name originally given to human-relations training in groups (Bradford, Gibb, and Benne, 1964), because of the assumed centrality in behavior change of increased awareness of self and others. Trainers placed primary emphasis upon observation and feedback of data on group processes, and accuracy in perceiving "social reality." The

first doctoral dissertation on sensitivity-training groups (Kelley, 1948) investigated the stability and determinants of first impressions. Kelley found, for instance, that changes in perceptions of trainers were a function of the self-assertiveness of the trainer and of his ability to fulfill the needs of individual participants.

An early goal of group leaders was to help participants to understand and predict the feelings, characteristics, or reactions of others. Research has demonstrated that the accuracy of such predictions can be improved through developing more valid subcultural stereotypes, greater sensitivity to assumed similarities, or more consistent response sets (Smith, 1966). Analysis has indicated that the methodological traps in such research are deceptive and multiple, and that demonstrated gains are often a function of methodological artifacts and statistical errors.

The problem has attracted the attention of numerous investigators. Seventeen of the studies in the bibliography have reported data on the influence of training on sensitivity to people and processes. Although fourteen report significant increases, as against only three that report no change, methodological ambiguities in the studies suggest tentativeness in interpreting the data.

Wedel (1957), Gage and Exline (1953), and Bennis, Burke, Cutter, Harrington, and Hoffman (1957) all found no change in the ability of participants to predict responses of other participants. Lohman, Zenger, and Weschler (1959) found that participants were better able, after training, to predict the leader's answers on a Gordon Personal Profile. However, participants took the same test twice, and there was no control group. Sikes (1964) found that participants were more accurate in predicting the responses of other members of a test discussion group than were members of a control group that had no training. They predicted how members ranked others in the discussion group. The results, however, were not confirmed in a second study of a different training group.

Findings regarding increases in sensitivity to group processes are somewhat more positive. Bass (1962a) found that participants became more sensitive to interpersonal relationships seen in the film "Twelve Angry Men" when filling out incomplete-sentence questionnaires. Using a Problem Analysis Questionnaire, Oshry and Harrison (1966) found that after training, participants saw "clearer connections between how well interpersonal needs are met and how well the work gets done." Miles, Cohen, and Whidman (1959) found a consistent improvement in "sensitivity to feelings," but not in sensitivity to other aspects of the social situation. Studies report increases, after training, in sensitivity to rankings of problem-solving technologies (Dietterich, 1961), in seeing other members in more interpersonal terms (Harrison, 1962), in more frequent use of interpersonal concepts to describe associates (Harrison, 1966), in sensitivity toward social factors in the interpersonal situation (Kelley and Pepitone, 1952), in sensitivity toward affective states in comparison to thought processes (Ford, 1964), and in sensitivity toward social factors in the work situation (Blansfield, 1962).

Several studies report data relevant to the question of whether participants learn to be more sensitive to the self. Wedel (1957) and Dietterich (1961) each report no significant change in the ability of participants to predict how they are seen by others. Three studies (Gibb, 1953; Burke and Bennis, 1961; Carson and Lakin, 1963) report a statistically significant increase, after training, in the ability to predict how they are seen by other participants in a ranking or in a semantic-differential measure. In somewhat less precise measures, others report greater insight into one's own role (Valiquet, 1964), increase in awareness of reactions of others to self (Blansfield, 1962), awareness of one's own role in one's own interpersonal problems (Culbert, 1966), and increased self-awareness, using a Problem Expression Scale (Clark and Culbert, 1965).

In a significant study, which provides the most convincing evidence for training effects upon sensitivity, Bunker (1965) studied a sample of 341 participants in two-week sensitivity training groups. He used a method devised by Miles (1960), in which a matched-pair control group was obtained by participant nomination. From 5 to 7 raters were asked to give open-ended behavior-change descriptions of each of the 229 trained subjects and each of the 112 controls. Though the data are subject to an indetermin-

able amount of bias due to the fact that the raters knew whether the ratee had participated in training, they show impressive consistency with other studies using other methods. The greatest differences shown between experimental and control groups had to do with the sensitivity-input set of variables, increased openness, greater "tolerance for new information," and greater acceptance of difference. This study bears out other findings that when changes do occur as a result of human relations training, they are likely to occur first in the sensitivity-input aspects of behavior change.

The input side of sensitivity has also been measured by means of attitude scales. Haiman (1963) devised an "open-mindedness" attitude scale, and administered it to 425 students before and after a human-relations training-group experience. The subjects were found to be more open-minded than a comparable group of 231 control subjects. Participants who are less dogmatic, more open-minded, and more "open" to incoming stimuli presumably are more "sensitive" to the world of people. D. R. Bunker (1965) and Oshry and Harrison (1966), among others, have found that those who are most open to ideas and to expression of feelings learn most from sensitivity training.

In spite of the increasing interest in the output side of sensitivity in the psychological and religious literature, and the increasingly frequent mention of authenticity, spontaneity, and transparency in the training journals, there have been surprisingly few studies of this presumably critical aspect of personal effectiveness. The evidence is very sketchy. Massarik and Carlson (1960) administered a California Psychological Inventory to 70 college students before and after sensitivity training. They found no statistically significant differences. The small differences they did find are in the predicted direction of increased spontaneity and less use of control. In the following section it will be seen that there is some evidence that training leads to greater expression of feeling. Gold (1967) found no statistically significant changes, when comparing experimental with control groups, in reactions to the Jourard self-disclosure questionnaires given three months after training. In the Bunker (1965) studies mentioned above, it is notable that there was no statistically significant improvement in the "sending" part of communication, but that there were significant differences in the "receiving" component. The communication processes in sensitivity training clearly warrant further study.

Managing Feelings

Among participants and practitioners there is common agreement that training is an emotional experience, and that many intense and varied feelings are aroused. The significant question is whether there is productive integration of these feelings into performance or into richer living, both during the group training and in work and group situations following training. Practitioners rely on clinical observations in making judgments about such subtle processes as greater awareness of one's feelings and greater congruence between feelings and behavior.

The most thorough and inventive studies of feeling management have been performed by a group of researchers at the University of Chicago working with Thelen. Thus, Ben-Zeev (1958b) found that members of T-groups who participated with those they liked showed a tendency on a Bionic projective test to express warmth and friendliness and to inhibit expressions of hostility and anger. A second group of people, who did not participate with those they liked, were found to have a tendency to express hostility and anger and to inhibit the expression of warmth and friendliness. Ben-Zeev (1958a), using a predictive test devised for the experimental program, was able to predict conditions under which work will be least suppressed and emotionality most suppressed. Liberman (1958d) studied the emotional predispositions to fight, withdraw, pair, or be dependent, and composed groups on the basis of these predisposition patterns. He found that members whose emotional habits were closely attuned to the prevailing group atmosphere seemingly had little pressure or opportunity to change. When behavior changes did occur in participants, they tended to occur in areas where an individual's affect was aroused, and where a person's predispositions were counter to the prevailing group atmosphere.

Bass (1962b) attempted to assess mood changes during the course of a ten-day training period. At each of five different times during the training, he asked members to check 27 different adjectives designating nine different moods. He found statistically significant trends in the development of four of the nine moods. Thus, depression and concentration increased and activation and skepticism decreased. Due to the repeated finding that learning is associated with affective dissonance among group members, it would seem that more carefully controlled research on feeling management would be helpful. The lack of carefully designed controls in the studies of feeling management makes it difficult to determine the possible effects of test administration, passage of time, or training intensity. Studies, for instance, have shown that control groups "improve," presumably due to factors unrelated to training, such as taking the experimental tests twice (See, for example, Gassner, Gold, and Snadowsky, 1964).

Several studies reported above (See especially Bunker and Knowles, 1967; Harrison, 1966) clearly indicate that feelings are the most salient stimuli in the group situation, and that changes in sensitivity, if they occur, take place in reference to feelings. Gibb, Smith, and Roberts (1955) provide data that indicate that defensive feelings (feelings that are inadequately "managed") are associated with task efficiency in an interdependent situation. Gibb and Gibb (1952) report that trained subjects, when placed as unknowns in test work groups, were rated by experienced observers as having higher "general emotional adjustment." Foster (1958) was able to make predictions from observed data on how participants managed affect to specific reactions in role playing. Argyris (1965b) reports that participants, after training, received higher ratings on the tendency to "own" one's feelings. The spontaneity studies reported above are relevant here. It is probable that one necessary step in greater personal growth is to make feelings available to the self and to others in relevant social interaction.

Managing Motivations

Practitioners have been interested in the degree to which participants have increased the capacity and motivation to take responsibility for one's own life, to be more assertive and inner-directed in initiating action in organizational positions, and to become more committed to one's own inner forces and to one's own actions. Changes in motivations can, of course, be inferred from other changes, particularly in interdependent behavior. Direct measures have been few. Kassarjian (1965) was interested in testing Riesman's theories of inner-directedness and outer-directedness. He used a forced-choice questionnaire that had been validated in other situations, and found no significant differences following training. Boyd and Elliss (1962) used a scale assessing the degree to which a person assumes responsibility for his own work situation. They found that both an increase and a decrease in personal responsibility were positively associated with on-the-job changes. The authors interpreted this finding as indicating that the managers made a more realistic assessment of their roles in the work situation. Livingston's (1951) finding that motivation in training groups was influenced by perceived structure, and that one's perceived power and influence was dependent upon the emergent structure in the group, is relevant.

Business management is very much interested in motivational changes in work. Twenty-six of the 106 studies listed have been performed directly in management-development programs. High management acceptance of programmed training is perhaps partly due to the presumably large effect of programmed training upon participant responsibility for one's own learning. Greiner (1965) made measurements on the effects of a Management Grid laboratory upon organizational change. He reports a 24 percent increase in the number of supervisors who described their work groups as highly motivated toward greater effort. He found that 80 new task groups were set up as a direct result of the training program. A greater number of supervisors rated their meetings as "lively" and interesting than before training. Supervisors initiated more activities and took greater risks. He also found a shift in top-management values toward greater acceptance of the initiation of new ideas by subordinates.

In an effort to encourage participants to take greater initiative and to "take charge of their own lives" to a greater degree, Byrd (1967) and his associates have invented a promising new training design. Byrd places people in a "nongroup," where each individual is maximally on his own, creates his own training designs, is responsible for his own learning, and "does his own thing" with a minimum of community and group coercion. He reports clinical and informal test evidence in the direction of much greater risk taking, greater variability in actions, and emergent feelings of responsibility.

There is evidence that participants learn from human relations training to be somewhat more self-determining. In view of the centrality of this self-generating process as a concept in many theories of personal growth, it is clear that more evidence is needed for an understanding of the training processes that are associated with such change.

Functional Attitudes Toward Self

Some investigators have attempted to determine changes in perceptions of the actual self and of the ideal self, as well as changes in degree of congruence between the two measures. Inasmuch as the investigators show that increase of congruence is a function of increase in positive view of the self rather than of a change in view of the ideal self, change in degree of congruence can be interpreted as a change in self-esteem or self-acceptance. Several studies have found that, following training, such congruence is increased, due to changes in the perceived actual self (G. L. Bunker, 1961; Burke and Bennis, 1961; Gassner, Gold, and Snadowsky, 1964; Grater, 1959; Peters, 1966). Gassner, Gold, and Snadowsky (1964) found statistically significant differences in congruence and self-acceptance following training, but found similar differences in the control groups. Burke and Bennis (1961) found significant differences, but did not use a control group. An earlier study by Bennis, Burke, Cutter, Harrington, and Hoffman (1957) showed no change following training. Lohman, Zenger, and Weschler (1959) predicted that students would see themselves as "more adequate" after training, and found no significant differences in the experimental group.

The most adequate studies are those performed by G. L. Bunker (1961) and by Peters (1966). Bunker (1961) used a Hilden Q sort to measure changes in self- and ideal concepts. He found a significant change in self-concept following group training in two-hour sessions twice a week over a period of sixteen weeks. Peters (1966) used a semantic differential test to measure self-concept and ideal concept before and after a two-week group training experience. A significant convergence of the self-concept and the ideal concept occurred during the training period. No such change occurred in the control group.

Several other studies are relevant. Zimet and Fine (1955) found an increase in positive attitudes toward the self. Clark and Miles (1954) report that administrators, after training, reported self-concept changes in the positive direction. In the Bunker and Knowles (1967) study, observer ratings of self-confidence showed significant changes after a two-week experience, and larger magnitude and even greater significance after a three-week experience. This last result is particularly critical, in the opinion of this reviewer, because of the careful design of the study and the fact that the trend with increased group-training experience is in line with predictions and with considerable clinical evidence reported by other investigators.

Some studies throw light on the dynamics of self-percept changes. Sherwood (1962, 1965), for instance, reports some evidence that self-concept (self-identity) is dependent upon a participant's subjectively held version of the peer group's actual ratings of him ("subjective public identity"), which is in turn a function of objective public identity. These data became more important as peers became seen as more important, as the data became communicated to the participant in feedback, and as the participants became involved in the group. Such perceptions play an important part in the potential that the group provides for learning. G. L. Bunker (1961), for instance, found that individuals ranked in the upper third of the group in perceived esteem will receive significantly more net positive feedback than will individuals ranked in the lower third in group perceived esteem.

Changes in perception of self may be a powerful mediator of other potential changes during group training. Stock (1952) made a detailed analysis of individuals undergoing group experience. She found that the persons who made few changes in perceptions of the self tended to make few changes in observable behavior. Those who did show more unstable perceptions of the self tended to make greater changes in behavior in the groups and following the group experience.

Many theorists have come back to Lewin's hypotheses about the important leverage effects of "unfreezing." It may be that one's feelings about oneself must undergo some disruption in order for major growth to take place. This unfreezing is apparently accompanied by a high degree of feeling about the group and about oneself, as is indicated in the research reported under the section on "management of feelings."

As the above evidence suggests, the training group can serve as a powerful reference group. Lieberman (1958b) found good evidence that stereotyped impressions of a "good group member" were developed during group interaction, and that these stereotypes influenced the ways that members saw themselves, and presumably influenced their attitudes toward items in the tests and their ratings of actual selves. Johnson (1966) found no significant changes from training in any of his measures except in changes in self-percept. It is possible that such change must preceed other changes. Again, the importance of phenomenal data and perceptual change is indicated in the research.

Functional Attitudes Toward Others

At least ten studies report significant trends, following training, toward less authoritarian, more democratic and participative attitudes (Argyris, 1962; Blake and Mouton, 1966; Bowers and Soar, 1961; Dietterich, 1961; Gassner, Gold, and Snadowsky, 1964; Seashore, 1955; Spector, 1958; Taylor, 1967; Wedel, 1957; Zimet and Fine, 1955). It is not surprising that participants would move in the direction of the values of the group leaders. Many pressures work in the same direction: group forces toward conformity, identification with important and relevant authority figures, desires to please the staff, knowledge of the "correct" test answer, and basic shifts in underlying values. By themselves, the data on attitude test scores are insignificant. Of more importance would be data on whether these changes in expressed attitude were embedded in deeper attitudes of trust toward others or whether they were accompanied by behaviors consistent with the attitudes.

Rubin (1967a, 1967b) found some evidence that high acceptance of self was related to high acceptance of others in the laboratory setting, and he proposes such training as a means of reducing prejudice. Some tests of attitude were more indirect and may have tapped deeper-lying attitudes. Thus, Carron (1964) found that group participants came to place a lower value on "structure" and a higher value on "considera-tion." Haiman (1963) found a significant increase in more positive attitudes toward open-mindedness. In the Ford (1964) study, partici-pants were found to value feelings more than thoughts, after training that presumably stressed the feeling component in interaction. Most training groups provide a climate where data on feelings are given high visibility. Baumgartel and Goldstein (1967) administered FIRO-B tests and found that training lowered religious values, increased wanted control, and decreased wanted affection. Smith (1964) showed that the dis-parity between own behavioral tendencies and those desired in others decreased after training, and that the largest changes occurred for those who initially showed strong control and weak affection tendencies and desired low control and high affection. Schutz and Allen (1966) used FIRO-B to measure possible attitude changes in 71 members of a training-laboratory set of groups and a control group of 30 students at the University of California at Berkeley. There were significantly greater changes in the experimental subjects than in the control subjects.

Several studies show no significant changes in attitude following training. Kernon (1963) found no significant changes in scores on the Ohio State Leadership Opinion Questionnaire on attitudes toward getting the work done (task orientation) and concern for human relations. Also using the Leadership Opinion Question-naire, Beer and Kleisath (1967) found significant changes when comparing scores on the test before and after training. The fact that no control group was used makes the results equivocal. Kassarjian (1965) measured inner-directedness and outer-directedness with an attitude test and found no significant differences. Zand, Steele,

and Zalkind (1967) measured attitudes toward McGregor's (1960) Theory Y and found no change after training.

Interdependent Behavior

Good evidence that participants learned to act more interdependently in various life and work situations would be critical to the assess-ment of training as a growth or therapeutic milieu.

Several studies have reported that participants after training have been rated by observers as performing more effectively. Bunker and Knowles (1967) report observer ratings of participants as having "increased interdepen-dence" and greater "functional flexibility." Gibb (1953) found that training produced significant differences on a "role flexibility" test, during which participants were required to take arbitrary roles and were rated on their performance. Members of a control group also showed significant differences, presumably from having taken the test twice. However, the experimental groups were given significantly higher scores on perceived "sincerity" measures, while members of the control groups were clearly seen as taking roles. Friedlander (1967) gave questionnaires to work groups six months after a program of human-relations team train-ing of the groups. Participants reported them-selves as having changed in the direction of greater participation, effectiveness in problem solving, and mutual influence. Bass (1962a), incidentally, had shown that his sensitivity scores, which increased with training, were significantly correlated with perceived influence in the small-group discussions.

Geitgey (1966) reported data on a study of the effects of training on the behavior of nurses. She found that the experimental group was significantly superior to the control groups on four measures: patient evaluation of nursing care, instructor evaluation of nursing care, interpersonal relations with peers (peer ratings), and interpersonal relations with instructors (ratings by instructors). Peer ratings and instructor ratings are presumably influenced to some degree by knowledge that the nurses had been given training. The patient evaluation of nursing care is presumably not influenced by such factors and seems to be especially good evidence that the behavior of the nurses changed in significant ways. In two other studies (Gibb and Gibb, 1952; Sikes, 1964), participants, after training, were placed with control subjects in test discussion groups several months after training. Observers rated effectiveness of participation, and the trained subjects were rated significantly higher than the controls. One limitation of the rating studies is that raters use all kinds of relatively superficial cues (such as higher participation rates and "sophisticated" words) in judging effectiveness of performance.

Argyris (1962) reported greater interpersonal competence of members of a trained management team, but noted that the new values and attitudes tended to wear off after six to nine months. Many experimenters have noted this phenomenon. The wearing-off seems to occur less when training is embedded in the organization (Argyris, 1962, 1965a; Gibb and Gibb, 1952) and when follow-up training is given at periodic intervals, the optimal length of which has not as yet been determined. Argyris (1965b) devised a complicated composite rating measure of "interpersonal competence" (including helping, experimenting, opening up, owning feelings, and the like). He found trained subjects to be significantly superior to members of matched control groups that had no training. Boyd and Elliss (1962) report that their experimental groups, when compared with two control groups, showed a significantly greater number of positive changes on the job (ratings by job associates), but also showed a significantly greater number of negative changes. Many of the "negative" changes might be coded as increased spontaneity (for example, an increase in irritability) and emotional expressiveness, and are part of the unfreezing process noted by other experimenters. Underwood (1965) also found that the trained managers made a significantly higher percentage of observed positive changes on the job, and a significantly higher number of observed unfavorable changes, than did a matched control group of supervisors. Although the possibilities of observer bias make this Underwood study inconclusive, the data are highly suggestive, and they highlight a chronic problem of doing depth training of normal adults in an organizational setting. The training, when effective, does apparently produce un-freezing, experimentation with new behavior, and many behavioral changes that may be seen as disruptive. Behavior that is counternorm or counterauthority may be functional for a period in the growth of the person, but may be seen as dysfunctional by work associates.

Greater job effectiveness is reported by a number of investigators. Clark and Miles (1954) report a detailed study of a sensitivity-training program for school administrators. Though no control group is provided and the data are subject to observer bias, they note improvement in long-range planning skills, skills in seeking and obtaining help, and ability in relating agenda formation to group work. Such changes have been consistently reported in later studies. Eight months following a training program for elementary-school principals, Miles (1965) obtained data on 34 participants in the training groups and 29 members of matched control groups. He asked subjects to report any changes that had occurred in the eight months, and also asked observers to report on noted changes. Reported and observed changes occurred in interdependent behavior, communication and leadership skills, and group problem-solving skills. Though changes were also reported for the control group, a significantly greater number of changes were both reported and observed for the trained group. As is usually found to be the case, observers saw less change than the participants reported. Sixteen members of five groups of managers were given team training in a management-development program studied by Nath (1964). Interviews and behavior observations indicate changes in a predicted direction, toward goal clarity, interpersonal skills, and greater two-way communication. No control groups were used.

Longitudinal Changes During Training

Research attempting to determine significant and predictable changes during the temporal course of the training group has been inconclusive. Practitioners and theorists have postulated "stages" of growth, for instance, based on clinical observations, but observed changes have been elusive, unpredictable, and dependent upon observer bias.

Several theories of training relate the change-inductive potential of the group experience to the relationship between personal growth and group growth along some critical dimensions (Bradford, Gibb, and Benne, 1964). One empirical issue is whether there are discernible and predictable trends in the temporal course of group development. Bennis and Shepard (1956) provide clinical data and a detailed theory that specifies the orderly development of the maturing group through the following stages: dependence-flight, counterdependence-flight, resolution-catharsis, enchantment-flight, disenchantment-flight, and a final consensual validation. Schutz (1958), with equal precision, postulates a two-cycle sequence in which the group goes through an "integrative" process of working out the inclusion, control, and affection concerns in order, and then a following "resolution" cycle, in which the group reworks the concerns in the opposite sequence, first affection, then control, and finally inclusion. Gibb (1964) reports clinical data showing that depth groups tend to work through a "contingency hierarchy" of four concerns in order—first acceptance, then data flow, then goal formation, and finally control. Tests of these theories have been elusive. Each of the above theorists assume that the dynamics that are most relevant to the growth-inductive properties of the training group occur at a latent level that is relatively unavailable to such techniques as behavior ratings, self-descriptions, role analysis, and the like.

Lakin and Carson (1964), for instance, obtained data from 29 persons in four T-groups over a 16-meeting sequence. Members of the groups provided ratings of intensity of group concern for each of eleven variables. What impressed the experimenters most was the variability in the data. The only two variables to show discernible trends were "competitiveness," which showed a linear decrease, and "cooperation," which showed a linear increase with time. Bass (1962b), in a study described above in the discussion of management of feelings, found that depression and concentration increased, and activation and skepticism decreased. Each of these studies, however, taps relatively superficial aspects of the processes postulated by the available theories. More promising are the methods used by Stock and Ben-Zeev (1958), who use Bionic categories of dependency, pairing, fight, and flight to analyze

in depth the sequential processes of a T-group. What they provide is a useful methodology for tapping the depth necessary for testing the available theories. Weschler and Reisel (1958) and Reisel (1959) demonstrate what can be done with a detailed clinical-diagnostic analysis of events and dynamics of a training group.

What we seem to have are some promising theories, some meager data, and some methodological innovations. We do not as yet have adequate tests of the theories of group growth.

RESEARCH ON TRAINING TECHNOLOGIES

Until we have more adequate measures and more rigorous studies of the general outcomes of training, it will be difficult to determine the relative power of training designs and leader interventions in producing behavior change. There is, however, some evidence as to differential effects of methods. This section will first examine each of the nine methods listed in Table 22.1 and then some selective aspects of methodology about which there is some empirical evidence.

Creativity-Growth Groups

Particularly in the last decade there has been a dramatic acceleration in training activities designed to "increase human potential" and to release creativity. This "growth potential movement" has been sparked by the phenomenal rise of "growth centers" around the country such as Esalen Institute at Big Sur, California; Shalal at Vancouver, B.C.; Kopavi at Minneapolis; Aureon in New York; and 108 others at current count. The quality of professional leadership is greatly varied, ranging from highly respected psychiatrists to laymen with no professional training. The methodology is an innovative and often undigested blending from various sources such as somatopsychic medicine, yoga, psychodrama, clinical psychology, and interpretive dance. The activities include kinetic theater, calligraphy, nude marathons, finger painting, psychedelic experiences, hypnotism, sensory awakening, breathing therapy, bioenergetic analysis, meditation, and transcendent experiences.

Unfortunately, there is as yet little published research available on the effects of such activities. The excitement generated among many competent professionals in clinical psychology and psychiatry suggests that new frontiers are being explored in a microenvironment that permits experimentation, innovation, and freedom from the usual restraints in the university, the clinic, or the private office. The activities are more controversial than the more respectable methods used in sensitivity training, and have created some concern among professional societies responsible for maintaining the standards of therapeutic and quasi-therapeutic practice.

Marathon Groups

The marathon format was devised partly to intensify the group experience. The original method (Stoller, 1968a) uses uninterrupted and deeply personal contact for periods of from 24 to 36 hours. A frequent professional impression is that sustained marathon experience is far more powerful as a change-inductive agent than is a comparable period of time in periodic training sessions.

Although the method has generated modifications in many human-relations training programs and some research that is now in progress, there is as yet little evaluation research available in the published literature. Several theories have been advanced to account for the apparent power of the method. It has been hypothesized that fatigue generates intensity of interaction and reduction of inhibition to disclosure; that persons who spend continuing energy in façade maintenance are physiologically incapable of maintaining the energy over marathon distance; and that sustained interpersonal depth contact creates intrinsic pressures toward self-disclosure.

Emergent Groups

As Mowrer (1964) and others have pointed out, there is a current rapid rise in the number of quasi-therapeutic and training groups that meet without appointed leaders or that meet with lay volunteers who have no special professional training as therapists or as trainers. As Gibb (1964; Gibb and Gibb, 1968a; 1968b) and others have demonstrated, essentially the same phenomena occur in these "emergent" groups

as occur in groups with skilled professional leaders (Berzon and Solomon, 1966; Hanson, Rothaus, Johnson, and Lyle, 1966). Groups sponsored by Alcoholics Anonymous, the Laymen's Movement, and Synanon, for example, are thought by some professionals who consult with the programs to have similar effects to those that accrue from human-relations training groups led by professionals. Unfortunately, the evidence is clinical and impressionistic, and there have been no studies of the effectiveness of these programs. There is, however, good evidence that training in groups without leaders produces changes in the behavior of group members (Gibb and Gibb, 1952; Johnson, Hanson, Rothaus, Morton, Lyle, and Moyer, 1965). Leaderless groups have become part of the standard methodology of team training in industry, religious organizations, and youth organizations (Gibb and Gibb, 1968a; Davis, 1967).

Authenticity Groups

Stemming from a growing accent in religion, therapy, management, and philosophy, upon authenticity, openness, transparency, encounter, and confrontation, the last decade has seen a rapid growth, particularly in California and other parts of the west, of quasi-therapeutic training groups that focus primarily on openness of communication of the person with himself and with others. Sometimes called "growth groups" or "encounter groups," these experiences are an extension of methods found to be effective in dyadic therapy and are, in a sense, "therapy for normals." Leaders, often coming to training groups from experience or training in individual or group therapy, rely upon time-tested methods of feeling-expression, personal feedback, mirroring, role playing, confrontation, and fantasy analysis. There is little available published research on training in these groups.

Sensitivity-Training Groups

The classic method of human relations training in depth in the small group is the "T-group" or "sensitivity-training group" (Bradford, Gibb, and Benne, 1964). In the first decade after their invention by the National Training Laboratories in 1947, these groups followed a fairly clear and consistent model. The group leader was a process observer and reporter, a relatively inactive trainer who attempted to keep attention on process rather than content and to keep interaction in the "here and now," continually dealing with perceptions and feelings that members generated about each other within the group setting. Since then the model has become considerably broadened to encompass a wide variety of "intervention styles," theories of leadership and behavior change, and most of the methods discussed in this chapter.

From the beginning, the practitioners of sensitivity training have been strongly research-oriented. Eighty-nine of the 106 studies reviewed here have been performed on sensitivity-training groups, 43 of which have gathered data on the standard heterogeneous groups in the relatively isolated "cultural islands" sponsored by the National Training Laboratories at Bethel, Maine, or at one of the regional centers.

Programmed Groups

Using programmed-learning and machine-teaching concepts as models, several experimenters have shown that tapes, training booklets, phonograph records, and data-gathering instruments can serve as functional leader surrogates. Professionals, through the use of such tools, can guide the goal formation, discussion content, and directional focus of the groups along lines suggested by their training theories.

The effects of programmed human relations training have been well demonstrated. Research at the Human Development Institute (Berlin, 1964), at the Western Behavioral Sciences Institute (Berzon and Solomon, 1966; Berzon, Pious, and Farson, 1963), with the Management Grid model (Blake, Mouton, Barnes, and Greiner, 1964; Greiner, 1965), and with hospitalized patients (Johnson, Hanson, Rothaus, Morton, Lyle, and Moyer, 1965; Rothaus, Johnson, Hanson, and Lyle, 1966) has clearly indicated the feasibility of doing programmed group training and has contributed to the research literature as indicated in various places in this review. There is no clear evidence as yet to indicate differential effects of programmed and nonprogrammed groups. The indication is very strong that they are as effective as groups led by professionals. Criticisms of these methods center around the potential

dangers and effects of manipulation of the group by trainers. In favor of the use of such methods are considerations such as the following: the potential economy of the designs if they prove to be as effective as groups with professionals; the inventiveness and adequacy of the theories underlying the designs; and the relative ease with which evaluative research can be related to training objectives.

Microexperience Groups

The classic weekend T-group (Bradford, Gibb and Lippitt, 1956) is a shortened version of the familiar Bethel laboratory. A variety of abbreviated experiences is provided by group professionals within the limits of 20 to 30 hours of training time over a weekend or a two-day period. Demands by organizations and by individual participants have caused practitioners to attempt to give training experiences in even less time than this. In what has sometimes been called a "micro-lab," the standard elements of the training "laboratory" have been encompassed into a variety of segments, each of which may last for from three to twelve minutes. Practitioners report favorable reactions of participants to a total experience that may last from two to five hours. While some clinical impressions of the effectiveness of such designs are very positive, we have as yet no research evaluating outcomes.

Inquiry Groups

What we have chosen to call "inquiry groups" in this review are relatively structured, focus upon the opportunity to practice interpersonal skills, integrate presentations of personality theory into the total experience, and make use of a number of training designs such as simulation, role playing, data collection, structured practice sessions, and demonstrations. The distinction made here between inquiry groups and sensitivity training groups is an arbitrary one, but one that may lead to clarification in the inconsistencies in the empirical literature. Unfortunately, it is often difficult to determine from the brief reports in the research literature what was actually done in the training sessions. The emphasis in the inquiry group is upon attaining skills of inquiry in group and team situations: gathering data, receiving help, communicating well, diagnosing group forces, and giving and receiving influence. Recent developments in the integration of research instruments into the training design, the use of videotapes as data-gathering tools (Stoller, 1968b), and the use of expressive behavior and nonverbal communication as tools of inquiry make possible the great enrichment of inquiry designs. Nonverbal methods have proved to be very productive. Recent evidence from a non-training setting (see, for instance, Delaney, 1966; Delaney and Heimann, 1966) that special training can sensitize people rather quickly to nonverbal communications bears out the clinical impressions from training groups.

Embedded Groups

Experiences in the past decade, particularly, have led practitioners to embed training into ongoing programs of organizational change, so that the training group is one of several events meshed into an integrated program designed for total impact. These programs often include testing, consulting, personal therapy, changed personnel practices, architectural design, re-organization of the sociotechnical system, and changed production technology. The program is usually system-oriented and clearly focused upon organizational change rather than directly upon personal growth or therapeutic change. Friedlander (1967), for instance, gives a clarifying statement of one embedded design that integrates training into an overall model. The bibliography at the end of the chapter includes several examples of embedded training.

Several studies (Bowers and Soar, 1961; Clark and Miles, 1954; Khanna, 1968; Schmuck, 1968) have reported on work directed toward modification of an educational system. Some studies have evaluated efforts to change personnel practices and increase production in an industrial system (for example, Argyris, 1962; Greiner, 1965; Nath, 1964).

Early research clearly indicated (Bradford, Gibb, and Benne, 1964) that induced change was more permanent when participants could relate to each other and "support" each other in the organizational environment. For this reason, attempts were made to train homo-geneous occupational groups. Thus, Dietterich (1961), Foster (1958), and Wedel (1957) report on training given to professional church leaders, with some success. Miles (1965) reports signi-ficant changes in members of a homogeneous population of elementary school principals. Batchelder and Hardy (1968) report studies on training within a large, loosely structured, national organization. Sensitivity training was administered to over half the professionals in the national YMCA as part of a program of executive development. Unfortunately, hard evidence on the effectiveness of these programs in changing organizational practices is lacking. The direct and indirect evidence from social psychological studies suggests strongly that when the group training is part of an integrated attempt to provide a supportive and congruent work environment, the effects are more enduring.

Composition

There is evidence that composition of the group makes a difference in its change-inductive properties. Watson (1953) used derivations from psychoanalytic theory to predict social behavior in the group. She found, for instance, that members with oral sadistic hostility were rated as aggressive in verbal behavior in the group, and that people with high anxiety scores were uncomfortable with minimal structure. She found that those showing greatest initial resis-tance to training showed more behavior change than those who showed little or no initial resistance. Lieberman (1958c) showed that Bionic modality predispositions would influence choice in a predictable way. He (1958d) used modality predispositions to compose differential groups, and found that composition influenced change in the affective area in which the change occurs. Mathis (1955) discovered that flight, dependency, and immobilization were negative indicators for trainability, and developed a trainability index using such measurements. Lieberman (1958c) determined that the kinds of behavior that group members could explore differed with the emotional subculture of the groups. Changes accompanying the training differed with the culture and with the "fit" of the group culture with the predispositions of the participant. It is possible to distinguish sub-groups in the group culture and to use these to predict behavioral reactions (Hill, 1955; Rosen-thal, 1952).

Harrison (1965) confirmed a hypothesis at satisfactory levels of significance that person-oriented members would be seen as behaving more expressively and warmly and that they would be more comfortable and feel stronger interpersonal ties within their homogeneous group than would the work-oriented members. He discusses some relevant hypotheses about group composition (Harrison, 1965).

Composing the training group of members of the same administrative or work team (Argyris, 1962; Kuriloff and Atkins, 1966) was thought in the early days of sensitivity training to violate the widely-held principles of heterogeneity and "culture island," and perhaps to be dangerous. Recent experience has caused practitioners to prefer team and unit training to work with heterogeneous groups. Research results are not conclusive, but certainly suggest strongly that such "team training" is effective. It is widely believed by professionals to be more effective than heterogeneous training.

Feedback

Trainers have usually seen as central to the effects of training the feedback of data on perceptions and feelings to participants. Lippitt (1959) demonstrated that counseling interviews focused upon what group members thought of the member and how they wanted him to change caused significant changes in the members getting feedback. This corroborates well-documented early evidence of the centrality of feedback in the learning process. There is some evidence concerning the conditions under which the effects of feedback can be optimized. Gibb, Smith, and Roberts (1955), for instance, found that persons given positive feedback outperformed persons given negative feedback on a situation task devised to measure task efficiency. They also found that feedback that emphasized feelings was more effective than feedback that focused on task. French, Sherwood, and Bradford (1966) report results from several tests of a formal theory specifying the conditions under which feedback is optimal. They demonstrated that a person's self-identity is influenced by the opinions that group members share with him; that the more that is communicated to the person, the more the change in his self-identity; and that the more that the person is dissatisfied

with his present self-perception (which is partly determined by the nature and amount of feedback), the more likely he is to change this self-perception.

Leader Behavior

The behavior of the leader is presumably a critical factor in determining the effect of the training group upon the behavior of its members and upon the permanence of their learnings. There is good evidence that the leader is a significant figure in the group. Peters (1966), for instance, found that members' self concepts, measured on semantic-differential scales, increasingly converged during training with their concepts of the trainer and also with the trainer's self-concept. Powers (1965) found that trainer style influenced effectiveness of the training. Homogeneous matchings of trainer orientations and behavior style of trainees produced higher learnings. Trainers perceived as having a "resource orientation" (high desire to give) were perceived more positively by participants than were trainers with high need orientation (high desire to receive).

Psathas and Hardert (1966) clearly show, from analysis of seven training groups, that trainer interventions contain implicit norm messages indicating to members what norms should be established in the group. Their norm-category systems provide a methodology for assessing trainer interventions on this dimension of norm communication. When considered in light of the work mentioned above on attitude change, this study provides a method for testing differential effects of trainer style.

Probably the most significant and suggestive study of trainer intervention is one by Culbert (1968). He gives data on the effects of early and late self-disclosure behavior on the part of group leaders, and suggests that the leader might well begin his participation in the group with a high rate of self-disclosure, and become more selective with time. Participants with more self-disclosing trainers more often entered into relationships with other group members. Members of groups that had trainers who were less self-disclosing tended to enter into relationships with the trainer. The study is limited in generalizability because of lack of representativeness of design, but the data are certainly suggestive of a hypothesis and a line of attack on the problem.

Duration of Training

Examination of the studies reported here indicates that there is a wide variation in the total amount of time spent in the basic group experience. Total time in group ranges from a minimum of 12 hours to a maximum of 150 hours. This difference is even greater when the total amount of continuous time is considered. There is a clear consensus among experienced trainers that continuous time, within indeterminable limits, is more powerful than time spent in short sessions spread out over long periods of time. The short groups are often made even less effective by spreading out a series of two-hour sessions, say, over a series of weekly meetings. Compared with the intensity of a three-week experience in groups meeting continuously for ten or twelve hours a day, the differential power of the groups is great. Though it is difficult to tell from some of the research reports exactly how much time was spent by participants in actual intensive participation in small groups, and therefore difficult to make a precise array of the data, it is clear that when the studies are arrayed simply in terms of amount of time in group, that greater differences are obtained from groups of longer duration than from short-term groups. The data most relevant on the question of the relative effectiveness of long-term groups is provided by the Bunker and Knowles (1967) study. They show that three weeks of laboratory training is clearly superior to two weeks of laboratory training in producing postlaboratory changes in behavior as seen both by participants and by panels of seven co-workers for each participant in the experimental groups. The improvement in the three-week training groups was especially noticed in overt behavioral changes.

Four other studies strongly suggest that time in group may produce some kind of accelerating effect within the learner such that learning actually increases over time rather than showing the usual decay or fallout effect after the termination of the training session. The studies suggest that short-term experiences may not bring changes to a critical point. It is likely that when changes are unstable and inadequately integrated into the behavioral systems of the learner, they show rapid loss over time. When changes become integrated into behavioral systems that are congruent with new attitudinal substrata in the person, the changes may actually increase over time. Thus, Harrison (1966) found that his significant effect on feeling-orientation appeared after three months but not after three weeks. Khanna (1968) found that the significant changes produced in scores on the Personal Orientation Inventory increased after a three-month interval. Gibb and Gibb (1968b) report that many of the changes induced in the training groups increase over time, especially when the initial training has been of long duration. Schutz and Allen (1966) show that changes that occurred on attitudes measured by FIRO-B administered immediately following a two-week session were increased when scales were administrated six months following the training.

IMPLICATIONS FOR PRACTICE

While the evidence for the therapeutic and behavior-change effects of human-relations training is certainly controversial and open to legitimate multiple interpretations, it seems clear to the reviewer that changes do occur in sensitivity, feeling management, directionality of motivation, attitudes toward self, attitudes toward others, and interdependence. Because these effects are closely related to hoped-for therapeutic outcomes, the evidence is strong that intensive group-training experiences have therapeutic effects. It is yet to be demonstrated whether the magnitude of the effects is sufficient to justify an increased use of extensive group training, or whether the effects are therapeutically significant in comparison with the effects of more conventional methods of therapy. The reviewer will attempt to state what seems to him to be a set of conservative implications from his review of the above evaluative research.

1. Educators, clinicians, and trainers can benefit from cross fertilization among the various disciplines that have implications for behavior change. For instance, it is surprising, in light of the wealth of evidence in the above

literature, to see less than two pages of a 1596-page handbook of clinical psychology (Wolman, 1965) devoted to a consideration of the array of methods and theories of group training. Helpful attempts to integrate theory and practice have been made by Bach (1954) in relating group dynamics and group therapy; by Whitaker and Lieberman (1964) in showing the implications for group therapy of the group training studies; by Durkin (1964) in relating the work on group growth to analytic therapy; by Bugental and Tannenbaum (1963), Lakin and Carson (1966), and Morton (1965) in relating personality theory to group process training; and by Fry (1961) in comparing adult education with human-relations training. The methods used in group training are currently enriching the practice of therapy, education, and executive development (Maier, Solem, and Maier, 1957; Hacon, 1961; Otto, 1968; Rothaus, Morton, Johnson, Cleveland, and Lyle, 1963).

2. Therapists and trainers are well advised to experiment with new theory and new methodology. One of the barriers to innovation in practice has been the widespread concern among lay and professional groups (for example, Dubin, 1961; Fry, 1961) about the reputed traumatic effects of group training. The evidence is clear that the reputed dangers of sensitivity training are greatly exaggerated. Typical of the evidence is a study reported by Batchelder and Hardy (1968), in which an effort was made to uncover harmful effects of group training upon approximately 1200 YMCA directors who had intensive experiences in sensitivity training. First, they found that executives who had not had such training reported widespread rumors of traumatic effects of such training upon YMCA directors they had heard about. The investigators were able to find only four out of 1200 cases that were supposed to be negative. Intensive interviewing revealed that three of these four cases turned out to be positive. Only one case still evaluated his experience as a "negative" one, and he continues to do an effective job in his position as a YMCA director.

3. When the trainer acts in such a way as to optimize group growth, the change-inductive properties of the training or therapy group are optimized. The evidence indicates that the group *qua* group can be a change-inductive milieu, and

that group training is something more than training individuals in a group setting. Groups grow under a variety of conditions, with or without leaders, and when this growth occurs, behavior change can happen. The above evidence indicates that the following optimal conditions for learning occur with group growth: feedback, behavior visibility, member-member interaction, feeling expression, and perceptual diversity.

4. The evidence indicates that the behavior of the trainer can make a difference. His influence is determined, in part, by the amount of self-disclosure, help-orientation, participation in person-oriented feedback, and process interventions. Measurements of the effects of training are as yet not sufficiently precise to permit differential measurement of the effects of trainer styles.

5. Practitioners might well focus their efforts upon training that is embedded in long-range programs aimed at changing organizations and institutions. This implies concentrating efforts upon the training of management teams, family-life training, organizational-change programs, continuing consultation, and follow-up training. It also means that training must integrate with, support, or change the management practices (Bass, 1967; Gibb, 1965; Steele, 1965, 1968), parental habits, or organizational procedures (Clark and Miles, 1954) of the subcultures in which training takes place.

6. Most human-relations training, as now practiced, is too short in duration to be of optimal enduring effect. The very significant findings that human-relations training, under some conditions, produces changes that seem to increase with time, seems to mean that initial periods of training must be long enough for persons to "learn to learn" from feedback or to reach a critical point at which internal organismic processes occur in the individual, which sustain change. How long training should be, and what temporal patterns of "booster shots" are optimal for long-range effects, are critical questions for investigators.

7. No clear guidelines for the leader in making decisions about composing groups can be derived from the available evidence. Studies do show that composition makes a difference with certain individuals and that we can make some

predictions about these effects (Harrison, 1965; Harrison and Lubin, 1965). No data exist that make it possible to make a judgment in favor of particular models of composition. Almost all of the studies cited here have been made on groups with maximum heterogeneity on several relevant variables. With the exception that it appears advantageous to form groups on the basis of team membership, the best guideline to follow is to compose on the basis of whatever heterogeneity is available. The question frequently arises as to whether some individuals should be restricted from participation in group training. Clinical judgment may guide a specific leader in a specific selection, but research evidence indicates no basis for making any restrictions as to group membership. Current methods have been used with the widest range of participants, including a wide range of different kinds of patients in mental hospitals, with no evidence of harm and no indication of

what kinds of persons profit most, or least, from group training.

8. Research efforts can be so planned as to be integrated into training aims and to aid the group members in their learning as training goes on. Morton and Bass (1964), for instance, show how data can be gathered on the participants in such a way as to be profitably fed back to them immediately. Some coding categories (Glad, 1959; Simon and Agazarian, 1967) emerge directly from group experiences in such a way as to be training-relevant to members as they learn to learn. Modern methods of data processing (Wagner, 1965) make possible computer analysis of data as the group engages in feedback sessions. Categories may be derived from depth psychology (for example, Lieberman, 1958a) to analyze "here-and-now" data. Ongoing research on management styles can be integrated directly into ongoing training. (Gibb and Gibb, 1968b; Greiner, 1965; Schutz, 1958).

REFERENCES

Argyris, C. *Interpersonal competence and organizational effectiveness.* Chicago: Irwin-Dorsey, 1962.

Argyris, C. Explorations in interpersonal competence—I. *Journal of Applied Behavioral Science*, 1965, **1**, 58–83. (a)

Argyris, C. Explorations in interpersonal competence—II. *Journal of Applied Behavioral Science*, 1965, **1**, 255–269. (b)

Bach, G. R. *Intensive group psychotherapy.* New York: Ronald Press, 1954.

Bales, R. F. *Interaction process analysis: A method for the study of small groups.* Cambridge, Mass.: Addison-Wesley, 1950.

Bass, B. M. Reactions to "12 Angry Men" as a measure of sensitivity training. *Journal of Applied Psychology*, 1962, **46**, 120–124. (a)

Bass, B. M. Mood changes during a management training laboratory. *Journal of Applied Psychology*, 1962, **46**, 361–364. (b)

Bass, B. M. The anarchist movement and the T group. *Journal of Applied Behavioral Science*, 1967, **3**, 211–226.

Batchelder, R. L., and Hardy, J. M. *Using sensitivity training and the laboratory method.* New York: Association Press, 1968.

Baumgartel, H., and Goldstein, J. W. Need and value shifts in college training groups. *Journal of Applied Behavioral Science*, 1967, **3**, 87–101.

Beer, M., and Kleisath, S. W. The effects of the Managerial Grid Lab on organizational and leadership dimensions. In S. S. Zalkind (Chm.), Research on the impact of using different laboratory methods for interpersonal and organizational change. Symposium presented at the American Psychological Association, Washington, D.C., September 1967.

Bennis, W., Burke, R., Cutter, H., Harrington, H., and Hoffman, J. A note on some problems of measurement and prediction in a training group. *Group Psychotherapy*, 1957, **10**, 328–341.

Bennis, W., and Shepard, H. A. A theory of group development. *Human Relations*, 1956, **9**, 415–438.

Ben-Zeev, S. Comparison of diagnosed behavioral tendencies with actual behavior. In D. Stock and H. A. Thelen (Eds.), *Emotional dynamics and group culture.* Washington, D.C.: National Training Laboratories, 1958. Pp. 26–34. (a)

Ben-Zeev, S. Sociometric choice and patterns of member participation. In D. Stock and H. A. Thelen (Eds.), *Emotional dynamics and group culture.* Washington, D.C.: National Training Laboratories, 1958. Pp. 84–91. (b)

Ben-Zeev, S., Gradolph, I. H., Gradolph, P., Stock, D., and Thelen, H. A. *Methods for studying work and emotionality in group operation*. Chicago: University of Chicago, Human Dynamics Laboratory, 1954.

Berlin, J. I. Program learning for personal and interpersonal improvement. *Acta Psychologica*, 1964, **13**, 321–335.

Berzon, B., Pious, C., and Farson, R. E. The therapeutic event in group psychotherapy: A study of subjective reports by group members. *Journal of Individual Psychology*, 1963, **19**, 204–212.

Berzon, B., and Solomon, L. N. Research frontier: The self-directed therapeutic group—three studies. *Journal of Counseling Psychology*, 1966, **13**, 491–497.

Blake, R. R., and Mouton, J. S. Some effects of managerial grid seminar training on union and management attitudes toward supervision. *Journal of Applied Behavioral Science*, 1966, **2**, 387–400.

Blake, R. R., Mouton, J. S., Barnes, L. B., and Greiner, L. E. Breakthrough in organization development. *Harvard Business Review*, 1964, **42**, 133–155.

Blansfield, M. G. Depth analysis of organizational life. *California Management Review*, 1962, **5**, 29–42.

Bowers, N. D., and Soar, R. S. *Evaluation of laboratory human relations training for classroom teachers.* Studies of human relations in the teaching-learning process. V. Final report. U.S. Office of Education Contract Number 8143. Columbia: University of South Carolina, 1961.

Boyd, J. B., and Elliss, J. D. *Findings of research into senior management seminars*. Toronto: Personnel Research Department, Hydro-Electric Power Commission of Ontario, 1962.

Bradford, L. P. *Explorations in human relations training*. Washington, D.C.: National Training Laboratories, 1953.

Bradford, L. P., Gibb, J. R., and Benne, K. D. *T group theory and laboratory method*. New York: Wiley, 1964.

Bradford, L. P., Gibb, J. R., and Lippitt, G. L. Human relations training in three days. *Adult Leadership*, 1956, **4**, 11–26.

Buchanan, P. C. Evaluating the effectiveness of laboratory training in industry. In *Explorations in Human Relations Training and Research*. No. 1. Washington, D.C.: National Training Laboratories, 1965.

Buchanan, P. C., and Brunstetter, P. H. A research approach to management development. Part II. *Journal of the American Society of Training Directors*, 1959, **13**, 18–27.

Bugental, J. F. T. *The search for authenticity*. New York: Holt, Rinehart and Winston, 1965.

Bugental, J. F. T., and Tannenbaum, R. Sensitivity training and being motivation. *Journal of Humanistic Psychology*, 1963, **3**, 76–85.

Bunker, D. R. Individual applications of laboratory training. *Journal of Applied Behavioral Science*, 1965, **1**, 131–148.

Bunker, D. R., and Knowles, E. S. Comparison of behavioral changes resulting from human relations training laboratories of different lengths. *Journal of Applied Behavioral Science*, 1967, **3**, 505–523.

Bunker, G. L. The effect of group perceived esteem on self and ideal concepts in an emergent group. Unpublished master's thesis, Brigham Young University, 1961.

Burke, R. L., and Bennis, W. G. Changes in perception of self and others during human relations training. *Human Relations*, 1961, **14**, 165–182.

Byrd, R. E. Training in a non-group. *Journal of Humanistic Psychology*, 1967, **7**, 18–27.

Campbell, J. P., and Dunnette, M. D. Effectiveness of T group experiences in managerial training and development. *Psychological Bulletin*, 1968, **70**, 73–104.

Carron, T. J. Human relations training and attitude change: A vector analysis. *Personnel Psychology*, 1964, **17**, 403–424.

Carson, R. C., and Lakin, M. Some effects of group sensitivity experience. Paper presented at the meeting of the Southeastern Psychology Association, Miami Beach, Florida, 1963.

Clark, J. V., and Culbert, S. A. Mutually therapeutic perception and self-awareness in a T group. *Journal of Applied Behavioral Science*, 1965, **1**, 180–194.

Clark, T. C., and Miles, M. B. Human relations training for school administrators. *Journal of Social Issues*, 1954, **10** (2), 25–39.

Culbert, S. A. Trainer self-disclosure and member growth in a T group. Unpublished doctoral dissertation, University of California, Los Angeles, 1966.

Culbert, S. A. Trainer self-disclosure and member growth in two T groups. *Journal of Applied Behavioral Science*, 1968, **4**, 47–73.

Davis, S. An organic problem-solving method of organizational change. *Journal of Applied Behavioral Science*, 1967, **3**, 3–21.

Delaney, D. J. A study of the effectiveness of sensitivity training on the perception of non-verbal communications in counselor education. Unpublished doctoral dissertation, Arizona State University, 1966.

Delaney, D. M., and Heimann, R. Z. Effectiveness of sensitivity training on the perception of non-verbal communications. *Journal of Counseling Psychology*, 1966, **13**, 436–440.

Dietterich, P. M. An evaluation of a group development laboratory approach to training church leaders. Unpublished doctoral dissertation, Boston University, 1961.

Dubin, R. Psyche, sensitivity, and social structure. In R. Tannenbaum, I. R. Weschler, and F. Massarik (Eds.), *Leadership and organization: A behavioral science approach*. New York: McGraw-Hill, 1961.

Durham, L. E., and Gibb, J. R. An annotated bibliography of research, 1947–1960. Research Reprint Series, Number 2. Washington, D.C.: National Training Laboratories, 1960.

Durkin, H. E. *The group in depth*. New York: International Universities Press, 1964.

Ford, J. D., Jr. Computer analysis of test for the measurement of social perception during human relations training. Document No. SP-1373/001/00, System Development Corporation, Santa Monica, California, 1964.

Foster, B. R. Some interrelationships between religious values, leadership concepts, and perception of group process of professional church workers. Unpublished doctoral dissertation, University of Michigan, 1958.

French, J. R. P., Jr., Sherwood, J. J., and Bradford, D. L. Change in self-identity in a management training conference. *Journal of Applied Behavioral Science*, 1966, **2**, 210–218.

Friedlander, F. The impact of organizational training laboratories upon the effectiveness and interaction of ongoing work groups. *Personnel Psychology*, 1967, **20**, 289–308.

Friedlander, F. A comparative study of consulting processes and group development. *Journal of Applied Behavioral Science*, 1968, **4**, 377–399.

Fry, J. R. *A hard look at adult Christian education*. Philadelphia: Westminster Press, 1961.

Gage, N. L., and Exline, R. V. Social perception and effectiveness in discussion groups. *Human Relations*, 1953, **6**, 381–396.

Gassner, S. M., Gold, J., and Snadowsky, A. M. Changes in the phenomenal field as a result of human relations training. *Journal of Psychology*, 1964, **58**, 33–41.

Geitgey, D. A. A study of some effects of sensitivity training on the performance of students in associate degree programs of nursing education. Unpublished doctoral dissertation, University of California, Los Angeles, 1966.

Gibb, J. R. Effects of role playing upon (a) role flexibility and upon (b) ability to conceptualize a new role. Paper presented at the meeting of the American Psychological Association, Cleveland, Ohio, 1953.

Gibb, J. R. Climate for trust formation. In L. P. Bradford, J. R. Gibb, and K. D. Benne (Eds.), *T group theory and laboratory method*. New York: Wiley, 1964. Pp. 279–309.

Gibb, J. R. Fear and façade: Defensive management. In R. E. Farson (Ed.), *Science and human affairs*. Palo Alto: Science and Behavior Books, 1965. Pp. 197–214.

Gibb, J. R., and Gibb, L. M. Leaderless groups: Growth-centered values and potentials. In H. A. Otto and J. Mann (Eds.), *Ways of growth: approaches to expanding awareness*. New York: Grossman, 1968. Pp. 101–114. (a)

Gibb, J. R., and Gibb, L. M. Emergence therapy: The TORI process in an emergent group. In G. M. Gazda (Eds.), *Innovations to group psychotherapy*. Springfield, Ill.: Thomas, 1968. Pp. 96–129. (b)

Gibb, J. R., Smith, E. E., and Roberts, A. H. Effects of positive and negative feedback upon defensive behavior in small problem-solving groups. Paper presented at the meeting of the American Psychological Association, San Francisco, California, September 1955.

Gibb, L. M., and Gibb, J. R. Effects of the use of "participative action" groups in a course in general psychology. Paper presented at the meeting of the American Psychological Association, Washington, D.C., September 1952.

Glad, D. D. *Operational values in psychotherapy*. New York: Oxford University Press, 1959.

Gold, J. S. An evaluation of a laboratory human relations training program for college undergraduates. Unpublished doctoral dissertation, Columbia University, 1967.

Grater, H. Changes in self and other attitudes in a leadership training group. *Personnel and Guidance Journal*, 1959, **37**, 493–496.

Greiner, L. E. Organizational change and development. Unpublished doctoral dissertation, Harvard University, 1965.

Hacon, R. J. *Management training: Aims and methods*. London: English Universities Press, 1961.

House, R. J. T group education and leadership effectiveness: A review of the empirical literature and a critical evaluation. *Personnel Psychology*, 1967, **20**, 1–32.

Jahoda, M. *Current concepts of positive mental health*. New York: Basic Books, 1958.

Johnson, D. L., Hanson, P. G., Rothaus, P., Morton, R. B., Lyle, F. A., and Moyer, R. Follow-up evaluation of human relations training for psychiatric patients. In E. H. Schein and W. G. Bennis (Eds.), *Personal and organizational change through group methods*. New York: Wiley, 1965. Pp. 152–168.

Johnson, L. K. The effect of trainer interventions on change in personal functioning through T group training. Unpublished doctoral dissertation, University of Minnesota, 1966.

Kassarjian, H. H. Social character and sensitivity training. *Journal of Applied Behavioral Science*, 1965, **1**, 433–440.

Kelley, H. H. First impressions in interpersonal relations. Unpublished doctoral dissertation, M.I.T., 1948.

Kelley, H., and Pepitone, A. An evaluation of a college course in human relations. *Journal of Educational Psychology*, 1952, **43**, 193–209.

Kernan, J. P. Laboratory human relations training: Its effect on the "personality" of supervisory engineers. Unpublished doctoral dissertation, New York University, 1963.

Khanna, J. L. A discovery learning approach to inservice training. Paper presented at the meeting of the American Psychological Association, San Francisco, September, 1968.

Knowles, E. S. A bibliography of research on human relations training since 1960. In *Explorations in Human Relations Training Research*. Washington, D.C.: National Training Laboratories, 1967.

Haiman, F. S. Effects of training in group processes on open-mindedness. *Journal of Communication*, 1963, **13**, 236–245.

Hampden-Turner, C. H. An existential "learning theory" and the integration of T group research. *Journal of Applied Behavioral Science*, 1966, **2**, 367–386.

Hanson, P. G., Rothaus, P., Johnson, D. L., and Lyle, F. A. Autonomous groups in human relations training for psychiatric patients. *Journal of Applied Behavioral Science*, 1966, **2**, 305–324.

Harrison, R. Impact of the laboratory on perceptions of others by the experimental group. In C. Argyris, *Interpersonal competence and organizational effectiveness.* Homewood, Ill.: Irwin, 1962. Pp. 261–271.

Harrison, R. Group composition models for laboratory design. *Journal of Applied Behavioral Science*, 1965, **1**, 409–432.

Harrison, R. Cognitive change and participation in a sensitivity training laboratory. *Journal of Consulting Psychology*, 1966, **30**, 517–520.

Harrison, R. Problems in the design and interpretation of research on human relations training. In *Explorations in Human Relations Training and Research*. No. 1. Washington, D.C.: National Training Laboratories, 1967.

Harrison, R., and Lubin, B. Personal style, group composition, and learning. *Journal of Applied Behavioral Science*, 1965, **1**, 286–301.

Hill, W. F. The influence of sub-groups on participation in human relations training groups. Unpublished doctoral dissertation, University of Chicago, 1955.

Hill, W. F. *HIM: Hill Interaction Matrix.* Los Angeles: Youth Study Center, University of Southern California, 1965.

Horwitz, M., and Cartwright, D. P. A projective method for the diagnosis of group properties. *Human Relations*, 1953, **6**, 397–410.

Kuriloff, A. H., and Atkins, S. T group for a work team. *Journal of Applied Behavioral Science*, 1966, **2**, 63–94.

Lakin, M., and Carson, R. C. Participant perception of group process in group sensitivity training. *International Journal of Group Psychotherapy*, 1964, **14**, 116–122.

Lakin, M., and Carson, R. C. A therapeutic vehicle in search of a theory of therapy. *Journal of Applied Behavioral Science*, 1966, **2**, 27–40.

Lieberman, M. A. The relationship between the emotional cultures of groups and individual change. Unpublished doctoral dissertation, University of Chicago, 1958. (a)

Lieberman, M. A. The relation of diagnosed behavioral tendencies to member-perceptions of self and of the group. In D. Stock and H. A. Thelen (Eds.), *Emotional dynamics and group culture.* Washington, D.C.: National Training Laboratories, 1958. Pp. 35–49. (b)

Lieberman, M. A. Sociometric choice related to affective approach. In D. Stock and H. A. Thelen (Eds.), *Emotional dynamics and group culture.* Washington, D.C.: National Training Laboratories, 1958. Pp. 71–83. (c)

Lieberman, M. A. The influence of group composition on change in affective approach. In D. Stock and H. A. Thelen (Eds.), *Emotional dynamics and group culture.* Washington, D.C.: National Training Laboratories, 1958. Pp. 131–139. (d)

Likert, R. *The human organization.* New York: McGraw-Hill, 1967.

Lippitt, G. L. Effects of information about group desire for change on members of a group. Unpublished doctoral dissertation, American University, 1959.

Livingston, D. G. The effects of varying group organization upon perception of power and benefit. Unpublished doctoral dissertation, University of Kansas, 1951.

Lohman, K., Zenger, J. H., and Weschler, I. R. Some perceptual changes during sensitivity training. *Journal of Educational Research*, 1959, **53**, 28–31.

Maier, N. R. F., Solem, A. R., and Maier, A. A. *Supervisory and executive development.* New York: Wiley, 1957.

Massarik, F., and Carlson, G. The California Psychological Inventory as an indicator of personality change in sensitivity training. Unpublished master's thesis, University of California, Los Angeles, 1960.

Mathis, A. G. Development and validation of a trainability index for laboratory training groups. Unpublished doctoral dissertation, University of Chicago, 1955.

McGregor, D. *The human side of enterprise.* New York: McGraw-Hill, 1960.

Miles, M. B. Human relations training: Processes and outcomes. *Journal of Counseling Psychology*, 7, 301–306.

Miles, M. B. Changes during and following laboratory training: A clinical-experimental study. *Journal of Applied Behavioral Science*, 1965, **1**, 215–242.

Miles, M. B., Cohen, S. K., and Whidman, F. L. *Changes in performance test scores after human relations training.* New York: Horace Mann-Lincoln Institute of School Experimentation, 1959.

Morton, R. B. The organization training laboratory: Some individual and organizational effects. *Journal of Advanced Management*, 1965, **30**, 58–67.

Morton, R. B., and Bass, B. M. The organizational training lab. *Journal of the American Society of Training Directors*, 1964, **18** (10), 2–15.

Mowrer, O. H. *The new group therapy.* Princeton: Van Nostrand, 1964.

Nath, R. Dynamics of organizational change: Some determinants of managerial problem solving and decision making competences. Unpublished doctoral dissertation, M.I.T., 1964.

Oshry, B. I., and Harrison, R. Transfer from here-and-now to there-and-then: Changes in organizational problem diagnosis stemming from T group training. *Journal of Applied Behavioral Science*, 1966, **2**, 185–198.

Otto, H. A. *Human potentialities: the challenge and the promise.* St. Louis: Green, 1968.

Otto, H. A., and Mann, J. *Ways of growth: Approaches to expanding awareness.* New York: Grossman, 1968.

Peters, D. R. Identification and personal change in laboratory training groups. Unpublished doctoral dissertation, M.I.T., 1966.

Powers, J. R. Trainer orientation and group composition in laboratory training. Unpublished doctoral dissertation, Case Institute of Technology, 1965.

Psathas, G., and Hardert, R. Trainer interventions and normative patterns in the T group. *Journal of Applied Behavioral Science*, 1966, **2**, 149–169.

Reisel, J. A search for behavior patterns in sensitivity training groups. Unpublished doctoral dissertation, U.C.L.A., 1959.

Rosenthal, D. Perceptions of some personality characteristics in members of a small group. Unpublished doctoral dissertation, University of Chicago, 1952.

Rothaus, P., Johnson, D. L., Hanson, P. G., and Lyle, F. A. Participation and sociometry in autonomous and trainer-led patient groups. *Journal of Counseling Psychology*, 1966, **13**, 68–76.

Rothaus, P., Morton, R. B., Johnson, D. L., Cleveland, S. E., and Lyle, F. A. Human relations training for psychiatric patients. *Archives of General Psychiatry*, 1963, **8**, 572–581.

Rubin, I. The reduction of prejudice through laboratory training. *Journal of Applied Behavioral Science*, 1967, **3**, 29–50. (a)

Rubin, I. Increased self-acceptance: A means of reducing prejudice. *Journal of Personality and Social Psychology*, 1967, **5**, 233–238. (b)

Schein, E. H., and Bennis, W. G. *Personal and organizational change through group methods.* New York: Wiley, 1965.

Schmuck, R. A. Helping teachers improve classroom group processes. *Journal of Applied Behavioral Science*, 1968, **4**, 401–435.

Schutz, W. C. *FIRO.* New York: Rinehart, 1958.

Schutz, W. C. *Joy: Expanding human awareness.* New York: Grove Press, 1967.

Schutz, W. C., and Allen, V. L. The effects of a T group laboratory on interpersonal behavior. *Journal of Applied Behavioral Science*, 1966, **2**, 265–286.

Seashore, C. N. Attitude and skill changes in participative action training groups. Unpublished master's thesis, University of Colorado, 1955.

Sherwood, J. J. Self identity and self-actualization: A theory and research. Unpublished doctoral dissertation, University of Michigan, 1962.

Sherwood, J. J. Self identity and referent others. *Sociometry*, 1965, **28**, 66–81.

Sikes, W. W. A study of some effects of a human relations training laboratory. Unpublished doctoral dissertation, Purdue University, 1964.

Simon, A., and Agazarian, Y. *Sequential analysis of verbal interaction.* Philadelphia: Research for Better Schools, Inc., 1967.

Smith, H. C. *Sensitivity to people.* New York: McGraw-Hill, 1966.

Smith, P. B. Attitude changes associated with training in human relations. *British Journal of Social and Clinical Psychology*, 1964, **3**, 104–112.

Spector, A. J. Changes in human relations attitudes. *Journal of Applied Psychology*, 1958, **42**, 154–157.

Steele, F. I. The relationship of personality to changes in interpersonal values effected by laboratory training. Unpublished doctoral dissertation, M.I.T., 1965.

Steele, F. I. Personality and the "laboratory style." *Journal of Applied Behavioral Science*, 1968, **4**, 25–45.

Stock, D. The relation between the sociometric structure of the group and certain personality characteristics of the individual. Unpublished doctoral dissertation, University of Chicago, 1952.

Stock, D. A survey of research on T groups. In L. P. Bradford, J. R. Gibb, and K. D. Benne (Eds.), *T group theory and laboratory method.* New York: Wiley, 1964. Pp. 395–441.

Stock, D., and Ben-Zeev, S. Changes in work and emotionality during group growth. In D. Stock and H. A. Thelen (Eds.), *Emotional dynamics and group culture.* Washington, D.C.: National Training Laboratories, 1958. Pp. 192–206.

Stoller, F. H. Marathon group therapy. In G. M. Gazda (Ed.), *Innovations to group psychotherapy.* Springfield, Ill.: Thomas, 1968. Pp. 42–95. (a)

Stoller, F. H. Focused feedback with video tape: Extending the group's functions. In G. M. Gazda (Ed.), *Innovations to group psychotherapy.* Springfield, Ill.: Thomas, 1968. Pp. 207–255. (b)

Taylor, F. C. Effects of laboratory training upon persons and their work groups. In S. S. Zalkind (Chm.), Research on the impact of using different laboratory methods for interpersonal and organizational change. Symposium presented at the meeting of the American Psychological Association, Washington, D.C., September 1967.

Underwood, W. J. Evaluation of laboratory-method training. *Training Directors Journal*, 1965, **19**, 34–40.

Valiquet, I. M. Contribution to the evaluation of a management development program. Unpublished master's thesis, M.I.T., 1964.

Wagner, A. B. The use of process analysis in business decision games. *Journal of Applied Behavioral Science*, 1965, **1**, 387–408.

Watson, J. Some social psychological correlates of personality: A study of the usefulness of psychoanalytic theory in predicting to social behavior. Unpublished doctoral dissertation, University of Michigan, 1953.

Wedel, C. C. A study of measurement in group dynamics laboratories. Unpublished doctoral dissertation, George Washington University, 1957.

Weschler, I. R., and Reisel, J. *Inside a sensitivity training group.* Los Angeles: Institute of Industrial Relations, University of California, Los Angeles, 1958.

Whitaker, D. S., and Lieberman, M. A. *Psychotherapy through the group process.* New York: Atherton Press, 1964.

Wolman, B. B. (Ed.) *Handbook of clinical psychology.* New York: McGraw-Hill, 1965.

Zand, D. E., Steele, F. I., and Zalkind, S. S. The impact of an organizational development program on perceptions of interpersonal, group and organizational functioning. In S. S. Zalkind (Chm.), Research on the impact of using different laboratory methods for interpersonal and organizational change. Symposium presented at the meeting of the American Psychological Association, Washington, D.C., September 1967.

Zimet, C. N., and Fine, H. J. Personality changes with a group therapeutic experience in a human relations seminar. *Journal of Abnormal and Social Psychology,* 1955, **51,** 68–73.

23

RESEARCH ON EDUCATIONAL AND VOCATIONAL COUNSELING

ROGER A. MYERS

COLUMBIA UNIVERSITY

The scope of this chapter has been purposely, self-consciously, and unsuccessfully limited to the research on counseling that is generally considered separate from that on psychotherapy. That the limitation is purposeful is natural enough because of the context in which the chapter appears, surrounded as it is by analyses of psychotherapy research from almost every conceivable point of view. The self-conscious aspect of the limitation derives from the writer's timidity before the task of culling from the literature studies of counseling-as-distinguished-from-psychotherapy, when so many have labored at the distinction without success. And finally, the limitation is unsuccessful because, regardless of the nature and number of criteria one applies to the task of separation, there are areas of the counseling and the psychotherapy research literature that are so clearly identical as to defy any rational attempts to separate them.

Though there are those who argue that there should be no differences between counseling and psychotherapy (for example, Patterson 1959, 1963a, 1966, 1969), it would be difficult to find a proponent for the position that there are no features of the two activities that permit a distinction, albeit an imperfect one. Many writers have treated the problem (Goldman, 1964; Hahn, 1953; Stefflre, 1965; Tyler, 1961; Wolberg, 1954; Vance and Volsky, 1962), and some have done so with considerable clarity. A recent example is Stefflre (1965), who summarized many previous attempts at making the distinction and classified the reasoning as to goals (the goals of counseling tend to be more limited, more growth-oriented, more focused on immediates, and more concerned with role functions); clients (counseling is more likely to go on with "normal" people); practitioners (counselors are likely to be less well trained); settings (counseling more often occurs in educational settings); and methods (counseling is more apt to be concerned with the present versus the past, with cognition versus affect, and with clarity versus ambiguity). Others have noted the importance of such things as length of treatment, instruments employed, and psychic discomfort—as distinguished from psychopathology—in working toward a distinction. Without depreciating the efforts of those who have worked with intelligence on this difficult problem of taxonomy, it is amusing how close we arrive to Hahn's 1953 conclusions that (a) counseling and psychotherapy cannot be distinguished clearly; (b) counselors practice what psychotherapists consider psychotherapy; (c) psychotherapists practice what counselors consider to be counseling; and (d) despite the above, they are different (p. 232).

The special aspects of the difference with which this chapter deals are related to the assertions that counseling is more frequently concerned with immediate decision making and with role functioning. Not unrelated to its frequent location in educational settings, a large portion of counseling activity is viewed as an instrumental endeavor to increase the efficacy of the client's planning activity, which is essential to his playing of productive social roles. The need for such an endeavor was created in an industrialized society with a diversified world of work, a well-developed division of labor, and a variety of social roles. The educational system that grew in support of such a society reflects this complexity by providing a variety of curricula that require of students—and of adults—a continuous series of more or less irreversible choices.

Thus, vocational counseling in educational settings grew, designed to assist students in the rather difficult task of picking their way through the maze of diversified offerings that lead to the more than 20,000 occupational opportunities waiting beyond the classroom. The decision-making requirements of such a system are enormous, especially since many decisions are required of youths quite early in their lives, before their experience prepares them for making choices of such consequence (Super and Overstreet, 1960). Cooley and Lohnes (1968), for example, have demonstrated that even though the essential choices be limited

to various combinations of two two-alternative decisions, that is, people versus things and college versus noncollege, the educational system requires that these choices be made during the junior-high-school years. The assertion that such choices are more or less irreversible is attested to by the fact that in all but the most enlightened of school systems, a student who changes his career objective in a major way pays for the change with lost time or some similar currency.

Such decision making is extremely important as an accommodation to an educational system that creates developmental tasks before students are equipped to deal with them. However, it is essential to bear in mind that such decisions are merely means to ends of considerably larger consequence. To illustrate this point, it is necessary to digress briefly in order to include small portions of the thinking of two major theorists in vocational development.

Super suggests that the choices one makes are attempts to implement one's self-concept by electing environmental circumstances most likely to permit self-expression. Once elected, a particular set of environmental circumstances provides the basis for reality testing through role playing. Choices continue throughout the person's life and are best viewed in a developmental frame of reference. For some of the particulars of this process, we quote a portion of the theoretical propositions in Super's own words:

1. Development through life stages can be guided, partly by facilitating the process of maturation of abilities and interests and partly by aiding in reality testing and in the development of self-concept.

2. The process of vocational development is essentially that of developing and implementing a self-concept: it is a compromise process in which the self-concept is a product of the interaction of inherited aptitudes, neural and endocrine makeup, opportunity to play various roles, and evaluations of the extent to which the results of the role playing meets with the approval of superiors and fellows.

3. The process of compromise between individual and social factors, between self-concept and reality, is one of role playing, whether the role is played in fantasy, in the counseling interview, or in real life activities such as school classes, clubs, part-time work and entry jobs.

4. Work satisfactions and life satisfactions depend upon the extent to which the individual finds adequate outlets for his abilities, interests, personality traits, and values; they depend upon his establishment in a type of work, a role which his growth and exploratory experiences have led him to consider congenial and appropriate (1953, pp. 189-190).

Even these brief glimpses of his thinking make clear the importance Super places on decision making as a part of the developmental process. The relationship of decision making to self-concept development is further elaborated in more recent work (Super, Starishevsky, Matlin, and Jordaan, 1963).

Tiedeman is another writer who has expanded upon the importance of the decision process in personal development. His thesis is that the particular style of linguistic analysis to be learned in the process of making educational and vocational decisions, a problem-solving style, can lead to an increase in the client's use of intelligent personal initiative, or a *sense of agency*. He has gone to great lengths to define this style (Tiedeman, 1966, 1967) and to demonstrate how it results from a well-designed decision-making context (Tiedeman, 1961; Tiedeman and O'Hara, 1963; Tiedeman and Dudley, 1967).

The making of educational and vocational decisions is viewed by many psychologists as the beginning, or at least an early stage, of a developmental process of considerable import. This view is shared, implicitly and explicitly, in the society at large, as is evidenced by the extensive degree to which it has been willing to support counseling activity to the end of enabling and fostering individual choices. There is, indeed, an enormous volume of counseling activity that takes place. Furthermore there are large national professional organizations, regulated training programs, and an extensive amount of theoretical, prescriptive, exhortative, and inspirational writing on the topic. Fortunately, there is also a growing research literature and a well-established tradition of research criticism (Berdie, 1954; Dressel, Pepinsky, and Shoben, 1950; Patterson,

1960; Schwebel, 1962; Williamson and Bordin, 1941).

The study of educational-vocational decision making and development is too extensive to be covered in a chapter of this size, and much of the research relevant to it falls outside the intended scope of this handbook. Therefore, the concentration here will be on that research dealing with the effects, the consequences, and the sequels of counseling intervention on these processes. For the most part, our attention will be addressed to the portion of the literature that is usually described by the label *outcome studies*. To accomplish this goal, the sections that follow have been organized according to the criteria employed by the investigators to assess the outcomes of their interventions. For the most part, these criteria fit into the two categories that are central to our concerns: educational-vocational decision making and effective role functioning.

STUDIES OF DECISION MAKING[1]

Accuracy of Self-Knowledge. The degree to which the client is aware of his own educationally and vocationally relevant characteristics has been a concern of those engaged in the guidance process since its very beginning. Frank Parsons (1909), widely recognized as the founder of the guidance movement, provided a logically appealing and simple prescription for guidance procedures which persists in influence despite the extensive and sophisticated theoretical advances that have occurred since his time (Calia, 1966). The elements of Parsons' procedure include individual analysis, knowledge of the conditions and requirements of work opportunities, and a rational treatment of the relationship between the two. The growth of differential psychology and its infusion into the history of the guidance movement added strength and substance to Parsons' prescription, especially the part dealing with individual analysis. Relevant personal characteristics could be measured, and the measurements could be communicated to the client to the end of

---

[1] For help with the completion of this section, I am deeply indebted to Guy T. Pilato, whose recent dissertation (1968) was a valuable guide.

increasing his self-insight and improving his ability to make rational decisions about his future.

Since much of the practice of guidance consisted of the communication of tests results to clients, it followed quite naturally that the effects of such activity should be seized upon as a useful criterion of counseling outcome. The usual paradigm for such research is to extract from the student some estimate of his personal characteristics, provide him with information on his test results, and then ask him to estimate his characteristics again. The difference between the pre- and postestimates provides the evidence for the impact of the treatment.

An impressive number of such studies were conducted during the 1950s, and the best of these have been critically reviewed by Goldman (1961, pp. 345–363). He found the group of studies to be rather mixed, scarcely comparable from one to another, replete with contradictory and noncomplementary findings, and characterized by a variety of methodological shortcomings. There were scattered results to suggest that accuracy of self-knowledge was not related to the certainty with which a client expressed his self-estimates; estimates of vocational interests were more susceptible to change (toward greater accuracy) than were those of intelligence or personality; group procedures for test interpretation showed slightly better results; effects were greatest when clients showed the greatest readiness to learn; and most changes in accuracy of self-knowledge were short-lived.

Goldman also identified a variety of methodological weaknesses in the studies he reviewed. He observed that posttreatment data collection frequently neglected concern for the permanence of the effects and for the possibility of broader implications of changes in self-knowledge. Furthermore, most of the studies failed to consider the influence of the nature of the subjects, whether they were recruits or volunteers, whether they were optimally concerned about the new data they were being given, and the extent to which gullibility or resistance influenced their reception of it. He was mildly critical of the short periods of time devoted to the treatments and suggested:

By the time they have reached high school, boys and girls have had many opportunities for reality testing, and they may have reached a crystallization of self-concept that is likely to resist change.

Finally, he repeatedly pointed to the fact that the actual methods of the treatment are inadequately specified—or not described at all—making it impossible to ascertain what elements of the process are related to the results.

Since Goldman's review appeared, a number of additional studies on the topic have been completed. As is so often the case, few of them have profited from his labors. However, some give evidence of an increasing level of methodological sophistication and are therefore worthy of mention.

For example, Holmes (1964) gave particularly careful attention to specifying the nature of the differential procedures used by counselors in presenting test information to male college freshmen. Her methods included (1) mailed reports to the students; (2) dominating and evaluative counselors; (3) dominating but reflective counselors; and (4) passive counselors eliciting student feelings about the tests. The students were given a test battery, provided with the results via the four methods, surveyed as to their attitudes about the counselors and the tests immediately and one week after the interviews, and asked to recall the results during the one-week follow-up. Because she was principally interested in the students' attitudes, Holmes concentrated her report on this aspect of the results and found no differences among counseling styles, except that students who received their results by mail valued the test information least. However, on recall of test information, the mail group did best of all. Holmes discounted the superiority of the mail group on the basis of probable cheating, and concluded that the passive but eliciting counselors produced the greatest accuracy of self-knowledge.

Wright's study (1963) also demonstrated that criticism about not specifying treatment methods had been heeded. He compared college freshmen who had been counseled individually and in groups with a no-treatment control group and found significant differences in accuracy of self-knowledge for the treated groups. The procedures of the one-interview test interpretations are carefully described, as are his criterion measures. Furthermore, his follow-up data collection took place three months after the treatment, and clearly demonstrated that the post-counseling gains persisted.

Lister and Ohlsen (1965) addressed themselves to some unexplored aspects of the problem by providing a precounseling training period on the meaning of the tests used, and by selecting subjects from grades 5, 7, 9, and 11. Strangely, they found that the pretraining was not related to increases in self-awareness, even though there were significant gains for both groups that received the test interpretations. Their results indicated some loss in accuracy of self-knowledge from immediately after counseling to the 60-day follow-up, but an overall gain from precounseling to follow-up remained. Since their concern was with students who were oriented and counseled, versus students who were counseled without previous orientation, they did not employ a no-treatment control group. They did, however, describe the treatment method in adequate detail.

Though none of these studies succeeded in overcoming all of the methodological difficulties of its forerunners, in two of them (Wright, 1963; Lister and Ohlsen, 1965) the investigators concerned themselves with the problem of duration of the effects, and all three took care to describe the treatment method in some detail. What emerges is some justification for a procedure that includes (a) causing the student to estimate his tested characteristics on a blank profile sheet; (b) providing him with test results which are then recorded on the same sheet; (c) eliciting the student's reactions to the similarities and discrepancies in the two sets of estimates; and (d) responding to the student's feelings resulting from such a procedure.

Wright's study further substantiated the efficacy of group procedures in test interpretation, and he and Lister and Ohlsen demonstrated that the gains in self-awareness do persist for a time, though not with their original strength.

In what is perhaps the most recent report on the topic, Tipton (1969) compared counselor-mediated test interpretation with a 69-frame Skinnerian linear-type program designed to accomplish the same purpose. His criterion was changes in concept measures on a semantic differential. He found the program to be slightly more effective in bringing about immediate changes. However, in his one-month follow-up, he found that the changes in meaning increased for the counseled group and decreased for those who used the programmed interpretation. The suitability of this kind of criterion for such studies has yet to be fully understood, but one can predict that more studies of technologically-based test interpretation methods are forthcoming.[2]

Appropriateness of Vocational Preference.
Though the procedural problems connected with the use of increased self-knowledge are sufficiently knotty, they appear minor when contrasted with the complex of difficulties related to the use of *appropriateness of vocational preference* as a criterion of counseling outcomes. Once again, the supporting rationale is simple and straightforward: professional assistance in educational-vocational decision making, if it is effective, should lead to client's selection of better goals for his vocational future. However, as the modern history of applied behavioral science consistently testifies, rational simplicity at the base often leads to—perhaps even dictates—complexity and confusion at the apex. The difficulties associated with operationalizing such a value-laden concept as "better goals" have been enormous, and so have the problems of instrumentation. Withal, the usual problems of identifying specific antecedents, establishing durability, and assessing relevance have persisted to haunt investigators and to make them increasingly wary of using the criterion at all.

Studies that use appropriateness of vocational preference as a criterion begin by assuming the possibility of matching men and jobs. Most of them proceed by eliciting a postcounseling vocational preference from the client and evaluating its appropriateness with respect to the congruence of the client's vocationally relevant characteristics and the requirements of the occupation for which he expresses a preference.

[2] The use of programmed materials for test interpretation was pioneered by William M. Gilbert and Thomas N. Ewing, whose unpublished report of their work (1965) is cited by Tipton.

The differences between pre- and postcounseling and/or between treatment and control groups on some measure of the congruence are the data of merit in assessing the treatment outcomes.

Pilato (1968, p. 19) has pointed out that appropriateness of vocational preference has been measured in three ways. The first, and least relevant, procedure is to compare a distribution of the preferences of a group of subjects to a distribution of actual employment opportunities. Movement from dissimilarity to similarity between the two types of distributions is presumed to represent movement toward greater realism of clients' preferences. Nick (1942) used this method to establish the efficacy of providing groups of 11th and 12th graders with information on employment opportunities, and Hutson and Webster (1943) used it to evaluate the counseling of 10th graders. In both studies the investigators reported changes in the desired direction and interpreted the results as supportive of the treatment practices. It is obvious that this procedure involves a number of difficult assumptions and completely neglects considerations of individual characteristics and changes, and therefore it has been virtually abandoned.

The second type of procedure for evaluating appropriateness of vocational preference has been by far the most popular scheme in studies of counseling outcomes. It involves the use of judges' ratings of the congruence of clients' characteristics, such as aptitudes and interests, and the characteristics of their preferred occupations. Though judging procedures have varied from study to study, the general approach is to rely on the judges' expertness about goodness of fit between the two sets of characteristics and to require relatively unrefined ratings from them.

Stone (1948) used judges' ratings to test the effects of courses in vocational orientation. He found that students who took the courses changed more in the direction of appropriateness than those who did not, and that those who had both the orientation and individual counseling showed substantial improvement. Speer and Jasker (1949) found that greater realism resulted when subjects were given either work experience or guided reading on occupations and discussions with counselors. The most

appropriate preferences, however, were made by those subjects who had both treatments. Bilovsky, McMasters, Shorr, and Singer (1953) found no differences between group and individual counseling in bringing about realistic preferences for 12th-grade boys. Hoyt (1955) also found no differences between individual and group treatment, but both groups improved significantly more than the no-treatment control group, a feature which the study of Bilovsky et al. lacked. Biersdorf (1958) found no differences on appropriateness ratings between treatment groups and controls when she provided two types of group test interpretation procedures.

Concerns about the validity of appropriateness of vocational preference as a criterion of counseling outcomes have affected the work of a number of investigators. For example, Gonyea (1962) obtained judges' ratings on clients' statements of vocational preference before, immediately after, and one year after counseling. The results indicated a significant increase in appropriateness from pre- to postcounseling and from precounseling to follow-up. However, the weakening of the effect observed from postcounseling to follow-up suggested the need for a second study. In it, Gonyea (1963) had judges rate students' vocational objectives stated (1) as college freshmen and (2) four to six years later. From this group he identified those students who had received vocational counseling at any time during the period and matched them with a no-treatment control group unmotivated for counseling. Neither group showed significant changes, and no significant differences in change of appropriateness were observable between them. His interpretation was that gains in appropriateness due to counseling do not persist. It is important to note however, that the second study did not include a measure of immediate postcounseling appropriateness, requiring that we assume that gains occurred in the first place in order to conclude that they did not persist.

Hewer is another investigator whose own research makes her uncomfortable and who reacts to the discomfort with further research. She set about to investigate the relative effects of individual counseling, and a "choosing your vocation" course on appropriateness of vocational preference (Hewer, 1959). She found no differences, but in the process she observed that the ratings of appropriateness were characterized by very low reliability, causing her to have doubts about the general validity of the criterion. In a subsequent study (Hewer, 1966), she obtained data on the actual employment of persons who had completed the vocations course seven to eight years earlier, and compared their work situations with the vocational preferences stated at the end of the course. Her premise was that the degree of congruence between the preferences stated in 1955–56 and the actual positions held seven years later would establish the degree of validity of the appropriateness concept. In fact, she found nearly two-thirds of the subjects doing what they had earlier planned to do, and concluded that appropriateness of vocational preference is a meaningful criterion for judging counseling effectiveness. Her data also led her to conclude that expert judgements immediately after counseling were not a satisfactory substitute for follow-up data in the assessment of appropriateness.

It should be noted that Hewer's follow-up dealt not with vocational *preference*, as do the studies previously cited, but with vocational *choice*, which describes a preference that has been acted upon. The terms are often used interchangeably, but ought not to be (Super, 1963, p. 83). Apostal (1960) also studied the appropriateness of actual vocational choices in order to assess the effectiveness of vocational counseling. He ascertained the occupations of former vocational-counseling clients six or seven years after counseling, and had judges rate the appropriateness of their choices on a 4-point scale. He found that 84 percent of the former clients held positions that the judges rated at the top two scale positions, "Appropriate" and "Borderline-Appropriate." The judgments were made in the context of six-year-old test results and case notes. Though this alone would have provided an argument for the efficacy of the treatment, Apostal went on to have other judges rate the adequacy of the vocational counseling that had taken place. He found no relationship between the judged adequacy of the counseling and the appropriateness of the later occupational position.

This sampling of studies provides a reasonable basis for evaluating the procedure of using judges' ratings as the criterion of appropriateness of vocational preference. Some investigators (Speer and Jasker, 1949; Stone, 1948) have succeeded in differentiating between different kinds of treatments with it, though others (Biersdorf, 1958; Bilovsky et al., 1953; Hewer, 1959; Hoyt, 1959) have not. Hoyt (1959) used it successfully in differentiating treatment from control groups, and Gonyea (1962) demonstrated precounseling, postcounseling, and follow-up differences. Hewer (1959) cast doubt about the reliability of the ratings in her study, and later (1966) demonstrated that the ratings were unrelated to a more nearly ultimate criterion. Though the algebraic sum of all of this is impossible to calculate, it is clear that there are problems in the use of judges' ratings that compound the problem of understanding the appropriateness phenomenon and of relating it to treatment antecedents. Though Apostal seems to have intended to, only Hewer has addressed herself to the properties of the ratings *per se*. Her discouraging results may have caused researchers to look for other procedures.

The third style for establishing appropriateness measures enables the investigator to obviate the assumption that an expert can reliably decide about the goodness of fit between personal characteristics and occupational requirements. It consists of an explicit comparison between vocationally relevant personal characteristics, that is, individual test results, and occupational norm group characteristics. Though this system is not as ample as one might hope, there is a basis for justifying the assumption that appropriateness can be judged from the congruence between (1) one's intelligence and the *level* of the occupation to which he aspires; and (2) one's measured interests and the *field of work* in which his vocational preference falls (Jordaan and Myers, 1970; Super and Crites, 1962, Tyler, 1964). In recent years, a number of investigators (Bidwell, 1969; Margolis, 1967; Milliken, 1962; Super, 1961) have employed this kind of procedure to establish an index of appropriateness without apparent procedural discomfort, but only one (Pilato, 1968) has used it as an outcome criterion for evaluating a treatment.

Pilato undertook his study as a preliminary test of a treatment strategy that was to be incorporated in a computer-based vocational orientation system. Therefore, his treatment conditions were highly specific and thoroughly described, though they cannot accurately be called counseling. Using groups of 11th-grade boys, he gave them an intelligence test and an interest test, had them make estimates of their standing on these two characteristics, and asked them to state their vocational preferences before, immediately after, and 55 days after treatment. The treatments included (1) feedback to the students about the accuracy of their self-knowledge; (2) teaching about the structure of the world of work: and (3) a combination of the two, all transmitted to groups of classroom size. A no-treatment control group was given a filler exercise. His findings are briefly summarized below:

1. The group receiving only accuracy-of-self-knowledge feedback increased the appropriateness of their most preferred occupations by revising them to more appropriate occupational levels.

2. The group receiving only information on the world of work showed no improvement.

3. The group receiving the combined treatment showed the most improvement, increasing the appropriateness of all their preferences and of their most preferred occupations.

4. All of the significant increases were found in the level dimension, and none were in the field dimension.

5. The increases in appropriateness did persist to the follow-up period, but with diminished strength.

The use of the explicit method of measuring appropriateness by comparing individual test results with normative characteristics of the preferred occupation is not without its complexities and its tenuous assumptions. In addition to the assumption of the relevance of the available occupational norms, decisions need to be made about which norms are to be used and how they are to be partitioned. The semantic slide from occupational norm group characteristics to occupational requirements to appropriateness of aspiration must be negotiated. The problem of overqualification, that is, of having higher intelligence scores than the norm of the occupation preferred, must be solved. And most important of all, a rational system for quantifying the relationships must be invented. Nevertheless, these problems appeared soluble in the several studies cited above, suggesting that the direct comparison procedure with its actuarial basis and its obviously greater reliability is clearly preferable to the use of judges' ratings for establishing a measure of the criterion appropriateness of vocational preference.

Of course, the decisions about the validity of the criterion itself are far from being definitively taken. Super (1961) reported that this criterion was not related to other measures of vocational maturity for 9th-grade boys, and later (Super, Kowalski, and Gotkin, 1967) reported that 9th-grade appropriateness measures, arrived at by direct comparisons, had no predictive value 10 years later and that measures taken in the 12th grade had relatively little. Apostal (1960) and Hewer (1966) attempted to illuminate the problem by studying actual choices 6, 7, and 8 years after treatment, and both found that treated groups made good choices after that much time. But Apostal had no immediate postcounseling measure to relate to his findings, and Hewer found that the early judges' ratings did not relate to the later implemented choices.

What remains then is a familiar residual dilemma: can our knowledge of treatment procedures be advanced by the use of an immediate criterion, no matter how well it is made, if it does not bear a substantial relationship to some relevant ultimate criterion? In view of the alternatives, the answer is clearly affirmative. To require of investigators that they invent and use criterion measures as flawless as those imagined by research critics would be to put an end to research on counseling outcomes. Despite the flaws contained in many of the studies completed to date, there is enough evidence to argue for continued investigation of the professional attempts to help clients make better decisions.

In examining the case of appropriateness of vocational preference, it must be recognized that it provides a criterion measure that has a logical validity for the goals of the participants and that can be reliably rendered. Though the studies in which it has been used as a criterion leave us far from our goal of connecting treatment procedures with treatment sequels, they have provided an increasingly illuminated path toward better understanding of the measure and toward generally more satisfactory research.

Instrumental Behavior. Notable among the more recent studies of the effects of counseling intervention on decision making are those of Krumboltz and his associates. This series of studies has been focused on the promotion of client behaviors, which are presumed to be instrumental to effective decision making, rather than on the decisions themselves. The rationale that has supported these studies is by no means a theory, but it is admirably explicit and systematic. Krumboltz (1966b) holds that client problems should be conceptualized as learning problems, that client goals should be defined in behavioral terms (Kumboltz, 1966a), and that the effects of counseling should be evaluated experimentally, inquiring into the relationship of specific counseling procedures to specific counseling goals. Since the entire framework characterizes the enterprise in learning terms, it is natural that the treatment procedures recommended are those derived from behavior theory applications to counseling and psychotherapy. They have been categorized by Krumboltz as operant learning, imitative learning, cognitive learning, and emotional learning (1966b, pp. 13–20).

The studies reported to date have concentrated on operant learning and imitative learning as a basis for treatment procedures. Ryan and Krumboltz (1964) used counselor verbal reinforcement in an attempt to influence clients' decision-making styles. In a single, twenty-minute interview, counselors used expressions of approval to reinforce deliberation statements for one group and decision statements for another. A control group received no reinforcements. Their results indicated that the two treatment groups significantly increased their reinforced classes of verbal behavior during the interview; and the group reinforced for decision statements made more such responses to a story-completion task after the interview, though the effects for the deliberation group did not generalize to the later task. Though the results were somewhat clouded by counselor differences—which were observed but not controlled—the surprisingly promising conclusion was that deliberation-decision behavior could be modified in such a short encounter.

For reasons which so far remain unexplained, Krumboltz and his associates have not followed up on this promising beginning in influencing deliberation-decision behavior. Instead, they turned their attention to another class of instrumental act in the decision-making context, information-seeking behavior. Thus, Krumboltz and Thoresen (1964) randomly distributed subjects to treatments that included individual counseling (two sessions), in which the counselor-reinforced statements that indicated that the client "had sought, was presently seeking or intended to seek information relevant to his own educational or vocational plans" (p. 326); group counseling (four clients, two sessions) with the same reinforcement strategy; individual counseling with a 15-minute audiotape of a model information-seeking male client followed by reinforcement; and a group form of the model-reinforcement treatment. Both an active and an inactive control group were used. The criterion was the frequency and amount of actual information-seeking behavior the clients engaged in during the three-week period following the treatment. They found that (1) all treatments were followed by more information seeking than was performed by the control groups; (2) the model-reinforcement procedure was more effective than reinforcement alone for the male clients (the model was a male); (3) group and individual treatments were equally effective; and (4) differential effects for counselors and schools were observable.

Krumboltz and Schroeder (1965) studied the same treatment strategies, used only in individual counseling sessions, and found that the treatment groups engaged in more postcounseling information seeking than the controls, that model reinforcement with the male model on the tape worked better for the males, and that reinforcement alone worked better for the females. It was also reported that seven of the nine counselors in the study were females which, coupled with the male model-male client results, led to an interest in client-counselor and client-model relationships.

Subsequently Thoresen, Krumboltz, and Varenhorst (1967) tried all possible combinations by varying the sex of the counselors, the model clients on a videotaped counseling session, the model counselors on the tape, and the clients. Again they found that the model-reinforcement treatment produced more information-seeking behavior than the controls exhibited. They also concluded that the male subjects (11th graders) responded best when all the roles were filled by males, while the female subjects were influenced more by the male counselors, using either all-male or all-female tapes. The same investigators (Krumboltz, Varenhorst, and Thoresen, 1967) explored the effects of simply observing the videotaped model counseling sessions, and again demonstrated that the treated groups engaged in more of the criterion behavior than either active or inactive control groups. They were not able, however, to demonstrate predicted differences in the effects of model counselors who varied in their attentiveness to the model client and in the degree of prestige attributed to them. In this study, the entire cast, save Krumboltz and Thoresen, was female.

As expressed in the Ryan and Krumboltz (1964) study, interest has continued in the relationship of in-counseling responses to post-counseling criterion behavior. Krumboltz and Schroeder (1964) found no relationships between number of information-seeking statements uttered by clients during counseling and later information-seeking behavior, but when they used a proportion of information-seeking talk to total talk, significant correlations of around .50 were observed. Thoresen and Krumboltz (1967) analyzed the talk from an earlier study, and did find a significant relationship with the number of client information-seeking statements, but none with the proportional index. They also found the criterion behavior related to the number of counselor cue responses and the number of counselor reinforcements of client information-seeking statements.

Though Krumboltz has already achieved more continuity and longevity in his work than most investigators of counseling outcomes have, it is clear that he is at the beginning of his series of investigations, and that is all to the good. His values are clearly stated and well executed in the

research in which he participates. The studies are well designed and carefully reported. There is little hedging in the conclusions, because the dangers of methodological obfuscation are minimized by the care that has been taken. The studies are models for their genre, because Krumboltz and his colleagues have negotiated the difficulties of doing research in the natural setting so expertly.

But perhaps these successes in the field could be augmented by the occasional use of laboratory approximations, especially those that might permit the use of outcome criteria of larger scope than information-seeking behavior. Further concentration on the deliberation-decision criterion, for example, would seem to be productive.

It seems mildly curious that Krumboltz' studies have never included a prestige-suggestion condition along with the treatments based on operant and imitative learning, especially since he is aware of its potential usefulness (Krumboltz, 1966b, p. 16). There is at least some likelihood that the use of the model condition is supplying the same thing, in view of the fact that it seems to work without the accompanying reinforcement (Krumboltz, et al., 1967), and the prestige-suggestion treatment would be vastly more economical.

To summarize the work reported to date, it seems firmly established that counselors can influence certain instrumental activities that may lead to better decision making, especially those having to do with seeking relevant information about imminent choices. That this class of behaviors is important is attested to by the findings of Super et al. (1967, Ch. VII), who report that the possession of certain types of occupational information in the 12th grade has predictive value for career behavior at age 25.

It is further established that, in working with high school students who volunteer for help in educational-vocational planning, the counselor's use of a planned reinforcement strategy during the interview is associated with subsequent increases in the target behavior after counseling and even after as few as two counseling sessions. The value of using models to enhance imitative behavior is established, and preliminary understandings about the relationship of the model to the client are provided.

To date, however, the most valuable contribution of this series of studies lies in their successful execution of well-designed experiments on specific counseling procedures and their sequels, conducted in the natural settings. Control procedures are exemplary, and statistical procedures are simple and appropriate. Most important of all, the details of the treatment conditions are clearly stated, rather than hidden under the label *counseling*, heretofore the most obscure of invisible role behaviors.

Implications for Future Research. In studies of counseling intervention in the service of better decision making we observe two classes, different enough from one another to be recognized as such. The first is the class of studies intended to evaluate services as they exist, yielding information valuable for helping service agencies decide about continuation, termination, or change in their methods for trying to help students. Aside from their local and administrative value, such studies advance the state of knowledge by uncovering, often exhibiting, the difficulties of method and procedure that one encounters when doing research on this topic. Furthermore, knowledge of criterion characteristics is advanced by the invention and frequent use of the various measures with which the investigators seek to operationalize their goals. What seldom benefits from this class of study is the knowledge of specific treatment procedures. Treatments, being ongoing service activities, are likely to be loosely described as counseling, courses in vocations, and the like, without explicit concern for what is being done behind the closed door.

For this type of gain we must look to the other class of studies, those that are experiments conducted to test the effectiveness of specific experiences or treatment procedures. In these studies, the investigators concentrate their interest in designing, defining, and describing that which the client does or that which is done to him and in relating the outcomes to it.

Though this difference is a natural one, it is clearly not a necessary one. "Service as rendered" need not be ambiguous or general or inexplicit. Investigators engaged in service evaluations could, with a little more effort, focus on the exact nature of the service and describe it better than they typically do. Instead of assuming that vocational counseling, for example, is the same process for all counselor-client pairs, it would be possible to find out exactly what each counselor in the treatment condition does and exactly how he does it. Though this would require more time and greater cooperation of the participants, the potential gains far outweigh the costs. Our current lack of understanding about the procedures and consequences of vocational counseling can in large measure be attributed to the fact that researchers—and, worse yet, reviewers—are so inclined to include all manner of treatments in a single category while trying to answer the unanswerable question: does treatment have any effect?

We are presently in possession of greater procedural sophistication, and the argument here is that it should be more widely shared. Especially in the area of promoting decision making, where the treatments are likely to be simple and of short duration, there is little excuse for perpetuating this fault.

Perhaps it is worth repeating the caution that clients involved in educational-vocational counseling have characteristic differences that deserve careful scrutiny and accurate description also. First there are differences in set, or readiness, that can be observed or inferred from the studies cited above. Some clients are willing to make themselves available for treatment because school regulations require it or because the guidance director has committed them to participation in a research project. Others volunteer when solicited in groups because peers are volunteering, because it might be interesting, and because it couldn't hurt. Still others actively seek help with their decision making because they perceive a need for help with an important developmental task. And even these last vary from those who consider their own response repertories inadequate for coping with a decision task to those who are intelligently and planfully using professional assistance as a part of their coping behavior.

More important are the client differences attributable to their developmental statuses at the time of treatment. Obviously, the decision requirements that confront the 9th grader are vastly different than those of the uncommitted college sophomore. Such criteria as accurate self-knowledge and appropriate vocational preferences do not serve all developmental stages in a unitary way, nor are such outcomes necessarily desirable at all stages of educational and vocational development. Clearly, then, the research on counseling practice—and, more important, the practice itself—must be planned in the context of where the client is in his growth process, what decision tasks are unique to his age and grade, and what treatment goals are appropriate at his stage. The hunger for generalization must not be fed by ignoring client developmental differences and summing research results that come from studies whose subjects are facing qualitatively different tasks.

Considering the fact that each investigator who hopes to study the outcomes of counseling must decide whether to proceed with inadequate criteria or switch focus and devote his life to the development of an adequate one, it is somewhat unfair to dwell on the shortcomings of the criterion measures employed. Furthermore, the characteristics of an ideal criterion have been frequently described and are generally understood. What bears repeating is the call for investigators to concentrate somewhat more attention to the metric properties of their criterion measures. Assigning numbers to complex behaviors remains a challenging part of studying counseling outcomes, and when the numbers approach isomorphism with the behaviors, investigators are inclined to consider the work of criterion-building finished. It is to be hoped that investigators will increasingly add another step to the process: that of observing the numbers as numbers. That is to say, once a concept such as accuracy of self-knowledge is scaled, the scalar properties that result deserve attention. Distributions need to be observed and more frequently reported, base rates require better understanding, and error components should cause more concern. In general, the point is that numbers behave too, and in their behavior lies the key to better understanding the behavior of the subjects.

There is one aspect of criterion adequacy that may be unique to studies of educational-vocational decision making, and that is the aspect of durability over time. In recent years investigators have, with reasonable consistency, assessed changes in the target behavior, not only at the end of treatment, but also at some later point in time. Their rationale is that behavioral changes associated with the treatment ought to have some permanence if the treatment is to be judged effective. If the treatment goals are well selected, then a goal achieved ought to be a goal possessed. However, in the enterprise of helping people make better decisions, a somewhat different strategy for connecting immediate to intermediate to ultimate criteria is indicated.

Let us consider first the rather grandiose notion that the brief, cognitively oriented treatments applied to help clients make better decisions can be presumed to have an indelible effect on a client's behavior from the point of treatment forward. Were this the assumption, it would not be appropriate to pursue the client for a long period, applying at intervals the same criterion measure used at the end of counseling. Once having established that, for example, the client was better able to describe his aptitudes and interests and that this improvement did not disappear immediately, there would be little value in submitting him to the same self-estimating task beyond the point in his life when accurate knowledge of these characteristics was important to his development. A more logical approach would be to investigate whether the client, having increased his awareness of his own aptitudes and interests, was able to sustain and amplify his style of knowing himself after counseling. Had the treatment introduced him to a new way of thinking about himself that persisted and grew, or was he merely given important facts about himself that he remembered? Were the notions of observing individual differences and comparing oneself to relevant norm groups retained and used in post-treatment life circumstances, or were they lost immediately?

What is recommended is that concerns for the persistence of treatment effects, given this assumption, be investigated, not by the repeated use of the immediate criterion measures, but rather by the invention of other measures that are logically consequent to the immediate criteria but more appropriate to the client's later life and broader in scope. If, as counseling proponents have frequently suggested, professional assistance not only helps the client with his immediate problem but also teaches problem-solving skills, this new learning and its amplified consequences should be amenable to investigation. Hewer's (1966) use of actual vocational implementation as a logical consequence of posttreatment appropriateness of vocational preference (albeit flawed) provides an excellent example.

A second possible assumption about the kinds of interventions studied in the investigations cited above is that they are truly—and simply—instrumental aids to immediate decision making. This assumption makes it unnecessary to expect and search for changes in client characteristics that persist in time. Instead, what is crucial is the influence of the intervention on the client's appropriate proximal decision. Under this assumption, one would not ask if the client's increase in accuracy of self-knowledge persisted for three to six months or if it generalized to broader areas of self-awareness. What would be important is the extent to which the increase influenced a subsequent curriculum choice. Concern about whether expressed vocational preferences remained appropriate from the end of treatment until a point several years later would be replaced by interest in the relationship of postcounseling preferences to the first necessary act of vocational-choice behavior that followed. The durability of a client's increased tendency to seek information about an imminent decision would be relevant only until that decision was reached.

Within the context of schools and colleges, relevant choice points are easily identified. Furthermore, the difficulties of evaluating choice behavior are no more serious than those of evaluating the appropriateness of intentions. Indeed, actual choice behavior may be easier to assess, since the accomplished act permits the inclusion of the client's internal responses to the consequences of his choice, that is, satisfaction measures, as well as interim measures of his success in the particular role he has elected.

Since educational and vocational development consists of a series of choice points, and since each choice is likely to exert a potent influence on the one that follows it, it is unlikely that short-term interventions could produce effects sufficiently robust to compete

with the choices themselves as major sources of variance in future choice behavior. The implication is that, no matter how much counselors may yearn to bring about lasting changes in their clients, investigators of counseling outcomes are better advised to limit their focus to the short-term considerations of the intervention and its effect on the decision task that follows it. More will be learned about how to help people make better decisions through counseling if the concerns of longer term are left to those who have the interests and the resources for longitudinal research on the developmental process.

STUDIES OF ROLE FUNCTIONING

Whether educational-vocational decisions are actively made by a student or imposed upon him by the characteristics of an educational system, they inevitably lead to a subsequent period of role enactment. Having entered a school, a university, or a particular curriculum, one proceeds to play the required role more or less well. Counseling in educational settings has frequently been directed toward the goal of increasing the effectiveness of such role functioning.

Though effective role functioning can be described along any number of dimensions, the dimensions most frequently chosen by investigators of counseling outcomes are those of general adjustment and academic performance, or grade-getting behavior. These choices are clearly justifiable on the grounds that the absence of serious maladjustments and the achievement of satisfactory grades are two central aspects of the role expectations imposed by educational settings. Furthermore, both are rather easily represented by convenient criterion measures.

Most investigators begin with the assumption that the two dimensions are related, perhaps even causally. Often the causal link is presumed to be that good adjustment leads to satisfactory academic performance, or at least, that improved adjustment will lead to improved performance. This assumption has two important consequences for the material that follows. The first is that the nature of the treatments described in the studies reviewed below is frequently based more heavily on the psychotherapeutic foundations of the counseling activity than on its vocational guidance foundations. The second is that, since many of the investigators employed both adjustment and performance criteria in a single study, the partitioning of sections according to outcome criteria does not serve us well. What follows, then, is divided according to the various educational levels of the clients and corresponds to the previously stated conviction that clients at differing developmental stages represent populations sufficiently different from each other to warrant separate consideration.

Elementary and Secondary School. While some people are uncertain about the wisdom of providing counseling services at the elementary-school level, others argue that psychological assistance with the developmental tasks at such an early age could be influential in reducing the frequency and intensity of difficulties encountered during the adolescent years. United States national policy was aligned with the latter group through the 1964 extension of the National Defense Education Act, which provided financial support for counseling and guidance services in the elementary schools. Since the passage of the 1964 extension, three outcome studies of counseling efforts with 4th-, 5th-, and 6th-grade pupils have appeared.

Kranzler, Mayer, Dyer, and Munger (1966) selected 4th-grade pupils who were rated lowest by their classmates on a sociometric instrument and assigned them randomly to three conditions. Eight subjects received eighteen group counseling sessions plus six individual sessions; four subjects were assigned to a teacher-guidance group, in which the counselors identified them to their teachers as problems and provided the teachers with suggestions for dealing with them; and seven subjects made up the control group. The treatment lasted for five months, after which the first sociometric posttest was administered. Seven months after the termination of the treatment, by which time the subjects had been promoted to the 5th grade, a second posttest was taken. Both of the treated groups showed significant improvement over

the controls at the end of the treatment, but at the follow-up, the counseled group had maintained their advantage, while the teacher-guided group had not. Considering their results unreliable because of the small number of subjects, Mayer, Kranzler, and Matthes (1967) used the same treatment conditions and the same sociometric device on a larger number of 5th and 6th graders and observed no differences in either sociometric status or teacher ratings of social skills. To improve the bet, the subjects in the second study were volunteers who knew about their low sociometric status, as compared to those in the first, who were assigned and naive. For reasons that are not explained, the treatment time for the second study was reduced from 18 sessions to 12 sessions. The combined results are inconclusive and not very encouraging.

Winkler, Teigland, Munger, and Kranzler (1965) identified 121 fourth-grade pupils who were underachievers and divided them among groups that received either individual counseling, group counseling, or reading instruction for 14 half-hour sessions over 11 weeks. None of the groups differed from active or inactive controls in GPA (grade-point average) improvement or in improved adjustment as measured by the California Test of Personality.

In studies with junior high school students, Caplan (1957) managed to increase self-acceptance and decrease school citizenship infractions of 34 nonvolunteer "problem" boys with 10 group-counseling sessions, but their grades remained unaffected. Laxer, Quarter, Isnor, and Kennedy (1967) found no influence on the adjustment of 42 male 9th-grade, nonvolunteer, problem students after 15 group sessions. Dolan (1964) improved attitudes toward reading and reading achievement for five 7th graders with reading problems through individual counseling plus a remedial reading program.

With senior high school students, Gilliland (1968) found that 36 group sessions led to improvements in the Cooperative English Achievement Tests and in vocational maturity for 14 Negro students in a predominantly white high school, but GPAs and self-concepts were not affected. Catron (1966) also found self-acceptance unaffected, except for rate of change, for 46 students who received from 10 to 14 group-counseling sessions.

Two studies of the treatment of underachievement deserve special mention because they are frequently cited in the introductions of the studies of underachievement that followed them. Broedel, Ohlsen, Proff, and Southhard (1960) devoted their attention to 9th-grade students who scored in the upper 10 percent of their class on an intelligence test, but who had achieved grades at the 9th decile or below. Before treatment, they met with the students and then met with the parents to explain what they were about to do. Of 34 students who met the underachievement criterion, 29 participated. The investigators later discovered that several of the students "participated as a consequence of parental pressure (1960, p. 164)," so we can conclude that not all subjects were volunteers. The subjects were assigned randomly to two group-counseling treatment groups (*E*s) and two wait-control groups (*C*s), who were counseled in the same way following the first post-testing. During the treatment period of the *E* groups, the *C* groups received no similar help through the school's regular guidance services. The treatment is only described as 16 sessions of group counseling, but we are told that the authors consider the terms counseling and psychotherapy to describe the same process.

The criteria were academic performance, measured by GPA and an achievement test battery; acceptance of self and others, revealed in a picture-story test; and interpersonal behavior as rated by the students themselves, the counselors, the parents, and the observers.

On the measure of acceptance of self and others, the gain for the *E* groups was significantly greater than that for the *C* groups while they were serving as controls. After treatment, the *C* groups did not improve, compared to their own control conditions. In rated interpersonal behaviors, both the *E*s and the *C*s improved after treatment, according to the ratings of others. That this improvement was maintained was demonstrated in an 18-month follow-up. Self-ratings for both groups, however, remained unchanged. In GPA, neither *E*s nor *C*s improved and, in fact, the GPAs of the *E* groups worsened significantly during the treatment period. No changes in the achievement battery were observed.

In another study, issuing from the same university at approximately the same time, Baymur and Patterson (1960) identified 32 underachieving 11th graders by selecting students whose grade-percentile ranks were 25 points or more below their percentile ranks on the Verbal and Abstract Reasoning tests of the Differential Aptitude Test battery. The nonvolunteer subjects were assigned to individual client-centered counseling (10 to 12 sessions), group client-centered counseling (9 sessions), a one-session "encouragement" group, and an inactive control group. Criteria were a *Q*-sort adjustment measure, a study habits inventory, and GPA in the immediate pretreatment semester and in the semester of treatment. An analysis of variance, the statistical treatment of choice, showed no differences among the groups, but post hoc *t* tests between the two counseled groups and the two groups not counseled, revealed the following:

1. The pre- and postcounseling differences in adjustment favored the two counseled groups, but the difference was due to gains in the group that received individual counseling.

2. No differences were found on the study habits inventory.

3. The counseled groups improved in GPA significantly more than the groups not counseled.

The authors found their results encouraging, despite their recognition that the group treatment did not proceed successfully.

One striking feature of these studies of counseling to improve the role functioning of students below the college level is that the clients were seldom self-initiated applicants for the services they received. Though presumably no student was treated against his expressed will, only Catron's study (1966) employed clients who sought the service being investigated. This is a natural phenomenon in work with students in the lower school years, because they tend to be less well informed about the availability of counseling service, naive to the techniques of seeking professional help, and even less likely to recognize their own need for help. In high school, however, this is less likely to be true, and indeed, many high school students do seek the help of counselors on their own initiative. Still, in all but one of the studies cited in this section, the clients were "identified," "selected," or "assigned."

That this is the state of things is not necessarily a cause for concern, since, to begin with, we are viewing efforts to improve role functioning. Both counselors and investigators are therefore logically drawn to problem students, to those who deviate from some standard of performance. The lament inheres in the fact that the advancement of understanding is seriously hindered by the lack of information about the effects of client motivation on the outcomes studied. Though some outcome studies are criticized for not including no-treatment control groups with a motivation to be helped, the issue may be even more complex when the treated groups are also lacking in such demonstrable motivation.

In these studies, the attempts to influence grade-getting behavior were noticeably unsuccessful. Several focused on academic underachievement as their main target (Baymur and Patterson, 1960; Broedel, et al., 1960; Winkler, et al., 1965), and applied treatments of considerable duration without success, except for Baymur and Patterson's second statistical pass over their data. As we shall see in the sections that follow, the highly appealing and wonderfully convenient criterion, GPA, has provided researchers with an outcome target that has not been consistently easy to hit.

College and University. In contrast to relatively few outcome studies on counseling with younger clients, there has been an impressive number of investigations on the effects of treating college-level students. This is undoubtedly due to the proliferation of college and university counseling centers in the 1950s and 1960s and to the greater likelihood that those who counsel students in college settings will investigate their work and publish their findings. For reasons that will be illustrated later, there seems to be an important qualitative difference between the studies of individual counseling and those of group-treatment procedures. Therefore, the two kinds of studies will be treated separately, despite the fact that there has been no

justification for doing this in previous sections of this chapter.

In general, there seems to be a basis for the conclusion that short-term treatment of students who do not initiate the request for help has little effect on their grade-getting behavior. Richardson (1960) invited 103 engineering freshmen who were likely to be dropped from college, held a one-interview counseling session, and found no subsequent effects in their academic performance. Searles (1962) found no effects from three interviews with superior freshmen who were assigned to counseling. Goodstein and Crites (1961) studied 19 "poor college risk" freshmen who were invited and who received from two to five sessions of educational and vocational counseling that was not associated with their subsequent grade performance. Marx (1959) found that, after from one to four interviews, 58 invited, underachieving, freshmen clients improved their GPAs in the following semester significantly more than similar clients seen in group counseling and more than those who did not respond to the invitation. However, Goodstein (1967) followed the same groups five years later and concluded that the gains did not persist. Moore and Popham (1960) studied the effects of three interviews of student-centered and content-center counseling on nonvolunteer clients and found no improvement in academic performance in the specific course with which they were concerned. Though none of these studies would qualify as the perfectly designed critical test of the effects of short-term counseling with nonvolunteer clients, the consistent absence of evidence of improved academic performance is strongly suggestive, if not surprising.

Several investigators have reported on the effects of counseling volunteer clients compared to nonmotivated control groups. Hill and Grieneeks (1966a) compared 479 students counseled—we do not know how or for how long—with unmotivated controls matched on admission test scores, freshman GPA, and sex. They found no differences in GPA or in graduations rates. The same investigators (Hill and Grieneeks, 1966b) also studied the effects of unspecified counseling on under- and overachievers as compared to unmotivated controls matched in a highly sophisticated manner, and still found no evidence of counseling effects. Richardson (1964) found no differences in grade patterns between 38 students seen 10 times or more in individual counseling and matched controls who were not motivated to seek counseling. The criterion grade patterns studied extended from two semesters prior to two semesters after the treatment semester. Instead of using a matching procedure, Ivey (1962) drew a random sample to serve as a nonmotivated control group and found that counseled students did improve more than the controls in grade-point average.

These last four studies are of the type previously indentified as conducted to evaluate existing services, and each was apparently conducted by analysis of records. As such, they are good examples of their type, but the difficulty of knowing how the counseled students would have performed without counseling is clearly present. The possibility that nonmotivated controls, more properly called comparison groups, represent a different population, exactly because they did not seek help, still exists. Information about the seeking of help as a source of relevant variance is not augmented.

On the topic of motivation, Ewing and Gilbert (1967) have contributed an interesting finding. They invited, and strongly urged the participation of, 255 superior freshmen in a counseling research project. Those who cooperated and were counseled improved their grades slightly more than those who cooperated and were assigned to a no-treatment control group. But the most striking differences occurred between the cooperative subjects, counseled or not, and those who did not cooperate. They concluded that their findings emphasize the importance of acceptance of counseling as a variable in counseling outcome.

One series of studies using general adjustment as an outcome criterion has attracted considerable attention because of its careful design, its generally positive results, and the short duration of the treatment studied. Williams (1962) compared 45 volunteer clients who received educational-vocational counseling consisting of an initial interview, aptitude and interest testing, and a second interview, with a motivated wait-control group of 46 and with a nonclient group of 30. The criterion was adjustment and concept congruence as measured by modifications of the Butler and Haigh (1954) and Dymond (1954) procedures. He found that (a) clients began counseling with lower adjustment levels and less concept congruence than nonclients; (b) clients improved in adjustment and congruence more than the wait controls and nonclients; (c) after counseling, wait controls also improved; and (d) the increases persisted over a period of four months.

This unusual success, considering the short treatment duration, was followed by a partial replication and extension. Williams and Hills (1962) extended the original study to determine if the improved adjustment could be attributed simply to the fact that the client had committed himself to the process of receiving help. One group replicated the first study, using a different counselor. A second group had the second administration of the Q-sort criterion instrument after the testing but before the second interview. Data for the wait controls and the nonclient controls were used from the first study. The group examined before the second interview increased in adjustment somewhat more than the controls, but significantly less than the group examined after the second interview. They concluded that the second interview was demonstrably important to the increase in adjustment. In a third study, Hills and Williams (1965) successfully demonstrated that the improvement in adjustment could not be attributed merely to the client's receipt of test information. Despite the fact that the use of the adjustment Q-sort as an outcome criterion is not without difficulties, the effectiveness of this counseling procedure, amply described by Williams (1962, pp. 19–20) and employed by these investigators, seems firmly demonstrated.

By far the most ambitious effort to study the outcomes of counseling on effective role functioning is that reported by Campbell (1965), who followed the treated and control groups used by Williamson and Bordin (1940) 25 years after they had been counseled. On many counts, Campbell's book is a major contribution to counseling outcome research. First, though he could not possibly describe the counseling as it occurred 25 years earlier, he has mustered considerable evidence on the professional mood of that time, including the writings of persons influential in the kind of counseling service that was being rendered. Secondly, with Herculean effort he managed to locate 99 percent of the 768 original subjects and to secure the cooperation of 90 percent of those who were still living. Thirdly, sensitive to the potential weakness of using a nonmotivated control group, he both reviewed all available evidence on the demonstrable differences between students who do and do not seek counseling and identified a "better" control group composed of students who were counseled subsequent to the termination of the original study.

The results of this complicated study are not easily summarized, but in general he found that the counseled group earned better grades, graduated with a higher frequency, received more academic honors, participated more in college activities during their postcounseling college careers, and achieved slightly more in the complex achievement criteria at the 25-year follow-up. The small differences found in happiness and satisfaction consistently indicated that the counseled groups were less contented with their adult lives.

It is doubtful that Campbell has succeeded in eradicating all reservations about the use of nonmotivated control groups in counseling outcome studies. In fact, both in the section comparing students who do and do not seek counseling (pp. 40–41) and in the report of the follow-up data (p. 70), he ventured the conclusion that the counseled groups demonstrated less emotional stability and contentment with life. However, for those investigators who are forced to use control groups that are without motivation to seek help, Campbell's skillful preoccupations with the problem are required reading.

Though Campbell's is the best-executed study of counseling outcomes after the fact, the most carefully preplanned study of its kind is that reported by Volsky, Magoon, Norman, and Hoyt (1965). For several years before their study was conducted, the investigators worked to develop a theoretical framework appropriate to the kinds of clients seen and the kind of service rendered at the university counseling center in which they were working. Their deliberations led them to hypothesize that counseling should result in decreasing anxiety and defensiveness and increasing problem-

solving abilities for the clients. Instruments for pre- and postcounseling measures of these three variables were carefully developed and validated. Of 100 volunteer clients, 80 were counseled and 20 were denied treatment. After counseling, the groups differed on the criterion behavior only insofar as the no-treatment group improved in problem-solving significantly more than the treated group. However, in three-, five-, and seven-year follow-up studies, the counseled students were shown to do significantly better in GPA and in graduation rate, presumably target behaviors that were important to the clients and counselors if not to the investigators.

To some degree, all the research on individual counseling suffers from the limitations of a set of assumptions that can be expressed as follows:

1. All clients within a given study who seek and/or receive counseling are more or less alike.
2. All counseling provided within a specified treatment condition of a given study is essentially the same thing.
3. The outcome criteria used in a given study are equally appropriate for all clients treated in a similar way.

Though few investigators would openly subscribe to assumptions like these, most of them have tacitly accepted them in employing the relatively standard research procedures that applied psychological specialties have inherited from their experimental ancestors.

Two important suggestions for improving this condition have been relatively unheeded. The first is Ford's (1959) suggestion that treatment effects will vary from client to client and "therefore, it is obviously a mistake to assume that a given variable should change in the same direction for all clients" (1959, p. 56). Within the realm of studies on counseling in educational settings, only Ewing (1964) attempted to follow Ford's advice, and his study provides a useful beginning toward a new investigative style.

The second important suggestion grows from Bergin's (1963) discovery that, at least in some psychotherapy studies, some clients improve but others worsen, cancelling effects when means on criterion measures are examined. Richardson (1964), Ivey (1962), and Ewing and Gilbert (1967) did take careful second looks at their treated groups and learned important things in the process. However, the practice of designing a study with the original intention of observing the treated group's variation on the outcome measure, rather than just its central tendency, remains rare.

It is encouraging that many of the recent investigations of the effects of group counseling on underachieving college students give evidence of the investigators' sensitivity to the inadequacy of the assumptions listed above. For example, Speilberger, Weitz, and Denny (1962) invited 112 highly anxious freshmen men to participate in a group counseling program. The 56 who responded were divided into matched experimental and motivated control groups. After group counseling of as much as 11 sessions, the counseled group improved significantly more than the group without treatment. To increase their confidence in the hypothesis that the counseling was instrumental to the improvement, they divided the counseled group in to High Attenders, that is, those who had attended 8 to 11 sessions; Middle Attenders, 6 to 7 sessions; and Low Attenders, 2 to 5 sessions. By a wide margin, the grade improvement of the High Attenders exceeded the other groups. Still not content, they matched the High Attenders with controls of similar MMPI profiles and still found robust differences. If the study has a flaw, it lies in the timing of the criterion measure, which was the difference between midterm (unofficial, advisory) grade reports and final grades in the semester of treatment. Nevertheless, they have successfully demonstrated that studies need not proceed from the assumptions that all the clients are alike and that all clients get the same treatment.

The matter of differences within the treatment condition was also given careful scrutiny by Dickenson and Truax (1966) in their study of underachieving college freshmen. Forty-eight students who responded to an invitation were randomly divided into treatment and control groups and given 24 sessions of group counseling over a period of 12 weeks. When the various measures of academic performance from pre- to postcounseling were compared, the counseled group improved significantly more. Dickenson and Truax also rated the recordings of the treatment sessions on the presence of accurate empathy, unconditional positive regard, and therapist genuiness. They found that those students whose group counseling was characterized by high levels of these conditions improved more than either the controls or those who received only moderate levels. The investigators' use of five highly correlated measures of academic improvement seems questionable—and turned out to be unnecessary—but the results are nonetheless valuable in both substantive and methodological ways.

Thelen and Harris (1968) showed recognition for the fact that all clients are not alike, in their study of freshmen underachievers. They sent letters to 127 students of this type whose grades were low and deviating downward from their predicted GPAs. From the responses they created groups of students who (1) took the 16PF and a self-ideal rating scale and were assigned to group counseling for a mean of 7.7 sessions; (2) took the tests but were denied counseling; or (3) took the tests but refused counseling. In the semester following treatment, the treated group improved more than the motivated controls, but not more than the "testing only" group. An examination of the relationship between GPA improvement and personality characteristics produced the conclusion that among the treated group, those highest in self-acceptance and in certain other positive personality traits improved the most. Furthermore, there were hints that the same personality characteristics bore relationships to improvement in the opposite direction for the two groups who did not receive treatment. The yield does not come up to useful advice on who should and who should not receive counseling, but the potential is suggested.

Three reports on the same treatment study (Chestnut, 1965; Gilbreath, 1967a, 1967b) have led to an interesting foretaste of the prospect of providing different kinds of underachievers with different kinds of treatments. From 683 male underachieving freshmen and sophomores who were sent invitations, 96 responded and 81 attended enough sessions of group counseling to be included in the study. Twenty-two students were assigned to group counseling described as leader-structured, in which the counselors initiated discussions on topics presumably related to underachievement. Twenty-six received group-structured counseling in which the students chose the topics, set the pace, and determined the degree of digression permitted, despite the presence of the counselor, who was described as an "active participant." Client response to a questionnaire established that the two types of treatment were indeed different on the intended dimension. Both treatments were offered in eight sessions of from 90 to 120 minutes in length. Thirty-three students were assigned to a motivated control group.

Chestnut (1965) compared the groups on a study-habits inventory, a need-achievement measure, and GPA before and after counseling, and found no differences. He did, however, detect differences in the rate of change in GPA and, from this, concluded that the leader-structured treatment was more effective. Gilbreath (1967b) later reported that the clients in the leader-structured treatment showed higher postcounseling ego strength than the controls, and the clients in the group-structured condition did not. He also demonstrated that the differences in rates of change of GPA persisted for three months beyond the observation of the first report, and that the leader-structured condition continued to produce the best results. The acceptability of ignoring the nonsignificant analysis of variance results and concluding effectiveness of the treatment on the basis of different rates of change is certainly open to question. The meaning of such a maneuver is made especially difficult to understand by the absence, from all three reports, of tables of means. Nevertheless, in the third attack on the data, Gilbreath (1967a) uncovered a finding of considerable interest.

Using the scores and the second-order factors from the Stern Activities Index and the GPAs, he concluded that academic improvement resulted when clients with high dependency needs were treated in leader-structured, high-authority groups and when clients with high autonomy needs were treated in group-structured, low-authority groups. As a guide for differential treatment of underachievers of differing personality types, the finding obviously needs further verification. But given the interest in underachievement and the inconsistent nature of successful treatment, it obviously deserves it.

Perhaps the strongest exhortation for differential diagnosis and differential treatment of the college underachiever is that advanced by Roth, who developed a set of constructs about the nature of the underachiever (Roth and Meyersburg, 1963) and a set of treatment procedures that derive directly from these constructs (Roth, Mauksch, and Peiser, 1967, pp. 395–396). The argument consists in the belief that there exists a *nonachievement syndrome* with an underlying set of dynamics that needs to be treated in a special way. To test the validity of the argument, Roth et al. (1967) studied 52 male students who were assumed to be underachievers because they were earning grades below the acceptable minimum. The students were informed by their academic deans that they would be dropped from the college unless they enrolled in a seminar in study habits, which was in fact, the group-counseling program. The groups met for two one-hour periods per week for an entire semester and received the counseling, which is well described. Attendance was mandatory. At the end of the treatment semester, their grades were compared with a matched group of probationary students who were neither dropped nor coerced into the counseling program. In the semester following the counseling, the treated group improved significantly more than the comparison group, and there was some evidence to indicate that the gain persisted for at least one additional semester.

The study has many flaws, not the least of which are the coercion to treatment and the lack of motivated controls. It is puzzling that the rhetoric so strongly urged considerations of homogeneity among clients and flexibility in treatment procedures while, on the other hand, the execution assumed that all of the students with low grades were examples of the nonachievement syndrome and treated them all with the same technique. Yet the technique did seem to work and its logic seems sound. At a future date someone may well profit from Roth's beginning by carefully identifying volunteer client underachievers who fit the syndrome and applying the prescribed treatment to them.

Implications for Future Research. One hardly needs to be reminded that counseling for adequate role functioning within the educational setting exists in a context different from that of psychotherapy in a private office or a walk-in clinic. In the former, the service and the counselors are necessarily perceived as a part of the social system in which the client's role enactment unfolds and is judged. Counselors may, and probably often do, succeed in disassociating themselves from the agents who judge the adequacy of client's role behavior, that is, grade-giving teachers, report-sending administrators and suspension-dispensing deans. Still, the fact that the counselor who offers help and the system that threatens disapprobation are in some way connected must necessarily produce a psychological climate for seeking and/or receiving help that is different from that of self-initiated applicant-client psychotherapy. Based on this assertion, some future studies of counseling for better role functioning might well be concentrated on the problem of client motivation.

Included in the studies reviewed above are clients who have been assigned, coerced, and invited to counseling, as well as those who have voluntarily sought it. Of these, no study in which clients have been assigned resulted in improved academic performance, except for that of Marx (1959), whose positive effects did not persist (Goodstein, 1967). The clients studied by Roth et al. (1967), who had to choose between being counseled or being dropped from college, did show improvement, but the comparison group was not clearly comparable in motivation. On adjustment criteria, assigned clients did frequently improve and, though these criteria were mostly reactive measures subject to various sources of bias, the improvements cannot be completely dismissed. The studies using clients who accepted invitations to counseling and who voluntarily sought it sum to a much higher frequency of success, although some of them also failed to produce better grade-getting behavior. Clearly, one cannot conclude from this accumulation of apples and oranges that invited and voluntary clients are helped, while assigned and coerced ones are not. The differences do, however, suggest that the manner in which the counselor-client contact is initiated deserves further study. What is obviously needed is a study in which all relevant conditions except the manner of initiating contact are controlled.

It is a source of encouragement that within the last decade investigators of counseling outcomes have fully accepted the need for using control groups to add meaning to the observed effects of treatment. Furthermore, the process of matching treated and nontreated groups on critical control variables such as age, sex, ability, class, and the like has been, in the main, well executed. A few investigators have taken precautions against the confounding of Hawthorne and placebo effects, and others have been diligent enough to follow the progress of groups composed of potential clients who refused treatment or those who began but did not continue for a sufficiently long period. Yet despite the acceptance of the need for control groups and the hints of increasing sophistication about their nature, the troublesome problem of identifying no-treatment controls with motivation to be helped continues to detract from the achievement of a more complete understanding of counseling outcomes.

As has been mentioned above, the issue of motivated controls interacts with concerns about the motivation of the treated groups. When clients are assigned to counseling and a similar group is merely observed on the criterion behaviors, the motivational equivalence of the two groups is unknown and perhaps unknowable. When nonmotivated controls are given pretests and posttests, a further confounding element is introduced.

At the other extreme, when clients are clearly volunteers and controls are clearly not, the meaning of the comparisons is equally enigmatic. For one thing, it is difficult to be assured that the no-treatment group has not received psychological help somewhere beyond the view of the investigator, as Bergin (1963) has warned and Le May and Christensen (1968) have demonstrated. For another, the possibility exists that control subjects who do not seek counseling are expressly motivated not to seek it, and the course of that which they are experiencing represents a further source of unknown variance. Finally, and most important, it is the frequently expressed belief that the acts of perceiving the need for and seeking counseling are evidence that the client is of a different nature from his opposite number in the nonmotivated control group, no matter how well they have been matched on other characteristics.

Clients and controls with equal motivation have been managed in two classes of the studies cited in this section. One is the type of study in which the clients are volunteers who are treated and the controls are volunteers who are denied treatment (for example, Williams, 1962; Volsky et al., 1965). This procedure can be easily adopted if the treatment duration is short and the time of the postcounseling observations is close to the end of treatment. If both conditions obtain, the wait-control procedure serves well. When these conditions do not obtain, the problem is more serious because, with few exceptions, counseling services do not find it easy to jeopardize their status with students and with administrators by turning away self-initiated help-seekers.

There does seem to be less reluctance to deny treatment to potential clients who have been invited to come for help, as seen in the second class of studies with clients and controls of equal motivation. Several investigators (for example, Chestnut, 1965; Dickenson and Truax, 1966; Ewing and Gilbert, 1967; Spielberger, et al., 1962) have employed this procedure with success, and in recent years it has become the preferred method of selecting subjects for outcome studies. Without belaboring the point, it should be remembered by investigators that responding to an invitation for counseling is not the same complex of acts as perceiving the need for help, finding out about the resources available, and propelling oneself to the reception desk. Whether these two modes of entry into treatment are different enough to influence the course and the consequence of counseling is an empirical question.

It is clear from the studies in this section that the academic underachiever is a likely candidate for selection as a subject in studies of counseling outcome. As a candidate for counseling he has, or is presumed to have, many qualifying characteristics: a behavior deficit in a salient area of role expectation; an imminent crisis of failure; a professed will to change; and a conflict. As a research subject he is similarly well equipped: he is available and responsive to threat; he has taken an academic aptitude test; and his criterion behavior is inexorably rated, carefully recorded, and easily retrieved. Though

investigators have plenty to do, clerks collect the data.

On the general topic of underachievement, a great deal has been written (for example, Kornrich, 1965; Farquhar, 1963; Taylor, 1964; Thorndike, 1963), and to review it here would be inefficient. It is strongly suggested, however, that anyone who selects underachievement as an object of investigative concern familiarize himself with the ample literature on this condition.

Of special relevance to future research on outcomes of counseling with underachievers is the matter of identifying the underachiever. The literature contains a wide variety of procedures for nominating underachievers, and sometimes the procedures are not even specified. In the sample of studies reviewed above, though all procedures are specified, there is considerable variation. To illustrate this variation, a few examples are presented below.

1. Winkler et al. (1965) used the correlation between a verbal IQ and GPA to compute a regression equation that permitted them to establish a predicted GPA for each student. Students whose actual GPAs were more than .8 of the standard error of estimate below the predicted GPA were selected. From a population of 700 they identified 121 underachievers.

2. Chestnut (1965) considered as an underachiever any freshman or sophomore student with a College Qualification Test score at the 50th percentile or higher and with a GPA of 2.00 (A = 4, B = 3, and so forth) or lower. The number so identified was 683, but the size of the original population was not reported.

3. Dickenson and Truax (1966) identified 109 underachieving freshman students whose first semester GPAs fell within the 1.49–2.00 range and whose predicted GPAs were 2.20 or higher.

4. Roth et al. (1967) assumed that any student at the Illinois Institute of Technology who did not achieve satisfactory grades was an underachiever, because of IIT's high admission standards. The size of the population and the number of underachievers identified are not reported.

There can be little doubt that the clients identified in these various ways had common characteristics. On the other hand, it would be irresponsible to suggest that the client population resulting from the application of one of these procedures was equal to that resulting from the use of another, even ignoring their differences on dimensions other than academic performance.

Farquhar and Payne (1964) have analyzed several different methods for identifying under-achievers and have concluded that the differing methods result in the selection of strikingly different samples. From their analysis they have derived a set of criteria for an ideal selection technique (1964, p. 876) that is a regression procedure and that includes, among others, recommendations for selecting students from the full range of ability, for building the selection model separately for the two sexes, and for controling regression effects. The selection procedure they developed to meet their own criteria is a sound one, and investigators who are truly interested in an orderly advance in knowledge about the effects of counseling an academic underachievement would be well advised to use it.

Perhaps a word is in order about the issue of timing with regard to studies of counseling intended to improve academic performance among college students. Many, but not all, such studies are conducted on client samples that are composed wholly or largely of freshmen. A common practice is to observe their first-term grades, counsel them during the second term, and then compare the grades earned in the second term with those from the first. The problem arises in the form of evidence that grades tend to rise after the first semester for all students, treated or not. De Sena (1964) argued, without evidence, that there is a period of adjustment that students must negotiate at the beginning of their college careers. Ofman (1964) considered the problem serious enough to include among his comparison groups a "base-line control" of students selected at random from the university where he was working. He observed the grades for eight semesters for groups that included counseled, motivated controls, wait controls, dropouts from counseling, and base-line controls. That his treatment worked was evident, but more interesting were the four-year grade patterns of these students with their various connections, and lack of connections, to the treatment process. His

respect for the importance of counseling effects over time is commended to the attention of future investigators.

Though there remains enough room for improvement to challenge researchers for some time to come, it can be concluded that research on the counseling process is growing toward greater adequacy. No longer can critics claim that studies of counseling employ barely trained, inexperienced counselors in their treatments. More studies of treatments of longer duration are appearing. The control group, as pointed out above, has become commonplace. Follow-up procedures of longer term are being used. Most important, the methodologically naive, totally inconclusive study that was the norm ten years ago is now hard to find.

As can be inferred from earlier remarks, the view of this writer is that continued improvement will depend on investigators' willingness and ingenuity in following some promising leads in two directions. The first is the style of investigation that goes beyond the assumption that counseling is professionally skillful benevolence, and pursues with rigor the differing things that occur within the consulting room. Among the studies reviewed above, those of Dickenson and Truax (1966) and Gilbreath (1967a) are promising beginnings. Perhaps the time has finally arrived for the process-outcome research style that Pepinsky and Pepinsky (1954, pp. 268–272) prescribed so long ago. The second direction is the derivative of Ford's (1959) idea that outcome criteria ought to be used in sufficient variety to reflect the diverse goals of separate client-counselor pairs, even though these pairs may exist within the same treatment condition. So far, only Ewing (1964) has ventured in this direction, but it is to be hoped that others will follow.

With progress in these two directions, we may someday arrive at a state of knowledge in which we know, to use Patterson's words, "what leads to what, [enabling] investigators to select methods or approaches that will lead to desired criteria or outcomes" (1963b, p. 222).

IMPLICATIONS FOR PRACTICE

While one might permit himself a qualified optimism about what yesterday's research on counseling outcomes has to say to today's researchers, it would be excessively sanguine to claim that this research provides an abundance of important directional messages for today's practitioners. Fortunately, there are few who expect that it will. It is generally well accepted that the lumbering pace that characterizes the progress of outcome research is no match for the fleet, multi-directional, undisciplined, often imaginative processes of change that counseling practitioners pursue. The researcher improves his techniques, awaits his long-term follow-up data, and endures the publication lag so he can speak with authority about the effects of relatively traditional treatment methods on well-socialized, middle-class, upward-striving, research-cooperating students. Meanwhile, the practitioner is fiddling with his videotape equipment, programming his computer, trying out confrontation groups, meddling in environmental manipulation, and scanning the news from Esalen in search of ways of becoming available and helpful to the "normal" student of today. And that "normal" student may be using consciousness-expanding drugs or threatening to burn the counseling center or, at the least, expecting to help decide whether there should be a counseling service.

This is the timely predicament, but it is unlikely that the situation has ever been seriously different. Counseling as a professional activity has never advanced behind a well-established body of scientific evidence that permitted its practitioners to select from methods and procedures whose differences in efficacy had been previously demonstrated. In fact, the flow of influence has been in the opposite direction, with the research following where the practice has led. Furthermore, there is no compelling reason to believe that the scientific aspect of counseling, tethered to its impedimenta of logical positivism, will ever catch up to and lead the more liberated artistic aspect. In this regard, the profession is obviously not unique.

To what use, then, can practitioners put the carefully documented experience of the researchers? There are two answers, and though they are highly related, they will be considered separately.

Treatment Procedures. One thing the studies of counseling outcomes provide for the practitioner is an array of treatment procedures of tentatively established worth. Though most of the procedures that compose this array have not been supported either by replications of tenability or by replications of generality,[3] they nevertheless represent procedures that have been tried under controlled conditions. Not only have they been tried, but also the consequences of the trials have been observed and reported. The resulting judgments about efficacy are limited by the samples used and by the idiosyncracies of the practitioners who applied the procedures, but these limitations detract from the worth of a procedure only insofar as they render it tentative. Any treatment procedure held in this condition of tentative worth has two characteristics of interest to practitioners: (1) it is available for reuse and for further trial, and (2) there is a favorable probability that it is not, under all circumstances, worthless. The practitioner is thereby aided in his search for and invention of procedures of value to his immediate problem situation.

From the studies reviewed above, a number of treatment procedures can be considered to be in this condition. Some of these are listed below as examples.

1. In an earlier part of this chapter, a procedure for interpreting test results was described that included the use of a blank profile for both obtaining the student's self-estimates and reporting his actual test results to him; eliciting his reactions to the two resulting profiles; and responding to the resulting feelings. The convergence of evidence from studies by Holmes (1964), Lister and Ohlsen (1965), and Wright (1963) suggests that this procedure leads to greater accuracy of self-knowledge, which tends to persist beyond the end of the treatment. The latter two studies supported the use of this procedure in groups.

2. Pilato (1968) found that 11th graders altered their vocational preferences to a more realistic level after the following procedure. He obtained self-estimates on intelligence and interest from the students, then provided them with a comparison of their estimates and their

---

[3] I am indebted to Robert Rosenthal (1969) for these ideas.

test results on the same profile sheet. He then taught them an occupational-classification structure, and related the structure to intelligence and interest. The treatment procedure, administered in classroom groups, did not affect the appropriateness of their choices as they related to interests, but did improve their choices as they related to intelligence. Pilato hypothesized that a memory factor influenced the differences between the subjects' subsequent use of intelligence (1 score) and of interests (10 scores).

3. In a 20-minute interview, Ryan and Krumboltz (1964) had counselors use 2 minutes to introduce the topic of educational and vocational plans; 6 minutes for giving cues without consciously giving reinforcement; 6 minutes for giving cues and reinforcing (with "good," "fine," "that's a good idea," and the like) client statements of decision responses; 6 minutes for an extinction period; and 3 minutes for closing. Decision responses were defined as client statements indicating a decision on a course of action, a goal selected, or an alternative eliminated. The procedure increased decision responses to a story-completion task given immediately after the close of the interview.

4. Krumboltz and Thoresen (1964) employed procedure in which the counselors introduced the topic of information seeking, gave frequent cues, and verbally reinforced client statements of an information-seeking nature during two interviews. In another condition, they began the first interview with an audiotape of a client talking with a counselor, who reinforced the model client's information-seeking statements. The 15-minute tape was followed by the counselor giving cues and reinforcing, as in the first condition. Second interviews were identical in both conditions, and both conditions were used in individual and group sessions. The clients subsequently increased their actual information-seeking behavior.

5. Williams (1962) used a relatively standard interview-testing-interview sequence to increase adjustment and concept congruence of his clients. Pretests were given, then clients were seen individually to discuss their concerns about indecision over educational and vocational plans; the discussion of personal-social problems was uncommon during these interviews. The first interview terminated with a discussion

of kinds of test information that might be helpful, and ability and interest tests were given in the two-to-four week period that followed. A second interview was then held, in which the test results were discussed and alternative plans were considered, but not worked out in great detail. The counselor described himself as "moderately nondirective." The posttest was administered within a day or two following termination. Adjustment scores and concept congruence increased, and a second counselor produced similar results in a replication (Williams and Hills, 1962).

6. Dickenson and Truax (1966) trained therapists to offer high levels of accurate empathy, unconditional positive regard, and therapist genuineness "with an integrated didactic and experiential approach." Clients were treated in groups of eight, for 24 one-hour sessions. The groups in which the therapist actually achieved high levels of these conditions improved their academic performance.

7 (a). The studies of Chestnut (1965) and Gilbreath (1967a, 1967b) used two procedures. In one, the counselor used eight group sessions to present a series of topics relevant to the dynamics of underachievement, each with a realistic example; elicited reactions to the topics; and "actively related personality variables to achievement." The topics were academic underachievement, goals and purposes, dependence-independence, self-feelings, expression of anger and hostility, and impulses and controls. Students with high dependency needs improved most in academic performance after this treatment.

7 (b). The second treatment, also carried out in eight sessions, relied heavily on material originating from the group, and the process of the sessions was determined by the groups. Though it was affectively oriented, it was described as less uncovering and less integrating than the first procedure. Students with high autonomy needs profited most from this treatment.

Obviously, there are other procedures included in these studies that can be considered in a condition of tentative worth, but these examples will serve to illustrate the point. Obviously excluded from this list is professionally competent counseling, tailored to the needs of the individual client, varying in duration according to those needs, and following in varying degrees the tenets of a particular theory. The evidence about such activities also suggests that they be regarded as having tentatively established worth, but while they are clearly treatment, they are not considered treatment procedures in the context of the present discussion.

Investigative Styles. The second, and more important, thing that outcomes studies provide for the practitioner is an array of investigative styles to assist him in implementing his intentions to become an inquiring practitioner. The aspiration to be an inquiring practitioner is one that is purposefully initiated in training programs, fostered by professional organizations, promoted in individual work settings, and generally shared among people who counsel. In fact, much of the research on counseling practice is produced by investigators who are themselves practitioners. Yet legions of counselors working at all educational levels fail to realize this aspiration.

The reasons for this failure are several, and are not particularly relevant to the present discussion. What is relevant is that the obvious lack of knowledge about counseling practice and its sequels is a salient influence on the practitioner's sense of competence, confidence, and general well-being. Though there is no reason to expect a large percentage of practitioners to contribute to the advance of basic knowledge about counseling, there is good reason to expect each practitioner to maintain an active search for better ways of understanding that which he does. Though understanding increases by way of several epistemological avenues, the vehicle of controlled, quantitative research is the means of travel most generally available and most widely endorsed.

Several styles for helping the practitioner investigate his own work are exhibited in the studies reviewed in this chapter. As has been noted earlier, many of these studies are the products of attempts to evaluate the counseling services as they were being rendered. Not all of the procedures employed in them are exemplary, but their use has been explored and, where appropriate, their faults have been pointed out. Specific issues, such as what kinds of outcome criteria should be used, have been engaged by the investigators, and despite the absence of complete satisfaction with their success, the practitioner who intends to inquire has an armamentarium at his disposal. Specific data-collection devices, such as searching academic records, have been demonstrated, and their strengths and weaknesses have been exposed.

If a practitioner is an imaginative and talented investigator who enjoys the challenge of converting conceptual schemes into empirical schemes, inquiring practice will surely result. If he is not, inquiry need not be blocked. The procedures of others are available and in the public domain. No practitioner can persuasively argue that he is not equipped to learn more and better about the effects of his life's work.

REFERENCES

Apostal, R. A. Two methods of evaluating vocational counseling. *Journal of Counseling Psychology*, 1960, **7**, 171–175.

Baymur, F. B., and Patterson, C. H. A comparison of three methods of assisting underachieving high school students. *Journal of Counseling Psychology*, 1960, **7**, 83–89.

Berdie, R. F. Changes in self-ratings as a method of evaluating counseling. *Journal of Counseling Psychology*, 1954, **1**, 49–54.

Bergin, A. E. The effects of psychotherapy: Negative results revisited. *Journal of Counseling Psychology*, 1963, **10**, 244–250.

Bidwell, G. P. Ego strength, self-knowledge, and vocational planning of schizophrenics. *Journal of Counseling Psychology*, 1969, **16**, 45–49.

Biersdorf, K. R. The effectiveness of two group vocational guidance treatments. Unpublished doctoral dissertation, University of Maryland, 1958.

Bilovsky, D., McMasters, W., Schorr, J. E., and Singer, S. L. Individual and group counseling. *Personnel and Guidance Journal*, 1953, **31**, 363–365.

Broedel, J., Ohlsen, M., Proff, F., and Southard, C. The effects of group counseling on gifted underachieving adolescents. *Journal of Counseling Psychology*. 1960, **7**, 163–170.

Butler, J. M., and Haigh, G. V. Changes in relation between self-concepts and ideal concepts consequent upon client-centered counseling. In C. R. Rogers and R. F. Dymond (Eds.), *Psychotherapy and personality change*. Chicago: University of Chicago Press, 1954. Pp. 76–84.

Calia, V. F. Vocational guidance: After the fall. *Personnel and Guidance Journal*, 1966, **45**, 320–327.

Campbell, D. P. *The results of counseling: Twenty-five years later*. Philadelphia: Saunders, 1965.

Caplan, S. W. The effect of group counseling on junior high school boys' concepts of themselves in school. *Journal of Counseling Psychology*, 1957, **4**, 124–128.

Catron, D. W. Educational-vocational group counseling: The effects on perception of self and others. *Journal of Counseling Psychology*, 1966, **13**, 202–207.

Chestnut, W. J. The effects of structured and unstructured group counseling on male college students' underachievement. *Journal of Counseling Psychology*, 1965, **12**, 388–394.

Cooley, W. W., and Lohnes, P. R. *Predicting development in young adults*. Interim Report 5 to the U.S. Office of Education, Cooperative Research Project No. 3051. Palo Alto: Project TALENT Office, American Institutes for Research and University of Pittsburgh, 1968.

DeSena, P. A. The role of consistency in identifying characteristics of three levels of achievement. *Personnel and Guidance Journal*, 1964, **43**, 145–149.

Dickenson, W. A., and Truax, C. B. Group counseling with college underachievers. *Personnel and Guidance Journal*, 1966, **45**, 243–247.

Dolan, G. K. Effects of individual counseling on selected test scores for delayed readers. *Personnel and Guidance Journal*, 1964, **42**, 914–919.

Dressel, P. L., Pepinsky, H. B., and Shoben, E. J., Jr. Research in counseling: A symposium. *Personnel and Guidance Journal*, 1953, **31**, 284–290.

Dymond, R. F. Adjustment changes over therapy from self-sorts. In C. R. Rogers and R. F. Dymond (Eds.), *Psychotherapy and personality change*. Chicago: University of Chicago Press, 1954. Pp. 76–84.

Ewing, T. N. Changes during counseling appropriate to the client's initial problem. *Journal of Counseling Psychology*, 1964, **11**, 146–150.

Ewing, T. N., and Gilbert, W. M. Controlled study of the effects of counseling on the scholastic achievements of students of superior ability. *Journal of Counseling Psychology*, 1967, **14**, 235–239.

Farquhar, W. W. *Motivation factors related to academic achievement*. Cooperative Research Project 846. East Lansing: Office of Research and Publications, College of Education, Michigan State University, 1963.

Farquhar, W. W., and Payne, D. A. A classification and comparison of techniques used in selecting over- and under-achievers. *Personnel and Guidance Journal*, 1964, **42**, 874–884.

Ford, D. H. Research approaches to psychotherapy. *Journal of Counseling Psychology*, 1959, **6**, 55–60.

Gilbert, W. M., and Ewing, T. N. A comparison of programmed and face to face counseling. Urbana: Student Counseling Service and Department of Psychology, University of Illinois. (Mimeo)

Gilbreath, S. H. Group counseling, dependence, and college male underachievement. *Journal of Counseling Psychology*, 1967, **14**, 449–453. (a)

Gilbreath, S. H. Group counseling with male underachieving college volunteers. *Personnel and Guidance Journal*, 1967, **45**, 469–476. (b)

Gilliland, B. E. Small group counseling with Negro adolescents in a public high school. *Journal of Counseling Psychology*, 1968, **15**, 147–152.

Goldman, L. *Using tests in counseling*. New York: Appleton-Century-Crofts, 1961.

Goldman, L. Another log. *American Psychologist*, 1964, **19**, 418–419.

Gonyea, G. G. Appropriateness-of-vocational-choice as a criterion of counseling outcome. *Journal of Counseling Psychology*, 1962, **9**, 213–219.

Gonyea, G. G. Appropriateness-of-vocational-choice of counseled and uncounseled college students. *Journal of Counseling Psychology*, 1963, **10**, 269–275.

Goodstein, L. D. Five-year follow-up of counseling effectiveness with probationary college students. *Journal of Counseling Psychology*, 1967, **14**, 436–439.

Goodstein, L., and Crites, J. O. Brief counseling with poor college risks. *Journal of Counseling Psychology*, 1961, **8**, 318–321.

Hahn, M. E. Conceptual trends in counseling. *Personnel and Guidance Journal*, 1953, **31**, 231–235.

Hewer, V. H. Group counseling, individual counseling, and a college class in vocations. *Personnel and Guidance Journal*, 1959, **37**, 660–665.

Hewer, V. H. Evaluation of a criterion: Realism of vocational choice. *Journal of Counseling Psychology*, 1966, **13**, 289–294.

Hill, A. H., and Grieneeks, L. Criteria in the evaluation of educational and vocational counseling in college. *Journal of Counseling Psychology*, 1966, **13**, 198–201. (a)

Hill, A. H., and Grieneeks, L. An evaluation of academic counseling of under- and over-achievers. *Journal of Counseling Psychology*, 1966, **13**, 325–328. (b)

Hills, D. A., and Williams, J. E. Effects of test information upon self-evaluation in brief educational-vocational counseling. *Journal of Counseling Psychology*, 1965, **12**, 275–281.

Holmes, J. E. The presentation of test information to college freshmen. *Journal of Counseling Psychology*, 1964, **11**, 54–58.

Hoyt, D. P. An evaluation of group and individual programs in vocational guidance. *Journal of Applied Psychology*, 1955, **39**, 26–30.

Hutson, P. W., and Webster, A. D. An experiment in the educational and vocational guidance of tenth-grade pupils. *Educational and Psychological Measurement*, 1943, **3**, 3–21.

Ivey, A. E. The academic performance of students counseled at a university counseling service. *Journal of Counseling Psychology*. 1962, **9**, 347–352.

Jordaan, J. P., and Myers, R. A. Individual differences in the world of work. In J. R. Davitz and S. Ball (Eds.), *Psychology of the educational process*. New York: McGraw-Hill, 1970.

Kornrich, M. *Underachievement*. Springfield, Ill.: Charles C. Thomas, 1965.

Kranzler, G. D., Mayer, G. R., Dyer, C. O., and Munger, P. F. Counseling with elementary school children: An experimental study. *Personnel and Guidance Journal*, 1966, **44**, 944–949.

Krumboltz, J. D. Behavioral goals for counseling. *Journal of Counseling Psychology*, 1966, **13**, 153–159. (a)

Krumboltz, J. D. Promoting adaptive behavior: New answers to familiar questions. In J. D. Krumboltz (Ed.), *Revolution in Counseling*. New York: Houghton Mifflin, 1966. (b)

Krumboltz, J. D., and Schroeder, W. W. Promoting career planning through reinforcement. *Personnel and Guidance Journal*, 1965, **44**, 19–25.

Krumboltz, J. D., and Thoresen, C. E. The effect of behavioral counseling in group and individual settings on information-seeking behavior. *Journal of Counseling Psychology*, 1964, **11**, 324–333.

Krumboltz, J. D., Varenhorst, B. B., and Thoresen, C. E. Non-verbal factors in the effectiveness of models in counseling. *Journal of Counseling Psychology*, 1967, **14**, 412–418.

Laxer, R. M., Quarter, J. J., Isnor, C., and Kennedy, D. R. Counseling small groups of behavior problem students in junior high schools. *Journal of Counseling Psychology*, 1967, **14**, 454–457.

LeMay, M. L., and Christensen, O. C., Jr. The uncontrollable nature of control groups. *Journal of Counseling Psychology*, 1968, **15**, 63–67.

Lister, J. L., and Ohlsen, M. M. The improvement of self-understanding through test interpretation. *Personnel and Guidance Journal*, 1965, **43**, 804–810.

Margolis, V. H. Kuder-Strong discrepancy in relation to conflict and congruence of vocational preference. Unpublished doctoral dissertation, Columbia University, 1967.

Marx, G. L. A comparison of the effectiveness of two methods of counseling with academic underachievers. Unpublished doctoral dissertation, University of Iowa, 1959.

Mayer, G. R., Kranzler, G. D., and Matthes, W. A. Elementary school counseling and peer relations. *Personnel and Guidance Journal*, 1967, **46**, 360–365.

Milliken, L. L. Realistic occupational appraisal by high school seniors. *Personnel and Guidance Journal*, 1962, **40**, 541–544.

Moore, M. R., and Popham, W. J. Effects of two interview techniques on academic achievement. *Journal of Counseling Psychology*, 1960, **7**, 176–179.

Nick, E. W. High school boys choose vocations. *Occupations*, 1942, **20**, 264–269.

Ofman, W. Evaluation of a group counseling procedure. *Journal of Counseling Psychology*, 1964, **11**, 152–159.

Parsons, F. *Choosing a vocation*. Boston: Houghton Mifflin, 1909.

Patterson, C. H. *Counseling and psychotherapy: Theory and practice*. New York: Harper & Row, 1959.

Patterson, C. H. Methodological problems in evaluation. *Personnel and Guidance Journal*, 1960, **39**, 270–274.

Patterson, C. H. Counseling and/or psychotherapy? *American Psychologist*, 1963, **18**, 667–669. (a)

Patterson, C. H. Program evaluation. *Review of Educational Research*, 1963, **33**, 214–224. (b)

Patterson, C. H. *Theories of Counseling and psychotherapy*. New York: Harper & Row, 1966.

Patterson, C. H. What is counseling psychology? *Journal of Counseling Psychology*, 1969, **16**, 23–29.

Pepinsky, H. B., and Pepinsky, P. N. *Counseling theory and practice*. New York: Ronald Press, 1954.

Pilato, G. T. The effects of three vocational guidance treatments on some aspects of vocational preference and self knowledge. Unpublished doctoral dissertation, Columbia University, 1968.

Richardson, L. H. Counseling the ambitious mediocre student. *Journal of Counseling Psychology*, 1960, **7**, 265–268.

Richardson, L. H. Grade patterns of counseled and non-counseled students. *Journal of Counseling Psychology*, 1964, **11**, 160–163.

Rosenthal, R. On not so replicated experiments and not so null results. *Journal of Consulting and Clinical Psychology*, 1969, **33**, 7–10.

Roth, R. M., Mauksch, H. O., and Peiser, K. The non-achievement syndrome, group therapy, and achievement change. *Personnel and Guidance Journal*, 1967, **46**, 393–398.

Roth, R. M., and Meyersburg, H. A. The non-achievement syndrome. *Personnel and Guidance Journal*, 1963, **41**, 535–540.

Ryan, T. A., and Krumboltz, J. D. Effect of planned reinforcement counseling on client decision-making behavior. *Journal of Counseling Psychology*, 1964, **11**, 315–323.

Schwebel, M. Some missing links in counseling theory and research. *Personnel and Guidance Journal*, 1962, **41**, 325–331.

Searles, A., Jr. The effectiveness of limited counseling in improving the academic achievement of superior college freshmen. *Personnel and Guidance Journal*, 1962, **50**, 630–633.

Speer, G. S., and Jasker, L. The influence of occupational information on occupational goals. *Occupations*, 1949, **28**, 15–17.

Spielberger, C. D., Weitz, H., and Denny, J. P. Group counseling and the academic performance of anxious college freshmen. *Journal of Counseling Psychology*, 1962, **9**, 195–204.

Stefflre, B. Function and present status of counseling theory. In Stefflre, B. (Ed.), *Theories of counseling*. New York: McGraw-Hill, 1965.

Stone, C. H. Are vocational orientation courses worth their salt? *Educational and Psychological Measurement*, 1948, **8**, 161–181.

Super, D. E. A theory of vocational development. *American Psychologist*, 1953, **8**, 185–190.

Super, D. E. Consistency and wisdom of vocational preferences as indices of vocational maturity in the ninth grade. *Journal of Educational Psychology*, 1961, **52**, 35–43.

Super, D. E. Vocational development in adolescence and early adulthood. In D. E. Super, R. Starishevsky, N. Matlin, and J. P. Jordaan, *Career development: Self-concept theory*. New York: College Entrance Examination Board Research Monograph No. 4, 1963.

Super, D. E., and Crites, J. O. *Appraising vocational fitness*. (Rev. ed.) New York: Harper & Row, 1962.

Super, D. E., Kowalski, R. S., and Gotkin, E. H. Floundering and trial after high school. Cooperative Research Project No. 1393, Teachers College, Columbia University, 1967.

Super, D. E., and Overstreet, P. L. *The vocational maturity of ninth-grade boys*. New York: Teachers College, Columbia University, Bureau of Publications, 1960.

Super, D. E., Starishevsky, R., Matlin, N., and Jordaan, J. P. *Career development: Self-concept theory*. New York: College Entrance Examination Board Research Monograph No. 4, 1963.

Taylor, R. G. Personality traits and discrepant achievement: A review. *Journal of Counseling Psychology*, 1964, **11**, 76–82.

Thelen, M. H., and Harris, C. S. Personality of college underachievers who improve with group psychotherapy. *Personnel and Guidance Journal*, 1968, **46**, 561–566.

Thoresen, C. E., and Krumboltz, J. D. Relationship of counselor reinforcement of selected responses to external behavior. *Journal of Counseling Psychology*, 1967, **14**, 140–144.

Thoresen, C. E., Krumboltz, J. D., and Varenhorst, B. Sex of counselors and models: Effect on client career exploration. *Journal of Counseling Psychology*, 1967, **14**, 503–508.

Thorndike, R. L. *The concepts of over- and under-achievement*. New York: Teachers College, Columbia University, Bureau of Publications, 1963.

Tiedeman, D. V. Decision and vocational development: A paradigm and its implications. *Personnel and Guidance Journal*, 1961, **40**, 15–20.

Tiedeman, D. V. Predicament, problem, and psychology: The case for paradox in life and in counseling psychology. *Journal of Counseling Psychology*, 1967, **14**, 1–8.

Tiedeman, D. V., and Dudley, G. A. Recent developments and current prospects in occupational fact mediation. Paper presented at the National Conference on Occupational Information in Vocational Guidance, Chicago, May, 1967.

Tiedeman, D. V. Liberation through education: A goal and theory of challenge to school counselors. Speech to International Guidance Conference Board, May 14, 1966. Cited in Cooley, W. W. and Lohnes, P. R., *Predicting development in young adults*. Palo Alto: Project TALENT Office, American Institutes for Research and University of Pittsburgh, 1968. Pp. 5–13 and 5–14.

Tiedeman, D. V., and O'Hara, R. P. *Career development: Choice and adjustment*. New York: College Entrance Examination Board Research Monograph No. 3, 1963.

Tipton, R. M. Relative effectiveness of two methods of interpreting ability test scores. *Journal of Counseling Psychology*, 1969, **16**, 75–80.

Tyler, L. E. The work of the counselor. (2nd ed.) New York: Appleton-Century-Crofts, 1961.

Tyler, L. E. Work and individual differences. In H. Borow (Ed.), *Man in a world at work*. Boston: Houghton Mifflin, 1964. Pp. 174–195.

Vance, F. L., and Volsky, T. C., Jr. Counseling and psychotherapy: Split personality or Siamese twins. *American Psychologist*, 1962, **17**, 565–570.

Volsky, T., Jr., Magoon, T. M., Norman, W. T., and Hoyt, D. P. *The outcomes of counseling and psychotherapy*. Minneapolis: University of Minnesota Press, 1965.

Williams, J. E. Changes in self and other perceptions following brief educational-vocational counseling. *Journal of Counseling Psychology*, 1962, **9**, 18–28.

Williams, J. E., and Hills, D. A. More on brief educational-vocational counseling. *Journal of Counseling Psychology*, 1962, **9**, 366–368.

Williamson, E. G., and Bordin, E. S. Evaluating counseling by means of a control-group experiment. *School and Society*, 1940, **52**, 434–440.

Williamson, E. G., and Bordin, E. S. The evaluation of vocational and educational counseling: A critique of the methodology of experiments. *Educational and Psychological Measurement*, 1941, **1**, 5–24.

Winkler, R. C., Teigland, J. J., Munger, P. F., and Kranzler, G. D. The effects of selected counseling and remedial techniques on underachieving elementary school students. *Journal of Counseling Psychology*, 1965, **12**, 384–387.

Wolberg, L. R. *The technique of psychotherapy*. New York: Grune & Stratton, 1954.

Wright, E. W. A comparison of individual and multiple counseling for test interpretation interviews. *Journal of Counseling Psychology*, 1963, **10**, 126–135.

PART V

EVALUATING THE TRAINING OF THERAPISTS

24

RESEARCH ON THE TEACHING AND LEARNING OF PSYCHOTHERAPEUTIC SKILLS

RUTH G. MATARAZZO

UNIVERSITY OF OREGON MEDICAL SCHOOL

INTRODUCTION

In a review of the same area written four years ago, the writer and her colleagues (R. G. Matarazzo, Wiens, and Saslow, 1966) began with a quote from Carl Rogers (1957): "Considering the fact that one-third of present-day psychologists have a special interest in the field of psychotherapy, we would expect that a great deal of attention might be given to the problem of training individuals to engage in the therapeutic process. . . . For the most part this field is characterized by a rarity of research and a plenitude of platitudes." Happily, today this state of affairs has begun to change, apparently in teaching programs of all theoretical persuasions, although progress is uneven among them.

The proponents of some orientations—especially the client-centred group—have shown a readiness to question basic assumptions regarding both the dimensions of effective therapeutic behavior and the correlated effectiveness of traditional teaching programs. Proponents of some other orientations appear less convinced of the necessity for definition and measurement of significant dimensions of therapist behavior, therapist change as a function of training, and patient improvement as a function of degree of therapeutic skill. Hence they tend to continue traditional teaching with minor modifications and apparent conviction that their students will be at least adequate practitioners of psychotherapy.

Some of the extraordinary difficulties in

conducting research on the effectiveness of training in psychotherapy are apparent when one considers that:

1. Descriptions of the attributes of the "ideal" therapist (one of the criterion variables) are diverse, poorly defined, and incredibly numerous; consist of dozens of adjectives (Krasner, 1963); and can boast very little research to substantiate their authors' assertions.

2. We are only beginning to define the dimensions of therapeutic behavior; we do not know which therapist behaviors or procedures are likely to produce specific behavioral changes; and it appears likely that different kinds of patients respond differentially to therapist characteristics and techniques (Goldstein, Heller, and Sechrest, 1966; Strupp and Bergin, 1969).

3. The change in student-therapist behaviors to be measured involve cognitive, experiential, and behavioral changes that are to be activated in a special kind of situation. Thus, verbal self-report, including attitude questionnaires, multiple-choice responses to interviewee statements, and the like, is not likely to reflect the complex behavioral learning required of the student. At the same time, subjective observer reports and ratings present their own distortions.

4. *The real proof of the pudding is not simply whether students' behaviors come to resemble more closely those which the supervisor believes to be therapeutic, but whether the students' patients or clients do, in fact, improve.* This necessitates *follow-up* studies, including both objective and subjective reports of patient improvement with regard to specific criteria (for example, the degree of improvement in the individuals' presenting complaints).

It is heartening to note that there has been a very marked increase in research activity in this area over the past few years. This movement is concomitant with the recent burgeoning of research aimed at stating more specifically what therapists do and what specific techniques lead to patient improvement. Such basic knowledge must necessarily precede effective training for the therapist role.

The remainder of this chapter will attempt primarily to describe and evaluate methods of teaching psychotherapeutic and/or counseling skills, and to summarize what appears to be the present state of knowledge and practice. Inasmuch as teaching programs vary according to theoretical orientation and professional identity, the chapter will be divided into sections according to these characteristics.

1. CONTRIBUTIONS FROM THE PSYCOANALYTIC SCHOOL

Psychoanalytic training programs seem to be less affected than others by the current trend to empiricism and self-examination and have retained, essentially unchanged, their hypothetical constructs and their teaching methods of didactic analysis, control analyses, and the case conference. The first two of these focus in large part upon the student's growth as a person (analysis of countertransference, and the like) and, in this sense, are similar to the aim of the T-group, the didactic-experiential group, and psychodrama. That is, they base their approach to teaching upon the fundamental assumption that the student's qualities as a human being are important to his therapeutic effectiveness, although these qualities, and changes in them, are not explicitly defined, and are assessed only by the supervisor. Hence, they are not open to objective measurement. The desired therapeutic qualities (freedom from neurotic blind spots and defenses) are assumed to evolve from training and to enable the therapist to provide the necessary therapeutic conditions. However, they have not been operationally defined, measured, or empirically related to patient improvement.

In psychoanalytic training, the case-conference method is one of the basic modes of teaching, and it apparently continues to use, primarily, discussion of case material as reconstructed by the student-therapist. This procedure continues currently, despite studies dating back to Covner (1944), in which it was shown that the verbal report of the student-therapist is likely to contain significant omissions and distortions. Other studies have suggested that it is a relatively ineffective method of producing student change (R. G. Matarazzo, Phillips, Wiens, and Saslow, 1965; R. G.

Matarazzo, Wiens, and Saslow, 1966). Indeed, from examination of bibliographies as well as of the articles themselves, one might conclude that a factor in the continuation of untested methods is that many psychoanalytic writers and teachers do not read nonpsychoanalytic literature.

Fleming and Hamburg (1958) have written a cogent analysis of the advantages and shortcomings of the several methods of presenting interview data for discussion in the case conference. They describe the "private" method (student presenting data from recall) as having the advantage of being spontaneous or unconstrained, but having the disadvantage of distortion. The semipublic methods (tape-recordings and observed interviews) are described as accurate but constrained, due to the participants' anxiety and the necessity for delaying discussion until the end of the hour. They have developed the dynamimetic interview (DMI) in which a student acts as therapist, interviewing the supervisor, who plays the role of a specific patient whom he knows well. It is then possible to interrupt and discuss interviewer tactics immediately; obtain a report of the interviewee's reactions; suggest a change of tactics; and note the results. This is an interesting technique, variants of which have become more widely used as psychodrama and role-playing have come into increasing prominence.

Muslin, Burstein, Gedo, and Sadow (1967) have recently conducted an evaluation of the student-presentation method in the psychoanalytic case conference. They had separate sets of judges make ratings of patient functioning on the basis of data from recordings of first-year psychiatric residents' interviews and on the basis of recordings of the residents' presentations in psychoanalytic supervisory sessions. They found that several manifest themes were missing from the students' presentations; that patient affect was inadequately reported; that the patient-therapist relationship was unclear; and that the student was unaware that he had cut off patient exploration in several areas. Furthermore, the supervisors concluded that their formulations, based on supervisory material, were in error. The authors concluded that student-therapists in the *early stages* of supervision are not reliable reporters.

One could legitimately ask whether firsthand data is not preferable at any stage in the learning process, and especially when the second-hand data must come from one who is reporting a series of events in which he is behaving and observing at the same time.

Saretsky (1966), in describing a psycho-analytically oriented postdoctoral program, describes the deleterious effect upon student learning and performance of an aspect of the control analysis requirement. The student is required to analyze one patient over a two-year period and, if the patient leaves therapy before that time has elapsed, the student must begin again with another patient. He describes the consequent felt necessity for the student to be ingratiating to the patient, and his reluctance to confront the patient even when it would be therapeutically useful.

Several books describe, in interesting detail, the process of psychoanalytic supervision (Ekstein & Wallerstein, 1958; Fleming & Benedek, 1966). Ekstein and Wallerstein describe the supervisory process and the student's problems in learning, which are defined as his neurotic defenses against change. There is internal consistency in analyzing the student's relationship to his supervisor as a means of teaching him his future role in analyzing patients' transferences to him. However, empirical confirmation of teaching efficacy is lacking, and student progress seems to be overly dependent upon the subjective judgment of a supervisor with whom he is expected to be involved in a "countertransference" relationship. Fleming and Benedek similarly emphasize the experiencing aspect of the supervisory process, with the supervisor acting as a catalyst to self-analysis in the student. They describe and give examples of the supervisors' evaluative function (regarding promotion, graduation, withdrawal from the program, and the like), and the difficulty in specifying and achieving consensus on what the student would be expected to learn. They reported that "steps of learning" were difficult to specify except as a reflection of progress in the patient under analysis. They state: "The evaluation of progress in learning, like evaluation of therapeutic change, remains for practical purposes confined to a scale of improved or not improved. More precise measurement must wait for further study by psychoanalytic educators (p. 206)." They recommended that supervisory reports include "critical incidents that correlate learning difficulties with learning objectives (p. 231)."

It appears to this author that some of the most critical thinkers and the most empirically inclined members of the psychoanalytic school are becoming increasingly aware of the subjective hazards in present methods of psychotherapeutic skills. They are gradually moving toward some "semipublic" methods. However, a theory and teaching tradition are especially slow to weaken in a school where there is no strong commitment to empiricism, measurement, or experimentation.

2. THE CLIENT-CENTERED ORIENTATION

From its inception, the client-centred group provided the strongest influence toward making psychotherapy observable, its practice and training techniques and attitudes specifiable, and its results measurable. Rogers and his collaborators were the first to develop brief, well-formulated workshops for the training of psychotherapists and to attempt to measure their effectiveness (Blocksma & Porter, 1947). They specified graded procedures for facilitating the kind of experiential learning that they deemed necessary for the psychotherapist, and defined the characteristics and behaviors required of him in order to develop a therapeutic relationship and effect patient change. Currently, some of the most interesting and systematic research on the teaching of psychotherapy can be traced to these origins.

Rogers' (1957) graded experiences consisted of the student's (a) listening to tape-recorded interviews of experienced therapists; (b) role-playing the therapist with fellow students; (c) observing a series of live demonstrations by the supervisor; (d) participating in group therapy or multiple therapy; (e) conducting individual psychotherapy and recording his own interviews for discussion with a facilitative, nondirective supervisor; and (f) undergoing personal therapy. Rogers had earlier discarded emphasis upon technique, which made the student behave in ways that were not genuine

for him. He emphasized the attitudinal, relationship aspects of the psychotherapist's behavior (Rogers, 1951), and was the first to emphasize that the student-therapist's attitudinal, experiential learning can take place only in a facilitative environment such as that which the effective therapist provides for his patient. He described the "necessary and sufficient" conditions for therapeutic change as the therapist's ability to communicate to his patient *empathic understanding* and *unconditional positive regard* while being, himself, *congruent or genuine* as a person. The supervisor must model these behaviors for his student and create a "facilitative" atmosphere for experiential learning (Rogers, 1957).

The facilitative conditions are held to be universally important in human interaction. Carkhuff (1967) effectively describes this orientation. Both counselors and clients are seen as varying on the same dimensions of interpersonal functioning, with high "therapeutic conditions" being the ingredients of effective living: "Facilitators communicate an accurately empathic understanding of deeper as well as the surface feelings of the second person(s); they are freely and deeply themselves in a nonexploitative relationship; they communicate a very deep respect . . .; and they are helpful in guiding the discussion of personally relevant feelings and experiences in specific and concrete terms." This is the *reverse* of the client in need of help who has a distorted frame of reference. His words are unrelated to his feelings, and when his responses are genuine to another, they are inclined to be *negative*. He has little positive regard for others and feelings are discussed on an abstract plane. These behaviors are typical of the ineffective person, be he counselor, counselee, parent or teacher, and improvement in his functioning would take place along the same dimensions. An individual who provides low conditions is hypothesized to be the product of a succession of retarding relationships that have left him without the developed capacities to engage in constructive encounters. Such an individual will require a long-term relationship with a facilitative person, whereas those functioning at higher levels often require only a brief therapeutic encounter to solve an immediate problem. Carkhuff hypothesizes that any individual functioning at a higher therapeutic level can help a person with lower facilitative skills through the processes of offering (1) an effective role model; (2) the experience of facilitative conditions; and (3) some direct teaching of facilitative behavior.

Bergin (1970) describes the effect of the teacher's warmth and empathy upon her class. These therapeutic conditions favor effective student learning and positive growth, whereas lack of these conditions can have a negative effect, encouraging blocks to learning and school phobias. Students having lower levels of interpersonal skill are probably more vulnerable to negative effects than are their classmates, and this seems to be the case with patients and therapy trainees as well. The programs described below are designed to produce therapists who are facilitators of this kind.

Studies Supporting the Theoretical Base of the Didactic-Experiential Training Program

The client-centred group has published a number of research studies suggesting that high therapist conditions, as described above, are associated with constructive patient change and that the absence of these conditions can lead to deterioration in patient functioning. Truax (1961) compared the level of therapist empathy (measured by the Truax Accurate Empathy Scale,) offered to 4 subsequently improved hospitalized patients, with 4 who showed deterioration following six months of psychotherapy. As judged from 384 2-minute samples of tape-recordings, it was found that the psychotherapists of the improved patients offered significantly higher levels of accurate empathy than did the therapists of the deteriorated patients ($p < .01$). Truax, Silber, and Carkhuff (1966) demonstrated the same effects of therapist empathy in therapy groups. Bergin and Solomon (1970) found that psychology graduate students' empathy in psychotherapy interviews was related to the student-therapists' general therapeutic competence, as judged by supervisors. Bergin (1963) also has reported that low empathy is related to client deterioration. Truax and Carkhuff (1967) have reviewed numerous other studies demonstrating these phenomena.

Earlier, Rogers and Truax (1962) found that degree of self-exploration in the second interview correlated .70 with final case outcome.

Anderson (1968) has shown that the therapists functioning at high levels of therapeutic conditions can confront clients without decreasing the depth of patient self-exploration, although confrontations by therapists functioning at lower facilitative levels had a deleterious effect upon self-exploration ($p < .05$). The high-functioning therapists also had a greater tendency to confront patients and, when they did so, confronted them with their *resources*. The lower-functioning therapists tended to confront patients with their *limitations*.

Piaget, Berenson, and Carkhuff (1967) tested the hypothesis that high therapist conditions are more important for low-functioning clients than for those patients who are more facilitative, themselves. Two counselors, one offering high levels and one offering low levels, interviewed four high- and four low-functioning clients. The counselors purposely lowered the level of facilitative conditions during the middle third of the interview, and found that depth of self-exploration among the low-functioning clients was affected, whereas self-exploration in the high-functioning clients was relatively independent of therapeutic conditions. Holder, Carkhuff, and Berenson (1967) demonstrated the same effect in a similar experiment.

Conversely, Alexik and Carkhuff (1967) suggest that counselors functioning at high levels are less likely to diminish the therapeutic level of their behavior when interviewing a non-cooperative patient than is the low-functioning counselor. One high- and one low-functioning counselor interviewed a standard client, who reduced her level of self-exploration during the middle third of the interview. The "low" counselor lowered his level of therapeutic facilitation during the second period of the interview ($p < .01$), whereas the high-functioning counselor increased his conditions during period 2 and again in period 3. Carkhuff and Alexik (1967) cross-validated these findings with 8 additional counselors. The standard client later described the counselors, finding those functioning at low therapeutic levels to be unimaginative, boring, pedestrian, and perfunctory. Those functioning at "high" levels were described as stimulating, exploring, and as having "left me feeling more hopeful and more courageous."

Kratochvil, Aspy, and Carkhuff (1967) found no relationship between therapist "conditions," as usually measured, and depth of client self-exploration. A second partly negative study is reported by Bergin and Jasper (1969), who found global supervisor ratings of patient outcome ($n = 24$) to be unrelated to therapist empathy, as rated on the Bergin-Solomon revision of the Truax Accurate Empathy Scale. They report that patient ratings of "feeling understood" correlated positively with patient outcome, as did two measures of therapist behavior from the Barrett-Lennard Relationship Inventory. These ratings were *not* related to scores on the Truax scale. The authors question the generalizability of Truax' results to non-client-centered therapy.

Somewhat equivocal results were obtained with a group of non-client-centered therapists. Four psychiatric residents treated 40 psychiatric outpatients at the Phipps Psychiatric Clinic (Truax, Wargo, Frank, Imber, Battle, Hoehn-Saric, Nash, and Stone, 1966). Accurate empathy, nonpossessive warmth, and genuineness were measured via application of the appropriate Truax scales to four three-minute samples from three interviews at the beginning, midway, and near termination of each 20-interview therapeutic series. Overall improvement was measured by global improvement scales filled out by both patient and therapist. Two more specific measures were filled out by the patient (discomfort scale and target improvement scale) and one by a posttherapy research interviewer (social ineffectiveness rating). The most striking result was that the patients who received high therapeutic conditions were given the most favorable global improvement ratings *by their therapists* ($p < .01$, two-tailed test). The patients' global ratings of their own improvement had a considerably lower, though significant, correlation with therapeutic conditions ($p < .05$, one-tailed test), but the more specific measures were not significantly related. Thus it appears that therapists who offered high therapeutic conditions tended to see greater improvement in their patients, and there was some evidence to confirm their perception. A factor possibly contributing to the lack of other significant relationships was a limited range in the level of therapeutic conditions.

Also, the authors used small samples of therapeutic behavior (only twelve three-minute samples from the entire therapy series), and interjudge ratings of conditions were not high ($r_{kk} = .59$ to .63). Additionally, in view of Bergin and Jasper's results, it may be that other measures of the same or similar variables, will turn out to be more useful than some of the Truax scales.

The above research is cohesive and nearly unanimous in suggesting that the conditions of warmth, accurate empathy, positive regard, and genuineness are important, although not the only, variables in determining depth of patient exploration and therapy outcome. They also appear to be important factors in determining the effectiveness of the supervisor-student relationship (see below). We shall now return to a description of some didactic-experiential programs and the degree of their apparent success in teaching trainees to offer these conditions in their own interviews.

The Didactic-Experiential Programs and Research Evaluations of Their Effectiveness

Truax, Carkhuff, and Douds (1964) and Truax and Carkhuff (1967) have added significant refinements to the earlier training procedures of Rogers and have carried out an ambitious research program to measure the effectiveness of their training program. The latter authors emphasize that theirs is "an integrated didactic and experiential approach to training" and that ... "this approach is an attempt to translate research and theory into effective practice by focusing on the experiential and didactic elements concurrently (p. 220)." They charge that most psychotherapy training programs have taught theory and patient psychodynamics rather than how to relate to a patient and conduct psychotherapy. They have been reinforced in the development of their training theory by research findings of others such as Barrett-Lennard (1962), Feifel and Eells (1963), Kamin and Caughlan (1963), Gardner (1964), Strupp, Wallach, and Wogan (1964), Lorr (1965), and Rice (1965), who found that patients were unimpressed with technique but valued the warmth, helpfulness, and human characteristics of the therapist. They also point out that therapist warmth and accurate empathy, in turn, have been related to such research-based variables as "depth of patient exploration" and patient outcome.

The three central elements of the training program are described as: "(1) a therapeutic context in which the supervisor himself provides high levels of therapeutic conditions; (2) highly specific didactic training in the implementation of the therapeutic conditions; and (3) a quasi-group therapy experience where the trainee can explore his own existence, and his individual therapeutic self can emerge (Truax & Carkhuff, 1967, p. 242)."

More specifically, the steps of the program are described as follows:

1. Students were given an extensive reading list followed by a "theory" examination.

2. They completed twenty-five hours' time listening to taped individual and group psychotherapy sessions to increase their response repertoire.

3. They rated excerpts from these tapes on the scales of "Accurate Empathy," "Nonpossessive Warmth" and "Genuineness." Some of the excerpts had already been rated by "experts," so that the student could obtain feedback (consensual validation) in the accuracy of his ratings.

4. They practiced making responses to tape-recorded patient statements (especially empathic responses). This was done in a group, competitively, and students were called upon randomly to assure vigilance and develop facility in verbalizing as well as in understanding. Training in warmth of tone was added as soon as empathy level was satisfactory.

5. Outside of class, pairs of students alternated playing "therapist" and "patient" roles in sessions that were recorded and brought to supervisory sessions. Parts of the tape were played back and rated on the therapeutic conditions scales by the supervisor and trainees, as a group, providing feedback for the individual student-therapist.

6. After achieving minimal levels of therapeutic conditions, the students had single interviews with real patients, with the goal of establishing "a good therapeutic relationship" and facilitating deep self-exploration. The interviews were tape recorded and samples were played back for rating by the student, his peers, and the supervisor, to promote the student's learning of what specific behaviors contributed to or detracted from his therapeutic relationship.

7. After the students achieved minimal levels of therapeutic conditions in single interviews, patients were assigned for continuing therapy. Sessions were tape recorded, and periodic samples were evaluated in the supervisory session.

8. On the sixth week of the program, quasi-group therapy was initiated with the students who met for two-hour sessions once a week (see below).

The authors stress that, throughout the training period, they encouraged the student-therapists to take part in decision-making, and that at all times the supervisors attempted to provide at least minimal levels of therapeutic conditions. By engaging in group decision-making under conditions fostering feelings of safety and freedom, the authors believe they enabled the students to expose new aspects of themselves and experiment with new modes of communicating and behaving. Truax and Carkhuff (1967) state: "The experiential base of the training program constituted the essential starting point for all other activities. If the trainees could not experience high levels of warmth and regard, understanding and genuineness from the supervisor, then they could not be expected to function at high therapeutic levels themselves (p. 272)." And ". . . although the experiential content served as a background for the classroom interactions, the experiential qualities came to the foreground in the quasi-group therapy experience, which provided a more concentrated therapeutic encounter (p. 271)."

The quasi-group therapy consisted of group discussion centered around the trainees' personal or emotional difficulties experienced *in their role as therapist*, and thus was not intended, broadly, to treat the student as a patient. "The aim of the quasi-group therapy experience was, first, to give trainees experiential meaning for the role of the therapist by their own participation as clients; and second, to provide an opportunity for self-exploration of their own goals, values, and experiences in relation to their emerging role as counselor or therapist (p. 273)."

The Truax and Carkhuff program, then (1) begins with a partial theory of the conditions essential to patient behavioral change; (2) has included the development and some testing of instruments for measuring those conditions; (3) cites some *research* to indicate that these conditions do foster constructive patient change, while their absence is a deterrent to constructive change; and (4) reflects, in its particular training steps, specific attempts to *foster the appropriate attitudes and behaviors* among the students. The authors also make use of ideas from social-learning theory, behavior-modification theory, and programmed instruction. For example, the following is from social learning and behavior modification theories:

The major implication of the present tentative analysis is that the therapists or counselors who are high in empathy, warmth, and genuineness are more effective in psychotherapy because they themselves are personally more potent positive reinforcers; *and* also because they elicit through reciprocal affect a high degree of positive affect in the patient, which increases the level of the patient's positive self-reinforcement, decreases anxiety, and increases the level of positive affect communicated to others, thereby reciprocally increasing the positive affect and positive reinforcement received from others. By contrast, counselors or therapists who are low in communicated accurate empathy, nonpossessive warmth and genuineness are ineffective and produce negative or deteriorative change in the patient because they are noxious stimuli who serve primarily as aversive reinforcers *and* also because they elicit negative affect in the patient (which increases the level of the patient's negative self-reinforcement, increases the level of negative affect communicated to others, and thus increases reciprocally the negative affect and negative reinforcement received from others p. 161–162).

Some ideas from programmed instruction can be seen in their attempt, as carefully as possible in this complex learning situation, to teach a few relatively simple behaviors at one time, provide immediate feedback, and gradually refine discriminations until a defined level of performance is reached and the student is considered ready for the next learning task. Feedback and reinforcement are probably made more potent by being administered in and by a group of peers as well as supervisors. Vigilance is maintained by uncertainty and aperiodic reinforcement; freedom from anxiety and freedom to experiment are maximized by high "therapeutic conditions." Increasing numbers of investigators are testing the effectiveness of this and similar programs, as shown by the sizable number of empirical studies measuring behavior change in student therapists, and studies testing the validity of the above constructs. Some of these investigations are described in the following paragraphs.

Carkhuff and Truax (1965a) evaluated two separate but similar and concurrent training programs. One involved 12 "advanced graduate students" and the other, 5 "volunteer but otherwise unselected lay hospital personnel." The classes met twice a week for 2-hour sessions over a 16-week semester. Students spent 2 additional hours listening, on their own, to tape recordings of therapy interviews. At the end of the semester, 6 four-minute excerpts from each student's taped interviews were rated by trained undergraduates for accurate empathy, unconditional positive regard, therapist self-congruence, and client depth of self-exploration. These ratings were compared with ratings of taped excerpts from experienced therapists and from the publicly dispersed tapes of 4 prominent therapists. The scores tended to rank the groups in the following order: experienced therapists, graduate students, and lay personnel. However, none of the differences was significant except in regard to the therapist self-congruence dimension. The authors conclude that, during 100 hours of training specifically directed toward variables empirically demonstrated to be necessary for therapist effectiveness, they can bring the performance of students and lay personnel to a level similar to that of experienced therapists. They found the ratings of both their lay and psychology graduate students to be superior to those reported by Bergin and Solomon (1970) of "postinternship fourth-year graduate students from a more didactically and psychoanalytically oriented clinical training program of a school of some repute in the field. . . ." In an additional study of the effectiveness of the above-mentioned lay personnel, Carkhuff and Truax (1965b) found that inpatients seen in 24 group-counseling sessions by the lay personnel made significantly greater constructive behavior change than did a control group of inpatients. They emphasize that the counselors were given instruction only in providing therapeutic conditions and had no theoretical background.

Berenson, Carkhuff, and Myrus (1966) attempted to measure the effect of different aspects of the integrated, didactic-experiential training program upon the functioning of undergraduate college students. Eighteen male and eighteen female volunteer students were randomly assigned to I, the training group proper, which received the total training, including quasi-group therapy; II, the training control group, which received the same program minus the use of the research scales and the quasi-group therapy; or III, a control group that received no training. Both training groups received 16 hours' training over 8 weeks. Group I had, in addition, 4 hours of group therapy, whereas Group II had 4 hours of discussion on typical college problems. The students were assessed, pre- and posttraining, in regard to empathy, positive regard, genuineness, concreteness, and degree of self-exploration elicited. These behaviors were assessed by means of tape-ratings; inventory reports of standard interviewees as well as significant others, and inventory self-reports. The greatest gain in interpersonal skill was made by Group I; Group II was intermediate; and the least gain was made by Group III, supporting the authors' belief that the total program would have the most effect.

Truax and Silber (1966), with 16 graduate student subjects, crossvalidated their previous demonstration of student change as a function of didactic-experiential training. They compared the students' "therapeutic conditions" early in training (after 14 class hours and 11 hours of listening to tape recordings) with the conditions provided by them after an additional 34 hours of training. From "early" to "late" training, there were significant increases in the level of accurate empathy ($p < .05$), and in the level of genuineness ($p < .01$), but the improvement in nonpossessive warmth was not significant.

Ivey, Normington, Miller, Morrill, and Haase (1968) have experimented with an ingenious brief variant of the "didactic-experiential" type of program. Their "microcounseling" technique is focused upon teaching specific counseling skills in prepracticum training. They report three studies in which they attempted to teach (a) attentiveness (1 hour) and the related concepts of (b) accurate reflection (2 hours) and (c) summarization of feeling (2 hours), respectively. In the study of attentiveness, they divided 38 dormitory counselors into experimental and control groups whose "clients" were 38 paid volunteers. The experimental procedure was as follows: (a) the trainee conducted a 5-minute videotaped interview with the instructions: "Go in and talk with this student; get to know him"; (b) he read the "Attending Behavior Manual"; (c) he viewed videotaped modeling of attending behavior by effective and less effective counselors, followed by discussion with his supervisor; (d) the trainee viewed his initial videotape and was asked to identify his own attending behavior; and (f) he recounseled the same "client" in a second, 5-minute, videotaped interview. As rated by 2 judges, the experimental students, after 1 hour's training, were significantly higher, post-instruction, in eye contact and in "verbal following" than the control group, whose members merely conducted 2 interviews with their clients, with no intervening training. For the experimental group, there was also a significantly greater increase in client ratings on the Semantic Differential Form and the Counselor Effectiveness Scale. Talk-time for the experimental group decreased from 47 percent to 33 percent of the total interview time.

The second (accurate reflection) and third (summarization of feelings) studies were similar, but had an additional 3-minute role-playing session and a third 5-minute interview. (Subjects were beginning counselors from the Department of Psychology, Counseling and Guidance; $n = 11$ and 10, respectively, for studies 2 and 3.) In each postinterview discussion, the supervisor was careful to reinforce the student's skills. In both the latter studies, there were significant increases in the appropriate skill (accurate reflection and accurate summarization, respectively); in client ratings; and in the student's self-confidence.

Effect of the Supervisory Relationship

Hansen and Barker (1964) measured the effect of the quality of the supervisory relationship upon the trainees' level of experiencing during an N.D.E.A. Counseling and Guidance Institute that extended over the course of an academic year. They hypothesized that the trainees who felt understood and accepted, and received genuineness from their supervisors, would have higher levels of experiencing, as measured by Gendlin and Tomlinson's (1963) Experiencing Scale. The 28 trainees were randomly divided into three groups and assigned to three different supervisors. After completion of the practicum, the trainees rated the supervisory relationship on the Relationship Inventory (Barrett-Lennard, 1962). At this time, supervisor 1 was given the highest relationship score, supervisor 3 was given the lowest, and supervisor 2 received an intermediate rating. Each trainee had a recorded interview with his supervisor, in which he was asked to discuss the significance of the practicum experiences for him. Three two-minute tape segments from each interview were analyzed by two judges, using Gendlin's Experiencing Scale. There was a significant relationship between the trainee's rating of the supervisory relationship and his level of experiencing. The trainees in group 1 had the highest relationship scores and the highest level of experiencing; group 2 was intermediate on both ratings; and group 3 was the lowest. This was interpreted to mean that students having the poorest supervisory relationship "were more remote from their experiencing and from their feelings, more likely to be cautious and defensive in this relationship."

Pagell, Carkhuff, and Berenson (1967) have reported that counselees who receive high levels of therapeutic conditions from the counselor will, when interviewing their own clients, offer higher levels than will counselees who, themselves, have received low levels of therapeutic conditions. They found that the level of *empathy* offered is the best predictor of the counselee's behavior. This study underscores the Rogerian contention that students should experience high facilitative conditions from their supervisors in order to be able to offer this therapeutic atmosphere to clients.

Pierce, Carkhuff, and Berenson (1967) studied the effects of a high- and a low-functioning supervisor upon 17 volunteers for a mental-health counselor training program. Eight trainees were assigned to a high-functioning supervisor (A) and 9 to a low-functioning supervisor (B). The previously described, integrated didactic and experiential training approach was used, and the students' interviews were assessed, pre- and posttraining, on the research scales of empathy, positive regard, genuineness, concreteness, and self-disclosure. All of the 8 trainees assigned to supervisor A continued their training to its conclusion, whereas, of the 9 assigned to B, only 4 remained, and 5 dropped out. A's group made significant gains during training ($p < .05$), but B's group had no significant change. The authors point out that the above dropout rate is similar to that reported for patients in psychotherapy. If cross-validated, this finding would underscore Truax and Carkhuff's (1967) statement regarding the ineffectiveness of some present training programs. "Part of the difficulty . . . clearly lies with the training institutions themselves. More often than not, they choose training and supervisory therapists on the basis of their academic research and theoretic contribution, ignoring to a large extent the effective professional therapist (p. 23)."

Personality Factors Associated with Therapeutic Effectiveness

Better selection of trainees is one way to improve the caliber or effectiveness of psychotherapists, but so far selection programs have been disappointing. Academic and/or intellectual criteria seem to be of limited usefulness, and few personality variables have been isolated, measured, and cross-validated.

Bergin and Solomon (1970) found that empathic ability was slightly negatively related to verbal intelligence and to the psychology subscale of the Graduate Record Examination. Personality measures seemed somewhat more promising, inasmuch as empathic ability was negatively related to the Pt and D scales of the MMPI, and positively related to the Dominance and Change subscales of the Edwards Personal Preference Inventory. In a recent replication (Bergin and Jasper, 1969), the MMPI D scale correlated $-.41$ and $-.31$ ($p < .06$ and

$p < .05$, respectively) with empathy; and the Pt scale correlated $-.54$ and $-.38$ with empathy ($p < .01$ and $p < .025$). The EPPI scale correlations were not replicated, and the authors have concluded that the previous correlation was a "chance" finding. Truax, Silber, and Wargo (1966) studied the personality inventory profiles of 16 graduate students who completed the didactic-experiential training in psychotherapy, and compared those who had gained the most in empathic skill during training with those who had changed the least. On the Edwards Personal Preference Inventory, the students who gained most scored significantly higher in the "Change" scale, both before and after training, than those who showed the least improvement. At the start, both groups were equivalent on the "Abasement" scale, but the high-gain students decreased in "Abasement," whereas the low-gain students increased. The Autonomy scale was the highest, and gained significantly among the high-gain students, but was significantly lower, and decreased among the low-gain students. The best students were also significantly lower on "Defensiveness" at the start, although both groups declined on "Defensiveness' during training. The authors conclude that their training program produces positive personality change in their students, as well as improving their ability to interact in a more therapeutic manner with patients. This conclusion seems premature, however.

Allen (1967) has concluded that, while no personality "types" or "profiles" are predictive, some higher-order concepts such as "openness" or degree of self-awareness may help to differentiate effective from relatively ineffective psychotherapists. He hypothesizes that this is a precondition for understanding others, and may also produce a "dyadic effect," the counselee's willingness to risk self-recognition being related to the counselor's willingness to do the same. "Openness," as measured by Rorschach performance (departures from vagueness and banality) were related ($p < .05$) to supervisor ratings of therapeutic effectiveness. "Open" counselors were rated as responding more to client feelings.

Whitely, Sprinthall, Mosher, and Donaghy (1967) investigated "cognitive flexibility" as a dimension of therapist effectiveness. Cognitive flexibility was defined as the ability to think and act simultaneously and appropriately, consisting of openmindedness, adaptability, resistance to premature closure, and the like. Nineteen students in a one-year guidance class were evaluated with the Rorschach, TAT, and Personal Differentiation Test. Predictions of counselor effectiveness from these scores correlated .78 and .73 with supervisor ratings, although intelligence scores correlated only .09 with such ratings. They found that some flexible students were better therapists at the beginning of the course than others were at the end; and that there was a small, tenacious minority with whom supervision was ineffectual. They suggest that research should be devoted toward improving the impact of training on the large middle group.

Bare (1967) studied the effect of counselor personality on client outcome. Forty-seven counselors and 208 clients took the Gordon Personal Profile, the Gordon Personal Inventory, and the Edwards Personal Preference Schedule. After 10 weeks of counseling, both counselors and clients rated the following items on a 4-point scale: "to what extent (a) has counseling been helpful, (b) has the counselor gotten to know the client, (c) has the client gotten to know the counselor, and (d) has the counselor shown empathy for the client's own perception of his problems." The author concluded that "counselor personality characteristics of high original thinking, high vigor, low ascendancy, low achievement needs, and low order needs seemed to be related to counselor helpfulness, empathy, and the facilitation of a close therapeutic relationship."

Although large-scale attempts to predict clinical success, such as those of Kelly and Fiske (1951) and Holt and Luborsky (1958), have been disappointing, there is some evidence to suggest that certain personality characteristics favor success as a psychotherapist. As yet, these characteristics are poorly defined, and perhaps one can only say that psychological good health, flexibility, openmindedness, positive attitudes towards people, and interpersonal skill seem to be associated with effectiveness as a therapist. Conversely, the lack of these attributes, or personality disturbance, appears to hinder the student's growth as a therapist, just as it would probably hinder his performance in any occupation requiring large amounts of interpersonal contact.

Studies Involving the Validity of Experimental Procedures and Concepts in Client-Centered Psychotherapy Research

Several researchers have attempted to define more clearly the therapist behaviors that are judged to be "warm," "empathic," and the like. If more operational definitions can be given to these variables, certainly they can be more easily taught and more reliably evaluated. It is not within the purview of this chapter to review these studies in detail, but several are very briefly described below.

Tomlinson and Stoler (1967) found that lay judges, who are often employed for ratings of therapy process, could differentiate patient "likeability" from dimensions of the therapeutic process. Zimmer and Park (1967) factor-analyzed therapist "*warmth*," which has been considered unidimensional. They found it to have several aspects, which they believe help to make its definition more operational. Some of these factors were described as (1) restating and understanding; (2) minimal activity; (3) open-ended questions; (4) supportive clarification; (5) eliciting clarification; (6) probing; and (7) cognitive-interpretive. Zimmer and Anderson (1968) examined the relationship between the dimensions of positive regard and empathy, and found them to be orthogonally related.

It would appear that such critical analytic studies will be helpful in increasing the teachability, meaningfulness, and usefulness of the concepts involved in the facilitative "conditions" used by the client-centred group.

Summary

This is an impressive body of research suggesting that warmth, empathy, and perhaps other relationship variables (a) are important in determining patient response to therapy and (b) can be taught to both lay and professional personnel in the kind of didactic-experiential program described. To date, this is the most comprehensive, sophisticated attempt to define some of the dimensions of effective therapeutic behavior; relate them, theoretically, to diverse research studies of others; develop research instruments to measure the dimensions; establish a program explicitly designed to teach students the presumed appropriate behavior on these dimensions; measure the effectiveness of teaching; and relate this to patient outcome. At the same time, one cannot assume that the above relationship variables are the only important ones in psychotherapy, particularly when they are derived from a single type of theory. As the authors suggest, these variables do not exhaust all the variance. In addition, they do not appear to be unitary; they will need more explicit, operational definition; and the presently used rating scales are undeniably crude. It is to be hoped that other researchers will attempt to make additional, independent replications of these studies. The possibility of the Rosenthal (1963) effect is troubling, especially inasmuch as most of the researchers' careers have been interrelated; the constructs have not been operationally defined; many studies present barely significant or not quite significant results; and the ratings of both therapist and patient performance are subjective.

3. TEACHING OF PSYCHOTHERAPY IN MEDICAL SCHOOLS

Prior to World War II, there was little training in interviewing or psychotherapy, even for psychiatrists, outside of psychoanalytic institutes. Subsequent to the war, a three-year residency program in psychiatry was instituted in most of this country's medical schools and in many psychiatric hospitals.

About twenty years ago, some psychiatrists in medical education began to emphasize the need for undergraduate medical students, throughout their four years, to learn some principles of interviewing and to practice, with supervision, the art of relating effectively to patients (Group for the Advancement of Psychiatry, 1948; Whitehorn, Jacobsen, Levine, and Lippard, 1952). Recently, Coggeshall (1965), in a blueprint for medical educators in the decade ahead, has emphasized the need for medical schools to turn out increasing numbers of students who are trained to practice in a manner quite different from that of their predecessors. More specifically, tomorrow's physician will probably need to screen larger numbers of patients, necessitating a warm and facilitating, yet often brief encounter. He will need to deal with increasing numbers of geriatric problems and to handle their special social-psychological problems; to relate to patients of increasingly diverse social-economic backgrounds; and to be able to teach and motivate patients to cooperate in the long-term care of their own chronic diseases. He will need to have interpersonal skills that will enable him to collaborate effectively and harmoniously with a team of medical specialists and allied health personnel. Thus, interviewing skill, constructive interpersonal attitudes, flexibility of role definition, and understanding of basic human behavior will be of increasing importance. Medical schools are experimenting with many individual programs in attempting to meet this challenge. Only certain aspects of these are relevant to the present chapter, that is, those attempting to teach skill in interviewing and/or psychotherapy. (None of the combined lecture-demonstration courses on human growth, behavior, and the like are reviewed here.)

In 1947 Coleman recommended that teaching psychotherapeutic skill could be a counterweight to the authoritarian, directive attitude fostered in medicine, and suggested specific, graded experiences of student-patient interaction. Gill, Newman, and Redlich (1954) were pioneers in reproducing, for distribution, the complete transcripts of three initial interviews, with a running commentary on the interviewer's behavior. In addition to making available recorded interviews of both "expert" therapists and a novice interviewer, with a commentary, they offered very specific behavioral suggestions for the interviewer. They also recommended that the interviewer listen to recordings of his own interviews, preferably with another person who could help him to identify emotions and attitudes.

At the University of Rochester, interviewing skill has been taught as part of a clerkship in comprehensive medicine (Engel, Green, Reichsman, Schmale, and Ashenburg, 1957). The instructors observe the students conducting initial interviews with unselected patients in order to help the medical student "master the basic techniques in human interaction as these are used in medical interviewing. . . ." Romano

(1962) observed that, although approximately one-quarter of American medical schools were beginning to teach in this fashion, interview or relationship skill was not emphasized in European medical schools at the time. Adams (1958) described a similar comprehensive clerkship at Western Reserve University, where a psychiatric consultant was available as needed. Werkman (1961) helped students with final, summing-up medical interviews through the use of an outline and role playing, with the supervisor as patient. Pfouts and Rader (1962) described a senior, full-time, five-week clerkship in the psychiatric outpatient clinic. The authors observed all initial interviews and discussed them with the students.

Lester, Gussen, Yamamoto, and West (1962) called for new teaching methods, pointing out that students' helplessness, anxiety, and hostility is a natural consequence of our inadequate teaching methods—and these attitudes are antitherapeutic. Heine, Aldrich, Draper, Meuser, Tippett, and Trosman (1962) have described a 17-week senior clerkship in the University of Chicago Psychiatry Outpatient Clinic, where the students conducted short-term psychotherapy under "intensive supervision." Between 80 percent and 90 percent of the students reported gains in insight, confidence, and sensitivity in their self-reports on a questionnaire. Not surprisingly, those students whose patients were rated as most improved had the most positive attitudes toward the course. The efforts reported above form an interesting collection of observations and subjective evaluations, but do not present objective data or evaluation of student performance.

Aldrich and Bernhardt (1963) described a new four-year sequence in psychiatry that included a three-fold increase in teaching time; seminar case-study instruction; and longer supervised patient contact. They compared the students of this program with those from the traditional program who had had less overall teaching time and less patient contact. There was no significant difference between the student groups on a Problem Cases Test, in which the students were asked to outline patient problems from seven vignettes, list additional information needed, and describe the action they would take. The authors believe the examination was inadequate, but one might question the efficiency of a teaching program that does not produce easily demonstrated differences in students who have experienced a three-fold increase in teaching time.

R. G. Matarazzo, Phillips, Wiens, and Saslow (1965), and R. G. Matarazzo, Wiens, and Saslow (1966), attempted to measure the interviewing behavior of sophomore medical students, pre- and postinstruction obtained during an eight-week summer psychiatry clerkship; and to measure the effect of three different methods of supervision given in the three clerkships. The six students enrolled in the 1960 clerkship interviewed the same six patients in counter-balanced order, pre- and postinstruction. Their interview behavior was rated on a "Check List of Therapist 'Error' Behavior" for verbalizations that were poor in focus or content; therapist role definition (authoritarian or social); and facilitation of communication. Also, the frequency and duration of single units of interviewer and interviewee speech and silence behavior (latency) were recorded on the Interaction Chronograph. There was a significant decrease in "errors" from pre- to posttraining, and errors were found to correlate $-.53$ with length of patient utterance, indicating that the decrease in errors, with training, produced demonstrable change in the patients' interview behavior. Pre-instruction, the students had particular difficulty in interviewing relatively quiet patients, and there was a significant association ($r = .43$ $p < .05$) between the length of the interview and the percentage of time that the patient talked. This relationship was not found post-instruction. Student talk-time decreased significantly, and patient talk-time increased significantly over the eight weeks ($p < .001$). Before training, the students' behaviors were inconsistent and seemed to be determined largely by the stimulus value of the patient whereas, after training, they had more stable, individual interviewing styles.

The 1961 and 1962 clerkship students were rated on the "error" scale only. Their errors, before instruction, were primarily in "facilitation of communication" (yes-no type of question, awkwardness, abruptness, structuring too much, and the like), suggesting that the student tended to prevent the patient from communicating freely. The greatest improvement took place in this category (from 54 percent to 28 percent). The students also improved in regard to focus on significant content, but made little change in faulty role definition (that is, the few students who were authoritarian or overly "social" in their patient relationship tended not to alter their roles). This is consistent with the results of Whitely et al., cited earlier, who described a "small, tenacious minority" of students who remained inflexible.

In 1962, the students had four sets of experimental interviews: one month prior to instruction; at the beginning of instruction; after one month of instruction; and at the end of the course. Little change was noted between interviews 1 and 2 (the control period); and the greatest improvement took place during the first month of instruction.

It was found that the classes of students made successively greater improvement each year, as the teaching program was altered. The mean number of errors per response at the end of training was .99, .74, and .65 for the years 1960, 1961, and 1962, respectively. This measure of improvement corresponded with the following teaching techniques. In 1960 the supervisors discussed therapy in the case conference style, with no observation. In 1961 the supervisor was not restricted from observing the students, and regularly used observation as part of the supervisory process. In 1962, the supervisor met with the students twice a week to observe interviews and involve the students in discussion of each other's interviews. Thus, discussion with no observation was least effective, and much observation followed by combined supervisor and peer discussion was the most potent method of improving interview skill.

Ornston, Cicchetti, and Fierman (1968) did not attempt to evaluate a training program, but compared the interview behavior of first-year psychiatric residents with that of experienced psychotherapists. Their results were similar to those of R. G. Matarazzo, Phillips, Wiens, and Saslow (1965) and R. G. Matarazzo, Wiens, and Saslow (1966), in that the novices used short, choppy questions and explored specific, narrow content areas. The experienced therapists tended to use more words per response, and tended to "say something" rather than "ask something."

Thurnblad and McCurdy (1967) summarized the medical school programs supported by the NIMH Human Behavior Grants during the year 1964–65. They pointed to the recent ferment in undergraduate medical education concerned with helping the student appreciate the diverse social, psychological, and biological etiological determinants of disease, and preparing him to administer comprehensive, holistic patient care. Twenty-two Human Behavior Grants were given during 1964–65, at an average cost of approximately $32,000 per year. The programs were diverse, usually involved the collaboration of several disciplines, and seemed to reflect the proclivities of those instructors who were involved in the planning and teaching. As the authors state: "The variety and volume of material which can be taught under the broad heading 'human behavior' have posed the common problems of what and how much to do." Most of the programs have used large-group lectures, but often supplement these with small-group discussions. Demonstration interviews, films, and videotapes are utilized. Unstructured student groups are often used as laboratories of human behavior, and for self-observation. As yet, there is no systematic comparison or evaluation of such programs. Apparently few if any of them have become directly involved with teaching the student himself how to interview and/or relate to patients, except as this may be implicit in lectures and "modeling" during demonstration interviews.

Summary

There is increasing conviction within medical education circles that future physicians must become more cognizant of factors affecting human behavior, including themselves as therapeutic agents, and that they must develop skill in practicing this new understanding. However, it is only within the past decade that most medical schools have fostered well-developed departments of psychiatry or behavioral science. Medical educators are still experimenting with diverse programs of undetermined value; often they have not adequately defined the behaviors they intend to foster in the student; and, partly as a result of the latter, they have not adequately measured changes in student performance. We

appear now to be on the brink of an era of somewhat more sophisticated and energetic attempts at self-evaluation. Again, it is unfortunate that there appears to be a literature barrier, with those teaching in psychiatric clerkships being relatively nonconversant with what has been appearing in psychology journals. To this writer, it seems imperative that the results of the research on the didactic-experiential program, and others, be evaluated and, as relevant, assimilated into medical programs.

Postgraduate Programs for the General Physician

In several medical schools, the departments of psychiatry have initiated postgraduate courses designed to help the medical practitioner increase his understanding of psychiatric disorders and to improve his interviewing skill and ability to relate to patients in a therapeutic manner. In part, these programs result from the fact that many practitioners, who are not recent graduates, did not have the benefit of such courses during their undergraduate years.

One of the first postgraduate programs in psychiatry was described by Whitaker (1949). He trained practitioners by involving them in multiple therapy in order to promote the "ability to develop a more therapeutic doctor-patient relationship" so that the practitioners could manage their own medical patients who had mild psychiatric disturbances. Balint (1954) described holding case conferences with six to eight physicians who discussed their day-to-day work with neurotic patients in their practice.

For many years, Enelow and his co-workers at the University of Southern California School of Medicine have experimented with different methods of teaching graduate physicians to deal with "the kinds of patients who might turn up in any physician's office." Enelow, Forde, and Gwartney (1962) described the initial program, in which case conferences were conducted with 8 to 10 physicians. Demonstration interviews were conducted and followed by group discussion of interview techniques and observations. Enelow, Adler, and Manning (1964) developed a teaching clinic that was designed to follow up the "basic psychiatry" course described above. This is a 4-hour clinic, of which 1½ hours are spent in conducting brief, 10- to 30-minute interviews. One of the physician-students is then observed while interviewing for half an hour; there is a half-hour demonstration interview conducted by the supervisor; and the last hour is spent in discussion. The psychiatrists' orientation is briefly described. The instructors' experience has led them to discontinue having students report on their patients as this seemed to involve recounting patient history to the exclusion of other relevant data. They also have come to spend increased amounts of time with their students and patients in the clinic, although they present no data to substantiate their belief that this activity is more valuable. Following the 32-week course, they gave an evaluation test, designed to measure gain in cognitive learning. Pre- and post-training, they also asked the 10 students to respond to two (alternate) sound movies of initial interviews. None of the investigators' hypotheses was substantiated over the full year. There was, however, throughout the course, a shift in the students' conception of the physician's role in the direction of lower regard for the use of authority and less reliance upon technical-medical skills in the physician-patient relationship.

Postgraduate courses for the physician, then, seem to appear sporadically on the medical scene and to reflect the special interest of a given department of psychiatry rather than a nationwide trend. The courses are usually eclectic in teaching method and theory, reasonably flexible in approach, but clearly neither innovative in method nor sophisticated in self-evaluation.

4. PROFESSIONAL PROGRAMS AND THE TRAINING OF LAY THERAPISTS

During the past decade there has been considerable soul-searching and dissatisfaction with the state of current training programs in clinical psychology. Kelly's (1961) conclusion from his survey of clinical psychologists was that . . . "a fairly large number of our members do not regard clinical training, as now offered, as an adequate preparation for clinical practice." He found that 50 percent of clinical psychologists

no longer believed in what they were doing and wished they had chosen another profession. As Mayman said of clinical psychologists at an APA symposium on professional training (Snyder, 1962). "Perhaps they no longer believe in what they are doing because they never learned to do it well." Fine (1966) points up one aspect of the difficulty when he states, "a careful examination of these training programs in clinical psychology reveals a situation similar to that in the residency training programs in psychiatry: the amount of training in psychotherapy varies from considerable to almost none. One result has been the establishment of postdoctoral training programs in psychotherapy, the first of which under university auspices has been begun by New York University." The 1965 Conference on the Professional Preparation of Clinical Psychologists (Hoch, Ross, and Winder, 1966) reached agreement that training in psychotherapy was a major training goal in clinical psychology. However, those attending the conference rejected the psychologist-psychotherapist as an adequate model, asserting that "competence in any single professional function . . . does not constitute clinical psychology." They were not able to recommend specific standards or experiences.

Difficulties in providing adequate psychotherapy training for psychologists are compounded by the universities' academic tradition and the fact that many professors neither have interest in nor approve of clinical application. Hence, universities often do not provide prestigious psychotherapist models for their students, nor are they interested in preparing students to become psychotherapists. As stated by Holt (in Snyder, 1962): "Well there is a paradox in the inadequacy of the Ph.D. training as a preparation for professional practice. Our graduates are hardly ready to do a passable job of diagnostic testing without supervision, much less psychotherapy." Clinical psychology appears to suffer, in its applied aspects, from its academic history. It is almost unique among the health professions in having been *first* an academic program, and having gradually developed practicum aspects. Its growing pains are therefore the reverse of those described by Weil and Parrish (1967), as they plead for better *academic* training for many kinds of allied health personnel. The latter state: "All health professions were established first on a preceptor basis, then, over a period of years, were developed in separate schools and hospitals, and finally were incorporated into college and university education."

One suggested solution has been the establishment of postdoctoral training programs, which have increased substantially in number over the past decade. They are diverse in purpose, ranging from those offering advanced training in general clinical psychology to those providing specialized training with a specific population or with a specific skill, including psychotherapy. Another suggested solution has been the establishment of a separate professional school for clinical psychologists (offering a "Doctor of Psychology" degree), or a separate professional school to train psychotherapists. It has often been pointed out that much of the professional training of those who do psychotherapy—from psychiatry, psychology, and social work—is irrelevant to their later role as psychotherapists. In addition, it has never been established that high levels of education and/or training are necessary to the development of an effective psychotherapist. As described earlier, Bergin and Solomon (1970) found that empathic skill is not related to intelligence or to performance on the "psychologist" subscale of the Graduate Record Examination, and Melloh (1964) noted that the level of accurate empathy provided by 28 postpracticum counselor trainees was unrelated to their practicum grades. It would appear, from these and numerous related studies, that academia's criteria for selecting students are often irrelevant to their aptitude for becoming psychotherapists, and that grading criteria may be equally unrelated to the clinical student's ability to function constructively as a therapist (see Kelly and Fiske, 1951; also Kelly and Goldberg, 1959).

Fine (1966) states that psychotherapy has become the domain of an independent profession, and that its insights have affected the respective disciplines from which it has emerged, more than vice versa. Although this seems to be an exaggeration of the present state of affairs, we may indeed be moving in that direction, with the mushrooming of brief programs to train lay personnel as therapists. The decline of the medical model and the growth of a social-learning-theory model of mental health appears to open the door for training diverse kinds of individuals to conduct psychotherapy, including the kind of "mental health professional" now being trained in associate degree programs by junior and senior colleges (Cowne, 1969). Schofield (1964) has suggested training psychotherapists, in two-year graduate programs, to deal with the garden variety of minor complaints that do not require the skill of a highly trained therapist.

Carkhuff (1968) takes clinical psychology programs to task, inasmuch as they "have not yet demonstrated the relevant evidence for the translation of their training efforts to client benefits." He considers these graduate programs to be nonusefully intellectual and to train "discriminators" rather than "communicators." Further, he concludes from his research (Carkhuff and Berenson, 1967) that experienced clinicians, including supervisors, are functioning at less than facilitative levels, although it has been shown (Pagell, Carkhuff, and Berenson, 1967; Pierce, Carkhuff, and Berenson, 1967) that the trainees of supervisors providing high levels of therapeutic conditions are likely to exhibit positive change and, conversely, students receiving low levels of conditions are likely to deteriorate.

He charges that (Carkhuff, 1968) "... The professional programs exhibit a drop in the level of trainee functioning over the course of graduate training, with the largest drop seeming to occur from the first to second year" (Carkhuff, Kratochvil, and Friel, 1968; Carkhuff, Piaget, and Pierce, 1968). He describes professional programs as consisting of a complex mixture of science, research, and practice. By contrast, he perceives lay training programs as directed toward the development of interpersonal skills and a change in trainee attitudes. Regarding the value of these programs, he states: "There is extensive evidence to indicate that lay persons can effect significant constructive changes in the clients whom they see."

Training of Lay Counselors

Rioch et al. (1965) described one of the pioneering projects in training lay therapists.

They carefully selected 8 college-educated homemakers and gave them an intensive 2-year training program in psychotherapy. The program included seminars, individual and group supervision, listening to their own tape recordings, and observing some of their supervisor's psychotherapy interviews. Four senior psychotherapists made blind ratings of the posttraining therapy interviews, and concluded that the trainees' performance was comparable to that of more highly trained psychotherapists. Sixty-one percent of their patients were rated as improved—a percentage comparable to that of many studies of psychotherapy outcome. Golann, Breiter, and Magoon (1967) measured the performance of the same students in responding to a 30-minute filmed interview developed by Stoller and Geertsma (1958). Briefly, lay therapists rated 109 items as being from "very characteristic" of the patient to "not characteristic" of the patient, and their performance was rated for accuracy, with the criterion being 5 psychiatrists' pooled ratings (satisfactory interrater reliability had been established). The lay therapists' performance was superior to that of hospital volunteer workers and freshman medical students and highly similar to that of senior medical students' postclerkship judgments. The relationship of such judgments to therapy skill and client benefit is, of course, unknown.

Beck, Kantor, and Gelineau (1963) demonstrated that college students, acting as "case-aide volunteers", could have a therapeutic effect upon chronic patients. Over an academic year, the students spent one hour per week with their patient, followed by one hour of group discussion and supervision with 8 to 10 other student case-aide volunteers. Thirty-one percent of the patients were able to leave the hospital while working with the students, although their average length of hospitalization had been 4.7 years. Those patients who were not released had a 12.4 years' mean length of hopitalization. The authors attributed the students' success to (1) the long-term dyadic relationship; (2) a loose role definition, freeing the student to do whatever seemed useful or most spontaneous; and (3) the fact that the relationship extended beyond the hospital, the student helping the patient with his job and family, as needed. They felt that continued group supervision was important in maintaining the students' morale and mitigating their anxiety.

Guerney (1964) and Stover and Guerney (1967) have effectively trained mothers to do nondirective play therapy (filial therapy) with their own children. From six to eight mothers are trained, in groups, to develop reflective, empathic skill during weekly half-hour play sessions with their own children. First the mother conducts an observed and tape-recorded, uninstructed, half-hour diagnostic play session with her child. Following diagnosis, the parents are interviewed again and filial therapy is recommended and described. The mothers in the two experimental groups then observed 3 to 5 demonstrations of following the child's lead, in initiating and directing activities, and in the expression of genuine empathy. Next, mothers demonstrated the above with their own child, and received comments from the trainer and the other mothers. The mothers' feelings about this reflective role were explored in group discussion, as were their reactions to the demonstrations and their growing awareness of their children's needs. The therapist attempted to be reflective and empathic, modeling the behaviors sought from the mothers. There were, altogether, 10 1½-hour sessions. The mothers made a marked gain in number of reflective statements and a drop in number of directive statements. There were large differences between the two experimental groups, which were taught by different clinicians, the more experienced clinician having the more pronounced effect. The mothers were more inclined to use restatement of content than clarification of feeling, which the authors believe is more difficult to master. The children's nonverbal and verbal aggression increased, with no change on the "leadership" and "dependency" dimensions. Thus, it appears that parents can be taught, by these means, to modify their own interaction behavior in the direction of becoming more like the client-centered therapist.

Stollak (1968) adapted Guerney's techniques in teaching college students to assume the role of play therapist (filial therapy). During a 10-week period, eighteen students were trained in 3 groups of 6. The first two sessions were spent in describing the therapist's role behaviors

—empathy, acceptance, non-directiveness, reflection, and the like. During sessions 3 to 5, the author demonstrated play techniques with "normal" children. The students observed, kept notes, and participated in discussion of the rationale, their feelings, and so on. During training sessions 6 to 10, each student played with a normal child. The play was observed and discussed, and feed-back was given by the other students. Twelve of the students then completed 10 sessions with a child "client." Their use of reflection increased over the 10 sessions. Clarification increased to session 5 and then declined. The children increased their expression of negative feeling to the 10th session. Their leadership scores increased to the 5th session, but dependency behavior did not change. The authors conclude that, despite the brevity of training, the students did significantly change their own behavior, and possibly effected the increased expression of negative feelings and leadership behavior among the children.

Harvey (1964) describes the selection and training of lay marriage counselors in Australia. Of about 270 counselors in the entire country, 235 are lay, part-time volunteers. By means of tests and interviews, the professional staff attempt to select mature, successful, intelligent people—usually housewives or underemployed individuals whose intelligence exceeds their education and occupation because of the depression or other external circumstances. Their training requires 2 years of attending classes that meet 1 or 2 evenings per week. The classes consist of introductory lectures on the family, child development, social psychology, personality theory, and the like, as well as practicum training. During the latter they study tape recordings, practice roleplaying, and discuss their own interviews from notes or tapes. The later stages of training are described as having much in common with therapy groups, and the supervisor-trainee relationship is described as "therapeutic." The author states: "After the training course and about two years of closely supervised counseling experience, the counselors become . . . remarkably skilled and sensitive in the use of this technique." No measurements of skill or patient outcome apparently are available.

It appears that the lay therapist training programs have in common (a) the selection of mature, presumably well-adjusted, socially skilled and successful people; (b) programs designed to teach, through appropriate practice, a specific[1] interpersonal role; and (c) a minimum of requirements unrelated to the specific relationship skills. Hence it would not be surprising to find that they teach this relationship skill at least as well as is done in graduate programs, where such skill is but one of many teaching goals and, in fact, explicitly does not have high priority.

Training of School Guidance Counselors

There have been numerous reports on training for relationship skill among school guidance counselors subsequent to the passage of the National Defense Education Act, which provided financial support for intensive counseling institutes. Dugan (1960) supported the need for such institutes in supplementing traditional university programs of which, at that time, less than half made provision for supervised counseling practicum. He stated that "this has represented perhaps the greatest single weakness in existing counselor preparation programs," and perceived that this lack was partly due to the costliness of practicum training in time, facilities, and staff-student ratio. His assertion was supported by the replies to Norris' (1960) questionnaire, which was sent to 379 counselors graduated from the master's level program at Michigan State University over a 12-year period. Fifty-five percent of the responders replied to an open-ended question asking for suggestions to improve the program. The answers most often stressed the need for greater emphasis on counseling *practicum* and *internship*, as well as courses in testing and statistics. The American Personnel and Guidance Association's *Standards for the Preparation of School Counselors* (1961) requires approximately 25 percent of the educational program to consist of supervised practice.

---

[1] This is reminiscent of the reports of brief training for specific skills (for example, tonsillectomy) being given to a new type of physician in the Soviet Union.

Jones (1963) measured attitude changes in 30 guidance counselors subsequent to a 7-week NDEA Summer Institute and found, as measured by responses to an opinionnaire, a significant increase in the number of counselors who endorsed a permissive atmosphere; the importance of an understanding and accepting atmosphere; and the need for considering with a student his total life situation rather than the immediate presenting problem only. Unfortunately, no behavioral or patient outcome measures were made.

Demos and Zuwaylif (1963) attempted to measure some of the effects of an NDEA six-week, intensive summer training program for counselors. In addition to course work, there was "extensive supervised counseling with secondary school students . . . considerable critiqueing of taped interviews—both individually and in small groups (and observing) counseling sessions." They administered Porter's (1950) written test pre- and posttraining. This test involves choosing the most appropriate of five responses to a given client statement. On all categories of the Porter test, the trainees made improvement that was significant at the .01 or .001 level of confidence. They were less evaluative, suggestive, and probing, and more understanding and interpretive. At the end of training, the counselors were rated as superior, average, or below average. Again, objective behavioral measures are lacking. It was found that the counselors who were rated "superior" had come to the institute with less evaluative and more understanding attitudes, and had made more movement than the "average" or "below average" counselors. The authors related this to Rogers' hypothesis that prognosis for client change is greatest among those already high on the "process scale." Conclusions must be tentative because of methodological limitations. However, the study appears to reinforce previously cited work regarding selection of students for psychotherapy training, and suggests that the selection procedures of the described lay counselor programs are more relevant than those of graduate programs.

Munger, Myers, and Brown (1963) also evaluated, with the Porter test, the persistence of attitude changes following an 8-week and a 16-week institute. In both institutes, practicum experience included the use of tape-recordings, one-way mirrors, and individual and group critiques of observed interviews. The students in each course demonstrated attitude changes but, after three months, the attitudes of the 8-week students had reverted. Following the 16-week course, the students' attitudes continued to change toward more "understanding" responses up to the last (six-month) follow-up. There was a significant difference between those who returned to work as counselors and those who had other positions. The counselors maintained their gain, whereas the noncounselors declined.

Rochester (1967) surveyed attitude changes among 126 counselor-trainees from 8 different one-year-long NDEA Counseling and Guidance Institutes. Attitudes were measured by the Porter Test and the Allport-Vernon-Lindzey Study of values pretraining, immediately posttraining, and after one year. A few changes were found, but these had reverted to pretraining attitudes at the time of follow-up.

Martin (1968) had counselors-in-training evaluate their own interviews on unconditional positive regard, accurate empathy, genuineness, and intensity or intimacy of relationship. In addition, during supervision the instructor rated tape segments on the same four scales. These counselors were found to improve more ($p < .01$) in accurate empathy than did a control group who received supervision but did not make self-ratings. Inexperienced counselors benefited somewhat more than experienced counselors. No differences were found between groups on the other three scales.

It is unfortunate that, in only one of the above studies, did the authors measure actual interview behaviors, and in none, client benefit. Porter (1950), himself, found that the test responses were not good predictors of interview behavior. For example, during posttraining evaluation, his students chose 89 percent reflective responses on the *written* test, but used only 11 percent reflective statements in a *test-interview*. The written test was also found to be unrelated to later job success as a counselor. It goes without saying that most supervisors of student-therapists are less concerned with purely *cognitive* changes than with verbal and nonverbal behavioral changes in therapist-client interaction. The apparent temporary effect of training suggests the need for follow-up workshops or inservice training.

Training of Rehabilitation Counselors

Miller and Lubin (1963) described the typical university program in rehabilitation counselor training, based upon questionnaire responses from thirty of the thirty-two programs approved by the Office of Vocational Rehabilitation (since August, 1967, restructured as Rehabilitation Services Administration). They pointed out that passage of Public Law 565 in 1954 provided great impetus to the establishment of university programs in vocational rehabilitation, and that 28 of the programs had been initiated since that date. Eleven schools offered the Ph.D. and 6 the Ed. D. All required an internship varying from 2 to 12 months, and were increasingly using a broader range of internship experience, including mental hospitals and sheltered workshops for the retarded. The schools rated the following learning activities as necessary for their students: participation in staff conferences on clients; the development of interviewing skills; supervised experience in personal counseling; and experience in placing clients in private industry.

Truax (1967) has reported the use of untrained but carefully selected support personnel in rehabilitation counseling at the Arkansas Rehabilitation Research and Training Center and the Hot Springs Rehabilitation Center. Selection (Truax, 1968) is made partially on the basis of psychological tests which appear to be correlated with the therapeutic conditions (MMPI and EPPS, see above). Applicants also conduct a group interview with prospective clients. The interviews are taped and rated, and successful applicants must average 4 or above on nonpossessive warmth and genuineness and 5 or above on accurate empathy. In the training of nonprofessional counselors, Truax emphasizes the importance of practicum or on-the-job training with *feedback*. The latter is recommended during the training process and also for maintaining quality control and improving performance over the years. Truax makes the interesting suggestion that such counselors have quarterly feedback in regard to (a) the level of interpersonal skill used in relating to clients and

(b) the average level of client benefit achieved in comparison with others.

In a research project designed to measure the effectiveness of these personnel, clients were randomly assigned to (1) a counselor working in the traditional manner; (2) a counselor assisted by a counselor aide, who received maximal supervision; or (3) a counselor aide functioning in the complete role of counselor, under supervision. Both counselors and counselor aides were randomly assigned to high and low case loads. The client's progress was rated from his vocational evaluation record, which included information regarding his productivity, cooperativeness, attitude, and dependability. The clients who were studied in this investigation spent "a majority of the year" in counseling. The best results were obtained by the aides, under supervision; the next best by the counselors, alone; and the least favorable, by the counselor and aide working together. The professional counselors worked best under low case loads and the aides under high case loads. With high case loads, the counselors spent less time per client, while the aides spent twice as much time with each client, on the average, under heavy case load. It appeared that the aides had greater enthusiasm and motivation, and communicated somewhat higher levels of warmth and empathy.

Truax interprets these results to confirm some of the contentions cited above: that graduate programs do not help students to greatly increase their interpersonal skills; that lifelong habits of relating are prepotent; that selection for interpersonal skill is important for improving client benefit; and that warmth and empathy are highly important variables in determining client benefit. He scores some telling points regarding professional training—for example, that one can obtain a Ph.D. and diplomate status without ever having demonstrated skill in relating to patients or in achievement of client benefit.

Training in Psychology Graduate Programs

There is no denying Carkhuff's (1968) complaint that psychology, as a profession, has done little to evaluate the degree of its success in training graduate students who can promote demonstrable, constructive client change. More studies have been conducted on the training outcome of students in counseling and guidance programs, and in medical school psychiatry practicum courses, although many of the studies are, unfortunately, unsophisticated in conceptualization and methodology and consequently of limited value. Paradoxically, some of the more sophisticated evaluations of these nonpsychologist programs have been conducted by psychologists. There is no question but that psychologists have been at the forefront in isolating some of the important dimensions of psychotherapy; devising instruments to measure them; attempting to establish the reliability and validity of the instruments; and relating the obtained measurements to outcome.

Why have psychologists for the most part so assiduously avoided evaluating the performance of their own graduate students? One can only conjecture, of course, but a few facts are worth consideration in this regard. Lubin's (1962) survey of one third of the members of the APA's (Clinical) Division 12 indicated that, although 41 percent of the respondees spent at least half of their time doing psychotherapy, 20 percent had had no supervised training in adult psychotherapy. Of those who had had supervised training, more than half had obtained most of it at the postdoctoral level, either through a formal program or by making individual arrangements. In addition, 59 percent had obtained their supervision from a psychiatrist rather than a psychologist. Thus, the supervision presumably was not entirely under the educational direction of psychologists and, as noted by the author, varied a great deal from one situation to another. One might conclude that often the psychology graduate student's training in psychotherapy has not been a required aspect of his predoctoral training; is loosely defined; and may not take place in a situation where it can be planned and evaluated by psychologists. This state of affairs was described by Albee (1964) as psychology's often being a guest in the house of psychiatry, a situation not conducive to the establishment of independent training programs. The practicum evaluation studies on graduate student populations have come from university counseling centers, summer workshops, and the like. Those

from medical settings have used medical-student therapist populations, primarily, and have usually had the goal of improving the student's diagnostic skill and, possibly, his ability to relate. Undoubtedly, the training of clinical psychologists has changed since the student days of those surveyed by Lubin in 1960. However, it appears that significant changes are just beginning to occur.

One of the few non-Rogerian descriptions of innovative methods in teaching psychotherapy to psychology graduate students has been written by Finney (1968), although he does not report any measures of its effectiveness. This program emphasizes experiential learning, but includes some didactic material. Each student is assigned to a fellow student who will act as his "client" and a (different) student who will act as his therapist. He meets with his therapist, or with his client, for one hour on alternate weeks. Each interview is completely transcribed by the therapist-student, the careful scrutiny required during typing being considered a learning experience in itself. The supervisor goes over the transcript and writes simple, direct comments that emphasize a few interviewing concepts such as "zip the lip," "don't change the subject," "keep your opinions out," and the like. By the end of the sixth or seventh interview ". . . they have learned to listen fairly perceptively, to reflect the important feelings, and to use open-ended questioning appropriately." The author believes that the experience of being a patient is useful and reports that, despite the complex transference situations that may arise, "there have been no episodes which seemed destructive." The professor demonstrates interviewing, using tape recordings of client interviews, and performing both role-playing and "real" interviews before the class, with the students as interviewees. Also, from time to time, the class is treated as a group-therapy situation. This is a bold program, which may be fraught with some dangers, but may also provide an unusual opportunity for intrapersonal exploration, in view of the presumed high similarity and high potential for empathic understanding between fellow graduate students. Hopefully, the author will evaluate change in student performance as a function of these training experiences. This would, of course, necessitate the explicit definition of the therapeutic dimensions along which he hopes to alter the students' behavior.

5. SPECIAL DEVICES FOR TEACHING AND EVALUATION OF TEACHING EFFECTIVENESS

A number of ingenious electronic devices, film adaptations of interviews, and the like have been constructed to help in the processes of supervision and evaluation of student learning.

Rogers' use of electrical recordings, 25 years ago, was a major breakthrough in first exposing the psychotherapeutic relationship to direct observation and measurement. The importance of this step can hardly be overestimated, as demonstrated by evidence of the omission and distortion of interview material which is presented for conference discussion by the student-therapist from memory. The one-way screen was a second breakthrough in exposing new dimensions of the therapeutic process to observation.

Videotapes and motion pictures have been used for demonstration purposes by Rogers; Gill, Newman, and Redlich; and others. Strupp and Jenkins (1963) developed sound motion pictures of therapy interviews with film stops at critical junctures where the viewer is asked for his response. They produced these filmed interviews in order to permit direct comparison of interviewer responses to the same stimulus situation, while maximizing the degree of realism. The films may have potential for measuring effects of training, although the authors are aware of the technique's shortcomings, especially that of lacking true *interaction* between the film patient and the therapist-viewer. This may be a fairly serious shortcoming, as evidenced by Porter's (1950) finding that students' interview behavior did not conform to their written responses.

Stoller and Geertsma (1958) filmed two 30-minute psychiatric interviews to be used as a standard situation to measure the student's ability to observe and evaluate patients subsequent to the senior psychiatric clerkship. To establish an "objective criterion" for the students' observations and evaluations of the patients, 5 instructors assigned ratings from 0 to 6 on 300 statements about the patient. The statements involved descriptive, evaluative, theoretical, and prognostic materials. The final criterion ratings were the instructors' average ratings on 100 statements having the highest interrater reliability. This may be a useful technique for examining the students' ability to observe and evaluate, but of course does not measure their ability to relate to patients or to elicit comparable material from patients by means of their own interview skills.

Korner and Brown (1962) developed a device called the Mechanical Third Ear that allows the supervisor to make comments to the student, during the course of an interview, unheard by the interviewee. The supervisor speaks into a microphone, from behind a one-way screen, and the student receives the message through a small hearing device. Ward (1960, 1962) developed a more sophisticated device (electronic preceptoring), which allows reception through a small radio receiver and obviates the necessity for an extended cord. He reports that students prefer the supervisor to react only at important junctures and with dynamics formulations, leaving the specific dialogue to the interviewer.

Those with a penchant for utilizing the latest communication equipment have used closed circuit television to allow large numbers of students to hear and observe single interviews, or the progress of psychotherapy.

Although the above instrumentation opens the possibility for improved and timely communication between teacher and student, there have been no carefully devised programs to measure the supervisors' possibly increased teaching effectiveness with their use. They do not appear as yet to have been used in conjunction with critical formulations of either the learning process or of what should be taught.

6. TEACHING THE TECHNIQUES OF BEHAVIOR MODIFICATION

In the last few years, there has been increasing enthusiasm for and use of operant conditioning and desensitization (classical conditioning) for populations that have been found to be relatively nonamenable to the more traditional forms of psychotherapy (for example, autistic and retarded children and chronic psychotics), as well as for removal of specific disturbing behaviors. Because of its recency, much of the reported work is in preliminary stages and in the form of case reports. However, as stated by Leff (1968), although there has been little opportunity for long-term follow-up, the latter would not be appropriate for many of the cases that are directed toward alteration of immediate behaviors. Similarly, statistical rates of improvement are seen as unnecessary to demonstrate that the procedures have real effects, because the evaluation of results is accomplished by means of successive experimentation with the same organism. "The subject thus becomes his own control in a program that has carefully specified target behaviors and modification goals. . . . Systematic variation of behavior in accordance with the changing experimental conditions provides conclusive evidence of efficacy (p. 398–399)."

There has been little specification of the techniques for training behavior therapists, perhaps because the methods are seen as simple and easily learned by nonprofessionals. Ullman (1967) points out that a wide range of normal people—parents, teachers and friends of the designated client—are involved in administering behavior therapy. Consequently, the psychologist's role shifts from therapist to consultant as he programs the environment and teaches the principles of behavior modification to others. In his role of teacher he must use the principles of "social learning" and "behavior influence." Ullman sees the *design* of the therapeutic situation, rather than its implementation, as crucial. However, he does not specify how to teach or evaluate the learning of either the psychologists' role of designer or the auxiliary therapists' role of implementation.

Lazarus (1968) agrees that the more important and complex skill is in learning to "extract the crucial and relevant problem areas . . . and thereafter to select the appropriate combination of techniques needed to quell the patient's discontent. The bulk of behavior therapy training should therefore be focused on these two central aspects—problem identification and the selection of appropriate techniques." In training *practitioners*—not scientist-practitioners—he recommends (a) the selection of kind and compassionate trainees, inasmuch as they have

been noted to have fewer patient dropouts and to produce more rapid patient change; (b) participation as co-therapist with several skilled therapists; and (c) behavior rehearsal. In the latter, the supervisor or other students may play the role of client; the interview is tape-recorded and played back; and the student receives feedback from the class and perhaps demonstration from the supervisor. Lazarus states that different skills and points of emphasis would be taught to the scientist-practitioner.

Leventhal and Pumroy (1968) describe the successful teaching of behavior modification techniques to a mature clinician through co-therapy. Sulzer (1968) has encouraged graduate students in educational psychology to undertake behavior modification projects in lieu of term papers. She has attempted to insure success (reinforcement) through having the students plan and specify their projects in detail, with clear definition of procedures, criterion performances, and goals.

Wolpe, Knopp, and Garfield (1966) have reported fairly large-scale training of practitioners who had already achieved professional status. They have provided three types of short-term programs for postgraduate professionals. The first kind of program was an intensive institute, involving daily training for a period of several weeks, in which there was theoretical discussion; demonstration of technique; supervised treatment of patients; and role-playing treatment situations with colleagues. The second type consisted of a running seminar, meeting weekly or biweekly over several months. Wolpe delivered five or six lectures, followed by case presentations and theory discussions. The third type of training is an apprenticeship. They consider this the training of choice, but it has the disadvantage that only a few people can be trained at one time.

Davison (1965) has trained undergraduates to be social reinforcers with autistic children. Four students were chosen on the basis of faculty recommendations and an interview assessment of their dependability and ingenuity. They had four, weekly lecture-and-discussion meetings regarding the rationale of behavior therapy and the operant-training paradigm; a functional analysis of the syndrome of early infantile autism; and the instrumental nature of various deviant behaviors and the implications for treatment. There were case discussions and the explication of both the use of play situations for differentially reinforcing compliant behavior and the importance of giving concomitant social reinforcement that would gradually replace the primary reinforcement. Readings from Bandura and Walters (1963) were also discussed. Following one month of studying the rationale, the author showed the students around and demonstrated the mechanics of treatment. After one session, they appeared able to carry on. Subsequent measures of student effectiveness suggested considerable improvement in the patients' compliance with their verbal commands, although certain experimental difficulties interfered with some of the planned measurements.

Bergin (1970) discusses the use of operant procedures by teachers in their classrooms. "It is argued by operant-conditioners that lack of control of classroom behavior is essentially a consequence of unwitting misapplication of reinforcement. . . ." He describes the procedure of training the teacher as follows:

Procedurally, a brief instruction period is conducted with the teacher in which she learns, via programmed instruction, how behavior is maintained by means of reinforcements paired with specific acts or patterns of action. Once this is accomplished, she and the consultant cooperate in conducting the behavioral assessment of the specific situation, usually with the assistance of an observer who makes frequency counts of the behaviors to be changed and the reinforcements occurring in the classroom that seem to be maintaining them.

It appears, then, that the behavior-modification student-therapist requires primarily didactic training, and a much smaller emphasis is placed upon the experiential or relationship aspects than is given to other forms of psychotherapy. The behavior therapist's task is one of observation, analysis, development of a program, and implementation of this program. The behavioral and attitudinal aspects of the program apparently are presumed to be sufficiently explicit that they depend less for their efficacy upon more general behavior characteristics of the particular behavioral engineer who administers them. Of the above writers, only Lazarus mentions the need to be "kind" or "compassionate." Perhaps the brief, relatively simple training procedures reflect the specificity of behaviors these therapists are attempting to modify, or the relatively primitive functioning of at least some of the groups to whom the techniques are applied. It may be anticipated that, as there are more follow-up studies of the effectiveness of treatment programs, it will be found that additional treatment factors do affect outcome. For example, dropout rate has not been adequately reported.

Conclusions

Research on the teaching of psychotherapy skill is still in its early stages, necessarily moving no faster than our knowledge of some of the important dimensions of psychotherapeutic behavior, as well as our ability to measure them and some of the significant dimensions of patient improvement. However, it is heartening to see a greatly increasing trend toward empiricism, improved techniques of measurement, and the application of theory and research-based concepts from the related areas of social learning, group dynamics, and classical and operant conditioning. In brief, the general area of psychotherapy has been enriched by its new conception as simply a particular kind of dyadic relationship to which our knowledge of dyadic interaction, generally, applies. By the same token, the supervision process in psychotherapy has been given new life by being conceptualized as a learning situation to which the principles from both didactic teaching and social learning apply.

The client-centered group has perhaps devoted more of its research to the development and evaluation of research in psychotherapy than has any other group of psychologists. Their dimensions of therapist behavior, including empathy, warmth, and the like, appear to make significant contributions to patient outcome; and their training programs apparently are able to teach these skills within a relatively small number of training hours.

It is unfortunate that there are no other systematic programs for teaching psychotherapeutic skill with measurement of training effects. As Bergin (1966) has suggested, some of the seemingly most important variables in the client-centered therapist's behavior may not turn out to be the most significant variables in the therapeutic behavior of eclectic or other therapists. Also, these studies have been accomplished by a relatively small number of researchers and should be verified by others who are less committed to the theories underlying the research.

Nevertheless, the client-centered research appears at present to be the most empirically based and internally logical training program thus far described in the literature. It is to be hoped that increasing numbers of others will abandon teaching techniques that have been shown to be relatively ineffective or inefficient; think in wider perspective about their programs; and objectively measure their effectiveness. We can improve only by searching for weaknesses and eliminating them, but sometimes it appears that we invest more effort in attempting to demonstrate to others that our present techniques are laudable.

Over the past decade, there has been considerable change in the philosophy underlying psychotherapy and the overall handling of social-emotional-behavioral disorders. The social-learning model has made large inroads into the clinical model for a large proportion of those outpatient clients who have behavioral deficits and/or maladaptive emotional responses. This conceptual change and the large unmet need for mental health workers, have promoted the teaching of mental health skills, including some forms of psychotherapy, to relatively large numbers of "lay" individuals. Mental health educators have devised relatively brief training programs and concerned themselves, to some extent, with the effectiveness of their programs. Most of the research studies attempting to evaluate training have been of limited value, partly due to the difficulties in defining and measuring the skills that the training was designed to improve. The few well-designed studies, as well as hints from those that are less definitive, suggest that lay counselors can be trained, in a relatively few hours, to change their interview behavior to become significantly more similar to that of trained therapists on a number of dimensions. Several studies also have shown that they effect patient improvement.

Some of the important variables in effective teaching programs appear to be *selection* of psychologically healthy individuals and combined *didactic* and *experiential* training for a specific, *well-defined* role. It appears that individuals who are already interpersonally sensitive and skillful can more quickly learn to become therapeutic. In the most effective programs, the desired attitudes and behaviors have been defined; taught singly, in some instances; and the degree of skill measured, with subsequent feedback. Peer observation and feedback seem to be effective in increasing the student-therapist's awareness of himself and motivating him to change. A warm and accepting supervisor relationship is also apparently a very important part of learning—both freeing the student to experiment with new behaviors, and serving as a model for appropriate, therapeutic behavior. Group experiential learning, with discussion of the students' attitudes and difficulties in the role of psychotherapist, also seems to promote learning.

Most medical schools have become concerned with teaching relationship skills to medical students, although usually these programs have combined and often confused the teaching of relationship and diagnostic skills. There has been little explicit definition of therapeutic dimensions, with consequent difficulty in establishing systematic training programs with built-in designs to measure the specific student-therapist skills acquired.

Psychology has not done as much as might be expected in developing training standards, experimental programs, and measurement of training effects with its own students. On the other hand, psychologists have made progress in defining some of the effective dimensions of psychotherapy, developing research instruments to measure these dimensions, and carrying out relatively sophisticated research in related areas. In regard to its own training programs, the field of clinical psychology has not given primary emphasis to development of skill in dyadic psychotherapy, seeing this as but one of many skills appropriate to the clinical psychologist. The greater emphasis upon more basic knowledge and research skill has begun to reap rewards, as demonstrated by the research above.

REFERENCES

Adams, W. R. The psychiatrist in an ambulatory clerkship for comprehensive medical care in a new curriculum. *Journal of Medical Education*, 1958, **33**, 211–220.

Albee, G. President's message: A declaration of independence for psychology. *Ohio Psychologist*, 1964, **10**, No. 4.

Aldrich, C. K., and Bernhardt, H. Evaluation of a change in teaching psychiatry to medical students. *American Journal of Orthopsychiatry*, 1963, **33**, 105–114.

Alexik, M., and Carkhuff R. R. The effects of the experimental manipulation of client self-exploration by high- and low-functioning therapists. *Journal of Clinical Psychology*, 1967, **23**, 210–212.

Allen, T. W. Effectiveness of counselor trainees as a function of psychological openness. *Journal of Counseling Psychology*, 1967, **14**, 35–40.

American Personnel and Guidance Association. A statement of policy: Standards for the preparation of school counselors. *Personnel and Guidance Journal*, 1961, **40**, 402–407.

Anderson, S. C. Effects of confrontation by high- and low-functioning therapists. *Journal of Counseling Psychology*, 1968, **15**, 411–416.

Balint, M. Method and technique in the teaching of medical psychology. II. Training general practitioners in psychotherapy. *British Journal of Medical Psychology*, 1954, **27**, 37–41.

Bandura, A., and Walters, R. H. *Social learning and personality development*. New York: Holt, Rinehart & Winston, 1963.

Bare, C. E. Relationship of counselor personality and counselor-client personality similarity to selected counseling success criteria. *Journal of Counseling Psychology*, 1967, **14**, 419–425.

Barrett-Lennard, G. T. Dimensions of therapist response as causal factors in therapeutic change. *Psychological Monographs: General and Applied*, 1962, **76** (43, Whole No. 562).

Beck, J. C., Kantor, D., and Gelineau, V. A. Follow-up study of chronic psychotic patients "treated" by college case-aid volunteers. *American Journal of Psychiatry*, 1963, **120**, 269–271.

Berenson, B. G., Carkhuff, R. R., and Myrus, P. The interpersonal functioning and training of college students. *Journal of Counseling Psychology*, 1966, **13**, 441–446.

Bergin, A. E. The effects of psychotherapy: Negative results revisited. *Journal of Counseling Psychology*, 1963, **10**, 244–250.

Bergin, A. E. Principles of personality and behavior change. In J. R. Davitz and S. Ball (Eds.), *Advanced Educational Psychology*, 1970.

Bergin, A. E., and Jasper, L. G. Correlates of empathy in psychotherapy: A replication. *Journal of Abnormal Psychology*, 1969, **74**, 477–481.

Bergin, A. E., and Solomon, S. Personality and performance correlates of empathic understanding in psychotherapy. In T. Tomlinson and J. Hart (Eds.), *New directions in client-centered therapy*. Boston: Houghton-Mifflin, 1970.

Blocksma, D. D., and Porter, E. H., Jr. A short-term training program in client-centered counseling. *Journal of Consulting Psychology*, 1947, **11**, 55–60.

Carkhuff, R. R. Toward a comprehensive model of facilitative inter-personal processes. *Journal of Counseling Psychology*, 1967, **14**, 67–72.

Carkhuff, R. R. Differential functioning of lay and professional helpers. *Journal of Counseling Psychology*, 1968, **15**, 117–126.

Carkhuff, R. R., and Alexik, M. Effect of client depth of self-exploration upon high- and low-functioning counselors. *Journal of Counseling Psychology*, 1967, **14**, 350–355.

Carkhuff, R. R., and Berenson, B. G. *Beyond counseling and psychotherapy*. New York: Holt, Rinehart, & Winston, 1967.

Carkhuff, R. R., Kratochvil, D., and Friel, T. Effects of professional training: Communication and discrimination of facilitative conditions. *Journal of Counseling Psychology*, 1968, **15**, 68–74.

Carkhuff, R. R., Piaget, G., and Pierce, R. The development of skills in interpersonal functioning. *Counselor Education and Supervision*, 1968, **7**, 102–106.

Carkhuff, R. R., and Truax, C. B. Training in counseling and psychotherapy: An evaluation of an integrated didactic and experiential approach. *Journal of Consulting Psychology*, 1965, **29**, 333–336. (a)

Carkhuff, R. R., and Truax, C. B. Lay mental health counseling—the effects of lay group counseling. *Journal of Consulting Psychology*, 1965, **29**, 426–431. (b)

Coggeshall, L. T. *Planning for medical progress through education*. Evanston, Ill.: Association of American Medical Colleges, 1965.

Coleman, J. V. The teaching of basic psychotherapy. *American Journal of Orthopsychiatry*, 1947, **17**, 622–627.

Covner, B. J. Studies in phonographic recordings of verbal material. III. The completeness and accuracy of counseling interview reports. *Journal of General Psychology*, 1944, **30**, 181–203.

Cowne, L. Approaches to the mental health manpower problem. *Mental Hygiene*, 1969, **53**, 176–187.

Davison, G. C. The training of undergraduates as social reinforcers for autistic children. In L. P. Ullman and L. Krasner (Eds.), *Case studies in behavior modification*. New York: Holt, Rinehart & Winston, 1965.

Demos, G. D., and Zuwaylif, F. H. Counselor movement as a result of an intensive six-week training program in counseling. *Personnel and Guidance Journal*, 1963, **42**, 125–128.

Dugan, W. E. The impact of NDEA upon counselor preparation. *Personnel and Guidance Journal*, 1960, **39**, 37–40.

Ekstein, R., and Wallerstein, R. S. *The teaching and learning of psychotherapy.* New York: Basic Books, 1958.

Enelow, A. J., Adler, L., and Manning, R. R. A supervised psychotherapy course for practicing physicians. *Journal of Medical Education*, 1964, **39**, 140–146.

Enelow, A. J., Forde, D. L., and Gwartney, R. H. Psychoanalytic medicine: An avenue for the psychiatric education of medical practitioners. *Diseases of the nervous system*, 1962, **23**, 1–3.

Engel, G. L., Green, W. L., Jr., Reichsman, F., Schmale, A., and Ashenburg, N. A graduate and undergraduate teaching program on the psychological aspects of medicine: A report of the liaison program between medicine and psychiatry at the University of Rochester School of Medicine. *Journal of Medical Education*, 1957, **32**, 157–169.

Feifel, H., and Eells, J. Patients and therapists assess the same psychotherapy. *Journal of Consulting Psychology*, 1963, **27**, 310–318.

Fine, R. Training the psychologist for psychotherapy. *Psychotherapy: Theory, Research and Practice*, 1966, **3**, 184–187.

Finney, B. C. Some techniques and procedures for teaching psychotherapy. *Psychotherapy: Theory, Research and Practice*, 1968, **5**, 115–119.

Fleming, J., and Benedek, T. *Psychoanalytic supervision.* New York: Grune & Stratton, 1966.

Fleming, J., and Hamburg, D. An analysis of methods for teaching psychotherapy with description of a new approach. *American Medical Association Archives of Neurology and Psychiatry*, 1958, **79**, 179–200.

Gardner, G. G. The psychotherapeutic relationship. *Psychological Bulletin*, 1964, **61**, 426–437.

Gendlin, E. T., and Tomlinson, T. M. "The Experiencing Scale" (Mathieu-Klein revision). Unpublished manual, 1963.

Gill, M., Newman, R., and Redlich, F. C. *The initial interview in psychoanalytic practice.* New York: International Universities, 1954.

Golann, S. E., Breiter, D. E., and Magoon, T. M. A filmed interview applied to the evaluation of mental health counselors. *Psychotherapy: Theory, Research and Practice*, 1967, **3**, 21–24.

Goldstein, A. P., Heller, K., and Sechrest, L. B. *Psychotherapy and the psychology of behavior change.* New York: Wiley, 1966.

Group for the Advancement of Psychiatry: Committee on Medical Education. *Report on Medical Education*, 1948, No. 3, 1–12.

Guerney, B. G., Jr. Filial therapy: description and rationale. *Journal of Consulting Psychology*, 1964, **28**, 304–310.

Hansen, J. C., and Barker, E. N. Experiencing and the supervisory relationship. *Journal of Counseling Psychology*, 1964, **11**, 107–111.

Harvey, L. V. The use of non-professional auxiliary counselors in staffing a counseling service. *Journal of Counseling Psychology*, 1964, **11**, 348–351.

Heine, R. W., Aldrich, C. K., Draper, E., Meuser, M., Tippett, J., and Trosman, H. *The student physician as psychotherapist.* Chicago: University of Chicago Press, 1962.

Hoch, E. L., Ross, A. O., and Winder, C. L. Conference on the professional preparation of clinical psychologists: A summary. *American Psychologist*, 1966, **21**, 42–51.

Holder, T., Carkhuff, R. R., and Berenson, B. G. Differential effects of the manipulation of therapeutic conditions upon high- and low-functioning clients. *Journal of Counseling Psychology*, 1967, **14**, 63–66.

Holt, R. R., and Luborsky, L. *Personality patterns of psychiatrists.* New York: Basic Books, 1958.

Ivey, A. E., Normington, C. J., Miller, D. C., Merrill, W. H., and Haase, R. F. Microcounseling and attending behavior: An approach to prepracticum counselor training. *Journal of Counseling Psychology*, 1968, **15** (Monogr. Suppl. 5).

Jones, V. Attitude changes in an NDEA Institute. *Personnel and Guidance Journal*, 1963, **42**, 387–392.

Kamin, I., and Caughlan, J. Patients report the subjective experience of outpatient psychotherapy: A follow-up study. *American Journal of Psychotherapy*, 1963, **17**, 660–668.

Kelly, E. L. Clinical psychology—1960: Report of survey findings. *Newsletter, Division of Clinical Psychology, American Psychological Association*, 1961, **14**, 1–11.

Kelly, E. L., and Fiske, D. W. *The prediction of performance in clinical psychology.* Ann Arbor: University of Michigan Press, 1951.

Kelly, E. L., and Goldberg, L. R. Correlates of later performance and specialization in psychology. *Psychological Monographs*, 1959, No. 482.

Korner, I. N., and Brown, W. H. The mechanical third ear. *Journal of Consulting Psychology*, 1952, **16**, 81–84.

Krasner, L. The therapist as a social reinforcer: Man or machine. Paper presented at the American Psychological Association Convention, Philadelphia, August, 1963.

Kratochvil, D., Aspy, D., and Carkhuff, R. R. The differential effects of absolute level and direction of growth in counselor functioning upon client level of functioning. *Journal of Clinical Psychology*, 1967, **23**, 216–217.

Lazarus, A. A. The content of behavior therapy training. Paper presented at the meeting of the Association for the Advancement of the Behavioral Therapies, San Francisco, August, 1968.

Leff, R. Behavior modification and the psychoses of childhood. *Psychological Bulletin*, 1968, **69**, 396–409.

Lester, B. K., Gussen, J., Yamamoto, J., and West, L. J. Teaching psychotherapy in a longitudinal curriculum. *Journal of Medical Education*, 1962, **37**, 28–32.

Leventhal, A. M., and Pumroy, D. K. Training in behavior therapy: A case study. Unpublished manuscript, University of Maryland, 1968.

Lorr, M. Client perception of therapists: A study of the therapeutic relation. *Journal of Consulting Psychology*, 1965, **29**, 146–149.

Lubin, B. Survey of psychotherapy training and activities of psychologists. *Journal of Clinical Psychology*, 1962, **18**, 252–255.

Martin, D. G. A method of self-evaluation for counselor education. U.S. Department of Health, Education and Welfare, Office of Education, Bureau of Research, 1968.

Matarazzo, R. G., Phillips, J. S., Wiens, A. N., and Saslow, G. Learning the art of interviewing: A study of what beginning students do and their pattern of change. *Psychotherapy: Theory, Research and Practice*, 1965, **2**, 49–60.

Matarazzo, R. G., Wiens, A. N., and Saslow, G. Experimentation in the teaching and learning of psychotherapy skills. In Gottschalk, L. K., and Auerbach, A. (Eds.), *Methods of Research in Psychotherapy*. New York: Appleton-Century-Crofts, 1966. Pp. 597–635.

Melloh, R. A. Accurate empathy and counselor effectiveness. Unpublished doctoral dissertation, University of Florida, 1964.

Miller, M. R., and Lubin, B. Rehabilitation counselor training in the United States. *Personnel and Guidance Journal*, 1963, **42**, 606–608.

Munger, P. F., Myers, R. A., and Brown, D. F. Guidance institutes and the persistence of attitudes: A progress report. *Personnel and Guidance Journal*, 1963, **41**, 415–419.

Muslin, H. L., Burstein, A. G., Gedo, J. E., and Sadow, L. Research on the supervisory process. I. Supervisor's appraisal of the interview data. *Archives of General Psychiatry*, 1967, **16**, 427–431.

Norris, W. More than a decade of training guidance and personnel workers. *Personnel and Guidance Journal*, 1960, **38**, 287–291.

Ornston, P. S., Cicchetti, J. L., and Fierman, L. B. Some parameters of verbal behavior that reliably differentiate novice from experienced psychotherapists. *Journal of Abnormal Psychology*, 1968, **73**, 240–244.

Pagell, W. A., Carkhuff, R. R., and Berenson, B. G. The predicted differential effects of the level of counselor functioning upon the level of functioning of outpatients. *Journal of Clinical Psychology*, 1967, **23**, 510–512.

Pfouts, J. H., and Rader, G. E. Instruction in interviewing technique in the medical school curriculum: Report of a trial program and some suggestions. *Journal of Medical Education*, 1962, **37**, 681–686.

Piaget, G. W., Berenson, B. G., and Carkhuff, R. R. Differential effects of the manipulation of therapeutic conditions by high- and moderate-functioning therapists upon high- and low-functioning clients. *Journal of Consulting Psychology*, 1967, **31**, 481–486.

Pierce, R., Carkhuff, R. R., and Berenson, B. G. The differential effects of high and low functioning counselors upon counselors-in-training. *Journal of Clinical Psychology*, 1967, **23**, 212–215.

Porter, E. H., Jr. *An introduction to therapeutic counseling*. Boston: Houghton Mifflin, 1950.

Rice, L. N. Therapists' style of participation and case outcome. *Journal of Consulting Psychology*, 1965, **29**, 155–160.

Rioch, M. J., Elkes, C., and Flint, A. A., Usdansky, B. S., Newman, R. G., and Silber, E. Pilot project in training mental health counselors. U.S. Department of Health, Education and Welfare, Public Health Service Publication No. 125, 1965.

Rochester, D. The persistence of attitudes and values of NDEA counselor trainees. *Journal of Counseling Psychology*, 1967, **14**, 535–537.

Rogers, C. R. *Client-centered therapy*. Boston: Houghton Mifflin, 1951.

Rogers, C. R. The necessary and sufficient conditions of therapeutic personality change. *Journal of Consulting Psychology*, 1957, **21**, 95–103.

Rogers, C. R., and Truax, C. B. The relationship between patient intrapersonal exploration in the first sampling interview and the final outcome criterion. *Brief Research Reports*, Wisconsin Psychiatric Institute, University of Wisconsin, 1962, **73**.

Romano, J. Comparative observations in the teaching of psychiatry to undergraduate medical students. *Perspectives in Biology*, 1962, **5**, 519–526.

Rosenthal, R. On the social psychology of the psychological experiment: The experimenter's hypothesis as unintended determinant of experimental results. *American Scientist*, 1963, **51**, 268–283.

Saretsky, T. Transference and counter-transference problems of the candidate analyst. *Psychotherapy: Theory, Research and Practice*, 1966, **3**, 188–189.

Schofield, W. *Psychotherapy: The purchase of friendship*. Englewood Cliffs, N J., Prentice-Hall, 1964.

Snyder, W. U. Professional training for clinical psychologists: A synthesis of a symposium. *Journal of Clinical Psychology*, 1962, **18**, 243–247.

Stollak, G. E. The experimental effects of training college students as play therapists. *Psychotherapy: Theory, Research and Practice*, 1968, **5**, 77–80.

Stoller, R. J., and Geertsma, R. H. Construction of a final examination to assess clinical judgment in psychiatry. *Journal of Medical Education*, 1958, **33**, 837–840.

Stover, L., and Guerney, B. G., Jr. The efficacy of training procedures for mothers in filial therapy. *Psychotherapy: Theory, Research and Practice*, 1967, **4**, 110–115.

Strupp, H. H., and Bergin, A. E. Some empirical and conceptual bases for coordinated research in psychotherapy: A critical review of issues, trends, and evidence. *International Journal of Psychiatry*, 1969, **7**, 18–90.

Strupp, H. H., and Jenkins, J. J. The development of six sound motion pictures simulating psychotherapeutic situations. *Journal of Nervous and Mental Disease*, 1963, **136**, 317–328.

Strupp, H. H., Wallach, M. S., and Wogan, M. Psychotherapy experience in retrospect: Questionnaire survey of former patients and their therapists. *Psychological Monographs: General and Applied*, 1964, **78** (11, Whole No. 588).

Sulzer, B. Student preparation for behavior modification projects. Paper presented at the meeting of the American Psychological Association, San Francisco, September, 1968.

Thurnblad, R. J., and McCurdy, R. L. Human behavior and the student physician. *Journal of Medical Education*, 1967, **42**, 158–162.

Tomlinson, T. M., and Stoler, N. The relationship between affective evaluation and ratings of therapy process and outcome with schizophrenics. *Psychotherapy: Theory, Research and Practice*, 1967, **4**, 14–18.

Truax, C. B. A program of psychotherapy with hospitalized schizophrenics. Symposium presented at the American Psychological Association Convention, New York, 1961.

Truax, C. B. The use of supportive personnel in rehabilitation counseling: Process and outcome. G. R. Leslie (Ed.), *Supportive personnel in rehabilitation centers: Current practices and future needs.* Washington, D.C.: Association of Rehabilitation Centers, Inc., 1967. Pp. 123–154.

Truax, C. B. Selection, training and utilization of nonprofessional personnel in rehabilitation counseling: The trained practical counselor. Unpublished manuscript, Arkansas Rehabilitation Research and Training Center, University of Arkansas, 1968.

Truax, C. B., and Carkhuff, R. R. *Toward effective counseling and psychotherapy: Training and practice.* Chicago: Aldine, 1967.

Truax, C. B., Carkhuff, R. R., and Douds, J. Toward an integration of the didactic and experiential approaches to training in counseling and psychotherapy. *Journal of Counseling Psychology*, 1964, **11**, 240–247.

Truax, C. B., and Silber, L. D. Personality and psychotherapeutic skills. Unpublished manuscript, University of Arkansas, 1966.

Traux, C. B., Silber, L. D., and Carkhuff, R. R. Accurate empathy, non-possessive warmth, genuineness and therapeutic outcome in lay group counseling. Unpublished manuscript, University of Arkansas, 1966.

Truax, C. B., Silber, L. D., and Wargo, D. G. Personality change and achievement in therapeutic training. Unpublished manuscript, Arkansas Rehabilitation Research and Training Center, University of Arkansas, 1966.

Truax, C. B., Wargo, D. G., Frank, J. D., Imber, S. D., Battle, C. C., Hoehn-Saric, R., Nash, E. H., and Stone, A. R. Therapist empathy, genuineness, and warmth and patient therapeutic outcome. *Journal of Consulting Psychology*, 1966, **30**, 395–401.

Ullman, L. The major concepts taught to behavior therapy trainees. Paper presented at the meeting of the American Psychological Association, Washington, D.C., September, 1967.

Ward, C. H. An electronic aide for teaching interviewing techniques. *Archives of General Psychiatry*, 1960, **3**, 357–358.

Ward, C. H. Electronic preceptoring in teaching beginning psychotherapy. *Journal of Medical Education*, 1962, **37**, 1128–1129.

Weil, T. P., and Parrish, H. M. Development of a coordinated approach for the training of allied health personnel. *Journal of Medical Education*, 1967, **42**, 651–659.

Werkman, S. L. Teaching the interpretive process to medical students. *American Journal of Psychiatry*, 1961. **117**, 897–902.

Whitaker, C. A. Teaching the practicing physician to do psychotherapy. *Southern Medical Jounral* 1949, **42**, 899–903.

Whitehorn, J. C., Jacobsen, C., Levine, M., and Lippard, V. W. (Eds.), *Psychiatry and medical education.* Report of the 1951 Conference on Psychiatric Education, Cornell University. Washington, D.C.: American Psychiatric Association, 1952.

Whitely, J. M., Sprinthall, N. A., Mosher, R. L., and Donaghy, R. T. Selection and evaluation of counselor effectiveness. *Journal of Counseling Psychology*, 1967, **14**, 226–234.

Wolpe, J , Knopp, W , and Garfield, Z. Post-graduate training in behavior therapy. *Excerpta Medica International Congress Series No. 150*, Proceedings of the IV World Congress of Psychiatry, Madrid, September, 1966.

Zimmer, J. M., and Anderson, S. Dimensions of positive regard and empathy. *Journal of Counseling Psychology*, 1968, **15**, 417–426.

Zimmer, J. M., and Park, P. Factor analysis of counselor communications. *Journal of Counseling Psychology*, 1967, **14**, 198–203.

AUTHOR INDEX

Aaronson, H. G., 510
Abeles, N., 356
Abelson, R. P., 682
Abramovitz, A., 210, 566
Abramson, H. A., 445, 446, 449
Abse, D. N., 41
Acheson, G. H., 522
Ackerman, N. W., 753
Ackerman, P. J., 552
Adams, H., 59
Adams, H. E., 721
Adams, J. K., 712
Adams, J. S., 166, 629
Adams, P. L., 486
Adelman, H. M., 584
Adler, A., 16, 314
Adler, L., 909
Adler, M. H., 198
Adorno, T. W., 826
Affleck, D. C., 277, 280, 282, 283, 284, 288, 290, 451, 454
Agard, F. B., 370
Agazarian, Y., 857
Agnew, J. W., Jr., 59
Agras, W. S., 134, 620
Ahmad, F. Z., 355, 721
Aiken, E. G., 169
Ainslie, J. D., 444
Albee, G. W., 795
Aldrich, C. K., 907
Alexander, F., 76, 219, 223, 410, 423, 453, 456, 460, 462, 710, 722
Alexander, J. F., 356
Alexander, L., 521
Alexik, M., 138, 139, 326, 362, 899
Allen, B. V., 352
Allen, C. K., 671
Allen, T. W., 905
Allen, V. L., 183, 846, 855
Allison, R. B., 273, 274, 277, 451, 460
Allport, G., 66-68, 200, 258
Alpern, G. D., 474
Alpern, H., 583
Anant, S., 580
Anant, S. S., 731

Anastasio, E. J., 96
Anderson, D. E., 763, 767
Anderson, D. L., 325
Anderson, O. D., 544, 553
Anderson, R. P., 822
Anderson, S. C., 360, 362, 899, 906
Anker, J. M., 816, 826
Ansell, S., 118
Apfelbaum, B., 422
Apostal, R. A., 869, 870
Appel, J. B., 583
Appel, K. E., 226, 236
Applegate, W., 372
Appleton, W. S., 504, 532
Appley, M. H., 802
Arbous, A. G., 188
Argyris, C., 840, 845, 847, 849, 853, 854
Armington, J., 454
Armitage, S. G., 618, 622, 633, 729
Armor, D. J., 795
Armstrong, H. E., 732, 733
Armstrong, M., 764
Armstrong, R. A., 780, 798
Arnold, C. B., 802
Arnold, C. R., 260, 765
Aronfreed, J., 656
Aronson, E., 168
Aronson, G. J., 518
Aronson, H., 230, 276, 283, 292, 354, 412
Arp, D. J., 366, 367, 371, 390
Arrington, W., 451-453
Artuso, A. A., 764, 769
Asch, S. E., 165
Ascough, J. C., 643
Ashby, J. D., 59, 130, 163, 170, 381
Ashem, B., 580, 732
Ashenberg, N., 907
Ashley, F. W., 446
Aspy, D., 334, 361, 900
Astin, A. W., 44
Astrachan, B. M., 357, 832
Astrup, C., 526
Atkins, S., 854

Atthowe, J. M., Jr., 638, 640
Auerbach, A. H., 357, 387, 417, 420
Auld, F., Jr., 49, 111, 279, 284, 345, 347, 348, 351, 363, 370, 371, 372, 378, 379, 380, 719
Austin, G. A., 716
Ax, A. F., 88, 92, 101
Ayllon, T., 655, 699
Azima, H., 503, 515, 517, 522
Azrin, N. H., 581, 582, 584, 619, 627, 638, 641, 643, 699

Bacal, H. A., 256, 258
Bach, G. R., 183, 856
Bachrach, A., 643, 727
Bachrach, H., 420, 421
Back, K. W., 162
Baehr, G. O., 816, 825
Baer, D. M., 654, 694
Bahn, A. K., 783
Bailey, M. A., 273, 278, 285
Bailey, P., 463
Baker, A. A., 449, 452, 453, 454
Baker, B., 602, 726
Baker, E., 59
Baker, F., 795, 804
Baker, G., 287
Baker, J. W., 114, 115
Bakker, C., 504
Baldridge, B. J., 522
Baler, L. A., 802
Bales, R. F., 184, 185, 186, 188, 355, 357, 358, 367, 415, 843
Balfour, F. H., 256, 258
Balint, M., 909
Balkin, J. L., 262
Bamberger, H., 364
Bancroft, J., 588
Bandura, A., 56-57, 135, 136, 171, 355, 381, 545, 614, 653-703, 716, 721, 722, 724, 919
Banks, G., 362
Bannazizi, A., 553
Barab, P. G., 694
Barber, T. X., 452, 454, 599
Barchilon, J., 448, 451, 453, 456
Barclay, J., 764, 765, 772

Bard, P., 102
Bardwick, J. M., 104
Bare, C. E., 905
Barends, J., 567
Barger, B., 823
Barker, E. N., 904
Barker, J. C., 588
Barker, R. G., 781
Barlow, D. H., 134, 620
Barnes, L. B., 852
Barrabee, E. L., 226, 260
Barratt, E. S., 98
Barrett, B. H., 619
Barrett-Lennard, G. T., 52, 353, 420, 900, 904
Barron, F., 227, 239, 242, 247, 286, 287, 525, 815, 819
Barry, J. R., 260, 288
Barten, H. H., 802
Bartholomew, D. J., 483
Bartlett, M. R., 226
Bass, B. M., 188, 843, 845, 848, 850, 856, 857
Bassin, A., 348, 367, 823, 824
Bastine, R., 330
Batchelder, R. L., 853, 856
Bateson, G., 355
Battig, W. F., 716
Battle, C. C., 260, 275, 290, 291, 303-325, 361, 451, 532, 722, 900
Bauer, M. L., 290
Baum, M., 564
Baum, N. C., 451-452, 460
Baum, O. E., 276, 292
Baumgartel, H., 848
Baymur, F. B., 877, 878
Beach, F. A., 588
Beal, A., 172
Bean, L. L., 797
Bechtel, G. G., 760
Beck, A. T., 41, 66, 762
Beck, J. C., 912
Beck, K. W., 257
Becker, L. A., 164
Becker, R. E., 357, 832
Becker, W. C., 260, 398, 757, 763, 764, 769
Beckett, P. G. S., 479
Beebe, G. W., 227
Beebe, J., 350, 351
Beech, H. R., 567, 570, 582, 600
Beecher, H. K., 442, 445, 446, 447, 449
Beer, M., 848
Beery, J. W., 57
Beguelin, J., 351
Beier, C. D., 97
Belanger, D., 105
Bell, G. B., 188
Bell, J. E., 753

Bellak, L., 41, 68, 387, 418, 430, 522
Bem, D. J., 177
Benedek, T., 897
Benjamin, J., 410
Benjamin, L. S., 95
Benne, K. D., 839, 840, 843, 850, 851, 853
Bennis, W. G., 839, 843, 844, 846, 850
Bennken, H. G., 83
Bentler, P. M., 444, 630
Ben-Zeer, S., 843, 845, 850
Berberich, J. P., 661, 663
Berdie, R. F., 865
Berelson, B., 346, 347, 348, 387
Berenson, B. G., 59, 64, 137, 239, 300, 331, 361, 362, 719, 899, 904
Berg, I. A., 354
Berg, W. K., 86
Berger, D. G., 805
Berger, H., 79
Berger, S., 825
Berger, S. E., 716
Berger, S. M., 691
Bergin, A. E., 40, 56, 149, 209, 211, 218, 228, 242, 246, 247, 249, 255, 327, 421, 477, 501, 525, 819, 880, 883, 896, 899, 900, 903, 904, 911, 919
Bergman, P., 360, 390, 423, 426, 428, 429, 453, 457, 460, 463
Bergman, R. L., 728
Berkowitz, L., 667
Berleman, W. C., 234, 249
Berlin, J. I., 59, 110, 842, 852
Berman, G., 374
Berman, L., 451, 453, 457, 460
Bernal, M., 755
Bernhardt, H., 907
Bernstein, A., 53, 289, 366, 367, 369
Bersh, P. J., 557, 671
Bertalanffy, L. von, 782
Berzins, J. I., 141
Berzon, B., 831, 840, 851, 852
Beskind, H., 478
Best, C. H., 78, 90
Betz, B. J., 51, 65, 140, 141, 236, 239, 302, 485, 506, 526
Bever, T. G., 387
Beverly, G. D., 172, 175
Beyer, N. L., 696
Bibring, E., 418, 419
Biddle, B., 130
Bidwell, G. P., 869
Bieber, I., 232
Bierer, J., 785
Biersdorf, K. R., 868-869
Bijou, S. W., 727, 752, 769

Bilovsky, D., 868, 869
Binder, A., 715
Bindra, D., 551
Binner, P. R., 803
Birdwhistell, R. L., 382
Birnbrauer, J. S., 769, 770
Birren, J. E., 104
Bishop, M. B., 446
Black, A. H., 669, 672
Black, S. M., 445-446
Blaine, G. B., Jr., 280, 451
Blake, B. G., 583, 587
Blake, R. R., 186, 188, 666, 695, 847, 852
Blakemore, C. B., 588
Blakiston, 440
Blanchard, E. B., 672-697
Blane, H. T., 723
Blansfield, M. G., 844
Blanton, R. L., 627, 720
Blick, B., 450
Block, S., 374
Block, W. E., 353
Blocksma, D. D., 898
Blockwood, 176
Blood, A. M., 499, 530, 532
Bloom, B. L., 776
Bloom, V., 363
Blum, R. H., 807
Blumenthal, I. J., 507, 509, 510, 511
Board, F. A., 234, 451, 452, 456, 457
Bobele, H. K., 350
Boe, E. E., 816
Bohn, M. J., Jr., 57, 64, 143, 147, 722
Bolles, R. C., 551, 583, 584
Bonato, R., 519
Bond, E. D., 226
Bontalvo, B., 803
Bonvallet, M., 101, 104
Booker, H. E., 118
Bookhammer, R. S., 526
Boomer, D. S., 372, 377, 382
Bordin, E. S., 53, 64, 128, 138, 160, 314, 316, 365, 418, 426, 865, 879
Boren, R., 452
Borgatta, E. F., 172, 188
Boring, E. G., 460
Boroczi, G., 582
Borodin, E. S., 456
Bostrum, 183
Bottrell, J., 599
Bower, E. M., 799
Bowers, N. D., 847, 853
Bown, O. H., 160
Boyd, J. B., 846, 849
Boyd, R. W., 232
Boyer, L. B., 41

Braaten, L. J., 348
Braaty, T., 451
Braceland, F. J., 226
Bradford, D. L., 842, 852
Bradford, L. P., 839, 840, 842, 843, 850, 851, 852, 853
Brady, J. V., 516, 585
Branch, C. H., 273, 274, 277, 451, 460
Brandon, S., 792
Brandt, L. W., 272, 273, 275, 284
Braucht, G. N., 247, 249
Brazier, M. A. B., 79, 98
Breer, P. E., 188
Breger, L., 44, 593, 710
Breggin, P. R., 794
Brehm, J. W., 176
Breiter, D. E., 912
Brekstad, A., 762
Brenman, M., 410, 418, 424, 454, 456, 460, 462
Brenner, J., 107
Brenner, M. S., 373
Brethower, D. M., 585
Breuer, J., 3, 18, 127, 451
Breuker, J., 567
Breznitz, S., 551
Bricker, W., 656, 698
Bridger, W. H., 552, 585, 671-672
Brill, N. Q., 49, 227, 232, 239, 241, 242, 249, 273, 278, 450, 451, 499, 501, 526, 533
Brissenden, A., 824
Broadhurst, P. L., 548, 554
Brock, T. C., 164
Brodkin, A. M., 230
Brodsky, G. D., 755, 762, 768
Brody, H. A., 698
Brody, J., 243
Broedel, J., 877, 878
Broen, W. E., 582
Brokaw, J. R., 356
Bronfenbrenner, U., 172
Brooks, G., 68
Brooks, S., 783
Brooks, S. H., 389
Brosin, H. W., 382
Brown, C. C., 77
Brown, D. F., 914
Brown, D. V., 816, 831
Brown, J., 765
Brown, J. B., 832
Brown, J. S., 583
Brown, P. T., 731, 733
Brown, W. H., 453, 456, 917
Bruner, J. S., 716
Brush, F. R., 551
Bryan, J. H., 630
Buber, M., 314

Buchanan, P. C., 842
Buchmueller, A. D., 799
Buchwald, J., 284, 450
Buckley, Nancy, 764
Buerney, B., Jr., 803
Bugental, J. F. T., 840, 856
Bull, J. P., 442
Bull, K., 98
Bunker, D. R., 844, 845, 846, 847, 848, 855
Bunker, G. L., 842, 846
Burdick, H. A., 162
Burgess, E. P., 632, 633
Burgess, M. N., 86, 114, 115
Burke, A., 478, 486
Burke, R. L., 843, 844, 846
Burkholder, R., 769
Burnes, A. J., 162, 789
Burns, B., 755
Burnstein, E., 689
Burnstein, J. W., 361
Burrow, T., 454, 460, 463
Burrows, V., 576
Burstein, A. G., 897
Burt, C., 559
Burton, R., 762
Burton, R. V., 762
Buss, A., 165
Buss, H., 92
Butler, J. M., 50, 60, 129, 261, 348, 363, 383, 879
Butler, J. R., 721
Butler, R. N., 449
Butler, S., 577
Byrd, R. E., 846
Byrne, D., 689

Cabeen, C. W., 815, 824
Cadman, W. H., 816, 831
Cahoon, D. P., 573
Calia, V. F., 865
Callahan, D. M., 140, 277, 282, 450
Callis, R., 371, 372
Calloway, E., 104
Calogeras, R., 367
Calverley, D. S., 454
Cameron, D. E., 384
Cameron, L., 551
Cameron, N. A., 172
Campbell, D., 732
Campbell, D. P., 879, 880
Campbell, D. T., 48, 142, 261, 694, 695, 828
Campbell, J., 762
Campbell, J. P., 842
Campbell, M., 517, 527
Campbell, R. E., 365, 387
Campos, J. J., 101, 111
Cannon, J. R., 361
Cannon, W. B., 102, 103

Canter, A. H., 234, 249
Cantor, A., 442, 444
Cantril, H., 67
Caplan, G., 293, 778, 801
Caplan, S. W., 876
Cappon, D., 234, 239, 240, 241
Caracena, P. F., 355, 356, 721
Carkhuff, R. R., 44, 47, 59, 64, 135, 137, 138, 139, 172, 218, 239, 245, 247, 253, 257, 261, 276, 284, 287, 291, 292, 300-301, 314, 319, 325-327, 330, 339-340, 360-362, 364, 420, 485, 501, 526, 551, 698, 719, 722, 818, 824, 900-904, 911-916
Carlin, A. S., 732, 733
Carlisle, J. M., 733
Carlsmith, J. M., 176
Carlson, A. R., 389
Carlson, D., 505
Carlson, G., 844
Carmichael, H. T., 219, 224, 390, 428, 429
Carmichael, R., 389, 390
Carmona, A., 553
Carota, N., 453, 454
Carrera, R., 725
Carroll, J. B., 370, 382
Carron, T. J., 848
Carse, J., 790
Carson, R. C., 64-65, 139, 140, 141, 142, 184, 290, 844, 850, 856
Cartwright, D. P., 843
Cartwright, D. S., 236, 239, 257, 262, 278, 287, 288, 292
Cartwright, R. D., 183, 230, 239, 247, 358, 415, 416, 451
Cassens, J., 350, 351
Cassotta, L., 369, 389
Castell, D., 731, 733
Castell, D. A., 205, 588
Castiglioni, 447
Catania, A., 613
Caton, R., 79
Catron, D. W., 876, 877
Cattell, R. B., 232, 257, 258, 262, 510, 558
Caudill, W., 791
Caughlan, J., 54, 900
Cautela, J., 581
Cautela, J. R., 619, 731, 733
Cauthen, N. R., 565, 726
Chafety, M. E., 723
Chance, E., 355, 422
Chapman, J., 165, 391
Chapple, E. D., 145, 351
Charms, R. de, 171, 696
Chase, H. H., 96, 98
Chassan, J. B., 45, 48, 67-68, 209,

255, 387, 388, 523
Chatterjee, B. B., 585, 671
Chazan, M., 486
Chein, I., 784
Chestnut, W. J., 881, 882, 884, 887
Chethik, M., 490
Chittenden, G. E., 171, 667
Chodoff, P., 453, 460
Christensen, O. C., Jr., 883
Christiansen, C., 287
Church, R. M., 583
Cicchetti, D. V., 142, 364
Cicchetti, J. L., 908
Clark, A. W., 631
Clark, D. F., 588
Clark, J. V., 350, 353, 842, 844
Clark, M., 769, 772
Clark, M. L., 444, 520
Clark, R. M., 565
Clark, T. C., 846, 849, 853, 856
Clausen, J. A., 798
Cleghorn, J. M., 374
Cleghorn, R. A., 515
Clement, P. W., 762
Clemes, S. R., 364
Cleveland, S. E., 856
Clifford, T., 716
Clifton, R. K., 98
Cobb, S., 354
Coburn, H., 130
Coggeshall, L. T., 906
Cohen, A. R., 176, 429
Cohen, G., 257, 260, 262
Cohen, M., 86, 429
Cohen, N. L., 645
Cohen, R., 726
Cohen, S. I., 92, 114, 115
Cohen, S. K., 843, 844
Cohn, B., 365
Colby, K. M., 38, 59, 143, 354, 377, 418, 426, 659
Cole, J. K., 489
Cole, J. O., 498, 515, 516, 519, 524, 532, 533
Cole, N., 451-453, 460
Cole, N. J., 273, 274, 277
Coleman, J. V., 907
Coleman, P. D., 583
Coleman, R., 110
Coles, E. M., 85
Collier, R. M., 585
Collins, B. E., 176
Collins, B. J., 630, 715
Collins, R. C., 762
Combs, A. W., 226
Condon, W. S., 384
Connor, W. H., 89, 98
Conrad, D. C., 354
Conrad, R., 354
Console, W. A., 414

Cook, S., 784
Cook, S. W., 585
Cooke, G., 134, 566, 569, 724
Cooley, W. W., 864
Coolidge, J. C., 487, 488
Coombs, A., 53
Coons, D., 792
Coons, W. H., 817, 824
Cooper, A. M., 522
Cooper, D., 59
Cooper, J. E., 571
Cooper, L., 379
Cooper, S., 789
Cordaro, L., 715
Coriat, I. H., 226
Corsini, R. J., 173, 666
Cosnier, J., 546
Cotter, L. H., 644
Covi, L., 498, 506, 507, 508, 509, 513, 523, 524, 525
Covner, B. J., 896
Cowan, P. A., 659
Cowden, R. C., 506, 509, 510, 817, 825
Cowen, E. L., 60, 130, 226, 800
Cowne, L., 911
Coyne, L., 388
Craig, K., 59
Craig, K. D., 599, 691
Crandall, V., 762
Cremerius, J., 578
Crider, A., 82, 107, 642
Crites, J. O., 869, 878
Cronbach, L. J., 37-38, 40, 55, 69, 252
Cross, H. J., 40, 229
Crowne, D. P., 49, 56
Culbert, S. A., 350, 352, 353, 842, 844, 854
Culbertson, F. M., 175
Cumming, E., 777, 786, 793, 808
Cumming, J., 273, 777, 786, 793
Curran, D., 219, 224
Cutler, R. L., 57, 364, 365, 381, 454
Cutter, H., 843, 846

Dahlstrom, W. G., 260
Dallett, K. M., 716
Dalsimer, J. S., 794
Danehy, J. J., 382
Danet, B., 377
D'Angelo, R., 488
Daniels, G., 268
Daniels, R. S., 374
Danskin, D. G., 364, 387
Darbonne, A. R., 293
Darrow, C. W., 83
Davids, A., 453, 456
Davidson, S., 487
Davies, B., 581, 588

Davis, D. R., 548
Davis, J. D., 59-60, 62, 146, 147, 366
Davis, J. F., 78
Davis, J. M., 498, 499
Davis, M., 673
Davis, R. C., 89, 97, 101, 110, 115
Davis, S., 851
Davison, G. C., 59, 133, 134, 199, 202, 205, 206, 208, 210, 255, 531, 565, 568, 724, 918
Davison, L. A., 105, 116
Davitz, J. R., 374
Dawson, M. E., 671
Dean, S. I., 278
Decker, J. B., 389
Deer, J., 189
De Fries, Z., 481
De Grazia, S., 448, 455
Delaney, D. J., 853
Delaney, D. M., 853
Delay, 517
Dell, P., 101, 104
Demos, G. D., 914
Demosthenes, 576
De Myer, M. K., 626
De Nike, L. D., 713
Deniker, P., 499, 517
Denker, P. G., 239, 241
Denny, J. P., 881
DeRidder, L. M., 350
De Sena, P. A., 885
Desiderato, O., 551
Detre, T., 357, 832
Deutsch, A., 789
De Verteuil, R., 503, 515
Dewey, J., 7, 9
Dews, P. B., 517
Deysach, R. E., 166
Diamond, S. A., 583
DiBennardo, F. R., 365
Dibner, A. S., 147, 374, 456
Di Cara, L. V., 107, 553
Dicke, 603
Dickel, H. A., 205
Dickenson, W. A., 310, 360, 881, 884, 885, 887
Dickinson, T. C., 716
Dieterich, P. M., 844, 845, 853
Dietze, D., 257
Dildy, L. W., 263
Di Mascio, A., 68, 516, 519
Dimmick, F. L., 544
Dinitz, S., 790
Dinoff, M., 59, 352
Dinsmoor, J. A., 582, 585
Dipboye, W. J., 364
Dittes, J. E., 147, 347, 451, 718
Dittmann, A. T., 112, 229, 365, 377, 383, 387, 390, 429

Diven, K., 551
Dixon, H. H., 205
Dixon, W. J., 523
Dobie, S., 450, 451, 460
Doering, C. R., 444, 446
Dohan, L. J., 442
Dohrenwend, B. S., 798, 799
Dolan, G. K., 876
Dollard, J., 49, 58, 114, 348, 371, 378, 379, 380, 390, 547, 556, 583, 691, 694-696
Domke, H. R., 799
Donaghy, R. T., 905
Donahue, W., 792
Donner, L., 581, 602, 732
Doob, L. W., 114
Dorfman, E., 353
Dostálek, Ctibor, 586
Douds, J., 239, 900
Draper, E., 907
Dreiblatt, I. S., 144
Dreikurs, R., 59, 234, 259
Dressel, P. L., 865
Drolette, M., 92
Droppleman, L. F., 519
Drvota, S., 565
Dubin, R., 956
Dudley, G. A., 865
Duffy, E., 103
Duffy, G., 554
Dugan, W. E., 913
Duhrssen, A., 414
Duke, J. D., 444
Dukes, W. F., 67, 408
Dulany, D. E., 370, 713
DuMas, F. M., 66
Dumont, D., 663
Dumont, M., 294
Duncan, A. D., 771
Duncan, D. B., 232, 249, 263
Duncan, S., Jr., 383
Dunette, M. D., 842
Dunham, H. W., 781, 797
Dunphy, D. C., 367, 371
Duran-Reynals, M. L., 442
Durea, M. A., 451
Durham, L. E., 842
Durkin, H. E., 183, 187, 189, 856
Durost, H. B., 515, 522
Duryee, J., 755
Dyer, C. O., 876
Dykman, R. A., 97
Dymond, R. F., 41, 227, 229, 239, 247, 252, 256, 261, 262, 289, 879
Dyrud, J. E., 631
D'Zmura, T., 374
D'Zurilla, T. J., 729

Easser, B. R., 222

Ebner, M., 762, 764, 767, 768
Edelberg, R., 82, 84, 85
Edinger, R. L., 621
Edison, C. B., 445, 446
Edlin, J. V., 587
Edwards, A. L., 40, 58, 253
Edwards, E. D., 173
Eells, J., 54, 230, 249, 900
Efran, J. S., 134, 725
Ehrenwald, K. J., 454
Ehrlich, H. J., 290
Eichler, M., 354
Eichler, R. M., 273, 278, 285
Eicker, W. F., 783
Eiduson, B. T., 389, 390, 784
Einstein, A., 603
Eisenberg, L., 475, 481, 486, 499, 527
Eissen, S. B., 449, 453
Eissler, K., 409
Ekman, P., 112, 376, 377, 449, 630
Ekstein, R., 897
Eldred, S. H., 374, 381, 383
Elenewski, J. J., 716
Elinson, J., 232, 249
Elkes, J., 497, 520, 521, 522, 527
Ellenberger, H., 453, 456
Elliode, M., 454, 455, 456
Elliott, R., 100, 101
Ellis, A., 234, 451, 719
Elliss, J. D., 846, 849
Ellson, D., 599
Elms, A. C., 175, 176, 177
Emerson, R., 824
Endicott, J., 230, 240, 241, 257
Endicott, N. A., 230, 240, 241, 391, 454
Endler, N. S., 261
Ends, E. J., 257, 451, 815
Enelow, A. J., 909
Engel, B. T., 100, 107, 118
Engel, G. L., 410, 416, 451, 453, 907
Engelhardt, D. M., 284, 444-446, 450, 790
Engleman, L., 523
Engler, R. E., 481
English, O. S., 391, 429
Eppel, H., 330
Eppinger, H., 91
Epstein, L. J., 451
Epstein, S., 112
Erbaugh, J. K., 762
Erickson, M. H., 199, 390, 429
Eriksen, C., 585
Eriksen, C. W., 108, 671, 713
Eron, L. S., 261, 279, 284
Erwin, W. J., 727
Escalona, S., 410

Esecover, H., 449
Essman, W. B., 583
Ester, S. G., 456
Estes, W. K., 583, 584
Etzioni, A., 807
Euler, U. S. V., 92
Evangelakis, M. G., 507, 509, 510
Evans, D. R., 579
Evans, F. J., 444
Evans, G. W., 762, 767
Evans, S. H., 96
Evans, W. I. M., 729
Ewalt, J. R., 508, 525, 526
Ewing, J. A., 387
Ewing, T. N., 867, 879, 880, 884, 885
Exener, J. E., 816, 831
Exline, R. V., 388, 843
Exner, J. E., Jr., 143
Eysenck, H. J., 40, 44, 66, 155, 198, 200, 207, 217-229, 239-240, 246, 252, 262, 301, 303, 414, 415, 460, 545, 546, 549, 551, 552, 555, 557, 558, 560, 561, 562, 565, 577, 578, 580, 616, 710, 734

Fabian, M., 522
Fahl, M. A., 728
Fahmy, S. A., 629
Fairweather, G., 239, 247, 257, 260, 524, 814, 815, 819, 825, 830
Farberow, N. L., 796
Faris, M. T., 523
Faris, R. E. L., 797
Farquhar, W. W., 885
Farrar, C. H., 581, 582
Farrell, B., 419
Farson, R. E., 852
Farwell, G. F., 356
Feder, B., 816
Feifel, H., 54, 230, 249, 816, 900
Feigenbaum, E. A., 716
Feld, S., 242, 245
Felder, F., 363
Feldman, F., 414
Feldman, J., 716
Feldman, M. P., 581, 589, 731, 733
Feldman, P. E., 449, 452, 454
Feldman, R., 234
Feldman, R. S., 622
Feldman, S., 370, 371
Feldstein, S., 369, 373, 389
Felzer, S. B., 276, 292
Fenichel, O., 52, 219, 220, 221, 223, 225, 414, 448, 451, 453, 455-456

Fenn, A., 130
Fenz, W. D., 113
Fere, C., 82
Ferenczi (1954), 451
Ferguson, R. E., 381
Fernandez, L. E., 677, 690
Ferster, C. B., 208, 613, 618, 626, 632
Festinger, L., 164, 169, 176, 682
Fey, W. F., 317, 323, 419
Fichtenbaum, L., 49, 379
Fiedler, F. E., 419, 451, 456
Fierman, L. B., 142, 364, 908
Fine, H. J., 332, 364, 367, 816, 824, 846, 847
Fine, R., 910, 911
Finesinger, J. E., 226, 260
Fink, M., 282, 369
Finney, B. C., 260, 916
Finney, R. C., 510
Firth, J. R., 382
Fish, B., 517, 527
Fisher, C., 451, 456
Fisher, D., 452, 642
Fisher, H. K., 445, 446, 447, 449
Fisher, S., 365, 519, 530
Fishman, J., 793
Fiske, D. W., 142, 232, 257, 287, 289, 292, 416, 905, 911
Fittkau, B., 330
Fivel, M. W., 716
Flanagan, B., 570
Flanagan, J. C., 384
Flanders, J. P., 694
Fleischmann, O., 390
Fleishman, J. M., 716
Fleming, D. E., 522
Fleming, J., 897
Fliess, W., 409
Flood, C., 268
Fode, K. L., 451, 453, 454
Fodor, J. A., 387
Foley, J. P., 548
Folkins, C. H., 134, 724
Fontana, A. F., 753
Ford, C. S., 588
Ford, D. H., 39, 41, 59, 130, 381, 880, 885
Ford, J. D., Jr., 844, 848
Forde, D. L., 909
Forehand, G. A., 807
Foreman, M. E., 453, 454
Forgy, E. W., 451
Forman, V. P., 362
Forrer, G. R., 442, 448
Forster, F. M., 118
Forsyth, R., 256, 260
Forsythe, A. B., 523
Foster, B. R., 845, 853
Foster, C. P., 360
Foulds, G., 442, 449, 454

Fowler, H., 584
Fox, B., 442, 454
Fox, R., 374
Frank, E. C., 374
Frank, G. H., 59, 287, 365
Frank, J. D., 48, 183, 236, 243, 247, 249, 252, 255, 257, 272, 273, 275, 276, 277, 278, 281, 289, 290, 291, 301, 302, 311, 325, 361, 442, 444, 454, 456, 457, 460, 461, 462, 463, 521, 532, 717, 719, 722, 732, 823, 825, 828, 830, 900
Frankie, G., 695
Franks, C. M., 586, 614, 732
Freedman, A. M., 515, 518
Freedman, N., 284, 376, 444, 445, 446, 450, 790
Freeman, E., 293
Freeman, G. L., 113
Freeman, H. E., 803, 807
Freeman, T., 593
Freitag, G., 626
Freitag, L., 664
French, J. R. P., Jr., 451, 842, 854
French, R. L., 188
French, T., 410
French, T. R., 169
Frenkel-Brunswik, E., 410, 826
Fretz, B. R., 375
Freud, A., 419
Freud, S., 3, 18, 39-40, 108, 126, 198, 288, 314, 408, 410, 421, 424, 426, 429, 432, 451, 460, 499, 500, 515, 715, 719, 734
Freund, K., 588, 590
Freyhan, F. A., 517, 521
Fried, M., 802
Friedlander, F., 454
Friedlander, F. A., 840, 848, 853
Friedlander, J., 234, 249
Friedman, C. J., 451, 454
Friedman, D., 566
Friedman, H. J., 289
Friedman, P. H., 700
Friel, T., 138, 139, 326, 362, 911
Friesen, W. V., 112, 376, 769
Friess, C., 226, 240, 241
Froehlich, A., 348, 356, 367, 823
Froelich, R. E., 356, 367
Frohlich, E. D., 93, 104
Fromm, E., 198, 353
Fromm-Reichmann, 314
Frostig, M., 381
Fruchter, B., 188
Frumkin, R. M., 817
Fry, J. R., 856
Fulkerson, S. C., 260, 288
Fuller, P. R., 616
Funkenstein, D. H., 92, 101, 115

Funkhouser, G. R., 388
Furst, W., 187

Gage, N. L., 843
Gagne, R. M., 38
Galanter, F., 66
Galen, 441
Galigher, D. L., 449, 450
Gallagher, J. J., 287
Gallant, D. M., 446
Gambaro, S., 115
Gamsky, N. R., 355
Gantt, W. H., 97, 449, 544
Ganzer, V. J., 135, 148, 665, 728
Garcia, J., 587
Gardner, E. A., 783
Gardner, G. E., 802
Gardner, G. G., 478, 900
Gardner, J. E., 207
Garetz, F. K., 449
Garfield, S. L., 272, 275, 278, 282, 283, 284, 285, 288, 290, 451, 454
Garfield, Z., 918
Garfield, Z. H., 566
Garland, L. H., 454
Garlington, W. K., 640
Garrison, F. H., 441, 463
Garrod, M., 219, 224
Gartner, C. J., 445, 446, 449, 450, 454
Gassner, S. M., 171, 172, 845, 846
Gaviria, B., 112
Gebhard, M. E., 239, 524, 815, 819, 830
Gedo, J. E., 897
Geer, J. A., 98, 108, 724
Geertsma, R. H., 912, 914
Geitgey, D. A., 848
Gelder, M. G., 59, 113, 260, 262, 564, 574, 580, 589, 590, 593, 602, 726
Gelfand, D. M., 696
Gelfand, S., 630
Gelineau, V. A., 912
Geller, M. H., 290
Gellhorn, E., 91
Gendlin, E. T., 49, 51, 59, 110, 137, 138, 230, 249, 253, 291, 301, 328, 349, 350, 417, 451, 456, 524, 526, 904
Geocaris, K., 170
George, A. L., 347
Gerard, H. B., 162
Gergen, K. J., 261
Gershon, E., 86
Gerst, M. S., 658
Getter, H., 287
Gibb, J. R., 839, 840, 842, 843, 844, 845, 848, 849, 850, 851,

852, 853, 854, 855, 856, 857
Gibb, L. M., 839, 840, 842, 843, 845, 848, 849, 850, 851, 855, 856, 857
Gibbens, T. C. N., 561
Gibbs, J. J., 509
Gibby, R. G., 277, 280, 284
Gibson, R. L., 257
Giebink, W., 728
Giedt, F. H., 829
Gilbert, W. M., 867, 879, 880, 884
Gilbreath, S. H., 881, 882, 885, 887
Gildea, E. F., 253
Gildea, M. C. L., 799
Gill, H. S., 391
Gill, M. G., 454, 456, 460, 462
Gill, M. M., 355, 391, 417, 418, 424, 425, 426, 427, 428, 429, 907
Gillan, P., 574
Gilligan, J., 498, 506
Gilliland, B. E., 876
Gilman, A., 90, 92, 115
Gilmer, B. von H., 807
Gilmore, J. B., 175, 176
Ginott, H. G., 476
Ginsberg, S. W., 451-453
Giovacchim, P. L., 41
Gittelman, M., 668
Glad, D. D., 381, 857
Glad, V. B., 381
Glaser, E. M., 449, 450
Glasscote, R. M., 777, 808
Glasser, W., 262, 484
Gleser, G., 824
Gleser, G. C., 374, 522
Glick (1967), 446
Glick, B. S., 284
Glidewell, J. C., 799
Gliedman, L. H., 227, 281, 289, 444-447, 449-450, 460, 521, 532, 816, 825
Globus, G., 112
Glover, E., 410, 414, 419, 448, 449, 451, 454, 456, 457, 460, 462, 463, 601
Gluck, M., 488
Glueck, B. C., Jr., 783
Glynn, J. D., 588
Gocka, E. F., 816
Goffman, E., 789
Goin, M. K., 289
Golann, S. E., 776, 912
Gold, S., 580, 731, 733
Gold, J., 844, 845, 846
Gold, V. J., 626
Goldberg, L. R., 911
Goldberg, N., 172
Goldberg, S. C., 519

Golde, P. J., 802
Golden, H., 421
Goldenberg, (1966), 603
Goldenberg, G. M., 379
Goldfried, M., 260
Goldiamond, I., 627, 631, 643
Goldman, A., 476
Goldman, D., 499
Goldman, G. D., 826
Goldman, L., 866
Goldman, M. J., 78
Goldstein, A. P., 37, 40, 45, 48, 127, 128, 149, 158, 173, 183, 184, 187, 188, 252, 254, 283, 289, 447-449-453, 456, 457, 460, 462, 463, 822, 828, 830, 896
Goldstein, H., 585
Goldstein, I., 158
Goldstein, J. W., 848
Goldstein, M. J., 517
Goldstein, N., 697
Goldstein, S. G., 352
Goldstein, W., 825
Golin, A. H., 551
Golin, S., 551
Gonyea, G. G., 868-869
Goodman, G., 232
Goodman, L. S., 90, 92, 115
Goodnow, J. J., 716
Goodrich, D. W., 372
Goodrich, G. A., 374
Goodstein, L., 878
Goodstein, L. D., 727, 878, 883
Goodwin, D. L., 764, 765
Goodwin, W., 768
Gordon, J. E., 60, 110, 130
Gordon, L. V., 451
Gordon, R. L., 162
Gordon, S., 275
Gorham, D. R., 506, 509, 510
Gorlow, L., 189
Gormeyano, I., 711
Gotkin, E. H., 870
Gottesfeld, H., 485
Gottesman, L. E., 792
Gottlieb, A. A., 232, 249
Gottschalk, L. A., 232, 249, 368, 369, 374, 377, 412, 496, 501, 521, 527, 530
Gough, H. G., 347
Gould, R. E., 294
Grad, J., 790
Gradolph, I. H., 843
Graham, D. T., 98, 105
Graham, F. K., 96, 98, 105
Graham, S. R., 234, 240, 241, 414
Grams, P., 484
Grande, P. P., 64, 365
Grater, H., 846

Grauer, H., 505
Gray, B., 265, 510
Green, W. L., Jr., 907
Greenacre, P., 451, 453, 455, 457, 460, 462
Greenbaum, C. W., 183
Greenberg, R., 165, 166
Greenblatt, M., 92, 110, 498, 503, 519, 795
Greenfield, N., 77
Greenson, R. R., 422
Greenspoon, J., 56-57, 132, 627, 628, 629, 712, 714, 715
Greenwald, H., 186, 367, 721
Greif, B., 421, 431
Greiner, L. E., 845, 852, 853, 857
Greiner, T., 454
Grieneeks, 878
Griffith, C. R., 785
Grimes, F. Z., 444, 446
Grindee, T., 767
Grings, W., 567, 585
Grings, W. W., 671, 691, 711
Grinker, R. R., 160
Grinspoon, L., 498, 503, 508, 525, 526
Grisell, J., 363
Gross, W. F., 350
Grossberg, J. M., 599, 614
Grossman, D., 59, 130
Grossman, K. G., 454
Grosz, H. J., 352-353, 454, 456
Grothe, M., 454, 456, 462
Gruenberg, E. M., 475, 792
Grummon, D. L., 60, 129
Grumpert, G., 448, 456, 460, 463
Grusec, J. E., 136, 658, 674, 688, 692, 716
Guerney, B. A., 602
Guerney, B. G., Jr., 59, 130, 245, 381, 481, 912
Guerney, L. F., 59, 130, 131, 381
Guilford, 558
Guillion, E. M., 755
Gundlach, R., 232, 249
Gurin, G., 242, 245
Gussen, J., 907
Guthrie, E. R., 563
Guthrie, G. M., 817
Guze, S. B., 351, 352, 521
Gwartney, R. H., 909
Gynther, M. D., 517

Hacon, R. J., 856
Haddock, J. N., 275, 334
Haefner, D. P., 452
Hagans, J. A., 444, 446
Haggard, E. A., 60, 129, 290, 364, 377, 380, 387, 391, 392, 412, 416, 428, 429, 762

Haggard, H. W., 441, 463
Hague, J. R., 510
Hahn, K. W., 599
Hahn, M. E., 863-864
Hahn, S. C., 668
Haigh, G., 261
Haigh, G. V., 879
Haiman, F. S., 844, 848
Hake, D. F., 582
Halas, E. S., 453, 454
Hale, B. H., 522
Haley, J., 199, 355, 448, 455, 460, 461, 740, 753
Halkides, G., 302, 451
Hall, B. H., 522
Hall, R. V., 763, 764, 765
Hallam, K. J., 520
Halperin, L., 825
Halpert, H. P., 806
Hambidge, G., Jr., 374, 522
Hamburg, D. A., 374, 412, 415, 897
Hamerlynck, L. A., 764
Hamilton, D. M., 219, 224
Hamilton, G. V., 548
Hamilton, M., 445-447, 496, 517, 519
Hammet, V. B. P., 451, 453, 459, 460
Hammond, K. R., 279, 286
Hampden-Turner, C. H., 842
Hanenson, I. B., 374
Haney, O. J., 456, 462
Hanf, C., 755
Hankoff, L. D., 284, 445, 446, 448, 450, 790, 796
Hanlon, T. E., 520
Hannon, A. E., 729
Hansen, J. C., 361, 702, 904
Hanson, P. G., 832, 851, 852
Haraguchi, R. S., 716
Harden, J. A., 64-65, 141, 142
Hardert, R., 854
Hardesty, A. S., 259
Harding, J., 522, 784
Hardy, J. M., 853, 856
Hare, A. P., 351, 367
Hargreaves, G. R., 446
Haring, N. G., 480, 767, 768, 769, 770, 771
Harmatz, M. G., 647
Harper, P., 588
Harrell, S., 59
Harrington, H., 843, 846
Harris, A., 236, 762
Harris, A. D., 454
Harris, C. S., 881
Harris, F. R., 207, 655, 661
Harris, M. R., 293
Harris, R. E., 287, 585
Harrison, R., 844, 845, 854,

855, 857
Harrow, G. S., 173
Harrow, M., 356, 357, 832
Hart, J., 111, 116
Hart, J. T., Jr., 302, 349, 417
Hartmann, E., 478, 489
Hartmann, H., 410
Harvey, L. V., 913
Harvey, O. J., 172, 175
Harway, N. I., 53, 365, 371, 389, 427
Hastings, A. S., 757
Hastings, D. W., 240, 241
Hastings, J. E., 106, 107, 643
Hatterer, L. J., 460, 463
Hauck, M. A., 767, 768
Haugen, G. B., 205
Haughton, E., 637, 764, 765
Havens, L. L., 517
Hawkins, H. L., 135, 482, 698, 699, 702
Hawkins, J. R., 445-447, 453
Hawkins, N., 757
Hawkins, R. P., 752
Hayes, A. S., 383
Hayne, M. L., 381
Hays, W. L., 365
Haythorn, W., 188
Healy, W., 474
Heath, E. S., 257, 258
Heath, H. A., 96, 449, 452
Heath, R. G., 277, 278
Hebb, D. O., 103
Heckel, R. L., 822
Heckel, R. V., 356, 368, 822, 830
Heilbrunn, G., 230
Heim, E., 112
Heim, R. B., 60
Heimann, R. Z., 853
Heine, R. W., 282, 283, 451-456, 460, 462
Heinicke, C. M., 475
Heller, K., 37, 40, 45, 48, 56-57, 59-60, 62, 127, 128, 132, 135, 136, 143, 146, 147, 148, 149, 158, 184, 187, 252, 254, 283, 323, 366, 367, 451, 453, 822, 830, 896
Helmreich, R. K., 176
Henderson, J. D., 635
Hendin, H., 368, 462
Hendry, D. P., 567
Heninger, G., 519
Henry, W. E., 234, 249
Herbert, M. C., 451
Heriat, J. T., 583
Hersch, C., 474, 482, 484
Hersov, L. A., 486
Herzberg, A., 544
Hess, H. F., 351

Hess, L., 91
Hetherington, E. M., 695
Hewer, V. H., 868-869, 870, 875
Hewett, F. M., 764, 765, 769, 770
Hicks, D. J., 696
Hiebel, G., 101, 104
Hiken, J. R., 391
Hiler, E. W., 277, 279, 281, 282, 285
Hilgard, E., 410
Hill, A. H., 878
Hill, F. A., 671
Hill, J. D. N., 98
Hill, J. H., 677
Hill, W. F., 843, 853
Hiller, E. W., 450
Hillmer, M. L., Jr., 689
Hills, D. A., 879, 887
Hippocrates, 284, 441
Hirsch, J., 38
Hirsch, M. W., 445
Hirsh, H., 502, 532
Hitchcock, J., 797
Hnatiow, M., 97, 98, 107, 108, 118
Hobbs, N., 451, 455, 460, 462, 479, 483, 791
Hoch, E. L., 189, 910
Hoch, P. H., 497, 501, 504, 526
Hockett, C. F., 382
Hoddinhoth, B. A., 659
Hodgson, R. J., 554
Hoehn-Saric, R., 276, 289, 290, 291, 292, 303, 312, 325, 361, 451, 532, 722
Hoffman, A. E., 365, 387
Hoffman, B., 629
Hoffman, J., 843, 846
Hoffman, S. P., 376
Hofling, C. K., 439, 442, 444, 448, 449
Hogan, R. A., 724
Hohmann, A. W., 104
Hoijer, H., 382
Hokanson, J. E., 86, 114, 115
Holder, T., 59, 64, 137, 138, 361, 362, 899
Holland, J. L., 239, 524, 815, 819, 830
Hollingshead, A. B., 49, 273, 460, 795, 798
Holman, D. C., 351
Holmes, F. B., 544, 574
Holmes, G. R., 368
Holmes, J. E., 866, 886
Holmes, J. S., 353
Holmquest, D., 82
Holsti, O. R., 346, 347, 389, 390
Holt, R. R., 160, 409, 413, 421, 432, 661, 905

Holtzman, W. H., 388
Holz, W. C., 581, 582, 584, 627
Holzberg, J. D., 794
Holzman, M., 362
Homme, L. D., 769
Honig, W. K., 613
Honigfeld, G., 372, 445, 451-453, 457, 509, 511
Hood-Williams, J., 475
Hope, M., 249
Hord, D. J., 98
Hordern, A., 504
Horne, D., 381
Horowitz, L., 330, 331
Horwitz, M., 843
Horwitz, W. A., 526
Hosford, R. E., 702
Hotchkiss, J. M., 763, 769, 770, 771, 772
House, R. J., 842
Houston, W. R., 449, 453
Hovland, C. I., 175
Howe, E. S., 50, 53, 365, 721
Hoyt, D. P., 239, 258, 868, 869, 880
Hsu, J., 587
Huang, C. L., 520
Huby, P. M., 454
Huddleson, J. H., 219, 224
Hudson, B. G., 583
Hull, C. L., 446, 552, 553
Humphrey, H. H., 453
Humphrey, J., 575, 664
Humphreys, L. G., 713
Humphries, O., 445-447
Hunt, E. B., 716
Hunt, H. F., 585
Hunt, J. McV., 160, 183, 252
Hunt, R. G., 278, 475
Hurd, W. S., 625
Hurvich, M., 522, 523
Huston, A. C., 695
Hutcheson, B. R., 783
Hutchinson, R. R., 619
Hutson, P. W., 868
Hutt, C., 660
Hutt, S. J., 660
Hyde, R., 172
Hyman, H. T., 219, 223, 224
Hyman, R., 44

Iacono, J. M., 374
Iflund, B., 698
Igersheimer, W., 367
Iker, H. P., 371, 389, 427
Imber, S. D., 227, 236, 242, 249, 258, 260, 276, 277, 281, 289, 290, 291, 303, 311, 325, 361, 444, 446, 450-451, 460, 521, 532, 722, 816, 825, 900
Imber, R. R., 567

Ince, L. P., 627, 634
Inwood, E. R., 374
Isaac, W., 627
Isaacs, K. S., 290, 364, 377, 380, 387, 391, 412, 416, 428
Isnor, C., 876
Ison, J. R., 715
Ivey, A. E., 879, 880
Ivey, M. E., 104, 903

Jack, L. M., 171
Jackson, D., 763
Jackson, D. D., 160, 354, 355, 381, 391, 429, 460
Jackson, E., 784
Jackson, J. K., 455
Jacob, T., 142
Jacobs, D., 522
Jacobs, R. C., 828
Jacobsen, C., 906
Jacobson, E., 106, 205, 565
Jacobson, E. A., 136, 148, 698
Jacobson, G. F., 293
Jacobson, L., 715
Jacobson, L. I., 712, 716, 728
Jaffe, J. H., 104, 368, 369, 373, 389, 391
Jahoda, M., 841
Jakubszak, L. F., 456, 696
James, B., 588
James, W., 101, 102
Janecek, J., 532
Janis, I. L., 172, 175, 176, 177, 178, 179, 181, 418
Jansen, M. J., 183
Jarvik, M. E., 445
Jasker, L., 868-869
Jasper, L. G., 420, 900, 904
Jaspers, K., 443, 451, 453, 455, 456, 460, 463
Jenkins, J. W., 57, 917
Jenkins, R. L., 618
Jenkins, W. O., 557
Jenny, R. H., 49
Jersild, A. T., 230, 455, 544, 574
Jessee, B. E., 334
Johnson, A., 486
Johnson, C. A., 454
Johnson, D. L., 136, 698, 832, 851, 852, 856
Johnson, J. A., 829
Johnson, K. E., 815
Johnson, L. C., 98, 111
Johnson, L. K., 847
Johnson, N. F., 387
Johnson, S. M., 134
Johnston, M. K., 661
Jonckheere, P., 229, 234, 242, 249
Jones, E., 219, 223
Jones, E. E., 146, 164, 173

Jones, F. D., 173, 817, 825
Jones, M. B., 444
Jones, M. C., 204, 544, 562, 574
Jones, N., 645
Jones, R., 767
Jones, R. T., 498
Jones, V., 914
Jordaan, J. P., 865, 869
Jorswieck, E., 414
Jourard, 844
Jourard, S. M., 327
Joyce, C. R. B., 454
Judd, L. L., 517
Jung, C., 560

Kabler, J. D., 105
Kadushin, C., 806
Kael, H. C., 56, 64, 715
Kagan, J., 723
Kahn, J. B., 522
Kahn, J. H., 487
Kahn, M., 601, 645, 726
Kahn, R. J., 519
Kahn, R. L., 369
Kalinowsky, L. B., 497
Kalis, B., 293
Kalish, H. I., 615, 731
Kamin, I., 54, 900
Kamin, L. J., 551, 563, 671
Kamiya, J., 107
Kanareff, V. T., 694, 696
Kanfer, F. H., 56, 59, 64, 132, 147, 260, 317, 323, 351, 352, 374, 483, 618, 627, 628, 729
Kanner, L., 474
Kanter, S. S., 391
Kantor, D., 912
Kantor, M. B., 799, 802
Kaplan, D. M., 801
Kaplan, F., 56, 64, 139
Kaplan, H. B., 111
Kaplan, S. M., 234, 249, 374, 522
Kapp, F., 824
Kapp, F. T., 522
Karmel, M., 205
Karn, H. W., 544
Karno, M., 451, 454, 456, 462
Karpman, B., 453, 460
Karsh, E. B., 583
Karush, A., 268, 522
Kashdon, B., 824
Kasl, S. V., 372
Kassarjian, H. H., 846, 848
Kassorla, I. C., 626, 663
Kaswan, J. W., 754
Katkin, E. S., 715
Katsch, 207
Katz, M. M., 281, 282, 528
Kaufman, E. L., 583
Kaufman, I. C., 790
Kaufman, M. R., 445

Kay, H., 450
Kaye, H., 284
Keele, C., 78, 90, 92, 104
Keen, R. E., 96
Keet, C. D., 60, 129, 410, 426
Keith-Spiegel, P., 54, 294
Keller, F. S., 613
Kelley, E. L., 905, 910, 911
Kelley, F. E., 227
Kelley, H. H., 165, 175, 843, 844
Kellner, R., 229, 238, 242
Kelly, G. A., 67, 665, 719
Kelly, J. A., 173
Kelly, J. G., 781-782
Kelly, M., 453, 454
Kelman, H. C., 174, 257
Kemp, D. E., 141
Kendall, J. W., Jr., 673
Kennedy, A., 461, 462
Kennedy, D. R., 876
Kennedy, W. A., 487
Kerenyi, A. B., 504
Kernan, J. P., 848
Kesner, L. S., 60
Kessel, L., 219, 223
Kety, S. S., 93, 454
Keutzer, C. S., 732
Kew, J. K., 352
Keynes, 639
Khanna, J. L., 853, 855
Kidder, J. D., 769
Kiesler, D. J., 40-41, 44-45, 48, 51, 53-54, 64, 132, 137, 138, 139, 218, 230, 236, 239, 246, 249, 252, 253, 256, 271, 279, 291, 300, 302, 328, 349, 350, 359, 360, 361, 387, 388, 524, 618
Kiev, A., 448, 452-457, 460, 463
Kilpatrick, F. P., 67
Kimble, G. A., 557, 563, 673
Kimmel, E., 642
Kimmel, H. D., 553, 642
King, B. T., 172, 174, 175, 176
King, D. L., 717
King, G. F., 618, 622, 633, 729
King, P. D., 510
King, S. H., 92
King, S. R., 449
Kirchner, J. H., 724
Kiresuk, T. J., 804
Kirkner, F. J., 287
Kirtner, W. L., 256, 287, 288, 289, 292, 417
Kissel, S., 688
Kissinger, D. R., 59, 64
Kitchener, H. L., 51, 290, 485
Kittleson, S., 825
Klein, A., 49
Klein, B., 712

Klein, D. C., 801
Klein, D. F., 517
Klein, H., 410, 411, 414
Klein, K., 98
Klein, M. H., 51, 53-54, 348, 350, 359, 388, 417
Klein, S. J., 138, 141
Klein, W., 793
Kleisath, S. W., 848
Klerman, G. L., 498, 503, 517, 519, 795
Kline, L. V., 56-57, 143, 146, 323
Klopfer, B., 287, 442, 447
Klynn, G. A., 663
Knapp, P. H., 112, 373, 410, 411, 414
Knapp, R. H., 794
Knapp, R. R., 257, 262
Knauss, J., 279
Knight, M. A., 441, 444, 446, 450
Knight, R. P., 219, 220, 222, 223, 225, 226, 414, 424, 571
Knopp, W., 918
Knowles, E. S., 842, 845, 846, 848, 855
Knowles, J. B., 445, 446, 449, 450, 454
Knowles, J. K., 641
Kodman, F., Jr., 135, 303, 360, 824
Koegler, R. R., 232, 239, 240, 241, 249, 251, 499, 507, 526, 533
Koenig, C. H., 754, 764, 765, 766, 767, 768
Kogan, W. S., 506, 509, 510
Kogang, W. S., 816
Kohn, H., 354
Kohn, M. N., 798
Kohn, P., 453, 454
Kolb, L. C., 448, 451, 526
Kolvin, I., 581
Kondas, O., 566, 569
Koppin, L. L., 806
Koranyi, E. K., 452, 453, 505
Korman, M., 50
Korner, I. N., 917
Kornetsky, C., 445-447
Kornreich, M., 229
Kornrich, M., 884
Koropsak, E., 114
Korr, I. M., 83
Kotin, J., 795
Kotkov, B., 280
Kounin, J. S., 130, 450, 769
Kowalski, R. S., 870
Kramer, E., 374, 377
Kramer, M. W., 522
Kranzler, G. D., 771, 876
Krasner, L., 47, 58, 132, 144,

173, 200, 253, 255, 444, 449, 451, 453-454, 456, 460, 462, 614, 618, 621, 622, 628, 629, 630, 638, 641, 642, 644, 645, 646, 710, 712, 715, 727, 896
Krasnogorski, N. I., 544
Kratochvil, D., 138, 326, 361, 362, 900, 911
Kraus, A. R., 813, 815
Krause, E. A., 783
Krause, M. S., 374
Krauss, H. H., 327
Kretschmer, E., 209
Kriegman, G., 226
Kringlen, E., 240, 241, 249
Kris, E., 410
Krumboltz, J. D., 323, 702, 764, 765, 871, 872, 887
Kruseman, A., 567
Kubie, L. S., 410, 419, 451, 453-454, 456, 460, 462, 515
Kuhn, T. S., 602
Kunzelmann, H., 769, 770, 771
Kuriloff, A. H., 854
Kurland, A. A., 445, 448, 453, 455, 520
Kurland, S. H., 275
Kurz, M., 272, 274, 275, 285
Kushner, M., 588, 733

La Barre, 448, 455
Laborit, 517
Lacey, B. C., 98, 99
Lacey, J. I., 95, 98, 99, 100, 101, 104, 105, 108, 111, 114, 670
Lacey, O. L., 85
Lackowicz, J., 769
Lader, M. H., 98, 112, 113, 563, 566
Laffal, J., 370, 371, 374
Lair, C. V., 727
Lakin, M., 184, 844, 850, 856
Lamb, R., 391
Lambert, H. L., 509, 510, 511
Lambert, N., 799
Land, J. M., 164
Landeen, J., 768
Landfield, A. W., 230, 249, 259
Landis, C. A., 219, 224, 239, 241
Laney, R. C., 331, 362
Lang, P. J., 76, 88, 97, 98, 106, 107, 108, 116, 117, 134, 199, 201, 208, 210, 260, 566, 568, 602, 643, 655, 723, 726
Lange, C. G., 102
Langer, T. S., 798
Langs, R. J., 445, 446
Langston, R. D., 796
Lanyon, R. I., 567
Lanzetta, J. T., 694, 696
La Polla, A., 517

Lapouse, R., 477
Lapuc, P. S., 647
Lasagna, L., 442, 445, 446, 447, 449, 450
Lasswell, H. D., 371
Latane, B., 103
Laties, V. G., 442
Latz, A., 516
Laufer, L. G., 364
Lauterbach, C. G., 509
Laverty, S. G., 732
La Vietes, R., 479
Lawrence, D. H., 169
Lawrence, L. E., 490
Lawson, F., 451, 454
Lawson, K. D., 134, 715, 724
Lawson, R., 712
Laxer, R. M., 876
Lazar, E., 230
Lazar, E. A., 455
Lazarus, A. A., 172, 181, 546, 566, 569, 571, 632, 666, 723, 726, 918
Lazarus, R. S., 105, 134, 201, 204, 206, 208, 210, 254, 255, 691, 723
Lazovik, A. D., 108, 116, 134, 201, 210, 260, 566, 567, 602, 655, 723
Leary, T. F., 227, 239, 242, 247, 261, 347, 355, 430, 525
Lebo, D., 372, 476
Lee, D., 660
Leff, J., 364
Leff, R., 738, 918
Lehner, G. F., Jr., 57
Lehrman, N. S., 501, 526
Leighton, A. H., 780, 798
Leighton, D. C., 780, 798
Leitenberg, H., 134, 620, 645
Le May, M. L., 883
Lemere, G., 586
Lemkau, P., 797, 805
Lennard, H. L., 53, 289, 366, 367, 369, 462
Leonard, R. C., 802
Lerivson, D. J., 456
Lerner, B., 230, 451
Leslie, A., 449
Lesse, S., 497, 500, 501, 502, 503, 504, 530, 531, 451, 453, 454, 456, 460, 462
Lesser, W. M., 290
Lessing, E. E., 489
Lester, B. K., 907
Letermendia, F. J. J., 454
Leuba, L., 599
Leury, T. F., 815, 819
Levenson, D. J., 460
Levenson, E. A., 487
Leventhal, A. M., 918

Leventhal, T., 486
Levey, A., 559
Levine, A., 445
Levine, D., 142
Levine, G. R., 757
Levine, J., 142, 364
Levine, M., 263, 906
Levine, R. A., 293
Levine, S., 551
Levinson, D. J., 1, 49, 795, 826
Levinson, P. K., 60, 130
Levinson, R., 290
Levinson, R. B., 51, 485
Levis, D. J., 725
Levitov, E. S., 380
Levitt, B. E., 301
Levitt, E. E., 289, 475, 477, 485
Levy, D. M., 686
Levy, L. H., 142
Levy, P., 98
Levy, W. H., 367
Lewin, 847
Lewin, K., 784, 826
Lewin, M. H., 59, 110, 143
Lewis, H. B., 374
Lewis, M., 169
Lewis, W. A., 334
Lewis, W. W., 474
Liberman, B., 171
Liberman, M. A., 856
Liberman, R., 445, 448, 453, 455, 593, 727
Liberty, P. G., Jr., 263
Libman, R. S., 452
Libo, L. M., 163, 785
Lichtenberg, J. D., 526
Lichtenstein, E., 290, 630
Lichtenstein, F. E., 552
Lidell, H. S., 544, 553
Lieberman, M. A., 845, 847, 853, 857
Lieberman, S., 172
Liebert, R. M., 677, 690
Lief, H. L., 277, 278
Lief, V. F., 277, 278
Light, B. H., 110, 371
Likert, R., 842
Lilley, D., 270
Lincoln, K., 421
Lindemann, E., 801
Lindley, R. H., 671
Lindquist, E. F., 65
Lindsley, D. B., 102
Lindsley, O. R., 614, 617, 618, 621, 622, 754, 755, 765
Ling, T. M., 249
Linn, E. L., 449
Linton, H. B., 445, 446, 448
Lipitt, G. L., 840, 852, 854
Lipkin, S., 226, 289
Lipman, R. S., 498, 506, 507,

508, 509, 513, 523, 524, 525
Lippard, V. W., 906
Lippert, W., 374
Lippit, R. E., 698, 799, 826
Lippold, O. C. J., 78
Lipsher, D. H., 56-57, 355, 721
Liroff, J. H., 716
Lisina, M. I., 107
Lister, J. L., 867, 886
Litrownick, A., 660
Littman, R. A., 656, 698
Litvak, S. B., 685
Liveright, A. A., 172
Liversedge, L. G., 582
Livingston, D. G., 846
Llewellyn, C. E., Jr., 290
Llewellyn, I., 112
Llewellyn, L. G., 387
Lloyd, E. N., 528
Lloyd, K. E., 640
Locke, N. M., 184, 187
Lockhart, R., 585
Lockhart, R. A., 671
Loenwald, H. W., 460
Lohman, K., 843, 846
Lohnes, P. R., 864
London, P., 38, 199, 455, 725, 728
Long, B. H., 388
Lorand, S., 414
Lord, E., 451
Lord, F. M., 96
Lordahl, D. S., 716
Lorenz, M., 354
Lorr, M., 140, 183, 230, 232, 234, 261, 277, 281, 282, 285, 450, 507, 509, 517, 900
Lourie, R. S., 793
Lovaas, O. I., 255, 626, 655, 659, 660, 661, 663, 664, 730
Love, L., 754
Lovell, J. T., 334
Lovibond, S. H., 557, 579, 580
Lowinger, P., 450-451, 460
Lowinger, P. L., 363
Lowrey, L. G., 184
Lubin, A., 98
Lubin, A. J., 548
Lubin, B., 857, 915, 916
Luborsky, L., 45, 160, 217, 239, 347, 353-354, 413, 415, 416, 417, 420, 421, 423, 424, 425, 430, 451, 460, 905
Lucas, C. J., 445, 446, 449, 450
Ludlow, N., 544
Luff, M. C., 219, 224
Luft, J., 451
Lukens, H. C., 714
Lund, D., 763
Lundberg, U., 92
Lundy, R. M., 59-60, 110, 143

Luria, Z., 68, 110, 371
Luria, Z. A., 815
Lustman, S. L., 410
Luthe, W., 106, 205
Luther, B., 95
Lykken, D. T., 85, 95, 98
Lyle, F. A., 832, 851, 852, 856
Lynch, M. D., 347
Lywood, D. W., 86

Maas, H. S., 481
Maas, J., 522
Maatsch, J. L., 583, 584
Mabry, J., 614
McAllister, D. E., 551
McAllister, W. D., 551
McArthur, C. C., 451
McClelland, D. C., 37
McClure, J., 351
McConnell, D., 715
Macculloch, M. J., 580, 587, 589, 733
McCurdy, R. L., 909
McDavid, J. W., 817
Macfarlane, J. W., 477
McFarland, R. L., 830
MacFarland, R. L., 451, 454, 630
McGaugh, J., 593
McGaugh, L. L., 710
McGee, R. K., 797
McGee, T. F., 454, 825
McGhie, A., 165
McGinies, E., 183
McGinnis, C. A., 815
McGregor, D., 842, 848
McGuegan, J. F., 454
McGuire, R., 579, 581, 587
McGuire, R. J., 733
McGuire, W. J., 716
Mack, R. A., 257, 262
Mack, R. L., 552
Mackay, J., 505
Mackie, R., 391
MacKinnon, D., 408
Mackler, 449, 451
Maclean, P. D., 102
MacLennan, B. W., 793
Macleod, J. A., 522
McMains, M. J., 677, 690
McMasters, W., 868
McMichael, J. S., 551
McNair, D. M., 140, 230, 232, 261, 277, 281, 285, 450, 452, 453, 507, 509, 517, 519
McNeal, S., 757
McQueen, Marjorie M., 768, 769
McQuown, N. A., 370, 382, 383, 384
McReynolds, P., 506, 509, 510
Maddi, S. R., 38, 41
Madigan, S. A., 716

Madison, P., 426
Madson, C. H., Jr., 260, 763, 764, 765
Magaret, A., 172
Magliocco, E. B., 374
Magnussen, M. G., 489
Magoon, T. M., 239, 258, 880, 912
Magoun, H. W., 102
Maher, B. A., 199, 200, 207
Mahl, G. F., 110, 163, 346, 347, 351, 366, 370, 372, 373, 374, 375, 376, 378, 388, 389, 390
Mahoney, M. J., 685
Maier, A. A., 856
Maier, N. R. F., 544, 856
Major, R. H., 441
Malan, D. H., 256, 258
Maley, M., 95
Malinowski, 447
Malitz, S., 449, 451
Mallin, A., 510
Malmo, R. B., 100, 103, 105, 110, 112
Mandel, A., 532
Mandel, I. J., 552, 585, 671-672
Madill, M. F., 732
Mandler, G., 716
Mangus, A. R., 799
Mann, C. H., 172
Mann, D., 445
Mann, J., 697, 840
Mann, J. H., 172, 178, 179, 180, 181, 183
Mann, R., 660
Mann, R. D., 380, 381, 387
Manning, R. R., 909
Manosevitz, M., 567
Maranon, G., 103
Marcia, J. E., 134, 725
Maree, J., 188
Margolis, R., 790
Margolis, V. H., 869
Marinn, J., 716
Markel, N. N., 383
Marks, I. M., 59, 113, 260, 262, 564, 571, 572, 573, 574, 580, 589, 593, 598, 602, 726
Marks, J., 641
Marlatt, G. A., 128, 132, 135, 136, 145, 698
Marmor, J., 454, 456, 462
Marsden, G., 228, 235, 351, 385
Marshall, H. R., 668
Marshall, W. E., 456
Marston, A. R., 56, 59, 64, 147, 317, 323, 628, 730
Martin, B., 59, 60, 143, 372, 583 754
Martin, D. G., 340, 914
Martin, I., 77, 83, 84, 85, 108,

110, 555, 562
Martin, J. C., 362
Martin, J. W., 764
Martin, L. K., 582
Martin, M., 769, 770
Martin, P. L., 618, 622
Marx, G. L., 878, 883
Masling, J., 451, 454
Mason, A., 234
Mason, A. S., 452
Mason, E. A., 801
Mason, J. W., 92
Mason, W. A., 688
Massarik, F., 844
Masserman, J. H., 219, 224, 451, 452, 454
Masserman, J. M., 544, 546, 582
Massimo, J. L., 234, 239, 240, 241, 257, 260, 261, 293, 484
Masters, J. C., 696
Matarazzo, J. D., 37, 53-54, 56, 59, 145, 147, 247, 292, 351, 352, 369, 488, 713, 714, 721
Matarazzo, R. G., 145, 147, 351, 352, 628, 897, 908
Materson, J. F., Jr., 240, 241
Mathieu, P. L., 51, 53-54, 138, 349, 350, 359, 388
Mathis, A. G., 853
Matlin, N., 865
Matthes, W. A., 876
Matthews, A. M., 564, 566
Mattson, R. H., 764
Matz, P. B., 219, 224, 301
Mauksch, H. O., 882
Max, L., 581, 588
May, H. L., 553
May, J. G., 696
May, P. R. A., 497, 498, 499, 503, 506, 508, 510, 511, 513, 517, 518, 521, 523, 526, 527
Mayer, G. R., 876
Mayerson, P., 232, 249
Mayo, C., 784
Mazo, B., 57
Mazurkiewicz, J. F., 59
Meadow, A., 280
Mechanick, P. G., 420
Medalia, N. Z., 168
Medeiros, D. C., 692
Mednick, S. A., 113, 280, 284
Meehl, P. E., 460, 525
Meerloo, J. A. M., 448, 451, 453-454, 560
Mefferd, R. B., 98
Megargee, E. I., 261
Meichenbaum, D. H., 621, 624
Meisel, J., 663
Melamed, B., 106, 111, 113, 116, 117, 208, 602
Melloh, R. A., 911

Meltzoff, J., 229
Mendel, G., 556
Mendelsohn, G. A., 290
Mendelson, M., 762
Mendelssohn, K., 594
Menlove, F. L., 136, 658, 674,
    676, 677, 688, 692, 716
Menninger, K., 457
Mensh, I. N., 253, 275, 799
Merbaum, M., 714, 721
Merrill, J. C., 347
Merrill, R. M., 60, 129, 426
Merrill, W. H., 903
Metz, A. S., 388
Meuser, M., 907
Meyers, R. W., 526
Meyersburg, H. A., 374
Mezaros, A. F., 449, 450
Michael, J., 637, 655
Michael, S. T., 798
Michaux, W. W., 230, 285, 509,
    517
Miles, H., 219, 224, 226, 260
Miles, M. B., 840, 842, 843, 844,
    846, 847, 849, 853, 856
Millenson, J. R., 567
Miller, C., 277, 280, 903
Miller, D. R., 277, 278, 279, 284
Miller, G. A., 716
Miller, H. E., 460
Miller, J. C., 357, 832
Miller, J. G., 454
Miller, M. R., 915
Miller, N. E., 58, 107, 114, 118,
    187, 199, 520, 545, 547, 553,
    556, 563, 581, 583, 584, 691,
    694, 695, 696, 710, 719, 721
Miller, P. E., 56-57, 355, 719
Millham, J., 716, 728
Milliken, L. L., 869
Millis, W., 332, 364
Mills, D. H., 356
Mills, J., 168
Mills, T. M., 367
Milmoe, S., 723
Milner, D. C., 762
Minard, J., 628
Minde, K. K., 768, 771
Mink, O. G., 239, 247
Minke, K. A., 768
Minsel, R., 330
Mintz, E., 258
Mintz, J., 417, 430, 431
Minuchin, S., 803
Mirsky, I. A., 691
Misback, L., 816, 831
Mischel, W., 108, 262, 618, 695
Mitchell, K. M., 247, 248, 267,
    300, 301-302, 325, 327, 330-
    332, 362
Mitchell, R. M., 332

Mock, J., 452
Mock, J. E., 762
Modell, W., 442, 444, 447, 449
Modlin, H. C., 313
Mohr, J. P., 727
Molde, D. A., 351
Moles, E. A., 135
Monk, M. A., 477
Montagu, J. D., 85
Montgomery, J., 448
Montgomery, R., 765
Moore, G. D., 361
Moore, M. R., 878
Moore, N., 569, 570
Moos, R. H., 364
Moravec, J., 331, 332, 362, 364
Mordkoff, A. M., 105
Moreno, J. L., 172, 666
Morgenstern, F., 581, 588
Morgenstern, F. S., 733
Morison, R. A. H., 445
Morrice, D. J., 136, 698
Morris, J. N., 779
Morris, R. I., 696
Morrison, A. P., 794
Morrison, G. G., 486
Morrissey, J. R., 803
Morse, E., 460
Morse, S. J., 261
Morton, R. B., 851, 852, 856,
    857
Moruzzi, G., 102
Mosak, H. H., 59, 234, 259
Mosely, E. C., 506, 509, 510
Moses, L., 268
Mosher, D., 56, 59, 64
Mosher, R. L., 905-906
Moss, C. S., 50
Moss, L. M., 232, 249, 250
Mosteller, F., 445
Motherby, G., 440
Mott, D. E. W., 677
Motto, R. L., 389, 783
Mouton, J. S., 847, 852
Mowrer, O. H., 58, 110, 114, 262,
    369, 371, 453, 455, 460, 546,
    551, 553, 557, 579, 585, 709,
    851
Moyer, K. E., 671
Moyer, R., 851, 852
Muench, G. A., 54
Muffley, R., 282
Muller, B. P., 445
Mulry, R. C., 454, 456, 462
Munger, P. F., 876, 914
Munzer, J., 186, 367
Murphy, G. E., 521
Murphy, J. M., 448, 455
Murphy, J. V., 691
Murphy, W. R. A., 460
Murray, E. J., 68, 245, 347, 351,

371, 373, 378, 709, 717, 718,
    719, 720, 721, 723, 734
Murray, H. A., 60, 111
Murray, J. H., 440
Murstein, B. I., 261
Muslin, H. L., 897
Mussen, P. H., 695
Myers, A., 187
Myers, J. K., 273, 275, 284, 460,
    797
Myers, J. M., 226, 236
Myers, R. A., 56-57, 60, 62, 143,
    146, 323, 366, 869, 914
Myersburg, H. A., 882
Myrus, P., 903

Nagel, K., 330
Napalkov, A. V., 551
Nash, E. H., 227, 236, 242, 249,
    258, 260, 276, 277, 281, 289,
    290, 291, 303, 312, 325, 361,
    521, 532, 722, 816, 825, 900
Nash, E. J., 444, 446, 450-451,
    460
Nath, R., 849, 853
Natsoulas, T., 689
Nawas, M. M., 267
Neil, E., 78
Nelson, C. L., 830
Nelson, F., 692
Nelson, K., 626, 664
Nelson, M. J., 226, 240, 241
Nemetz, S. I., 112
Nemiroff, R. A., 460, 462
Netter, F. H., 90
Neufeld, I., 580
Neufield, I. L., 731, 733
Neustadt, J. O., 442, 444
Neustatter, W. L., 219, 224
Newbrough, J. R., 528
Newcomb, T. M., 172
Newell, A., 716
Newman, R., 907, 909
Newman, S. S., 370
Newmark, L. D., 370
Nichols, R. C., 257
Nick, E. W., 868
Niland, T. M., 702
Nixon, S. B., 767
Noble, F., 186, 358, 367
Noblin, C. D., 56, 58, 64, 715,
    721
Nolen, P., 771
Norman, W. T., 239, 258, 880
Normington, C. J., 903
Norris, W., 913
North, R. C., 347, 387
Norton, E. A., 769
Norton, N., 377
Notterman, J. M., 671
Novick, J. I., 816, 825

Nowlis, V., 522
Nunberg, H., 414, 500
Nunnally, J. C., 803
Nursten, J. P., 487
Nuttin, J. M., Jr., 176

Oakes, W. F., 186
Ober, D. C., 732
Oberlander, M., 350, 351
Oberndorf, C. P., 414, 453, 460, 462
O'Brien, J. R., 446
Obrist, P. A., 98, 101
O'Connor, J. F., 234, 240, 241
O'Connor, R. D., 669, 688
Oelke, M. C., 354
Ofman, W., 885
Ogilvie, D. M., 367, 371
Ogle, 505
Ogston, W. D., 384
O'Hara, J. W., 444, 630
O'Hara, R. P., 865
Ohlsen, M., 354, 358, 365
Ohlsen, M. M., 867, 877, 886
Ojemann, R. H., 802
Oken, D., 96
O'Leary, K. D., 756, 769
O'Leary, S., 756
Olin, B. M., 445-447, 449
Oliveau, D. C., 134
Opler, M. K., 798
Opton, E. M., Jr., 105, 134
Opton, F. M., Jr., 724
Orgel, S. Z., 234, 240, 241
Orlando, R., 727
Orne, M. T., 452-454, 646
Ornstein, P. H., 522
Ornston, P. S., 142, 364, 908
Orth, M. H., 451
Osborn, R. R., 800
Osgood, C. E., 53, 68, 347, 370
Oshry, B. I., 844
Osler, S. F., 716
Ostow, M., 497, 501, 502, 515, 534
Ostwald, P. F., 112, 384
Otis, L. S., 520
Ottenstein, D., 789
Otto, H. A., 840, 856
Ounsted, C., 660
Overall, B., 276, 283, 292
Overstreet, P. L., 864

Page, C. W., 257, 815
Page, H. A., 564
Page, M. L., 171
Pagell, W. A., 361, 904, 911
Pahnke, W. N., 625
Paivio, A., 716
Pallone, N. J., 64, 365
Palmore, E., 367, 462

Panek, D. M., 110, 372, 621, 641
Papez, J. W., 102
Parad, H. J., 802
Pareis, E. N., 628, 713
Park, L. C., 452
Park, P., 364, 906
Parke, R. D., 456
Parker, A. L., 695
Parker, E. B., 388
Parker, G. V., 142, 261, 364
Parloff, M. B., 160, 184, 189, 230, 249, 257, 377, 416, 451, 452, 462, 697
Parmenter, R., 552
Parr, G., 98
Parrish, H. M., 910
Parsons, F., 865
Parsons, L. B., 142
Parsons, T., 447
Pasamanick, B., 790
Patchen, M., 689
Patterson, C. H., 38, 863, 865, 877, 878, 885
Patterson, G. R., 618, 656, 698, 699, 752, 754, 755, 757-762, 767, 768, 771
Paul, G. L., 113, 114, 116, 199, 201, 236, 241, 249, 252, 253, 255, 257, 260, 271, 569, 602, 618, 619, 646, 691, 697
Paul, I. H., 391, 420
Paul, L., 451, 453
Pavlov. I. P., 543, 544, 563
Payne, D. A., 885
Payson, G. E., 442, 444
Pearce, I. F., 733
Pearce, J., 581, 588
Pearl, A., 793, 795
Pearlin, L. J., 452, 453
Pearson, R. E., 365
Peiser, K., 882
Pentony, P., 697
Pepinsky, H. B., 865, 885
Pepitone, A., 844
Perez-Reyes, 101
Perkins, M. J., 757, 758
Perlin, S., 449
Perloff, B. F., 662, 685
Perrot, M. C., 614
Persinger, G. W., 453, 454, 456, 462
Persons, R. W., 230, 485, 815
Peterfreund, E., 432
Peters, A. N., 173
Peters, D. R., 846, 854
Peters, H. H., 825
Peters, H. N., 618
Peters, H. S., 828
Peterson, D. R., 728
Peterson, R. F., 694, 752
Pfeffer, A., 410

Pfeiffer, W. M., 205
Pfouts, J. H., 907
Phelps, R., 757
Phillips, E. L., 59, 66, 480, 483, 489
Phillips, J., 729
Phillips, J. S., 283, 351, 352, 896, 908
Phillips, L. F., 80
Piaget, G. W., 137, 361, 899, 907
Pierce, C. M., 522
Pierce, R., 284, 904, 911
Pierce, R. M., 361, 362, 904, 906
Pierce, W., 56, 59, 64
Pilato, G. T., 865, 868, 869-870, 886, 887
Pilisuk, M., 374
Pinschof, J. M., 589
Pinsky, 449, 451
Piotrowski, Z. A., 526
Pious, C., 852
Pisoni, S., 622, 629
Pittenger, R. E., 382
Pitts, F. N., 93
Platz, A., 372, 389
Plutarch, 576
Pokorny, A. D., 506, 509, 510
Polansky, N., 130, 450, 698
Polatin, P., 526
Polefka, D. A., 201
Pollack, R. H., 475
Pollard, J. C., 504
Pollin, W., 449
Pollock, G., 410
Polmantier, P. C., 371, 372
Pomeroy, D. S., 60
Pool, I., 346, 370, 382, 387
Pope, B., 50, 53, 148, 365, 366, 373
Popham, W. J., 878
Poppen, R. L., 673, 691
Porter, E. H., Jr., 898, 914, 917
Portnoy, S., 622
Poser, E., 245
Powdermaker, F. B., 830
Powell, B. J., 581, 582
Powell, T., 360
Powell, W. J., Jr., 59
Powers, E., 227, 239, 242, 247, 524, 526
Powers, J. R., 854
Preisler, L., 664
Prelinger, E., 522
Premack, D., 208, 631, 637
Preston, A., 762
Pribram, K. H., 103
Price, D. B., 383
Proctor, S., 692
Proff, F., 877
Proff, F. C., 358, 365, 371
Prokasy, W. F., 711

Pruett, H., 755
Psathas, G., 185, 366, 367, 371, 390, 854
Pumpian-Mindlin, W., 410
Pumroy, D. K., 918
Putyey, L. J., 666

Quarter, J. J., 876
Quay, H., 629
Quay, H. C., 763, 768, 769, 770
Querido, A., 790
Quigley, W. A., 643
Quinn, M. J., 456

Raab, E., 451-452, 460
Rabbie, J. M., 176
Rabin, A. I., 115
Rablen, 415, 417
Rablen, R. A., 348
Rabow, J., 365
Rachman, S., 210, 463, 550, 554, 559, 561, 566, 567, 574, 581, 585, 586, 589, 710, 723, 726, 731
Rader, G. E., 907
Ragland, R. E., 520
Raines, J., 450, 452-454, 566, 724, 726
Ramsay, R., 567
Ramsay, R. W., 733
Ramzy, I., 410
Rand, K., 822
Rand, K. H., 828
Rank, O., 199, 314
Rapaport, D., 410, 431, 432, 710
Rapoport, A., 409, 410
Rapoport, R. N., 791
Rapp, 762
Rashkis, H. A., 444, 446, 449, 450
Rashris, H. A., 815
Raskin, A., 230, 285, 451, 509, 517
Raskin, N. J., 420
Rasmussen, G., 162
Ratcliff, R. G., 733
Rathod, N. H., 449, 450, 582
Rau, L. C., 355, 721
Raush, H. L., 53, 316, 365, 807
Ray, A. A., 104, 134, 202, 725
Ray, E., 456
Ray, R., 699
Ray, Roberta, 752, 755, 757
Ray, W. S., 257, 520
Raymond, J. J., 588, 593
Raymond, M. J., 731
Rayner, R., 108, 543, 554, 613
Razran, G., 108, 585
Reahl, J. E., 239, 524, 814, 815, 830
Redlich, F. C., 49, 273, 390, 460,

795, 797, 907
Reeder, L. G., 802
Reens, R., 480
Rees, W. L., 733
Reese, E. P., 613
Reeves, R. B., 454
Rehm, L. P., 730
Rehm, R., 663
Reichman, F., 451
Reichsman, F., 907
Reid, J., 759, 760, 761, 762, 768
Reiff, R., 795
Reisel, J., 850
Reiser, M., 817
Reiser, M. F., 454
Rennecker, R., 377
Rennie, T. A., 798
Renzaglia, G. A., 356, 391
Rescorla, R. A., 669, 670, 693
Reynard, M. C., 58
Reynolds, D., 566, 568
Reynolds, D. J., 100, 116, 134, 723
Reynolds, G. S., 585, 613
Reznikoff, M., 453, 454
Rhudick, P. J., 509
Rice, C. E., 805
Rice, L. N., 50, 347, 348, 363, 383, 900
Richards, T. W., 449
Richardson, L. H., 878, 879, 880
Rickard, H. C., 59, 352
Rickels, K., 265, 451-453, 456, 460, 462, 499, 504, 510, 518, 519, 530, 532
Ricks, D., 257, 262
Riess, B. F., 232, 249, 272, 273, 275, 284
Riessman, F., 795
Rigler, D., 365
Rimland, B., 660
Rimm, D. C., 599, 685, 692
Rinkel, M., 519
Rinstock, W. A., 505
Rioch, M. J., 481, 911
Ripley, H. S., 455
Risk, R. T., 715
Riskin, J., 354
Risley, T., 659, 662, 769
Ritter, B., 566, 575, 672, 677, 679, 680, 685, 686, 688, 689, 690, 692, 693, 697, 725
Rivers, W. H. R., 448
Robbins, L. L., 522
Roberts, A. H., 845, 854
Roberts, A. J., 507, 509, 510
Roberts, B. H., 186
Roberts, J. M., 445-447
Roberts, L. K., 286
Roberts, R. B., Jr., 391
Robertson, M., 59

Robertson, R. J., 265
Robins, L. N., 484, 491
Robinson, A. J., 173
Robinson, F. P., 364, 387
Rochester, D., 914
Rodman, H., 484
Rodnick, E., 754
Rodnick, E. H., 517
Rodriguez, A., 487
Roeber, E. C., 371, 372
Roen, S. R., 789
Rogers, C. R., 39-41, 48, 51-54, 133, 137, 138, 160, 291, 302, 313, 314, 323, 327, 348, 349, 350, 351, 357, 358, 359, 360, 361, 363, 387, 389, 415, 417, 420, 451, 453-455, 519, 524, 525, 526, 643, 720, 722, 895, 898, 899
Rogers, J. M., 629
Rogers, L., 236
Rogers, L. S., 227, 229, 239, 242, 252, 253, 256, 258, 259, 262, 275. 279, 286
Rohovit, D. D., 374
Rokusin, J. M., 460
Rolland, J. C., 764
Romano, J., 907
Roose, L. J., 391
Rorschach, 451
Rose, R., 95
Rosekrans, M. A., 691
Rosen, B., 790
Rosen, J., 362
Rosen, J. N., 378
Rosen, S., 698
Rosenbaum, 183
Rosenbaum, G., 557
Rosenbaum, M., 234, 249
Rosenbaum, M. E., 171, 698
Rosenberg, M. J., 176
Rosenberg, P. P., 370
Rosenberg, S., 286, 522
Rosenblum, G., 789
Rosenblum, M. P., 509, 510, 511
Rosenhan, D., 522
Rosenman, S., 353
Rosenthal, D., 234, 236, 249, 272, 273, 275, 278, 289, 697, 723, 853
Rosenthal, R., 447, 451, 453, 454, 456, 457, 462, 715, 723, 762, 807, 814, 886, 906
Rosenzweig, S., 66, 217, 239, 408, 414
Rosman, B., 803
Ross, A. O., 910
Ross, D., 677, 696
Ross, L. E., 712
Ross, M., 796
Ross, S. A., 677, 696

Ross, T. A., 219, 224
Ross, T. Z., 301, 302
Ross, W. D., 374, 522
Rossi, A. M., 830
Roth, C. J., 167
Roth, I., 232, 509
Roth, R. M., 882, 883, 884
Rothaus, P., 645, 832, 851, 852, 856
Rothman, T., 452
Rotter, J. B., 709
Rottschafer, R. H., 356
Routtenberg, A., 105
Rubenstein, L., 384
Rubin, B. M., 134, 725
Rubin, I., 848
Rubinstein, E. A., 277, 281, 282
Ruch, T. C., 90
Rudolph, C., 273
Russell, J. C., 631
Russell, P. D., 57, 147
Russell, S. B., 234
Rutledge, E. F., 711
Ryan, T. A., 872, 887

Sabalis, R. F., 168
Sabatasso, A. P., 730
Sabshin, M., 449, 450, 452-454
Sacks, J. M., 452, 816
Sadow, L., 897
Sager, C. J., 232, 249
Sainsbury, P., 377, 790
Sair, C. V., 727
Sakata, R., 817
Salk, L., 522
Salter, A., 58, 209
Salzberg, H. C., 59, 356, 368, 830, 832
Salzinger, K., 347, 387, 622, 627-629, 712
Salzman, L., 41, 56, 374
Sampen, S., 757
Sampson, E. E., 451
Samuels, A., 830
Samuels, A. S., 445, 446
Sander, K., 330
Sanders, R., 239, 524, 793, 815, 819, 826
Sanderson, K. E., 732
Sandler, J., 429, 583, 733
Sanford, F. H., 168
Sangowicz, J., 515
Sapolsky, A., 160, 162, 171, 290, 451, 630, 715
Saporta, S., 382
Sarason, I. G., 135, 148, 628, 665, 728
Sarbin, T. R., 172, 183
Saretsky, 897
Sargant, W., 455, 456, 497, 499
Sarwer-Foner, G. H., 452, 453,

500, 504, 505, 515, 518, 519, 530, 532
Saslow, G., 145, 351, 352, 369, 618, 628, 713, 896, 908
Satir, V., 354
Savage, R. D., 557
Scarpitti, F. R., 790
Schachter, J., 76, 92, 101
Schachter, S., 76, 103, 104, 105, 202
Schaefer, H. H., 618, 622, 626
Schaeffer, B., 662
Schaeffer, L., 273, 274, 284, 460
Schafer, R., 373
Schaie, K. W., 114, 115
Schalock, H. D., 762
Scharaf, M. R., 456, 460
Scheflen, A. E., 226, 236, 367, 383, 384, 387, 389
Schein, E. H., 839
Schilder, P., 219, 224
Schildkraut, J. J., 93
Schill, T., 454
Schilling, F. H., 489
Schimek, J., 415
Schjelderup, H., 234, 414
Schlessinger, N., 410, 414
Schmale, A., 907
Schmidenberg, 448, 453-454, 456, 460, 461, 462, 463
Schmidt, E., 205, 588, 731, 733
Schmuck, R. A., 853
Schneider, L. A., 184
Schnore, M. M., 100
Schober, C. C., 526
Schoenfeld, W. N., 613, 671
Schoeninger, D. U., 54, 349, 360, 388
Schofield, W., 161, 481, 911
Schorer, C., 363
Schorr, J. E., 868
Schreber, D., 370
Schreibman, L., 663
Schroeder, W. W., 702, 871, 872
Schubot, E. D., 693
Schulberg, H. C., 795, 804
Schuldt, W. J., 355, 356, 828, 829
Schulz, R. W., 716
Schulman, R., 455
Schultz, J. H., 107, 205
Schulze, G., 257, 373, 374, 378
Schumer, F., 261, 803
Schutz, R. E., 769
Schutz, W. C., 170, 171, 387, 630, 848, 850, 855, 857
Schwartz, A. D., 826
Schwartz, A. H., 357
Schwartz, A. N., 135, 698, 699, 702
Schwartz, C. G., 807

Schwartz, E. K., 184, 187, 830
Schwartz, M., 791
Schwartz, M. S., 449, 807
Schwebel, M., 172, 865
Schweid, E., 752
Schwitzgebel, R., 625, 626, 642, 726
Scoles, P. E., 635
Scotch, N., 802
Scott, P. M., 762
Scott, W. A., 175, 388
Scriven, M., 253
Scundle, J., 588
Searles, A., Jr., 878
Sears, R. R., 114, 426, 762
Seashore, C. N., 847
Seashore, S. E., 162
Sebeok, T. A., 370, 382
Sechrest, L. B., 34, 40, 45, 48, 127, 128, 134, 149, 158, 184, 187, 252, 821-824, 830, 896
Secord, P. F., 165
Seelback, G. E., 584
Seeley, J. R., 799
Seeman, J., 451, 489
Seeman, W., 66
Segal, H. L., 451
Seidman, E., 142
Seitz, P. F. D., 430
Seleny, M. P., 110
Selye, H., 93
Semon, R. G., 816, 817, 825
Senior, K., 422, 423
Sergeant, 566
Sewall, L. G., 805
Shader, R. I., 505, 508, 516, 525, 526
Shagass, C., 110
Shah, S. A., 754
Shakow, D., 165, 390-391, 410, 428
Shalock, R., 641
Shamans, 452-454
Shannon, D. T., 569
Shanon, J., 374, 522
Shapiro, A. K., 439-442, 444-449, 451, 453-454, 456, 457, 458, 459
Shapiro, A. P., 447
Shapiro, D., 41, 82, 86, 107, 118, 643
Shapiro, J. G., 360, 375, 824
Shapiro, M. B., 68, 209, 255
Shapiro, T., 517, 527
Sharaf, M., 795
Shaskan, D. A., 509
Shaskon, D. A., 815
Shaw, D., 699
Shaw, D. A., 752, 767
Shaw, M. E., 666
Sheard, M. B., 451, 452, 456, 462

Shearn, D. W., 97, 107, 643
Sheldon, A., 804
Sheldon, M. Z., 828
Shellhase, L. J., 348
Shepard, H. A., 850
Shepherd, M., 476, 477, 489
Sherif, C. W., 187
Sherif, M., 187, 456, 462
Sherman, J. A., 665, 694, 700
Sherman, L. J., 452
Sherman, M., 622
Sherman, R. E., 804
Sherrington, C. S., 102
Sherwood, J. J., 842, 847, 854
Sherwood, S. L., 354
Shimkunas, A. M., 517
Shipman, W. G., 289, 452, 828
Shlien, J. M., 49, 59, 234, 249,
    259, 415
Shneidman, L. S., 796
Shoben, 314
Shoben, E. J., Jr., 709, 865
Shontz, F. C., 48, 55, 63, 66, 68
Shooter, J. R., 456
Shore, M. F., 234, 239, 240, 241,
    257, 260, 261, 293, 484
Shostrom, E. L., 257, 262
Shottstaedt, 449-451
Shows, W. D., 64-65, 141, 142
Sidman, M., 207, 618
Siegel, N., 282
Siegel, P. S., 85
Siegman, A. W., 148, 366, 373
Sikes, W. W., 843, 849
Silber, L. D., 310, 360, 899, 903,
    905
Sills, M., 486
Silvan, M., 522, 523
Silver, A. W., 189
Silver, H., 522
Silverman, A. J., 92, 115
Silverman, J., 289
Silverman, R. G., 585
Simmons, J. E., 474
Simmons, J. J., 757
Simmons, J. Q., 626
Simmons, O. G., 803, 807
Simon, A., 857
Simon, H. A., 716
Simon, J., 391, 416, 425, 427
Simon, R., 239, 524, 815, 819,
    830
Simonson, N. R., 166, 254
Singer, J. E., 76, 103, 202
Singer, J. L., 826
Singer, S. L., 868
Sipprelle, C. N., 59
Sjohelm, N. A., 715
Skard, A. G., 762
Skinner, B. F., 94, 207, 546, 583,
    612, 613, 615, 616, 617, 618,

621, 622, 629, 643, 714, 721,
    751
Skinner, D. F., 584
Skipper, J. K., 802
Sklansky, M. A., 380, 428
Slack, C. W., 625
Slater, E., 497
Slavson, S. R., 184, 187
Slavson, S. S., 831
Sloane, H., 757
Sloane, H. N., Jr., 662
Slobin, M. S., 509
Small, L., 41
Smarr, E. R., 444, 446, 449, 450
Smart, R. G., 546
Smith, A., 823
Smith, A. B., 348, 367
Smith, E. E., 843, 845, 848, 854
Smith, H. C., 843
Smith, H. L., Jr., 383
Smith, H. T., 762
Smith, K., 517
Smith, L., 777, 808
Smith, M. B., 387, 430
Smith, M. S., 367, 371
Smith, P. B., 848
Smith, R. S., 793
Smith, R. W., 356, 486
Snadowsky, A. M., 845, 846
Snell, J. E., 517
Snow, L. H., 456, 462
Snyder, B. J., 451, 453, 460
Snyder, R., 817
Snyder, W. U., 57, 131, 140, 147,
    160, 257, 356, 380, 451, 453,
    456, 457, 460, 910
Soar, R. S., 847, 853
Sokolov, E. N., 86, 98, 112
Solem, A. R., 856
Solomon, H. C., 92, 110
Solomon, L. N., 840, 851, 852
Solomon, P., 498
Solomon, R. L., 370, 552, 553,
    563, 583, 669, 670
Solomon, S., 421, 899, 900, 903,
    904, 911
Somers, R. K., 817, 825
Sommer, G. R., 57
Sonis, M., 474
Sonoda, B., 641
Southard, C., 877
Southwell, E. A., 714, 721
Spanner, M., 462
Spear, F. G., 826
Spector, A. J., 847
Speer, G. S., 869
Speisman, J. C., 52, 105, 365,
    381, 420
Spence, D. P., 417
Spence, J. T., 727, 732
Spence, K. W., 560, 585, 711

Sperber, Z., 365
Spiegel, D. E., 54, 294
Spiegler, M. D., 677, 690, 692
Spielberger, C. D., 628, 713, 715,
    881, 884
Spindler, J., 515
Spitzer, R. L., 257, 260, 262
Spivack, G., 262
Sprague, R. L., 768, 769
Springer, K. J., 374, 522
Sprinthall, N. A., 905-906
Sproles, J. A., 506, 509, 510
Srole, L., 798
Staats, A. W., 613, 619, 637, 763,
    768, 769, 772
Staats, C. K., 768, 770, 772
Stachnick, T., 614
Stampfl, T. G., 544, 563, 724
Stanley, J. C., 48
Stanton, A., 791
Stanton, A. H., 449
Starishevsky, R., 865
Stark, P., 284, 450
Starkweather, J. A., 384, 389, 390
Steele, F. I., 848, 856
Stefflre, B., 863
Stefflre, V., 522
Steffy, R. A., 113, 640
Stein, M. H., 460
Stein, N., 390, 733
Steinbook, R. M., 444, 446
Steinburn, T. W., 234, 249
Steinzor, B., 484
Stephens, J. H., 526
Stern, H., 352-353
Stern, J. A., 75
Stern, L. O., 268
Stern, M., 86
Sternbach, R. A., 77, 106
Sternberg, R. S., 391
Stevenson, T., 332
Stilwell, W. E., 702
Stock, D., 842, 843, 847, 850
Stoffer, D. L., 328
Stoler, N., 290, 349, 350, 451,
    906
Stollak, G. E., 912
Stoller, F. H., 840, 843, 850, 851,
    852
Stoller, G. E., 912, 914
Stolurow, L. M., 183
Stone, A. A., 504
Stone, A. P., 189
Stone, A. R., 227, 236, 242, 249,
    258, 260, 275, 277, 281, 289,
    290, 291, 361, 444, 450, 451,
    460, 521, 722, 816, 825, 900
Stone, C. H., 868-869
Stone, G. B., 239, 524, 815, 819,
    830

Stone, G. R., 583
Stone, L. J., 114, 115
Stone, P. J., 367, 371, 387, 388, 389, 390, 424, 427, 428, 716
Storms, L. H., 582
Storrow, H. A., 49, 273, 278, 450, 453, 462
Stotland, E., 689, 696
Stotsky, B. A., 277, 279, 284, 505
Stover, D. O., 728
Stover, L., 481, 912
Stoyva, J., 107, 205
Strachstein, H., 364
Strahley, D. F., 356, 655
Straughan, J. H., 754
Stretch, J. C., 777
Strickland, B. R., 49, 56
Strodtbeck, F. L., 184, 186, 367
Stroufe, L. A., 106, 107, 108, 643
Struening, E. L., 442, 445
Strupp, H. H., 40, 44-45, 49, 56-57, 140, 142, 149, 172, 209, 211, 217, 228, 230, 239, 246, 249, 251, 253, 255, 257, 347, 357, 377, 381, 387, 410, 414, 418, 419, 451-454, 455-457, 459, 460, 462, 476, 896, 900, 917
Stuart, H. M., 452
Stuart, R. B., 581, 633
Stukat, K., 444, 446
Sturm, I. E., 181, 666
Subotnik, L., 68
Suci, G. J., 387
Sullivan, H. S., 39, 353, 454, 456
Sullivan, P. L., 277, 280, 287
Sulyer, E. S., 728
Sulzer, B., 918
Sundland, D. M., 287
Super, D. E., 864-865, 869, 870, 872
Sussex, J. N., 777, 808
Sutherland, J. D., 391
Suttere, J. A., 101
Sward, K., 452
Sweetland, A., 365
Swenson, C. H., 291, 364
Swerdloff, B., 522
Sydenham, 442
Sylvester, J. D., 582
Syme, S. L., 802
Szasz, T. S., 460, 462

Taffel, C., 58, 628
Talbot, J. H., 711
Talland, G. A., 185, 367
Tannenbaum, R., 856
Tarachow, S., 41
Tarpy, R. M., 551

Tart, C. T., 452-454
Taulbee, E. X., 280
Tausch, R., 330
Tauson, V. B., 351
Taylor, E. W., 630
Taylor, F. C., 847
Taylor, F. D., 764, 769
Taylor, J. A., 712
Taylor, N. B., 78, 90, 112
Taylor, R. E., 352
Taylor, R. G., 884
Taylor, W., 451-452, 460
Teahan, J. E., 817
Teasdale, J. D., 581, 585, 587, 589, 593
Teele, J. E., 784
Teigland, J. J., 876
Teitelbaum, H. A., 449
Telchow, E. F., 189
Teuber, H. L., 524
Tharp, R. G., 754, 769
Thelen, H. A., 843, 845
Thelen, M. H., 881
Thibaut, J. W., 146, 164
Thoma, E., 817
Thomas, D. R., 260, 763, 764, 765
Thomas, P. E., 83
Thompson, C., 453
Thomson, I. G., 582
Thoresen, C. E., 702, 871, 872, 887
Thorn, W. F., 444
Thorndike, E. L., 544, 583
Thorndike, R. L., 884
Thorne, G. L., 754, 769
Thorpe, J., 588
Thorpe, J. G., 205, 449, 452, 453, 454, 731, 732
Thurnblad, R. J., 909
Tibbets, R. W., 445, 446, 447, 453
Ticho, E., 522
Ticho, G. R., 523
Tiedeman, D. V., 865
Tilton, J. R., 618, 622, 633, 729
Timmons, E. L., 715, 720
Timmons, E. O., 56, 58, 64, 352
Tippett, J., 907
Tipton, R. M., 867
Toffel, 715
Tokar, J. T., 522
Tolor, A., 59, 64
Tomlinson, T. M., 290, 349, 350, 417, 904, 906
Toomey, L. C., 453, 454
Tourney, G., 363
Traugott, M., 726
Trautman, G. E., 716
Troffer, S. A., 452-454
Trosman, H., 282, 451, 452, 453,

460, 907
Trouton, D. S., 445, 449
Trowill, J. A., 553
Truax, C. B., 44, 47, 51, 135, 137, 138, 160, 172, 187, 218, 230, 236, 239, 245, 247, 248, 249, 253, 257, 267, 276, 287, 291, 292, 300-319, 322-330, 331, 336, 337, 339, 349, 358, 361, 364, 388, 420, 421, 451, 476, 481, 485, 501, 524, 526, 551, 698, 720, 722, 729, 731, 733, 814, 815, 819, 824, 828, 829, 831, 881, 884-885, 887, 899-905, 915
Trumbull, R., 802
Tucker, J. E., 817
Tuma, A. H., 498, 506, 508, 510, 520
Turner, J. L., 794
Turner, L. H., 669
Tursky, B., 82, 86, 107, 643
Turtletaub, A., 724
Tyler, L. E., 392, 863, 869

Ubell, E., 453, 456
Uhlenhuth, E. H., 232, 249, 442, 444, 446, 451, 452, 498, 506, 507, 508, 509, 513, 523, 524-525, 532
Uhr, L., 454
Ullmann, L., 200, 253, 255, 614, 616, 621, 622, 623, 626, 630, 642, 710, 715, 727, 918
Ulrich, R., 614
Umbarger, C., 262
Umbarger, D. D., 794
Underwood, B. J., 717
Underwood, D. J., 48, 61-63
Underwood, W. J., 849
Uno, T., 567, 691
Urban, H. B., 39, 41

Vachon, L., 112
Valett, R. E., 764, 769
Valins, S., 134, 202, 532, 725, 738
Valiquet, I. M., 842, 844
Vallance, M., 581, 587
Vance, F. L., 863
Van Der Veen, 160, 261, 349, 350, 360, 361, 364
Vanderwater, S. L., 732
Van Kaam, A. L., 68
Van Maanen, E. F., 522
Vanney, I. H., 219, 224
van Sommers, P., 631
Van Velzen, V., 733
van Vlack, J., 390
Varble, D. L., 230, 249, 355, 721
Varenhorst, B., 702, 872

Vargas, M. J., 347
Venables, P. H., 77, 83, 84, 85
Verhave, T., 613
Veroff, J., 242, 245
Verplanck, W. S., 56-57
Vikan-Kline, L., 454, 456, 462
Viken, L. L., 454
Vlandis, 183
Voegtlin, W., 586
Vogel, J. L., 239
Vogel-Sprott, M., 576
Volgyesi, F. A., 449, 452
Volsky, T. C., Jr., 239, 247, 258,
863, 880, 884
Von Baeyer, W., 518
Von Felsinger, J. M., 445, 446,
447, 449
Von Mehring, O., 449
Vorster, D., 234, 240, 241
Voog, T., 327
Voth, V. M., 451

Waelder, R., 410, 430
Waife, S. O., 454
Wagner, A. B., 857
Wagner, A. R., 673
Wagner, B. R., 621
Wagner, M. K., 565, 726
Wagstaff, A. K., 50, 348, 364,
382
Wahler, R. G., 482, 755, 757,
758, 768, 770
Walder, L., 754, 757
Waldfogel, S., 802
Walker, A. M., 348, 417
Walker, H. M., 764, 769, 770, 771
Walker, R. G., 227
Wall, T. H., 219, 224
Wallace, J., 183
Wallach, M. S., 57, 230, 357, 451-
454, 456, 460, 462, 900
Wallerstein, R. S., 388, 410, 411,
414, 422, 429, 522, 587, 897
Walsh, J. F., 488
Walsh, R. P., 816
Walster, E., 164
Walter, W. G., 81
Walters, R. H., 135, 171, 456,
523, 665, 694, 698, 701, 919
Waltzer, H., 790, 796
Wang, G. H., 91
Ward, C. H., 392, 453, 454, 456,
463, 762, 917
Warden, C. J., 583
Wargo, D. G., 135, 236, 249, 291,
301, 303, 325, 330, 360, 361,
451, 476, 722, 824, 828, 829,
900, 905
Warne, M. M., 234, 249
Warren, C. O., 277
Warren, W., 478

Warshaw, L., 273, 277, 285
Waskow, I. E., 58, 360
Wasserman, L., 664
Watson, D. L., 371
Watson, J., 853
Watson, J. B., 108, 543, 554, 562,
613
Watson, P. D., 391
Watson, R. I., 253
Waxenberg, S. E., 364
Waxler, N., 351
Weatherall, M., 452, 453
Weatherly, D., 144
Webb, R. A., 101
Weber, J. J., 232, 249, 426
Webster, A. D., 868
Wedel, C. C., 843, 844, 847, 853
Weil, E., 374
Weil, T. P., 910
Weinberg, N. H., 655
Weiner, H., 111
Weiner, M., 712
Weingarten, E., 239, 524, 815,
819, 830
Weinman, B. S., 793
Weinman, J., 86
Weinstein, G. J., 507, 509, 510,
511, 517
Weinstein, L., 480, 483
Weinstein, M. S., 691
Weinstein, W. K., 712
Weintraub, W., 230, 354, 411,
412
Weise, C., 265, 510
Weiss, J. M., 259
Weiss, M., 476, 486
Weiss, R. L., 451, 618, 622, 630,
715
Weitman, M., 352
Weitz, H., 881
Weitzman, B., 198, 593, 654
Welsh, G. S., 260
Wenger, M. A., 76, 87, 91, 92,
103
Werkman, S. L., 907
Werry, J. S., 763, 768, 769, 771
Weschler, I. R., 843, 846, 850
Wessman, A. E., 262
West, L. J., 907
Wetzel, R. J., 754
Whalen, C., 136, 626, 664
Wheeler, L., 103, 202
Wheelis, A., 501, 526
Whidman, F. L., 843, 844
Whitaker, C. A., 909
Whitaker, D. S., 856
White, A. M., 49, 283, 370, 371,
378, 379, 719
White, G. J., 598
White, R. B., 451, 454
White, R. K., 826

Whitehorn, J. C., 140, 141, 301,
444, 446, 447, 485, 506, 526,
906
Whitely, J. M., 280, 905, 908
Whiteman, A., 544
Whitlow, G. C., 449, 450
Whitman, J. H., 444, 446
Whitman, R. M., 522
Whittier, J., 767
Wickens, D. S., 671
Wieland, B., 98
Wiener, M., 48, 60, 129
Wiens, A. N., 145, 351, 352, 369,
389, 895, 896, 908
Wiest, W. M., 710
Wigell, W. W., 354
Wiggins, S. L., 356
Wignall, C. M., 806
Wilcott, R. C., 83
Wilcox, G. T., 817
Wilde, G. J. S., 732
Wilder, J., 95, 219, 224
Wilder, S. N., 697
Wilensky, H., 442, 445
Wilkens, B., 509
Wilkins, B., 449
Wilkinson, A. E., 509
Willems, E. P., 807
Willers, K. R., 114
Williams, C. D., 753
Williams, J., 133, 365
Williams, J. E., 879, 884, 887
Williams, J. H., 627
Williams, M., 451, 453-454, 460,
817, 825
Williams, R., 475
Williams, R. H., 795
Williams, R. I., 627, 720
Williams, R. T., 94
Williams, T. A., 209
Williamson, E. G., 865, 879
Wilson, C. W. H., 454
Wilson, D. L., 817
Wilson, E. H., 691
Wilson, F. S., 623, 665, 701
Wilson, G. D., 579, 585, 598, 602
Wilson, G. T., 729
Wilson, M. E., Jr., 817
Wilson, W., 187
Winder, C. L., 355, 381, 721,
722, 910
Windle, C., 286
Wing, L., 98, 112, 113, 563
Winget, C. M., 374
Wingt, J., 824
Winitz, H., 664
Winkel, R., 148
Winkelman, N. W., 515, 518
Winkler, R., 639, 640
Winkler, R. C., 876, 878, 884
Wisham, W., 287

Wispe, L. G., 230, 249
Witkin, H. A., 374
Witmer, H., 227, 239, 242, 247
Wiznia, B., 234, 249
Wogan, M., 230, 451-452, 456, 462, 900
Wolberg, L. R., 41, 160, 357, 453, 460, 863
Wolcott, O., 645
Wolens, E., 456
Wolf, 655, 659, 661
Wolf, A., 184, 187, 830
Wolf, I., 723
Wolf, M. M., 207, 769
Wolf, S., 442, 444, 446, 449-451, 453
Wolff, H. H., 59, 260, 262, 564, 573
Wolff, H. N., 726
Wolff, W., 456, 460, 462
Wolman, B. B., 856
Wolpe, J., 39, 56, 58, 106, 133, 135, 201, 205, 206, 208, 210, 253, 545, 547, 563, 565, 571, 581, 593, 666, 681, 710, 723, 724, 726, 731, 741, 918
Wolpin, M., 283, 566, 724, 726
Wood, D. M., 101
Wood, E. C., 460

Wood, J., 391
Woodmansey, A., 445
Woodward, J. K., 370
Wooten, L. H., 226
Wright, B. A., 659
Wright, C. S., 352
Wright, D. J., 84
Wright, E. W., 866-867, 886
Wright, H. D., 761
Wright, M. A., 762, 767
Wylie, H. W., 374
Wynne, L. C., 383, 552, 553, 563, 582, 670
Wyrick, T. J., 332

Yalom, I. D., 822, 823, 824, 828, 829, 830
Yamamoto, J., 289, 907
Yanof, H. M., 80, 85, 87
Yarrow, M. R., 762
Yaskin, J. C., 219, 224
Yates, A. J., 211, 570
Yee, R., 265, 810
York, C., 577
Yorkston, 566
Young, A. J., 445
Young, B. G., 734
Young, H. H., 232, 356, 509
Yuille, J. C., 716

Zahn, D. A., 508
Zalkind, S. S., 848
Zand, D. E., 848
Zander, A., 162, 689
Zani, L. P., 702
Zaninovich, M. G., 347, 388
Zaslove, M., 655
Zausmer, D. M., 249
Zax, M., 49, 60, 130, 506, 509, 510, 800
Zeaman, D., 97
Zeilberger, J., 482, 757, 759
Zeisset, R. M., 134, 724, 726
Zeleny, M., 371
Zemach, M., 147
Zenger, J. H., 843, 846
Zerfas, P. G., 135
Zimbardo, P. G., 168, 175
Zimet, C. N., 367, 522, 815, 824, 847
Zimmer, H., 88
Zimmer, J. M., 360, 364, 906
Zimmerman, E. H., 764
Zimmerman, J., 637, 764, 768-769
Zimpfer, D. G., 381, 824
Zinnes, D. A., 347, 388
Zubin, J., 253, 261, 528
Zukerman, M., 456
Zuwaylif, F. H., 914

SUBJECT INDEX

A-B-A design, 207
Ability to relate, 337
Abnormal behavior, 616
Abreaction, 496, 497
A-B therapist categorization, 51,
    141-142, 300, 519, 526
Academic performance, 23, 875,
    877
Acceptance, 302, 316, 322
  of others, 323
  of self, 323
Accuracy, of interpretations and
    empathy, 419, 420
  of self-knowledge, 865, 866
Acetylcholine, 91
Achievement-motivation theory,
    353
Acquiescers, 518-519
Acoustical properties of speech,
    384
Acquisition, 712, 716
Acrophobic, 688
Acting out, 754
Action research, 779, 784, 785
Activation theory, 101-102
Activity, verbal, 348, 354, 357,
    365, 366, 373
Activity level, 25
Actuarial variables and termina-
    tion, 277, 278
Adequate role functioning, 882
Adjunctive therapy, 510
Adjustment, and concept congru-
    ence, 887
  general, 875, 879
Adolf Meyer Zone Center, 783
Adrenaline, 92
Adrenocorticotrophic hormone,
    93
Advantage score, 523
Affect, 348, 352, 354, 363, 364.
    368, 373, 374, 377, 381,
    382, 383, 506
Affection (love), 354, 378, 381
Affective arousal, 523
Affective change, 518
Affective dimensions, 823

Affect-oriented, 682
Affiliation, 356
Aftercare, 788
Aggression, laboratory instigated,
    114
  reduction of, 499
  scale of, 513
Aggressive psychic energy, 515
Agoraphobia, 572, 620
Aides, 327, 335-6
Alarm reaction, 93
Alcohol, 559
Alcoholics Anonymous, 851
Alcoholism, 575, 586
Alienation, social, 522
Allport-Vernon Study of Values,
    67
Alpha and beta receptors, 92
Alpha waves, 79, 102
Ambiguity, 133, 135, 147, 456
American Journal of Psychiatry,
    784
American Personnel and Guid-
    ance Association, 913
Amphetamine, 496, 497
Amplification, 25
Analogue studies, 46, 47, 60, 323
Analogue to digital conversion,
    87
Analogue-to-digital (A-D) con-
    verter, 88
Analytic Research Group of the
    Institute of the Pennsyl-
    vania Hospital, 428
Ancillary therapists, 182
Anger, 92
Anthropologic-linguistic matrix,
    522
Anticipatory avoidance, 589
Anti-psychotic drugs, 496, 499,
    513
Anxiety, 139, 140, 205-208,
    210, 363, 366, 372, 374,
    378, 383, 391, 447, 546,
    558, 583, 717-719, 721,
    723-726, 730, 736
  extinction, 322-323

level of, 496-499, 501, 502,
    503, 506, 507, 510, 516,
    517, 519
  paradoxical reaction of, 519
  reaction, 616
Anxiety-avoidance, 199
Anxiety scales, 506, 511
Anxiety theory, 12, 13
Apathy, 509, 618, 621, 638
Applied research, 655
Approach-avoidance, 57, 709,
    718, 721, 723, 733
Arousal, 561, 564
Arousal systems, 25, 28, 670
Arterial pressure, 86
Assertive behavior, 700
Assertive techniques, 737
Assessment, 618, 647
  traditional, 761
Assessment interviews, 259
Assignment of subjects, 828
Associative freedom, 418
Assumptive world, 719
Asthma, 207
Ataraxics, 15, 496, 502
Attention, 27, 354
Attentional processes, 657
Attention-placebo, 255
Attenuation, 25
Attitude, 313, 326, 353, 357,
    359, 453, 642
  of family as drug response
    factor, 518, 522
  of therapist as factor in out-
    come of treatment, 526
  to treatment, 452
Attitude change, 155, 158, 164,
    681, 682, 687
Attrition, 507, 509
Authenticity, 302, 840, 841, 851
Authoritarian, 108, 826
Autistic children, 207, 208, 527,
    626, 659, 660, 663, 755
Autogenic training, 204
Autonomic arousal, 670
Autonomic balance scores, 91
Autonomic control, 670

Autonomic feedback, 104, 106, 107
Autonomic function, 643
Autonomic lability scores, 95
Autonomic nervous system, 90
Aversion therapy, 561, 632, 723, 732, 733, 736, 739
Aversive conditioning, 17, 59, 204, 614
Avoidance conditioning, 17, 117, 201, 584
Awareness, 27, 714, 721, 727

Bakers Dozen Youth Center, 793
Barbiturates, 496
Barron Ego Strength Scale, 287
Base-line period, 765
Behavior, analysis and assessment, 203, 260
  change, 299-300, 319, 323
  control, 643
  drugs in children's, 527
  external, 257
  influence, 614, 615, 617, 618, 619, 627, 628, 629, 631, 637, 646, 647
  management programs, 756
  modification, 614, 615, 619, 635, 644
  oriented, 682
  rating scale, 480, 506
  rehearsal, 5, 18, 33, 180, 666, 700
  sampling, 325
Behavioral contagion, 698
Behavioral deficits, 665
Behavioral disorganization, 519
Behavioral inhibitions, 136
Behavioral Science Newsletter, 796
Behavioral selection, 187
Behavioral systems, 25
Behavioral toxicity, 516
Behaviorist, 5
Behavioristically oriented theorists, 314
Behavioristic models, 324
Behavior therapists, 15, 19, 32, 34, 253
Behavior therapy, 35, 159, 483, 546, 555, 613, 614, 615, 616, 617, 618, 619, 627, 632, 644
Beliefs, belief systems, 717, 719, 723, 725, 727, 733, 738, 739, 741
Berlin Psychoanalytic Institute, 414
Beta-adrenergic stimulation, 93
Bias, of therapist, 534
Bioelectric signals, 77

Biological systems, 23, 28
Biological transducer, 84
Bionic, 845, 850, 853
Body image, 519
Body integrity, 519
Boulder Conference, 154
Bounded variation, definition, 320
Brain systems, 26
Brain waves, 643
Bridge circuit, 83
Bridging, 128
Brief psychoanalysis, 15
Bromides, 496
Brookdale Hospital, 416, 427
Buckinghamshire Child Survey, 476
Butyrophenones, 496, 508

California Achievement Test, 480
California Psychological Inventory, 65, 844
California Test of Mental Maturity, 800
Cancellation effect, 819
Capsule effect, 507
Cartoon characters, 210
Case conference method, research evaluation, 896, 897, 907-909, 917
Case studies, 209, 632
Case-symptom controversy, 654
Catecholamines, 92
Catharsis, 115, 448, 456, 461, 667
Cathexis, 515
Causation, 325
CDAS Anxiety Scale, 511
CDAS Insight Scale, 512
Change in clinical status, 509
Change in symptoms, through drugs and psychotherapy, 519
Changes, multifactorial, 256
Chemical lobotomy theory, 517
Chemotherapy, *see* Drugs
Child, behavior, and achievement, 328
  deviant, 625, 753
  culturally deprived, 763
  guidance movement, 474
  middle class, 763
Children, autistic, and drug therapy, 527
  treatment of, using drugs, 520, 527
Children's day treatment center, 479
Chloral hydrate, 496
Chlordiazepoxide, 496, 507, 509-511, 519

Chlorpromazine, 496, 509, 510, 511, 516, 519, 528, 531
Choice behavior, 875
Classical conditioning, 613, 616, 645, 711, 712, 731
Classification, 11
Classroom, intervention in, 763
  token culture, 768
Classroom intervention programs, 756
"Clear Thinking," ratings of, in schizophrenia, 512, 513
Client behavior, 327, 332
  benefit, 338
  characteristics, 326, 335
  expectations, 282, 283, 289
  growth, 302, 327
  manipulation, 326
  motivation, 878
  pretherapy characteristics, 131
  progress in rehabilitation, 337
  self-evaluation, 256
  self-respect, 319
  variables and outcome, 204, 285-292
Client-centered theory, 302, 324, 349, 357-359, 360-363
Client-centered therapy, 17, 35, 253, 328, 347, 348, 353, 358-362, 378, 392, 451, 720, 738
Client-centered training, 898-904, 906, 910, 912, 918-920
Client-counselor relationship, 336
Client's exploration, 333
Clients rejection of psychotherapy, 272
Clients selection for psychotherapy, 272, 273
Clients social class, 273, 274, 277, 278, 283, 284
Client-therapist similarities, 290
Clinical experience, 197
Clinical experimentation, 196, 197, 211
Clinical impressions, 211
Clinical innovation, 196, 205
Clinical psychology, 620
  training in, 910-911, 915, 916, 918-920
Clinical status, change in, 506-508
Cloze procedure, 372
Clyde Mood Scale, 509, 511, 512
Coggeshall Report, 906
Cognitive dissonance, 51, 166, 176, 732
Cognitive flexibility, in relation to therapeutic effectiveness, 905
Cognitive rehearsal, 134, 135
Cognitive systems, 26, 28, 31

Cognitive variables, 197, 202, 206, 208, 346, 682, 710, 711, 713, 715, 717, 719, 723, 725, 728, 730, 731, 739, 741
College counselees, 310
College instructors, 332
College students, 327
Columbia University Psychoanalytic Clinic for Training and Research, 426
Commitment, 316, 458
Commonality, 128
Communities, experimental, 740
Community Adaptation Schedule, 789
Community mental health, 19, 32, 776, 777
Community Mental Health Centers Act, 777
Community mental health evaluation, 776
Community Mental Health Ideology Scale, 795
Community Transaction Audit (COMTA), 783
Complex, 557
Compulsive eating, 201
Computer Content Analyses, 351, 366, 369, 371, 373, 374, 389, 390
Computer usage, 782, 783
Concept congruence, 879
Conceptual disorganization, 506, 508
Conceptual units, 11
Concreteness, 331, 359
Conditionability, 560, 562
Conditioned reflex treatment, see Behavior therapy
Conditioning, 323, 448, 497, 516, 523, 711-715, 721
avoidance, 733
interoceptive, 585
vicarious, 695
Conflict, 13, 544, 733, 760
Confrontation, 331, 341
Congruence, 51
Connecticut Valley Hospital, 794
Conscience, 560
Conservation laws, 555
Consistency drive, 682
Consolidated effect, 170
Constitution type and drug effect in children, 527
Constructive personality change, 302, 310, 330
Constructive Personality Change Index, 312
Contact, 143
Content-Analysis Method, 21, 49,

345-347, 360, 369, 370, 373, 376, 378, 381
Content clues, 318
Context analysis, 370, 383, 384
Contingency analysis, 207, 370, 371, 387, 390
Contingency management, 20
Continuation in psychotherapy, 277-283
Continuity hypothesis, 474
Control, 61, 128, 302, 310, 312
analysis, 897
Control groups, 243, 246, 247, 253, 255, 301, 302, 310, 311, 328, 329, 524-526
Coordinate Index Reference Guide, 776
Cooperativeness, 668
Cooperative School and College Ability Tests (SCAT), 327
Core conditions, 302, 322
Cornell Index, 59
Correlational research, 55
Correlationists, 37, 46
Cortical slow wave, 88
Counseling, 4, 5, 17, 304, 863, 882
effective qualities of, 340
and information-seeking behavior, 871
intervention and decision making, 873
outcomes, 880
psychotherapy, 863
Counselor aides, 334, 336
education, 339
motivation, 337
Counselors, dormitory, 331-333
Counter-conditioning, 59, 133, 135, 379, 385, 386; see also Desensitization
Countertransference, 364, 391, 422, 504, 518, 531
Covariance, 95
Covert sensitization, 581, 733
Convulsive episodes, 17
Convulsive therapy, 497
Criminals, 559
"Crisis intervention," definition of, 801
Crisis theory, 801
Criteria of outcome, 45, 256-263, 460, 874
Custodial treatment, 19

Data Bank, use of, 806
Day treatment center, 479
Decision making, 864-865
Defense mechanisms, 332, 354, 373, 374, 375, 448, 515, 516, 761

Defensiveness, 316
Delinquency, 303, 310, 312, 332, 484, 625, 640, 665, 769
Delusional system, 206
Demand characteristics, 615, 646
Democratic group, 826
Demonstration projects, 785
Denial, 377
Dependency, 355, 378, 380, 502, 506
physical, 502, 503, 509-511
Depression, 147, 197, 258, 353, 357, 363, 373, 632, 633
scale of, 513
use of drugs and psychotherapy for, 496, 501, 506, 510, 512, 522
Deprivation, 618, 640
Desensitization, automatic, 116
contact, 680
group, 569
in vivo, 209
systematic, 59, 133, 135, 137, 149, 201, 204, 614, 615
vicarious, 575
Desensitization therapy, 17, 59, 113, 116, 134, 135, 199, 201, 208, 209, 319, 561, 562, 569, 614, 645-646, 655, 679, 681, 723-727, 732, 739
Designs, 252
Destructive effects on patients, 330
Detection of community mental health disorders, 799-800
Deterioration effect, 246-248, 250, 251, 300-303, 312, 329, 331, 476, 819, 820
Developmental, 12, 16, 29, 31, 34
Deviant behavior, 614, 615-618, 624, 626, 637
Diagnostic accuracy, 318
Diazepam, 519
Differential outcome, 237
Differential relaxation, 206
Digital computer, 88, 117
Direct analysis, 17, 718
Direct-coupled amplifiers, 81
Directiveness, 323, 363, 364
Disabled, 332
Discharge from treatment, 463
Discomfort-Relief Quotient (DRQ), 371, 372
Discrimination learning, 614, 711, 714
Disease entities, 621
model, 616
Disinhibitory effects, 656
Disorganization, 522
Disorganized thinking, 621

Doctor-patient relationship, 442
Doll play, 668
Dominance-submission, 364, 379, 462
Dreams, 522
  resulting from drug therapy, 522
Dropouts, premature, 221
Drug addiction, 575
Drug dosage, 531, 532, 533
Drug effect, 506, 518, 530, 531
Drug resistance, 503
Drug response, and IQ, 518
  and nonspecific factors, 518-520
  and personality factors, 518, 519, 531-532
  and specific factors, 516-521, 526-528, 530-534
  and therapist factors, 506, 516-518, 525, 526
Drugs, and group therapy, 496
  psychoanaleptic, 496
  and psychoanalysis, 497-499, 500, 513, 516, 522
  and psychotherapy, 497, 498, 500, 526, 529
  and suicide, 501
Drug therapy, for children, 519-521, 527
  for neuroses, 498, 499-502, 509-516, 526
  for schizophrenia, 495-501, 504-506, 515
  types, 496, 497, 506-511
Drug use, and hazards, 528-532
  and reduction of aggression, 499, 517
  and reduction of anxiety, 499, 501, 503, 507, 510, 516, 517, 519, 520
  withdrawal symptoms, 502, 508, 509-511, 518-520, 521-523, 533-534
Duchess County Unit, 792
Duncan Residence Hall Counselor Evaluation Scale, 333
Dyadic communication, 51, 133
Dynamically-oriented, 323
Dynamic psychotherapy, *see* Psychoanalytic treatment; Psychoanalysis analogues
Dynamimetic interview, 897
"Dysfunctioners," study of, 800
Dysthymics, 559, 560

Early detection and intervention, 799
Eclectic, 14
  psychotherapies, 226
Ecological psychology, 781

Ecology, 779, 781
Educational assessment of mental health, 799
Edwards Personal Preference Schedule, 64, 338, 356, 485, 904, 905
Effective role functioning, 879
Effects, of counseling and psycho-therapy, 229, 238, 301-303, 310, 327, 336
  of psychoanalysis, 225, 226, 230
Ego, 515, 517, 518, 521, 522
  and Milieu, 793
  Scale (IPAT), 509
Ego functions, objective assess-ment of, 522
Eigenwirkung, 518
Electrical artifact, 89
Electrical aversion therapy, 587
Electric shock therapy, 644
Electrocardiogram, 77, 376
Electroconvulsive therapy (ECT), 5, 497, 510, 511
Electrodes, 79
Electroencephalogram, 79
Electromyogram, 78
Electromyograph, 377
Electronic amplifiers, 80
Electrothermal fluctuations, 643
Elicitation, 714
Emotion, 103, 543, 548, 554, 717, 719, 723, 730, 741
Emotional arousal, 25
Emotional Crisis Center, 796
Emotional insight, 521-523
Emotional modulation and role of drugs, 515
Emotional response and its modi-fication, 105
Emotional words, 630
Emotive imagery, 210
Empathy, empathic understand-ing, accurate empathy, 51, 55, 137, 172, 300, 302, 303, 310, 312-315, 317-319, 322-341, 420, 720
  client's perception of, 330
  conjunctive, 420
  generative, 420
  scale, accurate, 338
  training, 339
Empiricism, trends toward, 919
Encounter, 302, 316, 322
Enuresis, 557, 575
Environmental adjustment, 814
Environmental systems, 28
Epidemiology, 779, 780
  analytic, 779
  descriptive, 779
Epileptic seizure, 118

Equilibrium, 185
Erotic psychic energy and drugs, 515
"Error" scale in relationship to teaching technique, 908
Evaluation, 20
Evaluational design, 44
Evaluative statements, 328
Evocative psychotherapy, 615
Evoked potential, 98
Excitation, 559
Excitement, as drug response, 519
  as scale of schizophrenia, 508
Existential, 5, 15, 35
Expectancy, expectation, 133-135, 141, 149, 715, 717, 719, 725, 735, 738, 739
Expectations, family, as drug re-sponse factor, 518
  patient, as drug response factor, 518
Experienced therapists, 142, 237
  versus inexperienced therapist behavior, 907, 908, 909
Experience level, 54, 142, 330
"Experiencing," 51, 52, 314, 315, 317, 318
  scale, 349, 350, 359, 903
Experiential, 257
Experimental client, 326
Experimental control, 127
Experimental manipulation, 226, 330
Experimental social psychology, 158
Experimenter bias, 454, 615, 617, 646
Experiments of nature, 54
Extensive research design, 67, 523
External behavior, 257
Extinction, 17, 59, 547, 553, 563, 567, 585, 614, 709, 711, 713, 714, 718, 725, 727, 736
  vicarious, 672, 674, 675
Extrapolatory research, 156
Extraversion, 353
Extrovert, 560
Eye-blink conditioning, 555

Facilitative condition, in teaching, 328
Factor analyses, 256-258
Fading, 759
Faith, 447
Family, as therapeutic agent, 530
  interview, 330, 355, 356
Family-centered, 32
Family therapy, 17, 488
Fantasy, 203, 204, 257
  as factor in drug therapy,

505, 532
Fear, 546
Fear Survey Schedule, 260
Feedback, 7, 25, 339, 340, 711,
    842, 843, 847, 854, 856,
    857
  from group ratings, 340
  from measurement of client
    benefits, 340
Feminine-identification, 519
Fetishism, 575, 588, 731
Filial therapy, 912
Finney Therapy Scale, 260
FIRO-B, 848, 855
First-impression formation, 165
Fixed-ratio schedule, 617
Fixed-role therapy, 173, 665
Focused group-therapy experi-
    ence, 339
Follow-up, 256, 303, 312, 324,
    328
Forgetting, 353, 354
Foster home care, 481
Franklin County, Ohio, study
    at, 790
Free-association, 4, 64, 133, 139,
    143, 147, 354, 522, 547
Frequency of contacts, 337
Freudian, conception of symp-
    tom, 12
Friendly, 131, 147
Frustration-observation sequence,
    197
  theory, 13
F scale, 390, 512
Functional, 208

Galvanic skin response, 643
Gastric motility, 87
General Inquirer, 366, 370, 387
Generalists, 37, 46
Generalizability, 128
Generalization, 545, 567, 581,
    630, 643, 709
General Systems Approach, 782
Genuineness, 302, 303, 310, 312-
    316, 319, 322, 324, 329,
    331-335, 338-341
  scale, 338
  training, 339
Goal objectives, 15
Goodenough Draw A Man Test,
    800
Gordon Personal Profile, 843
Grade-point average, 310, 327
Grandiosity, 506
Graylingwell Hospital, 790
Green Berets, 644
Grid model, 42, 69
Grief reaction, 801
Group cohesion, 186, 822

Group counseling, 334-335, 881
Group dynamics, 183, 822
Group for Advancement of Psy-
    chiatry (GAP), 409, 906
Group functioning and drugs, 522
Group growth, 840, 849, 850
Group leader role, 338
Group processes, 821-827
Group pychotherapy, 51, 303,
    310, 312, 324, 332, 338,
    348, 352-370, 381, 506,
    509-510, 736, 799, 878,
    887
Group sessions for education
    about drugs, 532, 533
Growth centers, 850
GSR, 21, 718, 725
Guidance, representational, 658
Guidance counselor training,
    APGA standards, 913
  effect of National Defense Edu-
    cation Act, 913-914
  measurement of counselor atti-
    tude change, 914
Guilt, 115, 506, 509, 510
Guttman scales, 786

Habituation, 98, 112, 553, 564
Haggerstown Study, 798
Hallucinations, 506
Harvard Medical School, 776
Harvard Need Affiliation diction-
    ary, 424
Hawthorne Effect, 807, 883
Healers and witches, 327
Health-Sickness Rating Scale, 412
Heart-rate, 643
  habituation, 116
Hebrew Bible, 440
Hempstead Index, 429
"Here-and-now," 840, 851, 857
Heredity as factor in drug re-
    sponse, 518
Heuristic, 200, 201
Homeostatic feedback, 95
Homosexuality, 205, 575, 588,
    589
Hooke's law of elasticity, 558
Hope, 447
Hormones, use of in treatment of
    psychosis, 500
Hospital adjustment, 508
Hospitalization, 302, 789-790
Hospital length of stay as related
    to drug therapy, 506, 508,
    510
Hospital treatment, goals for
    schizophrenics versus out-
    patient treatment, 530
Hostility, 355, 363, 364, 366,
    372, 373, 374, 376, 516,

    718, 721
Hudson River State Hospital,
    Duchess County Unit, 792
Human Development Institute,
    852
Human relationships, 300, 313,
    314, 320, 330, 337
Human relations training, 839,
    843, 844, 851, 855, 857
Hydrotherapy, 506, 507, 510
Hypnosis, 4, 105, 201, 496, 614,
    630
Hypnotics, sedative, 496, 519
Hypochondria, effect of on drug
    response, 518
Hypothalamus, 91
Hysterics, 559, 560

Iatroplacebogenesis, 457, 459,
    460, 463
  direct, 450
  indirect, 457-458
Id, 515
Identification, 315, 317, 546
Idiographic, 66, 199
IJR study, 489
Imagination, 599
Imipramine, 322, 497
Imitation, 135, 546, 661, 728; *see
    also* Modeling
Immediacy, 341
Implosive therapy, 544, 724
Impotent, 203
Improvement, 220, 239, 301,
    302, 303, 310, 325, 330,
    332
  rates of, 218, 224, 301-302
Impulsivity, 98
Incentive theory, 175
Incubation, 551, 553, 560
Indicant fallacy, 99
Indigenous change agents, 245,
    795
Individual differences, in drug re-
    sponse, 516-518, 527-528,
    528-530
  and integration of treatment
    methods, 311, 516, 533-
    534
  as treatment factor, 37, 528,
    529, 530, 533, 534, 545
Indoklon (Hexafluro-diethyl-
    ether), 497
Induced attraction, 163
Inequitable reward, 166
Inexperienced therapists, 237
Infantile autism, 625
Inference, 357, 366
Informational stimulus, process-
    ing and learning, informa-
    tion, 714, 716, 719, 723,

725, 728, 729, 731, 734, 737, 739
Information-seeking behavior, 702, 871-872
storage, 27, 33
Information influences, 686
Inhibition, 559
Inhibitory effects, 656
Initial level differences, 96
Innovation in psychotherapy, 197, 276, 293, 294
Insight, 17
outcome of psychotherapy, 512, 515, 521
ratings of, in schizophrenics, 511, 513, 517
Insomnia, use of sedatives for, 496
Instinct, effect of drugs on, 515
Instinctual energy, effect of drugs on, 41, 56
Institute, of Medical Psychology, 219, 224
of Living, 783
for Youth Studies, 793
Instruction, 714, 728, 732, 739
Instrumental behavior, 871
Insulin, 496, 497, 502, 506
Integrated, 31
Integration of treatment methods according to individual need, 529, 530
Intelligence, effect of drugs on, 516, 517
occupation level of, 869
Intensive research design, 209, 522, 523
Interaction, chronograph, 350, 908
Interaction matrix, 833
Interaction Process Analysis, 184, 355, 357, 358, 367
Interdisciplinary, 23, 34
Interest, 21
in the patient, 451, 455
Interference theory, 757
Intermittent reinforcement, 211, 618
Internal medicine, 442
states, 257
Interpersonal attraction, 51, 160
Interpersonal exchanges, 170
Interpersonal influence, 162
Interpersonal orientation, 630
Interpersonal relationship, 316, 710, 726, 729
Interpersonal skill, 302, 313, 318, 322, 337
as reinforcers, 322, 324
scales measuring, 322
Interposed tape review, 169

Interpretation, 52, 60, 133, 352, 357, 363, 365, 379, 380, 419, 420, 461, 462, 547, 549
Interrelationship, 5, 12, 23, 28, 31, 35
with environment, 28
Interruption, 352, 369, 379
Interstressor stereotype, 100
Intervention, in Community Mental Health Disorders, 799-802
hypothesis, 474
Interview, 653, 762
ambiguity, 147
importance of, prior to drug therapy, 531
Interviewer style, 146-149
Intrapersonal exploration, 822
Intrastressor stereotype, 100
Introspection, as measure of drug effect, 521, 522
Investigative styles, 888
Investigator characteristics effecting research results, 527
IPAT O-A Anxiety and Aggression, 509
IPAT Verbal Battery Ego Scale, 509
I.Q., as factor influencing drug response, 516-518

Jamesian theory, 102
Jenkins Symptom Rating Scale, 511
Johns Hopkins study, 303, 311
Judges and ratings, 868

Kings County Hospital, hospital avoidance study, 790
suicide prevention study, 790

Lability, 506
Laboratory analogues of psychological treatment, 116
Lactate level in anxiety neuroses, 93
Language acquisition, 661
Language impairment, drug effect, in autistic children, 527
in schizophrenics, 522
Latin Bible, 440
Lawful relationships, 39
Law of Effect, 483, 751
Law of initial values, 95, 480
Lay, personnel, 327
therapist training, 910, 911, 912, 913, 920
Leaderless groups, 851
Leadership Opinion Question-

naire, 848
Learning, 17, 448
theories of 28, 302, 314
theory of dual-process, 669, 670
Leary interpersonal scales, 788
Length of stay, and age of client, 277, 278
and client expectations, 282, 283
and education, 277
and IQ, 279, 284
and motivation, 282
and psychiatric diagnosis, 277
and psychological mindedness, 278
and sex of client, 272
and suggestibility, 281
and TR battery, 281
of treatment as outcome factor, 523-525; *see also* Hospital length of stay as related to drug therapy
Level of anxiety as factor in drug response, 516-618
Libido, 516
Likability, 349
Linguistics and drug effect, 522
Lithium, 497
Little Albert, 543
Locus of evaluation, 317
Love, 302
LSD, 17, 497

MACC, 511
Mahl's Ah Ratio, 373, 389
Mahl's Non-Ah Ratio, 3, 372, 377, 389
Manic-depression, use of lithium, 497
Manipulation, 156
Manipulative research, 61
Mannerism, psychotic, 506
"Manner of Relating" scale, 349
Marathon, 4, 17
Marlborough Experiment, 785
MAS, 558
Masculinity, 333
Masochism, 522
Massachusetts General Hospital, 776
Masturbation, 203
Matching, 170
Matrix algebra, 833
Maudsley Hospital Report, 219, 224
Meaningfulness, 416
Measured interests and the field of work, 869
Mechanisms, 654
Medfield State Hospital, 787-789

Mediated discrimination, 709
Medical ecology, 781
Medical history, 439, 457
Medical schools, NIMH Human
    Behavior grants, 909
  postgraduate training, 909-910
  teaching of psychotherapy in,
    906-909, 920
  undergraduate teaching of inter-
    view skill, 907-909
    effectiveness of, 907-909
    personality change during,
      907-909
Medication, 6, 31
Medicine, modern, 442
Meditation, 205
Memory, 26, 354, 527
Menninger Foundation Psycho-
    therapy Research Project,
    330, 410-414, 423, 429
Menninger Health-Sickness Scale,
    411, 511-513
Mental functioning, 814
Mental health administrator, 778
Mental hospital, 617, 622, 635,
    637, 644, 791
Mental patients, 303, 310, 328
Mental retardation, 615, 640
Mental status as scale of acute
    schizophrenia, 508, 516-
    518
Mephenesin, 566
Meprobamate, 496, 507, 509
Mescaline, 497
Methylamphetamine, 496
Methylphenidate, 496
Metrazol, 497
Microcounseling, 903
Midtown Study, 798
Midwest Psychological Field Sta-
    tion, 781
Milbank Fund, 779
Milieu therapy, 17, 507, 509,
    517, 530, 534, 740
Minnesota Counseling Inventory,
    485
Minnesota-Hartford Personality
    Assay and Automated Nurs-
    ing Notes, 783
MMPI, 258, 260, 261, 303, 337
  EPPS, selection devices, 337
  relationship to therapeutic skill,
    904
  scales, 512, 513
  Sc scale, 303, 330, 359
Mobility and mental health, 802
Modeling, 33, 135, 171, 181,
    317, 322, 615, 617, 623,
    625, 636, 754
  affective, 691
  effects of, 656

graduated, 672
group, 684
model, 136, 695, 716, 725,
    727, 729, 731, 736, 739
multiple, 676
participant, 681, 685, 687, 692
principles, 655
procedures, 656, 666
  with reinforced guided perform-
    ance or participation, 659,
    660, 680, 685, 687, 700
  self-administered, self-regulated,
    672, 677, 679
  supplemented with reinforce-
    ment, 700
  symbolic, 667-669, 676, 677,
    679, 692
Momentary forgetting, 424
Monoamine oxidase inhibitors
    (MAO), 497, 522
Mood scales, 262
Morphine, 520
Motivated controls, 883
Motivation, 353, 363, 370, 378,
    448, 879
  effect of drugs, 517
  as factor of drug response, 531
Motor disturbances as scale of
    schizophrenia, 508
Motoric reproduction process,
    658
Motor retardation, 506, 510
Motor system, 24, 28
Multifactorial, 256
Multivariate experimental design
    studies, 60
Muscle relaxation, 106
Muscular tension, 565

Napalkov phenomenon, 564
Narcissim in therapists, 504
Narcissistic tranquility and resist-
    ance to drug therapy, 503
Narcisstic withdrawal, 503
Narcosis, 17
  as a result of sedatives, 496
Narcosynthesis, 17
National Institute of Mental
    Health (NIMH), 416, 777
  Filmed Therapy Project, 428
  Psychotherapy Research Proj-
    ect, 423
National Training Laboratories,
    852
National Training School for
    Boys, 485
Naturalistic research, 47-48, 54
Natural therapeutic or interper-
    sonal skill, 338
Negative affect, 322
Negative and nonplacebo reac-

tion, 447
Negative practice, 614
Negative reactors, 445
Negative reinforcer, 621
Neuroeffector inhibition, 90
Neuroleptic drugs, 500, 505, 517
Neurophysiological explanation
    of the effects of drugs, 515
Neurosis, 301, 330, 332, 349,
    350, 353, 363, 378, 379,
    548
  factors in treatment outcome,
    526-527
  treatment, using tranquilizers,
    507-508
  using psychotherapy, 508,
    509, 526
  with ataraxic drugs, 499, 509-
    516, 526-528
Neurotics, non-specific factors of
    drug response, 519
Nitrous oxide, 496
Nomothetic, 66, 199
Nonachievement syndrome, 882
Nonconfirming experience, 735,
    736, 738
Nondirective therapy, *see* Client-
    centered therapy
Nonmotivated control groups,
    878, 880, 883
Nonpossessive warmth, 302-303,
    310, 312-314, 316-318,
    328-329, 331, 336, 338-
    340, 485
  scale, 338
Nonprofessionals in community
    mental health programs,
    327, 328, 793, 794
Nonreactors to drugs, 445
Nonspecific effects, 440, 730
Nonverbal communication, 317
Nonvocal behavior, 63
Noradrenaline, 91
Norepinephrine, 91
Normal behavior development, 16
Norman Vincent Peale tradition,
    64, 65
No-trial learning, 716
Nurturance, 356
Nutritional balance, 31

Obesity, 575
*Objective-Analytic Personality
    Factor Battery*, 262
Objectives, 9, 22, 27
Object-relations, 373, 374
  effects, as explanation of
    psychopharmacological
    events, 515, 522
Observation, 21
Observational learning, 135, 657;

see also Modeling
Observer bias, 762
Observer characteristics, 695
Occupation, 505
Ohio State Leadership Opinion Questionnaire, 848
Operant approach, 614, 615, 624, 626, 633, 635
Operant behavior, 613
Operant conditioning, 5, 17, 207, 612-631, 636, 642-647, 711, 713, 714, 716, 721, 739
Operant feedback control of EEG, 107
Operant feedback programs, 118
Operant shaping techniques, 107
Operant therapy, 612, 616-618, 644, 723, 727, 729, 736, 739
Operationalism, 157
Orienting and defense, 98
Oscilloscope, 87
Outcome, of child psychotherapy, 475
    of counseling, 879
    of psychoanalytic treatment, 414, 415
    of psychotherapy, client personality variables, 285, 287, 288
    evaluation of, 46, 228, 229, 236, 238, 241, 246, 252, 303, 348-351, 363-364, 371, 380, 386-387, 414, 734, 735, 814-820
    investigator factors, 527, 521-523
    length of treatment as factor, 525
    social class of patient and drugs, 518, 519
    therapist characteristics, 516-518, 524, 528
Outcome criteria, 49, 256-262, 332, 520, 521, 526, 814, 879, 885
Outliers in data analysis, 523
Outpatient, 303, 312, 330
    rehabilitation, 531-532
    treatment and factors, 530-533
Overlearning, 579
Own-control design, 620
Oxazepam, 519

Palmar sweat, 21, 373
    index, 113
Palo Alto Group Therapy Scale, 312, 332
Paradoxical discomfort, 141
Paradoxial reaction of anxiety,

519, 520
Paradoxical response to drugs, 519, 520
Paraldehyde, 496
Paranoid schizophrenic, 205-206
Paraprofessional, 5
Parasympathetic system, 90
Parental control, 759
Parents, 752
Partial reinforcement, 579
Participative management, 842
Passive-feminine identification, 519
Patient, 48, 57, 64
    adequacy of productions during psychoanalysis, 416
    behavior, classes of, 323-324
    checklists and self-ratings, 261
    expectations as drug response factor, 518
    experience with drugs as treatment factor, 531
    functioning, evaluation of, 340
    global improvement scale, 312
    individual needs as treatment factor, 533-534
    inner experience, 331
    liability or pathology, 331
    misinformation, 331
    motivation to change, 341
    outcome, 328, 331, 340
    personality, 445
    qualities of, most suitable to psychoanalysts, 412
    resources, 331
    selection of, 460
    variables, 444
    weakness, 331
Patient-therapist relationship, 443
Pavlovian conditioning, 613
    model, 13
Peer group, 763, 768
Peer ratings, 263
Penile reflexes, 554
Penis plethysmograph, 590
Perceptions, 26
Perceptual distortion, 509
Perphenazine, 522
Persistence of treatment, 874
Personal Constructs Scale, 349
Personality, 128, 138, 558
    and behavior change, 302, 303, 314, 814-818
    change during training, 905
    factors in therapeutic effectiveness, 904-905
    factors of drug response, 518, 519, 530-531
Personal Orientation Inventory, 262, 855
Persuasive potency, 332

Perversion, 202, 203
Pharmacotherapy, 458
Phase movement, 185
Phasic activity, 96
Phenobarbital, 507, 509, 522
Phenomenological, 5
Phenomenologically oriented psychoanalysts, 314
Phenothiazine, 496, 506-509, 516, 517, 528
Phenyltolaxamine, 519
Phobia, 59, 113, 201, 208, 544
Photoelectric transducer, 86
Physical rehabilitation, 634
Physician variables, 450
Pipradrol, 496, 522
Placebo, 202, 255, 439, 440, 445, 456, 459, 463, 646, 717, 732, 733, 735, 738
    adaptive, 443
    effect, clinical prognosis from, 445
    constancy of, 446
    history of, 442
    reactions, 444
    reactivity, 450
Placebogenesis, 443, 453
Play therapy, 17, 476, 489
Plethysmograph, 21, 86
Police as neighborhood social workers, 783
Polygraph, 87
Poor, New Careers for the, 795
Positive affect, 322-323
Positive change, 310
Positive reactors, 445
Positive regard, 51, 302, 331
Positive reinforcement, 620, 624, 632, 643, 645
Potency, 333, 341
Practical counselors, 338
Practice, 199, 208
Practicing clinician, 196, 208
Predelinquent boys, 769
Prediction of response to treatment, 303, 333, 527
Premature dropouts, 220, 221
Premorbid adjustment of schizophrenic as factor influencing drug effects, 516
Pre-post test, 813
Prescriptive Contextual Research, 779, 786, 787
Prestige of the investigator, 454
Preventive psychiatry, 33
    Caplan's definition, 778
Problem Analysis Questionnaire, 844
Problem-solving research, 22
Processing, storage, and retrieval of information, 26

Process studies, 45, 331, 423
Process variables, 301
Prochlorperazine, 507
Productivity of the patient, 416
Professional counselors, 336-338
Profit motive, 453
Progress in community mental health, 802
Projective techniques, 21, 446, 522
"Project Re-Ed" Program, 479, 791-792
Prostitution, 634
Pseudotherapy, 568
Psychiatric diagnosis, 446
Psychiatric epidemiology, 779
Psychiatric hospital as a small society, 791
Psychiatric status schedule, 257, 260
Psychic energy, drug effect as explanation of psychopharmacological events, 515
Psychoanalysis, 5, 17, 35, 330, 331, 354, 358, 383, 390, 416, 440, 463, 614, 720, 733, 741
  classical, 460, 462
  role of drugs in, 497-499, 500, 515-516, 522
Psychoanalytically oriented training, 324
Psychoanalytic libido theory, 353
Psychoanalytic supervisory process, 896-898
Psychoanalytic theory, early, 200
Psychoanalytic therapists, desirable qualities, 413
Psychoanalytic treatment analogues, 410, 426
Psychodrama, 4, 5, 17, 173, 352, 666
Psycholinguistics, 382-384
Psychological differentiation, 374
Psychological tests, 506, 509, 510
Psycho-noxious or harmful practitioners, 301, 476
Psychopaths, 559
  behavior exhibited under drugs, 496
Psychophysiological analysis of psychotherapy, 110
Psychosis, 269, 332, 370, 378, 381, 496, 499, 500, 617, 665
Psychosomatic disorder, 105, 108, 118, 643
Psychosomatic model, 13
Psychotherapeutic management, 498, 529
Psychotherapeutic relationship,

160
Psychotherapy, 451, 452, 619, 628, 630
  and drugs, 503, 507, 528-530
  effectiveness, 44
  formal definition, 498, 528-529
  and psychoanalysis, 459
Psychotomimetics, uses and types, 497
Psychotropic drugs, 521
Public health worker, 778
Punishment, 204, 583, 613-614, 618
Puppets, 4

Q-sort, 51, 67, 69, 261, 303, 312, 329, 332, 422
Quality control, 340
Quincy Aftercare Clinic, 788

Race as a factor in psychotherapy with children, 490
Racial differences, 361-362
Range correction, 95
Rapport, 365
Raters, 314, 319, 322
Rates of improvement, 218, 224
Ratings, behavioral and achievement, 328
  of insight in schizophrenics, 511-513, 517
  procedures, 322
  scales, 21
  tape-recorded samples, 328, 332
Rational-emotive psychotherapy, 17
Reading achievement, 334
Readmission rate, effect of drugs on, 506, 508, 510
Reality testing, 515, 517, 518
Reality therapy, 483
Reassurance, 461
Reciprocal affect, 322-323
Reciprocal inhibition, 17, 133, 547, 614
Reciprocally contingent relationships, 164
Reciprocal model of treatment interactions, 513
Recordings, audio tape, 319
  video tape, 319
Recordings therapy, 389, 390, 391
Recovery cycle, 96, 113
"Red Tag" studies, 800
Reeducative, 18
Reflective, 60
Regeneration, 521
Regression scale (IPAT), 509
Rehabilitation, client characteristics, 335

counseling, 335, 336
counselor, 334, 336
Rehabilitative, 33
Reinforce, 19
Reinforcement, 17, 33, 132, 135, 207-208, 322-324, 355, 361, 378, 709, 713-715, 720-721, 727-728, 730, 739
  differential, 324
  and motivational processes, 658
  negative, 324
  selective, 322, 667
  self, 730, 739
  social, 618, 622, 637, 643, 723, 735, 770
  verbal, 323, 630, 710, 714, 721, 727, 739
  and client's decision making, 871
  withdrawal, 615
Reinforcement schedules, 322, 667
Reinforcement theory, 752
Reinforcement therapy, 497, 516
Reinforcer, positive, negative, 713, 715, 720, 727, 728
Reinforcers, 614, 620-629, 631, 632, 635-639, 645
Reinforcer sampling, 619
Reinforcing stimulus, 614, 617
Reiss-Davis Child Study Center, 784
Relapses, 569, 578, 586
Relatability, 412
Relationship, 5
  intensity and intimacy, 316
  inventories, 52
  quality, 316
  questionnaires, 333, 338
Relaxation, 205, 206, 565-566, 615, 732
Release rate, effect of drugs on, 506, 508-510, 511-513
Reliability, 322, 378, 388, 389, 390, 822
Remainers in child treatment, 489
  dropouts, 50
Reminiscence, 551
Remission after drug therapy, factors of, 501
Replacement therapy, dependence on drugs as, 502
Repression, 60, 354, 377
Research, 128
  design, 47
  methods, 68
  models, 833
  in psychotherapy, 9, 22
Research Center for Mental Health of New York University, 427

Researcher, 778
Reserpine, 496, 506, 509, 510, 519, 522
Residential treatment, 17
  center, 479
Resistance, 363, 365, 366, 379
Resistance capacitance or R-C
  coupled amplifiers, 80
Respiration transducer, 85
Respondent behavior, 612
Respondent conditioning, 613
Response, 596
Response class, 629
Response duration, 352, 364, 365, 369, 374, 376
Response facilitation effects, 656, 700
Response frequency, 352, 355-356, 357, 364
Response hierarchy, 757
Response inhibition, 135
Response "shaping," 340
Response specificity, 99
  to treatment, 527, 534
Responsiveness, 132
Resultant attraction, 164
Retarded, 328
Retention processes, 657
Reticular formation, 102
Reverberating circuits, 515
Revisionism in psychotherapy, 154
Rewards, 613, 614, 617
Rochester Project on the Computer Analysis of Content, 427
Roger's Process Scale, 348-350, 358, 359, 360
Role, 133, 139
Role behavior, 146, 348, 360, 364, 365, 366, 376
Role Construct Repertory Test, 67
Role functioning, 864, 877
  college and university, 878
  elementary and secondary school, 876
Role induction interview
Role-playing, 4, 18, 33, 66, 158, 173, 340, 700, 845, 851, 852
  and change in clinically relevant behavior, 178
  in the laboratory, 176
  in psychotherapy, 173
Role relationships, 133
Roommate influence, 327
Rorschach Prognostic Rating Scale, 287
Rorshach Test, 506, 509
  and continuation in psycho-

therapy, 279, 280

Sado-masochistic, 203
Samples, coding of, 322
Sampling, method of, 319
SCAT scores, 333
Schachter's theory, 104
Schedule of reinforcement, 619
Schizophrenia, 51, 302, 310, 349, 351, 359, 370, 373, 382, 496, 616, 622-624
  ambulatory, 502
  and drug treatment, 496-501, 504-506, 514-516
  catatonic, 496
  primary symptoms and drug effect, 520-521
  secondary symptoms and drug effect, 520-521
  simple, 502
Schizophrenic behaviors, 622
Schizophrenic children, 626
Schizophrenic defenses, 515
Schizophrenic disorganization, 508
Schizophrenic language, 522
Schizophrenicsing, 826
Schizophrenic withdrawal, 515
School phobia, 201, 202, 485-486
School psychologists, 328
School refusal, 485
Scientism, 760
Screening interview, 324
Secobarbital, 519
"Secret Stories," use of, 799
Sedative, hypnotics, 320
Sedatives, 499, 506, 508, 510
  and narcosis, 496
  use of and reduction of anxiety, 496
Selection, processing and transforming of information, 26
  and training, 337
  of helping personnel, 337
Self, 841, 846-848, 854-856
Self-acceptance, regard and understanding, 315-317
Self-adjustment, 814
Self-awareness, 318, 347
Self-concept, 69, 303, 322, 730, 734, 738, 760, 864
  measures, 260
Self-congruence, 302
Self-control, 262
  of blood pressure, 118
Self-description, 142
Self-disclosure, 65, 136, 147
Self-esteem, 738
Self-evaluation, 29, 256, 340, 353, 382, 679
Self-exploration, 137-138, 317,

323-324, 326, 339, 360, 361
  depth of, 324, 326, 332
  scales, 330
Self-help, 246
Self-instruction, 711
Self-mastery, 354
Self-punitive behavior, 114
Self-reference, 348, 354, 392, 697
Self-regulation measures, 262
Self-regulatory functions, 703
Self-reinforcement, 322, 695
Self-stimulatory behavior, 660
Semantic differential, 21
  measures, 844, 847, 854
Sensitivity, 553, 840, 841, 843, 844, 845, 848
Sensitivity training, 17, 350, 740, 843-845, 850-854, 856
Sensory information, 26
Sensory systems, 24
Severity of initiation, 168
Set, 133
Sex, 202, 203, 366, 378
  of counselor, 332
Sex difference, 373, 375
Shaping, 656, 714
Sheltered workshop, 635
Shipley, V.I.Q., A.I.Q., 511, 512, 513
Short-term counseling, 878
Short-term therapy, 379
Side effects of drugs, 503, 530, 531, 532
Signal to noise ratio, 76
Silence, 351, 356, 362-363, 366, 368, 369, 370, 372, 374, 379, 389
Similarity, therapist-client, 133, 300
Simplification, 127, 128
Single case, 66-67, 601
Situational stereotype, 101
Situation variables, 449
Sixteen Personality Factor Questionnaire, 262
Skin, conductance response (SCR), 84
  potential response (SPR), 82
  resistance response (SRR), 83
Small group behavior, 155
Snake-phobic, 672
Social adjustment, 260
Social appearance schedule, 788
"Social-breakdown syndrome," study of, 792
Social class variables, implications for practice, 293, 294, 505, 518
Social engineering, 751
Social environment, 760

Social imitation, 545, 614
Social ineffectiveness, 260
Social influence, 133, 145, 149, 332, 714, 735, 741
Social interaction, 545
Social learning, 647, 763
  model of psychotherapy, 920
Social planning, 643
Social psychology, 155, 157, 352, 752
Social Rehabilitation Unit, 791
Social reward, 175
Social setting as non-specific factor in drug response, 518
Social therapy, 507
Social withdrawal, 622, 669
Social work, as therapeutic agent, 529-530
  ratings, 507
Social worker, 34
Socio-Economic Status, 349, 359, 375, 379
Sociogenic model, 13
Sociopathic personality, 616
Sociotherapy, 499, 516
Somatization, 506, 510
Somatogenic model, 13
Sound spectroscopy, 384
Southern California Psychoanalytic Institute, 414
South Shore Mental Health Center, 787
Spaced practice, 567
Special class, 480
Specific feedback, 340
Specific and non-specific treatment, 533-534
Specification in therapy theories, 132
Specificity, 45, 209, 590
Specific response to drugs, 516-517, 519, 527, 530-531, 534
Speech disturbance, 365, 366, 372, 373, 377, 378, 382
Speech-Disturbance Ratio, 366, 372, 373, 378
Speech duration, 351, 352; see also Response duration
Speech impairment as factor in drug effect, 517
Spontaneity, 316
Spontaneous activity, 98
Spontaneous remission, 44, 198, 239, 241, 242, 245, 246, 258, 303, 327, 456, 567
Spontaneous remission rates, 227, 240, 275
Spontaneous skin-conductance responses, 113
Stammerer, 631

Stammering, 631
Standard interviewer, 327-325
Standards for employment of helping personnel, 337
State hospital, 638
Status-spread effect, 167
Stimulants, 496-497
Stimulus, 596
  hunger, 456
  pull, 143
  variable, 444
Stimulus-response (S-R), 322
Stirling County Study, 780, 798
Stochastic models, 783
Street corner research, 625
Stress, 148
  tolerance to, 115
Strong Vocational Interest Blank, 51
Structured interview, 351, 352, 355-356, 376-377
Structuring, 162
Subjective anxiety, 506, 509-511
Subject variable, 444
Success-failure, 49
Successful, 50
Succorance, 65
Suggestibility, 444, 456
Suicide, 501, 522
Suicide Prevention Centers, 796
Super-ego, components, as related to drug, 515
Supervisor judgments, 300
Surgeons, 17
Suspicion (as sympton of psychosis), 506
Sweat gland activity, 83, 91
Symbolic meaning of drug, 531, 532
  control, 672
Sympathetic nervous system, 90
Symptom, 156, 209, 496, 502, 508, 510, 521
Symptom context methods, 423
Symptom removal, 3, 15, 200
Symptom specificity, 100, 112
Symptom substitution, 200, 616
Synanon, 851
Synchronous, synchrony, 145, 146, 147
Systematic desensitization, see Desensitization
System organization, 24
Systolic blood pressure, 92, 114
Systems, 23

Tailoring criteria, 258
Target behavior, 483
Target complaints, 260
Task Force on Juvenile Delinquency and Youth Crime of

the President's Commission on Law Enforcement and Administration of Justice, 484
TAT, 258, 261
Teacher, 763
  interpersonal characteristics of, 334
  interpersonal skills, 334
  personality characteristics, 334
  rated behavior problems, 328
  training, 764
Teacher-counselor, 483
Telemetry, 89
Tension, use of sedatives, 496, 506, 510
Tension-models, 13
Termination from psychotherapy, see Length, of stay
Test data, 331
Theoretic, 22
Theories of learning, 28, 302, 314
Theories of psychotherapy, 302
  client-centered, 302, 324
  eclectic, 302
  learning, 302, 314
  psychoanalytic, 302
Theory, 5, 6, 12, 199, 207, 842, 848
  early psychoanalytic, 200
Therapeutic "community" project, 791
Therapeutic conditions, facilitative and nonfacilitative, 137, 138, 324, 720, 734, 737
Therapeutic context, 339
Therapeutic effects, 229
Therapeutic Process Study (Mt. Zion Hospital and San Francisco Psychoanalytic Institute), 428
Therapeutic relationship, 729
Therapeutic result, 567
Therapeutic setting, 133
Therapeutic skill, Graduate Record Exam in, 904
Therapeutic techniques, 418
Therapist, ambiguity, 366
  anxiety, 331
  attraction, 172
  behavioral, 253, 319
  behavior of, 330
  bias, 533-534
  characteristics affecting treatment outcome, 516-518, 524, 525, 526
  conditions, 138, 221, 358, 359, 360-362, 388, 389
  effective, 302, 310
  evaluation, 256, 329
  evaluative statement, 330

experience, 124, 237, 300, 326, 355-365, 506, 524-525, 528
as expert, 341
genuineness, 314
global improvement scale, 312
immediacy, 302, 331
ineffective or harmful, 340
inexperienced, 237
in-patient, out-patient separation, 533-534
integration of treatments, factors of, 530
intellectual ability and expert knowledge, 318
mother as the, 481
personality characteristics, 59, 131, 140, 300, 341, 504
rating scales, 262
as reinforcer, 322
resistance to drug therapy, 506
skill, 330, 331
specificity, 365, 366, 369, 373
as technician, 341
technique, 59
traditional, 323
training, 352, 357, 362
type, 140-142
type of training, 326
warmth, 330-331
Therapist's experiencing, of patient, 331
of self, 331
Therapy analogue, 355, 357, 360-362, 364, 366, 386
duration of, 238
expectations, 353, 356, 368
Thorndike-Lorge List, 427
Thought disturbance, 362, 363, 374, 522
T-Group, *see* Sensitivity training
Time, 801
Time constant, 80
Time-limited therapy, 303, 330
"Time-out" procedures, 757, 770
Time spent counseling, 336
Token, 614, 618, 619, 621, 624, 626, 629, 634-641, 644, 645
Token economy, 615, 618, 622, 634, 637, 638, 640, 642, 645
Token reinforcement, 622, 624, 635, 641
Token systems, 769
Tonic and phasic activity, 94
Topical focus, 354, 364-366, 371, 373, 380
Toxic impairment of ego functioning, 530
Trainee personality characteristics, 338

Trainees, 340
personal values, goals, life style, 339
Training, 313, 327, 614
effective or harmful, 337-338
in the home, 756
to observe, 754
peers, 768
and practice, 339
program, 339
to reinforce, 755
Transactional response systems, 32
Transactional systems, 24
Transfer, 674, 684
Transference, 391, 501-502, 518, 521, 556, 726
cures, 521
as drug response factor, 518
effect, 333
effect of drugs on, 502
negative, 332
Tranquilizers, response to, 202, 496, 505-506, 517
Tranquilizing medication, 96
Transistors, 80
Transvestism, 575, 588
Transvestites, 592
Trauma model, 13
Traumatic conditioning, 553
Treatment defectors, 475
Treatment goals derived from research hospital versus outpatient, 528-529
Treatment interactions, reciprocal model, 513
Treatment plan, 16
Treatment response, prediction of, 527-528
Trifluoperazine, 519
Truancy, 486
rate of, 334
Type-Token Ration (TTR), 366, 369, 373, 389

Unconditional positive regard, 137, 302, 720
Unconscious conflicts, 201
Uncooperativeness as symptom of psychosis, 506
Underachievement, 877, 884, 887
Underachievers, 310-311, 317, 884, 885, 876, 881
Underachieving, 878
college students, 881
Underlying conflicts, 753
Understanding, 327, 328
Uniformity assumptions, 39
University of Illinois School of Medicine Psychotherapy Film Laboratory, 428

University of Minnesota, use of computers, 783
Unsuccessful, 50
Untrained community workers, 328
Untrained personnel, 328
Utopian society, 645

Validity, MMPI scale of, 513
Value inventories, 21
Valuing, 302
Variability, 310
in clients, 300
of criterion scores, 246
of outcome, 253
of results, 246
in therapists, 300-301, 320
Variable-interval reinforcement, 627
Variable-interval schedule, 617
Variation, bounded, 518-521
Variety versus uniformity in therapeutic techniques, 418
Verbal behavior, 323
and drug effect, 522, 526
Verbal conditioning, 58, 132, 137, 454, 615, 618, 625, 641, 642, 646
format, 148
Verbal influence procedures, 653
Verbal learning and conditioning, 711-716, 720, 729
Verbal productivity, 348, 363, 365, 366
Vicarious therapy pretraining, 276
Vicarious learning, 711, 724
Viet Cong, 644
Vigorous muscular activity, 210
Visceral feedback, 104
Visceral responses, 553
Vocational choice, 869
Vocational counselees, 323
Vocational preference, appropriateness of, 867, 869
Vocational rehabilitation process, 336
Voice quality, 348, 363, 383
Voluntary inhibitors, 712
Voluntary responders, 711
Volunteer community helpers, 328
Volunteers, 794

WAIS Similarities-Proverbs Scales, 511
Walden Two, 645
Warm, 131, 148, 300, 302, 326
Warmth, 172, 303, 312-315, 322-323, 325-329, 331-334, 337-341, 357, 360, 364,

366, 375
training of, 339
Way-of-life phobic, Type 2,
    487
Wellesley Human Relations
    Service, 801
Welsh Anxiety-Index, 303
Whitaker-Malone Method, 363
Winsorized data, 523
Wisconsin Study, 302, 310, 323,

328-329
Withdrawal, 506
    drug symptoms, 502, 515, 518-
        523
    from drug therapy, 533-534
Within-interview behavior, 49, 51
Word associations, 641
Word association test, 621
Word-counts, 351, 354, 358, 364,
    368, 389

Work, attitude, 335
    quantity, 335
World Health Organization, 796
    study of suicide, 796
Worthing Experiment, 790

YMCA, 853, 856
Yoga, 205
Young's modulus, 558
Ypsilanti State Hospital, 792